INFORMATION PLEASE ALMANAC®

ATLAS & YEARBOOK

1994

47TH EDITION

HOUGHTON MIFFLIN COMPANY BOSTON & NEW YORK

1994

Executive Editor
Otto Johnson
Associate Editor
Vera Dailey
Electronic Production Specialist
Christine Frantz
Manuscript Editor
Robert A.T. Scalza
Contributing Editors
Arthur Reed, Jr. (Current Events)
Thomas Nemeth, Ph.D. (World Countries)
Dennis M. Lyons (Sports)
Maps
Maps copyright © Hammond Incorporated.
Requests for map use should be sent to Hammond Incorporated, Maplewood, New Jersey 07040.
Front Cover
Photograph: Photo Library International 1994 ©/Westlight.

The Information Please Almanac invites comments and suggestions from readers. Because of the many letters received, however, it is not possible to respond personally to every correspondent. Nevertheless, all suggestions are most welcome, and the editors will consider them carefully. (Information Please Almanac does not rule on bets or wagers.)

ISBN (Hardcover): 0-395-67746-7
ISBN (Paperback): 0-395-67745-9
ISSN: 0073-7860

Previous editions of INFORMATION PLEASE were published from 1984–1992 by Houghton Mifflin Company, in 1982 by A&W Publishing Company, and in 1981, 1980, and 1979 by Simon & Schuster, in 1978 and 1977 by Information Please Publishing, Inc., and from 1947–1976 by Dan Golenpaul Associates.

New! The Information Please Almanac on floppy disk!

As this book is going to press, Houghton Mifflin Company is finalizing plans for a software edition of The 1994 Information Please Almanac. For more information, please send your name, address, and phone number to: Houghton Mifflin Company, 222 Berkeley Street, Boston, MA 02116. ATTN: Software Division—11th floor.

Copies of Information Please Almanac may be ordered directly by mail from: Customer Service Department, Houghton Mifflin Company, Burlington, Ma 01803. Phone toll-free, (800) 225-3362 for price and shipping information. In Massachusetts phone: 272-1500.

INFORMATION PLEASE ALMANAC®
Editorial Office
Houghton Mifflin Company
215 Park Avenue South
New York, N.Y. 10003

Printed in the United States of America

WP Pa BP Hbd 10 9 8 7 6 5 4 3 2 1

PROFILE OF THE UNITED STATES

GEOGRAPHY

Number of states: 50
Total area (1990): 3,787,425 sq mi.; land area, 3,536,341 sq mi.; water area, 251,083 sq mi. Share of world land area (1990): 6.2%
Comparative area: about one-third the size of Africa; about one-half the size of South America (or slightly larger than Brazil); slightly smaller than China; about two and one-half times the size of Western Europe.
Largest state: Alaska, total area, 656,424 sq mi.; land area, 570,374 sq mi.
Smallest state: Rhode Island, total area, 1,545 sq mi.; land area, 1,045 sq mi.
Northernmost point: Point Barrow, Alaska
Easternmost point: West Quoddy Head, Maine
Southernmost point: Ka Lae (South Cape), Hawaii
Westernmost point: Pochnoi Point, Alaska[1]
Geographic center: in Butte County, S.D. (44" 58' N. lat., 103" 46' W. long.)

1. The extreme points are measured from the geographic center of the United States (incl. Alaska and Hawaii), west of Castle Rock, S.D. 44° 58′ N. lat., 103° 46′ W. long. If measured from the prime meridian in Greenwich, England Pochnoi Point, Alaska would be the easternmost point.

POPULATION

Total (est. mid-1993): 258,300,000
Center of population (1990): 9.7 miles northwest of Steelville in Crawford County, Missouri.
Males (1990): 121,239,418
Females (1990): 127,470,455
White (1990): 199,686,070
Black (1990): 29,986,060
Hispanic origin (can be of any race) (1990): 22,354,059
American Indian, Eskimo, Aleut (1990): 22,354,059
Asian or Pacific Islander (1990): 7,273,662
Other race (1990): 9,804,443
Breakdown by age groups (1990):
  Under 5 years: 18,354,443
  5–17 years: 45,249,989
  18–20 years: 11,726,868
  21–24 years: 15,010,835
  25–44 years: 80,754,835
  45–54 years: 25,223,087
  55–59 years: 10,531,756
  60–64 years: 10,616,167
  65–74 years: 18,106,558
  75–84 years: 10,055,108
  85 and over: 3,080,165
Median age (1990): 32.9
Baby boomers (Nov. 1992): 77,000,000
Rural population (1990): 66,964,000
Metropolitan population (1990): 192,725,741
Total households (1990): 91,947,410
Family households (1990): 64,517,947
Non-family households (1990): 27,429,463
Average no. of persons per household (1990): 2.63
Average family size (1990): 3.17
No. of owner households (1990): 59,846,000
Est. homeless individuals any given night: 500,000–600,000; homeless families: 125,000–150,000.
Unmarried households (1990): 2,856,000
Single parent (1990): female, 6,599,000; male, 1,153,000
Families maintained by women only (1992): 11,692,000

Widows (1990): 11,477,000
Widowers (1990): 2,333,000
Childbearing: Never-married mothers 18–44 years (June 1992): 24%; African-American, 67%; Hispanic, 27%; White, 17%. Out of wedlock teenage births, 15–19 years: 65%; African-American, 94%; Hispanic, 60%; White, 56%.
Gays and lesbians: Official numbers not available. Surveys range from 1–10% of population. Gay and lesbian parents: Official figures not available. Children of gay and lesbian parents: estimates range from 1 to 40 to 1 in 70.

RELIGION

Protestant 61% (Baptist 21%, Methodist 12%, Lutheran 8%, Presbyterian 4%, Episcopalian 3%, other Protestant 13%), Roman Catholic 25%, Jewish 2%, other 5%, none 7%

VITAL STATISTICS

Births (est. 1992): 4,084,000. Births to unmarried women (1990): 1,165,400.
Deaths (est. 1992): 2,177,000
Leading cause of death (1990): heart disease, about 930,000 Americans
Marriages (est. 1992): 2,362,000. Married couples (March 1992): 52,457,000
Median age at first marriage (1992): male, 26.5; female, 24.4
Interracial marriages (1991): 994,000
Divorces (est. 1992): 1,215,000
Infant mortality rate (est. 1992): 10/1,000
Legal abortions (1988): 1,590,750
Life expectancy at birth (1992): 72 years male, 79 years female
Persons without health insurance (1990): 35 million (13% of population)
Total AIDS cases reported as of June 1993: 315,390, of these, 194,334 deaths reported.
Hate crimes officially reported (1991): 4,558
Child neglect and abuse (1987): 2,178,384 children reported; 1,404,242 families reports

CIVILIAN LABOR FORCE

Labor force (June 1993): 127,500,000
Nation's largest employer: U.S. Government, about 3 million Federal employees

(continued on page 6)

CONTENTS

SPECIAL SECTIONS

USING THIS ALMANAC

Information Please Almanac is divided topically into 55 major sections which cover the scope of the *Almanac*. Readers can quickly locate most of the facts they are seeking by turning directly to the appropriate section. For example, the TAXES section will contain the latest data on the Federal Income Tax. Information on Social Security and Medicare can be found in the SOCIAL SECURITY & AGING section. Current postage information can be located in the special POSTAGE section. In addition, the thumb tabs on the front and back covers permit fast access to the information you need.

To find a particular fact, date, or idea in the Comprehensive Index, one should begin by looking under the most specific word. For example, to find the population of Des Moines, one should start by looking for Des Moines. But that city is not listed separately. Therefore, the next step is to look under Iowa or Cities, U.S. Under Iowa, the designated page (761) gives the latest population for Des Moines. Under Cities, U.S., there is a sub-head, Population figures, with two alternatives: Largest (of which Des Moines is not one) and Largest by State (which refers back to Iowa).

For President George Washington, one should look under Washington, before checking President. Where general headings (such as Presidents, U.S.) are given, they refer to a section where the subject is treated at some length.

SPECIAL ARTICLES

PROFILE OF THE UNITED STATES

(continued from page 3)

Women in civilian labor force, 16 years and over (1992): 57,798,000; 45.5% of population
Unemployment rate (June 1993): 7.0%
Work at home (telecommuters, est. 1993): 7.6 million
Est. child care cost, families with working mothers (1988): $21 billion; avg. weekly cost per family: $54
Farms (est. 1992): 2,095,740; total acres: 980,063,000. Farm population (July 1991): 4,632,000; percent of civilian population, 1.8%
Small non-farm business establishments (1991): 6,199,339; with less than 10 employees, 4,613,125; employment, 92.8 million people; average annual salary, $23,200. Type of businesses: service, 32%; retail trade, 21.2%; manufacturing, 19.9%

INCOME AND CREDIT

The public debt (1992): $4,002,669 million; per capita: $15,650
Gross domestic product (1992): $5,950.7 billion
Per capita gross domestic product (1992): $23,296. U.S. trade deficit (July 1993): $10.34 billion; annual rate of deficit, $114.8 billion; deficit gap (1992): 84.5 billion
Federal budget (est. 1994): total receipts, $1,251.3 billion; total outlays, $1,517.2 billion; total deficit, $265.9 billion
Per capita personal income (prel. 1992): $19,841
Median family income (1992): $35,776
Median single-home price (1992): $103,700
Persons below poverty level (1991): 35.7 million (14.2%)
Tax freedom day (1993): May 3, when the average American will have worked 123 days to pay off his federal, state, and local taxes.

EDUCATION

School enrollment, public and private (Oct. 1992): Nursery school, 2,899,000; Kindergarten, 4,130,000; Grades 1–8, 30,153,000; Grades 9–12, 13,105,000; College, 14,035,000
High school dropouts, 14–19 years (Oct. 1992): 1,165,000
College graduates (1991–92 est.): 1,105,000
Average annual 4-year college fees (1993): Public colleges, $2,257; private colleges, $11,025
Estimated public school teachers (1993): 2,482,000; elementary, 1,414,000; secondary, 1,067,000; total, private, elementary, and secondary school teachers (1993): 365,000
Average salary for public school teachers (1991–92): $34,413
Literacy: 98% (male 97%, female 98%) age 25 and over having completed 5 or more years of schooling (1989). *Source: CIA World Factbook.* A 1993 study reported that 50% of Americans are functionally illiterate—unable to use basic educational skills in everyday life situations.

ENERGY

Total energy production (1992): 67 quadrillion Btu, down 1.2%. Total energy consumption (1992): a record level of 82 quadrillion Btu. Total energy consumption per capita (1992): 323 Btu, up one million Btu. Net imports of energy (1992): 14 quadrillion Btu, up 7.9%. Hydroelectric power (1992): 239 billion Kilowatt-hours, down 13% due to drought in western states.

CONVENIENCES

Radio sets (1988): households with, 99%; average no. of radio sets per household, 5.6
Radio stations (1991): 8,051
Television stations (1991): 1,367
Registered motor vehicles (est. 1992): 143,823,000. Automobiles leased (1992): 24% of total cars delivered
Households with telephones (1988): 85,300,000 (93%)
Newspaper circulation (morning and evening, Sept. 30, 1992): 60,164,499
Cable television subscribers (est. January 1993): 57,200,340
TV households (est. January 1993): 93,100,000; 2 or more sets, 59,584,000
Households with VCRs (1989): 58,000,000
Yearly avg. household TV viewing per day (1991–1992): 7 hours 40 minutes
Personal home computers (est. 1992): 30 to 35 million

DRUG USE

Americans spent (est. 1990): illegal drugs, $40.4 billion; on alcohol products, $44 billion; on tobacco products, $37 billion
Domestic cannabis production (est. 1987): 3,500 metric tons, about 25% of available marijuana

TRANSPORTATION

Railroads: 167,972 mi.
Highways: 3,955,578 mi. including 55,082 expressways
Inland waterways: 25,483 mi. of navigable inland channels, exclusive of the Great Lakes (est.)
Pipelines: 171,381 mi. petroleum, 189,713 natural gas (1985)
Merchant marine: 396 ships (1,000 gross register ton or over). In addition there are 231 government-owned vessels
Airports: 14,177 total, 12,417 usable.
Civil air: 8,252 commercial multiengine transport aircraft, including 6,036 jet, 831 turboprop, 1,382 piston (1989)

MOST POPULOUS STATES (1990 CENSUS)

1. California, 29,760,021; 2. New York, 17,990,455; 3. Texas, 16,986,510; 4. Florida, 12,937,926; 5. Pennsylvania, 11,881,643; 6. Illinois, 11,430,602; 7. Ohio, 10,847,115; 8. Michigan, 9,295,297; 9. New Jersey, 7,730,188; 10. North Carolina, 6,628,637

MOST POPULOUS CITIES (1990 CENSUS)

1. New York, N.Y., 7,322,564; 2. Los Angeles, Calif., 3,485,398; 3. Chicago, Ill., 2,783,726; 4. Houston, Texas, 1,630,553; 5. Philadelphia, Pa., 1,585,577; 6. San Diego, Calif., 1,110,549; 7. Detroit, Mich., 1,027,974; 8. Dallas, Texas, 1,006,877; 9. Phoenix, Ariz., 983,403; 10. San Antonio, Texas, 935,933

COMPREHENSIVE INDEX

A

B

C

D

E

F

G

H

I

J

K

L

Q

R

S

T

U

X

Y

Z

ELECTIONS

The Hundred and Third Congress

Composition of 102nd and 103rd Congresses

	103rd Congress[1]				102nd Congress[1]			
	Dem.	Rep.	Male	Female	Dem.	Rep.	Male	Fem
Senate	55	45	93	7	57	43	98	
House[2]	258	176	388	47	268	166	407	

1. One independent member in the House. 2. There is one vacancy in the House as of August 20, 1993.

The Senate

Senior Senator is listed first. The dates in the first column indicate period of service. The date given in parentheses a the Senator's name is year of birth. All terms are for six years and expire in January. Mailing address of Senators: Senate, Washington, D.C. 20510.

ALABAMA
1979–97 Howell T. Heflin (D) (1921)
1987–99 Richard Shelby (D) (1934)
ALASKA
1968–97 Ted Stevens (R) (1923)
1981–99 Frank H. Murkowski (R) (1933)
ARIZONA
1977–95 Dennis DeConcini (D) (1937)
1987–99 John McCain (R) (1936)
ARKANSAS
1975–99 Dale Bumpers (D) (1925)
1979–97 David H. Pryor (D) (1934)
CALIFORNIA
1993–95 Dianne Feinstein (D) (1933)
1993–99 Barbara Boxer (D) (1940)
COLORADO
1991–97 Hank Brown (R) (1940)
1993–99 Ben Nighthorse Campbell (D) (1933)
CONNECTICUT
1981–99 Christopher J. Dodd (D) (1944)
1989–95 Joseph I. Lieberman (D) (1942)
DELAWARE
1971–95 William V. Roth, Jr. (R) (1921)
1973–97 Joseph R. Biden, Jr. (D) (1942)
FLORIDA
1987–99 Bob Graham (D) (1936)
1989–95 Connie Mack III (R) (1940)
GEORGIA
1972–97 Sam Nunn (D) (1938)
1993–99 Paul Coverdell (R) (1939)
HAWAII
1963–99 Daniel K. Inouye (D) (1924)
1990–95 Daniel K. Akaka (D) (1924)
IDAHO
1991–97 Larry E. Craig (R) (1945)
1993–99 Dirk Kempthorne (R) (1951)
ILLINOIS
1985–97 Paul Simon (D) (1928)
1993–99 Carol Moseley Braun (D) (1947)
INDIANA
1977–95 Richard G. Lugar (R) (1932)
1989–99 Dan Coats (R) (1943)
IOWA
1981–99 Charles E. Grassley (R) (1933)
1985–97 Tom Harkin (D) (1939)
KANSAS
1969–99 Robert J. Dole (R) (1923)
1978–97 Nancy Landon Kassebaum (R) (1932)
KENTUCKY
1974–99 Wendell H. Ford (D) (1924)
1985–97 Mitch McConnell (R) (1942)
LOUISIANA
1972–97 J. Bennett Johnson (D) (1932)
1987–99 John B. Breaux (D) (1944)
MAINE
1979–97 William S. Cohen (R) (1940)
1980–95 George J. Mitchell (D) (1933)
MARYLAND
1977–95 Paul Sarbanes (D) (1933)
1987–99 Barbara A. Mikulski (D) (1936)
MASSACHUSETTS
1962–95 Edward M. Kennedy (D) (1932)
1985–97 John F. Kerry (D) (1943)
MICHIGAN
1976–95 Donald W. Riegle, Jr. (D) (1938)
1979–97 Carl Levin (D) (1934)
MINNESOTA
1978–95 David F. Durenberger (R) (1934)
1991–97 Paul Wellstone (D) (1944)
MISSISSIPPI
1978–97 Thad Cochran (R) (1937)
1989–95 Trent Lott (R) (1941)
MISSOURI
1976–95 John C. Danforth (R) (1936)
1987–99 Christopher S. (Kit) Bond (R) (1939)
MONTANA
1978–97 Max Baucus (D) (1941)
1989–95 Conrad Burns (R) (1935)
NEBRASKA
1979–97 J. James Exon (D) (1921)
1989–95 Robert Kerrey (D) (1943)
NEVADA
1987–99 Harry M. Reid (D) (1939)
1989–95 Dick Bryan (D) (1937)
NEW HAMPSHIRE
1991–97 Robert C. Smith (R) (1941)
1993–99 Judd Gregg (R) (1947)
NEW JERSEY
1979–97 Bill Bradley (D) (1943)
1982–95 Frank R. Lautenberg (D) (1924)
NEW MEXICO
1973–97 Pete V. Domenici (R) (1932)
1983–95 Jeff Bingaman (D) (1943)
NEW YORK
1977–95 Daniel P. Moynihan (D) (1927)
1981–99 Alfonse M. D'Amato (R) (1937)
NORTH CAROLINA
1973–97 Jesse Helms (R) (1921)
1993–99 Lauch Faircloth (R) (1928)
NORTH DAKOTA
1993–95 Kent Conrad (D) (1948)
1987–99 Byron Dorgan (D) (1942)

OHIO
1974–99 John H. Glenn, Jr. (D) (1921)
1976–95 Howard M. Metzenbaum (D) (1917)
OKLAHOMA
1979–97 David L. Boren (D) (1941)
1981–99 Don Nickles (R) (1948)
OREGON
1967–97 Mark O. Hatfield (R) (1922)
1969–99 Bob Packwood (R) (1932)
PENNSYLVANIA
1981–99 Arlen Specter (R) (1930)
1991–95 Harris Wofford (D) (1926)
RHODE ISLAND
1961–97 Claiborne Pell (D) (1918)
1976–95 John H. Chafee (R) (1922)
SOUTH CAROLINA
1956–97 Strom Thurmond (R) (1902)
1966–99 Ernest F. Hollings (D) (1922)
SOUTH DAKOTA
1979–97 Larry Pressler (R) (1942)
1987–99 Thomas A. Daschle (D) (1947)
TENNESSEE
1977–95 James R. Sasser (D) (1936)
1993–95 Harlan Mathews (D) (1927)
TEXAS
1993–95 Kathryn A.B. Huchison (R) (1943)
1985–97 Phil Gramm (R) (1942)
UTAH
1977–95 Orrin G. Hatch (R) (1934)
1993–99 Robert Bennett (R)
VERMONT
1975–99 Patrick J. Leahy (D) (1940)
1989–95 James M. Jeffords (R) (1934)
VIRGINIA
1979–97 John W. Warner (R) (1927)
1989–95 Charles Robb (D) (1939)
WASHINGTON
1989–95 Slade Gorton (R) (1928)
1993–99 Patty Murray (D) (1950)
WEST VIRGINIA
1959–95 Robert C. Byrd (D) (1918)
1985–97 John D. (Jay) Rockefeller IV (D) (1937)
WISCONSIN
1989–95 Herbert Kohl (D) (1935)
1993–99 Russell D. Feingold, Jr. (D) (1953)
WYOMING
1977–95 Malcolm Wallop (R) (1933)
1979–97 Alan K. Simpson (R) (1931)

The House of Representatives

The numerals indicate the Congressional Districts of the states; the designation AL means At Large. All terms end January 1993. Mailing address of Representatives: House of Representatives, Washington, D.C. 20515.

ALABAMA
(7 Representatives)
1. H.L. (Sonny) Callahan (R)
2. Terry Everett (R)
3. Glen Browder (D)
4. Thomas Bevill (D)
5. Bud Cramer (D)
6. Spencer Bachus (R)
7. Earl F. Hilliard (D)

ALASKA
(1 Representative)
AL Don Young (R)

ARIZONA
(6 Representatives)
1. Sam Coppersmith (D)
2. Ed Pastor (D)
3. Bob Stump (R)
4. Jon Kyl (R)
5. Jim Kolbe (R)
6. Karan English (D)

ARKANSAS
(4 Representatives)
1. Blanche Lambert (D)
2. Ray Thornton (D)
3. Tim Hutchinson (R)
4. Jay Dickey (R)

CALIFORNIA
(52 Representatives)
1. Dan Hamburg (D)
2. Wally Herger (R)
3. Vic Fazio (D)
4. John T. Doolittle (R)
5. Robert T. Matsui (D)
6. Lynn Woolsey (D)
7. George Miller (D)
8. Nancy Pelosi (D)
9. Ronald V. Dellums (D)
10. Bill Baker (R)
11. Richard W. Pombo (R)
12. Tom Lantos (D)
13. Pete Stark (D)
14. Anna G. Eshoo (D)
15. Norman Y. Mineta (D)
16. Don Edwards (D)
17. Sam Farr (D)
18. Gary Condit (D)
19. Richard H. Lehman (D)
20. Calvin Dooley (D)
21. Bill Thomas (R)
22. Michael Huffington (R)
23. Elton Gallegly (R)
24. Anthony C. Beilenson (D)
25. Howard P. "Buck" McKeon (R)
26. Howard L. Berman (D)
27. Carlos J. Moorhead (R)
28. David Dreier (R)
29. Henry A. Waxman (D)
30. Xavier Becerra (D)
31. Matthew G. Martinez (D)
32. Julian C. Dixon (D)
33. Lucille Roybal-Allard (D)
34. Esteban E. Torres (D)
35. Maxine Waters (D)
36. Jane Harman (D)
37. Walter R. Tucker (D)
38. Steve Horn (R)
39. Ed Royce (R)
40. Jerry Lewis (R)
41. Jay C. Kim (R)
42. George E. Brown Jr. (D)
43. Mark A. Takano (D)
44. Al McCandless (R)
45. Dana Rohrabacher (R)
46. Robert K. Dornan (R)
47. C. Christopher Cox (R)
48. Ron Packard (R)
49. Lynn Schenk (D)
50. Bob Filner (D)
51. Randy "Duke" Cunningham (R)
52. Duncan Hunter (R)

COLORADO
(6 Representatives)
1. Patricia Schroeder (D)
2. David E. Skaggs (D)
3. Scott McInnis (R)
4. Wayne Allard (R)
5. Joel Hefley (R)
6. Daniel L. Schaefer (R)

CONNECTICUT
(6 Representatives)
1. Barbara B. Kennelly (D)
2. Sam Gejdenson (D)
3. Rose DeLauro (D)
4. Christopher H. Shays (R)
5. Gary Franks (R)
6. Nancy L. Johnson (R)

DELAWARE
(1 Representative)
AL Michael N. Castle (R)

FLORIDA
(23 Representatives)
1. Earl D. Hutto (D)
2. Pete Peterson (D)
3. Corrine Brown (D)
4. Tillie Fowler (R)
5. Karen L. Thurman (D)
6. Cliff Stearns (R)
7. John L. Mica (R)
8. Bill McCollum (R)
9. Michael Bilirakis (R)
10. C.W. Bill Young (R)
11. Sam M. Gibbons (D)
12. Charles T. Canady (R)
13. Dan Miller (R)
14. Porter J. Goss (R)
15. Jim Bacchus (D)
16. Tom Lewis (R)
17. Carrie Meek (D)
18. Ileana Ros-Lehtineor (R)
19. Harry A. Johnston (D)
20. Peter Deutsch (D)
21. Lincoln Diaz-Balart (R)
22. E. Clay Shaw Jr. (R)
23. Alcee L. Hastings (D)

GEORGIA
(11 Representatives)
1. Jack Kingston (R)
2. Sanford Bishop (D)
3. Mac Collins (R)
4. John Linder (R)
5. John Lewis (D)
6. Newt Gingrich (R)
7. George (Buddy) Darden (D)
8. J. Roy Rowland (D)
9. Nathan Deal (D)
10. Don Johnson (D)
11. Cynthia McKinney (D)

HAWAII
(2 Representatives)
1. Neil Abercrombie (D)
2. Patsy T. Mink (D)

IDAHO
(2 Representatives)
1. Larry LaRocco (D)
2. Michael D. Crapo (R)

ILLINOIS
(20 Representatives)
1. Bobby L. Rush (D)
2. Mel Reynolds (D)
3. William C. Lipinski (D)
4. Luis V. Gutierrez (D)
5. Dan Rostenkowski (D)
6. Henry J. Hyde (R)
7. Cardiss Collins (D)
8. Phillip M. Crane (R)
9. Sidney R. Yates (D)
10. John Porter (R)
11. George E. Sangmeister (D)
12. Jerry F. Costello (D)
13. Harris F. Fawell (R)
14. Dennis Hastert (R)
15. Thomas W. Ewing (R)
16. Donald Manzullo (R)
17. Lane Evans (D)
18. Robert H. Michel (R)
19. Glen Poshard (D)
20. Richard J. Durbin (D)

INDIANA
(10 Representatives)
1. Peter Visclosky (D)
2. Philip R. Sharp (D)
3. Tim Roemer (D)
4. Jill L. Long (D)
5. Steve Buyer (R)
6. Daniel Burton (R)
7. John T. Meyers (R)
8. Frank McCloskey (D)
9. Lee H. Hamilton (D)
10. Andrew Jacobs, Jr. (D)

IOWA
(5 Representatives)
1. Jim Leach (R)
2. Jim Nussle (R)
3. Jim Ross Lightfoot (R)
4. Neal Smith (D)
5. Fred Grandy (R)

KANSAS
(4 Representatives)
1. Pat Roberts (R)
2. James Slattery (D)
3. Jan Meyers (R)
4. Dan Glickman (D)

KENTUCKY
(6 Representatives)
1. Tom Barlo (D)
2. William H. Natcher (D)
3. Romano L. Mazzoli (D)
4. Jim Bunning (R)
5. Harold Rogers (R)
6. Scotty Baesler

LOUISIANA
(7 Representatives)
1. Robert L. Livingston, Jr. (R)
2. William J. Jefferson (D)
3. W.J. "Billy" Tauzin (D)
4. Cleo Fields (D)
5. Jim McCrery (R)
6. Richard H. Baker (R)
7. Jimmy Hayes (D)

MAINE
(2 Representatives)
1. Thomas H. Andrews (D)
2. Olympia J. Snowe (R)

MARYLAND
(8 Representatives)
1. Wayne T. Gilchrest (R)
2. Helen Delich Bentley (R)
3. Benjamin L. Cardin (D)
4. Albert R. Wynn (D)
5. Steny H. Hoyer (D)
6. Roscoe G. Bartlett (R)
7. Kweisi Mfume (D)
8. Constance A. Morella (R)

MASSACHUSETTS
(10 Representatives)
1. John W. Olver (D)
2. Richard E. Neal (D)
3. Peter I. Blute (R)
4. Barney Frank (D)
5. Martin T. Meehan (D)
6. Peter G. Torkildsen (R)
7. Edward J. Markey (D)
8. Joseph P. Kennedy II (D)
9. Joe Moakley (D)
10. Gerry E. Studds (D)

MICHIGAN
(16 Representatives)
1. Bart Stupak (D)
2. Peter Hoekstra (R)
3. Vacancy
4. Dave Camp (R)
5. James A. Barcia (D)
6. Fred Upton (R)
7. Nick Smith (R)
8. Bob Carr (D)
9. Dale Kildee (D)
10. David E. Bonior (D)
11. Joe Knollenberg (R)
12. Sander M. Levin (D)
13. William D. Ford (D)
14. John Conyers, Jr. (D)
15. Barbara-Rose Collins (D)
16. John D. Dingell (D)

MINNESOTA
(8 Representatives)
1. Timothy J. Penny (D)
2. David Minge (D)
3. Jim Ramstad (R)
4. Bruce F. Vento (D)
5. Martin Olav Sabo (D)
6. Rod Grams (R)
7. Collin C. Peterson (D)
8. James L. Oberstar (D)

MISSISSIPPI
(5 Representatives)
1. Jamie L. Whitten (D)
2. Bennie Thompson (D)
3. G.V. "Sonny" Montgomery (D)
4. Mike Parker (D)
5. Gene Taylor (D)

MISSOURI
(9 Representatives)
1. William L. Clay (D)
2. James M. Talent (R)
3. Richard A. Gephardt (D)
4. Ike Skelton (D)
5. Alan Wheat (D)
6. Pat Danner (D)
7. Mel Hancock (R)
8. Bill Emerson (R)
9. Harold L. Volkmer (D)

MONTANA
(1 Representatives)
AL Pat Williams (D)

NEBRASKA
(3 Representatives)
1. Doug Bereuther (R)
2. Peter Hoagland (D)
3. Bill Barrett (R)

NEVADA
(2 Representatives)
1. James Bilbray (D)
2. Barbara Vucanovich (R)

NEW HAMPSHIRE
(2 Representatives)
1. Bill Zeliff (R)
2. Dick Swett (D)

NEW JERSEY
(13 Representatives)
1. Robert E. Andrews (D)
2. William J. Hughes (D)
3. H. James Saxton (R)
4. Christopher H. Smith (R)
5. Marge Roukema (R)
6. Frank Pallone, Jr. (D)
7. Bob Franks (R)
8. Herbert C. Klein (D)
9. Robert G. Torricelli (D)
10. Donald M. Payne (D)
11. Dean A. Gallo (R)
12. Dick Zimmer (R)
13. Robert Menendez (D)

NEW MEXICO
(3 Representatives)
1. Steve H. Schiff (R)
2. Joe Skeen (R)
3. Bill Richardson (D)

NEW YORK
(31 Representatives)
1. George J. Hochbreuckner (D)
2. Rick A. Lazio (R)
3. Peter T. King (R)
4. David A. Levy (R)
5. Gary L. Ackerman (D)
6. Floyd H. Flake (D)
7. Thomas J. Manton (D)
8. Jerrold Nadler (D)
9. Charles E. Schumer (D)
10. Edolphus Towns (D)
11. Major R. Owens (D)
12. Nydia M. Velazquez (D)
13. Susan Molinari (R)
14. Carolyn B. Maloney (D)
15. Charles B. Rangel (D)
16. Jose E. Serrano (D)
17. Eliot L. Engel (D)
18. Nita M. Lowey (D)
19. Hamilton Fish, Jr. (R)
20. Benjamin A. Gilman (R)
21. Michael R. McNulty (D)
22. Gerald B.H. Solomon (R)
23. Sherwood Boehlert (R)
24. John M. McHugh (R)
25. James T. Walsh (R)
26. Maurice D. Hinchey (D)
27. Bill Paxon (R)
28. Louise M. Slaughter (D)
29. John L. LaFalce (D)
30. Jack Quinn (R)
31. Amory Houghton (R)

NORTH CAROLINA
(12 Representatives)
1. Eve Clayton (D)
2. Tim Valentine (D)
3. H. Martin Lancaster (D)
4. David Price (D)
5. Stephen L. Neal (D)
6. Howard Coble (R)
7. Charlie Rose (D)
8. W.G. "Bill" Hefner (D)
9. Alex McMillan (R)
10. Cass Ballenger (R)
11. Charles H. Taylor (R)
12. Melvin Watt (D)

NORTH DAKOTA
(1 Representative)
AL Earl Pomeroy (D)

OHIO
(19 Representatives)
1. David Mann (D)
2. Rob Portman (R)
3. Tony P. Hall (D)
4. Michael G. Oxley (R)
5. Paul E. Gillmor (R)
6. Ted Strickland (D)
7. David L. Hobson (R)
8. John A. Boehner (R)
9. Marcy Kaptur (D)
10. Martin R. Hoke (R)
11. Louis Stokes (D)
12. John R. Kasich (R)
13. Sherrod Brown (D)
14. Tom Sawyer (D)
15. Deborah Pryce (R)
16. Ralph Regula (R)
17. James A. Traficant, Jr. (D)
18. Douglas Applegate (D)
19. Earl D. Fingerhut (D)

OKLAHOMA
(6 Representatives)
1. James M. Inhofe (R)
2. Mike Synar (D)
3. Bill Brewster (D)
4. Dave McCurdy (D)
5. Ernest Jim Istook (R)
6. Glenn English (D)

OREGON
(5 Representatives)
1. Elizabeth Furse (D)
2. Bob Smith (R)
3. Ron Wyden (D)
4. Peter A. De Fazio (D)
5. Mike Kopetski (D)

PENNSYLVANIA
(21 Representatives)
1. Thomas M. Foglietta (D)
2. Lucien E. Blackwell (D)
3. Robert A. Borski (D)
4. Ron Klink (D)
5. William F. Clinger (R)
6. Tim Holden (D)
7. Curt Weldon (R)
8. Jim Greenwood (R)
9. Bud Shuster (R)
10. Joseph M. McDade (R)
11. Paul E. Kanjorski (D)
12. John P. Murtha (D)
13. Marjorie Margolies Mezvinsky (D)
14. William J. Coyne (D)
15. Paul McHale (D)
16. Robert S. Walker (R)
17. George W. Gekas (R)
18. Rick Santorum (R)
19. Bill Goodling (R)
20. Austin J. Murphy (D)
21. Tom Ridge (R)

RHODE ISLAND
(2 Representatives)
1. Ronald Machtley (R)
2. John F. Reed (D)

SOUTH CAROLINA
(6 Representatives)
1. Arthur Ravenel, Jr. (R)
2. Floyd D. Spence (R)
3. Butler Derrick (D)
4. Bob Inglis (R)
5. John M. Spratt, Jr. (D)
6. James E. Clyburn (D)

SOUTH DAKOTA
(1 Representative)
AL Tim Johnson (D)

TENNESSEE
(9 Representatives)
1. James H. Quillen (R)
2. John J. "Jimmy" Duncan Jr. (R)
3. Marilyn Lloyd (D)
4. Jim Cooper (D)
5. Bob Clement (D)
6. Bart Gordon (D)
7. Don Sundquist (R)
8. John Tanner (D)
9. Harold E. Ford (D)

TEXAS
(30 Representatives)
1. Jim Chapman (D)
2. Charles Wilson (D)
3. Sam Johnson (R)
4. Ralph M. Hall (D)
5. John Bryant (D)
6. Joe L. Barton (R)
7. Bill Archer (R)
8. Jack Fields (R)
9. Jack Brooks (D)
10. J.J. Pickle (D)
11. Chet Edwards (D)
12. Pete Green (D)
13. Bill Sarpalius (D)
14. Greg Laughlin (D)
15. E. "Kika" de la Garza (D)
16. Ronald R. Coleman (D)
17. Charles W. Stenholm (D)
18. Craig Washington (D)
19. Larry Combest (R)
20. Henry B. Gonzalez (D)
21. Lamar Smith (R)
22. Tom DeLay (R)
23. Henry Bonilla (R)
24. Martin Frost (D)
25. Michael A. Andrews (D)
26. Richard Armey (R)
27. Solomon P. Ortiz (D)
28. Frank Tejeda (D)
29. Gene Green (D)
30. Eddie Bernice Johnson (D)

UTAH
(3 Representatives)
1. James V. Hansen (R)
2. Karen Shepherd (D)
3. Bill Orton (D)

VERMONT
(1 Representative)
AL Bernard Sanders (Ind)

VIRGINIA
(11 Representatives)
1. Herbert H. Bateman (R)
2. Owen B. Pickett (D)
3. Robert C. Scott (D)
4. Norman Sisisky (D)
5. Louis F. Payne (D)
6. Robert W. Goodlatte (R)
7. Thomas J. Bliley, Jr. (R)
8. James P. Moran, Jr. (D)
9. Rich Boucher (D)
10. Frank R. Wolf (R)
11. Leslie L. Byrne (D)

WASHINGTON
(9 Representatives)
1. Maria Cantwell (D)
2. Al Swift (D)
3. Jolene Unsoeld (D)
4. Jay Inslee (D)
5. Thomas S. Foley (D)
6. Norm Dicks (D)
7. Jim McDermott (D)
8. Jennifer Dunn (R)
9. Mike Kreidler (D)

WEST VIRGINIA
(3 Representatives)
1. Alan B. Mollohan (D)
2. Robert Wise (D)
3. Nick J. Rahall II (D)

WISCONSIN
(9 Representatives)
1. Peter Barca (D)
2. Scott L. Klug (R)
3. Steve Gunderson (R)
4. Gerald D. Kleczka (D)
5. Thomas M. Barrett (D)
6. Tom Petri (R)
7. David R. Obey (D)
8. Toby Roth (R)
9. F. James Sensenbrenner, Jr. (R)

WYOMING
(1 Representative)
AL Craig Thomas (R)

Characteristics of Voters in 1992 Presidential Election

(in thousands)

Characteristic	Persons of voting age	Persons reporting they voted: Total	Persons reporting they voted: Percent	Persons reporting they did not vote
Male	88,557	53,312	60.2	35,245
Female	97,126	60,554	62.3	36,573
White	157,837	100,405	63.6	57,432
Black	21,039	11,371	54.0	9,668
Hispanic origin[1]	14,688	4,238	28.9	10,450
Age: 18–20	9,727	3,749	38.5	5,979
21–24	14,644	6,693	45.7	7,951
25–34	41,603	22,120	53.2	19,483
35–44	39,716	25,269	63.6	14,447
45–54	28,058	19,292	68.8	8,766
55–64	21,089	15,107	71.6	5,982
65–74	18,445	13,607	73.8	4,839
75 and over	12,401	8,030	64.8	4,371

Characteristic	Persons of voting age	Persons reporting they voted: Total	Persons reporting they voted: Percent	Persons reporting they did not vote
Northeast	38,329	23,448	61.2	14,881
Midwest	44,410	29,830	67.2	14,580
South	63,659	37,590	59.0	26,068
West	39,286	22,997	58.5	16,289
Education				
8 years or less	15,391	5,406	30.3	9,985
9–11 years	20,970	8,638	41.2	12,332
12 years	65,281	37,517	57.5	27,765
16 or more	37,351	30,236	81.5	7,115
Employed	116,290	74,138	63.8	42,152
Unemployed	8,263	3,820	46.2	4,444
Not in labor force	61,131	35,908	58.7	25,223
Total	**185,684**	**113,866**	**61.3**	**71,818**

1. Persons of Hispanic origin may be of any race. *Source:* Department of Commerce, Bureau of Commerce, Bureau of the Census, *Current Population Reports,* April 1993..

Senate and House Standing Committees, 103rd Congress

Committees of the Senate

Agriculture, Nutrition, and Forestry (18 members)
Chairman: Patrick J. Leahy (Vt.)
Ranking Rep.: Richard G. Luger (Ind.)

Appropriations (29 members)
Chairman: Robert C. Byrd (W.Va.)
Ranking Rep.: Mark O. Hatfield (Ore.)

Armed Services (20 members)
Chairman: Sam Nunn (Ga.)
Ranking Rep.: Strom Thurmond (S.C.)

Banking, Housing, and Urban Affairs (20 members)
Chairman: Donald W. Riegle (Mich.)
Ranking Rep.: Alfonse M. D'Amato (N.Y.)

Budget (21 members)
Chairman: James R. Sasser (Tenn.)
Ranking Rep.: Pete V. Domenici (N.M.)

Commerce, Science, and Transportation (20 members)
Chairman: Ernest F. Hollings (S.C.)
Ranking Rep.: John C. Danforth (Mo.)

Energy and Natural Resources (20 members)
Chairman: J. Bennett Johnston (La.)
Ranking Rep.: Malcolm Wallop (Wyom.)

Environment and Public Works (17 members)
Chairman: Max Baucus (Mont.)
Ranking Rep.: John H. Chafee (R.I.)

Finance (20 members)
Chairman: Daniel P. Moynihan (N.Y.)
Ranking Rep.: Bob Packwood (Ore.)

Foreign Relations (19 members)
Chairman: Claiborne Pell (R.I.)
Ranking Rep.: Jesse Helms (N.C.)

Governmental Affairs (13 members)
Chairman: John Glenn (Ohio)
Ranking Rep.: William V. Roth, Jr. (Del.)

Judiciary (18 members)
Chairman: Joseph R. Biden, Jr. (Del)
Ranking Rep.: Orrin G. Hatch (Utah)

Labor and Human Resources (17 members)
Chairman: Edward M. Kennedy (Mass.)
Ranking Rep.: Nancy L. Kassebaum (Kan.)

Rules and Administration (16 members)
Chairman: Wendell H. Ford (Ky.)
Ranking Rep.: Ted Stevens (Alas.)

Small Business (18 members)
Chairman: Dale Bumpers (Ark.)
Ranking Rep.: Larry Pressler (S.D.)

Veterans' Affairs (12 members)
Chairman: John Rockefeller (W.V.)
Ranking Rep: Frank Murkowski (Alas.)

Select and Special Committees

Aging (21 members)
Chairman: David H. Pryor (Ark.)
Ranking Rep.: William S. Cohen (Me.)

Ethics (6 members)
Chairman: Richard Bryan (Nev.)
Ranking Rep.: Mitch McConnell (Ky.)

Indian Affairs (16 members)
Chairman: Daniel K. Inouye (Hawaii)
Ranking Rep.: John McCain (Ariz.)

Intelligence (15 members)
Chairman: Dennis DeConcini (Ariz.)
Ranking Rep.: John Warner (Va.)

Committees of the House

Agriculture (45 members)
Chairman: E. (Kika) de la Garza (Texas)
Ranking Rep.: Pat Roberts (Kan.)

Appropriations (60 members)
Chairman: William H. Natcher (Ky.)
Ranking Rep.: Joseph M. McDade (Pa.)

Armed Services (55 members)
Chairman: Ronald V. Dellums (Calif.)
Ranking Rep.: Floyd D. Spence (S.C.)

Banking, Finance, and Urban Affairs (50 members)
Chairman: Henry B. Gonzalez (Texas)
Ranking Rep.: Jim Leach (Iowa)

Budget (42 members)
Chairman: Martin O. Sabo (Mich.)
Ranking Rep.: John R. Kasich (Ohio)

District of Columbia (11 members)
Chairman: Pete Stark (Calif.)
Ranking Rep.: Thomas J. Bliley, Jr. (Va.)

Education and Labor (39 members)
Chairman: William D. Ford (Mich.)
Ranking Rep.: William F. Goodling (Pa.)

Energy and Commerce (44 members)
Chairman: John D. Dingell (Mich.)
Ranking Rep.: Carlos J. Moorhead (Calif.)

Foreign Affairs (44 members)
Chairman: Lee H. Hamilton (Ind.)
Ranking Rep.: Benjamin A. Gilman (N.Y.)

Government Operations (44 members)
Chairman: John Conyers, Jr. (Mich.)
Ranking Rep.: William F. Clinger (Pa.)

House Administration (19 members)
Chairman: Charlie Rose (N.C.)
Ranking Rep: William M. Thomas (Calif.)

Judiciary (35 members)
Chairman: Jack Brooks (Texas)
Ranking Rep.: Hamilton Fish, Jr. (N.Y.)

Merchant Marine and Fisheries (46 members)
Chairman: Gerry E. Studds (Mass.)
Ranking Rep.: Jack Fields (Texas)

Natural Resources (39 members)
Chairman: George Miller (Calif.)
Ranking Rep.: Don Young (Alas.)

Post Office and Civil Service (24 members)
Chairman: William (Bill) Clay (Mo.)
Ranking Rep.: John T. Myers (Ind.)

Public Works and Transportation (63 members)
Chairman: Norman Y. Mineta (Calif.)
Ranking Rep.: Bud Shuster (Pa.)

Rules (13 members)
Chairman: John Joseph Moakley (Mass.)
Ranking Rep.: Gerald B.H. Solomon (N.Y.)

Science, Space, and Technology (55 members)
Chairman: George E. Brown, Jr. (Calif.)
Ranking Rep.: Robert S. Walker (Pa.)

Small Business (45 members)
Chairman: John J. LaFalce (N.Y.)
Ranking Rep.: Jan Meyers (Kan.)

Standards of Official Conduct (14 members)
Chairman: James McDermott (Wash.)
Ranking Rep.: Fred Grandy (Iowa)

Veterans' Affairs (35 members)
Chairman: G. V. (Sonny) Montgomery (Miss.)
Ranking Rep.: Bob Stump (Ariz.)

Ways and Means (38 members)
Chairman: Dan Rostenkowski (Ill.)
Ranking Rep.: William Archer (Texas)

Select Committee

Intelligence (19 members)
Chairman: Dan Glickman (Kan.)
Ranking Rep.: Larry Combest (Texas)

Speakers of the House of Representatives

Dates served	Congress	Name and State	Dates served	Congress	Name and State
1789–1791	1	Frederick A. C. Muhlenberg (Pa.)	1869–1869	40	Theodore M. Pomeroy (N.Y.)[5]
1791–1793	2	Jonathan Trumbull (Conn.)	1869–1875	41–43	James G. Blaine (Me.)
1793–1795	3	Frederick A. C. Muhlenberg (Pa.)	1875–1876	44	Michael C. Kerr (Ind.)[6]
1795–1799	4–5	Jonathan Dayton (N.J.)[1]	1876–1881	44–46	Samuel J. Randall (Pa.)
1799–1801	6	Theodore Sedgwick (Mass.)	1881–1883	47	J. Warren Keifer (Ohio)
1801–1807	7–9	Nathaniel Macon (N.C.)	1883–1889	48–50	John G. Carlisle (Ky.)
1807–1811	10–11	Joseph B. Varnum (Mass.)	1889–1891	51	Thomas B. Reed (Me.)
1811–1814	12–13	Henry Clay (Ky.)[2]	1891–1895	52–53	Charles F. Crisp (Ga.)
1814–1815	13	Langdon Cheves (S.C.)	1895–1899	54–55	Thomas B. Reed (Me.)
1815–1820	14–16	Henry Clay (Ky.)[3]	1899–1903	56–57	David B. Henderson (Iowa)
1820–1821	16	John W. Taylor (N.Y.)	1903–1911	58–61	Joseph G. Cannon (Ill.)
1821–1823	17	Philip P. Barbour (Va.)	1911–1919	62–65	Champ Clark (Mo.)
1823–1825	18	Henry Clay (Ky.)	1919–1925	66–68	Frederick H. Gillett (Mass.)
1825–1827	19	John W. Taylor (N.Y.)	1925–1931	69–71	Nicholas Longworth (Ohio)
1827–1834	20–23	Andrew Stevenson (Va.)[4]	1931–1933	72	John N. Garner (Tex.)
1834–1835	23	John Bell (Tenn.)	1933–1934	73	Henry T. Rainey (Ill.)[7]
1835–1839	24–25	James K. Polk (Tenn.)	1935–1936	74	Joseph W. Byrns (Tenn.)[8]
1839–1841	26	Robert M. T. Hunter (Va.)	1936–1940	74–76	William B. Bankhead (Ala.)[9]
1841–1843	27	John White (Ky.)	1940–1947	76–79	Sam Rayburn (Tex.)
1843–1845	28	John W. Jones (Va.)	1947–1949	80	Joseph W. Martin, Jr. (Mass.)
1845–1847	29	John W. Davis (Ind.)	1949–1953	81–82	Sam Rayburn (Tex.)
1847–1849	30	Robert C. Winthrop (Mass.)	1953–1955	83	Joseph W. Martin, Jr. (Mass.)
1849–1851	31	Howell Cobb (Ga.)	1955–1961	84–87	Sam Rayburn (Tex.)[10]
1851–1855	32–33	Linn Boyd (Ky.)	1962–1971	87–91	John W. McCormack (Mass.)[11]
1855–1857	34	Nathaniel P. Banks (Mass.)	1971–1977	92–94	Carl Albert (Okla.)[12]
1857–1859	35	James L. Orr (S.C.)	1977–1987	95–99	Thomas P. O'Neill, Jr. (Mass.)[13]
1859–1861	36	Wm. Pennington (N.J.)	1987–1989	100–101	James C. Wright, Jr. (Tex.)[14]
1861–1863	37	Galusha A. Grow (Pa.)	1989–	101–	Thomas S. Foley (Wash.)
1863–1869	38–40	Schuyler Colfax (Ind.)			

1. George Dent (Md.) was elected Speaker pro tempore for April 20 and May 28, 1798. 2. Resigned during second session of 13th Congress. 3. Resigned between first and second sessions of 16th Congress. 4. Resigned during first session of 23rd Congress. 5. Elected Speaker and served the day of adjournment. 6. Died between first and second sessions of 44th Congress. During first session, there were two Speakers pro tempore: Samuel S. Cox (N.Y.), appointed for Feb. 17, May 12, and June 19, 1876, and Milton Sayler (Ohio), appointed for June 4, 1876. 7. Died in 1934 after adjournment of second session of 73rd Congress. 8. Died during second session of 74th Congress. 9. Died during third session of 76th Congress. 10. Died between first and second sessions of 87th Congress. 11. Not a candidate in 1970 election. 12. Not a candidate in 1976 election. 13. Not a candidate in 1986 election. 14. Resigned during first session of 101st Congress. *Source: Congressional Directory.*

Floor Leaders of the Senate

Democratic	Republican
Gilbert M. Hitchcock, Neb. (Min. 1919–20)	Charles Curtis, Kan. (Maj. 1925–29)
Oscar W. Underwood, Ala. (Min. 1920–23)	James E. Watson, Ind. (Maj. 1929–33)
Joseph T. Robinson, Ark. (Min. 1923–33, Maj. 1933–37)	Charles L. McNary, Ore. (Min. 1933–44)
Alben W. Barkley, Ky. (Maj. 1937–46, Min. 1947–48)	Wallace H. White, Jr., Me. (Min. 1944–47, Maj. 1947–48)
Scott W. Lucas, Ill. (Maj. 1949–50)	Kenneth S. Wherry, Neb. (Min. 1949–51)
Ernest W. McFarland, Ariz. (Maj. 1951–52)	Styles Bridges, N. H. (Min. 1951–52)
Lyndon B. Johnson, Tex. (Min. 1953–54, Maj. 1955–60)	Robert A. Taft, Ohio (Maj. 1953)
Mike Mansfield, Mont. (Maj. 1961–77)	William F. Knowland, Calif. (Maj. 1953–54, Min. 1955–58)
Robert C. Byrd, W. Va. (Maj. 1977–81, Min. 1981–86, Maj. 1987–88)	Everett M. Dirksen, Ill. (Min. 1959–69)
George John Mitchell, Me. (Maj. 1989–)	Hugh Scott, Pa. (Min. 1969–1977)
	Howard H. Baker, Jr., Tenn. (Min. 1977–81, Maj. 1981–84)
	Robert J. Dole, Kan. (Maj. 1985–86, Min. 1987–)

NOTE: Min. = Minority Leader; Maj. = Majority Leader. *Source:* United States Senate, Secretary for the Majority.

Presidential Election of 1992

Principal Candidates for President and Vice President
Republican: George H. Bush; J. Danforth Quayle
Democratic: William J. Clinton; Albert A. Gore, Jr.
Independent: H. Ross Perot; James B. Stockdale

State	Total	*Bush* Rep.	Percent	*Clinton* Dem.	Percent	*Perot* Ind.	Percent	Plurality	Electoral vote D	R	I
Alabama	1,688,060	804,283	48	690,080	41	183,109	11	114,203R	—	9	—
Alaska	258,506	102,000	39	78,294	30	73,481	28	23,706R	—	3	—
Arizona	1,486,975	572,086	38	543,050	37	353,741	24	29,036R	—	8	—
Arkansas	950,653	337,324	35	505,823	53	99,132	10	168,499D	6	—	—
California	11,131,721	3,630,574	33	5,121,325	46	2,296,006	21	1,490,751D	54	—	—
Colorado	1,569,180	562,850	36	629,681	40	366,010	23	66,831D	8	—	—
Connecticut	1,616,332	578,313	36	682,318	42	348,771	22	104,005D	8	—	—
Delaware	289,735	102,313	35	126,055	44	59,213	20	23,742D	3	—	—
D.C.	227,572	20,698	9	192,619	85	9,681	4	171,921D	3	—	—
Florida	5,314,492	2,173,310	41	2,072,798	39	1,053,067	20	100,512R	—	25	—
Georgia	2,321,125	995,252	43	1,008,966	43	309,657	13	13,714D	13	—	—
Hawaii	372,842	136,822	37	179,310	48	53,003	14	42,488D	4	—	—
Idaho	482,142	202,645	42	137,013	28	130,395	27	65,632R	—	4	—
Illinois	5,050,157	1,734,096	34	2,453,350	49	840,515	17	719,254D	22	—	—
Indiana	2,305,871	989,375	43	848,420	37	455,934	20	140,955R	—	12	—
Iowa	1,354,607	504,891	37	586,353	43	253,468	19	81,462D	7	—	—
Kansas	1,157,236	449,951	39	390,434	34	312,358	27	59,517R	—	6	—
Kentucky	1,492,900	617,178	41	665,104	45	203,944	14	47,926D	8	—	—
Louisiana	1,790,017	733,386	41	815,971	46	211,478	12	82,585D	9	—	—
Maine	679,499	206,504	30	263,420	39	206,820	30	56,600D	4	—	—
Maryland	1,985,046	707,094	36	988,571	50	281,414	14	281,477D	10	—	—
Massachusetts	2,773,664	805,039	29	1,318,639	48	630,731	23	513,600D	12	—	—
Michigan	4,274,673	1,554,940	36	1,871,182	44	824,813	19	316,242D	18	—	—
Minnesota	2,347,947	747,841	32	1,020,997	43	562,506	24	273,156D	10	—	—
Mississippi	981,793	487,793	50	400,258	41	85,626	9	87,535R	—	7	—
Missouri	2,391,565	811,159	34	1,053,873	44	518,741	22	242,714D	11	—	—
Montana	410,611	144,207	35	154,507	38	107,225	26	10,300D	3	—	—
Nebraska	739,283	344,346	47	217,344	29	174,687	24	127,002R	—	5	—
Nevada	506,318	175,828	35	189,148	37	132,580	26	13,320D	4	—	—
New Hampshire	537,945	202,484	38	209,040	39	121,337	23	6,556D	4	—	—
New Jersey	3,343,594	1,356,865	41	1,436,206	43	521,829	16	79,341D	15	—	—
New Mexico	569,986	212,824	37	261,617	46	91,895	16	48,793D	5	—	—
New York[1]	6,926,933	2,346,649	34	3,444,450	50	1,090,721	16	1,097,801D	33	—	—
North Carolina	2,611,850	1,134,661	43	1,114,042	43	357,864	14	20,619R	—	14	—
North Dakota	308,133	136,244	44	99,168	32	71,084	23	37,076R	—	3	—
Ohio	4,939,964	1,894,310	38	1,984,942	40	1,036,426	21	90,632D	21	—	—
Oklahoma	1,390,359	592,929	43	473,066	34	319,878	23	119,863R	—	8	—
Oregon	1,462,643	475,757	33	621,314	42	354,091	24	145,557D	7	—	—
Pennsylvania	4,959,810	1,791,841	36	2,239,164	45	902,667	18	447,323D	23	—	—
Rhode Island	453,478	131,605	29	213,302	47	105,051	23	81,697D	4	—	—
South Carolina	1,202,527	577,507	48	479,514	40	138,872	12	97,993R	—	8	—
South Dakota	336,254	136,718	41	124,888	37	73,295	22	11,830R	—	3	—
Tennessee	1,982,638	841,300	42	933,521	47	199,968	10	92,221D	11	—	—
Texas	6,154,018	2,496,071	41	2,281,815	37	1,354,781	22	214,256R	—	32	—
Utah	743,999	322,632	43	183,429	25	203,400	27	119,232R	—	5	—
Vermont	289,701	88,122	30	133,592	46	65,991	23	45,470D	3	—	—
Virginia	2,558,665	1,150,517	45	1,038,650	41	348,639	14	111,867R	—	13	—
Washington	2,288,228	731,235	32	993,039	43	541,801	24	261,804D	11	—	—
West Virginia	683,711	241,974	35	331,001	48	108,829	16	89,027D	5	—	—
Wisconsin	2,531,114	930,855	37	1,041,066	41	544,479	22	110,211D	11	—	—
Wyoming	200,587	79,347	40	68,160	34	51,263	26	11,187R	—	3	—
Total	**104,426,659**	**39,104,545**	**37**	**44,909,899**	**43**	**19,742,267**	**19**	**5,805,345D**	**370**	**168**	—

1. Bush figure is combined Republican, Conservative, and Right to Life Party votes; Clinton figure is combined Democratic and Liberal Party votes. NATIONAL TOTALS OF OTHER CANDIDATES FOR PRESIDENT: Andre Marrow, Libertarian, 291,628; James "Bo" Gritz, Populist/America First, 107,002; Lenora Fulani, New Alliance, 73,708; Howard Phillips, U.S. Taxpayers, 43,398; John Hagelin, Natural Law, 39,163; Ron Daniels, Independent, 27,969; Lyndon LaRouche, Independent, 26,334; James Mac Warren, Socialist Workers, 23,091; Drew Bradford, Independent, 4,749; Jack Herer, Grassroots, 3,875; John Quinn Brisben, Socialist, 3,064; Helen Halyard, Workers League, 3,050; John Yiamouyiannis, Independent, 2,199; Delbert Ehlers, Independent, 1,149; Earl Dodge, Prohibition, 961; Jim Boren, Apathy, 956; Eugene Hem, Third Party, 405; Isabelle Masters, Looking Back Group, 339; Robert J. Smith, American, 293; Gloria Estella La Riva, Workers World, 181; None of These Candidates, Nevada, 2,537; write-ins, 13,907. *Source:* Federal Election Commission.

The Governors of the Fifty States

State	Governor	Current term[1]	State	Governor	Current term[1]
Ala.	Jim Folson, Jr. (D)	1993–95	Mont.	Mark Racicot (R)	1993–97
Alaska	Walter Hickel (Ind.)	1990–94[2]	Neb.	Ben Nelson (D)	1991–95
Ariz.	Fife Symington (R)	1991–95	Nev.	Bob Miller (D)	1991–95
Ark.	Jim Guy Tucker (D)	1993–95	N.H.	Steve Merrill (R)	1993–95
Calif.	Pete Wilson (R)	1991–95	N.J.	James Florio (D)	1990–94
Colo.	Roy Romer (D)	1991–95	N.M.	Bruce King (D)	1991–95
Conn.	Lowell P. Weicker Jr. (Ind.)	1991–95	N.Y.	Mario M. Cuomo (D)	1991–95
Del.	Tom Carper (D)	1993–97	N.C.	Jim Hunt (D)	1993–97
Fla.	Lawton Chiles (D)	1991–95	N.D.	Ed Schafer (R)	1993–97
Ga.	Zell Miller (D)	1991–95	Ohio	George Voinovich (R)	1991–95
Hawaii	John Waihee (D)	1990–94[2]	Okla.	David Walters (D)	1991–95
Idaho	Cecil D. Andrus (D)	1991–95	Ore.	Barbara Roberts (D)	1991–95
Ill.	Jim Edgar (R)	1991–95	Pa.	Robert P. Casey (D)	1991–95
Ind.	B. Evan Bayh III (R)	1989–97	R.I.	Bruce Sundlun (D)	1991–93
Iowa	Terry E. Branstad (R)	1991–95	S.C.	Carroll A. Campbell, Jr. (R)	1991–95
Kan.	Joan Finney (D)	1991–95	S.D.	Walter Dale Miller (R)	1993–95
Ky.	Brereton C. Jones (D)	1991–95[2]	Tenn.	Ned McWherter (D)	1991–95
La.	Edwin W. Edwards (D)	1992–96	Tex.	Ann Richards (D)	1991–95
Me.	John R. McKernan, Jr. (R)	1991–95	Utah	Mike Leavitt (R)	1993–97
Md.	William Donald Schaefer (D)	1991–95	Vt.	Howard Dean (D)	1991–95
Mass.	William F. Weld (R)	1991–95	Va.	L. Douglas Wilder (D)	1990–94
Mich.	John Engler (R)	1991–95	Wash.	Mike Lowry (D)	1993–97
Minn.	Arne Carlson (R)	1991–95	W. Va.	Gaston Caperton (D)	1989–97
Miss.	Kirk Fordice (R)	1992–96	Wis.	Tommy G. Thompson (R)	1991–95
Mo.	Mel Carnahan (D)	1993–97	Wyo.	Mike J. Sullivan (D)	1991–95

1. Except where indicated, all terms begin in January. 2. December.

Black Elected Officials

Year	U.S. and State Legislatures[1]	City and County Offices[2]	Law Enforcement[3]	Education[4]	Total
1970 (Feb.)	182	715	213	362	1,472
1975 (Apr.)	299	1,878	387	939	3,503
1980 (July)	326	2,832	526	1,206	4,890
1981 (July)	343	2,863	549	1,259	5,014
1982 (July)	342	2,951	563	1,259	5,115
1983 (July)	366	3,197	607	1,369	5,559
1984 (Jan.)	396	3,259	636	1,363	5,654
1985 (Jan.)	407	3,517	661	1,431	6,016[5]
1986 (Jan.)	420	3,824	676	1,504	6,424[5]
1987 (Jan.)	440	3,966	728	1,547	6,681
1988 (July)	436	4,105	738	1,550	6,829
1989 (Jan.)	448	4,406	759	1,612	7,225
1990 (Jan.)	447	4,499	769	1,655	7,370
1991 (Jan.)	484	4,508	847	1,638	7,480
1992 (Jan.)	510	4,569	847	1,623	7,549[6]
1993 (Jan.)	571	4,825	923	1,694	8,016[6]

1. Includes elected State administrators and governors. 2. County commissioners and councilmen, mayors, vice mayors, aldermen, regional officials, and other. 3. Judges, magistrates, constables, marshals, sheriffs, justices of the peace, and other. 4. Members of State education agencies, college boards, school boards, and other. 5. Includes Black elected officials in the Virgin Islands. 6. Includes two statehood senators and one statehood representative, all non-voting, from the District of Columbia. *Source:* Joint Center for Political and Economic Studies, Washington, D.C., *Black Elected Officials: A National Roster,* Copyright.

1993 Annual Salaries of Federal Officials

President of the U.S.	$200,000[1]	Senators and Representatives	$133,600
Vice President of the U.S.	171,500[2]	President Pro Tempore of Senate	148,400
Cabinet members	148,400	Majority and Minority Leader of the Senate	148,400
Deputy Secretaries of State, Defense, Treasury	133,600	Majority and Minority Leader of the House	148,400
Deputy Attorney General	133,600	Speaker of the House	171,500
Secretaries of the Army, Navy, Air Force	133,600	Chief Justice of the United States	171,500
Under secretaries of executive departments	123,100	Associate Justices of the Supreme Court	164,100

1. Plus taxable $50,000 for expenses and a nontaxable sum (not to exceed $100,000 a year) for travel expenses. 2. Plus taxable $10,000 for expenses. NOTE: All salaries shown above are taxable. *Source:* Office of Personnel Management.

BUSINESS & ECONOMY

Telecommuting Comes of Age

More and more companies are installing high-tech telephone links to enable their employees to work at home and access the regular office computer. Benefits include reduced commuting costs and travel time, less fuel consumption and environmental pollution. Employers save on office space, utilities, and maintenance costs.

1993 Telecommuting Facts

Source: LINK Resources Corporation, 1993.

Total U.S. telecommuters	100%	7.6 million
Total U.S. telecommuter households	100%	5.8 million
Average annual growth rate		15% per year
Men (population total)	54%	4.1 million
Women (population total)	46%	3.5 million
Married/Couples (household total)	80%	4.6 million
Households with children under 18	49%	2.9 million
Selected occupational groups (population totals)		
All knowledge/ information workers	74%	5.6 million
Executives, managers	13%	1.0 million
Teachers	12%	910,000
Engineers, scientists	11%	858,000
Business professionals	11%	812,000
Households own PCs	55%	3.2 million
Households own modems	27%	1.5 million
Households own cellular phones	21%	1.2 million
Households own fax machines	14%	810,000

According to the annual LINK Resources National Work-at-Home Survey conducted in 1993, the number of company employees working at least part-time at home during normal business hours has reached 7.6 million. Known as "telecommuters," such employees typically spend one or two days per week working at home and rely increasingly on computers and telephone services to stay in touch with their regular offices. The trend grew 15% from 6.6 million found in LINK's 1992 annual telephone survey of 2,500 randomly selected U.S. households.

"Telecommuting continues to grow faster than any other form of work-at-home," said Thomas E. Miller, vice president of Home Office Research at LINK, commenting on the survey findings. "White collar participation is up, especially in mid-sized business, and use of computers has grown 27 percent.

LINK's latest data indicated that 6.1 percent of the adult U.S. work force now telecommute at least part-time, including 4.1 million men and 3.5 million women. Two-thirds of all telecommuter couples are dual career households. Just about 50 percent of the households involved in telecommuting have children under eighteen.

Information workers dominate the trend and comprise three-fourths of all telecommuters. The major increases in telecommuting noted in 1993 were among engineers, scientists, computer programmers, and teachers. By industry sector, the largest increases were in business and educational services.

Personal computers are now owned by over 55 percent of telecommuter households, or 3.2 million households. Altogether, LINK noted that telecommuters spent $4.7 billion for personal computers, fax machines, and telephone products, including telephone services.

Who Works at Home?

In 1993, the total number of homeworkers in the U.S. grew 5.4%, more than double the growth rate of the prior 12-month period. Individuals who began new home-based self-employment (either as a primary income source or part-time) totaled 3.1 million. Meanwhile, the number of homeworker households that own personal computers grew 27%, underscoring the importance of low-cost home office technologies in bolstering the work-at-home trend.

• **Primary Self-Employed Homeworkers—12.2 Million.** Self-employment is the primary source of income for these homeworkers, who typically operate home businesses or freelance as consultants and contract workers. Approximately 800,000 new homeworkers began in this workstyle segment in 1993, but 700,000 discontinued it due primarily to natural retirement or by returning to conventional employment.

• **Part-time Self-Employed Homeworkers—12.1 Million.** These homeworkers hold multiple jobs and work from home part of the time. Some 2.3 million *new* homeworkers began this form of home-based work in 1993, usually to supplement income, often as moonlighters. At the same time, some 1.9 million part-time self-employed homeworkers migrated either into full-time jobs or primary self-employment, resulting in a net workstyle gain of 400,000 in this segment over the past 12 months.

• **Telecommuters—7.6 Million.** Company employees who work from home part- or full-time *during normal business hours* are called "telecommuters." The net increase of 1 million telecommuters from 1992 reflects 15% average annual growth. LINK's studies confirm that most telecommuting is part-time and informal as knowledge workers in many industries look to gain added control over their work schedules. In 1993, mid-sized businesses doubled their share of telecommuting to 18% of the total.

• **High-Tech Corporate After-hours Homeworkers—9.2 Million.** This segment uses PCs, modems, fax machines, and/or extra phone lines to do company work at home *after* normal business hours. Healthy 7% annual growth in this segment reflects expanded after-hours business activity in the U.S. economy, spurring more briefcase workers to go "high tech." Personal computer penetration in this segment reached an astounding 70% level in 1993. □

Poverty in American History

Source: The Reader's Companion to American History.

Although Americans have long celebrated their nation's wealth and the abundance of its resources, poverty has been omnipresent in American history. From the colonial period to the present day, large numbers of Americans have been poor: they have lacked the resources to feed, clothe, and shelter themselves adequately according to socially defined standards. Just how many Americans have lived in poverty over the course of more than three centuries is impossible to gauge; not only are data scarce, but the definition of poverty has changed too often (and is too subject to debate) to permit precise measurement. Nonetheless, there can be no doubt that poverty, as a personal condition and as a social problem, has long been a prominent feature of the economic and social landscape.

Poverty was certainly widespread during the settlement decades of the seventeenth century. Most settlers in the New World had to contend with at least periodic material scarcity, and unfree laborers (slaves and indentured servants) always lived near the margins of subsistence. Seventeenth-century society also recognized the enduring presence of dependent and destitute individuals; by 1685, for example, the city of Boston had constructed an almshouse. Both the poor and the outright destitute (often the aged or infirm) were regarded as natural and inevitable components of our inherently hierarchical social order.

In the course of the eighteenth century, poverty became a more visible social problem, particularly in the port cities of the North. While farmers who lived on marginal lands continued to inhabit a world of scarcity, the urban centers witnessed a significant growth in the number of wage earners who became destitute whenever commerce flagged or serious economic dislocations occurred. In Boston, New York, and Philadelphia, for example, the number of people needing public assistance rose dramatically during and after the Seven Years' War. By the end of the century, according to some national estimates, virtually all African-Americans (slave and free) and between one-fifth and one-third of all whites lived in poverty.

Despite economic growth fueled by agricultural expansion and the Industrial Revolution, the problem of poverty did not become any less acute in the nineteenth century. Rural poverty persisted, particularly in the South; at the same time, the nation witnessed enormous population growth, rapid urbanization, and the formation of a large industrial working class most of whose members were either poor or could easily become so during hard times. It was in this century, particularly after 1870, that the social problem of poverty began to be identified primarily with urban society and crowded urban ghettos. In 1904, in his pioneering study, *Poverty,* Robert Hunter, citing Jacob Riis, noted that 10 percent of the people who died in New York City between 1885 and 1890 had been given a pauper's burial; he also claimed that 20 percent of the population of Boston lived in actual distress. In the nation as a whole, Hunter estimated that 10 million people, roughly12 percent of the population, were poor at the turn of the century. More recent analysts have concluded that Hunter's estimates—distressing as they may have been to contemporaries—were far too low, that, in fact, a broader definition of poverty would have embraced roughly 40 percent of all Americans in 1900.

The twentieth century witnessed a significant, yet unsteady, decline in the overall incidence of poverty (as well as a dramatic improvement in the acquisition of data bearing on the issue). Increases in real wages permitted many blue-collar Americans to cross the poverty line during the first quarter of the century, but the Great Depression reversed the gains that had been made. When Franklin D. Roosevelt proclaimed, in 1937, that "one-third" of the nation was "ill-housed, ill-clad, ill-nourished," he was understating the problem; in fact, the poverty rate was probably closer to 40 or 45 percent. After the Great Depression, however, the proportion of Americans living in poverty dropped sharply: according to government statistics, the figure stood at 30 percent in 1950, 20 percent in 1960, 13 percent in 1968, and 11 percent in 1973. Although these percentages meant that millions of people remained poor (23 million lived in official poverty in 1973), they suggested that the extraordinary growth of the economy between 1940 and the early 1970s was gradually eradicating the problem. Unfortunately, this benign statistical trend came to a halt in the 1970s and reversed itself after 1980. During the depression of the early 1980s, the poverty rate rose above 15 percent; in 1988, well after the depression had ended, it stood at 13 percent, reflecting the poverty of 32 million people—8 million more than had been officially poor a decade earlier.

Throughout these years, poverty afflicted some segments of the population far more than others. During the eighteenth and nineteenth centuries, more poor people lived in rural areas than in cities; although less visible and perhaps less dramatic, rural poverty was just as debilitating as its urban counterpart, and there were millions of rural families who experienced chronic or periodic distress well into the twentieth century. Many of these families eventually responded to their plight by migrating to the cities; indeed, after 1940, when technological transformations in agriculture precipitated a massive exodus from the land, the number of poor people living in rural areas declined substantially.

This exodus was most pronounced in the South, which had always been the nation's poorest region. In the late nineteenth century, poverty was far more widespread in all the southern states than in any others; as late as 1930, one-fourth of the population of the South lived in housing that typically lacked indoor plumbing, electricity, or running water. Only after World War II did the gap between the South and the rest of the country narrow noticeably, as a result both of the diversification of the Sunbelt economies and of the migration of poor southerners to other regions. This migration, indeed, symbolized the most pronounced cluster of changes in the United States: the problem has moved northward and from the countryside to the cities.

In both urban and rural America, poverty has always been more common among nonwhites than among whites; from the eighteenth century through the mid-twentieth century, most African-Americans were among the rural poor. And during key periods, poverty was also much more common among immigrants than among the native-born, particularly in cities: the poor, in nineteenth-century cities, tended to be disproportionately Irish, Italian, eastern European, or French Canadian. In key respects, these tendencies have proved to be durable; as recently as 1988, the poverty rates for African-Americans and for people of Hispanic background were roughly triple the rate for whites.

Two other dimensions of the distribution of poverty warrant mention. First, throughout the eighteenth and nineteenth centuries, the elderly constituted a relatively high percentage of the poor or, at least, the dependent poor. But in the mid-twentieth century, as a result of both private pension plans and the Social Security system, the incidence of poverty among the elderly declined. And second, at roughly the same time, the problem became increasingly rampant among women and children. In 1988, more than half of all poor families were headed by women, and nearly 40 percent of the nation's poor were children.

The most significant policy changes to occur in modern American history were those promulgated during the New Deal. Responsibility for providing aid to the poor was, to a considerable degree, shifted from municipalities and states to the federal government; the unemployed and the elderly were provided with social insurance; public assistance for some of the disabled and infirm, as well as dependent children, became an "entitlement." These programs vastly enlarged the support available to the poor and, coupled with the rapid economic growth that began in 1940, led many Americans to conclude that poverty was a problem of the past. The rediscovery of poverty amidst great plenty in the 1960s came then as a shock to middle-class Americans, a shock that helped launch attacks on poverty by the Kennedy and Johnson administrations. Lyndon B. Johnson's War on Poverty—an assembly of large-scale federal programs targeted at a variety of subpopulations—achieved some tangible results, but it did not come close to its widely publicized goal of conquering the problem. In its aftermath, few innovative or significant public policies were put into place.

Just why poverty has been so persistent—why more than 30 million people remain poor—is a much-debated issue. Some analysts have argued that the rate of economic growth has been insufficient to eradicate poverty, whereas others maintain that the cause resides more in the maldistribution of income. Some see the poor as lacking the skills or the will to escape their condition; others see the economy as dependent upon the poor to provide a low-wage labor force for industry and agriculture. Some critics have argued that government programs have not been sufficiently extensive or adequately funded to achieve their goals; others have claimed that such programs were always designed not to cure the problem but to discipline and regulate the poor. This lack of agreement, about the diagnosis and the prescription, has long been characteristic of twentieth-century public discourse about poverty. Yet, as the century drew to a close, both policy experts and the citizenry as a whole seemed to be less optimistic than they once were that the problem could, or would, be eradicated at all. □

Poverty Update

According to the U.S. Bureau of the Census, the average poverty threshold for a family of four was $13,924 in 1991. Average poverty thresholds varied from $6,932 for a person living alone to $27,942 for a family of nine or more members. The poverty definition is based on pre-tax money income only, excluding capital gains, and does not include the value of noncash benefits such as employer-provided health insurance, food stamps, or Medicaid.

The number of persons who were officially poor in 1991 was 35.7 million, representing 14.2% of the Nation's population.

Half of the Nation's poor were either children under 18 years old (40.2%) or elderly (10.6%). The poverty rates for Whites increased between 1990 and 1991. The poverty rates for Blacks and persons of Hispanic origin did not change significantly, nor did the rate for Asians and Pacific Islanders as a group.

The 1991 rates were 11.3% for Whites, 28.7% for persons of Hispanic origin, 32.7% for Blacks, and 13.8% for Asians and Pacific Islanders.

The number of poor families increased by 613,000 between 1990 and 1991. The increase in the number of poor families with a female householder accounted for 64.1% of the net increase in poor families between 1990 and 1991. Married couple families continue to have the lowest poverty rate (only 6%), followed by those headed by a male with no wife present (13%). Families headed by a female householder with no husband present had a 36% poverty rate.

Persons Below the Poverty Level, 1972–1991

(in thousands)

Year	All persons	White	Black	Hispanic origin[1]	Year	All persons	White	Black	Hispanic origin[1]
1972	24,460	16,203	7,710	—	1982	34,398	23,517	9,697	4,301
1973	22,973	15,142	7,388	2,366	1983	35,303	23,984	9,882	4,633
1974	23,370	15,736	7,182	2,575	1984	33,700	22,955	9,490	4,806
1975	25,877	17,770	7,545	2,991	1985	33,064	22,860	8,926	5,236
1976	24,975	16,713	7,595	2,783	1986	32,370	22,183	8,983	5,117
1977	24,720	16,416	7,726	2,700	1987	32,221	21,195	9,520	5,422
1978	24,497	16,259	7,625	2,607	1988	31,745	20,715	9,356	5,357
1979	26,072	17,214	8,050	2,921	1989	31,528	20,785	9,302	5,430
1980	29,272	19,699	8,579	3,491	1990	33,585	22,326	9,837	6,006
1981	31,822	21,553	9,173	3,713	1991	35,708	23,747	10,242	6,339

1. Persons of Hispanic origin may be of any race. *Source:* U.S. Department of Commerce, Bureau of the Census.

Consumer Price Indexes

(1982–84 = 100)

Year	All items	Energy	Food	Shelter	Apparel[1]	Transportation	Medical care	Fuel oil	Electricity	Utility (gas)	Telephone	Commodities
1960	29.6	22.4	30.0	25.2	45.7	29.8	22.3	13.5	29.9	17.6	58.3	33.6
1970	38.8	25.5	39.2	35.5	59.2	37.5	34.0	16.5	31.8	19.6	58.7	41.7
1975	53.8	42.1	59.8	48.8	72.5	50.1	47.5	34.9	50.0	31.1	71.7	58.2
1980	82.4	86.0	86.8	81.0	90.9	83.1	74.9	87.7	75.8	65.7	77.7	86.0
1990	130.7	104.5	132.4	140.0	124.1	120.5	162.8	n.a.	n.a.	n.a.	n.a.	n.a.
1991	136.2	106.7	136.3	146.3	128.7	123.8	177.0	n.a.	n.a.	n.a.	n.a.	n.a.
1992	140.3	108.1	137.9	151.2	131.9	126.5	190.1	n.a.	n.a.	n.a.	n.a.	n.a.

1. Includes upkeep. *Source: Monthly Labor Review, July 1993.*

Consumer Price Index for All Urban Consumers

(1982–84 = 100)

Group	March 1993	March 1992
All items	143.6	139.3
Food	140.1	138.1
Alcoholic beverages	149.4	146.7
Apparel and upkeep	136.2	133.4
Men's and boys' apparel	128.7	127.4
Women's and girls' apparel	138.4	133.6
Footwear	126.3	124.9
Housing, total	140.2	136.6
Rent	149.1	146.4
Gas and electricity	115.1	111.5
Fuel oil, coal, bottled gas	92.8	90.5
House operation[1]	118.7	117.7
House furnishings	109.3	109.4
Transportation	129.0	124.4
Medical care	198.6	187.3
Personal care	140.7	137.9
Tobacco products	236.3	213.5
Entertainment	144.8	141.2
Personal and educational expenses	206.3	193.5

1. Combines house furnishings and operation. *Source: Monthly Labor Review, May 1993.*

Per Capita Personal Income

Year	Amount	Year	Amount	Year	Amount	Year	Amount	Year	Amount
1935	$474	1965	$2,773	1978	$7,729	1983	$12,098	1988	$16,615
1945	1,223	1970	3,893	1979	8,638	1984	13,114	1989	17,696
1950	1,501	1975	5,851	1980	9,910	1985	13,896	1990	18,635
1955	1,881	1976	6,402	1981	10,949	1986	14,597	1991	19,091
1960	2,219	1977	7,043	1982	11,480	1987	15,638	1992[1]	19,841

1. Preliminary. *Source:* Department of Commerce, Bureau of Economic Analysis.

Per Capita Income and Personal Consumption Expenditures

(In current dollars)

				Personal Consumption Expenditures			
Year	Gross national product	Personal income	Disposable personal income	Durable goods	Nondurable goods	Services	Total
1950	$1,900	$1,504	$1,368	$203	$648	$416	$1,267
1955	2,456	1,901	1,687	235	755	570	1,560
1960	2,851	2,265	1,986	240	847	741	1,829
1965	3,268	2,840	2,505	327	987	954	2,268
1970	4,951	4,056	3,489	418	1,318	1,385	3,121
1975	7,401	6,081	5,291	627	1,927	2,135	4,689
1980	11,985	9,916	8,421	963	2,992	3,653	7,607
1985	16,776	13,895	11,861	1,555	3,807	5,622	10,985
1988	19,783	16,524	14,123	1,857	4,303	6,984	13,144
1989	20,903	17,621	14,973	1,908	4,541	7,417	13,866
1990	21,737	18,477	15,695	1,910	4,748	7,888	14,547
1991	22,500	19,100	16,700	1,800	5,000	8,700	15,400
1992	23,340	19,802	17,346	1,881	5,053	9,101	16,035

Source: U.S. Department of Commerce, *Survey of Current Business, June 1993.*

Total Family Income in 1991 CPI-U–XI Adjusted Dollars

(figures in percent)

Income range	White 1991	White 1990	White 1985	Black 1991	Black 1990	Black 1985	Hispanic[1] 1991	Hispanic[1] 1990	Hispanic[1] 1985
Families (thousands)[2]	57,224	56,803	54,991	7,716	7,471	6,921	5,177	4,981	4,206
Under $5,000	2.5	2.5	2.9	11.4	11.5	10.1	6.4	6.3	5.9
$5,000 to $9,999	4.8	4.7	5.6	15.0	14.1	15.7	12.4	12.3	13.6
$10,000 to $14,999	6.7	7.0	7.3	11.1	11.3	12.4	11.9	12.6	13.7
$15,000 to $24,999	15.7	16.0	17.0	18.4	19.5	21.2	21.5	21.7	20.9
$25,000 to $34,999	15.9	16.5	16.7	14.5	14.0	14.2	16.5	16.6	17.0
$35,000 to $49,999	20.3	20.8	21.1	14.8	15.0	14.2	15.0	15.7	15.1
$50,000 to $74,999	20.0	19.3	18.5	10.3	9.8	9.3	10.7	10.0	10.3
$75,000 to $99,999	8.0	7.3	6.3	3.1	3.4	2.1	3.2	2.9	2.4
$100,000 and over	6.1	5.9	4.5	1.4	1.3	0.9	2.3	1.9	1.2
Median income	$37,783	$36,915	$35,410	$21,548	$21,423	$20,390	$23,895	$23,431	$23,112

1. Persons of Hispanic origin may be of any race. 2. As of March 1992. *Source:* Department of Commerce, Bureau of the Census, *Current Population Reports, Consumer Income, Series P–60, No. 180.*

Median Weekly Earnings of Full-Time Workers by Occupation and Sex

Occupation	Men: Number of workers (in thousands)	Men: Median weekly earnings	Women: Number of workers (in thousands)	Women: Median weekly earnings	Total: Number of workers (in thousands)	Total: Median weekly earnings
Managerial and prof. specialty	12,082	$777	11,165	$562	23,246	$655
Executive, admin, and managerial	6,370	784	4,918	519	11,287	650
Professional specialty	5,712	770	6,247	587	11,959	659
Technical, sales, and admin. support	9,844	519	16,084	365	25,928	407
Technicians and related support	1,956	591	1,608	436	3,564	508
Sales occupations	4,663	523	3,240	313	7,903	432
Administrative support, incl. clerical	3,225	482	11,235	364	14,460	381
Service occupations	4,492	330	4,612	248	9,104	283
Private household	11	(1)	302	177	314	179
Protective service	1,548	501	256	399	1,805	486
Service, except private household and protective	2,932	283	4,053	248	6,985	263
Precision production, craft, and repair	9,581	503	854	336	10,435	491
Mechanics and repairers	3,625	496	124	523	3,749	496
Construction trades	3,193	495	44	(1)	3,237	494
Operators, fabricators, and laborers	10,618	393	3,383	279	14,000	357
Machine operators, assemblers, and inspectors	4,188	406	2,602	275	6,790	343
Transportation and material moving occupations	3,667	436	240	329	3,907	427
Handlers, equipment cleaners, helpers, and laborers	2,763	314	540	279	3,303	308
Farming, forestry, and fishing	1,260	269	170	223	1,430	263

1. Data not shown where base is less than 100,000. NOTE: Figures are for the year 1992. *Source:* U.S. Department of Labor, Bureau of Labor Statistics, "Employment and Earnings," January 1993.

Consumer Credit

(installment credit outstanding; in billions of dollars, not seasonally adjusted)

Holder	1992	1991	1990	1989	1988	1985	1980	1975
Commercial banks	331.9	340.7	347.1	342.8	324.8	245.1	147.0	82.9
Finance companies	117.1	121.9	133.3	138.9	144.7	111.7	62.3	32.7
Credit unions	97.6	92.7	93.1	93.1	88.3	72.7	44.0	25.7
Retailers[1]	42.1	39.8	43.5	44.2	48.4	43.0	28.7	18.2
Other[2]	47.8	50.3	57.0	67.2	67.1	53.8	20.1	9.2
Pools[3]	120.4	99.6	77.9	48.8	—	—	—	—
Total	**756.9**	**745.0**	**751.9**	**735.0**	**673.3**	**526.3**	**302.1**	**168.7**

1. Excludes 30-day charge credit held by retailers, oil and gas companies, and travel and entertainment companies. 2. Includes mutual savings banks, savings and loan associations, and gasoline companies. 3. Beginning 1989, outstanding balances of pools upon which securities have been issued; these balances are no longer on the balance sheets for the loan originators. Data are *not* available historically. *Source:* Federal Reserve Bulletin.

The Public Debt

Year	Gross debt: Amount (in millions)	Gross debt: Per capita	Year	Gross debt: Amount (in millions)	Gross debt: Per capita
1800 (Jan. 1)	$ 83	$ 15.87	1950	$256,087[1]	$1,688.30
1860 (June 30)	65	2.06	1955	272,807[1]	1,650.63
1865	2,678	75.01	1960	284,093[1]	1,572.31
1900	1,263	16.60	1965	313,819[1]	1,612.70
1920	24,299	228.23	1970	370,094[1]	1,807.09
1925	20,516	177.12	1975	533,189	2,496.90
1930	16,185	131.51	1980	907,701	3,969.55
1935	28,701	225.55	1985	1,823,103	7,598.51
1940	42,968	325.23	1990	3,233,313	12,823,28
1945	258,682	1,848.60	1992	4,002,669	15,650.00

1. Adjusted to exclude issues to the International Monetary Fund and other international lending institutions to conform to the budget presentation. *Source:* Department of the Treasury, Financial Management Service.

Gross Domestic Product or Expenditure[1]

(in billions)

Item	1992	1991	1990	1989	1988	1987	1985	1980	1970
Gross domestic product	5,950.7	5,667.5	5,513.8	5,244.0	4,900.4	4,539.9	4,038.7	2,708.0	1,010.7
GDP in constant (1987) dollars	4,922.8	4,821.0	4,884.9	4,836.9	4,718.6	4,540.0	4,279.8	3,776.3	2,875.8
Personal consumption expenditures	4,094.9	3,887.7	3,742.6	3,517.9	3,296.1	3,052.2	2,667.4	1,748.1	646.5
Durable goods	480.3	446.1	465.9	459.8	437.1	403.7	352.9	212.5	85.3
Nondurable goods	1,290.5	1,251.5	1,217.7	1,146.9	1,073.8	1,011.1	919.4	682.9	270.4
Services	2,324.0	2,190.1	2,059.0	1,911.2	1,785.2	1,637.4	1,395.1	852.7	290.8
Gross private domestic investment	770.9	721.1	802.6	837.6	793.6	749.3	714.5	467.6	150.3
Residential	217.8	190.3	215.7	230.9	232.0	225.2	185.9	123.3	41.4
Nonresidential	548.3	541.1	587.0	570.7	545.4	497.8	504.0	353.8	106.7
Change in business inventories	4.7	−10.2	0	36.0	16.2	26.3	24.6	−9.5	2.3
Net export of goods and services	−30.2	−21.8	−74.4	−82.9	−108.0	−143.1	−115.6	−14.7	1.2
Government purchases	1,115.2	1,090.5	1,042.9	971.4	918.7	881.5	772.3	507.1	212.7
Federal	449.2	447.3	424.9	401.4	387.0	384.9	344.3	209.1	100.1
State and local	666.0	643.2	618.0	570.0	531.7	496.6	428.1	298.0	112.6

1. Current dollars except as noted. *Source:* Department of Commerce, Bureau of Economic Analysis, *Survey of Current Business,* Vol. 73, No. 2, February 1993.

Producer Price Indexes by Major Commodity Groups

(1982 = 100)

Commodity	1992	1990	1985	1980	1975	1970
All commodities	117.2	116.3	103.2	89.8	58.4	38.1
Farm products	103.6	112.2	95.1	102.9	77.0	45.8
Processed foods and feeds	122.1	121.9	103.5	95.9	72.6	44.6
Textile products and apparel	117.8	114.9	102.9	89.7	67.4	52.4
Hides, skins, and leather products	140.4	141.7	108.9	94.7	56.5	42.0
Fuels and related products and power	80.4	82.2	91.4	82.8	35.4	15.3
Chemicals and allied products	125.9	123.6	103.7	89.0	62.0	35.0
Rubber and plastic products	115.1	113.6	101.9	90.1	62.2	44.9
Lumber and wood products	146.6	129.7	106.6	101.5	62.1	39.9
Pulp, paper, and allied products	145.2	141.3	113.3	86.3	59.0	37.5
Metals and metal products	119.2	123.0	104.4	95.0	61.5	38.7
Machinery and equipment	123.3	120.7	107.2	86.0	57.9	40.0
Furniture and household durables	122.2	119.1	107.1	90.7	67.5	51.9
Nonmetallic mineral products	117.3	114.7	108.6	88.4	54.4	35.3
Transportation equipment	130.4	121.5	107.9	82.9	56.7	41.9

Source: Department of Commerce, Bureau of Economic Analysis, *Survey of Current Businesses, July 1993.*

Weekly Earnings[1] of Full-Time Women Workers

Major occupation group	1992 weekly earnings	% Men's weekly earnings
Managerial and professional specialty	$562	72.3
Executive, administrative, and managerial	519	66.2
Professional specialty	587	76.2
Technical, sales, and administrative support	365	70.3
Technicians and related support	436	73.8
Sales occupations	313	59.8
Administrative support, including clerical	364	75.5
Service occupations	248	75.2
Precision production, craft, and repair	336	66.8
Operators, fabricators, and laborers	279	71.0
Machine operators, assemblers, and inspectors	275	67.7
Transportation and material moving	329	75.5
Handlers, equipment cleaners, helpers, and laborers	279	88.9
Farming, forestry, and fishing	223	82.9
All occupations	**$381**	**75.4**

1. Median usual weekly earnings. Half the workers earn more and half the workers usually earn less each week. *Source:* U.S. Department of Labor, Bureau of Labor Statistics.

Median Family Income

(in current dollars)

Year	Income	Percent change	Year	Income	Percent change
1980	$21,023	—	1987	$29,744	5.3
1981	22,388	6.5	1988	30,992	4.0
1982	23,433	4.7	1989	32,448	4.5
1983	24,580	4.9	1990	33,956	4.4
1984	25,948	5.1	1991	34,788	2.4
1985	27,144	5.0	1992	35,776	2.8
1986	28,236	4.0			

Source: U.S. Department of Labor, Bureau of Labor Statistics, *Employment and Earnings,* January 1993.

Expenditures for New Plant and Equipment[1]

(in billions of dollars)

Year	Manufacturing	Transportation[2]	Total nonmanufacturing	Total
1950	$7.73	$2.87	$18.08	$25.81
1955	12.50	3.10	24.58	37.08
1960	16.36	3.54	32.63	48.99
1965	25.41	5.66	45.39	70.79
1970	36.99	7.17	69.16	106.15
1975	53.66	9.95	108.95	162.60
1980	112.60	13.56	205.48	318.08
1985	152.88	14.57	302.05	454.93
1987	141.06	15.07	320.45	461.51
1988	163.45	16.63	344.77	508.22
1989	183.80	18.84	380.13	563.93
1990	192.61	21.47	399.34	591.96
1991	182.81	22.66	405.12	587.93
1992	173.90	22.78	433.28	607.19

1. Data exclude agriculture. 2. Transportation is included in total nonmanufacturing. NOTE: This series was revised in April 1993. *Source:* Department of Commerce, Bureau of the Census.

New Housing Starts[1] and Mobile Homes Shipped

(in thousands)

Year	No. of units started	Year	No. of units started	Year	Mobile homes shipped
1900	189	1970	1,469	1965	216
1910	387	1975	1,171	1970	401
1920	247	1980	1,313	1975	213
1925	937	1984	1,756	1980	222
1930	330	1985	1,745	1985	284
1935	221	1986	1,807	1986	244
1940	603	1987	1,623	1987	233
1945	326	1988[2]	1,488	1988	218
1950	1,952	1989	1,376	1989	198
1955	1,646	1990	1,193	1990	188
1960[1]	1,296	1991	1,014	1991	171
1965	1,510	1992	1,200	1992	211

1. Prior to 1960, starts limited to nonfarm housing; from 1960 on, figures include farm housing. 2. As of 1988 data for housing starts no longer include public housing starts and only include private housing starts. *Sources:* Department of Commerce, Housing Construction Statistics, 1900–1965, and Construction Reports, Housing Starts, 1970–to present, Manufactured Housing Institute, 1965–to present.

Life Insurance in Force

(in millions of dollars)

As of Dec. 31	Ordinary	Group	Industrial	Credit	Total
1915	$16,650	$100	$4,279	—	$21,029
1930	78,576	9,801	17,963	$ 73	106,413
1945	101,550	22,172	27,675	365	151,762
1950	149,116	47,793	33,415	3,844	234,168
1955	216,812	101,345	39,682	14,493	373,332
1960	341,881	175,903	39,563	29,101	586,448
1965	499,638	308,078	39,818	53,020	900,554
1970	734,730	551,357	38,644	77,392	1,402,123
1980	1,760,474	1,579,355	35,994	165,215	3,541,038
1985	3,247,289	2,561,595	28,250	215,973	6,053,107
1990	5,366,982	3,753,506	24,071	248,038	9,392,597
1992	5,941,810	4,240,919	20,973	202,090	10,405,792

Source: American Council of Life Insurance.

Farm Indexes

(1977 = 100)

Year	Prices paid by famers[1]	Prices rec'd by farmers[2]	Ratio
1950	37	56	151
1955	40	51	128
1960	44	52	118
1965	49	54	115
1970	56	60	109
1975	90	101	113
1980	138	134	97
1985	162	128	79
1990	184	150	82
1992	191	140	73

1. Commodities, interest, and taxes and wage rates. 2. All crops and livestock. *Source:* Department of Agriculture, National Agricultural Statistics Service.

Estimated Annual Retail and Wholesale Sales by Kind of Business

(in millions of dollars)

Kind of business	1992	1991
Retail trade, total	1,962,423	1,865,477
Building materials, hardware, garden supplies, and mobile home dealers	103,031	95,229
Automotive dealers	398,067	368,943
Furniture, home furnishings, and equipment stores	105,844	98,612
General merchandise group stores	247,354	228,473
Food stores	384,013	376,892
Gasoline service stations	133,000	134,100
Apparel and accessory stores	104,994	97,464
Eating and drinking places	201,866	196,875
Drug and proprietary stores	77,285	75,883
Liquor stores	25,619	23,990
Merchant wholesale trade, total	1,771,614	1,793,866
Durable goods, total	859,492	884,643
Motor vehicles and automotive parts and supplies	164,486	172,069
Furniture and home furnishings	32,306	33,933
Lumber and other construction materials	63,093	67,251
Electrical goods	117,009	117,840
Hardware, plumbing, heating, and supplies	46,651	50,174
Machinery, equipment, supplies	160,834	168,459
Professional and commercial equipment and supplies	121,038	112,060
Metals and minerals except petroleum	70,928	74,930
Miscellaneous durable goods	83,147	87,927
Nondurable goods, total	912,122	909,223
Paper and paper products	50,696	50,725
Drugs, drug proprietaries, and druggists' sundries	58,851	51,085
Apparel, piece goods, & notions	68,567	67,638
Groceries and related products	276,954	272,528
Beer, wine, distilled alcoholic beverages	54,995	51,669
Farm-product raw materials	105,756	108,220
Chemical and allied products	35,841	35,013
Petroleum and petroleum products	126,923	139,426
Miscellaneous nondurable goods	133,539	132,919

Source: Department of Commerce, Bureau of the Census.

Shareholders in Public Corporations

Characteristic	1990	1985	1983	1981	1980	1975	1970
Individual shareholders (thousands)	51,440	47,040	42,360	32,260	30,200	25,270	30,850
Adult shareowner incidence in population	1 in 4	1 in 4	1 in 4	1 in 5	1 in 5	1 in 6	1 in 4
Median household income	$43,800	$36,800	$33,200	$29,200	$27,750	$19,000	$13,500
Adult shareowners with household income: under $10,000 (thousands)	n.a.	2,151	1,460	2,164	1,742	3,420	8,170
$10,000 and over (thousands)	n.a.	40,999	36,261	26,913	25,715	19,970	20,130
$15,000 and over (thousands)	42,920	39,806	33,665	24,376	22,535	15,420	12,709
$25,000 and over (thousands)	38,230	32,690	25,086	17,547	15,605	6,642	4,114
$50,000 and over (thousands)	17,910	11,321	7,918	5,457	3,982	1,216	n.a.
Adult female shareowners (thousands)	17,750	17,547 [1]	20,385	14,154	13,696	11,750	14,290
Adult male shareowners (thousands)	30,220	27,446 [1]	19,226	15,785	14,196	11,630	14,340
Median age	43	44	45	46	46	53	48

NOTE: 1990 results are not strictly comparable with previous studies because of differences in methodologies. 1. Revised to correspond to 1990 methodology. n.a. = not available. *Source:* New York Stock Exchange. Data are latest available as of April 1992 publication.

50 Most Active Stocks in 1992

Stock	Share volume
General Motors (9)	435,774,600
Glaxo Holdings (10)	434,639,100
Philip Morris (2)	409,878,200
Telefonos de Mexico (14)	405,094,900
Int'l Business Machines (6)	393,457,200
RJR Nabisco Holdings (1)	376,215,600
American Tel. & Tel. (4)	366,884,800
Citicorp (7)	347,946,100
Ford Motor (20)	328,718,600
Chrysler Corporation (41)	321,835,200
Merck & Co., Inc.	308,540,100
Limited, Inc. (11)	275,522,600
American Express (5)	275,201,100
Coca-Cola Company (32)	264,698,000
Bristol-Myers Squibb (23)	264,190,500
PepsiCo., Inc. (3)	252,834,800
Chemical Banking Corp.	250,729,600
Unisys Corp.	233,112,300
General Electric (8)	227,903,100
Advanced Micro Devices (25)	226,833,400
Disney (Walt) Company	226,301,100
GTE Corp. (16)	226,100,100
Wal-Mart Stores (13)	223,066,900
Boeing Co. (12)	221,641,600
BankAmerica Corporation (22)	221,564,400
Exxon Corp. (18)	219,293,500
Syntex Corp. (40)	216,322,600
Waste Management (17)	213,343,800
Westinghouse Electric (15)	205,297,900
Abbot Laboratories	200,679,600
Johnson & Johnson (34)	196,637,400
COMPAQ Computer (24)	188,232,500
du Pont de Nemours (29)	187,583,600
Pfizer Inc. (39)	187,531,200
Hewlett-Packard (38)	186,195,700
Eastman Kodak (28)	182,046,500
Blockbuster Entertainment (21)	176,717,400
Home Depot Inc.	174,886,600
Federal National Mtg. Assn. (19)	173,865,600
USX-Marathon Group (26)	173,406,300
Sears Roebuck (50)	171,622,300
K mart Corp	171,295,900
Gap (The), Inc.	167,361,200
Toys "R" Us, Inc. (31)	166,548,100
McDonald's Corp. (27)	165,242,700
Unocal (49)	159,884,400
Union Carbide Corp.	159,593,000
Royal Dutch Petroleum (47)	158,512,100
British Petroleum, Ltd.	156,093,300
Chase Manhattan Corp. (44)	155,795,000

NOTE: 1991 ranking in parentheses, if among top 50. *Source:* New York Stock Exchange.

Geographic Distribution of Shareowners of Public Corporations (1990)

Metropolitan Area	Individuals	Households	Metropolitan area	Individuals	Households
New York	2,470,000	1,630,000	Pittsburgh	450,000	300,000
Los Angeles	1,850,000	1,230,000	Denver	440,000	290,000
Chicago	1,610,000	1,070,000	San Jose	420,000	280,000
Detroit	1,240,000	820,000	Cincinnati	410,000	270,000
Philadelphia	1,100,000	720,000	Riverside-San Bernardino	410,000	270,000
Washington D.C.	1,000,000	670,000	Bergan-Passaic, N.J.	400,000	270,000
Boston	940,000	620,000	Milwaukee	400,000	270,000
Houston	880,000	580,000	Kansas City	390,000	260,000
Nassau-Suffolk, N.Y.	750,000	500,000	Seattle	380,000	260,000
Dallas	670,000	440,000	Fort Worth	370,000	240,000
Phoenix	650,000	430,000	Fort Lauderdale	360,000	240,000
St. Louis	640,000	420,000	Columbus	330,000	220,000
Anaheim	630,000	420,000	Portland	310,000	210,000
Atlanta	630,000	410,000	Sacramento	310,000	210,000
Minneapolis	620,000	410,000	Hartford	310,000	210,000
Newark	600,000	400,000	Indianapolis	280,000	190,000
Cleveland	540,000	360,000	Norfolk	280,000	180,000
Baltimore	520,000	350,000	New Orleans	270,000	180,000
San Francisco	490,000	330,000	Orlando	270,000	180,000
Oakland	490,000	320,000	Charlotte	240,000	160,000
Tampa	480,000	320,000	Middlesex, N.J.	230,000	150,000
Miami	470,000	310,000	San Antonio	230,000	150,000
San Diego	450,000	300,000			

Source: New York Stock Exchange. Data are latest available as of April 1992 publication.

New York Stock Exchange Seat Sales for Cash, 1992

Month	Price High	Price Low	Number	Month	Price High	Price Low	Number
January	$475,000	$450,000	3	July	—	—	0
February	600,000	—	1	August	$460,000	$440,000	2
March	575,000	—	2	September	460,000	—	2
April	480,000	—	2	October	450,000	—	1
May	—	—	0	November	—	—	0
June	440,000	410,000	3	December	525,000	—	1

NOTE: In addition, there were 11 private seat sales, ranging from a high of $460,000 and a low of $375,000. *Source:* New York Stock Exchange.

Largest Businesses, 1992

(in millions of dollars)

50 LARGEST INDUSTRIAL CORPORATIONS

	Sales	Assets
General Motors	$132,774.9	$191,012.8
Exxon	103,547.0	85,030.0
Ford Motor	100,785.6	180,545.2
Int'l. Business Machines	65,096.0	86,705.0
General Electric	62,202.0	192,876.0
Mobil	57,389.0	40,561.0
Philip Morris	50,157.0	50,014.0
E.I. Du Pont de Nemours	37,643.0	38,870.0
Chevron	37,464.0	33,970.0
Texaco	37,130.0	25,992.0
Chrysler	36,897.0	40,653.0
Boeing	30,184.0	18,147.0
Procter & Gamble	29,890.0	24,025.0
Amoco	25,543.0	28,453.0
PepsiCo	22,083.7	20,951.2
United Technologies	22,032.0	15,928.0
Shell Oil	$21,702.0	$26,970.0
Conagra	21,219.0	9,758.7
Eastman Kodak	20,577.0	23,138.0
Dow Chemical	19,177.0	25,360.0
Xerox	18,261.0	34,051.0
Atlantic Richfield	18,061.0	24,256.0
McDonnell Douglas	17,513.0	13,781.0
Hewlett-Packard	16,427.0	13,700.0
USX	16,186.0	17,252.0
RJR Nabisco Holdings	15,734.0	32,041.0
Digital Equipment	14,027.0	11,284.3
Minnesota Mining & Mfg.	13,883.0	11,955.0
Johnson & Johnson	13,846.0	11,884.0
Tenneco	13,606.0	16,584.0
International Paper	13,600.0	16,459.0
Motorola	13,341.0	10,629.0
Sara Lee	13,321.0	9,989.0
Coca-Cola	13,238.0	11,052.0

	Sales	Assets
Westinghouse Electric	$12,100.0	$10,398.0
Allied-Signal	12,089.0	10,756.0
Phillips Petroleum	11,933.0	11,468.0
Goodyear Tire & Rubber	11,923.6	8,563.7
Georgia-Pacific	11,847.0	10,890.0
Bristol-Myers Squibb	11,805.0	10,804.0
Anheuser-Busch	11,400.8	10,537.9
IBP	11,129.7	1,499.4
Rockwell International	10,995.1	9,731.0
Caterpillar	10,194.0	13,935.0
Lockheed	10,138.0	6,754.0
Coastal	10,062.9	10,579.8
Merck	9,800.8	11,086.0
Ashland Oil	9,595.8	5,668.4
Aluminum Co. of America	9,588.4	11,023.1
Archer Daniels Midland	9,344.1	7,524.5

25 LARGEST RETAILING COMPANIES

	Sales	Assets
Sears Roebuck	$59,101.1	$83,533.0
Wal-Mart Stores	55,483.8	20,565.1
Kmart	37,724.0	18,931.0
Kroger	22,144.6	4,301.1
J.C. Penney	19,085.0	13,563.0
American Stores	19,051.2	6,545.0
Dayton Hudson	17,927.0	10,337.0
Safeway	15,151.9	5,225.8
Great Atlantic & Pacific Tea	11,592.5	3,212.8
May Department Stores	11,170.0	8,545.0
Melville	10,432.8	4,214.1
Winn-Dixie Stores	10,337.3	1,977.4
Albertson's	10,173.7	2,945.6
Woolworth	9,962.0	4,692.0
Price	7,511.8	1,923.7
Southland	7,477.1	2,044.0
Walgreen	7,475.0	2,373.5
Food Lion	7,195.9	2,521.5
Toys "R" Us	7,169.3	5,322.9
Home Depot	7,148.4	3,931.8
McDonald's	7,133.3	11,681.2
Federated Department Stores	7,079.9	7,019.8
Limited	6,900.0	3,846.4
Publix Super Markets	6,728.8	1,791.2
Costco Wholesale	6,629.6	1,648.5

10 LARGEST TRANSPORTATION COMPANIES

	Operating revenues	Assets
United Parcel Service	$16,541.1	$9,037.8
AMR	14,495.0	18,706.0
UAL	12,899.7	12,257.4
Delta Air Lines	10,836.8	10,161.6
CSX	8,734.0	13,049.0
Northwest Airlines	7,963.8	8,137.8
Federal Express	7,550.1	5,463.2
Union Pacific	7,294.0	14,098.0
USAir Group	6,696.3	6,594.5
Continental Airlines Holdings	5,575.2	3,327.8

10 LARGEST DIVERSIFIED FINANCIAL COMPANIES

	Assets	Revenues
Federal Nat'l Mortgage Assn.	$180,978.0	$14,559.0
American Express	175,752.0	26,961.0
Salomon	159,459.0	8,196.0
Merrill Lynch	107,024.2	13,428.3
Aetna Life & Casualty	89,928.2	17,497.2
Morgan Stanley Group	80,353.2	7,382.0
American International Group	79,835.2	18,388.6
CIGNA	69,827.0	18,582.0
Federal Home Loan Mortgage	59,502.0	4,461.0
ITT	58,764.0	21,651.0

10 LARGEST LIFE INSURANCE COMPANIES

	Assets	Premium and annuity income
Prudential of America	$154,779.4	$24,762.8
Metropolitan Life	118,178.3	19,934.0
Teachers Insurance & Annuity	61,776.7	3,158.1
Aetna Life	50,896.5	7,131.4
New York Life	46,925.0	8,595.0
Equitable Life Assurance	46,624.0	3,856.3
Connecticut General Life	44,075.5	3,488.5
Northwestern Mutual Life	39,666.3	4,912.3
John Hancock Mutual Life	39,146.1	7,304.7
Principal Mutual Life	35,124.8	8,102.1

10 LARGEST COMMERCIAL BANKS

	Assets	Deposits
Citicorp	$213,701.0	$144,175.0
BankAmerica Corp.	180,646.0	137,883.0
Chemical Banking Corp.	139,655.0	94,173.0
Nationsbank Corp.	118,059.3	82,726.5
J.P. Morgan & Co.	102,941.0	32,519.0
Chase Manhattan Corp.	95,862.0	67,224.0
Bankers Trust New York Corp.	72,448.0	25,071.0
Banc One Corp.	61,417.4	48,464.7
Wells Fargo & Co.	52,537.0	42,244.0
PNC Bank Corp.	51,379.9	29,469.5

10 LARGEST UTILITIES

	Assets	Operating revenues
GTE	$42,144.0	$19,984.0
Bellsouth	31,462.7	15,378.6
Bell Atlantic	28,099.5	12,647.0
US West	27,963.6	10,281.1
NYNEX	27,713.9	13,155.0
Pacific Gas & Electric	24,188.2	10,383.3
Southwestern Bell	23,810.0	10,015.4
Ameritech	22,817.7	11,153.0
Pacific Telesis Group	22,516.0	9,935.0
Southern	20,038.0	8,073.0

New Business Concerns and Business Failures

Formations and failures	1991[1]	1990	1989	1988	1987	1986	1985	1980
Business formations								
Index, net formations (1967 = 100)	115.4	120.7	124.7	124.1	121.2	120.4	120.	129.9
New incorporations (1,000)	629	647	677	685	685	702	663	534
Failures, number (1,000)	n.a.	60.0	50.4	57.1	61.1	61.6	57.1	11.7
Rate per 10,000 concerns	n.a.	75	65	98	102	120	115	42

1. Preliminary. *Sources:* U.S. Bureau of Economic Analysis and Dun & Bradstreet Corporation. From *Statistical Abstract of the United States 1992.* NOTE: Data are most recent available.

50 Leading Stocks in Market Value

Stock	Market value (millions)	Listed shares (millions)
Exxon Corp.	$110,582	1,813
General Electric Co.	78,754	927
Wal-Mart Stores	73,155	1,150
Morris (Philip) Co.	72,020	935
Coca-Cola Co.	70,848	1,692
American Telephone & Telegraph	67,604	1,326
Merck & Co.	59,459	1,367
Procter & Gamble	39,247	730
Johnson & Johnson	38,560	767
Bristol-Myers Squibb	35,863	532
PepsiCo. Inc.	35,689	863
GTE Corp.	32,836	945
du Pont de Nemours	31,781	674
International Business Machines	28,804	572
Mobil Corp.	27,755	440
American International Group	26,090	225
Abbott Laboratories	25,793	849
Bellsouth Corporation	24,862	489
Chevron Corp.	24,759	356
Amoco Corp.	24,189	496
Pfizer Inc.	24,100	332
American Home Products	23,897	355
Minnesota Mining & Manufacturing	23,748	236
Disney (Walt) Company	23,742	552
General Motors	22,781	706
Bell Atlantic	22,359	436
Home Depot Inc.	$22,288	331
Southwestern Bell	22,266	301
Federal National Mortgage Association	21,551	282
Ameritech Corp.	20,934	294
Kellogg Co.	20,695	310
McDonald's Corp.	20,239	415
Anheuser-Busch Companies	19,822	340
Waste Management	19,724	496
Pacific Telesis	19,153	433
Ford Motor	18,854	441
Dow Chemical	18,728	327
Atlantic Richfield	18,445	161
NYNEX Corp.	17,835	213
Lilly (Eli)	17,788	293
Hewlett-Packard Co.	17,587	252
Sears-Roebuck	17,556	387
Schlumberger Ltd.	17,436	306
Royal Dutch Petroleum	17,414	215
Schering-Plough Corp.	17,026	268
Texaco Inc.	16,389	274
US West	16,112	420
BankAmerica Corp.	16,070	346
Gillette Co.	15,774	277
Eastman Kodak	15,133	374
Total	**$1,514,096**	**27,521**

NOTE: As of Dec. 31, 1992. *Source:* New York Stock Exchange.

Top 50 Banks in the World

(in thousands of dollars)

Bank	Country	Assets (U.S. dollars)
Dai-ichi Kangyo Bank Ltd., Tokyo	Japan	$460,426,792
Fuji Bank, Ltd., Tokyo	Japan	458,674,996
Sumitomo Bank, Ltd., Osaka	Japan	452,811,639
Sanwa Bank Ltd., Osaka	Japan	449,770,095
Sakura Bank Ltd., Tokyo	Japan	441,735,163
Mitsubishi Bank, Ltd., Tokyo	Japan	428,013,635
Norinchukin Bank, Tokyo	Japan	371,727,700
Credit Lyonnais, Paris	France	350,811,485
Industrial Bank of Japan, Ltd., Tokyo	Japan	339,137,296
Deutsche Bank, AG, Frankfurt	Germany	305,922,898
Credit Agricole Mutuel, Paris	France	298,209,899
Mitsubishi Trust & Banking Corp., Tokyo	Japan	292,545,764
Banque Nationale de Paris	France	283,822,410
Long-Term Credit Bank of Japan, Ltd., Tokyo	Japan	274,035,005
Tokai Bank Ltd., Nagoya	Japan	272,929,933
Sumitomo Trust & Banking Co., Ltd., Osaka	Japan	268,997,744
Mitsui Trust & Banking Co., Ltd., Tokyo	Japan	257,223,751
Societe Generale, Paris	France	256,981,266
ABN-AMRO Bank, N.V., Amsterdam	Netherlands	252,708,543
Asahi Bank, Ltd., Tokyo[1]	Japan	249,166,903
Barclays Bank Plc, London	United Kingdom	225,764,652
Bank of Tokyo, Ltd.	Japan	222,864,221
National Westminster Bank Plc, London	United Kingdom	216,829,024
Daiwa Bank, Ltd., Osaka	Japan	212,228,884
Yasuda Trust & Banking Co., Ltd., Tokyo	Japan	201,328,709
Dresdner Bank, Frankfurt	Germany	200,328,051
Union Bank of Switzerland, Zurich	Switzerland	181,925,546
Toyo Trust & Banking Co., Ltd., Tokyo	Japan	$179,488,628
Westdeutsche Landesbank Girozentrale, Duesseldorf	Gemany	165,386,727
Citibank NA, New York	United States	162,044,000
Istituto Bancario San Paolo di Torino, Turin	Italy	161,018,790
Bayerische Vereinsbank, Munich	Germany	155,484,000
Nippon Credit Bank, Ltd., Tokyo	Japan	148,769,160
Commerzbank, Frankfurt	Germany	143,211,096
Shoko Chukin Bank, Tokyo	Japan	138,983,454
Swiss Bank Corp., Basel	Switzerland	137,014,482
Bayerische Hypotheken-und Wechsel-Bank, Munich	Germany	135,634,042
Bank of America, NT&SA, San Francisco	United States	132,166,000
Banque Paribas, Paris[2]	France	130,249,953
Rabobank Nederland, Utrecht	Netherlands	127,751,751
Deutsche Genossenschaftsbank, Frankfurt	Germany	127,586,962
Hongkong and Shanghai Banking Corp., Hongkong[3]	Hong Kong	125,486,040
Bayerische Landesbank Girozentrale, Munich	Germany	121,705,970
Zenshinren Bank, Tokyo	Japan	120,915,429
Credit Suisse, Zurich	Switzerland	118,011,234
Banca Nazionale del Lavoro, Rome	Italy	115,390,496
ING Bank, Amsterdam	Netherlands	109,186,218
Chemical Bank, New York	United States	107,615,000
Royal Bank of Canada, Montreal	Canada	106,840,136
Canadian Imperial Bank of Commerce, Toronto	Canada	106,562,872

NOTE: As of Dec. 31, 1992. Exceptions: Canadian bank data are for fiscal yearend October 31, 1992; all Japanese bank data are for fiscal yearend March 31, 1993. 1. Formerly Kyowa Saitama Bank, Ltd. Changed title on Sept. 21, 1992. 2. A subsidiary of the $203-billion-asset Compagnie Financiere de Paribas, the world's 27th largest banking company. 3. A subsidiary of $258-billion-asset HSBC Holdings, Plc, the world's 17th largest banking company. *Source: American Banker, July 29, 1993.* Reprinted by permission of American Banker/Bond Buyer.

National Labor Organizations With Membership Over 100,000

Members[1]	Union
861,658	Automobile, Aerospace and Agricultural Implement Workers of America; International Union, United
135,000	Bakery, Confectionery, and Tobacco Workers International Union
101,470	Bricklayers and Allied Craftsmen, International Union of
140,000	Bridge, Structural and Ornamental Iron Workers, International Association of
510,000	Carpenters and Joiners of America, United Brotherhood of
240,000	Clothing and Textile Workers Union, Amalgamated
600,000	Communications Workers of America
2,000,000	Education Association, National (Ind.)
845,000	Electrical Workers, International Brotherhood of
150,000	Electronic, Electrical, Salaried, Machine and Furniture Workers, International Union of
195,000	Fire Fighters, International Association of
1,300,000	Food and Commercial Workers International Union, United
210,000	Government Employees, American Federation of
175,000	Graphic Communications International Union
300,000	Hotel Employees and Restaurant Employees International Union
500,000	Laborers' International Union of North America
150,000	Ladies' Garment Workers' Union, International
307,000	Letter Carriers, National Association of
550,000	Machinists and Aerospace Workers, International Association of
171,000	Mine Workers of America, United
204,000	Nurses Association, American (Ind.)
140,000	Office and Professional Employees International Union
100,000	Oil, Chemical and Atomic Workers International Union
375,000	Operating Engineers, International Union of
135,000	Painters and Allied Trades, International Brotherhood of
250,000	Paper Workers International Union, United
315,000	Plumbing and Pipe Fitting Industry of the United States and Canada, United Association of Journeymen and Apprentices of the
365,000	Postal Workers Union, American
130,000	Retail, Wholesale, and Department Store Union
100,000	Rubber, Cork, Linoleum, and Plastic Workers of America, United
1,000,000	Service Employees International Union
147,000	Sheet Metal Workers' International Association
1,300,000	State, County and Municipal Employees, American Federation of
550,000	Steelworkers of America, United
830,000	Teachers, American Federation of
1,700,000	Teamsters, International Brotherhood of
160,000	Transit Union, Amalgamated
135,000	Transportation • Communications International Union
135,000	Transportation Union, United

1. Data are for 1993. Unless otherwise noted, unions are ALF-CIO affiliated.

Persons in the Labor Force

Year	Labor force[1] Number (thousands)	Labor force[1] % Working-age population	Percent in labor force in[2] Farm occupation	Percent in labor force in[2] Nonfarm occupation	Year	Labor force[1] Number (thousands)	Labor force[1] % Working-age population	Percent in labor force in[2] Farm occupation	Percent in labor force in[2] Nonfarm occupation
1840	5,420	46.6	68.6	31.4	1920	42,434	51.3	27.0	73.0
1850	7,697	46.8	63.7	36.3	1930	48,830	49.5	21.4	78.6
1860	10,533	47.0	58.9	41.1	1940	52,789	52.2	17.4	82.6
1870	12,925	45.8	53.0	47.0	1950	60,054	53.5	11.6	88.4
1880	17,392	47.3	49.4	50.6	1960	69,877	55.3	6.0	94.0
1890	23,318	49.2	42.6	57.4	1970	82,049	58.2	3.1	96.9
1900	29,073	50.2	37.5	62.5	1980	106,085	62.0	2.2	97.8
1910	37,371	52.2	31.0	69.0	1990	125,182	65.3	1.6	98.4

1. For 1830 to 1930, the data relate to the population and gainful workers at ages 10 and over. For 1940 to 1960, the data relate to the population and labor force at ages 14 and over; for 1970 and 1980, the data relate to the population and labor force at age 16 and over. For 1940 to 1980, the data include the Armed Forces. 2. The farm and nonfarm percentages relate only to the experienced civilian labor force. *Source:* Department of Commerce, Bureau of the Census.

Corporate Profits[1]

(in billions of dollars)

Item	1993[2]	1992	1991	1990	1985	1980	1975	1970
Domestic industries	316.4	300.2	249.5	236.4	190.8	161.9	107.6	62.4
Financial	64.1	56.8	41.7	18.7	21.0	26.9	11.8	12.1
Nonfinancial	252.3	243.5	207.7	217.7	169.7	134.9	95.8	50.2
Manufacturing	110.7	113.8	81.7	88.8	73.0	72.9	52.6	26.6
Wholesale and retail trade	51.9	47.7	45.8	41.5	49.7	23.6	21.3	9.5
Other	89.7	81.9	80.2	87.5	47.0	38.4	21.9	14.1
Rest of world	67.2	64.0	66.1	56.9	31.8	29.9	13.0	6.5
Total	**383.6**	**364.2**	**315.5**	**293.3**	**222.6**	**191.7**	**120.6**	**68.9**

1. Corporate profits before tax with inventory valuation adjustment. 2. First quarter (seasonally adjusted at annual rates). *Source:* U.S. Bureau of Economic Analysis, *Survey of Current Business.*

National Income by Type

(in billions of dollars)

Type of share	1992	1991	1990	1985	1980	1975	1970	1965	1960
National income	$4,743.4	$4,544.2	$4,459.6	$3,222.3	$2,121.4	$1,215.0	$800.5	$564.3	$414.5
Compensation of employees	3,525.2	3,390.8	3,290.3	2,368.2	1,596.5	931.1	603.9	393.8	294.2
Wages and salaries	2,916.6	2,812.2	2,738.9	1,965.8	1,343.6	805.9	542.0	358.9	270.8
Supplements to wages and salaries	608.6	578.7	551.4	402.4	252.9	125.2	61.9	35.0	23.4
Proprietors' income[1, 2]	404.5	368.0	373.2	254.4	130.6	87.0	66.9	57.3	46.2
Business and professional	364.9	332.2	330.7	225.2	107.2	63.5	50.0	42.4	34.2
Farm	39.5	35.8	42.5	29.2	23.4	23.5	16.9	14.8	12.0
Rental income of persons[1]	4.7	−10.4	−12.9	7.6[1]	31.8	22.4	23.9	19.0	15.8
Corporate profits[1, 2]	393.8	346.3	319.0	280.7	182.7	95.9	69.4	76.1	49.9
Net interest	415.2	449.5	490.1	311.4	179.8	78.6	36.4	18.2	8.4

1. Includes capital consumption adjustment. 2. Includes inventory valuation adjustment. *Source:* Department of Commerce, Bureau of Economic Analysis.

Per Capita Personal Income by States

State	1992[1]	1991	1990	1980	State	1992[1]	1991	1990	1980
Alabama	$16,220	$15,526	$14,998	$7,465	Montana	$16,062	$15,680	$15,304	$8,342
Alaska	21,603	21,144	21,646	13,007	Nebraska	19,084	17,780	17,490	8,895
Arizona	17,119	16,594	16,006	8,854	Nevada	20,266	19,812	19,049	10,848
Arkansas	15,439	14,636	14,176	7,113	New Hampshire	22,934	21,812	20,773	9,150
California	21,278	20,805	20,689	11,021	New Jersey	26,457	25,369	24,881	10,966
Colorado	20,124	19,395	18,860	10,143	New Mexico	15,353	14,709	14,254	7,940
Connecticut	26,979	25,968	25,395	11,532	New York	23,534	22,572	22,129	10,179
Delaware	21,451	20,935	20,095	10,059	North Carolina	17,667	16,848	16,266	7,780
D.C.	26,360	24,916	23,603	12,251	North Dakota	16,854	15,646	15,355	8,642
Florida	19,397	18,985	18,539	9,246	Ohio	18,624	17,767	17,568	9,399
Georgia	18,130	17,447	17,045	8,021	Oklahoma	16,198	15,570	15,451	9,018
Hawaii	21,218	21,062	20,361	10,129	Oregon	18,202	17,495	17,182	9,309
Idaho	16,067	15,366	15,250	8,105	Pennsylvania	20,253	19,313	18,679	9,353
Illinois	21,608	20,737	20,433	10,454	Rhode Island	20,299	19,201	18,809	9,227
Indiana	18,043	17,193	16,921	8,914	South Carolina	15,989	15,391	15,141	7,392
Iowa	18,287	17,251	17,301	9,226	South Dakota	16,558	16,095	15,890	7,800
Kansas	19,376	18,306	18,104	9,880	Tennessee	17,341	16,478	15,868	7,711
Kentucky	16,534	15,626	14,992	7,679	Texas	17,892	17,248	16,717	9,439
Louisiana	15,712	15,054	14,528	8,412	Utah	15,325	14,628	13,985	7,671
Maine	18,226	17,442	17,183	7,760	Vermont	18,834	17,960	17,506	7,957
Maryland	22,974	22,304	21,857	10,394	Virginia	20,629	20,046	19,701	9,413
Massachusetts	24,059	23,046	22,555	10,103	Washington	20,398	19,521	18,777	10,256
Michigan	19,508	18,642	18,378	9,801	West Virginia	15,065	14,315	13,744	7,764
Minnesota	20,049	19,130	18,731	9,673	Wisconsin	18,727	17,919	17,590	9,364
Mississippi	14,088	13,318	12,830	6,573	Wyoming	17,423	16,968	16,283	11,018
Missouri	18,835	17,980	17,479	8,812	**United States**	**19,841**	**19,091**	**18,696**	**9,494**

1. Preliminary. *Source:* U.S. Department of Commerce, Bureau of Economic Analysis, *Survey of Current Business.*

The Federal Budget—Receipts and Outlays

(in billions of dollars)

Description	1994[1]	1993	1992	Description	1994[1]	1993	1992
RECEIPTS BY SOURCE				Commerce & housing credit	22.6	61.0	46.8
Individual income taxes	560.0	515.3	476.0	Transportation	41.9	41.2	36.9
Corporate income taxes	120.3	106.3	100.3	Community development	9.0	11.2	12.3
Social insurance taxes and contributions	465.0	426.8	413.7	Education	57.0	55.8	48.7
				Health	115.8	109.0	92.6
Excise taxes	51.4	47.6	45.6	Medicare	147.3	134.7	133.6
Estate and gift taxes	12.7	12.6	11.1	Income security	218.7	215.8	200.6
Customs duties	21.3	19.2	17.4	Social security	322.3	306.7	289.5
Miscellaneous receipts	20.6	17.9	26.5	Veterans benefits	36.6	35.7	34.2
Total budget receipts	**1,251.3**	**1,145.7**	**1,090.5**	Administration of justice	16.3	15.2	14.8
OUTLAYS BY FUNCTION				General government	13.7	14.4	13.1
National Defense	263.3	272.8	295.0	Net interest	212.1	201.5	199.5
International affairs	19.6	31.0	21.2	Allowances	–0.8	—	—
Gen. science	18.4	17.4	17.3	Undistributed receipts	–37.5	–37.2	–39.3
Energy	4.0	4.2	6.1	**Total outlays**	**1,517.2**	**1,533.4**	**1,466.6**
Natural resources	20.2	22.6	21.3	**Total deficit**	**265.9**	**387.7**	**376.1**
Agriculture	16.8	20.5	22.4				

1. Estimated. NOTE: The fiscal year is from Oct. 1 to Sept. 30. *Source:* Executive Office of the President, Office of Management and Budget.

Foreign Assistance

(in millions of dollars)

	Non-military programs			Military programs		
Calendar years	**Net new grants**	**Net new credits**	**Net other assistance**	**Net grants**	**Net credits**	**Total net assistance[1]**
1945–1950[2]	$18,413	$8,086	—	$ 1,525	—	$28,023
1951–60	18,750	2,012	2,767	26,555	49	50,132
1961–70	18,192	14,776	12	21,591	176	54,747
1971–80	27,216	16,399	–1,011	22,602	9,003	74,209
1981–85	29,025	7,070	–2	9,295	10,836	56,225
1988	7,231	203	–35	3,576	–4,205	6,770
1989	7,365	–411	–2	3,802	–1,924	8,830
1990[3]	10,014	946	–33	6,717	–4,646	12,996
1991[3]	–32,242	–3,842	23	4,221	–1,556	–33,395
1992[3]	8,530	221	([4])	6,084	–52	14,784
Total postwar period	**127,840**	**43,093**	**1,699**	**113,223**	**9,227**	**295,082**

1. Excludes investment in international nonmonetary financial institutions of $23,840 million. 2. Includes transactions after V-J Day (Sept. 2, 1945). 3. Includes contributions received from coalition partners for Persian Gulf operations. 4. Less than $500,000. NOTE: Detail may not add to total due to rounding. *Source:* Department of Commerce, Bureau of Economic Analysis.

Women in the Civilian Labor Force

(16 years of age and over; in thousands)

Labor force status	1992	1991	1990	1989	1988	1987
In the labor force:	57,798	56,893	56,554	56,030	54,742	53,658
16 to 19 years of age	3,204	3,330	3,544	3,818	3,872	3,875
20 years and over	54,594	53,563	53,010	52,212	50,870	49,783
Employed	53,793	53,284	53,479	53,027	51,696	50,334
16 to 19 years of age	2,613	2,749	3,024	3,282	3,313	3,260
20 years and over	51,180	50,535	50,455	49,745	48,383	47,075
Unemployed	4,005	3,609	3,075	3,003	3,046	3,324
16 to 19 years of age	591	581	519	536	558	616
20 years and over	3,414	3,028	2,555	2,467	2,487	2,709
Not in the labor force:	42,237	42,321	41,845	41,601	42,014	42,195
Women as percent of labor force	45.5	45.4	45.3	45.2	45.0	44.8
Total civilian noninstitutional population	100,035	99,214	98,399	97,630	96,756	95,853

Source: Department of Labor, Bureau of Labor Statistics, annual averages.

Employed Persons 16 Years and Over, by Race and Major Occupational Groups

(number in thousands)

Race and occupational group	1992 Number	1992 Percent distribution	1991 Number	1991 Percent distribution
WHITE				
Managerial and professional specialty	27,948	27.5	27,943	27.7
Executive, administrative, & managerial	13,438	13.2	13,629	13.5
Professional specialty	14,510	14.3	14,313	14.2
Technical, sales, & administrative support	32,162	31.7	31,530	31.2
Technicians & related support	3,631	3.6	3,269	3.2
Sales occupations	12,564	12.4	12,581	12.5
Administrative support, including clerical	15,968	15.7	15,681	15.5
Service occupations	12,611	12.4	12,576	12.4
Precision production, craft, and repair	11,767	11.6	11,799	11.7
Operators, fabricators, and laborers	13,844	13.6	14,040	13.9
Farming, forestry, fishing	3,147	3.1	3,150	3.1
Total	**101,479**	**100.0**	**101,039**	**100.0**
BLACK				
Managerial and professional specialty	2,009	16.8	1,939	16.3
Executive, administrative, & managerial	855	7.2	858	7.2
Professional specialty	1,154	9.7	1,081	9.1
Technical, sales, & administrative support	3,337	28.0	3,354	28.3
Technicians & related support	410	3.4	337	2.8
Sales occupations	865	7.3	926	7.8
Administrative support, including clerical	2,062	17.3	2,091	17.6
Service occupations	2,809	23.5	2,755	23.2
Precision production, craft, and repair	996	8.4	1,022	8.6
Operators, fabricators, and laborers	2,556	21.4	2,569	21.7
Farming, forestry, and fishing	225	1.9	223	1.9
Total	**11,933**	**100.0**	**11,863**	**100.0**

Source: Department of Labor, Bureau of Labor Statistics.

Mothers Participating in Labor Force

(figures in percentage)

Year	Mother with children: Under 18 years	6 to 17 years	Under 6 years[1]
1955	27.0	38.4	18.2
1965	35.0	45.7	25.3
1975	47.4	54.8	38.9
1980	56.6	64.4	46.6
1983	58.9	66.3	50.5
1984	60.5	68.2	52.1
1985	62.1	69.9	53.5
1986	62.8	70.4	54.4
1987	64.7	72.0	56.7
1988	65.0	73.3	56.1
1989	n.a.	n.a.	n.a.
1990	66.7	74.7	58.2
1991	66.6	74.4	58.4
1992	67.2	75.9	58.0

1. May also have older children. NOTE: For 1955 data are for April; for 1965 and 1975–91, data are for March. *Source:* Department of Labor, Bureau of Labor Statistics. NOTE: Data are most recent available.

Women in the Civilian Labor Force

Year	Number[1] (thousands)	% Female population aged 16 and over[1]	% of Labor force population aged 16 and over[1]
1900	5,319	18.8	18.3
1910	7,445	21.5	19.9
1920	8,637	21.4	20.4
1930	10,752	22.0	22.0
1940	12,845	25.4	24.3
1950	18,389	33.9	29.6
1960[2]	23,240	37.7	33.4
1970	31,543	43.3	38.1
1980	45,487	51.5	42.5
1990	56,554	57.5	45.3
1991	56,893	57.3	45.4
1992	57,798	57.8	45.5

1. For 1900–1930, data relate to population and labor force aged 10 and over; for 1940, to population and labor force aged 14 and over; beginning 1950, to civilian population and labor force aged 16 and over. 2. Beginning in 1960, figures include Alaska and Hawaii. *Sources:* Department of Commerce, Bureau of the Census, and Department of Labor, Bureau of Labor Statistics.

Manufacturing Industries—Gross Average Weekly Earnings and Hours Worked

Industry	1992 Earnings	1992 Hours worked	1990 Earnings	1990 Hours worked	1985 Earnings	1985 Hours worked	1980 Earnings	1980 Hours worked	1975 Earnings	1975 Hours worked	1970 Earnings	1970 Hours worked
All manufacturing	$469.45	41.0	$442.27	40.8	$385.56	40.5	$288.62	39.7	$189.51	39.4	$133.73	39.8
Durable goods	498.83	41.5	468.76	41.3	415.71	41.2	310.78	40.1	205.09	39.9	143.07	40.3
Primary metal industries	587.81	43.0	550.83	42.7	484.72	41.5	391.78	40.1	246.80	40.0	159.17	40.5
Iron and steel foundries	525.46	43.0	484.99	42.1	429.62	40.8	328.00	40.0	220.99	40.4	151.03	40.6
Nonferrous foundries	446.35	41.1	413.48	40.3	388.74	41.8	291.27	39.9	190.03	39.1	138.16	39.7
Fabricated metal products	474.66	41.6	447.28	41.3	398.96	41.3	300.98	40.4	201.60	40.0	143.67	40.7
Hardware, cutlery, hand tools	464.32	41.2	440.08	40.9	396.42	40.7	275.89	39.3	187.07	39.3	132.33	40.1
Hardware	470.18	41.1	448.63	40.6	385.40	41.3	195.42	39.4	133.46	40.2		
Structural metal products	439.36	41.1	416.56	41.0	369.00	41.0	291.85	40.2	202.61	40.2	142.61	40.4
Electric and electronic equipment	453.61	41.2	420.65	40.8	384.48	40.6	276.21	39.8	180.91	39.5	130.54	39.8
Machinery, except electrical	524.55	42.2	494.34	42.0	427.04	41.5	328.00	41.0	219.22	40.9	154.95	41.1
Transportation equipment	633.69	41.8	592.20	42.0	542.72	42.7	379.61	40.6	242.61	40.3	163.22	40.3
Motor vehicles and equipment	649.99	42.4	619.46	42.4	584.64	43.5	394.00	40.0	262.68	40.6	170.07	40.3
Lumber and wood products	382.86	40.6	365.82	40.2	326.36	39.8	252.18	38.5	167.35	39.1	117.51	39.7
Furniture and fixtures	357.30	39.7	333.52	39.1	283.29	39.4	209.17	38.1	142.13	37.9	108.58	39.2
Nondurable goods	432.68	40.4	405.60	40.0	342.86	39.5	255.45	39.0	168.78	38.8	120.43	39.1
Textile mill products	353.46	41.1	320.40	40.0	266.39	39.7	203.31	40.1	133.28	39.2	97.76	39.9
Apparel and other textile products	258.54	37.2	239.88	36.4	208.00	36.3	161.42	35.4	111.97	35.1	84.37	35.3
Leather and leather products	281.20	38.0	258.43	37.4	217.09	37.3	169.09	36.7	120.80	37.4	92.63	37.2
Food and kindred products	413.71	40.6	392.90	40.8	341.60	40.0	271.95	39.7	184.17	40.3	127.98	40.5
Tobacco manufactures	644.23	38.6	645.23	39.2	448.26	37.2	294.89	38.1	171.38	38.0	110.00	37.8
Paper and allied products	570.72	43.6	532.59	43.3	466.34	43.1	330.85	42.2	207.58	41.6	144.14	41.9
Printing and publishing	447.68	38.1	426.38	37.9	365.31	37.7	279.36	37.1	198.32	37.0	147.78	37.7
Chemicals and allied products	622.80	43.1	576.80	42.6	484.78	41.9	344.45	41.5	219.63	40.9	153.50	41.6
Petroleum and allied products	782.71	43.8	723.86	44.6	603.72	43.0	422.18	41.8	267.07	41.6	182.76	42.7

Source: Department of Labor, Bureau of Labor Statistics.

Decade-Long Occupational Shift Reported

According to a Census Bureau report there have been significant shifts in the occupations held by the nation's work force since 1980.

The number of persons with skills or work experience in traditional fields such as agriculture; precision production, craft, and repair; and operators, fabricators, and laborers grew slowly or declined between 1980 and 1990.

Meanwhile some occupations grew at triple to quadruple the nation's population growth during the 1980s. Technicians and related support occupations grew by 43 percent; executive, administrative, and managerial occupations as well as sales occupations grew by 41 percent; and professional specialty occupations grew by 36 percent. Between 1980 and 1990, the nation's population increased by only 10 percent.

During the 1980s, the number of persons in the civilian work force increased by nearly twice the rate at which the population grew—18 percent versus 10 percent. Much of the growth in the work force came from the entry of women into the labor market. Women experienced a 27 percent growth in the participation rate compared to men's 12 percent.

Women continued to predominate in the administrative support, including clerical, occupations. Men comprised the majority in the occupations of precision productions, craft, and repair; farming, forestry, and fishing; and operators, fabricators, and laborers.

Nonmanufacturing Industries—Gross Average Weekly Earnings and Hours Worked

Industry	1992 Earnings	1992 Hours worked	1990 Earnings	1990 Hours worked	1985 Earnings	1985 Hours worked	1975 Earnings	1975 Hours worked	1970 Earnings	1970 Hours worked
Bituminous coal and lignite mining	$763.40	44.0	$740.52	44.0	$630.77	41.4	$284.53	39.2	$186.41	40.8
Metal mining	652.94	42.9	602.07	42.7	547.24	40.9	250.72	42.3	165.68	42.7
Nonmetallic minerals	550.92	44.9	524.12	45.3	451.68	44.5	213.09	43.4	155.11	44.7
Telephone communications	623.61	41.0	578.74	40.9	512.52	41.1	221.18	38.4	131.60	39.4
Radio and TV broadcasting	479.21	34.7	438.61	34.7	381.39	37.1	214.50	39.0	147.45	38.2
Electric, gas, and sanitary services	674.17	41.9	636.76	41.7	534.59	41.7	246.79	41.2	172.64	41.5
Local and suburban transportation	403.97	38.4	376.65	38.2	309.85	38.3	196.89	40.1	142.30	42.1
Wholesale trade	435.48	38.2	411.48	38.1	358.36	38.7	188.75	38.6	137.60	40.0
Retail trade	205.63	28.8	195.26	28.8	177.31	29.7	108.22	32.4	82.47	33.8
Hotels, tourist courts, motels	228.54	30.8	214.68	30.8	176.90	30.5	89.64	31.9	68.16	34.6
Laundries and dry cleaning plants	243.78	34.0	232.22	34.0	198.70	34.2	106.05	35.0	77.47	35.7
General building contracting	502.13	37.5	487.08	37.7	414.78	37.1	254.88	36.0	184.40	36.3

Source: Department of Labor, Bureau of Labor Statistics.

Median Income Comparisons of Year-Round Workers by Educational Attainment and Sex, 1991

(persons 25 years and over)

Years of school completed	Median income: Women	Median income: Men	Income gap in dollars	Women's income as a percent of men's	Percent men's income exceeded women's
Less than 9th grade	$11,637	$16,880	$5,243	69	45
High school:					
9th to 12th grade (no diploma)	13,538	20,944	7,406	65	55
Graduate (includes equivalency)	18,042	26,218	8,176	69	45
College:					
Some, no degree	21,328	31,034	9,706	69	45
Bachelor's degree	27,654	39,894	12,240	69	44

Source: Department of Commerce, Bureau of the Census. NOTE: Data are latest available.

Money Income of Households with Female Householder, 1991

(No husband present)

Income bracket	Number of Households: All	White	Black	Hispanic[1]
Less than $5,000	1,573,000	769,000	742,000	199,000
$5,000 to $9,999	2,230,000	1,272,000	896,000	329,000
$10,000 to $14,999	1,540,000	1,006,000	492,000	195,000
$15,000 to $19,999	1,323,000	890,000	391,000	143,000
$20,000 to $24,999	1,102,000	767,000	289,000	108,000
$25,000 to $29,999	905,000	671,000	208,000	73,000
$30,000 to $34,999	694,000	528,000	143,000	52,000
$35,000 to $39,999	594,000	460,000	114,000	40,000
$40,000 to $44,999	510,000	387,000	112,000	39,000
$45,000 to $49,999	299,000	235,000	60,000	19,000
$50,000 to $54,999	264,000	222,000	36,000	12,000
$55,000 to $59,999	164,000	134,000	20,000	9,000
$60,000 to $64,999	106,000	79,000	20,000	10,000
$65,000 to $69,999	90,000	78,000	11,000	13,000
$70,000 to $74,999	67,000	58,000	8,000	4,000
$75,000 to $79,999	46,000	41,000	4,000	2,000
$80,000 to $84,999	34,000	24,000	10,000	4,000
$85,000 to $89,999	24,000	18,000	4,000	2,000
$90,000 to $94,999	24,000	15,000	9,000	—
$95,000 to $99,999	18,000	12,000	—	—
$100,000 and over	85,000	61,000	12,000	7,000
Median income	$16,692	$19,547	$11,414	$12,132
Mean income	$21,946	$24,303	$16,528	$17,741

1. Persons of Hispanic origin may be of any race. *Source:* Department of Commerce, Bureau of the Census, *Current Population Reports, Consumer Income, Series P-60, No. 180.*

Unemployment by Marital Status, Sex, and Race[1]

Marital status and race	Men: Number	Men: Unemployment rate	Women: Number	Women: Unemployment rate
White, 16 years and over	4,121,000	6.9	2,926,000	6.0
Married, spouse present	1,775,000	4.7	1,324,000	4.7
Widowed, divorced, or separated	580,000	9.1	655,000	7.1
Single (never married)	1,766,000	11.3	947,000	8.4
Black, 16 years and over	1,046,000	15.2	912,000	13.0
Married, spouse present	260,000	8.3	187,000	7.8
Widowed, divorced, or separated	150,000	13.7	193,000	9.8
Single (never married)	636,000	24.0	532,000	20.2
Total, 16 years and over	5,380,000	7.8	4,005,000	6.9
Married, spouse present	2,124,000	5.0	1,584,000	5.0
Widowed, divorced, or separated	756,000	9.8	876,000	7.5
Single (never married)	2,499,000	13.1	1,545,000	10.7

1. 1992 Annual Averages. *Source: Employment and Earnings,* January 1993, U.S. Department of Labor, Bureau of Labor Statistics.

Earnings Distribution of Year-Round, Full-Time Workers, by Sex, 1991

(persons 15 years old and over as of March 1992)

Earnings group	Number: Women	Number: Men	Distribution (percent): Women	Distribution (percent): Men	Likelihood of a woman in each earnings group (percent)[1]
$2,499 or less	463,000	500,000	1.4	1.0	1.4
$2,500 to $4,999	314,000	292,000	1.0	0.6	1.7
$5,000 to $7,499	888,000	802,000	2.7	1.7	1.6
$7,500 to $9,999	1,601,000	1,282,000	4.9	2.7	1.8
$10,000 to $14,999	6,056,000	4,672,000	18.7	9.8	1.9
$15,000 to $19,999	6,129,000	5,469,000	18.9	11.4	1.7
$20,000 to $24,999	5,472,000	5,805,000	16.9	12.1	1.4
$25,000 to $49,999	10,130,000	20,586,000	31.2	43.0	0.7
$50,000 and over	1,380,000	8,480,000	4.3	17.7	0.2
Total	**32,436,000**	**47,888,000**	**100.0**	**100.0**	—

1. Figures obtained by dividing percentages for women by percentages for men. Percentages may not add to totals because of rounding. *Source:* Department of Commerce, Bureau of the Census.

Comparison of Median Earnings of Year-Round, Full-Time Workers 15 Years and Over, by Sex, 1960 to 1991

Year	Median earnings: Women	Median earnings: Men	Earnings gap in current dollars	Women's earnings as a percent of men's	Percent men's earnings exceeded women's	Earnings gap in constant 1991 CPI-U-xl adjusted dollars
1960	$3,257	$5,368	$2,111	60.7	64.8	8,929
1970	5,323	8,966	3,643	59.4	68.4	12,014
1980	11,197	18,612	7,415	60.2	66.2	12,271
1982	13,014	21,077	8,063	61.7	62.0	11,487
1983	13,915	21,881	7,966	63.6	57.2	10,893
1984	14,780	23,218	8,438	63.7	57.1	11,061
1985	15,624	24,195	8,571	64.7	54.9	10,849
1986	16,232	25,256	9,024	64.3	55.6	11,214
1987	16,911	25,946	9,035	65.2	53.4	10,832
1988	17,606	26,656	9,050	66.0	51.4	10,419
1989	18,778	27,430	8,652	68.5	46.1	9,503
1990	19,822	27,678	7,856	71.6	39.6	8,187
1991	20,553	29,421	8,868	69.9	43.1	8,868

Source: Department of Commerce, Bureau of the Census.

Occupations of Employed Women[1]

(16 years of age and over. Figures are percentage)

Occupations	1992	1991	1990	1989	1988	1987	1986
Managerial and professional	27.4	26.9	26.2	25.9	25.2	24.4	23.7
Technical, sales, administrative support	43.8	43.8	44.4	44.2	44.6	45.1	45.6
Service occupations	17.9	17.9	17.7	17.7	17.9	18.1	18.3
Precision production, craft and repair	2.1	2.1	2.2	2.2	2.3	2.3	2.4
Operators, fabricators, laborers	7.9	8.1	8,5	8.9	8.9	9.0	8.9
Farming, forestry, fishing	1.0	1.0	1.0	1.1	1.1	1.1	1.1

1. Annual averages. NOTE: Details may not add up to totals because of rounding. *Source:* Department of Labor.

Employed and Unemployed Workers by Full- and Part-Time Status, Sex, and Age: 1970 to 1992

(In thousands)

	1992	1991	1990	1989	1985	1980	1975	1970
Total 16 yr and over								
Employed	117,598	116,877	117,914	117,342	107,150	99,303	85,846	78,678
Full time	97,026	96,575	97,994	97,369	88,535	82,564	71,585	66,752
Part time	20,572	20,302	19,920	19,973	18,615	16,742	14,260	11,924
Unemployed	9,384	8,426	6,874	6,528	8,312	7,637	7,929	4,093
Full time	7,746	6,932	5,541	5,211	6,793	6,269	6,523	3,206
Part time	1,638	1,494	1,332	1,317	1,519	1,369	1,408	889
Men, 20 yr and over								
Employed	61,019	60,174	61,198	60,837	56,562	53,101	48,018	45,581
Full time	55,878	55,852	56,640	56,386	52,425	49,699	45,051	43,138
Part time	5,141	4,862	4,558	4,451	4,137	3,403	2,966	2,444
Unemployed	4,619	4,109	3,170	2,867	3,715	3,353	3,476	1,638
Full time	4,339	3,848	2,936	2,651	3,479	3,167	3,255	1,502
Part time	280	261	234	215	236	186	223	137
Women, 20 yr. and over								
Employed	51,181	50,535	50,455	49,745	44,154	38,492	30,726	26,952
Full time	39,409	38,854	39,036	38,408	33,604	29,391	23,242	20,654
Part time	11,772	11,681	11,419	11,337	10,550	9,102	7,484	6,297
Unemployed	3,413	3,028	2,555	2,467	3,129	2,615	2,684	1,349
Full time	2,794	2,463	2,044	1,963	2,536	2,135	2,210	1,077
Part time	620	565	511	504	593	480	474	271
Both sexes 16–19 yr.								
Employed	5,398	5,628	6,261	6,759	6,434	7,710	7,104	6,144
Full time	1,739	1.869	2,318	2,574	2,507	3,474	3,292	2,960
Part time	3,659	3,759	3,943	4,185	3,927	4,237	3,810	3,183
Unemployed	1,352	1,290	1,149	1,194	1,468	1,669	1,767	1,106
Full time	614	621	561	596	777	966	1,057	626
Part time	739	669	587	598	690	701	709	480

Source: U.S. Dept. of Labor, Bureau of Labor Statistics.

Work Stoppages Involving 1,000 Workers or More[1]

Year	Work stop-pages	Workers involved (thousands)	Man-days idle (thousands)	Year	Work stop-pages	Workers involved (thousands)	Man-days idle (thousands)
1950	424	1,698	30,390	1984	68	391	8,499
1960	222	896	13,260	1985	61	584	7,079
1965	268	999	15,140	1986	72	900	11,861
1970	381	2,468	52,761	1987	46	174	4,456
1975	235	965	17,563	1988	40	118	4,381
1980	187	795	20,844	1989	51	452	16,996
1981	145	729	16,908	1990	44	185	5,926
1982	96	656	9,061	1991	40	392	4,584
1983	81	909	17,461	1992	35	364	3,989

1. The number of stoppages and workers relate to stoppages that began in the year. Days of idleness include all stoppages in effect. Workers are counted more than once if they were involved in more than one stoppage during the year. *Source:* U.S. Department of Labor. Bureau of Labor Statistics, *Monthly Labor Review. July 1993.*

Leading Advertising Agencies in Worldwide Billings

(in thousands of dollars)

Agency	1991	1990
McCann-Erickson	$6,357,400[1]	$5,570,405[1]
FCB-Publicis	6,200,000[1]	5,790,000[1]
J. Walter Thompson	5,690,000[1]	4,957,000[1]
Saatchi & Saatchi Advertising	5,189,400[1]	5,189,400[1]
BBDO Worldwide	5,100,827[1]	4,400,000[2]
Ogilvy & Mather Worldwide	5,015,740[1]	4,831,338[1]
Young & Rubicam	4,981,134[1]	4,981,134[1]
Backer Spielvogel Bates Worldwide	4,730,658	4,492,000[2]
DDB Needham Worldwide	4,565,403	4,289,696[2]
Lintas Worldwide	4,422,981[1]	4,456,996

1. Estimated. 2. Restated pending acquisition or merger. *Source: ADWEEK Magazine,* Top 25 Worldwide Agencies, March 23, 1993 edition. © ADWEEK L.P. used with permission of *ADWEEK.*

Unemployment Rate, 1992

Race and age	Women[1]	Men[1]
All races:	6.9	7.8
16 to 19 years	18.5	21.5
20 years and over	10.1	10.4
White	6.0	6.9
16 to 19 years	15.7	18.4
20 years and over	5.4	6.3
Minority races:	12.4	13.5
16 to 19 years	38.4	35.3
20 years and over	11.1	12.0

1. Annual averages. *Source:* Bureau of Labor Statistics, Department of Labor.

Unemployment Rate in the Civilian Labor Force

Year	Unemployment rate	Year	Unemployment rate
1920	5.2	1982	9.7
1928	4.2	1983	9.6
1930	8.7	1984	7.5
1932	23.6	1985	7.2
1934	21.7	1986	7.0
1936	16.9	1987	6.2
1938	19.0	1988	5.4
1940	14.6	1989	5.3
1942	4.7	1990	5.5
1944	1.2	1991	6.7
1946	3.9	1992	7.4
1948	3.8	Jan.	7.1
1950	5.3	Feb.	7.3
1952	3.0	March	7.3
1954	5.5	April	7.3
1956	4.1	May	7.4
1958	6.8	June	7.7
1960	5.5	July	7.6
1962	5.5	Aug.	7.6
1964	5.2	Sept.	7.5
1966	3.8	Oct.	7.4
1968	3.6	Nov.	7.3
1970	4.9	Dec.	7.3
1972	5.6	1993	
1974	5.6	Jan.	7.1
1976	7.7	Feb.	7.0
1978	6.0	March	7.0
1980	7.1	April	7.0
1981	7.6		

NOTE: Estimates prior to 1940 are based on sources other than direct enumeration. *Source:* Department of Labor, Bureau of Labor Statistics.

Employment and Unemployment

(in millions of persons)

Category	1992	1991	1990	1985	1980	1975	1970	1950	1945	1932	1929
EMPLOYMENT STATUS[1]											
Civilian noninstitutional population	191.6	189.8	188.0	178.2	167.7	153.2	137.1	105.0	94.1	—	—
Civilian labor force	127.0	125.3	124.8	115.5	106.9	93.8	82.8	62.2	53.9	—	—
Civilian labor force participation rate	66.3	66.0	66.4	64.8	63.8	61.2	60.4	59.2	57.2	—	—
Employed	117.6	116.9	117.9	107.2	99.3	85.8	78.7	58.9	52.8	38.9	47.6
Employment-population ratio	61.6	61.6	62.7	60.1	59.2	56.1	57.4	56.1	56.1	—	—
Agriculture	3.2	3.2	3.2	3.2	3.4	3.4	3.5	7.2	8.6	10.2	10.5
Nonagricultural industries	114.4	113.6	114.7	104.0	95.9	82.4	75.2	51.8	44.2	28.8	37.2
Unemployed	9.4	8.4	6.9	8.3	7.6	7.9	4.1	3.3	1.0	12.1	1.6
Unemployment rate	7.4	6.7	5.5	7.2	7.1	8.5	4.9	5.3	1.9	23.6	3.2
Not in labor force	64.6	64.5	63.3	62.7	60.8	59.4	54.3	42.8	40.2	—	—
INDUSTRY[2]											
Total nonfarm employment	108.5	108.3	109.4	97.4	90.4	76.9	70.9	45.2	40.4	23.6	31.3
Goods-producing industries	23.1	23.7	24.9	24.8	25.7	22.6	23.6	18.5	17.5	8.6	13.3
Mining	0.6	0.7	0.7	0.9	1.0	0.8	0.6	0.9	0.8	0.7	1.1
Construction	4.5	4.7	5.1	4.7	4.3	3.5	3.6	2.4	1.1	1.0	1.5
Manufacturing: Durable goods	10.2	10.6	11.1	11.5	12.2	10.7	11.2	8.1	9.1	—	—
Nondurable goods	7.8	7.9	8.0	7.8	8.1	7.7	8.2	7.2	6.4	—	—
Services-producing industries	85.4	84.5	84.5	72.5	64.7	54.3	47.3	26.7	22.9	15.0	18.0
Transportation and public utilities	5.7	5.8	5.8	5.2	5.1	4.5	4.5	4.0	3.9	2.8	3.9
Trade, Wholesale	6.0	6.1	6.2	5.7	5.3	4.4	4.0	2.6	1.9	—	—
Retail	19.3	19.3	19.6	17.3	15.0	12.6	11.0	6.7	5.4	—	—
Finance, insurance, and real estate	6.6	6.7	6.7	5.9	5.2	4.2	3.6	1.9	1.5	1.3	1.5
Services	29.1	28.3	27.9	21.9	17.9	13.9	11.5	5.4	4.2	2.9	3.4
Federal government	3.0	3.0	3.1	2.9	2.9	2.7	2.7	1.9	2.8	0.6	0.5
State and local government	15.7	15.4	15.2	13.5	13.4	11.9	9.8	4.1	3.1	2.7	2.5

1. For 1929–45, figures on employment status relate to persons 14 years and over; beginning in 1950, 16 years and over.
2. Data for 1985–1992 have been revised. *Source:* U.S. Department of Labor, Bureau of Labor Statistics.

Livestock on Farms (in thousands)

Type	1993	1992	1991	1990	1985	1980	1975	1970	1965	1960
Cattle[1]	100,892	100,110	99,436	98,162	109,582	111,242	132,028	112,369	109,000	96,236
Dairy cows[1]	9,844	9,904	10,159	10,153	10,311	10,758	11,220	13,303	16,981	19,527
Sheep[1]	10,191	10,850	11,200	11,363	10,716	12,699	14,515	20,423	25,127	33,170
Swine[2]	58,340	56,974	52,360	51,150	54,073	67,318	54,693	57,046	56,106	59,026
Chickens[3]	6,753,170	6,499,971	6,223,623	5,873,923	4,689,973	4,201,706	3,173,820	3,220,085	2,535,141	1,976,737
Turkeys[4]	288,980	285,110	282,450	261,280	185,427	165,243	124,165	116,139	105,914	84,458

1. As of Jan. 1. 2. As of Jan. 1 of the previous year for 1950–60; Dec. 1 of the previous year for 1965–85 and 1992; as of March 1 for 1990–91. 3. Layers as of Jan. 1 of the previous year for 1950–60; Dec. of the previous year for 1965–93. 4. 1975–85 as of Dec. of previous year, 1990 total for calendar year. *Source:* Department of Agriculture, Statistical Reporting Service, Economic Research Service.

Agricultural Output by States, 1992 Crops

State	Corn (1,000 bu)	Wheat (1,000 bu)	Cotton (1,000 ba[1])	Potatoes (1,000 cwt)	Tobacco (1,000 lb)	Cattle[2] (1,000 head)	Swine[3] (1,000 head)
Alabama	30,080	4,180	610.0	1,733	—	1,770	370
Alaska	—	—	—	—	—	7.9	2
Arizona	1,870	7,700	857.0	1,800	—	890	106
Arkansas	12,350	39,100	1,700.0	—	—	1,710	810
California	23,925	46,365	3,080.0	14,972	—	4,500	250
Colorado	123,580	72,619	—	23,850	—	2,850	410
Connecticut	—	—	—	—	2,401	77	6
Delaware	19,159	4,060	—	1,380	—	33	46
Florida	8,250	840	80.0	9,370	19,608	1,950	115
Georgia	69,000	16,100	750.0	—	101,200	1,500	1,100
Hawaii	—	—	—	—	—	178	35
Idaho	4,290	100,000	—	121,380	—	1,680	60
Illinois	1,646,450	62,100	—	1,320	—	2,000	5,900
Indiana	877,590	22,500	—	989	18,900	1,220	4,600
Iowa	1,903,650	1,560	—	280	—	4,400	16,400
Kansas	259,500	363,800	0.9	—	—	5,890	1,440
Kentucky	171,600	23,100	—	—	508,870	2,600	870
Louisiana	37,080	6,120	1,290.0	—	—	1,000	55
Maine	—	—	—	22,400	—	116	9.1
Maryland	58,280	12,760	—	320	14,000	325	180
Massachusetts	—	—	—	855	624	71	27
Michigan	241,500	35,280	—	13,920	—	1,225	1,280
Minnesota	741,000	139,860	—	18,388	—	2,850	4,700
Mississippi	27,000	10,500	2,150.4	—	—	1,415	182
Missouri	324,000	64,800	548.0	1,764	2,960	4,600	2,850
Montana	2,750	139,581	—	2,465	—	2,450	215
Nebraska	1,066,500	55,500	—	3,298	—	5,900	4,650
Nevada	—	800	—	2,925	—	480	10
New Hampshire	—	—	—	—	—	52	9
New Jersey	9,840	1,400	—	840	—	75	28
New Mexico	11,360	11,220	70.0	3,247	—	1,370	23
New York	61,640	6,160	—	7,808	—	1,560	105
North Carolina	98,800	27,750	470.0	3,614	595,500	1,050	4,500
North Dakota	36,540	469,850	—	27,690	—	1,800	290
Ohio	507,650	59,095	—	1,440	22,680	1,610	1,800
Oklahoma	17,550	171,100	215.0	—	—	5,400	240
Oregon	2,250	47,800	—	19,450	—	1,350	70
Pennsylvania	118,800	10,175	—	4,940	20,840	1,850	950
Rhode Island	—	—	—	384	—	7	6
South Carolina	30,800	12,925	221.0	—	112,320	630	385
South Dakota	277,200	119,590	—	1,500	—	3,750	1,830
Tennessee	79,360	13,440	835.0	—	135,463	2,300	600
Texas	202,500	129,200	3,356.0	2,459	—	14,300	540
Utah	3,240	6,256	—	1,650	—	850	44
Vermont	—	—	—	—	—	300	4.7
Virginia	40,020	15,105	26.9	1,980	110,875	1,780	390
Washington	15,840	119,640	—	65,625	—	1,350	46
West Virginia	5,400	539	—	—	3,230	520	32
Wisconsin	306,800	2,640	—	25,160	14,360	3,950	1,210
Wyoming	3,920	5,720	—	440	—	1,350	35
U.S. Total	**9,478,914**	**2,458,830**	**16,260.2**	**411,636**	**1,683,831**	**100,892**	**59,815**

1. 480-lb net-weight bales. 2. Number on farms as of Jan. 1, 1993. 3. Number on farms as of Dec. 1, 1992. *Source:* Department of Agriculture, Statistical Reporting Service.

Farm Income

(in millions of dollars)

Year	Cash receipts from marketings: Crops	Livestock, livestock products	Government payments	Total cash income[1]
1930	$3,868	$5,187	—	$9,055
1935	2,977	4,143	$573	7,693
1940	3,469	4,913	723	9,105
1945	9,655	12,008	742	22,405
1950	12,356	16,105	283	28,764
1955	13,523	15,967	229	29,842
1960	15,023	18,989	703	34,958
1965	17,479	21,886	2,463	42,215
1970	20,977	29,532	3,717	54,768
1975	45,813	43,089	807	90,707
1980	71,746	67,991	1,285	143,295
1985	74,293	69,822	7,705	157,854
1987	65,851	75,993	16,747	158,591
1988	71,663	79,438	14,480	165,582
1989	76,879	84,148	10,887	171,914
1990	79,999	89,921	9,298	179,218
1991	80,547	86,745	8,214	175,506
1992	84,280[2]	85,996[2]	9,169[2]	n.a.

1. Includes items not listed. 2. Preliminary. *Source:* Department of Agriculture, Economic Research Service.

Per Capita Consumption of Principal Foods[1]

Food	1992	1991	1990
Red meat[2]	114.1	111.9	112.4
Poultry[2]	60.1	58.0	55.9
Fish and shellfish[2]	14.7	14.8	15.0
Eggs	30.2	30.0	30.1
Fluid milk and cream[3]	230.8	233.1	233.4
Ice cream	16.4	16.3	15.8
Cheese (excluding cottage)	26.0	25.0	24.6
Butter (actual weight)	4.2	4.2	4.4
Margarine (actual weight)	11.0	10.6	10.7
Total fats and oils[4]	65.6	63.8	62.2
Fruits (farm weight)[5]	262.9	264.7	261.3
Peanuts (shelled)	6.5	6.0	7.0
Vegetables (farm weight)	387.5	383.8	380.7
Sugar (refined)	64.5	63.7	64.4
Corn sweeteners (dry weight)	77.4	76.6	74.9
Flour and cereal products	187.0	185.4	183.5
Soft drinks (gal)	44.1	43.7	44.0
Coffee bean equivalent	10.6	10.5	10.3
Cocoa (chocolate liquor equivalent)	4.6	4.6	4.3

1. As of August 1993. Except where noted, consumption is from commercial sources and is in pounds retail weight. 2. Boneless, trimmed equivalent. 3. Includes milk and cream produced and consumed on farms. 4. Fat-content basis. 5. Excludes wine grapes.

Government Employment and Payrolls

Year and function	Employees (in thousands): Total	Federal[1]	State	Local	October payrolls (in millions): Total	Federal[1]	State	Local
1940	4,474	1,128	3,346		$566	177	$389	
1945	6,556	3,375	3,181		1,110	642	468	
1950	6,402	2,117	1,057	3,228	1,528	613	218	696
1955	7,432	2,378	1,199	3,855	2,265	846	326	1,093
1960	8,808	2,421	1,527	4,860	3,333	1,118	524	1,691
1965	10,589	2,588	2,028	5,973	4,884	1,484	849	2,551
1970	13,028	2,881	2,755	7,392	8,334	2,428	1,612	4,294
1975	14,973	2,890	3,271	8,813	13,224	3,584	2,653	6,987
1980	16,213	2,898	3,753	9,562	19,935	5,205	4,285	10,445
1982	15,841	2,848	3,744	9,249	23,173	5,959	5,022	12,192
1983	16,034	2,875	3,816	9,344	24,525	6,302	5,346	12,878
1984	16,436	2,942	3,898	9,595	26,904	7,137	5,815	13,952
1985	16,690	3,021	3,984	9,685	28,945	7,580	6,329	15,036
1986	16,933	3,019	4,068	9,846	30,670	7,561	6,810	16,298
1987	17,212	3,091	4,116	10,005	32,669	7,924	7,263	17,482
1988	17,588	3,112	4,236	10,240	34,203	7,976	7,842	18,385
1990	18,369	3,105	4,503	10,760	39,228	8,999	9,083	21,146
1991, total	18,554	3,103	4,521	10,934	41,237	9,687	9,437	22,117
National defense and international relations	1,019	1,019	(2)	(2)	3,294	3,294	(2)	(2)
Postal service	803	803	(2)	(2)	2,359	2,359	(2)	(2)
Education	8,086	14	1,999	6,074	15,724	41	3,551	12,132
Instructional employees	4,618	n.a.	624	3,995	11,057	n.a.	1,632	9,425
Highways	568	4	259	305	1,238	18	613	607
Health and hospitals	1,817	303	724	793	4,048	876	1,585	1,588
Police protection	844	83	87	674	2,253	304	205	1,699
Fire protection	341	(2)	(2)	341	771	(2)	(2)	771
Sewerage & solid waste management	241	(2)	3	238	518	(2)	7	510
Parks & recreation	342	26	44	271	489	66	69	353
Natural resources	433	233	162	39	1,150	732	349	70
Financial administration	508	147	149	212	1,119	400	343	376
All other	3,552	470	1,094	1,988	8,278	1,597	2,671	4,010

1. Civilians only. 2. Not applicable. NOTE: n.a. = not available. Detail may not add to totals because of rounding. Data are most recent available. *Source:* Department of Commerce, Bureau of the Census.

Receipts and Outlays of the Federal Government

(in millions of dollars)

From 1789 to 1842, the federal fiscal year ended Dec. 31; from 1844 to 1976, on June 30; and beginning 1977, on Sept. 30.

Year	Receipts: Customs (including tonnage tax)[1]	Internal revenue: Income and profits tax	Internal revenue: Other	Miscellaneous taxes and receipts	Total receipts	Net receipts[2]
1789–1791	$ 4	—	—	—	$ 4	$ 4
1800	9	—	$ –1	$ 1	11	11
1810	9	—	—	1	9	9
1820	15	—	—	3	18	18
1830	22	—	—	3	25	25
1840	14	—	—	6	20	20
1850	40	—	—	4	44	44
1860	53	—	—	3	56	56
1870	195	—	185	32	411	411
1880	187	—	124	23	334	334
1890	230	—	143	31	403	403
1900	233	—	295	39	567	567
1910	334	—	290	52	675	675
1915	210	$ 80	335	72	698	683
1929	602	2,331	607	493	4,033	3,862
1939	319	2,189	2,972	188	5,668	4,979
1944	431	34,655	7,030	3,325	45,441	43,563
1945	355	35,173	8,729	3,494	47,750	44,362
1950	423	28,263	11,186	1,439	41,311	36,422
1956[4]	705	56,639	20,564	389	78,297	74,547
1960	1,123	67,151	28,266	1,190	97,730	92,492
1965	1,478	79,792	39,996	1,598	122,863	116,833
1970	2,494	138,689	65,276	3,424	209,883	193,743
1975	3,782	202,146	108,371	6,711	321,010	280,997
1980	7,482	359,927	192,436	12,797	572,641	520,050
1985	12,079	474,074	311,092	18,576	815,821	733,996
1986	13,323	412,102	323,779	19,887	([5])	769,091
1987	15,085	476,483	343,268	19,307	([5])	854,143
1988	16,198	495,376	377,469	19,909	([5])	908,953
1989	16,334	549,273	402,200	22,800	([5])	990,691
1990	16,707	560,391	426,893	27,470	([5])	1,031,462
1991	15,949	565,913	449,577	22,846	([5])	1,054,265
1992	17,359	576,735	470,403	27,195	([5])	1,091,692

Year	Outlays: Department of Defense (Army, 1789–1950)	Department of the Navy	Interest on public debt	All other	Net outlays[3]	Surplus (+) or deficit (–)
1789–1791	$ 1	—	$ 2	$ 1	$ 4	—
1800	3	$ 3	3	1	11	—
1810	2	2	3	1	8	$ +1
1820	3	4	5	6	18	—
1830	5	3	2	5	15	+10
1840	7	6	—	11	24	–4
1850	9	8	4	18	40	+4
1860	16	12	3	32	63	–7
1870	58	22	129	101	310	+101
1880	38	14	96	120	268	+66
1890	45	22	36	215	318	+85
1900	135	56	40	290	521	+46
1910	190	123	21	359	694	–19
1915	202	142	23	379	746	–63
1929	426	365	678	1,658	3,127	+734
1939	695	673	941	6,533	8,841	–3,862
1944	49,438	26,538	2,609	16,401	94,986	–51,423

	Outlays					
Year	Department of Defense (Army, 1789–1950)	Department of the Navy	Interest on public debt	All other	Net outlays[3]	Surplus (+) or deficit (–)
1945	50,490	30,047	3,617	14,149	98,303	–53,941
1950	5,789	4,130	5,750	23,875	39,544	–3,122
1956[4]	35,693	—	6,787	27,981	70,460	+4,087
1960	43,969	—	9,180	39,075	92,223	+269
1965	47,179	—	11,346	59,904	118,430	–1,596
1970	78,360	—	19,304	98,924	196,588	–2,845
1975	87,471	—	32,665	205,969	326,105	–45,108
1980	136,138	—	74,860	368,013	579,011	–58,961
1985	244,054	—	178,945	513,810	936,809	–202,813
1986	273,369	—	135,284	581,136	989,789	–220,698
1987	282,016	—	138,519	581,612	1,002,147	–148,004
1988	290,349	—	151,711	621,995	1,064,055	–155,102
1989	303,600	—	169,100	649,943	1,142,643	–123,785
1990	299,355	—	183,790	768,725	1,251,850	–220,388
1991	273,292	—	194,541	855,924	1,323,757	–269,492
1992	298,188	—	199,422	884,285	1,381,895	–290,203

1. Beginning 1933, tonnage tax is included in "Other receipts." 2. Net receipts equal total receipts less (a) appropriations to federal old-age and survivors' insurance trust fund beginning fiscal year 1939 and (b) refunds of receipts beginning fiscal year 1933. 3. Includes Air Force 1950–65 (in millions): 1950—$3,521; 1956—$16,750; 1960—$19,065; 1965—$18,471. 4. Beginning 1956, computed on unified budget concepts; not strictly comparable with preceding figures. 5. Net receipts are now the total receipts. Public Law 99–177 moved two social security trust funds off-budget. *Source:* Department of the Treasury, Financial Management Service. NOTE: Totals figures may not add to totals because of rounding of some items.

Contributions to International Organizations

(for fiscal year 1990 in millions of dollars)

Organization	Amount[1]
United Nations and Specialized Agencies	
United Nations	$206.92
Food and Agriculture Organization	21.80
International Atomic Energy Agency	37.79
International Civil Aviation Organization	7.91
Joint Financing Program	2.46
International Labor Organization	53.16
International Telecommunication Union	5.32
United Nations Industrial Development Organization	19.11
World Health Organization	71.07
World Meteorological Organization	6.68
Others (5 Programs, less than $1 million)	2.38
Peacekeeping Forces	
United Nations Disengagement Observer Force (UNDOF) and UNIFIL	40.75
United Nations Force in Cyprus	8.84
United Nations Iran-Iraq Military Observer Group (UNIMOG)	12.49
United Nations Observer Group in Central America (ONUCA)	17.73
Multinational Force and Observers	23.73
Inter-American Organizations	
Organization of American States	46.33
Inter-American Institute for Cooperation on Agriculture	14.24
Inter-American Tropical Tuna Commission	2.84
Pan American Health Organization	39.20
Others (4 Programs, less than $1 million)	.58
Regional Organizations	
North Atlantic Assembly	1.03
NATO Civilian Headquarters	23.30
Organization for Economic Cooperation and Development	36.08
Others (2 Programs, less than $1 million)	.89
Other International Organizations	
Customs Cooperation Council	2.39
General Agreement on Tariffs and Trade	6.65
International Agency for Research on Cancer	1.25
International Criminal Police Organization	1.11
Others (34 Programs, less than $1 million)	6.17
Special Voluntary Programs	
Consultative Group on International Agricultural Research	40.00
International Atomic Energy Agency Technical Assistance Fund	21.55[2]
International Fund for Agricultural Development	34.40
International Organization for Migration	16.21
OAS Special Development Assistance Fund	3.93
OAS Special Multilateral Fund (Education and Science)	4.68
OAS Special Projects fund (Mar del Plata)	1.00
OAS Special Program	2.25
PAHO Special Health Promotion Funds	11.00
United Nations Children's Fund	63.95
United Nations Development Program	105.00
United Nations Environment Program	11.80
U.N. Afghanistan Emergency Trust Fund (UNOCA)	13.28
U.N. Capital Development Fund	1.48
U.N./FAO World Food Program	163.00[3]
U.N. Fund for Drug Abuse Control	4.00
U.N. High Commissioner for Refugees Program:	
Regular Programs (5)	74.32
Special Programs (7)	52.67
United Nations Relief and Works Agency:	
Regular Program	57.00
WHO Special Programs	40.00
WMO Voluntary Cooperation Program	1.97
Others (10 Programs, less than $1 million)	4.32
Total U.S. Contributions	**$1,448.01**

1. Estimated. 2. Includes cash, commodities and services, and $7.32 million for the Safeguards Program and other non-proliferation activities. 3. Includes cash, commodities and services, and $22.1 million for the International Emergency Food Reserve, and $55.9 million for WFP protracted refugee operations. NOTE: Data are most recent available.

Social Welfare Expenditures Under Public Programs

(in millions of dollars)

Year and source of funds	Social insurance	Public aid	Health and medical programs[1]	Veterans' programs	Education	Housing	Other social welfare	All health and medical care[2]	Total social welfare	Total social welfare as: Percent of gross domestic product	Total social welfare as: Percent of total gov't outlays
FEDERAL											
1980	191,162	48,666	12,886	21,254	13,452	6,608	8,786	68,989	303,276	11.5	53.2
1981	224,574	55,946	13,596	23,229	13,372	6,045	7,304	80,505	344,066	11.7	54.0
1982	250,551	52,485	14,598	24,463	11,917	7,176	6,500	90,776	367,691	11.8	52.5
1983	274,212	55,895	15,594	25,561	12,397	8,087	7,046	100,274	398,792	12.1	51.9
1984	288,743	58,480	16,622	25,970	13,010	10,226	7,349	103,927	420,399	11.4	50.2
1985	313,108	61,985	18,630	26,704	13,796	11,088	7,548	118,955	452,860	11.4	47.8
1986	326,588	65,615	19,926	27,072	15,022	10,164	7,977	125,730	472,364	11.2	47.6
1987	345,082	69,233	22,219	27,641	16,054	11,110	8,504	143,020	499,844	11.2	50.4
1988	358,412	74,137	22,681	28,845	16,952	14,006	8,112	149,102	523,144	11.0	49.1
1989	387,290	79,852	24,215	29,638	18,520	15,184	8,492	166,087	563,191	10.9	49.3
1990	419,337	92,650	27,515	30,428	18,374	16,612	8,905	187,430	613,821	11.2	51.1
STATE AND LOCAL											
1980	38,592	23,133	14,771	212	107,597	601	4,813	31,309	189,720	7.2	66.5
1981	42,821	26,477	17,124	212	114,773	688	4,679	36,327	206,774	7.0	63.1
1982	52,481	28,367	19,195	245	121,957	778	5,154	40,738	228,178	7.4	62.6
1983	56,846	29,935	20,382	265	129,416	1,003	5,438	42,854	243,285	7.4	60.1
1984	52,378	32,206	20,383	301	139,046	1,306	5,946	44,540	251,569	7.0	58.9
1985	59,420	34,792	22,430	338	152,622	1,540	6,398	48,587	277,540	7.1	59.0
1986	63,816	37,464	24,408	373	163,495	1,872	6,728	53,884	298,158	7.3	58.2
1987	69,941	41,462	25,400	410	188,486	2,129	6,773	60,566	344,601	7.5	59.6
1988	73,783	46,237	29,859	409	202,416	2,550	7,368	70,511	362,622	7.5	60.1
1989	80,765	47,623	32,651	465	220,111	2,943	8,117	75,559	392,676	7.6	60.2
1990	91,279	52,992	34,913	489	240,011	2,856	9,012	84,416	431,552	7.9	68.2
TOTAL											
1980	229,754	71,799	27,657	21,466	121,050	7,210	13,599	100,298	492,534	18.6	57.4
1981	267,395	82,424	30,720	23,441	128,145	6,734	11,983	116,832	550,841	18.7	56.9
1982	303,033	80,852	33,793	24,708	133,874	7,954	11,654	131,514	595,869	19.2	55.7
1983	331,058	85,830	35,976	25,826	141,813	9,090	12,484	143,128	642,077	19.6	54.5
1984	341,120	90,685	37,006	26,275	152,056	11,532	13,295	148,467	671,969	18.3	52.8
1985	372,529	96,777	41,060	27,042	166,418	12,627	13,946	167,542	730,399	18.4	51.2
1986	390,404	103,079	44,334	27,445	178,518	12,036	14,705	179,614	770,522	18.5	47.9
1987	415,023	110,695	47,619	28,051	204,540	13,240	15,278	203,586	834,446	18.7	53.5
1988	432,195	120,375	52,540	29,254	219,368	16,556	15,480	219,613	885,766	18.5	52.8
1989	468,055	127,475	56,866	30,103	238,631	18,127	16,609	241,646	955,867	18.5	53.0
1990	510,616	145,642	62,428	30,916	258,385	19,469	17,918	271,489	1,045,373	19.1	56.6
PERCENT OF TOTAL, BY TYPE											
1980	46.6	14.6	5.6	4.4	24.6	1.5	2.8	20.4	100.0	(3)	(3)
1984	50.9	13.4	5.6	3.9	22.6	1.5	2.0	23.1	100.0	(3)	(3)
1985	51.0	13.2	5.6	3.7	22.8	1.7	1.9	22.9	100.0	(3)	(3)
1986	50.7	13.4	5.8	3.6	23.2	1.6	1.9	23.3	100.0	(3)	(3)
1987	49.7	13.3	5.7	3.4	24.5	1.6	1.8	24.4	100.0	(3)	(3)
1988	48.8	13.6	5.9	3.3	24.8	1.9	1.7	24.8	100.0	(3)	(3)
1989	49.0	14.0	6.0	4.0	25.0	2.0	2.0	26.0	100.0	(3)	(3)
1990	48.0	13.0	5.0	2.0	24.0	1.0	1.0	25.0	100.0	(3)	(3)
FEDERAL PERCENT OF TOTAL											
1980	83.2	67.8	46.6	99.0	11.1	91.7	64.6	68.8	61.6	(3)	(3)
1984	84.7	64.2	43.6	99.0	8.5	87.4	54.7	70.0	62.4	(3)	(3)
1985	84.0	64.0	45.4	98.8	8.3	87.8	54.1	71.0	62.0	(3)	(3)
1986	83.6	63.7	44.9	98.6	8.4	84.4	54.2	70.0	61.3	(3)	(3)
1987	83.1	62.5	46.7	98.5	7.8	83.9	55.7	70.3	59.9	(3)	(3)
1988	82.9	61.6	43.2	98.6	7.7	84.6	52.4	67.9	59.1	(3)	(3)
1989	82.7	62.6	42.6	98.5	7.8	83.8	51.1	68.7	58.9	(3)	(3)
1990	82.1	63.6	44.1	98.4	7.1	85.3	49.7	69.2	58.7	(3)	(3)

1. Excludes program parts of social insurance, public aid, veterans, and other social welfare. 2. Combines health and medical programs with medical services provided in connection with social insurance, public aid, veterans, and other social welfare programs. 3. Not applicable. NOTE: Figures are latest available. *Source:* Department of Health and Human Services, Social Security Administration.

Distribution of Federal Funds by State and Territory: FY 1991

Million dollars. Detail may not add to total because of rounding.

State and Territory	Total	Grants to state and local governments	Salaries and wages[1, 2]	Direct payments for individuals[3]	Procurement[4]	Other programs[5]
United States, total	**1,096,493**	**153,350**	**156,350**	**541,963**	**207,702**	**37,128**
Alabama	18,464	2,347	2,917	9,325	3,461	413
Alaska	3,655	738	1,274	686	806	152
Arizona	15,491	1,810	2,124	8,116	3,098	343
Arkansas	9,053	1,439	971	5,727	486	429
California	127,684	16,885	18,519	56,631	32,101	3,549
Colorado	16,474	1,707	3,191	6,178	4,617	780
Connecticut	16,460	2,393	1,302	7,121	5,334	309
Delaware	2,435	386	415	1,404	190	39
District of Columbia	19,105	1,847	10,153	2,091	3,655	1,359
Florida	56,276	5,209	6,594	35,941	7,471	702
Georgia	23,739	3,553	5,174	11,990	2,500	522
Hawaii	6,162	739	2,318	2,216	761	128
Idaho	4,287	590	522	1,966	1,023	186
Illinois	40,767	5,954	4,990	24,587	3,973	1,264
Indiana	18,806	2,767	1,903	10,925	2,446	764
Iowa	10,306	1,475	777	6,118	720	1,216
Kansas	10,519	1,165	1,782	5,246	1,140	1,007
Kentucky	15,231	2,493	2,462	7,939	2,043	293
Louisiana	16,270	3,249	2,083	8,279	2,154	505
Maine	5,601	926	581	2,844	1,159	92
Maryland	29,507	2,557	6,485	10,778	7,384	2,302
Massachusetts	31,449	4,709	2,815	14,413	8,155	1,357
Michigan	31,565	5,246	2,534	20,624	2,304	676
Minnesota	16,366	2,559	1,404	8,108	2,117	2,178
Mississippi	11,240	1,822	1,340	5,711	2,060	307
Missouri	26,410	2,827	3,028	11,686	7,284	1,584
Montana	3,743	687	542	1,773	194	547
Nebraska	6,419	868	994	3,345	477	735
Nevada	4,922	544	699	2,494	1,132	53
New Hampshire	3,874	540	628	2,112	501	93
New Jersey	30,862	4,517	3,522	17,896	4,592	335
New Mexico	9,338	1,118	1,426	3,107	3,463	225
New York	76,790	17,226	6,797	40,935	9,881	1,951
North Carolina	23,243	3,447	4,284	12,814	2,154	544
North Dakota	3,253	533	532	1,345	243	599
Ohio	41,414	6,220	4,094	23,655	6,683	762
Oklahoma	12,973	1,788	2,453	7,048	1,033	652
Oregon	10,457	1,694	1,226	6,531	640	366
Pennsylvania	49,463	6,870	5,254	31,209	4,813	1,315
Rhode Island	4,604	908	579	2,548	462	107
South Carolina	14,907	2,078	2,598	6,801	3,242	187
South Dakota	3,106	539	520	1,484	212	350
Tennessee	20,890	3,129	2,164	10,406	4,871	319
Texas	64,472	7,837	9,848	31,479	13,152	2,155
Utah	6,694	839	1,486	2,721	1,433	214
Vermont	1,930	409	219	1,129	119	54
Virginia	38,674	2,432	11,344	13,676	9,963	1,259
Washington	21,529	2,832	3,911	10,244	3,570	972
West Virginia	7,465	1,284	643	4,826	627	85
Wisconsin	16,246	2,799	1,235	10,097	1,503	612
Wyoming	1,951	597	324	834	135	60
American Samoa	86	51	8	20	8	—
Guam	715	116	368	89	129	13
Northern Marianas	81	75	3	2	1	—
Puerto Rico	8,070	2,916	586	3,833	635	100
Virgini Islands	417	175	35	93	110	4
Undistributed	24,583	711	9	582	23,280	1

1. Recipients may not live in the State/territory in which salaries and wages are paid. 2. Federal employee salaries and wages. 3. Individual benefits such as Social Security, Medicare, and food stamps. 4. Contracts from the Defense Department and other departments and agencies. 5. Research grants, agricultural subsidies, and other purposes. *Source: Federal Expenditures by State for Fiscal Year 1991.*

Domestic Freight Traffic by Major Carriers

(in millions of ton-miles)[1]

Year	Railroads		Inland waterways[2]		Motor trucks		Oil pipelines		Air carriers	
	Ton-miles	% of total	Ton-miles	% of total	Ton-miles	% of total	Ton-miles	% of total	Ton-miles	% of total
1940	379,201	61.3	118,057	19.1	62,043	10.0	59,277	9.6	14	—
1945	690,809	67.3	142,737	13.9	66,948	6.5	126,530	12.3	91	—
1950	596,940	56.2	163,344	15.4	172,860	16.3	129,175	12.1	318	—
1955	631,385	49.5	216,508	17.0	223,254	17.5	203,244	16.0	481	—
1960	579,130	44.1	220,253	16.8	285,483	21.7	228,626	17.4	778	—
1965	708,700	43.3	262,421	16.0	359,218	21.9	306,393	18.7	1,910	0.1
1970	771,168	39.8	318,560	16.4	412,000	21.3	431,000	22.3	3,274	0.2
1975	759,000	36.7	342,210	16.5	454,000	22.0	507,300	24.6	3,732	0.2
1980	932,000	37.2	420,000	16.9	567,000	22.6	588,000	23.1	4,528	0.2
1985	895,000	36.4	382,000	15.6	610,000	24.9	564,000	22.9	6,080	0.2
1987	972,000	36.8	411,000	15.6	661,000	25.1	587,000	22.2	8,670	0.3
1988	1,028,000	37.0	438,000	15.8	699,000	25.1	601,000	21.6	9,300	0.3
1989	1,048,000	37.3	449,000	15.8	716,000	25.5	584,000	20.8	10,210	0.36
1990	1,071,000	37.4	464,000	16.2	735,000	25.7	583,000	20.4	10,420	0.36
1991	1,077,000	37.4	462,000	16.0	758,000	26.3	578,000	19.9	10,210	0.36
1992[3]	1,107,000	37.0	474,000	15.9	815,000	27.2	582,000	19.5	11,170	0.37

1. Mail and express included, except railroads for 1970. 2. Rivers, canals, and domestic traffic on Great Lakes. 3. Preliminary. *Source: Transportation in America,* Eno Foundation for Transportation (latest figures from 11th Edition, 1993).

Tonnage Handled by Principal U.S. Ports

(Over 10 million U.S. short tons (2,000 lbs per ton) annually; in thousands of tons)

Port	1991	1990	Port	1991	1990
Port of South Louisiana	189,374	193,042	Marcus Hook, Pa.	22,337	25,864
Houston	131,234	126,177	Chicago	21,767	22,533
New York	126,860	140,027	Seattle	20,897	21,569
Valdez, Alaska	99,616	95,953	Richmond, Calif.	19,919	21,155
Baton Rouge, La.	87,630	78,112	Tacoma, Wash.	19,544	21,433
New Orleans, La.	60,898	61,249	Boston	18,562	21,888
Corpus Christi, Texas	59,052	62,023	Huntington, W.V.	18,043	17,310
Port of Plaquemine, La.	53,782	56,527	Jacksonville, Fla.	15,780	14,597
Norfolk Harbor, Va.	53,473	53,722	Freeport, Texas	15,666	14,494
Long Beach, Calif.	52,891	52,425	Port Everglades, Fla.	14,499	14,144
Tampa, Fla.	49,548	51,579	Anacortes, Wash.	14,481	15,437
Los Angeles, Calif.	47,008	46,352	Detroit	14,321	17,734
Texas City, Texas	43,290	48,071	San Juan, P.R.	14,163	14,536
Mobile, Ala.	41,260	41,136	Indiana Harbor, Ind.	13,767	14,672
Lake Charles, La.	41,241	40,882	Lorain, Ohio	13,632	13,966
Baltimore, Md.	37,745	39,551	Cleveland	13,406	14,367
Duluth–Superior, Minn.	37,716	40,766	Savannah, Ga.	13,326	13,568
Philadelphia	37,257	41,836	Toledo, Ohio	12,538	14,667
Pittsburgh	31,277	35,492	Two Harbors, Minn.	12,501	n.a.
Port Arthur, Texas	29,835	30,679	Memphis, Tenn.	12,298	11,637
Pascagoula, Miss.	29,567	26,479	Cincinnati, Ohio	11,717	12,634
Portland, Ore.	29,299	27,475	Ashtabula, Ohio	11,276	11,852
St. Louis Metropolitan	29,263	27,108	Honolulu, Hawaii	11,208	11,341
Newport News, Va.	29,168	24,935	Galveston, Texas	10,858	n.a.
Paulsboro, N.J.	23,713	23,331	Oakland, Calif.	10,356	10,290
Beaumont, Texas	22,383	26,728			

n.a. = not available. *Source:* Department of the Army, Corps of Engineers.

Annual Railroad Carloadings[1]

Year	Total	Year	Total	Year	Total	Year	Total
1940	36,358,000	1965	28,344,381	1983	19,013,250	1988	22,599,993
1945	41,918,000	1970	27,015,020	1984	20,945,536	1989	21,226,015
1950	38,903,000	1975	22,929,843	1985	19,501,242	1990	21,884,649
1955	32,761,707	1980	22,223,000	1986	19,588,666	1991	20,868,297
1960	27,886,950	1982	18,584,760	1987	20,602,204	1992	21,205,530

1. Only Class 1 railroads after 1950. *Source:* Association of American Railroads.

Estimated Motor Vehicle Registration, 1992

(in thousands; including publicly owned vehicles)

State	Autos[1]	Trucks and buses	Motor-cycles	Total
Alabama	2,731	994	38	3,725
Alaska	295	175	10	470
Arizona	2,045	842	81	2,887
Arkansas	967	529	13	1,496
California	17,227	4,936	595	22,163
Colorado	2,202	816	85	3,018
Connecticut	2,428	142	50	2,570
Delaware	415	126	10	541
Dist. of Col.	223	18	2	241
Florida	8,072	2,109	195	10,181
Georgia	4,090	1,789	80	5,879
Hawaii	689	110	21	799
Idaho	646	410	30	1,056
Illinois	6,744	1,559	188	8,303
Indiana	3,279	1,198	97	4,477
Iowa	1,935	773	158	2,708
Kansas	1,205	657	53	1,862
Kentucky	1,969	1,049	33	3,018
Louisiana	2,010	1,069	34	3,079
Maine	768	219	36	987
Maryland	3,049	620	54	3,669
Massachusetts	3,102	506	52	3,608
Michigan	5,684	1,607	157	7,291
Minnesota	2,554	703	109	3,257
Mississippi	1,450	449	27	1,899
Missouri	2,816	1,184	59	4,000
Montana	443	311	20	754
Nebraska	953	488	21	1,441
Nevada	611	295	20	906
New Hampshire	694	198	36	892
New Jersey	5,010	451	85	5,461
New Mexico	834	500	31	1,334
New York	8,387	1,251	197	9,638
North Carolina	3,750	1,523	60	5,273
North Dakota	374	252	18	626
Ohio	7,137	1,666	240	8,803
Oklahoma	1,708	985	58	2,693
Oregon	1,928	640	60	2,568
Pennsylvania	6,489	1,631	161	8,120
Rhode Island	502	107	23	609
South Carolina	1,926	612	31	2,538
South Dakota	429	287	23	715
Tennessee	3,731	913	72	4,644
Texas	8,655	4,057	190	12,712
Utah	809	444	23	1,253
Vermont	321	117	19	438
Virginia	3,875	1,233	61	5,108
Washington	3,150	1,335	118	4,485
West Virginia	775	501	17	1,276
Wisconsin	2,500	1,253	214	3,753
Wyoming	237	232	16	469
Total	**143,823**	**45,871**	**4,081**	**189,694**

1. Includes taxicabs. NOTE: Figures are latest available. *Source:* Department of Transportation, Federal Highway Administration.

Passenger Car Production by Make

Companies and models	1992	1990	1985	1980	1975	1970
American Motors Corporation	—	—	109,919	164,725	323,704	276,127
Chrysler Corporation						
Plymouth	135,721	212,354	369,487	293,342	443,550	699,031
Dodge	263,539	361,769	482,388	263,169	354,482	405,699
Chrysler	116,765	136,339	414,193	82,463	102,940	158,614
Imperial	6,635	16,280	—	—	1,930	10,111
Total	**522,660**	**726,742**	**1,266,068**	**638,974**	**902,902**	**1,273,455**
Ford Motor Company						
Ford	922,488	933,466	1,098,627	929,627	1,301,414	1,647,918
Mercury	242,534	221,436	374,446	324,528	405,104	310,463
Lincoln	168,556	222,449	163,077	52,793	101,520	58,771
Total	**1,333,578**	**1,377,351**	**1,636,150**	**1,306,948**	**1,808,038**	**2,017,152**
General Motors Corporation						
Chevrolet	647,227	1,025,379	1,691,254	1,737,336	1,687,091	1,504,614
Pontiac	561,940	649,255	702,617	556,429	523,469	422,212
Oldsmobile	395,974	418,742	1,168,982	783,225	654,342	439,632
Buick	427,915	405,123	1,001,461	783,575	535,820	459,931
Cadillac	221,112	252,540	322,765	203,991	278,404	152,859
Saturn	212,122	4,245	—	—	—	—
Total	**2,466,290**	**2,755,284**	**4,887,079**	**4,064,556**	**3,679,126**	**2,979,248**
Volkswagen of America	—	—	96,458	197,106	—	—
Honda	458,254	435,437	238,159	145,337	—	—
Mazda	167,940	184,428	—	—	—	—
Nissan	171,404	95,844	43,810	—	—	—
Toyota	345,752	321,523	—	—	—	—
Diamond Star	139,783	148,379	—	—	—	—
Subaru Legacy	57,623	32,461	—	—	—	—
Industry total	**5,663,284**	**6,077,449**	**8,184,821**	**6,375,506**	**6,716,951**	**6,550,128**

Source: American Automobile Manufacturers Association.

Motor Vehicle Data

	1991	1990	1980	1970	1960
U.S. passenger cars and taxis registered (thousands)	142,956	143,550	121,724	89,280	61,671
Total mileage of U.S. passenger cars (millions)	1,533,668	1,513,184	1,111,596	916,700	588,083
Total fuel consumption of U.S. passenger cars (millions of gallons)	70,727	71,989	71,883	67,820	41,169
World registration of cars, trucks, and buses (thousands)	595,307	582,982	411,113	246,368	126,955
U.S. registration of cars, trucks, and buses (thousands)	188,372	188,655	155,796	108,418	73,858
U.S. share of world registration of cars, trucks, and buses	31.6%	32.4%	37.9%	44.0%	58.2%

Source: American Automobile Manufacturers Association.

Domestic Motor Vehicles Sales

(in thousands)

Type of Vehicle	1990	1989	1988	1987	1986	1985	1980	1975
Passenger Cars								
Passenger car factory sales	6,050	6,807	7,105	7,085	7,516	8,002	6,400	6,713
Passenger car (new) retail sales[1]	9,300	9,772	10,626	10,278	11,460	11,042	8,979	8,640
Domestic[2]	6,897	7,073	7,526	7,081	8,215	8,205	6,581	7,050
Subcompact[3]	n.a.	926	1,019	1,101	1,325	1,297	1,604	700
Compact[3]	n.a.	2,606	2,781	2,388	2,461	2,563	1,659	2,336
Standard[3]	n.a.	1,629	1,722	1,565	1,888	1,882	1,358	1,956
Intermediate[3]	n.a.	1,916	2,017	2,026	2,540	2,464	1,957	2,058
Imports[4]	2,403	2,699	3,100	3,197	3,245	2,838	2,398	1,587
Trucks								
Truck and bus factory sales	3,719	4,062	4,121	3,821	3,393	3,357	1,667	2,272
Truck and bus retail sales[5]	4,261	4,483	4,608	4,174	4,031	3,984	2,232	2,351
Light duty (up to 14,000 GVW)[6]	3,984	4,171	4,273	3,885	3,766	3,700	1,964	2,076
Med. duty (14,000–26,000 GVW)[6]	71	73	83	55	51	53	92	169
Heavy duty (over 26,000 GVW)[6]	207	239	251	234	214	231	176	106
Motorcycles								
Motorcycles (new) retail sales[7]	462	515	710	935	1,045	1,260	1,070	940
All-terrain vehicles	145	200	290	395	465	550	n.a.	n.a.
All-terrain vehicle imports	100	121	209	320	498	683	n.a.	n.a.
Motorcycle imports total[8]	169	253	287	318	550	733	1,120	948

1. Based on data from U.S. Dept. of Commerce. 2. Includes domestic models produced in Canada and Mexico. 3. Beginning 1980, cars produced in U.S. by foreign manufacturers are included. 4. Excludes domestic models produced in Canada. 5. Excludes motorcoaches and light-duty imports from foreign manufacturers. Includes imports sold by franchised dealers of U.S. manufacturers. Starting in 1986 includes sales of trucks over 10,000 lbs. GVW by foreign manufacturers. 6. Gross vehicle weight (fully loaded vehicles). 7. Estimates by Motorcycle Industry Council Inc., Costa Mesa, Calif. Includes all-terrain vehicles and scooters. Excludes mopeds/motorized bicycles. 8. *Source:* Motorcycle Industry Council Inc. Data from U.S. Dept. of Commerce. Excludes mopeds/motorized bicycles and all-terrain vehicles. NOTE: n.a. = not available. *Source: Statistical Abstract of the United States 1992.* NOTE: Data are most recent available.

Domestic and Export Factory Sales of Motor Vehicles

(in thousands)

	From plants in United States								
	Passenger cars			Motor trucks and buses			Total motor vehicles		
Year	Total	Domestic	Exports	Total	Domestic	Exports	Total	Domestic	Exports
1970	6,547	6,187	360	1,692	1,566	126	8,239	7,753	486
1975	6,713	6,073	640	2,272	2,003	269	8,985	8,076	909
1980	6,400	5,840	560	1,667	1,464	203	8,067	7,304	763
1985	8,002	7,337	665	3,464	3,234	231	11,467	10,571	896
1988	7,105	6,437	668	4,120	3,795	325	11,225	10,232	993
1989	6,807	6,181	626	4,062	3,752	310	10,869	9,933	936
1990	6,050	5,502	548	3,719	3,448	271	9,769	8,950	819
1991	5,407	4,874	533	3,375	3,038	338	8,783	7,912	871
1992	5,684	5,164	520	4,042	3,683	360	9,727	8,846	880

Source: American Automobile Manufacturers Association.

U.S. Direct Investment in EEC Countries, 1992

(in millions of dollars)

Countries	All industries	Petroleum	Manufacturing	Wholesale	Banking	Finance & insurance	Services	Other industries
Belgium	$10,771	$291	$5,940	$1,811	(1)	$2,072	$502	(1)
Denmark	1,707	(1)	315	503	(1)	351	116	13
France	23,257	(1)	13,975	3,750	337	2,363	1,075	(1)
Germany	35,393	2,111	20,951	3,328	2,001	4,666	790	1,545
Greece	429	(1)	129	65	(1)	(1)	(1)	0
Ireland	7,229	119	4,505	117	9	1,947	(1)	(1)
Italy	13,605	416	8,821	2,063	160	1,589	363	193
Luxembourg	1,863	17	852	1	201	779	3	9
Netherlands	19,114	1,465	7,216	3,043	133	4,931	1,600	726
Portugal	1,160	(1)	379	318	207	(1)	177	(2)
Spain	8,165	149	5,430	1,089	1,022	166	410	–101
United Kingdom	77,842	13,153	20,328	3,922	2,547	32,013	3,826	2,055
Total	**$200,535**	**$17,721**	**$88,791**	**$20,010**	**$6,617**	**$50,877**	**$8,862**	**$4,440**

1. Suppressed to avoid disclosure of data of individual companies. 2. Less than $500,000. *Source: Survey of Current Business,* June 1993.

Balance of International Payments

(in billions of dollars)

Item	1992	1991	1990	1985	1980	1975	1970	1965	1960
Exports of goods, services, and income	$730.5	$704.9	$652.9	$366.0	$343.2	$157.9	$68.4	$42.7	$30.5
Merchandise, adjusted, excluding military	440.1	416.0	389.5	214.4	224.0	107.1	42.5	26.5	19.7
Transfers under U.S. military agency sales contracts	11.0	10.7	9.8	9.0	8.2	3.9	1.5	0.8	0.3
Receipts of income on U.S. investments abroad	110.6	125.3	130.0	90.0	75.9	25.4	11.8	7.4	4.6
Other services	168.7	152.9	123.3	45.0	36.5	19.3	9.9	6.4	4.3
Imports of goods and services	–764.0	–716.6	–722.7	–461.2	–333.9	–132.6	–60.0	–32.8	–23.7
Merchandise, adjusted, excluding military	–536.3	–489.4	–497.6	–339.0	–249.3	–98.0	–39.9	–21.5	–14.8
Direct defense expenditures	–13.8	–16.2	–17.1	–12.0	–10.7	–4.8	4.9	–3.0	–3.1
Payments of income on foreign assets in U.S.	–104.4	–108.9	–118.1	–65.0	–43.2	–12.6	–5.5	–2.1	–1.2
Other services	–109.5	–102.1	–89.8	–46.0	–30.7	–17.2	–9.8	–6.2	–4.6
Unilateral transfers, excluding military grants, net	–32.9	8.0	–22.3	–15.0	–7.0	–4.6	–3.3	–2.9	–2.3
U.S. Government assets abroad, net	–1.6	3.4	2.9	–2.8	–5.2	–3.5	–1.6	–1.6	–1.1
U.S. private assets abroad, net	–53.3	–71.4	–58.5	–26.0	–71.5	–35.4	–10.2	–5.3	–5.1
U.S. assets abroad, net	–51.0	–62.2	–57.7	–27.7	–86.1	–39.7	–9.3	–5.7	–4.1
Foreign assets in U.S., net	129.6	67.0	86.3	127.1	50.3	15.6	6.4	0.7	2.3
Statistical discrepancy	–12.2	–1.1	63.5	23.0	29.6	5.5	–0.2	–0.5	–1.0
Balance on goods, services, and income	–33.5	–11.7	–69.7	–106.8	9.5	25.2	8.5	10.0	6.9
Balance on current account	–66.4	–3.7	–92.1	–118.0	3.7	18.4	2.4	5.4	2.8

NOTE: — denotes debits. *Source:* Department of Commerce, Bureau of Economic Analysis.

Foreign Investors in U.S. Business Enterprises

	Number				Investment outlays (millions of dollars)			
	1992[1]	1991	1990	1989	1992[1]	1991	1990	1989
Investments, total	690	1,091	1,617	1,580	$13,469	$25,538	$65,932	$71,16
Acquisitions	360	561	839	837	10,191	17,806	55,315	59,708
Establishments	330	530	778	743	3,278	7,732	10,617	11,455
Investors, total	732	1,220	1,768	1,742	13,469	25,538	65,932	71,163
Foreign direct investors	279	438	670	727	3,616	8,885	14,026	22,538
U.S. affiliates	453	782	1,098	1,015	9,853	16,653	51,906	48,625

1. Figures are preliminary. *Source:* U.S. Department of Commerce, *Survey of Current Business,* May 1993.

Imports of Leading Commodities
(value in millions of dollars)

Commodity	1992	1991
Food and agricultural commodities	**$21,864.2**	**$21,297.2**
Animal feeds	337.1	312.1
Cocoa	774.1	823.4
Coffee	1,566.4	1,738.1
Corn	68.5	39.2
Cotton, raw	11.4	16.3
Dairy products, eggs	506.6	452.4
Fish and preparations	5,656.8	5,637.6
Furskins, undressed	61.4	56.7
Hides and skins, undressed	124.4	109.7
Live animals	1,434.4	1,172.4
Meat and preparations	2,722.8	2,908.3
Oils and fats, animal	31.1	28.5
Oils and fats, vegetable	958.0	735.1
Rice	91.7	80.1
Soybeans	15.9	27.4
Sugar	667.7	713.2
Tobacco, unmanufactured	948.7	989.3
Vegetables and fruits	5,697.6	5,391.4
Wheat	189.6	66.0
Machinery and transport equipment	**150,018.3**	**136,720.3**
ADP equip.; office machinery	36,393.4	30,019.1
Airplanes	3,917.5	3,347.3
Airplane parts	3,396.8	4,046.0
Cars and trucks	55,776.0	53,045.5
Parts	15,840.6	14,066.5
Spacecraft	91.8	(—)
General industrial machinery	15,521.9	14,396.1
Metalworking machinery	3,170.3	3,605.0
Power generating machinery	15,910.0	14,194.8
Manufactured goods	**133,981.7**	**120,032.8**
Artwork and antiques	2,086.8	1,978.7
Chemicals—fertilizers	952.2	917.6
Chemicals—medicinal	3,812.1	3,046.9
Chemicals-organic and inorganic	12,665.8	11,429.3
Clothing and footwear	41,407.0	35,756.2
Gem diamonds	4,147.7	4,002.0
Glass	849.6	769.5
Iron and steel mill products	8,320.7	8,301.1
Metal manufactures	6,730.4	6,372.2
Paper and paperboard	7,998.5	8,020.6
Photographic equipment	3,849.4	3,640.9
Plastic articles	3,570.5	3,114.0
Pottery	1,402.8	1,242.3
Printed matter	1,876.0	1,701.6
Rubber articles	878.7	704.8
Scientific instruments	7,604.0	6,732.6
Textile yarns, fabric	7,840.3	6,981.1
Tires and tubes, automotive	2,512.2	2,308.8
Toys, games, sporting goods	10,747.1	8,820.9
Watches, clocks and parts	2,320.5	2,285.0
Wood manufactures	2,409.4	1,907.4
Mineral fuels and related products	**53,052.5**	**52,006.4**
Coal	419.2	310.0
Natural gas	2,807.5	2,482.5
Petroleum and petroleum products	49,825.8	49,213.9
Crude materials excluding agricultural products	**9,421.4**	**8,780.8**
Cork, wood and lumber	3,969.9	3,056.8
Pulp and waste paper	2,128.9	2,163.4
Metal ores, scrap	3,322.6	3,560.6
Tobacco excluding agricultural, beverages	**2,101.6**	**1,724.8**
Cigarettes	264.7	129.9
Distilled alcoholic beverages	1,836.9	1,594.9
All others	**162,058.9**	**145,566.7**
Total	**532,497.7**	**487,129.0**

Exports of Leading Commodities
(value in millions of dollars)

Commodity	1992	1991
Food and agricultural commodities	**39,139.7**	**36,026.8**
Animal feeds	3,521.0	3,192.3
Cocoa	31.1	22.7
Coffee	17.8	9.8
Corn	4,943.7	5,145.7
Cotton, raw	2,010.3	2,514.3
Dairy products, eggs	709.2	454.5
Fish and preparations	3,377.2	3,062.7
Furskins, undressed	95.2	106.5
Hides and skins, undressed	1,259.8	1,276.1
Live animals	608.4	687.6
Meat and preparations	4,205.4	3,629.6
Oils and fats, animal	521.4	446.8
Oils and fats, vegetable	826.7	596.2
Rice	725.0	735.5
Soybeans	4,416.4	3,994.9
Sugar	5.6	12.1
Tobacco, unmanufactured	1,650.6	1,429.6
Vegetables and fruits	5,718.5	5,341.7
Wheat	4,496.4	3,350.2
Machinery and transport equipment	**134,359.3**	**125,687.2**
ADP equip.; office machinery	26,987.8	24,978.8
Airplanes	26,412.6	24,335.1
Airplane parts	9,328.8	10,283.6
Cars and trucks	15,390.3	13,639.1
Parts	16,551.5	14,370.9
Spacecraft	269.6	257.3
General industrial machinery	18,436.2	17,152.8
Metalworking machinery	3,032.8	2,709.3
Power generating machinery	17,949.7	16,960.3
Manufactured goods	**81,404.2**	**77,521.1**
Artwork and antiques	1,075.7	1,239.4
Chemicals—fertilizers	2,372.0	2,977.3
Chemicals—medicinal	5,356.9	4,608.5
Chemicals—organic and inorganic	15,112.5	14,980.9
Clothing and footwear	4,696.3	3,757.7
Gem diamonds	367.5	209.3
Glass	1,193.7	1,144.6
Iron and steel milll products	3,595.4	4,210.8
Metal manufactures	5,491.0	5,188.8
Paper and paperboard	6,337.7	5,965.4
Photographic equipment	2,948.3	2,926.1
Plastic articles	2,773.2	2,240.1
Pottery	103.3	87.1
Printed matter	3,800.7	3,588.9
Rubber articles	616.3	579.1
Scientific instruments and parts	14,369.6	13,499.0
Textile yarns, fabric	5,756.2	5,481.9
Tires and tubes, automotive	1,407.9	1,274.0
Toys, games and sporting goods	2,435.9	2,087.0
Watches, clocks and parts	207.4	225.0
Wood manufactures	1,386.7	1,250.5
Mineral fuels and related products	**8,692.9**	**9,516.6**
Coal	4,324.8	4,775.6
Natural gas	351.1	308.2
Petroleum and petroleum products	4,017.0	4,432.8
Crude material excluding agricultural products	**12,568.5**	**12,752.9**
Cork, wood, lumber	5,297.6	5,113.8
Pulp and waste paper	3,849.9	3,600.4
Metal ores, scrap	3,421.0	4,0308.7
Tobacco, excluding agricultural, beverages	**4,535.3**	**4,517.1**
Cigarettes	4,192.0	4,238.1
Distilled alcoholic beverages	343.3	279.0
All other	**174,558.7**	**155,698.3**
Total	**448,156.3**	**421,730.0**

Source: Department of Commerce, Bureau of the Census, Foreign Trade Division. NOTE: (z) less than one half unit of measurement shown.

Small Business on the Rise

The nation's small businesses—those with one to 10 employees—grew in numbers during recession-plagued 1991, resisting the downturn experienced by medium and larger companies, according to a Census Bureau report.

This preliminary information, from the *1991 County Business Patterns* report series, shows that the number of small businesses increased up to one percent per year between 1987 and 1991. Larger businesses increased up to three percent per year through 1990, then declined in 1991; those with 10 to 100 employees were down 0.2 percent in 1991, while those with more than 100 fell 1.7 percent.

Businesses with more than 100 employees are concentrated in the manufacturing sector, which as recently as 1970 accounted for 35 percent of the workforce. By 1991, manufacturing workers made up less than 20 percent of the workforce. Conversely, the service sector, which includes both business and personal services, continues to add jobs and now employs more than 32 percent of the workforce. Service sector workers earn a significantly lower average salary than manufacturing employees.

Nationwide, the number of businesses increased 0.4 percent between 1990 and 1991, the smallest increase since the 0.2 percent gain reported in 1980. These 6.2 million non-farm businesses provided employment for 92.8 million people.

Number of Establishments and Employment[1] by Geographic Division and Employment-Size Class: 1990–1991

Area	1991P	1990
U.S. TOTAL		
Establishments	6,199,339	6,175,563
Less than 10 employees	4,613,125	4,584,041
10–99 employees	1,451,339	1,454,272
100 or more employees	134,875	137,250
Employment	92,795,447	93,476,087
Less than 10 employees	14,080,007	14,020,968
10–99 employees	37,688,867	37,765,615
100 or more employees	41,026,573	41,689,504
NEW ENGLAND		
Establishments	357,379	366,799
Less than 10 employees	268,709	273,539
10–99 employees	80,560	84,710
100 or more employees	8,110	8,550
Employment	5,483,679	5,726,808
Less than 10 employees	809,195	835,034
10–99 employees	2,075,074	2,181,969
100 or more employees	2,599,410	2,709,805
MIDDLE ATLANTIC		
Establishments	950,530	960,433
Less than 10 employees	720,985	724,992
10–99 employees	208,279	213,312
100 or more employees	21,266	22,129
Employment	14,558,683	14,894,060
Less than 10 employees	2,112,170	2,139,993
10–99 employees	5,425,078	5,556,152
100 or more employees	7,021,435	7,197,915
EAST NORTH CENTRAL		
Establishments	989,553	982,188
Less than 10 employees	715,668	709,758
10–99 employees	249,338	247,722
100 or more employees	24,547	24,708
Employment	16,319,523	16,403,879
Less than 10 employees	2,265,637	2,248,683
10–99 employees	6,540,013	6,497,630
100 or more employees	7,513,873	7,657,566
WEST NORTH CENTRAL		
Establishments	469,768	464,682
Less than 10 employees	350,278	346,722
10–99 employees	109,781	108,382
100 or more employees	9,709	9,578
Employment	6,809,844	6,746,269
Less than 10 employees	1,080,248	1,068,088
10–99 employees	2,813,297	2,777,459
100 or more employees	2,916,299	2,900,722
SOUTH ATLANTIC		
Establishments	1,108,705	1,104,420
Less than 10 employees	827,879	820,226
10–99 employees	257,064	259,721
100 or more employees	23,762	24,473
Employment	16,113,452	16,403,919
Less than 10 employees	2,542,209	2,540,031
10–99 employees	6,662,081	6,730,941
100 or more employees	6,909,162	7,132,947
EAST SOUTH CENTRAL		
Establishments	333,895	331,723
Less than 10 employees	246,796	245,060
10–99 employees	79,133	78,759
100 or more employees	7,966	7,904
Employment	5,161,415	5,121,436
Less than 10 employees	779,450	770,709
10–99 employees	2,056,490	2,046,769
100 or more employees	2,325,475	2,303,958
WEST SOUTH CENTRAL		
Establishments	618,740	610,844
Less than 10 employees	462,220	457,389
10–99 employees	143,304	140,596
100 or more employees	13,216	12,859
Employment	9,053,149	8,827,533
Less than 10 employees	1,423,202	1,403,273
10–99 employees	3,706,269	3,636,213
100 or more employees	3,923,678	3,788,047
MOUNTAIN		
Establishments	360,413	351,706
Less than 10 employees	273,242	266,373
10–99 employees	80,778	79,098
100 or more employees	6,393	6,235
Employment	4,782,833	4,663,921
Less than 10 employees	840,746	804,947
10–99 employees	2,043,279	2,000,790
100 or more employees	1,898,808	1,858,184
PACIFIC		
Establishments	1,010,356	1,002,768
Less than 10 employees	747,348	739,982
10–99 employees	243,102	241,972
100 or more employees	19,906	20,814
Employment	14,512,869	14,688,262
Less than 10 employees	2,227,150	2,210,210
10–99 employees	6,367,286	6,337,692
100 or more employees	5,918,433	6,140,360

1. Number of paid employees by size class estimated for 1991. P = Preliminary.

TAXES

History of the Income Tax in the United States

Source: Deloitte & Touche

The nation had few taxes in its early history. From 1791 to 1802, the United States Government was supported by internal taxes on distilled spirits, carriages, refined sugar, tobacco and snuff, property sold at auction, corporate bonds, and slaves. The high cost of the War of 1812 brought about the nation's first sales taxes on gold, silverware, jewelry, and watches. In 1817, however, Congress did away with all internal taxes, relying on tariffs on imported goods to provide sufficient funds for running the Government.

In 1862, in order to support the Civil War effort, Congress enacted the nation's first income tax law. It was a forerunner of our modern income tax in that it was based on the principles of graduated, or progressive, taxation and of withholding income at the source. During the Civil War, a person earning from $600 to $10,000 per year paid tax at the rate of 3%. Those with incomes of more than $10,000 paid taxes at a higher rate. Additional sales and excise taxes were added, and an "inheritance" tax also made its debut. In 1866, internal revenue collections reached their highest point in the nation's 90-year history—more than $310 million, an amount not reached again until 1911.

The Act of 1862 established the office of Commissioner of Internal Revenue. The Commissioner was given the power to assess, levy, and collect taxes, and the right to enforce the tax laws through seizure of property and income and through prosecution. His powers and authority remain very much the same today.

In 1868, Congress again focused its taxation efforts on tobacco and distilled spirits and eliminated the income tax in 1872. It had a short-lived revival in 1894 and 1895. In the latter year, the U.S. Supreme Court decided that the income tax was unconstitutional because it was not apportioned among the states in conformity with the Constitution.

By 1913, with the 16th Amendment to the Constitution, the income tax had become a permanent fixture of the U.S. tax system. The amendment gave Congress legal authority to tax income and resulted in a revenue law that taxed incomes of both individuals and corporations. In fiscal year 1918, annual internal revenue collections for the first time passed the billion-dollar mark, rising to $5.4 billion by 1920. With the advent of World War II, employment increased, as did tax collections—to $7.3 billion. The withholding tax on wages was introduced in 1943 and was instrumental in increasing the number of taxpayers to 60 million and tax collections to $43 billion by 1945.

In 1981, Congress enacted the largest tax cut in U.S. history, approximately $750 billion over six years. The tax reduction, however, was offset by two tax acts, in 1982 and 1984, which attempted to raise approximately $265 billion.

On Oct. 22, 1986, President Reagan signed into law one of the most far-reaching reforms of the United States tax system since the adoption of the income tax. The Tax Reform Act of 1986, as it was called, attempted to be revenue neutral by increasing business taxes and correspondingly decreasing individual taxes by approximately $120 billion over a five-year period.

Following the yearly tradition of new tax acts which began in 1986, the President signed into law the Revenue Reconciliation Act of 1990 on November 5, 1990. As with the '87, '88, and '89 acts, the 1990 act, while providing a number of substantive provisions, was small in comparison with the 1986 act. The emphasis of the 1990 act was increased taxes on the wealthy.

On August 10, 1993, President Clinton signed the Revenue Reconciliation Act of 1993 into law. The Act's purpose is to reduce by approximately $496 billion the Federal deficit that would otherwise accumulate in fiscal years 1994 through 1998. Approximately $241 billion of the deficit reduction will be accomplished through tax increases.

Internal Revenue Service

The Internal Revenue Service (IRS), a bureau of the U.S. Treasury Department, is the federal agency charged with the administration of the tax laws passed by Congress. The IRS functions through a national office in Washington, 7 regional offices, 63 district offices, and 10 service centers.

Operations involving most taxpayers are carried out in the district offices and service centers. District offices are organized into Resources Management, Examination, Collection, Taxpayer Service, Employee Plans and Exempt Organizations, and Criminal Investigation. All tax returns are filed with the service centers, where the IRS computer operations are located.

IRS service centers are processing an ever increasing number of returns and documents. In 1992 the number of returns and supplemental documents processed totaled 204 million.

Prior to 1987, all tax return processing was performed by hand. This process was time consuming and costly. In an attempt to improve the speed and efficiency of the manual processing procedure, the IRS began testing an electronic return filing system beginning with the filing of 1985 returns.

The two most significant results of the test were that refunds for the electronically filed returns were issued more quickly and the tax processing error rate was significantly lower when compared to paper returns.

Electronic filing of individual income tax returns with refunds became an operational program in selected areas for the 1987 processing year. This program is continually expanding. In 1991 7,565,755 individual returns were filed electronically. In 1992 10,924,000 individual returns were filed electronically.

In addition to expanding the program for the electronic filing of individual returns, the IRS has also implemented programs for the electronic filing of partnership, fiduciary, and employee benefit plan returns.

Internal Revenue Service

	1992	1991	1990	1989	1988	1970
U.S. population (in thousands)	256,167	252,901	251,329	249,412	246,329	204,878
Number of IRS employees	116,673	115,628	111,858	114,758	114,873	68,683
Cost to govt. of collecting $100 in taxes	$0.58	$0.56	$0.52	$0.51	$0.54	$0.45
Tax per capita	$4,375.27	$4,343.84	$4,203.12	$4,062.84	$3,792.15	$955.31
Collections by principal sources (in thousands of dollars)						
Total IRS collections	$1,120,799,558	$1,086,851,401	$1,056,365,652	$1,013,322,133	$935,106,594	$195,722,096
Income and profits taxes						
Individual	557,723,156	546,876,876	540,228,408	515,731,504	473,666,566	103,651,585
Corporation	117,950,796	113,598,569	110,016,539	117,014,564	109,682,554	35,036,983
Employment taxes	400,080,904	384,451,220	367,219,321	345,625,586	318,038,990	37,449,188
Estate and gift taxes	11,479,116	11,473,141	11,761,939	8,973,146	7,784,445	3,680,076
Alcohol taxes	NOTE 4	NOTE 4	NOTE 4	NOTE 4	NOTE 4	4,746,382
Tobacco taxes	NOTE 4	NOTE 4	NOTE 4	NOTE 4	NOTE 4	2,094,212
Manufacturers' excise taxes	NOTE 3	NOTE 3	NOTE 3	NOTE 3	NOTE 3	6,683,061
All other taxes	33,565,587	30,451,596	27,139,445	25,977,333	25,934,040	2,380,609

NOTE: For fiscal year ending September 30th. NOTE 2: Alcohol and tobacco tax collections are included in the "All other taxes" amount. NOTE 3: Manufacturers' excise taxes are included in the "All other taxes" amount. NOTE 4: Alcohol and tobacco tax collections are now collected and reported by the Bureau of Alcohol, Tobacco, and Firearms. *Source:* IRS 1992 Annual Report.

Auditing Tax Returns

Most taxpayers' contacts with the IRS arise through the auditing of their tax returns. The Service has been empowered by Congress to inquire about all persons who may be liable for any tax and to obtain for review the books and/or records pertinent to those taxpayers' returns. A wide-ranging audit operation is carried out in the 63 district offices by 15,894 revenue agents and 2,678 tax auditors.

Selecting Individual Returns for Audit

The primary method used by the IRS in selecting returns for audits is a computer program that measures the probability of tax error in each return. The higher the score, the greater the tax change potential. Other returns are selected for examination on the basis of claims for refund, multi-year audits, related return audits, and other audits initiated by the IRS as a result of informants' information, special compliance programs, and the information document matching program.

In 1992, the IRS recommended additional tax and penalties on 1,039,355 individual returns, totaling $6.0 billion.

The Appeals Process

The IRS attempts to resolve tax disputes through an administrative appeals system. Taxpayers who, after audit of their tax returns, disagree with a proposed change in their tax liabilities are entitled to an independent review of their cases. Taxpayers are able to seek an immediate, informal appeal with the Appeals Office. If, however, the dispute arises from a field audit and the amount in question exceeds $10,000, a taxpayer must submit a written protest. Alternatively, the taxpayer can wait for the examiner's report and then request consideration by the Appeals Office and file a protest if necessary. Taxpayers may represent themselves or be represented by an attorney, accountant, or any other advisor authorized to practice before the IRS. Taxpayers can forego their right to the above process and await receipt of a deficiency notice. At this juncture, taxpayers can either (1) not pay the deficiency and petition the Tax Court by a required deadline or (2) pay the deficiency and file a claim for refund with the District Director's office. If the claim is not allowed, a suit for refund may be brought either in the District Court or the Claims Court within a specified period.

Federal Individual Income Tax

Tax Brackets—1993 Taxable Income

Joint return	Single Taxpayer	Rate
$0–$36,900	$0–$22,100	15%
36,900–89,150	22,100–53,500	28%
89,150–140,000	53,500–115,000	31%[2]
140,000–250,000	115,000–250,000	36%[2]
250,000 and up[1]	250,000 and up[1]	39.6%[2]

1. The deduction for personal exemptions is phased out as the taxpayer's gross income exceeds $162,700 (for a joint return) and $108,450 for single taxpayers. 2. The tax rate is effectively increased because total otherwise allowable itemized deductions are reduced by 3% of the taxpayer's adjusted gross income in excess of $108,450.

The Federal individual income tax is levied on the world-wide income of U.S. citizens and resident aliens and on certain types of U.S. source income of non-residents. For a non-itemizer, "tax table income" is adjusted gross income (*see* below) less $2,350 for each personal exemption and the standard deduction (*see* below). If a taxpayer itemizes, tax table income is adjusted gross income minus total itemized deductions and personal exemptions. In addition, individuals may also be subject to the alternative minimum tax.

Who Must File a Return[1]

You must file a return if you are:	and your gross income is at least:
Single (legally separated, divorced, or married living apart from spouse with dependent child) and are under 65	$6,050
Single (legally separated, divorced, or married living apart from spouse with dependent child) and are 65 or older	$6,950
A person who can be claimed as a dependent on your parent's return, and who has taxable dividends, interest, or other unearned income	$600
Head of household under age 65	$7,800
Head of household over age 65	$8,700
Married, filing jointly, living together at end of year (or at date of death of spouse), and both are under 65	$10,900
Married, filing jointly, living together at end of year (or at date of death of spouse), and one is 65 or older	$11,600
Married, filing jointly, living together at end of year (or at date of death of spouse), and both are 65 or older	$12,300
Married, filing separate return, or married but not living together at end of year	$2,350
Married, filing separate return, or married but not living together at end of year over age 65	$2,350

1. In 1993.

Adjusted Gross Income

Gross income consists of wages and salaries, unemployment compensation, tips and gratuities, interest, dividends, annuities, rents and royalties, up to 1/2 of Social Security Benefits if the recipient's income exceeds a base amount, and certain other types of income. Among the items excluded from gross income, and thus not subject to tax, are public assistance benefits and interest on exempt securities (mostly state and local bonds).

Adjusted gross income is determined by subtracting from gross income: alimony paid, penalties on early withdrawal of savings, payments to an I.R.A. (reduced proportionately based upon adjusted gross income levels if taxpayer is an active participant in an employer maintained retirement plan), payments to a Keogh retirement plan and self-employed health insurance payments (25% limit). Employee business expenses and job related moving expenses are treated as itemized deductions.

Itemized Deductions

Taxpayers may itemize deductions or take the standard deduction. The standard deduction amounts for 1993 are as follows: Married filing jointly and surviving spouses, $6,200; Heads of household, $5,450; Single, $3,700; and Married filing separate returns, $3,100. Taxpayers who are age 65 or over or are blind are entitled to an additional standard deduction of $900 for single taxpayers and $700 for a married taxpayer.

In itemizing deductions, the following are major items that may be deducted in 1993: state and local income and property taxes, charitable contributions, employee moving expenses, medical expenses (exceeding 7.5% of adjusted gross income), casualty losses (only the amount over the $100 floor which exceeds 10% of adjusted gross income), mortgage interest, and miscellaneous deductions (deductible only to the extent by which cumulatively they exceed 2% of adjusted gross income).

Personal Exemptions

Personal exemptions are available to the taxpayer for himself, his spouse, and his dependents. The 1993 amount is $2,350 for each individual. No exemption is allowed to a taxpayer who can be claimed as a dependent on another taxpayer's return. Additional personal exemptions for taxpayers age 65 or over or blind have been eliminated.

Credits

Taxpayers can reduce their income tax liability by claiming the benefit of certain tax credits. Each dollar of tax credit offsets a dollar of tax liability. The following are a few of the available tax credits:

Certain low-income households with dependent children may claim an Earned Income Credit. The maximum Basic Earned Income Credit is $1,434 for taxpayers with one qualifying child and $1,511 for taxpayers with two or more qualifying children. In addition to the Basic Earned Income Credit, a taxpayer may also be eligible for a Health Insurance Credit which can be taken as a part of the total earned income credit. This maximum credit will be reduced if earned income or adjusted gross income exceeds $12,200, and the credit will be zero for families with incomes over $23,050. The earned income credit is a refundable credit.

A credit for Child and Dependent Care Expenses is available for amounts paid to care for a child or other dependent so that the taxpayer can work. The credit is between 20% and 30% (depending on adjusted gross income) of up to $2,400 of employment-related expenses for one qualifying child or dependent and up to $4,800 of expenses for two or more qualifying individuals.

The elderly and those under 65 who are retired under total disability may be entitled to a credit of up to $750 (if single) or $1,125 (if married and filing jointly). No credit is available if the taxpayer is single and has adjusted gross income of $17,500 or more, or $5,000 or more in nontaxable Social Security benefits. Similarly, the credit is unavailable to a married couple filing jointly if their adjusted gross income exceeds $25,000 or if their nontaxable Social Security benefits equal or exceed $7,500.

Free Taxpayer Publications

The IRS publishes over 100 free taxpayer information publications on various subjects. One of these, Publication 910, *Guide to Free Tax Services,* is a catalog of the free services the IRS offers. You can order these publications and any tax forms or instructions you need by calling the IRS toll-free at 1-800-829-3676.

Federal Income Tax Comparisons

Taxes at Selected Rate Brackets After Standard Deductions and Personal Exemptions[1]

Adjusted gross income	Single return listing no dependents				Joint return listing two dependents			
	1993	1992	1991	1975	1993	1992	1991	1975
$ 10,000	$ 593	$ 615	$ 668	$ 1,506	$-1,511	$-1,384[2]	$1,235[2]	$ 829
20,000	2,093	2,115	2,168	4,153	236	408	702	2,860
30,000	3,833	3,960	4,201	8,018	2,160	2,220	2,355	5,804
40,000	6,633	6,760	7,001	12,765	3,660	3,720	3,855	9,668
50,000	9,433	9,560	9,801	18,360	5,160	5,220	5,576	14,260

1. For comparison purposes, tax rate schedules were used. 2. Refund based on a basic earned income credit for families with dependent children.

Federal Corporation Taxes

Corporations are taxed under a graduated tax rate structure as shown in the chart. If a corporation has taxable income in excess of $100,000, the amount of tax shall be increased by the lesser of five percent of such excess or $11,750. When a corporation has taxable income in excess of $15,000,000 the amount of tax shall be increased by an additional amount equal to the lesser of three percent of such excess or $100,000.

If the corporation qualifies, it may elect to be an S corporation. If it makes this election, the corporation will not (with certain exceptions) pay corporate tax on its income. Its income is instead passed through and taxed to its shareholders. There are several requirements a corporation must meet to qualify as an S corporation including having 35 or fewer shareholders, and having only one class of stock.

Tax Brackets—1993

Taxable income	Tax rate
$0–$50,000	15%
$50,001–75,000	25
75,001–10,000,000	34
10,000,001 and up	35

State Corporation Income and Franchise Taxes

All states except Nevada, South Dakota, Washington, and Wyoming impose a tax on corporation net income. The majority of states impose the tax at flat rates ranging from 2.35% to approximately 12.5%. Several states have adopted a graduated basis of rates for corporations.

Nearly all states follow the federal law in defining net income. However, many states provide for varying exclusions and adjustments.

A state is empowered to tax all of the net income of its domestic corporations. With regard to non-resident corporations, however, it may only tax the net income on business carried on within its boundaries. Corporations are, therefore, required to apportion their incomes among the states where they do business and pay a tax to each of these states. Nearly all states provide an apportionment to their domestic corporations, too, in order that they not be unduly burdened.

Several states tax unincorporated businesses separately.

Federal Estate and Gift Taxes

A Federal Estate Tax Return must be filed for the estate of every U.S. citizen or resident whose gross estate, if the decedent died in 1993, exceeds $600,000. An estate tax return must also be filed for the estate of a non-resident, if the value of his gross estate in the U.S. is more than $60,000 at the date of death. The estate tax return is due nine months after the date of death of the decedent, but a reasonable extension of time to file may be obtained for good reason.

Under the unified federal estate and gift tax structure, individuals who made taxable gifts during the calendar year are required to file a gift tax return by April 15 of the following year.

A unified credit of $192,800 is available to offset both estate and gift taxes. Any part of the credit used to offset gift taxes is not available to offset estate taxes. As a result, although they are still taxable as gifts, lifetime transfers no longer cushion the impact of progressive estate tax rates. Lifetime transfers and transfers made at death are combined for estate tax rate purposes.

Gift taxes are computed by applying the uniform rate schedule to lifetime taxable transfers (after deducting the unified credit) and subtracting the taxes payable for prior taxable periods. In general, estate taxes are computed by applying the uniform rate schedule to cumulative transfers and subtracting the gift taxes paid. An appropriate adjustment is made for taxes on lifetime transfers—such as certain gifts within three years of death—in a decedent's estate.

Among the deductions allowed in computing the amount of the estate subject to tax are funeral expenditures, administrative costs, claims and bequests to religious, charitable, and fraternal organizations or government welfare agencies, and state inheritance taxes. For transfers made after 1981 during life or death, there is an unlimited marital deduction.

An annual gift tax exclusion is provided that permits tax-free gifts to each donee of $10,000 for each year. A husband and wife who agree to treat gifts to third persons as joint gifts can exclude up to $20,000 a year to each donee. An unlimited exclusion for medical expenses and school tuition paid for the benefit of any donee is also available.

Federal Estate and Gift Taxes

Unified Transfer Tax Rate Schedule, 1993[1]

If the net amount is:		Tentative tax is:		
From	To	Tax +	%	On excess over
$ 0	$ 10,000	$ 0	18	$ 0
10,001	20,000	1,800	20	10,000
20,001	40,000	3,800	22	20,000
40,001	60,000	8,200	24	40,000
60,001	80,000	13,000	26	60,000
80,001	100,000	18,200	28	80,000
100,001	150,000	23,800	30	100,000
150,001	250,000	38,800	32	150,000
250,001	500,000	70,800	34	250,000
500,001	750,000	155,800	37	500,000
750,001	1,000,000	248,300	39	750,000
1,000,001	1,250,000	345,800	41	1,000,000
1,250,001	1,500,000	448,300	43	1,250,000
1,500,001	2,000,000	555,800	45	1,500,000
2,000,001	2,500,000	780,800	49	2,000,000
2,500,001	3,000,000	1,025,800	53	2,500,000
3,000,001 and up	—	1,290,800	55	3,000,000

1. The estate and gift tax rates are combined in the single rate schedule effective for the estates of decedents dying, and for gifts made, after Dec. 31, 1976.

Tax Freedom Day

Tax Freedom Day is the day on which the American taxpayer will have earned enough money to pay his 1993 total taxes. Nineteen ninety-three's Tax Freedom Day was May 3rd

The largest and most visible tax for Americans is the income tax. Taxpayers will have worked almost six weeks (40 days) in 1993 to pay off their income tax obligations. The drain on social insurance payroll taxes will add more than 38 days to this total. In addition, there are sales and excise taxes, which require 17 days of work to pay off, and other property and business taxes, which take 16 days. Finally, almost ten days will go to pay corporate profits taxes, which are a "hidden" tax on individuals, since any business tax is passed on to individuals in one form or another. □

What if Your Tax Return is Examined?

Source: Internal Revenue Service.

If your return is selected for examination, it does not suggest that you are dishonest. The examination may or may not result in more tax. Your case may be closed without change. Or, you may receive a refund.

Many examinations are handled entirely by mail. For information on this, get Publication 1383, The Correspondence Process (Income Tax Accounts), available free by calling 1-800-829-3676. If the IRS notifies you that your examination is to be conducted through a face-to-face interview, or you request such an interview, you have the right to ask that the examination take place at a reasonable time and place that is convenient for both you and the IRS. If the time or place suggested by the IRS is not convenient, the examiner will try to work out something more suitable. However, in any case, the IRS makes the final determination of how, when, and where the examination will take place.

Throughout the examination, you may represent yourself, have someone else accompany you, or with proper written authorization, have someone represent you in your absence.

You may make a sound recording of the examination if you wish, provided you let the examiner know in advance so that he or she can do the same.

Repeat Examinations

The IRS tries to avoid repeat examinations of the same items, but this sometimes happens. If the IRS examined your tax return for the same items in either of the two previous years and proposed no change to your tax liability, you should contact the IRS as soon as possible so that the agency can see if it should discontinue the repeat examination.

Explanation of Changes

If the IRS proposes any changes to your return, they will explain the reasons for the changes. You should not hesitate to ask about anything that is unclear to you.

Interest

You must pay interest on additional tax that you owe. The interest is figured from the due date of the return. But if an IRS error caused a delay in your case, and this was grossly unfair, you may be entitled to a reduction in the interest. Only delays caused by procedural or mechanical acts that do not involve the exercise of judgment or discretion qualify. If you think the IRS caused such a delay, you should discuss it with the examiner and file a claim. □

State General Sales and Use Taxes[1]

State	Percent rate	State	Percent rate	State	Percent rate
Alabama	4	Louisiana	4	Ohio	5
Arizona	5	Maine	5	Oklahoma	4.5
Arkansas	4.5	Maryland	5	Pennsylvania	6
California	6	Massachusets	5	Rhode Island	7
Colorado	3	Michigan	4	South Carolina	5
Connecticut	6	Minnesota	6.5	South Dakota	4
D.C.	6	Mississippi	7	Tennessee	6
Florida	6	Missouri[2]	4.225	Texas	6.25
Georgia	4	Nebraska	5	Utah	5
Hawaii	4	Nevada	6.5	Vermont	5
Idaho	5	New Jersey	6	Virginia	3.5
Illinois	6.25	New Mexico	5	Washington	6.5
Indiana	5	New York[3]	4	West Virginia	6
Iowa	5	North Carolina	4	Wisconsin	5
Kansas	4.9	North Dakota	5	Wyoming	4
Kentucky	6				

1. Local and county taxes, if any, are additional. 2. State use tax 5.725%. 3. New York City, 8.25%. NOTE: Alaska, Delaware, Montana, New Hampshire, and Oregon have no state-wide sales and use taxes. *Source: Information Please Almanac* questionnaires to the states.

Imbalance of Federal Tax Burden by State

Source: Tax Foundation.

The uneven nature of federal tax payments among the fifty states was highlighted in economist Chris R. Edwards' latest *Special Report,* "The 1993 Federal Tax Burden by State." Some states' residents pay over $6,000 per capita to the federal Treasury each year, while others pay less than $3,000.

On the flip side, different states receive different levels of federal spending on everything from defense contracts to Social Security payments to residents.

Significant variations in federal tax burden occur between the states because of differences in income and other factors—including variations in consumption rates of federally taxed goods like gasoline.

By far the largest payment to the federal Treasury is made by residents of California, who will shoulder $148 billion, or 13.2 percent of all federal taxes in fiscal 1993. It would take the taxes attributable to all of the bottom-ranked 25 states and the District of Columbia to equal the amount of tax revenue generated from this single state. In contrast, Wyoming's $1.9 billion tax bill amounts to only 0.2 percent of the total.

A different picture emerges when taxes paid by each state are considered on a per capita basis. Connecticut residents have the highest per capita federal tax burden in the nation at $6,647. New Jersey residents are not far behind and face a per capita federal tax burden of $6,302.

At the other end of the scale, a number of mostly western and southern states have the lowest levels of per capita federal taxation. With a per capita tax burden of $2,703, Mississippi is the only remaining state where residents pay under $3,000, on average, to the federal Treasury. Mississippi is joined by West Virginia, Utah, New Mexico, and Arkansas to round out the five states that were lowest in per capita federal taxes. The gap between the highest-ranked state (Connecticut) and lowest-ranked (Mississippi) is close to $4,000 per person.

Over the past decade, Connecticut ranked as either the first or second highest-taxed state each year, while Mississippi managed to hold its place as the lowest-taxed state throughout the period. Some states, however, have moved substantially in the rankings. Texas, which had the 18th highest tax burden per capita in fiscal 1984, will fall to 32nd by fiscal 1994. North Dakota, originally ranking 23rd, will move down to 37th in the nation by fiscal 1994. The residents of Hawaii have moved in the opposite direction,

FY93 Federal Tax Burden Per Capita

Top and Bottom Ten States

State	Amount	Rank
Connecticut	$6,647	1
New Jersey	6,302	2
Alaska	5,502	3
Delaware	5,463	4
Massachusetts	5,316	5
New York	5,290	6
Maryland	5,120	7
Illinois	5,018	8
Hawaii	4,880	9
New Hampshire	4,757	10
Alabama	3,348	41
Louisiana	3,325	42
Kentucky	3,316	43
South Carolina	3,288	44
Idaho	3,249	45
Arkansas	3,189	46
New Mexico	3,153	47
Utah	3,080	48
West Virginia	3,078	49
Mississippi	2,703	50

Source: Tax Foundation.

from 24th in fiscal 1984 to 10th highest currently.

Federal taxes per capita for the county increased 23 percent over the decade [FY 1984–1994]. Differential changes in the tax burdens of each state primarily reflect changes in each state's economy and residents' incomes.

Only three states, Alaska, Oklahoma, and Wyoming, saw their real federal per capita tax burden fall over the period. A common factor for these states, as well as for Texas and Louisiana—states which also did not see increases in real federal tax burden—is the importance of the oil and gas industry to the states' economies.

In contrast, high-income states in the East, including New Jersey, Connecticut, Delaware, New York, Massachusetts, and New Hampshire, all saw their real per capita federal tax burdens increase by over 35 percent during the decade. □

Per Capita Property Tax Collections by State (in 1991 $)

	1980	1991	% change
Alabama	$ 79	$ 171	116 %
Alaska	900	1213	35
Arizona	352	662	88
Arkansas	134	242	81
California	274	639	133
Colorado	329	690	110
Connecticut	473	1138	141
Delaware	167	311	86
Florida	224	687	207
Georgia	199	506	155
Hawaii	193	430	123
Idaho	227	427	88
Illinois	367	785	114
Indiana	246	571	132
Iowa	360	686	91
Kansas	366	691	89
Kentucky	135	277	105
Louisiana	111	275	148
Maine	319	796	150
Maryland	288	617	114
Massachusetts	555	830	50
Michigan	413	894	116
Minnesota	324	718	122
Mississippi	141	344	144
Missouri	215	377	76
Montana	455	523	15
Nebraska	$ 401	$ 744	86 %
Nevada	256	456	78
New Hampshire	451	1341	197
New Jersey	499	1257	152
New Mexico	142	222	56
New York	501	1101	120
North Carolina	171	382	124
North Dakota	269	505	88
Ohio	281	541	93
Oklahoma	151	250	66
Oregon	382	877	123
Pennsylvania	249	562	126
Rhode Island	413	880	113
South Carolina	160	423	164
South Dakota	351	580	65
Tennessee	158	329	108
Texas	280	679	143
Utah	235	416	77
Vermont	377	925	145
Virginia	236	638	171
Washington	290	625	116
West Virginia	137	273	99
Wisconsin	361	797	121
Wyoming	552	912	65
Wash., D.C.	344	1475	329
U.S. Average	$ 300	$ 666	122 %

Source: Tax Foundation.

Comparing Gas Tax Burdens—U.S. Versus Other Nations

	Gas tax as of April '93[1] (U.S. cents/gallon)	Per-capita annual consumption (gal.)	Miles of freeway per capita	Persons per car	Per capita annual cost of 10¢ gas tax hike[2]
Italy	237¢	87	0.065	2.4	$ 8.70
Netherlands	260	83	0.086	2.8	8.30
France	241	127	0.073	2.5	12.70
Germany (Western)	232	159	0.087	2.1	15.90
Belgium	229	99	0.098	3.8	9.90
United Kingdom	176	152	0.032	2.9	15.20
Japan	187	94	0.022	4.0	9.40
United States	33	432	0.209	1.8	43.20

1. Federal and average state tax combined for the United States. 2. Extra costs assuming no behavior response. *Sources:* Tax Foundation computations based on data from Department of Commerce and Department of Transportation.

The tax rate per gallon of gas is lower in the U.S. than in most other large industrialized nations (*see* table). But a gas tax increase hits Americans far harder than citizens of other countries because of higher U.S. gasoline consumption. Higher consumption can be attributed, among other things, to low energy costs and the great distances between population centers in the United States. This means, for example, that while a 4.3-cent per gallon gas tax increase (as proposed recently by the administration) might cost the average Japanese citizen about $9.40 per year, a similar gas tax increase would cost the average American up to $43.20 per year. □

Federal Taxes vs. Federal Spending, 1992

Some States Give More to Uncle Sam Than They Get

	Taxes per capita	Taxes as % of U.S. avg.	Spending per capita	Spending as % of U.S. avg.	$ Paid/ $ Received[1]
Alabama	$3,177	76	$4,920	107	$0.72
Alaska	5,341	129	6,873	149	0.86
Arizona	3,385	82	4,309	94	0.87
Arkansas	3,019	73	4,151	90	0.81
California	4,525	109	4,526	98	1.11
Colorado	4,089	98	4,952	108	0.91
Connecticut	6,286	151	4,846	105	1.44
Delaware	5,230	126	3,897	85	1.49
Florida	4,105	99	4,648	101	0.98
Georgia	3,642	88	4,191	91	0.96
Hawaii	4,669	112	5,600	122	0.92
Idaho	3,099	75	4,425	96	0.78
Illinois	4,734	114	3,818	83	1.37
Indiana	3,659	88	3,529	77	1.15
Iowa	3,639	88	4,053	88	0.99
Kansas	3,981	96	4,442	97	0.99
Kentucky	3,135	75	4,139	90	0.84
Louisiana	3,127	75	4,340	94	0.80
Maine	3,417	82	5,291	115	0.72
Maryland	4,890	118	6,589	143	0.82
Massachusetts	5,025	121	5,474	119	1.02
Michigan	4,142	100	3,788	82	1.21
Minnesota	4,241	102	3,752	82	1.25
Mississippi	2,563	62	5,107	111	0.56
Missouri	3,776	91	5,025	109	0.83
Montana	3,234	78	4,967	108	0.72
Nebraska	3,801	92	4,281	93	0.98
Nevada	4,429	107	4,052	88	1.21
New Hampshire	4,558	110	3,853	84	1.31
New Jersey	5,966	144	4,405	96	1.50
New Mexico	3,025	73	6,572	143	0.51
New York	4,999	120	4,632	101	1.20
North Carolina	3,458	83	3,761	82	1.02
North Dakota	3,312	80	5,452	119	0.67
Ohio	3,910	94	3,950	86	1.10
Oklahoma	3,280	79	4,450	97	0.82
Oregon	3,843	93	3,934	86	1.08
Pennsylvania	4,226	102	4,640	101	1.01
Rhode Island	4,230	102	5,041	110	0.93
South Carolina	3,142	76	4,415	96	0.79
South Dakota	3,277	79	4,684	102	0.77
Tennessee	3,473	84	4,485	98	0.86
Texas	3,765	91	3,956	86	1.05
Utah	2,958	71	3,925	85	0.83
Vermont	3,721	90	3,801	83	1.08
Virginia	4,223	102	6,416	140	0.73
Washington	4,470	108	4,678	102	1.06
West Virginia	2,887	70	4,485	98	0.71
Wisconsin	3,891	94	3,563	77	1.21
Wyoming	3,870	93	4,506	98	0.95
D.C.	5,451	131	33,952	738	0.18
U.S. Average	$4,153	100	$4,599	100	$1.00

1. Taxes per capita are adjusted so that U.S. average taxes equals U.S. average spending. NOTE: Understanding this table. For example: New Jersey residents pay 144% of the U.S. average in Federal taxes and receive 96% of the U.S. average in Federal spending. That ratio adds up to $1.50 in Federal taxes for each dollar received in Federal spending. *Source:* Tax Foundation; U.S. Bureau of Census.

FIRST AID

Information Please Almanac is not responsible and assumes no responsibility for any action undertaken by anyone utilizing the first aid procedures which follow.

The Heimlich Maneuver[1]

Food-Choking

What to look for: Victim cannot speak or breathe; turns blue; collapses.

To perform the Heimlich Maneuver when the victim is standing or sitting:

1. Stand behind the victim and wrap your arms around his waist.
2. Place the thumb side of your fist against the victim's abdomen, slightly above the navel and below the rib cage.
3. Grasp your fist with the other hand and press your fist into the victim's abdomen with a quick upward thrust. Repeat as often as necessary.
4. If the victim is sitting, stand behind the victim's chair and perform the maneuver in the same manner.
5. After the food is dislodged, have the victim seen by a doctor.

When the victim has collapsed and cannot be lifted:

1. Lay the victim on his back.
2. Face the victim and kneel astride his hips.
3. With one hand on top of the other, place the heel of your bottom hand on the abdomen slightly above the navel and below the rib cage.
4. Press into the victim's abdomen with a quick upward thrust. Repeat as often as necessary
5. Should the victim vomit, quickly place him on his side and wipe out his mouth to prevent aspiration (drawing of vomit into the throat).
6. After the food is dislodged, have the victim seen by a doctor.

NOTE: If you start to choke when alone and help is not available, an attempt should be made to self-administer this maneuver.

Burns[2]

First Degree: Signs/Symptoms—reddened skin. **Treatment**—Immerse quickly in cold water or apply ice until pain stops.

Second Degree: Signs/Symptoms—reddened skin, blisters. **Treatment**—(1) Cut away loose clothing. (2) Cover with several layers of cold moist dressings or, if limb is involved, immerse in cold water for relief of pain. (3) Treat for shock.

Third Degree: Signs/Symtoms—skin destroyed, tissues damaged, charring. **Treatment**—(1) Cut away loose clothing (do not remove clothing adhered to skin). (2) Cover with several layers of sterile, cold, moist dressings for relief of pain and to stop burning action. (3) Treat for shock.

Poisons[2]

Treatment—(1) Dilute by drinking large quantities of water. (2) Induce vomiting except when poison is corrosive or a petroleum product. (3) Call the poison control center or a doctor.

Shock[2]

Shock may accompany any serious injury: blood loss, breathing impairment, heart failure, burns. Shock can kill—treat as soon as possible and continue until medical aid is available.

Signs/Symptoms—(1) Shallow breathing. (2) Rapid and weak pulse. (3) Nausea, collapse, vomiting. (4) Shivering. (5) Pale, moist skin. (6) Mental confusion. (7) Drooping eyelids, dilated pupils.

The Heimlich Maneuver

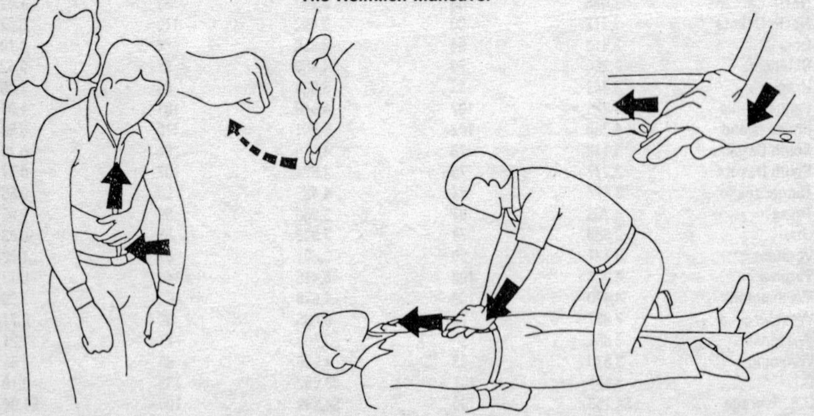

Treatment—(1) Establish and maintain an open airway. (2) Control bleeding. (3) Keep victim lying down. Exception: Head and chest injuries, heart attack, stroke, sun stroke. If no spine injury, victim may be more comfortable and breathe better in a semi-reclining position. If in doubt, keep the victim flat. Elevate the feet unless injury would be aggravated. Maintain normal body temperature. Place blankets under and over victim.

Nosebleed[2]

Nosebleeds are more often annoying than life threatening. They are more common during cold weather, when heated air dries out nasal passages.

Treatment—(1) Keep the victim quietly seated, leaning forward if possible. (2) Gently pinch the nostrils closed. (3) Apply cold compresses to the victim's nose and face. (4) If the person is conscious, it may be helpful to apply pressure beneath the nostril above the lip. (5) Instruct victim not to blow his/her nose for several hours after the bleeding has stopped, or clots could be dislodged and start the bleeding again.

Frostbite[2]

Most frequently frostbitten: toes, fingers, nose, and ears. It is caused by exposure to cold.

Signs/Symptoms—(1) Skin becomes pale or a grayish-yellow color. (2) Parts feel cold and numb. (3) Frozen parts feel doughy.

Treatment—(1) Until victim can be brought inside, he should be wrapped in woolen cloth and kept dry. (2) Do not rub, chafe, or manipulate frostbitten parts. (3) Bring victim indoors. (4) Place in warm water (102° to 105°) and make sure it remains warm. Test water by pouring on inner surface of your forearm. Never thaw if the victim has to go back out into the cold which may cause the affected area to be refrozen. (5) Do not use hot water bottles or a heat lamp, and do not place victim near a hot stove. (6) Do not allow victim to walk if feet are affected. (7) Once thawed, have victim gently exercise parts. (8) For serious frostbite, seek medical aid for thawing because pain will be intense and tissue damage extensive.

Heat Cramps[2]

Affects people who work or do strenous exercises in a hot environment. To prevent it, such people should drink large amounts of cool water and add a pinch of salt to each glass of water

Signs/Symptoms—(1) Painful muscle cramps in legs and abdomen. (2) Faintness. (3) Profuse perspiration.

Treatment—(1) Move victim to a cool place. (2) Give him sips of salted drinking water (one teaspoon of salt to one quart of water). (3) Apply manual pressure to the cramped muscle.

Heat Exhaustion[2]

Signs/Symptoms—(1) Pale and clammy skin. (2) Profuse perspiration. (3) Rapid and shallow breathing. (4) Weakness, dizziness, and headache.

Treatment—(1) Care for victim as if he were in shock. (2) Remove victim to a cool area, do not allow chilling. (3) If body gets too cold, cover victim.

Heat Stroke[2]

Signs/Symptoms—(1) Face is red and flushed. (2) Victim becomes rapidly unconscious. (3) Skin is hot and dry with no perspiration.

Treatment—(1) Lay victim down with head and shoulders raised. (2) Reduce the high body temperature as quickly as possible. (3) Apply cold applications to the body and head. (4) Use ice and fan if available. (5) Watch for signs of shock and treat accordingly. (6) Get medical aid as soon as possible.

Artificial Respiration[3]

(Mouth-to-Mouth Breathing—In Cases Like Drowning, Electric Shock or Smoke Inhalation.)

There is need for help in breathing when breathing movements stop or lips, tongue, and fingernails become blue. When in doubt, apply artificial respiration until you get medical help. No harm can result from its use and delay may cost the patient his life. Start immediately. Seconds count. Clear mouth and throat of any obstructions with your fingers.

For Adults: Place patient on back with face up.

Lift the chin and tilt the head back. If air passage is still closed, pull chin up by placing fingers behind the angles of the lower jaw and pushing forward.

Take deep breath, place you mouth over patient's mouth, making leak-proof seal.

Pinch patient's nostrils closed.

Blow into patient's mouth until you see his chest rise.

—OR—

Take deep breath, place your mouth over patient's nose, making leak-proof seal.

Seal patient's mouth with your hand.

Blow into patient's nose until you see his chest rise.

Remove your mouth and let patient exhale.

Repeat about 12 times a minute. (If the patient's stomach rises markedly, exert moderate hand pressure on the stomach just below the rib cage to keep it from inflating.)

For Infants and Small Children: Place your mouth over patient's mouth and nose. Blow into mouth and nose until you see patient's chest rise normally.

Repeat 20 to 30 times per minute. (Don't exaggerate the tilted position of an infant's head.)

NOTE: For emergency treatment of heart attack, cardiopulmonary resuscitation (CPR) is recommended. Instruction in CPR can be obtained through local health organizations or schools.

Sources: 1. New York City Department of Health. NOTE: Heimlich Maneuver, T.M. Pending. 2. *First Aid,* Mining Enforcement and Safety Administration, U.S. Department of the Interior. 3. *Health Emergency Chart,* Council on Family Health.

Genetically Engineered Foods: Fears and Facts

An interview with James Maryanski, biotechnology coordinator in FDA's Center for Food Safety and Applied Nutrition.

By FDA Consumer writer, Mary Alice Sudduth

Q: What is "new biotechnology" in reference to food plants, and how does it differ from old biotechnology?

A: All plant breeding involves genetic manipulation of plants. There are hundreds of new plant varieties introduced every year in the United States, and all have been genetically modified through traditional plant breeding techniques—such as cross-fertilization of selected plants—to produce desired traits. This is "old biotechnology."

The new biotechnology—known variously as gene splicing, recombinant DNA, or genetic engineering—is actually an extension of traditional plant breeding. It involves direct modification of DNA, a living thing's genetic material. This new technique is more precise, making it possible to direct and predict changes without introducing extraneous, undesirable traits. The new technique also will allow scientists to introduce genes from essentially any organism into a plant.

Q: Why do we need these plants and the foods they produce?

A: Plant breeders have a limited pool of genes—and, therefore, traits—available for use in improving plants. By looking at bacteria and animals, scientists can find other traits that may expand the number of potentially useful traits. These may include size, solids content, or resistance to certain viruses or fungi.

Q: Under what circumstances will FDA require labeling of genetically engineered foods?

A: One important area is that of potential allergens. If a gene from a food that commonly causes allergic reactions, like fish or peanuts, is inserted into tomatoes or corn, where people would not expect to find allergens, then the vegetables would have to be labeled to alert sensitive consumers. If companies can demonstrate scientifically that the allergenic component was not transferred to the vegetable, no special label will be required. FDA's policy states that proteins taken from commonly allergenic foods are presumed to be allergens unless demonstrated otherwise.

Labeling also could be required if the nutritional content of the food is changed. Tomatoes are a major source of vitamin C, and if someone develops a tomato that no longer contains vitamin C, then that will have to be disclosed. So we envision a number of circumstances where labeling will be necessary, and we'll use the same labeling regulations we've always used under the FD&C Act. We've invited public comment on this issue, because we anticipate consumers will have diverse opinions about genetic engineering and about what information should appear on labels.

Q: FDA has emphasized the importance of proper labeling of foods and has initiated legal action against certain products—Citrus Hill "fresh" orange juice, for example—because of misleading labeling. How does this differ from labeling biotechnology-derived foods? Isn't the fundamental issue the same—full disclosure?

A: The law says labeling for foods must disclose information that's material, as well as avoid false or misleading statements.

It's our view that the method by which a plant is developed by a plant breeder is not material information in the sense of the law. For example, we do not require sweet corn to be labeled "hybrid sweet corn" because it was developed through cross hybridization. And plant breeders have many other traditional techniques through which they coax nature to change genes that would not occur otherwise. A process called somoclonal variation allows breeders to take advantage of natural mutations in plant cells that produce desired traits. Through embryo rescue, breeders nurture embryos produced by crossing two plant varieties that would not breed naturally, producing potentially useful plants that would not have survived on their own. Historically, we have not required this information to be on labels. It would not be practical.

If genetic engineering or any other technique changes the composition of a tomato in a way that it's really not the same tomato anymore, then it would have to be called something different. It would have to have a different varietal name, or, if it was a significant difference, it may not even be called a tomato.

We are reviewing the comments from the public on this issue to see if there is a basis for modifying our policy. However, if we were to require labeling of all genetically engineered fruits and vegetables, it would not be merely a matter of putting a sticker on a tomato or a banana. Producers would have to segregate the genetically engineered foods from other varieties, whereas normally those are all just lumped into a barrel. And then what happens when you make tomato paste, and that tomato paste is used to make pizzas? Does the label have to follow along the food processing chain? It would increase the cost of these foods to consumers and would disrupt our complex food distribution system.

Q: Are there environmental risks involved in producing genetically altered foods?

A: Potential environmental risks from these crops are the same as those that occur in plants developed by traditional methods. There are many complex issues—such as potential transfer of traits to other plants and potential adverse effects on other organisms, particularly endangered species—that need to be taken into account. For example, if a plant has may wild relatives, it could pass a gene to one of those, resulting in an outcross plant species with some undesirable traits. The wild plants could develop into a fast-growing weed species, for instance. For some crops, like tomatoes, this really isn't a risk in the United States because there are few, if any, wild relatives of tomatoes that could be bred accidentally. But there are other plants, such as soybeans and squash, where there will be potential for an outcross species. Whether outcrossing is a problem depends on the trait that's introduced, as well.

Environmental risks are looked at during the research and development phase. Right now, crops developed using recombinant DNA methods are reviewed by the U.S. Department of Agriculture's Animal and Plant Health Inspection Service. If FDA acts on a food additive petition or GRAS [generally recognized as safe] petition for a new ingredient, we will do an environmental assessment. We will look at what the other agencies have done, and, to the extent possible, we will rely on their information. If there are other issues, they will have to be considered.

Q: How long will it be before most of the foods now being developed through new biotechnology are available to consumers?

A: That's a good question. People have this perception that all these things are just coming out of the sky and landing in the grocery stores next week, and that's just not true. There are products, like the Flavr Savr tomato, that are nearing commercialization. Assuming all the safety question are answered, it will probably be introduced within the next year [1994]. USDA has received a request to rule on whether a variety of virus-resistant squash may be grown without USDA oversight, so one would assume it's close to commercialization. But most of the products—such as insect-resistant produce, vegetables with increased amino acids, and low-caffeine coffee—are two to five years away. We're going to see a gradual introduction of these products over the next several years, not an avalanche.

Q: What about the possibility of plants containing animal genes?

A: Several experimental plants have been developed that have copies of genes found in animals, such as the "antifreeze protein" gene from the Arctic flounder that may make tomato paste freeze and thaw better.

However, there really aren't any plants with animal genes, that we know of, that are going to be marketed foods in the near future. So we have a good deal of time to think about the issue of animal genes. We believe the safety of the proteins produced by these genes should be evaluated based on their characteristics. If, for example, the flounder antifreeze protein is a component of fish fillet, it likely would be safe to eat as a component of tomato paste. But proteins derived from animals that have not been consumed safely will be treated as new food additives.

Q: Has FDA considered the ethnical or religious implications of injecting animal genes into plants? How will this affect vegetarians?

A: FDA is considering these issues. There are thousands of genes in a plant. When a scientists adds new genes from an animal, it gives that plant several new proteins. But these proteins would not seem to give animal characteristics to the vegetable.

A breeder does not actually take something from the animal and introduce it into the plant. For example, a scientist copies the fish "antifreeze protein" and modifies the gene. We know the characteristic of the fish gene, and we can tinker with it to make a different version. The copy is what is introduced into the plant, and the new gene works just like any other plant gene. So you don't really have pieces of animals in vegetables. You have pieces of plant DNA that are the same as, or nearly the same as, pieces of animal DNA.

One of the things people probably don't realize is that there are genes in humans and animals that are in plants. There is a gene that occurs in rice that also occurs in the human brain. Vegetarians would not avoid rice because of that.

Our current view is that these modifications will not result in foods that violate any ethical or religious considerations. However, we recognize people will have different views, and we specifically invited comment on this issue. We're also trying to get comments from various religious and other authoritative leaders so that we can get some sort of official opinion.

Q: What values will these genetically engineered plants have—more nutrients, better taste?

A: Both of those, and many agronomic values: better processing, freeze resistance. That's what using a flounder gene is all about—making a tomato freeze and thaw better. That protein also is being used as a model for developing a food additive to use in ice cream so ice crystals don't form.

In addition, scientists actually will be able to make food safer. They'll be able to reduce the natural toxins. We're already looking at ways to identify the allergenic proteins in foods like milk. But those things are many years in the future.

Right now, it's more a matter of giving fruits and vegetables better shelf life and shipping properties. Most of the traits will have economic values for farmers and processors. □

Alzheimer's Disease

Source: American Council on Science and Health.

Alzheimer's disease (AD) is named after Alois Alzheimer, a German physician, who first described the disease in one of his patients in 1906. This patient, a 51-year-old woman, suffered from memory loss, disorientation, depression, and hallucinations. She eventually suffered complete dementia and died five years later. Upon autopsy, her brain revealed extensive lesions of a type now considered characteristic of Alzheimer's disease.

Alzheimer's disease is tragic, not only because it causes untimely death, but because it involves mental deterioration and increases dependency on others. Victims are dependent on other people between 5 and 20 years before death occurs. Caring for an AD victim causes considerable emotional and economic hardship for the care givers, who are usually relatives. Many AD victims become so difficult to care for that they are eventually sent to nursing homes.

Familial Alzheimer's disease is less common than sporadic Alzheimer's disease. It can occur at an early age, as well as at later ages. *Sporadic* Alzheimer's disease, or dementia of the Alzheimer type, is much more common and occurs primarily over age 60, with the majority being age 85 and over. In one recent epidemiological community study, almost 50% of all persons over 75 had been diagnosed with probable Alzheimer's disease. This observation needs to be confirmed by other studies, because former estimates were significantly lower. Nevertheless AD increases exponentially with age. It is not clear whether familial or sporadic AD are one and the same disease or whether they represent two different diseases.

The causes of AD are not known. Inheritance seems to play a role in familial Alzheimer's disease. Defective genes or defective gene products may also play a role in sporadic AD. Treatment of AD focuses mainly on the alleviation of the symptoms. There is no known cure. □

The Global AIDS Situation Worsens

Source: World Health Organization (WHO).

Estimated Distribution of Cumulative HIV Infections in Adults, by Continent or Region: Mid-1993

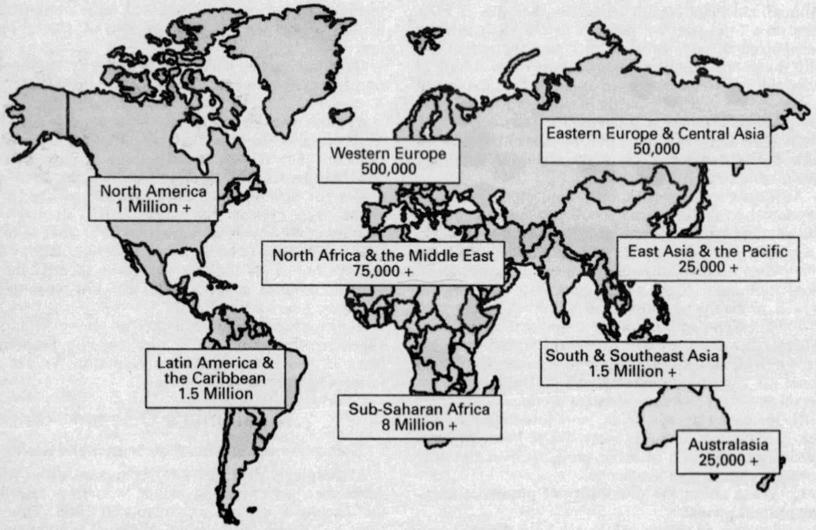

Global Total: 13 million +

As of June 30, 1993, 718,894 cumulative AIDS cases in adults and children have been reported to the Evaluation Unit, Office of Cooperation with National Programmes, World Health Organization Global Programme on AIDS.

WHO estimates that over 25 million cumulative AIDS cases have occurred to date. This estimate is based on the available data on the distribution, spread, and penetration of HIV throughout the World, and is consistent with the effect of under-diagnosis, underreporting, and delays in reporting of AIDS cases. Again as a consequence of such reporting biases, whereas over 50% of *reported* AIDS cases are from developed countries, about 80% of all *estimated* AIDS cases are from the developing world.

In the developing world, two-thirds of all estimated AIDS cases to date are thought to have occurred in sub-Saharan Africa; however, HIV infection trends have been rapid in South and South-East Asia, with over 1.5 million cumulative HIV infections estimated to have occurred to date. The worldwide total now exceeds 13 million adults HIV-infected since the pandemic's start, with an additional 1 million or more HIV-infected children. The distribution of adult HIV infections in other regions of the World is as follows: Australasia over 25,000; East Asia and the Pacific over 25,000; Eastern Europe and Central Asia about 50,000; Latin America and the Caribbean about 1.5 million; North Africa and the Middle East over 75,000; North America over 1 million infections; Western Europe about 500,000 HIV infections. The unstable political, social, and economic environment in Eastern Europe and Central Asia suggests that the evolution of HIV/AIDS in that part of the world may potentially be rapid; current estimates are based on relatively limited data. □

Understanding AIDS

The Acquired Immune Deficiency Syndrome, or AIDS, was first reported in the United States in mid-1981. The total AIDS cases in the United States (including U.S. territories) as of June 30, 1993, were 315,390, and of these cases, 194,334 deaths were reported, says the Center for Disease Control in Atlanta.

AIDS is characterized by a defect in natural immunity against disease. People who have AIDS are vulnerable to serious illnesses which would not be a threat to anyone whose immune system was functioning normally. These illnesses are referred to as "opportunistic" infections or diseases: in AIDS patients the most common of these are Pneumocystis carinii pneumonia (PCP), a parasitic infection of the lungs; and a type of cancer known as Kaposi's sarcoma

(KS). Other opportunistic infections include unusually severe infections with yeast, cytomegalovirus, herpes virus, and parasites such as Toxoplasma or Cryptosporidia. Milder infections with these organisms do not suggest immune deficiency.

AIDS is caused by a virus usually known as human immunodeficiency virus, or HIV. Symptoms of full-blown AIDS include a persistent cough, fever, and difficulty in breathing. Multiple purplish blotches and bumps on the skin may indicate Kaposi's sarcoma. The virus can also cause brain damage.

The credit for discovering the AIDS virus is jointly shared by Dr. Robert Gallo, a researcher at the National Cancer Institute, and Luc Montagnier of the Pasteur Institute, France.

People infected with the virus can have a wide range of symptoms—from none to mild to severe. At least a fourth to a half of those infected will develop AIDS within four to ten years. Many experts think the percentage will be much higher.

The national Centers for Disease Control and Prevention has changed its AIDS surveillance case definition for adolescents and adults to include HIV-infected people who have a CD4 T-lymphocyte (a white blood cell) count less than 200 cells per microliter (a millionth of a liter), or a CD4 percent less than 14. A normal adult has 800 to 1,200 CD4 cells in a microliter of blood. People with HIV infection lose all of the CD4 cells over time as their ability to produce them diminishes.

Also, CDC added recurrent pneumonia, pulmonary tuberculosis, and invasive cervical cancer in HIV-infected people to the 23 clinical conditions in the case definition published in 1987. According to CDC, the addition of these conditions reflects their documented or potential importance in the HIV epidemic. CDC reports, for instance, that cities with large numbers of AIDS cases have had parallel increases in TB rates, with the racial, ethnic, and age groups most affected by HIV having the greatest increase in TB incidence.

The expanded definition went into effect last Jan. 1. CDC estimates the expanded definition could increase AIDS reporting in 1993 by about 75 percent, possibly resulting in 80,000 to 90,000 case reports. Under the 1987 definition, 50,000 to 60,000 case reports would have been expected in 1993.

For a free single copy of "1992 Revised Classification System for HIV Infection and Expanded AIDS Surveillance Case Definition for Adolescents and Adults," contact the CDC National AIDS Clearinghouse, P.O. Box 6003, Rockville, Md. 20849-6003; telephone (1–800) 458-5231.

AIDS is spread by sexual contact, needle sharing, or less commonly through transfused blood or its components. The risk of infection with the virus is increased by having multiple sexual partners, either homosexual or heterosexual, and sharing of needles among those using illicit drugs. The occurrence of the syndrome in hemophilia patients and persons receiving transfusions provides evidence for transmission through blood. It may be transmitted from infected mother to infant before, during, or shortly after birth (probably through breast milk).

The AIDS virus can be spread by sexual intercourse whether you are male or female, heterosexual, bisexual, or homosexual. This happens because a person infected with the AIDS virus may have the virus in semen or vaginal fluids. The virus can enter the body through the vagina, penis, rectum or mouth. Anal intercourse, with or without a condom, is risky. The rectum is easily injured during anal intercourse.

Remember, AIDS is sexually transmitted, and the AIDS virus is not the only infection that is passed through intimate sexual contact.

Other sexually transmitted diseases, such as gonorrhea, syphilis, herpes, and chlamydia, can also be contracted through oral, anal, and vaginal intercourse.

Scientists have discovered how AIDS infects brain cells and have identified genes that affect the AIDS virus. But efforts to devise a treatment or vaccine are complicated by the fact that AIDS is caused by two, perhaps three, similar viruses, and that the virus mutates frequently.

With no cure in sight, prudence could save thousands of people in the U.S. who have yet to be exposed to the virus. Their fate will depend less on science than on the ability of large numbers of human beings to change their behavior in the face of growing danger. Experts believe that couples who have had a totally monogamous relationship for the past decade are safe. A negative blood test would be near-certain evidence of safety.

People who should be tested for AIDS include gay men and intravenous drug users, their sex partners, and anyone who has had several sex partners, if their sexual history is unknown, during any one of the last five years. Anyone who tests positive should see a physician immediately for a medical evaluation. Persons testing positive should inform their sex partners and should use a condom[1] during sex. (NOTE: According to the U.S. Food and Drug Administration, natural membrane condoms made from lambskin may not protect against the AIDS virus.) They should not donate blood, body organs, other tissue or sperm, nor should they share toothbrushes, razors, or other implements that could become contaminated with blood.

Information about where to go for confidential testing for the presence of the AIDS virus is provided by local and state health departments. There is a National AIDS Hot Line: (800) 342-2437 for recorded information about AIDS, or (800) 433-0366 for specific questions. □

Helping a Person With AIDS

No one will require more support and more love than your friend with AIDS. Feel free to offer what you can, without fear of becoming infected. You need to take precautions such as wearing rubber gloves only when blood is present.

If you don't know anyone with AIDS, but you'd still like to offer a helping hand, become a volunteer. You can be sure your help will be appreciated by a person with AIDS.

This might mean dropping by a supermarket to pick up groceries or just being there to talk. Above all, keep an upbeat attitude. It will help you and everyone face the disease more comfortably. □

Other Sexually Transmitted Diseases (STD)

Reliable data on the worldwide incidence of STD are not available. The World Health Organization's minimal estimates for the four major bacterial STD are: gonorrhoea, 25 million cases; genital chlamydial infections, 50 million cases; infectious syphilis, 3.5 million cases; and chancroid, 2 million cases. Rough estimates of genital herpes, a viral STD, is 20 million cases. □

1. Although condoms greatly reduce the risk of getting an AIDS infection, they are not guaranteed to be 100% effective. Considering that there is a 16% chance of failing when condoms are used as contraceptives it could also happen that a condom could fail in protecting against AIDS. The human sperm is many times larger than the AIDS virus. One sperm measures about 3,000 nanometers (a nanometer is one-billionth of a meter) and the AIDS virus is only 100 nanometers.—Ed.

Cancer Risks You Can Avoid

Source: National Cancer Institute, National Institutes of Health.

What is Cancer?

Cancer is really a group of diseases. There are more than 100 different types of cancer, but they all are a disease of some of the body's cells.

Healthy cells that make up the body's tissues grow, divide, and replace themselves in an orderly way. This process keeps the body in good repair. Sometimes, however, normal cells lose their ability to limit and direct their growth. They divide too rapidly and grow without any order. Too much tissue is produced and *tumors* begin to form. Tumors can be either *benign* or *malignant.*

Benign tumors are not cancer. They do not spread to other parts of the body and they are seldom a threat to life. Often, benign tumors can be removed by surgery, and they are not likely to return.

Malignant tumors are cancer. They can invade and destroy nearby tissue and organs. Cancer cells also can spread, or *metastasize,* to other parts of the body, and form new tumors.

Because cancer can spread, it is important for the doctor to find out as early as possible if a tumor is present and if it is cancer. As soon as a diagnosis is made, treatment can begin.

Signs and Symptoms of Cancer

Cancer and other illnesses often cause a number of problems you can watch for. The most common warning signs of cancer are:

Change in bowel or bladder habits;

A sore that does not heal;

Unusual bleeding or discharge;

Thickening or lump in the breast or elsewhere;

Indigestion or difficulty swallowing;

Obvious change in a wart or mole;

Nagging cough or hoarseness.

These signs and symptoms can be caused by cancer or by a number of other problems. They are *not* a sure sign of cancer. However, it is important to see a doctor if any problem lasts as long as 2 weeks. Don't wait for symptoms to become painful; pain is not an early sign of cancer.

Preventing Cancer

By choosing a lifestyle that avoids certain risks, you can help protect yourself from developing cancer. Many cancers are linked to factors that you can control.

Tobacco—Smoking and using tobacco in any form has been directly linked to cancer. Overall, smoking causes 30 percent of all cancer deaths. The risk of developing lung cancer is 10 times greater for smokers than for nonsmokers. The amount of risk from smoking depends on the number and type of cigarettes you smoke, how long you have been smoking, and how deeply you inhale. Smokers are also more likely to develop cancers of the mouth, throat, esophagus, pancreas, and bladder. And now there is emerging evidence that smoking can also cause cancer of the stomach and cervix.

The use of "smokeless" tobacco (chewing tobacco and oral snuff) increases the risk of cancer of the mouth and pharynx. Once you quit smoking or using smokeless tobacco, your risk of developing cancer begins to decrease right away.

Diet—What you eat may affect your chances of developing cancer. Scientists think there is a link between a high-fat diet and some cancers, particularly those of the breast, colon, endometrium, and prostate. Obesity is thought to be linked with increased death rates for cancers of the prostate, pancreas, breast, and ovary. Still other studies point to an increased risk of getting stomach cancer for those who frequently eat pickled, cured, and smoked foods. The National Cancer Institute believes that eating a well-balanced diet can reduce the risk of getting cancer. Americans should eat more high-fiber foods (such as whole-grain cereals and fruits and vegetables) and less fatty foods.

Sunlight—Repeated exposure to sunlight increases the risk of skin cancer, especially if you have fair skin or freckle easily. In fact, ultraviolet radiation from the sun is the main cause of skin cancer, which is the most common cancer in the United States. Ultraviolet rays are strongest from 11 a.m. to 2 p.m. during the summer, so that is when risk is greatest. Protective clothing, such as a hat and long sleeves, can help block out the sun's harmful rays. You can also use sunscreens to help protect yourself. Sunscreens with a number 15 on the label means most of the sun's harmful rays will be blocked out.

Alcohol—Drinking large amounts of alcohol (one or two drinks a day is considered moderate) is associated with cancers of the mouth, throat, esophagus, and liver. People who smoke cigarettes and drink alcohol have an especially high risk of getting cancers of the mouth and esophagus.

X-rays—Large doses of radiation increase cancer risk. Although individual x-rays expose you to very little radiation, repeated exposure can be harmful. Therefore, it is a good idea to avoid unnecessary x-rays. It's best to talk about the need for each x-ray with your doctor or dentist. If you do need an x-ray, ask if shields can be used to protect other parts of your body.

Industrial Agents and Chemicals—Being exposed to some industrial agents or chemicals increases cancer risk. Industrial agents cause damage by acting alone or together with another cancer-causing agent found in the workplace or with cigarette smoke. For example, inhaling asbestos fibers increases the risk of lung disease and cancer. This risk is especially high for workers who smoke. You should follow work and safety rules to avoid coming in contact with such dangerous materials.

Being exposed to large amounts of household solvent cleaners, cleaning fluids, and paint thinners should be avoided. Some chemicals are especially dangerous if inhaled in high concentrations, particularly in areas that are not well ventilated. In addition, inhaling or swallowing lawn and garden chemicals increases cancer risk. Follow label instructions carefully when using pesticides, fungicides, and other chemicals. Such chemicals should not come in contact with toys or other household items.

Hormones—Taking estrogen to relieve menopausal symptoms (such as hot flashes) has been associated with higher-than-average rates of cancer of the uterus. Numerous studies also have examined the relationship between oral contraceptives (the pill) and a variety of female cancers. Recent studies report that taking the pill does not increase a woman's chance of getting breast cancer. Also, pill users appear to have a lower-than-average risk of cancers of the endometrium and ovary. However, some researchers believe that there may be a higher risk of cancer of the cervix among pill users. Women taking hormones (either estrogens or oral contraceptives) should discuss the benefits and risks with their doctor.

Unavoidable Risks

Certain risk factors for cancer cannot be controlled, but people at high risk can help protect themselves by getting regular checkups. Some groups that have a higher-than-average risk of developing cancer are described below.

(1) Individuals who have close relatives with melanoma or cancer of the breast or colon. A small number of these cancers tend to occur more often in some families. If a close relative has been affected by one of these cancers, you should tell your doctor and be sure to have regular checkups to detect early problems.

(2) Persons who have had x-ray treatment to the head or neck when they were children or young adults. Exposure to these x-ray treatments may result in thyroid tumors, which have been associated with radiation given for an enlarged thymus gland, enlarged tonsils and adenoids, whooping cough, ringworm of the scalp, acne, and other head and neck conditions. Most thyroid tumors are not cancer. If thyroid cancer does develop, it usually can be cured. If you have had such x-rays, you should have a doctor examine your throat and neck every 1 or 2 years.

(3) Daughters and sons whose mothers took a drug called diethylstilbestrol (DES) to prevent miscarriages while they were pregnant with them. DES and some similar drugs given to mothers during pregnancy have been linked to certain unusual tissue formations in the vagina and cervix of their daughters. DES also has caused a rare type of vaginal and cervical cancer in a small number of exposed daughters. Women who took DES and DES-type drugs during pregnancy may themselves have a moderately increased risk of developing breast cancer. DES-exposed daughters and mothers should have examinations at least once a year that include pelvic and breast exams and Pap tests.

No link with cancer due to DES exposure before birth has been found in boys and men. However, there may be an increase in certain reproductive and urinary system problems in DES-exposed sons, who should also be examined regularly by a doctor. □

Dietary Guidelines for Americans

Source: U.S. Dept. of Agriculture, U.S. Dept. of Health and Human Services

Eat a Variety of Foods

You need more than 40 different nutrients for good health. Essential nutrients include vitamins, minerals, amino acids from protein, certain fatty acids from fat, and sources of calories (protein, carbohydrates, and fat).

These nutrients should come from a variety of foods, not from a few highly fortified foods or supplements. Any food that supplies calories and nutrients can be part of a nutritious diet. The content of the total diet over a day or more is what counts.

No single food can supply all nutrients in the amounts you need. For example, milk supplies calcium but little iron; meat supplies iron but little calcium. To have a nutritious diet, you must eat a variety of foods.

One way to assure variety—and with it, an enjoyable and nutritious diet—is to choose foods each day from the five major food groups.

Use Sugars Only in Moderation

Sugars and many foods that contain them in large amounts supply calories but are limited in nutrients. Thus, they should be used in moderation by most healthy people and sparingly by people with low calorie needs. For very active people with high calorie needs, sugars can be an additional source of calories.

Both sugars and starches—which break down into sugars—can contribute to tooth decay. Sugars and starches are in many foods that also supply nutrients—milk; fruits; some vegetables; and breads, cereals and other foods with sugars and starches as ingredients. The more often these foods—even small amounts—are eaten and the longer they are in the mouth before teeth are brushed, the greater the risk for tooth decay. Thus, eating such foods as frequent between-meal snacks may be more harmful to teeth than having them at meals.

Regular daily brushing with a fluoride toothpaste helps reduce tooth decay by getting fluoride to the teeth. Fluoridated water or other sources of fluoride that a doctor or dentist suggest are especially important for children whose unerupted teeth are forming and growing.

Use Salt and Sodium Only in Moderation

Table salt contains sodium and chloride—both are essential in the diet. However, most Americans eat more salt and sodium than they need. Food and beverages containing salt provide most of the sodium in our diets, much of it added during processing and manufacturing.

Drink Alcohol in Moderation

Alcoholic beverages supply calories but little or no nutrients. Drinking them has no net health benefit, is linked with many health problems, is the cause of many accidents, and can lead to addiction. Their consumption is not recommended. If adults elect to drink alcoholic beverages, they should consume them in moderate amounts.

Choose a Diet Low in Fat, Saturated Fat, and Cholesterol

Most health authorities recommend an American diet with less fat, saturated fat, and cholesterol. The higher levels of saturated fat and cholesterol in our diets are linked to our increased risk for heart disease.

A diet low in fat makes it easier for you to include the variety of foods you need for nutrients without exceeding your calorie needs because fat contains over twice the calories of an equal amount of carbohydrates or protein.

A diet low in saturated fat and cholesterol can help maintain a desirable level of blood cholesterol. For adults this level is below 200 mg/dl. As blood cholesterol increases above this level, greater risk for heart disease occurs. Risk can also be increased by high blood pressure, cigarette smoking, diabetes, a family history of premature heart disease, obesity, and being a male.

The way diet affects blood cholesterol varies among individuals. However, blood cholesterol does increase in most people when they eat a diet high in saturated fat and cholesterol and excessive in calories. Of these, dietary saturated fat has the greatest effect; dietary cholesterol has less.

Choose a Diet with Plenty of Vegetables, Fruits, Grain Products

This guideline recommends that adults eat at least three servings of vegetables and two servings of fruit daily. It recommends at least six servings of grain products, such as breads, cereals, pasta, and rice, with an emphasis on whole grains. Children should also be encouraged to eat plenty of these foods.

Vegetables, fruits, and grain products are emphasized in this guideline especially for their complex carbohydrates, dietary fiber, and other food components linked to good health.

These foods are generally low in fats. By choosing the suggested amounts of them, you are likely to increase carbohydrates and decrease fats in your diet, as health authorities suggest. You will also get more dietary fiber.

Maintain Healthy Weight

If you are too fat or too thin, your chances of developing health problems are increased.

Being too fat is common in the United States. It is linked with high blood pressure, heart disease, stroke, the most common type of diabetes, certain cancers, and other types of illness.

Being too thin is a less common problem. It occurs with anorexia nervosa and is linked with osteoporosis in women and greater risk of illness.

Whether your weight is "healthy" depends on how much of your weight is fat, where in your body the fat is located, and whether you have weight-related medical problems, such as high blood pressure, or a family history of such problems. □

Suggested Weights for Adults

Height[1]	Weight in pounds[2]	
	19 to 34 years	35 years and over
5'0"	[3]97—128	108—138
5'1"	101—132	111—143
5'2"	104—137	115—148
5'3"	107—141	119—152
5'4"	111—146	122—157
5'5"	114—150	126—162
5'6"	118—155	130—167
5'7"	121—160	134—172
5'8"	125—164	138—178
5'9"	129—169	142—183
5'10"	132—174	146—188
5'11	136—179	151—194
6'0"	140—184	155—199
6'1"	144—189	159—205
6'2"	148—195	164—210
6'3"	152—200	168—216
6'4"	156—205	173—222
6'5"	160—211	177—228
6'6"	164—216	182—234

1. Without shoes. 2. Without clothes. 3. The higher weights in the ranges generally apply to men, who tend to have more muscle and bone; the lower weights more often apply to women, who have less muscle and bone. Source: Derived from National Research Council, 1989.

The New Meat and Poultry Labels

Source: Food News For Consumers

New food labeling regulations were announced on January 6, 1993. While manufacturers have until July 1994 to meet the new requirements for processed meat and poultry products like hot dogs and chili, you are likely to see these new labels much sooner. However, consumers should be aware that not every food product will be required to carry a nutrition label. Companies can choose to volunteer information on raw, single-ingredient meat and poultry products like raw chicken legs.

The following are the new nutrient content claims and what their definitions mean:

Free. The product contains only a tiny or insignificant amount of fat, cholesterol, sodium, sugar, and/or calories. For example, a fat-free product will contain less than 0.5 grams of fat per serving.

Low. A food described as "low" in fat, saturated fat, cholesterol, sodium and/or calories could be eaten fairly often without exceeding dietary guidelines. So "low in fat" means no more than 3 grams of fat per serving.

Lean. "Lean" and "Extra Lean" are USDA terms for use on meat and poultry products. "Lean" means the product contains less than 10 grams of fat, 4 grams of saturated fat and 95 mg of cholesterol per serving. "Lean" is not as lean as "low."

Extra Lean. "Extra Lean" means that the product has less than 5 grams of fat, 2 grams of saturated fat, and 95 mg of cholesterol per serving. Leaner than "Lean," "Extra Lean" is still not as lean as "Low."

Reduced, Less, Fewer. Means a diet product contains 25% less of a nutrient or calories. For example, hot dogs might be labeled "25% less fat than our regular hot dogs."

Light/Lite. Means a diet product with 1/3 fewer calories or 1/2 the fat of the original. "Light in Sodium" means a product with 1/2 the usual sodium.

More. A food in which one serving has at least 10% of the Daily Value of a vitamin or mineral.

Good Source Of. One serving contains 10–19% of the Daily Value for a particular vitamin, mineral, or fiber. □

E. coli Alert

Source: Food News For Consumers

The FDA has raised the cooking temperature it recommends for cooking ground beef products. Ground beef products should now be cooked to heat all parts of the food to at least 155 degrees Fahrenheit. At this temperature, the ground beef will not be pink at the center, and juices will be clear.

The new recommendation was made as a result of a food-borne illness outbreak in January 1993 attributed to uncooked hamburgers contaminated with *Escherichia coli* 0157:H7 that was traced to a national food chain's outlets in Washington, Idaho, California, and Nevada.

E. coli 0157:H7 is related to other types of *E. coli* bacteria normally found in the intestines of humans and animals. It has been isolated from raw beef, pork, lamb, poultry, venison, unpasteurized milk, and water. This virulent strain can produce a toxin in the human digestive tract and cause an illness known as acute hemorrhagic colitis. The illness is characterized by severe abdominal cramps, followed by watery diarrhea that often contains blood. Occasionally, vomiting, nausea, and low-grade fever also occur.

Two to seven percent of people who get the illness develop a more serious, sometimes fatal disease—hemolytic uremic syndrome (HUS)—the leading cause of kidney failure in children. □

Heart Disease Leading Killer of Americans

What's the number one killer in America? Millions of people believe it's cancer. They're wrong. Cardiovascular disease holds that deadly distinction.

FACT: In 1990 heart and blood vessel diseases killed more than 930,000 Americans.

FACT: More than two of every five Americans dies of cardiovascular disease.

FACT: Of the current U.S. population of about 250 million, more than 70 million—more than one in four Americans—suffer some form of cardiovascular disease.

Make no mistake. Cancer and other diseases are a real threat. But let's put things in perspective. In 1990 about 506,000 Americans died of all forms of cancer. In the same year, 24,000 Americans died of AIDS. That's tragic, but the tragedy is compounded if Americans focus on these diseases and neglect a group of diseases that claims 400,000 more victims. Cardiovascular diseases are killers.

Heart and blood diseases aren't just a threat to the elderly, either. More than 161,000 Americans under age 65 die from cardiovascular diseases every year.

Modifying a methodology developed by the Centers for Disease Control to include data for people under age 75. "Total Cardiovascular Disease" accounted for 4,850,000 years of potential life lost in 1989. Next was cancer (4,360,000) and accidents (3,000,000).

Cardiovascular diseases demand attention. Too many people are dying. And many deaths may be preventable—the keys are to lower blood pressure, stop smoking, reduce the amount of cholesterol in the blood, stay physically active and know the warning signs. Education is vital.

Death rates from heart attack, stroke, and other cardiovascular diseases *are* declining. Advances in medical treatment and healthier lifestyles in recent years have undoubtedly played a part. But there's still a long way to go and no time for complacency. As the U.S. population ages, heart and blood vessel diseases will likely affect more people. And even now, despite the gains from research and the decline in death rates, a grim fact remains: Someone dies—from cardiovascular disease—every 34 seconds.

Prevalence

70,020,000 Americans have one or more forms of cardiovascular disease (CVD) according to current estimates.

- High blood pressure—63,640,000.
- Coronary heart disease—6,230,000.
- Stroke—3,020,000.
- Rheumatic heart disease—1,320,000.

Source: National Health and Nutrition Examination Survey II (NHANES II) (interview and examination data) and the AHA. Calculations based upon NHANES III data may differ.

- One in nine women aged 45–64 has some form of heart disease or stroke; this ratio soars to one in three at age 65 and beyond.
- One in six men aged 45–64 has some form of heart or blood vessel disease; in men aged 65 and over the ratio is one in eight. □

Leading Causes of Death, Males and Females

United States: 1989 Final Mortality

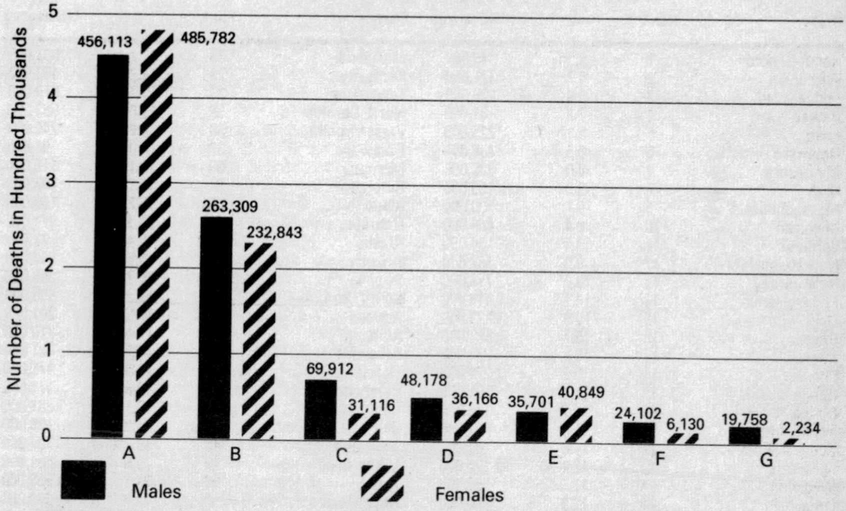

A Total Cardiovascular Diseases
B Cancer
C Accidents
D Chronic Obstructive Pulmonary Disease
E Pneumonia/Influenza
F Suicide
G AIDS

Source: National Center for Health Statistics and the American Heart Association.

Tuberculosis Cases Rising

In the 19th century, tuberculosis claimed more lives in this country than any other disease. The number of Americans who contracted TB declined sharply after 1900 due to a better understanding of the disease and improved hygiene, but the death rate was still high. Tuberculosis was responsible for five million deaths in the first half of the 20th century and as late as 1954, more than 110,000 beds were devoted to the care of TB patients alone in the United States.

In the past, TB testing was mandatory in schools throughout the United States but many of those programs were allowed to lapse because TB became less of a health threat. Now, this dormant problem is worrying health officials again.

26,673 cases of tuberculosis were reported to the U.S. Centers for Disease Control in Atlanta, Georgia, in 1992, up from 26,283 in 1991 and up 20% from 1985. What concerns public health authorities is that after decades of declining figures—22,201 cases in 1985, the lowest total in 60 years—the number of cases is beginning to creep up again.

Society's problems—AIDS, homelessness, alcohol and drug abuse, and other factors are reversing the downward trend.

It is estimated that 10 to 15 million Americans are among the 1.7 billion people worldwide who are TB carriers but are not infectious to others. About 90% of TB cases in this country occur when a dormant infection awakens and develops into active TB; only 10% result from a newly acquired infection. Of all infected people, 5% will develop the disease within a year, while another 5% will develop TB later on. Experts are not sure why it happens this way.

TB is usually caused by repeated exposure—usually at home or work—to droplets contaminated with tubercle bacilli that are expelled into the air when a person with active pulmonary TB coughs, sneezes, or even sings, speaks, or laughs.

TB was the most common cause of death in the Western world up to the time of the American Revolution.

Frédéric Chopin died of the disease, as did John Keats, Emily Brontë, Edgar Allan Poe, Henry David Thoreau, George Orwell, Vivien Leigh, Laurecne Sterne, and Anton Chekhov. Had Percy Bysshe Shelley not drowned in a boating accident at age 30, he would surely have died of TB, because he had an active case. Robert Louis Stevenson sought the cure at Saranac, then moved to Samoa, where he died at age 44. Ralph Waldo Emerson lost his first wife to the disease, as well as brothers and other family members, but successfully fought it himself. TB bedeviled Emerson descendants until antibiotics were discovered. TB also ran like wildfire through the Keats, Brontë, Thoreau, and Trollope families. Before Robert Koch, the eminent German bacteriologist, proved in 1882 that bacteria caused TB, many considered the disease to be hereditary.

In the early stages, TB is symptomless. Gradually, however, the TB patient feels tired, may run a fever, have night sweats, lose weight. This wasting away, in which the body is literally consumed by the disease, is the reason TB was once called consumption. As the disease progresses, the patient may cough up blood-tinged sputum. Chest pain is common, and shortness of breath develops when the lungs are heavily ravaged. And if a lung cavity erodes an artery, massive hemorrhage can occur. □

Rank, Percent, and Number of Health Care Uninsured, 1990

State	Rank	%	No. Uninsured	State	Rank	%	No. Uninsured
North Dakota	1	6.3	40,000	Maryland	26	12.7	601,000
Wisconsin	2	6.7	321,000	Kentucky	28	13.2	480,000
Connecticut	3	6.9	226,000	Tennessee	29	13.7	673,000
Hawaii	4	7.3	81,000	North Carolina	30	13.8	883,000
Iowa	5	8.1	225,000	West Virginia	30	13.8	249,000
Nebraska	6	8.5	138,000	Delaware	32	14.0	96,000
Minnesota	7	8.9	389,000	Montana	33	14.1	115,000
Utah	8	9.0	156,000	Colorado	34	14.7	495,000
Massachusetts	9	9.1	530,000	Idaho	35	15.2	159,000
Michigan	10	9.4	865,000	Georgia	36	15.3	971,000
Vermont	11	9.5	54,000	Alaska	37	15.4	77,000
New Hampshire	12	9.9	107,000	Arizona	38	15.5	547,000
New Jersey	13	10.0	773,000	Virginia	39	15.7	996,000
Pennsylvania	14	10.1	1,218,000	South Carolina	40	16.2	550,000
Ohio	15	10.3	1,123,000	Nevada	41	16.5	201,000
Indiana	16	10.7	587,000	Alabama	42	17.4	710,000
Kansas	17	10.8	272,000	Arkansas	42	17.4	421,000
Illinois	18	10.9	1,272,000	Florida	44	18.0	2,376,000
Rhode Island	19	11.1	105,000	Oklahoma	45	18.6	574,000
Maine	20	11.2	139,000	California	46	19.1	5,683,000
Washington	21	11.4	557,000	District of Columbia	47	19.2	109,000
South Dakota	22	11.6	81,000	Louisiana	48	19.7	797,000
New York	23	12.1	2,176,000	Mississippi	49	19.9	531,000
Wyoming	24	12.5	58,000	Texas	50	21.1	3,569,000
Oregon	24	12.5	360,000	New Mexico	51	22.2	339,000
Missouri	26	12.7	665,000	**Total U.S.**	—	**13.9**	**34,719,000**

Source: "The Vanishing Health Care Safety Net: New Data on Uninsured Americans" by David U. Himmelstein, M.D.; Steffie Woolhandler, M.D., M.P.H.; and Sidney M. Wolfe, M.D. The Center for National Health Program Studies, Harvard Medical School/The Cambridge Hospital.

HEADLINE HISTORY

In any broad overview of history, arbitrary compartmentalization of facts is self-defeating (and makes locating interrelated people, places, and things that much harder). Therefore, Headline History is designed as a "timeline"—a chronology that highlights both the march of time and interesting, sometimes surprising, juxtapositions.

Also see related sections of *Information Please,* particularly Inventions and Discoveries, Countries of the World, etc.

B.C.

Before Christ or Before Common Era (B.C.E.)

5 billion B.C. Planet Earth formed.

3 billion B.C. First signs of primeval life (bacteria and blue-green algae) appear in oceans.

600 million B.C. Earliest date to which fossils can be traced.

1.7 million B.C. First discernible hominids (*Australopithecus* and *Homo habilis*). Early hunters and food-gatherers.

500,000 B.C. *Homo erectus* (crude chopping tools).

70,000 B.C. Neanderthal man (use of fire and advanced tools).

35,000 B.C. Neanderthal man being replaced by later groups of *Homo sapiens* (i.e. Cro-Magnon man, etc.).

18,000 B.C. Cro-Magnons being replaced by later cultures.

15,000 B.C. Migrations across Bering Straits into the Americas.

10,000 B.C. Semi-permanent agricultural settlements in Old World.

10,000–4,000 B.C. Development of settlements into cities and development of skills such as the wheel, pottery and improved methods of cultivation in Mesopatamia and elsewhere.

Brontosaur

NOTE: For futher information on the geographic development in Earth's prehistory, see the Science section.

4500–3000 B.C. Sumerians in the Tigris and Euphrates valleys develop a city-state civilization; first phonetic writing (**c.3500 B.C.**). Egyptian agriculture develops. Western Europe is neolithic, without metals or written records. Earliest recorded date in Egyptian calendar (**4241 B.C.**). First year of Jewish calendar (**3760 B.C.**). Copper used by Egyptians and Sumerians.

3000–2000 B.C. Pharaonic rule begins in Egypt. Cheops, 4th dynasty (**2700–2675 B.C.**). The Great Sphinx of Giza. Earliest Egyptian mummies. Papyrus. Phoenician settlements on coast of what is now Syria and Lebanon. Semitic tribes settle in Assyria. Sargon, first Akkadian king, builds Mesopotamian empire. The Gilgamesh epic (**c.3000 B.C.**). Abraham leaves Ur (**c.2000 B.C.**). Systematic astronomy in Egypt, Babylon, India, China.

Moses

3000–1500 B.C. The most ancient civilization on the Indian subcontinent, the sophisticated and extensive Indus Valley civilization, flourishes in what is today Pakistan.

2000–1500 B.C. Hyksos invaders drive Egyptians from Lower Egypt (**17th century B.C.**). Amosis I frees Egypt from Hyksos (**c.1600 B.C.**). Assyrians rise to power—cities of Ashur and Nineveh. Twenty-four-character alphabet in Egypt. Israelites enslaved in Egypt. Cuneiform inscriptions used by Hittites. Peak of Minoan culture on Isle of Crete—earliest form of written Greek. Hammurabi, king of Babylon, develops oldest existing code of laws (**18th century B.C.**). In Britain, Stonehenge erected on some unknown astronomical rationale.

1500–1000 B.C. Ikhnaton develops monotheistic religion in Egypt (**c.1375 B.C.**). His successor, Tutankhamen, returns to earlier gods. Moses leads Israelites out of Egypt into Canaan—Ten Commandments. Greeks destroy Troy (**c.1193 B.C.**). End of Greek civilization in Mycenae with invasion of Dorians. Chinese civilization develops under Shang dynasty. Olmec civilization in Mexico—stone monuments; picture writing.

1000–900 B.C. Solomon succeeds King David, builds Jerusalem temple. After Solomon's death, kingdom divided into Israel and Judah. Hebrew elders begin to write Old Testament books of Bible. Phoenicians colonize Spain with settlement at Cadiz.

900–800 B.C. Phoenicians establish Carthage (**c.810 B.C.**). The *Iliad* and the *Odyssey,* perhaps composed by Greek poet Homer.

800–700 B.C. Prophets Amos, Hosea, Isaiah. First recorded Olympic games (**776 B.C.**). Legendary founding of Rome by Romulus (**753 B.C.**). Assyrian king

Egyptian chariots (1500 B.C.)

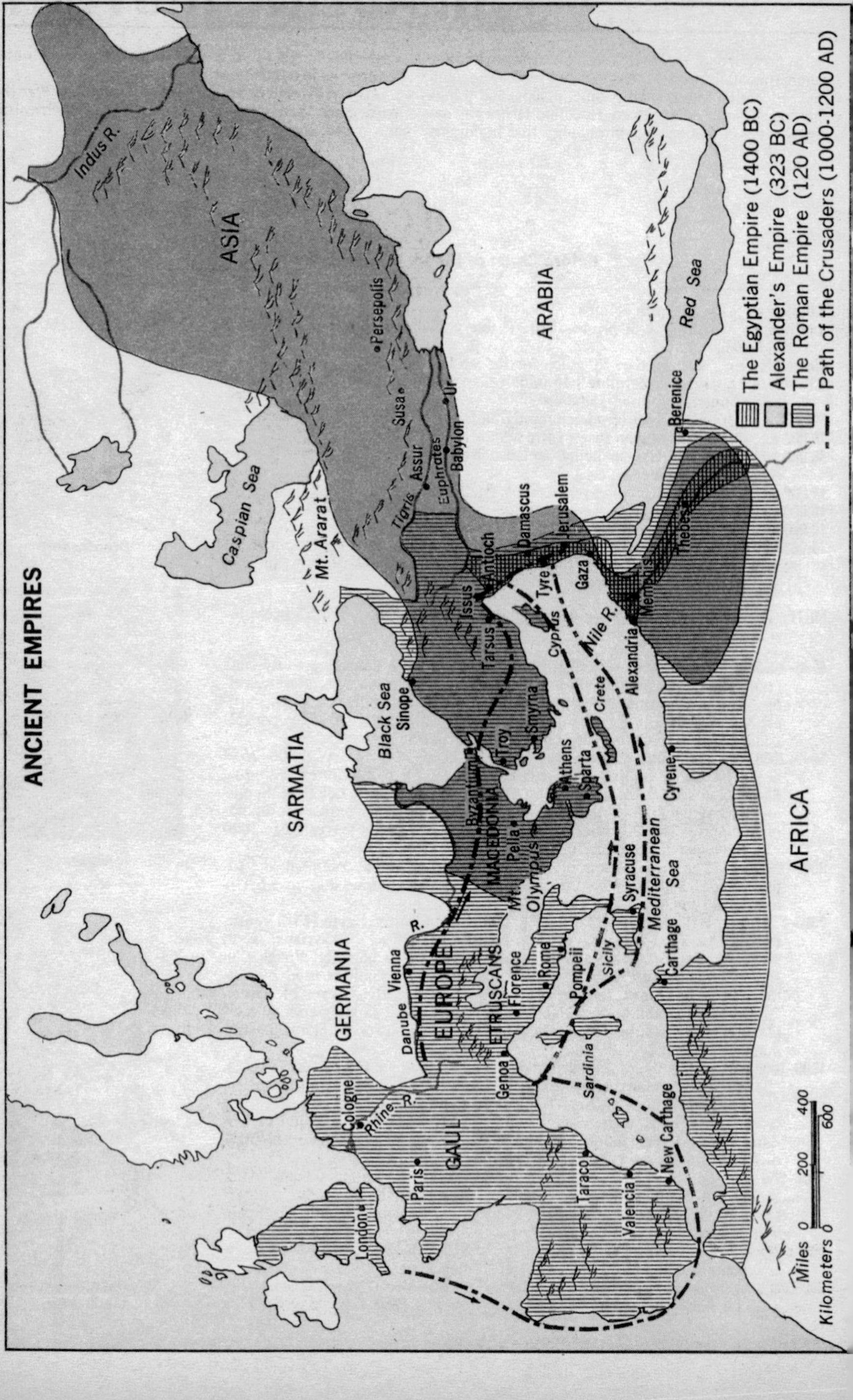
ANCIENT EMPIRES
The Egyptian Empire (1400 BC)
Alexander's Empire (323 BC)
The Roman Empire (120 AD)
Path of the Crusaders (1000-1200 AD)
Miles 0 200 400
Kilometers 0 600
ASIA
Indus R.
Persepolis
Susa
Ur
Babylon
Euphrates
Assur
Tigris
Caspian Sea
Mt. Ararat
ARABIA
Red Sea
Berenice
Thebes
Memphis
Jerusalem
Damascus
Antioch
Gaza
Tyre
Issus
Tarsus
Cyprus
Nile R.
Alexandria
Crete
Black Sea
Sinope
SARMATIA
Troy
Smyrna
Byzantium
Athens
Sparta
MACEDONIA
Pella
Mt. Olympus
Cyrene
Syracuse
Mediterranean Sea
AFRICA
GERMANIA
Vienna
Danube R.
EUROPE
ETRUSCANS
Florence
Rome
Pompeii
Sicily
Carthage
Genoa
Sardinia
Cologne
Rhine R.
GAUL
Paris
London
New Carthage
Taraco
Valencia

Some Ancient Civilizations

Name	Approximate dates	Location	Major cities
Akkadian	2350–2230 B.C.	Mesopotamia, parts of Syria, Asia Minor, Iran	Akkad, Ur, Erich
Assyrian	1800–889 B.C.	Mesopotamia, Syria	Assur, Nineveh, Calah
Babylonian	1728–1686 B.C. (old) 625–539 B.C. (new)	Mesopotamia, Syria, Palestine	Babylon
Cimmerian	750–500 B.C.	Caucasus, northern Asia Minor	—
Egyptian	2850–715 B.C.	Nile valley	Thebes, Memphis, Tanis
Etruscan	900–396 B.C.	Northern Italy	—
Greek	900–200 B.C.	Greece	Athens, Sparta, Thebes, Mycenae, Corinth
Hittite	1640–1200 B.C.	Asia Minor, Syria	Hattusas, Nesa
Indus Valley	3000–1500 B.C.	Pakistan, Northwestern India	—
Lydian	700–547 B.C.	Western Asia Minor	Sardis, Miletus
Mede	835–550 B.C.	Iran	Media
Minoan	3000–1100 B.C.	Crete	Knossos
Persian	559–330 B.C.	Iran, Asia Minor, Syria	Persepolis, Pasargadae
Phoenician	1100–332 B.C.	Palestine (colonies: Gibraltar, Carthage Sardinia)	Tyre, Sidon, Byblos
Phrygian	1000–547 B.C.	Central Asia Minor	Gordion
Roman	500 B.C.–A.D. 300	Italy, Mediterranean region, Asia Minor, western Europe	Rome, Byzantium
Scythian	800–300 B.C.	Caucasus	—
Sumerian	3200–2360 B.C.	Mesopotamia	Ur, Nippur

Sargon II conquers Hittites, Chaldeans, Samaria (end of Kingdom of Israel). Earliest written music. Chariots introduced into Italy by Etruscans.

700–600 B.C. End of Assyrian Empire (**616** B.C.)—Nineveh destroyed by Chaldeans (Neo-Babylonians) and Medes (**612** B.C.). Founding of Byzantium by Greeks (**c.660** B.C.). Building of the Acropolis in Athens. Solon, Greek lawgiver (**640–560** B.C.). Sappho of Lesbos, Greek poetess, Lao-Tse, Chinese philosopher and founder of Taoism (born **c.604** B.C.).

600–500 B.C. Babylonian king Nebuchadnezzar builds empire, destroys Jerusalem (**586** B.C.). Babylonian Captivity of the Jews (starting **587** B.C.). Hanging Gardens of Babylon. Cyrus the Great of Persia creates great empire, conquers Babylon (**539** B.C.), frees the Jews. Athenian democracy develops. Aeschylus, Greek dramatist (**525–465** B.C.). Confucius (**551–479** B.C.) develops philosophy-religion in China. Buddha (**563–483** B.C.) founds Buddhism in India.

500–400 B.C. Greeks defeat Persians: battles of Marathon (**490** B.C.), Thermopylae (**480** B.C.), Salamis (**480** B.C.). Peloponnesian Wars between Athens and Sparta (**431–404** B.C.)—Sparta victorious. Pericles comes to power in Athens (**462** B.C.). Flowering of Greek culture during the Age of Pericles (**450–400** B.C.). Sophocles, Greek dramatist (**496–c.406** B.C.). Hippocrates, Greek "Father of Medicine" (born **460** B.C.). Xerxes I, king of Persia (rules **485–465** B.C.).

400–300 B.C. Pentateuch—first five books of the Old Testament evolve in final form. Philip of Macedon assassinated (**336** B.C.) after conquering Greece; succeeded by son, Alexander the Great (**356–323** B.C.), who destroys Thebes (**335** B.C.), conquers Tyre and Jerusalem (**332** B.C.), occupies Babylon (**330** B.C.), invades India, and dies in Babylon. His empire is divided among his generals; one of them, Seleucis I, establishes Middle East empire with capitals at Antioch (Syria) and Seleucia (in Iraq). Trial and execution of Greek philosopher Socrates (**399** B.C.). Dialogues recorded by his student, Plato. Euclid's work on geometry (**323** B.C.). Aristotle, Greek philosopher (**384–322** B.C.). Demosthenes, Greek orator (**384–322** B.C.). Praxiteles, Greek sculptor (**400–330** B.C.).

300–251 B.C. First Punic War (**264–241** B.C.): Rome defeats the Carthaginians and begins its domination of the Mediterranean. Temple of the Sun at Teotihuacan, Mexico (**c.300** B.C.). Invention of Mayan calendar in Yucatán—more

Confucius (551-479 B.C.)

Plato (427?-347 B.C.)

Archimedes
(287-212 B.C.)

exact than older calendars. First Roman gladiatorial games (**264** B.C.). Archimedes, Greek mathematician (**287–212** B.C.).

250–201 B.C. Second Punic War (**219–201** B.C.): Hannibal, Carthaginian general (**246–142** B.C.), crosses the Alps (**218** B.C.), reaches gates of Rome (**211** B.C.), retreats, and is defeated by Scipio Africanus at Zama (**202** B.C.). Great Wall of China built (**c.215** B.C.).

200–151 B.C. Romans defeat Seleucid King Antiochus III at Thermopylae (**191** B.C.)—beginning of Roman world domination. Maccabean revolt against Seleucids (**167** B.C.).

150–101 B.C. Third Punic War (**149–146** B.C.): Rome destroys Carthage, killing 450,000 and enslaving the remaining 50,000 inhabitants. Roman armies conquer Macedonia, Greece, Anatolia, Balearic Islands, and southern France. Venus de Milo (**c.140** B.C.). Cicero, Roman orator (**106–43** B.C.).

100–51 B.C. Julius Caesar (**100–44** B.C.) invades Britain (**55** B.C.) and conquers Gaul (France) (**c.50** B.C.). Spartacus leads slave revolt against Rome (**71** B.C.). Romans conquer Seleucid empire. Roman general Pompey conquers Jerusalem (**63** B.C.). Cleopatra on Egyptian throne (**51–31** B.C.). Chinese develop use of paper (**c.100** B.C.). Virgil, Roman poet (**70–19** B.C.). Horace, Roman poet (**65–8** B.C.).

50–1 B.C. Caesar crosses Rubicon to fight Pompey (**50** B.C.). Herod made Roman governor of Judea (**47** B.C.). Caesar murdered (**44** B.C.). Caesar's nephew, Octavian, defeats Mark Antony and Cleopatra at Battle of Actium (**31** B.C.), and establishes Roman empire as Emperor Augustus—rules **27** B.C.—A.D. 14. Birth of Jesus Christ (variously given from **4** B.C. **to** A.D. **7**). Ovid, Roman poet (**43** B.C.—A.D. **18**).

A.D.

The Christian or Common Era (C.E.)

Jesus Christ
(4? B.C.-29? A.D.)

1–49 After Augustus, Tiberius becomes emperor (dies, **37**), succeeded by Caligula (assassinated, **41**), who is followed by Claudius. Crucifixion of Jesus (probably **30**). Han dynasty in China founded by Emperor Kuang Wu Ti. Buddhism introduced to China.

50–99 Claudius poisoned (**54**), succeeded by Nero (commits suicide, **68**). Missionary journeys of Paul the Apostle (**34–60**). Jews revolt against Rome; Jerusalem destroyed (**70**). Roman persecutions of Christians begin (**64**). Colosseum built in Rome (**71–80**). Trajan (rules **98–116**); Roman empire extends to Mesopotamia, Arabia, Balkans. First Gospels of St. Mark, St. John, St. Matthew.

100–149 Hadrian rules Rome (**117–138**); codifies Roman law, establishes postal system, builds wall between England and Scotland. Jews revolt under Bar Kokhba (**122–135**); final *Diaspora* (dispersion) of Jews begins.

150–199 Marcus Aurelius (rules Rome **161–180**). Oldest Mayan temples in Central America (**c.200**)., Mayan civilization develops writing, astronomy, mathematics.

200–249 Goths invade Asia Minor (**c.220**). Roman persecutions of Christians increase. Persian (Sassanid) empire re-established. End of Chinese Han dynasty.

250–299 Increasing invasions of the Roman empire by Franks and Goths. Buddhism spreads in China.

300–349 Constantine the Great (rules **312–337**) reunites eastern and western Roman empires, with new capital (Constantinople) on site of Byzantium (**330**); issues Edict of Milan legalizing Christianity (**313**); becomes a Christian on his deathbed (**337**). Council of Nicaea (**325**) defines orthodox Christian doctrine. First Gupta dynasty in India (**c.320**).

350–399 Huns (Mongols) invade Europe (**c.360**). Theodosius the Great (rules **392–395**)—last emperor of a united Roman empire. Roman empire permanently divided in **395**: western empire ruled from Rome; eastern empire ruled from Constantinople.

400–449 Western Roman empire disintegrates under weak emperors. Alaric, king of the Visigoths, sacks Rome (**410**). Attila, Hun chieftain, attacks Roman provinces (**433**). St. Patrick returns to Ireland (**432**). St. Augustine's *City of God* (**411**).

450–499 Vandals destroy Rome (**455**). Western Roman empire ends as Odoacer, German chieftain, overthrows last Roman emperor, Romulus Augustulus, and becomes king of Italy (**476**). Ostrogothic kingdom of Italy established by Theodoric the Great (**493**). Clovis, ruler of the Franks, is converted to Christianity (**496**). First schism between western and eastern churches (**484**). Peak of Mayan culture in Mexico (**c.460**).

500–549 Eastern and western churches reconciled (**519**). Justinian I, the Great

(483–565), becomes Byzantine emperor (527), issues his first code of civil laws (529), conquers North Africa, Italy, and part of Spain. Plague spreads through Europe (from 542). Arthur, semi-legendary king of the Britons (killed, c.537). Boëthius, Roman scholar (executed, 524).

550–599 Beginnings of European silk industry after Justinian's missionaries smuggle silkworms out of China (**553**). Mohammed, founder of Islam (**570–632**). Buddhism in Japan (**c.560**). St. Augustine of Canterbury brings Christianity to Britain (**597**). After killing about half the population, plague in Europe subsides (**594**).

600–649 Mohammed flees from Mecca to Medina (the *Hegira*); first year of the Muslim calendar (**622**). Muslim empire grows (**634**). Arabs conquer Jerusalem (**637**), destroy Alexandrian library (**641**), conquer Persians (**641**). Fatima, Mohammed's daughter (**606–632**).

650–699 Arabs attack North Africa (**670**), destroy Carthage (**697**). Venerable Bede, English monk (**672–735**).

700–749 Arab empire extends from Lisbon to China (by **716**). Charles Martel, Frankish leader, defeats Arabs at Tours/Poitiers, halting Arab advance in Europe (**732**). Charlemagne (**742–814**).

750–799 Caliph Harun al-Rashid rules Arab empire (**786–809**): the "golden age" of Arab culture. Vikings begin attacks on Britain (**790**), land in Ireland (**795**). Charlemagne becomes king of the Franks (**771**). City of Machu Picchu flourishes in Peru.

800–849 Charlemagne (Charles the Great) crowned first Holy Roman Emperor in Rome (**800**). Arabs conquer Crete, Sicily, and Sardinia (**826–827**). Charlemagne dies (**814**), succeeded by his son, Louis the Pious, who divides France among his sons (**817**).

850–899 Norsemen attack as far south as the Mediterranean but are repulsed (**859**), discover Iceland (**861**). Alfred the Great becomes king of Britain (**871**), defeats Danish invaders (**878**). Russian nation founded by Vikings under Prince Rurik, establishing capital at Novgorod (**855–879**).

900–949 Vikings discover Greenland (**c.900**). Arab Spain under Abd ar-Rahman III becomes center of learning (**912–961**).

950–999 Eric the Red establishes first Viking colony in Greenland (**982**). Mieczyslaw I becomes first ruler of Poland (**960**). Hugh Capet elected King of France in **987**; Capetian dynasty to rule until **1328**. Musical notation systematized (**c.990**). Vikings and Danes attack Britain (**988–999**). Holy Roman Empire founded by Otto I, King of Germany since **936**, crowned by Pope John XII in **962**.

Viking Discovery of Greenland (c.900)

11th century A.D.

c.1000 Hungary and Scandinavia converted to Christianity. Viking raider Leif Ericson discovers North America, calls it *Vinland*. Chinese invent gunpowder. *Beowulf*, Old English epic.

1009 Moslems destroy Holy Sepulchre in Jerusalem.

1013 Danes control England. Canute takes throne (**1016**), conquers Norway (**1028**), dies (**1035**); kingdom divided among his sons: Harold Harefoot (England), Sweyn (Norway), Hardecanute (Denmark).

1040 Macbeth murders Duncan, king of Scotland.

1053 Robert Guiscard, Norman invader, establishes kingdom in Italy, conquers Sicily (**1072**).

1054 Final separation between Eastern (Orthodox) and Western (Roman) churches.

1055 Seljuk Turks, Asian nomads, move west, capture Baghdad, Armenia (**1064**), Syria, and Palestine (**1075**).

1066 William of Normandy invades England, defeats last Saxon king, Harold II, at Battle of Hastings, crowned William I of England ("the Conqueror").

1073 Emergence of strong papacy when Gregory VII is elected. Conflict with English and French kings and German emperors will continue throughout medieval period.

1095 (*See* special material on "The Crusades.")

12th century A.D.

1150–67 Universities of Paris and Oxford founded in France and England.

1162 Thomas à Becket named Archbishop of Canterbury, murdered by Henry II's men (**1170**). Troubadours (wandering minstrels) glorify romantic concepts of feudalism.

1189 Richard I ("the Lionhearted") succeeds Henry II in England, killed in France (**1199**), succeeded by King John.

13th century A.D.

1211 Genghis Khan invades China, captures Peking (**1214**), conquers Persia (**1218**), invades Russia (**1223**), dies (**1227**).

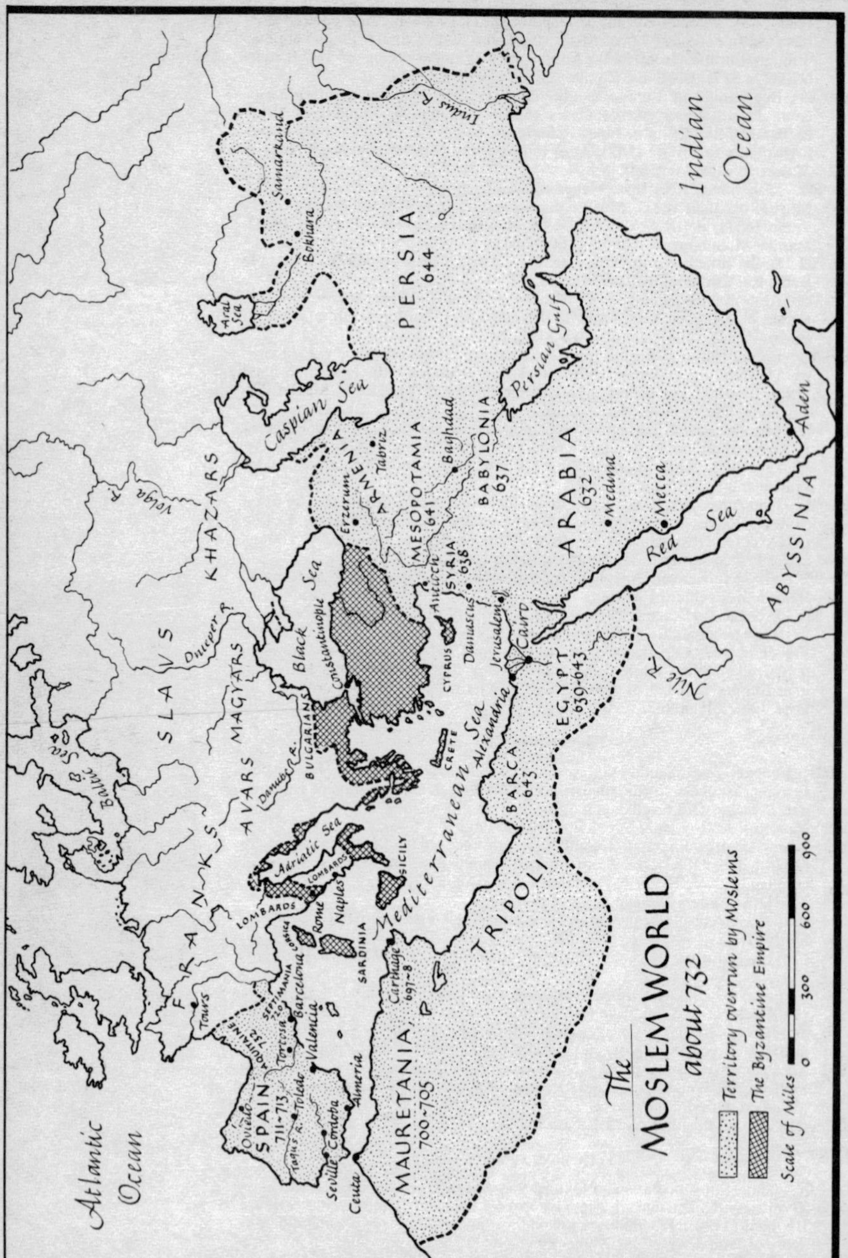
The MOSLEM WORLD about 732
Territory overrun by Moslems
The Byzantine Empire
Scale of Miles 0 300 600 900
Atlantic Ocean
Indian Ocean
SPAIN 711-713
Oviedo
Toledo
Tagus R.
Cordoba
Seville
Almeria
Valencia
Tortosa
Barcelona
SEPTIMANIA 720
AQUITAINE 732
Tours
Ceuta
MAURETANIA 700-705
Carthage 697-8
TRIPOLI
BARCA 643
EGYPT 639-643
Alexandria
Cairo
Nile R.
Jerusalem
Damascus
SYRIA 638
Antioch
CYPRUS
CRETE
SICILY
SARDINIA
CORSICA
Rome
Naples
LOMBARDS
Adriatic Sea
Mediterranean Sea
FRANKS
AVARS
MAGYARS
SLAVS
KHAZARS
BULGARIANS
Danube R.
Dnieper R.
Volga R.
Baltic Sea
Black Sea
Constantinople
Erzerum
ARMENIA
Tabriz
Caspian Sea
Aral Sea
MESOPOTAMIA 641
Baghdad
BABYLONIA 637
PERSIA 644
Bokhara
Samarkand
Indus R.
Persian Gulf
ARABIA 632
Medina
Mecca
Aden
Red Sea
ABYSSINIA

1215 King John forced by barons to sign Magna Carta at Runneymede, limiting royal power.

1233 The Inquisition begins as Pope Gregory IX assigns Dominicans responsibility for combatting heresy. Torture used **(1252).** Ferdinand and Isabella establish Spanish Inquisition **(1478).** Tourquemada, Grand Inquisitor, forces conversion or expulsion of Spanish Jews **(1492).** Forced conversion of Moors **(1499).** Inquisition in Portugal **(1531).** First Protestants burned at the stake in Spain **(1543).** Spanish Inquisition abolished **(1834).**

1241 Mongols defeat Germans in Silesia, invade Poland and Hungary, withdraw from Europe after Ughetai, Mongol leader, dies.

1251 Kublai Khan governs China, becomes ruler of Mongols (1259), establishes Yuan dynasty in China (1280), invades Burma (1287), dies (1294).

1271 Marco Polo of Venice travels to China, in court of Kublai Khan (1275–1292), returns to Genoa (1295) and writes *Travels.*

1295 English King Edward I summons the Model Parliament.

John Wycliffe (1320-1384)

14th century A.D.

1312–37 Mali Empire reaches its height in Africa under King Mansa Musa.

1337–1453 Hundred Years' War—English and French kings fight for control of France.

c.1325 The beginning of the Renaissance in Italy: writers Dante, Petrarch, Boccaccio; painter Giotto. Development of *No* drama in Japan. Aztecs establish capital on site of modern Mexico City. Peak of Moslem culture in Spain. Small cannon in use.

1347–1351 At least 25 million people die in Europe's "Black Death" (bubonic plague).

1368 Ming dynasty begins in China.

1376–82 John Wycliffe, pre-Reformation religious reformer and followers translate Latin Bible into English.

1378 The Great Schism (to 1417)—rival popes in Rome and Avignon, France, fight for control of Roman Catholic Church.

c.1387 Chaucer's *Canterbury Tales.*

Joan of Arc (1412-1431)

15th century A.D.

1415 Henry V defeats French at Agincourt. Jan Hus, Bohemian preacher and follower of Wycliffe, burned at stake in Constance as heretic.

1418–60 Portugal's Prince Henry the Navigator sponsors exploration of Africa's coast.

1428 Joan of Arc leads French against English, captured by Burgundians (1430) and turned over to the English, burned at the stake as a witch after ecclesiastical trial (1431).

1438 Inca rule in Peru.

1450 Florence becomes center of Renaissance arts and learning under the Medicis.

1453 Turks conquer Constantinople, end of the Byzantine empire. Hundred Years' War between France and England ends.

1455 The Wars of the Roses, civil wars between rival noble factions, begin in England (to 1485). Having invented printing with movable type at Mainz, Germany, Johann Gutenberg completes first Bible.

1462 Ivan the Great rules Russia until 1505 as first czar; ends payment of tribute to Mongols.

1492 Moors conquered in Spain by troops of Ferdinand and Isabella. Columbus discovers Caribbean islands, returns to Spain (1493). Second voyage to Dominica, Jamaica, Puerto Rico (1493–1496). Third voyage to Orinoco (1498). Fourth voyage to Honduras and Panama (1502–1504).

1497 Vasco da Gama sails around Africa and discovers sea route to India (1498). Establishes Portuguese colony in India (1502). John Cabot, employed by England, reaches and explores Canadian coast. Michelangelo's *Bacchus* sculpture.

Christopher Columbus (1451-1506)

THE CRUSADES (1096–1291)

In 1095 at Council of Clermont, Pope Urban II calls for war to rescue Holy Land from Moslem infidels. *First Crusade* (1096)—about 500,000 peasants led by Peter the Hermit prove so troublesome that Byzantine Emperor Alexius ships them to Asia Minor; only 25,000 survive return after massacre by Seljuk Turks. Followed by organized army, led by nobility, which reaches Constantinople (1097), conquers Jerusalem (1099), Acre (1104), establishes Latin Kingdom protected by Knights of St. John the Hospitaller (1100), and Knights Templar (1123). Seljuk Turks start series of counterattacks (1144). *Second Crusade* (1146) led by King Louis VIII of France and Emperor Conrad III. Crusaders perish in Asia Minor (1147).

Saladin controls Egypt (1171), unites Islam in Holy War *(Jihad)* against Christians, recaptures Jerusalem (1187). *Third Crusade* (1189) under kings of France, England, and Germany fails to reduce Saladin's power. *Fourth Crusade* (1200–1204)—French knights sack Greek Christian Constantinople, establish Latin empire in Byzantium. Greeks re-establish Orthodox faith (1262).

Children's Crusade (1212)—Only 1 of 30,000 French children and about 200 of 20,000 German children survive to return home. Other Crusades—against Egypt (1217), *Sixth* (1228), *Seventh* (1248), *Eighth* (1270). Mamelukes conquer Acre; end of the Crusades (1291).

16th century A.D.

Michelangelo Buonarroti (1475-1564)

Martin Luther (1483-1546)

Anthony Van Dyck (1559-1641)

1501 First black slaves in America brought to Spanish colony of Santo Domingo.

c.1503 Leonardo da Vinci paints the *Mona Lisa.*

1506 St. Peter's Church started in Rome; designed and decorated by such artists and architects as Bramante, Michelangelo, da Vinci, Raphael, and Bernini before its completion in **1626.**

1509 Henry VIII ascends English throne. Michelangelo paints the ceiling of the Sistine Chapel.

1517 Turks conquer Egypt, control Arabia. Martin Luther posts his 95 theses denouncing church abuses on church door in Wittenberg—start of the Reformation in Germany.

1519 Ulrich Zwingli begins Reformation in Switzerland. Hernando Cortes conquers Mexico for Spain. Charles I of Spain is chosen Holy Roman Emperor Charles V. Portuguese explorer Fernando Magellan sets out to circumnavigate the globe.

1520 Luther excommunicated by Pope Leo X. Suleiman I ("the Magnificent") becomes Sultan of Turkey, invades Hungary **(1521),** Rhodes **(1522),** attacks Austria **(1529),** annexes Hungary **(1541),** Tripoli **(1551),** makes peace with Persia **(1553),** destroys Spanish fleet **(1560),** dies **(1566).** Magellan reaches the Pacific, is killed by Philippine natives **(1521).** One of his ships under Juan Sebastián del Cano continues around the world, reaches Spain **(1522).**

1524 Verrazano, sailing under the French flag, explores the New England coast and New York Bay.

1527 Troops of the Holy Roman Empire attack Rome, imprison Pope Clement VII—the end of the Italian Renaissance. Castiglione writes *The Courtier.* The Medici expelled from Florence.

1532 Pizarro marches from Panama to Peru, kills the Inca chieftain, Atahualpa, of Peru **(1533).** Machiavelli's *Prince* published posthumously.

1535 Reformation begins as Henry VIII makes himself head of English Church after being excommunicated by Pope. Sir Thomas More executed as traitor for refusal to acknowledge king's religious authority. Jacques Cartier sails up the St. Lawrence River, basis of French claims to Canada.

1536 Henry VIII executes second wife, Anne Boleyn. John Calvin establishes Presbyterian form of Protestantism in Switzerland, writes *Institutes of the Christian Religion.* Danish and Norwegian Reformations. Michelangelo's *Last Judgment.*

1541 John Knox leads Reformation in Scotland, establishes Presbyterian church **(1560).**

1543 Publication of *On the Revolution of Heavenly Bodies* by Polish scholar Nicolaus Copernicus—giving his theory that the earth revolves around the sun.

1545 Council of Trent to meet intermittently until **1563** to define Catholic dogma and doctrine, reiterate papal authority.

1547 Ivan IV ("the Terrible") crowned as Czar of Russia, begins conquest of Astrakhan and Kazan **(1552),** battles nobles (boyars) for power **(1564),** kills his son **(1580),** dies, and is succeeded by a son who gives power to Boris Godunov **(1584).**

1553 Roman Catholicism restored in England by Queen Mary I, who rules until **1558.** Religious radical Michael Servetus burned as heretic in Geneva by order of John Calvin.

1554 Benvenuto Cellini completes the bronze *Perseus.*

1556 Akbar the Great becomes Mogul emperor of India, conquers Afghanistan **(1581),** continues wars of conquest (until **1605**).

1558 Queen Elizabeth I ascends the throne (rules to **1603**). Restores Protestantism, establishes state Church of England (Anglicanism). Renaissance will reach height in England—Shakespeare, Marlowe, Spenser.

1561 Persecution of Huguenots in France stopped by Edict of Orleans. French religious wars begin again with massacre of Huguenots at Vassy. St. Bartholomew's Day Massacre—thousands of Huguenots murdered **(1572).** Amnesty granted **(1573).** Persecution continues periodically until Edict of Nantes **(1598)** gives Huguenots religious freedom (until **1685**).

1568 Protestant Netherlands revolts against Catholic Spain; independence will be acknowledged by Spain in **1648.** High point of Dutch Renaissance—painters Rubens, Van Dyck, Hals, and Rembrandt.

1570 Japan permits visits of foreign ships. Queen Elizabeth I excommunicated by Pope. Turks attack Cyprus and war on Venice. Turkish fleet defeated at Battle of Lepanto by Spanish and Italian fleets **(1571).** Peace of Constantinople **(1572)** ends Turkish attacks on Europe.

1580 Francis Drake returns to England after circumnavigating the globe. Knighted by Queen Elizabeth I (**1581**). Montaigne's *Essays* published.
1583 William of Orange rules The Netherlands; assassinated on orders of Philip II of Spain (**1584**).
1587 Mary, Queen of Scots, executed for treason by order of Queen Elizabeth I. Monteverdi's *First Book of Madrigals.*
1588 Defeat of the Spanish Armada by English. Henry, King of Navarre and Protestant leader, recognized as Henry IV, first Bourbon king of France. Converts to Roman Catholicism in **1593** in attempt to end religious wars.
1590 Henry IV enters Paris, wars on Spain (**1595**), marries Marie de Medici (**1600**), assassinated (**1610**). Spenser's *The Faerie Queen,* El Greco's *St. Jerome.* Galileo's experiments with falling objects.
1598 Boris Godunov becomes Russian Czar. Tycho Brahe describes his astronomical experiments.

Francis Bacon (1561-1626)

17th century A.D.

1600 Giordano Bruno burned as a heretic. Ieyasu rules Japan, moves capital to Edo (Tokyo). Shakespeare's *Hamlet* begins his most productive decade. English East India Company established to develop overseas trade.
1607 Jamestown, Virginia, established—first permanent English colony on American mainland.
1609 Samuel de Champlain establishes French colony of Quebec.
1611 Gustavus Adolphus elected King of Sweden. King James Version of the Bible published in England. Rubens paints his *Descent from the Cross.*
1614 John Napier discovers logarithms.
1618 Start of the Thirty Years' War (to **1648**)—Protestant revolt against Catholic oppression; Denmark, Sweden, and France will invade Germany in later phases of war. Kepler proposes his Third Law of planetary motion.
1620 Pilgrims, after three-month voyage in *Mayflower,* land at Plymouth Rock. Francis Bacon's *Novum Organum.*
1633 Inquisition forces Galileo to recant his belief in Copernican theory.
1642 English Civil War. Cavaliers, supporters of Charles I, against Roundheads, parliamentary forces. Oliver Cromwell defeats Royalists (**1646**). Parliament demands reforms. Charles I offers concessions, brought to trial (**1648**), beheaded (**1649**). Cromwell becomes Lord Protector (**1653**). Rembrandt paints his *Night Watch.*
1644 End of Ming Dynasty in China—Manchus come to power. Descartes' *Principles of Philosophy.* John Milton's *Areopagitica* on the freedom of the press.
1648 End of the Thirty Years' War. German population about half of what it was in **1618** because of war and pestilence.
1658 Cromwell dies; his son, Richard, resigns and Puritan government collapses.
1660 English Parliament calls for the restoration of the monarchy; invites Charles II to return from France.
1661 Charles II is crowned King of England. Louis XIV begins personal rule as absolute monarch; starts to build Versailles.

Giordano Bruno (1548-1600)

George Washington (1732-1799)

THE FOUNDING OF THE AMERICAN NATION

Colonization of America begins: Jamestown, Va. (**1607**); Pilgrims in Plymouth (**1620**); Massachusetts Bay Colony (**1630**) New Netherland founded by Dutch West India Company (**1623**), captured by English (**1664**). Delaware established by Swedish trading company (**1638**), absorbed later by Penn family. Proprietorships by royal grants to Lord Baltimore (Maryland, **1632**); Captain John Mason (New Hampshire, **1635**); Sir William Berkeley and Sir George Carteret (New Jersey, **1663**); friends of Charles II (the Carolinas, **1663**); William Penn (Pennsylvania, **1682**); James Oglethorpe and others (Georgia, **1732**).

Increasing conflict between colonists and Britain on western frontier because of royal edict limiting western expansion (**1763**), and regulation of colonial trade and increased taxation of colonies (Writs of Assistance allow search for illegal shipments, **1761**; Sugar Act, **1764**; Currency Act, **1764**; Stamp Act, **1765**; Quartering Act, **1765**; Duty Act, **1767**.) Boston Massacre (**1770**). Lord North attempts conciliation (**1770**). Boston Tea Party (**1773**), followed by punitive measures passed by Parliament—the "Intolerable Acts."

First Continental Congress (**1774**) sends "Declaration of Rights and Grievances" to king, urges colonies to form Continental Association. Paul Revere's Ride and Lexington and Concord battle between Massachusetts minutemen and British (**1775**).

Second Continental Congress (**1775**), while sending "olive branch" to the king, begins to raise army, appoints Washington commander-in-chief, and seeks alliance with France. Some colonial legislatures urge their delegates to vote for independence. Declaration of Independence (**July 4, 1776**).

Major Battles of the Revolutionary War: *Long Island:* Howe defeats Putnam's division of Washington's Army in Brooklyn Heights, but Americans escape across East River (**1776**). *Trenton and Princeton:* Washington defeats Hessians at Trenton. British at Princeton, winters at Morristown (**1776–77**). Howe winters in Philadelphia; Washington at Valley Forge (**1777–78**). Burgoyne surrenders British army to General Gates at *Saratoga* (**1777**).

France recognizes American independence (**1778**). The War moves south: Savannah captured by British (**1778**); Charleston occupied (**1780**); Americans fight successful guerrilla actions under Marion, Pickens, and Sumter. In the West, George Rogers Clark attacks Forts Kaskaskia and Vincennes (**1778–1779**), defeating British in the region. Cornwallis surrenders at *Yorktown,* Virginia (**Oct. 19, 1781**). By **1782**, Britain is eager for peace because of conflicts with European nations. *Peace of Paris* (**1783**): Britain recognizes American independence.

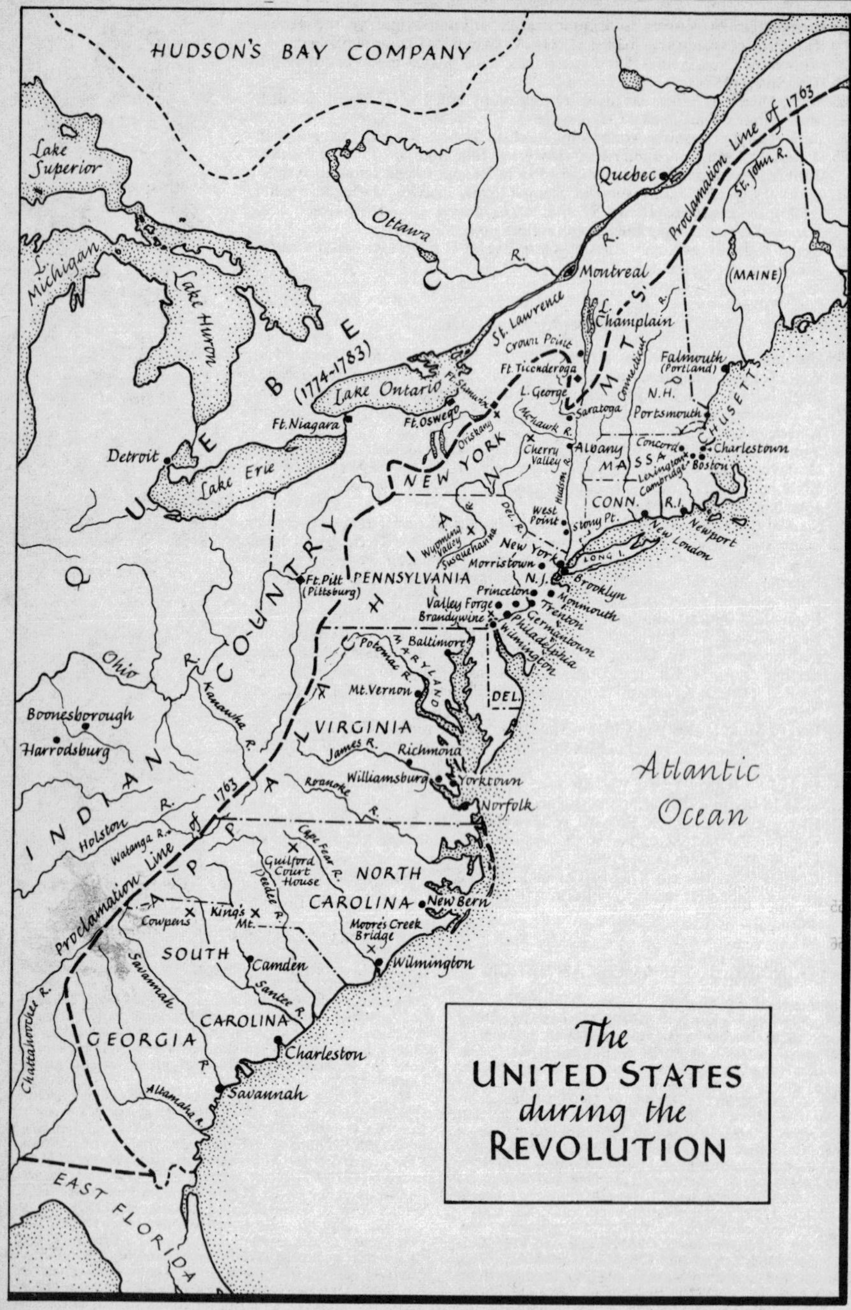
HUDSON'S BAY COMPANY
Lake Superior
L. Michigan
Lake Huron
Lake Ontario
Lake Erie
QUEBEC (1774-1783)
Quebec
Montreal
Ottawa R.
St. Lawrence R.
Proclamation Line of 1763
St. John R.
(MAINE)
L. Champlain
Crown Point
Ft. Ticonderoga
L. George
Saratoga
Ft. Stanwix
Oriskany
Ft. Oswego
Ft. Niagara
Detroit
Mohawk R.
Cherry Valley
Albany
Hudson R.
NEW YORK
Falmouth (Portland)
N.H.
Portsmouth
MASSACHUSETTS
Concord
Lexington
Cambridge
Charlestown
Boston
CONN.
R.I.
Newport
New London
West Point
Stony Pt.
LONG I.
New York
Brooklyn
Morristown
N.J.
Monmouth
Princeton
Trenton
Valley Forge
Brandywine
Germantown
Philadelphia
Wilmington
Wyoming Valley
Susquehanna R.
Del. R.
Ft. Pitt (Pittsburg)
PENNSYLVANIA
APPALACHIAN MTS.
INDIAN COUNTRY
Baltimore
MARYLAND
Potomac R.
Mt. Vernon
DEL.
Ohio R.
Kanawha R.
Boonesborough
Harrodsburg
VIRGINIA
James R.
Richmond
Williamsburg
Yorktown
Roanoke R.
Norfolk
Holston R.
Watauga R.
Cape Fear R.
Guilford Court House
Pee Dee R.
NORTH CAROLINA
New Bern
Cowpens
King's Mt.
Moore's Creek Bridge
SOUTH CAROLINA
Camden
Santee R.
Wilmington
Charleston
Savannah R.
Chattahoochee R.
GEORGIA
Altamaha R.
Savannah
EAST FLORIDA
Atlantic Ocean
The UNITED STATES during the REVOLUTION

1664 British take New Amsterdam from the Dutch. English limit "Nonconformity" with re-established Anglican Church. Isaac Newton's experiments with gravity.
1665 Great Plague in London kills 75,000.
1666 Great Fire of London. Molière's *Misanthrope.*
1683 War of European powers against the Turks (to **1699**). Vienna withstands three-month Turkish siege; high point of Turkish advance in Europe.
1685 James II succeeds Charles II in England, calls for freedom of conscience **(1687).** Protestants fear restoration of Catholicism and demand "Glorious Revolution." William of Orange invited to England and James II escapes to France **(1688).** William III and his wife, Mary, crowned. In France, Edict of Nantes of **1598,** granting freedom of worship to Huguenots (French Protestants), is revoked by Louis XIV; thousands of Protestants flee.
1689 Peter the Great becomes Czar of Russia—attempts to westernize nation and build Russia as a military power. Defeats Charles XII of Sweden at Poltava **(1709).** Beginning of the French and Indian Wars (to **1763**), campaigns in America linked to a series of wars between France and England for domination of Europe.
1690 William III of England defeats former King James II and Irish rebels at Battle of the Boyne in Ireland. John Locke's *Human Understanding.*

John Locke
(1632-1704)

18th century A.D.

1701 War of the Spanish Succession begins—the last of Louis XIV's wars for domination of the continent. The Peace of Utrecht (**1714**) will end the conflict and mark the rise of the British Empire. Called Queen Anne's War in America, it ends with the British taking New Foundland, Acadia, and Hudson's Bay Territory from France, and Gibraltar and Minorca from Spain.
1704 Deerfield (Mass.) Massacre of English colonists by French and Indians. Bach's first cantata. Jonathan Swift's *Tale of a Tub. Boston News Letter*—first newspaper in America.
1707 United Kingdom of Great Britain formed—England, Wales, and Scotland joined by parliamentary Act of Union.
1729 J. S. Bach's *St. Matthew Passion.* Isaac Newton's *Principia* translated from Latin into English.
1735 John Peter Zenger, New York editor, acquitted of libel in New York, establishing press freedom.
1740 Capt. Vitus Bering, Dane employed by Russia, discovers Alaska.
1746 British defeat Scots under Stuart Pretender Prince Charles at Culloden Moor. Last battle fought on British soil.
1751 Publication of the *Encyclopédie* begins in France, the "bible" of the Enlightenment.
1755 Samuel Johnson's *Dictionary* first published. Great earthquake in Lisbon, Portugal—over 60,000 die.
1756 Seven Years' War (French and Indian War in America) (to **1763**), in which Britain and Prussia defeat France, Spain, Austria, and Russia. France loses North American colonies; Spain cedes Florida to Britain in exchange for Cuba. In India, over 100 British prisoners die in "Black Hole of Calcutta."
1757 Beginning of British Empire in India as Robert Clive, British commander, defeats Nawab of Bengal at Plassey.
1759 British capture Quebec from French. Voltaire's *Candide.* Haydn's *Symphony No. 1.*
1762 Catherine II ("the Great") becomes Czarina of Russia. J. J. Rousseau's *Social Contract.* Mozart tours Europe as six-year-old prodigy.
1765 James Watt invents the steam engine.
1769 Sir William Arkwright patents a spinning machine—an early step in the Industrial Revolution.
1772 Joseph Priestley and Daniel Rutherford independently discover nitrogen. Partition of Poland—in **1772, 1793,** and **1795,** Austria, Prussia, and Russia divide land and people of Poland, end its independence.
1775 The American Revolution (*see* "The Founding of the American Nation"). Priestley discovers hydrochloric and sulfuric acids.
1776 Adam Smith's *Wealth of Nations.* Edward Gibbon's *Decline and Fall of the Roman Empire.* Thomas Paine's *Common Sense.* Fragonard's *Washerwoman.* Mozart's *Haffner Serenade.*
1778 Capt. James Cook discovers Hawaii. Franz Mesmer uses hypnotism.
1781 Immanuel Kant's *Critique of Pure Reason.* Herschel discovers Uranus.
1783 End of Revolutionary War (*see* special material on "The Founding of the

Catherine II
(1729-1796)

Napoleon Bonaparte
(1769-1821)

Thomas Jefferson
(1743-1826)

Alexander Hamilton
(1755-1804)

American Nation"). William Blake's poems. Beethoven's first printed works.

1784 Crimea annexed by Russia. John Wesley's *Deed of Declaration,* the basic work of Methodism.

1785 Russians settle Aleutian Islands.

1787 The Constitution of the United States signed. Lavoisier's work on chemical nomenclature. Mozart's *Don Giovanni.*

1788 French *Parlement* presents grievances to Louis XVI who agrees to convening of Estates-General in **1789**—not called since **1613.** Goethe's *Egmont.* Laplace's *Laws of the Planetary System.*

1789 French Revolution (*see* special material on the "French Revolution"). In U.S., George Washington elected President with all 69 votes of the Electoral College, takes oath of office in New York City. Vice President: John Adams. Secretary of State: Thomas Jefferson. Secretary of Treasury: Alexander Hamilton.

1790 H.M.S. *Bounty* mutineers settle on Pitcairn Island. Aloisio Galvani experiments on electrical stimulation of the muscles. Philadelphia temporary capital of U.S. as Congress votes to establish new capital on Potomac. U.S. population about 3,929,000, including 698,000 slaves. Lavoisier formulates *Table of 31 chemical elements.*

1791 U.S. Bill of Rights ratified. Boswell's *Life of Johnson.*

1794 Kosciusko's uprising in Poland quelled by the Russians. In U.S., Whiskey Rebellion in Pennsylvania as farmers object to liquor taxes. U.S. Navy and Post Office Department established.

1796 Napoleon Bonaparte, French general, defeats Austrians. In the U.S., Washington's Farewell Address **(Sept. 17);** John Adams elected President; Thomas Jefferson, Vice President. Edward Jenner introduces smallpox vaccination.

1798 Napoleon extends French conquests to Rome and Egypt.

1799 Napoleon leads coup that overthrows Directory, becomes First Consul—one of three who rule France.

19th century A.D.

1800 Napoleon conquers Italy, firmly establishes himself as First Consul in France. In the U.S., Federal Government moves to Washington. Robert Owen's social reforms in England. William Herschel discovers infrared rays. Alessandro Volta produces electricity.

1801 Austria makes temporary peace with France. United Kingdom of Great Britain and Ireland established with one monarch and one parliament; Catholics excluded from voting.

1803 U.S. negotiates Louisiana Purchase from France: For $15 million, U.S. doubles its domain, increasing its territory by 827,000 sq. mi. (2,144,500 sq km), from Mississippi River to Rockies and from Gulf of Mexico to British North America.

1804 Haiti declares independence from France; first black nation to gain freedom from European colonial rule. Napoleon proclaims himself emperor of France, systematizes French law under *Code Napoleon.* In the U.S., Alexander Hamilton is mortally wounded in duel with Aaron Burr. Lewis and Clark expedition begins exploration of what is now northwestern U.S.

1805 Lord Nelson defeats the French-Spanish fleets in the Battle of Trafalgar. Napoleon victorious over Austrian and Russian forces at the Battle of Austerlitz.

1807 Robert Fulton makes first successful steamboat trip on *Clermont* between New York City and Albany.

1808 French armies occupy Rome and Spain, extending Napoleon's empire. Britain begins aiding Spanish guerrillas against Napoleon in Peninsular War. In the U.S., Congress bars importation of slaves. Beethoven's *Fifth* and *Sixth Symphonies* performed.

1812 Napoleon's Grand Army invades Russia in June. Forced to retreat in winter, most of Napoleon's 600,000 men are lost. In the U.S., war with Britain

FRENCH REVOLUTION (1789–1799)

Revolution begins when Third Estate (Commons) delegates swear not to disband until France has a constitution. Paris mob storms Bastille, symbol of royal power **(July 14, 1789).** National Assembly votes for Constitution, Declaration of the Rights of Man, a limited monarchy, and other reforms **(1789–90).** Legislative Assembly elected, Revolutionary Commune formed, and French Republic proclaimed **(1792).** War of the First Coalition—Austria, Prussia, Britain, Netherlands, and Spain fight to restore French nobility **(1792–97).** Start of series of wars between France and European powers that will last, almost without interruption, for 23 years. Louis XVI and Marie Antoinette executed. Committee of Public Safety begins Reign of Terror as political control measure. Interfactional rivalry leads to mass killings. Danton and Robespierre executed. Third French Constitution sets up Directory government **(1795).**

declared over freedom of the seas for U.S. vessels. U.S.S. *Constitution* sinks British frigate. (*See* special material on the "War of 1812.")

1814 French defeated by allies (Britain, Austria, Russia, Prussia, Sweden, and Portugal) in War of Liberation. Napoleon exiled to Elba, off Italian coast. Bourbon King Louis XVIII takes French throne. George Stephenson builds first practical steam locomotive.

1815 Napoleon returns: "Hundred Days" begin. Napoleon defeated by Wellington at Waterloo, banished again to St. Helena in South Atlantic. Congress of Vienna: victorious allies change the map of Europe.

1817 Simón Bolívar establishes independent Venezuela, as Spain loses hold on South American countries. Bolívar named President of Colombia **(1819).** Peru, Guatemala, Panama, and Santo Domingo proclaim independence from Spain **(1821).**

1820 Missouri Compromise—Missouri admitted as slave state but slavery barred in rest of Louisiana Purchase north of 36°30′ N.

1822 Greeks proclaim a republic and independence from Turkey. Turks invade Greece. Russia declares war on Turkey **(1828).** Greece also aided by France and Britain. War ends and Turks recognize Greek independence **(1829).** Brazil becomes independent of Portugal. Schubert's *Eighth Symphony* ("The Unfinished").

1823 U.S. Monroe Doctrine warns European nations not to interfere in Western Hemisphere.

Charles Dickens (1812-1870)

1824 Mexico becomes a republic, three years after declaring independence from Spain. Beethoven's *Ninth Symphony.*

1825 First passenger-carrying railroad in England.

1830 French invade Algeria. Louis Philippe becomes "Citizen King" as revolution forces Charles X to abdicate. Mormon church formed in U.S. by Joseph Smith.

1831 Polish revolt against Russia fails. Belgium separates from the Netherlands. In U.S., Nat Turner leads unsuccessful slave rebellion.

1833 Slavery abolished in British Empire.

1834 Charles Babbage invents "analytical engine," precursor of computer. McCormick patents reaper.

1836 Boer farmers start "Great Trek"—Natal, Transvaal, and Orange Free State founded in South Africa. Mexican army besieges Texans in Alamo. Entire garrison, including Davy Crockett and Jim Bowie, wiped out. Texans gain independence from Mexico after winning Battle of San Jacinto. Dicken's *Pickwick Papers.*

1837 Victoria becomes Queen of Great Britain. Mob kills Elijah P. Lovejoy, Illinois abolitionist publisher.

1839 First Opium War (to **1842**) between Britain and China, over importation of drug into China.

1840 Lower and Upper Canada united.

1841 U.S. President Harrison dies **(April 4)** one month after inauguration; John Tyler becomes first Vice President to succeed to Presidency.

1844 Democratic convention calls for annexation of Texas and acquisition of Oregon ("Fifty-four-forty-or-fight"). Five Chinese ports opened to U.S. ships. Samuel F. B. Morse patents telegraph.

Henry Clay (1777-1852)

1845 Congress adopts joint resolution for annexation of Texas.

1846 Failure of potato crop causes famine in Ireland. U.S. declares war on Mexico. California and New Mexico annexed by U.S. Brigham Young leads Mormons to Great Salt Lake. W.T. Morton uses ether as anesthetic. Sewing machine patented by Elias Howe.

1848 Revolt in Paris: Louis Philippe abdicates; Louis Napoleon elected President of French Republic. Revolutions in Vienna, Venice, Berlin, Milan, Rome, and Warsaw. Put down by royal troops in **1848–49.** U.S.-Mexico War ends; Mexico cedes claims to Texas, California, Arizona, New Mexico, Utah, Nevada. U.S. treaty with Britain sets Oregon Territory boundary at 49th parallel. Karl Marx and Friedrich Engels' *Communist Manifesto.*

1849 California gold rush begins.

1850 Henry Clay opens great debate on slavery, warns South against secession.

1851 Herman Melville's *Moby Dick.* Harriet Beecher Stowe's *Uncle Tom's Cabin.*

1852 South African Republic established. Louis Napoleon proclaims himself Napoleon III ("Second Empire").

WAR OF 1812

British interference with American trade, impressment of American seamen, and "War Hawks" drive for western expansion lead to war. American attacks on Canada foiled; U.S. Commodore Perry wins battle of Lake Erie **(1813).** British capture and burn Washington **(1814)** but fail to take Fort McHenry at Baltimore. Andrew Jackson repulses assault on New Orleans after treaty of Ghent ends war **(1815).** War settles little but strengthens U.S. as independent nation.

Dred Scott (1795?-1858)

Abraham Lincoln (1809-1865)

Ulysses S. Grant (1822-1885)

1853 Crimean War begins as Turkey declares war on Russia. Commodore Perry reaches Tokyo.

1854 Britain and France join Turkey in war on Russia. In U.S., Kansas-Nebraska Act permits local option on slavery; rioting and bloodshed. Japanese allow American trade. Antislavery men in Michigan form Republican Party. Tennyson's *Charge of the Light Brigade*. Thoreau's *Walden*.

1855 Armed clashes in Kansas between pro- and anti-slavery forces. Florence Nightingale nurses wounded in Crimea. Walt Whitman's *Leaves of Grass*.

1856 Flaubert's *Madame Bovary*.

1857 Supreme Court, in Dred Scott decision, rules that a slave is not a citizen. Financial crisis in Europe and U.S. Great Mutiny (Sepoy Rebellion) begins in India. India placed under crown rule as a result.

1858 Pro-slavery constitution rejected in Kansas. Abraham Lincoln makes strong antislavery speech in Springfield, Ill.: ". . . this Government cannot endure permanently half slave and half free." Lincoln-Douglas debates. First trans-Atlantic telegraph cable completed by Cyrus W. Field.

1859 John Brown raids Harpers Ferry; is captured and hanged. Work begins on Suez Canal. Unification of Italy starts under leadership of Count Cavour, Sardinian premier. Joined by France in war against Austria. Edward Fitzgerald's *Rubaiyat of Omar Khayyam*. Charles Darwin's *Origin of Species*. J. S. Mill's *On Liberty*

1861 U.S. Civil War begins as attempts at compromise fail (*see* special material on "The Civil War"). Congress creates Colorado, Dakota, and Nevada territories; adopts income tax; Lincoln inaugurated. Serfs emancipated in Russia. Pasteur's theory of germs. Independent Kingdom of Italy proclaimed under Sardinian King Victor Emmanuel II.

1863 French capture Mexico City; proclaim Archduke Maximilian of Austria emperor.

1865 Lincoln fatally shot at Ford's Theater by John Wilkes Booth. Vice President Johnson sworn as successor. Booth caught and dies of gunshot wounds; four conspirators are hanged. Joseph Lister begins antiseptic surgery. Gregor Mendel's Law of Heredity. Lewis Carroll's *Alice's Adventures in Wonderland*.

1866 Alfred Nobel invents dynamite (patented in Britain 1867). Seven Weeks' War: Austria defeated by Prussia and Italy.

1867 Austria-Hungary Dual Monarchy established. French leave Mexico; Maximilian executed. Dominion of Canada established. U.S. buys Alaska from Russia for $7,200,000. South African diamond field discovered. Volume I of Marx's *Das Kapital*. Strauss's *Blue Danube*.

1868 Revolution in Spain; Queen Isabella deposed, flees to France. In U.S., Fourteenth Amendment giving civil rights to blacks is ratified. Georgia under military government after legislature expels blacks.

1869 First U.S. transcontinental rail route completed. James Fisk and Jay Gould attempt to control gold market causes Black Friday panic. Suez Canal opened. Mendeleev's periodic table of elements.

1870 Franco-Prussian War (to **1871**): Napoleon III capitulates at Sedan. Revolt in Paris; Third Republic proclaimed.

THE CIVIL WAR

(The War Between the States or the War of the Rebellion)

Apart from the matter of slavery, the Civil War arose out of both the economic and political rivalry between an agrarian South and an industrial North and the issue of the right of states to secede from the Union.

1861 After South Carolina secedes **(Dec. 20, 1860)**, Mississippi, Florida, Alabama, Georgia, Louisiana, and Texas follow, forming the Confederate States of America, with Jefferson Davis as president **(Jan.–March)**. War begins as Confederates fire on Fort Sumter **(April 12)**. Lincoln calls for 75,000 volunteers. Southern ports blockaded by superior Union naval forces. Virginia, Arkansas, Tennessee, and North Carolina secede to complete 11-state Confederacy. Union army advancing on Richmond repulsed at first Battle of Bull Run **(July)**.

1862 Edwin M. Stanton named Secretary of War **(Jan.)**. Grant wins first important Union victory in West, at Fort Donelson; Nashville falls **(Feb.)**. Ironclads, Union's *Monitor* and Confederate's *Virginia (Merrimac)* duel at Hampton Roads **(March)**. New Orleans falls to Union fleet under Farragut; city occupied **(April)**. Grant's army escapes defeat at Shiloh. Memphis falls as Union gunboats control upper Mississippi **(June)**. Confederate general Robert E. Lee victorious at second Battle of Bull Run **(Aug.)**. Union army under McClellan halts Lee's attack on Washington in the Battle of Antietam **(Sept.)**. Lincoln removes McClellan for lack of aggressiveness. Burnside's drive on Richmond fails at Fredericksburg **(Dec.)**. Union forces under Rosecrans chase Bragg through Tennessee; battle of Murfreesboro **(Oct.–Jan. 1863)**.

1863 Lee defeats Hooker at Chancellorsville; "Stonewall" Jackson, Confederate general, dies **(May)**. Confederate invasion of Pennsylvania stopped at Gettysburg by George Meade—Lee loses 20,000 men—the greatest battle of the War **(July)**. It and the Union victory at Vicksburg mark the war's turning point. Union general George H. Thomas, the "Rock of Chickamauga," holds Bragg's forces on Georgia-Tennessee border **(Sept.)**. Sherman, Hooker, and Thomas drive Bragg back to Georgia. Tennessee restored to the Union **(Nov.)**.

1864 Ulysses S. Grant named commander-in-chief of Union forces **(March)**. In the Wilderness campaign, Grant forces Lee's Army of Northern Virginia back toward Richmond **(May–June)**. Sherman's Atlanta campaign and "march to the sea" **(May–Sept.)**. Farragut's victory at Mobile Bay **(Aug.)**. Hood's Confederate army defeated at Nashville. Sherman takes Savannah **(Dec.)**.

1865 Sheridan defeats Confederates at Five Forks; Confederates evacuate Richmond **(April)**. On **April 9,** Lee surrenders to Grant at Appomattox.

1871 France surrenders Alsace-Lorraine to Germany; war ends. German Empire proclaimed with Prussian King as Kaiser Wilhelm I. Fighting with Apaches begins in American West. Boss Tweed corruption exposed in New York. The Chicago Fire, with 250 deaths and $196-million damage. Stanley meets Livingston in Africa.

1872 Congress gives amnesty to most Confederates. Jules Verne's *Around the World in 80 Days.*

1873 Economic crisis in Europe. U.S. establishes gold standard.

1875 First Kentucky Derby.

1876 Sioux kill Gen. George A. Custer and 264 troopers at Little Big Horn River. Alexander Graham Bell patents the telephone.

1877 After Presidential election of **1876,** Electoral Commission gives disputed Electoral College votes to Rutherford B. Hayes despite Tilden's popular majority. Russo-Turkish war (ends in **1878** with power of Turkey in Europe broken). Reconstruction ends in the American South. Thomas Edison patents phonograph.

1878 Congress of Berlin revises Treaty of San Stefano ending Russo-Turkish War; makes extensive redivision of southeastern Europe. First commercial telephone exchange opened in New Haven, Conn.

1880 U.S.-China treaty allows U.S. to restrict immigration of Chinese labor.

1881 President Garfield fatally shot by assassin; Vice President Arthur succeeds him. Charles J. Guiteau convicted and executed (in **1882**).

1882 Terrorism in Ireland after land evictions. Britain invades and conquers Egypt. Germany, Austria, and Italy form Triple Alliance. In U.S., Congress adopts Chinese Exclusion Act. Rockefeller's Standard Oil Trust is first industrial monopoly. In Berlin, Robert Koch announces discovery of tuberculosis germ.

1883 Congress creates Civil Service Commission. Brooklyn Bridge and Metropolitan Opera House completed.

1885 British Gen. Charles G. "Chinese" Gordon killed at Khartoum in Egyptian Sudan.

1886 Bombing at Haymarket Square, Chicago, kills seven policemen and injures many others. Eight alleged anarchists accused—three imprisoned, one commits suicide, four hanged. (In **1893,** Illinois Governor Altgeld, critical of trial, pardons three survivors.) Statue of Liberty dedicated. Geronimo, Apache Indian chief, surrenders.

1887 Queen Victoria's Golden Jubilee. Sir Arthur Conan Doyle's first Sherlock Holmes story, "A Study in Scarlet."

1888 Historic March blizzard in Northeast U.S.—many perish, property damage exceeds $25 million. George Eastman's box camera (the Kodak). J.B. Dunlop invents pneumatic tire. Jack the Ripper murders in London.

1889 Second (Socialist) International founded in Paris. Indian Territory in Oklahoma opened to settlement. Thousands die in Johnstown, Pa., flood. Mark Twain's *A Connecticut Yankee in King Arthur's Court.*

1890 Congress votes Sherman Antitrust Act. Sitting Bull killed in Sioux uprising.

1892 Battle between steel strikers and Pinkerton guards at Homestead, Pa.; union defeated after militia intervenes. Silver mine strikers in Idaho fight non-union workers; U.S. troops dispatched. Diesel engine patented.

1894 Sino-Japanese War begins (ends in **1895** with China's defeat). In France, Capt. Alfred Dreyfus convicted on false treason charge (pardoned in **1906**). In U.S., Jacob S. Coxey of Ohio leads "Coxey's Army" of unemployed on Washington. Eugene V. Debs calls general strike of rail workers to support Pullman Company strikers; strike broken, Debs jailed for six months. Thomas A. Edison's kinetoscope given first public showing in New York City.

1895 X-rays discovered by German physicist, Wilhelm Roentgen.

1896 Supreme Court's *Plessy v. Ferguson* decision—"separate but equal" doctrine. Alfred Nobel's will establishes prizes for peace, science, and literature. Marconi receives first wireless patent in Britain. William Jennings Bryan delivers "Cross of Gold" speech at Democratic Convention in

Geronimo (1829-1909)

Samuel Clemens (Mark Twain) (1835-1910)

Thomas A. Edison (1847-1931)

SPANISH-AMERICAN WAR (1898–1899)

War fires stoked by "jingo journalism" as American people support Cuban rebels against Spain. American business sees economic gain in Cuban trade and resources and American power zones in Latin America. Outstanding events: Submarine mine explodes U.S. battleship *Maine* in Havana Harbor **(Feb. 15)**; 260 killed; responsibility never fixed. Congress declares independence of Cuba **(April 19)**. Spain declares war on U.S. **(Apr. 24)**; Congress **(Apr. 25)** formally declares nation has been at war with Spain since Apr. 21. Commodore George Dewey wins seven-hour battle of Manila Bay **(May 1)**. Spanish fleet destroyed off Santiago, Cuba **(July 3)**; city surrenders **(July 17)**. Treaty of Paris (ratified by Senate **1899**) ends war. U.S. given Guam and Puerto Rico and agrees to pay Spain $20 million for Philippines. Cuba independent of Spain; under U.S. military control for three years until **May 20, 1902**. Yellow fever is eradicated and political reforms achieved.

Marie Curie (1867-1934)

Chicago. First modern Olympic games held in Athens, Greece.

1898 Chinese "Boxers," anti-foreign organization, established. They stage uprisings against Europeans in **1900;** U.S. and other Western troops relieve Peking legations. Spanish-American War (*see* special material on the "Spanish-American War"). Pierre and Marie Curie discover radium and polonium.

1899 Boer War (or South African War). Conflict between British and Boers (descendants of Dutch settlers of South Africa). Causes rooted in longstanding territorial disputes and in friction over political rights for English and other "uitlanders" following 1886 discovery of vast gold deposits in Transvaal. (British victorious as war ends in **1902.**) Casualties: 5,774 British dead, about 4,000 Boers. Union of South Africa established in **1908** as confederation of colonies; becomes British dominion in **1910.**

20th century A.D.

1900 Hurricane ravages Galveston, Tex.; 6,000 drown. Sigmund Freud's *The Interpretation of Dreams.*

1901 Queen Victoria dies; succeeded by son, Edward VII. As President McKinley begins second term, he is shot fatally by anarchist Leon Czolgosz. Theodore Roosevelt sworn in as successor.

1902 Enrico Caruso's first gramophone recording.

1903 Wright brothers, Orville and Wilbur, fly first powered, controlled, heavier-than-air plane at Kitty Hawk, N.C. Henry Ford organizes Ford Motor Company.

Theodore Roosevelt (1858-1919)

1904 Russo-Japanese War—competition for Korea and Manchuria: In **1905,** Port Arthur surrenders to Japanese and Russia suffers other defeats; President Roosevelt mediates Treaty of Portsmouth, N.H., ending war with concessions for Japan. *Entente Cordiale:* Britain and France settle their international differences. General theory of radioactivity by Rutherford and Soddy. New York City subway opened.

1905 General strike in Russia; first workers' soviet set up in St. Petersburg. Sailors on battleship *Potemkin* mutiny; reforms including first Duma (parliament) established by Czar's "October Manifesto." Albert Einstein's special theory of relativity and other key theories in physics. Franz Lehar's *Merry Widow.*

1906 San Francisco earthquake and three-day fire; 500 dead. Roald Amundsen, Norwegian explorer, fixes magnetic North Pole.

1907 Second Hague Peace Conference, of 46 nations, adopts 10 conventions on rules of war. Financial panic of **1907** in U.S.

1908 Earthquake kills 150,000 in southern Italy and Sicily. U.S. Supreme Court, in Danbury Hatters' case, outlaws secondary union boycotts.

1909 North Pole reached by American explorers Robert E. Peary and Matthew Henson.

1910 Boy Scouts of America incorporated.

1911 First use of aircraft as offensive weapon in Turkish-Italian War. Italy defeats Turks and annexes Tripoli and Libya. Chinese Republic proclaimed after revolution overthrows Manchu dynasty. Sun Yat-sen named president. Mexican Revolution: Porfirio Diaz, president since 1877, replaced by Francisco Madero. Triangle Shirtwaist Company fire in New York; 145 killed. Richard Strauss's *Der Rosenkavalier.* Irving Berlin's *Alexander's Ragtime Band.* Amundsen reaches South Pole.

Albert Einstein (1879-1955)

1912 Balkan Wars **(1912–13)** resulting from territorial disputes: Turkey defeated by alliance of Bulgaria, Serbia, Greece, and Montenegro; London peace treaty **(1913)** partitions most of European Turkey among the victors. In second war **(1913),** Bulgaria attacks Serbia and Greece and is defeated after Romania intervenes and Turks recapture Adrianople. *Titanic* sinks on maiden voyage; over 1,500 drown.

1913 Suffragettes demonstrate in London. Garment workers strike in New York and Boston; win pay raise and shorter hours. Sixteenth Amendment (income tax) and 17th (popular election of U.S. senators) adopted. Bill creating U.S. Federal Reserve System becomes law. Stravinsky's *The Rite of Spring.*

1914 World War I begins (*see* special material on "World War I"). Panama Canal officially opened. Congress sets up Federal Trade Commission, passes Clayton Antitrust Act. U.S. Marines occupy Veracruz, Mexico, intervening in civil war to protect American interests.

1915 U.S. protests German submarine actions and British blockade of Germany. U.S. banks lend $500 million to France and Britain. D. W. Griffith's film *Birth of a Nation.* Albert Einstein's *General Theory of Relativity.*

1916 Congress expands armed forces. Tom Mooney arrested for San Francisco bombing (pardoned in **1939**). Pershing fails in raid into Mexico in quest of

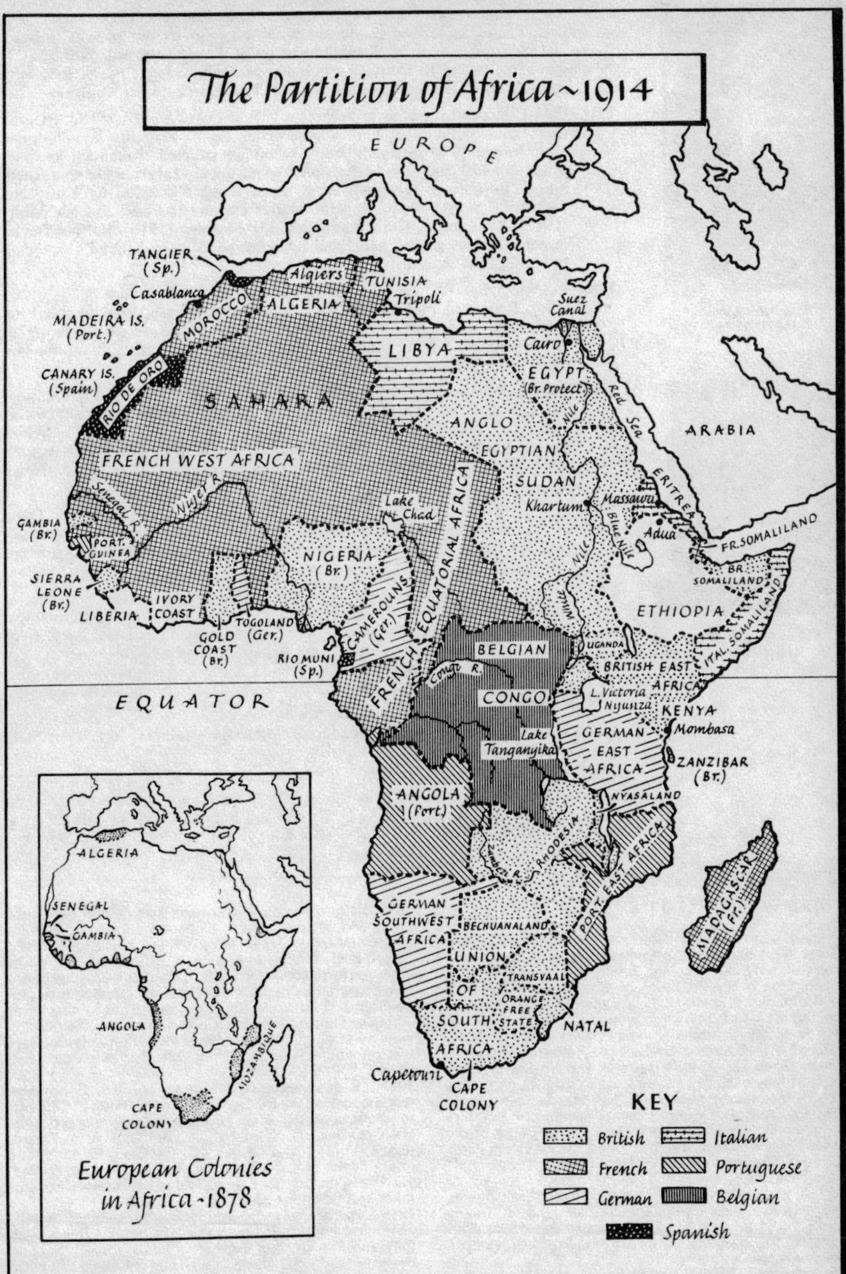
The Partition of Africa~1914
EUROPE
TANGIER (Sp.)
Casablanca
MADEIRA IS. (Port.)
CANARY IS. (Spain)
RIO DE ORO
MOROCCO
Algiers
ALGERIA
TUNISIA
Tripoli
LIBYA
Suez Canal
Cairo
EGYPT (Br. Protect.)
SAHARA
ANGLO EGYPTIAN SUDAN
Red Sea
Nile
ARABIA
FRENCH WEST AFRICA
Senegal R.
Niger R.
Lake Chad
FRENCH EQUATORIAL AFRICA
Khartum
Massawa
ERITREA
Adua
Blue Nile
FR. SOMALILAND
GAMBIA (Br.)
PORT. GUINEA
NIGERIA (Br.)
BR. SOMALILAND
SIERRA LEONE (Br.)
LIBERIA
IVORY COAST
GOLD COAST (Br.)
TOGOLAND (Ger.)
CAMEROUNS (Ger.)
White Nile
ETHIOPIA
ITAL. SOMALILAND
RIO MUNI (Sp.)
BELGIAN CONGO
Congo R.
UGANDA
BRITISH EAST AFRICA
L. Victoria Nyanza
KENYA
Mombasa
EQUATOR
Lake Tanganyika
GERMAN EAST AFRICA
ZANZIBAR (Br.)
ANGOLA (Port.)
NYASALAND
RHODESIA
Zambezi R.
PORT. EAST AFRICA
MADAGASCAR (Fr.)
GERMAN SOUTHWEST AFRICA
BECHUANALAND
UNION OF SOUTH AFRICA
TRANSVAAL
ORANGE FREE STATE
NATAL
Capetown
CAPE COLONY
ALGERIA
SENEGAL
GAMBIA
ANGOLA
MOZAMBIQUE
CAPE COLONY
European Colonies in Africa-1878
KEY
British
Italian
French
Portuguese
German
Belgian
Spanish

Vladimir Lenin (1870-1924)

Woodrow Wilson (1856-1924)

rebel Pancho Villa. U.S. buys Virgin Islands from Denmark for $25 million. President Wilson re-elected with "he kept us out of war" slogan. "Black Tom" explosion at munitions dock in Jersey City, N.J., $40,000,000 damages; traced to German saboteurs. Margaret Sanger opens first birth control clinic. Easter Rebellion in Ireland put down by British troops.

1917 First U.S. combat troops in France as U.S. declares war **(April 6).** Russian Revolution—climax of long unrest under czars. February Revolution—Czar forced to abdicate, liberal government created. Kerensky becomes prime minister and forms provisional government **(July).** In October Revolution, Bolsheviks seize power in armed coup d'état led by Lenin and Trotsky. Kerensky flees. Revolutionaries execute the czar and his family **(1918).** Reds set up Third International in Moscow **(1919).** Balfour Declaration promises Jewish homeland in Palestine. Sigmund Freud's *Introduction to Psychoanalysis.*

1918 Russian Civil War between Reds (Bolsheviks) and Whites (anti-Bolsheviks); Reds win in **1920.** Allied troops (U.S., British, French) intervene **(March);** leave in **1919.** Japanese hold Vladivostok until **1922.** World-wide influenza epidemic strikes; by **1920,** nearly 20 million are dead. In U.S. alone, 500,000 perish.

1919 Third International (Comintern) establishes Soviet control over international Communist movements. Paris peace conference. Versailles Treaty, incorporating Wilson's draft Covenant of League of Nations, signed by Allies and Germany; rejected by U.S. Senate. Congress formally ends war in **1921.** Eighteenth (Prohibition) Amendment adopted. Alcock and Brown make first trans-Atlantic non-stop flight.

1920 League of Nations holds first meeting at Geneva, Switzerland. U.S. Dept. of Justice "red hunt" nets thousands of radicals; aliens deported. Women's suffrage (19th) amendment ratified. First Agatha Christie mystery. Sinclair Lewis's *Main Street.*

1921 Reparations Commission fixes German liability at 132 billion gold marks. German inflation begins. Major treaties signed at Washington Disarmament Conference limit naval tonnage and pledge to respect territorial integrity of China. Irish Free State formed in southern Ireland as self-governing dominion of British Empire. In U.S., Nicola Sacco and Bartolomeo Vanzetti, Italian-born anarchists, convicted of armed robbery murder; case stirs world-wide protests; they are executed in **1927.**

1922 Mussolini marches on Rome; forms Fascist government. Irish Free State officially proclaimed.

1923 Adolf Hitler's "Beer Hall Putsch" in Munich fails; in **1924** he is sentenced to five years in prison where he writes *Mein Kampf;* released after eight months. Occupation of Ruhr by French and Belgian troops to enforce reparations payments. Widespread Ku Klux Klan violence in U.S. George Gershwin's *Rhapsody in Blue.*

WORLD WAR I (1914–1918)

Imperial, territorial, and economic rivalries lead to the "Great War" between the Central Powers (Austria-Hungary, Germany, Bulgaria, and Turkey) and the Allies (U.S., Britain, France, Russia, Belgium, Serbia, Greece, Romania, Montenegro, Portugal, Italy, Japan). About 10 million combatants killed, 20 million wounded.

1914 Austrian Archduke Francis Ferdinand and wife assassinated in Sarajevo by Serbian nationalist, Gavrilo Princip **(June 28).** Austria declares war on Serbia **(July 28).** Germany declares war on Russia **(Aug. 1),** on France **(Aug. 3),** invades Belgium **(Aug. 4).** Britain declares war on Germany **(Aug. 4).** Germans defeat Russians in Battle of Tannenberg on Eastern Front **(Aug.).** First Battle of the Marne **(Sept.).** German drive stopped 25 miles from Paris. By end of year, war on the Western Front is "positional" in the trenches.

1915 German submarine blockade of Great Britain begins **(Feb.).** Dardanelles Campaign—British land in Turkey **(April),** withdraw from Gallipoli **(Dec. to Jan. 1916).** Germans use gas at second Battle of Ypres **(April–May).** *Lusitania* sunk by German submarine—1,198 lost, including 128 Americans **(May 7).** On Eastern Front, German and Austrian "great offensive" conquers all of Poland and Lithuania; Russians lose 1 million men (by **Sept. 6).** "Great Fall Offensive" by Allies results in little change from 1914 **(Sept.–Oct.).** Britain and France declare war on Bulgaria **(Oct. 14).**

1916 Battle of Verdun—Germans and French each lose about 350,000 men **(Feb.).** Extended submarine warfare begins **(March).** British-German sea battle of Jutland **(May);** British lose more ships, but German fleet never ventures forth again. On Eastern front, the Brusilov offensive demoralizes Russians, costs them 1 million men **(June–Sept.).** Battle of the Somme—British lose over 400,000; French, 200,000; Germans, about 450,000; all with no strategic results **(July–Nov.).** Romania declares war on Austria-Hungary **(Aug. 27).** Bucharest captured **(Dec.).**

1917 U.S. declares war on Germany **(April 6).** Submarine warfare at peak **(April).** On Italian Front, Battle of Caporetto—Italians retreat, losing 600,000 prisoners and deserters **(Oct.–Dec.).** On Western Front, Battles of Arras, Champagne, Ypres (third battle), etc. First large British tank attack **(Nov.).** U.S. declares war on Austria-Hungary **(Dec. 7).** Armistice between new Russian Bolshevik government and Germans **(Dec. 15).**

1918 Great offensive by Germans **(March–June).** Americans' first important battle role at Château-Thierry—as they and French stop German advance **(June).** Second Battle of the Marne **(July–Aug.)**—start of Allied offensive at Amiens, St. Mihiel, etc. Battles of the Argonne and Ypres panic German leadership **(Sept.–Oct.).** British offensive in Palestine **(Sept.).** Germans ask for armistice **(Oct. 4).** British armistice with Turkey **(Oct.).** German Kaiser abdicates **(Nov.).** Hostilities cease on Western Front **(Nov. 11).**

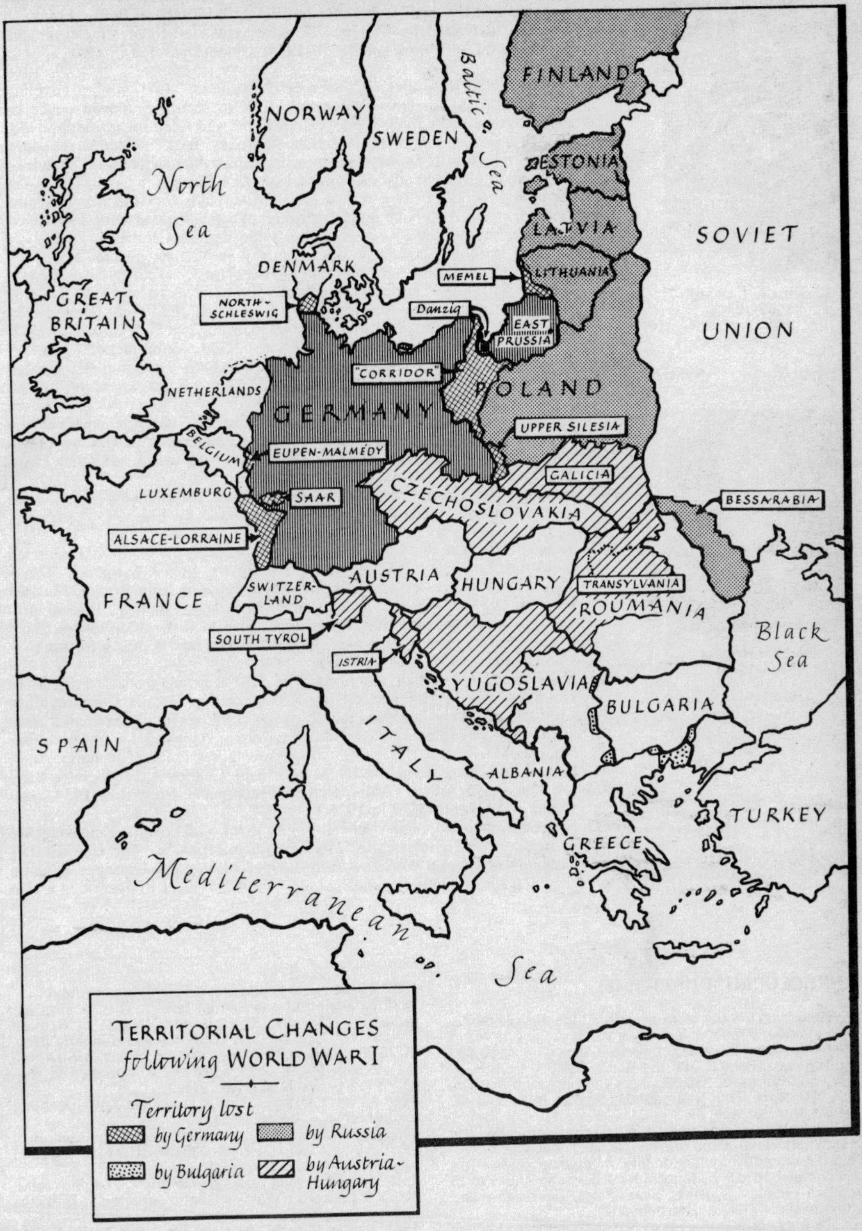

1924 Death of Lenin; Stalin wins power struggle, rules as Soviet dictator until death in **1953.** Italian Fascists murder Socialist leader Giacomo Matteotti. Interior Secretary Albert B. Fall and oilmen Harry Sinclair and Edward L. Doheny are charged with conspiracy and bribery in the Teapot Dome scandal, involving fraudulent leases of naval oil reserves. In **1931,** Fall is sentenced to year in prison; Doheny and Sinclair acquitted of bribery. Nathan

Charles A. Linbergh (1902-1974)

Herbert Hoover (1874-1964)

Leopold and Richard Loeb convicted in "thrill killing" of Bobby Franks in Chicago; defended by Clarence Darrow; sentenced to life imprisonment. (Loeb killed by fellow convict in **1936;** Leopold paroled in **1958,** dies in **1971.**)

1925 Nellie Tayloe Ross elected governor of Wyoming; first woman governor elected in U.S. Locarno conferences seek to secure European peace by mutual guarantees. John T. Scopes convicted and fined for teaching evolution in a public school in Tennessee "Monkey Trial"; sentence set aside. John Logie Baird, Scottish inventor, transmits human features by television. Adolf Hitler publishes Volume I of *Mein Kampf.*

1926 General strike in Britain brings nation's activities to standstill. U.S. marines dispatched to Nicaragua during revolt; they remain until **1933.** Gertrude Ederle of U.S. is first woman to swim English Channel.

1927 German economy collapses. Socialists riot in Vienna; general strike follows acquittal of Nazis for political murder. Trotsky expelled from Russian Communist Party. Charles A. Lindbergh flies first successful solo non-stop flight from New York to Paris. Ruth Snyder and Judd Gray convicted of murder of Albert Snyder; they are executed at Sing Sing prison in **1928.** *The Jazz Singer,* with Al Jolson, first part-talking motion picture.

1928 Kellogg-Briand Pact, outlawing war, signed in Paris by 65 nations. Alexander Fleming discovers penicillin. Richard E. Byrd starts expedition to Antarctic; returns in **1930.**

1929 Trotsky expelled from U.S.S.R. Lateran Treaty establishes independent Vatican City. In U.S., stock market prices collapse, with U.S. securities losing $26 billion—first phase of Depression and world economic crisis. St. Valentine's Day gangland massacre in Chicago.

1930 Britain, U.S., Japan, France, and Italy sign naval disarmament treaty. Nazis gain in German elections. Cyclotron developed by Ernest O. Lawrence, U.S. physicist.

1931 Spain becomes a republic with overthrow of King Alfonso XIII. German industrialists finance 800,000-strong Nazi party. British parliament enacts statute of Westminster, legalizing dominion equality with Britain. Mukden Incident begins Japanese occupation of Manchuria. In U.S., Hoover proposes one-year moratorium of war debts. Harold C. Urey discovers heavy hydrogen. Gangster Al Capone sentenced to 11 years in prison for tax evasion (freed in **1939;** dies in **1947**).

1932 Nazis lead in German elections with 230 Reichstag seats. Famine in U.S.S.R. In U.S., Congress sets up Reconstruction Finance Corporation to stimulate economy. Veterans march on Washington—most leave after Senate rejects payment of cash bonuses; others removed by troops under Douglas MacArthur. U.S. protests Japanese aggression in Manchuria. Amelia Earhart is first woman to fly Atlantic solo. Charles A. Lindbergh's baby son kidnapped, killed. (Bruno Richard Hauptmann arrested in **1934,** convicted in **1935,** executed in **1936.**)

1933 Hitler appointed German chancellor, gets dictatorial powers. Reichstag fire in Berlin; Nazi terror begins. (*See* special material on "The Holocaust.") Germany and Japan withdraw from League of Nations. Giuseppe Zangara executed for attempted assassination of President-elect Roosevelt in which

THE HOLOCAUST (1933–1945)

"Holocaust" is the term describing the Nazi annihilation of about 6 million Jews (two thirds of the pre-World War II European Jewish population), including 4,500,000 from Russia, Poland, and the Baltic; 750,000 from Hungary and Romania; 290,000 from Germany and Austria; 105,000 from The Netherlands; 90,000 from France; 54,000 from Greece, etc.

The Holocaust was unique in its being *genocide*—the systematic destruction of a people solely because of religion, race, ethnicity, nationality, or homosexuality—on an unmatched scale. Along with the Jews, another 9 to 10 million people—Gypsies, Slavs (Poles, Ukrainians, and Belorussians)—were exterminated.

The only comparable act of genocide in modern times was launched in April 1915, when an estimated 600,000 Armenians were massacred by the Turks.

1933 Hitler named German Chancellor **(Jan.)**. Dachau, first concentration camp, established **(March)**. Boycotts against Jews begin **(April)**.
1935 Anti-Semitic Nuremberg Laws passed by Reichstag **(Sept.)**.
1937 Buchenwald concentration camp opens **(July)**.
1938 Extension of anti-Semitic laws to Austria after annexation **(March)**. *Kristallnacht* (Night of Broken Glass)—anti-Semitic riots in Germany and Austria **(Nov. 9)**. 26,000 Jews sent to concentration camps; Jewish children expelled from schools **(Nov.)**. Expropriation of Jewish property and businesses **(Dec.)**.
1940 As war continues, Nazi acts against Jews extended to German-conquered areas.
1941 Deportation of German Jews begins; massacres of Jews in Odessa and Kiev—68,000 killed **(Nov.)**; in Riga and Vilna—almost 60,000 killed **(Dec.)**.
1942 Unified Jewish resistance in ghettos begins **(Jan.)**. 300,000 Jews from Warsaw Ghetto deported to Treblinka death camp **(July)**.
1943 Warsaw Ghetto uprisings **(Jan.** and **April)**; Ghetto exterminated **(May)**.
1944 476,000 Hungarian Jews sent to Auschwitz **(May–June)**. D-day **(June 6)**. Soviet Army liberates Maidanek death camp **(July)**. Nazis try to hide evidence of death camps **(Nov.)**.
1945 Americans liberate Buchenwald and British liberate Bergen-Belsen camps **(April)**. Nuremberg War Crimes Trial **(Nov. 1945** to **Oct. 1946)**.

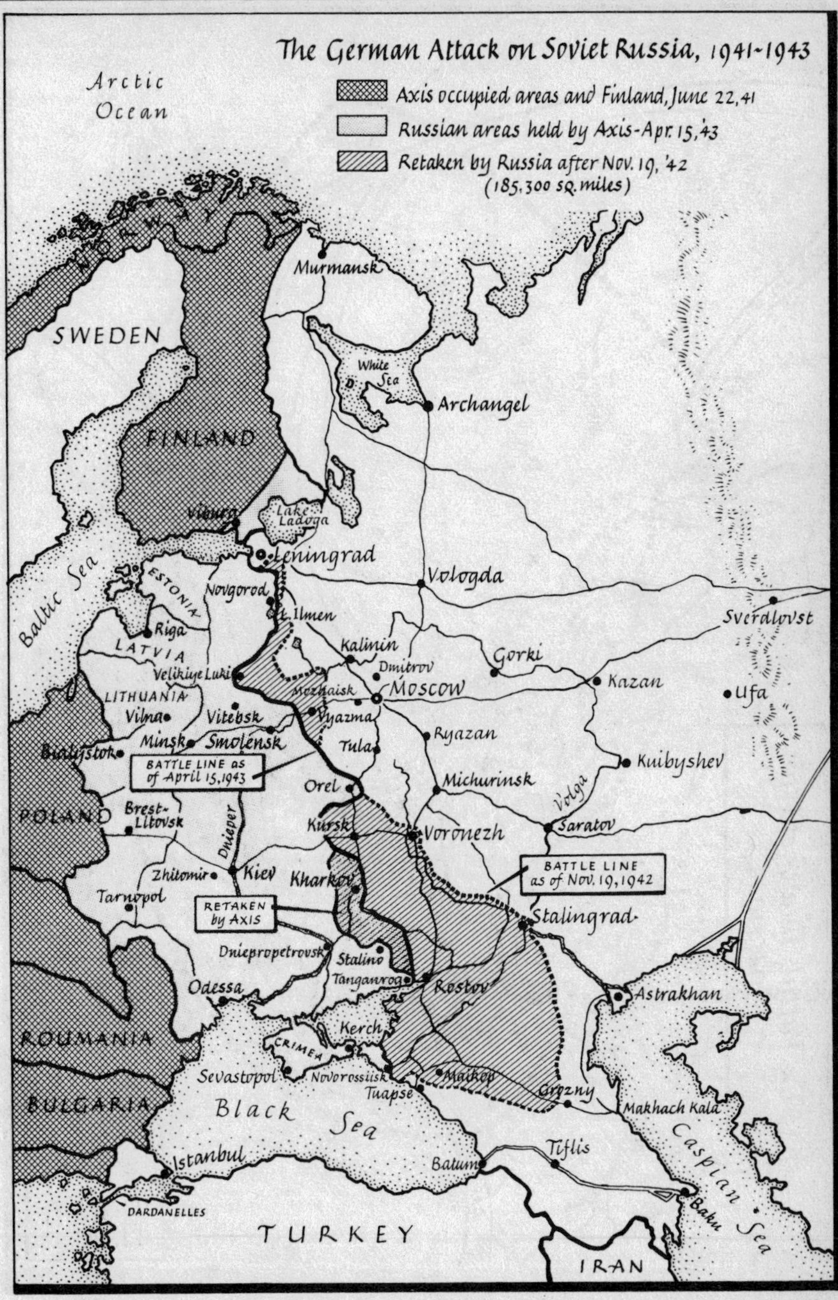

The German Attack on Soviet Russia, 1941-1943
Axis occupied areas and Finland, June 22, 41
Russian areas held by Axis-Apr. 15, '43
Retaken by Russia after Nov. 19, '42 (185,300 sq. miles)
Arctic Ocean
NORWAY
SWEDEN
FINLAND
Murmansk
White Sea
Archangel
Viborg
Lake Ladoga
Leningrad
Baltic Sea
ESTONIA
Novgorod
L. Ilmen
Vologda
Sverdlovst
Riga
LATVIA
Kalinin
Gorki
Velikiye Luki
Dmitrov
Kazan
LITHUANIA
Mozhaisk
Moscow
Ufa
Vilna
Vitebsk
Vyazma
Minsk
Smolensk
Ryazan
Bialystok
Tula
BATTLE LINE as of April 15, 1943
Kuibyshev
Orel
Michurinsk
POLAND
Brest-Litovsk
Volga
Dnieper
Kursk
Voronezh
Saratov
Zhitomir
Kiev
Kharkov
BATTLE LINE as of Nov. 19, 1942
Tarnopol
RETAKEN by AXIS
Stalingrad
Dniepropetrovsk
Stalino
Taganrog
Rostov
Astrakhan
Odessa
Kerch
CRIMEA
ROUMANIA
Sevastopol
Novorossiisk
Maikop
Tuapse
Grozny
BULGARIA
Black Sea
Makhach Kala
Caspian Sea
Istanbul
Batum
Tiflis
Baku
DARDANELLES
TURKEY
IRAN

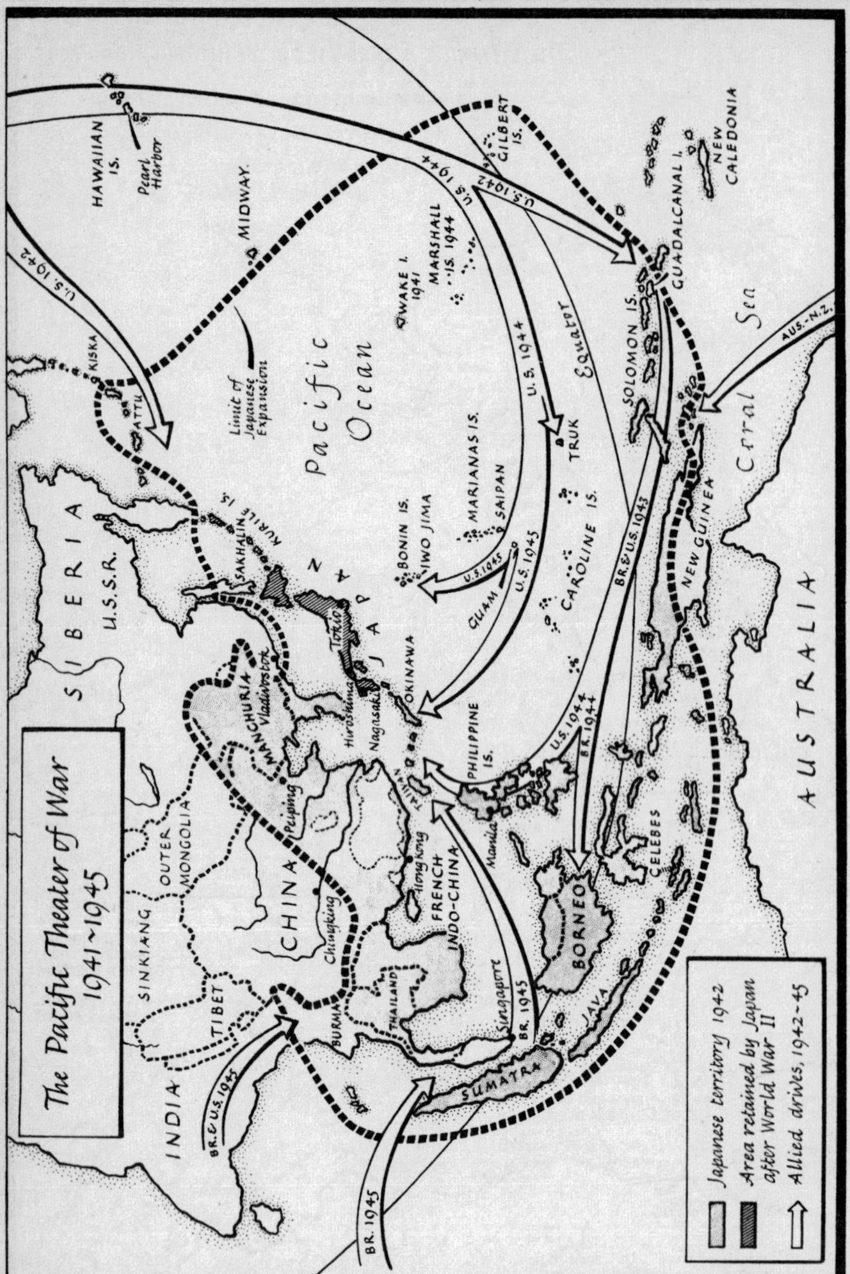
The Pacific Theater of War
1941~1945
Japanese territory 1942
Area retained by Japan after World War II
Allied drives, 1942–45
SIBERIA
U.S.S.R.
MANCHURIA
OUTER MONGOLIA
SINKIANG
TIBET
CHINA
INDIA
BURMA
THAILAND
FRENCH INDO-CHINA
JAPAN
AUSTRALIA
Pacific Ocean
Coral Sea
Equator
HAWAIIAN IS.
Pearl Harbor
MIDWAY
KISKA
ATTU
KURILE IS.
SAKHALIN
Vladivostok
Peiping
Chungking
Hong Kong
Tokio
Hiroshima
Nagasaki
OKINAWA
TAIWAN
Manila
PHILIPPINE IS.
BONIN IS.
IWO JIMA
MARIANAS IS.
SAIPAN
GUAM
TRUK
CAROLINE IS.
WAKE I. 1941
MARSHALL IS. 1944
GILBERT IS.
SOLOMON IS.
GUADALCANAL I.
NEW CALEDONIA
NEW GUINEA
CELEBES
BORNEO
JAVA
SUMATRA
Singapore
Limit of Japanese Expansion
U.S. 1942
U.S. 1944
U.S. 1945
BR. & U.S. 1943
BR. 1944
BR. 1945
BR. & U.S. 1945
AUS.-N.Z.

Chicago Mayor Cermak is fatally shot. Roosevelt inaugurated ("the only thing we have to fear is fear itself"); launches New Deal. Prohibition repealed. U.S.S.R. recognized by U.S.

1934 Chancellor Dollfuss of Austria assassinated by Nazis. Hitler becomes Führer. U.S.S.R. admitted to League of Nations. Dionne sisters, first quintuplets to survive beyond infancy, born in Canada.

1935 Saar incorporated into Germany after plebiscite. Nazis repudiate Versailles Treaty, introduce compulsory military service. Mussolini invades Ethiopia; League of Nations invokes sanctions. Roosevelt opens second phase of New Deal in U.S., calling for social security, better housing, equitable taxation, and farm assistance. Huey Long assassinated in Louisiana

1936 Germans occupy Rhineland. Italy annexes Ethiopia. Rome-Berlin Axis proclaimed (Japan to join in **1940**). Trotsky exiled to Mexico. King George V dies; succeeded by son, Edward VIII, who soon abdicated to marry American-born divorcée, and is succeeded by brother, George VI. Spanish civil war begins. (Franco's fascist forces defeat Loyalist forces by **1939,** when Madrid falls.) War between China and Japan begins, to continue through World War II. Japan and Germany sign anti-Comintern pact; joined by Italy in **1937.**

1937 Hitler repudiates war guilt clause of Versailles Treaty; continues to build German power. Italy withdraws from League of Nations. U.S. gunboat *Panay* sunk by Japanese in Yangtze River. Japan invades China, conquers most of coastal area. Amelia Earhart lost somewhere in Pacific on round-the-world flight.

1938 Hitler marches into Austria; political and geographical union of Germany and Austria proclaimed. Munich Pact—Britain, France, and Italy agree to let Germany partition Czechoslovakia. Douglas "Wrong-Way" Corrigan flies from New York to Dublin.

1939 Germany occupies Bohemia and Moravia; renounces pacts with Poland and England and concludes 10-year non-aggression pact with U.S.S.R. Russo-Finnish War begins; Finns to lose one-tenth of territory in **1940** peace treaty. World War II begins (*see* special material on "World War II"). In U.S., Roosevelt submits $1,319-million defense budget, proclaims U.S. neutrality, and declares limited emergency. Einstein writes FDR about feasibility of atomic bomb. New York World's Fair opens.

1940 Trotsky assassinated in Mexico. Estonia, Latvia, and Lithuania annexed by U.S.S.R. U.S. trades 50 destroyers for leases on British bases in Western Hemisphere. Selective Service Act signed.

Amelia Earhart (1898-1937)

WORLD WAR II (1939–1945)

Axis powers (Germany, Italy, Japan, Hungary, Romania, Bulgaria) *vs.* Allies (U.S., Britain, France, U.S.S.R., Australia, Belgium, Brazil, Canada, China, Denmark, Greece, Netherlands, New Zealand, Norway, Poland, South Africa, Yugoslavia).

1939 Germany invades Poland and annexes Danzig; Britain and France give Hitler ultimatum **(Sept. 1),** declare war **(Sept. 3)**. Disabled German pocket battleship *Admiral Graf Spee* blown up off Montevideo, Uruguay, on Hitler's orders **(Dec. 17)**. Limited activity ("Sitzkrieg") on Western Front.

1940 Nazis invade Netherlands, Belgium, and Luxembourg **(May 10)**. Chamberlain resigns as Prime Minister; Churchill takes over **(May 10)**. Germans cross French frontier **(May 12)** using air/tank/infantry "Blitzkrieg" tactics. Dunkerque evacuation—about 335,000 out of 400,000 Allied soldiers rescued from Belgium by British civilian and naval craft **(May 26–June 3)**. Italy declares war on France and Britain; invades France **(June 10)**. Germans enter Paris; city undefended **(June 14)**. France and Germany sign armistice at Compiègne **(June 22)**. Nazis bomb Coventry, England **(Nov. 14)**.

1941 Germans launch attacks in Balkans. Yugoslavia surrenders—General Mihajlovic continues guerrilla warfare; Tito leads left-wing guerrillas **(April 17)**. Nazi tanks enter Athens; remnants of British Army quit Greece **(April 27)**. Hitler attacks Russia **(June 22)**. Atlantic Charter—FDR and Churchill agree on war aims **(Aug. 14)**. Japanese attacks on Pearl Harbor, Philippines, Guam force U.S. into war; U.S. Pacific fleet crippled **(Dec. 7)**. U.S. and Britain declare war on Japan. Germany and Italy declare war on U.S.; Congress declares war on those countries **(Dec. 11)**.

1942 British surrender Singapore to Japanese **(Feb. 15)**. U.S. forces on Bataan peninsula in Philippines surrender **(April 9)**. U.S. and Filipino troops on Corregidor island in Manila Bay surrender to Japanese **(May 6)**. Village of Lidice in Czechoslovakia razed by Nazis **(June 10)**. U.S. and Britain land in French North Africa **(Nov. 8)**.

1943 Casablanca Conference—Churchill and FDR agree on unconditional surrender goal **(Jan. 14–24)**. German 6th Army surrenders at Stalingrad—turning point of war in Russia **(Feb. 1–2)**. Remnants of Nazis trapped on Cape Bon, ending war in Africa **(May 12)**. Mussolini deposed; Badoglio named premier **(July 25)**. Allied troops land on Italian mainland after conquest of Sicily **(Sept. 3)**. Italy surrenders **(Sept. 8)**. Nazis seize Rome **(Sept. 10)**. Cairo Conference: FDR, Churchill, Chiang Kai-shek pledge defeat of Japan, free Korea **(Nov. 22–26)**. Teheran Conference: FDR, Churchill, Stalin agree on invasion plans **(Nov. 28–Dec. 1)**.

1944 U.S. and British troops land at Anzio on west Italian coast and hold beachhead **(Jan. 22)**. U.S. and British troops enter Rome **(June 4)**. D-Day—Allies launch Normandy invasion **(June 6)**. Hitler wounded in bomb plot **(July 20)**. Paris liberated **(Aug. 25)**. Athens freed by Allies **(Oct. 13)**. Americans invade Philippines **(Oct. 20)**. Germans launch counteroffensive in Belgium—Battle of Bulge **(Dec. 16)**.

1945 Yalta Agreement signed by FDR, Churchill, Stalin—establishes basis for occupation of Germany, returns to Soviet Union lands taken by Germany and Japan; U.S.S.R. agrees to friendship pact with China **(Feb. 11)**. Mussolini killed at Lake Como **(April 28)**. Admiral Doenitz takes command in Germany; suicide of Hitler announced **(May 1)**. Berlin falls **(May 2)**. V-E Day—Germany signs unconditional surrender terms at Rheims **(May 7)**. Potsdam Conference—Truman, Churchill, Atlee (after **July 28**), Stalin establish council of foreign ministers to prepare peace treaties; plan German postwar government and reparations **(July 17–Aug. 2)**. A-bomb blasts Hiroshima **(Aug. 6)**. U.S.S.R. declares war on Japan **(Aug. 8)**. Nagasaki hit by A-bomb **(Aug. 9)**. Japan surrenders **(Aug. 14)**. V-J Day—Japanese sign surrender terms aboard battleship *Missouri* **(Sept. 2)**.

D-Day, June 6, 1944

Winston Churchill, Franklin D. Roosevelt, and Joseph V. Stalin at Yalta

Harry S. Truman (1884-1972)

1941 Japanese surprise attack on U.S. fleet at Pearl Harbor brings U.S. into World War II. Manhattan Project (atomic bomb research) begins. Roosevelt enunciates "four freedoms," signs lend-lease act, declares national emergency, promises aid to U.S.S.R.

1942 Declaration of United Nations signed in Washington. Women's military services established. Enrico Fermi achieves nuclear chain reaction. Japanese and persons of Japanese ancestry moved inland from Pacific Coast. Coconut Grove nightclub fire in Boston kills 491.

1943 President freezes prices, salaries, and wages to prevent inflation. Income tax withholding introduced.

1944 G.I. Bill of Rights enacted. Bretton Woods Conference creates International Monetary Fund and World Bank. Dumbarton Oaks Conference—U.S., British Commonwealth, and U.S.S.R. propose establishment of United Nations.

1945 Yalta Conference (Roosevelt, Churchill, Stalin) plans final defeat of Germany **(Feb.)**. Germany surrenders **(May 7)**. San Francisco Conference establishes U.N. **(April–June)**. FDR dies (April 12). Potsdam Conference (Truman, Churchill, Stalin) establishes basis of German reconstruction **(July–Aug)**. Japan signs surrender **(Sept. 2)**.

1946 First meeting of U.N. General Assembly opens in London **(Jan. 10)**. League of Nations dissolved **(April)**. Italy abolishes monarchy **(June)**. Verdict in Nuremberg war trial: 12 Nazi leaders (including 1 tried in absentia) sentenced to hang; 7 imprisoned; 3 acquitted **(Oct. 1)**. Goering commits suicide a few hours before 10 other Nazis are executed **(Oct. 15)**. Winston Churchill's "Iron Curtain" speech warns of Soviet expansion.

1947 Britain nationalizes coal mines **(Jan. 1)**. Peace treaties for Italy, Romania, Bulgaria, Hungary, Finland signed in Paris **(Feb. 10)**. Soviet Union rejects U.S. plan for U.N. atomic-energy control **(March 4)**. Truman Doctrine proposed—the first significant U.S. attempt to "contain" communist expansion **(March 12)**. Marshall Plan for European recovery proposed—a coordinated program to help European nations recover from ravages of war **(June)**. (By **1951**, this "European Recovery Program" had cost $11 billion.) India and Pakistan gain independence from Britain **(Aug. 15)**. Cominform (Communist Information Bureau) founded under Soviet auspices to rebuild contacts among European Communist parties, missing since dissolution of Comintern in **1943 (Sept.)**. (Yugoslav party expelled in **1948** and Cominform disbanded in **1956.**)

1948 Gandhi assassinated in New Delhi by Hindu fanatic **(Jan. 30)**. Communists seize power in Czechoslovakia **(Feb. 23–25)**. Burma and Ceylon granted independence by Britain. Organization of American States (OAS) Charter signed at Bogotá, Colombia **(April 30)**. Nation of Israel proclaimed; British end Mandate at midnight; Arab armies attack **(May 14)**. Berlin airlift begins **(June 21)**; ends **May 12, 1949.** Stalin and Tito break **(June 28)**. Independent Republic of Korea is proclaimed, following election supervised by U.N. **(Aug. 15)**. Verdict in Japanese war trial: Tojo and six others sentenced to hang (hanged Dec. 23); 18 imprisoned **(Nov. 12)**. United States of Indonesia established as Dutch and Indonesians settled conflict **(Dec. 27)**. Alger Hiss, former U.S. State Department official, indicted on perjury charges after denying passing secret documents to communist spy ring. Convicted in second trial **(1950)** and sentenced to five-year prison term.

1949 Cease-fire in Palestine **(Jan. 7)**. Truman proposes Point Four Program to help world's backward areas **(Jan. 20)**. Israel signs armistice with Egypt **(Feb. 24)**. Start of North Atlantic Treaty Organization (NATO)—treaty signed by 12 nations **(April 4)**. German Federal Republic (West Germany) established **(Sept. 21)**. Truman discloses Soviet Union has set off atomic explosion **(Sept. 23)**. Communist People's Republic of China formally proclaimed by Chairman Mao Zedong. **(Oct. 1)**.

1950 Truman orders development of hydrogen bomb **(Jan. 31)**. Korean War (*see* special material on the "Korean War"). Assassination attempt on President Truman by Puerto Rican nationalists **(Nov. 1)**. Brink's robbery in Boston; almost $3 million stolen **(Jan. 17)**.

KOREAN WAR (1950–1953)

1950 North Korean Communist forces invade South Korea (June 25). U.N. calls for cease-fire and asks U.N. members to assist South Korea (June 27). Truman orders U.S. forces into Korea (June 27). North Koreans capture Seoul (June 28). Gen. Douglas MacArthur designated commander of unified U.N. forces (July 8). Pusan Beachhead—U.N. forces counterattack and capture Seoul (Aug.–Sept.), capture Pyongyang, North Korean capital **(Oct.)**. Chinese Communists enter war **(Oct. 26)**, force U.N. retreat toward 39th parallel **(Dec.)**.

1951 Gen. Matthew B. Ridgeway replaces MacArthur after he threatens Chinese with massive retaliation **(April 11)**. Armistice negotiations **(July)** continue with interruptions until **June 1953**.

1953 Armistice signed **(June 26)**. Chinese troops withdraw from North Korea **(Oct. 26, 1958)**, but over 200 violations of armistice noted to **1959**.

1951 Six nations agree to Schuman Plan to pool European coal and steel **(March 19)**—in effect **Feb. 10, 1953.** Julius and Ethel Rosenberg sentenced to death for passing atomic secrets to Russians **(March).** Japanese peace treaty signed in San Francisco by 49 nations **(Sept. 8).** Color television introduced in U.S.

1952 George VI dies; his daughter becomes Elizabeth II **(Feb. 6).** NATO conference approves European army **(Feb.).** AEC announces "satisfactory" experiments in hydrogen-weapons research; eyewitnesses tell of blasts near Enewetak **(Nov.).**

1953 Gen. Dwight D. Eisenhower inaugurated President of United States **(Jan. 20).** Stalin dies **(March 5).** Malenkov becomes Soviet Premier; Beria, Minister of Interior; Molotov, Foreign Minister **(March 6).** Dag Hammarskjold begins term as U.N. Secretary-General **(April 10).** Edmund Hillary, of New Zealand, and Tenzing Norkay, of Nepal, reach top of Mt. Everest **(May 29).** East Berliners rise against Communist rule; quelled by tanks **(June 17).** Egypt becomes republic ruled by military junta **(June 18).** Julius and Ethel Rosenberg executed in Sing Sing prison **(June 19).** Korean armistice signed **(July 27).** Moscow announces explosion of hydrogen bomb **(Aug. 20).**

1954 First atomic submarine *Nautilus,* launched **(Jan. 21).** Five U.S. Congressmen shot on floor of House as Puerto Rican nationalists fire from spectators' gallery; all five recover **(March 1).** Army *vs.* McCarthy inquiry—Senate subcommittee report blames both sides **(Apr. 22–June 17).** Dien Bien Phu, French military outpost in Vietnam, falls to Vietminh army **(May 7).** (*see* special material on the "Vietnam War.") U.S. Supreme Court (in *Brown* v. *Board of Education of Topeka*) unanimously bans racial segregation in public schools **(May 17).** Eisenhower launches world atomic pool without Soviet Union **(Sept. 6).** Eight-nation Southeast Asia defense treaty (SEATO) signed at Manila **(Sept. 8).** West Germany is granted sovereignty, admitted to NATO and Western European Union **(Oct. 23).** Dr. Jonas Salk starts innoculating children against polio. Algerian War of Independence against France begins **(Nov.);** France struggles to maintain colonial rule until 1962 when it agrees to Algeria's independence.

1955 Nikolai A. Bulganin becomes Soviet Premier, replacing Malenkov **(Feb. 8).** Churchill resigns; Anthony Eden succeeds him **(April 6).** Federal Republic of West Germany becomes a sovereign state **(May 5).** Warsaw Pact,

Dwight D. Eisenhower (1890-1969)

Joseph Stalin (1879-1953)

VIETNAM WAR (1950–1975)

U.S., South Vietnam, and Allies versus North Vietnam and National Liberation Front (Viet Cong). Outstanding events:

1950 President Truman sends 35-man military advisory group to aid French fighting to maintain colonial power in Vietnam.

1954 After defeat of French at Dienbienphu, Geneva Agreements **(July)** provide for withdrawal of French and Vietminh to either side of demarcation zone (DMZ) pending reunification elections, which are never held. Presidents Eisenhower and Kennedy (from **1954** onward) send civilian advisors and, later, military personnel to train South Vietnamese.

1960 Communists from National Liberation Front in South.

1963 Ngo Dinh Diem, South Vietnam's premier, slain in coup **(Nov. 1).**

1961–1963 U.S. military advisors rise from 2,000 to 15,000.

1964 North Vietnamese torpedo boats reportedly attack U.S. destroyers in Gulf of Tonkin **(Aug. 2).** President Johnson orders retaliatory air strikes. Congress approves Gulf of Tonkin resolution **(Aug. 7)** authorizing President to take necessary steps to "maintain peace."

1965 U.S. planes begin combat missions over South Vietnam. In **June,** 23,000 American advisors committed to combat. By end of year over 184,000 U.S. troops in area.

1966 B-52s bomb DMZ, reportedly used by North Vietnam for entry into South **(July 31).**

1967 South Vietnam National Assembly approves election of Nguyen Van Thieu as President **(Oct. 21).**

1968 U.S. has almost 525,000 men in Vietnam. In Tet offensive **(Jan.–Feb.),** Viet Cong guerrillas attack Saigon, Hue, and some provincial capitals. President Johnson orders halt to U.S. bombardment of North Vietnam **(Oct. 31).** Saigon and N.L.F. join U.S. and North Vietnam in Paris peace talks.

1969 President Nixon announces Vietnam peace offer **(May 14)**—begins troop withdrawals **(June).** Viet Cong forms Provisional Revolutionary Government. U.S. Senate calls for curb on commitments **(June 25).** Ho Chi Minh, 79, North Vietnam president, dies **(Sept. 3);** collective leadership chosen. Some 6,000 U.S. troops pulled back from Thailand and 1,000 marines from Vietnam (announced **Sept. 30**). Massive demonstrations in U.S. protest or support war policies **(Oct. 15).**

1970 Nixon announces sending of troops to Cambodia **(April 30).** Last U.S. troops removed from Cambodia **(June 29).**

1971 Congress bars use of combat troops, but not air power, in Laos and Cambodia **(Jan. 1).** South Vietnamese troops, with U.S. air cover, fail in Laos thrust. Many American ground forces withdrawn from Vietnam combat. *New York Times* publishes Pentagon papers, classified material on expansion of war **(June).**

1972 Nixon responds to North Vietnamese drive across DMZ by ordering mining of North Vietnam ports and heavy bombing of Hanoi-Haiphong area **(April 1).** Nixon orders "Christmas bombing" of north to get North Vietnamese back to conference table **(Dec.).**

1973 President orders halt to offensive operations in North Vietnam **(Jan. 15).** Representatives of North and South Vietnam, U.S., and N.L.F. sign peace pacts in Paris, ending longest war in U.S. history **(Jan. 27).** Last American troops departed in their entirety **(March 29).**

1974 Both sides accuse each other of frequent violations of cease-fire agreement.

1975 Full-scale warfare resumes. Communists victorious **(April 30).** South Vietnam Premier Nguyen Van Thieu resigns **(April 21).** U.S. Marine Embassy guards and U.S. civilians and dependents evacuated **(April 30).** More than 140,000 Vietnamese refugees leave by air and sea, many to settle in U.S. Provisional Revolutionary Government takes control **(June 6).**

1976 Election of National Assembly paves way for reunification of North and South.

Yuri A. Gagarin
(1934-1968)

Fidel Castro
(Aug. 13, 1926)

east European mutual defense agreement, signed **(May 14).** Argentina ousts Perón **(Sept. 19).** President Eisenhower suffers coronary thrombosis in Denver **(Sept. 24).** Martin Luther King, Jr., leads black boycott of Montgomery, Ala., bus system **(Dec. 1)**; desegregated service begun **(Dec. 21).** AFL and CIO become one organization—AFL-CIO **(Dec. 5).**

1956 Nikita Khrushchev, First Secretary of U.S.S.R. Communist Party, denounces Stalin's excesses **(Feb. 24).** First aerial H-bomb tested over Namu islet, Bikini Atoll—10 million tons TNT equivalent **(May 21).** Worker's uprising against Communist rule in Poznan, Poland, is crushed **(June 28–30).** Egypt takes control of Suez Canal **(July 26).** Israel launches attack on Egypt's Sinai peninsula and drives toward Suez Canal **(Oct. 29).** British and French invade Egypt at Port Said **(Nov. 5).** Cease-fire forced by U.S. pressure stops British, French, and Israeli advance **(Nov. 6).** Revolt starts in Hungary—Soviet troops and tanks crush anti-Communist rebellion **(Nov.).**

1957 Eisenhower Doctrine calls for aid to Mideast countries which resist armed aggression from Communist-controlled nations **(Jan. 5).** Eisenhower sends troops to Little Rock, Ark., to quell mob and protect school integration **(Sept. 24).** Russians launch *Sputnik I,* first earth-orbiting satellite—the Space Age begins **(Oct. 4).**

1958 Army's Jupiter-C rocket fires first U.S. earth satellite, *Explorer I,* into orbit **(Jan. 31).** Egypt and Syria merge into United Arab Republic **(Feb. 1).** European Economic Community (Common Market) established by Rome Treaty becomes effective **Jan. 1, 1958.** Khrushchev becomes Premier of Soviet Union as Bulganin resigns **(Mar. 27).** Gen. Charles de Gaulle becomes French premier **(June 1),** remaining in power until **1969.** New French constitution adopted **(Sept. 28),** de Gaulle elected president of 5th Republic **(Dec. 21).** Eisenhower orders U.S. Marines into Lebanon at request of President Chamoun, who fears overthrow **(July 15).**

1959 Cuban President Batista resigns and flees—Castro takes over **(Jan. 1).** Tibet's Dalai Lama escapes to India **(Mar. 31).** St. Lawrence Seaway opens, allowing ocean ships to reach Midwest **(April 25).**

1960 American U-2 spy plane, piloted by Francis Gary Powers, shot down over Russia **(May 1).** Khrushchev kills Paris summit conference because of U-2 **(May 16).** Powers sentenced to prison for 10 years **(Aug. 19)**—freed in **February 1962** in exchange for Soviet spy. Top Nazi murderer of Jews, Adolf Eichmann, captured by Israelis in Argentina **(May 23)**—executed in Israel in **1962.** Communist China and Soviet Union split in conflict over Communist ideology. Belgium starts to break up its African colonial empire, gives independence to Belgian Congo (Zaire) on **June 30.** Cuba begins confiscation of $770 million of U.S. property **(Aug. 7).**

1961 U.S. breaks diplomatic relations with Cuba **(Jan. 3).** John F. Kennedy inaugurated President of U.S. **(Jan. 20).** Kennedy proposes Alliance for Progress—10-year plan to raise Latin American living standards **(Mar. 13).** Moscow announces putting first man in orbit around earth, Maj. Yuri A. Gagarin **(April 12).** Cuba invaded at Bay of Pigs by an estimated 1,200 anti-Castro exiles aided by U.S.; invasion crushed **(April 17).** First U.S. spaceman, Navy Cmdr. Alan B. Shepard, Jr., rockets 116.5 miles up in 302-mile trip **(May 5).** Virgil Grissom becomes second American astronaut, making 118-mile-high, 303-mile-long rocket flight over Atlantic **(July 21).** Gherman Stepanovich Titov is launched in Soviet spaceship *Vostok II:* makes 17 1/2 orbits in 25 hours, covering 434,960 miles before landing safely **(Aug. 6).** East Germans erect Berlin Wall between East and West Berlin to halt flood of refugees **(Aug. 13).** U.S.S.R. fires 50-megaton hydrogen bomb, biggest explosion in history **(Oct. 29).**

1962 Lt. Col. John H. Glenn, Jr., is first American to orbit earth—three times in 4 hr 55 min **(Feb. 20).** Adolf Eichmann hanged in Israel for his part in Nazi extermination of six million Jews **(May 31).** France transfers sovereignty to new republic of Algeria **(July 3).** Cuban missile crisis—U.S.S.R. to build missile bases in Cuba; Kennedy orders Cuban blockade, lifts blockade after Russians back down **(Aug.-Nov.).** James H. Meredith, escorted by Federal marshals, registers in University of Mississippi **(Oct. 1).** Pope John XXIII opens Second Vatican Council (Oct. 11)—Council holds four sessions, finally closing Dec. 8, 1965. Cuba releases 1,113 prisoners of 1961 invasion attempt **(Dec. 24).**

1963 France and West Germany sign treaty of cooperation ending four centuries of conflict **(Jan. 22).** Pope John XXIII dies **(June 3)**—succeeded June 21 by Cardinal Montini, who becomes Paul VI. U.S. Supreme Court rules no locality may require recitation of Lord's Prayer or Bible verses in public schools **(June 17).** Civil rights rally held by 200,000 blacks and whites in Washington, D.C. **(Aug. 28).** Washington-to-Moscow "hot line" communications link opens, designed to reduce risk of accidental war **(Aug. 30).** President Kennedy shot and killed by sniper in Dallas, Tex. Lyndon B.

Johnson becomes President same day **(Nov. 22).** Lee Harvey Oswald, accused assassin of President Kennedy, is shot and killed by Jack Ruby, Dallas nightclub owner **(Nov. 24).**

1964 U.S. Supreme Court rules that Congressional districts should be roughly equal in population **(Feb. 17).** Jack Ruby convicted of murder in slaying of Lee Harvey Oswald; sentenced to death by Dallas jury **(March 14)**—conviction reversed **Oct. 5, 1966;** Ruby dies **Jan. 3, 1967,** before second trial can be held. Three civil rights workers—Schwerner, Goodman, and Cheney—murdered in Mississippi **(June).** Twenty-one arrests result in trial and conviction of seven by Federal jury. President's Commission on the Assassination of President Kennedy issues Warren Report concluding that Lee Harvey Oswald acted alone.

John F. Kennedy (1917-1963)

1965 Rev. Dr. Martin Luther King, Jr., and more than 2,600 other blacks arrested in Selma, Ala., during three-day demonstrations against voter-registration rules **(Feb. 1).** Malcolm X, black-nationalist leader, shot to death at Harlem rally in New York City **(Feb. 21).** U.S. Marines land in Dominican Republic as fighting persists between rebels and Dominican army **(April 28).** Medicare, senior citizens' government medical assistance program, begins **(July 1).** Blacks riot for six days in Watts section of Los Angeles: 34 dead, over 1,000 injured, nearly 4,000 arrested, fire damage put at $175 million **(Aug. 11-16).** Power failure in Ontario plant blacks out parts of eight northeastern states of U.S. and two provinces of southeastern Canada **(Nov. 9).**

1966 Black teen-agers riot in Watts, Los Angeles; two men killed and at least 25 injured **(March 15).** Michael E. De Bakey implants artificial heart in human for first time at Houston hospital; plastic device functions and patient lives **(April 21).**

1967 Three Apollo astronauts—Col. Virgil I. Grissom, Col. Edward White II, and Lt. Cmdr. Roger B. Chaffee—killed in spacecraft fire during simulated launch **(Jan. 27).** Israeli and Arab forces battle; six-day war ends with Israel occupying Sinai Peninsula, Golan Heights, Gaza Strip, and east bank of Suez Canal **(June 5).** Red China announces explosion of its first hydrogen bomb **(June 17).** Racial violence in Detroit; 7,000 National Guardsmen aid police after night of rioting. Similar outbreaks occur in New York City's Spanish Harlem, Rochester, N.Y., Birmingham, Ala., and New Britain, Conn. **(July 23).** Thurgood Marshall sworn in as first black U.S. Supreme Court justice **(Oct. 2).** Dr. Christiaan N. Barnard and team of South African surgeons perform world's first successful human heart transplant **(Dec. 3)**—patient dies 18 days later.

Lyndon B. Johnson (1908-1973)

1968 North Korea seizes U.S. Navy ship *Pueblo;* holds 83 on board as spies **(Jan. 23).** President Johnson announces he will not seek or accept presidential renomination **(March 31).** Martin Luther King, Jr., civil rights leader, is slain in Memphis **(April 4)**—James Earl Ray, indicted in murder, captured in London on **June 8.** In **1969** Ray pleads guilty and is sentenced to 99 years. Sen. Robert F. Kennedy is shot and critically wounded in Los Angeles hotel after winning California primary **(June 5)**—dies **June 6.** Sirhan B. Sirhan convicted **1969.** Czechoslovakia is invaded by Russians and Warsaw Pact forces to crush liberal regime **(Aug. 20).**

1969 Richard M. Nixon is inaugurated 37th President of the U.S. **(Jan. 20).** Apollo 11 astronauts—Neil A. Armstrong, Edwin E. Aldrin, Jr., and Michael Collins—take man's first walk on moon **(July 20).** Sen. Edward M. Kennedy pleads guilty to leaving scene of fatal accident at Chappaquiddick, Mass. **(July 18)** in which Mary Jo Kopechne was drowned—gets two-month suspended sentence **(July 25).**

Martin Luther King, Jr. (1929-1968)

1970 Biafra surrenders after 32-month fight for independence from Nigeria **(Jan. 12).** Rhodesia severs last tie with British Crown and declares itself a racially segregated republic **(March 1).** Four students at Kent State University in Ohio slain by National Guardsmen at demonstration protesting April 30 incursion into Cambodia **(May 4).** Senate repeals Gulf of Tonkin resolution **(June 24).**

1971 Supreme Court rules unanimously that busing of students may be ordered to achieve racial desegregation **(April 20).** Anti-war militants attempt to disrupt government business in Washington **(May 3)**—police and military units arrest as many as 12,000; most are later released. Twenty-sixth Amendment to U.S. Constitution lowers voting age to 18. U.N. seats Communist China and expels Nationalist China **(Oct. 25).**

1972 President Nixon makes unprecedented eight-day visit to Communist China **(Feb.).** Britain takes over direct rule of Northern Ireland in bid for peace **(March 24).** Gov. George C. Wallace of Alabama is shot by Arthur H. Bremer at Laurel, Md., political rally **(May 15).** Five men are apprehended by police in attempt to bug Democratic National Committee headquarters in Washington D.C.'s Watergate complex—start of the Watergate scandal **(June 17).** Supreme Court rules that death penalty is unconstitutional

Richard M. Nixon
(Jan. 9, 1913)

(June 29). Eleven Israeli athletes at Olympic Games in Munich are killed after eight members of an Arab terrorist group invade Olympic Village; five guerrillas and one policeman are also killed (Sept. 5).

1973 Great Britain, Ireland, and Denmark enter European Common Market (Jan. 1). Nixon, on national TV, accepts responsibility, but not blame, for Watergate; accepts resignations of advisers H. R. Haldeman and John D. Ehrlichman, fires John W. Dean III as counsel. (April 30). Greek military junta abolishes monarchy and proclaims republic (June 1). U.S. bombing of Cambodia ends, marking official halt to 12 years of combat activity in Southeast Asia (Aug. 15). Fourth and biggest Arab-Israeli War begins as Egyptian and Syrian forces attack Israel as Jews mark Yom Kippur, holiest day in their calendar. (Oct. 6). Spiro T. Agnew resigns as Vice President and then, in Federal Court in Baltimore, pleads no contest to charges of evasion of income taxes on $29,500 he received in 1967, while Governor of Maryland. He is fined $10,000 and put on three years' probation (Oct. 10). In the "Saturday Night Massacre," Nixon fires special Watergate prosecutor Archibald Cox and Deputy Attorney General William D. Ruckelshaus; Attorney General Elliot L. Richardson resigns (Oct. 20). Egypt and Israel sign U.S.-sponsored cease-fire accord (Nov. 11).

1974 Patricia Hearst, 19-year-old daughter of publisher Randolph Hearst, kidnapped by Symbionese Liberation Army. (Feb. 5). House Judiciary Committee adopts three articles of impeachment charging President Nixon with obstruction of justice, failure to uphold laws, and refusal to produce material subpoenaed by the committee (July 30). Richard M. Nixon announces he will resign the next day, the first President to do so (Aug. 8). Vice President Gerald R. Ford of Michigan is sworn in as 38th President of the U.S. (Aug. 9). Ford grants "full, free, and absolute pardon" to ex-President Nixon (Sept. 8).

1975 John N. Mitchell, H. R. Haldeman, John D. Ehrlichman, and Robert C. Mardian found guilty of Watergate cover-up. Mitchell, Haldeman, and Ehrlichman are sentenced on Feb. 21 to 30 months-8 years in jail and Mardian to 10 months-3 years (Jan. 1). American merchant ship *Mayaguez,* seized by Cambodian forces, is rescued in operation by U.S. Navy and Marines, 38 of whom are killed (May 15). *Apollo* and *Soyuz* spacecraft take off for U.S.-Soviet link-up in space (July 15). President Ford escapes assassination attempt in Sacramento, Calif., (Sept. 5). President Ford escapes second assassination attempt in 17 days. (Sept. 22).

Viking I and II
(Launched 1975)

1976 Supreme Court rules that blacks and other minorities are entitled to retroactive job seniority (March 24). Ford signs Federal Election Campaign Act (May 11). Supreme Court rules that death penalty is not inherently cruel or unusual and is a constitutionally acceptable form of punishment (July 3). Nation celebrates Bicentennial (July 4). Israeli airborne commandos attack Uganda's Entebbe Airport and free 103 hostages held by pro-Palestinian hijackers of Air France plane; one Israeli and several Ugandan soldiers killed in raid (July 4). Mysterious disease that eventually claims 29 lives strikes American Legion convention in Philadelphia (Aug. 4). Jimmy Carter elected U.S. President (Nov. 2).

1977 First woman Episcopal priest ordained (Jan. 1). Scientists identify previously unknown bacterium as cause of mysterious "legionnaire's disease" (Jan. 18). Carter pardons Vietnam draft evaders (Jan. 21). Scientists report using bacteria in lab to make insulin (May 23). Supreme Court rules that states are not required to spend Medicaid funds on elective abortions (June 20). Deng Xiaoping, purged Chinese leader, restored to power as "Gang of Four" is expelled from Communist Party (July 22). Nuclear–proliferation pact, curbing spread of nuclear weapons, signed by 15 countries, including U.S. and U.S.S.R. (Sept. 21).

Voyager I and II
(Launched 1977)

1978 President chooses Federal Appeals Court Judge William H. Webster as F.B.I. Director (Jan. 19). Rhodesia's Prime Minister Ian D. Smith and three black leaders agree on transfer to black majority rule (Feb. 15). Former Italian Premier Aldo Moro kidnapped by leftwing terrorists, who kill five bodyguards (March 16); he is found slain (May 9). U.S. Senate approves Panama Canal neutrality treaty (March 16); votes treaty to turn canal over to Panama by year 2000 (April 18). Californians in referendum approve Proposition 13 for nearly 60% slash in property tax revenues (June 6). Supreme Court, in Bakke case, bars quota systems in college admissions but affirms constitutionality of programs giving advantage to minorities (June 28). Pope Paul VI, dead at 80, mourned (Aug. 6); new Pope, John Paul I, 65, dies unexpectedly after 34 days in office (Sept. 28); succeeded by Karol Cardinal Wojtyla of Poland as John Paul II (Oct. 16). "Framework for Peace" in Middle East signed by Egypt's President Anwar el-Sadat and Israel Premier Menachem Begin after 13-day conference at Camp David led by President Carter (Sept. 17).

1979 Oil spills pollute ocean waters in Atlantic and Gulf of Mexico (Jan. 1,

June 8, July 21). Ohio agrees to pay $675,000 to families of dead and injured in Kent State University shootings **(Jan. 4).** Vietnam and Cambodian insurgents it backs announce fall of Phnom Penh, Cambodian capital, and collapse of Pol Pot regime **(Jan. 7).** Shah leaves Iran after year of turmoil **(Jan. 16);** revolutionary forces under Moslem leader, Ayatollah Ruhollah Khomeini, take over **(Feb. 1** et seq.). Conservatives win British election; Margaret Thatcher new Prime Minister **(March 28).** Nuclear power plant accident at Three Mile Island, Pa:, releases radioactivity **(March 28).** Carter and Brezhnev sign SALT II agreement **(June 14).** Nicaraguan President Gen. Anastasio Somoza Debayle resigns and flees to Miami **(July 17);** Sandinistas form government **(July 19).** Earl Mountbatten of Burma, 79, British World War II hero, and three others killed by blast on fishing boat off Irish coast **(Aug. 27);** two I.R.A. members accused **(Aug. 30).** Iranian militants seize U.S. Embassy in Teheran and hold hostages **(Nov. 4).** Soviet invasion of Afghanistan stirs world protests **(Dec. 27).**

Margaret Thatcher
(Oct. 13, 1925)

1980 Six U.S. Embassy aides escape from Iran with Canadian help **(Jan. 29).** F.B.I.'s undercover operation "Abscam" (for Arab scam) implicates public officials **(Feb. 2).** U.S. breaks diplomatic ties with Iran **(April 7).** Eight U.S. servicemen are killed and five are injured as helicopter and cargo plane collide in abortive desert raid to rescue American hostages in Teheran **(April 25).** Supreme Court upholds limits on Federal aid for abortions **(June 30).** Shah of Iran dies at 60 **(July 27).** Anastasio Somoza Debayle, ousted Nicaragua ruler, and two aides assassinated in Asunción, Paraguay capital **(Sept. 17).** Iraq troops hold 90 square miles of Iran after invasion **(Sept. 19).** Ronald Reagan elected President in Republican sweep **(Nov. 4).** Three U.S. nuns and lay worker found shot in El Salvador **(Dec. 4).** John Lennon of Beatles shot dead in New York City **(Dec. 8).**

Sally K. Ride
(May 26, 1951)

1981 U.S.-Iran agreement frees 52 hostages held in Teheran since Nov. 4, 1979 **(Jan. 18);** hostages welcomed back in U.S. **(Jan. 25).** Ronald Reagan takes oath as 40th President **(Jan. 20).** President Reagan wounded by gunman, with press secretary and two law-enforcement officers **(March 30).** Pope John Paul II wounded by gunman **(May 14).** Supreme Court rules, 4-4, that former President Nixon and three top aides may be required to pay monetary damages for unconstitutional wiretap of home telephone of former national security aide **(June 22).** Reagan nominates Judge Sandra Day O'Connor, 51, of Arizona, as first woman on Supreme Court **(July 7).** More than 110 die in collapse of aerial walkways in lobby of Hyatt Regency Hotel in Kansas City; 188 injured **(July 18).** Air controllers strike, disrupting flights **(Aug. 3);** Government dismisses strikers **(Aug. 11).**

1982 British overcome Argentina in Falklands war **(April 2-June 15).** Israel invades Lebanon in attack on P.L.O. **(June 4).** John W. Hinckley, Jr. found not guilty because of insanity in shooting of President Reagan **(June 21).** Alexander M. Haig, Jr. resigns as Secretary of State **(June 25).** Equal rights amendment fails ratification **(June 30).** Lebanese Christian Phalangists kill hundreds of people in two Palestinian refugee camps in West Beirut **(Sept. 15).** Princess Grace, 52, dies of injuries when car plunges off mountain road; daughter, Stephanie, 17, suffers serious injuries **(Sept. 14).** Leonid I. Brezhnev, Soviet leader, dies at 75 **(Nov. 10).** Yuri V. Andropov, 68, chosen as successor **(Nov. 15).** Artificial heart implanted for first time in Dr. Barney B. Clark, 61, at University of Utah Medical Center in Salt Lake City **(Dec. 2);** Barney Clark dies **(March 23, 1983).**

1983 Pope John Paul II signs new Roman Catholic code incorporating changes brought about by Second Vatican Council **(Jan. 25).** Second space shuttle, *Challenger,* makes successful maiden voyage, which includes the first U.S. space walk in nine years **(April 4).** U.S. Supreme Court declares many local abortion restrictions unconstitutional **(June 15).** Sally K. Ride, 32, first U.S. woman astronaut in space as a crew member aboard space shuttle *Challenger* **(June 18).** U.S. admits shielding former Nazi Gestapo chief, Klaus Barbie, 69, the "butcher of Lyons," wanted in France for war crimes **(Aug. 15).** Benigno S. Aquino, Jr., 50, political rival of Philippines President Marcos, slain in Manila **(Aug. 21).** South Korean Boeing 747 jetliner bound for Seoul apparently strays into Soviet airspace and is shot down by a Soviet SU-15 fighter after it had tracked the airliner for two hours; all 269 aboard are killed, including 61 Americans **(Aug. 30).** Terrorist explosion kills 237 U.S. Marines in Beirut **(Oct. 23).** U.S. and Caribbean allies invade Grenada **(Oct. 25).**

Space Shuttle Columbia
(Launched April 12, 1981)

1984 Bell System broken up **(Jan. 1).** France gets first deliveries of Soviet natural gas **(Jan. 1).** Syria frees captured U.S. Navy pilot, Lieut. Robert C. Goodman, Jr. **(Jan. 3).** U.S. and Vatican exchange diplomats after 116-year hiatus **(Jan. 10).** Reagan orders U.S. Marines withdrawn from Beirut international peacekeeping force **(Feb. 7).** Yuri V. Andropov dies at 69; Konstantin U. Chernenko, 72, named Soviet Union leader **(Feb. 9).** Italy and Vatican agree to end Roman Catholicism as state religion **(Feb. 18).** Reagan ends U.S. role in Beirut by relieving Sixth Fleet from peacekeeping force **(March 30).** Con-

Indira Gandhi
(1917-1984)

gress rebukes President Reagan on use of federal funds for mining Nicaraguan harbors **(April 10).** Soviet Union withdraws from summer Olympic games in U.S., and other bloc nations follow **(May 7** et seq.). José Napoleón Duarte, moderate, elected president of El Salvador **(May 11).** Three hundred slain as Indian Army occupies Sikh Golden Temple in Amritsar **(June 6).** Thirty-ninth Democratic National Convention, in San Francisco, nominates Walter F. Mondale and Geraldine A. Ferraro **(July 16-19).** Thirty-third Republican National Convention, at Dallas, renominates President Reagan and Vice President Bush **(Aug. 20-25).** Brian Mulroney and Conservative party win Canadian election in landslide **(Sept. 4).** Indian Prime Minister Indira Gandhi assassinated by two Sikh bodyguards; 1,000 killed in anti-Sikh riots; son Rajiv succeeds her **(Oct. 31).** President Reagan re-elected in landslide with 59% of vote **(Nov. 7).** Toxic gas leaks from Union Carbide plant in Bhopal, India, killing 2,000 and injuring 150,000 **(Dec. 3).**

1985 Ronald Reagan, 73, takes oath for second term as 40th President **(Jan. 20).** New Zealand bars U.S. ship when Washington refuses to say whether she carries nuclear arms **(Feb. 4).** Worldwide Conservative Rabbinical Assembly approves women in clergy **(Feb. 14).** General Westmoreland settles libel action against CBS **(Feb. 18).** Prime Minister Margaret Thatcher addresses Congress, endorsing Reagan's policies **(Feb. 20).** U.S.S.R. leader Chernenko dies at 73 and is replaced by Mikhail Gorbachev, 54 **(March 11).** Secretary of Labor Raymond J. Donovan, facing New York fraud trial, resigns; first sitting Cabinet member to be indicted **(March 15).** Tens of thousands mark 40th anniversary of liberation of Buchenwald death camp **(April 13).** Reagan target of wide attacks by Jewish leaders and others over visit to Bitburg Cemetery, West Germany, where SS troops are buried **(April 18** et seq. **May 5).** Two Shiite Moslem gunmen capture TWA airliner with 133 aboard, 104 of them Americans **(June 14);** 39 remaining hostages freed in Beirut **(June 30).** Supreme Court, 5-4, bars public school teachers from parochial schools **(July 1).** Arthur James Walker, 50, retired naval officer, convicted by federal judge of participating in Soviet spy ring **(Aug. 9).** Thousands dead in Mexico earthquake **(Sept. 19).** P.L.O. terrorists hijack *Achille Lauro,* Italian cruise ship, with 80 passengers, plus crew **(Oct. 7);** American, Leon Klinghoffer, killed **(Oct. 8).** Italian government toppled by political crisis over hijacking of *Achille Lauro* **(Oct. 16).** John A. Walker and son, Michael I. Walker, 22, sentenced in Navy espionage case **(Oct. 28).** Volcano eruption leaves 25,000 dead and missing in Colombia **(Nov. 14).** Reagan and Gorbachev meet at summit **(Nov. 19);** agree to step up arms control talks and renew cultural contacts **(Nov. 21).** Terrorists seize Egyptian Boeing 737 airliner after takeoff from Athens **(Nov. 23);** 59 dead as Egyptian forces storm plane on Malta **(Nov. 24).** U.S. budget-balancing bill enacted **(Dec. 12).** Newfoundland plane crash kills 248 U.S. soldiers **(Dec. 12).** Terrorists kill 19 at Rome and Vienna airports **(Dec. 30).**

Ronald W. Reagan
(Feb. 6, 1911)

1986 Spain and Portugal join Common Market **(Jan. 1).** President freezes Libyan assets in U.S. **(Jan. 8).** Supreme Court bars racial bias in trial jury selection **(Jan. 14).** Britain and France plan Channel tunnel **(Jan. 20).** *Voyager 2* spacecraft reports secrets of Uranus **(Jan. 26).** Space shuttle *Challenger* explodes after launch at Cape Canaveral, Fla., killing all seven aboard **(Jan. 28).** Haiti President Jean-Claude Duvalier flees to France **(Feb. 7).** President Marcos flees Philippines after ruling 20 years, as newly elected Corazon Aquino succeeds him **(Feb. 26).** Prime Minister Olaf Palme of Sweden shot dead **(Feb. 28).** Kurt Waldheim service as Nazi army officer revealed **(March 3).** Union Carbide agrees to settlement with victims of Bhopal gas leak in India **(March 22).** Two scientific teams report finding AIDS viruses **(March 26).** Halley's Comet yields information on return visit **(April 10).** U.S. planes attack Libyan "terrorist centers" **(April 14).** Desmond Tutu elected Archbishop in South Africa **(April 14).** Major nuclear accident at Soviet Union's Chernobyl power station alarms world **(April 28** et seq.). Ex-Navy analyst, Jonathan Jay Pollard, 31, guilty as spy for Israel **(June 4).** Supreme Court reaffirms abortion rights **(June 11).** World Court rules U.S. broke international law in mining Nicaraguan waters **(June 27).** Supreme Court voids automatic provisions of budget-balancing law **(July 7).** Jerry A. Whitworth, ex-Navy radioman, convicted as spy **(July 24).** Moslem captors release Rev. Lawrence Martin Jenco **(July 26).** Senate Judiciary Committee approves William H. Rehnquist to be Chief Justice of U.S. **(Aug. 14).** Mexican police torture U.S. narcotics agent **(Aug. 14).** House votes arms appropriations bill rejecting Administration's "star wars" policy **(Aug. 15).** Three Lutheran church groups in U.S. set to merge **(Aug. 29).** Nicholas Daniloff, correspondent for *U.S. News & World Report,* detained in Moscow on espionage charges **(Aug. 30);** released and allowed to leave Soviet Union **(Sept. 29).** Congress overrides Reagan veto of stiff sanctions against South Africa **(Sept. 29** and **Oct. 2).** Congress approves immigration bill barring hiring of illegal aliens, with am-

Mikhail S. Gorbachev
(March 2, 1931)

nesty provision **(Oct. 17)**. Reagan signs $11.7-billion budget reduction measure **(Oct. 21)**. He approves sweeping revision of U.S. tax code **(Oct. 22)**. Democrats triumph in elections, gaining eight seats to win Senate majority **(Nov. 4)**. Secret initiative to send arms to Iran revealed **(Nov. 6** et seq.); Reagan denies exchanging arms for hostages and halts arms sales **(Nov. 19)**; diversion of funds from arms sales to Nicaraguan contras revealed **(Nov. 25)**. Walkers, father and son, sentenced in naval spy ring **(Nov. 6)**. Soviet lifts ban on Andrei D. Sakharov, rights activist **(Dec. 19)**. Hotel fire kills 96 in Puerto Rico **(Dec. 31)**.

1987 William Buckley, U.S. hostage in Lebanon, reported slain **(Jan. 20)**. U.S. charges three Wall Street traders with making millions in illegal inside trading **(Feb. 12)**. Reagan admits "mistake" in Iran-Contra affair **(March 4)**. F.D.A. approves drug AZT for treating AIDS victims **(March 20)**. Gene-altered bacteria tested in experiment to aid agriculture **(April 24)**. U.S. puts Austrian President Kurt Waldheim on list of those banned from country **(April 27)**. Quebec accepts Canadian Constitution as "distinct society" **(May 1)**. Supreme Court rules Rotary Clubs must admit women **(May 4)**. Thousands of aliens seek legal status under new amnesty law **(May 5)**. Ulster police slay nine attackers in police station battle **(May 8)**. Three-way heart transplant performed **(May 12)**. Soviet launches world's most powerful rocket **(May 16)**. Iraqi missiles kill 37 in attack on U.S. frigate *Stark* in Persian Gulf **(May 17)**; Iraqi president apologizes **(May 18)**. Prime Minister Thatcher wins rare third term in Britain **(June 11)**. Robert B. Anderson, 77, former Treasury Secretary, sentenced for tax evasion **(June 25)**. Supreme Court Justice Lewis F. Powell, Jr., retires **(June 26)**. Klaus Barbie, 73, Gestapo wartime chief in Lyons, sentenced to life by French court for war crimes **(July 4)**. Marine Lieut. Col. Oliver North, Jr., tells Congressional inquiry higher officials approved his secret Iran-Contra operations **(July 7–10)**. Admiral John M. Poindexter, former National Security Adviser, testifies he authorized use of Iran arms sale profits to aid Contras **(July 15–22)**. George P. Shultz testifies he was deceived repeatedly on Iran-Contra affair **(July 23–24)**. Defense Secretary Caspar W. Weinberger tells inquiry of official deception and intrigue **(July 31, Aug. 3)**. Hundreds killed in clashes at Moslem holy site of Mecca **(Aug. 1)**. Five regional presidents agree on peace accord for Central America **(Aug. 7)**. Reagan says Iran arms-Contra policy went astray and accepts responsibility **(Aug 12)**. Severe earthquake strikes Los Angeles, leaving 100 injured and six dead **(Oct. 1)**. Senate, 58–42, rejects Robert H. Bork as Supreme Court Justice **(Oct. 23)**

1988 U.S. and Canada reach free trade agreement **(Jan. 2)**. Supreme Court, 5–3, backs public school officials' power to censor student activities **(Jan. 13)**. Lyn Nofziger, former Reagan adviser, convicted of violating Federal ethics law **(Feb. 11)**. Marine Lieut. Col. William H. Higgins abducted in Lebanon **(Feb. 17)**. Nine killed in Soviet plane hijacking **(March 10)**. Robert C. McFarlane, former National Security Adviser, pleads guilty in Iran–Contra case **(March 11)**. Congress overrides Reagan veto of civil rights bill **(March 22)**. Arizona Gov. Evan Mecham removed from office after impeachment trial **(April 4)**. Gunmen hijack Kuwaiti airliner **(April 5** et seq.). Khalil al-Wazir, P.L.O. official, assassinated in Tunisia **(April 16)**. Israel court dooms John Demjanjuk, 68, "Ivan the Terrible," for Nazi war crimes **(April 25)**. Soviet court clears executed Bolsheviks **(June 13)**. Supreme Court rules against private-club membership restrictions **(June 20)**. U.S. Navy ship shoots down Iranian airliner in Persian Gulf, mistaking it for jet fighter; 290 killed **(July 3)**. Terrorists kill nine tourists on Aegean cruise **(July 11)**. Democratic convention nominates Gov. Michael Dukakis of Massachusetts for President and Texas Senator Lloyd Bentsen for Vice President **(July 17** et seq.). Reagan signs law to compensate interned Japanese-Americans **(Aug. 10)**. Republicans nominate George Bush for President and Indiana Senator Dan Quayle for Vice President **(Aug. 15** et seq.). Plane blast kills Pakistani President Mohammad Zia ul-Haq **(Aug. 17)**. Michael K. Deaver, Reagan friend, sentenced for lying about lobbying **(Sept. 23)**. Foes defeat Pinochet in Chile's Presidential plebiscite **(Oct. 5)**. Republicans sweep 40 states in election. Vice President Bush beats Gov. Dukakis **(Nov. 8)**. Soviet legislature approves political restructuring and new national legislature **(Dec. 1)**. Benazir Bhutto, first Islamic woman prime minister, chosen to lead Pakistan's government **(Dec. 1)**. Pan-Am 747 explodes from terrorist bomb and crashes in Lockerbie, Scotland, killing all 259 aboard and 11 on ground **(Dec. 21)**.

1989 U.S. planes shoot down two Libyan fighters over international waters in Mediterranean **(Jan. 4)**. Emperor Hirohito of Japan dead at 87 **(Jan. 7)**. George Herbert Walker Bush inaugurated as 41st U.S. President **(Jan. 20)**. Iran's Ayatollah Khomeini declares author Salman Rushdie's book "The Satanic Verses" offensive and sentences him and his publishers to death **(Feb. 14)**. Ruptured tanker *Exxon Valdez* sends 11 million gallons of crude

Corazon C. Aquino (Jan. 25, 1933)

Kurt Waldheim (Dec. 21, 1918)

George H. Bush (June 12, 1924)

L. Douglas Wilder (Jan. 17, 1931)

oil into Alaska's Prince William Sound (**March 24**). Tens of thousands of Chinese students take over Beijing's central square in rally for democracy (**April 19** et seq.). More than one million in Beijing demonstrate for democracy; chaos spreads across nation (**mid-May** et seq.). Mikhail S. Gorbachev named Soviet President (**May 25**). U.S. jury convicts Oliver L. North in Iran-Contra affair (**May 4**). Thousands killed as Chinese leaders take hard line toward demonstrators (**June 4** et seq.). Army Gen. Colin R. Powell is first black to become Chairman of Joint Chiefs of Staff (**Aug. 9**). P.W. Botha quits as South Africa's President (**Aug. 14**). *Voyager 2* spacecraft speeds by Neptune after making startling discoveries about the planet and its moons (**Aug. 29**). Hurricane Hugo devastates area from Caribbean to South Carolina (**Sept. 18**). L. Douglas Wilder, Democrat, is elected as first black governor of Virginia (**Nov. 7**). Deng Xiaoping resigns from China's leadership (**Nov. 9**). After 28 years, Berlin Wall is open to West (**Nov. 11**). Czech Parliament ends Communists' dominant role (**Nov. 30**). Romanian uprising overthrows Communist government (**Dec. 15** et seq.); President Ceausescu and wife executed (**Dec. 25**). U.S. troops invade Panama, seeking capture of Gen. Manuel Noriega (**Dec. 20**); resistance to U.S. collapses (**Dec. 24**).

1990 Gen. Manuel Noriega surrenders in Panama (**Jan. 3**). Yugoslav Communists end 45-year monopoly of power (**Jan. 22**). Richard V. Secord convicted in Iran–Contra affair (**Jan. 24**). Nicaraguan opposition crushes Sandinistas at polls (**Feb. 5**). Soviet Communists relinquish sole power (**Feb. 7**). South Africa frees Nelson Mandela, imprisoned 27 1/2 years (**Feb. 11**). Moscow admits Soviet secret police killed thousands in Katyn Forest massacre of 1940 (**April 13**). Violeta Barrios de Chamorro inaugurated as Nicaraguan President (**April 25**). Fire on Navy destroyer *Conynham* kills one and injures 12 (**May 8**). U.S.–Soviet summit reaches accord on armaments (**June 1**). South Africa lifts emergency decrees (**June 7**). Supreme Court upsets law banning flag burning (**June 11**). President Bush breaks with no-new-tax pledge in budget agreement (**June 26**). Imelda Marcos acquitted in New York of raiding Philippine Treasury (**July 2**). Western Alliance ends cold war and proposes joint action with Soviet Union and Eastern Europe (**July 6**). U.S. Appeals Court overturns Oliver North's Iran–Contra conviction (**July 20**). Iraqi troops invade Kuwait and seize petroleum reserves, setting off Persian Gulf War (**Aug. 2** et seq.) East and West Germany reunited (**Aug. 31** et seq.). Bush and Congressional leaders agree on drastic budget reduction plan (**Sept. 30**). Congress passes budget-reducing measure with new taxes and spending cuts (**Oct. 28**). Republicans set back in midterm elections (**Nov. 8**). Gorbachev assumes emergency powers (**Nov. 17**). Leaders of 34 nations in Europe and North America proclaim a united Europe (**Nov. 21**). Margaret Thatcher resigns as British Prime Minister (**Nov. 22**); John Major succeeds her (**Nov. 28**). Lech Walesa wins Poland's runoff Presidential election (**Dec. 9**). Twelve European nations move toward unified political ties (**Dec. 15**). Haiti elects leftist priest as President in first democratic election (**Dec. 17**).

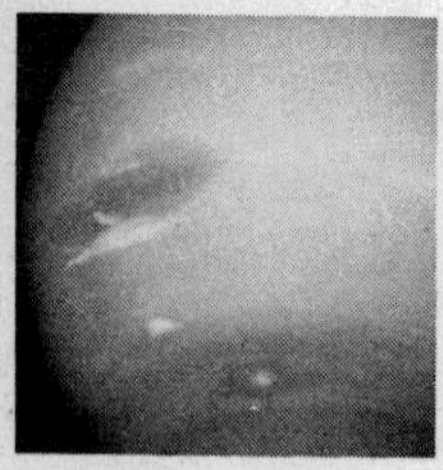
Neptune seen from Voyager 2

1991 Israelis open consulate in Moscow (**Jan. 3**). Lithuania Government resigns (**Jan. 8**). South Africa schools integrate (**Jan. 9**). Two P.L.O. leaders slain in Tunis (**Jan. 14**). U.S. and Allies at war with Iraq (**Jan. 15**). U.N. forces

THE PERSIAN GULF WAR (Aug. 2, 1990–April 6, 1991)

1990: Iraq invades its tiny neighbor, Kuwait, after talks break down over oil production and debt repayment. Iraqi Pres. Saddam Hussein later annexes Kuwait and declares it a 19th province of Iraq (**Aug. 2**). President Bush believes that Iraq intends to invade Saudi Arabia and take control of the region's oil supplies. He begins organizing a multinational coalition to seek Kuwait's freedom and restoration of its legitimate government. The U.N. Security Council authorizes economic sanctions against Iraq. Pres. Bush orders U.S. troops to protect Saudi Arabia at the Saudis' request and "Operation Desert Shield" begins (**Aug. 6**). 230,000 American troops arrive in Saudi Arabia to take defensive action, but when Iraq continues a huge military buildup in Kuwait, the President orders an additional 200,000 troops deployed to prepare for a possible offensive action by the U.S.-led coalition forces. He subsequently obtains a U.N. Security Council resolution setting a Jan. 15, 1991, deadline for Iraq to withdraw unconditionally from Kuwait (**Nov. 8**).

1991: Pres. Bush wins Congressional approval for his position with the most devastating air assault in history against military targets in Iraq and Kuwait (**Jan. 16**). He rejects a Soviet-Iraq peace plan for a gradual withdrawal that does not comply with all the U.N. resolutions and gives Iraq an ultimatum to withdraw from Kuwait by noon February 23 (**Feb. 22**). The President orders the ground war to begin (**Feb. 24**). In a brilliant and lightning-fast campaign, U.S. and coalition forces smash through Iraq's defenses and defeat Saddam Hussein's troops in only four days of combat. Allies enter Kuwait City (**Feb. 26**). Iraqi army sets fire to over 500 of Kuwait's oil wells as final act of destruction to Kuwait's infrastructure. Pres. Bush orders a unilateral cease-fire 100 hours after the ground offensive started (**Feb. 27**). Allied and Iraq military leaders meet on battlefield to discuss terms for a formal cease-fire to end the Gulf War. Iraq agrees to abide by all of the U.N. resolutions (**Mar. 3**). The first Allied prisoners of war are released (**Mar. 4**). Official cease-fire accepted and signed (**April 6**). 532,000 U.S. forces served in Operation Desert Storm. There were a total of 148 battle deaths during the Gulf War, 145 nonbattle deaths, and 467 wounded in action. Battle deaths by branch of service were: Army, 98; Navy, 6; Marines, 24; Air Force, 20. Nonbattle deaths: Army, 105; Navy, 8; Marines, 26; and Air Force, 6. No comprehensive casualty figures have been released by Iraq.

win Persian Gulf war (**Feb. 4** et seq.). Liberal priest becomes Haiti president (**Feb. 7**). Warsaw Pact dissolves military alliance (**Feb 25**). TV tape of Los Angeles police beating shocks nation (**March 3**). Baltic voters support independence from Soviet (**March 3**). Unrest breaks out in Yugoslavia (**March 9**). Britain to scrap unpopular poll tax (**March 21**). Supreme Court limits race in trial jury selection (**April 1**). Cease-fire ends Persian Gulf war (**April 3**). Thousands of Kurds flee Iraq (**April 3**). Europeans end sanctions on South Africa (**April 15**). Supreme Court limits death row appeals (**April 16**). Cholera epidemic spreads to Ecuador and Colombia, after killing 1,100 in Peru and making 50,000 ill (**April 18**). Senate rejects Social Security tax cut (**April 24**). Bush treated for abnormal heartbeat (**May 4**). William K. Smith, 30, nephew of Senator Edward Kennedy, accused of raping woman at Kennedy estate in Florida (**May 9**). Winnie Mandela sentenced in kidnapping (**May 13**). William H. Webster retires as Director of Central Intelligence; Robert H. Gates succeeds him (**May 14**). France agrees to sign 1968 treaty banning spread of atomic weapons (**June 3**). Communist Government of Albania resigns (**June 4**). Jiang Qing, widow of Mao, commits suicide (**June 4**). South African Parliament repeals apartheid laws (**June 5**). Volcano erupts in Philippines with mounting death toll (**June 18** et seq.). Berlin again becomes German capital (**June 20**). Warsaw Pact dissolved (**July 1**). Boris N. Yeltsin inaugurated as first freely elected president of Russian Republic (**July 10**). Bush-Gorbachev summit negotiates strategic arms reduction treaty (**July 31**). Hostages freed by abductors in Lebanon (**Aug. 8** et seq.). China accepts nuclear nonproliferation treaty (**Aug. 10**). Coup fails to unseat Gorbachev after Soviet hardliners seize him; he credits Yeltsin for rescue (**Aug. 18** et seq.). Gorbachev seals Communist Party doom, resigns as secretary-general (**Aug. 24**). Three Baltic republics win independence (**Aug. 25**); Bush recognizes them (**Sept. 2**). New Soviet ruling council recognizes independence of Lithuania, Estonia, and Latvia (**Sept. 6**). Charges against Oliver North dropped (**Sept. 15**). Yugoslav army moves on Croatia (**Sept. 30**). Haitian troops seize president in uprising (**Sept. 30**). U.S. suspends assistance to Haiti (**Oct. 1**). Woman professor accuses Judge Clarence Thomas of sexual harassment (**Oct. 6**); Senate, 52–48, confirms Thomas for Supreme Court after stormy hearings (**Oct. 15**). Israel and Soviet resume relations after 24 years (**Oct. 18**). First photo ever taken of an asteroid in space, *Gaspara* (**Oct. 29**). Robert Maxwell, 68, British press magnate, found dead in Atlantic (**Nov. 5**). European Community imposes economic sanctions on Yugoslavia (**Nov. 8**). U.S. indicts two Libyans in 1988 bombing of Pan Am Flight 103 over Lockerbie, Scotland (**Nov. 15**). Anglican envoy Terry Waite and U.S. Prof. Thomas M. Sutherland freed by Lebanese (**Nov. 18**). U.N. Security Council names Egyptian Deputy Prime Minister Boutros Boutros-Ghali as sixth Secretary-General (**Nov. 21**). Charles H. Keating, Jr., convicted of fraud in savings and loan crisis (**Dec. 4**). Last three U.S. hostages freed in Lebanon (**Dec. 2–4**). Kennedy nephew acquitted in Florida rape case (**Dec. 11**). Soviet Union breaks up after President Gorbachev's resignation; constituent republics form Commonwealth of Independent States, which U.S. and other nations move to recognize (**Dec. 25**). The 12-year-old civil war in El Salvador ends (**Dec. 31**).

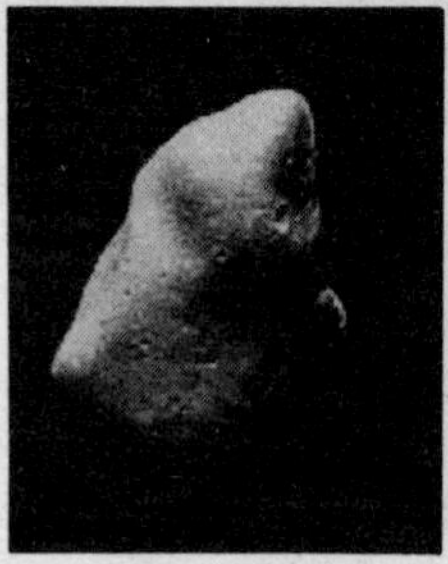

Asteroid *Gaspra*
(Oct. 29, 1991)

1992 Russians again observe Orthodox Christmas (**Jan. 6–7**). U.S. jobless rate at five-year high (**Jan. 10**). Yugoslav Federation broken up (**Jan. 15**). El Salvador Government and rebels sign peace treaty (**Jan. 16**). Bush and Yeltsin proclaim formal end to Cold War (**Feb. 1**). Bill Clinton reveals letter on draft status (**Feb. 12**). Milwaukee jury finds serial killer insane (**Feb. 15**). U.S. lifts trade sanctions against China (**Feb. 21**). Head of Arts Endowment forced out (**Feb. 21**). U.N. rebukes Iraq on disposal of weapons of mass destruction (**Feb. 27**). Bush apologizes for raising taxes (**March 3**). Blast kills 200 in Turkish coal mine (**March 4**). F.D.A. restricts use of silicone breast implants (**April 16**). South African whites vote for majority rule (**March 18**). I.M.F. endorses Russian economic reforms (**March 31**). Seven industrial democracies agree to aid Russia (**April 1**). U.S. recognizes three former Yugoslav republics (**April 7**). Gen. Noriega, former Panama leader, convicted in U.S. court (**April 9**). Charles H. Keating, Jr., financier, sentenced in fraud (**April 10**). Nearly 200 dead in Mexico explosion (**April 22**). U.N. imposes sanctions against Libya (**April 14**). Small new Yugoslavia proclaimed (**April 27**). Four officers acquitted in televised beating; violence erupts in Los Angeles (**April 29** et seq.). Supreme Court limits prisoner appeals (**May 4**). Scores dead in Thailand pro-democracy demonstrations (**May 17**). Six industrial nations plan nuclear cleanup for Eastern Europe (**May 20**). U.S. orders sanctions against Belgrade (**May 22**); U.N. votes sanctions (**May 30**). U.N. earth summit ends at Rio (**June 14**). Yeltsin successful in visit to West (**June 16** et seq.). Caspar W. Weinberger indicted in Iran-Contra affair (**Jun 16**).

William J. Clinton
(Aug. 19, 1946)

Last Western hostages freed in Lebanon (**June 17**). Opposition wins Israeli election (**June 23**). Supreme Court reaffirms right to abortion (**June 29**). House panel exonerates Bush in hostage-release inquiry (**July 1**). First food airlifted to Sarajevo (**July 1**). Gen. Noriega sentenced to 40 years on drug charges (**July 10**). Court clears *Exxon Valdez* skipper (**July 10**). Pan Am found liable in Flight 103 tragedy (**July 10**). Democrats nominate Bill Clinton and Al Gore (**July 11**). Israeli parliament approves Yitzhak Rabin's coalition government, dominated by Labor Party (**July 13**). Benign tumor removed from Pope's colon (**July 15**). Israel halts new settlements in occupied areas (**July 23**). Clark M. Clifford, 85, indicted in bank inquiry (**July 29**). Asian airliner crash kills more than 200 (**July 31**). Supreme Court upholds return of Haitians (**Aug. 1**). U.S. indicts four police officers in Los Angeles beating (**Aug. 5**). North American trade compact announced (**Aug. 12**). U.N. Council approves force to guard aid for Sarajevo (**Aug. 13**). Republicans renominate Bush and Quayle (**Aug. 20**). Allies agree to shoot down Iraqi planes (**Aug. 18**). Hurricane Andrew devastates South Florida; death toll high (**Aug. 24** et seq.). Neo-Nazis run amok in German Baltic seaport (**Aug. 25**). Bush pledges funds for hurricane rebuilding (**Sept. 1**). Fay Vincent quits as baseball commissioner (**Sept. 7**). Troops kill 24 in South African homeland (**Sept. 7**). Peru police capture fugitive Maoist rebel leader (**Sept. 13**). European currency markets in turmoil (**Sept. 14**). Floods kill 2,500 in North Pakistan and India (**Sept. 18**). U.N. expels Serbian-dominated Yugoslavia (**Sept. 22**). Death toll set at 167 in Nepal plane crash (**Sept. 28**). Brazilian President impeached in bribery inquiry (**Sept. 29**). Senate ratifies second Strategic Arms Limitation Treaty (**Oct. 1**). Serbs resume "ethnic cleansing" of Muslims (**Oct. 1**). U.S. missiles hit Turkish ship during NATO exercises (**Oct. 2**). China agrees to lower barriers to U.S. trade (**Oct. 9**). U.N. Council creates Bosnian "no-fly" zone (**Oct. 9**). Top Japanese leader, Shin Kanemaru, resigns in scandal (**Oct. 14**). British Government cancels plan to close down 31 of 50 coal mines (**Oct. 19**). Founder of German Green Party found slain (**Oct. 19**). Muslim extremists kill and wound tourists in Egypt (**Oct. 21**). Canadian voters reject constitutional reform package (**Oct. 26**). Pope admits Roman Catholic Church was wrong in condemning Galileo (**Oct. 31**). Bill Clinton elected U.S. President, Al Gore Vice President; Democrats keep control of Congress (**Nov. 3**). Russian parliament approves START treaty (**Nov. 4**). Irish coalition government collapses (**Nov. 5**). Church of England approves women priests (**Nov. 11**). Italian police seize 75 linked to Mafia (**Nov. 17**). U.S. and European Community compromise on farm subsidies (**Nov. 20**). Last U.S. forces leave Philippines, ending nearly a century of American military presence (**Nov. 24**). Ninety-three nations agree to move up ban on ozone-harming chemicals (**Nov. 25**). Czechoslovak Parliament approves separation into two nations (**Nov. 25**). Germany outlaws Neo-Nazi organization (**Nov. 27**). Supreme Court rebuffs Guam on abortion curbs (**Nov. 30**). U.N. approves U.S.-led force to guard food for Somalia (**Dec. 3**). Hindus destroy Indian mosque; sectarian conflict breaks out (**Dec. 6**). Swiss voters reject tie to European Community free trade zone (**Dec. 6**). Former C.I.A. official convicted in Iran-Contra scandal (**Dec. 9**). Russian President Yeltsin suffers setback in parliament; Gaidar out as premier (**Dec. 9**). Prince and Princess of Wales agree to separate (**Dec. 9**). Russian parliament confirms Chernomyrdin as premier in deal with Yeltsin (**Dec. 14**). Israel deports about 400 Palestinians (**Dec. 17**). New Yeltsin cabinet keeps reformist officials (**Dec. 23**). Bush pardons six former Reagan Administration officials involved in Iran-Contra affair (**Dec. 24**). U.S. downs Iraqi warplane (**Dec. 27**). U.S. and Russia agree on a second Strategic Arms Reduction Treaty (START II) (**Dec. 29**). Hard-liners oust Premier Panic of Yugoslavia (**Dec. 29**).

PICTURE CREDITS. The following credits list the names of organizations and individuals who have contributed illustrations to **HEADLINE HISTORY**. The editors wish to thank all of them for their assistance. The credits are arranged alphabetically by picture source, then picture title and page number in **HEADLINE HISTORY**. **Credits:** AIP Niels Bohr Library, **Marie Curie** and **Albert Einstein**, p. 108; British Information Services, **Margaret Thatcher**, p. 121; Embassy of The Philippines, **Corazon C. Aquino**, p. 123; Harry S. Truman Library, **Harry S. Truman**, p. 116; John Fitzgerald Kennedy Library, Boston, **John F. Kennedy**, p. 119; Matthew Kalmenott, **Brontosaur**, p. 93; NASA Photos, **Charles A. Lindbergh**, p. 112, **Voyager and Viking**, p. 120, **Space Shuttle Columbia**, p. 121; **Sally K. Ride**, p. 121 and **Asteroid *Gaspra***, p. 125; National Portrait Gallery, Smithsonian Institution, **Theodore Roosevelt**, p. 108; Novosti Photos, **Vladimir Lenin**, p. 110, **Yuri A. Gagarin**, p. 118; **Mikhail S. Gorbachev**, p. 122; The Library of Congress Picture Collection, **Christopher Columbus**, p. 99, **Dred Scott**, p. 106, **Geronimo**, p. 107, **Woodrow Wilson**, p. 110, **Herbert C. Hoover**, p. 112, **Amelia Earhart**, p. 115, **Dwight D. Eisenhower**, p. 117, **Lyndon B. Johnson**, p. 119, **Richard M. Nixon**, p. 120; The Permanent Mission of India to the U.N., **Indira Gandhi**, p. 122; Republican National Committee, **Ronald W. Reagan**, p. 122, **George H. Bush**, p. 123; U.S. Army Photos, **D-Day, Yalta Conference**, p. 116, **Joseph Stalin**, p. 117; AP/Wide World Photos, Inc., **Martin Luther King, Jr.**, p. 119, U.N. Photo, **Fidel Castro**, p. 118, U.N. Photo by D. Burnett, **Kurt Waldheim**, p. 123; Bob McNeely, The White House, **William J. Clinton**, p. 126. **MAP CREDITS:** Maps on pp. 94, 98, 102, 109, 111, 113, and 114 from *An Encyclopedia of World History*, by William L. Langer, The Fifth Edition, Copyright 1940, 1948, 1952, and © 1967, 1972 by Houghton Mifflin Company. Reprinted by permission of Houghton Mifflin Company.

A PROFILE OF THE WORLD

Source: The World Factbook, 1993.

GEOGRAPHY

Total area: 510.072 million sq km (196.93 million sq mi.). **Land area:** 148.94 million sq km (57.50 sq mi.). **Water area:** 361.132 million sq km (139.43 sq mi.). **Comparative area:** land area about 16 times the size of the United States. **Note:** 70.8% of the world is water, 29.2% is land

Land boundaries: The land boundaries in the world total 250,883.64 km (155,891.81 mi.) (not counting shared boundaries twice)

Maritime claims:
Contiguous zone: 24 nm (nautical miles) claimed by most but can vary. *Continental shelf:* 200-m (656 ft) depth claimed by most or to the depth of exploitation, others claim 200 nm or to the edge of the continental margin. *Exclusive fishing zone:* 200 nm claimed by most but can vary. *Exclusive economic zone:* 200 nm claimed by most but can vary. *Territorial sea:* 12 nm claimed by most but can vary

Note: Boundary situations with neighboring states prevent many countries from extending their fishing or economic zones to a full 200 nm; 42 nations and other areas that are landlocked include Afghanistan, Andorra, Armenia, Austria, Azerbaijan, Belarus, Bhutan, Bolivia, Botswana, Burkina Faso, Burundi, Central African Republic, Chad, Czech Republic, Ethiopia, Holy See (Vatican City), Hungary, Kazakhstan, Kyrgyzstan, Laos, Lesotho, Liechtenstein, Luxembourg, Macedonia, Malawi, Mali, Moldova, Mongolia, Nepal, Niger, Paraguay, Rwanda, San Marino, Slovakia, Swaziland, Switzerland, Tajikistan, Turkmenistan, Uganda, Uzbekistan, West Bank, Zambia, Zimbabwe

Climate: Two large areas of polar climates separated by two rather narrow temperate zones from a wide equatorial band of tropical to subtropical climates

Terrain: Highest elevation is Mt. Everest at 8,848 meters (29,028 ft) and lowest depression is the Dead Sea at 392 meters (1,286 ft) below sea level; greatest ocean depth is the Marianas Trench at 10,924 meters (35,840 ft)

Natural resources: The rapid using up of nonrenewable mineral resources, the depletion of forest areas and wetlands, the extinction of animal and plant species, and the deterioration in air and water quality (especially in Eastern Europe and the former USSR) pose serious long-term problems that governments and people are only beginning to address

Land use:
Arable land: 10%. *Permanent crops:* 1%. *Meadows and pastures:* 24%. *Forest and woodland:* 31%. *Other:* 34%. *Irrigated land:* N.A. square kilometers

Environment: Large areas subject to severe weather (tropical cyclones), natural disasters (earthquakes, landslides, tsunamis, volcanic eruptions), overpopulation, industrial disasters, pollution (air, water, acid rain, toxic substances), loss of vegetation (overgrazing, deforestation, desertification), loss of wildlife resources, soil degradation, soil depletion, erosion

PEOPLE

Population: 5,554,552,453 (July 1993 est.); **Growth rate:** 1.6% (1993 est.)
Birth rate: 25 births/1,000 population (1993 est.)
Death rate: 9 deaths/1,000 live births (1993 est.)
Infant mortality rate: 66 deaths/1,000 live births (1993 est.)
Life expectancy at birth:
Total population: 62 years. *Male:* 60 years. *Female:* 64 years (1993 est.)
Total fertility rate: 3.2 children born/woman (1993 est.)
Literacy: age 15 and over can read and write (1993 est.)
Combined: 74%. *Male:* 81%. *Female:* 67%.
Labor force: 2.24 billion (1992)

GOVERNMENT

Administrative divisions: 265 sovereign nations, dependent areas, other, and miscellaneous entries
Legal system: Varies by individual country; 182 are parties to the United Nations International Court of Justice (ICJ or World Court)

ECONOMY

Overview: Real global output—gross world product (GWP)—rose one-half of 1% in 1992, with results varying widely among regions and countries. Average growth of 1.5% in the GDP of industrialized countries (62% of GWP in 1992) and average growth of 5% in the GDP of less developed countries (30% of GWP) were offset by a further 15–20% drop in the GDP of the former Soviet–East European area (now only 8% of GWP). The United States accounted for 23% of GWP in 1992; the 12-member European Community[1] (EC), which established a single internal market on January 1, 1993, accounted for another 23%, and Japan accounted for 10%. These are the three "economic superpowers" presumably destined to compete for mastery in international markets on into the 21st century. In general, growth in the industrialized countries was sluggish in 1992, with unemployment typically at 7–11%. As for the less developed countries, China, India, and the Four Dragons—South Korea, Taiwan, Hong Kong, and Singapore—posted good records; however, many other countries, especially in Africa, suffered bitterly from drought, rapid population growth, and civil strife. The continued plunge in production in practically all the former Warsaw Pact economies strained the political and social fabric of these newly independent nations, in particular in Russia. The addition of nearly 100 million people each year to an already overcrowded globe is exacerbating the problems of pollution, desertification, underemployment, epidemics, and famine. Because of their own internal problems, the industrialized countries have inadequate resources to deal effectively with the poorer areas of the world, which, at least from the economic point of view, are becoming further marginalized.

1. 12 full members: Belgium, Denmark, France, Germany, Greece, Ireland, Italy, Luxembourg, Netherlands, Portugal, Spain, UK.

National product: GWP (gross world product)—purchasing power equivalent—$25.6 trillion (1992 est.)
National product real growth rate: 0.5% (1992 est.)
National product per capita: $4,600 (1992 est.)
Inflation rate (consumer prices):
Developed countries: 5% (1992 est.). *Developing countries:* 50% (1992 est.).
Note: these figures vary widely in individual cases
Unemployment rate: developed countries typically 7–11%; developing countries, extensive unemployment and underemployment (1992)
Exports: $3.64 trillion (f.o.b. 1992 est.) *Commodities:* the whole range of industrial and agricultural goods and services. *Partners:* in value, about 75% of exports from the developed countries.
Imports: $3.82 trillion (c.i.f., 1992 est.) *Commodities:* the whole range of industrial and agricultural goods and services. *Partners:* in value, about 75% of imports by the developed countries
External debt: $1 trillion for less developed countries (1992 est.)
Industrial production: growth rate –1% (1992 est.)
Electricity: 2,864,000,000 kW capacity; 11,450,000 million kWh produced, 2,150 kWh per capita (1990)
Industries: industry worldwide is dominated by the onrush of technology, especially in computers, robotics, telecommunications, and medicines and medical equipment; most of these advances take place in Organization for Economic Cooperation and Development[2] (OECD) nations; only a small portion of non-OECD countries have succeeded in rapidly adjusting to these technological forces, and the technological gap between the industrial nations and the less-developed countries continues to widen; the rapid development of new industrial (and agricultural) technology is complicating already grim environmental problems.

2. 24 full members: Australia, Austria, Belgium, Canada, Denmark, Finland, France, Germany, Greece, Iceland, Ireland, Italy, Japan, Luxembourg, Netherlands, New Zealand, Norway, Portugal, Spain, Sweden, Switzerland, Turkey, UK, US.

Agriculture: The production of major food crops has increased substantially in the last 20 years; the annual production of cereals, for instance, has risen by 50%, from about 1.2 billion metric tons to about 1.8 billion metric tons; production increases have resulted mainly from increased yields rather than increases in planted areas; while global production is sufficient for aggregate demand, about one-fifth of the world's population remains malnourished, primarily because local production cannot adequately provide for large and rapidly growing populations, which are too poor to pay for food imports; conditions are especially bad in Africa where drought in recent years has intensified the consequences of overpopulation

COMMUNICATIONS

Railroads: 148,775 mi. (239,430 km) of narrow gauge track; 441,642 mi. (710,754 km) of standard gauge track; 156,059 mi. (251,153 km) of broad gauge track; includes about 118,060 to 121,167 mi. (190,000 to 195,000 km) of electrified routes of which 91,814 mi. (147,760 km) are in Europe, 15,229 mi. (24,509 km) in the Far East, 6,866 mi. (11,050 km) in Africa, 2,624 mi. (4,223 km) in South America, and only 2,585 mi. (4,160 km) in North America; fastest speed in daily service is 186 mph (300 km/hr) attained by France's SNCF TGV-Atlantique line
Ports: Mina al Ahmadi (Kuwait), Chiba, Houston, Kawasaki, Kobe, Marseille, New Orleans, New York, Rotterdam, Yokohama
Merchant marine: 23,943 ships (1,000 GRT [gross register ton] or over) totaling 397,225,000 GRT/652,025,000 DWT (dead weight ton); includes 347 passenger-cargo, 12,581 freighters, 5,473 bulk carriers, and 5,542 tankers (January 1992)

DEFENSE FORCES

Branches: ground, maritime, and air forces at all levels of technology
Defense expenditures: $1.0 trillion, 4% of total world output; decline of 5–10% (1991 est.)

Area and Population by Country

Mid-1993 Estimates

Country	Area[1]	Population
Afghanistan	250,000	17,400,000
Albania	11,100	3,300,000
Algeria	919,590	27,300,000
Angola	481,350	9,500,000
Antigua and Barbuda	170	100,000
Argentina	1,068,300	33,500,000
Armenia	11,500	3,600,000
Australia	2,967,900	17,800,000
Austria	32,370	7,900,000
Azerbaijan	33,400	7,200,000
Bahamas	5,380	300,000
Bahrain	240	500,000
Bangladesh	55,600	113,900,000
Barbados	170	300,000
Belarus	80,200	10,300,000
Belgium	11,750	10,100,000
Belize	8,860	200,000
Benin	43,480	5,100,000
Bhutan	18,150	800,000
Bolivia	424,160	8,000,000
Bosnia-Herzegovina	19,740	4,000,000
Botswana	231,800	1,400,000
Brazil	3,268,470	152,000,000
Brunei	2,230	300,000
Bulgaria	42,820	9,000,000
Burkina Faso	105,870	10,000,000
Burundi	10,750	5,800,000
Cambodia	69,900	9,000,000
Cameroon	183,570	12,800,000
Canada	3,851,790	28,100,000
Cape Verde	1,560	400,000
Central African Republic	240,530	3,100,000
Chad	495,750	5,400,000
Chile	292,260	13,500,000
China, People's Republic of	3,705,390	1,178,500,000
Colombia	439,730	34,900,000
Comoros	690	500,000
Congo	132,050	2,400,000
Costa Rica	19,580	3,300,000
Côte d'Ivoire	124,500	13,400,000
Croatia	21,830	4,400,000
Cuba	44,420	11,000,000

Country	Area[1]	Population	Country	Area[1]	Population
Cyprus	3,570	700,000	Mozambique	309,490	15,300,000
Czech Republic	30,464	10,300,000	Myanmar	261,220	43,500,000
Denmark	16,630	5,200,000	Namibia	318,260	1,600,000
Djibouti	8,490	500,000	Nepal	54,360	20,400,000
Dominica	290	100,000	Netherlands	14,410	15,200,000
Dominican Republic	18,810	7,600,000	New Zealand	103,740	3,400,000
Ecuador	109,480	10,300,000	Nicaragua	50,190	4,100,000
Egypt	386,660	58,300,000	Niger	489,190	8,500,000
El Salvador	8,260	5,200,000	Nigeria	356,670	95,100,000
Equatorial Guinea	10,830	400,000	Norway	125,180	4,300,000
Estonia	17,410	1,600,000	Oman	82,030	1,600,000
Ethiopia	471,780	56,700,000	Pakistan	310,400	122,400,000
Fiji	7,050	800,000	Panama	29,760	2,500,000
Finland	130,130	5,100,000	Papua New Guinea	178,260	3,900,000
France	211,210	57,700,000	Paraguay	157,050	4,200,000
Gabon	103,350	1,100,000	Peru	496,220	22,900,000
Gambia	4,360	900,000	Philippines	115,830	64,600,000
Georgia	26,900	5,500,000	Poland	120,730	38,500,000
Germany	137,800	81,100,000	Portugal	35,550	9,800,000
Ghana	92,100	16,400,000	Qatar	4,250	500,000
Greece	50,940	10,500,000	Romania	91,700	23,200,000
Grenada	130	100,000	Russia	6,592,800	149,000,000
Guatemala	42,040	10,000,000	Rwanda	10,170	7,400,000
Guinea	94,930	6,200,000	St. Lucia	240	100,000
Guinea-Bissau	13,950	1,000,000	St. Vincent and the Grenadines	150	100,000
Guyana	83,000	800,000	Saudi Arabia	830,000	17,500,000
Haiti	10,710	6,500,000	Senegal	75,750	7,900,000
Honduras	43,280	5,600,000	Sierra Leone	27,700	4,500,000
Hungary	35,920	10,300,000	Singapore	220	2,800,000
Iceland	39,770	300,000	Slovakia	18,917	5,300,000
India	1,269,340	897,400,000	Slovenia	7,820	2,000,000
Indonesia	741,100	187,600,000	Solomon Islands	10,980	300,000
Iran	636,290	62,800,000	Somalia	246,200	9,500,000
Iraq	167,920	19,200,000	South Africa	471,440	39,000,000
Ireland	27,140	3,600,000	Spain	194,900	39,100,000
Israel	8,020	5,300,000	Sri Lanka	26,330	17,800,000
Italy	116,310	57,800,000	Sudan	967,490	27,400,000
Jamaica	4,240	2,400,000	Suriname	63,040	400,000
Japan	143,750	124,800,000	Swaziland	6,700	800,000
Jordan	35,480	3,800,000	Sweden	173,730	8,700,000
Kazakhstan	1,049,200	17,200,000	Switzerland	15,940	7,000,000
Kenya	224,960	27,700,000	Syria	71,500	13,500,000
Korea, North	46,540	22,600,000	Taiwan	12,460	20,900,000
Korea, South	38,020	44,600,000	Tajikistan	55,300	5,700,000
Kuwait	6,880	1,700,000	Tanzania	364,900	27,800,000
Kyrgyzstan	76,600	4,600,000	Thailand	196,460	57,200,000
Laos	91,430	4,600,000	Togo	21,930	4,100,000
Latvia	24,900	2,600,000	Trinidad and Tobago	1,980	1,300,000
Lebanon	4,020	3,600,000	Tunisia	63,170	8,600,000
Lesotho	11,720	1,900,000	Turkey	301,380	60,700,000
Liberia	43,000	2,800,000	Turkmenistan	188,500	4,000,000
Libya	679,360	4,900,000	Uganda	91,140	18,100,000
Lithuania	25,210	3,800,000	Ukraine	233,100	51,900,000
Luxembourg	990	400,000	United Arab Emirates	32,280	2,100,000
Macedonia	9,930	2,000,000	United Kingdom	94,530	58,000,000
Madagascar	226,660	13,300,000	United States	3,615,100	258,300,000
Malawi	45,750	10,000,000	Uruguay	68,040	3,200,000
Malaysia	127,320	18,400,000	Uzbekistan	172,700	21,700,000
Maldives	120	200,000	Vanuatu	5,700	200,000
Mali	478,760	8,900,000	Venezuela	352,140	20,700,000
Malta	120	400,000	Vietnam	127,240	71,800,000
Mauritania	397,950	2,200,000	Western Samoa	1,100	200,000
Mauritius	790	1,100,000	Yemen	203,850	11,300,000
Mexico	761,600	90,000,000	Yugoslavia	26,940	9,800,000
Moldova	13,000	4,400,000	Zaire	905,560	41,200,000
Mongolia	604,250	2,300,000	Zambia	290,580	8,600,000
Morocco	172,410	28,000,000	Zimbabwe	150,800	10,700,000

1. Square miles. *Source: 1993 World Population Data Sheet,* Population Reference Bureau, Inc., Washington, D.C.

World's Largest Cities by Rank

(Estimated Mid-Year Population in Thousands)

Rank in 1991	City	1991	1995	2000	Average Annual Growth Rate (%) 1991–95	Area (square miles)
1.	Tokyo-Yokohama, Japan	27,245	28,447	29,971	0.86	1,089
2.	Mexico City, Mexico	20,899	23,913	27,872	2.69	522
3.	São Paulo, Brazil	18,701	21,539	25,354	2.83	451
4.	Seoul, South Korea	16,792	19,065	21,976	2.54	342
5.	New York, United States	14,625	14,638	14,648	0.02	1,274
6.	Osaka–Kobe–Kyoto, Japan	13,872	14,060	14,287	0.27	495
7.	Bombay, India	12,109	13,532	15,357	2.22	95
8.	Calcutta, India	11,898	12,885	14,088	1.59	209
9.	Rio de Janeiro, Brazil	11,688	12,786	14,169	1.80	260
10.	Buenos Aires, Argentina	11,657	12,232	12,911	0.96	535
11.	Moscow, Russia	10,446	10,769	11,121	0.61	379
12.	Manila, Philippines	10,156	11,342	12,846	2.21	188
13.	Los Angeles, United States	10,130	10,414	10,714	0.55	1,110
14.	Cairo, Egypt	10,099	11,155	12,512	1.99	104
15.	Jakarta, Indonesia	9,882	11,151	12,804	2.42	76
16.	Tehran, Iran	9,779	11,681	14,251	3.55	112
17.	London, United Kingdom	9,115	8,897	8,574	–0.48	874
18.	Delhi, India	8,778	10,105	11,849	2.81	138
19.	Paris, France	8,720	8,764	8,803	0.10	432
20.	Karachi, Pakistan	8,014	9,350	11,299	3.08	190
21.	Lagos, Nigeria	7,998	9,799	12,528	4.06	56
22.	Essen, Germany	7,452	7,364	7,239	–0.24	704
23.	Shanghai, China	6,936	7,194	7,540	0.73	78
24.	Lima, Peru	6,815	7,853	9,241	2.83	120
25.	Taipei, Taiwan	6,695	7,477	8,516	2.21	138
26.	Istanbul, Turkey	6,678	7,624	8,875	2.65	165
27.	Chicago, United States	6,529	6,541	6,568	0.04	762
28.	Bangkok, Thailand	5,955	6,657	7,587	2.23	102
29.	Bogota, Colombia	5,913	6,801	7,935	2.80	79
30.	Madras, India	5,896	6,550	7,384	2.10	115
31.	Beijing, China	5,762	5,865	5,993	0.36	151
32.	Hong Kong, Hong Kong	5,693	5,841	5,956	0.51	23
33.	Santiago, Chile	5,378	5,812	6,294	1.55	128
34.	Pusan, South Korea	5,008	5,748	6,700	2.76	54
35.	Tianjin, China	4,850	5,041	5,298	0.77	49
36.	Bangalore, India	4,802	5,644	6,764	3.23	50
37.	Nagoya, Japan	4,791	5,017	5,303	0.92	307
38.	Milan, Italy	4,749	4,795	4,839	0.19	344
39.	St. Petersburg, Russia	4,672	4,694	4,738	0.09	139
40.	Madrid, Spain	4,513	4,772	5,104	1.11	66
41.	Dhaka, Bangladesh	4,419	5,296	6,492	3.62	32
42.	Lahore, Pakistan	4,376	4,986	5,864	2.61	57
43.	Shenyang, China	4,289	4,457	4,684	0.77	39
44.	Barcelona, Spain	4,227	4,492	4,834	1.22	87
45.	Baghdad, Iraq	4,059	4,566	5,239	2.36	97
46.	Manchester, United Kingdom	4,030	3,949	3,827	–0.40	357
47.	Philadelphia, United States	4,003	3,988	3,979	–0.08	471
48.	San Francisco, United States	3,987	4,104	4,214	0.58	428
49.	Belo Horizonte, Brazil	3,812	4,373	5,125	2.75	79
50.	Kinshasa, Zaire	3,747	4,520	5,646	3.75	57
51.	Ho Chi Minh City, Vietnam	3,725	4,064	4,481	1.74	31
52.	Ahmadabad, India	3,709	4,200	4,837	2.49	32
53.	Hyderabad, India	3,673	4,149	4,765	2.44	88
54.	Sydney, Australia	3,536	3,619	3,708	0.47	338
55.	Athens, Greece	3,507	3,670	3,866	0.91	116
56.	Miami, United States	3,471	3,679	3,894	1.16	448
57.	Guadalajara, Mexico	3,370	3,839	4,451	2.61	78
58.	Guangzhou, China	3,360	3,485	3,652	0.73	79
59.	Surabaya, Indonesia	3,248	3,428	3,632	1.08	43
60.	Caracas, Venezuela	3,217	3,338	3,435	0.74	54
61.	Wuhan, China	3,200	3,325	3,495	0.77	65
62.	Toronto, Canada	3,145	3,296	3,296	0.94	154
63.	Porto Alegre, Brazil	3,114	3,541	4,109	2.57	231
64.	Rome, Italy	3,033	3,079	3,129	0.30	69

Rank in 1990	City	1990	1995	2000	Average Annual Growth Rate (%) 1990–95	Area (square miles)
65.	Greater Berlin, Germany	3,021	3,018	3,006	–0.02	274
66.	Naples, Italy	2,978	3,051	3,134	0.48	62
67.	Casablanca, Morocco	2,973	3,327	3,795	2.25	35
68.	Detroit, United States	2,969	2,865	2,735	–0.71	468
69.	Alexandria, Egypt	2,941	3,114	3,304	1.14	35
70.	Monterrey, Mexico	2,939	3,385	3,974	2.83	77
71.	Montreal, Canada	2,916	2,996	3,071	0.54	164
72.	Melbourne, Australia	2,915	2,946	2,968	0.21	327
73.	Ankara, Turkey	2,872	3,263	3,777	2.55	55
74.	Rangoon, Burma	2,864	3,075	3,332	1.42	47
75.	Kiev, Ukraine	2,796	2,983	3,237	1.30	62
76.	Dallas, United States	2,787	2,972	3,257	1.28	419
77.	Singapore, Singapore	2,719	2,816	2,913	0.70	78
78.	Taegu, South Korea	2,651	3,201	4,051	3.77	(n.a.)
79.	Harbin, China	2,643	2,747	2,887	0.77	30
80.	Washington, United States	2,565	2,637	2,707	0.56	357
81.	Poona, India	2,547	2,987	3,647	3.19	(n.a.)
82.	Boston, United States	2,476	2,480	2,485	0.03	303
83.	Lisbon, Portugal	2,426	2,551	2,717	1.00	(n.a.)
84.	Tashkent, Uzbekistan	2,418	2,640	2,947	1.76	(n.a.)
85.	Chongqing, China	2,395	2,632	2,961	1.89	(n.a.)
86.	Chengdu, China	2,372	2,465	2,591	0.77	25
87.	Vienna, Austria	2,344	2,474	2,647	1.08	(n.a.)
88.	Houston, United States	2,329	2,456	2,651	1.06	310
89.	Budapest, Hungary	2,303	2,313	2,335	0.08	138
90.	Salvador, Brazil	2,298	2,694	3,286	3.18	(n.a.)
91.	Bucharest, Romania	2,163	2,214	2,271	0.47	52
92.	Birmingham, United Kingdom	2,162	2,130	2,078	–0.30	223
93.	Havana, Cuba	2,130	2,218	2,333	0.81	(n.a.)
94.	Kanpur, India	2,129	2,356	2,673	2.02	(n.a.)

Source: U.S. Bureau of the Census, 1991, International Data Base. NOTE: For this table cities are defined as population clusters of continuous built-up area with a population density of at least 5,000 persons per square mile. The boundary of the city was determined by examining detailed maps of each city in conjunction with the most recent official population statistics. Exclaves of areas exceeding the minimum population density were added to the city if the intervening gap was less than one mile. To the extent practical, nonresidential areas such as parks, airports, industrial complexes, and water were excluded from the area reported for each city, thus making the population density reflective of the concentrations in the residential portions of the city. By using a consistent definition for the city, it is possible to make comparisons of the cities on the basis of total population, area, and population density.

Political and administrative boundaries were disregarded in determining the population of a city.Detroit includes Windsor, Canada.

The population of each city was projected based on the proportion each city was of its country total at the time of the last two censuses and projected country populations.

Population figures for the nine cities with (n.a.) in the area column were derived by a less precise method, not involving the use of detailed maps. Thirty-four other cities are projected to have at least 2,000,000 inhabitants by midyear 2000. These population figures may not agree with those in the Countries of the World section as the source is different, and the basis for these figures is spelled out above.

Crude Marriage and Divorce Rates for Selected Countries

(per 1,000 population)

Country	Marriage Rate 1991	Marriage Rate 1990	Marriage Rate 1989	Divorce Rate 1991	Divorce Rate 1990	Divorce Rate 1989
Australia	6.6	6.8	7.0	n.a.	2.49	2.46
Austria	5.6	5.8	5.6	n.a.	2.11	2.03
Belgium	6.2	6.6	6.4	n.a.	n.a.	n.a.
Canada	n.a.	7.1	7.3	n.a.	n.a.	n.a.
Czechoslovakia	6.7	8.4	7.5	2.39[1]	2.61	2.54
Denmark	6.0	6.1	6.0	n.a.	n.a.	2.95
Finland	4.7	4.8	5.1	n.a.	n.a.	2.89
France	4.9	5.1	5.0	n.a.	1.87	1.87
Germany	6.3	6.5	6.7	n.a.	1.94	2.04
Greece	6.0	5.8	6.0	n.a.	n.a.	n.a.
Hungary	5.9	6.4	6.3	n.a.	2.40	2.40
Ireland	4.8	5.0	5.1	n.a.	n.a.	n.a.
Israel	6.5	7.0	7.0	n.a.	1.29	1.29
Italy	5.5	5.4	5.4	n.a.	0.48	0.53
Japan	6.0	5.8	5.8	n.a.	1.27	1.28
Luxembourg	6.7	6.2	5.8	n.a.	n.a.	2.27
Netherlands	6.3	6.4	6.1	1.88[1]	1.90	1.90
New Zealand	6.8	7.0	6.9	2.70[1]	2.70	2.58
Norway	n.a.	5.2	4.9	n.a.	2.40	2.18
Poland	6.2	6.7	6.8	0.91[1]	1.11	1.24
Portugal	6.8	7.3	7.4	1.01[1]	0.93	0.98
Spain	5.6	5.5	5.6	0.59[1]	n.a.	n.a.
Sweden	4.6	4.7	12.8	2.20[1]	2.26	2.22
Switzerland	6.8	6.9	6.8	n.a.	1.96	1.91
United Kingdom	6.5	6.8	6.1	n.a.	2.88	2.86
United States	9.4	9.8	9.7	4.73[1]	4.70	4.70
Yugoslavia	n.a.	6.3	6.7	n.a.	0.81	0.96

1. Provisional. n.a. = not available. *Sources:* Marriage rates: United Nations, *Monthly Bulletin of Statistics, June 1993.* Divorce rates: United Nations, *Demographic Yearbook 1991.*

World Population by Country, 1993–2025

(Covers countries with 10 million or more population in 1993)

Country	1993	2000[1]	2010	2025
Afghanistan	17,400,000	25,400,000	34,600,000	48,800,000
Algeria	27,300,000	32,700,000	38,200,000	46,800,000
Argentina	33,500,000	36,000,000	39,900,000	44,600,000
Australia	17,800,000	19,100,000	20,900,000	22,900,000
Bangladesh	113,900,000	146,600,000	164,800,000	211,200,000
Belarus	10,300,000	n.a.	10,800,000	11,000,000
Belgium	10,100,000	9,900,000	10,100,000	9,900,000
Brazil	152,000,000	179,500,000	185,600,000	205,300,000
Burkina Faso	10,000,000	12,500,000	17,200,000	26,200,000
Cameroon	12,800,000	14,500,000	21,200,000	32,600,000
Canada	28,100,000	29,300,000	32,700,000	35,700,000
Chile	13,500,000	15,300,000	17,000,000	19,800,000
China				
Mainland	1,178,500,000	1,280,000,000	1,397,800,000	1,546,300,000
Taiwan	20,900,000	22,100,000	23,800,000	25,200,000
Colombia	34,900,000	38,000,000	44,500,000	51,300,000
Côte d'Ivoire	13,400,000	18,500,000	23,700,000	37,900,000
Cuba	11,000,000	11,600,000	12,300,000	12,900,000
Czech Republic	10,300,000	n.a.	10,800,000	10,900,000
Ecuador	10,300,000	13,600,000	14,000,000	16,800,000
Egypt	58,300,000	69,000,000	82,500,000	104,600,000
Ethiopia[2]	56,700,000	70,800,000	94,500,000	140,800,000
France	57,700,000	57,900,000	58,800,000	58,700,000
Germany[3]	81,100,000	81,200,000	78,200,000	73,200,000
Ghana	16,400,000	20,400,000	26,600,000	38,000,000
Greece	10,500,000	10,200,000	10,900,000	10,500,000
Guatemala	10,000,000	11,800,000	15,800,000	21,700,000
Hungary	10,300,000	10,600,000	10,400,000	10,400,000
India	897,400,000	1,042,500,000	1,166,200,000	1,379,600,000
Indonesia	187,600,000	223,800,000	238,800,000	278,200,000
Iran	62,800,000	75,700,000	106,800,000	161,900,000
Iraq	19,200,000	27,200,000	34,500,000	52,600,000
Italy	57,800,000	58,600,000	56,400,000	51,900,000
Japan	124,800,000	127,500,000	130,400,000	125,800,000
Kazakhstan	17,200,000	n.a.	18,800,000	19,600,000
Kenya	27,700,000	35,100,000	45,200,000	61,900,000
Madagascar	13,300,000	16,600,000	22,400,000	33,700,000
Malawi	10,000,000	11,800,000	16,500,000	25,800,000
Malaysia	18,400,000	21,500,000	26,000,000	33,500,000
Mexico	90,000,000	107,200,000	118,500,000	137,500,000
Morocco	28,000,000	31,400,000	38,100,000	46,300,000
Mozambique	15,300,000	20,400,000	25,400,000	36,300,000
Myanmar	43,500,000	49,800,000	57,700,000	69,900,000
Nepal	20,400,000	24,300,000	30,500,000	41,000,000
Netherlands	15,200,000	15,300,000	16,700,000	17,200,000
Nigeria	95,100,000	n.a.	162,000,000	246,000,000
North Korea	22,600,000	24,900,000	28,500,000	32,100,000
Pakistan	122,400,000	149,100,000	190,700,000	275,100,000
Peru	22,900,000	26,400,000	30,100,000	35,600,000
Philippines	64,600,000	82,700,000	85,500,000	100,800,000
Poland	38,500,000	38,900,000	41,300,000	42,700,000
Romania	23,200,000	24,500,000	24,000,000	24,400,000
Russia	149,000,000	n.a.	153,000,000	152,300,000
Saudi Arabia	17,500,000	22,000,000	30,000,000	48,700,000
South Africa	39,000,000	51,500,000	55,900,000	70,000,000
South Korea	44,600,000	46,000,000	51,700,000	54,800,000
Spain	39,100,000	40,700,000	38,900,000	36,400,000
Sri Lanka	17,800,000	19,400,000	21,400,000	24,000,000
Sudan	27,400,000	33,600,000	43,000,000	60,600,000
Syria	13,500,000	18,000,000	24,200,000	36,500,000
Tanzania	27,800,000	36,500,000	47,500,000	73,000,000
Thailand	57,200,000	63,700,000	69,200,000	76,400,000
Turkey	60,700,000	69,000,000	81,800,000	98,700,000
Uganda	18,100,000	25,100,000	32,500,000	49,600,000
Ukraine	51,900,000	n.a.	52,300,000	51,500,000
United Kingdom	58,000,000	59,100,000	59,900,000	61,000,000
United States	258,300,000	268,300,000	298,600,000	334,700,000
Uzbekistan	21,700,000	n.a.	29,800,000	37,000,000

Country	1993	2000[1]	2010	2025
Venezuela	20,700,000	24,100,000	27,600,000	32,700,000
Vietnam	71,800,000	88,300,000	91,700,000	107,200,000
Yemen[4]	11,300,000	13,600,000	20,000,000	31,600,000
Zaire	41,200,000	50,300,000	68,600,000	104,500,000
Zimbabwe	10,700,000	13,100,000	16,500,000	22,500,000

1. Projection made in 1990. 2. Includes Eritrea. 3. Figure is the total of the populations of East and West Germany. 4. Figures are the total of the populations of North and South Yemen. NOTE: n.a. = not available. *Source: World Population Data Sheet 1990* and *1993,* Population Reference Bureau, Inc., Washington, D.C.

Estimates of World Population by Regions

	Estimated population in millions							
Year	North America[1]	Latin America[2]	Europe[3]	Former U.S.S.R.	Asia[4]	Africa	Oceania	World total
1650	1	7	103	([5])	257	100	2	470
1750	1	10	144	([5])	437	100	2	694
1850	26	33	274	([5])	656	100	2	1,091
1900	81	63	423	([5])	857	141	6	1,571
1950	166	164	392	180	1,380	219	13	2,513
1960	199	215	425	214	1,683	275	16	3,027
1970	226	283	460	244	2,091	354	19	3,678
1980	252	365	484	266	2,618	472	23	4,478
1985	264	410	492	278	2,831	566	24	4,865
1988	272	429	497	286	2,995	623	26	5,128
1989	275	438	499	289	3,061	646	26	5,234
1990	278	447	501	291	3,116	661	27	5,321
1991	280	451	502	292	3,155	677	27	5,384
1992	283	453	511[6]	284	3,207	654	28	5,420
1993	287	460	513	285	3,257	677	28	5,506

1. U.S. (including Alaska and Hawaii), Bermuda, Canada, Greenland, and St. Pierre and Miquelon. 2. Mexico, Central and South America, and Caribbean Islands. 3. Includes Russia 1650-1900. 4. Excludes Russia (U.S.S.R.). 5. Included in Europe. 6. Beginning with 1992, includes Estonia, Latvia, and Lithuania. NOTE: From 1930 on European Turkey included in Asia not Europe. *Sources:* W.F. Willcox, 1650-1900; United Nations, 1930-70. United States Department of Commerce, Bureau of the Census, 1980–85; *1988-1993 World Population Data Sheet,* Population Reference Bureau, Inc., Washington, D.C.

World's 20 Most Populous Countries: 1993 and 2025

1993			2025		
Rank	Country	Population	Rank	Country	Population
1.	China	1,178,500,000	1.	China	1,546,300,000
2.	India	897,400,000	2.	India	1,379,600,000
3.	United States	258,300,000	3.	United States	334,700,000
4.	Indonesia	187,600,000	4.	Indonesia	278,200,000
5.	Brazil	152,000,000	5.	Pakistan	275,100,000
6.	Russia	149,000,000	6.	Nigeria	246,000,000
7.	Japan	124,800,000	7.	Bangladesh	211,200,000
8.	Pakistan	122,400,000	8.	Brazil	205,300,000
9.	Bangladesh	113,900,000	9.	Iran	161,900,000
10.	Nigeria	95,100,000	10.	Russia	152,300,000
11.	Mexico	90,000,000	11.	Ethiopia[1]	140,800,000
12.	Germany	81,100,000	12.	Mexico	137,500,000
13.	Vietnam	71,800,000	13.	Japan	125,800,000
14.	Philippines	64,600,000	14.	Vietnam	107,200,000
15.	Iran	62,800,000	15.	Egypt	104,600,000
16.	Turkey	60,700,000	16.	Zaire	104,500,000
17.	Egypt	58,300,000	17.	Philippines	100,800,000
18.	United Kingdom	58,000,000	18.	Turkey	98,700,000
19.	Italy	57,800,000	19.	Tanzania	73,000,000
20.	France	57,700,000	20.	South Africa	70,000,000

1. Includes Eritrea. *Sources: 1993 World Population Data Sheet* of the Population Reference Bureau, Inc.

China and India Lead in Population

Ninety-two countries have higher birth rates than India, and 134 countries have higher birth rates than China. Nevertheless, more than one-third of the world's births occur in these countries. In 2000 China will rank first in population, as it does now, but in 2100 India will have overtaken it and rank first.

Expectation of Life by Age and Sex for Selected Countries

Country	Period	Average future lifetime in years at stated age											
		Males						Females					
		0	1	10	20	40	60	0	1	10	20	40	60
NORTH AMERICA													
U.S.	1989	71.80	71.60	62.80	53.30	35.10	18.60	78.60	78.30	69.50	59.70	40.50	22.70
Canada	1985–1987	73.02	72.64	63.87	54.26	35.51	18.40	79.79	79.33	70.52	60.71	41.27	23.24
Mexico	1979	62.10	—	—	—	—	—	66.00	—	—	—	—	—
Trinidad & Tobago	1980–1985	66.88	67.34	58.97	49.39	31.13	15.84	71.62	71.64	63.18	53.44	34.55	18.42
CENTRAL AND SOUTH AMERICA													
Brazil	1985–1990[1]	62.30	—	—	—	—	—	67.50	—	—	—	—	—
Chile	1985–1990	68.05	68.43	59.87	50.27	32.30	16.84	75.05	75.29	66.69	56.93	37.81	20.58
Costa Rica	1985–1990[1]	72.40	—	—	—	—	—	77.04	—	—	—	—	—
Ecuador	1985[2]	63.39	67.12	60.43	51.16	33.57	17.76	67.59	70.64	63.09	54.51	36.32	19.43
Guatemala	1979–1980	55.11	59.09	54.38	45.55	30.56	16.57	59.43	62.98	58.74	49.79	33.01	17.50
Panama	1985–1990[3]	70.15	70.92	63.00	53.58	35.43	18.80	74.10	74.65	66.62	57.03	38.28	20.81
Peru	1990[4]	62.93	67.37	60.55	51.16	33.06	16.69	66.58	70.67	63.86	54.36	35.94	18.46
Uruguay	1984–1986	68.43	69.67	61.03	51.40	32.68	16.65	74.88	75.89	67.24	57.46	38.27	21.01
Venezuela	1985[4]	66.68	68.45	60.31	50.92	33.07	17.30	72.80	74.16	65.90	56.23	37.31	20.30
EUROPE													
Austria	1990[5]	72.50	72.11	63.32	53.64	34.90	18.09	79.02	78.59	69.76	59.90	40.43	22.28
Belgium	1979–1982[5]	70.04	69.99	61.26	51.64	32.98	16.26	76.79	76.61	67.88	58.08	38.82	20.93
Cyprus	1985–1989	73.92	73.89	65.16	55.45	36.51	19.32	78.33	78.13	69.32	59.46	39.91	21.61
Czechoslovakia	1990[5]	67.25	67.14	53.43	48.62	30.01	14.69	75.81	75.54	66.73	56.90	37.45	19.59
Denmark[6]	1989–90[5]	71.98	71.60	62.80	53.10	34.30	17.50	77.70	77.20	68.40	58.60	39.20	21.70
Finland	1989[5]	70.85	70.33	61.48	51.87	33.43	17.08	78.90	78.33	69.48	59.62	40.19	21.89
France	1990[5]	72.75	72.36	63.56	53.87	35.51	19.02	80.94	80.44	71.61	61.77	42.45	24.19
Germany, Former East	1988–1989[5]	70.03	69.65	60.90	51.19	32.49	16.16	76.23	75.76	66.97	57.13	37.73	19.79
Germany	1985–1987[5]	71.81	71.52	62.73	53.01	34.07	17.26	78.37	77.97	69.15	59.30	39.87	21.72
Greece	1980[5]	72.15	72.82	54.13	54.48	35.58	18.17	76.35	76.78	68.24	58.43	38.95	20.63
Hungary	1990	65.13	65.22	56.45	46.78	28.84	14.72	73.71	73.69	64.91	55.10	36.05	19.02
Ireland	1985–1987[5]	71.01	70.67	61.88	52.18	33.12	15.98	76.70	76.28	67.46	57.60	38.05	20.06
Italy	1988[5]	73.18	72.92	64.09	54.37	35.36	18.07	79.70	79.35	70.50	60.63	41.09	22.65
Netherlands	1989–1990[5]	73.67	73.81	64.44	54.66	35.44	17.91	79.88	80.01	70.53	60.70	41.21	22.96
Norway	1990[5]	73.44	73.06	64.27	54.58	35.66	18.24	79.81	79.27	70.42	60.58	41.10	22.73
Poland	1990	66.51	66.69	57.97	48.32	30.22	15.31	75.49	75.53	66.76	56.93	37.58	19.96
Portugal	1990	70.13	70.05	61.41	51.97	33.73	17.21	77.17	77.01	68.30	58.53	39.25	21.15
Russia	1989	64.20	—	—	—	—	—	74.50	—	—	—	—	—
Spain	1985–1986[5]	73.27	73.00	64.26	54.57	35.76	18.69	79.69	79.32	70.53	60.70	41.22	22.71
Sweden	1990[5]	74.81	74.31	65.47	55.70	36.66	19.08	80.41	79.84	70.95	61.09	41.60	23.27
Switzerland	1989–1990[5]	74.00	73.60	64.80	55.10	36.60	19.10	80.00	80.40	71.50	61.70	42.30	23.90
United Kingdom	1987–1989	72.42	72.16	63.35	53.63	34.51	17.21	78.03	77.63	68.79	58.94	39.44	21.44
Yugoslavia	1988–1990[5]	68.64	69.42	60.78	51.07	32.35	16.33	74.48	75.20	66.55	56.73	37.36	19.50
ASIA													
Bangladesh	1988	56.91	63.66	58.73	49.53	31.58	15.50	55.97	61.50	57.26	48.30	31.44	15.76
India	1981–1985	55.40	60.81	56.08	46.99	29.39	14.61	55.67	61.11	57.98	49.18	32.12	16.42
Iran	1976	55.75	60.78	53.87	45.19	29.19	14.58	55.04	60.14	54.38	44.97	30.47	15.39
Israel[7]	1989	74.54	74.31	65.54	55.76	36.62	18.96	78.09	77.83	69.04	59.18	39.67	21.32
Japan	1990[8]	75.86	75.24	66.47	56.71	37.52	19.95	81.81	81.15	72.32	62.44	42.90	24.29
Korea, South	1989	66.92	66.66	58.18	48.56	30.30	14.87	74.96	74.75	66.23	56.54	37.50	19.87
Pakistan	1976–1978	59.04	66.46	61.34	52.30	34.77	19.25	59.20	65.58	60.68	51.98	35.23	19.27
Sri Lanka	1981	67.78	68.99	60.99	51.64	33.19	17.74	71.66	72.67	64.75	55.36	36.96	19.57
Syria	1981	64.42	68.48	61.18	51.69	33.28	16.61	68.05	71.73	64.12	54.85	36.07	18.32
AFRICA													
Egypt	1985–1990[1]	57.80	—	—	—	—	—	60.30	—	—	—	—	—
Kenya	1985–1990[1]	56.50	—	—	—	—	—	60.50	—	—	—	—	—
South Africa	1985–1990[1]	57.50	—	—	—	—	—	63.50	—	—	—	—	—
OCEANIA													
Australia	1990[5, 9]	73.86	73.54	64.76	55.09	36.38	18.82	80.01	79.60	70.76	60.93	41.49	23.14
New Zealand	1988–1990	71.94	71.75	63.04	53.55	35.04	17.80	77.96	77.61	68.81	59.06	39.75	21.94

1. Estimates prepared in the Population Division of the United Nations. 2. Excluding nomadic Indian tribes. 3. Excluding tribal Indian population. 4. Excluding Indian jungle population. 5. Complete life table. 6. Excluding the Faeroe Islands and Greenland. 7. Including data for East Jerusalem and Israeli residents in certain other territories. 8. For Japanese nationals in Japan only. 9. Excluding full-blooded aborigines. NOTE: Figures are latest available as of August 1993. *Source:* United Nations *Demographic Yearbook, 1991.*

Crude Birth and Death Rates for Selected Countries

(per 1,000 population)

Country	Birth rates 1991	1990	1985	1980	1975	Death rates 1991	1990	1985	1980	1975
Australia	14.8	15.4	15.7	15.3	16.9	6.9	7.0	7.5	7.4	7.9
Austria	12.0	11.6	11.6	12.0	12.5	10.6	10.6	11.9	12.2	12.8
Belgium	12.8	12.6	11.5	12.7	12.2	10.7	10.6	11.2	11.6	12.2
Canada	15.2	5.2	14.8	15.4	15.8	7.3	n7.2	7.2	7.2	7.4
Cuba	16.2	17.6	18.0	14.1	n.a.	6.6	6.8	6.4	5.7	n.a.
Former Czechoslovakia	13.3	13.4	14.5	16.4	19.6	11.5	11.7	11.8	12.1	11.5
Denmark	12.5	12.4	10.6	11.2	14.2	11.6	11.9	11.4	10.9	10.1
Finland	13.1	13.2	12.8	13.1	13.9	9.8	10.0	9.8	9.3	9.3
France	13.3	13.5	13.9	14.8	14.1	9.2	9.3	10.1	10.2	10.6
Germany[1]	11.3	11.4	9.6	10.0	9.7	11.1	11.2	11.5	11.6	12.1
Greece	n.a.	10.2	11.7	15.4	15.7	n.a	9.3	9.4	9.1	8.9
Hong Kong	n.a.	11.7	14.0	16.9	n.a.	n.a	4.9	4.6	5.1	n.a.
Hungary	12.3	12.1	12.2	13.9	18.4	14.0	14.1	13.9	13.6	12.4
Ireland	15.0	15.1	17.6	21.9	21.5	8.9	9.1	9.4	9.7	10.6
Israel	21.4	22.2	23.5	24.1	28.2	6.3	6.2	6.6	6.7	7.1
Italy	9.9	9.8	10.1	11.2	14.8	9.7	9.4	9.5	9.7	9.9
Japan	9.8	9.9	11.9	13.7	17.2	6.7	6.7	6.2	6.2	6.4
Luxembourg	12.9	13.3	11.2	11.5	11.2	9.7	10.1	11.0	11.5	12.2
Malta	15.2	15.2	16.8	16.0	18.3	7.8	7.7	8.5	8.8	8.8
Mauritius	20.7	21.0	18.8	27.0	25.1	6.6	6.5	6.8	7.2	8.1
Netherlands	13.2	13.3	12.3	12.8	13.0	8.6	8.6	8.5	8.1	8.3
New Zealand	17.8	18.0	15.6	n.a.	18.4	7.8	7.9	8.4	n.a.	8.1
Norway	14.2	14.3	12.3	12.5	14.1	10.5	10.7	10.7	10.1	9.9
Panama	n.a.	23.9	26.6	26.8	32.3	n.a.	n.a.	n.a.	n.a.	n.a.
Poland	14.3	14.3	18.2	19.5	18.9	10.6	10.2	10.3	9.8	8.7
Portugal	11.8	11.8	12.8	16.4	19.1	9.7	10.4	9.6	9.9	10.4
Romania	11.9	13.6	15.8	n.a.	n.a.	10.9	10.6	10.9	n.a.	n.a.
Singapore	17.8	17.0	16.6	17.3	17.8	5.0	n.a.	5.2	5.2	5.1
Spain	9.9	10.2	11.7	16.1	19.1	8.7	8.5.	8.0	7.7	8.2
Sweden	14.4	14.5	11.8	11.7	12.6	11.0	11.	11.3	11.0	10.8
Switzerland	12.6	12.5	11.6	11.3	12.3	9.0	9.5	9.2	9.2	8.7
Tunisia	n.a.	25.8	31.3	35.2	36.6	n.a.	n.a.	n.a.	n.a.	n.a.
United Kingdom	13.7	13.9	13.3	13.5	12.5	11.2	11.2	11.8	11.8	11.9
United States	16.3	16.7	15.7	16.2	14.0	8.6	8.6	8.7	8.9	8.9
Former Yugoslavia	n.a.	14.0	15.9	17.0	18.2	n.a.	9.0	9.1	9.0	8.7

1. All data pertaining to Germany prior to1990, are for West Germany. NOTE: n.a. = not available. *Source:* United Nations, *Monthly Bulletin of Statistics,* May 1993.

Legal Abortions in Selected Countries, 1982–1990

Country	1982	1983	1984	1985	1986	1987	1988	1989	1990
Bulgaria	147,791	134,165	131,140	132,041	134,686	133,815	—	132,021	144,644
Canada	66,254	61,750	62,291	60,956	62,406	63,585	—	70,705	—
Cuba	126,745	116,956	139,588	138,671	160,926	152,704	155,325	151,146	—
Czechoslovakia	107,638	108,662	113,802	119,325	124,188	158,451	164,730	160,285	159,705
Denmark	21,462	20,791	20,742	19,919	20,067	20,830	21,199	21,456	—
Finland	13,861	13,360	13,645	13,832	13,310	13,000[1]	12,995	12,658	—
France	181,122	182,862	180,789	173,335	166,797	161,036	163,000	165,199	161,646
Germany, West	91,064	86,529	86,298	83,538	84,274	88,540	83,784	75,297	78,808
Greece	—	220	193	180[1]	—	—	—	—	—
Hungary	78,682	78,599	82,191	81,970	83,586	84,547	87,106	90,508	90,394
Iceland	613	687	745	705	684	691	673	670	714
India	500,624	492,696	561,033	583,704	—	—	534,870	582,161	596,345
Israel	16,829	15,593	18,948	18,406	17,469	15,290	16,181	15,216	—
Italy	231,308	231,061	228,377	210,192	196,969	187,618	175,541	165,456	—
Netherlands	20,187	19,700	18,700[1]	17,300[1]	—	—	—	—	—
New Zealand	6,903	7,198	7,275	7,130	8,056	8,789	10,000[1]	10,200	—
Norway	13,496	13,646	14,070	14,599	15,474	15,422	15,852	16,208	15,551
Poland	141,177	130,980	132,844	135,564	129,720	122,536	105,333	80,127	59,417
Singapore	15,548	19,100	22,190	23,512	21,374	21,226	—	—	—
Sweden	32,604	31,014	30,755	30,838	33,090	34,707	37,585	37,920	37,489
United Kingdom	171,417	170,620	179,102	180,983	157,168	165,542	178,426	180,622	184,092
United States	1,304,000	1,269,000	1,333,500	1,328,600	1,328,000[1]	1,354,000[1]	—	—	—

1. Provisional. NOTE: Data latest available as of August 1993. *Source:* United Nations, *Demographic Yearbook, 1991.*

Cost of Living of United Nations Personnel in Selected Cities as Reflected by Index of Retail Prices, 1992

(New York City, December 1992 = 100)

City	Index	City	Index	City	Index
Abu Dhabi	89	Dar es Salaam	78[1]	Nassau	120
Addis Ababa	80[1]	Geneva	123	New Delhi	80
Algiers	92	Guatemala City	77	Panama City	88
Amman	82	The Hague	99	Paris	109
Ankara	85	Helsinki	96	Port-au-Prince	84
Athens	84	Islamabad	77	Quito	84
Baghdad	133	Jakarta	84	Rabat	81
Bangkok	87	Kabul	68	Rome	97
Beirut	98	Kathmandu	74	Roseau	94
Belgrade	89[2]	Kingston	92	San Salvador	83
Bogota	84	Kinshasa	94[1]	Santiago	81
Bonn	106	La Paz	82	Seoul	99
Brazzaville	103[1]	Lagos	93[1]	Sofia	82
Brussels	93	Lima	96	Sydney	76
Budapest	88	London	95	Tokyo	155
Buenos Aires	108	Madrid	110	Tripoli	128[1]
Cairo	86	Managua	90	Tunis	85
Caracas	86	Manila	89	Valetta	85
Colombo	78	Mexico City	94	Vienna	109
Copenhagen	106	Montevideo	97	Warsaw	85
Dhaka	79	Montreal	82	Washington, D.C.	90
Dakar	103	Nairobi	74	Yangon	101

1. Calculated on the basis of cost of Government or subsidized housing which is normally lower than prevailing rentals.
2. Indexes frozen. *Source:* United Nations, *Monthly Bulletin of Statistics, March 1993.*

Consumer Price Indexes for All Items for Selected Countries, 1992

(1980 = 100)

Country	Index	Country	Index	Country	Index
Australia	227.3	Greece	789.6	Philippines	165.6
Austria	151.9	Hong Kong	265.8	Singapore	132.2
Canada	190.9	Indonesia	132.2	South Africa	528.2[1]
Chile	893.3	Italy	280.6	Spain	273.4
Cyprus	180.0	Japan	128.6	Sri Lanka	396.1
Czechoslovakia, former	216.7	Jordan	227.3	Sweden	232.3
Denmark	185.5	Korea, South	213.0	Turkey	1,283.1
Egypt	649.3	Mexico	21,334.8	United Kingdom	207.2
Finland	204.8	Morocco	231.0[1]	United States	170.3
France	194.4	Netherlands	137.1	Uruguay	38,861.8
Germany	139.3	Norway	220.6		

1. As of Sept. 1992. *Source:* International Labour Office from *Monthly Bulletin of Statistics, July 1993*

Labor Force Participation Rates by Sex[1]

Country	Females				Males				Females as percent of total labor force			
	1990	1989	1985	1980	1990	1989	1985	1980	1990	1989	1985	1980
Canada	53.7	53.3	48.8	46.2	69.8	71.1	68.7	73.0	44.7	44.1	42.7	39.7
France	40.4[2]	40.1[2]	39.6	40.1	61.3[2]	61.0[2]	62.3	68.5	42.3[2]	42.3[2]	41.4	39.5
Germany[3]	40.2[2]	39.5[2]	37.1	37.7	65.3[2]	65.6[2]	66.4	70.9	40.8[2]	40.2[2]	39.0	38.0
Italy	29.0[2]	28.6	27.8	27.9	60.5[2]	59.9	62.5	66.0	34.5[2]	34.3	32.8	31.7
Japan	48.0	47.4	46.3	45.7	75.4	75.1	75.9	77.9	40.3	40.1	39.4	38.4
Sweden	62.8[2]	62.6	59.7	58.0	71.8[2]	71.9	70.5	73.6	47.8[2]	47.8	47.2	45.2
United Kingdom	49.8[2]	49.1[2]	44.3	44.8	70.4[2]	70.5[2]	67.1	72.8	43.5[2]	43.1[2]	42.0	40.4
United States	54.4	54.3	50.4	47.7	71.9	72.5	70.9	72.0	45.4	45.2	44.1	42.4

1. Labor force of all ages as percent of population, 15-64 years old. 2. Break in series. 3. Former West Germany (prior to unification) *Source:* U.S. Bureau of Labor Statistics, *Comparative Labor Force Statistics for Ten Countries, 1959–1990, November 1991.* From *Statistical Abstract of the United States 1992.* NOTE: Data are most recent available.

Unemployment Figures for Selected Countries: 1987–1992

(In thousands except for percentages)

	1992		1991		1990		1989		1988		1987	
Country	**No.**	**%**	**No.**	**%**	**No.**	**%**	**No.**	**%**	**No.**	**%**	**No.**	**%**
Australia	933.1	10.8	821.0	9.6	587.1	6.9	509.1	6.2	576.2	7.2	628.8	8.1
Austria[1]	193.1	5.9	185.0	5.8	165.8	5.4	149.2	5.0	158.6	5.3	164.5	5.6
Belgium[1]	472.9	11.2	429.5	10.4	402.8	9.8	419.3	10.1	459.4	10.9	500.8	11.9
Canada	1,556.0	11.3	1,417.0	10.3	1,109.0	8.1	1,018.0	7.5	1,047.0	7.8	1,167.0	8.9
Chile[2]	n.a.	n.a.	253.7	5.3	281.3	5.6	249.8	n.a.	285.8	8.1	343.6	7.9
Denmark[1]	314.7	11.3	293.9	10.5	269.1	9.6	264.9	9.4	243.9	8.7	219.4	8.0
Finland	328.0	13.1	193.0	7.6	88.0	3.4	89.0	3.5	116.0	4.5	130.0	5.1
Germany, West[1]	1,820.6	6.7	1,689.4	6.3	1,872.0	7.2	2,032.0	7.9	2,236.6	8.7	2,232.5	8.9
Hong-Kong	54.7	2.0	50.3	1.8	37.0	1.3	30.0	1.1	37.9	1.4	47.5	1.7
Ireland[3, 4]	283.1	n.a.	253.9	19.1	224.7	17.4	231.6	17.9	241.4	18.6	247.3	19.0
Israel	207.5	11.2	187.4	10.6	157.9	9.6	142.5	n.a.	100.0	6.4	90.0	6.1
Italy	2,799.0	11.5	2,653.0	10.9	2,621.0	11.0	2,865.0	12.0	2,885.0	12.0	2,832.0	12.0
Japan	1,420.8	2.1	1,370.0	2.1	1,340.0	2.1	1,420.0	2.3	1,550.0	2.5	1,730.0	2.9
Korea, South	463.4	2.4	436.0	2.3	451.0	2.5	459.0	2.6	435.0	2.5	519.0	3.1
Netherlands[1, 5]	303.0	4.2	319.0	4.5	346.0	4.9	390.0	5.8	433.0	6.5	685.5	11.5
New Zealand[1]	n.a.	n.a.	195.1	n.a.	164.0	7.7	153.6	n.a.	120.9	n.a.	86.1	6.6
Norway	126.0	5.9	116.0	5.5	112.0	4.3	106.0	3.8	69.3	3.2	45.0	2.1
Portugal	186.9	4.1	198.6	4.1	220.1	4.7	232.8	5.0	262.2	5.7	319.6	7.1
Puerto Rico[6]	n.a.	n.a.	176.0	16.0	152.0	14.2	155.0	14.6	158.0	15.0	171.0	16.8
Sweden	214.0	4.8	122.0	2.7	69.0	1.6	61.0	1.4	72.0	1.6	84.0	1.9
Switzerland[1]	92.3	n.a.	39.2	1.3	18.1	0.6	17.5	0.6	22.2	0.7	24.7	0.8
United Kingdom[1, 7]	2,778.6	9.8	2,291.9	8.1	1,664.5	5.9	1,800.5	6.4	2,370.4	8.4	2,953.4	10.6
United States	9,384.0	7.4	8,426.0	6.7	6,874.0	5.5	6,528.0	5.3	6,701.0	5.5	7,425.0	6.2
Yugoslavia[1]	n.a.	n.a.	1,501.5	19.5	1,308.5	16.4	1,201.2	14.9	1,131.8	14.1	1,080.6	13.6

1. Employment office statistics. All others labor force sample surveys unless otherwise indicated. 2. Average of less than 12 months. 3. Excluding agriculture, fishing and private domestic services. 4. Compulsory unemployment insurance statistics. 5. Based on labor force sample surveys beginning 1988 and scope of series revised. 6. Excluding persons temporarily laid off. 7. Excluding persons temporarily laid off. Excluding adult students registered for vacation employment. NOTE: n.a.= not available. *Source:* United Nations, *Monthly Bulletin of Statistics, July 1993.*

Non-Agricultural Employment for Selected Countries, 1986–1992

(in thousands)

Country	1992	1991	1990	1989	1988	1987	1986
Australia[1, 2, 3]	—	7,284.0	7,413.7	7,299.8	6,907.3	6,665.6	6,491.2
Canada[3, 4]	11,674.6	11,556.0	12,040.0	11,949.0	11,804.0	11,372.0	11,045.0
Chile[3]	3,913.2	3,674.2	3,574.6	3,568.0	3,401.2	3,252.0	3,093.8
Czechoslovakia[1, 5]	—	5,071.0	6,374.0	6,775.0	6,786.0	6,764.0	6,739.0
Finland[3]	1,987.0	2,154.0	2,260.0	2,252.0	2,193.0	2,172.0	2,165.0
Germany[4, 6]	—	—	26,985.0	26,133.0	25,740.0	25,502.0	25,255.0
Hungary[5]	1,585.7	1,916.1	2,249.9	2,483.3	2,614.9	2,686.5	2,735.3
Israel	1,659.8	1,551.9	1,415.5	1,263.3	1,259.3	1,242.6	1,195.8
Italy[3]	19,710.0	19,769.0	19,409.0	19,058.0	19,045.0	18,667.0	18,615.0
Japan[3, 4]	60,249.2	59,410.0	57,990.0	56,650.0	55,360.0	54,220.0	53.580.0
Korea, South[3, 4]	15,896.0	15,473.0	14,744.0	14,094.0	13,386.0	12,774.0	11,843.0
New Caledonia	46.4	45.9	44.4	42.2	38.0	36.7	32.2
New Zealand[7]	—	1,294.6	1,315.9	1,310.8	1,346.7	1,393.3	1,380.1
Norway[3, 8]	1,894.0	1,894.0	1,901.0	1,917.0	1,980.0	1,987.0	1,934.0
Portugal[3]	3,850.6	3,831.8	3,700.7	3,566.0	3,413.8	3,265.2	3,193.9
Puerto Rico[3, 4]	—	892.0	887.0	872.0	866.0	816.0	771.0
Spain[3]	10,933.5	11,264.3	11,093.3	10,660.4	10,078.4	9,647.1	9,079.9
Sweden[4]	—	4,287.0	4,358.0	4,307.0	4,231.0	4,166.0	4,090.0
Switzerland[9]	102.3	—	106.4	105.1	103.7	102.5	101.1
United States[3, 4, 10]	114,391.0	113,644.0	114,728.0	114,142.0	111,800.0	109,232.0	106,434.0

1. Annual averages: one month of each year (Czechoslovakia, former: 31 Dec.). 2. Excluding armed forces. 3. Persons aged 15 years and over (Finland: 15–74; Italy: 14; South Korea: prior to July 1986: 14; Norway and Sweden: 16–74, Puerto Rico, Spain, and U.S.A.: 16 years; Portugal: 12 years). 4. Civilian labor force. 5. Socialized sector. 6. All data shown for Germany prior to October 3 are based on its territories as West Germany at the time indicated. 7. Annual averages: average of less than 12 months. 8. Revised scope. 9. Base: third quarter 1985 = 100. 10. Including forestry and fishing. *Source:* United Nations, *Monthly Bulletin of Statistics, July 1993.*

Energy, Petroleum, and Coal, by Country

Country	Energy consumed[1] (coal equiv.): Total (mil. metric tons) 1989	Total 1980	Per capita (kilograms) 1989	Per capita 1980	Electric energy production[2] (bil. kwh) 1989	1980	Crude petroleum production[3] (mil. metric tons) 1989	1980	Coal production[4] (mil. metric tons) 1989	1980
Algeria	22.7	24.8	936	1,322	15.4	7.1	34.1	47.4	(Z)	(Z)
Argentina	60.6	49.1	1,899	1,739	50.4	39.7	23.5[6]	25.3	0.4[6]	0.4
Australia[7]	120.0	91.4	7,208	6,222	147.8	96.1	22.5	19.8[6]	147.8	72.5
Austria	30.4	31.2	4,014	4,138	50.2	41.6	1.2	1.5	—	—
Bahrain	7.8	4.4	15,601	12,615	3.5	1.7	1.9	2.4	n.a.	n.a.
Bangladesh[8]	7.8	4.0	69	45	7.4	2.7	(Z)	(Z)	(X)	(X)
Belgium	57.0	62.3	5,787	6,320	66.9	53.1	(X)	(X)	3.6[9]	6.3
Brazil	116.6	92.4	791	762	221.7	139.5	29.8	9.1	n.a.	n.a.
Bulgaria	45.5	47.5	5,052	5,360	44.3	34.8	0.1	0.3[6]	0.2	0.3
Canada	287.4	251.4	10,927	10,457	499.5	377.5	76.5	70.4	38.8	20.2
Chile	15.6	11.4	1,206	1,021	17.8	11.8	0.9	1.6	1.9	1.0
China	902.5	545.5	819	557	582.0	300.6	137.5	105.9	1,054.0	595.8
Colombia	25.0	20.2	773	753	34.6	20.6	20.4	6.5	18.9	4.1
Cuba	16.1	13.7	1,532	1,412	15.2	10.0	0.7	0.3	(X)	(X)
Czechoslovakia	93.8	95.2	6,003	6,215	87.5	72.7	0.1	0.1	25.1[9]	28.3[9]
Denmark	22.7	27.7	4,413	5,398	22.8	27.1	5.5	0.3	(X)	(X)
Ecuador	6.8	5.7	662	699	5.7	3.4	14.6	10.4	n.a.	n.a.
Egypt	37.9	20.9	739	512	39.3	18.9	43.0	29.4	(X)	(X)
Ethiopia	1.2	0.8	24	21	0.9	0.7	(X)	(X)	n.a.	n.a.
Finland	29.0	25.7	5,839	5,384	53.9[5]	38.7[5]	(X)	(X)	(X)	(X)
France[12]	219.1	242.9	3,915	4,506	406.3[5]	245.7[5]	3.2	1.2	12.3[9]	20.2[9]
Germany, East	124.5	120.6	7,631	7,208	119.0	98.8	(Z)	0.1	—	—
Germany, West	330.3	371.6	5,391	6,036	437.0	367.5	5.4	5.2	77.5	94.5
Greece	31.2	20.2	3,113	2,098	34.5	22.7	0.9	—	(X)	(X)
Hong Kong	11.5	7.3	1,996	1,447	27.4	12.6	n.a.	n.a.	(X)	(X)
Hungary	39.1	40.9	3,697	3,815	29.6	23.9	2.0	2.0	2.1[9]	3.1[9]
India[10]	256.3	139.3	307	202	266.2	119.3	33.7	9.4	198.7	109.2
Indonesia	56.2	36.1	311	239	41.8	14.2	69.3	77.6	4.6	0.3
Iran[13]	88.1	45.7	1,650	1,174	42.3	22.4	140.4	72.7	1.2	0.9[6]
Iraq	19.4	10.7	1,059	802	28.9	11.4	136.6	130.1	n.a.	n.a.
Ireland	13.4	11.4	3,632	3,361	13.8	10.6	(X)	(X)	(Z)	0.1
Israel	13.8	8.8	3,040	2,277	20.3	12.5	(Z)	(Z)	(X)	(X)
Italy[14]	217.8	188.9	3,813	3,346	207.5	183.5	4.7	1.8	0.1	—
Japan	491.3	433.4	3,995	3,710	798.8	577.5	0.5	0.4	10.2	18.0
Korea, North	60.1	48.5	2,814	2,658	53.5	35.0	(X)	(X)	40.7[6]	36.0[6]
Korea, South	93.1	51.4	2,195	1,349	102.9	40.1	(X)	(X)	20.8	18.6
Kuwait[15]	17.4	12.0	8,825	8,735	20.5	9.4	74.1	84.1	n.a.	n.a.
Libya	18.8	7.3	4,286	2,399	18.0	4.8	54.3	88.3	(X)	(X)
Malaysia	22.3	11.3	1,278	821	21.7	10.1	28.0	13.4	0.1	(X)
Mexico	150.6	117.1	1,736	1,663	118.1[5]	67.0[5]	130.7	99.9	11.5[6]	7.0
Morocco	8.9	6.5	366	336	9.1	4.9	(Z)	(Z)	0.5	0.7
Myanmar[10]	2.5	2.0	62	60	2.5	1.5	0.9	1.6	(Z)	(Z)
Netherlands	98.6	98.5	6,639	6,965	73.1	64.8	3.4	1.3	—	—
New Zealand[16]	17.0	10.0	5,053	3,208	29.5	22.0	1.7	0.3	2.5	2.0
Nigeria	21.7	12.0	207	153	9.9	7.2	85.2	104.2	0.1[6]	0.2
Norway[17]	30.2	26.5	7,181	6,476	118.8	83.6	72.6	24.6	0.4	0.3
Pakistan[8]	31.5	16.6	265	195	40.3	15.0	2.3	0.5	2.6	1.6
Peru	10.7	11.0	505	637	13.4	10.0	7.0	9.7	0.1[6]	(Z)
Philippines	18.0	15.9	295	330	25.9	18.0	0.3	0.5	1.4	0.3
Poland	173.1	176.8	4,531	4,969	145.5	121.9	0.2	0.3	177.6	193.1
Portugal	18.6	12.5	1,811	1,281	25.5	15.3	(X)	(X)	0.3	0.2
Romania	103.9	103.0	4,486	4,637	75.9	67.5	9.2	11.5	8.3	8.1
Saudi Arabia[15]	86.5	25.3	6,362	2,703	46.3	18.9	252.4	495.9	n.a.	n.a.
South Africa[18]	105.7	84.3	2,644	2,604	162.3	89.6	(X)	(X)	174.7	116.6
Soviet Union	1,877.2	1,507.5	6,553	5,677	1,722.0	1,293.9	601.5	603.2	577.0	492.9
Spain	97.1	87.1	2,485	2,321	146.6	109.2	1.0	1.6	14.5[9]	13.1[9]
Sudan	1.6	1.5	64	81	1.3	0.9	(X)	(X)	n.a.	n.a.
Sweden	42.7	44.2	5,070	5,318	143.9	96.3	(Z)	(Z)	—	(Z)
Switzerland[19]	24.2	24.3	3,662	3,834	53.8[5]	47.1[5]	(X)	(X)	(X)	(X)
Syria	11.8	8.6	978	981	10.3	3.8	18.3	9.2	(X)	(X)
Taiwan[11]	62.1	37.8	3,074	2,126	n.a.	n.a.	0.1	0.2	0.8	2.6
Tanzania	0.9	0.9	36	46	0.9	0.8	(X)	(X)	(Z)	(Z)
Thailand	35.0	17.3	637	371	39.1	15.1	1.1	(Z)	—	—
Trinidad and Tobago	7.8	7.5	6,160	6,901	3.5	2.1	7.7	11.0	n.a.	n.a.

Country	Energy consumed[1] (coal equiv.) Total (mil. metric tons) 1989	1980	Per capita (kilograms) 1989	1980	Electric energy production[2] (bil. kwh) 1989	1980	Crude petroleum production[3] (mil. metric tons) 1989	1980	Coal production[4] (mil. metric tons) 1989	1980
Tunisia	6.1	4.1	761	643	5.0	2.8	4.9	5.6	(X)	(X)
Turkey	56.2	31.1	1,027	699	52.0	23.3	2.9	2.3	3.0	3.6
United Arab Emirates	31.5	9.9	20,361	9,749	13.3	6.3	89.3	82.8	n.a.	n.a.
United Kingdom	289.0	271.8	5,043	4,809	313.8	283.7	87.4	78.9	98.3[9]	130.1[9]
United States	2,504.0	2,364.4	10,124	10,381	2,985.2[5]	2,354.4[5]	382.7	424.2	810.0	710.4
Venezuela	58.0	49.2	3,012	3,278	59.3	35.9	100.1	114.8	2.1	(Z)
Vietnam	8.6	6.7	132	126	7.8	4.2	1.5	(X)	3.9	5.3
Yugoslavia	62.9	47.9	2,656	2,145	86.3	59.4	3.8[6]	4.2	0.3	0.4
Zaire	2.3	2.0	67	75	6.1	4.4	1.4	1.0	0.1[6]	0.1
Zambia	1.6	2.3	198	396	6.7[5]	9.2[5]	(X)	(X)	0.4	0.6
World, total	**10,270.8**	**8,593.1**	**1,975**	**1,932**	**11,449.8**	**8,236.9**	**2,956.4**	**2,982.4**	**3,562.2**	**2,728.0**

n.a. = not available. X = Not applicable. Z = Less than 50,000 metric tons. 1. Based on apparent consumption of coal, lignite, petroleum products, natural gas, and hydro, nuclear, and geothermal electricity. 2. Comprises production by utilities generating primarily for public use, and production by industrial establishments generating primarily for own use. Relates to production at generating centers, including station use and transmission losses. 3. Includes shale oil, but excludes natural gasoline. 4. Excludes lignite and brown coal, except as noted. 5. Net production, i.e., excluding station use. 6. Provisional. 7. For year ending June 30 of year shown. 8. For year ending June of year shown. 9. Includes slurries. 10. For year ending April of year shown. 11. *Source:* U.S. Bureau of Census. Data from Republic of China publications. 12. Includes Monaco. 13. For year ending March 20 for year shown. 14. Includes San Marino. 15. Includes share of production and consumption in the Neutral Zone. 16. For year ending March 31 for year shown. 17. Includes Svalbard and Jan Mayen Islands. 18. Includes Botswana, Lesotho, Namibia, and Swaziland. 19. Includes Liechtenstein. *Source:* Except as noted, Statistical Office of the United Nations, New York, N.Y., *Energy Statistics Yearbook,* annual (copyright). From: *Statistical Abstract of the United States, 1992.* NOTE: Data are most recent available.

Wheat, Rice, and Corn—Production for Selected Countries

(in thousands of metric tons)

Country	Wheat 1989	1988	1987	Rice 1989	1988	1987	Corn 1989	1988	1987
Argentina	10,000[1]	7,800	9,000	469	415	371	4,260	9,200	9,250
Australia	14,200	14,054	12,369	748	751	613	217	221	206
Belgium[2]	1,478	1,293	1,078	n.a.	n.a.	n.a.	62	54	40
Brazil	5,407	5,751	6,035	11,107	11,806	10,419	26,508	24,750	26,803
Canada	24,383	15,996	25,992	n.a.	n.a.	n.a.	6,400	5,369	7,015
China: Mainland[3]	91,002[1]	85,435	85,845	179,403[1]	171,368	176,958	75,840[1]	77,671	79,457
Egypt	3,148[1]	2,839[1]	2,721[1]	2,680[1]	2,132[1]	2,406[1]	3,748[1]	4,087[1]	3,019
France	31,817	29,677	27,415	97	65	54	12,926	14,120	12,470
Germany, West	11,065	11,922	9,932	n.a.	n.a.	n.a.	1,574	1,535	1,217
Greece	2,005	2,183	2,213	110	116	137	1,700	1,750	2,156
Hungary	6,559	7,026	5,748	45	47	40	6,949	6,256	7,234
India	53,995[1]	46,169	44,323	107,500[1]	106,385	85,339	7,800[1]	8,332	5,721
Indonesia	n.a.	n.a.	n.a.	43,566	41,676	40,078	6,324	6,652	5,155
Iran	5,800	7,265	7,600	1,200	1,419	1,803	40[3]	55[3]	60[1]
Iraq	491[1]	929	722	140[3]	141	196	70[3]	77	61
Italy	7,408	7,952	9,381	1,130[1]	1,094	1,064	6,251[1]	6,289	5,764
Japan	985[3]	1,021	864	12,934[1]	12,419	13,284	1	1[3]	1[3]
Korea, South	2[1]	2	4	8,200[1]	8,260	7,596	118[1]	106	127
Mexico	3,900[1]	3,665	4,415	441[1]	456	591	9,900[1]	10,600	11,607
Myanmar	230	157	192	13,581[1]	13,162[1]	13,636	270[3]	259	224
Pakistan	14,419	12,675	12,016	4,796	4,800	4,861	1,120	1,204	1,127
Soviet Union	90,500	84,445	83,312	2,525	2,866	2,683	17,000[3]	16,030	14,808
Sweden	1,764[1]	1,296	1,558	n.a.	n.a.	n.a.	n.a.	n.a.	n.a.
Thailand	n.a.	n.a.	n.a.	21,300[1]	21,263	18,428	4,456	4,675	2,781
United Kingdom	13,900	11,640	11,941	n.a.	n.a.	n.a.	n.a.	n.a.	n.a.
United States	55,407	49,303	57,363	7,007	7,253	5,879	191,197	125,193	181,142
Vietnam	n.a.	n.a.	n.a.	18,100[1]	16,860	15,550	900[3]	815	561
Yugoslavia	5,599	6,304	5,345	30[1]	24	49	9,415	7,700	8,863
World, total	**538,056**	**506,968**	**510,482**	**506,291**	**490,768**	**465,780**	**470,318**	**400,892**	**451,086**

1. Unofficial figure. 2. Includes Luxembourg. 3. FAO estimate. NOTES: Rice data cover rough and paddy. Data for each country pertain to the calendar year in which all or most of the crop was harvested. n.a. = not available. *Source:* Food and Agriculture Organization of the United Nations, Rome, Italy. *FAO Production Yearbook,* (copyright). From: *Statistical Abstract of the United States, 1991.* NOTE: Data are most recent available.

Wheat, Rice and Corn Exports and Imports, 1980–1989

(In millions of dollars. Countries listed are the 10 leading exporters or importers in 1989)

Exporters	1980	1985	1989	Importers	1980	1985	1989
WHEAT				**WHEAT**			
United States	6,587	3,781	6,187	China: Mainland	2,437	909	2,573
France	2,542	2,650	3,152	Soviet Union	3,189	3,019	2,297
Canada	3,423	2,838	2,236	Egypt	1,035	1,393	1,758
Australia	2,440	2,233	1,746	Italy	774	793	1,428
West Germany	409	253	852	Japan	1,236	991	1,188
Argentina	825	1,146	661	Algeria	690	752	881
United Kingdom	279	306	568	Iran	252	351	760
Italy	280	345	460	Iraq	531	373	652
Saudi Arabia	2	8	303	West Germany	343	509	502
Soviet Union	455	243	242	South Korea	369	442	436
RICE				**RICE**			
Thailand	953	830	1,769	Iran	209	171	310
United States	1,285	665	983	China: Mainland	40	36	304
Vietnam	10	15	372	Soviet Union	265	83	221
Pakistan	422	220	310	United Arab Emirates	123	65	216
Italy	289	304	305	France	154	146	209
Belgium–Luxembourg	91	114	156	Iraq	217	175	196
India	173	188	150	United Kingdom	98	126	192
Australia	145	94	122	India	1	14	175
China: Mainland	450	227	94	Saudi Arabia	230	204	174
United Arab Emirates	84	39	90	Hong Kong	158	115	160
CORN				**CORN**			
United States	8,571	5,312	6,691	Japan	2,011	1,937	2,262
France	869	815	1,592	Soviet Union	1,508	2,315	2,257
China: Mainland	17	742	438	South Korea	376	422	854
Argentina	513	766	236	Taiwan	437	424	617
Thailand	352	280	159	Netherlands	626	422	508
Spain	1	1	112	Mexico	589	255	476
Yugoslavia	86	146	77	West Germany	443	327	327
Netherlands	135	26	68	United Kingdom	547	266	318
Hungary	27	39	56	Belgium–Luxembourg	473	293	276
Kenya	(Z)	3	45	Spain	668	495	238

Z = less than $500,000. *Source:* U.S. Dept. of Agriculture, Economic Research Service, *World Agriculture—Trends and Indicators*. From *Statistical Abstract of the United States*. NOTE: Data are most recent available.

Passenger Car Production[1]

(in thousands, monthly averages)

Country	1991	1990	1989	1988	1987	1986	1985
Argentina[2]	—	9.5	9.5	10.4	13.0	1.7	9.6
Australia[2]	25.9	30.1	27.7	26.2	25.2	26.5	31.8
Austria	1.2	1.2	0.6	0.6	0.6	0.6	0.6
Brazil[2]	24.4	22.3	26.1	32.9	33.1	39.9	38.3
Canada	74.2	78.4	82.0	84.0	67.5	88.4	89.6
Czechoslovakia	14.7	15.9	15.7	13.7	14.5	15.4	15.2
France	260.1	246.9	284.5	261.5	248.5	227.7	232.0
Germany, East[3]	—	—	18.2	18.2	18.1	18.2	17.5
Germany, West[3]	355.8	384.9	378.6	359.1	361.7	356.1	347.1
India	16.1	17.8	14.8	14.5	12.9	10.8	7.8
Italy	135.6	156.1	164.2	157.0	142.7	136.9	112.8
Japan	813.0	829.0	697.5	683.3	657.6	650.9	637.1
Korea, South[2]	94.3	79.8	70.6	72.3	64.8	38.1	21.8
Mexico[2]	61.1	51.2	37.9	29.0	19.0	16.5	23.8
Netherlands	7.1	10.3	11.2	10.0	10.4	9.9	9.0
Poland	13.9	22.2	23.8	24.5	24.5	24.2	23.6
Romania	6.2	—	10.0	10.0	10.8	10.3	11.2
Spain	152.5	144.7	141.3	131.3	119.3	108.2	101.4
Sweden	—	28.0[4]	32.0[4]	—	34.7	34.6	33.4
Former U.S.S.R.	98.7	104.9	101.4	105.1	108.3	109.9	111.0
United Kingdom	106.5	108.0	108.3	102.2	95.2	84.9	87.3
United States[5]	450.6	504.3	567.3	592.1	590.4	626.3	666.8
Yugoslavia	18.2	24.3[2]	26.0[2]	25.8[2]	25.8[2]	17.5	19.1

1. Vehicles built on imported chassis or assembled from imported parts are excluded except for those countries marked. 2. Including assembly. 3. Unification of Germany occurred on October 3, 1990. All data which pertain to Germany prior to that date are indicated separately for East and West Germany. 4. Provisional, preliminary or estimated figure. 5. Factory sales. *Source:* United Nations, *Monthly Bulletin of Statistics, January 1993.*

Meat—Production by Country

(in thousands of metric tons)

Country	1989	1985	1980	Country	1989	1985	1980
Argentina	3,325	3,588	3,622	Japan	3,634	3,461	3,046
Australia[1]	2,773	2,461	2,672	Mexico	3,644	2,933	2,537
Brazil	5,976	4,621	4,551	Soviet Union	19,936	17,131	15,094
Canada	2,896	2,758	2,556	United Kingdom	3,314	3,343	3,070
China	26,400	19,913	13,744	United States	28,384	26,016	24,599
France	5,509	5,328	5,300	West Germany	5,241	5,245	5,199
Italy	3,897	3,723	3,571	**World**	**169,887**	**151,215**	**134,407**

1. Year ending June 30. NOTE: Covers beef and veal (incl. buffalo meat), pork (incl. bacon and ham), and mutton and lamb (incl. goat meat). Refers to meat from animals slaughtered within the national boundaries irrespective of origin of animals, and relates to commercial and farm slaughter. Excludes lard, tallow, and edible offals. NOTE: Data are most recent available. *Source:* U.S. Department of Agriculture, Economic Research Service, *World Agriculture—Trends and Indicators.* From: *Statistical Abstract of the United States 1992.*

Crude Steel Production

(in thousands of metric tons)

Country	1991	1990	1989	Country	1991	1990	1989
Argentina	248	302	324	Japan	9,137	9,194	8,992
Australia	518	557	559	Korea, South	2,234	2,039	1,975
Austria	367	379	417	Luxembourg	282	290	310
Belgium	941	952	913	Mexico	643	685	616
Brazil	1,884	1,715	2,176	Netherlands	431	451	473
Bulgaria	135	182	242	Poland	870	1,135	1,258
Canada	1,987	1,807	1,288	Portugal	48	62	63
China	5,880	5,388	5,351	Romania	593	518	791
Czechslovakia, former	1,006	1,239	1,289	South Africa	745	719	788
Finland	241	238	243	Spain	1,047	1,052	1,047
France	1,536	1,585	1,609	Sweden	353	371	391
Germany, East	n.a.	n.a.	652	Turkey	775	784	654
Germany	3,232	3,203	3,423	USSR, former	11,660	12,868	13,341
Greece	82	83	80	United Kingdom	1,386	1,372	1,562
Hungary	155	234	276	United States	7,287	8,168	7,366
India	1,366	1,247	1,073	Venezuela	259	265	284
Italy	2,086	2,121	2,098	Yugoslavia	n.a.	n.a.	375

NOTE: Production data cover ingots and steel for casting. Wrought (puddled) iron is included. n.a. = not available. *Source:* United Nations, *Monthly Bulletin of Statistics, July 1993.*

Railway Freight Traffic for Selected Countries

(Net ton-kilometers in millions)

Country	1991	1990	1989	Country	1991	1990	1989
Argentina	455	n.a.	686	Korea, South	1,208	1,123	1,123
Austria[1]	1,072	1,057	987	Luxembourg	59	60	56
Belgium	679	696	671	Mexico	2,749	3,032	3,176
Bulgaria[2]	724	1,177	1,420	Netherlands	252	213	200
Chile	225	230	246	Norway[7]	223	196	226
China	n.a.	88,343	86,441	Poland	5,429	6,961	9,184
Czechoslovakia, former	4,161	5,360	5,998	Portugal	149	132	143
Finland	636	696	663	Romania	3,154	4,771	6,761
France	4,299	4,294	4,439	Spain	876	934	968
Germany	6,719	n.a.	n.a.	Sweden	1,524	1,457	1,574
Greece[3]	50	54	55	Turkey	n.a.	659	631
Hong Kong	5	6	6	USSR, former	275,978	309,751	320,973
Hungary	995	1,398	1,617	United Kingdom[8]	1,289	1,319	1,437
India[2, 4, 5]	20,440	19,441	18,887	United States[9]	127,173	126,148	123,502
Ireland	47	45	43	Venezuela	4	3	3
Italy[6]	1,796	1,825	1,738	Yugoslavia	n.a.	2,037	2,150
Japan	2,279	2,221	2,064	Zimbabwe[1, 6]	909	475	441

1. Federal railroads only. 2. Including service traffic. 3. Including military and government traffic. 4. Government railways: broad meter and narrow gauges only. 5. Annual figures: 12 months beginning April 1. 6. Excluding livestock. 7. Average of two months. 8. British railways only. Excluding Northern Ireland. 9. Class I railways only. n.a. = not available. *Source:* United Nations, *Monthly Bulletin of Statistics, July 1993.*

Value of Exports and Imports

(in millions of U.S. dollars)

Country	Exports[1]	Imports[1]
Afghanistan	$ 235[2]	$ 937[2]
Algeria	13,306[2]	10,122[2]
Argentina	11,978[3]	8,275[3]
Australia	42,417	40,696
Austria	44,430	54,116
Bahamas	2,678[2]	2,920[2]
Bahrain	3,404[3]	4,066[3]
Bangladesh	1,674[3]	3,407[3]
Barbados	202[3]	695[3]
Belgium–Luxembourg	123,066	125,058
Bolivia	858[3]	942[3]
Brazil	36,148	20,501
Bulgaria	3,835[3]	3,017[3]
Burkina Faso	95[4]	322[4]
Burundi	91[3]	256[3]
Cameroon	2,019[2]	1,650[2]
Canada	134,223	122,477
Central African Republic	74[3]	145[3]
Chile	9,986	10,129
China	84,635	80,315
Colombia	7,269[3]	4,967[3]
Congo	976[2]	600[2]
Costa Rica	1,746	2,453
Côte d'Ivoire	2,931[4]	2,185[4]
Cuba	3,585[3]	3,690[3]
Cyprus	1,002	3,289
Czechoslovakia (former)	11,656	12,530
Denmark	39,577	33,613
Dominican Republic	651[3]	1,721[3]
Ecuador	3,008	2,491
Egypt	3,104	8,357
El Salvador	412[2]	902[2]
Ethiopia	189[3]	472[3]
Fiji	435	624
Finland	23,530	20,756
France	231,948	238,911
Gabon	1,599[4]	767[4]
Gambia	43[3]	222[3]
Germany	430,315	408,358
Ghana	1,024[4]	1,275[4]
Greece	8,653[3]	21,582[3]
Guatemala	1,058	2,463
Guyana	255[2]	512[2]
Haiti	103[3]	374[3]
Honduras	782[3]	880[3]
Hong Kong	119,511	123,428
Hungary	10,680	11,122
Iceland	1,553[3]	1,762[3]
India	17,479[3]	20,295[3]
Indonesia	29,142[3]	25,869[3]
Ireland	28,333	22,478
Israel	11,889[3]	16,906[3]
Italy	178,471	188,712
Jamaica	1,145[3]	1,799[3]
Japan	340,483	233,548
Jordan	1,194	3,257
Kazakhstan	1,398	469
Kenya	1,125[3]	1,802[3]
Korea, South	76,332	81,775
Kuwait	11,502[4]	6,297[4]
Liberia	396[5]	272[5]
Libya	6,683[5]	5,879[5]
Madagascar	$ 306[3]	$ 441[3]
Malawi	376	699
Malaysia	40,711	39,964
Mali	271[4]	500[4]
Malta	1,238[3]	2,114[3]
Mauritania	437[4]	222[4]
Mauritius	1,290	1,626
Mexico	27,531	48,138
Morocco	3,977	7,356
Myanmar	533	653
Netherlands	139,944	134,475
New Zealand	9,829	9,205
Nicaragua	300[6]	923[6]
Nigeria	12,912[2]	4,318[2]
Norway	35,150	26,076
Oman	5,428	3,769
Pakistan	7,273	9,365
Panama	510	2,019
Papua-New Guinea	1,812	1,522
Paraguay	1,163[4]	695[4]
Peru	3,379[3]	2,955[3]
Philippines	8,840[3]	12,051[3]
Poland	14,460[3]	14,261[3]
Portugal	17,905	29,726
Romania	4,031	5,394
Russia	38,100	35,000
Rwanda	68	288
Saudi Arabia	44,417[2]	24,069[2]
Senegal	606[6]	1,023[6]
Sierra Leone	166	131
Singapore	63,516	72,216
Solomon Islands	70[2]	92[2]
Somalia	104[6]	132[6]
South Africa	22,072	18,236
Spain	64,329	99,766
Sri Lanka	2,354	3,513
Sudan	509[5]	1,060[5]
Suriname	473[2]	472[2]
Sweden	56,021	49,835
Switzerland	65,783	65,924
Syria	3,143[3]	3,151[3]
Tanzania	331	698
Thailand	32,437	40,883
Togo	245[4]	472[4]
Tonga	14[3]	59[3]
Trinidad and Tobago	1,869	1,431
Tunisia	4,042	6,415
Turkey	14,883	22,507
Uganda	201[3]	197[3]
United Arab Emirates	15,837[7]	6,422[7]
U.K.	190,052	222,655
U.S.	448,164	532,665
Uruguay	1,590[3]	1,619[3]
Uzbekistan	869	929
Vanuatu	20[3]	83[3]
Venezuela	13,173	12,946
Western Samoa	6	113
Yemen	101[6]	1,378[6]
Yugoslavia (former)	9,548[3]	11,804[3]
Zaire	832[3]	713[3]
Zambia	899[2]	1,243[2]
Zimbabwe	826[2]	1,850[2]

1. 1992 unless otherwise indicated. 2. 1990. 3. 1991. 4. 1989. 5. 1988. 6. 1987. 7. 1986. *Source:* United Nations, *Monthly Bulletin of Statistics, July 1993.*

COUNTRIES OF THE WORLD

***Major sources: Information Please Almanac* questionnaires to the individual countries; C.I.A. *World Factbook*; Population Reference Bureau, Inc. (As of August 1, 1993. For later reports, *see* Current Events of 1993.)**

Definitions: Gross domestic product (GDP): The value of all goods and services produced domestically; Gross national product (GNP): the value of all goods and services produced domestically plus income earned abroad, minus income earned by foreigners from domestic production; c.i.f.: cost, insurance, and freight; f.o.b.: free on board; inflation: based on consumer prices; literacy: There are no universal definitions and standards of literacy. Literacy rates are those supplied by the individual countries or else taken from the World Fact Book. The standards that each country uses to assess the ability to read and write is beyond the scope of this almanac.

AFGHANISTAN

Islamic State of Afghanistan
President: Burhanuddin Rabbani (1992)
Prime Minister: Gulbuddin Hekmatyar (1993)
Area: 250,000 sq mi. (647,500 sq km).
Population (est. mid-1993): 17,400,000 (Average annual rate of natural increase: 2.8%); birth rate: 49/1000; infant mortality rate: 168/1000; density per square mile: 69
Capital: Kabul; **Largest cities (est. 1988):** Kabul, 1,424,400; Kandahar, 225,500; Herat, 177,300; **Monetary unit:** Afghani; **Languages:** Pushtu, Dari Persian, other Turkic and minor languages; **Religion:** Islam (Sunni, 84%; Shiite, 15%; other 1%); **National name:** Jamhouri Afghanistan; **Literacy rate:** 29%
Economic summary: Gross domestic product (1989): $3 billion, $200 per capita. Average annual growth rate (1989 est.): .0%. Inflation (est. 1991): over 90%. Arable land: 12%; labor force: 4,980,000. Principal products: wheat, cotton, fruits, nuts, wool. Labor force in industry: 10.2%. Major industrial products: carpets and textiles. Natural resources: natural gas, oil, coal, copper, sulfur, lead, zinc, iron, salt, precious and semi-precious stones. Exports: $236 million (f.o.b., FY91 est.): fresh and dried fruits, nuts, natural gas, carpets. Imports: $874 million (c.i.f., FY91 est.): petroleum products and food supplies. Major trading partners: Eastern Europe and C.I.S. countries, Japan, and China. Illicit drugs: Afghanistan is the world's second largest opium producer (after Myanmar) and a major source of hashish.

Geography. Afghanistan, approximately the size of Texas, is bordered on the north by Turkmenistan, Uzbekistan, and Tajikistan, on the extreme northeast by China, on the east and south by Pakistan, and Iran in the west. The country is split east to west by the Hindu Kush mountain range, rising in the east to heights of 24,000 feet (7,315 m). With the exception of the southwest, most of the country is covered by high snow-capped mountains and is traversed by deep valleys.

Government. With the fall of the Marxist Najibullah regime in April 1992 the victorious insurgents established a 50-member ruling council of guerrillas, religious leaders and intellectuals, who announced the creation of an Islamic republic and promised free elections.

History. Darius I and Alexander the Great were the first conquerors to use Afghanistan as the gateway to India. Islamic conquerors arrived in the 7th century and Genghis Khan and Tamerlane followed in the 13th and 14th centuries.

In the 19th century, Afghanistan became a battleground in the rivalry of imperial Britain and Czarist Russia for the control of Central Asia. The Afghan Wars (1838–42 and 1878–81) fought against the British by Dost Mohammed and his son and grandson ended in defeat.

Afghanistan regained autonomy by the Anglo-Russian agreement of 1907 and full independence by the Treaty of Rawalpindi in 1919. Emir Amanullah founded the kingdom in 1926.

After a coup in 1978, Noor Taraki's attempts to create a Marxist state with Soviet aid brought armed resistance from conservative Muslim opposition.

Taraki was eventually succeeded by Babrak Karmal, who called for Soviet troops under a mutual defense treaty.

The Soviet invasion was met with unanticipated fierce resistance from the Afghan population, resulting in a bloody war. Soviet troops had to fight Afghan tribesmen who called themselves "mujahedeen," or "holy warriors." In the early fighting, many of the guerrillas were armed only with flintlock rifles, but later they acquired more modern weapons, including rockets that they used to attack Soviet installations.

In April 1988, the U.S.S.R., U.S.A., Afghanistan, and Pakistan signed accords calling for an end to outside aid to the warring factions, in return for Soviet withdrawal by 1989. This took place in February of that year.

An agreement signed in September 1991 between the USSR and the USA called for an end to all outside military assistance to the warring factions. By mid-April 1992 then-President Najibullah was ousted as Islamic rebels advanced on the capital. Almost immediately the various rebel groups began fighting each other for control. Only after three weeks into a cease-fire was it deemed safe enough in June 1993 for a coalition government to be sworn into office.

ALBANIA

The Republic of Albania
President: Sali Berisha (1992)
Prime Minister: Alesander Meksi (1992)
Area: 11,100 sq mi. (28,748 sq km)
Population (est. mid-1993): 3,300,000 (average annual rate of natural increase: 2.0%); birth rate: 25/1000; infant mortality rate: 28.3/1000; density per square mile: 314
Capital and largest city (1989): Tirana, 238,100; **Monetary unit:** Lek; **Language:** Albanian, Greek; **Religions (1980):** Sunni Moslem, 70%; Roman Catholic, 10%; Orthodox, 20%; **Literacy rate** 75%
Economic summary: Gross national product (1991 est.): $2.7 billion; per capita, $820; real growth rate, –35%; inflation, 100%; unemployment, 40%. Arable land: 21%; labor force: 1,500,000 (1987). Principal agricultural products: wheat, corn, potatoes, sugar beets, cotton, tobacco. Labor force in industry and commerce: 40%. Major products: textiles, timber, construction materials, fuels, semi-processed minerals.

Exports: $80 million (f.o.b., 1991 est.): asphalt, petroleum products, metals and metallic ores, electricity, crude oil, vegetables, fruits, and tobacco. Imports: $147 million (f.o.b., 1991 est.): machinery, machine tools, iron and steel products, textiles, chemicals, pharmaceuticals. Major trading partners: Greece, Yugoslavia, Czech and Slovak Republics, Poland, Hungary, Bulgaria, Romania, Germany, France, Italy

Geography. Albania is situated on the eastern shore of the Adriatic Sea, with Yugoslavia to the north and east and Greece to the south. Slightly larger than Maryland, it is a mountainous country, mostly over 3,000 feet (914 m) above sea level, with a narrow, marshy coastal plain crossed by several rivers. The centers of population are contained in the interior mountain plateaus and basins.

Government. A multi-party system was installed in March 1991. Elections in March 1992 gave the Democratic Party 92 of the 140 parliamentary seats, thus assuring it the two-thirds majority for enacting constitutional reform. Election of the president is by parliamentary majority.

History. Albania proclaimed its independence on Nov. 28, 1912, after a history of Roman, Byzantine, and Turkish domination.

Largely agricultural, Albania is one of the poorest countries in Europe. A battlefield in World War I, after the war it became a republic in which a conservative Moslem landlord, Ahmed Zogu, proclaimed himself President in 1925, and then proclaimed himself King Zog I in a monarchy in 1928. He ruled until Italy annexed Albania in 1939. Communist guerrillas under Enver Hoxha seized power in 1944, near the end of World War II.

Hoxha was succeeded by Ramiz Alia, 59, who had been President since 1982.

The elections in March 1991 gave the Communists a decisive majority. But a general strike and street demonstrations soon forced the all-Communist cabinet to resign. In June 1991 the Communist Party of Labor renamed itself the Socialist Party and renounced its past ideology. The opposition Democratic Party won a landslide victory in 1992 elections. The Socialist Party made significant gains in local elections of July 26.

ALGERIA

Democratic and Popular Republic of Algeria
President: A collegial presidency headed by Ali Kafi.
Prime Minister: Belaid Abdesalam (1992)
Area: 919,595 sq mi. (2,381,751 sq km)
Population (est. mid-1993): 27,300,000 (average annual rate of natural increase: 2.7%); birth rate: 34/1000; infant mortality rate: 61/1000; density per square mile: 30
Capital: Algiers; **Largest cities (1987):** Algiers, 1,507,241; Oran, 628,558; Constantine, 440,842; Annaba, 305,526; **Monetary unit:** Dinar; **Languages:** Arabic (official), French, Berber dialects; **Religion:** 99% Islam (Sunni); **National name:** République Algérienne Democratique et Populaire—El Djemhouria El Djazaïria Demokratia Echaabia; **Literacy rate** (1987): 50%
Economic summary: Gross domestic product (1992): $45 billion; $1,698 per capita; real growth rate (1990), 2.5%; inflation (1991), 30%; unemployment (1991 est.), 30%. Arable land: 3%; labor force: 3,700,000. Principal agricultural products: wheat, barley, oats, wine, citrus fruits, olives, livestock. Labor force in industry: 40%. Major industrial products: petroleum, gas, petrochemicals, fertilizers, iron and steel, textiles, transport equipment. Natural resources: petroleum, natural gas, iron ore, phosphates, lead, zinc, mercury, uranium. Exports: $11.7 billion (f.o.b., 1991 est.): petroleum and gas, iron, wine, phosphates. Imports: $9 billion (f.o.b., 1991 est.): food, capital and consumer goods. Major trading partners: Netherlands, Spain, Germany, U.K., Russia, Italy, France, U.S.

Geography. Nearly four times the size of Texas, Algeria is bordered on the west by Morocco and on the east by Tunisia and Libya. To the south are Mauritania, Mali, and Niger. Low plains cover small areas near the Mediterranean coast, with 68% of the country a plateau between 2,625 and 5,250 feet (800 and 1,600 m) above sea level. The highest point is Mount Tahat in the Sahara, which rises 9,850 feet (3,000 m).

Government. A military-backed government run by a five-member High State Council headed by the president.

History. As ancient Numidia, Algeria became a Roman colony at the close of the Punic Wars (145 B.C.). Conquered by the Vandals about A.D. 440, it fell from a high state of civilization to virtual barbarism, from which it partly recovered after invasion by the Moslems about 650.

In 1492 the Moors and Jews, who had been expelled from Spain, settled in Algeria. Falling under Turkish control in 1518, Algiers served for three centuries as the headquarters of the Barbary pirates. The French took Algeria in 1830 and made it a part of France in 1848.

On July 5, 1962, Algeria was proclaimed independent. In October 1963, Ahmed Ben Bella was elected President. He began to nationalize foreign holdings and aroused opposition. He was overthrown in a military coup on June 19, 1965, by Col. Houari Boumediène, who suspended the Constitution and sought to restore financial stability.

Boumediène died in December 1978 after a long illness. Chadli Bendjedid, Secretary-General of the National Liberation Front, took the presidency in a smooth transition of power.

Nationwide riots in 1988 led the government to introduce democratic reforms. In December 1991 in the first parliamentary elections ever held in Algeria a militant Islamic fundamentalist party won. In an apparent effort to thwart the electoral results senior army commanders arranged the resignation of President Benjedid. The government then canceled the continuation of the electoral process. In late June President Boudiaf was assassinated.

In June 1993 the government presented a plan to change the constitution in two to three years, promising the introduction of democracy and free-market economics.

ANDORRA

Principality of Andorra
Head of Government: Oscar Ribas Reig (1991)
Area: 175 sq mi. (453 sq km)
Population (1991): 55,400 (average annual growth rate: 2.2%); density per square mile: 306.1
Capital (1990): Andorra la Vella, 20,437; **Monetary units:** French franc and Spanish peseta; **Languages:** Catalán

(official); French, Spanish; **Religion:** Roman Catholic; **National names:** Les Vallées d'Andorre-Valls d'Andorra; **Literacy rate** 100%

Economic summary: Gross domestic product (1990 est): $727 million; per capita, $14,000. Arable land: 2%; labor force: NA. Principal agricultural products: oats, barley, cattle, sheep. Major industrial products: tobacco products and electric power; tourism. Natural resources: water power, mineral water. Major trading partners: Spain and France.

Geography. Andorra lies high in the Pyrenees Mountains on the French-Spanish border. The country is drained by the Valira River.

Government. A new constitution, their first, was approved on March 14, 1993 which redefined Andorra as a parliamentary co-principality and sharply differentiated the three branches of government.

History. An autonomous and semi-independent coprincipality, Andorra has been under the joint suzerainty of the French state and the Spanish bishops of Urgel since 1278.

In 1990 Andorra approved a customs union treaty with the E.C. permitting free movement of industrial goods between the two, but Andorra would apply the E.C.'s external tariffs to third countries. This treaty went into effect on July 1, 1991.

ANGOLA

People's Republic of Angola

President: José Eduardo dos Santos (1979)

Area: 481,350 sq mi. (1,246,700 sq km)

Population (est. mid-1993): 9,500,000 (average annual rate of natural increase: 3.1); birth rate: 51/1000; infant mortality rate: 131/1000; density per square mile: 20

Capital and largest city (est. 1990): Luanda, 1,544,000; **Monetary unit:** Kwanza; **Languages:** Bantu, Portuguese (official); **Religions:** 47% Indigenous, 38% Roman Catholic, 15% Protestant (est.); **Literacy rate:** 42%

Economic summary: Gross domestic product (1991 est.): $8.3 billion, $950 per capita; real growth rate 1.7%; inflation (1990 est). 6.1%. Arable land: 2%. Labor force: 2,783,000; Labor force in agriculture: 85%. Principal agricultural products: coffee, sisal, corn, cotton, sugar, tobacco, bananas, cassava. Major industrial products: oil, diamonds, processed fish, tobacco, textiles, cement, processed food and sugar, brewing. Natural resources: diamonds, gold, iron, oil. Exports: $3.9 billion (f.o.b., 1990 est.): oil, coffee, diamonds, fish and fish products, iron ore, timber, corn. Imports: $1.5 billion (f.o.b., 1990 est.): machinery and electrical equipment, bulk iron, steel and metals, textiles, clothing, food. Major trading partners: Brazil, C.I.S., Cuba, Portugal, U.S.

Geography. Angola, more than three times the size of California, extends for more than 1,000 miles (1,609 km) along the South Atlantic in southwestern Africa. Zaire is to the north and east, Zambia to the east, and South-West Africa (Namibia) to the south. A plateau averaging 6,000 feet (1,829 m) above sea level rises abruptly from the coastal lowlands. Nearly all the land is desert or savanna, with hardwood forests in the northeast.

Government. President José Eduardo dos Santos, head of the Popular Movement for the Liberation of Angola–Workers Party, won a U.N. certified election in September 1992 against the guerilla organization UNITA led by Jonas Savimbi. The U.S. recognized the new democratic Angolan administration on May 8, 1993.

History. Discovered by the Portuguese navigator Diego Cao in 1482, Angola became a link in trade with India and the Far East. Later it was a major source of slaves for Portugual's New World colony of Brazil. Development of the interior began after the Treaty of Berlin in 1885 fixed the colony's borders, and British and Portuguese investment pushed mining, railways, and agriculture.

Following World War II, independence movements began but were sternly suppressed by military force. The April revolution of 1974 brought about a reversal of Portugal's policy, and the next year President Francisco da Costa Gomes signed an agreement to grant independence to Angola. The plan called for election of a constituent assembly and a settlement of differences by the MPLA and the National Front for the Liberation of Angola (FNLA) and the National Union for the Total Independence of Angola (UNITA).

The Organization of African Unity recognized the MPLA government led by Agostinho Neto on Feb. 11, 1976, and the People's Republic of Angola became the 47th member of the organization.

Although militarily victorious, Neto's regime had yet to consolidate its power in opposition strongholds in the east and south.

In March 1977 and May 1978, Zairean refugees in Angola invaded Zaire's Shaba Province, bringing charges by Zairean President Mobutu Sese Seko that the unsucessful invasions were Soviet-backed with Angolan help. Angola, the U.S.S.R., and Cuba denied complicity.

Neto died in Moscow of cancer on Sept. 10, 1979. The Planning Minister, José Eduardo dos Santos, was named President.

The South-West Africa People's Organization, or Swapo, the guerrillas fighting for the independence of the disputed territory south of Angola also known as Namibia, fought from bases in Angola and the South African armed forces also maintained troops there both to fight the SWAPO guerrillas and to assist the UNITA guerrillas against Angolan and Cuban troops.

In December 1988, Angola, Cuba, and South Africa signed agreements calling for Cuban withdrawal from Angola and South African withdrawal from Namibia by July 1991 and independence for Namibia.

Elections in late September 1992 gave the MPLA the most votes with UNITA second. A runoff was set when UNITA's Savimbi withdrew charging the election was unfair. Fighting resumed between the government and UNITA in October. Within a month the latter had taken control over two-thirds of the country.

ANTIGUA AND BARBUDA

Sovereign: Queen Elizabeth II (1952)

Governor-General: Sir Wilfred E. Jacobs (1981)

Prime Minister: Vere C. Bird, Sr. (1976)

Land area: 171 sq mi. (442 sq km)

Population (est. mid-1993): 100,000 (average annual growth rate: 1.2%); birth rate: 18/1000; infant mortality rate: 20/1000; density per square mile: 584

Capital and largest city (est. 1986): St. John's, 36,000. Capital of Barbuda is the village of Cordrington, est. pop. 1,000; **Monetary unit:** East Caribbean dollar;

Language: English; **Religions:** Anglican and Roman Catholic; **Literacy rate:** 90%
Member of Commonwealth of Nations
Economic summary: Gross domestic product (1990 est.): $360.7 million, per capita $5,600; real growth rate 4.2%; inflation rate 7%; unemployment rate (est. 1989) 3.0%. Arable land: 18%; Labor force: 30,000; Labor force in industry (1990): 19.7%; principal product: cotton, bananas, coconuts, cucumbers, mangoes. Major industry: tourism which accounts for 60% of economic activity and over half of the GNP. Exports: $33.2 billion (f.o.b., 1990): petroleum products, manufactures, machinery and transport equipment. Imports: $325.9 million (c.i.f., 1990): fuel, food, machinery. Major trading partners: U.K., U.S., Canada, Caribbean community and Common Market members.

Geography. Antigua, the larger of the two main islands located 295 miles (420 km) south-southeast of San Juan, P.R., is low-lying except for a range of hills in the south that rise to their highest point at Boggy Peak (1,330 ft; 405 m). As a result of its relative flatness, Antigua suffers from cyclical drought, despite a mean annual rainfall of 44 inches. Barbuda (formally known as Dulcina) is a coral island, well-wooded.

Antigua is 108 sq. miles (280 sq km), and the island dependences of Redonda (an uninhabited rocky islet) and Barbuda are 0.5 sq miles (1.30 sq km) and 62 sq miles (161 sq km), respectively.

Government. Executive power is held by the Cabinet, presided over by Prime Minister Vere C. Bird, Sr. A 17-member Parliament is elected by universal suffrage. The Antigua Labour Party, led by Prime Minister Bird, holds 15 seats.

History. Antigua was discovered by Christopher Columbus in 1493 and named for the Church of Santa Maria la Antigua in Seville. Colonized by Britain in 1632, it joined the West Indies Federation in 1958. With the breakup of the Federation, it became one of the West Indies Associated States in 1967, self-governing in internal affairs. Full independence was granted Nov. 1, 1981.

The opposition in 1992 continued its attacks on the prime minister alleging a scandal. The three chief opposition parties merged under the name United Progressive Party. Bird has said he would step down by the time of the next general election in 1994.

ARGENTINA

Argentine Republic
President: Carlos S. Menem (1989)
Area: 1,072,067 sq mi. (2,776,654 sq km)
Population (est. mid-1993): 33,500,000 (average annual rate of natural increase: 1.3%); birth rate: 21/1000; infant mortality rate: 25.6/1000; density per square mile: 32
Capital: Buenos Aires (plans to move to Viedma by 1990 indefinitely postponed); **Largest cities (est. 1983):** Buenos Aires, 3,000,000; Córdoba, 1,000,000; Rosario, 950,000; La Plafa, 450,000; San Miguel de Tucumán, 400,000; **Monetary unit:** Peso; **Language:** Spanish, English, Italian, German, French; **Religion:** Predominantly Roman Catholic (nominally); **National name:** República Argentina; **Literacy rate** 94%
Economic summary: Gross national product (1991 est.): $101.2 billion; $3,100 per capita; real growth rate 5.5%; inflation 83.8%; unemployment (Oct. 91) 6.4%. Arable land: 9%; labor force: est. 12,000,000. Principal products: grains, oilseeds, livestock products. Labor force in industry: 31%. Major products: processed foods, motor vehicles, consumer durables, textiles, chemicals. Natural resources: minerals, lead, zinc, tin, copper, iron, manganese, oil, uranium. Exports: $12 billion (f.o.b., 1991): meats, corn, wheat, wool, hides and oilseed. Imports: $8 billion (c.i.f., 1991): machinery, fuel and lubricating oils, iron and steel, chemical products. Major trading partners: U.S., Brazil, Italy, Germany, Netherlands, Japan, former Soviet republics.

Geography. With an area slightly less than one third of the United States and second in South America only to its eastern neighbor, Brazil, in size and population, Argentina is a plain, rising from the Atlantic to the Chilean border and the towering Andes peaks. Aconcagua (23,034 ft.; 7,021 m) is the highest peak in the world outside Asia. It is bordered also by Bolivia and Paraguay on the north, and by Uruguay on the east.

The northern area is the swampy and partly wooded Gran Chaco, bordering on Bolivia and Paraguay. South of that are the rolling, fertile pampas, rich for agriculture and grazing and supporting most of the population. Next southward is Patagonia, a region of cool, arid steppes with some wooded and fertile sections.

Government. Argentina is a federal union of 22 provinces, one national territory, and the Federal District. Under the Constitution of 1853 (restored by a Constituent National Convention in 1957), the President and Vice President are elected every six years by popular vote through an electoral college. The President appoints his Cabinet. The Vice President presides over the Senate but has no other powers. The Congress consists of two houses: a 46-member Senate and a 254-member Chamber of Deputies.

History. Discovered in 1516 by Juan Díaz de Solis, Argentina developed slowly under Spanish colonial rule. Buenos Aires was settled in 1580; the cattle industry was thriving as early as 1600.

Invading British forces were expelled in 1806–07, and when Napoleon conquered Spain, the Argentinians set up their own government in the name of the Spanish King in 1810. On July 9, 1816, independence was formally declared.

As in World War I, Argentina proclaimed neutrality at the outbreak of World War II, but in the closing phase declared war on the Axis on March 27, 1945, and became a founding member of the United Nations. Juan D. Perón, an army colonel, emerged as the strongman of the postwar era, winning the Presidential elections of 1946 and 1951.

Opposition to Perón's increasing authoritarianism, led to a coup by the armed forces that sent Perón into exile in 1955. Argentina entered a long period of military dictatorships with brief intervals of constitutional government.

The former dictator returned to power in 1973 and his wife was elected Vice-President.

After Peron's death in 1974, his widow became the hemisphere's first woman chief of state, but was deposed in 1976 by a military junta.

In December 1981. Lt. Gen. Leopoldo Galtieri, commander of the army, was named president.

On April 2, 1982, Galtieri landed thousands of troops on the Falkland Islands and reclaimed the Malvinas, their Spanish name, as national territory. By May 21, 5,000 British marines and paratroops landed from the British armada, and regained control of the islands.

Galtieri resigned three days after the surrender of the island garrison on June 14. Maj. Gen. Reynaldo Bignone, took office as President on July 1.

In the presidential election of October 1983, Raúl Alfonsín, leader of the middle-class Radical Civic Union, handed the Peronist Party its first defeat since its founding.

Twin economic problems of growing unemployment and quadruple-digit inflation led to a Peronist victory in the elections of May 1989. Inflation of food prices led to riots that induced Alfonsin to step down in June 1989, six months early, in favor of the Peronist, Carlos Menem.

A group of army leaders and their followers attempted an uprising on December 3, 1990. Most commanders, however, stood by the legitimate government, and the insurrection was suppressed in less than 24 hours.

In 1991 President Menem hammered out a vast deregulation of the economy designed to reverse decades of state intervention and protectionism.

In 1992 and early 1993 attention centered on Menem's lifestyle and his campaign to alter the constitution to permit him to run for another term.

ARMENIA

President: Levon A. Ter-Petrossian (1990)
Prime Minister: Hrant Bagratyan (1993)
Vice President: Gaguik G. Haroutunian
Area: 11,500 sq mi. (29,800 sq km)
Population (est. mid-1993): 3,600,000 (average annual rate of increase: 1.6%) (Armenian, 93%; others, Kurds, Ukrainians, and Russians); birth rate: 23/1000; infant mortaility rate: 22/1000, density per square mile: 312
Capital and largest city (1992): Yerevan, 1,400,000; other large cities: Gyumri (Leninakan), 120,000; Kirovakan, 169,000; **Money:** Ruble; **Language:** Armenian; **Religion:** Adopted Christianity in A.D. 301
Economic summary: Per capita GNP (1989): $4,710. The republic is rich in mineral resources, chiefly copper. It has little coal or iron. Manufacturing products include nonferrous metallurgy, electrical equipment, chemicals, textiles, and cognac. Its agricultural crops include wine grapes, fruits, wheat, sugar beets, cotton, and tobacco. Exports: $176 million (f.o.b., 1990). Imports: $1.5 billion (c.i.f., 1990).

Geography. Soviet Armenia is located in the southern Caucasus and is the smallest of the Soviet republics. It is bounded by Georgia on the north, Azerbaijan on the east, Iran on the south, and Turkey on the west. It is a land of rugged mountains and extinct volcanoes. Mt. Aragats, 13,435 ft (4,095 m) is the highest point. Although the terrain is rugged and dry with few trees, it has excellent pastures. The largest lake, Sevan, 541 sq mi, is the main source of the republic's vast irrigation system and hydroelectric power.

Government: A constitutional republic.

History: Armenia has been the scene of struggle throughout its long history with the Greeks, Romans, Persians, Mongols, and Turks. Russia acquired the present day Armenia S.S.R. from Persia in 1828. Armenia joined Azerbaijan and Georgia in 1917 to form the anti-Bolshevik Transcaucasian Federation, but it was dissolved in 1918. Armenia's independence was short-lived and it was annexed by the Red Army in 1920. On March 12, 1922, the Soviets joined Georgia, Armenia, and Azerbaijan to form the Transcaucasian Soviet Socialist Republic which became part of the U.S.S.R. In 1936, after a reorganization, Armenia became a separate constituent republic of the U.S.S.R.

Since 1983, Armenia has been involved in a territorial dispute with Azerbaijan over the enclave of Nagorno-Karabakh which both republics lay claim to. The autonomous region of Nagorno-Karabahk lies entirely within Azerbaijan. The majority population of the enclave are Armenian Christians who want to secede from Azerbaijan and join with Armenia.

The political disruption in Azerbaijan in June 1993 led to significant military advances for the Armenian forces, leaving them in control of much of the disputed region as well as a corridor to Armenia proper.

AUSTRALIA

Commonwealth of Australia
Sovereign: Queen Elizabeth II (1952)
Governor-General: William Hayden (1989)
Prime Minister: Paul Keating (1991)
Area: 2,966,150 sq mi. (7,682,300 sq km)
Population (est. mid-1993): 17,800,000 (average annual rate of natural increase: 0.8%); birth rate: 15/1000; infant mortality rate: 6.9/1000; density per square mile: 6
Capital (est. 1990): Canberra, 310,100; **Largest cities (1990):** Sydney, 3,656,500; Melbourne, 3,080,000; Brisbane, 1,301,700; Adelaide, 1,049,100; Perth, 1,193,100; **Monetary unit:** Australian dollar; **Language:** English; **Religions:** 26.1% Anglican, 26.0% Roman Catholic, 24.3% other Christian; **Literacy rate:** 100%
Member of Commonwealth of Nations
Economic summary: Gross domestic product (1991 est.): $280.8 billion; per capita $16,200; real growth rate –0.6%; inflation (Sept. 1991): 3.3%; unemployment (Jan. 93): 11.7%. Arable land: 6%. Principal products: wool, meat, cereals, sugar, sheep, cattle, dairy products. Labor force (Sept. 91): 8,630,000; finance and services, 33.8%; public and community services, 22.3%; wholesale and retail trade, 20.1%; manufacturing, 16.2%. Natural resources: iron ore, bauxite, zinc, lead, tin, coal, oil, gas, copper, nickel, uranium. Exports: $41.7 billion (f.o.b., FY91): metals, minerals, coal, wool, cereals, meat, manufacturers. Imports: $37.8 billion (f.o.b., FY91): manufactured raw materials, capital equipment, consumer goods. Major trading partners: Japan, U.S., U.K., New Zealand, Germany, South Korea, Singapore.

Geography. The continent of Australia, with the island state of Tasmania, is approximately equal in area to the United States (excluding Alaska and Hawaii), and is nearly 50% larger than Europe (excluding the U.S.S.R.).

Mountain ranges run from north to south along the east coast, reaching their highest point in Mount Kosciusko (7,308 ft; 2,228 m). The western half of the continent is occupied by a desert plateau that rises into barren, rolling hills near the west coast. It includes the Great Victoria Desert to the south and the Great Sandy Desert to the north. The Great Barrier Reef, extending about 1,245 miles (2,000 km), lies along the northeast coast.

The island of Tasmania (26,178 sq mi.; 67,800 sq km) is off the southeastern coast.

Government. The Federal Parliament consists of a bicameral legislature. The House of Representatives has 146 members elected for three years by popular vote. The Senate has 76 members elected by popular vote for six years. One half of the Senate is elected every three years. Voting is compulsory at 18. Supreme federal judicial power is vested in the High Court of Australia in the Federal Courts, and in the State Courts invested by Parliament with Federal jurisdiction. The High Court consists of seven justices, appointed by the Governor-General in Council. Each of the states has its own judicial system.

History. Dutch, Portuguese, and Spanish ships sighted Australia in the 17th century; the Dutch landed at the Gulf of Carpentaria in 1606. Australia was called New Holland, Botany Bay, and New South Wales until about 1820.

Captain James Cook, in 1770, claimed possession for Great Britain. A British penal colony was set up at what is now Sydney, then Port Jackson, in 1788, and about 161,000 transported English convicts were settled there until the system was suspended in 1839.

Free settlers established six colonies: New South Wales (1786), Tasmania (then Van Diemen's Land) (1825), Western Australia (1829), South Australia (1834), Victoria (1851), and Queensland (1859).

The six colonies became states and in 1901 federated into the Commonwealth of Australia with a Constitution that incorporated British parliamentary tradition and U.S. federal experience. Australia became known for liberal legislation: free compulsory education, protected trade unionism with industrial conciliation and arbitration, the "Australian" ballot facilitating selection, the secret ballot, women's suffrage, maternity allowances, and sickness and old age pensions.

In the election of 1983, Robert Hawke, head of the Labor Party, became Prime Minister. The Labor government was reelected in a Federal election in December 1984.

Amid a deep recession Hawke was ousted by Paul Keating in 1991—the first time an Australian prime minister was removed from office by his own party.

March 1993 general elections returned Prime Minister Keating and his Labour Party to power. The campaign centered on the economy and Keating's pledge to sponsor a referendum on Queen Elizabeth's status as head of state.

Australian External Territories

Norfolk Island (13 sq mi.; 36.3 sq km) was placed under Australian administration in 1914. Population, 2,620 (July 1992); growth rate, 1.7%.

The Ashmore and Cartier Islands (.8 sq mi.), situated in the Indian Ocean off the northwest coast of Australia, came under Australian administration in 1934. In 1938 the islands were annexed to the Northern Territory. On the attainment of self-government by the Northern Territory in 1978, the islands which are uninhabited were retained as Commonwealth Territory.

The Australian Antarctic Territory (2,360,000 sq mi.; 6,112,400 sq km), comprises all the islands and territories, other than Adélie Land, situated south of lat. 60°S and lying between long. 160° to 45°E. It came under Australian administration in 1936.

Heard Island and the McDonald Islands (158 sq mi.; 409.2 sq km), lying in the sub-Antarctic, were placed under Australian administration in 1947. The islands are uninhabited.

Christmas Island (52 sq mi.; 134.7 sq km) is situated in the Indian Ocean. It came under Australian administration in 1958. Population 929 (July 92).

Coral Sea Islands (400,000 sq mi.; 1,036,000 sq km, but only a few sq mi. of land) became a territory of Australia in 1969. There is no permanent population on the islands.

Cocos (Keeling) Islands. The territory of the Cocos comprises a group of 27 small coral islands in two separate atolls in the Indian Ocean, 1,721 miles (2,768 kilometers) northwest of Perth. West Island is the largest, about 6.2 miles (10 kilometers) long. The islands became an Australian territory in 1955. Population 597 (July 92); growth rate –0.5%.

AUSTRIA

Republic of Austria
President: Thomas Klestil (1992)
Chancellor: Franz Vranitzky (1986)
Area: 32,375 sq mi. (83,851 sq km)
Population (est. mid-1993): 7,900,000 (average annual rate of natural increase: 0.2%); birth rate: 12/1000; infant mortality rate: 7.5/1000; density per square mile: 249
Capital and largest city (1991): Vienna, 1,600,000; **Other large cities (est. 1991):** Graz, 232,150; Linz, 203,000; Salzburg, 144,000; Innsbruck, 115,000; **Monetary unit:** Schilling; **Languages:** German. Slovene, Croatian, Hungarian; **Religion:** Roman Catholic, 89%; **Literacy rate:** 98%
National name: Republik Österreich
Economic summary: Gross domestic product (1991): $167.0 billion; per capita $20,985; real growth rate (1992): 2.5%; inflation rate (1991): 3.3%; unemployment (1991): 5.8%. Arable land: 17%. Labor force: 3,037,000; 56.4% in services; principal agricultural products: livestock, forest products, grains, sugar beets, potatoes. Principal products: iron and steel, chemicals, machinery, paper and pulp. Natural resources: iron ore, petroleum, timber, magnesite, aluminum, coal, lignite, cement, copper, hydropower. Exports: $40 billion (1991): iron and steel products, timber, paper, textiles, chemical products. Imports: $50 billion (1991): machinery, chemicals, foodstuffs, textiles and clothing, petroleum. Major trading partners: Germany, Italy, Switzerland, U.S., Eastern Europe.

Geography. Slightly smaller than Maine, Austria includes much of the mountainous territory of the eastern Alps (about 75% of the area). The country contains many snowfields, glaciers, and snowcapped peaks, the highest being the Grossglockner (12,530 ft; 3,819 m). The Danube is the principal river. Forests and woodlands cover about 40% of the land area.

Almost at the heart of Europe, Austria has as its neighbors Italy, Switzerland, Germany, Czech Republic, Hungary, Slovenia, and Liechtenstein.

Government. Austria is a federal republic composed of nine provinces (Bundesländer), including Vienna. The President is elected by the people for a term of six years. The bicameral legislature consists of the Bundesrat, with 58 members chosen by the provincial assemblies, and the Nationalrat, with 183 members popularly elected for four years. Presidency of the Bundesrat revolves every six months, going to the provinces in alphabetical order.

History. Settled in prehistoric times, the Central European land that is now Austria was overrun in pre-Roman times by various tribes, including the Celts. Charlemagne conquered the area in 788 and encouraged colonization and Christianity. In 1252, Ottokar, King of Bohemia, gained possession, only to lose the territories to Rudolf of Hapsburg in 1278. Thereafter, until World War I, Austria's history was largely that of its ruling house, the Hapsburgs.

Austria emerged from the Congress of Vienna in 1815 as the Continent's dominant power. The *Ausgleich* of 1867 provided for a dual sovereignty, the empire of Austria and the kingdom of Hungary, under Francis Joseph I, who ruled until his death on Nov. 21, 1916. He was succeeded by his grandnephew, Charles I.

During World War I, Austria-Hungary was one of the Central Powers with Germany, Bulgaria, and Turkey, and the conflict left the country in political chaos and economic ruin. Austria, shorn of Hungary, was proclaimed a republic in 1918, and the monarchy was dissolved in 1919.

A parliamentary democracy was set up by the Constitution of Nov. 10, 1920. To check the power of Nazis advocating union with Germany, Chancellor Engelbert Dolfuss in 1933 established a dictatorship, but was assassinated by the Nazis on July 25, 1934. Kurt von Schuschnigg, his successor, struggled to keep Austria independent but on March 12, 1938, German troops occupied the country, and Hitler proclaimed its *Anschluss* (union) with Germany, annexing it to the Third Reich.

After World War II, the U.S. and Britain declared the Austrians a "liberated" people. But the Russians prolonged the occupation. Finally Austria concluded a state treaty with the U.S.S.R. and the other occupying powers and regained its independence on May 15, 1955. The second Austrian republic, established Dec. 19, 1945, on the basis of the 1920 Constitution (amended in 1929), was declared by the federal parliament to be permanently neutral.

On June 8, 1986, former UN Secretary-General Kurt Waldheim was elected to the ceremonial office of President in a campaign marked by controversy over his alleged links to Nazi war-crimes in Yugoslavia.

The chief of Austria's diplomatic corps. Thomas Klestil, handily won election to the Presidency, paving the way for a normalization of relations strained during Waldheim's term.

The government in 1992 actively pursued negotiations concerning admission to the European Community.

AZERBAIJAN

Republic of Azerbaijan
Acting President: Heydar Aliyev (1993)
Prime Minister: Surat Husseinov (1993)
Area: 33,400 sq mi. (86,600 sq km)
Population (est. mid-1993): 7,200,000 (average annual rate of natural increase: 2.1%); (Azerbaijanis, 83%; major minorities, Russians, and Armenians). The republic is noted for the longevity of its population. Forty-eight out of every 100,000 residents are over 100 years old. Birth rate: 27/1000; infant mortality rate: 33/1000; density per square mile: 214
Capital and largest city (1991): Baku, 1,713,300, a port on the Caspian Sea. Other large cities: Gyandzha (Kirovabad) (1989), 278,000; Sumgait, 231,000
Monetary unit: Ruble
Languages: Azeri, 82%; Russian, 7%; Armenian, 5%
Religion: Moslem, 87%; Russian Orthodox, 5.6%; Armenian Orthodox, 5.6%
Economic summary: Azerbaijan's Apsheron peninsula is an oil-rich area but is now in decline. Industries: petroleum and natural gas, petroleum products, oilfield equipment, steel, iron ore, cement, chemicals and petrochemicals and textiles. Agricultural production includes cotton, wheat, tobacco, fruit, wine grapes, potatoes, sheep and other livestock. Labor force: 2,789,000 (1990): agriculture and forestry, 32%; industry and construction, 26%. Exports: $780 million (f.o.b., 1991). Imports: $2.2 billion (c.i.f., 1990).

Geography: Azerbaijan is located on the western shore of the Caspian Sea at the southeastern extremity of the Caucasus. The region is a mountainous country. About 7% of it is arable land. The Kira River Valley is the area's major agricultural zone. The republic is bounded on the north by Russia, by the Caspian Sea in the east, by Iran in the south, and by Georgia and Armenia in the west.

Government: A constitutional republic in transition.

History: Azerbaijan was known in ancient times as Albania. The area was the site of many conflicts involving Arabs, Kazars, and the Turks. After the 11th century, the territory became dominated by the Turks and eventually became a stronghold of the Shi'ite Muslim religion and Islamic culture.

The territory of Soviet Azerbaijan was acquired by Russia from Persia through the Treaty of Gulistan in 1813 and the Treaty of Turkamanchai in 1828.

After the Bolshevik Revolution, Azerbaijan declared its independence from Russia in May 1918. The republic was reconquered by the Red Army in 1920, and was annexed into the Transcaucasian Soviet Federated Socialist Republic in 1922. It was later reestablished as a separate Soviet Republic on Dec. 5, 1936.

Since 1983, the rival republics of Azerbaijan and Armenia have been feuding over the enclave of Nagorno-Karabakh located within Azerbaijan. Both nations claim this autonomous region. The majority of the enclave's residents are both Armenians and Christians and they are agitating to secede from the predominantly Muslim Azerbaijan and join with Armenia.

Campaigning on a platform calling for the country to break from the CIS and retain Nagorno-Karabakh, Popular Front leader Elchibey won more than 60% of the June 1992 vote.

A power struggle in June 1993 sent Elchibey fleeing when rebel forces advanced on the capital. These events were set against a worsening of the economy and major reverses in the war with Armenia.

BAHAMAS

Commonwealth of the Bahamas
Sovereign: Queen Elizabeth II (1952)
Governor-General: Sir Clifford Darling (1992)
Prime Minister: Hubert Ingraham (1992)
Area: 5,380 sq mi. (13,939 sq km)
Population (est. mid-1993): 300,000 (average annual rate of natural increase: 1.4%); birth rate: 20/1000; infant mortality rate: 28.4/1000; density per square mile: 55.7
Capital and largest city (1991 census): Nassau, 171,542; **Monetary unit:** Bahamian dollar; **Language:** English; **Religions:** Baptist, 29%; Anglican, 23%; Roman Catholic, 22%, others; **Literacy rate:** 95%

Member of Commonwealth of Nations
Economic summary: Gross domestic product (1990): $2.8 billion; $11,055 per capita; real growth rate 5.6%; inflation rate (est. 1991): 7.3%; unemployment (1991): 16%. Labor force: 132,600; Principal agricultural products: fruits, vegetables. Major industrial products: fish, refined petroleum, pharmaceutical products; tourism. Natural resources: salt, aragonite, timber. Exports: $306 million (f.o.b., 1991 est.) rum, crawfish, pharmaceuticals, cement, rum. Imports: $1.14 billion (c.i.f., 1991 est.): foodstuffs, manufactured goods, fuels. Major trading partners: U.S., U.K., Nigeria, Canada, Iran.

Geography. The Bahamas are an archipelago of about 700 islands and 2,400 uninhabited islets and cays lying 50 miles off the east coast of Florida. They extend from northwest to southeast for about 760 miles (1,223 km). Only 22 of the islands are inhabited; the most important is New Providence (80 sq mi.; 207 sq km), on which Nassau is situated. Other islands include Grand Bahama, Abaco, Eleuthera, Andros, Cat Island, San Salvador (or Watling's Island), Exuma, Long Island, Crooked Island, Acklins Island, Mayaguana, and Inagua.

The islands are mainly flat, few rising above 200 feet (61 m). There are no fresh water streams. There are several large brackish lakes on several islands including Inagua and New Providence.

Government. The Bahamas moved toward greater autonomy in 1968 after the overwhelming victory in general elections of the Progressive Liberal Party, led by Prime Minister Lynden O. Pindling. The black leader's party won 29 seats in the House of Assembly to only 7 for the predominantly white United Bahamians, who had controlled the islands for decades before Pindling became Premier in 1967.

With its new mandate from the 85%-black population, Pindling's government negotiated a new Constitution with Britain under which the colony became the Commonwealth of the Bahama Islands in 1969. On July 10, 1973, The Bahamas became an independent nation as the Commonwealth of the Bahamas. The islands established diplomatic relations with Cuba in 1974.

In the 1992 election, the Free National Movement won 32 of 49 seats in Parliament; the Progressive Liberal Party, 17. Hubert A. Ingraham was sworn in as Prime Minister on Aug. 20, 1992, ending 25 years of rule by the Progressive Liberal Party.

Several days later Hurricane Andrew came ashore causing extensive property damage.

History. The islands were reached by Columbus in October 1492, and were a favorite pirate area in the early 18th century. The Bahamas were a crown colony from 1717 until they were granted internal self-government in 1964.

BAHRAIN

State of Bahrain
Emir: Sheik Isa bin-Sulman al-Khalifa (1961)
Prime Minister: Sheik Khalifa bin Sulman al-Khalifa (1970)
Area: 240 sq mi. (620 sq km)
Population (est. mid-1993): 500,000 (average annual rate of natural increase: 2.4%); birth rate: 27/1000; infant mortality rate: 20/1000; density per square mile: 2,087
Capital (est. 1988): Manama, 151,500; **Monetary unit:** Bahrain dinar; **Languages:** Arabic (official), English, Farsi, Urdu; **Religion:** Islam; **Literacy rate** : 80%
Economic summary: Gross domestic product (1989): $3.4 billion, $7,000 per capita; real growth rate (1988): 0%; inflation (1989) 1.5%; unemployment (1989) 8–10%. Labor force (1982): 140,000; labor force in industry and commerce: 85%. Principal agricultural products: eggs, vegetables, fruits. Major industries: petroleum processing and refining, aluminum smelting, offshore banking, ship repairing. Natural resources: oil, fish. Exports: $3.7 billion (f.o.b., 1990 est.): petroleum and petroleum products, 80%; aluminum, 7%. Imports: $3.7 billion (f.o.b., 1989 est.): machinery, oil-industry equipment, motor vehicles, foodstuffs. Major trading partners: Saudi Arabia, U.S., U.K., Japan.

Geography. Bahrain is an archipelago in the Persian Gulf off the coast of Saudi Arabia. The islands for the most part are level expanses of sand and rock.

Government. A new Constitution was approved in 1973. It created the first elected parliament in the country's history. Called the National Council, it consisted of 30 members elected by male citizens for four-year terms, plus up to 16 Cabinet ministers as ex-officio members. In August 1975, the Amir dissolved the National Council.

History. A sheikdom that passed from the Persians to the al-Khalifa family from Arabia in 1782, Bahrain became, by treaty, a British protectorate in 1820. It has become a major Middle Eastern oil center and, through use of oil revenues, is one of the most developed of the Persian Gulf sheikdoms. The Emir, Sheik Isa bin-Sulman al-Khalifa, who succeeded to the post in 1961, is a member of the original ruling family. Bahrain announced its independence on Aug. 14, 1971.

The country's territorial dispute with Qatar was taken to the International Court of Justice in 1992 with the latter saying it would seek ICJ arbitration.

BANGLADESH

People's Republic of Bangladesh
President: Abdur Rahman Biswas
Prime Minister: Begum Khaleda Zia (1991)
Area: 55,598 sq mi. (143,998 sq km)
Population (est. mid-1993): 113,900,000 (average annual rate of natural increase: 2.4%); birth rate: 37/1000; infant mortality rate: 116/1000; density per square mile: 2,087
Capital and largest city (est. 1991): Dhaka, 3,400,000; other large cities: Chittagong, 1,364,000; Khulna, 546,000; **Monetary unit:** Taka; **Principal languages:** Bangla (official), English; **Religions:** Islam, (official) 83%; Hindu, 16%; **Literacy rate:** 36%
Member of Commonwealth of Nations
Economic summary: Gross domestic product (1991–92): $23.67 billion; per capita $210; real growth rate (FY91): 3.2%; unemployment rate (est. FY90): 30%; inflation rate (est. FY91): 8.9%. Arable land: 67%. Agriculture accounts for 40% of GDP and 70% of employment. Principal products: rice, jute, tea, sugar, potatoes, beef. Labor force: 35,100,000, 11% in industry and commerce. Major industrial products: jute goods, textiles, sugar, fertilizer, paper, processed foods. Natural resources: natural gas, uranium, timber. Exports: $1.7 billion (FY91 est.): jute, tea, leather, garments. Imports: $3.5 billion (FY91 est.): food grains, fuels, raw cotton, manufactured goods. Major trading partners: U.S., Japan, Middle East, Europe.

Geography. Bangladesh, on the northern coast of the Bay of Bengal, is surrounded by India, with a small common border with Burma in the southeast. It is approximately the size of Wisconsin. The country is low-lying riverine land traversed by the many branches and tributaries of the Ganges and Brahmaputra rivers. Elevations averages less than 600 feet (183 m) above sea level. Tropical monsoons and frequent floods and cyclones inflict heavy damage in the delta region.

Government. Khaleda Zia, widow of assassinated President Ziaur Rahman, and her Bangladesh Nationalist Party won the election of late-February 1991. P.M. Zia returned Bangladesh to the parliamentary system. In a referendum in September 1991 the electorate voted to reduce the president to a figurehead.

History. The former East Pakistan was part of imperial British India until Britain withdrew in 1947. The two Pakistans were united by religion (Islam), but their peoples were separated by culture, physical features, and 1,000 miles of Indian territory. Bangladesh consists primarily of East Bengal (West Bengal is part of India and its people are primarily Hindu) plus the Sylhet district of the Indian state of Assam. For almost 25 years after independence from Britain, its history was as part of Pakistan (*see* Pakistan).

The East Pakistanis unsuccessfully sought greater autonomy from West Pakistan. The first general elections in Pakistani history, in December 1970, saw virtually all 171 seats of the region (out of 300 for both East and West Pakistan) go to Sheik Mujibur Rahman's Awami League.

Attempts to write an all-Pakistan Constitution to replace the military regime of Gen. Yahya Khan failed. Yahya put down a revolt in March 1971. An estimated one million Bengalis were killed in the fighting or later slaughtered. Ten million more took refuge in India.

In December 1971, India invaded East Pakistan, routed the West Pakistani occupation forces, and created Bangladesh. In February 1974, Pakistan agreed to recognize the independence of Bangladesh.

On March 24, 1982, Gen. Hossain Mohammad Ershad, army chief of staff, took control in a bloodless coup. Ershad assumed the office of President in 1983.

Gen. Ershad resigned on December 6, 1990 amidst protests and numerous allegations of corruption.

Democracy gained a breathing spell in 1992 with the military staying outside politics. Refugees from Myanmar fleeing persecution placed a heavy burden on the already impoverished nation.

BARBADOS

Sovereign: Queen Elizabeth II
Governor-General: Dame Nita Barrow (June 1990)
Prime Minister: L. Erskine Sandiford (1987)
Area: 166 sq. mi. (431 sq km)
Population (est. mid-1993): 300,000; growth rate: .8%.; birth rate: 16;/1000 infant mortality rate: 11.8/1000; density per square mile: 1,566
Capital and largest city (est. 1988): Bridgetown (urban area), 102,000; **Monetary unit:** Barbados dollar; **Language:** English; **Religions:** Anglican, 40%; Methodist, 7%; Pentecostal, 8%; Roman Catholic, 4%; **Literacy rate:** 99%
Member of Commonwealth of Nations
Economic summary: Gross domestic product (1990): $1.7 billion; per capita $6,500; real growth rate –3.1%; inflation, 3.4%; unemployment (1991), 18%. Arable land: 77%. Principal products: sugar cane, subsistence foods. Labor force (1991): 120,900; 37% services and government. Major industrial products: light manufactures, sugar milling, tourism. Tourism industry is major employer of labor force. Exports: $210.6 million (f.o.b., 1990): sugar and sugar cane byproducts, clothing, electrical parts. Imports: $704 million (c.i.f., 1990): foodstuffs, crude oil, manufactured goods. Major trading partners: U.S., Caribbean nations, U.K., Canada, Japan.

Geography. An island in the Atlantic about 300 miles (483 km) north of Venezuela, Barbados is only 21 miles long (34 km) and 14 miles across (23 km) at its widest point. It is circled by fine beaches and narrow coastal plains. The highest point is Mount Hillaby (1,105 ft; 337 m) in the north central area.

Government. The Barbados legislature dates from 1627. It is bicameral, with a Senate of 21 appointed members and an Assembly of 28 elected members. The major political parties are the Democratic Labor Party (18 seats in Assembly), led by Prime Minister L. Erskine Sandiford; Barbados Labor Party (10 seats), led by Owen Arthur and National Democratic Party (0 seats) led by Richie Haynes.

History. Barbados, with a population 90% black, was settled by the British in 1627. It became a crown colony in 1885. It was a member of the Federation of the West Indies from 1958 to 1962. Britain granted the colony independence on Nov. 30, 1966, and it became a parliamentary democracy.

Prime Minister Sandiford handily won a second five-year term as a result of parliamentary elections in January 1991.

During 1992 the economy faced a number of setbacks. The IMF ordered higher interest rates, privatization and cuts in government expenditures. Sugar production fell to a record low.

BELARUS

Republic of Belarus
Chairman of the Supreme Soviet: Stanislav S. Sushkevich
Prime Minister: Vyacheslau F. Kebich
Area: 80,200 sq mi. (207,600 sq km)
Population (est. mid-1993): 10,300,000 (average annual rate of natural increase: .2%) (In 1989: Belarusian, 77.9%; Russian, 13.2%; Polish, 4.1%; Ukrainian, 2.9%; Jewish, 1.1%); birth rate: 13/1000; infant mortality rate: 15/1000; density per square mile: 128
Capital and largest city (1991): Mensk (Minsk), 1,658,000. Other large cities (1989): Gomel, 500,000; Vitebsk, 350,000; Grodno, 270,000; Brest, 255,000; Orsha, 123,000; Pinsk, 119,000; **Monetary unit:** Belarusian ruble; **Language:** Belarusian (white Russian); **Religion:** Orthodoxy is predominant
Economic summary: Per capita GNP (1991), $3,110; inflation (1991): 81%. Industry accounts for about two-thirds of the country's income. Major industries include tractors, trucks, agricultural machinery, textiles, timber, chemical products including fertilizers, light manufacturing including TV sets, refrigerators, and computers, and food processing. Belarus's land is not well suited for farming. One-quarter of the republic's work force is employed in agriculture. High-yield agricultural crops are potatoes and vegetables, flax, rye, oats, other grains, sugar beets, fruit, and considerable quantities of meat, milk, and eggs. Exports: $4.3 billion (f.o.b., 1990). Imports: $5.6 billion (c.i.f., 1990).

Geography: Much of Belarus (formerly Byelorussia) is a hilly lowland with forests, swamps, and numerous rivers and lakes. There are wide rivers emptying into the Baltic and the Black Seas. Its forests cover over one-third of the land and its peat marshes are a valuable natural resource. The largest lake is Narach, 31 sq mi. (79.6 sq km). The republic borders Latvia and Lithuania on the north, Ukraine on the south, Russia on the east, and Poland on the west.

Government: A constitutional republic.

History: In the 5th century, Belarus (also known as White Russia) was colonized by east Slavic tribes and was dominated by Kiev from the 9th to 12th centuries. After the destruction of Kiev by the Mongols in the 13th century, the territory was conquered by the dukes of Lithuania. Belarus became part of the Grand Duchy of Lithuania which merged with Poland in 1569.

Following the partitions of Poland in 1772, 1793, and the final partition which divided Poland between Russia, Prussia, and Austria, Belarus became part of the Russian empire.

The peace Treaty of Riga in March 1921 ending the Polish-Soviet War ceded west Belarus to Poland. The eastern part of the country was joined to the U.S.S.R. in 1922. In 1939, the Soviet Union took back West Belarus under the secret protocol of the Nazi-Soviet Nonaggression Pact and incorporated it into the Byelorussian Soviet Socialist Republic.

Following the end of World War II, Belarus was given membership in the United Nations in 1945.

Belarus declared its sovereignty in July 1990 and its independence in August 1991.

The Belarus president, Nikolai Dementei, a communist hard-liner, was forced to resign under pressure following the August 1991 attempted coup and Stanislav S. Shushkevich, First Deputy Chairman of the Parliament, assumed leadership of the country.

Belarus became a co-founder of the Commonwealth of Independent States (CIS) on Dec. 8, 1991, and its capital Minsk became the seat of the new union's government. On Dec. 21, 1991, Belarus formally proclaimed its membership in the Commonwealth of Independent States along with ten other former Soviet republics.

The first Strategic Arms Reduction Treaty (START 1) was ratified by parliament in February 1993, leaving Ukraine as the only holdout.

BELGIUM

Kingdom of Belgium
Sovereign: King Albert II (1993)
Prime Minister: Jean-Luc Dehaene (1992)
Area: 11,781 sq mi. (30,513 sq km)
Population (est. mid-1993): 10,100,000 (average annual rate of natural increase: .2%); birth rate: 13/1000; infant mortality rate: 8.4/1000; density per square mile: 857
Capital: Brussels; **Largest cities (1991):** Brussels, 954,045; Antwerp, 467,518; Ghent, 230,246; Charleroi, 206,214; Liege, 194,956; Bruges, 117,063; **Monetary Unit:** Belgian franc; **Languages:** Flemish (Dutch), 56%; French, 32%; bilingual (Brussels), 11%; German, 1%.; **Religion:** Roman Catholic, 75%; **Literacy rate:** 98%
National name: Royaume de Belgique—Koningkrijk van België
Economic summary: Gross domestic product (est. 1991): $171.8 billion; per capita $17,300; real growth rate 1.4%; inflation rate 3.2%; unemployment rate (est. 1991): 9.4%. Arable land: 46%. Agricultural products: pork, beef, milk, fruits and vegetables, ornamental plants, meals, sugar beets, eggs, dairy products. Labor force (1988): 4,200,000; services, 69%; industry, 28%; agriculture, 3%. Major products: fabricated metal, iron and steel, machinery, textiles, chemicals, food processing. Exports: $118 billion (f.o.b., 1990): (Belg.-Luxembourg Econ. Union) iron and steel products, chemicals, pharmaceuticals, textile products. Imports: $120 billion (c.i.f., 1990): (Belg.-Luxembourg Econ. Union) nonelectrical machinery, motor vehicles, textiles, chemicals, fuels. Major trading partners: European Communities, U.S., Eastern Europe.

Geography. A neighbor of France, Germany, the Netherlands, and Luxembourg, Belgium has about 40 miles of seacoast on the North Sea at the Strait of Dover. In area, it is approximately the size of Maryland. The northern third of the country is a plain extending eastward from the seacoast. North of the Sambre and Meuse Rivers is a low plateau; to the south lies the heavily wooded Ardennes plateau, attaining an elevation of about 2,300 feet (700 m).

The Schelde River, which rises in France and flows through Belgium, emptying into the Schelde estuaries, enables Antwerp to be an ocean port.

Government. Belgium, a parliamentary democracy under a constitutional monarch, consists of nine provinces. Its bicameral legislature has a Senate, with its 184 members elected for four years—106 by general election, 50 by provincial councillors and 25 by the Senate itself. The 212-member Chamber of Representatives is directly elected for four years by proportional representation. There is universal suffrage, and those who do not vote are fined.

Belgium joined the North Atlantic Alliance in 1949 and is a member of the European Community. NATO and the European Community have their headquarters in Brussels.

The sovereign, Baudouin I, was born Sept. 7, 1930, the son of King Leopold III and Queen Astrid. He became King on July 17, 1951, after the abdication of his father. He married Doña Fabiola de Mora y Aragón on Dec. 15, 1960. Since he has no children, his brother, Prince Albert, is heir to the throne.

History. Belgium occupies part of the Roman province of Belgica, named after the Belgae, a people of ancient Gaul. The area was conquered by Julius Caesar in 57–50 B.C., then was overrun by the Franks in the 5th century. It was part of Charlemagne's empire in the 8th century, then in the next century was absorbed into Lotharingia and later into the Duchy of Lower Lorraine. In the 12th century it was partitioned into the Duchies of Brabant and Luxembourg, the Bishopric of Liège, and the domain of the Count of Hainaut, which included Flanders.

In the 16th century, Belgium, with most of the area of the Low Countries, passed to the Duchy of Burgundy and was the marriage portion of Archduke Maximilian of Hapsburg and the inheritance of his grandson, Charles V, who incorporated it into his empire. Then, in 1555, they were united with Spain.

By the treaty of Utrecht in 1713, the country's sovereignty passed to Austria. During the wars that followed the French Revolution, Belgium was occupied and later annexed to France. But with the downfall of Napoleon, the Congress of Vienna in 1815 gave the country to the Netherlands. The Belgians revolted in 1830 and declared their independence.

Germany's invasion of Belgium in 1914 set off World War I. The Treaty of Versailles (1919) gave the areas of Eupen, Malmédy, and Moresnet to Belgium. Leopold III succeeded Albert, King during World War I, in 1934. In World War II, Belgium was overwhelmed by Nazi Germany, and Leopold III was made prisoner. When he attempted to return in 1950, Socialists and Liberals revolted. He abdicated July 16, 1951, and his son, Baudouin, became King the next day.

Despite the increasingly strong divisions between the French- and Flemish-speaking communities, a Christian Democrat-Liberal coalition that took office in December 1981 came close to setting a record for longevity among the 32 governments that had ruled Belgium since World War II. In national elections of November 1991 the environmental and far-right parties made significant gains. Political instability in Zaire following riots there led to Belgian troops supervising an exodus of foreigners in September 1991.

The dominant political issues in 1992 were the reform of the state into a true federalism and a reduction in the budget deficit to the norms specified in the Maastrict treaty.

BELIZE

Sovereign: Queen Elizabeth II (1952)
Governor-General: Dame Minita Gordon (1981)
Prime Minister: Manuel Esquivel (1993)
Area: 8,867 sq mi. (22,965 sq km)
Population (est. mid-1993): 200,000 (average annual rate of natural increase: 3.3%); birth rate: 38/1000; infant mortality rate: 23/1000.; density per sq mi.: 23
Capital (est. 1990): Belmopan, 5,256; **Largest city (est. 1990):** Belize City, 43,621; **Monetary unit:** Belize dollar; **Languages:** English (official) and Spanish, Maya, Carib; **Religions:** Roman Catholic, 62%; Protestant, 30%;; **Literacy rate:** 91% (est.)
Member of Commonwealth of Nations
Economic summary: Gross domestic product (1990 est.): $373 million, per capita $1,635; real growth rate 10%). Arable land: 2%. Principal products: sugar cane, citrus fruits, corn, molasses, rice, bananas, livestock. Labor force: 51,500; 10.3% in manufacturing. Major products: timber, processed foods, furniture, rum, soap. Natural resource: timber, fish. Exports: $134 million (f.o.b., 1991 est.): sugar, molasses, clothing, lumber, citrus fruits, fish. Imports: $194 million (c.i.f., 1991 est.): fuels, transportation equipment, foodstuffs, textiles, machinery. Major trading partners: U.S., U.K., Trinidad and Tobago, Canada, Netherlands Antilles, Mexico.

Geography. Belize (formerly British Honduras) is situated on the Caribbean Sea south of Mexico and east and north of Guatemala. In area, it is about the size of New Hampshire. Most of the country is heavily forested with various hardwoods. Mangrove swamps and cays along the coast give way to hills and mountains in the interior. The highest point is Victoria Peak, 3,681 feet (1,122 m).

Government. Formerly the colony of British Honduras, Belize became a fully independent commonwealth on Sept. 21, 1981, after having been self-governing since 1964. Executive power is nominally wielded by Queen Elizabeth II through an appointed Governor-General but effective power is held by the Prime Minister, who is responsible to a 29-member parliament elected by universal suffrage.

History. Once a part of the Mayan empire, the area was deserted until British timber cutters began exploiting valuable hardwoods in the 17th century. Efforts by Spain to dislodge British settlers, including a major naval attack in 1798, were defeated. The territory was formally named a British colony in 1862 but administered by the Governor of Jamaica until 1884.

Guatemala has long made claims to the territory. A tentative agreement was reached between Britain, Belize, and Guatemala in March 1981 that would offer access to the Caribbean through Belizean territory for Guatemala. The agreement broke down, however.

The prime minister and his People's United Party easily defeated the opposition United Democratic Party in the general elections of Septemebr 1989.

Guatemala recognized Belize's sovereignty in September 1991 and abandoned its territorial claim.

In February 1992 former members of the opposition UDP formed a new political party.

BENIN

Republic of Benin
President: Nicephore Soglo (1991)
Area: 43,483 sq mi. (112,622 sq km)
Population (est. mid-1993): 5,100,000 (average annual rate of natural increase: 3.0%); birth rate: 49/1000; infant mortality rate: 89/1000; density per square mile: 119
Capital (est. 1984): Porto-Novo, 208,000; **Largest city (est. 1982):** Cotonou, 490,000; **Monetary unit:** Franc CFA; **Ethnic groups:** Fons and Adjas, Baribas, Yorubas, Mahis; **Languages:** French, African languages; **Religions:** indigenous, 70%; Christian, 15%; Islam, 15%; **National name:** Republique du Benin; **Literacy rate (1990 est.):** 23%
Economic summary: Gross domestic product (1991): $2 billion; $410 per capita; real growth rate (1990): 3%; inflation rate 3%. Arable land: 12%. Principal agricultural products: palm oils, peanuts, cotton, coffee, tobacco, corn, rice, livestock, fish. Labor force: 1,900,000; 60% in agriculture. Major industrial products: processed palm oil, palm kernel oil, textiles, beverages. Natural resources: limestone, some offshore oil, marble, timber. Exports: palm and agricultural products. Imports: beverages, tobacco, consumer goods, fuels, foodstuffs, machinery. Major trading partners: France and other Western European countries, Japan, U.S.

Geography. This West African nation on the Gulf of Guinea, between Togo on the west and Nigeria on the east, is about the size of Tennessee. It is bounded also by Burkina Faso and Niger on the north. The land consists of a narrow coastal strip that rises to a swampy, forested plateau and then to highlands in the north. A hot and humid climate blankets the entire country.

Government. The change in name from Dahomey to Benin was announced by President Mathieu Kerekou on November 30, 1975. Benin commemorates an African kingdom that flourished in the 17th century. At the same time, Kerekou announced the formation of a political organization, the Party of the People's Revolution of Benin, to mark the first anniversary of his declaration of a "new society" guided by Marxist-Leninist principles. Kérékou repudiated Marxism-Leninism in 1989.

History. One of the smallest and most densely populated states in Africa, Benin was annexed by the French in 1893. The area was incorporated into French West Africa in 1904. It became an autonomous republic within the French Community in 1958, and on Aug. 1, 1960, was granted its independence within the Community.

Gen. Christophe Soglo deposed the first president, Hubert Maga, in an army coup in 1963. He dismissed the civilian government in 1965, proclaiming himself chief of state. A group of young army officers seized power in December 1967, deposing Soglo. They promulgated a new Constitution in 1968.

In December 1969, Benin had its fifth coup of the decade, with the army again taking power. In May 1970, a three-man presidential commission was created to take over the government. The commission had a six-year term. In May 1972, yet another army coup ousted the triumvirate and installed Lt. Col. Mathieu Kerekou as President.

Student protests and widespread strikes in 1989 and 1990 moved Benin toward multiparty democracy. In March 1991 Prime Minister Soglo won the first free presidential election.

A coup attempt by army officers was thwarted in May 1992, and an army mutiny in July was suppressed.

BHUTAN

Kingdom of Bhutan

Ruler: King Jigme Singye Wangchuck (1972)
Area: 18,000 sq mi. (46,620 sq km)
Population (est. mid-1993): 800,000 (average annual rate of natural increase: 2.3%); birth rate: 40/1000; infant mortality rate: 130/1000; density per square mile: 43
Capital (est. 1985): Thimphu, 20,000; **Monetary unit:** Ngultrum; **Language:** Dzongkha (official); **Religions:** Buddhist, 75%; Hindu, 25%; **National name:** Druk-yul; **Literacy rate:** not available
Economic summary: Gross domestic product (1991 est.): $320 million; per capita $200; real growth rate 3.1%; inflation (FY90) 12%. Arable land: 3%. Labor force in agriculture: 95%. Principal products: rice, barley, wheat, potatoes, fruit. Major industrial product: cement. Natural resources: timber, hydroelectric power. Exports: $74 million (f.o.b., FY91): cardamom, gypsum, timber, handicrafts, cement, fruit. Imports: $106.4 million (c.i.f., FY91 est.): fuels, machinery, vehicles. Major trading partner: India.

Geography. Mountainous Bhutan, half the size of Indiana, is situated on the southeast slope of the Himalayas, bordered on the north and east by Tibet and on the south and west and east by India. The landscape consists of a succession of lofty and rugged mountains running generally from north to south and separated by deep valleys. In the north, towering peaks reach a height of 24,000 feet (7,315 m).

Government. Bhutan is a constitutional monarchy. The King rules with a Council of Ministers and a Royal Advisory Council. There is a National Assembly (Parliament), which meets semiannually, but no political parties.

History. British troops invaded the country in 1865 and negotiated an agreement under which Britain undertook to pay an annual allowance to Bhutan on condition of good behavior. A treaty with India in 1949 increased this subsidy and placed Bhutan's foreign affairs under Indian control.

In the 1960s, Bhutan undertook modernization, abolishing slavery and the caste system, emancipating women and enacting land reform. In 1985, Bhutan made its first diplomatic links with non-Asian countries.

A pro-democracy campaign emerged in 1991 that the government claimed was composed largely of Nepalese immigrants. Some 70,000 Nepalese civil servants in 1992 fled the country as part of the pro-democracy campaign.

BOLIVIA

Republic of Bolivia

President: Gonzalo Sanchez de Lozada (1993)
Area: 424,162 sq mi. (1,098,581 sq km)
Population (est. mid-1993): 8,000,000 (average annual rate of natural increase: 2.7%); birth rate: 37/1000; infant mortality rate: 89/1000; density per square mile: 19
Judicial capital (est. 1989): Sucre, 105,800; **Administrative capital (est. 1989):** La Paz; **Largest cities (est. 1989):** La Paz, 669,400; Santa Cruz, 529,200; Cochabamba, 403,600; Oruro, 176,700; **Monetary unit:** Boliviano; **Languages:** Spanish, Quechua, Aymara; **Religion:** Roman Catholic, 95%; **National name:** República de Bolivia; **Literacy rate:** 78%
Economic summary: Gross domestic product (1991): $4.6 billion; per capita, $630; real growth rate, 4%; inflation rate, 15%; unemployment rate (est. 1991), 7%. Arable land: 3%. Labor force: 1,700,000; labor force in agriculture: 50%. Principal agricultural products: potatoes, corn, rice, sugar cane, bananas, coffee. Labor force in manufacturing: 10%. Major industrial products: refined petroleum, processed foods, tin, textiles, clothing. Natural resources: petroleum, natural gas, tin, lead, zinc, copper, tungsten, bismuth, antimony, gold, sulfur, silver, iron ore. Exports: $970 million (f.o.b., 1991): tin, lead, zinc, silver, antimony, coffee, sugar, cotton, soya beans, leather, citrus, natural gas. Imports: $760 million (c.i.f., 1991): foodstuffs, petroleum, consumer goods. Illicit drugs: Is world's second largest producer of coca (after Peru), est. 47,900 hectares under cultivation. Major trading partners: U.S., Argentina.

Geography. Landlocked Bolivia, equal in size to California and Texas combined, lies to the west of Brazil. Its other neighbors are Peru and Chile on the west and Argentina and Paraguay on the south.

The country is a low alluvial plain throughout 60% of its area toward the east, drained by the Amazon and Plata river systems. The western part, enclosed by two chains of the Andes, is a great plateau—the Altiplano, with an average altitude of 12,000 feet (3,658 m). More than 80% of the population lives on the plateau, which also contains La Paz. At an altitude of 11,910 feet (3,630 m), it is the highest administrative capital city in the world.

Lake Titicaca, half the size of Lake Ontario, is one of the highest large lakes in the world, at an altitude of 12,507 feet (3,812 m). Islands in the lake hold ruins of the ancient Incas.

Government. The Bolivian Constitution provides for a democratic, representative, unitary republic, with a government made up of three branches: legislative, executive, and judicial. Executive power is exercised by the president, elected by a direct vote for a four-year term. Legislative power is vested in the National Congress, consisting of the Chamber of Deputies and the Senate. Judicial power is in the hands of the Supreme Court.,

History. Famous since Spanish colonial days for its mineral wealth, modern Bolivia was once a part of the ancient Incan Empire. After the Spaniards defeated the Incas in the 16th century, Bolivia's predominantly Indian population was reduced to slavery. The country won its independence in 1825 and was named after Simón Bolívar, the famed liberator.

Harassed by internal strife, Bolivia lost great slices of territory to three neighbor nations. Several thousand square miles and its outlet to the Pacific were taken by Chile after the War of the Pacific (1879–84). In 1903 a piece of Bolivia's Acre province, rich in rubber, was ceded to Brazil. And in 1938, after a war with Paraguay, Bolivia gave up claim to nearly 100,000 square miles of the Gran Chaco.

In 1965 a guerrilla movement mounted from Cuba and headed by Maj. Ernesto (Ché) Guevara began a revolutionary war. With the aid of U.S. military advisers, the Bolivian army, helped by the peasants, smashed the guerrilla movement, wounding and capturing Guevara on Oct. 8, 1967, and shooting him to death the next day.

Faltering steps toward restoration of civilian government were halted abruptly on July 17, 1980, when Gen. Luis Garcia Meza Tejada seized power. A series of military leaders followed before the military moved, in 1982, to return the government to civilian rule. Hernán Siles Zuazo was inaugurated President on Oct. 10, 1982.

Under Siles' left-of-center government, the country was regularly shut down by work stoppages, the bulk of Bolivia's natural resources—natural gas, gold, lithium, potassium and tungsten—were either sold on the black market or left in the ground, the country had the lowest per-capita income in South America, and inflation approached 3,000 percent. In 1985, the 73-year-old Siles decided he was unable to carry on and quit a year early.

As in 1985 the inconclusive presidential election of 1989 was decided in Congress, where the second place finisher Bánzer threw his support to Paz Zamora, who finished third, in exchange for naming a majority of the new cabinet.

The presidential elections of June 1993 gave the post to a millionaire mining entrepreneur who ran on a platform calling for free market policies and privatization. His running mate was an Aymara Indian and is expected to give that group greater political clout.

BOPHUTHATSWANA

See South Africa

BOSNIA AND HERCEGOVINA

Republic of Bosnia and Hercegovina
President: Alija Izetbegovic (1990)
Area: 19,741 sq mi. (51,129 sq km)
Population (pre-war, 1991 census): 4,400,000; **(est. mid-1993):** 4,000,000 (average annual rate of natural increase: .8%), Muslims 40%; Serbs, 33%; Croats, 18%. Birth rate: 14/1000; infant mortality rate: 15.2/1000; density per square mile: 203
Capital and largest city (1991): Sarajevo (Bosnia) 525,980; Banja Luka (Bosnia), 195,139.. Mostar is capital of Herzegovina; **Monetary unit:** Dinar; **Language:** Bosnian, written in Latin and Cyrillic; **Religions:** Slavic Muslim, 40%; Orthodox, 31%; Catholic, 15%; Protestant, 4%
Economic summary: Gross domestic product (1991): $14 billion, real growth rate –37%; inflation 80%; unemployment (Feb. 92 est.): 28%. Labor force: 1,026,254 (1991 est.): 2% agriculture; 45% industry. Industries: steel production, mining (coal, iron ore, lead, zinc, manganese, and bauxite); vehicle assembly, textiles, tobacco products, wooden furniture, domestic appliances, oil refining. Agriculture: orchards, vineyards, livestock, some wheat and corn. Exports: $2,054 million. Imports: $1,891 million (1990).

Geography: Bosnia and Hercegovina is a roughly triangular-shaped republic about one-half the size of the state of Kentucky. The Bosnian region in the north is mountainous and covered with thick forests. The Hercegovina region in the south is largely a rugged and flat farm land. The republic is bordered on the east by Serbia, the southeast by Montenegro, and in the north and west by the Republic of Croatia. It has a narrow coastline without natural harbors stretching 13 miles (20 km) along the Adriatic Sea. The Sava and Drina Rivers form much of the country's northern and eastern boundaries with Croatia and Serbia, respectively. The Sava and its tributaries are the nation's chief rivers.

Government: Democratic republic with bicameral legislature. The parties of the three ethnic groups share power in the legislature.

History: Bosnia and Hercegovina were once part of the Roman provinces of Illyricum and Pannonia. Serbs first settled in the land during the 7th century A.D. and by the end of the 10th century, Bosnia became an independent state. Later Bosnia came under Hungarian rule in the middle of the 12th century.

Medieval Bosnia reached the height of its power and prestige during the 14th century when it controlled many of the surrounding territories including Hercegovina. During this period, religious strife arose among the Roman Catholic, Orthodox, and Muslim populations which weakened the country and in 1463, Ottoman Turks conquered the disunited nation.

At the Congress of Berlin in 1878 following the end of the Russo-Turkish War (1877–78), Austria was given a mandate to occupy and govern Bosnia and Hercegovina. Although the provinces were still officially part of the Ottoman Empire, they were annexed into the Austro-Hungarian empire on Oct. 7, 1908. As a result, relations with Serbia, which had claims on Bosnia and Hercegovina, became embittered. The hostile tension between the two countries climaxed in the assassination of Austrian archduke Francis Ferdinand at Sarajevo on June 28, 1914 by a Serbian nationalist. This event precipitated the start of World War I (1914–1918).

Bosnia and Hercegovina were annexed to Serbia as part of the newly formed Kingdom of Serbs, Croats, and Slovenes on Oct. 26, 1918. The name was later changed to Yugoslavia in 1929.

When Germany invaded Yugoslavia in 1941, Bosnia and Hercegovina were made part of a Croatian state that was controlled by a Fascist dictatorship. During the German and Italian occupation of their land Bosnian and Hercegovinan resistance fighters fought a fierce guerrilla warfare against the Fascist troops.

After the defeat of Germany in 1945, Bosnia and Hercegovina were reunited into a single state as one of the six republics of the newly reestablished Yugoslavia.

In December 1991, Bosnia and Hercegovina declared their independence from Yugoslavia and asked for recognition by the 12 member nations of the European Community (E.C.). The E.C. said that before it could recommend recognition, Bosnia and Hercegovina should hold a referendum on independence.

Most Bosnian voters chose independence during a referendum held in March 1992 and President Izetbegovic again declared the nation an independent state.

Attempting to carve out enclaves for themselves the Serbian minority, with the help of the largely Serbian Yugoslav army, took the offensive and laid siege, particularly on Sarajevo, resulting in countless deaths.

By the end of August, rebel Bosnian Serbs had conquered over 60% of Bosnia and Hercegovina.

The Vance-Owens peace plan was rejected in May 1993 by the self-styled Bosnian Serb parliament. Instead it submitted the accord to a popular referendum, which again overwhelmingly rejected it. The western European nations consistently opposed lifting the ban on sending arms to Bosnia.

BOTSWANA

Republic of Botswana
President: Quett K.J. Masire (1980)
Area: 231,800 sq mi. (600,360 sq km)
Population (est. mid-1993): 1,400,000 (average annual rate of natural increase: 2.8%); birth rate: 37/1000; infant mortality rate: 45/1000; density per square mile: 6
Capital and largest city (est. 1991): Gaborone, 133,791; **Monetary unit:** Pula; **Languages:** English, Setswana; **Religions:** Christian, 48%; traditional, 49%; **Member of Commonwealth of Nations; Literacy rate:** 23%
Economic summary: Gross domestic product (est. 1991): $3.6 billion, per capita $2,800; real growth rate 6.3%; inflation 12.6%; unemployment (1989): 25%. Arable land: 2%. Principal agricultural products: livestock, sorghum, corn, millet, cowpeas, beans. Labor force: 400,000; 198,500 formal sector employees, most others involved in cattle raising and subsistence agriculture. Major industrial products: diamonds, copper, nickel, salt, soda ash, potash, coal, frozen beef; tourism. Natural resources: diamonds, copper, nickel, salt, soda ash, potash, coal, natural gas. Exports: $1.8 billion (f.o.b., 1990): diamonds, cattle, animal products, copper, nickel. Imports: $1.6 billion (c.i.f., 1990): foodstuffs, vehicles, textiles, petroleum products. Major trading partners: South Africa, U.K., U.S., Switzerland.

Geography. Twice the size of Arizona, Botswana is in south central Africa, bounded by Namibia, Zambia, Zimbabwe, and South Africa. Most of the country is near-desert, with the Kalahari occupying the western part of the country. The eastern part is hilly, with salt lakes in the north.

Government. The Botswana Constitution provides, in addition to the unicameral National Assembly, for a House of Chiefs, which has a voice on bills affecting tribal affairs. There is universal suffrage. The major political parties are the Democratic Party (31 of 34 elective seats in 36-man Legislative Assembly), led by President Quett Masire; National Front (4 seats), led by Kenneth Koma; People's Party (1 seat), led by Kenneth Nkhwa.

History. Botswana is the land of the Batawana tribes, which, when threatened by the Boers in Transvaal, asked Britain in 1885 to establish a protectorate over the country, then known as Bechuanaland. In 1961, Britain granted a Constitution to the country. Self-government began in 1965, and on Sept. 30, 1966, the country became independent. Since 1975, it has been an associate member of the European Common Market.

Owing to a land scandal the vice president and the minister of agriculture were forced to resign in March 1992. The minister of finance was selected to be the new vice president.

BRAZIL

Federative Republic of Brazil
President: Itamar Franco (1992)
Area: 3,286,470 sq mi. (8,511,957 sq km)
Population (est. mid-1993): 152,000,000 (average annual rate of natural increase: 1.5%); birth rate: 23/1000; infant mortality rate: 63/1000; density per square mile: 47
Capital (est. 1985): Brasilia; **Largest cities (est. 1985):** São Paulo, 10,099,086; Rio de Janeiro, 5,615,149; Salvador, 1,811,367; Belo Horizonte, 2,122,073; Brasilia, 1,576,657; Recife, 1,289,627; Porto Alegre, 1,275,483; **Monetary unit:** Novo cruzado; **Language:** Portuguese; **Religion:** Roman Catholic, 90% (nominal); **National name:** República Federativa de Brasil; **Literacy rate:** 81%
Economic summary: Gross domestic product (1991): $358 billion; per capita $2,300; inflation 478.5%; unemployment 4.3%. Arable land: 7%. Principal products: world's largest producer of coffee. Sugar cane, oranges, cocoa, soybeans, tobacco, cattle. Labor force (1990 est.): 57,409,975; 27% in industry. Major industrial products: steel, chemicals, petrochemicals, machinery, motor vehicles, cement, lumber. Natural resources: iron ore, manganese, bauxite, nickel, other industrial metals, hydropower, timber. Exports: $31.6 billion (1991): coffee, iron ore, soybeans, sugar, beef, transport equipment, footwear, orange juice. Imports: $21 billion (1991): crude oil, capital goods, chemical products, foodstuffs, coal. Major trading partners: U.S., Japan, Saudi Arabia, Africa, E.C. countries.

Geography. Brazil covers nearly half of South America, extends 2,965 miles (4,772 km) north-south, 2,691 miles (4,331 km), east-west, and borders every nation on the continent except Chile and Ecuador.

More than a third of Brazil is drained by the Amazon and its more than 200 tributaries. The Amazon is navigable for ocean steamers to Iquitos, Peru, 2,300 miles (3,700 km) upstream. Southern Brazil is drained by the Plata system—the Paraguay, Uruguay, and Paraná Rivers. The most important stream entirely within Brazil is the São Francisco, navigable for 1,000 miles (1,903 km), but broken near its mouth by the 275-foot (84 m) Paulo Afonso Falls.

Government. A federal republic. The president is elected for a five-year term through direct, compulsory and secret suffrage. The National Congress maintains a bicameral structure—a Senate, whose members serve eight-year terms, and a Chamber of Deputies, elected for four-year terms. Brazil has had a democratically-elected president since March 1990.

History. Brazil is the only Latin American nation deriving its language and culture from Portugal. Adm. Pedro Alvares Cabral claimed the territory for the Portuguese in 1500. He brought to Portugal a cargo of wood, pau-brasil, from which the land received its name. Portugal began colonization in 1532 and made the area a royal colony in 1549.

During the Napoleonic wars, King João VI, then Prince Regent, fled the country in 1807 in advance of the French armies and in 1808 set up his court in Rio de Janeiro. João was drawn home in 1820 by a revolution, leaving his son as Regent. When Portugal sought to reduce Brazil again to colonial status, the prince declared Brazil's independence on Sept. 7, 1822, and became Pedro I, Emperor of Brazil.

Harassed by his parliament, Pedro I abdicated in 1831 in favor of his five-year-old son, who became Emperor in 1840 as Pedro II. The son was a popular monarch, but discontent built up and, in 1889, following a military revolt, he had to abdicate. Although a republic was proclaimed, Brazil was under two military dictatorships during the next four years. A revolt permitted a gradual return to stability under civilian Presidents.

The President during World War I, Wenceslau Braz, cooperated with the Allies and declared war on Germany.

In World War II, Brazil cooperated with the Western Allies, welcoming Allied air bases, patrolling the South Atlantic, and joining the invasion of Italy after declaring war on the Axis.

Gen. João Baptista de Oliveira Figueiredo, became President in 1979 and pledged a return to democracy in 1985.

The electoral college's choice of Tancredo Neves on Jan. 15, 1985, as the first civilian President since 1964 brought a nationwide wave of optimism, but the 75-year-old President-elect was hospitalized and underwent a series of intestinal operations. The civilian government was inaugurated on schedule on March 15, but only Neves' Vice Presidential running mate, José Sarney, was sworn in, and he was widely distrusted because he had previously been a member of the governing military regime's political party. When Neves died on April 21, Sarney became President.

Economically, Brazil's $93-billion foreign debt was the Third World's largest, and inflation reached a staggering 229% annual rate in 1984, almost double the 115% rate in 1983.

Collor de Mello won the election of late 1989 and took office in March 1990 despite his lack of support from a major party. In the campaign he pledged to lower the chronic hyperinflation following the path of free-market economics. Yet an economic recession still saw the inflation rate running at about 400% during the president's first year in office.

On the basis of a corruption scandal Collor in 1992 faced impeachment by Congress. Just minutes after the trial began on December 29 the president resigned, and the vice president assumed the presidency.

BRUNEI DARUSSALAM

State of Brunei Darussalam
Sultan: Hassanal Bolkiah
Area: 2,226 sq mi. (5,765 sq km)
Population (est. mid-1993): 300,000 (annual rate of natural increase: 2.6%); birth rate: 29/1000; infant mortality rate: 9/1000; density per square mile: 136
Capital and largest city (est. 1988): Bandar Seri Begawan, 52,3000; **Monetary unit:** Brunei dollar; **Ethnic groups:** 64% Malay, 20% Chinese, 16% other; **Languages:** Malay (official), Chinese, English; **Religions:** Islam (official religion), 63%; Christian, 8%; Buddhist, 14%; indigenous beliefs and other, 15%; **Literacy rate:** 77%
Economic summary: Gross domestic product (1990 est.): $3.5 billion, per capita $8,800; real growth rate 1%; inflation (1989) 1.3%; unemployment 3.7%. Arable land: 1%; principle agricultural products: fruit, rice, pepper, buffaloes. Labor force (including Army): 89,000; 47.5% production of oil, natural gas, services, and construction; 41.9% in agriculture, forestry, fishing. Major industrial products: crude petroleum, liquified natural gas. Natural resources: petroleum, natural gas, timber. Exports: $2.26 billion (f.o.b., 1990 est.): crude petroleum, liquified natural gas. Imports: $1.76 billion (c.i.f., 1990 est.): machinery, transport equipment, manufactured goods, foodstuffs. Major trading partners: Japan, Thailand, U.S., U.K., Singapore.

Geography. About the size of Delaware, Brunei is an independent sultanate on the northwest coast of the island of Borneo in the South China Sea, wedged between the Malaysian states of Sabah and Sarawak. Three quarters of the thinly populated country is covered with tropical rain forest; there are rich oil and gas deposits.

Government. Sultan Hassanal Bolkiah is ruler of the state, a former British protectorate which became fully sovereign and independent on New Year's Day, 1984, presiding over a Privy Council and Council of Ministers appointed by himself.

History. Brunei (pronounced broon-eye) was a powerful state from the 16th to the 19th century, ruling over the northern part of Borneo and adjacent island chains. But it fell into decay and lost Sarawak in 1841, becoming a British protectorate in 1888 and a British dependency in 1905.

The Sultan regained control over internal affairs in 1959, but Britain retained responsibility for the state's defense and foreign affairs until the end of 1983, when the sultanate became fully independent.

Sultain Bolkiah was crowned in 1968 at the age of 22, succeeding his father, Sir Omar Ali Saifuddin, who had abdicated. During his reign, exploitation of the rich Seria oilfield has made the sultanate wealthy.

Warning against opposition to his government, the Islamic religion and himself, the sultan in 1990 said that the laws of the sultanate would be restructured into conformity with Islamic law.

In February 1992 diplomatic relations were established with Vietnam, and in September the country joined the non-aligned movement.

BULGARIA

Republic of Bulgaria
Prime Minister: Prof. Lyuben Berov (1992)
President: Zhelyu Zhelev (1992)
Area: 42,823 sq mi. (110,912 sq km)
Population (est. mid-1993): 9,000,000 (average annual rate of natural increase: –0.2%); birth rate: 11/1000; infant mortality rate: 16.7/1000; density per square mile: 210
Capital: Sofia; **Largest cities (1989):** Sofia, 1,136,875; Plovdiv, 364,162; Varna, 306,300; Burgas, 200,464; Ruse, 190,432; **Monetary unit:** Lev; **Language:** Bulgarian; **Religions:** Bulgarian Orthodox, 90%; Muslim, Catholic, Protestant, Judaic, Armeno-Gerogorian; **National name:** Narodna Republika Bulgariya; **Literacy rate:** 95%

Economic summary: Gross national product (1991 est.): $36.4 billion, per capita $4,100; real growth rate –22%; inflation 420%; unemployment 10%. Arable land: 34%. Principal products: grains, tobacco, fruits, vegetables. Labor force: 4,300,000, 33% in industry; 33% in agriculture. Major products: processed agricultural products, machinery, electronics, chemicals. Natural resources: metals, minerals, timber. Exports: $8.4 billion (f.o.b., 1990): machinery and transport equipment, fuels, minerals, raw materials, agricultural products. Imports: $9.6 billion (f.o.b., 1990): machinery and transportation equipment, fuels, raw materials, metals, agricultural raw materials. Major trading partners: C.I.S., U.S.,, Eastern European countries, EEC.

Geography. Two mountain ranges and two great valleys mark the topography of Bulgaria, a country the size of Tennessee. Situated on the Black Sea in the eastern part of the Balkan peninsula, it shares borders with Serbia, Macedonia, Romania, Greece, and Turkey. The Balkan belt crosses the center of the country, almost due east-west, rising to a height of 6,888 feet (2,100 m). The Rhodope, Rila and Pirin mountains straightens out along the western and southern border. Between the two ranges, is the valley of the Maritsa, Bulgaria's principal river. Between the Balkan range and the Danube, which forms most of the northern boundary with Romania, is the Danubian tableland.

Southern Dobruja, a fertile region of 2,900 square miles (7,511 sq km), below the Danube delta, is an area of low hills, fens, and sandy steppes.

Government. An emerging democracy. The National Assembly, consisting of 240 members is the legislative body. Direct elections for president and vice president were held in January 1992.

History. The first Bulgarians, a tribe of wild horsemen akin to the Huns, crossed the Danube from the north in A.D. 679 and subjugated the Slavic population of Moesia. They adopted a Slav dialect and Slavic customs and twice conquered most of the Balkan peninsula between 893 and 1280. After the Serbs subjected their kingdom in 1330, the Bulgars gradually fell prey to the Turks, and from 1396 to 1878 Bulgaria was a Turkish province. In 1878, Russia forced Turkey to give the country its independence; but the European powers, fearing that Bulgaria might become a Russian dependency, intervened. By the Treaty of Berlin in 1878, Bulgaria became autonomous under Turkish sovereignty.

In 1887, Prince Ferdinand of Saxe-Coburg-Gotha was elected ruler of Bulgaria; on Oct. 5, 1908, he declared the country independent and took the title of Tsar.

Bulgaria joined Germany in World War I and lost. On Oct. 3, 1918, Tsar Ferdinand abdicated in favor of his son, Tsar Boris III. Boris assumed dictatorial powers in 1934–35. When Hitler awarded Bulgaria southern Dobruja, taken from Romania in 1940, Boris joined the Nazis in war the next year and occupied parts of Yugoslavia and Greece. Later the Germans tried to force Boris to send his troops against the Russians. Boris resisted and died under mysterious circumstances on Aug. 28, 1943. Simeon II, infant son of Boris, became nominal ruler under a regency. Russia declared war on Bulgaria on Sept. 5, 1944. An armistice was agreed to three days later, after Bulgaria had declared war on Germany. Russian troops streamed in the next day and under an informal armistice a coalition "Fatherland Front" cabinet was set up under Kimon Georgiev.

A Soviet-style people's Republic was established in 1947 and Bulgaria acquired the reputation of being the most slavishly loyal to Moscow of all the East European Communist countries.

Zhikov resigned in 1989 after 35 years in power. His successor, Peter Mladenov, purged the Politburo, ended the Communist monopoly on power and held free elections in May 1990 that led to a surprising victory for the Communists, renamed the Bulgarian Socialist Party. Mladenov was forced to resign in July 1990.

Parliamentary elections in October 1991 resulted in a victory for the opposition Union of Democratic Forces. In the presidential election of January 1992 UDF leader Zhelev won 53.5% of the vote. The principally Turkish party, the Movement for Rights and Freedoms, joined with the Socialists in 1992 to pass a no-confidence motion. Later in the year a non-Turk nominated by the MRF became prime minister.

BURKINA FASO

President: Blaise Compaore (1991)
Area: 105,870 sq mi. (274,200 sq km)
Population (est. mid-1993): 10,000,000 (average annual rate of natural increase: 3.4%); birth rate: 50/1000; infant mortality rate: 119/1000; density per square mile: 94
Capital and largest city (est. 1990): Ouagadougou, 500,000; **Monetary unit:** Franc CFA; **Ethnic groups:** Mossis, Bobos, Lobis, Fulanis; **Languages:** French, Tribal languages; **Religions:** Animist, 65%; Islam, 25%; Roman Catholic, 10%; **National name:** Burkina Faso; **Literacy rate:** 26.9%
Economic summary: Gross domestic product (1990 est.): $2.9 billion, per capita $320; real growth rate 1.3%; inflation (1989) –0.5%. Arable land: 10%. Labor force: 3,300,000; in agriculture, 82%. Principal products: millet, sorghum, corn, rice, livestock, peanuts, sugar cane, cotton. Major industrial products: processed agricultural products, light industrial items, brick, brewed products. Natural resources: manganese, limestone, marble, gold, uranium, bauxite, copper. Exports: $262 million (f.o.b., 1989): oilseeds, cotton, live animals, gold. Imports: $619 million (f.o.b., 1989): grain, dairy products, petroleum, machinery. Major trading partners: E.C., China, Côte d'Ivoire, Africa.

Geography. Slightly larger than Colorado, Burkina Faso, formerly known as Upper Volta, is a landlocked country in West Africa. Its neighbors are the Ivory Coast, Mali, Niger, Benin, Togo, and Ghana. The country consists of extensive plains, low hills, high savannas, and a desert area in the north.

Government. The presidential election in December 1991 was boycotted by the main opposition parties. A 20-man transitional government is to guide the country to multi-party democracy. A National Reconciliation Forum was convened in 1992 after negotiations with opposition leaders.

History. The country, called Upper Volta by the French, consists chiefly of the lands of the Mossi Empire, where France established a protectorate over the Kingdom of Ouagadougou in 1897. Upper Volta became a separate colony in 1919, was partitioned among Niger, the Sudan, and the Ivory Coast in 1933 and was reconstituted in 1947. An autonomous republic within the French Community, it became independent on Aug. 5, 1960.

President Maurice Yameogo was deposed on Jan. 3, 1966, by a military coup led by Col. Sangoulé Lamizana, who dissolved the National Assembly and suspended the Constitution. Constitutional rule returned in 1978 with the election of an Assembly and a presidential vote in June in which Gen. Lamizana won by a narrow margin over three other candidates.

On Nov. 25, 1980, there was a bloodless coup which placed Gen. Lamizana under house arrest. Col. Sayé Zerbo took charge as the President of the Military Committee of Reform for National Progress. Maj. Jean-Baptiste Ouedraogo toppled Zerbo in another coup on Nov. 7, 1982. Captain Thomas Sankara, in turn, deposed Ouedraogo a year later. His government changed the country's name on Aug. 3, 1984, to Burkina Faso (the "land of upright men") to sever ties with its colonial past. He was overthrown and killed by Blaise Compaore in 1987.

In June 1991 voters approved a draft constitution providing for three branches of government and presidential elections every seven years. The president's party won a majority of the legislative seats in elections of May 1992.

BURMA

See Myanmar

BURUNDI

Republic of Burundi
President: Melchior Ndadaye (1993)
Prime Minister: Adrien Sibomana (1988)
Area: 10,747 sq mi. (27,834 sq km)
Population (est. mid-1993): 5,800,000 (average annual rate of natural increase: 3.2%); birth rate: 47/1000; infant mortality rate: 109/1000; density per square mile: 589
Capital and largest city (1990): Bujumbura, 226,628; **Monetary unit:** Burundi franc; **Languages:** Kirundi and French (official), Swahili; **Religions:** Roman Catholic, 62%; Protestant, 5%; indigenous, 32%; **National name:** Republika Y'Uburundi; **Literacy rate:** 50%
Economic summary: Gross domestic product (1990 est.): $1.13 billion, per capita $200; real growth rate 3.4%; inflation 7.1%. Arable land: 43%; Principal agricultural products: coffee, tea, cotton, bananas, sorghum. Labor force: 1,900,000 (1983 est.); 93% in agriculture. Major industrial products: light consumer goods. Natural resources: nickel, uranium, rare earth oxide, peat, cobalt, copper, unexploited platinum, vanadium. Exports: $74.7 million (f.o.b., 1990): coffee, tea, cotton, hides and skins. Imports: $234.6 million (c.i.f., 1990): food, petroleum products, capital goods, consumer goods. Major trading partners: U.S., Western Europe, Asia.

Geography. Wedged among Tanzania, Zaire, and Rwanda in east central Africa, Burundi occupies a high plateau divided by several deep valleys. It is equal in size to Maryland.

Government. A republic. Legislative and executive power is vested in the president.

A new Constitution adopted by referendum on March 9, 1992, established a multi-party system.

History. Burundi was once part of German East Africa. An integrated society developed among the Watusi, a tall, warlike people and nomad cattle raisers, and the Bahutu, a Bantu people, who were subject farmers. Belgium won a League of Nations mandate in 1923, and subsequently Burundi, with Rwanda, was transferred to the status of a United Nations trust territory.

In 1962, Burundi gained independence and became a kingdom under Mwami Mwambutsa IV. His son deposed him in 1966 to rule as Ntaré V. He was overthrown by Premier Micombero.

One of Africa's worst tribal wars, which became genocide, occurred in Burundi in April 1972, following the return of Ntare V. He was given a safe-conduct promise in writing by President Micombero but was "judged and immediately executed" by the Burundi leader. His return was apparently attended by an invasion of exiles of Burundi's Hutu tribe. Whether Hutus living in Burundi joined the invasion is unclear, but after it failed, the victorious Tutsis proceeded to massacre some 100,000 persons in six weeks, with possibly 100,000 more slain by summer.

On Nov. 1, 1976, Lt. Col. Jean-Baptiste Bagaye led a coup and assumed the presidency. He suspended the Constitution, and announced that a 30-member Supreme Revolutionary Council would be the governing body.

Bagaza was elected head of the only legal political party in 1979 and was overthrown as party chieftain in 1987.

The Burundi Democracy Front's candidate Melchior Ndadaye won the first democratic presidential elections held on June 2, 1993.

CAMBODIA

President: Prince Norodom Sihanouk (1991)
Prime Minister: Hun Sen
Area: 69,884 sq mi. (181,000 sq km)
Population (est. mid-1993): 9,000,000 (average annual rate of natural increase: 2.5%); birth rate: 41/1000; infant mortality rate: 123/1000; density per square mile: 132
Capital and largest city (est. 1989 for metropolitan area): Phnom Penh, 800,000; **Monetary unit:** Riel; **Ethnic groups:** Khmer, 90%; Chinese, 5%; other minorities 5%; **Languages:** Khmer (official), French; **Religion:** Theravada Buddhist, 5% others; **Literacy rate:** 35%
Economic summary: Gross domestic product (1991 est.): $930 million, per capita $130; real growth rate n.a. Arable land: 16%. Principal agricultural products: rice, rubber, corn. Labor force: 2.5–3.0 million; 80% in agriculture. Major industrial products: fish, wood and wood products, milled rice, rubber, cement. Natural resources: timber, gemstones, iron ore, manganese, phosphate. Exports: $32 million (f.o.b., 1988): natural rubber, rice, pepper, wood. Imports: $147 million (c.i.f., 1988): foodstuffs, fuel, consumer goods. Major trading partners: Vietnam, C.I.S., Eastern Europe, Japan, India.

Geography. Situated on the Indochinese peninsula, Cambodia is bordered by Thailand and Laos on the north and Vietnam on the east and south. The Gulf of Siam is off the western coast. The country, the size of Missouri, consists chiefly of a large alluvial plain ringed in by mountains and on the east by the Mekong River. The plain is centered on Lake Tonle Sap, which is a natural storage basin of the Mekong.

Government. On June 15, 1993, the Parliament gave Prince Norodom Sihanouk broad powers to restore peace and solve the nation's problems. On June 16, 1993, Prince Sihanouk and Mr. Hun Sen agreed to share power equally as co-presidents with Prince Sihanouk remaining as head of state. The interim coalition government will rule until the 120-member National Assembly drafts a constitution.

The power sharing arrangement was unanimously approved by the Cambodian assembly on July 1, 1993.

History. Cambodia came under Khmer rule about A.D. 600. Under the Khmers, magnificent temples were built at Angkor. The Khmer kingdom once ruled over most of Southeast Asia, but attacks by the Thai and the Vietnamese almost annihilated the empire until the French joined Cambodia, Laos, and Vietnam into French Indochina.

Under Norodom Sihanouk, enthroned in 1941, and particularly under Japanese occupation during World War II, nationalism revived. After the ouster of the Japanese, the Cambodians sought independence, but the French returned in 1946, granting the country a Constitution in 1947 and independence within the French Union in 1949. Sihanouk won full military control during the French--Indochinese War in 1953. He abdicated in 1955 in favor of his parents, remaining head of the government, and when his father died in 1960, becamechief of state without returning to the throne. In 1963, he sought a guarantee of Cambodia's neutrality from all parties to the Vietnam War.

On March 18, 1970, while Sihanouk was abroad trying to get North Vietnamese and the Vietcong out of border sanctuaries near Vietnam, anti-Vietnamese riots occurred, and Sihanouk was overthrown.

The Vietnam peace agreement of 1973 stipulated withdrawal of foreign forces from Cambodia, but fighting continued between Hanoi-backed insurgents and U.S.-supplied government troops.

Fighting climaxed in April 1975 when the Lon Nol regime was overthrown by Pot Pol, leader of the communist Khmer Rouge forces.

In the next two years, from 2 million to 4 million Cambodians are estimated to have died under the brutality of the Pol Pot regime. Border clashes with Vietnam developed into a Vietnamese invasion and Pot Pol was ousted by Vietnamese forces on Jan. 8, 1979 and a new government led by Heng Samrin was installed.

While Sihanouk remained in exile, about 9,000 noncommunist troops loyal to him and another 15,000 under Son Sann joined about 35,000 communist Pol Pot forces fighting the 170,000 Vietnamese troops supporting the Heng Samrin government. The Cambodian insurgents suffered a major defeat in March 1985 when Vietnamese forces overran their camps in Cambodia and forced them into Thailand.

The Vietnamese plan originally called for them to withdraw by early 1990 and negotiate a political settlement. The talks, however, stalled through 1990 on into 1991. In 1992 a UN agreement was signed in Paris under which Prince Sihanouk was to be the leader of a Supreme National Council that was to run the country until free elctions in 1993.

Free elections in May 1993 saw the defeat of the ruling party. In June the victors, the royalist opposition, completed a power sharing deal with the ruling party.

CAMEROON

Republic of Cameroon
President: Paul Biya (1988)
Prime Minister: Simon Achidi Achu (1992)
Area: 183,569 sq mi. (475,442 sq km)
Population (est. mid-1993): 12,800,000 (average annual rate of natural increase: 2.9%); birth rate: 41/1000; infant mortality rate: 82/1000; density per square mile: 71
Capital: Yaoundé; **Largest cities (est. 1991):** Douala, 908,000; Yaoundé, 730,000; **Monetary unit:** Franc CFA; **Languages:** French and English (both official); 24 major African language groups; **Religions:** 51% indigenous beliefs, 33% Christian, 16% Muslim; **National name:** République du Cameroun; **Literacy rate:** 56.2%
Economic summary: Gross domestic product (1990): $11.5 billion, per capita $1,040; real growth rate 0.7%. Arable land: 13%. Agriculture: coffee, cocoa, timber, corn, peanuts. Labor force in agriculture: 74.4%. Industries: crude oil products, food processing, light consumer goods, textiles, sawmills. Natural resources: timber, some oil, bauxite, hydropower potential. Exports: $2.1 billion (f.o.b., 1990 est.): cocoa, coffee, timber, petroleum. Imports: $2.1 billion (c.i.f., 1990 est.): machines and electrical equipment, transport equipment, chemical products, consumer goods. Major trading partners: France, U.S., Western European nations, particularly the Netherlands.

Geography. Cameroon is a West African nation on the Gulf of Guinea, bordered by Nigeria, Chad, the Central African Republic, the Congo, Equatorial Guinea, and Gabon. It is nearly twice the size of Oregon.

The interior consists of a high plateau, rising to 4,500 feet (1,372 m), with the land descending to a lower, densely wooded plateau and then to swamps and plains along the coast. Mount Cameroon (13,350 ft.; 4,069 m), near the coast, is the highest elevation in the country. The main rivers are the Benue, Nyong, and Sanaga.

Government. After a 1972 plebiscite, a unitary nation was formed out of East and West Cameroon to replace the former Federal Republic. At present the country is a multiparty democracy with a one house legislative body, the National Assembly, holding 180 seats.

History. The Republic of Cameroon is inhabited by Hamitic and Semitic peoples in the north, where Islam is the principal religion, and by Bantu peoples in the central and southern regions, where native animism prevails. The tribes were conquered by many invaders.

The land escaped colonial rule until 1884, when treaties with tribal chiefs brought the area under German domination. After World War I, the League of Nations gave the French a mandate over 80% of the area, and the British 20% adjacent to Nigeria. After World War II, when the country came under a U.N. trusteeship in 1946, self-government was granted, and the Cameroun People's Union emerged as the dominant party by campaigning for reunification of French and British Cameroon and for independence. Accused of being under Communist control, it waged a campaign of revolutionary terror from 1955 to 1958, when it was crushed. In British Cameroon, unification was pressed also by the leading party, the Kamerun National Democratic Party, led by John Foncha.

France set up Cameroon as an autonomous state in 1957, and the next year its legislative assembly voted for independence by 1960. In 1959 a fully autonomous government of Cameroon was formed under Ahmadou Ahidjo. Cameroon became an independent republic on Jan. 1, 1960.

The president's Cameroon People's Democratic Movement held onto power after the first parliamentary elections in more than three decades by entering into an alliance with a smaller party. Biya won the presidential election in October 1992 but by a narrow margin.

CANADA

Sovereign: Queen Elizabeth II (1952)
Governor General: Raymond John Hnatyshyn (1990)
Prime Minister: Kim Campbell (1993)
Area: 3,851,809 sq mi. (9,976,186 sq km)
Population (est. mid-1992): 27,400,000 (average annual rate of natural increase: 0.8%); birth rate: 15/1000; infant mortality rate: 7.1/1000; density per square mile: 7
Capital: Ottawa, Ont.; **Largest cities (1991 census; metropolitan areas):** Toronto, 3,893,046; Montreal, 3,127,242; Vancouver: 1,602,502; Ottawa/Hull, 920,857; Edmonston, 839,924; Calgary, 754,033; Winnipeg, 652,354; Quebec, 645,550; Hamilton, 599,760; London, 381,522; St. Catherines-Niagara, 364,552; **Monetary Unit:** Canadian dollar; **Languages:** English, French; **Religions:** 46% Roman Catholic, 16% United Church, 10% Anglican; **Literacy rate:** 99%
Economic Summary: Gross domestic product (1991 est.): $521.5 billion, per capita $19,400; real growth rate −1.9%; inflation 4.2%; unemployment (Nov. 91) 10.4%. Arable land: 7.47%. Principal products; wheat, barley, oats, livestock. Labor force (1990): 13,681,000; 75% in manufacturing. Major industrial products; transportation equipment, petroleum, chemicals, wood products. Exports: $124 billion (f.o.b., 1991): newsprint, wood pulp, timber, crude petroleum, machinery, natural gas, aluminum, motor vehicles and parts, telecommunications equipment. Imports: $118 billion (c.i.f., 1991): crude petroleum, chemicals, motor vehicles and parts, durable consumer goods, computers, telecommunications equipment and parts. Major trading partners: U.S., Japan, U.K., C.I.S. nations, Germany, Mexico, South Korea, Taiwan.

Geography. Covering most of the northern part of the North American continent and with an area larger than that of the United States, Canada has an extremely varied topography. In the east the mountainous maritime provinces have an irregular coastline on the Gulf of St. Lawrence and the Atlantic. The St. Lawrence plain, covering most of southern Quebec and Ontario, and the interior continental plain, covering southern Manitoba and Saskatchewan and most of Alberta, are the principal cultivable areas. They are separated by a forested plateau rising from lakes Superior and Huron.

Westward toward the Pacific, most of British Columbia, Yukon, and part of western Alberta are covered by parallel mountain ranges including the Rockies. The Pacific border of the coast range is ragged with fiords and channels. The highest point in Canada is Mount Logan (19,850 ft; 6,050 m), which is in the Yukon.

Canada has an abundance of large and small lakes. In addition to the Great Lakes on the U.S. border, there are 9 others that are more than 100 miles long (161 km) and 35 that are more than 50 miles long (80 km). The two principal river systems are the Mackenzie and the St. Lawrence. The St. Lawrence, with its tributaries, is navigable for over 1,900 miles (3,058 km).

Government. Canada, a self-governing member of the Commonwealth of Nations, is a federation of 10 provinces (Alberta, British Columbia, Manitoba, New Brunswick, Newfoundland, Nova Scotia, Ontario, Prince Edward Island, Quebec, and Saskatchewan) and two territories (Northwest Territories and Yukon) whose powers were spelled out in the British North America Act of 1867. With the passing of the Constitution Act of 1981, the act and the Constitutional amending power were transferred from the British Parliament to Canada so that the Canadian Constitution is now entirely in the hands of the Canadians.

Actually the Governor General acts only with the advice of the Canadian Prime Minister and the Cabinet, who also sit in the federal Parliament. The Parliament has two houses: a Senate of 104 members appointed for life, and a House of Commons of 295 members apportioned according to provincial population. Elections are held at least every five years or whenever the party in power is voted down in the House of Commons or considers it expedient to appeal to the people. The Prime Minister is the leader of the majority party in the House of Commons—or, if no single party holds a majority, the leader of the party able to command the support of a majority of members of the House. Laws must be passed by both houses of Parliament and signed by the Governor General in the Queen's name.

The 10 provincial governments are nominally headed by Lieutenant Governors appointed by the federal government, but the executive power in each actually is vested in a Cabinet headed by a Premier, who is leader of the majority party. The provincial legislatures are composed of one-house assemblies whose members are elected for four-year terms. They are known as Legislative Assemblies, except in Newfoundland, where it is the House of Assembly, and in Quebec, where it is the National Assembly.

The judicial system consists of a Supreme Court in Ottawa (established in 1875), with appellate jurisdiction, and a Supreme Court in each province, as well as county courts with limited jurisdiction in most of the provinces. The Governor General in Council appoints these judges.

History. The Norse explorer Leif Ericson probably reached the shores of Canada (Labrador or Nova Scotia) in A.D. 1000, but the history of the white man in the country actually began in 1497, when John Cabot, an Italian in the service of Henry VII of England, reached Newfoundland or Nova Scotia. Canada was taken for France in 1534 by Jacques Cartier. The actual settlement of New France, as it was then called, began in 1604 at Port Royal in what is now Nova Scotia; in 1608, Quebec was founded. France's colonization efforts were not very successful, but French explorers by the end of the 17th century had penetrated beyond the Great Lakes to the western prairies

Population by Provinces and Territories

Province	1981 (Census)	1991 (Census)
Alberta	2,237,724	2,545,553
British Columbia	2,744,467	3,282,061
Manitoba	1,026,241	1,091,942
New Brunswick	696,403	723,900
Newfoundland	567,681	568,474
Nova Scotia	847,442	899,942
Ontario	8,625,107	10,084,885
Prince Edward Island	122,506	129,765
Quebec	6,438,403	6,895,963
Saskatchewan	968,313	988,928
Northwest Territories	45,471	57,649
Yukon Territory	23,153	27,797
Total	**24,343,181**	**27,296,859**

Source: Statistics Canada.

Canadian Governors General and Prime Ministers Since 1867

Term of Office	Governor General	Term	Prime Minister	Party
1867–1868	Viscount Monck[1]	1867–1873	Sir John A. Macdonald	Conservative
1869–1872	Baron Lisgar	1873–1878	Alexander Mackenzie	Liberal
1872–1878	Earl of Dufferin	1878–1891	Sir John A. Macdonald	Conservative
1878–1883	Marquess of Lorne	1891–1892	Sir John J. C. Abbott	Conservative
1883–1888	Marquess of Lansdowne	1892–1894	Sir John S. D. Thompson	Conservative
1888–1893	Baron Stanley of Preston	1894–1896	Sir Mackenzie Bowell	Conservative
1893–1898	Earl of Aberdeen	1896	Sir Charles Tupper	Conservative
1898–1904	Earl of Minto	1896–1911	Sir Wilfrid Laurier	Liberal
1904–1911	Earl Grey	1911–1917	Sir Robert L. Borden	Conservative
1911–1916	Duke of Connaught	1917–1920	Sir Robert L. Borden	Unionist
1916–1921	Duke of Devonshire	1920–1921	Arthur Meighen	Unionist
1921–1926	Baron Byng of Vimy	1921–1926	W. L. Mackenzie King	Liberal
1926–1931	Viscount Willingdon	1926	Arthur Meighen	Conservative
1931–1935	Earl of Bessborough	1926–1930	W. L. Mackenzie King	Liberal
1935–1940	Baron Tweedsmuir	1930–1935	Richard B. Bennett	Conservative
1940–1946	Earl of Athlone	1935–1948	W. L. Mackenzie King	Liberal
1946–1952	Viscount Alexander	1948–1957	Louis S. St. Laurent	Liberal
1952–1959	Vincent Massey	1957–1963	John G. Diefenbaker	Conservative
1959–1967	George P. Vanier	1963–1968	Lester B. Pearson	Liberal
1967–1973	Roland Michener	1968–1979	Pierre Elliott Trudeau	Liberal
1974–1979	Jules Léger	1979–1980	Charles Joseph Clark	Conservative
1979–1984	Edward R. Schreyer	1980–1984	Pierre Elliott Trudeau	Liberal
1984–1990	Jeanne Sauvé	1984–1984	John Turner	Liberal
1990–	Raymond John Hnatyshyn	1984–1993	Brian Mulroney	Conservative
		1993–	Kim Campbell	Conservative

1. Became Governor General of British North America in 1861.

and south along the Mississippi to the Gulf of Mexico. Meanwhile, the English Hudson's Bay Company had been established in 1670. Because of the valuable fisheries and fur trade, a conflict developed between the French and English; in 1713, Newfoundland, Hudson Bay, and Nova Scotia (Acadia) were lost to England.

During the Seven Years' War (1756–63), England extended its conquest, and the British Maj. Gen. James Wolfe won his famous victory over Gen. Louis Montcalm outside Quebec on Sept. 13, 1759. The Treaty of Paris in 1763 gave England control.

At that time the population of Canada was almost entirely French, but in the next few decades, thousands of British colonists emigrated to Canada from the British Isles and from the American colonies. In 1849, the right of Canada to self-government was recognized. By the British North America Act of 1867, the Dominion of Canada was created through the confederation of Upper and Lower Canada, Nova Scotia, and New Brunswick. Prince Edward Island joined the Dominion in 1873.

In 1869 Canada purchased from the Hudson's Bay Company the vast middle west (Rupert's Land) from which the provinces of Manitoba (1870), Alberta, and Saskatchewan (1905) were later formed. In 1871, British Columbia joined the Dominion. The country was linked from coast to coast in 1885 by the Canadian Pacific Railway.

During the formative years between 1866 and 1896, the Conservative Party, led by Sir John A. Macdonald, governed the country, except during the years 1873–78. In 1896, the Liberal Party took over and, under Sir Wilfrid Laurier, an eminent French Canadian, ruled until 1911.

By the Statute of Westminster in 1931 the British Dominions, including Canada, were formally declared to be partner nations with Britain, "equal in status, in no way subordinate to each other," and bound together only by allegiance to a common Crown.

Newfoundland became Canada's 10th province on March 31, 1949, following a plebiscite. Canada includes two territories—the Yukon Territory, the area north of British Columbia and east of Alaska, and the Northwest Territories, including all of Canada north of 60° north latitude except Yukon and the northernmost sections of Quebec and Newfoundland. This area includes all of the Arctic north of the mainland, Norway having recognized Canadian sovereignty over the Svendrup Islands in the Arctic in 1931.

The Liberal Party, led by William Lyon Mackenzie King, dominated Canadian politics from 1921 until 1957, when it was succeeded by the Progressive Conservatives. The Liberals, under the leadership of Lester B. Pearson, returned to power in 1963. Pearson remained Prime Minister until 1968, when he retired and was replaced by a former law professor, Pierre Elliott Trudeau. Trudeau maintained Canada's defensive alliance with the United States, but began moving toward a more independent policy in world affairs.

Trudeau's election was considered in part a response to the most serious problem confronting the country, the division between French- and English-speaking Canadians, which had led to a separatist movement in the predominantly French province of Quebec. Trudeau, himself a French Canadian, supported programs for bilingualism and an increased measure of provincial autonomy, although he would not tolerate the idea of separatism. In 1974, the provincial government voted to make French the official language of Quebec.

Despite Trudeau's removal of price and wage controls in 1978, continuing inflation and a high rate of unemployment caused him to delay elections until May 22, 1979. The delay gave Trudeau no advantage—the Progressive Conservatives under Charles Joseph Clark defeated the Liberals everywhere except in Quebec, New Brunswick, and Newfoundland.

Clark took office as the head of Canada's fifth minority government in the last 20 years.

His government collapsed after only six months when a motion to defeat the Tory budget carried by 139–133 on Dec. 13, 1979. On the same day, the Quebec law making French the exclusive official language of the province—an issue which had been expected to provide Clark's first major internal test—was voided by the Canadian Supreme Court.

In national elections Feb. 18, 1980, the resurgent Liberals under Trudeau scored an unexpectedly big victory.

Resolving a dispute that had occupied Trudeau since the beginning of his tenure, Queen Elizabeth II, in Ottawa on April 17, 1982, signed the Constitution Act, cutting the last legal tie between Canada and Britain. Since 1867, the British North America Act required British Parliament approval for any Canadian constitutional change.

The new charter was approved by the federal House of Commons, 246–24, on Dec. 2, 1981, and by a 59–23 vote of the Senate six days later. The Constitution retains Queen Elizabeth as Queen of Canada and keeps Canada's membership in the Commonwealth.

In the national election on Sept. 4, 1984, the Progressive Conservative Party scored an overwhelming victory, fundamentally changing the country's political landscape. The Conservatives, led by Brian Mulroney, a 45-year-old corporate lawyer, won the highest political majority in Canadian history, Mulroney was sworn in as Canada's 18th Prime Minister on Sept. 17.

The dominant foreign issue was a free trade pact with the U.S., a treaty bitterly opposed by the Liberal and New Democratic parties. The conflict led to elections in Nov. 1988 that solidly re-elected Mulroney and gave him a mandate to proceed with the agreement.

The issue of separatist sentiments in French-speaking Quebec flared up again in 1990 with the failure of the Meech Lake accord. The accord was designed to ease the Quebecers' fear of losing their identity within the English-speaking majority by giving Quebec constitutional status as a "distinct society." In an attempt to keep Canada united, the three major political parties came to an agreement in February 1992 on constitutional reforms.

Voters in the Northwest Territories authorized the division of their region in two, creating a homeland for Eskimos.

Also in 1992 Canada announced its decision to withdraw its combat units from NATO command. The economy continued to be mired in a long recession many blamed on the free trade agreement.

A national referendum was held in October 1992 on the proposal to change the constitution to insure greater representation in parliament for the more populous regions and thereby the French-speaking Quebecers. The referendum, however was defeated.

Brian Mulroney's popularity continued to slump in 1992 and early 1993, leading to his decision to retire prior to the required November election. The governing Progressive Conservative Party chose Defense Minister Kim Campbell as its leader in June making her the first female prime minister in Canadian history.

CAPE VERDE

Republic of Cape Verde
President: Antonio Mascarenhas Monteiro (1991)
Premier: Carlos Wahnon Veiga (1991)
Area: 1,557 sq mi. (4,033 sq km)
Population: (est. mid-1993): 400,000 (average annual rate of natural increase: 2.9%); birth rate: 36/1000; infant mortality rate: 47/1000; density per square mile: 254
Capital (1990): Praia; **Largest cities (est. 1982):** Praia, 61,797; Mindelo, 50,000; **Monetary unit:** Cape Verdean escudo; **Language:** Portuguese, Criuolo; **Religion:** Roman Catholic fused with indigenous beliefs; **National name:** República de Cabo Verde; **Literacy rate:** 66%
Economic summary: Gross domestic product (1990 est.): $310 million, per capita $800; real growth rate 4%; inflation 10%; unemployment (1988) 25%. Arable land: 9%. Labor force in agriculture: 57%. Principal agricultural products: bananas, corn, sugar cane, beans. Major industry: fishing, salt mining. Natural resources: salt, siliceous rock. Exports: $10.9 million (f.o.b., 1989 est.): fish, bananas, salt. Imports: $107.8 million (c.i.f., 1989): petroleum, foodstuffs, consumer goods, industrial products. Major trading partners: Portugal, Angola, Algeria, Belgium/Luxembourg, Italy, Netherlands, Spain, France, U.S., Germany.

Geography: Cape Verde, only slightly larger than Rhode Island, is an archipelago in the Atlantic 385 miles (620 km) west of Dakar, Senegal.

The islands are divided into two groups: Barlavento in the north, comprising Santo Antão (291 sq mi.; 754 sq km), Boa Vista (240 sq mi.; 622 sq km), São Nicolau (132 sq mi.; 342 sq km), São Vicente (88 sq mi.; 246 sq km), Sal (83 sq mi.; 298 sq km), and Santa Luzia (13 sq mi.; 34 sq km); and Sotavento in the south, consisting of São Tiago (383 sq mi.; 992 sq km), Fogo (184 sq mi.; 477 sq km), Maio (103 sq mi.; 267 sq km), and Brava (25 sq mi.; 65 sq km). The islands are mostly mountainous, with the land deeply scarred by erosion. There is an active volcano on Fogo.

Government. The islands became independent on July 5, 1975, under an agreement negotiated with Portugal in 1974. Elections of January 13, 1991 resulted in the ruling African Party for the Independence of Cape Verde losing its majority in the 79-seat parliament. The big winner was the Movement for Democracy, whose candidate, Antonio Monteiro, won the subsequent presidential election on February 17. These were the first free elections since independence in 1975.

History. Uninhabited upon their discovery in 1456, the Cape Verde islands became part of the Portuguese empire in 1495. A majority of their modern inhabitants are of mixed Portuguese and African ancestry.

The former opposition MPD that had won the parliamentary and the presidential elections early in 1991 also won 10 out of 14 councils in the country's first local elections.

The government in 1992 embarked on a plan to privatize a number of state companies.

CENTRAL AFRICAN REPUBLIC

Head of Government: Gen. André Kolingba (1986)
Prime Minister: Timothée Malendoma (1992)
Area: 241,313 sq mi. (625,000 sq km)
Population (est. mid-1993): 3,100,000 (average annual rate of natural increase: 2.6%); birth rate: 44/1000; infant mortality rate: 140/1000; density per square mile: 13

Capital and largest city (1988): Bangui, 596,776; **Monetary unit:** Franc CFA; **Ethnic groups:** Baya, Banda, Sara, Mandjia, Mboum, M'Baka, 6,500 Europeans; **Languages:** French (official), Sangho, Arabic, Hansa, Swahili; **Religions:** 24% indigenous beliefs, 50% Protestant and Roman Catholic with animist influence, 15% Muslim, 11% other; **National name:** République Centrafricaine; **Literacy rate:** 33%

Economic summary: Gross domestic product (1990 est.): $1.3 billion, per capita $440; real growth rate 2.0%; inflation –3.0%; unemployment (1988 est.): 30% in Bangui. Arable land: 3%. Principal products: cotton, coffee, peanuts, food crops, livestock. Labor force (1986 est.): 775,413; 85% in agriculture. Major industrial products: timber, textiles, soap, cigarettes, diamonds, processed food, brewed beverages. Natural resources: diamonds, uranium, timber. Exports: $151.3 million (1990 est.): diamonds, cotton, timber, coffee. Imports: $214.5 million (1990 est.): machinery and electrical equipment, petroleum products, textiles. Major trading partners: France, Belgium, Italy, Japan, U.S., Western Europe, Algeria, Yugoslavia.

Geography. Situated about 500 miles north (805 km) of the equator, the Central African Republic is a landlocked nation bordered by Cameroon, Chad, the Sudan, Zaire, and the Congo. Twice the size of New Mexico, it is covered by tropical forests in the south and semidesert land in the east. The Ubangi and Shari are the largest of many rivers.

Government. The Central African Republic has been ruled since 1981 by General André Kolingba who came to power in a bloodless coup and was elected to a six-year term as President in 1986. A Constitution was adopted on November 21, 1987 establishing a unicameral National Assembly. The following year the Central African Democracy Party (R.D.C.) was formed as the only political party. Since April 1991 other political parties legally registered by the Ministry of the Interior are allowed to compete for legislative and presidential elections scheduled for 1992 but then postponed.

There are now 15 registered parties and efforts to move toward political liberalization have been promised, although little progress occurred in 1992.

History. As the colony of Ubangi-Shari, what is now the Central African Republic was united with Chad in 1905 and joined with Gabon and the Middle Congo in French Equatorial Africa in 1910. After World War II a rebellion in 1946 forced the French to grant self-government. In 1958 the territory voted to become an autonomous republic within the French Community, but on Aug. 13, 1960, President David Dacko proclaimed the republic's independence from France.

Dacko undertook to move the country into Peking's orbit, but was overthrown in a coup on Dec. 31, 1965, by the then Col. Jean-Bédel Bokassa, Army Chief of Staff.

On Dec. 4, 1976, the Central African Republic became the Central African Empire. Marshal Jean-Bédel Bokassa, who had ruled the republic since he took power in 1965, was declared Emperor Bokassa I. He was overthrown in a coup on Sept. 20, 1979. Former President David Dacko, returned to power and changed the country's name back to the Central African Republic. An army coup on Sept. 1, 1981, deposed President Dacko again.

Although President Kolingba in 1991, under pressure, announced a move toward multi-party democracy no specifics were given, leading to further civil unrest. A general strike called for in August resulted in the legalization of three opposition parties. Refusing to convene a national assembly in 1992 the government proposed the opening of a "national debate" for August 1992, which was boycotted by many opposition groups.

CHAD

Republic of Chad
President: Col. Idriss Deby (1991)
Prime Minister: Dr. Fidéle Moungar (1993)
Area: 495,752 sq mi. (1,284,000 sq km)
Population (est. mid-1993): 5,400,000 (average annual rate of natural increase, 2.5%); birth rate: 44/1000; infant mortality rate: 127/1000; density per square mile: 11

Capital and largest city (est. 1991): N'Djamena, 500,000; **Monetary unit:** Franc CFA; **Ethnic groups:** Baguirmiens, Kanembous, Saras, Massas, Arabs, Toubous, others; **Languages:** French and Arabic (official), many tribal languages; **Religions:** Islam, 44%; Christian, 33%; traditional, 23%; **National name:** République du Tchad; **Literacy rate:** 17%

Economic summary: Gross domestic product (1989 est.): $1.1 billion, per capita $205; real growth rate 0.9%; inflation –4.9%. Arable land: 2%; principal agricultural products: cotton, cattle, sugar, subsistence crops. Labor force in agriculture: 85%. Major products: livestock and livestock products, beer, food processing, textiles, cigarettes. Natural resources: petroleum, unexploited uranium, kaolin. Exports: $174 million (f.o.b., 1990 est.): cotton, livestock and animal products, fish. Imports: $264 million (c.i.f., 1990 est.): food, motor vehicles and parts, petroleum products, machinery, cement, textiles. Major trading partners: France, Nigeria, U.S., Cameroon.

Geography. A landlocked country in north central Africa, Chad is about 85% the size of Alaska. Its neighbors are Niger, Libya, the Sudan, the Central African Republic, Cameroon, and Nigeria. Lake Chad, from which the country gets its name, lies on the western border with Niger and Nigeria. In the north is a desert that runs into the Sahara.

Government. Hissen Habré was overthrown by Col. Idriss Deby in December 1990.

History. Chad was absorbed into the colony of French Equatorial Africa, as part of Ubangi-Shari, in 1910. France began the country's development after 1920, when it became a separate colony. In 1946, French Equatorial Africa was admitted to the French Union. By referendum in 1958 the Chad territory became an autonomous republic within the French Union.

A movement led by the first Premier and President, François (later Ngarta) Tombalbaye, achieved complete independence on Aug. 11, 1960.

Tombalbaye was killed in the 1975 coup and was succeeded by Gen. Félix Malloum, who faced a Libyan-financed rebel movement throughout his tenure in office. A ceasefire backed by Libya, Niger, and the Sudan early in 1978 failed to end the fighting.

Nine rival groups meeting in Lagos, Nigeria, in March 1979 agreed to form a provisional government headed by Goukouni Oueddei, a former rebel leader. Fighting broke out again in Chad in March 1980, when Defense Minister Hissen Habré challenged Goukouni and seized the capital. By the year's end, Libyan troops supporting Goukouni recaptured

N'djamena, and Libyan President Muammar el-Qaddafi, in January 1981, proposed a merger of Chad with Libya.

The Libyan proposal was rejected and Libyan troops withdrew from Chad but in 1983 poured back into the northern part of the country in support of Goukouni. France, in turn, sent troops into southern Chad in support of Habré.

A Qaddafi-Goukouni break in Nov. 1986 led to the defection of his troops. Government troops then launched an offensive in early 1987 that drove the Libyans out of most of the country.

After the overthrow of Habré's government, Deby, a former defense minister, declared himself president, dissolved the legislature (elected the previous July), and suspended the constitution. Moves toward a multi-party system were "postponed." In early 1992 at least 450 were killed in an abortive coup attempt.

CHILE

Republic of Chile
President: Patricio Aylwin (1990)
Area: 292,132 sq mi. (756,622 sq km)
Population (est. mid-1993): 13,500,000 (average annual rate of natural increase: 1.6%); birth rate: 21/1000; infant mortality rate: 15.4/1000; density per square mile: 47
Capital: Santiago; **Largest cities (1990):** Santiago, 5,236,361; Concepción, 307,626; Valparaiso, 289,951; Talcahuano, 247,311; Temuco, 245,757; Antofagasta, 219,291; **Monetary unit:** Peso; **Language:** Spanish; **Religion:** Roman Catholic, 89%; Protestant, 11%; small Jewish and Muslim populations.; **National name:** República de Chile; **Literacy rate:** 94%
Economic summary: Gross domestic product (1991): $32.0 billion; $2,500 per capita; 5.5% real growth rate; inflation 18.7%; unemployment 6.5%. Arable land: 7%. Principal products: wheat, corn, sugar beets, vegetables, wine, livestock. Labor force: 31.3% in industry. Major industrial products: processed fish, iron and steel, pulp, paper. Natural resources: copper, timber, iron ore, nitrates. Exports: $8.9 billion (f.o.b., 1991): copper, iron ore, paper and wood products, fruits. Imports: $7.4 billion (f.o.b., 1991): wheat, vehicles, petroleum, capital goods, spare parts, raw materials. Major trading partners: U.S., Japan, European Community, Brazil.

Geography. Situated south of Peru and west of Bolivia and Argentina, Chile fills a narrow 1,800-mile (2,897 km) strip between the Andes and the Pacific. Its area is nearly twice that of Montana.

One third of Chile is covered by the towering ranges of the Andes. In the north is the mineral-rich Atacama Desert, between the coastal mountains and the Andes. In the center is a 700-mile-long (1,127 km) valley, thickly populated, between the Andes and the coastal plateau. In the south, the Andes border on the ocean.

At the southern tip of Chile's mainland is Punta Arenas, the southernmost city in the world, and beyond that lies the Strait of Magellan and Tierra del Fuego, an island divided between Chile and Argentina. The southernmost point of South America is Cape Horn, a 1,390-foot (424-m) rock on Horn Island in the Wollaston group, which belongs to Chile. Chile also claims sovereignty over 482,628 sq mi (1,250,000 sq km) of Antarctic territory.

The Juan Fernández Islands, in the South Pacific about 400 miles (644 km) west of the mainland, and Easter Island, about 2,000 miles (3,219 km) west, are Chilean possessions.

Government. The President serves an eight-year term (with the exception of the 1990–1994 term). There is a bicameral legislature, the National Congress.

History. Chile was originally under the control of the Incas in the north and the fierce Araucanian people in the south. In 1541, a Spaniard, Pedro de Valdivia, founded Santiago. Chile won its independence from Spain in 1818 under Bernardo O'Higgins and an Argentinian, José de San Martin. O'Higgins, dictator until 1823, laid the foundations of the modern state with a two-party system and a centralized government.

The dictator from 1830 to 1837, Diego Portales, fought a war with Peru in 1836–39 that expanded Chilean territory. The Conservatives were in power from 1831 to 1861. Then the Liberals, winning a share of power for the next 30 years, disestablished the church and limited presidential power. Chile fought the War of the Pacific with Peru and Bolivia from 1879 to 1883, winning Antofagasta, Bolivia's only outlet to the sea, and extensive areas from Peru. A revolt in 1890 led by Jorge Montt overthrew, in 1891, José Balmaceda and established a parliamentary dictatorship that existed until a new Constitution was adopted in 1925. Industrialization began before World War I and led to the formation of Marxist groups.

Juan Antonio Ríos, President during World War II, was originally pro-Nazi but in 1944 led his country into the war on the side of the U.S.

A small abortive army uprising in 1969 raised fear of military intervention to prevent a Marxist, Salvador Allende Gossens, from taking office after his election to the presidency on Sept. 4, 1970. Dr. Allende was the first President in a non-Communist country freely elected on a Marxist-Leninist program.

Allende quickly established relations with Cuba and the People's Republic of China and nationalized several American companies.

Allende's overthrow and death in an army assault on the presidential palace in September 1973 ended a 46-year era of constitutional government in Chile.

The takeover was led by a four-man junta headed by Army Chief of Staff Augusto Pinochet Ugarte, who assumed the office of President.

Committed to "exterminate Marxism," the junta embarked on a right-wing dictatorship. It suspended parliament, banned political activity, and broke relations with Cuba.

In 1977, Pinochet, in a speech marking his fourth year in power, promised elections by 1985 if conditions warranted. Earlier, he had abolished DINA, the secret police, and decreed an amnesty for political prisoners.

Pinochet was inaugurated on March 11, 1981, for an eight-year term as President, at the end of which, according to the Constitution adopted six months earlier, the junta would nominate a civilian as successor, although Pinochet announced that he might serve another eight-year term. He stepped down in January 1990 in favor of Patricio Aylwin who was elected Dec. 1989 as the head of a 17-party coalition.

Local elections in June 1992 gave the ruling coalition parties more than 53% of the vote, which the president hailed as a mandate to implement constitutional reforms. The right-wing, however, still in control of the Senate warned against any abrupt changes.

CHINA

People's Republic of China
President: Jiang Zemin (1993)
Premier: Li Peng (1987)
Area: 3,691,521 sq mi. (9,561,000 sq km)[1]
Population (est. mid-1993): 1,178,500,000 (average rate of natural increase: 1.2%); birth rate: 18/1000; infant mortality rate: 53/1000; density per square mile: 327. China has 56 ethnic groups. In 1991, the Han people accounted for 92% of the population.
Capital: Beijing; **Largest cities (est. 1991):** Shanghai, 7,500,000; Beijing (Peking) 5,700,000; Tianjin (Tientsin) 4,575,000; Canton, 2,914,000; Wuhan, 3,284,200; Shenyang (Mukden), 3,604,000; Nanjing (Nanking), 2,100,000; Chongqing (Chongking), 2,267,000; Harbin, 2,443,400; **Monetary unit:** Yuan; **Languages:** Chinese, Mandarin, also local dialects; **Religions:** Officially atheist but traditional religion contains elements of Confucianism, Taoism, Buddhism; **National name:** Zhonghua Renmin Gongheguo; **Literacy rate:** 73%
Economic summary: Latest GNP n.a.; per capita, n.a. Gross national product (1989 est.); $413 billion; $370 per capita; 5% real growth rate; inflation rate (1991): 2.1%; unemployment rate (1991) in urban areas: 4.0%. Arable land: 10%. Principal agricultural products: rice, wheat, grains, cotton. Labor force: 553,000,000; 60% in agriculture and forestry. Major industrial products: iron and steel, textiles, armaments, petroleum. Natural resources: coal, natural gas, limestone, marble, metals, hydropower potential. Exports: $71.9 billion (f.o.b., 1991): agricultural products, oil, minerals, metals, manufactured goods. Imports: $63.8 billion (c.i.f., 1991): grains, chemical fertilizer, steel, industrial raw materials, machinery and equipment. Major trading partners: Japan, Hong Kong, U.S., Germany, Singapore, C.I.S. countries.

1. Including Manchuria and Tibet.

Geography. China, which occupies the eastern part of Asia, is slightly larger in area than the U.S. Its coastline is roughly a semicircle. The greater part of the country is mountainous, and only in the lower reaches of the Yellow and Yangtze Rivers are there extensive low plains.

The principal mountain ranges are the Tien Shan, to the northwest; the Kunlun chain, running south of the Taklimakan and Gobi Deserts; and the Trans-Himalaya, connecting the Kunlun with the borders of China and Tibet. Manchuria is largely an undulating plain connected with the north China plain by a narrow lowland corridor. Inner Mongolia contains the relatively fertile southern and eastern portions of the Gobi. The large island of Hainan (13,200 sq mi.; 34,300 sq km) lies off the southern coast.

Hydrographically, China proper consists of three great river systems. The northern part of the country is drained by the Yellow River (Huang Ho), 2,109 miles long (5,464 km) and mostly unnavigable. The central part is drained by the Chang Jiang (Yangtze Kiang), the third longest river in the world 2,432 miles (6,300 km). The Zhujiang (Si Kiang) in the south is 848 miles long (2,197 km) and navigable for a considerable distance. In addition, the Amur (1,144 sq mi.; 2,965 km) forms part of the northeastern boundary.

Government. With 2,978 deputies, elected for four-year terms by universal suffrage, the National People's Congress is the chief legislative organ. A State Council has the executive authority. The Congress elects the Premier and Deputy Premiers. All ministries are under the State Council, headed by the Premier.

The Communist Party controls the government.

History. By 2000 B.C. the Chinese were living in the Huang Ho basin, and they had achieved an advanced stage of civilization by 1200 B.C. The great philosophers Lao-tse, Confucius Mo Ti, and Mencius lived during the Chou dynasty (1122–249 B.C.). The warring feudal states were first united under Emperor Ch'in Shih Huang Ti, during whose reign (246–210 B.C.) work was begun on the Great Wall. Under the Han dynasty (206 B.C.–A.D. 220), China prospered and traded with the West.

In the T'ang dynasty (618–907), often called the golden age of Chinese history, painting, sculpture, and poetry flourished, and printing made its earliest known appearance.

The Mings, last of the native rulers (1368–1644), overthrew the Mongol, or Yuan, dynasty (1280–1368) established by Kublai Khan. The Mings in turn were overthrown in 1644 by invaders from the north, the Manchus.

China closely restricted foreign activities, and by the end of the 18th century only Canton and the Portuguese port of Macao were open to European merchants. Following the Anglo-Chinese War of 1839–42, however, several treaty ports were opened, and Hong Kong was ceded to Britain. Treaties signed after further hostilities (1856–60) weakened Chinese sovereignty and removed foreigners from Chinese jurisdiction. The disastrous Chinese-Japanese War of 1894–95 was followed by a scramble for Chinese concessions by European powers, leading to the Boxer Rebellion (1900), suppressed by an international force.

The death of the Empress Dowager Tzu Hsi in 1908 and the accession of the infant Emperor Hsüan T'ung (Pu-Yi) were followed by a nation-wide rebellion led by Dr. Sun Yat-sen, who became first President of the Provisional Chinese Republic in 1911. The Manchus abdicated on Feb. 12, 1912. Dr. Sun resigned in favor of Yuan Shih-k'ai, who suppressed the republicans but was forced by a serious rising in 1915–16 to abandon his intention of declaring himself Emperor. Yuan's death in June 1916 was followed by years of civil war between rival militarists and Dr. Sun's republicans.

Nationalist forces, led by Gen. Chiang Kai-shek and with the advice of Communist experts, soon occupied most of China, setting up a Kuomintang regime in 1928. Internal strife continued, however, and Chiang broke with the Communists.

An alleged explosion on the South Manchurian Railway on Sept. 18, 1931, brought invasion of Manchuria by Japanese forces, who installed the last Manchu Emperor, Henry Pu-Yi, as nominal ruler of the puppet state of "Manchukuo." Japanese efforts to take China's northern provinces in July 1937 were resisted by Chiang, who meanwhile had succeeded in uniting most of China behind him. Within two years, however, Japan seized most of the ports and railways. The Kuomintang government retreated first to Hankow and then to Chungking, while the Japanese set up a puppet government at Nanking headed by Wang Jingwei.

Japan's surrender in 1945 touched off civil war between Nationalist forces under Chiang and Communist forces led by Mao Zedong, the party chairman. Despite U.S. aid, the Chiang forces were overcome by the Maoists, backed by the Soviet bloc, and were expelled from the mainland. The Mao regime, established in Peking as the new capital, proclaimed the People's Republic of China on Oct. 1, 1949, with Zhou Enlai as Premier.

Provinces and Regions of China

Name	Area (sq mi.)	Area (sq km)	Capital
Provinces			
Anhui (Anhwei)	54,015	139,900	Hefei (Hofei)
Fujian (Fukien)	47,529	123,100	Fuzhou (Fukien)
Gansu (Kansu)	137,104	355,100	Lanzhou (Lanchow)
Guangdong (Kwangtung)	76,100	197,100	Canton
Guizhou (Kweichow)	67,181	174,000	Guiyang (Kweiyang)
Hainan	13,200	34,300	Haikou
Hebei (Hopei)	81,479	211,030	Shijiazhuang (Shitikiachwang)
Heilongjiang (Heilungkiang)[1]	178,996	463,600	Harbin
Henan (Honan)	64,479	167,000	Zhengzhou (Chengchow)
Hubei (Hupeh)	72,394	187,500	Wuhan
Hunan	81,274	210,500	Changsha
Jiangsu (Kiangsu)	40,927	106,000	Nanjing (Nanking)
Jiangxi (Kiangsi)	63,629	164,800	Nanchang
Jilin (Kirin)[1]	72,201	187,000	Changchun
Liaoning[1]	53,301	138,050	Shenyang
Quinghai (Chinghai)	278,378	721,000	Xining (Sining)
Shaanxi (Shensi)	75,598	195,800	Xian (Sian)
Shandong (Shantung)	59,189	153,300	Jinan (Tsinan)
Shanxi (Shansi)	60,656	157,100	Taiyuan
Sichuan (Szechwan)	219,691	569,000	Chengdu (Chengtu)
Yunnan	168,417	436,200	Kunming
Zhejiang (Chekiang)	39,305	101,800	Hangzhou (Hangchow)
Autonomous Region			
Guangxi Zhuang (Kwangsi Chuang)	85,096	220,400	Nanning
Nei Monggol (Inner Mongolia)[1]	454,633	1,177,500	Hohhot (Huhehot)
Ningxia Hui	30,039	77,800	Yinchuan (Yinchwan)
Xinjiang Uygur (Sinkiang Uighur)[1]	635,829	1,646,800	Urumqi (Urumchi)
Xizang (Tibet)	471,660	1,221,600	Lhasa

1. Together constitute (with Taiwan) what has been traditionally known as Outer China, the remaining territory forming the historical China Proper. NOTE: Names are in Pinyin, with conventional spelling in parentheses.

After the Korean War began in June 1950, China led the Communist bloc in supporting North Korea, and on Nov. 26, 1950, the Mao regime intervened openly.

In 1958, Mao undertook the "Great Leap Forward" campaign, which combined the establishment of rural communes with a crash program of village industrialization but it failed and was abandoned.

China exploded its first atomic (fission) bomb in 1964 and produced a fusion bomb in 1967.

Mao moved to Shanghai, and from that base he and his supporters waged what they called a Cultural Revolution. In the spring of 1966 the Mao group formed Red Guard units dominated by youths and students, closing the schools to free the students for agitation.

The Red Guards campaigned against "old ideas, old culture, old habits, and old customs." Often they were no more than uncontrolled mobs, and brutality was frequent. Early in 1967 efforts were made to restore control. The Red Guards were urged to return home. Schools started opening.

Persistent overtures by the Nixon Administration resulted in the dramatic announcement in July that Henry Kissinger, President Richard M. Nixon's national security adviser, had secretly visited Peking and reached agreement on a visit by the President to China.

The movement toward reconciliation, which signaled the end of the U.S. containment policy toward China, provided irresistible momentum for Chinese admission to the U.N. Despite U.S. opposition to expelling Taiwan (Nationalist China), the world body overwhelmingly ousted Chiang in seating Peking.

President Nixon went to Peking for a week early in 1972, meeting Mao as well as Zhou. The summit ended with a historic communiqué on February 28, in which both nations promised to work toward improved relations. Full diplomatic relations were barred by China as long as the U.S. continued to recognize Nationalist China.

On Jan. 8, 1976, Zhou died. His successor, Vice Premier Deng Xiaoping was supplanted within a month by Hua Guofeng, former Minister of Public Security. Hua became permanent Premier in April. In October he was named successor to Mao as Chairman of the Communist Party.

After Mao died on Sept. 10, a campaign against his widow, Jiang Qing, and three of her "radical" colleagues began. The "Gang of Four" was denounced for having undermined the party, the government, and the economy. They were tried and convicted in 1981.

At the Central Committee meeting of 1977, Deng was reinstated as Deputy Premier, Chief of Staff of the Army, and member of the Central Committee of the Politburo.

At the same time, Jiang Qing, Wang Hongwen, Zhang Chunqiao, and Yao Wenyuan—the notorious "Gang of Four"—were removed from all official posts and banished from the party.

In May 1978, expulsion of ethnic Chinese by Vietnam produced an open rupture. Peking sided with Cambodia in the border fighting that flared between Vietnam and Cambodia, charging Hanoi with aggression.

Peking and Washington announced that they would open full diplomatic relations on Jan. 1, 1979 and the Carter Administration abrogated the Taiwan defense treaty. Deputy Premier Deng sealed the agreement with a visit to the U.S. that coincided with the opening of embassies in both capitals on March 1.

On Deng's return from the U.S. Chinese troops invaded Vietnam to avenge alleged violations of Chinese territory. The action was seen as a reaction to Vietnam's invasion of Cambodia.

After the Central Committee meeting of June 27–29, 1981, Hu Yaobang, a Deng protégé, was elevated to the party chairmanship, replacing Hua Guofeng. Deng became chairman of the military commission of the central committee, giving him control over the army. The committee's 215 members concluded the session with a statement holding Mao Zedong responsible for the "grave blunder" of the Cultural Revolution.

Under Deng Xiaoping's leadership, meanwhile, China's Communist idealogy was almost totally reinterpreted and sweeping economic changes were set in motion in the early 1980s. The Chinese scrapped the personality cult that idolized Mao Zedong, muted Mao's old call for class struggle and exportation of the Communist revolution, and imported Western technology and management techniques to replace the Marxist tenets that retarded modernization.

Also under Deng's leadership, the Chinese Communists worked out an arrangement with Britain for the future of Hong Kong after 1997. The flag of China will be raised but the territory will retain its present social, economic and legal system.

The removal of Hu Yaobang as party chairman in January 1987 was a sign of a hard-line resurgence. He was replaced by former Premier Zhao Ziyang. Conflict between hard-liners and moderates continued and reached a violent climax in 1989. Student demonstrations calling for accelerated liberalization were crushed by military force in June, resulting in several hundred deaths. This was followed by a purge of moderates, including party leader Zhao Ziyang, who was replaced with Jiang Zemin.

The rubber-stamp National People's Congress concluded its April 1992 session with a call to guard against "leftism," widely interpreted as a sign of consolidation and a call for accelerating the drive for economic reform. Nevertheless, several hard-liners remained in their conspicuous positions.

China settled its long-running feud with Vietnam and normalized its relations with Japan during 1991. China pragmatically recognized the Baltic States and the individual members of the CIS at an early date.

The annual session of the National People's Congress in March 1993 was widely seen as an effort by Deng Xiaoping, the paramount leader, to maintain China's moves toward a market economy while retaining political authoritarianism. Communist Party leader Jiang Zemin was elected president, while hard-liner Li Peng was reelected to another five-year term as prime minister despite, but perhaps because of, his politics.

A protest demonstration by hundreds of Tibetans against Chinese rule in May 1993 met with a barrage of tear gas and the detention of foreigners.

COLOMBIA

Republic of Colombia
President: César Gaviria Trujillo (1990)
Area: 439,735 sq mi. (1,138,910 sq km)
Population (est. mid-1993): 34,900,000 (average annual rate of natural increase, 2.1%); birth rate: 26/1000; infant mortality rate: 34/1000; density per square mile: 87
Capital: Bogotá; **Largest cities (est. 1989):** Bogotá, 4,819,696; Medellín, 1,638,637; Cali, 1,637,000; Barranquilla, 1,029,478; Cartagena, 563,949; **Monetary unit:** Peso; **Language:** Spanish; **Religion:** 95% Roman Catholic; **National name:** República de Colombia; **Literacy rate (1990 est.):** 87%
Economic summary: Gross domestic product (1990 est.): $45 billion, per capita $1,300 real growth rate 3.7%; inflation (1991) 26.8%; unemployment (1991) 10.5%. Arable land: 4%. Principal agricultural products: coffee, bananas, rice, corn, sugar cane, cotton, tobacco, oilseeds. Labor force: 11,000,000; 53% in services. Major industrial products: textiles, processed food, beverages, chemicals, cement. Natural resources: petroleum, natural gas, coal, iron ore, nickel, gold, copper, emeralds. Exports: $7.5 billion (f.o.b., 1991): coffee, fuel oil, coal, bananas, fresh cut flowers. Imports: $6.1 billion (c.i.f., 1991): machinery, paper products, chemical products, metals and metal products, transportation equipment. Major trading partners: U.S., E.C., Japan, Venezuela, Netherlands, Brazil, Sweden. Illicit drugs: Major supplier of cocaine to U.S. and other international drug markets.

Geography. Colombia, in the northwestern part of South America, is the only country on that continent that borders on both the Atlantic and Pacific Oceans. It is nearly equal to the combined areas of California and Texas.

Through the western half of the country, three Andean ranges run north and south, merging into one at the Ecuadorean border. The eastern half is a low, jungle-covered plain, drained by spurs of the Amazon and Orinoco, inhabited mostly by isolated, tropical-forest Indian tribes. The fertile plateau and valley of the eastern range are the most densely populated parts of the country.

Government. Colombia's President, who appoints his own Cabinet, serves for a four-year term. The Senate, the upper house of Congress, has 102 members elected for four years by direct vote. The House of Representatives of 162 members is directly elected for four years.

History. Spaniards in 1510 founded Darien, the first permanent European settlement on the American mainland. In 1538 the Spaniards established the colony of New Granada, the area's name until 1861. After a 14-year struggle, in which Simón Bolívar's Venezuelan troops won the battle of Boyacá in Colombia on Aug. 7, 1819, independence was attained in 1824. Bolívar united Colombia, Venezuela, Panama, and Ecuador in the Republic of Greater Colombia (1819–30), but lost Venezuela and Ecuador to separatists. Bolívar's Vice President, Francisco de Paula Santander, founded the Liberal Party as the Federalists while Bolívar established the Conservatives as the Centralists.

Santander's presidency (1832–36) re-established order, but later periods of Liberal dominance (1849–57 and 1861–80), when the Liberals sought to disestablish the Roman Catholic Church, were marked by insurrection and even civil war. Rafael Nuñez, in a 15-year-presidency, restored the power of the central government and the church, which led in 1899 to a bloody civil war and the loss in 1903 of Panama over ratification of a lease to the U.S. of the Canal Zone. For 21 years, until 1930, the Conservatives held power as revolutionary pressures built up.

The Liberal administrations of Enrique Olaya Herrera and Alfonso López (1930–38) were marked by social reforms that failed to solve the country's problems, and in 1946, insurrection and banditry broke out, claiming hundreds of thousands of lives by 1958. Laureano Gómez (1950–53); the Army Chief of Staff, Gen. Gustavo Rojas Pinilla (1953–56), and a military junta (1956–57) sought to curb disorder by repression.

Government efforts to stamp out the Movement of April 19 (M–19), an urban guerrilla organization, intensified in 1981 with the capture of some of the leaders. The Liberals won a solid majority in 1982, but a party split enabled Belisario Betancur Cuartas, the Conservative candidate, to win the presidency on May 31. After his inauguration, he ended the state of siege that had existed almost continuously for 34 years and renewed the general amnesty of 1981.

In an official war against drug trafficking Colombia became a public battleground with bombs, killings and kidnapping. In 1989 a leading presidential candidate, Luis Carlos Galán, was murdered. In an effort to quell the terror President Gaviria proposed lenient punishment in exchange for surrender by the leading drug dealers. In addition in 1991 the constitutional convention voted to ban extradition. In July 1992 Pablo Escobar of the Medellin drug cartel escaped from prison in an operation that left six dead.

A new constitution adopted in July 1991 provided for direct election of the state governors. In national legislative elections of October the governing Liberal Party retained a slight majority, though the voter turnout was low.

Peace talks between the government and guerrilla groups collapsed in 1992 leading in November to a declaration of a state of emergency.

COMOROS

Federal Islamic Republic of the Comoros
President: Said Mohammed Djohar (1989)
Area: 690 sq mi. (1,787 sq km)
Population (est. mid-1993): 500,000 (average annual rate of natural increase: 3.5%); birth rate: 48/1000; infant mortality rate: 89/1000; density per square mile: 712
Capital and largest city (est. 1988): Moroni (on Grande Comoro), 22,000; **Monetary unit:** Franc CFA; **Languages:** Shaafi Islam (Swahili dialect), Malagasu, French, Arabic; **Religions:** Sunni Muslim, 86%; Roman Catholic, 14%.; **National name:** République Fédéral Islamique des Comores; **Literacy rate (1981):** 45%
Economic summary: Gross domestic product (1991): \$260 million; \$540 per capita; real growth rate 2.7%; inflation 4%; unemployment (1988): over 16%. Arable land: 35%. Labor force: 140,000 (1982); 80% in agriculture. Principal agricultural products: perfume essences, copra, coconuts, cloves, vanilla, cassava, bananas. Major industrial products: perfume distillations. Exports: \$16 million (f.o.b., 1990 est.): perfume essences, vanilla, copra, cloves. Imports: \$41 million (f.o.b., 1990 est.): foodstuffs, cement, petroleum products, consumer goods. Major trading partners: France, Germany, U.S., Africa, Pakistan.

Geography. The Comoros Islands—Grande Comoro, Anjouan, Mohéli, and Mayotte (which retains ties to France)—are an archipelago of volcanic origin in the Indian Ocean between Mozambique and Madagascar.

Government. Democratic elections were held in March 1990. The interim president Said Djohar won from among a field of eight candidates. The constitution dates from October 1, 1978, and the country is an Islamic republic with a 42-member unicameral legislature.

History. Under French rule since 1886, the Comoros declared themselves independent July 6, 1975. However, Mayotte, with a Christian majority, voted against joining the other, mainly Islamic, islands, in the move to independence and remains French.

A month after independence, Justice Minister Ali Soilih staged a coup with the help of mercenaries, overthrowing the new nation's first president, Ahmed Abdallah. He was overthrown on May 13, 1978, when a small boatload of French mercenaries, some of whom had aided him three years earlier, seized government headquarters.

Voters approved a new constitution in a referendum of June 1992. Violence disrupted multiparty legislative elections in November.

CONGO

Republic of the Congo
President: Prof. Pascal Lissouba (1992)
Prime Minister: Claude Antoine Dacosta (1992)
Area: 132,046 sq mi. (342,000 sq km)
Population (est. mid-1993): 2,400,000 (average annual rate of natural increase: 2.8%); birth rate: 42/1000; infant mortality rate: 114/1000. Density per sq mile: 18
Capital and largest city (est. 1990): Brazzaville, 760,300; **Monetary unit:** Franc CFA; **Ethnic groups:** About 15 Bantu groups, Europeans; **Languages:** French, Lingala, Kikongo, others; **Religions:** 50% Christian, 48% animist, 2% Muslim; **National name:** République Populaire du Congo; **Literacy rate:** 57%
Economic summary: Gross domestic product (1990 est.): \$2.4 billion, per capita \$1,070; real growth rate 0.5%; inflation (1989 est.) 4.6%. Arable land: 2%. Principal agricultural products: cassava, rice, corn, peanuts, coffee, cocoa. Labor force: 79,100; 75% in agriculture. Major industrial products: crude oil, cigarettes, cement, beverages, milled sugar. Natural resources: wood, potash, petroleum, natural gas. Exports: \$751 million (f.o.b., 1988): oil, lumber, coffee, cocoa, sugar, diamonds. Imports: \$564 million (c.i.f., 1988): foodstuffs, consumer goods, intermediate manufactures, capital equipment. Major trading partners: France, U.S., Italy, Spain, Brazil, Germany, Japan.

Geography. The Congo is situated in west Central Africa astride the Equator. It borders on Gabon, Cameroon, the Central African Republic, Zaire, and the Angola exclave of Cabinda, with a short stretch of coast on the South Atlantic. Its area is nearly three times that of Pennsylvania.

Most of the inland is tropical rain forest, drained by tributaries of the Zaire (Congo) River, which flows south along the eastern border with Zaire to Stanley Pool. The narrow coastal plain rises to highlands separated from the inland plateaus by the 200-mile-wide Niari River Valley, which gives passage to the coast.

History. The inhabitants of the former French Congo, mainly Bantu peoples with Pygmies in the north, were subjects of several kingdoms in earlier times.

The Frenchman Pierre Savorgnan de Brazza signed a treaty with Makoko, ruler of the Bateke people, in 1880, which established French control. The area, with Gabon and Ubangi-Shari, was constituted the colony of French Equatorial Africa in 1910. It joined Chad in supporting the Free French cause in World War II. The Congo proclaimed its independence without leaving the French Community in 1960.

Maj. Marien Ngouabi, head of the National Council of the Revolution, took power as president on Jan. 1, 1969. He was sworn in for a second five-year term in 1975.

A four-man commando squad assassinated Ngouabi in Brazzaville on March 18, 1977.

Col. Joachim Yhombi-Opango, Army Chief of Staff, assumed the presidency on April 4. Yombhi-Opango resigned on Feb. 4, 1979, and was replaced by Col. Denis Sassou-Neguessou.

In July 1990 the leaders of the ruling party voted to end the one-party system. A national political conference, hailed as a model for sub-Saharan Africa, in 1991 renounced Marxism, and scheduled the country's first free elections for 1992. The national conference ending in June 1991 rewrote the constitution.

Voters in March 1992 approved the new constitution. Legislative elections took place in June–July, and presidential voting in August. After the government lost a vote of confidence in October the president dissolved the legislature. A new government was formed to prepare for general elections.

COSTA RICA

Republic of Costa Rica
President: Rafael Calderón Fournier (1990)
Area: 19,652 sq mi. (50,898 sq km)
Population (est. mid-1993): 3,300,000 (average annual rate of natural increase: 2.4%); birth rate: 27/1000; infant mortality rate: 15.3/1000; density per square mile: 166
Capital and largest city (est. 1990): San José, 294,167; **Monetary unit:** Colón; **Language:** Spanish; **Religion:** 95% Roman Catholic; **National name:** República de Costa Rica; **Literacy rate (1984):** 93%
Economic summary: Gross domestic product (1991 est.): $5.9 billion; per capita $1,900; real growth rate 2.5%; inflation 27%; unemployment 4.6%. Arable land: 6%. Principal products: bananas, coffee, sugar cane, rice, corn, livestock. Labor force: 868,300; 35.1% in industry and commerce. Major products: processed foods, textiles and clothing, construction materials, fertilizer. Natural resource: hydropower potential. Exports: $1.5 billion (f.o.b., 1991 est.): coffee, bananas, beef, sugar, cocoa. Imports: $1.8 billion (c.i.f., 1991 est.): machinery, chemicals, foodstuffs, fuels, fertilizer. Major trading partners: U.S., Central American countries, Germany, Japan, United Kingdom.

Geography. This Central American country lies between Nicaragua to the north and Panama to the south. Its area slightly exceeds that of Vermont and New Hampshire combined.

Most of Costa Rica is tableland, from 3,000 to 6,000 feet (914 to 1,829 m) above sea level. Cocos Island (10 sq mi.; 26 sq km), about 300 miles (483 km) off the Pacific Coast, is under Costa Rican sovereignty.

Government. Under the 1949 Constitution, the president and the one-house Legislative Assembly of 57 members are elected for terms of four years.

The army was abolished in 1949. There is a civil guard and a rural guard.

History. Costa Rica was inhabited by 25,000 Indians when Columbus discovered it and probably named it in 1502. Few of the Indians survived the Spanish conquest, which began in 1563. The region was administered as a Spanish province. Costa Rica achieved independence in 1821 but was absorbed for two years by Agustín de Iturbide in his Mexican Empire. It was established as a republic in 1848.

Except for the military dictatorship of Tomás Guardia from 1870 to 1882, Costa Rica has enjoyed one of the most democratic governments in Latin America.

Rodrigo Carazo Odio, leader of a four-party coalition called the Unity Party, won the presidency in February 1978. His tenure was marked by a disastrous decline in the economy.

On Feb. 2, 1986, Oscar Arias Sanchez won the national elections on a neutralist platform. Arias initiated a policy of preventing contra usage of Costa Rican territory. Rafael Calderón won the presidential election of February 4, 1990 with 51% of the vote, his party winning 29 seats in the Assembly. Calderón promised to continue the economic policies of the previous administration.

Armed captors seized 18 supreme court justices and five others in April 1993. The authorities managed to free all the hostages unharmed and arrest the captors.

CÔTE D'IVOIRE

Republic of Côte d'Ivoire
President: Félix Houphouët-Boigny (1960)
Area: 124,502 sq mi. (322,462 sq km)
Population (est. mid-1993): 13,400,000 (average annual rate of natural increase: 3.5%); birth rate: 50/1000; infant mortality rate: 95/1000; density per square mile: 109
Capital (est. 1984): Yamoussoukro[1] (since March 1983), 120,000; **Monetary unit:** Franc CFA; **Ethnic groups:** 60 different groups: principals are Baoule, Bete, Senoufou, Malinke, Agni; **Languages:** French and African languages (Diaula esp.); **Religions:** 60% indigenous, 17% Christian, 23% Islam; **National name:** République de la Côte d'Ivoire; **Literacy rate:** 54%
Economic summary: Gross domestic product (1990): $10 billion; per capita $800; real growth rate –2.9%; inflation –0.8%; unemployment (1985) 14%. Arable land: 9%; Labor force: 5,718,000; over 85% in agriculture. Principal products: coffee, cocoa, corn, beans, timber. Major industrial products: food, wood, refined oil, textiles, fertilizer. Natural resources: diamonds, iron ore, crude oil, manganese, cobalt, bauxite, copper. Exports: $2.5 billion (f.o.b., 1989): coffee, cocoa, tropical woods. Imports: $1.4 billion (f.o.b., 1989): raw materials, consumer goods, fuels. Major trading partners: France, U.S., Western European countries, Nigeria.

1. Not recognized by U.S. which recognizes Abidjan.

Geography. Côte d'Ivoire (also known as the Ivory Coast), in western Africa on the Gulf of Guinea, is a little larger than New Mexico. Its neighbors are Liberia, Guinea, Mali, Burkina Faso, and Ghana.

The country consists of a coastal strip in the south, dense forests in the interior, and savannas in the north. Rainfall is heavy, especially along the coast.

Government. The government is headed by a President who is elected every five years by popular vote, together with a National Assembly of 175 members.

History. Côte d'Ivoire attracted both French and Portuguese merchants in the 15th century. French traders set up establishments early in the 19th century, and in 1842, the French obtained territorial concessions from local tribes, gradually extending their influence along the coast and inland. The area was organized as a territory in 1893, became an autonomous republic in the French Union after World War II, and achieved independence on Aug. 7, 1960.

The Côte d'Ivoire formed a customs union in 1959 with Dahomey (Benin), Niger, and Burkina Faso.

Roman Catholic Pres. Houphouët-Boigny ordered the building of the largest Christian church in the world, Notre Dame de la Pax, in the capital city, which he periodically paid for.

Falling cocoa and coffee prices made this nation the largest per capita debtor in Africa. Massive protests by students, farmers and professionals forced the president to legalize opposition parties and hold the first contested presidential election. In October 1990 Houphouët-Boigny won 81% of the vote and is currently serving his seventh consecutive five-year term. In the first multiparty legislative elections in November the president's Democratic Party won 163 of the 175 seats.

Negotiations with the IMF over aid were suspended in July 1992 when the government refused to consider reducing public expenditures.

CROATIA

Republic of Croatia
President: Franjo Tudjman
Area: 21,829 sq mi. (56,537 sq km)
Population (est. mid-1993): 4,400,000 (average annual rate of natural increase: 0.1%), predominantly Croats, about 12% Serbs. Birth rate: 12/1000; infant mortality rate: 10.6/1000; density per square mile: 203
Capital (1991): Zagreb, 930,753. Other large cities (1981): Split, 169,322; Rijeka (Fiume), 159,433; Osijek, 104,775; **Monetary unit:** Yugoslav dinar replaced with Croatian currency; **Languages:** Croatian written with Roman characters; **Literacy rate:** est. 90%; **Religion:** predominantly Roman Catholic
Economic summary: Gross domestic product (1991 est.): $26.3 billion; $5,600 per capita; real growth rate –25%; inflation (March 92): 14.3%; unemployment (Dec. 91): 20%. Industries: chemicals, plastics, machine tools, fabricated metals, electronics, pig iron and rolled steel products, aluminum reduction, wood products, building materials, petroleum and petroleum refining, food processing, and beverages. Before the current war, shipbuilding was a major industry. Agriculture: wheat, corn, oats, sugar beets, potatoes, livestock breeding and dairy farming. Exports: $2.9 billion (1990). Imports: $4.4 billion (1990).

Geography: Croatia is about half the size of the state of Louisiana. It is bounded in the north by the Republic of Slovenia, in the east by Hungary, in the east and south by Yugoslavia, and in the west by the Adriatic Sea. Part of Croatia is a barren, rocky region lying in the Dinaric Alps. The Zagorje region north of the capital, Zagreb, is a land of rolling hills, and the fertile agricultural region of the Pannonian Plain is bordered by the Drava, Danube, and Sava Rivers in the east. Over one-third of Croatia is forested.

Government: A parliamentary democracy with two legislative houses.

History: The original home of the Slavic Croats was in an area that was part of the Republic of Ukraine. Other tribes arrived in the region during the 6th century A.D, which was then part of the Roman province of Pannonia. The Croats converted to Christianity between the 7th and 9th centuries and adopted the Roman alphabet.

In 925 A.D. the Croats defeated Byzantine and Frankish invaders and established their own independent kingdom which reached its peak during the 11th century.

A civil war ensued in 1089 which later led to the country being conquered by the Hungarians in 1091. The signing of the *Pacta Conventa* by Croatian tribal chiefs and the Hungarian king in 1102 united the two nations politically under the Hungarian monarch.

When the Hungarians were defeated by the Turks in 1526, most of Croatia fell under Ottoman rule until the end of the 17th century. The rest of Croatia elected Ferdinand of Austria as their king and became associated with the Hapsburgs of Austria.

After the establishment of the Austro-Hungarian kingdom in 1867, Croatia and Slovenia became part of Hungary until the collapse of Austria-Hungary in 1918 following their defeat in World War I.

On Oct. 29, 1918, Croatia proclaimed its independence and joined in union with Montenegro, Serbia, and Slovenia to form the Kingdom of Serbs, Croats, and Slovenes. The name was changed to Yugoslavia in 1929.

When Germany invaded Yugoslavia in 1941, an independent Croatian state was created that was controlled by a Fascist dictatorship. After Germany was defeated in 1945, Croatia was made into a republic of the newly reestablished nation of Yugoslavia.

In May 1991, Croatian voters supported a referendum calling for their republic's independence and when the Croatian parliament passed a declaration of independence from Yugoslavia in June, a six-month civil war followed with the Serbian-dominated Yugoslavian army. The war claimed thousands of lives and wrought mass destruction on the land.

A UN cease-fire was arranged on Jan. 2, 1992. The Security Council in February approved sending a 14,000-member peacekeeping force to monitor the cease-fire and protect the minority Serbs in Croatia.

By the end of August, rebel Serbs in Croatia still controlled a third of that republic.

Elections in February 1992 for the 63-seat upper house of parliament produced a victory for the nationalist party of President Tudjman. A six-month old government resigned in March over economics and a political dispute within the ruling party.

CUBA

Republic of Cuba
President: Fidel Castro Ruz (1976)
Area: 44,218 sq mi. (114,524 sq km)
Population (est. mid-1993): 11,000,000 (average annual rate of natural increase: 1.0%); birth rate: 16/1000; infant mortality rate: 10.7/1000; density per square mile: 258
Capital: Havana; **Largest cities (est. 1989):** Havana, 2,077,938; Santiago de Cuba, 397,024; Camagüey, 278,958 Holguin, 222,794; Santa Clara, 190,735; **Monetary unit:** Peso; **Language:** Spanish; **Religion:** at least 85% nominally Roman Catholic before Castro assumed power; **National name:** República de Cuba; **Literacy rate:** 94%
Economic summary: Gross national product (1991 est.): $17 billion, per capita $1,580; real growth rate –20%. Arable land: 23%. Principal agricultural products: sugar, tobacco, coffee, rice, fruits. Labor force: 3,578,800; 30% in services and government. Major industrial products: processed sugar and tobacco, refined oil products, textiles, chemicals, paper and wood products, metals, consumer products. Natural resources: metals, primarily nickel, timber. Exports: $3.6 billion (f.o.b., 1991 est.): coffee, sugar, nickel, shellfish, tobacco. Imports: $3.7 billion (c.i.f., 1991 est.): capital goods, industrial raw materials, petroleum, foodstuffs. Trading partners: C.I.S. countries, China, Canada, Japan, Italy, Argentina, Spain, Mexico.

Geography. The largest island of the West Indies group (equal in area to Pennsylvania), Cuba is also the westernmost—just west of Hispaniola (Haiti and the Dominican Republic), and 90 miles (145 km) south of Key West, Fla., at the entrance to the Gulf of Mexico.

The island is mountainous in the southeast and south central area (Sierra Maestra). Elsewhere it is flat or rolling.

Government. Since 1976, elections have been held every five years to elect the National Assembly, which in turn elects the 31-member Council of States, its President, First Vice-President, five Vice-Presidents, and Secretary. Fidel Castro is President of the Council of State and of the government and First Secretary of the Communist Party of Cuba, the only political party.

History. Arawak Indians inhabiting Cuba when Columbus discovered the island in 1492 died off from diseases brought by sailors and settlers. By 1511, Spaniards under Diego Velásquez were founding settlements that served as bases for Spanish exploration. Cuba soon after served as an assembly point for treasure looted by the conquistadores, attracting French and English pirates.

Black slaves and free laborers were imported to work sugar and tobacco plantations, and waves of chiefly Spanish immigrants maintained a European character in the island's culture. Early slave rebellions and conflicts between colonials and Spanish rulers laid the foundation for an independence movement that turned into open warfare from 1867 to 1878. The poet, José Marti, in 1895 led the struggle that finally ended Spanish rule, thanks largely to U.S. intervention in 1898 after the sinking of the battleship *Maine* in Havana harbor.

A treaty in 1899 made Cuba an independent republic under U.S. protection. The U.S. occupation, which ended in 1902, suppressed yellow fever and brought large American investment. From 1906 to 1909, Washington invoked the Platt Amendment to the treaty, which gave it the right to intervene in order to suppress any revolt. U.S. troops came back in 1912 and again in 1917 to restore order. The Platt Amendment was abrogated in 1934.

Fulgencio Batista, an army sergeant, led a revolt in 1933 that overthrew the regime of President Gerado Machado.

Batista's Cuba was a police state. Corrupt officials took payoffs from American gamblers who operated casinos, demanded bribes from Cubans for various public services and enriched themselves with raids on the public treasury. Dissenters were murdered and their bodies dumped in gutters.

Fidel Castro Ruz, a hulking, bearded attorney in his 30s, landed in Cuba on Christmas Day 1956 with a band of 12 fellow revolutionaries, evaded Batista's soldiers, and set up headquarters in the jungled hills of the Sierra Maestra range. By 1958 his force had grown to about 2,000 guerrillas, for the most part young and middle class. Castro's brother, Raul, and Ernesto (Ché) Guevara, an Argentine physician, were his top lieutenants. Businessmen and landowners who opposed the Batista regime gave financial support to the rebels. The United States, meanwhile, cut off arms shipments to Batista's army.

The beginning of the end for Batista came when the rebels routed 3,000 government troops and captured Santa Clara, capital of Las Villas province 150 miles from Havana, and a trainload of Batista reinforcements refused to get out of their railroad cars. On New Year's Day 1959, Batista flew to exile in the Dominican Republic and Castro took over the government. Crowds cheered the revolutionaries on their seven-day march to the capital.

The United States initially welcomed what looked like the prospect for a democratic Cuba, but a rude awakening came within a few months when Castro established military tribunals for political opponents, jailed hundreds, and began to veer leftward. Castro disavowed Cuba's 1952 military pact with the United States. He confiscated U.S. investments in banks and industries and seized large U.S. landholdings, turning them first into collective farms and then into Soviet-type state farms. The United States broke relations with Cuba on Jan. 3, 1961. Castro thereupon forged an alliance with the Soviet Union.

From the ranks of the Cuban exiles who had fled to the United States, the Central Intelligence Agency recruited and trained an expeditionary force, numbering less than 2,000 men, to invade Cuba, with the expectation that the invasion would spark an uprising of the Cuban populace against Castro. The invasion was planned under the Eisenhower administration and President John F. Kennedy gave the go-ahead for it in the first months of his administration, but rejected a CIA proposal for U.S. planes to provide air support. The landing at the Bay of Pigs on April 17, 1961, was a fiasco. Not only did the invaders fail to receive any support from the populace, but Castro's tanks and artillery made short work of the small force.

A Soviet attempt to change the global power balance by installing in Cuba medium-range missiles—capable of striking targets in the United States with nuclear warheads—provoked a crisis between the superpowers in 1962 that had the potential of touching off World War III. After a visit to Moscow by Cuba's war minister, Raul Castro, work began secretly on the missile launching sites.

Denouncing the Soviets for "deliberate deception," President Kennedy on Oct. 22 announced that the U.S. navy would enforce a "quarantine" of shipping to Cuba and search Soviet bloc ships to prevent the missiles themselves from reaching the island. After six days of tough public statements on both sides and secret diplomacy, Soviet Premier Nikita Khrushchev on Oct. 28 ordered the missile sites dismantled, crated and shipped back to the Soviet Union, in return for a U.S. pledge not to attack Cuba. Limited diplomatic ties were re-established on Sept. 1, 1977.

Emigration increased dramatically after April 1, 1980, when Castro, irritated by the granting of asylum to would-be refugees by the Peruvian embassy in Havana, removed guards and allowed 10,000 Cubans to swarm into the embassy grounds.

As an airlift began taking the refugees to Costa Rica, Castro opened the port of Mariel to a "freedom flotilla" of ships and yachts from the United States, many of them owned or chartered by Cuban-Americans to bring out relatives. It wasn't until after they had reached the United States that it was discovered that the regime had opened prisons and mental hospitals to permit criminals, homosexuals and others unwanted in Cuba to join the refugees.

For most of President Ronald Reagan's first term, U.S.-Cuban relations were frozen, with Secretary of State Alexander Haig calling Havana the "source" of troubles in Central America. But late in 1984, an agreement was reached between the two countries. Cuba would take back more than 2,700 Cubans who had come to the United States in the Mariel exodus but were not eligible to stay in the country under U.S. immigration law because of criminal or psychiatric disqualification. Castro cancelled it when the U.S. began the Radio Marti broadcasts in May 1985 to bring a non-Communist view to the Cuban people.

In the face of sweeping changes in Eastern Europe and the Soviet Union itself, Cuba has reaffirmed its adherence to Marxism-Leninism.

With the collapse of Communism in Eastern Europe Cuba's foreign trade plummeted as did aid from Russia, producing the worst economic crisis in the island's history. The sharp drop in imports made the government further control already rationed consumption. In hope of increasing the number of visiting tourists, and thereby the flow of hard currency, the government refurbished many older resorts and supported other projects aimed at the tourist trade.

CYPRUS

Republic of Cyprus

President: Glafcos Clerides (1993)

Area: 3,572 sq mi (9,251 sq km)

Population (est. mid-1992): 733,522; Greek Cypriots, 601,722; Turkish Cypriots, 131,800. (average annual rate of natural increase: 1.0%); birth rate: 19/1000; infant mortality rate: 11/1000; density per square mile: 204

Capital and largest city (est. 1992): Nicosia (in government controlled area), 177,410; **Monetary unit:** Cyprus pound; **Languages:** Greek, Turkish (official), English; **Religions:** Greek Orthodox, 78%; Sunni Moslem, 18%; Maronite Latin, Armenian; **National name:** Kypriaki Dimokratia—Kibris Cumhuriyeti; **Member of Commonwealth of Nations; Literacy rate (1993):** 99%

Economic summary: Gross domestic product (Greek area, 1990): $5.5 billion, per capita $9,600; real growth rate 6%; inflation rate 1.8%; unemployment rate in Greek area (1990): 1.8%. Arable land: 40%. Principal agricultural products: vine products, citrus, potatoes, other vegetables. Labor force: 251,406; 33% in industry. Major industrial products: beverages, footwear, clothing, cement, asbestos mining. Natural resources: copper, asbestos, gypsum, timber, marble, clay, salt. Exports: $847 million (f.o.b., 1990): citrus, potatoes, grapes, wine, cement, clothing, footwear. Imports: $2.3 billion (f.o.b., 1990): consumer goods, petroleum and lubricants, food and feed grains, machinery. Major trading partners: EEC (61%), Middle East, North Africa, U.S., Japan

Geography. The third largest island in the Mediterranean (one and one half times the size of Delaware), Cyprus lies off the southern coast of Turkey and the western shore of Syria. Most of the country consists of a wide plain lying between two mountain ranges that cross the island. The highest peak is Mount Olympus at 6,406 feet (1,953 m).

Government. The president is elected for a five-year term and exercises executive power through an appointed Council of Ministers. Under the Republic's constitution, for the protection of the Turkish minority, the vice president as well as three of the 10 cabinet ministers must be from the Turkish community.

Legislative power lies with the House of Representatives which comprises 80 members elected for five years. 56 members are Greek-Cypriots elected by the Greek-Cypriot community; 24 are Turkish-Cypriots elected by the Turkish-Cypriot community. Since the Turkish-Cypriot ministers and other officials withdrew from their posts in 1963, the 24 seats allotted to the Turkish Cypriots remain vacant. The Cypriot House assembly has been functioning only with its 56 Greek Cypriot members. Representatives from the Maronite, Armenian, and Latin minorities are also elected as observers. Mediation efforts by the U.N. seek to achieve reunification of the island under one federated system of government.

History. Cyprus was the site of early Phoenician and Greek colonies. For centuries its rule passed through many hands. It fell to the Turks in 1571, and a large Turkish colony settled on the island.

In World War I, on the outbreak of hostilities with Turkey, Britain annexed the island. It was declared a crown colony in 1925.

For centuries the Greek population, regarding Greece as its mother country, has sought self-determination and reunion with it *(enosis)*. The resulting quarrel with Turkey threatened NATO. Cyprus became an independent nation on Aug. 16, 1960, with Britain, Greece, and Turkey as guarantor powers.

Archbishop Makarios, president since 1959, was overthrown July 15, 1974, by a military coup led by the Cypriot National Guard. The new regime named Nikos Giorgiades Sampson as president and Bishop Gennadios as head of the Cypriot Church to replace Makarios.

Diplomacy failed to resolve the crisis. Turkey invaded Cyprus by sea and air July 20, 1974, asserting its right to protect the Turkish Cypriote minority.

Geneva talks involving Greece, Turkey, Britain, and the two Cypriote factions failed in mid-August, and the Turks subsequently gained control of 40% of the island. Greece made no armed response to the superior Turkish force, but bitterly suspended military participation in the NATO alliance.

The tension continued after Makarios returned to become President on Dec. 7, 1974. He offered self-government to the Turkish minority, but rejected any solution "involving transfer of populations and amounting to partition of Cyprus."

Turkish Cypriots proclaimed a separate state under Rauf Denktas in the northern part of the island in Nov. 1983, and proposed a "biregional federation."

Makarios died on Aug. 3, 1977, and Spyros Kyprianou was elected to serve the remainder of his term. Kyprianou was subsequently re-elected in 1978, 1983, and 1985. In 1988, George Vassiliou defeated Kyprianou.

Despite several attempts in 1991 by the UN to resolve the dispute little if any progress was made.

Then-President Vassiliou won a plurality in the presidential election of February 1993 but fell short of a majority. A 73-year-old conservative and critic of UN proposals to reunify Cyprus narrowly won the second round of elections to become president

Northern Cyprus—On Nov. 15, 1983, the Turkish Cypriot Parliament proclaimed the northern part of Cyprus as the Turkish Republic of Northern Cyprus (TRNC) which is recognized by Turkey. However, the Greek area controlled by the Cypriot government is the only internationally recognized government of Cyprus.

In June 1985, Rauf R. Denktas was elected president of TRNC and was reelected in April 1990. Both sides have publicly called for the resolution of inter-communal differences and the creation of a new federal system of government. Diplomacy by the United Nations has failed to settle the dispute between the two de facto autonomous states.

NORTHERN CYPRUS

Turkish Republic of Northern Cyprus
President: Rauf Denktas (1990)
Area: 1,295 sq mi. (3,355 sq km)
Population (est. 1991): Turkish Cypriots, 172,288; Greek Cypriots, 544; Maronites, 250 (1992); (average annual rate of natural increase: 1.1%); birth rate: 20.5/1,000; infant mortality rate: 8/1000; density per square km: 52.20
Capital and largest city (1990): Nicosia North (Lefkosa), 40,009; **Monetary unit:** Turkish lira; **Official language:** Turkish; **Religions:** Moslem, 99%; others, 1%; **National name:** Kuzey Kibris Türk Cumhuriyeti (Turkish Republic of Northern Cyprus); **Literacy rate (1991):** 100%
Economic summary: Gross national product (1991): $532.5 million; per capita $3,065. Average rate of growth (1975–1990): 6.4%. Arable land (1990): 66%. Principal agricultural products: citrus, potatoes, tobacco, vegetables. Labor force (1991): 71,941; 26.2% in agriculture; 11.2% in industry. Major industrial products: concentrated citrus, hides, leathers, P.V.C. covered electric cables, footwear, clothing, cosmetics. Natural resources: gypsum, pyrite mine. Exports: dairy products, citrus, live animals, potatoes, ready-made clothing, tobacco, carobs, hides and leathers. Imports: consumer goods, petroleum and lubricants, food, machinery and transport equipment, chemicals. Major trading partners: EC countries (mainly U.K. and Germany) and Turkey are the largest trading partners.

Geography. The Turkish Republic of Northern Cyprus covers the northern part of the island of Cyprus. North Cyprus consists of the coastal plains, the Besparmak (Five-Finger) Mountains (the highest peak is Mount Selvili at 3,360 feet), and the interior plains.

Government. The Constitution envisages a Parliamentary democracy. The legislative power is exercised by an Assembly composed of 50 deputies elected for five years. The President is Head of State and represents the unity of the state. He appoints the Prime Minister from among the deputies.

CZECH REPUBLIC

President: Vaclav Havel (1993)
Premier: Vaclav Klaus (1992)
Area: 30,464 sq mi. (78,902 sq km)
Population (est. mid-1993): 10,300,000 (average annual rate of natural increase: 0.1%); birth rate: 13/1000; infant mortality rate: 10.4/1000; density per square mile: 338
Capital: Prague (1993): 1,500,000. Other large cities (1991): Brno, 387,986; Ostrava, 327,553; Plzen, 173,129; Olomouc, 105,690; **Monetary unit:** Koruna; **Language:** Czech; **Religions:** Roman Catholic major; other: Protestant, Orthodox; **Literacy rate:** 99%
Economic summary: Per capita GNP (est. 1991)[1]: $6,900; real growth rate, –15%; inflation 52%; unemployment, nearly 70%. The Czech Republic has a developed but deteriorating industrialized economy—much of its plant equipment is among the oldest in Europe. Major natural resources are coal (brown and hard), timber, and uranium. Principal industries are heavy and general machine building, motor vehicles, iron and steel production, metalworking, chemicals, electronics, textiles, shoes, glassware, beer-brewing, ceramics, and pharmaceuticals. Main agricultural products are sugar beets, fodder roots, corn, potatoes, wheat, barley, hops, flax, dairy farming, beef cattle, hogs, and poultry. Major trading partners are C.I.S., Bulgaria, Yugoslavia, Germany, Hungary, Poland, Austria, and Switzerland.

1. 1991 data for the former united Czechoslovakia.

Geography. The Czech Republic lies in central Europe. It is bordered on the north by Poland, on the east by Slovakia, on the south by Austria, and on the west and northwest by Germany. The two principal regions are Bohemia and Moravia. The Bohemian landscape consists of rolling hills and plateaus surrounded by low mountains to the north, west, and south. Moravia is bordered on the north by mountains and generally has more hills than Bohemia. The Principal rivers are the Elbe and the Vltava which are vital to the nation's waterborne and agricultural commerce. The Czech Republic is about the size of the state of South Carolina.

Government. A parliamentary democracy headed by the president. The parliament consists of two chambers—the 200-member House, elected for four-year terms, and the 81-member Senate, elected for six-year terms. The president is elected for a five-year term by both chambers of parliament.

History. Probably about the 5th century A.D., Slavic tribes from the Vistula basin settled in the region of the traditional Czech lands of Bohemia, Moravia, and Silesia. The Czechs founded the kingdom of Bohemia, the Premyslide dynasty, which ruled Bohemia and Moravia from the 10th to the 16th century.

One of the Bohemian kings, Charles IV, Holy Roman Emperor, made Prague an imperial capital and a center of Latin scholarship. The Hussite movement founded by Jan Hus (1369?–1415) linked the Slavs to the Reformation and revived Czech nationalism, previously under German domination. A Hapsburg, Ferdinand I, ascended the throne in 1526. The Czechs rebelled in 1618. Defeated in 1620, they were ruled for the next 300 years as part of the Austrian Empire. Full independence from the Hapsburgs was not achieved until the end of World War I following the collapse of the Austrian-Hungarian Empire.

A union of the Czech lands and Slovakia was proclaimed in Prague on Nov. 14, 1918, and the Czech nation became one of the two component parts of the newly formed Czechoslovakian state.

In March 1939, German troops occupied Czechoslovakia and Czech Bohemia and Moravia became German protectorates for the duration of World War II. The former government returned in April 1945 when the war ended and the country's pre-1938 boundaries were restored.

When elections were held in 1946, the Communists became the dominant political party and gained control of the Czechoslovakian government in 1948. Thereafter, the former democracy was turned into a Soviet-style state.

Nearly 42 years of Communist rule ended when Vaclav Havel was elected president of Czechoslovakia in 1989. The return of democratic political reform saw a strong Slovak nationalist movement emerge by the end of 1991 which sought independence for Slovakia as a sovereign nation and the breakup of the two Czechoslovakian republics.

When the general elections of June 1992 failed to resolve the continuing coexistence of the two republics within the Federation, Czech and Slovak political leaders agreed to separate their states into two fully independent nations. On Aug. 26, 1992 they announced their intentions to disolve the Czechoslovakian federation on Jan. 1, 1993.

Havel was elected for a 5-year term as president in January 1993 by the 200-member parliament.

DENMARK

Kingdom of Denmark
Sovereign: Queen Margrethe II (1972)
Prime Minister: Poul Rasmussen (1993)
Area: 16,631 sq mi. (43,075 sq km[1]
Population (est. mid-1993): 5,200,000 (average annual rate of natural increase: 0.1%); birth rate: 13/1000; infant mortality rate: 7.5/1000; density per square mile: 317
Capital: Copenhagen; **Largest cities (1988):** Copenhagen, 1,343,916; Aarhus, 198,047; Odense, 137,082; Alborg, 112,620; **Monetary unit:** Krone; **Language:** Danish, Faroese, Greenlandic (an Eskimo dialect), small German-speaking minority; **Religion:** 92% Evangelical Lutheran; **National name:** Kongeriget Danmark; **Literacy rate:** 99%
Economic summary: Gross domestic product (1991): $91.1 billion; $17,700 per capita; real growth rate, 2.0%; inflation rate 2.4%; unemployment rate (1991): 10.6%. Arable land: 61%. Principal agricultural products: meat, dairy products, fish, grains. Labor force: 2,581,400. Government services, 30.2%; private services, 36.4%; manufacturing and mining, 20%. Major industrial products: processed foods, machinery and equipment, textiles. Natural resources: crude oil, natural gas, fish, salt, limestone. Exports: $37.8 billion (f.o.b., 1991): meat and dairy products, fish, industrial machinery, chemical products, transportation equipment. Imports: $31.6 billion (c.i.f., 1991): machinery and equipment, transport equipment, petroleum, chemicals, grains and foodstuffs, textiles, paper. Major trading partners: Germany, Sweden, France, U.K., U.S., Norway, Japan.

1. Excluding Faeroe Islands and Greenland.

Geography. Smallest of the Scandinavian countries (half the size of Maine), Denmark occupies the Jutland peninsula, which extends north from Germany between the tips of Norway and Sweden. To the west is the North Sea and to the east the Baltic.

The country also consists of several Baltic islands; the two largest are Sjaelland, the site of Copenhagen, and Fyn. The narrow waters off the north coast are called the Skagerrak and those off the east, the Kattegat.

Government. Denmark has been a constitutional monarchy since 1849. Legislative power is held jointly by the Sovereign and parliament. The Constitution of 1953 provides for a unicameral parliament called the Folketing, consisting of 179 popularly elected members who serve for four years. The Cabinet is presided over by the Sovereign, who appoints the Prime Minister.

The Sovereign, Queen Margrethe II, was born April 16, 1940, and became Queen—the first in Denmark's history—Jan. 15, 1972, the day after her father, King Frederik IX, died at 72 in the 25th year of his reign. Margrethe was the eldest of his three daughters (by Princess Ingrid of Sweden). The nation's Constitution was amended in 1953 to permit her to succeed her father in the absence of a male heir to the throne. (Denmark was ruled six centuries ago by Margrethe I, but she was never crowned Queen since there was no female right of succession.)

History. Denmark emerged with establishment of the Norwegian dynasty of the Ynglinger in Jutland at the end of the 8th century. Danish mariners played a major role in the raids of the Vikings, or Norsemen, on Western Europe and particularly England. The country was Christianized by St. Ansgar and Harald Blaatand (Bluetooth)—the first Christian king—in the 10th century. Harald's son, Sweyn, conquered England in 1013. His son, Canute the Great, who reigned from 1014 to 1035, united Denmark, England, and Norway under his rule; the southern tip of Sweden was part of Denmark until the 17th century. On Canute's death, civil war tore the country until Waldemar I (1157–82) re-established Danish hegemony over the north.

In 1282, the nobles won the Great Charter, and Eric V was forced to share power with parliament and a Council of Nobles. Waldemar IV (1340–75) restored Danish power, checked only by the Hanseatic League of north German cities allied with ports from Holland to Poland. His daughter, Margrethe, in 1397 united under her rule Denmark, Norway, and Sweden. But Sweden later achieved autonomy and in 1523, under Gustavus I, independence.

Denmark supported Napoleon, for which it was punished at the Congress of Vienna in 1815 by the loss of Norway to Sweden. In 1864, Bismarck, together with the Austrians, made war on the little country as an initial step in the unification of Germany. Denmark was neutral in World War I.

In 1940, Denmark was invaded by the Nazis. King Christian X reluctantly cautioned his countrymen to accept the occupation, but there was widespread resistance against the Nazis. In 1944, Iceland declared its independence from Denmark, ending a union that had existed since 1380.

Liberated by British troops in May 1945, the country staged a fast recovery in both agriculture and manufacturing and was a leader in liberalizing trade. It joined the United Nations in 1945 and NATO in 1949.

Disputes over economic policy led to elections in 1981 that led to Poul Schlüter coming to power in early 1982. Further disputes over his pro-NATO posture led to elections in May, 1988 that marginally confirmed his position.

In a referendum of early June 1992 the voters narrowly rejected the Maastricht accord on European union, which effectively vetoed the treaty.

A second referendum on the accord in May 1993 passed with 56.8 percent of the vote but confidence in European monetary and political unity was waning in other European community countries.

Outlying Territories of Denmark

FAEROE ISLANDS

Status: Autonomous part of Denmark
Chief of State: Queen Margrethe II (1972)
High Commissioner: Bent Klinte
Prime Minister: Atli P. Dam (1991)
Lagmand (President): Jogran Sundstein (1989)
Area: 540 sq mi. (1,399 sq km)
Population (July 1992): 48,588 (average annual growth rate: 0.9%); density per square mile: 90
Capital (est. 1990): Thorshavn, 14,767; **Monetary unit:** Faeroese krone; **Literacy rate:** 99%
Economic summary: Gross domectic product (1989 est.): $662 million, per capita $14,000; real growth rate 3%; inflation (1988) 2%; unemployment (1991 est.) 5–6%. Arable land: 2%; principal agricultural products: sheep, vegetables. Labor force: 17,585, largely engaged in fishing manufacturing, transportation and commerce. Major industrial products: fish, ships, handicrafts. Exports: $386 million (f.o.b., 1990 est.): fish and fish products. Imports: $322 million (c.i.f., 1990 est.): machinery and transport equipment, foodstuffs, petroleum and petroleum products. Major trading partners: Denmark, U.S., U.K., Germany, Canada, France, Japan.

This group of 18 islands, lying in the North Atlantic about 200 miles (322 km) northwest of the Shetland Islands, joined Denmark in 1386 and has since been part of the Danish kingdom. The islands were occupied by British troops during World War II, after the German occupation of Denmark.

The Faeroes have home rule under a bill enacted in 1948; they also have two representatives in the Danish Folketing.

GREENLAND

Status: Autonomous part of Denmark
Chief of State: Queen Margrethe II (1972)
High Commissioner: Bent Klinte
Premier: Lars Emil Johansen (1991)
Area: 840,000 sq mi. (incl. 708,069 sq mi. covered by ice-cap) (2,175,600 sq km)
Population (July 1992): 57,407 (growth rate: 1.1%); density per square mile: 14.6. Ethnic divisions: Greenlander (Eskimos and Greenland-born Caucasians), 86%; Danish, 14%
Capital (1990): Godthaab, 12,217; **Monetary unit:** Krone; **Literacy rate:** 99%
Economic summary: Gross national product (1988): $500 million, per capita $9,000; real growth rate 5%; inflation (1991) 1.6%; unemployment (1990 est.) 9%. Arable land: 0%; principal agricultural products: hay, sheep, garden produce. Labor force: 22,800, largely engaged in fishing, hunting, sheep breeding. Major industries: fish processing, lead and zinc processing, handicrafts. Natural resources: metals, cryolite, iron ore, coal, uranium, fish. Exports: $435 million (f.o.b., 1990 est.): fish and fish products, metalic ores and concentrates. Imports: $420 million (c.i.f., 1990 est.): petroleum and petroleum products, machinery and transport equipment, foodstuffs. Major trading partners: Denmark, U.S., Germany, Sweden, Japan, Norway.

Greenland, the world's largest island, was colonized in 985–86 by Eric the Red. Danish sovereignty, which covered only the west coast, was extended over the whole island in 1917. In 1941 the U.S. signed an agreement with the Danish minister in Washington, placing it under U.S. protection during World War II but maintaining Danish sovereignty. A definitive agreement for the joint defense of Greenland within the framework of NATO was signed in 1951. A large U.S. air base at Thule in the far north was completed in 1953.

Under 1953 amendments to the Danish Constitution, Greenland became part of Denmark, with two representatives in the Danish Folketing. On May 1, 1979, Greenland gained home rule, with its own local parliament (Landsting), replacing the Greenland Provincial Council.

In February 1982, Greenlanders voted to withdraw from the European Community, which they had joined as part of Denmark in 1973. Danish Premier Anker Jørgensen said he would support the request, but with reluctance.

An election in early March 1991 gave the Siumut Party 11 of the 27 available seats. The early election was called after a scandal allegedly involving overspending by government officials on entertainment.

DJIBOUTI

Republic of Djibouti
President: Hassan Gouled Aptidon (1977)
Prime Minister: Barkat Gourad Hamadou (1978)
Area: 8,490 sq mi. (22,000 sq km)
Population (1993): 525,000 (average annual rate of natural increase: 3%); birth rate: 47/1000; infant mortality rate: 117/1000; density per square mile: 54
Capital (1992 est.): Djibouti, 395,000; **Monetary unit:** Djibouti franc; **Languages:** Arabic, French, Afar, Somali; **Religions:** Muslim, 94%; Christian, 6%; **National name:** Jumhouriyya Djibouti; **Literacy rate:** 48%
Economic summary: Gross domestic product (1989 est.): $340 million, $1,030 per capita; real growth rate –1.0%; inflation 3.7%; unemployment over 30%. Arable land: 0%; principal agricultural products: goats, sheep, camels. Labor force: NA. Industries: small-scale enterprises such as dairy products and mineral- water bottling. Exports: $190 million (f.o.b., est. 1990): hides, skins, coffee (in transit from Ethiopia). Imports: $311 million (f.o.b., 1990 est.): petroleum, transport equipment, foodstuffs. Major trading partners: Middle East, Africa, Europe, Bahrain, Asia.

Geography. Djibouti lies in northeastern Africa on the Gulf of Aden at the southern entrance to the Red Sea. It borders on Ethiopia and Somalia. The country, the size of Massachusetts, is mainly a stony desert, with scattered plateaus and highlands.

Government. On May 8, 1977, the population of the French Territory of the Afars and Issas voted by more than 98% for independence. Voters also approved a 65-member interim Constituent Assembly. France transferred sovereignty to the new nation of Djibouti on June 27. Later in the year it became a member of the Organization of African Unity and the Arab League.

History. The territory that is now Djibouti was acquired by France between 1843 and 1886 by treaties with the Somali sultans. Small, arid, and sparsely populated, Djibouti is important chiefly because of the capital city's port, the terminal of the Djibouti-Addis Ababa railway that carries 60% of Ethiopia's foreign trade.

Originally known as French Somaliland, the colony voted in 1958 and 1967 to remain under French rule. It was renamed the Territory of the Afars and Issas in 1967 and took the name of its capital city on attaining independence.

The two principal opposition groups in exile banded to form a common front in early 1990.

A referendum in 1992 approved a new constitution permitting a multiparty system. The general elections in December, however, gave all 65 seats to the ruling Popular Rally for Progress.

DOMINICA

Commonwealth of Dominica
President: Sir Clarence Seignoret (1985)
Prime Minister: Mary Eugenia Charles (1980)
Area: 290 sq mi. (751 sq km)
Population: (est. mid-1993): 100,000 (average annual rate of natural increase: 1.2%); birth rate: 20/1000; infant mortality rate: 18.4/1000; density per square mile: 245
Capital and largest city (est. 1987): Roseau, 22,000; **Monetary unit:** East Caribbean dollar; **Languages:** English and French patois; **Religions:** Roman Catholic, 77%; Protestant, 15%; **Member of Commonwealth of Nations; Literacy rate:** 94%

Economic summary: Gross domestic product (1991): $175.8 million, per capita $2,046; real growth rate 2.1%; inflation 4.7%; unemployment (1989 est.) 10%. Arable land: 9%. Principal products: bananas, citrus fruits, coconuts, plantains. Labor force: 30,600 (1989); 32% in industry and commerce. Major industries: agricultural processing; tourism. Exports: $59.9 million (f.o.b., 1990): bananas, coconuts, soap, pre-fab buildings. Imports: $103.9 million (c.i.f., 1990): manufactured goods classified chiefly by materials. Major trading partners: U.K., Caribbean countries, U.S.

Geography. Dominica is an island of the Lesser Antilles in the Caribbean south of Guadeloupe and north of Martinique.

Government. Dominica is a republic, with a president elected by the House of Assembly as head of state and a prime minister appointed by the president on the advice of the Assembly. The Freedom Party (11 of 21 seats in the Assembly) is led by Prime Minister Mary Eugenia Charles. The Opposition United Workers Party holds six seats and the United Dominica Labor Party holds four seats.

History. Visited by Columbus in 1493, Dominica was claimed by Britain and France until 1815, when Britain asserted sovereignty. Dominica, along with other Windward Isles, became a self-governing member of the West Indies Associated States in free association with Britain in 1967.

Dissatisfaction over the slow pace of reconstruction after Hurricane David struck the island in September 1979 brought a landslide victory for the Freedom Party in July 1980. The vote gave the prime ministership to Mary Eugenia Charles, a strong advocate of free enterprise. The Freedom Party won again in 1985 elections, giving Miss Charles a second five-year term as prime minister. She and her party won a third term in elections on May 28, 1990, though with a greatly reduced mandate.

In 1992 the issue of granting citizenship to foreign businessmen in order to promote investment from abroad became divisive and led to demonstrations.

DOMINICAN REPUBLIC

President: Joaquin Balaguer (1986)
Vice President: Carlos Morales Troncoso (1986)
Area: 18,704 sq mi. (48,442 sq km)
Population (est. mid-1993): 7,600,000 (average annual rate of natural increase: 2.2%); birth rate: 28/1000; infant mortality rate: 43/1000; density per square mile: 408
Capital: Santo Domingo; **Largest cities (1990):** Santo Domingo, 2,200,000; Santiago de los Caballeros, 500,000; **Monetary unit:** Peso; **Language:** Spanish, English widely spoken; **Religion:** 90% Roman Catholic; **National name:** República Dominicana; **Literacy rate:** 83%
Economic summary: Gross domestic product (est. 1991): $7 billion, $950 per capita, –2% real growth rate; inflation rate 9%; unemployment rate (1991 est): 30%. Arable land: 23%. Principal agricultural products: sugar cane, coffee, cocoa, tobacco, beef, fruit and vegetables. Agriculture accounts for 15% of GDP and 49% of labor force. Labor force (1986): 2,300,000–2,600,000; 18% in industry. Major industries: tourism, sugar processing, ferronickel and gold mining, textiles, cement, tobacco. Natural resources: nickel, bauxite, gold, silver. Exports: $775 million (f.o.b., 1991 est.): sugar, coffee, cocoa, gold, ferronickel. Imports: $1.8 billion (c.i.f., 1991 est.): foodstuffs, petroleum, cotton and fabrics, chemicals, and pharmaceuticals. Major trading partners: U.S., including Puerto Rico.

Geography. The Dominican Republic in the West Indies, occupies the eastern two thirds of the island of Hispaniola, which it shares with Haiti. Its area equals that of Vermont and New Hampshire combined.

Crossed from northwest to southeast by a mountain range with elevations exceeding 10,000 feet (3,048 m), the country has fertile, well-watered land in the north and east, where nearly two thirds of the population lives. The southwest part is arid and has poor soil, except around Santo Domingo.

Government. The president is elected by direct vote every four years. Legislative powers rest with a Senate and a Chamber of Deputies, both elected by direct vote, also for four years. All citizens must vote when they reach 18 years of age, or even earlier if they are married.

History. The Dominican Republic was discovered by Columbus in 1492. He named it La Española, and his son, Diego, was its first viceroy. The capital, Santo Domingo, founded in 1496, is the oldest European settlement in the Western Hemisphere. Spain ceded the colony to France in 1795, and Haitian blacks under Toussaint L'Ouverture conquered it in 1801.

In 1808 the people revolted and the next year captured Santo Domingo, setting up the first republic. Spain regained title to the colony in 1814. In 1821 the people overthrew Spanish rule, but in 1822 they were reconquered by the Haitians. They revolted again in 1844, threw out the Haitians, and established the Dominican Republic, headed by Pedro Santana. Uprisings and Haitian attacks led Santana to make the country a province of Spain from 1861 to 1865. The U.S. Senate refused to ratify a treaty of annexation. Disorder continued until the dictatorship of Ulíses Heureaux; in 1916, when disorder broke out again, the U.S. sent in a contingent of marines, who remained until 1934.

A sergeant in the Dominican army trained by the marines, Rafaél Leonides Trujillo Molina, overthrew Horacio Vásquez in 1930 and established a dictatorship that lasted until his assassination 31 years later.

Leftists rebelled April 24, 1965, and President Lyndon Johnson sent in marines and troops. After an OAS ceasefire request May 6, a compromise installed Hector Garcia-Godoy as provisional president. Joaquin Balaguer won in free elections in 1966 against Bosch, and a peacekeeping force of 9,000 U.S. troops and 2,000 from other countries withdrew. Balaguer restored political and economic stability.

In 1978, the army suspended the counting of ballots when Balaguer trailed in a fourth-term bid. After a warning from President Jimmy Carter, however, Balaguer accepted the victory of Antonio Guzmán of the opposition Dominican Revolutionary Party.

Salvador Jorge Blanco of the Dominican Revolutionary Party was elected President on May 16, 1982, defeating Balaguer and Bosch. Austerity measures imposed by the International Monetary Fund, including sharply higher prices for food and gasoline, provoked rioting in the spring of 1984 that left more than 50 dead.

Saying he feared they would provoke "some kind of revolution," Blanco dragged his feet about putting into effect further IMF demands for higher prices and taxes and devaluation of the peso, and came within weeks of defaulting on several big loans.

Balaguer was elected President in May 1986 and aimed economic policy at diversifying the economy. On May 16, 1990 Balaguer won a sixth presidential term in elections following a non-violent campaign.

A new Labour Code was signed into law in 1992 and led to a split in the opposition Dominican Liberation Party over the issue. The disaffected elements formed a new party, the Alliance for Democracy, although they said they would back a coalition to oppose the president's reelection.

ECUADOR

Republic of Ecuador
President: Sixto Durán Ballén (1992)
Area: 106,927 sq mi. (276,840 sq km)
Population (est. mid-1993): 10,300,000 (average annual rate of natural increase: 2.5%); birth rate: 31/1000; infant mortality rate: 53/1000; density per square mile: 96
Capital: Quito
Largest cities (1992): Guayaquil, 1,475,118; Quito, 1,094,318; Cuenca, 195,738
Monetary unit: Sucre
Languages: Spanish (by 90% of population), Quéchua
Religion: Roman Catholic, 95%
National name: República del Ecuador
Literacy rate: 92%
Economic summary: Gross domestic product (1991). $11.5 billion, per capita $1,070; real growth rate 2.5%; inflation 49%; unemployment 8%. Arable land: 6%; principal agricultural products: bananas, cocoa, coffee, sugar cane, manioc, plantains, potatoes, rice. Labor force (1982): 2,800,000; 21% in manufacturing; major industries: food processing, textiles, chemicals, fishing, timber, petroleum. Exports: $2.9 billion (f.o.b., 1991): petroleum, coffee, bananas, cocoa products, shrimp, fish products. Imports: $1.95 billion (f.o.b., 1991): transport equipment, vehicles, machinery, chemicals, petroleum. Major trading partners: U.S., Latin America, EEC, Caribbean, Japan.

Geography. Ecuador, about equal in area to Nevada, is in the northwest part of South America fronting on the Pacific. To the north is Colombia and to the east and south is Peru. Two high and parallel ranges of the Andes, traversing the country from north to south, are topped by tall volcanic peaks. The highest is Chimborazo at 20,577 feet (6,272 m).

The Galápagos Islands (or Colón Archipelago) (3,029 sq mi.; 7,845 sq km), in the Pacific Ocean about 600 miles (966 km) west of the South American mainland, became part of Ecuador in 1832.

Government. A 1978 Constitution returned Ecuador to civilian government after eight years of military rule. The President is elected to a term of four years and a House of Representatives of 71 members is popularly elected for the same period.

History. The tribes in the northern highlands of Ecuador formed the Kingdom of Quito around A.D. 1000. It was absorbed, by conquest and marriage, into the Inca Empire. Pizarro conquered the land in 1532, and through the 17th century a thriving colony was built by exploitation of the Indians. The first revolt against Spain occurred in 1809. Ecuador then joined Venezuela, Colombia, and Panama in a confederacy known as Greater Colombia.

On the collapse of this union in 1830, Ecuador became independent. Subsequent history was one of revolts and dictatorships; it had 48 presidents during the first 131 years of the republic. Conservatives ruled until the Revolution of 1895 ushered in nearly a half century of Radical Liberal rule, during which the church was disestablished and freedom of worship, speech, and press was introduced.

In 1988, Rodrigo Borja was elected President. He was also able to form a coalition in the House, confirming a leftward shift in the government and promising smoother executive-legislative relations.

Blamed for econommic conditions the governing Social Democrats were defeated in elections of May 1992 by right-wing parties promising free-market reforms.

In the runoff presidential election of July 5, 1992 Sixto Duran Ballen captured 58% of the vote. A devaluation of the currency and the elimination of energy price subsidies led to a national strike in September.

Ecuador withdrew from the OPEC oil cartel in November 1992 citing what it considered exorbitant dues.

EGYPT

Arab Republic of Egypt
President: Hosni Mubarak (1981)
Premier: Dr. Atef Sedky (1986)
Area: 386,900 sq. mi. (1,002,000 sq km)
Population (est. mid-1993): 58,300,000 (average annual rate of natural increase: 2.3%); birth rate: 31/1000; infant mortality rate: 56/1000; density per square mile: 152
Capital: Cairo; **Largest cities (est. 1990):** City of Cairo, 6,513,000; Greater Cairo, 12,560,000; Alexandria, 3,183,000; (est 1987): Giza, 1,670,800; Shubra el Khema, 533,300; El Mahalla el Kubra, 385,300; **Monetary unit:** Egyptian pound; **Language:** Arabic; **Religions:** Islam, 94%; Christian (mostly Coptic), 6%; **Literacy rate:** 50.2%
Economic summary: Gross domestic product (1991): $39.2 billion; $720 per capita; 2% real growth rate; inflation rate 17%; unemployment rate (est. 1991): 15%. Arable land: 3%. Principal agricultural products: cotton, wheat, rice, corn, beans. Labor force: 15,000,000; 20% in privately owned services and manufacturing. Major industries: textiles, food processing, tourism, chemicals, petroleum, construction, cement, metals. Natural resources: crude oil, natural gas, iron ore, phosphates, manganese, limestone, gypsum, talc, asbestos, lead, zinc. Exports: $4.5 billion (f.o.b., 1991 est.): cotton, petroleum, yarn, textiles. Imports: $11.7 billion (f.o.b., 1991 est.): foodstuffs, machinery, fertilizers, woods. Major trading partners: U.S., Western Europe, Japan, Eastern Europe.

Geography. Egypt, at the northeast corner of Africa on the Mediterranean Sea, is bordered on the west by Libya, on the south by the Sudan, and on the east by the Red Sea and Israel. It is nearly one and one half times the size of Texas.

The historic Nile flows through the eastern third of the country. On either side of the Nile valley are desert plateaus, spotted with oases. In the north, toward the Mediterranean, plateaus are low, while south of Cairo they rise to a maximum of 1,015 feet (309 m) above sea level. At the head of the Red Sea is the Sinai Peninsula, between the Suez Canal and Israel.

Navigable throughout its course in Egypt, the Nile is used largely as a means of cheap transport for heavy goods. The principal port is Alexandria.

The Nile delta starts 100 miles (161 km) south of the Mediterranean and fans out to a sea front of 155 miles between the cities of Alexandria and Port Said. From Cairo north, the Nile branches into many streams, the principal ones being the Damietta and the Rosetta.

Except for a narrow belt along the Mediterranean, Egypt lies in an almost rainless area, in which high daytime temperatures fall quickly at night.

Government. Executive power is held by the President, who is elected every six years and can appoint one or more Vice Presidents.

The National Democratic Party, led by President Hosni Mubarak, is the dominant political party. Elections on Nov. 29, 1990 confirmed its huge majority. There is also one opposition party and some independents in the parliament—there are a total of 12 parties actively engaged in the political process.

History. Egyptian history dates back to about 4000 B.C., when the kingdoms of upper and lower Egypt, already highly civilized, were united. Egypt's "Golden Age" coincided with the 18th and 19th dynasties (16th to 13th centuries B.C.), during which the empire was established. Persia conquered Egypt in 525 B.C.; Alexander the Great subdued it in 332 B.C.; and then the dynasty of the Ptolemies ruled the land until 30 B.C., when Cleopatra, last of the line, committed suicide and Egypt became a Roman province. From 641 to 1517 the Arab caliphs ruled Egypt, and then the Turks took it for their Ottoman Empire.

Napoleon's armies occupied the country from 1798 to 1801. In 1805, Mohammed Ali, leader of a band of Albanian soldiers, became Pasha of Egypt. After completion of the Suez Canal in 1869, the French and British took increasing interest in Egypt.

British troops occupied Egypt in 1882, and British resident agents became its actual administrators, though it remained under nominal Turkish sovereignty. In 1914, this fiction was ended, and Egypt became a protectorate of Britain.

Egyptian nationalism forced Britain to declare Egypt an independent, sovereign state on Feb. 28, 1922, although the British reserved rights for the protection of the Suez Canal and the defense of Egypt. In 1936, by an Anglo-Egyptian treaty of alliance, all British troops and officials were to be withdrawn, except from the Suez Canal Zone. When World War II started, Egypt remained neutral. British imperial troops finally ended the Nazi threat to Suez in 1942 in the battle of El Alamein, west of Alexandria.

In 1951, Egypt abrogated the 1936 treaty and the 1899 Anglo-Egyptian condominium of the Sudan (*See* Sudan). Rioting and attacks on British troops in the Suez Canal Zone followed, reaching a climax in January 1952. The army, led by Gen. Mohammed Naguib, seized power on July 23, 1952. Three days later, King Farouk abdicated in favor of his infant son. The monarchy was abolished and a republic proclaimed on June 18, 1953, with Naguib holding the posts of Provisional President and Premier. He relinquished the latter in 1954 to Gamal Abdel Nasser, leader of the ruling military junta. Naguib was deposed seven months later and Nasser confirmed as President in a referendum on June 23, 1956.

Nasser's policies embroiled his country in continual conflict. In 1956, the U.S. and Britain withdrew their pledges of financial aid for the building of the Aswan High Dam. In reply, Nasser nationalized the Suez Canal and expelled British oil and embassy officials. Israel, barred from the Canal and exasperated by terrorist raids, invaded the Gaza Strip and the Sinai Peninsula. Britain and France, after demanding Egyptian evacuation of the Canal Zone, attacked Egypt on Oct. 31, 1956. Worldwide pressure forced Britain, France, and Israel to halt the hostilities. A U.N. emergency force occupied the Canal Zone, and all troops were evacuated in the spring of 1957.

On June 5, 1967, Israel invaded the Sinai Peninsula, the East Bank of the Jordan River, and the zone around the Gulf of Aqaba. A U.N. ceasefire on June 10 saved the Arabs from complete rout.

Nasser declared the 1967 cease-fire void along the Canal in April 1969 and began a war of attrition. The U.S. peace plan of June 19, 1970, resulted in Egypt's agreement to reinstate the cease-fire for at least three months, (from August) and to accept Israel's existence within "recognized and secure" frontiers that might emerge from U.N.-mediated talks. In return, Israel accepted the principle of withdrawing from occupied territories.

Then, on Sept. 28, 1970, Nasser died, at 52, of a heart attack. The new President was Anwar el-Sadat, an associate of Nasser and a former newspaper editor.

In July 1972, Sadat ordered the expulsion of Soviet "advisors and experts" from Egypt because the Russians had not provided the sophisticated weapons he felt were needed to retake territory lost to Israel in 1967.

The fourth Arab-Israeli war broke out Oct. 6, 1973, while Israelis were commemorating Yom Kippur, the Jewish high holy day. Egypt swept deep into the Sinai, while Syria strove to throw Israel off the Golan Heights.

A U.N.-sponsored truce was accepted on October 22. In January 1974, both sides agreed to a settlement negotiated by U.S. Secretary of State Henry A. Kissinger that gave Egypt a narrow strip along the entire Sinai bank of the Suez Canal. In June, President Nixon made the first visit by a U.S. President to Egypt and full diplomatic relations were established. The Suez Canal was cleared and reopened on June 5, 1975.

In the most audacious act of his career, Sadat flew to Jerusalem at the invitation of Prime Minister Menachem Begin and pleaded before Israel's Knesset on Nov. 20, 1977, for a permanent peace settlement. The Arab world reacted with fury—only Morocco, Tunisia, Sudan, and Oman approved.

Egypt and Israel signed a formal peace treaty on March 26, 1979. The pact ended 30 years of war and established diplomatic and commercial relations.

Egyptian and Israeli officials met in the Sinai desert on April 26, 1979, to implement the peace treaty calling for the phased withdrawal of occupation forces from the peninsula. By mid-1980, two thirds of the Sinai was transferred, but progress here was not matched—the negotiation of Arab autonomy in the Gaza Strip and the West Bank.

Sadat halted further talks in August 1980 because of continued Israeli settlement of the West Bank. On October 6 1981, Sadat was assassinated by extremist Muslim soldiers at a parade in Cairo. Vice President Hosni Mubarak, a former Air Force chief of staff, was confirmed by the parliament as president the next day.

Although feared unrest in Egypt did not occur in the wake of the assassination, and Israel completed the return of the Sinai to Egyptian control on April 25, 1982, Mubarak was unable to revive the autonomy talks. Israel's invasion of Lebanon in June imposed a new strain on him, and brought a marked cooling in Egyptian-Israeli relations, but not a disavowal of the peace treaty.

While President Mubarak's stand during the Persian Gulf war won wide praise in the West, domestically this position proved far less popular. Nevertheless Egypt emerged with new clout and respect in the international community as evidenced by the election of the Deputy Prime Minister as secretary-general of the U.N., which further contributed to the country's international prestige.

During 1991 Egypt pressed ahead with economic reforms promised in exchange for IMF assistance. For its stance during the Gulf War Egypt's almost 56 billion military debt to the U.S. was written off.

The government in 1993 continued its crackdown on the extremist Islamic movement announcing the first execution on charges of terrorism of a member since 1982.

Suez Canal. The Suez Canal, in Egyptian territory between the Arabian Desert and the Sinai Peninsula, is an artificial waterway about 100 miles (161 km) long between Port Said on the Mediterranean and Suez on the Red Sea. Construction work, directed by the French engineer Ferdinand de Lesseps, was begun April 25, 1859, and the Canal was opened Nov. 17, 1869. The cost was 432,807,882 francs. The concession was held by an Egyptian joint stock company, *Compagnie Universelle du Canal Maritime de Suez,* in which the British government held 353,504 out of a total of 800,000 shares. The concession was to expire Nov. 17, 1968, but the company was nationalized July 26, 1956, by unilateral action of the Egyptian government.

The Canal was closed in June 1967 after the Arab-Israeli conflict. With the help of the U.S. Navy, work was begun on clearing the Canal in 1974, after the cease-fire ending the Arab-Israeli war. It was reopened to traffic June 5, 1975.

The government in 1993 continued its crackdown on the extremist Islamic movement announcing the first execution on charges of terrorism of a member since 1982.

EL SALVADOR

Republic of El Salvador
President: Alfredo Cristiani (1989)
Area: 8,260 sq mi. (21,393 sq km)
Population (est. mid-1993): 5,200,000 (average annual rate of natural increase: 2.6%); birth rate: 34/1000; infant mortality rate: 53/1000; density per square mile: 644
Capital: San Salvador; **Largest cities (est. 1987):** San Salvador, 477,959; Santa Ana, 144,835; Mejicanos, 95,919; San Miguel, 92,891; **Monetary unit:** Colón; **Language:** Spanish; **Religion:** Roman Catholic; **National name:** República de El Salvador; **Literacy rate:** 73%
Economic summary: Gross domestic product (1991 est.): $5.5 billion; $1,010 per capita; real growth rate 3%; inflation 19%; unemployment (1989) 10%. Arable land: 27%. Principal agricultural products: coffee, cotton, corn, sugar, rice, sorghum. Labor force: 1,700,000; 40% in agriculture. Major industrial products: processed foods, clothing and textiles, petroleum products. Natural resources: hydro- and geothermal power, crude oil. Exports: $580 million (f.o.b., 1990 est.): coffee, cotton, sugar, shrimp. Imports: $1.2 billion (c.i.f., 1990 est.): machinery, construction materials, petroleum, foodstuffs, fertilizer. Major trading partners: U.S., Guatemala, Japan, Germany, Mexico, Venezuela, Costa Rica.

Geography. Situated on the Pacific coast of Central America, El Salvador has Guatemala to the west and Honduras to the north and east. It is the smallest of the Central American countries, its area equal to that of Massachusetts, and the only one without an Atlantic coastline.

Most of the country is a fertile volcanic plateau about 2,000 feet (607 m) high. There are some active volcanoes and many scenic crater lakes.

Government. The President is elected for a nonrenewable, five-year term, and legislative power is in a unicameral 84-member National Assembly elected by universal suffrage and proportional representation.

History. Pedro de Alvarado, a lieutenant of Cortés, conquered El Salvador in 1525. El Salvador, with the other countries of Central America, declared its independence from Spain on Sept. 15, 1821, and was part of a federation of Central American states until that union was dissolved in 1838. Its independent career for decades thereafter was marked by numerous revolutions and wars against other Central American republics.

On Oct. 15, 1979, a junta deposed the President, Gen. Carlos Humberto Romero, seeking to halt increasingly violent clashes between leftist and rightist forces.

On Dec. 4, 1980, three American nuns and an American lay worker were killed in an ambush near San Salvador, causing the Carter Administration to suspend all aid pending an investigation. The naming of José Napoleón Duarte, a moderate civilian, as head of the governing junta brought a resumption of U.S. aid.

In an election closely monitored by American and other foreign observers, Duarte was elected President in May 1984.

Duarte's Christian Democratic Party scored an unexpected electoral triumph in national legislative and municipal elections held in March 1985, a winning majority in the new National Assembly. The rightist parties that had been dominant in the previous Constituent Assembly demanded that the vote be nullified, but the army high command rejected their assertion that the voting had been fraudulent.

At the same time, U.S. officials said that while the rebels still were far from being defeated, there had been marked improvement in the effectiveness of government troops in the civil war against anti-government guerrillas that has been waged mainly in the countryside. Talks with the rebels broke down in September 1986. Duarte's inability to find solutions led to the rightwing ARENA party controlling half the seats in the National Assembly, in the elections of March, 1988. The decisive victory of Alfredo Cristiani, the ARENA candidate for president, gives the right-wing party effective control of the country, given their political control of most of the municipalities.

On January 16, 1992 the government signed a peace treaty with the guerrilla forces formally ending a 12-year civil war that had claimed 75,000 lives. Under the terms of the treaty each side was expected to make significant concessions.

Demobilization of the guerrilla forces proceeded, though slowly on the grounds that the government was failing to meet its obligations. On December 14 the completion of the demobilization was marked with a ceremony in San Salvador.

EQUATORIAL GUINEA

Republic of Equatorial Guinea
President: Col. Teodoro Obiang Nguema Mbasogo (1979)
Prime Minister: Don Silvestre Siale Bileka (1992)
Area: 10,830 sq mi. (28,051 sq km)
Population (est. mid-1993): 400,000 (average annual rate of natural increase: 2.6%); birth rate: 43/1000; infant mortality rate: 112/1000; density per square mile: 35
Capital and largest city (1983): Malabo, 30,418; **Monetary unit:** CFA Franc; **Languages:** Spanish (official), pidgin English, Fang, Bubi, Creole; **Religions:** Roman Catholic, Protestant, traditional; **National name:** Républica de Guinea Ecuatorial; **Literacy rate:** 50%
Economic summary: Gross domestic product (1988 est.): $156 million; $400 per capita. Arable land: 8%. Principal products: cocoa, wood, coffee, rice, yams. Natural resources: wood, crude oil. Exports: $37 million (f.o.b., 1990 est.): cocoa, wood, coffee. Imports: $68.3 million (c.i.f., 1990): petroleum, foodstuffs, textiles, machinery. Major trading partners: Spain, Italy, France, the Netherlands, Germany.

Geography. Equatorial Guinea, formerly Spanish Guinea, consists of Rio Muni (10,045 sq mi.; 26,117 sq km), on the western coast of Africa, and several islands in the Gulf of Guinea, the largest of which is Bioko (formerly Fernando Po) (785 sq mi.; 2,033 sq km). The other islands are Annobón, Corisco, Elobey Grande, and Elobey Chico. The total area is twice that of Connecticut.

Government. A Supreme Military Council, headed by the president, exercises all power. Political parties were banned until May 1982.

History. Fernando Po and Annobón came under Spanish control in 1778. From 1827 to 1844, with Spanish consent, Britain administered Fernando Po, but in the latter year Spain reclaimed the island. Río Muni was given to Spain in 1885 by the Treaty of Berlin.

Negotiations with Spain led to independence on Oct. 12, 1968.

In 1969, anti-Spanish incidents in Río Muni, including the tearing down of a Spanish flag by national troops, caused 5,000 Spanish residents to flee for their safety, and diplomatic relations between the two nations became strained. A month later, President Masie Nguema Biyogo Negue Ndong charged that a coup had been attempted against him. He seized dictatorial powers and arrested 80 opposition politicians and even several of his Cabinet ministers and the secretary of the National Assembly.

A coup on Aug. 3, 1979, deposed Masie, and a junta led by Lieut. Col. Teodoro Obiang Nguema Mbasogo took over the government. Obiang expelled Soviet technicians and reinstated cooperation with Spain.

In January 1992 the president established a transitional government toward a supposedly multiparty system. However, in successive months a number of opposition figures were arrested and one beaten to death. Some activists then called for foreign intervention to oust the government.

ERITREA

President: Isaias Afewerki (1993)
Area: 36,170 sq mi. (93,679 sq km)
Population (est. 1992): 3,317,611
Capital and largest city (1988): Asmara, 344,101. Other major cities: the ports of Massawa and Assab; **Monetary unit:** Birr. **Languages:** Tigrinya and Amharic. **Major religions:** Muslim and Christian Ethiopian Orthodox. **Literacy rate:** 62%.
Economic summary: The economy and infrastructure were severely damaged by the long civil war and natural disasters. It is estimated that massive aid in excess of $2 billion is needed from the international community to rebuild the country. Major manufacturing industries are textiles, leather, and food products. Most Eritreans are employed in agriculture and important crops are cotton, wheat, and coffee. Major mineral resources are salt and copper. There is potential for the development of a fishing industry. Important trading partners are Italy, Germany, U.S., and the U.K.

Geography. Eritrea was formerly the northernmost province of Ethiopia and is about the size of Indiana. Much of the country is mountainous. Its narrow Red Sea coastal plain is one of the hottest and driest places in Africa. The cooler central highlands have fertile valleys that support agriculture. Eritrea is bordered by the Sudan on the north and west, the Red Sea on the north and east, and Ethiopia and Djibouti on the south. The country controls land-locked Ethiopia's only access to the Red Sea.

Government. A transitional government committed to a democratic system.

History. Eritrea was part of the first Ethiopian kingdom of Askum until its decline in the 8th century A.D. It came under control of the Ottoman Empire in the 16th century, and later the Egyptians. The Italians captured the coastal areas in 1885, and the Treaty of Uccialli (May 2, 1889) gave Italy sovereignty over part of Eritrea. The Italians named their colony after the Roman name for the Red Sea—*Mare Erythraeum*—and ruled it up until World War II.

The British captured Eritrea in 1941 and later administered it as a U.N. Trust Territory until it became federated with Ethiopia on Sept. 15, 1952. It was made an Ethiopian province on Nov. 14, 1962.

A civil war broke out against the Ethiopian government led by rebel groups who opposed the union and wanted independence for Eritrea. The bitter conflict raged on for 17 years against the hard-line communist regime of the Ethiopian dictator, Mengistu Haile Mariam until he was overthrown in May 1991.

The Eritrean People's Liberation Front (EPLF) took control of Eritrea and shared power in a multi-party government in Addis Ababa with the Ethiopian People's Revolutionary Democratic Front (EPRDF). They agreed to hold a referendum on Eritrean independence within two years and on April 23–25, 1993, Eritrean voters almost unanimously opted for an independent republic. Ethiopia recognized Eritrea's sovereignty on May 3, 1993, and sought a new era of cooperation between the two countries.

ESTONIA

Republic of Estonia
President: Lennart Meri (1992)
Prime Minister: Mart Laar (1992)
Area: 18,370 sq mi. (47,549 sq km)
Population: (est. mid-1993): 1,600,000 (average annual rate of natural increase: 0%); (Estonians, 61.5%;

Russians, 30.3%; Ukrainians, 3.1%; Byelorussians, 1.8%; Finns, 1.1%); birth rate: 12/1000; infant mortality rate: 14/1000; density per square mile: 89

Capital and largest city (1991): Tallinn, 500,000. Other important cities: Tartu, Kohtla-Järve, Narva, and Pärnu; **Monetary unit:** Kroon; **Languages:** Estonian is official; also Russian; **Religions (1937):** Lutheran, 78%; Orthodox, 19%; **National name:** Eesti; **Literacy:** (n.a., there was a 100% literacy rate before the Soviet occupation)

Economic summary: Gross national product, n.a.; per capita GNP (1991): $3,830; real growth rate (1992): –11%. Labor force (1990): 796,000, industry and construction, 42%; agriculture and forestry, 13%. Estonia is suffering through a difficult transitional period—between a collapsed command economic structure and a still-to-be-built market structure. Exports: $186 million (f.o.b., 1990): machinery, 30%; food, 17%; chemicals, 11%; electric power, 9%. Imports $1.2 billion (c.i.f., 1990): machinery, 45%; oil, 13%; chemicals, 12%. Trades with over 93 countries.

Geography. Estonia borders on the Baltic Sea in the west, the gulfs of Riga and Finland in the southwest and north, respectively, Latvia in the south, and Russia in the east. It is mainly a lowland country with numerous lakes. Lake Peipus is the largest and is important to the fishing and shipping industries.

Government. Parliamentary democracy.

History. Born out of World War I, this small Baltic state enjoyed a mere two short decades of independence before it was absorbed again by its powerful neighbor, Russia. In the 13th century, the Estonians had been conquered by the Teutonic Knights of Germany, who reduced them to serfdom. In 1526, the Swedes took over, and the power of the German (Balt) landowning class was curbed somewhat. But after 1721, when Russia succeeded Sweden as the ruling power, the Estonians were subjected to a double bondage—the Balts and the tsarist officials. The oppression lasted until the closing months of World War I, when Estonia finally achieved independence after a victorious War of Independence (1918–20).

Shortly after the start of World War II, the nation was occupied by Russian troops and was incorporated as the 16th republic of the U.S.S.R. in 1940. Germany occupied the nation from 1941 to 1944, when it was retaken by the Russians.

Soon after Lithuania's declaration of independence from the Soviet Union in March 1990, the Estonian congress renamed its country on May 8 and omitted the words "Soviet Socialist" and adopted the former (1918) Coat of Arms of the Republic of Estonia. Thereafter, the government cautiously promoted national autonomy.

After the attempted Soviet coup to remove President Gorbachev failed, Estonia formally declared its independence from the U.S.S.R. on August 20, 1991. Recognition by European and other countries followed. The Soviet Union recognized Estonia's independence on September 6 and it received UN membership on Sept. 17, 1991.

Despite rampant inflation and a falling GDP the first free elections took place in September 1992 giving a slight majority to right-wing parties. Only Estonians were allowed to vote, excluding 38% of the population, who are chiefly ethnic Russians.

ETHIOPIA

Transitional Government of Ethiopia

President: Meles Zenawi (1991)

Prime Minister: Tamirat Laynie (1991)

Area: 446,952 sq mi. (1,157,585 sq km)

Population (est. mid-1993): 56,700,000 (average annual rate of natural increase: 2.8%); birth rate: 47/1000; infant mortality rate: 127/1000; density per square mile: 133

Capital and largest city (est. 1986): Addis Ababa, 1,495,266; **Monetary unit:** Birr; **Languages:** Amharic (official), English, Orominga, Tigrigna; **Religions:** Ethiopian Orthodox, 35–40%; Islam, 40–45%; animist, 15-20%; other, 5%; **Literacy rate:** 62%

Economic summary: Gross domestic product (FY90 est.): $6.6 billion; $130 per capita; real growth rate –0.4%; inflation (1989): 5.2%. Arable land: 12%. Principal agricultural products: coffee, barley, wheat, corn, sugar cane, cotton, oilseeds, livestock. Major industrial products: cement, textiles, processed foods, refined oil. Natural resources: potash, gold, platinum, copper. Exports: $780 million (f.o.b., 1991): coffee, hides and skins, oilseeds. Imports: $2.2 billion (c.i.f., 1990): petroleum, foodstuffs. Major trading partners: C.I.S. countries, U.S., Germany, Italy, Japan, Djibouti, South Yemen, France, Saudi Arabia.

Geography. Ethiopia is in east central Africa, bordered on the west by the Sudan, the east by Somalia and Djibouti, the south by Kenya, and northeast by Eritrea. It is nearly three times the size of California.

Over its main plateau land, Ethiopia has several high mountains, the highest of which is Ras Dashan at 15,158 feet (4,620 m). The Blue Nile, or Abbai, rises in the northwest and flows in a great semicircle east, south, and northwest before entering the Sudan. Its chief reservoir, Lake Tana, lies in the northwestern part of the plateau.

Government. A transitional government committed to a democratic system. A new constitution is being written and national elections will be held in 1994.

History. Black Africa's oldest state, Ethiopia can trace 2,000 years of recorded history. Its now deposed royal line claimed descent from King Menelik I, traditionally believed to have been the son of the Queen of Sheba and King Solomon. The present nation is a consolidation of smaller kingdoms that owed feudal allegiance to the Ethiopian Emperor.

Hamitic peoples migrated to Ethiopia from Asia Minor in prehistoric times. Semitic traders from Arabia penetrated the region in the 7th century B.C. Its Red Sea ports were important to the Roman and Byzantine Empires. Coptic Christianity came to the country in A.D. 341, and a variant of that communion became Ethiopia's state religion.

Ancient Ethiopia reached its peak in the 5th century, then was isolated by the rise of Islam and weakened by feudal wars. Modern Ethiopia emerged under Emperor Menelik II, who established its independence by routing an Italian invasion in 1896. He expanded Ethiopia by conquest.

Disorders that followed Menelik's death brought his daughter to the throne in 1917, with his cousin, Tafari Makonnen, as Regent, heir presumptive, and strongman. When the Empress died in 1930, Tafari was crowned Emperor Haile Selassie I.

As Regent, Haile Selassie outlawed slavery. As Emperor, he worked for centralization of his diffuse realm, in which 70 languages are spoken, and for moderate reform. In 1931, he granted a Constitution, revised in 1955, that created a parliament with an appointed Senate and an elected Chamber of Deputies, and a system of courts. But basic power remained with the Emperor.

Bent on colonial empire, fascist Italy invaded Ethiopia on Oct. 3, 1935, forcing Haile Selassie into exile in May 1936. Ethiopia was annexed to Eritrea, then an Italian colony, and Italian Somaliland to form Italian East Africa, losing its independence for the first time in recorded history. In 1941, British troops routed the Italians, and Haile Selassie returned to Addis Ababa.

In August 1974, the Armed Forces Committee nationalized Haile Selassie's palace and estates and directed him not to leave Addis Ababa. On Sept. 12, 1974, he was deposed after nearly 58 years as Regent and Emperor. The 82-year-old "Lion of Judah" was placed under guard. Parliament was dissolved, the Constitution suspended and Ethiopia was proclaimed a socialist state.

On Aug. 27, 1975, Haile Selassie died in a small apartment in his former Addis Ababa palace where he had been treated as a state prisoner. He was 83.

Lt. Col. Mengistu Haile Mariam was named head of state, Feb. 2, 1977, and when a communist regime was established on Sept. 10, 1984, Mengistu became party leader.

A cut-off of Soviet aid led to mass animosity, and a rebel offensive began in February 1991. Mengistu resigned and fled the country in May. A group called the Ethiopian People's Revolutionary Democratic Front seized the capital. Also in May a separatist guerrilla organization, the Eritrean People's Liberation Front, took control of the province of Eritrea. The two groups agreed in early July that Eritrea would have an internationally supervised referendum on independence. This election took place in April 1993 with an almost unanimous support for Eritrean independence. Ethiopia accepted and recognized Eritrea as an independent state within a few days.

FIJI

Republic of Fiji
President: Ratu Sir Penaia Ganilau (1987)
Prime Minister: Maj. Gen. Sitiveni Rabuka (1992)
Area: 7,078 sq mi. (18,333 sq km)
Population (est. mid-1993): 800,000 (average annual rate of natural increase: 2.0%); birth rate: 25/1000; infant mortality rate: 10/1000; density per square mile: 107
Capital (1986): Suva (on Viti Levu), 69,665; **Monetary unit:** Fiji dollar; **Languages:** Fijian, Hindustani, English; **Religions:** Christian, 52%; Hindu, 38%; Islam, 8%; other, 2%; **Literacy rate:** 80%
Economic summary: Gross domestic product (1991): $1.3 billion; $1,700 per capita; real growth rate 3.5%; inflation rate 7.0%; unemployment rate (est. 1991): 5.9%. Arable land: 8%. Principal products: sugar, copra, rice, ginger. Labor force (1987): 235,000; 67% subsistence agriculture; 18% wage earners; salary earners, 15%. Major industrial products: refined sugar, gold, lumber. Natural resources: timber, fish, gold, copper. Exports: $646 million (f.o.b., 1991 est.): sugar, copra, processed fish, lumber. Imports: $840 million (c.i.f., 1991 est.): foodstuffs, machinery, manufactured goods, fuels, chemicals. Major trading partners: U.K., Australia, Japan, New Zealand, U.S.

Geography. Fiji consists of more than 330 islands in the southwestern Pacific Ocean about 1,960 miles (3,152 km) from Sydney, Australia. The two largest islands are Viti Levu (4,109 sq mi.; 10,642 sq km) and Vanua Levu (2,242 sq mi.; 5,807 sq km). The island of Rotuma (18 sq mi.; 47 sq km), about 400 miles (644 km) to the north, is a province of Fiji. Overall, Fiji is nearly as large as New Jersey.

The largest islands in the group are mountainous and volcanic, with the tallest peak being Mount Victoria (4,341 ft; 1,323 m) on Viti Levu. The islands in the south have dense forests on the windward side and grasslands on the leeward.

Government. Military coup leader Major General Sitiveni Rabuka formerly declared Fiji a republic on Oct. 6, 1987. The Sept. 23, 1988 constitution provided for a bicameral parliament consisting of a 342-member Senate and a 70-member House of Representatives.

The new constitution of July 1990 ensured ethnic Fijians a majority of seats in the parliament as well as the presidency, prime ministership and other central positions.

History. In 1874, an offer of cession by the Fijian chiefs was accepted, and Fiji was proclaimed a possession and dependency of the British Crown.

During World War II, the archipelago was an important air and naval station on the route from the U.S. and Hawaii to Australia and New Zealand.

Fiji became independent on Oct. 10, 1970. The next year it joined the five-island South Pacific Forum, which intends to become a permanent regional group to promote collective diplomacy of the newly independent members.

In Oct., 1987, then Brig. Gen. Sitiveni Rabuka, the coup leader, declared Fiji a republic and removed it from the British Commonwealth.

In elections of May 1992 Rabuka, as leader of the Fijian Politial Party, became prime minister.

FINLAND

Republic of Finland
President: Mauno H. Koivisto (1982)
Premier: Esko Aho (1991)
Area: 130,119 sq mi. (337,009 sq km)
Population (est. mid-1993): 5,100,000 (average annual rate of natural increase: 0.3%); birth rate: 13/1000; infant mortality rate: 5.8/1000; density per square mile: 43
Capital: Helsinki; **Largest cities (est. 1992):** Helsinki, 496,300; Tampere, 174,250; Turku, 159,500; Espoo, 175,800; **Monetary unit:** Markka; **Languages:** Finnish, Swedish; **Religions:** Evangelical Lutheran, 90%; Greek Orthodox, 0.1%; **National name:** Suomen Tasavalta—Republiken Finland; **Literacy rate:** 100%
Economic summary: Gross domestic product (1992): $98 billion; $21,678 per capita GDP; inflation rate (1991): 2.9%; unemployment rate (1991): 7.6%). Arable land: 8%. Principal products: dairy and meat products, cereals, sugar beets, potatoes. Labor force: 2,556,000; 22.9% mining and manufacturing. Major products: metal manufactures, forestry and wood products, refined copper, ships, electronics. Natural resource: timber. Exports: $22.9 billion (f.o.b., 1991): timber, paper and pulp, ships, machinery, clothing, footwear. Imports: $21.6 billion (c.i.f., 1991): petroleum and petroleum products, chemicals, transportation equipment, machinery, textile yarns, foodstuffs, fodder grain. Major trading partners: Germany, Sweden, U.K., U.S., France, Japan.

Geography. Finland stretches 700 miles (1,127 km) from the Gulf of Finland on the south to Petsamo, north of the Arctic Circle. Russia extends along the entire eastern frontier while Norway is on her northern border and Sweden lies on her western border. In area, Finland is three times the size of Ohio.

Off the southwest coast are the Aland Islands, controlling the entrance to the Gulf of Bothnia. Finland has more than 200,000 lakes.

The Swedish-populated Aland Islands (581 sq mi.; 1,505 sq km) have an autonomous status under a law passed in 1921.

Government. The president, chosen for six years by popular vote, appoints the Cabinet. The one-chamber Diet, the Eduskunta, consists of 200 members elected for four-year terms by proportional representation.

History. At the end of the 7th century, the Finns came to Finland from their Volga settlements, taking the country from the Lapps, who retreated northward. The Finns' repeated raids on the Scandinavian coast impelled Eric IX, the Swedish King, to conquer the country in 1157 and bring it into contact with Western Christendom. By 1809 the whole of Finland was conquered by Alexander I of Russia, who set up Finland as a Grand Duchy.

The first period of Russification (1809–1905) resulted in a lessening of the powers of the Finnish Diet. The Russian language was made official, and the Finnish military system was superseded by the Russian. The pace of Russification was intensified from 1908 to 1914. When Russian control was weakened as a consequence of the March Revolution of 1917, the Diet on July 20, 1917, proclaimed Finland's independence, which became complete on Dec. 6, 1917.

Finland rejected Soviet territorial demands, and the U.S.S.R. attacked on Nov. 30, 1939. The Finns made an amazing stand of three months and finally capitulated, ceding 16,000 square miles (41,440 sq km) to the U.S.S.R. Under German pressure, the Finns joined the Nazis against Russia in 1941, but were defeated again and ceded the Petsamo area to the U.S.S.R. In 1948, a 20-year treaty of friendship and mutual assistance was signed by the two nations and renewed for another 20 years in 1970.

Premier Mauno Koivisto, leader of the Social Democratic Party, was elected President on Jan. 26, 1982, winning decisively over a conservative rival with support from Finnish Communists.

Elections in March 1991 made the Center Party the largest single party in parliament.

Although the country has set 1995 as the target date for membership in the European Community the latter has said that Finland's agricultural and defense policy could prove to be a major stumbling block. Economically Finland's debt grew and the currency devalued again in September 1992.

FRANCE

French Republic

President: François Mitterrand (1981)

Premier: Édouard Balladur (1993)

Area: 212,918 sq mi. (547,026 sq km)

Population (est. mid-1993): 57,700,000 (average annual rate of natural increase: 0.4%); birth rate: 13/1000; infant mortality rate: 7.3/1000; density per square mile: 272

Capital: Paris; **Largest cities (1990):** Paris, 2,152,000 (10,650,600, Paris region); Marseilles, 801,000; Lyons, 415,000; Toulouse, 359,000; Nice, 342,000; Strasbourg, 252,000; Nantes, 245,000; Bordeaux, 201,000; **Monetary unit:** French Franc; **Language:** French, declining regional dialects; **Religion:** Roman Catholic, 81%; Protestant, 1.7%; Muslim, 5%; Jewish, 1.2%; **National name:** République Française; **Literacy rate:** 99%

Economic summary: Gross domestic product (1991 est.): $1,033.7 billion; $18,300 per capita; 1.4% real growth rate; inflation 3.3%; unemployment (end '91) 9.8%. Arable land: 32%. Principal products: cereals, feed grains, livestock and dairy products, wine, fruits, vegetables, potatoes. Labor force (1987): 24,170,000: services 61.5%, industry 31.3%. Major products: chemicals, automobiles, processed foods, iron and steel, aircraft, textiles, clothing. Natural resources: coal, iron ore, bauxite, fish, forests. Exports: $209.5 billion (f.o.b., 1990): textiles and clothing, chemicals, machinery and transport equipment, agricultural products. Imports: $232.5 billion (c.i.f., 1990): machinery, crude petroleum, chemicals, agricultural products. Major trading partners: Germany, Italy, U.S., Belgium-Luxembourg, U.K., Netherlands.

Geography. France is about 80% the size of Texas. In the Alps near the Italian and Swiss borders is Europe's highest point—Mont Blanc (15,781 ft; 4,810 m). The forest-covered Vosges Mountains are in the northeast, and the Pyrenees are along the Spanish border.

Except for extreme northern France, which is part of the Flanders plain, the country may be described as four river basins and a plateau. Three of the streams flow west—the Seine into the English Channel, the Loire into the Atlantic, and the Garonne into the Bay of Biscay. The Rhône flows south into the Mediterranean. For about 100 miles (161 km), the Rhine is France's eastern border.

West of the Rhône and northeast of the Garonne lies the central plateau, covering about 15% of France's area and rising to a maximum elevation of 6,188 feet (1,886 m). In the Mediterranean, about 115 miles (185 km) east-southeast of Nice, is Corsica (3,367 sq mi.; 8,721 sq km).

Government. The president is elected for seven years by universal suffrage. He appoints the premier, and the Cabinet is responsible to Parliament. The president has the right to dissolve the National Assembly or to ask Parliament for reconsideration of a law. The Parliament consists of two houses: the National Assembly and the Senate.

History. The history of France, as distinct from ancient Gaul, begins with the Treaty of Verdun (843), dividing the territories corresponding roughly to France, Germany, and Italy among the three grandsons of Charlemagne. Julius Caesar had conquered part of Gaul in 57–52 B.C., and it remained Roman until Franks invaded it in the 5th century.

Charles the Bald, inheritor of *Francia Occidentalis,* founded the Carolingian dynasty, which ruled over a kingdom increasingly feudalized. By 987, the crown passed to Hugh Capet, a princeling who controlled only the Ile-de-France, the region surrounding Paris. For 350 years, an unbroken Capetian line added to its domain and consolidated royal authority until the accession in 1328 of Philip VI, first of the Valois line. France was then the most powerful nation in Europe, with a population of 15 million.

Rulers of France

Name	Born	Ruled[1]
CAROLINGIAN DYNASTY		
Pepin the Short	c. 714	751–768
Charlemagne[2]	742	768–814
Louis I the Debonair[3]	778	814–840
Charles I the Bald[4]	823	840–877
Louis II the Stammerer	846	877–879
Louis III[5]	c. 863	879–882
Carloman[5]	?	879–884
Charles II the Fat[6]	839	884–887 [7]
Eudes (Odo), Count of Paris	?	888–898
Charles III the Simple[8]	879	893–923 [9]
Robert I[10]	c. 865	922–923
Rudolf (Raoul), Duke of Burgundy	?	923–936
Louis IV d'Outremer	c. 921	936–954
Lothair	941	954–986
Louis V the Sluggard	c. 967	986–987
CAPETIAN DYNASTY		
Hugh Capet	c. 940	987–996
Robert II the Pious[11]	c. 970	996–1031
Henry I	1008	1031–1060
Philip I	1052	1060–1108
Louis VI the Fat	1081	1108–1137
Louis VII the Young	c.1121	1137–1180
Philip II (Philip Augustus)	1165	1180–1223
Louis VIII the Lion	1187	1223–1226
Louis IX (St. Louis)	1214	1226–1270
Philip III the Bold	1245	1270–1285
Philip IV the Fair	1268	1285–1314
Louis X the Quarreler	1289	1314–1316
John I[12]	1316	1316
Philip V the Tall	1294	1316–1322
Charles IV the Fair	1294	1322–1328
HOUSE OF VALOIS		
Philip VI	1293	1328–1350
John II the Good	1319	1350–1364
Charles V the Wise	1337	1364–1380
Charles VI the Well-Beloved	1368	1380–1422
Charles VII	1403	1422–1461
Louis XI	1423	1461–1483
Charles VIII	1470	1483–1498
Louis XII the Father of the People	1462	1498–1515
Francis I	1494	1515–1547
Henry II	1519	1547–1559
Francis II	1544	1559–1560
Charles IX	1550	1560–1574
Henry III	1551	1574–1589
HOUSE OF BOURBON		
Henry IV of Navarre	1553	1589–1610
Louis XIII	1601	1610–1643
Louis XIV the Great	1638	1643–1715
Louis XV the Well-Beloved	1710	1715–1774
Louis XVI	1754	1774–1792 [13]
Louis XVII (Louis Charles de France)[14]	1785	1793–1795
FIRST REPUBLIC		
National Convention	—	1792–1795
Directory (Directoire)	—	1795–1799
CONSULATE		
Napoleon Bonaparte[15]	1769	1799–1804
FIRST EMPIRE		
Napoleon I	1769	1804–1815 [16]
RESTORATION OF HOUSE OF BOURBON		
Louis XVIII le Désiré	1755	1814–1824
Charles X	1757	1824–1830 [17]
BOURBON-ORLEANS LINE		
Louis Philippe ("Citizen King")	1773	1830–1848 [18]
SECOND REPUBLIC		
Louis Napoleon[19]	1808	1848–1852
SECOND EMPIRE		
Napoleon III (Louis Napoleon)	1808	1852–1870 [20]
THIRD REPUBLIC (PRESIDENTS)		
Louis Adolphe Thiers	1797	1871–1873
Marie E. P. M. de MacMahon	1808	1873–1879
François P. J. Grévy	1807	1879–1887
Sadi Carnot	1837	1887–1894
Jean Casimir-Périer	1847	1894–1895
François Félix Faure	1841	1895–1899
Émile Loubet	1838	1899–1906
Clement Armand Fallières	1841	1906–1913
Raymond Poincaré	1860	1913–1920
Paul E. L. Deschanel	1856	1920–1920
Alexandre Millerand	1859	1920–1924
Gaston Doumergue	1863	1924–1931
Paul Doumer	1857	1931–1932
Albert Lebrun	1871	1932–1940
VICHY GOVERNMENT (CHIEF OF STATE)		
Henri Philippe Pétain	1856	1940–1944
PROVISIONAL GOVERNMENT (PRESIDENTS)		
Charles de Gaulle	1890	1944–1946
Félix Gouin	1884	1946–1946
Georges Bidault	1899	1946–1947
FOURTH REPUBLIC (PRESIDENTS)		
Vincent Auriol	1884	1947–1954
René Coty	1882	1954–1959
FIFTH REPUBLIC (PRESIDENTS)		
Charles de Gaulle	1890	1959–1969
Georges Pompidou	1911	1969–1974
Valéry Giscard d'Estaing	1926	1974–1981
François Mitterrand	1916	1981–

1. For Kings and Emperors through the Second Empire, year of end of rule is also that of death, unless otherwise indicated. 2. Crowned Emperor of the West in 800. His brother, Carloman, ruled as King of the Eastern Franks from 768 until his death in 771. 3. Holy Roman Emperor 814–840. 4. Holy Roman Emperor 875–877 as Charles II. 5. Ruled jointly 879–882. 6. Holy Roman Emperor 881–887 as Charles III. 7. Died 888. 8. King 893–898 in opposition to Eudes. 9. Died 929. 10. Not counted in regular line of Kings of France by some authorities. Elected by nobles but killed in Battle of Soissons. 11. Sometimes called Robert I. 12. Posthumous son of Louis X; lived for only five days. 13. Executed 1793. 14. Titular King only. He died in prison according to official reports, but many pretenders appeared during the Bourbon restoration. 15. As First Consul, Napoleon held the power of government. In 1804, he became Emperor. 16. Abdicated first time June 1814. Re-entered Paris March 1815, after escape from Elba; Louis XVIII fled to Ghent. Abdicated second time June 1815. He named as his successor his son, Napoleon II, who was not acceptable to the Allies. He died 1821. 17. Died 1836. 18. Died 1850. 19. President; became Emperor in 1852. 20. Died 1873.

The missing pieces in Philip's domain were the French provinces still held by the Plantagenet kings of England, who also claimed the French crown. Beginning in 1338, the Hundred Years' War eventually settled the contest. English longbows defeated French armored knights at Crécy (1346) and the English also won the second landmark battle at Agincourt (1415), but the final victory went to the French at Castillon (1453).

Absolute monarchy reached its apogee in the reign of Louis XIV (1643–1715), the Sun King, whose brilliant court was the center of the Western world.

Revolution plunged France into a blood bath beginning in 1789 and ending with a new authoritarianism under Napoleon Bonaparte, who had successfully defended the infant republic from foreign attack and then made himself First Consul in 1799 and Emperor in 1804.

The Congress of Vienna (1815) sought to restore the pre-Napoleonic order in the person of Louis XVIII, but industrialization and the middle class, both fostered under Napoleon, built pressure for change, and a revolution in 1848 drove Louis Phillipe, last of the Bourbons, into exile.

A second republic elected as its president Prince Louis Napoleon, a nephew of Napoleon I, who declared the Second Empire in 1852 and took the throne as Napoleon III. His opposition to the rising power of Prussia ignited the Franco-Prussian War (1870–71), ending in his defeat and abdication.

A new France emerged from World War I as the continent's dominant power. But four years of hostile occupation had reduced northeast France to ruins. The postwar Third Republic was plagued by political instability and economic chaos.

From 1919, French foreign policy aimed at keeping Germany weak through a system of alliances, but it failed to halt the rise of Adolf Hitler and the Nazi war machine. On May 10, 1940, mechanized Nazi troops attacked, and, as they approached Paris, Italy joined with Germany. The Germans marched into an undefended Paris and Marshal Henri Philippe Pétain signed an armistice June 22. France was split into an occupied north and an unoccupied south, the latter becoming a totalitarian state with Pétain as its chief.

Allied armies liberated France in August 1944. The French Committee of National Liberation, formed in Algiers in 1943, established a provisional government in Paris headed by Gen. Charles de Gaulle. The Fourth Republic was born Dec. 24, 1946.

The Empire became the French Union; the National Assembly was strengthened and the presidency weakened; and France joined the North Atlantic Treaty Organization. A war against communist insurgents in Indochina was abandoned after the defeat at Dien Bien Phu. A new rebellion in Algeria threatened a military coup, and on June 1, 1958, the Assembly invited de Gaulle to return as premier with extraordinary powers. He drafted a new Constitution for a Fifth Republic, adopted Sept. 28, which strengthened the presidency and reduced legislative power. He was elected president Dec. 21.

De Gaulle took France out of the NATO military command in 1967 and expelled all foreign-controlled troops from the country. He later went on to attempt to achieve a long-cherished plan of regional reform. This, however, aroused wide opposition. He decided to stake his fate on a referendum. At the voting in April 1969, the electorate defeated the plan.

His successor Georges Pompidou continued the de Gaulle policies of seeking to expand France's influence in the Mideast and Africa.

Socialist François Mitterrand attained a stunning victory in the May 10, 1981, Presidential election over the Gaullist alliance that had held power since 1958.

The victors immediately moved to carry out campaign pledges to nationalize major industries, halt nuclear testing, suspend nuclear power plant construction, and impose new taxes on the rich. On Feb. 11, 1982, the nationalization bills became law.

The Socialists' policies during Mitterrand's first two years created a 12% inflation rate, a huge trade deficit, and devaluations of the franc. In early 1983, Mitterrand embarked on an austerity program to control inflation and reduce the trade deficit. He increased taxes and slashed government spending. A halt in economic growth, declining purchasing power for the average Frenchman, and an increase in unemployment to 10% followed. Mitterrand sank lower and lower in the opinion polls.

In March 1986, a center-right coalition led by Jacques Chirac won a slim majority in legislative elections. Chirac became Premier initiating a period of "co-habitation" between him and the Socialist President, Mitterrand, a cooperation marked by sparring over Chirac's plan to denationalize major industries and effect a harder line on security issues.

Mitterrand's decisive reelection in May 1987, led to Chirac being replaced as Premier by Michel Rocard, a Socialist. Mitterrand called legislative elections for June, 1987 that gave the Socialists a plurality.

Relations, however, cooled with Rocard, and in May 1991 he was replaced with Edith Cresson, France's first female prime minister and like Mitterrand a Socialist.

The conservative coalition won a resounding victory in the March 1993 parliamentary elections forcing the Socialist Party to oust its leader Laurent Fabius.

A new law enacted in June authorized police to make random identity checks in an effort to curb illegal immigration.

Overseas Departments

Overseas Departments elect representatives to the National Assembly, and the same administrative organization as that of mainland France applies to them.

FRENCH GUIANA (including ININI)

Status: Overseas Department
Prefect: Jean-François Di Chiara
Area: 35,126 sq mi. (90,976 sq km)
Population (July 1992): 127,505; growth rate (1992): 4.6%; birth rate 27/1000; infant mortality rate 17/1000
Capital (1990): Cayenne, 41,067; **Monetary unit:** Franc; **Language:** French; **Religion:** Roman Catholic; **Literacy rate:** 73%
Economic summary: Gross domestic product (1985): $186 million; $2,240 per capita; inflation (1987): 4.1%; unemployment (1987): 15%. Arable land: negligible; principal agricultural products: rice, cassava, bananas, sugar cane. Labor force: 23,265; 21.2% in industry. Major industrial products: timber, rum, rosewood essence, gold mining, processed shrimp. Natural resources: bauxite, timber, cinnabar, kaolin. Exports: $54 million (f.o.b., 1987): shrimp, timber, rum, rosewood essence. Imports: $394 million (c.i.f., 1987): food, consumer and producer goods, petroleum. Major trading partners: U.S., France, Japan.

French Guiana, lying north of Brazil and east of Suriname on the northeast coast of South America, was first settled in 1604. Penal settlements, embracing the area around the mouth of the Maroni River and the Iles du Salut (including Devil's Island), were founded in 1852; they have since been abolished.

During World War II, French Guiana at first adhered to the Vichy government, but the Free French took over in 1943. French Guiana accepted in 1958 the new Constitution of the French Fifth Republic and remained an Overseas Department of the French Republic.

GUADELOUPE

Status: Overseas Department
Prefect: France Pekiez
Area: 687 sq mi. (1,779 sq km)
Population (est. mid-1993): 400,000 (average annual growth rate: 1.3%); birth rate: 19/1000; infant mortality rate: 9.9/1000; density per square mile: 621
Capital (1990): Basse-Terre, 14,000; **Largest city (1987):** Pointe-à-Pitre, over 25,312; **Monetary unit:** Franc; **Language:** French, Creole patois; **Religions:** Roman Catholic; **Literacy rate:** over 70%
Economic summary: Gross domestic product (1987): $1.1 billion; $3,300 per capita; n.a. real growth rate; inflation (1987): 2.3%; unemployment (1987): 38%. Arable land: 18%; principal agricultural products: sugar cane, bananas, eggplant, flowers. Labor force: 120,000; 25.8% industry. Major industries: construction, public works, sugar, rum, tourism. Exports: $153 million (f.o.b., 1988): sugar, rum, bananas, eggplant, flowers. Imports: $1.2 billion (c.i.f., 1988): foodstuffs, clothing, consumer goods, construction materials, petroleum products. Major trading partner: France.

Guadeloupe, in the West Indies about 300 miles (483 km) southeast of Puerto Rico, was discovered by Columbus in 1493. It consists of the twin islands of Basse-Terre and Grande-Terre and five dependencies—Marie-Galante, Les Saintes, La Désirade, St. Barthélemy, and the northern half of St. Martin. The volcano Soufrière (4,813 ft; 1,467 m), also called La Grande Soufrière, is the highest point on Guadeloupe. Violent activity in 1976 and 1977 caused thousands to flee their homes.

French colonization began in 1635. In 1958, Guadeloupe voted in favor of the new Constitution of the French Fifth Republic and remained an Overseas Department of the French Republic.

MARTINIQUE

Status: Overseas Department
Prefect: Jean Claude Raire
Area: 431 sq mi. (1,116 sq km)
Population (est. mid-1993): 400,000 (average annual growth rate: 1.2%); birth rate: 18/1000; infant mortality rate: 9/1000; density per square mile: 907
Capital (1990): Fort-de-France, 101,540; Other cities: Le Lamentin, 26,683; Sainte-Marie, 18,533; **Monetary unit:** Franc; **Languages:** French, Creole patois; **Religion:** Roman Catholic; **Literacy rate:** over 70%
Economic summary: Gross domestic product (1986): $2 billion; $6,000 per capita; inflation (1989): 2.9%; unemployment (1988): 30%. Average annual growth rate n.a. Arable land: 10%; principal agricultural products: sugar cane, bananas, rum, pineapples. Labor force: 100,000; 31.7% in service industry. Major industries: sugar, rum, refined oil, cement, tourism. Natural resources: coastal scenery and beaches. Exports: $196 million (f.o.b., 1988): bananas, refined petroleum products, rum, sugar, pineapples. Imports: $1.3 billion (c.i.f., 1988): foodstuffs, clothing and other consumer goods, petroleum products, construction materials. Major trading partners: France, U.S.

Martinique, lying in the Lesser Antilles about 300 miles (483 km) northeast of Venezuela, was probably discovered by Columbus in 1502 and was taken for France in 1635. Following the Franco-German armistice of 1940, it had a semiautonomous status until 1943, when authority was relinquished to the Free French. The area, administered by a Prefect assisted by an elected council, is represented in the French Parliament. In 1958, Martinique voted in favor of the new Constitution of the French Fifth Republic and remained an Overseas Department of the French Republic.

RÉUNION

Status: Overseas Department
Prefect: Jacques Dewatre
Area: 970 sq mi. (2,510 sq km)
Population (est. mid-1993): 600,000 (average annual growth rate, 1.8%); birth rate: 24/1000; infant mortality rate: 8/1000; density per square mile: 657
Capital (1990): Saint-Denis (metropolitan area), 142,000. Other cities: Saint-Paul, 58,494; Saint-Pierre, 50,419; Le Tampon, 41,305; Saint-Louis, 32,045; **Monetary unit:** Franc; **Languages:** French, Creole; **Religion:** Roman Catholic
Economic summary: Gross domestic product (1987 est.): $3.37 billion; $6,000 per capita; inflation (1988) 1.3%; unemployment (Feb. 91) 35%. Arable land: 20%; principal agricultural products: rum, vanilla, bananas, perfume plants. Major industrial products: rum, cigarettes, processed sugar. Exports: $166 million (f.o.b., 1988): sugar, perfume essences, rum, molasses. Imports: $1.7 billion (c.i.f., 1988): manufactured goods, foodstuffs, beverages, machinery and transportation equipment, petroleum products. Major trading partners: France, Mauritius, Bahrain, South Africa, Italy.

Discovered by Portuguese navigators in the 16th century, the island of Réunion, then uninhabited, was taken as a French possession in 1642. It is located about 450 miles (724 km) east of Madagascar, in the Indian Ocean. In 1958, Réunion approved the Constitution of the Fifth French Republic and remained an Overseas Department of the French Republic.

ST. PIERRE AND MIQUELON

Status: Overseas Department
Prefect: Jean-Pierre Marquie
Area: 93 sq mi. (242 sq km)
Population (July 1992): 6,513; growth rate 0.4%; birth rate 9/1000; infant mortality rate 10/1000
Capital (1990): Saint Pierre, 5,683
Economic summary: Gross domestic product (1991 est.): $60 million; $9,500 per capita; unemployment (1990) 9.6%. Major industries: fishing, canneries. Exports: $25.5 million (f.o.b., 1990): fish, pelts. Imports: $87.2 million (c.i.f., 1990): meat, clothing, fuel, electrical equipment, machinery, building materials. Major trading partners: Canada, France, U.S., U.K., the Netherlands.

The sole remnant of the French colonial empire in North America, these islands were first occupied by the French in 1604. Their only importance arises from proximity to the Grand Banks, located 10 miles south of Newfoundland, making them the center of the French Atlantic cod fisheries. On July 19, 1976, the islands became an Overseas Department of the French Republic.

Overseas Territories

Overseas Territories are comparable to Departments, except that their administrative organization includes a locally-elected government.

FRENCH POLYNESIA

Status: Overseas Territory
President of the Territorial Government: Gaston Plosse (1991)
Area: 1,544 sq mi. (4,000 sq km)
Population (mid-1993): 200,000 (average annual growth rate: 2.3%); birth rate: 28/1000; infant mortality rate: 16/1000; density per square mile: 149
Capital (1988): Papeete (on Tahiti), 23,555; **Monetary unit:** Pacific financial community franc; **Language:** French; **Religions:** Protestant, 55%; Roman Catholic, 32%
Economic summary: Gross national product (1991 est.): $1.2 billion; $6,000 per capita; inflation (1989) 2.9%; unemployment (1988 est.) 14.9%. Principal agricultural product: copra. Major industries: tourism, maintenance of French nuclear test base. Exports: $88.9 million (f.o.b., 1989): coconut products, mother of pearl, vanilla. Imports: $765 million (c.i.f., 1989): fuels, foodstuffs, equipment. Major trading partners: France, U.S.

The term French Polynesia is applied to the scattered French possessions in the South Pacific—Mangareva (Gambier), Makatea, the Marquesas Islands, Rapa, Rurutu, Rimatara, the Society Islands, the Tuamotu Archipelago, Tubuai, Raivavae, and the island of Clipperton—which were organized into a single colony in 1903. There are 120 islands, of which 25 are uninhabited.

The President of the Territorial Government is assisted by a Council of Government and a popularly elected Territorial Assembly. The principal and most populous island—Tahiti, in the Society group—was claimed as French in 1768. In 1958, French Polynesia voted in favor of the new Constitution of the French Fifth Republic and remained an Overseas Territory of the French Republic. The natives are mostly Maoris.

The Pacific Nuclear Test Center on the atoll of Mururoa, 744 miles (1,200 km) from Tahiti, was completed in 1966.

MAYOTTE

Status: Territorial collectivity
Prefect: Akli Khides
Area: 146 sq mi. (378 sq km)
Population (July 1992): 86,628; growth rate (1992) 3.8%; birth rate 50/1000; infant mortality rate 84/1000
Capital (1985): Dzaoudzi (Mamoudzou), 7,325
Economic summary: Exports (1984): $4 million (f.o.b.). Imports $21.8 million (f.o.b., 1984). Principal products: vanilla, ylang-ylang, coffee, copra

The most populous of the Comoro Islands in the Indian Ocean, with a Christian majority, Mayotte voted in 1974 and 1976 against joining the other, predominantly Moslem islands, in declaring themselves independent. It continues to retain its ties to France.

NEW CALEDONIA AND DEPENDENCIES

Status: Overseas Territory
High Commissioner: Alain Christnacht (1991)
Area: 7,374 sq mi. (19,103 sq km)[1]
Population (mid-1993): 200,000 (average annual growth rate: 1.9%); birth rate: 25/1000; infant mortality rate: 15/1000; density per square mile: 25
Capital (1989): Nouméa, 65,110; **Monetary unit:** Pacific financial community franc; **Languages:** French, Melanesian and Polynesian dialects; **Religion:** Roman Catholic, 60%; Protestant, 30%; **Literacy rate:** Not known
Economic summary: Gross national product (1989 est): $860 million; average annual growth rate 2.4%; per capita income $5,810; inflation 4.1%;, unemployment 16%. Principal agricultural products: coffee, copra, beef, wheat, vegetables. Major industrial product: nickel. Natural resources: nickel, chromite, iron ore. Exports: $671 million (f.o.b., 1989): nickel, chrome. Imports: $764 million (c.i.f., 1989): mineral fuels, machinery, electrical equipment, foodstuffs. Major trading partners: France, Japan, U.S., Australia.

1. Including dependencies.

New Caledonia (6,466 sq mi.; 16,747 sq km), about 1,070 miles (1,722 km) northeast of Sydney, Australia, was discovered by Capt. James Cook in 1774 and annexed by France in 1853. The government also administers the Isle of Pines, the Loyalty Islands (Uvéa, Lifu, and Maré), the Belep Islands, the Huon Island group, and Chesterfield Islands.

The natives are Melanesians; about one third of the population is white and one fifth Indochinese and Javanese. The French National Assembly on July 31, 1984, voted a bill into law that granted internal autonomy to New Caledonia and opened the way to possible eventual independence. This touched off ethnic tensions and violence between the natives and the European settlers, with the natives demanding full independence and sovereignty while the settlers wanted to remain part of France. In June 1988, France resumed direct administration of the territory and promised a referendum on self-determination in 1998. This was agreed to by organizations representing the natives and the French settlers.

SOUTHERN AND ANTARCTIC LANDS

Status: Overseas Territory
Administrator: Christian Dors (1991)
Area: 3,004 sq mi. (7,781 sq km, excluding Adélie Land)
Capital: Port-au-Français

This territory is uninhabited except for the personnel of scientific bases. It consists of Adélie Land (166,752 sq mi.; 431,888 sq km) on the Antarctic mainland and the following islands in the southern Indian Ocean: the Kerguelen and Crozet archipelagos and the islands of Saint-Paul and New Amsterdam.

WALLIS AND FUTUNA ISLANDS

Status: Overseas Territory
Administrator: Jacques de Llenoff
Area: 106 sq mi. (274 sq km)
Population (July 1992): 17,095; growth rate 3% (1992); birth rate 27/1000; infant mortality rate 29/1000.
Capital (1983): Mata-Utu, 815
Economic summary: Gross domestic product (1991 est.): $25 million; $1,500 per capita. Exports: negligible. Imports (1984, c.i.f.): $13.3 million: foodstuffs, manufactured goods, transport equipment, fuel.

The two islands groups in the South Pacific between Fiji and Samoa were settled by French missionaries at the beginning of the 19th century. A protectorate was established in the 1880s. Following a referendum by the Polynesian inhabitants, the status was changed to that of an Overseas Territory in 1961.

GABON

Gabonese Republic
President: Omar Bongo (1967)
Premier: Oyé Mba Casimir (1990)
Area: 103,346 sq mi. (267,667 sq km)
Population (est. mid-1993): 1,100,000 (average annual rate of natural increase: 2.4%); birth rate: 41/1000; infant mortality rate: 99/1000; density per square mile: 11
Capital and largest city (est. 1987): Libreville, 352,000; **Monetary unit:** Franc CFA; **Ethnic groups:** Bateke, Obamba, Bakota, Shake, Pongwés, Adumas, Chiras, Punu, and Lumbu; **Languages:** French (official) and Bantu dialects; **Religions:** Christian, 55–75%; Muslim, less than 1%; remainder animist; **National name:** République Gabonaise; **Member of French Community; Literacy rate:** 61%
Economic summary: Gross domestic product (1990 est.): $3.3 billion; $3,090 per capita; real growth rate 13%. Arable land: 1%. Principal agricultural products: cocoa, coffee, wood, palm oil. Labor force: 120,000 salaried; 65% in agriculture. Major industrial products: petroleum, natural gas, processed wood, manganese, uranium. Natural resources: wood, petroleum, iron ore, manganese, uranium. Exports: $1.16 billion (f.o.b., 1989): crude petroleum, wood and wood products, minerals. Imports: $0.78 billion (c.i.f., 1989): mining and road-building machinery, electrical equipment, foodstuffs, textiles, transport vehicles. Major trading partners: France, U.S., Germany, Japan, U.K.

Geography. This West African land with the Atlantic as its western border is also bounded by Equatorial Guinea, Cameroon, and the Congo. Its area is slightly less than Colorado's.

From mangrove swamps on the coast, the land becomes divided plateaus in the north and east and mountains in the north. Most of the country is covered by a dense tropical forest.

Government. The president is elected for a seven-year term. Legislative powers are exercised by a 120-seat National Assembly, which is elected for a seven-year term. After his conversion to Islam in 1973, President Bongo changed his given name, Albert Bernard, to Omar. The Rassemblement Social Démocrate Gabonais is led by President Bongo. He was re-elected without opposition in 1973 and in 1980.

History. Little is known of Gabon's history, even in oral tradition, but Pygmies are believed to be the original inhabitants. Now there are many tribal groups in the country, the largest being the Fang people who constitute a third of the population.

Gabon was first visited by the Portuguese navigator Diego Cam in the 15th century. In 1839, the French founded their first settlement on the left bank of the Gabon Estuary and gradually occupied the hinterland during the second half of the 19th century. It was organized as a French territory in 1888 and became an autonomous republic within the French Union after World War II and an independent republic on Aug. 17, 1960.

Following strikes and riots the president called a national conference in March 1990. In May it adopted a transitional constitution legalizing political parties and calling for free elections. Although the legislative elections in March 1991 were accompanied by violence, process was upheld. Nevertheless, the president remained in firm control while the opposition bickered among themselves. The country's international image rose.

GAMBIA

Republic of the Gambia
President: Sir Dawda K. Jawara (1970)
Area: 4,093 sq mi. (10,600 sq km)
Population (est. mid-1993): 900,000 (average annual rate of natural increase: 2.5%); birth rate: 46/1000; infant mortality rate: 138/1000; density per square mile: 241
Capital (1986): Banjul, 44,188
Monetary unit: Dalasi
Languages: Native tongues, English (official)
Religions: Islam, 90%; Christian, 9%; traditional, 1%
Literacy rate: 25.1%
Member of Commonwealth of Nations
Economic summary: Gross domestic product (FY91 est.): $207 million; per capita $235; real growth rate 3%; inflation 6%. Arable land: 16%. Principal products: peanuts, rice, palm kernels. Labor force: 400,000; 18.9% in industry, commerce and services. Major industrial products: processed peanuts, fish, and hides. Natural resources: fish. Exports: $116 million (f.o.b., FY90): peanuts and peanut products, fish. Imports: $147 million (f.o.b., FY90): foodstuffs, fuel, machinery, transport equipment. Major trading partners: U.S., E.C., Asia.

Geography. Situated on the Atlantic coast in westernmost Africa and surrounded on three sides by Senegal, Gambia is twice the size of Delaware. The Gambia River flows for 200 miles (322 km) through Gambia on its way to the Atlantic. The country, the smallest on the continent, averages only 20 miles (32 km) in width.

Government. The president's five-year term is linked to the 35-member unicameral House of Representatives, from which he appoints his Cabinet members and the vice president.

The major political party is the People's Progressive Party (27 seats in House of Representatives), led by President Jawara.

History. During the 17th century, Gambia was settled by various companies of English merchants. Slavery was the chief source of revenue until it was abolished in 1807. Gambia became a crown colony in 1843 and an independent nation within the Commonwealth of Nations on Feb. 18, 1965.

Full independence was approved in a 1970 referendum, and on April 24 of that year Gambia proclaimed itself a republic.

President Dawda K. Jawara won overwhelming re-election to his fifth term on May 5, 1982.

Elections of April 29, 1992 returned Jawara for a fifth term. His People's Progressive Party won 25 of the 36 seats in the House of Representatives.

GEORGIA

Republic of Georgia
State Council Chairman: Eduard Shevardnadze (1992)
Acting Prime Minister: Tengiz Sigua (1992)
Area: 26,900 sq mi. (167,700 sq km)
Population (est. mid-1993): 5,500,000 (Georgians, 70%; largest minorities: Armenians, other: Russians and Azerbaijanis); average annual rate of natural increase: 0.7%; birth rate: 15/1000; infant mortality rate: 16/1000; density per square mile: 204
Capital and largest city (1991): Tbilisi, 1,279,000. Other cities (1989): Kutaisa, 235,000; Batumi, 136,000; and Sukhumi, 121,000; **Monetary unit:** Ruble, to be replaced by the "maneti"; **Language:** Georgian (official), 71%; Russian, 9%; Armenian, 7%; Azerbaijani, 6%; **Religion:** Georgian Orthodox, 65%; Russian Orthodox, 10%; Armenian Orthodox, 8%; Muslim, 11%
Economic summary: Per capita gross national product (1990): $1,640. Labor force (1988): 2,834,000: agriculture, 29.1%; industry, 17.8%. Industries: heavy industrial products include raw steel, rolled steel, cement, lumber, machine tools, foundry equipment, electric locomotives, tower cranes, welding equipment, meat packing, dairy and fishing, farm machinery. Agriculture: citrus fruits, grapes, sugar, vegetables, grains, cattle, sheep, goats, pigs, and poultry. Exports: $176 million (f.o.b., 1990). Imports: $1.5 billion (c.i.f., 1990).

Geography. Georgia is a land of snow-capped mountains, turbulent rivers, dense forests, and fertile valleys. Mt. Kazbet, 16,541 ft (5,042 m) is the country's tallest peak. Georgia's principal rivers, Kura Mtkvari and the Rioni and their tributaries are harnessed to provide an abundance of hydroelectric power for the country. Georgia is bordered by the Black Sea in the west, by Turkey and Armenia in the south, by Azerbaijan in the east, and Russia in the north. The republic also includes the Abkhaz and Adzhar autonomous republics and the Yugo-Ossetian Autonomous Oblast.

Government. A republic. On March 10, 1992, a temporary legislative and executive body called the State Council was established which is headed by Eduard Shevardnadze.

History. Georgia became a kingdom about 4 B.C. and reached its greatest period of expansion in the 12th century when its territory included the whole of Transcaucasia. The country was the scene of a struggle between Persia and Turkey from the 16th century on, and in the 18th century became a vassal to Russia in exchange for protection from the Turks.

Georgia joined Azerbaijan and Armenia in 1917 to establish the anti-Bolshevik Transcaucasian Federation, and upon its dissolution, proclaimed its independence in 1918. In 1922, the Red Army invaded Georgia and replaced the republic with a Soviet government. In 1922, Georgia, Armenia, and Azerbaijan were annexed and formed into the Transcaucasian Soviet Socialist Republic affiliated with the U.S.S.R. In 1936, it became a separate Soviet republic.

Zviad Gamsakhurdia won the first directly elected Soviet presidency in 1990 with 86.5% of the vote, pledging to lead Georgia toward independence. Georgia proclaimed its independence on April 9, 1990.

Gamsakhurdia was later accused of dictatorial policies, the jailing of opposition leaders, human rights abuses, and clamping down on the media. A two week civil war centered in the capital of Tbilisi ensued and Gamsakhurdia was forced to flee to Azerbaijan and later to Armenia. A ruling military council was established by the opposition until a civilian authority can be restored.

During 1993 the government continued to fight separatists in Abkhazia. Shevardnadze accused Russia of aiding the Abkhazian forces and a virtual state of war existed with Russia over the region. Russia denied taking sides although admitted that some of its soldiers had to defend themselves.

GERMANY

Federal Republic of Germany
President: Richard von Weizsäcker (1984)
Chancellor: Helmut Kohl (1982)
Area: 137,838 sq mi. (357,000 sq km)
Population (est. mid-1993): 81,100,000 (average annual growth rate: –0.1%; birth rate: 10/1000; infant mortality rate: 6.7/1000; density per square mile: 601
Capital (June 1989): Berlin, 3,376,800; seat of parliament and government: Bonn[1], 283,700 (1988); **Largest cities (1990):** Hamburg, 1,640,000; Munich, 1,219,600; Cologne, 950,200; Frankfurt, 641,300; Essen, 626,100; Dortmund, 597,400; Stuttgart, 576,600; Dusseldorf, 575,100; Bremen, 548,900; Duisberg, 533,600; Leipzig, 513,600; Hanover, 509,800; Dresden, 493,200; **Monetary unit:** Deutsche Mark; **Language:** German; **Religions:** Protestant, 49%; Roman Catholic, 45%; **National name:** Bundesrepublik Deutschland; **Literacy rate:** 99%
Economic summary (est. 1992): United Germany GNP $1,643 billion; per capita, $19,943; real GNP growth, 3.1%. **Western Germany:** inflation rate (1991): West 3.5%; East n.a.; unemployment rate (1991): West 6.3%; East 11%. Exports: (f.o.b., 1989): West—$324.3 billion. Imports: (f.o.b., 1989): West—$346.5 billion. Eastern Germany's share of all-Germany GDP in 1991 was only about 7% and eastern productivity is just 30% of the west. Arable land: 30%. Principal products: grains, potatoes, sugar beets. Labor force: 27,790,000; 41.6% in industry. Major products: chemicals, machinery, vehicles, electronics, food and beverages, iron, steel, coal, and cement. Natural resources: iron ore, timber, coal. Exports: machines and precision tools, chemicals, motor vehicles, iron and steel products. Imports: manufactured and agricultural products, raw materials, fuels. Major trading partners: France, Netherlands, Italy, Belgium-Luxembourg, U.S., U.K.
Eastern Germany: Arable land: 45%; principal products: grains, potatoes, sugar beets, meat and dairy products. Labor force: 8,960,000; 37.5% in industry; major products: metal fabrication, shipbuilding, chemicals, machinery, food and beverages, textiles, petroleum refining, and agriculture. Natural resources: brown coal, potash, bauxite. Exports: machinery and equipment, chemical products, textiles, clothing. Imports: raw materials, fuels, agricultural products, machinery and equipment

1. At present, seat of government will eventually move to the traditional capital of Berlin.

Rulers of Germany and Prussia

Name	Born	Ruled[1]
KINGS OF PRUSSIA		
Frederick I[2]	1657	1701–1713
Frederick William I	1688	1713–1740
Frederick II the Great	1712	1740–1786
Frederick William II	1744	1786–1797
Frederick William III	1770	1797–1840
Frederick William IV	1795	1840–1861
William I	1797	1861–1871 [3]
EMPERORS OF GERMANY		
William I	1797	1871–1888
Frederick III	1831	1888–1888
William II	1859	1888–1918 [4]
HEADS OF THE REICH		
Friedrich Ebert[5]	1871	1919–1925
Paul von Hindenburg[5]	1847	1925–1934
Adolf Hitler[6, 7]	1889	1934–1945
Karl Doenitz[6]	1891	1945–1945

Name	Born	Ruled[1]
GERMAN FEDERAL REPUBLIC (WEST) (CHANCELLORS)		
Konrad Adenauer	1876	1949–1963
Ludwig Erhard	1897	1963–1966
Kurt Georg Kiesinger	1904	1966–1969
Willy Brandt	1913	1969–1974
Helmut Schmidt	1918	1974–1984
Helmut Kohl	1930	1984–1990
GERMAN DEMOCRATIC REPUBLIC (EAST)		
Wilhelm Pieck[5]	1876	1949–1960
Walter Ulbricht[8]	1893	1960–1973
Willi Stoph[9]	1914	1973–1976
Erich Honecker[9]	1912	1976–1989
Egon Krenz[9]	1937	1989–1989
Manfred Gerlach[9]		1989–1990
Sabine Bergman-Pohl[9]		1990–1990
GERMAN FEDERAL REPUBLIC CHANCELLORS		
Helmut Kohl	1930	1991–

1. Year of end of rule is also that of death, unless otherwise indicated. 2. Was Elector of Brandenburg (1688–1701) as Frederick III. 3. Became Emperor of Germany in 1871. 4. Died 1941. 5. President. 6. Führer. 7. Named Chancellor by President Hindenburg in 1933. 8. Chairman of Council of State. Died 1973. 9. Chairman of Council of State.

Geography. The Federal Republic of Germany occupies the western half of the central European area historically regarded as German. This was the part of Germany occupied by the United States, Britain, and France after World War II, when the eastern half of prewar Germany was split roughly between a Soviet-occupied zone, which became the German Democratic Republic, and an area annexed by Poland. After being divided for more than four decades, the two Germanys were reunited on Oct. 3, 1990. The united Federal Republic is about the size of Montana.

Germany's neighbors are France, Belgium, Luxembourg, and the Netherlands on the west, Switzerland and Austria on the south, Czechoslovakia and Poland on the east, and Denmark on the north.

The northern plain, the central hill country, and the southern mountain district constitute the main physical divisions of West Germany, which is slightly smaller than Oregon. The Bavarian plateau in the southwest averages 1,600 feet (488 m) above sea level, but it reaches 9,721 feet (2,962 m) in the Zugspitze Mountains, the highest point in the country.

Important navigable rivers are the Danube, rising in the Black Forest and flowing east across Bavaria into Austria, and the Rhine, which rises in Switzerland and flows across the Netherlands in two channels to the North Sea and is navigable by ocean-going and coastal vessels as far as Cologne. The Elbe, which also empties into the North Sea, is navigable within Germany for smaller vessels. The Weser, flowing into the North Sea, and the Main and Mosel (Moselle), both tributaries of the Rhine, are also important. In addition, the Oder and Neisse Rivers form the border with Poland.

Government. Under the Constitution of May 23, 1949, the Federal Republic was established as a parliamentary democracy. The Parliament consists of the Bundesrat, an upper chamber representing and appointed by the Länder, or states, and the Bundestag, a lower house elected for four years by universal suffrage. A federal assembly composed of Bundestag deputies and deputies from the state parliaments elects the President of the Republic for a five-year-term; the Bundestag alone chooses the Chancellor, or Prime Minister. Each of the 16 Länder have a legislature popularly elected for a four-year or five-year term.

The major political parties are the Christian Democratic Union-Christian Social Union (268 and Christian Socialist Union, 51 of 662 seats in the Bundestag), led by Chancellor Helmut Kohl; Social Democratic Party (239 seats); and the Free Democratic Party (78 seats), led by Otto Count Larbsdorff, the Alliance 90/Greens (8 seats) and Party of Democratic Socialism (17 seats). Kohl's government is a coalition with the Free Democrats.

History. Immediately before the Christian era, when the Roman Empire had pushed its frontier to the Rhine, what is now Germany was inhabited by several tribes believed to have migrated from Central Asia between the 6th and 4th centuries B.C. One of these tribes, the Franks, attained supremacy in western Europe under Charlemagne, who was crowned Holy Roman Emperor A.D. 800. By the Treaty of Verdun (843), Charlemagne's lands east of the Rhine were ceded to the German Prince Louis. Additional territory acquired by the Treaty of Mersen (870) gave Germany approximately the area it maintained throughout the Middle Ages. For several centuries after Otto the Great was crowned King in 936, the German rulers were also usually heads of the Holy Roman Empire.

Relations between state and church were changed by the Reformation, which began with Martin Luther's 95 theses, and came to a head in 1547, when Charles V scattered the forces of the Protestant League at Mühlberg. Freedom of worship was guaranteed by the Peace of Augsburg (1555), but a Counter Reformation took place later, and a dispute over the succession to the Bohemian throne brought on the Thirty Years' War (1618–48), which devastated Germany and left the empire divided into hundreds of small principalities virtually independent of the Emperor.

Meanwhile, Prussia was developing into a state of considerable strength. Frederick the Great (1740–86) reorganized the Prussian army and defeated Maria Theresa of Austria in a struggle over Silesia. After the defeat of Napoleon at Waterloo (1815), the struggle between Austria and Prussia for supremacy in Germany continued, reaching its climax in the defeat of Austria in the Seven Weeks' War (1866) and the formation of the Prussian-dominated North German Confederation (1867).

The architect of German unity was Otto von Bismarck, a conservative, monarchist, and militaristic Prussian Junker who had no use for "empty phrase-making and constitutions." From 1862 until his retirement in 1890 he dominated not only the German but also the entire European scene. He unified all Germany in a series of three wars against Denmark (1864), Austria (1866), and France (1870–71), which many historians believe were instigated and promoted by Bismarck in his zeal to build a nation through "blood and iron."

On Jan. 18, 1871, King Wilhelm I of Prussia was proclaimed German Emperor in the Hall of Mirrors at Versailles. The North German Confederation, created in 1867, was abolished, and the Second German Reich, consisting of the North and South German states, was born. With a powerful army, an efficient bureaucracy, and a loyal bourgeoisie, Chancellor Bismarck consolidated a powerful centralized state.

Wilhelm II dismissed Bismarck in 1890 and embarked upon a "New Course," stressing an intensified colonialism and a powerful navy. His chaotic foreign policy culminated in the diplomatic isolation of Germany and the disastrous defeat in World War I (1914–18).

The Second German Empire collapsed following the defeat of the German armies in 1918, the naval mutiny at Kiel, and the flight of the Kaiser to the Netherlands on November 10. The Social Democrats, led by Friedrich Ebert and Philipp Scheidemann, crushed the Communists and established a moderate republic with Ebert as President.

The Weimar Constitution of 1919 provided for a President to be elected for seven years by universal suffrage and a bicameral legislature, consisting of the Reichsrat, representing the states, and the Reichstag, representing the people. It contained a model Bill of Rights. It was weakened, however, by a provision that enabled the President to rule by decree.

President Ebert died Feb. 28, 1925, and on April 26, Field Marshal Paul von Hindenburg was elected president.

The mass of Germans regarded the Weimar Republic as a child of defeat, imposed upon a Germany whose legitimate aspirations to world leadership had been thwarted by a world conspiracy. Added to this were a crippling currency debacle, a tremendous burden of reparations, and acute economic distress.

Adolf Hitler, an Austrian war veteran and a fanatical nationalist, fanned discontent by promising a Greater Germany, abrogation of the Treaty of Versailles, restoration of Germany's lost colonies, and destruction of the Jews. When the Social Democrats and the Communists refused to combine against the Nazi threat, President Hindenburg made Hitler chancellor on Jan. 30, 1933.

With the death of Hindenburg on Aug. 2, 1934, Hitler repudiated the Treaty of Versailles and began full-scale rearmament. In 1935 he withdrew Germany from the League of Nations, and the next year he reoccupied the Rhineland and signed the anti-Comintern pact with Japan, at the same time strengthening relations with Italy. Austria was annexed in March 1938. By the Munich agreement in September 1938 he gained the Czech Sudetenland, and in violation of this agreement he completed the dismemberment of Czechoslovakia in March 1939. But his invasion of Poland on Sept. 1, 1939, precipitated World War II.

On May 8, 1945, Germany surrendered unconditionally to Allied and Soviet military commanders, and on June 5 the four-nation Allied Control Council became the *de facto* government of Germany.

(For details of World War II, *see* Headline History.)

At the Berlin (or Potsdam) Conference (July 17–Aug. 2, 1945) President Truman, Premier Stalin, and Prime Minister Clement Attlee of Britain set forth the guiding principles of the Allied Control Council. They were Germany's complete disarmament and demilitarization, destruction of its war potential, rigid control of industry, and decentralization of the political and economic structure. Pending final determination of territorial questions at a peace conference, the three victors agreed in principle to the ultimate transfer of the city of Königsberg (now Kaliningrad) and its adjacent area to the U.S.S.R. and to the administration by Poland of former German territories lying generally east of the Oder-Neisse Line.

For purposes of control Germany was divided in 1945 into four national occupation zones, each headed by a Military Governor.

The Western powers were unable to agree with the U.S.S.R. on any fundamental issue. Work of the Allied Control Council was hamstrung by repeated Soviet vetoes; and finally, on March 20, 1948, Russia walked out of the Council. Meanwhile, the U.S. and Britain had taken steps to merge their zones economically (Bizone); and on May 31, 1948, the U.S., Britain, France, and the Benelux countries agreed to set up a German state comprising the three Western Zones.

The U.S.S.R. reacted by clamping a blockade on all ground communications between the Western Zones and Berlin, an enclave in the Soviet Zone. The Western Allies countered by organizing a gigantic airlift to fly supplies into the beleaguered city, assigning 60,000 men to it. The U.S.S.R. was finally forced to lift the blockade on May 12, 1949.

The Federal Republic of Germany was proclaimed on May 23, 1949, with its capital at Bonn. In free elections, West German voters gave a majority in the Constituent Assembly to the Christian Democrats, with the Social Democrats largely making up the opposition. Konrad Adenauer became chancellor, and Theodor Heuss of the Free Democrats was elected first president.

When the Federal Republic of Germany was established in West Germany, the East German states adopted a more centralized constitution for the Democratic Republic of Germany, and it was put into effect on Oct. 7, 1949. The U.S.S.R. thereupon dissolved its occupation zone but Soviet troops remained. The Western Allies declared that the East German Republic was a Soviet creation undertaken without self-determination and refused to recognize it. It was recognized only within the Soviet bloc.

The area that was occupied by East Germany, as well as adjacent areas in Eastern Europe, consists of Mecklenburg, Brandenburg, Lusatia, Saxony, and Thuringia. Soviet armies conquered the five territories by 1945. In the division of 1945 they were allotted to the U.S.S.R. Soviet forces created a State controlled by the secret police with a single party, the Socialist Unity (Communist) Party. The Russians appropriated East German plants to restore their war-ravaged industry.

By 1973, normal relations were established between East and West Germany and the two states entered the United Nations.

The 25-year diplomatic hiatus between East Germany and the U.S. ended Sept. 4, 1974, with the establishment of formal relations.

THE BERLIN WALL (1961–1990)

Major anti-Communist riots broke out in East Berlin in June 1953 and, on Aug. 13, 1961, the Soviet Sector was sealed off by a Communist-built wall, 26 1/2 miles (43 km) long, running through the city. It was built to stem the flood of refugees seeking freedom in the West, 200,000 having fled in 1961 before the wall was erected.

On Nov. 9, 1989, several weeks after the resignation of East Germany's long-time Communist leader, Erich Honecker, the wall's designer and chief defender, the East German government opened its borders to the West and allowed thousands of its citizens to pass freely through the Berlin Wall. They were cheered and greeted by thousands of West Berliners, and many of the jubilant newcomers celebrated their new freedom by climbing on top of the hated wall.

The following day, East German troops began dismantling parts of the wall. It was ironic that this wall was built to keep the citizens from leaving and, 28 years later, it was being dismantled for the same reason.

On Nov. 22, new passages were opened at the north and south of the Brandenburg Gate in an emotional ceremony attended by Chancellor Helmut Kohl of West Germany and Chancellor Hans Modrow of East Germany. The opening of the Brandenburg Gate climaxed the ending of the barriers that had divided the German people since the end of World War II. By the end of 1990, the entire wall had been removed.

Agreements in Paris in 1954 giving the Federal Republic full independence and complete sovereignty came into force on May 5, 1955. Under it, West Germany and Italy became members of the Brussels treaty organization created in 1948 and renamed the Western European Union. West Germany also became a member of NATO. In 1955 the U.S.S.R. recognized the Federal Republic. The Saar territory, under an agreement between France and West Germany, held a plebiscite and despite economic links to France voted to rejoin West Germany. It became a state of West Germany on Jan. 1, 1957.

In 1963, Chancellor Adenauer concluded a treaty of mutual cooperation and friendship with France and then retired. He was succeeded by his chief inner-party critic, Ludwig Erhard, who was followed in 1966 by Kurt Georg Kiesinger. He, in turn, was succeeded in 1969 by Willy Brandt, former mayor of West Berlin.

The division between West Germany and East Germany was intensified when the Communists erected the Berlin Wall in 1961. In 1968, the East German Communist leader, Walter Ulbricht, imposed restrictions on West German movements into West Berlin. The Soviet-bloc invasion of Czechoslovakia in August 1968 added to the tension.

A treaty with the U.S.S.R. was signed in Moscow in August 1970 in which force was renounced and respect for the "territorial integrity" of present European states declared.

Three months later, West Germany signed a similar treaty with Poland, renouncing force and setting Poland's western border as the Oder-Neisse Line. It subsequently resumed formal relations with Czechoslovakia in a pact that "voided" the Munich treaty that gave Nazi Germany the Sudetenland.

Both German states were admitted to the United Nations in 1973.

Brandt, winner of a Nobel Peace Prize for his foreign policies, was forced to resign in 1974 when an East German spy was discovered to be one of his top staff members. Succeeding him was a moderate Social Democrat, Helmut Schmidt.

Helmut Schmidt, Brandt's successor as chancellor, staunchly backed U.S. military strategy in Europe nevertheless, staking his political fate on the strategy of placing U.S. nuclear missiles in Germany unless the Soviet Union reduced its arsenal of intermediate missiles.

The chancellor also strongly opposed nuclear freeze proposals and won 2–1 support for his stand at the convention of Social Democrats in April. The Free Democrats then deserted the Socialists after losing ground in local elections and joined with the Christian Democrats to unseat Schmidt and install Helmut Kohl as chancellor in 1982. An economic upswing in 1986 led to Kohl's re-election.

The fall of the Communist government in East Germany left only Soviet objections to German reunification to be dealt with. This was resolved in July 1990. Soviet objections to a reunified Germany belonging to NATO were dropped in return for German promises to reduce their military and engage in wide-ranging economic cooperation with the Soviet Union.

In ceremonies beginning on the evening of Tuesday, Oct. 2, 1990, and continuing throughout the next day, the German Democratic Republic acceded to the Federal Republic and Germany became a united and sovereign state for the first time since 1945. Some one million people gathered at midnight Oct. 2 at the Reichstag in Berlin. At midnight, a replica of the Liberty Bell, a gift from the United States, rang, and unity was officially proclaimed.

Following unification, the Federal Republic became the second largest country in Europe, after the Soviet Union. A reunited Berlin serves as the official capital, although the government will initially remain in Bonn.

During the national election campaign of late 1990 the central issue remained the cost of unification, including the modernization of the former East German economy. The ruling Christian Democrats promised no tax increases would be needed, while the opposition Social Democrats argued that this was mere wishful thinking.

In the December 2 election the Christian Democrats emerged as the strongest group, taking 43.8% of the vote. Analysts generally considered the vote to be an expression of thanks and support to the Chancellor for his forceful drive for political unity. The Party of Democratic Socialism, formerly the Communist Party, won 17 seats in Parliament.

The new Parliament convened in January 1991 reelecting Helmut Kohl chancellor. Nevertheless it soon became clear that previous official estimates of the cost and time required to absorb eastern Germany were considerably understated. The number of failed enterprises in the east continued to grow, and the exodus of personnel to western Germany ceased to abate.

On June 20, 1991 the German Parliament officially voted in favor of moving the seat of the federal government to Berlin, although given the huge expense of such a move it would be done slowly and require 12 years before Berlin would be a fully functional federal capital.

The leader of the opposition Social Democrats resigned in May 1993 as a result of a lie about an old scandal. His party was forced to seek a new candidate for the chancellorship at a time when the governing party seemed particularly vulnerable.

Also in May the lower house of parliament voted to tighten Germany's liberal asylum law. The country's highest court also ruled a new abortion law as unconstitutional. and in effect restricting abortion.

GHANA

Republic of Ghana
President: His Excellency Flt. Lt. (rtd.) Jerry John Rawlings
Area: 92,100 sq mi. (238,537 sq km)
Population (est. mid-1993): 16,400,000 (average annual rate of natural increase: 3.1%); birth rate: 43/1000; infant mortality rate: 86/1000; density per square mile: 185
Capital: Accra; **Largest cities (est. 1988):** Accra, 949,100; Kumasi, 385,200 Tamale, 151,100; **Monetary unit:** Cedi; **Languages:** English (official), Native tongues (Brong Ahafo, Twi, Fanti, Ga, Ewe, Dagbani); **Religions:** indigenous belief, 38%; Islam, 30%; Christian, 24%; **Literacy rate:** 50%
Member of Commonwealth of Nations
Economic summary: Gross domestic product (1991 est.): $6.2 billion; per capita $400; real growth rate 5%; inflation 10%; unemployment 10%. Arable land: 5%. Principal products: cocoa, coconuts, coffee, cassava, yams, rice, rubber. Labor force (1983): 3,700,000; 18.7% in industry. Major products: mining products, cocoa products, aluminum. Natural resources: gold, industrial diamonds, bauxite, manganese, timber, fish. Exports: $843 million (f.o.b., 1991 est.): cocoa beans and products, gold, timber, tuna, bauxite, and aluminum. Imports: $1.2 billion (c.i.f., 1991 est.): petroleum, consumer goods, foods, intermediate goods, capital equipment. Major trading partners: U.K., U.S., Germany, France, Japan, South Korea.

Geography. A West African country bordering on the Gulf of Guinea, Ghana is bounded by Côte d'Ivoire to the west, Burkina Faso to the north, Togo to the east and the Atlantic Ocean to the south. It compares in size to Oregon.

The coastal belt, extending about 270 miles (435 km), is sandy, marshy, and generally exposed. Behind it is a gradually widening grass strip. The forested plateau region to the north is broken by ridges and hills. The largest river is the Volta.

Government. A republic. Presidential and Parliamentary elections were held Nov. 3, 1992 and ushered in the Fourth Republic on Jan. 7, 1993.

History. Created an independent country on March 6, 1957, Ghana is the former British colony of the Gold Coast. The area was first seen by Portuguese traders in 1470. They were followed by the English (1553), the Dutch (1595), and the Swedes (1640). British rule over the Gold Coast began in 1820, but it was not until after quelling the severe resistance of the Ashanti in 1901 that it was firmly established. British Togoland, formerly a colony of Germany, was incorporated into Ghana by referendum in 1956. As the result of a plebiscite, Ghana became a republic on July 1, 1960.

Premier Kwame Nkrumah attempted to take leadership of the Pan-African Movement, holding the All-African People's Congress in his capital, Accra, in 1958 and organizing the Union of African States with Guinea and Mali in 1961. But he oriented his country toward the Soviet Union and China and built an autocratic rule over all aspects of Ghanaian life.

In February 1966, while Nkrumah was visiting Peking and Hanoi, he was deposed by a military coup led by Gen. Emmanuel K. Kotoka.

A series of military coups followed and on June 4, 1979, Flight Lieutenant Jerry Rawlings overthrew Lt. Gen. Frederick Akuffo's military rule. Rawlings permitted the election of a civilian president to go ahead as scheduled the following month, and Hilla Limann, candidate of the People's National Party, took office. Charging the civilian government with corruption and repression, Rawlings staged another coup on Dec. 31, 1981. As chairman of the Provisional National Defense Council, Rawlings instituted an austerity program and reduced budget deficits.

On July 11, 1985, a relative of Rawlings, Michael Agbotui Soussoudis, 39, and Sharon M. Scranage, 29, who had been a low-level clerk in the Central Intelligence Agency station in the West African country, were arrested in the United States on espionage charges.

In a referendum of May 1992 over 92% of the voters approved a new constitution, which provided for a multi-party system.

In the elections of late 1992 Rawlings won a majority of the votes for president, and the opposition's boycott of the legislative elections gave Rawlings' supporters almost all the available seats.

GREECE

Hellenic Republic
President: Constantine Karamanlis (1990)
Premier: Constantine Mitsotakis (1990)
Area: 50,961 sq mi. (131,990 sq km)
Population (est. mid-1993): 10,500,000 (average annual rate of natural increase: 0.1%); birth rate: 10/1000; infant mortality rate: 10/1000; density per square mile: 207
Capital: Athens; **Largest cities (1991 est.):** Athens, 748,000; Salonika, 378,000; Piraeus, 170,000; Patras, 155,000; Heraklion, 117,000; Larissa, 113,500; **Monetary unit:** Drachma; **Language:** Greek; **Religion:** Greek Orthodox, 98%; Muslim, 1.3%; **National name:** Elliniki Dimokratia; **Literacy rate:** 93%
Economic summary: Gross domestic product (1991): $77.6 billion; $7,730 per capita; 1.0% real growth rate; inflation 17.8%; unemployment 8.6%. Arable land: 23%. Principal agricultural products: grains, fruits, vegetables, olives, olive oil, tobacco, cotton, livestock, dairy products. Labor force (1988): 3,657,000; 44% services, 27% agriculture, 20% mining and manufacturing. Major industrial products: textiles, chemicals, food processing. Natural resources: bauxite, lignite, magnesite, crude oil, marble. Exports: $6.4 billion (f.o.b., 1990): manufactured goods, food and live animals, fuels and lubricants, raw materials. Imports:

$18.7 billion (c.i.f., 1990): machinery and automotive equipment, petroleum, consumer goods, chemicals, foodstuffs. Major trading partners: Germany, Italy, France, U.S.A., U.K., Netherlands.

Geography. Greece, on the Mediterranean Sea, is the southernmost country on the Balkan Peninsula in southern Europe. It is bordered on the north by Albania, Yugoslavia, and Bulgaria; on the west by the Ionian Sea; and on the east by the Aegean Sea and Turkey. It is slightly smaller than Alabama.

North central Greece, Epirus, and western Macedonia all are mountainous. The main chain of the Pindus Mountains rises to 10,256 feet (3,126 m) in places, separating Epirus from the plains of Thessaly. Mt. Olympus, rising to 9,570 feet (2,909 m) in the north near the Aegean Sea, is the highest point in the country. Greek Thrace is mostly a lowland region separated from European Turkey by the lower Evros River.

Among the many islands are the Ionian group off the west coast; the Cyclades group to the southeast; other islands in the eastern Aegean, including the Dodecanese Islands, Euboea, Lesbos, Samos, and Chios; and Crete, the fourth largest Mediterranean island.

Government. A referendum in December 1974, five months after the collapse of a military dictatorship, ended the Greek monarchy and established a republic. Ceremonial executive power is held by the president; the Premier heads the government and is responsible to a 300-member unicameral Parliament.

History. Greece, with a recorded history going back to 766 B.C., reached the peak of its glory in the 5th century B.C., and by the middle of the 2nd century B.C., it had declined to the status of a Roman province. It remained within the Eastern Roman Empire until Constantinople fell to the Crusaders in 1204.

In 1453, the Turks took Constantinople, and by 1460 Greece was a Turkish province. The insurrection made famous by the poet Lord Byron broke out in 1821, and in 1827 Greece won independence with sovereignty guaranteed by Britain, France, and Russia.

The protecting powers chose Prince Otto of Bavaria as the first king of modern Greece in 1832 to reign over an area only slightly larger than the Peloponnese Peninsula. Chiefly under the next king, George I, chosen by the protecting powers in 1863, Greece acquired much of its present territory. During his 57-year reign, a period in which he encouraged parliamentary democracy, Thessaly, Epirus, Macedonia, Crete, and most of the Aegean islands were added from the disintegrating Turkish empire. An unsuccessful war against Turkey after World War I brought down the monarchy, to be replaced by a republic in 1923.

Two military dictatorships and a financial crisis brought George II back from exile, but only until 1941, when Italian and German invaders defeated tough Greek resistance. After British and Greek troops liberated the country in October 1944, Communist guerrillas staged a long campaign in which the government received U.S. aid under the Truman Doctrine, the predecessor of the Marshall Plan.

A military junta seized power in April 1967, sending young King Constantine II into exile December 14. Col. George Papadopoulos, as premier, converted the government to republican form in 1973 and as President ended martial law. He was moving to restore democracy when he was ousted in November of that year by his military colleagues. The regime of the "colonels," which had tortured its opponents and scoffed at human rights, resigned July 23, 1974, after having bungled an attempt to seize Cyprus.

Former Premier Karamanlis returned from exile to become premier of Greece's first civilian government since 1967.

On Jan. 1, 1981, Greece became the 10th member of the European Community.

Double-digit inflation and scandals in the Socialist government led to them losing their majority in the elections of June 1989. The opposition New Democracy Party did not gain a majority, however, leading to the creation of a NDP-Communist coalition that initiated an investigation of the scandals. The coalition government was short-lived. Elections in April 1990 finally gave the conservative New Democracy Party a one-seat majority in parliament. Soon afterwards Karamanlis, the founder of that party, was elected president by parliament.

During 1992 the government vigorously campaigned internationally to stop the former Yugoslav republic across its borders from using the name "Macedonia."

GRENADA

State of Grenada
Sovereign: Queen Elizabeth II
Governor General: Sir Reginald Palmer (1992)
Prime Minister: Nicholas Braithwaite (1990)
Area: 133 sq mi. (344 sq km)
Population (est. mid-1993): 100,000 (average annual growth rate, 2.5%); birth rate: 33/1000; infant mortality rate: 15.9/1000; density per square mile: 708
Capital and largest city (1991): St. George's, 4,439; **Monetary unit:** East Caribbean dollar; **Ethnic groups:** Blacks and Indians; **Language:** English; **Religions:** Roman Catholic, 64%; Anglican, 21%; **Literacy rate:** 98%; **Member of Commonwealth of Nations**
Economic summary: Gross domestic product (1990): $200.7 million; $2,390 per capita; 5.4% real growth rate; inflation rate 7.0%; est. unemployment rate 25%. Arable land: 15%. Principal products: spices, cocoa, bananas. Tourism is the leading foreign exchange earner followed by agricultural exports. Exports: $26 million (f.o.b., 1990 est.): nutmeg, cocoa beans, bananas, mace. Imports: $105 million (f.o.b., 1989 est.): foodstuffs, machinery, manufactured goods, petroleum. Labor force: 36,000; 31% in services. Major trading partners: U.K., Trinidad and Tobago, U.S., Japan, Canada.

Geography. Grenada (the first "a" is pronounced as in "gray") is the most southerly of the Windward Islands, about 100 miles (161 km) from the South American coast. It is a volcanic island traversed by a mountain range, the highest peak of which is Mount St. Catherine (2,756 ft.; 840 m).

Government. A Governor-General represents the sovereign, Elizabeth II. The Prime Minister is the head of government, chosen by a 15-member House of Representatives elected by universal sufferage every five years.

History. Grenada was discovered by Columbus in 1498. After more than 200 years of British rule, most recently as part of the West Indies Associated States, it became independent Feb. 7, 1974, with Eric M. Gairy as Prime Minister.

Prime Minister Maurice Bishop, a protégé of Cuba's President Castro, was killed in a military coup on Oct. 19, 1983. At the request of five members of the Organization of Eastern Caribbean States, President Reagan ordered an invasion of Grenada on Oct. 25 involving over 1,900 U.S. troops and a small military force from Barbados, Dominica, Jamaica, St. Lucia, and St. Vincent. The troops met strong resistance from Cuban military personnel on the island.

A centrist coalition led by Herbert A. Blaize, a 66-year-old lawyer, won 14 of the 15 seats in Parliament in an election in December 1984, and Blaize became Prime Minister.

None of the four main parties won a clear victory in the election of March 1990. Negotiations led to the National Democratic Congress forming a government with the support of several members from other parties.

The government pursued attempts to reduce the size of the civil service and diminish the number of nationalized enterprises.

GUATEMALA

Republic of Guatemala

President: Ramiro de Leon Carpio (1993)

Area: 42,042 sq mi. (108,889 sq km)

Population (est. mid-1993): 10,000,000 (average annual rate of natural increase: 3.1%); birth rate: 39/1000; infant mortality rate: 54/1000; density per square mile: 240

Capital and largest city (est. 1993): Guatemala City, 2,000,000; **Monetary unit:** Quetzal; **Languages:** Spanish, Indian dialects; **Religion:** Roman Catholic, Protestant, Mayan.; **National name:** República de Guatemala; **Literacy rate:** 55%

Economic summary: Gross domestic product (1991 est.): $11.7 billion; per capita $1,260; real growth rate 3%; inflation 40%. Arable land: 12%. Principal products: corn, beans, coffee, cotton, cattle, sugar, bananas, fruits and vegetables. Labor force: 2,500,000; 14% in manufacturing. Principal products: sugar, textiles and clothing, furniture, chemicals, petroleum, metals, rubber. Natural resources: nickel, crude oil, rare woods, fish, chicle. Exports: $1.16 billion (f.o.b., 1990): coffee, sugar, bananas, beef. Imports: $1.66 billion (c.i.f., 1990): fuel and petroleum products, machinery, grain, fertilizers, motor vehicles. Major trading partners: U.S., Central- American nations, Caribbean, Mexico.

Geography. The northernmost of the Central American nations, Guatemala is the size of Tennessee. Its neighbors are Mexico on the north and west, and Belize, Honduras, and El Salvador on the east. The country consists of three main regions—the cool highlands with the heaviest population, the tropical area along the Pacific and Caribbean coasts, and the tropical jungle in the northern lowlands. The principal mountain range rises to the highest elevation in Central America and contains many volcanic peaks. Volcanic eruptions are frequent.

The Petén region in the north contains important resources and archaeological sites of the Mayan civilization.

Government. On June 5, 1993, the Congress elected Ramiro de Leon Carpio as President to end Jorge Seranno's term after he stepped down following the failure of a self-attempted coup d'etat. Presently the constitutional structure is in transition.

History. Once the site of the ancient Mayan civilization, Guatemala, conquered by Spain in 1524, set itself up as a republic in 1839. From 1898 to 1920, the dictator Manuel Estrada Cabrera ran the country, and from 1931 to 1944, Gen. Jorge Ubico Castaneda was the strongman.

Jacobo Arbenz Guzmán won the 1950 election. He expropriated the large estates, including plantations of the United Fruit Company. With covert U.S. backing, a revolt was led by Col. Carlos Castillo Armas, and Arbenz took refuge in Mexico. Castillo Armas became president but was assassinated in 1957. Gen. Miguel Ydigoras Fuentes was elected president in 1957.

A wave of terrorism, by left and right, began in 1967. Fear of anarchy led to the election in 1970 of Army Chief of Staff Carlos Araña Osorio. Araña, surprisingly, pledged social reforms when he took office. Another military candidate, Gen. Kjell Laugerud, won the presidency in 1974 amid renewed political violence.

The administration of Gen. Romeo Lucas Garcia, elected president in 1978, ended in a coup by a three-man military junta on March 23, 1982. Lucas Garcia was charged by Amnesty International with responsibility for at least 5,000 political murders in a reign of brutality and corruption that brought a cutoff of U.S. military aid in 1978. Hopes for improvement under the junta faded when Gen. José Efraín Ríos Montt took sole power in June.

President Oscar Mejía Victores, another general, seized power from Rios Montt in an August 1983 coup and pledged to turn over power to an elected civilian President in 1985. A constituent assembly was elected on July 1, 1984, to write a new Constitution.

Jorge Serrano Elias presided over seven years of democratic rule until in May 1993 he moved to dissolve congress and the supreme court and suspend constitutional rights. Under strong foreign and domestic pressure the military deposed Serrano on June 1 and allowed the inauguration of de Leon Carpio, the former Attorney General of Human Rights and no particular friend of the military.

GUINEA

Republic of Guinea

President: Brig. Gen. Lansana Conté (1984)

Area: 94,925 sq mi. (245,857 sq km)

Population (est. mid-1993): 6,200,000 (average annual rate of natural increase: 2.5%); birth rate: 47/1000; infant mortality rate: 149/1000; density per square mile: 66

Capital and largest city (1983): Conakry, 705,280; **Monetary unit:** Guinean franc; **Languages:** French (official), native tongues (Malinké, Susu, Fulani); **Religions:** Islam, 85%; 7% indigenous, 8% Christian ; **National name:** République de Guinée; **Literacy rate:** 24% in French; 48% in local languages

Economic summary: Gross domestic product (1990 est.): $3 billion; per capita $410; real growth rate 4.3%; inflation 19.6%.. Arable land: 6%. Principal agricultural products: rice, cassava, millet, corn, coffee, bananas, pineapples. Labor force: 2,400,000 (1983); 11% in industry and commerce. Major industrial products: bauxite, alumina, light manufactured and processed goods, diamonds. Natural resources: bauxite, iron ore, diamonds, gold, water power. Exports: $788 million (f.o.b., 1990 est.): bauxite, alumina, diamonds, pineapples, bananas, coffee. Imports: $692 million (c.i.f., 1990 est): petroleum, machinery, transport equipment, foodstuffs, textiles. Major trading partners: U.S., Canada, Eastern Europe, France, Brazil, Germany.

Geography. Guinea, in West Africa on the Atlantic, is also bordered by Guinea-Bissau, Senegal, Mali, the Ivory Coast, Liberia, and Sierra Leone. Slightly smaller than Oregon, the country consists of a coastal plain, a mountainous region, a savanna interior, and a forest area in the Guinea Highlands. The highest peak is Mount Nimba at 5,748 ft (1,752 m).

Government. Military government headed by President Lansana Conté, who promoted himself from colonel to brigadier general after a 1984 coup. In 1989, President Conté announced that Guinea would move to a multi-party democracy.

A new constitution approved in a nationwide referendum, December 1990, provided for the establishment of a directly elected multi-party parliament (five-year terms) and a popularly elected president for a maximum of two five-year terms, and a judiciary to be independent of either the presidency or the legislature. A transitional Committee for National Recovery (CTRN) replaced the military committee to guide implementation of the new constitution.

History. Previously part of French West Africa, Guinea achieved independence by rejecting the new French Constitution, and on Oct. 2, 1958, became an independent state with Sékou Touré as president. Touré led the country into being the first avowedly Marxist state in Africa. Diplomatic relations with France were suspended in 1965, with the Soviet Union replacing France as the country's chief source of economic and technical assistance.

Prosperity came in 1960 after the start of exploitation of bauxite deposits. Touré was re-elected to a seven-year term in 1974 and again in 1981.

After 26 years as President, Touré died in the United States in March 1984, following surgery. A week later, a military regime headed by Col. Lansana Conté took power with a promise not to shed any more blood after Touré's harsh rule. Conté became President and his co-conspirator in the coup, Col. Diara Traoré, became Prime Minister, but Conté later demoted Traoré to Education Minister. Traoré tried to seize power on July 4, 1985, while Conté was out of the country, but his attempted coup was crushed by troops loyal to Conté.

In 1991 voters approved a new constitution that would lead the country to democracy. Under mounting popular pressure Conté declared in April 1992 that constitutional rule would begin, but he set no timetable for elections.

IMF imposed austerity measures resulted in domestic unrest, which frightened foreign investors.

GUINEA-BISSAU

Republic of Guinea-Bissau
President of the Council of State: João Bernardo Vieira (1980)
Area: 13,948 sq mi. (36,125 sq km)
Population (est. mid-1993): 1,000,000 (average annual rate of natural increase: 2.1%); birth rate: 43/1000; infant mortality rate: 146/1000; density per square mile: 95
Capital and largest city (est. 1988): Bissau, 125,000; **Monetary unit:** Guinea-Bissau peso; **Language:** Portugese Criolo, African languages; **Religions:** traditional, 65%; Islam, 30%; Christian, 5%; **National name:** República da Guiné-Bissau; **Literacy rate:** 36% (1990 est.)
Economic summary: Gross domestic product (1989): $162 million; $160 per capita; real growth rate 5.0%; inflation (1990 est.): 25%. Arable land: 9%. Principal products: palm kernels, cotton, cashew nuts, peanuts. Labor force: 403,000 (est.). Major industries: food processing, beer, soft drinks. Natural resources: unexploited deposits of bauxite, petroleum, phosphates; fish and timber. Exports: $14.2 million (f.o.b., 1989 est.): peanuts, cashews, fish, palm kernels. Imports: $68.9 million (f.o.b., 1989 est.): capital equipment, consumer goods, semiprocessed goods, foods, petroleum. Major trading partners: Portugal, Spain, and other European countries, Senegal, U.S.

Geography. A neighbor of Senegal and Guinea in West Africa, on the Atlantic coast, Guinea-Bissau is about half the size of South Carolina.

The country is a low-lying coastal region of swamps, rain forests, and mangrove-covered wetlands, with about 25 islands off the coast. The Bijagos archipelago extends 30 miles (48 km) out to sea. Internal communications depend mainly on deep estuaries and meandering rivers, since there are no railroads. Bissau, the capital, is the main port.

Government. After the overthrow of Louis Cabral in November 1980, the nine-member Council of the Revolution formed an interm government. In 1982, they formed a new government consisting of the President, 2 Vice-Presidents, 18 ministers and 10 state secretaries.

History. Guinea-Bissau was discovered in 1446 by the Portuguese Nuno Tristao, and colonists in the Cape Verde Islands obtained trading rights in the territory. In 1879 the connection with the Cape Verde Islands was broken. Early in the 1900s the Portuguese managed to pacify some tribesmen, although resistance to colonial rule remained.

The African Party for the Independence of Guinea-Bissau and Cape Verde was founded in 1956 and several years later began guerrilla warfare that grew increasingly effective. By 1974 the rebels controlled most of the countryside, where they formed a government that was soon recognized by scores of countries. The military coup in Portugal in April 1974 brightened the prospects for freedom, and in August the Lisbon government signed an agreement granting independence to the province as of Sept. 10. The new republic took the name Guinea-Bissau.

In November 1980, Prémier João Bernardo Vieira headed a coup that deposed Luis Cabral, President since 1974. A Revolutionary Council assumed the powers of government, with Vieira as its head. An extraordinary congress of the ruling party in January 1991 approved a multi-party system. In June the constitution was amended to allow for opposition parties.

GUYANA

Cooperative Republic of Guyana
President: Dr. Cheddi Jagan (1992)
Area: 83,000 sq mi. (214,969 sq km)
Population (est. mid-1993): 800,000 (average annual rate of natural increase: 1.8%); birth rate: 25/1000; infant mortality rate: 48/1000; density per square mile: 11
Capital and largest city (est. 1986): Georgetown, 150,368; **Monetary unit:** Guyana dollar; **Languages:** English (official), Amerindian dialects; **Religions:** Hindu, 34%; Protestant, 18%; Islam, 9%; Roman Catholic, 18%; Anglican, 16%; **Member of Commonwealth of Nations; Literacy rate:** 85%

Economic summary: Gross domestic product (1991 est.): $250 million; $300 per capita; real growth rate 6%; inflation (1990): 75%; unemployment (1990 est.): 12–15%. Arable land: 3%. Principal products: sugar, rice. Labor force (1985): 268,000; 44.5% industry and commerce. Major products: bauxite, alumina. Natural resources: bauxite, gold, diamonds, hardwood timber, shrimp. Exports: $189 million (f.o.b., 1990 est.): sugar, bauxite, rice, timber, shrimp, gold, molasses, rum. Imports: $246 million (c.i.f., 1991): petroleum, food, machinery. Major trading partners: U.K., U.S., Canada.

Geography. Guyana is situated on the northern coast of South America east of Venezuela, west of Suriname, and north of Brazil. The country consists of a low coastal area and the Guiana Highlands in the south. There is an extensive north-south network of rivers. Guyana is the size of Idaho.

Government. Guyana, formerly British Guiana, proclaimed itself a republic on Feb. 23, 1970, ending its tie with Britain while remaining in the Commonwealth.

Guyana has a unicameral legislature, the National Assembly, with 53 members directly elected for five-year terms and 12 elected by local councils. A 17-member Cabinet is headed by the President.

History. British Guiana won internal self-government in 1952. The next year the People's Progressive Party, headed by Cheddi B. Jagan, an East Indian dentist, won the elections and Jagan became Prime Minister. British authorities deposed him for alleged Communist connections. A coalition ousted Jagan in 1964, installing a moderate Socialist, Forbes Burnham, a black, as Prime Minister. On May 26, 1966, the country became an independent member of the Commonwealth and resumed its traditional name, Guyana.

After ruling Guyana for 21 years, Burnham died on Aug. 6, 1985, in a Guyana hospital after a throat operation. Desmond Hoyte, the country's Prime Minister succeeded him under the Guyanese constitution.

Jagan's People's Progressive Party won a majority in the general election of October 1992.

HAITI

Republic of Haiti
Prime Minister: Robert Malval (1993)
Area: 10,714 sq mi. (27,750 sq km)
Population (est. mid-1993): 6,500,000 (average annual rate of natural increase: 2.8%); birth rate: 43/1000; infant mortality rate: 105/1000; density per square mile: 614
Capital and largest city (est. 1989): Port-au-Prince, 514,438
Monetary unit: Gourde
Languages: French, Creole
Religion: Roman Catholic, 80%; Protestant, 16%
National name: République d'Haïti
Literacy rate: 53%
Economic summary: Gross domestic product (1990 est.): $2.7 billion; $440 per capita; –3.0% real growth rate; inflation 20%; unemployment 25–50%. Arable land: 20%. Principal agricultural products: coffee, sugar cane, rice, corn, sorghum. Labor force: 2,300,000; 66% in agriculture. Major industrial products: refined sugar, textiles, flour, cement, light assembly products. Natural resource: bauxite. Exports: $169 million (f.o.b., 1990 est.): coffee, light industrial products, agricultural products. Imports: $348 million (c.i.f., 1990 est.): machines and manufactures, food and beverages, petroleum products, fats and oils, chemicals. Major trading partner: U.S., Italy, France, Japan.

Geography. Haiti, in the West Indies, occupies the western third of the island of Hispaniola, which it shares with the Dominican Republic. About the size of Maryland, Haiti is two thirds mountainous, with the rest of the country marked by great valleys, extensive plateaus, and small plains. The most densely populated region is the Cul-de-Sac plain near Port-au-Prince.

Government. A republic with a bicameral assembly consisting of an upper house or Senate and a lower house, the House of Deputies. The National Assembly consists of 27 senate seats and 83 deputies.

Democratically-elected Pres. Aristide was replaced by an interim president following a military coup on Sept. 30, 1991. Under a U.N. accord, Aristide is scheduled to resume his presidential duties on Oct. 30, 1993.

History. Discovered by Columbus, who landed at Môle Saint Nicolas on Dec. 6, 1492, Haiti in 1697 became a French possession known as Saint Domingue. An insurrection among a slave population of 500,000 in 1791 ended with a declaration of independence by Pierre-Dominique Toussaint l'Ouverture in 1801. Napoleon Bonaparte suppressed the independence movement, but it eventually triumphed in 1804 under Jean-Jacques Dessalines, who gave the new nation the aboriginal name Haiti.

Its prosperity dissipated in internal strife as well as disputes with neighboring Santo Domingo during a succession of 19th-century dictatorships, a bankrupt Haiti accepted a U.S. customs receivership from 1905 to 1941. Direct U.S. rule from 1915 to 1934 brought a measure of stability and a population growth that made Haiti the most densely populated nation in the hemisphere.

In 1949, after four years of democratic rule by President Dumarsais Estimé, dictatorship returned under Gen. Paul Magloire, who was succeeded by François Duvalier in 1957.

Duvalier established a dictatorship based on secret police, known as the "Ton-ton Macoutes," who gunned down opponents of the regime. Duvalier's son, Jean-Claude, or "Baby Doc," succeeded his father in 1971 as ruler of the poorest nation in the Western Hemisphere. Duvalier fled the country in 1986 after strong unrest.

Following the election of December 6, 1990 which he won, Jean-Bertrand Aristide, a Roman Catholic priest, was sworn in as president on February 7, 1991—the country's first freely elected chief executive.

In September 1991 elements of the military seized the President and took control of the government. Although the OAS attempted to have Aristide reinstated the Army forced the Assembly officially to depose him. The OAS call for economic blockade led to a sharp downturn in an already poor economy. Many Haitians fled their country by whatever means was available.

The population largely ignored parliamentary elections the following January many saw as intended to pack the legislature with Aristide's foes. During the early months of 1993 the economy continued to deteriorate. In July Aristide and the army signed an accord to return the exiled president to power.

HONDURAS

Republic of Honduras
President: Rafael L. Callejas (1990)
Area: 43,277 sq mi. (112,088 sq km)
Population (est. mid-1993): 5,600,000 (average annual rate of natural increase: 3.1%); birth rate: 39/1000; infant mortality rate: 61/1000; density per square mile: 130
Capital and largest city (est. 1989): Tegucigalpa, 571,400; **Monetary unit:** Lempira; **Languages:** Spanish, some Indian dialects, English in Bay Islands Department; **Religion:** Roman Catholic about 97%, small Protestant minority; **National name:** República de Honduras; **Literacy rate:** 73%
Economic summary: Gross domestic product (1991 est.): $5.2 billion; $1,050 per capita; real growth rate –0.3%; inflation 26%; unemployment (1989) 15%. Arable land: 14%. Principal products: bananas, coffee, timber, beef, shrimp, citrus. Labor force (1985): 1,300,000; agriculture 62%; services 20%. Major industrial products: processed agricultural products, textiles and clothing, wood products. Natural resources: timber, gold, silver, copper, lead, zinc, iron ore, antimony. Exports: $1 billion (f.o.b., 1991): bananas, coffee, lumber, shrimp and lobster, minerals. Imports: $1.3 billion (c.i.f., 1991): manufactured goods, machinery, transportation equipment, chemicals, petroleum. Major trading partners: U.S., Caribbean countries, Western Europe, Japan, Latin America.

Geography. Honduras, in the north central part of Central America, has a 400-mile (644-km) Caribbean coastline and a 40-mile (64-km) Pacific frontage. Its neighbors are Guatemala to the west, El Salvador to the south, and Nicaragua to the east. Honduras is slightly larger than Tennessee. Generally mountainous, the country is marked by fertile plateaus, river valleys, and narrow coastal plains.

Government. The President serves a four-year term. There is a 134-member National Congress.

History. Columbus discovered Honduras on his last voyage in 1502. Honduras, with four other countries of Central America, declared its independence from Spain in 1821 and was part of a federation of Central American states until 1838. In that year it seceded from the federation and became a completely independent country.

In July 1969, El Salvador invaded Honduras after Honduran landowners had deported several thousand Salvadorans. The fighting left 1,000 dead and tens of thousands homeless. By threatening economic sanctions and military intervention, the OAS induced El Salvador to withdraw.

Although parliamentary democracy returned with the election of Roberto Suazo Córdova as President in 1982 after a decade of military rule, Honduras faced severe economic problems and tensions along its border with Nicaragua. "Contra" rebels, waging a guerrilla war against the Sandinista regime in Nicaragua, used Honduras as a training and staging area. At the same time, the United States used Honduras as a site for military exercises and built bases to train both Honduran and Salvadoran troops.

In the first democratic transition of power since 1932 Rafael Callejas became president in January 1990. The immediate task was to deal with a deficit caused in part by reduced U.S. aid and the previous government's fiscal policies.

In 1992 the passage of the Agriculture Modernization Law, intended to encourage foreign investment and crop development, increased tensions in the countryside.

HUNGARY

Republic of Hungary
President: Arpad Goncz (1990)
Premier: József Antall (1990)
Area: 35,919 sq mi. (93,030 sq km)
Population (est. mid-1993): 10,300,000 (average annual rate of natural increase: –0.2%); birth rate: 12/1000; infant mortality rate: 15.1/1000; density per square mile: 289
Capital: Budapest; **Largest cities (1991 est.):** Budapest, 2,018,000; Debrecen, 213,930; Miskolc, 194,000; Szeged, 176,100; Péces, 170,000; Györ, 129,600; **Monetary unit:** Forint; **Language:** Magyar; **Religions:** Roman Catholic, 67.5%; Protestant, 25%; atheist and others, 7.5%; **National name:** Magyar Köztársaság; **Literacy rate:** 99%
Economic summary: Gross domestic product (1991 est.): $60.1 billion; $5,700 per capita; –7% real growth rate; inflation rate 34%; unemployment rate 8.0%. Arable land: 54%. Principal agricultural products: corn, wheat, potatoes, sugar beets, sun flowers, livestock, dairy products. Labor force: 4,860,000; 43.2% in services, trade and government. Major industrial products: steel, chemicals, pharmaceuticals, textiles, transport equipment. Natural resources: bauxite, coal, natural gas. Exports: $10.2 billion (f.o.b., 1991): machinery and tools, industrial and consumer goods, raw materials. Imports: $11.7 billion (f.o.b., 1991): machinery and transport, fuels, chemical products, manufactured consumer goods. Major trading partners: C.I.S. countries, Eastern Europe.

Geography. This central European country the size of Indiana is bordered by Austria to the west, Czechoslovakia to the north, Ukraine and Romania to the east, and Yugoslavia to the south.

Most of Hungary is a fertile, rolling plain lying east of the Danube River and drained by the Danube and Tisza rivers. In the extreme northwest is the Little Hungarian Plain. South of that area is Lake Balaton (250 sq mi.; 648 sq km).

Government. Hungary is a Republic with legislative power vested in the unicameral National Assembly, whose 386 members are elected directly for four-year terms. The National Assembly elects the President. The supreme body of state power is the 21-member Presidential Council elected by the National Assembly. The supreme administrative body is the Council of Ministers, headed by the Premier.

The major political parties are the Socialist Party, the Hungarian Democratic Forum, the Alliance of Free Democrats, the Independent Socialist Party and the Independent Smallholder's Party.

History. About 2,000 years ago, Hungary was part of the Roman provinces of Pannonia and Dacia. In A.D. 896 it was invaded by the Magyars, who founded a kingdom. Christianity was accepted during the reign of Stephen I (St. Stephen) (997–1038).

The peak of Hungary's great period of medieval power came during the reign of Louis I the Great (1342–82), whose dominions touched the Baltic, Black, and Mediterranean seas.

War with the Turks broke out in 1389, and for more than 100 years the Turks advanced through the Balkans. When the Turks smashed a Hungarian army in 1526, western and northern Hungary accepted Hapsburg rule to escape Turkish occupation. Transylvania became independent under Hungarian princes. Intermittent war with the Turks was waged until a peace treaty was signed in 1699.

After the suppression of the 1848 revolt against Hapsburg rule, led by Louis Kossuth, the dual monarchy of Austria-Hungary was set up in 1867.

The dual monarchy was defeated with the other Central Powers in World War I. After a short-lived republic in 1918, the chaotic Communist rule of 1919 under Béla Kun ended with the Romanians occupying Budapest on Aug. 4, 1919. When the Romanians left, Adm. Nicholas Horthy entered the capital with a national army. The Treaty of Trianon of June 4, 1920, cost Hungary 68% of its land and 58% of its population. Meanwhile, the National Assembly had restored the legal continuity of the old monarchy; and, on March 1, 1920, Horthy was elected Regent.

Following the German invasion of Russia on June 22, 1941, Hungary joined the attack against the Soviet Union, but the war was not popular and Hungarian troops were almost entirely withdrawn from the eastern front by May 1943. German occupation troops set up a puppet government after Horthy's appeal for an armistice with advancing Soviet troops on Oct. 15, 1944, had resulted in his overthrow. The German regime soon fled the capital, however, and on December 23 a provisional government was formed in Soviet-occupied eastern Hungary. On Jan. 20, 1945, it signed an armistice in Moscow. Early the next year, the National Assembly approved a constitutional law abolishing the thousand-year-old monarchy and establishing a republic.

By the Treaty of Paris (1947), Hungary had to give up all territory it had acquired since 1937 and to pay \$300 million reparations to the U.S.S.R., Czechoslovakia, and Yugoslavia. In 1948 the Communist Party, with the support of Soviet troops seized control. Hungary was proclaimed a People's Republic and one-party state in 1949. Industry was nationalized, the land collectivized into state farms, and the opposition terrorized by the secret police.

The terror, modeled after that of the U.S.S.R., reached its height with the trial of József Cardinal Mindszenty, Roman Catholic primate. He confessed to fantastic charges under duress of drugs or brainwashing and was sentenced to life imprisonment in 1949. Protests were voiced in all parts of the world.

On Oct. 23, 1956, anti-Communist revolution broke out in Budapest. To cope with it, the Communists set up a coalition government and called former Premier Imre Nagy back to head it. But he and most of his ministers were swept by the logic of events into the anti-Communist opposition, and he declared Hungary a neutral power, withdrawing from the Warsaw Treaty and appealing to the United Nations for help.

One of his ministers, János Kádár, established a counter-regime and asked the U.S.S.R. to send in military power. Soviet troops and tanks suppressed the revolution in bloody fighting after 190,000 people had fled the country and Mindszenty, freed from jail, had taken refuge in the U.S. Embassy.

Kádár was succeeded as Premier, but not party secretary, by Gyula Kallai in 1965. Continuing his program of national reconciliation, Kádár emptied prisons, reformed the secret police, and eased travel restrictions.

Following local and parliamentary elections in October 1990, József Antall's Hungarian Democratic Forum and its conservative coalition parties held 60% of the parliamentary seats. The last Soviet troops left Hungary in June 1991, thereby ending almost 47 years of military presence.

The transition to a market economy was proving difficult, but Western influence appeared secure in that Hungary received over half of all foreign investment in the region. Hungary strengthened its ties with Poland and Czechoslovakia but grew concerned about the fate of ethnic Hungarians in neighboring countries.

Hungary cautiously watched the birth of Slovakia and its treatment of a large ethnic Hungarian minority. The country also feared becoming involved in the wars in the break-up of neighboring Yugoslavia.

The ruling party's vocal right-wing faction proved embarrassingly controversial, leading in June 1993 to their expulsion from the party.

ICELAND

Republic of Iceland
President: Mrs. Vigdis Finnbogadottir (1980)
Prime Minister: David Oddsson (1991)
Area: 39,709 sq mi. (102,846 sq km)[1]
Population (est. mid-1993): 300,000 (average annual rate of natural increase: 1.1%); birth rate: 18/1000; infant mortality rate: 5.5/1000; density per square mile: 7
Capital and largest city (est. 1990): Reykjavik, 97,569; **Monetary unit:** M.N. króna; **Language:** Icelandic; **Religion:** Evangelical Lutheran; **National name:** Lydveldid Island; **Literacy rate:** 100%
Economic summary: Gross domestic product (1991): \$4.2 billion; \$16,200 per capita; real growth rate 0.3%; inflation 7.5%; unemployment 1.8%. Arable land: NEGL%; principal agricultural products: livestock, potatoes and turnips. Labor force: 134,429; 55.4% in commerce, finance and services. Major products: processed aluminum, fish. Natural resources: fish, diatomite, hydroelectric and geothermal power. Exports: \$1.6 billion (f.o.b., 1991): fish, animal products, aluminum, diatomite. Imports: \$1.7 billion (c.i.f., 1991): petroleum products, machinery and transportation equipment, food, textiles. Major trading partners: European Communities (EC) countries, European Free Trade Association (EFTA) countries, U.S., Japan, and Denmark,.

1. Including some offshore islands.

Geography. Iceland, an island about the size of Kentucky, lies in the north Atlantic Ocean east of Greenland and just touches the Arctic Circle. It is one of the most volcanic regions in the world.

Small fresh-water lakes are to be found throughout the island, and there are many natural phenomena, including hot springs, geysers, sulfur beds, canyons, waterfalls, and swift rivers. More than 13% of the area is covered by snowfields and glaciers, and most of the people live in the 7% of the island comprising fertile coastlands.

Government. The president is elected for four years by popular vote. Executive power resides in the prime minister and his Cabinet. The Althing (Parliament) is composed of 63 members.

History. Iceland was first settled shortly before 900, mainly by Norse. A Constitution drawn up about 930 created a form of democracy and provided for an Althing, or General Assembly.

In 1262–64, Iceland came under Norwegian rule and passed to ultimate Danish control through the formation of the Union of Kalmar in 1483. In 1874, Icelanders obtained their own Constitution. In 1918, Denmark recognized Iceland as a separate state with unlimited sovereignty but still nominally under the Danish king.

On June 17, 1944, after a popular referendum, the Althing proclaimed Iceland an independent republic.

The British occupied Iceland in 1940, immediately after the German invasion of Denmark. In 1942, the U.S. took over the burden of protection. Iceland refused to abandon its neutrality in World War II and thus forfeited charter membership in the United Nations, but it cooperated with the Allies throughout the conflict. Iceland joined the North Atlantic Treaty Organization in 1949.

Iceland unilaterally extended its territorial waters from 12 to 50 nautical miles in 1972, precipitating a running dispute with Britain known as the "cod war."

Elections to the Althing in April 1991 gave the opposition Independence Party 26 of the 63 seats, up from 18. Prime Minister Hermannson resigned allowing David Oddsson of the Independence Party to enter into talks with the Social Democrats about a coalition government. None of the parties is interested in Iceland pursuing membership in the E.C., although it is a member of the European Free Trade Association.

GNP fell by 3% in 1992 largely owing to declining fish stocks and resulting in increased unemployment. In response new public construction projects were started and the deficit was allowed to grow.

INDIA

Republic of India
President: Dr. Shankar Dayal Sharma (1992)
Prime Minister: P.V. Narasimha Rao (1991)
Area: 1,229,737 sq mi. (3,185,019 sq km)
Population (est. mid-1993): 897,400,000 (average annual rate of natural increase: 2.1%); birth rate: 31/1000; infant mortality rate: 91/1000; density per square mile: 782
Capital (1991): New Delhi, 294,149; **Largest cities (1992):** Greater Bombay, 12,916,272; Calcutta, 10,916,272; Delhi, 8,375,188; Madras, 5,361,468; Ahmedabad, 4,775,670; Bangalore, 4,807,019; Kanpur, 2,284,000; **Monetary unit:** Rupee; **Principal languages;** Hindi (official), English (official), Bengali, Gujarati, Kashmiri, Malayalam, Marathi, Oriya, Punjabi, Tamil, Telugu, Urdu, Kannada, Assamese, Sanskrit, Sindhi (all recognized by the Constitution). Dialects, 1,652; **Religions:** Hindu, 82.6%; Islam, 11.3%; Christian, 2.4%; Sikh, 2%; Buddhists, 0.71%; Jains, 0.48%; **National name:** Bharat; **Literacy rate:** 52.11%; **Member of Commonwealth of Nations**
Economic summary: Gross domestic product (FY92 est.): $328 billion; $380 per capita; real growth rate 2.11%; inflation (1991) 12%; unemployment (1991 est.) 20%. Arable land: 55%. Principal products: rice, wheat, oilseeds, cotton, tea, opium poppy (for pharmaceuticals). Labor force (1992): 314,903,642; 67% in agriculture. Major industrial products: jute, processed food, steel, machinery, transport machinery, cement. Natural resources: iron ore, coal, manganese, mica, bauxite, limestone, textiles. Exports: $20.2 billion (f.o.b., FY91): tea, coffee, iron ore, fish products, chemicals, engineering goods, textiles, gems and jewelry. Imports: $25.2 billion (c.i.f., FY91): petroleum, edible oils, capital goods, uncut gems and jewelry, chemicals, iron and steel. Major trading partners: U.S., C.I.S. nations, Japan, E.C., Middle East

Geography. One third the area of the United States, the Republic of India occupies most of the subcontinent of India in south Asia. It borders on China in the northeast. Other neighbors are Pakistan on the west, Nepal and Bhutan on the north, and Burma and Bangladesh on the east.

The country contains a large part of the great Indo-Gangetic plain, which extends from the Bay of Bengal on the east to the Afghan frontier and the Arabian Sea on the west. This plain is the richest and most densely settled part of the subcontinent. Another distinct natural region is the Deccan, a plateau of 2,000 to 3,000 feet (610 to 914 m) in elevation, occupying the southern portion of the subcontinent.

Forming a part of the republic are several groups of islands—the Laccadives (14 islands) in the Arabian Sea and the Andamans (204 islands) and the Nicobars (19 islands) in the Bay of Bengal.

India's three great river systems, all rising in the Himalayas, have extensive deltas. The Ganges flows south and then east for 1,540 miles (2,478 km) across the northern plain to the Bay of Bengal; part of its delta, which begins 220 miles (354 km) from the sea, is within the republic. The Indus, starting in Tibet, flows northwest for several hundred miles in the Kashmir before turning southwest toward the Arabian Sea; it is important for irrigation in Pakistan. The Brahmaputra, also rising in Tibet, flows eastward, first through India and then south into Bangladesh and the Bay of Bengal.

Government. India is a federal republic. It is also a member of the Commonwealth of Nations, a status defined at the 1949 London Conference of Prime Ministers, by which India recognizes the Queen as head of the Commonwealth. Under the Constitution effective Jan. 26, 1950, India has a parliamentary type of government.

The constitutional head of the state is the President, who is elected every five years. He is advised by the Prime Minister and a Cabinet based on a majority of the bicameral Parliament, which consists of a Council of States (Rajya Sabha), representing the constituent units of the republic and a House of the People (Lok Sabha), elected every five years by universal suffrage.

History. The Aryans who invaded India between 2400 and 1500 B.C. from the northwest found a land already well civilized. Buddhism was founded in the 6th century B.C. and spread through northern India, most notably by one of the greatest ancient kings, Asoka (c. 269–232 B.C.), who also unified most of the Indian subcontinent.

In 1526, Moslem invaders founded the great Mogul empire, centered on Delhi, which lasted, at least in name, until 1857. Akbar the Great (1542–1605) strengthened and consolidated this empire. The long reign of his great-grandson, Aurangzeb (1658–1707), represents both the greatest extent of the Mogul empire and the beginning of its decay.

Vasco da Gama, the Portuguese explorer, visited India first in 1498, and for the next 100 years the Portuguese had a virtual monopoly on trade with the subcontinent. Meanwhile, the English founded the East India Company, which set up its first factory at Surat in 1612 and began expanding its influence, fighting the Indian rulers and the French, Dutch, and Portuguese traders simultaneously.

Bombay, taken from the Portuguese, became the seat of English rule in 1687. The defeat of French and Islamic armies by Lord Clive in the decade ending in 1760 laid the foundation of the British Empire in India. From then until 1858, when the administration of India was formally transferred to the British Crown following the Sepoy Mutiny of native troops in 1857, the East India Company suppressed native uprisings and extended British rule.

After World War I, in which the Indian states sent more than 6 million troops to fight beside the Allies, Indian nationalist unrest rose to new heights under the leadership of a little Hindu lawyer, Mohandas K. Gandhi, called Mahatma Gandhi. His tactics called for nonviolent revolts against British authority. He soon became the leading spirit of the All-India Congress Party, which was the spearhead of revolt. In 1919 the British gave added responsibility to Indian officials, and in 1935 India was given a federal form of government and a measure of self-rule.

In 1942, with the Japanese pressing hard on the eastern borders of India, the British War Cabinet tried and failed to reach a political settlement with nationalist leaders. The Congress Party took the position that the British must quit India. In 1942, fearing mass civil disobedience, the government of India carried out widespread arrests of Congress leaders, including Gandhi.

Gandhi was released in 1944 and negotiations for a settlement were resumed. Finally, in February 1947, the Labor government announced its determination to transfer power to "responsible Indian hands" by June 1948 even if a Constitution had not been worked out.

Lord Mountbatten as Viceroy, by June 1947, achieved agreement on the partitioning of India along religious lines and on the splitting of the provinces of Bengal and the Punjab, which the Moslems had claimed.

The Indian Independence Act, passed quickly by the British Parliament, received royal assent on July 18, 1947, and on August 15 the Indian Empire passed into history.

Jawaharlal Nehru, leader of the Congress Party, was made Prime Minister. Before an exchange of populations could be arranged, bloody riots occurred among the communal groups, and armed conflict broke out over rival claims to the princely state of Jammu and Kashmir. Peace was restored only with the greatest difficulty. In 1949 a Constitution, along the lines of the U.S. Constitution, was approved making India a sovereign republic. Under a federal structure the states were organized on linguistic lines.

The dominance of the Congress Party contributed to stability. In 1956 the republic absorbed the former French settlements. Five years later, it forcibly annexed the Portuguese enclaves of Goa, Damao, and Diu.

Nehru died in 1964. His successor, Lal Bahadur Shastri, died on Jan. 10, 1966. Nehru's daughter, Indira Gandhi, became Prime Minister, and she continued his policy of nonalignment.

In 1971 the Pakistani Army moved in to quash the independence movement in East Pakistan that was supported by clandestine aid from India, and some 10 million Bengali refugees poured across the border into India, creating social, economic, and health problems. After numerous border incidents, India invaded East Pakistan and in two weeks forced the surrender of the Pakistani army. East Pakistan was established as an independent state and renamed Bangladesh.

In the summer of 1975, the world's largest democracy veered suddenly toward authoritarianism when a judge in Allahabad, Mrs. Gandhi's home constituency, found her landslide victory in the 1971 elections invalid because civil servants had illegally aided her campaign. Amid demands for her resignation, Mrs. Gandhi decreed a state of emergency on June 26 and ordered mass arrests of her critics, including all opposition party leaders except the Communists.

In 1976, India and Pakistan formally renewed diplomatic relations.

Despite strong opposition to her repressive measures and particularly the resentment against compulsory birth control programs, Mrs. Gandhi in 1977 announced parliamentary elections for March. At the same time, she freed most political prisoners.

The landslide victory of Morarji R. Desai unseated Mrs. Gandhi.

Mrs. Gandhi staged a spectacular comeback in the elections of January 1980.

In 1984, Mrs. Gandhi ordered the Indian Army to root out a band of Sikh holy men and gunmen who were using the holiest shrine of the Sikh religion, the Golden Temple in Amritsar, as a base for terrorist raids in a violent campaign for greater political autonomy in the strategic Punjab border state. The perceived sacrilege to the Golden Temple kindled outrage among many of India's 14 million Sikhs and brought a spasm of mutinies and desertions by Sikh officers and soldiers in the army.

On Oct. 31, 1984, Mrs. Gandhi was assassinated by two men identified by police as Sikh members of her bodyguard. The ruling Congress I Party chose her older son, Rajiv Gandhi, to succeed her as Prime Minister.

One week after the resignation of Prime Minister Shekhar, India's president in March 1991 called for national elections. While at an election rally on May 22 former prime minister Rajiv Gandhi was assassinated. Final phases of the election were postponed a month. When they were resumed the Congress Party and its allies won 236 seats in the lower house, 20 short of a majority. P.V. Narasimha Rao was chosen to form a new government. In elections for 15 parliamentary seats in November 1991 Rao's government won more votes than expected, largely interpreted as a sign of willingness to move closer toward a free-market economy.

Communal strife and violence in early 1993 led to a cabinet shakeup. The destruction of a mosque in a northern town was followed by nationwide disturbances in which more than 1,200 people died.

Native States. Most of the 560-odd native states and subdivisions of pre-1947 India acceded to the new nation, and the central government pursued a vigorous policy of integration. This took three forms: merger into adjacent provinces, conversion into centrally administered areas, and grouping into unions of states. Finally, under a controversial reorganization plan effective Nov. 1, 1956, the unions of states were abolished and merged into adjacent states, and India became a union of 15 states and 8 centrally administered areas. A 16th state was added in 1962, and in 1966, the Punjab was partitioned into two states. Today India consists of 25 states and 7 Union Territories.

Resolution of the territorial dispute over Kashmir grew out of peace negotiations following the two-week India-Pakistan war of 1971. After sporadic skirmishing, an accord reached July 3, 1972, committed both powers to withdraw troops from a temporary cease-fire line after the border was fixed. Agreement on the border was reached Dec. 7, 1972.

In April 1975, the Indian Parliament voted to make the 300-year-old kingdom of Sikkim a full-fledged Indian state, and the annexation took effect May 16.

Situated in the Himalayas, Sikkim was a virtual dependency of Tibet until the early 19th century. Under an 1890 treaty between China and Great Britain, it became a British protectorate, and was made an Indian protectorate after Britain quit the subcontinent.

INDONESIA

Republic of Indonesia

President: Soeharto (1969)[1]

Area: 735,268 sq mi. (1,904,344 sq km)[2]

Population (est. mid-1993): 187,600,000 (average annual rate of natural increase: 1.7%); birth rate: 26/1000; infant mortality rate: 68/1000; density per square mile: 266

Capital: Jakarta; **Largest cities (est. 1985):** Jakarta, 9,404,477; Surabaya, 2,345,000; Medan, 2,110,000; Bandung, 1,633,000; Semarang (1984), 1,077,000; **Monetary unit:** Rupiah; **Languages:** Bahasa Indonesia (official), Dutch, English, and more than 583 languages, and dialects; **Religions:** Islam, 87%; Christian, 9%; Hindu, 2%; other, 2%; **National name:** Republik Indonesia; **Literacy rate:** 86.3%

Economic summary: Gross domestic product (1991 est.): $122 billion; $630 per capita; real growth rate 6%; inflation 10%; unemployment 3%. Arable land: 8%. Principal agricultural products: rice, cassava, peanuts, rubber, coffee. Labor force: 67,000,000; 10% in manufacturing. Major industrial products: petroleum, timber, textiles, cement, fertilizer, rubber. Natural resources: oil, timber, nickel, natural gas, tin, bauxite, copper. Exports: $25.7 billion (f.o.b., 1990): petroleum and liquid natural gas, timber, rubber, coffee, textiles. Imports: $21.8 billion (f.o.b., 1990): chemicals, machinery, manufactured goods. Major trading partners: Japan, U.S., Singapore, E.C.

1. General Soeharto served as Acting President of Indonesia from 1967. He was elected President in March 1968. 2. Includes West Irian (former Netherlands New Guinea), renamed Irian Jaya in March 1973 (159,355 sq mi.; 412,731 sq km), and former Portuguese Timor (5,763 sq mi.; 14,925 sq km), annexed in 1976.

Geography. Indonesia is part of the Malay archipelago in Southeast Asia with an area nearly three times that of Texas. It consists of the islands of Sumatra, Java, Bali, Madura, Borneo (except Sarawak and Brunei in the north), the Celebes, the Moluccas, Irian Jaya, and about 30 smaller archipelagos, totaling 13,677 islands, of which about 6,000 are inhabited. Its neighbor to the north is Malaysia and to the east Papua New Guinea.

A backbone of mountain ranges extends throughout the main islands of the archipelago. Earthquakes are frequent, and there are many active volcanoes.

Government. The President is elected by the People's Consultative Assembly, whose 1,000 members include the functioning legislative arm, the 500-member House of Representatives. Meeting at least once every five years, the Assembly has broad policy functions. The House, 100 of whose members are appointed from the armed forces, meets at least once annually. General Soeharto was elected unopposed to a sixth five-year term in 1993.

History. Indonesia is inhabited by Malayan and Papuan peoples ranging from the more advanced Javanese and Balinese to the more primitive Dyaks of Borneo. Invasions from China and India contributed Chinese and Indian admixtures.

During the first few centuries of the Christian era, most of the islands came under the influence of Hindu priests and traders, who spread their culture and religion. Moslem invasions began in the 13th century, and most of the area was Moslem by the 15th. Portuguese traders arrived early in the 16th century but were ousted by the Dutch about 1595. After Napoleon subjugated the Netherlands homeland in 1811, the British seized the islands but returned them to the Dutch in 1816. In 1922 the islands were made an integral part of the Netherlands kingdom.

During World War II, Indonesia was under Japanese military occupation with nominal native self-government. When the Japanese surrendered to the Allies, President Sukarno and Mohammed Hatta, his Vice President, proclaimed Indonesian independence from the Dutch on Aug. 17, 1945. Allied troops—mostly British Indian troops—fought the nationalists until the arrival of Dutch troops. In November 1946, the Dutch and the Indonesians reached a draft agreement contemplating formation of a Netherlands-Indonesian Union, but differences in interpretation resulted in more fighting between Dutch and Indonesian forces.

On Nov. 2, 1949, Dutch and Indonesian leaders agreed upon the terms of union. The transfer of sovereignty took place at Amsterdam on Dec. 27, 1949. In February 1956 Indonesia abrogated the Union with the Netherlands and in August 1956 repudiated its debt to the Netherlands. In 1963, Netherlands New Guinea was transferred to Indonesia and renamed West Irian. In 1973 it became Irian Jaya.

Hatta and Sukarno, the co-fathers of Indonesian independence, split after it was achieved over Sukarno's concept of "guided democracy." Under Sukarno, the country's leading political figure for almost a half century, the Indonesian Communist Party gradually gained increasing influence.

After an attempted coup was put down by General Soeharto, the army chief of staff, and officers loyal to him, thousands of Communist suspects were sought out and killed all over the country. Soeharto took over the reins of government, gradually eased Sukarno out of office, and took full power in 1967.

Soeharto permitted national elections, which moved the nation back to representative government. He also ended hostilities with Malaysia. Under President Soeharto, Indonesia has been strongly anticommunist. It also has been politically stable and has made progress in economic development.

Indonesia invaded the former Portuguese half of the island of Timor in 1975, and annexed the territory in 1976. More than 100,000 Timorese, a sixth of the mostly Catholic population, were reported to have died from famine, disease, and fighting since the annexation.

Several new pro-democracy groups were formed in 1991 amid speculation over Soeharto's plans for a new five-year term. The government continued its reform program, cutting tariffs and barriers to foreign investment.

In November 1991 Indonesian troops killed numerous mourners at a funeral in East Timor.

In March 1993 the 1,000 member People's Consultative Assembly, a body which meets every five years for the express purpose of choosing a president, reelected Soeharto, who ran unopposed.

IRAN

Islamic Republic of Iran
President: Hashemi Rafsanjani (1989)
Area: 636,293 sq mi. (1,648,000 sq km)
Population (est. mid-1993): 62,800,000 (average annual rate of natural increase: 3.5%); birth rate: 45/1000; infant mortality rate: 76/1000; density per square mile: 99
Capital: Teheran; **Largest cities (1986):** Teheran, 6,042,584; Mashed, 1,463,508; Isfahan, 986,753; Tabriz, 971,482; **Monetary unit:** Rial; **Languages:** Farsi (Persian), Kurdish, Arabic; **Religions:** Shi'ite Moslem, 95%; Sunni Moslem, 4%; **Literacy rate:** 48% (est.)
Economic summary: Gross national product (1991 est.): $90 billion; $1,500 per capita; real growth rate 10%; inflation 18%; unemployment (1989) 30%. Arable land: 8%. Principal agricultural products: wheat, barley, rice, sugar beets, cotton, dates, raisins, sheep, goats. Labor force: 15,400,000; 33% in agriculture. Major industrial products: crude and refined oil, textiles, petrochemicals, cement, processed foods, steel and copper fabrication. Natural resources: oil, gas, iron, copper. Exports: $17.8 billion (f.o.b., 1990): petroleum, carpets. Imports: $15.9 billion (c.i.f., 1990): machinery, military supplies, foodstuffs, pharmaceuticals. Major trading partners: Japan, Germany, Netherlands, U.K., Italy, Spain, Turkey.

Geography. Iran, a Middle Eastern country south of the Caspian Sea and north of the Persian Gulf, is three times the size of Arizona. It shares borders with Iraq, Turkey, the U.S.S.R., Afghanistan, and Pakistan.

In general, the country is a plateau averaging 4,000 feet (1,219 m) in elevation. There are also maritime lowlands along the Persian Gulf and the Caspian Sea. The Elburz Mountains in the north rise to 18,603 feet (5,670 m) at Mt. Damavend. From northwest to southeast, the country is crossed by a desert 800 miles (1,287 km) long.

Government. The Pahlavi dynasty was overthrown on Feb. 11, 1979, by followers of the Ayatollah Ruhollah Khomeini. After a referendum endorsed the establishment of a republic, Khomeini drafted a Constitution calling for a President to be popularly elected every four years, an appointed Prime Minister, and a unicameral National Consultative Assembly, popularly elected every four years. A constitutional amendment in 1989 eliminated the post of Prime Minister.

Khomeini also instituted a Revolutionary Council to insure the adherence to Islamic principles in all phases of Iranian life. The Council formally handed over its powers to the Assembly after the organization of the legislature in July 1980, but continued to exercise power behind the scenes. The parliament consists of 270 seats.

History. Oil-rich Iran was called Persia before 1935. Its key location blocks the lower land gate to Asia and also stands in the way of traditional Russian ambitions for access to the Indian Ocean. After periods of Assyrian, Median, and Achaemenidian rule, Persia became a powerful empire under Cyrus the Great, reaching from the Indus to the Nile at its zenith in 525 B.C. It fell to Alexander in 331–30 B.C. and to the Seleucids in 312–02 B.C., and a native Persian regime arose about 130 B.C. Another Persian regime arose about A.D. 224, but it fell to the Arabs in 637. In the 12th century, the Mongols took their turn ruling Persia, and in the early part of the 18th century, the Turks occupied the country.

An Anglo-Russian convention of 1907 divided Persia into two spheres of influence. British attempts to impose a protectorate over the entire country were defeated in 1919. Two years later, Gen. Reza Pahlavi seized the government and was elected hereditary Shah in 1925. Subsequently he did much to modernize the country and abolished all foreign extraterritorial rights.

Increased pro-Axis activity led to Anglo-Russian occupation of Iran in 1941 and deposition of the Shah in favor of his son, Mohammed Reza Pahlavi.

Ali Razmara became premier in 1950 and pledged to restore efficient and honest government, but he was assassinated after less than nine months in office and Mohammed Mossadegh took over. Mossadegh was ousted in August 1953, by Fazollah Zahedi, whom the Shah had named premier.

Opposition to the Shah spread, despite the imposition of martial law in September 1978, and massive demonstrations demanded the return of the exiled Ayatollah Ruhollah Khomeini. Riots and strikes continued despite the appointment of an opposition leader, Shahpur Bakhtiar, as premier on Dec. 29. The Shah and his family left Iran on Jan. 16, 1979, for a "vacation," leaving power in the hands of a regency council.

Khomeini returned on Feb. 1 to a nation in turmoil as military units loyal to the Shah continued to support Bakhtiar and clashed with revolutionaries. Khomeini appointed Mehdi Bazargan as premier of the provisional government and in two days of fighting, revolutionaries forced the military to capitulate on Feb. 11.

The new government began a program of nationalization of insurance companies, banks, and industries both locally and foreign-owned. Oil production fell amid the political confusion.

Khomeini, ignoring opposition, proceeded with his plans for revitalizing Islamic traditions. He urged women to return to the veil, or chador; banned alcohol and mixed bathing, and prohibited music from radio and television broadcasting, declaring it to be "no different from opium."

Revolutionary militants invaded the U.S. Embassy in Teheran on Nov. 4, 1979, seized staff members as hostages, and precipitated an international crisis.

Khomeini refused all appeals, even a unanimous vote by the U.N. Security Council demanding immediate release of the hostages.

Iranian hostility toward Washington was reinforced by the Carter administration's economic boycott and deportation order against Iranian students in the U.S., the break in diplomatic relations and ultimately an aborted U.S. raid in April aimed at rescuing the hostages.

As the first anniversary of the embassy seizure neared, Khomeini and his followers insisted on their original conditions: guarantee by the U.S. not to interfere in Iran's affairs, cancellation of U.S. damage claims against Iran, release of $8 billion in frozen Iranian assets, an apology, and the return of the assets held by the former imperial family.

These conditions were largely met and the 52 American hostages were released on Jan. 20, ending 444 days in captivity.

From the release of the hostages onward, President Bani-Sadr and the conservative clerics of the dominant Islamic Republican Party clashed with growing frequency. He was stripped of his command of the armed forces by Khomeini on June 6 and ousted as President on June 22. On July 24, Prime Minister Mohammed Ali Rajai was elected overwhelmingly to the Presidency.

Rajai and Prime Minister Mohammed Javad Bahonar were killed on Aug. 30 by a bomb in Bahonar's office. Hojatolislam Mohammed Ali Khamenei, a clergyman, leader of the Islamic Republican Party and spokesman for Khomeini, was elected President on Oct. 2, 1981.

The sporadic war with Iraq regained momentum in 1982, as Iran launched an offensive in March and regained much of the border area occupied by Iraq in late 1980.

Iran continued to be at war with Iraq well into 1988. Although Iraq expressed its willingness to cease fighting, Iran stated that it would not stop the war until Iraq agreed to make payment for war damages to Iran, and punish the Iraqi government leaders involved in the conflict.

On July 20, 1988, Khomeini, after a series of Iranian military reverses, agreed to cease-fire negotiations with Iraq. A cease-fire went into effect Aug. 20, 1988.

Khomeini died in June 1989.

By early 1991 the Islamic Revolution appeared to have lost much of its militancy. Attempting to revive a stagnant economy President Rafsanjani took measures to decentralize the command system and introduce free-market mechanisms.

Rafsanjani won reelection in June 1993 but in the four-way race he obtained only 63% of the vote with 56% of the electorate casting ballots, which was interpreted as due to popular frustration and apathy.

IRAQ

Republic of Iraq
President: Saddam Hussein (1979)
Area: 167,920 sq mi. (434,913 sq km)
Population (est. mid-1993): 19,200,000 (average annual rate of natural increase: 3.7%); birth rate: 45/1000; infant mortality rate: 79/1000; density per square mile: 113
Capital: Baghdad; **Largest cities (est. 1985):** Baghdad, 4,648,609; Basra, 616,700; Mosul, 570,926; **Monetary unit:** Iraqi dinar; **Languages:** Arabic (official) and Kurdish; **Religions:** Islam, 95%; Christian or other, 5%; **National name:** Jumbouriyat Al Iraq; **Literacy rate:** 55–65% (est.)
Economic summary: Gross national product (1989 est.): $35 billion, $1,940 per capita; 5% real growth rate; inflation (1989): 45%. Arable land: 12%. Principal products: dates, livestock, wheat, barley, cotton, rice. Labor force: 3,400,000 (1984); 28% in industry. Major products: petroleum, chemicals, textiles,, construction materials. Natural resources: oil, natural gas, phosphates, sulfur. Exports: $10.4 billion (f.o.b., 1990): petroleum and refined products, machinery, chemicals, dates. Imports: $6.6 billion (c.i.f., 1990): manufactured goods, food. Major trading partners: France, Italy, Japan, Germany, Brazil, U.K., U.S., Turkey, C.I.S. countries.

Geography. Iraq, a triangle of mountains, desert, and fertile river valley, is bounded on the east by Iran, on the north by Turkey, the west by Syria and Jordan, and the south by Saudi Arabia and Kuwait. It is twice the size of Idaho.

The country has arid desertland west of the Euphrates, a broad central valley between the Euphrates and Tigris, and mountains in the northeast. The fertile lower valley is formed by the delta of the two rivers, which join about 120 miles (193 km) from the head of the Persian Gulf. The gulf coastline is 26 miles (42 km) long. The only port for seagoing vessels is Basra, which is on the Shatt-al-Arab River near the head of the Persian Gulf.

Government. Since the coup d'etat of July 1968, Iraq has been governed by the Arab Ba'ath Socialist Party through a Council of Command of the Revolution headed by the President. There is also a Council of Ministers headed by the President.

History. From earliest times Iraq was known as Mesopotamia—the land between the rivers—for it embraces a large part of the alluvial plains of the Tigris and Euphrates.

An advanced civilization existed by 4000 B.C. Sometime after 2000 B.C. the land became the center of the ancient Babylonian and Assyrian empires. It was conquered by Cyrus the Great of Persia in 538 B.C., and by Alexander in 331 B.C. After an Arab conquest in A.D. 637–40, Baghdad became capital of the ruling caliphate. The country was cruelly pillaged by the Mongols in 1258, and during the 16th, 17th, and 18th centuries was the object of repeated Turkish-Persian competition.

Nominal Turkish suzerainty imposed in 1638 was replaced by direct Turkish rule in 1831. In World War I, an Anglo-Indian force occupied most of the country, and Britain was given a mandate over the area in 1920. The British recognized Iraq as a kingdom in 1922 and terminated the mandate in 1932 when Iraq was admitted to the League of Nations. In World War II, Iraq generally adhered to its 1930 treaty of alliance with Britain, but in 1941, British troops were compelled to put down a pro-Axis revolt led by Premier Rashid Ali.

Iraq became a charter member of the Arab League in 1945, and Iraqi troops took part in the Arab invasion of Palestine in 1948.

Faisal II, born on May 2, 1935, succeeded his father, Ghazi I, who was killed in an automobile accident on April 4, 1939. Faisal and his uncle, Crown Prince Abdul-Illah, were assassinated in July 1958 in a swift revolutionary coup that brought to power a military junta headed by Abdul Karem Kassim. Kassim, in turn, was overthrown and killed in a coup staged March 8, 1963, by the Ba'ath Socialist Party.

Abdel Salam Arif, a leader in the 1958 coup, staged another coup in November 1963, driving the Ba'ath members of the revolutionary council from power. He adopted a new constitution in 1964. In 1966, he, two Cabinet members, and other supporters died in a helicopter crash. His brother, Gen. Abdel Rahman Arif, assumed the presidency, crushed the opposition, and won an indefinite extension of his term in 1967. His regime was ousted in July 1968 by a junta led by Maj. Gen. Ahmed Hassan al-Bakr.

A long-standing dispute over control of the Shatt al-Arab waterway between Iraq and Iran broke into full-scale war on Sept. 20, 1980. Iraqi planes attacked Iranian airfields and the Abadan refinery, and Iraqi ground forces moved into Iran.

Despite the smaller size of its armed forces, Iraq took and held the initiative by seizing Abadan and Khurramshahr together with substantial Iranian territory by December and beating back Iranian counterattacks in January. Peace efforts by the Islamic nations, the nonaligned, and the United Nations failed as 1981 wore on and the war stagnated.

In 1982, the Iraqis fell back to their own country and dug themselves in behind sandbagged defensive fortifications. From the beginning of the war in September 1980 to September 1984, foreign military analysts estimated that more than 100,000 Iranians and perhaps 50,000 Iraqis had been killed.

The Iraqis clearly wanted to end the war, but the Iranians refused.

In February 1986, Iranian forces gained on two fronts; but Iraq retook most of the lost ground in 1988 and the war continued a stalemate. In August, Iraq and Iran agreed to hold direct talks after a cease-fire takes effect.

In July 1990, President Hussein claimed that Kuwait was flooding world markets with oil and forcing down prices. A mediation attempt by Arab leaders failed, and on Aug. 2, 1990, over this and territorial claims, Iraqi troops invaded Kuwait and set up a puppet government.

After the Gulf War, Saddam Hussein was still in power. The U.N. Security Council affirmed an embargo against military supplies to that country and a trade embargo was still in place, pending claims of compensation for damage to Kuwait.

The Gulf War allies imposed a no-fly zone south of the 32nd parallel for Iraqi aircraft in August 1992. The UN sanctions continued in effect during 1992.

IRELAND

President: Mary Robinson (1990)
Taoiseach (Prime Minister): Albert Reynolds (1992)
Area: 27,136 sq mi. (70,282 sq km)
Population (est. mid-1993): 3,600,000 (average annual rate of natural increase: 0.6%); birth rate: 15/1000; infant mortality rate: 8.6/1000; density per square mile: 134
Capital: Dublin; **Largest cities (1991):** Dublin, 1,024,429; Cork, 282,790; Limerick, 109,816; **Monetary unit:** Irish pound (punt); **Languages:** Irish, English; **Religions:** Roman Catholic, 94%; Anglican, 4%; other, 2%; **National name:** Ireland, or Eire in the Irish language; **Literacy rate:** 99%
Economic summary: Gross national product (1992 est.): $38.95 billion; $11,128 per capita; real growth rate 2%; inflation (1991) 3.8%; unemployment 20.4%. Arable land: 14%. Principal products: cattle and dairy products, pigs, poultry and eggs, sheep and wool, horses, barley, sugar beets. Labor force: 1,334,000 est.; 28.6% in manufacturing and construction. Major products: processed foods, brews, textiles, clothing, chemicals, pharmaceuticals, machinery, transportation equipment, glass and crystal. Natural resources: zinc, lead, natural gas, crude oil, barite, copper, gypsum, limestone, dolomite, peat, silver. Exports: $27.8 billion (f.o.b., 1991): livestock, dairy products, machinery, chemicals, data processing equipment. Imports: $24.5 billion (c.i.f., 1991): food, animtal feed, chemicals, petroleum products, machinery, textile clothing. Major trading partners: U.K., Western European countries, U.S.

Geography. Ireland is situated in the Atlantic Ocean and separated from Britain by the Irish Sea. Half the size of Arkansas, it occupies the entire island except for the six counties which make up Northern Ireland.

Ireland resembles a basin—a central plain rimmed with mountains, except in the Dublin region. The mountains are low, with the highest peak, Carrantuohill in County Kerry, rising to 3,415 feet (1,041 m).

The principal river is the Shannon, which begins in the north central area, flows south and southwest for about 240 miles (386 km), and empties into the Atlantic.

Government. Ireland is a parliamentary democracy. The National Parliament (Oireachtas) consists of the president and two Houses, the House of Representatives (Dáil éireann) and the Senate (Seanad éireann), whose members serve for a maximum term of five years. The House of Representatives has 166 members elected by proportional representation; the Senate has 60 members of whom 11 are nominated by the prime minister, 6 by the universities and the remaining 43 from five vocational panels. The prime minister (Taoiseach), who is the head of government, is appointed by the president on the nomination of the House of Representatives, to which he is responsible.

History. In the Stone and Bronze Ages, Ireland was inhabited by Picts in the north and a people called the Erainn in the south, the same stock, apparently, as in all the isles before the Anglo-Saxon invasion of Britain. About the fourth century B.C., tall, red-haired Celts arrived from Gaul or Galicia. They subdued and assimilated the inhabitants and established a Gaelic civilization.

By the beginning of the Christian Era, Ireland was divided into five kingdoms—Ulster, Connacht, Leinster, Meath, and Munster. St. Patrick introduced Christianity in 432 and the country developed into a center of Gaelic and Latin learning. Irish monasteries, the equivalent of universities, attracted intellectuals as well as the pious and sent out missionaries to many parts of Europe and, some believe, to North America.

Norse depredations along the coasts, starting in 795, ended in 1014 with Norse defeat at the Battle of Clontarf by forces under Brian Boru. In the 12th century, the Pope gave all Ireland to the English Crown as a papal fief. In 1171, Henry II of England was acknowledged "Lord of Ireland," but local sectional rule continued for centuries, and English control over the whole island was not reasonably absolute until the 17th century. By the Act of Union (1801), England and Ireland became the "United Kingdom of Great Britain and Ireland."

A steady decline in the Irish economy followed in the next decades. The population had reached 8.25 million when the great potato famine of 1846–48 took many lives and drove millions to emigrate to America. By 1921 it was down to 4.3 million.

In the meantime, anti-British agitation continued along with demands for Irish home rule. The advent of World War I delayed the institution of home rule and resulted in the Easter Rebellion in Dublin (April 24–29, 1916), in which Irish nationalists unsuccessfully attempted to throw off British rule. Guerrilla warfare against British forces followed proclamation of a republic by the rebels in 1919.

The Irish Free State was established as a dominion on Dec. 6, 1922, with the six northern counties as part of the United Kingdom. Ireland was neutral in World War II.

In 1948, Eamon de Valera, American-born leader of the Sinn Fein, who had won establishment of the Free State in 1921 in negotiations with Britain's David Lloyd George, was defeated by John A. Costello, who demanded final independence from Britain. The Republic of Ireland was proclaimed on April 18, 1949. It withdrew from the Commonwealth but in 1955 entered the United Nations.

Through the 1960s, two antagonistic currents dominated Irish politics. One sought to bind the wounds of the rebellion and civil war. The other was the effort of the outlawed extremist Irish Republican Army to bring Northern Ireland into the republic.

In the elections of June 11, 1981, Garret M. D. FitzGerald, leader of the Fine Gael, was elected Prime Minister. FitzGerald resigned Jan. 27, 1982, after his presentation of an austerity budget aroused the opposition of independents who had backed him previously. Former Prime Minister Haughey was sworn in on March 9 and presented a budget with nearly a $1 billion deficit. FitzGerald was re-elected Prime Minister on Dec. 14, 1982 but was unable to solve the problem of unemployment and the elections of 1987 brought Haughey back into power on March 10.

Three candidates vied in the November 1990 presidential election. Although Brian Lenihan of Fianna Fail led in the first round, Mary Robinson, supported by the Labour Party and the Workers Party, won the second round with 52.8% of the vote, becoming the first non-Fianna Fail president since 1945.

Amid allegations of scandal Prime Minister Haughey resigned in early 1992. Reynolds was chosen by a majority of his Fianna Fail party to become the next prime minister. In March the Irish Supreme Court broadened the grounds for legal abortion.

In November Reynolds lost a vote of confidence. The general election later that month saw Reynolds's Fianna Fail receive a plurality requiring the formation of another coalition government.

ISRAEL

State of Israel
President: Ezer Weizman (1993)
Prime Minister: Yitzhak Rabin (1992)
Area: 8,020 sq mi. (20,772 sq km)
Population (est. mid-1993): 5,300,000[1] (average annual rate of natural increase: 1.5%); birth rate: 21/1000; infant mortality rate: 9.4/1000; density per square mile: 671
Capital: Jerusalem[2]; **Largest cities (est. 1990):** Jerusalem, 504,100[3]; Tel Aviv, 321,700; Haifa, 223,600; **Monetary unit:** Shekel; **Languages:** Hebrew, Arabic, English; **Religions:** Judaism, 82%; Islam, 14%; Christian, 2%; others, 2%; **National name:** Medinat Yisra'el; **Literacy rate:** 92%
Economic summary: Gross national product (1991 est.): $54.6 billion; $12,000 per capita; real growth rate 5%; inflation 18%; unemployment 11%. Arable land: 17%. Principal agricultural products: citrus and other fruits, vegetables, beef, dairy and poultry products. Labor force: (1989): 1,348,000; 29.3% in public services. Major industrial products: processed foods, cut diamonds, clothing and textiles, chemicals, metal products, transport and electrical equipment, high-technology electronics. Natural resources: sulfur, copper, phosphates, potash, bromine. Exports: $12.1 billion (f.o.b., 1991 est.): polished diamonds, citrus and other fruits, clothing and textiles, processed foods, electronics, military hardware, fertilizer and chemical products. Imports: $18.1 billion (c.i.f., 1991 est.): rough diamonds, chemicals, oil, machinery, iron and steel, cereals, textiles, vehicles, ships. Major trading partners: U.S., E.C., Switzerland, Japan, Hong Kong, Canada, South Africa.

1. Includes West Bank, Gaza Strip, East Jerusalem. 2. Not recognized by U.S. which recognizes Tel Aviv. 3. Includes East Jerusalem.

Geography. Israel, slightly smaller than Massachusetts, lies at the eastern end of the Mediterranean Sea. It is bordered by Egypt on the west, Syria and Jordan on the east, and Lebanon on the north. Northern Israel is largely a plateau traversed from north to south by mountains and broken by great depressions, also running from north to south.

The maritime plain of Israel is remarkably fertile. The southern Negev region, which comprises almost half the total area, is largely a wide desert steppe area. The National Water Project irrigation scheme is now transforming it into fertile land. The Jordan, the only important river, flows from the north through Lake Hule (Waters of Merom) and Lake Kinneret (Sea of Galilee or Sea of Tiberias), finally entering the Dead Sea, 1,290 feet (393 m) below sea level. This "sea," which is actually a salt lake (394 sq mi.; 1,020 sq km), has no outlet, its water balance being maintained by evaporation.

Government. Israel, which does not have a written constitution, has a republican form of government headed by a president elected for a five-year term by the Knesset. The president may serve no more than two terms. The Knesset has 120 members elected by universal suffrage under proportional representation for four years. The government is administered by the Cabinet, which is headed by the prime minister.

The Knesset decided in June 1950 that Israel would acquire a constitution gradually through the years by the enactment of fundamental laws. Israel grants automatic citizenship to every Jew who desires to settle within its borders, subject to control of the Knesset.

History. Palestine, cradle of two great religions and homeland of the modern state of Israel, was known to the ancient Hebrews as the "Land of Canaan." Palestine's name derives from the Philistines, a people who occupied the southern coastal part of the country in the 12th century B.C.

A Hebrew kingdom established in 1000 B.C. was later split into the kingdoms of Judah and Israel; they were subsequently invaded by Assyrians, Babylonians, Egyptians, Persians, Macedonians, Romans, and Byzantines. The Arabs took Palestine from the Byzantine Empire A.D. 634–40. With the exception of a Frankish Crusader kingdom from 1099 to 1187, Palestine remained under Moslem rule until the 20th century (Turkish rule from 1516), when British forces under Gen. Sir Edmund Allenby defeated the Turks and captured Jerusalem Dec. 9, 1917. The League of Nations granted Britain a mandate to govern Palestine, effective in 1923.

Jewish colonies—Jews from Russia established one as early as 1882—multiplied after Theodor Herzl's 1897 call for a Jewish state. The Zionist movement received official approval with the publication of a letter Nov. 2, 1917, from Arthur Balfour, British Foreign Secretary, to Lord Rothschild, a British Jewish leader. Balfour promised support for the establishment of a Jewish homeland in Palestine on the understanding that the civil and religious rights of non-Jewish Palestinians would be safeguarded.

A 1937 British proposal called for an Arab and a Jewish state separated by a mandated area incorporating Jerusalem and Nazareth. Arabs opposed this, demanding a single state with minority rights for Jews, and a 1939 British White Paper retreated, offering instead a single state with further Jewish immigration to be limited to 75,000. Although the White Paper satisfied neither side, further discussion ended on the outbreak of World War II, when the Jewish population stood at nearly 500,000, or 30% of the total. Illegal and legal immigration during the war brought the Jewish population to 678,000 in 1946, compared with 1,269,000 Arabs. Unable to reach a compromise, Britain turned the problem over to the United Nations in 1947, which on November 29 voted for partition—despite strong Arab opposition.

Britain did not help implement the U.N. decision and withdrew on expiration of its mandate May 14, 1948. Zionists had already seized control of areas designated as Jewish, and, on the day of British departure, the Jewish National Council proclaimed the State of Israel.

U.S. recognition came within hours. The next day, Jordanian and Egyptian forces invaded the new nation. At the cease-fire Jan. 7, 1949, Israel increased its original territory by 50%, taking western Galilee, a broad corridor through central Palestine to Jerusalem, and part of modern Jerusalem. (In April 1950, Jordan annexed areas of eastern and central Palestine that had been designated for an Arab state, together with the old city of Jerusalem).

Chaim Weizmann and David Ben-Gurion became Israel's first president and prime minister. The new government was admitted to the U.N. May 11, 1949.

The next clash with Arab neighbors came when Egypt nationalized the Suez Canal in 1956 and barred Israeli shipping. Coordinating with an Anglo-French force, Israeli troops seized the Gaza Strip and drove through the Sinai to the east bank of the Suez Canal, but withdrew under U.S. and U.N. pressure. In 1967, Israel threatened retaliation against Syrian border raids, and Syria asked Egyptian aid. Egypt demanded the removal of U.N. peace-keeping forces from Suez, staged a national mobilization, closed the Gulf of Aqaba, and moved troops into the Sinai. Starting with simultaneous air attacks against Syrian, Jordanian, and Egyptian air bases on June 5, Israel during a six-day war totally defeated its Arab enemies. Expanding its territory by 200%, Israel at the cease-fire held the Golan Heights, the West Bank of the Jordan River, the Old City, and all of the Sinai and the east bank of the Suez Canal.

Israel insisted that Jerusalem remain a unified city and that peace negotiations be conducted directly, something the Arab states had refused to do because it would constitute a recognition of their Jewish neighbor.

Egypt's President Gamal Abdel Nasser renounced the 1967 cease-fire in 1969 and began a "war of attrition" against Israel, firing Soviet artillery at Israeli forces on the east bank of the canal. Nasser died of a heart attack on Sept. 28, 1970, and was succeeded by Anwar el-Sadat.

In the face of Israeli reluctance even to discuss the return of occupied territories, the fourth Mideast war erupted Oct. 6, 1973, with a surprise Egyptian and Syrian assault on the Jewish high holy day of Yom Kippur. Initial Arab gains were reversed when a cease-fire took effect two weeks later, but Israel suffered heavy losses in manpower.

U.S. Secretary of State Henry A. Kissinger arranged a disengagement of forces on both the Egyptian and Syrian fronts. Geneva talks, aimed at a lasting peace, foundered, however, when Israel balked at inclusion of the Palestine Liberation Organization.

A second-stage Sinai withdrawal signed by Israel and Egypt in September 1975 required Israel to give up the strategic Mitla and Gidi passes and to return the captured Abu Rudeis oil fields. Egypt guaranteed passage of Israeli cargoes through the reopened Suez Canal, and both sides renounced force in the settlement of disputes. Two hundred U.S. civilian technicians were stationed in a widened U.N. buffer zone to monitor and warn either side of truce violations.

A dramatic breakthrough in the tortuous history of Mideast peace efforts occurred Nov. 9, 1977, when Egypt's President Sadat declared his willingness to go anywhere to talk peace. Prime Minister Menachem Begin on Nov. 15 extended an invitation to the Egyptian leader to address the Knesset. Sadat's arrival in Israel four days later raised worldwide hopes. But optimism ebbed even before Begin was invited to Ismailia by Sadat, December 25–26.

An Israeli peace plan unveiled by Begin on his return, and approved by the Knesset, offered to end military administration in the West Bank and the Gaza Strip, with a degree of Arab self-rule but no relinquishment of sovereignty by Israel. Sadat severed talks on Jan. 18 and, despite U.S. condemnation, Begin approved new West Bank settlements by Israelis.

On March 14, 1979, after a visit by Carter, the Knesset approved a final peace treaty, and 12 days later Begin and Sadat signed the document, together with Carter, in a White House ceremony. Israel began its withdrawal from the Sinai on May 25 by handing over the coastal town of El Arish and the two countries opened their border on May 29.

One of the most difficult periods in Israel's history began with a confrontation with Syria over the placing by Syria of Soviet surface-to-air missiles in the Bekaa Valley of Lebanon in April 1981. President Reagan dispatched Philip C. Habib to prevent a clash. While Habib was seeking a settlement, Begin ordered a bombing raid against an Iraqi nuclear reactor on June 7, invoking the theory of preemptive self-defense because he said Iraq was planning to make nuclear weapons to attack Israel.

Although Israel withdrew its last settlers from the Sinai in April 1982 and agreed to a Sinai "peace patrol" composed of troops from four West European nations, the fragile peace engineered by Habib in Lebanon was shattered on June 9 by a massive Israeli assault on southern Lebanon. The attack was in retaliation for what Israel charged was a PLO attack that critically wounded the Israeli ambassador to London six days earlier.

Israeli armor swept through UNIFIL lines in southern Lebanon, destroyed PLO strongholds in Tyre and Sidon, and reached the suburbs of Beirut on June 10. As Israeli troops ringed Moslem East Beirut, where 5,000 PLO guerrillas were believed trapped, Habib sought to negotiate a safe exit for them.

A U.S.-mediated accord between Lebanon and Israel, signed on May 17, 1983, provided for Israeli withdrawal from Lebanon. Israeli withdrawal was conditioned on withdrawal of Syrian troops from the Bekaa Valley, however, and the Syrians refused to leave. Israel eventually withdrew its troops from the Beirut area, but kept them in southern Lebanon. Lebanon, under pressure from Syria, canceled the accord in March 1984.

Prime Minister Begin resigned on Sept. 15, 1983. On Oct. 10, Likud Party stalwart Yitzhak Shamir was elected Prime Minister.

After a close election, the two major parties worked out a carefully balanced power-sharing agreement and the Knesset, on Sept. 14, 1984 approved a national unity government including both the Labor Alignment and the Likud bloc.

In one hopeful development, the coalition government declared an economic emergency on July 1 and imposed sweeping austerity measures intended to break the country's 260% inflation. Key elements were an 18.8% devaluation of the shekel, price increases in such government-subsidized products as gasoline, dismissal of 9,000 government employees, government spending cuts and a wage and price freeze. By the end of Peres' term in October, 1986, the shekel had been revalued and stabilized and inflation was down to less than 20%.

In Dec. 1987, riots by Gazan Palestinians led to the current general uprising throughout the occupied territories which consists of low-level violence and civil disobedience. As a consequence, in 1988 the PLO formally declared an independent state. Also, in response to their ostensible recognition of Israel in that year, the U.S. established low-level diplomatic contacts with the PLO.

A deadlock in the elections of Dec. 1988 led to a continuation of the Likud-Labor national unity government. This collapsed in 1990, leading to Shamir forming a right-wing coalition that included the religious parties.

The relaxation of Soviet emigration rules resulted in a massive wave of Jews entering Israel. Citing for one the severe housing shortage, but probably owing as much to political considerations, Israel embarked on constructing new settlements in the West Bank, angering the U.S. Hopes for quick progress on a general Israel-Arab peace after the Persian Gulf War dimmed as many parties to the dispute resumed traditional stances.

Elections in late June 1992 scored a major victory for Rabin's Labor Party but without a parliamentary majority, forcing the new prime minister to search for coalition partners.

The Israeli parliament in January 1993 lifted a ban on contacts with the PLO. In April Israel closed the West Bank and Gaza Strip sharply limiting the number of Palestinians allowed into Israel to work. The government hoped this would curb violence against its citizens.

ITALY

Italian Republic
President: Oscar Luigi Scalfaro (1992)
Prime Minister: Carlo Azeglio Ciampi (1993)
Area: 116,500 sq mi. (301,278 sq km)
Population (est. mid-1993): 57,800,000 (average annual rate of natural increase: 0%); birth rate: 10/1000; infant mortality rate: 8.3/1000; density per square mile: 509
Capital: Rome; **Largest cities (est. 1991):** Rome, 2,800,000; Milan, 1,432,200; Naples, 1,206,000; Turin, 992,000; Palermo, 734,250; Genoa, 710,000; Bologna, 411,800; Florence, 408,400; Catania, 364,200; Bari, 353,000; **Monetary unit:** Lira; **Language:** Italian; **Religion:** Roman Catholic, almost 100%; **National name:** Repubblica Italiana; **Literacy rate:** 97%
Economic summary: Gross domestic product (1992): $1.02 trillion, $17,600 per capita; 1.2% real growth rate; inflation rate (1991) 6.5%; unemployment rate (1991 est.) 11.0%. Arable land: 32%. Principal agricultural products: grapes, olives, citrus fruits, vegetables, wheat, corn. Labor force: 21,569,000; 58.7% in services. Major industrial products: machinery, iron and steel, autos, textiles, shoes, chemicals. Natural resources: mercury, potash, sulfur, fish, gas, marble. Exports: $209 billion (f.o.b., 1991): textiles, wearing apparel, metals, transport equipment, chemicals. Imports: $222 billion (c.i.f., 1991): petroleum, industrial machinery, chemicals, food, metals. Major trading partners: United States, E.C., OPEC

Geography. Italy is a long peninsula shaped like a boot bounded on the west by the Tyrrhenian Sea and on the east by the Adriatic. Slightly larger than Arizona, it has for neighbors France, Switzerland, Austria, and Yugoslavia.

Approximately 600 of Italy's 708 miles (1,139 km) of length are in the long peninsula that projects into the Mediterranean from the fertile basin of the Po River. The Apennine Mountains, branching off from the Alps between Nice and Genoa, form the peninsula's backbone, and rise to a maximum height of 9,560 feet (2,912 m) at the Gran Sasso d'Italia (Corno). The Alps form Italy's northern boundary.

Several islands form part of Italy. Sicily (9,926 sq mi.; 25,708 sq km) lies off the toe of the boot, across the Strait of Messina, with a steep and rockbound northern coast and gentler slopes to the sea in the west and south. Mount Etna, an active volcano, rises to 10,741 feet (3,274 m), and most of Sicily is more than 500 feet (3,274 m) in elevation. Sixty-two miles (100 km) southwest of Sicily lies Pantelleria (45 sq mi.; 117 sq km), and south of that are Lampedusa and Linosa. Sardinia (9,301 sq mi.; 24,090 sq km), which is just south of Corsica and about 125 miles (200 km) west of the mainland, is mountainous, stony, and unproductive.

Italy has many northern lakes, lying below the snow-covered peaks of the Alps. The largest are Garda (143 sq mi.; 370 sq km), Maggiore (83 sq mi.; 215 sq km), and Como (55 sq mi.; 142 sq km).

The Po, the principal river, flows from the Alps on Italy's western border and crosses the Lombard plain to the Adriatic.

Government. The president is elected for a term of seven years by Parliament in joint session with regional representatives. The president nominates the premier and, upon the premier's recommendations, the members of the Cabinet. Parliament is composed of two houses: a Senate with 315 elective members and a Chamber of Deputies of 630 members elected by the people for a five-year term.

History. Until A.D. 476, when the German Odoacer became head of the Roman Empire in the west, the history of Italy was largely the history of Rome. From A.D. 800 on, the Holy Roman Emperors, Popes, Normans, and Saracens all vied for control over various segments of the Italian peninsula. Numerous city states, such as Venice and Genoa, and many small principalities flourished in the late Middle Ages.

In 1713, after the War of the Spanish Succession, Milan, Naples, and Sardinia were handed over to Austria, which lost some of its Italian territories in 1735. After 1800, Italy was unified by Napoleon, who crowned himself King of Italy in 1805; but with the Congress of Vienna in 1815, Austria once again became the dominant power in Italy.

Austrian armies crushed Italian uprisings in 1820–1821, and 1831. In the 1830s Giuseppe Mazzini, brilliant liberal nationalist, organized the Risorgimento (Resurrection), which laid the foundation for Italian unity.

Disappointed Italian patriots looked to the House of Savoy for leadership. Count Camille di Cavour (1810–61), Premier of Sardinia in 1852 and the architect of a united Italy, joined England and France in the Crimean War (1853–56), and in 1859, helped France in a war against Austria, thereby obtaining

Lombardy. By plebiscite in 1860, Modena, Parma, Tuscany, and the Romagna voted to join Sardinia. In 1860, Giuseppe Garibaldi conquered Sicily and Naples and turned them over to Sardinia. Victor Emmanuel II, King of Sardinia, was proclaimed King of Italy in 1861.

Allied with Germany and Austria-Hungary in the Triple Alliance of 1882, Italy declared its neutrality upon the outbreak of World War I on the ground that Germany had embarked upon an offensive war. In 1915, Italy entered the war on the side of the Allies.

Benito (Il Duce) Mussolini, a former Socialist, organized discontented Italians in 1919 into the Fascist Party to "rescue Italy from Bolshevism." He led his Black Shirts in a march on Rome and, on Oct. 28, 1922, became premier. He transformed Italy into a dictatorship, embarking on an expansionist foreign policy with the invasion and annexation of Ethiopia in 1935 and allying himself with Adolf Hitler in the Rome-Berlin Axis in 1936. He was executed by Partisans on April 28, 1945 at Dongo on Lake Como.

Following the overthrow of Mussolini's dictatorship and the armistice with the Allies (Sept. 3, 1943), Italy joined the war against Germany as a co-belligerent. King Victor Emmanuel III abdicated May 9, 1946, and left the country after having installed his son as King Humbert II. A plebiscite rejected monarchy, however, and on June 13, King Humbert followed his father into exile.

The peace treaty of Sept. 15, 1947, required Italian renunciation of all claims in Ethiopia and Greece and the cession of the Dodecanese to Greece and of five small Alpine areas to France. Much of the Istrian Peninsula, including Fiume and Pola, went to Yugoslavia.

The Trieste area west of the new Yugoslav territory was made a free territory (until 1954, when the city and a 90-square-mile zone were transferred to Italy and the rest to Yugoslavia).

Scandal brought the long reign of the Christian Democrats to an end when Italy's 40th premier since World War II, Arnaldo Forlani, was forced to resign in the wake of disclosure that many high-ranking Christian Democrats and civil servants belonged to a secret Masonic lodge known as "P-2."

When the Socialists deserted the coalition, Forlani was forced to resign on May 26, 1981, leaving to Giovanni Spadolini of the small Republican Party the task of forming a new government.

In early February 1991 the Italian Communist Party officially changed its name to the Democratic Party of the Left. Though still the second largest party, it has three bitter factions. A political crisis in March led Prime Minister Andreotti to fashion a new coalition in April, Italy's 50th postwar government.

In elections of April 1992 the Christian Democrats obtained less than one-third of the vote, its lowest ever but still making it the largest party. Andreotti routinely handed in his resignation but to compound matters President Cossiga also did so shortly afterwards.

During the early months of 1993 the nation was riveted by a political scandal of a seemingly ever-growing size involving the Mafia and many government leaders. In a referendum in mid-April voters approved changing the current proportional system of representation in the Senate for one utilizing majority voting. In the aftermath of the vote a search began for a government stable and untainted by scandal to see the reforms enacted.

JAMAICA

Sovereign: Queen Elizabeth II
Governor-General: H.E. The Most Hon. Sir Howard F.H. Cooke (1991)
Prime Minister: The Rt. Hon. Percival J. Patterson (1992)
Area: 4,411 sq mi. (11,424 sq km)
Population (est. mid-1993): 2,400,000 (average annual rate of natural increase: 1.9%); birth rate: 25/1000; infant mortality rate: 17/1000; density per square mile: 581
Capital and largest city (est. 1991): Kingston, 104,000; **Monetary unit:** Jamaican dollar; **Language:** English, Jamaican Creole; **Religions:** Protestant, 55.9%; Roman Catholic, 5%; other, 39.1%; **Member of Commonwealth of Nations; Literacy rate:** 98%
Economic summary: Gross domestic product (1991 est.): $3.6 billion; $1,400 per capita; real growth rate 1%; inflation 80%; unemployment 15.1%. Arable land: 19%. Principal products: sugar cane, citrus fruits, bananas, coffee, potatoes, livestock. Labor force (1991): 1,072,500; services, 41%; agriculture, 22.5%; industry, 19%. Industries: Tourism, bauxite mining, textiles, processed foods, light manufactures. Natural resources: bauxite, gypsum. Exports: $1.2 billion (f.o.b., 1991): alumina, bauxite, sugar, bananas. Imports: $1.86 billion (c.i.f., 1991): fuels, machinery, consumer goods, construction goods, food. Major trading partners: U.S., U.K., Canada, Norway, Trinidad and Tobago, Venezuela, Japan.

Geography. Jamaica is an island in the West Indies, 90 miles (145 km) south of Cuba and 100 miles (161 km) west of Haiti. It is a little smaller than Connecticut.

The island is made up of a plateau and the Blue Mountains, a group of volcanic hills, in the east. Blue Mountain (7,402 ft.; 2,256 m) is the tallest peak.

Government. The legislature is a 60-member House of Representatives elected by universal suffrage and an appointed Senate of 21 members. The Prime Minister is appointed by the Governor-General and must, in the Governor-General's opinion, be the person best able to command the confidence of a majority of the members of the House of Representatives.

History. Jamaica was inhabited by Arawak Indians when Columbus visited it in 1494 and named it St. Iago. It remained under Spanish rule until 1655, then became a British possession. The island prospered from wealth brought by buccaneers to their base, Port Royal, the capital, until the city disappeared in the sea in 1692 after an earthquake. The Arawaks died off from disease and exploitation, and slaves, mostly black, were imported to work sugar plantations. Abolition of the slave trade (1807), emancipation of the slaves (1833), and a gradual drop in sugar prices led to depressed economic conditions that resulted in an uprising in 1865.

The following year Jamaica's status was changed to that of a colony, and conditions improved considerably. Introduction of banana cultivation made the island less dependent on the sugar crop for its well-being.

On May 5, 1953, Jamaica attained internal autonomy, and in 1958 it led in organizing the West Indies Federation. This effort at Caribbean unification failed. A nationalist labor leader, Sir Alexander Bustamente, led a campaign for withdrawal from the Federation. As the result of a popular referendum in 1961, Jamaica became independent on Aug. 6, 1962.

Michael Manley became Prime Minister in 1972 and initiated a socialist program.

The Labor Party defeated Manley's People's National Party in 1980 and its capitalist-oriented leader, Edward P.G. Seaga, became Prime Minister. He instituted measures to encourage private investment.

Like other Caribbean countries, Jamaica was hard-hit by the 1981–82 recession. By 1984, austerity measures that Seaga instituted in the hope of bringing the economy back into balance included elimination of government subsidies. Devaluation of the Jamaican dollar made Jamaican products more competitive on the world market and Jamaica achieved record growth in tourism and agriculture. Manufacturing also grew. But at the same time, the cost of many foods went up 50% to 75% and thousands of Jamaicans fell deeper into poverty.

The PNP decisively won local elections in mid-July, 1987, signaling a weakening in Seaga's position. In 1989, Manley swept back into power with a clear-cut victory. He indicated that he would pursue more centrist policies than he did in his previous administration.

The PNP again decisively won local elections in March 1990. Nevertheless Seaga retained his leadership position in the Labor Party.

Manley stepped down in 1992 for reasons of health being replaced by a British-trained P.J. Patterson.

Parliamentary elections in March 1993 were marred by violence in which 11 died. The PNP received 53 of the 60 seats in parliament.

JAPAN

Emperor: Akihito (1989)
Prime Minister: Morihiro Hosokawa (1993)
Area: 145,874 sq mi. (377,815 sq km)
Population (est. Oct. 1992): 124,450,000 (average annual rate of natural increase: .3%); birth rate: 10/1000; infant mortality rate: 4.4/1000; density per square mile: 853
Capital: Tokyo; **Largest cities (Jan. 1993):** Tokyo, 8,112,000; Yokohama, 3,276,000; Osaka 2,601,000; Nagoya, 2,162,000; Sapporo, 1,719,000; Kobe, 1,501,000; Kyoto, 1,456,000; Fukuoka, 1,263,000; Kawasaki, 1,196,000; Hiroshima, 1,099,000; **Monetary unit:** Yen; **Language:** Japanese; **Religions:** Shintoist, 111.8 million; Buddhist, 93.1 million; Christian, 1.4 million; other, 11.4 million; **National name:** Nippon; **Literacy rate:** 99.9%
Economic summary: Gross national product (1992): $3,705.5 billion; $29,774 per capita; real growth rate 1.5%; inflation (1991) 3.3%; unemployment (1991) 2.1%. Arable land: 13%. Principal agricultural products: rice, vegetables, fruits, sugar beets. Labor force: 65,050,000; 54% in trade and services. Major industrial products: machinery and equipment, metals and metal products, textiles, autos, consumer electronics, chemicals, electrical and electronic equipment. Natural resource: fish. Exports: $314.3 billion (f.o.b., 1991): machinery and equipment, automobiles, metals and metal products, consumer electronics. Imports: $236,6 billion (c.i.f., 1991): fossil fuels, metal ore, raw materials, foodstuffs. Major trading partners: U.S., Middle East, Western Europe, Southeast Asia

Geography. An archipelago extending in an arc more than 1,744 miles (2,790 km) from northeast to southwest in the Pacific, Japan is separated from the east coast of Asia by the Sea of Japan. It is approximately the size of Montana.

Japan's four main islands are Honshu, Hokkaido, Kyushu, and Shikoku. The Ryukyu chain to the southwest was U.S.-occupied and the Kuriles to the northeast are Russian-occupied. The surface of the main islands consists largely of mountains separated by narrow valleys. There are about 60 more or less active volcanoes, of which the best-known is Mount Aso. Mount Fuji, seen on postcards, is not active.

Government. Japan's Constitution, promulgated on Nov. 3, 1946, replaced the Meiji Constitution of 1889. The 1946 Constitution, sponsored by the U.S. during its occupation of Japan, brought fundamental changes to the Japanese political system, including the abandonment of the Emperor's divine rights. The Diet (Parliament) consists of a House of Representatives of 511 members, elected for four years, and a House of Councilors of 252 members, half of whom are elected every three years for six-year terms. Executive power is vested in the Cabinet, which is headed by a Prime Minister, nominated by the Diet from its members.

On Jan. 7, 1989, Emperor Hirohito, Japan's longest-reigning monarch died and was succeeded by his son, Akihito (born 1933). He was married in 1959 to Michiko Shoda (the first time a crown prince married a commoner).

History. A series of legends attributes creation of Japan to the sun goddess, from whom the later emperors were allegedly descended. The first of them was Jimmu Tenno, supposed to have ascended the throne in 660 B.C.

Recorded Japanese history begins with the first contact with China in the 5th century A.D. Japan was then divided into strong feudal states, all nominally under the Emperor, but with real power often held by a court minister or clan. In 1185, Yoritomo, chief of the Minamoto clan, was designated Shogun (Generalissimo) with the administration of the islands under his control. A dual government system—Shogun and Emperor—continued until 1867.

First contact with the West came about 1542, when a Portuguese ship off course arrived in Japanese waters. Portuguese traders, Jesuit missionaries, and Spanish, Dutch, and English traders followed. Suspicious of Christianity and of Portuguese support of a local Japanese revolt, the shoguns prohibited all trade with foreign countries; only a Dutch trading post at Nagasaki was permitted. Western attempts to renew trading relations failed until 1853, when Commodore Matthew Perry sailed an American fleet into Tokyo Bay.

Japan now quickly made the transition from a medieval to a modern power. Feudalism was abolished and industrialization was speeded. An imperial army was established with conscription. The shogun system was abolished in 1868 by Emperor Meiji, and parliamentary government was established in 1889. After a brief war with China in 1894–95, Japan acquired Formosa (Taiwan), the Pescadores Islands, and part of southern Manchuria. China also recognized the independence of Korea (Chosen), which Japan later annexed (1910).

In 1904–05, Japan defeated Russia in the Russo-Japanese War, gaining the territory of southern Sakhalin (Karafuto) and Russia's port and rail rights in Manchuria. In World War I Japan seized Germany's Pacific islands and leased areas in China. The Treaty of Versailles then awarded it a mandate over the islands

At the Washington Conference of 1921–22, Japan agreed to respect Chinese national integrity. The series of Japanese aggressions that was to lead to the nation's downfall began in 1931 with the invasion of Manchuria. The following year, Japan set up this area as a puppet state, "Manchukuo," under Emperor Henry Pu-Yi, last of China's Manchu dynasty. On Nov. 25, 1936, Japan joined the Axis by signing the anti-Comintern pact. The invasion of China came the next year and the Pearl Harbor attack on the U.S. on Dec. 7, 1941.

(For details of World War II (1939–45), *see* Headline History.)

Japan surrendered formally on Sept. 2, 1945, aboard the battleship *Missouri* in Tokyo Bay after atomic bombs had hit Hiroshima and Nagasaki. Southern Sakhalin and the Kurile Islands reverted to the U.S.S.R., and Formosa (Taiwan) and Manchuria to China. The Pacific islands remained under U.S. occupation. General of the Army Douglas MacArthur was appointed Supreme Commander for the Allied Powers on Aug. 14, 1945.

A new Japanese Constitution went into effect in 1947. In 1949, many of the responsibilities of government were returned to the Japanese. Full sovereignty was granted to Japan by the Japanese Peace Treaty in 1951.

Following the visit of Prime Minister Eisaku Sato to Washington in 1969, the U.S. agreed to return Okinawa and other Ryukyu Islands to Japan in 1972, and both nations renewed the security treaty in 1970.

The general election of July 1989 for the upper house of parliament scored a loss for the ruling Liberal Democratic Party, the first in 35 years. The following month, however, the party's president, Toshiki Kaifu, was elected prime minister.

Kaifu pledged to provide $9 billion to the U.S. to help defray the expense of the latter's operations in the Persian Gulf. Kaifu's general stance in support of the U.S. drew considerable domestic criticism. The government attempted to push legislation that would have permitted Japan to send a military contingent to the Gulf in noncombat roles. This was defeated amid public outcry against it.

During Soviet President Gorbachev's visit to Tokyo in April 1991 he and Prime Minister Kaifu attempted to resolve a territorial dispute arising out of the last days of World War II. No breakthrough resulted, and the issue still remained at an impasse.

Miyazawa became prime minister in November 1991 and set off a storm of protest for appointing a cabinet of veteran politicans with past links to bribery and scandal.

Parliament approved a bill in June 1992 that would allow Japanese troops to be sent abroad for limited use in international peace-keeping operations.

Rebellious legislators in June 1993 joined with the opposition to force a vote of no confidence in the government. In its wake Miyazawa dissolved parliament. Many of the rebels quit the ruling Liberal Democrats to form three new parties.

The elections of July saw the largest loss for the Liberal Democrats since its creation. Yet it managed to retain 223 of the 511 seats, making it the largest single party and insuring it a large role in the next government.

JORDAN

The Hashemite Kingdom of Jordan
Ruler: King Hussein I (1952)
Prime Minister: Abdel Salam Al-Majali
Area: 34,573 sq mi (89,544 sq km) excludes West Bank
Population (est. mid-1993): 3,800,000 (average annual rate of natural increase: 3.6%); birth rate: 40/1000; infant mortality rate: 34/1000; density per square mile: 111
Capital: Amman; **Largest cities (est. 1990):** Amman, 1,047,870; Zarka, 420,900; Irbid, 280,000; Salt, 143,600; **Monetary unit:** Jordanian dinar; **Languages:** Arabic (official), English; **Religions:** Islam, 96%; Christian, 4%; **National name:** Al Mamlaka al Urduniya al Hashemiyah; **Literacy rate:** 82%
Economic summary: Gross national product (1990): $4.6 billion; $1,400 per capita; –15% real growth rate (1986). Arable land: 4%. Principal products: wheat, fruits, vegetables, olive oil. Labor force (1991): 650,000; 20% in manufacturing and mining. Major products: phosphate, refined petroleum products, cement. Natural resources: phosphate, potash. Exports: phosphates, fruits, and vegetables, shale oil, fertilizer. Imports: petroleum products, textiles, capital goods, motor vehicles, foodstuffs. Major trading partners: U.S., Japan, Saudi Arabia, Iraq, E.C., China.

Geography. The Middle East kingdom of Jordan is bordered on the west by Israel and the Dead Sea, on the north by Syria, on the east by Iraq, and on the south Saudi Arabia. It is comparable in size to Indiana.

Arid hills and mountains make up most of the country. The southern section of the Jordan River flows through the country.

Government. Jordan is a constitutional monarchy with a bicameral parliament.

The upper house consists of 40 members appointed by the king and the lower house is composed of 80 members elected by popular vote. The Constitution guarantees freedom of religion, speech, press, association, and private property.

Political parties were legalized in 1991.

History. In biblical times, the country that is now Jordan contained the lands of Edom, Moab, Ammon, and Bashan. In A.D. 106 it became part of the Roman province of Arabia and in 633–36 was conquered by the Arabs.

Taken from the Turks by the British in World War I, Jordan (formerly known as Transjordan) was separated from the Palestine mandate in 1920, and in 1921, placed under the rule of Abdullah ibn Hussein.

In 1923, Britain recognized Jordan's independence, subject to the mandate. In 1946, grateful for Jordan's loyalty in World War II, Britain abolished the mandate. That part of Palestine occupied by Jordanian troops was formally incorporated by action of the Jordanian Parliament in 1950.

King Abdullah was assassinated in 1951. His son Talal was deposed as mentally ill the next year. Talal's son Hussein, born Nov. 14, 1935, succeeded him.

From the beginning of his reign, Hussein had to steer a careful course between his powerful neighbor to the west, Israel, and rising Arab nationalism, frequently a direct threat to this throne. Riots erupted when he joined the Central Treaty Organization (the Baghdad Pact) in 1955, and he incurred further unpopularity when Britain, France, and Israel attacked the Suez Canal in 1956, forcing him to place his army under nominal command of the United Arab Republic of Egypt and Syria.

The 1961 breakup of the UAR eased Arab national pressure on Hussein, who was the first to recognize Syria after it reclaimed its independence. Jordan was swept into the 1967 Arab-Israeli war, however, and lost the old city of Jerusalem and all of its territory west of the Jordan river, the West Bank. Embittered Palestinian guerrilla forces virtually took over sections of Jordan in the aftermath of defeat, and open warfare broke out between the Palestinians and government forces in 1970.

Despite intervention of Syrian tanks, Hussein's Bedouin army defeated the Palestinians, suffering heavy casualties. A U.S. military alert and Israeli armor massed on the Golan Heights contributed psychological weight, but the Jordanians alone drove out the Syrians and invited the departure of 12,000 Iraqui troops who had been in the country since the 1967 war. Ignoring protests from other Arab states, Hussein by mid-1971 crushed Palestinian strength in Jordan and shifted the problem to Lebanon, where many of the guerrillas had fled.

In October 1974, Hussein concurred in an Arab summit resolution calling for an independent Palestinian state and endorsing the Palestine Liberation Organization as the "sole legitimate representative of the Palestinian people." This apparent reversal of policy changed with the growing disillusion of Arab states with the P.L.O., however, and by 1977 Hussein referred again to the unity of people on both banks of the Jordan.

As Egypt and Israel neared final agreement on a peace treaty early in 1979, Hussein met with Yassir Arafat, the PLO leader, on March 17 and issued a joint statement of opposition. Although the U.S. pressed Jordan to break Arab ranks on the issue, Hussein elected to side with the great majority, cutting ties with Cairo and joining the boycott against Egypt.

In September 1980, Jordan declared itself with Iraq in its conflict with Iran and, despite threats from Syria, opened ports to war shipments for Iraq.

Jordan's stance during the Persian Gulf war strained relations with the U.S. and led to the termination of aid to the former. The signing of a national charter by King Hussein and leaders of the main political groups in June 1991 meant political parties were permitted in exchange for acceptance of the constitution and the monarchy.

Still smarting from its stance during the Gulf War unemployment soared. The King's decision to join the Middle East peace talks in mid-1991 helped his country's relations with the U.S.

In May 1993 Jordan broke with Iraq when King Hussein declared that he favored the introduction of a pluralistic government there.

KAZAKHSTAN

Republic of Kazakhstan
President: Nursultan A. Nazarbaev (1990)
Vice President: Erik M. Asanbaev
Prime Minister: Sergei A. Tereshchenko
Area: 1,049,000 sq mi. (2,717,300 sq km)
Population (est. mid-1993): 17,200,000 (Kazaks, 38%; Russians, 36%; Germans, 5.5%; Ukranians, 5.3%; other minorities: Tatars, Izbeks, Belarus, and Koreans); average annual rate of natural increase: 1.3%; birth rate: 21/1000; infant mortality rate, 32/1000; density per square mile: 16
Capital and largest city (1991): Alma-Ata, 1,156,200. Other large cities: Karaguada, 608,600; (1989): Chimkent, 393,000; Semipalatinsk, 334,000; Ust-Kamenogorsk, 324,000; Aktyubinsk, 253,000; Temiratau, 212,000; **Monetary unit:** Tanga; **Language:** Kazakh (Qazaq) official language, Russian; **Religion:** Muslim, 47%; Russian Orthodox; Lutheran
Economic summary: Per capita GNP (1991): $2,470; real growth rate –7%; inflation 83%. Industries: extractive industries (oil, coal, iron ore, manganese, bauxite, gold, silver, phosphates, sulfur), iron and steel, nonferrous metals, tractors and other agricultural machinery, electric motors, construction materials. Agriculture employs 30% of the labor force: grains, spring wheat, meat, cotton, and wool. Exports: $4.2 billion (f.o.b., 1990). Imports: n.a.. Trading partners: Russia, Ukraine, Uzbekistan, and other former Soviet republics.

Geography: Kazakhstan lies in the north of the central Asian republics and is bounded by Russia in the north, China in the east, the Kyrgyzstan and Uzbekistan in the south, and the Caspian Sea and part of Turkmenistan in the west. It has almost 15,000 miles of coastline on the Caspian Sea. Kazakhstan is the second largest republic of the Commonwealth of Independent States in area and is slightly more than twice the size of Texas. The territory is mostly steppe land with hilly plains and plateaus.

Government: A constitutional republic.

History: The indigenous Kazakhs were a nomadic Turkic people who belonged to several divisions of Kazakh hordes. They grouped together in settlements and lived in dome-shaped tents made of felt called "yurts." Their tribes migrated seasonally to find pastures for their herds of sheep, horses, and goats. Although they had chiefs, the Kazakhs were rarely united as a single nation under one great leader. Their tribes fell under Mongol rule in the 13th century and they were dominated by Tartar Khanates until the area was conquered by Russia in the 18th century.

Kazakhstan became a constituent republic of the Soviet Union in 1936 and collective farming and modern industrial production methods were instituted.

The world's first fast-breeder nuclear reactor was built in the republic and the main space center for the Commonwealth of Independent States is located in Baikonuy.

Kazakhstan sought greater political autonomy but delayed seeking independence from the former Soviet Union.

Kazakhstan proclaimed its membership in the Commonwealth of Independent States on Dec. 21, 1991, along with ten other former Soviet republics.

A draft constitution was adopted in June 1992 that guaranteed political pluralism.

In May 1992 the country agreed to remove all strategic nuclear weapons within two years.

KENYA

Republic of Kenya
President: Daniel arap Moi (1978)
Area: 224,960 sq mi. (582,646 sq km)
Population (est. mid-1993): 27,700,000 (average annual rate of natural increase: 3.7%); birth rate: 45/1000; infant mortality rate: 72/1000; density per square mile: 126
Capital: Nairobi; **Largest cities (est. 1990):** Nairobi, 1,200,000; Mombasa, 800,000; **Monetary unit:** Kenyan shilling; **Languages:** English (official), Swahili (national), and several other languages spoken by 40 ethnic groups; **Religions:** Protestant, 38%; Roman Catholic, 28%; traditional, 26%; Islam, 6%; **Literacy rate:** 69%; **Member of Commonwealth of Nations; National name:** Jamhuri ya Kenya

Economic summary: Gross domestic product (1990 est.): $9.7 billion; $385 per capita; real growth rate (1991 est.): 2.3%; inflation 14.3%. Arable land: 3%. Principal agricultural products: coffee, sisal, tea, pineapples, livestock. Labor force: 9.2 million: services, 54.8%; industry, 26.2%; agriculture, 19%. Major industrial products: textiles, processed foods, consumer goods, refined oil. Natural resources: gold, limestone, minerals, wildlife. Exports: $1.0 billion (f.o.b., 1991 est.): coffee, tea, refined petroleum. Imports: $1.9 billion (f.o.b., 1991 est.): machinery, transport equipment, crude oil, iron and steel products. Major trading partners: Western European countries, Far East, U.S., Africa, Middle East

Geography. Kenya lies on the equator in east central Africa on the coast of the Indian Ocean. It is twice the size of Nevada. Kenya's neighbors are Tanzania, Uganda, the Sudan, Ethiopia, and Somalia.

In the north, the land is arid; the southwestern corner is in the fertile Lake Victoria Basin; and a length of the eastern depression of Great Rift Valley separates western highlands from those that rise from the lowland coastal strip. Large game reserves have been developed.

Government. Under its Constitution Kenya has a one-house National Assembly of 188 members, elected for five years by universal suffrage and 12 nominated and 2 ex-officio, for a total of 202. Since 1969, the president has been chosen by a general election.

The Kenya African National Union (KANU), led by the president, is the only political party allowed.

History. Kenya, formerly a British colony and protectorate, was made a crown colony in 1920. The whites' domination of the rich plateau area, the White Highlands, long regarded by the Kikiyu people as their territory, was a factor leading to native terrorism, called the Mau Mau movement, in 1952. In 1954 the British began preparing the territory for African rule and independence. In 1961 Jomo Kenyatta was freed from banishment to become leader of the Kenya African National Union.

Internal self-government was granted in 1963; Kenya became independent on Dec. 12, 1963, with Kenyatta the first president.

Moi's tenure has been marked by a consolidation of power which has included the harassment of political opponents and the banning of secret ballots.

In reluctant elections of December 1992 Moi won reelection, although the opposition disputed the results.

The government reimposed price controls and broke with the IMF and World Bank in March 1993, threatening a break in Western aid. The opposition boycotted the opening of parliament in protest.

KIRIBATI

Republic of Kiribati
President: Teatao Teannaki (1991)
Area: 280 sq mi. (726 sq km)
Population (July 1992): 74,788 (average annual growth rate: –2.1%); density per square mile: 267
Capital (1990): Tarawa, 25,154; **Monetary unit:** Australian dollar; **Language:** English; **Religions:** Roman Catholic, 52.6%; Protestant, 40.9%; **Member of Commonwealth of Nations; Literacy rate:** 90%
Economic summary: Gross domestic product (1990 est.): $36.8 million; $525 per capita; 1% real growth rate; inflation 4%. Arable land: NEGL%: Principal agricultural products: copra, vegetables. Exports: $5.8 million (f.o.b., 1990 est.): fish, copra. Imports: $26.7 million (c.i.f., 1990 est.): foodstuffs, fuel, transportation equipment. Major trading partners: New Zealand, Australia, Japan, American Samoa, U.K., U.S.

Geography. Kiribati, formerly the Gilbert Islands, consists of three widely separated main groups of Southwest Pacific islands, the Gilberts on the equator, the Phoenix Islands to the east, and the Line Islands further east. Ocean Island, producer of phosphates until it was mined out in 1981, is also included in the two million square miles of ocean, which give Kiribati an important fishery resource.

Government. The president holds executive power. The legislature consists of a House Assembly with 39 members.

History. A British protectorate since 1892, the Gilbert and Ellice Islands became a colony in 1915–16. The two island groups were separated in 1975 and given internal self-government.

Tarawa and others of the Gilbert group were occupied by Japan during World War II. Tarawa was the site of one of the bloodiest battles in U.S. Marine Corps history when Marines landed in November 1943 to dislodge the Japanese defenders.

Princess Anne, representing Queen Elizabeth II, presented the independence documents to the new government on July 12, 1979.

President Tabai resigned in July 1991 after the maximum 12 years in office, being succeeded by his vice president.

In 1992 the only female member of parliament was forced to resign over electoral improprieties.

KOREA, NORTH

Democratic People's Republic of Korea
President: Marshal Kim Il Sung (1972)
Premier: Kang Song San (1992)
Area: 46,768 sq mi. (121,129 sq km)
Population (est. mid-1993): 22,600,000 (average annual rate of natural increase: 1.9%); birth rate: 24/1000; infant mortality rate: 30/1000; density per square mile: 487
Capital and largest city (est. 1987): Pyongyang, 2,355,000; **Monetary unit:** Won; **Language:** Korean; **Religions:** Buddhism and Confucianism, religious activities almost nonexistent; **National name:** Choson Minjujuui Inmin Konghwaguk; **Literacy rate:** 95% (est.)
Economic summary: Gross national product (1991 est.): $23.3 billion; $1,100 per capita; real growth rate –2%. Arable land: 18%. Principal agricultural products: corn, rice, vegetables. Labor force: 9,615,000; 64% nonagricultural. Major industrial products: machines, electric power, chemicals, textiles, processed food, metallurgical products. Natural resources: coal, iron ore, hydroelectric power. Exports: $2.02 billion (f.o.b., 1990): minerals, metallurgical products, agricultural products. Imports: $2.62 billion (f.o.b., 1990 est.): machinery and equipment, petroleum, grain, coking coal. Major trading partners: C.I.S. countries, China, Japan, Hong Kong, Germany, Singapore.

Geography. Korea is a 600-mile (966 km) peninsula jutting from Manchuria and China (and a small portion of the U.S.S.R.) into the Sea of Japan and the Yellow Sea off eastern Asia. North Korea occupies an area slightly smaller than Pennsylvania north of the 38th parallel.

The country is almost completely covered by a series of north-south mountain ranges separated by narrow valleys. The Yalu River forms part of the northern border with Manchuria.

Government. The elected Supreme People's Assembly, as the chief organ of government, chooses a Presidium and a Cabinet. The Cabinet, which exercises executive authority, is subject to approval by the Assembly and the Presidium.

The Korean Workers (Communist) Party, led by President Kim Il Sung, is the only political party.

History. According to myth, Korea was founded in 2333 B.C. by Tangun. In the 17th century, it became a vassal of China and was isolated from all but Chinese influence and contact until 1876, when Japan forced Korea to negotiate a commercial treaty, opening the land to the U. S. and Europe. Japan achieved control as the result of its war with China (1894–95) and with Russia (1904–05) and annexed Korea in 1910. Japan developed the country but never won over the Korean nationalists.

After the Japanese surrender in 1945, the country was divided into two occupation zones, the U.S.S.R. north of and the U.S. south of the 38th parallel. When the cold war developed between the U.S. and U.S.S.R., trade between the zones was cut off. In 1948, the division between the zones was made permanent with the establishment of separate regimes in the north and south. By mid-1949, the U.S. and U.S.S.R. withdrew all troops. The Democratic People's Republic of Korea (North Korea) was established on May 1, 1948. The Communist Party, headed by Kim II Sung, was established in power.

On June 25, 1950, the North Korean army launched a surprise attack on South Korea. On June 26, the U.N. Security Council condemned the invasion as aggression and ordered withdrawal of the invading forces. On June 27, President Harry S. Truman ordered air and naval units into action to enforce the U.N. order. The British government did the same, and soon a multinational U.N. command was set up to aid the South Koreans. The North Korean invaders took Seoul and pushed the South Koreans into the southeast corner of their country.

Gen. Douglas MacArthur, U.N. commander, made an amphibious landing at Inchon on September 15 behind the North Korean lines, which resulted in the complete rout of the North Korean army. The U.N. forces drove north across the 38th parallel, approaching the Yalu River. Then Communist China entered the war, forcing the U.N. forces into headlong retreat. Seoul was lost again, then regained; ultimately the war stabilized near the 38th parallel but dragged on for two years while the belligerents negotiated. An armistice was agreed to on July 27, 1953.

Formerly strenuously opposed to separate membership for the two Koreas in the U.N., the North in May 1991 announced it would, albeit reluctantly, apply for such membership.

Tension mounted in 1993 when the country said it was withdrawing from the international treaty banning nuclear weapons. Later it "suspended" the move and continued to allow international inspections of some, though not all, of its nuclear sites.

KOREA, SOUTH

Republic of Korea
President: Kim Young Sam (1993)
Prime Minister: Hwang In Sung (1993)
Area: 38,031 sq mi. (98,500 sq km)
Population (est. mid-1993): 44,600,000 (average annual rate of natural increase: 1.0%); birth rate: 16/1000; infant mortality rate: 15/1000; density per square mile: 1,170
Capital: Seoul; **Largest cities (est. 1990):** Seoul, 10,628,000; Pusan, 3,798,000; Taegu, 2,229,000; Inchon, 1,818,000; **Monetary unit:** Won; **Language:** Korean; **Religions (1989):** Buddhist, 46.9%; Confucianist, 2.8%; Catholic, 10.8%; Protestant, 37.7%; **National name:** Taehan Min'guk; **Literacy rate:** 96%
Economic summary: Gross national product (1991): $270 billion; $6,253 per capita; 8.6% real growth rate; inflation 9.7%; unemployment 2.4%. Arable land: 21%. Principal acricultural products: rice, barley. Labor force: 16,900,000; 27% in mining and manufacturing. Major products: clothing and textiles, processed foods, automobiles, steel, electronics equipment. Natural resources: molybdenum, lead, tungsten, graphite, coal, hydropower. Exports: $71.9 billion (f.o.b., 1991): footwear, clothing, fish, textiles, automobiles, electric and electronics, ships, and steel. Imports: $81.6 billion (c.i.f., 1991): transport equipment, organic chemicals, textiles, steel, oil, grains, chemicals, machinery, electronics. Major trading partners: U.S., Japan.

Geography. Slightly larger than Indiana, South Korea lies below the 38th parallel on the Korean peninsula. It is mountainous in the east; in the west and south are many harbors on the mainland and offshore islands.

Government. Constitutional amendments enacted in Sept. 1987 called for direct election of a President, who would be limited to a single five-year term, and increased the powers of the National Assembly *vis a vis* the President.

The National Assembly was expanded from 276 to 299 seats, filled by proportional representation.

History. South Korea came into being in the aftermath of World War II as the result of a 1945 agreement making the 38th parallel the boundary between a northern zone occupied by the U.S.S.R. and a southern zone occupied by U.S. forces. (For details, *see* North Korea.)

Elections were held in the U.S. zone in 1948 for a national assembly, which adopted a republican Constitution and elected Syngman Rhee president. The new republic was proclaimed on August 15 and was recognized as the legal government of Korea by the U.N. on Dec. 12, 1948.

On June 25, 1950, South Korea was attacked by North Korean Communist forces. U.S. armed intervention was ordered on June 27 by President Harry S. Truman, and on the same day the U.N. invoked military sanctions against North Korea. Gen. Douglas MacArthur was named commander of the U.N. forces. U.S. and South Korean troops fought a heroic holding action but, by the first week of August, they had been forced back to a 4,000-square-mile beachhead in southeast Korea.

There they stood off superior North Korean forces until September 15, when a major U.N. amphibious attack was launched far behind the Communist lines at Inchon, port of Seoul. By September 30, U.N. forces were in complete control of South Korea. They then invaded North Korea and were nearing the Manchurian and Siberian borders when several hundred thousand Chinese Communist troops entered the conflict in late October. U.N. forces were then forced to retreat below the 38th parallel.

On May 24, 1951, U.N. forces recrossed the parallel and had made important new inroads into North Korea when truce negotiations began on July 10. An armistice was finally signed at Panmunjom on July 27, 1953, leaving a devastated Korea in need of large-scale rehabilitation.

The U.S. and South Korea signed a mutual-defense treaty on Oct. 1, 1953.

Rhee, president since 1948, resigned in 1960 in the face of rising disorders. PoSun Yun was elected to succeed him, but political instability continued. In 1961, Gen. Park Chung Hee took power and subsequently built up the country. The U.S. stepped up military aid, building up South Korea's armed forces to 600,000 men. The South Koreans sent 50,000 troops to Vietnam, at U.S. expense.

Park's assassination on Oct. 26, 1979, by Kim Jae Kyu, head of the Korean Central Intelligence Agency, brought a liberalizing trend as Choi Kyu Hah, the new President, freed imprisoned dissidents. The release of opposition leader Kim Dae jung in February 1980 generated anti-government demonstrations that turned into riots by May. Choi resigned on Aug. 16. Chun Doo Wha, head of a military Special Committee for National Security Measures, was the sole candidate as the electoral college confirmed him as President on Aug. 27.

Elected to a full seven-year term on Feb. 11, Chun had visited Washington on Feb. 2 to receive President Reagan's assurance that U.S. troops would remain in South Korea.

Debate over the Presidential succession in 1988 was the main dispute in 1986–87 with Chun wanting election by the electoral college and the opposition demanding a direct popular vote, charging that Chun could manipulate the college. On April 13, 1987, Chun declared a close on the debate but when, in June, he appointed Roh Toe Woo, the DJP chairman as his successor, violent protests broke out. Roh, and later, Chun, agreed that direct elections should be held. A split in the opposition led to Roh's election on Dec. 16, 1987, with 36.6% of the vote.

Weeks of anti-government protests in May 1991 led to the resignation of then-Prime Minister Ro Ja Bong.

In early 1991 the Soviet Union announced it would not oppose South Korea's application for U.N. membership.

The presidential election of December 1992 gave the ruling party's candidate, Kim Young Sam, a plurality of votes. He had earlier run for the presidency as an opposition figure.

KUWAIT

State of Kuwait
Emir: Sheik Jaber al-Ahmad al-Sabah (1977)
Prime Minister: Sheik Sa'ad Abdullah al-Salim (1978)
Area: 6,880 sq mi. (17,820 sq km)
Population (est. mid-1993): 1,700,000 (average annual rate of natural increase: 3.0%); birth rate: 32/1000; infant mortality rate: 14/1000; density per square mile: 247
Capital (est. 1990): Kuwait, 151,060; **Largest city (est. 1985):** as-Salimiyah, 153,220; **Monetary unit:** Kuwaiti dinar; **Languages:** Arabic and English; **Religions:** Islam; **National name:** Dawlat al Kuwayt; **Literacy rate:** 74%
Economic summary: Gross domestic product (1991 est.): $8.75 billion; $6,200 per capita; real growth rate –50%. Labor force: 566,000 (1986); 45% in services. Major products: crude and refined oil, petrochemicals, building materials, salt. Natural resources: petroleum, fish, shrimp. Exports: $11.4 billion (f.o.b., 1989): oil 90%. Imports: $6.6 billion (f.o.b., 1989): foodstuffs, automobiles, building materials, machinery, textiles. Major trading partners: U.S., Japan, Italy, Germany, U.K..

Geography. Kuwait is situated northeast of Saudi Arabia at the northern end of the Persian Gulf, south of Iraq. It is slightly larger than Hawaii. The low-lying land is mainly sandy and barren.

Government. Sheik Jaber al-Ahmad al-Sabah rules as Emir of Kuwait and appoints the Prime Minister, who appoints his Cabinet (Council of Ministers). National elections were held in 1992 and the National Assembly (legislative branch), dissolved in 1986 was reinstated. There are no political parties in Kuwait.

History. Kuwait obtained British protection in 1897 when the Sheik feared that the Turks would take over the area. In 1961, Britain ended the protectorate, giving Kuwait independence, but agreed to give military aid on request. Iraq immediately threatened to occupy the area and Sheik Sabah al-Salem al-Sabah called in British troops in 1961. Soon afterward the Arab League sent in troops, replacing the British. The prize was oil.

Oil was discovered in the 1930s. Kuwait proved to have 20% of the world's known oil resources. It has been a major producer since 1946, the world's second largest oil exporter. The Sheik, who gets half the profits, devotes most of them to the education, welfare, and modernization of his kingdom. In 1966, Sheik Sabah designated a relative, Jaber al-Ahmad al-Sabah, as his successor.

By 1968, the sheikdom had established a model welfare state, and it sought to establish dominance among the sheikdoms and emirates of the Persian Gulf.

In July 1990, Iraq President Hussein blamed Kuwait for falling oil prices. After a failed Arab mediation attempt to solve the dispute peacefully, Iraq invaded Kuwait on Aug. 2, 1990, and set up a pro-Iraqi provisional government.

A coalition of Arab and Western military forces drove Iraqi troops from Kuwait in February 1991. The Emir returned to his country from Saudi Arabia in mid-March. Martial law, in effect since the end of the Gulf war, ended in late June.

The U.S. sent 2,400 troops to the country in August 1992 as part of a training exercise but this was widely interpreted as a show of strength to Saddam Hussein.

The general election of October 1992 was widely interpreted as a success for supporters of a return to Islamic law. A political independent was named speaker of the parliament, and the opposition held 31 of the 50 seats. The franchise was, however, limited to males who could trace citizenship back to at least 1920.

In May 1993 Kuwait announced its plans to build a deep ditch along its entire land border with Iraq.

KYRGYZSTAN

The Kyrgyz Republic
President: Askar Akaev (1990)
Prime Minister: Tursunbek Chyngyshev (1990)
Area: 76,000 sq mi. (198,500 sq km)
Population (est. mid-1993): 4,600,000; (Kyrgyz, 52%; Russian, 22%); (average annual rate of natural increase: 2.2%); birth rate: 29/1000; infant mortality rate: 40/1000; density per square mile: 60
Capital and largest city (1991): Bishkek (Frunze), 631,300. Other (1989): Osh, 213,000; **Monetary unit:** The Som; **Language:** Kyrgyz (of Turkic group); **Religion:** Muslim, 70%; Russian Orthodox
Economic summary: Important natural resources are rare earth metals and gold. Industrial production includes electrical engineering, hydroelectric power, agricultural machine building, washing machines, furniture, cement, paper, and brick. Agricultural products are food grains including wheat, cotton, grapes, sugar beets, tobacco, and livestock raising, especially sheep. Labor force: 1,894,000 (1989): agriculture, 33%; industry, 18%. Exports: $115 million (c.i.f., 1990). Imports: $1.5 million (c.i.f., 1990). Trading partners: Russia, 70%; others Ukraine, Uzbekistan, Kazakhstan.

Geography: Kyrgyzstan (formerly Kirghizia) is a rugged country with the Tien Shan mountain range covering approximately 95 percent of the whole territory. The mountain tops are covered with perennial snow and glaciers. Kyrgyzstan borders Kazakhstan on the north and northwest, Uzbekistan in the southwest, Tajikistan in the south, and China in the southeast. The republic is the same size in area as the state of Nebraska.

Government: A constitutional republic.

History: The native Kyrgyz are a Turkic people who in ancient times first settled in the Tien Shan mountains. They were traditionally pastoral nomads. There was extensive Russian colonization in the 1900s and Russian settlers were given much of the best agricultural land. This led to an unsuccessful and disastrous revolt by the Kyrgyz people in 1916. Kyrgyzstan became part of the Soviet Federated Socialist Republic in 1924, and was made an autonomous republic in 1926. Kyrgyzstan became a constituent republic of the U.S.S.R. in 1936. The Soviets forced the Kyrgyz to abandon their nomadic culture and brought modern farming and industrial production techniques into their society. It has greatly changed their traditional way of life.

President Askar Akaev supported Soviet President Gorbachev's reform programs and promoted them in his country.

Kyrgyzstan proclaimed its independence from the Soviet Union on Aug. 31, 1991.

On Dec. 21, 1991, Kyrgyzstan joined with ten other former Soviet republics as members of the Commonwealth of Independent States.

The country joined the UN and the IMF in 1992 and adopted a shock-therapy economic program.

LAOS

Lao People's Democratic Republic
President: Nouhak Phoumsavane (1992)
Premier: Khamtai Siphandon (1991)
Area: 91,429 sq mi. (236,800 sq km)
Population (est. mid-1993): 4,600,000 (average annual rate of natural increase: 2.9%); birth rate: 45/1000; infant mortality rate: 110/1000; density per square mile: 51
Capital and largest city (1990): Vientiane, 442,000; **Monetary unit:** Kip; **Languages:** Lao (official), French, English; **Religions:** Buddhist, 85%; animist and other, 15%; **Literacy rate:** 85%
Economic summary: Gross domestic product: (1991): $912 million; $220 per capita; 4% real growth rate; inflation rate (Dec. 1991): 10.4%; unemployment rate (1989 est.): 21%. Arable land: 4%. Principal agricultural products: rice, corn, vegetables. Labor force: 1–1.5 million; 85–90% in agriculture. Major industrial products: tin, timber, electric power. Natural resources: tin, timber, hydroelectric power. Exports: $72 million (f.o.b., 1990 est.): electric power, forest products, tin concentrates, coffee. Imports: $238 million (c.i.f., 1990 est.): rice, foodstuffs, petroleum products, machinery, transport equipment. Major trading partners: Thailand, Malaysia, Vietnam, C.I.S. countries, Japan, France, U.S., Hong Kong, Singapore.

Geography. A landlocked nation in Southeast Asia occupying the northwestern portion of the Indochinese peninsula, Laos is surrounded by China, Vietnam, Cambodia, Thailand, and Burma. It is twice the size of Pennsylvania.

Laos is a mountainous country, especially in the north, where peaks rise above 9,000 feet (2,800 m). Dense forests cover the northern and eastern areas. The Mekong River, which forms the boundary with Burma and Thailand, flows entirely through the country for 932 miles (1,500 km) of its course.

Government. Laos is a people's democratic republic with executive power in the hands of the premier. The monarchy was abolished Dec. 2, 1975, when the Pathet Lao ousted a coalition government and King Sisavang Vatthana abdicated. The King was appointed "Supreme Adviser" to the President, the former Prince Souphanouvong. Former Prince Souvanna Phouma, Premier since 1962, was made an "adviser" to the government. The Lao People's Revolutionary Party (Pathet Lao) is the only political party.

History. Laos became a French protectorate in 1893, and the territory was incorporated into the union of Indochina. A strong nationalist movement developed during World War II, but France reestablished control in 1946 and made the King of Luang Prabang constitutional monarch of all Laos. France granted semiautonomy in 1949 and then, spurred by the Viet Minh rebellion in Vietnam, full independence within the French Union in 1950. In 1951, Prince Souphanouvong organized the Pathet Lao, a Communist independence movement, in North Vietnam. The Viet Minh in 1953 established the Pathet Lao in power at Samneua. Viet Minh and Pathet Lao forces invaded central Laos, and civil war resulted.

By the Geneva agreements of 1954 and an armistice of 1955, two northern provinces were given the Pathet Lao, the royal regime the rest. Full sovereignty was given the kingdom by the Paris agreements of Dec. 29, 1954. In 1957, Prince Souvanna Phouma, the royal Premier, and the Pathet Lao leader, Prince Souphanouvong, the Premier's half-brother, agreed to reestablishment of a unified government, with Pathet Lao participation and integration of Pathet Lao forces into the royal army. The agreement broke down in 1959, and armed conflict broke out again.

In 1960, the struggle became three-way as Gen. Phoumi Nosavan, controlling the bulk of the royal army, set up in the south a pro-Western revolutionary government headed by Prince Boun Gum. General Phoumi took Vientiane in December, driving Souvanna Phouma into exile in Cambodia. The Soviet bloc supported Souvanna Phouma. In 1961, a cease-fire was arranged and the three princes agreed to a coalition government headed by Souvanna Phouma.

But North Vietnam, the U.S. (in the form of Central Intelligence Agency personnel), and China remained active in Laos after the settlement. North Vietnam used a supply line (Ho Chi Minh trail) running down the mountain valleys of eastern Laos into Cambodia and South Vietnam, particularly after the U.S.-South Vietnamese incursion into Cambodia in 1970 stopped supplies via Cambodian seaports.

An agreement, reached in 1973 revived coalition government. The Communist Pathet Lao seized complete power in 1975, installing Souphanouvong as president and Kaysone Phomvihane as premier. Since then other parties and political groups have been moribund and most of their leaders have fled the country.

The Supreme People's Assembly in August 1991 adopted a new constitution that dropped all references to socialism but retained the one-party state. In addition to implementing market-oriented policies, the country has passed laws governing property, inheritance and contracts. Laos agreed to trade with Moscow and Hanoi in hard currency.

The death of Kaysone Phoumvihan in November 1992 saw the presidency pass to his old friend Nouhak Phoumsavan, while the prime minister became party chairman.

LATVIA

The Republic of Latvia
President: Guntis Ulmanis (1993)
Prime Minister: Valdis Birkavs (1993)
Area: 25,400 sq mi. (65,786 sq km)
Population (est. mid-1993): 2,600,000 (Latvian, 53%; Russian, 33%; Ukrainians, Byelorussians, other 14%);)average annual rate of natural increase: –0.2%); birth rate: 12/1000; infant mortality rate: 17/1000; density per square mile: 106
Capital and largest city (1990): Riga, 915,000. Other important cities: Daugavpils, 127,000; Liepaja, 114,000; **Monetary unit:** Latvian ruble and "Lats."; **Language:** Latvian; **Religions:** Lutheran, Catholic, and Baptist; **National name:** Latvija; **Literacy:** very high
Economic survey: Most industrialized of the Baltic states. Latvia is in the process of reforming a central planned economy into a market economy. Gross domestic product n.a.; per capita GNP (1991): $3,410; real growth rate (1991): –8%; inflation rate (1991): approximately 200%. Labor force (1992): industries 33.2%, agriculture 23%. Latvia's industries are highly diversified. They produce buses, trains, street and railroad cars, synthetic fibres, agricultural machinery, fertilizers, pharmaceuticals, washing machines, radios, electronics, processed foods, and textiles. Agricultures is principally dairy farming and livestock raising. Exports: $239 million (f.o.b., 1990). Imports: $9 billion (c.i.f., 1989): machinery, 35%; petroleum products, 13%; chemicals, 9%. Natural resources: Peat, sapropel, timber, limestone, dolomite, and clay. Major trading partners are Russia, 50%; Ukraine, 15%; other former Soviet Republics, 30%; also Poland, Germany, Sweden, and Czechoslovakia.

Geography: Latvia borders Estonia on the north, Lithuania in the south, the Baltic Sea with the Gulf of Riga in the west, Russia in the east, and Byelorussia in the southeast. Latvia is largely a fertile lowland with numerous lakes and hills to the east.

Government: Latvia is a parliamentary democracy.

History: Descended from Aryan stock, the Latvians were early tribesmen who settled along the Baltic Sea and, lacking a central government, fell an easy prey to more powerful peoples. The German Teutonic knights first conquered them in the 13th century and ruled the area, consisting of Livonia and Courland, until 1562.

Poland conquered the territory in 1562 and ruled until 1795 in Courland; control of Livonia was disputed between Sweden and Poland from 1562 to 1629. Sweden controlled Livonia from 1629 to 1721. Russia took over Livonia in the latter year and Courland after the third partition of Poland in 1795.

From that time until 1918, the Latvians remained Russian subjects, although they preserved their language, customs, and folklore. The Russian Revolution of 1917 gave them their opportunity for freedom, and the Latvian republic was proclaimed on Nov. 18, 1918.

The republic lasted little more than 20 years. It was occupied by Russian troops in 1939 and incorporated into the Soviet Union in 1940. German armies occupied the nation from 1941 to 1943–44, when they were driven out by the Russians. Most countries, including the United States, refused to recognize the Soviet annexation of Latvia.

When the coup against Soviet President Mikhail Gorbachev failed, the Baltic nations saw a historic opportunity to free themselves from Soviet domination and, following the actions of Lithuania and Estonia, Latvia declared its independence on Aug. 21, 1991.

European and most other nations quickly recognized their independence, and on Sept. 2, 1991, President Bush announced full diplomatic recognition for Latvia, Estonia, and Lithuania. The Soviet Union recognized Latvia's independence on September 6, and UN membership followed on Sept. 17, 1991.

In addition to severe economic problems the issue of citizenship loomed explosive as almost half the population is non-Latvian.

In the first post-Soviet parliamentary elections in June 1993 an alliance of former Communists and emigres made a strong showing. The franchise, however, was by and large not extended to the non-ethnic-Latvian minority.

Russia agreed to withdraw its troops from Latvia by 1995 if the latter extends the rights of the resident ethnic Russians and agrees to other conditions.

LEBANON

Republic of Lebanon
President: Rafiq Hariri (1992)
Premier: Rafik al-Hariri (1992)
Area: 4,015 sq mi. (10,400 sq km)
Population (est. mid-1993): 3,600,000 (average annual rate of natural increase: 2.1%); birth rate: 28/1000; infant mortality rate: 46/1000; density per square mile: 899

Capital: Beirut; **Largest cities (est. 1990):** Beirut, 1,100,000; Tripoli, 240,000; Sidon, 110,000; Tyre, 60,000; Zahleh, 55,000; **Monetary unit:** Lebanese pound; **Languages:** Arabic (official), French, English; **Religions:** Islam, 60%; Christian, 40% (17 recognized sects); Judaism Negl. % (1 sect); **National name:** Al-Joumhouriya al-Lubnaniya; **Literacy rate:** 80%

Economic summary: Gross domestic product (1991 est.): $4.8 billion; $1,400 per capita; real growth rate: n.a.; inflation (1991): 30%; unemployment (1991 est.): 35%. Arable land: 21%; principal agricultural products: citrus fruits, vegetables, potatoes, tobacco, olives, shrimp. Labor force (1985): 650,000; 79% in industry, commerce and services. Major industrial products: processed foods, textiles, cement, chemicals, refined oil. Exports: $700 million (f.o.b., 1990 est.): fruits, vegetables, textiles. Imports: $1.8 billion (c.i.f., 1990 est.): metals, machinery, foodstuffs. Major trading partners: U.S., Western European and Arab countries.

Geography. Lebanon lies at the eastern end of the Mediterranean Sea north of Israel and west of Syria. It is four fifths the size of Connecticut.

The Lebanon Mountains, which parallel the coast on the west, cover most of the country, while on the eastern border is the Anti-Lebanon range. Between the two lies the Bekaa Valley, the principal agricultural area.

Government. Lebanon is governed by a President, elected by Parliament for a six-year term, and a Cabinet of Ministers appointed by the President but responsible to Parliament.

The unicameral Parliament has 108 members elected for a four-year term by universal suffrage and chosen by proportional division of religious groups.

History. After World War I, France was given a League of Nations mandate over Lebanon and its neighbor Syria, which together had previously been a single political unit in the Ottoman Empire. France divided them in 1920 into separate colonial administrations, drawing a border that separated predominantly Moslem Syria from the kaleidoscope of religious communities in Lebanon in which Maronite Christians were then dominant. After 20 years of the French mandate regime, Lebanon's independence was proclaimed on Nov. 26, 1941, but full independence came in stages. Under an agreement between representatives of Lebanon and the French National Committee of Liberation, most of the powers exercised by France were transferred to the Lebanese government on Jan. 1, 1944. The evacuation of French troops was completed in 1946.

Civil war broke out in 1958, with Moslem factions led by Kamal Jumblat and Saeb Salam rising in insurrection against the Lebanese government headed by President Camille Chamoun, a Maronite Christian. At Chamoun's request, President Eisenhower on July 15 sent U.S. troops to reestablish the government's authority.

Clan warfare between various factions in Lebanon goes back centuries. The hodgepodge includes Maronite Christians, who since independence have dominated the government; Sunni Moslems, who have prospered in business and shared political power; the Druse, a secretive Islamic splinter group; and at the bottom of the heap until recently, Shiite Moslems.

A new—and bloodier—Lebanese civil war that broke out in 1975 resulted in the addition of still another ingredient in the brew—the Syrians. In the fighting between Lebanese factions, 40,000 Lebanese were estimated to have been killed and 100,000 wounded between March 1975 and November 1976. At that point, a Syrian-dominated Arab Deterrent Force intervened and brought large-scale fighting to a halt.

Palestinian guerrillas staging raids on Israel from Lebanese territory drew punitive Israeli raids on Lebanon, and two large-scale Israeli invasions. The Israelis withdrew in June after the U.N. Security Council created a 6,000-man peacekeeping force for the area, called UNIFIL. As they departed, the Israelis turned their strongpoints over to a Christian militia that they had organized, instead of to the U.N. force.

The second Israeli invasion came on June 6, 1982, and this time it was a total one. It was in response to an assassination attempt by Palestinian terrorists on the Israeli ambassador in London.

A U.S. special envoy, Philip C. Habib, negotiated the dispersal of most of the PLO to other Arab nations and Israel pulled back some of its forces. The violence seemed to have come to an end when, on Sept. 14, Bashir Gemayel, the 34-year-old President-elect, was killed by a bomb that destroyed the headquarters of his Christian Phalangist Party.

The day after Gemayel's assassination, Israeli troops moved into west Beirut in force. On Sept. 17 it was revealed that Christian militiamen had massacred hundreds of Palestinians in two refugee camps but Israel denied responsibility.

On Sept. 20, Amin Gemayel, older brother of Bashir Gemayel, was elected President by the parliament.

The massacre in the refugee camps prompted the return of a multinational peacekeeping force composed of U.S. Marines and British, French, and Italian soldiers. Their mandate was to support the central Lebanese government, but they soon found themselves drawn into the struggle for power between different Lebanese factions. During their stay in Lebanon, 260 U.S. Marines and about 60 French soldiers were killed, most of them in suicide bombings of the Marine and French Army compounds on Oct. 23, 1983. The multinational force left in the spring of 1984.

During 1984, Israeli troops remained in southern Lebanon and Syrian troops remained in the Bekaa Valley. By the third anniversary of the invasion, June 6, 1985, all Israeli troops had withdrawn except for several hundred "advisers" to a Christian militia trained and armed by the Israelis.

In July 1986, Syrian observers took position in Beirut to monitor a peacekeeping agreement. The agreement broke down and fighting between Shiite and Druze militia in West Beirut became so intense that Syrian troops moved in force in February 1987, suppressing militia resistance.

Amin Gemayel's Presidency expired on Sept. 23, 1988. The impossibility of setting up elections led Gemayel to designate a government under army chief Gen. Michael Aoun. Aoun's government was rejected by Prime Minister Selim al-Hoss who established a rival government in Muslim West Beirut.

In October 1989, Lebanese Christian and Moslem deputies approved a tentative peace accord and the new National Assembly selected a President.

In early 1991 the Lebanese government, backed by Syria, attempted to regain control over the south and disband all private militias, thereby ending the 16-year civil war. This led in July to clashes with PLO guerrillas, who on July 4 agreed to hand over their weapons. Israel, however, announced it would not withdraw from its self-proclaimed security zone in the south, as Beirut had hoped.

In the general elections of August 1992 most Christians abstained from voting demanding that Syrian forces first leave the country. The new legislature consisted of mostly pro-Syrian members. The largest Christian party was further weakened when in January 1993 it appeared to split into two factions.

his son was sworn in as King Letsie III.

Lekhanya, the chairman of the Military Counccil, was himself forced to resign in April 1991. Col. Ramaema became the new chairman in May.

In 1992 the country established full relations with South Africa, being only the third country to do so.

LESOTHO

Kingdom of Lesotho
Sovereign: King Letsie III (1990)
Prime Minister: Dr. Ntsu Mokhehle
Area: 11,720 sq mi. (30,355 sq km)
Population (est. mid-1993): 1,900,000 (average annual rate of natural increase: 2.5%); birth rate: 35/1000; infant mortality rate: 84/1000; density per square mile: 161
Capital and largest city (1992): Maseru (1992), 170,000; **Monetary unit:** Loti; **Languages:** English and Sesotho (official); also Zulu and Xhosa; **Religions:** Christian, 80%; indigenous beliefs; Muslim; and Bahai; **Member of Commonwealth of Nations; Literacy rate:** 59% (1989)
Economic summary: Gross domestic product (1990 est.): $420 million; $240 per capita; 4% real growth rate; inflation 15%; unemployment (1991 est.): 55% among adult males. Arable land: 10%. Principal products: corn, wheat, sorghum, barley. Labor force: 689,000; 86.2% in subsistence agriculture. Natural resources: diamonds. Exports: $59 million (f.o.b., 1990): wool, mohair, wheat, cattle, hides and skins. Imports: $604 million (f.o.b., 1990): foodstuffs, building materials, clothing, vehicles, machinery. Major trading partner: South Africa, E.C., North and South America.

Geography. Mountainous Lesotho, the size of Maryland, is surrounded by the Republic of South Africa in the east central part of that country except for short borders on the east and south with two discontinuous units of the Republic of Transkei. The Drakensberg Mountains in the east are Lesotho's principal chain. Elsewhere the region consists of rocky tableland.

Government. A constitutional monarchy. The executive power is with the prime minister and the cabinet (Council of Ministers).

History. Lesotho (formerly Basutoland) was constituted a native state under British protection by a treaty signed with the native chief Moshesh in 1843. It was annexed to Cape Colony in 1871, but in 1884 it was restored to direct control by the Crown.

The colony of Basutoland became the independent nation of Lesotho on Oct. 4, 1966.

In the 1970 elections, Ntsu Mokhehle, head of the Basutoland Congress Party, claimed a victory, but Jonathan declared a state of emergency, suspended the Constitution, and arrested Mokhehle. Jonathan jailed 45 opposition politicians and declared the King had "technically abdicated" by siding with the opposition party.

The King returned after a compromise with Jonathan in which the new Constitution would name him head of state but forbid his participation in politics.

After the King refused to approve the replacements in February 1990 of individuals dismissed by Lekhanya, the latter stripped the King of his executive power. Then in early March Lekhanya sent the King into exile. In November the King was dethroned, and

LIBERIA

Republic of Liberia
President: Amos Sawyer (interim) (1990)
Area: 43,000 sq mi. (111,370 sq km)
Population (est. mid-1993): 2,800,000 (average annual rate of natural increase: 3.2%); birth rate: 47/1000; infant mortality rate: 134/1000; density per square mile: 77
Capital and largest city (est. 1984): Monrovia, 425,000; **Monetary unit:** Liberian dollar; **Languages:** English (official) and tribal dialects; **Religions:** traditional, 70%; Christian, 10%; Islam, 20%; **Literacy rate:** 40%
Economic summary: Gross domestic product (1988): $988 million; $395 per capita; 1.5% real growth rate; inflation (1989): 12%; unemployment (1988): 43% urban. Arable land: 1%. Principal agricultural products: rubber, rice, palm oil, cassava, coffee, cocoa. Labor force: 510,000; 70.5% in agriculture. Major industrial products: iron ore, diamonds, processed rubber, processed food, construction materials. Natural resources: iron ore, gold, timber, diamonds. Exports: $505 million (f.o.b., 1989 est.): iron ore, rubber, timber, coffee. Imports: $394 million (c.i.f., 1989 est.): machinery, petroleum products, transport equipment, foodstuffs. Major trading partners: U.S., E.C., Netherlands, Japan, China.

Geography. Lying on the Atlantic in the southern part of West Africa, Liberia is bordered by Sierra Leone, Guinea, and the Ivory Coast. It is comparable in size to Tennessee.

Most of the country is a plateau covered by dense tropical forests, which thrive under an annual rainfall of about 160 inches a year.

Government. A five-nation West African peacekeeping force installed an interim government in October 1990 and in November made Amos Sawyer interim president. The National Patriotic Front led by Charles Taylor controls most of the country.

History. Liberia was founded in 1822 as a result of the efforts of the American Colonization Society to settle freed American slaves in West Africa. In 1847, it became the Free and Independent Republic of Liberia.

The government of Africa's first republic was modeled after that of the United States, and Joseph J. Roberts of Virginia was elected the first president. He laid the foundations of a modern state and initiated efforts, never too successful but pursued for more than a century, to bring the aboriginal inhabitants of the territory to the level of the emigrants. The English-speaking descendants of U.S. blacks, known as Americo-Liberians, were the intellectual and ruling class. The indigenous inhabitants, divided, constitute 99% of the population.

After 1920, considerable progress was made toward opening up the interior, a process that was spurred in 1951 by the establishment of a 43-mile (69-km) railroad to the Bomi Hills from Monrovia.

In July 1971, while serving his sixth term as president, William V. S. Tubman died following surgery and was succeeded by his long-time associate, Vice President William R. Tolbert, Jr.

Tolbert was ousted in a military coup carried out April 12, 1980, by army enlisted men led by Master Sgt. Samuel K. Doe. Tolbert and 27 other high officials were executed.

A rebellion led by Charles Taylor, a former Doe aide, started in December 1989 and, by mid-July 1990, had taken most of Liberia's key population and economic centers and surrounded the capital.

A West African peacekeeping force intervened in Liberia and effectively partitioned the country into two zones: One, containing the capital of Monrovia, led by President Sawyer, is backed by virtually all West African nations. The other, led by Mr. Taylor, constitutes about 95% of the territory. A national conference in March 1991 failed to reach an agreement but reelected Sawyer interim president.

Despite a 1991 peace factional fighting continued at times in the country's civil war. In July 1993 the disputants reached a peace agreement that included a cease-fire, the establishment of an interim government and democratic elections.

LIBYA

Socialist People's Libyan Arab Jamahiriya
Head of State: Col. Muammar el-Qaddafi (1969)
Secretary of the General People's Committee: Abuzeid Omar Dorda (1990)
Area: 679,536 sq mi. (1,759,998 sq km)
Population (est. mid-1993): 4,900,000 (average annual rate of natural increase: 3.4%); birth rate: 42/1000; infant mortality rate: 68/1000; density per square mile: 7
Capital: Tripoli; **Largest cities (est. 1988):** Tripoli, 591,062; Benghazi, 446,250; **Monetary unit:** Libyan dinar; **Language:** Arabic, Italian and English widely understood in major cities; **Religion:** Islam; **National name:** Socialist People's Libyan Arab Jamahiriya; **Literacy rate:** 64%
Economic summary: Gross national product (1990 est.): $28.9 billion; $6,800 per capita; real growth rate 9%; unemployment (1988 est.) 2%. Arable land: 1%. Principal products: wheat, barley, olives, dates, citrus fruits, peanuts. Labor force: 1,000,000; 31% in industry. Major products: petroleum, processed foods, textiles, handicrafts, cement. Natural resources: petroleum, natural gas. Exports: $11 billion (f.o.b., 1990 est.): petroleum, peanuts, hides. Imports: $7.6 billion (f.o.b., 1990 est.): machinery, foodstuffs, manufactured goods. Major trading partners: Italy, Germany, U.K., France, Spain, Japan.

Geography. Libya stretches along the northeastern coast of Africa between Tunisia and Algeria on the west and Egypt on the east; to the south are the Sudan, Chad, and Niger. It is one sixth larger than Alaska.

A greater part of the country lies within the Sahara. Along the Mediterranean coast and farther inland is arable plateau land.

Government. In a bloodless coup d'etat on Sept. 1, 1969, the military seized power in Libya. King Idris I, who had ruled since 1951, was deposed and the Libyan Arab Republic proclaimed. The official name was changed in 1977 to the Socialist People's Libyan Arab Jamahiriya—Jamahiriya (a state of the masses): in theory, governed by the populace through local councils; in fact, a military dictatorship. The Revolutionary Council that had governed since the coup was renamed the General Secretariat of the General People's Congress. The Arab Socialist Union Organization is the only political party.

History. Libya was a part of the Turkish dominions from the 16th century until 1911. Following the outbreak of hostilities between Italy and Turkey in that year, Italian troops occupied Tripoli; Italian sovereignty was recognized in 1912.

Libya was the scene of much desert fighting during World War II. After the fall of Tripoli on Jan. 23, 1943, it came under Allied administration. In 1949, the U.N. voted that Libya should become independent by 1952.

Discovery of oil in the Libyan Desert promised financial stability and funds for economic development.

On Aug. 19, 1981, two U.S. Navy F-14's shot down two Soviet-made SU-22's of the Libyan air force that had attacked them in air space above the Gulf of Sidra, claimed by Libya but held to be international by the U.S. In December, Washington asserted that Libyan "hit squads" had been dispatched to the U.S. and security was drastically tightened around President Reagan and other officials. When the Mobil Oil Company abandoned its operations in April 1982, only four U.S. firms were still in Libya, using Libyan or third-country personnel.

Qaddafi's troops also supported rebels in Chad but suffered major military reverses in 1987.

On March 24, 1986, U.S. and Libyan forces skirmished in the Gulf of Sidra, with two Libyan patrol boats being sunk.

On April 14, after a Libyan-backed attack on a West Berlin disco in which two people, including an American serviceman, were killed, Reagan ordered an air raid on Libyan military installations.

A two-year-old U.S. covert policy to destabilize the Libyan government with U.S.-trained Libyan ex-P.O.W.s ended in failure in December 1990 when a Libyan-supplied guerrilla force assumed power in Chad, where the commandos were based, and asked the band to leave.

For its refusal to extradite two Libyans accused of involvement in an airline bombing back in 1988 the UN imposed sanctions in April 1992.

Relations with Chad improved as the two nations signed an agreement of mutual cooperation. The border dispute with Chad, however, was sent to the International Court in The Hague.

LIECHTENSTEIN

Principality of Liechtenstein
Ruler: Prince Hans Adam (1989)
Prime Minister: Markus Büchel (1993)
Area: 61 sq mi. (157 sq km)
Population (mid-1993): 30,000 (average annual growth rate: 0.8%); birth rate: 14/1000; infant mortality rate: 2.7/1000; density per square mile: 486
Capital and largest city (est. 1990): Vaduz, 4,874; **Monetary unit:** Swiss franc; **Language:** German; **Religions:** Roman Catholic, 87.3%; Protestant, 8,.3%; other 4.4%; **Literacy rate:** 100%
Economic summary: Gross domestic product (1990 est.): $630 million; $22,300 per capita; inflation 5.4%; unemployment 1.5%. Arable land: 25%. Principal agricultural products: livestock, vegetables, corn, wheat, potatoes, grapes. Labor force: Labor force: 19,905 (11,933 are foreigners); industry, 53%; service, 45%.

Major industrial products: electronics, metal products, textiles, ceramics, pharmaceuticals, food products, precision instruments. Natural resource: hydroelectric power. Exports: $1.6 billion: small specialty machinery, dental products, stamps, hardware, pottery. Imports: $n.a.: machinery, processed foods, metal goods, textiles, motor vehicles. Major trading partners: Switzerland and other Western European countries.

Geography. Tiny Liechtenstein, not quite as large as Washington, D.C., lies on the east bank of the Rhine River south of Lake Constance between Austria and Switzerland. It consists of low valley land and Alpine peaks. Falknis (8,401 ft; 2,561 m) and Naafkopf (8,432 ft; 2,570 m) are the tallest.

Government. The Constitution of 1921, amended in 1972, provides for a legislature, the Landtag, of 25 members elected by direct suffrage.

History. Founded in 1719, Liechtenstein was a member of the German Confederation from 1815 to 1866, when it became an independent principality. It abolished its army in 1868 and has managed to stay neutral and undamaged in all European wars since then. In a referendum on July 1, 1984, male voters granted women the right to vote, a victory for Prince Hans Adam.

The country became the smallest member of the UN in 1990.

A June 1992 referendum to lower the voting age from 20 to 18 was rejected.

LITHUANIA

Republic of Lithuania
President: Algirdas Mykolas Brazamskos (1993)
Prime Minister: Adolfas Slezevicius (1993)
Area: 25,174 sq mi. (64,445 sq km)
Population (1993): 3,751,000 (Lithuanian, 80.6%; Russian, 8.9%); (average annual rate of natural increase: 0.4%); birth rate: 15/1000; infant mortality rate: 14/1000; density per square mile: 152
Capital and largest city (1992): Vilnius, 590,100; **Monetary unit:** Litas; **Languages:** Lithuanian; **Religion (1939):** Catholic, 85%; **National name:** Lietuva; **Literacy:** very high
Economic survey: Gross domestic product (1992): $545 million; per capita gross national product (1991): $2,710; real growth rate –13%; inflation 200%. Labor force (1990): 1,886,000. Natural resources: peat. Industries: metal cutting, electric motors, TV sets, refrigerators and freezers, petroleum refining, shipbuilding, furniture, textiles, food processing, electronic components, computers. Agriculture (36% of labor force): Most developed are the livestock and dairy branches. Lithuania is a net exporter of meat, milk, and eggs. Exports (1989): electronics, petroleum products, food, chemicals. Imports (1990): oil, machinery, chemicals, grain. Major trading parters: CIS nations about 75%.

Geography: Lithuania is situated on the eastern shore of the Baltic Sea and borders Latvia on the north, Belarus on the east and south, Poland and the Kaliningrad region of Russia on the southwest. It is a country of gently rolling hills, many forests, rivers and streams, and lakes. Its principal natural resource is agricultural land.

Government: Lithuania is a democracy. The head of state is the directly-elected President. The president nominates the prime minister who is then approved by the parliament (Stimas).

History: Southernmost of the three Baltic states, Lithuania in the Middle Ages was a grand duchy joined to Poland through royal marriage. Poles and Lithuanians merged forces to defeat the Teutonic knights of Germany at Tannenberg in 1410 and extended their power far into Russian territory. In 1795, however, following the third partition of Poland, Lithuania fell into Russian hands and did not regain its independence until 1918, toward the end of the first World War.

The republic was occupied by the Soviet Union in June 1940 and annexed in August 1940. From June 1941 to 1944 it was occupied by German troops and then was retaken by Russia. Western countries, including the United States, never recognized the Russian annexation of Lithuania.

Nineteen eighty-eight saw a re-emergence of the Lithuanian independence movement. Elections were held on Feb. 24, 1990, and Vytautas Landsbergis, the non-communist head of the largest Lithuanian popular movement (Sajudis) was elected to parliament that day, and on March 11, 1990, the parliament elected him as its president. On the same day, the Supreme Council rejected Soviet rule and declared the restoration of Lithuania's independence, the first Baltic republic to take this action.

Confrontation with the Soviet Union ensued along with economic sanctions, but they were lifted after both sides agreed to a face-saving compromise.

After an abortive coup to depose Soviet President Mikhail Gorbachev, President Landsbergis called his country's independence a formality.

Lithuania's independence was quickly recognized by major European and other nations, and on Sept. 2, 1991, President Bush announced full diplomatic recognition for the Baltic republics. The Soviet Union finally recognized the independence of the Baltic states on September 6. UN admittance followed on Sept. 17, 1991.

Elections in February 1993 made Brazauskas, a former Communist Party leader, president. He renounced his past and promised to move ahead with privatization and encourage foreign investment.

LUXEMBOURG

Grand Duchy of Luxembourg
Ruler: Grand Duke Jean (1964)
Premier: Jacques Santer (1984)
Area: 999 sq mi. (2,586 sq km)
Population (est. mid-1993): 400,000 (average annual rate of natural increase: 0.3%); birth rate: 13/1000; infant mortality rate: 9.2/1000; density per square mile: 404
Capital and largest city (1991): Luxembourg, 75,622; **Monetary unit:** Luxembourg franc; **Languages:** Luxembourgish, French, German; **Religion:** Mainly Roman Catholic; **National name:** Grand-Duché de Luxembourg; **Literacy rate:** 100%
Economic summary: Gross national product (1991 est.): $7.83 billion; $20,200 per capita; real growth rate 2.5%; inflation (1990): 3.7%; unemployment (1990): 1.3%. Arable land: 24%. Principal agricultural products: livestock, dairy products, wine. Labor force (1988): 177,300; one-third are foreign workers. Services, 65%; industry, 31.6%; agriculture, 3.4%. Major industrial products: banking, steel, processed food, chemicals,

metal products, tires, glass. Natural resource: Iron ore. Exports: $6.3 billion (f.o.b., 1990): steel, chemicals, rubber products, glass, aluminum. Imports: $7.5 billion (c.i.f., 1990): minerals, metals, foodstuffs, consumer goods. Major trading partners: European Common Market countries.

Geography. Luxembourg is a neighbor of Belgium on the west, Germany on the east, and France on the south. The Ardennes Mountains extend from Belgium into the northern section of Luxembourg.

Government. Luxembourg's unicameral legislature, the Chamber of Deputies, consists of 60 members elected for five years.

History. Sigefroi, Count of Ardennes, an offspring of Charlemagne, was Luxembourg's first sovereign ruler. In 1060, the country came under the rule of the House of Luxembourg. From the 15th to the 18th century, Spain, France, and Austria held it in turn. The Congress of Vienna in 1815 made it a Grand Duchy and gave it to William I, King of the Netherlands. In 1839 the Treaty of London ceded the western part of Luxembourg to Belgium.

The eastern part, continuing in personal union with the Netherlands and a member of the German Confederation, became autonomous in 1848 and a neutral territory by decision of the London Conference of 1867, governed by its Grand Duke. Germany occupied the duchy in World Wars I and II. Allied troops liberated the enclave in 1944.

In 1961, Prince Jean, son and heir of Grand Duchess Charlotte, was made head of state, acting for his mother. She abdicated in 1964, and Prince Jean became Grand Duke. Grand Duchess Charlotte died in 1985.

By a customs union between Belgium and Luxembourg, which came into force on May 1, 1922, to last for 50 years, customs frontiers between the two countries were abolished. On Jan. 1, 1948, a customs union with Belgium and the Netherlands (Benelux) came into existence. On Feb. 3, 1958, it became an economic union.

Luxembourg's parliament approved the "Maastricht Accord" in July 1992, with the proviso that the country negotiate an exemption to the clause granting foreigners the vote.

MACEDONIA[1]

Republic of Macedonia
President: Kiro Gilgorov
Prime Minister: Branko Crvenkovski (1992)
Area: 9,928 sq mi. (25,713 sq km)
Population (1991 census): 2,033,964; Macedonians, 65.3%; Albanians, 21.7%; Turks, 3.8%; Rhomas, 2.5%; Vlachs, 0.3%; Other, 6.4%. (Average annual rate of natural increase: 1.0%); birth rate: 17/1000; infant mortality rate: 35.3/1000; density per square mile: 205
Capital and largest city (1991 est.): Skopje, 448,229. Other large cities: Bitola, 84,002; Kumanovo, 69,231; Prelep, 70,152; Tetovo, 51,472; Titov Veles, 47,326; Ohrid, 42,903; Sitip, 42,826; **Monetary unit:** Dinar; **Languages:** Macedonian, 70%; Albanian, 21%; Turkish, 3%; other, 6%; **Religions:** Eastern Orthodox, 59%; Muslim, 26%; other Christian
Economic summary: Gross domestic product (1991 est.): $7.1 billion; $3,100 per capita; real growth rate, –18%; inflation (March 1992): 4,500%; unemployment (1991 est.): 20%. Industries: low level technology (basic fuels) mining, basic textiles, wood products, and tobacco. Agriculture: rice, tobacco, wheat, corn, millet, cotton, citrus fruits, and vegetables. Exports (1991): $1,095 million. Imports (1991): $1,274 million. Major trading partners: Germany, Albania, Bulgaria, former Yugoslav republics.

1. The U.N. recognized the Republic of Macedonia on April 8, 1993 under the temporary name the Former Yugoslav Republic of Macedonia.

Geography: Macedonia is a landlocked state in the heart of the Balkans and is slightly smaller than the state of Vermont. It is a mountainous country with small basins of agricultural land linked by rivers. It borders the Yugoslavian Republic of Serbia in the north, Bulgaria in the east, Greece in the south, and Albania in the west. The three major rivers are the Aliakmon, the Vardar, and the Strymon. The Vardar is the largest and most important river.

Government: A democratic republic with two legislative houses—the National Assembly consisting of 120 deputies, each elected for a four-year term. The assembly's president and vice presidents are elected from among its members.

History: The Republic of Macedonia occupies the western half of the ancient Kingdom of Macedonia. Historic Macedonia was defeated by Rome in 146 B.C. and became a Roman province in 148 B.C.

After the Roman Empire was divided in A.D. 395, Macedonia was intermittently ruled by the Byzantine Empire until Turkey took possession of the land in 1389. The Ottoman Turks dominated Macedonia for the next five centuries up until 1913.

During the 19th and 20th centuries, there was a constant struggle by the Balkan powers to possess Macedonia for its economic and strategic military corridors.

The Treaty of San Stefano in 1878 ending the Russo-Turkish War gave the largest part of Macedonia to Bulgaria. Bulgaria lost much of its Macedonian territory when it was defeated by the Greeks and Serbs in the Second Balkan War of 1913. Most of Macedonia went to Serbia and the remainder was divided among Greece and Bulgaria.

In 1914, Serbia, which included Macedonia, joined in union with Croatia, Slovenia, and Montenegro to form the Kingdom of Serbs, Croats, and Slovenes which was renamed Yugoslavia in 1929.

Bulgaria joined the Axis powers in World War II and occupied parts of Yugoslavia including Macedonia in 1941. During the occupation of their country, Macedonian resistance fighters fought a guerrilla warfare against the invading troops.

The Yugoslavian Republic was re-established after the defeat of Germany in 1945, and in 1946, the government removed Macedonia from Serbian control and made it an autonomous Yugoslavian republic. Later, when President Tito recognized the Macedonian people as a separate nation, the Macedonians strove to develop their own culture and language separate from Bulgaria and Serbia.

In January 1992, Macedonia declared its independence from Yugoslavia and asked for recognition from the European Community nations. While the E.C. approved the move in principle, it requested that the republic hold a referendum on independence.

Bulgaria strongly supported a Macedonian state as a safeguard against Serbian expansion in the area.

The U.S. and the E.C. in July 1992 refused recognition of the republic under a name that includes "Macedonia."

MADAGASCAR

Democratic Republic of Madagascar
President and Head of State: Didier Ratsiraka (1975)
Prime Minister: Guy Razanamasy
Area: 226,660 sq mi. (587,050 sq km)
Population (est. mid-1993): 13,300,000 (average annual rate of natural increase: 3.3%); birth rate: 46/1000; infant mortality rate: 93/1000; density per square mile: 59
Capital and largest city (est. 1990): Antananarivo, 802,390; **Monetary unit:** Malagasy franc; **Languages:** Malagasy, French; **Ethnic groups:** Merina (or Hova), Betsimisaraka, Betsileo, Tsimihety, Antaisaka, Sakalava, Antandroy; **Religions:** traditional, 52%; Christian, 41%; Islam, 7%; **National name:** Repoblika Demokratika Malagasy; **Literacy rate:** 80%
Economic summary: Gross domestic product (1991 est.): $2.4 billion; $200 per capita; 3.8% real growth rate. Arable land: 4%. Principal agricultural products: rice, livestock, coffee, vanilla, sugar, cloves, cardamom, beans, bananas. Labor force: 4,900,000; 90% in subsistence agriculture. Major industrial products: processed food, textiles, assembled automobiles, soap, cement. Natural resources: graphite, chromium, bauxite, semiprecious stones. Exports: $290 million (f.o.b., 1990 est.): coffee, cloves, vanilla, sugar, petroleum products. Imports: $436 million (f.o.b., 1990 est.): consumer goods, foodstuffs, crude petroleum. Major trading partners: France, U.S., Japan, Italy, Germany, U.K. and other E.C.

Geography. Madagascar lies in the Indian Ocean off the southeast coast of Africa opposite Mozambique. The world's fourth-largest island, it is twice the size of Arizona. The country's low-lying coastal area gives way to a central plateau. The once densely wooded interior has largely been cut down.

Government. The Constitution of Dec. 30, 1975, approved by referendum following a military coup, provides for direct election by universal suffrage of a president for a seven-year term, a Supreme Council of the Revolution as a policy-making body, a unicameral People's National Assembly of 137 members (elected for five-year terms), and a military Committee for Development. The new constitution followed a period of martial rule that began with the suspension of the republic's original bicameral legislature in 1972.

A decree of March 1990 permitted the formation of political parties. Three new groupings immediately appeared.

History. The present population is of black and Malay stock, with perhaps some Polynesian, called Malagasy. The French took over a protectorate in 1885, and then in 1894–95 ended the monarchy, exiling Queen Rànavàlona III to Algiers. A colonial administration was set up, to which the Comoro Islands were attached in 1908, and other territories later. In World War II, the British occupied Madagascar, which retained ties to Vichy France.

An autonomous republic within the French Community since 1958, Madagascar became an independent member of the Community in 1960. In May 1973, an army coup led by Maj. Gen. Gabriel Ramanantsoa ousted Philibert Tsiranana, president since 1959.

On June 15, 1975, Comdr. Didier Ratsiraka was named President. He announced that he would follow a socialist course and, after nationalizing banks and insurance companies, declared all mineral resources nationalized.

In July 1991 opposition leaders named an alternative government. After a 15-day strike the president offered a referendum on a multiparty constitution and named a new prime minister. An interim government was formed in May that included the opposition and would prepare constitutional changes.

The first round of the presidential election gave Albert Zafy slightly less than half the vote necessitating another round. Irregularities, however, forced postponement of the second round into 1993.

MALAWI

Republic of Malawi
President: Hastings Kamuzu Banda (1966)
Area: 45,747 sq mi. (118,484 sq km)
Population (est. mid-1993): 10,000,000 (average annual rate of natural increase: 3.4%); birth rate: 53/1000; infant mortality rate: 138/1000; density per square mile: 276
Capital (1987): Lilongwe, 233,973; **Largest city (1987):** Blantyre, 331,588; **Monetary unit:** Kwacha; **Languages:** English and Chichewa (National); **Religions:** Christian, 75%; Islam, 20%; **Member of Commonwealth of Nations; Literacy rate:** 41.2%
Economic summary: Gross domestic product (1991 est.): $1.9 billion; $200 per capita; growth rate 4.2%; inflation rate 9%. Arable land: 25%. Agriculture accounts for 40% of GDP and 90% of export revenues. Principal agricultural products: tobacco, tea, sugar, corn, cotton. Labor force: 428,000 wage earners; 43% in agriculture. Major industrial products: food, tobacco, cement, processed wood, consumer goods. Natural resources: limestone, uranium, coal, bauxite. Exports: $390 million (f.o.b., 1990 est.): tobacco, sugar, tea, coffee, peanuts. Imports: $560 million (c.i.f., 1990 est.): transport equipment, food, petroleum, consumer goods. Major trading partners: U.K., U.S., Japan, Germany, South Africa, Zambia, Zimbabwe.

Geography. Malawi is a landlocked country the size of Pennsylvania in southeastern Africa, surrounded by Mozambique, Zambia, and Tanzania. Lake Malawi, formerly Lake Nyasa, occupies most of the country's eastern border. The north-south Rift Valley is flanked by mountain ranges and high plateau areas.

Government. Under a Constitution that came into effect on July 6, 1966, the president is the sole head of state; there is neither a prime minister nor a vice president. The National Assembly has 141 members.

There is only one national party—the Malawi Congress Party led by President Hastings K. Banda, who was designated President for life in 1970.

History. The first European to make extensive explorations in the area was David Livingstone in the 1850s and 1860s. In 1884, Cecil Rhodes's British South African Company received a charter to develop the country. The company came into conflict with the Arab slavers in 1887–89. After Britain annexed the Nyasaland territory in 1891, making it a protectorate in 1892, Sir Harry Johnstone, the first high commissioner, using Royal Navy gunboats, wiped out the slavers.

Nyasaland became the independent nation of Malawi on July 6, 1964. Two years later, it became a republic within the Commonwealth of Nations.

Dr. Hastings K. Banda, Malawi's first Prime Minister, became its first President. He pledged to follow a policy of "discretionary nonalignment." Banda alienated much of black Africa by maintaining good relations with South Africa. He argued that his landlocked country had to rely on South Africa for access to the sea and trade.

The results of a referendum in June 1993 on Banda's one-party rule gave 63% in favor of a multiparty democracy. The opposition promptly demanded that the president step aside, clearing the way for a coalition government and early elections by Christmas.

MALAYSIA

Paramount Ruler: Azlan Muhibuddin Shah, Sultan of Perak (1989)
Prime Minister: D.S. Mahathir bin Mohamad (1981)
Area: 128,328 sq mi. (332,370 sq km)
Population (est. mid-1993): 18,400,000 (average annual rate of natural increase: 2.3%); birth rate: 28/1000; infant mortality rate: 14/1000; density per square mile: 145
Capital: Kuala Lumpur; **Largest cities (1988):** Kuala Lumpur, 1,181,490 (1980); George Town (Pinang), 248,241 Ipoh, 293,849; **Monetary unit:** Ringgit; **Languages:** Malay (official), Chinese, Tamil, English; **Ethnic divisions:** 59% Malay and other indigenous; 32% Chinese; 9% Indian; **Religions:** Malays all Muslim, Chinese predominantly Buddhists, Indians predominantly Hindu; **Member of Commonwealth of Nations; Literacy rate:** 78%
Economic summary: Gross domestic product (1991 est.): $48 billion; $2,670 per capita; real growth rate 8.6%; unemployment 5.8%. Arable land: 3%. Principal agricultural products: rice, rubber, palm products. Labor force (1990): 7,258,000. Major industrial products: processed rubber, timber, and palm oil, tin, petroleum, light manufactures, electronics equipment. Natural resources: tin, oil, copper, timber. Exports: $35.4 billion (f.o.b., 1991): natural rubber, palm oil, tin, timber, petroleum, electronics. Imports: $38.7 billion (c.i.f., 1991): food, crude oil, capital equipment, chemicals. Major trading partners: Japan, Singapore, U.S., Western European countries. Illicit drugs: Transit point for Golden Triangle heroin going to the U.S., Western Europe, and the Third World.

Geography. Malaysia is on the Malay Peninsula in southeast Asia. The nation also includes Sabah and Sarawak on the island of Borneo to the east. Its area slightly exceeds that of New Mexico.

Most of Malaysia is covered by forest, with a mountain range running the length of the peninsula. Extensive forests provide ebony, sandalwood, teak, and other woods.

Government. Malaysia is a sovereign constitutional monarchy within the Commonwealth of Nations. The Paramount Ruler is elected for a five-year term by the hereditary rulers of the states from among themselves. He is advised by the prime minister and his cabinet. There is a bicameral legislature. The Senate, whose role is comparable more to that of the British House of Lords than to the U.S. Senate, has 68 members, partly appointed by the Paramount Ruler to represent minority and special interests, and partly elected by the legislative assemblies of the various states.

The House of Representatives, is made up of 180 members, who are elected for five-year terms.

History. Malaysia came into existence on Sept. 16, 1963, as a federation of Malaya, Singapore, Sabah (North Borneo), and Sarawak. In 1965, Singapore withdrew from the federation. Since 1966, the 11 states of former Malaya have been known as West Malaysia, and Sabah and Sarawak have been known as East Malaysia.

The Union of Malaya was established April 1, 1946, being formed from the Federated Malay States of Negri Sembilan, Pahang, Perak, and Selangor; the Unfederated Malay States of Johore, Kedah, Kelantan, Perlis, and Trengganu; and two of the Straits Settlements—Malacca and Penang. The Malay states had been brought under British administration during the late 19th and early 20th centuries.

It became the Federation of Malaya on Feb. 1, 1948, and the Federation attained full independence within the Commonwealth of Nations in 1957.

Sabah, constituting the extreme northern portion of the island of Borneo, was a British protectorate administered under charter by the British North Borneo Company from 1881 to 1946, when it assumed the status of a colony. It was occupied by Japanese troops from 1942 to 1945.

Sarawak extends along the northwestern coast of Borneo for about 500 miles (805 km). In 1841, part of the present territory was granted by the Sultan of Brunei to Sir James Brooke. Sarawak continued to be ruled by members of the Brooke family until the Japanese occupation.

From 1963, when Malaysia became independent, it was the target of guerrilla infiltration from Indonesia, but beat off invasion attempts. In 1966, when Sukarno fell and the Communist Party was liquidated in Indonesia, hostilities ended.

In the late 1960s, the country was torn by communal rioting directed against Chinese and Indians, who controlled a disproportionate share of the country's wealth. Beginning in 1968, the government moved to achieve greater economic balance through a rural development program.

Malaysia felt the impact of the "boat people" fleeing Vietnam early in 1978. Because the refugees were mostly ethnic Chinese, the government was apprehensive about any increase of a minority that previously had been the source of internal conflict in the country. In April 1988, it announced that starting in April 1989 it would accept no more refugees.

General elections were held in October 1990 producing another victory for Prime Minister Mahathir and his Barisan National coalition, which won 127 of the 180 parliamentary seats.

Frictions developed in 1992 between the dominant partner in the governing coalition and the country's nine hereditary rulers.

MALDIVES

Republic of Maldives
President: Maumoon Abdul Gayoom (1978)
Area: 115 sq mi. (298 sq km)
Population (est. mid-1993): 200,000 (average annual rate of natural increase: 3.4%); birth rate: 41/1000; infant mortality rate: 34/1000; density per square mile: 2,055
Capital and largest city (1990): Malé, 55,130; **Monetary unit:** Maldivian rufiyaa; **Language:** Dhivehi; **Religion:** Islam; **Literacy rate:** 98%
Economic summary: Gross domestic product (1992): $157.9 million; $684 per capita; real growth rate 6.3%; inflation (1990): 10.7%. Arable land: 10%. Principal agricultural products: coconuts, corn, sweet potatoes. Labor force: 66,000; 80% in fishing. Major products: fish, processed coconuts, handicraft. Natural resource: fish. Tourism is also an important sector of the economy. Export: $52 million (f.o.b., 1990): fish,

clothing. Imports: $128.9 million (c.i.f., 1990): intermediate and capital goods, consumer goods, petroleum products. Major trading partners: Thailand, U.S., Singapore, U.K.

Geography. The Republic of Maldives is a group of atolls in the Indian Ocean about 417 miles (671 km) southwest of Sri Lanka. Its 1,190 coral islets stretch over an area of 35,200 square miles (90,000 sq km). With concerns over global warming and the shrinking of the polar ice caps, Maldives felt directly threatened as none of its islands rises more than six feet above sea level.

Government. The 11-member Cabinet is headed by the president. The Majlis (Parliament) is a unicameral legislature consisting of 48 members. Eight of these are appointed by the president. The others are elected for five-year terms, 2 from the capital island of Malé and 2 from each of the 19 administrative atolls.

There are no political parties in the Maldives.

History. The Maldives (formerly called the Maldive Islands) are inhabited by an Islamic seafaring people. Originally the islands were under the suzerainty of Ceylon. They came under British protection in 1887 and were a dependency of the then colony of Ceylon until 1948. The independence agreement with Britain was signed July 26, 1965.

For centuries a sultanate, the islands adopted a republican form of government in 1952, but the sultanate was restored in 1954. In 1968, however, as the result of a referendum, a republic was again established in the islands.

Ibrahim Nasir, president since 1968, was removed from office by the Majlis in November 1978 and replaced by Maumoon Abdul Gayoom.

Despite the imposition of press censorship in 1991 opposition to the government continued.

MALI

Republic of Mali
President of the Republic: Alpha Oumar Konaré (1992)
Area: 478,819 sq mi. (1,240,142 sq km)
Population (est. mid-1993): 8,900,000 (average annual rate of natural increase: 3%); birth rate: 52/1000; infant mortality rate: 111/1000; density per square mile: 19
Capital and largest city (1992 est.): Bamako, 746,000; **Monetary unit:** Franc CFA; **Ethnic groups:** Bambara, Peul, Soninke, Malinke, Songhai, Dogon, Senoufo, Minianka, Berbers, and Moors; **Languages:** French (official), African languages; **Religions:** Islam, 90%; traditional, 9%; Christian, 1%; **National name:** République de Mali; **Literacy rate:** 32%
Economic summary: Gross domestic product (1990 est.): $2.2 billion; $265 per capita; real growth rate 2.2%; inflation –1.6%. Arable land: 2%; Principal agricultural products: millet, corn, rice, cotton, peanuts, livestock. Labor force: 2,666,000; 80% in agriculture. Major industrial products: consumer goods, phosphates, gold, fish. Natural resources: bauxite, iron ore, manganese, phosphate, salt, limestone, gold. Exports: $285 million (f.o.b., 1989 est.): livestock, peanuts, dried fish, cotton, skins. Imports: $513 million (f.o.b., 1989 est.): textiles, vehicles, petroleum products, machinery, sugar, cereals. Major trading partners: Western Europe.

Geography. Most of Mali, in West Africa, lies in the Sahara. A landlocked country four fifths the size of Alaska, it is bordered by Guinea, Senegal, Mauritania, Algeria, Niger, Burkina Faso, and the Ivory Coast.

The only fertile area is in the south, where the Niger and Senegal Rivers provide irrigation.

Government. The army overthrew the government on Nov. 19, 1968, and formed a provisional government. The Military Committee of National Liberation consists of 14 members and forms the decision-making body.

Soldiers promising a multiparty democracy overthrew the dictatorship of General Traoré in March 1991.

The present government is a multiparty democracy with one parliamentary house of 129 seats, 13 of which are designated for Malians abroad.

History. Subjugated by France by the end of the 19th century, this area became a colony in 1904 (named French Sudan in 1920) and in 1946 became part of the French Union. On June 20, 1960, it became independent and, under the name of Sudanese Republic, was federated with the Republic of Senegal in the Mali Federation. However, Senegal seceded from the Federation on Aug. 20, 1960, and the Sudanese Republic then changed its name to the Republic of Mali on September 22.

In the 1960s, Mali concentrated on economic development, continuing to accept aid from both Soviet bloc and Western nations, as well as international agencies. In the late 1960s, it began retreating from close ties with China. But a purge of conservative opponents brought greater power to President Modibo Keita, and in 1968 the influence of the Chinese and their Malian sympathizers increased.

Mali, with Mauritania, the Ivory Coast, Senegal, Dahomey (Benin), Niger, and Burkina Faso signed a treaty establishing the Economic Community for West Africa.

Mali and Burkina Faso fought a brief border war from December 25 to 29, 1985.

The leader of the March 1991 coup, Lieut. Col. Amadou Toumani Touré, promised the army would return to the barracks. There were at least 59 casualties after the overnight coup, which France welcomed. A failed coup attempt by Major Lamine Diabira, a member of the ruling council, resulted in his arrest in July.

Multiparty elections in 1992 gave the Alliance for Democracy in Mali 76 of the 116 parliamentary seats, and the presidency went to that party's candidate Konaré with 70% of the vote.

MALTA

Malta
President: Dr. Vincent Tabone (1989)
Prime Minister: Dr. Edward Fenech Adami (1987)
Area: 122 sq mi. (316 sq km)
Population (est. mid-1993): 400,000 (average annual rate of natural increase: 0.7%); birth rate: 15/1000; infant mortality rate: 9.1/1000; density per square mile: 2,946
Capital (est. 1991): Valletta, 9,196; **Largest city (est. 1987):** Sliema; **Monetary unit:** Maltese lira; **Languages:** Maltese and English; **Religion:** Roman Catholic; **National name:** Malta; **Member of Commonwealth of Nations; Literacy rate:** 84%
Economic summary: Gross domestic product (1991 est.): $2.5 billion; $7,000 per capita; real growth rate (1990) 5.5%; inflation (1990) 3.0%; unemployment (1990) 3.8%.

Arable land: 38%. Principal agricultural products: potatoes, wheat, barley, citrus, vegetables, hogs, poultry. Labor force: 125,674; 27% in manufacturing. Major manufacturing products are high-tech semiconductors, electrical switchgear, gold and silver items, rubber products, and textiles. The same products are exported. Tourism is also important to the economy. Exports: $1.1 billion (f.o.b., 1990). Imports: $2.0 billion (f.o.b., 1990): food, petroleum, machinery, and semimanufactured goods. Major trading partners: E.C. countries, U.S.

Geography. The five Maltese islands—with a combined land area smaller than Philadelphia—are in the Mediterranean about 60 miles (97 km) south of the southeastern tip of Sicily.

Government. The government is headed by a Prime Minister, responsible to a 65-member House of Representatives elected by universal suffrage.

The major political parties are the Nationalists (35 of 65 seats in the House,) led by Prime Minister Dr. Dr. Edward Fenech-Adami; Malta Labor Party (31 seats), led by Dr. Alfred Sant.

History. The strategic importance of Malta was recognized by the Phoenicians, who occupied it, as did in their turn the Greeks, Carthaginians, and Romans. The apostle Paul was shipwrecked there in A.D. 58.

The Knights of St. John (Malta), who obtained the three habitable Maltese islands of Malta, Gozo, and Comino from Charles V in 1530, reached their highest fame when they withstood an attack by superior Turkish forces in 1565.

Napoleon seized Malta in 1798, but the French forces were ousted by British troops the next year, and British rule was confirmed by the Treaty of Paris in 1814.

Malta was heavily attacked by German and Italian aircraft during World War II, but was never invaded by the Axis.

Malta became an independent nation on Sept. 21, 1964, and a republic Dec. 13, 1974, but remained in the British Commonwealth. The Governor-General, Sir Anthony Mamo, was sworn in as first president and Dom Mintoff became prime minister.

Malta applied for membership in the E.C. in July 1990 and expects to be admitted in the next enlargement.

Fenech Adami won reelection in February 1992 when his party won an absolute majority of three seats in the parliament.

MARSHALL ISLANDS

Republic of the Marshall Islands
President: Amata Kabua (1979)
Total land area: 70 sq mi (181.3 sq km), includes the atolls of Bikini, Eniwetok, and Kwajalein
Population (July 1992): 50,004; growth rate 3.9%; birth rate 47/1000; infant mortality rate 52/1000; density per square mile: 714.
Capital and largest city (1988): Majuro, 17,649; **Government:** Constitutional government in free association with the United States; **Ethnic divisions:** almost entirely Micronesian; **Religion:** predominantly Christian, mostly Protestant; **Literacy rate:** 93%; **Language:** Both Marshallese and English are official languages. Marshallese is a dialect of the Malayo-Polynesian family
Net migration rate (1992): 0 migrant/1000 population
Comparative land area: slightly larger than Washington, D.C.
Economic summary: Gross domestic product (1989 est.): $63 million; per capita, $1,500; real growth rate, n.a. Total exports from the Marshall Islands are some $2 million annually, of which copra products account for some 90 percent. Agriculture, marine resources, and tourism are the top development priorities for the Republic of the Marshall Islands (RMI). The government of the RMI is the largest employer with some 2,000 workers. Direct U.S. aid under the Compact of Free Association accounted for some two-thirds of the RMI's 1990 budget of $69 million. The United States and Japan are major trading partners.

The Government of the United States and the RMI signed a Compact of Free Association on October 15, 1986, which became effective as of October 21, 1986. The termination of the Trusteeship Agreement became effective on November 3, 1986. The Marshall Islands were admitted to the United Nations on Sept. 17, 1991.

The Marshall Islands, east of the Carolines, are divided into two chains: the western or Ralik group, including the atolls Jaluit, Kwajalein, Wotho, Bikini, and Eniwetok; and the eastern or Ratak group, including the atolls Mili, Majuro, Maloelap, Wotje, and Likiep. The islands are of the coral-reef type and rise only a few feet above sea level.

President Amata Kabua won reelection by the national legislature in January 1992, although some cabinet ministers were defeated in the general elections of November 1991.

MAURITANIA

Islamic Republic of Mauritania
Chief of State and Head of Government: Pres. Maaouye Ould Sidi Ahmed Taya (1984)
Area: 397,953 sq mi. (1,030,700 sq km)
Population (est. mid-1993): 2,200,000 (average annual rate of natural increase: 2.8%); birth rate: 46/1000; infant mortality rate: 122/1000; density per square mile: 6
Capital and largest city (est. 1990): Nouakchott, 500,000; **Monetary unit:** Ouguyia; **Ethnic groups:** Moors, Black/moor mix, 70%; Blacks, 30%. ; **Languages:** Arabic (official) and French; **Religion:** Islam; **National name:** République Islamique de Mauritanie; **Literacy rate:** 34%
Economic summary: Gross domestic product (1991 est.): $1.1 billion; $535 per capita; real growth rate 3.0%; inflation (1990) 6.5%; unemployment (1991 est.) 20%. Arable land: 1%; Principal agricultural products: livestock, millet, maize, wheat, dates, rice. Labor force: 465,000 (1981 est.); 45,000 wage earners; 14% in industry and commerce. Major industrial products: iron ore, processed fish. Natural resources: copper, iron ore, gypsum, fish. Exports: $436 million (f.o.b., 1990): iron ore, fish, gum arabic, gypsum. Imports: $389 million (c.i.f., 1990): foodstuffs, petroleum, capital goods. Major trading partners: E.C., Japan, Côte d'Ivoire.

Geography. Mauritania, three times the size of Arizona, is situated in northwest Africa with about 350 miles (592 km) of coastline on the Atlantic Ocean. It is bordered by Morocco on the north, Algeria and Mali on the east, and Senegal on the south.

The country is mostly desert, with the exception of the fertile Senegal River valley in the south and grazing land in the north.

Government. An Army coup on July 10, 1978, deposed Moktar Ould Daddah, who had been President since Mauritania's independence in 1960. President Mohammed Khouna Ould Haldala, who seized power in the 1978 coup, was in turn deposed in a Dec. 12, 1984, coup by army chief of staff Maaouye Ould Sidi Ahmed Taya, who assumed the title of President.

In the January 1992 elections Pres. Taya won 62% of the electorate vote.

History. Mauritania was first explored by the Portuguese. The French organized the area as a territory in 1904.

Mauritania became an independent nation on Nov. 28, 1960, and was admitted to the United Nations in 1961 over the strenuous opposition of Morocco, which claimed the territory. With Moors, Arabs, Berbers, and blacks frequently in conflict, the government in the late 1960s sought to make Arab culture dominant to unify the land.

Mauritania acquired administrative control of the southern part of the former Spanish Sahara when the colonial administration withdrew in 1975, under an agreement with Morocco and Spain.

Increased military spending and rising casualties in Western Sahara contributed to the discontent that brought down the civilian government of Ould Daddah in 1978. A succession of military rulers has followed.

In 1989 Mauritania fought a border war with Senegal. Although the country voted in the U.N. to support the embargo against Iraq, the government actually leaned the other way.

The government in April 1991 announced a transition to a multiparty system. A constitutional reform embodying these changes won approcal in a referendum in July.

The opposition's call for a boycott of the March parliamentary elections reduced turnout to no more than 40%. Yet Taya's party won 67 of the 79 available seats.

MAURITIUS

President: Cassam Uteem (1992)
Prime Minister: Aneerood Jugnauth (1982)
Area: 787 sq mi. (2,040 sq km)
Population (est. mid-1993): 1,100,000 (average annual rate of natural increase: 1.4%); birth rate: 21/1000; infant mortality rate: 18.6/1000; density per square mile: 1,526
Capital and largest city (est. 1990): Port Louis, 141,870; **Monetary unit:** Mauritian rupee; **Languages:** English (official), French, Creole, Hindi, Urdu, Hakka, Bojpoori; **Religions:** Hindu, 52%, Christian, 28.3%; Islam, 16.6%; other, 3.1%; **Member of Commonwealth of Nations; Literacy rate:** 82.8%
Economic summary: Gross domestic product (FY 1991 est.): $2.5 billion; $2,300 per capita; real growth rate, 6.1%; inflation 13.2%; unemployment 2.4%. Arable land: 54%. Principal products: sugar cane, tea. Labor force: 335,000; 22% in manufacturing; 29% in government services; 27% in agriculture and fishing. Major products: processed sugar, wearing apparel, chemical products, textiles. Natural resources: fish. Exports: $1.2 billion (f.o.b., 1990): sugar, light manufactures, textiles. Imports: $1.6 billion (f.o.b., 1990): foodstuffs, manufactured goods. Major trading partners: E.C., S. Africa, U.S.

Geography. Mauritius is a mountainous island in the Indian Ocean east of Madagascar.

Government. Mauritius is a republic within the British Commonwealth. The unicameral Legislative Assembly has 70 members, 62 of whom are elected by direct suffrage. The remaining 8 are chosen from among the unsuccessful candidates.

History. After a brief Dutch settlement, French immigrants who came in 1715 gave the name of Isle de France to the island and established the first road and harbor infrastructure, as well as the sugar industry, under the leadership of Gov. Mahe de Labourdonnais. Negroes from Africa and Madagascar came as slaves to work in the cane fields. In 1810, the British captured the island and in 1814, by the Treaty of Paris, it was ceded to Great Britain along with its dependencies.

Indian immigration which followed the abolition of slavery in 1835 changed rapidly the fabric of Mauritian society, and the country flourished with the increased cultivation of sugar cane.

Mauritius became independent on March 12, 1968.

The Labor Party government of Sir Seewoosagur Ramgoolam, who had ruled Mauritius since independence, was toppled in a 1982 election by the Movement Militant Mauricien, which had campaigned for recovery of Diego Garcia island, separated from Mauritius during the colonial period and leased by Britain to the United States for a naval base. But an Alliance Party coalition, including the Labor Party, regained power at the end of 1983 and brought back Ramgoolam as Prime Minister. He was succeeded by Aneerood Jugnauth of his party in 1982.

A transformation of the nation from a constitutional monarchy into a republic was attempted in mid-1990 on the understanding that opposition party leader Paul Bérenger would be named president. Public dissent for the move, however, arose, and the required parliamentary vote was never taken.

The country formally broke ties with the British crown in March 1992 becoming a republic. The president was elected by the Legislative Assembly on June 30.

MEXICO

United Mexican States
President: Carlos Salinas de Gortari (1988)
Area: 761,600 sq mi. (1,972,547 sq km)
Population (July 1992): 92,380,721 (average annual rate of natural increase: 2.3%); birth rate: 29/1000; infant mortality rate: 30/1000; density per square mile: 121
Capital: Federal District (Mexico City); **Largest cities (1989):** Federal District, 19,479,000; Guadalajara, 3,186,500; Monterey, 2,858,800; Puebla, 1,707,000; Leon, 1,006,700; **Monetary unit:** Peso; **Languages:** Spanish, Indian languages; **Religion:** nominally Roman Catholic, 97%; Protestant, 3%; **Official name:** Estados Unidos Mexicanos; **Literacy rate:** 88%
Economic summary: Gross domestic product (1991 est.): $289 billion; $3,200 per capita; real growth rate 4%; inflation 18.8%; unemployment 14–17%. Arable land: 12%;principal products: corn, cotton, fruits, wheat, beans, coffee, tomatoes, rice. Labor force: 24,063,283 (1990); 27.9% in manufacturing; 22.6% in agriculture;

46.1% in services. Major products: processed foods, chemicals, basic metals and metal products, petroleum. Natural resources: petroleum, silver, copper, gold, lead, zinc, natural gas, timber. Exports: $27.4 billion (f.o.b., 1991 est.): motor vehicles, consumer electronics, cotton, shrimp, coffee, petroleum, petroleum products, engines. Imports: $36.7 billion (c.i.f., 1991 est.): grain, metal manufactures, agricultural machinery, electrical equipment. Major trading partners: U.S., Japan, Western European countries.

Geography. The United States' neighbor to the south, Mexico is about one fifth its size. Baja California in the west, an 800-mile (1,287-km) peninsula, forms the Gulf of California. In the east are the Gulf of Mexico and the Bay of Campeche, which is formed by Mexico's other peninsula, the Yucatán.

The center of Mexico is a great, high plateau, open to the north, with mountain chains on east and west and with ocean-front lowlands lying outside of them.

Government. The President, who is popularly elected for six years and is ineligible to succeed himself, governs with a Cabinet of secretaries. Congress has two houses—a 500-member Chamber of Deputies, elected for three years, and a 64-member Senate, elected for six years half of which is renewed every three years. Popularly elected officials (President, members of Congress, mayors, etc.) cannot seek reelection.

Each of the 31 states has considerable autonomy, with a popularly elected governor, a legislature, and a local judiciary. The President of Mexico appoints the mayor of the Federal District.

History. At least two civilized races—the Mayas and later the Toltecs—preceded the wealthy Aztec empire, conquered in 1519–21 by the Spanish under Hernando Cortés. Spain ruled for the next 300 years until 1810 (the date was Sept. 16 and is now celebrated as Independence Day), when the Mexicans first revolted. They continued the struggle and finally won independence in 1821.

From 1821 to 1877, there were two emperors, several dictators, and enough presidents and provisional executives to make a new government on the average of every nine months. Mexico lost Texas (1836), and after defeat in the war with the U.S. (1846–48) it lost the area comprising the present states of California, Nevada, and Utah, most of Arizona and New Mexico, and parts of Wyoming and Colorado.

In 1855, the Indian patriot Benito Juárez began a series of liberal reforms, including the disestablishment of the Catholic Church, which had acquired vast property. A subsequent civil war was interrupted by the French invasion of Mexico (1861), the crowning of Maximilian of Austria as Emperor (1864), and then his overthrow and execution by forces under Juárez, who again became President in 1867.

The years after the fall of the dictator Porfirio Diaz (1877–80 and 1884–1911) were marked by bloody political-military strife and trouble with the U.S., culminating in the punitive expedition into northern Mexico (1916–17) in unsuccessful pursuit of the revolutionary Pancho Villa. Since a brief period of civil war in 1920, Mexico has enjoyed a period of gradual agricultural, political, and social reforms. Relations with the U.S. were again disturbed in 1938 when all foreign oil wells were expropriated. Agreement on compensation was finally reached in 1941.

During 1983 and 1984, Mexico suffered its worst financial crisis in 50 years, leading to critically high unemployment and an inability to pay its foreign debt. The collapse of oil prices in 1986 cut into Mexico's export earnings and worsened the situation.

Although the ruling Institutional Revolutionary Party's candidate, Carlos Salinas de Gortari, won the presidential election of 1988, the opposition parties on the left and the right showed unprecedented strength.

In the economic sphere Mexico decided to apply for membership in the Organization for Economic Cooperation & Development and talks began on a comprehensive North American free-trade agreement. The national telephone company was privatized.

Mid-term elections in 1991 were broadly supportive of the ruling PRI. In September 1991 a free-trade agreement was signed with Chile. Talks continued on the North American free trade agreement. Constitutional changes permitted religious institutions and parochial schools. The PRI also performed well in gubernatorial elections of mid-1992.

MICRONESIA

Federated States of Micronesia
President: Bailey Olter (1991)
Total area: 271 sq mi (703 sq km). Land area, same (includes islands of Pohnpei, Truk, Yap, and Kosrae.
Population (est. mid-1993): 100,000 (average annual rate of natural increase: 2.3%); birth rate: 30/1000; infant mortality rate: 41/1000; density per square mile: 409.9
Capital: Kolonia (on the island of Pohnpei. A new capital is being built about 6.2 miles (10 km) southwest in the Palikir valley.; **Ethnic divisions:** Nine ethnic Micronesian and Polynesian groups.; **Language:** English is the official and common language; major indigenous languages are Trukese, Pohnpeian, Yapase, and Kosrean.; **Literacy rate:** 90%
Government: A constitutional government in free association with the United States since November 1986.
Economic summary: Gross national product (1989 est.): $150 million, per capita, $1,500. Financial assistance from the U.S. is the primary source of revenue, with the U.S. pledged to spend $1 billion in the islands in the 1990s. Micronesia also earns about $4 million a year in fees from foreign fishing concerns. Economic activity consists primarily of subsistence farming and fishing. Unemployment rate: 80% **Aid:** Under the terms of the Compact of Free Association, the U.S. will provide $1.3 billion in grand aid during the period 1986–2001.

On April 2, 1947, the United Nations Security Council created the Trust Territory of the Pacific Islands under which the Northern Mariana, Caroline, and Marshall Islands were placed under the administration of the United States. These islands comprised what is now called the Federated States of Micronesia and only the Republic of Palau is still administered as a Trust Territory. Micronesia was admitted to the United Nations on September 17, 1991.

The Micronesian islands vary geologically from high mountainous islands to low, coral atolls; volcanic outcroppings on Pohnpei, Kosrae, and Truk. The climate is tropical with heavy, year-round rainfall. The islands are located 3,200 miles (5,150 km) west-southwest of Honolulu in the North Pacific Ocean, about three-quarters of the way between Hawaii and Indonesia.

MOLDOVA

Republic of Moldova
President: Mircea I. Snegur (1990)
Prime Minister: Andrei Sangheli (1992)
Area: 13,000 sq mi. (33,700 sq km)
Population (est. mid-1993): 4,400,000 (Moldovans, 65.5%; Ukrainians, 13.9%; Russians, 13.0%; Gagauz, 3.5%; Bulgarians, 2.0%; Jews, 1.5%); (average annual rate of natural increase: 0.6%); birth rate: 17/1000; infant mortality rate: 23/1000, density per square mile: 309
Capital and largest city (1991): Chisinau (Kishinyov), 676,700. Other large cities (est. 1991): Tiraspol, 186,000; Beltsy, 165,000; Bendery (Tighina), 141,500; **Monetary unit:** Ruble; **Language:** Romanian official language since 1989
Economic summary: Per capita GNP (1991): $2,170; real growth rate –12%. Agriculture and food processing are the main industries. Others include power engineering, textiles, metalworking, building materials, machine-building, TV sets, washing machines and other consumer goods, and manufacturing of electrical equipment. Agricultural products are wheat, corn, barley, sugar beets, fruits, and wine grapes, soybeans, tobacco, and animal husbandry. Eighty-five percent of all the land is cultivated. Exports: $400 million rubles (f.o.b., 1990). Imports: $1.9 billion rubles (c.i.f., 1990).

Geography: Moldova (formerly Moldavia) is a landlocked republic of hilly plains lying in the southwestern part of the former Soviet Union between the Prut and Dnestr (Dneister) Rivers. The Prut River separates it from Romania in the west and Ukraine borders it in the north, east, and south. The area is a very fertile region with rich black soil (chernozem) covering three-quarters of the territory.

Government: A democratic republic in transition with a parliament made up of 370 deputies. The working body of the parliament is the 21-member Presidium.

History: Most of Moldova was an independent principality in the 14th century. In the 16th century it came under Ottoman Turkish rule. Russia acquired Moldovan territory in 1791, and in 1812 (The Treaty of Bucharest) when Turkey gave up the province of Bessarabia[1] to Russia. Turkey held the rest of Moldova but it was passed to Romania in 1918. Russia did not recognize the cession of this territory.

In 1924, the U.S.S.R. established Moldova as an Autonomous Soviet Socialist Republic of the Ukraine. As a result of the Nazi-Soviet Nonaggression Pact of 1939, Romania was forced to cede all of Bessarabia to the Soviet Union in 1940 and the Moldovan A.S.S.R. was merged with the Romanian-speaking districts of Bessarabia to form the former Moldovan Soviet Socialist Republic.

During World War II, Romania joined Germany in the attack on the Soviet Union and reconquered Bessarabia. Soviet troops retook the territory in 1944 and reestablished the Moldovan S.S.R.

For many years, a controversy existed between Romania and the U.S.S.R. over Bessarabia. Following the aborted coup against Soviet President Mikhail Gorbachev, Moldova proclaimed its independence in September 1991, but did not plan to seek integration with Romania for several years until a satisfactory arrangement with the Soviet Union could be worked out.

Following the demise of the Soviet Union, Moldova joined the Commonwealth of Independent States along with ten other former Soviet republics on Dec. 21, 1991.

Conflict between ethnic Romanians and Slavs in Trans-Dniester has erupted since independence. The prime minister and most of his Cabinet resigned in early June 1992 because of the continued strife. Russia and Moldova agreed in July 1992 to send a joint peace-keeping force to the region and outlined guarantees for its future.

1. The area between the Prut and Dnestr Rivers.

MONACO

Principality of Monaco
Ruler: Prince Rainier III (1949)
Minister of State: Jacques Dupont (1991)
Area: 0.73 sq mi. (465 acres)
Population (July 1992): 29,965 (average annual growth rate: 0.9%); birth rate 7/1000; infant mortality rate: 8/1000; density per square mile: 40,701
Capital: Monaco-Ville; **Monetary unit:** French franc; **Languages:** French, Monégasque, Italian; **Religion:** Roman Catholic, 95%; **National name:** Principauté de Monaco; **Literacy rate:** 99%
Economic summary: Gross domestic product: (1991 est.): $475 million; $16,000 per capita; real growth rate, n.a. About 50% of Monaco's revenues come from value-added taxes on hotels, banks, and industrial sector. About 25% of revenues comes from tourism.

Geography. Monaco is a tiny, hilly wedge driven into the French Mediterranean coast nine miles east of Nice.

Government. Prince Albert of Monaco gave the principality a Constitution in 1911, creating a National Council of 18 members popularly elected for five years. The head of government is the Minister of State.

Prince Rainier III, born May 31, 1923, succeeded his grandfather, Louis II, on the latter's death, May 9, 1949. Rainier was married April 18, 1956, to Grace Kelly, U.S. actress. A daughter, Princess Caroline Louise Margueritte, was born on Jan. 23, 1957 (married to Philippe Junot June 28, 1978 and divorced in 1980; married to Stefano Casiraghi Dec. 29, 1983, and gave birth to a son, Andrea Albert, June 9, 1984); a son, Prince Albert Louis Pierre, on March 14, 1958; and Princess Stéphanie Marie Elisabeth, on Feb. 1, 1965. Princess Grace died Sept. 14, 1982, of injuries received the day before when the car she was driving went off the road near Monte Carlo. She was 52.

The special significance attached to the birth of descendants to Prince Rainier stems from a clause in the Treaty of July 17, 1919, between France and Monaco stipulating that in the event of vacancy of the Crown, the Monégasque territory would become an autonomous state under a French protectorate.

The National and Democratic Union (all 18 seats in National Council), led by Auguste Medecin, is the only political party.

History. The Phoenicians, and after them the Greeks, had a temple on the Monacan headland honoring Hercules. From *Monoikos*, the Greek surname for this mythological strong man, the principality took its name. After being independent for 800 years, Monaco was annexed to France in 1793 and was placed under Sardinia's protection in 1815. In 1861, it went under French guardianship but continued to be independent.

By a treaty in 1918, France stipulated that the French government be given a veto over the succession to the throne.

Monaco is a little land of pleasure with a tourist business that runs as high as 1.5 million visitors a year. It had popular gaming tables as early as 1856. Five years later, a 50-year concession to operate the games was granted to François Blanc, of Bad Homburg. This concession passed into the hands of a private company in 1898.

Monaco's practice of providing a tax shelter for French businessmen resulted in a dispute between the countries. When Rainier refused to end the practice, France retaliated with a customs tax. In 1967, Rainier took control of the Société des Bains de Mer, operator of the famous Monte Carlo gambling casino, in a program to increase hotel and convention space.

With the recent tragedies in the royal family speculation has centered on Rainier's grooming of his son Prince Albert to assume the duties of chief of state.

The country was admitted to the UN in May 1993, making it the smallest country represented there.

MONGOLIA

Mongolia
President: Punsalmaagiin Ochirbat (1990)
Prime Minister: Puntsagiyn Jasray (1992)
Area: 604,250 sq mi. (1,565,000 sq km)
Population (est. mid-1993): 2,300,000 (average annual rate of natural increase: 2.7%); birth rate: 36/1000; infant mortality rate: 50/1000; density per square mile: 4
Capital and largest city (est. 1990): Ulan Bator, 550,000; **Monetary unit:** Tugrik; **Language:** Mongolian, 90%; also Turkic, Russian, and Chinese; **Religion:** predominantly Tibetan Buddhist; Islam about 4%; **Literacy rate:** 90% (est.)
Economic summary: Gross domestic product (1991 est.): $2.1 billion; $900 per capita; real growth rate –13%; inflation, 100%; unemployment 15%. Arable land: 1%. Principal agricultural products: livestock, wheat, potatoes, forage, barley. Mongolia has the highest number of livestock per person in the world. Major industrial products: coal, copper and molybdenum concentrate. Natural resources: coal, copper, molybdenum, iron, oil, lead, gold, and tungsten. Exports: $279 million (f.o.b., 1991): copper, cashmere, livestock, animal products, wool, nonferrous metals. Imports: $360 million (f.o.b., 1991): fuels, food products, industrial consumer goods, chemicals, building materials, machinery and equipment. Major trading partners: C.I.S. nations, China, Japan.

Geography. Mongolia lies in central Asia between Siberia on the north and China on the south. It is slightly larger than Alaska.

The productive regions of Mongolia—a tableland ranging from 3,000 to 5,000 feet (914 to 1,524 m) in elevation—are in the north, which is well drained by numerous rivers, including the Hovd, Onon, Selenga, and Tula.

Much of the Gobi Desert falls within Mongolia.

Government. In January 1992, the Great People's Hural (parliament) approved a new constitution which entered into force Feb. 12, 1992, and changed the name of the former communist state to Mongolia. Mongolia became an independent sovereign republic now in transition from communism. The highest organ of state power is the State Great Hural (SGH). The SGH has one chamber consisting of 76 members. Its chairman and vice-chairman are elected for a term of four years.

History. The State of Mongolia was formerly known as Outer Mongolia. It contains the original homeland of the historic Mongols, whose power reached its zenith during the 13th century under Kublai Khan. The area accepted Manchu rule in 1689, but after the Chinese Revolution of 1911 and the fall of the Manchus in 1912, the northern Mongol princes expelled the Chinese officials and declared independence under the Khutukhtu, or "Living Buddha."

In 1921, Soviet troops entered the country and facilitated the establishment of a republic by Mongolian revolutionaries in 1924 after the death of the last Living Buddha. China, meanwhile, continued to claim Outer Mongolia but was unable to back the claim with any strength. Under the 1945 Chinese-Russian Treaty, China agreed to give up Outer Mongolia, which, after a plebiscite, became a nominally independent country.

Allied with the U.S.S.R. in its dispute with China, Mongolia has mobilized troops along its borders since 1968 when the two powers became involved in border clashes on the Kazakh-Sinkiang frontier to the west and on the Amur and Ussuri Rivers. A 20-year treaty of friendship and cooperation, signed in 1966, entitled Mongolia to call upon the U.S.S.R. for military aid in the event of invasion.

Free elections were held in August 1990 that produced a multiparty government, though still largely Communist. As a result Mongolia has decided to move toward a market economy.

The former Communist Party won a landslide victory in parliamentary elections of June 1992, causing considerable consternation in the democratic forces.

Moves toward a market economy continued in 1992 despite disruptions in energy supplies from Russia.

MOROCCO

Kingdom of Morocco
Ruler: King Hassan II (1961)
Prime Minister: Mohamed Karim Lamrani (1992)
Area: 172,413 sq mi. (446,550 sq km)
Population (est. mid-1993): 28,000,000 (average annual rate of natural increase: 2.4%); birth rate: 31/1000; infant mortality rate: 57/1000; density per square mile: 162
Capital: Rabat; **Largest cities:** Casablanca, 3,500,000; Rabat-Sale, 1,000,000; Fez, 600,000; Marrakesh, 500,000; Laayoune, 100,000; **Monetary unit:** Dirham; **Languages:** Arabic, French, Berber dialects, Spanish; **Religions:** Islam, 98.7%, Christian, 1.1%; Jewish, 0.2%; **National name:** al-Mamlaka al-Maghrebia; **Literacy rate:** 50%
Economic summary: Gross domestic product (1991): $27.3 billion; $1,060 per capita; real growth rate 4.2%; inflation 8.1%; unemployment 16%. Arable land: 20%. Products: barley, wheat, citrus fruits, vegetables. Labor force (1985): 7,400,000: agriculture 50%; services 26%. Major products: textiles, processed food, phosphates, leather goods. Natural resources: phosphates, lead, manganese, fisheries. Exports: $4.1 billion (f.o.b., 1991): food and beverages, semiprocessed goods, consumer goods, phosphates. Imports: $6 billion (f.o.b., 1991): capital goods, fuels, foodstuffs, raw materials, consumer goods. Major trading partners: E.C., C.I.S. nations, Japan, U.S.

Geography. Morocco, about one tenth larger than California, is just south of Spain across the Strait of Gibraltar and looks out on the Atlantic from the northwest shoulder of Africa. Algeria is to the east and Mauritania to the south.

On the Atlantic coast there is a fertile plain. The Mediterranean coast is mountainous. The Atlas Mountâins, running northeastward from the south to the Algerian frontier, average 11,000 feet (3,353 m) in elevation.

Government. A constitutional monarchy. The King, after suspending the 1962 Constitution and dissolving Parliament in 1965, promulgated a new Constitution in 1972. He continued to rule by decree until June 3, 1977, when the first free elections since 1962 took place. The National Assembly has 333 seats. Morocco has 14 political parties, 8 of whom are represented in the House of Representatives.

History. Morocco was once the home of the Berbers, who helped the Arabs invade Spain in A.D. 711 and then revolted against them and gradually won control of large areas of Spain for a time after 739.

The country was ruled successively by various native dynasties and maintained regular commercial relations with Europe, even during the 17th and 18th centuries when it was the headquarters of the famous Salé pirates. In the 19th century, there were frequent clashes with the French and Spanish. Finally, in 1904, France and Spain divided Morocco into zones of French and Spanish influence, and these were established as protectorates in 1912.

Meanwhile, Morocco had become the object of big-power rivalry, which almost led to a European war in 1905 when Germany attempted to gain a foothold in the rich mineral country. By terms of the Algeciras Conference (1906), Morocco was internationalized economically, and France's privileges were limited.

The Tangier Statute, concluded by Britain, France, and Spain in 1923, created an international zone at the port of Tangier, permanently neutralized and demilitarized. In World War II, Spain occupied the zone, ostensibly to ensure order, but was forced to withdraw in 1945.

Sultan Mohammed V was deposed by the French in 1953 and replaced by his uncle, but nationalist agitation forced his return in 1955. On his death on Feb. 26, 1961, his son, Hassan, became King.

France and Spain recognized the independence and sovereignty of Morocco in 1956.

In 1975, tens of thousands of Moroccans crossed the border into Spanish Sahara to back their government's contention that the northern part of the territory was historically part of Morocco. At the same time, Mauritania occupied the southern half of the territory in defiance of Spanish threats to resist such a takeover. Abandoning its commitment to self-determination for the territory, Spain withdrew, and only Algeria protested.

When Mauritania signed a peace treaty with the Algerian-backed Polisario Front in August 1979, Morocco occupied and assumed administrative control of the southern part of the Western Sahara, in addition to the northern part it already occupied. Under pressure from other African leaders, Hassan agreed in mid-1981 to a cease-fire with a referendum under international supervision to decide the fate of the Sahara territory, but the referendum was never carried out.

King Hassan became the second Arab leader to meet with an Israeli leader when, on July 21, 1986, Israeli Prime Minister Shimon Peres came to Morocco. Libyan criticism of the meeting led to King Hassan's abrogation of the treaty with Libya.

Morocco became the first Arab state to condemn the 1990 Iraqi invasion of Kuwait and promised to send an 1,100-men contingent to Saudi Arabia. Public opinion, however, as evidenced by sanctioned marches in Rabat, mounted against Moroccan involvement and demanded withdrawal from the U.S.-led alliance.

Owing to delays and disputes in implementing a UN peacekeeping plan a referendum in the disputed Western Sahara has been delayed indefinitely.

The opposition was victorious in June 1993 parliamentary elections, although observers believed King Hassam's rule was secure owing to the need for a coalition and the limited powers of the Assembly.

MOZAMBIQUE

Republic of Mozambique
President: Joaquim Chissano (1986)
Prime Minister: Dr. Mario Machungo (1986)
Area: 303,073 sq mi. (799,380 sq km)
Population (est. mid-1993): 15,300,000 (average annual rate of natural increase: 2.7%); birth rate: 45/1000; infant mortality rate: 151/1000; density per square mile: 51
Capital and largest city (1989): Maputo, 1,069,727; **Monetary unit:** Metical; **Languages:** Portuguese (official), Bantu languages; **Religions:** traditional, 60%; Christian, 30%; Islam, 10%; **National name:** República Popular de Moçambique; **Literacy rate:** 33%
Economic summary: Gross domestic product (1991 est.): $1.7 billion; $120 per capita; real growth rate 1%; inflation (1990 est.) 40.5%; unemployment (1989 est.) 50%. Arable land: 4%. Principal agricultural products: cotton, cashew nuts, sugar, tea, shrimp. Labor force: 90% in agriculture. Major industrial products: processed foods, petroleum products, beverages, textiles, tobacco. Natural resources: coal, titanium. Exports: $117 million (f.o.b., 1990 est.): cashew nuts, sugar, shrimp, copra, citrus. Imports: $870 million (c.i.f., 1990 est.) incl. aid: refined petroleum, food, clothing, farm equipment. Major trading partners: U.S., Western Europe, Japan, C.I.S. countries.

Geography. Mozambique stretches for 1,535 miles (2,470 km) along Africa's southeast coast. It is nearly twice the size of California. Tanzania is to the north; Malawi, Zambia, and Zimbabwe to the west; and South Africa and Swaziland to the south.

The country is generally a low-lying plateau broken up by 25 sizable rivers that flow into the Indian Ocean. The largest is the Zambezi, which provides access to central Africa. The principal ports are Maputo and Beira, which is the port for Zimbabwe.

Government. After having been under Portuguese colonial rule for 470 years, Mozambique became independent on June 25, 1975. The first President, Samora Moises Machel, headed the National Front for the Liberation of Mozambique (FRELIMO) in its 10-year guerrilla war for independence. He died in a plane crash on Oct. 19, 1986, and was succeeded by his Foreign Minister, Joaquim Chissano.

History. Mozambique was discovered by Vasco da Gama in 1498, although the Arabs had penetrated into the area as early as the 10th century. It was first colonized in 1505, and by 1510, the Portuguese had control of all the former Arab sultanates on the east African coast.

FRELIMO was organized in 1963. Guerrilla activity had become so extensive by 1973 that Portugal was forced to dispatch 40,000 troops to fight the rebels. A cease-fire was signed in September 1974, when Portugal agreed to grant Mozambique independence.

On Jan. 25, 1985, Mozambique's celebration of a decade of independence from Portugal was not a happy one. The government was locked in a five-year-old, stalemated, paralyzing war with anti-government guerrillas, known as the MNR, backed by the white minority government in South Africa.

President Chissano decided to abandon Marxism-Leninism in 1989. A new constitution was drafted calling for three branches of government and granting civil liberties.

A cease-fire agreement was signed in October 1992 between the government and the MNR to end 16 years of civil war.

MYANMAR

Union of Myanmar

Head of State (Chairman): Senior Gen. Than Shwe (1992)
Area: 261,220 sq mi. (676,560 sq km)
Population (est. mid-1993): 43,500,000 (average annual rate of natural increase: 1.9%); birth rate: 30/1000; infant mortality rate: 72/1000; density per square mile: 171
Capital: Yangon; **Largest cities (est. 1983):** Yangon, 2,458,712; Mandalay, 532,895; **Monetary unit:** Kyat; **Language:** Myanmar, minority languages; **Religions:** Buddhist, 85%; animist, Islam, Christian, or other, 15%; **National name:** Pyidaungsu Myanmar Naingngandau; **Literacy rate:** 81%
Economic summary: Gross domestic product (1991): $22.2 billion; $530 per capita; real growth rate 5.6%; inflation 40%; unemployment (FY89 est.): 9.6% in urban areas. Arable land: 15%. Principal products: oilseed, pulses, sugar cane, corn, rice. Labor force (FY89 est.): 16,036,000: 65.2% agriculture, 14.3% industry. Major products: textiles, footwear, processed agricultural products, wood and wood products, refined petroleum. Natural resources: timber, tin, antimony, zinc, copper, precious stones, crude oil and natural gas. Exports (1991): $568 million: rice, teak, oilseeds, metals, rubber, gems. Imports (1991): $1.6 billion: machinery, transportation equipment, chemicals, food products. Major trading partners: Japan, E.C., China, Southeast Asia. Illicit drugs: Myanmar is the world's largest illicit producer of opium poppy.

Geography. Myanmar occupies the northwest portion of the Indochinese peninsula. India lies to the northwest and China to the northeast. Bangladesh, Laos, and Thailand are also neighbors. The Bay of Bengal touches the southwestern coast.

Slightly smaller than Texas, the country is divided into three natural regions: the Arakan Yoma, a long, narrow mountain range forming the barrier between Myanmar and India; the Shan Plateau in the east, extending southward into Tenasserim; and the Central Basin, running down to the flat fertile delta of the Irrawaddy in the south. This delta contains a network of intercommunicating canals and nine principal river mouths.

Government. A military regime. On March 2, 1962, the government of U Nu was overthrown and replaced by a Revolutionary Council, which assumed all power in the state. Gen. U Ne Win, as chairman of the Revolutionary Council, became the chief executive. In 1972, Ne Win and his colleagues resigned their military titles. In 1974, Ne Win dissolved the Revolutionary Council and became President under the new Constitution. He voluntarily relinquished the presidency on Nov. 9, 1981. A military coup led by Gen. Saw Maung overthrew the civilian government in 1988.

History. In 1612, the British East India Company sent agents to Burma, but the Burmese long resisted efforts of British traders, and Dutch and Portuguese as well, to establish posts on the Bay of Bengal. By the Anglo-Burmese War in 1824–26 and two following wars, the British East India Company expanded to the whole of Burma by 1886. Burma was annexed to India. It became a separate colony in 1937.

During World War II, Burma was a key battleground; the 800-mile Burma Road was the Allies' vital supply line to China. The Japanese invaded the country in December 1941, and by May 1942 had occupied most of it, cutting off the Burma Road. After one of the most difficult campaigns of the war, Allied forces liberated most of Burma prior to the Japanese surrender in August 1945.

Burma became independent on Jan. 4, 1948. In 1951 and 1952 the Socialists achieved power, and Burma became the first Asian country to introduce social legislation.

In 1968, after the government had made headway against the Communist and separatist rebels, the military regime adopted a policy of strict nonalignment and followed "the Burmese Way" to socialism. But the insurgents continued active.

In July 1988, Ne Win announced his resignation from the Burmese Socialist Program Party (BSPP), the only legal political party.

The civilian government was overthrown in Sept. 1988 by a military junta led by General Saw Maung, an associate of U Ne Win.

The new government held elections in May 1990 and the opposition National League for Democracy won in a landslide despite its leaders being in jail or under house arrest.

Under increasing international pressure and economic failure Saw Maung resigned in April 1992. The military government then released a dozen political prisoners and promised to allow a conference in preparation for writing a new constitution. In September martial law was lifted.

NAMIBIA

President: Sam Nujoma (1990)
Status: Independent Country
Area: 318,261 sq mi. (824,296 sq km)
Population (est. mid-1993): 1,600,000 (average annual growth rate: 3.1%); birth rate: 43/1000; infant mortality rate: 75/1000; density per square mile: 5
Capital (est. 1990): Windhoek, 160,000; **Summer capital (est. 1980):** Swakopmund, 17,500; **Monetary unit:**

South African rand[1]; **Languages:** Afrikaans, German, English (official), several indigenous; **Religion:** Predominantly Christian; **National name:** Republic of Namibia; **Literacy rate:** 58%

Economic summary: Gross domestic product (1991 est.): $2 billion; $1,400 per capita; real growth rate 5.1%; inflation 17%; unemployment over 25%. Arable land: 1%. Principal products: corn, millet, sorghum, livestock. Labor force: 500,000; 60% in agriculture, 19% in industry and commerce. Major products: canned meat, dairy products, tanned leather, textiles, clothing. Natural resources: diamonds, copper, lead, zinc, uranium, fish. Exports: $1,021 million (f.o.b., 1989): diamonds, copper, lead, zinc, beef cattle, karakul pelts, marble, semi-precious stones, uranium, beef. Imports: $894 million (f.o.b., 1989): construction materials, fertilizer, grain, foodstuffs. Major trading partners: South Africa, France, Germany, Switzerland, U.S., Japan.

1. Namibian dollar to replace Rand in 1993.

Geography. Namibia, bounded on the north by Angola and Zambia and on the east by Botswana and South Africa in the south. The Portuguese explorer Bartholomius Diaz was the first European to visit Namibia in the late 15th century. It is for the most part a portion of the high plateau of southern Africa with a general elevation of from 3,000 to 4,000 feet.

Government. Namibia became independent in 1990 after its new constitution was ratified. A multi-party democracy with an independent judiciary was established.

History. The territory became a German colony in 1884 but was taken by South African forces in 1915, becoming a South African mandate by the terms of the Treaty of Versailles in 1920.

South Africa's application for incorporation of the territory was rejected by the U.N. General Assembly in 1946 and South Africa was invited to prepare a trusteeship agreement instead. By a law passed in 1949, however, the territory was brought into much closer association with South Africa—including representation in its Parliament.

In 1969, South Africa extended its laws to the mandate over the objection of the U.N., particularly its black African members. When South Africa refused to withdraw them, the Security Council condemned it.

Under a 1974 Security Council resolution, South Africa was required to begin the transfer of power to the Namibians by May 30, 1975, or face U.N. action, but 10 days before the deadline Prime Minister Balthazar J. Vorster rejected U.N. supervision. He said, however, that his government was prepared to negotiate Namibian independence, but not with the South-West African People's Organization, the principal black separatist group. Meanwhile, the all-white legislature of South-West Africa eased several laws on apartheid in public places.

Despite international opposition, the Turnhalle Conference in Windhoek drafted a constitution to organize an interim government based on racial divisions, a proposal overwhelmingly endorsed by white voters in the territory in 1977. At the urging of ambassadors of the five Western members of the Security Council—the U.S., Britain, France, West Germany, and Canada—South Africa on June 11 announced rejection of the Turnhalle constitution and acceptance of the Western proposal to include the South-West Africa People's Organization (SWAPO) in negotiations.

Although negotiations continued between South Africa, the western powers, neighboring black African states, and internal political groups, there was still no agreement on a final independence plan. A new round of talks aimed at resolving the 18-year-old conflict ended in a stalemate on July 25, 1984.

As policemen wielding riot sticks charged demonstrators in a black, South-West Africa township, South Africa handed over limited powers to a new, multiracial administration in the former German colony on June 17, 1985. Installation of the new government ended South Africa's direct rule, but South Africa retained an effective veto over the new government's decisions along with responsibility for the territory's defense and foreign policy, and South Africa's efforts to quell the insurgents seeking independence continued.

An agreement between South Africa, Angola, and Cuba arranged for elections for a Constituent Assembly in Nov. 1989 to establish a new government. SWAPO won 57% of the vote, a majority but not enough to dictate a constitution unilaterally. In February 1990, SWAPO leader Sam Nujoma was elected President and took office when Namibia became independent on March 21, 1990.

The growth of the economy slowed in 1992 principally because of a prolonged drought and the lowered prices for uranium and diamonds on the world market.

NAURU

Republic of Nauru

President: Bernard Dowiyogo (1989)

Area: 8.2 sq mi. (21 sq km)

Population (July 1992): 9,460; average annual growth rate: 1.3%; birth rate 18/1000; infant mortality rate 41/1000; density per square mile: 1,086

Capital (1983): Yaren, 559; **Monetary unit:** Australian dollar; **Languages:** Nauruan and English; **Religions:** Protestant, 58%; Roman Catholic, 24%; Confucian and Taoist, 8%; **Special relationship within the Commonwealth of Nations; Literacy rate:** 99%

Economic summary: Gross national product (1989): more than $90 million; $10,000 per capita. Major industrial products: phosphates. Natural resources: phosphates. Exports: $93 million (f.o.b., 1984): phosphates. Imports: $73 million (c.i.f., 1984): foodstuffs, fuel, machinery. Major trading partners: Australia, New Zealand, U.K., Japan.

Geography. Nauru (pronounced NAH oo roo) is an island in the Pacific just south of the equator, about 2,500 miles (4,023 km) southwest of Honolulu.

Government. Legislative power is invested in a popularly elected 18-member Parliament, which elects the President from among its members. Executive power rests with the President, who is assisted by a five-member Cabinet.

History. Nauru was annexed by Germany in 1888. It was placed under joint Australian, New Zealand, and British mandate after World War I, and in 1947 it became a U.N. trusteeship administered by the same three powers. On Jan. 31, 1968, Nauru became an independent republic.

In elections on December 9, 1989, Bernard Dowiyogo was elected and took office three days later.

NEPAL

Kingdom of Nepal
Ruler: King Birendra Bir Bikram Shah Deva (1972)
Prime Minister: Girija Prasad Koirala (1991)
Area: 54,463 sq mi. (141,059 sq km)
Population (mid-1993): 20,400,000 (average annual rate of natural growth: 2.5%); birth rate: 41/1000; infant mortality rate: 107/1000; density per square mile: 386
Capital and largest city (1991): Kathmandu, 414,264; **Monetary unit:** Nepalese rupee; **Languages:** Nepali (official), Newari, Bhutia, Maithali; **Religions:** Hindu, 90%; Buddhist, 5%; Islam, 3%; **Literacy rate:** 36%
Economic summary: Gross domestic product (FY91): $3.2 billion; $165 per capita; real growth rate 3.5%; inflation (Dec. 91) 15%; unemployment (1987) 5%. Arable land: 17%. Labor force: 4,100,000. Principal products: rice, maize, wheat, millet, jute, sugar cane, oilseed, potatoes. Agriculture is the mainstay of the economy accounting for 60% of the GDP and 90% of the work force. Major products: sugar, textiles, jute, cigarettes, cement. Natural resources: water, timber, hydroelectric potential. Exports: $180 million (f.o.b., FY91): clothing, carpets, leather goods, grain. Imports: $545 million (c.i.f., FY91 est.): petroleum products, fertilizer, machinery. Major trading partners: India, Japan, U.S., Europe.

Geography. A landlocked country the size of Arkansas, lying between India and the Tibetan Autonomous Region of China, Nepal contains Mount Everest (29,108 ft; 8,872 m), the tallest mountain in the world. Along its southern border, Nepal has a strip of level land that is partly forested, partly cultivated. North of that is the slope of the main section of the Himalayan range, including Everest and many other peaks higher than 20,000 feet (6,096 m).

Government. In November, 1990, King Birendra promulgated a new constitution and introduced a multiparty democracy in Nepal. In the May elections of 1991, the Nepali Congress Party won an absolute majority and Mr. Girija Prasad Koirala became the Prime Minister. Parliament consists of two houses: the higher with 60 members and a lower house with 205.

History. The Kingdom of Nepal was unified in 1768 by King Prithwi Narayan Shah. A commercial treaty was signed with Britain in 1792, and in 1816, after more than a year's hostilities, the Nepalese agreed to allow British residents to live in Katmandu, the capital. In 1923, Britain recognized the absolute independence of Nepal. Between 1846 and 1951, the country was ruled by the Rana family, which always held the office of prime minister. In 1951, however, the King took over all power and proclaimed a constitutional monarchy.

Mahendra Bir Bikram Shah became King in 1955. After Mahendra, who had ruled since 1955, died of a heart attack in 1972, Prince Birendra, at 26, succeeded to the throne.

In the first election in 22 years, on May 2, 1980, voters approved the continued autocratic rule by the King with the advice of a partyless Parliament. The King, however, permitted the election of a new legislature, in May 1986, to which the Prime Minister and Cabinet are responsible.

In 1990, pro-democracy movement forced King Birendra to lift the ban on political parties and appoint an opposition leader to head an interim government as Prime Minister.

The first free election in three decades provided a victory for the liberal Nepali Congress Party in 1991, although the Communists made a strong showing.

In April 1992 a demonstration against corruption and inflation sponsored by the United Nepal Communist Party left at least seven dead.

THE NETHERLANDS

Kingdom of the Netherlands
Sovereign: Queen Beatrix (1980)
Premier: Ruud Lubbers (1982)
Area: 16,041 sq mi. (41,548 sq km)
Population (est. mid-1993): 15,200,000 (average annual rate of natural increase: 0.5%); birth rate: 13/1000; infant mortality rate: 6.5/1000; density per square mile: 1,164
Capital: Amsterdam; seat of government: The Hague; **Largest cities (est. 1991):** Amsterdam, 702,444; Rotterdam, 582,266; 's-Gravenhage, 444,242; Utrecht, 231,231; Eindhoven, 192,895; **Monetary unit:** Guilder; **Language:** Dutch; **Religions:** Roman Catholic, 36%; Protestant, 27%; other, 4%; unaffiliated, 33%; **National name:** Koninkrijk der Nederlanden; **Literacy rate:** 99%
Economic summary: Gross domestic product (1991 est.): $249.6 billion; $16,600 per capita; real growth rate 2.2%; inflation 3.6%; unemployment 6.2%. Arable land; 25%. Principal products: wheat, barley, sugar beets, potatoes, meat and dairy products. Labor force: 6,955,000; 50.1% in services, 28.2% in manufacturing and construction. Major products: metal fabrication, electrical machinery and equipment, chemicals, electronic equipment, petroleum, fishing. Exports: $131.5 billion (f.o.b., 1990): foodstuffs, natural gas, chemicals, metal products, textiles. Imports: $125.9 billion (c.i.f., 1990): raw materials, consumer goods, transportation equipment, food products, crude petroleum. Major trading partners: Germany, Belgium, France, U.K., U.S.

Geography. The Netherlands, on the coast of the North Sea, has Germany to the east and Belgium to the south. It is twice the size of New Jersey.

Part of the great plain of north and west Europe, the Netherlands has maximum dimensions of 190 by 160 miles (360 by 257 km) and is low and flat except in Limburg in the southeast, where some hills rise to 300 feet (92 m). About half the country's area is below sea level, making the famous Dutch dikes a requisite to the use of much land. Reclamation of land from the sea through dikes has continued through recent times.

All drainage reaches the North Sea, and the principal rivers—Rhine, Maas (Meuse), and Schelde—have their sources outside the country. The Rhine is the most heavily used waterway in Europe.

Government. The Netherlands and its former colony of the Netherlands Antilles form the Kingdom of the Netherlands.

The Netherlands is a constitutional monarchy with a bicameral Parliament. The Upper Chamber has 75 members elected for six years by representative bodies of the provinces, half of the members retiring every three years. The Lower Chamber has 150 members elected by universal suffrage for four years. The two Chambers have the right of investigation and interpellation; the Lower Chamber can initiate legislation and amend bills.

The Sovereign, Queen Beatrix Wilhelmina Armgard, born Jan. 31, 1938, was married on March 10, 1966, to Claus von Amsberg, a former West German diplomat. The marriage drew public criticism because of the bridegroom's service in the German army during World War II. In 1967, Beatrix gave birth to a son, Willem-Alexander Claus George Ferdinand, the first male heir to the throne since 1884. She also has two other sons, Johan Friso Bernhard Christian David, born in 1968, and Constantijn Christof Frederik Aschwin, born the next year.

History. Julius Caesar found the low-lying Netherlands inhabited by Germanic tribes—the Nervii, Frisii, and Batavi. The Batavi on the Roman frontier did not submit to Rome's rule until 13 B.C., and then only as allies.

A part of Charlemagne's empire in the 8th and 9th centuries A.D., the area later passed into the hands of Burgundy and the Austrian Hapsburgs, and finally in the 16th century came under Spanish rule.

When Philip II of Spain suppressed political liberties and the growing Protestant movement in the Netherlands, a revolt led by William of Orange broke out in 1568. Under the Union if Utrecht (1579), the seven northern provinces became the Republic of the United Netherlands.

The Dutch East India Company was established in 1602, and by the end of the 17th century Holland was one of the great sea and colonial powers of Europe.

The nation's independence was not completely established until after the Thirty Years' War (1618–48), after which the country's rise as a commercial and maritime power began. In 1814, all the provinces of Holland and Belgium were merged into one kingdom, but in 1830 the southern provinces broke away to form the Kingdom of Belgium. A liberal Constitution was adopted by the Netherlands in 1848.

In spite of its neutrality in World War II, the Netherlands was invaded by the Nazis in May 1940, and the East Indies were later taken by the Japanese. The nation was liberated in May 1945. In 1948, after a reign of 50 years, Queen Wilhelmina resigned and was succeeded by her daughter Juliana.

In 1949, after a four-year war, the Netherlands granted independence to the East Indies, which became the Republic of Indonesia. In 1963, it turned over the western half of New Guinea to the new nation, ending 300 years of Dutch presence in Asia. Attainment of independence by Suriname on Nov. 25, 1975, left the Dutch Antilles as the Netherlands' only overseas territory.

Prime Minister Van Agt lost his narrow majority in elections on May 26, 1981, in which the major issue was the deployment of U.S. cruise missiles on Dutch soil. Van Agt lost his centrist coalition in May 1982 in a dispute over economic policy, and was succeeded by Ruud Lubbers as Premier.

Lubbers formed his third government, a center-left coalition, in November 1989. The Netherlands participated in the Persian Gulf war by sending two marine frigates to the Gulf.

In February 1993 the country's parliament approved a new law that sanctioned euthanasia under certain strict conditions.

Netherlands Autonomous Countries

NETHERLANDS ANTILLES

Status: Part of the Kingdom of the Netherlands
Governor: Mr. J. M. Saleh (1990)
Premier: Maria Liberia Peters
Area: 313 sq mi. (800 sq km)
Population (mid-1993): 200,000 (average annual growth rate: 1.3%); birth rate: 18/1000; infant mortality rate: 6.3/1000; density per square mile: 636
Capital (est. 1985): Willemstad, 125,000; **Literacy rate:** 95%
Economic summary: Gross domestic product (1990 est.): $1.4 billion; $7,600 per capita; real growth rate 1.5%; inflation 5%; unemployment 21% (1991). Arable land: 8%. Principal agricultural products: aloes, sorghum, peanuts. Labor force: 89,000; 28% industry and commerce (1983). Major industries: oil refining, tourism. Natural resource: phosphate. Export: $1.1 billion (f.o.b., 1988): petroleum products. Imports: $1.4 billion (c.i.f., 1988): crude petroleum, food. Major trading partners: U.S., Venezuela.

Geography. The Netherlands Antilles comprise two groups of Caribbean islands 500 miles (805 km) apart: one, about 40 miles (64 km) off the Venezuelan coast, consists of Curaçao (173 sq mi.; 448 sq km), Bonaire (95 sq mi.; 246 sq km), the other, lying to the northeast, consists of three small islands with a total area of 34 square miles (88 sq km).

Government. There is a constitutional government formed by the Governor and Cabinet and an elected Legislative Council. The area has complete autonomy in domestic affairs.

ARUBA

Status: Part of the Kingdom of the Netherlands
Governor: F. B. Tromp
Prime Minister: Nelson Oduber
Area: 75 sq mi. (193 sq km)
Population: (July 1992): 64,692; growth rate 0.7%; **Capital: (1986):** Oranjestad, 19,800; **Literacy rate:** 95%
Economic summary: Gross domestic product (1990 est.): $854 million; $13,600 per capita; real growth rate 10%; inflation 8%; unemployment (1991 est.) 3%. Little agriculture. Major industries: tourism, light manufacturing (tobacco, beverages, consumer goods. Exports: $134.4 billion (f.o.b., 1990): mostly petroleum products. Imports: $488 million (f.o.b., 1990): food, consumer goods, manufacturers.

Geography. Aruba, an island slightly larger than Washington D.C., lies 18 miles (28.9 km) off the coast of Venezuela in the southern Caribbean.

Government. The governmental structure comprises the Governor, appointed by the Queen for a term of six years; the Legislature consisting of 21 members elected by universal suffrage for terms not exceeding four years; and the Council of Ministers, presided over by the Prime Minister, which holds executive power.

NEW ZEALAND

Sovereign: Queen Elizabeth II
Governor-General: Dame Catherine Tizard (1990)
Prime Minister: Hon. Jon Bolger (1990)
Area: 103,884 sq mi. (269,062 sq km) (excluding dependencies)
Population (est. mid-1993): 3,435,000 (average annual growth rate: 1.0%); birth rate: 18/1000; infant mortality rate: 8.3/1000; density per square mile: 33
Capital: Wellington; **Largest cities (1991):** Auckland, 885,600; Wellington, 325,700; Christchurch, 307,200; **Monetary unit:** New Zealand dollar; **Languages:** English, Maori; **Religions:** Christian, 81%; none or unspecified, 18%; Hindu, Confucian, and other, 1%; **Member of Commonwealth of Nations; Literacy rate:** 99%
Economic summary: Gross domestic product (1991 est.): $46.2 billion; $14,000 per capita; real growth rate –0.4%; inflation (Sept. 1991) 1.0%; unemployment (Sept. 1991) 10.7%. Arable land: 2%. Principal products: wool, meat, dairy products, livestock. Labor force (June 1991): 1,603,500; services 67.4%; manufacturing 19.8%. Major products: processed foods, textiles, machinery, transport equipment, wood and paper products, financial services. Natural resources: forests, natural gas, iron ore, coal, gold. Exports: $9.4 billion (f.o.b., FY91): meat, dairy products, wool. Imports: $8.4 billion (f.o.b., FY91): consumer goods, petroleum, motor vehicles, industrial equipment. Major trading partners: Japan, Australia, E.C., U.S.

Geography. New Zealand, about 1,250 miles (2,012 km) southeast of Australia, consists of two main islands and a number of smaller, outlying islands so scattered that they range from the tropical to the antarctic. The country is the size of Colorado.

New Zealand's two main components are North Island and South Island, separated by Cook Strait, which varies from 16 to 190 miles (26 to 396 km) in width. North Island (44,281 sq mi.; 114,688 sq km) is 515 miles (829 km) long and volcanic in its south-central part. This area contains many hot springs and beautiful geysers. South Island (58,093 sq mi.; 150,461 sq km) has the Southern Alps along its west coast, with Mount Cook (12,283.3 ft; 3,744 m) the highest point.

The largest of the outlying islands are the Auckland Islands (234 sq mi.; 606 sq km), Campbell Island (44 sq mi.; 114 sq km), the Antipodes Islands (24 sq mi.; 62 sq km), and the Kermadec Islands (13 sq mi.; 34 sq km).

Government. New Zealand was granted self-government in 1852, a full parliamentary system and ministries in 1856, and dominion status in 1907. The Queen is represented by a Governor-General, and the Cabinet is responsible to a unicameral Parliament of 97 members, who are elected by popular vote for three years.

In the first of a two-part referendum in September 1992, voters approved a mixed-member proportional representation system in which each voter would vote once for an MP and cast another vote for a political party.

History. New Zealand was discovered and named in 1642 by Abel Tasman, a Dutch navigator. Captain James Cook explored the islands in 1769. In 1840, Britain formally annexed them.

From the first, the country has been in the forefront in instituting social welfare legislation. It adopted old age pensions (1898); a national child welfare program (1907); social security for the aged, widows, and orphans, along with family benefit payments; minimum wages; a 40-hour week and unemployment and health insurance (1938); and socialized medicine (1941).

In the general elections of October 1990 the opposition National Party captured 49% of the vote, winning a 39-seat majority in Parliament. Shortly after becoming the new prime minister, Jim Bolger, abandoning campaign promises, in an effort to revive the economy began severe cutbacks in government social benefits, reductions in health-care coverage and introduced legislation to weaken the country's strong labor unions.

Cook Islands and Overseas Territories

The Cook Islands (93 sq mi.; 241 sq km) were placed under New Zealand administration in 1901. They achieved self-governing status in association with New Zealand in 1965. Population (July 1992): 17,977; growth rate 0.5%; birth rate: 22/1000; infant mortality rate: 25/1000; density per square mile: 193. The seat of government is on Rarotonga Island.

Economic summary: Gross domestic product (1988): $40 million; $2,200 per capita. Exports: $4.0 million (f.o.b., 1988): citrus juice, clothing, canned fruit, and pineapple juice. Imports: $38.7 million (c.i.f., 1988): foodstuffs, textiles, fuels, timber. Nearly all of the trade is with New Zealand, some with Japan, Australia, and U.S.

Niue (100 sq mi.; 259 sq km) was formerly administered as part of the Cook Islands. It was placed under separate New Zealand administration in 1901 and achieved self-governing status in association with New Zealand in 1974. The capital is Alofi. **Population (July 1992):** 1,751; growth rate (1992): -6.4%. **Economic summary:** Gross national product (1989 est.): $2.1 million; per capita, $1,000. Exports: $175,274 (f.o.b., 1985): canned coconut cream, copra, honey, passion fruit products, pawpaw, root crops, limes, footballs, stamps, handicrafts. Imports: $3.8 million: food, live animals, manufactured goods, machinery, fuels, chemicals, lubricants, drugs. Major trading partners: New Zealand, 59%; Fiji, 20%; Japan, 13%.

The Ross Dependency (160,000 sq mi.; 414,400 sq km), an Antarctic region, was placed under New Zealand administration in 1923.

Tokelau (4 sq mi.; 10 sq km) was formerly administered as part of the Gilbert and Ellice Islands colony. It was placed under New Zealand administration in 1925. Its population is about 1,600.

NICARAGUA

Republic of Nicaragua
President: Violeta Barrios de Chamorro (1990)
Area: 50,180 sq mi. (130,000 sq km)
Population (est. mid-1993): 4,100,000 (average annual rate of natural increase: 3.0%); birth rate: 38/1000; infant mortality rate: 59/1000; density per square mile: 89
Capital and largest city (est. 1985): Managua, 682,111; **Monetary unit:** Cordoba; **Language:** Spanish; **Religion:** Roman Catholic, 95%; Protestant, 5%; **National name:** República de Nicaragua; **Literacy rate:** 57%
Economic summary: Gross domestic product (1991 est.): $1.6 billion; $425 per capita; real growth rate –1%; inflation 766%; unemployment 13%. Arable land: 9%.

Principal products: cotton, coffee, sugar cane, rice, corn, beans, cattle. Labor force: 1,086,000; 13% in industry (1986). Major products: processed foods, chemicals, metal products, clothing and textiles, beverages, footwear. Natural resources: timber, fisheries, gold, silver, copper, tungsten, lead, zinc. Exports: $342 million (f.o.b., 1991 est.): coffee, cotton, seafood, bananas, sugar, meat, chemicals. Imports: $738 million (c.i.f., 1991 est.): machinery, chemicals, food, clothing, petroleum. Major trading partners: Latin America, U.S., C.I.S. countries, Eastern Europe.

Geography. Largest but most sparsely populated of the Central American nations, Nicaragua borders on Honduras to the north and Costa Rica to the south. It is slightly larger than New York State.

Nicaragua is mountainous in the west, with fertile valleys. A plateau slopes eastward toward the Caribbean.

Two big lakes—Nicaragua, about 100 miles long (161 km), and Managua, about 38 miles long (61 km)—are connected by the Tipitapa River. The Pacific coast is volcanic and very fertile. The Caribbean coast, swampy and indented, is aptly called the "Mosquito Coast."

Government. A republic. The president is chief of state and head of government. The National Assembly is the legislative branch.

History. Nicaragua, which established independence in 1838, was first visited by the Spaniards in 1522. The chief of the country's leading Indian tribe at that time was called Nicaragua, from whom the nation derived its name. A U.S. naval force intervened in 1909 after two American citizens had been executed, and a few U.S. Marines were kept in the country from 1912 to 1925. The Bryan-Chamorro Treaty of 1916 (terminated in 1970) gave the U.S. an option on a canal route through Nicaragua, and naval bases. Disorder after the 1924 elections brought in the marines again.

A guerrilla leader, Gen. César Augusto Sandino, began fighting the occupation force in 1927. He fought the U.S. troops until their withdrawal in 1933. Gen. Anastasio Somoza García emerged and ruled as dictator from 1936 until his assassination in 1956. He was succeeded by his son Luis, who alternated with trusted family friends in the presidency until his death in 1967. Another son, Maj. Gen. Anastasio Somoza Debayle, became President in 1967.

Sandinista guerrillas, leftists who took their name from Gen. Sandino, launched an offensive in May 1979. After seven weeks of fighting, Somoza fled the country on July 17, 1979. The Sandinistas assumed power on July 19, promising to maintain a mixed economy, a non-aligned foreign policy, and a pluralist political system. However, the prominence of Cuban President Fidel Castro at the celebration of the first anniversary of the revolution and a five-year delay in holding elections increased debate over the true political color of the Sandinistas.

On Jan. 23, 1981, the Reagan Administration suspended U.S. aid, charging that Nicaragua, with the aid of Cuba and the Soviet Union, was supplying arms to rebels in El Salvador. The Sandinistas denied the charges. Later that year, Nicaraguan guerrillas known as "contras," began a war to overthrow the Sandinistas.

The elections were finally held on Nov. 4, 1984, with Daniel Ortega Saavedra, the Sandinista junta coordinator, winning 63% of the votes cast for President. He began a six-year term on Jan. 10, 1985.

The war intensified in 1986–87, with the resupplied contras establishing themselves inside the country. Negotiations sponsored by the Contadora (neutral Latin American) nations, but a peace plan sponsored by Arias, the Costa Rican president, led to a treaty signed by the Central American leaders in August 1987, that called for an end to outside aid to guerrillas and negotiations between hostile parties.

In 1989, an accord established a one-year advance in general elections to Feb. 1990.

Violetta Chamorro, owner of the opposition paper *La Prensa*, led a broad anti-Sandinista coalition to victory in the presidential and legislative elections, ending 11 years of Sandinista rule.

After a year in office Pres. Chamorro found herself besieged. Business groups were dissatisfied with the pace of reforms; Sandinistas with what they regarded as the dismantling of their earlier achievements and threatened to take up arms again. In Feb. 1991 the president brought the military under her direct command.

By early 1993 relations between the president and the coalition that backed her had soured over charges of corruption and the continuing influence of the Sandinistas in the government and the army.

NIGER

Republic of Niger
President: Mahamane Ousmane (1993)
Prime Minister: Mahamadou Issoufou (1993)
Area: 489,206 sq mi. (1,267,044 sq km)
Population (est. mid-1993): 8,500,000 (average annual rate of natural increase: 3.2%); birth rate: 52/1000; infant mortality rate: 123/1000; density per square mile: 17
Capital and largest city (1988): Niamey, 398,265; **Other large cities:** Zinder, 120,900; Maradi, 112,970; **Monetary unit:** Franc CFA; **Ethnic groups:** Hausa, 54%; Djerma and Songhai, 24%; Peul, 11%; **Languages:** French (official); Hausa, Songhai; Arabic; **Religions:** Islam, 80%; Animist and Christian, 20%; **National name:** République du Niger; **Literacy rate:** 28%
Economic summary: Gross domestic product (1991): $2.4 billion; $300 per capita; real growth rate –3.4%. Arable land: 3%. Principal products: peanuts, cotton, livestock, millet, sorghum, cassava, rice. Labor force: 2,500,000 (1982); 90% in agriculture. Major industrial products: uranium, cement, bricks, light industrial products. Natural resources: uranium, coal, iron ore, tin, phosphates. Exports: $320 million (f.o.b., 1990): uranium, cowpeas, livestock, hides, skins. Imports: $439 million (c.i.f., 1990): fuels, machinery, transport equipment, foodstuffs, consumer goods. Major trading partners: France, Nigeria, Japan, Algeria, U.S.

Geography. Niger, in West Africa's Sahara region, is four-fifths the size of Alaska. It is surrounded by Mali, Algeria, Libya, Chad, Nigeria, Benin, and Burkina Faso.

The Niger River in the southwest flows through the country's only fertile area. Elsewhere the land is semiarid.

Government. Niger held its first democratic elections in April 1993 and formed a new coalition government on April 23, 1993. Eighty-three representatives from its different political parties formed a national assembly. The U.S. supports the new Nigerian government and its new democratic institutions.

History. Niger was incorporated into French West Africa in 1896. There were frequent rebellions, but when order was restored in 1922, the French made the area a colony. In 1958, the voters approved the French Constitution and voted to make the territory an autonomous republic within the French Community. The republic adopted a Constitution in 1959 and the next year withdrew from the Community, proclaiming its independence.

The 1974 army coup ousted President Hamani Diori, who had held office since 1960. An estimated 2 million people were starving in Niger, but 200,000 tons of imported food, half U.S.-supplied, substantially ended famine conditions by the year's end. The new President, Lt. Col. Seyni Kountché, Chief of Staff of the army, installed a 12-man military government. A predominantly civilian government was formed by Kountché in 1976.

A national conference convened in July 1991 and proclaimed its sovereignty against government objections.

The country's first multiparty election in February 1993 resulted in the need for a runoff for the presidency in March. Ousmane Mahamane, the candidate of the biggest opposition party, won.

NIGERIA

Federal Republic of Nigeria

Head, Interim Government: Ernest Shonekan (1993)
Area: 356,700 sq mi. (923,853 sq km)
Population (est. mid-1993): 95,100,000; average annual rate of natural increase: 3.1%; birth rate: 45/1000; infant mortality rate: 84/1000; density per square mile: 270
Capital: Abuja; **Largest cities (est. 1991):** Lagos, 1,340,000; Ibadan, 1,263,000; Ogbomosho, 644,200; Kano, 594,800; **Monetary unit:** Naira; **Languages:** English (official) Hausa, Yoruba, Ibo; **Religions:** Islam, 50%; Christian, 40%; indigenous, 10%; **Member of Commonwealth of Nations; Literacy rate:** 51%
Economic summary: Gross national product (1990 est.): $30 billion; $250 per capita; real growth rate 5.2%; inflation 40%. Arable land: 31%. Principal products: peanuts, rubber, cocoa, grains, fish, yams, cassava, livestock. Labor force (1985): 42,844,000, 54% in agriculture; 15% in government; 19% in industry, commerce and services. Major products: crude oil, natural gas, coal, tin, processed rubber, cotton, petroleum, hides, textiles, cement, chemicals. Natural resources: petroleum, tin, columbite, iron ore, coal, limestone, lead. Exports: $13.6 billion (f.o.b., 1990): oil, cocoa, palm products, rubber. Imports: $6.9 billion (c.i.f., 1990): consumer goods, capital equipment, raw materials, chemicals. Major trading partners: Western European countries, U.S., Japan

Geography. Nigeria, one-third larger than Texas and black Africa's most populous nation, is situated on the Gulf of Guinea in West Africa. Its neighbors are Benin, Niger, Cameroon, and Chad.

The lower course of the Niger River flows south through the western part of the country into the Gulf of Guinea. Swamps and mangrove forests border the southern coast; inland are hardwood forests.

Government. A military government since Dec. 31, 1983. The government annulled the results of the June 12, 1993 presidential election and suspended the return to civilian rule. Gen. Ibrahim Babangida resigned Aug. 26, 1993 and appointed a civilian leader of the interim government.

History. Between 1879 and 1914, private colonial developments by the British, with reorganizations of the Crown's interest in the region, resulted in the formation of Nigeria as it exists today. During World War I, native troops of the West African frontier force joined with French forces to defeat the German garrison in the Cameroons.

Nigeria became independent on Oct. 1, 1960.

Organized as a loose federation of self-governing states, the independent nation faced an overwhelming task of unifying a country with 250 ethnic and linguistic groups.

Rioting broke out again in 1966, the military commander was seized, and Col. Yakubu Gowon took power. Also in that year, the Moslem Hausas in the north massacred the predominantly Christian Ibos in the east, many of whom had been driven from the north. Thousands of Ibos took refuge in the Eastern Region. The military government there asked Ibos to return to the region and, in May 1967, the assembly voted to secede from the federation and set up the Republic of Biafra. Civil war broke out.

In January 1970, after 31 months of civil war, Biafra surrendered to the federal government.

Gowon's nine-year rule was ended in 1975 by a bloodless coup that made Army Brigadier Muritala Rufai Mohammed the new chief of state.

The return of civilian leadership was established with the election of Alhaji Shehu Shagari, as president in 1979.

A coup on December 31, 1983, restored military rule. The military regime headed by Maj. Gen. Mohammed Buhari was overthrown in a bloodless coup on Aug. 27, 1985, led by Maj. Gen. Ibrahim Babangida, who proclaimed himself president.

The presidential election of June 1993 was almost immediately voided by the government. Violence soon erupted. In July the two legal parties agreed to form an interim government that would organize new elections.

NORWAY

Kingdom of Norway

Sovereign: King Harald V (1991)
Prime Minister: Gro Harlem Brundtland (1991)
Area: 125,049 sq mi. (323,877 sq km)
Population (est. mid-1993): 4,300,000 (average annual growth rate: 0.4%); birth rate: 14/1000; infant mortality rate: 7.8/1000; density per square mile: 36
Capital: Oslo; **Largest cities (1990):** Oslo, 457,818; Bergen, 211,866; Trondheim, 137,408; Stavanger, 97,716; **Monetary unit:** Krone; **Language:** Norwegian; **Religion:** Evangelical Lutheran (state), 94%; other Protestant and Roman Catholic, 4%; **National name:** Kongeriket Norge; **Literacy rate:** 100%
Economic summary: Gross domestic product (1991 est.): $72.9 billion; $17,100 per capita; real growth rate 4.1%; inflation 3.5%; unemployment 5.4%. Labor force (Sept. 90): 2,167,000; services, 34.7%; commerce, 18%; mining and manufacturing, 16.6%:. Arable land: 3%. Principal products: dairy products, livestock, grain, potatoes, furs, wool. Major products: oil and gas, fish, pulp and paper, ships, aluminum, iron, steel, nickel, fertilizers, transportation equipment, hydroelectric power, petrochemicals. Natural resources: fish, timber, hydroelectric power, ores, oil, gas. Exports: $34.2 billion (f.o.b., 1991): oil, natural gas, fish products, ships, pulp and paper, aluminum. Imports: $25.1 billion (c.i.f., 1991): machinery, fuels and lubricants, transportation equipment, chemicals foodstuffs, and clothing. Major trading partners: U.K., Sweden, Germany, U.S., Denmark, Netherlands, Japan.

Geography. Norway is situated in the western part of the Scandinavian peninsula. It extends about 1,100 miles (1,770 km) from the North Sea along the Norwegian Sea to more than 300 miles (483 km) above the Arctic Circle, the farthest north of any European country. It is slightly larger than New Mexico. Sweden borders on most of the eastern frontier, with Finland and the U.S.S.R. in the northeast.

Nearly 70% of Norway is uninhabitable and covered by mountains, glaciers, moors, and rivers. The hundreds of deep fiords that cut into the coastline give Norway an overall oceanfront of more than 12,000 miles (19,312 km). Nearly 50,000 islands off the coast form a breakwater and make a safe coastal shipping channel.

Government. Norway is a constitutional hereditary monarchy. Executive power is vested in the King together with a Cabinet, or Council of State, consisting of a Prime Minister and at least seven other members. The Storting, or Parliament, is composed of 165 members elected by the people under proportional representation. The Storting discusses and votes on political and financial questions, but divides itself into two sections (Lagting and Odelsting) to discuss and pass on legislative matters. The King cannot dissolve the Storting before the expiration of its term.

The sovereign is Harald V, born in 1937, son of Olav V and Princess Martha of Sweden. He succeeded to the throne upon the death of his father in January 1991. He married Sonja Haraldsen, a daughter of a merchant, in 1968.

History. Norwegians, like the Danes and Swedes, are of Teutonic origin. The Norsemen, also known as Vikings, ravaged the coasts of northwestern Europe from the 8th to the 11th century.

In 1815, Norway fell under the control of Sweden. The union of Norway, inhabited by fishermen, sailors, merchants, and peasants, and Sweden, an aristocratic country of large estates and tenant farmers, was not a happy one, but it lasted for nearly a century. In 1905, the Norwegian Parliament arranged a peaceful separation and invited a Danish prince to the Norwegian throne—King Haakon VII. A treaty with Sweden provided that all disputes be settled by arbitration and that no fortifications be erected on the common frontier.

When World War I broke out, Norway joined with Sweden and Denmark in a decision to remain neutral and to cooperate in the joint interest of the three countries. In World War II, Norway was invaded by the Germans on April 9, 1940. It resisted for two months before the Nazis took over complete control. King Haakon and his government fled to London, where they established a government-in-exile. Maj. Vidkun Quisling, whose name is now synonymous with traitor or fifth columnist, was the most notorious Norwegian collaborator with the Nazis. He was executed by the Norwegians on Oct. 24, 1945.

Despite severe losses in the war, Norway recovered quickly. The country led the world in social experimentation. It entered the North Atlantic Treaty Organization in 1949.

The Conservative government of Jan Syse resigned in October 1990 over the issue of Norway's future relationship to the E.C. A minority Labor government headed by Gro Brundtland was installed a few days later. Norway is a member of the European Free Trade Association.

The country's currency remained relatively stable in 1992 when others faltered. However in December the krone was allowed to float and suffered a 5% devaluation.

In November 1992 the parliament voted to apply to join the European Community.

Dependencies of Norway

Svalbard (24,208 sq mi.; 62,700 sq km), in the Arctic Ocean about 360 miles north of Norway, consists of the Spitsbergen group and several smaller islands, including Bear Island, Hope Island, King Charles Land, and White Island (or Gillis Land). The capital is Longyearbyen. It came under Norwegian administration in 1925. Population (July 1992): 3,181; growth rate –3.9%. **Economic summary (1991):** Coal mining is major economic activity. There is also some trapping of seal, polar bear, fox, and walrus.

Bouvet Island (23 sq mi.; 60 sq km), in the South Atlantic about 1,600 miles south-southwest of the Cape of Good Hope, came under Norwegian administration in 1928. It is uninhabited.

Jan Mayen Island (147 sq mi.; 380 sq km), in the Arctic Ocean between Norway and Greenland, came under Norwegian administration in 1929. There are no permanent inhabitants.

Peter I Island (96 sq mi.; 249 sq km), lying off Antarctica in the Bellinghausen Sea, came under Norwegian administration in 1931.

Queen Maud Land, a section of Antarctica, came under Norwegian administration in 1939.

OMAN

Sultanate of Oman
Sultan: Qabus Bin Said (1970)
Area: 82,030 sq mi. (212,458 sq km)[1]
Population (est. mid-1993): 1,600,000 (average annual rate of natural increase: 3.5%); birth rate: 42/1000; infant mortality rate: 44/1000; density per square mile: 20
Capital and largest city (est. 1991): Muscat, 350,000;
Monetary unit: Omani Rial; **Language:** Arabic (official); also English and Indian languages; **Religion:** Islam, 95%; **National name:** Saltonat Uman; **Literacy rate:** 65.8%
Economic summary: Gross domestic product (1990): $10.6 billion; $6,925 per capita; real growth rate (1989): 0.5%; inflation (1989) 1.3%. Principal agricultural products: dates, fruit, cereal, livestock. Labor force: 430,000; 60% in agriculture. Major industries: petroleum drilling, fishing, construction. Natural resources: oil, marble, copper, limestone. Exports: $5.5 billion (f.o.b., 1990): oil. Imports: $2.5 billion (f.o.b., 1990): machinery and transport equipment, food, manufactured goods, livestock, lubricants. Major trading partners: U.K., U.S., Germany, Japan.

1. Excluding the Kuria Muria Islands.

Geography. Oman is a 1,000-mile-long (1,700-km) coastal plain at the southeastern tip of the Arabian peninsula lying on the Arabian Sea and the Gulf of Oman. The interior is a plateau. The country is the size of Kansas.

Government. The Sultan of Oman (formerly called Muscat and Oman), an absolute monarch, is assisted by a council of ministers, seven specialized councils, a Majllis Ashura, and personal advisers.

There are no political parties.

History. Although Oman is an independent state under the rule of the Sultan, it has been under British protection since the early 19th century.

Muscat, the capital of the geographical area known as Oman, was occupied by the Portuguese from 1508 to 1648. Then it fell to Persian princes and later was regained by the Sultan.

In a palace coup on July 23, 1970, the Sultan, Sa'id bin Taimur, who had ruled since 1932, was overthrown by his son, who promised to establish a modern government and use new-found wealth to aid the people of this very isolated state.

A long border dispute with Yemen ended in late October 1992 when the Sultan signed an agreement with the Yemeni president.

PAKISTAN

Islamic Republic of Pakistan
Acting President: Wasim Sajjad (1993)
Acting Prime Minister: Moeen Qureshi (1993)
Area: 310,400 sq mi. (803,936 sq km)[1]
Population (est. mid-1993): 122,400,000 (average annual growth rate: 3.1%); birth rate: 44/1000; infant mortality rate: 109/1000; density per square mile: 411
Capital (1981 census): Islamabad, 201,000; **Largest cities (1981 census for metropolitan area):** Karachi, 5,208,100; Lahore, 2,952,700; Faisalabad, (Lyallpur) 1,920,000; Rawalpindi, 920,000; Hyderabad, 795,000; **Monetary unit:** Pakistan rupee; **Principal languages:** Urdu (national), English (official), Punjabi, Sindhi, Pashtu, and Baluchi; **Religions:** Islam, 97%; Hindu, Christian, Buddhist, Parsi; **Literacy rate:** 35%
Economic summary: Gross national product (FY91 est.): $45.4 billion; $380 per capita; real growth rate 4.8%; inflation 12.3%; unemployment 10%. Arable land: 26%. Principal products: wheat, rice, cotton, sugarcane. Labor force (1987): 28,900,000; agriculture, 54%; services, 33%. Major products: cotton textiles, processed foods, petroleum products, construction materials. Natural resources: natural gas, limited petroleum, iron ore. Exports: $6 billion (FY91, f.o.b.): cotton, rice, textiles, clothing. Imports: $7.9 billion (f.o.b., FY91): edible oil, crude oil, machinery, chemicals, transport equipment. Major trading partners: U.S., E.C., Japan.

1. Excluding Kashmir and Jammu.

Geography. Pakistan is situated in the western part of the Indian subcontinent, with Afghanistan and Iran on the west, India on the east, and the Arabian Sea on the south. The name "Pakistan" is derived from two Persian words "Pak" (meaning pure) and "stan" (meaning country).

Nearly twice the size of California, Pakistan consists of towering mountains, including the Hindu Kush in the west, a desert area in the east, the Punjab plains in the north, and an expanse of alluvial plains. The 1,000-mile-long (1,609 km) Indus River flows through the country from the Kashmir to the Arabian Sea.

Government. Pakistan is a federal republic with a bicameral legislature—a 217-member National Assembly and an 87-member Senate.

History. Pakistan was one of the two original successor states to British India. For almost 25 years following independence in 1947, it consisted of two separate regions East and West Pakistan, but now comprises only the western sector. It consists of Sind, Baluchistan, the former North-West Frontier Province, western Punjab, the princely state of Bahawalpur, and several other smaller native states.

The British became the dominant power in the region in 1757 following Lord Clive's military victory, but rebellious tribes kept the northwest in turmoil. In the northeast, the formation of the Moslem League in 1906 estranged the Moslems from the Hindus. In 1930, the league, led by Mohammed Ali Jinnah, demanded creation of a Moslem state wherever Moslems were in the majority. He supported Britain during the war. Afterward, the league received almost a unanimous Moslem vote in 1946 and Britain agreed to the formation of Pakistan as a separate dominion.

Pakistan was proclaimed a republic March 23, 1956. The election of 1970 set the stage for civil war when Sheik Muuibur told East Pakistanis to stop paying taxes to the central government. West Pakistan troops moved in and fighting began. The independent state of Bangladesh, or Bengali nation, was proclaimed March 26, 1971. The intervention of Indian troops protected the new state and brought President Yahya Kahn down. Bhutto took over and accepted Bangladesh as an independent entity.

Diplomatically, 1976 saw the resumption of formal relations between India and Pakistan.

Pakistan's first elections under civilian rule took place in March 1977 and provoked bitter opposition protest when Bhutto's party was declared to have won 155 of the 200 elected seats in the 216-member National Assembly. A rising tide of violent protest and political deadlock led to a military takeover on July 5. Gen. Mohammed Zia ul-Haq became Chief Martial Law Administrator.

Bhutto was tried and convicted for the 1974 murder of a political opponent, and despite worldwide protests was executed on April 4, 1979, touching off riots by his supporters. Zia declared himself President on Sept. 16, 1978, a month after Fazel Elahi Chaudhry left office upon the completion of his 5-year term.

A measure of representative government was restored with the election of a new National Assembly in February 1985, although leaders of opposition parties were banned from the election and it was unclear what powers Zia would yield to the legislature.

On December 30, 1985, Zia ended martial law.

On August 19, 1988, President Zia was killed in a mid-air explosion of a Pakistani Air Force plane.

Elections at the end of 1988 brought longtime Zia opponent Benazir Bhutto, daughter of Zulfikar Bhutto, into office as Prime Minister.

In August 1990, Pakistan's President dismissed Prime Minister Bhutto on charges of corruption and incompetence and dissolved parliament. Sharif's coalition, the Islamic Democratic Alliance, won the elections of October 1990. Fulfilling a campaign promise, parliament decreed in May 1991 that Islamic law would take precedence over civil legislation.

In April 1993 the president dismissed the prime minister on charges of corruption and dissolved the parliament. A month later, however, the country's supreme court overturned the order. The next day parliament gave the prime minister a vote of confidence. In July, however, the army demanded a resolution of the standoff. The president and the prime minister resigned and new elections were called for October.

PANAMA

Republic of Panama
President: Guillermo Endara Galimany (1990)
Area: 29,761 sq mi. (77,082 sq km)
Population (est. mid-1993): 2,500,000 (average annual rate of natural increase: 2.0%); birth rate: 25/1000; infant mortality rate: 21/1000; density per square mile: 84
Capital and largest city (1990): Panama City, 411,549; **Monetary unit:** Balboa; **Language:** Spanish (official); many bilingual in English; **Religions:** Roman Catholic, over 93%; Protestant, 6%; **National name:** República de Panamá; **Literacy rate:** 88%
Economic summary: Gross domestic product (1991 est.): $5 billion; $2,040 per capita; real growth rate 9.3%; inflation 2%; unemployment 17%. Arable land: 6%. Principal agricultural products: bananas, corn, sugar, rice, coffee. Labor force: 770,472 (1987); 27.9% in government and community services. Major industrial products: refined petroleum, sugar, cement, paper products. Natural resources: copper, mahogany, shrimp. Exports: $380 million (f.o.b., 1991 est.): bananas, refined petroleum, sugar, shrimp, coffee. Imports: $1.5 billion (f.o.b., 1991 est.): petroleum, manufactured goods, machinery and transportation equipment, food. Major trading partners: U.S., Central America and the Caribbean, Western Europe, Mexico.

Geography. The southernmost of the Central American nations, Panama is south of Costa Rica and north of Colombia. The Panama Canal bisects the isthmus at its narrowest and lowest point, allowing passage from the Caribbean Sea to the Pacific Ocean.

Panama is slightly smaller than South Carolina. It is marked by a chain of volcanic mountains in the west, moderate hills in the interior, and a low range on the east coast. There are extensive forests in the fertile Caribbean area.

Government. Panama is a centralized republic. The executive power is vested in the president and two vice presidents who exercise power jointly with a cabinet of 12 ministers of state appointed by the president. Presidents and vice presidents are elected for five-year terms and may not succeed themselves. The legislative function is exercised through the National Assembly. The legislators are elected for five-year terms by direct vote and can be reelected.

History. Visited by Columbus in 1502 on his fourth voyage and explored by Balboa in 1513, Panama was the principal transshipment point for Spanish treasure and supplies to and from South and Central America in colonial days. In 1821, when Central America revolted against Spain, Panama joined Colombia, which already had declared its independence. For the next 82 years, Panama attempted unsuccessfully to break away from Colombia. After U.S. proposals for canal rights over the narrow isthmus had been rejected by Colombia, Panama proclaimed its independence with U.S. backing in 1903.

For canal rights in perpetuity, the U.S. paid Panama $10 million and agreed to pay $250,000 each year, increased to $430,000 after devaluation of the U.S. dollar in 1933 and was further increased under a revised treaty signed in 1955. In exchange, the U.S. got the Canal Zone—a 10-mile-wide strip across the isthmus—and a considerable degree of influence in Panama's affairs.

Panama and the U.S. agreed in 1974 to negotiate the eventual reversion of the canal to Panama, despite strongly expressed opposition in the U.S. Congress. The texts of two treaties—one governing the transfer of the canal and the other guaranteeing its neutrality after transfer—were negotiated by August 1977 and were signed by Pres. Omar Torrijos Herara and President Carter in Washington on September 7. A Panamanian referendum approved the treaties by more than two thirds on October 23, but further changes were insisted upon by the U.S. Senate.

The principal change was a reservation specifying that despite the neutrality treaty's specification that only Panama shall maintain forces in its territory after transfer of the canal Dec. 31, 1999, the U.S. should have the right to use military force to keep the canal operating if it should become obstructed. The Senate approved the treaties in March-April 1978.

Nicolas Ardito Barletta, Panama's first directly elected President in 16 years, was inaugurated on Oct. 11, 1984, for a five-year term. He lacked the necessary support to solve the country's economic crisis and resigned September 28, 1985. He was replaced by Vice President Eric Arturo Delvalle.

In June 1986, reports surfaced that the behind-the-scenes strongman, Gen. Manuel Noriega, was involved in drug trafficking and the murder of an opposition leader. In 1987, Noriega was accused by his ex-Chief of Staff of assassinating Torrijos in 1981. He was indicted in the U.S. for drug trafficking but when Delvalle attempted to fire him, he forced the National Assembly to replace Delvalle with Manuel Solis Palma.

The crisis continued when Noriega called presidential elections for when the current term expired. Despite massive fraud by Noriega, the opposition seemed headed to a landslide. Noriega annulled the elections and suppressed protests by the opposition.

In December 1989, the Assembly named Noriega the "maximum leader" and declared the U.S. and Panama to be in a state of war. A further series of incidents led to a U.S. invasion overthrowing Noriega, who was brought to the U.S. to stand trial for drug trafficking. Guillermo Endara, who probably would have won the election suppressed by Noriega, was instated as President.

A military revolt in December 1990 was easily suppressed, although the leaders eluded capture. The U.S. has pledged to use its troops in Panama if necessary to foil any coup attempt.

A referendum in November 1992 on a package of 58 proposed reforms went down to defeat although less than half of those eligible voted.

Panama Canal. First conceived by the Spaniards in 1524, when King Charles V of Spain ordered a survey of a waterway across the Isthmus, a construction concession was granted by the Colombian government in 1878 to St. Lucien N. B. Wyse, representing a French company. Two years later, the French Canal Company, inspired by Ferdinand de Lesseps, began construction of what was to have been a sea-level canal. The effort ended in bankruptcy nine years later and the United States ultimately paid the French $40 million for their rights and assets.

The U.S. project, built on territory controlled by the United States, and calling for the creation of an interior lake connected to both oceans by locks, got under way in 1904. Completed in 1914, the Canal is 50.7 miles long and lifts ships 85 feet above sea level through a series of three locks on the Pacific and Atlantic sides. Enlarged in later years, each lock now measures 1,000 feet in length, 110 feet in width, and 40 feet in depth of water.

PAPUA NEW GUINEA

Sovereign: Queen Elizabeth II
Governor General: Wina Korowi
Prime Minister: Paias Wingti (1992)
Area: 178,704 sq mi. (462,840 sq km)
Population (est. mid-1993): 3,900,000 (average annual rate of natural increase: 2.3%); birth rate: 35/1000; infant mortality rate: 99/1000; density per square mile: 23
Capital and largest city (est. 1987): Port Moresby, 152,100; **Monetary unit:** Kina; **Languages:** English, Melanesian pidgin, Hiri Motu, and 717 distinct native languages; **Religions:** over half Christian, remainder indigenous; **Member of Commonwealth of Nations; Literacy rate:** 52%
Economic summary: Gross domestic product (1991): $3.1 billion; $800 per capita; 9% real growth rate; inflation 6.8% est.; unemployment (1988) 5%. Principal products: coffee, copra, palm oil, cocoa, tea, coconuts. Major industrial products: coconut oil, plywood, wood chips, gold, silver. Natural resources: copper, gold, silver, timber, natural gas. Exports: $1.14 billion (f.o.b., 1990): gold, copper, coffee, palm oil, copra, timber. Imports: $1.18 billion (c.i.f., 1990): food, machinery, transport equipment, fuels. Major trading partners: Australia, U.K., Japan, Germany, Singapore, Spain, New Zealand, U.S.

Geography. Papua New Guinea occupies the eastern half of the island of New Guinea, just north of Australia, and many outlying islands. The Indonesian province of Irian Jaya is to the west. To the north and east are the islands of Manus, New Britain, New Ireland, and Bougainville, all part of Papua New Guinea.

Papua New Guinea is about one-tenth larger than California. Its mountainous interior has only recently been explored. The high-plateau climate is temperate, in contrast to the tropical climate of the coastal plains. Two major rivers, the Sepik and the Fly, are navigable for shallow-draft vessels.

Government. Papua New Guinea attained independence Sept. 16, 1975, ending a United Nations trusteeship under the administration of Australia. Parliamentary democracy was established by a Constitution that invests power in a 109-member national legislature.

History. The eastern half of New Guinea was first visited by Spanish and Portuguese explorers in the 16th century, but a permanent European presence was not established until 1884, when Germany declared a protectorate over the northern coast and Britain took similar action in the south. Both nations formally annexed their protectorates and, in 1901, Britain transferred its rights to a newly independent Australia. Australian troops invaded German New Guinea in World War I and retained control under a League of Nations mandate that eventually became a United Nations trusteeship, incorporating a territorial government in the southern region, known as Papua.

Australia granted limited home rule in 1951. Autonomy in internal affairs came nine years later.

In February 1990 guerrillas of the Bougainville Revolutionary Army (BRA) attacked plantations, forcing the evacuation of numerous workers. In May the BRA declared Bougainville's independence, whereupon the government blockaded the island until January 1991, when a peace treaty was signed.

A general election of June 1992 saw the defeat of the incumbent prime minister. In December he was charged with misappropriation of government funds.

PARAGUAY

Republic of Paraguay
President: Juan Carlos Wasmosy (1993)
Area: 157,047 sq mi. (406,752 sq km)
Population (est. mid-1993): 4,200,000 (average annual rate of natural increase: 2.7%); birth rate: 34/1000; infant mortality rate: 48/1000; density per square mile: 28
Capital and largest city (est. 1990): Asunción, 607,700; **Monetary unit:** Guaraní; **Languages:** Spanish (official), Guaraní; **Religion:** Roman Catholic, 90%; **National name:** República del Paraguay; **Literacy rate:** 90%
Economic summary: Gross domestic product (1991 est.): $7 billion; $1,460 per capita; real growth rate 3.0%; inflation 15%; unemployment 14%. Arable land: 20%. Principal agricultural products: soybeans, cotton, timber, cassava, tobacco, corn, rice, sugar cane. Labor force: 1,300,000; 44% agricultural. Major industrial products: packed meats, crushed oilseeds, beverages, textiles, light consumer goods, cement. Natural resources: iron ore, timber, manganese, limestone, hydropower. Exports: $642 million (f.o.b., 1991): cotton, soybeans, meat products, timber, coffee, tung oil. Imports: $1.85 billion (c.i.f., 1991): fuels and lubricants, machinery and motors, motor vehicles, beverages, tobacco, foodstuffs. Major trading partners: Argentina, Brazil, U.S., E.C., Japan.

Geography. California-size Paraguay is surrounded by Brazil, Bolivia, and Argentina in south central South America. Eastern Paraguay, between the Paraná and Paraguay Rivers, is upland country with the thickest population settled on the grassy slope that inclines toward the Paraguay River. The greater part of the Chaco region to the west is covered with marshes, lagoons, dense forests, and jungles.

Government. The President is elected by popular vote for five years. The legislature is bicameral, consisting of a Senate of 45 members and a Chamber of Representatives of 80 members. There is also a Council of State, whose members are nominated by the government.

History. In 1526 and again in 1529, Sebastian Cabot explored Paraguay when he sailed up the Paraná and Paraguay Rivers. From 1608 until their expulsion from the Spanish dominions in 1767, the Jesuits maintained an extensive establishment in the south and east of Paraguay. In 1811, Paraguay revolted against Spanish rule and became a nominal republic under two Consuls.

Actually, Paraguay was governed by three dictators during the first 60 years of independence. The third, Francisco López, waged war against Brazil and Argentina in 1865–70, a conflict in which the male population was almost wiped out. A new Constitution in 1870, designed to prevent dictatorships and internal strife, failed to do so, and not until 1912 did a period of comparative economic and political stability begin.

After World War II, politics became particularly unstable.

Stroessner ruled under a state of siege until 1965, when the dictatorship was relaxed and exiles returned. The Constitution was revised in 1967 to permit Stroessner to be re-elected.

The Stroessner regime was criticized by the U.S. State Department during the Carter administration as a violator of human rights, but unlike Argentina and Uruguay, Paraguay did not suffer cuts in U.S. military aid.

Stroessner was overthrown by an army leader, Gen. Andres Rodriguez, in 1989. Rodriguez won in Paraguay's first multi-candidate elections in decades. He has promised to hand over power to an elected civilian successor in 1993.

The National Assembly in June 1991 approved a reform of the constitution. Constituent Assembly elections in December gave the ruling Colorado Party a victory, but voter turnout was low.

The country's first ever democratic presidential election took place in May 1993. Wasmosy, a wealthy businessman and the candidate of the governing Colorado Party won a five-year term in an election that despite irregularities was regarded as reliable.

PERU

Republic of Peru
President: Alberto Fujimori (1990)
Premier: Dr. Oscar De la Puente Raygada
Area: 496,222 sq mi. (1,285,216 sq km)
Population (est. mid-1993): 22,900,000 (average annual rate of natural increase: 2.0%); birth rate: 28/1000; infant mortality rate: 81/1000; density per square mile: 46
Capital: Lima; **Largest cities (est. 1990):** Lima, 5,826,000; Arequipa, 634,500; Callao, 589,000; Trujillo, 532,000; Chiclayo, 426,300; **Monetary unit:** Nuevo Sol (1991); **Languages:** Spanish, Quéchua, Aymara, and other native languages; **Religion:** Roman Catholic; **National name:** República del Perú; **Literacy rate:** est. 80%
Economic summary: Gross domestic product (1991 est.): $20.6 billion; $920 per capita; real growth rate 2.4%; inflation 139%; unemployment 15%. Arable land: 3%. Principal products: wheat, potatoes, beans, rice, sugar, cotton, coffee. Labor force: 6,800,000 (1986); 19% in industry (1988 est.). Major products: processed minerals, fish meal, refined petroleum, textiles. Natural resources: silver, gold, iron, copper, fish, petroleum, timber. Exports: $3.3 billion (f.o.b., 1991 est.): copper, fish products, cotton, sugar, coffee, lead, silver, zinc, oil, iron ore. Imports: $3.5 billion (f.o.b., 1991 est.): machinery, foodstuffs, chemicals, pharmaceuticals. Major trading partners: U.S., Japan, Western European, and Latin American countries.

Geography. Peru, in western South America, extends for nearly 1,500 miles (2,414 km) along the Pacific Ocean. Colombia and Ecuador are to the north, Brazil and Bolivia to the east, and Chile to the south.

Five-sixths the size of Alaska, Peru is divided by the Andes Mountains into three sharply differentiated zones. To the west is the coastline, much of it arid, extending 50 to 100 miles (80 to 160 km) inland. The mountain area, with peaks over 20,000 feet (6,096 m), lofty plateaus, and deep valleys, lies centrally. Beyond the mountains to the east is the heavily forested slope leading to the Amazonian plains.

Government. A republic in transition. The president was elected in 1990 by universal suffrage for a five-year term and holds executive power. On Nov. 22, 1992, an 80-member Constituent Congress was elected by universal suffrage. It is drafting a new constitution which will be submitted to the people for approval by a national referendum. The congress will continue legislating and overseeing the government's functions until July 1995.

History. Peru was once part of the great Incan empire and later the major vice-royalty of Spanish South America. It was conquered in 1531–33 by Francisco Pizarro. On July 28, 1821, Peru proclaimed its independence, but the Spanish were not finally defeated until 1824. For a hundred years thereafter, revolutions were frequent, and a new war was fought with Spain in 1864–66.

Peru emerged from 20 years of dictatorship in 1945 with the inauguration of President José Luis Bustamente y Rivero after the first free election in many decades. But he served for only three years and was succeeded in turn by Gen. Manual A. Odria, Manuel Prado y Ugarteche, and Fernando Belaúnde Terry. On Oct. 3, 1968, Belaúnde was overthrown by Gen. Juan Velasco Alvarado.

Velasco nationalized the nation's second biggest bank and turned two large newspapers over to Marxists in 1970, but he also allowed a new agreement with a copper-mining consortium of four American firms.

In 1975, Velasco was replaced in a bloodless coup by his Premier, Gen. Francisco Morales Bermudez, who promised to restore civilian government. In elections held on May 18, 1980, Belaunde Terry, the last previous civilian President and the candidate of the conservative parties that have traditionally ruled Peru, was elected President again.

But Peru's fragile democracy survived this period of stress and when he left office in 1985 Belaunde Terry was the first elected President to turn over power to a constitutionally elected successor since 1945.

In the June run-off to the April 1990 elections Alberto Fujimori won 56.5% of the vote. A newcomer to national politics, Fujimori is the son of Japanese immigrants. Nevertheless, two guerrilla groups working separately declared war on the government.

Citing continuing terrorism, drug trafficking and corruption Fujimori in April 1992 dissolved Congress, suspended the constitution and imposed censorship. Three days later the Congress, meeting secretly, voted to impeach the President.

In September the police arrested Abimael Guzman, leader of the Maoist Shining Path.

THE PHILIPPINES

Republic of the Philippines
President: Fidel V. Ramos (1992)
Vice President: Joseph Estrada (1992)
Area: 115,830 sq mi. (300,000 sq km)
Population (est. mid-1993): 64,600,000 (average annual rate of natural increase: 2.5%); birth rate: 32/1000; infant mortality rate: 43/1000; density per square mile: 562
Capital: Manila; **Largest cities (1990):** Manila, 1,587,000[1]; Quezon City, 1,632,000; Cebu, 610,000; **Monetary unit:** Peso; **Languages:** Filipino (based on Tagalog), English; regional languages: Tagalog, Ilocano, Cebuano, others; **Religions:** Roman Catholic, 83%; Protestant, 9%; Islam, 5%; Buddhist and other, 3%; **National name:** Republika ng Pilipinas; **Literacy rate:** 90% (est.)
Economic summary: Gross domestic product (1991 est.): $47 billion; $720 per capita; real growth rate 0.1%; inflation 17.6%; unemployment 10%. Arable land: 26%. Principal products: rice, corn, coconuts, sugar cane, bananas, pineapple. Labor force (1989): 24,120,000; agriculture, 46%; services, 18.5%; industry and commerce, 16%. Major products: textiles, pharmaceuticals, chemicals, food processing, electronics assem-

bly. Natural resources: forests, crude oil, metallic and non-metallic minerals. Exports: $8.7 billion (f.o.b., 1991 est.): electrical equipment, coconut products, chemicals, logs and lumber, copper concentrates, nickel. Imports: $12.3 billion (c.i.f., 1991 est.): petroleum, industrial equipment, raw materials. Major trading partners: U.S., Japan, E.C.

1. Metropolitan area population is 7,832,000.

Geography. The Philippine Islands are an archipelago of over 7,000 islands lying about 500 miles (805 km) off the southeast coast of Asia. The overall land area is comparable to that of Arizona. The northernmost island, Y'Ami, is 65 miles (105 km) from Taiwan, while the southernmost, Saluag, is 40 miles (64 km) east of Borneo.

Only about 7% of the islands are larger than one square mile, and only one third have names. The largest are Luzon in the north (40,420 sq mi.; 104,687 sq km), Mindanao in the south (36,537 sq mi.; 94,631 sq km), Samar (5,124 sq mi.; 13,271 sq km).

The islands are of volcanic origin, with the larger ones crossed by mountain ranges. The highest peak is Mount Apo (9,690 ft; 2,954 m) on Mindanao.

Government. On February 2, 1987, the Filipino people voted for a new Constitution that established a 24-seat Senate and a 250-seat House of Representatives and gave President Aquino a six-year term. It limits the powers of the President, who can't be re-elected.

History. Fernando Magellan, the Portuguese navigator in the service of Spain, discovered the Philippines in 1521. Twenty-one years later, a Spanish exploration party named the group of islands in honor of Prince Philip, later Philip II of Spain. Spain retained possession of the islands for the next 350 years.

The Philippines were ceded to the U.S. in 1899 by the Treaty of Paris after the Spanish-American War. Meanwhile, the Filipinos, led by Emilio Aguinaldo, had declared their independence. They continued guerrilla warfare against U.S. troops until the capture of Aguinaldo in 1901. By 1902, peace was established except among the Moros.

The first U.S. civilian Governor-General was William Howard Taft (1901–04). The Jones Law (1916) provided for the establishment of a Philippine Legislature composed of an elective Senate and House of Representatives. The Tydings-McDuffie Act (1934) provided for a transitional period until 1946, at which time the Philippines would become completely independent.

Under a Constitution approved by the people of the Philippines in 1935, the Commonwealth of the Philippines came into being, with Manuel Quezon y Molina as President.

On Dec. 8, 1941, the Philippines were invaded by Japanese troops. Following the fall of Bataan and Corregidor, Quezon established a government-in-exile, which he headed until his death in 1944. He was succeeded by Vice President Sergio Osmeña.

U.S. forces led by Gen. Douglas MacArthur reinvaded the Philippines in October 1944 and, after the liberation of Manila in February 1945, Osmeña re-established the government.

The Philippines achieved full independence on July 4, 1946. Manual A. Roxas y Acuña was elected first president. Subsequent presidents have been Elpidio Quirino (1948–53), Ramón Magsaysay (1953–57). Carlos P. García (1957–61), Diosdado Macapagal (1961–65), Ferdinand E. Marcos (1965–86).

Marcos, who had freed the last of the national leaders still in detention, former Senator Benigno S. Aquino, Jr., in 1980 and permitted him to go to the United States, ended eight years of martial law on January 17, 1981.

Despite having been warned by First Lady Imelda Marcos that he risked being killed if he came back, opposition leader Aquino returned to the Philippines from self-exile on Aug. 21, 1983. He was shot to death as he was being escorted from his plane by military police at Manila International Airport. The government contended the assassin was a small-time hoodlum allegedly hired by communists, who was in turn shot dead by Filipino troops, but there was widespread suspicion that the Marcos government was involved in the murder.

In an attempt to re-secure American support, Marcos set Presidential elections for Feb. 7, 1986. With the support of the Catholic church, Corazon Aquino, widow of Benigno Aquino, declared her candidacy. Marcos was declared the winner, but the vote was widely considered to be rigged and anti-Marcos protests continued. The defection of Defense Minister Juan Enrile and Lt. Gen. Fidel Ramos signaled an end of military support for Marcos, who fled into exile in the U.S. on Feb. 25, 1986.

The Aquino government survived coup attempts by Marcos supporters and other right-wing elements including one, in November, by Enrile. Legislative elections on May 11, 1987, gave pro-Aquino candidates a large majority.

Negotiations on renewal of leases for U.S. military bases threatened to sour relations between the two countries. The volcanic eruptions from Mount Pinatubo, however, severely damaged Clark Air Base. In July 1991 the U.S. decided simply to abandon the base.

In elections of May 1992 Gen. Fidel Ramos, who had the support of outgoing Corazon Aquino, won the presidency in a seven-way race. The opposition gained control of the Congress.

The U.S. Navy turned over the Subic Bay naval base to the Philippines in September, ending a long U.S. military presence.

POLAND

Republic of Poland
President: Lech Walesa (1990)
Prime Minister: Hanna Suchocka (1992)
Area: 120,727 sq mi. (312,683 sq km)
Population (est. mid-1993): 38,500,000 (average annual rate of natural increase: 0.3%); birth rate: 13/1000; infant mortality rate: 14.4/1000; density per square mile: 327
Capital: Warsaw; **Largest cities (est. 1991):** Warsaw, 1,655,000; Lodz, 846,500; Krakow, 750,600; Wroclaw, 643,000; Poznan, 590,000; Gdansk, 465,400; Szczecin, 413,600; **Monetary unit:** Zloty; **Language:** Polish; **Religions:** Roman Catholic, 95%; Russian Orthodox, Protestant, and other, 5%; **National name:** Rzeczpospolita Polska; **Literacy rate:** 98%
Economic summary: Gross national product (1991 est.): $162.7 billion; $4,300 per capita; real growth rate –5%; inflation (est. 1991) 60%; unemployment (Dec. 1991) 11.4%. Arable land: 46%. Principal products: rye, rapeseed, potatoes, hogs and other livestock. Labor force: 17,104,000 (1989); 36.1% in agriculture; 27.3% in industry and construction. Major products: iron and

steel, chemicals, textiles, processed foods, machine building. Natural resources: coal, sulfur, copper, natural gas. Exports: $12.8 billion (f.o.b., 1991 est.): coal, machinery and equipment, industrial products. Imports: $12.9 billion (f.o.b., 1991 est.): machinery and equipment, fuels, raw materials, agricultural and food products. Major trading partners: Germany, Czech Republic, Slovak Republic.

Geography. Poland, a country the size of New Mexico in north central Europe, borders on Germany to the west, Czech and Slovak Republics to the south, and Ukraine, Balarus, Lithuania, and Russia to the east. In the north is the Baltic Sea.

Most of the country is a plain with no natural boundaries except the Carpathian Mountains in the south and the Oder and Neisse Rivers in the west. Other major rivers, which are important to commerce, are the Vistula, Warta, and Bug.

Government. Parliament adopted a new temporary constitution, Oct. 17, 1992, which describes Poland as the Republic of Poland. Work on a permanent constitution continues. The supreme organ of state authority is the Sejm (Parliament), which is composed of 460 members elected for four years and a 100-member Senate (Senat).

History. Little is known about Polish history before the 11th century, when King Boleslaus I (the Brave) ruled over Bohemia, Saxony, and Moravia. Meanwhile, the Teutonic knights of Prussia conquered part of Poland and barred the latter's access to the Baltic. The knights were defeated by Wladislaus II at Tannenberg in 1410 and became Polish vassals, and Poland regained a Baltic shoreline. Poland reached the peak of power between the 14th and 16th centuries, scoring military successes against the Russians and Turks. In 1683, John III (John Sobieski) turned back the Turkish tide at Vienna.

An elective monarchy failed to produce strong central authority, and Prussia and Austria were able to carry out a first partition of the country in 1772, a second in 1792, and a third in 1795. For more than a century thereafter, there was no Polish state, but the Poles never ceased their efforts to regain their independence.

Poland was formally reconstituted in November 1918, with Marshal Josef Pilsudski as Chief of State. In 1919, Ignace Paderewski, the famous pianist and patriot, became the first premier. In 1926, Pilsudski seized complete power in a coup and ruled dictatorially until his death on May 12, 1935, when he was succeeded by Marshal Edward Smigly-Rydz.

Despite a 10-year nonaggression pact signed in 1934, Hitler attacked Poland on Sept. 1, 1939. Russian troops invaded from the east on September 17, and on September 28 a German-Russian agreement divided Poland between Russia and Germany. Wladyslaw Raczkiewicz formed a government-in-exile in France, which moved to London after France's defeat in 1940.

All of Poland was occupied by Germany after the Nazi attack on the U.S.S.R. in June 1941.

The legal Polish government soon fell out with the Russians, and, in 1944, a Communist-dominated Polish Committee of National Liberation received Soviet recognition. Moving to Lublin after that city's liberation, it proclaimed itself the Provisional Government of Poland. Some former members of the Polish government in London joined with the Lublin government to form the Polish Government of National Unity, which Britain and the U.S. recognized.

On Aug. 2, 1945, in Berlin, President Harry S. Truman, Joseph Stalin, and Prime Minister Clement Attlee of Britain established a new *de facto* western frontier for Poland along the Oder and Neisse Rivers. (The border was finally agreed to by West Germany in a nonagression pact signed Dec. 7, 1970.) On Aug. 16, 1945, the U.S.S.R. and Poland signed a treaty delimiting the Soviet-Polish frontier. Under these agreements, Poland was shifted westward. In the east it lost 69,860 square miles (180,934 sq km) with 10,772,000 inhabitants; in the west it gained (subject to final peace-conference approval) 38,986 square miles (100,973 sq km) with a prewar population of 8,621,000.

A New Constitution in 1952 made Poland a "people's democracy" of the Soviet type. In 1955, Poland became a member of the Warsaw Treaty Organization, and its foreign policy became identical with that of the U.S.S.R. The government undertook persecution of the Roman Catholic Church as a remaining source of opposition.

Wladyslaw Gomulka was elected leader of the United Workers (Communist) Party in 1956. He denounced the Stalinist terror, ousted many Stalinists, and improved relations with the church. Most collective farms were dissolved, and the press became freer.

A strike that began in shipyards and spread to other industries in August 1980 produced a stunning victory for workers when the economically hard-pressed government accepted for the first time in a Marxist state the right of workers to organize in independent unions.

Led by Solidarity, a free union founded by Lech Walesa, workers launched a drive for liberty and improved conditions. A national strike for a five-day week in January 1981 led to the dismissal of Premier Pinkowski and the naming of the fourth Premier in less than a year, Gen. Wojciech Jaruzelski.

Antistrike legislation was approved on Dec. 2 and martial law declared on Dec. 13, when Walesa and other Solidarity leaders were arrested.

Martial law was formally ended in 1984 but the government retained emergency powers. On July 21, 1984, the Parliament marked the 40th anniversary of Communist rule in Poland by enacting an amnesty bill authorizing the release of 652 political prisoners—virtually all except for those charged with high treason, espionage, and sabotage—and 35,000 common criminals. On September 10, 1986, the government freed all 225 remaining political prisoners.

Increasing opposition to the government because of the failing economy led to a new wave of strikes in 1988. Unable to totally quell the dissent, it relegalized Solidarity and allowed them to compete in elections.

Solidarity won a stunning victory, taking almost all the seats in the Senate and all of the 169 seats they were allowed to contest in the Sejm. This has given them substantial influence in the new government. Taduesz Mazowiecki was appointed prime minister.

The presidential election of 1990 was essentially a three-way race between Mazowiecki, Solidarity-leader Lech Walesa and an almost unknown businessman Stanislaw Tyminski. In the second round Walesa received 74% of the vote.

In 1991, the first fully free parliamentary election since WW II resulted in representation for 29 political parties.

The government of Poland's first female prime minister lost a vote of confidence in May 1993. President Walesa asked Suchocka to head a caretaker government until new elections could be held.

PORTUGAL

Republic of Portugal
President: Mario Soares (1986)
Prime Minister: Anibal Cavaco Silva (1987)
Area: 35,550 sq mi. (92,075 sq km)
Population (est. mid-1993): 9,800,000 (average annual rate of natural increase: 0.1%); birth rate: 12/1000; infant mortality rate: 10.8/1000; density per square mile: 277
Capital: Lisbon; **Largest cities (est. 1986):** Lisbon, 829,600; Opporto, 347,300; **Monetary unit:** Escudo; **Language:** Portuguese; **Religion:** Roman Catholic 97%, 1% Protestant, 2% other; **National name:** República Portuguesa; **Literacy rate:** 85%
Economic summary: Gross domestic product (1991 est.): $87.3 billion; $8,400 per capita; real growth rate 2.7%; inflation 12%; unemployment 4%. Arable land: 32%. Principal products: grains, potatoes, olives, wine grapes. Labor force (1988): 4,605,700; 45% in services, 20% in agriculture, 35% in industry. Major products: textiles, footwear, wood pulp, paper, cork, metal products, refined oil, chemicals, canned fish, wine. Natural resources: fish, cork, tungsten, iron ore. Exports: $16.4 billion (f.o.b., 1990): cotton, textiles, cork and cork products, canned fish, wine, timber and timber products, resin. Imports: $25.1 billion (c.i.f., 1990): petroleum, cotton, foodgrains, industrial machinery, iron and steel, chemicals. Major trading partners: Western European countries, U.S.

Geography. Portugal occupies the western part of the Iberian Peninsula, bordering on the Atlantic Ocean to the west and Spain to the north and east. It is slightly smaller than Indiana.

The country is crossed by many small rivers, and also by three large ones that rise in Spain, flow into the Atlantic, and divide the country into three geographic areas. The Minho River, part of the northern boundary, cuts through a mountainous area that extends south to the vicinity of the Douro River. South of the Douro, the mountains slope to the plains about the Tejo River. The remaining division is the southern one of Alentejo.

The Azores, stretching over 340 miles (547 km) in the Atlantic, consist of nine islands divided into three groups, with a total area of 902 square miles (2,335 sq km). The nearest continental land is Cape da Roca, Portugal, about 900 miles (1,448 km) to the east. The Azores are an important station on Atlantic air routes, and Britain and the U.S. established air bases there during World War II. Madeira, consisting of two inhabited islands, Madeira and Porto Santo, and two groups of uninhabited islands, lie in the Atlantic about 535 miles (861 km) southwest of Lisbon. The Madeiras are 307 square miles (796 sq km) in area.

Government. A republic. The president is elected for a five-year term. The unicameral legislature, the Assembly of the Republic, for four years.

History. Portugal was a part of Spain until it won its independence in the middle of the 12th century. King John I (1385–1433) unified his country at the expense of the Castilians and the Moors of Morocco. The expansion of Portugal was brilliantly coordinated by John's son, Prince Henry the Navigator. In 1488, Bartolomew Diaz reached the Cape of Good Hope, proving that the Far East was accessible by sea. In 1498, Vasco da Gama reached the west coast of India. By the middle of the 16th century, the Portuguese Empire was in West and East Africa, Brazil, Persia, Indochina, and Malaya.

In 1581, Philip II of Spain invaded Portugal and held it for 60 years, precipitating a catastrophic decline of Portuguese commerce. Courageous and shrewd explorers, the Portuguese proved to be inefficient and corrupt colonizers. By the time the Portuguese dynasty was restored in 1640, Dutch, English, and French competitors began to seize the lion's share of the world's colonies and commerce. Portugal retained Angola and Mozambique in Africa, and Brazil (until 1822).

The corrupt King Carlos, who ascended the throne in 1889, made Joao Franco the Premier with dictatorial power in 1906. In 1908, Carlos and his heir were shot dead on the streets of Lisbon. The new King, Manoel II, was driven from the throne in the Revolution of 1910 and Portugal became a French-style republic.

Traditionally friendly to Britain, Portugal fought in World War I on the Allied side in Africa as well as on the Western Front. Weak postwar governments and a revolution in 1926 brought Antonio Oliveira Salazar to power. He kept Portugal neutral in World War II but gave the Allies naval and air bases after 1943.

Portugal lost the tiny remnants of its Indian empire—Goa, Daman, and Diu—to Indian military occupation in 1961, the year an insurrection broke out in Angola. For the next 13 years, Salazar, who died in 1970, and his successor, Marcello Caetano, fought independence movements amid growing world criticism. Leftists in the armed forces, weary of a losing battle, launched a successful revolution on April 25, 1974.

In late 1985, a PSP-PSD split ended the Soares coalition government. Cavaco Silva, an advocate of free-market economics, was the Social Democratic candidate.

In July 1987, the governing Social Democratic Party was swept back into office with 50.22% of the popular vote, giving Portugal its first majority Government since democracy was restored in 1974.

Mario Soares easily won a second five-year term as president in January 1991 elections.

The general elections of October 1991 gave an absolute majority in the Assembly to the prime minister's Social Democratic Party.

The Assembly in December 1992 ratified the Maastricht Treaty by a vote of 207–22 bypassing a popular referendum

Portuguese Overseas Territory

After the April 1974 revolution, the military junta moved to grant independence to the territories, beginning with Portuguese Guinea in September 1974, which became the Republic of Guinea-Bissau.

Mozambique and Angola followed, leaving only Portuguese Timor and Macao of the former empire. Despite Lisbon's objections, Indonesia annexed Timor.

MACAO

Status: Territory
Governor: Vasco Rocha Vieira (1991)
Area: 6 sq mi. (15.5 sq km)
Population (est. mid-1993): 400,000 (average annual growth rate: 1.2%); birth rate: 15/1000; infant mortality rate: 8/1000; density per square mile: 53,766
Capital (1986 est.): Macao, 416,200; **Monetary unit:** Patacá; **Languages:** Portuguese official; Cantonese is language of commerce; **Religion:** Buddhist, 45%; Roman Caholic, 7%; Protestant, 1%; **Literacy rate (1981):** al

most 100% among Portuguese and Macanese, no data on Chinese
Economic summary: Gross domestic product (1991 est.): $3.1 billion; $6,900 per capita; real growth rate 6%; inflation 8.8%. Principal agricultural products: rice and vegetables. Major industrial products: clothing, textiles, plastics, furniture. Exports: $1.5 billion (1990 est.): textiles, clothing, toys. Imports: $1.8 billion (1990 est.). raw materials, foodstuffs, capital goods. Major trading partners: Hong Kong, China, U.S., Germany, France.

Macao comprises the peninsula of Macao and the two small islands of Taipa and Colôane on the South China coast, about 35 miles (53 km) from Hong Kong. Established by the Portuguese in 1557, it is the oldest European outpost in the China trade, but Portugal's sovereign rights to the port were not recognized by China until 1887. The port has been eclipsed in importance by Hong Kong, but it is still a busy distribution center and also has an important fishing industry. Portugal will return Macao to China in 1999.

QATAR

State of Qatar
Emir: Sheikh Khalifa bin Hamad al-Thani (1972)
Area: 4,000 sq mi. (11,437 sq km)
Population (est. mid-1993): 500,000 (average annual rate of natural increase: 2.1%); birth rate: 23/1000; infant mortality rate: 26/1000; density per square mile: 117
Capital (est. 1990): Doha, 300,000; **Monetary unit:** Qatari riyal; **Language:** Arabic; English is also widely spoken; **Religion:** Islam, 95%; **Literacy rate:** 76%
Economic summary: Gross domestic product (1990): $7.4 billion; $15,000 per capita; inflation (1988 est.): 4.9%. Labor force: 104,000. Major industrial product: oil. Natural resources: oil, gas. Exports: $3.2 billion (f.o.b., 1990 est.): oil. Imports: $1.5 billion (f.o.b., 1990 est.): foodstuffs, animal and vegetable oils, chemicals, machinery and equipment. Major trading partners: Japan, Western Europe, U.S., Australia, Arab countries.

Geography. Qatar occupies a small peninsula that extends into the Persian Gulf from the east side of the Arabian Peninsula. Saudi Arabia is to the west and the United Arab Emirates to the south. The country is mainly barren.

Government. For a long time, Qatar was under Turkish protection, but in 1916, the Emir accepted British protection. After the discovery of oil in the 1940s and its exploitation in the 1950s and 1960s, political unrest spread to the sheikhdoms. Qatar declared its independence in 1971. The next year the current Sheikh, Khalifa bin Hamad al-Thani, ousted his cousin in a bloodless coup.

History. The emir agreed to the deployment of Arab and Western forces in Qatar following the Iraqi invasion of Kuwait.

A border dispute with Saudi Arabia pushed Qatar somewhat closer to Iran. The dispute was settled in December 1992.

In June Qatar signed a defense pact with the U.S., becoming the third Gulf state to do so.

ROMANIA

Republic of Romania
President: Ion Iliescu (1990)
Prime Minister: Nicolae Vacaroiu (1992)
Area: 91,700 sq mi. (237,500 sq km)
Population (est. mid-1993): 23,200,000 Romanian, 88.1%; Magyar, 7.9%; German, 1.6%; (average annual rate of natural increase: 0.1%); birth rate: 12/1000; infant mortality rate: 22.7/1000; density per square mile: 261
Capital: Bucharest; **Largest cities (1991):** Bucharest, 2,318,889; Brasov, 352,640; Timisoara, 333,365; Cluj Napoca, 317,914; Constanta, 315,917; Galati, 307,376; Ploiesti, 247,502; **Monetary unit:** Leu; **Languages:** Romanian, Magyar; **Religions:** Romanian Orthodox, 70%; Reformed Church (Protestant), 6%; Roman Catholic, 6%; Greek Catholic (Uniate) Church, 3%; unaffiliated, 15%; **National name:** Republica Socialista România; **Literacy rate:** 98%
Economic summary: Gross national product (1991 est.): $71.9 billion; $3,100 per capita; real growth rate –12%; inflation 21.5%; unemployment 4%. Arable land: 43%. Principal products: corn, wheat, livestock. Labor force (1989): industry, 38%; agriculture, 28%. Major products: timber, metal production and processing, chemicals, food processing, petroleum. Natural resources: oil, timber, natural gas, coal, iron ore. Exports: $4 billion (f.o.b., 1991 est.): machinery, minerals and metals, foodstuffs, lumber, fuel, manufactures. Imports: $5.4 billion (f.o.b., 1991 est.): machinery, minerals, fuels, agricultural products, consumer goods. Major trading partners: C.I.S. countries, Germany, Italy, U.K., U.S.

Geography. A country in southeastern Europe slightly smaller than Oregon, Romania is bordered on the west by Hungary and Yugoslavia, on the north and east by Moldova and Ukraine, on the east by the Black Sea, and on the south by Bulgaria.

The Carpathian Mountains divide Romania's upper half from north to south and connect near the center of the country with the Transylvanian Alps, running east and west.

North and west of these ranges lies the Transylvanian plateau, and to the south and east are the plains of Moldavia and Walachia. In its last 190 miles (306 km), the Danube River flows through Romania only. It enters the Black Sea in northern Dobruja, just south of the border with the Soviet Union.

Government. A multiparty republic with a bicameral Parliament consisting of an upper house or Senate and a lower house or House of Deputies.

History. Most of Romania was the Roman province of Dacia from about A.D. 100 to 271. From the 6th to the 12th century, wave after wave of barbarian conquerors overran the native Daco-Roman population. By the 16th century, the main Romanian principalities of Moldavia and Walachia had become satellites within the Ottoman Empire, although they retained much independence. After the Russo-Turkish War of 1828–29, they became Russian protectorates. The nation became a kingdom in 1881 after the Congress of Berlin.

King Ferdinand ascended the throne in 1914. At the start of World War I, Romania proclaimed its neutrality, but later joined the Allied side and in 1916 declared war on the Central Powers. The armistice of Nov. 11, 1918, gave Romania vast territories from Russia and the Austro-Hungarian Empire.

The gains of World War I, making Romania the largest Balkan state, included Bessarabia, Transylvania, and Bukovina. The Banat, a Hungarian area, was divided with Yugoslavia.

In 1925, Crown Prince Carol renounced his rights to the throne, and when King Ferdinand died in 1927, Carol's son, Michael (Mihai) became King under a regency. However, Carol returned from exile in 1930, was crowned King Carol II, and gradually became a powerful political force in the country. In 1938, he abolished the democratic Constitution of 1923.

In 1940, the country was reorganized along Fascist lines, and the Fascist Iron Guard became the nucleus of the new totalitarian party. On June 27, the Soviet Union occupied Bessarabia and northern Bukovina. By the Axis-dictated Vienna Award of 1940, two-fifths of Transylvania went to Hungary, after which Carol dissolved Parliament and granted the new premier, Ion Antonescu, full power. He abdicated and again went into exile.

Romania subsequently signed the Axis Pact on Nov. 23, 1940, and the following June joined in Germany's attack on the Soviet Union, reoccupying Bessarabia. Following the invasion of Romania by the Red Army in August 1944, King Michael led a coup that ousted the Antonescu government. An armistice with the Soviet Union was signed in Moscow on Sept. 12, 1944.

A Communist-dominated government bloc won elections in 1946, Michael abdicated on Dec. 30, 1947, and Romania became a "people's republic." In 1955, Romania joined the Warsaw Treaty Organization and the United Nations. Despite his liberal international record, at home Ceausescu harshly suppressed dissidents calling for freedom of expression in the wake of the Helsinki agreements.

An army-assisted rebellion in Dec. 1989 led to Ceausescu's overthrow. He was tried and executed. Elections in May 1990 led to the head of the interim government, Ion Iliescu, being elected President.

The government remains torn between introducing free-market reforms and its pledges to hold down unemployment and reduce shortages. While some, though few, measures have been implemented, price reforms in November 1990 led to strikes and demonstrations. The opposition remains weak and fragmented.

General elections in September 1992 saw the president returned for a second term and his party became the largest single party in parliament.

Although the government made moves toward a market economy much nationalized property remained in its hands. The UN embargo against was seen as hurting Romania's economic growth.

RUSSIA

Russian Federation

President: Boris N. Yeltsin (1991)

Vice President: Aleksandr V. Rutskoi

Prime Minister: Viktor Chernomyrdin (1992)

Area: 6,592,800 sq mi. (17,075,400 sq km)

Population (est. mid-1993): 149,000,000 (Russian, 82%. Minorities: Tartars, Ukrainians, and Chuvashes); (average annual rate of natural increase: 0.1%); birth rate: 12/1000; infant mortality rate: 20/1000; density per square mile: 23

Capital and largest city (1991): Moscow, 8,801,500. ; **Other large cities:** St. Petersburg, 4,466,800; Novosibirsk, 1,446,300; Samara (Kuybyshev), 1,257,300; Chelyabinsk, 1,148,300; Rostov-na-Donu, 1,127,600; Volgograd (Stalingrad), 1,007,300; Krasnoyarsk, 924,400; Vladivostok, 648,000; Irkutsk, 640,500; Yaroslavl, 638,100; Krasnodar, 631,200; Khabarovsk, 613,300; Barnaul, 606,800; Novo Kuznetsk, 601,900; **Monetary unit:** Ruble; **Religion:** Mainly Eastern Orthodoxy; **Language:** Russian

Economic summary: Russia is a highly industrialized-agrarian republic. Its vast mineral resources include oil and natural gas, coal, iron, zinc, lead, nickel, aluminum, molybdenum, gold, platinum, and other nonferrous metals. Russia has the world's largest oil and natural gas reserves. Three-quarters of the republic's mineral wealth is concentrated in Siberia and the Far East. Approximately ten million people are engaged in agriculture and they produce half of the region's grain, meat, milk, and other dairy products. The largest granaries are located in the North Caucasus and the Volga and Amur regions. Per capita GDP (1991): $3,220; real growth rate –9%; inflation 89%. Exports: $58.7 billion (f.o.b., 1991): petroleum and petroleum products, natural gas, wood and wood products, coal, nonferrous metals, chemicals, civilian and military manufacturers. Imports: $43.5 billion (c.i.f., 1991): machinery and equipment, chemicals, consumer goods, grain, meat, semifinished metal products. Foreign investment in Russia (1993 est.): $500 million.

Geography: The Russian Federation is the largest republic of the Commonwealth of Independent States. It is about one and four-fifths of the land area of the United States and occupies most of eastern Europe and north Asia. Russia stretches from the Baltic Sea in the west to the Pacific Ocean in the east and from the Arctic Ocean in the north to the Black Sea and the Caucasus, the Altai, and Sayan Mountains, and the Amur and Ussuri Rivers in the south. It is bordered by Norway and Finland in the northwest, Estonia, Latvia, Belarus and Ukraine in the west, Georgia and Azerbaijan in the southwest, and Kazakhstan, Mongolia, and China along the southern border. The federation comprises 21 republics.

Government: A constitutional republic. The supreme legislature is the Congress of People's Deputies with 1,033 members. Of these, one-quarter or 256 members are elected to the bicameral Supreme Soviet or parliament. The Supreme Soviet has two chambers—the Soviet of the Republic and the Soviet of Nationalities—and is accountable to the Congress of People's Deputies.

History. Tradition says the Viking Rurik came to Russia in A.D. 862 and founded the first Russian dynasty in Novgorod. The various tribes were united by the spread of Christianity in the 10th and 11th centuries; Vladimir "the Saint" was converted in 988. During the 11th century, the grand dukes of Kiev held such centralizing power as existed. In 1240, Kiev was destroyed by the Mongols, and the Russian territory was split into numerous smaller dukedoms, early dukes of Moscow extended their dominions through their office of tribute collector for the Mongols.

In the late 15th century, Duke Ivan III acquired Novgorod and Tver and threw off the Mongol yoke. Ivan IV, the Terrible (1533–84), first Muscovite Tsar, is considered to have founded the Russian state. He crushed the power of rival princes and boyars (great landowners), but Russia remained largely medieval until the reign of Peter the Great (1689–1725), grandson of the first Romanov Tsar, Michael (1613–45). Peter made extensive reforms aimed at westernization and, through his defeat of Charles XII of Sweden at the Battle of Poltava in 1709, he extended Russia's boundaries to the west.

Catherine the Great (1762–96) continued Peter's westernization program and also expanded Russian territory, acquiring the Crimea and part of Poland. During the reign of Alexander I (1801–25), Napoleon's attempt to subdue Russia was defeated (1812–13), and new territory was gained, including Finland (1809) and Bessarabia (1812). Alexander originated the Holy Alliance, which for a time crushed Europe's rising liberal movement.

Alexander II (1855–81) pushed Russia's borders to the Pacific and into central Asia. Serfdom was abolished in 1861, but heavy restrictions were imposed on the emancipated class. Revolutionary strikes following Russia's defeat in the war with Japan forced Nicholas II (1894–1917) to grant a representative national body (Duma), elected by narrowly limited suffrage. It met for the first time in 1906, little influencing Nicholas in his reactionary course.

World War I demonstrated tsarist corruption and inefficiency and only patriotism held the poorly equipped army together for a time. Disorders broke out in Petrograd (renamed Leningrad now St. Petersburg) in March 1917, and defection of the Petrograd garrison launched the revolution. Nicholas II was forced to abdicate on March 15, 1917, and he and his family were killed by revolutionists on July 16, 1918.

A provisional government under the successive premierships of Prince Lvov and a moderate, Alexander Kerensky, lost ground to the radical, or Bolshevik, wing of the Socialist Democratic Labor Party. On Nov. 7, 1917, the Bolshevik revolution, engineered by N. Lenin[1] and Leon Trotsky, overthrew the Kerensky government and authority was vested in a Council of People's Commissars, with Lenin as Premier.

The humiliating Treaty of Brest-Litovsk (March 3, 1918) concluded the war with Germany, but civil war and foreign intervention delayed Communist control of all Russia until 1920. A brief war with Poland in 1920 resulted in Russian defeat.

Emergence of the U.S.S.R.

The Union of Soviet Socialist Republics was established as a federation on Dec. 30, 1922.

The death of Lenin on Jan. 21, 1924, precipitated an intraparty struggle between Joseph Stalin, General Secretary of the party, and Trotsky, who favored swifter socialization at home and fomentation of revolution abroad. Trotsky was dismissed as Commissar of War in 1925 and banished from the Soviet Union in 1929. He was murdered in Mexico City on Aug. 21, 1940, by a political agent.

Stalin further consolidated his power by a series of purges in the late 1930s, liquidating prominent party leaders and military officers. Stalin assumed the premiership May 6, 1941.

Soviet foreign policy, at first friendly toward Germany and antagonistic toward Britain and France and then, after Hitler's rise to power in 1933, becoming anti-Fascist and pro-League of Nations, took an abrupt turn on Aug. 24, 1939, with the signing of a nonaggression pact with Nazi Germany. The next month, Moscow joined in the German attack on Poland, seizing territory later incorporated into the Ukrainian and Byelorussian S.S.R.'s. The war with Finland, 1939–40, added territory to the Karelian S.S.R. set up March 31, 1940; the annexation of Bessarabia and Bukovina from Romania became part of the new Moldavian S.S.R. on Aug. 2, 1940; and the annexation of the Baltic republics of Estonia, Latvia, and Lithuania in June 1940 created the 14th, 15th, and 16th Soviet Republics. The illegal annexation of the Baltic republics was never recognized by the U.S. for the 51 years leading up to Soviet recognition of Estonia, Latvia and Lithuania's independence on September 6, 1991.

The Soviet-German collaboration ended abruptly with a lightning attack by Hitler on June 22, 1941, which seized 500,000 square miles of Russian territory before Soviet defenses, aided by U.S. and British arms, could halt it. The Soviet resurgence at Stalingrad from November 1942 to February 1943 marked the turning point in a long battle, ending in the final offensive of January 1945.

Then, after denouncing a 1941 nonaggression pact with Japan in April 1945, when Allied forces were nearing victory in the Pacific, the Soviet Union declared war on Japan on Aug. 8, 1945, and quickly occupied Manchuria, Karafuto, and the Kurile islands.

The U.S.S.R. built a cordon of Communist states running from Poland in the north to Albania and Bulgaria in the south, including East Germany, Czechoslovakia, Hungary, and Romania, composed of the territories Soviet troops occupied at the war's end. With its Eastern front solidified, the Soviet Union launched a political offensive against the non-Communist West, moving first to block the Western access to Berlin. The Western powers countered with an airlift, completed unification of West Germany, and organized the defense of Western Europe in the North Atlantic Treaty Organization.

Stalin died on March 6, 1953, and was succeeded the next day by G. M. Malenkov as Premier.

The new power in the Kremlin was Nikita S. Khrushchev, First Secretary of the party.

Khrushchev formalized the Eastern European system into a Council for Mutual Economic Assistance (Comecon) and a Warsaw Pact Treaty Organization as a counterweight to NATO.

The Soviet Union exploded a hydrogen bomb in 1953, developed an intercontinental ballistic missile by 1957, sent the first satellite into space (Sputnik I) in 1957, and put Yuri Gagarin in the first orbital flight around the earth in 1961.

Khrushchev's downfall stemmed from his decision to place Soviet nuclear missiles in Cuba and then, when challenged by the U.S., backing down and removing the weapons. He was also blamed for the ideological break with China after 1963.

Khrushchev was forced into retirement on Oct. 15, 1964, and was replaced by Leonid I. Brezhnev as First Secretary of the Party and Aleksei N. Kosygin as Premier.

Carter and the ailing Brezhnev signed the SALT II treaty in Vienna on June 18, 1979, setting ceilings on each nation's arsenal of intercontinental ballistic missiles. Doubts about Senate ratification grew, and became a certainty on Dec. 27, when Soviet troops invaded Afghanistan. Despite protests from the Moslem and Western worlds, Moscow insisted that Afghan President Hafizullah Amin had asked for aid in quelling a rebellion.

In the face of evidence that Amin had been liquidated by Soviet advisers before the troops arrived, the Soviet Union vetoed a Security Council resolution on Jan. 7, 1980, that called for a withdrawal. Carter ordered a freeze on grain exports and high-technology equipment.

On Jan. 20, Carter called for a world boycott of the Summer Olympic Games scheduled for Moscow. The boycott, less than complete, nevertheless marred the first Olympics to be held in Moscow as the United States, Canada, Japan, and to a partial extent all the western allies except France and Italy shunned the event.

1. N. Lenin was the pseudonym taken by Vladimir Ilich Ulyanov. It is sometimes given as Nikolai Lenin or V. Lenin.

Rulers of Russia Since 1533

Name	Born	Ruled[1]
Ivan IV the Terrible	1530	1533–1584
Theodore I	1557	1584–1598
Boris Godunov	c.1551	1598–1605
Theodore II	1589	1605–1605
Demetrius I[2]	?	1605–1606
Basil IV Shuiski	?	1606–1610 [3]
"Time of Troubles"	—	1610–1613
Michael Romanov	1596	1613–1645
Alexis I	1629	1645–1676
Theodore III	1656	1676–1682
Ivan V[4]	1666	1682–1689 [5]
Peter I the Great[4]	1672	1682–1725
Catherine I	c.1684	1725–1727
Peter II	1715	1727–1730
Anna	1693	1730–1740
Ivan VI	1740	1740–1741 [6]
Elizabeth	1709	1741–1762
Peter III	1728	1762–1762
Catherine II the Great	1729	1762–1796
Paul I	1754	1796–1801
Alexander I	1777	1801–1825
Nicholas I	1796	1825–1855
Alexander II	1818	1855–1881
Alexander III	1845	1881–1894
Nicholas II	1868	1894–1917 [7]
PROVISIONAL GOVERNMENT (PREMIERS)		
Prince Georgi Lvov	1861	1917–1917
Alexander Kerensky	1881	1917–1917
POLITICAL LEADERS OF U.S.S.R.		
N. Lenin	1870	1917–1924
Aleksei Rykov	1881	1924–1930
Vyacheslav Molotov	1890	1930–1941
Joseph Stalin[8]	1879	1941–1953
Georgi M. Malenkov	1902	1953–1955
Nikolai A. Bulganin	1895	1955–1958
Nikita S. Khrushchev	1894	1958–1964
Leonid I. Brezhnev	1906	1964–1982
Yuri V. Andropov	1914	1982–1984
Konstantin U. Chernenko	1912	1984–1985
Mikhail S. Gorbachev	1931	1985–1991
PRESIDENT OF RUSSIA		
Boris Yeltsin	1931	1991–

1. For Tsars through Nicholas II, year of end of rule is also that of death, unless otherwise indicated. 2. Also known as Pseudo-Demetrius. 3. Died 1612. 4. Ruled jointly until 1689, when Ivan was deposed. 5. Died 1696. 6. Died 1764. 7. Killed 1918. 8. General Secretary of Communist Party, 1924–53.

Despite the tension between Moscow and Washington, Strategic Arms Reduction Talks (START) began in Geneva between U.S. and Soviet delegations in mid-1982. Negotiations on intermediate missile reduction also continued in Geneva.

On November 10, 1982, Soviet radio and television announced the death of Leonid Brezhnev. Yuri V. Andropov, who formerly headed the K.G.B., was chosen to succeed Brezhnev as General Secretary. By mid-June 1983, Andropov had assumed all of Brezhnev's three titles.

The Soviet Union broke off both the START talks and the parallel negotiations on European-based missiles in November 1983 in protest against the deployment of medium-range U.S. missiles in Western Europe.

After months of illness, Andropov died in February 1984. Konstantin U. Chernenko, a 72-year-old party stalwart who had been close to Brezhnev, succeeded him as General Secretary and, by mid-April, had also assumed the title of President. In the months following Chernenko's assumption of power, the Kremlin took on a hostile mood toward the West of a kind rarely seen since the height of the cold war 30 years before. Led by Moscow, all the Soviet bloc countries except Romania boycotted the 1984 Summer Olympic Games in Los Angeles—tit-for-tat for the U.S.-led boycott of the 1980 Moscow Games, in the view of most observers.

After 13 months in office, Chernenko died on March 10, 1985. He had been ill much of the time and left only a minor imprint on Soviet history.

Chosen to succeed him as Soviet leader was Mikhail S. Gorbachev, at 54 the youngest man to take charge of the Soviet Union since Stalin. Under Gorbachev, the Soviet Union began its long-awaited shift to a new generation of leadership. Unlike his immediate predecessors, Gorbachev did not also assume the title of President but wielded power from the post of party General Secretary. In a surprise move, Gorbachev elevated Andrei Gromyko, 75, for 28 years the Soviet Union's stony-faced Foreign Minister, to the largely ceremonial post of President. He installed a younger man with no experience in foreign affairs, Eduard Shevardnadze, 57, as Foreign Minister.

A new round of U.S. Soviet arms reduction negotiations began in Geneva in March 1985, this time involving three types of weapons systems.

The Soviet Union took much criticism in early 1986 over the April 24 meltdown at the Chernobyl nuclear plant and its reluctance to give out any information on the accident.

In June 1987, Gorbachev obtained the support of the Central Committee for proposals that would loosen some government controls over the economy and in June 1988, an unusually open party conference approved several resolutions for changes in the structure of the Soviet system. These included a shift of some power from the Party to local soviets, a ten-year limit on the terms of elected government and party officials, and an alteration in the office of the President to give it real power in domestic and foreign policy. Gorbachev was elected President in 1989. The elections to the Congress were the first competitive elections in the Soviet Union since 1917. Dissident candidates won a surprisingly large minority although pro-Government deputies maintained a strong lock on the Supreme Soviet.

The possible beginning of the fragmentation of the Communist party took place when Boris Yeltsin, leader of the Russian S.S.R. who urges faster reform, left the Communist party along with other radicals.

In March 1991 the Soviet people were asked to vote on a referendum on national unity engineered by President Gorbachev. The resultant victory for the federal government was tempered by the separate approval in Russia for the creation of a popularly-elected republic presidency. In addition, six republics boycotted the vote.

The bitter election contest for the Russian presidency principally between Yeltsin and a Communist loyalist resulted in a major victory for Yeltsin. He took the oath of office for the new position on July 10.

Reversing his relative hard-line position adopted in the autumn of 1990, Gorbachev together with leaders of nine Soviet republics signed an accord, called the Union Treaty, which was meant to preserve the unity of the nation. In exchange the federal government would have turned over control of industrial and natural resources to the individual republics.

An attempted coup d'état took place on August 19 orchestrated by a group of eight senior officials calling itself the State Committee on the State of Emergency. Boris Yeltsin, held up in the Russian Parliament building, defiantly called for a general strike. The next day huge crowds demonstrated in Leningrad, and Yeltsin supporters fortified barricades surrounding the Parliament building. On August 21 the coup committee disbanded, and at least some of its members attempted to flee Moscow. The Soviet Parliament formally reinstated Gorbachev as President. Two days later he resigned from his position as General Secretary of the Communist Party and recommended that its Central Committee be disbanded. On August 29 the Parliament approved the suspension of all Communist Party activities pending an investigation of its role in the failed coup.

At the time of the attempted coup, the republic's President Boris Yeltsin was the most popular political figure in the lands comprising the former Soviet Union. A leading reformer, he became the first directly elected leader in Russian history and received 60% of the vote for President of the Russian Republic.

During the attempted coup in August 1991 by hard-line Communists to dislodge Mikhail Gorbachev, Yeltsin risked his life and rallied the opposition against the coup leaders. His heroism won him worldwide acclaim when the coup failed and he gained new stature and influence.

Yeltsin championed the cause for national reconstruction and the adoption of a Union Treaty with the other republics to create a free-market economic association.

Dissolution of the U.S.S.R.

On Dec. 12, 1991, the Russian parliament ratified Yeltsin's plea to establish a new commonwealth of independent nations open to all former members of the Soviet Union. The new union was created with the governments of Ukraine and Belarus who along with Russia were the three original cofounders of the Soviet Union in 1922.

After the end of the Soviet Union, Russia and ten other Soviet republics joined in a Commonwealth of Independent States on Dec. 21, 1991.

At the start of 1992, Russia embarked on a series of dramatic economic reforms, including the freeing of prices on most goods, which led to an immediate downturn. Tensions arose with Ukraine on the pace of these reforms and on the division of military units, particularly the large Black Sea fleet. Relations with the West improved dramatically but were still chilly with Japan in the absence of a settlement concerning the Kurile Islands.

A national referendum on confidence in Yeltsin and his economic program took place in April 1993. To the surprise of many the president and his shock-therapy program won by a resounding margin. The voters, however, expressed the wish for early parliamentary elections. Yeltsin used the results to move ahead with the writing of a new constitution.

The conflict with Ukraine over the Black Sea fleet was resolved with each country agreeing to take half.

RWANDA

Rwandese Republic

President: Maj. Gen. Juvénal Habyarimana (1973)
Prime Minister: Dismas Nsengiyaremye
Area: 10,169 sq mi. (26,338 sq km)
Population (est. mid-1993): 7,400,000 (average annual rate of natural increase: 2.3%); birth rate: 40/1000; infant mortality rate: 110/1000; density per square mile: 777
Capital and largest city (1990): Kigali, 300,000; **Monetary unit:** Rwanda franc; **Languages:** Kinyarwanda and French; **Religions:** Roman Catholic, 56%; Protestant, 18%; Islam, 1%; Animist, 25%; **National name:** Repubulika y'u Rwanda; **Literacy rate:** 5%
Economic summary: Gross domestic product (1990): $2.1 billion; $300 per capita; real growth rate –6.8%; inflation 4.2%. Arable land: 29%. Principal products: coffee, tea, bananas, yams, beans. Labor force 3,600,000; in agriculture, 93%; in industry: 2%. Major products: processed foods, light consumer goods, minerals. Natural resources: gold, cassiterite, wolfram. Exports: $111.7 million (f.o.b., 1990 est.): coffee, tea, tungsten, tin, pyrethrum. Imports: $279.2 million (f.o.b., 1990 est.): textiles, foodstuffs, machinery, and equipment. Major trading partners: Belgium, Germany, Kenya, Japan, France, U.S.

Geography. Rwanda, in east central Africa, is surrounded by Zaire, Uganda, Tanzania, and Burundi. It is slightly smaller than Maryland.

Steep mountains and deep valleys cover most of the country. Lake Kivu in the northwest, at an altitude of 4,829 feet (1,472 m) is the highest lake in Africa. Extending north of it are the Virunga Mountains, which include Volcan Karisimbi (14,187 ft; 4,324 m), Rwanda's highest point.

Government. Grégoire Kayibanda was President from 1962 until he was overthrown in a bloodless coup on July 5, 1973, by the military led by Gen. Juvénal Habyarimana.

In a plebiscite in December 1978, Habyarimana was elected to a five-year term as president and a new constitution adopted that provides for an elected Assembly and a single official party, the National Revolutionary Development Movement.

In 1988, Habyarimana was elected to a third five-year term.

The constitution was revised in 1991 to implement a multiparty system and schedule new elections.

History. Rwanda, which was part of German East Africa, was first visited by European explorers in 1854. During World War I, it was occupied in 1916 by Belgian troops. After the war, it became a Belgian League of Nations mandate, along with Burundi, under the name of Ruanda-Urundi. The mandate was made a U.N. trust territory in 1946. Until the Belgian Congo achieved independence in 1960, Ruanda-Urundi was administered as part of that colony.

Ruanda became the independent nation of Rwanda on July 1, 1962.

In August 1992 a formal agreement was signed ending the civil war between the government and the Rwandan Patriotic Front. In October another agreement was signed that would bring all political parties into the cabinet.

ST. KITTS AND NEVIS

Federation of St. Kitts and Nevis
Sovereign: Queen Elizabeth II
Governor General: Sir Clement Athelston Arrindell (1985)
Prime Minister: Kennedy Alphonse Simmonds (1980)
Area: St. Kitts 65 sq mi. (169 sq km); Nevis 35 sq mi. (93 sq km)
Total population (est. mid-1993): 40,000 (average annual rate of natural increase: 1.2%); birth rate: 23/1000; infant mortality rate: 22.2/1000; density per square mile: 288
Capital: Basseterre (on St. Kitts), 19,000; **Largest town on Nevis:** Charlestown, 1,771; **Monetary unit:** East Caribbean dollar
Economic summary: Gross domestic product (1990): $146.6 million; per capita $3,650; real growth rate 2.1%; inflation 4.2%; unemployment (1989) 15%. Arable land: 22%. Principal agricultural products: sugar, rice, yams. Labor force: 20,000 (1981). Major industries: tourism, sugar processing, salt extraction. Exports: $24.6 million (f.o.b., 1990): sugar, manufactures, postage stamps. Imports: $103.2 million (f.o.b., 1990): foodstuffs, manufactured goods, machinery, fuels. Major trading partners: U.S., U.K., Japan, Trinidad and Tobago, Canada.

St. Christopher-Nevis, preferably St. Kitts and Nevis, was formerly part of the West Indies Associated States which were established in 1967 and consisted of Antigua and St. Kitts-Nevis-Anguilla of the Leeward Islands, and Dominica, Grenada, St. Lucia, and St. Vincent of the Windward Islands. Statehood for St. Vincent was held up until 1969 because of local political uncertainties. Anguilla's association with St. Christopher-Nevis ended in 1980.

St. Christopher-Nevis, now St. Kitts and Nevis, became independent on September 19, 1983.

The premier of Nevis in 1990 announced that he intended to seek an end to the federation with St. Kitts by the end of 1992.

A victory for the Concerned Citizens Movement in a local election in June 1992 removed the threat of succession of Nevis from the federation for now.

ST. LUCIA

Sovereign: Queen Elizabeth II
Governor-General: Sir Stanislaus A. James (1989)
Prime Minister: John Compton (1982)
Area: 238 sq mi. (616 sq km)
Population (1992): 138,151 (average annual rate of natural increase: 1.7%); birth rate: 23/1000; infant mortality rate: 20.8/1000; density per square mile: 659
Capital (1989): Castries, 51,246; **Monetary unit:** East Caribbean dollar; **Languages:** English and patois; **Religions:** Roman Catholic, 90%; Protestant, 7%; Anglican, 3%; **Member of Commonwealth of Nations; Literacy rate:** 90%
Economic summary: Gross domestic product (1990 est.): $295 million; $1,930 per capita; real growth rate 4.0%; inflation 5.65% (1992); unemployment (1988) 16%. Arable land: 8%. Principal products: bananas, coconuts, cocoa, citrus fruit. Major industrial products: clothing, assembled electronics, beverages. Exports: $127 million (f.o.b., 1990 est.): bananas, cocoa. Imports: $270 million (c.i.f., 1990): foodstuffs, machinery and equipment, fertilizers, petroleum products. Major trading partners: U.K., U.S., Caribbean countries, Japan.

Geography. One of the Windward Isles of the Eastern Caribbean, St. Lucia lies just south of Martinique. It is of volcanic origin. A chain of wooded mountains runs from north to south, and from them flow many streams into fertile valleys.

Government. A Governor-General represents the sovereign, Queen Elizabeth II. A Prime Minister is head of government, chosen by a 17-member House of Assembly elected by universal suffrage for a maximum term of five years.

History. Discovered by Spain in 1503 and ruled by Spain and then France, St. Lucia became a British territory in 1803. With other Windward Isles, St. Lucia was granted home rule in 1967 as one of the West Indies Associated States. On Feb. 22, 1979, St. Lucia achieved full independence in ceremonies boycotted by the opposition St. Lucia Labor Party, which had advocated a referendum before cutting ties with Britain.

Unrest and a strike by civil servants forced Prime Minister John Compton to hold elections in July, in which his United Workers Party lost its majority for the first time in 15 years.

A Labor Party government was ousted in turn by Compton and his followers, in elections in May 1982.

Formerly dependent on a single crop, bananas, St. Lucia has sought to lower its chronic unemployment and payments deficit. The government provided tax incentives to a U.S. corporation, Amerada Hess, to facilitate location of a $150-million oil refinery and transshipment terminal on the island.

Elections of April 1992 returned the prime minister and his party once again to office.

ST. VINCENT AND THE GRENADINES

Sovereign: Queen Elizabeth II
Governor-General: David Jack (1989)
Prime Minister: James Mitchell (1984)
Area: 150 sq mi. (389 sq km)
Population (est. mid-1993): 100,000 (average annual rate of natural increase: 1.8%); birth rate: 24/1000; infant mortality rate: 21.7/1000; density per square mile: 757
Capital and largest city (1989): Kingstown, 19,274; **Monetary unit:** East Caribbean dollar; **Language:** English, some French patois; **Religions:** Anglican, 47%; Methodist, 28%; Roman Catholic, 13%; **Member of Commonwealth of Nations; Literacy rate:** 96%
Economic summary: Gross domestic product (1989 est.): $146 million; $1,315 per capita; 5.9% real growth rate. Arable land: 38%. Principal products: bananas, arrowroot, coconuts. Labor Force: 67,000 (1984 est.). Major industry: food processing. Exports: $75 million (f.o.b., 1990): bananas, arrowroot, copra. Imports: $130 million (f.o.b., 1990 est.): foodstuffs, machinery and equipment, chemicals, fuels, minerals. Major trading partners: U.K., U.S., Caribbean nations.

Geography. St. Vincent, chief island of the chain, is 18 miles (29 km) long and 11 miles (18 km) wide. One of the Windward Islands in the Lesser Antilles, it is 100 miles (161 km) west of Barbados. The island is mountainous and well forested. The Grenadines, a chain of nearly 600 islets with a total area of only 17 square miles (27 sq km), extend for 60 miles (96 km) from northeast to southwest between St. Vincent and Grenada, southernmost of the Windwards.

St. Vincent is dominated by the volcano La Soufrière, part of a volcanic range running north and south, which rises to 4,048 feet (1,234 m). The volcano erupted over a 10-day period in April 1979, causing the evacuation of the northern two-thirds of the island. (There is also a volcano of the same name on Basse-Terre, Guadeloupe, which became violently active in 1976 and 1977.)

Government. A Governor-General represents the sovereign, Queen Elizabeth II. A Prime Minister, elected by a 15-member unicameral legislature, holds executive power.

History. Discovered by Columbus in 1498, and alternately claimed by Britain and France, St. Vincent became a British colony by the Treaty of Paris in 1783. The islands won home rule in 1969 as part of the West Indies Associated States and achieved full independence Oct. 26, 1979. Prime Minister Milton Cato's government quelled a brief rebellion Dec. 8, 1979, attributed to economic problems following the eruption of La Soufrière in April 1979. Unlike a 1902 eruption which killed 2,000, there was no loss of life but widespread losses to agriculture.

Parliament approved plans in mid-1992 for a massive boat yard and marina that would be a joint venture with an Italian company.

SAN MARINO

Most Serene Republic of San Marino
Co-Regents: Two selected every six months by Grand and General Council
Area: 23.6 sq mi. (62 sq km)
Population (mid-1993): 20,000 (average annual growth rate: 0.5%); birth rate: 12/1000; infant mortality rate: 3.8/1000; density per square mile: 1,036
Capital and largest city (est. 1991): San Marino, 2,339; **Monetary unit:** Italian lira; **Language:** Italian; **Religion:** Roman Catholic; **National name:** Repubblica di San Marino; **Literacy rate:** 96%
Economic summary: Gross domestic product (1991): $400 million; $17,000 per capita; real growth rate, n.a.; inflation (1990) 6%; unemployment (1985) 6.5%. Arable land: 17%. Principal products: wheat and other grains, grapes, olives, cheese. Labor force: approx. 4,300. Major industrial products: textiles, leather, cement, wine, olive oil. Exports: building stone, lime, chestnuts, wheat, hides, baked goods. Imports: manufactured consumer goods. Major trading partner: Italy.

Geography. One-tenth the size of New York City, San Marino is surrounded by Italy. It is situated in the Apennines, a little inland from the Adriatic Sea near Rimini.

Government. The country is governed by two co-regents. Executive power is exercised by ten ministers. In 1959, the Grand Council granted women the vote. San Marino is a member of the Conference on Security and Cooperation in Europe.

History. According to tradition, San Marino was founded about A.D. 350 and had good luck for centuries in staying out of the many wars and feuds on the Italian peninsula. It is the oldest republic in the world.

A person born in San Marino remains a citizen and can vote no matter where he lives.

In February 1992 the U.N. Security Council unanimously supported the republic's application for admission to the U.N. In September the country joined the IMF and the Social Democrats entered into a coalition with the Christian Democrats.

SÃO TOMÉ AND PRÍNCIPE

Democratic Republic of São Tomé and Príncipe
President: Miguel Trovoada (1991)
Prime Minister: H.E. Norberto Costa Alegre (1992)
Area: 370 sq mi. (958 sq km)
Population (est. mid-1993): 100,000 (average annual growth rate: 2.5%); birth rate: 35/1000; infant mortality rate: 71.9/1000; density per square mile: 359
Capital and largest city (est. 1984): São Tomé, 34,997; **Monetary unit:** Dobra; **Language:** Portuguese; **Religions:** Roman Catholic, Evangelical Protestant, Seventh-Day Adventist; **Literacy rate:** 57% (est.)
Economic summary: Gross domestic product (1989): $46.0 million; $380 per capita; 1.5% annual growth rate. Arable land: 1%. Principal agricultural products: cocoa, copra, coconuts, palm oil, coffee, bananas. Labor force: 21,096 (1981): mostly in subsistence agriculture. Major industrial products: shirts, soap, beer, processed fish and shrimp. Exports: $4.4 million (f.o.b., 1990 est.): cocoa, coffee, copra, palm oil. Imports: $21.3 million (f.o.b., 1990 est.): textiles, machinery, electrical equipment, fuels, food products. Major trading partners: Netherlands, Portugal, Germany, China.

Geography. The tiny volcanic islands of São Tomé and Príncipe lie in the Gulf of Guinea about 150 miles (240 km) off West Africa. São Tomé (about 330 sq mi.; 859 sq km) is covered by a dense mountainous jungle, out of which have been carved large plantations. Príncipe (about 40 sq mi.; 142 sq km) consists of jagged mountains. Other islands in the republic are Pedras Tinhosas and Rolas.

Government. The Constitution grants supreme power to a 55-seat People's Assembly composed of members elected for four years. In 1990 a referendum approved a new constitution paving the way for a multi-party democracy.

History. São Tomé and Príncipe were discovered by Portuguese navigators in 1471 and settled by the end of the century. Intensive cultivation by slave labor made the islands a major producer of sugar during the 17th century but output declined until the introduction of coffee and cacao in the 19th century brought new prosperity. The island of São Tomé was the world's largest producer of cacao in 1908 and the crop is still the most important. An exile liberation movement was formed in 1953 after Portuguese landowners quelled labor riots by killing several hundred African workers.

The Portuguese revolution of 1974 brought the end of the overseas empire and the new Lisbon government transferred power to the liberation movement on July 12, 1975.

President Pinto da Costa's ruling party was defeated in multi-party elections in January 1991. A former prime minister and dissident Miguel Trovoada was elected president in March after the withdrawal of the two other candidates.

SAUDI ARABIA

Kingdom of Saudi Arabia

Ruler and Prime Minister: King Fahd bin 'Abdulaziz (1982)

Area: 865,000 sq mi. (2,250,070 sq km)

Population (est. mid-1993): 17,500,000 (average annual rate of natural increase: 3.2%); birth rate: 39/1000; infant mortality rate: 65/1000; density per square mile: 21

Capital: Riyadh; **Largest cities (est. 1980):** Riyadh, 1,500,000; Jeddah, 1,500,000; Makkah (Mecca,) 750,000; Damman, 350,000; **Monetary unit:** Riyal; **Language:** Arabic, English widely spoken; **Religion:** Islam, 100%; **National name:** Al-Mamlaka al-'Arabiya as-Sa'udiya; **Literacy rate:** 62%

Economic summary: Gross domestic product (1991 est.): $104 billion; $5,800 per capita; real growth rate 1.5%; inflation 3%; unemployment (1989 est.): 0%. Arable land: 1%. Principal agricultural products: dates, grains, livestock, wheat, fish, flowers. Labor force: 4,200,000; about 45% are foreign workers; 28% in industry and oil. Major industrial products: petroleum, cement, plastic products, steel, packaged goods. Natural resources: oil, natural gas, iron ore. Exports: $44.3 billion (f.o.b., 1990): petroleum and petroleum products. Imports: $21.5 billion (f.o.b., 1990): manufactured goods, transport equipment, construction materials, processed food. Major trading partners: U.S., Germany, Great Britain and other Western European countries, South Korea, Taiwan, Japan.

Geography. Saudi Arabia occupies most of the Arabian Peninsula, with the Red Sea and the Gulf of Aqaba to the west, the Arabian Gulf to the east. Neighboring countries are Jordan, Iraq, Kuwait, Qatar, the United Arab Emirates, the Sultanate of Oman, Yemen, and Bahrain, connected to the Saudi mainland by a causeway.

A narrow coastal plain on the Red Sea rims a mountain range that spans the length of the western coastline. These mountains gradually rise in elevation from north to south. East of these mountains is a massive plateau which slopes gently downward to ward the Arabian Gulf. Part of this plateau is covered by the world's largest continuous sand desert, the Rub Al-Khali, or Empty Quarter. Saudi Arabia's oil region lies primarily in the eastern province along the Arabian Gulf, but significant recent discoveries have also been made in the interior south of Riyadh.

Government. Saudi Arabia is a monarchy based on the Sharia (Islamic law), as revealed in the Koran (the holy book) and the Hadith (teachings and sayings of the prophet Mohammed). A Council of Ministers was formed in 1953, which acts as a Cabinet under the leadership of the King. There are 21 Ministries.

Royal and ministerial decrees account for most of the promulgated legislation, treaties, and conventions. There are no political parties.

In March 1992 King Fahd announced a new constitution that called for the creation of a 60-member Consultative Council to propose and review laws. The Cabinet, composed largely of members of the Saudi royal family, passes laws.

History. Mohammed united the Arabs in the 7th century, and his followers, led by the caliphs, founded a great empire, with its capital at Medina. Later, the caliphate capital was transferred to Damascus and then Baghdad, but Arabia retained its importance because of the holy cities of Mecca and Medina. In the 16th and 17th centuries, the Turks established at least nominal rule over much of Arabia, and in the middle of the 18th century, it was divided into separate principalities.

The Kingdom of Saudi Arabia is almost entirely the creation of King Ibn Saud (1882–1953). A descendant of earlier Wahabi rulers, he seized Riyadh, the capital of Nejd, in 1901 and set himself up as leader of the Arab nationalist movement. By 1906 he had established Wahabi dominance in Nejd. He conquered Hejaz in 1924–25, consolidating it and Nejd into a dual kingdom in 1926. In 1932, Hejaz and Nejd became a single kingdom, which was officially named Saudi Arabia. A year later the region of Asir was incorporated into the kingdom.

Oil was discovered in 1936, and commercial production began during World War II. Saudi Arabia was neutral until nearly the end of the war, but it was permitted to be a charter member of the United Nations. The country joined the Arab League in 1945 and took part in the 1948–49 war against Israel.

On Ibn Saud's death in 1953, his eldest son, Saud, began an 11-year reign marked by an increasing hostility toward the radical Arabism of Egypt's Gamal Abdel Nasser. In 1964, the ailing Saud was deposed and replaced by the Premier, Crown Prince Faisal, who gave vocal support but no military help to Egypt in the 1967 Mideast war.

Faisal's assassination by a deranged kinsman in 1975 shook the Middle East, but failed to alter his kingdom's course. His successor was his brother, Prince Khalid. Khalid gave influential support to Egypt during negotiations on Israeli withdrawal from the Sinai desert.

King Khalid died of a heart attack June 13, 1982, and was succeeded by his half-brother, Prince Fahd bin 'Abdulaziz, 60, who had exercised the real power throughout Khalid's reign. King Fahd, a pro-Western modernist, chose his 58-year-old half-brother, Abdullah, as Crown Prince.

Saudi Arabia and the smaller, oil-rich Arab states on the Persian Gulf, fearful that they might become Ayatollah Ruhollah Khomeini's next targets if Iran conquered Iraq, made large financial contributions to the Iraqi war effort. They began being dragged into the conflict themselves in the spring of 1984, when Iraq and Iran extended their ground war to attacks on Gulf shipping. First, Iraq attacked tankers loading at Iran's Kharg Island terminal with air-to-ground missiles, then Iran struck back at tankers calling at Saudi Arabia and other Arab countries.

At the same time, cheating by other members of the Organization of Petroleum Exporting Countries, competition from nonmember oil producers, and conservation efforts by consuming nations combined to drive down the world price of oil. Saudi Arabia has one-third of all known oil reserves, but falling demand and rising production outside OPEC combined to reduce its oil revenues from $120 billion in 1980 to $43 billion in 1984 to less the $25 billion in 1985, threatening the country with domestic unrest and undermining its influence in the Gulf area.

Saudi Arabia broke relations with Iran in April 1988 over the issues of riots by Iranian pilgrims in Mecca in July, 1987 and Iranian naval attacks on Saudi vessels in the Persian Gulf.

Fearing the spread of Islamic fundamentalism the government in 1993 passed measures to tighten the political system and crack down on dissidents.

SENEGAL

Republic of Senegal
President: Abdou Diouf (1981)
Area: 75,954 sq mi. (196,722 sq km)
Population (est. mid-1993): 7,900,000 (average annual rate of natural increase: 2.7%); birth rate: 44/1000; infant mortality rate: 84/1000; density per square mile: 107
Capital and largest city (1988): Dakar, 1,490,450; **Monetary unit:** Franc CFA; **Ethnic groups:** Wolofs, Sereres, Peuls, Tukulers, and others; **Languages:** French (official); Wolof, Serer, other ethnic dialects; **Religions:** Islam, 92%; indigenous, 6%; Christian, 2%; **National name:** République du Sénegal; **Literacy rate:** 38%
Economic summary: Gross domestic product (1990): $5 billion; $615 per capita; real growth rate 3.6%; inflation 2%; unemployment (1987) 3.5%. Arable land: 27%. Principal agricultural products: peanuts, millet, corn, rice, sorghum. Labor force: 2,509,000; 77% subsistence agriculture workers. Major industrial products: processed food, phosphates, refined petroleum, cement, and fish. Natural resources: fish, phosphate, iron ore. Exports: $814 million (f.o.b., 1990 est.): peanuts, phosphate rock, canned fish, petroleum products. Imports: $1.05 billion (c.i.f., 1990 est.): foodstuffs, consumer goods, machinery, transport equipment, petroleum. Major trading partners: U.S., Western European countries, African neighbors, Japan, China, India.

Geography. The capital of Senegal, Dakar, is the westernmost point in Africa. The country, slightly smaller than South Dakota, surrounds Gambia on three sides and is bordered on the north by Mauritania, on the east by Mali, and on the south by Guinea and Guinea-Bissau.

Senegal is mainly a low-lying country, with a semi-desert area in the north and northeast and forests in the southwest. The largest rivers include the Senegal in the north and the Casamance in the south tropical climate region.

Government. There is a National Assembly of 120 members, elected every five years. There is universal suffrage and a constitutional guarantee of equality before the law.

History. The Portuguese had some stations on the banks of the Senegal River in the 15th century, and the first French settlement was made at Saint-Louis about 1650. The British took parts of Senegal at various times, but the French gained possession in 1840 and organized the Sudan as a territory in 1904. In 1946, together with other parts of French West Africa, Senegal became part of the French Union. On June 20, 1960, it became an independent republic federated with the Sudanese Republic in the Mali Federation, from which it withdrew two months later.

In 1973, Senegal joined with six other states to create the West African Economic Community.

In elections of February 21, 1993 President Diouf was reelected although the results were not made official for three weeks pending the opposition's charge of vote rigging.

SEYCHELLES

Republic of Seychelles
President: France-Albert René (1977)
Area: 175 sq mi. (453 sq km)
Population (est. mid-1993): 100,000 (average annual rate of natural increase: 1.7%); birth rate: 25/1000; infant mortality rate: 13/1000; density per square mile: 691
Capital: Victoria, 24,000; **Monetary unit:** Seychelles rupee; **Languages:** English and French (official); Creole; **Religions:** Roman Catholic, 90%; Anglican, 8%; **Member of Commonwealth of Nations; Literacy rate:** 58%
Economic summary: Gross domestic product (1991 est.): $350 million; $5,200 per capita; real growth rate –4.5%; inflation (1990 est.) 1.8%; unemployment (1987) 9%. Arable land: 4%. Principal agricultural products: vanilla, coconuts, cinnamon. Labor force: 27,700; 31% in industry and commerce. Major industrial products: processed coconut and vanilla, coir rope. Exports: $40 million (f.o.b., 1990 est.): cinnamon, fish, copra. Imports: $186 million (f.o.b., 1990 est.): food, tobacco, manufactured goods, machinery, petroleum products, transport equipment. Major trading partners: U.K., France, Japan, Pakistan, Reunion, South Africa.

Geography. Seychelles consists of an archipelago of about 100 islands in the Indian Ocean northeast of Madagascar. The principal islands are Mahé (55 sq mi.; 142 sq km), Praslin (15 sq mi.; 38 sq km), and La Digue (4 sq mi.; 10 sq km). The Aldabra, Farquhar, and Desroches groups are included in the territory of the republic.

Government. Seized from France by Britain in 1810, the Seychelles Islands remained a colony until June 29, 1976. The state is an independent republic within the Commonwealth.

On June 5, 1977, Prime Minister Albert René ousted the islands' first President, James Mancham, suspending the Constitution and the 25-member National Assembly. Mancham, whose "lavish spending" and flamboyance were cited by René in seizing power, charged that Soviet influence was at work. The new president denied this and, while more left than his predecessor, pledged to keep the Seychelles in the nonaligned group of countries.

An unsuccessful attempted coup against René attracted international attention when a group of 50 South African mercenaries posing as rugby players attacked the Victoria airport on Nov. 25, 1981. They caused extensive damage before they hijacked an Air India plane and returned to South Africa, where all but five were freed. Only after widespread international protest did the Pretoria government, which denied any responsibility for the attack, reverse the decision and order all the mercenaries tried as hijackers.

Despite the president's continued support for a one-party state during 1990, in December 1991 the ruling party approved adopting a multiparty system without specifying a date for elections.

An election was held in July 1992 for members of a commission to write a new constitution. 14 of the 23 seats went to the president's Seychelles People's Progressive Party. The draft constitution that emerged, however, was defeated in a referendum in November, failing to get the 60% of the vote needed for adoption. Opposition forces and the Catholic Church had urged a rejection.

SIERRA LEONE

Republic of Sierra Leone
President: Capt. Valentine Strasser (1992)
Area: 27,700 sq mi. (71,740 sq km)
Population (est. mid-1993): 4,500,000 (average annual rate of natural increase: 2.6%); birth rate: 48/1000;

infant mortality rate: 148/1000; density per square mile: 163

Capital and largest city (1985): Freetown, 469,776; **Monetary unit:** Leone; **Languages:** English (official), Mende, Temne, Krio; **Religions:** Islam, 30%; indigenous, 30%; Christian, 10%; other, 30%; **Member of Commonwealth of Nations; Literacy rate:** 21%

Economic summary: Gross domestic product (FY 1991 est.): $1.4 billion; $330 per capita; real growth rate 3%; inflation (1990) 110%. Arable land: 25%; principal agricultural products: coffee, cocoa, palm kernels, rice. Labor force: 1,369,000 (est.); 65% in agriculture. Major industrial products: diamonds, bauxite, rutile, beverages, cigarettes, textiles, footwear. Natural resources: diamonds, bauxite, iron ore. Exports: $138 million (f.o.b., 1990): diamonds, rutile, bauxite, cocoa, coffee. Imports: $146 million (c.i.f., 1990): food, petroleum, products, capital goods. Major trading partners: U.K., U.S., Western European countries, Japan.

Geography. Sierra Leone, on the Atlantic Ocean in West Africa, is half the size of Illinois. Guinea, in the north and east, and Liberia, in the south, are its neighbors.

Mangrove swamps lie along the coast, with wooded hills and a plateau in the interior. The eastern region is mountainous.

Government. Sierra Leone became an independent nation on April 27, 1961, and declared itself a republic on April 19, 1971.

Sierra Leone became a one party state under the aegis of the All People's Congress Party in April 1978.

History. The coastal area of Sierra Leone was ceded to English settlers in 1788 as a home for blacks discharged from the British armed forces and also for runaway slaves who had found asylum in London. The British protectorate over the hinterland was proclaimed in 1896.

After elections in 1967, the British Governor-General replaced Sir Albert Margai, head of SLPP, which had held power since independence, with Dr. Stevens, head of APC, as prime minister. The Army took over the government; then another coup in April 1968 restored civilian rule and put the military leaders in jail.

A coup attempt early in 1971 by the army commander was apparently foiled by loyal army officers, but the then Prime Minister Stevens called in troops of neighboring Guinea's army, under a 1970 mutual defense pact, to guard his residence. After perfunctorily blaming the U.S. for the coup attempt, Stevens switched Governors-General, changed the Constitution, and ended up with a republic, of which he was first president. Dr. Stevens' picked successor, Major-General Joseph Saidu Momoh was elected unopposed on Oct. 1, 1985.

Rebel soldiers in April 1992 toppled the government, voicing support for democracy. A few days later the ruling junta arrested their leader, placing in charge their second-in-command.

SINGAPORE

Republic of Singapore

Prime Minister: Goh Chok Tong (1990)

Area: 246.7 sq mi. (639 sq km)

Population (est. mid-1993): 2,800,000 (average annual rate of natural increase: 1.3%); birth rate: 17/1000; infant mortality rate: 5.5/1000; density per square mile: 11;982

Capital (1990): Singapore, 2,690,100; **Monetary unit:** Singapore dollar; **Languages:** Malay, Chinese (Mandarin), Tamil, English; **Religions:** Islam, Christian, Buddhist, Hindu, Taoist; **Member of Commonwealth of Nations; Literacy rate:** 91%

Economic summary: Gross domestic product (1991 est.): $38.3 billion; $13,900 per capita; real growth rate 6.5%; inflation 3.4%; unemployment 1.5%. Arable land: 4%. Principal agricultural products: poultry, rubber, copra, vegetables, fruits. Labor force (1990): 1,619,600; financial, business, other services 30.2%; manufacturing 28.4%; commerce 22%. Major industries: petroleum refining, ship repair, electronics, financial and business services, biotechnology. Exports: $57.8 billion (f.o.b., 1991 est.): petroleum products, rubber, manufactured goods, electrical and electronics, computers and computer peripherals. Imports: $65.8 billion (c.i.f., 1991 est.): machinery and equipment, manufactured goods, crude petroleum and petroleum products. Major trading partners: U.S., Malaysia, Japan, Hong Kong.

Geography. The Republic of Singapore consists of the main island of Singapore, off the southern tip of the Malay Peninsula between the South China Sea and the Indian Ocean, and 58 nearby islands.

There are extensive mangrove swamps extending inland from the coast, which is broken by many inlets.

Government. There is a Cabinet, headed by the Prime Minister, and a Parliament of 81 members elected by universal suffrage.

History. Singapore, founded in 1819 by Sir Stamford Raffles, became a separate crown colony of Britain in 1946, when the former colony of the Straits Settlements was dissolved. The other two settlements—Penang and Malacca—were transferred to the Union of Malaya, and the small island of Labuan was transferred to North Borneo. The Cocos (or Keeling) Islands were transferred to Australia in 1955 and Christmas Island in 1958.

Singapore attained full internal self-government in 1959. On Sept. 16, 1963, it joined Malaya, Sabah (North Borneo), and Sarawak in the Federation of Malaysia. It withdrew from the Federation on Aug. 9, 1965, and proclaimed itself a republic the next month.

A law of January 1991 expanded the powers of the presidency. In August the ruling People's Action Party won 36 of the 40 contested parliamentary seats.

The government announced in 1992 that monies would be distributed on a priority basis to those wards where a majority had voted for the ruling party. The sale of chewing gum was also banned.

SLOVAKIA

Republic of Slovakia

President: Michal Kovac (1993)

Prime Minister: Vladimir Meciar (1992)

Area: 18,917 sq mi. (48,995 sq km)

Population (est. mid-1993): 5,300,000; 90% Slovaks, other: Hungarians, Czechs. (Average annual rate of natural increase: 0.5%); birth rate: 15/1000; infant mortality rate: 13.2/1000; density per square mile: 284

Capital and largest city (1991): Bratislava, 441,453. Other large city (1990): Kosice, 234,840; **Monetary unit:** Slovak Korena; **Language:** Slovak, also Czech, Hungarian; **Religion:** Roman Catholic major, other religions: Protestant, Orthodox Jewish; **Literacy rate:** 99%

Economic summary: Per capita income (est. 1990)[1]: $7,700; real growth rate: –2.9%. Important industries are iron and nonferrous mining, metal processing, and shipbuilding. Other industries are construction materials, consumer appliances, and leather goods. Major agricultural products: grains, potatoes, sugar beets, fruit, vegetables, forestry. Livestock: pigs, cattle, poultry, sheep. Land use: 37% forest and woodland, 13% meadows and pastures, 1% permanent crops, 9% other.

1. 1990 data for the former united Czechoslovakia.

Geography. Slovakia is bordered by Poland in the north, Ukraine in the east, Hungary in the south, Austria in the southwest, and the Czech Republic in the west. The land has rugged mountains, rich in mineral resources, with vast forests and pastures. Southern Slovakia is a river island called "Zitny Ostrov," with fertile soil. Slovakia is about twice the size of the state of Maryland.

Government. A federal republic. The National Council (parliament) has 150 members. The coalition government is dominated by the Movement for a Democratic Slovakia (MDS) and Prime Minister Meciar is the party chairman.

History. Present day Slovakia was settled by Slavic Slovaks about the 5th century A.D. They were politically united in the Moravian empire in the 9th century. In 907, the Germans and the Magyars conquered the Moravian state and the Slovaks fell under Hungarian control from the 10th century up until 1918.

When the Hapsburg state collapsed in 1918 following World War I, the Slovaks joined the Czech lands of Bohemia, Moravia, and part of Silesia to form the new joint state of Czechoslovakia.

In March 1939, Germany occupied Czechoslovakia, established a German "protectorate," and created a puppet state out of Slovakia with Monsignor Josef Tiso as premier. The country was liberated from the Germans by the Soviet army in the spring of 1945, and Slovakia was restored to its pre-war status and rejoined to a new Czechoslovakian state.

After the Communist party took power in February 1948, Slovakia was again subjected to a centralized Czech-dominated government and antagonism between the two republics developed. On January 1969, the nation became the Slovak Socialist Republic of Czechoslovakia.

Nearly 42 years of Communist rule for Slovakia ended when Vaclav Havel became president of Czechoslovakia in 1989 and democratic political reform began. However, with the demise of Communist power, a strong Slovak nationalist movement resurfaced and the rival relationship between the two states increased.

By the end of 1991, tensions heightened between Slovak and Czech political leaders following a debate over a Declaration of Slovak Sovereignty proclaimed by the Slovak parliament. Various attempts to resolve the issue by both parties failed. A crisis developed over whether the Czech and Slovak republics should continue to coexist within the federal structure or divide into two independent states. A draft treaty between both republics "to live in a common state" was rejected by the Slovak parliament in February 1992.

The results of the general election in June 1992 failed to affirm the continuing coexistence of the Czech and Slovak Republics within a federal state and resulted in the Czech and Slovak political leaders agreeing to separate their nations into two fully independent republics. The Republic of Slovakia came into existence on January 1, 1993. The parliament in February elected Michael Kovac president.

SLOVENIA

Republic of Slovenia
President: Milan Kucan
Prime Minister: Janez Drnovsek
Area: 7,819 sq mi. (20,251 sq km)
Population (est. mid-1993): 2,000,000. Major ethnic groups: 87.6% Slovenes, 2.7% Croats, 2.4% Serbs, 1.4% Muslims; (average annual rate of natural increase: 0.3%); birth rate: 13/1000; infant mortality rate: 8.9/1000; density per square mile: 256
Capital (est. 1991): Ljubljana, 323,291. Other large city: Maribor, 106,113; **Monetary unit:** Slovenian Tolar; **Languages:** Slovenian; most can also speak Serbo-Croatian; **Religions:** predominantly Roman Catholic; **Literacy rate:** est. 96%
Economic summary: (1991 est.) Gross domestic product: $21 billion; $10,700 per capita; real growth rate –10%; inflation 15–20%; unemployment (April 1992): 10%. Principal products are corn, rye, oats, potatoes, fruit, livestock raising, and forestry. Mineral resources include coal, iron, and mercury. Major manufactured products are automobiles, iron and steel, cement, chemicals, and textiles. Exports: $4,120 million (f.o.b., 1990): machinery and transport equipment, 38%; other manufactured goods, 44%; chemicals, 9%; food and live animals, 4.6%; raw materials, 3%. Imports: $4,679 million (c.i.f., 1990): machinery and transport equipment, 35%; other manufactured goods, 26.7%; chemicals, 14.5%; raw materials, 9.4%; fuels and lubricants, 7%. Trading partners: Germany, U.S., Hungary, Austria, Italy, former Yugoslavia and U.S.S.R. republics.

Geography: Slovenia occupies an area about the size of the state of Massachusetts. It borders Austria on the north, Hungary in the northeast, the Republic of Croatia in the south, and Italy and the Adriatic Sea in the west. It is largely a mountainous republic and almost half of the land is forested, with hilly plains spread across the central and eastern regions. Mount Triglav, the highest peak, rises to 9,393 ft (2,864 m).

Government: A parliamentary democracy with two legislative houses consisting of an 80-member National Assembly and 40-member State Council.

History: The Slovenes were a south-Slavic group that settled in the region during the 6th century A.D. During the 7th century, they established the Slavic state of Samu which owed its allegiance to the Avars, who dominated the Hungarian plain until Charlemagne defeated them in the late 8th century.

In the 11th century, Slovenia was a separate province of the Kingdom of Hungary. When the Hungarians were defeated by the Turks in 1526, Hungary accepted Austrian Hapsburg rule in order to escape Turkish domination. Thus, Slovenia and Croatia became part of the Austro-Hungarian kingdom when the dual-monarchy was established in 1857.

After 1848, nationalism was revived in Slovenia and following the defeat and collapse of Austria-Hungary in World War I, Slovenia declared its independence. It formally joined with Montenegro, Serbia, and Croatia on Dec. 4, 1918, to form the new nation called the Kingdom of the Serbs, Croats, and Slovenes. The name was later changed to Yugoslavia in 1929.

During World War II, Germany occupied Yugoslavia and Slovenia was divided among Germany, Italy, and Hungary. For the duration of the war many Slovenes fought a guerrilla warfare against the Nazis under the leadership of the Croatian-born communist re-sistance leader, Marshal Tito. After the final defeat of the Axis powers in 1945, Slovenia was again made into a republic of the newly established nation of Yugoslavia.

Slovenia declared its independence from Yugoslavia on June 25, 1991. The Serbian-dominated Yugoslavian army tried to keep Slovenia in line and some brief fighting took place, but the Yugoslavian army withdrew its forces and, unlike neighboring Croatia, Slovenia was able to maintain a peaceful status.

Elections in December 1992 gave the presidency to a former Communist. In January a coalition government was formed chiefly of former Communists.

SOLOMON ISLANDS

Sovereign: Queen Elizabeth II
Governor-General: Sir George Lepping (1988)
Prime Minister: Solomon Mamaloni (1989)
Area: 11,500 sq mi. (29,785 sq km)
Population (est. mid-1993): 300,000 (average annual rate of natural increase: 3.2%); birth rate: 39/1000; infant mortality rate: 44/1000; density per square mile: 32
Capital and largest city (986): Honiara (on Guadalcanal), 30,499; **Monetary unit:** Solomon Islands dollar; **Languages:** English, Pidgin, 80 other languages and dialects; **Religions:** Anglican; Roman Catholic; South Seas Evangelical; Seventh-Day Adventist, United (Methodist) Church, other Protestant; **Member of British Commonwealth; Literacy rate:** 30%
Economic summary: Gross domestic product (1990 est.): $200 million; $600 per capita; real growth rate 6%; inflation 10.2%. Arable land: 1%. Principal agricultural products: coconuts, palm oil, rice, cocoa, yams, pigs. Labor force (1984): 23,448; agriculture, forestry, fishing 32.4%; services 25%. Major industrial products: processed fish, copra. Natural resources: fish, timber, gold, bauxite. Exports: $67.3 million (f.o.b., 1990): fish, timber, copra, palm oil. Imports: $86 million (c.i.f., 1990): machinery and transport equipment, foodstuffs, fuel. Major trading partners: Japan, EEC, Australia, U.K., Thailand, Singapore.

Geography. Lying east of New Guinea, this island nation consists of the southern islands of the Solomon group: Guadalcanal, Malaita, Santa Isabel, San Cristóbal, Choiseul, New Georgia, Santa Cruz group, and numerous smaller islands.

Government. After 85 years of British rule, the Solomons achieved independence July 7, 1978. The Crown is represented by a Governor-General and legislative power is vested in a unicameral legislature of 38 members, led by the Prime Minister.

History. Discovered in 1567 by Alvaro de Mendana, the Solomons were not visited again for about 200 years. In 1886, Great Britain and Germany divided the islands between them. In 1914, Australian forces took over the German islands and the Solomons became an Australian mandate in 1920. In World War II, most of the islands were occupied by the Japanese. American forces landed on Guadalcanal on Aug. 7, 1942.

Mamaloni in 1990 revamped his government to include several opposition members and back benchers from his own party.

A border dispute with Papua New Guinea was the dominant political issue in 1992.

SOMALIA

Somali Democratic Republic
President: Ali Mahdi Mohammed (interim 1991)
Prime Minister: Omar Artan Qalib (1991)
Area: 246,199 sq mi. (637,655 sq km)
Population (est. mid-1993): 9,500,000 (average annual rate of natural increase: 3.1%); birth rate: 50/1000; infant mortality rate: 127/1000; density per square mile: 39
Capital and largest city (est. 1985): Mogadishu, 700,000; **Monetary unit:** Somali shilling; **Language:** Somali (official), Arabic, English, Italian; **Religion:** Islam (Sunni); **National name:** Al Jumhouriya As-Somalya al-Dimocradia; **Literacy rate:** 24%
Economic summary: Political turmoil in 1991–92 resulted in widespread famine and a substantial drop in economic output. Gross domestic product (1988): $1.7 billion; $210 per capita; –1.4% real growth rate. Arable land: 2%. Principal agricultural products: livestock, bananas, sorghum, cereals, sugar cane, maize. Labor force: 2,200,000; very few are skilled laborers. A few small industries: sugar refining, textiles, petroleum refining. Natural resources: uranium. Exports: livestock, skins and hides, bananas. Imports: textiles, foodstuffs, construction materials and equipment, petroleum products. Major trading partners: Saudi Arabia, Italy, U.S., U.K., Germany, Italy.

Geography. Somalia, situated in the Horn of Africa, lies along the Gulf of Aden and the Indian Ocean. It is bounded by Djibouti in the northwest, Ethiopia in the west, and Kenya in the southwest. In area it is slightly smaller than Texas.

Generally arid and barren, Somalia has two chief rivers, the Shebelle and the Juba.

Government. None. Last president was overthrown in January 1991 and Somalia was plunged into anarchy.

History. From the 7th to the 10th century, Arab and Persian trading posts were established along the coast of present-day Somalia. Nomadic tribes occupied the interior, occasionally pushing into Ethiopian territory. In the 16th century, Turkish rule extended to the northern coast and the Sultans of Zanzibar gained control in the south.

After British occupation of Aden in 1839, the Somali coast became its source of food. The French established a coaling station in 1862 at the site of Djibouti and the Italians planted a settlement in Eritrea. Egypt, which for a time claimed Turkish rights in the area, was succeeded by Britain. By 1920, a British protectorate and an Italian protectorate occupied what is now Somalia. The British ruled the entire area after 1941, with Italy returning in 1950 to serve as United Nations trustee for its former territory.

In mid-1960, Britain and Italy granted independence to their respective sectors, enabling the two to join as the Republic of Somalia on July 1. Somalia broke diplomatic relations with Britain in 1963 when the British granted the Somali-populated Northern Frontier District of Kenya to the Republic of Kenya.

On Oct. 15, 1969, President Abdi Rashid Ali Shermarke was assassinated and the army seized power, dissolving the legislature and arresting all government leaders. Maj. Gen. Mohamed Siad Barre, as President of a renamed Somali Democratic Republic, leaned heavily toward the U.S.S.R.

In 1977, Somalia openly backed rebels in the easternmost area of Ethiopia, the Ogaden desert, which had been seized by Ethiopia at the turn of the century.

Somalia acknowledged defeat in an eight-month war against the Ethiopians, having lost much of its 32,000-man army and most of its tanks and planes. In 1988, guerrillas in the north went on the offensive and threatened the northern regional capital.

President Siad Barre fled the country in late January 1991. His departure left Somalia in the hands of a number of clan-based guerrilla groups, none of which trust each other. The installation of Ali Mahdi Mohammed as interim president by the United Somali Congress, based on the Hawye clan, won the disapproval of other groups, who refused to attend a proposed conference in the capital.

U.S. troops were sent in to protect the delivery of food in December 1992. Somali leaders agreed in March 1993 to a compromise that called for a transitional national council, but the solidity of the agreement was unclear. In May the U.N. took control of the relief efforts from the U.S.

SOUTH AFRICA

Republic of South Africa
President: F.W. de Klerk (1989)
Area: 471,440 sq mi. (1,221,030 sq km)
Population (est. mid-1993): 39,000,000 (average annual rate of natural increase: 2.6%); birth rate: 34/1000; infant mortality rate: 51/1000; density per square mile: 83
Administrative capital: Pretoria; **Legislative capital:** Cape Town; **Judicial capital:** Bloemfontein; **Largest metropolitan areas:** Cape Peninsula (Cape Town and surroundings), 1,911,500; Johannesburg/Randburg, 1,609,500; East Rand (Springs, Germiston and surroundings), 1,038,000; Durban/Pinetown/Inanda, 982,075; Pretoria/Wonderboom/Shoshanguve, 822,900; **Monetary unit:** Rand; **Languages:** English, Afrikaans (official); Xhosa, Zulu, other African tongues; **Religions:** Christian; Hindu; Islam; **National name:** Republic of South Africa; **Literacy rate:** 76%
Economic summary: Gross domestic product (1991 est.): $104 billion; $2,600 per capita; –0.5% real growth rate; inflation (March 1992) 15.7%; unemployment (1991) 40%. Arable land: 11.59%. Principal agricultural products: corn, wool, wheat, sugar cane, fruits, vegetables. Labor force: 11,000,000; 34% in services, 30% agriculture, 29% industry and commerce. Major industrial products: gold, chromium, diamonds, assembled automobiles, machinery, textiles, iron and steel, chemicals, fertilizer. Natural resources: gold, diamonds, platinum, uranium, coal, iron ore, phosphates, manganese. Exports: $24 billion (f.o.b., 1991): gold, diamonds, minerals and metals, food, chemicals. Imports: $18.8 billion (c.i.f., 1991): motor vehicle parts, machinery, metals, chemicals, textiles, scientific instruments. Major trading partners: U.S., Germany, other E.C., Japan, U.K., Hong Kong.

Geography. South Africa, on the continent's southern tip, is washed by the Atlantic Ocean on the west and by the Indian Ocean on the south and east. Its neighbors are Namibia in the northwest, Zimbabwe and Botswana in the north, and Mozambique and Swaziland in the northeast. The kingdom of Lesotho forms an enclave within the southeastern part of South Africa. Bophuthatswana, Transkei, Ciskei, and Venda are independent states within South Africa, which occupies an area nearly three times that of California.

The country has a high interior plateau, or veld, nearly half of which averages 4,000 feet (1,219 m) in elevation.

There are no important mountain ranges, although the Great Escarpment, separating the veld from the coastal plain, rises to over 11,000 feet (3,350 m) in the Drakensberg Mountains in the east. The principal river is the Orange, rising in Lesotho and flowing westward for 1,300 miles (2,092 km) to the Atlantic.

The southernmost point of Africa is Cape Agulhas, located in Cape Province about 100 miles (161 km) southeast of the Cape of Good Hope.

Government. A new Constitution in 1984 replaced the unicameral legislature with a three-chamber Parliament; racially divided to provide for representation by whites, Indians, and coloreds (mixed race). A new office of Executive State President was created. An Electoral College, constituted of representatives from the three Parliamentary chambers, select the President.

In 1989, Frederick Willem de Klerk was elected State President. He stepped up constitutional reform which was initiated by this predecessor, P.W. Botha, and in February 1990 all outlawed political parties were unbanned including the South African Communist Party. All political prisoners, including African National Congress leader Nelson Mandela, were released.

By 1991, the last remaining laws supporting the infamous Apartheid policy, were scrapped. In December of 1991, multilateral negotiations were initiated to determine a new non-racial democratic constitution, based on universal franchise. Possible re-integration of the four nominally sovereign black states is one of the discussion points of the negotiation forum, commonly known as CODESA-Conference for a Democratic South Africa.

In April 1993, CODESA was reformed into the multi-party forum with 26 political organizations participating. Issues to be negotiated in the forum include transitional executive authority, an election commission, an election date, and a transitional constitution.

History. The Dutch East India Company landed the first settlers on the Cape of Good Hope in 1652, launching a colony that by the end of the 18th century numbered only about 15,000. Known as Boers or Afrikaners, speaking a Dutch dialect known as Afrikaans, the settlers as early as 1795 tried to establish an independent republic.

After occupying the Cape Colony in that year, Britain took permanent possession in 1814 at the end of the Napoleonic wars, bringing in 5,000 settlers. Anglicization of government and the freeing of slaves in 1833 drove about 12,000 Afrikaners to make the "great trek" north and east into African tribal territory, where they established the republics of the Transvaal and the Orange Free State.

The discovery of diamonds in 1867 and gold nine years later brought an influx of "outlanders" into the republics and spurred Cecil Rhodes to plot annexation. Rhodes's scheme of sparking an "outlander" rebellion to which an armed party under Leander Starr Jameson would ride to the rescue misfired in

1895, forcing Rhodes to resign as prime minister of the Cape colony. What British expansionists called the "inevitable" war with the Boers eventually broke out on Oct. 11, 1899.

The defeat of the Boers in 1902 led in 1910 to the Union of South Africa, composed of four provinces, the two former republics and the old Cape and Natal colonies. Louis Botha, a Boer, became the first Prime Minister.

Jan Christiaan Smuts brought the nation into World War II on the Allied side against Nationalist opposition, and South Africa became a charter member of the United Nations in 1945, but refused to sign the Universal Declaration of Human Rights. Apartheid—racial separation—dominated domestic politics as the Nationalists gained power and imposed greater restrictions on Bantus, Coloreds, and Asians.

Afrikaner hostility to Britain triumphed in 1961 with the declaration on May 31 of the Republic of South Africa and the severing of ties with the Commonwealth. Nationalist Prime Minister H. F. Verwoerd's government in 1963 asserted the power to restrict freedom of those who opposed rigid racial laws. Three years later, amid increasing racial tension and criticism from the outside world, Verwoerd was assassinated. His Nationalist successor, Balthazar J. Vorster, launched a campaign of conciliation toward conservative black African states, offering development loans and trade concessions.

A scandal led to Vorster's resignation on June 4, 1978. Pieter W. Botha succeeded him as Prime Minister, and became President on Sept. 14, 1984.

Elections on May 7, 1987, increased the power of Botha's Nationalist party while enabling the far-right Conservative Party to replace the liberal Progressives as the official opposition. The results of the whites-only vote indicated a strong conservative reaction against Botha's policy of limited reform.

A stroke led Botha to step down as leader of his party in 1989 in favor of Frederick de Klerk. De Klerk has accelerated the pace of reform. He unbanned the African National Congress, the principal anti-apartheid organization, and released Nelson Mandela, the ANC deputy chief, after 27 1/2 years imprisonment. Negotiations between the government and the ANC have commenced.

On June 5, 1991 the parliament scrapped the country's apartheid laws concerning property ownership. On June 17 the parliament did the same for the Population Registration Act of 1950, which classified all South Africans at birth by race.

A referendum in March 1992 gave the president a mandate to continue negotiations with blacks on ending minority rule.

In February 1993 the ANC approved a plan that would allow minority parties to participate in the government for five years after the end of white rule. Also in February the first nonwhites entered the cabinet in an apparent bid to broaden the base of the ruling National Party. The first universal elections are expected by April 1994.

BOPHUTHATSWANA

Republic of Bophuthatswana
President: Kgosi Lucas Mangope (1977)
Area: 15,573 sq mi. (40,333 sq km)
Population (est. 1991): 2,002,000 (average annual growth rate: 2.8%); **Density per square mile:** 83.5
Capital: Mmabatho; **Largest city (est. 1987):** Mabopane, 100,000; **Monetary unit:** South African rand; **Languages:** Setswana, English, Afrikaans; **Religions:** Methodist, Lutheran, Anglican, Presbyterian, Dutch Reformed, Roman Catholic, A.M.E.

Geography. Bophuthatswana consists of six discontinuous areas within the boundaries of South Africa. Most of them share a common border with Botswana.

Government. The republic has a 108-member Legislative Assembly, three quarters of whom are elected and the other 24 nominated by regional authorities. President Mangope's Democratic Party is the majority party.

History. Bophuthatswana was given independence by South Africa on Dec. 6, 1977, following Transkei as the second "homeland" to opt for independence. The new state and Transkei are recognized only by South Africa and each other.

Mangope, as chief minister in the pre-independence period, sought linkage of the seven units into a consolidated area, and has succeeded because Marico Corridor and adjoining farmers have been added and many more farms will be released. A second issue, the citizenship of Batswana in South Africa who wished to remain South African nationals, was settled by enabling them to have citizenship in South African homelands not yet independent.

About two-thirds of the population of Bophuthatswana live permanently in Bophuthatswana and thousands commute daily to South Africa.

Economy. Bophuthatswana is richer than many other South African homelands, as it has more than half of the republic's platinum deposits. All foreign trade is included with South Africa's, and it is economically interdependent at present with that country.

CISKEI

Republic of Ciskei
Head of State: Brig. Gen. Oupa Gqozo (1990)
Area: 3,282 sq mi. (8,500 sq km)
Population (est. 1991): 862,000; **Density per square mile:** 205.7
Capital (est. 1980): Zwelitsha, 30,750; **Largest city (1986):** Mdantsane, 242,823; **Monetary unit:** South African rand; **Languages:** Xhosa (official) and English; **Religions:** Methodist, Lutheran, Anglican, and Bantu Christian

Geography. Ciskei is surrounded by South Africa on three sides, with the Indian Ocean on the south. From a subtropical coastal strip, the land rises through grasslands to the mountainous escarpment that edges the South African interior plateau.

Government. Ruled by a military council installed after Gen Oupa Gqozo seized power in a March 1990 coup. South Africa's State President retains the power to legislate by proclamation and has veto power over the budget.

History. Oral tradition ascribes the origin of the Cape Nguni peoples to the central lakes area of Africa. They arrived in what is now Ciskei in the mid-17th century. White settlers from the Cape Colony first entered the territory a century later, but the Dutch East India Colony sought unsuccessfully to discourage white penetration. Nine wars between whites and the inhabitants, by now known as Xhosas, occurred between 1779 and 1878.

A Ciskeian territorial authority was established in 1961, with 84 chiefs and an executive council exercising limited self-government. In 1972, 20 elected members were added to the legislative assembly and a chief minister and six cabinet members elected by the assembly to function as an executive.

A proposed Constitution was approved by referendum on Oct. 30, 1980, and independence ceremonies held on Dec. 4. No government outside South Africa recognized the new state.

Two coup attacks were suppressed in 1991 leading South Africa to station some troops of its own there.

Economy. A subsistence agricultural economy has been superseded by commuter and migratory labor, which accounted for 64% of national income in 1977. There is some light industry and a potential for exploitation of limestone and other minerals.

TRANSKEI

Republic of Transkei
President: Chief Tutor N. Ndamase (1986)
Head of Military Council: Maj. Gen. Bantu Holomisa (1987)
Area: 15,831 sq mi. (41,002 sq km)
Population (est. 1991): 3,373,000 (growth rate: 2.2%); **Density per square mile:** 151.6
Capital (1989): Umtata, 57,796; **Monetary unit:** South African rand; **Languages:** English, Xhosa, Southern Sotho; **Religions:** Christian, 66%; tribal, 24%
Economic summary: Gross domestic product: $150 million. Per capita income: $86. Principal agricultural products: tea, corn, sorghum, dry beans. Major industrial products: timber, textiles. Natural resource: timber. Exports: timber, tea, sacks. Imports: foodstuffs, machines, equipment. Major trading partner: South Africa.

Geography. Transkei occupies three discontinuous enclaves within southeast South Africa that add up to twice the size of Massachusetts. It has a 270-mile (435 km) coastline on the Indian Ocean. The capital, Umtala, is connected by rail to the South African port of East London, 100 miles (161 km) to the southwest.

Government. Transkei was granted independence by South Africa as of Oct. 26, 1976. A constitution called for organization of a parliament composed of 77 chiefs and 75 elected members, with a ceremonial president and executive power in the hands of a prime minister.

The Organization of African States and the chairman of the United Nations Special Committee Against Apartheid denounced the new state as a sham and urged governments not to recognize it.

History. British rule was established over the Transkei region between 1866 and 1894, and the Transkeian Territories were formed in 1903. Under the Native Land Act of 1913, the Territories were reserved for black occupation. In 1963, Transkei was given internal self-government and a legislature that elected Paramount Chief Kaiser Matanzima as Chief Minister, a post he retained in elections in 1968 and 1973. Instability led to a coup in Dec. 1987.

Economy. Some 60% of Transkei is cultivated, producing corn, wheat, beans, and sorghum. Grazing is important. Some light industry has been established.

VENDA

Republic of Venda
Chairman of the Council of National Unity: Col. Gabriel Mutheiwana Ramushwana (1990)
Area: 2,510 sq mi. (6,500 sq km)
Population (est. 1991): 529,000 (average annual growth rate: 2.4%); **Density per square mile:** 214.5
Capital and largest city (1985): Thohoyandou, 10,166; **Monetary unit:** South African rand; **Languages:** Venda, English, Afrikaans; **Religions:** Christian, tribal
Economic summary: Gross domestic product: $156 million. Per capita income: $312. Principal agricultural products: meat, tea, fruit, sisal, corn. Major industrial products: timber, graphite, magnetite.

Geography. Venda is composed of two noncontiguous territories in northeast South Africa with a total area of about half that of Connecticut. It is mountainous but fertile, well-watered land, with a climate ranging from tropical to subtropical.

Government. The third of South Africa's homelands to be granted independence, Venda became a separate republic on Sept. 13, 1979, unrecognized by any government other than South Africa and its sister homelands, Transkei and Bophuthatswana. The President is popularly elected. An 84-seat legislature is half elected, half appointed.

History. The first European reached Venda in 1816, but the isolation of the area prevented its involvement in the wars of the 19th century between blacks and whites and with other tribes. Venda came under South African administration after the Boer War in 1902. Limited home rule was granted in 1962. Chief Patrick R. Mphephu, leader of one of the 27 tribes that historically made up the Venda nation, became Chief Minister of the interim government in 1973 and President upon independence in 1979. There has been a military regime in power since April 5, 1990.

SPAIN

Kingdom of Spain
Ruler: King Juan Carlos I (1975)
Prime Minister: Felipe González Márquez (1982)
Area: 194,884 sq mi. (504,750 km)[1]
Population (est. mid-1993): 39,100,000 (average annual growth rate: 0.1%); birth rate: 10/1000; infant mortality rate: 7.8/1000; density per square mile: 203
Capital: Madrid; **Largest cities (est. 1990):** Madrid, 3,120,732; Barcelona, 1,707,286; Valencia, 758,738; Seville, 678,218; **Monetary unit:** Peseta; **Languages:** Spanish, Basque, Catalan, Galician; **Religion:** Roman Catholic, 99%; **National name:** Reino de España; **Literacy rate:** 97%
Economic summary: Gross domestic product (1991 est.): $487.5 billion; $12,400 per capita; real growth rate 2.5%; inflation 5.9%; unemployment 16%. Arable land: 31%. Principal agricultural products: cereals, vegetables, citrus fruits, wine, olives and olive oil, livestock. Labor force (1988): 14,621,000: services 53%; 24% in industry. Major industrial products: processed foods, textiles, footwear, petro-chemicals, steel, automobiles, ships. Natural resources: coal, lignite, water power, uranium, mercury, pyrites, fluorospar, gypsum, iron ore, zinc, lead, tungsten, copper. Exports: $60.1 billion (f.o.b., 1991): foodstuffs, live animals, wood,

footwear, machinery, chemicals. Imports: $93.1 billion (c.i.f., 1990): machinery and transportation equipment, chemicals, petroleum, timber, iron, steel. Major trading partners: Western European nations, U.S., Middle Eastern countries. Illicit drugs: Key European gateway country for Latin American cocaine entering the European market.

1. Including the Balearic and Canary Islands.

Geography. Spain occupies 85% of the Iberian Peninsula in southwestern Europe, which it shares with Portugal; France is to the northeast, separated by the Pyrenees. The Bay of Biscay lies to the north, the Atlantic Ocean to the west, and the Mediterranean Sea to the south and east: Africa is less than 10 miles (16 km) south at the Strait of Gibraltar.

A broad central plateau slopes to the south and east, crossed by a series of mountain ranges and river valleys.

Principal rivers are the Ebro in the northeast, the Tajo in the central region, and the Guadalquivir in the south.

Off Spain's east coast in the Mediterranean are the Balearic Islands (1,936 sq mi.; 5,014 sq km), the largest of which is Majorca. Sixty miles (97 km) west of Africa are the Canary Islands (2,808 sq mi.; 7,273 sq km).

Government. A parliamentary monarchy.

The Cortes, or Parliament, consists of a Chamber of Deputies of 350 members and a Senate of 208, all elected by universal suffrage.

History. Spain, originally inhabited by Celts, Iberians, and Basques, became a part of the Roman Empire in 206 B.C., when it was conquered by Scipio Africanus. In A.D. 412, the barbarian Visigothic leader Ataulf crossed the Pyrenees and ruled Spain, first in the name of the Roman emperor and then independently. In 711, the Moslems under Tariq entered Spain from Africa and within a few years completed the subjugation of the country. In 732, the Franks, led by Charles Martel, defeated the Moslems near Poitiers, thus preventing the further expansion of Islam in southern Europe. Internal dissension of Spanish Islam invited a steady Christian conquest from the north.

Aragon and Castile were the most important Spanish states from the 12th to the 15th century, consolidated by the marriage of Ferdinand II and Isabella I in 1469. The last Moslem stronghold, Granada, was captured in 1492. Roman Catholicism was established as the official state religion and the Jews (1492) and the Moslems (1502) expelled.

In the era of exploration, discovery, and colonization, Spain amassed tremendous wealth and a vast colonial empire through the conquest of Peru by Pizarro (1532–33) and of Mexico by Cortés (1519–21). The Spanish Hapsburg monarchy became for a time the most powerful in the world.

In 1588, Philip II sent his Invincible Armada to invade England, but its destruction cost Spain its supremacy on the seas and paved the way for England's colonization of America. Spain then sank rapidly to the status of a second-rate power and never again played a major role in European politics. Its colonial empire in the Americas and the Philippines vanished in wars and revolutions during the 18th and 19th centuries.

In World War I, Spain maintained a position of neutrality. In 1923, Gen. Miguel Primo de Rivera became dictator. In 1930, King Alfonso XIII revoked the dictatorship, but a strong antimonarchist and republican movement led to his leaving Spain in 1931. The new Constitution declared Spain a workers' republic, broke up the large estates, separated church and state, and secularized the schools. The elections held in 1936 returned a strong Popular Front majority, with Manuel Azaña as President.

On July 18, 1936, a conservative army officer in Morocco, Francisco Franco Bahamonde, led a mutiny against the government. The civil war that followed lasted three years and cost the lives of nearly a million people. Franco was aided by Fascist Italy and Nazi Germany, while Soviet Russia helped the Loyalist side. Several hundred leftist Americans served in the Abraham Lincoln Brigade on the side of the republic. The war ended when Franco took Madrid on March 28, 1939.

Franco became head of the state, national chief of the Falange Party (the governing party), and Premier and Caudillo (leader). In a referendum in 1947, the Spanish people approved a Franco-drafted succession law declaring Spain a monarchy again. Franco, however, continued as Chief of State.

In 1969, Franco and the Cortes designated Prince Juan Carlos Alfonso Victor María de Borbón (who married Princess Sophia of Greece on May 14, 1962) to become King of Spain when the provisional government headed by Franco came to an end.

Franco died of a heart attack on Nov. 20, 1975, after more than a year of ill health, and Juan Carlos was proclaimed King seven days later.

Under pressure from Catalonian and Basque nationalists, Premier Adolfo Suárez granted home rule to these regions in 1979, but centrists backed by him did poorly in the 1980 elections for local assemblies in the two areas. Economic problems persisted, along with new incidents of terrorism, and Suárez resigned on Jan. 29, 1981 and was succeeded by Leopoldo Calvo Sotelo.

With the overwhelming election of Prime Minister Felipe González Márquez and his Spanish Socialist Workers Party in the Oct. 20, 1982, parliamentary elections, the Franco past was finally buried. The thrust of González, a pragmatic moderate, was to modernize rather than radicalize Spain.

A treaty admitting Spain, along with Portugal, to the European Economic Community took effect on Jan. 1, 1986. Later that year, in June, Spain voted to remain in NATO, but outside of its military command.

General elections of June 1993 returned the Socialist Party to power although by reduced margins. The major issue in the election was the over 21% unemployment rate and negative economic growth.

SRI LANKA

Democratic Socialist Republic of Sri Lanka
President: H.E.D.B. Wijetunga (1993)
Prime Minister: Hon. Ranil Wickremasinghe (1993)
Area: 25,332 sq mi. (65,610 sq km)
Population (est. mid-1993): 17,800,000 (average annual rate of natural increase: 1.4%); birth rate: 20/1000; infant mortality rate: 19/1000; density per square mile: 715
Capital: Sri Jayewardenepura Kotte (Colombo); **Largest cities (est. 1990):** Colombo, 1,262,000; Kandy, 200,000; Jafna, 250,000; Galle, 170,000; **Monetary unit:** Sri Lanka rupee; **Languages:** Sinhala, Tamil, English; **Religions:** Buddhist, 69%; Hindu, 15%; Islam, 8%; Christian, 8%; **Member of Commonwealth of Nations; Literacy rate:** 91%

Economic summary: Gross domestic product (1991 est.): $7.2 billion; $410 per capita; real growth rate 5%; inflation 10%; unemployment 14%. Arable land: 16%. Principal products: tea, coconuts, rubber, rice, spices. Labor force: 6,600,000; 13.3% in mining and manufacturing. Major products: processed rubber, tea, coconuts, textiles, cement, refined petroleum. Natural resources: limestone, graphite, gems. Exports: $2.3 billion (f.o.b., 1991): textiles, tea, rubber, petroleum products, gems and jewelry. Imports: $3.0 billion (c.i.f., 1991): petroleum, machinery, transport equipment, sugar. Major trading partners: Egypt, Iraq, Saudi Arabia, U.S., U.K., Germany, Japan, Singapore, India.

Geography. An island in the Indian Ocean off the southeast tip of India, Sri Lanka is about half the size of Alabama. Most of the land is flat and rolling; mountains in the south central region rise to over 8,000 feet (2,438 m).

Government. Ceylon became an independent country in 1948 after British rule and reverted to the traditional name (resplendent island) on May 22, 1972. A new constitution adopted in 1978 set up the National State Assembly, a 225-member unicameral legislature that serves for six years unless dissolved earlier.

History. Following Portuguese and Dutch rule, Ceylon became an English crown colony in 1798. The British developed coffee, tea, and rubber plantations and granted six Constitutions between 1798 and 1924. The Constitution of 1931 gave a large measure of self-government.

Ceylon became a self-governing dominion of the Commonwealth of Nations in 1948.

Presidential elections were held in December 1982, and won by J.R. Jayewardene.

Tension between the Tamil minority and the Sinhalese majority continued to build and erupted in bloody violence in 1983 that has grown worse since. There are about 2.6 million Tamils in Sri Lanka, while the Sinhalese make up about three-quarters of the 17-million population. Tamil extremists are fighting for a separate nation.

The civil war continued during 1990 after a 13-month cease-fire collapsed. The president ruled month to month. The Tamil guerrillas announced a unilateral cease-fire to take effect on January 1, 1991, and the government, too, suspended operations. The cease-fire broke down ten days later. In the early months of 1991 the rebel forces suffered severe casualties.

India had sent soldiers in July 1987 to help enforce an accord granting the Tamil minority limited autonomy. The agreement failed, and Indian troops withdrew at the end of 1989.

President Premadasa was assassinated at a May Day political rally in 1993 when a Tamil rebel detonated explosives strapped to himself. The country's leading opposition figure had been gunned down the previous week.

SUDAN

Republic of the Sudan

Prime Minister: Brig. Omar Hassam Ahmed Bashir (1989)

Area: 967,491 sq mi. (2,505,802 sq km)

Population (est. mid-1993): 27,400,000 (average annual rate of natural increase: 3.1%); birth rate: 45/1000; infant mortality rate: 87/1000; density per square mile: 30

Capital: Khartoum; **Largest cities (est. 1988):** Khartoum, 817,000; Omdurman, 527,000; Port Sudan, 207,000; **Monetary unit:** Sudanese pound; **Languages:** Arabic, English, tribal dialects; **Religions:** Islam, 70% (Sunni); indigenous, 20%; Christian, 5%; **National name:** Jamhuryat es-Sudan; **Literacy rate:** 27%

Economic summary: Gross domestic product (FY91 est.): $12.1 billion; $450 per capita; real growth rate 0%; inflation 95%; unemployment 15%. Arable land: 5%. Principal agricultural products: cotton, oil seeds, gum arabic, sorghum, wheat, millet, sheep. Labor force: 6,500,000; 80% in agriculture. Major industrial products: cement, textiles, pharmaceuticals, shoes, soap, refined petroleum. Natural resources: crude oil, some iron ore, copper, chrome, industrial metals. Exports: $325 million (f.o.b., FY91 est.): cotton, peanuts, gum arabic, sesame. Imports: $1.40 billion (c.i.f., FY91 est.): petroleum products, machinery and equipment, medicines and chemicals. Major trading partners: Western Europe, Saudi Arabia, Eastern Europe, Japan, U.S.

Geography. The Sudan, in northeast Africa, is the largest country on the continent, measuring about one fourth the size of the United States. Its neighbors are Chad and the Central African Republic on the west, Egypt and Libya on the north, Ethiopia on the east, and Kenya, Uganda, and Zaire on the south. The Red Sea washes about 500 miles of the eastern coast.

The country extends from north to south about 1,200 miles (1,931 km) and west to east about 1,000 miles (1,609 km). The northern region is a continuation of the Libyan Desert. The southern region is fertile, abundantly watered, and, in places, heavily forested. It is traversed from north to south by the Nile, all of whose great tributaries are partly or entirely within its borders.

Government. On January 31, 1991, a criminal code became law that applied Islamic law in the predominantly Moslem north. The ruling military council passed a decree on February 4 dividing the country into nine states each administered by a governor and a cabinet of ministers.

History. The early history of the Sudan (known as the Anglo-Egyptian Sudan between 1898 and 1955) is linked with that of Nubia, where a powerful local kingdom was formed in Roman times with its capital at Dongola. After conversion to Christianity in the 6th century, it joined with Ethiopia and resisted Mohammedanization until the 14th century. Thereafter the area was broken up into many small states until 1820–22, when it was conquered by Mohammed Ali, Pasha of Egypt. Egyptian forces were evacuated during the Mahdist revolt (1881–98), but the Sudan was reconquered by the Anglo-Egyptian expeditions of 1896–98, and in 1899 became an Anglo-Egyptian condominium, which was reaffirmed by the Anglo-Egyptian treaty of 1936.

Egypt and Britain agreed in 1953 to grant self-government to the Sudan under an appointed Governor-General. An all-Sudanese Parliament was elected in November-December 1953, and an all-Sudanese government was formed. In December 1955, the Parliament declared the independence of the Sudan, which, with the approval of Britain and Egypt, was proclaimed on Jan. 1, 1956.

In October 1969, Maj. Gen. Gaafar Mohamed Nimeiri, the president of the Council for the Revolution, took over as prime minister. He was elected the nation's first president in 1971.

In 1976, a third coup was attempted against Nimeiri. Nimeiri accused President Muammar el Qaddafi of

Libya of having instigated the attempt and broke relations with Libya.

On April 6, 1985, while out of the country on visits to the United States and Egypt, Nimeiri lost power in the same way he gained it 16 years previously—by a military coup headed by his Defense Minister, Gen. Abdel Rahman Siwar el-Dahab.

Among the problems that the new government faced were a debilitating civil war with rebels in the south of the country, other sectarian and tribal conflicts, and a famine.

During 1992 the government attempted to impose militant Islam throughout the nation as well as initiate capitalistic economic reforms, including the lifting of subsidies on basic commodities. The civil war continued during the year with no accommodation in sight as the largely Christian and animist south insisted on self-determination.

SURINAME

Republic of Suriname
President: Ronald Venetiaan (1991)
Vice President and Prime Minister: Jules Adjodhia (1991)
Area: 63,251 sq mi. (163,820 sq km)
Population (est. mid-1993): 400,000 (average annual rate of natural increase: 1.7%); birth rate: 24/1000; infant mortality rate: 27/1000; density per square mile: 7
Capital and largest city (1986): Paramaribo, 77,558; **Monetary unit:** Suriname guilder; **Languages:** Dutch, Surinamese (lingua franca), English widely spoken; **Religions:** Protestant, 25.2%; Roman Catholic, 22.8%; Hindu, 27.4%; Islam, 19.6%; indigenous, about 5%; **Literacy rate:** 95%
Economic summary: Gross domestic product (1989 est.): $1.4 billion; $3,400 per capita; real growth rate 2.0%; inflation (1989 est.) 50%; unemployment (1990) 33%. Arable land: NEGL %. Principal products: rice. Work force: 104,000. Major products: aluminum, alumina, processed foods, lumber. Natural resources: bauxite, iron ore, timber, fish, shrimp. Exports: $549 million (f.o.b, 1989 est.): bauxite, alumina, aluminum, rice, shrimp, lumber and wood products. Imports: $331 million (f.o.b., 1989 est.): capital equipment, petroleum, cotton, foodstuffs, consumer goods.Major trading partners: U.S., Trinidad, Netherlands, Norway, Germany, Brazil, U.K., Japan, Netherlands Antilles.

Geography. Suriname lies on the northeast coast of South America, with Guyana to the west, French Guiana to the east, and Brazil to the south. It is about one-tenth larger than Michigan. The principal rivers are the Corantijn on the Guyana border, the Marowijne in the east, and the Suriname, on which the capital city of Paramaribo is situated. The Tumuc-Humac Mountains are on the border with Brazil.

Government. Suriname, formerly known as Dutch Guiana, became an independent republic on Nov. 25, 1975. The executive branch consists of the president, vice-president and prime minister, Cabinet of Ministers, and Council of State. The legislative branch consists of a unicameral National Assembly with 51 members.

History. England established the first European settlement on the Suriname River in 1650 but transferred sovereignty to the Dutch in 1667 in the Treaty of Breda, by which the British acquired New York. Colonization was confined to a narrow coastal strip, and until the abolition of slavery in 1863, African slaves furnished the labor for the plantation economy. After 1870, laborers were imported from British India and the Dutch East Indies.

In 1948, the colony was integrated into the Kingdom of the Netherlands and two years later was granted full home rule in other than foreign affairs and defense. After race rioting over unemployment and inflation, the Netherlands offered complete independence in 1973.

During much of the 1980s Suriname has been under the control of Lieut. Col. Dési Bouterse, who in late December 1990 resigned as commander of the armed forces. The following night Pres. Shenkar was ousted in a bloodless coup. A few days later interim president Johan Krug acted to reinstate Bouterse.

A deadlocked parliament in 1991 gave way to an assembly, consisting of members of parliament and elected representatives of local councils, convened to select Venetiaan as president.

In 1992 a draft peace treaty was signed between the government and several guerrilla groups that included a general amnesty and integration of the guerrilla forces into the police.

SWAZILAND

Kingdom of Swaziland
Ruler: King Mswati III (1986)
Prime Minister: Obed Dlamini (1989)
Area: 6,704 sq mi. (17,363 sq km)
Population (est. mid-1993): 800,000 (average annual rate of natural increase: 3.2%); birth rate: 44/1000; infant mortality rate: 101/1000; density per square mile: 123
Capital (1986): Mbabane, 38,290; **Monetary unit:** Lilangeni; **Languages:** English and Swazi (official); **Religions:** Christian, 60%; indigenous, 40%; **Member of Commonwealth of Nations; Literacy rate:** 55%
Economic summary: Gross national product (1990): $563 million; $670 per capita; 5.0% real growth rate; inflation (1990) 13%. Arable land: 8%. Principal agricultural products: corn, livestock, sugar cane, citrus fruits, cotton, sorghum, peanuts. Labor force: 195,000; about 92,000 wage earners with 14% in manufacturing. Major industrial products: milled sugar, ginned cotton, processed meat and wood. Natural resources: asbestos, diamonds. Exports: $557 million (f.o.b., 1990): sugar, wood pulp, asbestos, citrus fruits. Imports: $632 million (f.o.b., 1990): motor vehicles, transport equipment, petroleum products, foodstuffs, chemicals. Major trading partners: South Africa, U.K., U.S.

Geography. Swaziland, 85% the size of New Jersey, is surrounded by South Africa and Mozambique. The country consists of a high veld in the west and a series of plateaus descending from 6,000 feet (1,829 m) to a low veld of 1,500 feet (457 m).

Government. In 1967, a new Constitution established King Sobhuza II as head of state and provided for an Assembly of 24 members elected by universal suffrage, together with a Senate of 12 members—half appointed by the Assembly and half by the King. In 1973, the King renounced the Constitution, suspended political parties, and took total power for himself. In 1977, he replaced the Parliament with an assembly of tribal leaders. The Parliament reconvened in 1979.

History. Bantu peoples migrated southwest to the area of Mozambique in the 16th century. A number of clans broke away from the main body in the 18th century and settled in Swaziland. In the 19th century they organized as a tribe, partly because they were in constant conflict with the Zulu. Their ruler, Mswazi, applied to the British in the 1840s for help against the Zulu. The British and the Transvaal governments guaranteed the independence of Swaziland in 1881.

South Africa held Swaziland as a protectorate from 1894 to 1899, but after the Boer War, in 1902, Swaziland was transferred to British administration. The Paramount Chief was recognized as the native authority in 1941.

In 1963, the territory was constituted a protectorate, and on Sept. 6, 1968, it became the independent nation of Swaziland.

The king in October 1992 dissolved parliament and announced plans for a new constitution allowing a multiparty democracy, with elections to be held sometime in 1993.

SWEDEN

Kingdom of Sweden
Sovereign: King Carl XVI Gustaf (1973)
Prime Minister: Carl Bildt (1991)
Area: 173,800 sq mi. (449,964 sq km)
Population (est. mid-1993): 8,700,000 (average annual rate of natural increase: 0.3%); birth rate: 14/1000; infant mortality rate: 6.2/1000; density per square mile: 55
Capital: Stockholm; **Largest cities (1990):** Stockholm, 1,491,726; Göteborg, 730,867; Malmö, 475,224; **Monetary unit:** Krona; **Language:** Swedish; **Religions:** Evangelical Lutheran, 93.5%; Roman Catholic, 1%; other, 5.5%; **National name:** Konungariket Sverige; **Literacy rate:** 99%
Economic summary: Gross domestic product (1991): $147.6 billion; $17,200 per capita; real growth rate –1.1%; inflation 8%; unemployment 2.7%. Arable land: 7%. Principal agricultural products: dairy products, grains, sugar beets, potatoes. Labor force: 4,572,000 (1990); 37.4% in government services; 23.1% in mining, manufacturing, electricity, and water service; 22.2% in private services. Major products: iron and steel, precision equipment, wood pulp and paper products, automobiles. Natural resources: forests, iron ore, hydroelectric power, zinc, uranium. Exports: $54.5 billion (f.o.b., 1991 est.): machinery, motor vehicles, wood pulp, paper products, chemicals, petroleum and petroleum products, iron and steel products. Imports: $50.2 billion (c.i.f., 1991 est.): machinery, clothing, petroleum and petroleum products, foodstuffs, iron and steel, chemicals. Major trading partners: Norway, Germany, U.K., Denmark, U.S.

Geography. Sweden occupies the eastern part of the Scandinavian peninsula, with Norway to the west, Finland and the Gulf of Bothnia to the east, and Denmark and the Baltic Sea in the south. Sweden is the fourth largest country in Europe and is one-tenth larger than California.

The country slopes eastward and southward from the Kjólen Mountains along the Norwegian border, where the peak elevation is Kebnekaise at 6,965 feet (2,123 m) in Lapland. In the north are mountains and many lakes. To the south and east are central lowlands and south of them are fertile areas of forest, valley, and plain.

Along Sweden's rocky coast, chopped up by bays and inlets, are many islands, the largest of which are Gotland and Öland.

Government. Sweden is a constitutional monarchy. Under the 1975 Constitution, the Riksdag is the sole governing body. The prime minister is the political chief executive.

In 1967, agreement was reached on part of a new Constitution after 13 years of work. It provided for a single-house Riksdag of 350 members (later amended to 349 seats) to replace the 104-year old bicameral Riksdag. The members are popularly elected for three years. One hundred fifteen present members of the Riksdag are women.

The King, Carl XVI Gustaf, was born April 30, 1946, and succeeded to the throne Sept. 19, 1973, on the death at 90 of his grandfather, Gustaf VI Adolf. Carl Gustaf was married on June 19, 1976, to Silvia Sommerlath, a West German commoner. They have three children: Princess Victoria, born July 14, 1977; Prince Carl Philip, born May 13, 1979; and Princess Madeleine, born June 10, 1982. Under the new Act of Succession, effective Jan. 1, 1980, the first child of the reigning monarch, regardless of sex, is heir to the throne.

History. The earliest historical mention of Sweden is found in Tacitus' *Germania,* where reference is made to the powerful king and strong fleet of the Suiones. Toward the end of the 10th century, Olaf Skóttkonung established a Christian stronghold in Sweden. Around 1400, an attempt was made to unite the northern nations into one kingdom, but this led to bitter strife between the Danes and the Swedes.

In 1520, the Danish King, Christian II, conquered Sweden and in the "Stockholm Bloodbath" put leading Swedish personalities to death. Gustavus Vasa (1523–60) broke away from Denmark and fashioned the modern Swedish state.

Sweden played a leading role in the second phase (1630–35) of the Thirty Years' War (1618–48). By the Treaty of Westphalia (1648), Sweden obtained western Pomerania and some neighboring territory on the Baltic. In 1700, a coalition of Russia, Poland, and Denmark united against Sweden and by the Peace of Nystad (1721) forced it to relinquish Livonia, Ingria, Estonia, and parts of Finland.

Sweden emerged from the Napoleonic Wars with the acquisition of Norway from Denmark and with a new royal dynasty stemming from Marshal Jean Bernadotte of France, who became King Charles XIV (1818–44). The artificial union between Sweden and Norway led to an uneasy relationship, and the union was finally dissolved in 1905.

Sweden maintained a position of neutrality in both World Wars.

An elaborate structure of welfare legislation, imitated by many larger nations, began with the establishment of old-age pensions in 1911. Economic prosperity based on its neutralist policy enabled Sweden, together with Norway, to pioneer in public health, housing, and job security programs.

Forty-four years of Socialist government were ended in 1976 with the election of a conservative coalition headed by Thorbjörn Fälldin, a 50-year-old sheep farmer.

Fälldin resigned on Oct. 5, 1978, when his conservative parties partners demanded less restrictions on nuclear power, and his successor, Ola Ullsten, resigned a year later after failing to achieve a consensus on the issue. Returned to office by his coalition partners, Fälldin said he would follow the course directed by a national referendum.

Olaf Palme and the Socialists were returned to power in the election of 1982.

In February 1986, Palme was killed by an unknown assailant.

In July 1991 Sweden formally filed an application for membership in the European Community.

Elections in September 1991 ousted the Social Democrats from power. The new coalition of four conservative parties pledged to cut taxes and cut back on the welfare state but not alter Sweden's traditional neutrality.

After coming to power the government has reduced unemployment benefits and injury compensations and raised the eligibility age for full pensions. Cuts have also been made in a number of other social service programs.

SWITZERLAND

Swiss Confederation
President: Ogi Adolf (1993)
Vice President: Stich Otto (1993)
Area: 15,941 sq mi. (41,288 sq km)
Population (est. mid-1993): 7,000,000 (average annual rate of natural increase: 0.3%); birth rate: 13/1000; infant mortality rate: 6.9/1000; density per square mile: 453
Capital: Bern; **Largest cities (1992):** Zurich, 345,000; Basel, 174,000; Geneva, 170,000; Bern, 136,000; Lausanne, 125,000; **Monetary unit:** Swiss franc; **Languages:** German, 65%; French, 18%; Italian, 10%; Romansch, 1%; **Religions:** Roman Catholic, 49%; Protestant, 48%; **National name:** Schweiz/Suisse/Svizzera/Svizra; **Literacy rate:** 99%
Economic summary: Gross domestic product (1991 est.): $147.4 billion; $21,700 per capita; real growth rate –0.2%; inflation 5.9%; unemployment 1.3%. Arable land: 10%. Principal products: cheese and other dairy products, livestock. Labor force (1989): 3,310,000; 904,095 foreign workers, mostly Italian; 50% in industry and crafts. Major products: watches and clocks, precision instruments, machinery, chemicals, pharmaceuticals, textiles. Natural resources: water power, timber, salt. Exports: $62.2 billion (f.o.b., 1991 est.): machinery and equipment, precision instruments, textiles, foodstuffs, metal products. Imports: $68.5 billion (c.i.f., 1991 est.): transport equipment, foodstuffs, chemicals, textiles, construction material. Major trading partners: U.S., E.C., Japan

Geography. Switzerland, in central Europe, is the land of the Alps. Its tallest peak is the Dufourspitze at 15,203 feet (4,634 m) on the Swiss side of the Italian border, one of 10 summits of the Monte Rose massif in the Apennines. The tallest peak in all of the Alps, Mont Blanc (15,771 ft; 4,807 m), is actually in France.

Most of Switzerland comprises a mountainous plateau bordered by the great bulk of the Alps on the south and by the Jura Mountains on the northwest. About one-fourth of the total area is covered by mountains and glaciers.

The country's largest lakes—Geneva, Constance (Bodensee), and Maggiore—straddle the French, German-Austrian, and Italian borders, respectively.

The Rhine, navigable from Basel to the North Sea, is the principal inland waterway. Other rivers are the Aare and the Rhône.

Switzerland, twice the size of New Jersey, is surrounded by France, West Germany, Austria, Liechtenstein, and Italy.

Government. The Swiss Confederation consists of 23 sovereign cantons, of which three are divided into six half-cantons. Federal authority is vested in a bicameral legislature. The Ständerat, or State Council, consists of 46 members, two from each canton. The lower house, the Nationalrat, or National Council, has 200 deputies, elected for four-year terms.

Executive authority rests with the Bundesrat, or Federal Council, consisting of seven members chosen by parliament. The parliament elects the President, who serves for one year and is succeeded by the Vice President. The federal government regulates foreign policy, railroads, postal service, and the national mint. Each canton reserves for itself important local powers.

A constitutional amendment adopted in 1971 by referendum gave women the vote in federal elections and the right to hold federal office. An equal rights amendment was passed in a national referendum June 14, 1981, barring discrimination against women under canton as well as federal law.

A referendum in March 1990 gave 18-year olds the right to vote in federal elections. A similar referendum failed to pass in 1979.

History. Called Helvetia in ancient times, Switzerland in the Middle Ages was a league of cantons of the Holy Roman Empire. Fashioned around the nucleus of three German forest districts of Schwyz, Uri, and Unterwalden, the Swiss Confederation slowly added new cantons. In 1648 the Treaty of Westphalia gave Switzerland its independence from the Holy Roman Empire.

French revolutionary troops occupied the country in 1798 and named it the Helvetic Republic, but Napoleon in 1803 restored its federal government. By 1815, the French- and Italian-speaking peoples of Switzerland had been granted political equality.

In 1815, the Congress of Vienna guaranteed the neutrality and recognized the independence of Switzerland. In the revolutionary period of 1847, the Catholic cantons seceded and organized a separate union called the *Sonderbund.* In 1848 the new Swiss Constitution established a union modeled upon that of the U.S. The Federal Constitution of 1874 established a strong central government while maintaining large powers of control in each canton.

National unity and political conservatism grew as the country prospered from its neutrality. Its banking system became the world's leading repository for international accounts. Strict neutrality was its policy in World Wars I and II. Geneva was the seat of the League of Nations (later the European headquarters of the United Nations) and of a number of international organizations.

Voters in May 1992 approved Switzerland joining the IMF and the World Bank.

A referendum in December on merging the European Community with the 7 nation European Free Trade Association was narrowly defeated, but was expected to be resubmitted to the electorate soon.

SYRIA

Syrian Arab Republic
President: Hafez al-Assad (1971)
Premier: Mahmoud al-Zubi (1987)
Area: 71,498 sq mi. (185,180 sq km)
Population (est. mid-1993): 13,500,000 (average annual rate of natural increase: 3.8%); birth rate: 45/1000; infant mortality rate: 48/1000; density per square mile: 189
Capital: Damascus; **Largest cities (est. 1989):** Damascus, 1,361,000; Aleppo, 1,308,000; Homs, 464,000; Hama, 229,000; Latakia, 258,000; **Monetary unit:** Syrian pound; **Language:** Arabic; **Religions:** Islam, 90%; Christian, 10%; **National name:** Al-Jamhouriya al Arabiya As-Souriya; **Literacy rate:** 64%
Economic summary: Gross domestic product (1991 est.): $30 billion; $2,300 per capita; real growth rate 11%; inflation 25%. Arable land: 28%. Principal agricultural products: Cotton, wheat, barley, lentils, sheep, goats. Labor force: 2,400,000; 32% in industry. Major industrial products: textiles, phosphate, petroleum, processed food. Natural resources: chrome, manganese, asphalt, iron ore, rock salt, phosphate, oil, gypsum. Exports: $3.6 billion (f.o.b., 1991 est.): petroleum, textiles, phosphates. Imports: $2.7 billion (f.o.b., 1991 est.): machinery and metal products, fuels, foodstuffs. Major trading partners: Italy, Romania, C.I.S. countries, U.S., EC, Arab countries.

Geography. Slightly larger than North Dakota, Syria lies at the eastern end of the Mediterranean Sea. It is bordered by Lebanon and Israel on the west, Turkey on the north, Iraq on the east, and Jordan on the south.

Coastal Syria is a narrow plain, in back of which is a range of coastal mountains, and still farther inland a steppe area. In the east is the Syrian Desert, and in the south is the Jebel Druze Range. The highest point in Syria is Mount Hermon (9,232 ft; 2,814 m) on the Lebanese border.

Government. A republic under a military regime since March 1963 with a unicameral legislature, the People's Council. The ruling party is the Arab Socialist Resurrectionist (Ba'th) Party.

History. Ancient Syria was conquered by Egypt about 1500 B.C., and after that by Hebrews, Assyrians, Chaldeans, Persians, and Greeks. From 64 B.C. until the Arab conquest in A.D. 636, it was part of the Roman Empire except during brief periods. The Arabs made it a trade center for their extensive empire, but it suffered severely from the Mongol invasion in 1260 and fell to the Ottoman Turks in 1516. Syria remained a Turkish province until World War I.

A secret Anglo-French pact of 1916 put Syria in the French zone of influence. The League of Nations gave France a mandate over Syria after World War I, but the French were forced to put down several nationalist uprisings. In 1930, France recognized Syria as an independent republic, but still subject to the mandate. After nationalist demonstrations in 1939, the French High Commissioner suspended the Syrian Constitution. In 1941, British and Free French forces invaded Syria to eliminate Vichy control. During the rest of World War II, Syria was an Allied base.

Again in 1945, nationalist demonstrations broke into actual fighting, and British troops had to restore order. Syrian forces met a series of reverses while participating in the Arab invasion of Palestine in 1948. In 1958, Egypt and Syria formed the United Arab Republic, with Gamal Abdel Nasser of Egypt as President. However, Syria became independent again on Sept. 29, 1961, following a revolution.

In the war of 1967, Israel quickly vanquished the Syrian army. Before acceding to the U.N. cease-fire, the Israeli forces took over control of the fortified Golan Heights commanding the Sea of Galilee.

Syria joined Egypt in attacking Israel in October 1973 in the fourth Arab-Israeli war, but was pushed back from initial successes on the Golan Heights to end up losing more land. However, in the settlement worked out by U.S. Secretary of State Henry A. Kissinger in 1974, the Syrians recovered all the territory lost in 1973 and a token amount of territory, including the deserted town of Quneitra, lost in 1967.

Syrian troops, in Lebanon since 1976 as part of an Arab peacekeeping force whose other members subsequently departed, intervened increasingly during 1980 and 1981 on the side of Moslem Lebanese in their clashes with Christian militants supported by Israel. When Israeli jets shot down Syrian helicopters operating in Lebanon in April 1981, Syria moved Soviet-built surface-to-air (SAM 6) missiles into Lebanon's Bekaa Valley. Israel demanded that the missiles be removed because they violated a 1976 understanding between the governments. The demand, backed up by bombing raids, prompted the Reagan Administration to send veteran diplomat Philip C. Habib as a special envoy to avert a new conflict between the nations.

Habib's carefully engineered cease-fire was shattered by a new Israeli invasion in June 1982, when Israeli aircraft bombed Bekaa Valley missile sites.

Nevertheless, while the Israelis overran most of the rest of Lebanon, the Syrians retained their positions in the Bekaa Valley. As the various Lebanese factions fought each other, the Syrians became the dominant force in the country, both militarily and politically.

The first Arab country to condemn Iraq's invasion of Kuwait, Syria sent troops to help defend Saudi Arabia from possible Iraq attack. After the Gulf war hope for peace negotiations between Israel and Arab states, particularly Syria, rose then floundered.

In 1990 President Assad ruled out any possibility of legalizing opposition political parties. According to official sources, voters in December 1991 approved Assad staying on for a fourth term in office, giving him 99.98% of the vote. In April 1992 Syria lifted a travel ban on its Jewish population.

According to official sources, voters in December 1991 approved Assad staying on for a fourth term in office, giving him 99.98% of the vote. In April 1992 Syria lifted a travel ban on its Jewish population.

TAIWAN

Republic of China
President: Lee Teng-Hui (1988)
Premier: Lien Chan (1993)
Area: 13,895 sq mi. (35,988 sq km)
Population (end 1992): 20,742,389 (average annual rate of natural increase: 1.1%); birth rate: 16/1000; infant mortality rate: 5.1/1000; density per square mile: 1,501
Capital: Taipei; **Largest cities (1992):** Taipei, 2,697,977; Kaohsiung, 1,403,647; Tai Chung, 790,670; Tainan, 693,585; Chilung (Keelung), 358,336; **Monetary unit:** New Taiwan dollar; **Languages:** Chinese (Mandarin) and various dialects; **Religions (1991):** Buddhist, 4.86 million; Taoist, 3.3 million; Protestant, 422,000; Catholic, 304,000; **Literacy rate:** 94%

Economic summary: Gross national product (1992): $210.5 billion; per capita income $9,313; real growth rate 6.11%; inflation (1991 est.) 3.8%; unemployment (1991 est.): 1.5%. Arable land: 24%; principal products: rice, yams, sugar cane, bananas, pineapples, citrus fruits. Labor force (1992): 8,765,000; 40% in industry; 13% in agriculture; 47% in services. Major products: textiles, clothing, chemicals, processed foods, electronic equipment, cement, ships, plywood. Natural resources: coal, natural gas, limestone, marble. Exports: textiles, electrical machinery, plywood. Imports: machinery, basic metals, crude oil, chemicals. Major trading partners: U.S., Japan, Hong Kong, Germany.

Geography. The Republic of China today consists of the island of Taiwan, an island 100 miles (161 km) off the Asian mainland in the Pacific; two off-shore islands, Kinmen (Quemoy) and Matsu; and the nearby islets of the Pescadores chain. It is slightly larger than the combined areas of Massachusetts and Connecticut.

Taiwan is divided by a central mountain range that runs from north to south, rising sharply on the east coast and descending gradually to a broad western plain, where cultivation is concentrated.

Government. The President and the Vice President are elected by the National Assembly for a term of six years. There are five major governing bodies called Yuans: Executive, Legislative, Judicial, Control, and Examination. Taiwan's internal affairs are administered by the Taiwan Provincial Government under the supervision of the Provincial Assembly, which is popularly elected.

The majority and ruling party is the Kuomintang (KMT) (Nationalist Party) led by President Lee Teng-Hui. The main opposition party is the Democratic Progressive Party (DPP).

History. Taiwan was inhabited by aborigines of Malayan descent when Chinese from the areas now designated as Fukien and Kwangtung began settling it beginning in the 7th century, becoming the majority.

The Portuguese explored the area in 1590, naming it The Beautiful (Formosa). In 1624 the Dutch set up forts in the south, the Spanish in the North. The Dutch threw out the Spanish in 1641 and controlled the island until 1661, when the Chinese General Koxinga took it over, established an independent kingdom, and expelled the Dutch. The Manchus seized the island in 1683 and held it until 1895, when it passed to Japan after the first Sino-Japanese War. Japan developed and exploited it, and it was heavily bombed by American planes during World War II, after which it was restored to China.

After the defeat of its armies on the mainland, the Nationalist Government of Generalissimo Chiang Kai-shek retreated to Taiwan in December 1949. With only 15% of the population consisting of the 1949 immigrants, Chiang dominated the island, maintaining a 600,000-man army in the hope of eventually recovering the mainland. Japan renounced its claim to the island by the San Francisco Peace Treaty of 1951.

By stationing a fleet in the Strait of Formosa the U.S. prevented a mainland invasion in 1953.

The "China seat" in the U.N., which the Nationalists held with U.S. help for over two decades was lost in October 1971, when the People's Republic of China was admitted and Taiwan ousted by the world body.

Chiang died at 87 of a heart attack on April 5, 1975. His son, Chiang Ching-kuo, continued as Premier and dominant power in the Taipei regime. He assumed the presidency in 1978, and Sun Yun-hsuan became Premier.

Martial law was lifted in 1987. In April 1991 President Lee Teng-Hui formally declared an end to emergency rule, yet without abandoning his government's claim to be the sole legitimate government of China.

In the first full election in many decades the governing Kuomintang in December 1991 won 71% of the vote, affirming the party's opposition to independence in principle from China.

In February 1993 the president, himself a native Taiwanese, nominated Lien Chan, another native to be prime minister marking a further generational shift away from mainland exiles. In April China and Taiwan concluded their first high level meeting by signing four agreements. One of the agreements provided for establishing a regular dialogue between the two antagonists.

TAJIKISTAN

Republic of Tajikistan
Chairman, Supreme Council: Rakhmond Emomali
Prime Minister: Abdulladjanov Abdumalic
Area: 55,300 sq mi. (143,100 sq km)
Population (est. mid-1993): 5,700,000 (1989: Tajiks, 62.3%; Uzbeks, 23.5%; Russians, 7.6%; Tatars, 1.4%; Kyrgyz, 1.3%); (average annual rate of natural inmcrease: 3.4%); birth rate, 40/1000; infant motality rate: 50/1000; density per square mile: 102
Capital and largest city (1991): Dushaube, 592,000; (1989): Khodzhent (Leninabad), 160,000; **Monetary unit:** Ruble; **Religion:** Sunni Moslem, 80%; **Language:** Tajik
Economic summary: Per capita GNP (1991): $1,050; real growth rate –9%; inflation 84%; unemployment 25%. Arable land: 6%. Labor force: 1,938,000. Industries: Aluminum, zinc, lead, cement, vegetable oil, metal cutting machine tools, refrigerators and freezers. Agriculture: cotton, grain, fruits, and grapes. Exports: $706 million (1990): aluminum, cotton, fruits, vegetable oil, textiles. Imports: $1.3 billion (1990): chemicals, machinery and transport equipment, textiles, foodstuffs. Trading partners: Russia, Kazakhstan, Ukraine, and Uzbekistan.

Geography: Ninety-three percent of Tajikistan's territory is mountainous and the mountain glaciers are the source of its rivers. Tajikistan is an earthquake-prone area. The republic is bounded by China in the east, Afghanistan to the south, Uzbekistan and Kirghizia to the west and north. The central Asian republic also includes the Gorno-Badakh Shan Autonomous region. Tajikistan is slightly larger than the state of Illinois in area.

Government: A parliamentary republic governed by a Supreme Council.

History: The name Tadzhikstan (now Tajikistan) dates from the 1920s when the territory became an official Russian administrative area. The Tajiks had an ancient nomadic culture and were ruled at different times by Afghanistan and Persia.

Tajikistan declared its sovereignty in August 1990. In 1991, the republic's Communist leadership supported the attempted coup against Soviet President Mikhail Gorbachev. Shortly afterward pro-Communist president Makhkamov was forced to resign by mounting pressure from pro-democracy groups and the Tajikistan parliament restored an earlier ban on the Communist Party. The ban was rescinded in late September but again restored. The election of November 24 went to Nabiev, former head of the local Communist Party.

Tajikistan joined with ten other former Soviet republics in the Commonwealth of Independent States on Dec. 21, 1991. A parliamentary republic was proclaimed and presidential rule abolished on November 1992. Former Communists dominated the government.

TANZANIA

United Republic of Tanzania
President: Ali Hassan Mwinyi (1985)
Prime Minister: John Malecela (1990)
Area: 364,879 sq mi. (945,037 sq km)[1]
Population (est. mid-1993): 27,800,000 (average annual rate of natural increase: 3.1%); birth rate: 46/1000; infant mortality rate: 104/1000; density per square mile: 81
Capital and largest city (1988): Dar es Salaam, 1,360,850; **Monetary unit:** Tanzanian shilling; **Languages:** Swahili, English, local languages; **Religions:** Christian, 33%; Islam, 33%; indigenous beliefs, 33%; **Member of Commonwealth of Nations; Literacy rate:** 46%
Economic summary: Gross domestic product (1989 est.): $6.9 billion; $260 per capita; 4.5% real growth rate; inflation (1991 est.) 16.5%. Arable land: 5%. Principal agricultural products: tobacco, corn, cassava, wheat, cotton, coffee, sisal, cashew nuts, pyrethrum, cloves. Labor force: 732,200; 90% in agriculture. Major industrial products: textiles, wood products, refined oil, processed agricultural products, diamonds, cement, fertilizer. Natural resources: hydroelectric potential, phosphates, iron and coal. Exports: $478 million (f.o.b., FY91 est.): coffee, cotton, sisal, diamonds, cloves, cashew nuts. Imports: $1.5 billion (c.i.f., FY91 est.): manufactured goods, machinery and transport equipment, crude oil, foodstuffs. Major trading partners: Germany, U.K., U.S., Japan, Italy, Denmark, Kenya.

1. Including Zanzibar.

Geography. Tanzania is in East Africa on the Indian Ocean. To the north are Uganda and Kenya; to the west, Burundi, Rwanda, and Zaire; and to the south, Mozambique, Zambia, and Malawi. Its area is three times that of New Mexico.

Tanzania contains three of Africa's best-known lakes—Victoria in the north, Tanganyika in the west, and Nyasa in the south. Mount Kilimanjaro in the north, 19,340 feet (5,895 m), is the highest point on the continent.

Government. Under the republican form of government, Tanzania has a President elected by universal suffrage who appoints the Cabinet ministers. The 244-member National Assembly is composed of 119 elected members from the mainland, 50 elected from Zanzibar, 10 members appointed by the President (from both Tanganyika and Zanzibar), 5 national members (elected by the National Assembly after nomination by various national institutions), 20 members elected by Zanzibar's House of Representatives, 25 Regional Commissioners sitting as *ex officio* members, and 15 seats reserved for women (elected by the National Assembly).

The Tanganyika African National Union, the only authorized party on the mainland, and the Afro-Shirazi Party, the only party in Zanzibar and Pemba, merged in 1977 as the Revolutionary Party (Chama Cha Mapinduzi) and elected Julius K. Nyerere as its head.

History. Arab traders first began to colonize the area in A.D. 700. Portuguese explorers reached the coastal regions in 1500 and held some control until the 17th century, when the Sultan of Oman took power. With what are now Burundi and Rwanda, Tanganyika became the colony of German East Africa in 1885. After World War I, it was administered by Britain under a League of Nations mandate and later as a U.N. trust territory.

Although not mentioned in old histories until the 12th century, Zanzibar was believed always to have had connections with southern Arabia. The Portuguese made it one of their tributaries in 1503 and later established a trading post, but they were driven out by Arabs from Oman in 1698. Zanzibar was declared independent of Oman in 1861 and, in 1890, it became a British protectorate.

Tanganyika became independent on Dec. 9, 1961; Zanzibar, on Dec. 10, 1963. On April 26, 1964, the two nations merged into the United Republic of Tanganyika and Zanzibar. The name was changed to Tanzania six months later.

An invasion by Ugandan troops in November 1978 was followed by a counterattack in January 1979, in which 5,000 Tanzanian troops were joined by 3,000 Ugandan exiles opposed to President Idi Amin. Within a month, full-scale war developed.

Nyerere kept troops in Uganda in open support of former Ugandan President Milton Obote, despite protests from opposition groups, until the national elections in December 1980.

In November 1985, Nyerere stepped down as President. Ali Hassan Mwinyi, his Vice-President, succeeded him. Nyerere remained chairman of the party. Nyerere resigned as head of the party in August 1990, being replaced by President Mwinyi. Running unopposed Mwinyi was elected president in October. Shortly thereafter plans were announced to study the benefits of instituting a multi-party democracy.

A special congress of the ruling Revolutionary Party of Tanzania unanimously supported a move towards a multiparty system although there had been little pressure, domestic or foreign, in this direction.

THAILAND

Kingdom of Thailand
Ruler: King Bhumibol Adulyadej (1946)
Prime Minister: Chuan Leekpai (1992)
Area: 198,455 sq mi. (514,000 sq km)
Population (est. mid-1993): 57,200,000 (average annual rate of natural increase: 1.4%); birth rate: 21/1000; infant mortality rate: 40/1000; density per square mile: 290
Capital and largest city (est. 1989): Bangkok, 5,876,000; **Monetary unit:** Baht; **Languages:** Thai (Siamese), Chinese, English; **Religions:** Buddhist, 94.4%; Islam, 4%; Hinduism, 1.1%; Christian, 0.5%; **National name:** Thailand; **Literacy rate:** 93%
Economic summary: Gross national product (1991 est.): $192.6 billion; $1,630 per capita; real growth rate 8%; inflation 5.6%; unemployment 4.1%. Arable land: 34%. Principal agricultural products: rice, rubber, corn, tapioca, sugar, coconuts. Labor force (1989 est.): 30,870,000; 62% in agriculture; 13% in commerce; 11% in services, including government. Major industrial

products: processed food, textiles, furniture, cement, tin, tungsten, jewelry. Natural resources: fish, natural gas, forests, fluorite, tin, tungsten. Exports: $27.5 billion (f.o.b., 1991): rice, tapioca, fishing products, tin, textiles, jewelry. Imports: $39 billion (c.i.f., 1991): machinery and parts, petroleum products, iron and steel, electrical appliances, chemicals. Major trading partners: Japan, U.S., Singapore, Malaysia, Netherlands, U.K., France, China, Hong Kong, Germany.

Geography. Thailand occupies the western half of the Indochinese peninsula and the northern two-thirds of the Malay peninsula in southeast Asia. Its neighbors are Myanmar on the north and west, Laos on the north and northeast, Cambodia on the east, and Malaysia on the south. Thailand is about the size of France.

Most of the population is supported in the fertile central alluvial plain, which is drained by the Chao Phraya River and its tributaries.

Government. A constitutional monarchy. The government is run by an elected civilian coalition of political parties. King Bhumibol Adulyadej, who was born Dec. 5, 1927, second son of Prince Mahidol of Songkhla, succeeded to the throne on June 9, 1946. He was married on April 28, 1950, to Queen Sirikit; their son, Vajiralongkorn, born July 28, 1952, is the Crown Prince.

History. The Thais first began moving down into their present homeland from the Asian continent in the 6th century A.D. and by the end of the 13th century ruled most of the western portion. During the next 400 years, the Thais fought sporadically with the Cambodians and the Burmese. The British obtained recognition of paramount interest in Thailand in 1824, and in 1896 an Anglo-French accord guaranteed the independence of Thailand.

A coup in 1932 changed the absolute monarchy into a representative government with universal suffrage. After five hours of token resistance on Dec. 8, 1941, Thailand yielded to Japanese occupation and became one of the springboards in World War II for the Japanese campaign against Malaya.

After the fall of its pro-Japanese puppet government in July 1944, Thailand pursued a policy of passive resistance against the Japanese, and after the Japanese surrender, Thailand repudiated the declaration of war it had been forced to make against Britain and the U.S. in 1942.

Thailand's major problem in the late 1960s was suppressing guerrilla action by Communist invaders in the north.

Although Thailand had received $2 billion in U.S. economic and military aid since 1950 and had sent troops (paid by the U.S.) to Vietnam while permitting U.S. bomber bases on its territory, the collapse of South Vietnam and Cambodia in the spring of 1975 brought rapid changes in the country's diplomatic posture.

At the Thai government's insistence, the U.S. agreed to withdraw all 23,000 U.S. military personnel remaining in Thailand by March 1976. Diplomatic relations with China were established in 1975.

After three years of civilian government ended with a military coup on Oct. 6, 1976, Thailand reverted to military rule. Political parties, banned after the coup, gained limited freedom in 1980. The same year, the National Assembly elected Gen. Prem Tinsulanonda as prime minister. General elections on April 18, 1983, and July 27, 1986, resulted in Prem continuing as prime minister over a coalition government.

Refugees from Laos, Cambodia, and Vietnam flooded into Thailand in 1978 and 1979, and despite efforts by the United States and other Western countries to resettle them, a total of 130,000 Laotian and Vietnamese refugees were living in camps along the Cambodian border in mid-1980. A drive by Vietnamese occupation forces on western Cambodian areas loyal to the Pol Pot government, culminating in invasions of Thai territory in late June, drove an estimated 100,000 Cambodians across the line as refugees, adding to the 200,000 of their countrymen already in Thailand.

On April 3, 1981, a military coup against the Prem government failed. Another coup attempt on Sept. 9, 1985, was crushed by loyal troops after 10 hours of fighting in Bangkok. Four persons were killed and about 60 wounded.

In February 1991 a nonviolent military coup led by Gen. Suchinda Kraprayoon overthrew the democratic government charging corruption. The junta leaders declaring a state of emergency and martial law dismissed the houses of Parliament and abolished the Constitution. The following week the military appointed a well-known businessman and former ambassador, Anand Panyarachun to serve as interim prime minister. Under terms of an interim constitution the junta serves as an equal partner in an administration otherwise dominated by experienced technocrats and diplomats.

Parliamentary elections in March 1992 gave more than half the seats at stake to pro-military parties. In April the top military commander was appointed prime minister. Violent street clashes ensued between pro-democracy civilians and the military leading to the King's rebuke of the government. Panyarachun was again made interim Prime Minister in June and was replaced by Chuan Leekpai in September.

TOGO

Republic of Togo
President: Gen. Gnassingbé Eyadema (1967)
Prime Minister: Joseph Koffigoh (1991)
Area: 21,925 sq mi. (56,785 sq km)
Population (est. mid-1993): 4,100,000 (average annual rate of natural increase: 3.6%); birth rate: 49/1000; infant mortality rate: 96/1000; density per square mile: 195
Capital and largest city (1983): Lomé, 366,476; **Monetary unit:** Franc CFA; **Languages:** Ewé, Mina (south), Kabyé, Cotocoli (north), French (official), and many dialects; **Religions:** Indigenous beliefs, 70%; Christian, 20%; Islam, 10%; **National name:** République Togolaise; **Literacy rate:** 43%
Economic summary: Gross domestic product (1990 est.): $1.5 billion; $400 per capita; real growth rate 2%; inflation 1%; unemployment (1987) 2%. Arable land: 25%. Principal agricultural products: yams, cotton, millet, sorghum, cocoa, coffee, rice. Labor force: 78% in agriculture. Major industrial products: phosphate, textiles, processed food. Natural resources: marble, phosphate, limestone. Exports: $396 million (f.o.b., 1990): phosphate, cocoa, coffee. Imports: $502 million (f.o.b., 1990): consumer goods, fuels, machinery, foodstuffs. Major trading partners: E.C., Japan, U.S., Africa

Geography. Togo, twice the size of Maryland, is on the south coast of West Africa bordering on Ghana to the west, Burkina Faso to the north and Benin to the east.

The Gulf of Guinea coastline, only 32 miles long (51 km), is low and sandy. The only port is at Lomé. The Togo hills traverse the central section.

Government. The government of Nicolas Grunitzky was overthrown in a bloodless coup on Jan. 13, 1967, led by Lt. Col. Etienne Eyadema (now Gen. Gnassingbé Eyadema). A National Reconciliation Committee was set up to rule the country. In April, however, Eyadema dissolved the Committee and took over as President. In December 1979, a 67-member National Assembly was voted in by national referendum. The Assembly of the Togolese People is the only political party.

History. Freed slaves from Brazil were the first traders to settle in Togo. Established as a German colony (Togoland) in 1884, the area was split between the British and the French as League of Nations mandates after World War I and subsequently administered as U.N. trusteeships. The British portion voted for incorporation with Ghana.

Togo became independent on April 27, 1960.

Although political parties were legalized in 1991, violent protests continued. The president convened a national conference in July which declared itself sovereign.

In October 1992 troops loyal to Eyadema took the National Assembly building. In January 1993 police fired on demonstrators campaigning for democracy killing at least 20.

TONGA

Kingdom of Tonga
Sovereign: King Taufa'ahau Tupou IV (1965)
Prime Minister: Baron Vaea (1991)
Area: 290 sq mi. (751 sq km)
Population (July 1992): 103,114 (average annual growth rate: 0.8%); birth rate: 26/1000; infant mortality rate: 22/1000; density per square mile: 356.
Capital (1986): Nuku'alofa, 21,383; **Monetary unit:** Pa'anga; **Languages:** Tongan, English; **Religions:** Christian; Free Wesleyan Church claims over 30,000 adherents; **Member of Commonwealth of Nations; Literacy rate:** 100%
Economic summary: Gross domestic product (FY90 est.): $92 million; $900 per capita; real growth rate 2.5%; inflation about 8.9%. Arable land: 25%. Principal agricultural products: vanilla, coffee, ginger, black pepper, coconuts, bananas, copra. Labor force: 70% in agriculture. Natural resources: fish, copra. Exports: $9.6 million (f.o.b., FY90 est.): copra, coconut products, bananas. Imports: $59.9 million (c.i.f., FY90 est.): foodstuffs, machinery and transport equipment, fuels, chemicals, building materials. Major trading partners: New Zealand, Australia, Fiji, U.S., Japan, E.C.

Geography. Situated east of the Fiji Islands in the South Pacific, Tonga (also called the Friendly Islands) consists of some 150 islands, of which 36 are inhabited.

Most of the islands contain active volcanic craters; others are coral atolls.

Government. Tonga is a constitutional monarchy. Executive authority is vested in the Sovereign, a Privy Council, and a Cabinet headed by the Prime Minister. Legislative authority is vested in the Legislative Assembly. Nine seats are reserved for commoners; the others filled by appointees of the king.

History. The present dynasty of Tonga was founded in 1831 by Taufa'ahau Tupou, who took the name George I. He consolidated the kingdom by conquest and in 1875 granted a Constitution.

In 1900, his great-grandson, George II, signed a treaty of friendship with Britain, and the country became a British protected state. The treaty was revised in 1959.

Tonga became independent on June 4, 1970.

Moves were made in 1992 to form a political party independent of the hereditary nobility that dominates the parliament.

TRANSKEI

See South Africa

TRINIDAD AND TOBAGO

Republic of Trinidad and Tobago
President: Noor Hassanali (1987)
Prime Minister: Patrick Manning (1991)
Area: 1,980 sq mi. (5,128 sq km)
Population (est. mid-1993): 1,300,000 (average annual rate of natural increase: 1.4%); birth rate: 21/1000; infant mortality rate: 10.2/1000; density per square mile: 646
Capital and largest city (1990): Port-of-Spain, 50,878; **Monetary unit:** Trinidad and Tobago dollar; **Languages:** English (official); Hindi, French, Spanish; **Religions:** Christian, 60.6%; Hindu, 24.3%; Islam, 6%; **Member of Commonwealth of Nations; Literacy rate:** 98%
Economic summary: Gross domestic product (1990): $4.9 billion; $3,600 per capita; real growth rate 0.7%; inflation 11.1%; unemployment 20.1%. Arable land: 14%. Principal products: sugar cane, cocoa, coffee, citrus. Labor force: 463,900; 14.8% in manufacturing, mining, and quarrying. Major industrial products: petroleum, processed food, cement; tourism. Natural resources: petroleum, natural gas, asphalt. Exports: $2 billion (f.o.b., 1990): petroleum, chemicals, fertilizer. Imports: $1.2 billion (c.i.f., 1990): raw materials, capital goods, consumer goods. Major trading partners: U.S., Caribbean, Latin America, Western Europe, UK, Canada.

Geography. Trinidad and Tobago lies in the Caribbean Sea off the northeast coast of Venezuela. The area of the two islands is slightly less than that of Delaware.

Trinidad, the larger, is mainly flat and rolling, with mountains in the north that reach a height of 3,085 feet (940 m) at Mount Aripo. Tobago is heavily forested with hardwood trees.

Government. A parliamentary democracy. The legislature consists of a 24-member Senate and a 36-member House of Representatives. The political parties are the Peoples National Movement led by Prime Minister Mr. Patrick Manning (21 seats in the House of Representatives); the United National Congress led by Mr. Basdeo Panday (19 seats); and the National Alliance for Reconstruction led by Mr. Selby Wilson (2 seats).

History. Trinidad was discovered by Columbus in 1498 and remained in Spanish possession, despite raids by other European nations, until it capitulated to the British in 1797 during a war between Britain and Spain.

Trinidad was ceded to Britain in 1802, and in 1899 it was united with Tobago as a colony. From 1958 to 1962, Trinidad and Tobago was a part of the West Indies Federation, and on Aug, 31, 1962, it became independent.

On Aug. 1, 1976, Trinidad and Tobago cut its ties wit Britain and became a republic, remaining within the Commonwealth and recognizing Queen Elizabeth II only as head of that organization.

The People's National Movement won a landslide victory in elections of December 1991, making Manning prime minister.

The PNM did well in local elections in September 1992. The ANR, however, held sway over the Tobago House of Assembly in December elections.

TUNISIA

Republic of Tunisia
President: Gen. Zine al-Abidine Ben Ali (1987)
Prime Minister: Hamed Karoui (1989)
Area: 63,379 sq mi. (164,152 sq km)
Population (est. mid-1993): 8,600,000 (average annual rate of natural increase: 1.9%); birth rate: 25/1000; infant mortality rate: 43/1000; density per square mile: 143
Capital and largest city (1991): Tunis, 834,629; **Monetary unit:** Tunisian dinar; **Languages:** Arabic, French; **Religion:** Islam (Sunni), 98%; Christian, 1%; Jewish, less than 1%; **National name:** Al-Joumhouria Attunisia; **Literacy rate:** 65%
Economic summary: Gross domestic product (1991): $13.5 billion; $1,700 per capita; real growth rate 8.5%; inflation 8.2%; unemployment 15%. Arable land: 20%. Principal agricultural products: wheat, olives, oranges, grapes, dates. Labor force: 2,250,000; 32% in agriculture. Major industrial products: textiles, and leather, chemical fertilizers, petroleum, phosphate, iron ore. Natural resources: oil, phosphates, iron ore, lead, zinc. Exports: $3.7 billion (f.o.b., 1991): petroleum, phosphates and chemicals. Imports: $4.9 billion (f.o.b., 1991): machinery and equipment, consumer goods, foodstuffs. Major trading partners: E.C., C.I.S. countries, Middle East, U.S., Turkey, China.

Geography. Tunisia, at the northernmost bulge of Africa, thrusts out toward Sicily to mark the division between the eastern and western Mediterranean Sea. Twice the size of South Carolina, it is bordered on the west by Algeria and by Libya on the south.

Coastal plains on the east rise to a north-south escarpment which slopes gently to the west. Saharan in the south, Tunisia is more mountainous in the north, where the Atlas range continues from Algeria.

Government. Executive power is vested by the Constitution in the president, elected for five years and eligible for re-election to two additional terms. Legislative power is vested in a House of Deputies elected by universal suffrage.

In 1975, the National Assembly amended the Constitution to make Habib Bourguiba president for life. At 71, Bourguiba was re-elected to a fourth five-year term when he ran unopposed in 1974. He was deposed by Gen. Zine Ben Ali in 1987. Ben Ali was elected to a five-year term in April 1989.

History. Tunisia was settled by the Phoenicians and Carthaginians in ancient times. Except for an interval of Vandal conquest in A.D. 439–533, it was part of the Roman Empire until the Arab conquest of 648–69. It was ruled by various Arab and Berber dynasties until the Turks took it in 1570–74. French troops occupied the country in 1881, and the Bey signed a treaty acknowledging a French protectorate.

Nationalist agitation forced France to grant internal autonomy to Tunisia in 1955 and to recognize Tunisian independence and sovereignty in 1956. The Constituent Assembly deposed the Bey on July 25, 1957, declared Tunisia a republic, and elected Habib Bourguiba as president.

Bourguiba maintained a pro-Western foreign policy that earned him enemies. Tunisia refused to break relations with the U.S. during the Israeli-Arab war in June 1967.

Tunisia ended its traditionally neutral role in the Arab world when it joined with the majority of Arab League members to condemn Egypt for concluding a peace treaty with Israel.

Developments in 1986–87 were characterized by a consolidation of power by the 84-year-old Bourguiba and his failure to arrange for a successor. This issue was settled when the then-Prime Minister, Gen. Ben Ali, deposed Bourguiba.

In a surprise move to Western observers President Ben Ali in 1990 expressed his disapproval of U.S.-led actions leading up to the Gulf war.

Concerned with Islamic fundamentalist plots against the state, the government stepped up efforts to eradicate the movement including censorship and frequent detention of suspects.

TURKEY

Republic of Turkey
President: Suleyman Demirel (1993)
Prime Minister: Tansu Ciller (1993)
Area: 300,947 sq mi. (incl. 9,121 in Europe) (779,452 sq km)
Population (est. mid-1993): 60,700,000 (average annual rate of natural increase: 2.2%); birth rate: 29/1000; infant mortality rate: 59/1000; density per square mile: 204
Capital: Ankara; **Largest cities (1990 census):** Istanbul, 6,620,241; Ankara, 2,559,471; Izmir, 1,757,414; Adana, 916,150; Bursa, 834,576; Gaziantep, 603,434; **Monetary unit:** Turkish Lira; **Language:** Turkish; **Religion:** Islam (mostly Sunni), 98%; **National name:** Türkiye Cumhuriyeti; **Literacy rate:** 90.7%
Economic summary: Gross national product (1992): $107 billion; $2,100 per capita; real growth rate 5.9%; inflation (1991): 71.1%; unemployment (1991 est.): 11.1%. Arable land: 20%. Principal agricultural products: cotton, tobacco, cereals, sugar beets, fruits, olives. Labor force: 19,000,000; industry, 25.8%; trade, 18.8%; agriculture, 15.6%; transportation, 12.2%. Major industrial products: textiles, coal, minerals, processed foods, steel, petroleum. Natural resources: coal, chromite, copper, borate, sulfur, petroleum. Exports: $13 billion (f.o.b., 1990): agricultural products, textiles, leather, glass. Imports: $22.3 billion (c.i.f., 1990): crude oil, machinery, motor vehicles, metals, mineral fuels, fertilizer, chemicals. Major trading partners: Germany, France, Italy, U.S., U.K., Iran, Japan.

Geography. Turkey is at the northeastern end of the Mediterranean Sea in southeast Europe and southwest Asia. To the north is the Black Sea and to the west the Aegean Sea. Its neighbors are Greece and Bulgaria to the west, Russia and Ukraine to the north (through the Black Sea), Georgia, Armenia, Azerbaijain, and Iran to the east, and Syria and Iraq to the south.

The Dardanelles, the Sea of Marmara, and the Bosporus divide the country.

Turkey in Europe comprises an area about equal to the state of Massachusetts. It is hilly country drained by the Maritsa River and its tributaries.

Turkey in Asia, or Anatolia, about the size of Texas, is roughly a rectangle in shape with its short sides on the east and west. Its center is a treeless plateau rimmed by mountains.

Government. The President is elected by the Grand National Assembly for a seven-year term and is not eligible for re-election.

The Prime Minister and his Council of Ministers hold the executive power although the President has the right to veto legislation.

History. The Ottoman Turks first appeared in the early 13th century in Anatolia, subjugating Turkish and Mongol bands pressing against the eastern borders of Byzantium. They gradually spread through the Near East and Balkans, capturing Constantinople in 1453 and storming the gates of Vienna two centuries later. At its height, the Ottoman Empire stretched from the Persian Gulf to western Algeria.

Defeat of the Turkish navy at Lepanto by the Holy League in 1571 and failure of the siege of Vienna heralded the decline of Turkish power. By the 18th century, Russia was seeking to establish itself as the protector of Christians in Turkey's Balkan territories. Russian ambitions were checked by Britain and France in the Crimean War (1854–56), but the Russo-Turkish War (1877–78) gave Bulgaria virtual independence and Romania and Serbia liberation from their nominal allegiance to the Sultan.

Turkish weakness stimulated a revolt of young liberals known as the Young Turks in 1909. They forced Sultan Abdul Hamid to grant a constitution and install a liberal government. Reforms were no barrier to further defeats, however, in a war with Italy (1911–12) and the Balkan Wars (1912–13). Under the influence of German military advisors, Turkey signed a secret alliance with Germany on Aug. 2, 1914, that led to a declaration of war by the Allied powers and the ultimate humiliation of the occupation of Turkish territory by Greek and other Allied troops.

In 1919, the new Nationalist movement, headed by Mustafa Kemal, was organized to resist the Allied occupation and, in 1920, a National Assembly elected him President of both the Assembly and the government. Under his leadership, the Greeks were driven out of Smyrna, and other Allied forces were withdrawn.

The present Turkish boundaries (with the exception of Alexandretta, ceded to Turkey by France in 1939) were fixed by the Treaty of Lausanne (1923) and later negotiations. The caliphate and sultanate were separated, and the sultanate was abolished in 1922. On Oct. 29, 1923, Turkey formally became a republic, with Mustafa Kemal, who took the name Kemal Atatürk, as its first President. The caliphate was abolished in 1924, and Atatürk proceeded to carry out an extensive program of reform, modernization, and industrialization.

Gen. Ismet Inönü was elected to succeed Atatürk in 1938 and was re-elected in 1939, 1943, and 1946. Defeated in 1950, he was succeeded by Celâl Bayar. In 1939, a mutual assistance pact was concluded with Britain and France. Neutral during most of World War II Turkey, on Feb. 23, 1945, declared war on Germany and Japan, but took no active part in the conflict.

Turkey became a full member of NATO in 1952.

Turkey invaded Cyprus by sea and air July 20, 1974, following the failure of diplomatic efforts to resolve the crisis caused by the ouster of Archbishop Makarios.

Talks in Geneva involving Greece, Turkey, Britain, and Greek Cypriot and Turkish Cypriot leaders broke down in mid-August. Turkey unilaterally announced a cease-fire August 16, after having gained control of 40% of the island. Turkish Cypriots established their own state in the north on Feb. 13, 1975.

In July 1975, after a 30-day warning, Turkey took over control of all the U.S. installations except the big joint defense base at Incirlik, which it reserved for "NATO tasks alone."

The establishment of military government in September 1980 stopped the slide toward anarchy and brought some improvement in the economy.

A Constituent Assembly, consisting of the six-member National Security Council and members appointed by them, drafted a new Constitution that was approved by an overwhelming (91.5%) majority of the voters in a Nov. 6, 1982, referendum. Prime Minister Turgut Özal's Motherland Party came to power in parliamentary elections held in late 1983. Özal was re-elected in November 1987.

The ruling Anap Party chose a new leader in June 1991, Mesut Yilmaz, who reorganized the government, replacing 20 members of the former cabinet.

In general elections in October 1991 Yilmaz's party was defeated. In November Demirel and his True Path Party formed a coalition government with the Social Democrats.

The sudden death of Turgut Ozal in April 1993 led to Demirel assuming the presidency in May. In June the True Path Party chose Tansu Ciller as its new leader leading to her appointment as Turkey's first female prime minister.

TURKMENISTAN

Republic of Turkmenistan
President: Saparmurad A. Niyazov (1990)
Prime Minister: Khan Akhmedov (1992)
Head of the Government: Saparmurad A. Niyazov
Area: 188,500 sq mi. (488,100 sq km)
Population (est. mid-1993): 4,000,000 (Turkmen, 72%; Russian, 10%; other minorities, Uzbeks, Kazakhs, Ukrainians); (average annual rate of natural increase: 2.7%); birth rate: 34/100; infant mortality rate: 56/100; density per square mile: 21
Capital and largest city (1989): Ashkhabad, 398,000;
Languages: Turkmen, 72%; Russian, 12%; Uzbek, 9%;
Religions: Islam, 85%; Eastern Orthodox, 10%
Economic summary: Per capita GNP (1991): $1,700; real growth rate –6%; inflation 85%; unemployment 20–25%. Labor force: 1,542,000: agriculture and forestry, 42%; industry and construction, 21%. Industries: oil and gas, petrochemicals, fertilizers, food processing, textiles. Agriculture: cotton, fruits, vegetables. Exports: $239 million (1990): natural gas, oil, chemicals, cotton, textiles, carpets. Imports: $970 million (1990): machinery and parts, plastics and rubber, consumer durables, textiles.

Geography. Turkmenistan (formerly Turkmenia) lies between the Caspian Sea in the west and is bounded by Kazakhstan in the north, Uzbekistan in the east, and Iran and Afghanistan in the south. Eighty percent of the republic's territory is desert. The largest desert is the Kara-Kum (Black Sand) approximately 138,966 sq mi. (360,000 sq km) in area. A 684 mil (1,100 km) long canal runs across the Kara-Kum Desert and it supplies water from the Amu Darya River for irrigation and hydroelectric power.

Government. A constitutional republic. The constitution allows for a strong presidential rule. The president heads the Cabinet of Ministers, whose members he appoints with the consent of the Meglis (parliament).

History. Turkmenistan was once part of the ancient Persian empire. The Turkmen people were originally pastoral nomads and some of them continued their unsettled way of life up into the 20th century, living in transportable dome-shaped felt tents. The territory was ruled by the Seljuk Turks in the 11th century. The Mongols of Ghenghis Khan conquered the land in the 13th century and dominated the area for the next two centuries until they were deposed in the late 15th century by invading Uzbeks.

Prior to the 19th century, Turkmenia was divided into two lands, one belonging to the Khanate of Khiva and the other belonging to the Khanate of Bukhara. In 1868, the Khanate of Khiva was made part of the Russian empire and Turkmenia became known as the Transcaspia Region of Russian Turkistan. Turkmenistan was later formed out of the Turkistan Autonomous Soviet Socialist Republic, founded in 1922, and was made an independent Soviet Socialist Republic on May 13, 1925.

Turkmenistan declared its sovereignty in August 1990 and became a member of the Commonwealth of Independent States on Dec. 21, 1991 together with ten other former Soviet republics.

In the presidential election of June 1992 voters reelected Niyazov in a one-candidate race. A new constitution was adopted in May 1992 making it the first Central Asian state to do so.

TUVALU

Sovereign: Queen Elizabeth II
Governor-General: Toaripi Lauti
Prime Minister: Bikenibeu Paeniu (1989)
Area: 10 sq mi. (26 sq km)
Population (July 1992): 9,494; (1992): growth rate 1.8%; birth rate, 28/1000; infant mortality rate, 34/1000; density per square mile: 95
Capital and largest city (1985): Funafuti, 2,810; **Monetary unit:** Australian dollar; **Languages:** Tuvaluan, English; **Religion:** Church of Tuvalu (Congregationalist), 97%; **Member of the Commonwealth of Nations; Literacy rate:** less than 50%
Economic summary: Gross national product (1989 est.): $4.6 million. Per capita Income: $530. Principal agricultural products: copra and coconuts. Export: copra. Imports: food, fuels, machinery. Major trading partners: Australia, Fiji, New Zealand

Geography. Formerly the Ellice Islands, Tuvalu consists of nine small islands scattered over 500,000 square miles of the western Pacific, just south of the equator.

Government. Official executive power is vested in a Governor-General, representing the Queen, who is appointed by her on the recommendation of the Tuvalu government. Actual executive power lies with a Prime Minister, who is responsible to a House of Assembly composed of eight elected members.

History. The Ellice Islands became a British protectorate in 1892 and were annexed by Britain in 1915–16 as part of the Gilbert and Ellice Islands Colony. The Ellice Islands were separated in 1975, given home rule, and renamed Tuvalu. Full independence was granted on Sept. 30, 1978.

Concerned with global warming, Tuvalu became one of the first to sign the Rio de Janeiro conventions in June 1992.

UGANDA

Republic of Uganda
President: Yoweri Museveni (1986)
Prime Minister: George Kosmas Adyebo (1991)
Area: 91,459 sq mi. (236,880 sq km)
Population (est. mid-1993): 18,100,000 (average annual rate of natural increase: 3.1%); birth rate: 51/1000; infant mortality rate: 106/1000; density per square mile: 192
Capital and largest city (est. 1990): Kampala, 1,008,707
Monetary unit: Ugandan shilling
Languages: English (official), Swahili, Luganda, Ateso, Luo
Religions: Christian, 66%; Islam, 16%
Member of Commonwealth of Nations
Literacy rate: 48%
Economic summary: Gross domestic product (1991 est.): $5.6 billion; $300 per capita; real growth rate 4.5%; inflation 35%. Arable land: 23%. Principal agricultural products: coffee, tea, cotton, sugar. Labor force: 4,500,000 (est.); 94% in subsistence activities. Major industrial products: refined sugar, beer, tobacco, cotton textiles, cement. Natural resources: copper, cobalt, limestone, salt. Exports: $208 million (f.o.b., 1990): coffee, cotton, tea. Imports: $209 million (c.i.f., 1990): petroleum products, machinery, transport equipment, metals, food. Major trading partners: U.S., U.K., Kenya, Italy, France, Spain.

Geography. Uganda, twice the size of Pennsylvania, is in east Africa. It is bordered on the west by Zaire, on the north by the Sudan, on the east by Kenya, and on the south by Tanzania and Rwanda.

The country, which lies across the Equator, is divided into three main areas—swampy lowlands, a fertile plateau with wooded hills, and a desert region. Lake Victoria forms part of the southern border.

Government. The country has been run by the National Resistance Movement (NRM) since January, 1986.

History. Uganda was first visited by European explorers as well as Arab traders in 1844. An Anglo-German agreement of 1890 declared it to be in the British sphere of influence in Africa, and the Imperial British East Africa Company was chartered to develop the area. The company did not prosper financially, and in 1894 a British protectorate was proclaimed.

Uganda became independent on Oct. 9, 1962.

Sir Edward Mutesa was elected the first President and Milton Obote the first Prime Minister of the newly independent country. With the help of a young army officer, Col. Idi Amin, Prime Minister Obote seized control of the government from President Mutesa four years later.

On Jan. 25, 1971, Col. Amin deposed President Obote. Obote went into exile in Tanzania. Amin expelled Asian residents and launched a reign of terror against Ugandan opponents, torturing and killing tens of thousands. In 1976, he had himself proclaimed President for Life. In 1977, Amnesty International estimated that 300,000 may have died under his rule, including church leaders and recalcitrant cabinet ministers.

After Amin held military exercises on the Tanzanian border, angering Tanzania's President Julius Nyerere, a combined force of Tanzanian troops and Ugandan exiles loyal to former President Obote invaded Uganda and chased Amin into exile.

After a series of interim administrations, President Obote led his People's Congress Party to victory in 1980 elections that opponents charged were rigged.

On July, 27, 1985, army troops staged a coup taking over the government. Obote fled into exile. The military regime installed Gen. Tito Okello as chief of state.

The National Resistance Army (NRA), an anti-Obote group led by Yoweri Musevni, kept fighting after being excluded from the new regime. They seized Kampala on January 29, 1986, and Musevni was declared President but strife still continues in the northern part of the country.

In 1992 the president still adamantly opposed any move to a multiparty system saying the country needed a respite. A security agreement with Rwanda signed in August aroused hopes that border clashes between the two countries would end.

UKRAINE

Ukraine
President: Leonid M. Kravchuk (1991)
Prime Minister: Leonid D. Kuchma (1992)
Area: 233,000 sq mi. (603,700 sq km)
Population (est. mid-1993): 51,900,000 (Ukrainians, 73%; Russians, 22%; Jews, Poles, Moldovians, Bulgarians); (average annual rate of natural increase: –0.1%): birth rate: 12/1000; infant mortality rate: 18/1000; density per square mile: 223
Capital: Kyiv (Kiev); **Largest cities:** Kyiv, 2,637,000; Kharkiv, 1,622,000; Donetske, 1,121,000; Odessa, 1,104,000; Lviv, 803,000; **Monetary unit:** The Hyrnia; **Language:** Ukrainian; **Religion:** Orthodox, 76%; Urkainian Catholic, 13.5%; Jewish, 2.3%; Baptist, Mennonite, Protestant, and Moslem, 8.2%; **Literacy rate (1992):** 99%
Economic summary: Gross national product (1990): $47.6 billion; per capita GNP (1991): $2,340; real growth rate (1991 est.): –10%; inflation (1991 est.): 83%. Labor force (1990): 25,277,000; industry and construction, 41%; agriculture and forestry, 19%; health, education, and culture, 18%; trade and distribution, 8%; transport and communication, 7%. Mineral resources are iron ore, coal, manganese, natural gas, oil, salt, sulfur, graphite, titanium, magnesium, kaolin, nickel, mercury, and timber. Important agricultural crops are grain, vegetables, meat, and milk. Exports: $13.5 billion (1990): coal, electric power, ferrous and nonferrous metals, chemicals, machinery and transportation equipment, grain and meat. Imports: $16.7 billion (1990): machinery and parts, transportation equipment, chemicals, and textiles. Major trading partners: Russia, Belarus, and Kazakhstan.

Geography. Located in southeastern Europe, the country consists largely of fertile black soil steppes. Mountainous areas include the Carpathians in the southwest and the Crimean chain in the south. There are forest lakes in the north. It is bordered by Belarus on the north and the Russian Federation on the northeast and east, by Poland on the west, by Romania, and Moldova in the southwest, by Hungary, Slovakia, and Poland on the west, and the Baltic Sea and the Sea of Azov in the south.

Government. A constitutional republic.

History. Ukraine was known as "Rus" (from which Russia is a derivative) up until the 16th century. In the 9th century, Kiev was the major political and cultural center in eastern Europe. Kievian Rus reached the height of its power in the 10th century and adopted Byzantine Christianity and the Cyrillic alphabet during that period.

The Mongol conquest in 1240 ended Kievian power. From the 13th to the 16th century, Kiev was under the influence of Poland and western Europe. In 1654, Ukraine asked the czar of Moscovy for protection against Poland and the Treaty of Pereyasav signed that year recognized the suzerainty of Moscow. The agreement was interpreted by Moscow as an invitation to take over Kiev and the Ukrainian state was eventually absorbed into the Russian empire.

After the Russian revolution, Ukraine declared its independence from Russia on Jan. 28, 1918 and several years of warfare ensued with several groups. The Red Army finally was victorious over Kiev and in 1920, Ukraine became a Soviet republic. In 1922, Ukraine became one of the founders of the United Soviet Socialist Republics.

Ukraine was one of the most devastated Soviet republics during World War II.

On April 15, 1986, the nation's nuclear power plant at Chernobyl was the site of the world's worst nuclear accident. On Oct. 29, 1991, the Ukrainian parliament voted to shut down the reactor within two years' time and asked for international assistance in dismantling it.

When president Leonid Kravchuk was elected by the Ukrainian parliament in 1990, he vowed to seek Ukrainian sovereignty. Ukraine declared its independence on Aug. 24, 1991.

New elections were held Dec. 1, 1991 and Mr. Kravchuk was elected president with 61.5% of the vote. Voters also overwhelmingly approved a referendum to establish full independence from the Soviet Union.

On December 8, 1991, Ukrainian, Russian, and Belarus leaders cofounded a new Commonwealth of Independent States with the new capital to be situated in Minsk, Belarus. The Commonwealth was formally established on Dec. 21, 1991 with ten other former Soviet republics.

After independence Ukraine sought to affirm and exercise its territorial claim on the Crimea, which was legally transferred from Russian jurisdiction in 1954. Tensions immediately arose with Russia over this as well as over control of the Black Sea Fleet.

In June 1993 the presidents of Russia and Ukraine agreed to split the contentious Black Sea fleet. Russia also agreed to give Ukraine security guarantees. The dissolution of the CIS joint military command in June left Ukraine's nuclear arms under the control of Russia's Strategic Forces.

UNITED ARAB EMIRATES

President: Sheik Zayed Bin Sultan Al-Nahayan (1971)
Prime Minister: Sheik Maktum ibn Rashid al-Maktum (1990)
Area: 32,000 sq mi. (82,880 sq km)
Population (est. mid-1993): 2,100,000 (average annual rate of natural increase: 2.8%); birth rate: 31/1000; infant mortality rate: 25/1000; density per square mile: 65
Capital and largest city (est. 1989): Abu Dhabi, 363,432
Monetary unit: Dirham
Language: Arabic; Farsi and English widely spoken
Religion: Islam (Sunni, 80%; Shiite, 16%); other, 4%
Literacy rate: 68%
Economic summary: Gross domestic product (1990): $33.7 billion; $14,100 per capita; real growth rate (1989) 11%; inflation (1990 est.) 5.5%. Arable land: negligible%. Principal agricultural products: vegetables, dates, poultry, fish. Labor force: 580,000 (1986 est.) 80% is foreign; 85% in industry and commerce. Major industrial products: light manufactures, petroleum, construction materials. Natural resource: oil. Exports: $21.3 billion (f.o.b., 1990 est.): petroleum, dates, fish. Imports: $11 billion (f.o.b, 1990 est.): consumer goods, food. Major trading partners: Japan, Western Europe, U.S.

Geography. The United Arab Emirates, in the eastern part of the Arabian Peninsula, extends along part of the Gulf of Oman and the southern coast of the Persian Gulf. The nation is the size of Maine. Its neighbors are Saudi Arabia in the west and south, Qatar in the north, and Oman in the east. Most of the land is barren and sandy.

Government. The United Arab Emirates was formed in 1971 by seven emirates known as the Trucial States—Abu Dhabi (the largest), Dubai, Sharjah, Ajman, Fujairah, Ras al Khaimah and Umm al-Qaiwain.

The loose federation allows joint policies in foreign relations, defense, and development, with each member state keeping its internal local system of government headed by its own ruler. A 40-member legislature consists of eight seats each for Abu Dhabi and Dubai, six seats each for Ras al Khaimah and Sharjah, and four each for the others. It is a member of the Arab League.

History. Originally the area was inhabited by a seafaring people who were converted to Islam in the seventh century. Later, a dissident sect, the Carmathians, established a powerful sheikdom, and its army conquered Mecca. After the sheikdom disintegrated, its people became pirates.

Threatening the sultanate of Muscat and Oman early in the 19th century, the pirates provoked the intervention of the British, who in 1820 enforced a partial truce and in 1853 a permanent truce. Thus what had been called the Pirate Coast was renamed the Trucial Coast.

A crisis with Iran over sovereignty of three islands near the Strait of Hormuz arose in 1992. Despite efforts to resolve the issue little progress was made.

UNITED KINGDOM

United Kingdom of Great Britain and Northern Ireland
Sovereign: Queen Elizabeth II (1952)
Prime Minister: John Major (1990)
Area: 94,247 sq mi. (244,100 sq km)
Population (est. mid-1993): 58,000,000 (average annual rate of natural increase: 0.3%); birth rate: 14/1000; infant mortality rate: 7.1/1000; density per square mile: 622
Capital: London, England; **Largest cities (1991 census):** London, 6,377,900 (metropolitan area); Manchester, 406,900; Birmingham, 934,900; Glasgow, (est.) 696,577; Leeds, 674,400; Sheffield, 499,700; Liverpool, 448,300; Bradford, 449,100; Edinburgh, (est.) 434,520; Bristol, 370,300; **Monetary unit:** Pound sterling (£); **Languages:** English, Welsh, Scots Gaelic; **Religions:** Church of England (established church); Church of Wales (disestablished); Church of Scotland (established church—Presbyterian); Church of Ireland (disestablished); Roman Catholic; Methodist; Congregational; Baptist; Jewish; **Literacy rate:** 99%
Economic summary: Gross domestic product (1991 est.): $915.5 billion; $15,900 per capita; real growth rate –1.9%; inflation 5.8%; unemployment 8.1%. Arable land: 29%. Principal agricultural products: wheat, barley, potatoes, sugar beets, livestock, dairy products. Labor force (June 1991): 26,117,000: services, 60.6%; mfg. and construction, 27.2%. Major industrial products: machinery and transport equipment, metals, processed food, paper, textiles, chemicals, clothing. Natural resources: coal, oil, gas. Exports: $186.4 billion (f.o.b., 1991): machinery, transport equipment, chemicals, petroleum. Imports: $211.9 billion (c.i.f., 1991): foodstuffs, machinery, manufactured goods, semifinished goods. Major trading partners: Western European nations, U.S.

Geography. The United Kingdom, consisting of England, Wales, Scotland, and Northern Ireland, is twice the size of New York State. England, in the southeast part of the British Isles, is separated from Scotland on the north by the granite Cheviot Hills; from them the Pennine chain of uplands extends south through the center of England, reaching its highest point in the Lake District in the northwest. To the west along the border of Wales—a land of steep hills and valleys—are the Cambrian Mountains, while the Cotswolds, a range of hills in Gloucestershire, extend into the surrounding shires.

The remainder of England is plain land, though not necessarily flat, with the rocky sand-topped moors in the southwest, the rolling downs in the south and southeast, and the reclaimed marshes of the low-lying fens in the east central districts.

Scotland is divided into three physical regions—the Highlands, the Central Lowlands, containing two-thirds of the population, and the Southern Uplands. The western Highland coast is intersected throughout by long, narrow sea-lochs, or fiords. Scotland also includes the Outer and Inner Hebrides and other islands off the west coast and the Orkney and Shetland Islands off the north coast.

Wales is generally hilly; the Snowdon range in the northern part culminates in Mount Snowdon (3,560 ft, 1,085 m), highest in both England and Wales.

Important rivers flowing into the North Sea are the Thames, Humber, Tees, and Tyne. In the west are the Severn and Wye, which empty into the Bristol Channel and are navigable, as are the Mersey and Ribble.

Government. The United Kingdom is a constitutional monarchy, with a Queen and a Parliament that has two houses: the House of Lords with about 830 hereditary peers, 26 spiritual peers, about 270 life peers and peeresses, and 9 law-lords, who are hereditary, or life, peers, and the House of Commons, which has 650 popularly elected members. Supreme

Rulers of England and Great Britain

Name	Born	Ruled[1]
SAXONS[2]		
Egbert[3]	c.775	828–839
Ethelwulf	?	839–858
Ethelbald	?	858–860
Ethelbert	?	860–866
Ethelred I	?	866–871
Alfred the Great	849	871–899
Edward the Elder	c.870	899–924
Athelstan	895	924–939
Edmund I the Deed-doer	921	939–946
Edred	c.925	946–955
Edwy the Fair	c.943	955–959
Edgar the Peaceful	943	959–975
Edward the Martyr	c.962	975–979
Ethelred II the Unready	968	979–1016
Edmund II Ironside	c.993	1016–1016
DANES		
Canute	995	1016–1035
Harold I Harefoot	c.1016	1035–1040
Hardecanute	c.1018	1040–1042
SAXONS		
Edward the Confessor	c.1004	1042–1066
Harold II	c.1020	1066–1066
HOUSE OF NORMANDY		
William I the Conqueror	1027	1066–1087
William II Rufus	c.1056	1087–1100
Henry I Beauclerc	1068	1100–1135
Stephen of Boulogne	c.1100	1135–1154
HOUSE OF PLANTAGENET		
Henry II	1133	1154–1189
Richard I Coeur de Lion	1157	1189–1199
John Lackland	1167	1199–1216
Henry III	1207	1216–1272
Edward I Longshanks	1239	1272–1307
Edward II	1284	1307–1327
Edward III	1312	1327–1377
Richard II	1367	1377–1399 [4]
HOUSE OF LANCASTER		
Henry IV Bolingbroke	1367	1399–1413
Henry V	1387	1413–1422
Henry VI	1421	1422–1461 [5]

Name	Born	Ruled[1]
HOUSE OF YORK		
Edward IV	1442	1461–1483 [5]
Edward V	1470	1483–1483
Richard III	1452	1483–1485
HOUSE OF TUDOR		
Henry VII	1457	1485–1509
Henry VIII	1491	1509–1547
Edward VI	1537	1547–1553
Jane (Lady Jane Grey)[6]	1537	1553–1553
Mary I ("Bloody Mary")	1516	1553–1558
Elizabeth I	1533	1558–1603
HOUSE OF STUART		
James I[7]	1566	1603–1625
Charles I	1600	1625–1649
COMMONWEALTH		
Council of State	—	1649–1653
Oliver Cromwell[8]	1599	1653–1658
Richard Cromwell[8]	1626	1658–1659 [9]
RESTORATION OF HOUSE OF STUART		
Charles II	1630	1660–1685
James II	1633	1685–1688 [10]
William III[11]	1650	1689–1702
Mary II[11]	1662	1689–1694
Anne	1665	1702–1714
HOUSE OF HANOVER		
George I	1660	1714–1727
George II	1683	1727–1760
George III	1738	1760–1820
George IV	1762	1820–1830
William IV	1765	1830–1837
Victoria	1819	1837–1901
HOUSE OF SAXE-COBURG[12]		
Edward VII	1841	1901–1910
HOUSE OF WINDSOR[12]		
George V	1865	1910–1936
Edward VIII	1894	1936–1936 [13]
George VI	1895	1936–1952
Elizabeth II	1926	1952–

1. Year of end of rule is also that of death, unless otherwise indicated. 2. Dates for Saxon kings are still subject of controversy. 3. Became King of West Saxons in 802; considered (from 828) first King of all England. 4. Died 1400. 5. Henry VI reigned again briefly 1470–71. 6. Nominal Queen for 9 days; not counted as Queen by some authorities. She was beheaded in 1554. 7. Ruled in Scotland as James VI (1567–1625). 8. Lord Protector. 9. Died 1712. 10. Died 1701. 11. Joint rulers (1689–1694). 12. Name changed from Saxe-Coburg to Windsor in 1917. 13. Was known after his abdication as the Duke of Windsor, died 1972.

legislative power is vested in Parliament, which sits for five years unless sooner dissolved.

The executive power of the Crown is exercised by the Cabinet, headed by the Prime Minister. The latter, normally the head of the party commanding a majority in the House of Commons, is appointed by the Sovereign, with whose consent he or she in turn appoints the rest of the Cabinet. All ministers must be members of one or the other house of Parliament; they are individually and collectively responsible to the Crown and Parliament. The Cabinet proposes bills and arranges the business of Parliament, but it depends entirely on the votes in the House of Commons. The Lords cannot hold up "money" bills, but they can delay other bills for a maximum of one year.

By the Act of Union (1707), the Scottish Parliament was assimilated with that of England, and Scotland is now represented in Commons by 71 members. The Secretary of State for Scotland, a member of the Cabinet, is responsible for the administration of Scottish affairs.

Ruler. Queen Elizabeth II, born April 21, 1926, elder daughter of King George VI and Queen Elizabeth, succeeded to the throne on the death of her father on Feb. 6, 1952; married Nov. 20, 1947, to Prince Philip, Duke of Edinburgh, born June 10, 1921; their children are Prince Charles[1] (heir presumptive), born Nov. 14, 1948; Princess Anne, born Aug. 15, 1950; Prince Andrew, born Feb. 19, 1960; and Prince Edward, born March 10, 1964. The Queen's sister is Princess Margaret, born Aug. 21, 1930. Prince William Arthur Philip Louis, son of the Prince and Princess of Wales and second in line to the throne, was born June 21, 1982. A second son, Prince Henry Charles Albert David, was born Sept. 15, 1984, and is third in line.

History. Roman invasions of the 1st century B.C. brought Britain into contact with the Continent. When the Roman legions withdrew in the 5th century A.D., Britain fell easy prey to the invading hordes of Angles, Saxons, and Jutes from Scandinavia and the Low Countries. Seven large kingdoms were established, and the original Britons were forced into Wales and Scotland. It was not until the 10th century that the country finally became united under the kings of Wessex. Following the death of Edward the Confessor (1066), a dispute about the succession arose, and William, Duke of Normandy, invaded England, defeating the Saxon King, Harold II, at the Battle of Hastings (1066). The Norman conquest introduced Norman law and feudalism.

The reign of Henry II (1154–89), first of the Plantagenets, saw an increasing centralization of royal power at the expense of the nobles, but in 1215 John (1199–1216) was forced to sign the Magna Carta, which awarded the people, especially the nobles, certain basic rights. Edward I (1272–1307) continued the conquest of Ireland, reduced Wales to subjection, and made some gains in Scotland. In 1314, however, English forces led by Edward II were ousted from Scotland after the Battle of Bannockburn. The late 13th and early 14th centuries saw the development of a separate House of Commons with tax-raising powers.

Edward III's claim to the throne of France led to the Hundred Years' War (1338–1453) and the loss of almost all the large English territory in France. In England, the great poverty and discontent caused by the war were intensified by the Black Death, a plague that reduced the population by about one-third. The Wars of the Roses (1455–85), a struggle for the throne between the House of York and the House of Lancaster, ended in the victory of Henry Tudor (Henry VII) at Bosworth Field (1485).

During the reign of Henry VIII (1509–47), the Church in England asserted its independence from the Roman Catholic Church. Under Edward VI and Mary, the two extremes of religious fanaticism were reached, and it remained for Henry's daughter, Elizabeth I (1558–1603), to set up the Church of England on a moderate basis. In 1588, the Spanish Armada, a fleet sent out by Catholic King Philip II of Spain, was defeated by the English and destroyed during a storm. During Elizabeth's reign, England became a world power.

Elizabeth's heir was a Stuart—James VI of Scotland—who joined the two crowns as James I (1603–25). The Stuart kings incurred large debts and were forced either to depend on Parliament for taxes or to raise money by illegal means. In 1642, war broke out between Charles I and a large segment of the Parliament; Charles was defeated and executed in 1649, and the monarchy was then abolished. After the death in 1658 of Oliver Cromwell, the Lord Protector, the Puritan Commonwealth fell to pieces and Charles II was placed on the throne in 1660. The struggle between the King and Parliament continued, but Charles II knew when to compromise. His brother, James II (1685–88), possessed none of his ability and was ousted by the Revolution of 1688, which confirmed the primacy of Parliament. James's daughter, Mary, and her husband, William of Orange, were now the rulers.

1. The title Prince of Wales, which is not inherited, was conferred on Prince Charles by his mother on July 26, 1958. The investiture ceremony took place on July 1, 1969. The previous Prince of Wales was Prince Edward Albert, who held the title from 1911 to 1936 before he became Edward VIII.

Area and Population of United Kingdom

Subdivision	Area sq mi.	Area sq km	Population 1991 (census) preliminary)
England and Wales	58,381	151,207	48,960,000
Scotland	30,414	78,772	4,957,000
Northern Ireland	5,452	14,121	1,583,000
Total	**94,247**	**244,100**	**55,500,000**

Queen Anne's reign (1702–14) was marked by the Duke of Marlborough's victories over France at Blenheim, Oudenarde, and Malplaquet in the War of the Spanish Succession. England and Scotland meanwhile were joined by the Act of Union (1707). Upon the death of Anne, the distant claims of the elector of Hanover were recognized, and he became King of Great Britain and Ireland as George I.

The unwillingness of the Hanoverian kings to rule resulted in the formation by the royal ministers of a Cabinet, headed by a Prime Minister, which directed all public business. Abroad, the constant wars with France expanded the British Empire all over the globe, particularly in North America and India. This imperial growth was checked by the revolt of the American colonies (1775–81).

Struggles with France broke out again in 1793 and during the Napoleonic Wars, which ended at Waterloo in (1815).

The Victorian era, named after Queen Victoria (1837–1901), saw the growth of a democratic system of government that had begun with the Reform Bill of 1832. The two important wars in Victoria's reign were the Crimean War against Russia (1853–56) and the Boer War (1899–1902), the latter enormously extending Britain's influence in Africa.

Increasing uneasiness at home and abroad marked the reign of Edward VII (1901–10). Within four years after the accession of George V in 1910, Britain entered World War I when Germany invaded Belgium. The nation was led by coalition Cabinets, headed first by Herbert Asquith and then, starting in 1916, by the Welsh statesman David Lloyd George. Postwar labor unrest culminated in the general strike of 1926.

King Edward VIII succeeded to the throne on Jan. 20, 1936, at his father's death, but abdicated on Dec. 11, 1936 (in order to marry an American divorcee, Wallis Warfield Simpson) in favor of his brother, who became George VI.

The efforts of Prime Minister Neville Chamberlain to stem the rising threat of Nazism in Germany failed with the German invasion of Poland on Sept. 1, 1939, which was followed by Britain's entry into World War II on September 3. Allied reverses in the spring of 1940 led to Chamberlain's resignation and the formation of another coalition war Cabinet by the Conservative leader, Winston Churchill, who led Britain through most of World War II. Churchill resigned shortly after V-E Day, May 7, 1945, but then formed

British Prime Ministers Since 1770

Name	Term
Lord North (Tory)	1770–1782
Marquis of Rockingham (Whig)	1782–1782
Earl of Shelburne (Whig)	1782–1783
Duke of Portland (Coalition)	1783–1783
William Pitt, the Younger (Tory)	1783–1801
Henry Addington (Tory)	1801–1804
William Pitt, the Younger (Tory)	1804–1806
Baron Grenville (Whig)	1806–1807
Duke of Portland (Tory)	1807–1809
Spencer Perceval (Tory)	1809–1812
Earl of Liverpool (Tory)	1812–1827
George Canning (Tory)	1827–1827
Viscount Goderich (Tory)	1827–1828
Duke of Wellington (Tory)	1828–1830
Earl Grey (Whig)	1830–1834
Viscount Melbourne (Whig)	1834–1834
Sir Robert Peel (Tory)	1834–1835
Viscount Melbourne (Whig)	1835–1841
Sir Robert Peel (Tory)	1841–1846
Earl Russell (Whig)	1846–1852
Earl of Derby (Tory)	1852–1852
Earl of Aberdeen (Coalition)	1852–1855
Viscount Palmerston (Liberal)	1855–1858
Earl of Derby (Conservative)	1858–1859
Viscount Palmerston (Liberal)	1859–1865
Earl Russell (Liberal)	1865–1866
Earl of Derby (Conservative)	1866–1868
Benjamin Disraeli (Conservative)	1868–1868
William E. Gladstone (Liberal)	1868–1874
Benjamin Disraeli (Conservative)	1874–1880
William E. Gladstone (Liberal)	1880–1885
Marquis of Salisbury (Conservative)	1885–1886
William E. Gladstone (Liberal)	1886–1886
Marquis of Salisbury (Conservative)	1886–1892
William E. Gladstone (Liberal)	1892–1894
Earl of Rosebery (Liberal)	1894–1895
Marquis of Salisbury (Conservative)	1895–1902
Arthur James Balfour (Conservative)	1902–1905
Sir H. Campbell–Bannerman (Liberal)	1905–1908
Herbert H. Asquith (Liberal)	1908–1915
Herbert H. Asquith (Coalition)	1915–1916
David Lloyd George (Coalition)	1916–1922
Andrew Bonar Law (Conservative)	1922–1923
Stanley Baldwin (Conservative)	1923–1924
James Ramsay MacDonald (Labor)	1924–1924
Stanley Baldwin (Conservative)	1924–1929
James Ramsay MacDonald (Labor)	1929–1931
James Ramsay MacDonald (Coalition)	1931–1935
Stanley Baldwin (Coalition)	1935–1937
Neville Chamberlain (Coalition)	1937–1940
Winston Churchill (Coalition)	1940–1945
Clement R. Attlee (Labor)	1945–1951
Sir Winston Churchill (Conservative)	1951–1955
Sir Anthony Eden (Conservative)	1955–1957
Harold Macmillan (Conservative)	1957–1963
Sir Alec Frederick Douglas–Home (Conservative)	1963–1964
Harold Wilson (Labor)	1964–1970
Edward Heath (Conservative)	1970–1974
Harold Wilson (Labor)	1974–1976
James Callaghan (Labor)	1976–1979
Margaret Thatcher (Conservative)	1979–1990
John Major (Conservative)	1990–

a "caretaker" government that remained in office until after the parliamentary elections in July, which the Labor Party won overwhelmingly. The government formed by Clement R. Attlee began a moderate socialist program.

For details of World War II (1939–45), *see* Headline History.

In 1951, Churchill again became Prime Minister at the head of a Conservative government. George VI died Feb. 6, 1952, and was succeeded by his daughter Elizabeth II.

Churchill stepped down in 1955 in favor of Sir Anthony Eden, who resigned on grounds of ill health in 1957, and was succeeded by Harold Macmillan and Sir Alec Douglas-Home. In 1964, Harold Wilson led the Labor Party to victory.

A lagging economy brought the Conservatives back to power in 1970. Prime Minister Edward Heath won Britain's admission to the European Community.

Margaret Thatcher became Britain's first woman Prime Minister as the Conservatives won 339 seats on May 3, 1979.

An Argentine invasion of the Falkland Islands on April 2, 1982, involved Britain in a war 8,000 miles from the home islands. Although Argentina had long claimed the Falklands, known as the Malvinas in Spanish, negotiations were in progress until a month before the invasion.

When more than 11,000 Argentine troops on the Falklands surrendered on June 14, 1982, Mrs. Thatcher declared her intention to garrison the islands indefinitely, together with a naval presence.

Although there were continuing economic problems and foreign policy disputes, an upswing in the economy in 1986–87 led Thatcher to call elections for June 11 in which she won a near-unprecedented third consecutive term.

Through much, if not all, of 1990 the Conservatives were losing the confidence of the electorate. The unpopularity of her poll tax together with an uncompromising position toward further European integration eroded support within her own party. When John Major won the Conservative Party leadership in November, Mrs. Thatcher resigned, paving the way for the Queen to ask Mr. Major to form a government. In the ensuing months the prime minister revamped the nation's tax system.

In the middle of a long recession John Major called a national election for April 1992. Confounding many political observers the Conservatives won but by a far narrower margin than previously.

After months of political maneuvering the House of Commons in May 1993 passed a bill ratifying the Maastrict Treaty. The prime minister made clear, however, that the UK had no intention to rejoin the Exchange Rate Mechanism.

NORTHERN IRELAND

Status: Part of United Kingdom
Secretary of State: Sir Patrick Mayhew (1992)
Area: 5,452 sq mi. (14,121 sq km)
Population (est. 1991): 1,583,000; **Density per square mile:** 279.7
Capital and largest city (mid-1990): Belfast, 295,100

Monetary unit: British pound sterling; **Languages:** English, Gaelic; **Religions:** Roman Catholic, 28%; Presbyterian, 22.9%; Church of Ireland, 19%; Methodist, 4%

Geography. Northern Ireland comprises the counties of Antrim, Armagh, Down, Fermanagh, Londonderry, and Tyrone, which make up predominantly Protestant Ulster and form the northern part of the island of Ireland, westernmost of the British Isles. It is slightly larger than Connecticut.

Government. Northern Ireland is an integral part of the United Kingdom (it has 12 representatives in the British House of Commons), but under the terms of the government of Ireland Act in 1920, it had a semi-autonomous government. But in 1972, after three years of internal strife which resulted in over 400 dead and thousands injured, Britain suspended the Ulster parliament. The Ulster counties became governed directly from London after an attempt to return certain powers to an elected Assembly in Belfast.

The Northern Ireland Assembly was dissolved in 1975 and a Constitutional Convention was elected to write a Constitution acceptable to Protestants and Catholics. The convention failed to reach agreement and closed down the next year.

History. Ulster was part of Catholic Ireland until the reign of Elizabeth I (1558–1603) when, after crushing three Irish rebellions, the crown confiscated lands in Ireland and settled in Ulster the Scot Presbyterians who became rooted there. Another rebellion in 1641–51, crushed as brutally by Oliver Cromwell, resulted in the settlement of Anglican Englishmen in Ulster. Subsequent political policy favoring Protestants and disadvantaging Catholics encouraged further settlement in Northern Ireland.

But the North did not separate from the South until William Gladstone presented in 1886 his proposal for home rule in Ireland as a means of settling the Irish Question. The Protestants in the North, although they had grievances like the Catholics in the South, feared domination by the Catholic majority. Industry, moreover, was concentrated in the north and dependent on the British market.

When World War I began, civil war threatened between the regions. Northern Ireland, however, did not become a political entity until the six counties accepted the Home Rule Bill of 1920. This set up a semiautonomous Parliament in Belfast and a Crown-appointed Governor advised by a Cabinet of the Prime Minister and eight ministers, as well as a 12-member representation in the House of Commons in London.

As the Republic of Ireland gained its sovereignty, relations improved between North and South, although the Irish Republican Army, outlawed in recent years, continued the struggle to end the partition of Ireland. In 1966–69, communal rioting and street fighting between Protestants and Catholics occurred in Londonderry, fomented by extremist nationalist Protestants, who feared the Catholics might attain a local majority, and by Catholics demonstrating for civil rights.

Rioting, terrorism, and sniping killed more than 2,200 people from 1969 through 1984 and the religious communities, Catholic and Protestant, became hostile armed camps. British troops were brought in to separate them but themselves became a target of Catholics.

In 1973, a new British charter created a 78-member Assembly elected by proportional representation that gave more weight to Catholic strength. It created a Province Executive with committee chairmen of the Assembly heading all government departments except law enforcement, which remained under London's control. Assembly elections in 1973 produced a majority for the new Constitution that included Catholic assemblymen.

Ulster's leaders agreed in 1973 to create an 11-member Executive Body with six seats assigned to Unionists (Protestants) and four to members of Catholic parties. Unionist leader Brian Faulkner headed the Executive. Also agreed to was a Council of Ireland, with 14 seats evenly divided between Dublin and Belfast, which could act only by unanimous vote.

Although the Council lacked real authority, its creation sparked a general strike by Protestant extremists in 1974. The two-week strike caused Faulkner's resignation from the Executive and resumption of direct rule from London.

In April 1974, London instituted a new program that responded to some Catholic grievances, but assigned more British troops to cut off movement of arms and munitions to Ulster's violence-racked cities.

Violence continued unabated, with new heights reached early in 1976 when the British government announced the end of special privileges for political prisoners in Northern Ireland. British Prime Minister James Callaghan visited Belfast in July and pledged that Ulster would remain part of the United Kingdom unless a clear majority wished to separate.

In October 1977, the 1976 Nobel Prize for Peace was awarded to Mairead Corrigan and Betty Williams for their campaign for peace in Northern Ireland. Intermittent violence continued, however, and on Aug. 27, 1979, an I.R.A. bomb killed Earl Mountbatten as he was sailing off southern Ireland.

New talks aimed at a restoration of home rule in Northern Ireland began and quickly ended in January 1980. In May, Mrs. Thatcher met with the new Prime Minister of the Irish Republic, Charles Haughey, but she insisted that the future of Ulster must be decided only by its people and the British Parliament. Haughey declared that an internal solution "cannot and will not succeed."

On November 15, 1985, Mrs. Thatcher signed an agreement with Irish Prime Minister Garrett Fitzgerald giving Ireland a consultative role in the affairs of Northern Ireland. It was met with intense disapproval by the Ulster Unionists.

Talks began in June 1991 between leaders of four major Ulster political parties. The hope was that these talks would lead to some degree of home rule in Northern Ireland. On July 3, however, they collapsed.

Dependencies of the United Kingdom

ANGUILLA

Status: Dependency
Governor: A.W. Shave (1992)
Area: 35 sq mi. (91 sq km)
Population (1992 census): 8,800
Capital (1992): The Valley, 1,400; **Monetary unit:** East Caribbean dollar; **Literacy:** 95%

Anguilla was originally part of the West Indies Associated States as a component of St. Kitts-Nevis-Anguilla.

In 1967, Anguilla declared its independence from the St. Kitts-Nevis-Anguilla federation. Britain however, did not recognize this action. In February 1969,

Anguilla voted to cut all ties with Britain and become an independent republic. In March, Britain landed troops on the island and, on March 30, a truce was signed. In July 1971, Anguilla became a dependency of Britain and two months later Britain ordered the withdrawal of all its troops.

A new Constitution for Anguilla, effective in February 1976, provides for separate administration and a government of elected representatives. The Associated State of St. Kitts-Nevis-Anguilla ended Dec. 19, 1980.

BERMUDA

Status: Self-governing dependency
Governor: Lord Waddington (1992)
Premier: John Swan (1982)
Area: 20 sq mi. (52 sq km)
Population (July 1992): 60,213
Capital (1990): Hamilton, 2,000; **Monetary unit:** Bermuda dollar; **Literacy rate:** 98%
Economic summary: Gross domestic product (1989 est.): $1.3 billion; $23,000 per capita; 2.0% real growth rate. Arable land: 0%. Principal agricultural products: bananas, vegetables, citrus fruits, dairy products. Labor force: 32,000; 47% clerical and in services. Major industrial products: structural concrete, paints, pharmaceuticals. Natural resource: limestone. Exports: semi-tropical produce, light manufactures. Imports: foodstuffs, fuel, machinery. Major trading partners: U.S., U.K., Canada.

Bermuda is an archipelago of about 360 small islands, 580 miles (934 km) east of North Carolina. The largest is (Great) Bermuda, or Long Island. Discovered by Juan de Bermúdez, a shipwrecked Spaniard, early in the 16th century, the islands were settled in 1612 by an offshoot of the Virginia Company and became a crown colony in 1684.

In 1940, sites on the islands were leased for 99 years to the U.S. for air and navy bases. Bermuda is also the headquarters of the West Indies and Atlantic squadron of the Royal Navy.

In 1968, Bermuda was granted a new Constitution, its first Prime Minister, and autonomy, except for foreign relations, defense, and internal security. The predominantly white United Bermuda Party has retained power in four elections against the opposition—the black-led Progressive Laborites—although Bermuda's population is 60% black.

The 1991 budget called for tax increases and control of the island's offshore banking sector was tightened.

BRITISH ANTARCTIC TERRITORY

Status: Dependency
Commissioner: Peter M. Newton
Area: 500,000 sq mi. (1,395,000 sq km)
Population (1990): no permanent residents

The British Antarctic Territory consists of the South Shetland Islands, South Orkney Islands, and nearby Graham Land on the Antarctic continent, largely uninhabited. They are dependencies of the British crown colony of the Falkland Islands but received a separate administration in 1962, being governed by a British-appointed High Commissioner who is Governor of the Falklands.

BRITISH INDIAN OCEAN TERRITORY

Status: Dependency
Commissioner and Administrator: T.G. Harris
Administrative headquarters: Victoria, Seychelles
Area: 85 sq mi. (220 sq km)

This dependency, consisting of the Chagos Archipelago and other small island groups, was formed in 1965 by agreement with Mauritius and the Seychelles. There is no permanent civilian population in the territory.

BRITISH VIRGIN ISLANDS

Status: Dependency
Governor: Peter Alfred Penfold (1992)
Area: 59 sq mi. (153 sq km)
Population (July 1992): 12,555
Capital (est. 1989): Road Town (on Tortola): 2,479; **Monetary unit:** U.S. dollar

Some 36 islands in the Caribbean Sea northeast of Puerto Rico and west of the Leeward Islands, the British Virgin Islands are economically interdependent with the U.S. Virgin Islands to the south. They were formerly part of the administration of the Leeward Islands. They received a separate administration in 1956 as a crown colony. In 1967 a new Constitution was promulgated that provided for a ministerial system of government headed by the Governor. The principal islands are Tortola, Virgin Gorda, Anegada, and Jost Van Dyke.

CAYMAN ISLANDS

Status: Dependency
Governor: Michael E.J. Gore (1992)
Area: 100 sq mi. (259 sq km)
Population (July 1992): 29,139
Capital (1989): George Town (on Grand Cayman), 12,921; **Monetary unit:** Cayman Islands dollar

This dependency consists of three islands—Grand Cayman (76 sq mi.; 197 sq km), Cayman Brac (22 sq mi.; 57 sq km), and Little Cayman (20 sq mi.; 52 sq km)—situated about 180 miles (290 km) northwest of Jamaica. They were dependencies of Jamaica until 1959, when they became a unit territory within the Federation of the West Indies. In 1962, upon the dissolution of the Federation, the Cayman Islands became a British dependency.

The islands' chief export is turtle products.

CHANNEL ISLANDS

Status: Crown dependencies
Lieutenant Governor of Jersey: Air Marshall Sir John Sutton (1990)
Lieutenant Governor of Guernsey: Lt. Gen. Sir Michael Wilkins (1990)
Area: 120 sq mi. (311 sq km)
Populations (July 1992): Jersey, 85,026; Guernsey, 57,949
Capital of Jersey (1986): St. Helier, 27,083' **Capital of Guernsey (1986):** St. Peter Port, 16,085' **Monetary units:** Guernsey pound; Jersey pound

This group of islands, lying in the English Channel off the northwest coast of France, is the only portion of the Duchy of Normandy belonging to the

English Crown, to which it has been attached since the conquest of 1066. It was the only British possession occupied by Germany during World War II.

For purposes of government, the islands are divided into the Bailiwick of Jersey (45 sq mi.; 117 sq km) and the Bailiwick of Guernsey (30 sq mi.; 78 sq km), including Alderney (3 sq mi.; 7.8 sq km); Sark (2 sq mi.; 5.2 sq km), Herm, Jethou, etc. The islands are administered according to their own laws and customs by local governments. Acts of Parliament in London are not binding on the islands unless they are specifically mentioned. The Queen is represented in each Bailiwick by a Lieutenant Governor.

FALKLAND ISLANDS AND DEPENDENCIES

Status: Dependency
Governor: David Evarard Tatham (1992)
Chief Executive: R. Sampson
Area: 4,700 sq mi. (12,173 sq km)
Population (July 1992): 1,900
Capital (1991): Stanley (on East Falkland), 1,643
Monetary unit: Falkland Island pound

This sparsely inhabited dependency consists of a group of islands in the South Atlantic, about 250 miles (402 km) east of the South American mainland. The largest islands are East Falkland and West Falkland. Dependencies are South Georgia Island (1,450 sq mi.; 3,756 sq km), the South Sandwich Islands, and other islets. Three former dependencies—Graham Land, the South Shetland Islands, and the South Orkney Islands—were established as a new British dependency, the British Antarctic Territory, in 1962.

The chief industry is sheep raising and, apart from the production of wool, hides and skins, and tallow, there are no known resources. The whaling industry is carried on from South Georgia Island.

The chief export is wool.

GIBRALTAR

Status: Self-governing dependency
Governor: Admiral Sir Derek Reffell
Chief Minister: J. Bossano
Area: 2.25 sq mi. (5.8 sq km)
Population (July 1992): 29,651; growth rate: 0.1%
Monetary unit: Gibraltar pound; **Literacy rate:** 99% (est.)
Economic summary: Gross national product (FY87 est.): $182 million; $4,600 per capita. Exports: $82 million (f.o.b., 1988): re-exports of tobacco, petroleum, wine. Imports: $258 million (c.i.f., 1988): manufactured goods, fuels, foodstuffs. Major trading partners: U.K., Morocco, Portugal, Netherlands, Spain, U.S.

Gibraltar, at the south end of the Iberian Peninsula, is a rocky promontory commanding the western entrance to the Mediterranean. Aside from its strategic importance, it is also a free port, naval base, and coaling station. It was captured by the Arabs crossing from Africa into Spain in A.D. 711. In the 15th century, it passed to the Moorish ruler of Granada and later became Spanish. It was captured by an Anglo-Dutch force in 1704 during the War of the Spanish Succession and passed to Great Britain by the Treaty of Utrecht in 1713. Most of the inhabitants of Gibraltar are of Spanish, Italian, and Maltese descent.

Spanish efforts to recover Gibraltar culminated in a referendum in 1967 in which the residents voted overwhelmingly to retain their link with Britain. Spain sealed Gibraltar's land border in 1969 and did not open communications until April 1980, after the two governments had agreed to solve their dispute in keeping with a United Nations resolution calling for restoration of the "Rock" to Spain.

The last British military battalion on the "Rock" was withdrawn in March 1991. Spain suggested a form of joint control, but the U.K. refused.

HONG KONG

Status: Dependency
Governor: Christopher Patten (1992)
Area: 398 sq mi. (1,031 sq km)
Population (est. mid-1993): 5,800,000 (average annual rate of natural increase: 0.7%); birth rate: 12/1000; infant mortality rate: 6.7/1000; density per square mile: 15,142
Capital (1976 census): Victoria (Hong Kong Island), 501,700; **Monetary unit:** Hong Kong dollar; **Literacy rate:** 77%
Economic summary: Gross domestic product (1991 est.): $80.9 billion: $13,800 per capita; real growth rate 3.8%; inflation 12%; unemployment 2%. Arable land: 7%. Principal agricultural products: vegetables, rice, dairy products. Labor force (1990): 2,800,000: 28.5% manufacturing; 27.9%, wholesale, retail, hotels, restaurants. Major industrial products: textiles, clothing, toys, transistor radios, watches, electronic components. Exports: $82 billion (f.o.b., 1990): clothing, textiles, toys, watches, electrical appliances, footwear. Imports: $82.4 billion (c.i.f., 1990): raw materials, transport equipment, food. Major trading partners: U.S., U.K., Japan, Germany, China, Taiwan.

The crown colony of Hong Kong comprises the island of Hong Kong (32 sq mi.; 83 sq km), Stonecutters' Island, Kowloon Peninsula, and the New Territories on the adjoining mainland. The island of Hong Kong, located at the mouth of the Pearl River about 90 miles (145 km) southeast of Canton, was ceded to Britain in 1841.

Stonecutters' Island and Kowloon were annexed in 1860, and the New Territories, which are mainly agricultural lands, were leased from China in 1898 for 99 years. Hong Kong was attacked by Japanese troops Dec. 7, 1941, and surrendered the following Christmas. It remained under Japanese occupation until August 1945.

After two years of painstaking negotiation, authorities of Britain and the People's Republic of China agreed in 1984 that Hong Kong would return to Chinese sovereignty on June 30, 1997, when Britain's lease on the New Territories expires. They also agreed that the vibrant capitalist enclave on China's coast would retain its status as a free port and its social, economic, and legal system as a special administrative region of China. Current laws will remain basically unchanged.

Under a unique "One Country, Two Systems" arrangement, the Chinese government promised that Hong Kong's lifestyle would remain unchanged for 50 years, and that freedoms of speech, press, assembly, association, travel, right to strike, and religious belief would be guaranteed by law. However, the chief executive and some of the legislature will be appointed by Beijing.

Hong Kong will continue to have its own finances and issue its own travel documents, and Peking will not levy taxes.

The crackdown by hard-liners in China has led to apprehension that Hong Kong's autonomy won't be respected.

ISLE OF MAN

Status: Self-Governing Crown Dependency
Lieutenant Governor: Air Marshall Sir Laurence Jones
Area: 227 sq mi. (588 sq km)
Population (1991 census): 69,788; growth rate 0.1%
Capital (1991): Douglas, 22,214; **Monetary unit:** Isle of Man pound

Situated in the Irish Sea, equidistant from Scotland, Ireland, and England, the Isle of Man is administered according to its own laws by a government composed of the Lieutenant Governor, a Legislative Council, and a House of Keys, one of the most ancient legislative assemblies in the world.

The chief exports are beef and lamb, fish, and livestock.

LEEWARD ISLANDS

See British Virgin Islands; Montserrat

MONTSERRAT

Status: Dependency
Chief Minister: Reuben Meade (1991)
Area: 38 sq mi. (98 sq km)
Population (July 1992): 12,617; growth rate 0.4%
Capital (est. 1988): Plymouth, 3,000
Monetary unit: East Caribbean dollar

The island of Montserrat is in the Lesser Antilles of the West Indies. Until 1956, it was a division of the Leeward Islands. It did not join the West Indies Associated States established in 1967.

The chief exports are cattle, potatoes, cotton, lint, recapped tires, mangoes, and tomatoes.

PITCAIRN ISLAND

Status: Dependency
Governor: David Joseph Moss
Island Magistrate: J. Warren
Area: 1.75 sq mi. (4.5 sq km)
Population (July 1992): 52
Capital: Adamstown

Pitcairn Island, in the South Pacific about midway between Australia and South America, consists of the island of Pitcairn and the three uninhabited islands of Henderson, Duicie, and Oeno. The island of Pitcairn was settled in 1790 by British mutineers from the ship *Bounty*, commanded by Capt. William Bligh. It was annexed as a British colony in 1838. Overpopulation forced removal of the settlement to Norfolk Island in 1856, but about 40 persons soon returned.

The colony is governed by a 10-member Council presided over by the Island Magistrate, who is elected for a three-year term.

ST. HELENA

Status: Dependency
Governor: A.N. Hoole (1991)
Area: 120 sq mi. (310 sq km)
Population (July 1992): 6,698; growth rate 0.3%
Capital (1987): Jamestown, 1,332
Monetary unit: Pound sterling

St. Helena is a volcanic island in the South Atlantic about 1,100 miles (1,770 km) from the west coast of Africa. It is famous as the place of exile of Napoleon (1815–21).

It was taken for England in 1659 by the East India Company and was brought under the direct government of the Crown in 1834.

St. Helena has two dependencies: Ascension (34 sq mi.; 88 sq km), an island about 700 miles (1,127 km) northwest of St. Helena; and Tristan da Cunha (40 sq mi.; 104 sq km), a group of six islands about 1,500 miles (2,414 km) south-southwest of St. Helena.

TURKS AND CAICOS ISLANDS

Status: Dependency
Governor: Michael Bradley (1987)
Area: 193 sq mi. (500 sq km)
Population (July 1992): 12,697; growth rate: 3.3%
Capital (1990): Cockburn Town, 3,720
Monetary unit: U.S. dollar

These two groups of islands are situated at the southeast end of the Bahamas. The principal islands in the Turks group are Grand Turk and Salt Cay; the principal ones in the Caicos group are South Caicos, East Caicos, Middle (or Grand) Caicos, North Caicos, Providenciales, and West Caicos.

The Turks and Caicos Islands were dependencies of Jamaica until 1959, when they became a unit territory within the Federation of the West Indies. In 1962, when Jamaica became independent, the Turks and Caicos became a British crown colony. The present Constitution has been in force since 1969.

Chief exports in 1974 were crayfish (73%) and conch (25%).

VIRGIN ISLANDS

See British Virgin Islands

UNITED STATES

The United States of America
President: William J. Clinton (1993)
Vice President: Albert A. Gore, Jr. (1993)
Land area: 3,536,341 sq mi. (9,159,123 sq km)
Population (est. mid-1993): 258,300,000; **(1990 census):** 248,709,873 (% change 1980–1990: +9.80). White: 199,686,070 (80.3%); Black: 29,986,060 (12.1%); American Indian, Eskimo, or Aleut: 1,959,234 (0.8%); Asian or Pacific Islander: 7,273,662 (2.9%); Other Race: 9,804,847 (3.9%); Hispanic Origin[1]: 22,354,059 (9.0%); (average annual rate of natural increase: 0.8%); birth rate: 16/1000; infant mortality rate: 8.6/1000; density per square mile: 73
Capital (1990 census.): Washington, D.C., 606,900; **Largest cities (1990 census):** New York, 7,322,564; Los Angeles, 3,485,398; Chicago, 2,783,726; Houston, 1,630,553; Philadelphia, 1,585,577; San Diego, 1,110,549; Detroit, 1,027,974; Dallas, 1,006,877; Phoenix, 983,403; San Antonio, 935,933; **Monetary unit:** Dollar; **Languages:** predominantly English, sizable Spanish-speaking minority; **Religions:** Protestant, 61%; Roman Catholic, 25%; Jewish, 2%; other, 5%; none, 7%; **Literacy rate:** 97%
Economic summary: Gross domestic product (1992): $5,950 billion; per capita personal income (1992 est.): $19,841. Civilian labor force (June 1993): 127,500,000 Arable land: 20%. Principal products: corn, wheat, barley, oats, sugar, potatoes, soybeans, fruits, beef,

veal, pork. Labor force: 125,557,000. Major industrial products: petroleum products, fertilizers, cement, pig iron and steel, plastics and resins, newsprint, motor vehicles, machinery, natural gas, electricity. Natural resources: coal, oil, copper, gold, silver, minerals, timber. Exports: machinery, chemicals, aircrafts, military equipment, cereals, motor vehicles, grains. Imports: crude and partly refined petroleum, machinery, automobiles. Major trading partners: Canada, Japan, Western Europe.

1. Persons of Hispanic origin can be of any race.

Government. The president is elected for a four-year term and may be re-elected only once. In 1993, the bicameral Congress consisted of the 100-member Senate (55 Democrats, 45 Republicans), elected to a six-year term with one-third of the seats becoming vacant every two years, and the 435-member House of Representatives (258 Democrats, 176 Republicans, 1 Independent), elected every two years. The minimum voting age is 18.

URUGUAY

Oriental Republic of Uruguay
President: Luis Alberto Lacalle (1990)
Area: 68,040 sq mi. (176,224 sq km)
Population (est. mid-1993): 3,200,000 (average annual rate of natural increase: 0.9%); birth rate: 19/1000; infant mortality rate: 20/1000; density per square mile: 47
Capital and largest city (est. 1992): Montevideo, 1,500,000; **Monetary unit:** Peso; **Language:** Spanish; **Religion:** Roman Catholic, 66%; Protestant, 2%; Jewish, 2%; **National name:** Republica Oriental del Uruguay; **Literacy rate:** 94%
Economic summary: Gross domestic product (1992): $11.5 billion: $3,643 per capita; real growth rate 2.3%; inflation (1992 est.) 60%; unemployment (1991) 8.5%. Arable land: 8%. Principal products: livestock, grains. Labor force (1991 est.): 1,355,000: government, 25%; manufacturing, 19%; commerce, 12%; agriculture, 11%. Major products: processed meats, wool and hides, textiles, shoes, handbags and leather wearing apparel, cement, refined petroleum. Natural resources: hydroelectric power potential. Exports: $1.6 billion (f.o.b., 1991): meat, hides, wool, fish. Imports: $1.3 billion (f.o.b., 1991): crude petroleum, transportation equipment, chemicals, machinery, metals. Major trading partners: U.S., Brazil, Argentina, Germany.

Geography. Uruguay, on the east coast of South America south of Brazil and east of Argentina, is comparable in size to the State of Oklahoma.

The country consists of a low, rolling plain in the south and a low plateau in the north. It has a 120-mile (193 km) Atlantic shore line, a 235-mile (378 km) frontage on the Rio de la Plata, and 270 miles (435 km) on the Uruguay River, its western boundary.

Government. A republic. Presidents serve a single five-year term. The bicameral Congress, the General Assembly, consists of the Chamber of Senators and the Chamber of Representatives.

History. Juan Díaz de Solis, a Spaniard, discovered Uruguay in 1516, but the Portuguese were first to settle it when they founded Colonia in 1680. After a long struggle, Spain wrested the country from Portugal in 1778. Uruguay revolted against Spain in 1811, only to be conquered in 1817 by the Portuguese from Brazil. Independence was reasserted with Argentine help in 1825, and the republic was set up in 1828.

Independence, however, did not restore order, and a revolt in 1836 touched off nearly 50 years of factional strife, with occasional armed intervention from Argentina and Brazil.

Uruguay, made prosperous by meat and wool exports, founded a welfare state early in the 20th century. A decline began in the 1950s as successive governments struggled to maintain a large bureaucracy and costly social benefits. Economic stagnation and political frustration followed.

A military coup ousted the civilian government in 1973. The military dictatorship that followed used fear and terror to demoralize the population, taking thousands of political prisoners, probably the highest proportion of citizens jailed for political reasons anywhere in the world.

After ruling for 12 years, the military regime permitted election of a civilian government in November 1984 and relinquished rule in March 1985.

Luis Lacalle became president in March 1990, becoming the first Blanco Party member to assume that office in 23 years.

Attempts at belt-tightening led to general strikes in 1991 and early 1992, but a special poll in July failed to receive enough votes to force a referendum.

UZBEKISTAN

Republic of Uzbekistan
President: Islam A. Karimov (1990)
Prime Minister: Abdulkhashim Mutalov
Area: 172,700 sq mi. (447,400 sq km)
Population (est. mid-1993): 21,700,000 (Uzbeks, 71%; Russians, 8%; other minorities: Tajiks, Kazakhs, and Tartars); (average annual rate of natural increase: 2.8%); birth rate: 35/1000; infant mortality rate: 44/1000; density per square mile: 126
Capital and largest city (1991): Tashkent, 2,113,300. Other: Samarkand, 370,500; **Language:** Uzbek, 85%; Russian, 5%; **Religion:** Muslim (mostly Sunnis) 75–80%
Economic summary: Per capita GNP (1991): $1,350; real growth rate –0.9%; inflation 83%. Labor force (1990): 7,941,000: agriculture and forestry, 39%; industry and construction, 24%. Natural resources: natural gas, petroleum, coal, gold, uranium, silver, copper, lead and zinc, tungsten, molybdenum. Agriculture: major crop is cotton. Exports (1990): $1.5 billion: cotton, gold, textiles, chemicals, mineral fertilizers, vegetable oil. Imports (1990): $3.5 billion: machinery and parts, consumer durables, grain, and other food. Trading partners: Former Soviet republics.

Geography. Uzbekistan is situated in the former Soviet Central Asia between the Amu Darya and Syr Darya Rivers, the Aral Sea, and the slopes of the Tien Shan Mountains. It is bounded by Kazakhstan in the north and northwest, Kyrgyzstan and Tajikistan in the east and southeast, and Turkmenistan in the southwest. The republic also includes the Kara-Kalpak Autonomous S.S.R. since 1936 with its capital, Nukus, 1987 population, 152,000. The land is made up of deserts, oases, and mountains with valleys. Two-thirds of the territory are occupied by deserts and semi-deserts. The country is about one-tenth larger in area than the state of California.

Government. A constitutional republic.

History. The Uzbekistan land was once part of the ancient Persian empire and was later conquered by Alexander the Great in 4 B.C. During the 8th century, the nomadic Turkic tribes living there were converted to Islam by invading Arab forces who dominated the area. The Mongols under Ghengis Khan took over the region from the Seljuk Turks in the 13th century and it later became part of Tamerlane the Great's empire and his successors until the 16th century.

The Uzbeks invaded the territory in the early 16th century and merged with the other inhabitants in the area. Their empire broke up into separate Uzbek principalities, the khanates of Khiva, Bukhara, and Kokand. These city-states resisted Russian expansion into the area, but were conquered by the Russian forces in the mid-19th century.

The territory was made into the Uzbek Republic in 1924 and became the independent Uzbekistan Soviet Socialist Republic in 1925.

Uzbekistan joined with ten other former Soviet republics on Dec. 21, 1991, in the Commonwealth of Independent States.

In February 1992, Karimov, a former Communist Party boss, affirmed his commitment to democracy and human rights. An election in December 1991 had given him 85% of the vote, but the main opposition parties were not allowed to field candidates.

Opposition forces in mid-1993 formed a coalition. However the government closed their headquarters and arrested the leaders. The criminal code was amended to impose stricter penalties for antigovernment activity.

VANUATU

Republic of Vanuatu
President: Fred Timakata (1989)
Prime Minister: Maxime Carlot (1991)
Area: 5,700 sq mi. (14,763 sq km)
Population (est. mid-1993): 200,000 (average annual rate of natural increase: 3.3%); birth rate: 40/1000; infant mortality rate: 65/1000; density per square mile: 35
Capital (est. 1987): Port Vila, 15,100; **Monetary unit:** Vatu; **Religions:** Presbyterian, 36.7%; Roman Catholic, 15%; Anglican, 15%; other Christian, 10%; indigenous beliefs, 7.6%, other, 15.7%; **Literacy rate:** 53%
Economic Summary: Gross domestic product (1989 est.): $137 million, $860 per capita; real growth rate: 4.3%; inflation (1990) 5%. Arable land: 1%. Principal agricultural products: copra, cocoa, coffee. Exports: $15.6 million (f.o.b., 1990 est.): copra, cocoa, coffee, frozen fish. Imports: $60.4 million (f.o.b., 1990 est.): machines and vehicles, food, raw materials, fuel. Major trading partners: France, New Zealand, Japan, Australia, Netherlands.

Geography. Formerly known as the New Hebrides, Vanuatu is an archipelago of some 80 islands lying between New Caledonia and Fiji in the South Pacific. Largest of the islands is Espiritu Santo (875 sq mi.; 2,266 sq km); others are Efate, Malekula, Malo, Pentecost, and Tanna. The population is largely Melanesian of mixed blood.

Government. The constitution by which Vanuatu achieved independence on July 30, 1980, vests executive authority in a President, elected by an electoral college for a five-year term. A unicameral legislature of 46 members exercises legislative power.

History. The islands were discovered by Pedro Fernandes de Queiros of Portugal in 1606 and were charted and named by the British navigator James Cook in 1774. Conflicting British and French interests were resolved by a joint naval commission that administered the islands from 1887. A condominium government was established in 1906.

The islands' plantation economy, based on imported Vietnamese labor, was prosperous until the 1920s, when markets for its products declined. The New Hebrides escaped Japanese occupation in World War II and the French population was among the first to support the Gaullist Free French movement.

A brief rebellion by French settlers and plantation workers on Espiritu Santo led by Jimmy Stevens in May 1980 threatened the scheduled independence of the islands. Britain sent a company of Royal Marines and France a contingent of 50 policemen to quell the revolt, which the new government said was financed by the Phoenix Foundation, a right-wing U.S. group. With the British and French forces replaced by soldiers from Papua New Guinea, independence ceremonies took place on July 30. The next month it was reported that Stevens had been arrested and the revolt quelled.

Disaffection with Prime Minister Lini in August 1991 led to his dismissal as head of his party. Lini formed another to contest the November general elections. The Union of Moderate Parties won and formed an alliance with Lini's.

VATICAN CITY STATE

Ruler: Pope John Paul II (1978)
Area: 0.17 sq mi. (0.44 sq km)
Population (July 1992): 802; density per square mile: 4,424
Monetary unit: Lira; **Languages:** Latin, Italian, and various other languages; **Religion:** Roman Catholic
Labor force: High dignataries, priests, nuns, guards, and 3,000 lay workers who live outside the Vatican
National name: Stato della Città del Vaticano
Budget (1992): Revenues $92 million; expenditures $178 million including capital expenditures. Projected deficit for 1993: $91.7 million. American Catholics contribute $13.9 million to the Vatican.

Geography. The Vatican City State is situated on the Vatican hill, on the right bank of the Tiber River, within the commune of Rome.

Government. The Pope has full legal, executive, and judicial powers. Executive power over the area is in the hands of a Commission of Cardinals appointed by the Pope. The College of Cardinals is the Pope's chief advisory body, and upon his death the cardinals elect his successor for life. The cardinals themselves are created for life by the Pope.

In the Vatican the central administration of the Roman Catholic Church throughout the world (Holy See) is carried on by the Secretariat of State, nine Congregations, three tribunals, twelve councils, and five offices. In its diplomatic relations, the Holy See is represented by the Papal Secretary of State.

History. The Vatican City State, sovereign and independent, is the survivor of the papal states that in

1859 comprised an area of some 17,000 square miles (44,030 sq km). During the struggle for Italian unification, from 1860 to 1870, most of this area became part of Italy.

By an Italian law of May 13, 1871, the temporal power of the Pope was abrogated, and the territory of the Papacy was confined to the Vatican and Lateran palaces and the villa of Castel Gandolfo. The Popes consistently refused to recognize this arrangement and, by the Lateran Treaty of Feb. 11, 1929, between the Vatican and the Kingdom of Italy, the exclusive dominion and sovereign jurisdiction of the Holy See over the city of the Vatican was again recognized, thus restoring the Pope's temporal authority over the area.

The first session of Ecumenical Council Vatican II was opened by John XXIII on Oct. 11, 1962, to plan and set policies for the modernization of the Roman Catholic Church. Pope Paul VI continued the Council, opening the second session on Sept. 29, 1963.

On Aug. 26, 1978, Cardinal Albino Luciani was chosen by the College of Cardinals to succeed Paul VI, who had died of a heart attack on Aug. 6. The new Pope, who took the name John Paul I, was born on Oct. 17, 1912, at Forno di Canale in Italy.

(For a listing of all the Popes, *see* the Index.)

Only 34 days after his election, John Paul I died of a heart attack, ending the shortest reign in 373 years. On Oct. 16, Cardinal Karol Wojtyla, 58, was chosen Pope and took the name John Paul II.

On May 13, 1981, a Turkish terrorist shot the Pope in St. Peter's Square, the first assassination attempt against the Pontiff in modern times. Mehmet Ali Agca was sentenced on July 22 to life imprisonment by an Italian Court.

On June 3, 1985, the Vatican and Italy ratified a new church-state treaty, known as a concordat, replacing the Lateran Pact of 1929. The new accord affirmed the independence of Vatican City but ended a number of privileges the Catholic Church had in Italy, including its status as the state religion. The treaty ended Rome's status as a "sacred city."

Relations, diplomatic and ecclesiastical, with Eastern Europe have improved dramatically with the fall of communism. Relations with the Soviet Union, while improving, have not yet reached the ambassadorial level.

During 1991 diplomatic relations with the Baltic states were resumed and ties established with Albania.

Diplomatic relations were established in 1992 with a host of new countries including Croatia, Slovenia, Armenia, Azerbaijan and Ukraine and reestablished with Mexico after 125 years.

VENEZUELA

Republic of Venezuela
Acting President: Ramon J. Velasquez (1993)
Area: 352,143 sq mi. (912,050 sq km)
Population (est. mid-1993): 19,886,504 (average annual rate of natural increase: 2.6%); birth rate: 30/1000; infant mortality rate: 20.4/1000; density per square mile: 61
Capital: Caracas; **Largest cities (est. 1990):** Caracas, 1,290,087; Maracaibo, 1,206,726; Valencia, 616,000; Barquisimento, 723,587; **Monetary unit:** Bolivar; **Language:** Spanish, Indian dialects in interior; **Religion:** Roman Catholic; **National name:** Republica de Venezuela; **Literacy rate:** 85.6%
Economic summary: Gross domestic product (1991 est.): $52.3 billion, $2,590 per capita; real growth rate 9.2%; inflation 30.7%; unemployment 9.3%. Arable land: 3%. Principal agricultural products: rice, coffee, corn, cacao, sugar, bananas, dairy and meat products. Labor force: 5,800,000; 56% in services, 28% in industry. Principal industrial products: refined petroleum products, aluminum, iron and steel, cement, textiles, transport equipment. Natural resources: petroleum, natural gas, iron ore, hydroelectric power. Exports: $15.1 billion (f.o.b., 1991 est.): petroleum, iron ore, bauxite. Imports: $10.2 billion (f.o.b., 1991 est.): industrial machinery and equipment, manufactures, chemicals, foodstuffs. Major trading partners: U.S., Japan, Germany, Brazil, Italy.

Geography. Venezuela, a third larger than Texas, occupies most of the northern coast of South America on the Caribbean Sea. It is bordered by Colombia to the west, Guyana to the east, and Brazil to the south.

Mountain systems break Venezuela into four distinct areas: (1) the Maracaibo lowlands; (2) the mountainous region in the north and northwest; (3) the Orinoco basin, with the llanos (vast grass-covered plains) on its northern border and great forest areas in the south and southeast; (4) the Guiana Highlands, south of the Orinoco, accounting for nearly half the national territory. About 80% of Venezuela is drained by the Orinoco and its tributaries.

Government. Venezuela is a federal republic consisting of 22 states, the Federal District, and 72 islands in the Caribbean. There is a bicameral Congress, the 50 members of the Senate and the 199 members of the Chamber of Deputies being elected by popular vote to five-year terms. The President is also elected for five years. He must be a Venezuelan by birth and over 30 years old. He is not eligible for re-election until 10 years after the end of his term.

History. Columbus discovered Venezuela on his third voyage in 1498. A subsequent Spanish explorer gave the country its name, meaning "Little Venice." There were no important settlements until Caracas was founded in 1567. Simón Bolívar, who led the liberation of much of the continent from Spain, was born in Caracas in 1783. With Bolívar taking part, Venezuela was one of the first South American colonies to revolt against Spain, in 1810, but it was not until 1821 that independence was won. Federated at first with Colombia and Ecuador, the country set up a republic in 1830 and then sank for many decades into a condition of revolt, dictatorship, and corruption.

From 1908 to 1935, Gen. Juan Vicente Gómez was an absolute dictator. A military junta ruled after his death in 1935. Dr. Rómulo Betancourt and the liberal Acción Democrática Party won a majority of seats in a constituent assembly to draft a new Constitution in 1946. A well-known writer, Rómulo Gallegos, candidate of Betancourt's party, easily won the presidential election of 1947. But, the army ousted Gallegos the next year and instituted a military junta.

The country overthrew the dictatorship in 1958 and thereafter enjoyed democratic government. Rafael Caldera Rodríguez, President from 1969 to 1974, legalized the Communist Party and established diplomatic relations with Moscow.

In 1974, President Carlos Andrés took office. In 1976, Venezuela nationalized 21 oil companies, mostly subsidiaries of U.S. firms, offering compensation of $1.28 billion. Oil income in that year was $9.9 billion, and although production decreased 2.2%, revenue remained at the same level in 1977 because of higher prices, largely financing an ambitious social welfare program.

Despite difficulties at home, Pérez continued to play an active foreign role in extending economic aid to Latin neighbors, in backing the human-rights policy of President Carter, and in supporting Carter's return of the Panama Canal to Panama.

Opposition Christian Democrats capitalized on Pérez's domestic problems to elect Luis Herrera Campíns President in Venezuela's fifth consecutive free election, on Dec. 3, 1978.

Herrera Campins at first supported U.S. policy in Central America, lining up behind the government of El Salvador but he later shifted toward a "political solution" that would include the insurgents. In March 1982, he assailed Reagan's policy as "interventionalist."

When the Falklands war broke out, Venezuela became one of the most vigorous advocates of the Argentine cause and one of the sharpest critics of the U.S. decision to back Britain.

In the presidential election of December 1988 former president Carlos Andres Perez of the Democratic Action party easily won.

Loyal soldiers put down an attempted coup in February 1992.

President Perez surrendered his powers in May 1993 in order to defend himself in impeachment proceedings arising out of corruption charges. Ramon Velasquez was elected by Congress to serve as acting president pending the outcome of the impeachment proceedings.

VIETNAM

Socialist Republic of Vietnam
President: Le Duc Anh (1992)
Premier: Vo Van Kiet (1991)
Area: 127,246 sq mi. (329,566 sq km)
Population (est. mid-1993): 71,800,000 (average annual rate of natural increase: 2.2%); birth rate: 30/1000; infant mortality rate: 45/1000; Density per square mile: 571
Capital: Hanoi; **Largest cities (1992):** Ho Chi Minh City (Saigon),[1] 4,000,000; Hanoi, 2,000,000. Other large cities (1989): Haiphong, 456,049; Da Nang, 370,670; Nha Trang, 213,687; Qui Nho'n, 160,091; Hué 211,085; **Monetary unit:** Dong; **Languages:** Vietnamese (official), French, English, Khmer, Chinese; **Religions:** Buddhist, Roman Catholic, Islam, Taoist, Confucian, Animist; **National name:** Công Hòa Xa Hôi Chú Nghia Viêt Nam; **Literacy rate:** 88%
Economic summary: Gross national product (1991 est.): $15 billion; $220 per capita; inflation 80%; unemployment 30%. Arable land: 22%. Principal agricultural products: rice, rubber, fruits and vegetables, corn, sugar cane, fish. Labor force: 32,700,000; 65% in agriculture. Major industrial products: processed foods, textiles, cement, chemical fertilizers, glass, tires. Natural resources: phosphates, forests, coal. Exports: $1.8 billion (f.o.b., 1991): agricultural products, coal, minerals. Imports: $1.9 billion (c.i.f., 1991): petroleum, steel products, railroad equipment, chemicals, medicines, raw cotton, fertilizer, grain. Major trading partners: C.I.S. countries, Singapore, Japan, Eastern Europe.

1. Includes suburb of Cholon.

Geography. Vietnam occupies the eastern and southern part of the Indochinese peninsula in Southeast Asia, with the South China Sea along its entire coast. China is to the north and Laos and Cambodia to the west. Long and narrow on a north-south axis, Vietnam is about twice the size of Arizona.

The Mekong River delta lies in the south and the Red River delta in the north. Heavily forested mountain and plateau regions make up most of the country.

Government. Less than a year after the capitulation of the former Republic of Vietnam (South Vietnam) on April 30, 1975, a joint National Assembly convened with 249 deputies representing the North and 243 representing the South. The Assembly set July 2, 1976, as the official reunification date. Hanoi became the capital.

A new constitution was adopted in April 1992 which called for the creation of a presidency and a prime ministry. The document affirmed the free-market economy and the role of the Communist Party is limited to that of guidance. Foreign assets are guaranteed against nationalization. The assembly has 395 members.

History. The Vietnamese are descendants of Mongoloid nomads from China and migrants from Indonesia. They recognized Chinese suzerainty until the 15th century, an era of nationalistic expansion, when Cambodians were pushed out of the southern area of what is now Vietnam.

A century later, the Portuguese were the first Europeans to enter the area. France established its influence early in the 19th century and within 80 years conquered the three regions into which the country was then divided—Cochin-China in the south, Annam in the center, and Tonkin in the north.

France first unified Vietnam in 1887, when a single governor-generalship was created, followed by the first physical links between north and south—a rail and road system. Even at the beginning of World War II, however, there were internal differences among the three regions.

Japan took over military bases in Vietnam in 1940 and a pro-Vichy French administration remained until 1945. A veteran Communist leader, Ho Chi Minh, organized an independence movement known as the Vietminh to exploit a confused situation. At the end of the war, Ho's followers seized Hanoi and declared a short-lived republic, which ended with the arrival of French forces in 1946.

Paris proposed a unified government within the French Union under the former Annamite emperor, Bao Dai. Cochin-China and Annam accepted the proposal, and Bao Dai was proclaimed emperor of all Vietnam in 1949. Ho and the Vietminh withheld support, and the revolution in China gave them the outside help needed for a war of resistance against French and Vietnamese troops armed largely by the U.S.

A bitter defeat at Dien Bien Phu in northwest Vietnam on May 5, 1954, broke the French military campaign and brought the division of Vietnam at the conference of Geneva that year.

In the new South, Ngo Dinh Diem, Premier under Bao Dai, deposed the monarch in 1955 and established a republic with himself as President. Diem used strong U.S. backing to create an authoritarian regime that suppressed all opposition but could not eradicate the Northern-supplied Communist Viet Cong.

Skirmishing grew into a full-scale war, with escalating U.S. involvement. A military coup, U.S.-inspired in the view of many, ousted Diem Nov. 1, 1963, and a kaleidoscope of military governments followed. The most savage fighting of the war occurred in early 1968, during the Tet holidays.

Although the Viet Cong failed to overthrow the Saigon government, U.S. public reaction to the apparently endless war forced a limitation of U.S. troops to

550,000 and a new emphasis on shifting the burden of further combat to the South Vietnamese. Ho Chi Minh's death on Sept. 3, 1969, brought a quadrumvirate to replace him but no flagging in Northern will to fight.

U.S. bombing and invasion of Cambodia in the summer of 1970—an effort to destroy Viet Cong bases in the neighboring state—marked the end of major U.S. participation in the fighting. Most American ground troops were withdrawn from combat by mid-1971 as heavy bombing of the Ho Chi Minh trail from North Vietnam appeared to cut the supply of men and matériel to the South.

Secret negotiations for peace by Secretary of State Henry A. Kissinger with North Vietnamese officials during 1972 after heavy bombing of Hanoi and Haiphong brought the two sides near agreement in October. When the Northerners demanded the removal of the South's President Nguyen Van Thieu as their price, President Nixon ordered the "Christmas bombing" of the North. The conference resumed and a peace settlement was signed in Paris on Jan. 27, 1973. It called for release of all U.S. prisoners, withdrawal of U.S. forces, limitation of both sides' forces inside South Vietnam, and a commitment to peaceful reunification.

An armored attack across the 17th parallel in January 1975 panicked the South Vietnamese army and brought the invasion within 40 miles of Saigon by April 9. Thieu resigned on April 21 and fled, to be replaced by Vice President Tran Van Huong, who quit a week later, turning over the office to Gen. Duong Van Minh. "Big Minh" surrendered Saigon on April 30, ending a war that took 1.3 million Vietnamese and 56,000 American lives, at the cost of $141 billion in U.S. aid.

On May 3, 1977, the U.S. and Vietnam opened negotiations in Paris to normalize relations. One of the first results was the withdrawal of U.S. opposition to Vietnamese membership in the United Nations, formalized in the Security Council on July 20. Two major issues remained to be settled, however: the return of the bodies of some 2,500 U.S. servicemen missing in the war and the claim by Hanoi that former President Nixon had promised reconstruction aid under the 1973 agreement. Negotiations failed to resolve these issues.

The new year also brought an intensification of border clashes between Vietnam and Cambodia and accusations by China that Chinese residents of Vietnam were being subjected to persecution. Peking cut off all aid and withdrew 800 technicians.

Hanoi was undoubtedly preoccupied with a continuing war in Cambodia, where 60,000 Vietnamese troops were aiding the Heng Samrin regime in suppressing the last forces of the pro-Chinese Pol Pot regime. In early 1979, Vietnam was conducting a two-front war, defending its northern border against a Chinese invasion and at the same time supporting its army in Cambodia.

The Hanoi government agreed in July 1984 to resume technical talks with U.S. officials on the possible whereabouts of the 2,490 Americans still listed as missing, most of them believed dead.

Economic troubles continued, with the government seeking to reschedule its $1.4-billion foreign hard-currency debt, owed mainly to Japan and the International Monetary Fund. In late 1987, a shuffle of the Vietnamese Politburo brought in new leaders who are expected to slightly relax the government grip on the economy and crack down on corruption within the party.

In 1988, Vietnam also began limited troop withdrawals from Laos and Cambodia.

Economic reform continued during 1991 and 1992, although the Communist Party retained its role in politics and socialism remained enshrined in the official ideology. Vietnam supported the Cambodian peace agreement signed in October 1991.

General elections in July 1992 saw 601 candidates competing for the 395 seats in the assembly.

(For a Vietnam War chronology, see Headline History.)

WESTERN SAMOA

Independent State of Western Samoa
Head of State: Malietoa Tanumafili II (1962)
Prime Minister: Tofilau Eti Alesana (1988)
Area: 1,093 sq mi. (2,831 sq km)
Population (est. mid-1993): 200,000 (average annual growth rate: 2.8%); birth rate: 34/1000; infant mortality rate: 43/1000; density per square mile: 183
Capital and largest city (1981): Apia, 33,170; **Monetary unit:** Tala; **Languages:** Samoan and English; **Religions:** Christian, 99.7%; **National name:** Western Samoa; **Member of Commonwealth of Nations; Literacy rate:** 90%
Economic summary: Gross domestic product (1990 est.): $115 million; $620 per capita; –4.5% real growth rate; inflation 15%. Arable land: 19%. Principal agricultural products: copra, coconuts, cocoa, bananas, taro, yams. Labor force (1987): 38,000; 22,000 employed in agriculture. Agriculture accounts for 50% of GDP. Major industrial products: timber, processed food, fish. Natural resource: timber. Exports: $9 million (f.o.b., 1990): copra, cocoa, coconut oil and cream, timber. Imports: $75 million (c.i.f., 1990): food, manufactured goods, machinery. Major trading partners: New Zealand, EC, Australia, U.S., Fiji, Japan

Geography. Western Samoa, the size of Rhode Island, is in the South Pacific Ocean about 2,200 miles (3,540 km) south of Hawaii midway to Sydney, Australia, and about 800 miles (1,287 km) northeast of Fiji. The larger islands in the Samoan chain are mountainous and of volcanic origin. There is little level land except in the coastal areas, where most cultivation takes place.

Government. Western Samoa has a 49-member Legislature, consisting mainly of the titleholders (chiefs) of family groups, with two non-title members. All members are elected by universal suffrage. When the present Head of State dies, successors will be elected by the Legislature for five-year terms.

History. The Samoan islands were discovered in the 18th century and visited by Dutch and French traders. Toward the end of the 19th century, conflicting interests of the U.S., Britain, and Germany resulted in a treaty signed in 1899. It recognized the paramount interests of the U.S. in those islands east of 171° west longitude (American Samoa) and Germany's interests in the other islands (Western Samoa).

New Zealand occupied Western Samoa in 1914, and was granted a League of Nations mandate. In 1947, the islands became a U.N. trust territory administered by New Zealand.

Western Samoa became independent on Jan. 1, 1962.

A referendum of 1990 gave most women the right to vote for the first time. The April 1991 election gave the ruling Human Rights Protection Party a narrow victory.

REPUBLIC OF YEMEN

President: Ali Abdullah Saleh
Prime Minister: Haidar Abu Bakr al-Attas
Area: 203,850 sq mi. (527,970 sq km)
Population (est. mid-1993): 11,300,000 (average annual rate of natural increase: 3.2%); birth rate: 53/1000; infant mortality rate: 131/1000; density per square mile: 56
Capital: San'a'; **Largest cities (1986):** San'a', 427,185; (est. 1984): Aden, 318,000; **Monetary unit:** Both Dinar and Rial ; **Language:** Arabic ; **Religion:** Islam (Sunni and Shiite) **Literacy rate:** 38%
Economic summary: Gross domestic product (1990 est.): $5.3 billion; $545 per capita; real growth rate n.a. Principal agricultural products: wheat, sorghum, cattle, sheep, cotton, fruits, coffee, dates. Principal industrial products: crude and refined oil, textiles, leather goods, handicrafts, fish. Exports: (North) $606 million (f.o.b., 1989); (South) $113.8 million (f.o.b., est.): cotton, coffee, hides, vegetables, dried fish; Imports: (North) $1.3 billion (f.o.b., 1989); (South) $553.9 million (f.o.b., est.): textiles, manufactured consumer goods, foodstuffs, sugar, grain, flour. Major trading partners: U.K., Japan, Saudi Arabia, Australia, U.S.

Geography. Formerly known as the states of Peoples Democratic Republic of Yemen and the Yemen Arab Republic, the Republic of Yemen occupies the southwestern tip of the Arabian Peninsula on the Red Sea opposite Ethiopia, and extends along the southern part of the Arabian Peninsula on the Gulf of Aden and the Indian Ocean. Saudi Arabia is to the north and Oman is to the east. The country is about the size of France.

It has a 700-mile (1,130-km) narrow coastal plain in the south that gives way to a mountainous region and then a plateau area. Some of the interior highlands in the west attain a height of 12,000 feet (3,660 m).

Government. Parliamentary. There is a five-man ruling Presidential Council consisting of the President, Vice-President, and three other members. They are Salem Saleh Mohammed, the former deputy to the new vice-president, Abdel-Karim al-Arshi, former speaker of Yemen's parliament, and Abdel-Aziz Abdulghani, former Prime Minister of the Yemen Arab Republic.

History. The history of Yemen dates back to the Minaean kingdom (1200–650 B.C.). It accepted Islam in A.D. 628, and in the 10th century came under the control of the Rassite dynasty of the Zaidi sect. The Turks occupied the area from 1538 to 1630 and from 1849 to 1918. The sovereign status of Yemen was confirmed by treaties signed with Saudi Arabia and Britain in 1934.

In 1962, a military revolt of elements favoring President Gamal Abdel Nasser of Egypt broke out. A ruling junta proclaimed a republic, and Yemen became an international battleground, with Egypt and the U.S.S.R. supporting the revolutionaries, and King Saud of Saudi Arabia and King Hussein of Jordan the royalists. The civil war continued until the war between the Arab states and Israel broke out in June 1967. Nasser had to pull out many of his troops and agree to a cease-fire and withdrawal of foreign forces. The war finally ended with the defeat of the royalists in mid-1969.

The People's Republic of Southern Yemen was established Nov. 30, 1967, when Britain granted independence to the Federation of South Arabia. This Federation consisted of the state (once the colony) of Aden and 16 of the 20 states of the Protectorate of South Arabia (once the Aden Protectorate). The four states of the Protectorate that did not join the Federation later became part of Southern Yemen.

The Republic of Yemen was established on May 23, 1990, when pro-western Yemen and Marxist Yemen Arab Republic merged after 300 years of separation to form the new nation. The union had been approved by both governments in November 1989.

The new president, Ali Abdullah Salen of Yemen, was elected by the parliaments of both countries. The parliaments also chose South Yemen's Ali Salem al-Baidh, secretary general of the ruling socialist party, to be the new vice-president.

Since unification a coalition of the People's Congress Party, which ruled in the north, and the Yemen Socialist Party, which ruled in the south, has governed the country.

In the Gulf War, Yemen favored Iraq. Consequently, many expatriates in Saudi Arabia were forced to return. A referendum in May 1992 on a constitution resulted in a landslide in favor of it.

A 25-year-old border dispute with Oman ended with the signing of an agreement in October 1992.

YUGOSLAVIA

Federal Republic of Yugoslavia
Acting President: Milos Radulovic (1993)
Prime Minister: Radoje Kontic (1993)
Area: 26,940 sq mi. (69,774.6 sq km)[1]
Population (est. mid-1993): 9,800,000; (average annual rate of natural increase: 0.5%); birth rate: 14/1000; infant mortality rate: 15.4/1000; density per square mile: 366
Capital: Belgrade (in Serbia); **Largest cities (1991):** Belgrade, 5,753,825; Titograd (in Montenegro), 616,327; **Monetary unit:** Yugoslav new Dinar **Languages:** Serbo-Croatian 100%; **Religions:** Orthodox, 65%; Muslim, 19%; Christian religions, 5%; **National name (former Yugoslavia):** Socijalisticka Federativna Republika Jugoslavija' **Literacy rate:** 90.5%
Economic summary (Serbia and Montenegro): Gross domestic product (1990): $44 billion; per capita $4,200; inflation 60% per month; unemployment 25–40%. Labor force (1990): 2,640,909; industry and mining, 40%; agriculture, 5%. Industries: machine building (incl. aircraft, trucks, automobiles), nonferrous metallurgy, consumer goods, electronics, chemicals, petroleum products, pharmaceuticals. Exports: $4.4 billion (f.o.b., 1990): machinery and transportation equipment, manufactured goods and articles, chemicals, food, and live animals. Imports: $6.4 billion (c.i.f., 1990): machinery and transport equipment, fuels and lubricants, other manufacturers, chemicals, raw materials, food, and animals. Trading partners: C.I.S. countries, E.C., U.S., Eastern European countries.

Geography. Yugoslavia consists of the two states of Serbia and Montenegro. The nation is bordered by Hungary in the north, Romania and Bulgaria in the east, Macedonia in the south, Albania and the Adriatic Sea in the west, and the former Yugoslavian republics of Bosnia-Herzegovina and Croatia in the west. Yugoslavia is about the size of the state of Kentucky.

Yugoslavia is largely a mountainous country. The northeastern section of Serbia is part of the rich, fertile Danubian Plain drained by the Danube, Tisa, Sava, and Morava River systems. Montenegro is a jumbled mass of mountains, containing also some grassy slopes and fertile river valleys.

Government. Yugoslavia (Serbia and Montenegro) is a federal republic in transition. Actual administration is carried out by the Federal Executive Council and its secretaries. NOTE: The U.S. does not formally recognize the union of Serbia and Montenegro as a joint-independent state. The U.S. view is that the Socialist Federal Republic of Yugoslavia has dissolved and that none of its successor republics represents its continuation.

History. Yugoslavia was formed Dec. 4, 1918, from the patchwork of Balkan states and territories where World War I began with the assassination of Archduke Ferdinand of Austria at Sarajevo on June 28, 1914. The new Kingdom of Serbs, Croats, and Slovenes included the former kingdoms of Serbia and Montenegro; Bosnia-Herzegovina, previously administered jointly by Austria and Hungary; Croatia-Slavonia, a semi-autonomous region of Hungary, and Dalmatia, formerly administered by Austria. King Peter I of Serbia became the first monarch, his son acting as Regent until his accession as Alexander I on Aug. 16, 1921.

Croatian demands for a federal state forced Alexander to assume dictatorial powers in 1929 and to change the country's name to Yugoslavia. Serbian dominance continued despite his efforts, amid the resentment of other regions. A Macedonian associated with Croatian dissidents assassinated Alexander in Marseilles, France, on Oct. 9, 1934, and his cousin, Prince Paul, became Regent for the King's son, Prince Peter.

Paul's pro-Axis policy brought Yugoslavia to sign the Axis Pact on March 25, 1941, and opponents overthrew the government two days later. On April 6 the Nazis occupied the country, and the young King and his government fled. Two guerrilla armies —the Chetniks under Draza Mihajlovic supporting the monarchy and the Partisans under Tito (Josip Broz) leaning toward the U.S.S.R.—fought the Nazis for the duration of the war. In 1943, Tito established an Executive National Committee of Liberation to function as a provisional government.

Tito won the election held in the fall of 1945, as monarchists boycotted the vote. A new Assembly abolished the monarchy and proclaimed the Federal People's Republic of Yugoslavia, with Tito as Prime Minister. Ruthlessly eliminating opposition, the Tito government executed Mihajlovic in 1946.

Tito broke with the Soviet bloc in 1948 and Yugoslavia followed a middle road, combining orthodox Communist control of politics and general overall economic policy with a varying degree of freedom in the arts, travel, and individual enterprise. Tito became President in 1953 and President for life under a revised Constitution adopted in 1963.

After Tito's death on May 4, 1980, a rotating presidency designed to avoid internal dissension was put into effect immediately, and the feared clash of Yugoslavia's multiple nationalities and regions appeared to have been averted.

Demonstrations by ethnic Albanians in Kosovo for freedom from Serb rule were met with a forcible response from Serb authorities under the direction of Serb leader Slobodan Miloslovic. Miloslovic mobilized Serb sentiment not only against the Albanians but also against the central government, raising the spectre of further divisiveness within Yugoslavia. In 1990, elections in the states of Croatia and Slovenia were won by parties advocating greater autonomy.

In May 1991 Croatian voters supported a referendum calling for their republic to become an independent nation. A similar referendum passed in December in Slovenia. In June the respective parliaments in both republics passed declarations of independence. Ethnic violence flared almost immediately. The largely Serbian-led Yugoslav military pounded break-away Bosnia and Herzegovina, leading the U.N. Security Council in May 1992 to impose economic sanctions on the Belgrade government.

When it became clear in May 1993 that the West would not intervene militarily in Bosnia Serbian leaders said they would not accept international monitoring of their border with Bosnia. In early June President Cosic, considered too moderate, was voted out of office by Parliament.

ZAIRE

Republic of Zaire
President: Mobutu Sese Seko (1965)
Prime Minister: Faustin Birindwa (1993)
Area: 905,365 sq mi. (2,344,885 sq km)
Population (est. mid-1993): 41,200,000 (average annual rate of natural increase: 3.3%); birth rate: 48/1000; infant mortality rate: 98/1000; density per square mile: 47
Capital: Kinshasa; **Largest cities (est. 1990):** Kinshasa, 3,562,122; Lubumbashi, 683,056; Mbuji-Mayi, 508,469; Kananga, 301,349; **Monetary unit:** Zaire; **Languages:** French (official), English, Bantu dialects, mainly Swahili, Lingala, Ishiluba, and Kikongo; **Religions:** Roman Catholic 50%, Protestant 20%, Kimbanguist 10%, Islam 10%; syncretic and traditional, 10%; **Ethnic groups:** Bantu, Sudanese, Nilotics, Pygmies, Hamites; **National name:** République du Zaïre; **Literacy rate:** 72%
Economic summary: Gross domestic product (1990 est.): $6.6 billion; $180 per capita; –2% real growth rate. Arable land: 3%. Principal agricultural products: coffee, palm oil, rubber, quinine, cassava, bananas, plantains, vegetables, fruits. Labor force: 15,000,000; 13% in industry. Major industrial products: processed and unprocessed minerals, consumer goods. Natural resources: copper, cobalt, zinc, industrial diamonds, manganese, tin, gold, silver, bauxite, iron, coal, crude oil, hydroelectric potential. Exports: copper, cobalt, diamonds, petroleum, coffee. Imports: consumer goods, foodstuffs, mining and other machinery, transport equipment. Major trading partners: Belgium, France, U.S., Germany, South Africa.

Geography. Zaire is situated in west central Africa and is bordered by the Congo, the Central African Republic, the Sudan, Uganda, Rwanda, Burundi, Tanzania, Zambia, Angola, and the Atlantic Ocean. It is one quarter the size of the U.S.

The principal rivers are the Ubangi and Bomu in the north and the Zaire (Congo) in the west, which flows into the Atlantic. The entire length of Lake Tanganyika lies along the eastern border with Tanzania and Burundi.

Government. A republic with a multiparty unicameral legislature. The president and the legislature are elected by universal suffrage for five-year terms.

History. Formerly the Belgian Congo, this territory was inhabited by ancient Negrito peoples (Pygmies), who were pushed into the mountains by Bantu and Nilotic invaders. The American correspondent Henry M. Stanley navigated the Congo River in 1877 and opened the interior to exploration. Commissioned by King Leopold II of the Belgians, Stanley made treaties with native chiefs that enabled the King to obtain personal title to the territory at the Berlin Conference of 1885.

Criticism of forced labor under royal exploitation prompted Belgium to take over administration of the Congo, which remained a colony until agitation for independence forced Brussels to grant freedom on June 30, 1960. Moise Tshombe, Premier of the then Katanga Province seceded from the new republic on July 11, and another mining province, South Kasai, followed. Belgium sent paratroopers to quell the civil war, and with President Joseph Kasavubu and Premier Patrice Lumumba of the national government in conflict, the United Nations flew in a peacekeeping force.

Kasavubu staged an army coup in 1960 and handed Lumumba over to the Katangan forces. A U.N. investigating commission found that Lumumba had been killed by a Belgian mercenary in the presence of Tshombe. Dag Hammarskjold, U.N. Secretary-General, died in a plane crash en route to a peace conference with Tshombe on Sept. 17, 1961.

U.N. Secretary-General U Thant submitted a national reconciliation plan in 1962 that Tshombe rejected. Tshombe's troops fired on the U.N. force in December, and in the ensuing conflict Tshombe capitulated on Jan. 14, 1963. The peacekeeping force withdrew, and, in a complete about-face, Kasavubu named Tshombe Premier to fight a spreading rebellion. Tshombe used foreign mercenaries and, with the help of Belgian paratroops airlifted by U.S. planes, defeated the most serious opposition, a Communist-backed regime in the northeast.

Kasavubu abruptly dismissed Tshombe in 1965 and was himself ousted by Gen. Joseph-Desiré Mobutu, Army Chief of Staff. The new President nationalized the Union Minière, the Belgian copper mining enterprise that had been a dominant force in the Congo since colonial days. The plane carrying the exiled Tshombe was hijacked in 1967 and he was held prisoner in Algeria until his death from a heart attack was announced June 29, 1969.

Mobutu eliminated opposition to win election in 1970 to a term of seven years, which was renewed in a 1977 election. In 1975, he nationalized much of the economy, barred religious instruction in schools, and decreed the adoption of African names.

On March 8, 1977, invaders from Angola calling themselves the Congolese National Liberation Front pushed into Shaba and threatened the important mining center of Kolwezi. France and Belgium responded to Mobutu's pleas for help with weapons, but the U.S. gave only nonmilitary supplies.

In April, France flew 1,500 Moroccan troops to Shaba to defeat the invaders, who were, Mobutu charged, Soviet-inspired, and Cuban-led. U.S. intelligence sources, however, confirmed Soviet and Cuban denials of any participation and identified the rebels as former Katanga gendarmes who had fled to Angola after their 1963 defeat.

In April 1990 Mobutu announced he intended to introduce multiparty democracy, but that elections in January 1991 would reduce the number of political parties to two besides his own. Opposition leaders denounced the scheme as giving Mobutu's party an unfair advantage.

A national conference was scheduled for July 1991, but in June three opposition groups announced a boycott and that they would form a parallel government of national union. The conference was postponed.

The conference finally convened in August, but, boycotted by the main opposition parties, it was adjourned without achieving anything. Mobutu offered the prime ministerial post to an opposition leader. The ensuing power struggle led to his dismissal in October. In November Mobutu appointed Mr. Nguza, another opposition figure, to the post. An attempted coup in January was crushed. Constitutional talks resumed in April 1992.

In early 1993 Mobutu rejected Western demands that he yield power and announced plans to regroup his one-party parliament dismissing the main opposition leader Prime Minister Tshisekedi. A special "political enclave" in March chose a new prime minister.

ZAMBIA

Republic of Zambia
President: Frederick T.J. Chiluba (1991)
Vice President: Levy Mwanawasa (1991)
Area: 290,586 sq mi. (752,618 sq km)
Population (est. mid-1993): 8,600,000 (average annual rate of natural increase: 3.1%); birth rate: 48/1000; infant mortality rate: 107/1000; density per square mile: 30
Capital: Lusaka; **Largest cities (est. 1988):** Lusaka, 870,030; Kitwe, 472,260; Ndola, 442,670; Chingola, 194,350; **Monetary unit:** Kwacha; **Languages:** English and local dialects; **Religions:** Christian, 50–75%; Islam and Hindu, 1%; remainder indigenous beliefs; **Member of Commonwealth of Nations; Literacy rate:** 75.7%
Economic summary: Gross domestic product (1991): $4.7 billion; $600 per capita; real growth rate –2%; inflation 100%. Arable land: 7%. Principal agricultural products: corn, tobacco, rice, sugar cane. Labor force: 2,455,000; Agriculture 85%. Major industrial products: copper, textiles, chemicals, zinc, fertilizers. Natural resources: copper, zinc, lead, cobalt, coal. Exports: $1.1 billion (f.o.b., 1991): copper, zinc, lead, cobalt, tobacco. Imports: $1.3 billion (c.i.f., 1991): manufactured goods, machinery and transport equipment, foodstuffs. Major trading partners: Western Europe, Japan, South Africa, U.S.

Geography. Zambia, a landlocked country in south central Africa, is about one-tenth larger than Texas. It is surrounded by Angola, Zaire, Tanzania, Malawi, Mozambique, Zimbabwe, Botswana, and Namibia (formerly South-West Africa). The country is mostly a plateau that rises to 8,000 feet (2,434 m) in the east.

Government. A multiparty system. Zambia (formerly Northern Rhodesia) is governed by a president, elected by universal suffrage, and a unicameral Legislative Assembly, consisting of 150 members elected by universal suffrage.

History. Empire builder Cecil Rhodes obtained mining concessions in 1889 from King Lewanika of the Barotse and sent settlers to the area soon thereafter. It was ruled by the British South Africa Company, which he established, until 1924, when the British government took over the administration.

From 1953 to 1964, Northern Rhodesia was federated with Southern Rhodesia and Nyasaland in the Federation of Rhodesia and Nyasaland. On Oct. 24, 1964, Northern Rhodesia became the independent nation of Zambia.

Kenneth Kaunda, the first president, kept Zambia within the Commonwealth of Nations. The country's economy, dependent on copper exports, was threatened when Rhodesia declared its independence from British rule in 1965 and defied U.N. sanctions, which Zambia supported, an action that deprived Zambia of its trade route through Rhodesia. The U.S., Britain, and Canada organized an airlift in 1966 to ship gasoline into Zambia. In 1967, Britain agreed to finance new trade routes for Zambia.

Kaunda visited China in 1967, and China later agreed to finance a 1,000-mile railroad from the copper fields to Dar es Salaam in Tanzania. A pipeline was opened in 1968 from Ndola in Zambia's copper belt to the Indian Ocean at Dar es Salaam, ending the three-year oil drought.

In 1969, Kaunda announced the nationalization of the foreign copper-mining industry, with Zambia to take 51% (over $1 billion, estimated), and an agreement was reached with the companies on payment. He then announced a similar takeover of foreign oil producers.

With a soaring debt and inflation rate the government in 1990 turned to the International Monetary Fund and the World Bank, with whom an agreement was reached in exchange for economic reforms. Soaring prices in June 1990 led to riots in Lusaka, resulting in a number of killings. Mounting domestic pressure forced Kaunda to move Zambia toward multi-party democracy.

National elections on October 31, 1991 brought a stunning defeat to the long-serving President Kaunda and a repudiation of his long belief in a one-party state. The newly-elected chief executive, Chiluba, called for sweeping economic reforms including privatization and the establishing of a stock market.

The United National Independence Party in early January 1992 announced the resignation of Kaunda from his post as party leader.

ZIMBABWE

Republic of Zimbabwe
Executive President: Robert Mugabe (1987)
Area: 150,698 sq mi. (390,308 sq km)
Population (est. mid-1993): 10,700,000 (average annual rate of natural increase: 3.0%); birth rate: 41/1000; infant mortality rate: 59/1000; density per square mile: 72
Capital: Harare; **Largest cities (est. 1983 for metropolitan area):** Harare, 681,000; Bulawayo, 429,000; **Monetary unit:** Zimbabwean dollar; **Languages:** English (official), Ndebele, Shona; **Religions:** Christian, 25%; Animist, 24%; Syncretic, 50%; **Literacy rate:** 74%
Economic summary: Gross domestic product (1991 est.): $7.1 billion; $660 per capita; real growth rate 3.5%; inflation 25%; unemployment, at least 30%. Arable land: 7%. Principal agricultural products: tobacco, corn, sugar, cotton, livestock. Labor force: 3,100,000; 74% in agriculture; 16%, transport and services. Major industrial products: steel, textiles, chemicals, vehicles, gold, copper. Natural resources: gold, copper, chrome, nickel, tin, asbestos. Exports: $1.8 billion (f.o.b., 1991 est.): gold, tobacco, asbestos, copper, meat, chrome, nickel, corn, sugar. Imports: $1.6 billion (c.i.f., 1991 est.): machinery, petroleum products, transport equipment. Major trading partners: South Africa, E.C., U.S.

Geography. Zimbabwe, a landlocked country in south central Africa, is slightly smaller than California. It is bordered by Botswana on the west, Zambia on the north, Mozambique on the east, and South Africa on the south.

A high veld up to 6,000 feet (1,829 m) crosses the country from northeast to southwest. This is flanked by a somewhat lower veld that contains ranching country. Tropical forests that yield hardwoods lie in the southeast.

In the north, on the border with Zambia, is the 175-mile-long (128-m) Kariba Lake, formed by the Kariba Dam across the Zambezi River. It is the site of one of the world's largest hydroelectric projects.

Government. A parliamentary democracy with a 150-seat unicameral legislature, the House of Assembly. The Executive President is chief of state and head of government. There are two co-vice presidents.

History. Zimbabwe was colonized by Cecil Rhodes's British South Africa Company at the end of the 19th century. In 1923, European settlers voted to become the self-governing British colony of Southern Rhodesia rather than merge with the Union of South Africa. After a brief federation with Northern Rhodesia and Nyasaland in the post-World War II period, Southern Rhodesia chose to remain a colony when its two partners voted for independence in 1963.

On Nov. 11, 1965, the white-minority government of Rhodesia unilaterally declared its independence from Britain.

In 1967, the U.N. imposed mandatory sanctions against Rhodesia. The country moved slowly toward meeting the demands of black Africans. The white-minority regime of Prime Minister Ian Smith withstood British pressure, economic sanctions, guerrilla attacks, and a right-wing assault.

On March 1, 1970, Rhodesia formally proclaimed itself a republic, and within the month nine nations, including the U.S., closed their consulates there.

Heightened guerrilla war and a withdrawal of South African military aid—particularly helicopters—marked the beginning of the collapse of Smith's 11 years of resistance in the spring of 1976. Under pressure from South Africa, Smith agreed with the U.S. that majority rule should come within two years.

In the fall, Smith met with black nationalist leaders in Geneva. The meeting broke up six weeks later when the Rhodesian Premier insisted that whites must retain control of the police and armed forces during the transition to majority rule. A British proposal called for Britons to take over these powers.

Divisions between Rhodesian blacks—Bishop Abel Muzorewa of the African National Congress and Ndabaningi Sithole as moderates versus Robert Mugabe and Joshua Nkomo of the Patriotic Front as advocates of guerrilla force—sharpened in 1977 and no agreement was reached. In July, with white residents leaving in increasing numbers and the economy showing the strain of war, Smith rejected outside mediation and called for general elections in order to work out an "internal solution" of the transfer of power.

On March 3, 1978, Smith, Muzorewa, Sithole, and Chief Jeremiah Chirau signed an agreement to transfer power to the black majority by Dec. 31, 1978. They constituted themselves an Executive Council, with chairmanship rotating but Smith retaining the title of Prime Minister. Blacks were named to each cabinet ministry, serving as co-ministers with the whites already holding these posts. African nations and the Patriotic Front leaders immediately denounced the action, but Western governments were more reserved, although none granted recognition to the new regime.

White voters ratified a new constitution on Jan. 30, 1979, enfranchising all blacks, establishing a black majority Senate and Assembly, and changing the country's name to Zimbabwe Rhodesia.

Muzorewa agreed to negotiate with Mugabe and Nkomo in British-sponsored talks beginning Sept. 9. By December, all parties accepted a new draft constitution, a cease-fire, and a period of British administration pending a general election.

In voting completed on Feb. 29, 1980, Mugabe's ZANU-Patriotic Front party won 57 of the 80 Assembly seats reserved for blacks. In an earlier vote on Feb. 14, the Rhodesian Front won all 20 seats reserved for whites in the Assembly.

At a ceremony on April 18, Prince Charles of Britain handed to President-elect Rev. Canaan Banana the symbols of independence.

On April 18, 1980, Britain formally recognized the independence of Zimbabwe.

In January 1981, Mugabe dismissed Nkomo as Home Minister and his onetime rival left the government in protest. At the same time, the Prime Minister discharged Edgar Z. Tekere, Manpower and Planning Minister, who had been tried and acquitted of the murder of a white farmer.

Mugabe survived both tests and scored an unprecedented triumph when, in response to his appeal for economic aid, Western nations pledged $1.8 billion for the next three years.

The 1985 harvest was good in Zimbabwe and the country could feed itself. But political turmoil and civil strife continued. In what Western analysts viewed as a free and fair election, President Mugabe's African National Union increased its sizeable majority in the House of Assembly but Mugabe was frustrated because it did not win the 70 seats he sought to cement one-party rule. After the election, Mugabe cracked down on Nkomo's ZAPU-Patriotic Front party.

In April 1990, Mugabe was re-elected and his ZANU(PF) party given virtual unanimity in the Assembly.

In December 1990 the parliament voted by 113 to 3 to amend the original 1980 constitution to allow the compulsory acquisition of white-owned farmland at government-set prices. Indeed, white farmers would have no judiciary recourse. Britain and the U.S. warned that forceful land acquisitions would deter foreign investments and further depress the country.

A split in the opposition Zimbabwe Unity Movement in June 1991 reduced pressure on the ruling ZANU(PF). At that time the latter deleted all references to Marxism-Leninism and scientific socialism from its constitution.

A long drought in southern Africa and government miscalculation on the expected maize harvest the previous year resulted in a shortage of that grain in 1992.

The Land Acquisition Act was amended in 1992 to permit compensation for compulsorily acquired land.

(For late reports, see Current Events of 1993)

Highlights of the 1993 Amnesty International Report

Appalling human rights catastrophes shocked the world in 1992. As international attention focused on the carnage in the former Yugoslavia and Somalia, in many other countries, torture, "disappearances," and political killings continued at horrifying levels. The following summary covers events from January to December 1992.

Asia and the Pacific

Prisoners of conscience. Thousands of prisoners of conscience, jailed solely for the peaceful exercise of their human rights, were held in at least 14 countries, including Myanmar, Indonesia and East Timor, and China.

Administrative detention. Thirteen countries between them held many thousands of political prisoners without charge or trial, particularly China and Sri Lanka.

Releases. Thousands of political prisoners, including prisoners of conscience, were freed in nine countries, including Afghanistan, Myanmar, Cambodia, and Sri Lanka.

Unfair trials. In at least 11 countries, including China, Indonesia and East Timor, Myanmar, and Pakistan, political prisoners were held after unfair trials in 1992 and in at least three countries, including China and Indonesia and East Timor, after unfair trials in previous years.

"Disappearances." Hundreds of people "disappeared" in six countries including India, the Philippines, and Sri Lanka, and tens of thousands of people who "disappeared" in previous years remained unaccounted for.

Political killings. Hundreds of people were apparently extrajudicially executed by government security forces or by "death squads" said to be linked to them in 12 countries, including India, Indonesia and East Timor, the Philippines, Cambodia, Sri Lanka, and Myanmar.

Torture or ill-treatment. Torture or ill-treatment of prisoners were reported in 20 countries, including China, Indonesia and East Timor, India, Myanmar, Sri Lanka, and Pakistan. In at least eight countries—including Bangladesh, China, India, Indonesia and East Timor, and Pakistan—people died in custody, apparently as a result of torture. Women were raped or sexually abused by security forces in eight countries, including India, Pakistan, Myanmar, and the Philippines.

Summary of Human Rights Abuses, 1992

Prisoners. Prisoners of conscience—jailed solely for the peaceful exercise of their basic human rights—were held in some 62 countries. Possible prisoners of conscience were held in 32 countries. The number of known prisoners of conscience in those countries totalled more than 4,400. At least 300,000 political prisoners were detained without charge or trial or under administrative detention in more than 60 countries.

Unfair trials. More than 1,500 political prisoners were imprisoned after unfair trials in at least 30 countries. Political prisoners in 30 countries were still in prison after unfair trials in previous years.

Torture and ill-treatment. Detainees were tortured or ill-treated in prisons, police stations, or secret detention centers in at least 110 countries. Over 500 people died apparently as a result of torture or inhuman prison conditions or in "suspicious" circumstances in some 48 countries.

Political killings. Suspected government opponents, members of targeted ethnic groups, or people living in opposition strongholds were apparently victims of extrajudicial execution in some 48 countries.

"Disappearances." At least 950 people were reported to have "disappeared" after arrest by security forces in some 25 countries and many others remained "disappeared" in at least 27 countries after "disappearing" in previous years.

Death penalty. 1,708 prisoners are known to have been executed in 35 countries and 2,697 people were sentenced to death in 62 countries. The true figures are certainly higher. At the end of 1992, 44% of countries have abolished the death penalty in law or practice. 47 countries have abolished it for all offenses and 16 for all but exceptional offenses, such as war crimes. A further 20 countries and territories, while retaining the penalty in law, have not carried out any executions for at least ten years. 106 countries and territories retain and use the death penalty for ordinary crimes. China and Iran account for 82% of all known executions.

Women. Women were victims of a range of human rights violations, including rape by security forces, in at least 45 countries.

Children. Some 35 countries violated the basic human rights of children and juveniles.

Indigenous peoples. People from indigenous communities were targeted for human rights violations in at least 40 countries.

Death penalty. The death penalty was imposed in 13 countries, and thousands of people remained on death row. Executions were carried out in 11 countries in the region. In China alone, Amnesty International knows of over 1,000 executions in 1992 and over 1,800 death sentences passed by the courts.

Other abuses. Armed opposition groups committed human rights abuses, such as torture or deliberate and arbitrary killings, in at least eight countries, including Bhutan, Cambodia, Sri Lanka, India, and Myanmar.

Africa

Political killings. Several thousand people were victims or possible victims of extrajudicial execution by security forces in 14 countries, including Sierra Leone, Angola, Chad, Zaire, and South Africa.

"Disappearances." Some 108 people were reported to have "disappeared" in five countries and the fate of close to 2,863 others from nine countries was still unknown after their "disappearance" in previous years. The countries included Sudan, Chad, Mauritania, and Mozambique.

Torture and ill-treatment. Detainees were tortured or ill-treated in prison, police stations, or special secret detention centers in 30 countries, including Cameroon and Malawi. More than 420 people died apparently from beatings and other torture in some 18 countries, including Chad, Djibouti, Sierra Leone, and South Africa. Prisoners in at least eight countries including Côte d'Ivoire and Kenya had to endure harsh prison conditions which amounted to cruel, inhuman, or degrading treatment.

Prisoners. Prisoners of conscience or possible prisoners of conscience, detained solely for the peaceful exercise of their human rights, were held in at least 17 countries in the region. A total of more than 337 prisoners of conscience were held in those countries which included Chad, Malawi, and Sudan. A further 401 possible prisoners of conscience were held in eight countries including Cameroon, Guinea, Ghana, and Gambia.

More than 3,920 people were held in administrative detention—without charge or trial—in some 24 countries, including Cameroon, Chad, Burundi, Nigeria, and Malawi. At least 4,000 political prisoners, including some prisoners of conscience and others, that were held without charge or trial, were released in 24 countries including Ghana.

Unfair trials. More than 170 political prisoners were imprisoned after unfair trials in six countries, including Djibouti and Burundi. More than 1,459 political prisoners were still held after unfair trials in previous years in seven countries.

Death penalty. Over 31 people were executed by hanging, firing squad, or other methods in four countries including Sierra Leone and Sudan. More than 1,329 people in 20 countries including Cameroon, South Africa, and Kenya, were on death row, either after death sentences passed in 1992 or previous years.

Other abuses. Armed opposition groups committed human rights abuses such as torture or deliberate and arbitrary killings in at least 17 countries including Angola, Sierra Leone, Sudan, and Somalia.

Europe

Torture and ill-treatment. Detainees were tortured or ill-treated in prison, police stations, or other detention centers in 22 countries including Bosnia-Hercegovina, Croatia, Georgia, Tajikistan, Yugoslavia, and Turkey. More than 30 people died apparently from beatings by police and other torture in some six countries.

Prisoners. Thousands of prisoners of conscience or possible prisoners of conscience were held in 15 countries in the region, including Bosnia-Hercegovina, Greece, France, and Switzerland.

Political killings. More than 500 extrajudicial executions or possible extrajudicial executions were reported in six countries—Turkey, Croatia, Azerbaijan, Tajikistan, Georgia, and Yugoslavia. Hundreds, possibly thousands, of civilians and captured or wounded combatants were deliberately and arbitrarily killed in the course of conflict in Bosnia-Hercegovina.

Death penalty. Some 68 people were known to have been executed in Albania, Georgia, Latvia, Turkmenistan, Kyrgyzstan, Kazakhstan, Russia, Belarus, and Ukraine and an additional 125 were sentenced to death or remained on death row in 14 countries.

Other abuses. Armed opposition groups committed human rights abuses, such as torture or deliberate and arbitrary killings in at least eight countries, including Spain, United Kingdom, and Turkey.

Middle East

Political killings. At least 500 people were victims or possible victims of extrajudicial execution by security forces in six countries, including Algeria, Iraq, and Israel and the Occupied Territories.

"Disappearances." Hundreds of people were reported to have disappeared in Iraq. The fate of many thousands of others was still unknown after their "disappearance" in previous years in six countries including Iraq, Kuwait, Lebanon, Morocco, and Western Sahara.

Torture and ill-treatment. Detainees were tortured or ill-treated in prisons, police stations, or special secret detention centers in virtually every country in the region including Kuwait, Morocco, Israel and the Occupied Territories, Iran, and Iraq. People died apparently from beatings and other torture in five countries, including Saudi Arabia, Syria, and Tunisia.

Prisoners. Prisoners of conscience, or possible prisoners of conscience, were held in at least 11 countries in the region: some 1,500 prisoners of conscience in 11 countries and a further 2,000 possible prisoners of conscience. More than 14,000 people were held in administrative detention, without charge or trial, in at least 12 countries in the region. Over 5,000 political prisoners, including some prisoners of conscience and others held without charge or trial, were released in nine countries.

Unfair trials. Hundreds of political prisoners were imprisoned after unfair trials in 11 countries, including Iran, Jordan, and Kuwait. Over 3,500 political prisoners were still held after unfair trials in previous years in nine countries, including Bahrain, Libya, and Tunisia.

Death penalty. More than 400 people were executed by hanging, firing squad, or other method in seven countries—at least 330 in Iran. Over 500 people in nine countries including Algeria and Morocco were on death row, either after death sentences passed in 1992 or previous years.

Other abuses. Armed opposition groups committed human rights abuses, such as torture or deliberate and arbitrary killings, in at least five countries—Algeria, Egypt, Iraq, Israel and the Occupied Territories, and Lebanon.

The Americas

"Disappearances." People "disappeared" or remained unaccounted for in 18 countries. Hundreds of people "disappeared" in Colombia and Peru, hundreds more remained unaccounted for from past years in countries including Argentina, El Salvador, Uruguay, and Mexico.

Political killings. At least 3,700 people were apparently extrajudicially executed by government security forces or by "death squads" said to be linked to them in 11 countries, notably Brazil, Colombia, Guatemala, and Haiti. There were prison massacres by security forces in Peru, Brazil, and Venezuela in which more than 100 people were killed.

Torture or ill-treatment. Torture or ill-treatment of prisoners was reported in 26 countries, including Argentina, Brazil, Chile, Ecuador, Haiti, and Peru. Women were allegedly raped or sexually abused by security forces in 13 countries, including Bolivia, Brazil, Colombia, Guatemala, and Haiti.

Prisoners. Hundreds of prisoners of conscience, jailed solely for the peaceful exercise of their human rights, were held in many countries in the region, including Cuba, Haiti, and Venezuela. Other political prisoners were held after unfair trials or held without charge or trial in several countries including Peru, Cuba, and Haiti.

Death penalty. The death penalty was imposed in ten countries and thousands of people remained on death row, notably in the United States, Jamaica, and Trinidad and Tobago. Some 33 executions were carried out in two countries in the region, 31 of them in the United States.

Other abuses. Armed opposition groups committed human rights abuses, such as torture or deliberate and arbitrary killings, in at least eight countries, including Peru, Bolivia, and Colombia.

World's Largest Labor Force Is in Developing Countries

According to the U.S. Census Bureau, the labor force in developing countries is significantly larger than in developed nations and most of the increase in the world labor force by the year 2010 will be in developing countries.

The visible world labor force is expected to grow from 2.4 billion persons in 1990 to 3.2 billion in 2010, a 35% increase. The figure excludes many women, workers in subsistence agriculture, and others in the informal sector. If these "invisible" workers were included, the contrast between developed and developing countries probably would be even greater.

For example, in Bangladesh, 90% of the female population is engaged in agriculture. In Africa, 60 to 80% of all agricultural work is done by women. In the developing countries as a whole, rural women account for at least 50% of food production. Yet women's work is not recognized and is usually omitted from the economically active count.

The labor force will grow very little in developed countries. The main change is that the labor force will become older as fewer young men and women enter. As a result, some countries may experience a labor shortage.

By contrast, the labor force in developing countries will grow rapidly—doubling in countries with rapid population growth. Unless the economies of these countries also grow rapidly, it is difficult to imagine how jobs can be created for many new potential workers. □

The World's 20 Oldest Countries: 1992

(Percent of population 65 years and over)

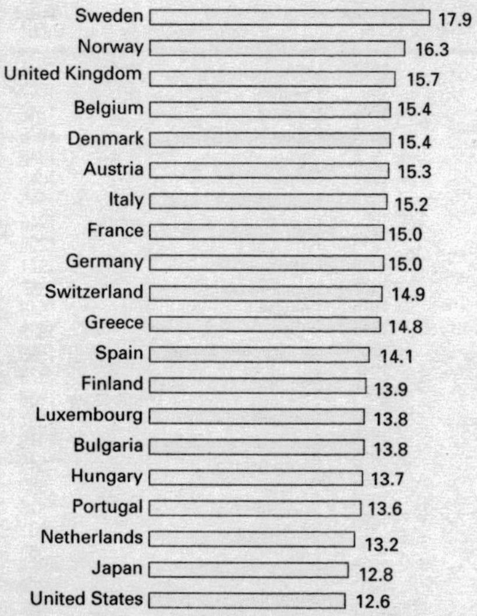

Source: U.S. Bureau of the Census, Center for International Research, International Data Base on Aging.

Percent Distribution of World Population, 80 Years and Over: 1990

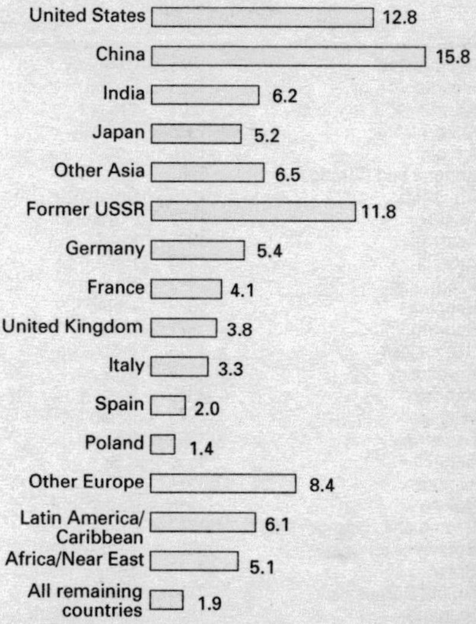

Source: U.S. Bureau of the Census, Center for International Research, International Data Base on Aging.

The Dimensions of An Aging World

A 1993 Census Bureau report revealed that one of the major successes of the 20th century is that populations have the luxury of aging. In fact, the study found that the coming growth of the oldest old, those 80 years and over, will be stunning. Most notably:

• The global population aged 65 and over is estimated to be 342 million persons (6.2% of the world's total population in 1992). This is an increase of 2.7 million elderly people since 1991.

• The world's elderly population is increasing by 800,000 persons each month. By the year 2010, projections suggest the worldwide growth of the elderly will be over 1.1 million people a month.

• The elderly population is growing at the fastest rate in developing countries. Sixty-two percent of the world's monthly net increase in elderly individuals, half a million persons, occurs in developing countries.

• The fastest growing portion of the elderly population is those aged 80 and over. Nearly 40% of the world's population 80 years and over live in the People's Republic of China, the United States, and the lands encompassing the former Soviet Union combined. Cynthia Tauber, co-author with Kevin Kinsella of the report, "An Aging World II," said, "The population 80 years and over are 22 percent of the elderly in developed nations and 12 percent in developing nations. These proportions probably won't change too much in most countries, but the numbers may increase rapidly. This could be a challenge for developing nations where families traditionally provide all care for frail elderly."

Tauber also noted that "The projected increase in the world's elderly population is primarily the result of high fertility after World War II. Other nations have Baby-Boom generations just like the United States."

"The increase is secondarily the result of reduced death rates at all ages so that more people reach old age. In most nations of the world, there have been major reductions in infectious and parasitic diseases, reductions in infant and maternal mortality, and improved nutrition in this century," Kinsella added.

Other notable findings from the report:

• Based on the mortality experience of 1990, Japan's life expectancy of 79 years is the world's highest. However, Europe is the world's oldest region.

• In 1992, Sweden was the world's oldest country, with 17.9% of the population aged 65 and over, followed by Norway at 16.3%, and the United Kingdom at 15.7%. Japan and the United States rank 19th and 20th, respectively, with both having 12.8% of their populations aged 65 and over.

• In most nations, elderly women outnumber elderly men.

• Elderly men tend to be married, while elderly women tend to be widowed.

• In developing nations, the majority of elderly live with others. In developed nations, 40% of Sweden's elderly lived alone (the highest) compared with only 10% in Japan (the lowest).

For additional reading, *see* "Sixty-Five Plus in America," page 459.

UNITED NATIONS

The 184 Members of the United Nations

Country	Joined U.N.[1]
Afghanistan	1946
Albania	1955
Algeria	1962
Andorra	1993
Angola	1976
Antigua and Barbuda	1981
Argentina	1945
Armenia	1992
Australia	1945
Austria	1955
Azerbaijan	1992
Bahamas	1973
Bahrain	1971
Bangladesh	1974
Barbados	1966
Belarus	1945
Belgium	1945
Belize	1981
Benin	1960
Bhutan	1971
Bolivia	1945
Bosnia and Hercegovina	1992
Botswana	1966
Brazil	1945
Brunei Darussalam	1984
Bulgaria	1955
Burkina Faso	1960
Burundi	1962
Cambodia	1955
Cameroon	1960
Canada	1945
Cape Verde	1975
Central African Republic	1960
Chad	1960
Chile	1945
China[2]	1945
Colombia	1945
Comoros	1975
Congo	1960
Costa Rica	1945
Côte d'Ivoire	1960
Croatia	1992
Cuba	1945
Cyprus	1960
Czech Republic[3]	1993
Denmark	1945
Djibouti	1977
Dominica	1978
Dominican Republic	1945
Ecuador	1945
Egypt	1945
El Salvador	1945
Equatorial Guinea	1968
Eritrea	1993
Estonia	1991
Ethiopia	1945
Fiji	1970
Finland	1955
France	1945
Gabon	1960
Gambia	1965
Georgia	1992
Germany	1973
Ghana	1957
Greece	1945
Grenada	1974
Guatemala	1945
Guinea	1958
Guinea-Bissau	1974
Guyana	1966
Haiti	1945
Honduras	1945
Hungary	1955
Iceland	1946
India	1945
Indonesia	1950
Iran	1945
Iraq	1945
Ireland	1955
Israel	1949
Italy	1955
Jamaica	1962
Japan	1956
Jordan	1955
Kazakhstan	1992
Kenya	1963
Korea, North	1991
Korea, South	1991
Kuwait	1963
Kyrgyzstan	1992
Laos	1955
Latvia	1991
Lebanon	1945
Lesotho	1966
Liberia	1945
Libya	1955
Liechtenstein	1990
Lithuania	1991
Luxembourg	1945
Madagascar	1960
Malawi	1964
Malaysia	1957
Maldives	1965
Mali	1960
Malta	1964
Marshall Islands	1991
Mauritania	1961
Mauritius	1968
Mexico	1945
Micronesia	1991
Moldova	1992
Monaco	1993
Mongolia	1961
Morocco	1956
Mozambique	1975
Myanmar	1948
Namibia	1990
Nepal	1955
Netherlands	1945
New Zealand	1945
Nicaragua	1945
Niger	1960
Nigeria	1960
Norway	1945
Oman	1971
Pakistan	1947
Panama	1945
Papua New Guinea	1975
Paraguay	1945
Peru	1945
Philippines	1945
Poland	1945
Portugal	1955
Qatar	1971
Romania	1955
Russian Federation	1945
Rwanda	1962
St. Kitts and Nevis	1983
St. Lucia	1979
St. Vincent and the Grenadines	1980
San Marino	1992
São Tomé and Príncipe	1975
Saudi Arabia	1945
Senegal	1960
Seychelles	1976
Sierra Leone	1961
Singapore	1965
Slovak Republic[3]	1993
Slovenia	1992
Solomon Islands	1978
Somalia	1960
South Africa	1945
Spain	1955
Sri Lanka	1955
Sudan	1956
Suriname	1975
Swaziland	1968
Sweden	1946
Syria	1945
Tajikistan	1992
Tanzania	1961
Thailand	1946
The former Yugoslav Republic of Macedonia[4]	1993
Togo	1960
Trinidad and Tobago	1962
Tunisia	1956
Turkey	1945
Turkmenistan	1992
Uganda	1962
Ukraine	1945
United Arab Emirates	1971
United Kingdom	1945
United States	1945
Uruguay	1945
Uzbekistan	1992
Vanuatu	1981
Venezuela	1945
Vietnam	1977
Western Samoa	1976
Yemen, Republic of	1947
Yugoslavia	1945
Zaire	1960
Zambia	1964
Zimbabwe	1980

1. The U.N. officially came into existence on Oct. 24, 1945. 2. On Oct. 25, 1971, the U.N. voted membership to the People's Republic of China, which replaced the Republic of China (Taiwan) in the world body. 3. Czechoslovakia was an original member of the United Nations from Oct. 24, 1945. As of December 31, 1992 it ceased to exist and the Czech Republic and the Slovak Republic as successor States were admitted January 19, 1993. 4. The General Assembly on April 8, 1993 decided to admit the State provisionally being referred to as "The former Yugoslav Republic of Macedonia" pending settlement of the difference that has arisen over its name.

Member Countries' Assessments to U.N. Budget, 1993

Country	Total
Afghanistan	$102,051
Albania	102,051
Algeria	1,632,818
Angola	102,051
Antigua and Barbuda	102,051
Argentina	5,816,914
Armenia	1,326,665
Australia	15,409,719
Austria	7,653,843
Azerbaijan	2,245,124
Bahamas	204,102
Bahrain	306,154
Bangladesh	102,051
Barbados	102,051
Belarus	4,898,454
Belgium	10,817,419
Belize	102,051
Benin	102,051
Bhutan	102,051
Bolivia	102,051
Bosnia and Hercegovina	408,205
Botswana	102,051
Brazil	16,226,128
Brunei Darussalam	306,154
Bulgaria	1,326,665
Burkina Faso	102,051
Burundi	102,051
Cambodia	102,051
Cameroon	102,051
Canada	31,743,607
Cape Verde	102,051
Central African Republic	102,051
Chad	102,051
Chile	816,409
China	7,857,936
Colombia	1,326,665
Comoros	102,051
Congo	102,051
Costa Rica	102,051
Côte d'Ivoire	204,102
Croatia	1,326,665
Cuba	918,460
Cyprus	204,102
Denmark	6,633,323
Djibouti	102,051
Dominica	102,051
Dominican Republic	204,102
Ecuador	306,154
Egypt	714,357
El Salvador	102,051
Equatorial Guinea	102,051
Estonia	714,357
Ethiopia	102,051
Fiji	102,051
Finland	5,816,914
France	61,230,672
Gabon	204,102
Gambia	102,051
Georgia	2,143,073
Germany	91,131,650
Ghana	102,051
Greece	3,571,790
Grenada	102,051
Guatemala	204,102
Guinea	102,051
Guinea-Bissau	102,051
Guyana	102,051
Haiti	102,051
Honduras	102,051
Hungary	1,836,921
Iceland	306,154
India	3,673,841
Indonesia	1,632,818
Iran	7,857,936
Iraq	1,326,665
Ireland	1,836,921
Israel	2,347,175
Italy	43,779,930
Jamaica	102,051
Japan	127,053,643
Jordan	102,051
Kazakhstan	3,571,790
Kenya	102,051
Korea, North	510,256
Korea, South	7,041,527
Kuwait	2,551,278
Kyrgyzstan	612,307
Laos	102,051
Latvia	1,326,665
Lebanon	102,051
Lesotho	102,051
Liberia	102,051
Libya	2,449,227
Liechtenstein	102,051
Lithuania	1,530,767
Luxembourg	612,307
Madagascar	102,051
Malawi	102,051
Malaysia	1,224,613
Maldives	102,051
Mali	102,051
Malta	102,051
Marshall Islands	102,051
Mauritania	102,051
Mauritius	102,051
Mexico	8,980,498
Micronesia	102,051
Mongolia	102,051
Morocco	306,154
Mozambique	102,051
Myanmar	102,051
Namibia	102,051
Nepal	102,051
Netherlands	15,307,668
New Zealand	2,449,227
Nicaragua	102,051
Niger	102,051
Nigeria	2,041,023
Norway	5,612,811
Oman	306,154
Pakistan	612,307
Panama	204,102
Papua New Guinea	102,051
Paraguay	204,102
Peru	612,307
Philippines	714,357
Poland	4,796,403
Portugal	2,041,023
Qatar	510,256
Romania	1,734,869
Russian Federation	68,476,301
Rwanda	102,051
St. Kitts and Nevis	102,051
St. Lucia	102,051
St. Vincent & the Grenadines	102,051
San Marino	102,051
São Tomé and Príncipe	102,051
Saudi Arabia	9,796,908
Senegal	102,051
Seychelles	102,051
Sierra Leone	102,051
Singapore	1,224,613
Slovenia	918,460
Solomon Islands	102,051
Somalia	102,051
South Africa	4,184,096
Spain	20,206,121
Sri Lanka	102,051
Sudan	102,051
Suriname	102,051
Swaziland	102,051
Sweden	11,327,675
Syria	408,205
Tajikistan	510,256
Tanzania	102,051
Thailand	1,122,562
Togo	102,051
Trinidad and Tobago	510,256
Tunisia	306,154
Turkey	2,768,430
Turkmenistan	612,307
Uganda	102,051
Ukraine	19,083,559
United Arab Emirates	2,143,073
United Kingdom	51,229,662
United States	309,922,958
Uruguay	408,205
Uzbekistan	2,653,329
Vanuatu	102,051
Venezuela	5,000,505
Vietnam	102,051
Western Samoa	102,051
Yemen	102,051
Yugoslavia	1,632,818
Zaire	102,051
Zambia	102,051
Zimbabwe	102,051
TOTAL	**$1,070,018,454**

Preamble of the United Nations Charter

The Charter of the United Nations was adopted at the San Francisco Conference of 1945. The complete text may be obtained by writing to the United Nations Sales Section, United Nations, New York, N.Y. 10017, and enclosing $1.

We the peoples of the United Nations determined to save succeeding generations from the scourge of war, which twice in our lifetime has brought untold sorrow to mankind, and

To reaffirm faith in fundamental human rights, in the dignity and worth of the human person, in the equal rights of men and women and of nations large and small, and

To establish conditions under which justice and respect for the obligations arising from treaties and other sources of international law can be maintained, and

To promote social progress and better standards of life in larger freedom, and for these ends

To practice tolerance and live together in peace with one another as good neighbors, and

To unite our strength to maintain international peace and security, and

To insure, by the acceptance of principles and the institution of methods, that armed force shall not be used, save in the common interest, and

To employ international machinery for the promotion of the economic and social advancement of all peoples, have resolved to combine our efforts to accomplish these aims.

Accordingly, our respective Governments, through representatives assembled in the city of San Francisco, who have exhibited their full powers found to be in good and due form, have agreed to the present Charter of the United Nations and do hereby establish an international organization to be known as the United Nations.

Principal Organs of the United Nations

Secretariat

This is the directorate on U.N. operations, apart from political decisions. All members contribute to its upkeep. Its staff of about 5,000 specialists is recruited from member nations on the basis of as wide a geographical distribution as possible. The staff works under the Secretary-General, whom it assists and advises.

Secretaries-General

Boutros Boutros-Ghali, Egypt, Jan. 1, 1992.
Javier Pérez de Cuéllar, Peru, Jan. 1, 1982, to Dec. 31, 1991.
Kurt Waldheim, Austria, Jan. 1, 1972, to Dec. 31, 1981.
U Thant, Burma, Nov. 3, 1961, to Dec. 31, 1971.
Dag Hammarskjöld, Sweden, April 11, 1953, to Sept. 17, 1961.
Trygve Lie, Norway, Feb. 1, 1946, to April 10, 1953.

General Assembly

The General Assembly is the world's forum for discussing matters affecting world peace and security, and for making recommendations concerning them. It has no power of its own to enforce decisions.

The Assembly is composed of the 51 original member nations and those admitted since, a total of 183. Each nation has one vote. On important questions including international peace and security, a two-thirds majority of those present and voting is required. Decisions on other questions are made by a simple majority.

The Assembly's agenda can be as broad as the Charter. It can make recommendations to member nations, the Security Council, or both. Emphasis is given on questions relating to international peace and security brought before it by any member, the Security Council, or nonmembers.

The Assembly also maintains a broad program of international cooperation in economic, social, cultural, educational, and health fields, and for assisting in human rights and freedoms.

Among other duties, the Assembly has functions relating to the trusteeship system, and considers and approves the U.N. Budget. Every member contributes to operating expenses according to its means.

Security Council

The Security Council is the primary instrument for establishing and maintaining international peace. Its main purpose is to prevent war by settling disputes between nations.

Under the Charter, the Council is permitted to dispatch a U.N. force to stop aggression. All member nations undertake to make available armed forces, assistance, and facilities to maintain international peace and security.

Any member may bring a dispute before the Security Council or the General Assembly. Any nonmember may do so if it accepts the charter obligations of pacific settlement.

The Security Council has 15 members. There are five permanent members: the United States, the Russian Federation, Britain, France, and China; and 10 temporary members elected by the General Assembly for two-year terms, from five different regions of the world.

Voting on procedural matters requires a nine-vote majority to carry. However, on questions of substance, the vote of each of the five permanent members is required.

Current temporary members are (term expires Dec. 31, 1993): Cape Verde, Hungary, Japan, Morocco, and Venezuela; (term expires Dec. 31, 1994): Brazil, Djibouti, New Zealand, Pakistan, and Spain.

Economic and Social Council

This council is composed of 54 members elected by the General Assembly to 3-year terms. It works closely with the General Assembly as a link with groups formed within the U.N. to help peoples in such fields as education, health, and human rights. It insures that there is no overlapping and sets up commissions to deal with economic conditions and collect facts and figures on conditions over the world. It issues studies and reports and may make recommendations to the Assembly and specialized agencies.

Functional Commissions

Statistical Commission; Population Commission; Commission for Social Development; Commission on Human Rights; Commission on the Status of Women; Commission on Narcotic Drugs; Commission on Sustainable Development.

Regional Commissions

Economic Commission for Europe (ECE); Economic and Social Commission for Asia and the Pacific (ESCAP); Economic Commission for Latin America and the Caribbean (ECLAC); Economic Commission for Africa (ECA); Economic and Social Commission for Western Asia (ESCWA).

Trusteeship Council

This council supervises territories administered by various nations and placed under an international trusteeship system by the United Nations. Each nation is charged with developing the self-government of the territory and preserving and advancing the cultural, political, economic, and other forms of welfare of the people.

The Trusteeship Council is currently composed of 5 members: 1 member—the United States—that administers a trust territory, and 4 members—China, France, the Russian Federation, and the United Kingdom—that are permanent members of the Security Council but do not administer trust territories.

The following countries ceased to be administering members because of the independence of territories they had administered: Italy and France in 1960, Belgium in 1962, New Zealand and the United Kingdom in 1968 and Australia in 1975. France and the U.K. became nonadministering members.

As of December 1985, there was only one trust territory: the Trust Territory of the Pacific Islands. As of December 1990, only Palau remained of the four entities under United States administration.

International Court of Justice

The International Court of Justice sits at The Hague, the Netherlands. Its 15-judge bench was established to hear disputes among states, which must agree to accept its verdicts. Its judges, charged with administering justice under international law, deal with cases ranging from disputes over territory to those concerning rights of passage.

Following are the members of the Court and the years in which their terms expire on Feb. 5:

President: Sir Robert Yewdall Jennings, United Kingdom (1994 as president; 2000 term)
Vice President: Shigeru Oda, Japan (1994)
Bola Ajibola, Nigeria (1994)
Jens Evensen, Norway (1997)
Ni Zhengyu, China (1994)
Geza Herczegh, Hungary (1994)
Roberto Ago, Italy (1997)
Mohamed Shahabuddeen, Guyana (1997)
Stephen Schwebel, United States (1997)
Mohammed Bedjaoui, Algeria (2000)
Nikolai Tarassov, Russian Federation (1997)
Gilbert Guillaume, France (2000)
Andres Aguilar, Venezuela (2000)
Raymond Ranjeva, Madagascar (2000)
Christopher Gregory Weeramantry, Sri Lanka (2000)

Agencies of the United Nations

INTL. ATOMIC ENERGY AGENCY (IAEA)

Established: Statute for IAEA, approved on Oct. 26, 1956, at a conference held at U.N. Headquarters, New York, came into force on July 29, 1957. The Agency is under the aegis of the U.N., but unlike the following, it is not a specialized agency.

Purpose: To promote the peaceful uses of atomic energy; to ensure that assistance provided by it or at its request or under its supervision or control is not used in such a way as to further any military purpose.

Headquarters: Vienna International Center, P.O. Box 100, Wargramer Strasse 5, A-1400 Vienna, Austria

FOOD AND AGRICULTURE ORGANIZATION OF THE UNITED NATIONS (FAO)

Established: October 16, 1945, when constitution became effective.

Purpose: To raise nutrition levels and living standards; to secure improvements in production and distribution of food and agricultural products.

Headquarters: Via delle Terme di Caracalla, 00100, Rome, Italy.

GENERAL AGREEMENT ON TARIFFS AND TRADE (GATT)

Established: Jan. 1, 1948.

Purpose: An International Trade Organization (ITO) was originally planned. Although this agency has not materialized, some of its objectives have been embodied in an international commercial treaty, the General Agreement on Tariffs and Trade. Its purpose is to sponsor trade negotiations.

Headquarters: Centre William Rappard, 154 Rue de Lausanne, CH-1211, Geneva 21, Switzerland.

INTERNATIONAL BANK FOR RECONSTRUCTION AND DEVELOPMENT (IBRD) (WORLD BANK)

Established: December 27, 1945, when Articles of Agreement drawn up at Bretton Woods Conference in July 1944 came into force. Began operations on June 25, 1946.

Purpose: To assist in reconstruction and development of economies of members by facilitating capital investment and by making loans to governments and furnishing technical advice.

Headquarters: 1818 H St., N.W., Washington, D.C. 20433.

INTL. CIVIL AVIATION ORGANIZATION (ICAO)

Established: April 4, 1947, after working as a provisional organization since June 1945.

Purpose: To study problems of international civil aviation; to establish international standards and regulations; to promote safety measures, uniform regulations for operation, simpler procedures at international borders, and the use of new technical methods and equipment. It has evolved standards for meteorological services, traffic control, communications, radio beacons and ranges, search and rescue organization, and other facilities. It has brought about much simplification of customs, immigration, and public health regulations as they apply to international air transport. It drafts international air law conventions, and is concerned with economic aspects of air travel.

Headquarters: 1000 Sherbrooke St. West, Montreal, Quebec, H3A 2R2, Canada.

INTL. DEVELOPMENT ASSOCIATION (IDA)

Established: Sept. 24, 1960. An affiliate of the World Bank, IDA has the same officers and staff as the Bank.

Purpose: To further economic development of its members by providing finance on terms which bear less heavily on balance of payments of members than those of conventional loans.

Headquarters: 1818 H St., N.W., Washington, D.C. 20433.

INTERNATIONAL FINANCE CORPORATION (IFC)

Established: Charter of IFC came into force on July 20, 1956. Although IFC is affiliated with the World Bank, it is a separate legal entity, and its funds are entirely separate from those of the Bank. However, membership in the Corporation is open only to Bank members.

Purpose: To further economic development by encouraging the growth of productive private enterprise in its member countries, particularly in the less developed areas; to invest in productive private enterprises in association with private investors, without government guarantee of repayment where sufficient private capital is not available on reasonable terms; to serve as a clearing house to bring together investment opportunities, private capital (both foreign and domestic), and experienced management.

Headquarters: 1818 H St., N.W., Washington, D.C. 20433.

INTERNATIONAL FUND FOR AGRICULTURAL DEVELOPMENT (IFAD)

Established: June 18, 1976. Began operations in December 1977.

Purpose: To mobilize additional funds for agricultural and rural development in developing countries through projects and programs directly benefiting the poorest rural populations.

Headquarters: 107 Via del Serafico, 00142, Rome, Italy.

INTERNATIONAL LABOR ORGANIZATION (ILO)

Established: April 11, 1919, when constitution was adopted as Part XIII of Treaty of Versailles. Became specialized agency of U.N. in 1946.

Purpose: To contribute to establishment of lasting peace by promoting social justice; to improve labor conditions and living standards through international action; to promote economic and social stability. The U.S. withdrew from the ILO in 1977 and resumed membership in 1980.

Headquarters: 4, Route des Morillons, CH-1211 Geneva 22, Switzerland.

INTERNATIONAL MARITIME ORGANIZATION (IMO)

Established: March 17, 1958.

Purpose: To give advisory and consultative help to promote international cooperation in maritime navigation and to encourage the highest standards of safety and navigation. Its aim is to bring about a uniform system of measuring ship tonnage; systems now vary widely in different parts of the world. Other activities include cooperation with other U.N. agencies on matters affecting the maritime field.

Headquarters: 4 Albert Embankment, London SE 1 7SR England.

INTERNATIONAL MONETARY FUND (IMF)

Established: Dec. 27, 1945, when Articles of Agreement drawn up at Bretton Woods Conference in July 1944 came into force. Fund began operations on March 1, 1947.

Purpose: To promote international monetary cooperation and expansion of international trade; to promote exchange stability; to assist in establishment of multilateral system of payments in respect of currency transactions between members.

Headquarters: 700 19th St., N.W., Washington, D.C. 20431.

INTERNATIONAL TELECOMMUNICATION UNION (ITU)

Established: 1865. Became specialized agency of U.N. in 1947.

Purpose: To extend technical assistance to help members keep up with present day telecommunication needs; to standardize communications equipment and procedures; to lower costs. It also works for orderly sharing of radio frequencies and makes studies and recommendations to benefit its members.

Headquarters: Place des Nations, 1211 Geneva 20, Switzerland.

UNITED NATIONS EDUCATIONAL, SCIENTIFIC, AND CULTURAL ORGANIZATION (UNESCO)

Established: Nov. 4, 1946, when twentieth signatory to constitution deposited instrument of acceptance with government of U.K.

Purpose: To promote collaboration among nations through education, science, and culture in order to further justice, rule of law, and human rights and freedoms without distinction of race, sex, language, or religion.

Headquarters: UNESCO House. 7, Place de Fontenoy, 75007 Paris, France.

UNITED NATIONS INDUSTRIAL DEVELOPMENT ORGANIZATION (UNIDO)

Established: Nov. 17, 1966. Became specialized agency of the U.N. in 1985.

Purpose: To promote and accelerate the industrialization of the developing countries.

Headquarters: UNIDO, Vienna International Centre, P.O. Box 300, A-1400 Vienna, Austria.

UNIVERSAL POSTAL UNION (UPU)

Established: Oct. 9, 1874. Became specialized agency of U.N. in 1947.

Purpose: To facilitate reciprocal exchange of correspondence by uniform procedures by all UPU members; to help governments modernize and speed up mailing procedures.

Headquarters: Weltpoststrasse 4, Berne, Switzerland.

WORLD HEALTH ORGANIZATION (WHO)

Established: April 7, 1948, when 26 members of the U.N. had accepted its constitution, adopted July 22, 1946, by the International Health Conference in New York City.

Purpose: To aid attainment by all people of highest possible level of health.

Headquarters: 20 Avenue Appia, 1211 Geneva 27, Switzerland.

WORLD INTELLECTUAL PROPERTY ORGANIZATION (WIPO)

Established: April 26, 1970, when its Convention came into force. Originated as International Bureau of Paris Union (1883) and Berne Union (1886), later succeeded by United International Bureau for the Protection of Intellectual Property (BIRPI). Became a specialized agency of the U.N. in December 1974.

Purpose: To promote legal protection of intellectual property, including artistic and scientific works, artistic performances, sound recordings, broadcasts, inventions, trademarks, industrial designs, and commercial names.

Headquarters: 34 Chemin des Colombettes, CH-1211 Geneva 20, Switzerland.

WORLD METEOROLOGICAL ORGANIZATION (WMO)

Established: March 23, 1950, succeeding the International Meteorological Organization, a non-governmental organization founded in 1878.

Purpose: To promote international exchange of weather reports and maximum standardization of observations; to help developing countries establish weather services for their own economic needs; to fill gaps in observation stations; to promote meterological investigations affecting jet aircraft, satellites, energy resources, etc.

Headquarters: 41, Avenue Giuseppe-Motta, CH-1211 Geneva 2, Switzerland.

STRUCTURES

The Seven Wonders of the World

(Not all classical writers list the same items as the Seven Wonders, but most of them agree on the following.)

The Pyramids of Egypt. A group of three pyramids, *Khufu, Khafra,* and *Menkaura* at Giza, outside modern Cairo, is often called the first wonder of the world. The largest pyramid, built by Khufu (Cheops), a king of the fourth Dynasty, had an original estimated height of 482 ft (now approximately 450 ft). The base has sides 755 ft long. It contains 2,300,000 blocks; the average weight of each is 2.5 tons. Estimated date of construction is 2800 B.C. Of all the Seven Wonders, the pyramids alone survive.

Hanging Gardens of Babylon. Often listed as the second wonder, these gardens were supposedly built by Nebuchadnezzar about 600 B.C. to please his queen, Amuhia. They are also associated with the mythical Assyrian Queen, Semiramis. Archeologists surmise that the gardens were laid out atop a vaulted building, with provisions for raising water. The terraces were said to rise from 75 to 300 ft.

The Walls of Babylon, also built by Nebuchadnezzar, are sometimes referred to as the second (or the seventh) wonder instead of the Hanging Gardens.

Statue of Zeus (Jupiter) at Olympia. The work of Phidias (5th century B.C.), this colossal figure in gold and ivory was reputedly 40 ft high. All trace of it is lost, except for reproductions on coins.

Temple of Artemis (Diana) at Ephesus. A beautiful structure, begun about 350 B.C. in honor of a non-Hellenic goddess who later became identified with the Greek goddess of the same name. The temple, with Ionic columns 60 ft high, was destroyed by invading Goths in A.D. 262.

Mausoleum at Halicarnassus. This famous monument was erected by Queen Artemisia in memory of her husband, King Mausolus of Caria in Asia Minor, who died in 353 B.C. Some remains of the structure are in the British Museum. This shrine is the source of the modern word "mausoleum."

Colossus at Rhodes. This bronze statue of Helios (Apollo), about 105 ft high, was the work of the sculptor Chares, who reputedly labored for 12 years before completing it in 280 B.C. It was destroyed during an earthquake in 224 B.C.

Pharos of Alexandria. The seventh wonder was the Pharos (lighthouse) of Alexandria, built by Sostratus of Cnidus during the 3rd century B.C. on the island of Pharos off the coast of Egypt. It was destroyed by an earthquake in the 13th century.

Famous Structures

Ancient

The *Great Sphinx of Egypt,* one of the wonders of ancient Egyptian architecture, adjoins the pyramids of Giza and has a length of 240 ft. It was built in the 4th dynasty.

Other Egyptian buildings of note include the *Temples of Karnak* and *Edfu* and the *Tombs at Beni Hassan.*

The *Parthenon of Greece,* built on the Acropolis in Athens, was the chief temple to the goddess Athena. It was believed to have been completed by 438 B.C. The present temple remained intact until the 5th century A.D. Today, though the Parthenon is in ruins, its majestic proportions are still discernible.

Other great structures of ancient Greece were the *Temples at Paestum* (about 540 and 420 B.C.); the *Temple of Poseidon* (about 460 B.C.); the *Temple of Apollo* at Corinth (about 540 B.C.); the *Temple of Apollo* at Bassae (about 450–420 B.C.); the famous *Erechtheum* atop the Acropolis (about 421–405 B.C.); the *Temple of Athena Niké* at Athens (about 426 B.C.); the *Olympieum* at Athens (174 B.C.–A.D. 131); the *Athenian Treasury* at Delphi (about 515 B.C.); the *Propylaea* of the Acropolis at Athens (437–432 B.C.); the *Theater of Dionysus* at Athens (about 350–325 B.C.); the *House of Cleopatra* at Delos (138 B.C.) and the *Theater* at Epidaurus (about 325 B.C.).

The *Colosseum (Flavian Amphitheater) of Rome,* the largest and most famous of the Roman amphitheaters, was opened for use A.D. 80. Elliptical in shape, it consisted of three stories and an upper gallery, rebuilt in stone in its present form in the third century A.D. Its seats rise in tiers, which in turn are buttressed by concrete vaults and stone piers. It could seat between 40,000 and 50,000 spectators. It was principally used for gladiatorial combat.

The *Pantheon* at Rome, begun by Agrippa in 27 B.C. as a temple, was rebuilt in its present circular form by Hadrian (A.D. 110–25). Literally the Pantheon was intended as a temple of "all the gods." It is remarkable for its perfect preservation today, and it has served continuously for 20 centuries as a place of worship.

Famous Roman arches include the *Arch of Constantine* (about A.D. 315) and the *Arch of Titus* (about A.D. 80).

Later European

St. Mark's Cathedral in Venice (1063–67), one of the great examples of Byzantine architecture, was begun in the 9th century. Partly destroyed by fire in 976, it was later rebuilt as a Byzantine edifice.

Other famous Byzantine examples of architecture are *St. Sophia* in Istanbul (A.D. 532–37); *San Vitale* in Ravenna (542); *St. Paul's Outside the Walls,* Rome (5th century); *Assumption Cathedral* in the Kremlin, Moscow (begun in 1475); and *St. Lorenzo Outside the Walls,* Rome, begun in 588.

The *Cathedral Group* at Pisa (1067–1173), one of the most celebrated groups of structures built in Romanesque-style, consists of the cathedral, the cathedral's baptistery, and the *Leaning Tower.* This trio forms a group by itself in the northwest corner of the city. The cathedral and baptistery are built in varicolored marble. The campanile *(Leaning Tower)* is 179 ft. high and leans more than 16 ft out of the perpendicular. There is little reason to believe that the architects intended to have the tower lean.

Other examples of Romanesque architecture include the *Vézelay Abbey* in France (1130); the *Church of Notre-Dame-du-Port* at Clermont-Ferrand in France (1100); the *Church of San Zeno* (begun in 1138) at Verona, and *Durham Cathedral* in England.

The *Alhambra* (1248–1354), located in Granada, Spain, is universally esteemed as one of the greatest masterpieces of Moslem architecture. Designed as a palace and fortress for the Moorish monarchs of Granada, it is surrounded by a heavily fortified wall more than a mile in perimeter. The location of the Alhambra in the Sierra Nevada provides a magnificent setting for this jewel of Moorish Spain.

The *Tower of London* is a group of buildings and towers covering 13 acres along the north bank of the Thames. The central *White Tower,* begun in 1078 during the reign of William the Conqueror, was originally a fortress and royal residence, but was later used as a prison. The *Bloody Tower* is associated with Anne Boleyn and other notables.

Westminster Abbey, in London, was begun in 1045 and completed in 1065. It was rebuilt and enlarged in 1245–50.

Notre-Dame de Paris (begun in 1163), one of the great examples of Gothic architecture, is a twin-towered church with a steeple over the crossing and immense flying buttresses supporting the masonry at the rear of the church.

Other famous Gothic structures are *Chartres Cathedral* (12th century); *Sainte Chapelle,* Paris (1246–48); *Laon Cathedral,* France (1160–1205); *Reims Cathedral* (about 1210–50; rebuilt after its almost complete destruction in World War I); *Rouen Cathedral* (13th–16th centuries); *Amiens Cathedral* (1218–69); *Beauvais Cathedral* (begun 1247); *Salisbury Cathedral* (1220–60); *York Minster* or the *Cathedral of St. Peter* (begun in the 7th century); *Milan Cathedral* (begun 1386); and *Cologne Cathedral* (13th–19th centuries); badly damaged in World War II.

The Duomo (cathedral) in Florence was founded in 1298, completed by Brunelleschi and consecrated in 1436. The oval-shaped dome dominates the entire structure.

The *Vatican* is a group of buildings in Rome comprising the official residence of the Pope. The *Basilica of St. Peter,* the largest church in the Christian world, was begun in 1450. The *Sistine Chapel,* begun in 1473, is noted for the art masterpieces of Michelangelo, Botticelli, and others. The *Basilica of the Savior* (known as *St. John Lateran*) is the first-ranking Catholic Church in the world, for it is the cathedral of the Pope.

Other examples of Renaissance architecture are the *Palazzo Riccardi,* the *Palazzo Pitti* and the *Palazzo Strozzi* in Florence; the *Farnese Palace* in Rome; *Palazzo Grimani* (completed about 1550) in Venice; the *Escorial* (1563–93) near Madrid; the *Town Hall* of Seville (1527–32); the *Louvre,* Paris; the *Château* at Blois, France; *St. Paul's Cathedral,* London (1675–1710; badly damaged in World War II); the *École Militaire,* Paris (1752); the *Pazzi Chapel,* Florence, designed by Brunelleschi (1429); the Palace of *Fontainebleau* and the *Château de Chambord* in France.

The *Palace of Versailles,* containing the famous Hall of Mirrors, was built during the reign of Louis XIV and served as the royal palace until 1793.

Outstanding European buildings of the 18th and 19th centuries are the *Superga* at Turin, the *Hôtel-Dieu* in Lyons, the *Belvedere Palace* at Vienna, the *Royal Palace* of Stockholm, the *Opera House* of Paris (1863–75); the *Bank of England,* the *British Museum,* the *University of London,* and the *Houses of Parliament,* all in London; the *Panthéon,* the *Church of the Madeleine,* the *Bourse,* and the *Palais de Justice* in Paris.

The *Eiffel Tower,* in Paris, was built for the Exposition of 1889 by Alexandre Eiffel. It is 984 ft high.[1]

1. 1,056 ft, including the television tower.

Asiatic and African

The *Taj Mahal* (1632–50), at Agra, India, built by Shah Jahan as a tomb for his wife, is considered by some as the most perfect example of the Mogul style and by others as the most beautiful building in the world. Four slim white minarets flank the building, which is topped by a white dome; the entire structure is of marble.

Other examples of Indian architecture are the temples at Benares and Tanjore.

Among famed Moslem edifices are the *Dome of the Rock* or *Mosque of Omar,* Jerusalem (A.D. 691); the *Citadel* (1166), and the *Tombs of the Mamelukes* (15th century), in Cairo; the *Tomb of Humayun* in Delhi; the *Blue Mosque* (1468) at Tabriz, and the *Tamerlane Mausoleum* at Samarkand.

Angkor Wat, outside the city of Angkor Thom, Cambodia, is one of the most beautiful examples of Cambodian or Khmer architecture. The sanctuary was built during the 12th century.

Great Wall of China (228 B.C.?), designed specifically as a defense against nomadic tribes, has large watch towers which could be called buildings. It was erected by Emperor Ch'in Shih Huang Ti and is 1,400 miles long. Built mainly of earth and stone, it varies in height between 18 and 30 ft.

Typical of Chinese architecture are the pagodas or temple towers. Among some of the better-known pagodas are the *Great Pagoda of the Wild Geese* at Sian (founded in 652); *Nan t'a* (11th century) at Fang Shan; the *Pagoda of Sung Yueh Ssu* (A.D. 523) at Sung Shan, Honan.

Other well-known Chinese buildings are the *Drum Tower* (1273), the *Three Great Halls* in the Purple Forbidden City (1627), *Buddha's Perfume Tower* (19th century), the *Porcelain Pagoda,* and the *Summer Palace,* all at Beijing.

United States

Rockefeller Center, in New York City, extends from 5th Ave. to the Avenue of the Americas between 48th and 52nd Sts. (and halfway to 7th Ave. between 47th and 51st Sts.). It occupies more than 22 acres and has 19 buildings.

The Cathedral of St. John the Divine, at 112th St. and Amsterdam Ave. in New York City, was begun in 1892 and is now in the final stages of completion. When completed, it will be the largest cathedral in the world: 601 ft long, 146 ft wide at the nave, 320 ft wide at the transept. The east end is designed in Romanesque-Byzantine style, and the nave and west end are Gothic.

St. Patrick's Cathedral, at Fifth Ave. and 50th St. in New York City, has a seating capacity of 2,500. The nave was opened in 1877, and the cathedral was dedicated in 1879.

Louisiana Superdome, in New Orleans, is the largest arena in the history of mankind. The main area can accommodate up to 95,000 people. It is the world's largest steel-constructed room. Unobstructed by posts, it covers 13 acres and reaches 27 stories at its peak.

World Trade Center, in New York City, was dedicated in 1973. Its twin towers are 110 stories high (1,350 ft), and the complex contains over 9 million sq ft of office space. A restaurant is on the 107th floor of the North Tower.

World's Highest Dams

Name	River, Country or State	Structural height		Gross reservoir capacity		Year completed
		feet	meters	thousands of acre feet	millions of cubic meters	
Rogun	Vakhsh, Tajikistan	1066	325	9,404	11,600	1985
Nurek	Vakhsh, Tajikistan	984	300	8,512	10,500	1980
Grande Dixence	Dixence, Switzerland	935	285	324	400	1962
Inguri	Inguri, Georgia	892	272	801	1,100	1984
Chicoasén	Grijalva, Mexico	869	265	1,346	1,660	1981
Vaiont	Vaiont, Italy	869	265	137	169	1961
Tehri	Bhagirathi, India	856	261	2,869	3,540	UC
Kinshau	Tons, India	830	253	1,946	2,400	1985
Guavio	Orinoco, Colombia	820	250	811	1,000	1989
Mica	Columbia, Canada	794	242	20,000	24,670	1972
Sayano-Shushensk	Yenisei, Russia	794	242	25,353	31,300	1980
Mihoesti	Aries, Romania	794	242	5	6	1983
Chivor	Batá, Colombia	778	237	661	815	1975
Mauvoisin	Drance de Bagnes, Switzerland	777	237	146	180	1957
Oroville	Feather, California	770	235	3,538	4,299	1968
Chirkey	Sulak, Ukraine	764	233	2,252	2,780	1977
Bhakra	Sutlej, India	741	226	8,002	9,870	1963
El Cajón	Humuya, Honduras	741	226	4,580	5,650	1984
Hoover	Colorado, Arizona/Nevada	726	221	28,500	35,154	1936
Contra	Verzasca, Switzerland	722	220	70	86	1965
Dabaklamm	Dorferbach, Austria	722	220	191	235	UC
Mratinje	Piva, Herzegovina	722	220	713	880	1973
Dworshak	N. Fk. Clearwater, Idaho	717	219	3,453	4,259	1974
Glen Canyon	Colorado, Arizona	710	216	27,000	33,304	1964
Toktogul	Naryn, Kyrgyzstan	705	215	15,800	19,500	1978
Daniel Johnson	Manicouagan, Canada	703	214	115,000	141,852	1968
San Roque	Agno, Philippines	689	210	803	990	UC
Luzzone	Brenno di Luzzone, Switzerland	682	208	71	87	1963
Keban	Firat, Turkey	679	207	25,110	31,000	1974
Dez	Dez, Abi, Iran	666	203	2,707	3,340	1963
Almendra	Tormes, Spain	662	202	2,148	2,649	1970
Kölnbrein	Malta, Austria	656	200	166	205	1977
Kārūn	Karun, Iran	656	200	2,351	2,900	1976
Altinkaya	Kizil Irmak, Turkey	640	195	4,672	5,763	1986
New Bullards Bar	No. Yuba, California	637	194	960	1,184	1968
Lakhwar	Yamuna, India	630	192	470	580	1985
New Melones	Stanislaus, California	625	191	2,400	2,960	1979
Itaipu	Paraná, Brazil/Paraguay	623	190	23,510	29,000	1982
Kurobe 4	Kurobe, Japan	610	186	162	199	1964
Swift	Lewis, Washington	610	186	756	932	1958
Mossyrock	Cowlitz, Washington	607	185	1,300	1,603	1968
Oymopinar	Manavgat, Turkey	607	185	251	310	1983
Atatürk	Firat, Turkey	604	184	39,482	48,700	1990
Shasta	Sacramento, California	602	183	4,550	5,612	1945
Bennett WAC	Peace, Canada	600	183	57,006	70,309	1967
Karakaya	Firat, Turkey	591	180	7,767	9,580	1986
Tignes	Isère, France	591	180	186	230	1952
Amir Kabir (Karad)	Karadj, Iran	591	180	166	205	1962
Tachien	Tachia, Taiwan	591	180	188	232	1974
Dartmouth	Mitta-Mitta, Australia	591	180	3,243	4,000	1978
Özköy	Gediz, Turkey	591	180	762	940	1983
Emosson	Barberine, Switzerland	590	180	184	225	1974
Zillergrūndl	Ziller, Austria	590	180	73	90	1986
Los Leones	Los Leones, Chile	587	179	86	106	1986
New Don Pedro	Tuolumne, California	585	178	2,030	2,504	1971
Alpa-Gera	Cormor, Italy	584	178	53	65	1965

Name	River, Country or State	Structural height		Gross reservoir capacity		Year completed
		feet	meters	thousands of acre feet	millions of cubic meters	
Kopperston Tailings 3	Jones Branch, West Virginia	580	177	—	—	1963
Takase	Takase, Japan	577	176	62	76	1979
Nader Shah	Marun, Iran	574	175	1,313	1,620	1978
Hasan Ugurlu	Yesil Irmak, Turkey	574	175	874	1,078	1980
Pauti-Mazar	Mazar, Ecuador	540	165	405	500	1984
Hungry Horse	S.Fk., Flathead, Montana	564	172	3,470	4,280	1953
Longyangxia	Huanghe, China	564	172	20,025	24,700	1983
Cabora Bassa	Zambezi, Mozambique	561	171	51,075	63,000	1974
Maqarin	Yarmuk, Jordan	561	171	259	320	1987
Amaluza	Paute, Ecuador	558	170	81	100	1982
Idikki	Periyar, India	554	169	1,618	1,996	1974
Charvak	Chirchik, Uzbekistan	552	168	1,620	2,000	1970
Gura Apelor Retezat	Riul Mare, Romania	552	168	182	225	1980
Grand Coulee	Columbia, Washington	550	168	9,390	11,582	1942
Boruca	Terraba, Costa Rica	548	167	12,128	14,960	UC
Vidraru	Arges, Romania	545	166	380	465	1965
Kremasta (King Paul)	Achelöus, Greece	541	165	3,850	4,750	1965

NOTE: UC = under construction. *Source:* Department of the Interior, Bureau of Reclamation and *International Water Power and Dam Construction.*

World's Largest Dams

Dam	Location	Volume (thousands)		Year completed
		Cubic meters	Cubic yards	
New Cornelia Tailings	Arizona	209,500	274,015	1973
Poti (Chapetón)	Argentina	200,000	261,590	UC
Tarbela	Pakistan	121,720	159,203	1976
Fort Peck	Montana	96,049	125,628	1940
Atatürk	Turkey	84,500	110,522	1990
Yacyretá-Apipe	Paraguay/Argentina	81,000	105,944	UC
Guri (Raul Leoni)	Venezuela	78,000	102,014	1986
Rogun	Tajikistan	75,500	98,750	1985
Oahe	South Dakota	70,339	92,000	1963
Mangla	Pakistan	65,651	85,872	1967
Gardiner	Canada	65,440	85,592	1968
Afsluitdijk	Netherlands	63,400	82,927	1932
Oroville	California	59,639	78,008	1968
San Luis	California	59,405	77,700	1967
Nurek	Tajikistan	58,000	75,861	1980
Garrison	North Dakota	50,843	66,500	1956
Cochiti	New Mexico	48,052	62,850	1975
Tabka (Thawra)	Syria	46,000	60,168	1976
Bennett W.A.C.	Canada	43,733	57,201	1967
Tucuruii	Brazil	43,000	56,242	1984
Boruca	Costa Rica	43,000	56,242	UC
High Aswan (Sadd-el-Aali)	Egypt	43,000	56,242	1970
San Roque	Philippines	43,000	56,242	UC
Kiev	Russia	42,841	56,034	1964
Dantiwada Left Embankment	India	41,040	53,680	1965
Saratov	Russia	40,400	52,843	1967
Mission Tailings 2	Arizona	40,088	52,435	1973
Fort Randall	South Dakota	38,227	50,000	1953
Kanev	Ukraine.	37,860	49,520	1976
Mosul	Iraq	36,000	47,086	1982
Kakhovka	Ukraine	35,640	46,617	1955
Itumbiara	Brazil	35,600	46,563	1980
Lauwerszee	Netherlands	35,575	46,532	1969
Beas	India	35,418	46,325	1974
Oosterschelde	Netherlands	35,000	45,778	1986

NOTE: UC = under construction. *Source:* Department of the Interior, Bureau of Reclamation and *International Water Power and Dam Construction.*

World's Largest Hydroelectric Plants

Name of Dam	Location	Rated capacity (MW) Present	Ultimate	Year of initial operation
Itaipu	Brazil/Paraguay	1,400	12,600	1984
Grand Coulee	Washington	6,480	10,080	1942
Guri (Raul Leoni)	Venezuela	2,800	10,060	1968
Tucuruíi	Brazil	—	7,500	1985
Sayano-Shushensk	Former U.S.S.R.	—	6,400	1980
Krasnoyarsk	Russia	6,096	6,096	1968
Corpus-Posadas	Argentina/Paraguay	—	6,000	UC
LaGrande 2	Canada	5,328	5,328	1982
Churchill Falls	Canada	5,225	5,225	1971
Bratsk	Siberia	4,100	4,600	1964
Ust'—Ilimsk	Russia	3,675	4,500	1974
Cabora Bassa	Mozambique	2,075	4,150	1974
Yacyretá-Apipe	Argentina/Paraguay	—	4,050	UC
Rogun	Tajikistan	—	3,600	1985
Paulo Afonso	Brazil	3,409	3,409	1954
Salto Santiago	Brazil	1,332	3,333	1980
Pati (Chapetón)	Argentina	—	3,300	UC
Brumley Gap	Virginia	3,200	3,200	1973
Ilha Solteira	Brazil	3,200	3,200	1973
Inga I	Zaire	360	2,820	1974
Gezhouba	China	965	2,715	1981
John Day	Oregon/Washington	2,160	2,700	1969
Nurek	Tajikistan	900	2,700	1976
Revelstoke	Canada	900	2,700	1984
Sáo Simao	Brazil	2,680	2,680	1979
LaGrande 4	Canada	2,637	2,637	1984
Mica	Canada	1,736	2,610	1976
Volgograd—22nd Congress	Russia	2,560	2,560	1958
Fos do Areia	Brazil	2,511	2,511	1983
Itaparica	Brazil	—	2,500	1985
Bennett W.A.C.	Canada	2,116	2,416	1969
Chicoasén	Mexico	—	2,400	1980
Atatürk	Turkey	—	2,400	1990
LaGrande 3	Canada	2,310	2,310	1982
Volga—V.I. Lenin	Russia	2,300	2,300	1955
Iron Gates I	Romania/Yugoslavia	2,300	2,300	1970
Iron Gates II	Romania/Yugoslavia	270	2,160	1983
Bath County	Virginia	—	2,100	1985
High Aswan (Saad-el-Aali)	Egypt	2,100	2,100	1967
Tarbela	Pakistan	1,400	2,100	1977
Piedra del Aquila	Argentina	—	2,100	UC
Itumbiara	Brazil	2,080	2,080	1980
Chief Joseph	Washington	2,069	2,069	1956
McNary	Oregon	980	2,030	1954
Green River	North Carolina	—	2,000	1980
Tehri	India	—	2,000	UC
Cornwall	New York	—	2,000	1978
Ludington	Michigan	1,979	1,979	1973
Robert Moses—Niagara	New York	1,950	1,950	1961
Salto Grande	Argentina/Uruguay	—	1,890	1979

Note: MW = Megawatts, UC = under construction. *Source:* Department of the Interior, Bureau of Reclamation and *International Water Power and Dam Construction.*

Notable U.S. Skyscrapers

City	Building	Stories	Height ft	m	City	Building	Stories	Height ft	m
Chicago	Sears Tower	110	1,454	443	New York	Chrysler	77	1,046	319
New York	World Trade Center	110	1,377	419	Los Angeles	First Interstate World Center	73	1,017	310
New York	Empire State	102	1,250	381	Atlanta	Nations Plaza	55	1,025	312
Chicago	AMOCO	80	1,136	346	Houston	Texas	75	1,002	305
Chicago	John Hancock Center	100	1,127	343	Houston	Allied Bank	71	985	300

Chicago	311 South Wacker Drive	65	969	295
New York	American International	66	952	290
Cleveland	Society Tower	57	948	289
Philadelphia	One Liberty Place	62	945	288
Seattle	Columbia Seafirst Center	76	943	287
New York	Citicorp Center	59	915	279
Atlanta	One Peachtree Center	60	902	275
New York	40 Wall Tower	71	900	274
Chicago	Two Prudential Center	64	900	274
Seattle	Two Union Square	56	886	270
Philadelphia	Mellon Bank Center	56	880	268
Charlotte	NationsBank Corporate Center	60	875	267
Chicago	Water Tower Place	74	859	262
Los Angeles	First Interstate Bank	62	858	261
San Francisco	Transamerica Pyramid	61	853	260
Chicago	First National Bank	60	851	259
New York	RCA	70	850	259
Seattle	Washington Mutual Tower	56	849	259
Philadelphia	Two Liberty Place	52	845	257
Pittsburgh	USX Tower	64	841	256
Atlanta	One Atlantic Center	50	825	251
New York	Chase Manhattan	60	813	248
New York	Pan Am	59	808	246
New York	Woolworth	55	792	241
Boston	John Hancock Tower	60	790	241
San Francisco	Bank of America	52	779	237
Minneapolis	IDS Tower	57	775	236
New York	One Liberty Plaza	54	775	236
Chicago	Three First National Plaza	57	775	236
New York	One Penn Plaza	57	774	236
Minneapolis	Norwest Center	57	772	235
Minneapolis	First Bank Place	56	770	235
Miami	Southeast Finan. Ctr.	55	765	233
Atlanta	Westin Peachtree Plaza	73	754	230
New York	Exxon	54	750	229
Boston	Prudential Tower	52	750	229
Dallas	First Interst. Bank Tower	60	744	227
Los Angeles	Security Pacific Plaza	55	743	226
Los Angeles	Wells Fargo Center	54	743	227
Atlanta	Georgia-Pacific Center	52	741	226
Atlanta	191 Peachtree Tower	50	740	225
New York	One Astor Plaza	54	730	222
Chicago	Olympia Centre	63	727	222
Houston	Gulf Tower	52	725	221
New York	Marine Midland	52	724	221
Los Angeles	Mitsui (North Tower) Fudosan Tower	52	716	218
Pittsburgh	One Mellon Bank Center	54	715	218
Houston	One Shell Plaza	50	714	218
Detroit	Detroit Westin Hotel	73	712	220
Indianapolis	Banc One Center Tower	51	711	216
Dallas	Renaissance Tower	56	710	216
Cleveland	Terminal Tower	52	708	216
New York	Union Carbide	52	707	215
New York	General Motors	50	705	215
Seattle	AT&T Gateway Tower	62	702	214
New York	Metropolitan Life	50	700	213
Philadelphia	Blue Cross Tower	50	700	213
Chicago	Leo Burnett Building	46	700	213

NOTE: Height does not include TV towers and antennas. *Source: Information Please* questionnaires.

Notable Tunnels

Name	Location	Length mi.	Length km	Year completed
Railroad, excluding subways				
Seikan	Tsugara Strait, Japan	33.1	53.3	1983
Simplon (I and II)	Alps, Switzerland-Italy	12.3	19.8	1906 & 1922
Apennine	Bologna-Florence, Italy	11.5	18.5	1934
St. Gotthard	Swiss Alps	9.3	14.9	1881
Lötschberg	Swiss Alps	9.1	14.6	1911
Mont Cénis	French Alps	8.5[1]	13.7	1871
New Cascade	Cascade Mountains, Washington	7.8	12.6	1929
Vosges	Vosges, France	7.0	11.3	1940
Arlberg	Austrian Alps	6.3	10.1	1884
Moffat	Rocky Mountains, Colorado	6.2	9.9	1928
Shimuzu	Shimuzu, Japan	6.1	9.8	1931
Rimutaka	Wairarapa, New Zealand	5.5	8.9	1955
Vehicular				
St. Gotthard	Alps, Switzerland	10.2	16.4	1980
Mt. Blanc	Alps, France-Italy	7.5	12.1	1965
Mt. Ena	Japan Alps, Japan	5.3	8.5	1976[2]
Great St. Bernard	Alps, Switzerland-Italy	3.4	5.5	1964
Mount Royal	Montreal, Canada	3.2	5.1	1918
Lincoln	Hudson River, New York-New Jersey	2.5	4.0	1937
Queensway Road	Mersey River, Liverpool, England	2.2	3.5	1934
Brooklyn-Battery	East River, New York City	2.1	3.4	1950
Holland	Hudson River, New York-New Jersey	1.7	2.7	1927
Fort McHenry	Baltimore, Maryland	1.7	2.7	1985
Hampton Roads	Norfolk, Virginia	1.4	2.3	1957
Queens-Midtown	East River, New York City	1.3	2.1	1940
Liberty Tubes	Pittsburgh, Pennsylvania	1.2	1.9	1923
Baltimore Harbor	Baltimore, Maryland	1.2	1.9	1957
Allegheny Tunnels	Pennsylvania Turnpike	1.2	1.9	1940[3]

1. Lengthened to its present 8.5 miles in 1881. 2. Parallel tunnel begun in 1976. 3. Parallel tunnel built in 1965, twin tunnel in 1966. NOTE: UC = under construction. *Source:* American Society of Civil Engineers and International Bridge, Tunnel & Turnpike Association.

Notable Modern Bridges

Name	Location	Length of main span ft	Length of main span m	Year completed
Suspension				
Humber	Hull, Britain	4,626	1,410	1981
Verrazano-Narrows	Lower New York Bay	4,260	1,298	1964
Golden Gate	San Francisco Bay	4,200	1,280	1937
Mackinac Straits	Michigan	3,800	1,158	1957
Bosporus	Istanbul	3,524	1,074	1973
George Washington	Hudson River at New York City	3,500	1,067	1931
Ponte 25 de Abril	Tagus River at Lisbon	3,323	1,013	1966
Second Bosporus Bridge	Turkey	3,322	1,012	1988
Forth Road	Queensferry, Scotland	3,300	1,006	1964
Severn	Severn River at Beachley, England	3,240	988	1966
Tacoma Narrows	Puget Sound at Tacoma, Wash.	2,800	853	1950
Kanmon Strait	Kyushu-Honshu, Japan	2,336	712	1973
Angostura	Orinoco River at Ciudad Bolivar, Venezuela	2,336	712	1967
Transbay (twin spans)	San Francisco Bay	2,310	704	1936
Bronx-Whitestone	East River, New York City	2,300	701	1939
Pierre Laporte	St. Lawrence River at Quebec, Canada	2,190	668	1970
Delaware Memorial (twin bridges)	Delaware River near Wilmington, Del.	2,150	655	1951, 1968
Seaway Skyway	St. Lawrence River at Ogdensburg, N.Y.	2,150	655	1960
Gas Pipe Line	Atchafalaya River, Louisiana	2,000	610	1951
Walt Whitman	Delaware River at Philadelphia	2,000	610	1957
Tancarville	Seine River at Tancarville, France	1,995	608	1959
Lillebaelt	Lillebaelt Strait, Denmark	1,969	600	1970
Ambassador International	Detroit River at Detroit	1,850	564	1929
Throgs Neck	East River, New York City	1,800	549	1961
Benjamin Franklin	Delaware River at Philadelphia	1,750	533	1926
Skjomen	Narvik, Norway	1,722	525	1972
Kvalsund	Hammerfest, Norway	1,722	525	1977
Kleve-Emmerich	Rhine River at Emmerich, Germany	1,640	500	1965
Bear Mountain	Hudson River at Peekskill, N.Y.	1,632	497	1924
Wm. Preston Lane, Jr., Memorial (twin bridges)	Near Annapolis, Md.	1,600	488	1952, 1973
Williamsburg	East River, New York City	1,600	488	1903
Newport	Narragansett Bay at Newport, R.I.	1,600	488	1969
Brooklyn	East River, New York City	1,595	486	1883
Cantilever				
Quebec Railway	St. Lawrence River at Quebec, Canada	1,800	549	1917
Forth Railway (twin spans)	Queensferry, Scotland	1,710	521	1890
Minato Ohashi	Osaka, Japan	1,673	510	1974
Commodore John Barry	Chester, Pa.	1,644	501	1974
Greater New Orleans (twin spans)	Mississippi River, Louisiana	1,576	480	1958
Howrah	Hooghly River at Calcutta	1,500	457	1943
Transbay Bridge	San Francisco Bay	1,400	427	1936
Baton Rouge	Mississippi River, Louisiana	1,235	376	1968
Tappan Zee	Hudson River at Tarrytown, N.Y.	1,212	369	1955
Longview	Columbia River at Longview, Wash.	1,200	366	1930
Patapsco River	Baltimore Outer Harbor Crossing	1,200	366	1976
Queensboro	East River, New York City	1,182	360	1909
Steel Arch				
New River Gorge	Fayetteville, W. Va.	1,700	518	1977
Bayonne	Kill Van Kull at Bayonne, N.J.	1,675	510	1931
Sydney Harbor	Sydney, Australia	1,670	509	1932
Fremont	Portland, Ore.	1,255	383	1973
Zdákov	Vltava River, Czechoslovakia	1,244	380	1967
Port Mann	Fraser River at Vancouver, British Columbia	1,200	366	1964
Thatcher Ferry	Panama Canal, Panama	1,128	344	1962
Laviolette	St. Lawrence River, Trois Rivieres, Quebec	1,100	335	1967
Runcorn-Widnes	Mersey River, England	1,082	330	1961
Birchenough	Sabi River at Fort Victoria, Rhodesia	1,080	329	1935

Name	Location	Length of main span ft	m	Year completed
Cable-Stayed				
Ikuchi	Honshu-Shikoku, Japan	1,608	490	1991
Alex Fraser	Vancouver, B.C., Canada	1,525	465	1986
Yokohama-ko-odan	Kanagawa, Japan	1,509	460	1989
Second Hooghly	Calcutta, India	1,500	457	UC
Chao Phya	Thailand	1,476	450	1986
Barrios de Luna	Spain	1,444	440	1983
Hitshuishi-jima and Iwakuro-jima	Honshu-Shikoku, Japan	1,378	420	1988
Meiko Nishi	Aichi, Japan	1,329	405	1985
St. Nazaire	Loire River, St. Nazaire, France	1,325	404	1975
Rande	Rande, Spain	1,312	400	1977
Dame Point	Jacksonville, Florida	1,300	396	1988
Houston Ship Channel	Baytown, Texas	1,250	381	1991
Hale Boggs Memorial	Luling, Louisiana	1,222	373	1983
Dusseldorf Flehe	Germany	1,207	368	1979
Tjörn	Sweden	1,200	366	1981
Sunshine Skyway	Tampa, Florida	1,200	366	1987
Continuous Truss				
Mark Clark Expressway I-526	Cooper River, at Charleston, S.C.	1,600	487	1992
Astoria	Columbia River at Astoria, Oregon	1,232	376	1966
Oshima	Oshima Island, Japan	1,066	325	1976
Croton Reservoir	Croton, N.Y.	1,052	321	1970
Tenmon	Kumamoto, Japan	984	300	1966
Kuronoseto	Nagashima-Kyushu, Japan	984	300	1974
Ravenswood	Ohio River, Ravenswood, W. Va.	902	275	1981
Dubuque	Mississippi River at Dubuque, Iowa	845	258	1943
Braga Memorial	Taunton River at Somerset, Mass.	840	256	1966
Graf Spee	Germany	839	256	1936
Concrete Arch				
KRK	Zagreb, Croatia	1,280	390	1979
Gladesville	Parramatta River at Sydney, Australia	1,000	305	1964
Amizade	Paraná River at Foz do Iguassu, Brazil	951	290	1964
Arrábida	Porto, Portugal	886	270	1963
Sandö	Angerman River at Kramfors, Sweden	866	264	1943
Shibenik	Krka River, Yugoslavia	808	246	1966
Fiumarella	Catanzaro, Italy	758	231	1961
Zaporozhe	Old Dnepr River, Ukraine	748	228	1952
Novi Sad	Danube River, Croatia	692	211	1961
Segmental Congrete Box Girder				
Jesse H. Jones Memorial	Houston Ship Channel, Texas	750	228	1982

NOTE: UC = under construction. *Source: Encyclopaedia Britannica,* American Society of Civil Engineers, and Bridge Division, Federal Highway Administration.

Famous Ship Canals

Name	Location	Length (miles)[1]	Width (feet)	Depth (feet)	Locks	Year opened
Albert	Belgium	80.0	53.0	16.5	6	1939
Amsterdam-Rhine	Netherlands	45.0	164.0	41.0	3	1952
Beaumont-Port Arthur	United States	40.0	200.0	34.0	—	1916
Chesapeake and Delaware	United States	19.0	250.0	27.0	—	1927
Houston	United States	50.0	[2]	40.0	—	1914
Kiel (Nord-Ostsee Kanal)	Germany	61.3	144.0	36.0	4	1895
Panama	Canal Zone	50.7	110.0	41.0	12	1914
St. Lawrence Seaway	U.S. and Canada	2,400.0[3]	([4])	—	—	1959
Montreal to Prescott	U.S. and Canada	11.5	80.0	30.0	7	1959
Welland	Canada	27.5	80.0	27.0	8	1931
Sault Ste. Marie	Canada	1.2	60.0	16.8	1	1895
Sault Ste. Marie	United States	1.6	80.0	25.0	4	1915
Suez	Egypt	100.6[5]	197.0	36.0	—	1869

1. Statute miles. 2. 300–400 feet. 3. From Montreal to Duluth. 4. 442–550 feet; there are 11.5 miles of locks, 80 feet wide and 30 feet deep. 5. From Port Said lighthouse to entrance channel in Suez roads. *Source:* American Society of Civil Engineers.

MEDIA

Leading Magazines: United States and Canada

Magazine	Circulation[1]
American Health—Fitness of Body and Mind	895,668
Beckett Baseball Card Monthly	890,797
Better Homes and Gardens	8,002,585
Bon Appetit	1,231,327
Business Week (North America)	886,229
Car and Driver	1,019,630
Chatelaine	911,477
Conde Nast Traveler	1,020,592
Consumers Digest	1,003,558
Cooking Light	1,025,511
Cosmopolitan	2,705,224
Country America	940,064
Country Home	1,095,721
Country Living	1,839,363
Discover	1,014,152
Ebony	1,791,536
Elle	901,619
Entertainment Weekly	866,431
Essence	906,034
Family Circle	5,283,660
The Family Handyman	1,047,679
Field & Stream	2,007,234
Food & Wine	777,453
Glamour	2,083,849
Globe	1,102,335
Golf Digest	1,421,883
Golf Magazine	1,183,684
Good Housekeeping	5,139,355
Gourmet	915,171
Harper's Bazaar	772,715
Health	1,013,428
Home	1,013,182
Home Mechanix	1,013,963
Hot Rod	856,774
House Beautiful	1,002,458
Jet	909,014
Kiplinger's Personal Finance Magazine	1,116,539
Ladies Home Journal	5,041,143
Life	1,777,087
Mademoiselle	1,219,159
McCall's	4,704,772
Midwest Living	752,112
Money	2,146,410
Motor Trend	943,441
National Enquirer	3,401,263
National Geographic Magazine	9,708,254
Nation's Business	861,581
New Woman	1,313,181
Newsweek	3,240,131
Organic Gardening	786,373
Outdoor Life	1,502,542
Parents Magazine	1,749,322
PC Magazine	1,004,235
PC/Computing	803,306
Penthouse	1,254,207
People Weekly	3,506,816
Playboy	3,402,630
Popular Mechanics	1,642,081
Popular Science	1,812,019
Prevention	3,234,901
Reader's Digest	16,258,476
Reader's Digest (Canadian English Edition)	1,266,518
Redbook	3,395,029
Road & Track	758,255
Rolling Stone	1,211,586
Self	1,408,975
Seventeen	1,915,426
Smithsonian	2,211,552
Soap Opera Digest	1,396,346
Southern Living	2,374,530
Sport	816,990
Sports Illustrated	3,432,044
Star	2,931,305
Sunset, The Magazine of Western Living	1,452,086
'Teen	1,188,257
Tennis	758,991
Time	4,203,991
Travel & Leisure	1,092,414
True Story	785,183
True Story Plus	1,225,347
TV Guide	14,498,341
TV Guide (Canada)	810,156
U.S. News & World Report	2,307,569
US	1,102,783
Vanity Fair	1,151,887
Victoria	886,661
Vogue	1,284,193
Weight Watchers Magazine	1,006,397
Woman's Day	4,810,445
The Workbasket	890,006
Workbench	831,751
Working Woman	866,816
YM	1,340,415

1. Average total paid circulation for the six-month period ending December 31, 1992. The table lists magazines with combined newsstand and subscription circulation of over 750,000. *Source:* Audit Bureau of Circulations. Publishers' Statements for six-month period ending December 31, 1992.

Major U.S. Daily Newspapers[1]

City and Newspaper	Net paid circulation			
	Morning[1, 2]	All-Day[2]	Evening[2]	Sunday
Akron, Ohio: *Beacon Journal*	160,577		—	229,377
Albany, N.Y.: *Times-Union* (M & S)	103,072		—	164,864
Albuquerque, N.M.: *Journal* (M & S); *Tribune* (E)	119,362[4]		36,248[4]	168,410[4]
Allentown, Pa.: *Call* (M & S)	137,726		—	188,276
Amarillo, Tex.: *News* (M); *Globe-Times* (E); *News-Globe* (S)	44,367		21,725[3]	78,883
Anchorage, Alaska: *News*	76,064		—	98,831

City and Newspaper	Net paid circulation			
	Morning[1, 2]	All-Day[2]	Evening[2]	Sunday
Atlanta: *Constitution* (M); *Journal* (E); *Journal and Constitution* (S)	314,506[3]		149,996[3]	719,411
Atlantic City, N.J.: *Press*	77,384		—	98,820
Augusta, Ga.: *Chronicle* (M); *Herald* (E); *Chronicle—Herald* (S)	72,593[3]		10,217[3]	102,496
Austin, Tex.: *American-Statesman*	176,194		—	233,924
Bakersfield, Calif.: *Californian*	75,923			91,233
Baltimore: *Sun*	234,864[3]		108,344[3]	488,183
Bangor, Me.: *News*	73,946[3]		—	92,041[5]
Baton Rouge, La.: *Advocate* (M & S)	100,861[3]		—	140,138
Bergen County (Hackensack), N.J.; *Record*	160,084[4]		—	225,196[4]
Beaumont, Tex.: *Enterprise*	68,258		—	85,011
Binghamton, N.Y.: *Press & Sun-Bulletin* (M & S)	70,907		—	93,365
Birmingham, Ala.: *Post-Herald* (M); *News* (E & S)	64,960[3]		169,625[3]	217,278
Boston: *Globe*	504,869[3]		—	811,409
Herald	337,543[3]		—	233,507
Christian Science Monitor	107,871[3]		—	—
Bridgeport, Conn: *Post*	70,690		—	91,025
Buffalo, N.Y.: *News*	—	312,614[3]	—	388,891
Camden, N.J.: *Courier-Post*	89,327[4]		—	99,923[4]
Canton, Ohio: *Repository*	—		62,002[4]	80,817[4]
Cedar Rapids, Iowa: *Gazette Post*	70,790		—	84,441
Charleston, S.C.: *Post & Courier* (M); *Post–Courier* (S)	112,827		—	128,504
Charleston, W. Va.: *Gazette* (M); *Mail* (E); *Gazette-Mail* (S)	55,780		49,656	108,920
Charlotte, N.C.: *Observer*	233,560		—	299,842
Chattanooga, Tenn.: *Times* (M); *News-Free Press* (E & S)	41,547		43,197	113,763
Chicago: *Tribune*	691,941[3]		—	1,117,816
Sun-Times	553,355[3]		—	549,038
Herald	123,091		—	119,686
Cincinnati: *Enquirer* (M & S); *Post* (E)	203,259		97,892	358,519
Cleveland: *Plain Dealer*	408,829		—	548,789
Colorado Springs, Colo.: *Gazette Telegraph*	101,955		—	120,047
Columbia, S.C.: *State*	138,273		—	169,915
Columbus, Ohio: *Dispatch*	266,968		—	404,890
Corpus Christi, Tex.: *Caller* (M): *Caller-Times* (S)	68,988[4]		—	97,901[4]
Dallas: *News*	504,313		—	834,035
Wall Street Journal (Southwest edition)	176,562[3]		—	—
Davenport, Iowa: *Quad City Times*	54,758[3]		—	86,370
Dayton, Ohio: *News*	174,585		—	230,957
Daytona Beach, Fla.: *News-Journal*	104,013		—	121,304
Denver: *Post*	283,412		—	438,205
Rocky Mountain News	363,272		—	444,333
Des Moines, Iowa: *Register*	189,885		—	323,748
Detroit: *Free Press* (M); *News* (E); *News & Free Press* (S)	574,817[3]		389,073[3]	1,179,197
Duluth, Minn.: *News-Tribune*	57,202		—	82,376
Erie, Pa.: *News* (M); *Times* (E); *Times-News* (S)	32,108[3]		40,229[3]	107,126
El Paso, Tex.: *Times* (M & S); *Herald-Post* (E)	67,766[3,4]		26,168[3,4]	101,854[3,4]
Eugene, Ore.: *Register-Guard*	75,423[3]		—	80,567
Evansville, Ind.: *Courier* (M); *Press* (E); *Courier & Press* (S)	64,455		31,319	120,263
Fayetteville, N.C.: *Observer-Times* (S)	72,510[4]		—	82,037[4]
Flint, Mich.: *Journal*	—		103,622	123,694
Fort Lauderdale, Fla.: *Sun-Sentinel* (M); *News* (E); *News & Sun-Sentinel* (S)	278,086		—	376,764
Fort Myers, Fla.: *News-Press*	105,434		—	130,901
Fort Wayne, Ind.: *Journal-Gazette* (M & S); *News-Sentinel* (E)	63,027		54,910	138,179
Fort Worth: *Star-Telegram*	—	254,140	—	356,131
Fresno, Calif.: *Bee*	150,674[4]		—	185,436[4]
Gary, Ind.: *Post-Tribune*	73,347		—	86,100
Grand Rapids, Mich.: *Press*	—		149,821	196,048
Green Bay, Wis.: *Press-Gazette*	—		60,369	85,983
Greensboro, N.C.: *News & Record*	109,935		—	130,551
Greensburg, Pa.: *Tribune-Review*	76,012		—	166,237
Greenville, S.C.: *News* (M); *Piedmont* (E); *News & Piedmont* (S)	95,726[3]		25,073[3]	142,766
Harrisburg, Pa.: *Patriot* (M); *News* (E); *Patriot-News* (S)	63,061[3]		44,223[3]	179,552
Hartford, Conn.: *Courant*	234,686		—	327,339

City and newspaper	Net paid circulation: Morning[1, 2]	All-Day[2]	Evening[2]	Sunday
Honolulu: *Advertiser* (M); *Star-Bulletin* (E); *Star-Bulletin & Advertiser* (S)	108,021		87,531	198,934
Houston: *Chronicle*	—	423,256	—	608,429
Post	292,764		—	337,656
Huntsville, Ala.: *News* (M); *Times* (E & S)	17,551[3]		58,758[3]	83,683
Indianapolis: *Star* (M & S); *News* (E)	230,465[4]		95,598[4]	411,219[4]
Jackson, Miss.: *Clarion-Ledger*	110,322		—	129,716
Jacksonville, Fla.: *Times-Union*	184,554		—	258,101
Kalamazoo, Mich.: *Gazette*	—		65,476[3]	82,139
Kansas City, Mo.: *Star* (M & S)	290,568[3]		—	435,689
Knoxville, Tenn.: *News-Sentinel* (M & S)	127,196		—	185,702
Lake Co., Ind.: *Times* (M & S)	68,873		—	75,513
Lakeland, Fla.: *Ledger*	91,465[4]		—	110,282[4]
Lancaster, Pa.: *Intelligencer-Journal* (M); *New Era* (E); *News* (S)	44,961[4]		52,952[4]	106,636[4]
Lansing, Mich.: *State-Journal*	71,576		—	96,074
Las Vegas, Nev.: *Review-Journal* (M); *Review–Journal–Sun* (E & S)	139,459[3]		39,615[3]	207,503
Levittown–Bristol–Langhorne, Pa.: *Bucks County Courier-Times* (M & S)	70,253[3]		—	76,741
Lexington, Ky.: *Herald-Leader*	127,373		—	169,106
Lincoln, Neb.: *Star* (M); *Journal* (E); *Journal & Star* (S)	42,015[3]		40,315[3]	86,157
Little Rock, Ark.: *Democrat–Gazette*	180,189		—	301,359
Long Beach, Calif.: *Press-Telegram*	125,893[3]		—	142,073
Long Island (Melville), N.Y.: *Newsday*	—	762,043[3]	—	851,685
Los Angeles: *Times*	1,138,353[3]		—	1,521,197
News	212,255[3]		—	232,665
Louisville, Ky.: *Courier-Journal*	240,636		—	331,692
Lubbock, Tex.: *Avalanche-Journal*	66,319		—	77,121
Macon, Ga.: *Telegraph*	75,442		—	105,011
Madison, Wis.: *State Journal* (M & S); *Capital Times* (E)	85,244[3]		23,512[3]	164,763
Melbourne, Fla.: *Today*	89,141		—	117,761
Memphis, Tenn.: *Commercial Appeal*	185,215[6]		—	287,620
Miami, Fla.: *Herald*	414,216		—	542,450
Middletown, N.Y.: *Times Herald-Record* (M); *Record* (S)	86,017[4]		—	101,552[4]
Milwaukee: *Sentinel* (M); *Journal* (E & S)	172,594[3]		239,768[3]	490,134
Minneapolis: *Star–Tribune*	413,603		—	695,710
Mobile, Ala.: *Register* (M); *Press* (E); *Press-Register* (S)	65,148[3, 4]		40,243[3, 4]	117,012[4]
Modesto, Calif.: *Bee*	83,680[4]		—	92,310[4]
Montgomery, Ala. *Advertiser* (M); *Journal* (E); *Journal & Advertiser* (S)	53,093		11,499	80,581
Naperville, Ill.: *Wall Street Journal* (Midwest edition)	509,549[3]		—	—
Nashville, Tenn.: *Tennessean* (M & S); *Banner* (E)	144,623[3]		59,182[3]	278,577
New Haven, Conn.: *Register*	100,443		—	128,328
New Orleans: *Times-Picayune*	—	266,977[3, 4]	—	325,009[4]
New York: *News*	769,801[3]		—	977,599
Times	1,230,461[3]		—	1,812,458
Post	427,319		—	359,388[7]
Wall Street Journal (Eastern edition)	778,584[3]		—	—
Women's Wear Daily	n.a.			
Newark, N.J.: *Star-Ledger*	483,012[3, 4]		—	728,579[4]
Newport News–Hampton, Va.: *Press*	102,946[4]		—	125,130[4]
Norfolk-Portsmouth-Virginia Beach-Chesapeake, Va.: *Virginian-Pilot* (M); *Ledger-Star* (E); *Virginian-Pilot/Ledger-Star* (S)	156,679[3, 4]		52,950[3, 4]	235,997[4]
Oakland, Calif.: *Tribune* (M & S)	n.a.			n.a.
Oklahoma City: *Oklahoman* (M & S)	224,451[3]		—	323,107
Omaha, Neb.: *World-Herald*	133,738[3]		95,645[3]	290,532
Orange County (Santa Ana), Calif.: *Register*	—	351,498	—	411,965
Orlando, Fla.: *Sentinel*	—	279,772	—	397,643
Palo Alto, Calif.: *Wall Street Journal* (Western edition)	388,272[3]		—	—
Peninsula Times Tribune			n.a.	n.a.
Pensacola, Fla.: *News-Journal*	63,095[3, 4]		—	86,141[4]
Peoria, Ill.: *Journal Star*	—	83,477[3]	—	110,618
Philadelphia: *Inquirer*	502,740[3]		—	965,350
Daily News	197,481[3]		—	111,892[7]
Phoenix, Ariz.: *Republic* (M & S); *Gazette* (E)	397,118[4]		86,216[4]	612,041[4]
Pittsburgh: *Post-Gazette, Sun-Telegraph* (M); *Press* (E & S)	n.a.		n.a.	n.a.
Pontiac, Mich.: *Oakland Press*	73,060		—	81,656

City and newspaper	Net paid circulation: Morning[1, 2]	All-Day[2]	Evening[2]	Sunday
Portland, Me.: *Press-Herald*	72,913		—	—
Telegram	—		—	137,555
Portland, Or.: *Oregonian*	—	345,985[3]	—	444,853
Providence, R.I.: *Journal Bulletin;* Journal (S)	—	190,010[3]	—	268,805
Quincy, Mass.: *Patriot-Ledger*	—		87,033[3, 4]	100,583[4, 7]
Raleigh, N.C.: *News & Observer* (M & S)	150,574[4]		—	195,413[4]
Reading, Pa.: *Times* (M); *Eagle* (E & S)	48,520[3]		25,983[3]	111,571
Reno, Nev.: *Gazette Journal*	66,460		—	83,963
Richmond, Va.: *Times-Dispatch* (M & S)	217,790		—	254,384
Riverside, Calif.: *Press-Enterprise* (M & S)	158,673		—	167,206
Roanoke, Va.: *Times & World-News*	116,421		—	127,154
Rochester, N.Y.: *Democrat & Chronicle* (M & S); *Times-Union* (E)	135,981[3]		71,598[3]	260,871
Rockford, Ill.: *Register Star*	76,967		—	90,777
Sacramento, Calif.: *Bee*	266,053[4]		—	342,262[4]
Union	n.a.			n.a.
St. Louis: *Post-Dispatch*	349,209[3]		—	569,857
St. Paul: *Pioneer Press*	210,753[3]		—	274,919
St. Petersburg, Fla.: *Times*	384,283[4]		—	498,216[4]
Salt Lake City, Utah: *Tribune* (M & S);	121,764		—	154,079
Deseret News (E & S)	—		63,604	69,012
San Antonio: *Express News*	—	211,625[8]	—	330,770
San Bernardino, Calif.: *Sun*	87,993		—	100,220
San Bernardino (county): *Inland Valley Bulletin*	84,750		—	89,547
San Diego, Calif.: *Union–Tribune*	—	390,331[4]	—	464,734[4]
San Francisco: *Chronicle* (M); *Examiner* (E); *Examiner & Chronicle* (S)	564,374[3]		132,776[3]	715,299
San Jose, Calif.: *Mercury-News*	—	273,973[3]	—	337,247
Santa Rosa, Calif.: *Press Democrat*	96,425		—	101,451
Sarasota, Fla.: *Herald-Tribune* (M & S)	140,817[4]		—	174,536[4]
Savannah, Ga.: *News* (M & S); *Press* (E)	56,715[3]		16,439[3]	84,185
Scranton, Pa.: *Tribune* (M); *Times* (E & S)	30,432[3, 4]		43,510[3, 4]	82,266[4]
Seattle: *Post-Intelligencer* (M); *Times* (E); combined (S)	206,936[3]		237,665[3]	520,453
Shreveport, La.: *Times* (M & S)	82,646[4]		—	103,231[4]
South Bend-Mishawaka, Ind.: *Tribune*	—		86,883	124,553
Spokane, Wash.: *Spokesman-Review* (M & S)	121,664[3]		—	154,375
Springfield, Ill.: *State Journal-Register*	67,904		—	77,514
Springfield, Mass.: *Union News; Republican* (S)	109,020		—	158,102
Springfield, Mo.: *News-Leader*	61,168[4]		—	103,793[4]
Staten Island, N.Y.: *Advance* (E&S)	—		78,155	95,394
Syracuse, N.Y.: *Post-Standard* (M); *Herald-Journal* (E); *Herald-American* (S)	88,392		85,842	217,302
Tacoma, Wash.: *News-Tribune*	127,689[4]		—	147,284[4]
Tallahassee, Fla.: *Democrat*	58,696		—	79,752
Tampa, Fla.: *Tribune* (M); *Tribune & Times* (S)	302,327[4]		—	401,473[4]
Toledo, Ohio: *Blade*	150,410		—	208,199
Trenton, N.J.: *Times* (M&S)	85,057		—	95,912
Trentonian (M & S)	75,757[3]		—	60,998
Tucson, Ariz.: *Star* (M & S); *Citizen* (E)	103,575[4]		52,378[4]	184,086[4]
Tulsa, Okla.: *World* (M & S)	177,383[4]		—	247,817[4]
Walnut Creek, Calif.: *Contra Costa Times*	91,155		—	103,003
Washington, D.C.: *Post*	855,171[3]		—	1,170,150
Times	92,205		—	69,208
USA Today	1,632,345[8]		—	2,003,620[9]
West Palm Beach, Fla.: *Post*	188,752		—	239,168
Wichita, Kan.: *Eagle*	119,364		—	195,518
Wilmington, Del.: *News Journal*	—	125,550[4]	—	147,426[4]
Winston-Salem, N.C.: *Journal*	92,199		—	108,486
Worcester, Mass.: *Telegram Gazette; Telegraph* (S)	—	111,285[4]	—	139,828[4]
York, Pa.: *Record* (M); *Dispatch* (E); *News* (S)	41,166[3]		40,114[3]	87,833
Youngstown, Ohio: *Vindicator*	—		90,227[4]	134,821[4]

1. Listing is of cities in which any one edition of a newspaper exceeds an average net paid circulation of 75,000; newspapers of smaller circulation in those cities are also included. 2. Unless otherwise indicated, figures are average Monday-through-Saturday circulation for six-month period ending March 31, 1991. 3. Average Monday-through-Friday circulation. 4. Three-month average. 5. Week-end edition. 6. Monday, Tuesday, and Thursday. 7. Saturday edition. 8. Monday-Thursday. 9. Friday morning. n.a. = not available. *Source:* Audit Bureau of Circulations.

English Language Daily and Sunday U.S. Newspapers

(number of newspapers as of Feb. 1, 1993; circulation as reported for Sept. 30, 1992)

State	Morning papers and circulation		Evening papers and circulation		Total M and E and circulation		Sunday papers and circulation	
Alabama	16	325,730	11	435,670	27	761,400	20	767,937
Alaska	5	109,743	2	10,042	7	119,785	4	138,604
Arizona	9	517,582	13	243,221	22	760,803	14	844,736
Arkansas	10	347,210	21	128,815	31	476,025	16	529,878
California[1]	61	5,017,102	50	1,410,434	108	6,427,536	71	6,709,914
Colorado	13	887,264	16	150,596	29	1,037,860	11	1,208,810
Connecticut[1]	12	655,497	9	168,248	19	823,745	11	840,302
Delaware[1]	3	91,585	1	62,045	3	153,630	2	175,766
District of Columbia	2	894,057	0	0	2	894,057	2	1,211,089
Florida[1]	31	2,907,067	11	249,502	41	3,156,569	35	3,988,471
Georgia	14	676,288	21	425,645	35	1,101,933	18	1,293,165
Hawaii	2	112,470	4	131,524	6	243,994	5	262,197
Idaho	7	135,621	5	80,931	12	216,552	10	266,711
Illinois[1]	16	1,837,569	54	762,947	69	2,600,516	28	2,760,115
Indiana	14	697,429	59	799,583	73	1,497,012	22	1,377,127
Iowa	11	438,047	26	265,435	37	703,482	10	722,723
Kansas	7	279,338	40	238,936	47	518,274	17	477,514
Kentucky	7	458,652	16	208,118	23	666,770	12	682,904
Louisiana[1]	12	502,334	14	251,071	25	753,405	21	892,833
Maine	5	237,346	2	26,602	7	263,948	2	188,639
Maryland	10	452,354	5	203,736	15	656,090	7	671,684
Massachusetts[1,2]	9	1,199,241	31	717,692	39	1,916,933	14	1,780,191
Michigan	11	768,826	41	1,425,967	52	2,194,793	27	2,421,701
Minnesota	13	803,757	12	153,707	25	957,464	14	1,184,043
Mississippi	6	213,712	16	189,848	22	403,560	15	381,397
Missouri	11	811,894	34	233,859	45	1,045,753	21	1,350,634
Montana	6	152,525	5	38,315	11	190,840	7	201,839
Nebraska	5	223,706	15	247,876	20	471,582	7	439,142
Nevada	3	202,880	5	61,508	8	264,388	4	308,354
New Hampshire	3	103,989	7	129,473	10	233,462	5	184,982
New Jersey	13	1,279,039	8	337,154	21	1,616,193	17	1,935,995
New Mexico	5	188,749	13	118,789	18	307,538	13	295,079
New York[1,2]	28	5,674,783	48	1,309,885	73	6,984,668	44	5,700,215
North Carolina	15	939,151	34	471,625	49	1,410,776	36	1,495,634
North Dakota	6	164,679	4	22,605	10	187,284	7	189,824
Ohio	15	1,582,609	69	1,128,186	84	2,710,795	37	2,940,436
Oklahoma	10	432,052	37	233,264	47	665,316	42	875,451
Oregon[1]	5	321,784	15	366,351	19	688,135	10	716,336
Pennsylvania[1]	41	2,032,790	49	974,389	89	3,007,179	32	2,839,671
Rhode Island[1]	2	120,341	5	161,666	6	282,007	3	308,659
South Carolina	11	582,089	5	85,173	16	667,262	14	750,462
South Dakota	4	113,793	7	55,109	11	168,902	4	139,348
Tennessee[1]	11	623,128	17	287,362	27	910,490	17	1,106,950
Texas[1]	36	2,303,376	60	877,743	93	3,181,119	87	4,199,226
Utah	1	117,858	5	180,211	6	298,069	6	338,801
Vermont	4	95,946	4	32,926	8	128,872	3	104,863
Virginia[1,2]	19	2,334,313	13	272,765	30	2,607,078	16	980,620
Washington	10	692,018	14	510,200	24	1,202,218	16	1,284,699
West Virginia	10	257,871	13	168,432	23	426,303	11	414,303
Wisconsin	10	405,449	26	703,865	36	1,109,314	20	1,208,786
Wyoming	6	65,180	4	27,640	10	92,820	4	71,211
Totals	**596**	**42,387,813**	**996**	**17,776,686**	**1,570**	**60,164,499**	**891**	**62,159,971**
Total U.S., Sept. 30, 1991	571	41,469,756	1,042	19,217,369	1,586	60,687,125	875	62,067,820
Total U.S., Sept. 30, 1990	559	41,311,167	1,084	21,016,795	1,611	62,327,962	863	62,634,512
Total U.S., Sept. 30, 1989	530	40,759,016	1,125	21,890,202	1,626	62,649,218	847	62,008,154
Total U.S., Sept. 30, 1988	520	40,452,815	1,141	22,242,001	1,642	62,694,816	840	61,474,189
Total U.S., Sept. 30, 1987	511	39,123,807	1,166	23,702,466	1,645	62,826,273	820	60,111,863
Total U.S., Sept. 30, 1986	499	37,441,125	1,188	25,060,911	1,657	62,502,036	802	58,924,518
Total U.S., Sept. 30, 1985	482	36,361,561	1,220	26,404,671	1,676	62,766,232	798	58,825,978
Total U.S., Sept. 30, 1984	458	35,424,418	1,257	27,657,322	1,688	63,081,740	783	57,573,979
Total U.S., Sept. 30, 1983	446	33,842,142	1,284	28,802,461	1,701	62,644,603	722	56,747,436

1. "All-day" newspapers are listed in morning and evening columns but only once in the total, and their circulations are divided between morning and evening figures. Adjustments have been made in state and U.S. total figures. 2. Includes nationally circulated daily. Circulation counted only in the state indicated. *Source: Editor and Publisher International Yearbook, 1993.*

See **the Entertainment and Culture section for additional Media information.**

WHERE TO FIND OUT MORE

Reference Books and Other Sources

This cannot be a record of all the thousands of available sources of information. Nevertheless, these selected references will enable the reader to locate additional facts about many subjects covered in the *Information Please Almanac*. The editors have chosen sources that they believe will be helpful to the general reader.

General References

Encyclopedias are a unique category, since they attempt to cover most subjects quite thoroughly. The most valuable multivolume encyclopedias are the **Encyclopaedia Britannica** and the **Encyclopedia Americana.** Useful one-volume encyclopedias are **The Columbia Encyclopedia 5th Edition** (Houghton Mifflin) and the **Random House Encyclopedia.**

Dictionaries and similar "word books" are also unique: **The American Heritage Dictionary, Second College Edition,** containing 200,000 definitions and specialized usage guidance; **The American Heritage Illustrated Encyclopedic Dictionary,** containing 180,000 entries, 275 boxed encyclopedic features, and 175 colored maps of the world; **Webster's Third New International Dictionary, Unabridged; Webster's II New Riverside University Dictionary,** containing 200,000 definitions plus hundreds of word history paragraphs; and the multivolume **Oxford English Dictionary,** providing definitions in historical order. **Roget's II The New Thesaurus,** containing thousands of synonyms grouped according to meaning, assists writers in choosing just the right word. The quick reference set—**The Word Book III** (over 40,000 words spelled and divided), **The Right Word III** (a concise thesaurus), and **The Written Word III** (a concise guide to writing, style, and usage)—are based on **The American Heritage Dictionary** and are intended for the busy reader needing information fast. Two excellent books of quotations are **Bartlett's Familiar Quotations** and **The Oxford Dictionary of Quotations.**

There are a number of useful atlases: the **New York Times Atlas of the World,** a number of historical atlases (Penguin Books), **Oxford Economic Atlas of the World, Rand McNally Cosmopolitan World Atlas: New Census Edition,** and **Atlas of the Historical Geography of the United States** (Greenwood). Many contemporary road atlases of the United States and foreign countries are also available.

A source of information on virtually all subjects is the United States Government Printing Office (GPO). For information, write: Superintendent of Documents, Washington, D.C. 20402.

For help on any subject, consult: **Subject Guide to Books in Print, The New York Times Index,** and the **Reader's Guide to Periodical Literature** in your library.

Specific References

AIDS Answer Book (ETR Assoc.)
America Votes (Congressional Quarterly, Inc.)
American Indian, Reference Encyclopedia of the (Todd Publications)
American Recipe Collection (Lifetime)
American Revolution, The (Houghton Mifflin)
Anatomy, Gray's (Churchill)
Antiques and Collectibles Price List, 1993 Kovels' (Crown)
Architectural & Building Technology, Dictionary of (Elsevier)
Architecture, Encyclopedia of World (Orient Book Distributors)
Art, History of (Abrams)
Art, Oxford Companion to (Oxford University Press)
Art, Who's Who in American (R.R. Bowker)
Art Directory, American (R.R. Bowker)
Associations, Encyclopedia of (Gale Research Co.)
Astronomy, Peterson First Guide (Houghton Mifflin)
Authors, 1000–1900, European (H.W. Wilson)
Authors, Twentieth Century (H.W. Wilson)
Automobile Facts and Figures (Kallman)
Automotive Yearbook (Wards Communication)
Ballet, Concise Oxford Dictionary of (Oxford University Press)
Banking and Finance, Encyclopedia of (Bank Administrators Institute)
Baseball Encyclopedia (Macmillan)
Biographical Dictionary, Cambridge (Cambridge University Press)
Biography Yearbook, Current (H.W. Wilson)
Birds, Field Guide to the, Peterson Field Guide Series (Houghton Mifflin)
Black Americans, Who's Who Among (Gale)
Book Review Digest, 1905– (H.W. Wilson)
Business Almanac and Desk Reference, 1994 Information Please (Houghton Mifflin)
Catholic Encyclopedia, New (Publishers Guild)
Chemistry, Encyclopedia of (VanNostrand Rinehold)
Chemistry, Lange's Handbook of, 13th Edition (McGraw Hill)
Christian Church, Oxford Dictionary of the (Oxford University Press)
College Cost Book, 1993, The (The College Board)
Composers, Great 1300–1900 (H.W. Wilson)
Composers Since 1900 (H .W. Wilson)
Computer Science and Technology, Encyclopedia of (Dekker)
Computer Software (McGraw Hill)
Computer Terms, Dictionary of (Barron)
Condo and Co-op Information Book, Complete (Houghton Mifflin)
Consumer Reports (Consumers Union)
Costume, The Dictionary of (Macmillan)
Drama As You Like It (DOK Publications)
Cultural Literacy, The Dictionary of (Houghton Mifflin)
Drama, 20th Century, England, Ireland, the United States (McGraw Hill)
Ecology (Wiley)
Energy: Facts and Future (CRC Printing)
Environmental Almanac, The 1994 Information Please (Houghton Mifflin)
Environmental Politics and Policy, 2nd Edition (Congressional Quarterly)
Environmental Science, 4th Edition (Macmillan)
Europa World Year Book (Taylor & Francis)
Fact Books, The Rand McNally (Macmillan)
Facts, Famous First (H.W. Wilson)

Facts on File (Facts on File, Inc.)
Film: A Reference Guide (Greenwood)
(Film) **Leonard Maltin's Movie & Video Guide 1993** (Signet)
(Finance) **Touche Ross Guide to Personal Financial Management** (Prentice-Hall)
Football Made Easy (Jonathan David)
Games, Book of (Jazz Press)
Gardening, Wyman's Encyclopedia of: Updated Edition (Macmillan)
Gardening, Taylor's Pocket Guides (Houghton Mifflin)
Geography, Dictionary of (Penguin Books)
Government Manual, U.S. (U.S. Office of the Federal Register, Government Printing Office)
History, Album of American (Macmillan)
History, Dictionary of American (Littlefield)
History, Documents of American (Prentice-Hall)
History, Encyclopedia of Latin-American (Greenwood)
History, Encyclopedia of World (Houghton Mifflin)
Hockey, the Illustrated History: An Official Publication of the National Hockey League (Doubleday)
Homosexuality: Lesbian and Gay Lifestyles (Irvington Publishers, N.Y.); **Understanding Homosexuality** (Crossroad Publishing Co., N.Y.)
How the World Works, A Guide to Science's Greatest Discoveries (Quill/William Morrow)
Infomania, The Guide to Essential Electronic Services (Houghton Mifflin Company)
Islam, Dictionary of (Orient Book Distributors)
Jazz in the Seventies, Encyclopedia of (Da Capo)
Jewish Concepts, Encyclopedia of (Hebrew Publishers)
Legal Word Book, The (Houghton Mifflin)
Libraries, World Guide to (K. G. Saur)
Library Directory, American (R.R. Bowker)
Literary Market Place (R. R. Bowker)
Literature, Oxford Companion to American (Oxford University Press)
Literature, Oxford Companion to Classical (Oxford University Press)
Literature, Oxford Companion to English (Oxford University Press)
(Literature) **Reader's Adviser: A Layman's Guide to Literature** (R.R. Bowker)
Medical Encyclopedia, Home (Bern Porter)
Medical & Health Sciences Word Book (Houghton Mifflin)
Museums of the World (K.G. Saur)
Music and Musicians, Handbook of American (Da Capo)
Music, Concise Oxford Dictionary of (Oxford University Press)
Music, Harvard Dictionary of (Harvard University Press)
Musical Terms, Dictionary of (Gordon Press)
Mystery Writers, Twentieth Century Crime and (St. Martin's Press)
Mythology (Little, Brown and Co.)
National Park Guide (Prentice-Hall)
New Nations: A Student Handbook (Shoe String)
Numismatist's Fireside Companion, Vol. 2 (Bowers & Merena)
Occupational Outlook Handbook (U.S. Bureau of Labor Statistics, Government Printing Office)
Operas, New Milton Cross Complete Stories of the Great (Doubleday)
Performing Arts Information (Kansas State University)
Physics (Wiley)
Pocket Data Book, U.S.A. (U.S. Department of Commerce, Bureau of the Census, Government Printing Office)
Poetry, Granger's Index to (Columbia University Press)
Politics, Almanac of American (National Journal)
Politics, Who's Who in American (R.R. Bowker)
Popular Music, American, Vol. 2 The Age of Rock (Bowling Green University)
Prescription & Non-Prescription Drugs, Complete Guide to, 1993 Edition (Putnam)
Private Schools of the United States [Council for American Private Education (CAPE) Schools]
Radon, A Citizen's Guide to (Government Printing Office)
Religions, The Facts on File Dictionary of (Facts on File)
Robert's Rules of Order Revised (Morrow & Co.)
Science, American Men and Women of (R.R. Bowker)
Science and Technology, Asimov's Biographical Encyclopedia of (Doubleday)
Scientific Encyclopedia, VanNostrand's (VanNostrand Reinhold)
Secretary's Handbook, The Professional (Houghton Mifflin)
Senior Citizens Information Resources, Encyclopedia of (Gale Research Co.)
Shakespeare, The Riverside (Houghton Mifflin)
Ships, Boats, & Vessels, Illustrated Encyclopedia of (Overlook Press)
Social Security Handbook (USGPO)
Sports Almanac, 1994 Information Please (Houghton Mifflin)
Stamp Collecting for Beginners (Wilshire)
Stars and Planets, Field Guide to the (Houghton Mifflin)
States, Book of the (Council of State Governments)
Statesman's Year-Book (St. Martin's)
Theater, Oxford Companion to the (Oxford University Press)
United Nations, Demographic Yearbook (Unipub)
United Nations, Statistical Yearbook of the (Unipub)
United States, Historical Statistics of the Colonial Times to 1970 (Revisionist Press)
United States, Statistical Abstract of the (U.S. Department of Commerce, Bureau of the Census, Government Printing Office)
Vitamin Book: A No-Nonsense Consumer Guide (Bantam)
Washington Information Directory (Congressional Quarterly, Inc.)
The Way Things Work (Houghton Mifflin)
Who's Who in America (Marquis)
Wines & Spirits, Alexis Lichine's New Encyclopedia of (Knopf)
Women, Notable American (Harvard University Press)
World War I (Houghton Mifflin)
World War II (Houghton Mifflin)
Writer's Market (Writers Digest)
Zip Code and Post Office Directory, National (U.S. Postal Service, Government Printing Office)

See the full range of publications of Dun & Bradstreet and Standard & Poor's for corporate financial and stockholder information.

For detailed information on American colleges and universities, see the many publications of the **American Council on Education.**

Also see many other specialized **Who's Who** volumes not listed here for biographies of famous people in many fields.

THE DC-3 OF SPACE. An artist's depiction of the nose-cone-shaped Delta Clipper at an altitude of 35,000 feet. Like the famed Douglas DC-3 airliner which helped establish air travel as a normal means of transportation in the 1930s, the Delta Clipper promises significantly to enhance space travel by offering a safe, low-cost transfer of people and cargo to and from orbit.

The Delta Clipper Promises Low Cost Space Flights

The McDonnell Douglas Clipper is a totally new reusable spacecraft being developed for the Ballistic Missile Defense Organization (BMDO). It is not a NASA project. Unlike the space shuttle, the Delta Clipper is a reusable single-stage-to-orbit (SSTO) spacecraft. This new technology means that it can take off and land with the same vehicle, the takeoffs and landings are performed vertically, it can operate with or without a crew, and can remain in orbit from seven to fourteen days. Its advanced engineering design gives it the capability to abort a launch and return safely to base even if its engines fail.

Initial testing of the Delta Clipper Experimental (DC-X) engines made in the spring of 1993 were successful and indicated the feasibility of building single-stage-to-orbit rockets.

Demonstration flight tests of the DC-X, a one-third size experimental vehicle, are planned at the White Sands Missile Range in New Mexico. The results from ground and flight tests will be used in a follow-up program which could develop a full-scale prototype of the Clipper called the DC-Y.

If built, the Delta Clipper will resemble a giant nose cone approximately 130 feet tall and 40 feet in diameter at its base, powered by eight rocket engines. This remarkable vehicle will be capable of placing a 20,000-pound payload into an easterly low earth orbit or 10,000 pounds in polar orbit at the amazingly low cost of $10 million per flight, perhaps as low as $1–2 million per flight! The Delta Clipper will use liquid oxygen and liquid hydrogen as the propellant for its main engine.

The spacecraft is named "Delta" after the famous Thor/Delta launch vehicle and "Clipper" after the renowned Yankee Clipper ships that opened the sea trade routes more than two centuries ago.

Mars Observer Mission

The first NASA mission to study the surface, atmosphere, interior, and magnetic field of Mars for a full Martian Year began on Sept. 25, 1992. Called the *Mars Observer,* it was the first in a planned series of Planetary Observer missions that would use a new class of spacecraft derived from Earth-orbiter designs. These missions will be of modest cost and are intended to explore objects of the inner solar system such as Venus, the Moon, Mars, and near-Earth asteroids and comets.

The *Mars Observer* continued NASA's exploration of the red planet, which began with the *Mariner 4* mission in 1964–65, and continued with *Mariners 6* and *7* in 1969 and *Mariner 9* in 1971–72. This program reached its peak with the *Viking* orbiters and landers of 1975–82.

The new global studies of the planet's geology and atmosphere are expected to give scientists more information about the planet's evolution. One subject of particular interest is the role that water once played on Mars. While there is no liquid water on the surface of Mars now, the *Mariner* and *Viking* missions found ample evidence that liquid flowed there long ago.

At Cape Canaveral on Sept. 25, 1992, an expendable commercial *Titan III* launch vehicle carried the *Mars Observer* and its booster into Earth orbit. From there, the Transfer Orbit Stage boosted the spacecraft into an interplanetary orbit leading to Mars.

After an 11-month cruise, *Mars Observer* arrived at the red planet on Aug. 24, 1993, and was to be placed in a special orbit that would circle above Mars about every two hours. Communications with the spacecraft were lost and by the end of August efforts to reestablish contact had failed, dooming the mission.

The mission will last for one Martian year (almost 687 Earth days) to allow the spacecraft to examine the planet through its four seasons.

The scientific objectives of the Mars mission were to: determine the global elemental and mineralogical character of the surface material; define the global topography and gravitational field; establish the nature of the magnetic field; determine the time and space distribution, abundance, sources and sinks of volatile material and dust over a seasonal cycle; and to explore the structure and aspects of the circulation of the atmosphere.

In addition, *Mars Observer* was to participate in an ambitious international Mars investigation through an agreement with France and the former Soviet Union. The Russian government is expected to pick up the old Soviet space programs. However, due to severe economic problems in the former Soviet state, budget cuts may force changes or delays in their programs. The participation is the Mars Balloon Relay Experiment.

The former Soviet *Mars '94* mission has been changed to a split *'94/'96* mission due to financial difficulties. A Mars orbiter will be launched in 1994 and a second orbiter and descent module will be launched in 1996. The *Mars Balloon* will be deployed during the 1996 mission. The balloon will carry instrument packages in the atmosphere of Mars. (*See The Mars Balloon* in this section.) □

ULYSSES

Ulysses is an international project to study the poles of the Sun and interstellar space above and below the poles. The 814-lb (370-kg) spacecraft will be put into an orbit at right angles to the solar system's ecliptic plane. (The ecliptic is the plane in which the Earth and most of the planets orbit the Sun). This special orbit will allow the spacecraft to examine for the first time the regions of the Sun's north and south poles. Besides examining the Sun's energy fields, instruments on *Ulysses* will study other phenomena from the Milky Way and beyond.

While scientists have studied the Sun for centuries, they know very little about matter reaching the solar system from other nearby stars. This is because particles reaching the Sun's magnetic field from beyond the solar system are greatly changed by the Sun's magnetic field and by collision with particles flowing outward from the Sun. No spacecraft has ever left the solar system to make actual measurements of the interstellar medium.

The *Ulysses* spacecraft was launched from the space shuttle *Discovery* on Oct. 6, 1990, and will make its first solar encounter between June to October 1994. A second encounter will take place from June to September 1995.

On Feb. 8, 1992, *Ulysses* flew past Jupiter at 61,249 mph, using the planet's gravity as a slingshot to send it toward the Sun. During the flyby (Jan. 31–Feb. 16, 1992), the spacecraft studied unexplored portions of Jupiter's huge magnetic field.

THE CASSINI MISSION

The ringed planet Saturn, its major moon Titan, and a complex system of at least 18 other satellites[1] will be the destinations for NASA's and the European Space Agency's Cassini Mission. Cassini is named for the Italian-French astronomer, Gian Domenico Cassini (1625–1712), who discovered four of Saturn's major moons and a dark, narrow gap ("Cassini's Division") splitting the planet's rings.

The mission to Saturn is scheduled for launch in 1997. Cassini is to arrive at Saturn in June 2004. The cost of the mission is approximately $1.9 billion.

Early during the spacecraft's four-year tour orbiting Saturn, it will launch a parachuted probe descending through Titan's dense atmosphere to the surface of the satellite which has unique organic-like chemistry that could provide clues to the origin of life on Earth.

In order to reach Saturn, Cassini will first execute flybys of the Earth and Jupiter to gain "gravity assist" boosts in velocity to send it on its way. The first flyby of Earth will take place 26 months after launch, followed by the Jupiter flyby some 19 months later. During the first leg of its trip, before its first Earth flyby, Cassini will navigate through part of the asteroid belt and could perform an encounter with the asteroid Maja. Maja is a carbonaceous, or "C" type asteroid about 50 miles (78 kilometers) in diameter. Two small asteroids are being considered as possible additional targets, but only one of them can be visited.

The spacecraft's final encounter before proceeding to Saturn will be with Jupiter, which it will pass at a distance of about 2.2 million miles (3.6 million kilometers). Its flight path will take it for 130 days down through a region that no spacecraft has explored more than briefly—the giant planet's magnetotail. Cassini will fly down the magnetotail[2] of Jupiter, performing studies complementing the Galileo mission to Jupiter.

Upon reaching Saturn, the spacecraft will begin the first of some three dozen highly elliptical orbits during the remainder of its mission. Eighty-five days later, it will release its probe to Titan. Eleven days later, the probe will enter Titan's dense atmosphere and descend to the surface by parachute.

The $260-million probe is called *Huygens* after the famous Dutch astronomer Christiaan Huygens (1629–1695) who was the first to correctly interpret the rings of Saturn. He was also the discoverer of Saturn's largest satellite, *Titan.*

Because of the dense atmosphere shrouding the moon Titan, little is known of its surface. Scientists hope to gain a better understanding of the abundances of elements and compounds in its atmosphere, winds, and temperatures, and its surface state and composition.

After relaying to Earth data from the Titan probe's experiments, Cassini will continue with orbits of Saturn and flybys of most of the planet's 16 or more moons. In addition to 36 close encounters with Titan, the spacecraft's orbits will allow it to study Saturn's polar regions after examining the planet's equatorial zone. □

1. The International Astronomical Union has officially recognized 18 Saturnian moons. Photographs from *Voyager* flybys suggest that others may exist. 2. A tube of Jupiter's energy field, which trails away from the sun for several million miles.

GALILEO

Galileo is a project to orbit Jupiter and send an instrumented probe into the giant planet's atmosphere. The Galileo mission will allow scientists to study—at close range and for almost two years—the largest planet in the solar system, its satellites and massive energy field. The project is named after the Italian astronomer Galileo Galilei, who on Jan. 7, 1610, discovered three of Jupiter's moons and later on January 13th discovered a fourth satellite. These four "Galilean" satellites—Io, Europa, Ganymede, and Callisto, are major targets for the mission. The spacecraft will study the chemical composition and physical state of Jupiter's atmosphere and the four moons, as well as the structure and dynamics of the Jovian magnetosphere.

During the 22–month life of the mission, the orbiter will complete 10 orbits of Jupiter while making a close flyby of at least one Galilean satellite on each orbit.

The spacecraft was carried aloft by the space shuttle *Atlantis* and launched toward Jupiter on Oct. 18, 1989. After a six-year journey, it will reach the planet Dec. 7, 1995.

Using special maneuvers to gain speed with gravity assists, Galileo passed Venus in Feb. 1990, Earth in Dec. 1990, and made one last fly-by of Earth on Dec. 8, 1992, passing about 186 miles (300 kilometers) above Earth at a speed of 8.7 miles per second (14.1 kilometers per second).

On Oct. 29, 1991, Galileo took a historic photograph of asteroid 951 *Gaspera* from a distance of 10,000 miles (16,200 kilometers). It was the first close-up photo ever taken of an asteroid in space. Galileo will encounter asteroid *Ida* on Aug. 28, 1993.

A problem with opening Galileo's main antenna developed in April 1991.

Numerous attempts were made to deploy the antenna but they were unsuccessful. As a result, Galileo is expected to accomplish 70% of its mission and may return only several thousand photographs of the planet.

MAGELLAN
Venus Radar Mapper

On May 4, 1989, NASA'S unmanned spacecraft *Magellan* was launched from the shuttle *Discovery.* It was the first time a space probe was launched from a shuttle. *Magellan* is a spacecraft equipped with an imaging radar system designed to "see" through Venus' thick cloud-like cover and obtain detailed photographlike images of 90% or more of the planet's surface. *Magellan* reached Venus on Aug. 10, 1990, and although there were problems with its radio transmissions, it began taking the sharpest images of the planet ever seen. The spacecraft was placed in an elliptical orbit, circling Venus once every 3.1 hours and the radar was planned to operate once each orbit for approximately 40 minutes, from an altitude of 190 to 1060 miles (300 to 1,700 kilometers). The mapping was scheduled for 243 days.

The spacecraft's first objective in radar probing Venus was completed on May 15, 1991, after 1,789 orbits during which 84% of the planet's surface was mapped in fantastic detail.

Magellan's mapping revealed a surface covered with enormous lava flows, thousands of craters, and unusual features not found on Earth. Over 600 large craters were found on Venus. The largest crater yet found was a double-ring basin, 170.8 miles (275 kilometers) across. It has been proposed that it be named after Margaret Mead, the American anthropologist.

Magellan began surveying Venus for the second time in January 1992. During its mission,the spacecraft discovered a sinuous channel 4,200 miles (6,800 kilometers) long making it the longest known channel in the solar system. The craft ended its radar and emissions mapping in September 1992 after covering 98% of the Venusian surface.

Although NASA planned to use the spacecraft into 1995, budget cuts will shut the probe down in 1993 and the remaining funding will go to other programs. □

Is There Ice on the Moon?

Unlike the rest of the Moon's surface, the temperature of its polar regions remains permanently about –390° to –315° F and some of its craters remain perpetually in the dark. Some scientists have speculated that ice may have accumulated in the dark craters over long eons of time. □

The Mars Balloon

The ambitious Mars '94/'96 program calls for two launches, one in October 1994 for arrival in September 1995 and the other in 1996. During the '96 mission, the spacecraft will drop one or two balloons which will carry several scientific packages for analyzing Martian meteorological and surface conditions over a wide range of the planet.

The balloon segment of the mission is a joint undertaking by Russia, France, and the United States, which has greatly benefitted from the successful balloon deployed at Venus in 1985 under the Soviet VEGA program.

The American effort is being led by the Planetary Society and Titan Systems, Inc.

The balloon will carry both a suspended payload (gondola) and a distributed payload (SNAKE) which will come into contact with the planet's surface as the balloon descends during the Martian night. The SNAKE will carry its own instruments to investigate the Martian surface. The sun's light will heat the gases within the lightweight balloon during the daytime, causing the balloon to rise and drift with the winds above the planet's surface. At night, the gases will cool, causing the balloon to descend and rest on the Martian soil.

The French Space Agency, The Centre National d'Etudes Spatials (CENES) is building the balloon that will carry the SNAKE.

The total mass of the balloon system is targeted for 60 to 65 kilograms (130 to 134 pounds). The gondola will weigh about 15 kilograms (33 pounds). □

The Dawning of the Space Age

On Oct. 4, 1957, the Soviet Union put the world's first artificial satellite, *Sputnik I,* into Earth orbit and ushered in the modern space age. *Sputnik* ("traveling companion") was spherical in shape with four antennas about 8 to 9 feet in length, 23 inches in diameter, and weighed 183.4 pounds. It circled the globe every 96 minutes at a speed of 18,000 miles per hour for 92 days until Jan. 4, 1958, when it re-entered the atmosphere and burned up.

Sputnik I orbited the Earth between 156 miles at its perigee (low point) and 560 miles at its apogee (high point). Its two radio transmitters marked the first time in history that man-made radio signals were sent from space to the Earth.

A month later on Nov. 3, 1957, the Soviet Union launched *Sputnik II,* the world's first satellite put into orbit with an animal housed aboard, an 11 lb mongrel dog named *Laika* ("barker"). She died a week later after the oxygen supply ran out. The satellite carried more sophisticated instrumentation, weighed 1,120 lbs and circled the Earth every 103.7 minutes. Its orbit was approximately 145 miles at its perigee and 1,056 miles at its apogee. The satellite burned up after being in orbit for 162 days.

U.S. Unmanned Planetary and Lunar Programs

Lunar Orbiter. Series of spacecraft designed to orbit the Moon, taking pictures and obtaining data in support of the subsequent manned Apollo landings. The U.S. launched five *Lunar Orbiters* between Aug. 10, 1966 and Aug. 2, 1967.

Mariner. Designation for a series of spacecraft designed to fly past or orbit the planets, particularly Mercury, Venus, and Mars. *Mariners* provided the early information on Venus and Mars. *Mariner 9,* orbiting Mars in 1971, returned the most startling photographs of that planet and helped pave the way for a *Viking* landing in 1976. *Mariner 10* explored Venus and Mercury in 1973 and was the first probe to use a planet's gravity to whip it toward another.

Pioneer. Designation for the United States' first series of sophisticated interplanetary spacecraft. *Pioneers 10* and *11* reached Jupiter in 1973 and 1974 and continued on to explore Saturn and the other outer planets. *Pioneer 11,* renamed *Pioneer Saturn,* examined the Saturn system in September 1979. Significant discoveries were the finding of a small new moon and a narrow new ring. In 1986, *Pioneer 10* was the first man-made object to escape the solar system. *Pioneer Venus 1* and *2* reached Venus in 1978 and provided detailed information about that planet's surface and atmosphere.

Ranger. NASA's earliest Moon exploration program. Spacecraft were designed for a crash landing on the Moon, taking pictures and returning scientific data up to the moment of impact. Provided the first closeup views of the lunar surface. The *Rangers* provided more than 17,000 closeup pictures, giving us more information about the Moon in a few years than in all the time that had gone before.

Surveyor. Series of unmanned spacecraft designed to land gently on the Moon and provide information on the surface in preparation for the manned lunar landings. Their legs were instrumented to return data on the surface hardness of the Moon. *Surveyor* dispelled the fear that Apollo spacecraft might sink several feet or more into the lunar dust.

Viking. Designation for two spacecraft designed to conduct detailed scientific examination of the planet Mars, including a search for life. *Viking 1* landed on July 20, 1976; *Viking 2,* Sept. 3, 1976. More was learned about the Red Planet in a few short months than in all the time that had gone before. But the question of life on Mars remains unresolved.

Voyager. Designation for two spacecraft designed to explore Jupiter and the other outer planets. *Voyager 1* and *Voyager 2* passed Jupiter in 1979 and sent back startling color TV images of that planet and its moons. They took a total of about 33,000 pictures. *Voyager 1* passed Saturn November 1980. *Voyager 2* passed Saturn August 1981 and Uranus in January 1986.

It encountered Neptune on August 29, 1989 and made many startling discoveries. Found four rings around the planet, six new moons, a Giant Spot, and evidence of volcanic-like activity on its largest moon, Triton. The spacecraft sent back over 9,000 pictures of the planet and its system.

On February 13, 1990, at a distance of 3.7 billion miles, *Voyager 1* took its final pictures—the Sun and six of its planets as seen from deep space. NASA released the extraordinary images to the public on June 6, 1990. Only Mercury, Mars, and Pluto were not seen.

Notable Unmanned Lunar and Interplanetary Probes

Spacecraft	Launch date	Destination	Remarks
Pioneer 3 (U.S.)	Dec. 6, 1958	Moon	Max. alt.: 66,654 mi. Discovered outer Van Allen layer.
Luna 2 (U.S.S.R.)	Sept. 12, 1959	Moon	Impacted on Sept. 14. First space vehicle to reach moon.
Luna 3 (U.S.S.R.)	Oct. 4, 1959	Moon	Flew around Moon and transmitted first pictures of lunar far side, Oct. 7.
Mariner 2 (U.S.)	Aug. 27, 1962	Venus	Venus probe. Successful mid-course correction. Passed 21,648 mi. from Venus Dec. 14, 1962. Reported 800°F. surface temp. Contact lost Jan. 3, 1963 at 54 million mi.
Mariner 4 (U.S.)	Nov. 28, 1964	Mars	Transmitted first close-up pictures on June 14, 1965, from altitude of 6,000 mi.
Ranger 7 (U.S.)	July 28, 1964	Moon	Impacted near Crater Guericke 68.5 h after launch. Sent 4,316 pictures during last 15 min of flight as close as 1,000 ft above lunar surface.
Luna 9 (U.S.S.R.)	Jan. 31, 1966	Moon	3,428 lb. Instrument capsule of 220 lb soft-landed Feb. 3, 1966. Sent back about 30 pictures.
Surveyor 1 (U.S.)	May 30, 1966	Moon	Landed June 2, 1966. Sent almost 10,400 pictures, a number after surviving the 14-day lunar night.
Lunar Orbiter 1 (U.S.)	Aug. 10, 1966	Moon	Orbited Moon Aug. 14. 21 pictures sent.
Surveyor 3 (U.S.)	April 17, 1967	Moon	Soft-landed 65 h after launch on Oceanus Procellarum. Scooped and tested lunar soil.

Spacecraft	Launch date	Destination	Remarks
Venera 4 (U.S.S.R.)	June 12, 1967	Venus	Arrived Oct. 17. Instrument capsule sent temperature and chemical data.
Surveyor 5 (U.S.)	Sept. 8, 1967	Moon	Landed near lunar equator Sept. 10. Radiological analysis of lunar soil. Mechanical claw for digging soil.
Surveyor 7 (U.S.)	Jan. 6, 1968	Moon	Landed near Crater Tycho Jan. 10. Soil analysis. Sent 3,343 pictures.
Pioneer 9 (U.S.)	Nov. 8, 1968	Sun Orbit	Achieved orbit. Six experiments returned solar radiation data.
Venera 5 (U.S.S.R.)	Jan. 5, 1969	Venus	Landed May 16, 1969. Returned atmospheric data.
Mariner 6 (U.S.)	Feb. 24, 1969	Mars	Came within 2000 mi. of Mars July 31, 1969. Sent back data & TV pictures.
Luna 16 (U.S.S.R.)	Sept. 12, 1970	Moon	Soft-landed Sept. 20, scooped up rock, returned to Earth Sept. 24.
Luna 17 (U.S.S.R.)	Nov. 10, 1970	Moon	Soft-landed on Sea of Rains Nov. 17. Lunokhod 1, self-propelled vehicle, used for first time. Sent TV photos, made soil analysis, etc.
Mariner 9 (U.S.)	May 30, 1971	Mars	First craft to orbit Mars, Nov. 13. 7,300 pictures, 1st close-ups of Mars' moon. Transmission ended Oct. 27, 1972.
Luna 20 (U.S.S.R.)	Feb. 14, 1972	Moon	Soft-landed Feb. 21 in Sea of Fertility. Returned Feb. 25 with rock samples.
Pioneer 10 (U.S.)	March 3, 1972	Jupiter	620-million-mile flight path through asteroid belt passed Jupiter Dec. 3, 1973, to give man first closeup of planet. In 1986, it became first man-made object to escape solar system.
Luna 21 (U.S.S.R.)	Jan. 8, 1973	Moon	Soft-landed Jan. 16. Lunokhod 2 (moon-car) scooped up soil samples, returned them to Earth Jan. 27.
Mariner 10 (U.S.)	Nov. 3, 1973	Venus, Mercury	Passed Venus Feb. 5, 1974. Arrived Mercury March 29, 1974, for man's first closeup look at planet. First time gravity of one planet (Venus) used to whip spacecraft toward another (Mercury).
Viking 1 (U.S.)	Aug. 20, 1975	Mars	Carrying life-detection labs. Landed July 20, 1976, for detailed scientific research, including pictures. Designed to work for only 90 days, it operated for almost 6 1/2 years before it went silent in November 1982.
Viking 2 (U.S .)	Sept. 9, 1975	Mars	Like Viking 1. Landed Sept. 3, 1976. Functioned 3 1/2 years.
Luna 24 (U.S.S.R.)	Aug. 9, 1976	Moon	Soft-landed Aug. 18, 1976. Returned soil samples Aug. 22, 1976.
Voyager 1 (U.S.)	Sept. 5, 1977	Jupiter, Saturn	Fly-by mission. Reached Jupiter in March 1979; passed Saturn Nov. 1980; passed Uranus 1986.
Voyager 2 (U.S.)	Aug. 20, 1977	Jupiter, Saturn, Uranus	Launched before *Voyager 1*. Encountered Jupiter in July 1979; flew by Saturn Aug. 1981; passed Uranus January 1986; and passed Neptune in August 1989.
Pioneer Venus 1 (U.S.)	May 20, 1978	Venus	Arrived Dec. 4 and orbited Venus, photographing surface and atmosphere. Crashed into planet's surface mid-October 1992 after circling Venus for 14 years.
Pioneer Venus 2 (U.S.)	Aug. 8, 1978	Venus	Four-part multi-probe, landed Dec. 9.
Venera 13 (U.S.S.R.)	Oct. 30, 1981	Venus	Landed March 1, 1982. Took first X-ray fluorescence analysis of the planet's surface. Transmitted data 2 hours 7 minutes.
VEGA 1 (U.S.S.R.)	Deployed on Venus, June 10, 1985	Encounter with	In flyby over Venus while enroute to encounter with Halley's Comet, VEGA 1 and 2 dropped scientific capsules onto
VEGA 2 (U.S.S.R.)	Deployed on Venus, June 14, 1985	Halley's comet	Venus to study atmosphere and surface material. Encountered Halley's Comet on March 6 and March 9, 1986. Took TV pictures and studied comet's dust particles.
Suisei (Japan)	Encountered Halley's Comet March 8, 1986	Halley's Comet	Spacecraft made fly-by of comet and studied atmosphere with ultraviolet camera. Observed rotation nucleus.
Sakigake (Japan)	Encountered Halley's Comet March 10, 1986	Halley's Comet	Spacecraft made fly-by to study solar wind and magnetic fields. Detected plasma waves.
Giotto (ESA)	Encountered Halley's Comet March 13, 1986	Halley's Comet	European Space Agency spacecraft made closest approach to comet. Studied atmosphere and magnetic fields. Sent back best pictures of nucleus. Flew by comet Grigg-Skjellerup, July 10, 1992. Unable to send pictures.
Phobos Mission (U.S.S.R.)	July 7 and July 12, 1988	Mars and Phobos	Two spacecraft to probe Martian moon Phobos starting April 1989. Were to study orbit, soil chemistry, send TV pictures and data of planet. Contact was lost with Phobos 1 in August 1988 and later with Phobos 2 in March 1989 after it reached the Martian moon.
Magellan (U.S.)	May 4, 1989	Venus	Arrived at Venus on Aug. 10, 1990 and made a geologic map of planet with a powerful radar.
Galileo (U.S.)	Oct. 18, 1989	Jupiter	To study Jupiter's atmosphere and its moons during 22-month mission. It will reach the planet in 1995.

Spacecraft	Launch date	Destination	Remarks
Hiten (Japan)	Jan. 24, 1990	Moon	First Japanese unmanned spacecraft carried two small satellites without scientific instruments. One satellite placed in lunar orbit called *Hagoromo;* its transmitter later failed. The other in Earth orbit for future missions but contact was lost. Project was a practice test for later scientific missions in the 1990s.
Hubble Space Telescope (U.S., E.S.A.)[1]	April 25, 1990	Earth Orbit	Studies distant stars and galaxies and searches for evidence of planets in other solar systems. Crew of the 8-day shuttle mission Endeavour STS-61, scheduled for December 1993 will try to repair the flawed telescope.
Ulysses (U.S., ESA)	Oct. 6, 1990	The Sun	To study the poles of the Sun and interstellar space above and below the poles. First solar encounter to be in 1994. Second encounter to be in 1995.
Gamma-Ray Observatory (U.S.)	April 7, 1991	Earth Orbit	To make first survey of gamma ray sources across the whole sky, studying explosive energic sources such as supernovae, quasars, neutron stars, pulsars, and black holes.
Mars Observer (U.S.)	Sept. 25, 1992	Mars	Spacecraft to arrive at Mars Aug. 1993 and orbit the planet for one full Martian year to study atmosphere and surface change during the planet's seasons.
Mars '94/'96 (Russia)	Oct. 1994[1]	Mars	Two spacecraft to study Mars over an 18-month period. Will investigate Martian surface and deploy a balloon-borne package during second mission to study the planet's atmosphere.

1. European Space Agency (E.S.A.), responsible for furnishing the solar arrays, the Faint Object Camera, and participation in flight operations aspects of the mission.

U.S. Manned Space Flights

Mercury. *Project Mercury,* initiated in 1958 and completed in 1963, was the United States' first man-in-space program. It was designed to further knowledge about man's capabilities in space.

In April 1959, seven military jet test pilots were introduced to the public as America's first astronauts. They were: Lt. M. Scott Carpenter, USN; Capt. L. Gordon Cooper, Jr., USAF; Lt. Col. John H. Glenn, Jr., USMC; Cap. Virgil I. Grissom, USAF; Lt. Comdr. Walter M. Shirra, Jr., USN; Lt. Comdr. Alan B. Shepard, Jr., USN; and Capt. Donald K. Slayton, USAF. Six of the original seven would make a Mercury flight. Slayton was grounded for medical reasons, but remained a director of the astronaut office. He returned to flight status in 1975 as Docking Module Pilot on the Apollo-Soyuz flight.

Flight Summary

Each astronaut named his capsule and added the numeral 7 to denote the teamwork of the original astronauts.

May 5, 1961. Alan B. Shepard, Jr., makes a suborbital flight in *Freedom 7* and becomes the first American in space. Time: 15 minutes, 22 seconds.

July 21, 1961. Virgil I. Grissom makes the second successful suborbital flight in *Liberty Bell 7*, but spacecraft sank shortly after splashdown. Time: 15 minutes, 37 seconds. Grissom was later killed in *Apollo 1* fire, Jan. 27, 1967.

February 20, 1962. John H. Glenn, Jr., makes a three-orbit flight and becomes the first American in orbit. Time: 4 hours, 55 minutes.

May 24, 1962. M. Scott Carpenter duplicates Glenn's flight in *Aurora 7*. Time: 4 hours, 56 minutes.

October 3, 1962. Walter M. Schirra, Jr., makes a six-orbit engineering test flight in *Sigma 7*. Time: 9 hours, 13 minutes.

May 15–16, 1963. L. Gordon Cooper, Jr., performs the last *Mercury* mission and completes 22 orbits in *Faith 7* to evaluate effects of one day in space. Time: 34 hours, 19 minutes.

Gemini. *Gemini* was an extension of *Project Mercury,* to determine the effects of prolonged space flight on man—two weeks or longer—the time it takes to reach the Moon and return. "Walks in space" provided invaluable information for astronauts' later walks on the Moon. The *Gemini* spacecraft, twice as large as the *Mercury* capsule, accommodated two astronauts. Its crew named the project *Gemini* for the third constellation of the Zodiac and its twin stars, Castor and Pollux. The capsule differed from the *Mercury* spacecrafts in that it had hatches above the capsules so that the astronauts could leave the spacecraft and perform spacewalks or extra vehicular activities (EVAs).

There were ten manned flights in the *Gemini* program, starting with *Gemini 3* on March 23, 1965, and ending with the *Gemini 12* mission on Nov. 15, 1966. *Gemini 1* and *2* were unmanned test flights of the equipment.

When the *Gemini* program ended, U.S. astronauts had perfected rendezvous and docking maneuvers with other orbiting vehicles.

Apollo. *Apollo* was the designation for the United States' effort to land a man on the Moon and return him safely to Earth. The goal was successfully accomplished with *Apollo 11* on July 20, 1969, culminating eight years of rehearsal and centuries of dreaming. Astronauts Neil A. Armstrong and Col. Edwin E. Aldrin, Jr., scooped up and brought back the first lunar rocks ever seen on Earth—about 47 pounds.

Tragedy struck Jan. 27, 1967, on the launch pad during a preflight test of what would have become *Apollo 1*, the first manned mission. Astronauts Lt. Col. Virgil "Gus" Grissom, Lt. Col. Edward H. White, and Lt. Cdr. Roger Chafee lost their lives when a fire swept through the command module.

Six *Apollo* flights followed, ending with *Apollo 17* in December, 1972. The last three *Apollos* carried mechanized vehicles called lunar rovers for wide-ranging surface exploration of the Moon by astronauts. The rendezvous and docking of an *Apollo* spacecraft with a Russian *Soyuz* craft in Earth orbit on July 18, 1975, closed out the *Apollo* program.

Remembering the Great Adventure: Apollo 11

July 20, 1994, marks the 25th anniversary of one of the greatest human achievements in this century—the landing of the first men on another celestial body—240,000 miles from home. Over the years, public interest in U.S. space achievements has waned, but on that momentous day in the tumultuous sixties, an estimated one billion people were mesmerized as they listened to and followed broadcasts of the awesome accomplishment. Over 100 million Americans stayed up all night viewing the progress of the lunar explorers, and people at home and as far away as Japan prayed for the astronauts' safe return to Earth.

The decision to win the space race with the former Soviet Union and put the first men on the Moon was made by President John F. Kennedy after days of extensive study and expert scientific analysis. He announced the plan to put the first men on the Moon by the end of the decade to Congress on May 25, 1961, and 2,978 days later on July 20, 1969, at 4:17:40 p.m., E.D.T., the perilous mission was accomplished. The lunar lander *Eagle* carrying Neil Armstrong and "Buzz" Aldrin set down safely on the rock-strewn plain of the *Sea of Tranquility.*

Hours later, at 10:56 p.m. E.D.T., enthralled TV viewers saw the white-space-suited Neil Armstrong descend the ladder from the fragile, four-legged lunar module and slowly place his size 9-1/2 boot firmly on the lunar soil. He flubbed his famous first words and proclaimed *"That's one small step for man, one giant step for mankind,"* when he had intended to say *"That's one small step for a man . . "* To his worldwide viewing audience, it really didn't matter anyway. It was a great irony that while millions on Earth could view the historic event, Col. Michael Collins, orbiting the Moon in the command ship *Columbia,* was unable to watch them and could only learn about their progress on his radio.

The three space flight veterans chosen for the hazardous task were all born in 1930. They were the civilian mission commander, Neil A. Armstrong, 38, born in Wapakoneta, Ohio, on August 5; the command module pilot, Air Force Lieut. Col. Michael Collins, 38, born on October 31 in Rome, Italy, where his father was a military attache; and the lunar module pilot, Air Force Col. Edwin E. "Buzz" Aldrin, Jr., 39, born in Montclair, N.J., on January 20. Neil Armstrong had an early love of flying and received his pilot's license as a teenager before he obtained a driver's license. He was a Navy pilot during the Korean War and flew 78 missions. Armstrong was the command pilot for the March 1966 *Gemini 8* mission. Michael Collins graduated from West Point in 1952 and entered the Air Force. He was the pilot for the July 1966 *Gemini 10* mission. Edwin Aldrin graduated 3rd in his class at the U.S. Military Academy and had been a combat pilot flying missions in Korea. He was the pilot for the November 1966 *Gemini 12* mission.

Twelve *Apollo* missions to the moon were planned but only nine took place. The last three lunar missions were cancelled in 1970 when NASA's budget was cut and the funding went to develop the more economical space shuttle.

The *Apollo* flights to the Moon were never without unexpected problems and the astronauts always faced potential dangers on each voyage. It is remarkable that no fatal accidents occurred during the nine lunar missions. The *Information Please Almanac* pays tribute to the memory of the *Apollo 11* expedition and all the thousands of dedicated people who overcame innumerable obstacles to make this extraordinary feat possible—*Ed.*

During the Apollo project, the following 12 astronauts explored the lunar terrain:

Col. Edwin E. "Buzz" Aldrin, Jr., and Neil A. Armstrong, *Apollo 11;* Cdr. Alan L. Bean and Cdr. Charles Conrad, Jr., *Apollo 12;* Edgar D. Mitchell and Alan B. Shepard, *Apollo 14*; Lt. Col. James B. Irwin (1930–1991) and Col. David R. Scott, *Apollo 15*; Col. Charles M. Duke, Jr., and Capt. John W. Young, *Apollo 16*; and Capt. Eugene A. Cernan and Dr. Harrison H. Schmitt, *Apollo 17.*

Apollo was a three-part spacecraft: the command module (CM), the crew's quarters and flight control section; the service modules (SM) for the propulsion and spacecraft support systems (when together, the two modules were called CSM); and the lunar module (LM) to take two of the crew to the lunar surface, support them on the Moon, and return them to the CSM in orbit. The crews that made the lunar flights where both command modules and lunar modules were involved selected call names for the vehicles. The call names for the spacecraft in the six lunar landing missions with the command module and lunar module designations respectively were:

Apollo 11, Columbia and *Eagle; Apollo 12, Yankee Clipper* and *Intrepid;* (NOTE: The third lunar attempt, *Apollo 13*, April 11–17, 1970, 5 days, 22.9 hours, was aborted after the service module oxygen tank ruptured. The *Apollo 13* crew members were James A. Lovell, Jr., John L. Swigert, Jr., and Fred W. Haise, Jr. The mission was classified as a "Successful failure," because the crew was rescued. The call names for their spacecraft were *Odyssey* (CM) and *Aquarius* (LM).) *Apollo 14, Kitty Hawk* and *Antares; Apollo 15, Endeavor* and *Falcon; Apollo 16, Casper* and *Orion;* and *Apollo 17, America* and *Challenger.*

Skylab. America's first Earth-orbiting space station. *Project Skylab* was designed to demonstrate that men can work and live in space for prolonged periods without ill effects. Originally the spent third stage of a Saturn 5 moon rocket, *Skylab* measured 118 feet from stem to stern, and carried the most varied assortment of experimental equipment ever assembled in a single spacecraft. Three three-man crews visited the space stations, spending more than 740 hours observing the Sun and bringing home more than 175,000 solar pictures. These were the first recordings of solar activity above Earth's obscuring atmosphere. *Skylab* also evaluated systems designed to gather information on Earth's resources and environmental conditions. *Skylab*'s biomedical findings indicated that man adapts well to space for at least a period of three months, provided he has a proper diet and adequately programmed exercise, sleep, work, and recreation periods. *Skylab* orbited Earth at a distance of about 300 miles. Five years after the last *Skylab* mission, the 77-ton space station's orbit began to deteriorate faster than expected, owing to unexpectedly high sunspot activity. On July 11, 1979, the parts of *Skylab* that did not burn up in the atmosphere came crashing down on parts of Australia and the Indian Ocean. No one was hurt.

Space Shuttle. The *Shuttle* is a manned rocket which, after depositing its payload in space, can be flown back to Earth like a conventional airplane and be available for re-use. NASA originally hoped to launch as many as 40 missions a year, but in practice, 12 missions a year are the maximum capability. The NASA orbiter is 122.2 feet long and has a wingspan of 78.6 feet.

The *Space Shuttle Columbia* was successfully launched on April 12, 1981. It made five flights (the first four were test runs), the last completed on November 16, 1982. The second shuttle, *Challenger,* made its maiden flight on April 4, 1983. In April 1984, crew members of the *Challenger* captured, repaired, and returned the Solar Max satellite to orbit, making it the first time a disabled satellite had been repaired in space. The third shuttle, *Discovery,* made its first flight on August 30, 1984. The fourth space shuttle, *Atlantis,* made its maiden flight on Oct. 3, 1985.

A tragedy occurred on Jan. 28, 1986, when the shuttle *Challenger* exploded, killing the crew of seven 73 seconds after takeoff. It was the world's worst space flight disaster.

The first U.S. space mission since the *Challenger* disaster was launched 32 months later on Sept. 29, 1988, with the flight of *Discovery.* It had a crew of five and deployed a TDRS (Tracking Data Relay Satellite) communications satellite.

Six shuttle launches were made during 1991. The last flight occurred on Nov. 24, 1991 when the *Atlantis* deployed an Air Force satellite during its seven-day mission. It brought the total of shuttle flights to 44 by the end of 1991, of which nine were exclusively used for military payloads.

The fifth and last orbiter, *Endeavour,* was built as a replacement for *Challenger*. It was named after the British explorer James Cook's first ship. *Endeavour* was launched on its maiden voyage on May 7, 1992 with a crew of seven astronauts. They made four spacewalks and retrieved a disabled Intelsat-6 communications satellite. During the mission, Dr. Kathryn Thornton became the second American woman to walk in space.

The shuttle *Columbia* set a record 14-days in space, June 25 to July 9, 1992.

The crew of the 50th mission aboard the *Endeavour,* launched Sept. 12, 1992, included the first black woman astronaut, Dr. Mae C. Jemison, the first married couple to fly together in space, Air Force Lt. Col. Mark C. Lee and Dr. N. Jan Davis, and Dr. Mamoru Mohri, the first Japanese astronaut to fly aboard an American spacecraft.

American and Russian space engineering teams are working on modifications to *Atlantis* to enable the shuttle to dock in orbit with the *Mir* space station in late 1994 or 1995. Plans call for a Russian astronaut to join the crew of a U.S. space shuttle mission in November 1993 and to place an American astronaut aboard the *Mir* space station for a 90-day mission in 1995.

Notable Manned Space Flights

Designation and country	Date	Astronauts	Flight time (h/min)	Remarks
Vostok 1(U.S.S.R.)	April 12, 1961	Yuri A. Gagarin	1/48	First manned orbital flight
MR III (U.S.)	May 5, 1961	Alan B. Shepard, Jr.	0/15	Range 486 km (302 mi.), peak 187 km (116.5 mi); capsule recovered. First American in space.
Vostok 2 (U.S.S.R.)	Aug. 6–7, 1961	Gherman S. Titov	25/18	First long-duration flight
MA VI (U.S.)	Feb. 20, 1962	John H. Glenn, Jr.	4/55	First American in orbit
MA IX (U.S.)	May 15–16, 1963	L. Gordon Cooper, Jr.	34/20	Longest Mercury flight
Vostok 6 (U.S.S.R.)	June 16–19, 1963	Valentina V. Tereshkova	70/50	First orbital flight by female cosmonaut
Voskhod 1 (U.S.S.R.)	Oct. 12, 1964	Vladimir M. Komarov; Konstantin P. Feoktistov; Boris G. Yegorov	24/17	First 3-man orbital flight; also first flight without space suits
Voskhod 2 (U.S.S.R.)	March 18, 1965	Alexei A. Leonov; Pavel I. Belyayev	26/2	First "space walk" (by Leonov), 10 min
GT III (U.S.)	March 23, 1965	Virgil I. Grissom; John W. Young	4/53	First manned test of Gemini spacecraft
GT IV (U.S.)	June 3–7, 1965	James A. McDivitt; Edward H. White, 2d	97/48	First American "space walk" (by White), lasting slightly over 20 min
GT VIII (U.S.)	March 16–17, 1966	Neil A. Armstrong; David R. Scott	10/42	First docking between manned spacecraft and an unmanned space vehicle (an orbiting Agena rocket).
Apollo 7 (U.S.)	Oct. 11–22, 1968	Walter M. Schirra, Jr.; Donn F. Eisele; R. Walter Cunningham	260/9	First manned test of Apollo command module; first live TV transmissions from orbit
Soyuz 3 (U.S.S.R.)	Oct. 26–30, 1968	Georgi T. Bergeovoi	94/51	First manned rendezvous and possible docking by Soviet cosmonaut
Apollo 8 (U.S.)	Dec. 21–27, 1968	Frank Borman; James A. Lovell, Jr.; William A. Anders	147/00	First spacecraft in circumlunar orbit; TV transmissions from this orbit. The three astronauts were also the first men to view the Earth whole.
Apollo 9 (U.S.)	Mar. 3–13, 1969	James A. McDivitt; David R. Scott; Russell L. Schweikart	241/1	First manned flight of Lunar Module
Apollo 10 (U.S.)	May 18–26, 1969	Thomas P. Stafford; Eugene A. Cernan; John W. Young	192/3	First descent to within 9 miles of moon's surface by manned craft
Apollo 11 (U.S.)	July 16–24, 1969	Neil A. Armstrong; Edwin E. Aldrin, Jr, Michael Collins	195/18	First manned landing and EVA on Moon; soil and rock samples collected; experiments left on lunar surface

Designation and country	Date	Astronauts	Flight time (h/min)	Remarks
Soyuz 6 (U.S.S.R.)	Oct. 11–16, 1969	Gorgiy Shonin; Valriy Kabasov	118/42	Three spacecraft and seven men put into earth orbit simultaneously for first time
Apollo 12 (U.S.)	Nov. 14–24, 1969	Charles Conrad, Jr.; Richard F. Gordon, Jr.; Alan Bean	244/36	Manned lunar landing mission; investigated Surveyor 3 spacecraft; collected lunar samples. EVA time: 15 h 30 min
Apollo 13 (U.S.)	April 11–17, 1970	James A. Lovell, Jr.; Fred W. Haise, Jr.; John L. Swigert, Jr.	142/54	Third manned lunar landing attempt; aborted due to pressure loss in liquid oxygen in service module and failure of fuel cells
Apollo 14 (U.S.)	Jan. 31–Feb. 9, 1971	Alan B. Shepard; Stuart A. Roosa; Edgar D. Mitchell	216/42	Third manned lunar landing: returned largest amount of lunar material
Soyuz 11 (U.S.S.R.)	June 6–30, 1971	Georgiy Tomofeyevich Dobrovolskiy; Vladislav Nikolayevich Volkov; Viktor Ivanovich Patsyev	569/40	Linked up with first space station, Salyut 1. Astronauts died just before re-entry due to loss of pressurization in spacecraft
Apollo 15 (U.S.)	July 26–Aug. 7, 1971	David R. Scott; James B. Irwin; Alfred M. Worden	295/12	Fourth manned lunar landing; first use of Lunar Rover propelled by Scott and Irving; first live pictures of LM lift-off from Moon; exploration time: 18 hours
Apollo 16 (U.S.)	April 16–27, 1972	John W. Young; Thomas K. Mattingly; Charles M. Duke, Jr.	265/51	Fifth manned lunar landing; second use of Lunar Rover Vehicle, propelled by Young and Duke Total exploration time on the Moon was 20 h 14 min, setting new record. Mattingly's in-flight "walk in space" was 1 h 23 min. Approximately 213 lb of lunar rock returned
Apollo 17 (U.S.)	Dec. 7–19, 1972	Eugene A. Cernan; Ronald E. Evans; Harrison H. Schmitt	301/51	Sixth and last manned lunar landing; third to carry lunar rover. Cernan and Schmitt, during three EVA's, completed total of 22 h 05 min 3 sec. USS Ticonderoga recovered crew and about 250 lbs of lunar samples
Skylab SL-2 (U.S.)	May 25–June 22, 1973	Charles Conrad, Jr.; Joseph P. Kerwin; Paul J. Weitz	672/50	First manned Skylab launch. Established Skylab Orbital Assembly and conducted scientific and medical experiments
Skylab SL-3 (U.S.)	July 28–Sept. 25, 1973	Alan L. Bean, Jr.; Jack R. Lousma; Owen K. Garriott	1427/9	Second manned Skylab launch. New crew remained in space for 59 days, continuing scientific and medical experiments and earth observations from orbit
Skylab SL-4 (U.S.)	Nov. 16, 1973–Feb. 8, 1974	Gerald Carr; Edward Gibson; William Pogue	2017/16	Third manned Skylab launch; obtained medical data on crew for use in extending the duration of manned space flight; crews "walked in space" 4 times, totaling 44 h 40 min. Longest space mission yet—84 d 1 h 16 min. Splashdown in Pacific, Feb. 9, 1974
Apollo/Soyuz Test Project (U.S. and U.S.S.R.)	July 15–24, 1975 (U.S.)	U.S.: Brig. Gen. Thomas P. Stafford, Vance D. Brand, Donald K. Slayton	216/05	World's first international manned rendezvous and docking in space; aimed at developing a space rescue capability
	July 15–21, 1975 (U.S.S.R.)	U.S.S.R.: Col. A. A. Leonov, V. N. Kubasov	223/35	Apollo and Soyuz docked and crewmen exchanged visits on July 17, 1975. Mission duration for Soyuz: 142 h 31 min. For Apollo: 217 h, 28 min.
Columbia (U.S.)	April 12–14, 1981	Capt. Robert L. Crippen; John W. Young	54/20	Maiden voyage of *Space Shuttle,* the first spacecraft designed specifically for re-use up to 100 times
Salyut 7 (U .S.S.R.)	Feb. 8, 1984–Oct. 2, 1985	Leonid Kizim; Vladimir Solovyov; Oleg Atkov	237 days	Record Soviet team endurance flight in orbiting space station
Mir (U.S.S.R.)	Feb. 8, 1987–Dec. 29, 1987	Yuri V. Romanenko[2]	326.5 days	Record Soviet single endurance flight in orbiting space station.
Mir (U.S.S.R.)	Dec. 21, 1988–Dec. 21, , 1988	Col. Vladimir Titov and Musa Manarov[3]	366 days	Record Soviet team endurance flight in orbiting space station.
Endeavour (U.S.)	May 13, 1992	Richard J. Hieb; Thomas D. Akers; Pierre J. Thugt	8 /20	Absolute record for extravehicular duration in space.
Columbia (U.S.)	June 25–July 9, 1992	Capt. Richard N. Richards; Lt. Cmdr. Kenneth D. Bowersox; Ellen S. Baker; Carl J. Meade; Lawrence J. DeLucas; Eugene H. Trinh	13 days, 19/30/ 4 sec	Longest aerospace mission in duration and in orbital missions with more than 2 astronauts

1. Approximate time. NOTE: The letters MR stand for Mercury (capsule) and Redstone (rocket); MA, for Mercury and Atlas (rocket); GT, for Gemini (capsule) and Titan-II (rocket). The first astronaut listed in the Gemini and Apollo flights is the command pilot. The Mercury capsules had names: MR-III was *Freedom 7,* MR-IV was *Liberty Bell 7,* MA-VI was *Friendship 7,* MA-VII was *Aurora 7,* MA-VIII was *Sigma 7,* and MA-IX was *Faith 7.* The figure 7 referred to the fact that the first group of U.S. astronauts numbered seven men. Only one Gemini capsule had a name: GT-III was called *Molly Brown* (after the Broadway musical *The Unsinkable Molly Brown*); thereafter the practice of naming the capsules was discontinued. 2. Returned to earth with two fellow cosmonauts, Aleksandr P. Aleksandrov and Anatoly Levchenko, who had spent a shorter stay aboard the *Mir.* 3. Also returned to earth with French astronaut Jean-Loup Chrétien who spent 3-1/2 weeks aboard the *Mir.*

Soviet Manned Space Flight Programs

Vostok. The Soviets' first manned capsule, roughly spherical, used to place the first six cosmonauts in Earth orbit (1961–65).

Voskhod. Adaptation of the *Vostok* capsule to accommodate two and three cosmonauts. *Voskhod 1* orbited three persons, and *Voskhod 2* orbited two persons performing the world's first manned extra-vehicular activity.

Soyuz. Late-model manned spacecraft with provisions for three cosmonauts and a "working compartment" accessible through a hatch. Soyuz is the Russian word for "union". Since 1973, all *Soyuz* spacecraft have carried two cosmonauts. *Soyuz 19,* launched July 15, 1975, docked with the American *Apollo* spacecraft.

Salyut. Earth-orbiting space station intended for prolonged occupancy and re-visitation by cosmonauts. They are usually launched by Soviet Proton rockets. *Salyut 1* was launched April 19, 1971. *Salyut 2,* launched April 3, 1973, malfunctioned in orbit and was never occupied. *Salyut 3* was launched June 25, 1974. *Salyut 4* was launched Dec. 26, 1974. *Salyut 5* was launched June 22, 1976. *Salyut 6* was launched on Sept. 29, 1977. *Salyut 7* was launched on April 19, 1982. A record breaking Russian endurance flight was set (Feb. 8, 1984–Oct. 2, 1985) when Soviet astronauts spent 237 days in orbit aboard *Salyut 7. Salyut 7* re-entered the atmosphere and crashed into the Atlantic Ocean on Feb. 6, 1991.

Mir. The former Soviet Union's space station was launched into orbit on Feb. 20, 1986. Since that time, two space endurance records have been set in the *Mir.* On Dec. 29, 1987, Col. Yuri Romanenko set a single-mission record of 326.5 days in space. On Dec. 21, 1989, Col. Vladimir Titov and Musa Manarov returned to Earth after spending 366 days aboard the orbiting space station.

The U.S. and Russia are planning a joint U.S. space shuttle–*Mir* space station docking in 1995.

The Russian Space Shuttle *Buran*

The successful test flight of the former Soviet Union's first reusable space shuttle *Buran* (Russian for "snowstorm") was made on Nov. 15, 1988. The unmanned flight circled the Earth for two orbits and lasted 3 hr 25 min.

The Russian and American space shuttles closely resemble each other in size and appearance and have similar delta wings and vertical tail structures. Some major differences between the two shuttles are that the Russian craft has no large rocket engines of its own. It uses the giant disposable *Energiya* rocket for most of its propulsion, and has only small rockets for maneuvering.

Unlike the American version, the *Buran* is designed for fully automatic flight, from takeoff to landing, a difficult engineering feat.

The crew cabin of *Buran* can accommodate two to four astronauts and has seats for six passengers or other crew members.

The Russian craft is 19 ft (5.6 m) in diameter compared with NASA's shuttle, 17 ft (5.2 m). The wingspan is 79.2 ft (24 m). NASA's orbiter is 78.6 ft (23.79 m). *Buran's* length is 119 ft (36 m), the U.S. shuttle is 122.2 ft long (37.24 m).

Russia plans to make a second unpiloted test flight of *Buran* in 1994. Once *Buran* is in orbit, it will automatically dock with the space station *Mir.* Crew members from *Mir* are to work aboard *Buran* for seven days and then return to their space station. Russian engineers will automatically return the shuttle to its base on earth without a crew as it did in 1988.

Our Forgotten Astronaut Programs

Nowadays, when we think of American astronauts, we tend to think of NASA's Moon landing missions, Skylab, and the space shuttle crews. However, NASA once had three other astronaut programs in which participants could achieve the astronaut rating using the standard definition of having flown above 50 miles or 264,000 feet (80 kilometers). These were the NASA/Navy/Air Force X-15 program from 1952 to 1969, the Air Force/NASA Dyna-Soar program from 1956 to 1963, and the Dept. of Defense Manned Orbiting Laboratory program from 1963 to 1969.

The North American X-15 was a sophisticated rocket-propelled research aircraft that could fly at hypersonic speeds (over 4,500 miles per hour or 7,200 kilometers per hour) and attain ultra high altitudes (over 350,000 feet or 107 kilometers). It was slung under a B-52 bomber "mother aircraft" and taken up into the atmosphere and released for each flight. Only the X-15 actually went through the flight testing phase before the programs were cancelled due to budget cuts.

Dyna-Soar (X-20) was primarily a military research effort to develop a small, piloted glider that could be boosted into space flight and capable of maneuverable re-entry from orbit to a conventional controlled landing. It was intended to explore the problems of hypersonic flight beyond the range of the X-15.

The Manned Orbiting Laboratory (MOL) was to be designed to accommodate two men in orbit for thirty days.

During the nine years that the X-15 was flown (1959 through 1968) 199 flights were completed. The highest altitude reached was 354,200 feet (108 kilometers) by Joseph Walker on Aug. 22, 1963. Walker died on June 8, 1966, in a mid-air collision between the F-104 fighter he was piloting and an experimental aircraft. The fastest speed recorded was Mach 6.70 (4,520 miles or 7,270 kilometers per hour) by William "Pete" Knight on Oct. 3, 1967.

Eight of the twelve men who flew the X-15 achieved astronaut status. One test pilot, Michael J. Adams, was killed on Nov. 15, 1967 in an X-15 crash. On his last flight, he attained an altitude of 266,000 feet (81.8 kilometers) thus achieving the astronaut title. One of the former X-15 test pilots was Neil A. Armstrong who made seven flights and reached an altitude of 207,500 feet. Although attaining this height did not qualify him as an astronaut, he later became the Command Pilot for the Gemini 8 spacecraft mission and, during the Apollo 11 spaceflight, became the first man to walk on the Moon, July 20, 1969.

ASTRONOMY

Astronomical Terms

Planet is the term used for a body in orbit around the Sun. Its origin is Greek; even in antiquity it was known that a number of "stars" did not stay in the same relative positions to the others. There were five such restless "stars" known—Mercury, Venus, Mars, Jupiter, and Saturn—and the Greeks referred to them as *planetes,* a word which means "wanderers." That the earth is one of the planets was realized later. The additional planets were discovered after the invention of the telescope.

Satellite (or *moon*) is the term for a body in orbit around a planet. As long as our own Moon was the only moon known, there was no need for a general term for the moons of planets. But when Galileo Galilei discovered the four main moons of the planet Jupiter, Johannes Kepler (in a letter to Galileo) suggested "satellite" (from the Latin *satelles,* which means attendant) as a general term for such bodies. The word is used interchangeably with "moons": astronomers speak and write about the moons of Neptune, Saturn, etc. A satellite may be any size.

Orbit is the term for the path traveled by a body in space. It comes from the Latin *orbis,* which means circle, circuit, etc., and *orbita,* which means a rut or a wheel track. Theoretically, four mathematical figures are possible orbits: two are open (hyperbola and parabola) and two are closed (ellipse and circle), but in reality all closed orbits are ellipses. These ellipses can be nearly circular, as are the orbits of most planets, or very elongated, as are the orbits of most comets. In these orbits, the Sun is in one focal point of the ellipse, and the other focal point is empty. In the orbits of satellites, the planet stands in one focal point of the orbit. The *primary* of an orbit is the body in the focal point. For planets, the point of the orbit closest to the Sun is the *perihelion,* and the point farthest from the Sun is the *aphelion.* For orbits around the Earth, the corresponding terms are *perigee* and *apogee;* for orbits around other planets, corresponding terms are coined when necessary.

Two heavenly bodies are in *inferior* or *superior conjunction* when they have the same Right Ascension, or are in the same meridian; that is, when one is due north or south of the other. If the bodies appear near each other as seen from the Earth, they will rise and set at the same time. They are in *opposition* when they are opposite each other in the heavens: when one rises as the other is setting. *Greatest elongation* is the greatest apparent angular distance from the Sun, when a planet is most favorably suited for observation. Mercury can be seen with the naked eye only at about this time. An *occultation* of a planet or star is an eclipse of it by some other body, usually the Moon.

Stars are the basic units of population in the universe. Our Sun is the nearest star. Stars are very large (our Sun has a diameter of 865,400 miles—a comparatively small star). Stars are composed of intensely hot gasses, deriving their energy from nuclear reactions going on in their interiors.

Galaxies are immense systems containing billions of stars. All that you can see in the sky (with a very few exceptions) belongs to our galaxy—a system of roughly 200 billion stars. The few exceptions are other galaxies. Our own galaxy, the rim of which we see as the "Milky Way," is about 100,000 light-years in diameter and about 10,000 light-years in thickness. Its shape is roughly that of a thick lens; more precisely it is a "spiral nebula," a term first used for other galaxies when they were discovered and before it was realized that these were separate and distant galaxies. The spiral galaxy nearest to ours is in the constellation Andromeda. It is somewhat larger than our own galaxy and is visible to the naked eye.

Recent developments in radio astronomy have revealed additional celestial objects that are still incompletely understood.

Quasars ("quasi-stellar" objects), originally thought to be peculiar stars in our own galaxy, are now believed to be the most remote objects in the Universe. Spectral studies of quasars indicate that some are 9 billion light years away and moving away from us at the incredible rate of 150,000 miles per second. Quasars emit tremendous amounts of light and microwave radiation. Although they appear to be far smaller than ordinary galaxies, some quasars emit as much as 100 times more energy. Some astronomers believe that quasars are the cores of violently exploding galaxies.

Pulsars are believed to be rapidly spinning neutron stars, so crushed by their own gravity that a million tons of their matter would hardly fill a thimble. Pulsars are so named because they emit bursts of radio energy at regular intervals.

Pulsar *Geminga,* estimated to be within 300 light years from Earth, is the closest known pulsar to the solar system. In 1993, astronomers reported the discovery of a pulsar about 400 light years from Earth.

A *black hole* is the theoretical end-product of the total gravitational collapse of a massive star or group of stars. Crushed even smaller than an incredibly dense neutron star, such a body may become so dense that not even light can escape its gravitational field. It has been suggested that black holes may be detectable in proximity to normal stars when they draw matter away from their visible neighbors. Strong sources of X-rays in our galaxy and beyond may also indicate the presence of black holes. One possible black hole now being studied is the invisible companion to a supergiant star in the constellation Cygnus.

Origin of the Universe

Evidence tends to confirm that the universe began its existence about 15 billion years ago as a dense, hot globule of gas expanding rapidly outward. At that time, the universe contained nothing but hydrogen and a small amount of helium. There were no stars and no planets. The first stars probably began to condense out of the primordial hydrogen when the universe was about 100 million years old and continued to form as the universe aged. The Sun arose in this way 4.6 billion years ago. Many stars came into being before the Sun was formed; many others formed after the Sun appeared. This process continues, and through telescopes we can now see stars forming out of compressed pockets of hydrogen in outer space.

The Gamma Ray Observatory

The Gamma Ray Observatory (GRO) launched from the space shuttle *Atlantis* April 7, 1991, is the second and may be the last of the four "Great Observatories" NASA had planned for studying the Universe in this decade. The first of the "Great Observatories" was the Hubble Space Telescope, launched April 24, 1990. The others were the Advanced X-ray Astrophysics Facility (AXAF) expected to launch in 1997 but budget cuts delayed the project, and the Space Infrared Telescope Facility (SIRTF) which was curtailed due to budget problems.

Unlike visible radiation and radio waves, gamma rays cannot be focused with telescopes. Instead, gamma rays are detected when they interact with matter. Their passage through the detectors on the GRO convert the rays to flashes of visible light which are counted and measured. From those flashes, scientists can determine their energy level and source. Gamma rays cannot be detected on Earth because they do not penetrate the atmosphere.

The $617-million spacecraft was built by TRW and measures 70 feet (21 meters) between the tips of its solar arrays. The solar arrays provide 1800 watts of electrical power required for the operation of the observatory. The spacecraft was designed to have a minimum life of two years, but it is expected to operate for at least six years.

Gamma rays are the highest energy radiations in the electromagnetic spectrum, ranging from tens of thousands to tens of billions of electron volts (eV). An eV is a measure of the amount of energy impacted to an electron when subjected to an electrical potential of 1 volt. In contrast, visible light corresponds to only a few electron volts. These gamma rays provide a means of studying some of the primary forces of change in the astrophysical processes.

Gamma rays are thought to originate with the "Big Bang" and subsequent expansion of the universe we witness today. Through these gamma-ray observations, we may witness the birth of elements and deaths of stars, gain clues into the mysteries of quasars, pulsars, neutron stars, and get a glimpse into the spacetime precipice of a black hole. In all these cases, large amounts of energy are released and gamma rays produced.

Gamma rays are generated by **supernovas** and by their very dense remains, **neutron stars.** These stars spin very rapidly, some—perhaps all—emit radiation in pulses and are known as pulsars. Pulsars are thought to be remnants of supernova explosions. One of the fastest known **pulsars** makes 643 complete rotations in one second. How these stars convert their rotational energy to gamma rays is not known. Since the first pulsar was discovered in 1968, we now have located more than 500 of them.

Quasi-stellar objects (**quasars** for short) are the most energetic objects in the universe. No other entity emits more energy. They also flicker, and their radiation can change from day to day. Astronomers are uncertain about the nature of quasars. One quasar has been observed emitting vast numbers of gamma rays, and many others may do so as well.

The **Milky Way Galaxy** emits a glow of gamma rays, although the sources of this glow is not fully understood.

Active galaxies, unlike the Milky Way, shine brightest in radio waves, X-rays, or even gamma rays, and the intensity of their radiation may change from week to week. Scientists want to know why these galaxies vary so much.

Bursters and other **transient sources** also produce gamma rays. These intense bursts are particularly hard to study because they cannot be predicted and last a very short time. In 1979 one gamma-ray burst observed near the Large Magellanic Cloud, our nearest galactic neighbor, unleashed in just one-tenth of a second more gamma-ray energy than our sun can pump out in every form over the next 1,000 years. It is not known why these bursts occur.

Black holes are theoretical points of space where gravity is so strong that even light cannot escape. Scientists think that, if black holes do exist, matter drawn into them will give off gamma rays just as it disappears.

In 1992, instruments aboard the Cosmic Background Explorer (COBE) satellite, launched in 1989, showed that 99.97% of the radiant energy of the universe was released within the first year of the primeval explosion. This evidence seems to confirm the Big Bang theory which holds that the universe originated from a single violent explosion (a *big bang*) of a very small agglomeration of matter of extremely high density and temperatures. Astronomers also theorize that 99% of the matter in the universe is invisible or *dark matter* composed of some kind of matter that they cannot yet detect.

Birth and Death of a Star

When a star begins to form as a dense cloud of gas, the individual hydrogen atoms fall toward the center of the cloud under the force of the star's gravity. As they fall, they pick up speed, and their energy increases. The increase in energy heats the gas. When this process has continued for some millions of years, the temperature reaches about 20 million degrees Fahrenheit. At this temperature, the hydrogen within the star ignites and burns in a continuing series of nuclear reactions in which all the elements in the universe are manufactured from hydrogen and helium. The onset of these reactions marks the birth of a star. When a star begins to exhaust its hydrogen supply, its life nears an end. The first sign of old age is a swelling and reddening of its outer regions. Such an aging, swollen star is called a red giant. The Sun, a middle-aged star, will probably swell to a red giant in 5 billion years, vaporizing the earth and any creatures that may be left on its surface. When all its fuel has been exhausted, a star cannot generate sufficient pressure at its center to balance the crushing force of gravity. The star collapses under the force of its own weight; if it is a small star, it collapses gently and remains collapsed. Such a collapsed star, at its life's end, is called a white dwarf. The Sun will probably end its life in this way. A different fate awaits a large star. Its final collapse generates a violent explosion, blowing the innards of the star out into space. There, the materials of the exploded star

Astronomical Constants

Light–year (distance traveled by light in one year)	5,880,000,000,000 mi.
Parsec (parallax of one second, for stellar distances)	3.259 light-yrs.
Velocity of light	186,281.7 mi./sec.
Astronomical unit (A.U.), or mean distance earth-to-sun	ca. 93,000,000 mi.[1]
Mean distance, earth to moon	238,860 mi.
General precession	50″.26
Obliquity of the ecliptic	23° 27′8″.26–0″.4684(t–1900)[2]
Equatorial radius of the earth	3963.34 statute mi.
Polar radius of the earth	3949.99 statute mi.
Earth's mean radius	3958.89 statute mi.
Oblateness of the earth	1/297
Equatorial horizontal parallax of the moon	57′ 2″.70
Earth's mean velocity in orbit	18.5 mi./sec.
Sidereal year	365d.2564
Tropical year	365d.2422
Sidereal month	27d.3217
Synodic month	29d.5306
Mean sidereal day	23h56m4s.091 of mean solar time
Mean solar day	24h3m56s.555 of sidereal time

1. Actual mean distance derived from radar bounces: 92,935,700 mi. The value of 92,897,400 mi. (based on parallax of 8,.80) is used in calculations. 2. *t* refers to the year in question, for example, 1994.

mix with the primeval hydrogen of the universe. Later in the history of the galaxy, other stars are formed out of this mixture. The Sun is one of these stars. It contains the debris of countless other stars that exploded before the Sun was born.

Supernovas

On Feb. 24, 1987, Canadian astronomer Ian Shelter at the Las Campas Observatory in Chile discovered a supernova—an exploding star—from a photograph taken on Feb. 23 of the Large Magellanic Cloud, a galaxy some 160,000 light years away from Earth. Astronomers believe that the dying star was Sanduleak –69°202, a 10-million-year-old blue supergiant.

Supernova 1987A was the closest and best studied supernova in almost 400 years. One was previously observed by Johannes Kepler in 1604, four years before the telescope was invented.

In April 1992, researchers observed the most distant supernova explosion, 5 billion light-years away from Earth.

Formation of the Solar System

The sun's age was calculated in 1989 to be 4.49 billion years old, less than the 4.7 billion years previously believed. It was formed from a cloud of hydrogen mixed with small amounts of other substances that had been manufactured in the bodies of other stars before the Sun was born. This was the parent cloud of the solar system. The dense hot gas at the center of the cloud gave rise to the Sun; the outer regions of the cloud—cooler and less dense—gave birth to the planets.

Our solar system consists of one star (the Sun), nine planets and all their moons, several thousand minor planets called asteroids or planetoids, and an equally large number of comets.

The Sun

All the stars, including our Sun, are gigantic balls of superheated gas, kept hot by atomic reactions in their centers. In our Sun, this atomic reaction is hydrogen fusion: four hydrogen atoms are combined to form one helium atom. The temperature at the core of our Sun must be 20 million degrees centigrade, the surface temperature averages 6,000 degrees centigrade, or about 11,000 degrees Fahrenheit. The diameter of the sun is 865,400 miles, and its surface area is approximately 12,000 times that of the Earth. Compared with other stars, our Sun is just a bit below average in size and temperature, and is a yellow dwarf star. Its fuel supply (hydrogen) is estimated to last for another 5 billion years.

Our Sun is not motionless in space; in fact it has two proper motions. One is a seemingly straight-line motion in the direction of the constellation Hercules at the rate of about 12 miles per second. But since the Sun is a part of the Milky Way system and since the whole system rotates slowly around its own center, the Sun also moves at the rate of 175 miles per second as part of the rotating Milky Way system.

In addition to this motion, the Sun rotates on its axis. Observing the motion of sun spots (darkish areas which look like enormous whirling storms) and solar flares, which are usually associated with sun spots, has shown that the rotational period of our Sun is just short of 25 days. But this figure is valid for the Sun's equator only; the sections near the Sun's poles seem to have a rotational period of 34 days. Naturally, since the Sun generates its own heat and light, there is no temperature difference between poles and equator.

What we call the Sun's "surface" is technically known as the photosphere. Since the whole Sun is a ball of very hot gas, there is really no such thing as a surface; it is a question of visual impression. The next layer outside the photosphere is known as the chromosphere, which extends several thousand miles beyond the photosphere. It is in steady motion, and often enormous prominences can be seen to burst from it, extending as much as 100,000 miles into space. Outside the chromosphere is the corona. The corona consists of very tenuous gases (essentially hydrogen) and makes a magnificent sight when the Sun is eclipsed.

The Moon

Mercury and Venus do not have any moons. Therefore, the Earth is the planet nearest the Sun to be orbited by a moon.

THE MILKY WAY GALAXY. Our sun is one of 200-billion stars banded together by gravity in an enormous spiral disk called the Milky Way Galaxy. The arrow indicates our position three-fifths of the way out from the center. It takes light 100,000 years to traverse our Galaxy, one of billions of galaxies in the universe. Copyright Hansen Planetarium, Salt Lake City, Utah. Reproduced with Permission.

The next planet farther out, Mars, has two very small moons. Jupiter has four major moons and twelve minor ones. Saturn, the ringed planet, has eighteen known moons (and possibly more), of which one (Titan) is larger than the planet Mercury. Uranus has fifteen moons, (four of them large) as well as rings, while Neptune has one large and seven small moons. Pluto has one moon, discovered in 1978. Some astronomers still consider Pluto to be a "runaway moon" of Neptune.

Our own Moon, with a diameter of 2,160 miles, is one of the larger moons in our solar system and is especially large when compared with the planet that it orbits. In fact, the common center of gravity of the Earth-Moon system is only about 1,000 miles below the Earth's surface. The closest our Moon can come to us (its perigee) is 221,463 miles; the farthest it can go away (its apogee) is 252,710 miles. The period of rotation of our Moon is equal to its period of revolution around the Earth. Hence from Earth we can see only one hemisphere of the Moon. Both periods are 27 days, 7 hours, 43 minutes and 11.47 seconds. But while the rotation of the Moon is constant, its velocity in its orbit is not, since it moves more slowly in apogee than in perigee. Consequently, some portions near the rim which are not normally visible will appear briefly. This phenomenon is called "libration," and by taking advantage of the librations, astronomers have succeeded in mapping approximately 59% of the lunar surface. The other 41% can never be seen from the earth but has been mapped by American and Russian Moon-orbiting spacecraft.

Though the Moon goes around the Earth in the time mentioned, the interval from new Moon to new Moon is 29 days, 12 hours, 44 minutes and 2.78 seconds. This delay of nearly two days is due to the fact that the Earth is moving around the Sun, so that the Moon needs two extra days to reach a spot in its orbit where no part is illuminated by the Sun, as seen from Earth.

If the plane of the Earth's orbit around the Sun (the ecliptic) and the plane of the Moon's orbit around the Earth were the same, the Moon would be eclipsed by the Earth every time it is full, and the Sun would be eclipsed by the Moon every time the Moon is "new" (it would be better to call it the "black Moon" when it is in this position). But because the two orbits do not coincide, the Moon's shadow normally misses the Earth and the Earth's shadow misses the Moon. The inclination of the two orbital planes to each other is 5 degrees. The tides are, of course, caused by the Moon with the help of the Sun, but in the open ocean they are surprisingly low, amounting to about one yard. The very high tides which can be observed near the shore in some places are due to funnelling effects of the shorelines. At new Moon and at full Moon the tides raised by the Moon are reinforced by the Sun; these are the "spring tides." If the Sun's tidal power acts at right angles to that of the Moon (quarter moons) we get the low "neap tides."

Our Planet Earth

The Earth, circling the Sun at an average distance of 93 million miles, is the fifth largest planet and the third from the Sun. It orbits the Sun at a speed of 67,000 miles per hour, making one revolution in 365 days, 5 hours, 48 minutes, and 45.51 seconds. The Earth completes one rotation on its axis every 23 hours, 56 minutes, and 4.09 seconds. Actually a bit pear-shaped rather than a true sphere, the Earth has a diameter of 7,927 miles at the Equator and a few miles less at the poles. It has an estimated mass of about 6.6 sextillion tons, with an average density of 5.52 grams per cubic centimeter. The Earth's surface area encompasses 196,949,970 square miles of which about three-fourths is water.

The Brightest Stars

Star	Constellation	Mag.	Dist. (l.-y.)
Sirius	Canis Major	−1.6	8
Canopus	Carina	−0.9	650
Alpha Centauri	Centaurus	+0.1	4
Vega[1]	Lyra	0.1	23
Capella	Auriga	0.2	42
Arcturus	Boötes	0.2	32
Rigel	Orion	0.3	545
Procyon	Canis Minor	0.5	10
Achernar	Eridanus	0.6	70
Beta Centauri	Centaurus	0.9	130
Altair	Aquila	0.9	18
Betelgeuse	Orion	0.9	600
Aldebaran	Taurus	1.1	54
Spica	Virgo	1.2	190
Pollux	Gemini	1.2	31
Antares	Scorpius	1.2	170
Fomalhaut	Piscis Austrinus	1.3	27
Deneb	Cygnus	1.3	465
Regulus	Leo	1.3	70
Beta Crucis	Crux	1.5	465
Eta Carinae	Carina	1–7	—
Alpha-one Crucis	Crux	1.6	150
Castor	Gemini	1.6	44
Gamma Crucis	Crux	1.6	—
Epsilon Canis Majoris	Canis Major	1.6	325
Epsilon Ursae Majoris	Ursa Major	1.7	50
Bellatrix	Orion	1.7	215
Lambda Scorpii	Scorpius	1.7	205
Epsilon Carinae	Carina	1.7	325
Mira	Cetus	2–10	250

1. In 1984, the discovery of a possible planetary system around Vega was reported.

Origin of the Earth. The Earth, along with the other planets, is believed to have been born 4.5 billion years ago as a solidified cloud of dust and gases left over from the creation of the Sun. For perhaps 500 million years, the interior of the Earth stayed solid and relatively cool, perhaps 2000° F. The main ingredients, according to the best available evidence, were iron and silicates, with small amounts of other elements, some of them radioactive. As millions of years passed, energy released by radioactive decay—mostly of uranium, thorium, and potassium—gradually heated the Earth, melting some of its constituents. The iron melted before the silicates, and, being heavier, sank toward the center. This forced upward the silicates that it found there. After many years, the iron reached the center, almost 4,000 miles deep, and began to accumulate. No eyes were around at that time to view the turmoil which must have taken place on the face of the Earth—gigantic heaves and bubbling of the surface, exploding volcanoes, and flowing lava covering everything in sight. Finally, the iron in the center accumulated as the core. Around it, a thin but fairly stable crust of solid rock formed as the Earth cooled. Depressions in the crust were natural basins in which water, rising from the interior of the planet through volcanoes and fissures, collected to form the oceans. Slowly the Earth acquired its present appearance.

The Earth Today. As a result of radioactive heating over millions of years, the Earth's molten *core* is probably fairly hot today, around 11,000° F. By comparison, lead melts at around 800° F. Most of the Earth's 2,100-mile-thick core is liquid, but there is evidence that the center of the core is solid. The liquid outer portion, about 95% of the core, is constantly in motion, causing the Earth to have a magnetic field that makes compass needles point north and south. The details are not known, but the latest evidence suggests that planets which have a magnetic field probably have a solid core or a partially liquid one.

Outside the core is the Earth's *mantle,* 1,800 miles thick, and extending nearly to the surface. The mantle is composed of heavy silicate rock, similar to that brought up by volcanic eruptions. It is somewhere between liquid and solid, slightly yielding, and therefore contributing to an active, moving Earth. Most of the Earth's radioactive material is in the thin *crust* which covers the mantle, but some is in the mantle and continues to give off heat. The crust's thickness ranges from 5 to 25 miles.

Scientists recently discovered that the Earth's core is not a perfect sphere. X-ray like images of inside the Earth show that there are vast mountains six to seven miles high and deep valleys on the core. These features are in an upside down relationship to the Earth's surface.

Continental Drift. A great deal of recent evidence confirms the theory that the continents of the Earth, made mostly of relatively light granite, float in the slightly yielding mantle, like logs in a pond. For many years it had been noticed that if North and South America could be pushed toward western and southern Europe and western Africa, they would fit like pieces in a jigsaw puzzle. Today, there is little question—the continents have drifted widely and continue to do so.

In 10 million years, the world as we know it may be unrecognizable, with California drifting out to sea, Florida joining South America, and Africa moving farther away from Europe and Asia.

The Earth's Atmosphere. The thin blanket of atmosphere that envelops the Earth extends several hundred miles into space. From sea level—the very bottom of the ocean of air—to a height of about 60 miles, the air in the atmosphere is made up of the same gases in the same ratio: about 78% nitrogen, 21% oxygen, and the remaining 1% being a mixture of argon, carbon dioxide, and tiny amounts of neon, helium, krypton, xenon, and other gases. The atmosphere becomes less dense with increasing altitude: more than three-fourths of the Earth's huge envelope is concentrated in the first 5 to 10 miles above the surface. At sea level, a cubic foot of the atmosphere weighs about an ounce and a quarter. The entire atmosphere weighs 5,700,000,000,000,000 tons, and the force with which gravity holds it in place causes it to exert a pressure of nearly 15 pounds per square inch. Going out from the Earth's surface, the atmosphere is divided into five regions. The regions, and the heights to which they extend, are: *Troposphere,* 0 to 7 miles (at middle latitudes); *stratosphere,* 7 to 30 miles; *mesosphere,* 30 to 50 miles; *thermosphere,* 50 to 400 miles; and *exosphere,* above 400 miles. The boundaries between each of the regions are known

(Continued on page 335)

PLANET SIZES. Shown from left to right: Mercury, Venus, Earth, Mars, Jupiter, Saturn, Uranus, Neptune, and Pluto.

Basic Planetary Data

	Mercury	Venus	Earth	Mars	Jupiter
Mean distance from Sun (Millions of kilometers)	57.9	108.2	149.6	227.9	778.3
(Millions of miles)	36.0	67.24	92.9	141.71	483.88
Period of revolution	88 days	224.7 days	365.2 days	687 days	11.86 yrs
Rotation period	59 days	243 days retrograde	23 hr 56 min 4 sec	24 hr 37 min	9 hr 55 min 30 sec
Inclination of axis	Near 0°	3°	23°27′	25°12′	3°5′
Inclination of orbit to ecliptic	7°	3.4°	0°	1.9°	1.3°
Eccentricity of orbit	.206	.007	.017	.093	.048
Equatorial diameter (Kilometers)	4,880	12,100	12,756	6,794	142,800
(Miles)	3,032.4	7,519	7,926.2	4,194	88,736
Atmosphere (Main components)	Virtually none	Carbon dioxide	Nitrogen oxygen	Carbon dioxide	Hydrogen helium
Satellites	0	0	1	2	16
Rings	0	0	0	0	1

	Saturn	Uranus	Neptune	Pluto
Mean distance from Sun (Millions of kilometers)	1,427	2,870	4,497	5,900
(Millions of miles)	887.14	1,783.98	2,796.46	3,666
Period of revolution	29.46 yrs	84 yrs	165 yrs	248 yrs
Rotation period	10 hr 40 min 24 sec	16.8 hr(?) retrograde	16 hr 11 min(?)	6 days 9 hr 18 mins retrograde
Inclination of axis	26°44′	97°55′	28°48′	60° (?)
Inclination of orbit to ecliptic	2.5°	0.8°	1.8°	17.2°
Eccentricity of orbit	.056	.047	.009	.254
Equatorial diameter (Kilometers)	120,660	51,810	49,528	2,290 (?)
(Miles)	74,978	32,193	30,775	1,423 (?)
Atmosphere (Main components)	Hydrogen helium	He lium hydrogen methane	Hydrogen helium methane	None detected
Satellites	18+[1]	15	8	1
Rings	1,000 (?)	11	4	?

1. 1981 S13 discovered from *Voyager* photos in 1990. *Source:* Basic NASA data and other sources.

THE SOLAR SYSTEM

THE SOLAR SYSTEM. Orbiting around the Sun are Mercury, Venus, Earth, Mars, Jupiter, Saturn, Uranus, Neptune, and Pluto. Our Solar System was born nearly five billion years ago out of a cloud of interstellar gas and dust. Gravity caused this nebula to contract and flatten into a spinning disk. Near the center, where the density was greatest, a body formed which was so massive that its internal pressures ignited and sustained a nuclear reaction, creating a star we call the Sun. Elsewhere in the cloud, smaller bodies coalesced and cooled—nine planets, perhaps fifty moons, millions of asteroids, and billions of comets. Within our Milky Way Galaxy, there may be billions of other solar systems. Copyright Hansen Planetarium, Salt Lake City, Utah. Reproduced with permission.

(Continued from page 332)

respectively as the *tropopause, stratopause, mesopause*, and *thermopause*. Alternate terms often used for the layers above the troposphere are *ozonosphere* (for stratosphere) and *ionosphere* for the remaining upper layers.

The Seasons. Seasons are caused by the 23.4 degree tilt of the Earth's axis, which alternately turns the North and South Poles toward the Sun. Times when the Sun's apparent path crosses the Equator are known as *equinoxes*. Times when the Sun's apparent path is at the greatest distance from the Equator are known as *solstices*. The lengths of the days are most extreme at each solstice. If the Earth's axis were perpendicular to the plane of the Earth's orbit around the Sun, there would be no seasons, and the days always would be equal in length. Since the Earth's axis is at an angle, the Sun strikes the Earth directly at the Equator only twice a year: in March (vernal equinox) and September (autumnal equinox). In the Northern Hemisphere, spring begins at the vernal equinox, summer at the summer solstice, fall at the autumnal equinox, and winter at the winter solstice. The situation is reversed in the Southern Hemisphere.

Mercury

Mercury is the planet nearest the Sun. Appropriately named for the wing-footed Roman messenger of the gods, Mercury whizzes around the Sun at a speed of 30 miles per second completing one circuit in 88 days. The days and nights are long on Mercury. It takes 59 Earth days for Mercury to make a single rotation. It spins at a rate of about 10 kilometers (about 6 miles) per hour, measured at the equator, as compared to the Earth's spin of about 1,600 kilometers (about 1,000 miles) per hour at the equator.

The photographs *Mariner 10* (1974–75) radioed back to Earth revealed an ancient, heavily cratered surface on Mercury, closely resembling our own Moon. The pictures showed huge cliffs, or scarps, crisscrossing the planet. These apparently were created when Mercury's interior cooled and shrank, compressing the planet's crust. The cliffs are as high as two kilometers (1.2 miles) and as long as 1,500 kilometers (932 miles). Another unique feature is the Caloris Basin, a large impact crater about 1,300 kilometers (808 miles) in diameter.

Mercury, like the Earth, appears to have a crust of light silicate rock. Scientists believe it has a heavy iron-rich core that makes up about half of its volume.

Instruments onboard *Mariner 10* discovered that the planet has a weak magnetic field and a trace of atmosphere—a trillionth the density of the Earth's and composed chiefly of argon, neon, and helium. The spacecraft reported temperatures ranging from 510° C (950° F) on Mercury's sunlit side to –210° C (–346° F) on the dark side. Mercury literally bakes in daylight and freezes at night.

Until the *Mariner 10* probe, little was known about the planet. Even the best telescopic views from Earth showed Mercury as an indistinct object lacking any surface detail. The planet is so close to the Sun that it is usually lost in the Sun's glare.

Radar images taken by astronomers at Jet Propulsion Laboratories and California Institute of Technology during the summer of 1991 suggest that the polar regions of Mercury may be covered with patches of water ice. Although this seems impossible due to the planet's sizzling heat, the polar regions receive very little sunlight and may get as cold as –235° F. The radar images showed bright patterns at the poles which are characteristic of ice reflecting the radar signals. Other explanations may be offered for this unexpected discovery.

Mercury is a naked eye object at morning or evening twilight when it is at greatest elongation.

Venus

Although Venus is Earth's closest neighbor, very little is known about the planet because it is permanently covered by thick clouds. In 1962, Soviet and American space probes, coupled with Earth-based radar and infrared spectroscopy, began slowly unraveling some of the mystery surrounding Venus. Twenty-eight years later, the *Magellan* spacecraft sent by the United States arrived at Venus in August 1990 and began radar-mapping the planet's surface in greater detail.

According to the latest results, Venus' atmosphere exerts a pressure at the surface 94.5 times greater than Earth's. Walking on Venus would be as difficult as walking a half-mile beneath the ocean. Because of a thick blanket of carbon dioxide, a "greenhouse effect" exists on Venus. Venus intercepts twice as much of the Sun's light as does the Earth. The light enters freely through the carbon dioxide gas and is changed to heat radiation in molecular collisions. But carbon dioxide prevents the heat from escaping. Consequently, the temperature of the surface of Venus is over 800° F, hot enough to melt lead.

The atmospheric composition of Venus is about 96% carbon dioxide, 4% nitrogen, and minor amounts of water, oxygen, and sulfur compounds. There are at least four distinct cloud and haze layers that exist at different altitudes above the planet's surface. The haze layers contain small aerosol particles, possibly droplets of sulfuric acid. A concentration of sulfur dioxide above the cloud tops has been observed to be decreasing since 1978. The source of sulfur dioxide at this altitude is unknown; it may be injected by volcanic explosions or atmospheric overturning.

Measurements of the Venusian atmosphere and its cloud patterns reveal nearly constant high-speed zonal winds, about 100 meters per second (220 miles per hour) at the equator. The winds decrease toward the poles so that the atmosphere at cloud-top level rotates almost like a solid body. The wind speeds at the equator correspond to Venus' rotation period of four to five days at most latitudes. The circulation is always in the same direction—east to west—as Venus' slow retrograde motion. Earth's winds blow from west to east, the same direction as its rotation.

Venus is quite round, very different from the other planets and from the Moon. Venus has neither polar flattening nor an equatorial bulge. The diameter of Venus is 12,100 kilometers (7,519 miles). Venus has a retrograde axial rotation period of 243.1 Earth days. The surface atmospheric pressure is 1,396 pounds per square inch (95 Earth atmospheres). The planet's mean distance from the Sun is 108.2 million kilometers (67.2 million miles). The period of its revolution around the Sun is 224.7 days.

The highest point on Venus is the summit of Maxwell Montes, 10.8 kilometers (6.71 miles) above the mean level, more than a mile taller than Mount Everest. There is some evidence that this huge mountain is an active volcano. The lowest point is in the rift valley, Diana Chasma, 2.9 kilometers (1.8 miles) below the mean level. This point is about one-fifth the greatest depth on Earth in the Marianas Trench.

Venus has an extreme lowland basin, Atalanta Planitia, which is about the size of Earth's North Atlan-

(Continued on page 337)

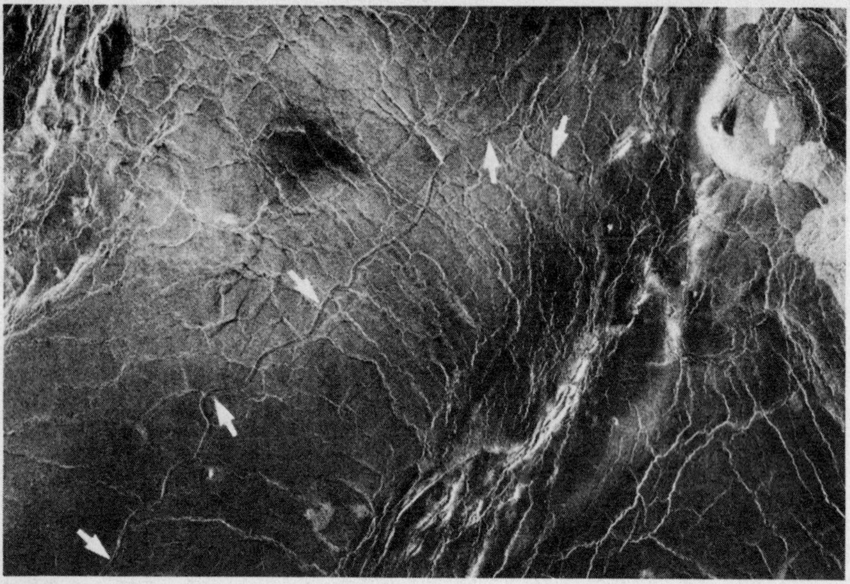

LARGEST CHANNEL IN SOLAR SYSTEM. ***Magellan*** **took the above image of the largest known channel on Venus. At 4,200 miles (6,800 kilometers) long and an average of 1.1 miles (1.8 kilometers) in width, it is longer than the Nile River, Earth's longest river, making it the longest known channel in the solar system. The channel was originally discovered by the Soviet** ***Venera 15*** **and** ***16*** **spacecraft orbiters. NASA.**

Magellan **radar image of Golubkina Crater on Venus. The impact crater is 20.4 miles (34 kilometers) in diameter. NASA.**

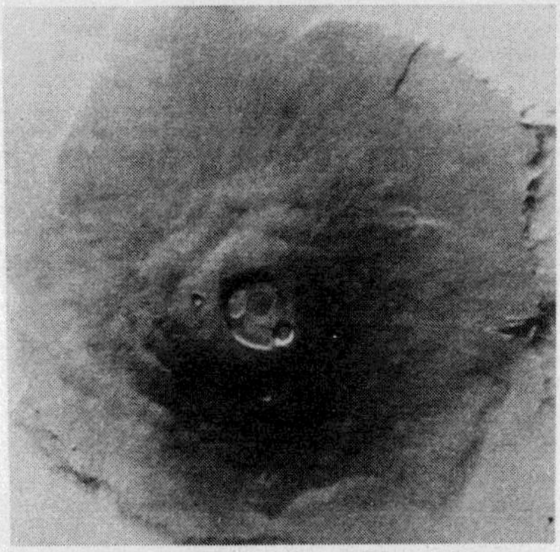

Giant Olympus Mons, the tallest volcano on Mars, is also the highest mountain in the solar system. It is 540 kilometers (336 miles) across and rises 10 miles higher than Mount Everest. NASA photo.

(Continued from page 335)

tic Ocean basin. The smooth surface of the Atalanta Planitia resembles the mare basins of the Moon.

There are only two highland or continental masses on Venus: Ishtar Terra and Aphrodite Terra. Ishtar Terra is 11 kilometers (6.8 miles) at its highest points (the highest peaks on Venus) and those of Aphrodite Terra rise to about 5 kilometers (3.10 miles) above the planet. Ishtar Terra is about the size of the continental United States and Aphrodite Terra is about the size of Africa.

The unmanned NASA spacecraft *Magellan* was launched on May 4, 1989, from the shuttle *Atlantis* and arrived at Venus Aug. 10, 1990, to map most of the planet. Despite some problems with its radio transmissions, the results of the radar mapping delighted scientists and provided them with the sharpest images ever taken of the planet's surface. Images taken from *Magellan* show ten times more detail than ever seen before.

The radar images provided scientists with compelling evidence that the planet has been dominated by volcanism on a global scale. The photos also showed that the planet's second highest mountain, Maat Mons, rising five miles (eight kilometers) above the Venusian plains, appears to be covered with fresh lava and is possibly an active volcano.

Magellan discovered the longest known channel in the solar system on Venus. It is 4,200 miles (6,800 kilometers) long and averages slightly over a mile (1.8 kilometers) wide. Its origin is puzzling to scientists because high temperature lava is unlikely to have caused such a long distance flow on the surface and there are no known substances that could remain liquid long enough under the planet's atmospheric pressure and temperature to have carved out this snake-like feature. The channel is slightly longer than the Nile River, the longest river on Earth. *Magellan* ended its radar and emissions mapping in September 1992 after covering 98% of the planet's surface. (Also see *Magellan* in the Space Section.)

• Venus is the brightest of all the planets and is often visible in the morning or evening, when it is frequently referred to as the Morning Star or Evening Star. At its brightest, it can sometimes be seen with the naked eye in full daylight, if one knows where to look.

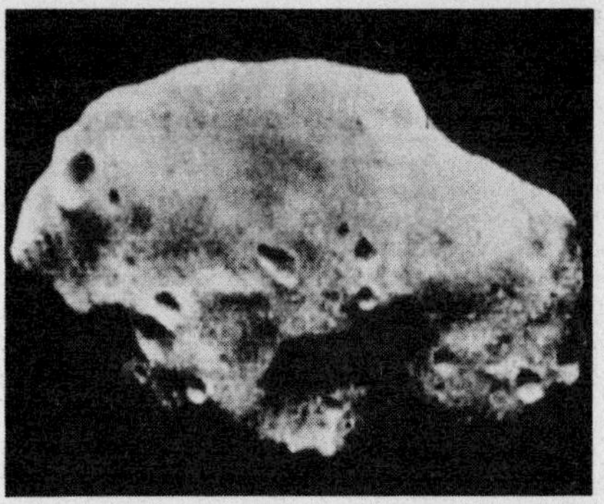

Phobos, Mars' tiny inner moon, is covered with a large number of craters.

Mars

Mars, on the other side of the Earth from Venus, is Venus' direct opposite in terms of physical properties. Its atmosphere is cold, thin, and transparent, and readily permits observation of the planet's features. We know more about Mars than any other planet except Earth. Mars is a forbidding, rugged planet with huge volcanoes and deep chasms. The largest volcano, Olympus Mons (Olympic Mountain) rises 78,000 feet above the surface, higher than Mount Everest. The plains of Mars are pockmarked by the hits of thousands of meteors over the years.

Most of our information about Mars comes from the Mariner 9 spacecraft, which orbited the planet in 1971. Mariner 9, photographing 100% of the planet, uncovered spectacular geological formations, including a Martian Grand Canyon that dwarfs the one on Earth. Called Valles Marineris (Mariner Valley) it stretches more than 3,000 miles along the equatorial region of Mars and is over 4 kilometers (2.5 miles) deep in places and 80 to 100 kilometers (50 to 62 miles) wide. The spacecraft's cameras also recorded what appeared to be dried riverbeds, suggesting the onetime presence of water on the planet. The latter idea gives encouragement to scientists looking for life on Mars, for where there is water, there may be life. However, to date, no evidence of life has been found. Temperatures near the equator range from –17 degrees F. in the daytime to –130 degrees F. at night.

None of these probes have clearly shown whether Mars has its own magnetic field. Scientists hoped that the failed *Mars Observer,* launched Sept. 25, 1992, would provide a conclusive answer. (See *Mars Observer* in Space Section.)

Mars rotates upon its axis in nearly the same period as Earth—24 hours, 37 minutes—so that a Mars day is almost identical to an Earth day. Mars takes 687 days to make one trip around the Sun. Because of its eccentric orbit Mars' distance from the Sun can vary by about 36 million miles. Its distance from Earth can vary by as much as 200 million miles. The atmosphere of Mars is much thinner than Earth's; atmospheric pressure is about 1% that of our planet. Its gravity is one-third of Earth's. Major constituents are carbon dioxide and nitrogen. Water vapor and oxygen are minor constituents. Mars' polar caps, composed mostly of frozen carbon dioxide (dry ice), recede and advance according to the Martian seasons.

Scientists have not yet determined if the Martian snow (as water ice or carbon dioxide particles) actually crystallizes on the polar caps or whether it falls from the clouds over them.

Mars has four seasons like Earth, but they are much longer. For example, in the northern hemisphere, the Martian spring is 198 days, and the winter season lasts 158 days.

Mars was named for the Roman god of war, because when seen from Earth its distinct red color reminded the ancient people of blood. We know now that the reddish hue reflects the oxidized (rusted) iron in the surface material. The landing of two robot Viking spacecraft on the surface of Mars in 1976 provided more information about Mars in a few months than in all the time that has gone before.

The Martian Moons

Mars has two very small elliptical-shaped moons, Deimos and Phobos—the Greek names for the companions of the God Mars: Deimos (Terror) and Phobos (Fear). They were discovered in August 1877 by the American astronomer Asaph Hall (1829–1907) of the U.S. Naval Observatory in Washington, D.C.

The inner satellite Phobos is 27 kilometers (16.78 miles) long and it revolves around the planet in 7.6 hours. The outer moon, Deimos, is 15 kilometers (9.32 miles) long and it circles the planet in 30.35 hours. The short orbital period of Phobos means that the satellite travels around Mars twice in a Martian day. If an observer were suitably situated on the planet, he would see Phobos rise and set twice in a day.

Recent studies of Phobos indicate that its orbit is slowly decreasing downward and that in approximately 40 million years, it will crash into the planet's surface.

In 1988, the Soviet Union launched two spacecraft to study the geology, climate, and atmosphere of Mars, and explore its moon, Phobos. The attempt was unsuccessful as contact was lost with both spacecraft.

The Soviet Union plans to make unmanned studies of the Martian atmosphere and surface during 1994 to 1996. (*Also see* Space Section.)

Meteorites From Mars

Our knowledge of the origin and history of Mars has been greatly enhanced by recent research showing that a group of eight meteorites, labeled SNC[1] (named for towns where they were found: Shergotty, India, in 1865; Nakhla, Egypt, in 1911; and Chassigny, France, in 1815), are probably samples of Mars. This hypothesis is based largely on the composition of noble gases (particularly argon and xenon) trapped in the meteorites, and the Shergottites in particular, which resemble measurements of the Martian atmosphere made by the *Viking* spacecraft. Major element compositions of the SNCs are also similar to Martian soil analyses made by *Viking*.

Jupiter's ring. A line has been drawn around a photograph of Jupiter to show the position of the extremely thin faint ring. NASA photo.

These meteorites suggest that the Martian mantle is two to four times richer than Earth in moderately volatile elements such as potassium, rubidium, chlorine, bromine, sodium, zinc, and lead. In contrast, nitrogen, carbon dioxide, and the noble gases are more depleted than expected in the Martian atmosphere, suggesting an episode of severe atmospheric loss at some time in its history.

The relatively young isotopic ages of the SNC meteorites (1.3 billion years or less) suggest that Mars has been volcanically active during its recent past.

In 1991, a ninth meteorite, LEW 88516, was identified as having reached Earth from Mars some 180 million years ago. It was discovered in December 1988 near Lewis Cliff in Antarctica. The meteorite is very small with a dark pitted surface and weighs 13.2 grams (less than half an ounce).

Scientists do not know how the meteorites were thrown off the Martian surface.

1. Pronounced "snick."

Jupiter

Jupiter is the largest planet in the solar system—a gaseous world as large as 1,300 Earths. Its equatorial diameter is 142,800 kilometers (88,736 miles), while from pole to pole, Jupiter measures only 133,500 kilometers (84,201 miles). For comparison, the diameter of the Earth is 12,756 kilometers (7,926.2 miles). The massive planet rotates at a dizzying speed—once every 9 hours and 55 minutes. It takes Jupiter almost 12 Earth years to complete a journey around the Sun.

The giant planet appears as a banded disk of turbulent clouds with all of its stripes running parallel to its bulging equator. Large dusky gray regions surround each pole. Darker Gray or brown stripes called belts intermingle with lighter, yellow-white stripes called zones. The belts are regions of descending air masses and the zones are rising cloudy air masses. The strongest winds—up to 400 kilometers (250 miles) per hour—are found at boundaries between the belts and zones.

This uniquely colorful atmosphere is mainly hydrogen and helium. It contains small amounts of methane, ammonia, ethane, acetylene, phosphene, germanium tetrahydride, and possibly hydrogen cyanide.

Cloud-type lightning bolts similar to those on Earth have been found in the Jovian atmosphere. At the polar regions, auroras have been observed. A very thin ring of material less than one kilometer (0.6 mile) in thickness and about 6,000 kilometers (4,000 miles) in radial extent has been observed circling the planet about 55,000 kilometers (35,000 miles) above the cloud tops.

The most prominent feature on Jupiter is its Great Red Spot, an oval larger than the planet Earth. It is a tremendous atmospheric storm that rotates counter-clockwise with one revolution every six days at the outer edge, while at the center almost no motion can be seen. The Spot is about 25,000 kilometers (16,000 miles) on its long axis, and would cover three Earths. The outer rim shows streamline shapes of 360-kilometer (225-mile) winds. Wind currents on the top flow east to west and currents on the top flow east to west and currents on the bottom flow west to east. The color of the Great Red Spot may indicate that it extends deep into the Jovian atmosphere.

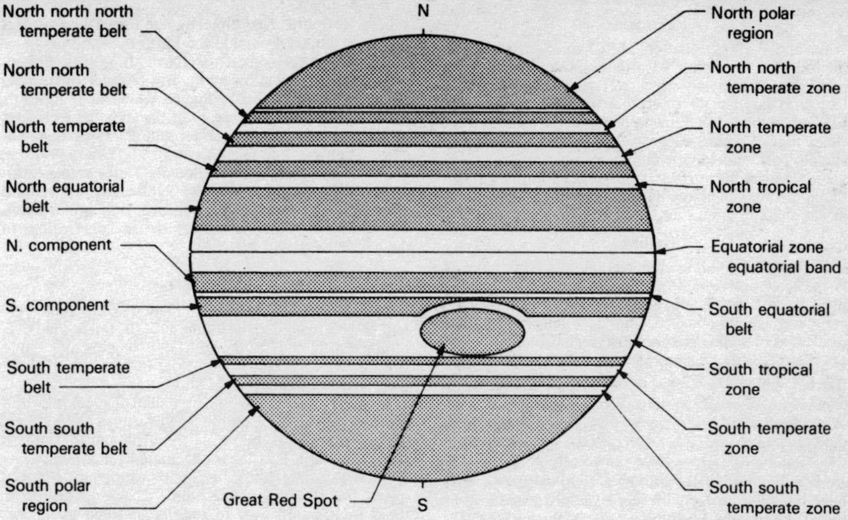

Schematic diagram of Jupiter's major features. NASA illustration.

Ganymede, Jupiter's largest satellite and also the largest known moon in the solar system. Its diverse surface indicates several periods of geologic activity.

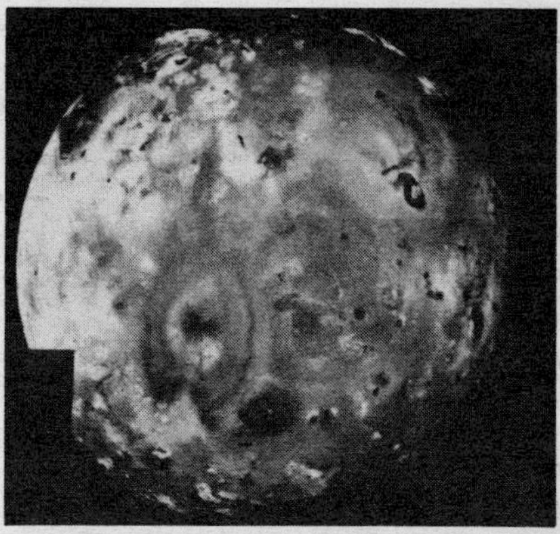

A computer-generated image of Io, the most volcanically active planetary body known in the solar system. Io's volcanoes and lava lakes cover the landscape and continually reface it, so that many impact craters have disappeared. NASA photo.

The Spot was first seen more than three centuries ago. During the years, it has changed its color and size, and it escaped detection for nearly 50 years in the 1700s. *Voyager 1* and *2* found the Great Red Spot to be cooler at the top than the surrounding clouds, indicating that the Spot may tower above them.

Jupiter emits 67% more heat than it absorbs from the Sun. This heat is thought to be accumulated during the planet's formation several billion years ago.

Jovian Moons

The four great moons of Jupiter were discovered by Galileo Galilei (1564–1642) in January 1610, and are called the Galilean satellites after their discoverer. Their names are Io, Europa, Ganymede, and Callisto. Like our Moon, the satellites always keep the same face turned toward the Earth. Jupiter has 16 known satellites.

Ganymede

Ganymede, 5,270 kilometers (3,275 miles) in diameter, is Jupiter's largest moon, and also it is the largest satellite in the solar system. Ganymede is about one and one-half times the size of our Moon. It is heavily cratered and probably has the greatest variety of geologic process recorded on its surface. Ganymede is half water and half rock, resulting in a density about two-thirds that of Europa, an ice-coated satellite. No atmosphere has been detected on it.

Europa

Europa, 3,130 kilometers (1,945 miles) in diameter, the brightest of Jupiter's Galilean satellites, may have a surface of thin ice crust overlying water or softer ice, with large-scale fracture and ridge systems appearing in the crust. Europa has a density about three times that of water, suggesting that it is a mixture of silicate rock and some water. Very few impact craters are visible on the surface, implying a continual resurfacing process, perhaps by the production of fresh ice or snow along cracks and cold glacier-like flows.

Callisto

Callisto, 4,840 kilometers (3,008 miles) in diameter, is the least active geologically of the Galilean satellites. Its icy, dirt-laden surface appears to be very ancient and heavily cratered. Callisto's density (less than twice that of water) is very close to that of Ganymede, yet there is little or no evidence of the crustal motion and internal activity that is visible on Ganymede.

Io

Io, 3,640 kilometers (2,262 miles) in diameter, is the most spectacular of the Galilean moons. Its brilliant colors of red, orange, and yellow set it apart from any other planet. Eight active volcanoes have been detected on Io, with some plumes extending up to 320 kilometers (200 miles) above the surface. The relative smoothness of Io's surface and its volcanic activity suggest that it has the youngest surface of Jupiter's moons. Its surface is composed of large amounts of sulfur and sulfur-dioxide frost, which account for the primarily yellow-orange surface color.

The volcanoes seem to eject a sufficient amount of sulfur dioxide to form a doughnut-shaped ring (torus) of ionized sulfur and oxygen atoms around Jupiter near Io's orbit. The Jovian magnetic field lines that go through the torus allow particles to precipitate into the polar regions of Jupiter, resulting in intense ultraviolet and visible auroras.

Amalthea

Amalthea, Jupiter's most innermost satellite, was discovered in 1892. It is so small—265 kilometers (165 miles) long and 150 kilometers (90 miles) wide—that it is extremely difficult to observe from Earth. Amalthea is an elongated, irregularly shaped satellite of reddish color. It orbits the planet every 12 hours and is in synchronous rotation, with its long axis always oriented toward Jupiter.

The Magnetosphere

Perhaps the largest structure in the solar system is the magnetosphere of Jupiter. This is the region of space which is filled with Jupiter's magnetic field and is bounded by the interaction of that magnetic field with the solar wind, which is the Sun's outward flow of charged particles. The plasma of electrically charged particles that exists in the magnetosphere is flattened into a large disk more than 4.8 million kilometers (3 million miles) in diameter, is coupled to the magnetic field, and rotates around Jupiter. The Galilean satellites are located in the inner regions of the magnetosphere and are subjected to intense radiation bombardment.

The intense radiation field that surrounds Jupiter is fatal to humans. If astronauts were one day able to approach the planet as close as the *Voyager 1* spacecraft did, they would receive a dose of 400,000 rads or roughly 1,000 times the lethal dose for humans.

In 1989, evidence from ground-based infrared spectra of Io indicated that the Jovian moon has hydrogen sulfide (H_2S) on its surface and in its atmosphere. It is the first time that the presence of H_2S has been detected outside the Earth.

• Even when nearest the Earth, Jupiter is still almost 400 million miles away. But because of its size, it may rival Venus in brilliance when near. Jupiter's four large moons may be seen through field glasses, moving rapidly around Jupiter and changing their position from night to night.

The United States launched its *Galileo* spacecraft toward Jupiter on Oct. 18, 1989. The unmanned spacecraft will reach Jupiter in 1995 and make a 22-month study of the planet. (Also see *Galileo* in the Space Section.)

Saturn

Saturn, the second largest planet in the solar system, is the least dense. Its mass is 95 times the mass of the Earth and its density is 0.70 gram per cubic centimeter, so that it would float in an ocean if there were one big enough to hold it.

Saturn radiates more energy than it receives from the Sun, about 80% more. However, the excess thermal energy cannot be primarily attributed to Saturn's primordial heat loss, as is speculated for Jupiter.

Saturn's diameter is 120,660 kilometers (74,978 miles) but 10% less at the poles, a consequence of its rapid rotation. Its axis of rotation is tilted by 27 degrees and the length of its day is 10 hours, 39 minutes, and 24 seconds.

Saturn is composed primarily of liquid metallic hydrogen (about 80%) and the second most common element is believed to be helium.

Saturn's atmospheric appearance is very similar to Jupiter's with dark and light cloud markings and swirls, eddies, and curling ribbons; the belts and zones are more numerous and a thick haze mutes the markings. The temperature ranges from 80° K to 90° K (176° F to –203° F).

Winds blow at extremely high speeds on Saturn. Near the equator, the *Voyagers* measured winds of about 500 meters per second (1,100 miles per hour). The winds blow primarily in an eastward direction.

Saturn's Rings

Saturn's spectacular ring system is unique in the solar system, with uncountable billions of tiny particles of water ice (with traces of other material) in orbit around the planet. The ring particles range in size from smaller than grains of sugar to as large as a house. The main rings stretch out from about 7,000 kilometers (4,350 miles) to above the atmosphere of the planet out to the F ring, a total span of 74,000 kilometers (45,984 miles). Saturn's rings can be likened to a phonograph, rings within rings numbering in the hundreds, and spokes in the B rings, and shepherding satellites controlling the F ring.

The main rings are called the A, B, and C rings moving from outside to inside. The gap between the A and B rings is called the Cassini Division and is named for the Italian-French astronomer, Gian Domenico Cassini, who discovered four of Saturn's major moons and the dark, narrow gap, "Cassini's Division," splitting the planet's rings.

Saturn's magnetic field has well-defined north and south magnetic poles, and is aligned with Saturn's axis of rotation to within one degree.

Saturn's Moons

Saturn has 18 recognized moons and there is evidence for several more. The five largest moons, Tethys, Dione, Rhea, Titan, and Iapetus, range from 1060 to 5150 kilometers (650 to 3,200 miles) in di-

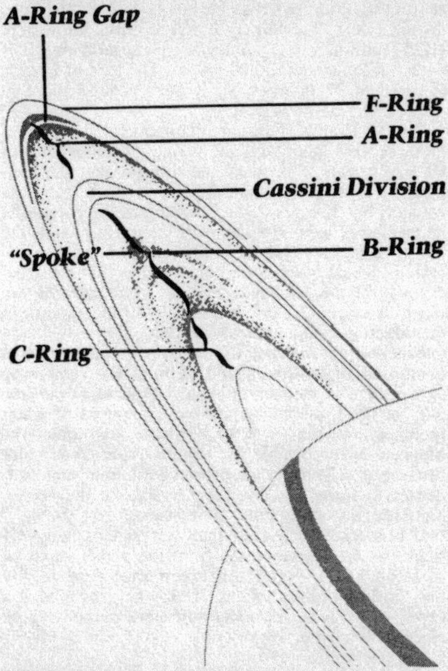

NASA illustration of the divisions in Saturn's ring system.

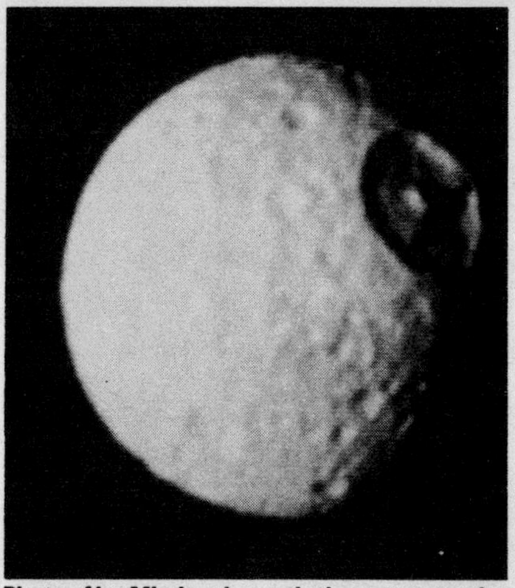

Photo of icy Mimias shows the largest meteorite crater which is about one-quarter the diameter of the entire moon. A huge mountain can be seen rising up almost 20,000 feet from the center of the crater. The crater's walls average 16,000 feet in height. NASA photo.

ameter. The planet's outstanding satellite is Titan, first discovered by the Dutch astronomer Christiaan Huygens in 1656.

Titan

Titan is remarkable because it is the only known moon in the solar system that has a substantial atmosphere—largely nitrogen with a minor amount of methane and a rich variety of other hydrocarbons. Its surface is completely hidden from view (except at infrared and radio wavelengths) by a dense, hazy atmosphere.

The diameter of Titan is 5,150 kilometers (3,200 miles) and it is the second largest satellite in the solar system after Jupiter's Ganymede. Titan is larger than the planet Mercury.

Titan's surface temperature is about –175° C (–280° F) and its surface pressure is about 50% greater than the surface pressure of the Earth. After the Voyager I flyby in 1980, scientists hypothesized that Titan may have an ocean of liquid hydrogen covering its surface. However, in 1990 it was shown that Titan's surface reflects and scatters radio waves, suggesting that the satellite has a solid surface with the possibility of small hydrocarbon lakes or ponds on the surface.

The data were obtained by using NASA's 70-meter antenna in California to transmit powerful radio waves to Titan, and the Very Large Array in New Mexico as the receiver of the reflected waves.

NASA plans to send a scientific probe to the surface of Titan in August 2002 as part of its Cassini Mission. The probe will be provided by the European Space Agency (ESA).

Other Notable Saturnian Moons

The other four largest moons of Saturn are: Tethys, Dione, Rhea, and Iapetus.

Tethys is 1,060 kilometers (650 miles) in diameter. Its surface is heavily cratered and it has a huge, globe-girdling canyon, Ithaca Chasma. Part of the canyon stretches over three-quarters of the satellite's surface. Ithaca Chasma is about 2,500 kilometers (1,550 miles) long. It has an average width of about 100 kilometers (62 miles) and a depth of 3 to 5 kilometers (1.8 to 3.1 miles).

Tethys also has a huge impact crater named Odysseus, 400 kilometers (244 miles) in diameter, or more than one-third its diameter.

Dione is slightly larger than Tethys, 1,120 kilometers (696 miles) and is more than half composed of water ice. It has bright, wispy markings resembling thin veils covering its features.

Rhea, the largest of the inner satellites, is 1,530 kilometers (951 miles) in diameter. It is composed mainly of water ice, causing its reflective surface to present an almost uniform white appearance.

Iapetus is the outermost of Saturn's icy satellites. Its appearance is unique because it has one dark and one bright hemisphere. The origin of the black coating of its dark face is unknown. Iapetus has a diameter of 1,460 kilometers (907 miles).

Other notable moons of Saturn are Mimas, Enceladus, Hyperion, and Phoebe.

Mimas is small, only 329 kilometers (244 miles) in diameter. It has a huge impact crater, Herschel, nearly one-third of its diameter. The crater is about 130 kilometers (81 miles) wide and its icy peak rises almost 10 kilometers (6.2 miles) above the floor.

Mimas is believed to be composed mainly of water ice and to contain between 20 to 50% rock.

Enceladus is remarkable in that its surface shows signs of extensive and recent geological activity. There may be active water volcanism. The surface is extremely bright, reflecting more than 90% of incident sunlight. This suggests that its surface is com-

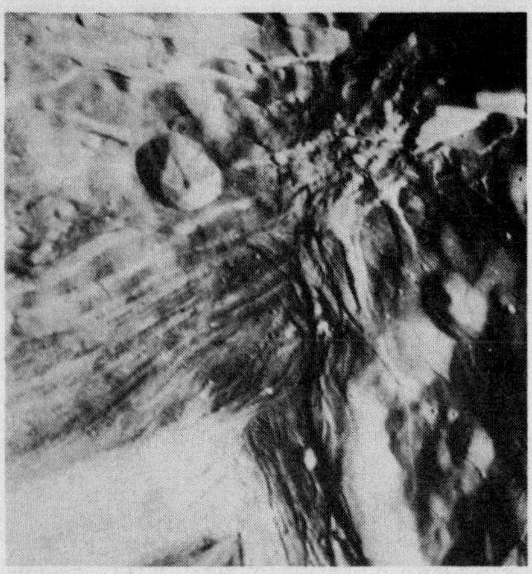

The Uranian moon Miranda is one of the strangest objects in the solar system. Photo shows some of its complex surface terrain. NASA photo.

posed of extremely pure ice without dust or rocks to contaminate it. Enceladus has a diameter of 500 kilometers (310 miles).

Hyperion orbits between Iapetus and Titan. It is irregular in shape, measuring about 400 by 250 by 200 kilometers (248 by 155 by 124 miles). It may be a remnant of a much larger object which was shattered by impact with another space body. It appears that Hyperion is composed primarily of water ice.

Hyperion orbits Saturn in a random-like motion ("chaotic tumbling").

Phoebe is Saturn's outermost satellite. It travels in a retrograde orbit at a distance of over 10 million kilometers (6.2 million miles) away from the planet. It is the darkest moon of Saturn and is the planet's only known satellite that does not keep the same face always turned to Saturn. It has been speculated that it is an asteroid that was captured by the planet. Phoebe rotates in about nine hours and orbits Saturn in 406 days. It has a diameter of 200 kilometers (124 miles).

Pan was discovered in 1990 from *Voyager 2* photos taken in 1981. An official name, Pan, is to be approved by the International Astronomical Union. The satellite is estimated to be about 20 kilometers (12.43 miles) in diameter, which makes it the planet's smallest known moon. It orbits within the Encke Gap, a 325-kilometer (202 mile) division in Saturn's A ring. It was identified by Johann Franz Encke (1791–1865) in 1837.

The remaining eight moons range from 25 to 190 kilometers (15 to 120 miles) in diameter. They are all non-spherical in shape.

If NASA's planned Cassini Mission to Saturn in the later 1990s takes place, it will shed more light on the planet's mysteries. (*See* Cassini Mission in the Space Section.)

• Saturn is the last of the planets visible to the naked eye. Saturn is never an object of overwhelming brilliance, but it looks like a bright star. The rings can be seen with a small telescope.

Uranus

Uranus, the first planet discovered in modern times by Sir William Herschel in 1781, is the seventh planet from the Sun, twice as far out as Saturn. Its mean distance from the Sun is 2,869 million kilometers (1,783 million miles). Uranus's equatorial diameter is 51,810 kilometers (32,200 miles). The axis of Uranus is tilted at 97 degrees, so it goes around the Sun nearly lying on its side.

Due to Uranus' unusual inclination, the polar regions receive more sunlight during a Uranus year of 84 Earth years. Scientists had thought that the temperature of its poles would be warmer than that at its equator, but *Voyager 2* discovered that the equatorial temperatures were similar to the temperatures at the poles, –209° C (–344° F), implying that some redistribution of heat toward the equatorial region must occur within the atmosphere. The wind patterns are much like Saturn's, flowing parallel to the equator in the direction of the planet's rotation.

Ninety-eight percent of the upper atmosphere is composed of hydrogen and helium; the remaining two percent is methane. Scientists speculate that the bulk of the lower atmosphere is composed of water (perhaps as much as 50%), methane, and ammonia. Methane is responsible for Uranus' blue-green color because it selectively absorbs red sunlight and condenses to form clouds of ice crystals in the cooler, higher regions of Uranus' atmosphere.

It was also discovered that the planet's magnetic field was 60 degrees tilted from the planet's axis of rotation and offset from the planet's center by one-third of Uranus' radius. It may be generated at a depth where water is under sufficient pressure to be electrically conductive.

The Uranian Rings

Voyager 2 also expanded the body of information pertaining to the rings and moons of Uranus. *Voyager*'s cameras obtained the first images of nine previously known narrow rings and discovered at least two new rings, one narrow and one broadly diffused, bringing the total known rings to eleven. It was found that a highly structured distribution of fine dust exists throughout the ring system.

The outermost (epsilon) ring contains nothing smaller than fist-sized particles. It is flanked by two small moons discovered interior to the orbit of the Uranian moon Miranda. The moons exert a shepherding influence on the epsilon ring and on the outer edges of the gamma and delta rings.

All of the rings lie within one planetary radius[1] of Uranus' cloud tops. Most of Uranus' rings are narrow, ranging in width from 1 to 93 kilometers (0.6 to 58 miles) and are only a few kilometers thick. The Uranian rings are colorless and extremely dark. The dark material may be either irradiated methane ice or organic-rich minerals mixed with water-impregnated, silicon-based compounds. There is evidence that incomplete rings, or "ring arcs," exist at Uranus.

The Uranian Moons

There are 15 known moons of Uranus. In order of decreasing distance from the planet, the moons are Oberon, Titania, Umbriel, Ariel, Miranda, Puck, Belinda, Cressida, Portia, Rosalind, Desdemona, Juliet, Bianca, Ophelia, and Cordelia. Nine of the new moons range in size from 26 to 108 kilometers (16 to 67 miles) in diameter and, being closer to the planet, have faster periods of revolution (8 to 15 hours) than their more distant relatives.

1. The equatorial radius of Uranus is 25,560 kilometers (15,880 miles) at a pressure of 1 bar.

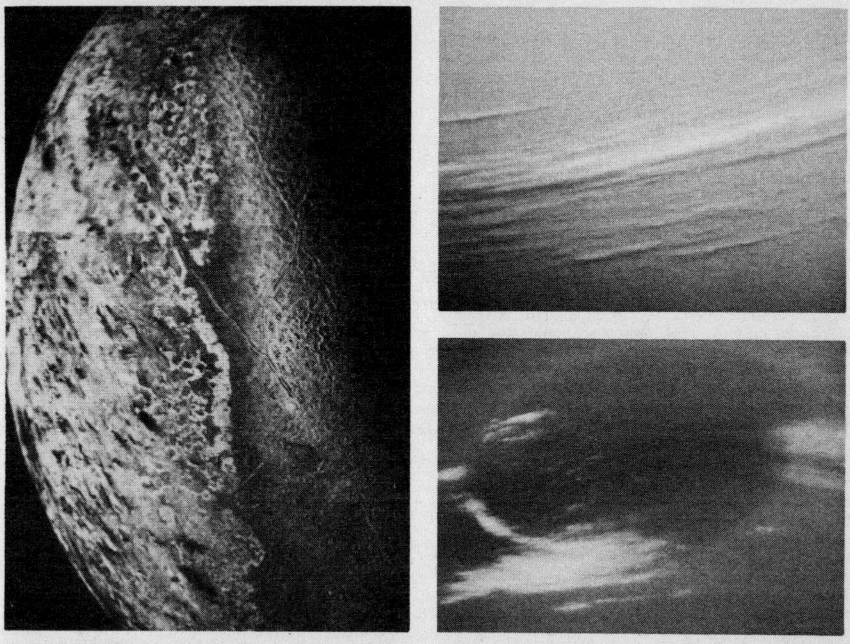

ABOVE LEFT: The rugged terrain of Triton, Neptune's largest moon. *Voyager 2* photographed geyser-like eruptions of nitrogen gas on Triton. ABOVE RIGHT: High-altitude clouds in Neptune's atmosphere. BELOW RIGHT: The Great Dark Spot is the most prominent feature in the planet's atmosphere. It is a counter-clockwise storm about the size of the Earth.

Oberon and Titania

The two largest moons, Oberon, 1,516 kilometers (942 miles) in diameter, and Titania (1,580 kilometers (982 miles) in diameter, are less than half the diameter of Earth's moon. Titania, the reddest of Uranus' moons, may have endured global tectonics as evidenced by complex valleys and fault lines etched into its surface. Smooth sections indicate that volcanic resurfacing has taken place.

Umbriel and Ariel

Umbriel and Ariel are roughly three-fourths the size of Oberon and Titania. Umbriel is the darkest of the large moons with huge craters peppering its surface. Umbriel has a paucity of what are known as bright ray craters, which are formed on an older darker surface when bright submerged ice is excavated and sprayed by meteoroid impacts.

In contrast, the surface of Ariel, the brightest of the Uranian moons, is relatively free of pockmarks due to volcanism which periodically erases the damage done by foreign projectiles. However, there are several extremely deep cuts on Ariel's surface.

Miranda

The smallest of Uranus' large moons, Miranda, 472 kilometers (293 miles) in diameter, has been described as "the most bizarre body in the solar system," with the most geologically complex surface. Miranda's remarkable terrain consists of rolling, heavily cratered plains (the oldest known in the Uranian system) adjoined by three huge, 200 to 300 kilometer (120 to 180 mile) oval-to-trapezoidal regions known as coronae, which are characterized by networks of concentric canyons.

Puck

Puck was the first new moon discovered by *Voyager*, and is 154 kilometers (96 miles) in diameter and makes a trip around Uranus every 18 hours. Puck is shaped somewhat like a potato with a huge impact crater marring roughly one-fourth of its surface.

• Uranus can—on rare occasions—become bright enough to be seen with the naked eye, if one knows exactly where to look; normally, a good set of field glasses or a small portable telescope is required.

Neptune

Little was known about Neptune until August 1989, when NASA's *Voyager 2* became the first spacecraft to observe the planet. Passing about 4,950 kilometers (3,000 miles) above Neptune's north pole, *Voyager 2* made its closest approach to any planet since leaving Earth twelve years prior. The spacecraft passed about 40,000 kilometers (25,000 miles) from Neptune's largest moon, Triton, the last solid body that *Voyager 2* will have studied.

Nearly 4.5 billion kilometers (3 billion miles) from the Sun, Neptune orbits the Sun once in 165 years, and therefore has made not quite a full circle around the Sun since it was discovered.[1]

With an equatorial diameter of 49,528 kilometers (30,775 miles), Neptune is the smallest of our solar system's four gas giants.[2] Even so, its volume could hold nearly 60 Earths. Neptune is also denser than the other gas giants—Jupiter, Saturn, and Uranus, about 64% heavier than if it were composed entirely of water.

Neptune has a blue color as a result of methane in its atmosphere. Methane preferentially absorbs the longer wavelengths of sunlight (those near the red end of the spectrum). What are left to be reflected are colors at the blue end of the spectrum.

The atmosphere of Neptune is mainly composed of hydrogen, with helium and traces of methane and ammonia.

Neptune is a dynamic planet even though it receives only three percent as much sunlight as Jupiter does. Several large, dark spots are prominent features on the planet. The largest spot is about the size of the Earth and was designated the "Great Dark Spot" by its discoverers. It appears to be an anticyclone similar to Jupiter's Great Red Spot. While Neptune's Great Dark Spot is comparable in size, relative to the planet, and at the same latitude (22° south latitude) as Jupiter's Great Red Spot, it is far more variable in size and shape than its Jovian counterpart. Bright, wispy "cirrus-type" clouds overlay the Great Dark Spot at its southern and northeastern boundaries.

At about 42° south, a bright, irregularly shaped, eastward-moving cloud circles much faster than does the Great Dark Spot, "scooting" around Neptune in about 16 hours. This "scooter" may be a cloud plume rising between cloud decks.

Another spot, designated "D2," is located far to the south of the Great Dark Spot at 55° S latitude. It is almond-shaped, with a bright central core, and moves eastward around the planet in about 16 hours.

The atmosphere above Neptune's clouds is hotter near the equator, cooler in the mid-latitudes, and warm again at the south pole. Temperatures in the stratosphere were measured to be 750 kelvins (900° F), while at the 100 millibar pressure level, they were measured to be 55° K (–360° F).

Long, bright clouds, reminiscent of cirrus clouds on Earth, were seen high in Neptune's atmosphere. They appear to form above most of the methane, and consequently are not blue.

At northern low latitudes (27° N), *Voyager* captured images of cloud streaks casting their shadows on cloud decks estimated to be about 50 to 100 kilometers (30 to 60 miles) below. The widths of these cloud streaks range from 50 to 200 kilometers (30 to 125 miles). Cloud streaks were also seen in the southern polar regions (71° S) where the cloud heights were about 50 kilometers (30 miles).

Most of the winds on Neptune blow in a westward direction, which is retrograde, or opposite to the rotation of the planet. Near the Great Dark Spot, there are retrograde winds blowing up to 1,500 miles an hour—the strongest winds measured on any planet.

1. Astronomers have studied Neptune since Sept. 23, 1846, when Johann Gottfried Galle, of the Berlin Observatory, and Louis d'Arrest, an astronomy student, discovered the eighth planet on the basis of mathematical predictions by Urbain Jean Joseph Le Verrier. Similar predictions were made independently by John Couch Adams. Galileo Galilei had seen Neptune during several nights of observing Jupiter, in January 1613, but didn't realize he was seeing a new planet.

2. These four planets are about 4 to 12 times greater in diameter than Earth. They have no solid surfaces, but possess massive atmospheres that contain substantial amounts of hydrogen and helium with traces of other gases.

The Magnetic Field

Neptune's magnetic field is tilted 47 degrees from the planet's rotation axis, and is offset at least 0.55 radii (about 13,500 kilometers or 8,500 miles) from the physical center. The dynamo electric currents produced within the planet, therefore, must be relatively closer to the surface than for Earth, Jupiter, or Saturn. Because of its unusual orientation, and the tilt of the planet's rotation axis, Neptune's magnetic field goes through dramatic changes as the planet rotates in the solar wind.

Voyager's planetary radio astronomy instrument measured the periodic radio waves generated by the magnetic field and determined that the rotation rate of the interior of Neptune is 16 hours 7 minutes.

Voyager also detected auroras, similar to the northern and southern lights on Earth, in Neptune's atmosphere. Unlike those on Earth, due to Neptune's complex magnetic field, the auroras are extremely complicated processes that occur over wide regions of the planet, not just near the planet's magnetic poles.

Neptune's Moons

Triton

The largest of Neptune's eight known satellites, Triton is different from all other icy moons that *Voyager* has studied. Triton circles Neptune in a tilted, circular, retrograde orbit, completing an orbit in 5.875 days at an average distance of 330,000 kilometers (205,000 miles) above the planet's cloud tops.

Triton shows evidence of a remarkable geologic history, and *Voyager 2* images show active geyser-like eruptions spewing invisible nitrogen gas and dark dust particles 2 to eight kilometers (1 to 5 miles) into space.

Triton is about three-quarters the size of Earth's moon and has a diameter of about 2,705 kilometers (1,680 miles), and a mean density of about 2.066 grams per cubic centimeter. (The density of water is 1.0 gram per cubic centimeter.) This means that Triton contains more rock in its interior than the icy satellites of Saturn and Uranus do.

The relatively high density and the retrograde orbit offer strong evidence that Triton did not originate near Neptune, but is a captured object.

An extremely thin atmosphere extends as much as 800 kilometers (500 miles) above the satellite's surface. Tiny nitrogen ice particles may form thin clouds a few kilometers above the surface. Triton is very bright, reflecting 60 to 95% of the sunlight that strikes it. (By comparison, Earth's moon reflects only 11 percent.)

The atmospheric pressure at Triton's surface is about 14 microbars, a mere 1/70,000th the surface pressure on Earth. Temperature at the surface is about 38 kelvins (–391° F), making it the coldest surface of any body yet visited in the solar system.

The Smaller Satellites

In addition to the previously known moons Triton and Nereid, *Voyager 2* found six more satellites, making the total eight.

Nereid

Nereid was discovered in 1948 through Earth-based telescopes. Little is known about Nereid, which is slightly smaller than Proteus, having a diameter of 340 kilometers (211 miles). The satellite's surface reflects about 14% of the sunlight that strikes it. Nereid's orbit is the most eccentric in the solar system, ranging from about 1,353,600 km (841,100 miles) to 9,623,700 (5,980,200 mi.).

Proteus

Like all six of Neptune's recently discovered small satellites, it is one of the darkest objects in the solar system—"as dark as soot" is a good description. It reflects only 6% of the sunlight that strikes it. Proteus is an ellipsoid about 258 kilometers (415 miles) in diameter, larger than Nereid. It circles Neptune at a distance of about 92,800 kilometers (57,700 miles) above the cloud tops, and completes one orbit in 26 hours 54 minutes. Scientists say that it is about as large as a satellite can be without being pulled into a spherical shape by its own gravity.

Larissa

This object is only about 48,800 kilometers (30,300 miles) from Neptune and circles the planet in 13 hours 18 minutes. Its diameter is 190 kilometers (120 miles).

Despina

The satellite is 27,700 kilometers (17,200 miles) from Neptune's clouds and makes one orbit every 8 hours. Its diameter is about 150 kilometers (90 miles).

Galatea

It lies 37,200 kilometers (23,100 miles) from Neptune. Its diameter is 180 kilometers (110 miles) and it completes an orbit in 10 hours 18 minutes.

Thalassa

The satellite appears to be about 80 kilometers (50 miles) in diameter. It orbits Neptune in 7 hours 30 minutes some 25,200 kilometers (15,700 miles) above the cloud tops.

Naiad

The last satellite discovered, it is about 60 kilometers (37 miles) in diameter and orbits Neptune about 23,200 kilometers (14,400 miles) above the clouds in 7 hours 6 minutes.

Proteus and its tiny companions are cratered and irregularly shaped—they are not round—and show no signs of any geologic modifications. All circle the planet in the same direction as Neptune rotates, and remain close to Neptune's equatorial plane.

Neptune's Rings

Voyager found four rings and evidence of ring *arcs* or incomplete rings. The "Main Ring" orbits Neptune at about 38,100 kilometers (23,700 miles) above the cloud tops. The "Inner Ring " is about 28,400 kilometers (17,700 miles) from Neptune's cloud tops. An "Inside Diffuse Ring"—a complete ring—is located about 17,100 kilometers (10,600 miles) from the planet's cloud tops. Some scientists suspect that this ring may extend all the way down to Neptune's cloud tops. An area called "the Plateau" is a broad, diffuse sheet of fine material just outside the so-called "Inner Ring." The fine material is approximately the size of smoke particles. All other rings contain a greater proportion of larger material.

Pluto

Pluto, the outermost and smallest planet in the solar system, is the only planet not visited by an exploring spacecraft. So little is known about it, that it is difficult to classify. Its distance is so great that the Hubble Space Telescope cannot reveal its surface features. Appropriately named for the Roman god of the underworld, it must be frozen, dark, and dead. Pluto's mean distance from the Sun is 5,900 million kilometers (3,666 million miles).

In 1978, light curve studies gave evidence of a moon revolving around Pluto with the same period as Pluto's rotation. Therefore, it stays over the same point on Pluto's surface. In addition, it keeps the same face toward the planet. The satellite was later named Charon and is estimated to be about 1,284 kilometers (798 miles) in diameter. Recent estimates indicate Pluto's diameter is about about 2,290 kilometers (1,423 miles), making the pair more like a double planet than any other in the solar system. Previously, the Earth-Moon system held this distinction. The density of Pluto is slightly greater than that of water.

There is evidence that Pluto has an atmosphere containing methane and polar ice caps that increase and decrease in size with the planet's seasons. It is not known to have water.

Pluto was predicted by calculation when Percival Lowell (1855–1916) noticed irregularities in the orbits of Uranus and Neptune. Clyde Tombaugh (1906–) discovered the planet in 1930, precisely where Lowell predicted it would be. The name Pluto was chosen because the first two letters represent the initials of Percival Lowell.

• Pluto has the most eccentric orbit in the solar system, bringing it at times closer to the Sun than Neptune. Pluto approached the perihelion of its orbit on Sept. 5, 1989, and for the rest of this century will be closer to the Sun than Neptune. Even then, it can be seen only with a large telescope.

The Asteroids

Between the orbits of Mars and Jupiter are an estimated 30,000 pieces of rocky debris, known collectively as the asteroids, or planetoids. The first and, incidentally, the largest (Ceres) was discovered during the New Year's night of 1801 by the Italian astronomer Father Piazzi (1746–1826), and its orbit was calculated by the German mathematician Karl Friedrich Gauss (1777–1855). Gauss invented a new method of calculating orbits on that occasion. A German amateur astronomer, the physician Olbers (1748–1840), discovered the second asteroid, Pallas. The number now known, catalogued, and named is over 5,000 and could reach 10,000 by the end of the 20th century. A few asteroids do not move in orbits beyond the orbit of Mars, but in orbits which cross the orbit of Mars. The first of them was named Eros because of this peculiar orbit. It had become the rule to bestow female names on the asteroids, but when it was found that Eros crossed the orbit of a major planet, it received a male name. Since then around two dozen orbit-crossers have been discovered, and they are often referred to as the "male asteroids." A few of them—Albert, Adonis, Apollo, Amor, and Icarus—cross the orbit of the Earth, and two of them may come closer than our Moon; but the crossing is like a bridge crossing a highway, not like two highways intersecting. Hence there is very little danger of collision from these bodies. They are all small, three to five miles in diameter, and therefore very difficult objects to identify, even when quite close. Some scientists believe the asteroids represent the remains of an exploded planet. Asteroid 1992 AD, discovered January 1992, is the outermost asteroid known. It takes 93 years to orbit the Sun. This minor planet's orbit crosses the paths of Saturn, Uranus, and Neptune.

On Oct. 29, 1991, the Galileo spacecraft took a historic photograph of asteroid 951 *Gaspra* from a

The First Ten Minor Planets (Asteroids)

Name	Year of discovery	Mean Distance from sun (millions of miles)	Orbital period (years)	Diameter (miles)	Magnitude
1. Ceres	1801	257.0	4.60	485	7.4
2. Pallas	1802	257.4	4.61	304	8.0
3. Juno	1804	247.8	4.36	118	8.7
4. Vesta	1807	219.3	3.63	243	6.5
5. Astraea	1845	239.3	4.14	50	9.9
6. Hebe	1847	225.2	3.78	121	8.5
7. Iris	1847	221.4	3.68	121	8.4
8. Flora	1847	204.4	3.27	56	8.9
9. Metis	1848	221.7	3.69	78	8.9
10. Hygeia	1849	222.6	5.59	40 (?)	9.5

distance of 10,000 miles (16,200 kilometers) away. It was the first close-up photo ever taken of an asteroid in space.

Gaspra was discovered to be an irregular, potato-shaped object about 12.5 mi (20 km) by 7.5 mi (12 km) by 7 mi (11 km) in size. Its surface is covered with a layer of loose rubble and its terrain is covered with several dozen small craters.

Scientists believe that *Gaspra* is a fragment of a larger body which was shattered from collisions with other asteroids.

The asteroid was named after a Black Sea retreat favored by Russian astronomer Grigoriy N. Neujmin who discovered it in 1916.

Comets

Comets, according to the noted astronomer, Fred L. Whipple (1906–   ), are enormous "snowballs" of frozen gases (mostly carbon dioxide, methane, and water vapor) and contain very little solid material. The whole behavior of comets can then be explained as the behavior of frozen gas being heated by the Sun. When the comet Kohoutek made its first appearance to man in 1973, its behavior seemed to confirm this theory and later, the international study by five spacecraft that encountered Comet Halley in March 1986 confirmed Whipple's idea of the make-up of comets.

Since comets appear in the sky without any warning, people in classical times and especially during the Middle Ages believed that they had a special meaning, which, of course, was bad. Since a natural catastrophe of some sort of a military conflict occurs every year, it was quite simple to blame the comet that happened to be visible. But even in the past, there were some people who used logical reasoning. When, in Roman times, a comet was blamed for the loss of a battle and hence was called a "bad omen," a Roman writer observed that the victors in the battle probably did not think so.

Up until the middle of the sixteenth century, comets were believed to be phenomena of the upper atmosphere; they were usually "explained" as "burning vapors" which had risen from "distant swamps." That nobody had ever actually seen burning vapors rise from a swamp did not matter.

But a large comet which appeared in 1577 was carefully observed by Tycho Brahe (1546–1601), a Danish astronomer who is often, and with the best of reasons, called "eccentric" but who insisted on precise measurements for everything. It was Tycho Brahe's accumulation of literally thousands of precise measurements which later enable his younger collaborator, Johannes Kepler (1571–1630), to discover the laws of planetary motion. Measuring the motion of the comet of 1577, Tycho Brahe could show that it had been far beyond the atmosphere, even though he could not give figures for the distance. Tycho Brahe's work proved that comets were astronomical and not meteorological phenomena.

In 1682, the second Astronomer Royal of Great Britain, Dr. Edmond Halley (1656–1742), checked the orbit of a bright comet that was in the sky then and compared it with earlier comet orbits which were known in part. Halley found that the comet of 1682 was the third to move through what appeared to be the same orbit. And the three appearances were roughly 76 years apart. Halley concluded that this was the same comet, moving around the Sun in a closed orbit, like the planets. He predicted that it would reappear in 1758 or 1759. Halley himself died in 1742, but a large comet appeared sixteen years after his death as predicted and was immediately referred to as "Halley's comet."

In the Spring of 1973, the discovery of comet Kohoutek, apparently headed for a close-Christmastime rendezvous with the Sun, created worldwide excitement. The comet was a visual disappointment, but turned out to be a treasure trove of information on these little-understood celestial objects. Given an unprecedented advance notice of nine months on the advent of the fiery object, scientists were able to study the comet in visible, ultraviolet and infrared light; with optical telescopes, radio telescopes, and radar. They observed it from the ground, from high-flying aircraft, with instruments aboard unmanned satellites, with sounding rockets, and telescopes and cameras on the Earth-orbiting Skylab space station.

Halley's Comet appeared again in 1986, sparking a worldwide effort to study it up close. Five satellites in all took readings from the comet at various distances. Two Soviet craft, *Vega 1* and *Vega 2,* went in close to provide detailed pictures of the comet, including the first of the comet's core. The European Space Agency's craft, *Giotto,* entered the comet itself, coming to within 450 miles of the comet's center and successfully passing through its tail. In addition, two Japanese craft, the *Suisei* and the *Sakigake,* passed at a longer distance in order to analyze the cloud and tail of the comet and the effect of solar radiation upon it. The United States declined to launch a similar mission, citing budgetary constraints imposed by the shuttle program. A space telescope was to study Halley's Comet but was destroyed in the *Challenger* disaster.

The information gained included measurements of the size of the nucleus, an idea of its configuration and the rate of its rotation. The gas and dust of the comet were analyzed as was the material of the tail. This information is considered important because comets are believed to be debris from the formation of the solar system and to have changed little since then.

Astronomers refer to comets as "periodic" or as "non-periodic" comets, but the latter term does not mean that these comets have no period; it merely means that their period is not known. The actual periods of comets run from 3.3 years (the shortest known) to many thousands of years. Their orbits are elliptical, like those of the planets, but they are very eccentric, long and narrow ellipses. Only comet Schwassmann-Wachmann has an orbit which has such a low eccentricity (for a cometary orbit) that it could be the orbit of a minor planet.

When a comet, coming from deep space, approaches the Sun, it is at first indistinguishable from a minor planet. Somewhere between the orbits of Mars and Jupiter its outline becomes fuzzy; it is said to develop a "coma" (the word used here is the Latin word *coma*, which means "hair," not the phonetically identical Greek word which means "deep sleep"). Then, near the orbit of Mars, the comet develops its tail, which at first trails behind. This grows steadily as the comet comes closer and closer to the Sun. As it rounds the Sun (as first noticed by Girolamo Fracastoro, 1483–1553) the tail always points away from the Sun so that the comet, when moving away from the Sun, points its tail ahead like the landing lights of an airplane.

The reason for this behavior is that the tail is pushed in these directions by the radiation pressure of the Sun. It sometimes happens that a comet loses its tail at perihelion; it then grows another one. Although the tail is clearly visible against the black of the sky, it is very tenuous. It has been said that if the tail of Halley's comet could be compressed to the density of iron, it would fit into a small suitcase.

Although very low in mass, comets are among the largest members of the solar system. The nucleus of a comet may be up to 10,000 miles in diameter; its coma between 10,000 and 50,000 miles in diameter; and its tail as long as 28 million miles.

Meteors and Meteorites

The term "meteor" for what is usually called a "shooting star" bears an unfortunate resemblance to the term "meteorology," the science of weather and weather forecasting. This resemblance is due to an ancient misunderstanding which wrongly considered meteors an atmospheric phenomenon. Actually, the streak of light in the sky that scientists call a meteor is essentially an astronomical phenomenon: the entry of a small piece of cosmic matter into our atmosphere.

The distinction between "meteors" and "fireballs" (formerly also called "bolides") is merely one of convenience; a fireball is an unusually bright meteor. Incidentally, it also means that a fireball is larger than a faint meteor.

Bodies which enter our atmosphere become visible when they are about 60 miles above the ground. The fact that they grow hot enough to emit light is not due to the "friction" of the atmosphere, as one can often read. The phenomenon responsible for the heating is one of compression. Unconfined air cannot move faster than the speed of sound. Since the entering meteorite moves with 30 to 60 times the speed of sound, the air simply cannot get out of the way. Therefore, it is compressed like the air in the cylinder of a Diesel engine and is heated by compression. This heat—or part of it—is transferred to the moving body. The details of this process are now fairly well understood as a result of re-entry tests with ballistic-missile nose cones.

The average weight of a body producing a faint "shooting star" is only a small fraction of an ounce. Even a bright fireball may not weigh more than 2 or 3 pounds. Naturally, the smaller bodies are worn to dust by the passage through the atmosphere; only rather large ones reach the ground. Those that are found are called meteorites. (The "meteor," to repeat, is the term for the light streak in the sky.)

The largest meteorite known is still imbedded in the ground near Grootfontein in SW Africa and is estimated to weight 70 tons. The second largest known is the 34-ton Anighito (on exhibit in the Hayden Planetarium, New York), which was found by Admiral Peary in 1892 at Cape York in Greenland. The largest meteorite found in the United States is the Willamette meteorite (found in Oregon, weight ca. 15 tons), but large portions of this meteorite weathered away before it was found. Its weight as it struck the ground may have been 20 tons.

All these are iron meteorites (an iron meteorite normally contains about 7% nickel), which form one class of meteorites. The other class consists of the stony meteorites, and between them there are the so-called "stony irons." The so-called "tektites" consist of glass similar to our volcanic glass obsidian, and because of the similarity, there is doubt in a number of cases whether the glass is of terrestrial or of extra-terrestrial origin.

Though no meteorite larger than the Grootfontein is actually known, we do know that the Earth has, on occasion, been struck by much larger bodies. Evidence for such hits are the meteorite craters, of which an especially good example is located near the Cañon Diablo in Arizona. Another meteor crater in the United States is a rather old crater near Odessa, Texas. A large number of others are known, especially in eastern Canada; and for many "probables," meteoric origin has now been proved.

Some scientists theorize that the mass extermination of dinosaurs from the face of the Earth 65 million years ago was due to a large meteor that struck out planet at that time.

The meteor showers are caused by multitudes of very small bodies travelling in swarms. The Earth travels in its orbit through these swarms like a car driving through falling snow. The point from which the meteors seem to emanate is called the *radiant* and is named for the constellation in that area. The Perseid meteor shower in August is the most spectacular of the year, boasting at peak roughly 60 meteors per hour under good atmospheric conditions. The presence of a bright moon diminishes the number of visible meteors.

The Constellations

Constellations are groupings of stars which form patterns that can be easily recognized and remembered, for example, Orion and the Big Dipper. The Big Dipper is actually an asterism, not a constellation, because it is only part of the constellation Ursa Major (the Big Bear). Actually, the stars of the majority of all constellations do not "belong together." Usually they are at greatly varying distances from the Earth and just happen to lie more or less in the same line of sight as seen from our solar system. But in a few cases the stars of a constellation are actually as-

The 88 Recognized Constellations

In astronomical works, the Latin names of the constellations are used. The letter N or S following the Latin name indicates whether the constellation is located to the north or south of the Zodiac. The letter Z indicates that the constellation is within the Zodiac.

Latin name	Letter	English version
Andromeda	N	Andromeda
Antlia	S	Airpump
Apus	S	Bird of Paradise
Aquarius	Z	Water Bearer
Aquila	N	Eagle
Ara	S	Altar
Aries	Z	Ram
Auriga	N	Charioteer
Boötes	N	Herdsmen
Caelum	S	Sculptor's Tool
Camelopardalis	N	Giraffe
Cancer	Z	Crab
Canes Venatici	N	Hunting Dogs
Canis Major	S	Great Dog
Canis Minor	S	Little Dog
Capricornus	Z	Goat (or Sea-Goat)
Carina	S	Keel (of Argo)[1]
Cassiopeia	N	Cassiopeia
Centaurus	S	Centaur
Cepheus	N	Cepheus
Cetus	S	Whale
Chameleon	S	Chameleon
Circinus	S	Compasses
Columba	S	Dove
Coma Berenices	N	Berenice's Hair
Corona Australis	S	Southern Crown
Corona Borealis	N	Northern Crown
Corvus	S	Crow (Raven)
Crater	S	Cup
Crux	S	Southern Cross
Cygnus	N	Swan

Latin name	Letter	English version
Delphinus	N	Dolphin
Dorado	S	Swordfish (Goldfish)
Draco	N	Dragon
Equuleus	N	Filly
Eridanus	S	Eridanus (river)
Fornax	S	Furnace
Gemini	Z	Twins
Grus	S	Crane
Hercules	N	Hercules
Horologium	S	Clock
Hydra	N	Sea Serpent
Hydrus	S	Water Snake
Indus	S	Indian
Lacerta	N	Lizard
Leo	Z	Lion
Leo Minor	N	Little Lion
Lepus	S	Hare
Libra	Z	Scales
Lupus	S	Wolf
Lynx	N	Lynx
Lyra	N	Lyre (Harp)
Mensa	S	Table (mountain)
Microscopium	S	Microscope
Monoceros	S	Unicorn
Musca	S	Southern Fly
Norma	S	Rule (straightedge)
Octans	S	Octant
Ophiuchus	N	Serpent-Bearer
Orion	S	Orion

Latin name	Letter	English version
Pavo	S	Peacock
Pegasus	N	Pegasus
Perseus	N	Perseus
Phoenix	S	Phoenix
Pictor	S	Painter (or his Easel)
Pisces	Z	Fishes
Piscis Austrinus	S	Southern Fish
Puppis	S	Poop (of Argo)[1]
Pyxis	S	Mariner's Compass
Reticulum	S	Net
Sagitta	N	Arrow
Sagittarius	Z	Archer
Scorpius	Z	Scorpion
Sculptor	S	Sculptor
Scutum	N	Shield
Serpens	N	Serpent
Sextans	S	Sextant
Taurus	Z	Bull
Telescopium	S	Telescope
Triangulum	N	Triangle
Triangulum Australe	S	Southern Triangle
Tucana	S	Toucan
Ursa Major	N	Big Dipper
Ursa Minor	N	Little Dipper
Vela	S	Sail (of Argo)[1]
Virgo	Z	Virgin
Volans	S	Flying Fish
Vulpecula	N	Fox

1. The original constellation Argo Navis (the Ship Argo) has been divided into Carina, Puppis, and Vela. Normally the brightest star in each constellation is designated by alpha, the first letter of the Greek alphabet, the second brightest by beta, the second letter of the Greek alphabet, and so forth. But the Greek letters run through Carina, Puppis, and Vela as if it were still one constellation.

sociated; most of the bright stars of the Big Dipper travel together and form what astronomers call an open cluster.

If you observe a planet, say Mars, for one complete revolution, you will see that it passes successively through twelve constellations. All planets (except Pluto at certain times) can be observed only in these twelve constellations, which form the so-called Zodiac, and the Sun also moves through the Zodiacal signs, though the Sun's apparent movement is actually caused by the movement of the Earth.

Although the constellations are due mainly to the optical accident of line of sight and have no real significance, astronomers have retained them as reference areas. It is much easier to speak of a star in Orion than to give its geometrical position in the sky. During the Astronomical Congress of 1928, it was decided to recognize 88 constellations. A description of their agreed-upon boundaries was published at Cambridge, England, in 1930, under the title *Atlas Céleste.*

The Auroras

The "northern lights" *(Aurora borealis)* as well as the "southern lights" *(Aurora australis)* are upper-atmosphere phenomena of astronomical origin. The auroras center around the magnetic (not the geographical) poles of the Earth, which explains why, in the Western Hemisphere, they have been seen as far to the south as New Orleans and Florida while the equivalent latitude in the Eastern Hemisphere never sees an aurora. The northern magnetic pole happens to be in the Western Hemisphere.

The lower limit of an aurora is at about 50 miles. Upper limits have been estimated to be as high as 400 miles. Since about 1880, a connection between the auroras on Earth and the sun spots has been suspected and has gradually come to be accepted. It was said that the sun spots probably eject "particles" (later the word *electrons* was substituted) which on striking the Earth's atmosphere, cause the auroras. But this explanation suffered from certain difficulties. Sometimes a very large sun spot group on the Sun, with individual spots bigger than the Earth itself, would not cause an aurora. Moreover, even if a sun spot caused an aurora, the time that passed between the appearance of the one and the occurrence of the other was highly unpredictable.

This problem of the time lag is, in all probability, solved by the discovery of the Van Allen layer by artificial satellite *Explorer I.* The Van Allen layer[1] is

1. Named after the American physicist, James Alfred Van Allen (1914–   ) who discovered the broad bands of intense radiation surrounding the Earth in 1958.

a double layer of charged sub-atomic particles around the Earth. The inner layer, with its center some 1,500 miles from the ground, reaches from about 40° N. to about 40° S. and does not touch the atmosphere. The outer layer, much larger and with its center several thousand miles from the ground, does touch the atmosphere in the vicinity of the magnetic poles.

It seems probable that the "leakage" of electrons from the outer Van Allen layer causes the auroras. A new burst of electrons from the Sun seems to be caught in the outer layer first. Under the assumption that all electrons are first caught in the outer layer, the time lag can be understood. There has to be an "overflow" from the outer layer to produce an aurora.

The Atmosphere

Astronomically speaking, the presence of our atmosphere is deplorable. Though reasonably transparent to visible light, the atmosphere may absorb as much as 60% of the visible and near-visible light. It is opaque to most other wave-lengths, except certain fairly short radio waves. In addition to absorbing much light, our atmosphere bends light rays entering at a slant (for a given observer) so that the true position of a star close to the horizon is not what it seems to be. One effect is that we see the Sun above the horizon before it actually is. And the unsteady movement of the atmosphere causes the "twinkling" of the stars, which may be romantic but is a nuisance when it comes to observing.

The composition of our atmosphere near the ground is 78% nitrogen and 21% oxygen, the remaining 1% consisting of other gases, most of it argon. The composition stays the same to an altitude of at least 70 miles (except that higher up two impurities, carbon dioxide and water vapor, are missing), but the pressure drops very fast. At 18,000 feet, half of the total mass of the atmosphere is below, and at 100,000 feet, 99% of the mass of the atmosphere is below. The upper limit of the atmosphere is usually given as 120 miles; no definitive figure is possible, since there is no boundary line between the incredibly attenuated gases 120 miles up and space.

Astronomical Telescopes

Optical telescopes used in astronomy are of two basic kinds: refracting and reflecting. In the *refractor telescope,* a lens is used to collect light from a distant object and bring it to a focus. A second lens, the eyepiece, then magnifies the image which may be examined visually or photographed directly. The *reflector telescope* uses a concave mirror instead of a lens, which reflects the light rays back toward the upper end of the telescope where they are magnified and observed or photographed. Most large optical telescopes now being built are reflectors.

Radio telescopes are used to study radio waves coming from outside the Earth's atmosphere. The waves are gathered by an antenna or "dish," which is a parabolic reflecting surface made of metal or finely meshed wire. Radio signals have been received from the Sun, Moon, and planets, and from the center of our galaxy and other galaxies. Radio signals are the means by which the distant and mysterious quasars and pulsars were discovered.

Searching for the Big Broadcast

An extensive, ten-year international search for intelligent life beyond the solar system began on Oct. 12, 1992, using the world's largest radio telescopes. They include those of the Arecibo Observatory, the Greenbank 140-foot telescope, NASA's 112-foot Goldstone radio antenna, and the Parks Radio Observatory in Australia.

Astronomers hope to uncover interstellar messages that may have been transmitted from other intelligent life forms that may exist in an area of some 1,000 Milky Way stars within 80 light years of the Earth. □

Some Giant Telescopes

• The world's largest fixed-dish radio telescope (1963) is located near Arecibo, Puerto Rico. It is 1,000 ft (35 m) in diameter and spans some 25 acres.

• The Very Large Array (VLA) telescope (1980) near Socorro, N.M. is the world's most powerful radio telescope. It is Y-shaped and has 27 separate mobile antennas (each 82 ft in diameter) and is spread out over about a 25-mile area.

• The world's largest fully-steerable radio telescope (1972) located at Effelsberg, Germany, has a 100-meter (328 ft) antenna.

• The Very Long Baseline Array (VLBA) radio telescope was scheduled for operation in August 1993. The VLBA is a system linking ten widely scattered radio dishes—across the continental U.S., Hawaii, and the U.S. Virgin Islands—that will act as a single telescope. Each of the ten dish-shaped antenna is 82 feet (25.29 meters) in diameter. The VLBA is controlled by a "correlator" computer system located at Socorro, New Mexico.

The Very Long Baseline Array will study the most far out violent phenomena and exotic objects in the universe such as quasars, pulsars, and colliding galaxies with unprecedented accuracy. It should have a "seeing" ability that is 500 times better than the Hubble space telescope after it is repaired to operate in perfect condition.

• The Very Large Telescope of the European Southern Observatory (ESO) located at La Silla, Chile, will be the world's largest ground-based reflector when it is completed around the year 2000. It will consist of four 8-meter (26.24 ft) telescopes whose mirrors will combine their images to simulate a single 16 meter (52.49 ft) diameter telescope thereby giving it the power of a 630-inch primary mirror.

• The W.M. Keck Telescope (1991) at Mauna Kea, Hawaii, is the world's most powerful reflector telescope. It has a primary mirror composed of 36 hexagonal segments, each 1.8 meters in size. The Keck Telescope has a light gathering power four times greater than the 200-inch Hale.

• The 200-inch (5 meter) Hale telescope at Mount Palomar, Calif. (1948) is the second largest reflector in use.

• The 236-inch Special Astrophysical Observatory (1976) at Zelenchukskaya on the northern slopes of the Caucasus Mountains in the Russian Federation is the world's largest reflector telescope in use. However, problems with it make it less useful than the 200-inch Hale.

• The 40-inch (1.01 meter) telescope at Yerkes Observatory (1897) at Williams Bay, Wisc. is the world's largest refracting telescope.

• The Edwin P. Hubble Space Telescope was released by the space shuttle *Discovery* on April 25, 1990. It is able to peer far out in space and back in time, producing imagery of unprecedented clarity, of galaxies, star systems, and some of the universe's more intriguing objects: quasars, pulsars, and exploding galaxies. It can distinguish fine details—in planetary atmospheres or nearby star fields—with ten times the clarity of the best ground observatories. When pointed at Jupiter, for example, the telescope provides images comparable to those from Voyager flybys.

The $1.6-billion Space Telescope has a primary mirror 2.4 m (94 inches) in diameter. The mirror is almost half the diameter of the 5-m (200 inch) telescope at Mt. Palomar, the most powerful ground-based telescope in the western world.

After it was placed in orbit at 380 miles (611.5 km) altitude, the Hubble Telescope became the principal tool for exploring the universe through this decade and the next.

The Space telescope can view galaxies and quasars over distances up to 14 billion light years. Seeing that far will show us the universe as it was early in its lifetime and will reveal how matter has evolved over the eons. It will also teach us more about the large structure of the universe, providing clues as to whether the universe will continue to expand.

It was discovered in June 1990 that there was a spherical aberration in one of the telescope's mirrors. In 1991, two of the craft's six gyroscopes failed, and a third failed on Nov. 18, 1992, causing additional problems. In the meantime, observations are continuing with the equipment that is working correctly.

NASA plans to have the space shuttle *Endeavour* rendezvous with Hubble in December 1993 and have crew members repair the telescope. The repair mission will cost $630 million. If a second mission is needed, it would be scheduled for six months to a year later.

Phenomena, 1994

Configurations of Sun, Moon, and Planets

NOTE: The hour listings are in Universal Time. For conversion to United States time zones, see conversion table on next page.

JANUARY

d	h	
2	06	Earth at perihelion
3	20	Mercury in superior conjunction
5	00	LAST QUARTER
6	01	Moon at perigee
6	22	Jupiter 3° N of Moon
11	08	Neptune in conjunction with Sun
11	23	NEW MOON
12	17	Uranus in conjunction with Sun
15	00	Saturn 7° S of Moon
17	02	Venus in superior conjunction
19	05	Moon at apogee
19	20	FIRST QUARTER
27	13	FULL MOON
31	04	Moon at perigee

FEBRUARY

2	04	Mercury 1°.3 N of Saturn
3	08	Jupiter 3° N of Moon
3	08	LAST QUARTER
4	21	Mercury greatest elong. E (18°)
8	08	Neptune 3° S of Moon
8	12	Uranus 5° S of Moon
10	14	NEW MOON
10	18	Mercury stationary
16	02	Moon at apogee
18	18	FIRST QUARTER
20	08	Mercury in inferior conjunction
21	17	Saturn in conjunction with Sun
23	14	Juno stationary
26	01	FULL MOON
27	01	Mercury 4° N of Mars
27	22	Moon at perigee
28	21	Jupiter stationary

MARCH

2	16	Jupiter 2° N of Moon
4	01	Pluto stationary
4	12	Mercury stationary
4	17	LAST QUARTER
7	16	Neptune 4° S of Moon
7	21	Uranus 5° S of Moon
10	04	Mercury 5° S of Moon
10	23	Mars 7° S of Moon
11	04	Saturn 7° S of Moon
12	07	NEW MOON
13	17	Venus 5° S of Moon
14	10	Mars 0°.4 N of Saturn
15	17	Moon at apogee
19	02	Mercury greatest elong W (28°)
20	03	Pallas in conjunction with Sun
20	12	FIRST QUARTER
20	20	Equinox
24	08	Mercury 0°.3 S of Saturn
27	11	FULL MOON
28	06	Moon at perigee
29	23	Jupiter 2° N of Moon

APRIL

3	03	LAST QUARTER
3	22	Neptune 4° S of Moon
4	02	Mercury 1°.5 S of Mars
4	04	Uranus 5° S of Moon
7	16	Saturn 7° S of Moon
9	02	Mars 6° S of Moon
9	11	Mercury 7° S of Moon
11	00	NEW MOON
12	00	Moon at apogee
12	23	Venus 1°.0 S of Moon (Occn.)
15	01	Juno at opposition
19	03	FIRST QUARTER
25	09	Neptune stationary
25	17	Moon at perigee
25	20	FULL MOON
26	05	Jupiter 3° N of Moon
28	05	Vesta in conjunction with Sun
30	09	Jupiter at opposition
30	10	Mercury in superio conjunction

MAY

1	01	Uranus stationary
1	06	Neptune 4° S of Moon
1	12	Uranus 5° S of Moon
2	15	LAST QUARTER
5	00	Venus 6° N of Aldebaran
5	03	Saturn 7° S of Moon
8	04	Mars 4° S of Moon
9	02	Moon at apogee
10	17	NEW MOON (Eclipse)
13	06	Venus 4° S of Moon
15	11	Mercury 8° N of Aldebaran
17	20	Pluto at opposition
18	13	FIRST QUARTER
23	11	Jupiter 3° N of Moon
24	03	Moon at perigee
25	04	FULL MOON (Eclipse)
28	14	Neptune 4° S of Moon
28	20	Uranus 5° S of Moon
30	07	Mercury greatest elong. E (23°)

JUNE

1	04	LAST QUARTER
1	12	Saturn 7° S of Moon
5	13	Moon at apogee
6	05	Mars 2° S of Moon
8	03	Ceres in conjunction with Sun
9	08	NEW MOON
10	05	Venus 5° S of Pollux
11	00	Mercury 3° N of Moon
11	15	Juno stationary
12	12	Mercury stationary
12	13	Venus 7° N of Moon
16	20	FIRST QUARTER
19	16	Jupiter 3° N of Moon
21	07	Moon at perigee
21	15	Solstice
23	12	FULL MOON
24	04	Saturn stationary
24	23	Neptune 4° S of Moon
25	05	Uranus 5° S of Moon
25	10	Mercury in inferior conjunction
28	21	Saturn 7° S of Moon
30	20	LAST QUARTER

Conversion of Universal Time (U. T.) to Civil Time

U.T.	E.D.T.[1]	E.S.T.[2]	C.S.T.[3]	M.S.T.[4]	P.S.T.[5]	U.T.	E.D.T.[1]	E.S.T.[2]	C.S.T.[3]	M.S.T.[4]	P.S.T.[5]
00	*8P	*7P	*6P	*5P	*4P	12	8A	7A	6A	5A	4A
01	*9P	*8P	*7P	*6P	*5P	13	9A	8A	7A	6A	5A
02	*10P	*9P	*8P	*7P	*6P	14	10A	9A	8A	7A	6A
03	*11P	*10P	*9P	*8P	*7P	15	11A	10A	9A	8A	7A
04	M	*11P	*10P	*9P	*8P	16	N	11A	10A	9A	8A
05	1A	M	*11P	*10P	*9P	17	1P	N	11A	10A	9A
06	2A	1A	M	*11P	*10P	18	2P	1P	N	11A	10A
07	3A	2A	1A	M	*11P	19	3P	2P	1P	N	11A
08	4A	3A	2A	1A	M	20	4P	3P	2P	1P	N
09	5A	4A	3A	2A	1A	21	5P	4P	3P	2P	1P
10	6A	5A	4A	3A	2A	22	6P	5P	4P	3P	2P
11	7A	6A	5A	4A	3A	23	7P	6P	5P	4P	3P

1. Eastern Daylight Time. 2. Eastern Standard Time, same as Central Daylight Time. 3. Central Standard Time, same as Mountain Daylight Time. 4. Mountain Standard Time, same as Pacific Daylight Time. 5. Pacific Standard Time. NOTES: *denotes previous day. N = noon. M = midnight.

JULY

2 16 Jupiter stationary
3 05 Moon at apogee
5 05 Mars 0°.3 N of Moon (Occn.)
5 19 Earth at aphelion
6 20 Mercury stationary
7 13 Mercury 1°.3 S of Moon
8 22 NEW MOON
10 17 Venus °.1 N of Regulus
12 12 Venus 7° N of Moon
14 16 Neptune at opposition
16 01 FIRST QUARTER
16 23 Jupiter 3° N of Moon
17 04 Uranus at opposition
17 14 Mercury greatest elong. W (21°)
18 18 Moon at perigee
18 21 Mars 5° N of Aldebaran
22 07 Neptune 4° S of Moon
22 12 Uranus 5° S of Moon
22 20 FULL MOON
26 04 Saturn 7° S of Moon
30 13 LAST QUARTER
30 23 Moon at apogee
31 07 Mercury 6° S of Pollux

AUGUST

3 04 Mars 3° N of Moon
7 09 NEW MOON
9 14 Pluto stationary
10 23 Venus 3° N of Moon
12 23 Moon at perigee
13 01 Mercury in superior conjunction
13 07 Jupiter 2° N of Moon
14 06 FIRST QUARTER
18 14 Neptune 4° S of Moon
18 18 Uranus 5° S of Moon
21 07 FULL MOON
22 10 Saturn 7° S of Moon
24 23 Venus greatest elong. E (46°)
27 18 Moon at apogee
29 07 LAST QUARTER
31 04 Vesta 0°.7 S of Moon (Occn.)
31 21 Venus 0°.7 S of Spica

SEPTEMBER

1 03 Mars 4° N of Moon
1 17 Saturn at opposition
5 19 NEW MOON
7 09 Mercury 3° N of Moon
8 14 Moon at perigee
9 01 Venus 2° S of Moon
9 20 Jupiter 1°.4 N of Moon
12 12 FIRST QUARTER
14 19 Neptune 4° S of Moon
14 23 Uranus 5° S of Moon
18 13 Saturn 7° S of Moon
19 20 FULL MOON
21 13 Mercury 0°.1 S of Spica
23 06 Equinox
24 12 Moon at apogee
24 15 Mars 6° S of Pollux
26 16 Mercury greatest elong. E (26°)
28 00 LAST QUARTER
28 03 Vesta 0°.06 N of Moon (Occn.)
28 22 Venus greatest brilliancy
29 22 Mars 6° N of Moon

OCTOBER

2 03 Uranus stationary
2 14 Neptune stationary
5 04 NEW MOON
6 14 Moon at perigee
6 18 Mercury 3° S of Moon
7 05 Pallas stationary
7 10 Venus 7° S of Moon
7 12 Jupiter 0°.7 N of Moon (Occn.)
9 09 Mercury stationary
11 19 FIRST QUARTER
12 01 Neptune 4° S of Moon
12 04 Uranus 5° S of Moon
12 23 Venus stationary
15 16 Saturn 7° S of Moon
19 12 FULL MOON
21 05 Mercury in inferior conjunction
22 02 Moon at apogee
25 19 Vesta 0°.6 N of Moon (Occn.)
27 17 LAST QUARTER
28 13 Mars 7° N of Moon
29 17 Mercury stationary

NOVEMBER

2 10 Mercury 4° N of Moon
2 23 Venus in inferior conjunction
3 01 Mercury 4° N of Spica
3 14 NEW MOON (Eclipse)
4 00 Moon at perigee
6 01 Mercury greatest elong. W (19°)
6 15 Vesta stationary
8 08 Neptune 4° S of Moon
8 12 Uranus 6° S of Moon
8 20 Pallas at opposition
9 21 Saturn stationary
10 06 FIRST QUARTER
11 21 Saturn 7° S of Moon
12 18 Mercury 5° N of Venus
17 20 Jupiter in conjunction with Sun
18 05 Moon at apogee
18 07 FULL MOON (Penumbral Eclipse)
18 17 Juno in conjunction with Sun
20 13 Pluto in conjunction with Sun
21 16 Venus stationary
22 00 Vesta 1°.0 N of Moon (Occn.)
25 20 Mars 8° N of Moon
26 07 LAST QUARTER
30 14 Venus 2° N of Moon

DECEMBER

2 12 Moon at perigee
3 00 NEW MOON
5 19 Neptune 4° S of Moon
6 00 Uranus 6° S of Moon
8 08 Mars 2° N of Regulus
9 05 Saturn 7° S of Moon
9 11 Venus greatest brilliancy
9 21 FIRST QUARTER
14 03 Mercury in superior conjunction
15 08 Moon at apogee
18 02 FULL MOON
22 02 Solstice
23 15 Mars 9° N of Moon
24 17 Ceres stationary
25 02 Vesta at opposition
25 19 LAST QUARTER
29 05 Venus 3° N of Moon
30 00 Jupiter 1°.1 S of Moon (Occn.)
30 23 Moon at perigee

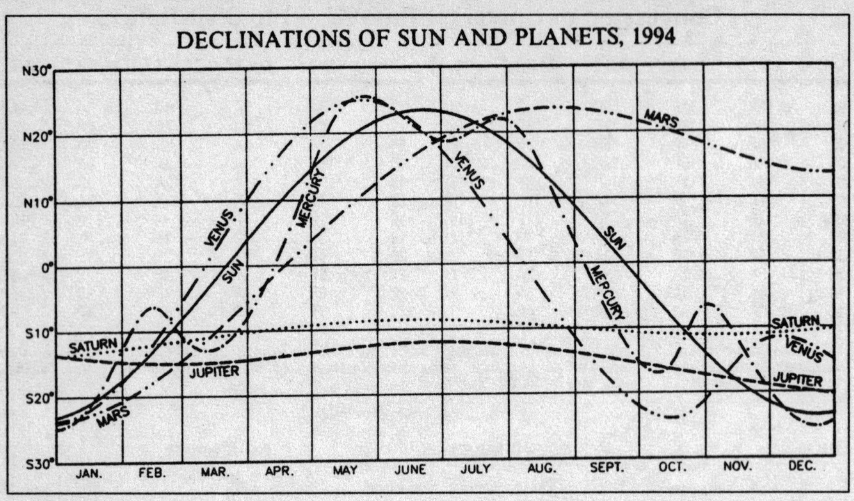

Visibility of Planets, 1994

The planet diagram on page 353 shows, in graphical form for any date during the year, the local mean times of meridian passage of the Sun, of the five planets, Mercury, Venus, Mars, Jupiter, and Saturn, and of every 2^h of right ascension. Intermediate lines, corresponding to particular stars, may be drawn in by the user if desired. The diagram is intended to provide a general picture of the availability of planets and stars for observation during the year.

On each side of the line marking the time of meridian passage of the Sun, a band 45^m wide is shaded to indicate that planets and most stars crossing the meridian within 45^m of the Sun are generally too close to the Sun for observation.

For any date the diagram provides immediately the local mean time of meridian passage of the Sun, planets and stars, and thus the following information:

(a) whether a planet or star is too close to the Sun for observation;

(b) visibility of a planet or star in the morning or evening;

(c) location of a planet or star during twilight;

(d) proximity of planets to stars or other planets.

When the meridian passage of a body occurs at midnight, it is close to opposition to the Sun and is visible all night, and may be observed in both morning and evening twilights. As the time of meridian passage decreases, the body ceases to be observable in the morning, but its altitude above the eastern horizon during evening twilight gradually increases until it is on the meridian at evening twilight. From then onwards the body is observable above the western horizon, its altitude at evening twilight gradually decreasing, until it becomes too close to the Sun for observation. When it again becomes visible, it is seen in the morning twilight, low in the east. Its altitude at morning twilight gradually increases until meridian passage occurs at the time of morning twilight, then as the time of meridian passage decreases to 0^h, the body is observable in the west in the morning twilight with a gradually decreasing altitude, until it once again reaches opposition.

Notes on the visibility of the principal planets in morning and evening twilight are given on page 355. Further information on the visibility of planets may be obtained from the diagram above which shows, in graphical form for any date during the year, the declinations of the bodies plotted on the planet diagram on page 353.

Mercury can only be seen low in the east before sunrise, or low in the west after sunset (about the time of the beginning or end of civil twilight). It is visible in the mornings between the following approximate dates: February 27 to April 22, July 4 to August 5, and October 28 to November 27. The planet is brighter at the end of each period, (the best conditions in northern latitudes occur around the first week of November, and in southern latitudes from mid-March to early April). It is visible in the evenings between the following approximate dates: January 18 to February 14, May 8 to June 16, August 23 to October 15 and December 30 and 31. The planet is brighter at the beginning of each period, (the best conditions in northern latitudes occur during the first week of February and, especially in low northern latitudes, during the last two weeks of May and southern latitudes from the beginning of September until towards mid-October).

Venus is too close to the Sun for observation until the end of February when it appears as a brilliant object in the evening sky. By late October it again becomes too close to the Sun for observation until mid-November when it reappears in the morning sky. Venus is in conjunction with Mercury on November 12.

(Continued on page 354)

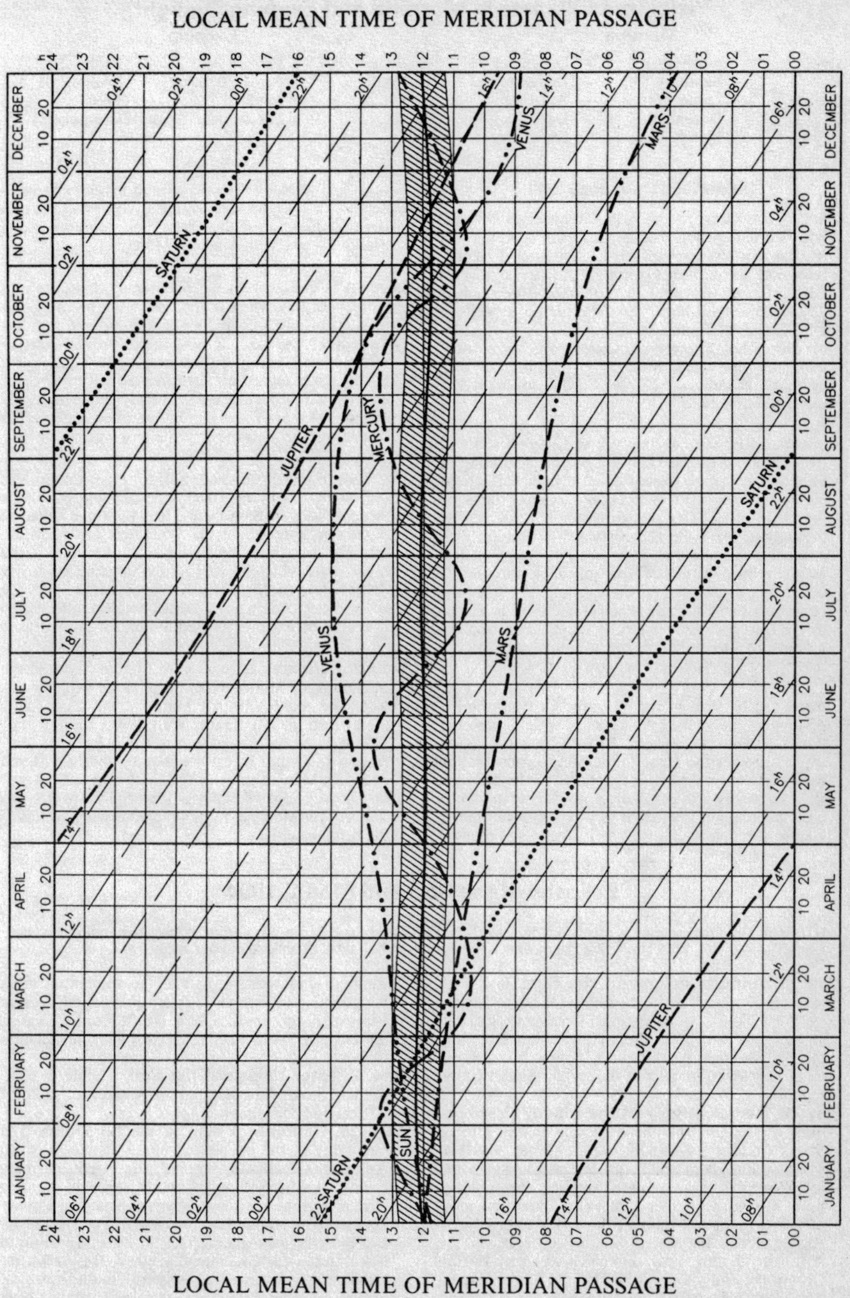
LOCAL MEAN TIME OF MERIDIAN PASSAGE
JANUARY
FEBRUARY
MARCH
APRIL
MAY
JUNE
JULY
AUGUST
SEPTEMBER
OCTOBER
NOVEMBER
DECEMBER
SUN
MERCURY
VENUS
MARS
JUPITER
SATURN
LOCAL MEAN TIME OF MERIDIAN PASSAGE

Visibility of Planets in Morning and Evening Twilight

Morning				Evening			
Venus	November 9	—	December 31	Venus	February 28	—	October 29
Mars	February 28	—	December 31	Jupiter	April 30	—	November 5
Jupiter	January 1	—	April 30	Saturn	January 1	—	February 4
	December 1	—	December 31		September 1	—	December 31
Saturn	March 11	—	September 1				

(Continued from page 352)

Mars is too close to the Sun for observation until late February when it appears in the morring sky in Capricornus. Its westward elongation gradually increases as it passes through Aquarius, Pisces, Aries, Taurus (passing 5° N of *Aldebaran* on July 18), Gemini (passing 6° S of *Pollux* on September 24), Cancer and into Leo (passing 2° N of *Regulus* on December 8), where it can be seen for more than half the night. Mars is in conjunction with Mercury on February 27 and April 4 and with Saturn on March 14.

Jupiter can be seen in the morning sky in Libra at the beginning of the year and by the beginning of February it can be seen for more than half of the night. Its westward elongation increases until on April 30 it is at opposition when it is visible throughout the night. Its eastward elongation then gradually decreases as it passes into Virgo in late May; in mid-August it passes back into Libra where it can be seen in the evening sky until the beginning of November when it becomes too close to the Sun for observation. It reappears at the beginning of December in the morning sky passing into Scorpius in mid-December.

Saturn can be seen in the evening sky from the beginning of the year in Aquarius in which constellation it remains throughout the year. In early February it becomes too close to the Sun for observation until early March when it reappears in the morning sky. Its westward elongation gradually increases until September 1 when it is at opposition and is visible throughout the night. Its eastward elongation then gradually decreases and by early December it can only be seen in the evening sky. Saturn is in conjunction with Mercury on February 2 and March 24 and with Mars on March 14.

Uranus is too close to the Sun for observation until early February when it appears in the morning sky in Sagittarius, in which constellation it remains throughout the year. It is at opposition on July 17 when it can be seen throughout the night, after which its eastward elongation gradually decreases and from mid-October it can only be seen in the evening sky until late December when it again becomes too close to the Sun for observation.

Neptune is too close to the Sun for observation until the beginning of February when it appears in the morning sky in Sagittarius, in which constellation it remains throughout the year. It is at opposition on July 14 when it can be seen throughout the night, after which its eastward elongation gradually decreases and from mid-October it can only be seen in the evening sky until late December when it again becomes too close the Sun for observation.

Do not confuse (1) Mars with Mercury around the beginning of March when Mars is the brighter object. The reddish tint of Mars should assist in its identification. (2) Saturn with Mars around mid-March when Saturn is the brighter object. (3) Mercury with Saturn in early February and late March and with Mars at the end of March and early April; on all occasions Mercury is the brighter object. (4) Venus with Mercury mid-November when Venus is the brighter object. □

Eclipses of the Sun and Moon, 1994

NOTE: The day of an eclipse is given in Universal Time (U.T.) and may start a day earlier or later depending on your time zone. See Phenomena, 1994 table to find time of eclipse in your area.

May 10. Annular eclipse of the Sun. Visible in extreme northeast Asia, North and Central America, West Indies, Arctic regions, Greenland, Iceland, and Europe except in the southeast but including the British Isles, northwestern Africa, and the extreme northwestern part of the former Soviet Union republics.

May 25. Partial eclipse of the Moon. The beginning of the umbral phase visible in the United States (except for the far west, Alaska, and Hawaii), southeastern and south central Canada, Mexico, Central America, South America, the southern tip of Greenland, Iceland, most of Antarctica, most of Africa, most of Europe, the southeastern North Pacific Ocean, the eastern South Pacific Ocean, the Atlantic Ocean, and the southwestern Indian Ocean; the end visible in the United States (except Alaska and Hawaii), Canada (except for the northwest), Mexico, Central America, South America, the southern tip of Greenland, most of Antarctica, southern and western Africa, the southern United Kingdom, southern and western France, the Iberian Peninsula, the southeastern North Pacific Ocean, the eastern South Pacific Ocean, and the Atlantic Ocean.

Nov. 3. Total eclipse of the Sun. Visible in Central and South America, part of Antarctica, south of Africa, and Madagascar.

Nov. 18. Penumbral eclipse of the Moon. The beginning of the penumbral phase visible in North America, Greenland, Iceland, the Arctic regions, Central America, South America, Hawaii, western Africa, Europe, extreme western Asia, the Palmer Peninsula of Antarctica, the eastern Pacific Ocean, and most of the Atlantic Ocean; the end visible in North America, Greenland, Iceland, the Arctic regions, Central America, western South America, Hawaii, northeastern Asia, eastern Australia, New Zealand, the Pacific Ocean, and the western North Atlantic Ocean.

A Lesson in Astronomy—The Celestial Sphere

Illustration by Tony Moller, Courtesy U.S. Naval Observatory.

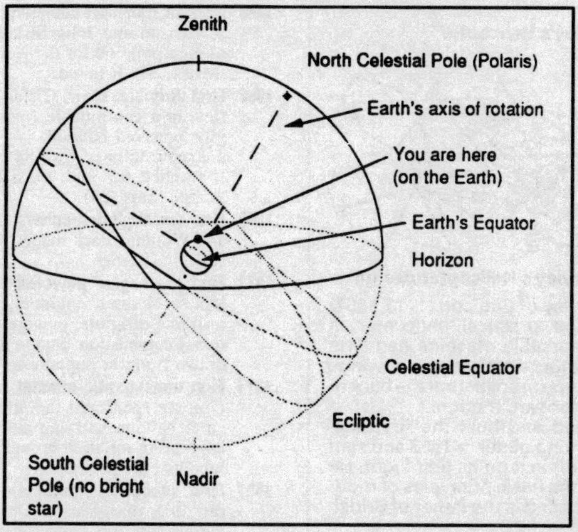

To understand where things are in the sky, and how the locations of the planets relate to each other, you have to understand one of the most basic things about astronomy—the *celestial sphere.*

Imagine, if you will, all the things in the sky—the Sun, Moon, planets, stars, etc.—no matter how far away they actually are, being on a gigantic transparent sphere, with the Earth at its center. The early Greeks believed this celestial sphere to be made out of some crystalline material, at a very great distance from the Earth.

From here things get easy. As the Earth rotates on its axis, we perceive the celestial sphere to be moving, and not the Earth. The sphere has two points around which it rotates, and we call them the celestial poles. The celestial poles are where the Earth's axis penetrates the celestial sphere. The north celestial pole is marked by Polaris, the North Star, which is relatively close to the pole. The south celestial pole has no bright star nearby to mark its place in the sky. Now, if we extend the Earth's equator on to the celestial sphere, we get the celestial equator. The celestial equator is 90° from the celestial poles. Straight up from where you happen to be is called the zenith, and straight down is called the nadir. The zenith forms the apex of the hemisphere of the celestial sphere that is above your horizon at any given time.

Now for something not so easy. As we watch the Sun rise and set on any given day it marks a path in the sky called a diurnal circle. In fact, any object on the celestial sphere will make a diurnal circle—the apparent path of an object made through the course of a day. If you marked the position of the Sun (in Right Ascension and Declination) against the background of stars through the course of a year you would see another path on the celestial sphere—we call it the ecliptic. The ecliptic is the apparent path the Sun makes on the celestial sphere due to the Earth's revolution around the Sun. The ecliptic also represents the plane of the solar system. The inclination of the orbits of all other objects in the solar system are measured against it.

How do astronomers measure things on the celestial sphere? There are two ways. The first way is probably most familiar, called the altitude-azimuth, or horizon system. Altitude is the object's position in degrees above the horizon, and azimuth is the object's direction, measured in degrees from north (0°), moving east (just like a compass, east is 90°, south is 180°, etc.). Altitude-azimuth is always measured from the observer's position, and does not give you a universal position for an object. The best way to mark an object's position in the heavens is to use a fixed set of coordinates, much like the Earth's latitude and longitude. The celestial coordinate system most used is the Right Ascension and Declination system.

Right Ascension is measured in hours, not degrees, starting at the vernal equinox, a zero point equivalent to 0° longitude on the Earth, and is marked in one hour increments, measured east. Each one hour increment equals 15°, and there are 24 hours of Right Ascension. Declination is a measurement of degrees north or south of the celestial equator. Positive is above the celestial equator, and negative is below. For example, the bright star Sirius in the winter sky has a position of 6 hours, 44 minutes Right Ascension, and –16 degrees, 42 minutes Declination (abbreviated 6h 44m and –16° 42′).

The orientation of the observer to the celestial sphere is an important factor you cannot overlook. The first thing you should do is find the North Star. Once you have that in your sights, everything else will fall into place. If you know your latitude, you're in good shape, because your latitude marks your position north of the equator (if you are in the northern hemisphere). Your latitude is equal to the altitude of the North Star above the northern horizon. Subtract your latitude from 90° and you will have the altitude of the celestial equator above your southern horizon. It is best to have a star chart handy during an evening observing session, as most will have the ecliptic charted among the evening constellations.—*Reprinted by courtesy of the U.S. Naval Observatory* □

AVIATION

Famous Firsts in Aviation

Cayley's Helicopter

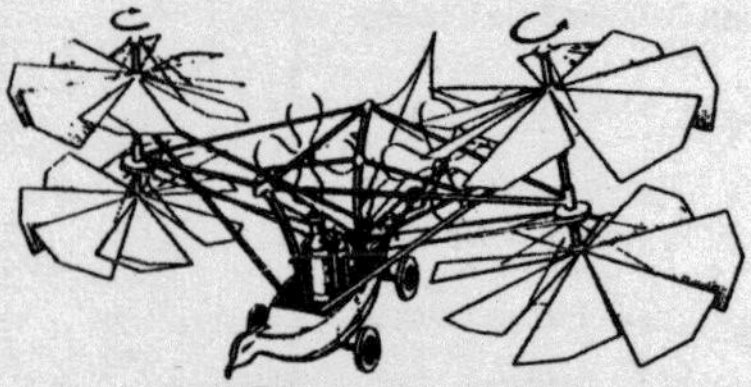

Sir George Cayley's Helicopter design

Sir George Cayley of England (1773-1857) designed the first practical helicopter in 1842-43. His remarkable machine had twin contra-rotating rotors which served as wings and two pusher-type propellers at the back to give the aircraft forward motion.

Cayley designed and built the first successful man-carrying glider in 1853 and sent his coachman aloft in it on its first flight. He also formulated the basic principles of modern aerodynamics and is the father of British aeronautics.

1782 **First balloon flight.** Jacques and Joseph Montgolfier of Annonay, France, sent up a small smoke-filled balloon about mid-November.

1783 **First hydrogen-filled balloon flight.** Jacques A. C. Charles, Paris physicist, supervised construction by A. J. and M. N. Robert of a 13-ft diameter balloon that was filled with hydrogen. It got up to about 3,000 ft and traveled about 16 mi. in a 45-min flight (Aug. 27).

First human balloon flights.A Frenchman, Jean Pilâtre de Rozier made the first captive-balloon ascension (Oct. 15). With the Marquis d'Arlandes, Pilâtre de Rozier made the first free flight, reaching a peak altitude of about 500 ft, and traveling about 5 1/2 mi. in 20 min (Nov. 21).

1784 **First powered balloon.** Gen. Jean Baptiste Marie Meusnier developed the first propeller-driven and elliptically-shaped balloon—the crew cranking three propellers on a common shaft to give the craft a speed of about 3 mph.

First woman to fly. Mme. Thible, a French opera singer (June 4).

1793 **First balloon flight in America.** Jean Pierre Blanchard, a French pilot, made it from Philadelphia to near Woodbury, Gloucester County, N.J., in a little over 45 min (Jan. 9).

1794 **First military use of the balloon.** Jean Marie Coutelle, using a balloon built for the French Army, made two 4-hr observation ascents. The military purpose of the ascents seems to have been to damage the enemy's morale.

1797 **First parachute jump.** André-Jacques Garnerin dropped from about 6,500 ft over Monceau Park in Paris in a 23-ft diameter parachute made of white canvas with a basket attached (Oct. 22).

1843 **First air transport company.** In London, William S. Henson and John Stringfellow filed articles of incorporation for the Aerial Transit Company (March 24). It failed.

1852 **First dirigible.** Henri Giffard, a French engineer, flew in a controllable (more or less) steam-engine powered balloon, 144 ft long and 39 ft in diameter, inflated with 88,000 cu ft of coal gas. It reached 6.7 mph on a flight from Paris to Trappe (Sept. 24).

1860 **First aerial photographers.** Samuel Archer King and William Black made two photos of Boston, still in existence.

1872 **First gas-engine powered dirigible.** Paul Haenlein, a German engineer, flew in a semi-rigid-frame dirigible, powered by a 4-cylinder internal-combustion engine running on coal gas drawn from the supporting bag.

1873 **First transatlantic attempt.** *The New York Daily Graphic* sponsored the attempt with a 400,000 cu ft balloon carrying a lifeboat. A rip in the bag during inflation brought collapse of the balloon and the project.

1897 **First successful metal dirigible.** An all-metal dirigible, designed by David Schwarz, a Hungarian, took off from Berlin's Tempelhof Field and, powered by a 16-hp Daimler engine, got several miles before leaking gas caused it to crash (Nov. 13).

1900 **First Zeppelin flight.** Germany's Count Ferdinand von Zeppelin flew the first of his long series of rigid-frame airships. It attained a speed of 18 mi. per h and got 3 1/2 mi. before its steering gear failed (July 2).

1903 **First successful heavier-than-air machine flight.** Aviation was really born on the sand dunes at Kitty Hawk, N.C., when Orville Wright crawled to his prone position between the wings of the biplane he and his brother Wilbur had built, opened the throttle of their homemade 12-hp engine and took to the air. He covered 120 ft in 12 sec. Later that day, in one of four flights, Wilbur stayed up 59 sec and covered 852 ft (Dec. 17).

Did the Wrights Fly First?

Supporters of Gustave A. Whitehead are seeking to prove that the German-born inventor flew a powered-batwing aircraft on Aug. 14, 1901, in Bridgeport, Conn., two years before the Wright Brothers made their first powered flight.

While photographs of Whitehead's plane exist, none of them show it flying, nor is there much useful evidence to prove or disprove this claim.

Although Whitehead supporters have built what they claim is a replica of his plane and have flown it on several short hops in 1986, it should be noted that blueprints of Whitehead's actual craft do not exist.

The current opinion of the Smithsonian is that none of Gustave Whitehead's planes actually flew and the controversy remains.

Dec. 17, 1903. Orville Wright at the controls, Wilbur runs alongside him. (National Air and Space Museum, Smithsonian Institution)

1904 **First airplane maneuvers.** Orville Wright made the first turn with an airplane (Sept. 15); 5 days later his brother Wilbur made the first complete circle.

1905 **First airplane flight over half an hour.** Orville Wright kept his craft up 33 min 17 sec (Oct. 4).

1906 **First European airplane flight.** Alberto Santos-Dumont, a Brazilian, flew a heavier-than-air machine at Bagatelle Field, Paris (Sept. 13).

1908 **First airplane fatality.** Lt. Thomas E. Selfridge, U.S. Army Signal Corps, was in a group of officers evaluating the Wright plane at Fort Myer, Va. He was up about 75 ft with Orville Wright when the propeller hit a bracing wire and was broken, throwing the plane out of control, killing Selfridge and seriously injuring Wright (Sept. 17).

1909 **First cross-Channel flight.** Louis Blériot flew in a 25-hp Blériot VI monoplane from Les Baraques near Calais, France, and landed near Dover Castle, England, in a 26.61-mi. (38-km) 37-min flight across the English Channel (July 25).

First International Aviation Competition Meeting. American Glenn Curtis narrowly beats France's Louis Blériot in main event and wins the Gordon Bennett Cup. Meet held at Rheims, France (Aug. 22–28).

1910 **First licensed woman pilot.** Baroness Raymonde de la Roche of France, who learned to fly in 1909, received ticket No. 36 on March 8.

First flight from shipboard. Lt. Eugene Ely, USN, took a Curtiss plane off from the deck of cruiser *Birmingham* at Hampton Roads, Va., and flew to Norfolk (Nov. 14). The following January, he reversed the process, flying from Camp Selfridge to the deck of the armored cruiser *Pennsylvania* in San Francisco Bay (Jan. 18).

First aircraft to take off from water. Henri Fabrer in Gnome-powered floatplane, at Martigues, France (March 28).

1911 **First U.S. woman pilot.** Harriet Quimby, a magazine writer, got ticket No. 37, making her the second licensed female pilot in the world.

1912 **First woman's cross-Channel flight.** Harriet Quimby flew from Dover, England, across the English Channel, and landed at Hardelot, France (25 mi. south of Calais) in a Blériot monoplane loaned to her by Louis Blériot (April 16). She was later killed in a flying accident over Dorchester Bay during a Harvard-Boston aviation meet on July 1, 1912.

Harriet Quimby was the leading woman aviator of her day. (Leslie's Weekly Illustrated Newspaper)

First parachute jump from a powered airplane. Albert Berry jumps in a test over Jefferson Barracks military post, St. Louis (March 1). Some sources credit Grant Morton as making first jump in 1911.

1913 **First multi-engined aircraft.** Built and flown by Igor Ivan Sikorsky while still in his native Russia.

1914 **First aerial combat.** In August, Allied and German pilots and observers started shooting at each other with pistols and rifles—with negligible results.

1915 **First air raids on England.** German Zeppelins started dropping bombs on four English communities (Jan. 19).

1918 **First U.S. air squadron.** The U.S. Army Air Corps made its first independent raids over enemy lines, in DH-4 planes (British-designed) powered with 400-hp American-designed Liberty engines (April 8).

First regular airmail service. Operated for the Post Office Department by the Army, the first regular service was inaugurated with one round trip a day (except Sunday) between Washington, D.C., and New York City (May 15).

1919 First transatlantic flight. The NC-4, one of four Curtiss flying boats commanded by Lt. Comdr. Albert C. Read, reached Lisbon, Portugal, (May 27) after hops from Trepassy Bay, Newfoundland, to Horta, Azores (May 16–17), to Ponta Delgada (May 20). The Liberty-powered craft was piloted by Walter Hinton.

First nonstop transatlantic flight. Capt. John Alcock and Lt. Arthur Whitten Brown, British World War I flyers, made the 1,900 mi. from St. John's, Newfoundland, to Clifden, Ireland, in 16 h 12 min in a Vickers-Vimy bomber with two 350-hp Rolls-Royce engines (June 15–16).

First lighter-than-air transatlantic flight. The British dirigible R-34, commanded by Maj. George H. Scott, left Firth of Forth, Scotland, (July 2) and touched down at Mineola, L.I., 108 h later. The eastbound trip was made in 75 h (completed July 13).

First scheduled London-Paris passenger service (using airplanes). Aircraft Travel and Transport inaugurated London-Paris service (Aug. 25). Later the company started the first trans-channel mail service on the same route (Nov. 10).

First free-fall parachute jump. Leslie Irvin jumps over McCook Field, Dayton, Ohio, to prove that you won't lose consciousness during a delayed free-fall using a manually-operated parachute (April 28).

1921 First naval vessel sunk by aircraft. Two battleships being scrapped by treaty were sunk by bombs dropped from Army planes in demonstration put on by Brig. Gen. William S. Mitchell (July 21).

First helium balloon. The C-7, non-rigid Navy dirigible was first to use non-inflammable helium as lifting gas, making a flight from Hampton Roads, Va., to Washington, D.C. (Dec. 1).

1922 First member of Caterpillar Club. Lt. (later Maj. Gen.) Harold Harris bailed out of a crippled plane he was testing at McCook Field, Dayton, Ohio (Oct. 20), and became the first man to join the Caterpillar Club—those whose lives have been saved by parachute.

1923 First nonstop transcontinental flight. Lts. John A. Macready and Oakley Kelly flew a single-engine Fokker T-2 nonstop from New York to San Diego, a distance of just over 2,500 mi. in 26 h 50 min (May 2–3).

First autogyro flight. Juan de la Cierva, a brilliant Spanish mathematician, made the first successful flight in a rotary wing aircraft in Madrid (June 9).

1924 First round-the-world flight. Four Douglas Cruiser biplanes of the U.S. Army Air Corps took off from Seattle under command of Maj. Frederick Martin (April 6). 175 days later, two of the planes (Lt. Lowell Smith's and Lt. Erik Nelson's) landed in Seattle after a circuitous route—one source saying 26,345 mi., another saying 27,553 mi.

1926 First polar flight. Then-Lt. Cmdr. Richard E. Byrd, acting as navigator, and Floyd Bennett as pilot, flew a trimotor Fokker from Kings Bay, Spitsbergen, over the North Pole and back in 15 1/2 h (May 8–9).

1927 First solo, nonstop transatlantic flight. Charles Augustus Lindbergh lifted his Wright-powered Ryan monoplane, *Spirit of St. Louis,* from Roosevelt Field, L.I., to stay aloft 33 h 39 min and travel 3,600 mi. to Le Bourget Field outside Paris (May 20–21).

Charles A. Lindbergh and *The Spirit of St. Louis.* (National Air and Space Museum, Smithsonian Institution)

First transatlantic passenger. Charles A. Levine was piloted by Clarence D. Chamberlin from Roosevelt Field, L.I., to Eisleben, Germany, in a Wright-powered Bellanca (June 4–5).

1928 First east-west transatlantic crossing. Baron Guenther von Huenefeld, piloted by German Capt. Hermann Koehl and Irish Capt. James Fitzmaurice, left Dublin for New York City (April 12) in a single-engine all-metal Junkers-monoplane. Some 37 h later, they crashed on Greely Island, Labrador. Rescued.

First U.S.-Australia flight. Sir Charles Kingsford-Smith and Capt. Charles T. P. Ulm, Australians, and two American navigators, Harry W. Lyon and James Warner, crossed the Pacific from Oakland to Brisbane. They went via Hawaii and the Fiji Islands in a trimotor Fokker (May 31–June 8).

First transarctic flight. Sir Hubert Wilkins, an Australian explorer and Carl Ben Eielson, who served as pilot, flew from Point Barrow, Alaska, to Spitsbergen (mid-April).

1929 First of the endurance records. With Air Corps Maj. Carl Spaatz in command and Capt. Ira Eaker as chief pilot, an Army Fokker, aided by refueling in the air, remained aloft 150 h 40 min at Los Angeles (Jan. 1–7).

First round-the-world airship flight. The LZ-127, known as the *Graf Zeppelin,* flew 21,300 miles in 20 days and 4 hours. Also set distance record (August).

First blind flight. James H. Doolittle proved the feasibility of instrument-guided flying when he took off and landed entirely on instruments (Sept. 24).

First rocket-engine flight. Fritz von Opel, a German auto maker, stayed aloft in his small rocket-powered craft for 75 sec, covering nearly 2 mi. (Sept. 30).

First South Pole flight. Comdr. Richard E. Byrd, with Bernt Balchen as pilot, Harold I. June, radio operator, and Capt. A. C. McKinley, photographer, flew a trimotor Fokker from the Bay of Whales, Little America, over the South Pole and back (Nov. 28–29).

1930 First Paris-New York nonstop flight. Dieudonné Coste and Maurice Bellonte, French pilots, flew a Hispano-powered Breguet biplane from Le Bourget Field to Valley Stream, L.I., in 37 h 18 min. (Sept. 2–3).

1931 First flight into the stratosphere. Auguste Piccard, a Swiss physicist, and Charles Knipfer ascended in a balloon from Augsburg, Germany, and reached a height of 51,793 ft in a 17-h flight that terminated on a glacier near Innsbruck, Austria (May 27).

First nonstop transpacific flight. Hugh Herndon and Clyde Pangborn took off from Sabishiro Beach, Japan, dropped their landing gear, and flew 4,860 mi. to near Wenatchee, Wash., in 41 h 13 min. (Oct. 4–5).

1932 **First woman's transatlantic solo.** Amelia Earhart, flying a Pratt & Whitney Wasp-powered Lockheed Vega, flew alone from Harbor Grace, Newfoundland, to Ireland in approximately 15 h (May 20–21).

First westbound transatlantic solo. James A. Mollison, a British pilot, took a de Havilland Puss Moth from Portmarnock, Ireland, to Pennfield, N.B. (Aug. 18).

First woman airline pilot. Ruth Rowland Nichols, first woman to hold three international records at the same time—speed, distance, altitude—was employed by N.Y.-New England Airways.

1933 **First round-the-world solo.** Wiley Post took a Lockheed Vega, *Winnie Mae,* 15,596 mi. around the world in 7 d 18 h 49 1/2 min (July 15–22).

1937 **First successful helicopter.** Hanna Reitsch, a German pilot, flew Dr. Heinrich Focke's FW-61 in free, fully controlled flight at Bremen (July 4).

1939 **First turbojet flight.** Just before their invasion of Poland, the Germans flew a Heinkel He-178 plane powered by a Heinkel S3B turbojet (Aug. 27).

1940 **First wartime use of military gliders.** German commandos make successful glider assault on Belgium's Fort Eben-Emael during WW II (May 10).

1941–1945 **Most combat missions flown by a pilot in any war.** Captain Hans-Ulrich Rudel of Germany flew 2,530 combat missions during WW II while flying a JU-87 Stuka dive bomber. He survived the war.

1942–1945 **Top scoring fighter pilot of any war.** German Luftwaffe ace Maj. Erich Hartmann scored 352 victories all while flying a Messerschmitt BF 109 during WW II. He was involved in 800 dogfights, and flew 1,425 missions. Maj. Hartmann survived the war.

1942 **First American jet plane flight.** Robert Stanley, chief pilot for Bell Aircraft Corp., flew the Bell XP-59 *Airacomet* at Muroc Army Base, Calif. (Oct. 1).

1944 **The first production stage rocket-engine fighter plane,** the German Messerschmitt Me 163B *Komet* (test flown 1941) becomes operational in June 1944. Some 350 of these delta-wing fighters were built before WW II in Europe ended.

1947 **First piloted supersonic flight in an airplane.** Capt. Charles E. Yeager, U.S. Air Force, flew the X-1 rocket-powered research plane built by Bell Aircraft Corp., faster than the speed of sound at Muroc Air Force Base, California (Oct. 14).

1949 **First round-the-world nonstop flight.** Capt. James Gallagher and USAF crew of 13 flew a Boeing B-50A Superfortress around the world nonstop from Ft. Worth, returning to same point: 23,452 mi. in 94 h 1 min, with 4 aerial refuelings enroute (Feb. 27–March 2).

1950 **First nonstop transatlantic jet flight.** Col. David C. Schilling (USAF) flew 3,300 mi. from England to Limestone, Maine, in 10 h 1 min (Sept. 22).

Chuck Yeager alongside the Bell X-1 named *Glamorous Glennis* after his wife. (National Air and Space Museum, Smithsonian Institution)

1951 **First solo across North Pole.** Charles F. Blair, Jr., flew a converted P-51 (May 29).

1952 **First jetliner service.** De Havilland Comet flight inaugurated by BOAC between London and Johannesburg, South Africa (May 2). Flight, including stops, took 23 h 38 min.

First transatlantic helicopter flight. Capt. Vincent H. McGovern and 1st Lt. Harold W. Moore piloted 2 Sikorsky H-19s from Westover, Mass., to Prestwick, Scotland (3,410 mi.). Trip was made in 5 steps, with flying time of 42 h 25 min (July 15–31).

First transatlantic round trip in same day. British Canberra twin-jet bomber flew from Aldergrove, Northern Ireland, to Gander, Newfoundland, and back in 7 h 59 min flying time (Aug. 26).

1955 **First transcontinental round trip in same day.** Lt. John M. Conroy piloted F-86 Sabrejet across U.S. (Los Angeles-New York) and back—5,085 mi.—in 11 h 33 min 27 sec (May 21).

1957 **First round-the-world, nonstop jet plane flight.** Maj. Gen. Archie J. Old, Jr., USAF, led a flight of 3 Boeing B-52 bombers, powered with 8 10,000-lb. thrust Pratt & Whitney Aircraft J57 engines around the world in 45 h 19 min; distance 24,325 mi.; average speed 525 mph. (Completed Jan. 18.)

1958 **First transatlantic jet passenger service.** BOAC, New York to London (Oct. 4). Pan American started daily service, N.Y. to Paris (Oct. 26).

First domestic jet passenger service. National Airlines inaugurated service between New York and Miami (Dec. 10).

1968 **Prototype of world's first supersonic** airliner, the Soviet-designed Tupolev Tu-144 made first flight, Dec. 31. It first achieved supersonic speed on June 5, 1969.

1973 **First female pilot of a U.S. major scheduled airline.** Emily H. Warner became employed by Frontier Airlines on January 29 as second officer on a Boeing 737.

1976 **First regularly-scheduled commercial supersonic transport (SST) flights begin.** Air France and British Airways inaugurate service (January 21). Air France flies the Paris-Rio de Janeiro route; B.A., the London-Bahrain. Both airlines begin SST service to Washington, D.C. (May 24).

1977 **First successful man-powered aircraft.** Paul MacCready, an aeronautical engineer from Pasadena, Calif., was awarded the Kremer Prize for creating the world 's first successful man-powered aircraft. The *Gossamer Condor* was flown by Bryan Allen over the required 3-mile course on Aug. 23.

World's 25 Busiest Airports in 1992

Airport	Total passengers	92/91 % Chg	Cargo (metric tons)	92/91 % Chg	Aircraft movements	92//91 % Chg
1. Chicago–O'Hare, US	64,441,087	7.7	1,115,116	12.9	841,013	3.3
2. Dallas/Ft. Worth Airport, US	51,943,567	7.8	577,318	5.9	764,242	3.8
3. Los Angeles–Int'l, US	46,964,555	2.8	1,238,198	8.5	680,489	3.5
4. London–Heathrow, GB	45,234,993	11.7	834,916	13.4	406,433	6.5
5. Tokyo–Haneda, JP	42,638,852	1.5	489,743	0.1	191,750	–0.8
6. Atlanta, US	42,032,988	10.9	649,294	8.3	621,365	5.4
7. San Francisco, US	31,789,021	1.9	602,741	4.0	409,352	–2.2
8. Denver, US	30,877,180	9.2	327,264	7.8	503,546	3.7
9. Frankfurt, DE	30,746,463	9.9	1,399,802	2.5	340,468	6.5
10. New York–JF Kennedy Int'l, US	27,760,912	5.8	1,317,961	4.8	321,498	15.9
11. Miami, US	26,483,717	–0.4	1,002,464	14.2	496,822	4.6
12. Paris–Ch De Gaulle, FR	25,198,420	14.7	658,325	6.9	296,194	14.7
13. Paris–Orly, FR	25,170,204	7.9	306,991	3.6	214,543	6.8
14. New York–Newark, US	24,286,986	9.0	587,753	21.2	410,996	8.5
15. Osaka, JP	23,516,231	0.1	482,439	–3.4	132,070	1.0
16. Boston, US	22,988,717	7.2	371,536	6.8	476,982	10.8
17. Minneapolis/St. Paul, US	22,907,490	11.2	301,607	12.5	413,502	8.2
18. Detroit, US	22,840,643	7.2	235,586	11.8	425,013	7.3
19. Hong Kong, HK	22,663,388	14.8	956,908	12.6	140,791	7.6
20. Honolulu, US	22,608,188	1.7	380,852	–0.3	403,630	0.0
21. Phoenix, US	22,111,555	–0.1	161,471	18.3	492,739	–0.7
22. Tokyo–Narita, JP	22,030,102	6.4	1,335,871	–3.4	122,580	–1.5
23. Seoul, KR	21,231,468	15.0	743,397	5.5	145,731	18.9
24. Orlando, US	21,147,888	14.9	168,410	16.0	304,084	11.5
25. St. Louis, US	20,984,782	9.6	111,680	5.9	427,755	3.5

Source: Airport Operators Council International.

1978 First successful transatlantic balloon flight. Three Albuquerque, N.M., men, Ben Abruzzo, Larry Newman, and Maxie Anderson, completed the crossing (Aug. 16. Landed, Aug. 17) in their helium-filled balloon, *Double Eagle II.*

1979 First man-powered aircraft to fly across the English Channel. The Kremer Prize for the Channel crossing was won by Bryan Allen who flew the *Gossamer Albatross* from Folkestone, England to Cap Gris-Nez, France, in 2 h 55 min (June 12).

1980 First successful balloon flight over the North Pole. Sidney Conn and his wife Eleanor, in hot-air balloon *Joy of Sound* (April 11).

First nonstop transcontinental balloon flight, and also record for longest overland voyage in a balloon. Maxie Anderson and his son, Kris, completed four-day flight from Fort Baker, Calif., to successful landing outside Matane, Quebec, on May 12 in their helium-filled balloon, *Kitty Hawk.*

First long-distance solar-powered flight. Janice Brown, 98-lb former teacher, flew tiny experimental solar-powered aircraft, *Solar Challenger* six miles in 22-min near Marana, Ariz. (Dec. 3). The craft was powered by a 2.75-hp engine.

First solar-powered aircraft to fly across the English Channel. Stephen R. Ptacek flew the 210-lb *Solar Challenger* at the average speed of 30 mph from Cormeilles-en-Vexin near Paris to the Royal Manston Air Force Base on England's southeastern coast in 5 h 30 min (July 7).

1984 First solo transatlantic balloon flight. Joe W. Kittinger landed Sept. 18 near Savona, Italy, in his helium-filled balloon *Rosie O'Grady's Balloon of Peace* after a flight of 3,535 miles from Caribou, Me.

1986 First nonstop flight around the world without refueling. From Edwards AFB, Calif., Dick Rutan and Jeana Yeager flew in *Voyager* around the world (24,986.727 mi.), returning to Edwards in 216 h 3 min 44 s (Dec. 14–23).

1987 First transatlantic hot-air balloon flight. Richard Branson and Per Lindstrand flew 2,789.6 miles from Sugarloaf Mt., Maine, to Ireland in the hot-air balloon *Virgin Atlantic Flyer* (July 2–4).

1991 First transpacific hot-air balloon flight. Richard Branson and Per Lindstrand flew about 6,700 miles from Miyakonyo, Japan, to 150 miles west of Yellowknift, Northwest Territories, Canada (Jan. 15–17). Record pending verification.

1992 World's longest balloon flight. Americans Richard Abruzzo and Troy Bradley made a flight of 3,318.23 miles from Bangor, Maine to Sidi Amar El Kadmiri, Ben Slimane, Morocco in 144 hours and 16 minutes in Cameron R-77 (Sept. 16–22).

1993 First woman to co-pilot a commercial supersonic plane. Barbara Harmer, British Airways, flew as first officer on the Concorde from London to New York City (March 25).

World Class Helicopter Records

Selected records. *Source:* National Aeronautic Association.

Great Circle Distance Without Landing

International: 2,213.04 mi.; 3,561.55 km.

Robert G. Ferry (U.S.) in Hughes YOH-6A helicopter powered by Allison T-63-A-5 engine; from Culver City, Calif., to Ormond Beach, Fla., April 6–7, 1966.

Distance, Closed Circuit

International: 1,739.96 mi.; 2,800.20 km.

Jack Schweibold (U.S.) in Hughes YOH-6A helicopter powered by Allison T-62-A-5 engine; Edwards Air Force Base, Calif., March 26, 1966.

Altitude Without Payload

International: 40,820 ft; 12,442 m.

Jean Boulet (France) in Alouette SA 315-001 "Lama" powered by Artouste IIIB 735 KW engine; Istres, France, June 21, 1972.

Altitude in Horizontal Flight
International: 36,122 ft; 11,010 m.
CWO James K. Church, (U.S.) in Sikorsky CH-54B helicopter powered by 2 P&W JFTD-12 engines; Stratford, CT., Nov. 4, 1971.
Speed Around the World
35.40 mph; 56.97 kph.
H. Ross Perot, Jr., pilot; J.W. Coburn, co-pilot (U.S.) in Bell 206 L-II Long Ranger, powered by one Allison 250-C28B of 435 hp. Elapsed time: 29 days 3 h 8 min 13 sec, Sept. 10–30, 1982.

Some Memorable Record Flights of 1992

Source: National Aeronautic Association.

• Jumping from six different airplanes, 200 skydivers joined together over Myrtle Beach, S.C., for the largest freefall formation. This record, set on October 23, broke the previous record of 150.

• Climbing to 9,000 meters (nearly 30,000 feet) in 2 minutes, 11 seconds, members of the 319th Wing of the United States Air Force flew the Rockwell B-1B to this and 11 additional time-to-climb records. These records were set on February 28 and 29, and March 18 in Grand Forks, N.D.

• Starting in San Jose, Calif., and flying westbound in a Piper Aerostar 601P—via the Pacific Islands, Brunei, Bombay, Qatar, Greece, Azores, and Washington, D.C.—Hamad Al-Thani returned to San Jose 12 days later, setting a 'round-the-world speed record of 82 mph. This record, set April 17–29, broke the previous record of 37 mph.

• Burning only 3-1/2 pounds of fuel, Maynard Hill's piston-engine, radio controlled model airplane flew for 33 hours, 39 minutes. This duration record, set October 1–3 in Hagerstown, Md., broke the previous record of 24 hours, 4 minutes (also set by Hill).

Active Pilot Certificates Held[1]

(as of January 1)

Year	Total	Airline transport	Commercial	Private
1970	720,028	31,442	176,585	299,491
1980	814,667	63,652	182,097	343,276
1985	722,376	79,192	155,929	320,086
1990	702,659	107,732	149,666	299,111
1991	692,095	112,167	148,365	293,306
1992	682,959	115,855	146,385	288,078

1. Includes other pilot categories—helicopter, glider and recreational (18,044), and students (114,597). *Source:* Department of Transportation, Federal Aviation Administration.

THE WORLD'S FASTEST AIRCRAFT. The Lockheed SR-71 A/B "Blackbird" first produced in January 1966 was moth-balled in 1989. It is the world's fastest and highest flying production aircraft built. The Blackbird was unarmed and had a crew of two seated in tandem. The dimensions are: span 55 ft 7 in.; length 107 ft 5 in.; and height 18 ft 6 in. Its estimated maximum speed at 78,750 feet is over Mach 3, and its operational ceiling is above 80,000 feet. In a reconnaissance mission, the SR-71 could cover up to a 100,000 sq.-mi. area in one hour. One of the SR-71s set a transcontinental speed record on March 6, 1990: distance: 2,404 miles, time: 1 hr 7 min 53.69 seconds, speed: 2,124.51 miles per hour.

Since their retirement from military service, Blackbirds are being tested as scientific research vehicles for use in daytime astronomy and the observation of ultraviolet radiation. □

Absolute World Records

(Maximum Performance in Any Class)

Source: National Aeronautic Association

These official Absolute World Records are the supreme achievements of all the hundreds of records open to flying machines. They are the most outstanding of all the major types, and thus warrant the highest respect.

All types of airplanes are eligible for these few very special records. Airplanes may be powered by piston, turboprop, turbojet, rocket engines or a combination. They may be landplanes, seaplanes or amphibians; they may be lightplanes, business planes, military or commercial airplanes.

Over the years, many different categories of aircraft have held these records. In the past, the cost of developing high-performance aircraft has been so great that only airplanes created for military purposes have held these records. There have been two exceptions to this situation.

Most recently and most dramatically, the Rutan designed "Voyager" shattered the theory that only a complicated military behemoth could hold an Absolute World Record. The Voyager team and its nonstop, non-refueled flight around the world proved that the dreams of dedicated individuals, combined with creative engineering, new technology, and hard work, could conquer the world.

The other exception was the X-15 rocket-powered research airplane. Holder of one record, it was used for both civilian and military research during its highly productive lifetime.

Speed Around the World, Nonstop, Nonrefueled

Speed (mph)	Date	Type Plane	Pilots	Place
115.65	Dec. 14-23, 1986	*Voyager*	Dick Rutan & Jeana Yeager (U.S.)	Edwards AFB, Calif.—Edwards AFB, Calif.

Distance, Great Circle Without Landing, also Distance, Closed Circuit Without Landing

Distance (mi.)	Date	Pilots	Place
24,986.727	Dec. 14-23, 1986	Dick Rutan & Jeana Yeager (U.S.)	Edwards AFB, Calif.—Edwards AFB, Calif.

Speed Over a Straight Course

Speed (mph)	Date	Type Plane	Pilot	Place
2,193.16	July 28, 1976	Lockheed SR-71A	Capt. Eldon W. Joersz (USAF)	Beale AFB, Calif.

Speed Over A Closed Circuit

Speed (mph)	Date	Type Plane	Pilot	Place
2,092.294	July 27,1976	Lockheed SR-71A	Maj. Adolphus H. Bledsoe, Jr. (USAF)	Beale, AFB, Calif.

Altitude

Height (ft)	Date	Type Plane	Pilot	Place
123,523.58	Aug. 31, 1977	MIG-25, E-266M	Alexander Fedotov (U.S.S.R.)	U.S.S.R.

Altitude in Horizontal Flight

Height (ft)	Date	Pilot	Place
85,068.997	July 28, 1976	Capt. Robert C. Helt (USAF)	Beale AFB, Calif.

Altitude, Aircraft Launched From A Carrier Airplane

Height (ft)	Date	Type Plane	Pilot	Place
314,750.00	July 17, 1962	N. American X-15-1	Maj. Robert White (USAF)	Edwards AFB, Calif.

The Speed of Sound

Source: Air & Space/Smithsonian.

The speed of sound varies with temperature. At sea level Mach 1 is around 742 mph. It decreases with altitude until it reaches about 661 mph at 36,000 feet, then remains at that speed in a band of steady temperature up to 60,000 feet. Because of the variation, it is possible for an airplane flying supersonic at high altitude to be slower than a subsonic flight at sea level. The transsonic band extends from around Mach .8—when the first supersonic shock waves form on the wing—to Mach 1.2, when the entire wing has gone supersonic.

Emergency Help for Americans Abroad

Source: U.S. Department of State, Bureau of Consular Affairs.

The Citizens Emergency Center deals with emergencies involving Americans abroad—Americans who die, become destitute, get sick, disappear, have accidents, or get arrested.

In addition to individual emergencies, the Citizens Emergency Center is also the State Department's focal point for major disasters involving Americans abroad: plane crashes, hijackings, natural disasters, terrorist incidents, etc.

The Citizens Emergency Center's telephone number is: (202) 647-5225. The Center is open 8:15 a.m. to 10:00 p.m. Monday through Friday, and 9:00 a.m. to 3:00 p.m. Saturday. At other times, including holidays, a duty officer can be reached through the State Department's main number: (202) 647-4000.

Emergency assistance generally falls into four categories: deaths, arrests, financial/medical problems, and welfare/whereabouts queries. The Citizens Emergency Center, working through American embassies and consulates abroad, is a link between the citizen in distress and his or her family in the U.S. The Citizens Emergency Center is also responsible for the Department's consular information program consisting of Consular Information Sheets and Travel Warnings.

Deaths

Americans traveling abroad on business, pleasure, or a study program rarely think about death. Nevertheless, approximately 6,000 Americans do die outside the U.S. each year. Of those, the Citizens Emergency Center assists with the return to the U.S. of the remains of approximately 2,000 each year.

When an American dies abroad, a consular officer notifies the American's family and informs them about options and costs for disposition of remains. Costs for preparing and returning a body to the U.S. are high and are the responsibility of the family. Often local laws and procedures make returning a body to the U.S. for burial a lengthy process.

Arrests

About 3,000 Americans are arrested abroad each year. Over 30% of these arrests are drug related. Over 70% of drug-related arrests involve marijuana or cocaine.

The rights an American enjoys in this country do **not** travel abroad. Each country is sovereign, and its laws apply to everyone who enters regardless of nationality. The U.S. Government cannot "spring" Americans from foreign jails.

However, a consul will insist on prompt access to the arrested American, provide a list of reputable attorneys, provide information on the host country's legal system, offer to contact the arrested American's family or friends, visit on a regular basis, protest mistreatment, monitor jail conditions, provide dietary supplements if needed, and keep the State Department informed.

The Citizens Emergency Center is the point of contact in the U.S. for family members and others who are concerned about an American arrested abroad.

Welfare/Whereabouts

The Citizens Emergency Center receives approximately 12,000 inquiries a year concerning the welfare or whereabouts of an American abroad. Many inquiries are from worried relatives who have not heard from the traveler. Others are attempts to notify the traveler about a family crisis at home.

Most welfare/whereabouts inquiries are successfully resolved. However, occasionally, a person truly is missing. It is the responsibility of local authorities to investigate. (The State Department and U.S. consuls abroad do not conduct investigations.) As in the U.S., sometimes missing persons are never found.

Financial Assistance

If destitute, Americans can turn to a U.S. consular officer abroad for help. The Citizens Emergency Center will help by contacting the destitute person's family, friends, or business associates to raise private funds. It will help transmit these funds to destitute Americans.

The Citizens Emergency Center transfers approximately $3,000,000 a year in private emergency funds. It can approve small government loans to destitute Americans abroad to tide them over until private funds arrive.

Also, the Citizens Emergency Center can approve repatriation loans to pay for destitute Americans' direct return to the U.S. Each year over $500,000 are loaned to destitute Americans.

Medical Assistance

The Citizens Emergency Center works with U.S. consuls abroad to assist Americans who become physically or mentally ill while traveling. The Center locates family members, guardians, and friends in the U.S., assists in transmitting private funds, and, when necessary, assists in the return of ill or injured Americans to the U.S. by commercial carrier.

Travel Information

The Citizens Emergency Center issues Consular Information Sheets for all countries. They describe unusual entry or currency regulations, health conditions, the crime and security situation, political disturbances, areas of instability, and drug penalties. In addition, when the situation in a country is dangerous enough for the Department of State to recommend that Americans defer travel to the country, a Travel Warning is issued for the country.

Consular Information Sheets and Travel Warnings may be heard by calling the Citizens Emergency Center 24 hours a day at (202) 647-5225 from a touch-tone phone. They are posted at the 13 regional passport agencies across the U.S. and are available at U.S. embassies and consulates abroad. Consular Information Sheets and Travel Warnings can also be accessed through many electronic bulletin boards, including the Consular Affairs Bulletin Board (CABB). The number for the CABB is (202) 647-9225—set software at 8-N-1. □

U.S. Passport and Customs Information

Source: Department of State, Bureau of Consular Affairs and Department of the Treasury, Customs Service.

Passports

With a few exceptions, a passport is required for all U.S. citizens to depart and enter the United States and to enter most foreign countries. A valid U.S. passport is the best documentation of U.S. citizenship available. Persons who travel to a country where a U.S. passport is not required should be in possession of documentary evidence of their U.S. citizenship and identity to facilitate reentry into the United States. Travelers should check passport and visa requirements with consular officials of the countries to be visited well in advance of their departure date.

Application for a passport may be made at a passport agency; to a clerk of any Federal court or State court of record; or a judge or clerk of any probate court accepting applications; or at a post office selected to accept passport applications. Passport agencies are located in Boston, Chicago, Honolulu, Houston, Los Angeles, Miami, New Orleans, New York, Philadelphia, San Francisco, Seattle, Stamford, Conn., and Washington, D.C.

All persons are required to obtain individual passports in their own names. Neither spouses nor children may be included in each others' passports. Applicants age 13 years and older must appear in person before the clerk or agent executing the application. For children under the age of 13, a parent or legal guardian may execute an application for them.

First time passport applicants must apply in person. Applicants must present evidence of citizenship (e.g., a certified copy of birth certificate), personal identification (e.g., a valid driver's license), two identical black and white or color photographs taken within six months (2 × 2 inches, with the image size measured from the bottom of the chin to the top of the head [including hair] not less than 1 inch nor more than 1 3/8 inches on a plain white or off–white background, vending machine photographs not acceptable), plus a completed passport application (DSP–11). If you were born abroad, you may also use as proof of citizenship: a Certificate of Naturalization, a Certificate of Citizenship, a Report of Birth Abroad of a Citizen of the United States of America or a Certification of Birth. A fee of $55 plus a $10 execution fee is charged for adults 18 years and older for a passport valid for ten years from the date of issue. The fee for minor children under 18 years of age is $30 for a five–year passport plus $10 for the execution of the application.

You may apply for a passport by mail if you have been the bearer of a passport issued within 12 years prior to the date of a new application, are able to submit your most recent U.S. passport with your new application, and your previous passport was not issued before your 18th birthday. If you are eligible to apply by mail, include your previous passport, a completed, signed, and dated DSP–82 "Application for Passport by Mail," new photographs, and the passport fee of $55. The $10 execution fee is not required when applying by mail. Mail the application and attachments in accordance with the instructions on the form.

Passports may be presented for amendment to show a married name or legal change of name or to correct descriptive data. Any alterations to the passport by the bearer other than in the spaces provided for change of address and next of kin data are forbidden.

Loss, theft or destruction of a passport should be reported to Passport Services, 1425 K Street, N.W., Washington, D.C. 20524 immediately, or to the nearest passport agency. If you are overseas, report loss to the nearest U.S. Embassy or consulate and to local police authorities. Your passport is a valuable citizenship and identity document. It should be carefully safeguarded. Its loss could cause you unnecessary travel complications as well as significant expense. It is advisable to photocopy the data page of your passport and keep it in a place separate from your passport to facilitate the issuance of a replacement passport should one be necessary.

Portsmouth National Passport Center

The Department of State has opened the largest passport processing center in the United States at Portsmouth, New Hampshire. Known as the National Passport Center, the facility is capable of issuing 6,000 passports per day but can be expanded to issue 9,000 passports per day. The Center represents the Department's commitment to meeting an expected passport renewal workload surge. The increase is anticipated because of a 1983 statutory change extending the validity of passports issued to persons over age 18 from five years to ten years. With the first of the 10-year passports expiring in 1993, the Department expects to issue 4.3 million passports this coming year. About 1.1 million of these applications are expected to be mail renewals.

The Center is now processing passport mail renewal applications from around the United States. Passport fees are deposited in Pittsburgh, with the applications subsequently express mailed to Portsmouth for processing. The other passport agencies will process first-time applications and any other requests for passport services presented in person.

To renew a passport by mail, applicants must:

1. Obtain an "Application for Passport by Mail" (Form DSP-82) from a passport acceptance facility (post office, court house or passport agency);
2. Complete and sign the application and attach the most recent passport issued not more than 12 years ago but after the applicant's 18th birthday, two identical 2″ × 2″ passport photographs, and a check or money order for $55.
3. Mail the above items to the National Passport Center, Post Office Box 371971, Pittsburgh, Pennsylvania 15250-7971.

Customs

United States residents must declare all articles acquired abroad and in their possession at the time of their return. In addition, articles acquired in the U.S. Virgin Islands, American Samoa, or Guam and not accompanying you must be declared at the time of your return. The wearing or use of an article acquired abroad does *not* exempt it from duty. Customs declaration forms are distributed on vessels and planes, and should be prepared in advance of arrival for presentation to the customs inspectors.

If you have not exceeded the duty–free exemption allowed, you may make an oral declaration to the customs inspector. However, the inspector can request a written declaration and may do so. A written declaration is necessary when (1) the total fair retail value of articles exceeds the personal exemption of $400; (2) over 1 liter of liquor, 200 cigarettes, or 100 cigars are included; (3) items are not intended for your personal or household use, or articles brought home for another person; (4) when a customs duty or internal

revenue tax is collectible on any article in your possession; and (5) if your personal exemption was used in the last 30 days.

An exception to the above are regulations applicable to articles purchased in the U.S. Virgin Islands, American Samoa, or Guam where you may receive a customs exemption of $1,200. Not more than $400 of this exemption may be applied to merchandise obtained elsewhere than in these islands or $600 if acquired in a beneficiary country. Five liters of alcoholic beverages and 1000 cigarettes may be included provided not more than one liter and 200 cigarettes were acquired elsewhere than in these islands. Articles acquired in and sent from these islands to the United States may be claimed under your duty–free personal exemption if properly declared at the time of your return. For information on rules applying to beneficiary countries and a list of them check with your customer officer or write for the pamphlet "GSP and the Traveler" from the Department of the Treasury, U.S. Customs Services, Washington, D.C. 20229. Since rules change it is always wise to check with customs before leaving, to get information pertinent to the areas you will be visiting.

Articles accompanying you, in excess of your personal exemption, up to $1000 will be assessed at a flat rate of duty of 10% based on fair retail value in country of acquisition. (If articles were acquired in the insular possessions, the flat rate of duty is 5% and these goods may accompany you or be shipped home.) These articles must be for your personal use or for use as gifts and not for sale. This provision may be used every 30 days, excluding the day of your last arrival. Any items which have a "free" duty rate will be excluded before duty is calculated.

Other exemptions include in part: automobiles, boats, planes, or other vehicles taken abroad for noncommercial use. Foreign–made personal articles (e.g., watches, cameras, etc.) taken abroad should be registered with Customs before departure. Customs will register anything with a serial number identifying marks or documented by sales receipt or insurance document. Gifts of not more than $50 can be shipped back to the United States tax and duty free ($100 if mailed from the Virgin Islands, American Samoa, or Guam). Household effects and tools of trade which you take out of the United States are duty free at time of return.

Prohibited and restricted articles include in part: absinthe, narcotics and dangerous drugs, obscene articles and publications, seditious and treasonable materials, hazardous articles (e.g., fireworks, dangerous toys, toxic and poisonous substances, and switchblade knives), biological materials of public health or veterinary importance, fruit, vegetables and plants, meats, poultry and products thereof, birds, monkeys, and turtles. You can get additional information on this subject from the publication *Pets, Wildlife, U.S. Customs.* For a free copy write to the U.S. Customs Service, P.O. Box 7407, Washington, D.C. 20044.

If you understate the value of an article you declare, or if you otherwise misrepresent an article in your declaration, you may have to pay a penalty in addition to payment of duty. Under certain circumstances, the article could be seized and forfeited if the penalty is not paid.

If you fail to declare an article acquired abroad, not only is the article subject to seizure and forfeiture, but you will be liable for a personal penalty in an amount equal to the value of the article in the United States. In addition, you may also be liable to criminal prosecution.

If you carry more than $10,000 into or out of the United States in currency (either United States or foreign money), negotiable instruments in bearer form, or travelers checks, a report must be filed with United States Customs at the time you arrive or depart with such amounts.

Foreign Embassies in the United States

Source: U.S. Department of State.

Embassy of the Republic of Afghanistan, 2341 Wyoming Ave., N.W., Washington, D.C. 20008. Phone: (202) 234–3770, 3771.

Embassy of the Republic of Albania, 1150 18th St., N.W., Washington, D.C. 20036. Phone: (202) 223-4942.

Embassy of the Democratic & Popular Republic of Algeria, 2118 Kalorama Rd., N.W., Washington, D.C. 20008. Phone: (202) 265–2800.

Embassy of Antigua & Barbuda, 3400 International Dr., N.W., Suite 4M, Washington, D.C. 20008. Phone: (202) 362–5211, 5166, 5122.

Embassy of the Argentine Republic, 1600 New Hampshire Ave., N.W., Washington, D.C. 20009. Phone: (202) 939–6400 to 6403, inclusive.

Embassy of the Republic of Armenia, 122 C St., N.W., Suite 360, Washington, D.C. 20001. Phone: (202) 628-5766.

Embassy of Australia, 1601 Massachusetts Ave., N.W., Washington, D.C. 20036. Phone: (202) 797–3000.

Embassy of Austria,3524 International Court, N.W., Washington, D.C. 20008. Phone: (202) 895-6700.

Embassy of The Commonwealth of The Bahamas, 2220 Massachusetts Ave., N.W., Washington, D.C. 20008. Phone: (202) 319-2660.

Embassy of the State of Bahrain, 3502 International Dr., N.W., Washington, D.C. 20008. Phone: (202) 342–0741, 0742.

Embassy of the People's Republic of Bangladesh, 2201 Wisconsin Ave., N.W., Washington, D.C. 20007. Phone: (202) 342–8372 to 8376.

Embassy of Barbados, 2144 Wyoming Ave., N.W., Washington, D.C. 20008. Phone: (202) 939–9200 to 9202.

Embassy of the Republic of Belarus, 1511 K St., N.W., Suite 619, Wash[illegible] (202) 638-2954.

Embassy of Belgium, 3330 Garfield St., N.W., Washington, D.C. 20008. Phone: (202) 333–6900.

Embassy of Belize, 2535 Massachusetts Ave., N.W., Washington, D.C. 20008. Phone: (202) 332-9636.

Embassy of the Republic of Benin, 2737 Cathedral Ave., N.W., Washington, D.C. 20008. Phone: (202) 232–6656 to 6658.

Embassy of Bolivia, 3014 Massachusetts Ave., N.W., Washington, D.C. 20008. Phone: (202) 483–4410 to 4412.

Embassy of the Republic of Botswana, 3400 International Dr., N.W., Suite 7M, Washington, D.C. 20008. Phone: (202) 244–4990, 4991.

Brazilian Embassy, 3006 Massachusetts Ave., N.W., Washington, D.C. 20008. Phone: (202) 745–2700.

Embassy of the State of Brunei Darussalam, Watergate, 2600 Virginia Ave., N.W., Suite 300, Washington, D.C. 20037. Phone: (202) 342–0159.

Embassy of the Republic of Bulgaria, 1621 22nd St., N.W., Washington, D.C. 20008. Phone: (202) 387–7969.

Embassy of Burkina Faso, 2340 Massachusetts Ave., N.W., Washington, D.C. 20008. Phone: (202) 332–5577, 6895.

Embassy of the Republic of Burundi, 2233 Wisconsin Ave., N.W., Suite 212, Washington, D.C. 20007. Phone: (202) 342–2574.

Embassy of the Republic of Cameroon, 2349 Massachusetts Ave., N.W., Washington, D.C. 20008. Phone: (202) 265–8790 to 8794.

Embassy of Canada, 501 Pennsylvania Ave., N.W., Washington, D.C. 20001. Phone: (202) 682–1740.

Embassy of the Republic of Cape Verde, 3415 Massachusetts Ave., N.W., Washington, D.C. 20007. Phone: (202) 965–6820.

Embassy of Central African Republic, 1618 22nd St. N.W., Washington, D.C. 20008. Phone: (202) 483–7800, 7801.

Embassy of the Republic of Chad, 2002 R St., N.W., Washington, D.C. 20009. Phone: (202) 462–4009.

Embassy of Chile, 1732 Massachusetts Ave., N.W., Washington, D.C. 20036. Phone: (202) 785–1746.

Embassy of the People's Republic of China, 2300 Connecticut Ave., N.W., Washington, D.C. 20008. Phone: (202) 328–2500 to 2502.

Embassy of Colombia, 2118 Leroy Pl., N.W., Washington, D.C. 20008. Phone: (202) 387–8338.

Embassy of the Federal and Islamic Republic of Comoros, c/o Permanent Mission of the Federal and Islamic Republic of Comoros to the United Nations, 336 E. 45th St., 2nd floor, New York, N.Y. 10017. Phone: (212) 972–8010.

Embassy of the Republic of Congo, 4891 Colorado Ave., N.W., Washington, D.C. 20011. Phone: (202) 726–5500, 5501.

Embassy of Costa Rica, 1825 Connecticut Ave., N.W., Suite 211, Washington, D.C. 20009. Phone: (202) 234–2945 to 2947.

Embassy of the Republic of Cote d'Ivoire, 2424 Massachusetts Ave., N.W., Washington, D.C. 20008. Phone: (202) 797–0300.

Embassy of the Republic of Croatia, 236 Massachusetts Ave., N.E., Washington, D.C. 20002. Phone: (202) 543-5580.

Cuban Interests Section, 2630 and 2639 16th St., N.W., Washington, D.C. 20009. Phone: (202) 797–8518 to 8520, 8609, 8610.

Embassy of the Republic of Cyprus, 2211 R St. N.W., Washington, D.C. 20008. Phone: (202) 462–5772.

Embassy of the Czech Republic, 3900 Spring of Freedom St., N.W., Washington, D.C. 20008. Phone: (202) 363–6315, 6316.

Royal Danish Embassy, 3200 Whitehaven St., N.W., Washington, D.C. 20008. Phone: (202) 234–4300.

Embassy of the Republic of Djibouti, 1156 15th St., N.W., Suite 515, Washington, D.C. 20005. Phone: (202) 331-0270.

Embassy of the Dominican Republic, 1715 22nd St., N.W., Washington, D.C. 20008. Phone: (202) 332–6280.

Embassy of Ecuador, 2535 15th St., N.W., Washington, D.C. 20009. Phone: (202) 234–7200.

Embassy of the Arab Republic o f Egypt, 2310 Decatur Pl., N.W., Washington, D.C. 20008. Phone: (202) 232–5400.

Embassy of El Salvador, 2308 California St., N.W., Washington, D.C. 20008. Phone: (202) 265–9671, 9672.

Embassy of Equatorial Guinea, 57 Magnolia Ave., Mount Vernon, N.Y. 10553. Phone: (914) 738-9584 and 667-6913.

Embassy of Estonia, 1030 15th St., N.W., Suite 1000, Washington, D.C. 20005. Phone: (202) 789-9223,

Embassy of Ethiopia, 2134 Kalorama Rd., N.W., Washington, D.C. 20008. Phone: (202) 234–2281, 2282.

Embassy of The Republic of Fiji, 2233 Wisconsin Ave., N.W., Suite 240, Washington, D.C. 20007. Phone: (202) 337–8320.

Embassy of Finland, 3216 New Mexico Ave., N.W., Washington, D.C. 20016. Phone: (202) 363–2430.

Embassy of France, 4101 Reservoir Rd., N.W., Washington, D.C. 20007. Phone: (202) 944–6000.

Embassy of the Gabonese Republic, 2034 20th St., N.W., Washington, D.C. 20009. Phone: (202) 797–1000.

Embassy of The Gambia, 1155 15th St., N.W., Suite 1000, Washington, D.C. 20005. Phone: (202) 785-1399, 1379, 1425.

Embassy of the Federal Republic of Germany, 4645 Reservoir Rd., N.W., Washington, D.C. 20007. Phone: (202) 298–4000.

Embassy of Ghana, 3512 International Dr., N.W., Washington, D.C. 20008 (202) 686–4520.

Embassy of Greece, 2221 Massachusetts Ave., N.W., Washington, D.C. 20008. Phone (202) 939–5800.

Embassy of Grenada, 1701 New Hampshire Ave., N.W., Washington, D.C. 20009. Phone: (202) 265–2561.

Embassy of Guatemala, 2220 R St., N.W., Washington, D.C. 20008. Phone: (202) 745–4952 to 4954.

Embassy of the Republic of Guinea, 2112 Leroy Pl., N.W., Washington, D.C. 20008. Phone: (202) 483–9420.

Embassy of the Republic of Guinea–Bissau, 918 16th St., N.W., Mezzanine Suite, Washington, D.C. 20006. Phone: (202) 872-4222.

Embassy of Guyana, 2490 Tracy Pl., N.W. Washington, D.C. 20008. Phone: (202) 265–6900 to 6903.

Embassy of the Republic of Haiti, 2311 Massachusetts Ave., N.W., Washington, D.C. 20008. Phone: (202) 332–4090 to 4092.

Apostolic Nunciature of the Holy See, 3339 Massachusetts Ave., N.W., Washington, D.C. 20008. Phone: (202) 333–7121.

Embassy of Honduras, 3007 Tilden St., N.W., Washington, D .C. 20008. Phone: (202) 966–7702, 2604, 5008, 4596.

Embassy of the Republic of Hungary, 3910 Shoemaker St., N.W., Washington, D.C. 20008. Phone: (202) 362–6730.

Embassy of Iceland, 2022 Connecticut Ave., N.W., Washington, D.C. 20008. Phone: (202) 265–6653 to 6655.

Embassy of India, 2107 Massachusetts Ave., N.W., Washington, D.C. 20008. Phone: (202) 939–7000.

Embassy of the Republic of Indonesia, 2020 Massachusetts Ave., N.W., Washington, D.C. 20036. Phone: (202) 775–5200.

Iranian Interests Section, 2209 Wisconsin Ave., N.W., Washington, D.C. 20007. Phone: (202) 965-4990.

Iraqi Interests Section, 1801 P St., N.W., Washington, D.C. 20036. Phone: (202) 483–7500.

Embassy of Ireland, 2234 Massachusetts Ave., N.W., Washington, D.C. 20008. Phone: (202) 462–3939.

Embassy of Israel, 3514 International Dr., N.W., Washington, D.C. 20008. Phone: (202) 364–5500.

Embassy of Italy, 1601 Fuller St., N.W., Washington, D.C. 20009. Phone: (202) 328–5500.

Embassy of Jamaica, 1850 K St., N.W., Suite 355, Washington, D.C. 20006. Phone: (202) 452–0660.

Embassy of Japan, 2520 Massachusetts Ave., N.W., Washington, D.C. 20008. Phone: (202) 939–6700.

Embassy of the Hashemite Kingdom of Jordan, 3504 International Dr., N.W., Washington, D.C. 20008. Phone: (202) 966–2664.

Embassy of the Republic of Kenya, 2249 R St., N.W., Washington, D.C. 20008. Phone: (202) 387–6101.

Embassy of Korea, 2450 Massachusetts Ave., N.W., Washington, D.C. 20008. Phone: (202) 939–5600.

Embassy of the State of Kuwait, 2940 Tilden St., N.W., Washington, D.C. 20008. Phone: (202) 966–0702.

Embassy of the Republic of Kyrgystan, 1511 K St., N.W., Suite 705, Washington, D.C. 20005. Phone: (202) 347-3732, 3733, and 3718.

Embassy of the Lao People's Democratic Republic, 2222 S St., N.W., Washington, D.C. 20008. Phone: (202) 332–6416, 6417.

Embassy of Latvia, 4325 17th St., N.W., Washington, D.C. 20011. Phone: (202) 726–8213, 8214.

Embassy of Lebanon, 2560 28th St., N.W., Washington, D.C. 20008. Phone: (202) 939–6300.

Embassy of the Kingdom of Lesotho, 2511 Massachusetts Ave., N.W., Washington, D.C. 20008. Phone: (202) 797–5533 to 5536.

Embassy of the Republic of Liberia, 5201 16th St., N.W., Washington, D.C. 20011. Phone: (202) 291–0761.

Embassy of the Republic of Lithuania, 2622 16th St., N.W., Washington, D.C. 20009. Phone: (202) 234–5860, 2639.

Embassy of Luxembourg, 2200 Massachusetts Ave., N.W., Washington, D.C. 20008. Phone: (202) 265–4171.

Embassy of the Democratic Republic of Madagascar, 2374 Massachusetts Ave., N. W., Washington, D.C. 20008. Phone: (202) 265–5525, 5526.

Malawi Embassy, 2408 Massachusetts Ave., N.W., Washington, D.C. 20008. Phone: (202) 797–1007.

Embassy of Malaysia, 2401 Massachusetts Ave., N.W., Washington, D.C. 20008. Phone: (202) 328–2700.

Embassy of the Republic of Mali, 2130 R St., N.W., Washington, D.C. 20008. Phone: (202) 332–2249; (202) 939–8950.

Embassy of Malta, 2017 Connecticut Ave., N.W., Washington, D.C. 20008. Phone: (202) 462–3611, 3612.

Embassy of the Republic of the Marshall Islands, 2433 Massachusetts Ave., N.W., Washington, D.C. 20008. Phone: (202) 234-5414.

Embassy of the Islamic Republic of Mauritania, 2129 Leroy Pl., N.W., Washington, D.C. 20008. Phone: (202) 232–5700.

Embassy of Mauritius, 4301 Connecticut Ave., N.W., Suite 441, Washington, D.C. 20008. Phone: (202) 244–1491, 1492.

Embassy of Mexico, 1911 Pennsylvania Ave., N.W., 20006, Washington, D.C. Phone: (202) 728–1600.

Embassy of the Federated States of Micronesia, 1725 N St., N.W., Washington, D.C. 20036. Phone: (202) 223-4383.

Embassy of Mongolia, 2833 M St., N.W., Washington, D.C. 20007. Phone: (202) 333-7117.

Embassy of the Kingdom of Morocco, 1601 21st St., N.W., Washington, D.C. 20009. Phone: (202) 462–7979 to 7982, inclusive.

Embassy of the Republic of Mozambique, 1990 M St., N.W., Suite 570, Washington, D.C. 20036. Phone: (202) 293–7146.

Embassy of the Union of Myanmar, 2300 S St., N.W., Washington, D.C. 20008. Phone: (202) 332–9044, 9045.

Embassy of the Republic of Namibia, 1605 New Hampshire Ave., N.W., Washington, D.C. 20009. Phone: (202) 986-0540.

Royal Nepalese Embassy, 2131 Leroy Pl., N.W., Washington, D.C. 20008. Phone: (202) 667–4550.

Embassy of the Netherlands, 4200 Linnean Ave., N.W., Washington, D.C. 20008. Phone: (202) 244–5300; after 6 p.m. (202) 244–5304.

Embassy of New Zealand, 37 Observatory Circle, N.W., Washington, D.C. 20008. Phone: (202) 328–4800.

Embassy of Nicaragua, 1627 New Hampshire Ave., N.W., Washington, D.C. 20009. Phone: (202) 939–6570.

Embassy of the Republic of Niger, 2204 R St., N.W., Washington, D.C. 20008. Phone: (202) 483–4224 to 4227, inclusive.

Embassy of the Federal Republic of Nigeria, 2201 M St., N.W., Washington, D.C. 20037. Phone: (202) 822–1500.

Royal Norwegian Embassy, 2720 34th St., N.W., Washington, D.C. 20008. Phone: (202) 333–6000.

Embassy of the Sultanate of Oman, 2342 Massachusetts Ave., N.W., Washington, D.C. 20008. Phone: (202) 387–1980 to 1982.

Embassy of Pakistan, 2315 Massachusetts Ave., N.W., Washington, D.C. 20008. Phone: (202) 939–6205.

Embassy of the Republic of Panama, 2862 McGill Terrace, N.W., Washington, D.C. 20008. Phone: (202) 483–1407.

Embassy of Papua New Guinea, 1615 New Hampshire Ave., N.W., 3rd floor, Washington, D.C. 20009. Phone: (202) 745-3680.

Embassy of Paraguay, 2400 Massachusetts Ave., N.W., Washington, D.C. 20008. Phone: (202) 483–6960 to 6962.

Embassy of Peru, 1700 Massachusetts Ave., N.W., Washington, D.C. 20036. Phone: (202) 833–9860 to 9869.

Embassy of the Philippines, 1617 Massachusetts Ave., N.W., Washington, D.C. 20036. Phone: (202) 483–1414.

Embassy of the Republic of Poland, 2640 16th St., N.W., Washington, D.C. 20009. Phone: (202) 234–3800 to 3802.

Embassy of Portugal, 2125 Kalorama Rd., N.W., Washington, D.C. 20008. Phone: (202) 328–8610.

Embassy of the State of Qatar, 600 New Hampshire Ave., N.W., Suite 1180, Washington, D.C. 20037. Phone: (202) 338–0111.

Embassy of Romania, 1607 23rd St., N.W., Washington, D.C. 20008. Phone: (202) 332-4846, 4848, 4851; after hours 332-4848.

Embassy of the Russian Federation, 1125 16th St., N.W., Washington, D.C. 20036. Phone: (202) 628-7551, 8548.

Embassy of the Republic of Rwanda, 1714 New Hampshire Ave., N.W., Washington, D.C. 20009. Phone: (202) 232–2882.

Embassy of Saint Kitts and Nevis, 2100 M St., N.W., Suite 608, Washington, D.C. 20037. Phone: (202) 833-3550.

Embassy of Saint Lucia, 2100 M St., N.W., Suite 309, Washington, D.C. 20037. Phone: (202) 463–7378, 7379.

Embassy of Saint Vincent and the Grenadines, 1717 Massachusetts Ave., N.W., Suite 102, Washington, D.C. 20036. Phone: (202) 462-7806, 7846.

Embassy of São Tomé and Príncipe, 801 Second Ave., Suite 603, New York, N.Y. 10017 (temporary address). Phone: (212) 697–4211.

Embassy of Saudi Arabia, 601 New Hampshire Ave., N.W., Washington, D.C. 20037. Phone: (202) 342–3800.

Embassy of the Republic of Senegal, 2112 Wyoming Ave., N.W., Washington, D.C. 20008. Phone: (202) 234–0540, 0541.

Embassy of the Republic of Seychelles, c/o Permanent Mission of Seychelles to the United Nations, 820 Second Ave., Suite 900F, New York, N.Y. 10017. Phone: (212) 687–9766/9767.

Embassy of Sierra Leone, 1701 19th St., N.W., Washington, D.C. 20009. Phone: (202) 939–9261.

Embassy of the Republic of Singapore, 1824 R St., N.W., Washington, D.C. 20009. Phone: (202) 667–7555.

Embassy of the Slovak Republic, 4828 Linnean Ave., N.W., Washington, D.C. 20008. Phone: (202) 363-6315.

Embassy of the Republic of Slovenia, 1300 19th St., N.W., Suite 410, Washington, D.C. 20036. Phone: (202) 818-1650.

Embassy of South Africa, 3051 Massachusetts Ave., N.W., Washington, D.C. 20008. Phone: (202) 232–4400.

Embassy of Spain, 2700 15th St., N.W., Washington, D.C. 20009. Phone: (202) 265–0190, 0191.

Embassy of the Democratic Socialist Republic of Sri Lanka, 2148 Wyoming Ave., N.W., Washington, D.C. 20008. Phone: (202) 483–4025 to 4028.

Embassy of the Republic of the Sudan, 2210 Massachusetts Ave., N.W., Washington, D.C. 20008. Phone: (202) 338–8565 to 8570.

Embassy of the Republic of Suriname, 4301 Connecticut Ave., N.W., Suite 108, Washington, D.C. 20008. Phone: (202) 244–7488, 7490 to 7492.

Embassy of the Kingdom of Swaziland, 3400 International Drive, N.W., Washington, D.C. 20008. Phone: (202) 362–6683, 6685.

Embassy of Sweden, 600 New Hampshire Ave., N.W., Suites 1200 and 715, Washington, D.C. 20037. Phone: (202) 944–5600.

Embassy of Switzerland, 2900 Cathedral Ave., N.W., Washington, D.C. 20008. Phone: (202) 745–7900.

Embassy of the Syrian Arab Republic, 2215 Wyoming Ave., N.W., Washington, D.C. 20008. Phone: (202) 232–6313.

Embassy of the United Republic of Tanzania, 2139 R St., N.W., Washington, D.C. 20008. Phone: (202) 939–6125.

Embassy of Thailand, 2300 Kalorama Rd., N.W., Washington, D.C. 20008. Phone: (202) 483–7200.

Embassy of the Republic of Togo, 2208 Massachusetts Ave., N.W., Washington, D.C. 20008. Phone: (202) 234–4212, 4213.

Embassy of Trinidad and Tobago, 1708 Massachusetts Ave., N.W., Washington, D.C. 20036. Phone: (202) 467–6490.

Embassy of Tunisia, 1515 Massachusetts Ave., N.W., Washington, D.C. 20005. Phone: (202) 862–1850.

Embassy of the Republic of Turkey, 1714 Massachusetts Ave. N.W., Washington, D.C. 20036. Phone: (202) 659–8200.

Embassy of the Republic of Uganda, 5909 16th St., N.W., Washington, D.C. 20011. Phone: (202) 726–7100 to 7102, 0416.

Embassy of Ukraine, 1828 L St., N.W., Suite 711, Washington, D.C. 20036. Phone: (202) 333-0606.

Embassy of the United Arab Emirates, 600 New Hampshire Ave., N.W., Suite 740, Washington, D.C. 20037. Phone: (202) 338–6500.

United Kingdom of Great Britain & Northern Ireland—British Embassy, 3100 Massachusetts Ave., N.W., Washington, D.C. 20008. Phone: (202) 462–1340.

Embassy of Uruguay, 1 918 F St., N.W., Washington D.C. 20006. Phone: (202) 331–1313 to 1316, inclusive.

Embassy of the Republic of Venezuela, 1099 30th St., N.W., Washington D.C. 20007. Phone: (202) 342-2214.

Embassy of Western Samoa, 820 Second Ave., Suite 800, New York, N.Y. 10017. Phone: (212) 599-6196, 6197.

Embassy of the Republic of Yemen, 2600 Virginia Ave., N.W. Suite 705, Washington, D.C. 20037. Phone: (202) 965–4760, 4761.

Embassy of the Socialist Federal Republic of Yugoslavia, 2410 California St., N.W., Washington, D.C. 20008. Phone: (202) 462–6566.

Embassy of the Republic of Zaire, 1800 New Hampshire Ave., N.W., Washington, D.C. 20009. Phone: (202) 234–7690, 7691.

Embassy of the Republic of Zambia, 2419 Massachusetts Ave., N.W., Washington, D.C. 20008. Phone: (202) 265–9717 to 9721.

Embassy of the Republic of Zimbabwe, 1608 New Hampshire Ave., N.W., Washington, D.C. 20009. Phone: (202) 332–7100.

Diplomatic Personnel To and From the U.S.

Country	U.S. Representative to[1]	Rank	Representative from[2]	Rank
Afghanistan	—	—	Abdul Rahim	Cd'A.
Albania	William E. Ryerson	Amb.	Roland Bimo	Amb.
Algeria	Mary Ann Casey	Amb.	Nourredine Yazid Zerhouni	Amb.
Antigua and Barbuda	Bryant J. Salter	Cd'A.	Dr. Patrick Albert Lewis	Amb.
Argentina	Terence A. Todman	Amb.	Carlos Ortiz de Rozas	Amb.

Country	U.S. Representative to[1]	Rank	Representative from[2]	Rank
Armenia	Thomas L. Price	CdA.	Rouben Robert Shugarian	Amb.
Australia	Edward Perkins	Amb.	Michael John Cook	Amb.
Austria	(Vacancy)	Amb.	Helmut Tuerk	Amb.
Azerbaijan	Richard Miles	Cd'A.	Hafiz Mir Jalal Oglu Pashayev	Amb.
Bahamas	(Vacancy)	Amb.	Timothy Baswell Donaldson	Amb.
Bahrain	(Vacancy)	Amb.	Abdul Rahman bin Fares Al-Khalifa	Amb.
Bangladesh	William B. Milam	Amb.	Abul Ahsan	Amb.
Barbados	G. Philip Hughes	Amb.	Rudi Valentine Webster	Amb.
Belarus	David Swartz	Cd'A.	Serguei Nikolaevich Martynov	Consl.
Belgium	Bruce S. Gelb	Amb.	Juan Cassiers	Amb.
Belize	Eugene L. Scassa	Amb.	James V. Hyde	Amb.
Benin	Ruth A. Davis	Amb.	Candide Pierre Ahouansou	Amb.
Bolivia	Charles R. Bowers	Amb.	Jorge Crespo–Velasco	Amb.
Botswana	David Passage	Amb.	Botsweletse Kingsley Sebele	Amb.
Brazil	Richard H. Melton	Amb.	Rubens Ricupero	Amb.
Brunei	Donald B. Ensenat	Amb.	Dato Haji Mohammad Kassim	Amb.
Bulgaria	Hugh Kenneth Hill	Amb.	Ognian Raytchev Pishev	Amb.
Burkina Faso	Edward P. Byrnn	Amb.	Thomas Yara Kambou	Consl.
Burundi	(Vacancy)	Amb.	Julien Kavakure	Amb.
Cameroon	(Vacancy)	Amb.	Paul Pondi	Amb.
Canada	(Vacancy)	Amb.	John J.D. deChastelain	Amb.
Cape Verde	Joseph M. Segars	Amb.	Carlos Alberto Santos Silva	Amb.
Central African Republic	Richard E. Gribbon III	Amb.	Jean–Pierre Sohahong–Kombet	Amb.
Chad	Richard W. Bogosian	Amb.	Lemayel Favitsou-Boulandi	Cd'A.
Chile	Curtis W. Kamman	Amb.	Patricio Silva	Amb.
China	J. Stapleton Roy	Amb.	Li Daoyu	Amb.
Colombia	Morris D. Busby	Amb.	Jaime Garcia-Parra	Amb.
Comoros	Kenneth N. Peltier	Amb.	Amini Ali Moumin	Amb.
Congo, People's Republic of	James D. Phillips	Amb.	Roger Issombo	Amb.
Costa Rica	Luis Guinot, Jr.	Amb.	Gonzalo J. Facio	Amb.
Côte d'Ivoire	Hume A. Horan	Amb.	Charles Gomis	Amb.
Croatia	(Vacancy)	Amb.	Peter A. Sarcevic	Amb.
Cyprus	Robert E. Lamb	Amb.	Michael E. Sherifis	Amb.
Czech Republic	Adrian A. Basora	Amb.	Michael Zantovsky	Amb.
Denmark	Richard B. Stone	Amb.	Peter P. Dyvig	Amb.
Djibouti	Charles R. Baquet III	Amb.	Roble Olhaye	Amb.
Dominica	—	—	Edward I. Watty	Amb.
Dominican Republic	Robert S. Pastorino	Amb.	Jose del Carmen Ariza	Amb.
Ecuador	(Vacancy)	Amb.	Edgar Teran-Teran	Amb.
Egypt	Robert H. Pelletreau, Jr.	Amb.	Ahmed Maher El Sayed	Amb.
El Salvador	(Vacancy)	Amb.	Miguel Angel Salaverria	Amb.
Equatorial Guinea	John E. Bennett	Amb.	Damaso Obiang Ndong	Amb.
Estonia	Robert C. Frasure	Amb.	Eerik-Niiles Kross	Cd'A.
Ethiopia	Marc. A. Baas	Cd'A.	Berhane Gebre-Christos	Amb.
Fiji	(Vacancy)	Amb.	Pita Kewa Nacuva	Amb.
Finland	John H. Kelly	Amb.	Jukka Valtasaari	Amb.
France	Pamela C. Harriman	Amb.	Jacques Andreani	Amb.
Gabon	Joseph C. Wilson IV	Amb.	Fidele Nguembi Moussavou	Cd'A.
Gambia	Arlene Render	Amb.	Ousman A. Sallah	Amb.
Georgia	Kent N. Brown	Cd'A.	—	—
Germany	Richard C. Holbrooke	Amb.	Immo Stabreit	Amb.
Ghana	Kenneth L. Brown	Amb.	Dr. Joseph L.S. Abbey	Amb.
Greece	Thomas M.T. Niles	Amb.	Christos Zacharakis	Amb.
Grenada	Annette T. Veler	Cd'A.	Denneth Modeste	Amb.
Guatemala	(Vacancy)	Amb.	Edmond Mulet	Amb.
Guinea	Dane F. Smith, Jr.	Amb.	Elhadj Boubarcar Barry	Amb.
Guinea–Bissau	Roger A. McGuire	Amb.	Alfredo Lopes Cabral	Amb.
Guyana	George F. Jones	Amb.	June Angela Persaud	Cd'A.
Haiti	Leslie M. Alexander	Cd'A.	Jean Casimir	Amb.
Holy See	Raymond L. Flynn	Amb.	Most Rev. Agostino Cacciavillan	Pro–Nuncio
Honduras	Cresencio S. Arcos, Jr.	Amb.	Rene Arturo Bendana-Valenzuela	Amb.
Hungary	Melvyn Levitsky	Amb.	Pal Tar	Amb.
Iceland	Parker W. Borg	Amb.	Tomas A. Tomasson	Amb.
India	Stephen J. Solarz	Amb.	Siddhartha S. Ray	Amb.
Indonesia	Robert L. Barry	Amb.	Abdul Rachman Ramly	Amb.
Ireland	Jean Kennedy Smith	Amb.	Dermot A. Gallagher	Amb.
Israel	(Vacancy)	Amb.	Itamar Rabinovich	Amb.
Italy	Reginald Bartholomew	Amb.	Boris Biancheri	Amb.
Jamaica	(Vacancy)	Amb.	Richard Leighton Bernal	Amb.
Japan	Walter F. Mondale	Amb.	Takakazu Kuriyama	Amb.
Jordan	Roger G. Harrison	Amb.	Fayez A. Tarawneh	Amb.

Country	U.S. Representative to[1]	Rank	Representative from[2]	Rank
Kazakhstan	William Courtney	Cons. Gen.	Alim Sh. Djambourchine	Amb.
Kenya	(Vacancy)	Amb.	Denis D. Afande	Amb.
Korea, South	James T. Laney	Amb.	Seung-Soo Han	Amb.
Kuwait	Edward W. Gnehm, Jr.	Amb.	Mohammed Sabah Al-Salim Al-Sabah	Amb.
Kyrgyzstan	Edward Hurwitz	Cd'A.	Roza Otunbayeva	Amb.
Laos	Victor Tomseth	Amb.	Hiem Phommachanh	Amb.
Latvia	Ints M. Silins	Amb.	Ojars Eriks Kalnins	Amb.
Lebanon	Ryan C. Crocker	Amb.	Simon Massoud Karam	Amb.
Lesotho	(Vacancy)	Amb.	Teboho E. Kitleli	Amb.
Liberia	William P. Twaddell	Cd'A.	Konah K. Blackett	Cd'A.
Lithuania	Darryl N. Johnson	Amb.	Stasys Lozoraitis	Amb.
Luxembourg	Edward M. Rowell	Amb.	Alphonse Berns	Amb.
Madagascar	Dennis P. Barrett	Amb.	Pierrot J. Rajaonarivelo	Amb.
Malawi	Michael T.F. Pistor	Amb.	Robert B. Mbaya	Amb.
Malaysia	John S. Wolf	Amb.	Dato Abdul Maji Mohamed	Amb.
Mali	Herbert Donald Gelber	Amb.	Siragatou Ibrahim Cisse	Amb.
Malta	(Vacancy)	Amb.	Albert Borg Olivier De Puget	Amb.
Marshall Islands	David C. Fields	Amb.	Wilfred I. Kendall	Amb.
Mauritania	Gordon S. Brown	Amb.	Mohamed Fall Ainina	Amb.
Mauritius	(Vacancy)	Amb.	Chitmansing Jesseramsing	Amb.
Mexico	James R. Jones	Amb.	Jorge Montano	Amb.
Micronesia	Aurelia E. Brazeal	Amb.	Jesse B. Marehalau	Amb
Moldova	Mary C. Pendleton	Cd'A.	—	—
Mongolia	Joseph E. Lake	Amb.	Luvsandorj Dawagiv	Amb.
Morocco	(Vacancy)	Amb.	Mohamed Benaissa	Amb.
Mozambique	Townsend B. Friedman, Jr.	Amb.	Hipolito Pereira Zozimo Patricio	Amb.
Myanmar (Burma)	(Vacancy)	Amb.	U Thaung	Amb.
Namibia	(Vacancy)	Amb.	Tuliameni Kalomoh	Amb.
Nepal	Julia Chang Bloch	Amb.	Yog Prasad Upadhyay	Amb.
Netherlands	(Vacancy)	Amb.	Adriaan Pieter Roetert Jacobovits	Amb.
New Zealand	(Vacancy)	Amb.	Denis Bazeley Gordon McLean	Amb.
Nicaragua	(Vacancy)	Amb.	Roberto Genaro Mayorga-Cortes	Amb.
Niger	Jennifer C. Ward	Amb.	Adamou Seydou	Amb.
Nigeria	William L. Swing	Amb.	Zubair Mahmud Kazaure	Amb.
Norway	(Vacancy)	Amb.	Kjeld Vibe	Amb.
Oman	David J. Dunford	Amb.	Awadh Bader Al-Shanfari	Amb.
Pakistan	John C. Monjo	Amb.	Ali Sarwar Naqvi	Amb.
Panama	Deane R. Hinton	Amb.	Jaime Ford Boyd	Amb.
Papua New Guinea	Robert W. Farrand	Amb.	Margaret Taylor	Amb.
Paraguay	Jon David Glassman	Amb.	Juan Esteban Aguirre	Amb.
Peru	(Vacancy)	Amb.	Ricardo V. Luna	Amb.
Philippines	John D. Negroponte	Amb.	Franklin M. Ebdalin	Min.
Poland	(Vacancy)	Amb.	Kazimierz Dziewanowski	Amb.
Portugal	Everett Ellis Briggs	Amb.	Francisco Jose Laco Treichler Knopfli	Amb.
Qatar	Kenton W. Keith	Amb.	Abdulrahman bin Saud Al-Thaxi	Amb.
Romania	John R. Davis, Jr.	Amb.	Aurel-Dragos Munteanu	Amb.
Russia	Thomas Pickering	Amb.	Vladimir Petrovich Lukin	Amb.
Rwanda	Robert A. Flaten	Amb.	Aloys Uwimana	Amb.
Saint Kitts and Nevis	—		Aubrey Eric Hart	Min.
Saint Lucia	—		Dr. Joseph Edsel Edmunds	Amb.
Saint Vincent and the Grenadines	—	—	Kingsley C.A. Layne	Amb.
Saudi Arabia	(Vacancy)	Amb.	Prince Bandar Bin Sultan	Amb.
Senegal	(Vacancy)	Amb.	Ibra Deguene Ka	Amb.
Seychelles	(Vacancy)	Amb.	Marc R. Marengo	2nd Secy.
Sierra Leone	Lauralee M. Peters	Amb.	Thomas Kahota Kargbo	Amb.
Singapore	Jon M. Huntsman, Jr.	Amb.	S.R. Nathan	Amb.
Slovak Republic	Paul Hacker	P.O.	Milan Erban	Min. Consl.
Slovenia	Allan Wendt	Cd'A.	Dr. Ernest Petric	Amb.
Solomon Islands	Robert W. Farrand	Amb.	—	—
South Africa	Princeton N. Lyman	Amb.	Harry Heinz Schwarz	Amb.
Spain	Richard N. Gardner	Amb.	Jaime de Ojeda	Amb.
Sri Lanka	Teresita C. Schaffer	Amb.	Anada W.P. Guruge	Amb.
Sudan	Donald K. Petterson	Amb.	Abdalla Ahmed Abdalla	Amb.
Suriname	John P. Leonard	Amb.	Willem A. Udenhout	Amb.
Swaziland	Stephen H. Rogers	Amb.	Absalom Vusani Mamba	Amb.
Sweden	(Vacancy)	Amb.	Carl Henrik Sihver Liljegren	Amb.
Switzerland	(Vacancy)	Amb.	Edouard Brunner	Amb.
Syria	Christopher W.S. Ross	Amb.	Walid Al-Moualem	Amb.
Tajikistan	Stanley Escudero	Cd'A,	—	—
Tanzania	Peter Jon de Vos	Amb.	Charles Musama Nyirabu	Amb.

Country	U.S. Representative to[1]	Rank	Representative from[2]	Rank
Thailand	David F. Lambertson	Amb.	M.L. Birabhongse Kasemsri	Amb.
Togo	Harmon E. Kirby	Amb.	Edem Frederic Hegbe	Consl.
Trinidad and Tobago	Sally G. Cowal	Amb.	Corinne Averille McKnight	Amb.
Tunisia	John T. McCarthy	Amb.	Ismail Khelil	Amb.
Turkey	Richard C. Barkley	Amb.	Nuzhet Kandemir	Amb.
Turkmenistan	Joseph S. Hulings III	Cd'A.	—	—
Uganda	Johnnie Carson	Amb.	Stephen Kapimpina Katenta–Apuli	Amb.
Ukraine	Roman Popadiuk	Cd'A.	Oleh H. Bilorus	Amb.
United Arab Emirates	William A. Rugh	Amb.	Mohammad bin Hussein Al-Shaali	Amb.
United Kingdom	Raymond G.H. Seitz	Amb.	Sir Robin Renwick	Amb.
Uruguay	Richard C. Brown	Amb.	Dr. Eduardo MacGillycuddy	Amb.
Uzbekistan	Henry L. Clarke	Amb.	Mukhamed Bobir Malikou	Amb.
Venezuela	Michael M. Skol	Amb.	Simon Alberto Consalvi	Amb.
Western Samoa	(Vacancy)	Amb.	Tuiloma Neroni Slade	Amb.
Yemen	Arthur H. Hughes	Amb.	Mohsin A. Alaini	Amb.
Yugoslavia (Bosnia-Hercegovina)	Victor Jackovich	Cd'A.	Ivan Zivkovic	Min. Consl.
Zaire	(Vacancy)	Amb.	Tatanene Manata	Amb.
Zambia	Gordon L. Streeb	Amb.	Dunstan Weston Kamana	Amb.
Zimbabwe	E. Gibson Lanpher	Amb.	Amos Bernhard Muvengwa Midzi	Amb.

1. As of Spring 1993. 2. As of May 1993. NOTE: Amb.=Ambassador; Cd'A.=Charge d'Affaires; Secy.=Secretary; Consl.=Counselor; Min.=Minister; P.O.=Principal Officer. *Source:* U.S. Department of State.

Preventing Traveler's Ailments

Source: FDA Consumer.

Traveler's Diarrhea

Some 20 to 50 percent of Americans visiting the tropics get what is called "Montezuma's revenge," the "skitters" or, in Spanish-speaking countries, "turista." Its symptoms include loose and watery stools, nausea, bloating, abdominal cramps, and sometimes fever and malaise. Fortunately, it is a self-limiting disease. Even if untreated, its symptoms usually go away in three or four days. If diarrhea last more than four days or is accompanied by severe cramps, bloody stools, or foul-smelling gas, the individual should see a physician.

Most travelers' diarrhea is caused by a special strain of the common intestinal bacteria *Escherichia coli.* This strain of *E. coli,* as it is usually known, accounts for at least 40 percent of all travelers' diarrhea. Other bacteria, such as the ones responsible for salmonellosis and shigellosis, can also cause diarrhea, as can such parasitic conditions as giardiasis and amebiasis.

Whatever the cause, the best way to treat travelers' diarrhea, the experts say, is to prevent it. Most diarrhea-causing organisms are water-borne, passed on in untreated water or by food handlers who have not washed their hands adequately.

Savvy tourists will avoid using untreated or suspect water in areas where travelers' diarrhea is common. This includes not drinking tap water or using it to brush your teeth (even in good hotels), not using ice in sodas or alcoholic drinks, and not mixing alcohol with water. It's also smart to skip milk and other dairy products unless you are sure they have been pasteurized.

For brushing your teeth or drinking in your hotel room, boil the water you intend to use for at least five minutes or add water purification tablets. Avoid bottled water unless it is carbonated—the carbonation process inhibits bacterial growth. Drink carbonated beverages, beer, wine, and coffee or tear. And wipe off bottle or can tops before drinking from them.

Also be cautious about food, especially in developing countries. Don't eat raw vegetables, fruits, meats, or seafood. Avoid cold buffets left in the sun for several hours, garden or potato salads, and food from street vendors. Eat only hot cooked meals, fruits you have peeled yourself, and packaged foods.

If, despite all your best efforts, travelers' diarrhea strikes, medical experts and experienced travelers alike recommend drinking plenty of fluids to replace water and adding oral rehydration packets to fluids to replace lost minerals. Additionally, several prescription and over-the-counter drugs will relieve diarrhea's symptoms or kill bacteria that cause the disease.

Malaria

If travelers' diarrhea is the disease most likely to strike Americans abroad, malaria is the most serious ailment they are likely to encounter. Once thought to be under control and perhaps even close to eradication, malaria has made a remarkable comeback in the past decade or two.

Malaria is caused by a single-cell blood parasite called plasmodium. The parasite is usually transmitted to people by the bite of an infected *Anopheles* mosquito. Symptoms start with a listless feeling, loss of appetite, muscle aches, and a low fever. After a few days, the classic symptoms appear: a fever that can reach 105 degrees Fahrenheit and teeth-rattling chills that can last 20 to 60 minutes. The fever may break and then return again on a 48-to-72-hour cycle, and it may be accompanied by nausea, diarrhea and vomiting. Fortunately, malaria can still be prevented and cured in most cases if diagnosed properly.

As with travelers' diarrhea, the best treatment for malaria is prevention. Americans are advised to avoid the mosquitoes that transmit the disease. Stay inside at dusk and dawn, wear long pants or long-sleeved shirts when in mosquito-infested areas, sleep in well-screened rooms or under mosquito nets, and use an insect repellent such as DEET (N, N-diethyl-m-tolumide) on exposed skin.

Other Diseases

Most other diseases or medical conditions to which American travelers are likely to be exposed are rare and easily avoided. Schistosomiasis, for example, occurs in much of Africa, the Middle East, northeastern South America, and some Caribbean islands. Also called bilharzia or snail fever, it is caused by a freshwater snail-borne parasite. Schistosomiasis can be prevented by staying out of freshwater lakes and streams in infested areas. Salt water and adequately chlorinated swimming pools are okay, though.

Typhoid is caused by the bacterial organism *Salmonella typhi,* usually transmitted through contaminated food or water. Rare in the United States, most of the 400 to 500 typhoid cases a year reported in this country have been contracted abroad, usually in less developed areas where sanitation is poor. Immunization is therefore recommended, but only for travelers going to areas where the disease is common.

The Centers for Disease Control maintains a recorded telephone message system with general and geographic-specific information on travelers' diseases. The number is (404) 332-4559. Information on malaria and other specific diseases can be obtained by calling (404) 332-4555. □

State and City Tourism Offices

The following is a selected list of state tourism offices. Where a toll-free 800 number is available, it is given. However, the numbers are subject to change.

ALABAMA
Bureau of Tourism & Travel
401 Adams Ave., Suite 126
P.O. Box 4309
Montgomery, AL 36104-4331
205–242–4169 or 1–800–ALABAMA

ALASKA
Alaska Division of Tourism
P.O. Box 110801
Juneau, AK 99811-0801
907–465–2010

ARIZONA
Arizona Office of Tourism
1100 West Washington
Phoenix, AZ 85007
602 542–TOUR or 1–800–842–8257

ARKANSAS
Arkansas Department of Parks and Tourism
1 Capitol Mall
Little Rock, AR 72201
501–682–7777 or 1–800–NATURAL
(to receive literature both in and out of state)

CALIFORNIA
California Office of Tourism
P.O. Box 1499
Sacramento, CA 95812–1499
1–800–862–2543 U.S. only

COLORADO
Colorado Tourism Board
1625 Broadway, Suite 1700
Denver, CO 80202
303–592–5410
For a vacation planning kit, call Toll–Free
1–800–COLORADO (265–6723)

CONNECTICUT
Tourism Promotion Service
CT Dept. of Economic Development
865 Brook Street
Rocky Hill, CT 06067–3405
203–258–4355 or 800–CT BOUND (nationwide)

DELAWARE
Delaware Tourism Office
Delaware Development Office
99 Kings Highway
P.O. Box 1401
Dover, DE 19903
302–739–4271 or 1–800–441–8846
(both in and out of state)

DISTRICT OF COLUMBIA
Washington Convention and Visitors Association
1212 New York Ave., NW Suite 600
Washington, D.C. 20005–3992
202–789–7000

FLORIDA
Department of Commerce Visitors Inquiry
126 Van Buren St.
Tallahassee, FL 32399–2000
904–487–1462

GEORGIA
Tourist Division
P.O. Box 1776
Atlanta, GA 30301-1776
404–656–3590
1-800-VISIT GA
(1-800-847-4842)

HAWAII
Hawaii Visitors Bureau
2270 Kalakaua Ave., Suite 801
Honolulu, HI 96815
808–923–1811

IDAHO
Department of Commerce
700 W. State St. Second Floor
Boise, ID 83720
208–334–2470 or 1–800–635–7820

ILLINOIS
Illinois Bureau of Tourism
100 W. Randolph, Suite 3–400
Chicago, IL 60601
312–814–4732

INDIANA
Indiana Dept. of Commerce
Tourism & Film Development Division
One North Capitol
Suite 700
Indianapolis, IN 46204–2288
317–232–8860 or 1–800–289–6646

IOWA
Iowa Department of Economic Development
Division of Tourism
200 East Grand Avenue
Des Moines, IA 50309
515–242-4705
1-800-345-IOWA

KANSAS
Kansas Department of Commerce & Housing
Travel & Tourism Development Division
700 SW Harrison St., Suite 1300
Topeka, KS 66603–3712
913–296–2009
1–800–2KANSAS

KENTUCKY
Department of Travel Development
Dept. MR
P.O. Box 2011
Frankfort, KY 40602
1–800–225–TRIP
(From the United States and Canadian provinces of Ontario and Quebec)

LOUISIANA
Office of Tourism
P.O. Box 94291
Baton Rouge, LA 70804–9291
504–342–8119 or 1–800–33GUMBO

Average Daily Temperatures (°F) in Tourist Cities

Location	January High	January Low	April High	April Low	July High	July Low	October High	October Low
U.S. CITIES (See Weather and Climate Section)								
CANADA								
Ottawa	21	3	51	31	81	58	54	37
Quebec	18	2	45	29	76	57	51	37
Toronto	30	16	50	34	79	59	56	40
Vancouver	41	32	58	40	74	54	57	44
MEXICO								
Acapulco	85	70	87	71	89	75	88	74
Mexico City	66	42	78	52	74	54	70	50
OVERSEAS								
Australia (Sydney)	78	65	71	58	60	46	71	56
Austria (Vienna)	34	26	57	41	75	59	55	44
Bahamas (Nassau)	77	65	81	69	88	75	85	73
Bermuda (Hamilton)	68	58	71	59	85	73	79	69
Brazil (Rio de Janeiro)	84	73	80	69	75	63	77	66
Denmark (Copenhagen)	36	29	50	37	72	55	53	42
Egypt (Cairo)	65	47	83	57	96	70	86	65
France (Paris)	42	32	60	41	76	55	59	44
Germany (Berlin)	35	26	55	38	74	55	55	41
Greece (Athens)	54	42	67	52	90	72	74	60
Hong Kong	64	56	75	67	87	78	81	73
India (Calcutta)	80	55	97	76	90	79	89	74
Italy (Rome)	54	39	68	46	88	64	73	53
Israel (Jerusalem)	55	41	73	50	87	63	81	59
Japan (Tokyo)	47	29	63	46	83	70	69	55
Nigeria (Lagos)	88	74	89	77	83	74	85	74
Netherlands (Amsterdam)	40	34	52	43	69	59	56	48
Puerto Rico (San Juan)	81	67	84	69	87	74	87	73
South Africa (Cape Town)	78	60	72	53	63	45	70	52
Spain (Madrid)	47	33	64	44	87	62	66	48
United Kingdom (London)	44	35	56	40	73	55	58	44
United Kingdom (Edinburgh)	43	35	50	39	65	52	53	44
Russia (Moscow)	21	9	47	31	76	55	46	34
Venezuela (Caracas)	75	56	81	60	78	61	79	61
Yugoslavia (Belgrade)	37	27	64	45	84	61	65	47

MAINE
Maine Publicity Bureau
P.O. Box 2300
Hallowell, ME 04347–2300
207–582–9300

MARYLAND
Office of Tourism Development
217 E. Redwood St.
Baltimore, MD 21202
410–333–6611 Business Office
1–800–543–1036—Maryland Travel Kit

MASSACHUSETTS
Executive Office of Economic Affairs
Office of Travel and Tourism
100 Cambridge St., 13th Floor
Boston, MA 02202
617–727–3201

MICHIGAN
Travel Bureau
Department of Commerce
P.O. Box 30226
Lansing, MI 48909
1–800–5432–YES

MINNESOTA
Minnesota Office of Tourism
100 Metro Square
121 Seventh Place E
St. Paul, MN 55101-2112
612–296–5029 or 1–800–657–3700

MISSISSIPPI
Department of Economic and Community Development
Tourism Development
P.O. Box 22825
Jackson, MS 39205-2825
601–359–3297 or 1–800–647–2290

MISSOURI
Missouri Division of Tourism
Truman State Office Bldg.
301 W. High St.
P.O. Box 1055
Jefferson City, MO 65102
314–751–4133

MONTANA
Department of Commerce
Travel Montana
1424 9th Avenue
Helena, MT 59620
406–444–2654 or
1–800–541–1447

NEBRASKA
Dept. of Economic Development
Division of Travel and Tourism
P.O. Box 98913
Lincoln, NE 68509
402–471–3744 or
1–800–228–4307
(In-state or out of state)

NEVADA
Commission on Tourism
Capitol Complex
Carson City, NV 89710
1–800–Nevada–8

NEW HAMPSHIRE
Office of Vacation Travel
P.O. Box 856
Concord, NH 03302
603–271–2666
or for recorded weekly events, ski conditions, foliage reports
1–800–258–3608

NEW JERSEY
Division of Travel and Tourism
CN–826
Trenton, NJ 08625
1–800–JERSEY–7

NEW MEXICO
New Mexico Department of Tourism
Lamy Bldg.
491 Old Santa Fe Trail
Santa Fe, NM 87503
505–827–7400 or 1–800–545–2040

NEW YORK
Division of Tourism
1 Commerce Plaza
Albany, NY 12245
Toll free from anywhere in the U.S. and its territorial possessions
1–800–225–5697. From Canada, call (518) 474–4116

NORTH CAROLINA
Travel and Tourism Division
Department of Commerce
430 North Salisbury St.
Raleigh, NC 27611
919–733–4171 or
1–800–VISIT NC

NORTH DAKOTA
North Dakota Tourism Promotion
Liberty Memorial Building
Capitol Grounds
604 E. Boulevard
Bismarck, ND 58505
701–224–2525 or
1–800–435–5663

OHIO
Ohio Division of Travel and Tourism
P.O. Box 1001
Columbus, OH 43266–0001
614–466–8844 (Business Office)
1–800–BUCKEYE (National Toll–Free Travel Hotline)

OKLAHOMA
Oklahoma Tourism and Recreation Dept.
Literature Distribution Center
P.O. Box 60789
Oklahoma City, OK 73146–9910
405–521–2409 (In Oklahoma City area) or nationwide at
1–800–652–6552

OREGON
Tourism Division
Oregon Economic Development Dept.
775 Summer St. NE
Salem, OR 97310
503–373–1270 or 1–800–547–7842 (Out of state and in–state)

PENNSYLVANIA
Office of Travel Marketing
453 Forum Building
Harrisburg, PA 17120
717–787–5453 (Business Office)
1–800–VISIT PA, ext. 257
(To order single free copy of PA Travel Guide)

RHODE ISLAND
Rhode Island Tourism Division
7 Jackson Walkway
Providence, RI 02903
401–277–2601 or
1–800–556–2484
U.S. and Canada

SOUTH CAROLINA
South Carolina Division of Tourism
Box 71
Columbia, SC 29202
803–734–0235

SOUTH DAKOTA
Department of Tourism
711 E. Wells Ave.
Pierre, South Dakota 57501
605–773–3301 or
1–800–S–DAKOTA

TENNESSEE
Department of Tourist Development
P.O. Box 23170
Nashville, TN 37202
615–741–2158

TEXAS
Travel Information Services
Texas Department of Transportation
P.O. Box 5064
Austin, TX 78763–5064
512–483–3705
1–800–452–9292

UTAH
Utah Travel Council
Council Hall, Capitol Hill
Salt Lake City, UT 84114
801–538–1030

VERMONT
Department of Travel and Tourism
134 State St.
Montpelier, VT 05602–9848
802–828–3236

VIRGINIA
Virginia Department of Economic Development
Division of Tourism
1021 East Cary St.
Richmond, VA 23219
804–786–4484
1–800-VISIT-VA

WASHINGTON
Washington State Dept. of Trade and Economic Development
101 General Administration Bldg.
P.O. Box 42500
Olympia, WA 98504–2500
206–753–5630

WASHINGTON, D.C.
See District of Columbia

WEST VIRGINIA
Division of Tourism and Parks
2101 Washington St. E.
Charleston, WV 25305
304–558–2286 or
1–800–CALL–WVA

WISCONSIN
Travel Information
Division of Tourism
Box 7606
Madison, WI 53707
Toll free in WI and neighbor states 1–800–372–2737
others: 608–266–2161
Nationally 1–800–432–TRIP

WYOMING
Wyoming Division of Tourism
I–25 at College Drive
Cheyenne, WY 82002
307–777–7777 or
1–800–225–5996

Passport Travel Tips

The American Society of Travel Agents (ASTA) advises those traveling abroad to photocopy important pages in their passports, especially the pages featuring their photos and passport numbers, and dates and places of issue. Also copy those pages containing visas of countries you plan to visit.

In the case of a lost passport, U.S. embassies will usually accept photocopies as proof that you actually possess a passport. Losing a passport abroad can be a time–consuming and expensive process to replace.

Keep a list of your credit cards and other important numbers (driver's license, traveler's cheques) in a separate location from your cards in case they are lost. □

Road Mileages Between U.S. Cities[1]

Cities	Birming-ham	Boston	Buffalo	Chicago	Cleveland	Dallas	Denver
Birmingham, Ala.	—	1,194	947	657	734	653	1,318
Boston, Mass.	1,194	—	457	983	639	1,815	1,991
Buffalo, N.Y.	947	457	—	536	192	1,387	1,561
Chicago, Ill.	657	983	536	—	344	931	1,050
Cleveland, Ohio	734	639	192	344	—	1,205	1,369
Dallas, Tex.	653	1,815	1,387	931	1,205	—	801
Denver, Colo	1,318	1,991	1,561	1,050	1,369	801	—
Detroit, Mich.	754	702	252	279	175	1,167	1,301
El Paso, Tex.	1,278	2,358	1,928	1,439	1,746	625	652
Houston, Tex.	692	1,886	1,532	1,092	1,358	242	1,032
Indianapolis, Ind.	492	940	510	189	318	877	1,051
Kansas City, Mo.	703	1,427	997	503	815	508	616
Los Angeles, Calif.	2,078	3,036	2,606	2,112	2,424	1,425	1,174
Louisville, Ky.	378	996	571	305	379	865	1,135
Memphis, Tenn.	249	1,345	965	546	773	470	1,069
Miami, Fla.	777	1,539	1,445	1,390	1,325	1,332	2,094
Minneapolis, Minn.	1,067	1,402	955	411	763	969	867
New Orleans, La.	347	1,541	1,294	947	1,102	504	1,305
New York, N.Y.	983	213	436	840	514	1,604	1,780
Omaha, Neb.	907	1,458	1,011	493	819	661	559
Philadelphia, Pa.	894	304	383	758	432	1,515	1,698
Phoenix, Ariz.	1,680	2,664	2,234	1,729	2,052	1,027	836
Pittsburgh, Pa.	792	597	219	457	131	1,237	1,411
St. Louis, Mo.	508	1,179	749	293	567	638	871
Salt Lake City, Utah	1,805	2,425	1,978	1,458	1,786	1,239	512
San Francisco, Calif.	2,385	3,179	2,732	2,212	2,540	1,765	1,266
Seattle, Wash.	2,612	3,043	2,596	2,052	2,404	2,122	1,373
Washington, D.C.	751	440	386	695	369	1,372	1,635

Cities	Detroit	El Paso	Houston	Indian-apolis	Kansas City	Los Angeles	Louisville
Birmingham, Ala.	754	1,278	692	492	703	2,078	378
Boston, Mass.	702	2,358	1,886	940	1,427	3,036	996
Buffalo, N.Y.	252	1,928	1,532	510	997	2,606	571
Chicago, Ill.	279	1,439	1,092	189	503	2,112	305
Cleveland, Ohio	175	1,746	1,358	318	815	2,424	379
Dallas, Tex.	1,167	625	242	877	508	1,425	865
Denver, Colo.	1,310	652	1,032	1,051	616	1,174	1,135
Detroit, Mich.	—	1,696	1,312	290	760	2,369	378
El Paso, Tex.	1,696	—	756	1,418	936	800	1,443
Houston, Tex.	1,312	756	—	1,022	750	1,556	981
Indianapolis, Ind.	290	1,418	1,022	—	487	2,096	114
Kansas City, Mo.	760	936	750	487	—	1,609	519
Los Angeles, Calif.	2,369	800	1,556	2,096	1,609	—	2,128
Louisville, Ky.	378	1,443	981	114	519	2,128	—
Memphis, Tenn.	756	1,095	586	466	454	1,847	396
Miami, Fla.	1,409	1,957	1,237	1,225	1,479	2,757	1,111
Minneapolis, Minn.	698	1,353	1,211	600	466	2,041	716
New Orleans, La.	1,101	1,121	365	839	839	1,921	725
New York, N.Y.	671	2,147	1,675	729	1,216	2,825	785
Omaha, Neb.	754	1,015	903	590	204	1,733	704
Philadelphia, Pa.	589	2,065	1,586	647	1,134	2,743	703
Phoenix, Ariz.	1,986	402	1,158	1,713	1,226	398	1,749
Pittsburgh, Pa.	288	1,778	1,395	360	847	2,456	416
St. Louis, Mo.	529	1,179	799	239	255	1,864	264
Salt Lake City, Utah	1,721	877	1,465	1,545	1,128	728	1,647
San Francisco, Calif.	2,475	1,202	1,958	2,299	1,882	403	2,401
Seattle, Wash.	2,339	1,760	2,348	2,241	1,909	1,150	2,355
Washington, D.C.	526	1,997	1,443	565	1,071	2,680	601

1. These figures represent estimates and are subject to change.

Road Mileages Between U.S. Cities

Cities	Memphis	Miami	Minne-apolis	New Orleans	New York	Omaha	Phila-delphia
Birmingham, Ala.	249	777	1,067	347	983	907	894
Boston, Mass.	1,345	1,539	1,402	1,541	213	1,458	304
Buffalo, N.Y.	965	1,445	955	1,294	436	1,011	383
Chicago, Ill.	546	1,390	411	947	840	493	758
Cleveland, Ohio	773	1,325	763	1,102	514	819	432
Dallas, Tex.	470	1,332	969	504	1,604	661	1,515
Denver, Colo.	1,069	2,094	867	1,305	1,780	559	1,698
Detroit, Mich.	756	1,409	698	1,101	671	754	589
El Paso, Tex.	1,095	1,957	1,353	1,121	2,147	1,015	2,065
Houston, Tex.	586	1,237	1,211	365	1,675	903	1,586
Indianapolis, Ind.	466	1,225	600	839	729	590	647
Kansas City, Mo.	454	1,479	466	839	1,216	204	1,134
Los Angeles, Calif.	1,847	2,757	2,041	1,921	2,825	1,733	2,743
Louisville, Ky.	396	1,111	716	725	785	704	703
Memphis, Tenn.	—	1,025	854	401	1,134	658	1,045
Miami, Fla.	1,025	—	1,801	892	1,328	1,683	1,239
Minneapolis, Minn.	854	1,801	—	1,255	1,259	373	1,177
New Orleans, La.	401	892	1,255	—	1,330	1,043	1,241
New York, N.Y.	1,134	1,328	1,259	1,330	—	1,315	93
Omaha, Neb.	658	1,683	373	1,043	1,315	—	1,233
Philadelphia, Pa.	1,045	1,239	1,177	1,241	93	1,233	—
Phoenix, Ariz.	1,464	2,359	1,644	1,523	2,442	1,305	2,360
Pittsburgh, Pa.	810	1,250	876	1,118	386	932	304
St. Louis, Mo.	295	1,241	559	696	968	459	886
Salt Lake City, Utah	1,556	2,571	1,243	1,743	2,282	967	2,200
San Francisco, Calif.	2,151	3,097	1,997	2,269	3,036	1,721	2,954
Seattle, Wash.	2,363	3,389	1,641	2,606	2,900	1,705	2,818
Washington, D.C.	902	1,101	1,114	1,098	229	1,170	140

Cities	Phoenix	Pitts-burgh	St. Louis	Salt Lake City	San Francisco	Seattle	Wash-ington
Birmingham, Ala.	1,680	792	508	1,805	2,385	2,612	751
Boston, Mass.	2,664	597	1,179	2,425	3,179	3,043	440
Buffalo, N.Y.	2,234	219	749	1,978	2,732	2,596	386
Chicago, Ill.	1,729	457	293	1,458	2,212	2,052	695
Cleveland, Ohio	2,052	131	567	1,786	2,540	2,404	369
Dallas, Tex.	1,027	1,237	638	1,239	1,765	2,122	1,372
Denver, Colo.	836	1,411	871	512	1,266	1,373	1,635
Detroit, Mich.	1,986	288	529	1,721	2,475	2,339	526
El Paso, Tex.	402	1,778	1,179	877	1,202	1,760	1,997
Houston, Tex.	1,158	1,395	799	1,465	1,958	2,348	1,443
Indianapolis, Ind.	1,713	360	239	1,545	2,299	2,241	565
Kansas City, Mo.	1,226	847	255	1,128	1,882	1,909	1,071
Los Angeles, Calif.	398	2,456	1,864	728	403	1,150	2,680
Louisville, Ky.	1,749	416	264	1,647	2,401	2,355	601
Memphis, Tenn.	1,464	810	295	1,556	2,151	2,363	902
Miami, Fla.	2,359	1,250	1,241	2,571	3,097	3,389	1,101
Minneapolis, Minn.	1,644	876	559	1,243	1,997	1,641	1,114
New Orleans, La.	1,523	1,118	696	1,743	2,269	2,626	1,098
New York, N.Y.	2,442	386	968	2,282	3,036	2,900	229
Omaha, Neb.	1,305	932	459	967	1,721	1,705	1,178
Philadelphia, Pa.	2,360	304	886	2,200	2,954	2,818	140
Phoenix, Ariz.	—	2,073	1,485	651	800	1,482	2,278
Pittsburgh, Pa.	2,073	—	599	1,899	2,653	2,517	241
St. Louis, Mo.	1,485	599	—	1,383	2,137	2,164	836
Salt Lake City, Utah	651	1,899	1,383	—	754	883	2,110
San Francisco, Calif.	800	2,653	2,137	754	—	817	2,864
Seattle, Wash.	1,482	2,517	2,164	883	817	—	2,755
Washington, D.C.	2,278	241	836	2,110	2,864	2,755	—

Air Distances Between U.S. Cities in Statute Miles

Cities	Birming-ham	Boston	Buffalo	Chicago	Cleveland	Dallas	Denver
Birmingham, Ala.	—	1,052	776	578	618	581	1,095
Boston, Mass.	1,052	—	400	851	551	1,551	1,769
Buffalo, N. Y.	776	400	—	454	173	1,198	1,370
Chicago, Ill.	578	851	454	—	308	803	920
Cleveland, Ohio	618	551	173	308	—	1,025	1,227
Dallas, Tex.	581	1,551	1,198	803	1,025	—	663
Denver, Colo.	1,095	1,769	1,370	920	1,227	663	—
Detroit, Mich.	641	613	216	238	90	999	1,156
El Paso, Tex.	1,15 2	2,072	1,692	1,252	1,525	572	557
Houston, Tex.	567	1,605	1,286	940	1,114	225	879
Indianapolis, Ind.	433	807	435	165	263	763	1,000
Kansas City, Mo.	579	1,251	861	414	700	451	558
Los Angeles, Calif.	1,802	2,596	2,198	1,745	2,049	1,240	831
Louisville, Ky.	331	826	483	269	311	726	1,038
Memphis, Tenn.	217	1,137	803	482	630	420	879
Miami, Fla.	665	1,255	1,181	1,188	1,087	1,111	1,726
Minneapolis, Minn.	862	1,123	731	355	630	862	700
New Orleans, La.	312	1,359	1,086	833	924	443	1,082
New York, N. Y.	864	188	292	713	405	1,374	1,631
Omaha, Neb.	732	1,282	883	432	739	586	488
Philadelphia, Pa.	783	271	279	666	360	1,299	1,579
Phoenix, Ariz.	1,456	2,300	1,906	1,453	1,749	887	586
Pittsburgh, Pa.	608	483	178	410	115	1,070	1,320
St. Louis, Mo.	400	1,038	662	262	492	547	796
Salt Lake City, Utah	1,466	2,099	1,699	1,260	1,568	999	371
San Francisco, Calif.	2,013	2,699	2,300	1,858	2,166	1,483	949
Seattle, Wash.	2,082	2,493	2,117	1,737	2,026	1,681	1,021
Washington, D.C.	661	393	292	597	306	1,185	1,494

Cities	Detroit	El Paso	Houston	Indian-apolis	Kansas City	Los Angeles	Louisville
Birmingham, Ala.	641	1,152	567	433	579	1,802	331
Boston, Mass.	613	2,072	1,605	807	1,251	2,596	826
Buffalo, N. Y.	216	1,692	1,286	435	861	2,198	483
Chicago, Ill.	238	1,252	940	165	414	1,745	269
Cleveland, Ohio	90	1,525	1,114	263	700	2,049	311
Dallas, Tex.	999	572	225	763	451	1,240	726
Denver, Colo.	1,156	557	879	1,000	558	831	1,038
Detr oit, Mich.	—	1,479	1,105	240	645	1,983	316
El Paso, Tex.	1,479	—	676	1,264	839	701	1,254
Houston, Tex.	1,105	676	—	865	644	1,374	803
Indianapolis, Ind.	240	1,264	865	—	453	1,809	107
Kansas City, Mo.	645	839	644	453	—	1,356	480
Los Angeles, Calif.	1,983	701	1,374	1,809	1,356	—	1,829
Louisville, Ky.	316	1,254	803	107	480	1,829	—
Memphis, Tenn.	623	976	484	384	369	1,603	320
Miami, Fla.	1,152	1,643	968	1,024	1,241	2,339	919
Minneapolis, Minn.	543	1,157	1,056	511	413	1,524	605
New Orleans, La.	939	983	318	712	680	1,673	623
New York, N. Y.	482	1,905	1,420	646	1,097	2,451	652
Omaha, Neb.	669	878	794	525	166	1,315	580
Philadelphia, Pa.	443	1,836	1,341	585	1,038	2,394	582
Phoenix, Ariz.	1,690	346	1,017	1,499	1,049	357	1,508
Pittsburgh, Pa.	205	1,590	1,137	330	781	2,136	344
St. Louis, Mo.	455	1,034	679	231	238	1,589	242
Salt Lake City, Utah	1,492	689	1,200	1,356	925	579	1,402
San Francisco, Calif.	2,091	995	1,645	1,949	1,506	347	1,986
Seattle, Wash.	1,938	1,376	1,891	1,872	1,506	959	1,943
Washington, D.C.	396	1,728	1,220	494	945	2,300	476

Source: National Geodetic Survey.

Air Distances Between U.S. Cities in Statute Miles

Cities	Memphis	Miami	Minne-apolis	New Orleans	New York	Omaha	Phila-delphiae
Birmingham, Ala.	217	665	862	312	864	732	783
Boston, Mass.	1,137	1,255	1,123	1,359	188	1,282	271
Buffalo, N. Y.	803	1,181	731	1,086	292	883	279
Chicago, Ill.	482	1,188	355	833	713	432	666
Cleveland, Ohio	630	1,087	630	924	405	739	360
Dallas, Tex.	420	1,111	862	443	1,374	586	1,299
Denver, Colo.	879	1,726	700	1,082	1,631	488	1,579
Detroit, Mich.	623	1,152	543	939	482	669	443
El Paso, Tex.	976	1,643	1,157	983	1,905	878	1,836
Houston, Tex.	484	968	1,056	318	1,420	794	1,341
Indianapolis, Ind.	384	1,024	511	712	646	525	585
Kansas City, Mo.	369	1,241	413	680	1,097	166	1,038
Los Angeles, Calif.	1,603	2,339	1,524	1,673	2,451	1,315	2,394
Louisville, Ky.	320	919	605	623	652	580	582
Memphis, Tenn.	—	872	699	358	957	529	881
Miami, Fla.	872	—	1,511	669	1,092	1,397	1,019
Minneapolis, Minn.	699	1,511	—	1,051	1,018	290	985
New Orleans, La.	358	669	1,051	—	1,171	847	1,089
New York, N. Y.	957	1,092	1,018	1,171	—	1,144	83
Omaha, Neb.	529	1,397	290	847	1,144	—	1,094
Philadelphia, Pa.	881	1,019	985	1,089	83	1,094	—
Phoenix, Ariz.	1,263	1,982	1,280	1,316	2,145	1,036	2,083
Pittsburgh, Pa.	660	1,010	743	919	317	836	259
St. Louis, Mo.	240	1,061	466	598	875	354	811
Salt Lake City, Utah	1,250	2,089	987	1,434	1,972	833	1,925
San Francisco, Calif.	1,802	2,594	1,584	1,926	2,571	1,429	2,523
Seattle, Wash.	1,867	2,734	1,395	2,101	2,408	1,369	2,380
Washington, D.C.	765	923	934	966	205	1,014	123

Cities	Phoenix	Pitts-burgh	St. Louis	Salt Lake City	San Francisco	Seattle	Wash-ington
Birmingham, Ala.	1,456	608	400	1,466	2,013	2,082	661
Boston, Mass.	2,300	483	1,038	2,099	2,699	2,493	393
Buffalo, N. Y.	1,906	178	662	1,699	2,300	2,117	292
Chicago, Ill.	1,453	410	262	1,260	1,858	1,737	597
Cleveland, Ohio	1,749	115	492	1,568	2,166	2,026	306
Dallas, Tex.	887	1,070	547	999	1,483	1,681	1,185
Denver, Colo.	586	1,320	796	371	949	1,021	1,494
Detroit, Mich.	1,690	205	455	1,492	2,091	1,938	396
El Paso, Tex.	346	1,590	1,034	689	995	1,376	1,728
Houston, Tex.	1,017	1,137	679	1,200	1,645	1,891	1,220
Indianapolis, Ind.	1,499	330	231	1,356	1,949	1,872	494
Kansas City, Mo.	1,049	781	238	925	1,506	1,506	945
Los Angeles, Calif.	357	2,136	1,589	579	347	959	2,300
Louisville, Ky.	1,508	344	242	1,402	1,986	1,943	476
Memphis, Tenn.	1,263	660	240	1,250	1,802	1,867	765
Miami, Fla.	1,982	1,010	1,061	2,089	2,594	2,734	923
Minneapolis, Minn.	1,280	743	466	987	1,584	1,395	934
New Orleans, La.	1,316	919	598	1,434	1,926	2,101	966
New York, N. Y.	2,145	317	875	1,972	2,571	2,408	205
Omaha, Neb.	1,036	836	354	833	1,429	1,369	1,014
Philadelphia, Pa.	2,083	259	811	1,925	2,523	2,380	123
Phoenix, Ariz.	—	1,828	1,272	504	653	1,114	1,983
Pittsburgh, Pa.	1,828	—	559	1,668	2,264	2,138	192
St. Louis, Mo.	1,272	559	—	1,162	1,744	1,724	712
Salt Lake City, Utah	504	1,668	1,162	—	600	701	1,848
San Francisco, Calif.	653	2,264	1,744	600	—	678	2,442
Seattle, Wash.	1,114	2,138	1,724	701	678	—	2,329
Washington, D.C.	1,983	192	712	1,848	2,442	2,329	—

Source: National Geodetic Survey.

Air Distances Between World Cities in Statute Miles

Cities	Berlin	Buenos Aires	Cairo	Calcutta	Cape Town	Caracas	Chicago
Berlin	—	7,402	1,795	4,368	5,981	5,247	4,405
Buenos Aires	7,402	—	7,345	10,265	4,269	3,168	5,598
Cairo	1,795	7,345	—	3,539	4,500	6,338	6,129
Calcutta	4,368	10,265	3,539	—	6,024	9,605	7,980
Cape Town, South Africa	5,981	4,269	4,500	6,024	—	6,365	8,494
Caracas, Venezuela	5,247	3,168	6,338	9,605	6,365	—	2,501
Chicago	4,405	5,598	6,129	7,980	8,494	2,501	—
Hong Kong	5,440	11,472	5,061	1,648	7,375	10,167	7,793
Honolulu, Hawaii	7,309	7,561	8,838	7,047	11,534	6,013	4,250
Istanbul	1,078	7,611	768	3,638	5,154	6,048	5,477
Lisbon	1,436	5,956	2,363	5,638	5,325	4,041	3,990
London	579	6,916	2,181	4,947	6,012	4,660	3,950
Los Angeles	5,724	6,170	7,520	8,090	9,992	3,632	1,745
Manila	6,132	11,051	5,704	2,203	7,486	10,620	8,143
Mexico City	6,047	4,592	7,688	9,492	8,517	2,232	1,691
Montreal	3,729	5,615	5,414	7,607	7,931	2,449	744
Moscow	1,004	8,376	1,803	3,321	6,300	6,173	4,974
New York	3,965	5,297	5,602	7,918	7,764	2,132	713
Paris	545	6,870	1,995	4,883	5,807	4,736	4,134
Rio de Janeiro	6,220	1,200	6,146	9,377	3,773	2,810	5,296
Rome	734	6,929	1,320	4,482	5,249	5,196	4,808
San Francisco	5,661	6,467	7,364	7,814	10,247	3,904	1,858
Shanghai, China	5,218	12,201	5,183	2,117	8,061	9,501	7,061
Stockholm	504	7,808	2,111	4,195	6,444	5,420	4,278
Sydney, Australia	10,006	7,330	8,952	5,685	6,843	9,513	9,272
Tokyo	5,540	11,408	5,935	3,194	9,156	8,799	6,299
Warsaw	320	7,662	1,630	4,048	5,958	5,517	4,667
Washington, D.C.	4,169	5,218	5,800	8,084	7,901	2,059	597

Cities	Hong Kong	Honolulu	Istanbul	Lisbon	London	Los Angeles	Manila
Berlin	5,440	7,309	1,078	1,436	579	5,724	6,132
Buenos Aires	11,472	7,561	7,611	5,956	6,916	6,170	11,051
Cairo	5,061	8,838	768	2,363	2,181	7,520	5,704
Calcutta	1,648	7,047	3,638	5,638	4,947	8,090	2,203
Cape Town, South Africa	7,375	11,534	5,154	5,325	6,012	9,992	7,486
Caracas, Venezuela	10,167	6,013	6,048	4,041	4,660	3,632	10,620
Chicago	7,793	4,250	5,477	3,990	3,950	1,745	8,143
Hong Kong	—	5,549	4,984	6,853	5,982	7,195	693
Honolulu, Hawaii	5,549	—	8,109	7,820	7,228	2,574	5,299
Istanbul	4,984	8,109	—	2,012	1,552	6,783	5,664
Lisbon	6,853	7,820	2,012	—	985	5,621	7,546
London	5,982	7,228	1,552	985	—	5,382	6,672
Los Angeles, Calif.	7,195	2,574	6,783	5,621	5,382	—	7,261
Manila	693	5,299	5,664	7,546	6,672	7,261	—
Mexico City	8,782	3,779	7,110	5,390	5,550	1,589	8,835
Montreal	7,729	4,910	4,789	3,246	3,282	2,427	8,186
Moscow	4,439	7,037	1,091	2,427	1,555	6,003	5,131
New York	8,054	4,964	4,975	3,364	3,458	2,451	8,498
Paris	5,985	7,438	1,400	904	213	5,588	6,677
Rio de Janeiro	11,021	8,285	6,389	4,796	5,766	6,331	11,259
Rome	5,768	8,022	843	1,161	887	6,732	6,457
San Francisco	6,897	2,393	6,703	5,666	5,357	347	6,967
Shanghai, China	764	4,941	4,962	6,654	5,715	6,438	1,150
Stockholm	5,113	6,862	1,348	1,856	890	5,454	5,797
Sydney, Australia	4,584	4,943	9,294	11,302	10,564	7,530	3,944
Tokyo	1,794	3,853	5,560	6,915	5,940	5,433	1,866
Warsaw	5,144	7,355	863	1,715	899	5,922	5,837
Washington, D.C.	8,147	4,519	5,215	3,562	3,663	2,300	8,562

Source: Encyclopaedia Britannica.

Air Distances Between World Cities in Statute Miles

Cities	Mexico City	Montreal	Moscow	New York	Paris	Rio de Janeiro	Rome
Berlin	6,047	3,729	1,004	3,965	545	6,220	734
Buenos Aires	4,592	5,615	8,376	5,297	6,870	1,200	6,929
Cairo	7,688	5,414	1,803	5,602	1,995	6,146	1,320
Calcutta	9,492	7,607	3,321	7,918	4,883	9,377	4,482
Cape Town, South Africa	8,517	7,931	6,300	7,764	5,807	3,773	5,249
Caracas, Venezuela	2,232	2,449	6,173	2,132	4,736	2,810	5,196
Chicago	1,691	744	4,974	713	4,134	5,296	4,808
Hong Kong	8,782	7,729	4,439	8,054	5,985	11,021	5,768
Honolulu	3,779	4,910	7,037	4,964	7,438	8,285	8,022
Istanbul	7,110	4,789	1,091	4,975	1,400	6,389	843
Lisbon	5,390	3,246	2,427	3,364	904	4,796	1,161
London	5,550	3,282	1,555	3,458	213	5,766	887
Los Angeles	1,589	2,427	6,003	2,451	5,588	6,331	6,732
Manila	8,835	8,186	5,131	8,498	6,677	11,259	6,457
Mexico City	—	2,318	6,663	2,094	5,716	4,771	6,366
Montreal	2,318	—	4,386	320	3,422	5,097	4,080
Moscow	6,663	4,386	—	4,665	1,544	7,175	1,474
New York	2,094	320	4,665	—	3,624	4,817	4,281
Paris	5,716	3,422	1,544	3,624	—	5,699	697
Rio de Janeiro	4,771	5,097	7,175	4,817	5,699	—	5,684
Rome	6,366	4,080	1,474	4,281	697	5,684	—
San Francisco	1,887	2,539	5,871	2,571	5,558	6,621	6,240
Shanghai, China	8,022	7,053	4,235	7,371	5,754	11,336	5,677
Stockholm	5,959	3,667	762	3,924	958	6,651	1,234
Sydney, Australia	8,052	9,954	9,012	9,933	10,544	8,3 06	10,136
Tokyo	7,021	6,383	4,647	6,740	6,034	11,533	6,135
Warsaw	6,365	4,009	715	4,344	849	6,467	817
Washington, D.C.	1,887	488	4,858	205	3,829	4,796	4,434

Cities	San Francisco	Shanghai	Stockholm	Sydney	Tokyo	Moscow	Wash-ington
Berlin	5,661	5,218	504	10,006	5,540	320	4,169
Buenos Aires	6,467	12,201	7,808	7,330	11,408	7,662	5,218
Cairo	7,364	5,183	2,111	8,952	5,935	1,630	5,800
Calcutta	7,814	2,117	4,195	5,685	3,194	4,048	8,084
Cape Town, South Africa	10,247	8,061	6,444	6,843	9,156	5,958	7,901
Caracas, Venezuela	3,904	9,501	5,420	9,513	8,799	5,517	2,059
Chicago	1,858	7,061	4,278	9,272	6,299	4,667	597
Hong Kong	6,897	764	5,113	4,584	1,794	5,144	8,147
Honolulu	2,393	4,941	6,862	4,943	3,853	7,355	4,519
Istanbul	6,703	4,962	1,348	9,294	5,560	863	5,215
Lisbon	5,666	6,654	1,856	11,302	6,915	1,715	3,562
London	5,357	5,715	890	10,564	5,940	899	3,663
Los Angeles	347	6,438	5,454	7,530	5,433	5,922	2,300
Manila	6,967	1,150	5,797	3,944	1,866	5,837	8,562
Mexico City	1,887	8,022	5,959	8,052	7,021	6,365	1,887
Montreal	2,539	7,053	3,667	9,954	6,383	4,009	488
Moscow	5,871	4,235	762	9,012	4,647	715	4,858
New York	2,571	7,371	3,924	9,933	6,740	4,344	205
Paris	5,558	5,754	958	10,544	6,034	849	3,829
Rio de Janeiro	6,621	11,336	6,651	8,306	11,533	6,467	4,796
Rome	6,240	5,677	1,234	10,136	6,135	817	4,434
San Francisco	—	6,140	5,361	7,416	5,135	5,841	2,442
Shanghai, China	6,140	—	4,825	4,899	1,097	4,951	7,448
Stockholm	5,361	4,825	—	9,696	5,051	501	4,123
Sydney, Australia	7,416	4,899	9,696	—	4,866	9,696	9,758
Tokyo	5,135	1,097	5,051	4,866	—	5,249	6,772
Warsaw	5,841	4,951	501	9,696	5,249	—	4,457
Washington, D.C.	2,442	7,448	4,123	9,758	6,772	4,457	—

Source: Encyclopaedia Britannica.

50 Years Ago: Remembering The Valor of D-Day, 1944

The future of the whole European continent hung in the outcome of the Allied invasion of Normandy

The greatest amphibious assault in history took place at dawn on June 6, 1944, when the first wave of Allied soldiers hit the beaches of Normandy, France. There had never been anything like it before and there would never be anything like it again. Volumes of books and articles have been written about the horror, the bloodshed, and tragedy of D-Day.

This daring gamble, code named "Overlord," began when an Allied invasion force of over 5,000 ships, carrying more than 200,000 soldiers and seamen, sailed from England during the pre-dawn hours to the coast of northern France. At 6:30 a.m., the first of the American, British, and Canadian troops began to storm the heavily defended, mined, and booby-trapped beaches of Normandy to defeat the German army and destroy Adolf Hitler's Third Reich.

Five beaches on the Normandy coast were assaulted, two by the Americans code-named Omaha and Utah, and three by the British and Canadians, called Gold, Juno, and Sword. The overall ground command was given to British General Sir Bernard L. Montgomery and the American forces were led by Lt. General Omar N. Bradley.

The amphibious invasion was preceded at 1:30 a.m. by paratroopers from the U.S. 101st and 82nd Airborne Divisions, who were dropped low, over the moonlit Normandy coast. The 82nd Airborne division landed at Ste.-Mere-Eglise to take the town and bridges. The 101st mission was to capture the town of Carentan. Both of these towns were located inland behind Utah and Omaha beaches. Because it was difficult for the pilots to locate their targets at night under a heavy cloud cover, the airdrops were a near disaster. The troopers were scattered over a wide area, many of their supplies were lost, some drowned after landing in flooded fields and others were killed in accidents.

At Ste-Mere-Eglise, a strong wind blew some of the men over the town square which was lit-up by the flames of a burning building. As they helplessly floated down, they were machine-gunned by German soldiers. Two of the unfortunate men fell right into the inferno and perished. Both U.S. airborne units lost some 1,200 men each before the day was over.

The British 6th Airborne Division was dropped about the same time east of the Orne River to capture the Pegasus Bridge and protect the eastern flank of the landings. They accomplished their mission with great daring and heavy fighting. The total number of American and British paratroopers and airborne glider troops used in the attacks that day were 17,000 men.

When the Americans attempted their landing at Omaha Beach, they discovered that the German gun batteries had not been destroyed by an intense Allied naval bombardment. They struggled towards the open beaches in deep water under heavy shelling and murderous machine gun fire, and many of the wounded drowned in the rising tide. Many of the flimsy landing craft floundered and were swamped in the heavy sea, others were blown-up by enemy shells and mortars.

Twenty-eight tanks equipped with special flotation devices that did not work sank into the rough sea and most of their crews drowned. The heaviest fighting of the day occurred at Omaha Beach and some units there had casualties as high as fifty percent. For a while, the assault seemed to be a disaster, and the local German commanders reported to their headquarters that they had repelled the attack. With great courage and personal leadership, the exhausted men at "Bloody Omaha" were able to overcome their desperate situation and they managed to advance two miles inland by nightfall. They had lost almost 2,500 men but 34,000 others made it ashore.

Because of different tidal conditions, the British and Canadians did not face the same difficulties that the Americans had in their landings and were able to fight their way inland and linkup with their British airborne units.

The American casualties at Utah Beach were lighter, 200 killed and about 23,000 got to the beachhead. The British and Canadian forces lost about 4,000 men that day.

It was a hazardous undertaking from the start and the logistics of continuously supplying the huge invasion force staggers the mind. The invasion planners expected that the foul weather the troops had landed in would soon turn worse, making it difficult to supply them. Yet they accomplished a technical miracle under the most difficult conditions and within one week had landed over 260,000 men, 50,000 vehicles, and over 100,000 tons of supplies.

The Allies were also up against one of the best organized and combat experienced armies in the world. Although the German defenders were outnumbered, outgunned, and were practically without air support to protect them, they fought fiercely to repel the assault.

It was remarkable that the Allied armies took the Germans by complete surprise. The Germans knew than an invasion was imminent, but did not know when and where. In order to deceive the Germans, the Allies created a vast phantom invasion force with dummy planes, equipment, landing craft, tent encampments, and phony radio messages, which they established across the English Channel from Calais. The German intelligence service and Hitler fell for this elaborate hoax and were convinced that the major invasion force would come ashore in the Pais-de-Calais area. This belief caused Hitler to make a monumental blunder on D-Day. He refused to send vital reinforcements to Normandy because he thought it was only a diversionary attack.

It was also remarkable that German intelligence had known the secret code message that would be broadcast to the French Resistance alerting them to mobilize and begin their sabotage operations when the invasion would take place within 48-hours. When this secret message was broadcast and intercepted by German intelligence, the German high command did not take it seriously and failed to take appropriate measures to defend Normandy.

A bloody tragedy began at 7:00 a.m. that morning at Pointe du Huc, when the U.S. Army's second and fifth Ranger Battalions started scaling 100-foot cliffs, to silence a massive enemy gun emplacement with their ropes, grappling hooks, and ladders. Although the Germans kept firing straight down at them, threw grenades, pushed their ladders, and cut their ropes, the Rangers kept climbing. Their casualties were enormous and out of the 225 Rangers that made the assault, only 90 made it to the top. They had lost 135 men in the heroic attack only to find out that guns were not there.

The Normandy invasion was one of the most momentous events in history and the importance of D-Day should never be forgotten. If the Allied invasion had failed, Hitler could have concentrated more of his might against the Soviet Union and may have been able to defeat it and bring the whole of Europe under Nazi domination. The Allies still had a tough war with Japan to fight and needed all of their remaining resources to win it. It may have taken a long time before they could attempt another invasion of Europe, if they were willing to attempt it again, at all.—*Ed.*

Highest Ranking Officers in the Armed Forces

ARMY

Generals; Colin L. Powell[1], Chairman of the Joint Chiefs of Staff; Gordon R. Sullivan, Chief of Staff; Dennis J. Reimer, Vice Chief of Staff; John R. Galvin, Supreme Allied Commander, Europe and Commander-in-Chief, U.S. European Command; Edwin H. Burba, Jr.; Frederick M. Franks, Jr.; George A. Joulwan; Robert W. Riscassi; Jimmy D. Ross; Crosbie E. Saint; Carl W. Stiner.

AIR FORCE

Generals: Merril A. McPeak, Chief of Staff; George L. Butler; Michael P.C. Carns; John M. Loh; James P. McCarthy; Robert C. Oaks; James B. Davis; Ronald W. Yates.

NAVY

Admirals: David E. Jeremiah (Vice Chairman, JCS); Frank B. Kelso II, Chief of Naval Operations; Stanley R. Arthur; Bruce DeMars; Charles R. Larson; Henry H. Mauz, Jr.; Paul D. Miller; William D. Smith; Robert J. Kelly; Jeremy M. Boorda.

MARINE CORPS

Generals: Carl E. Mundy, Jr., Commandant of the Marine Corps; Walter E. Boomer, Assistant Commandant of the Marine Corps and Chief of Staff; Joseph P. Hoar, Commander in Chief, U.S. Central Command.

Lieutenant Generals: William Keys, Walter Boomer, Robert A. Tiebout, Royal Moore, Jr., Robert B. Johnston, Henry C. Stackpole, III, Martin Brandtner.

COAST GUARD

Admiral: Adm. J. William Kime, Commandant.

Vice Admirals: Vice Adm. Robert T. Nelson, Vice Commandant; Vice Adm. Paul A. Welling, Commander Atlantic Area; Vice Adm. Martin H. Daniell, Jr., Commander Pacific Area.

1. Gen. Powell retired in September 1993. Pres. Clinton named Army Gen. John Shalikashvili to replace him. *See* Current Events, September, 1993.

History of the Armed Services

Source: Department of Defense.

U.S. Army

On June 14, 1775, the Continental Congress "adopted" the New England Armies—a mixed force of volunteers besieging the British in Boston—appointing a committee to draft "Rules and regulations for the government of the Army" and voting to raise 10 rifle companies as a reinforcement. The next day, it appointed Washington commander-in-chief of the "Continental forces to be raised for the defense of liberty," and he took command at Boston on July 3, 1775. The Continental Army that fought the Revolution was our first national military organization, and hence the Army is the senior service. After the war, the army was radically reduced but enough survived to form a small Regular Army of about 700 men under the Constitution, a nucleus for expansion in the 1790s to successfully meet threats from the Indians and from France. From these humble beginnings, the U.S. Army has developed, normally expanding rapidly by absorbing citizen soldiers in wartime and contracting just as rapidly after each war.

U.S. Navy

The antecedents of the U.S. Navy go back to September 1775, when Gen. Washington commissioned 8 schooners and brigantines to prey on British supply vessels bound for the Colonies or Canada. On Oct. 13, 1775, a resolve of the Continental Congress called for the purchase of 2 vessels for the purpose of intercepting enemy transports. With its passage a Naval Committee of 7 men was formed, and they rapidly obtained passage of legislation calling for procurement of additional vessels. The Continental Navy was supplemented by privateers and ships operated as state navies, but soon after the war ended, it was disestablished.

In 1794, because of dissatisfaction with the payment of tribute to the Barbary pirates, Congress authorized construction of 6 frigates. The first, *United States,* was launched May 10, 1797, but the Navy still remained under the control of the Secretary of War until April 1798, when the Navy Department was created under the Secretary of the Navy with Cabinet rank.

U.S. Air Force

Until creation of the National Military Establishment in September 1947, which united the services under one department, military aviation was a part of the U.S. Army. In the Army, aeronautical operations came under the Signal Corps from 1907 to 1918, when the Army Air Service was established. In 1926, the Army Air Corps came into being and remained until 1941, when the Army Air Forces succeeded it as the Army's air arm. On Sept. 18, 1947, the U.S. Air Force was established as an independent military service under the National Military Establishment. At that time, the name "Army Air Forces" was abolished.

U.S. Coast Guard

Our country's oldest continuous seagoing service, the U.S. Coast Guard, traces its history back to 1790, when the first Congress authorized the construction of ten vessels for the collection of revenue. Known first as the Revenue Marine, and later as the Revenue Cutter Service, the Coast Guard received its present name in 1915 under an act of Congress combining the Revenue Cutter Service with the Life-Saving Service. In 1939, the Lighthouse Service was also consolidated with this unit. The Bureau of Marine Inspection and Navigation was transferred temporarily to the Coast Guard in 1942, permanently in 1946. Through its antecedents, the Coast Guard is one of the oldest organizations under the federal government and, until the Navy Department was established in 1798, served as the only U.S. armed force afloat. In times of peace, it operates under the Department of Transportation, serving as the nation's primary agency for promoting marine safety and enforcing federal maritime laws. In times of war, or on direction of the President, it is attached to the Navy Department.

U.S. Marine Corps

Founded in 1775 and observing its official birthday on Nov. 10, the U.S. Marine Corps was developed to serve on land, on sea, and in the air.

Marines have fought in every U.S. war. From an initial two battalions in the Revolution, the Corps reached a peak strength of six divisions and five aircraft wings in World War II. Its present strength is three active divisions and aircraft wings and a Reserve division/aircraft wing team. Marine units deploy for operations as fully integrated Marine air-ground task forces.

Service Academies

U.S. Military Academy

Source: U.S. Military Academy.

Established in 1802 by an act of Congress, the U.S. Military Academy is located on the west bank of the Hudson River some 50 miles north of New York City. To gain admission a candidate must first secure a nomination from an authorized source. These sources are:

Congressional Sources

Representatives
Senators
Other: Vice Presidential
  District of Columbia
  Puerto Rico
  Am. Samoa, Guam, Virgin Is.

Military-Service-Connected Sources

Presidential—Sons or daughters of active duty or retired service members
Enlisted members of Army
Enlisted members of Army Reserve/National Guard
Sons and daughters of deceased and disabled veterans
Honor military, naval schools and ROTC
Sons and daughters of persons awarded the Medal of Honor

Any number of applicants can meet the requirements for a *nomination* in these categories. *Appointments* (offers of admission), however, can only be made to a much smaller number, about 1,200 each year.

Candidates may be nominated for vacancies during the year preceding the day of admission, which occurs in late June or early July. The best time to apply is during the junior year in high school.

Candidates must be citizens of the U.S., be unmarried, be at least 17 but not yet 22 years old on July 1 of the year admitted, have a secondary-school education or its equivalent, and be able to meet the academic, medical, and physical aptitude requirements. Academic qualification is determined by an analysis of entire scholastic record, and performance on either the American College Testing (ACT) Assessment Program Test or the College Entrance Examination Board Scholastic Assessment Tests (SAT). Entrance requirements and procedures for appointment are described in the Admissions Bulletin and the Admissions Prospectus, available without charge from Admissions, U.S. Military Academy, West Point, N.Y. 10996-1797. Telephone: (914) 938-4041.

Cadets are members of the U.S. Army. As such they receive full scholarships and annual salaries from which they pay for their uniforms, textbooks, and incidental expenses. Upon successful completion of the four-year course, the graduate receives the degree of Bachelor of Science and is commissioned a second lieutenant in the U.S. Army with a requirement to serve as an officer for a minimum of six years.

U.S. Naval Academy

Source: U.S. Naval Academy.

The Naval School, established in 1845 at Fort Severn, Annapolis, Md., was renamed the U.S. Naval Academy in 1850. A four-year course was adopted a year later. The "Yard" as the campus is referred to, blends French Renaissance and modern architecture with many new academic, athletics, and laboratory facilities.

The Superintendent is a rear admiral. A civilian academic dean heads the academic program. A captain heads the 4,200 members of the Brigade of Midshipmen and military, professional, and physical training. The faculty is half military and half civilian, with 650 members; 95% of the civilian faculty hold PhD's. The faculty-student ratio at 1:7 is one of the lowest in the nation and provides for classes that rarely exceed seventeen.

Eighteen majors are offered, including chemistry, math, computer science, economics, general engineering, history, English, ocean engineering, aerospace engineering, electrical engineering, oceanography, political science, mechanical engineering, marine engineering, physics, and naval architecture. Graduates are awarded the Bachelor of Science or Bachelor of Science in Engineering and are commissioned as officers in the U.S. Navy or Marine Corps.

To have basic eligibility for admission, candidates must be citizens of the U.S., of good moral character, at least 17 and not more than 22 years of age on July 1 of their entering year, and unmarried.

The Admissions Board at the Naval Academy examines each candidate's school record, College Board or ACT scores, recommendations from school officials, extracurricular activities, and evidence from other sources concerning his or her character, leadership potential, academic preparation, and physical fitness. Qualification for admission is based on all of the above factors.

Tuition, board, lodging, and medical and dental care are provided. Midshipmen receive over $540 a month for books, uniforms, and personal needs.

For general information or answers to specific questions, write: Director of Candidate Guidance, U.S. Naval Academy, Annapolis, Md. 21402-5018, or call 1-800-638-9156.

U.S. Air Force Academy

Source: U.S. Air Force Academy.

The bill establishing the Air Force Academy was signed by President Eisenhower on April 1, 1954. The first class of 306 cadets was sworn in on July 11, 1955, at Lowry Air Force Base, Denver, the Academy's temporary location. The Cadet Wing moved into the Academy's permanent home north of Colorado Springs, Colorado, in 1958.

Cadets receive four years of academic, military, and physical education to prepare them for leadership as officers in the Air Force. The Academy is authorized a total of 4,000 cadets by 1995. Each new class averages 1,300. The candidates for the Academy must be at least 17 and not have passed their 22nd birthday on July 1 of the year for which they enter the Academy, must be a United States citizen, never married, and be able to meet the mental and physical requirements. International students authorized admission are exempt from the U.S. citizenship requirement. A candidate is required to take the following examinations and tests: (1) the Service Academies' Qualifying Medical Examination; (2) either the American College Testing (ACT) Assessment Program test or the College Entrance Examination Board Scholastic Aptitude Test (SAT); and (3) a Candidate Fitness Test.

Cadets receive their entire education at government expense and, in addition, are paid more than $540 per month base pay. From this sum, they pay for their uniforms, textbooks, tailoring, laundry, entertainment tickets, etc. Upon completion of the four-year program, leading to a Bachelor of Science degree, a cadet who meets the qualifications is commissioned a second lieutenant in the U.S. Air Force. For details on admissions, write: HQ USAFA/RRS, 2304 Cadet Drive, Suite 200, USAF Academy, CO 80840-5025.

U.S. Coast Guard Academy

Source: U.S. Coast Guard Academy.

The U.S. Coast Guard Academy, New London, Conn., was founded on July 31, 1876, to serve as the "School of Instruction" for the Revenue Cutter Service, predecessor to the Coast Guard.

The J.C. Dobbin, a converted schooner, housed the first Coast Guard Academy, and was succeeded in 1878 by the barque Chase, a ship built for cadet training. First winter quarters were in a sail loft at New Bedford, Mass. The school was moved in 1900 to Arundel Cove, Md., to provide a more technical education, and in 1910 was moved back to New England to Fort Trumbull, New London, Conn. In 1932 the Academy moved to its present location in New London.

The Academy today offers a four-year curriculum for the professional and academic training of cadets, which leads to a Bachelor of Science degree and a commission as ensign in the Coast Guard.

The U.S. Coast Guard Academy is the only one of the five federal service academies that offers appointments solely on the basis of an annual nationwide competition; there are no congressional nominations or geographical quotas involved. Competition is open to any young American who meets the basic eligibility requirements, which consist of satisfactory Scholastic Aptitude Test (SAT) or American College Testing Program examination (ACT) results, high school standing, and leadership potential. Either the SAT or the ACT must be completed prior to or during the December test administration of the year of application. All cadets must have reached their 17th but not their 22nd birthday by July 1 of the year of entrance to the Academy. All cadets must pass a rigid medical examination before being accepted.

Women were first admitted to the Coast Guard Academy in 1976 and first graduated in 1980. Cadets must be unmarried upon entry and must remain unmarried until after graduation. As ensigns, they must serve a five-year obligation following graduation. Cadets receive a stipend to cover incidentals and uniform expenses. Meals and quarters are provided.

A catalog can be obtained by writing to: Director of Admissions, U.S. Coast Guard Academy, 15 Mohegan Ave., New London, Conn. 06320-4195, or call (203) 444-8501 or (800) 424-8883.

U.S. Merchant Marine Academy

Source: U.S. Merchant Marine Academy.

The U.S. Merchant Marine Academy, situated at Kings Point, N.Y., on the north shore of Long Island, was dedicated Sept. 30, 1943. It is maintained by the Department of Transportation under direction of the Maritime Administration.

The Academy has a complement of approximately 890 men and women representing every state, D.C., the Canal Zone, Puerto Rico, Guam, American Samoa, and the Virgin Islands. It is also authorized to admit up to 12 candidates from the Western Hemisphere and 30 other foreign students at any one time.

Candidates are nominated by Senators and members of the House of Representatives. Nominations to the Academy are governed by a state and territory quota system based on population and the results of the College Entrance Examination Board tests.

A candidate must be a citizen not less than 17 and not yet 22 years of age by July 1 of the year in which admission is sought. Fifteen high school credits, including 3 units in mathematics (from algebra, geometry and/or trigonometry), 1 unit in science (physics or chemistry) and 3 in English are required.

The course is four years and includes one year of practical training aboard a merchant ship. Study includes marine engineering, navigation, satellite navigation and communications, electricity, ship construction, naval science and tactics, economics, business, languages, history, etc.

Upon completion of the course of study, a graduate receives a Bachelor of Science degree, a license as a merchant marine deck or engineering officer, and a commission as an Ensign in the Naval Reserve. □

U.S. Casualties in Major Wars

War	Branch of service	Numbers engaged	Battle deaths	Other deaths	Total deaths	Wounds not mortal	Total casualties[1]
Revolutionary War 1775 to 1783	Army	n.a.	4,044	n.a.	n.a.	6,004	n.a.
	Navy	n.a.	342	n.a.	n.a.	114	n.a.
	Marines	n.a.	49	n.a.	n.a.	70	n.a.
	Total	**n.a.**	**4,435**	**n.a.**	**n.a.**	**6,188**	**n.a.**
War of 1812 1812 to 1815	Army	n.a.	1,950	n.a.	n.a.	4,000	n.a.
	Navy	n.a.	265	n.a.	n.a.	439	n.a.
	Marines	n.a.	45	n.a.	n.a.	66	n.a.
	Total	**286,730**	**2,260**	**n.a.**	**n.a.**	**4,505**	**n.a.**
Mexican War 1846 to 1848	Army	n.a.	1,721	11,550	13,271	4,102	17,373
	Navy	n.a.	1	n.a.	n.a.	3	n.a.
	Marines	n.a.	11	n.a.	n.a.	47	n.a.
	Total	**78,718**	**1,733**	**n.a.**	**n.a.**	**4,152**	**n.a.**
Civil War[2] 1861 to 1865	Army	2,128,948	138,154	221,374	359,528	280,040	639,568
	Navy	84,415	2,112	2,411	4,523	1,710	6,233
	Marines		148	312	460	131	591
	Total	**2,213,363**	**140,414**	**224,097**	**364,511**	**281,881**	**646,392**
Spanish-American War 1898	Army	280,564	369	2,061	2,430	1,594	4,024
	Navy	22,875	10	0	10	47	57
	Marines	3,321	6	0	6	21	27
	Total	**306,760**	**385**	**2,061**	**2,446**	**1,662**	**4,108**
World War I 1917 to 1918	Army	4,057,101	50,510	55,868	106,378	193,663	300,041
	Navy	599,051	431	6,856	7,287	819	8,106
	Marines	78,839	2,461	390	2,851	9,520	12,371
	Total	**4,734,991**	**53,402**	**63,114**	**116,516**	**204,002**	**320,518**
World War II 1941 to 1946	Army[3]	11,260,000	234,874	83,400	318,274	565,861	884,135
	Navy	4,183,466	36,950	25,664	62,614	37,778	100,392
	Marines	669,100	19,733	4,778	24,511	67,207	91,718
	Total	**16,112,566**	**291,557**	**113,842**	**405,399**	**670,846**	**1,076,245**
Korean War 1950 to 1953	Army	2,834,000	27,704	9,429	37,133	77,596	114,729
	Navy	1,177,000	458	4,043	4,501	1,576	6,077
	Marine	424,000	4,267	1,261	5,528	23,744	29,272
	Air Force	1,285,000	1,200	5,884	7,084	368	7,452
	Total	**5,720,000**	**33,629**	**20,617**	**54,246**	**103,284**	**157,530**
War in Southeast Asia[4]	Army	4,386,000	30,904	7,270	38,174	96,802	134,976
	Navy[5]	1,842,000	1,634	916	2,552	4,178	6,730
	Marines	794,000	13,079	1,750	14,829	51,392	66,221
	Air Force	1,740,000	1,765	815	2,580	931	3,511
	Total	**8,744,000**	**47,382**	**10,753**	**58,135**	**153,303**	**211,438**

1. Excludes captured or interned and missing in action who were subsequently returned to military control. 2. Union forces only. Totals should probably be somewhat larger as data or disposition of prisoners are far from complete. Final Confederate deaths, based on incomplete returns, were 133,821, to which should be added 26,000–31,000 personnel who died in Union prisons. 3. Army data include Air Force. 4. As of Nov. 11, 1986. 5. Includes a small number of Coast Guard of which 5 were battle deaths. NOTE: All data are subject to revision. For wars before World War I, information represents best data from available records. However, due to incomplete records and possible difference in usage of terminology, reporting systems, etc., figures should be considered estimates. n.a. = not available. *Source:* Department of Defense.

Female Military Personnel on Active Duty

Year	Army	Air Force	Navy	Marine Corps	Total
1970	16,724	13,654	8,683	2,418	41,479
1980	69,338	60,394	34,980	6,706	171,418
1985	79,247	70,061	52,603	9,695	211,606
1989	86,494	77,103	59,518	9,708	232,823
1990	83,621	74,134	59,907	9,356	227,018
1991	80,306	72,436	59,391	9,005	221,138
1992	73,430	68,789	59,305	8,524	210,048

Data as of September 30th.

The National Guard

Source: Departments of the Army and the Air Force, National Guard Bureau.

The National Guard is unique among the United States reserve military forces, filling both federal and state missions. In peacetime, the National Guard is commanded by the governors of the states and territories and may be called to state active duty by the governor in response to natural disasters, civil disturbances, or other state emergencies. During a war or national emergency, the National Guard may be called to active duty by the President or Congress, and serves as the primary source of augmentation for the active Army and active Air Force.

The men and women of the National Guard are described as citizen soldiers and airmen. They have full-time civilian careers, but, each month they meet with their unit for military training. National Guard members receive the same training, use the same equipment, and wear the same uniform as their active duty counterparts.

The foundation for the National Guard's dual state and federal mission can be traced to the earliest militias of the 13 original colonies. The oldest units were organized in the Massachusetts Bay Colony in 1636, and have been in continuous existence ever since. Framers of the U.S. Constitution provided for the continuation of the militia, a principle that has been further developed through subsequent legislation.

From its colonial beginnings, the militia system has evolved into today's Army National Guard and Air National Guard, our nation's community-based defense force of modern military units that serve their respective states and are part of the nation's overall military forces. In addition to countless call-ups for state duty, the National Guard has fought in every American war, from the Pequot War in 1637 to Operation DESERT STORM in which 75,000 members of the National Guard were called to active duty.

As a reserve component of the U.S. military, the National Guard makes up a significant part of what is called the Total Force—active duty service members, the reserve components, and the civilians who are employed by the Department of Defense. The other federal reserve components include the Army Reserve, Naval Reserve, Marine Corps Reserve, Air Force Reserve, and Coast Guard Reserve. Members in all of these organizations are trained and equipped in units which are available for full-time duty in case of war or national emergency. However, the other federal reserve components of the military services, unlike the National Guard, are legally and operationally linked only to the active duty services, not the states. This distinction of having both federal and state missions makes the National Guard unique.

The Army National Guard is made up of more than 3,000 units located in 2,635 communities throughout the 50 states, Puerto Rico, Guam, the Virgin Islands, and the District of Columbia. The U.S. Army's primary source of combat reserve units, the Army National Guard provides roughly 45 percent of the Army's total combat capability and approximately 30 percent of its combat support and combat service support units. Units are provided modern military equipment including M-1 tanks, Bradley Fighting Vehicles, and Blackhawk helicopters.

The Air National Guard has 92 flying units and 1,508 support units at 200 locations. This represents approximately one-third of the U.S. Air Force's fighter and air transport assets. Air National Guard units fly F-16 fighters, KC-135 tankers, and C-130 transports, among other aircraft.

As part of the nation's total military force, Army and Air National Guard units are trained and equipped to mesh with active duty and other federal reserve component forces. Typically, members of the National Guard report for training duty one weekend per month, along with a minimum of 15 days of continuous unit training each year. Weekend training usually is performed at the unit's community armory or nearby military training facility. The annual training usually is performed at a large military training base or overseas location, frequently in cooperation with active duty and other reserve units. In recent years, Army National Guard units have trained in more than 30 nations, including locations in Central America, Europe, Asia, and Africa. Air National Guard units train with active Air Force and Air Force Reserve units on a regular basis at worldwide locations.

Approximately one-half of the National Guard's members join their units with no previous military experience. They complete basic military training and a technical school at an active duty training base and then return to their unit. The balance of the National Guard's membership consists of personnel who have had prior active duty in any U.S. military service.

National Guard members receive a full day's pay at their military rank for each unit training assembly they attend, for the 15 days of annual training, and for any military school or special assignment they may complete. All such training counts toward retirement. A member who has 20 or more years of qualifying military service begins to collect retired pay at age 60.

The National Guard offers its members a broad range of educational opportunities beyond the training and on-the-job experiences they receive for their military specialties. These benefits include participation in the Montgomery GI Bill and additional enlistment incentives for select military career fields. Members of the National Guard have access to active duty military shopping centers in addition to participation in many other active duty military benefit programs. Many states offer additional benefits and civilian educational incentives.

For 1993, the numerical strength of the Army National Guard was authorized at 423,000, and the Air National Guard 119,000. The 1993 federal budget for the Army National Guard was $6.4 billion, the Air National Guard $4.4. States and territories provide additional funds to support state missions, recruiting and training administration, armory construction, and funding for state-salaried employees.

Additional information about the National Guard may be obtained from local units or from the National Guard Bureau in Washington, D.C. 20310-2500.

Veterans' Benefits

Veterans have been provided for by the individual states and the federal government since Colonial days, including disability compensation, allotments for dependents, life insurance, and vocational rehabilitation. In the 1940s, benefits for veterans were broadened in scope and value. On March 15, 1989, the Veterans Administration, the federal agency that administers benefits for veterans, became the Department of Veterans Affairs.

The following benefits available to veterans generally require certain minimum periods of active duty during qualifying periods of service and are applicable only to those whose discharges are not dishonorable. Certain types of discharges are subject to special adjudication to determine eligibility.

For information or assistance in applying for veterans benefits, write, call, or visit a VA Regional Office. Consult your local telephone directory under United States Government, Department of Veterans Affairs (VA) for the address and telephone number. Toll-free telephone service is available in all 50 States: 1-800-827-1000.

Unemployment allowances. The Department of Veterans Affairs provides job referral assistance through the Department of Labor and state employment agencies. Disabled veterans are provided a full range of assistance, including training, education, and placement.

Loan Guaranty. VA will guarantee loans for a variety of purposes, such as: to buy or build a home; to purchase a manufactured home with or without a lot; and to refinance a home presently owned and occupied by the veteran. When the purpose of a refinancing loan is to lower the interest rate on an existing guaranteed loan then prior occupancy by the veteran or spouse will suffice. VA will guarantee the lender against loss up to 50% on loans of $45,000 or less, the lesser of $36,000 or 40% (never less than $22,500) on loans of more than $45,000, and the lesser of $46,000 or 25% on loans of more than $144,000. On manufactured home loans, the amount of the guarantee is 40% of the loan to a maximum of $20,000. The interest rate may not exceed the maximum rate set by VA and in effect when the loan is made.

Disability compensation. Veterans with permanent service-connected disabilities are provided with from $85 to $1,730 per month, depending upon the extent of disability. For special conditions, an additional $4,943 a month may be paid, plus allowances for dependents when the disability is 30 percent or more.

Vocational Rehabilitation. VA provides professional counseling, training and other assistance to help compensably service-disabled veterans, rated 10 percent or more, who have an employment handicap to achieve maximum independence in daily living and, to the extent possible, to obtain and maintain suitable employment. Generally, a veteran may receive up to 48 months of this assistance within the 12 years from the date he or she is notified of entitlement to VA compensation. All the expenses of a veteran's rehabilitation program are paid by VA. In addition, the veteran receives a subsistence allowance which varies based on the rate of training and number of dependents. For example, a single veteran training full time would receive about $366 (exact amount not yet calculated for period after Oct. 1, 1993) monthly.

Vocational Training for VA Pension Recipients. Veterans who are awarded pension during the period from February 1, 1985, and December 31, 1995, may participate in a program of vocational training essentially identical to that provided in VA's vocational rehabilitation program. Certain veterans awarded pension before February 1, 1985, may also participate in this program. Work income will affect the continuing receipt of pension.

Medical and dental care. Free medical care may be provided in VA and, in certain instances, in non-VA, or other federal hospitals. It also covers outpatient treatment at a VA field facility or, in some cases, by an approved private physician or dentist. Full domiciliary care also may be provided to veterans with low incomes. Nursing home care may be provided at certain VA medical facilities or in approved community nursing homes. Hospital and other medical care may also be provided for the spouse and child dependents of a veteran who is permanently and totally disabled due to a service-connected disability; or for survivors of a veteran who dies from a service-connected disability; or for survivors of a veteran who at the time of death had a total disability, permanent in nature, resulting from a service-connected disability. These latter benefits are usually provided in nonfederal facilities. Eligibility criteria for veterans' medical benefits vary. Veterans must agree to make a copayment for the care they receive from VA if their incomes exceed levels that vary with number of dependents and they do not have a service-connected disability or service in certain early war periods. Veterans and/or their dependents or survivors should always apply in advance. Contact the nearest VA medical facility for eligibility.

Readjustment Counseling. VA provides readjustment counseling to veterans of the Vietnam Era or the war or conflict zones of Lebanon, Grenada, Panama, or the Persian Gulf theaters in need of assistance in resolving post-war readjustment problems in the areas of family, education, and personal readjustment including post-traumatic stress disorder. Services are provided at community-based Vet Centers and at VA Medical Centers in certain locations. Services include individual, family and group counseling, employment and educational counseling, and assistance in obtaining referrals to various governmental and nongovernmental agencies. Contact the nearest Vet Center or VA facility.

Dependents compensation. Payments are made to surviving dependents of veterans who died while on active duty or, after discharge, of a service-connected injury or disease. Beginning January 1, 1993, all surviving spouses of veterans who died on or after that date will receive $750 a month. In certain cases, parents and children may be eligible for additional payments.

Dependents' educational assistance. VA pays a maximum of $404 a month for up to 45 months of schooling to spouses and children of veterans who died of service-connected causes or who were permanently and totally disabled from service-connected causes or died while permanently and totally disabled or who are currently missing in action, captured in the line of duty, or forcibly detained or interned in line of duty by a foreign power for more than 90 days.

Montgomery GI Bill. This Act provides education benefits for individuals entering the military after June 30, 1985. Servicepersons entering active duty after that date will have their basic pay reduced by $100 a month for the first 12 months of their service, unless they specifically elect not to participate in the program. Servicepersons eligible for post-Korean GI Bill benefits as of December 31, 1989, and who serve 3 years in active duty service after July 1, 1985, are also eligible for the new program, but will not have their basic pay reduced. Servicepersons who, after December 31, 1976, received commissions as officers from service academies or scholarship senior ROTC programs are not eligible for this program.

Active duty for three years (two years, if the initial obligated period of active duty is less than three years), or two years active duty plus four years in the Selected Reserve or National Guard will entitle an individual to $350 a month basic benefits. Those who enlist for less than three years will receive $275 a month. VA pays an additional amount, commonly called a "kicker," if directed by the Defense Department.

An educational entitlement program is also available for members of the Selected Reserve. Eligibility applies to individuals who, after June 30, 1985 enlist, re-enlist, or extend an enlistment for a six-year period. Benefits may be paid to eligible members of the Selected Reserve who complete their initial period of active duty training. Full-time payments are $170 a month for 36 months.

Pensions. Pension benefits ranging from $7,619 (pensions are similar to disability compensation, but of lesser amounts) a year may be payable to wartime veterans permanently and totally disabled from non-service-connected causes. These benefits are based on need. Surviving spouses and children of wartime veterans are eligible for Nonservice-Connected Death Pensions that range from $5,106 a year, based on the veteran's honorable wartime service and their need.

Insurance. The VA life insurance programs have approximately 6.5 million policyholders with total coverage of about $510 billion. Detailed information on NSLI (National Service Life Insurance), USGLI (United States Government Life Insurance), SGLI (Servicemen's Group Life Insurance) and VGLI (Veterans Group Life Insurance) may be obtained by calling 1-800-669-8477.

Burial benefits. Burial is provided in any VA national cemetery with available grave space to any deceased veteran of wartime or peacetime service who was discharged under conditions other than dishonorable. Also eligible for burial in a national cemetery are the veteran's spouse, widow, widower, minor children, and under certain conditions, unmarried adult children.

Headstone or marker. A government headstone or marker is furnished for any deceased veteran of wartime or peacetime service, who was discharged under conditions other than dishonorable and is interred in a national, state veterans', or private cemetery. VA also will furnish markers to veterans' eligible dependents interred in a national or state veterans' cemetery.

War's Accidental Deaths

During the Gulf War, 35 Americans were killed and 72 wounded by their own forces. The accidental deaths, termed "friendly fire," are as old as warfare itself. On the evening of the United States' entry into World War II, Dec. 7, 1941, following the Japanese attack on Pearl Harbor, four U.S. Naval carrier planes coming in to help the U.S. defenders were fired upon by American antiaircraft guns as they approached the island. Three were shot down and killed and the pilot of the fourth was wounded. It was the first "friendly fire" incident of the war.

Combat is not a normal experience for those involved in it and it induces a heightened sense of danger that can play tricks on one's mind. During Operation Desert Storm, the troops were fighting in a sweeping, fast moving battle, much of it at night, in inclement weather and with poor visibility which gave rise to misidentification of friend and foe.

Military service is a hazardous occupation and hundreds of accidental deaths occur each year even in peacetime. Other people in life threatening occupations such as police work also fall victim to "friendly fire." For example, during 1991, nearly half of all the wounded police officers in one of our nation's largest cities were accidentally shot by other officers or by themselves. This doesn't excuse "friendly fire" but shows that it occurs in other high tension, life threatening situations.

Living Veterans in the United States

There were an estimated 20,280,000 living veterans in 1991. This figure includes one living Spanish-American War veteran and an indeterminate number of Mexican Border period veterans.

For the same period, there were 65,000 World War I veterans.

There were 8,443,000 World War II veterans, including 269,000 who served in the Vietnam era, Korean conflict, and World War II. Also included are 649,000 who served in both World War II, and the Korean conflict.

There were 4,693,000 Korean conflict vets including 269,000 who served in the Vietnam era, Korean conflict, and World War II. This also includes 649,000 who served in both World War II and the Korean conflict.

There were 8,269,000 Vietnam era veterans, including 269,000 who served in the Vietnam era and the Korean conflict, and World War II. It also includes 339,000 who served both in the Korean conflict and the Vietnam era. This figure excludes reservists.

There were 263,000 Persian Gulf War veterans excluding reservists, but including 47,000 who served both in the Vietnam era and the Persian Gulf War.

Casualties in World War I

Country	Total mobilized forces	Killed or died[1]	Wounded	Prisoners or missing	Total Casualties
Austria-Hungary	7,800,000	1,200,000	3,620,000	2,200,000	7,020,000
Belgium	267,000	13,716	44,686	34,659	93,061
British Empire[2]	8,904,467	908,371	2,090,212	191,652	3,190,235
Bulgaria	1,200,000	87,500	152,390	27,029	266,919
France[2]	8,410,000	1,357,800	4,266,000	537,000	6,160,800
Germany	11,000,000	1,773,700	4,216,058	1,152,800	7,142,558
Greece	230,000	5,000	21,000	1,000	27,000
Italy	5,615,000	650,000	947,000	600,000	2,197,000
Japan	800,000	300	907	3	1,210
Montenegro	50,000	3,000	10,000	7,000	20,000
Portugal	100,000	7,222	13,751	12,318	33,291
Romania	750,000	335,706	120,000	80,000	535,706
Russia	12,000,000	1,700,000	4,950,000	2,500,000	9,150,000
Serbia	707,343	45,000	133,148	152,958	331,106
Turkey	2,850,000	325,000	400,000	250,000	975,000
United States	4,734,991	116,516	204,002	—	320,518

1. Includes deaths from all causes. 2. Official figures. NOTE: For additional U.S. figures, *see* the table on U.S. Casualties in Major Wars in this section.

Casualties in World War II

Country	Men in war	Battle deaths	Wounded
Australia	1,000,000	26,976	180,864
Austria	800,000	280,000	350,117
Belgium	625,000	8,460	55,513[1]
Brazil[2]	40,334	943	4,222
Bulgaria	339,760	6,671	21,878
Canada	1,086,343[7]	42,042[7]	53,145
China[3]	17,250,521	1,324,516	1,762,006
Czechoslovakia	—	6,683[4]	8,017
Denmark	—	4,339	—
Finland	500,000	79,047	50,000
France	—	201,568	400,000
Germany	20,000,000	3,250,000[4]	7,250,000
Greece	—	17,024	47,290
Hungary	—	147,435	89,313
India	2,393,891	32,121	64,354
Italy	3,100,000	149,496[4]	66,716
Japan	9,700,000	1,270,000	140,000
Netherlands	280,000	6,500	2,860
New Zealand	194,000	11,625[4]	17,000
Norway	75,000	2,000	—
Poland	—	664,000	530,000
Romania	650,000[5]	350,000[6]	—
South Africa	410,056	2,473	—
U.S.S.R.	—	6,115,000[4]	14,012,000
United Kingdom	5,896,000	357,116[4]	369,267
United States	16,112,566	291,557	670,846
Yugoslavia	3,741,000	305,000	425,000

1. Civilians only. 2. Army and Navy figures. 3. Figures cover period July 7, 1937–Sept. 2, 1945, and concern only Chinese regular troops. They do not include casualties suffered by guerrillas and local military corps. 4. Deaths from all causes. 5. Against Soviet Russia; 385,847 against Nazi Germany. 6. Against Soviet Russia; 169,822 against Nazi Germany. 7. National Defense Ctr., Canadian Forces Hq., Director of History. NOTE: The figures in this table are unofficial estimates obtained from various sources.

Merchant Marine Casualties in World War II

In 1988, the U.S. Government conferred official veterans status on those who served aboard oceangoing merchant ships in World War II. The officers and crews played a key role in transporting the troops and war material that enabled the United States and its allies to defeat the Axis powers.

During the war, merchant seamen died as a result of enemy attacks at a rate that proportionately exceeded all branches of the armed services, with the exception of the U.S. Marine Corps.

Enemy action sank more than 700 U.S.-flag merchant ships and claimed the lives of over 6,000 civilian seafarers. Untold thousands of additional seamen were wounded or injured during these attacks, and nearly 600 were made prisoners of war. □

U.S. Military Actions Other Than Declared Wars

Hawaii (1893): U.S. Marines, ordered to land by U.S. Minister John L. Stevens, aided the revolutionary Committee of Safety in overthrowing the native government. Stevens then proclaimed Hawaii a U.S. protectorate. Annexation, resisted by the Democratic administration in Washington, was not formally accomplished until 1898.

China (1900): Boxers (a group of Chinese revolutionists) occupied Peking and laid siege to foreign legations. U.S. troops joined an international expedition which relieved the city.

Panama (1903): After Colombia had rejected a proposed agreement for relinquishing sovereignty over the Panama Canal Zone, revolution broke out, aided by promoters of the Panama Canal Co. Two U.S. warships were standing by to protect American privileges. The U.S. recognized the Republic of Panama on November 6.

Dominican Republic (1904): When the Dominican Republic failed to meet debts owed to the U.S. and foreign creditors, President Theodore Roosevelt declared the U.S. intention of exercising "international police power" in the Western Hemisphere whenever necessary. The U.S. accordingly administered customs and managed debt payments of the Dominican Republic from 1905 to 1907.

Nicaragua (1911): The possibility of foreign control over Nicaragua's canal route led to U.S. intervention and agreement. The U.S. landed Marines in Nicaragua (Aug. 14, 1912) to protect American interests there. A small detachment remained until 1933.

Mexico (1914): Mexican dictator Victoriano Huerta, opposed by President Woodrow Wilson, had the support of European governments. An incident involving unarmed U.S. sailors in Tampico led to the landing of U.S. forces on Mexican soil. Veracruz was bombarded by the Navy to prevent the landing of munitions from a German vessel. At the point of war, both powers agreed to mediation by Argentina, Brazil, and Chile. Huerta abdicated, and Venustiano Carranza succeeded to the presidency.

Haiti (1915): U.S. Marines imposed a military occupation. Haiti signed a treaty making it a virtual protectorate of the U.S. until troops were withdrawn in 1934.

Mexico (1916): Raids by Pancho Villa cost American lives on both sides of the border. President Carranza consented to a punitive expedition led by Gen. John J. Pershing, but antagonism grew in Mexico. Wilson withdrew the U.S. force when war with Germany became imminent.

Dominican Republic (1916): Renewed intervention in the Dominican Republic with internal administration by U.S. naval officers lasted until 1924.

Korea (1950): In this undeclared war, which terminated with the July 27, 1953, truce at Panmunjom and the establishment of a neutral nations' supervisory commission, the U.S. and 15 member-nations of the U.N. came to the aid of the Republic of South Korea, whose 38th-parallel border was crossed by the invading Russian Communist-controlled North Koreans, who were later joined by the Chinese Communists.

Lebanon (1958 and 1983): Fearful of the newly formed U.A.R. abetting the rebels of his politically and economically torn country, President Camille Chamoun appealed to the U.S. for military assistance. U.S. troops landed in Beirut in mid-July and left before the end of the year, after internal and external quiet were restored. In September 1983, President Reagan ordered Marines to join an international peacekeeping force in Beirut. On October 23, 241 were killed in the terrorist bombing of the Marine compound. On February 7, 1984, Reagan ordered the Marine contingent withdrawn. He ended the U.S. role in Beirut on March 30 by releasing the Sixth Fleet from the international force.

Dominican Republic (1965): On April 28, when a political coup-turned-civil war endangered the lives of American nationals, President Lyndon B. Johnson rushed 400 marines into Santo Domingo, the beginning of an eventual U.S. peak-commitment of 30,000 troops, constituting the preponderant military strength of the OAS-created Inter-American Peace Force, and 6,500 troops, including 5,000 Americans, remained until after the peaceful inauguration of President Joaquín Balaguer on July 1, 1966, and the entire force left the country on September 20.

Vietnam: This longest war in U.S. history began with economic and technical assistance after 1954 Geneva accords ending the Indochinese War. By 1964 it had escalated into a major conflict.

This involvement spanning the administrations of five Presidents led to domestic discontent in the late 1960s. By April 1969, U.S. troop strength reached a peak of 543,400. Peace negotiations began in Paris in 1968 but proved fruitless. Finally, on Jan. 27, 1973, a peace accord was signed in Paris by the U.S., North and South Vietnam, and the Vietcong. Within 60 days, U.S. POWs were returned, and the U.S. withdrew all military forces from South Vietnam.

Grenada (1983): A left-wing military coup resulted in the intervention of a 1,900-man United States contingent, supported by token forces from Caribbean allies, which engaged an 800-man Cuban Force and secured the island within a few days. The American combat force was brought home two months later although a small non-combat unit was left behind to assist in peacekeeping functions.

Panama (1989): On Dec. 15, the Panamanian legislature proclaimed dictator Gen. Manuel Noriega the nation's "maximum leader," and declared a "state of war" with the United States. On Dec. 20th, following several attacks on Americans, Pres. George Bush ordered over 20,000 U.S. military forces into action in Panama to protect the lives of 35,000 American citizens he considered in "grave danger," to apprehend Gen. Noriega for trial in the U.S. on federal drug trafficking charges, to secure the safety of the Canal, and to defend democracy in Panama. Noriega surrendered to U.S. troops the first week in January 1990.

Persian Gulf War (1990): *See* Headline History, page 124.

The Medal of Honor

Often called the Congressional Medal of Honor, it is the Nation's highest military award for "uncommon valor" by men and women in the armed forces. It is given for actions that are above and beyond the call of duty in combat against an armed enemy. The medal was first awarded by the Army on March 25, 1863, and then by the Navy on April 3, 1863. In April 1991, President Bush awarded posthumously the Medal of Honor to World War I veteran, Army Cpl. Freddie Stowers. He was the first black soldier to receive the nation's highest honor for valor in either World War.

Recipients of the medal receive $200 per month for life, a right to burial at Arlington National Cemetery, admission for them or their children to a service academy if they qualify and quotas permit, and free travel on government aircraft to almost anywhere in the world, on a space-available basis.

In 1989, medals were restored to William F. Cody (Buffalo Bill) and four other scouts who had them revoked in 1917 due to a new ruling.

Medal of Honor Recipients[1]

	Total	Army	Navy	Marines	Air Force	Coast Guard
Civil War	1,520	1,196	307	17	—	—
Indian Wars (1861-98)	428	428	—	—	—	—
Korean Expedition (1871)	15	—	9	6	—	—
Spanish-American War	109	30	64	15	—	—
Philippines/Samoa (1899-1913)	91	70	12	9	—	—
Boxer Rebellion (1900)	59	4	22	33	—	—
Dominican Republic (1904)	3	—	—	3	—	—
Nicaragua (1911)	2	—	—	2	—	—
Mexico (Veracruz) (1914)	55	—	46	9	—	—
Haiti (1915)	6	—	—	6	—	—
Misc. (1865-1920)	166	1	161	4	—	—
World War I	124	96	21	7	—	—
Haitian Action (1919-20)	2	—	—	2	—	—
Misc. (1920-1940)	18	2	15	1	—	—
World War II	433	294	57	81	—	1
Korean War	131	78	7	42	4	—
Vietnam War	238	155	14	57	12	—
Total	**3,400***	**2,354**	**735**	**294**	**16**	**1**

1. Total number of actual medals awarded is 3,418. This includes nine awarded to Unknown Soldiers, and some soldiers received more than one medal. *Source:* The Congressional Medal of Honor Society, New York, N.Y.

Active Military Duty Personnel, 1940–1992[1]

Year	Total	Army[2]	Navy	Marine Corps	Air Force[2, 3]
1940	458,365	269,023	160,997	28,345	
1945	12,055,884	8,266,373	3,319,586	469,925	
1950	1,459,462	593,167	380,739	74,279	411,277
1955	2,935,107	1,109,296	660,695	205,170	959,946
1960	2,475,438	873,078	616,987	170,621	814,752
1965	2,653,926	969,066	669,985	190,213	824,662
1970	3,064,760	1,322,548	691,126	259,737	791,349
1975	2,128,120	784,333	535,085	195,951	612,751
1980	2,050,627	777,036	527,153	188,469	557,969
1985	2,151,032	780,787	570,705	198,025	601,515
1990	2,043,705	732,403	579,417	196,652	535,233
1991	1,985,555	710,821	570,262	194,040	510,432
1992	1,807,177	610,450	541,883	184,529	470,315

1. Military personnel on extended or continuous active duty. Excludes reserves on active duty for training. Prior year totals have been corrected. 2. Represents "Command Strength" prior to June 30, 1956. 3. Army Air Forces and its predecessors for period prior to September 18, 1947. *Source:* Department of Defense.

WEATHER & CLIMATE

Climate of 100 Selected U.S. Cities

City	Average Monthly Temperature (°F)[1]				Precipitation		Snowfall	
	Jan.	April	July	Oct	Average (in.)[1]	annual (days)[2]	Average annual (in.)[2]	Years[2]
Albany, N.Y.	21.1	46.6	71.4	50.5	35.74	134	65.5	38
Albuquerque, N.M.	34.8	55.1	78.8	57.4	8.12	59	10.6	45
Anchorage, Alaska	13.0	35.4	58.1	34.6	15.20	115	69.2	41[3]
Asheville, N.C.	36.8	55.7	73.2	56.0	47.71	124	17.5	20
Atlanta, Ga.	41.9	61.8	78.6	62.2	48.61	115	1.9	50
Atlantic City, N.J.	31.8	51.0	74.4	55.5	41.93	112	16.4	40[3]
Austin, Texas	49.1	68.7	84.7	69.8	31.50	83	0.9	43
Baltimore, Md.	32.7	54.0	76.8	56.9	41.84	113	21.8	34
Baton Rouge, La.	50.8	68.4	82.1	68.2	55.77	108	0.1	34[3]
Billings, Mont.	20.9	44.6	72.3	49.3	15.09	96	57.2	50
Birmingham, Ala.	42.9	62.8	80.1	62.6	54.52	117	1.3	41
Bismark, N.D.	6.7	42.5	70.4	46.1	15.36	96	40.3	45
Boise, Idaho	29.9	48.6	74.6	51.9	11.71	92	21.4	45
Boston, Mass.	29.6	48.7	73.5	54.8	43.81	127	41.8	49[3]
Bridgeport, Conn.	29.5	48.6	74.0	56.0	41.56	117	26.0	36
Buffalo, N.Y.	23.5	45.4	70.7	51.5	37.52	169	92.2	41
Burlington, Vt.	16.6	42.7	69.6	47.9	33.69	153	78.2	41
Caribou, Maine	10.7	37.3	65.1	43.1	36.59	160	113.3	45
Casper, Wyom.	22.2	42.1	70.9	47.1	11.43	95	80.5	34
Charleston, S.C.	47.9	64.3	80.5	65.8	51.59	113	0.6	42
Charleston, W.Va.	32.9	55.3	74.5	55.9	42.43	151	31.5	37
Charlotte, N.C.	40.5	60.3	78.5	60.7	43.16	111	6.1	45
Cheyenne, Wyom.	26.1	41.8	68.9	47.5	13.31	98	54.1	49
Chicago, Ill.	21.4	48.8	73.0	53.5	33.34	127	40.3	26
Cleveland, Ohio	25.5	48.1	71.6	53.2	35.40	156	53.6	43
Columbia, S.C.	44.7	63.8	81.0	63.4	49.12	109	1.9	37
Columbus, Ohio	27.1	51.4	73.8	53.9	36.97	137	28.3	37[3]
Concord, N.H.	19.9	44.1	69.5	48.3	36.53	125	64.5	43
Dallas–Ft. Worth, Texas	44.0	65.9	86.3	67.9	29.46	78	3.1	31
Denver, Colo.	29.5	47.4	73.4	51.9	15.31	88	59.8	50
Des Moines, Iowa	18.6	50.5	76.3	54.2	30.83	107	34.7	45
Detroit, Mich.	23.4	47.3	71.9	51.9	30.97	133	40.4	26
Dodge City, Kan.	29.5	54.3	80.0	57.7	20.66	78	19.5	42
Duluth, Minn.	6.3	38.3	65.4	44.2	29.68	135	77.4	41[3]
El Paso, Texas	44.2	63.6	82.5	63.6	7.82	47	5.2	45
Fairbanks, Alaska	–12.7	30.2	61.5	25.1	10.37	106	67.5	33
Fargo, N.D.	4.3	42.1	70.6	46.3	19.59	100	35.9	42
Grand Junction, Colo.	25.5	51.7	78.9	54.9	8.00	72	26.1	38
Grand Rapids, Mich.	22.0	46.3	71.4	50.9	34.35	143	72.4	21
Hartford, Conn.	25.2	48.8	73.4	52.4	44.39	127	50.0	30
Helena, Mont.	18.1	42.3	67.9	45.1	11.37	96	47.9	44
Honolulu, Hawaii	72.6	75.7	80.1	79.5	23.47	100	0.0	38[3]
Houston, Texas	51.4	68.7	83.1	69.7	44.76	105	0.4	50
Indianapolis, Ind.	26.0	52.4	75.1	54.8	39.12	125	23.1	53[3]
Jackson, Miss.	45.7	65.1	81.9	65.0	52.82	109	1.2	21
Jacksonville, Fla.	53.2	67.7	81.3	69.5	52.76	116	T	43
Juneau, Alaska	21.8	39.1	55.7	41.8	53.15	220	102.8	41
Kansas City, Mo.	28.4	56.9	80.9	59.6	29.27	98	20.0	43
Knoxville, Tenn .	38.2	59.6	77.6	59.5	47.29	127	12.3	42
Las Vegas, Nev.	44.5	63.5	90.2	67.5	4.19	26	1.4	36
Lexington, Ky.	31.5	55.1	75.9	56.8	45.68	131	16.3	40
Little Rock, Ark.	39.9	62.4	82.1	63.1	49.20	104	5.4	42
Long Beach, Calif.	55.2	60.9	72.8	67.5	11.54	32	T	41[3]
Los Angeles, Calif.	56.0	59.5	69.0	66.3	12.08	36	T	49
Louisville, Ky.	32.5	56.6	77.6	57.7	43.56	125	17.5	37
Madison, Wisc.	15.6	45.8	70.6	49.5	30.84	118	40.8	36
Memphis, Tenn.	39.6	62.6	82.1	62.9	51.57	107	5.5	34
Miami, Fla.	67.1	75.3	82.5	77.9	57.55	129	0.0	42
Milwaukee, Wisc.	18.7	44.6	70.5	50.9	30.94	125	47.0	44

City	Average Monthly Temperature (°F)[1]				Precipitation		Snowfall	
	Jan.	April	July	Oct	Average (in.)[1]	annual (days)[2]	Average annual (in.)[2]	Years[2]
Minneapolis–St. Paul, Minn.	11.2	46.0	73.1	49.6	26.36	115	48.9	46
Mobile, Ala.	50.8	68.0	82.2	68.5	64.64	123	0.3	43
Montgomery, Ala.	46.7	65.2	81.7	65.3	49.16	108	0.3	40
Mt. Washington, N.H.	5.1	22.4	48.7	30.5	89.92	209	246.8	52
Nashville, Tenn.	37.1	59.7	79.4	60.2	48.49	119	11.1	43
Newark, N.J.	31.2	52.1	76.8	57.2	42.34	122	28.2	43
New Orleans, La.	52.4	68.7	82.1	69.2	59.74	114	0.2	38[3]
New York, N.Y.	31.8	51.9	76.4	57.5	42.82	119	26.1	40[3]
Norfolk, Va.	39.9	58.2	78.4	61.3	45.22	115	7.9	36
Oklahoma City, Okla.	35.9	60.2	82.1	62.3	30.89	82	9.0	45
Olympia, Wash.	37.2	47.3	63.0	50.1	50.96	164	18.0	43
Omaha, Neb.	20.2	52.2	77.7	54.5	30.34	98	31.1	49[3]
Philadelphia, Pa.	31.2	52.9	76.5	56.5	41.42	117	21.9	42[3]
Phoenix, Ariz.	52.3	68.1	92.3	73.4	7.11	36	T	47[3]
Pittsburgh, Pa.	26.7	50.1	72.0	52.5	36.30	154	44.6	32
Portland, Maine	21.5	42.8	68.1	48.5	43.52	128	72.4	44
Portland, Ore.	38.9	50.4	67.7	54.3	37.39	154	6.8	44
Providence, R.I.	28.2	47.9	72.5	53.2	45.32	124	37.1	31
Raleigh, N.C.	39.6	59.4	77.7	59.7	41.76	112	7.7	40
Reno, Nev.	32.2	46.4	69.5	50.3	7.49	51	25.3	42
Richmond, Va.	36.6	57.9	77.8	58.6	44.07	113	14.6	47
Roswell, N.M.	41.4	61.9	81.4	61.7	9.70	52	11.4	37[3]
Sacramento, Calif.	45.3	58.2	75.6	63.9	17.10	58	0.1	36[3]
Salt Lake City, Utah	28.6	49.2	77.5	53.0	15.31	90	59.1	56
San Antonio, Texas	50.4	69.6	84.6	70.2	29.13	81	0.4	42
San Diego, Calif.	56.8	61.2	70.3	67.5	9.32	43	T	44
San Francisco, Calif.	48.5	54.8	62.2	60.6	19.71	63	T	57
Savannah, Ga.	49.1	66.0	81.2	66.9	49.70	111	0.3	34
Seattle–Tacoma, Wash.	39.1	48.7	64.8	52.4	38.60	158	12.8	40
Sioux Falls, S.D.	12.4	46.4	74.0	49.4	24.12	96	39.9	39
Spokane, Wash.	25.7	45.8	69.7	47.5	16.71	114	51.5	37
Springfield, Ill.	24.6	53.3	76.5	56.0	33.78	114	24.5	37
St. Louis, Mo.	28.8	56.1	78.9	57.9	33.91	111	19.8	48[3]
Tampa, Fla.	59.8	71.5	82.1	74.4	46.73	107	T	38
Toledo, Ohio	23.1	47.8	71.8	51.7	31.78	137	38.3	29
Tucson, Ariz.	51.1	64.9	86.2	70.4	11.14	52	1.2	44
Tulsa, Okla.	35.2	61.0	83.2	62.6	38.77	89	9.0	46
Vero Beach, Fla.	61.9	71.7	81.1	75.2	51.41	n.a.	n.a.	0
Washington, D.C.	35.2	56.7	78.9	59.3	39.00	112	17.0	41[3]
Wilmington, Del.	31.2	52.4	76.0	56.3	41.38	117	20.9	37
Wichita, Kan.	29.6	56.3	81.4	59.1	28.61	85	16.4	31

1. Based on 30 year period 1951–80. Data latest available. 2. Data through 1984 based on number of years as indicated in Years column. 3. For snowfall data where number of years differ from that for precipitation data. T = trace. n.a. = not available. *Source:* National Oceanic and Atmospheric Administration.

Wind Chill Factors

Wind speed (mph)	Thermometer reading (degrees Fahrenheit)															
	35	30	25	20	15	10	5	0	–5	–10	–15	–20	–25	–30	–35	–40	–45
5	33	27	21	19	12	7	0	–5	–10	–15	–21	–26	–31	–36	–42	–47	–52
10	22	16	10	3	–3	–9	–15	–22	–27	–34	–40	–46	–52	–58	–64	–71	–77
15	16	9	2	–5	–11	–18	–25	–31	–38	–45	–51	–58	–65	–72	–78	–85	–92
20	12	4	–3	–10	–17	–24	–31	–39	–46	–53	–60	–67	–74	–81	–88	–95	–103
25	8	1	–7	–15	–22	–29	–36	–44	–51	–59	–66	–74	–81	–88	–96	–103	–110
30	6	–2	–10	–18	–25	–33	–41	–49	–56	–64	–71	–79	–86	–93	–101	–109	–116
35	4	–4	–12	–20	–27	–35	–43	–52	–58	–67	–74	–82	–89	–97	–105	–113	–120
40	3	–5	–13	–21	–29	–37	–45	–53	–60	–69	–76	–84	–92	–100	–107	–115	–123
45	2	–6	–14	–22	–30	–38	–46	–54	–62	–70	–78	–85	–93	–102	–109	–117	–125

NOTES: This chart gives equivalent temperatures for combinations of wind speed and temperatures. For example, the combination of a temperature of 10° Fahrenheit and a wind blowing at 10 mph has a cooling power equal to –9° F. Wind speeds of higher than 45 mph have little additional cooling effect.

World and U.S. Extremes of Climate

Highest recorded temperature

	Place	Date	Degree Fahrenheit	Degree Centigrade
World (Africa)	El Azizia, Libya	Sept. 13, 1922	136	58
North America (U.S.)	Death Valley, Calif.	July 10, 1913	134	57
Asia	Tirat Tsvi, Israel	June 21, 1942	129	54
Australia	Cloncurry, Queensland	Jan. 16, 1889	128	53
Europe	Seville, Spain	Aug. 4, 1881	122	50
South America	Rivadavia, Argentina	Dec. 11, 1905	120	49
Canada	Midale and Yellow Grass, Saskatchewan	July 5, 1937	113	45
Persian Gulf (sea–surface)		August 5, 1924	96	36
South Pole		Dec. 27, 1978	7.5	–14
Antarctica	Vanda Station	Jan. 5, 1974	59	15

Lowest recorded temperature

	Place	Date	Degree Fahrenheit	Degree Centigrade
World (Antarctica)	Vostok	July 21, 1983	–129	–89
Asia	Verkhoyansk/Oimekon	Feb. 6, 1933	–90	–68
Greenland	Northice	Jan. 9, 1954	–87	–66
North America (excl. Greenland)	Snag, Yukon, Canada	Feb. 3, 1947	–81	–63
Alaska	Prospect Creek, Endicott Mts.	Jan. 23, 1971	–80	–62
U.S., excluding Alaska	Rogers Pass, Mont.	Jan. 20, 1954	–70	–56.5
Europe	Ust'Shchugor, U.S.S.R.	n.a.	–67	–55
South America	Sarmiento, Argentina	Jan. 1, 1907	–27	–33
Africa	Ifrane, Morocco	Feb. 11, 1935	–11	–24
Australia	Charlotte Pass, N.S.W.	July 22, 1947	–8	–22
United States	Prospect Creek, Alaska	Jan. 23, 1971	–80	–62

Greatest rainfalls

	Place	Date	Inches	Centimeters
1 minute (World)	Unionville, Md.	July 4, 1956	1.23	3.1
20 minutes (World)	Curtea–de–Arges, Romania	July 7, 1889	8.1	20.5
42 minutes (World)	Holt, Mo.	June 22, 1947	12	30.5
12 hours (World)	Foc–Foc, La Réunion	Jan. 7–8, 1966	45	114
24 hours (World)	Foc–Foc, La Réeunion	Jan. 7–8, 1966	72	182.5
24 hours (N. Hemisphere)	Paishih, Taiwan	Sept. 10–11, 1963	49	125
24 hours (Australia)	Bellenden Ker, Queensland	Jan. 4, 1979	44	114
24 hours (U.S.)	Alvin, Texas	July 25–26, 1979	43	109
24 hours (Canada)	Ucluelet Brynnor Mines, British Columbia	Oct. 6, 1967	19	49
5 days (World)	Commerson, La Réunion	Jan. 23–28, 1980	156	395
1 month (World)	Cherrapunji, India	July 1861	366	930
12 months (World)	Cherrapunji, India	Aug. 1860–Aug. 1861	1,042	2,647
12 months (U.S.)	Kukui, Maui, Hawaii	Dec. 1981–Dec. 1982	739	1878

Greatest snowfalls

	Place	Date	Inches	Centimeters
1 month (U.S.)	Tamarack, Calif.	Jan. 1911	390	991
24 hours (N. America)	Silver Lake, Colo.	April 14–15, 1921	76	192.5
24 hours (Alaska)	Thompson Pass	Dec. 29, 1955	62	157.5
19 hours (France)	Bessans	April 5–6, 1969	68	173
1 storm (N. America)	Mt. Shasta Ski Bowl, Calif.	Feb. 13–19, 1959	189	480
1 storm (Alaska)	Thompson Pass	Dec. 26–31, 1955	175	445.5
1 season (N. America)	Paradise Ranger Sta., Wash.	1971–1972	1,122	2,850
1 season (Alaska)	Thompson Pass	1952–1953	974.5	2,475
1 season (Canada)	Revelstoke Mt. Copeland, British Columbia	1971–1972	964	2,446.5

Source: U.S. Army Corps of Engineers, Engineer Topographic Laboratories.

Tropical Storms and Hurricanes, 1886–1992

	Jan.–April	May	June	July	Aug.	Sept.	Oct.	Nov.	Dec.	Total
Number of tropical storms (incl. hurricanes)	4	14	56	69	216	308	188	43	6	904
Number of tropical storms that reached hurricane intensity	1	3	23	36	150	193	96	22	3	527

Other Recorded Extremes

Highest average annual mean temperature (World): Dallol, Ethiopia (Oct. 1960–Dec. 1966), 94° F (35° C). **(U.S.):** Key West, Fla. (30–year normal), 78.2° F (25.7° C).

Lowest average annual mean temperature (Antarctica): Plateau Station –70° F (–57° C). **(U.S.):** Barrow, Alaska (30–year normal), 9.3° F (–13° C).

Greatest average yearly rainfall (U.S.): Mt. Waialeale, Kauai, Hawaii (32–year avg), 460 in. (1,168 cm). **(India):** Cherrapunji (74–year avg), 450 in. (1,143 cm).

Minimum average yearly rainfall (Chile): Arica (59–year avg), 0.03 in. (0.08 cm) (no rainfall for 14 consecutive years). **(U.S.):** Death Valley, Calif. (42–year avg), 1.63 in. (4.14 cm). Bagdad, Calif., holds the U.S. record for the longest period with no measurable rain, 767 days, from Oct. 3, 1912 to Nov. 8, 1914).

Hottest summer avg in Western Hemisphere (U.S.): Death Valley, Calif., 98° F (36.7° C).

Longest hot spell (W. Australia): Marble Bar, 100° F (38° C) (or above) for 162 consecutive days, Oct. 30, 1923–Apr. 7, 1924.

Largest hailstone (U.S.): Coffeyville, KS, 17.5 in. (44.5 cm), Sept. 3, 1979.

Weather Glossary

blizzard: storm characterized by strong winds, low temperatures, and large amounts of snow.

blowing snow: snow lifted from ground surface by wind; restricts visibility.

cold wave warning: indicates that a change to abnormally cold weather is expected; greater than normal protective measures will be required.

cyclone: circulation of winds rotating counterclockwise in the northern hemisphere and clockwise in the southern hemisphere. Hurricanes and tornadoes are both examples of cyclones.

drifting snow: strong winds will blow loose or falling snow into significant drifts.

drizzle: uniform close precipitation of tiny drops with diameter of less than .02 inch.

flash flood: dangerous rapid rise of water levels in streams, rivers, or over land area.

freezing rain or drizzle: rain or drizzle that freezes on contact with the ground or other objects forming a coating of ice on exposed surfaces.

gale warning: winds in the 33–48 knot (38–55 mph) range forecast.

hail: small balls of ice falling separately or in lumps; usually associated with thunderstorms and temperatures that may be well above freezing.

hazardous driving warnings: indicates that drizzle, freezing rain, snow, sleet, or strong winds make driving conditions difficult.

heavy snow warnings: issued when 4 inches or more of snow are expected to fall in a 12–hour period or when 6 inches or more are anticipated in a 24–hour period.

hurricane: devastating cyclonic storm; winds over 74 mph near storm center; usually tropical in origin; called cyclone in Indian Ocean, typhoon in the Pacific.

hurricane warning: winds in excess of 64 knots (74 mph) in connection with hurricane.

rain: precipitation of liquid particles with diameters larger than .02 inch.

sleet: translucent or transparent ice pellets; frozen rain; generally a winter phenomenon.

small craft warning: indicates winds as high as 33 knots (38 mph) and sea conditions dangerous to small boats.

snow flurries: snow falling for a short time at intermittent periods; accumulations are usually small.

snow squall: brief, intense falls of snow, usually accompanied by gusty winds.

storm warnings: winds greater than 48 knots (55 mph) are forecast.

temperature–humidity index (THI): measure of personal discomfort based on the combined effects of temperature and humidity. Most people are uncomfortable when the THI is 75. A THI of 80 produces acute discomfort for almost everyone.

tidal waves: series of ocean waves caused by earthquakes; can reach speeds of 600 mph; they grow in height as they reach shore and can crest as high as 100 feet.

thunder: the sound produced by the rapid expansion of air heated by lightning.

tornado: dangerous whirlwind associated with the cumulonimbus clouds of severe thunderstorms; winds up to 300 mph.

tornado warning: tornado has actually been detected by radar or sighted in designated area.

tornado watch: potential exists in the watch area for storms that could contain tornadoes.

travelers' warning: *see* hazardous driving warning.

tsunami: *see* tidal waves.

wind–chill factor: combined effect of temperature and wind speed as compared to equivalent temperature in calm air .

During a Hurricane

Source: Federal Emergency Management Agency and NOAA.

Remain indoors during a hurricane. Blowing debris can injure and kill. Travel is extremely dangerous. Be especially wary of the "eye" of the hurricane. If the storm center passes directly overhead, there will be a lull in the wind lasting from a few minutes to half-an-hour or more. At the other side of the "eye" the winds will increase rapidly to hurricane force, and will come from the opposite direction.

Record Highest Temperatures by State

State	Temp. °F	Temp °C	Date	Station	Elevation, feet
Alabama	112	44	Sept. 5, 1925	Centerville	345
Alaska	100	38	June 27, 1915	Fort Yukon	est. 420
Arizona	127	53	July 7, 1905*	Parker	345
Arkansas	120	49	Aug. 10, 1936	Ozark	396
California	134	57	July 10, 1913	Greenland Ranch	–178
Colorado	118	48	July 11, 1888	Bennett	5,484
Connecticut	105	41	July 22, 1926	Waterbury	400
Delaware	110	43	July 21, 1930	Millsboro	20
D.C.	106	41	July 20, 1930	Washington	410
Florida	109	43	June 29, 1931	Monticello	207
Georgia	113	45	May 27, 1978	Greenville	860
Hawaii	100	38	Apr. 27, 1931	Pahala	850
Idaho	118	48	July 28, 1934	Orofino	1,027
Illinois	117	47	July 14, 1954	E. St. Louis	410
Indiana	116	47	July 14, 1936	Collegeville	672
Iowa	118	48	July 20, 1934	Keokuk	614
Kansas	121	49	July 24, 1936*	Alton (near)	1,651
Kentucky	114	46	July 28, 1930	Greensburg	581
Louisiana	114	46	Aug. 10, 1936	Plain Dealing	268
Maine	105	41	July 10, 1911*	North Bridgton	450
Maryland	109	43	July 10, 1936*	Cumberland & Frederick	623;325
Massachusetts	107	42	Aug. 2, 1975	New Bedford & Chester	120;640
Michigan	112	44	July 13, 1936	Mio	963
Minnesota	114	46	July 6, 1936*	Moorhead	904
Mississippi	115	46	July 29, 1930	Holly Springs	600
Missouri	118	48	July 14, 1954*	Warsaw & Union	687;560
Montana	117	47	July 5, 1937	Medicine Lake	1,950
Nebraska	118	48	July 24, 1936*	Minden	2,169
Nevada	122	50	June 23, 1954*	Overton	1,240
New Hampshire	106	41	July 4, 1911	Nashua	125
New Jersey	110	43	July 10, 1936	Runyon	18
New Mexico	116	47	July 14, 1934*	Orogrande	4,171
New York	108	42	July 22, 1926	Troy	35
North Carolina	110	43	Aug. 21, 1983	Fayetteville	81
North Dakota	121	49	July 6, 1936	Steele	1,857
Ohio	113	45	July 21, 1934*	Gallipolis (near)	673
Oklahoma	120	49	July 26, 1943*	Tishomingo	670
Oregon	119	48	Aug. 10, 1898	Pendleton	1,074
Pennsylvania	111	44	July 10, 1936*	Phoenixville	100
Rhode Island	104	40	Aug. 2, 1975	Providence	51
South Carolina	111	44	June 28, 1954*	Camden	170
South Dakota	120	49	July 5, 1936	Gannvalley	1,750
Tennessee	113	45	Aug. 9, 1930*	Perryville	377
Texas	120	49	Aug. 12, 1936	Seymour	1,291
Utah	117	47	July 5, 1895	Saint George	2,880
Vermont	105	41	July 4, 1911	Vernon	310
Virginia	110	43	July 15, 1954	Balcony Falls	725
Washington	118	48	Aug. 5, 1961*	Ice Harbor Dam	475
West Virginia	112	44	July 10, 1936*	Martinsburg	435
Wisconsin	114	46	July 13, 1936	Wisconsin Dells	900
Wyoming	114	46	July 12, 1900	Basin	3,500

*Also on earlier dates at the same or other places. *Source:* National Climatic Data Center, Asheville, N.C., and Storm Phillips, STORMFAX, INC.

Record Lowest Temperatures by State

State	Temp. °F	Temp °C	Date	Station	Elevation, feet
Alabama	–27	–33	Jan. 30, 1966	New Market	760
Alaska	–80	–62	Jan. 23, 1971	Prospect Creek	1,100
Arizona	–40	–40	Jan. 7, 1971	Hawley Lake	8,180
Arkansas	–29	–34	Feb. 13, 1905	Pond	1,250
California	–45	–43	Jan. 20, 1937	Boca	5,532
Colorado	–60	–51	Jan. 1, 1979*	Maybell	5,920
Connecticut	–32	–36	Feb. 16, 1943	Falls Village	585
Delaware	–17	–27	Jan. 17, 1893	Millsboro	20
D.C.	–15	–26	Feb. 11, 1899	Washington	410
Florida	–2	–19	Feb. 13, 1899	Tallahassee	193
Georgia	–17	–27	Jan. 27, 1940	CCC Camp F–16	est. 1,000
Hawaii	14	–11	Jan. 2, 1961	Haleakala, Maui Is	9,750
Idaho	–60	–51	Jan. 18, 1943	Island Park Dam	6,285
Illinois	–35	–37	Jan. 22, 1930	Mount Carroll	817
Indiana	–35	–37	Feb. 2, 1951	Greensburg	954
Iowa	–47	–44	Jan. 12, 1912	Washta	1,157
Kansas	–40	–40	Feb. 13, 1905	Lebanon	1,812
Kentucky	–34	–37	Jan. 28, 1963	Cynthiana	684
Louisiana	–16	–27	Feb. 13, 1899	Minden	194
Maine	–48	–44	Jan. 19, 1925	Van Buren	510
Maryland	–40	–40	Jan. 13, 1912	Oakland	2,461
Massachusetts	–34	–37	Jan. 18, 1957	Birch Hill Dam	840
Michigan	–51	–46	Feb. 9, 1934	Vanderbilt	785
Minnesota	–59	–51	Feb. 16, 1903*	Pokegama Dam	1,280
Mississippi	–19	–28	Jan. 30, 1966	Corinth	420
Missouri	–40	–40	Feb. 13, 1905	Warsaw	700
Montana	–70	–57	Jan. 20, 1954	Rogers Pass	5,470
Nebraska	–47	–44	Feb. 12, 1899	Camp Clarke	3,700
Nevada	–50	–46	Jan. 8, 1937	San Jacinto	5,200
New Hampshire	–46	–43	Jan. 28, 1925	Pittsburg	1,575
New Jersey	–34	–37	Jan. 5, 1904	River Vale	70
New Mexico	–50	–46	Feb. 1, 1951	Gavilan	7,350
New York	–52	–47	Feb. 18, 1979*	Old Forge	1,720
North Carolina	–29	–37	Jan. 30, 1966	Mt. Mitchell	6,525
North Dakota	–60	–51	Feb. 15, 1936	Parshall	1,929
Ohio	–39	–39	Feb. 10, 1899	Milligan	800
Oklahoma	–27	–33	Jan. 18, 1930	Watts	958
Oregon	–54	–48	Feb. 10, 1933*	Seneca	4,700
Pennsylvania	–42	–41	Jan. 5, 1904	Smethport	est. 1,500
Rhode Island	–23	–31	Jan. 11, 1942	Kingston	100
South Carolina	–20	–28	Jan. 18, 1977	Caesars Head	3,100
South Dakota	–58	–50	Feb. 17, 1936	McIntosh	2,277
Tennessee	–32	–36	Dec. 30, 1917	Mountain City	2,471
Texas	–23	–31	Feb. 8, 1933*	Seminole	3,275
Utah	–50	–51	Jan. 5, 1913*	Strawberry Tunnel	7,650
Vermont	–50	–46	Dec. 30, 1933	Bloomfield	915
Virginia	–29	–34	Feb. 10, 1899	Monterey	—
Washington	–48	–44	Dec. 30, 1968	Mazama & Winthrop	2,120;1,765
West Virginia	–37	–38	Dec. 30, 1917	Lewisburg	2,200
Wisconsin	–54	–48	Jan. 24, 1922	Danbury	908
Wyoming	–63	–53	Feb. 9, 1933	Moran	6,770

*Also on earlier dates at the same or other places. *Source:* National Climatic Data Center, Asheville, N.C., and Storm Phillips, STORMFAX, INC.

Record High and Low Temperature in U.S. for Each Month

Source: National Climatic Data Center, Asheville, N.C., and Storm Phillips, STORMFAX, Inc.
NOTE: for the conterminous states only.

January

The highest temperature ever recorded for the month of January occurred on January 17, 1936, again in 1954, in Laredo, Tex. (elevation 421 ft) where the temperature reached 98° F.

The lowest temperature ever recorded for the month of January occurred on January 20, 1954, in Rogers Pass, Mont. (elevation 5,470 ft) where the temperature fell to –70° F.

February

The highest temperature ever recorded for the month of February occurred on February 3, 1963, in Montezuma, Ariz. (elevation 735 ft) where the temperature reached 105° F.

The lowest temperature ever recorded for the month of February occurred on February 9, 1933, at the Riverside Ranger Station in Montana (elevation 6,700 ft) where the temperature fell to –66° F.

March

The highest temperature ever recorded for the month of March occurred on March 31, 1954, in Rio Grande City, Tex. (elevation 168 ft) where the temperature reached 108° F.

The lowest temperature ever recorded for the month of March occurred on March 17, 1906, in Snake River, Wyo. (elevation 6,862 ft) where the temperature dropped to –50° F.

April

The highest temperature ever recorded for the month of April occurred on April 25, 1898, at Volcano Springs, Calif. (elevation –220 ft) where the temperature reached 118° F.

The lowest temperature ever recorded for the month of April occurred on April 5, 1945, in Eagle Nest, N. Mex. (elevation 8,250 ft) where the temperature dropped to –36° F.

May

The highest temperature ever recorded for the month of May occurred on May 27, 1896, in Salton, Calif. (elevation –263 ft) where the temperature reached 124° F.

The lowest temperature ever recorded for the month of May occurred on May 7, 1964, in White Mountain 2, Calif. (elevation 12,470 ft) where the temperature dropped to –15° F.

June

The highest temperature ever recorded for the month of June occurred on June 15, 1896, at Fort Mohave, Ariz. (elevation 555 ft) where the temperature reached 127° F.

The lowest temperature ever recorded for the month of June occurred on June 13, 1907, in Tamarack, Calif. (elevation 8,000 ft) where the temperature dropped to 2° F.

July

The highest temperature ever recorded for the month of July occurred on July 10, 1913, at Greenland Ranch, Calif. (elevation –178 ft) where the temperature reached 134° F.

The lowest temperature ever recorded for the month of July occurred on July 21, 1911, at Painter, Wyo. (elevation 6,800 ft) where the temperature fell to 10° F.

August

The highest temperature ever recorded for the month of August occurred on August 12, 1933, at Greenland Ranch, Calif. (elevation –178 ft) where the temperature reached 127° F.

The lowest temperature ever recorded for the month of August occurred on August 25, 1910, in Bowen, Mont. (elevation 6,080 ft) where the temperature fell to 5° F.

September

The highest temperature ever recorded for the month of September occurred on September 2, 1950, in Mecca, Calif. (elevation –175 ft) where the temperature reached 126° F.

The lowest temperature ever recorded for the month of September occurred on September 24, 1926, at Riverside Ranger Station, Mont. (elevation 6,700 ft) where the temperature fell to –9 F.

October

The highest temperature ever recorded for the month of October occurred on October 5, 1917, in Sentinel, Ariz. (elevation 685 ft) where the temperature reached 116° F.

The lowest temperature ever recorded for the month of October occurred on October 29, 1917, in Soda Butte, Wyo. (elevation 6,600 ft) where the temperature fell to –33° F.

November

The highest temperature ever recorded for the month of November occurred on November 12, 1906, in Craftonville, Calif. (elevation 1,759 ft) where the temperature reached 105° F.

The lowest temperature ever recorded for the month of November occurred on November 16, 1959, at Lincoln, Mont. (elevation 5,130 ft) where the temperature fell to –53° F.

December

The highest temperature ever recorded for the month of December occurred on December 8, 1938, in La Mesa, Calif. (elevation 539 ft) where the temperature reached 100° F.

The lowest temperature ever recorded for the month of December occurred on December 19, 1924, at Riverside Ranger Station, Mont. (elevation 6,700 ft) where the temperature fell to –59° F.

Temperature Extremes in The United States

Source: National Oceanic and Atmospheric Administration, Environmental Data and Information Service, and National Climatic Center

The Highest Temperature Extremes

Greenland Ranch, California, with 134° F on July 10, 1913, holds the record for the highest temperature ever officially observed in the United States. This station was located in barren Death Valley, 178 feet below sea level. Death Valley is about 140 miles long, four to six miles wide, and oriented north to south in southwestern California. Much of the valley is below sea level and is flanked by towering mountain ranges with Mt. Whitney, the highest landmark in the 48 conterminous states, rising to 14,495 feet above sea level, less than 100 miles to the west. Death Valley has the hottest summers in the Western Hemisphere, and is the only known place in the United States where nightime temperatures sometimes remain above 100° F.

The highest annual normal (1941–70 mean) temperature in the United States, 78.2° F, and the highest summer (June–August) normal temperature, 92.8° F, are for Death Valley, California. The highest winter (December–February) normal temperature is 72.8° F for Honolulu, Hawaii.

Amazing temperature rises of 40° to 50° F in a few minutes occasionally may be brought about by chinook winds.[1]

Some Outstanding Temperature Rises

In 12 hours: 83° F, Granville, N.D., Feb. 21, 1918, from –33° F to 50° F from early morning to late afternoon.

In 15 minutes: 42° F, Fort Assiniboine, Mont., Jan. 19, 1892, from –5° F to 37° F.

In seven minutes: 34° F, Kipp, Mont., Dec. 1, 1896. The observer also reported that a total rise of 80° F occurred in a few hours and that 30 inches of snow disappeared in one–half day.

In two minutes: 49° F, Spearfish, S.D., Jan. 22, 1943 from –4° F at 7:30 a.m. to 45° F at 7:32 a.m.

The Lowest Temperature Extremes

The lowest temperature on record in the United States, –79.8° F, was observed at Prospect Creek Camp in the Endicott Mountains of northern Alaska (latitude 66° 48′N, longitude 150° 40′W) on Jan. 23, 1971. The lowest ever recorded in the conterminous 48 states, –69.7° F, occurred at Rogers Pass, in Lewis and Clark County, Mont., on Jan. 20, 1954. Rogers Pass is in mountainous and heavily forested terrain about one–half mile east of and 140 feet below the summit of the Continental Divide.

The lowest annual normal (1941–70 mean) temperature in the United States is 9.3° F for Barrow, Alaska, which lies on the Arctic coast. Barrow also has the coolest summers (June–August) with a normal temperature of 36.4° F. The lowest winter (December–February) normal temperature, is –15.7° F for Barter Island on the arctic coast of northeast Alaska.

In the 48 conterminous states, Mt. Washington, N.H. (elevation 6,262 feet) has the lowest annual normal temperature 26.9° F and the lowest normal summer temperature, 46.8° F. A few stations in the northeastern United States and in the upper Rocky Mountains have normal annual temperatures in the 30s; summer normal temperatures at these stations are in the low 50s. Winter normal temperatures are lowest in northeastern North Dakota, 5.6° F for Langdon Experiment Farm, and in northwestern Minnesota, 5.3° F for Hallock.

Some Outstanding Temperature Falls

In 24 hours: 100° F, Browing, Mont., Jan. 23–24, 1916, from 44° to –56° F.

In 12 hours: 84° F, Fairfield, Mont., Dec. 24, 1924, from 63° at noon to –21° F at midnight.

In 2 hours: 62° F, Rapid City, S.D., Jan. 12, 1911, from 49° F at 6:00 a.m. to –13° F at 8:00 a.m.

In 27 minutes: 58° F, Spearfish, S.D., Jan. 22, 1943, from 54° F at 9:00 a.m. to –4° F at 9:27 a.m.

In 15 minutes: 47° F, Rapid City, S.D., Jan. 10, 1911, from 55° F at 7:00 a.m. to 8° F. at 7:15 a.m.

1. A warm, dry wind that descends from the eastern slopes of the Rocky Mountains, causing a rapid rise in temperature.

Winter Indoor Comfort and Relative Humidity

Compared to summer when the moisture content of the air (relative humidity) is an important factor of body discomfort, air moisture has a lesser effect on the human body during outdoor winter activities. But it is a big factor for winter indoor comfort because it has a direct bearing on health and energy consumption.

The colder the outdoor temperature, the more heat must be added indoors for body comfort. However, the heat that is added will cause a drying effect and lower the indoor relative humidity, unless an indoor moisture source is present.

While a room temperature between 71° and 77° F may be comfortable for short periods of time under very dry conditions, prolonged exposure to dry air has varying effects on the human body and usually causes discomfort. The moisture content of the air is important, and by increasing the relative humidity to above 50% within the above temperature range, 80% or more of all average dressed persons would feel comfortable.

Effects of Dry Air on the Body

Studies have shown that dry air has four main effects on the human body:

1. Breathing dry air is a potential health hazard which can cause such respiratory ailments as asthma, bronchitis, sinusitis, and nosebleeds, or general dehydration since body fluids are depleted during respiration.

2. Skin moisture evaporation can cause skin irritations and eye itching.

3. Irritative effects, such as static electricity which causes mild shocks when metal is touched, are common when the air moisture is low.

Average Indoor Relative Humidity, %, for January

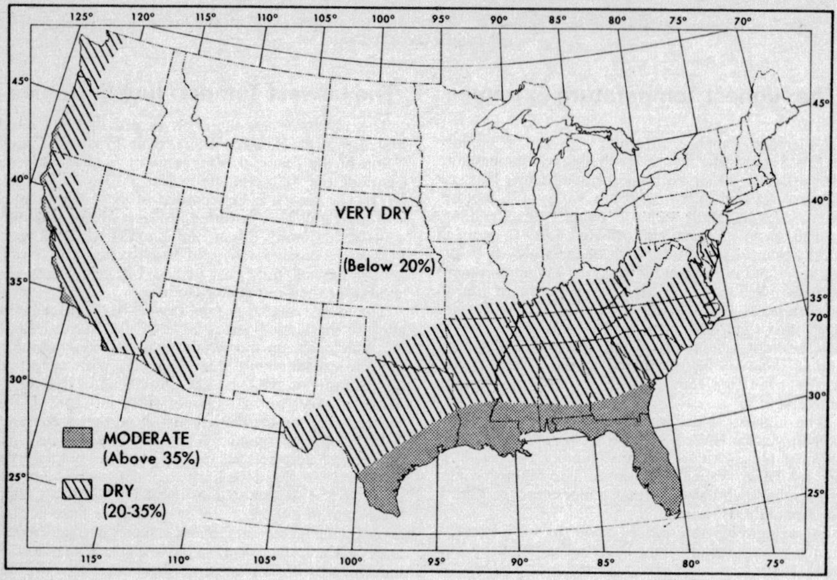

Source: National Oceanic and Atmospheric Administration, Environmental Data and Information Service, National Climatic Center.

4. The "apparent temperature" of the air is lower than what the thermometer indicates, and the body "feels" colder.

These problems can be reduced by simply increasing the indoor relative humidity. This can be done through use of humidifiers, vaporizers, steam ge nerators, sources such as large pans, or water containers made of porous ceramics. Even wet towels or water in a bathtub will be of some help. The lower the room temperature the easier the relative humidity can be brought to its desired level. A relative humidity indicator (hygrometer) may be of assistance in determining the humidity in the house.

Referring to item 4, a more detailed discussion is necessary. While the indoor temperature as read from a thermometer may be 75° F, the apparent temperature (what it feels like) may be warmer or colder depending on the moisture content of the air. Apparent temperature can vary as much as 8° F within a relative humidity range of 10 to 80 percent (these limits are generally possible in a closed room). Because of evaporation the human body cools when exposed to dry air, and the sense of coldness increases as the humidity decreases. With a room temperature of 70° F, for example, a person will feel colder in a dry room than in a moist room; this is especially noticeable when entering a dry room after bathing.

The table on the following page gives apparent temperatures for various combinations of room temperature and relative humidity. As an example of how to read the table, a room temperature of 70° F combined with a relative humidity of 10% feels like 64° F, but at 80% it feels like 71° F.

Although degrees of comfort vary with age, health, activity, clothing, and body characteristics, the table can be used as a general guideline when raising the apparent temperature and the level of comfort through an increase in room moisture, rather than by an addition of heat to the room. This method of changing the apparent temperature can give the direct benefit of reducing heating costs because comfort can be maintained with a lower thermostat setting if moisture is added. For example, an apparent comfortable temperature can be maintained with a thermostat setting of 75° F with 20% relative humidity or with a 70° F setting with 80 percent humidity. A relative humidity of 20 percent is common for homes without a humidifier during winter in the northern United States. □

Hurricane Advisories and Warnings

Source: Federal Emergency Management Agency and NOAA.

Thanks to modern detection and tracking devices, the National Weather Service can usually provide 12 to 24 hours of advance warning. Advisories are issued by the Weather Service if NOAA hurricanes approach land.

A "hurricane watch" is issued whenever a hurricane becomes a threat to coastal areas. Everyone in the area covered by the "watch" should listen for further advisories and be prepared to act promptly if a hurricane warning is issued.

A "hurricane warning" is issued when hurricane winds of 74 miles an hour or higher, or a combination of dangerously high water and very rough seas, are expected in a specific coastal area within 24 hours. Precautionary actions should begin immediately. □

Apparent Temperature for Values of Room Temperature and Relative Humidity

ROOM TEMPERATURE (F)	RELATIVE HUMIDITY (%) 0	10	20	30	40	50	60	70	80	90	100
75	68	69	71	72	74	75	76	76	77	78	79
74	66	68	69	71	72	73	74	75	76	77	78
73	65	67	68	70	71	72	73	74	75	76	77
72	64	65	67	68	70	71	72	73	74	75	76
71	63	64	66	67	68	70	71	72	73	74	75
70	63	64	65	66	67	68	69	70	71	72	73
69	62	63	64	65	66	67	68	69	70	71	72
68	61	62	63	64	65	66	67	68	69	70	71
67	60	61	62	63	64	65	66	67	68	68	69
66	59	60	61	62	63	64	65	66	67	67	68
65	59	60	61	61	62	63	64	65	65	66	67
64	58	59	60	60	61	62	63	64	64	65	66
63	57	58	59	59	60	61	62	62	63	64	64
62	56	57	58	58	59	60	61	61	62	63	63
61	56	57	57	58	59	59	60	60	61	61	62
60	55	56	56	57	58	58	59	59	60	60	61

Source: National Oceanic and Atmospheric Administration, Environmental Data and Information Service and National Climatic Center.

GREAT DISASTERS

The following lists are not all-inclusive due to space limitations. Only disasters involving great loss of life and/or property, historical interest, or unusual circumstances are listed. Data as of Aug. 1, 1993. For later disasters see *Current Events*.

Earthquakes and Volcanic Eruptions

A.D. 79 **Aug. 24, Italy:** eruption of Mt. Vesuvius buried cities of Pompeii and Herculaneum, killing thousands.

1556 **Jan. 24, Shaanxi (Shensi) Province, China:** most deadly earthquake in history; 830,000 killed.

1755 **Nov. 1, Portugal:** one of the most severe of recorded earthquakes leveled Lisbon and was felt as far away as southern France and North Africa; 10,000–20,000 killed in Lisbon.

1883 **Aug. 26–28, Netherlands Indies:** eruption of Krakatau; violent explosions destroyed two thirds of island. Sea waves occurred as far away as Cape Horn, and possibly England. Estimated 36,000 dead.

1902 **May 8, Martinique, West Indies:** Mt. Pelée erupted and wiped out city of St. Pierre; 40,000 dead.

1908 **Dec. 28, Messina, Sicily:** about 85,000 killed and city totally destroyed.

1915 **Jan. 13, Avezzano, Italy:** earthquake left 29,980 dead.

1920 **Dec. 16, Gansu (Kansu) Province, China:** earthquake killed 200,000.

1923 **Sept. 1, Japan:** earthquake destroyed third of Tokyo and most of Yokohama; more than 140,000 killed.

1933 **March 10, Long Beach, Calif.:** 117 left dead by earthquake.

1935 **May 31, India:** earthquake at Quetta killed an estimated 50,000.

1939 **Jan. 24, Chile:** earthquake razed 50,000 sq mi.; about 30,000 killed.

Dec. 27, Northern Turkey: severe quakes destroyed city of Erzingan; about 100,000 casualties.

1950 **Aug. 15, India:** earthquake affected 30,000 sq mi. in Assam; 20,000–30,000 believed killed.

1963 **July 26, Skoplje, Yugoslavia:** four fifths of city destroyed; 1,011 dead, 3,350 injured.

1964 **March 27, Alaska:** strongest earthquake ever to strike North America hit 80 miles east of Anchorage; followed by seismic wave 50 feet high that traveled 8,445 miles at 450 miles per hour; 117 killed.

1970 **May 31, Peru:** earthquake left 50,000 dead, 17,000 missing.

1972 **April 10, Iran:** 5,000 killed in earthquake 60 0 miles south of Teheran.

Dec. 22, Managua, Nicaragua: earthquake devastated city, leaving up to 6,000 dead.

1976 **Feb. 4, Guatemala:** earthquake left over 23,000 dead.

July 28, Tangshan, China: earthquake devastated 20-sq-mi. area of city leaving estimated 242,000 dead.

Aug. 17, Mindanao, Philippines: earthquake and tidal wave left up to 8,000 dead or missing.

1977 **March 4, Bucharest:** earthquake razed most of downtown Bucharest; 1,541 reported dead, over 11,000 injured.

1978 **Sept. 16, Tabas, Iran:** earthquake destroyed city in eastern Iran, leaving 25,000 dead.

1980 **Nov. 23, Naples, Italy:** 2,735 killed when earthquake struck southern Italy.

1982 **Dec. 13, Yemen:** 2,800 reported dead in earthquake.

1985 **Sept. 19–20, Mexico:** earthquake registering 8.1 on Richter scale struck central and southwestern regions, devastating part of Mexico City and three coastal states. An estimated 25,000 killed.

Nov. 14–16, Colombia: eruption of Nevada del Ruiz, 85 miles northwest of Bogotá, caused mud slides which buried most of the town of Armero and devastated Chinchiná. An estimated 25,000 were killed.

1988 **Dec. 7, Armenia:** an earthquake measuring 6.9 on the Richter scale killed nearly 25,000, injured 15,000, and left at least 400,000 homeless.

1989 **Oct. 17, San Francisco Bay Area:** an earthquake measuring 7.1 on the Richter Scale killed 67 and injured over 3,000. The quake damaged or destroyed over 100,000 buildings and caused billions of dollars of damage.

1990 **June 21, Northwestern Iran:** an earthquake measuring 7.7 on the Richter Scale destroyed cities, towns, and villages in Caspian Sea area. At least 50,000 dead, over 60,000 injured, and 400,000 homeless.

July 16, Luzon Island, The Philippines: an earthquake measuring 7.7 on the Richter scale claimed the lives of over 1,600 people and injured nearly 3,000 others.

Major U.S. Epidemics

1793 **Philadelphia.** More than 4,000 residents died from yellow fever.

1832 **July–August, New York City.** Over 3,000 people killed in a cholera epidemic. **October, New Orleans.** Cholera took the lives of 4,340 persons.

1848 **New York City.** More than 5,000 deaths caused by cholera.

1853 **New Orleans.** Yellow fever killed 7,790 residents.

1867 **New Orleans.** 3,093 persons perished from yellow fever.

1878 **Southern States.** Over 13,000 people died from yellow fever in lower Mississippi Valley.

1916 **Nationwide.** Over 7,000 deaths occurred and 27,363 cases were reported of polio (infantile paralysis) in America's worst polio epidemic.

1918 **March–November, Nationwide.** Outbreak of influenza killed over 500,000 people in the worst single U.S. epidemic.

1949 **Nationwide.** 2,720 deaths occurred from polio and 42,173 cases were reported.

1952 **Nationwide.** Polio killed 3,300; 57,628 cases reported; worst epidemic since 1916.

1981 **To present.** The Center for Disease Control projects that between 330,000 to 385,000 persons in the U.S. will have died of AIDS by 1995. The CDC estimates that approximately one in 250 Americans are infected with HIV.

WORST UNITED STATES DISASTERS

Aircraft

1979 **May 25, Chicago:** American Airlines DC-10 lost left engine upon take-off and crashed seconds later, killing all 272 persons aboard and three on the ground in worst U.S. air disaster.

Dam

1928 **March 12, Santa Paula, Calif.:** collapse of St. Francis Dam left 450 dead.

Drought

1930s **Many states:** longest drought of the 20th century. Peak periods were 1930, 1934, 1936, 1939, and 1940. During 1934, dry regions stretched solidly from New York and Pennsylvania across the Great Plains to the California coast. A great "dust bowl" covered some 50 million acres in the south central plains during the winter of 1935–1936.

Earthquake

1906 **April 18, San Francisco:** earthquake accompanied by fire razed more than 4 sq mi.; more than 500 dead or missing.

Epidemic

1918 **Nationwide:** Spanish influenza killed over 500,000 Americans.

Explosion

1947 **April 16–18, Texas City, Texas:** Most of the city destroyed by a fire and subsequent explosion on the French freighter *Grandcamp* carrying a cargo of ammonium nitrate. At least 516 were killed and over 3,000 injured.

Fire

1871 **Oct. 8, Peshtigo, Wis.:** over 1,200 lives lost and 2 billion trees burned in forest fire.

Flood

1889 **May 31, Johnstown, Pa.:** more than 2,200 died in flood.

Hurricane

1900 **Aug. 27–Sept. 15, Galveston, Tex.:** over 6,000 died from devastation due to both winds and tidal wave.

Marine

1865 **April 27, *Sultana*:** boiler explosion on Mississippi River steamboat near Memphis, 1,547 killed.

Mine

1907 **Dec. 6, Monongha, W. Va.:** coal mine explosion killed 361.

Oil Spill

1989 **Mar. 24, Prince William Sound, Alaska:** Tanker, *Exxon Valdez,* hit an undersea reef and released 10 million plus gallons of oil into the waters, causing the worst oil spill in U.S. history.

Railroad

1918 **July 9, Nashville, Tenn.:** 101 killed in a two-train collision near Nashville.

Submarine

1963 **April 10, *Thresher*:** atomic-powered submarine sank in North Atlantic: 129 dead.

Tornado

1925 **March 18, Great Tri-State Tornado:** Missouri, Illinois, and Indiana; 695 deaths. Eight additional tornadoes in Kentucky, Tennessee, and Alabama raised day's toll to 792 dead.

Winter Storm

1888 **March 11–14, East Coast:** The Blizzard of 1888. 400 people died, as much as 5 feet of snow. Damage was estimated at $20 million.

Floods, Avalanches, and Tidal Waves

1228 **Holland:** 100,000 persons reputedly drowned by sea flood in Friesland.

1642 **China:** rebels destroyed Kaifeng seawall; 300,000 drowned.

1896 **June 15, Sanriku, Japan:** earthquake and tidal wave killed 27,000.

1953 **Northwest Europe:** storm followed by floods devastated North Sea coastal areas. Netherlands was hardest hit with 1,794 dead.

1959 **Dec. 2, Frejus, France:** flood caused by collapse of Malpasset Dam left 412 dead.

1960 **Agadir, Morocco:** 10, 000–12,000 dead as earthquake set off tidal wave and fire, destroying most of city.

1962 **Jan. 10, Peru:** avalanche down Huascaran, extinct Andean volcano, killed more than 3,000 persons.

1963 **Oct. 9, Italy:** landslide into the Vaiont Dam; flood killed about 2,000.

1966 **Oct. 21, Aberfan, Wales:** avalanche of coal, waste, mud, and rocks killed 144 persons, including 116 children in school.

1969 **Jan. 18–26, Southern California:** floods and mudslides from heavy rains caused widespread property damage; at least 100 dead. Another downpour (Feb. 23–26) caused further floods and mudslides; at least 18 dead.

1970 **Nov. 13, East Pakistan:** 200,000 killed by cyclone-driven tidal wave from Bay of Bengal. Over 100,000 missing.

1971 **Sept. 29, Orissa State, India:** cyclone and tidal wave off Bay of Bengal killed as many as 10,000.

1972 **Feb. 26, Man, W. Va.:** more than 118 died when slag-pile dam collapsed under pressure of torrential rains and flooded 17-mile valley.

June 9–10, Rapid City, S.D.: flash flood caused 237 deaths and $160 million in damage.

June 20, Eastern Seaboard: tropical storm Agnes, in 10-day rampage, caused widespread flash floods. Death toll was 129, 115,000 were left homeless, and damage estimated at $3.5 billion.

1976 **Aug. 1, Loveland, Colo.:** Flash flood along Route 34 in Big Thompson Canyon left 139 dead.

1977 **Nov. 19, Andhra Pradesh State, India:** cyclone and flood from Bay of Bengal left 7,000–10,000 dead.

1988 August-September, Bangladesh: Heaviest monsoon in 70 years innundates three-fourths of country, killing more than 1,300 people and leaving 30 million homeless. Damage is estimated at over $1 billion.

1993 June–August, Ill., Iowa, Kan., Ky., Minn., Mo., Neb., N.D., S.D., Wis.: Two months of heavy rain caused Mississippi River and its tributaries to flood in ten states, causing almost 50 deaths and an estimated $12 billion in damage to property and agriculture in the Midwest. Almost 70,000 people left homeless. For a state-by-state summary, *see* "The Great Flood of 1993," page 791.

Tropical Storms

Cyclones, typhoons, and hurricanes are the same kind of tropical storms but are called by different names in different areas of the world. For example: a typhoon is a severe tropical hurricane that occurs in the western Pacific and China Sea.

Cyclones

1864 Oct. 5, India: most of Calcutta denuded by cyclone; 70,000 killed.

1942 Oct. 16, India: cyclone devastated Bengal; about 40,000 lives lost.

1960 Oct. 10, East Pakistan: cyclone and tidal wave killed about 6,000.

1963 May 28–29, East Pakistan: cyclone killed about 22,000 along coast.

1965 May 11–12 and June 1–2, East Pakistan: cyclones killed about 47,000.
Dec. 15, Karachi, Pakistan: cyclone killed about 10,000.

1970 Nov. 12–13, East Pakistan: cyclone and tidal waves killed 200,000 and another 100,000 were reported missing.

1971 Sept. 29, Orissa State, India: cyclone and tidal wave off Bay of Bengal killed as many as 10,000.

1974 Dec. 25, Darwin, Australia: cyclone destroyed nearly the entire city, causing mass evacuation; 50 reported dead.

1977 Nov. 19, Andhra Pradesh, India: cyclone and tidal wave claimed lives of 20,000.

1991 April 30, southeastern Bangladesh: cyclone killed over 131,000 and left as many as 9 million homeless. Thousands of survivors died from hunger and water borne disease.

U.S. Hurricanes

(U.S. deaths only, except where noted)

1775 Sept. 2–Sept. 9, North Carolina to Nova Scotia: called the "Hurricane of Independence," it is believed that 4,170 in the U.S. and Canada died in the storm.

1856 Aug. 11, Last Island, La.: 400 died.

1893 Aug. 28, Savannah, Ga., Charleston, S.C., Sea Islands, S.C.: at least 1,000 died.

1900 Aug. 27–Sept. 15, Galveston, Tex. and Texas Gulf Coast: more than 6,000 died in hurricane and tidal wave.

1909 Sept. 10–21, Louisiana and Mississippi: 350 deaths.

1915 Aug. 5–23, East Texas and Louisiana: 275 killed.

1919 Sept. 2–15, Florida, Louisiana and Texas: 287 deaths, and 488 deaths at sea.

1926 Sept. 11–22, Florida and Alabama: 243 deaths.

1928 Sept. 6–20, Southern Florida: 1,836 died and 1,870 injured.

1935 Aug. 29–Sept. 10, Southern Florida: 408 killed.

1938 Sept. 10–22, Long Island and Southern New England: 600 deaths; 1,764 injured.

1944 Sept. 9–16, North Carolina to New England: 46 deaths, and 344 deaths at sea.

1947 Sept. 4–21, Florida and Mid-Gulf Coast: 51 killed.

1954 Aug. 25–31, North Carolina to New England: "Carol" killed 60 and injured 1,000 in Long Island–New England area.
Oct. 5–18, South Carolina to New York: "Hazel" killed 95 in U.S.; about 400-1000 in Haiti; 78 in Canada.

1955 Aug. 7–21, North Carolina to New England: "Diane" took 184 lives.

1957 June 25–28. Texas to Alabama: "Audrey" wiped out Cameron, La., causing 390 deaths.

1960 Aug. 29–Sept. 13, Florida to New England: "Donna" killed 50 in the United States. 115 deaths in Antilles—mostly from flash floods in Puerto Rico.

1961 Sept. 3–15, Texas coast: "Carla" devastated Texas gulf cities, taking 46 lives.

1965 Aug. 27–Sept. 12, Southern Florida and Louisiana: "Betsy" killed 75 people.

1969 Aug. 14–22, Mississippi, Louisiana, Alabama, Virginia, W. Virginia: 256 killed and 68 persons missing as a result of "Camille."

1972 June 14–23, Florida to New York: "Agnes" caused 117 deaths (50 in Pennsylvania).

1979 Aug. 25–Sept. 7, Caribbean Islands to New England: "David" caused 5 U.S. deaths; 1,200 in the Dominican Republic.

1980 Aug. 3–10, Caribbean Islands to Texas Gulf: "Allen" killed 28 in the U.S.; over 200 killed in Caribbean.

1989 Sept. 10–22, Caribbean Sea and South and North Carolina: "Hugo" claimed 49 U.S. lives (71 killed overall) and $4.2 billion were paid in insurance claims.

1992 Aug. 22–26, South Florida, Louisiana, and Bahamas: Gulf Coast Hurricane Andrew with damage in South Florida alone estimated at $20.6 billion (est. $7.3 billion in private insurance claims) is most costly U.S. hurricane.

Other Hurricanes

1926 Oct. 20, Cuba: worst hurricane in 80 years, 650 reported dead.

1930 Sept. 3 Santo Domingo: hurricane killed about 2,000 and injured 6,000.

1934 Sept. 21, Japan: hurricane killed more than 4,000 on Honshu.

1955 Sept. 19, Mexico: Hurricane "Hilda" took 200 lives.
Sept. 22–28, Caribbean: Hurricane "Janet" killed 200 in Honduras and 300 in Mexico.

1961 Oct. 31, British Honduras: Hurricane "Hattie" devastated capital Belize, killed at least 400.

1963 Oct. 2–7, Caribbean: Hurricane "Flora" killed up to 7,000 in Haiti and Cuba.

1966 Sept. 24–30, Caribbean area: Hurricane "Inez" killed 293.

1974 Sept. 20, Honduras: Hurricane "Fifi" struck northern section of country, leaving 8,000 dead, 100,000 homeless.

1988 Sept. 12–17, Caribbean Sea and Gulf of Mexico: Hurricane "Gilbert," worst Atlantic storm ever recorded, took at least 260 lives and caused some 39 tornadoes in Texas.

Nuclear Power Plant Accidents

1952 **Dec. 12, Chalk River, near Ottawa, Canada:** A partial meltdown of the reactor's uranium fuel core resulted after the accidental removal of four control rods. Although millions of gallons of radioactive water accumulated inside the reactor, there were no injuries.

1957 **Oct. 7, Windscale Pile No. 1, north of Liverpool, England:** Fire in a graphite-cooled reactor spewed radiation over the countryside, contaminating a 200 sq mi area.
South Ural Mountains: Explosion of radioactive wastes at Soviet nuclear weapons factory 12 miles from city of Kyshtym forces the evacuation of over 10,000 people from a contaminated area. No casualties were reported by Soviet officials.

1976 **near Greifswald, East Germany.** Radioactive core of reactor in the Lubmin nuclear power plant nearly melted down due to the failure of safety systems during a fire.

1979 **March 28, Three Mile Island, near Harrisburg, Pa.:** One of two reactors lost its coolant, which caused the radioactive fuel to overheat and caused a partial meltdown. Some radioactive material was released.

1986 **April 26, Chernobyl, near Kiev, U.S.S.R.:** Explosion and fire in the graphite core of one of four reactors released radioacti ve material which spread over part of the Soviet Union, Eastern Europe, Scandinavia, and later Western Europe, in the worst such accident to date.

Tornadoes

1884 **Feb. 19:** tornadoes in Mississippi, Alabama, North and South Carolina, Tennessee, Kentucky and Indiana caused estimated 800 deaths.

1925 **Mar. 18:** tornadoes in Missouri, Illinois, Indiana, Kentucky, Tennessee, and Alabama killed 792.

1932 **March 21:** outbreak of tornadoes in Alabama, Mississippi, Georgia, and Tennessee killed 268.

1936 **April 5–6:** series of tornadoes in Arkansas, Alabama, Tennessee, Georgia, and South Carolina killed 498.

1952 **March 21–22:** tornadoes in Arkansas, Tennessee, Missouri, Mississippi, Alabama, and Kentucky caused 343 deaths.

1953 **May 11:** a single tornado struck Wako, Texas, killing 114.
June 8: another tornado killed 116 in Flint, Michigan.

1965 **April 11:** Tornadoes in Iowa, Illinois, Indiana, Ohio, Michigan, and Wisconsin caused 256 deaths.

1974 **April 3–4:** a series of tornadoes in East, South, and Midwest killed approximately 315.

Typhoons

1906 **Sept. 18, Hong Kong:** typhoon with tsunami killed an estimated 10,000 persons.

1949 **Dec. 5, Off Korea:** typhoon struck fishing fleet; several thousand men reported dead.

1959 **Aug. 20, Fukien Province, China:** Typhoon "Iris" killed 2,334.
Sept. 27, Honshu, Japan: Typhoon "Vera" killed an estimated 4,464.

1960 **June 9, Fukien Province, China:** Typhoon "Mary" caused at least 1,600 deaths.

1984 **Sept. 2–3, Philippines:** Typhoon "Ike" hit seven major islands leaving 1,300 dead.

1991 **Nov. 5, Central Philippines:** Flash floods triggered by tropical storm Thelma killed about 3,000 people. Leyte city of Ormoc was worst hit.

Fires and Explosions

1666 **Sept. 2, England:** "Great Fire of London" destroyed St. Paul's Church, etc. Damage £10 million.

1835 **Dec. 16, New York City:** 530 buildings destroyed by fire.

1871 **Oct. 8, Chicago:** the "Chicago Fire" burned 17,450 buildings, killed 250 persons; $196 million damage.

1872 **Nov. 9, Boston:** fire destroyed 800 buildings; $75-million damage.

1876 **Dec. 5, New York City:** fire in Brooklyn Theater killed more than 300.

1881 **Dec. 8, Vienna:** at least 620 died in fire at Ring Theatre.

1894 **Sept. 1, Minnesota:** forest fire over 480-square-mile area destroyed six towns and killed 480 people.

1900 **May 1, Scofield, Utah:** explosion of blasting powder in coal mine killed 200.
June 30, Hoboken, N.J.: piers of North German Lloyd Steamship line burned; 326 dead.

1903 **Dec. 30, Chicago:** Iroquois Theatre fire killed 602.

1906 **March 10, France:** explosion in coal mine in Courrières killed 1,060.

1907 **Dec. 19, Jacobs Creek, Pa.:** explosion in coal mine left 239 dead.

1909 **Nov. 13, Cherry, Ill.:** explosion in coal mine killed 259.

1911 **March 25, New York City:** fire in Triangle Shirtwaist Factory fatal to 145.

1913 **Oct. 22, Dawson, N.M.:** coal mine explosion left 263 dead.

1917 **April 10, Eddystone, Pa.:** explosion in munitions plant killed 133.
Dec. 6, Canada: 1,600 people died when French ammunition ship *Mont Blanc* collided with Belgium steamer in Halifax Harbor.

1930 **April 21, Columbus, Ohio:** fire in Ohio State Penitentiary killed 320 convicts.

1937 **March 18, New London, Tex.:** explosion destroyed schoolhouse; 294 killed.

1942 **April 26, Manchuria:** explosion in Honkeiko Colliery killed 1,549.
Nov. 28, Boston: Cocoanut Grove nightclub fire killed 491.

1944 **July 6, Hartford, Conn.:** fire and ensuing stampede in main tent of Ringling Brothers Circus killed 168, injured 487.
July 17, Port Chicago, Calif.: 322 killed as ammunition ships explode.
Oct. 20, Cleveland: liquid-gas tanks exploded, killing 130.

1946 **Dec. 7, Atlanta:** fire in Winecoff Hotel killed 119.

THE WORST MARINE DISASTER IN U.S. HISTORY.

The Mississippi sidewheeler *Sultana* had a total capacity of 376 passengers and crew. On this occasion, the ship was jammed with some 2,400 Union soldiers who had recently been released from Confederate prison camps. The Civil War had ended several weeks before and the troops were cheerfully looking forward to returning home. There were about 100 civilian passengers aboard, men, women, and children, who occupied first-class cabins. The boat also had a cargo of horses, mules, hogs, and, surprisingly, a live ten-foot alligator that was kept in a wooden crate. On April 27, 1865, eight miles out of Memphis, Tennessee, the boiler exploded and the ship burst into flames. During the night, the *Sultana* burned down to the water line, while its survivors clung to floating debris. Some passengers were trapped aboard the flaming ship and died in the inferno. During the shipboard fire, one desperate individual managed to kill the alligator with a knife and used the crate to float to safety. Exactly how many people died in the disaster is not known. At least 1,547 lives were lost, exceeding the total of 1,513 for the 1912 sinking of the *Titanic*. Illustration: Courtesy of Mariners' Museum, Newport News, Virginia.

1948 Dec. 3, Shanghai: Chinese passenger ship *Kiangya*, carrying refugees fleeing Communist troops during civil war, struck an old mine, exploded, and sank off Shanghai. Over 3,000 people are believed killed.

1949 Sept. 2, China: fire on Chongqing (Chungking) waterfront killed 1,700.

1954 May 26, off Quonset Point, R.I.: explosion and fire aboard aircraft carrier *Bennington* killed 103 crewmen.

1956 Aug. 7, Colombia: about 1,100 reported killed when seven army ammunition trucks exploded at Cali.

Aug. 8, Belgium: 262 died in coal mine fire at Marcinelle.

1960 Jan. 21, Coalbrook, South Africa: coal mine explosion killed 437.

Nov. 13, Syria: 152 children killed in moviehouse fire.

1961 Dec. 17, Niteroi, Brazil: circus fire fatal to 323.

1962 Feb. 7, Saarland, West Germany: coal mine gas explosion killed 298.

1963 Nov. 9, Japan: explosion in coal mine at Omuta killed 447.

1965 May 28, India: coal mine fire in state of Bihar killed 375.

June 1, near Fukuoka, Japan: coal mine explosion killed 236.

1967 May 22, Brussels: fire in L'Innovation, major department store, left 322 dead.

July 29, off North Vietnam: fire on U.S. carrier *Forrestal* killed 134.

1969 Jan. 14, Pearl Harbor, Hawaii: nuclear aircraft carrier *Enterprise* ripped by explosions; 27 dead, 82 injured.

1970 Nov. 1, Saint-Laurent-du-Pont, France: fire in dance hall killed 146 young people.

1972 May 13, Osaka, Japan: 118 people died in fire in nightclub on top floor of Sennichi department store.

June 6, Wankie, Rhodesia: explosion in coal mine killed 427.

1973 Nov. 29, Kumamoto, Japan: fire in Taiyo department store killed 101.

1974 Feb. 1, Sao Paulo, Brazil: fire in upper stories of bank building killed 189 persons, many of whom leaped to death.

1975 Dec. 27, Dhanbad, India: explosion in coal mine followed by flooding from nearby reservoir left 372 dead.

1977 May 28, Southgate, Ky.: fire in Beverly Hills Supper Club; 167 dead.

Space Accidents

1967 Jan. 27, Apollo 1: A fire aboard the space capsule on the ground at Cape Kennedy, Fla. killed astronauts Virgil I. Grissom, Edward H. White, and Roger Chaffee.

April 23–24, Soyuz 1: Vladimir M. Komarov was killed when his craft crashed after its parachute lines, released at 23,000 feet for re-entry, became snarled.

1971 June 6–30, Soyuz 11: Three cosmonauts, Georgi T. Dolrovolsky, Vladislav N. Volkov, and Viktor I. Patsayev, found dead in the craft after its automatic landing. Apparently the cause of death was loss of pressurization in the space craft during re-entry into the earth's atmosphere.

1980 March 18, U.S.S.R. A Vostok rocket exploded on its launch pad while being refueled, killing 50 at the Plesetsk Space Center.

1986 Jan 28, Challenger Space Shuttle: Exploded 73 seconds after lift off, killing all seven crew members. They were: Christa McAuliffe, Francis R. Scobee, Michael J. Smith, Judith A. Resnick, Ronald E. McNair, Ellison S. Onizuka, and Gregory B. Jarvis. A booster leak ignited the fuel, causing the explosion.

1978 July 11, Tarragona, Spain: 140 killed at coastal campsite when tank truck carrying liquid gas overturned and exploded.

Aug. 20, Abadan, Iran: nearly 400 killed when arsonists set fire to crowded theater.

1982 Dec. 18–21, Caracas, Venezuela: power-plant fire leaves 128 dead.

1986 Dec. 31, San Juan, P. R.: arson fire in Dupont Plaza Hotel set by three hotel employees kills 96.

1989 April 19, off Puerto Rico: A gun turret on the battleship *Iowa* exploded during a test-firing while participating in training excercises in the Atlantic about 330 miles northeast of Puerto Rico; 47 crew members were killed.

June 3, Ural Mountains: Liquified petroleum gas leaking from a pipeline running alongside the Trans-Siberian railway near Uta, 720 miles east of Moscow, exploded and destroyed two passing passenger trains. About 500 travelers were killed and 723 injured of an estimated 1,200 passengers on both trains.

Oct. 23, Pasadena, Texas. A huge explosion followed by a series of others and a raging fire at a plastics manufacturing plant owned by Phillips Petroleum Co. killed 22 and injured more than 80 persons. A large leak of ethylene was presumed to be the cause.

1990 Jan. 14, Zaragoza, Spain. A fire at a discotheque killed 43 with poisonous smoke fumes.

March 25, New York City. Arson fire in illegal *Happy Land Social Club*, Bronx, killed 87.

1991 Oct. 20–23, Oakland–Berkeley, Calif.: Brush fire in drought-stricken area destroyed over 3,000 homes and apartments. At least 24 persons died, damage estimated at $1.5 billion.

Shipwrecks

1833 May 11, *Lady of the Lake:* bound from England to Quebec, struck iceberg; 215 perished.

1853 Sept. 29 *Annie Jane:* emigrant vessel off coast of Scotland; 348 died.

1898 Nov. 26, *City of Portland:* Loss of 157 off Cape Cod.

1904 June 15, *General Slocum:* excursion steamer burned in East River, New York; 1,021 perished.

1912 March 5, *Principe de Asturias:* Spanish steamer struck rock off Sebastien Point; 500 drowned.

April 15, *Titanic:* sank after colliding with iceberg; 1,513 died.

1914 May 29, *Empress of Ireland:* sank after collision in St. Lawrence River; 1,024 perished.

1915 July 24, *Eastland:* Great Lakes excursion steamer overturned in Chicago River; 812 died.

1928 Nov. 12, *Vestris:* British steamer sank in gale off Virginia; 110 died.

1931 June 14: French excursion steamer overturned in gale off St. Nazaire; approximately 450 died.

1934 Sept. 8, *Morro Castle:* 134 killed in fire off Asbury Park, N.J.

1939 May 23, *Squalus:* submarine with 59 men sank off Hampton Beach, N.H.; 33 saved.

June 1, Submarine *Thetis:* sank in Liverpool Bay, England; 99 perished.

1942 Oct. 2, *Queen Mary:* rammed and sank a British cruiser; 338 aboard the cruiser died.

1945 April 9: U.S. ship, loaded with aerial bombs, exploded at Bari, Italy; at least 360 killed.

1947 November, Yingkow: Unidentified Chinese troopship evacuating Nationalist troops from Manchuria sank, killing an estimated 6,000 persons.

1949 Sept. 17, *Noronic:* Canadian Great Lakes cruise ship burned at Toronto dock; about 130 died.

1952 April 26, *Hobson:* minesweeper collided with aircraft carrier *Wasp* and sank during night maneuvers in mid-Atlantic; 176 persons lost.

1953 Jan. 9, *Chang Tyong-Ho:* South Korean ferry foundered off Pusan; 249 reported dead.

Jan. 31, *Princess Victoria:* British ferry sank in Irish Sea; 133 lost.

1956 July 25, *Andrea Doria:* Italian liner collided with Swedish liner *Stockholm* off Nantucket Island, Mass., sinking next day; 52, mostly passengers on Italian ship, dead or unaccounted for; over 1,600 rescued.

1962 April 8, *Dara,* British liner, exploded and sank in Persian Gulf; 236 persons dead. Caused by time bomb.

1963 May 4: U.A.R. ferry capsized and sank in upper Nile; over 200 died.

1968 Late May, *Scorpion:* nuclear submarine sank in Atlantic 400 miles S.W. of Azores; 99 dead. (Located Oct. 31.)

1970 Dec. 15: ferry in Korean Strait capsized; 261 lost.

1976 Oct. 20, Luling, La.: *George Prince,* Mississippi River ferry, rammed by Norwegian tanker *Frosta;* 77 dead.

1983 May 25, *10th of Ramadan,* Nile steamer, caught fire and sank in Lake Nasser, near Aswan, Egypt; 272 dead and 75 missing.

1987 March 9, Belgium: British ferry capsizes after leaving Belgian port of Zeebrugge with 500 abroad; 134 drowned. Water rushing through open bow is believed to be probable cause.

1987 Dec. 20. Manila: Over 1,500 people killed when passenger ferry *Dona Paz* collided with oil tanker *Victor* off Mindoro Is., 110 miles south of Manila.

1989 April 7, Norwegian Sea: Fourty-two seamen died when Soviet Mike-class nuclear-powered submarine sank more than 300 miles off coast of Norway after an undersea accident and fire. Twenty-seven crew members were rescued.

1990 April 7, Skagerrak Strait off Norway. Suspected arson fire aboard Danish-owned North Sea ferry, *Scandinavian Star,* kills at least 110 passengers.

April 7, Myanmar (Burma). Double-decker ferry sinks in Gyaing River during a storm and 215 persons are believed drowned.

1991 Dec. 14, off coast of Safaga, Egypt: Ferry carrying 569 passengers sank in Red Sea after hitting a coral reef. Over 460 people believed drowned.

1993 Feb. 17, off southern peninsula, Haiti: Tripledeck ferry *Neptune* capsized during a squall. Over 1,000 passengers believed drowned. About 300 survived the sinking.

Aircraft Accidents

1921 Aug. 24, England: *AR-2* British dirigible, broke in two on trial trip near Hull; 62 died.

1925 Sept. 3, Caldwell, Ohio: U.S. dirigible *Shenandoah* broke apart; 14 dead.

1930 Oct. 5, Beauvais, France: British dirigible R 101 crashed, killing 47.

1933 April 4, New Jersey Coast: U.S. dirigible *Akron* crashed; 73 died.

1937 May 6, Lakehurst, N.J.: German zeppelin *Hindenburg* destroyed by fire at tower mooring; 36 killed.

1945 July 28, New York City: U.S. Army bomber crashed into Empire State Building; 13 dead.

1952 Jan. 22, Elizabeth, N.J.: 29 killed, including former Secretary of War Robert P. Patterson, when airliner hit apartments; seven of dead were on ground.

1953 June 18, near Tokyo: crash of U.S. Air Force "Globemaster" killed 129 servicemen.

1960 Dec. 16, New York City: United and Trans World planes collided in fog, crashed in two boroughs, killing 134 in air and on ground.

1961 Feb. 15, near Brussels: 72 on board and farmer on ground killed in crash of Sabena plane; U.S. figure skating team wiped out.

1966 March 5, Japan: British airliner caught fire and crashed into Mt. Fuji; 124 dead.

Dec. 24, Binh Thai, South Vietnam: crash of military-chartered plane into village killed 129.

1970 Nov. 14, Huntington, W. Va.: chartered plane carrying 43 players and coaches of Marshall University football team crashed; 75 dead.

1971 July 30, Morioka, Japan: Japanese Boeing 727 and F-86 fighter collided in mid-air; toll was 162.

Sept. 4, near Juneau, Alaska: Alaska Airlines Boeing 727 crashed into Chilkoot Mountains; 111 killed.

1972 Aug. 14, East Berlin, East Germany: Soviet-built East German Ilyushin plane crashed, killing 156.

Dec. 3, Santa Cruz de Tenerife, Canary Islands: Spanish charter jet carrying West German tourists crashed on take-off; all 155 aboard killed.

Dec. 30, Miami, Fla.: Eastern Airlines Lockheed 1011 TriStar Jumbo jet crashed into Everglades; 101 killed, 75 survived.

1973 Jan. 22, Kano, Nigeria: 171 Nigerian Moslems returning from Mecca and five crewmen died in crash.

1973 Feb. 21: Civilian Libyan Arab Airlines Boeing 727 shot down by Israeli fighters over Sinai after it had strayed off course; 108 died, five survived. Officials claimed that the pilot had ignored fighters' warnings to land.

April 10, Hochwald, Switzerland: British airliner carrying tourists to Swiss fair crashed in blizzard; 106 dead.

July 11, Paris: Boeing 707 of Varig Airlines, en route to Rio de Janeiro, crashed near airport, killing 122 of 134 passengers.

1974 March 3, Paris: Turkish DC-10 jumbo jet crashed in forest shortly after take-off; all 346 passengers and crew killed.

Dec. 4, Colombo, Sri Lanka: Dutch DC-8 carrying Moslems to Mecca crashed on landing approach, killing all 191 persons aboard.

1975 April 4, near Saigon, Vietnam: Air Force Galaxy C-5A crashed after take-off, killing 172, mostly Vietnamese children.

Aug. 3, Agadir, Morocco: Chartered Boeing 707, returning Moroccan workers home after vacation in France, plunged into mountainside; all 188 aboard killed.

1976 Sept. 10, Zagreb, Yugoslavia: midair collision between British Airways Trident and Yugoslav charter DC-9 fatal to all 176 persons aboard; worst mid-air collision on record.

1977 March 27, Santa Cruz de Tenerife, Canary Islands: Pan American and KLM Boeing 747s collided on runway. All 249 on KLM plane and 333 of 394 aboard Pan Am jet killed. Total of 582 is highest for any type of aviation disaster.

1978 Jan. 1, Bombay: Air India 747 with 213 aboard exploded and plunged into sea minutes after takeoff.

Sept. 25, San Diego, Calif.: Pacific Southwest plane collided in midair with Cessna. All 135 on airliner, 2 in Cessna, and 7 on ground killed for total of 144.

Nov. 15, Colombo, Sri Lanka: Chartered Icelandic Airlines DC-8, carrying 249 Moslem pilgrims from Mecca, crashed in thunderstorm during landing approach; 183 killed.

1979 Nov. 26, Jidda, Saudi Arabia: Pakistan International Airlines 707 carrying pilgrims returning from Mecca crashed on take-off; all 156 aboard killed.

Nov. 28, Mt. Erebus, Antarctica: Air New Zealand DC-10 crashed on sightseeing flight; 257 killed.

1980 March 14, Warsaw: LOT Polish Airlines Ilyushin 62 crashed while attempting landing; 22 boxers and officials of a U.S. amateur boxing team killed along with 65 others.

April 25, Santa Cruz de Tenerife, Canary Islands: Chartered Boeing 727 carrying 138 British vacationers and crew of 8 crashed into mountain while approaching for landing; all killed.

Aug. 19, Riyadh, Saudi Arabia: all 301 aboard Saudi Arabian jet killed when burning plane made safe landing but passengers were unable to escape.

1981 Dec. 1, Ajaccio, Corsica: Yugoslav DC-9 Super 80 carrying tourists crashed into mountain on landing approach, killing all 178 aboard.

1983 June 28, near Cuenca, Ecuador, Ecuadorean jetliner crashed in mountains, killing 119.

Aug. 30, near island of Sakhalin off Siberia, South Korean civilian jetliner shot down by Soviet fighter after it strayed off course into Soviet airspace. All 269 people aboard killed.

Nov. 26, Madrid: A Columbian Avianca Boeing 747 crashed near Mejorada del Campó Airport killing 183 persons aboard. Eleven people survived the accident.

1985 June 23: Air-India Boeing 747 exploded over the Atlantic off the coast of Ireland, all 329 aboard killed.

Aug. 12, Japan Air Lines Boeing 747 crashed into a mountain, killing 520 of the 524 aboard.

Dec. 12, A chartered Arrow Air DC-8, bringing American soldiers home for Christmas, crashed on takeoff from Gander, Newfoundland. All 256 aboard died.

1987 May 9, Poland: Polish airliner, Ilyushin 62M on charter flight to New York, crashes after takeoff from Warsaw killing 183.

Aug. 16, Detroit: Northwest Airlines McDonnell Douglas MD-30 plunges to heavily traveled boulevard, killing 156. Girl 4, only survivor.

Nov. 26: South African Airways Boeing 747 goes down south of Mauritius in rough seas; 160 die.

Nov. 29: Korean Air Boeing 747 jetliner explodes from bomb planted by North Korean agents and crashes into sea off Burma, killing all 115 aboard.

1988 July 3, Persian Gulf: U.S. Navy cruiser *Vincennes* shot down Iran Air A300 Airbus, killing 290 persons, after mistaking it for an attacking jet fighter.

Aug. 28, Ramstein Air Force Base, West Germany: Three jets from Italian Air Force acr obatic team collided in mid-air during air show and crashed, killing 70 persons, including the pilots and spectators on the ground. It is worst air-show disaster in history.

Dec. 21, Lockerbie, Scotland: A New-York-bound Pan-Am Boeing 747 exploded in flight from a terrorist bomb and crashed into Scottish village, killing all 259 aboard and 11 persons on the ground. Passengers included 38 Syracuse University students and many U.S. military personnel.

1989 June 7, Paramaribo, Suriname: A Surinam Airways DC-8 carrying 174 passengers and nine crew members crashed into the jungle while making a third attempt to land in a thick fog, killing 168 aboard.

1991 July 11, Jedda, Saudi Arabia: Canadian-chartered DC-8 carrying pilgrims returning to Nigeria crashes after takeoff, killing 261 persons.

Railroad Accidents

NOTE: Very few passengers were killed in a single U.S. train wreck up until 1853. These early trains ran slowly, made short trips, night travel was rare, and there were not many of them in operation.

1831 June 17: The boiler exploded on America's first passenger locomotive, *The Best Friend of Charleston,* killing the fireman. He was the first person in America to be killed in a railroad accident.

1833 Nov. 8, near Heightstown, N.J.: the world's first train wreck and the first passenger fatalities recorded. A 24-passenger Camden & Amboy train was derailed due to a broken axle, killing two passengers and injuring all others. Former president, John Quincy Adams and Cornelius Vanderbilt, who later made a fortune in railroads, were aboard the train.

1853 May 6, Norwalk, Conn: a New Haven Railroad train ran through an open drawbridge and plunged into the Norwalk River. Forty-six passengers were crushed to death or drowned. This was the first major drawbridge accident.

1856 July 17, Camp Hill, Pa.: two Northern Penn trains crashed head-on. Sixty-six church school children bound for a picnic died in the flaming wreckage.

1876 Dec. 29, Ashtabula, Ohio: a Lake Shore train fell into the Ashtabula River when a bridge it was crossing collapsed during a snowstorm. Ninety-two were killed.

1887 Aug. 10, near Chatsworth, Ill.: a burning railroad trestle collapsed while a Toledo, Peoria & Western train was crossing, killing 81 and injuring 372.

1904 Aug. 7, Eden, Colo.: Train derailed on bridge during flash flood; 96 killed.

1910 March 1, Wellington, Wash.: two trains swept into canyon by avalanche; 96 dead.

1915 May 22, Gretna, Scotland: two passenger trains and troop train collided; 227 killed.

1917 Dec. 12, Modane, France: nearly 550 killed in derailment of troop train near mouth of Mt. Cenis tunnel.

1918 Nov. 1, New York City: derailment of subway train in Malbone St. tunnel in Brooklyn left 92 dead.

1926 March 14, Virilla River Canyon, Costa Rica: An over-crowded train carrying pilgrims was derailed while crossing the Colima Bridge, killing over 300 people and injuring hundreds more.

1939 Dec. 22, near Magdeburg, Germany: more than 125 killed in collision; 99 killed in another wreck near Friedrichshafen.

1943 Dec. 16, near Rennert, N.C.: 72 killed in derailment and collision of two Atlantic Coast Line trains.

1944 March 2, near Salerno, Italy: 521 suffocated when Italian train stalled in tunnel.

1949 Oct. 22, near Nowy Dwor, Poland: more than 200 reported killed in derailment of Danzig-Warsaw express.

1950 Nov. 22, Richmond Hill, N.Y.: 79 died when one Long Island Rail Road commuter train crashed into rear of another.

1951 Feb. 6, Woodbridge, N.J.: 85 died when Pennsylvania Railroad commuter train plunged through temporary overpass.

1952 Oct. 8, Harrow-Wealdstone, England: two express trains crashed into commuter train; 112 dead.

1953 Dec. 24, near Sakvice, Czechoslovakia: two trains crashed; over 100 dead.

1957 **Sept. 1, near Kendal, Jamaica:** about 175 killed when train plunged into ravine.

Sept. 29, near Montgomery, West Pakistan: express train crashed into standing oil train; nearly 300 killed.

Dec. 4, St. John's, England: 92 killed, 187 injured as one commuter train crashed into another in fog.

1960 **Nov. 14, Pardubice, Czechoslovakia:** two trains collided; 110 dead, 106 injured.

1962 **May 3, near Tokyo:** 163 killed and 400 injured when train crashed into wreckage of collision between inbound freight train and outbound commuter train.

1963 **Nov. 9, near Yokohama, Japan:** two passenger trains crashed into derailed freight, killing 162.

1964 **July 26, Custoias, Portugal:** passenger train derailed; 94 dead.

1970 **Feb. 4, near Buenos Aires:** 236 killed when express train crashed into standing commuter train.

1972 **July 21, Seville, Spain:** head-on crash of two passenger trains killed 76.

Oct. 6, near Saltillo, Mexico: train carrying religious pilgrims derailed and caught fire, killing 204 and injuring over 1,000.

Oct. 30, Chicago: two Illinois Central commuter trains collided during morning rush hour; 45 dead and over 200 injured.

1974 **Aug. 30, Zagreb, Yugoslavia:** train entering station derailed, killing 153 and injuring over 60.

1981 **June 6, Near Mansi, India:** Driver of train carrying over 500 passengers, braked to avoid hitting cow, causing train to plunge off a bridge into Baghmati River; 268 passengers were reported killed, but at least 300 more were missing.

1982 **July 11, Tepic, Mexico:** Nogales-Guadalajara train plunges down mountain gorge killing 120.

1989 **Jan. 15, Maizdi Khan, Bangladesh:** A train carrying Muslim pilgrims crashed head-on with a mail train killing at least 110 persons and injuring as many as 1,000. Many people were riding on the roof of the trains and between the cars.

1989 **Aug. 10, near Los Mochis, Mexico:** A second-class passenger train traveling from Mazatlán to Mexicali, plunged off a bridge at Puente del Rio Bamoa into the river and killed an estimated 85 people and injured 107.

1990 **Jan. 4, Sangi village, Sindh province, Pakistan:** An overcrowded sixteen-car passenger train was switched to the wrong track and rammed into a standing freight train. At least 210 persons were killed and 700 were believed injured in what is said to be Pakistan's worst train disaster.

Oil Spills

1978 **March 16, off Portsall, France:** Wrecked supertanker *Amoco Cadiz* spilled 68 million gallons causing widespread environmental damage over 100 miles of coast of Brittany. Is world's largest tanker disaster.

1979 **June 8, Gulf of Mexico:** Exploratory oil well, Ixtoc 1, blew out, spilling an estimated 140 million gallons of crude into the open sea. Although it is the largest known oil spill, it had a low environmental impact.

1989 **Dec. 19. Off Las Palmas, the Canary Islands.** An explosion in Iranian supertanker, the *Kharg-5*, tore through its hull and caused 19 million gallons of crude oil to spill out into the Atlantic Ocean about 400 miles north of Las Palmas, forming a 100-square-mile oil slick.

Wartime Spills

1991 **Jan. 25, Southern Kuwait:** during the Persian Gulf War, Iraq deliberately released an estimated 460 million gallons of crude oil into the Persian Gulf from tankers at Mina al-Ahmadi and Sea Island Terminal 10 miles off Kuwait. Spill had little military significance. On Jan. 27, U.S. warplanes bombed pipe systems to stop the flow of oil.

Sports

1955 **June 11, Le Mans, France:** Racing car in Grand Prix hurtled into grandstand, killing 82 spectators.

1964 **May 24, Lima, Peru:** More than 300 soccer fans killed and over 500 injured during riot and panic following unpopular ruling by referee in Peru vs. Argentina soccer game. It is worst soccer disaster on record.

1971 **Jan. 2, Glasgow, Scotland:** Sixty-six persons killed in a crush at the Glasgow Rangers home stadium when fans trying to leave encountered fans trying to return to the stadium after hearing that a late goal had been scored.

1982 **Oct. 20, Moscow:** According to *Sovietsky Sport*, as many as 340 persons were killed at Lenin Stadium when exiting soccer fans collided with returning fans after final goal was scored. All the fans had been crowded into one section of stadium by police.

1985 **May 11, Bradford, England:** 56 persons burned to death and over 200 injured when fire engulfed the main grandstand at Bradford's soccer stadium.

May 29, Brussels, Belgium: Drunken group of British soccer fans supporting Liverpool club stormed stand filled with Italian supporters of Juventus team before European Champion's Cup final. While British fans attacked rival spectators at the Heysel Stadium, concrete retaining wall collapsed and 39 persons were crushed or trampled to death, 32 of them Italians. More than 400 persons were injured.

1988 **March 12, Katmandu, Nepal:** Some 80 soccer fans seeking cover during a violent hail storm at the national stadium were trampled to death in a stampede because the stadium doors were locked.

1989 **April 15, Sheffield, England:** Ninety-four people were killed and 170 injured at Hillsborough stadium when throngs of Liverpool soccer fans, many without tickets, collapsed a stadium barrier in a mad rush to see the game between Liverpool and Nottingham Forest. It was Britain's worst soccer disaster.

Terrorist Attacks in U.S.

1920 **Sept. 16, New York City:** TNT bomb planted in unattended horse-drawn wagon exploded on Wall Street opposite House of Morgan, killing 35 persons and injuring hundreds more. Bolshevist or anarchist terrorists believed responsible but crime never solved.

1975 **Jan. 24, New York City:** Bomb set off in historical Fraunces Tavern killed four and injured more than 50 persons. Puerto Rican nationalist group (FALN) claimed responsibility and police tied 13 other bombings to them.

Dec. 29, New York City: Bomb exploded in locker area of main terminal at La Guardia Airport, killing 11 persons and injuring 75 others. Puerto Rican nationalist group (FALN) was the prime suspect.

1993 **Feb. 26, New York City:** Bomb exploded in basement garage of World Trade Center; killed 6 persons and injured at least 1,040 others. Worst terrorist bombing on U.S. soil.

Miscellaneous

1958 **January–October, Austria, France, Germany, Italy, and Switzerland:** 283 people were killed in mountain climbing accidents in Alps Mountains.

1980 **Jan. 20, Sincelejo, Colombia:** Bleachers at a bullring collapsed, leaving 222 dead.

March 30, Stavanger, Norway: Floating hotel in North Sea collapsed, killing 123 oil workers.

1981 **July 18, Kansas City, Mo.:** suspended walkway in Hyatt Regency Hotel collapses; 113 dead, 186 injured.

1984 **Dec. 3, Bhopal, India:** Toxic gas, methyl isocyanate, seeped from Union Carbide insecticide plant, killing more than 2,000; injuring about 150,000.

1987 **Sept. 18. Goiânia, Brazil:** 244 people contaminated with cesium-137 removed from steel cylinder taken from cancer-therapy machine in abandoned clinic and sold as scrap. Four people died in worst radiation disaster in Western Hemisphere.

1988 **July 6, North Sea off Scotland:** 166 workers killed in explosion and fire on Occidental Petroleum's Piper Alpha rig in North Sea off Scottish coast; 64 survivors rescued. It is the world's worst offshore oil disaster.

1990 **July 2, Mecca, Saudi Arabia:** a stampede in a 1,800 foot-long pedestrian tunnel leading from Mecca to a tent city for pilgrims, killed 1,426 pilgrims who were trampled to death.

1991 **Nov. 29, near Coalinga, Calif.:** A massive traffic accident occurred during a severe dust storm involving 104 vehicles in a pileup on Interstate 5; 17 persons killed.

Wartime Disasters

1915 **May 6:** Despite German warnings in newspapers, the Cunard Liner *Lusitania* sailed from New York for Liverpool, England, on May 1st and was sunk off the coast of Ireland by a German submarine. 1,198 passengers and crew, 128 of them Americans, died. Unknown to the passengers, the ship was carrying a cargo of small arms. The disaster contributed to the entry of the United States into World War I.

1916 **Feb. 26:** 3,100 people died when the French cruiser *Provence* was sunk by a German submarine in the Mediterranean.

1940 **Sept. 13.** The luxury liner *S.S. City of Benares* sailed from Liverpool with over 90 British children who were being evacuated to Canada to escape harm during World War II. About 600 miles out to sea, the ship was torpedoed by a German submarine during the night and only 13 of the children survived the disaster.[1]

1943 **Dec., Bari Harbor, Italy:** U.S. ship, damaged during German bombing attack, leaked mustard gas into harbor, killing 83 U.S. servicemen and nearly 1,000 civilians.

1944 **Sept. 12, South China Sea:** U.S. submarines torpedoed and sank two Japanese troop ships[2], the *Kachidoki Maru* and the *Rakuyo Maru.* Unknown to the submarines, the Japanese, in disregard for the rules of treatment of prisoners of war, had forced 2,000 British, Australian, and American POWs into the holds of the ships which were designed to hold only 300 troops. Later, when the subs discovered the tragedy, they sought to rescue as many survivors as possible. Japanese vessels picked up most of *Kachidoki Maru*'s prisoners but abandoned those from the *Rakuyo Maru,* taking only the Japanese survivors. Of the 1,300 POWs aboard the *Rakuyo Maru,* 159 were rescued, but only seven lived.

Oct. 24, South China Sea: The *Arisan Maru*[2] carrying 1,800 American prisoners was torpedoed by a U.S. submarine and sunk. The Japanese destroyer escort rescued Japanese military and civilian personnel and left the POWs to their fate. It is estimated that only ten prisoners survived the disaster.

Dec. 17–18, Philippine Sea: A typhoon struck U.S. Third Fleet's Task Force 38, sank three destroyers, damaged seven other ships, destroyed 186 aircraft, and killed 800 officers and men.

1945 **Jan. 30:** 7,700 persons died in world's largest marine disaster when the Nazi passenger ship *Wilhelm Gustoff* car rying Germans fleeing Poland was torpedoed in the Baltic by a Soviet submarine.

May 3, *Cap Arcona:* Several days before World War II ended in Europe, the German passenger ship carrying about 6,000, of which an estimated 5,000 were concentration camp prisoners, was sunk by British aircraft. An estimated 5,000 persons were killed, most of them prisoners who were about to gain their freedom.

July 29, near Leyte Gulf: The heavy cruiser *Indianapolis* was torpedoed and sunk by a Japanese submarine. Of the crew of 1,199 men, only 316 survived. Several days earlier, the *Indianapolis* had delivered a lead cylinder containing uranium (U-235) and the firing mechanism for the first atomic bomb to Tinian Island. Had the ship been sunk earlier while delivering its special cargo, WW II would have ended differently.

1991 **February, Kuwait:** during the Persian Gulf War, Iraqi troops systematically dynamited and set fire to 650 of Kuwait's 950 oil wells, causing the world's worst man-made environmental disaster. A total of 749 wells were damaged including those set ablaze. The last of the oil fires was extinguished on Nov. 6, 1991.

1. During the war (1939-1945), some 10,000 children were evacuated to say with foster parents in the United States and Canada. The sinking of the *City of Benares* ended the British government's evacuation program.
2. The ships had no identification that they were transporting prisioners of war.

RELIGION

Major Religions of the World

Judaism

The determining factors of Judaism are: descendance from Israel, the *Torah*, and Tradition.

The name Israel (Jacob, a patriarch) also signifies his descendants as a people. During the 15th–13th centuries B.C., Israelite tribes, coming from South and East, gradually settled in Palestine, then inhabited by Canaanites. They were held together by Moses, who gave them religious unity in the worship of *Jahweh*, the God who had chosen Israel to be his people.

Under Judges, the 12 tribes at first formed an amphictyonic covenant. Saul established kingship (circa 1050 B.C.), and under David, his successor (1000–960 B.C.), the State of Israel comprised all of Palestine with Jerusalem as religio-political center. A golden era followed under Solomon (965–926 B.C.), who built *Jahweh* a temple.

After Solomon's death, the kingdom separated into Israel in the North and Judah in the South. A period of conflicts ensued, which ended with the conquest of Israel by Assyria in 722 B.C. The Babylonians defeated Judah in 586 B.C., destroying Jerusalem and its temple, and deporting many to Babylon.

The era of the kings is significant also in that the great prophets worked in that time, emphasizing faith in *Jahweh* as both God of Israel and God of the universe, and stressing social justice.

When the Persians permitted the Jews to return from exile (539 B.C.), temple and cult were restored in Jerusalem. The Persian rulers were succeeded by the Seleucides. The Maccabaean revolt against these Hellenistic kings gave independence to the Jews in 128 B.C., which lasted till the Romans occupied the country.

Important groups that exerted influence during these times were the Sadducees, priests in the temple in Jerusalem; the Pharisees, teachers of the Law in the synagogues; Essenes, a religious order (from whom Dead Sea Scrolls, discovered in 1947, came); Apocalyptists, who were expecting the heavenly Messiah; and Zealots, who were prepared to fight for national independence.

When the latter turned against Rome in A.D. 66, Roman armies under Titus suppressed the revolt, destroying Jerusalem and its temple in A.D. 70. The Jews were scattered in the *diaspora* (Dispersion), subject to oppressions until the Age of the Enlightenment (18th century) brought their emancipation, although persecutions did not end entirely.

Estimated Membership of the Principal Religions of the World

Statistics of the world's religions are only very rough approximations. Aside from Christianity, few religions, if any, attempt to keep statistical records; and even Protestants and Catholics employ different methods of counting members. All persons of whatever age who have received baptism in the Catholic Church are counted as members, while in most Protestant Churches only those who "join" the church are numbered. The compiling of statistics is further complicated by the fact that in China one may be at the same time a Confucian, a Taoist, and a Buddhist. In Japan, one may be both a Buddhist and a Shintoist.

Religion	Africa	Asia	Europe[1]	Latin America	Northern America	Oceania	World
Christians	327,204,000	285,365,000	523,010,000	435,811,000	239,004,000	22,628,000	1,833,022,000
Roman Catholics	122,907,000	123,597,000	268,228,000	405,623,000	97,022,000	8,208,000	1,025,585,000
Protestants	87,332,000	81,476,000	83,797,000	17,263,000	93,212,000	7,518,000	373,698,000
Orthodox	28,549,000	3,655,000	129,870,000	1,764,000	6,008,000	576,000	170,422,000
Anglicans	26,863,000	707,000	32,956,400	1,300,000	7,338,000	5,719,000	74,883,400
Other Christians	61,553,000	75,930,000	8,158,600	9,861,000	32,324,000	607,000	188,433,600
Muslims	278,250,800	636,976,000	51,803,900	1,350,500	2,847,000	100,500	971,328,700
Nonreligious	1,896,000	691,144,000	137,477,000	17,159,000	25,265,000	3,291,000	876,232,000
Hindus	1,475,000	728,118,000	706,000	884,000	1,269,000	360,000	732,812,000
Buddhists	21,000	313,114,000	679,000	541,000	558,000	26,000	314,939,000
Atheists	316,000	161,414,000	73,502,000	3,224,000	1,319,000	535,000	240,310,000
Chinese folk religionists	13,000	186,817,000	61,000	73,000	122,000	21,000	187,107,000
New-Religionists	21,000	141,382,000	51,000	530,000	1,421,000	10,000	143,415,000
Tribal religionists	70,588,000	24,948,000	1,000	936,000	41,000	67,000	96,581,000
Sikhs	26,000	18,272,000	231,500	8,000	254,000	9,000	18,800,500
Jews	337,000	5,587,000	3,705,000	1,092,000	7,003,000	98,000	17,822,000
Shamanists	1,000	10,233,000	256,000	1,000	1,000	1,000	10,493,000
Confucians	1,000	5,994,000	4,000	2,000	26,000	1,000	6,028,000
Baha'is	1,496,000	2,680,000	98,000	801,000	365,000	77,000	5,517,000
Jains	53,000	3,717,000	15,000	4,000	4,000	1,000	3,794,000
Shintoists	200	3,220,000	600	500	1,000	500	3,222,800
Other religionists	433,000	12,292,000	1,802,000	3,570,000	485,000	4,000	18,586,000
Total Population	**682,132,000**	**3,231,273,000**	**793,403,000**	**465,987,000**	**279,985,000**	**27,230,000**	**5,480,010,000**

1. Includes the former U.S.S.R. Reprinted with permission from *1993 Britannica Book of the Year.* © 1993 Encyclopaedia Britannica, Inc.

The fall of the Jerusalem temple was an important event in the religious life of the Jews, which now developed around *Torah* (Law) and synagogue. Around A.D. 100 the Sacred Scriptures were codified. Synagogue worship became central, with readings from *Torah* and prophets. Most important prayers are the *Shema* (Hear) and the Prayer of the 18 Benedictions.

Religious life is guided by the commandments contained in the *Torah:* circumcision and *Sabbath,* as well as other ethical and ceremonial commandments.

The *Talmud,* based on the *Mishnah* and its interpretations, took shape over many centuries in the Babylonian and Palestinian Schools. It was a strong binding force of Judaism in the Dispersion.

In the 12th century, Maimonides formulated his "13 Articles of Faith," which carried great authority. Fundamental in this creed are: belief in God and his oneness *(Sherma),* belief in the changeless *Torah,* in the words of Moses and the prophets, belief in reward and punishment, the coming of the Messiah, and the resurrection of the dead.

Judaism is divided into theological schools, the main divisions of which are Orthodox, Conservative, and Reform.

Christianity

Christianity is founded upon Jesus Christ, to whose life the New Testament writings testify. Jesus, a Jew, was born in about 7 B.C. and assumed his public life, after his 30th year, in Galilee. The Gospels tell of many extraordinary deeds that accompanied his ministry. He proclaimed the Kingdom of God, a future reality that is at the same time already present. Nationalistic-Jewish expectations of the Messiah he rejected. Rather, he referred to himself as the "Son of Man," the Christ, who has power to forgive sins now and who shall also come as Judge at the end of time. Jesus set forth the religio-ethical demands for participation in the Kingdom of God as change of heart and love of God and neighbor.

At the Last Supper he signified his death as a sacrifice, which would inaugurate the New Covenant, by which many would be saved. Circa A.D. 30 he died on a cross in Jerusalem. The early Church carried on Jesus' proclamation, the apostle Paul emphasizing his death and resurrection.

The person of Jesus is fundamental to the Christian faith since it is believed that in his life, death, and resurrection, God's revelation became historically tangible. He is seen as the turning point in history, and man's relationship to God as determined by his attitude to Jesus.

Historically Christianity thus arose out of Judaism, claiming fulfillment of the promises of the Old Testament in Jesus. The early Church designated itself as "the true Israel," which expected the speedy return of Jesus. The mother church was at Jerusalem, but churches were soon founded in many other places. The apostle Paul was instrumental in founding and extending a Gentile Christianity that was free from Jewish legalism.

The new religion spread rapidly throughout the eastern and western parts of the Roman Empire. In coming to terms with other religious movements within the Empire, Christianity began to take definite shape as an organization in its doctrine, liturgy, and ministry circa A.D. 200. In the 4th century the Catholic Church had taken root in countries stretching from Spain in the West to Persia and India in the East. Christians had been repeatedly subject to persecution by the Roman state, but finally gained tolerance under Constantine the Great (A.D. 313). Since that time, the Church became favored under his successors and in 380 the Emperor Theodosius proclaimed Christianity the State religion. Paganism was suppressed and public life was gradually molded in accordance with Christian ethical demands.

It was in these years also that the Church was able to achieve a certain unity of doctrine. Due to differences of interpretation of basic doctrines concerning Christ, which threatened to divide the Catholic Church, a standard Christian Creed was formulated by bishops at successive Ecumenical Councils, the first of which was held in A.D. 325 (Nicaea). The chief doctrines formulated concerned the doctrine of the Trinity, i.e., that there is one God in three persons: Father, Son, and Holy Spirit (Constantinople, A.D. 381); and the nature of Christ as both divine and human (Chalcedon, A.D. 541).

Through differences and rivalry between East and West the unity of the Church was broken by schism in 1054. In 1517 a separation occurred in the Western Church with the Reformation. From the major Protestant denominations [Lutheran, Presbyterian, Anglican (Episcopalian)], many Free Churches separated themselves in an age of individualism.

In the 20th century, however, the direction is toward unity. The Ecumenical Movement led to the formation of the World Council of Churches in 1948 (Amsterdam), which has since been joined by many Protestant and Orthodox Churches.

Through its missionary activity Christianity has spread to most parts of the globe.

Eastern Orthodoxy

Eastern Orthodoxy comprises the faith and practice of Churches stemming from ancient Churches in the Eastern part of the Roman Empire. The term covers Orthodox Churches in communion with the See of Constantinople and Nestorian and Monophysite Churches.

The Orthodox, Catholic, Apostolic Church is the direct descendant of the Byzantine State Church and consists of a series of independent national churches that are united by Doctrine, Liturgy, and Hierarchical organization (deacons and priests, who may either be married or be monks before ordination, and bishops, who must be celibates). The heads of these Churches

U.S. Religious Bodies with Members Over 2,000,000

Religious body	Members
Roman Catholic Church	58,267,424
Southern Baptist Convention	15,232,347
United Methodist Church	8,785,135
National Baptist Convention, U.S.A.	8,000,000
Jewish congregations[1]	5,981,000
Church of God in Christ	5,499,875
Evangelical Lutheran Church in America	5,245,177
Church of Jesus Christ of Latter-day Saints	4,336,000
Presbyterian Church in America	3,778,358
African Methodist Episcopal Church	3,500,000
National Baptist Convention of America (DAARB)	3,500,000
Lutheran Church–Missouri Synod	2,607,309
National Missionary Baptist Convention of America	2,500,000
Progressive National Baptist Convention	2,500,000
Episcopal Church	2,471,880
Assemblies of God	2,334,708

1. Includes Orthodox, Conservative, and Reform. *Source:* Yearbook of American & Canadian Churches, 1993.

are patriarchs or metropolitans; the Patriarch of Constantinople is only "first among equals." Rivalry between the Pope of Rome and the Patriarch of Constantinople, aided by differences and misunderstandings that existed for centuries between the Eastern and Western parts of the Empire, led to a schism in 1054. Repeated attempts at reunion have failed in past centuries. The mutual excommunication pronounced in that year was lifted in 1965, however, and because of greater interaction in theology between Orthodox Churches and those in the West, a climate of better understanding has been created in the 20th century. First contacts were with Anglicans and Old Catholics. Orthodox Churches belong to the World Council of Churches.

The Eastern Orthodox Churches recognize only the canons of the seven Ecumenical Councils (325–787) as binding for faith and they reject doctrines that have been added in the West.

The central worship service is called the Liturgy, which is understood as representation of God's acts of salvation. Its center is the celebration of the Eucharist, or Lord's Supper.

In their worship icons (sacred pictures) are used that have a sacramental meaning as representation. The Mother of Christ, angels, and saints are highly venerated.

The number of sacraments in the Orthodox Church is the same as in the Western Catholic Church.

Orthodox Churches are found in the Balkans and the Soviet Union also, since the 20th century, in Western Europe and other parts of the world, particularly in America.

Eastern Rite Churches

These include the Uniate Churches that recognize the authority of the Pope but keep their own traditional liturgies and those Churches dating back to the 5th century that emanicipated themselves from the Byzantine State Church: the Nestorian Church in the Near East and India and the Monophysite Churches (Coptic, Ethiopian, Syrian, Armenian, and the Mar Thoma Church in India).

Roman Catholicism

Roman Catholicism comprises the belief and practice of the Roman Catholic Church. The Church stands under the authority of the Bishop of Rome, the Pope, and is ruled by him and bishops who are held to be, through ordination, successors of Peter and the Apostles, respectively. Fundamental to the structure of the Church is the juridical aspect: doctrine and sacraments are bound to the power of jurisdiction and consecration of the hierarchy. The Pope, as the head of the hierarchy of archbishops, bishops, priests, and deacons, has full ecclesiastical power, granted him by Christ, through Peter. As successor to Peter, he is the Vicar of Christ. The powers that others in the hierarchy possess are delegated.

Roman Catholics believe their Church to be the one, holy, catholic, and apostolic Church, possessing all the properties of the one, true Church of Christ.

The faith of the Church is understood to be identical with that taught by Christ and his Apostles and contained in Bible and Tradition, i.e. the original deposit of faith, to which nothing new may be added. New definitions of doctrines, such as the Immaculate Conception of Mary (1854) and the bodily Assumption of Mary (1950), have been declared by Popes, however, in accordance with the principle of development (implicit-explicit doctrine).

At Vatican Council I (1870) the Pope was proclaimed "endowed with infallibility, *ex cathedra,* i.e., when exercising the office of Pastor and Teacher of all Christians."

The center of Roman Catholic worship is the celebration of the Mass, the Eucharist, which is the commemoration of Christ's sacrificial death and of his resurrection. Other sacraments are Baptism, Confirmation, Confession, Matrimony, Ordination, and Extreme Unction, seven in all. The Virgin Mary and saints, and their relics, are highly venerated and prayers are made to them to intercede with God, in whose presence they are believed to dwell.

The Roman Catholic Church is the largest Christian organization in the world, found in most countries.

Since Vatican Council II (1962–65), and the effort to "update" the Church, many interesting changes and developments have been taking place.

Protestantism

Protestantism comprises the Christian churches that separated from Rome during the Reformation in the 16th century, initiated by an Augustinian monk, Martin Luther. "Protestant" was originally applied to followers of Luther, who protested at the Diet of Spires (1529) against the decree which prohibited all further ecclesiastical reforms. Subsequently, Protestantism came to mean rejection of attempts to tie God's revelation to earthly institutions, and a return to the Gospel and the Word of God as sole authority in matters of faith and practice. Central in the biblical message is the justification of the sinner by faith alone. The Church is understood as a fellowship and the priesthood of all believers stressed.

The Augsburg Confession (1530) was the principal statement of Lutheran faith and practice. It became a model for other Confessions of Faith, which in their turn had decisive influence on Church policy. Major Protestant denominations are the Lutheran, Reformed (Calvinist), Presbyterian, and Anglican (Episcopal). Smaller ones are the Mennonite, Schwenkfeldians, and Unitarians. In Great Britain and America there are the Congregationalists, Baptists, Quakers, Methodists, and other free church types of communities. (In regarding themselves as being faithful to original biblical Christianity, these Churches differ from such religious bodies as Unitarians, Mormons, Jehovah's Witnesses, and Christian Scientists, who either teach new doctrines or reject old ones.)

Since the latter part of the 19th century, national councils of churches have been established in many countries, e.g. the Federal Council of Churches of Christ in America in 1908. Denominations across countries joined in federations and world alliances, beginning with the Anglican Lambeth Conference in 1867.

Protestant missionary activity, particularly strong in the last century, resulted in the founding of many younger churches in Asia and Africa. The Ecumenical Movement, which originated with Protestant missions, aims at unity among Christians and churches.

Islam

Islam is the religion founded in Arabia by Mohammed between 610 and 632. There are an estimated 2.6 million Moslems in Northern America and 950 million Moslems worldwide.

Mohammed was born in A.D. 570 at Mecca and belonged to the Quraysh tribe, which was active in caravan trade. At the age of 25 he joined the caravan trade from Mecca to Syria in the employment of a rich widow, Khadiji, whom he married. Critical of the idolatry of the inhabitants of Mecca, he began to lead a contemplative life in the deserts. There he received a series of revelations. Encouraged by Khadiji, he gradually became convinced that he was given a God-appointed task to devote himself to the reform of religion and society. Idolatry was to be abandoned.

The *Hegira (Hijra)* (migration) of Mohammed from Mecca, where he was not honored, to Medina, where he was well received, occurred in 622 and marks the beginning of the Muslim era. In 630 he marched on Mecca and conquered it. He died at Medina in 632. His grave there has since been a place of pilgrimage.

Mohammed's followers, called Moslems, revered him as the prophet of *Allah* (God), beside whom there is no other God. Although he had no close knowledge of Judaism and Christianity, he considered himself succeeding and completing them as the seal of the Prophets. Sources of the Islamic faith are the *Qur'an,* regarded as the uncreated, eternal Word of God, and Tradition *(hadith)* regarding sayings and deeds of the prophet.

Islam means surrender to the will of *Allah.* He is the all-powerful, whose will is supreme and determines man's fate. Good deeds will be rewarded at the Last Judgment in paradise and evil deeds will be punished in hell.

The Five Pillars, primary duties, of Islam are: witness; confessing the oneness of God and of Mohammed, his prophet; prayer, to be performed five times a day; almsgiving to the poor and the mosque (house of worship); fasting during daylight hours in the month of Ramadan; and pilgrimage to Mecca at least once in the Moslem's lifetime.

Islam, upholding the law of brotherhood, succeeded in uniting an Arab world that had disintegrated into tribes and castes. Disagreements concerning the succession of the prophet caused a great division in Islam between *Sunnis* and *Shias.* Among these, other sects arose *(Wahhabi).* Doctrinal issues also led to the rise of different schools of thought in theology. Nevertheless, since Arab armies turned against Syria and Palestine in 635, Islam has expanded successfully under Mohammed's successors. Its rapid conquests in Asia and Africa are unsurpassed in history. Turning against Europe, Moslems conquered Spain in 713. In 1453 Constantinople fell into their hands and in 1529 Moslem armies besieged Vienna. Since then, Islam has lost its foothold in Europe.

In modern times it has made great gains in Africa.

Hinduism

Hinduism is the major religion of India where there are over 550 million adherents. In contrast to other religions, it has no founder. Considered the oldest religion in the world, it dates back, perhaps, to prehistoric times.

Hinduism is hard to define, there being no common creed, no one doctrine to bind Hindus together. Intellectually there is complete freedom of belief, and one can be monotheist, polytheist, or atheist.

The most important sacred texts of the Hindu religion are written in Sanskrit and called the *Vedas* (*Veda*-knowledge). There are four Vedic books, of which the *Rig-Veda* is the oldest. It speaks of many gods and also deals with questions concerning the universe and creation. The dates of these works are unknown (1000 B.C.?).

The *Upanishads* (dated 1000–300 B.C.), commentaries on the Vedic texts, have philosophical speculations on the origin of the universe, the nature of deity, of *atman* (the human soul), and its relationship to *Brahman* (the universal soul).

Brahman is the principle and source of the universe who can be indicated only by negatives. As the divine intelligence, he is the ground of the visible world, a presence that pervades all beings. Thus the many Hindu deities came to be understood as manifestations of the one *Brahman* from whom everything proceeds and to whom everything ultimately returns. The religio-social system of Hinduism is based on the concept of reincarnation and transmigration in which all living beings, from plants below to gods above, are caught in a cosmic system that is an everlasting cycle of becoming and perishing.

Life is determined by the law of *karma,* according to which rebirth is dependent on moral behavior in a previous phase of existence. In this view, life on earth is regarded as transient *(maya)* and a burden. The goal of existence is liberation from the cycle of rebirth and redeath and entrance into the indescribable state of what in Buddhism is called *nirvana* (extinction of passion).

Further important sacred writings are the Epics *(ithasas),* which contain legendary stories about gods and men. They are the *Mahabharata* (composed between 200 B.C. and A.D. 200) and the *Ramayana.* The former includes the poem *Bhagavad-Gita* (Song of the Lord).

The practice of Hinduism consists of rites and ceremonies centering on the main socio-religious occasions of birth, marriage, and death. There are many Hindu temples, which are dwelling places of the deities and to which people bring offerings. There are also places of pilgrimages, the chief one being Benares on the Ganges, most sacred among the rivers in India.

Orthodox Hindu society in India was divided into four major hereditary casts: 1) Brahmans (priestly and learned class); 2) Kshatriyas (military, professional, rulers and governing occupations); 3) Vaisyas (landowners, merchants, and business occupations); and 4) Sudras (artisans, laborers, and peasants). Below the Sudras was a fifth group, the untouchables (lowest menial occupations and no social standing). The Indian government banned discrimination against the untouchables in 1949.

In modern times work has been done to reform and revive Hinduism. One of the outstanding reformers was Ramakrishna (1836–86), who inspired many followers, one of whom founded the Ramakrishna mission. The mission is active both in India and in other countries and is known for its scholarly and humanitarian works.

Buddhism

Founded in the 6th century B.C. in northern India by Gautama Buddha, who was born in southern Nepal as son to a king. His birth is surrounded by many legends, but Western scholars agree that he lived from 563 to 483 B.C. Warned by a sage that his son would become an ascetic or a universal monarch, the king confined him to his home. He was able to escape and began the life of a homeless wanderer in search of peace, passing through many disappointments until he finally came to the Tree of Enlightenment, under which he lived in meditation till enlightenment came to him and he became a Buddha (enlightened one).

Now he understood the origin of suffering, summarized in the *Four Noble Truths,* which constitutes the foundation of Buddhism. The Four are the truth of suffering, which all living beings must endure; of the origin of suffering, which is craving and which leads to rebirth; that it can be destroyed; and of the way that leads to cessation of pain, i.e., the *Noble Eightfold Way,* which is the rule of practical Buddhism:

right views, right intention, right speech, right action, right livelihood, right effort, right concentration, and right ecstasy.

Nirvana is the goal of all existence, the state of complete redemption, into which the redeemed enters. Buddha's insight can free every man from the law of reincarnation through complete emptying of the self.

The nucleus of Buddha's church or association was originally formed by monks and lay-brothers, whose houses gradually became monasteries used as places for religious instruction. The worship service consisted of a sermon, expounding of Scripture, meditation, and confession. At a later stage pilgrimages to the holy places associated with the Buddha came into being, as well as veneration of relics.

In the 3rd century B.C., King Ashoka made Buddhism the State religion of India but, as centuries passed, it gradually fell into decay through splits, persecutions, and the hostile Brahmans. Buddhism spread to countries outside India, however.

At the beginning of the Christian era, there occurred a split that gave rise to two main types: *Hinayana* (Little Vehicle), or southern Buddhism, and *Mahayana* (Great Vehicle), or northern Buddhism. The former type, more individualistic, survived in Ceylon and southern Asia. *Hinayana* retained more closely the original teachings of the Buddha, which did not know of a personal god or soul. *Mahayana*, more social, polytheistic, and developing a pluralistic pompous cult, was strong in the Himalayas, Tibet, Mongolia, China, Korea, and Japan.

In the present century, Buddhism has found believers also in the West and there are an estimated 554,000 Buddhists in Northern America.

Confucianism

Confucius (K'ung Fu-tzu), born in the state of Lu (northern China), lived from 551 to 479 B.C. Tradition, exaggerating the importance of Confucius in life, has depicted him as a great statesman but, in fact, he seems to have been a private teacher. Anthologies of ancient Chinese classics, along with his own Analects *(Lun Yu)*, became the basis of Confucianism. These Analects were transmitted as a collection of his sayings as recorded by his students, with whom he discussed ethical and social problems. They developed into men of high moral standing, who served the State as administrators.

In his teachings, Confucius emphasized the importance of an old Chinese concept *(li)*, which has the connotation of proper conduct. There is some disagreement as to the religious ideas of Confucius, but he held high the concepts handed down from centuries before him. Thus he believed in Heaven *(T'ien)* and sacrificed to his ancestors. Ancestor worship he indeed encouraged as an expression of filial piety, which he considered the loftiest of virtues.

Piety to Confucius was the foundation of the family as well as the State. The family is the nucleus of the State, and the "five relations," between king and subject, father and son, man and wife, older and younger brother, and friend and friend, are determined by the virtues of love of fellow men, righteousness, and respect.

An extension of ancestor worship may be seen in the worship of Confucius, which became official in the 2nd century B.C. when the emperor, in recognition of Confucius' teachings as supporting the imperial rule, offered sacrifices at his tomb.

Mencius (Meng Tse), who lived around 400 B.C., did much to propagate and elaborate Confucianism in its concern with ordering society. Thus, for two millennia, Confucius' doctrine of State, with its emphasis on ethics and social morality, rooted in ancient Chinese tradition and developed and continued by his disciples, has been standard in China and the Far East.

With the revolution of 1911 in China, however, students, burning Confucius in effigy, called for the removal of "the old curiosity shop."

Shintoism

Shinto, the Chinese term for the Japanese *Kami no Michi*, i.e., the Way of the Gods, comprises the religious ideas and cult indigenous to Japan. *Kami*, or gods, considered divine forces of nature that are worshipped, may reside in rivers, trees, rocks, mountains, certain animals, or, particularly, in the sun and moon. The worship of ancestors, heroes, and deceased emperors was incorporated later.

After Buddhism had come from Korea, Japan's native religion at first resisted it. Then there followed a period of compromise and amalgamation with Buddhist beliefs and ceremonies, resulting, since the 9th century A.D., in a syncretistic religion, a Twofold Shinto. Buddhist deities came to be regarded as manifestations of Japanese deities and Buddhist priests took over most of the Shinto shrines.

In modern times Shinto regained independence from Buddhism. Under the reign of the Emperor Meiji (1868–1912) it became the official State religion, in which loyalty to the emperor was emphasized. The line of succession of emperors is traced back to the first Emperor Jimmu (660 B.C.) and beyond him to the Sun-goddess *Amaterasuomikami.*

The centers of worship are the shrines and temples in which the deities are believed to dwell and believers approach them through *torii* (gateways). Most important among the shrines is the imperial shrine of the Sun-goddess at Ise, where state ceremonies were once held in June and December. The *Yasukuni* shrine of the war dead in Tokyo is also well known.

Acts of worship consist of prayers, clapping of hands, acts of purification, and offerings. On feast days processions and performances of music and dancing take place and priests read prayers before the gods in the shrines, asking for good harvest, the well-being of people and emperor, etc. In Japanese homes there is a god-shelf, a small wooden shrine that contains the tablets bearing the names of ancestors. Offerings are made and candles lit before it.

After World War II the Allied Command ordered the disestablishment of State Shinto. To be distinguished from State Shinto is Sect Shinto, consisting of 13 recognized sects. These have arisen in modern times. Most important among them is *Tenrikyo* in Tenri City (Nara), in which healing by faith plays a central role.

Taoism

Taoism, a religion of China, was, according to tradition, founded by Lao Tse, a Chinese philosopher, long considered one of the prominent religious leaders from the 6th century B.C.

Data about him are for the most part legendary, however, and the *Tao Te Ching* (the classic of the Way and of its Power), traditionally ascribed to him, is now believed by many scholars to have originated in the 3rd century B.C. The book is composed in short chapters, written in aphoristic rhymes. Central are the word *Tao*, which means way or path and, in a deeper sense, signifies the principle that underlies the reality of this world and manifests itself in nature and in the lives of men, and the word *Te* (power).

The virtuous man draws power from being absorbed in *Tao*, the ultimate reality within an ever-changing world. By non-action and keeping away from human striving it is possible for man to live in harmony with the principles that underlie and govern the universe. *Tao* cannot be comprehended by reason and knowledge, but only by inward quiet.

Besides the *Tao Te Ching*, dating from approximately the same period, there are two Taoist works, written by Chuang Tse and Lieh Tse.

Theoretical Taoism of this classical philosophical movement of the 4th and 3rd centuries B.C. in China differed from popular Taoism, into which it gradually degenerated. The standard of theoretical Taoism was maintained in the classics, of course, and among the upper classes it continued to be alive until modern times.

Religious Taoism is a form of religion dealing with deities and spirits, magic and soothsaying. In the 2nd century A.D. it was organized with temples, cult, priests, and monasteries and was able to hold its own in the competition with Buddhism that came up at the same time.

After the 7th century A.D., however, Taoist religion further declined. Split into numerous sects, which often operate like secret societies, it has become a syncretistic folk religion in which some of the old deities and saints live on.

Roman Catholic Pontiffs

St. Peter, of Bethsaida in Galilee, Prince of the Apostles, was the first Pope. He lived first in Antioch and then in Rome for 25 years. In AD 64 or 67, he was martyred. St. Linus became the second Pope.

		Reigned	
Name	**Birthplace**	**From**	**To**
St. Linus	Tuscia	67	76
St. Anacletus (Cletus)	Rome	76	88
St. Clement	Rome	88	97
St. Evaristus	Greece	97	105
St. Alexander I	Rome	105	115
St. Sixtus I	Rome	115	125
St. Telesphorus	Greece	125	136
St. Hyginus	Greece	136	140
St. Pius I	Aquileia	140	155
St. Anicetus	Syria	155	166
St. Soter	Campania	166	175
St. Eleutherius	Epirus	175	189
St. Victor I	Africa	189	199
St. Zephyrinus	Rome	199	217
St. Callistus I	Rome	217	222
St. Urban I	Rome	222	230
St. Pontian	Rome	230	235
St. Anterus	Greece	235	236
St. Fabian	Rome	236	250
St. Cornelius	Rome	251	253
St. Lucius I	Rome	253	254
St. Stephen I	Rome	254	257
St. Sixtus II	Greece	257	258
St. Dionysius	Unknown	259	268
St. Felix I	Rome	269	274
St. Eutychian	Luni	275	283
St. Caius	Dalmatia	283	296
St. Marcellinus	Rome	296	304
St. Marcellus I	Rome	308	309
St. Eusebius	Greece	309[1]	309[1]
St. Meltiades	Africa	311	314
St. Sylvester I	Rome	314	335
St. Marcus	Rome	336	336
St. Julius I	Rome	337	352
Liberius	Rome	352	366
St. Damasus I	Spain	366	384
St. Siricius	Rome	384	399
St. Anastasius I	Rome	399	401
St. Innocent I	Albano	401	417
St. Zozimus	Greece	417	418
St. Boniface I	Rome	418	422
St. Celestine I	Campania	422	432
St. Sixtus III	Rome	432	440
St. Leo I (the Great)	Tuscany	440	461
St. Hilary	Sardinia	461	468
St. Simplicius	Tivoli	468	483
St. Felix III (II)[2]	Rome	483	492
St. Gelasius I	Africa	492	496
Anastasius II	Rome	496	498
St. Symmachus	Sardinia	498	514
St. Hormisdas	Frosinone	514	523
St. John I	Tuscany	523	526
St. Felix IV (III)	Samnium	526	530
Boniface II	Rome	530	532
John II	Rome	533	535
St. Agapitus I	Rome	535	536
St. Silverius	Campania	536	537
Vigilius	Rome	537	555
Pelagius I	Rome	556	561
John III	Rome	561	574
Benedict I	Rome	575	579
Pelagius II	Rome	579	590
St. Gregory I (the Great)	Rome	590	604
Sabinianus	Tuscany	604	606
Boniface III	Rome	607	607
St. Boniface IV	Marsi	608	615
St. Deusdedit (Adeodatus I)	Rome	615	618
Boniface V	Naples	619	625
Honorius I	Campania	625	638
Severinus	Rome	640	640
John IV	Dalmatia	640	642
Theodore I	Greece	642	649
St. Martin I	Todi	649	655
St. Eugene I[3]	Rome	654	657
St. Vitalian	Segni	657	672
Adeodatus II	Rome	672	676
Donus	Rome	676	678
St. Agatho	Sicily	678	681
St. Leo II	Sicily	682	683
St. Benedict II	Rome	684	685
John V	Syria	685	686
Conon	Unknown	686	687
St. Sergius I	Syria	687	701
John VI	Greece	701	705
John VII	Greece	705	707
Sisinnius	Syria	708	708
Constantine	Syria	708	715
St. Gregory II	Rome	715	731
St. Gregory III	Syria	731	741
St. Zachary	Greece	741	752
Stephen II (III)[4]	Rome	752	757
St. Paul I	Rome	757	767

Name	Birthplace	Reigned From	To
Stephen III (IV)	Sicily	768	772
Adrian I	Rome	772	795
St. Leo III	Rome	795	816
Stephen IV (V)	Rome	816	817
St. Paschal I	Rome	817	824
Eugene II	Rome	824	827
Valentine	Rome	827	827
Gregory IV	Rome	827	844
Sergius II	Rome	844	847
St. Leo IV	Rome	847	855
Benedict III	Rome	855	858
St. Nicholas I (the Great)	Rome	858	867
Adrian II	Rome	867	872
John VIII	Rome	872	882
Marinus I	Gallese	882	884
St. Adrian III	Rome	884	885
Stephen V (VI)	Rome	885	891
Formosus	Portus	891	896
Boniface VI	Rome	896	896
Stephen VI (VII)	Rome	896	897
Romanus	Gallese	897	897
Theodore II	Rome	897	897
John IX	Tivoli	898	900
Benedict IV	Rome	900	903
Leo V	Ardea	903	903
Sergius III	Rome	904	911
Anastasius III	Rome	911	913
Landus	Sabina	913	914
John X	Tossignano	914	928
Leo VI	Rome	928	928
Stephen VII (VIII)	Rome	928	931
John XI	Rome	931	935
Leo VII	Rome	936	939
Stephen VIII (IX)	Rome	939	942
Marinus II	Rome	942	946
Agapitus II	Rome	946	955
John XII	Tusculum	955	964
Leo VIII[5]	Rome	963	965
Benedict V[5]	Rome	964	966
John XIII	Rome	965	972
Benedict VI	Rome	973	974
Benedict VII	Rome	974	983
John XIV	Pavia	983	984
John XV	Rome	985	996
Gregory V	Saxony	996	999
Sylvester II	Auvergne	999	1003
John XVII	Rome	1003	1003
John XVIII	Rome	1004	1009
Sergius IV	Rome	1009	1012
Benedict VIII	Tusculum	1012	1024
John XIX	Tusculum	1024	1032
Benedict IX[6]	Tusculum	1032	1044
Sylvester III	Rome	1045	1045
Benedict IX (2nd time)	—	1045	1045
Gregory VI	Rome	1045	1046
Clement II	Saxony	1046	1047
Benedict IX (3rd time)	—	1047	1048
Damasus II	Bavaria	1048	1048
St. Leo IX	Alsace	1049	1054
Victor II	Germany	1055	1057
Stephen IX (X)	Lorraine	1057	1058
Nicholas II	Burgundy	1059	1061
Alexander II	Milan	1061	1073
St. Gregory VII	Tuscany	1073	1085
Bl. Victor III	Benevento	1086	1087
Bl. Urban II	France	1088	1099
Paschal II	Ravenna	1099	1118

Name	Birthplace	Reigned From	To
Gelasius II	Gaeta	1118	1119
Callistus II	Burgundy	1119	1124
Honorius II	Flagnano	1124	1130
Innocent II	Rome	1130	1143
Celestine II	Città di Castello	1143	1144
Lucius II	Bologna	1144	1145
Bl. Eugene III	Pisa	1145	1153
Anastasius IV	Rome	1153	1154
Adrian IV	England	1154	1159
Alexander III	Siena	1159	1181
Lucius III	Lucca	1181	1185
Urban III	Milan	1185	1187
Gregory VIII	Benevento	1187	1187
Clement III	Rome	1187	1191
Celestine III	Rome	1191	1198
Innocent III	Anagni	1198	1216
Honorius III	Rome	1216	1227
Gregory IX	Anagni	1227	1241
Celestine IV	Milan	1241	1241
Innocent IV	Genoa	1243	1254
Alexander IV	Anagni	1254	1261
Urban IV	Troyes	1261	1264
Clement IV	France	1265	1268
Bl. Gregory X	Piacenza	1271	1276
Bl. Innocent V	Savoy	1276	1276
Adrian V	Genoa	1276	1276
John XXI[7]	Portugal	1276	1277
Nicholas III	Rome	1277	1280
Martin IV[8]	France	1281	1285
Honorius IV	Rome	1285	1287
Nicholas IV	Ascoli	1288	1292
St. Celestine V	Isernia	1294	1294
Boniface VIII	Anagni	1294	1303
Bl. Benedict XI	Treviso	1303	1304
Clement V	France	1305	1314
John XXII	Cahors	1316	1334
Benedict XII	France	1334	1342
Clement VI	France	1342	1352
Innocent VI	France	1352	1362
Bl. Urban V	France	1362	1370
Gregory XI	France	1370	1378
Urban VI	Naples	1378	1389
Boniface IX	Naples	1389	1404
Innocent VII	Sul mona	1404	1406
Gregory XII	Venice	1406	1415
Martin V	Rome	1417	1431
Eugene IV	Venice	1431	1447
Nicholas V	Sarzana	1447	1455
Callistus III	Jativa	1455	1458
Pius II	Siena	1458	1464
Paul II	Venice	1464	1471
Sixtus IV	Savona	1471	1484
Innocent VIII	Genoa	1484	1492
Alexander VI	Jativa	1492	1503
Pius III	Siena	1503	1503
Julius II	Savona	1503	1513
Leo X	Florence	1513	1521
Adrian VI	Utrecht	1522	1523
Clement VII	Florence	1523	1534
Paul III	Rome	1534	1549
Julius III	Rome	1550	1555
Marcellus II	Montepulciano	1555	1555
Paul IV	Naples	1555	1559
Pius IV	Milan	1559	1565
St. Pius V	Bosco	1566	1572
Gregory XIII	Bologna	1572	1585
Sixtus V	Grottammare	1585	1590
Urban VII	Rome	1590	1590
Gregory XIV	Cremona	1590	1591

Name	Birthplace	Reigned From	To	Name	Birthplace	Reigned From	To
Innocent IX	Bologna	1591	1591	Clement XIII	Venice	1758	1769
Clement VIII	Florence	1592	1605	Clement XIV	Rimini	1769	1774
Leo XI	Florence	1605	1605	Pius VI	Cesena	1775	1799
Paul V	Rome	1605	1621	Pius VII	Cesena	1800	1823
Gregory XV	Bologna	1621	1623	Leo XII	Genga	1823	1829
Urban VIII	Florence	1623	1644	Pius VIII	Cingoli	1829	1830
Innocent X	Rome	1644	1655	Gregory XVI	Belluno	1831	1846
Alexander VII	Siena	1655	1667	Pius IX	Senegallia	1846	1878
Clement IX	Pistoia	1667	1669	Leo XIII	Carpineto	1878	1903
Clement X	Rome	1670	1676	St. Pius X	Riese	1903	1914
Bl. Innocent XI	Como	1676	1689	Benedict XV	Genoa	1914	1922
Alexander VIII	Venice	1689	1691	Pius XI	Desio	1922	1939
Innocent XII	Spinazzola	1691	1700	Pius XII	Rome	1939	1958
Clement XI	Urbino	1700	1721	John XXIII	Sotto il Monte	1958	1963
Innocent XIII	Rome	1721	1724	Paul VI	Concesio	1963	1978
Benedict XIII	Gravina	1724	1730	John Paul I	Forno di Canale	1978	1978
Clement XII	Florence	1730	1740	John Paul II	Wadowice, Poland	1978	
Benedict XIV	Bologna	1740	1758				

1. Or 310. 2. He should be called Felix II, and his successors of the same name should be numbered accordingly. The discrepancy was caused by the erroneous insertion in some lists of the name of St. Felix of Rome, Martyr. 3. He was elected during the exile of St. Martin I, who endorsed him as Pope. 4. After St. Zachary died, a Roman priest named Stephen was elected but died before his consecration as Bishop of Rome. His name is not included in all lists for this reason. In view of this historical confusion, the *National Catholic Almanac* lists the true Stephen II as Stephen II (III), the true Stephen III as Stephen III (IV), etc. 5. Confusion exists concerning the legitimacy of claims. If the deposition of John was invalid, Leo was an antipope until after the end of Benedict's reign. If the deposition of John was valid, Leo was the legitimate Pope and Benedict an antipope. 6. If the triple removal of Benedict IX was not valid, Sylvester III, Gregory VI, and Clement II were antipopes. 7. Elimination was made of the name of John XX in an effort to rectify the numerical designation of Popes named John. The error dates back to the time of John XV. 8. The names of Marinus I and Marinus II were construed as Martin. In view of these two pontificates and the earlier reign of St. Martin I, this pontiff was called Martin IV. *Source: National Catholic Almanac,* from *Annuarto Pontificio.*

Basic Beliefs of Major U.S. Religions

Source: "Religion in America, 1992–1993," Copyright © by The Princeton Religion Research Center.

Over the years we have asked the American public in various ways if they believe in God, and always with the result that most people do. Some may think of God in the anthropomorphic image of the painters of the Renaissance, others may believe God is female. To some God is an abstract life force or universal spirit. Most believe in a personal God who rewards or punishes them for their actions. Very few people in this country say they are atheists, or even agnostics.

The proportion of Americans saying they believe in God or a universal spirit has ranged from 94–99 percent over the years, with the rate holding constant at about 94 percent in recent years.

Teen-agers continue this level of belief, with 95 percent saying they believe in God or a universal spirit. The level of belief dips somewhat during the college years (to 89 percent in a 1988 study) but after this temporary hiatus, belief generally gradually returns to the usual high levels.

Even though some may call God a universal spirit, very few view him as an abstract idea (5 percent) or as an impersonal creator (2 percent). Most see him as the heavenly father of the Bible who can be reached by prayers (84 percent).

Three in four teen-agers (76 percent) believe in a personal God who observes their actions and rewards or punishes them for them. Even more significantly, most teens (93 percent) truly believe that God loves them.

And God is not just something that one reads or hears about: a majority of Americans (54 percent) say they have been aware of or influenced by an outside force which is different from their everyday selves. Already by the teen years, three young people in 10 (29 percent) say they personally have experienced the presence of God.

Son of God

Christianity of course is the predominant religious faith in America. Over the years we have asked people about their belief in the divinity of Jesus Christ. For the past four decades we have found that at least three persons in four believe Jesus Christ either is God or the son of God. Six in 10 in a 1981 study said it is completely true that they believe in the divinity of Jesus Christ. An additional 25 percent wavered from stating the matter absolutely and said they thought the statement is "mostly true." Just 15 percent denied or doubted in any way his divinity. Similarly, 86 percent of teens in a 1991 Gallup Youth Survey said they believed Jesus Christ is God or the son of God.

In the strongest question wording used to date, in 1991, we asked if people believe that the only assurance of eternal life is personal faith in Jesus Christ, and six in 10 said they agreed completely with the statement, while an additional 17 percent agreed somewhat.

The Bible

One of the most dramatic shifts in religious beliefs we have witnessed is how people view the Bible. As recently as in 1963, two persons in three viewed the

Paranormal Beliefs—Members of Major U.S. Denominations

Believe in:	Protestant	Baptist	Lutheran	Methodist	Presbyterian	Catholic
Déjà vu	51%	48%	50%	61%	48%	63%
ESP	46	43	52	52	50	52
Clairvoyance	22	23	15	25	24	30
Telepathy	33	28	38	37	39	38
Telekinesis	14	16	16	14	14	15
The devil	62	66	56	51	56	51
Possession by the devil	54	61	42	45	48	43
Witches	14	11	7	9	12	13
Life after death	74	72	79	79	81	84
Communicating with the dead	14	14	10	12	16	23
Channeling	11	9	4	8	6	10
Psychic healing	44	40	36	52	45	48
Pyramids	5	7	—	3	6	6
Rock crystals	3	3	6	3	1	5
Other life in the universe	42	36	46	53	40	52
UFOs	40	30	56	49	33	53
Extraterrestrial visitors	24	21	36	27	26	34
Astrology	25	25	20	33	31	27
Number of interviews	**(702)**	**(224)**	**(81)**	**(107)**	**(65)**	**(284)**

Bible as the *actual* word of God, to be taken literally, word for word. Today, only one person in three still holds to that interpretation. Instead, most people (49 percent) view the Bible as the *inspired* word of God, and that everything in it should not be taken literally. Only 16 percent of the American public believe the Bible is totally humanistic in origin; i.e., is only an ancient book of fables, legends, history, and moral precepts.

Origin and Descent of Man

There is a fairly even division of opinion concerning the origin and descent of man, with 46 percent of the public taking the literal Genesis account of man's origin, and 40 percent believing that the process took millions of years, but under God's guidance. Just nine percent maintain God played no role in the matter.

Recent surveys suggest there is a new religious environmental ethic: About nine Americans in 10 (93 percent) say that nature is God's creation and therefore it is our duty to take care of it; furthermore, 87 percent feel humans have a moral obligation to protect all living things. Just 13 percent subscribe to the view that God intended nature to be used by humans, and so we should not worry too much if our actions harm the environment. □

Books of the Bible

NEW TESTAMENT

Matthew
Mark
Luke
John
Acts
Romans
1 Corinthians
2 Corinthians
Galatians
Ephesians
Phillipians
Colossians
1 Thessalonians
2 Thessalonians
1 Timothy
2 Timothy
Titus
Philemon
Hebrews
James
1 Peter
2 Peter
1 John
2 John
3 John
Jude
Revelation

OLD TESTAMENT

Genesis
Exodus
Leviticus
Numbers
Deuteronomy
Joshua
Judges
Ruth
I Samuel
2 Samuel
I Kings
2 Kings
I Chronicles
2 Chronicles
Ezra
Nehemiah
[1]Tobit
[1]Judith
Esther
[1]1 Maccabees
[1]2 Maccabees
Job
Psalms
Proverbs
Ecclesiastes
Song of Songs/Solomon
[1]Wisdom
[1]Sirach/Ecclesiasticus
Isaiah
Jeremiah
Lamentations
[1]Baruch
Ezekiel
Daniel
Hosea
Joel
Amos
Obadiah
Jonah
Micah
Nahum
Habakkuk
Zephaniah
Haggai
Zechariah
Malachi

1. These books are generally not accepted in the Protestant canon of Scripture, and Protestants refer to them as "Apocrypha." Catholic bibles include these books and refer to them as "Deuterocanonical." These disputed books were included in pre-Reformation Bibles.

A Concise Guide to Style

This section discusses and illustrates the basic conventions of American capitalization, punctuation, and italicization.

Capitalization

Capitalize the following: **1.** the first word of a sentence: Some spiders are poisonous; others are not. Are you my new neighbor?

2. the first word of a direct quotation, except when the quotation is split: Joyce asked, "Do you think that the lecture was interesting?" "No," I responded, "it was very boring." Tom Paine said, "The sublime and the ridiculous are often so nearly related that it is difficult to class them separately."

3. the first word of each line in a poem in traditional verse: Half a league, half a league,/Half a league onward,/All in the valley of Death/Rode the six hundred.—Alfred, Lord Tennyson

4. the names of people, of organizations and their members, of councils and congresses, and of historical periods and events: Marie Curie, Benevolent and Protective Order of Elks, an Elk, Protestant Episcopal Church, an Episcopalian, the Democratic Party, a Democrat, the Nuclear Regulatory Commission, the U.S. Senate, the Middle Ages, World War I, the Battle of Britain.

5. the names of places and geographic divisions, districts, regions, and locales: Richmond, Vermont, Argentina, Seventh Avenue, London Bridge, Arctic Circle, Eastern Hemisphere, Continental Divide, Middle East, Far North, Gulf States, East Coast, the North, the South Shore.

Do not capitalize words indicating compass points unless a specific region is referred to: Turn north onto Interstate 91.

6. the names of rivers, lakes, mountains, and oceans: Ohio River, Lake Como, Rocky Mountains, Atlantic Ocean.

7. the names of ships, aircraft, satellites, and space vehicles: U.S.S. *Arizona, Spirit of St. Louis,* the spy satellite Ferret-D, Voyager II, the space shuttle Challenger.

8. the names of nationalities, races, tribes, and languages: Spanish, Maori, Bantu, Russian.

9. words derived from proper names, except in their extended senses: the Byzantine Empire. *But:* byzantine office politics.

10. words indicating family relationships when used with a person's name as a title: Aunt Toni and Uncle Jack. *But:* my aunt and uncle, Toni and Jack Walker.

11. a title (i.e., civil, judicial, military, royal and noble, religious, and honorary) when preceding a name: Justice Marshall, General Jackson, Mayor Daley, Queen Victoria, Lord Mountbatten, Pope John Paul II, Professor Jacobson, Senator Byrd.

12. all references to the President and Vice President of the United States: The President has entered the hall. The Vice President presides over the Senate.

13. all key words in titles of literary, dramatic, artistic, and musical works: the novel *The Old Man and the Sea,* the short story "Notes from Underground," an article entitled "On Passive Verbs," James Dickey's poem "In the Tree House at Night," the play *Cat on a Hot Tin Roof,* Van Gogh's *Wheat Field and Cypress Trees,* Beethoven's *Emperor Concerto.*

14. *the* in the title of a newspaper if it is a part of the title: *The Wall Street Journal. But:* the New York *Daily News.*

15. the first word in the salutation and in the complimentary close of a letter: My dear Carol, Yours sincerely.

16. epithets and substitutes for the names of people and places: Old Hickory, Old Blood and Guts, The Oval Office, the Windy City.

17. words used in personifications: When is not Death at watch/Within those secret waters?/What wants he but to catch/Earth's heedless sons and daughters?—Edmund Blunden

18. the pronoun *I:* I told them that I had heard the news.

19. names for the Deity and sacred works: God, the Almighty, Jesus, Allah, the Supreme Being, the Bible, the Koran, the Talmud.

20. days of the week, months of the year, holidays, and holy days: Tuesday, May, Independence Day, Passover, Ramadan, Christmas.

21. the names of specific courts: The Supreme Court of the United States, the Massachusetts Appeals Court, the United States Court of Appeals for the First Circuit.

22. the names of treaties, accords, pacts, laws, and specific amendments: Panama Canal Treaty, Treaty of Paris, Geneva Accords, Warsaw Pact countries, Sherman Antitrust Law, Labor Management Relations Act, took the Fifth Amendment.

23. registered trademarks and service marks: Day-Glo, Comsat.

24. the names of geologic eras, periods, epochs, and strata and the names of prehistoric divisions: Paleozoic Era, Precambrian, Pleistocene, Age of Reptiles, Bronze Age, Stone Age.

25. the names of constellations, planets, and stars: Milky Way, Southern Crown, Saturn, Jupiter, Uranus, Polaris.

26. genus but not species names in binomial nomenclature: *Rana pipiens.*

27. New Latin names of classes, families, and all groups higher than genera in botanical and zoological nomenclature: Nematoda.

But do not capitalize derivatives from such names: nematodes.

28. many abbreviations and acronyms: Dec., Tues., Lt. Gen., M.F.A., UNESCO, MIRV.

Italicization

Use italics to:

1. indicate titles of books, plays, and epic poems:

War and Peace, The Importance of Being Earnest, Paradise Lost.

2. indicate titles of magazines and newspapers: *New York* magazine, *The Wall Street Journal,* the New York *Daily News.*

3. set off the titles of motion pictures and radio and television programs: *Star Wars, All Things Considered, Masterpiece Theater.*

4. indicate titles of major musical compositions: Handel's *Messiah,* Adam's *Giselle.*

5. set off the names of paintings and sculpture: *Mona Lisa, Pietà.*

6. indicate words, letters, or numbers that are referred to: The word *hiss* is onomatopoeic. *Can't* means *won't* in your lexicon. You form your *n*'s like *u*'s. A *6* looks like an inverted *9.*

7. indicate foreign words and phrases not yet assimilated into English: *C'est la vie* was the response to my complaint.

8. indicate the names of plaintiff and defendant in legal citations: *Roe* v. *Doe.*

9. emphasize a word or phrase: When you appear on the national news, you are *somebody.*

Use this device sparingly.

10. distinguish New Latin names of genera, species, subspecies, and varieties in botanical and zoological nomenclature: *Homo sapiens.*

11. set off the names of ships and aircraft but not space vehicles: U.S.S. *Arizona, Spirit of St. Louis,* Voyager II, the space shuttle Challenger, the spy satellite Ferret-D.

Punctuation

Apostrophe. 1. indicates the possessive case of singular and plural nouns, indefinite pronouns, and surnames combined with designations such as *Jr., Sr.,* and *II:* my sister's husband, my three sisters' husbands, anyone's guess, They answer each other's phones, John Smith, Jr.'s car.

2. indicates joint possession when used with the last of two or more nouns in a series: Doe and Roe's report.

3. indicates individual possession or authorship when used with each of two or more nouns in a series: Smith's, Roe's, and Doe's reports.

4. indicates the plurals of words, letters, and figures used as such: 60's and 70's; *x*'s, *y*'s, and *z*'s.

5. indicates omission of letters in contractions: aren't, that's, o'clock.

6. indicates omission of figures in dates: the class of '63.

Brackets.

1. enclose words or passages in quoted matter to indicate insertion of material written by someone other than the author: A tough but nervous, tenacious but restless race [the Yankees]; materially ambitious, yet prone to introspection. . . .—Samuel Eliot Morison

2. enclose material inserted within matter already in parentheses: (Vancouver [B.C.] January 1, 19—).

Colon.

1. introduces words, phrases, or clauses that explain, amplify, or summarize what has gone before: Suddenly I realized where we were: Rome.

"There are two cardinal sins from which all the others spring: impatience and laziness."—Franz Kafka

2. introduces a long quotation: In his original draft of the *Declaration of Independence,* Jefferson wrote: "We hold these truths to be sacred and undeniable; that all men are created equal and independent, that from that equal creation they derive rights inherent and inalienable. . . ."

3. introduces a list: We need the following items: pens, paper, pencils, blotters, and erasers.

4. separates chapter and verse numbers in Biblical references: James 1:4.

5. separates city from publisher in footnotes and bibliographies: Chicago: Riverside Press, 1983.

6. separates hour and minute(s) in time designations: 9:30 a.m., a 9:30 meeting.

7. follows the salutation in a business letter: Gentlemen:

Comma. 1. separates the clauses of a compound sentence connected by a coordinating conjunction: A difference exists between the musical works of Handel and Haydn, and it is a difference worth noting.

The comma may be omitted in short compound sentences: I heard what you said and I am furious. I got out of the car and I walked and walked.

2. separates *and* or *or* from the final item in a series of three or more: Red, yellow, and blue may be mixed to produce all colors.

3. separates two or more adjectives modifying the same noun if *and* could be used between them without altering the meaning: a solid, heavy gait. *But:* a polished mahogany dresser.

4. sets off nonrestrictive clauses or phrases (i.e., those that if eliminated would not affect the meaning of the sentences): The burglar, who had entered through the patio, went straight to the silver chest.

The comma should not be used when a clause is restrictive (i.e., essential to the meaning of the sentence): The burglar who had entered through the patio went straight to the silver chest; the other burglar searched for the wall safe.

5. sets off words or phrases in apposition to a noun or noun phrase: Plato, the famous Greek philosopher, was a student of Socrates.

The comma should not be used if such words or phrases precede the noun: The Greek philosopher Plato was a student of Socrates.

6. sets off transitional words and short expressions that require a pause in reading or speaking: Unfortunately, my friend was not well traveled. Did you, after all, find what you were looking for? I live with my family, of course.

7. sets off words used to introduce a sentence: No, I haven't been to Paris. Well, what do you think we should do now?

8. sets off a subordinate clause or a long phrase that precedes a principal clause: By the time we found the restaurant, we were starved. Of all the illustrations in the book, the most striking are those of the tapestries.

9. sets off short quotations and sayings: The candidate said, "Actions speak louder than words." "Talking of axes," said the Duchess, "chop off her head"—Lewis Carroll

10. indicates omission of a word or words: To err is human; to forgive, divine.

11. sets off the year from the month in full dates: Nicholas II of Russia was shot on July 16, 1918.

But note that when only the month and the year are used, no comma appears: Nicholas II of Russia was shot in July 1918.

12. sets off city and state in geographic names: Atlanta, Georgia, is the transportation center of the South. 34 Beach Drive, Bedford, VA 24523.

13. separates series of four or more figures into thousands, millions, etc.: 67,000; 200,000.

14. sets off words used in direct address: "I tell you, folks, all politics is applesauce."—Will Rogers Thank you for your expert assistance, Dolores.

15. Separates a tag question from the rest of a sentence: You forgot your keys again, didn't you?

16. sets off sentence elements that could be misunderstood if the comma were not used: Some time after, the actual date for the project was set.

17. follows the salutation in a personal letter and the complimentary close in a business or personal letter: Dear Jessica, Sincerely yours.

18. sets off titles and degrees from surnames and from the rest of a sentence: Walter T. Prescott, Jr.; Gregory A. Rossi, S.J.; Susan P. Green, M.D., presented the case.

Dash.

1. indicates a sudden break or abrupt change in continuity: "If—if you'll just let me explain—" the student stammered. And the problem—if there really is one—can then be solved.

2. sets apart an explanatory, a defining, or an emphatic phrase: Foods rich in protein—meat, fish, and eggs—should be eaten on a daily basis.

More important than winning the election, is governing the nation. That is the test of a political party—the acid, final test.—Adlai E. Stevenson

3. sets apart parenthetical matter: Wolsey, for all his faults—and he had many—was a great statesman, a man of natural dignity with a generous temperament. . . .—Jasper Ridley

4. marks an unfinished sentence: "But if my bus is late—" he began.

5. sets off a summarizing phrase or clause: The vital measure of a newspaper is not its size but its spirit—that is its responsibility to report the news fully, accurately, and fairly.—Arthur H. Sulzberger

6. sets off the name of an author or source, as at the end of a quotation: A poet can survive everything but a misprint.—Oscar Wilde

Ellipses.

1. indicate, by three spaced points, omission of words or sentences within quoted matter: Equipped by education to rule in the nineteenth century, . . . he lived and reigned in Russia in the twentieth century.—Robert K. Massie

2. indicate, by four spaced points, omission of words at the end of a sentence: The timidity of bureaucrats when it comes to dealing with . . . abuses is easy to explain. . . .—*New York*

3. indicate, when extended the length of a line, omission of one or more lines of poetry:

Roll on, thou deep and dark blue
    ocean—roll!

. . . .

Man marks the earth with ruin—his
    control
Stops with the shore.—Lord Byron

4. are sometimes used as a device, as for example, in advertising copy:

To help you Move and Grow
    with the Rigors of
Business in the 1980's . . .
    and Beyond.—*Journal of Business Strategy*

Exclamation Point.

1. terminates an emphatic or exclamatory sentence: Go home at once! You've got to be kidding!

2. terminates an emphatic interjection: Encore!

Hyphen. 1. indicates that part of a word of more than one syllable has been carried over from one line to the next:

During the revolution, the nation was
beset with problems—looting, fight-
ing, and famine.

2. joins the elements of some compounds: great-grandparent, attorney-at-law, ne'er-do-well.

3. joins the elements of compound modifiers preceding nouns: high-school students, a fire-and-brimstone lecture, a two-hour meeting.

4. indicates that two or more compounds share a single base: four- and six-volume sets, eight- and nine-year olds.

5. separates the prefix and root in some combinations; check the Dictionary when in doubt about the spelling: anti-Nazi, re-elect, co-author, re-form/reform, re-cover/recover, re-creation/recreation.

6. substitutes for the word *to* between typewritten inclusive words or figures: pp. 145–155, the Boston-New York air shuttle.

7. punctuates written-out compound numbers from 21 through 99: forty-six years of age, a person who is forty-six, two hundred fifty-nine dollars.

Parentheses. 1. enclose material that is not essential to a sentence and that if not included would not alter its meaning: After a few minutes (some say less) the blaze was extinguished.

2. often enclose letters or figures to indicate subdivisions of a series: A movement in sonata form consists of the following elements: (1) the exposition, (2) the development, and (3) the recapitulation.

3. enclose figures following and confirming written-out numbers, especially in legal and business documents: The fee for my services will be two thousand dollars ($2,000.00).

4. enclose an abbreviation for a term following the written-out term, when used for the first time in a text: The patient is suffering from acquired immune deficiency syndrome (AIDS).

Period. 1. terminates a complete declarative or mild imperative sentence: There could be no turning back as war's dark shadow settled irrevocably across the continent of Europe.—W. Bruce Lincoln. Return all the books when you can. Would you kindly affix your signature here.

2. terminates sentence fragments: Gray clouds—and what looks like a veil of rain falling behind the East German headland. A pair of ducks. A tired or dying swan, head buried in its back feathers, sits on the sand a few feet from the water's edge.—Anthony Bailey

3. follows some abbreviations: Dec., Rev., St., Blvd., pp., Co.

Question Mark. 1. punctuates a direct question: Have you seen the new play yet? Who goes there? *But:* I wonder who said "Nothing is easy in war." I asked if they planned to leave.

2. indicates uncertainty: Ferdinand Magellan (1480?–1521), Plato (427?–347 B.C.).

Quotation Marks. 1. Double quotation marks enclose direct quotations: "What was Paris like in the Twenties?" our daughter asked. "Ladies and Gentlemen," the Chief Usher said, "the President of the United States." Robert Louis Stevenson said that "it is better to be a fool than to be dead." When advised not to become a lawyer because the profession was already overcrowded, Daniel Webster replied, "There is always room at the top."

2. Double quotation marks enclose words or phrases to clarify their meaning or use or to indicate that they are being used in a special way: This was the border of what we often call "the West" or "the Free World." "The Windy City" is a name for Chicago.

3. Double quotation marks set off the translation of a foreign word or phrase: *die Grenze,* "the border."

4. Double quotation marks set off the titles of series of books, of articles or chapters in publications, of essays, of short stories and poems, of individual radio and television programs, and of songs and short musical pieces: "The Horizon Concise History" series; an article entitled "On Reflexive Verbs in

English"; Chapter Nine, "The Prince and the Peasant"; Pushkin's "The Queen of Spades"; Tennyson's "Ode on the Death of the Duke of Wellington"; "The Bob Hope Special"; Schubert's "Death and the Maiden."

5. Single quotation marks enclose quotations within quotations: The blurb for the piece proclaimed, "Two years ago at Geneva, South Vietnam was virtually sold down the river to the Communists. Today the spunky little . . . country is back on its own feet, thanks to "a mandarin in a sharkskin suit who's upsetting the Red timetable.' "—Frances FitzGerald

Put commas and periods inside quotation marks; put semicolons and colons outside. Other punctuation, such as exclamation points and question marks, should be put inside the closing quotation marks only if part of the matter quoted.

Semicolon. 1. separates the clauses of a compound sentence having no coordinating conjunction: Do not let us speak of darker days; let us rather speak of sterner days.—Winston Churchill

2. separates the clauses of a compound sentence in which the clauses contain internal punctuation, even when the clauses are joined by conjunctions: Skis in hand, we trudged to the lodge, stowed our lunches, and donned our boots; and the rest of our party waited for us at the lifts.

3. separates elements of a series in which items already contain commas: Among those at the diplomatic reception were the Secretary of State; the daughter of the Ambassador to the Court of St. James's, formerly of London; and two United Nations delegates.

4. separates clauses of a compound sentence joined by a conjunctive adverb, such as *however, nonetheless,* or *hence:* We insisted upon a hearing; however, the Grievance Committee refused.

5. may be used instead of a comma to signal longer pauses for dramatic effect: But I want you to know that when I cross the river my last conscious thought will be of the Corps; and the Corps; and the Corps.—General Douglas MacArthur

Virgule. 1. separates successive divisions in an extended date: fiscal year 1983/84.

2. represents *per:* 35 km/hr, 1,800 ft/sec.

3. means *or* between the words *and* and *or:* Take water skis and/or fishing equipment when you visit the beach this summer.

4. separates two or more lines of poetry that are quoted and run in on successive lines of a text: The student actress had a memory lapse when she came to the lines "Double, double, toil and trouble/Fire burn and cauldron bubble/Eye of newt and toe of frog/Wool of bat and tongue of dog" and had to leave the stage in embarrassment.

Forms of Address[1]

Source: Webster's II New Riverside University Dictionary. Copyright © 1984 by Houghton Mifflin Company.

Academics

Dean, college or university. *Address:* **Dean** _____. *Salutation:* Dear Dean _____

President. *Address:* President _____ _____. *Salutation:* Dear President _____.

Professor, college or university. *Address:* Professor _____ _____. *Salutation:* Dear Professor _____.

Clerical and Religious Orders

Abbot. *Address:* The Right Reverend _____ _____ O.S.B. Abbot of _____. *Salutation:* Right Reverend Abbot or Dear Father Abbot.

Archbishop, Eastern Orthodox. *Address:* The Most Reverend Joseph, Archbishop of _____. *Salutation:* Your Eminence.

Archbishop, Roman Catholic. The Most Reverend _____ _____, Archbishop of _____. *Salutation:* Your Excellency.

Archdeacon, Episcopal. *Address:* The Venerable _____ _____, Archdeacon of _____. *Salutation:* Venerable Sir or Dear Archdeacon _____.

Bishop, Episcopal. *Address;* The Right Reverend _____ _____, Bishop of _____. *Salutation:* Right Reverend Sir or Dear Bishop _____.

Bishop, other Protestant. *Address:* The Reverend _____ _____. *Salutation:* Dear Bishop _____.

Bishop, Roman Catholic. *Address:* The Most Reverend _____ _____, Bishop of _____. *Salutation:* Your Excellency or Dear Bishop _____.

Brotherhood, Roman Catholic. *Address:* Brother _____ _____, C.F.C. *Salutation:* Dear Brother or Dear Brother Joseph.

Brotherhood, superior of. *Address:* Brother Joseph C.F.C. Superior. *Salutation:* Dear Brother Joseph.

Cardinal. *Address:* His Eminence Joseph Cardinal Stone. *Salutation:* Your Eminence.

Clergyman/woman, Protestant. *Address:* The Reverend _____ _____ or The Reverend _____ _____, D.D. *Salutation:* Dear Mr./Ms. _____ or Dear Dr. _____.

Dean of a cathedral, Episcopal. *Address:* The Very Reverend _____ _____, Dean of _____. *Salutation:* Dear Dean _____.

Monsignor. *Address:* The Right Reverend Monsignor _____ _____. *Salutation:* Dear Monsignor.

Patriarch, Greek Orthodox. *Address:* His All Holiness Patriarch Joseph. *Salutation:* Your All Holiness.

Patriarch, Russian Orthodox. *Address:* His Holiness the Patriarch of _____. *Salutation:* Your Holiness.

Pope. *Address:* His Holiness The Pope. *Salutation:* Your Holiness or Most Holy Father.

Priest, Roman Catholic. *Address:* The Reverend _____ _____, S.J. *Salutation:* Dear Reverend Father or Dear Father.

Rabbi, man or woman. *Address:* Rabbi _____ _____ or _____ _____ D.D.. *Salutation:* Dear Rabbi _____ or Dear Dr. _____.

Sisterhood, Roman Catholic. *Address:* Sister _____ _____, C.S.J. *Salutation:* Dear Sister or Dear Sister _____.

Sisterhood, superior of. *Address:* The Reverend Mother Superior, S.C. *Salutation:* Reverend Mother.

Diplomats

Ambassador, U.S. *Address:* The Honorable _____ _____ The Ambassador of the United States. *Salutation:* Sir/Madam or Dear Mr./Madam Ambassador.

Ambassador to the U.S. *Address:* His/Her Excellency _____ _____, The Ambassador of _____. *Salutation:* Excellency or Dear Mr./Madam Ambassador.

Chargé d'Affaires, U.S. *Address:* The Honorable _____ _____, United States Chargé d'Affaires. *Salutation:* Dear Mr./Ms. _____.
Consul, U.S. *Address:* _____ _____, Esq., United States Consul. *Salutation:* Dear Mr./Ms. _____.
Minister, U.S. or to U.S. *Address:* The Honorable _____ _____, The Minister of _____. *Salutation:* Sir/Madam or Dear Mr./Madame Minister.
Secretary General, United Nations. *Address:* His/Her Excellency _____ _____, Secretary General of the United Nations. *Salutation:* Dear Mr./Madam/Madame Secretary General.
United Nations Representative (Foreign). *Address:* His/Her Excellency _____ _____ Representative of _____ to the United Nations. *Salutation:* Excellency or My dear Mr./Madame _____.
United Nations Representative (U.S.) *Address:* The Honorable _____ _____, United States Representative to the United Nations. *Salutation:* Sir/Madam or Dear Mr./Ms. _____.

Government Officials

Assemblyman. *Address:* The Honorable _____ _____. *Salutation:* Dear Mr./Ms. _____.
Associate Justice, U.S. Supreme Court. *Address:* Mr./Madam Justice _____. *Salutation:* Dear Mr./Madam Justice or Sir/Madam.
Attorney General, U.S. *Address:* The Honorable _____ _____, Attorney General of the United States. *Salutation:* Dear Mr./Madam or Attorney General.
Cabinet member: *Address:* The Honorable _____ _____, Secretary of _____. *Salutation:* Sir/Madam or Dear Mr./Madam Secretary.
Chief Justice, U.S. Supreme Court. *Address:* The Chief Justice of the United States. *Salutation:* Dear Mr. Chief Justice.
Commissioner (federal, state, local). *Address:* The Honorable _____ _____. *Salutation:* Dear Mr./Ms. _____.
Governor. *Address:* The Honorable _____ _____, Governor of _____. *Salutation:* Dear Governor _____.
Judge, Federal: *Address:* The Honorable _____ _____, Judge of the United States District Court for the _____, District of _____. *Salutation:* Sir/Madam or Dear Judge _____.
Judge, state or local. *Address:* The Honorable _____ _____, Judge of the Court of _____. *Salutation:* Dear Judge _____.
Lieutenant Governor. *Address:* The Honorable _____ _____, Lieutenant Governor of _____. *Salutation:* Dear Mr./Ms. _____.
Mayor. *Address:* The Honorable _____ _____, Mayor of _____. *Salutation:* Dear Mayor _____.
President, U.S. *Address:* The President. *Salutation:* Dear Mr. President.
President, U.S., former. *Address:* The Honorable _____ _____. *Salutation:* Dear Mr. _____.
Representative, state. *Address:* The Honorable _____ _____. *Salutation:* Dear Mr./Ms. _____.
Representative, U.S. *Address:* The Honorable _____ _____, United States House of Representatives. *Salutation:* Dear Mr./Ms. _____.
Senator, state. *Address:* The Honorable _____ _____, The State Senate, State Capitol. *Salutation:* Dear Senator _____.
Senator, U.S. *Address:* The Honorable _____ _____, United States Senate. *Salutation:* Dear Senator _____.
Speaker, U.S. House of Representatives. *Address:* The Honorable _____ _____, Speaker of the House of Representatives. *Salutation:* Dear Mr./Madam Speaker.
Vice President, U.S. *Address:* The Vice President of the United States. *Salutation:* Sir or Dear Mr. Vice President.

Military and Naval Officers

Rank. *Address:* Full rank, USN (or USCG, USAF, USA, USMC). *Salutation:* Dear (full rank) _____.

Professions

Attorney. *Address:* Mr./Ms. _____ _____, Attorney at law or _____ _____, Esq. *Salutation:* Dear Mr./Ms. _____.
Dentist. *Address:* _____ _____, D.D.S. *Salutation:* Dear Dr. _____.
Physician. *Address:* _____ _____, M.D. *Salutation:* Dear Dr. _____.
Veterinarian. *Address:* _____ _____, D.V.M. *Salutation:* Dear Dr. _____.

1. Forms of address do not always follow set guidelines; the type of salutation is often determined by the relationship between correspondents or by the purpose and content of the letter. However, a general style applies to most occasions. In highly formal salutations, when the addressee is a woman, "Madam" should be substituted for "Sir." When the salutation is informal, "Ms.," "Miss," or "Mrs." should be substituted for "Mr." If a woman addressee has previously indicated a preference for a particular form of address, that form should be used.

Selecting Child Care

Choosing child care is an important issue for parents. Here are some questions parents may want to ask when looking for child care:

1. What are the licensing laws for day care providers in your city, county, or state? Your local consumer protection office is a good place to check for this information.
2. Do caregivers have references? What about special training in child development and education? How many children does each adult look after?
3. Is the home or center clean? Is there enough space inside and outside for the children to play? Is the playground fenced?
4. If the center is large, do visitors and children sign in and out? What are the safety precautions in case of fire or other emergencies?
5. What about sick children? Do they stay home? What if a child needs medical help?
6. How does the staff discipline children? How much of each day is filled with planned activities? Are activities geared to children's ages and development?
7. What are the fees for half-days, overtime, or sick children?
8. Are kids' pictures or projects hung up and changed often?
9. Do caregivers tell you what your child did that day? How he or she is doing overall?

After your child is in a program, you may wish to ask:

1. Does your child talk happily about the program?
2. Do you know new employees? Do they talk to your child?

WEIGHTS & MEASURES

Measures and Weights

Source: Department of Commerce, National Bureau of Standards.

The International System (Metric)

The International System of Units is a modernized version of the metric system, established by international agreement, that i.e. provides a logical and interconnected framework for all measurements in science, industry, and commerce. The system is built on a foundation of seven basic units, and all other units are derived from them. (Use of metric weights and measures was legalized in the United States in 1866, and our customary units of weights and measures are defined in terms of the meter and kilogram.)

Length. Meter. Up until 1893, the meter was defined as 1,650,764.73 wavelengths in vacuum of the orange-red line of the spectrum of krypton-86. Since then, it is equal to the distance traveled by light in a vacuum in 1/299,792,458 of a second.

Time. Second. The second is defined as the duration of 9,192,631,770 cycles of the radiation associated with a specified transition of the cesium 133 atom.

Mass. Kilogram. The standard for the kilogram is a cylinder of platinum-iridium alloy kept by the International Bureau of Weights and Measures at Paris. A duplicate at the National Bureau of Standards serves as the mass standard for the United States. The kilogram is the only base unit still defined by a physical object.

Temperature. Kelvin. The kelvin is defined as the fraction 1/273.16 of the thermodynamic temperature of the triple point of water; that is, the point at which water forms an interface of solid, liquid and vapor. This is defined as 0.01°C on the Centigrade or Celsius scale and 32.02°F on the Fahrenheit scale. The temperature 0°K is called "absolute zero."

Electric Current. Electric current. The ampere is defined as that current that, if maintained in each of two long parallel wires separted by one meter in free space, would produce a force between the two wires (due to their magnetic fields) of 2×10^{-7} newton for each meter of length. (A newton is the unit of force which when applied to one kilogram mass would experience an acceleration of one meter per second per second.)

Luminous Intensity. Candela. The candela is defined as the luminous intensity of 1/600,000 of a square meter of a cavity at the temperature of freezing platinum (2,042K).

Amount of Substance. Mole. The mole is the amount of substance of a system that contains as many elementary entities as there are atoms in 0.012 kilogram of carbon-12.

Tables of Metric Weights and Measures

LINEAR MEASURE

10 millimeters (mm) =	1 centimeter (cm)
10 centimeters =	1 decimeter (dm) = 100 millimeters
10 decimeters =	1 meter (m) = 1,000 millimeters
10 meters =	1 dekameter (dam)
10 dekameters =	1 hectometer (hm) = 100 meters
10 hectometers =	1 kilometer (km) = 1,000 meters

AREA MEASURE

100 square millimeters (mm^2) =	1 sq centimeter (cm^2)
10,000 square centimeters =	1 sq meter (m^2) = 1,000,000 sq millimeters
100 square meters =	1 are (a)
100 ares =	1 hectare (ha) = 10,000 sq meters
100 hectares =	1 sq kilometer (km^2) = 1,000,000 sq meters

VOLUME MEASURE

10 milliliters (ml) =	1 centiliter (cl)
10 centiliters =	1 deciliter (dl) = 100 milliliters
10 deciliters =	1 liter (l) = 1,000 milliliters
10 liters =	1 dekaliter (dal)
10 dekaliters =	1 hectoliter (hl) = 100 liters
10 hectoliters =	1 kiloliter (kl) = 1,000 liters

CUBIC MEASURE

1,000 cubic millimeters (mm^3) =	1 cu centimeter (cm^3)
1,000 cubic centimeters =	1 cu decimeter (dm^3) = 1,000,000 cu millimeters
1,000 cubic decimeters =	1 cu meter (m^3) = 1 stere = 1,000,000 cu centimeters = 1,000,000,000 cu millimeters

WEIGHT

10 milligrams (mg) =	1 centigram (cg)
10 centigrams =	1 decigram (dg) = 100 milligrams
10 decigrams =	1 gram (g) = 1,000 milligrams
10 grams =	1 dekagram (dag)
10 dekagrams =	1 hectogram (hg) = 100 grams
10 hectograms =	1 kilogram (kg) = 1,000 grams
1,000 kilograms =	1 metric ton (t)

Tables of Customary U.S. Weights and Measures

LINEAR MEASURE

12 inches (in.) =	1 foot (ft)
3 feet =	1 yard (yd)
5 1/2 yards =	1 rod (rd), pole, or perch (16 1/2 ft)
40 rods =	1 furlong (fur) = 220 yds = 660 ft
8 furlongs =	1 statute mile (mi.) = 1,760 yds = 5,280 ft
3 land miles =	1 league
5,280 feet =	1 statute or land mile
6,076.11549 feet =	1 international nautical mile

AREA MEASURE

144 square inches =	1 sq ft
9 square feet =	1 sq yd = 1,296 sq in.
30 1/4 square yards =	1 sq rd = 272 1/4 sq ft
160 square rods =	1 acre = 4,840 sq yds = 43,560 sq ft
640 acres =	1 sq mi.
1 mile square =	1 section (of land)
6 miles square =	1 township = 36 sections = 36 sq mi.

CUBIC MEASURE

1,728 cubic inches =	1 cu ft
27 cubic feet =	1 cu yd

LIQUID MEASURE

When necessary to distinguish the liquid pint or quart from the dry pint or quart, the word "liquid" or the abbreviation "liq" should be used in combination with the name or abbreviation of the liquid unit.

4 gills (gi) =	1 pint (pt) (= 28.875 cu in.)
2 pints =	1 quart (qt) (= 57.75 cu in.)
4 quarts =	1 gallon (gal) (= 231 cu in.) = 8 pts = 32 gills

APOTHECARIES' FLUID MEASURE

60 minims (min.) =	1 fluid dram (fl dr) (= 0.2256 cu in.)
8 fluid drams =	1 fluid ounce (fl oz) (= 1.8047 cu in.)
16 fluid ounces =	1 pt (= 28.875 cu in.) = 128 fl drs
2 pints =	1 qt (= 57.75 cu in.) = 32 fl oz = 256 fl drs
4 quarts =	1 gal (= 231 cu in.) = 128 fl oz = 1,024 fl drs

DRY MEASURE

When necessary to distinguish the dry pint or quart from the liquid pint or quart; the word "dry" should be used in combination with the name or abbreviation of the dry unit.

2 pints =	1 qt (=67.2006 cu in.)
8 quarts =	1 peck (pk) (=537.605 cu in.) = 16 pts
4 pecks =	1 bushel (bu) (= 2,150.42 cu in.) = 32 qts

AVOIRDUPOIS WEIGHT

When necessary to distinguish the avoirdupois dram from the apothecaries dram, or to distinguish the avoirdupois dram or ounce from the fluid dram or ounce, or to distinguish the avoirdupois ounce or pound from the troy or apothecaries, ounce or pound, the word "avoirdupois" or the abbreviation "avdp" should be used in combination with the name or abbreviation of the avoirdupois unit. (The "grain" is the same in avoirdupois, troy, and apothecaries weights.)

27 11/32 grains =	1 dram (dr)
16 drams =	1 oz = 437 1/2 grains
16 ounces =	1 lb = 256 drams = 7,000 grains
100 pounds =	1 hundredweight (cwt)[1]
20 hundredweights =	1 ton (tn) = 2,000 lbs[1]

In "gross" or "long" measure, the following values are recognized:

112 pounds =	1 gross or long cwt[1]
20 gross or long hundredweights =	1 gross or long ton = 2,240 lbs[1]

1. When the terms "hundredweight" and "ton" are used unmodified, they are commonly understood to mean the 100–pound hundredweight and the 2,000–pound ton, respectively; these units may be designated "net" or "short" when necessary to distinguish them from the corresponding units in gross or long measure.

UNITS OF CIRCULAR MEASURE

Second (″) =	—
Minute (′) =	60 seconds
Degree (°) =	60 minutes
Right angle =	90 degrees
Straight angle =	180 degrees
Circle =	360 degrees

TROY WEIGHT

24 grains =	1 pennyweight (dwt)
20 pennyweights =	1 ounce troy (oz t) = 480 grains
12 ounces troy =	1 pound troy (lb t) = 240 pennyweights = 5,760 grains

APOTHECARIES' WEIGHT

20 grains =	1 scruple (s ap)
3 scruples =	1 dram apothecaries' (dr ap) = 60 grains
8 drams apothecaries =	1 ounce apothecaries' (oz ap) = 24 scruples = 480 grains
12 ounces apothecaries =	1 pound apothecaries' (lb ap) = 96 drams apothecaries' = 288 scruples = 5,760 grains

GUNTER'S OR SURVEYOR'S CHAIN MEASURE

7.92 inches =	1 link (li)
100 links =	1 chain (ch) = 4 rods = 66 ft
80 chains =	1 statute mile = 320 rods = 5,280 ft

Metric and U.S. Equivalents

1 angstrom[1] (light wave measurement)	0.1 millimicron 0.000 1 micron 0.000 000 1 millimeter 0.000 000 004 inch
1 cable's length	120 fathoms 720 feet 219.456 meters
1 centimeter	0.3937 inch
1 chain (Gunter's or surveyor's)	66 feet 20.1168 meters
1 decimeter	3.937 inches
1 dekameter	32.808 feet
1 fathom	6 feet 1.8288 meters
1 foot	0.3048 meter
1 furlong	10 chains (surveyor's) 660 feet 220 yards 1/8 statute mile 201.168 meters

1 inch	2.54 centimeters
1 kilometer	0.621 mile
1 league (land)	3 statute miles 4.828 kilometers
1 link (Gunter's or surveyor's)	7.92 inches 0.201 168 meter
1 meter	39.37 inches 1.094 yards
1 micron	0.001 millimeter 0.000 039 37 inch
1 mil	0.001 inch 0.025 4 millimeter
1 mile (statute or land)	5,280 feet 1.609 kilometers
1 mile (nautical international)	1.852 kilometers 1.151 statute miles 0.999 U.S. nautical miles
1 millimeter	0.03937 inch
1 millimicron (m+GRKm)	0.001 micron 0.000 000 039 37 inch
1 nanometer	0.001 micrometer or 0.000 000 039 37 inch
1 point (typography)	0.013 837 inch 1/72 inch (approximately) 0.351 millimeter
1 rod, pole, or perch	16 1/2 feet 5.0292 meters
1 yard	0.9144 meter

AREAS OR SURFACES

1 acre	43,560 square feet 4,840 square yards 0.405 hectare
1 are	119.599 square yards 0.025 acre
1 hectare	2.471 acres
1 square centimeter	0.155 square inch
1 square decimeter	15.5 square inches
1 square foot	929.030 square centimeters
1 square inch	6.4516 square centimeters
1 square kilometer	0.386 square mile 247.105 acres
1 square meter	1.196 square yards 10.764 square feet
1 square mile	258.999 hectares
1 square millimeter	0.002 square inch
1 square rod, square pole or square perch	25.293 square meters
1 square yard	0.836 square meters

CAPACITIES OR VOLUMES

1 barrel, liquid	31 to 42 gallons[2]
1 barrel, standard for fruits, vegetables, and other dry commodities except cranberries	7,056 cubic inches 105 dry quarts 3.281 bushels, struck measure
1 barrel, standard, cranberry	5.286 cubic inches 86 45/64 dry quarts 2.709 bushels, struck measure
1 bushel (U.S.) struck measure	2,150.42 cubic inches 35.238 liters
1 bushel, heaped (U.S.)	2,747.715 cubic inches 1.278 bushels, struck measure[3]
1 cord (firewood)	128 cubic feet
1 cubic centimeter	0.061 cubic inch
1 cubic decimeter	61.024 cubic inches
1 cubic foot	7.481 gallons 28.316 cubic decimeters
1 cubic inch	0.554 fluid ounce 4.433 fluid drams 16.387 cubic centimeters
1 cubic meter	1.308 cubic yards
1 cubic yard	0.765 cubic meter
1 cup, measuring	8 fluid ounces 1/2 liquid pint
1 dram, fluid or liquid (U.S.)	1/8 fluid ounces 0.226 cubic inch 3.697 milliliters 1.041 British fluid drachms
1 dekaliter	2.642 gallons 1.135 pecks
1 gallon (U.S.)	231 cubic inches 3.785 liters 0.833 British gallon 128 U.S. fluid ounces
1 gallon (British Imperial)	277.42 cubic inches 1.201 U.S. gallons 4.546 liters 160 British fluid ounces
1 gill	7.219 cubic inches 4 fluid ounces 0.118 liter
1 hectoliter	26.418 gallons 2.838 bushels
1 liter	1.057 liquid quarts 0.908 dry quart 61.024 cubic inches
1 milliliter	0.271 fluid dram 16.231 minims 0.061 cubic inch
1 ounce, fluid or liquid (U.S.)	1.805 cubic inch 29.574 milliliters 1.041 British fluid ounces

1 peck	8.810 liters
1 pint, dry	33.600 cubic inches 0.551 liter
1 pint, liquid	28.875 cubic inches 0.473 liter
1 quart, dry (U.S.)	67.201 cubic inches 1.101 liters 0.969 British quart
1 quart, liquid (U.S.)	57.75 cubic inches 0.946 liter 0.833 British quart
1 quart (British)	69.354 cubic inches 1.032 U.S. dry quarts 1.201 U.S. liquid quarts
1 tablespoon, measuring	3 teaspoons 4 fluid drams 1/2 fluid ounce
1 teaspoon, measuring	1/3 tablespoon 1 1/3 fluid drams
1 assay ton[4]	29.167 grams
1 carat	200 milligrams 3.086 grains
1 dram, apothecaries'	60 grains 3.888 grams
1 dram, avoirdupois	27 11/32 (=27.344) grains 1.772 grams
1 grain	64.798 91 milligrams
1 gram	15.432 grains 0.035 ounce, avoirdupois
1 hundredweight, gross or long[5]	112 pounds 50.802 kilograms
1 hundredweight, net or short	100 pounds 45.359 kilograms
1 kilogram	2.205 pounds
1 microgram [μg (the Greek letter mu in combination with the letter g)]	0.000 001 gram
1 milligram	0.015 grain
1 ounce, avoirdupois	437.5 grains 0.911 troy or apothecaries, ounce 28.350 grams
1 ounce, troy or apothecaries	480 grains 1.097 avoirdupois ounces 31.103 grams
1 pennyweight	1.555 grams
1 point	0.01 carat 2 milligrams
1 pound, avoirdupois	7,000 grains 1.215 troy or apothecaries pounds 453.592 37 grams
1 pound, troy or apothecaries	5,760 grains 0.823 avoirdupois pound 373.242 grams
1 ton, gross or long[5]	2,240 pounds 1.12 net tons 1.016 metric tons
1 ton, metric	2,204.623 pounds 0 .984 gross ton 1.102 net tons
1 ton, net or short	2,000 pounds 0.893 gross ton 0.907 metric ton

1. The angstrom is basically defined as 10^{-10} meter. 2. There is a variety of "barrels" established by law or usage. For example, federal taxes on fermented liquors are based on a barrel of 31 gallons; many state laws fix the "barrel for liquids" at 31 1/2 gallons; one state fixes a 36–gallon barrel for cistern measurement; federal law recognizes a 40–gallon barrel for "proof spirits"; by custom, 42 gallons comprise a barrel of crude oil or petroleum products for statistical purposes, and this equivalent is recognized "for liquids" by four states. 3. Frequently recognized as 1 1/4 bushels, struck measure. 4. Used in assaying. The assay ton bears the same relation to the milligram that a ton of 2,000 pounds avoirdupois bears to the ounce troy; hence the weight in milligrams of precious metal obtained from one assay ton of ore gives directly the number of troy ounces to the net ton. 5. The gross or long ton and hundredweight are used commercially in the United States to only a limited extent, usually in restricted industrial fields. These units are the same as the British "ton" and "hundredweight."

Miscellaneous Units of Measure

Acre: An area of 43,560 square feet. Originally, the area a yoke of oxen could plow in one day.

Agate: Originally a measurement of type size (5 1/2 points). Now equal to 1/14 inch. Used in printing for measuring column length.

Ampere: Unit of electric current. A potential difference of one volt across a resistance of one ohm produces a current of one ampere.

Astronomical Unit (A.U.): 93,000,000 miles, the average distance of the earth from the sun. Used for astronomy.

Bale: A large bundle of goods. In the U.S., the approximate weight of a bale of cotton is 500 pounds. The weight varies in other countries.

Board Foot (fbm): 144 cubic inches (12 in. × 12 in. × 1 in.). Used for lumber.

Bolt: 40 yards. Used for measuring cloth.

Btu: British thermal unit. Amount of heat needed to increase the temperature of one pound of water by one degree Fahrenheit (252 calories).

Carat (c): 200 milligrams or 3.086 grains troy. Originally the weight of a seed of the carob tree in the Mediterranean region. Used for weighing precious stones. *See also* Karat.

Chain (ch): A chain 66 feet or one–tenth of a furlong in length, divided into 100 parts called links. One mile is equal to 80 chains. Used in surveying and sometimes called Gunter's or surveyor's chain.

Cubit: 18 inches or 45.72 cm. Derived from distance between elbow and tip of middle finger.

Decibel: Unit of relative loudness. One decibel is the smallest amount of change detectable by the human ear.

Ell, English: 1 1/4 yards or 1/32 bolt. Used for measuring cloth.

Freight, Ton (also called Measurement Ton): 40 cubic feet of merchandise. Used for cargo freight.

Great Gross: 12 gross or 1728.

Gross: 12 dozen or 144.

Hand: 4 inches or 10.16 cm. Derived from the width of the hand. Used for measuring the height of horses at withers.

Hertz: Modern unit for measurement of electromagnetic wave frequencies (equivalent to "cycles per second").

Hogshead (hhd): 2 liquid barrels or 14,653 cubic inches.

Horsepower: The power needed to lift 33,000 pounds a distance of one foot in one minute (about 1 1/2 times the power an average horse can exert). Used for measuring power of steam engines, etc.

Karat (kt): A measure of the purity of gold, indicating how many parts out of 24 are pure. For example: 18 karat gold is 3/4 pure. Sometimes spelled *carat.*

Knot: Not a distance, but the rate of speed of one nautical mile per hour. Used for measuring speed of ships.

League: Rather indefinite and varying measure, but usually estimated at 3 miles in English-speaking countries.

Light-Year: 5,880,000,000,000 miles, the distance light travels in a vacuum in a year at the rate of 186,281.7 miles (299,792 kilometers) per second. (If an astronomical unit were represented by one inch, a light-year would be represented by about one mile.) Used for measurements in interstellar space.

Magnum: Two-quart bottle. Used for measuring wine, etc.

Ohm: Unit of electrical resistance. A circuit in which a potential difference of one volt produces a current of one ampere has a resistance of one ohm.

Parsec: Approximately 3.26 light-years of 19.2 million miles. Term is combination of first syllables of *par*allax and *sec*ond, and distance is that of imaginary star when lines drawn from it to both earth and sun form a maximum angle or parallax of one second (1/3600 degree). Used for measuring interstellar distances.

Pi (π): 3.14159265+. The ratio of the circumference of a circle to its diameter. For practical purposes, the value is used to four decimal places: 3.1416.

Pica: 1/6 inch or 12 points. Used in printing for measuring column width, etc.

Pipe: 2 hogsheads. Used for measuring wine and other liquids.

Point: .013837 (approximately 1/72) inch or 1/12 pica. Used in printing for measuring type size.

Quintal: 100,000 grams or 220.46 pounds avoirdupois.

Quire: Used for measuring paper. Sometimes 24 sheets but more often 25. There are 20 quires to a ream.

Ream: Used for measuring paper. Sometimes 480 sheets, but more often 500 sheets.

Roentgen: International Unit of radiation exposure produced by X-rays.

Score: 20 units.

Sound, Speed of: Usually placed at 1,088 ft per second at 32°F at sea level. It varies at other temperatures and in different media.

Span: 9 inches or 22.86 cm. Derived from the distance between the end of the thumb and the end of the little finger when both are outstretched.

Square: 100 square feet. Used in building.

Stone: Legally 14 pounds avoirdupois in Great Britain.

Therm: 100,000 Btu's.

Township: U.S. land measurement of almost 36 square miles. The south border is 6 miles long. The east and west borders, also 6 miles long, follow the meridians, making the north border slightly less than 6 miles long. Used in surveying.

Tun: 252 gallons, but often larger. Used for measuring wine and other liquids.

Watt: Unit of power. The power used by a current of one ampere across a potential difference of one volt equals one watt.

Kelvin Scale

Absolute zero, –273.16° on the Celsius (Centigrade) scale, is 0° Kelvin. Thus, degrees Kelvin are equivalent to degrees Celsuis plus 273.16. The freezing point of water, 0°C. and 32°F., is 273.16°K. The conversion formula is K° = C° + 273.16.

Conversion of Miles to Kilometers and Kilometers to Miles

Miles	Kilometers	Miles	Kilometers	Miles	Kilometers	Kilometers	Miles	Kilometers	Miles	Kilometers	Miles
1	1.6	8	12.8	60	96.5	1	0.6	8	4.9	60	37.2
2	3.2	9	14.4	70	112.6	2	1.2	9	5.5	70	43.4
3	4.8	10	16.0	80	128.7	3	1.8	10	6.2	80	49.7
4	6.4	20	32.1	90	144.8	4	2.4	20	12.4	90	55.9
5	8.0	30	48.2	100	160.9	5	3.1	30	18.6	100	62.1
6	9.6	40	64.3	1,000	1609	6	3.7	40	24.8	1,000	621
7	11.2	50	80.4			7	4.3	50	31.0		

Bolts and Screws: Conversion from Fractions of an Inch to Millimeters

Inch	mm	Inch	mm	Inch	mm	Inch	mm
1/64	0.40	17/64	6.75	33/64	13.10	49/64	19.45
1/32	0.79	9/32	7.14	17/32	13.50	25/32	19.84
3/64	1.19	19/64	7.54	35/64	13.90	51/64	20.24
1/16	1.59	5/16	7.94	9/16	14.29	13/16	20.64
5/64	1.98	21/64	8.33	37/64	14.69	53/64	21.03
3/32	2.38	11/32	8.73	19/32	15.08	27/32	21.43
7/64	2.78	23/64	9.13	39/64	15.48	55/64	21.83
1/8	3.18	3/8	9.53	5/8	15.88	7/8	22.23
9/64	3.57	25/64	9.92	41/64	16.27	57/64	22.62
5/32	3.97	13/32	10.32	21/32	16.67	29/32	23.02
11/64	4.37	27/64	10.72	43/64	17.06	59/64	23.42
3/16	4.76	7/16	11.11	11/64	17.46	15/16	23.81
13/64	5.16	29/64	11.51	45/64	17.86	61/64	24.21
7/32	5.56	15/32	11.91	23/32	18.26	31/32	24.61
15/64	5.95	31/64	12.30	47/64	18.65	63/64	25.00
1/4	6.35	1/2	12.70	3/4	19.05	1	25.40

U.S.—Metric Cooking Conversions

U.S. customary system				Metric			
Capacity		Weight		Capacity		Weight	
1/5 teaspoon	1 milliliter	1 fluid oz	30 milliliters	1 milliliter	1/5 teaspoon	1 gram	.035 ounce
1 teaspoon	5 ml		28 grams	5 ml	1 teaspoon	100 grams	3.5 ounces
1 tablespoon	15 ml	1 pound	454 grams	15 ml	1 tablespoon	500 grams	1.10 pounds
1/5 cup	50 ml			34 ml	1 fluid oz	1 kilogram	2.205 pounds
1 cup	240 ml						
2 cups (1 pint)	470 ml			100 ml	3.4 fluid oz		35 oz
4 cups (1 quart)	.95 liter			240 ml	1 cup		
4 quarts (1 gal.)	3.8 liters			1 liter	34 fluid oz		
					4.2 cups		
					2.1 pints		
					1.06 quarts		
					0.26 gallon		

Cooking Measurement Equivalents

16 tablespoons =	1 cup
12 tablespoons =	3/4 cup
10 tablespoons + 2 teaspoons =	2/3 cup
8 tablespoons =	1/2 cup
6 tablespoons =	3/8 cup
5 tablespoons + 1 teaspoon =	1/3 cup
4 tablespoons =	1/4 cup
2 tablespoons =	1/8 cup
2 tablespoons + 2 teaspoons =	1/6 cup
1 tablespoon =	1/16 cup
2 cups =	1 pint
2 pints =	1 quart
3 teaspoons =	1 tablespoon
48 teaspoons =	1 cup

Prefixes and Multiples

Prefix	Suffix	Equivalent	Multiple/ submultiple
atto	a	quintillionth part	10^{-18}
femto	f	quadrillionth part	10^{-15}
pico	p	trillionth part	10^{-12}
nano	n	billionth part	10^{-9}
micro	µ	millionth part	10^{-6}
milli	m	thousandth part	10^{-3}
centi	c	hundredth part	10^{-2}
deci	d	tenth part	10^{-1}
deka	da	tenfold	10
hecto	h	hundredfold	10^{2}
kilo	k	thousandfold	10^{3}
mega	M	millionfold	10^{6}
giga	G	billionfold	10^{9}
tera	T	trillionfold	10^{12}

Common Formulas

Circumference

Circle: $C = \pi d$, in which π is 3.1416 and *d* the diameter.

Area

Triangle: $A = \frac{ab}{2}$, in which *a* is the base and *b* the height.

Square: $A = a^2$, in which *a* is one of the sides.

Rectangle: $A = ab$, in which *a* is the base and *b* the height.

Trapezoid: $A = \frac{h(a+b)}{2}$, in which *h* is the height, *a* the longer parallel side, and *b* the shorter.

Regular pentagon: $A = 1.720a^2$, in which *a* is one of the sides.

Regular hexagon: $A = 2.598a^2$, in which *a* is one of the sides.

Regular octagon: $A = 4.828a^2$, in which *a* is one of the sides.

Circle: $A = \pi r^2$, in which π is 3.1416 and *r* the radius.

Volume

Cube: $V = a^3$, in which *a* is one of the edges.

Rectangular prism: $V = abc$, in which *a* is the length, *b* is the width, and *c* the depth.

Pyramid: $V = \frac{Ah}{3}$, in which *A* is the area of the base and *h* the height.

Cylinder: $V = \pi r^2 h$, in which π is 3.1416, *r* the radius of the base, and *h* the height.

Cone: $V = \frac{\pi r^2 h}{3}$, in which π is 3.1416, *r* the radius of the base, and *h* the height.

Sphere: $V = \frac{4 \pi r^3}{3}$, in which π is 3.1416 and *r* the radius.

Miscellaneous

Distance in feet traveled by falling body: $d = 16t^2$, in which *t* is the time in seconds.

Speed in sound in feet per second through any given temperature of air:

$$V = \frac{1087\sqrt{273+t}}{16.52}$$

in which *t* is the temperature Centigrade.

Cost in cents of operration of electrical device: $C = \frac{Wtc}{1000}$, in which *W* is the number of watts, *t* the time in hours, and *c* the cost in cents per hilo-watt-hour.

Conversion of matter into energy (Einstein's Theorem): $E = mc^2$, in which *E* is the energy in ergs, *m* the mass of the matter in grams, and *c* the speed of light in centimeters per second ($c^2 = 3 \times 10^{20}$).

Decimal Equivalents of Common Fractions

1/2	.5000	1/10	.1000	2/7	.2857	3/11	.2727	5/9	.5556	7/11	.6364
1/3	.3333	1/11	.0909	2/9	.2222	4/5	.8000	5/11	.4545	7/12	.5833
1/4	.2500	1/12	.0833	2/11	.1818	4/7	.5714	5/12	.4167	8/9	.8889
1/5	.2000	1/16	.0625	3/4	.7500	4/9	.4444	6/7	.8571	8/11	.7273
1/6	.1667	1/32	.0313	3/5	.6000	4/11	.3636	6/11	.5455	9/10	.9000
1/7	.1429	1/64	.0156	3/7	.4286	5/6	.8333	7/8	.8750	9/11	.8182
1/8	.1250	2/3	.6667	3/8	.3750	5/7	.7143	7/9	.7778	10/11	.9091
1/9	.1111	2/5	.4000	3/10	.3000	5/8	.6250	7/10	.7000	11/12	.9167

Conversion Factors

To change	To	Multiply by
acres	hectares	.4047
acres	square feet	43,560
acres	square miles	.001562
atmospheres	cms. of mercury	76
BTU	horsepower-hour	.0003931
BTU	kilowatt-hour	.0002928
BTU/hour	watts	.2931
bushels	cubic inches	2150.4
bushels (U.S.)	hectoliters	.3524
centimeters	inches	.3937
centimeters	feet	.03281
circumference	radians	6.283
cubic feet	cubic meters	.0283
cubic meters	cubic feet	35.3145
cubic meters	cubic yards	1.3079
cubic yards	cubic meters	.7646
degrees	radians	.01745
dynes	grams	.00102
fathoms	feet	6.0
feet	meters	.3048
feet	miles (nautical)	.0001645
feet	miles (statute)	.0001894
feet/second	miles/hour	.6818
furlongs	feet	660.0
furlongs	miles	.125
gallons (U.S.)	liters	3.7853
grains	grams	.0648
grams	grains	15.4324
grams	ounces avdp	.0353
grams	pounds	.002205
hectares	acres	2.4710
hectoliters	bushels (U.S.)	2.8378
horsepower	watts	745.7
hours	days	.04167
inches	millimeters	25.4000
inches	centimeters	2.5400
kilograms	pounds avdp or t	2.2046
kilometers	miles	.6214
kilowatts	horsepower	1.341
knots	nautical miles/hour	1.0
knots	statute miles/hour	1.151
liters	gallons (U.S.)	.2642
liters	pecks	.1135
liters	pints (dry)	1.8162
liters	pints (liquid)	2.1134
liters	quarts (dry)	.9081
liters	quarts (liquid)	1.0567
meters	feet	3.2808
meters	miles	.0006214
meters	yards	1.0936
metric tons	tons (long)	.9842
metric tons	tons (short)	1.1023
miles	kilometers	1.6093
miles	feet	5280
miles (nautical)	miles (statute)	1.1516
miles (statute)	miles (nautical)	.8684
miles/hour	feet/minute	88
millimeters	inches	.0394
ounces avdp.	grams	28.3495
ounces	pounds	.0625
ounces (troy)	ounces (avdp)	1.09714
pecks	liters	8.8096
pints (dry)	liters	.5506
pints (liquid)	liters	.4732
pounds ap or t	kilograms	.3782
pounds avdp	kilograms	.4536
pounds	ounces	16
quarts (dry)	liters	1.1012
quarts (liquid)	liters	.9463
radians	degrees	57.30
rods	meters	5.029
rods	feet	16.5
square feet	square meters	.0929
square kilometers	square miles	.3861
square meters	square feet	10.7639
square meters	square yards	1.1960
square miles	square kilometers	2.5900
square yards	square meters	.8361
tons (long)	metric tons	1.016
tons (short)	metric tons	.9072
tons (long)	pounds	2240
tons (short)	pounds	2000
watts	Btu/hour	3.4129
watts	horsepower	.001341
yards	meters	.9144
yards	miles	.0005682

Fahrenheit and Celsius (Centigrade) Scales

Zero on the Fahrenheit scale represents the temperature produced by the mixing of equal weights of snow and common salt.

	F	C
Boiling point of water	212°	100°
Freezing point of water	32°	0°
Absolute zero	–459.6°	–273.1°

Absolute zero is theoretically the lowest possible temperature, the point at which all molecular motion would cease.

To convert Fahrenheit to Celsius (Centigrade), subtract 32 and multiply by 5/9.

To convert Celsius (Centigrade) to Fahrenheit, multiply by 9/5 and add 32.

°Centigrade	°Fahrenheit	°Centigrade	°Fahrenheit
–273.1	–459.6	30	86
–250	–418	35	95
–200	–328	40	104
–150	–238	45	113
–100	–148	50	122
–50	–58	55	131
–40	–40	60	140
–30	–22	65	149
–20	–4	70	158
–10	14	75	167
0	32	80	176
5	41	85	185
10	50	90	194
15	59	95	203
20	68	100	212
25	77		

Roman Numerals

Roman numerals are expressed by letters of the alphabet and are rarely used today except for formality or variety.

There are three basic principles for reading Roman numerals:

1. A letter repeated once or twice repeats its value that many times (XXX = 30, CC = 200, etc.).

2. One or more letters placed after another letter of greater value increases the greater value by the amount of the smaller. (VI = 6, LXX = 70, MCC = 1200, etc.).

3. A letter placed before another letter of greater value decreases the greater value by the amount of the smaller. (IV = 4, XC = 90, CM = 900, etc.).

Letter	Value	Letter	Value	Letter	Value	Letter	Value	Letter	Value
I	1	VII	7	XXX	30	LXXX	80	$\overline{V}$	5,000
II	2	VIII	8	XL	40	XC	90	$\overline{X}$	10,000
III	3	IX	9	L	50	C	100	$\overline{L}$	50,000
IV	4	X	10	LX	60	D	500	$\overline{C}$	100,000
V	5	XX	20	LXX	70	M	1,000	$\overline{D}$	500,000
VI	6							$\overline{M}$	1,000,000

Mean and Median

The mean, also called the average, of a series of quantities is obtained by finding the sum of the quantities and dividing it by the number of quantities. In the series 1, 3, 5, 18, 19, 20, 25, the mean or average is 13—i.e., 91 divided by 7.

The median of a series is that point which so divides it that half the quantities are on one side, half on the other. In the above series, the median is 18.

The median often better expresses the common-run, since it is not, as is the mean, affected by an excessively high or low figure. In the series 1, 3, 4, 7, 55, the median of 4 is a truer expression of the common-run than is the mean of 14.

Prime Numbers Between 1 and 1,000

	2	3	5	7	11	13	17	19	23
29	31	37	41	43	47	53	59	61	67
71	73	79	83	89	97	101	103	107	109
113	127	131	137	139	149	151	157	163	167
173	179	181	191	193	197	199	211	223	227
229	233	239	241	251	257	263	269	271	277
281	283	293	307	311	313	317	331	337	347
349	353	359	367	373	379	383	389	397	401
409	419	421	431	433	439	443	449	457	461
463	467	479	487	491	499	503	509	521	523
541	547	557	563	569	571	577	587	593	599
601	607	613	617	619	631	641	643	647	653
659	661	673	677	683	691	701	709	719	727
733	739	743	751	757	761	769	773	787	797
809	811	821	823	827	829	839	853	857	859
863	877	881	883	887	907	911	919	929	937
941	947	953	967	971	977	983	991	997	(1009)

Definitions of Gold Terminology

The term "fineness" defines a gold content in parts per thousand. For example, a gold nugget containing 885 parts of pure gold, 100 parts of silver, and 15 parts of copper would be considered 885-fine.

The word "karat" indicates the proportion of solid gold in an alloy based on a total of 24 parts. Thus, 14-karat (14K) gold indicates a composition of 14 parts of gold and 10 parts of other metals.

The term "gold-filled" is used to describe articles of jewelry made of base metal which are covered on one or more surfaces with a layer of gold alloy. No article having a gold alloy portion of less than one twentieth by weight may be marked "gold-filled." Articles may be marked "rolled gold plate" provided the proportional fraction and fineness designations are also shown.

Electroplated jewelry items carrying at least 7 millionths of an inch of gold on significant surfaces may be labeled "electroplate." Plate thicknesses less than this may be marked "gold-flashed" or "gold-washed."

Portraits and Designs of U.S. Paper Currency[1]

Currency	Portrait	Design on back
$1	Washington	ONE between obverse and reverse of Great Seal of U.S.
$2[2]	Jefferson	Monticello
$2[3]	Jefferson	"The Signing of the Declaration of Independence"
$5	Lincoln	Lincoln Memorial
$10	Hamilton	U.S. Treasury Building
$20	Jackson	White House

Currency	Portrait	Design on back
$50	Grant	U.S. Capitol
$100	Franklin	Independence Hall
$500	McKinley	Ornate FIVE HUNDRED
$1,000	Cleveland	Ornate ONE THOUSAND
$5,000	Madison	Ornate FIVE THOUSAND
$10,000	Chase	Ornate TEN THOUSAND
$100,000[4]	Wilson	Ornate ONE HUNDRED THOUSAND

1. Denominations of $500 and higher were discontinued in 1969. 2. Discontinued in 1966. 3. New issue, April 13, 1976. 4. For use only in transactions between Federal Reserve System and Treasury Department.

The articles and opinions in this section are for general information only and are not intended to provide specific advice or recommendations for any individual.

Basic Points About Bond Mutual Funds

By The Investment Company Institute

What are bond mutual funds? Bond mutual funds are pools of bonds managed by professionals and owned by their shareholders. The investment manager of a bond fund pools the money received from the sale of new shares and purchases fixed-income securities (debt obligations that pay a stated periodic rate of interest), collects the interest payments earned by these bonds, and pays out the earnings to each shareholder in the form of dividends.

What is a bond? A bond is like an IOU. The holder of a bond (the investor) lends money to the issuer (a corporation or a government entity) in return for the promise of a periodic payment of interest and the return of the principal on a specified date. For instance, state and local governments may issue bonds to finance the construction of highways or other parts of the community infrastructure. Treasury bonds issued by the U.S. government are considered to be the safest. Corporate bonds range from very safe to extremely chancy, depending on the financial strength and business prospects of the company.

Is there much variety among the bond mutual funds? Currently there are more than 1,500 bond funds, with considerable differences among them. Some stick to taxable U.S. government or corporate bonds, and others invest in tax-free municipal bonds. Funds vary in the average maturity of their holdings and the degree of credit risk they accept. Each fund's investment profile—its objective, related risks, expenses, fees and services—is spelled out in its prospectus.

What risks are associated with bonds and bond funds? All bonds are subject to interest rate, or market, risk. Daily changes in rates cause the price of bonds and bond funds (the investor's principal) to rise or fall in value. Bonds fluctuate in price daily because general interest rates do. When interest rates rise, bond prices decline. When interest rate decline, bond prices rise. Thus, an investor's principal investment as well as the fund's total return can rise or fall. In general, the shorter the maturity of a bond or the average weighted maturity of a fund's portfolio, the smaller is the degree of risk that its shareholders are exposed to in the per-share price. Some debt securities adjust their interest payments periodically to conform to market interest rates, thus reducing this type of risk. The so-called adjustable rate funds invest in securities having these features.

Are there other risks? Yes. Investors in bonds and bond funds are also subject to credit risk—the possibility that the issuer of a debt obligation will not be able to pay interest or repay the principal when due. Only the U.S. Treasury's bonds, notes and bills are considered free of credit risk. Investors in foreign bonds or in mutual funds that invest in foreign bonds must contend with currency risk—the risk that changes in various foreign currency values will affect the value of foreign assets and of income originating abroad, which could produce either a loss or a gain when "translated" into dollars. Also, investors in certain mortgage market funds (such as Ginnie Mae funds) face the risk that borrowers, in an environment of falling interest rates, will repay home loans ahead of schedule. That would reduce returns to investors in those funds, since the returned principal could only be reinvested at the lower rates then prevailing in the market.

Why do bond prices fall when interest rates climb and vice versa? Between the time a bond is issued and the time it reaches maturity, bond prices will move up or down in response to changing interest rates. For example, a newly issued 10-year bond with a 7 percent coupon (interest) rate and a $1,000 face, or par, value pays $70 a year until the bond matures in 10 years, when the $1,000 par value is due and must be repaid. If interest rates rise fo 8 percent, for instance, the existing bond's coupon rate of 7 percent would make the bond less desirable to investors. Therefore, market forces put downward pressure on the bond's current value until its price falls enough for investors to be attracted by its yield. On the other hand, interest rates could fall. If market interest rates fell from 7 percent to 6 percent, the existing bond's coupon rate would make the bond more desirable, and its current value would increase.

Another factor influencing a bond's price volatility is the amount of time remaining before its principal is due. The market value is much more stable for a bond nearing its repayment date.

Why does the per-share value of a bond fund fluctuate? The per-share value of a bond fund is subject to fluctuation because the individual bonds and other securities held by the fund fluctuate in price. Mutual funds, including bond funds, are priced daily, to reflect the true market value of the holdings in their portfolios.

How do bond funds work? When investors buy shares of a bond fund, the fund manager uses the money to purchase debt obligations. The mix depends, among other things, on the fund's investment objective, such market conditions as current supply and demand, and the market's assessment about the future stability of prices and interest rates. A bond fund's payments to its shareholders, called the fund's "distribution rate" may include repayment of principal by the borrowers that issued the securities, capital gains from trading the securities in the portfolio, and interest earned on the securities in the portfolio.

What is total return? There are several components of total return on a bond fund. The first is income earned on the fund's investments. This income may come from interest and/or capital gains. Another major component of a fund's total return is any change in the per-share price of the fund, that is, its net asset value. The total return is the amount of income and capital gains distributed to shareholders, plus or minus any increase or decrease in the fund's net asset value.

What advantages are there buying a bond mutual fund rather than individual bonds? An investor receives immediate diversification in a bond fund. When an investor buys an individual bond, he or she is totally exposed to both credit risk and interest rate risk. By investing in a bond fund, however, an investor buys a diversified portfolio of bonds. Because it is unlikely that all the bonds in a fund's portfolio will default, the investor's exposure to credit risk is reduced. And because a fund may hold bonds with a variety of maturities, the exposure to market risk may be somewhat reduced.

Another important advantage of bond funds is their modest initial investment requirement. An investor with an initial investment of $1,000 or $2,000, for example, receives a degree of diversification that would otherwise require many thousands of dollars. In addition, the funds provide professional investment management to evaluate changes in economic conditions and make strategic and tactical decisions regarding portfolio securities. Another benefit is liquidity, which means an investor can redeem shares at any time. Most funds also provide for automatic reinvestment of dividends, which gives investors the benefit of compounded growth.

There are some important differences between owning shares of an actively managed portfolio of bonds and direct ownership of individual bonds. For example, bond fund investors cannot lock in yields, because yields rise or fall in response to market conditions. Also, funds do not promise that investors will get back their principal, or original, amount invested. The contents of a bond fund's portfolio are constantly changing, and yields and per-share prices may change every day.

Are bond mutual funds insured by the government? Bond funds do not have federal deposit insurance coverage. Only federally insured depository institutions, such as banks, credit unions and savings and loans offer federal deposit insurance. Although mutual funds are not federally insured, they are strictly regulated by the Securities and Exchange Commission under federal securities laws, in order to provide safeguards. For instance, federal regulations generally require that the assets of a fund be held by a separate custodian for safekeeping, or by the fund under strict conditions. In addition, all fund employees who handle investors' money must be bonded. Also, some bond funds invest only in securities backed by a government agency or insured by a commercial insurance company, thereby reducing the credit risk of owning those bonds.

What is the attraction of bond funds? Bond funds aim to provide a higher total return to investors than they would get from alternative investments that carry less risk, such as money market mutual funds or other savings vehicles. As interest rates began declining in 1991, large numbers of investors purchased shares in long-term bond funds in order to obtain relatively higher yields. Doing so, these investors accepted greater risk. Where investments are concerned, risk and reward go hand in hand. Usually, higher risk is required in order to get higher rewards.

Why not avoid risk entirely? Those who want to avoid all investment risks should probably stay in certificates or deposits or U.S. savings bonds. However, even these instruments do not avoid what some call "inflation risk." Suppose inflation were just 3 percent a year. Even if a risk-averse person stashed $1,000 in cash in a secret hiding place for 10 years, inflation would have whittled $256 from the true value of the stash by the time it is retrieved.

Basic Facts on Money Market Mutual Funds

By The Investment Company Institute

What money market funds are—Money market mutual fund are professionally managed pools of short-term securities whose shares are offered to the public. These funds are managed with the objective of maintaining a stable principal, or net asset value, usually $1 per share, while providing competitive money market yields. The funds are open-end investment companies, commonly known as mutual funds. As such, they stand ready to redeem, or buy back, investors' shares at any time. Money market mutual funds were introduced in 1972, and now have over $500 billion in assets, representing over half the assets of all mutual funds. It is important to remember that money market funds are pools of securities, and are structured and regulated differently than money market deposit accounts offered by banks.

How money market funds work—When investors buy shares of a money market fund, the fund's manager uses the money to purchase short-term debt instruments, known as money market securities. A money market instrument or security is a short-term obligation issued by any of a variety of borrowers, ranging from the U.S. Treasury to banks and individual companies. Included are federal government securities, such as Treasury bills, and instruments issued by U.S. Government agencies, such as obligations of the Federal National Mortgage Association. Other examples include short-term loans to corporations, known as commercial paper, and negotiable certificates of deposit at banks.

Not all money market funds are the same—Depending on the objective of the particular fund as spelled out in its prospectus, the manager may buy money market instruments, such as short-term paper issued by the U.S. Treasury or other federal agencies, banks and corporations, or, in the case of tax-exempt funds, state and local governments. (Some funds in the tax-exempt category buy only the short-term paper issued by authorities in a single state.) Some funds limit their holdings to U.S. Treasury bills. Others hold mixtures of several types of money-market instruments, while some concentrate on corporations' commercial paper.

Risk and safety—Although money market funds are not federally insured, they are heavily regulated by the U.S. Securities and Exchange Commission and state regulators. Money market funds are considered among the safest of investments because the securities they hold are of high quality and are short-term, thus reducing investors' exposure to the risk of changing interest rates or possible deterioration of the financial strength of the issuers or money market securities. In addition, most funds diversify their holdings to limit their exposure to risk of default by a single borrower. As is the case with all mutual funds, a money market fund's investments are held by a custodian (an organization separate from the people doing the investing, usually a bank), and all employees who work with investors' money are bonded. Despite these various factors that reduce the risk of money market funds, they are not insured or guaranteed, and therefore are not entirely risk-free.

Limited maturity—Short-term money market instruments are considered safer than longer-term debt securities because there is less time for borrowers' situations to change before the time comes for repayment or for a dramatic change in interest rates, which could affect the market value of money market fund securities. Generally, money market funds may purchase only securities with maturities of one year or less. Under U.S. Securities and Exchange Commission rules, most fund portfolios may not have an average maturity of more than 90 days. In fact, most funds' actual maturity is far shorter. For taxable funds, recently it was 54 days on average, on an industrywide basis. Tax-exempt funds had an average maturity of 45 days.

Diversification—Most money market mutual funds have policies which require them to maintain a diversified portfolio. This limits exposure to the risk that an issuer of short-term paper might default. Under new SEC rules no more than 5 percent of a fund's assets may be invested in the securities of a single borrower, except the federal government.

Quality—Under the new SEC rules money market fund managers may purchase commercial paper and other securities that have been rated in the top category of creditworthiness by nationally recognized securities rating organizations (such as those rated A-1 by Standard & Poor's and P-1 by Moody's Investors Service), except for 5 percent of the portfolio, which may be in second tier paper, such as A-2 or P-2. If unrated, the paper must be determined to be of similar high quality. In addition, fund managers must make their own evaluations to determine that each security purchased by the fund presents a minimal credit risk.

Effect of a default—Each fund's yield and share value is calculated on the basis that each of its holdings will pay the promised interest rate and be redeemed at face value at maturity. If a commercial paper issuer defaults, this assumption is obviously affected. Depending upon the size of the fund's holding of that issuer's obligations, the fund's yield, its net asset value or both may change. If the fund's holding is relatively small, fund management may be able to offset the loss to the fund by temporarily reducing the fund's dividends and, therefore, its yield. If the position is more significant, the fund may have to reduce share value. In such a case, the fund's share value would probably fall from $1 per share to 99 or 98 cents. The shareholder's annual return would remain positive, although possibly reduced from perhaps 4 or 5 percent to 3 percent, as the other securities in the portfolio would continue to have earnings, which would be passed on to shareholders. The amount of decline in assets and reduction in return would depend on the individual portfolio's exposure to the defaulted paper. A default by one issuer would not affect any of the fund's other holdings. The fund's management could then decide to leave its share value at the lower level and could continue to pay a competitive yield or the dividend could be reduced allowing undistributed income retained by the fund to offset the capital loss. This strategy would gradually increase the fund's net asset value. Once it returned to the $1 level, the normal dividend level would be resumed.

Risks vary—To a great extent, risk is determined by the investment policy of the fund. It is up to investors to decide whether a particular fund is suitable with respect to risk. Each fund's prospectus tells investors what degree of relative risk the specific money market has been authorized to take. However, the securities which the funds purchase are all required to be of high quality.

Yield—Money market mutual funds are required by law to distribute their net earnings to investors, and that amount determines the yield. The investment return on money market mutual funds is uniformly calculated, as prescribed by the SEC, so investors can compare yields among funds.

Liquidity—Like any other type of mutual fund, an investment in a money market fund is liquid (easily converted into cash). By law, money market funds must stand ready to redeem (buy back) investors' shares on any business day. In addition, most money market funds provide for redemptions through check-writing privileges. Most funds specify a minimum amount for checks—typically, $250, or $500.

Protection of shareholders—In addition to quality and limited maturity, federal securities laws provide protection against fraud, misrepresentation and unsound practices. Some of the other areas covered by SEC regulations include fund registration, organization, operation, recordkeeping, pricing, sale and redemption of shares.

Advantages—In return for assuming a degree of risk beyond that of federally insured savings, investors usually receive attractive yields at low cost. They also have convenient access to their money through check writing or wire transfer or both. Moreover, many money market mutual funds are part of fund families, many of which allow investors to easily exchange investments among funds within the family, and in some cases to take advantage of dollar-cost-averaging programs.

Initial investment—Before money market funds were introduced in the 1970s, institutional investors and wealthy individuals were the main buyers of money market securities. The advent of money market funds provided a means for small investors to participate in the risks and rewards of the nation's money markets with a smaller initial investment than would be required for investing directly in those money markets. Whereas the minimum of $10,000 to $1 million required for direct investment in the money markets is prohibitive for most investors, most money market mutual funds require a much smaller initial investment, often as little as $250 to $1,000.

General information—Contact fund sponsors for an application and prospectus or request information through a broker. Advertisements of money market mutual funds appear in numerous periodicals. Individuals can write for a free copy of the pamphlet "Money Market Mutual Funds: A Part of Every Financial Plan" which is published by the Investment Company Institute, 1600 M Street N.W., Washington, D.C. 20036. □

Free Mutual Fund Investment Information

Source: The Investment Company Institute.

The Investment Company Institute, the national association of the U.S. mutual fund industry, publishes a variety of consumer educational materials on the basics of mutual fund investing. These materials are provided free of charge to individuals who write for them. Multiple copies also are provided free to schools, clubs, and public libraries.

What Is A Mutual Fund?—Concise, illustrated leaflet presents key features of a mutual fund investment. Includes table showing how to read mutual fund share quotes and chart illustrating the tradeoff between risk and reward.

Eight Basics of Bond Fund Investing—20-page booklet explains how bond mutual funds work, differences between bonds and bond funds, how shares are priced, risk/reward tradeoff, various types of risk, and government protections for investors.

Money Market Mutual Funds—Plain-English explanation of money market mutual funds—the investment vehicle that changed the way Americans handle their money. Examines the ways money market funds provide safety, liquidity and yield.

Reading the Mutual Fund Prospectus—30-page investor's guide that helps investors decipher "legalese" of mutual fund prospectuses. Illustrated text provides a guided tour of the most important items investors are likely to find in prospectuses.

Planning for College?—Brochure offers practical insights for those preparing to meet the rising costs of college education, outlines the major advantages of using mutual funds to meet those costs. Includes information on the latest tax rules for minors.

Discipline—Colorful leaflet explains dollar-cost averaging, the strategy of buying more shares when the price is low and fewer shares when the price is high. Shows how dollar-cost averaging works when the market fluctuates, declines or rises.

Investing: Start Now!—Crisp explanation of how money and time can be made to work together in systematic investment programs. Illustrates the sizeable advantage of starting early on a long-term investment program.

To receive a free copy of any of these publications, write: Consumer Brochures, Investment Company Institute, P.O. Box 66140, Washington, D.C. 20035-6140. No one who requests these free materials will be placed on any mailing lists.

Housing Affordability for the United States, 1970–1992

Year	Median priced single-family home	Monthly mortgage rate[1]	Monthly principal and interest payment	Payment as % income	Median family income	Qualifying income[2]	Affordability Index: Composite	Affordability Index: Fixed	Affordability Index: Adjustable rate mortgage
1970	$23,000	8.35%	$140	17.0%	$ 9,867	$ 6,697	147.3	147.3	147.3
1975	35,300	9.21	232	20.2	13,719	11,112	123.5	123.5	123.5
1980	62,200	12.95	549	31.3	21,023	26,328	79.9	79.9	79.9
1985	75,500	11.74	609	26.2	27,735	29,243	94.8	89.6	100.6
1989	93,100	10.11	660	23.6	33,600	31,662	106.1	101.8	112.3
1990	95,500	10.04	673	22.8	35,353	32,286	109.5	106.5	118.3
1991	100,300	9.30	663	22.1	35,939	31,825	112.9	109.9	124.2
1992	103,700	8.11	615	20.0	36,837	29,523	124.8	120.2	145.1

1. Effective rate on loans closed on existing homes—Federal Housing Finance Board. 2. Based on current lending requirements of the Federal National Mortgage Association using a 20 percent down payment. *Source:* National Association of Realtors. © 1993 National Association of Realtors.

Housing Expense Guidelines

How much should families spend for housing? The banking and housing industries provide individuals and families with guidelines for determining how much they can afford for housing. Banks have traditionally suggested that homeowners borrow no more than 2-1/2 times the family income for a home mortgage. For example, a family with a total annual before-tax income of $50,000 should plan to allocate no more than $125,000 toward a home mortgage. Renters should typically plan to spend about one week's take-home pay each month for rent.

The National Association of Realtors publishes housing affordability indexes showing the median income American families need to qualify for a mortgage on a median-priced existing single-family home or a first-time buyer starter home. (*See* above table.)

The Federal National Mortgage Association (FNMA) states that monthly housing payments (principal and interest, taxes, insurance, and associated costs) for a conventional loan cannot exceed 28% of gross monthly family income, and total family debt cannot exceed 36% of that amount. □

How to Measure the Shrinking Value of the Dollar

Source: Martin Lefkowitz, economist, U.S. Chamber of Commerce.

How to use this table. The value of a dollar is given for any year relative to the 1993 dollar. For example: What weekly salary would you need to earn in 1993 to equal the purchasing power of a weekly salary of $100 in 1960? Take the 1960 multiplier, 4.92, times $100 and you would need to earn $492 a week in 1993 to achieve the same salary.

Again, what income would you need in 1993 to equal the purchasing power of $1000 in 1983? The 1983 multiplier, 1.46, time $1000, equals $1,460 needed to stay even with inflation during those past ten years.

Year	Value of dollar in 1993 dollars	Year	Value of dollar in 1993 dollars	Year	Value of dollar in 1993 dollars
1946	7.46	1962	4.82	1978	2.23
1947	6.25	1963	4.76	1979	2.00
1948	6.04	1964	4.69	1980	1.77
1949	6.12	1965	4.62	1981	1.60
1950	6.04	1966	4.49	1982	1.51
1951	5.60	1967	4.36	1983	1.46
1952	5.49	1968	4.18	1984	1.40
1953	5.45	1969	3.97	1985	1.35
1954	5.41	1970	3.75	1986	1.33
1955	5.43	1971	3.59	1987	1.28
1956	5.35	1972	3.48	1988	1.23
1957	5.18	1973	3.28	1989	1.17
1958	5.04	1974	2.95	1990	1.11
1959	5.00	1975	2.71	1991	1.07
1960	4.92	1976	2.56	1992	1.03
1961	4.87	1977	2.40	1993	1.00

The Biweekly Mortgage

An Easy, Affordable Way To Own Your Own Home

Source: Fannie Mae.

How It Works

The biweekly mortgage gets its name from the frequency of its payments, which occur every two weeks. Each payment, however, is equivalent to *half* the amount of a comparable monthly payment.

A traditional 30-year fixed-rate mortgage has 12 monthly mortgage payments a year. A biweekly mortgage, on the other hand, with payments due every 2 weeks, requires an average of 26 payments over the course of a year. The 26 biweekly payments are equivalent to 13 monthly payments a year—or, in effect, one "extra monthly payment" as compared with a traditional 30-year fixed-rate mortgage.

The biweekly's "extra monthly payment," along with its more frequent application of payments to the loan balance (or amortizaton), greatly increases the speed with which the loan pays off and results in several significant advantages for you.

The Biweekly's Advantages

Fast Equity Build-up. The extra payments under the biweekly mortgage, along with the more frequent payment schedule, pay the loan off much faster than a traditional 30-year fixed-rate monthly payment. Loans that ordinarily take 30 years to amortize will pay off in as few as 19 to 21 years when paid on a biweekly basis. This means that you can own your home a lot sooner.

Interest Savings. Because of its faster amortization,the biweekly mortgage offers you significant interest savings. With the loan being paid off faster, you pay interest on a smaller balance. And because the loan amortizes so fast, you also pay interest for a shorter period of time—closer to 20 rather than 30 years. Over the life of the loan, this adds up to significant savings for you.

The actual term and interest savings for a biweekly mortgage depend on the interest rate of the loan. The higher the rate of the loan, the shorter the term of the biweekly. Check the chart at the end of this article to see the actual term and interest savings for various mortgage amounts.

Affordable Payments. The biweekly mortgage, for all its benefits, costs about one monthly payment more per year than a fixed-rate mortgage. And because the two to three extra biweekly payments are distributed throughout the year, the extra cost is easier to manage.

This combination of advantages is attracting a great deal of interest to the biweekly mortgage.

Commonly Asked Questions

Why does the biweekly pay off so much faster than a 30-year fixed-rate mortgage?

The biweekly pays off faster than a 30-year fixed-rate mortgage because of:

• the two or three extra biweekly payments each year, and,

• the biweekly, as opposed to monthly, amortization of the loan.

These two factors, over the life of the loan, account for a dramatic reduction in the biweekly's loan term and interest expense.

Is qualifying for a biweekly mortgage any different than for a 30-year fixed-rate mortgage?

Because of the two or three additional biweekly payments each year, the income requirements for the biweekly mortgage are higher than for a comparable 30-year fixed-rate mortgage.

The following table illustrates just how well the biweekly mortgage compares with a 30-year fixed-rate mortgage.

Biweekly Mortgage Comparison

($70,000 Mortgage)

	30-year FRM	Biweekly
Interest rate	10.5%	10.5%
Payment amount	$640	$320[1]
Qualifying income[2]	$27,429	$29,714

1. Biweekly payment equivalent to one-half of fixed-rate monthly payment. 2. Based on 28 percent payment-to-income underwriting ratio (or 1/12 of total annual biweekly payments) cannot exceed 28 percent of your gross monthly income.

Why does a biweekly mortgage with a higher interest rate have a shorter loan term than a biweekly with a lower interest rate?

As the interest rate increases, so does the biweekly payment amount, and a greater portion of the biweekly payment is applied to the principal balance. This results in faster payoff of the mortgage. The chart at the end of this article illustrates the various loan terms (in months) for different interest rates.

How does the biweekly compare with the 15-year fixed-rate mortgage?

The biweekly mortgage and the 15-year mortgage are two alternatives to the traditional 30-year fixed-rate mortgage. Both offer faster equity build-up and reduced interest costs. The biweekly has a longer term than the 15-year fixed-rate mortgage, but the payments are more affordable.

For more information on the 15-year fixed-rate mortgage, refer to Fannie Mae's brochure, "A Mortgage You Can Bank On: How a 15-year mortgage can help you save for the future." To receive your copy, ask your lender or write: Fannie Mae 15-Year Mortgage Consumer Brochure, P.O. Box 2335, Baltimore, Md. 21203.

The table below illustrates the amount of time it takes to pay off a biweekly mortgage and the total amount of interest saved when compared with a 30-year fixed-rate mortgage based on varying mortgage amounts and interest rates.

Are all biweekly mortgage programs alike?

No. You should be aware that some programs call themselves "biweekly" because they draft your account every two weeks, but they apply only one payment per month to your loan's unpaid principal balance. With "true" biweekly mortgages, including those purchased by Fannie Mae, funds are applied directly to your loan's unpaid principal balance as they are drafted from your account.

For more information on how a biweekly mortgage can meet your home financing needs, see your Fannie Mae-approved mortgage lender. □

Fannie Mae

Fannie Mae's position as the nation's largest single investor in conventional home mortgages enables it to offer a broad range of mortgage products to local lenders.

Fannie Mae does not lend money to consumers, but buys mortgages from a national network of 4,000 approved lenders who do originate mortgage loans, including mortgage bankers, savings and loan institutions, and commercial banks.

Biweekly Payment Amount and Total Interest Saved*

	$60,000		$80,000		$100,000		$120,000	
Interest Rate, Term in Months	Biweekly Payment Amount	Total Interest Savings[1]	Biweekly Payment Amount	Total Interest Savings[1]	Biweekly Payment Amount	Total Interest Savings[1]	Biweekly Payment Amount	Total Interest Savings[1]
9.00%[2] 264 mos.[3]	241	36,244	322	48,332	402	60,417	483	72,500
9.50%[2] 258 mos.[3]	252	40,994	336	54,668	420	68,329	505	82,003
10.00%[2] 252 mos.[3]	263	46,088	351	61,450	439	76,806	527	92,180
10.50%[2] 246 mos.[3]	274	51,503	366	68,663	457	85,843	549	103,014
11.00%[2] 240 mos.[3]	286	57,229	381	76,318	476	95,396	571	114,480
11.50%[2] 234 mos.[3]	297	63,264	396	84,353	495	105,442	594	126,550
12.00%[3] 229 mos.[3]	309	69,596	411	92,770	514	115,975	617	139,190
12.50%[2] 223 mos.[3]	320	76,166	427	101,572	534	126,962	640	152,364
13.00%[2] 217 mos.[3]	332	83,016	442	110,688	553	138,360	664	166,033

1. As compared with a 30-year fixed-rate mortgage. 2. Interest rate. 3. Length of loan term (in months). *All figures are approximate.

Mortgage Highlights

Type	Description	Considerations
Fixed rate mortgage	Fixed interest rate, usually long–term; equal mnthly payments of principl and interest until debt is paid in full.	Offers stability and long–term tax advantages. Interest rates may be higher than other types of financing. New fixed rates are rarely assumable.
Fifteen–year mortgage	Fixed interest rate. Requires down payment or monthly payments higher than 30–year loan. Loan is fully repaid over 15–year term.	Frequently offered at slightly reduced interest rate. Offers faster accumulation of equity than traditional fixed rate mortgage but has higher monthly payments. Involves paying less interest but this may result in fewer tax deductions.
Adjustable rate mortgage	Interest rate changes over the life of the loan, resulting in possible changes in your monthly payments, loan term, and/or principal. Some plans have rate or interest caps.	Starting interest rate is slightly below market, but payments can increase sharply and frequently if index increases. Payment caps prevent wide fluctuations in payments but may cause negative amortization. Rate caps limit total amount debt can expand
Renegotiable rate mortgage (roll–over)	Interest rate and monthly payments are constant for several years; changes possible thereafter. Long–term mortgage.	Less frequent changes in interest rate offer some stability.
Balloon mortgage	Monthly payments based on fixed interest rate; usually short–term; payments may cover interest only with principal due in full at term end.	Offers low monthly payments but possibly no equity until loan is fully paid. When due, loan must be paid off or refinanced. Refinancing poses high risk if rates climb.
Graduated payment mortgage	Lower monthly payments rise gradually (usually over 5–10 years), then level off for duration of term. With adjustable interest rate, additional payment changes possible if index changes.	Easier to qualify for. Buyer's income must be able to keep pace with scheduled payment increases. With an adjustable rate, payment increases beyond the graduated payments can result in additional negative amortization..
Shared appreciation mortgage	Below–market interest rate and lower monthly payments, in exchange for a share of profits when property is sold or on a specified date. Many variations.	If home appreciates greatly, total cost of loan jumps. If home fails to appreciate, projected increase in value may still be due, requiring refinancing at possibly higher rates.
Assumable mortgage	Buyer takes over seller's original, below–market rate mortgage.	Lowers monthly payments. May be prohibited if "due on sale" clause is in original mortgage. Not permitted on most new fixed rate mortgages.
Seller take–back	Seller provides all or part of financing with a first or second mortgage.	May offer a below–market interest rate; may have a balloon payment requiring full payment in a few years or refinancing at market rates, which could sharply increase debt.
Wraparound	Seller keeps original low rate mortgage. Buyer makes payments to seller who forwards a portion to the lender holding original mortgage. Offers lower effective interest rate on total transation.	Lender may call in old mortgage and require higher rate. If buyer defaults, seller must take legal action to collect debt.
Growing equity mortgage (rapid payoff mortgage)	Fixed interest rate but monthly payments may vary according to agreed–upon sschedule or index.	Permits rapid payoff of debt because payment increases reduce principal. Buyer's income must be able to keep up with payment increases.
Land contract	Seller retains original mortgage. No transfer of title until loan is fully paid. Equal monthly payments based on below–market interest rate with unpaid principal due at loan end.	May offer no equity until loan is fully paid. Buyer has few protections if conflict arises during loan.
Buy–down	Developer (or other party) provides an interest subsidy which lowers monthly payments during the first few years of the loan. Can have fixed or adjustable interest rate.	Offers a break from higher payments during early years. Enables buyer with lower income to qualify. With adjustable rate mortgage, payments may jump substantially at end of subsidy. Developer may increase selling price.
Rent with option	Renter pays "option fee" for right to purchase property at specified time and agreed–upon price. Rent may or may not be applied to sales price.	Enables renter to buy time to obtain down payment and decide whether to purchase. Locks in price during inflationary times. Failure to take option means loss of option fee and rental payments.
Reverse annuity mortgage (equity conversion)	Borrower owns mortgage–free property and needs income. Lender makes monthly payments to borrower, using property as collateral.	Can provide homeowners with needed cash. At end of term, borrower must have money available to avoid selling property or refinancing.

Source: The Mortgage Money Guide, Federal Trade Commission.

Mortgage Payment Tables

Source: The Mortgage Money Guide, Federal Trade Commission.

8% Annual Percentage Rate

Amount Financed	Monthly payments (principal and interest)* 5 Years	10 Years	15 Years	20 Years	25 Years	30 Years
$ 25,000	506.91	303.32	238.91	209.11	192.95	183.44
30,000	608.29	363.98	286.70	250.93	231.54	220.13
35,000	709.67	424.65	334.48	292.75	270.14	256.82
40,000	811.06	485.31	382.26	334.58	308.73	293.51
45,000	912.44	545.97	430.04	376.40	347.32	330.19
50,000	1013.82	606.64	477.83	418.22	385.91	366.88
60,000	1216.58	727.97	573.39	501.86	463.09	440.26
70,000	1419.35	849.29	668.96	585.51	540.27	513.64
80,000	1622.11	970.62	764.52	669.15	617.45	587.01
90,000	1824.88	1091.95	860.09	752.80	694.63	660.39
100,000	2027.64	1213.28	955.65	836.44	771.82	733.76

9% Annual Percentage Rate

Amount Financed	Monthly payments (principal and interest)* 5 Years	10 Years	15 Years	20 Years	25 Years	30 Years
$ 25,000	518.96	316.69	253.57	224.93	209.80	201.16
30,000	622.75	380.03	304.28	269.92	251.76	241.39
35,000	726.54	443.36	354.99	314.90	293.72	281.62
40,000	830.33	506.70	405.71	359.89	335.68	321.85
45,000	934.13	570.04	456.42	404.88	377.64	362.08
50,000	1037.92	633.38	507.13	449.86	419.60	402.31
60,000	1245.50	760.05	608.56	539.84	503.52	482.77
70,000	1453.08	886.73	709.99	629.81	587.44	563.24
80,000	1660.67	1013.41	811.41	719.78	671.36	643.70
90,000	1868.25	1140.08	912.84	809.75	755.28	724.16
100,000	2075.84	1266.76	1014.27	899.73	839.20	804.62

10% Annual Percentage Rate

Amount Financed	Monthly payments (principal and interest)* 5 Years	10 Years	15 Years	20 Years	25 Years	30 Years
$ 25,000	531.18	330.38	268.65	241.26	227.18	219.39
30,000	637.41	396.45	322.38	289.51	272.61	263.27
35,000	743.65	462.53	376.11	337.76	318.05	307.15
40,000	849.88	528.60	429.84	386.01	363.48	351.03
45,000	956.12	594.68	483.57	434.26	408.92	394.91
50,000	1062.35	660.75	537.30	482.51	454.35	438.79
60,000	1274.82	792.90	644.76	579.01	545.22	526.54
70,000	1487.29	925.06	752.22	675.52	636.09	614.30
80,000	1699.76	1057.20	859.68	772.02	726.96	702.06
90,000	1912.23	1189.36	967.14	868.52	817.83	789.81
100,000	2124.70	1321.51	1074.61	965.02	908.70	877.57

Losing Ground

Source: The Mortgage Money Guide, Federal Trade Commission.

Repaying debt gradually through payments of principal and interest is called amortization. Today's economic climate has given rise to a reverse process called negative amortization.

Negative amortization means that you are losing—not gaining—value, or equity. This is because your monthly payments may be too low to cover the interest rate agreed upon in the mortgage contract. Instead of paying the full interest costs now, you'll pay them later—either in larger payments or in more payments. You will also be paying interest on that interest.

In other words, the lender postpones collection of the money you owe by increasing the size of your debt. In extreme cases, you may even lose the equity

11% Annual Percentage Rate

Amount Financed	Monthly payments (principal and interest)* 5 Years	10 Years	15 Years	20 Years	25 Years	30 Years
$ 25,000	543.56	344.38	284.15	258.05	245.03	238.08
30,000	652.27	413.25	340.98	309.66	294.03	285.70
35,000	760.98	482.13	397.81	361.27	343.04	333.31
40,000	869.70	551.00	454.64	412.88	392.05	380.93
45,000	978.41	619.88	511.47	464.48	441.05	428.55
50,000	1087.12	688.75	568.30	516.09	490.06	476.16
60,000	1304.54	826.50	681.96	619.31	588.07	571.39
70,000	1521.97	964.25	795.62	722.53	686.08	666.63
80,000	1739.39	1102.00	909.28	825.75	784.09	761.86
90,000	1956.81	1239.75	1022.94	928.97	882.10	857.09
100,000	2174.24	1377.50	1136.60	1032.19	980.11	952.32

12% Annual Percentage Rate

Amount Financed	Monthly payments (principal and interest)* 5 Years	10 Years	15 Years	20 Years	25 Years	30 Years
$ 25,000	556.11	358.68	300.05	275.28	263.31	257.16
30,000	667.33	430.42	360.06	330.33	315.97	308.59
35,000	778.56	502.15	420.06	385.39	368.63	360.02
40,000	889.78	573.89	480.07	440.44	421.29	411.45
45,000	1001.00	645.62	540.08	495.49	473.96	462.88
50,000	1112.22	717.36	600.09	550.55	526.62	514.31
60,000	1334.67	860.83	720.11	660.66	631.93	617.17
70,000	1557.11	1004.30	840.12	770.77	737.26	720.03
80,000	1779.56	1147.77	960.14	880.87	842.58	822.90
90,000	2002.00	1291.24	1080.15	990.98	947.90	925.75
100,000	2224.44	1434.71	1200.17	1101.09	1053.23	1028.62

13% Annual Percentage Rate

Amount Financed	Monthly payments (principal and interest)* 5 Years	10 Years	15 Years	20 Years	25 Years	30 Years
$ 25,000	568.83	373.28	316.32	292.90	281.96	276.55
30,000	682.60	447.94	379.58	351.48	338.36	331.86
35,000	796.36	522.59	442.84	410.06	394.75	387.17
40,000	910.13	597.25	506.10	468.64	451.14	442.48
45,000	1023.89	671.90	569.36	527.21	507.53	497.79
50,000	1137.66	746.56	632.63	585.79	563.92	553.10
60,000	1365.19	895.87	759.15	702.95	676.71	663.72
70,000	1592.72	1045.18	885.67	820.11	789.49	774.34
80,000	1820.25	1194.49	1012.20	937.27	902.27	884.96
90,000	2047.78	1343.80	1138.72	1054.42	1015.05	995.58
100,000	2275.31	1493.11	1265.25	1171.58	1127.84	1106.20

you purchased with your down payment, leaving you in worse financial shape a few years after you purchase your home than when you bought it.

Suppose you signed an adjustable rate mortgage for $50,000 in 1978. The index established your initial rate at 9.15%. It nearly doubled to 17.39% by 1981. If your monthly payments had kept pace with the index, they would have risen from $408 to $722. But because of a payment cap they stayed at $408. By 1981 your mortgage had swelled from $50,000 to $58,350, even though you had dutifully paid $408 every month for 48 months. In other words, you paid out $20,000 but you were $8,000 more in debt than you were three years earlier. During the next few years, despite the fact that the index fell gradually, you were still paying off the increases made to your principal from earlier years.

Certain loans, such as graduated payment mortgages, are structured so that you regain the lost ground with payments that eventually rise high enough to fully pay off your debt. And you may also be able to pay off the extra costs if your home is gaining rapidly in value or if your income is rising fast enough to meet the increased obligation. But if it isn't, you may realize a loss if, for example, you sign a below-market adjustable rate mortgage in January and try to sell the home in August when interest rates are higher. You could end up owing more than you'd make on the sale. □

14% Annual Percentage Rate

Amount Financed	Monthly payments (principal and interest)* 5 Years	10 Years	15 Years	20 Years	25 Years	30 Years
$ 25,000	581.71	388.17	332.94	310.89	300.95	296.22
30,000	698.05	465.80	399.53	373.06	361.13	355.47
35,000	814.39	543.44	466.11	435.24	421.32	414.71
40,000	930.74	621.07	532.70	497.41	481.51	473.95
45,000	1047.08	698.70	599.29	559.59	541.70	533.20
50,000	1163.42	776.34	665.88	621.77	601.89	592.44
60,000	1396.10	931.60	799.05	746.12	722.26	710.93
70,000	1628.78	1086.87	932.22	870.47	842.64	829.42
80,000	1861.47	1242.14	1065.40	994.82	963.01	947.90
90,000	2094.14	1397.40	1198.57	1119.17	1083.38	1066.38
100,000	2326.83	1552.67	1331.75	1243.53	1203.77	1184.88

15% Annual Percentage Rate

Amount Financed	Monthly payments (principal and interest)* 5 Years	10 Years	15 Years	20 Years	25 Years	30 Years
$ 25,000	594.75	403.34	349.90	329.20	320.21	316.12
30,000	713.70	484.01	419.88	395.04	384.25	379.34
35,000	832.65	564.68	489.86	460.88	448.30	442.56
40,000	951.60	645.34	559.84	526.72	512.34	505.78
45,000	1070.55	726.01	629.82	592.56	576.38	569.00
50,000	1189.50	806.68	699.80	658.40	640.42	632.23
60,000	1427.40	968.01	839.76	790.08	768.50	758.67
70,000	1665.30	1129.35	979.72	921.76	896.59	885.12
80,000	1903.20	1290.68	1119.67	1053.44	1024.67	1011.56
90,000	2141.09	1452.01	1259.63	1185.11	1152.75	1138.00
100,000	2379.00	1613.35	1399.59	1 316.79	1280.84	1264.45

*For loans that fully pay off the debt over the loan term.

Know Homebuying Lingo

Source: National Association of Realtors

Amortization. The gradual repayment of a mortgage by periodic installments.

Annual percentage rate (APR). The total finance charge (interest, loan fees, points) expressed as a percentage of the loan amount.

Assessed value. The valuation placed on property by a public tax assessor as the basis of property taxes.

Binder. An agreement, accompanied by a deposit, whereby the buyer evidences good faith.

Cap. The maximum amount an interest or monthly payment can change, either at adjustment time or over the life of the mortgage.

Closing. The final step in transferring ownership of a property from the seller to the buyer.

Closing costs. Fees and expenses, not including the price of the home, payable by the sell er and the buyer at the closing (e.g. brokerage commissions, title insurance premiums, and inspection, appraisal, recording, and attorney's fees).

Deed. A legal document conveying title to a property.

Escrow. The placement of money or documents with a third party for safekeeping pending the fulfillment or performance of a specified act or condition.

Lien. A legal claim against a property that must be paid when the property is sold.

Loan–to–value–ratio. The relationship between the amount of a home loan and the total value of the property. Lenders may limit their maximum loan to 80–95 percent of value.

Lock–in rate. A commitment made by lenders on a mortgage loan to "lock in" a certain rate pending loan approval. Lock–in periods vary.

Points. A dollar amount paid to the lender as a consideration for making the loan. A point is one percent of the loan amount; also called discount points.

Principal, interest, taxes, and insurance (PITI) payment. A periodic (typically monthly) payment that includes the principal and interest payment plus a contribution to the escrow account established by the lender to pay insurance premiums and property taxes on the mortgaged property.

Private mortgage insurance (PMI). Insurance issued to a lender by a private company to protect the lender against loss on a defaulted mortgage loan. Its use is usually limited to loans with high loan–to–value ratios. The borrower pays the premiums.

Shared equity mortgage. A home loan in which an investor is granted a share of the equity, thereby allowing the investor to participate in the proceeds from resale.

Title. A document that's evidence of ownership.

Title insurance. Protection for lenders and homeowners against financial loss resulting from legal debts in the title.

Sexual Harassment in the Global Work Force

According to the most recent report by the International Labour Organization (ILO), entitled "Combating Sexual Harassment at Work," November 1992, many thousands of women are victims of sexual harassment at the workplace in the industrialized world every year. Some studies reveal that sexual harassment caused between 6 to 8 percent of women surveyed to change their jobs. Many of them were involuntarily dismissed. It may well be that the proportion of one out of 12 women being forced out of a job after being sexually harassed could apply to many countries worldwide.

Between 15 to 30 percent of working women questioned in some surveys say they have been subjected to frequent, serious sexual harassment—unwanted touching, pinching, offensive remarks, and unwelcome requests for sexual intercourse. While expressing concern at these figures, the ILO cautions that the surveys, limited to 23 countries and using varied definitions, methods, and sample groups, are not comparable and should not be interpreted as representing the global situation. The full picture is also incomplete because a large percentage of cases go unreported in every country. According to one report, 60 percent of victims of sexual harassment ignore it, believing that complaining will not resolve the problem but instead will cause further economic and psychological harm. Men may also be harassed, although to a lesser extent than women. In a British survey in 1991, for example, 14 percent of men said they had been harassed, compared to 47 percent of women.

Summary

Surveys reveal great differences among the 23 countries, both in the legal remedies available against sexual harassment and in the voluntary steps that have been taken. A sampling of the surveys reveals the following:

The United States: The term "sexual harassment" was first devised in the United States, where concrete steps to deal with the problem were first taken. In 1980, the federal Merit Systems Protection Board conducted the most extensive American survey up to that time on the issue, covering some 23,000 federal employees. Of the women surveyed, 42 percent reported some form of sexual harassment. Approximately 1 percent reported rape or sexual assault on the job; 10 percent reported demands for sexual favors; 20 percent pressure for unwanted dates; 25 percent deliberate touching, pinching, leaning over, or sexual comments; and 35 percent sexual remarks, teasing jokes, or questions. Federal courts first recognized sexual harassment as a prohibited form of sex discrimination in 1975.

Australia: The federal Human Rights and Equal Opportunities Commission found that most sexual harassment claims are from young women in small businesses of less than 100 employees. It said 75 percent of the complaints that proceeded to a public hearing involved women under the age of 20. Sexual harassment complaints accounted for 36.3 percent of the total number of sex discrimination complaints filed under the federal Sex Discrimination Act of 1984.

Austria: A 1986 survey by the Federal Ministry of Labour and Social Affairs showed that 30.5 percent of women reported serious incidents of sexual harassment. Legislation is under consideration.

Czechoslovakia: A survey showed that 17.5 percent of women had been sexual harassed physically, 35.8 percent verbally. No court cases have dealt with the issue. However, provisions contained in the labor and penal codes and the Charter of Basic Rights and Freedoms could potentially be applicable to sexual harassment.

Denmark: A 1991 survey by the Danish Gallop Institute disclosed that 11 percent of 1,350 women questioned said they had been sexually harassed at work. While in 65 percent of the cases there were no tangible consequences, eight percent of the victims had been dismissed.

France: A study commissioned by the Secretary of State for Women's and Consumer's Rights in 1991 found that 21 percent of 1,300 women surveyed had personally experienced sexual harassment. In recently adopted amendments to the penal and labor code, sexual harassment is limited to acts carried out by a person in a position of authority in order to obtain sexual favors; such acts will become illegal.

Germany: The first in-depth study of sexual harassment in the workplace was carried out in 1990 at the request of the Ministry of Youth, Family, Women and Health, finding that the issue was a serious problem. Six percent of all women interviewed had resigned from at least one job as a result of being sexually harassed. Only 6 percent of their alleged harassers had received a warning from their employer. There are no specific federal laws covering sexual harassment at work, but trade unions have included the subject in their educational programs.

Japan: In 1990, a women's organization named Santama No Kai surveyed 1,131 female alleged victims of sexual harassment, known in Japanese as "seku hara." Of that total, 23.5 percent said their direct superiors were the harassers, while 14 percent identified a man in a superior position, 15.8 percent identified a colleague, 4.4 percent a customer, 4.2 percent a business client, and 19.6 percent said the advances came from others. There are no statutory provisions which explicitly outlaw sexual harassment in Japan, but in April 1992 a woman, relying on provisions of the nation's Civil Code, won the first sexual harassment case to be brought in Japan.

Netherlands: There is no legal definition of "sexual harassment" and case law has not developed a definition of the term. A 1986 Government survey showed that 58 percent of women questioned had experienced sexual harassment at work. Employers' and workers' organizations, however, are treating the problem seriously: about a third of all workers are covered by a collective agreement that calls for the prevention of sexual harassment.

Norway: Sexual harassment is not explicitly referred to in any Norwegian law. A 1988 survey found that 41 percent of the women had been subjected to unwanted sexual touching many times, 40 percent sometimes, 9 percent once, and 9 percent never; also, 38 percent said they had sometimes experienced pressure to have sex on the job, and 9 percent said they had received that pressure many times.

Equal Rights Amendment

Next to abortion, the Equal Rights Amendment (ERA) was perhaps the most widely debated feminist issue of the 1970s. The ERA, which would provide for the legal equality of the sexes, was first proposed by the National Women's party in 1923. In its most recent form the amendment declared, "Equality of rights under the law shall not be denied or abridged by the United States or any State on account of sex." The amendment was approved by the requisite two-thirds vote of the House of Representatives in October 1971 and by the Senate in March 1972. Spurred by the revival of feminism in the late 1960s and 1970s, the ERA received much early support as thirty states ratified it within one year of its Senate approval. But it ultimately failed to achieve ratification by the required thirty-eight states, even though the deadline for ratification was extended to June 30, 1982. The defeat of the ERA was spearheaded by Phyllis Schlafly and her organization Stop ERA, which benefited from the conservative backlash that gained momentum in the mid-1970s. Nonetheless, despite its defeat, public support for the amendment never fell below 54%, and as late as 1976 support for its passage was included in the platforms of both major political parties.

Opponents of the women's movement thought that the ERA would challenge traditional gender roles and ruin the stability of the family. They maintained that the ERA was unnecessary because women's rights were already protected. They also claimed that the ERA would lead to a draft of women into the military, abolish separate-sex public restrooms, and end alimony payments to divorced women.

In the view of ERA opponents, if men and women were equal in the eyes of the law, women would be as responsible as men for the support of the family. Therefore, a husband could not be held fully responsible for support of his wife and children.

Spain: In 1989, the Spanish Government adopted a provision for protection against sexual harassment in the workplace. In a 1986 survey, 84 percent of women workers said that sexual commentary and jokes had been made to them on the job, while 55 percent had experienced sexual looks or gestures. Some 4 percent said they were subjected to attempted sexual intercourse, and 27 percent received strong verbal advances and unwanted touching.

Sweden: The Equal Opportunity Ombudsman carried out the first study of sexual harassment in the workplace in 1987, which showed that 17 percent of women had experienced some form of sexual harassment. The Equal Opportunities Act of 1991 created a new legal principle in Sweden, putting the responsibility on employers to take affirmative action to combat sexual harassment in the workplace.

Switzerland: The National Commission for Women of the Swiss Union of Public Service Employees said in 1987 that 7 percent of its female members have lost their jobs as a result of sexual harassment, 2 percent of whom were dismissed, and 5 percent who resigned. No Swiss law explicitly defines sexual harassment, but cases have been brought to court.

United Kingdom: Sexual harassment is not specifically mentioned in any British law, but courts have held it to be prohibited under the Sexual Discrimination Act of 1975. A 1987 survey by the Labour Research Department found that 74 percent of those responding reported some form of sexual harassment in their workplace. In 1991, the Trade Union Council issued guidelines, urging unions to negotiate preventive policies with employers and to undertake educational activities internally. □

Remarriage After Divorce

Remarriage in the United States has become a relatively common event. Currently, more than four out of ten marriages in the U.S. involve a second or higher-order marriage for the bride, the groom, or both. In 1990, about 3.1 million women 15 to 65 years old had ended their first two marriages in divorce. These women represented five percent of all ever-married women and 29% of all women who remarried after their first divorce. By contrast, 17.2 million women, about 28%, had ended a first marriage by divorce.

Remarriage following a divorce is more frequent for women who were divorced at a young age—in their twenties or thirties—and who were divorced for a relatively short time. Seventy-five percent of those who divorced in their twenties had remarried compared with about 50% in their late thirties. This data seems to hold true for white women, black women, and women of Hispanic origin.

In 1990, the median duration of a divorce before a woman married again was 2.5 years. □

Percent of Women Whose First Marriage Ended in Divorce and May Eventually End in Divorce: June 1990

Age	Divorced by June 1990	May end in divorce	
		1975 to 1980	1985 to 1990
20 to 24	12.5	49.2	37.6
25 to 29	19.2	46.4	39.0
30 to 34	28.1	46.2	40.8
35 to 39	34.1	44.8	42.0
40 to 44	35.8	41.9	39.9
45 to 49	35.2	38.7	36.2
50 to 54	29.5	32.0	30.2

Source: U.S. Bureau of the Census.

Percent of Women Whose Second Marriage Ended in Redivorce and May Eventually End in Redivorce: June 1990

Age	Redivorced by June 1990	May end in redivorce	
		1980 to 1985	1985 to 1990
20 to 24	13.1	62.1	46.8
25 to 29	17.8	57.1	42.4
30 to 34	22.7	57.6	42.8
35 to 39	28.5	55.6	40.1
40 to 44	30.6	49.4	38.5
45 to 49	36.4	49.8	40.9
50 to 54	34.5	45.7	38.3
55 to 59	31.1	38.3	31.1
60 to 65	27.0	(X)	(X)

X = Not applicable. *Source:* U.S. Bureau of the Census.

Family and Medical Leave Act

By Elizabeth E. Janice

The traditional 40-hour workweek was designed with men in mind, back in the days when gender roles were clearly defined. Today, however, more than half of American women over age 16 are in the work force. And each year, two million of them have babies. Caught in the middle of work and family responsibilities, more and more American women have been demanding a family leave policy.

Until President Bill Clinton signed the Family and Medical Leave Act in February 1993, the United States was the only industrialized nation without a family leave policy. The act, which went into effect August 5, requires companies to give all but their top employees up to 12 weeks of unpaid leave during any 12-month period for the birth, adoption, or placement of a foster child; the serious illness of a child, spouse, or parent; or an employee's own serious health condition.

Employers must also continue to provide pre-existing health benefits, although they are entitled to recover premiums paid for the leave period if the employee does not return to work and guarantee that employees will return to equivalent jobs.

To be eligible for leave under the new law workers must have been employed by the company for at least 12 months and must have worked 1,250 hours during the year before the leave begins. If paid leave is available, the employer may require the employee to substitute the paid leave for part of the 12 weeks.

The act applies only to companies with 50 or more employees—and therefore won't protect the majority of working women, who work for small businesses. Nonetheless, it does set a standard for American businesses, since the vast majority of working women will get pregnant sometime during their careers.

Until now, women who took maternity leave often lost their jobs as a result. Researchers who examined cases from the Ohio Civil Rights Commission found that nearly 25% of the women who had filed complaints found their jobs missing when they tried to return to work after childbirth. Furthermore, they discovered that a woman on pregnancy leave is 10 times more likely to lose her job than one on medical leave for other reasons.

Still, some fear that the family leave act may hinder—rather than help—women. A 1991 Gallup poll found that nearly half of small-business owners would hesitate to hire young women if a family leave act became law.

The act's hidden costs may be exaggerated, however. The Family and Work Institute studied the effect of parental-leave in four states that already have such laws: Minnesota, Rhode Island, Oregon, and Wisconsin. Most of the employers surveyed reported "no increase" in operating costs, a third found the regulations "easy to comply with," and only 9 percent found the law to be "difficult."

The average woman today works the double shift: full-time professional and full-time mother. In order to attract good workers, corporations will have to design a more flexible work environment. □

The Male-Female Wage Gap

By Elizabeth E. Janice

Led by young baby boomers, record numbers of women flooded the workplace in the early 1970s. Armed with degrees, many of them entered traditionally male-dominated professions. Today, 44 percent of adult working women are college-educated, compared with only 20 percent in 1965. Women now receive over half of all master's degrees and one-third of all doctorates.

Conventional wisdom had it that as women entered so-called male professions, the wage gap between men and women would narrow. Yet, women still earn less than men—in virtually every job category. The average female college graduate today earns less than a man with a high school diploma.

The size of the gap varies from one profession to another. In fields where women are the majority, such as teaching and nursing, the gap is lower. Female secretaries, for example, make 97¢ for every dollar male secretaries make. However, female-dominated fields tend to be low-paying to begin with.

In male-dominated fields, the gap is wider. Female lawyers and engineers earn only 75% and 84%, respectively, of what their male counterparts make. The Department of Labor lists only one field where women make more than men: postal clerk.

Apparently, wage discrimination occurs even in the White House. A recent list published by a congressional subcommittee revealed that, in 1991, some men in the White House were making more than women with similar positions: male deputy press secretary, 42% more; male deputy assistant to the President, 65% more.

The wage gap between men and women was actually narrower in 1955 than in the mid-1980s. The average woman in 1955 earned 63.9¢ for every dollar a man made; in 1984, she earned slightly less, 63.7¢. After 1984, women's pay began to inch up again—but progress has been painfully slow: However slight, these gains may be illusional. Women started to catch up just as men started to lose ground. In the 1980s, as the nation's manufacturing base eroded and high-paying union jobs disappeared, men's wages fell. As men did worse, women seemed to do better.

If women's salaries had continued to rise each year, pay parity would have been reached by the year 2017. But in 1991, women's wages again started to slide, falling two cents. Today, women earn 70¢ for every dollar earned by men.

The older a woman gets, the wider the gap. Women ages 25 to 34 earn 79.6¢ for every dollar earned by men in the same age group. But for women in the 45-to-54 age group, their share is only 61.4¢.

The effects of the wage gap extend far beyond the workplace. Women represent the majority of all poor adults. Almost two-thirds of workers earning the minimum wage are women. And despite the common depiction of the media of the fast-track "superwoman"—who has it all—nearly three-quarters of all female workers still earn less than $20,000 a year. □

Roe v. Wade

Source: The Reader's Companion To American History

This 1973 Supreme Court ruling proved to be one of the most controversial in the Court's history. "Roe" was Norma McGorvey, who was denied the right under Texas law to abort a fetus she did not want to bear. She sued the state, and the case came before the U.S. Supreme Court. The Court ruled 7–2 that women had an unrestricted right to abort a fetus during the first trimester of pregnancy, but that the state had an interest in protecting the fetus after that, when it became "viable" or able to live outside the womb.

The opinion extended the "right to privacy" enunciated in *Griswold* v. *Connecticut* (1965), in which the Court ruled that a state could not prohibit married couples from using contraceptives; this right to privacy was implied in the First Amendment guarantee of free speech, the Ninth Amendment's reference to "certain rights," and the Fourteenth Amendment's guarantee of due process of law.

The ruling continues to cause controversy. Early in the 1980s, the "right-to-life" movement, with help from politicians such as President Ronald Reagan, pushed for a constitutional amendment prohibiting abortion except in cases of rape, incest, or a threat to the mother's life. Although antiabortionists were unable to pass the amendment, they did secure a ban on federal and, in many cases, state financing of abortions. The Roman Catholic church and many Protestant fundamentalist groups strongly opposed abortion. In response, women's groups such as the National Organization for Women stepped up their efforts to elect prochoice candidates. The abortion issue had evolved into a "litmus test" for both liberals and conservatives and had become a trying issue for many political candidates and judicial appointees.

A History of Abortion in the United States

Source: The Reader's Companion To American History

Abortion has been practiced in the United States since the founding of the Republic, but both its social character and its legal status have varied considerably. Through the early decades of the nineteenth century, Americans regarded abortion primarily as the recourse of women wronged by duplicitous suitors or pregnant as the result of illicit relationships, though records exist of married women having abortions. Americans tolerated the practice, which had long been legal under colonial common law and remained legal under American common law, provided the pregnancy was terminated before quickening: the first perception of fetal movement by the woman. Quickening generally occurs near the midpoint of gestation.

As married women moved to lower their fertility rates after 1830, abortion became a widespread practice in the United States. Abortionists advertised in the daily press and pharmaceutical firms competed in a lucrative market of purported abortifacients. Women spoke to each other and to their doctors in straightforward terms about their abortions. When physicians estimated American abortion rates in the 1860s and 1870s, they used figures strikingly close to those of the 1960s and 1970s: approximately one abortion for every four live births.

In the middle decades of the nineteenth century several state legislatures began to restrict the increasingly common practice of abortion. Some lawmakers feared for the safety of women undergoing abortions. Others reacted negatively to what they considered indecent advertising. Concerned about falling birthrates, many opposed all forms of fertility control, not just abortion. But the greatest pressure for legal change came from the American Medical Association (AMA), founded in 1847.

Led by Horatio Robinson Storer, a Boston physician, the AMA and its affiliated medical societies worked in state capitals throughout the nation during the 1860s and 1870s to outlaw abortion at any stage of gestation, except when doctors themselves determined the procedure to be necessary. Though the physicians put forward scientific, social, and moral arguments their professional aspirations to upgrade and regulate American medical practice also loomed large. The legal status of abortion was altered by state legislatures after the Civil War not in a religious context but in the context of who would be allowed to do what to whom in the practice of medicine.

The antiabortion laws and legal decisions of the second half of the nineteenth century, though seldom and selectively enforced, drove the practice of abortion underground. Substantial numbers of women, especially immigrant women with limited access to other (also illegal) methods of fertility control, nonetheless continued to have abortions. Surveys conducted under the auspices of the AMA and the federal government confirmed the persistence of widespread abortion in the United States through the 1930s.

By the late 1950s significant portions of the population began to call for repeal of the regulations that proscribed abortion. . . . Nineteenth-century commitments to life of any sort under any conditions were being questioned as a result of heightened sensitivities to what was called the quality of life. Even so, three additional factors stood out.

First was a profound shift in the role of American women. Abortion had always been a women's issue, but not until the 1960s did significant numbers of women address it in an overtly public and political fashion. Control over their own reproductive processes, including the right to terminate an unwanted pregnancy, became for many women one of the fundamental demands of modern feminism. Second was a perception of inequality. While the wealthy and well connected arranged discreet abortions under favorable conditions, the poor and the unsophisticated often suffered. Third was an almost complete reversal of opinion within the medical establishment. By 1967, according to a national survey, 87 percent of American doctors favored liberalization of the antiabortion laws that their professional predecessors had fought to enact a century earlier.

In January 1973 the Supreme Court in *Roe* v. *Wade* ruled that women, as part of their constitutional right to privacy, could choose to terminate a pregnancy prior to the point at which the fetus reached a stage of development that would allow it to survive outside the womb. This ruling, and its subsequent refinements, effectively struck antiabortion laws from state criminal codes and returned the United States, in a rough sense, to standards functionally similar to those of the early Republic. After the *Roe* decision, abortion became a divisive and intensely emotional public issue. □

The New Patterns of Family Life

The traditional American family of a working father and a mother at home raising children is waning and single-parent households, cohabiting couples, and domestic partnerships are rising

Source: The Reader's Companion to American History.

At the end of the nineteenth century many Americans feared that the family was disintegrating. Three momentous developments contributed to the sense of crisis: a declining birthrate, a rising divorce rate, and mounting evidence that younger women were no longer content to remain within their "sphere of domesticity."

Between 1800 and 1900, the birthrate fell 40% overall and even more sharply among the middle class. At the century's beginning, a typical wife gave birth to her first child at twenty-three and bore children every two years until menopause; in 1900 she bore her last child at thirty-three. The birthrate dropped in part because children, in an increasingly commercial society, were no longer economic assets who could be employed in household industries or bound out as apprentices and partly because many women were eager to break the unending cycle of pregnancy, birth, and nursing. The sharp rise in the divorce rate also generated anxiety. Despite efforts late in the century to restrict divorce by reducing legal grounds and lengthening residence requirements, the rate jumped fifteenfold between 1870 and 1920. A further source of alarm was the changing role of women. Increasing numbers were going to college, joining women's organizations, and taking jobs outside the home.

Many educators, scholars, and social workers responded to these developments by popularizing a new ideal—the "companionate family," which emphasized equal rights, sexual attraction, and companionship. Spouses would be "friends and lovers," parents and children, "pals." To achieve this ideal, influential groups recommended liberalized divorce laws, marriage counseling, sex education, access to birth-control information, and permissive child-rearing practices that stressed affection and encouraged self-expression rather than self-control. The full impact of this new ideal was delayed by the Great Depression and World War II, but the concept resurfaced after the war.

In the meantime, during the depression, unemployment or part-time work, lower wages, and demands of needy relatives tore at the fabric of family life, forcing many to share living quarters with relatives, delay marriages, and put off having children. The divorce rate fell, for the simple reason that fewer people could afford one, but the rate of desertion soared. By 1940, over 1.5 million married couples were living apart. Families sought to cope by pooling incomes and planting gardens, canning food, and making clothing. Children took part-time jobs and wives earned supplementary income by taking in sewing or laundry, setting up parlor groceries, or housing lodgers.

World War II also subjected the social order to severe strain. During the war, one-sixth of the nation's families suffered prolonged separation from sons or fathers. Five million "war widows" ran their homes and cared for children alone, and thousands went to work in war industries. Wartime migration added to the strain, as more than 15 million civilians moved about in search of work. Families faced a severe shortage of housing and a lack of schools, hospitals, and child-care facilities. These stresses contributed to a dramatic upsurge in the divorce rate and to severe problems among the young. Tens of thousands became unsupervised "latchkey" children, and rates of juvenile delinquency, venereal disease, and truancy all rose.

The next decade witnessed a sharp reaction to the stresses of the depression and war. The divorce rate slowed and couples married earlier than their parents had. Women bore more children, at younger ages, and closer together than in the past. As the housing shortage eased, millions of people moved to new single-family homes in the suburbs.

Since 1960, the American family has undergone further radical changes. In little more than a decade, the divorce rate doubled, as did the proportion of working mothers; the number of single-parent households tripled; the number of couples living together outside of wedlock quadrupled; and the birthrate fell by half. Forces for change have included a massive influx of women into the work force, propelled by a rapidly rising cost of living; increased control over fertility, which has permitted many women to pursue careers more readily; heightened emphasis on self-gratification and self-fulfillment, which has helped reduce the stigma attached to divorce; and the rise of feminism, which has challenged the idea that child care and housework are the apex of a women's accomplishments and her sole means of fulfillment.

Black families have experienced particularly intense strain. In 1960, 21% of black families were headed by women and 24% of black children were born outside of marriage. By the end of the 1980s, nearly half of all black children lived in female-headed households, more than half were born outside of wedlock, and over half were growing up in poverty. Low wages, unstable jobs, high levels of unemployment, and welfare policies that permitted many states to deny benefits to two-parent households contributed to the breakup of many impoverished families. □

Baby Boomer Marriages

Baby boomers have delayed entry into marriage and are more likely to dissolve a marriage than were previous generations. Both developments are indicative of how baby boomers followed a different course than did their parents.

In 1960, the median age for marriage for women was 20.3. By 1975 it had risen to 21.1. For men, median age at first marriage rose from 22.8 in 1960 to 23.5 in 1975. In an era of women's liberation, changing sexual mores, and greater tolerance for nonconforming behaviors, the norm for early age at marriage weakened. [In 1991, the median age at first marriage for women was 24.1, for men 26.3.]

The 1960s also marked the beginning of a sharp increase in the divorce rate. Initially, the growing number of divorces in the early 1960s occurred among older couples (age 45 or older), not to baby boomers. But by the 1970s, three of every four divorces were to people in their 20s and 30s—that is, the baby boomers. The number of divorces passed the 1 million mark for the first time in 1975 and the divorce rate hit an all-time high of 5.8 divorces per 1,000 marriages in 1979. Although the divorce rate declined to 4.7 by 1988, about 60% of first marriages are now likely to end in divorce. [In 1991, the divorce rate was estimated at 4.7.]

This high level of marital instability challenged old norms and created new patterns of family life. A snapshot of the marital status of baby boomers in 1990 reflects a pattern quite different from their counterparts in the 1960s. Among the baby-boom generation, nearly two-thirds are married, one in eight are currently divorced, and one in five have never married. This pattern is far different from the marital status of young adults (ages 25 to 44) 30 years ago.

There are substantial differences within the generation along lines of race and gender. Two-thirds of white baby boomers are currently married, whereas less than half (43%) of black baby boomers are. Almost twice the percentage of black boomers (36%) as white boomers (19%) have never married. Similarly, baby-boom women are more likely than baby-boom men to be married or divorced. One in four baby-boom men never married compared with only one in six baby-boom women.

Cohabitation

Source: Population Reference Bureau, Inc.

Prior to 1960, most young adults lived in their parents' home until they got married. The social and sexual revolutions of the 1960s indelibly changed this pattern.

During the 1960s, society's strict disapproval of unmarried men and women living together weakened. The fear of having a child out-of-wedlock was greatly reduced by the introduction of the birth control pill, and the changing sexual mores of the times encouraged many young men and women of the baby-boom generation to live together before marriage. Only 8% of first marriages in the late 1960s were preceded by cohabitation, but nearly half of all couples who married in the mid-1980s had cohabited. The number of cohabiting couples doubled between 1960 and 1977 from fewer than 500,000 to almost 1 million and grew rapidly from that time. Most of this sharp increase reflected the behavior of people under age 25.

In 1990, 2.9 million households consisted of unmarried adults living together. Over half (58%) were baby boomers (ages 25–44) and another quarter (28%) were persons under age 25. Persons who had never married made up the largest share of cohabiting partners, followed by those who had been divorced. Nearly one-third of these households had children under age 15. □

Reprinted from "The Baby Boom—Entering Midlife," Leon F. Bouvier and Carol J. De Vita, Population Bulletin, Vol. 46, No. 3 (Washington, D.C.: Population Reference Bureau, Inc., November 1991).

Who's Supporting the Kids?

The number of women living with children whose father was absent was 9,955,000 as of spring 1990, an increase of 39% in a little more than a decade. Approximately 16 million children lived in these households. At present, 26% of all children are born to unmarried mothers.

According to the latest Census Bureau report on Child Support and Alimony published in 1991, about 5.7 million women had been awarded child support from the children's father, leaving a large number of them without financial support from the children's father. Consequently, 3.2 million of these women, about one in three, lived in poverty. The number of never-married women with children from an absent father was three million, more than double the number reported in 1979. □

Interracial Married Couples

According to the Census Bureau, a very small proportion of all married couples are interracial, and there has been very little increase in this percent over the past two decades. In 1991, there were 994,000 interracial married couples, representing only 1.9 percent of all married couples. A 1991 census report on Marital Status and Living Arrangements published in 1992 showed 231,000 Black married to White couples in 1991, 720,000 White married to "other" (other than White or Black), and 43,000 Black married to "other" couples. Between 1970 and 1991, the number of interracial married couples increased from 310,000 to 994,000. This increase is partially attributable to the difference between the sampling variability of the two census surveys [Current Population Survey (CPS) versus Decennial census]. □

Gay Marriages

In a case brought up by three homosexual couples, the Hawaiian State Supreme Court ruled three to one on May 5, 1993, that a ban on marriages between couples of the same sex may violate the State Constitution's prohibition against sex discrimination. However, the court did not overturn the ban.

No state currently permits same sex couples to marry. If Hawaii eventually permitted same sex couples to marry, the union would have to be recognized nationwide because marriages in one state are legally recognized in all states. □

Domestic Partnerships

The newest category of family, called domestic partnerships, has been sanctioned by over 25 cities or counties in the United States to grant some of the rights of traditional married couples to unmarried heterosexual, homosexual, elderly, and disabled couples who share the traditional bond of a family.

In March 1993, New York City became the latest to legally acknowledge domestic partnerships. To become recognized as domestic partners in New York, unmarried, unrelated couples over 18 years of age register at the City Clerk's office with two proofs of identification and place of residence and swear that they have a close committed personal relationship and have been living together on a continuing basis. They receive a notarized affidavit similar to a marriage license. To divorce from the partnership, couples simply have to advise the city that they no longer live together as couples.

The rights granted include the same unpaid leave that married city workers receive and the same standing as married couples in qualifying for apartments. A proposal to grant registered domestic partners the same health benefits that married city workers receive is being considered. □

The Dimensions of Family Violence

Source: Public Health Reports, 1993, based on a keynote address by James O. Mason, MD, DrPH, Assistant Secretary for Health, Head, Public Health Service, to the Second Annual Utah Conference on Violence, 1992.

Violence is not only as American as apple pie, it is often as homemade. For example, the majority of people who are murdered are not killed by a stranger during a hold-up or similar crime but are killed by someone they know, 16 percent of the time by a family member.

Gang fights and drive-by shootings get more attention, but homegrown suicides, child abuse, elder abuse, and spouse abuse are at least as important and have long-range emotional and disabling repercussions. Richard Gelles, the director of the Family Violence Research Program at the University of Rhode Island, says that just considering the medical costs and productivity losses resulting from family violence, "It's not out of bounds to talk about $5–10 billion a year."

One-fifth to one-third of all women are physically abused during their lifetime. Ten percent of the time the injury is serious enough to require hospitalization or emergency room treatment.

Studies on domestic violence also find:

- 25–50 percent of homeless families headed by women left home to escape domestic violence.
- Half of the murdered women in the United States are killed by a current or former partner. Women who are divorced, separated, or otherwise estranged from their partners are at the highest risk of assault.
- A Texas survey found that 34 percent of domestic violence calls to police were repeat calls. A similar study in Kansas found that 85 percent of calls to police were repeat offenses. Fifty percent of the time it was the fifth or more offense.
- Pregnancy is a particularly dangerous time for women. Approximately 37 percent are physically abused by their partner. Blows and kicks are often directed toward the abdomen. Younger pregnant women are at higher risk than older pregnant women.

In the home, women are about as violent as men—they hit, bite, and kick just as often as men—but they don't do as much damage. Men inflict more harm because of their generally greater size and strength. In addition, violence by women is often in retaliation or self-defense. Women commit only 8 percent of all homicides in this country, but 51 percent of them are against partners with a history of wife abuse.

In one recent year, nearly 1 million children experienced demonstrable harm as a result of abuse or neglect. Some 1,100 died from abuse or neglect. Another 40,000 children were sexually abused with rape by a caregiver. And a higher number were sexually molested without rape. According to a survey, 1.9 out of every 1,000 children were sexually molested by a parent or guardian.

We know less about the incidence of elder abuse than about child and spouse abuse. The term was not even coined until the early 1980s. One study of 2,000 elderly persons in Boston showed that between 2.5 and 3.9 percent of the elderly who were interviewed were abused or neglected, physically or emotionally. When we project the Boston experience nationwide, between 700,000 and 1 million-plus elderly are abused or neglected.

Victims of elder abuse tend to be the "old-old, the frail elderly." Nearly all live with the assailant who is likely to be financially dependent on the victim. Some research has provided evidence that abusers of the elderly are more likely to be developmentally disabled, mentally ill, or alcoholic.

Children who are abused or witness domestic violence are stunted in social and emotional development. They experience phobias, nightmares, and eating disorders. They can be withdrawn or overly aggressive. They have lower self-esteem and lower performance on standardized IQ tests.

In one study of men who had been abused as children, half had subsequently been convicted of a serious crime, become alcoholic, mentally ill, or died unusually young.

Like abused children, battered women and elders suffer many complex psychological problems. Victims undergo psychological changes—a sort of "learned helplessness" and acceptance. They become confused, increasingly dependent, and powerless.

Battered women experience a higher rate of alcoholism—as many as half of all female alcoholics are battered women—and once a woman is battered, the risk of drug abuse is nine times higher. Between 35 and 40 percent of battered women attempt suicide. □

Child Abuse and Neglect

Source: Administration for Children and Families, Department of Health and Human Services.

In recent years, experts have declared the child abuse and neglect problem an epidemic; cases have overflowed our hospitals, foster care homes, social worker case loads and court dockets.

The Extent of the Problem

- Child abuse was formally recognized by the medical profession in 1961 as the "battered-child syndrome."
- An estimated 2.4 million cases of suspected child abuse, child sexual abuse and child neglect are reported to child protective agencies each year. Since 1980, reports of child abuse have quadrupled.
- Investigations have confirmed over 1.5 million cases of child abuse and neglect in 1990. And more than three children die each day in the United States from abuse and neglect.
- The link between substance abuse and child abuse has strengthened over the years. Parental abuse of alcohol and use of other drugs has been identified as a major factor contributing to child maltreatment and death. It is estimated that nearly 10 million children under age 18 are affected in some way by the substance abuse of their parents.
- Child maltreatment often has negative short and long term effects on children's mental health and development. For example, abused and neglected children frequently suffer drops in IQ and an increase in learning disabilities, depression and drug use.
- The effects of child abuse are sometimes obvious even decades later. The effects are often pervasive: mental, physical *and* social in nature. Suicide, violence, delinquency, drug and alcohol abuse and other forms of criminality are frequently child-abuse related.
- Studies of adults show that 15 percent to 38 percent of women report experiences of various types of sexual victimization during childhood and adolescence, and about 10 percent of men report sexual abuse during childhood and adolescence. □

Need Help in Collecting Child Support?

You can contact the Organization for the Enforcement of Child Support, Inc. (OECS), at 1712 Deer Park Road, Finksburg, MD 21048. Phone: (410) 876-1826. When writing, please enclose a stamped, self-addressed envelope. The OECS is a nonprofit group of volunteers established in July 1979 to address the numerous problems of child support enforcement.

The following suggestions were provided by the OECS:

Pitfalls, Problems, and Solutions

Reviewing Your Legal Papers: Always read any legal document you receive—carefully—checking for errors. Be sure that the Court Order or Decree specifies the amount of support to be paid and the payment intervals. Otherwise you may not be able to enforce it if the payments are skipped or reduced. Verbal agreements are unenforceable, even if stipulated in court, unless they are in the written Order or Decree. Do not depend upon a lawyer or support enforcement agent to take care of this for you, regardless of how high a fee you paid. Check your own papers carefully! If there are errors, a Petition to Revise the Decree must be filed with the Court within 30 days. (This may vary from state-to-state.) After 30 days, the Court still has continuing jurisdiction if it can be proven that a party was guilty of fraud or if there is a mistake or irregularity in the Order which fails to conform with the meaning of the parties.

Do You Have a Court Order? A Separation Agreement is NOT a Court Order. It is simply a contract between two parties. It must be reduced to a Court Order as soon as possible. Separation Agreements are only enforceable by law suits. Without a Court Order you cannot proceed with other enforcement mechanisms. Do not delay! If you have no Court Order for support (which may be in your Divorce Decree) then file a Petition for one immediately. Such a Petition can, and should, be filed the day the non-custodial parent leaves.

Providing the Obligor's Address: Enforcement agencies, courts, and lawyers request that you furnish the absent parent's current address before any action can be taken. This is bad advice, because any delay in filing will result in a delay in receipt of the child's support. But, most importantly, Statutes of Limitations must be considered, and the child may lose any claim to arrearages. Some laws allow child support to be ordered retroactively to the date a Petition was filed in Court. Therefore, file immediately. If you don't know the obligor's address, use his/her last-known address.

Establishing Paternity: It is essential to your child's future that you legally establish paternity and obtain a Court Order for support. Some mothers may feel that it is easier to raise a child alone than to hassle with the problems of child support enforcement. But remember, 18 years is a long time. Who knows what the mother's financial and emotional circumstances may be in the future. Every child needs and deserves a father and every father should nurture and love his child. If paternity is not determined, the child loses all inheritance rights. He also loses a loving parental relationship. The best time to start proceedings is now! See your local child support enforcement agency for help.

Using the Federal Court: In interstate cases, if the responding state (the state in which the obligor resides) fails to cooperate, ask to have the case taken into Federal Court. This Court has jurisdiction over *all* states.

Shaken Baby Syndrome

Source: Administration for Children and Families, Department of Health and Human Services.

The term "Shaken Baby Syndrome" (SBS) describes the consequences which occur when a young child's head is whiplashed back and forth during shaking. Babies can be easily injured when shaken. Their neck muscles aren't strong enough to control head movements, and rapid movement of the head can result in the brain being bruised from banging against the skull wall. Bleeding behind the eyes and in and around the brain occurs and can cause serious injury. Depending upon the vulnerability of the child and the severity of the shaking, consequences may include seizures, partial or total blindness, paralysis, mental retardation, or death. In cases of less violent and sometimes chronic shaking of a young child, long-term outcomes can include attention deficits and learning disabilities.

With the recent introduction of a technological instrument called a Magnetic Resonance Imager (MRI), more and more cases of SBS are being identified. In the past, these cases may have gone undetected or been misdiagnosed as Sudden Infant Death Syndrome (SIDS). As more cases of SBS have been identified medically, criminal investigation of, and prosecution for, possible child abuse have increased. A concomitant rise in media attention to the problem is in part responsible for a greater emphasis on prevention efforts.

Five studies conducted between 1982 and 1990 revealed that 25–50% of teenagers and adults did **not** know that shaking a baby is dangerous. These data clearly dispute the assumption that knowing about the dangers of shaking is just common sense. The need for education has never been more clear.

The following recent case examples illustrate the nature of the problem:

- In November, 1991, an 18-year-old man shook a 7-week-old infant for whom he was baby-sitting because he wanted him to stop crying. The infant died the next day.
- In July, 1991, a 29-year-old man shook his girlfriend's 9-month-old boy on two different occasions. The baby had recurring vomiting and seizures, but survived. The boyfriend admitted shaking the baby but said he didn't mean to harm him.
- In January, 1991, a 32-year-old mother shook her one-month-old son to death. She blamed her 2-year-old daughter for injuring the baby.
- In October, 1990, a 32-year-old man shook his 4-month-old daughter violently. She died three days later.
- In June, 1990, a 29-year-old man shook his girlfriend's 13-month-old to stop her from crying. She suffered partial paralysis, visual impairment, and speech delay. □

SOCIAL SECURITY & AGING

Social Security

The original Social Security Act was passed in 1935 and amended in 1939, 1946, 1950, 1952, 1954, 1956, 1958, 1960, 1961, 1965, 1967, 1969, 1972, 1974, 1977, 1980-1984, 1986, and 1988-1989.

The act is administered by the Social Security Administration and the Health Care Financing Administration, and other agencies within the Department of Health and Human Services.

For purposes of clarity, the explanations given below will describe the provisions of the act as amended.

Social Security Contribution and Rate Schedule

(percent of covered earnings)

Year	Retirement survivors, and disability insurance	Hospital insurance	Year
EMPLOYERS AND EMPLOYEES			
1978	4.95%	1.10%	6.05%
1979-80	5.08	1.05	6.13
1981	5.35	1.30	6.65
1982-83	5.40	1.30	6.70
1984	5.70	1.30	7.00
1985	5.70	1.35	7.05
1986-87	5.70	1.45	7.15
1988-89	6.06	1.45	7.51
1990 & later	6.20	1.45	7.65
SELF-EMPLOYED			
1978	7.00%	1.10%	8.10%
1979-80	7.05	1.05	8.10
1981	8.00	1.30	9.30
1982	8.05	1.30	9.35
1983	8.05	1.30	9.35
1984	11.40	2.60	*14.00
1985	11.40	2.70	*14.10
1986-87	11.40	2.90	*14.30
1988-89	12.12	2.90	*15.02
1990 & later	12.40	2.90	*15.30

*The law provides credit against self-employment tax liability in the following manner: 2.7% in 1984; 2.3% in 1985; 2.09% 1986-1989 and, beginning with the 1990 taxable year, the credit is replaced.

Old Age, Disability, and Survivors Insurance

Practically everyone who works fairly regularly is covered by social security. Most state and local government employees are covered under voluntary agreements between states and the Secretary of Health and Human Services. Workers not covered include most federal civilian employees hired prior to January 1984, career railroad workers, and a few other exceptions.

Cash tips count for Social Security if they amount to $20 or more in a month from employment with a single employer.

To qualify for benefits or make payments possible for your survivors, you must be in work covered by the law for a certain number of "quarters of coverage." Before 1978, a quarter of coverage was earned if a worker was paid $50 or more wages in a 3-month calendar quarter. A self-employed person got 4 "quarters of coverage" for a year in which his net earnings were $400 or more.

In 1978, a worker, whether employed or self-employed, received one quarter of coverage for each $250 of covered annual earnings up to a maximum of four for a year. The quarter of coverage measure was increased to $260 in 1979 and $290 in 1980, $310 in 1981, $340 in 1982, $370 in 1983, $390 in 1984, $410 in 1985, $440 in 1986, $460 in 1987, $470 in 1988, $500 in 1989, $520 in 1990, $540 in 1991, $570 in 1992, $590 in 1993, and will increase automatically in future years to keep pace with increases in average wages. The number of quarters needed differs for different persons and depends on the date of your birth; in general, it is related to the number of years after 1950, or after the year you reach 21, if later, and up to the year you reach 62, become disabled, or die. One "quarter of coverage" is required for each such year in order for you or your family to get benefits. No one will need more than 40 quarters. Your local Social Security office can tell you how long you need to work.

Who Pays for the Insurance?

Both workers and their employers pay for the workers' insurance. Self-employed persons pay their own social security contributions annually along with their income tax. The rates include the cost of Medicare hospital insurance. The contribution and benefit base is $57,600 for 1993 for retirement, survivor and disability coverage, and $135,000 for 1993 for Medicare coverage, and will increase automatically in future years as earnings levels rise. The contribution rate schedules under present law are shown in a table in this section.

The separate payroll contribution to finance hospital insurance is placed in a separate trust fund in the U.S. Treasury. In addition, the medical insurance premiums, currently $36.60 a month in 1993, and the government's shares go into another separate trust fund.

How to Apply for Benefits

You apply for benefits by filing a claim either in person, by mail, or by telephone at any social security office. You can get the address of your nearest office either from the post office, from the phone book under the listing, United States Government—Department of Health and Human Services—Social Security Administration, or by calling Social Security's toll-free number 1–800–772–1213. You will need certain kinds of proof, depending upon the type of benefit you are claiming. If it is a retirement benefit, you should provide your social security number and a birth certificate or religious record. If you are unable to get these documents, other old documents showing your age or date of birth—such as census records, school records, early naturalization certificate,

Delayed Retirement Credit Rates

Age 62	Monthly percentage	Yearly percentage
Prior to 1979	1/12 of 1%	1%
1979-1986	1/4 of 1%	3%
1987-1988	7/24 of 1%	3.5%
1989-1990	1/3 of 1%	4%
1991-1992	3/8 of 1%	4.5%
1993-1994	5/12 of 1%	5%
1995-1996	11/24 of 1%	5.5%
1997-1998	1/2 of 1%	6%
1999-2000	13/24 of 1%	6.5%
2001-2002	7/12 of 1%	7%
2003-2004	5/8 of 1%	7.5%
2005 or later	2/3 of 1%	8%

etc.—may be acceptable. A widow, or widower, 60 or older who is claiming widow's benefits based on his/her spouse's earnings should have his/her own social security number, his/her spouse's social security number, proof of age and a copy of the marriage certificate. A child claiming child's benefits should provide a birth certificate, his/her own social security number, and the social security number of the parent on whose record benefits are being claimed. If formal proof is not available, the Social Security office will tell you what kinds of information will be acceptable. Do not delay applying even if you do not have the necessary information or proofs.

What Does Social Security Offer?

The Social Security contribution you pay gives you four different kinds of protection: (1) retirement benefits, (2) survivors' benefits, (3) disability benefits, and (4) Medicare hospital insurance benefits.

Retirement benefits. Currently, a worker becomes eligible for the full amount of his retirement benefits at age 65, if he has retired under the definition in the law. A worker may retire at 62 and get 80% of his full benefit. The closer he is to age 65 when he starts collecting his benefit, the larger is the fraction of his full benefit that he will get.

The amount of the retirement benefit you are entitled to at 65 is the key to all other benefits under the program. The retirement benefit is based on covered earnings, generally those after 1950. Your covered earnings will be updated (indexed) to the second year before you reach age 62, become disabled, or die, and will reflect the increases in average wages that have occurred since the earnings were paid.

A worker who delays his retirement past age 65, or who does not receive a benefit for some months after age 65 because of high earnings will get a special credit that can mean a larger benefit. The credit adds to a worker's benefits 1% (3% for workers age 62 from 1979–1986) for each year (1/12 of 1% for each month) from age 65 to age 70 for which he did not get benefits. (*See* table.)

The law provides a special minimum benefit at retirement for people who worked under Social Security for many years. The provision will help people who had low incomes, but above a specific level, in their working years. The amount of the special minimum depends on the number of years of coverage. For a worker retiring at 65 in Jan. 1993 with 30 or more years of coverage, the special minimum benefit would be $492.50. These benefits are reduced if a worker is under 65 and are increased automatically for increases in the cost of living.

If you retired at age 65 in Jan. 1993 with average earnings, you would get a benefit of $794.00.

If your spouse is also 65, then he or she will get a spouse's benefit that is equal to half your benefit. So if your benefit is $819.00, your spouse gets $409.00.

If your spouse is between ages 62 and 65, he or she can draw a reduced benefit; the amount depends on the number of months before 65 that he or she starts getting checks. If he or she draws his or her benefit when he or she is 62, he or she will get about 3/8 of your basic benefit, or $307.00. (He or she will get this amount for the rest of his or her life, unless you should die first; then he or she can start getting widow's or widower's benefits, described below.)

If the spouse is entitled to a worker's retirement benefit on his or her own earnings, he or she can draw whichever amount is larger. If the spouse is entitled to a retirement benefit which is less than the spouse's benefit, he or she will receive his or her own retirement benefit plus the difference between the retirement benefit and the spouse's benefit.

If you have children under 18 or a child under age 19 in full-time attendance at an elementary or secondary school or a son or daughter who became totally disabled prior to reaching age 22, when you retire they will get a benefit equal to half your full retirement benefits (subject to maximum payments that can be made to a family). If your spouse is caring for a child who is under 16 or who became disabled before 22 (and getting benefits too), he or she is eligible for benefits, even if he or she is under 62.

In general, the highest retirement check that can be paid to a worker who retired at 65 in Jan. 1993 is about $1128.00 a month. Maximum payment to the family of this retired worker is about $1,974.00 in Jan. 1993. When your children reach age 18, their benefits will stop except for children under age 19 attending an elementary or secondary school and except for a benefit that is going to a son or daughter who became totally disabled before attaining age 22. Such a person can continue to get his benefits as long as his disability meets the definition in the law.

If you are divorced, you can get Social Security benefits (the same as a spouse or widow, or widower), based on your ex-spouse's earnings record if you were married at least 10 years and if your ex-spouse has retired, become disabled, or died. If a divorced spouse has been divorced for at least 2 years, the spouse may be eligible for benefits even if the worker is not receiving benefits. However, both the worker and spouse must be age 62 or over and the worker must be fully insured.

Survivor benefits. This feature of the social security program gives your family valuable life insurance protection—in some cases benefits to a family could amount to $100,000 or more over a period of years. The amount of protection is again geared to what the worker would be entitled to if he had been age 65 when he died. Your survivors could get:

1. A one-time cash payment. [NOTE: There is no restriction on the use of the lump-sum death payment.] This "lump-sum death payment" is $255.

2. A benefit for each child until he reaches 18, or 19 if the child is in full-time attendance at an elementary or secondary school or at any age if disabled before 22. Each eligible child receives 75% of the basic benefit (subject to reduction for the family maximum). (A disabled child can continue to collect benefits after age 22.) If certain conditions are met, dependent grandchildren of insured workers can receive survivor or dependent benefits.

3. A benefit for your widow(er) at any age, if she/he has children under 16 or disabled in care. Her/his benefit is also 75% of the basic benefit. She/he can collect this as long as she/he has a child under 16 or disabled now "in care." Payments stop then (they will start again upon application when she/he is 60 at a slightly lower amount).

Total family survivor benefits are estimated to be as high as $2,320.00 a month if the worker dies in 1993.

4. If there are no children either under 16 or disabled, your spouse or divorced spouse can get a widow's, widower's, or surviving divorced spouse's benefit starting at age 60. This would come to 71 1/2% of the basic amount at age 60. A widow, or widower, who first becomes entitled at 65 or later may get 100% of his or her deceased spouse's basic amount (provided neither he nor she ever drew reduced benefits).

5. Dependent parents can sometimes collect survivors' benefits. They are usually eligible if: (a) they were getting at least half their support from the deceased worker at (1) the time of the worker's death if the worker did not qualify for disability benefits before death, or (2) if the worker had been entitled to disability benefits which had not been terminated before death either at the beginning of the period of disability or at the time of death; (b) they have reached 62; and (c) they are not eligible for a greater retirement benefit based on their own earnings. A single surviving parent can then get 82 1/2% of the basic benefit. If two parents are eligible, each would get 75%.

Here is an example of survivors' benefits in one family situation: John Jones died at age 29 in June 1993 leaving a wife and two children aged one and three. He had average covered earnings under Social Security. Family survivors' benefits would include: (1) a cash lump-sum death payment of $255, and (2) a total monthly benefit of $1,488 for the family. When the children reach 18, their benefits stop unless they are attending an elementary or secondary school full time, in which case payments continue up to age 19. When the older child no longer collects benefits, the widow and younger child continue to get benefits until that child is 16. He will still get a benefit until age 18 (or age 19, if he continues in elementary or secondary school), but Mrs. Jones' checks will stop. When Mrs. Jones becomes 60 (assuming she has not remarried), she will be able to get a reduced widow's benefit if she so chooses, or she can wait until age 65 to get a full benefit.

If in addition to your Social Security benefit as a wife, husband, divorced spouse, widow, widower, or surviving divorced spouse you receive a pension based on your work in employment not covered by Social Security, your benefit as a spouse or survivor will be reduced by 2/3rds of the amount of that pension. Under an exception in the law, your government pension will not affect your spouse's or survivor's benefit if you became eligible for that pension before December 1982 and if, at the time you apply or become entitled to your social security benefit as a spouse or survivor, you could have qualified for that benefit if the law in effect in January 1977 had remained in effect (e.g., at that time, men had to prove they were dependent upon their wives for support to be eligible for benefits as a spouse or survivor.) There are also several other exceptions in the law. Your government pension, however, currently will not affect any Social Security benefit based on your own work covered by social security.

Work Credit for Disabilty Benefits

Born after 1929, become disabled at age	Born before 1930, become disabled before 62 in	Years of work credit you need
42 or younger	1971	5
44	1973	5 1/2
46	1975	6
48	1977	6 1/2
50	1979	7
51	1980	7 1/4
52	1981	7 1/2
54	1983	8
56	1985	8 1/2
58	1987	9
60	1989	9 1/2
62 or older	1991 or later	10

NOTE: Five years of this credit must have been earned in the 10 years ending when you became disabled; years need not be continuous or in units of full years.

Disability Benefits. Disability benefits can be paid to several groups of people:

Disabled workers under 65 and their families.

Persons disabled before 22 who continue to be disabled. These benefits are payable as early as 18 when a parent (or grandparent under certain circumstances) receives social security retirement or disability benefits or when an insured parent dies.

Disabled widows and widowers and (under certain conditions) disabled surviving divorced spouses of workers who were insured at death. These benefits are payable as early as 50.

A disabled person is eligible for Medicare after being entitled to disability payments for 24 months.

If you are a worker and become severely disabled, you will be eligible for monthly benefits if you have worked under Social Security long enough and recently enough. The amount of work you will need depends on your age when you become disabled:

Before 24: You need credit for 1 1/2 years of work in the 3-year period ending when your disability begins.

24 through 30: You need credit for having worked half the time between 21 and the time you become disabled.

31 or older: All workers disabled at 31 or older—except the blind—need the amount of credit shown in the chart.

To be considered disabled under the social security law you must be: (1) unable to engage in any substantial activity because of any medically determinable physical or mental impairment which can be expected to result in death or has lasted for 12 continuous months, or (2) blind. A person whose vision is no better than 20/200 even with glasses, or who has a limited visual field of 20 degrees or less, is considered "blind" under the social security law.

If you meet these conditions, you may be able to get payments even if your recovery from the disability is expected.

The medical evidence from your physician or other sources will show the severity of your condition and the extent to which it prevents you from doing substantial gainful work. Your age, education, training, and work experience also may be considered in deciding whether you are able to work. If you can't do your regular work but can do other substantial gainful work, you will not be considered disabled.

While you are receiving benefits as a disabled worker, payments can also be made to certain members of your family. These family members include:

Your unmarried children under 18.

Your children under 19 if they are unmarried and attending an elementary or secondary school full time.

Your unmarried children 18 or older who were disabled before reaching 22 and continue to be disabled.

Your spouse at any age if she/he has in-care a child who is under 16 or disabled and who is getting benefits based on your social security record.

Your spouse 62 or older even if there are no children entitled to benefits.

A child may be eligible on a grandparent's social security record only if the child's parents are disabled or deceased and the child was living with and receiving 1/2 support from the grandparent at the time the grandparent qualified for benefits.

Benefits begin after a waiting period of 5 full calendar months. No benefits can be paid for these first 5 months of disability; therefore, the first payment is for the 6th full month. If you are disabled more than 6 full months before you apply, back benefits may be payable, but not before the 6th full month of disability. It is important to apply soon after the disability starts because back payments are limited to the 12 months preceding the month you apply.

Certain disabled people under 65 are eligible for Medicare. They include disabled workers at any age, persons who became disabled before age 22, and disabled widows and widowers age 50 or over who have been entitled to disability checks for 2 years or more.

Medicare protection generally ends when monthly disability benefits end, and can continue an additional 3 years after benefits stop because an individual returns to gainful work. (Under certain circumstances, former disability beneficiaries may purchase continued Medicare coverage. *See* "Do You Qualify for Hospital Insurance?" in this section.)

If a person becomes entitled to disability benefits again, Medicare coverage starts at the same time if a worker becomes disabled again within 5 years after benefits end (or within 7 years for a disabled widow, widower, or person disabled before age 22).

Benefits to workers disabled after 1978 and their dependents are based, in part, on earnings that have been adjusted to take account of increases in average wages since they were earned. The adjusted earnings are averaged together and a formula is applied to the adjusted average to figure the benefit rate.

Monthly benefits in Jan. 1993 or later can be as high as $1,345.00 for a worker and as high as $2,071.00 for a worker with a family. Once a person starts receiving benefits, the amount will increase automatically in future years to keep pace with the rising cost of living.

If you receive benefits as a disabled worker, an adult disabled since childhood, or a disabled widow or widower, you are not subject to the general rule under which some benefits are withheld if you have substantial earnings. There are special rules, which include medical considerations, for determining how any work you do might affect your disability payments.

If one of your dependents who is under 65 and who is not disabled works and earns more than $7,680 in 1993, some of the dependent's benefits may be withheld. In general, $1 in benefits is withheld for each $2 over $7,680. Different rules apply to your dependents who are 65 or over. A person 65 or over can earn $10,560 in 1993 without having benefits withheld. For persons 65 or over, $1 in benefits is withheld for $3 in earnings over $10,560.

The amount a person can earn without having any benefits withheld will increase in future years as the level of average wages rises.

If you are receiving disability benefits, you are required by law to let the Social Security Administration know if your condition improves or if you return to work no matter how little you earn.

If at any time medical evidence shows that you no longer meet the requirements for entitlement to disability benefits, you will still receive benefits for a 3-month period of adjustment. Benefits will then be stopped.

Whether or not you report a return to work or that your condition has improved, Social Security will review your claim periodically to see if you continue to meet the requirements for benefits.

If you are a disabled worker or a person disabled in childhood and you return to work in spite of a severe condition, your benefits may continue to be paid during a trial work period of up to 9 months—not necessarily consecutive months. This will give you a chance to test your ability to work. If after 9 service months it is decided that you are able to do substantial gainful work, your benefits will be paid for an adjustment period of 3 additional months.

Thus, if you go to work in spite of your disability, you may continue to receive disability benefits for up to 12 months, even though the work is substantial gainful work. If it is decided that the work you are able to do is not substantial and gainful, you may continue to receive benefits. Of course, should you no longer meet the requirements for entitlement to disability, your benefits would be stopped after a 3-month adjustment period even though your trial work period might not be over.

Disabled widows and widowers also can have a trial work period. If your benefits are stopped because you return to work and you become unable to continue working within the next 33 months, your benefits can be restarted automatically. You do not have to file a new disability application.

You Can Earn Income Without Losing Benefits

If you are 70 or over you can earn any amount and still get all your benefits. If you are under 70, you can receive all benefits if your earnings do not exceed the annual exempt amount. The annual amount for 1993 is $10,560 for people 65 or over and $7,680 for people under 65.

If your earnings go over the annual amount, $1 in benefits is withheld for each $2 ($3 if age 65-69) of earnings above the limit.

The monthly measure used for 1977 and earlier years to determine whether benefits could be paid for any month during which they earned 1/12 or less of the annual exempt amount and did not perform substantial work in their business has been eliminated. A person can now use the monthly test only in the first year that he or she has a month in which earnings do not exceed 1/12 of the annual exempt amount or does not perform substantial services in self-employment. If such a month occurs in 1993, a benefit can be paid for any month in which you earn $880 or less (if 65 or older) or $640 or less (if under 65) and don't perform substantial services in self-employment even though your total yearly earnings exceed the annual amount.

The annual exempt amount will increase automatically as the level of average wages rises.

If a worker's earnings exceed the exempt amount, social security benefits to his dependents may be reduced. However, a dependent's benefits will not be reduced if another dependent has excess earnings.

Anyone earning over the annual exempt amount a year while receiving benefits (and under age 70) must report these earnings to the Social Security Administration. If you continue to work after you have applied for social security, your additional earnings may increase the amount of your monthly payment. This will be done automatically by the Social Security Administration. You need not ask for it.

Medicare

The Medicare program is administered by the Health Care Financing Administration.

Most people 65 and over and many under 65 who have been entitled to disability checks for at least 2 years have Medicare protection. So do insured people and their dependents who need a kidney transplant or dialysis treatment because of permanent kidney failure.

The hospital insurance part of Medicare helps pay the cost of inpatient hospital care and certain kinds of follow-up care. The medical insurance part helps pay for the cost of doctors' services, outpatient hospital services, and for certain other medical items and services.

A person who is eligible for monthly benefits at 65 gets hospital insurance automatically and does not have to pay a premium. He does pay a monthly premium for medical insurance.

Supplemental Security Income

The supplemental security income (SSI) program is a federally funded program administered by the Social Security Administration. Its basic purpose is to assure a minimum level of income to people who are elderly (65 or over), blind or disabled, and who have limited income and resources.

In 1993, the maximum Federal SSI payment was $434 a month for an individual and $652 a month for a couple. But in many States, SSI payments are much higher because the State adds to the Federal payment.

Countable resources must be valued at $2,000 or less for an individual or $3,000 or less for a couple. But not all the things people own count for SSI. For instance, the house a person lives in and the land around it, and usually, one car does not count.

Generally, depending on the State, people who get SSI can also get Medicaid to pay for their health care costs as well as food stamps and other social services. And in many States an application for SSI is an application for Medicaid, so people do not have to make separate applications. Certain people can also apply for food stamps at the same Social Security office where they apply for SSI.

Social Security representatives will need information about the income and resources and the citizenship or alien status of people applying for benefits. If the person is living with a spouse, or the application is for a disabled child living with parents, the same information is needed about the spouse/parents.

People who are age 65 or over will need proof of their age such as a birth certificate, or religious record. And if a person who is filing is disabled or blind, Social Security will need information about the impairment and its treatment history.

It helps if people have this information and evidence with them when they talk to their Social Security representative. But they do not need to have **any** of these things to **start** their application. All they need to do is to call Social Security to find out if they are eligible for SSI payments and the other benefits that come with it. Benefits are not retroactive, so delay can cost money.

The Social Security representative will explain just what information/evidence is needed for the SSI claim, and will provide help in getting it if help is needed. Most Social Security offices will make an appointment for an office visit or for a telephone interview if that is more convenient. Or people can just walk in, and wait until someone is free to help them.

Over 5 million people receive SSI benefits now. Many receive both SSI and Social Security. Do not wait. Call 1-800-772-1213, and find out more about SSI. Even the call is free!

How to Protect Your Social Security Record

Always show your Social Security card when you start a new job. In that way you will be sure that your earnings will be credited to *your* Social Security record and not someone else's. If you lose your Social Security card, contact Social Security to find out how to apply for a new one. When a woman marries, she should apply for a new card showing her married name (and the same number).

Public Assistance

The Federal government makes grants to the states to help them provide financial assistance, medical care, and social services to certain persons in need, including children dependent because of the death, absence from home, incapacity, or (in some states) unemployment of a parent. In addition, some help is provided from only state and/or local funds to some other needy persons.

Federal sharing in state cash assistance expenditures made in accordance with the Social Security Act is based on formulas which are set forth in the Act. The Social Security Act gives the states the option of using one of two formulas, whichever is to its benefit. One formula limits the amount of assistance payment in which there is federal sharing. The other formula permits federal sharing without a limit on the amount of assistance payment. Administrative costs in all the programs are shared equally by the federal and state governments.

Within these and other general patterns set by the requirements of the Social Security Act and their administrative interpretations, each state initiates and administers its own public assistance programs, including the determination of who is eligible to receive assistance, and how much can be granted and under what conditions. Assistance is in the form of cash payments made to recipients, except that direct payments are used for medical care, and restricted payments may be used in cases of mismanagement. Other social services are provided, in some instances, to help assistance recipients increase their capacity for self-care and self-support or to strengthen family life.

In the medical assistance Medicaid program, federal funds pay 50% to 83% of the costs for medical care. If it is to a state's benefit, it may use the Medicaid formula for federal sharing for its money payment programs, ignoring the maximum on dollar amounts per recipient.

Medicare Program

The Medicare program is a federal health-insurance program for persons 65 and over, disabled people under 65 who have been entitled to social security disability benefits at least 24 months, or have worked long enough in Federal employment to be insured for Medicare, and insured workers and their dependents at any age who need dialysis treatment or a kidney transplant because of permanent kidney failure.

Enacted under the Social Security Amendments of 1965, Medicare's official name is Title XVIII of the Social Security Act. These amendments also carried Title XIX, providing federal assistance to state medical-aid programs, which has come to be known as Medicaid.

Medicare

It will be helpful to your understanding of the Medicare program if you keep the following points in mind:

- The federal health-insurance program does not of itself offer medical services. It helps pay hospital, doctor, and other medical bills. You choose your own doctor, who prescribes your treatment and place of treatment. But, you should always make sure that health care facilities or persons who provide you with treatment or services are participating in Medicare. Usually, Medicare cannot pay for care from non-participating health care organizations.
- There are two parts of the program: (1) The hospital insurance part for the payment of most of the cost of covered care provided by participating hospitals, skilled nursing facilities, home health agencies, and hospices. (2) The medical insurance part which helps pay doctors' bills and certain other expenses.
- Another important point to remember: While Medicare pays the major share of the costs of many illnesses requiring hospitalization, it does not offer adequate protection for long-term illness or mental illness.
- Therefore, it may be advisable not to cancel any private health insurance you now carry. You may wish to cancel a policy whose benefits are duplicated by the federal program, and consider a new policy that will provide for the payment of costs not covered by the federal program. Private insurance companies offer policies supplementing the protection offered by the federal program.
- If you want help in deciding whether to buy private supplemental insurance, ask at any social security office for the pamphlet, *Guide to Health Insurance for People with Medicare.* This free pamphlet describes the various types of supplemental insurance available.

Do You Qualify for Hospital Insurance?

If you're entitled to monthly social security or railroad retirement checks (as a worker, dependent, or survivor), you have hospital insurance protection automatically when you're 65. People 65 or older who are not entitled to monthly benefits must have worked long enough under Social Security or the railroad retirement system or in covered Federal, state, and local employment to get hospital insurance without paying a monthly premium. If they do not have enough work, they can buy hospital insurance. The premium is $221 a month in 1993. Disabled people under 65 will have hospital insurance automatically after they have been entitled to social security disability benefits for 24 months. Effective July 1, 1990, former disability beneficiaries will be able to purchase hospital insurance if their premium-free coverage stops due to work activity. Federal, state, or local employees who are disabled before 65 may be eligible on the basis of their government employment. (Disabled people who get railroad annuities must meet special requirements.) People are eligible at any age if they need maintenance dialysis or a kidney transplant for permanent kidney failure and are getting monthly Social Security or railroad retirement benefits or have worked long enough.

To be sure your protection will start the month you reach 65, apply for Medicare insurance 3 months before reaching 65, even if you don't plan to retire.

Do You Qualify for Medicare Medical Insurance?

The medical insurance plan is a vital supplement to the hospital plan. It helps pay for doctors' and other medical services. Many people have not been able to obtain such insurance from private companies because they could not afford it or because of their medical histories.

One difference between the hospital insurance plan and the medical insurance plan is that you do not have to be covered under the social security or railroad retirement systems to enroll in the medical plan. Almost anyone who is 65 or older or who is eligible for hospital insurance can enroll in medical insurance.

People who get social security benefits or retirement benefits under the railroad retirement system will be enrolled automatically for medical insurance—unless they say they don't want it—when they become entitled to hospital insurance. Automatic enrollment does not apply to people who plan to continue working past 65, who are disabled widows or widowers between 50 and 65 who aren't getting disability checks, who are 65 but have not worked long enough to be eligible for hospital insurance, who have permanent kidney failure, who are eligible for Medicare on the basis of government employment, or who live in Puerto Rico or foreign countries. These people have to apply for medical insurance if they want it. People who have medical insurance pay a monthly premium covering part of the cost of this protection. The other part is paid from general federal revenues. The basic premium for enrollees is $36.60 a month in 1993.

Is Other Insurance Necessary?

As already indicated, Medicare provides only partial reimbursement. Therefore, you should know how much medical cost you can bear and perhaps arrange for other insurance.

In 1993, for the first 60 days of inpatient hospital care in each benefit period, hospital insurance pays for all covered services except for the first $676. For the 61st through 90th day of a covered inpatient hospital stay, hospital insurance pays for all covered services except for $169 a day. People who need to be in a hospital for more than 90 days in a benefit period can use some or all of their 60 lifetime reserve days. Hospital insurance pays for all covered services except for $338 a day for each reserve day used. Hospital insurance also does not pay the full cost of an inpatient stay in a skilled nursing facility.

Under medical insurance, the patient must meet an annual deductible. In 1993, the annual deductible is $100. After the patient has met the deductible, each year, medical insurance generally pays 80% of the approved amounts for any additional covered services the patient receives during the rest of the year.

How You Obtain Coverage

If you are receiving Social Security or railroad retirement monthly benefits, you will receive from the government information concerning Medicare about 3 months before you become eligible for hospital insurance.

All other eligible people have to file an application for Medicare. They should contact a social security office to apply for Medicare.

New Medicare Benefits

Breast Cancer Screening (Mammography): Medicare medical insurance now helps pay for X-ray screenings to detect breast cancer. Women 65 or older can use the benefit ever other year. Younger disabled women covered by Medicare can use it more frequently. Medicare will pay 80 percent of up to $58.29 for each screening in 1993.

Physician Payment Reforms: In 1993, physicians who do not accept assignment may not charge you for office and hospital visits more than 115 percent of the Medicare approved amount. Physicians who knowingly charge more than these amounts are subject to sanctions.

You no longer have to file claims to Medicare for covered medical insurance services. Doctors, suppliers, and other providers of services must submit the claims to Medicare within one year of providing the service to you or be subject to certain penalties. □

Sixty-Five Plus in America

Source: Current Population Reports, Bureau of the Census.

In 1990, the Baby Boom generation was nearly one-third of the American population and in their economically productive years. They were also raising families, the Baby Echo.[1] The elderly population was one-eighth of the total population and numbered 31.1 million.

The oldest old are a small but rapidly growing group in the United States. In 1900, 374,000 people were 80 years or older compared with 1990 when nearly 7 million were at that age. The 1990 census counted about 3 million seniors who were 85 years or older and nearly 1 million elderly who reported their age as 90 years or older. Centenarians, persons who had reached the exceptional age of 100 or older, numbered 36,000 persons in 1990. That is more than double the number estimated in 1980. About four out of every five centenarians are women.

Overall, the age group 85 and over is projected to be the fastest growing part of the elderly population into the next century. Since 1960, this group increased 232 percent compared with an increase of 89 percent for the population 65 years and over and 39 percent for the total population. While such growth rates are extremely high, those attaining 85 years and over are a relatively small group, just over 1 percent of the American population. Their size is already sufficient, however, to have a major impact on the nation's health and social service systems. Longer life expectancy has not necessarily translated into better health for the oldest old.

The experience and problems of the young old caring for the oldest old will become more and more familiar throughout society. The physician condition of the young old may become a serious issue as they try to help frail elderly move from beds to chairs to baths and toilets. Need for a greater diversity of home aids and increased demands for access to public buildings for the disabled are likely.

1. A Baby Boomlet or Baby Echo are terms for the children of persons born during the Baby Boom. Baby Boomers are those born between 1946 and 1964.

By 2010, the Baby Boom will be aged 45 to 64. After that, growth of the elderly population will be more dramatic as the Baby Boom becomes the Grandparent Boom (to a certain extent, we are talking about a Grandma Boom assuming women continue to outnumber men significantly). From 2010 to 2030, they will be the young old and the aged (65 to 74 years old and 75 to 84 years old). Women are expected to outnumber men 3 to 2. During these two decades, the population aged 65 to 84 years would grow 73 percent under middle series projections while the population aged 85 and over would grow 33 percent. The population under age 675 would decrease almost 3 percent.

After 2030, we will see the final phase of the gerontological explosion. The growth of the young old would decelerate as the cohort born after the Baby Boom, from 1965 to 1984, will be ages 65 through 84 in 2050. That age group would decrease from 57 million in 2030 to 53 million in 2050. It is the size of the oldest old population that we will notice most as the aging of the aged, the Great-Grandparent Boom begins. The population aged 85 and over would more than double, from 3 million in 1990 to 8 million in 2030. This group would nearly double in size again by 2050, to over 15 million, as the survivors of the Baby-Boom cohort reach the oldest ages. The oldest old would be then 5 percent of the total population in 2050.

If mortality levels continue on the same course as we are experiencing now, by the middle of the next century, about 8 million Americans would be 90 years or older compared with just under 1 million in 1990. If mortality rates decrease at a faster rate among the oldest old than is projected, the numbers will be much higher. If fertility rates decrease further, the elderly would become a larger proportion of the population than now. With such demographic facts staring us in the face, some (especially policy makers and businesses) are becoming more attentive to the implications of not just an older population, but of an aging society. □

ENERGY

Energy Overview

Source: Annual Energy Review, 1992.

Production

Historically, three fossil fuels have accounted for the bulk of domestic energy production, which by 1992 totaled 67 quadrillion Btu. Coal accounted for the largest share of domestic energy production in 1949–1951 and, after a long hiatus, again in 1982 and in 1984–1992. In the interim, first crude oil and then natural gas dominated domestic production. In 1992, coal production totaled 22 quadrillion Btu. Dry natural gas production totaled 18 quadrillion Btu and crude oil production totaled 15 quadrillion Btu. Natural gas plant liquids accounted for another 2.4 quadrillion Btu.

Electricity net generation increased throughout the 1949–1992 period, registering only two year-to-year declines (during the 1982 recession and again in 1992). However, the rate of growth of electricity net generation slowed during the 44-year period. From 1949 through 1979, the annual growth rate averaged 7.1%, whereas from 1980 through 1992, the annual growth rate averaged 1.7 percent. After the mid-1970s, coal and nuclear fuels provided increasing shares of fuel input for electricity generation, displacing substantial quantities of both petroleum and natural gas. Nuclear power used for electricity generation increased to the record level of 6.7 quadrillion Btu in 1992.

Hydroelectric generation accounted for over 1.4 quadrillion Btu of electricity in 1949 and from the 1970s through 1987 usually provided about 3 quadrillion Btu per year. However, in 1988, the second year of a drought, hydroelectric generation totaled only 2.3 quadrillion Btu. From 1989 through 1991, hydroelectric generation averaged about 2.9 quadrillion Btu per year. In 1992, a year of persistent drought in the West, the annual total fell to 2.5 quadrillion Btu. Renewable energy sources (other than hydroelectric generation) also contributed to the domestic energy supply. In 1992, electric utilities' generation of electricity from renewable sources such as geothermal, biofuel, and solar energy totaled 0.2 quadrillion Btu.

Consumption

Energy consumption more than doubled during the 1949–1973 period, increasing from 30 quadrillion Btu in 1949 to 74 quadrillion Btu in 1973, and the U.S. economy grew at about the same rate. The domestic energy market was dominated by rapid growth in petroleum and natural gas consumption, which more than tripled during the period. After the 1973 oil price shock, energy consumption fluctuated, influenced by dramatic changes in oil prices, changes in the rate of growth of the domestic economy, and factors such as concerns about the effect of energy use on the environment. The post-1973 low point of energy consumption, 71 quadrillion Btu, occurred in 1983 during a period of very high oil prices. The highest level of energy consumption, 82 quadrillion Btu, occurred in 1992, when oil prices were low.

The composition of demand after 1973 reflected a shift away from petroleum and, to a lesser extent, natural gas toward electricity generated by other fuels. In 1973, petroleum and natural gas accounted for 77 percent of total energy consumption; by 1992, their share had declined to 65 percent.

Industrial sector consumption proved to be the most responsive to the turmoil in energy markets after the 1973–1974 embargo. In 1979, it peaked at 33 quadrillion Btu. In the early 1980s, a stagnant economy restrained industrial consumption, which declined to a 16-year low of 26 quadrillion Btu in 1983. In 1988 and 1989, economic growth spurred demand for energy in the industrial sector, and industrial energy consumption in 1989 rose to 29 quadrillion Btu. Despite slower economic growth in 1990, industrial energy consumption rose modestly to 30 quadrillion Btu, but the economic recession in 1991 led to a 0.3-quadrillion Btu decline. In 1992, industrial use of petroleum and natural gas increased by 0.9 quadrillion Btu, while industrial use of electricity grew little and use of coal declined slightly.

Much of the growth in energy consumption during the 1949–1992 period occurred in the residential and commercial sector. Residential and commercial consumption leveled off in response to higher energy prices in the late 1970s and early 1980s, but lower prices in the 1986-to-1991 period played a role in boosting residential and commercial energy consumption to the record level of 29 quadrillion Btu in 1991.

Energy consumption by the transportation sector was primarily petroleum consumption. Over the 44-year period, the transportation sector's consumption of petroleum more than tripled, but growth was slower during the 1980s than in previous decades. In 1992, consumption of petroleum in the transportation sector totaled 22 quadrillion Btu, up about 1 percent from the 1991 level.

Changing Patterns of Trade

From 1958 forward, the United States consumed more energy than it produced, and the difference was met by energy imports. Net imports of energy (primarily petroleum) grew rapidly through 1973, as demand for cheap foreign oil eroded quotas on petroleum imports. The Arab oil embargo of 1973–1974, coupled with the increase in the price of crude oil, interrupted growth in petroleum net imports, but nevertheless they climbed to a peak of 18 quadrillion Btu in 1977. A second round of price increases, in 1979–1981, suppressed demand for foreign oil. In 1985, petroleum net imports totaled 9.0 quadrillion Btu, and U.S. dependence fell to 27% of consumption. Subsequently, petroleum net imports increased every year through 1989, when U.S. dependence on foreign sources of crude oil reached 42% of consumption. In 1992, U.S. dependence equaled 41%.

Natural gas trade was limited to border countries until the advent of shipping natural gas in liquefied form in the late 1960s. In 1992, natural gas net imports reached the record level of 1.8 quadrillion Btu. Throughout the 1949-to-1992 period, the United States was a net exporter of coal. In 1992, coal net exports totaled 2.6 quadrillion Btu. □

Energy Consumption and Consumption per Capita by State, 1991

Rank	State	Consumption Trillion Btu	Rank	State	Consumption per capita Million Btu
1.	Texas	9,785.1	1.	Alaska	1,030.9
2.	California	7,161.9	2.	Wyoming	849.5
3.	Ohio	3,686.9	3.	Louisiana	815.4
4.	New York	3,558.5	4.	Texas	564.0
5.	Illinois	3,513.0	5.	North Dakota	504.4
6.	Pennsylvania	3,491.6	6.	West Virginia	434.2
7.	Louisiana	3,468.9	7.	Indiana	431.5
8.	Florida	3,021.9	8.	Montana	422.9
9.	Michigan	2,753.9	9.	Kansas	416.4
10.	Indiana	2,421.0	10.	Oklahoma	404.1
11.	New Jersey	2,299.7	11.	Kentucky	397.7
12.	Georgia	2,057.0	12.	Washington	392.1
13.	Washington	1,965.1	13.	Alabama	388.8
14.	North Carolina	1,961.6	14.	New Mexico	379.6
15.	Virginia	1,848.4	15.	Idaho	372.7
16.	Tennessee	1,746.5	16.	Mississippi	366.2
17.	Alabama	1,590.7	17.	Tennessee	352.6
18.	Missouri	1,512.6	18.	Delaware	347.9
19.	Kentucky	1,476.5	19.	South Carolina	339.7
20.	Wisconsin	1,411.7	20.	Ohio	337.0
21.	Minnesota	1,363.7	21.	Iowa	335.4
22.	Massachusetts	1,313.1	22.	Nebraska	327.7
23.	Oklahoma	1,283.0	23.	Oregon	326.3
24.	Maryland	1,215.3	24.	Arkansas	324.3
25.	South Carolina	1,209.3	25.	Utah	320.0
26.	Kansas	1,038.9	26.	Nevada	311.9
27.	Colorado	964.2	27.	Georgia	310.6
28.	Oregon	953.4	28.	Minnesota	307.7
29.	Mississippi	949.6	29.	Illinois	304.4
30.	Iowa	937.4	30.	New Jersey	296.6
31.	Arizona	923.6	31.	Virginia	294.3
32.	West Virginia	782.9	32.	District of Columbia	294.3
33.	Arkansas	769.6	33.	Maine	293.6
34.	Connecticut	732.0	34.	Michigan	293.6
35.	New Mexico	588.0	35.	Missouri	293.3
36.	Alaska	587.6	36.	Pennsylvania	292.0
37.	Utah	566.3	37.	North Carolina	291.2
38.	Nebraska	522.0	38.	South Dakota	291.2
39.	Nevada	400.2	39.	Colorado	285.4
40.	Wyoming	390.8	40.	Wisconsin	284.8
41.	Idaho	387.7	41.	Maryland	250.1
42.	Maine	362.3	42.	Arizona	246.4
43.	Montana	342.1	43.	Hawaii	238.9
44.	North Dakota	320.3	44.	California	235.7
45.	Hawaii	271.6	45.	Vermont	233.7
46.	New Hampshire	238.7	46.	Florida	227.8
47.	Delaware	236.6	47.	Connecticut	222.6
48.	Rhode Island	214.5	48.	Massachusetts	219.0
49.	South Dakota	205.0	49.	New Hampshire	216.2
50.	District of Columbia	175.1	50.	Rhode Island	213.4
51.	Vermont	132.5	51.	New York	197.1
	United States	**81,119.0**		**United States**	**321.7**

Source: Energy Information Administration, *State Energy Data Report 1991, Consumption Eestimates* (May 1993).

Households That Burn Wood

Household characteristic	1980	1981	1982	1984	1987	1990
Households That Burn Wood						
Numbers of households (millions)	21.6	22.8	21.4	22.9	22.5	22.9
Share of all U.S. households (percent)	26.4	27.4	25.6	26.6	24.8	24.3
Wood energy consumed (trillion Btu)	854	881	971	981	853	582
Households That Burn Wood as Main Heating Fuel						
Number of households (millions)	4.7	5.3	5.6	6.4	5.0	3.9
Share of all U.S. households (percent)	5.8	6.4	6.7	7.5	5.6	4.1
Number of cords burned (millions)	22.4	24.7	28.7	29.4	23.5	15.0
Wood energy consumed (trillion Btu)	448	493	574	589	470	300

Source: Energy Information Administration, Form EIA–457, "Residential Energy Consumption Survey."

Selected Type of Heating in Occupied Housing Units, Percent

Year	Coal[1]	Natural gas	Liquefied gas	Distillate fuel oil	Kerosene	Electricity	Wood	Solar
1950	33.8	26.0	2.3	22.1	(2)	0.6	9.7	n.a.
1960	12.2	43.1	5.1	32.4	(2)	1.8	4.2	n.a.
1970	2.9	55.2	6.0	26.0	(2)	7.7	1.3	n.a.
1975	0.8	56.4	5.7	22.5	(2)	12.6	1.2	n.a.
1980	0.4	55.4	5.2	18.1	0.5	17.7	1.7	n.a.
1983[3]	0.5	55.2	4.6	14.9	0.5	18.5	4.8	n.a.
1985	0.5	51.3	4.1	14.1	1.2	20.8	7.1	0.1
1987	0.4	50.6	4.0	14.0	1.2	22.7	6.0	0.1
1989	0.4	50.6	3.9	13.3	1.1	24.6	4.9	(4)
1991	0.3	50.5	4.2	12.3	1.1	25.5	4.8	(4)

1. Includes coal coke. 2. Included in distillate fuel oil. 3. Since 1983, the *American Housing Survey for the United States* has been a biennial survey. 4. Less than 0.1 percent. n.a. = Not available. NOTES: Includes mobile homes and individual housing units in apartment buildings. Housing units with more than one type of heating system are classified according to the principal type of heating system. *Sources:* 1950, 1960, and 1970—Bureau of the Census, *Census of Population and Housing.* 1973 and forward—Bureau of the Census, *American Housing Survey for the United States in 1991,* Table 2–5.

Households With Selected Appliances

Appliance	Percent of households					
	1980	1981	1982	1984	1987	1990
Type of Appliances						
Electric Appliances						
Television set (color)	82	82	85	88	93	96
Television set (B/W)	51	48	47	43	36	31
Clothes washer	75	74	72	74	76	76
Range (stove-top burner)	54	54	53	54	57	58
Oven, regular or microwave	59	58	59	63	79	88
Oven, microwave	14	17	21	34	61	79
Clothes dryer	47	45	45	46	51	53
Separate freezer	38	38	37	37	34	35
Dishwasher	37	37	36	38	43	45
Dehumidifier	9	9	9	9	10	12
Waterbed heaters[1]	n.a.	n.a.	n.a.	10	14	15
Window or ceiling fan	n.a.	n.a.	28	35	46	51
Whole house fan	n.a.	n.a.	8	8	9	10
Evaporative cooler	4	4	4	4	3	4
Personal computer	n.a.	n.a.	n.a.	n.a.	n.a.	16
Pump for well water	n.a.	n.a.	n.a.	n.a.	n.a.	15
Swimming pool pump[2]	4	4	4	4	3	5
Gas Appliances[3]						
Range (stove-top or burners)	46	46	47	45	43	42
Oven	42	40	42	42	41	41
Clothes dryer	14	16	15	16	15	16
Outdoor gas grill	9	9	11	13	20	26
Outdoor gas light	2	2	2	1	1	1
Swimming pool heater[4]	n.a.	n.a.	n.a.	1	1	2
Refrigerators[5]						
One	86	87	86	88	86	84
Two or more	14	13	13	12	14	15
Air Conditioning (A/C)						
Central[6]	27	27	28	30	36	39
Individual room units[6]	30	31	30	30	30	29
None	43	42	42	40	36	32
Portable kerosene heaters	(1)	1	3	6	6	5

1. Less than 0.5 percent. 2. All reported swimming pools were assumed to have an electric pump for filtering and circulating the water. 3. Includes natural gasd or liquefied petroleum gases (LPG). 4. In 1984, 1987, and 1990, also includes heaters for jacuzzis and hot tubs. 5. Fewer than 0.5 percent of the households do not have a refrigerator. 6. Households with both central and individual room units are counted only under central. n.a. = Not available. NOTE: No data are available for years not shown. *Sources:* 1978 and 1979—Energy Information Administration (EIA), Form EIA-84, "Residential Energy Consumption Survey;" 1980 forward—EIA, Form EIA-457, "Residential Energy Consumption Survey."

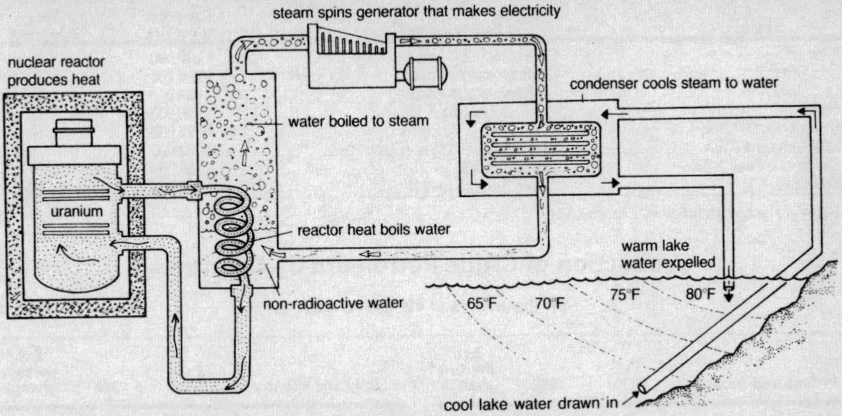

Simplified diagram of a nuclear reactor. Laurel Cook, Boston, MA.

Largest Nuclear Power Plants in the United States

(over a million kilowatts)

Plant	Operating utility	Capacity (kilowatts)	Year operative
South Texas 1, TX	Houston Lighting & Power	1,250,000	1988
South Texas 2	Houston Lighting	1,250,000	1989
Palo Verde 1, AZ	Arizona Public Service	1,221,000	1986
Palo Verde 2, AZ	Arizona Public Service	1,221,000	1986
Palo Verde 3, AZ	Arizona Public Service	1,221,000	1988
Perry 1, OH	Cleveland Electric Illumination	1,205,000	1987
Sequoyah 1, TN	Tennessee Valley Authority	1,148,000	1981
Sequoyah 2, TN	Tennessee Valley Authority	1,148,000	1982
Callaway, MO	Union Electric	1,145,000	1984
Grand Gulf 1, MS	System Energy Resources	1,142,000	1985
Millstone 3, CT	Northeast Nuclear Energy	1,142,000	1986
Catawba 1, SC	Duke Power Co.	1,129,000	1985
Catawba 2, SC	Duke Power Co.	1,129,000	1986
McGuire 1, NC	Duke Power Co.	1,129,000	1981
McGuire 2, NC	Duke Power Co.	1,129,000	1984
Wolf Creek 1, KS	Wolf Creek Nuclear Operating	1,128,000	1985
Braidwood 1, IL	Commonwealth Edison	1,120,000	1988
Braidwood 2, IL	Commonwealth Edison	1,120,000	1988
Salem 1, DE	Public Service Electric & Gas	1,106,000	1977
Salem 2, DE	Public Service Electric & Gas	1,106,000	1981
Byron 1, IL	Commonwealth Edison	1,105,000	1985
Byron 2, IL	Commonwealth Edison	1,105,000	1987
Vogtle 2	Georgia Power	1,083,000	1989
Trojan, OR	Portland General Electric	1,095,000	1976
Fermi 2, OH	Detroit Edison	1,093,000	1988
Diablo Canyon 2	Pacific Gas & Electric	1,087,000	1986
Nine Mile Point 2, NY	Niagara Mohawk Power	1,080,000	1988
San Onofre 3, CA	Southern California Edison	1,080,000	1984
Vogtle 1, GA	Georgia Power	1,079,000	1987
Waterford 3, LA	Louisiana Power & Light	1,075,000	1985
Diablo Canyon 1, CA	Pacific Gas & Electric	1,073,000	1985
San Onofre 2, CA	Southern California Edison	1,070,000	1983
Hope Creek 1, DE	Public Service Electric & Gas	1,067,000	1986
Browns Ferry 1, AL	Tennessee Valley Authority	1,065,000	1974
Browns Ferry 2, AL	Tennessee Valley Authority	1,065,000	1975
Browns Ferry 3, AL	Tennessee Valley Authority	1,065,000	1977
Limerick 2	Philadelphia Elec	1,065,000	1990
Cook 2, MI	Indiana & Michigan Power	1,060,000	1978
Limerick 1, PA	Philadelphia Electric	1,055,000	1986
Peach Bottom 2, PA	Philadelphia Electric	1,051,000	1974
Zion 1, IL	Commonwealth Edison	1,040,000	1973

Plant	Operating utility	Capacity (kilowatts)	Year operative
Zion 2, IL	Commonwealth Edison	1,040,000	1974
La Salle 1, IL	Commonwealth Edison	1,036,000	1984
La Salle 2, IL	Commonwealth Edison	1,036,000	1984
Peach Bottom 3, PA	Philadelphia Gas & Electric	1,035,000	1974
Susquehanna 1, PA	Pennsylvania Power & Light	1,032,000	1983
Susquehanna 2, PA	Pennsylvania Power & Light	1,032,000	1985
Comanche Peak 1, TX	Texas Utilities	1,159,000	1990
Seabrook 1, NH	Public Service of N.H.	1,150,000	1990

Source: Nuclear Regulatory Commission.

Production of Crude Petroleum by Countries

(in thousands of 42–gallon barrels)

Area and country	Est. 1993[1]	1992[1]	Est. percent change
Western Hemisphere	5,804,230	5,892,195	–1.5
Argentina	203,670	193,450	5.3
Bolivia	7,665	7,300	5.0
Brazil	234,695	230,315	1.9
Canada	572,685	577,430	–0.8
Chile	5,110	5,475	–6.7
Columbia	182,500	167,900	8.7
Ecuador	119,355	113,515	5.1
Mexico	952,650	969,805	–1.8
Peru	45,260	39,420	14.8
Trinidad	45,625	52,560	–13.2
United States	2,556,460	2,689,320	–4.9
Venezuela	868,335	836,580	3.8
Western Europe	1,642,500	1,692,505	–3.0
Austria	9,125	9,125	0.0
Denmark	58,765	59,130	–0.6
France	20,075	21,170	–5.2
Germany	21,900	23,725	–7.7
Italy	29,200	35,405	–17.5
Netherlands	16,425	21,170	–22.4
Norway	759,200	773,435	–1.8
Spain	5,110	7,665	–33.3
Turkey	29,200	28,835	1.3
United Kingdom	688,755	707,370	–2.6
Eastern Europe	3,142,285	3,543,420	–11.3
Albania	5,840	6,205	–5.9
Hungary	12,045	12,045	0.0
Romania	50,005	48,545	3.0
C.I.S.[2]	3,048,480	3,450,710	–11.7
Croatia	15,695	15,695	0.0
Serbia	8,030	8,030	0.0
Middle East	6,681,690	6,230,915	7.2
Bahrain	39,420	39,785	–0.9
Iran	1,355,245	1,254,140	8.1
Iraq	155,125	156,950	–1.2
Kuwait	605,535	170,820	254.5
Oman	273,750	265,720	3.0
Qatar	162,425	120,815	34.4
Saudi Arabia	2,994,825	3,096,295	–3.3
Syria	204,400	180,675	13.1
United Arab Emirates	825,625	880,015	–6.2
Yemen	65,700	65,700	0.0
Asia Pacific	2,396,590	2,376,515	0.8
Australia	189,800	191,625	–1.0
Brunei	62,780	62,050	1.2
China	1,050,470	1,039,520	1.1
India	192,355	217,540	–11.6
Indonesia	498,225	516,475	–3.5
Japan	5,840	6,570	–11.1
Malaysia	234,695	241,265	–2.7
New Zealand	14,600	13,140	11.1
Pakistan	25,550	27,375	–6.7
Papua New Guinea	51,100	365	13,900.0
Thailand	18,980	18,250	4.0
Vietnam	41,975	36,500	15.0
Africa	2,318,480	2,325,780	–0.3
Algeria	281,050	288,715	–2.7
Angola	190,895	186,150	2.5
Cameroon	47,450	54,750	–13.3
Congo	76,650	62,050	23.5
Egypt	317,550	317,915	–0.1
Gabon	109,500	104,390	4.9
Libya	524,870	567,940	–7.6
Nigeria	719,050	690,215	4.2
Tunisia	37,595	42,340	–11.2
Zaire	9,125	9,125	0.0
World Total	**21,985,775**	**22,054,030**	**–0.3**

1. Based on Jan.–Feb. average. 2. Formerly the U.S.S.R. Totals may not add up due to rounding.

Energy Equivalents

(*Source:* Energy Information Administration.)

1 Btu of energy: one match tip, 250 calories (International Steam Table), or 0.25 kilocalories (food calories).

1,000 Btu of energy: two five–ounce glasses of table wine; 250 kilocalories (food calories), or 0.80 peanut butter and jelly sandwiches.

1 million Btu of energy: 90 pounds of coal, 120 pounds of oven dried hardwood, 8 gallons of motor gasoline, 10 therms of natural dry gas, 11 gallons of propane, 1.2 days of U.S. energy consumption per capita (1984), or two months dietary intake of a laborer.

1 barrel of crude oil: 14 days U.S. petroleum consumption per capita, 5.6 thousand cubic feet of dry natural gas, 0.26 short tons (520 pounds) of coal, or 1,700 kilowatts of electricity.

1 short ton of coal: 102 days of U.S. petroleum consumption per capita, 3.8 barrels of crude oil, 21 thousand cubic feet of dry natural gas, or 6,500 kilowatt-hours of electricity. □

Petroleum Imports by Selected Countries of Origin

(Thousand barrels per day)

	OPEC[1]						Non-OPEC			
Year	Algeria	Indonesia	Nigeria	Saudi Arabia	Vene-zuela	Arab OPEC[2]	Canada	Mexico	United Kingdom	Virgin Is. and Puerto Rico
1970	8	70	50	30	989	196	766	42	11	271
1975	282	390	762	715	702	1,383	846	71	14	496
1980	488	348	857	1,261	481	2,551	455	533	176	476
1985	187	314	293	168	605	472	770	816	310	275
1988	300	205	618	1,073	794	1,839	999	747	315	264
1989	269	183	815	1,224	873	2,130	931	767	215	353
1990	280	114	800	1,339	1,025	2,244	934	755	189	315
1991	[R]253	111	[R]703	[R]1,802	[R]1,035	[R]2,064	[R]1,033	[R]807	[R]138	[R]270
1992[P]	197	78	681	1,716	1,162	1,971	1,049	827	230	274

1. Organization of Petroleum Exporting Countries. 2. Algeria, Iraq, Kuwait, Libya, Qatar, Saudi Arabia, and United Arab Emirates. Imports from the Neutral Zone are included in imports from "Arab OPEC." R = Revised data. P = Preliminary data. NOTES: Data include imports for the Strategic Petroleum Reserve, which began in 1977. *Sources:* 1960–1975—Bureau of Mines, *Minerals Yearbook,* "Crude Petroleum and Petroleum Products" Chapter. 1976–1980—Energy Information Administration (EIA), Energy Data Reports, *P.A.D. Districts Supply/Demand Annual.* 1981–1991—EIA, *Petroleum Supply Annual.* 1992—EIA, *Petroleum Supply Monthly,* February 1993.

Petroleum Exports by Country of Destination

(Thousand Barrels per Day)

Year	Canada	Mexico	Japan	Nether-lands	Belgium[1]	Italy	U.K.	France	Brazil	Puerto Rico	Virgin Islands
1970	31	33	69	15	5	10	12	5	7	1	([2])
1975	22	42	27	23	9	10	7	6	6	5	7
1980	108	28	32	23	20	14	7	11	4	86	134
1985	74	61	108	44	26	30	14	11	3	26	135
1988	84	70	124	26	25	29	9	12	3	21	126
1989	92	89	122	36	23	37	9	11	5	18	123
1990	91	89	92	54	20	48	11	17	2	11	90
1991	70	99	95	72	22	55	13	27	13	10	107
1992[P]	64	124	100	52	22	38	12	9	20	7	88

1. Including Luxembourg. 2. Less than 500 barrels per day. P – Preliminary data. *Sources:* 1960–1975—Bureau of Mines, Mineral Industry Surveys, *Petroleum Statement Annual.* 1976–1980—Energy Information Administration (EIA), Energy Data Reports, *Petroleum Statement Annual.* 1981–1991—EIA, *Petroleum Supply Annual.* 1992—EIA, *Petroleum Supply Monthly,* February 1993.

U.S. Motor Vehicle Fuel Consumption and Related Data

(1991 estimate)

Type of vehicle	Total travel (million vehicle miles)	Number of registered vehicles	Average miles traveled per vehicle	Fuel consumed (thousand gallons)	Average fuel consumption per vehicle (gallons)
All passenger vehicles	1,548,589	147,763,939	10,480	71,775,106	486
Total personal passenger vehicles	1,542,846	147,132,660	10,486	70,910,679	482
Cars	1,533,668	142,955,623	10,728	70,727,119	495
Motorcycles	9,178	4,177,037	2,197	183,560	44
All buses	5,743	631,279	9,097	864,427	1,369
All cargo vehicles	623,625	44,785,033	13,925	56,849,158	1,269
Single unit trucks	526,676	43,180,698	12,197	39,684,160	919
Combination	96,949	1,604,335	60,429	17,164,998	10,699
All motor vehicles	2,172,214	192,548,972	11,281	128,624,264	668

Source: Department of Transportation, Federal Highway Administration.

DRUG USE AND ABUSE

Drugs in America: Historical Highlights

Source: From the exhibition, *Altered States: Alcohol and Other Drugs in America,* mounted by the Strong Museum, Rochester, New York.

1611 Jamestown colonists plant tobacco. European explorers saw Indians smoking tobacco and brought the habit back to the Old World, where it quickly spread. Initially, rulers banned tobacco, but the demand for the addictive weed grew so great that a lucrative drug trade in tobacco evolved. Besides being addicted to nicotine, people in the seventeenth century smoked and chewed tobacco because they believed it had medicinal benefits. This view developed from European observations of Native Americans who used tobacco topically to treat rheumatism, wounds, and toothaches, and who smoked it to relieve the common cold.

1656 First rum distillery opens in Boston. Immigrants introduced beer, hard cider, wine, brandy, rum, and gin to North America. Alcohol was both food and medicine. Most people believed that it nourished the body, eased its pains, cheered the heart, and prolonged life. The Puritan minister Increase Mather pronounced drink "a good Creature of God." Water, on the other hand, was often unsafe. Milk was scarce. Tea, coffee, and chocolate were luxuries.

Early 19th century: Dram drinking. In the early 19th century, many men began the day with a small shot or dram of whiskey measuring one-eighth of an ounce. Business transactions also began and ended with drams. Workers regularly stopped at 11:00 a.m. and 4:00 p.m. for whiskey breaks. Many employers paid workers in both cash and liquor rations—as much as eight ounces a day.

1820–1850 The temperance movement and "teetotaling." A temperance movement swelled between 1820 and 1850. Many societies were formed, aimed at curbing or eliminating alcohol consumption. Some temperance societies offered members a choice between swearing off alcohol altogether, or just strong drink. Total abstainers received a "T" for "total" abstinence—"teetotalers."

1840–1870 Opium imports increase seven times faster than the population growth. Aggressive advertising boosted patent medicine sales. Opium, morphine, or alcohol was usually the active ingredient. Because manufacturers were not yet required to label a product's ingredients, many people unknowingly became dependent upon tonics and elixirs that promised a quick fix. They simply knew that they felt fine if they took their medicine and unwell if they didn't. Other Americans smoked hashish or visited opium dens, using drugs solely for their pleasurable effects. In the 1870s and 1880s, the press shocked the public with exposés on the widespread use of opiates and other drugs for both medical and recreational use.

The Alcoholic Republic, 1800–1855

Americans steadily drank more and more whiskey during the early 1800s as supply increased and price tumbled. The annual per capita consumption of distilled spirits in 1830 was five gallons—nearly five times the amount people consume today. Like rum, whiskey was legal tender. People bartered with whiskey, paid their taxes with whiskey, and on some occasions, paid their ministers' salaries with whiskey. It was also a dietary staple because the supply of other beverages was unreliable and water sometimes carried disease.

Liquor and socializing were closely entwined. Taverns and inns served as important community centers. They sheltered and fed travelers and often served as the local trading post, post office, auction house, courtroom, polling place, recruiting and militia office, stage coach depot, and liquor retailer. As community gathering spots, they encouraged patrons to drink and smoke—often and in great quantities.

As whiskey consumption accelerated, drunkenness increased so markedly that it caused widespread community complaint and commentary. Family violence also became a more visible fact of life. Accounts of inebriate mothers neglecting their children spread, but these stories were outnumbered by incidents of wife and child beating.

These social ills coupled with rising incidents of alcohol-related illnesses alarmed many Americans, giving rise to a temperance movement between 1820 and 1850. The cries for temperance—moderate use of alcohol—and for complete abstinence swept across the United States with a wave of religious revivals. Secular societies also organized, including the Washingtonians, a support group similar to today's Alcoholics Anonymous. As a result of the temperance movement, drinking rates sharply dropped from five gallons per capita in 1830 to less than two gallons in 1840.

1860–1900 Bitters. Many Americans drank bitters, a concoction of alcohol and herbs, to aid digestion and health. Some manufacturers slyly increased the alcohol content of their products to 84 proof, or 42% alcohol. But because it was "medicine," even some temperance supporters who frowned upon drinking willingly dosed themselves with bitters.

1870 Hypodermic injection revolutionized drug use. Hypodermic injection allowed drugs such as morphine to enter the bloodstream directly. When injected, opiates killed pain quickly and caused an intense "high." This tempted some to repeatedly inject the drug despite the equally intense "down" or withdrawal that followed.

1881 Cigarette rolling machines invented. James Bonsack, a Virginia teenager, changed how Americans used tobacco. His machine could roll 70,000 cigarettes a day, the work of forty hand rollers. People could smoke more cheaply. Later Bonsack rollers produced 120,000 cigarettes a day, each delivering a measured dose of addicting nicotine.

1898 Bayer markets heroin cough syrup. Heroin is a semi-synthetic derivative of morphine and twice as potent. At first, people thought heroin was a non-addictive miracle drug. Some doctors even used heroin to treat morphine, alcohol, and cocaine addictions.

1920 Eighteenth Amendment forbids alcohol production and sales. The Eighteenth Amendment—Prohibition—was impossible to enforce. The Prohibition Bureau initially estimated it would cost $5 million to implement; by 1923, estimates rose to $28 million because so many ignored the law. Prohibition agents even took to the skies to spot illicit stills.

1921 Cigarette prohibition enacted in 14 states. By 1921, some states prohibited or restricted the sale of cigarettes, but supply and demand soared in the 1920s. Annual cigarette consumption rose from 2.5 billion in 1900 to 118.6 billion in 1919. Ads aimed at "the modern woman" portrayed the cigarette as a stylish and sexy accessory, persuading many to begin smoking cigarettes.

1933 Repeal of Prohibition/rise of the cocktail party. After the repeal of Prohibition, the cocktail party became a respectable social ritual suitable to smaller, servantless homes and apartments. It was a convenient way to entertain large numbers in small spaces without providing individual seating or dinner. Etiquette developed for dress, behavior, and the serving of "finger foods," allowing one to gracefully snack while holding a glass in one hand.

1956 Narcotic Control Act toughens penalties for marijuana and heroin sale and possession. Punitive action peaked with the Narcotics Control Act which stiffened penalties for drug users, provided lengthy mandatory minimum sentences, and the death sentence for persons over 18 convicted of selling heroin to persons under 18. The tough Narcotics Control Act reflected two fears of the 1950s: the fear of communism and the fear of racial minorities. Narcotics Commissioner Harry Anslinger and FBI Director J. Edgar Hoover were convinced that Chinese communists were controlling the drug trade to subvert America. Stiff penalties for users and drug dealers were designed to control potentially restive inner-city minorities.

1960 Timothy Leary experiments with LSD. In the early 1960s, Harvard psychology professor Timothy Leary became an apostle for LSD. He advised young people to "turn on, tune in, and drop out." "Acid" users who followed him wryly appropriated the advertising slogan, "better living through chemistry." They argued that LSD experiences opened up compelling inner vistas that, once viewed, would end social ills as varied as war, violence, and alcoholism. Dealers soaked LSD into blotter paper, sugar cubes, and animal crackers.

1964 Surgeon General reports smoking may be hazardous to health.

1965 Cigarette sales increase.

1967 Vietnam War escalates—marijuana use increases. For some Americans, marijuana represented a counterculture rejection of traditional values and the Vietnam War. In the 1950s and 60s, Americans became intrigued with Eastern culture and the enlightenment promised by Eastern philosophies. Many perceived marijuana and hashish as a harmless alternative to alcohol, a drug linked with aggression and the older generation. By 1979, about 50 million people had tried marijuana.

1971 Nixon declares war on drugs. Heroin use greatly increased between 1965 and 1970. After the army's 1968 anti-marijuana campaign, some soldiers serving in Vietnam turned to heroin. Many Americans incorrectly feared that vets would return addicted. Consequently, President Nixon declared "war on drugs." He created the National Institute on Drug Abuse, the DEA, and research programs on opioid addiction and treatment.

1985 Crack hits the streets. Cheap, smokable "crack" cocaine flooded west coast cities in the mid-1980s. Los Angeles street gangs, the Crips and the Bloods, acted as couriers and dealers.

1986 The Reagans declare war on drugs. On August 4, 1986, President Ronald Reagan declared war on drugs allocating nearly $4 billion for drug control. Using moral suasion, Mrs. Reagan later addressed the nation, calling upon citizens to "just say no" to drugs.

1992 Smokable heroin marketed in New York City. Researchers predict smokable heroin will be the drug of the 1990s as Americans, frightened of acquiring the AIDS virus through intravenous injection, will "chase the dragon" instead. Southeast Asia and Mexico, the source of "black tar," a crudely processed heroin, remain primary suppliers of the American market, although Colombia has increased its poppy cultivation.

Drug use today. Although overall drug use has declined, the rate of illicit drug use remains higher for American youth than for the youth of any other industrialized country. President Bush declared another war on drugs in his first televised speech as president in 1989. By 1992, the federal government's spending on drug control approximated $12 billion. □

Commonly Abused Drugs

NARCOTICS

The term narcotic in its medical meaning refers to opium and opium derivatives or synthetic substitutes.[1]

Under medical supervision, narcotics are administered orally or by intramuscular injection. As drugs of abuse, however, they also are sniffed, smoked, or self-administered by the more direct routes of subcutaneous ("skin-popping") and intravenous ("mainlining") injection.

The relief of suffering, whether of physical or psychological origin, may result in a short-lived state of euphoria. The initial effects, however, are often unpleasant, leading many to conclude that those who persist in their illicit use may have latent personality disturbances.

To the extent that the response may be felt to be pleasurable, its intensity may be expected to increase with the amount of the dose administered. Repeated use, however, will result in increasing tolerance: the user must administer progressively larger doses to attain the desired effect, thereby reinforcing the compulsive behavior known as drug dependence.

Since addicts tend to become preoccupied with the daily ritual of obtaining and taking drugs, they often neglect themselves and may suffer from malnutrition, infections, and unattended diseases or injuries. Among the hazards of narcotic addiction are toxic reactions to contaminants, such as quindine, sugars, and talcum power, as well as unsterile needles and injection techniques, resulting in abscesses, blood poisoning, hepatitis, and AIDS.

NARCOTICS OF NATURAL ORIGIN

The poppy *Papaver somniferum* is the main source of the nonsynthetic narcotics. It was grown in the Mediterranean region as early as 300 B.C. and has since been cultivated in countries around the world, such as Hungary, Turkey, India, Burma, China, Lebanon, Pakistan, Afghanistan, Laos, and Mexico.

Opium

There were no legal restrictions on the importation or use of opium until the early 1900s. In those days, patent medicines often contained opium without any warning label. Today, there are state, federal, and international laws governing the production and distribution of narcotics substances, and there is little abuse of opium in the United States.

Although a small amount of opium is used to make antidiarrheal preparations, such as paregoric, virtually all the opium imported into this country is broken down into its alkaloid constituents, principally morphine and codeine.

Morphine

The principal constituent of opium, ranging in concentration from 4 to 21 percent, morphine is one of the most effective drugs known for the relief of pain. It is marketed in the form of white crystals, hypodermic tablets, and injectable preparations. Its licit use is restricted primarily to hospitals. Morphine is odorless, tastes bitter, and darkens with age. It may be administered subcutaneously, intramuscularly, or intravenously, the latter method being the one most frequently resorted to by addicts.

Codeine

This alkaloid is found in raw opium in concentrations ranging from 0.7 to 2.5 percent. It was first isolated in 1832 as an impurity in a batch of morphine. Although it occurs naturally, most codeine is produced from morphine.

SEMI-SYNTHETIC NARCOTICS

Heroin

First synthesized from morphine in 1874, heroin was not extensively used in medicine until the beginning of this century. While it received widespread acceptance, the medical profession for years remained unaware of its potential for addiction. The first comprehensive control of heroin in the United States was established with the Harrison Narcotic Act of 1914.

Pure heroin is a white powder with a bitter taste. Illicit heroin may vary in both form and color. Most illicit heroin is a powder which may vary in color from white to dark brown because of impurities left from the manufacturing process or the presence of additives, such as food coloring, cocoa, or brown sugar.

Pure heroin is rarely sold on the street. A "bag"—slang for a single dosage unit of heroin—may weigh about 100 mg, usually containing about five percent heroin. To increase the bulk of the material sold to the addict, diluents are mixed with the heroin in ratios ranging from 9 to 1 to as much as 99 to 1. Sugars, starch, powdered milk, and quinine are among the diluents used.

Hydromorphone

Most commonly sold as Dilaudid, hydromorphone is the second oldest semi-synthetic narcotic analgesic. Marketed both in tablet and injectable form, it is shorter acting and more sedating than morphine, but its potency is from two to eight times as great. It is, therefore, a highly abusable drug, much sought after by narcotic addicts, who usually obtain it through fraudulent prescription or theft.

Oxycodone

Oxycodone is synthesized from thebaine. It is similar to codeine, but more potent and with a higher dependence potential. It is effective orally and is marketed in combination with aspirin as Percodan for the relief of pain. Addicts take Percodan orally or dissolve tablets in water, filter out the insoluble material, and "mainline" the active drug.

SYNTHETIC NARCOTICS

In contrast to pharmaceutical products derived directly or indirectly from narcotics of natural origin, synthetic narcotics are produced entirely within the laboratory. A continuing search for a product that will retain the analgesic properties of morphine without the consequent dangers of tolerance and dependence has yet to yield a drug that is not susceptible to abuse. The two that are most widely available are meperidine and methadone.

1. Cocaine, ecgonine, and coca leaves, classified as narcotics under the Controlled Substances Act (CSA), are discussed in the text on stimulants.

Drug Usage Trends Among Students

Drug use rises among eighth-grade students. LSD may be making a comeback. Twelfth graders' use continues to decline.

	Annual %		
	1991	1992	'91–'92 change
Marijuana/Hashish			
8th grade	6.2	7.2	+1.0 s
10th grade	16.5	15.2	–1.3
12th grade	23.9	21.9	–2.0 s
Inhalants[a, b]			
8th grade	9.0	9.5	+0.5
10th grade	7.1	7.5	+0.4
12th grade	6.6	6.2	–0.4
Hallucinogens[b]			
8th grade	1.9	2.5	+0.6 ss
10t grade	4.0	4.3	+0.3
12th grade	5.8	5.9	+0.1
LSD			
8th grade	1.7	2.1	+0.4 s
10th grade	3.7	4.0	+0.3
12th grade	5.2	5.6	+0.4
Hallucinogens other than LSD			
8th grade	0.7	1.1	+0.4 ss
10th grade	1.3	1.4	+0.1
12th grade	2.0	1.7	–0.3
Cocaine			
8th grade	1.1	1.5	+0.4 s
10th grade	2.2	1.9	–0.3
12th grade	3.5	3.1	–0.4

	Annual %		
	1991	1992	'91–'92 change
Crack			
8th grade	0.7	0.9	+0.2
10th grade	0.9	0.9	0.0
12th grade	1.5	1.5	0.0
Other cocaine[c]			
8th grade	1.0	1.2	+0.2
10th grade	2.1	1.7	–0.4
12th grade	3.2	2.6	–0.6 s
Heroin			
8th grade	0.7	0.7	0.0
10th grade	0.5	0.6	+0.1
12th grade	0.4	0.6	+0.2
Stimulants[d]			
8th grade	6.2	6.5	+0.3
10th grade	8.2	8.2	0.0
12th grade	8.2	7.1	–1.1 s
Tranquilizers[d]			
8th grade	1.8	2.0	+0.2
10th grade	3.2	3.5	+0.3
12th grade	3.6	2.8	–0.8 s
Alcohol			
Any use			
8th grade	54.0	53.7	–0.3
10th grade	72.3	70.2	–2.1 s
12th grade	77.7	76.8	–0.9

NOTE: Level of significance of difference between the two most recent classes: S = .05, ss = 0.1. Any apparent inconsistency between the change estimate and the prevalence estimates for the recent classes is due to rounding error. Approx. N = 8th grade = 17,500 in 1991; 18,600 in 1992. 10th grade = 14,800 in 1991; 14,800 in 1992. 12th grade = 15,000 in 1991; 15,800 in 1992. a. 12th grade only: Data based on five questionnaire forms. N is five-sixths of N indicated. b. 12th grade only: Unadjusted for underreporting of certain drugs. c. 12th grade only: Data based on four questionnaire forms. N is four-sixths of N indicated. d. 12th grade only: Only drug use which was not under a doctor's orders is included here. *Source:* The University of Michigan annual study "Monitoring the Future," conducted under a series of research grants from the National Institute on Drug Abuse to the U–M Institute for Social Research.

Meperidine (Pethidine)

The first synthetic narcotic, meperidine, is chemically dissimilar to morphine but resembles it in its analgesic effect. It is probably the most widely used drug for the relief of moderate to severe pain. Available in pure form as well as in products containing other medicinal ingredients, it is administered either orally or by injection, the latter method being the most widely abused. Tolerance and dependence develop with chronic use, and large doses can result in convulsions or death.

Methadone

German scientists synthesized methadone during World War II because of a shortage of morphine. Although chemically unlike morphine or heroin, it produces many of the same effects. Introduced into the United States in 1947, it became widely used in the 1960s in the treatment of narcotic addicts. The effects of methadone differ from morphine-based drugs in that they have a longer duration of action, lasting up to 24 hours, thereby permitting administration only once a day in heroin detoxification and maintenance programs. Moreover, methadone is almost as effective when administered orally as it is by injection. But tolerance and dependence may develop, and withdrawal symptoms, though they develop more slowly and are less severe, are more prolonged. Ironically, methadone, designed to control narcotic addiction, has emerged in some metropolitan areas as a major cause of overdose deaths.

DEPRESSANTS

Depressants have a potential for abuse associated with both physical and psychological dependence. Taken as prescribed as a physician, depressants may be beneficial for the relief of anxiety, irritability, and tension, and for the symptomatic treatment of insomnia. In excessive amounts, however, they produce a state of intoxication that is remarkably similar to that of alcohol.

Tolerance to the intoxicating effects develops rapidly, leading to a progressive narrowing of the margin of safety between an intoxicating and lethal dose. The person who is unaware of the dangers of increasing dependence will often increase the daily dose up to 10 or 20 times the recommended therapeutic level. The source of supply may be no farther than the family medicine cabinet. Depressants are also frequently obtained by theft, illegal prescription, or purchase on the illicit market.

In the world of illicit drug use, depressants often are used as self-medication to soothe jangled nerves brought on by the use of stimulants, to quell the anxiety of "flashbacks" resulting from prior use of hallucinogens, or to ease withdrawal from heroin. The dangers, it should be stressed, are compounded when depressants are used in combination with alcohol or other drugs. Chronic intoxication, though it affects every age group, is not common in middle age. The problem often remains unrecognized until the user exhibits recurrent confusion or an obvious inability to function.

Barbiturates

Among the drugs most frequently prescribed to induce sedation and sleep by both physicians and veterinarians are the barbiturates. About 2,500 derivatives of barbituric acid have been synthesized, but of these only about 15 remain in medical use. Small therapeutic doses tend to calm nervous conditions, and larger dozes cause sleep 20 to 60 minutes after oral administration. As in the case of alcohol, some individuals may experience a sense of excitement before sedation takes effect. If dosage is increased, however, the effects of the barbiturates may progress through successive stages of sedation, sleep, and coma to death from respiratory arrest and cardiovascular complications.

STIMULANTS

The two most prevalent stimulants are nicotine in tobacco products and caffeine, the active ingredient of coffee, tea, and some bottled beverages that are sold in every supermarket. When used in moderation, these stimulants tend to relieve fatigue and increase alertness. They are an accepted part of our culture.

Users tend to rely on stimulants to feel stronger, more decisive, and self-possessed. Because of the cumulative effects of the drugs, chronic users often follow a pattern of taking "uppers" in the morning and "downers," such as alcohol or sleeping pills, at night. Such chemical manipulation interferes with normal body processes and can lead to mental and physical illness.

Cocaine

The most potent stimulant of natural origin, cocaine is extracted from the leaves of the coca plant (Erythroxylon coca), which has been grown in the Andean highlands of South America since prehistoric times. The leaves of the plant are chewed in the region for refreshment and relief from fatigue.

Pure cocaine, the principal psychoactive ingredient, was first isolated in the 1880s. It was used as an anesthetic in eye surgery for which no previously known drug had been suitable. It became particularly useful in surgery of the nose and throat because of its ability to anesthetize tissue while simultaneously constricting blood vessels and limiting bleeding. Many of its therapeutic applications are now obsolete because of the development of safer drugs as local anesthetics.

Illicit cocaine is usually distributed as a white crystalline powder, often diluted by a variety of other ingredients, the most common of which are sugars such as lactose, inositol, mannitol, and local anesthetics such as lidocaine. The frequent adulteration is to increase volume and thus to multiply profits.

The drug is most commonly administered by being "snorted" through the nasal passages. Symptoms of repeated use in this manner may resemble the congested nose of a common cold.

The intensity of the psychological effects of cocaine, as with many psychoactive drugs, depends on the rate of entry into the blood. Intravenous injection or smoking produces an almost immediate intense experience. Cocaine hydrochloride, the usual form in which cocaine is sold, while soluble in water and sometimes injected, is fairly insensitive to heat. Conversion of cocaine hydrochloride to cocaine base yields a substance that will become volatile when heated. "Crack," or cocaine base in the form of chips, chunks or "rocks," is usually vaporized in a pipe or smoked with plant material in a cigarette or a "joint." Inhalation of the cocaine fumes produces effects that are very fast in onset, very intense, and are quickly over. These intense effects are often followed within minutes by a dysphoric "crash," leading to frequently repeated doses and rapid addiction.

Excessive doses of cocaine may cause seizures and death from, for example, respiratory failure, stroke, cerebral hemorrhage, or heart failure. There is no specific treatment for cocaine overdose. Nor does tolerance develop to the toxic effects of cocaine. In fact, there are studies which indicate that repeated use lowers the dose at which toxicity occurs. There is no "safe" dose of cocaine.

COCAINE

The Office of National Drug Control Policy (ONDCP) reported that, in 1990 alone, 215,000 pounds of cocaine with a street value of $3 billion were seized by law enforcement agencies. The ONDCP has estimated that the world supply of cocaine in 1990 was 1,000 metric tons or about 2.2 million pounds.

Many of the chemicals used to produce illicit drugs are common substances in international trade and thousands of tons are shipped annually to foreign ports for industrial purposes. In fact, most of the cocaine smuggled into the United States is processed with chemicals exported by American and Western European companies.

Just as money laundering can be traced through financial records, so can illicit drug products be traced through the records of manufacturers and dealers of raw materials used in drug production.

Amphetamines

Amphetamine, dextroamphetamine, and methamphetamine are so similar in the effects they induce that they can be differentiated from one another only by laboratory analysis. Amphetamine was first used clinically in the mid-1930s to treat narcolepsy, a rare disorder resulting in an uncontrollable tendency to sleep. After the introduction of the amphetamines into medical practice, the number of conditions for which they were prescribed multiplied, as did the quantities made available.

For a time, they were sold without prescription in inhalers and other over-the-counter preparations. Abuse became popular. Many segments of the population, especially those concerned with extensive or irregular hours, were among those who used amphetamines orally in excessive amounts. "Speed freaks," who injected amphetamines, became known for their bizarre and often violent behavior. Over-the-counter availability (except inhalers) was terminated and amphetamines now are available only by prescription. Inhalers still are available over-the-counter.

Their illicit use closely parallels that of cocaine in the range of its short-term and long-term effects. Despite broad recognition of the risks, clandestine laboratories produce vast quantities of amphetamines, particularly methamphetamine, for distribution on the illicit market.

Methamphetamine Abusers

Abuse patterns suggest an estimated two- to four-year latency period from first use to full addiction. Most treatment clients interviewed initiated use by intranasal snorting, but then turned to intravenous (IV) administration. Compulsive abuse accelerates with IV use because of the drug's rapid onset of action in a pattern similar to crack cocaine abuse. Although crack is not injected, inhalation of its vapors provides a rapid pulmonary delivery of the drug in concentrated dose to the brain promoting an intensified onset of action. This method, like IV methamphetamine use, triggers an initial, short-term jolt which compels the user to repeat drug use again and again in a futile attempt to re-experience the drug's exhilarating effects.

CANNABIS

Cannabis sativa L., the hemp plant, grows wild throughout most of the tropic and temperate regions of the world. It is a single species. This plant has long been cultivated for the tough fiber of the stem, the seed used in feed mixtures, and the oil as an ingredient of paint, as well as for its biologically active substances, most highly concentrated in the leaves and resinous flowering tops.

The plant material has been used as a drug for centuries. In 1839, it entered the annals of western medicine with the publication of an article surveying its therapeutic potential, including possible uses as an analgesic and anticonvulsant agent. It was alleged to be effective in treating a wide range of physical and mental ailments during the remainder of the 19th century. With the introduction of many new synthetic drugs in the 20th century, interest in it as a medication waned.

The controls imposed with the passage of the Marijuana Tax Act of 1937 further curtailed its use in treatment, and by 1941 it had been deleted from the *U.S. Pharmacopoeia* and the *National Formulary*, the official compendia of drugs.

Cannabis products are usually smoked in the form of loosely rolled cigarettes ("joints"). They may be used alone or in combination with other substances. They may also be administered orally, but are reported to be about three times more potent when smoked. The effects are felt within minutes, reach their peak in 10 to 30 minutes, and may linger for 2 or 3 hours.

A condensed description of these effects is apt to be inadequate or even misleading. So much depends upon the experience and expectations of the individual as well as the activity of the drug itself. Low doses tend to induce restlessness and an increasing sense of well-being, followed by a dreamy state of relaxation, and frequently hunger, especially a craving for sweets. Changes of sensory perception—a more vivid sense of sight, smell, touch, taste, and hearing—may be accompanied by subtle alterations in thought formation and expression. Stronger doses intensify reactions. The individual may experience shifting sensory imagery, rapidly fluctuating emotions, a flight of fragmentary thoughts with disturbed associations, an altered sense of self-identity, impaired memory, and a dulling of attention despite an illusion of heightened insight. This state of intoxication may not be noticeable to an observer. High doses may result in image distortion, a loss of personal identity, and fantasies and hallucination. Very high doses may result in a toxic psychosis.

Marijuana

The term marijuana is used in this country to refer to the cannabis plant and to any part or extract of it that produces somatic or psychic changes in humans. A tobacco-like substance produced by drying the leaves and flowering tops of the plant, marijuana varies significantly in its potency, depending on the source and selectivity of plant materials used. Most wild U.S. cannabis is considered inferior because of a low concentration of THC[1], usually less than 0.5 percent. Jamaican, Colombian, and Mexican varieties range between 0.5 and 7 percent. The most selective produce is reputed to be sinsemilla (Spanish, *sin semilla:* without seed), prepared from the unpollinated female cannabis plant, samples of which have been found to contain up to 20 percent THC.

HALLUCINOGENS

Hallucinogenic drugs, both natural and synthetic, are substances that distort the perception of objective reality. They induce a state of excitation of the central nervous system, manifested by alterations of mood, usually euphoric, but sometimes severely depressive. Under the influence of hallucinogens, the senses of direction, distance, and time becomes disoriented. A user may speak of "seeing" sounds and "hearing" colors. If taken in a large enough dose, the drug produces delusions and visual hallucinations. Occasionally, depersonalization and depression are so severe that suicide is possible, but the most common danger is impaired judgment, leading to rash decisions and accidents. Persons in hallucinogenic states should, therefore, be closely supervised and upset as little as possible to keep them from harming themselves and others. Acute anxiety, restlessness, and sleeplessness are common until the drug wears off.

Long after hallucinogens are eliminated from the body, users may experience flashbacks—fragmentary recurrences of psychedelic effects—such as the intensification of a perceived color, the apparent motion of a fixed object, or the mistaking of one object for another. Recurrent use produces tolerance, which tends to encourage resorting to greater amounts. Although no evidence of physical dependence is detectable when the drugs are withdrawn, recurrent use tends to produce psychic dependence, varying according to the drug, the dose, and the individual user. It should be stressed that the hallucinogens are unpredictable in their effects each time they are used.

Peyote and Mescaline

The primary active ingredient of the peyote cactus is the hallucinogen *mescaline*. It is derived from the fleshy parts or buttons of this plant, which has been employed by Indians in northern Mexico from the earliest recorded time as a part of traditional religious rites. Peyote, or mescal buttons, and mescaline should not be confused with mescal, the colorless Mexican

1. Delta-9-tetrahydro-cannabinol, believed to be responsible for most of its characteristic psychoactive effects.

liquor distilled from the leaves of maguey plants. Usually ground into a powder, peyote is taken orally. Mescaline can also be produced synthetically. A dose of 350 to 500 mg of mescaline produces illusions and hallucinations lasting from 5 to 12 hours.

LSD (LSD-25, lysergide)

LSD is an abbreviation of the German expression for lysergic acid diethylamide. It is produced from lysergic acid, a substance derived from the ergot fungus which grows on rye or from lysergic acid amide, a chemical found in morning glory seeds.

LSD was first synthesized in 1938. Its psychotomimetic effects were discovered in 1943 when a chemist accidentally took some LSD. As he began to experience the effects now known as a "trip," he was aware of vertigo and an intensification of light. Closing his eyes, he saw a stream of fantastic images of extraordinary vividness accompanied by a kaleidoscopic play of colors. This condition lasted for about two hours.

Because of the extremely high potency of LSD, its structural relationship to a chemical which is present in the brain, and its similarity in effects to certain aspects of psychosis, LSD was used as a tool of research to study the mechanism of mental illness.

LSD is usually sold in the form of tablets, thin squares of gelatin ("window panes"), or impregnated paper ("blotter acid"), The average effective oral dose is from 30 to 50 micrograms, but the amount per dosage unit varies greatly. The effects of higher doses persist for 10 to 12 hours. Tolerance develops rapidly.

Phencyclidine (PCP)

PCP is sold under at least 50 other names, including Angel Dust, Crystal, Supergrass, Killer Weed, Embalming Fluid, and Rocket Fuel, that reflect the range of its bizarre and volatile effects. It is also frequently misrepresented as mescaline, LSD, or THC. In its pure form, it is a white crystalline powder that readily dissolves in water. Most PCP now contains contaminants resulting from its makeshift manufacture, causing the color to range from tan to brown and the consistency from a powder to a gummy mass. Although sold in tablets and capsules, as well as in powder and liquid form, it is commonly applied to a leafy material, such as parsley, mint, oregano, or marijuana, and smoked.

The drug is as variable in its effects as it is in its appearance. A moderate amount often produces in the user a sense of detachment, distance, and estrangement from the surroundings. Numbness, slurred or blocked speech, and a loss of coordination may be accompanied by a sense of strength and invulnerability. A blank stare, rapid and involuntary eye movements, and an exaggerated gait are among the more common observable effects. Auditory hallucinations, image distortion as in a fun-house mirror, and severe mood disorders may also occur, producing in some acute anxiety and a feeling of impending doom, in others paranoia and violent hostility. PCP is unique among popular drugs of abuse in its power to produce psychoses indistinguishable from schizophrenia.

ALCOHOL

Source: U.S. Department of Education.

Effects.—Alcohol consumption causes a number of marked changes in behavior. Even low doses significantly impair the judgment and coordination required to drive a car safely, increasing the likelihood that the driver will be involved in an accident. Low to moderate doses of alcohol also increase the incidence of a variety of aggressive acts, including spouse and child abuse. Moderate to high doses of alcohol cause marked impairments in higher mental functions, severely altering a person's ability to learn and remember information. Very high doses cause respiratory depression and death. If combined with other depressants of the central nervous system, much lower doses of alcohol will produce the effects just described.

Repeated use of alcohol can lead to dependence. Sudden cessation of alcohol intake is likely to produce withdrawal symptoms, including severe anxiety, tremors, hallucinations, and convulsions. Alcohol withdrawal can be life-threatening. Long-term consumption of large quantities of alcohol, particularly when combined with poor nutrition, can also lead to permanent damage to vital organs such as the brain and the liver.

Mothers who drink alcohol during pregnancy may give birth to infants with fetal alcohol syndrome. These infants have irreversible physical abnormalities and mental retardation. In addition, research indicates that children of alcoholic parents are at greater risk than other youngsters of becoming alcoholics.

TOBACCO

Source: U.S. Department of Education.

Effects.—The smoking of tobacco products is the chief avoidable cause of death in our society. Smokers are more likely than nonsmokers to contract heart disease—some 170,000 die each year from smoking-related coronary heart disease. Lung, larynx, esophageal, bladder, pancreatic, and kidney cancers also strike smokers at increased rates. Some 30 percent of cancer deaths (130,000 per year) are linked to smoking. Chronic obstructive lung diseases such as emphysema and chronic bronchitis are 10 times more likely to occur among smokers than among nonsmokers.

Smoking during pregnancy also poses serious risks. Spontaneous abortion, preterm birth, low birth weights, and fetal and infant deaths are all more likely to occur when the pregnant woman/mother is a smoker.

Perhaps the most dangerous substance in tobacco smoke is nicotine. Although it is implicated in the onset of heart attacks and cancer, its most dangerous role is reinforcing and strengthening the desire to smoke. Because nicotine is highly addictive, addicts find it very difficult to stop smoking. Of 1,000 typical smokers, fewer than 20 percent succeed in stopping on the first try.

Although the harmful effects of smoking cannot be questioned, people who quit can make significant strides in repairing damage done by smoking. For pack-a-day smokers, the increased risk of heart attack dissipates after 10 years. The likelihood of contracting lung cancer as a result of smoking can also be greatly reduced by quitting.

Sources of Information

American Council for Drug Education.—This organization provides information on drug use, develops media campaigns, reviews scientific findings, publishes books and a newsletter, and offers films and curriculum materials for preteens. 204 Monroe St., Rockville, Md. 20850. Telephone (301) 294-0600.

U.S. Clearinghouse.—(A publication list is available on request, along with placement on a mailing list for new publications. Single copies are free.) National Clearinghouse for Alcohol and Drug Information (NCADI), P.O. Box 2345, Rockville, Md. 20852. Telephone (301) 468-2600

World Geography

Explorations

(All years are A.D. unless B.C. is specified.)

Country or place	Event	Explorer	Date
AFRICA			
Sierra Leone	Visited	Hanno, Carthaginian seaman	c. 520 B.C.
Zaire River (Congo)	Mouth visited[1]	Diogo Cão, Portuguese	c. 1484
Cape of Good Hope	Rounded	Bartolomeu Diaz, Portuguese	1488
Gambia River	Explored	Mungo Park, Scottish explorer	1795
Sahara	Crossed	Dixon Denham and Hugh Clapperton, English explorers	1822–23
Zambezi River	Visited[1]	David Livingstone, Scottish explorer	1851
Sudan	Explored	Heinrich Barth, German explorer	1852–55
Victoria Falls	Visited[1]	Livingstone	1855
Lake Tanganyika	Visited[1]	Richard Burton and John Speke, British explorers	1858
Zaire River (Congo)	Traced	Sir Henry M. Stanley, British explorer	1877
ASIA			
Punjab (India)	Visited	Alexander the Great	327 B.C.
China	Visited	Marco Polo, Italian traveler	c. 1272
Tibet	Visited	Odoric of Pordenone, Italian monk	c. 1325
Southern China	Explored	Niccolò dei Conti, Venetian traveler	c. 1440
India	Visited (Cape route)	Vasco da Gama, Portuguese navigator	1498
Japan	Visited	St. Francis Xavier of Spain	1549
Arabia	Explored	Carsten Niebuhr, German explorer	1762
China	Explored	Ferdinand Richthofen, German scientist	1868
Mongolia	Explored	Nikolai M. Przhevalsky, Russian explorer	1870–73
Central Asia	Explored	Sven Hedin, Swedish scientist	1890–1908
EUROPE			
Shetland Islands	Visited	Pytheas of Massilia (Marseille)	c. 325 B.C.
North Cape	Rounded	Ottar, Norwegian explorer	c. 870
Iceland	Colonized	Norwegian noblemen	c. 890–900
NORTH AMERICA			
Greenland	Colonized	Eric the Red, Norwegian	c. 985
Labrador; Nova Scotia(?)	Visited[1]	Leif Ericson, Norse explorer	1000
West Indies	Visited[1]	Christopher Columbus, Italian	1492
North America	Coast visited[1]	Giovanni Caboto (John Cabot), for British	1497
Pacific Ocean	Sighted[1]	Vasco Núñez de Balboa, Spanish explorer	1513
Florida	Explored	Ponce de León, Spanish explorer	1513
Mexico	Conquered	Hernando Cortés, Spanish adventurer	1519–21
St. Lawrence River	Visited[1]	Jacques Cartier, French navigator	1534
Southwest U. S.	Explored	Francisco Coronado, Spanish explorer	1540–42
Colorado River	Visited[1]	Hernando de Alarcón, Spanish explorer	1540
Mississippi River	Visited[1]	Hernando de Soto, Spanish explorer	1541
Frobisher Bay	Visited[1]	Martin Frobisher, English seaman	1576
Maine Coast	Explored	Samuel de Champlain, French explorer	1604

Country or place	Event	Explorer	Date
Jamestown, Va.	Settled	John Smith, English colonist	1607
Hudson River	Explored	Henry Hudson, English navigator	1609
Hudson Bay (Canada)	Visited[1]	Henry Hudson	1610
Baffin Bay	Visited[1]	William Baffin, English navigator	1616
Lake Michigan	Navigated	Jean Nicolet, French explorer	1634
Arkansas River	Visited[1]	Jacques Marquette and Louis Jolliet, French explorers	1673
Mississippi River	Explored	Sieur de La Salle, French explorer	1682
Bering Strait	Visited[1]	Vitus Bering, Danish explorer	1728
Alaska	Visited[1]	Vitus Bering	1741
Mackenzie River (Canada)	Visited[1]	Sir Alexander Mackenzie, Scottish–Canadian explorer	1789
Northwest U. S.	Explored	Meriwether Lewis and William Clark	1804–06
Northeast Passage (Arctic Ocean)	Navigated	Nils Nordenskjöld, Swedish explorer	1879
Greenland	Explored	Robert Peary, American explorer	1892
Northwest Passage	Navigated	Roald Amundsen, Norwegian explorer	1906
SOUTH AMERICA			
Continent	Visited	Columbus, Italian	1498
Brazil	Visited[1]	Pedro Alvarez Cabral, Portuguese	1500
Peru	Conquered	Francisco Pizarro, Spanish explorer	1532–33
Amazon River	Explored	Francisco Orellana, Spanish explorer	1541
Cape Horn	Visited[1]	Willem C. Schouten, Dutch navigator	1615
OCEANIA			
Papua New Guinea	Visited	Jorge de Menezes, Portuguese explorer	1526
Australia	Visited	Abel Janszoon Tasman, Dutch navigator	1642
Tasmania	Visited[1]		
Australia	Explored	John McDouall Stuart, English explorer	1828
Australia	Explored	Robert Burke and William Wills, Australian explorers	1861
New Zealand	Sighted (and named)	Abel Janszoon Tasman	1642
New Zealand	Visited	James Cook, English navigator	1769
ARCTIC, ANTARCTIC, AND MISCELLANEOUS			
Ocean exploration	Expedition	Magellan's ships circled globe	1519–22
Galápagos Islands	Visited	Diego de Rivadeneira, Spanish captain	1535
Spitsbergen	Visited	Willem Barents, Dutch navigator	1596
Antarctic Circle	Crossed	James Cook, English navigator	1773
Antarctica	Visited[1]	Nathaniel Palmer, U. S. whaler (archipelago) and Fabian Gottlieb von Bellingshausen, Russian admiral (mainland)	1820–21
Antarctica	Explored	Charles Wilkes, American explorer	1840
North Pole	Reached	Robert E. Peary, American explorer	1909
South Pole	Reached	Roald Amundsen, Norwegian explorer	1911

1. First European to reach the area.

The Continents

A continent is defined as a large unbroken land mass completely surrounded by water, although in some cases continents are (or were in part) connected by land bridges.

The hypothesis first suggested late in the 19th century was that the continents consist of lighter rocks that rest on heavier crustal material in about the same manner that icebergs float on water. That the rocks forming the continents are lighter than the material below them and under the ocean bottoms is now established. As a consequence of this fact, Alfred Wegener (for the first time in 1912) suggested that the continents are slowly moving, at a rate of about one yard per century, so that their relative positions are not rigidly fixed. Many geologists that were originally skeptical have come to accept this theory of Continental Drift.

When describing a continent, it is important to remember that there is a fundamental difference between a deep ocean, like the Atlantic, and shallow seas, like the Baltic and most of the North Sea, which are merely flooded portions of a continent. Another and entirely different point to remember is that political considerations have often overridden geographical facts when it came to naming continents.

Geographically speaking, Europe, including the British Isles, is a large western peninsula of the continent of Asia; and many geographers, when referring to Europe and Asia, speak of the Eurasian Continent. But traditionally, Europe is counted as a separate continent, with the Ural and the Caucasus mountains forming the line of demarcation between Europe and Asia.

To the south of Europe, Asia has an odd-shaped peninsula jutting westward, which has a large number of political subdivisions. The northern section is taken up by Turkey; to the south of Turkey there are Syria, Iraq, Israel, Jordan, Saudi Arabia, and a number of smaller Arab countries. All this is part of Asia. Traditionally, the island of Cyprus in the Mediterranean is also considered to be part of Asia, while the island of Crete is counted as European.

The large islands of Java, Borneo, and Sumatra and the smaller islands near them are counted as part of "tropical Asia," while New Guinea is counted as related to Australia. In the case of the Americas, the problem arises as to whether they should be considered one or two continents. There are good arguments on both sides, but since there is now a land bridge between North and South America (in the past it was often flooded) and since no part of the sea east of the land bridge is deep ocean, it is more logical to consider the Americas as one continent.

Politically, based mainly on history, the Americas are divided into North America (from the Arctic to the Mexican border), Central America (from Mexico to Panama, with the Caribbean islands), and South America. Greenland is considered a section of North America, while Iceland is traditionally counted as a European island because of its political ties with the Scandinavian countries.

The island groups in the Pacific are often called "Oceania," but this name does *not* imply that scientists consider them the remains of a continent.

The seven continents are North America, South America, Europe, Asia, Africa, Australia, and Antarctica.

Volcanoes of the World

About 500 volcanoes have had recorded eruptions within historical times. Almost two thirds of these are in the Northern Hemisphere. Most volcanoes occur at the boundaries of the earth's crustal plates, such as the famous "Ring of Fire" that surrounds the Pacific Ocean plate. Of the world's active volcanoes, about 60% are along the perimeter of the Pacific, about 17% on mid-oceanic islands, about 14% in an arc along the south of the Indonesian islands, and about 9% in the Mediterranean area, Africa, and Asia Minor. Many of the world's volcanoes are submarine and have unrecorded eruptions.

Pacific "Ring of Fire"

NORTHWEST

Japan: At least 33 active vents.

Aso (5,223 ft; 1,592 m), on Kyushu, has one of the largest craters in the world.

Asama (over 8,300 ft; 2,530 m), on Honshu, is continuously active; violent eruption in 1783.

Azuma (nearly 7,700 ft; 2,347 m), on Honshu, erupted in 1900.

Chokai (7,300 ft; 2,225 m), on Honshu, erupted in 1974 after having been quiescent since 1861.

Fujiyama (Fujisan) (12,385 ft; 3,775 m), on Honshu, southwest of Tokyo. Symmetrical in outline, snow-covered. Regarded as a sacred mountain.

On-take (3,668 ft; 1,118 m), on peninsula of Kyushu. Strong smoke emissions and explosions began November 1973 and continued through 1974.

Mt. Unzen (4,500 ft; 1,371 m), on Kyushu erupted on June 3, 1991. Last eruption was in 1792.

U.S.S.R.: Kamchatka peninsula, 14–18 active volcanoes. Klyuchevskaya (Kluchev) (15,500 ft; 4,724 m) reported active in 1974.

Kurile Islands: At least 13 active volcanoes and several submarine outbreaks.

SOUTHWEST

New Zealand: Mount Tarawera (3,645 ft; 1,112 m), on North Island, had a severe eruption in 1886 that destroyed the famous Pink and White sinter terraces of Rotomahana, a hot lake.

Ngauruhoe (7,515 ft; 2,291 m), on North Island, emits steam and vapor constantly. Erupted 1974.

Papua New Guinea: Karkar Island (4,920 ft; 1,500 m). Mild eruptions 1974.

Philippine Islands: About 100 eruptive centers; Hibok Hibok, on Camiguin, erupted September 1950 and again in December 1951, when about 750 were reported killed or missing; eruptions continued during 1952–53.

Taal (4,752 ft; 1,448 m), on Luzon. Major eruption in 1965 killed 190; erupted again, 1968.

Mt. Pinatubo (4,795 ft; 1,462 m), on Luzon erupted on June 9, 1991. Last major eruption in 1380.

Volcano Islands: Mount Suribachi (546 ft; 166 m), on Iwo Jima. A sulfurous steaming volcano. Raising of U.S. flag over Mount Suribachi was one of the dramatic episodes of World War II.

NORTHEAST

Alaska: Mount Wrangell (14,163 ft; 4,317 m) and Mount Katmai (about 6,700 ft; 2,042 m). On June 6, 1912, a violent eruption (Nova Rupta) of Mount Katmai occurred, during which the "Valley of Ten Thousand Smokes" was formed.

Aleutian Islands: There are 32 active vents known and numerous inactive cones. Akutan Island (over 4,000 ft; 1,220 m) erupted in 1974, with ash and debris rising over 300 ft.

Great Sitkin (5,741 ft; 1,750 m). Explosive activity February-September 1974, accompanied by earthquake originating at volcano that registered 2.3 on Richter scale.

Augustine Island: Augustine volcano (4,000 ft; 1,220 m) erupted March 27, 1986. It last erupted in 1976.

California, Oregon, Washington: Lassen Peak (10,453 ft; 3,186 m) in California is one of two observed active volcanoes in the U.S. outside Alaska and Hawaii. The last period of activity was 1914–17. Mt. St. Helens (9,677 ft; 2,950 m) in the Cascade Range of southwest Washington became active on March 27, 1980, and erupted on May 18 after being inactive since 1857. From April 15 through May 1, 1986, weak activity began for the first time in two years. Other mountains of volcanic origin include Mount Shasta (California), Mount Hood (Oregon), Mount Mazama (Oregon)—the mountain containing Crater Lake, Mount Rainier (Washington), and Mount Baker (Washington), which has been steaming since

Continued on page 478

The Pacific Ocean "Ring of Fire"

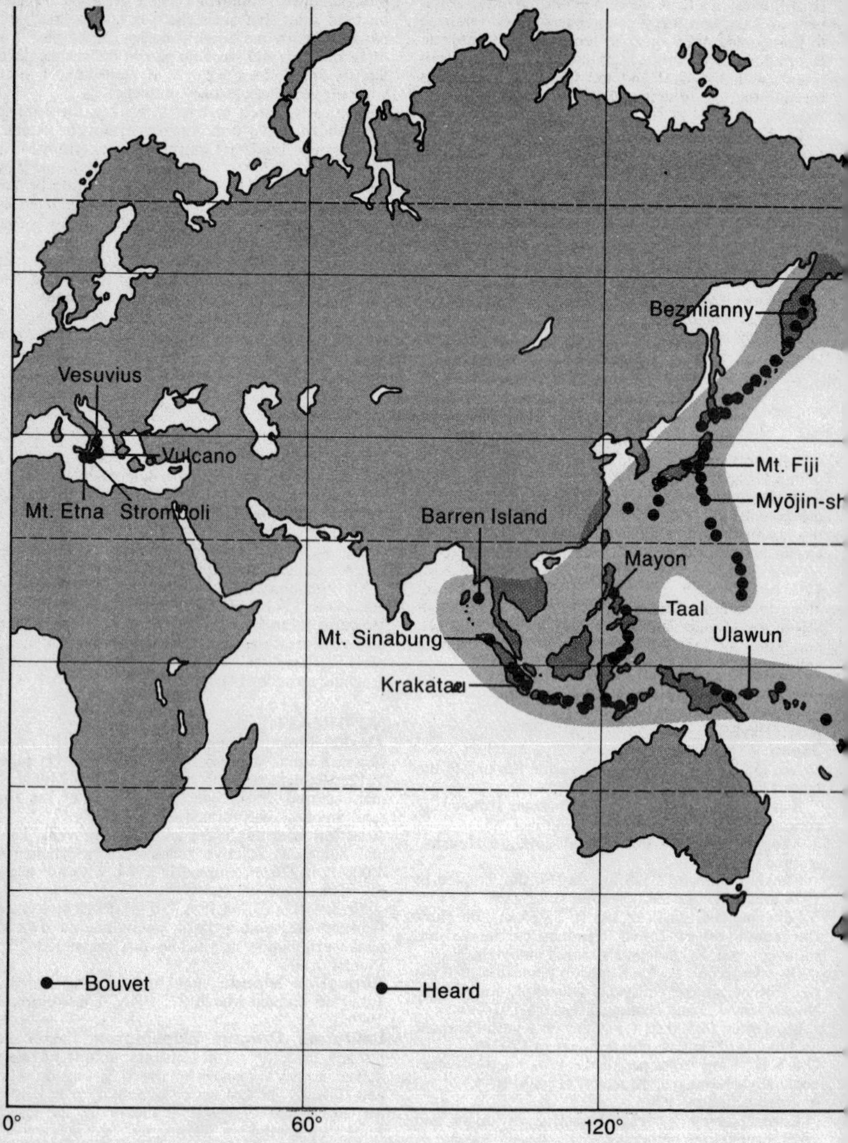

U.S. Geological Information Sources

The U.S. Geological Survey (USGS) is a diverse agency that has responsibilities for national and international geologic and hydrologic studies and publishes a variety of maps. Topographic maps are, perhaps, their best known publications.

The Minerals Information Offices (MIOs) of the USGS are staffed by professionals who will respond to inquiries about mineral resources of the U.S. and beyond.

Minerals Information Offices

Main Office. Interior Bldg., Rm. 2647, 18th & C Sts., NW, Washington, D.C. 20240. (202) 208-5512.

Field Offices. USGS, Corbett Bldg., 340 N. 6th Ave., Tucson, Ariz. 85705 (602) 670-5544. USGS c/o Mackay School of Mines, Scrugham Engineering

Source: U.S. Department of the Interior, U.S. Geological Survey.

Mines Bldg., UNR, Reno, Nev. 89557-0047 (702) 784-5552. USGS, Rm. 651 US Courthouse Bldg., W. 920 Riverside Dr., Spokane, Wash. 99201 (509) 353-2649.

Publications Sales

Books and Open-File Reports Section. Federal Center, Box 25425, Denver, Colo. 80225. (303) 236-7476.

Map Sales. Federal Center, Box 25286, Denver, Colo. 80225 (303) 236-7477.

Other USGS (headquarters) Offices. Public Affairs: 703-648-4460. Geologic Inquiries Group: 703-648-4383. Earth Science Information Center: 703-648-6045. Water Resources Inquiries Group: 703-648-5669.

(Continued from p. 475)

October 1975, but gives no sign of an impending eruption.

SOUTHEAST

Chile and Argentina: About 25 active or potentially active.

Colombia: Huila (nearly 18,900 ft; 5,760 m), a vapor-emitting volcano, and Tolima (nearly 18,500 ft; 5,640 m). Eruption of Puracé (15,600 ft; 4,755 m) in 1949 killed 17 people. Nevado del Ruiz (16,200 ft; 4,938 m.), erupted Nov. 13, 1985, sending torrential floods of mud and water engulfing the town of Armero and killing more than 22,000 people.

Ecuador: Cayambe (nearly 19,000 ft; 5,791 m). Almost on the equator.

Cotopaxi (19,344 ft; 5,896 m). Perhaps highest active volcano in the world. Possesses a beautifully formed cone.

Reventador (11,434 ft; 3,485 m). Observed in active state in late 1973.

El Salvador: Izalco ("beacon of Central America") (7,830 ft; 2,387 m) first appeared in 1770 and is still growing (erupted in 1950, 1956; last erupted in October-November 1966). San Salvador (6,187 ft; 1,886 m) had a violent eruption in 1923. Conchagua (about 4100 ft; 1,250 m) erupted with considerable damage early in 1947.

Guatemala: Santa Maria Quezaltenango (12,361 ft; 3,768 m). Frequent activity between 1902–08 and 1922–28 after centuries of quiescence. Most dangerously active vent of Central America. Other volcanoes include Tajumulco (13,814 ft; 4,211 m) and Atitlán (11,633 ft; 3,546 m).

Mexico: Boquerón ("Big Mouth"), on San Benedicto, about 250 mi. south of Lower California.
Newest volcano in Western Hemisphere, discovered September 1952.

Colima (about 14,000 ft; 4,270 m), in group that has had frequent eruptions.

Orizaba (Citlaltépetl) (18,701 ft; 5,700 m).

Parícutin (7,450 ft; 2,270 m). First appeared in February 1943. In less than a week, a cone over 140 ft high developed with a crater one quarter mile in circumference. Cone grew more than 1,500 ft (457 m) in 1943. Erupted 1952.

Popocatépetl (17,887 ft; 5,452 m). Large, deep, bell-shaped crater. Not entirely extinct; steam still escapes.

El Chinchonal (7,300 ft; 1,005.6 m) about 15 miles from Pichucalco. Long inactive, it erupted in March 1982.

Nicaragua: Volcanoes include Telica, Coseguina, and Momotombo. Between Momotombo on the west shore of Lake Managua and Coseguina overlooking the Gulf of Fonseca, there is a string of more than 20 cones, many still active. One of these, Cerro Negro, erupted in July 1947, with considerable damage and loss of life, and again in 1971.

Concepción (5,100 ft; 1,555 m). Ash eruptions 1973–74.

Mid-oceanic Islands

Canary Islands: Pico de Teide (12,192 ft; 3,716 m), on Tenerife.

Cape Verde Islands: Fogo (nearly 9,300 ft; 2,835 m). Severe eruption in 1857; quiescent until 1951.

Caribbean: La Soufrière (4,813 ft; 1,467 m), on Basse-Terre, Guadeloupe. Also called La Grande Soufrière. Violent activity in July-August 1976 caused evacuation of 73,000 people; renewed activity in April 1977 again caused thousands to flee their homes.

La Soufrière (4,048 ft; 1,234 m), on St. Vincent. Major eruption in 1902 killed over 1,000 people. Eruptions over 10-day period in April 1979 caused evacuation of northern two thirds of island.

Comoros: One volcano, Karthala (nearly 8,000 ft; 2,440 m), is visible for over 100 miles. Last erupted in 1904.

Hawaii: Mauna Loa ("Long Mountain") (13,680 ft; 4,170 m), on Hawaii, discharges from its high side vents more lava than any other volcano. Largest volcanic mountain in the world in cubic content. Area of crater is 3.7 sq mi. Violent eruption in June 1950, with lava pouring 25 miles into the ocean. Last major eruption in March 1984.

Mauna Kea (13,796 ft; 4,205 m), on Hawaii. Highest mountain in state.

Kilauea (4,090 ft; 1,247 m) is a vent in the side of Mauna Loa, but its eruptions are apparently independent. One of the most spectacular and active craters. Crater has an area of 4.14 sq mi. Earthquake in July 1975 caused major eruption. Eruptions began in September 1977 and reached a height of 980 ft (300 m). Activity ended Oct. 1. Became active again in January 1983, exploding in earnest in March 1983 forming the volcanic cone Pu'u O which has erupted periodically ever since. By May 1990, the lava flow had traveled 20 miles, obliterating the community of Kalapana on the southeast coast. By summer it had reached the Pacific Ocean.

Iceland: At least 25 volcanoes active in historical times. Very similar to Hawaiian volcanoes. Askja (over 4,700 ft; 1,433 m) is the largest. Hekla, one of the most active volcanoes in Iceland, erupted on Jan. 17, 1990 after 10 years of repose.

Lesser Antilles (West Indian Islands): Mount Pelée (over 4,500 ft; 1,370 m), northwestern Martinique. Eruption in 1902 destroyed town of St. Pierre and killed approximately 40,000 people.

Réunion Island (east of Madagascar): Piton de la Fournaise (Le Volcan) (8,610 ft; 2,624 m). Large lava flows. Last erupted in 1972.

Samoan archipelago: Savai'i Island had an eruption in 1905 that caused considerable damage. Niuafoo (Tin Can), in the Tonga Islands, has a crater that extends 6,000 feet below and 600 feet above water.

Indonesia

Sumatra: Ninety volcanoes have been discovered; 12 are now active. The most famous, Krakatau, is a small volcanic island in the Sunda Strait. Numerous volcanic discharges occurred in 1883. One extremely violent explosion caused the disappearance of the highest peak and the northern part of the island. Fine dust was carried around the world in the upper atmosphere. Over 36,000 persons lost their lives in resultant tidal waves that were felt as far away as Cape Horn. Active in 1972.

Mediterranean Area

Italy: Mount Etna (10,902 ft; 3,323 m), eastern Sicily. Two new craters formed in eruptions of February-March 1947. Worst eruption in 50 years occurred November 1950–January 1951. Erupted again in 1974, 1975, 1977, 1978, 1979, 1983, December 1991, and lava flows continued into April 1992.

Stromboli (about 3,000 ft; 914 m), Lipari Islands (north of Sicily). Called "Lighthouse of the Mediterranean." Reported active in 1971.

Mount Vesuvius (4,200 ft; 1,280 m), southeast of Naples. Only active volcano on European mainland. Pompeii buried by an eruption, A.D. 79.

Antarctica

The discovery of two small active volcanoes in 1982 brings to five the total number known on Antarctica. The new ones, 30 miles apart, are on the Weddell Sea side of the Antarctic Peninsula. The largest, Mount Erebus (13,000 ft; 3,962 m), rises from McMurdo Sound. Mount Melbourne (9,000 ft; 2,743 m) is in Victoria Land. The fifth, off the northern tip of the Antarctic Peninsula, is a crater known as Deception Island.

Principal Types of Volcanoes

(*Source:* U.S. Dept. of Interior, Geological Survey.)

The word "volcano" comes from the little island of Vulcano in the Mediterranean Sea off Sicily. Centuries ago, the people living in this area believed that Vulcano was the chimney of the forge of Vulcan—the blacksmith of the Roman gods. They thought that the hot lava fragments and clouds of dust erupting from Vulcano came from Vulcan's forge. Today, we know that volcanic eruptions are not supernatural but can be studied and interpreted by scientists.

Geologists generally group volcanoes into four main kinds—cinder cones, composite volcanoes, shield volcanoes, and lava domes.

Cinder Cones

Cinder cones are the simplest type of volcano. They are built from particles and blobs of congealed lava ejected from a single vent. As the gas-charged lava is blown violently into the air, it breaks into small fragments that solidify and fall as cinders around the vent to form a circular or oval cone. Most cinder cones have a bowl-shaped crater at the summit and rarely rise more than a thousand feet or so above their surroundings. Cinder cones are numerous in western North America as well as throughout other volcanic terrains of the world.

Composite Volcanoes

Some of the Earth's grandest mountains are composite volcanoes—sometimes called *stratovolcanoes.* They are typically steep-sided, symmetrical cones of large dimension built of alternating layers of lava flows, volcanic ash, cinders, blocks, and bombs and may rise as much as 8,000 feet above their bases. Some of the most conspicuous and beautiful mountains in the world are composite volcanoes, including Mount Fuji in Japan, Mount Cotopaxi in Ecuador, Mount Shasta in California, Mount Hood in Oregon, and Mount St. Helens and Mount Rainier in Washington.

Most composite volcanoes have a crater at the summit which contains a central vent or a clustered group of vents. Lavas either flow through breaks in the crater wall or issue from fissures on the flanks of the cone. Lava, solidified within the fissures, forms *dikes* that act as ribs which greatly strengthen the cone.

The essential feature of a composite volcano is a conduit system through which magma from a reservoir deep in the Earth's crust rises to the surface. The volcano is built up by the accumulation of material erupted through the conduit and increases in size as lava, cinders, ash, etc., are added to its slopes.

Shield Volcanoes

Shield volcanoes, the third type of volcano, are built almost entirely of fluid lava flows. Flow after flow pours out in all directions from a central summit vent, or group of vents, building a broad, gently sloping cone of flat, domical shape, with a profile much like that of a warrior's shield. They are built up slowly by the accretion of thousands of flows of highly fluid basaltic (from *basalt,* a hard, dense dark volcanic rock) lava that spread widely over great distances, and then cool as thin, gently dipping sheets. Lavas also commonly erupt from vents along fractures (rift zones) that develop on the flanks of the cone. Some of the largest volcanoes in the world are shield volcanoes. In northern California and Oregon, many shield volcanoes have diameters of 3 or 4 miles and heights of 1,500 to 2,000 feet. The Hawaiian Islands are composed of linear chains of these volcanoes, including Kilauea and Mauna Loa on the island of Hawaii.

In some shield-volcano eruptions, basaltic lava pours out quietly from long fissures instead of central vents and floods the surrounding countryside with lava flow upon lava flow, forming broad plateaus. Lava plateaus of this type can be seen in Iceland, southeastern Washington, eastern Oregon, and southern Idaho.

Lava Domes

Volcanic or lava domes are formed by relatively small, bulbous masses of lava too viscous to flow any great distance; consequently, on extrusion, the lava piles over and around its vent. A dome grows largely by expansion from within. As it grows its outer surface cools and hardens, then shatters, spilling loose fragments down its sides. Some domes form craggy knobs or spines over the volcanic vent, whereas others form short, steep-sided lava flows known as "coulees." Volcanic domes commonly occur within the craters or on the flanks of large composite volcanoes. The nearly circular Novarupta Dome that formed during the 1912 eruption of Katmai Volcano, Alaska, measures 800 feet across and 200 feet high. The internal structure of this dome—defined by layering of lava fanning upward and outward from the center—indicates that it grew largely by expansion from within. Mount Pelée in Martinique, West Indies, and Lassen Peak and Mono domes in California, are examples of lava domes.

Submarine Volcanoes

Submarine volcanoes and volcanic vents are common features on certain zones of the ocean floor. Some are active at the present time and, in shallow water, disclose their presence by blasting steam and rock-debris high above the surface of the sea. Many others lie at such great depths that the tremendous weight of the water above them results in high, confining pressure and prevents the formation and release of steam and gases. Even very large, deepwater eruptions may not disturb the ocean floor.

The famous black sand beaches of Hawaii were created virtually instantaneously by the violent interaction between hot lava and sea water.

Plate-Tectonics Theory—The Lithosphere Plates of the Earth

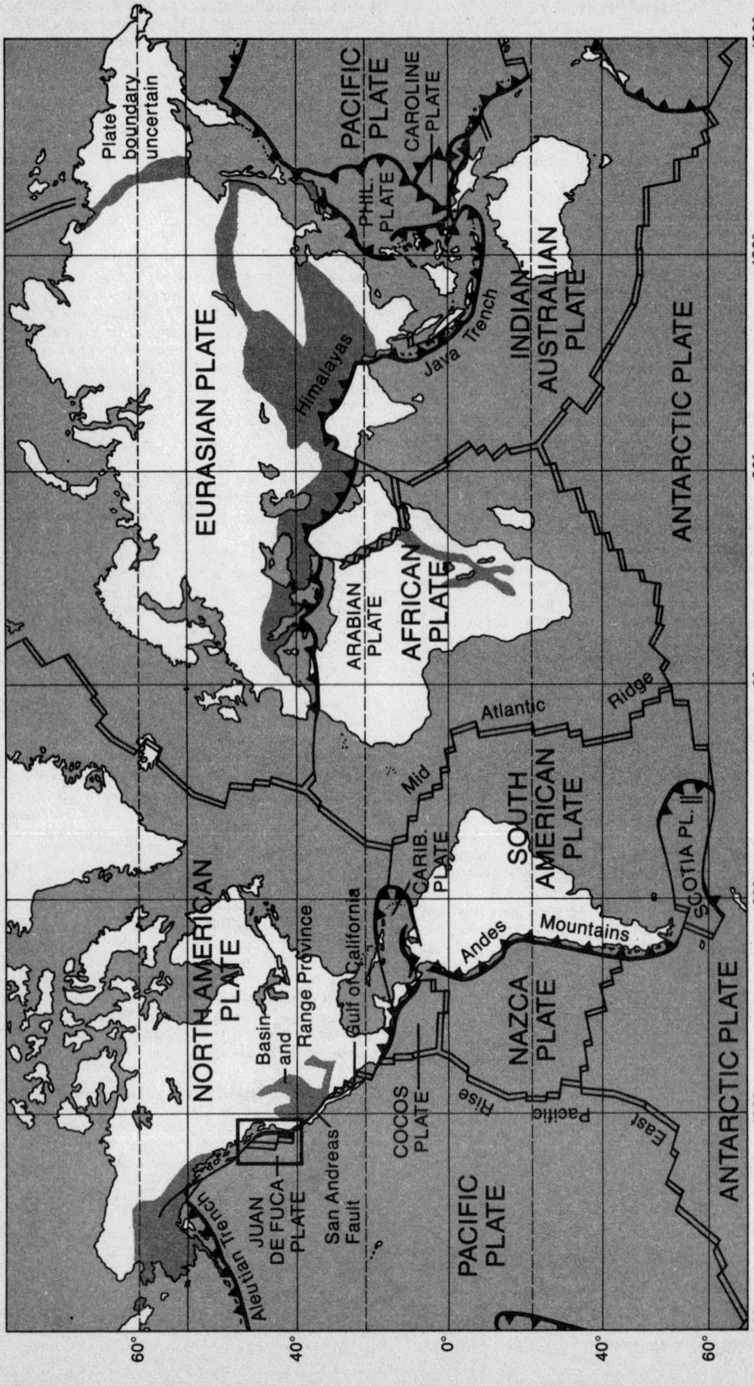

Source: U.S. Department of the Interior, U.S. Geological Survey.

World Population, Land Areas, and Elevations

Area	Estimated population, mid-1993	Approximate Land area sq mi.	Percent of total land area	Population density per sq mi.	Elevation, feet: Highest	Elevation, feet: Lowest
WORLD	5,506,000,000	58,433,000	100.0	94.2 [1]	Mt. Everest, Asia, 29,028	Dead Sea, Asia, 1,290 below sea level
ASIA, incl. Philippines, Indonesia, and European and Asiatic Turkey; excl. Asiatic former U.S.S.R	3,257,000,000	10,644,000	18.2	306.0	Mt. Everest, Tibet-Nepal, 29,108	Dead Sea, Israel-Jordan, 1,290 below sea level
AFRICA	677,000,000	11,707,000	20.0	58.0	Mt. Kilimanjaro, Tanzania, 19,340	Lake Assal, Djibouti, 571 below sea level
NORTH AMERICA, including Hawaii, Central America, and Caribbean region	443,000,000	9,360,000	16.0	47.3	Mt. McKinley; Alaska, 20,320	Death Valley, Calif., 282 below sea level
SOUTH AMERICA	305,000,000	6,883,000	11.8	44.3	Mt. Aconcagua, Arg.-Chile, 23,034	Valdes Peninsula, 131 below sea level
ANTARCTICA	—	6,000,000	10.3	—	Vinson Massif, Sentinel Range, 16,863	Sea level
EUROPE, incl. Iceland; excl. European former U.S.S.R. and European Turkey	513,000,000	1,905,000	3.3	269.3	Mont Blanc, France, 15,781	Sea level
OCEANIA, incl. Australia, New Zealand, Melanesia, Micronesia, and Polynesia[2]	28,000,000	3,284,000	5.6	8.5	Wilhelm, Papua New Guinea, 14,793	Lake Eyre, Australia, 38 below sea level
Former U.S.S.R., both European and Asiatic	285,000,000	8,647,000	14.8	33.0	Communism Peak, Pamir, 24,590	Caspian Sea, 96 below sea level

1. In computing density per square mile, the area of Antarctica is omitted. 2. Although Hawaii is geographically part of Oceania, its population is included in the population figure for North America. *Source:* Population Reference Bureau, Inc. NOTE: The land area of Asia including the Asiatic portion of the former U.S.S.R. is 17,240,000 sq miles according to the *Rand McNally Cosmopolitan World Atlas.*

Plate-Tectonics Theory

(*Source:* U.S. Dept. of the Interior, Geological Survey.)

According to the generally accepted "plate-tectonics" theory, scientists believe that the Earth's surface is broken into a number of shifting slabs or plates, which average about 50 miles in thickness. These plates move relative to one another above a hotter, deeper, more mobile zone at average rates as great as a few inches per year. Most of the world's active volcanoes are located along or near the boundaries between shifting plates and are called "plate-boundary" volcanoes. However, some active volcanoes are not associated with plate boundaries, and many of these so-called "intra-plate" volcanoes form roughly linear chains in the interior of some oceanic plates. The Hawaiian Islands provide perhaps the best example of an "intra-plate" volcanic chain, developed by the northwest-moving Pacific plate passing over an inferred "hot spot" that initiates the magma-generation and volcano-formation process. The peripheral areas of the Pacific Ocean Basin, containing the boundaries of several plates, are dotted by many active volcanoes that form the so-called "Ring of Fire." The "Ring" provides excellent examples of "plate-boundary" volcanoes, including Mount St. Helens.

The accompanying figure on page 464 shows the boundaries of lithosphere plates that are active at present. The double lines indicate zones of spreading from which plates are moving apart. The lines with barbs show zones of underthrusting (subduction), where one plate is sliding beneath another. The barbs on the lines indicate the overriding plate. The single line defines a strike-slip fault along which plates are sliding horizontally past one another. The stippled areas indicate a part of a continent, exclusive of that along a plate boundary, which is undergoing active extensional, compressional, or strike-slip faulting.

The Severity of an Earthquake

(*Source:* U.S. Dept. of the Interior, Geological Survey.)

The Richter Magnitude Scale

The Richter magnitude scale was developed in 1935 by Charles F. Richter of the California Institute of Technology as a mathematical device to compare the size of earthquakes. The magnitude of an earthquake is determined from the logarithm of the amplitude of waves recorded by seismographs. Adjustments are included in the magnitude formula to compensate for the variation in the distance between the various seismographs and the epicenter of the earthquakes. On the Richter Scale, magnitude is expressed in whole numbers and decimal fractions. For example, a magnitude of 5.3 might be computed for a moderate earthquake, and a strong earthquake might be rated as magnitude 6.3.

Because of the logarithmic basis of the scale, each whole-number increase in magnitude represents a tenfold increase in measured amplitude; as an estimate of energy, each whole number step in the magnitude scale corresponds to the release of about 31 times more energy than the amount associated with the preceding whole number value.

Earthquakes with magnitudes of about 2.0 or less are usually called microearthquakes; they are not commonly felt by people and are generally recorded only on local seismographs. Events with magnitudes of about 4.5 or greater—there are several thousand such shocks annually—are strong enough to be recorded by sensitive seismographs all over the world.

Great earthquakes, such as the 1906 earthquake in San Francisco, have magnitudes of 8.0 or higher. On the average, one earthquake of such size occurs somewhere in the world each year. Although the Richter Scale has no upper limit, the largest known shocks have had magnitudes in the 8.8 to 8.9 range.

The Richter Scale is not used to express damage. An earthquake in a densely populated area which results in many deaths and considerable damage may have the same magnitude as a shock in a remote area that does nothing more than frighten the wildlife. Large-magnitude earthquakes that occur beneath the oceans may not even be felt by humans.

The Modified Mercalli Intensity Scale

The effect of an earthquake on the Earth's surface is called the intensity. The intensity scale consists of a series of certain key responses such as people awakening, movement of furniture, damage to chimneys, and finally—total destruction. Although numerous *intensity scales* have been developed over the last several hundred years to evaluate the effects of earthquakes, the one currently used in the United States is the Modified Mercalli (MM) Intensity Scale. It was developed in 1931 by the American seismologists Harry Wood and Frank Neumann. This scale, composed of 12 increasing levels of intensity that range from imperceptible shaking to catastrophic destruction, is designated by Roman numerals. It does not have a mathematical basis; instead it is an arbitrary ranking based on observed effects.

The Modified Mercalli Intensity value assigned to a specific site after an earthquake has a more meaningful measure of severity to the nonscientist than the magnitude because intensity refers to the effects actually experienced at that place. After the occurrence of widely-felt earthquakes, the Geological Survey mails questionnaires to postmasters in the disturbed area requesting the information so that intensity values can be assigned. The results of this postal canvass and information furnished by other sources are used to assign an intensity value, and to compile isoseismal maps that show the extent of various levels of intensity within the felt area. The maximum observed intensity generally occurs near the epicenter.

The *lower* numbers of the intensity scale generally deal with the manner in which the earthquake is felt by people. The *higher* numbers of the scale are based on observed structural damage. Structural engineers usually contribute information for assigning intensity values of VIII or above.

The Mexico City earthquake on September 19, 1985, was assigned an intensity of IX on the Mercalli Scale.

The following is an abbreviated description of the 12 levels of Modified Mercalli intensity.

I. Not felt except by a very few under especially favorable conditions.

II. Felt only by a few persons at rest, especially on upper floors of buildings. Delicately suspended objects may swing.

III. Felt quite noticeably by persons indoors, especially on upper floors of buildings. Many people do not recognize it as an earthquake. Standing motor cars may rock slightly. Vibration similar to the passing of a truck. Duration estimated.

IV. Felt indoors by many, outdoors by few during the day. At night, some awakened. Dishes, windows, doors disturbed; walls make cracking sound. Sensation like heavy truck striking building. Standing motor cars rocked noticeably.

V. Felt by nearly everyone; many awakened. Some dishes, windows broken. Unstable objects overturned. Pendulum clocks may stop.

VI. Felt by all, many frightened. Some heavy furniture moved; a few instances of fallen plaster. Damage slight.

VII. Damage negligible in buildings of good design and construction; slight to moderate in well-built ordinary structures; considerable damage in poorly built or badly designed structures; some chimneys broken.

VIII. Damage slight in specially designed structures; considerable damage in ordinary substantial buildings with partial collapse. Damage great in poorly built structures. Fall of chimneys, factory stacks, columns, monuments, walls. Heavy furniture overturned.

IX. Damage considerable in specially designed structures; well-designed frame structures thrown out of plumb. Damage great in substantial buildings, with partial collapse. Buildings shifted off foundations.

X. Some well-built wooden structures destroyed; most masonry and frame structures destroyed with foundations. Rails bent.

XI. Few, if any (masonry) structures remain standing. Bridges destroyed. Rails bent greatly.

XII. Damage total. Lines of sight and level are distorted. Objects thrown into the air.

Latitude and Longitude of World Cities

(and time corresponding to 12:00 noon, eastern standard time)

City	Lat. °	Lat. ′	Long. °	Long. ′	Time
Aberdeen, Scotland	57	9 n	2	9 w	5:00 p.m.
Adelaide, Australia	34	55 s	138	36 e	2:30 a.m.[1]
Algiers	36	50 n	3	0 e	6:00 p.m.
Amsterdam	52	22 n	4	53 e	6:00 p.m.
Ankara, Turkey	39	55 n	32	55 e	7:00 p.m.
Asunción, Paraguay	25	15 s	57	40 w	1:00 p.m.
Athens	37	58 n	23	43 e	7:00 p.m.
Auckland, New Zealand	36	52 s	174	45 e	5:00 a.m.[1]
Bangkok, Thailand	13	45 n	100	30 e	midnight[1]
Barcelona	41	23 n	2	9 e	6:00 p.m.
Beijing	39	55 n	116	25 e	1:00 a.m.[1]
Belém, Brazil	1	28 s	48	29 w	2:00 p.m.
Belfast, Northern Ireland	54	37 n	5	56 w	5:00 p.m.
Belgrade, Yugoslavia	44	52 n	20	32 e	6:00 p.m.
Berlin	52	30 n	13	25 e	6:00 p.m.
Birmingham, England	52	25 n	1	55 w	5:00 p.m.
Bogotá, Colombia	4	32 n	74	15 w	12:00 noon
Bombay	19	0 n	72	48 e	10:30 p.m.
Bordeaux, France	44	50 n	0	31 w	6:00 p.m.
Bremen, Germany	53	5 n	8	49 e	6:00 p.m.
Brisbane, Australia	27	29 s	153	8 e	3:00 a.m.[1]
Bristol, England	51	28 n	2	35 w	5:00 p.m.
Brussels	50	52 n	4	22 e	6:00 p.m.
Bucharest	44	25 n	26	7 e	7:00 p.m.
Budapest	47	30 n	19	5 e	6:00 p.m.
Buenos Aires	34	35 s	58	22 w	2:00 p.m.
Cairo	30	2 n	31	21 e	7:00 p.m.
Calcutta	22	34 n	88	24 e	10:30 p.m.
Canton, China	23	7 n	113	15 e	1:00 a.m.[1]
Cape Town, South Africa	33	55 s	18	22 e	7:00 p.m.
Caracas, Venezuela	10	28 n	67	2 w	1:00 p.m.
Cayenne, French Guiana	4	49 n	52	18 w	1:00 p.m.
Chihuahua, Mexico	28	37 n	106	5 w	11:00 a.m.
Chongqing, China	29	46 n	106	34 e	1:00 a.m.[1]
Copenhagen	55	40 n	12	34 e	6:00 p.m.
Córdoba, Argentina	31	28 s	64	10 w	2:00 p.m.
Dakar, Senegal	14	40 n	17	28 w	5:00 p.m.
Darwin, Australia	12	28 s	130	51 e	2:30 a.m.[1]
Djibouti	11	30 n	43	3 e	8:00 p.m.
Dublin	53	20 n	6	15 w	5:00 p.m.
Durban, South Africa	29	53 s	30	53 e	7:00 p.m.
Edinburgh, Scotland	55	55 n	3	10 w	5:00 p.m.
Frankfurt	50	7 n	8	41 e	6:00 p.m.
Georgetown, Guyana	6	45 n	58	15 w	1:15 p.m.
Glasgow, Scotland	55	50 n	4	15 w	5:00 p.m.
Guatemala City, Guatemala	14	37 n	90	31 w	11:00 a.m.
Guayaquil, Ecuador	2	10 s	79	56 w	12:00 noon
Hamburg	53	33 n	10	2 e	6:00 p.m.
Hammerfest, Norway	70	38 n	23	38 e	6:00 p.m.
Havana	23	8 n	82	23 w	12:00 noon
Helsinki, Finland	60	10 n	25	0 e	7:00 p.m.
Hobart, Tasmania	42	52 s	147	19 e	3:00 a.m.[1]
Iquique, Chile	20	10 s	70	7 w	1:00 p.m.
Irkutsk, Russia	52	30 n	104	20 e	1:00 a.m.
Jakarta, Indonesia	6	16 s	106	48 e	0:30 a.m.[1]
Johannesburg, South Africa	26	12 s	28	4 e	7:00 p.m.
Kingston, Jamaica	17	59 n	76	49 w	12:00 noon
Kinshasa, Zaire	4	18 s	15	17 e	6:00 p.m.
La Paz, Bolivia	16	27 s	68	22 w	1:00 p.m.
Leeds, England	53	45 n	1	30 w	5:00 p.m.
Lima, Peru	12	0 s	77	2 w	2:00 noon
Lisbon	38	44 n	9	9 w	5:00 p.m.
Liverpool, England	53	25 n	3	0 w	5:00 p.m.
London	51	32 n	0	5 w	5:00 p.m.
Lyons, France	45	45 n	4	50 e	6:00 p.m.
Madrid	40	26 n	3	42 w	6:00 p.m.
Manchester, England	53	30 n	2	15 w	5:00 p.m.
Manila	14	35 n	120	57 e	1:00 a.m.[1]
Marseilles, France	43	20 n	5	20 e	6:00 p.m.
Mazatlán, Mexico	23	12 n	106	25 w	10:00 a.m.
Mecca, Saudi Arabia	21	29 n	39	45 e	8:00 p.m.
Melbourne	37	47 s	144	58 e	3:00 a.m.[1]
Mexico City	19	26 n	99	7 w	11:00 a.m.
Milan, Italy	45	27 n	9	10 e	6:00 p.m.
Montevideo, Uruguay	34	53 s	56	10 w	2:00 p.m.
Moscow	55	45 n	37	36 e	8:00 p.m.
Munich, Germany	48	8 n	11	35 e	6:00 p.m.
Nagasaki, Japan	32	48 n	129	57 e	2:00 a.m.[1]
Nagoya, Japan	35	7 n	136	56 e	2:00 a.m.[1]
Nairobi, Kenya	1	25 s	36	55 e	8:00 p.m.
Nanjing (Nanking), China	32	3 n	118	53 e	1:00 a.m.[1]
Naples, Italy	40	50 n	14	15 e	6:00 p.m.
Newcastle-on-Tyne, England	54	58 n	1	37 w	5:00 p.m.
Odessa, Ukraine	46	27 n	30	48 e	8:00 p.m.
Osaka, Japan	34	32 n	135	30 e	2:00 a.m.[1]
Oslo	59	57 n	10	42 e	6:00 p.m.
Panama City, Panama	8	58 n	79	32 w	12:00 noon
Paramaribo, Surinam	5	45 n	55	15 w	1:30 p.m.
Paris	48	48 n	2	20 e	6:00 p.m.
Perth, Australia	31	57 s	115	52 e	1:00 a.m.[1]
Plymouth, England	50	25 n	4	5 w	5:00 p.m.
Port Moresby, Papua New Guinea	9	25 s	147	8 e	3:00 a.m.[1]
Prague	50	5 n	14	26 e	6:00 p.m.
Reykjavik, Iceland	64	4 n	21	58 w	4:00 p.m.
Rio de Janeiro	22	57 s	43	12 w	2:00 p.m.
Rome	41	54 n	12	27 e	6:00 p.m.
Salvador, Brazil	12	56 s	38	27 w	2:00 p.m.
Santiago, Chile	33	28 s	70	45 w	1:00 p.m.
St. Petersburg	59	56 n	30	18 e	8:00 p.m.
Sao Paulo, Brazil	23	31 s	46	31 w	2:00 p.m.
Shanghai, China	31	10 n	121	28 e	1:00 a.m.[1]
Singapore	1	14 n	103	55 e	0:30 a.m.[1]
Sofia, Bulgaria	42	40 n	23	20 e	7:00 p.m.
Stockholm	59	17 n	18	3 e	6:00 p.m.
Sydney, Australia	34	0 s	151	0 e	3:00 a.m.[1]
Tananarive, Madagascar	18	50 s	47	33 e	8:00 p.m.
Teheran, Iran	35	45 n	51	45 e	8:30 p.m.
Tokyo	35	40 n	139	45 e	2:00 a.m.[1]
Tripoli, Libya	32	57 n	13	12 e	7:00 p.m.
Venice	45	26 n	12	20 e	6:00 p.m.
Veracruz, Mexico	19	10 n	96	10 w	11:00 a.m.
Vienna	48	14 n	16	20 e	6:00 p.m.
Vladivostok, Russia	43	10 n	132	0 e	3:00 a.m.[1]
Warsaw	52	14 n	21	0 e	6:00 p.m.
Wellington, New Zealand	41	17 s	174	47 e	5:00 a.m.[1]
Yangon, Myanmar	16	50 n	96	0 e	11:30 p.m.
Zürich	47	21 n	8	31 e	6:00 p.m.

1. On the following day.

Highest Mountain Peaks of the World

(For U.S. peaks, see Index)

Mountain peak	Range	Location	Height feet	Height meters
Everest	Himalayas	Nepal-Tibet	29,028[1]	8,848
Godwin Austen (K-2)	Karakoram	Kashmir	28,250[1]	8,611
Kanchenjunga	Himalayas	Nepal-Sikkim	28,208	8,598
Lhotse	Himalayas	Nepal-Tibet	27,890	8,501
Makalu	Himalayas	Tibet-Nepal	27,790	8,470
Dhaulagiri I	Himalayas	Nepal	26,810	8,172
Manaslu	Himalayas	Nepal	26,760	8,156
Cho Oyu	Himalayas	Nepal	26,750	8,153
Nanga Parbat	Himalayas	Kashmir	26,660	8,126
Annapurna I	Himalayas	Nepal	26,504	8,078
Gasherbrum I	Karakoram	Kashmir	26,470	8,068
Broad Peak	Karakoram	Kashmir	26,400	8,047
Gasherbrum II	Karakoram	Kashmir	26,360	8,033
Gosainthan	Himalayas	Tibet	26,291	8,013
Gasherbrum III	Karakoram	Kashmir	26,090	7,952
Annapurna II	Himalayas	Nepal	26,041	7,937
Gasherbrum IV	Karakoram	India	26,000	7,925
Kangbachen	Himalayas	Nepal	25,925	7,902
Gyachung Kang	Himalayas	Nepal	25,910	7,897
Himal Chuli	Himalayas	Nepal	25,895	7,893
Disteghil Sar	Karakoram	Kashmir	25,868	7,885
Nuptse	Himalayas	Nepal	25,850	7,829
Kunyang Kish	Karakoram	Kashmir	25,760	7,852
Dakum (Peak 29)	Himalayas	Nepal	25,760	7,852
Masherbrum	Karakoram	Kashmir	25,660	7,821
Nanda Devi	Himalayas	India	25,645	7,817
Chomolonzo	Himalayas	Nepal-Tibet	25,640	7,815
Rakaposhi	Karakoram	Kashmir	25,550	7,788
Batura	Karakoram	Kashmir	25,540	7,785
Kanjut Sar	Karakoram	Kashmir	25,460	7,760
Kamet	Himalayas	India-Tibet	25,447	7,756
Namche Barwa	Himalayas	Tibet	25,445	7,756
Dhaulagiri II	Himalayas	Nepal	25,427	7,750
Saltoro Kangri	Karakoram	India	25,400	7,742
Gurla Mandhata	Himalayas	Tibet	25,355	7,728
Ulugh Muztagh	Kunlun	Tibet	25,341	7,724
Trivor	Karakoram	Kashmir	25,330	7,721
Jannu	Himalayas	Nepal	25,294	7,710
Tirich Mir	Hindu Kush	Pakistan	25,230	7,690
Saser Kangri	Karakoram	India	25,170	7,672
Makalu II	Himalayas	Nepal	25,130	7,660
Chogolisa	Karakoram	India	25,110	7,654
Dhaulagiri IV	Himalayas	Nepal	25,064	7,639
Fang	Himalayas	Nepal	25,013	7,624
Kula Kangri	Himalayas	Bhutan	24,783	7,554
Changtse	Himalayas	Tibet	24,780	7,553
Muztagh Ata	Muztagh Ata	China	24,757	7,546
Skyang Kangri	Himalayas	Kashmir	24,750	7,544
Communism Peak	Pamir	Tajikstan	24,590	7,495
Victory Peak	Pamir	Tajikistan	24,406	7,439
Sia Kangri	Himalayas	Kashmir	24,340	7,419
Chamlang	Himalayas	Nepal	24,012	7,319
Alung Gangri	Himalayas	Tibet	23,999	7,315
Chomo Lhari	Himalayas	Tibet-Bhutan	23,996	7,314
Muztagh (K-5)	Kunlun	China	23,891	7,282
Amne Machin	Kunlun	China	23,490	7,160
Gaurisankar	Himalayas	Népal-Tibet	23,440	7,145
Lenin Peak	Tien-Shan	Tajikistan/Kyrgyzstan	23,405	7,134
Korzhenevski Peak	Pamir	Tajikistan	23,310	7,105
Kangto	Himalayas	Tibet	23,260	7,090
Dunagiri	Himalayas	India	23,184	7,066
Pauhunri	Himalayas	India-Tibet	23,180	7,065
Aconcagua	Andes	Argentina-Chile	23,034	7,021
Revolution Peak	Pamir	Tajikistan	22,880	6,974
Kangchenjhan	Himalayas	India	22,700	6,919
Siniolchu	Himalayas	India	22,620	6,895

Mountain peak	Range	Location	Height feet	Height meters
Ojos des Salado	Andes	Argentina-Chile	22,588	6,885
Bonete	Andes	Argentina-Chile	22,546	6,872
Simvuo	Himalayas	India	22,346	6,811
Tup	Andes	Argentina	22,309	6,800
Kungpu	Himalayas	Bhutan	22,300	6,797
Falso-Azufre	Andes	Argentina-Chile	22,277	6,790
Moscow Peak	Pamir	Tajikistan	22,260	6,785
Veladero	Andes	Argentina	22,244	6,780
Pissis	Andes	Argentina	22,241	6,779
Mercedario	Andes	Argentina-Chile	22,211	6,770
Huascarán	Andes	Peru	22,198	6,766
Tocorpuri	Andes	Bolivia-Chile	22,162	6,755
Karl Marx Peak	Pamir	Tajikistan	22,067	6,726
Llullaillaco	Andes	Argentina-Chile	22,057	6,723
Libertador	Andes	Argentina	22,047	6,720
Kailas	Himalayas	Tibet	22,027	6,714
Lingtren	Himalayas	Nepal-Tibet	21,972	6,697
Incahuasi	Andes	Argentina-Chile	21,719	6,620
Carnicero	Andes	Peru	21,689	6,611
Kurumda	Pamir	Tajikistan	21,686	6,610
Garmo Peak	Pamir	Tajikistan	21,637	6,595
Sajama	Andes	Bolivia	21,555	6,570
Ancohuma	Andes	Bolivia	21,490	6,550
El Muerto	Andes	Argentina-Chile	21,456	6,540
Nacimiento	Andes	Argentina	21,302	6,493
Illimani	Andes	Bolivia	21,184	6,457
Antofalla	Andes	Argentina-Chile	21,129	6,440
Coropuña	Andes	Peru	21,079	6,425
Cuzco (Ausangate)	Andes	Peru	20,995	6,399
Toro	Andes	Argentina-Chile	20,932	6,380
Parinacota	Andes	Bolivia-Chile	20,768	6,330
Chimboraso	Andes	Ecuador	20,702	6,31
Salcantay	Andes	Peru	20,575	6,271
General Manuel Belgrano	Andes	Argentina	20,505	6,250
Chañi	Andes	Argentina	20,341	6,200
Caca Aca	Andes	Bolivia	20,328	6,196
McKinley	Alaska	Alaska	20,320	6,194
Vudor Peak	Pamir	Tajikistan	20,118	6,132
Condoriri	Andes	Bolivia	20,095	6,125
Solimana	Andes	Peru	20,069	6,117
Nevada	Andes	Argentina	20,023	6,103

1. India gives the height as 29,028 feet (8,848 meters), however, in 1987, an Italian expedition recalculated its height to be 29,108 feet and K-2 to be 29,064 feet.

Oceans and Seas

Name	Area sq mi.	Area sq km	Average depth feet	Average depth meters	Greatest known depth feet	Greatest known depth meters	Place greatest known depth
Pacific Ocean	64,000,000	165,760,000	13,215	4,028	36,198	11,033	Mariana Trench
Atlantic Ocean	31,815,000	82,400,000	12,880	3,926	30,246	9,219	Puerto Rico Trough
Indian Ocean	25,300,000	65,526,700	13,002	3,963	24,460	7,455	Sunda Trench
Arctic Ocean	5,440,200	14,090,000	3,953	1,205	18,456	5,625	77° 45′ N; 175° W
Mediterranean Sea[1]	1,145,100	2,965,800	4,688	1,429	15,197	4,632	Off Cape Matapan, Greece
Caribbean Sea	1,049,500	2,718,200	8,685	2,647	22,788	6,946	Off Cayman Islands
South China Sea	895,400	2,319,000	5,419	1,652	16,456	5,016	West of Luzon
Bering Sea	884,900	2,291,900	5,075	1,547	15,659	4,773	Off Buldir Island
Gulf of Mexico	615,000	1,592,800	4,874	1,486	12,425	3,787	Sigsbee Deep
Okhotsk Sea	613,800	1,589,700	2,749	838	12,001	3,658	146° 10′ E; 46° 50′ N
East China Sea	482,300	1,249,200	617	188	9,126	2,782	25° 16′ N; 125° E
Hudson Bay	475,800	1,232,300	420	128	600	183	Near entrance
Japan Sea	389,100	1,007,800	4,429	1,350	12,276	3,742	Central Basin
Andaman Sea	308,100	797,700	2,854	870	12,392	3,777	Off Car Nicobar Island
North Sea	222,100	575,200	308	94	2,165	660	Skagerrak
Red Sea	169,100	438,000	1,611	491	7,254	2,211	Off Port Sudan
Baltic Sea	163,000	422,200	180	55	1,380	421	Off Gotland

1. Includes Black Sea and Sea of Azov. NOTE: For Caspian Sea, *see* Large Lakes of World elsewhere in this section.

World's Greatest Man-Made Lakes[1]

Name of dam	Location	Millions of cubic meters	Thousands of acre-feet	Year completed
Owen Falls	Uganda	204,800	166,000	1954
Kariba	Zimbabwe	181,592	147,218	1959
Bratsk	Siberia	169,270	137,220	1964
High Aswan (Sadd-el-Aali)	Egypt	168,000	136,200	1970
Akosombo	Ghana	148,000	120,000	1965
Daniel Johnson	Canada	141,852	115,000	1968
Guri (Raul Leoni)	Venezuela	136,000	110,256	1986
Krasnoyarsk	Siberia	73,300	59,425	1967
Bennett W.A.C.	Canada	70,309	57,006	1967
Zeya	Russia	68,400	55,452	1978
Cabora Bassa	Mozambique	63,000	51,075	1974
LaGrande 2	Canada	61,720	50,037	1982
LaGrande 3	Canada	60,020	48,659	1982
Ust'-Ilimsk	Russia	59,300	48,075	1980
Volga-V.I. Lenin	Russia	58,000	47,020	1955
Caniapiscau	Canada	53,790	43,608	1981
Poti (Chapetón)	Argentina	53,700	43,535	UC
Upper Wainganga	India	50,700	41,103	1987
Sáo Felix	Brazil	50,600	41,022	1986
Bukhtarma	Former U.S.S.R.	49,740	40,325	1960
Atatürk (Karababa)	Turkey	48,700	39,482	1990
Cerros Colorados	Argentina	48,000	38,914	1973
Irkutsk	Russia	46,000	37,290	1956
Tucuruí	Brazil	36,375	29,489	1984
Vilyuy	Russia	35,900	29,104	1967
Sanmenxia	China	35,400	28,700	1960
Hoover	Nevada/Arizona	35,154	28,500	1936
Sobridinho	Brazil	34,200	27,726	1981
Glen Canyon	Arizona	33,304	27,000	1964
Jenpeg	Canada	31,790	25,772	1975

1. Formed by construction of dams. NOTE: UC = under construction, *Source:* Department of the Interior, Bureau of Reclamation and *International Water Power and Dam Construction.*

Large Lakes of the World

Name and location	Area sq mi.	Area km	Length mi.	Length km	Maximum depth feet	Maximum depth meters
Caspian Sea, Azerbaijan-Kazakhstan-Turkmenistan-Iran[1]	152,239	394,299	745	1,199	3,104	946
Superior, U.S.-Canada	31,820	82,414	383	616	1,333	406
Victoria, Tanzania-Uganda	26,828	69,485	200	322	270	82
Aral, Kazakhstan-Uzbekistan	25,659	66,457	266	428	223	68
Huron, U.S.-Canada	23,010	59,596	247	397	750	229
Michigan, U.S.	22,400	58,016	321	517	923	281
Tanganyika, Tanzania-Zaire	12,700	32,893	420	676	4,708	1,435
Baikal, Russia	12,162	31,500	395	636	5,712	1,741
Great Bear, Canada	12,000	31,080	232	373	270	82
Nyasa, Malawi-Mozambique-Tanzania	11,600	30,044	360	579	2,316	706
Great Slave, Canada	11,170	28,930	298	480	2,015	614
Chad,[2] Chad-Niger-Nigeria	9,946	25,760	—	—	23	7
Erie, U.S.-Canada	9,930	25,719	241	388	210	64
Winnipeg, Canada	9,094	23,553	264	425	204	62
Ontario, U.S.-Canada	7,520	19,477	193	311	778	237
Balkhash, Kazakhstan	7,115	18,428	376	605	87	27
Ladoga, Russia	7,000	18,130	124	200	738	225
Onega, Russia	3,819	9,891	154	248	361	110
Titicaca, Bolivia-Peru	3,141	8,135	110	177	1,214	370
Nicaragua, Nicaragua	3,089	8,001	110	177	230	70
Athabaska, Canada	3,058	7,920	208	335	407	124
Rudolf, Kenya	2,473	6,405	154	248	—	—
Reindeer, Canada	2,444	6,330	152	245	—	—
Eyre, South Australia	2,400[3]	6,216	130	209	varies	varies
Issyk-Kul, Kyrgyzstan	2,394	6,200	113	182	2,297	700
Urmia,[2] Iran	2,317	6,001	81	130	49	15
Torrens, South Australia	2,200	5,698	130	209	—	—
Vänern, Sweden	2,141	5,545	87	140	322	98

Name and location	Area sq mi.	Area km	Length mi.	Length km	Maximum depth feet	Maximum depth meters
Winnipegosis, Canada	2,086	5,403	152	245	59	18
Mobutu Sese Seko, Uganda	2,046	5,299	100	161	180	55
Nettilling, Baffin Island, Canada	1,950	5,051	70	113	—	—
Nipigon, Canada	1,870	4,843	72	116	—	—
Manitoba, Canada	1,817	4,706	140	225	22	7
Great Salt, U.S.	1,800	4,662	75	121	15/25	5/8
Kioga, Uganda	1,700	4,403	50	80	about 30	9
Koko-Nor, China	1,630	4,222	66	106	—	—

1. The Caspian Sea is called "sea" because the Romans, finding it salty, named it *Mare Caspium*. Many geographers, however, consider it a lake because it is land-locked. 2. Figures represent high-water data. 3. Varies with the rainfall of the wet season. It has been reported to dry up almost completely on occasion.

Principal Rivers of the World

(For other U.S. rivers, see Index)

River	Source	Outflow	Approx. length miles	Approx. length km
Nile	Tributaries of Lake Victoria, Africa	Mediterranean Sea	4,180	6,690
Amazon	Glacier-fed lakes, Peru	Atlantic Ocean	3,912	6,296
Mississippi-Missouri-Red Rock	Source of Red Rock, Montana	Gulf of Mexico	3,880	6,240
Yangtze Kiang	Tibetan plateau, China	China Sea	3,602	5,797
Ob	Altai Mts., Russia	Gulf of Ob	3,459	5,567
Huang Ho (Yellow)	Eastern part of Kunlan Mts., west China	Gulf of Chihli	2,900	4,667
Yenisei	Tannu-Ola Mts., western Tuva, Russia	Arctic Ocean	2,800	4,506
Paraná	Confluence of Paranaiba and Grande rivers	Río de la Plata	2,795	4,498
Irtish	Altai Mts., Russia	Ob River	2,758	4,438
Zaire (Congo)	Confluence of Lualab and Luapula rivers, Zaire	Atlantic Ocean	2,716	4,371
Heilong (Amur)	Confluence of Shilka (Russia) and Argun (Manchuria) rivers	Tatar Strait	2,704	4,352
Lena	Baikal Mts., Russia	Arctic Ocean	2,652	4,268
Mackenzie	Head of Finlay River, British Columbia, Canada	Beaufort Sea (Arctic Ocean)	2,635	4,241
Niger	Guinea	Gulf of Guinea	2,600	4,184
Mekong	Tibetan highlands	South China Sea	2,500	4,023
Mississippi	Lake Itasca, Minnesota	Gulf of Mexico	2,348	3,779
Missouri	Confluence of Jefferson, Gallatin, and Madison rivers, Montana	Mississippi River	2,315	3,726
Volga	Valdai plateau, Russia	Caspian Sea	2,291	3,687
Madeira	Confluence of Beni and Maumoré rivers, Bolivia-Brazil boundary	Amazon River	2,012	3,238
Purus	Peruvian Andes	Amazon River	1,993	3,207
São Francisco	Southwest Minas Gerais, Brazil	Atlantic Ocean	1,987	3,198
Yukon	Junction of Lewes and Pelly rivers, Yukon Territory, Canada	Bering Sea	1,979	3,185
St. Lawrence	Lake Ontario	Gulf of St. Lawrence	1,900	3,058
Rio Grande	San Juan Mts., Colorado	Gulf of Mexico	1,885	3,034
Brahmaputra	Himalayas	Ganges River	1,800	2,897
Indus	Himalayas	Arabian Sea	1,800	2,897
Danube	Black Forest, Germany	Black Sea	1,766	2,842

River	Source	Outflow	Approx. length miles	km
Euphrates	Confluence of Murat Nehri and Kara Su rivers, Turkey	Shatt-al-Arab	1,739	2,799
Darling	Central part of Eastern Highlands, Australia	Murray River	1,702	2,739
Zambezi	11°21′S, 24°22′E, Zambia	Mozambique Channel	1,700	2,736
Tocantins	Goiás, Brazil	Pará River	1,677	2,699
Murray	Australian Alps, New South Wales	Indian Ocean	1,609	2,589
Nelson	Head of Bow River, western Alberta, Canada	Hudson Bay	1,600	2,575
Paraguay	Mato Grosso, Brazil	Paraná River	1,584	2,549
Ural	Southern Ural Mts., Russia	Caspian Sea	1,574	2,533
Ganges	Himalayas	Bay of Bengal	1,557	2,506
Amu Darya (Oxus)	Nicholas Range, Pamir Mts., Turkmenistan	Aral Sea	1,500	2,414
Japurá	Andes, Colombia	Amazon River	1,500	2,414
Salween	Tibet, south of Kunlun Mts.	Gulf of Martaban	1,500	2,414
Arkansas	Central Colorado	Mississippi River	1,459	2,348
Colorado	Grand County, Colorado	Gulf of California	1,450	2,333
Dnieper	Valdai Hills, Russia	Black Sea	1,419	2,284
Ohio-Allegheny	Potter County, Pennsylvania	Mississippi River	1,306	2,102
Irrawaddy	Confluence of Nmai and Mali rivers, northeast Burma	Bay of Bengal	1,300	2,092
Orange	Lesotho	Atlantic Ocean	1,300	2,092
Orinoco	Serra Parima Mts., Venezuela	Atlantic Ocean	1,281	2,062
Pilcomayo	Andes Mts., Bolivia	Paraguay River	1,242	1,999
Xi Jiang (Si Kiang)	Eastern Yunnan Province, China	China Sea	1,236	1,989
Columbia	Columbia Lake, British Columbia, Canada	Pacific Ocean	1,232	1,983
Don	Tula, Russia	Sea of Azov	1,223	1,968
Sungari	China-North Korea boundary	Amur River	1,215	1,955
Saskatchewan	Canadian Rocky Mts.	Lake Winnipeg	1,205	1,939
Peace	Stikine Mts., British Columbia, Canada	Great Slave River	1,195	1,923
Tigris	Taurus Mts., Turkey	Shatt-al-Arab	1,180	1,899

Highest Waterfalls of the World

Waterfall	Location	River	Height feet	m
Angel	Venezuela	Tributary of Caroni	3,281	1,000
Tugela	Natal, South Africa	Tugela	3,000	914
Cuquenán	Venezuela	Cuquenán	2,000	610
Sutherland	South Island, N.Z.	Arthur	1,904	580
Takkakaw	British Columbia	Tributary of Yoho	1,650	503
Ribbon (Yosemite)	California	Creek flowing into Yosemite	1,612	491
Upper Yosemite	California	Yosemite Creek, tributary of Merced	1,430	436
Gavarnie	Southwest France	Gave de Pau	1,384	422
Vettisfoss	Norway	Mörkedola	1,200	366
Widows' Tears (Yosemite)	California	Tributary of Merced	1,170	357
Staubbach	Switzerland	Staubbach (Lauterbrunnen Valley)	984	300

Waterfall	Location	River	Height feet	m
Middle Cascade (Yosemite)	California	Yosemite Creek, tributary of Merced	909	277
King Edward VIII	Guyana	Courantyne	850	259
Gersoppa	India	Sharavati	829	253
Kaieteur	Guyana	Potaro	822	251
Skykje	Norway	In Skykjedal (valley of Inner Hardinger Fjord)	820	250
Kalambo	Tanzania-Zambia	—	720	219
Fairy (Mount Rainier Park)	Washington	Stevens Creek	700	213
Trummelbach	Switzerland	Trummelbach (Lauterbrunnen Valley)	700	213
Aniene (Teverone)	Italy	Tiber	680	207
Cascata delle Marmore	Italy	Velino, tributary of Nera	650	198
Maradalsfos	Norway	Stream flowing into Ejkisdalsvand (lake)	643	196
Feather	California	Fall River	640	195
Maletsunyane	Lesotho	Maletsunyane	630	192
Bridalveil (Yosemite)	California	Yosemite Creek	620	189
Multnomah	Oregon	Multnomah Creek, tributary of Columbia	620	189
Vøringsfos	Norway	Bjoreia	597	182
Nevada (Yosemite)	California	Merced	594	181
Skjeggedal	Norway	Tysso	525	160
Marina	Guyana	Tributary of Kuribrong, tributary of Potaro	500	152
Tequendama	Colombia	Funza, tributary of Magdalena	425	130
King George's	Cape of Good Hope, South Africa	Orange	400	122
Illilouette (Yosemite)	California	Illilouette Creek, tributary of Merced	370	113
Victoria	Rhodesia-Zambia boundary	Zambezi	355	108
Handöl	Sweden	Handöl Creek	345	105
Lower Yosemite	California	Yosemite	320	98
Comet (Mount Rainier Park)	Washington	Van Trump Creek	320	98
Vernal (Yosemite)	California	Merced	317	97
Virginia	Northwest Territories, Canada	South Nahanni, tributary of Mackenzie	315	96
Lower Yellowstone	Wyoming	Yellowstone	310	94

NOTE: Niagara Falls (New York-Ontario), though of great volume, has parallel drops of only 158 and 167 feet.

Large Islands of the World

Island	Location and status	Area sq mi.	sq km
Greenland	North Atlantic (Danish)	839,999	2,175,597
New Guinea	Southwest Pacific (Irian Jaya, Indonesian, west part; Papua New Guinea, east part)	316,615	820,033
Borneo	West mid-Pacific (Indonesian, south part, Brunei and Malaysian, north part)	286,914	743,107
Madagascar	Indian Ocean (Malagasy Republic)	226,657	587,042
Baffin	North Atlantic (Canadian)	183,810	476,068
Sumatra	Northeast Indian Ocean (Indonesian)	182,859	473,605
Honshu	Sea of Japan-Pacific (Japanese)	88,925	230,316
Great Britain	Off coast of NW Europe (England, Scotland, and Wales)	88,758	229,883
Ellesmere	Arctic Ocean (Canadian)	82,119	212,688
Victoria	Arctic Ocean (Canadian)	81,930	212,199
Celebes	West mid-Pacific (Indonesian)	72,986	189,034
South Island	South Pacific (New Zealand)	58,093	150,461
Java	Indian Ocean (Indonesian)	48,990	126,884
North Island	South Pacific (New Zealand)	44,281	114,688

Island	Location and status	Area sq mi.	Area sq km
Cuba	Caribbean Sea (republic)	44,218	114,525
Newfoundland	North Atlantic (Canadian)	42,734	110,681
Luzon	West mid-Pacific (Philippines)	40,420	104,688
Iceland	North Atlantic (republic)	39,768	102,999
Mindanao	West mid-Pacific (Philippines)	36,537	94,631
Ireland	West of Great Britain (republic, south part; United Kingdom, north part)	32,597	84,426
Hokkaido	Sea of Japan—Pacific (Japanese)	30,372	78,663
Hispaniola	Caribbean Sea (Dominican Republic, east part; Haiti, west part)	29,355	76,029
Tasmania	South of Australia (Australian)	26,215	67,897
Sri Lanka (Ceylon)	Indian Ocean (republic)	25,332	65,610
Sakhalin (Karafuto)	North of Japan (Russia)	24,560	63,610
Banks	Arctic Ocean (Canadian)	23,230	60,166
Devon	Arctic Ocean (Canadian)	20,861	54,030
Tierra del Fuego	Southern tip of South America (Argentinian, east part; Chilean, west part)	18,605	48,187
Kyushu	Sea of Japan—Pacific (Japanese)	16,223	42,018
Melville	Arctic Ocean (Canadian)	16,141	41,805
Axel Heiberg	Arctic Ocean (Canadian)	15,779	40,868
Southampton	Hudson Bay (Canadian)	15,700	40,663

Principal Deserts of the World

Desert	Location	Approximate size	Approx. elevation, ft
Atacama	North Chile	400 mi. long	7,000–13,500
Black Rock	Northwest Nevada	About 1,000 sq mi.	2,000–8,500
Colorado	Southeast California from San Gorgonio Pass to Gulf of California	200 mi. long and a maximum width of 50 mi.	Few feet above to 250 below sea level
Dasht-e-Kavir	Southeast of Caspian Sea, Iran	—	2,000
Dasht-e-Lut	Northeast of Kerman, Iran	—	1,000
Gobi (Shamo)	Covers most of Mongolia	500,000 sq mi.	3,000–5,000
Great Arabian	Most of Arabia	1,500 mi. long	—
An Nafud (Red Desert)	South of Jauf	400 mi. by avg of 140 mi.	3,000
Dahna	Northeast of Nejd	400 mi. by 30 mi.	—
Rub' al-Khali	South portion of Nejd	Over 200,000 sq. mi.	—
Syrian (Al-Hamad)	North of lat. 30°N	—	1,850
Great Australian	Western portion of Australia	About one half the continent	600–1,000
Great Salt Lake	West of Great Salt Lake to Nevada—Utah boundary	About 110 mi. by 50 mi.	4,500
Kalahari	South Africa—South-West Africa	About 120,000 sq mi.	Over 3,000
Kara Kum (Desert of Kiva)	Southwest Turkmenistan	115,000 sq mi.	—
Kyzyl Kum	Uzbekistan and Kazakhstan	Over 100,000 sq. mi.	160 near Lake Aral to 2,000 in southeast
Libyan	Libya, Egypt, Sudan	Over 500,000 sq mi.	—
Mojave	North of Colorado Desert and south of Death Valley, southeast California	15,000 sq mi.	2,000
Nubian	From Red Sea to great west bend of the Nile, Sudan	—	2,500
Painted Desert	Northeast Arizona	Over 7,000 sq mi.	High plateau, 5,000
Sahara	North Africa to about lat. 15°N and from Red Sea to Atlantic Ocean	3,200 mi. greatest length along lat. 20°N; area over 3,500,000 sq mi.	440 below sea level to 11,000 above; avg elevation, 1,400–1,600
Takla Makan	South central Sinkiang, China	Over 100,000 sq mi.	—
Thar (Indian)	Pakistan-India	Nearly 100,000 sq mi.	Over 1,000

Interesting Caves and Caverns of the World

Aggtelek. In village of same name, northern Hungary. Large stalactitic cavern about 5 miles long.

Altamira Cave. Near Santander, Spain. Contains animal paintings (Old Stone Age art) on roof and walls.

Antiparos. On island of same name in the Grecian Archipelago. Some stalactites are 20 ft long. Brilliant colors and fantastic shapes.

Blue Grotto. On island of Capri, Italy. Cavern hollowed out in limestone by constant wave action. Now half filled with water because of sinking coast. Name derived from unusual blue light permeating the cave. Source of light is a submerged opening, light passing through the water.

Carlsbad Caverns. Southeast New Mexico. Largest underground labyrinth yet discovered. Three levels: 754, 900, and 1,320 ft below the surface.

Fingal's Cave. On island of Staffa off coast of western Scotland. Penetrates about 200 ft inland. Contains basaltic columns almost 40 ft high.

Ice Cave. Near Dobsina, Czechoslovakia. Noted for its beautiful crystal effects.

Jenolan Caves. In Blue Mountain plateau, New South Wales, Australia. Beautiful stalactitic formations.

Kent's Cavern. Near Torquay, England. Source of much information on Paleolithic man.

Luray Cavern. Near Luray, Va. Has large stalactitic and stalagmitic columns of many colors.

Mammoth Cave. Limestone cavern in central Kentucky. Cave area is about 10 miles in diameter but has over 300 miles of irregular subterranean passageways at various levels. Temperature remains fairly constant at 54°F.

Peak Cavern or Devil's Hole. Derbyshire, England. About 2,250 ft into a mountain. Lowest part is about 600 ft below the surface.

Postojna (Postumia) Grotto. Near Postumia in Julian Alps, about 25 miles northeast of Trieste. Stalactitic cavern, largest in Europe. Piuca (Pivka) River flows through part of it. Caves have numerous beautiful stalactites.

Singing Cave. Iceland. A lava cave; name derived from echoes of people singing in it.

Wind Cave. In Black Hills of South Dakota. Limestone caverns with stalactites and stalagmites almost entirely missing. Variety of crystal formations called "boxwork."

Wyandotte Cave. In Crawford County, southern Indiana. A limestone cavern with five levels of passages; one of the largest in North America. "Monumental Mountain," approximately 135 ft high, is believed to be one of the world's largest underground "mountains."

U.S. Geography

Miscellaneous Data for the United States

Source: Department of the Interior, U.S. Geological Survey.

Highest point: Mount McKinley, Alaska	20,320 ft (6,198 m)
Lowest point: Death Valley, Calif.	282 ft (86 m) below sea level
Approximate mean altitude	2,500 ft (763 m)
Points farthest apart (50 states):	5,859 mi. (9,429 km)
Log Point, Elliot Key, Fla., and Kure Island, Hawai	
Geographic center (50 states):	44° 58′ N. lat.103° 46′ W. long.
In Butte County, S.D. (west of Castle Rock)	
Geographic center (48 conterminous states):	39° 50′ N. lat.98° 35′ W. long.
In Smith County, Kan. (near Lebanon)	
Boundaries:	
Between Alaska and Canada	1,538 mi. (2,475 km)
Between the 48 conterminous states and Canada (incl. Great Lakes)	3,987 mi. (6,416 km)
Between the United States and Mexico	1,933 mi. (3,111 km)

Extreme Points of the United States (50 States)

Extreme point	Latitude	Longitude	Distance[1] mi.	Distance[1] km
Northernmost point: Point Barrow, Alaska	71°23′ N	156°29′ W	2,507	4,034
Easternmost point: West Quoddy Head, Me.	44°49′ N	66°57′ W	1,788	2,997
Southernmost point: Ka Lae (South Cape), Hawaii	18°55′ N	155°41′ W	3,463	5,573
Westernmost point: Cape Wrangell, Alaska (Attu Island)	52°55′ N	172°27′ E	3,625	5,833

1. From geographic center of United States (incl. Alaska and Hawaii), west of Castle Rock, S.D., 44°58′ N. lat., 103°46′ W long. If measured from the prime meridian in Greenwich, England, Cape Wrangell, Attu Island, Alaska would be the easternmost point.

Highest, Lowest, and Mean Elevations in the United States

State	Elevation ft[1]	Highest point	Elevation ft[1]	Lowest point	Elevation ft[1]
Alabama	500	Cheaha Mountain	2,405	Gulf of Mexico	Sea level
Alaska	1,900	Mount McKinley	20,320	Pacific Ocean	Sea level
Arizona	4,100	Humphreys Peak	12,633	Colorado River	70
Arkansas	650	Magazine Mountain	2,753	Ouachita River	55
California	2,900	Mount Whitney	14,494[2]	Death Valley	282[3]
Colorado	6,800	Mount Elbert	14,433	Arkansas River	3,350
Connecticut	500	Mount Frissell, on south slope	2,380	Long Island Sound	Sea level
Delaware	60	On Ebright Road	448	Atlantic Ocean	Sea level
D.C.	150	Tenleytown, at Reno Reservoir	410	Potomac River	1
Florida	100	Sec. 30, T6N, R20W[4]	345	Atlantic Ocean	Sea level
Georgia	600	Brasstown Bald	4,784	Atlantic Ocean	Sea level
Hawaii	3,030	Puu Wekiu, Mauna Kea	13,796	Pacific Ocean	Sea level
Idaho	5,000	Borah Peak	12,662	Snake River	710
Illinois	600	Charles Mound	1,235	Mississippi River	279[5]
Indiana	700	Franklin Township, Wayne County	1,257	Ohio River	320[5]
Iowa	1,100	Sec. 29, T100N, R41W[6]	1,670	Mississippi River	480
Kansas	2,000	Mount Sunflower	4,039[7]	Verdigris River	679
Kentucky	750	Black Mountain	4,139	Mississippi River	257[5]
Louisiana	100	Driskill Mountain	535	New Orleans	8[3]
Maine	600	Mount Katahdin	5,267	Atlantic Ocean	Sea level
Maryland	350	Backbone Mountain	3,360	Atlantic Ocean	Sea level
Massachusetts	500	Mount Greylock	3,487	Atlantic Ocean	Sea level
Michigan	900	Mount Arvon	1,979	Lake Erie	572[5]
Minnesota	1,200	Eagle Mountain	2,301	Lake Superior	600
Mississippi	300	Woodall Mountain	806	Gulf of Mexico	Sea level
Missouri	800	Taum Sauk Mountain	1,772	St. Francis River	230[5]
Montana	3,400	Granite Peak	12,799	Kootenai River	1,800
Nebraska	2,600	Johnson Township, Kimball County	5,424	Missouri River	840
Nevada	5,500	Boundary Peak	13,140	Colorado River	479
New Hampshire	1,000	Mount Washington	6,288	Atlantic Ocean	Sea level
New Jersey	250	High Point	1,803[7]	Atlantic Ocean	Sea level
New Mexico	5,700	Wheeler Peak	13,161	Red Bluff Reservoir	2,842
New York	1,000	Mount Marcy	5,344	Atlantic Ocean	Sea level
North Carolina	700	Mount Mitchell	6,684	Atlantic Ocean	Sea level
North Dakota	1,900	White Butte	3,506	Red River	750
Ohio	850	Campbell Hill	1,549	Ohio River	455[5]
Oklahoma	1,300	Black Mesa	4,973	Little River	289
Oregon	3,300	Mount Hood	11,239	Pacific Ocean	Sea level
Pennsylvania	1,100	Mount Davis	3,213	Delaware River	Sea level
Rhode Island	200	Jerimoth Hill	812	Atlantic Ocean	Sea level
South Carolina	350	Sassafras Mountain	3,560	Atlantic Ocean	Sea level
South Dakota	2,200	Harney Peak	7,242	Big Stone Lake	966
Tennessee	900	Clingmans Dome	6,643	Mississippi River	178[5]
Texas	1,700	Guadalupe Peak	8,749	Gulf of Mexico	Sea level
Utah	6,100	Kings Peak	13,528	Beaverdam Wash	2,000
Vermont	1,000	Mount Mansfield	4,393	Lake Champlain	95
Virginia	950	Mount Rogers	5,729	Atlantic Ocean	Sea level
Washington	1,700	Mount Rainier	14,410	Pacific Ocean	Sea level
West Virginia	1,500	Spruce Knob	4,861	Potomac River	240
Wisconsin	1,050	Timms Hill	1,951	Lake Michigan	579[5]
Wyoming	6,700	Gannett Peak	13,804	Belle Fourche River	3,099
United States	2,500	Mount McKinley (Alaska)	20,320	Death Valley (California)	282[3]

1. Approximate mean altitude. 2. National Geodetic Survey. 3. Below sea level. 4. Walton County. 5. Corps of Engineers 6. Osceola County. 7. State Surveys *Source:* Department of the Interior, U.S. Geological Survey.

The Continental Divide

The Continental Divide is a ridge of high ground which runs irregularly north and south through the Rocky Mountains and separates eastward-flowing from westward-flowing streams. The waters which flow eastward empty into the Atlantic Ocean, chiefly by way of the Gulf of Mexico; those which flow westward empty into the Pacific.

Mason and Dixon's Line

Mason and Dixon's Line (often called the Mason-Dixon Line) is the boundary between Pennsylvania and Maryland, running at a north latitude of 39°43′19.11″. The greater part of it was surveyed from 1763–67 by Charles Mason and Jeremiah Dixon, English astronomers who had been appointed to settle a dispute between the colonies. As the line was partly the boundary between the free and the slave states, it has come to signify the division between the North and the South.

Latitude and Longitude of U.S. and Canadian Cities

(and time corresponding to 12:00 noon, eastern standard time)

City	Lat. °	Lat. ′	Long. °	Long. ′	Time	City	Lat. °	Lat. ′	Long. °	Long. ′	Time
Albany, N.Y.	42	40	73	45	12:00 noon	Memphis, Tenn	35	9	90	3	11:00 a.m.
Albuquerque, N.M.	35	05	106	39	10:00 a.m.	Miami, Fla.	25	46	80	12	12:00 noon
Amarillo, Tex.	35	11	101	50	11:00 a.m.	Milwaukee	43	2	87	55	11:00 a.m.
Anchorage, Alaska	61	13	149	54	8:00 a.m.	Minneapolis	44	59	93	14	11:00 a.m.
Atlanta	33	45	84	23	12:00 noon	Mobile, Ala.	30	42	88	3	11:00 a.m.
Austin, Tex.	30	16	97	44	11:00 a.m.	Montgomery, Ala.	32	21	86	18	11:00 a.m.
Baker, Ore.	44	47	117	50	9:00 a.m.	Montpelier, Vt.	44	15	72	32	12:00 noon
Baltimore	39	18	76	38	12:00 noon	Montreal, Que.	45	30	73	35	12:00 noon
Bangor, Me.	44	48	68	47	12:00 noon	Moose Jaw, Sask.	50	37	105	31	10:00 a.m.
Birmingham, Ala.	33	30	86	50	11:00 a.m.	Nashville, Tenn.	36	10	86	47	11:00 a.m.
Bismarck, N.D.	46	48	100	47	11:00 a.m.	Nelson, B.C.	49	30	117	17	9:00 a.m.
Boise, Idaho	43	36	116	13	10:00 a.m.	Newark, N.J.	40	44	74	10	12:00 noon
Boston	42	21	71	5	12:00 noon	New Haven, Conn.	41	19	72	55	12:00 noon
Buffalo, N.Y.	42	55	78	50	12:00 noon	New Orleans	29	57	90	4	11:00 a.m.
Calgary, Alberta	51	1	114	1	10:00 a.m.	New York	40	47	73	58	12:00 noon
Carlsbad, N.M.	32	26	104	15	10:00 a.m.	Nome, Alaska	64	25	165	30	8:00 a.m.
Charleston, S.C.	32	47	79	56	12:00 noon	Oakland, Calif.	37	48	122	16	9:00 a.m.
Charleston, W. Va.	38	21	81	38	12:00 noon	Oklahoma City	35	26	97	28	11:00 a.m.
Charlotte, N.C.	35	14	80	50	12:00 noon	Omaha, Neb.	41	15	95	56	11:00 a.m.
Cheyenne, Wyo.	41	9	104	52	10:00 a.m.	Ottawa, Ont.	45	24	75	43	12:00 noon
Chicago	41	50	87	37	11:00 a.m.	Philadelphia	39	57	75	10	12:00 noon
Cincinnati	39	8	84	30	12:00 noon	Phoenix, Ariz.	33	29	112	4	10:00 a.m.
Cleveland	41	28	81	37	12:00 noon	Pierre, S.D.	44	22	100	21	11:00 a.m.
Columbia, S.C.	34	0	81	2	12:00 noon	Pittsburgh	40	27	79	57	12:00 noon
Columbus, Ohio	40	0	83	1	12:00 noon	Port Arthur, Ont.	48	30	89	17	12:00 noon
Dallas	32	46	96	46	11:00 a.m.	Portland, Me.	43	40	70	15	12:00 noon
Denver	39	45	105	0	10:00 a.m.	Portland, Ore.	45	31	122	41	9:00 a.m.
Des Moines, Iowa	41	35	93	37	11:00 a.m.	Providence, R.I.	41	50	71	24	12:00 noon
Detroit	42	20	83	3	12:00 noon	Quebec, Que.	46	49	71	11	12:00 noon
Dubuque, Iowa	42	31	90	40	11:00 a.m.	Raleigh, N.C.	35	46	78	39	12:00 noon
Duluth, Minn.	46	49	92	5	11:00 a.m.	Reno, Nev.	39	30	119	49	9:00 a.m.
Eastport, Me.	44	54	67	0	12:00 noon	Richfield, Utah	38	46	112	5	10:00 a.m.
El Centro, Calif.	32	38	115	33	9:00 a.m.	Richmond, Va.	37	33	77	29	12:00 noon
El Paso	31	46	106	29	10:00 a.m.	Roanoke, Va.	37	17	79	57	12:00 noon
Eugene, Ore.	44	3	123	5	9:00 a.m.	Sacramento, Calif.	38	35	121	30	9:00 a.m.
Fargo, N.D.	46	52	96	48	11:00 a.m.	St. John, N.B.	45	18	66	10	1:00 p.m.
Flagstaff, Ariz.	35	13	111	41	10:00 a.m.	St. Louis	38	35	90	12	11:00 a.m.
Fort Worth, Tex.	32	43	97	19	11:00 a.m.	Salt Lake City, Utah	40	46	111	54	10:00 a.m.
Fresno, Calif.	36	44	119	48	9:00 a.m.	San Antonio	29	23	98	33	11:00 a.m.
Grand Junction, Colo.	39	5	108	33	10:00 a.m.	San Diego, Calif.	32	42	117	10	9:00 a.m.
Grand Rapids, Mich.	42	58	85	40	12:00 noon	San Francisco	37	47	122	26	9:00 a.m.
Havre, Mont.	48	33	109	43	10:00 a.m.	San Jose, Calif.	37	20	121	53	9:00 a.m.
Helena, Mont.	46	35	112	2	10:00 a.m.	San Juan, P.R.	18	30	66	10	1:00 p.m.
Honolulu	21	18	157	50	7:00 a.m.	Santa Fe, N.M.	35	41	105	57	10:00 a.m.
Hot Springs, Ark.	34	31	93	3	11:00 a.m.	Savannah, Ga.	32	5	81	5	12:00 noon
Houston, Tex.	29	45	95	21	11:00 a.m.	Seattle	47	37	122	20	9:00 a.m.
Idaho Falls, Idaho	43	30	112	1	10:00 a.m.	Shreveport, La.	32	28	93	42	11:00 a.m.
Indianapolis	39	46	86	10	12:00 noon	Sioux Falls, S.D.	43	33	96	44	11:00 a.m.
Jackson, Miss.	32	20	90	12	11:00 a.m.	Sitka, Alaska	57	10	135	15	9:00 a.m.
Jacksonville, Fla.	30	22	81	40	12:00 noon	Spokane, Wash.	47	40	117	26	9:00 a.m.
Juneau, Alaska	58	18	134	24	8:00 a.m.	Springfield, Ill.	39	48	89	38	11:00 a.m.
Kansas City, Mo.	39	6	94	35	11:00 a.m.	Springfield, Mass.	42	6	72	34	12:00 noon
Key West, Fla.	24	33	81	48	12:00 noon	Springfield, Mo.	37	13	93	17	11:00 a.m.
Kingston, Ont.	44	15	76	30	12:00 noon	Syracuse, N.Y.	43	2	76	8	12:00 noon
Klamath Falls, Ore.	42	10	121	44	9:00 a.m.	Tampa, Fla.	27	57	82	27	12:00 noon
Knoxville, Tenn.	35	57	83	56	12:00 noon	Toledo, Ohio	41	39	83	33	12:00 noon
Las Vegas, Nev.	36	10	115	12	9:00 a.m.	Toronto, Ont.	43	40	79	24	12:00 noon
Lewiston, Idaho	46	24	117	2	9:00 a.m.	Tulsa, Okla.	36	09	95	59	11:00 a.m.
Lincoln, Neb.	40	50	96	40	11:00 a.m.	Victoria, B.C.	48	25	123	21	9:00 a.m.
London, Ont.	43	2	81	34	12:00 noon	Virginia Beach, Va.	36	51	75	58	12:00 noon
Long Beach, Calif.	33	46	118	11	9:00 a.m.	Washington, D.C.	38	53	77	02	12:00 noon
Los Angeles	34	3	118	15	9:00 a.m.	Wichita, Kan.	37	43	97	17	11:00 a.m.
Louisville, Ky.	38	15	85	46	12:00 noon	Wilmington, N.C.	34	14	77	57	12:00 noon
Manchester, N.H.	43	0	71	30	12:00 noon	Winnipeg, Man.	49	54	97	7	11:00 a.m.

Named Summits in the U.S. Over 14,000 Feet Above Sea Level

Name	State	Height	Name	State	Height	Name	State	Height
Mt. McKinley	Alaska	20,320	Castle Peak	Colo.	14,265	Mt. Eolus	Colo.	14,083
Mt. St. Elias	Alaska	18,008	Quandary Peak	Colo.	14,265	Windom Peak	Colo.	14,082
Mt. Foraker	Alaska	17,400	Mt. Evans	Colo.	14,264	Mt. Columbia	Colo.	14,073
Mt. Bona	Alaska	16,500	Longs Peak	Colo.	14,255	Mt. Augusta	Alaska	14,070
Mt. Blackburn	Alaska	16,390	Mt. Wilson	Colo.	14,246	Missouri Mtn.	Colo.	14,067
Mt. Sanford	Alaska	16,237	White Mtn.	Calif.	14,246	Humboldt Peak	Colo.	14,064
Mt. Vancouver	Alaska	15,979	North Palisade	Calif.	14,242	Mt. Bierstadt	Colo.	14,060
South Buttress	Alaska	15,885	Mt. Cameron	Colo.	14,238	Sunlight Peak	Colo.	14,059
Mt. Churchill	Alaska	15,638	Mt. Shavano	Colo.	14,229	Split Mtn.	Calif.	14,058
Mt. Fairweather	Alaska	15,300	Crestone Needle	Colo.	14,197	Handies Peak	Colo.	14,048
Mt. Hubbard	Alaska	14,950	Mt. Belford	Colo.	14,197	Culebra Peak	Colo.	14,047
Mt. Bear	Alaska	14,831	Mt. Princeton	Colo.	14,197	Mt. Lindsey	Colo.	14,042
East Buttress	Alaska	14,730	Mt. Yale	Colo.	14,196	Ellingwood Point	Colo.	14,042
Mt. Hunter	Alaska	14,573	Mt. Bross	Colo.	14,172	Little Bear Peak	Colo.	14,037
Browne Tower	Alaska	14,530	Kit Carson Mtn.	Colo.	14,165	Mt. Sherman	Colo.	14,036
Mt. Alverstone	Alaska	14,500	Mt. Wrangell	Alaska	14,163	Redcloud Peak	Colo.	14,034
Mt. Whitney	Calif.	14,494[1]	Mt. Shasta	Calif.	14,162	Mt. Langley	Calif.	14,027
University Peak	Alaska	14,470	El Diente Peak	Colo.	14,159	Conundrum Peak	Colo.	14,022
Mt. Elbert	Colo.	14,433	Point Success	Wash.	14,158	Mt. Tyndall	Calif.	14,019
Mt. Massive	Colo.	14,421	Maroon Peak	Colo.	14,156	Pyramid Peak	Colo.	14,018
Mt. Harvard	Colo.	14,420	Tabeguache Mtn.	Colo.	14,155	Wilson Peak	Colo.	14,017
Mt. Rainier	Wash.	14,410	Mt. Oxford	Colo.	14,153	Wetterhorn Peak	Colo.	14,015
Mt. Williamson	Calif.	14,370	Mt. Sill	Calif.	14,153	North Maroon Peak	Colo.	14,014
La Plata Peak	Colo.	14,361	Mt. Sneffels	Colo.	14,150	San Luis Peak	Colo.	14,014
Blanca Peak	Colo.	14,345	Mt. Democrat	Colo.	14,148	Middle Palisade	Calif.	14,012
Uncompahgre Peak	Colo.	14,309	Capitol Peak	Colo.	14,130	Mt. Muir	Calif.	14,012
Crestone Peak	Colo.	14,294	Liberty Cap	Wash.	14,112	Mt. of the Holy Cross	Colo.	14,005
Mt. Lincoln	Colo.	14,286	Pikes Peak	Colo.	14,110	Huron Peak	Colo.	14,003
Grays Peak	Colo.	14,270	Snowmass Mtn.	Colo.	14,092	Thunderbolt Peak	Calif.	14,003
Mt. Antero	Colo.	14,269	Mt. Russell	Calif.	14,088	Sunshine Peak	Colo.	14,001
Torreys Peak	Colo.	14,267						

1. National Geodetic Survey. *Source:* Department of the Interior, U.S. Geological Survey.

Rivers of the United States

(350 or more miles long)

Alabama-Coosa (600 mi.; 966 km): From junction of Oostanula and Etowah R. in Georgia to Mobile R.

Altamaha-Ocmulgee (392 mi.; 631 km): From junction of Yellow R. and South R., Newton Co. in Georgia to Atlantic Ocean.

Apalachicola-Chattahoochee (524 mi.; 843 km): From Towns Co. in Georgia to Gulf of Mexico in Florida.

Arkansas (1,459 mi.; 2,348 km): From Lake Co. in Colorado to Mississippi R. in Arkansas.

Brazos (923 mi.; 1,490 km): From junction of Salt Fork and Double Mountain Fork in Texas to Gulf of Mexico.

Canadian (906 mi.; 1,458 km): From Las Animas Co. in Colorado to Arkansas R. in Oklahoma.

Cimarron (600 mi.; 966 km): From Colfax Co. in New Mexico to Arkansas R. in Oklahoma.

Colorado (1,450 mi.; 2,333 km): From Rocky Mountain National Park in Colorado to Gulf of California in Mexico.

Colorado (862 mi.; 1,387 km): From Dawson Co. in Texas to Matagorda Bay.

Columbia (1,243 mi.; 2,000 km): From Columbia Lake in British Columbia to Pacific Ocean (entering between Oregon and Washington).

Colville (350 mi.; 563 km): From Brooks Range in Alaska to Beaufort Sea.

Connecticut (407 mi.; 655 km): From Third Connecticut Lake in New Hampshire to Long Island Sound in Connecticut.

Cumberland (720 mi.; 1,159 km): From junction of Poor and Clover Forks in Harlan Co. in Kentucky to Ohio R.

Delaware (390 mi.; 628 km): From Schoharie Co. in New York to Liston Point, Delaware Bay.

Gila (649 mi.; 1,044 km): From Catron Co. in New Mexico to Colorado R. in Arizona.

Green (360 mi.; 579 km): From Lincoln Co. in Kentucky to Ohio R. in Kentucky.

Green (730 mi.; 1,175 km): From Sublette Co. in Wyoming to Colorado R. in Utah.

Illinois (420 mi.; 676 km): From St. Joseph Co. in Indiana to Mississippi R. at Grafton in Illinois.

James (sometimes called *Dakota*) (710 mi.; 1,143 km): From Wells Co. in North Dakota to Missouri R. in South Dakota.

Kanawha-New (352 mi.; 566 km): From junction of North and South Forks of New R. in North Carolina, through Virginia and West Virginia (New River becoming Kanawha River), to Ohio River.

Kansas (743 mi.; 1,196 km) From source of Arikaree R. in Elbert Co., Colorado, to Missouri R. at Kansas City, Kansas.

Koyukuk (470 mi.; 756 km): From Brooks Range in Alaska to Yukon R.

Kuskokwim (724 mi.; 1,165 km): From Alaska Range in Alaska to Kuskokwim Bay.

Licking (350 mi.; 563 km): From Magoffin Co. in Kentucky to Ohio R. at Cincinnati in Ohio.

Little Missouri (560 mi.; 901 km): From Crook Co. in Wyoming to Missouri R. in North Dakota.

Milk (625 mi.; 1,006 km): From junction of forks in Alberta Province to Missouri R.

Mississippi (2,340 mi.; 3,766 km): From Lake Itasca in Minnesota to mouth of Southwest Pass in La.

Coastline of the United States

State	General coastline[1]	Tidal shoreline[2]
Atlantic Coast:		
Maine	228	3,478
New Hampshire	13	131
Massachusetts	192	1,519
Rhode Island	40	384
Connecticut	—	618
New York	127	1,850
New Jersey	130	1,792
Pennsylvania	—	89
Delaware	28	381
Maryland	31	3,190
Virginia	112	3,315
North Carolina	301	3,375
South Carolina	187	2,876
Georgia	100	2,344
Florida (Atlantic)	580	3,331
Total Atlantic coast	2,069	28,673
Gulf Coast:		
Florida (Gulf)	770	5,095
Alabama	53	607
Mississippi	44	359
Louisiana	397	7,721
Texas	367	3,359
Total Gulf coast	1,631	17,141
Pacific Coast:		
California	840	3,427
Oregon	296	1,410
Washington	157	3,026
Hawaii	750	1,052
Alaska (Pacific)	5,580	31,383
Total Pacific coast	7,623	40,298
Arctic Coast:		
Alaska (Arctic)	1,060	2,521
Total Arctic coast	1,060	2,521
States Total	**12,383**	**88,633**

Lengths, statute miles.

1. Figures are lengths of general outline of seacoast. Measurements made with unit measure of 30 minutes of latitude on charts as near scale of 1:1,200,000 as possible. Coastline of bays and sounds is included to point where they narrow to width of unit measure, and distance across at such point is included. 2. Figures obtained in 1939–40 with recording instrument on largest-scale maps and charts then available. Shoreline of outer coast, offshore islands, sounds, bays, rivers, and creeks is included to head of tidewater, or to point where tidal waters narrow to width of 100 feet. *Source:* Department of Commerce, National Oceanic and Atmospheric Administration, National Ocean Service.

Mississippi-Missouri-Red Rock (3,710 mi.; 5,970 km): From source of Red Rock R. in Montana to mouth of Southwest Pass in Louisiana.
Missouri (2,315 mi.; 3,726 km): From junction of Jefferson R., Gallatin R., and Madison R. in Montana to Mississippi R. near St. Louis.
Missouri-Red Rock (2,540 mi.; 4,090 km): From source of Red Rock R. in Montana to Mississippi R. near St. Louis.
Mobile-Alabama-Coosa (645 mi.; 1,040 km): From junction of Etowah R. and Oostanula R. in Georgia to Mobile Bay.
Neosho (460 mi.; 740 km): From Morris Co. in Kansas to Arkansas R. in Oklahoma.
Niobrara (431 mi.; 694 km): From Niobrara Co. in Wyoming to Missouri R. in Nebraska.
Noatak (350 mi.; 563 km): From Brooks Range in Alaska to Kotzebue Sound.
North Canadian (800 mi.; 1,290 km): From Union Co. in New Mexico to Canadian R. in Oklahoma.
North Platte (618 mi.; 995 km): From Jackson Co. in Colorado to junction with So. Platte R. in Nebraska to form Platte R.
Ohio (981 mi.; 1,579 km): From junction of Allegheny R. and Monongahela R. at Pittsburgh to Mississippi R. between Illinois and Kentucky.
Ohio-Allegheny (1,306 mi.; 2,102 km): From Potter Co. in Pennsylvania to Mississippi R. at Cairo in Illinois.
Osage (500 mi.; 805 km): From east-central Kansas to Missouri R. near Jefferson City in Missouri.
Ouachita (605 mi.; 974 km): From Polk Co. in Arkansas to Red R. in Louisiana.
Pearl (411 mi.; 661 km): From Neshoba County in Mississippi to Gulf of Mexico (Mississippi-Louisiana).
Pecos (926 mi.; 1,490 km): From Mora Co. in New Mexico to Rio Grande in Texas.
Pee Dee-Yadkin (435 mi.; 700 km): From Watauga Co. in North Carolina to Winyah Bay in South Carolina.
Pend Oreille-Clark Fork (531 mi.; 855 km): Near Butte in Montana to Columbia R. on Washington-Canada border.
Platte (990 mi.; 1,593 km) From source of Grizzly Creek in Jackson Co., Colorado, to Missouri R. south of Omaha, Nebraska.
Porcupine (569 mi.; 916 km): From Yukon Territory, Canada, to Yukon R. in Alaska.
Potomac (383 mi.; 616 km): From Garrett Co. in Md. to Chesapeake Bay at Point Lookout in Md.
Powder (375 mi.; 603 km): From junction of forks in Johnson Co. in Wyoming to Yellowstone R. in Montana.
Red (1,290 mi.; 2,080 km): From source of Tierra Blanca Creek in Curry County, New Mexico to Mississippi R. in Louisiana.
Red (also called *Red River of the North*) (545 mi.; 877 km): From junction of Otter Tail R. and Bois de Sioux R. in Minnesota to Lake Winnipeg in Manitoba.
Republican (445 mi.; 716 km): From junction of North Fork and Arikaree R. in Nebraska to junction with Smoky Hill R. in Kansas to form the Kansas R.
Rio Grande (1,900 mi.; 3,060 km): From San Juan Co. in Colorado to Gulf of Mexico.
Roanoke (380 mi.; 612 km): From junction of forks in Montgomery Co. in Virginia to Albemarle Sound in North Carolina.
Sabine (380 mi.; 612 km): From junction of forks in Hunt Co. in Texas to Sabine Lake between Texas and Louisiana.
Sacramento (377 mi.; 607 km): From Siskiyou Co. in California to Suisun Bay.
Saint Francis (425 mi.; 684 km): From Iron Co. in Missouri to Mississippi R. in Arkansas.
Salmon (420 mi.; 676 km): From Custer Co. in Idaho to Snake R.
San Joaquin (350 mi.; 563 km): From junction of forks in Madera Co. in California to Suisun Bay.
San Juan (360 mi.; 579 km): From Archuleta Co. in Colorado to Colorado R. in Utah.
Santee-Wateree-Catawba (538 mi.; 866 km): From McDowell Co. in North Carolina to Atlantic Ocean in South Carolina.
Smoky Hill (540 mi.; 869 km): From Cheyenne Co. in Colorado to junction with Republican R. in Kansas to form Kansas R.

Snake (1,038 mi.; 1,670 km): From Ocean Plateau in Wyoming to Columbia R. in Washington.
South Platte (424 mi.; 682 km): From Park Co. in Colorado to junction with North Platte R. in Nebraska to form Platte R.
Stikine (379 mi.; 610 km) From British Columbia in Canada to Stikine Strait near Wrangell, Alaska.
Susquehanna (444 mi.; 715 km): From Otsego Lake in New York to Chesapeake Bay in Maryland.
Tanana (659 mi.; 1,060 km): From Wrangell Mts. in Yukon Territory, Canada, to Yukon R. in Alaska.
Tennessee (652 mi.; 1,049 km): From junction of Holston R. and French Broad R. in Tennessee to Ohio R. in Kentucky.
Tennessee-French Broad (886 mi.; 1,417 km): From Transylvania Co. in North Carolina to Ohio R. at Paducah in Kentucky.
Tombigbee (525 mil; 845 km): From junction of forks in Itawamba Co. in Mississippi to Mobile R. in Alabama.
Trinity (360 mi.; 579 km): From junction of forks in Dallas Co. in Texas to Galveston Bay.
Wabash (512 mi.; 824 km): From Darke Co. in Ohio to Ohio R. between Illinois and Indiana.
Washita (500 mi.; 805 km): From Hemphill Co. in Texas to Red R. in Oklahoma.
White (722 mi.; 1,160 km): From Madison Co. in Arkansas to Mississippi R.
Wisconsin (430 mi.; 692 km): From Vilas Co. in Wisconsin to Mississippi R.
Yellowstone (692 mi.; 1,110 km): From Park Co. in Wyoming to Missouri R. in North Dakota.
Yukon (1,979 mi.; 3,185 km): From source of McNeil R. in Yukon Territory, Canada, to Bering Sea in Alaska.

Geysers in The United States

Geysers are natural hot springs that intermittently eject a column of water and steam into the air. They exist in many parts of the volcanic regions of the world such as Japan and South America but their greatest development is in Iceland, New Zealand, and Yellowstone National Park.

There are 120 named geysers in Yellowstone National Park, Wyoming, and perhaps half that numebr unnamed. Most of the geysers and the 4,000 or more hot springs are located in the western portion of the park. The most important are the following:

Norris Geyser Basin has 24 or more active geysers; the number varies. There are scores of steam vents and hot springs. *Valentine* is highest, erupting 50–75 ft at intervals varying from 18 hr to 3 days or more. *Minuté* erupts 15–20 ft high, several hours aprt. Others include *Steamboat, Fearless, Veteran, Vixen, Corporal, Whirligig, Little Whirligig,* and *Pinwheel.*

Lower Geyser Basin has at least 18 active geysers. *Fountain* throws water 50–75 ft in all directions at unpredictable intervals. *Clepsydra* erupts violently from four vents up to 30 ft. *Great Fountain* plays every 8 to 15 hr in spurts from 30 to 90 ft high.

Midway Geyser Basin has vast steaming terraces of red, orange, pink and other colors; there are pools and springs, including the beautiful *Grand Prismatic Spring. Excelsior* crater discharges boiling water into Firehole River at the rate of 6 cu ft per second.

Giant erupts up to 200 ft at intervals of 2 1/2 days to 3 mo; eruptions last about 1 1/2 hr. *Daisy* sends water up to 75 ft but is irregular and frequently inactive.

Old Faithful sends up a column varying from 116 to 175 ft at intervals of about 65 min, varying from 33 to 90 min. Eruptions last about 4 min, during which time about 12,000 gal are discharged.

Giantess seldom erupts, but during its active period sends up streams 150–200 ft.

Lion Group: *Lion* plays up to 60 ft every 2–4 days when active; *Little Cub* up to 10 ft every 1–2 hr. *Big Cub* and *Lioness* seldom erupt.

Mammoth Hot Springs: There are no geysers in this area. The formation is travertine. Sides of a hill are steps and terraces over which flow the steaming waters of hot springs laden with minerals. Each step is tinted by algae to many shades of orange, pink, yellow, brown, green, and blue. Terraces are white where no water flows.

One Lake or Two?

It is a widely accepted fact that Lake Superior, with an area of 31,820 square miles is the world's largest freshwater lake. However this fact is based on an historical inaccuracy in the naming of Lake Huron and Lake Michigan. What should have been considered one body of water, Lake Michigan-Huron with an area of 45,410 square miles, was mistakenly given two names, one for each lobe. The explorers in colonial times incorrectly believed each lobe to be a separate lake because of its great size.

Why should the two lakes be considered one? The Huron Lobe and the Michigan Lobe are at the same elevation and are connected by the 120-foot deep Mackinac Strait, also at the same elevation. Lakes are separated from each other by streams and rivers. The Strait of Mackinac is not a river. It is 3.6 to 5 miles wide, wider than most lakes are long. In essence, it is just a narrowing, not a separation of the two lobes of Lake Michigan-Huron.

The flow between the two lakes can reverse. Because of the large connecting channel, the two can equalize rapidly whenever a water level imbalance occurs. Gage records for the lakes clearly show them to have identical water level regimes and mean long-term behavior; that is, Lake Michigan and Lake Huron act as one lake for many purposes. Hydrologically they are considered one lake.

Historical names are not easily changed. The separate names for the lake are a part of history and are also legally institutionalized since Lake Michigan is treated as American and Lake Huron is bisected by the international boundary between the United States and Canada.

Of all the world's freshwater lakes, North America's Great Lakes are unique. Their five basins combine to form a single watershed with one common outlet to the ocean. The total volume of the lakes is about 5,475 cubic miles, more than 6,000 trillion gallons.

The Great Lakes are: Superior with an area of 31,820 square miles (82,414 km) shared by the United States and Canada; Huron with an area of 23,010 square miles (59,596 sq km) shared by the United States and Canada; Michigan with an area of 22,400 square miles (58,016 sq km) entirely in the United States; Erie with an area of 9,930 square miles (25,719 km) shared by the United States and Canada; and Ontario with an area of 7,520 square miles (19,477 km) shared by the United States and Canada.

The United States also has another large lake, Great Salt Lake in Utah with an area of 1,800 square miles (4,662 sq km). However it is not a freshwater lake.

NORTH AMERICA
LAMBERT AZIMUTHAL EQUAL-AREA PROJECTION
SCALE OF MILES
0 200 400 600 800 1000
SCALE OF KILOMETERS
0 200 400 600 800 1000
Capitals
International Boundaries
Canals
© Copyright HAMMOND INCORPORATED, Maplewood, N. J.
ARCTIC OCEAN
North Pole
GREENLAND SEA
Jan Mayen (Nor.)
GREENLAND (KALAALLIT NUNAAT) (Den.)
PEARY LAND
KING CHRISTIAN X LAND
KING CHRISTIAN IX LAND
FREDERIK VI COAST
PRUDHOE LAND
ICELAND
Reykjavík
Ammassalik
Str. of Denmark
C. Farewell
Qaqortoq
Nuuk (Godthåb)
Disko I.
Thule Air Base
Baffin Bay
Davis Strait
Lincoln Sea
Ellesmere I.
Axel Heiberg I.
SVERDRUP IS.
QUEEN ELIZABETH IS.
Devon I.
Lancaster Sd.
Prince Patrick I.
Melville I.
M'Clure Str.
Parry Channel
Banks I.
Victoria I.
M'Clintock Chan.
G. of Boothia
Boothia Pen.
Melville Pen.
Baffin I.
Foxe Basin
Pangnirtung
Cumberland Sd.
Amundsen Gulf
BEAUFORT SEA
ASIA
Anadyr'
Arctic Circle
Wrangel I.
Bering Str.
BERING SEA
St. Lawrence I.
Norton Sd.
Nome
Seward Pen.
Pt. Barrow
Koyukuk
Yukon
Kuskokwim
Fairbanks
ALASKA
UNITED STATES
Bristol Bay
Anchorage
Alaska Pen.
Kodiak I.
G. of Alaska
ALEXANDER ARCH.
Juneau
Ketchikan
Dixon Entr.
QUEEN CHARLOTTE IS.
Prince Rupert
Aklavik
Inuvik
Dawson
Whitehorse
Norman Wells
Mackenzie
Ft. Simpson
Liard
Port Radium
Great Bear L.
Yellowknife
Great Slave L.
Ft. Smith
L. Athabasca
Fort McMurray
Peace
Athabasca
Chesterfield Inlet
Wager Bay
Southampton I.
Coats I.
Mansel I.
Hudson Str.
C. Chidley
Ungava Bay
Labrador
Hamilton Inlet
Battle Harbour
Str. of Belle Isle
Newfoundland
St. John's
C. Race
Goose Bay
Hudson Bay
BELCHER IS.
James Bay
Grande-Rivière de la Baleine
La Grande-Rivière
CANADA
Churchill
Reindeer L.
Nelson
Saskatchewan
Edmonton
Calgary
Saskatoon
Prince Albert
Regina
Lethbridge
Medicine Hat
L. Manitoba
L. Winnipeg
Winnipeg
Albany
Moosonee
Nottaway
L. Nipigon
Timmins
Thunder Bay
L. Superior
Sault Ste. Marie
Québec
Montréal
Ottawa
St. Lawrence
G. of St. Lawrence
Charlottetown
Saint John
Halifax
Sydney
C. Breton I.
C. Sable
Fraser
Vancouver I.
Vancouver
Victoria
Str. of Juan de Fuca
ROCKY MOUNTAINS
Tacoma
Seattle
Spokane
Portland
Columbia
Butte
Great Falls
Yellowstone
Bismarck
Fargo
Duluth
St. Paul
Minneapolis
Milwaukee
L. Michigan
L. Huron
Detroit
Toronto
L. Ontario
L. Erie
Buffalo
Albany
Portland
Boston
C. Cod
Providence
New York
Philadelphia
Baltimore
Pittsburgh
Cleveland
Columbus
Washington
Richmond
Norfolk
C. Hatteras
Winston-Salem
Charlotte
Charleston
Savannah
Jacksonville
Atlanta
Chattanooga
Nashville
Louisville
Cincinnati
Indianapolis
Ohio
Chicago
Peoria
Des Moines
Boise
Snake
Pocatello
C. Mendocino
Great Salt Lake
Salt Lake City
Cheyenne
Casper
Platte
Pierre
Missouri
Sioux City
Omaha
Reno
Sacramento
San Francisco
Oakland
Denver
Pueblo
Colorado
Kansas City
St. Louis
UNITED STATES
Wichita
Tulsa
Oklahoma City
Arkansas
Little Rock
Memphis
Mississippi
Birmingham
Jackson
Mobile
Los Angeles
San Diego
Albuquerque
Amarillo
Phoenix
Tucson
El Paso
Fort Worth
Dallas
Red
Brazos
Austin
Houston
San Antonio
New Orleans
Ciudad Juárez
Hermosillo
Chihuahua
Rio Grande
Yaqui
Lower California
Gulf of California
Guadalupe I. (Mex.)
I. Cedros
Tropic of Cancer
Monterrey
Torreón
Durango
C. San Lucas
Mazatlán
San Luis Potosí
Tampico
Aguascalientes
Guadalajara
C. Corrientes
Santiago
Mexico City
Veracruz Llave
MEXICO
Revillagigedo Is. (Mex.)
Balsas
Villahermosa
Oaxaca
Acapulco
Gulf of Mexico
Tampa
Miami
C. Canaveral
Strs. of Florida
Florida
BAHAMAS
Nassau
Bermuda (U.K.) Hamilton
Havana
CUBA
I. de la Juventud
Camagüey
Santiago de Cuba
Yucatán Chan.
Mérida
Yucatán Pen.
Belmopan
BELIZE
JAMAICA
Kingston
HAITI
Port-au-Prince
DOMINICAN REP.
Santo Domingo
Windward Pass.
Mona Pass.
San Juan
PUERTO RICO (U.S.)
WEST INDIES
Guatemala
GUATEMALA
HONDURAS
Tegucigalpa
C. Gracias a Dios
CARIBBEAN SEA
San Salvador
EL SALVADOR
Managua
NICARAGUA
San José
CENTRAL AMERICA
COSTA RICA
Panama Canal
Panamá
PANAMA
G. of Panamá
Maracaibo
Medellín
Bogotá
SOUTH AMERICA
Quito
Guayaquil
Equator
Clipperton I. (Fr.)
Cocos I. (C.R.)
GALÁPAGOS IS. (Ecuador)
PACIFIC OCEAN
ATLANTIC OCEAN
Longitude 100° West of Greenwich 90°

PACIFIC OCEAN
WASHINGTON
OREGON
CALIFORNIA
NEVADA
IDAHO
MONTANA
WYOMING
UTAH
COLORADO
ARIZONA
NEW MEXICO
NORTH DAKOTA
SOUTH DAKOTA
NEBRASKA
KANSAS
TEXAS
CANADA
MEXICO
ROCKY MOUNTAINS
CASCADE R.
SIERRA NEVADA
Vancouver Island
Str. of Juan de Fuca
Vancouver
Victoria
Calgary
Saskatoon
Regina
Moose Jaw
Swift Current
Medicine Hat
Lethbridge
Seattle
Tacoma
Olympia
Spokane
Yakima
Walla Walla
Portland
Salem
Eugene
Medford
Klamath Falls
Boise
Pocatello
Twin Falls
Idaho Falls
Butte
Helena
Missoula
Great Falls
Billings
Bozeman
Miles City
Sheridan
Casper
Cheyenne
Laramie
Rock Springs
Ogden
Salt Lake City
Provo
Great Salt Lake
Reno
Carson City
Elko
Ely
Sacramento
San Francisco
Oakland
San Jose
Fresno
Bakersfield
Los Angeles
Long Beach
San Diego
Las Vegas
Denver
Colorado Springs
Pueblo
Grand Junction
Flagstaff
Phoenix
Tucson
Yuma
Albuquerque
Santa Fe
Las Cruces
El Paso
Amarillo
Lubbock
Odessa
Midland
Rapid City
Pierre
Bismarck
Mt. Rainier 14,410 ft. (4392 m.)
Mt. Shasta 14,162 ft. (4317 m.)
Mt. Whitney 14,494 ft. (4418 m.)
Mt. Elbert 14,433 ft. (4399 m.)
Pikes Peak 14,110 ft. (4301 m.)
Gannett Pk. 13,804 ft. (4207 m.)
Borah Pk. 12,662 ft. (3859 m.)
Wheeler Peak 13,161 ft. (4011 m.)
Blanca Pk. 14,317 ft. (4364 m.)
Mt. Wilson 14,246 ft. (4342 m.)
YELLOWSTONE NAT'L. PARK
GLACIER NAT'L. PARK
YOSEMITE NAT'L. PARK
GRAND CANYON NAT'L. PARK
OLYMPIC NAT'L. PARK
Death Valley
Lower California
Gulf of California
ARCTIC OCEAN
RUSSIA
ALASKA
BERING SEA
Brooks Range
Alaska Range
Mt. McKinley 20,320 ft. (6194 m.)
Mt. St. Elias 18,008 ft. (5489 m.)
Fairbanks
Anchorage
Nome
Juneau
Kodiak
Gulf of Alaska
Aleutian Is.
Same scale as Alaska map
Longitude West of Greenwich 156°
HAWAII
Kauai
Oahu
Molokai
Lanai
Maui
Hawaii
Honolulu
Hilo
Mauna Kea 13,796 ft. (4205 m.)
Mauna Loa 13,677 ft. (4169 m.)
Midway Is. (U. S.)
Tropic of Cancer
PACIFIC OCEAN

UNITED STATES
POLYCONIC PROJECTION
SCALE OF MILES
0 50 100 200 300 400
SCALE OF KILOMETERS
0 100 200 300 400
Capitals of Countries
State Capitals
International Boundaries
© Copyright HAMMOND INCORPORATED, Maplewood, N. J.
Longitude 95° West of H Greenwich 90° J 85° K 80° L 75°
ATLANTIC
OCEAN
GULF OF MEXICO
BAHAMAS
CUBA
Tropic of Cancer
N

CANADA
CONIC PROJECTION
SCALE OF MILES
0 100 200 300 400 500
SCALE OF KILOMETERS
0 100 200 300 400 500
Capitals of Countries
Provincial & Territorial Capitals
Administrative Centers
© Copyright HAMMOND INCORPORATED, Maplewood, N.J.
ATLANTIC OCEAN
PACIFIC OCEAN
HUDSON BAY
UNITED STATES
GREENLAND

MIDDLE AMERICA
BONNE PROJECTION
Copyright by C. S. HAMMOND & Co., N. Y.
SCALE OF MILES
0 200 400 600
KILOMETERS
0 200 400 600
Capitals of Countries
Other Capitals
International Boundaries
UNITED STATES
MEXICO
CENTRAL AMERICA
GUATEMALA
BELIZE
HONDURAS
EL SALVADOR
NICARAGUA
COSTA RICA
PANAMA
CUBA
BAHAMAS
JAMAICA
HAITI
DOMINICAN REP.
PUERTO RICO (U.S.)
COLOMBIA
VENEZUELA
GUYANA
ECUADOR
PERU
BRAZIL
ATLANTIC OCEAN
PACIFIC OCEAN
CARIBBEAN SEA
Gulf of Mexico
Sargasso Sea
Bay of Campeche
Gulf of California
Lower California
WEST INDIES
GREATER ANTILLES
LESSER ANTILLES
NETH. ANTILLES
Tropic of Cancer
Equator
Longitude West of Greenwich
San Diego
Mexicali
Tijuana
Phoenix
Tucson
Heroica Nogales
Albuquerque
Roswell
El Paso
Ciudad Juárez
Oklahoma City
Wichita Falls
Tulsa
Little Rock
Memphis
Nashville
Knoxville
Chattanooga
Durham
Charlotte
Columbia
Wilmington
C. Hatteras
Dallas
Ft. Worth
Shreveport
Odessa
Waco
Austin
San Antonio
Houston
Galveston
Baton Rouge
Birmingham
Atlanta
Jackson
Montgomery
Macon
Mobile
Pensacola
Tallahassee
Charleston
Savannah
Jacksonville
New Orleans
Daytona Beach
C. Canaveral
Tampa
L. Okeechobee
Ft. Myers
Miami
Key West
Strs. of Florida
Gd. Bahama
Nassau
Andros
San Salvador (Watling I.)
Bermuda (U.K.)
Laredo
Corpus Christi
Brownsville
Matamoros
Hermosillo
Guaymas
Sta. Rosalía
Cedros I.
C. San Lázaro
La Paz
Navojoa
Topolobampo
Culiacán
Chihuahua
Ciudad Camargo
Torreón
Durango
Mazatlán
C. Falso
Sa. Madre Occidental
Sa. Madre Oriental
Nuevo Laredo
Saltillo
Monterrey
Matehuala
Ciudad Victoria
Zacatecas
San Luis Potosí
Cárdenas
Tampico
Tres Marías Is.
C. Corrientes
Tepic
León
Querétaro
Tuxpan
Guadalajara
Morelia
Pachuca
Mexico City
Puebla
Popocatépetl
Veracruz Llave
Manzanillo
Colima
Balsas
Taxco
Chilpancingo
Acapulco de Juárez
Oaxaca
Tehuantepec
Villahermosa
Coatzacoalcos
Tuxtla Gutiérrez
G. of Tehuantepec
Ciudad de las Casas
Revillagigedo Is. (Mex.)
Clipperton I. (Fr.)
Campeche
Progreso
Mérida
Cancún
Yucatán Pen.
Cozumel I.
Yucatán Chan.
Belmopan
G. of Honduras
Bay Is.
Is. Santanilla (Hond.)
Cobán
La Ceiba
Quezaltenango
Guatemala
Tegucigalpa
San José
San Salvador
San Miguel
León
Managua
Granada
L. Nicaragua
Coco
Mosquito Coast
C. Gracias a Dios
Corn Is.
Bluefields
Providencia (Col.)
San Andrés (Col.)
Puntarenas
San José
Limón
Golfito
David
Panama Canal
Colón
Panama
G. of Panamá
G. de Urabá
Cocos I. (C. R.)
Malpelo I. (Col.)
Galápagos Is. (Ecuador)
Havana
Pinar del Río
I. de la Juventud
Matanzas
Sta. Clara
Cienfuegos
Camagüey
Holguín
Santiago de Cuba
Cayman Is. (U.K.)
Montego Bay
Kingston
Windward Pass.
Hispaniola
Port-au-Prince
Santo Domingo
Mona Pass.
San Juan
TURKS & CAICOS IS. (U.K.)
Charlotte Amalie
Virgin Is. (U.S. & U.K.)
ST. KITTS & NEVIS
ANTIGUA & BARBUDA
St. Johns
Guadeloupe (Fr.)
Basse-Terre
DOMINICA
Martinique (Fr.)
Ft-de-France
ST. LUCIA
BARBADOS
Bridgetown
ST. VINC. & GRENS.
GRENADA
St. George's
Tobago
TRINIDAD & TOBAGO
Port of Spain
Trinidad
ARUBA (Neth.)
Curaçao
Guajira Pen.
G. of Venezuela
Barranquilla
Cartagena
Maracaibo
L. Maracaibo
Coro
Valencia
La Guaira
Caracas
Barcelona
Barquisimeto
Calabozo
Orinoco
Ciudad Bolívar
Cuyuni
Mérida
Barinas
Monteria
Cúcuta
Bucaramanga
Magdalena
Arauca
Medellín
Manizales
Tunja
Bogotá
Cauca
Pto. Ayacucho
San Fernando de Atabapo
Roraima
Sa. Pacaraima
Buenaventura
Cali
Neiva
Guaviare
Popayán
Boa Vista
Branco
Tumaco
Pasto
Esmeraldas
Quito
Vaupés
Mitú
Negro
Barcelos
Andes
Llanos

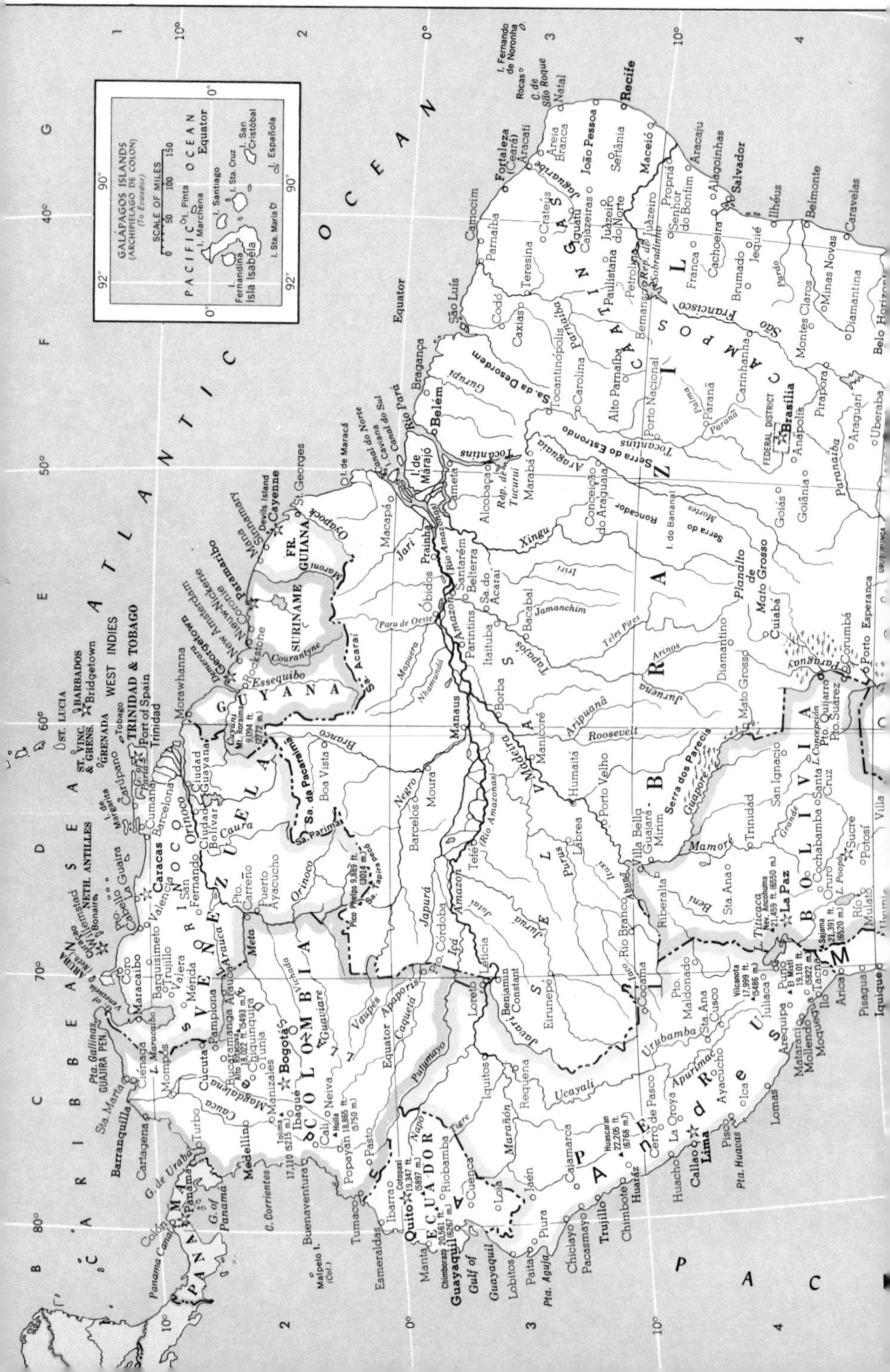

CARIBBEAN SEA
ATLANTIC OCEAN
PACIFIC OCEAN
Equator
GALÁPAGOS ISLANDS (ARCHIPIÉLAGO DE COLÓN) (To Ecuador)
SCALE OF MILES
BRAZIL
VENEZUELA
COLOMBIA
GUYANA
SURINAME
FR. GUIANA
ECUADOR
PERU
BOLIVIA
PANAMA
NETH. ANTILLES
ARUBA
TRINIDAD & TOBAGO
WEST INDIES
BARBADOS
ST. LUCIA
ST. VINC. & GRENS.
GRENADA
Caracas
Bogotá
Quito
Lima
La Paz
Sucre
Brasília
Georgetown
Paramaribo
Cayenne
Belém
Manaus
Recife
Salvador
Fortaleza
São Luís
Guayaquil
Maracaibo
Medellín
Cali
Amazon
Orinoco
Madeira
Negro
Xingu
Tapajós
Tocantins
Araguaia
São Francisco
Mato Grosso
Planalto de Mato Grosso
Serra dos Parecis
Serra do Roncador
L. Titicaca
I. de Marajó
Gulf of Guayaquil
I. Fernando de Noronha

SOUTH AMERICA
LAMBERT AZIMUTHAL EQUAL-AREA PROJECTION
SCALE OF MILES
0 100 200 400 600
SCALE OF KILOMETERS
0 100 200 400 600
Capitals of Countries
International Boundaries
Canals
Copyright by C. S. HAMMOND & CO., N.Y.
Tropic of Capricorn
Longitude 60° West of Greenwich
A T L A N T I C
O C E A N
P A C I F I C
O C E A N
RIO DE JANEIRO
SÃO PAULO
Campos
C. de São Tomé
Cabo Frio
Niterói
Angra dos Reis
Petrópolis
Juiz de Fora
I. S. Sebastião
Santos
Campinas
São João
Araraquara
Sorocaba
Juquiá
Curitiba
Paranaguá
Florianópolis
I. de Santa Catarina
Laguna
Joinville
Londrina
Castro
Porto Alegre
L. dos Patos
Rio Grande
L. Mirim
Pelotas
Cáxias do Sul
Santana do Livramento
Bagé
Cruz Alta
Uruguaiana
Posadas
Encarnación
Villarrica
Iguaçu Falls
Itaipu Res.
Concepción
Pto. Casado
Asunción
PARAGUAY
URUGUAY
Montevideo
Rocha
Melo
Florida
Rivera
Salto
Paysandú
Mercedes
Río de la Plata
C. San Antonio
Mar del Plata
La Plata
BUENOS AIRES
Avellaneda
Dolores
Tandil
Quequén
Bahía Blanca
Pergamino
Chivilcoy
Rosario
Santa Fe
Paraná
Concordia
Corrientes
Resistencia
Formosa
Reconquista
Córdoba
Villa María
Río Cuarto
San Luis
Mendoza
San Rafael
Victorica
Sta. Rosa
Gral. Acha
Viedma
Golfo San Matías
Pen. Valdés
Rawson
Puerto Madryn
Las Plumas
Camarones
Comodoro Rivadavia
Golfo San Jorge
Colonia Las Heras
C. Tres Puntas
Puerto Deseado
San Julián
Santa Cruz
Bahía Grande
Río Gallegos
Punta Arenas
Tierra del Fuego
Ushuaia
C. San Diego
I. de los Estados (Staten I.)
Bahía Nassau
Cape Horn (Cabo de Hornos)
I. Hoste
FALKLAND ISLANDS (IS. MALVINAS) (U.K.—claimed by Arg.)
Stanley
West Falkland
East Falkland
Neuquén
Zapala
San Carlos de Bariloche
Norquincó
Chubut
Colorado
Negro
Salado
Dulce
Mar Chiquita
Bermejo
Pilcomayo
Yacuiba
Orán
Embarcación
Jujuy
La Quiaca
Salta
S. Antonio
Rosario
S. Miguel de Tucumán
Santiago del Estero
Catamarca
La Rioja
Tinogasta
Chilecito
Jachal
San Juan
Nev. Ojos del Salado 22,572 ft. (6880 m.)
Vol. Llullaillaco 22,057 ft. (6723 m.)
Cerro Aconcagua 22,831 ft. (6959 m.)
Maipo 17,454 ft. (5320 m.)
Santiago
Valparaíso
Viña del Mar
Los Vilos
Ovalle
Coquimbo
La Serena
Vallenar
Huasco
Copiapó
Caldera
Chañaral
Taltal
Antofagasta
Tocopilla
Calama
Talca
Chillán
Constitución
Talcahuano
Concepción
Arauco
Temuco
Villarrica
Valdivia
Pto. Montt
Ancud
Castro
Isla de Chiloé
G. del Corcovado
ARCHIPIÉLAGO de los CHONOS
PEN. TAITAO
C. Tres Montes
G. de Penas
I. Campana
I. Wellington
I. Madre de Dios
I. Hanover
Pto. Natales
Strait of Magellan
I. Desolación
I. Sta. Inés
I. Clarence
L. Buenos Aires
L. San Martín
L. Viedma
L. Argentino
Deseado
Chico
JUAN FERNÁNDEZ IS. (Chile)
I. Robinson Crusoe
I. Alejandro Selkirk
I. San Félix (Chile)
I. San Ambrosio (Chile)
General Alvear
N

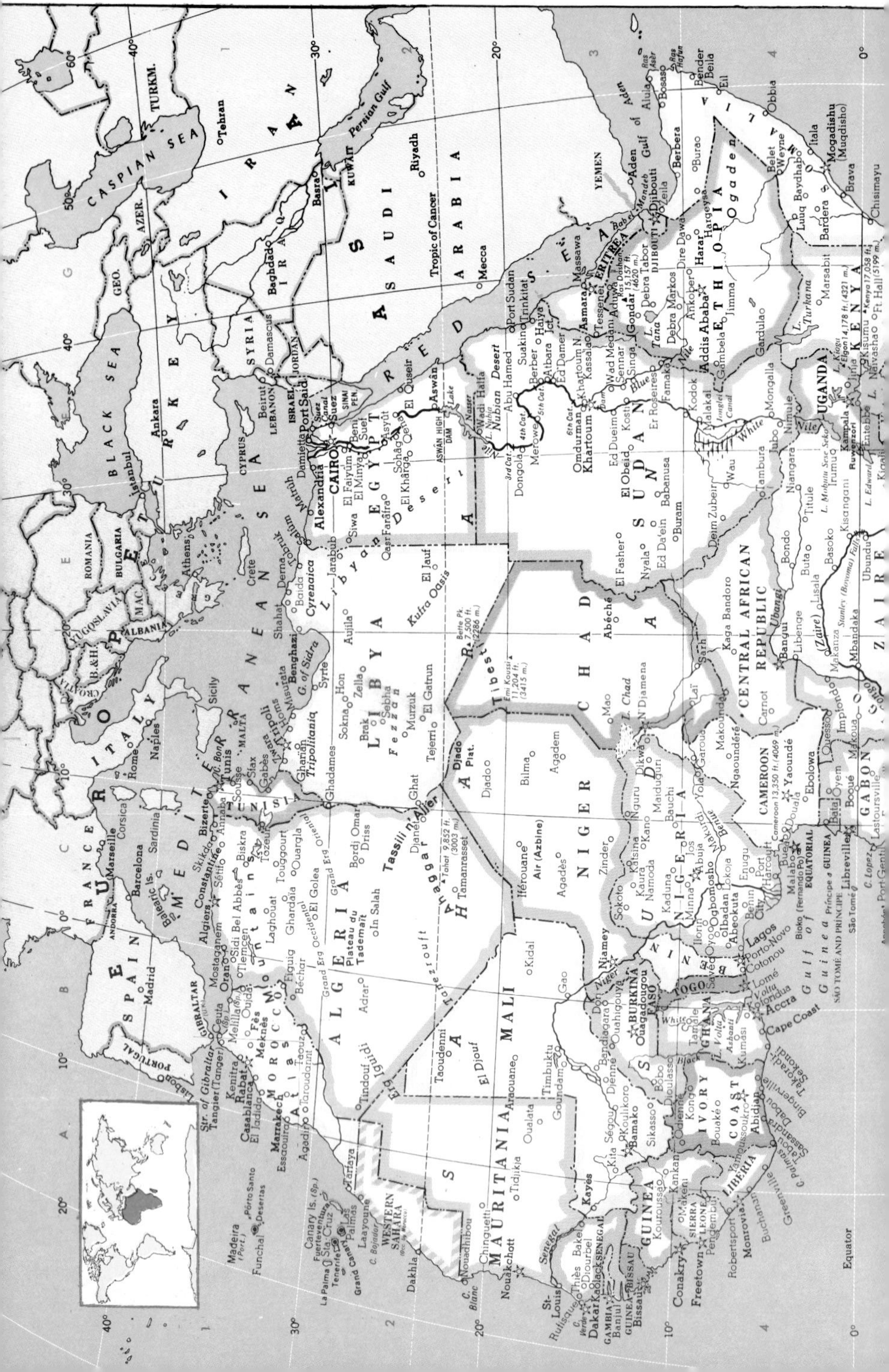
CASPIAN SEA
BLACK SEA
MEDITERRANEAN SEA
RED SEA
Persian Gulf
Gulf of Aden
Tropic of Cancer
Equator
IRAN
TURKEY
SAUDI ARABIA
IRAQ
SYRIA
JORDAN
ISRAEL
LEBANON
KUWAIT
YEMEN
CYPRUS
EGYPT
LIBYA
ALGERIA
MOROCCO
TUNISIA
SUDAN
CHAD
NIGER
MALI
MAURITANIA
WESTERN SAHARA
NIGERIA
CAMEROON
CENTRAL AFRICAN REPUBLIC
ETHIOPIA
ERITREA
DJIBOUTI
SOMALIA
KENYA
UGANDA
ZAIRE
GABON
CONGO
GHANA
TOGO
BENIN
BURKINA FASO
IVORY COAST
LIBERIA
SIERRA LEONE
GUINEA
GUINEA-BISSAU
GAMBIA
SENEGAL
EQUATORIAL GUINEA
SÃO TOMÉ AND PRINCIPE
SPAIN
PORTUGAL
FRANCE
ITALY
GREECE
ALBANIA
BULGARIA
ROMANIA
YUGOSLAVIA
CROATIA
B.&H.
MAC.
GEO.
AZER.
TURKM.
ANDORRA
GIBRALTAR
MALTA
SAHARA
Tehran
Riyadh
Mecca
Baghdad
Basra
Damascus
Beirut
Ankara
Istanbul
Athens
Cairo
Alexandria
Port Said
Suez
Aswān
Khartoum
Omdurman
Port Sudan
Addis Ababa
Asmara
Djibouti
Aden
Mogadishu
Nairobi
Kampala
Tripoli
Benghazi
Tunis
Algiers
Rabat
Casablanca
Marrakech
Fès
Madrid
Lisbon
Barcelona
Marseille
Rome
Naples
Dakar
Nouakchott
Bamako
Niamey
Ouagadougou
Accra
Lomé
Lagos
Abuja
N'Djamena
Bangui
Yaoundé
Libreville
Malabo
Freetown
Monrovia
Conakry
Bissau
Banjul
Abidjan
Timbuktu
Canary Is.
Madeira
Tibesti
Ahaggar
L. Chad
L. Nasser
Nile
Sicily
Sardinia
Corsica
Crete
Balearic Is.

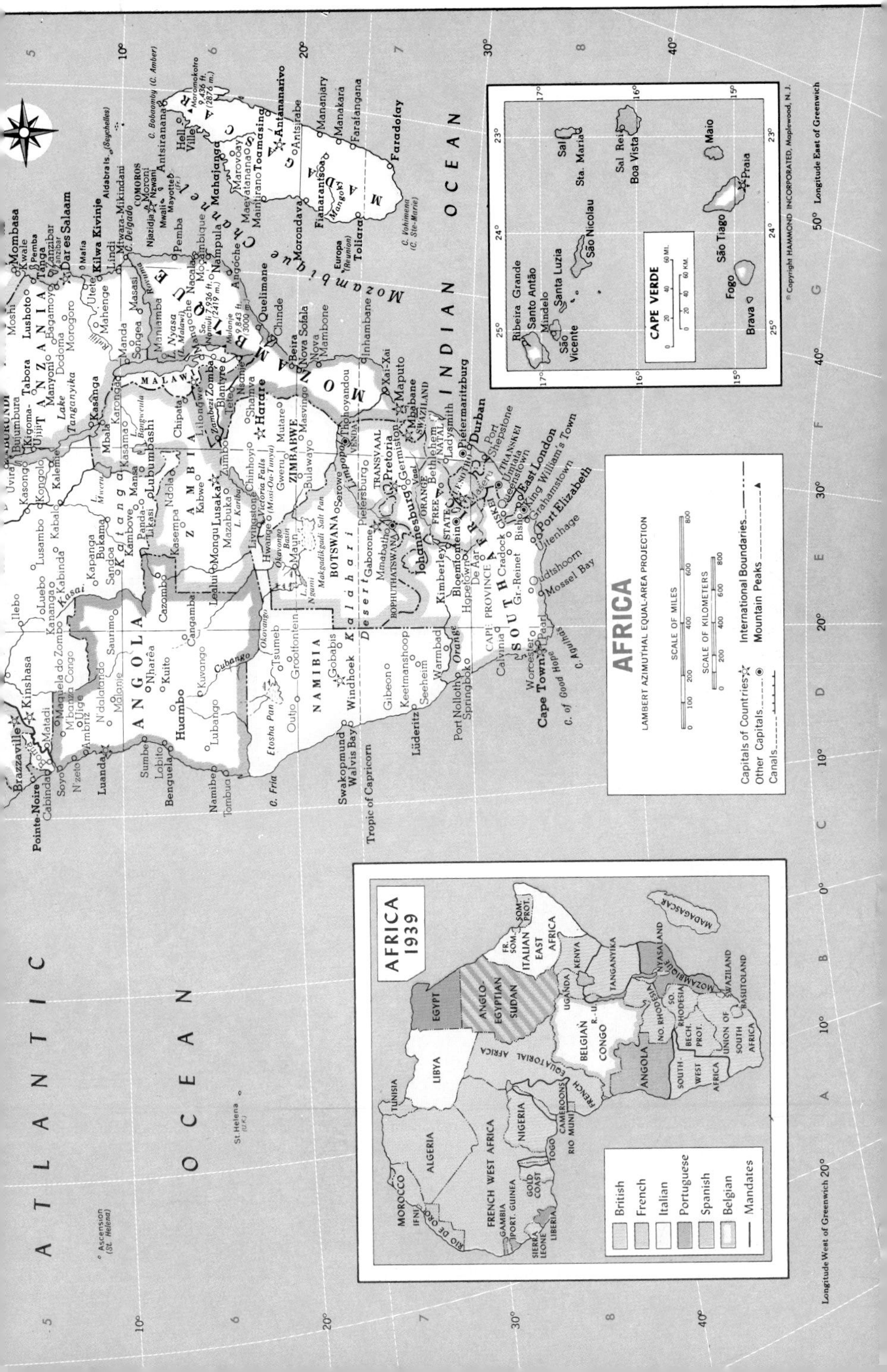
AFRICA
LAMBERT AZIMUTHAL EQUAL-AREA PROJECTION
SCALE OF MILES
0 100 200 400 600 800
SCALE OF KILOMETERS
0 200 400 600 800
Capitals of Countries
Other Capitals
Canals
International Boundaries
Mountain Peaks
ATLANTIC OCEAN
INDIAN OCEAN
Mozambique Channel
ANGOLA
NAMIBIA
BOTSWANA
ZIMBABWE
ZAMBIA
MALAWI
TANZANIA
MOZAMBIQUE
MADAGASCAR
SOUTH AFRICA
Tropic of Capricorn
CAPE VERDE
AFRICA 1939
British
French
Italian
Portuguese
Spanish
Belgian
Mandates
© Copyright HAMMOND INCORPORATED, Maplewood, N. J.
Longitude West of Greenwich 20°
Longitude East of Greenwich 50°

40° A 30° B 20° C 10° D 0° E 10° F
60°
50°
40°
70°
2
3
4
5
Jan Mayen (Nor.)
NORWEGIAN SEA
Arctic Circle
Horn
Breidhafjördhur
Húnaflói
Reykjavík
ICELAND
Akureyri
Fontur
Seydhisfjördhur
Hekla
Hornafjördhur
ATLANTIC OCEAN
Faroe Is. (Den.)
Tórshavn
Trondheimsfjorden
Namsos
Kristiansund
Ålesund
Trondheim
Östersund
Senja
Vesterålen
Lofoten
Vestfjorden
Mo
Ångerman
Shetland Is.
Lerwick
Sognefjorden
Lillehammer
Sundsvall
Söderhamn
Falun
Gäv
Rockall (U.K.)
Orkney Is.
Kirkwall
Pentland Firth
Hebrides
The Minch
Moray Firth
Bergen
Hardangerfjorden
Haugesund
Stavanger
Oslo
Drammen
Fredrikstad
Larvik
Arendal
Karlstad
Uppsala
Västerås
Vänern
Örebro
Eskilst
Norrköp
Linköpin
Halden
Lindesnes
Kristiansand
Skagerrak
Göteborg
Vättern
Borås
Jönköping
Visby
Öland
Inverness
GREAT BRITAIN
UNITED KINGDOM
Aberdeen
SCOTLAND
Glasgow
Dundee
Edinburgh
NORTH SEA
Donegal Bay
NO. IRELAND
North Channel
Belfast
IRELAND
Dundalk
Galway
Limerick (Luimneach)
Dublin
Isle of Man
Great Britain
Carlisle
Newcastle upon Tyne
Manchester
IRISH SEA
Leeds
Hull
Liverpool
Sheffield
Waterford
Cork
Cobh
C. Clear
St. George's Chan.
WALES
ENGLAND
Birmingham
The Wash
Swansea
Cardiff
LONDON
Bristol
Plymouth
Southampton
Portsmouth
Land's End
English Channel
DENMARK
Ålborg
Kattegat
Århus
Copenhagen
Esbjerg
Odense
Hälsingborg
Lund
Malmö
Karlskrona
BALTIC
Bornholm
Flensburg
Helgoland
Frisian Is.
Lübeck
Kiel
Rostock
Stralsund
Stupsk
Kołobrzeg
Amsterdam
The Hague
NETHERLANDS
Bremen
Hamburg
Weser
Elbe
Szczecin (Stettin)
Bydgo
Rotterdam
Antwerp
Utrecht
Münster
Hannover
BERLIN
Poznan
Essen
Braunschweig
Magdeburg
Oder
Warta
Łód
Ghent
Dortmund
GERMANY
Calais
Brussels
Kassel
Halle
Leipzig
Boulogne
BELGIUM
Düsseldorf
Dresden
Wrocław (Breslau)
Cherbourg
Le Havre
Channel Is. (Br.)
Lille
Liège
Cologne
Erfurt
Ushant I.
Brest
Amiens
Aachen
Bonn
Plauen
Częstochowa
Rouen
LUX.
Mainz
Wiesbaden
Chemnitz
Zabrze
Frankfurt
Mannheim
Prague (Praha)
Ostrava
Rennes
Seine
Marne
Versailles
PARIS
Reims
Saarbrücken
Rhine
Belle Isle
Angers
Orléans
Nancy
Karlsruhe
Nürnberg
Plzeň
CZECH REP.
Olomouc
St-Nazaire
Loire
Strasbourg
Stuttgart
Danube
Regensburg
Brno
Nantes
Tours
Mulhouse
Augsburg
VIENNA (Wien)
Bratislav
Bay of Biscay
La Rochelle
I. d'Oléron
FRANCE
Dijon
Freiburg
Munich
Linz
Basel
Zürich
L. of Constance
Salzburg
Győr
El Ferrol
La Coruña
C. Finisterre
Limoges
Vichy
LIECHTENSTEIN
Innsbruck
AUSTRIA
Sopron
Bern
SWITZERLAND
Alps
Graz
HUN
Bordeaux
Clermont-Ferrand
Lyon
Geneva
L. Geneva
Mt. Blanc
Maribor
Balaton L.
Gijón
Oviedo
Santander
San Sebastián
Biarritz
Dordogne
St-Étienne
Grenoble
Trento
Bolzano
Ljubljana
Pécs
Vigo
Miño
Bilbao
Garonne
Brescia
Venice
Trieste
SLOVENIA
Zagreb
Drava
Porto (Oporto)
Braga
León
Bayonne
Montauban
Milan
Verona
Padua
Rijeka
Valladolid
Burgos
Pyrenées
Turin (Torino)
Po
Coimbra
Douro
Ebro
Toulouse
Nîmes
Rhône
Genoa
Parma
Ferrara
PORTUGAL
Salamanca
Duero
Saragossa
ANDORRA
Nice
Modena
Bologna
Banja Luka
Sava
Sa de Guadarrama
Montpellier
MONACO
La Spezia
Florence (Firenze)
Zadar
BOSNIA AND HERCEGOVINA
Sarajevo
Lisbon (Lisboa)
Tejo
MADRID
G. of Lions
Marseille
Toulon
Livorno
SAN MARINO
Ancona
ADRIATIC
Mostar
Tagus (Tajo)
SPAIN
Barcelona
Siena
Perugia
Split
Dubrov
Setúbal
Guadiana
Toledo
Tarragona
Corsica (Corse)
Elba
Tiber
ITALY
Évora
Badajoz
Ajaccio
ROME
Cetinje
C. St. Vincent
Sierra Morena
Albacete
Valencia
Balearic Is.
VATICAN CITY
Shkodë
Córdoba
Sassari
Olbia
Durrë
Guadalquivir
Palma
Minorca
Sardinia (Sardegna)
Foggia
Vesuvius
Bari
G. of Cádiz
Cádiz
Seville
Murcia
Lorca
Ibiza
Majorca
Naples (Napoli)
Taranto
Brindis
Str. of Gibraltar
Jerez
Sa Nevada
Granada
Alicante
Iglesias
G. of Taranto
Kérki
Tangier
Málaga
GIBRALTAR (U.K.)
Almería
Cartagena
MEDITERRANEAN
TYRRHENIAN SEA
Cagliari
Catanzaro
Kenitra
Ceuta (Sp.)
IONIAN SEA
Casablanca
Rabat
Melilla (Sp.)
Oran
Algiers
Skikda
Bizerte
Palermo
Messina
Reggio di Calabria
Fès (Fez)
Constantine
Annaba
C. Bon
Etna
Sicily (Sicilia)
Catania
Meknès
ALGERIA
TUNISIA
Tunis
Pantelleria
Syracuse
MOROCCO
Marrakech
Biskra
Sousse
MALTA
Valletta
Longitude West D of Greenwich
Longitude East E of Greenwich
0°
10°
F

EUROPE
LAMBERT AZIMUTHAL EQUAL AREA PROJECTION
SCALE OF MILES
0 100 200 300 400 500
SCALE OF KILOMETERS
0 100 200 300 400 500
Capitals of Countries
International Boundaries
Canals
Copyright by C. S. HAMMOND & CO., N.Y.
BARENTS SEA
Nordkapp (North Cape)
Kolguyev I.
KANIN PEN.
Cheshskaya Bay
Bay of Mezen'
White Sea
KOLA PEN.
Murmansk
Pechenga
Vadsø
L. Inari
Tana
Kirovsk
Kandalaksha
Kem'
Archangel
Mezen'
Naryan Mar
Pechora
Ust Tsilma
Vorkuta
Usa
Salekhard
Berezovo
Ob'
Surgut
Khanty-Mansiysk
Tobol'sk
Irtysh
Tobol
Kurgan
Tyumen'
Yekaterinburg
Krasnoural'sk
Nizhniy Tagil
Kirovgrad
Chelyabinsk
Troitsk
Qostanay
Magnitogorsk
Zlatoust
Ufa
Belaya
Naberezhnye Chelny
Perm'
Kama
Kama Res.
Berezniki
Votkinsk Res.
Izhevsk
Sarapul
Vyatka
Kotel'nich
Syktyvkar
Northern Dvina
Kotlas
Velikiy Ustyug
Nyandoma
Onega
L. Onega
Petrozavodsk
Joensuu
Sortavala
L. Ladoga
Vyborg
Kotka
Helsinki
Gulf of Finland
St. Petersburg
(Leningrad)
Cherepovets
Vologda
Rybinsk Res.
Kostroma
Gor'kiy Res.
Rybinsk
Yaroslavl
Ivanovo
Balakhna
Dzerzhinsk
Nizh. Novgorod
(Gor'kiy)
Volga
Kazan
Kuybyshev
Simbirsk
Res.
Samara
(Kuybyshev)
Orenburg
Aqtöbe
Oral
Ural
Temir
Emba
Shalqar
KAZAKHSTAN
UZBEKISTAN
TURKMENISTAN
Atyrau
Aqtau
G. of Kara Bogaz
Krasnovodsk
CASPIAN SEA
Baku
AZERBAIJAN
Tbilisi
GEORGIA
ARMENIA
Yerevan
Gymri
Nakhichevan
Dzhul'fa
Araks
Caucasus
Makhachkala
Groznyy
Vladikavkaz
El'brus 18,510 ft. (5642 m.)
Karachayevsk
Kislovodsk
Pyatigorsk
Armavir
Elista
L. Manych-Gudilo
Astrakhan
Volgograd
(Stalingrad)
Tsimlyansk Res.
Saratov
Engel's
Volgograd Res.
Penza
Tambov
Michurinsk
Voronezh
Don
Donets
Millerovo
Lugansk
Shakhty
Rostov
Taganrog
Makeyevka
Donetsk
Kramatorsk
Dneprodzerzhinsk
Zaporozh'ye
Dnepropetrovsk
Kremenchug
Poltava
Khar'kov
Kursk
Orel
Bryansk
Kaluga
Tula
Oka
Serpukhov
MOSCOW
(Moskva)
Orekhovo Zuyevo
Tver'
(Kalinin)
L. Il'men
Kingisepp
Narva
Tallinn
ESTONIA
Tartu
L. Peipus
Pärnu
G. of Riga
Riga
Cēsis
LATVIA
Rēzekne
Jelgava
Šiauliai
Panevėžys
Daugavpils
LITHUANIA
Kaunas
Vilnius
Kaliningrad
Pskov
Velikiye Luki
Vitebsk
Smolensk
Minsk
Negoreloye
BELARUS
Grodno
Stolbtsy
Białystok
Pinsk
Gomel'
Brest
Bug
Lublin
Wisła
Rovno
Zhitomir
Kiev
Kiev Res.
Dnieper
Shepetovka
UKRAINE
Przemyśl
L'viv
Ivano-Frankovsk
Vinnitsa
Kirovograd
Krivoy Rog
Nikolayev
Kakhovka Res.
Mariupol'
Sea of Azov
Kherson
Odessa
Tiraspol
Chişinău
Bendery
MOLDOVA
Dniester
Chernovtsy
Mukachevo
Satu Mare
Debrecen
Oradea
Cluj-Napoca
Iaşi
Roman
Siret
Prut
Arad
ROMANIA
Timişoara
Sibiu
Braşov
Brăila
Galaţi
Ploieşti
Bucharest
Iron Gate
Craiova
Danube
Belgorod Dnestrovskiy
Sulina
Constanţa
CRIMEA
Kerch
Simferopol
Sevastopol
Yalta
Krasnodar
Novorossiysk
Maykop
Tuapse
Sochi
Sukhumi
Kutaisi
Batumi
BLACK SEA
Varna
Burgas
Ruse
Pleven
Sliven
BULGARIA
Sofia
Plovdiv
Stara Zagora
Niš
Morava
Skopje
MACEDONIA
Bitola
Rhodope
Edirne
ISTANBUL
Bosporus
Tekirdağ
Sea of Marmara
Dardanelles
Bursa
Eskişehir
Sinop
Samsun
Trabzon
Erzurum
Ereğli
Kizilirmak
Ankara
Sivas
TURKEY
Kayseri
Maraş
Afyonkarahisar
Konya
Manisa
İzmir
Tarsus
Adana
Mersin
Antalya
Antakya
Aleppo
Latakia
SYRIA
Nicosia
CYPRUS
Larnaca
IRAN
Thessaloníki
Kavála
GREECE
Ioánnina
Lárisa
Vólos
Tríkkala
Lamía
Euboea
Khalkís
Athens
Piraiév
Corinth
Pátrai
Kalámai
Taínaron
Lésvos
Khíos
Sámos
AEGEAN SEA
Rhodes
Crete
Khania
Iráklion
Tornio
Oulu
L. Oulu
Kuopio
Vaasa
Tampere
FINLAND
URAL MOUNTAINS
RUSSIA
Mezen'
Pechora
Belaya
70°
60°
50°
40°
30°
80°
G H J K L M
2 3 5

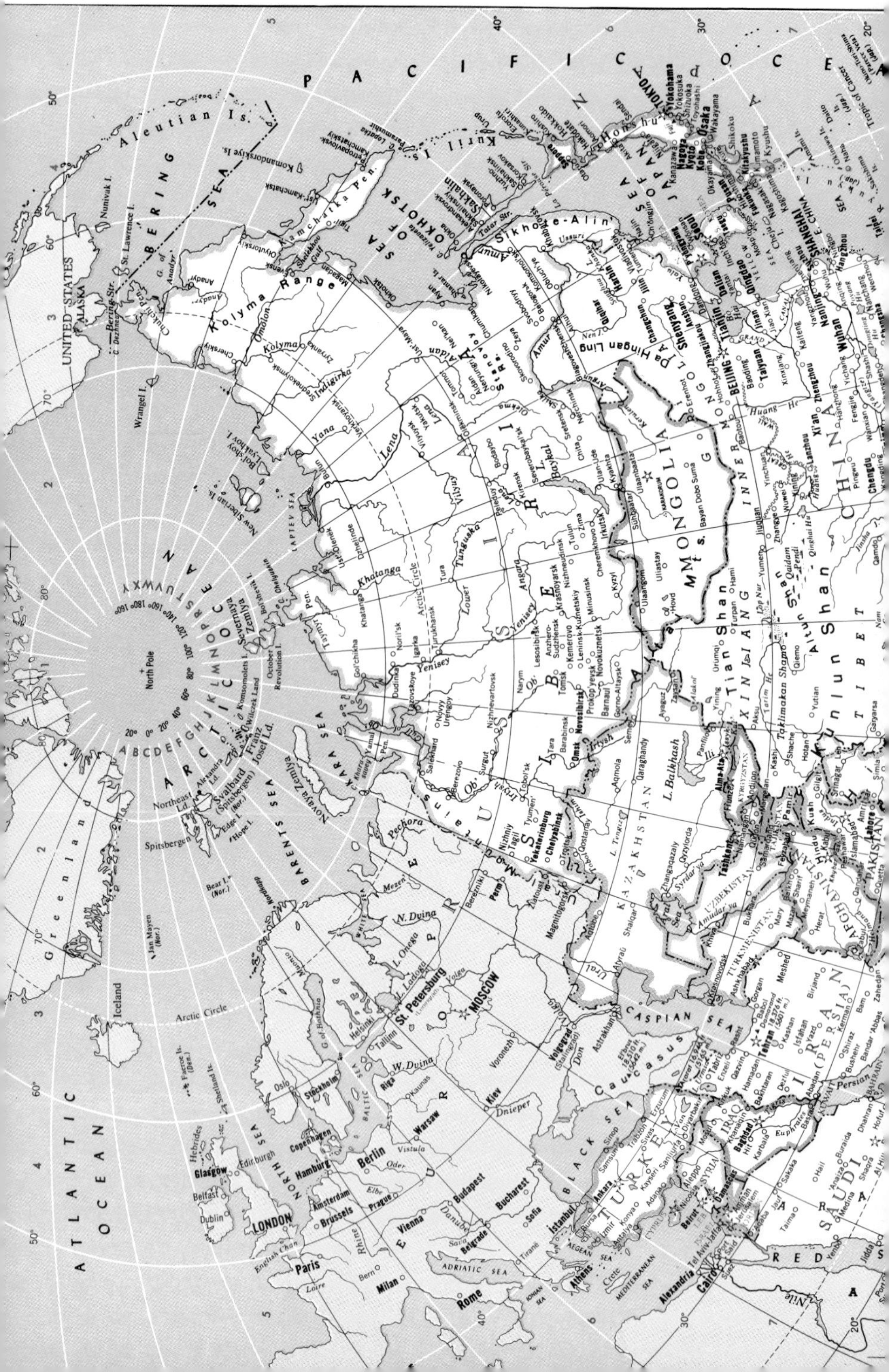
PACIFIC OCEAN
ATLANTIC OCEAN
ARCTIC OCEAN
BERING SEA
SEA OF OKHOTSK
SEA OF JAPAN
BARENTS SEA
KARA SEA
LAPTEV SEA
NORTH SEA
BALTIC SEA
BLACK SEA
CASPIAN SEA
MEDITERRANEAN SEA
ADRIATIC SEA
AEGEAN SEA
RED SEA
Aleutian Is.
Kuril Is.
Kamchatka Pen.
Komandorskiye Is.
UNITED STATES
ALASKA
Bering Str.
Wrangel I.
New Siberian Is.
Severnaya Zemlya
Franz Josef Ld.
Svalbard (Spitsbergen) (Nor.)
Spitsbergen
Novaya Zemlya
Greenland
Iceland
North Pole
Arctic Circle
Kolyma Range
Sikhote-Alin'
Sakhalin
Hokkaido
Honshu
JAPAN
TOKYO
Yokohama
Osaka
Sapporo
Seoul
Pyongyang
Harbin
Shenyang
Dalian
Tianjin
BEIJING
Qingdao
SHANGHAI
Nanjing
Wuhan
Chengdu
Xi'an
Lanzhou
Da Hinggan Ling
MONGOLIA
Ulaanbaatar
INNER MONGOLIA
CHINA
XINJIANG
TIBET
Tian Shan
Kunlun Shan
Altun Shan
Taklimakan Shamo
SIBERIA
Lena
Yenisey
Ob
Irtysh
Amur
Angara
Lower Tunguska
Kolyma
Indigirka
Yana
Khatanga
Vilyuy
Aldan
L. Baykal
Irkutsk
Krasnoyarsk
Novosibirsk
Omsk
KAZAKHSTAN
L. Balkhash
Alma-Ata
Tashkent
UZBEKISTAN
TURKMENISTAN
KYRGYZSTAN
TAJIKISTAN
AFGHANISTAN
PAKISTAN
Kabul
Islamabad
Lahore
IRAN (PERSIA)
Tehran
Meshed
Isfahan
IRAQ
Baghdad
SAUDI ARABIA
SYRIA
Damascus
TURKEY
Ankara
Istanbul
Aral Sea
Ural Mts.
Ural
Volga
Volgograd (Stalingrad)
Yekaterinburg
Chelyabinsk
Perm
MOSCOW
St. Petersburg
L. Ladoga
L. Onega
N. Dvina
W. Dvina
Dnieper
Kiev
Caucasus
Pechora
EUROPE
Helsinki
Stockholm
Oslo
Riga
Tallinn
Copenhagen
Berlin
Warsaw
Hamburg
Amsterdam
Brussels
LONDON
Paris
Prague
Vienna
Budapest
Bucharest
Belgrade
Sofia
Athens
Rome
Milan
Bern
Glasgow
Belfast
Dublin
Beirut
Cairo
Alexandria
Nile
Euphrates
Danube
Rhine
Elbe
Oder
Vistula
Tropic of Cancer

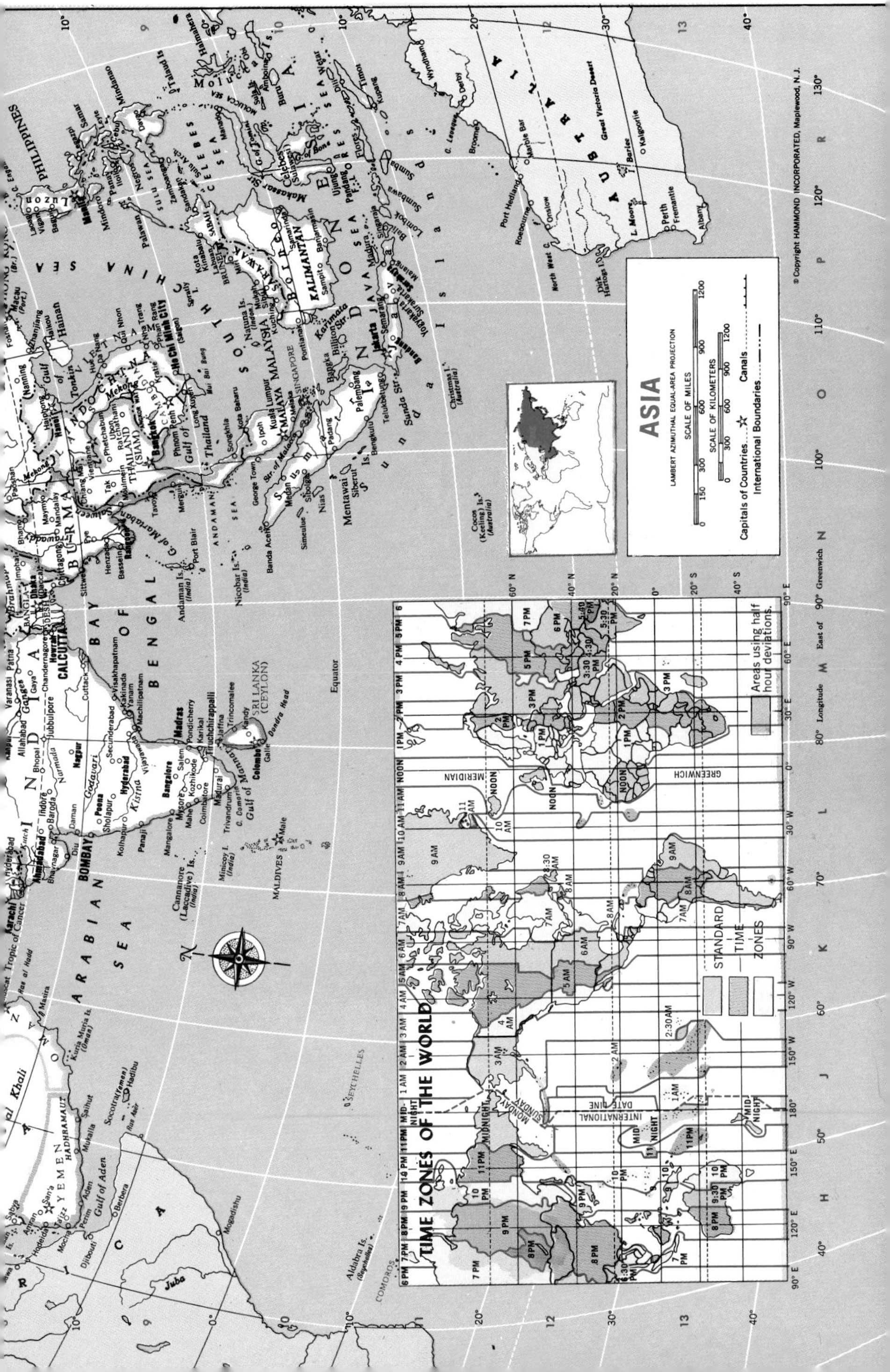
ASIA
LAMBERT AZIMUTHAL EQUAL-AREA PROJECTION
SCALE OF MILES
0 150 300 600 900 1200
SCALE OF KILOMETERS
0 300 600 900 1200
Capitals of Countries
International Boundaries
Canals
TIME ZONES OF THE WORLD
STANDARD TIME ZONES
Areas using half hour deviations.
INTERNATIONAL DATE LINE
GREENWICH MERIDIAN
MONDAY
SUNDAY
© Copyright HAMMOND INCORPORATED, Maplewood, N.J.
PHILIPPINES
SOUTH CHINA SEA
BAY OF BENGAL
ARABIAN SEA
INDIA
BURMA
THAILAND (SIAM)
INDOCHINA
AUSTRALIA
MALAYSIA
SINGAPORE
SRI LANKA (CEYLON)
MALDIVES
SEYCHELLES
COMOROS
YEMEN
HADHRAMAUT
Gulf of Aden
Socotra (Yemen)
Sumatra
JAVA
Borneo
KALIMANTAN
SARAWAK
SABAH
BRUNEI
Celebes
Sulawesi
CELEBES SEA
SULU SEA
MOLUCCA SEA
Moluccas
BANDA SEA
FLORES SEA
TIMOR SEA
JAVA SEA
ANDAMAN SEA
Great Victoria Desert
Tropic of Cancer
Equator
Indian Ocean
CALCUTTA
BOMBAY
Madras
Bangkok
Ho Chi Minh City (Saigon)
Jakarta
Manila
Colombo
Karachi
Hainan
Luzon
Mindanao
Andaman Is. (India)
Nicobar Is. (India)
Cocos (Keeling) Is. (Australia)
Christmas I. (Australia)
Aldabra Is. (Seychelles)

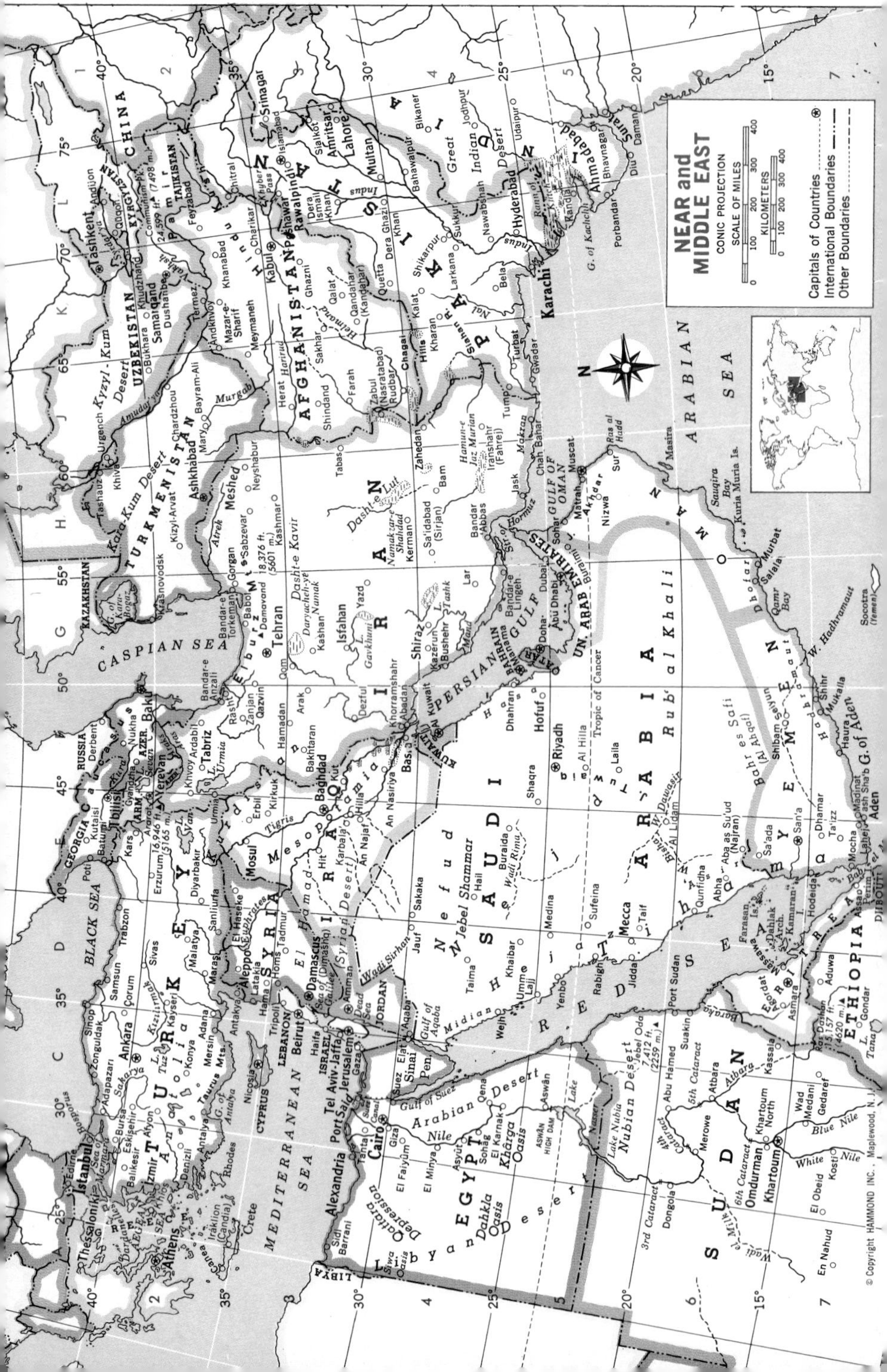
NEAR and
MIDDLE EAST
CONIC PROJECTION
SCALE OF MILES
0 100 200 300 400
KILOMETERS
0 100 200 300 400
Capitals of Countries
International Boundaries
Other Boundaries
© Copyright HAMMOND INC., Maplewood, N.J.

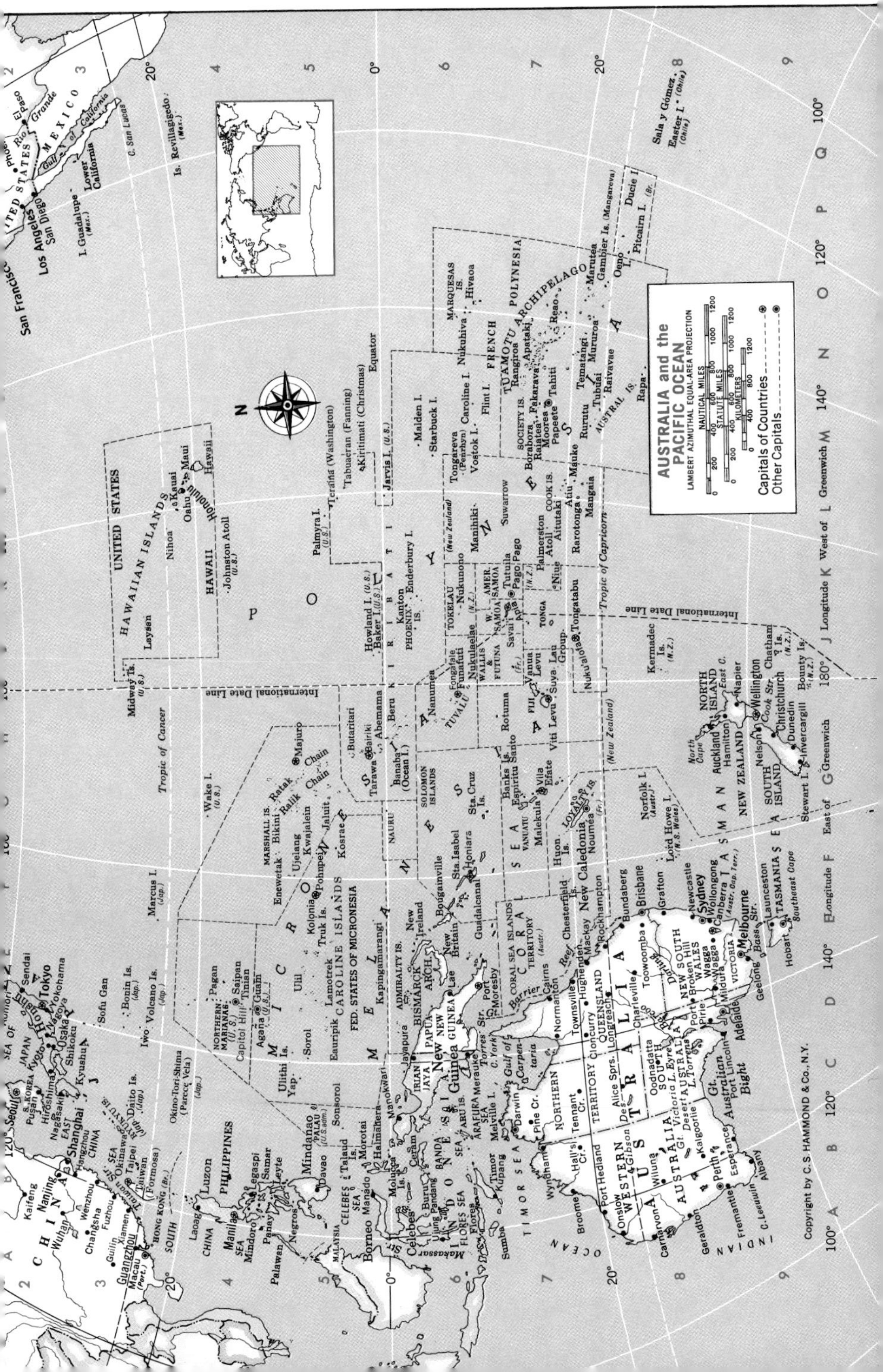
AUSTRALIA and the PACIFIC OCEAN
LAMBERT AZIMUTHAL EQUAL-AREA PROJECTION
NAUTICAL MILES
STATUTE MILES
KILOMETERS
Capitals of Countries
Other Capitals
Copyright by C.S. HAMMOND & Co., N.Y.
AUSTRALIA
NEW ZEALAND
NEW GUINEA
PHILIPPINES
JAPAN
CHINA
HAWAIIAN ISLANDS
UNITED STATES
MEXICO
MICRONESIA
MELANESIA
POLYNESIA
FRENCH POLYNESIA
TUAMOTU ARCHIPELAGO
CAROLINE ISLANDS
FED. STATES OF MICRONESIA
MARSHALL IS.
SOLOMON ISLANDS
CORAL SEA
TASMAN SEA
ARAFURA SEA
TIMOR SEA
INDIAN OCEAN
International Date Line
Tropic of Cancer
Tropic of Capricorn
Sydney
Melbourne
Brisbane
Adelaide
Perth
Darwin
Auckland
Wellington
Christchurch
Tokyo
Shanghai
Manila
Honolulu
Los Angeles
San Francisco
Tahiti
Noumea
Great Barrier Reef
Longitude West of Greenwich
Longitude East of Greenwich

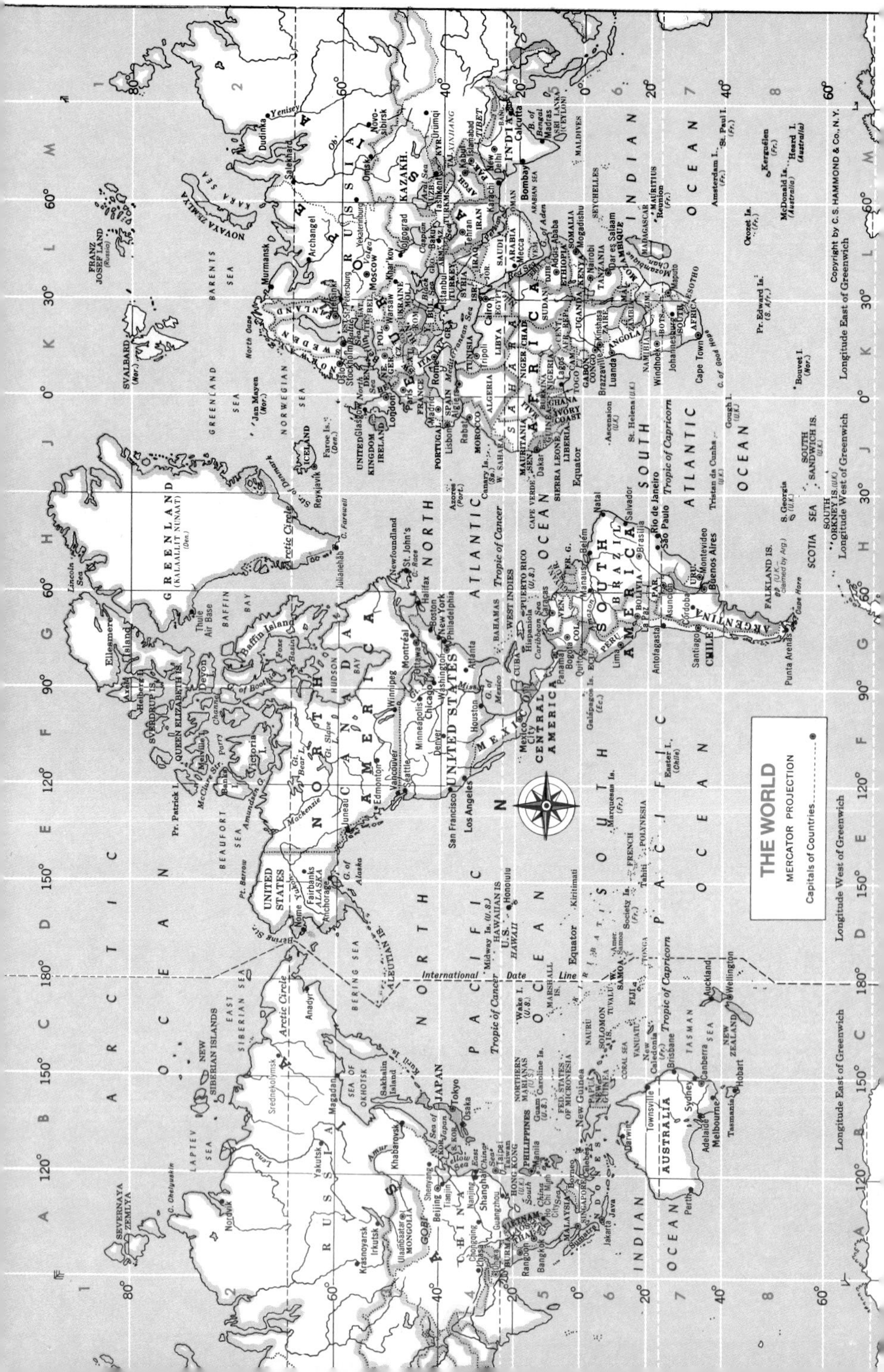
THE WORLD
MERCATOR PROJECTION
Capitals of Countries
Copyright by C. S. HAMMOND & Co., N. Y.
Longitude East of Greenwich
Longitude West of Greenwich
ARCTIC OCEAN
NORTH PACIFIC OCEAN
SOUTH PACIFIC OCEAN
NORTH ATLANTIC OCEAN
SOUTH ATLANTIC OCEAN
INDIAN OCEAN
NORTH AMERICA
SOUTH AMERICA
AFRICA
EUROPE
ASIA
AUSTRALIA
International Date Line
Tropic of Cancer
Tropic of Capricorn
Equator
Arctic Circle

THE YEAR IN PICTURES

PHOTO CREDITS: All photos in this section are credited to AP/Wide World Photos unless otherwise noted.

SWEARING IN—William Clinton takes the oath of office from Chief Justice William Rehnquist, as daughter Chelsea and wife Hillary watch.

INAUGURAL POET—President Clinton reaches out to hug Maya Angelou after she recited her inaugural poem.

IN TRIBUTE—Mourners file past the coffin of former Supreme Court Justice Thurgood Marshall during his lying-in-state in the Great Hall of the Supreme Court.

ON PATROL—A U.S. Marine M-1 Abrams tank takes to the streets of Mogadishu, Somalia, following the shooting of a marine.

RELIEF—Delighted residents of besieged Gorazde, Bosnia, tear open a U.S. airdrop food package.

FACING CONGRESS—President Clinton presents his economic plan to a joint session of Congress.

NORTHEAST STORM—Morning commuters in midtown Manhattan cope with the aftermath of "the storm of the century."

RIOT—Thousands of militant Hindus face Indian riot police near New Delhi railway station as they seek the government's ouster.

TERROR—Police survey bomb damage at the parking garage beneath the World Trade Center in New York City.

TALE OF TWO CITIES—Forensic experts inspect heavy damage from a bomb explosion in London's financial district (left) and others view bomb damage outside the Uffizi Gallery in Florence, Italy (right). That explosion killed five people.

TAKING THE OATH—Supreme Court Justice Byron White administers the oath of office to Janet Reno, making her the first woman to be Attorney General. Her niece holds the Bible as the President looks on.

WELCOME HOME—President Clinton inspects troops who have just returned from their relief mission in Somalia.

PROTEST—Riot police clash with diehard Communist demonstrators in Moscow on May Day.

SUPPORT—Pro-Yeltsin supporters rally at Moscow's Red Square.

BEFORE—This aerial photo shows the compound of the Branch Davidian sect in Waco, Texas, as it was before the siege began.

AFTER—Following the disastrous fire, this is all that remains of the compound.

GAYS MARCH—From around the country, gay and lesbian marchers gather at the Lincoln Memorial in Washington, D.C., to demand the end to the ban on gays in the military and for equal rights.

VANCOUVER SUMMIT—President Clinton and Russian President Boris Yeltsin talk and stroll on the grounds of the University of British Columbia at their first summit.

RESTORATION—Haiti's exiled president Jean-Bertrand Aristide, right, and U.N. aide Leonardo Despouy take a break during negotiations to restore him to power.

WORKING ON THE LEVEE—St. Joseph, Mo., residents form a human chain to pass sand bags along a Missouri River levee when the river was inches from topping it.

NOMINATED—President presents Judge Ruth Bader Ginsburg to the press as his choice to sit on the Supreme Court. The Senate subsequently confirmed her appointment.

FLOODING—Water from the Missouri River engulfs Elwood, Kans., after a levee north of town broke.

VICTOR—Senator Carol Mosley-Braun relaxes after her triumph on the Senate floor over the use of the Confederate flag by a women's organization.

ADVOCATE—First lady Hillary Rodham Clinton makes her case for health care reform to members of the Johns Hopkins School of Medicine.

NEWLY-WEDS—Crown Prince Naruhito of Japan and his bride Princess Masako radiate happiness after the ceremony.

PAPAL VISIT—Pope John Paul II enters Mile High Stadium in Denver in his bulletproof Popemobile for his World Youth Day address amid welcoming crowd.

BREAKING GROUND—Dignitaries take part in a ground-breaking ceremony for the Vietnam Women's Memorial. A model of the memorial appears in the foreground.

BEACHED—Illegal Asian immigrants huddle wrapped in blankets on a beach in the Rockaway section of New York City after the freighter carrying them ran aground.

BILL SIGNING—Vice President Gore, whose Senate vote was crucial to its passage, looks on as President Clinton signs the Budget bill.

IN LINE OF SUCCESSION—Retiring Chairman of the Joint Chiefs General Colin Powell, left, congratulates his replacement, Army General John Shalikashvili, as President Clinton looks on.

CROSSWORD PUZZLE GUIDE

First Aid to Crossword Puzzlers

We cannot begin to list all the odd words you will meet with in your daily and Sunday crossword puzzles, for such words run into many thousands. But we have tried to include those that turn up most frequently, as well as many others that should be of help to you when you are unable to go any further.

Also, we do not guarantee that the definitions in your puzzle will be exactly the same as ours, although we have checked every word with a standard dictionary and have followed its definition.

In nearly every case, we have used as the key word the principal noun of the definition, rather than any adjective, adjective phrase, or noun used as an adjective. And, to simplify your searching, we have grouped the words according to the number of spaces you have to fill.

For a list of Foreign Phrases, *see* Index. For Rulers of England and Great Britain, France, Germany and Prussia, and Russia, *see* Countries of the World.

Words of Two Letters

Ambary, DA
And (French, Latin), ET
Article (Arabic), AL
(French), LA, LE, UN
(Spanish), EL, LA, UN
At the (French), AU
(Spanish), AL
Behold, LO
Bird: Hawaiian, OO
Birthplace: Abraham's, UR
Bone, OS
Buddha, FO
Butterfly: Peacock, IO
Champagne, AY
Chaos, NU
Chief: Burmese, BO
Coin: Roman, AS
Siamese, AT
Concerning, RE
Dialect: Chinese, WU
Double (Egy. relig.), KA
Drama: Japanese, NO
Egg (comb. form), OO
Esker, OS
Eye (Scotch), EE
Factor: Amplification, MU
Fifty (Greek), NU
Fish: Carplike, ID
Force, OD
Forty (Greek), MU
From (French, Latin, Spanish), DE
(Latin prefix), AB
From the (French), DU
God: Babylonian, EA, ZU
Egyptian sun, RA
Hindu unknown, KA
Semitic, EL
Goddess: Babylonian, AI
Greek earth, GE
Gold (heraldry), OR
Gulf: Arctic, OB
Heart (Egy. relig.), AB
Indian: South American, GE
King: Of Bashan, OG
Language: Artificial, RO
Assamese, AO
Lava: Hawaiian, AA
Letter: Greek, MU, NU, PI, XI
Hebrew, HE, PE
Lily: Palm, TI
Measure: Annamese, LY
Chinese, HO, HU, KO, LI, MU, PU, TO, TU
Japanese, GO, JO, MO, RI, SE, TO
Metric land, AR
Netherlands, EL
Portuguese, PE
Siamese, WA
Swedish, AM
Type, EM, EN
Monk: Buddhist, BO
Month: Jewish, AB
Mouth, OS
Mulberry: Indian, AL
Native: Burmese, WA
Note: Of Scale, DO, FA, MI, LA, RE, TI
Of (French, Latin, Spanish), DE
Of the (French), DU
One (Scotch), AE
Pagoda: Chinese, TA
Plant: East Indian fiber, DA
Ridge: Sandy, AS, OS
River: Russian, OB
Sloth: Three-toed, AI
Soul (Egy. relig.), BA
Sound: Hindu mystic, OM
Suffix: Comparative, ER
The. *See* Article
To the: French, AU
Spanish, AL
Tree: Buddhist sacred, BO
Tribe: Assamese, AO
Type: Jumbled, PI
Weight: Annamese, TA
Chinese, LI
Danish, ES
Japanese, MO
Roman, AS
Whirlwind: Faeroe Is., OE
Yes (German), JA
(Italian, Spanish), SI
(Russian), DA

Words of Three Letters

Adherent: IST
Again, BIS
Age, ERA
Antelope: African, GNU, KOB
Apricot: Japanese, UME
Article (German), DAS, DEM, DEN, DER, DES, DIE, EIN
(French), LES, UNE
(Spanish), LAS, LOS, UNA
Banana: Polynesian, FEI
Barge, HOY
Bass: African, IYO
Beak, NEB, NIB
Beard: Grain, AWN
Beetle: June, DOR
Being, ENS
Berry: Hawthorn, HAW
Beverage: Hawaiian, AVA
Bird: Australian, EMU
Crowlike, JAY
Extinct, MOA
Fabulous, ROC
Frigate, IWA
Parson, POE, TUE, TUI
Sea, AUK
Blackbird, ANI, ANO
Born, NEE
Bronze: Roman, AES
Bugle: Yellow, IVA
By way of, VIA
Canton: Swiss, URI
Cap: Turkish, FEZ
Catnip, NEP
Character: In "Faerie Queene," UNA
Coin: Afghan, PUL
Albanian, LEK
British Guiana, BIT
Bulgarian, LEV, LEW
French, ECU, SOU
Indian, PIE
Japanese, SEN, YEN
Korean, WON
Lithuanian, LIT
Macao, Timor, AVO
Palestinian, MIL
Persian, PUL
Peruvian, SOL
Rumanian, BAN, LEU, LEY
Scandinavian, ORE
Siamese, ATT
See also Money of account
Collection: Facts, ANA
Commune: Belgian, ANS, ATH
Netherlands, EDE, EPE
Community: Russian, MIR
Constellation: Southern, ARA
Contraction: Poetic, EEN, EER, OER
Covering: Apex of roof, EPI
Crab: Fiddler, UCA
Crag: Rocky, TOR
Cry: Crow, rook, raven, CAW
Cup: Wine, AMA
Cymbal, Oriental, TAL, ZEL

Disease: Silkworm, UJI
Division: Danish territorial, AMT
 Geologic, EON
Doctrine, ISM
Dowry, DOT
Dry (French), SEC
Dynasty: Chinese, CHI, HAN, SUI, WEI, YIN
Eagle: Sea, ERN
Earth (comb. form), GEO
Egg: Louse, NIT
Eggs: Fish, ROE
Emmet, ANT
Enzyme, ASE
Equal (comb. form), ISO
Extension: building, ELL
Far (comb. form), TEL
Farewell, AVE
Fiber: Palm, TAL
Finial, EPI
Fish: Carplike, IDE
 Pikelike, GAR
Flatfish, DAB
Fleur-de-lis, LIS, LYS
Food: Hawaiian, POI
Formerly, NEE
Friend (French), AMI
Game: Card, LOO
Garment: Camel-hair, ABA
Gateway, DAR
Gazelle: Tibetan, GOA
Genus: Ducks, AIX
 Grasses, POA
 Grasses (maize), ZEA
 Herbs or shrubs, IVA
 Lizards, UTA
 Rodents (incl. house mice), MUS
 Ruminants (incl. cattle), BOS
 Swine, SUS
Gibbon: Malay, LAR
God: Assyrian, SIN
 Babylonian, ABU, ANU, BEL, HEA, SIN, UTU
 Irish sea, LER
 Phrygian, MEN
 Polynesian, ORO
Goddess: Babylonian, AYA
 Etruscan, UNI
 Hindu, SRI, UMA, VAC
 Teutonic, RAN
Governor: Algerian, DEY
 Turkish, BEY
Grampus, ORC
Grape, UVA
Grass: Meadow, POA
Gypsy, ROM
Hail, AVE
Hare: Female, DOE
Hawthorn, HAW
Hay: Spread for drying, TED
Herb: Japanese, UDO
 Perennial, PIA
 Used for blue dye, WAD
Herd: Whales, GAM, POD
Hero: Spanish, CID
High (music), ALT
Honey (pharm.), MEL
Humorist: American, ADE
I (Latin), EGO
I love (Latin), AMO
Indian: Algonquian, FOX, SAC, WEA
 Chimakuan, HOH
 Keresan, SIA
 Mayan, MAM
 Shoshonean, UTE
 Siouan, KAW, OTO
 South American, ITE, ONA, URO, URU, YAO
 Tierra del Fuego, ONA
 Wakashan, AHT
Ingot, PIG
Inlet: Narrow, RIA
Island: Cyclades, IOS
 Dodecanese, COS, KOS
 (French), ILE
 River, AIT

Jackdaw, DAW
John (Gaelic), IAN
Keelbill, ANI, ANO
Kiln, OST
King: British legendary LUD
Kobold, NIS
Lace: To make, TAT
Lamprey, EEL
Language: Artificial, IDO
 Bantu, ILA
 Siamese, LAO, TAI
Leaf: Palm, OLA, OLE
Leaving, ORT
Left: Cause to turn, HAW
Letter: Greek, CHI, ETA, PHI, PSI, RHO, TAU
 Hebrew, MEM, NUN, SIN, TAV, VAU
Lettuce, COS
Life (comb. form), BIO
Lily: Palm, TOI
Lizard, EFT
Louse: Young, NIT
Love (Anglo-Irish), GRA
Lute: Oriental, TAR
Macaw: Bralizian, ARA
Marble, TAW
Match: Shooting (French), TIR
Meadow, LEA
Measure: Abyssinian, TAT
 Algerian, PIK
 Annamese, GON, MAU, NGU, VUO, SAO, TAO, TAT
 Arabian, DEN, SAA
 Belgian, VAT
 Bulgarian, OKA, OKE
 Chinese, FEN, TOU, YIN
 Cloth, ELL
 Cyprus, OKA, OKE, PIK
 Czech, LAN, SAH
 Danish, FOD, MIL, POT
 Dominican Republic, ONA
 Dutch, old, AAM
 East Indian, KIT
 Egyptian, APT, HEN, PIK, ROB
 Electric, MHO, OHM
 Energy, ERG
 English, PIN
 Estonian, TUN
 French, POT
 German, AAM
 Greek, PIK
 Hebrew, CAB, HIN, KOR, LOG
 Hungarian, AKO
 Icelandic, FET
 Indian, GAZ, GUZ, JOW, KOS
 Japanese, BOO, CHO, KEN, RIN, SHO, SUN, TAN
 Malabar, ADY
 Metric land, ARE
 Netherlands, KAN, KOP, MUD, VAT, ZAK
 Norwegian, FOT, POT
 Persian, GAZ, GUZ, MOU, ZAR, ZER
 Polish, CAL
 Rangoon, DHA, LAN
 Roman, PES, URN
 Russian, FUT, LOF
 Scotch, COP
 Siamese, KEN, NIU, RAI, SAT, SEN, SOK, WAH, YOT
 Somaliland, TOP
 Spanish, PIE
 Straits Settlements, PAU, TUN
 Swedish, ALN, FOT, MIL, REF, TUM
 Swiss, POT
 Tunisian, SAA
 Turkish, OKA, OKE, PIK
 Wire, MIL
 Württemberg, IMI
 Yarn, LEA
 Yugoslavian, OKA, RIF
Milk, LAC
Milkfish, AWA
Moccasin, PAC
Money: Yap stone, FEI
Money of Account: Anglo-Saxon, ORA, ORE
 French, SOU
 Indian, LAC
 Japanese, RIN
 Oman, GAJ
 Virgin Islands, BIT
 See also Coin
Monkey: Capuchin, SAI
Morsel, ORT
Mother: Peer Gynt's, ASE
Mountain: Asia Minor, IDA
Mulberry: Indian, AAL, ACH, AWL
Muttonbird: New Zealand, OII
Nahoor, SNA
Native: Mindanao, ATA
Neckpiece, BOA
Newt, EFT
No (Scotch), NAE
Note: Guido's highest, ELA
 Of scale, SOL
Nursemaid: Oriental, AMA, IYA
Ocher: Yellow, SIL
One (Scotch), YIN
Ornament: Pagoda, TEE
Oven: Polynesian, UMU
Ox: Tibetan, YAK
Pagoda: Chinese, TAA
Parrot: Hawk, HIA
 New Zealand, KEA
Part: Footlike, PES
Particle: Electrified, ION
Pasha, DEY
Pass: Mountain, COL
Paste: Rice, AME
Pea: Indian split, DAL
Peasant: Philippine, TAO
Penpoint, NEB, NIB
Piece out, EKE
Pigeon, NUN
Pine: Textile screw, ARA
Pistol (slang), GAT
Pit: Baking, IMU
Plant: Pepper, AVA
Play: By Capek, RUR
Poem: Old French, DIT
Porgy: Japanese, TAI
Priest: Biblical high, ELI
Prince Ethiopian, RAS
Pseudonym: Dickens', BOZ
Queen: Fairy, MAB
Quince: Bengal, BEL
Record: Ship's, LOG
Refuse: Flax (Scotch), PAB, POB
Resin, LAC
Resort, SPA
Revolver (slang), GAT
Right: Cause to turn, GEE
River: Scotch or English, DEE
 (Spanish), RIO
 Swiss, AAR
Room: Harem, ODA
Rootstock: Fern, ROI
Rose (Persian), GUL
Ruff: Female, REE
Rule: Indian, RAJ
Sailor, GOB, TAR
Saint: Female (abbr.), STE
 Mohammedan, PIR
Salt, SAL
Sash: Japanese, OBI
Scrap, ORT
Seed: Poppy, MAW
 Small, PIP
Self, EGO
Serpent: Vedic sky, AHI
Sesame, TIL
Sheep: Female, EWE
 Indian, SHA
 Male, RAM
Sheepfold (Scotch), REE
Shelter, LEE
Shield, ECU
Shooting match (French), TIR
Shrew: European, ERD
Shrub: Evergreen, YEW
Silkworm, ERI

Snake, ASP, BOA
Soak, RET
Son-in-law: Mohammed's, ALI
Sorrel: Wood, OCA
Spade: Long, narrow, LOY
Spirit: Malignant, KER
Spot: Playing-card, PIP
Spread for drying, TED
Spring: Mineral, SPA
Sprite: Water, NIX
Statesman: Japanese, ITO
Stern: Toward, AFT
Stomach: Bird's, MAW
Street (French), RUE
Summer (French), ETE
Sun, SOL
Swamp, BOG, FEN
Swan: Male, COB
Tea: Chinese, CHA
Temple: Shinto, SHA
The. *See* Article
Thing (law), RES
Title: Etruscan, LAR
 Monk's, FRA
 Portuguese, DOM
 Spanish, DON
 Turkish, AGA, BEY
Tool: Cutting, ADZ, AXE
 Mining, GAD
 Piercing, AWL
Tree: Candlenut, AMA
 Central American, EBO
 East Indian, SAJ, SAL
 Evergreen, YEW
 Hawaiian, KOA, KOU
 Indian, BEL, DAR
 Linden, LIN
 New Zealand, AKE
 Philippine, DAO, TUA, TUI
 Rubber, ULE
 South American, APA
Tribe: New Zealand, ATI
Turmeric, REA
Twice, BIS
Twin: Siamese, ENG
Uncle (dialect), EAM, EME
Veil: Chalice, AER, AIR
Vessel: Wine, AMA
Vestment: Ecclesiastical, ALB
Vetch: Bitter, ERS
Victorfish, AKU
Vine: New Zealand, AKA
 Philippine, IYO
Wallaba, APA
Wapiti, ELK
Water (French), EAU
Waterfall, LIN
Watering place: Prussian, EMS
Weave: Designating plain, UNI
Weight: Annamese, CAN
 Bulgarian, OKA, OKE
 Burmese, MOO, VIS
 Chinese, FEN, HAO, KIN, SSU, TAN, YIN
 Cyprus, OKA, OKE
 Danish, LOD, ORT, VOG
 East Indian, TJI
 Egyptian, KAT, OKA, OKE
 English, for wool, TOD
 German, LOT
 Greek, MNA, OKA, OKE
 Indian, SER
 Japanese, FUN, KIN, RIN, SHI
 Korean, KON
 Malacca, KIP
 Mongolian, LAN
 Netherlands, ONS
 Norwegian, LOD
 Polish, LUT
 Rangoon, PAI
 Roman, BES
 Russian, LOT
 Siamese, BAT, HAP, PAI
 Swedish, ASS, ORT
 Turkish, OKA, OKE
 Yugoslavian, OKA, OKE
Whales: Herd, GAM, POD
Wildebeest, GNU
Wing, ALA
Witticism, MOT
Wolframite, CAL
Worm: African, LOA
Wreath: Hawaiian, LEI
Yale, ELI
Yam: Hawaiian, HOI
Yes (French), OUI
Young: Bring forth, EAN
Z (letter), ZED

Words of Four Letters

Aborigine: Borneo, DYAK
Agave, ALOE
Animal: Footless, APOD
Ant: White, ANAI, ANAY
Antelope: African, ASSE, BISA, GUIB,KOBA, KUDU, ORYX, POKU, PUKU, TOPI, TORA
Apoplexy: Plant, ESCA
Apple, POME
Apricot, ANSU
Ardor, ELAN
Armadillo, APAR, PEBA, PEVA, TATU
Ascetic: Mohammedan, SUFI
Association: Chinese, TONG
Astronomer: Persian, OMAR
Avatar: Of Vishnu, RAMA
Axillary, ALAR
Band: Horizontal (heraldry), FESS
Barracuda, SPET
Bark: Mulberry, TAPA
Base: Column, DADO
Bearing (heraldry), ORLE
Beer: Russian, KVAS
Beige, ECRU
Being, ESSE
Beverage: Japanese rice, SAKE
Bird: Asian, MINA, MYNA
 Egyptian sacred, IBIS
 Extinct, DODO, MAMO
 Flightless, KIWI
 Gull-like, TERN
 Hawaiian, IIWI, MAMO
 Parson, KOKO
 Unfledged, EYAS
Birds: As class, AVES
Black, EBON
 (French), NOIR
Blackbird: European, MERL
Boat: Flat-bottomed, DORY
Bone: Forearm, ULNA
Bones, OSSA
Box, Japanese, INRO
Bravo (rare), EUGE
Buffalo: Indian wild, ARNA
Bull (Spanish), TORO
Burden, ONUS
Cabbage: Sliced, SLAW
Caliph: Mohammedan, OMAR
Canoe: Malay, PRAU, PROA
Cap: Military, KEPI
Cape, NESS
Capital: Ancient Irish, TARA
Case: Article, ETUI
Cat: Wild, BALU, EYRA
Chalcedony, SARD
Chamber: Indian ceremonial, KIVA
Channel: Brain, ITER
Cheese: Dutch, EDAM
Chest: Sepulchral stone, CIST
Chieftain: Arab, EMIR
Church: Part of, APSE, NAVE
 (Scotch), KIRK
Claim (law), LIEN
Cluster: Flower, CYME
Coin: Chinese, TAEL, YUAN
 German, MARK
 Indian, ANNA
 Iranian, RIAL
 Italian, LIRA
 Moroccan, OKIA
 Siamese, BAHT
 South American, PESO
 Spanish, DURO, PESO
 Turkish, PARA
Commune: Belgian, AATH
Composition: Musical, OPUS
Compound: Chemical, DIOL
Constellation: Southern, PAVO
Council: Russian, DUMA
Counsel, REDE
Covering: Seed, ARIL
Cross: Egyptian, ANKH
Cry: Bacchanalian, EVOE
Cup (Scotch), TASS
Cupbearer, SAKI
Dagger, DIRK
 Malay, KRIS
Dam: River, WEIR
Dash, ELAN
Date: Roman, IDES
Dawn: Pertaining to, EOAN
Dean: English, INGE
Decay: In fruit, BLET
Deer: Sambar, MAHA
Disease: Skin, ACNE
Disk: Solar, ATEN
Dog: Hunting, ALAN
Drink: Hindu intoxicating, SOMA
Duck, SMEE, SMEW, TEAL
Dynasty: Chinese, CHEN, CHIN, CHOU, CHOW, HSIA, MING, SUNG, TANG, TSIN
 Mongol, YUAN
Eagle: Biblical, GIER
 Sea, ERNE
Egyptian: Christian, COPT
Ear: Pertaining to, OTIC
Entrance: Mine, ADIT
Esau, EDOM
Escutcheon: Voided, ORLE
Eskers, OSAR
Evergreen: New Zealand, TAWA
Fairy: Persian, PERI
Family: Italian, ESTE
Far (comb. form), TELE
Farewell, VALE
Father (French), PERE
Fennel: Philippine, ANIS
Fever: Malarial, AGUE
Fiber: East Indian, JUTE
Firn, NEVE
Fish: Carplike, DACE
 Hawaiian, ULUA
 Herringlike, SHAD
 Mackerellike, CERO
 Marine, HAKE
 Sea, LING, MERO, OPAH
 Spiny-finned, GOBY
Food: Tropical, TARO
Foot: Metric, IAMB
Formerly, ERST
Founder: Of Carthage, DIDO
France: Southern, MIDI
Furze, ULEX
Gaelic, ERSE
Gaiter, SPAT
Game: Card, FARO, SKAT
Garlic: European wild, MOLY
Garment: Hindu, SARI
 Roman, TOGA
Gazelle, CORA

Gem, JADE, ONYX, OPAL, RUBY
Genus: Amphibians (incl. frogs), RANA
  Amphibians (incl. tree toads), HYLA
  Antelopes, ORYX
  Auks, ALCA, URIA
  Bees, APIS
  Birds (American ostriches), RHEA
  Birds (cranes), CRUS
  Birds (magpies), PICA
  Birds (peacocks), PAVO
  Cetaceans, INIA
  Ducks (incl. mallards), ANAS
  Fishes (burbots), LOTA
  Fishes (incl. bowfins), AMIA
  Geese (snow geese), CHEN
  Gulls, XEMA
  Herbs, ARUM, GEUM
  Insects (water scorpions), NEPA
  Lilies, ALOE
  Mammals (mankind), HOMO
  Orchids, DISA
  Owls, ASIO, BUBO, OTUS
  Palms, NIPA
  Sea birds, SULA
  Sheep, OVIS
  Shrubs, Eurasian, ULEX
  Shrubs (hollies), ILEX
  Shrubs (incl. Virginia Willow), ITEA
  Shrubs, tropical, EVEA
  Snakes (sand snakes), ERYX
  Swans, OLOR
  Trees, chocolate, COLA
  Trees (ebony family), MABA
  Trees (incl. maples), ACER
  Trees (olives), OLEA
  Trees, tropical, EVEA
  Turtles, EMYS
Goat: Wild, IBEX, KRAS, TAHR, TAIR, THAR
God: Assyrian, ASUR
  Babylonian, ADAD, ADDU, ENKI, ENZU, IRRA, NABU, NEBO, UTUG
  Celtic, LLEU, LLEW
  Hindu, AGNI, CIVA, DEVA, DEWA, KAMA, RAMA, SIVA, VAYU
  Phrygian, ATYS
  Semitic, BAAL
  Teutonic, HLER
Goddess: Babylonian, ERUA, GULA
  Hawaiian, PELE
  Hindu, DEVI, KALI, SHRI, VACH
Gooseberry: Hawaiian, POHA
Gourd, PEPO
Grafted (heraldry), ENTE
Grandfather (obsolete), AIEL
Grandparents: Pertaining to, AVAL
Grass: Hawaiian, HILO
Gray (French), GRIS
Green (heraldry), VERT
Groom: Indian, SYCE
Half (prefix), DEMI, HEMI, SEMI
Hamlet, DORP
Hammer-head: Part of, PEEN
Handle, ANSA
Harp: Japanese, KOTO
Hartebeest, ASSE, TORA
Hautboy, OBOE
Hawk: Taken from nest (falconry), EYAS
Hearing (law), OYER
Heater: For liquids, ETNA
Herb: Aromatic, ANET, DILL
  Fabulous, MOLY
  Perennial, GEUM, SEGO
  Pot, WORT
  Used for blue dye, WADE, WOAD
Hill: Flat-topped, MESA
  Sand, DENE, DUNE
Hoarfrost, RIME
Hog: Immature female, GILT
Holly, ILEX
House: Cow, BYRE
  (Spanish), CASA
Ice: Floating, FLOE
Image, ICON, IKON
Incarnation: Of Vishnu, RAMA
Indian: Algonquian, CREE, SAUK
  Central American, MAYA
  Iroquoian, ERIE
  Mexican, CORA
  Peruvian, CANA, INCA, MORO
  Shoshonean, HOPI
  Siouan, OTOE
  Southwestern, HOPI, PIMA,
YUMA, ZUNI
Insect: Immature, PUPA
Instrument: Stringed, LUTE, LYRE
Ireland, EIRE, ERIN
Jacket: English, ETON
Jail (British), GAOL
Jar, OLLA
Judge: Mohammedan, CADI
Juniper: European, CADE
Kiln, OAST, OVEN
King: British legendary, LUDD, NUDD
Kiss, BUSS
Knife: Philippine, BOLO
Koran: Section of, SURA
Laborer: Spanish American, PEON
Lake: Mountain, TARN
  (Scotch), LOCH
Lamp: Miner's, DAVY
Landing place: Indian, GHAT
Language: Buddhist, PALI
  Japanese, AINU
Latvian, LETT
Layer: Of iris, UVEA
Leaf: Palm, OLAY, OLLA
Legislature: Ukrainian, RADA
Lemur, LORI
Leopard, PARD
Let it stand, STET
Letter: Greek, BETA, IOTA, ZETA
  Hebrew, AYIN, BETH, CAPH, KOPH, RESH, SHIN, TETH, YODH
  Papal, BULL
Lily, ALOE
Literature: Hindu sacred, VEDA
Lizard, GILA
  Monitor, URAN
Loquat, BIWA
Magistrate: Genoese or Venetian, DOGE
Man (Latin), HOMO
Mark: Omission, DELE
armoset: South American, MICO
Meadow: Fertile, VEGA
Measure: Electric, VOLT, WATT
  Force, DYNE
  Hebrew, OMER
  Printing, PICA
  Spanish or Portuguese, VARA
  Swiss land, IMMI
Medley, OLIO
Merganser, SMEW
Milk (French), LAIT
Molding, GULA
  Curved, OGEE
Mongoose: Crab-eating, URVA
Monk: Tibetan, LAMA
Monkey: African, MONA, WAAG
  Ceylonese, MAHA
  Cochin-China, DOUC
  South American, SAKI, TITI
Monkshood, ATIS
Month: Jewish, ADAR, ELUL, IYAR
Mother (French), MERE
Mountain: Thessaly, OSSA
Mouse: Meadow, VOLE
Mythology: Norse, EDDA
Nail (French), CLOU
Native: Philippine, MORO
Nest: Of pheasants, NIDE
Network, RETE
No (German), NEIN
Noble: Mohammedan, AMIR
Notice: Death, OBIT
Novel: By Zola, NANA
Nursemaid: Oriental AMAH, AYAH, EYAH
Nut: Philippine, PILI
Oak: Holm, ILEX
Oil (comb. form), OLEO
Ostrich: American, RHEA
Oven, KILN, OAST
Owl: Barn, LULU
Ox: Celebes wild, ANOE
  Extinct wild, URUS
Palm, ATAP, NIPA, SAGO
Parliament, DIET
Parrot: New Zealand, KAKA
Pass: Indian mountain, GHAT
Passage: Closing (music), CODA
Peach: Clingstone, PAVY
Peasant: Indian, RYOT
  Old English, CARL
Pepper: Australasian, KAVA
Perfume, ATAR
Persia, IRAN
Person: Extraordinary, ONER
Pickerel or pike, ESOX
Pitcher, EWER
Plant: Aromatic, NARD
  Century, ALOE
  Indigo, ANIL
  Pepper, KAVA
Platform: Raised, DAIS
Plum: Wild, SLOE
Pods: Vegetable, OKRA, OKRO
Poem: Epic, EPOS
Poet: Persian, OMAR
  Roman, OVID
Poison, BANE
  Arrow, INEE
Porkfish, SISI
Portico: Greek, STOA
Premium, AGIO
Priest: Mohammedan, IMAM
Prima donna, DIVA
Prong: Fork, TINE
Pseudonym: Lamb's, ELIA
Queen: Carthaginian, DIDO
  Hindu, RANI
Rabbit, CONY
Race: Of Japan, AINU
Rail: Ducklike, COOT
  North American, SORA
Redshank, CLEE
Refuse: After pressing, MARC
Regiment: Turkish, ALAI
Reliquary, ARCA
Resort: Italian, LIDO
Ridges: Sandy, ASAR, OSAR
River: German, ELBE, ODER
  Italian, ADDA
  Siberian, LENA
Road: Roman, ITER
Rockfish: California, RENA
Rodent: Mouselike, VOLE
  South American, PACA
Rootstock, TARO
Salamander, NEWT
Salmon: Silver, COHO
  Young, PARR
Same (Greek), HOMO
  (Latin), IDEM
Sauce: Fish, ALEC
School: English, ETON
Seaweed, AGAR, ALGA, KELP
Secular, LAIC
Sediment, SILT
Seed: Dill, ANET
  Of vetch, TARE
Serf, ILOT
Sesame, TEEL
Settlement: Eskimo, ETAH
Shark: Atlantic, GATA
  European, TOPE
Sheep: Wild, UDAD
Sheltered, ALEE
Shield, EGIS
Ship: Jason's, ARGO
  Left side of, PORT
  Two-masted, BRIG
Shrine: Buddhist, TOPE
Shrub: New Zealand, TUTU

Sign: Magic, RUNE
Silkworm, ERIA
Skin: Beaver, PLEW
Skink: Egyptian, ADDA
Slave, ESNE
Sloth: Two-toed, UNAU
Smooth, LENE
Snow: Glacial, NEVE
Soapstone, TALC
Society: African secret, EGBO, PORO
Son: Of Seth, ENOS
Song (German), LIED
  Unaccompanied, GLEE
Sound: Lung, RALE
Sour, ACID
Sow: Young, GILT
Spike: Brad-shaped, BROB
Spirit: Buddhist evil, MARA
Stake: Poker, ANTE
Star: Temporary, NOVA
Starch: East Indian, SAGO
Stone: Precious, OPAL
Strap: Bridle, REIN
Strewn (heraldry), SEME
Sweetsop, ATES, ATTA
Sword: Fencing, EPEE, FOIL
Tambourine: African, TAAR
Tapir: Brazilian, ANTA
Tax, CESS
Tea: South American, MATE
Therefore (Latin), ERGO
Thing: Extraordinary, ONER
Three (dice, cards, etc.), TREY
Thrush: Hawaiian, OMAO
Tide, NEAP
Tipster: Racing, TOUT
Tissue, TELA
Title: Etruscan, LARS
  Hindu, BABU
  Indian, RAJA
  Mohammedan, EMIR, IMAM
  Persian, BABA
  Spanish, DONA
  Turkish, AGHA, BABA
Toad: Largest-known, AGUA
  Tree, HYLA
Tool: Cutting, ADZE
Track: Deer, SLOT
Tract: Sandy, DENE
Tree: Apple, SORB
  Central American, EBOE
  East Indian, TEAK
  Eucalyptus, YATE
  Guiana and Trinidad, MORA
  Javanese, UPAS
  Linden, LIME, LINN, TEIL, TILL
  Sandarac, ARAR
  Sassafras, AGUE
  Tamarisk salt, ATLE
Tribe: Moro, SULU
Trout, CHAR
Urchin: Street, ARAB
Vessel: Arab, DHOW
Vestment: Ecclesiastical, COPE
Vetch, TARE
Vine: East Indian, SOMA
Violinist: Famous, AUER
Vortex, EDDY
Wampum, PEAG
Wapiti, STAG
Waste: Allowance for, TRET
Watchman: Indian, MINA
Water (Spanish), AGUA
Waterfall, LINN
Wavy (heraldry), ONDE, UNDE
Wax, CERE
  Chinese, PELA
Weed: Biblical, TARE
Weight: Ancient, MINA
  Danish (pl.), ESER
  East Asian, TAEL
  Greek, MINA
  Siamese, BAHT
Well done (rare), EUGE
Whale, CETE
  Killer, ORCA
  White, HUSE, HUSO
Whirlpool, EDDY
Wife: Of Geraint, ENID
Willow: Virginia, ITEA
Wine, PORT
Winged, ALAR
  (Heraldry), AILE
Wings, ALAE
Withered, SERE
Without (French), SANS
Wool: To comb, CARD
Work, OPUS
Wrong: Civil, TORT
Young: Bring forth, YEAN

Words of Five Letters

Abode of dead: Babylonian, ARALU
Aborigine: Borneo DAYAK
Aftersong, EPODE
Aloe, AGAVE
Animal: Footless, APODE
Ant, EMMET
Antelope: African, ADDAX, BEISA, CAAMA, ELAND,
  GUIBA, ORIBI, TIANG
  Goat, GORAL, SEROW
  Indian, SASIN
  Siberian, SAIGA
Arch: Pointed, OGIVE
Armadillo, APARA, POYOU, TATOU
Arrowroot, ARARU
Artery: Trunk, AORTA
Association: Russian, ARTEL
  Secret, CABAL
Author: English, READE
Automaton, GOLEM, ROBOT
Award: Motion-picture, OSCAR
Basket: Fishing, CREEL
Beer: Russian, KVASS
Bible: Mohammedan, KORAN
Bird: Asian, MINAH, MYNAH
  Indian, SHAMA
  Larklike, PIPIT
  Loonlike, GREBE
  Oscine, VIREO
  South American, AGAMI
  Swimming, GREBE
Black: (French), NOIRE
  (Heraldry), SABLE
Blackbird: European, MERLE, OUSEL, OUZEL
Block: Glacial, SERAC
Blue (heraldry), AZURE
Boat: Eskimo, BIDAR, UMIAK
Bobwhite, COLIN, QUAIL
Bone (comb. form), OSTEO
  Leg, TIBIA
  Thigh, FEMUR
Broom: Twig, BESOM
Brother (French), FRERE
  Moses, AARON
Canoe: Eskimo, BIDAR, KAYAK
Cape: Papal, FANON, ORALE
Caravansary, SERAI
Card: Old playing, TAROT
Caterpillar: New Zealand, AWETO
Catkin, AMENT
Cavity: Stone, GEODE
Cephalopod, SQUID
Cetacean, WHALE
Chariot, ESSED
Cheek: Pertaining to, MALAR
Chieftain: Arab, EMEER
Child (Scotch), BAIRN
Cigar, CLARO
Coating: Seed, TESTA
Cockatoo: Palm, ARARA
Coin: Costa Rican, COLON
  Danish, KRONE
  Ecuadorian, SUCRE
  English, GROAT, PENCE
  French, FRANC
  German, KRONE, TALER
  Hungarian, PENGO
  Icelandic, KRONA
  Indian, RUPEE
  Iraqi, DINAR
  Norwegian, KRONE
  Polish, ZLOTY
  Russian, COPEC, KOPEK, RUBLE
  Swedish, KRONA
  Turkish, ASPER
  Yugoslav, DINAR
Collar: Papal, FANON, ORALE
  Roman, RABAT
Commune: Italian, TREIA
Composition: Choral, MOTET
Compound: Chemical, ESTER
Conceal (law), ELOIN
Council: Ecclesiastical, SYNOD
Court: Anglo-Saxon, GEMOT
  Inner, PATIO
Crest: Mountain, ARETE
Crown: Papal, TIARA
Cuttlefish, SEPIA
Date: Roman, NONES
Decree: Mohammedan, IRADE
  Russian, UKASE
Deposit: Loam, LOESS
Desert: Gobi, SHAMO

Devilfish, MANTA
Disease: Cereals, ERGOT
Disk, PATEN
Dog: Wild, DHOLE, DINGO
Dormouse, LEROT
Drum, TABOR
Duck: Sea, EIDER
Dynasty: Chinese, CHING, LIANG, SHANG
Earthquake, SEISM
Eel, ELVER, MORAY
Ermine: European, STOAT
Ether: Crystalline, APIOL
Fabric: Velvetlike, PANNE
Fabulist, AESOP
Family: Italian, CENCI
Fiber: West Indian, SISAL
Fig: Smyrna, ELEME, ELEMI
Figure: Of speech, TROPE
Finch: European, SERIN
Fish: American small, KILLY
Flower: Garden, ASTER
Friend (Spanish), AMIGO
Fruit: Tropical, MANGO
Fungus: Rye, ERGOT
Furze, GORSE
Gateway, TORAN, TORII
Gem, AGATE, BERYL, PEARL, TOPAZ
Genus: Barnacles, LEPAS
  Bears, URSUS
  Birds (loons), GAVIA
  Birds (nuthatches), SITTA
  Cats, FELIS
  Dogs, CANIS
  Fishes (chiros), ELOPS
  Fishes (perch), PERCA
  Geese, ANSER
  Grasses, STIPA
  Grasses (incl. oats), AVENA
  Gulls, LARUS
  Hares, rabbits, LEPUS
  Hawks, BUTEO
  Herbs, old world, INULA
  Herbs, trailing or climbing, APIOS
  Herbs, tropical, TACCA, URENA
  Horses, EQUUS
  Insects (olive flies), DACUS
  Lice, plant, APHIS
  Lichens, USNEA
  Lizards, AGAMA
  Moles, TALPA
  Mollusks, OLIVA
  Monkeys, CEBUS
  Palms, ARECA
  Pigeons, GOURA
  Plants (amaryllis family), AGAVE
  Ruminants (goats), CAPRA
  Shrubs, Asiatic, SABIA
  Shrubs (heath), ERICA
  Shrubs (incl. raspberry), RUBUS
  Shrubs, tropical, IXORA, TREMA, URENA
  Ticks, ARGAS
  Trees (of elm family), TREMA, ULMUS
  Trees, tropical, IXORA, TREMA
Goat: Bezoar, PASAN
God: Assyrian, ASHIR, ASHUR, ASSUR
  Babylonian, DAGAN, SIRIS
  Gaelic, DAGDA
  Hindu, BHAGA, INDRA, SHIVA
  Japanese, EBISU
  Philistine, DAGON
  Phrygian, ATTIS
  Teutonic, AEGIR, GYMIR
  Welsh, DYLAN
Goddess: Babylonian, ISTAR, NANAI
  Hindu, DURGA, GAURI, SHREE
Group: Of six, HEXAD
Grove: Sacred to Diana, NEMUS
Growing out, ENATE
Guitar: Hindu, SITAR
Gull: PEWEE, PEWIT
Hartebeest, CAAMA
Headdress: Jewish or Persian, TIARA
  Liturgical, MITER, MITRE
Heath, ERICA
Herb: Grasslike marsh, SEDGE
Heron, EGRET
Hog: Young, SHOAT, SHOTE
Image, EIKON
Indian: Cariban, ARARA
  Iroquoian, HURON
  Mexican, AZTEC, OPATA, OTOMI
  Muskhogean, CREEK
  Siouan, OSAGE, TETON
  Spanish American, ARARA, CARIB
Inflorescence: Racemose, AMENT
Insect: Immature, LARVA
Intrigue, CABAL
Iris: Yellow, SEDGE
Juniper, GORSE, RETEM
Kidneys: Pertaining to, RENAL
King: British legendary, LLUDD
Kite: European, GLEDE
Kobold, NISSE
Land: Cultivated, ARADA, ARADO
Landholder (Scotch), LAIRD, THANE
Language: Dravidian, TAMIL
Lariat, LASSO, REATA
Laughing, RIANT
Lawgiver: Athenian, DRACO, SOLON
Leaf: Calyx, SEPAL
  Fern, FROND
Lemur, LORIS
Letter: English, AITCH
  Greek, ALPHA, DELTA, GAMMA, KAPPA, OMEGA, SIGMA, THETA
Hebrew, ALEPH, CHETH, GIMEL, SADHE, ZAYIN
Lichen, USNEA
Lighthouse, PHARE
Lizard: Old World, AGAMA
Loincloth, DHOTI
Louse: Plant, APHID
Macaw: Brazilian, ARARA
Mahogany: Philippine, ALMON
Mammal: Badgerlike, RATEL
  Civetlike, GENET
  Giraffelike, OKAPI
  Raccoonlike, COATI
Man (French), HOMME
Marble, AGATE
Mark: Insertion, CARET
Market place: Greek, AGORA
Marsupial: Australian, KOALA
Measure: Electric, FARAD, HENRY
  Energy, JOULE
  Metric, LITER, STERE
  Printing, AGATE
  Russian, VERST
Mixture: Smelting, MATTE
Mohicans: Last of, UNCAS
Molding: Convex, OVOLO, TORUS
Mole, TALPA
Monkey: African, PATAS
  Capuchin, SAJOU
  Howling, ARABA
Monkshood, ATEES
Month: Jewish, NISAN, SIVAN, TEBET
Museum (French), MUSEE
Musketeer, ATHOS
Native: Aleutian, ALEUT
  New Zealand, MAORI
Neckpiece: Ecclesiastical, AMICE
Nerve (comb. form), NEURO
Nest: Eagle's or hawk's, AERIE
  Insect's, NIDUS
Net: Fishing, SEINE
Newsstand, KIOSK
Nitrogen, AZOTE
Noble: Mohammedan, AMEER
Nodule: Stone, GEODE
Nostrils, NARES
Notched irregularly, EROSE
Nymph: Mohammedan, HOURI
Official: Roman, EDILE
Oleoresin, ELEMI
Opening: Mouthlike, STOMA
Oration: Funeral, ELOGE
Ostiole, STOMA
Page: Left-hand, VERSO
  Right-hand, RECTO
Palm, ARECA, BETEL

Park: Colorado, ESTES
Perfume, ATTAR
Philosopher: Greek, PLATO
Pillar: Stone, STELA, STELE
Pinnacle: Glacial, SERAC
Plain, LLANO
Plant: Century, AGAVE
  Climbing, LIANA
  Dwarf, CUMIN
  East Asian perennial, RAMIE
  Medicinal, SENNA
  Mustard family, CRESS
Plate: Communion, PATEN
Poem: Lyric, EPODE
Point: Lowest, NADIR
Poplar, ABELE, ALAMO, ASPEN
Porridge: Spanish American, ATOLE
Post: Stair, NEWEL
Priest: Mohammedan, IMAUM
Protozoan, AMEBA
Queen: (French), REINE
  Hindu, RANEE
Rabbit, CONEY
Rail, CRAKE
Red (heraldry), GULES
Religion: Moslem, ISLAM
Resin, ELEMI
Revoke (law), ADEEM
Rich man, MIDAS, NABOB
Ridge: Sandy, ESKAR, ESKER
River: French, LOIRE, SEINE
Rockfish: California, REINA
Rootstock: Fragrant, ORRIS
Ruff: Female, REEVE
Sack: Pack, KYACK
Salt: Ethereal, ESTER
Saltpeter, NITER, NITRE
Salutation: Eastern, SALAM
Sandpiper: Old World, TEREK
Scented, OLENT
School: Fish, SHOAL
  French public, LYCEE
Scriptures: Mohammedan, KORAN
Seaweeds, ALGAE
Seed: Aromatic, ANISE
Seraglio, HAREM, SERAI
Serf, HELOT
Sheep: Wild, AUDAD
Sheeplike, OVINE
Shield, AEGIS
Shoe: Wooden, SABOT
Shoots: Pickled bamboo, ACHAR
Shot: Billiard, CAROM, MASSE
Shrine: Buddhist, STUPA
Shrub: Burning bush, WAHOO
  Ornamental evergreen, TOYON
  Used in tanning, SUMAC
Silk: Watered, MOIRE
Sister (French), SOEUR
  (Latin), SOROR
Six: Group of, HEXAD
Skeleton: Marine, CORAL
Slave, HELOT
Snake, ABOMA, ADDER, COBRA, RACER
Soldier: French, POILU
  Indian, SEPOY
Sour, ACERB
Spirit: Air, ARIEL
Staff: Shepherd's, CROOK
Starwort, ASTER
Steel (German), STAHL
Stockade: Russian, ETAPE
Stop (nautical), AVAST
Storehouse, ETAPE
Subway: Parisian, METRO
Tapestry, ARRAS
Tea: Paraguayan, YERBA
Temple: Hawaiian, HEIAU
Terminal: Positive, ANODE
Theater: Greek, ODEON, ODEUM
Then (French), ALORS
Thread: Surgical, SETON
Thrush: Wilson's, VEERY
Title: Hindu, BABOO
  Indian, RAJAH, SAHEB, SAHIB
  Mohammedan, EMEER, IMAUM
Tree: Buddhist sacred, PIPAL
  East Indian cotton, SIMAL
  Hickory, PECAN
  Light-wooded, BALSA
  Malayan, TERAP
  Mediterranean, CAROB
  Mexican, ABETO
  Mexican pine, OCOTE
  New Zealand, MAIRE
  Philippine, ALMON
  Rain, SAMAN
  South American, UMBRA
  Tamarack, LARCH
  Tamarisk salt, ATLEE
  West Indian, ACANA
Trout, CHARR
Troy, ILION, ILIUM
Twin: Siamese, CHANG
Vestment: Ecclesiastical, STOLE
Violin: Famous, AMATI, STRAD
Volcano: Mud, SALSE
Wampum, PEAGE
War cry: Greek, ALALA
Wavy (heraldry), UNDEE
Weight: Jewish, GERAH
Wen, TALPA
Wheat, SPELT
Wheel: Persian water, NORIA
Whitefish, CISCO
Willow, OSIER
Window: Bay, ORIEL
Wine, MEDOC, RHINE, TINTA, TOKAY
Winged, ALATE
Woman (French), FEMME
Year: Excess of solar over lunar, EPACT
Zoroastrian, PARSI

Words of Six or More Letters

Agave, MAGUEY
Alkaloid: Crystalline, ESERIN, ESERINE
Alligator, CAYMAN
Amphibole, EDENITE, URALITE
Ant: White, TERMITE
Antelope: African, DIKDIK, DUIKER, GEMSBOK, IMPALA, KOODOO
  European, CHAMOIS
  Indian, NILGAI, NILGAU, NILGHAI, NILGHAU
Ape: Asian or East Indian, GIBBON
Appendage: Leaf, STIPEL, STIPULE
Armadillo, PELUDO, TATOUAY
Arrowroot, ARARAO
Ascetic: Jewish, ESSENE
Ass: Asian wild, ONAGER
Avatar: Of Vishnu, KRISHNA
Babylonian, ELAMITE
Badge: Shoulder, EPAULET
Baldness, ALOPECIA
Barracuda, SENNET
Bark: Aromatic, SINTOC
Bearlike, URSINE
Beetle, ELATER
Bible: Zoroastrian, AVESTA
Bird: Sea, PETREL
  South American, SERIEMA
  Wading, AVOCET, AVOSET
Bone: Leg, FIBULA
Branched, RAMATE
Brother (Latin), FRATER
Bunting: European, ORTOLAN
Call: Trumpet, SENNET
Canoe: Eskimo, BAIDAR, OOMIAK
Caravansary, IMARET
Cat: Asian or African, CHEETAH
  Leopardlike, OCELOT
Cenobite: Jewish, ESSENE
Centerpiece: Table, EPERGNE

Cetacean, DOLPHIN, PORPOISE
Chariot, ESSEDA, ESSEDE
Chief: Seminole, OSCEOLA
Claim: Release as (law), REMISE
Clock: Water, CLEPSYDRA
Cloud, CUMULUS, NIMBUS
Coach: French hackney, FIACRE
Coin: Czech, KORUNA
  Ethiopian, TALARI
  Finnish, MARKKA
  German, THALER
  Greek, DRACHMA
  Haitian, GOURDE
  Honduran, LEMPIRA
  Hungarian, FORINT
  Indo-Chinese, PIASTER
  Netherlands, GUILDER
  Panamanian, BALBOA
  Paraguayan, GUARANI
  Portuguese, ESCUDO
  Russian, COPECK, KOPECK, ROUBLE
  Spanish, PESETA
  Venezuelan, BOLIVAR
Communion: Last holy, VIATICUM
Conceal (law), ELOIGN
Confection, PRALINE
Construction: Sentence, SYNTAX
Convexity: Shaft of column, ENTASIS
Court: Anglo-Saxon, GEMOTE
Cow: Sea, DUGONG, MANATEE
Cylindrical, TERETE
Dagger, STILETTO
  Malay, CREESE, KREESE
Date: Roman, CALENDS, KALENDS
Deer, CARIBOU, WAPITI
Disease: Plant, ERINOSE
Doorkeeper, OSTIARY
Dragonflies: Order of, ODANATA
Drink: Of gods, NECTAR
Drum: TABOUR
  Moorish, ATABAL, ATTABAL
Duck: Fish-eating, MERGANSER
  Sea, SCOTER
Dynasty: Chinese, MANCHU
Eel, CONGER
Edit, REDACT
Envelope: Flower, PERIANTH
Eskimo, AMERIND
Ether: Crystalline, APIOLE
Excuse (law), ESSOIN
Eyespots, OCELLI
Fabric, ESTAMENE, ESTAMIN, ETAMINE
Falcon: European, KESTREL
Figure: Used as column, CARYATID, TELAMON
Fine: For punishment, AMERCE
Fish: Asian fresh-water, GOURAMI
  Pikelike, BARRACUDA
Five: Group of, PENTAD
Fly: African, TSETSE
Foot: Metric, ANAPEST, IAMBUS
Foxlike, VULPINE
Frying pan, SPIDER
Fur, KARAKUL
Galley: Greek or Roman, BIREME, TRIREME
Game: Card, ECARTE
Garment: Greek, CHLAMYS
Gateway, GOPURA, TORANA
Genus: Birds (ravens, crows), CORVUS
  Eels, CONGER
  Fishes, ANABAS
  Foxes, VULPES
  Herbs, ANEMONE
  Insects, CICADA
  Lemurs, GALAGO
  Mints (incl. catnip), NEPETA
  Mollusks, ANOMIA, ASTARTE, TEREDO
  Mollusks (incl. oysters), OSTREA
  Monkeys (spider monkeys), ATELES
  Thrushes (incl. robins), TURDUS
  Trees (of elm family), CELTIS
  Trees (inc. dogwood), CORNUS
  Trees, tropical American, SAPOTA
  Wrens, NANNUS
Gibbon, SIAMANG, WOUWOU
Gland: Salivary, RACEMOSE

Goat: Bezoar, PASANG
Goatlike, CAPRINE
God: Assyrian, ASHSHUR, ASSHUR
  Babylonian, BABBAR, MARDUK, MERODACH, NANNAR, NERGAL, SHAMASH
  Hindu, BRAHMA, KRISHNA, VISHNU
  Tahitian, TAAROA
Goddess: Babylonian, ISHTAR
  Hindu, CHANDI, HAIMAVATI, LAKSHMI, PARVATI, SARASVATI, SARASWATI
Government, POLITY
Governor: Persian, SATRAP
Grandson (Scotch), NEPOTE
Group: Of five, PENTAD
  Of nine, ENNEAD
  Of seven, HEPTAD
Hare: in first year, LEVERET
Harpsichord, SPINET
Herb: Alpine, EDELWEISS
  Chinese, GINSENG
  South African, FREESIA
Hermit, EREMITE
Hero: Legendary, PALADIN
Heron, BITTERN
Horselike, EQUINE
Hound: Short-legged, BEAGLE
House (French), MAISON
Idiot, CRETIN
Implement: Stone, NEOLITH
Incarnation: Hindu, AVATAR
Indian, APACHE, COMANCHE, PAIUTE, SENECA
Inn: Turkish, IMARET
Insects: Order of, DIPTERA
Instrument: Japanese banjolike, SAMISEN
  Musical, CLAVIER, SPINET
Interstice, AREOLA
Ironwood, COLIMA
Juniper: Old Testament, RAETAM
Kettledrum, ATABAL
King: Fairy, OBERON
Kneecap, PATELLA
Knife, MACHETE
Langur: Sumatran, SIMPAI
Legislature: Spanish, CORTES
Lemur: African, GALAGO
  Madagascar, AYEAYE
Letter: Greek, EPSILON, LAMBDA, OMICRON, UPSILON
  Hebrew, DALETH, LAMEDH, SAMEKH
Lighthouse, PHAROS
Lizard, IGUANA
Llama, ALPACA
Lockjaw, TETANUS
Locust, CICADA, CICALA
Macaw: Brazilian, MARACAN
Maid: Of Astolat, ELAINE
Mammal: Madagascar, TENDRAC, TENREC
Man (Spanish), HOMBRE
Marmoset: South American, TAMARIN
Marsupial, BANDICOOT, WOMBAT
Massacre, POGROM
Mayor: Spanish, ALCALDE
Measure: Electric, AMPERE, COULOMB, KILOWATT
Medicine: Quack, NOSTRUM
Member: Religious order, CENOBITE
Molasses, TREACLE
Monkey: African, GRIVET, NISNAS
  Asian, LANGUR
  Philippine, MACHIN
  South American, PINCHE, SAIMIRI, SAMIRI, SAPAJOU
Monster, CHIMERA, GORGON
  (Comb. form), TERATO
  Cretan, MINOTAUR
Month: Jewish, HESHVAN, KISLEV, SHEBAT, TAMMUZ, TISHRI, VEADAR
Mountain: Asia Minor, ARARAT
Mulct, AMERCE
Musketeer, ARAMIS, PORTHOS
Nearsighted, MYOPIC
Net, TRAMMEL
New York City, GOTHAM
Nine: Group of, ENNEAD
Nobleman: Spanish, GRANDEE
Official: Roman, AEDILE
Onyx: Mexican, TECALI
Order: Dragonflies, ODANATA

Insects, DIPTERA
Organ: Plant, PISTIL
Ornament: Shoulder, EPAULET
Overcoat: Military, CAPOTE
Ox: Wild, BANTENG
Oxidation: Bronze or copper, PATINA
Paralysis: Incomplete, PARESIS
Pear: Alligator, AVOCADO
Persimmon: Mexican, CHAPOTE
Pipe: Peace, CALUMET
Plaid (Scotch), TARTAN
Plain, PAMPAS, STEPPE, TUNDRA
Plant: Buttercup family, ANEMONE
  Century, MAGUEY
  On rocks, LICHEN
Plowing: Fit for, ARABLE
Poem: Heroic, EPOPEE
  Six-lined, SESTET
Point: Highest, ZENITH
Potion: Love, PHILTER, PHILTRE
Protozoan, AMOEBA
Punish, AMERCE
Purple (heraldry), PURPURE
Queen: Fairy, TITANIA
Race: Skiing, SLALOM
Rat, BANDICOOT, LEMMING
Retort, RIPOST, RIPOSTE
Ring: Harness, TERRET
  Little, ANNULET
Rodent: Jumping, JERBOA
  Spanish American, AGOUTI, AGOUTY
Sailor: East Indian, LASCAR
Salmon: Young, GRILSE
Salutation: Eastern, SALAAM
Sandpiper, PLOVER
Sandy, ARENOSE
Sapodilla, SAPOTA, SAPOTE
Saw: Surgical, TREPAN
Seven: Group of, HEPTAD
Sexes: Common to both, EPICENE
Shawl: Mexican, SERAPE
Sheathing: Flower, SPATHE
Sheep: Wild, AOUDAD, ARGALI
Shipworm, TEREDO
Shoes: Mercury's winged, TALARIA
Shortening: Syllable, SYSTOLE
Shrub, SPIRAEA
Sickle-shaped, FALCATE
Silver (heraldry), ARGENT
Snake, ANACONDA
Speech: Loss of, APHASIA
Spiral, HELICAL
Staff: Bishop's, CROSIER, CROZIER
Stalk: Plant, PETIOLE
State: Swiss, CANTON
Studio, ATELIER
Swan: Young, CYGNET
Swimming, NATANT
Sword-shaped, ENSATE
Terminal: Negative, CATHODE
Third (music), TIERCE
Thrust: Fencing, RIPOST, RIPOSTE
Tile: Pertaining to, TEGULAR
Tomb: Empty, CENOTAPH
Tooth (comb. form), ODONTO
Tower: Mohammedan, MINARET
Tree: African timber, BAOBAB
  Black gum, TUPELO
  East Indian, MARGOSA
  Locust, ACACIA
  Malayan, SINTOC
  Marmalade, SAPOTE
Urn: Tea, SAMOVAR
Vehicle, LANDAU, TROIKA
Verbose, PROLIX
Viceroy: Egyptian, KHEDIVE
Vulture: American, CONDOR
Warehouse (French), ENTREPOT
Whale: White, BELUGA
Whirlpool, VORTEX
Will: Addition to, CODICIL
  Having left, TESTATE
Wind, CHINOOK, MONSOON, SIMOOM, SIMOON, SIROCCO
Window: In roof, DORMER
Wine, BARBERA, BURGUNDY, CABERNET, CHABLIS, CHIANTI, CLARET, MUSCATEL, RIESLING, SAUTERNE, SHERRY, ZINFANDEL
Wolfish, LUPINE
Woman: Boisterous, TERMAGANT
Woolly, LANATE
Workshop, ATELIER
Zoroastrian, PARSEE

Old-Testament Names

(We do not pretend that this list is all-inclusive. We include only those names which in our opinion one meets most often in crossword puzzles.)

Aaron: First high priest of Jews; son of Amram; brother of Miriam and Moses; father of Abihu, Eleazer, Ithamar, and Nadab.

Abel: Son of Adam; slain by Cain.

Abigail: Wife of Nabal; later, wife of David.

Abihu: Son of Aaron.

Abimelech: King of Gerar.

Abner: Commander of army of Saul and Ishbosheth; slain by Joab.

Abraham (or Abram): Patriarch; forefather of the Jews; son of Terah; husband of Sarah; father of Isaac and Ishmael.

Absalom: Son of David and Maacah; revolted against David; slain by Joab.

Achish: King of Gath; gave refuge to David.

Achsa (or Achsah): Daughter of Caleb; wife of Othniel.

Adah: Wife of Lamech.

Adam: First man; husband of Eve; father of Cain, Abel, and Seth.

Adonijah: Son of David and Haggith.

Agag: King of Amalek; spared by Saul; slain by Samuel.

Ahasuerus: King of Persia; husband of Vashti and, later, Esther; sometimes identified with Xerxes the Great.

Ahijah: Prophet; foretold accession of Jeroboam.

Ahinoam: Wife of David.

Amasa: Commander of army of David; slain by Joab.

Amnon: Son of David and Ahinoam; ravished Tamar; slain by Absalom.

Amram: Husband of Jochebed; father of Aaron, Miriam and Moses.

Asenath: Wife of Joseph.

Asher: Son of Jacob and Zilpah.

Balaam: Prophet; rebuked by his donkey for cursing God.

Barak: Jewish captain; associated with Deborah.

Baruch: Secretary to Jeremiah.

Bathsheba: Wife of Uriah; later, wife of David.

Belshazzar: Crown prince of Babylon.

Benaiah: Warrior of David; proclaimed Solomon King.

Ben-Hadad: Name of several kings of Damascus.

Benjamin: Son of Jacob and Rachel.

Bezaleel: Chief architect of tabernacle.

Bilbah: Servant of Rachel; mistress of Jacob.

Bildad: Comforter of Job.

Boaz: Husband of Ruth; father of Obed.

Cain: Son of Adam and Eve; slayer of Abel; father of Enoch.

Cainan: Son of Enos.

Caleb: Spy sent out by Moses to visit Canaan; father of Achsa.

Canaan: Son of Ham.

Chilion: Son of Elimelech; husband of Orpah.

Cush: Son of Ham; father of Nimrod.

Dan: Son of Jacob and Bilhah.

Daniel: Prophet; saved from lions by God.

Deborah: Hebrew prophetess; helped Israelites conquer Canaanites.

Delilah: Mistress and betrayer of Samson.

Elam: Son of Shem.

Eleazar: Son of Aaron; succeeded him as high priest.

Eli: High priest and judge; teacher of Samuel; father of Hophni and Phinehas.
Eliakim: Chief minister of Hezekiah.
Eliezer: Servant of Abraham.
Elihu: Comforter of Job.
Elijah (or Elias): Prophet; went to heaven in chariot of fire.
Elimelech: Husband of Naomi; father of Chilion and Mahlon.
Eliphaz: Comforter of Job.
Elisha (or Eliseus): Prophet; successor of Elijah.
Elkanah: Husband of Hannah; father of Samuel.
Enoch: Son of Cain.
Enoch: Father of Methuselah.
Enos: Son of Seth; father of Cainan.
Ephraim: Son of Joseph.
Esau: Son of Isaac and Rebecca; sold his birthright to his brother Jacob.
Esther: Jewish wife of Ahasuerus; saved Jews from Haman's plotting.
Eve: First woman; created from rib of Adam.
Ezra (or Esdras): Hebrew scribe and priest.
Gad: Son of Jacob and Zilpah.
Gehazi: Servant of Elisha.
Gideon: Israelite hero; defeated Midianites.
Goliath: Philistine giant; slain by David.
Hagar: Handmaid of Sarah; concubine of Abraham; mother of Ishmael.
Haggith: Mother of Adonijah.
Ham: Son of Noah; father of Cush, Mizraim, Phut, and Canaan.
Haman: Chief minister of Ahasuerus; hanged on gallows prepared for Mordecai.
Hannah: Wife of Elkanah; mother of Samuel.
Hanun: King of Ammonites.
Haran: Brother of Abraham; father of Lot.
Hazael: King of Damascus.
Hephzi-Bah: Wife of Hezekiah; mother of Mannaseh.
Hiram: King of Tyre.
Holofernes: General of Nebuchadnezzar; slain by Judith.
Hophni: Son of Eli.
Isaac: Hebrew patriarch; son of Abraham and Sarah; half brother of Ishmael; husband of Rebecca; father of Esau and Jacob.
Ishmael: Son of Abraham and Hagar; half brother of Isaac.
Issachar: Son of Jacob and Leah.
Ithamar: Son of Aaron.
Jabal: Son of Lamech and Adah.
Jabin: King of Hazor.
Jacob: Hebrew patriarch, founder of Israel; son of Isaac and Rebecca; husband of Leah and Rachel; father of Asher, Benjamin, Dan, Gad, Issachar, Joseph, Judah, Levi, Naphtali, Reuben, Simeon, and Zebulun.
Jael: Slayer of Sisera.
Japheth: Son of Noah.
Jehoiada: High priest; husband of Jehoshabeath; revolted against Athaliah and made Joash King of Judah.
Jehoshabeath (or Jehosheba): Daughter of Jehoram of Judah; wife of Jehoiada.
Jephthah: Judge in Israel; sacrificed his only daughter because of vow.
Jesse: Son of Obed; father of David.
Jethro: Midianite priest; father of Zipporah.
Jezebel: Phoenician princess; wife of Ahab; mother of Ahaziah, Athaliah, and Jehoram.
Joab: Commander in chief under David; slayer of Abner, Absalom, and Amasa.
Job: Patriarch; underwent many afflictions; comforted by Bildad, Elihu, Eliphaz and Zophar.
Jochebed: Wife of Amram.
Jonah: Prophet; cast into sea and swallowed by great fish.
Jonathan: Son of Saul; friend of David.
Joseph: Son of Jacob and Rachel; sold into slavery by his brothers; husband of Asenath; father of Ephraim and Manassah.
Joshua: Successor of Moses; son of Nun.
Jubal: Son of Lamech and Adah.
Judah: Son of Jacob and Leah.
Judith: Slayer of Holofernes.
Kish: Father of Saul.
Laban: Father of Leah and Rachel.
Lamech: Son of Methuselah; father of Noah.
Lamech: Husband of Adah and Zillah; father of Jabal, Jubal, and Tubal-Cain.
Leah: Daughter of Laban; wife of Jacob.
Levi: Son of Jacob and Leah.
Lot: Son of Haran; escaped destruction of Sodom.
Maacah: Mother of Absalom and Tamar.
Mahlon: Son of Elimelech; first husband of Ruth.
Manasseh: Son of Joseph.
Melchizedek: King of Salem.
Methuselah: Patriarch; son of Enoch; father of Lamech.
Michal: Daughter of Saul; wife of David.
Miriam: Prophetess; daughter of Amram; sister of Aaron and Moses.
Mizraim: Son of Ham.
Mordecai: Uncle of Esther; with her aid, saved Jews from Haman's plotting.
Moses: Prophet and lawgiver; son of Amram; brother of Aaron and Miriam; husband of Zipporah.
Naaman: Syrian captain; cured of leprosy by Elisha.
Nabal: Husband of Abigail.
Naboth: Owner of vineyard; stoned to death because he would not sell it to Ahab.
Nadab: Son of Aaron.
Nahor: Father of Terah.
Naomi: Wife of Elimelech; mother-in-law of Ruth.
Naphtali: Son of Jacob and Bilhah.
Nathan: Prophet; reproved David for causing Uriah's death.
Nebuchadnezzar (or Nebuchadrezzar): King of Babylon; destroyer of Jerusalem.
Nehemiah: Jewish leader; empowered by Artaxerxes to rebuild Jerusalem.
Nimrod: Mighty hunter; son of Cush.
Noah: Patriarch; Son of Lamech; escaped Deluge by building Ark; father of Ham, Japheth and Shem.
Nun (or Non): Father of Joshua.
Obed: Son of Boaz; father of Jesse.
Og: King of Bashan.
Orpah: Wife of Chilion.
Othniel: Kenezite; judge of Israel; husband of Achsa.
Phinehas: Son of Eleazer.
Phinehas: Son of Eli.
Phut (or Put): Son of Ham.
Potiphar: Egyptian official; bought Joseph.
Rachel: Wife of Jacob.
Rebecca (or Rebekah): Wife of Isaac.
Reuben: Son of Jacob and Leah.
Ruth: Wife of Mahlon, later of Boaz; daughter-in-law of Naomi.
Samson: Judge of Israel; famed for strength; betrayed by Delilah.
Samuel: Hebrew judge and prophet; son of Elkanah.
Sarah (or Sara, Sarai): Wife of Abraham.
Sennacherib: King of Assyria.
Seth: Son of Adam; father of Enos.
Shem: Son of Noah; father of Elam.
Simeon: Son of Jacob and Leah.
Sisera: Canaanite captain; slain by Jael.
Tamar: Daughter of David and Maachah; ravished by Amnon.
Terah: Son of Nahor; father of Abraham.
Tubal-Cain: Son of Lamech and Zillah.
Uriah: Husband of Bathsheba; sent to death in battle by David.
Vashti: Wife of Ahasuerus; set aside by him.
Zadok: High priest during David's reign.
Zebulun (or Zabulon): Son of Jacob and Leah.
Zillah: Wife of Lamech.
Zilpah: Servant of Leah; mistress of Jacob.
Zipporah: Daughter of Jethro; wife of Moses.
Zophar: Comforter of Job.

Kings of Judah and Israel

Kings Before Division of Kingdom

Saul: First King of Israel; son of Kish; father of Ish-Bosheth, Jonathan and Michal.

Ish-Bosheth (or Eshbaal): King of Israel; son of Saul.

David: King of Judah; later of Israel; son of Jesse; husband of Abigail, Ahinoam, Bathsheba, Michal, etc.; father of Absalom, Adonijah, Amnon, Solomon, Tamar, etc.

Solomon: King of Israel and Judah; son of David; father of Rehoboam.

Rehoboam: Son of Solomon; during his reign the kingdom was divided into Judah and Israel.

Kings of Judah (Southern Kingdom)

Rehoboam: First King.

Abijah (or Abijam or Abia): Son of Rehoboam.

Asa: Probably son of Abijah.

Jehoshaphat: Son of Asa.

Jehoram (or Joram): Son of Jehoshaphat; husband of Athaliah.

Ahaziah: Son of Jehoram and Athaliah.

Athaliah: Daughter of King Ahab of Israel and Jezebel; wife of Jehoram.

Joash (or Jehoash): Son of Ahaziah.

Amaziah: Son of Joash.

Uzziah (or Azariah): Son of Amaziah.

Jotham: Regent, later King; son of Uzziah.

Ahaz: Son of Jotham.

Hezekiah: Son of Ahaz; husband of Hephzi-Bah.

Manasseh: Son of Hezekiah and Hephzi-Bah.

Amon: Son of Manasseh.

Josiah (or Josias): Son of Amon.

Jehoahaz (or Joahaz): Son of Josiah.

Jehoiachin: Son of Jehoiakim.

Jehoiakim: Son of Josiah.

Zedekiah: Son of Josiah; kingdom overthrown by Babylonians under Nebuchadnezzar.

Kings of Israel (Northern Kingdom)

Jeroboam I: Led secession of Israel.

Nadab: Son of Jeroboam I.

Baasha: Overthrew Nadab.

Elah: Son of Baasha.

Zimri: Overthrew Elah.

Omri: Overthrew Zimri.

Ahab: Son of Omri; husband of Jezebel.

Ahaziah: Son of Ahab.

Jehoram (or Joram): Son of Ahab.

Jehu: Overthrew Jehoram.

Jehoahaz (or Joahaz): Son of Jehu.

Jehoash (or Joash): Son of Jehoahaz.

Jeroboam II: Son of Jehoash.

Zechariah: Son of Jeroboam II.

Shallum: Overthrew Zechariah.

Menahem: Overthrew Shallum.

Pekahiah: Son of Menahem.

Pekah: Overthrew Pekahiah.

Hoshea: Overthrew Pekah; kingdom overthrown by Assyrians under Sargon II.

Prophets

Major.—Isaiah, Jeremiah, Ezekiel, Daniel.

Minor.—Hosea, Obadiah, Nahum, Haggai, Joel, Jonah, Habakkuk, Zechariah, Amos, Micah, Zephaniah, Malachi.

Greek and Roman Mythology

(Most of the Greek deities were adopted by the Romans, although in many cases there was a change of name. In the list below, information is given under the Greek name; the name in parentheses is the Latin equivalent. However, all Latin names are listed with cross references to the Greek ones. In addition, there are several deities which were exclusively Roman.)

Acheron: *See* Rivers.

Achilles: Greek warrior; slew Hector at Troy; slain by Paris, who wounded him in his vulnerable heel.

Actaeon: Hunter; surprised Artemis bathing; changed by her to stag and killed by his dogs.

Admetus: King of Thessaly; his wife, Alcestis, offered to die in his place.

Adonis: Beautiful youth loved by Aphrodite.

Aeacus: One of three judges of dead in Hades; son of Zeus.

Aeëtes: King of Colchis; father of Medea; keeper of Golden Fleece.

Aegeus: Father of Theseus; believing Theseus killed in Crete, he drowned himself, Aegean Sea named for him.

Aegisthus: Son of Thyestes; slew Atreus; with Clytemnestra, his paramour, slew Agamemnon; slain by Orestes.

Aegyptus: Brother of Danaus; his sons, except Lynceus, slain by Danaides.

Aeneas: Trojan; son of Anchises and Aphrodite; after fall of Troy, led his followers eventually to Italy; loved and deserted Dido.

Aeolus: *See* Winds.

Aesculapius: *See* Asclepius.

Aeson: King of Ioclus; father of Jason; overthrown by his brother Pelias; restored to youth by Medea.

Aether: Personification of sky.

Aethra: Mother of Theseus.

Agamemnon: King of Mycenae; son of Atreus; brother of Menelaus; leader of Greeks against Troy; slain on his return home by Clytemnestra and Aegisthus.

Agiaia: *See* Graces.

Ajax: Greek warrior; killed himself at Troy because Achilles' armor was awarded to Odysseus.

Alcestis: Wife of Admetus; offered to die in his place but saved from death by Hercules.

Alcmene: Wife of Amphitryon; mother by Zeus of Hercules.

Alcyone: *See* Pleiades.

Alecto: *See* Furies.

Alectryon: Youth changed by Ares into cock.

Althaea: Wife of Oeneus; mother of Meleager.

Amazons: Female warriors in Asia Minor; supported Troy against Greeks.

Amor: *See* Eros.

Amphion: Musician; husband of Niobe; charmed stones to build fortifications for Thebes.

Amphitrite: Sea goddess; wife of Poseidon.

Amphitryon: Husband of Alcmene.

Anchises: Father of Aeneas.

Ancile: Sacred shield that fell from heavens; palladium of Rome.

Andraemon: Husband of Dryope.

Andromache: Wife of Hector.

Andromeda: Daughter of Cepheus; chained to cliff for monster to devour; rescued by Perseus.

Anteia: Wife of Proetus; tried to induce Bellerophon to elope with her.

Anteros: God who avenged unrequited love.

Antigone: Daughter of Oedipus; accompanied him to Colonus; performed burial rite for Polynices and hanged herself.

Antinoüs: Leader of suitors of Penelope; slain by Odysseus.

Aphrodite (Venus): Goddess of love and beauty; daughter of Zeus; mother of Eros.

Apollo: God of beauty, poetry, music; later identified with Helios as Phoebus Apollo; son of Zeus and Leto.
Aquilo: *See* Winds.
Arachne: Maiden who challenged Athena to weaving contest; changed to spider.
Ares (Mars): God of war; son of Zeus and Hera.
Argo: Ship in which Jason and followers sailed to Colchis for Golden Fleece.
Argus: Monster with hundred eyes; slain by Hermes; his eyes placed by Hera into peacock's tail.
Ariadne: Daughter of Minos; aided Theseus in slaying Minotaur; deserted by him on island of Naxos and married to Dionysus.
Arion: Musician; thrown overboard by pirates but saved by dolphin.
Artemis (Diana): Goddess of moon; huntress; twin sister of Apollo.
Asclepius (Aesculapius): Mortal son of Apollo; slain by Zeus for raising dead; later deified as god of medicine. Also known as Asklepios.
Astarte: Phoenician goddess of love; variously identified with Aphrodite, Selene, and Artemis.
Astraea: Goddess of Justice; daughter of Zeus and Themis.
Atalanta: Princess who challenged her suitors to a foot race; Hippomenes won race and married her.
Athena (Minerva): Goddess of wisdom; known poetically as Pallas Athene; sprang fully armed from head of Zeus.
Atlas: Titan; held world on his shoulders as punishment for warring against Zeus; son of Iapetus.
Atreus: King of Mycenae; father of Menelaus and Agamemnon; brother of Thyestes, three of whose sons he slew and served to him at banquet; slain by Aegisthus.
Atropos: *See* Fates.
Aurora: *See* Eos.
Auster: *See* Winds.
Avernus: Infernal regions; name derived from small vaporous lake near Vesuvius which was fabled to kill birds and vegetation.
Bacchus: *See* Dionysus.
Bellerophon: Corinthian hero; killed Chimera with aid of Pegasus; tried to reach Olympus on Pegasus and was thrown to his death.
Bellona: Roman goddess of war.
Boreas: *See* Winds.
Briareus: Monster of hundred hands; son of Uranus and Gaea.
Briseis: Captive maiden given to Achilles; taken by Agamemnon in exchange for loss of Chryseis, which caused Achilles to cease fighting, until death of Patroclus.
Cadmus: Brother of Europa; planter of dragon seeds from which first Thebans sprang.
Calliope: *See* Muses.
Calypso: Sea nymph; kept Odysseus on her island Ogygia for seven years.
Cassandra: Daughter of Priam; prophetess who was never believed; slain with Agamemnon.
Castor: *See* Dioscuri.
Celaeno: *See* Pleiades.
Centaurs: Beings half man and half horse; lived in mountains of Thessaly.
Cephalus: Hunter; accidentally killed his wife Procris with his spear.
Cepheus: King of Ethiopia; father of Andromeda.
Cerberus: Three-headed dog guarding entrance to Hades.
Ceres: *See* Demeter.
Chaos: Formless void; personified as first of gods.
Charon: Boatman on Styx who carried souls of dead to Hades; son of Erebus.
Charybdis: Female monster; personification of whirlpool.
Chimera: Female monster with head of lion, body of goat, tail of serpent; killed by Bellerophon.
Chiron: Most famous of centaurs.
Chronos: Personification of time.
Chryseis: Captive maiden given to Agamemnon; his refusal to accept ransom from her father Chryses caused Apollo to send plague on Greeks besieging Troy.
Circe: Sorceress; daughter of Helios; changed Odysseus' men into swine.
Clio: *See* Muses.
Clotho: *See* Fates.
Clytemnestra: Wife of Agamemnon, whom she slew with aid of her paramour, Aegisthus; slain by her son Orestes.
Cocytus: *See* Rivers.
Creon: Father of Jocasta; forbade burial of Polynices; ordered burial alive of Antigone.
Creüsa: Princess of Corinth, for whom Jason deserted Medea; slain by Medea, who sent her poisoned robe; also known as Glaüke.
Creusa: Wife of Aeneas; died fleeing Troy.
Cronus (Saturn): Titan; god of harvests; son of Uranus and Gaea; dethroned by his son Zeus.
Cupid: *See* Eros.
Cybele: Anatolian nature goddess; adopted by Greeks and identified with Rhea.
Cyclopes: Race of one-eyed giants (singular: Cyclops).
Daedalus: Athenian artificer; father of Icarus; builder of Labyrinth in Crete; devised wings attached with wax for him and Icarus to escape Crete.
Danae: Princess of Argos; mother of Perseus by Zeus, who appeared to her in form of golden shower.
Danaïdes: Daughters of Danaüs; at his command, all except Hypermnestra slew their husbands, the sons of Aegyptus.
Danaüs: Brother of Aegyptus; father of Danaïdes; slain by Lynceus.
Daphne: Nymph; pursued by Apollo; changed to laurel tree.
Decuma: *See* Fates.
Deino: *See* Graeae.
Demeter (Ceres): Goddess of agriculture; mother of Persephone.
Diana: *See* Artemis.
Dido: Founder and queen of Carthage; stabbed herself when deserted by Aeneas.
Diomedes: Greek hero; with Odysseus, entered Troy and carried off Palladium, sacred statue of Athena.
Diomedes: Owner of man-eating horses, which Hercules, as ninth labor, carried off.
Dione: Titan goddess; mother by Zeus of Aphrodite.
Dionysus (Bacchus): God of wine; son of Zeus and Semele.
Dioscuri: Twins Castor and Pollux; sons of Leda by Zeus.
Dis: *See* Hades.
Dryads: Wood nymphs.
Dryope: Maiden changed to Hamadryad.
Echo: Nymph who fell hopelessly in love with Narcissus; faded away except for her voice.
Electra: Daughter of Agamemnon and Clytemnestra; sister of Orestes; urged Orestes to slay Clytemnestra and Aegisthus.
Electra: *See* Pleiades.
Elysium: Abode of blessed dead.
Endymion: Mortal loved by Selene.
Enyo: *See* Graeae.
Eos (Aurora): Goddess of dawn.
Epimetheus: Brother of Prometheus; husband of Pandora.
Erato: *See* Muses.
Erebus: Spirit of darkness; son of Chaos.
Erinyes: *See* Furies.
Eris: Goddess of discord.
Eros (Amor or Cupid): God of love; son of Aphrodite.
Eteocles: Son of Oedipus, whom he succeeded to rule alternately with Polynices; refused to give up throne at end of year; he and Polynices slew each other.
Eumenides: *See* Furies.
Euphrosyne: *See* Graces.
Europa: Mortal loved by Zeus, who, in form of white bull, carried her off to Crete.
Eurus: *See* Winds.
Euryale: *See* Gorgons.
Eurydice: Nymph; wife of Orpheus.
Eurystheus: King of Argos; imposed twelve labors on Hercules.
Euterpe: *See* Muses.

Fates: Goddesses of destiny; Clotho (Spinner of thread of life), Lachesis (Determiner of length), and Atropos (Cutter of thread); also called Moirae. Identified by Romans with their goddesses of fate; Nona, Decuma, and Morta; called Parcae.

Fauns: Roman deities of woods and groves.

Faunus: *See* Pan.

Favonius: *See* Winds.

Flora: Roman goddess of flowers.

Fortuna: Roman goddess of fortune.

Furies: Avenging spirits; Alecto, Megaera, and Tisiphone; known also as Erinyes or Eumenides.

Gaea: Goddess of earth; daughter of Chaos; mother of Titans; known also as Ge, Gea, Gaia, etc.

Galatea: Statue of maiden carved from ivory by Pygmalion; given life by Aphrodite.

Galatea: Sea nymph; loved by Polyphemus.

Ganymede: Beautiful boy; successor to Hebe as cupbearer of gods.

Glaucus: Mortal who became sea divinity by eating magic grass.

Glauke: *See* Creüsa.

Golden Fleece: Fleece from ram that flew Phrixos to Colchis; Aeëtes placed it under guard of dragon; carried off by Jason.

Gorgons: Female monsters; Euryale, Medusa, and Stheno; had snakes for hair; their glances turned mortals to stone. *See* Medusa.

Graces: Beautiful goddesses: Aglaia (Brilliance), Euphrosyne (Joy), and Thalia (Bloom); daughters of Zeus.

Graeae: Sentinels for Gorgons; Deino, Enyo, and Pephredo; had one eye among them, which passed from one to another.

Hades (Dis): Name sometimes given Pluto; also, abode of dead, ruled by Pluto.

Haemon: Son of Creon; promised husband of Antigone; killed himself in her tomb.

Hamadryads: Tree nymphs.

Harpies: Monsters with heads of women and bodies of birds.

Hebe (Juventas): Goddess of youth; cupbearer of gods before Ganymede; daughter of Zeus and Hera.

Hecate: Goddess of sorcery and witchcraft.

Hector: Son of Priam; slayer of Patroclus; slain by Achilles.

Hecuba: Wife of Priam.

Helen: Fairest woman in world; daughter of Zeus and Leda; wife of Menelaus; carried to Troy by Paris, causing Trojan War.

Heliades: Daughters of Helios; mourned for Phaëthon and were changed to poplar trees.

Helios (Sol): God of sun; later identified with Apollo.

Helle: Sister of Phrixos; fell from ram of Golden Fleece; water where she fell named Hellespont.

Hephaestus (Vulcan): God of fire; celestial blacksmith; son of Zeus and Hera; husband of Aphrodite.

Hera (Juno): Queen of heaven; wife of Zeus.

Hercules: Hero and strong man; son of Zeus and Alcmene; performed twelve labors or deeds to be free from bondage under Eurystheus; after death, his mortal share was destroyed, and he became immortal. Also known as Herakles or Heracles. Labors: (1) killing Nemean lion; (2) killing Lernaean Hydra; (3) capturing Erymanthian boar; (4) capturing Cerynean hind; (5) killing man-eating Stymphalian birds; (6) procuring girdle of Hippolyte; (7) cleaning Augean stables; (8) capturing Cretan bull; (9) capturing man-eating horses of Diomedes; (10) capturing cattle of Geryon; (11) procuring golden apples of Hesperides; (12) bringing Cerberus up from Hades.

Hermes (Mercury): God of physicians and thieves; messenger of gods; son of Zeus and Maia.

Hero: Priestess of Aphrodite; Leander swam Hellespont nightly to see her; drowned herself at his death.

Hesperus: Evening star.

Hestia (Vesta): Goddess of hearth; sister of Zeus.

Hippolyte: Queen of Amazons; wife of Theseus.

Hippolytus: Son of Theseus and Hippolyte; falsely accused by Phaedra of trying to kidnap her; slain by Poseidon at request of Theseus.

Hippomenes: Husband of Atalanta, whom he beat in race by dropping golden apples, which she stopped to pick up.

Hyacinthus: Beautiful youth accidentally killed by Apollo, who caused flower to spring up from his blood.

Hydra: Nine-headed monster in marsh of Lerna; slain by Hercules.

Hygeia: Personification of health.

Hyman: God of marriage.

Hyperion: Titan; early sun god; father of Helios.

Hypermnestra: Daughter of Danaüs; refused to kill her husband Lynceus.

Hypnos (Somnus): God of sleep.

Iapetus: Titan; father of Atlas, Epimetheus, and Prometheus.

Icarus: Son of Daedalus; flew too near sun with wax-attached wings and fell into sea and was drowned.

Io: Mortal maiden loved by Zeus; changed by Hera into heifer.

Iobates: King of Lycia; sent Bellerophon to slay Chimera.

Iphigenia: Daughter of Agamemnon; offered as sacrifice to Artemis at Aulis; carried by Artemis to Tauris where she became priestess; escaped from there with Orestes.

Iris: Goddess of rainbow; messenger of Zeus and Hera.

Ismene: Daughter of Oedipus; sister of Antigone.

Iulus: Son of Aeneas.

Ixion: King of Lapithae; for making love to Hera he was bound to endlessly revolving wheel in Tartarus.

Janus: Roman god of gates and doors; represented with two opposite faces.

Jason: Son of Aeson; to gain throne of Ioclus from Pelias, went to Colchis and brought back Golden Fleece; married Medea; deserted her for Creüsa.

Jocasta: Wife of Laius; mother of Oedipus; unwittingly became wife of Oedipus; hanged herself when relationship was discovered.

Juno: *See* Hera.

Jupiter: *See* Zeus.

Juventas: *See* Hebe.

Lachesis: *See* Fates.

Laius: Father of Oedipus, by whom he was slain.

Laocoön: Priest of Apollo at Troy; warned against bringing wooden horse into Troy; destroyed with his two sons by serpents sent by Athena.

Lares: Roman ancestral spirits protecting descendants and homes.

Lavinia: Wife of Aeneas after defeat of Turnus.

Leander: Swam Hellespont nightly to see Hero; drowned in storm.

Leda: Mortal loved by Zeus in form of Swan; mother of Helen, Clytemnestra, Dioscuri.

Lethe: *See* Rivers.

Leto (Latona): Mother by Zeus of Artemis and Apollo.

Lucina: Roman goddess of childbirth; identified with Juno.

Lynceus: Son of Aegyptus; husband of Hypermnestra; slew Danaüs.

Maia: Daughter of Atlas; mother of Hermes.

Maia: *See* Pleiades.

Manes: Souls of dead Romans, particularly of ancestors.

Mars: *See* Ares.

Marsyas: Shepherd; challenged Apollo to music contest and lost; flayed alive by Apollo.

Medea: Sorceress; daughter of Aeëtes; helped Jason obtain Golden Fleece; when deserted by him for Creüsa, killed her children and Creüsa.

Medusa: Gorgon; slain by Perseus, who cut off her head.

Megaera: *See* Furies.

Meleager: Son of Althaea; his life would last as long as brand burning at his birth; Althaea quenched and saved it but destroyed it when Meleager slew his uncles.

Melpomene: *See* Muses.

Memnon: Ethiopian king; made immortal by Zeus; son of Tithonus and Eos.

Menelaus: King of Sparta; son of Atreus; brother of Agamemnon; husband of Helen.

Mercury: *See* Hermes.

Merope: *See* Pleiades.

Mezentius: Cruel Etruscan king; ally of Turnus against Aeneas; slain by Aeneas.

Midas: King of Phrygia; given gift of turning to gold all he touched.

Minerva: *See* Athena.

Minos: King of Crete; after death, one of three judges of dead in Hades; son of Zeus and Europa.

Minotaur: Monster, half man and half beast, kept in Labyrinth in Crete; slain by Theseus.
Mnemosyne: Goddess of memory; mother by Zeus of Muses.
Moirae: *See* Fates.
Momus: God of ridicule.
Morpheus: God of dreams.
Mors: *See* Thanatos.
Morta: *See* Fates.
Muses: Goddesses presiding over arts and sciences: Calliope (epic poetry), Clio (history), Erato (lyric and love poetry), Euterpe (music), Melpomene (tragedy), Polymnia or Polyhymnia (sacred poetry), Terpsichore (choral dance and song), Thalia (comedy and bucolic poetry), Urania (astronomy); daughters of Zeus and Mnemosyne.
Naiads: Nymphs of waters, streams, and fountains.
Napaeae: Wood nymphs.
Narcissus: Beautiful youth loved by Echo; in punishment for not returning her love, he was made to fall in love with his image reflected in pool; pined away and became flower.
Nemesis: Goddess of retribution.
Neoptolemus: Son of Achilles; slew Priam; also known as Pyrrhus.
Neptune: *See* Poseidon.
Nereids: Sea nymphs; attendants on Poseidon.
Nestor: King of Pylos; noted for wise counsel in expedition against Troy.
Nike: Goddess of victory.
Niobe: Daughter of Tantalus; wife of Amphion; her children slain by Apollo and Artemis; changed to stone but continued to weep her loss.
Nona: *See* Fates.
Notus: *See* Winds.
Nox: *See* Nyx.
Nymphs: Beautiful maidens; inferior deities of nature.
Nyx (Nox): Goddess of night.
Oceanids: Ocean nymphs; daughters of Oceanus.
Oceanus: Eldest of Titans; god of waters.
Odysseus (Ulysses): King of Ithaca; husband of Penelope; wandered ten years after fall of Troy before arriving home.
Oedipus: King of Thebes; son of Laius and Jocasta; unwittingly murdered Laius and married Jocasta; tore his eyes out when relationship was discovered.
Oenone: Nymph of Mount Ida; wife of Paris, who abandoned her; refused to cure him when he was poisoned by arrow of Philoctetes at Troy.
Ops: *See* Rhea.
Oreads: Mountain nymphs.
Orestes: Son of Agamemnon and Clytemnestra; brother of Electra; slew Clytemnestra and Aegisthus; pursued by Furies until his purification by Apollo.
Orion: Hunter; slain by Artemis and made heavenly constellation.
Orpheus: Famed musician; son of Apollo and Muse Calliope; husband of Eurydice.
Pales: Roman goddess of shepherds and herdsmen.
Palinurus: Aeneas' pilot; fell overboard in his sleep and was drowned.
Pan (Faunus): God of woods and fields; part goat; son of Hermes.
Pandora: Opener of box containing human ills; mortal wife of Epimetheus.
Parcae: *See* Fates.
Paris: Son of Priam; gave apple of discord to Aphrodite, for which she enabled him to carry off Helen; slew Achilles at Troy; slain by Philoctetes.
Patroclus: Great friend of Achilles; wore Achilles' armor and was slain by Hector.
Pegasus: Winged horse that sprang from Medusa's body at her death; ridden by Bellerophon when he slew Chimera.
Pelias: King of Ioclus; seized throne from his brother Aeson; sent Jason for Golden Fleece; slain unwittingly by his daughters at instigation of Medea.
Pelops: Son of Tantalus; his father cooked and served him to gods; restored to life; Peloponnesus named for him.
Penates: Roman household gods.
Penelope: Wife of Odysseus; waited faithfully for him for ten years while putting off numerous suitors.
Pephredo: *See* Graeae.
Periphetes: Giant; son of Hephaestus; slain by Theseus.
Persephone (Proserpine): Queen of infernal regions; daughter of Zeus and Demeter; wife of Pluto.
Perseus: Son of Zeus and Danaë; slew Medusa; rescued Andromeda from monster and married her.
Phaedra: Daughter of Minos; wife of Theseus; caused the death of her stepson, Hippolytus.
Phaethon: Son of Helios; drove his father's sun chariot and was struck down by Zeus before he set world on fire.
Philoctetes: Greek warrior who possessed Hercules' bow and arrows; slew Paris at Troy with poisoned arrow.
Phineus: Betrothed of Andromeda; tried to slay Perseus but turned to stone by Medusa's head.
Phlegethon: *See* Rivers.
Phosphor: Morning star.
Phrixos: Brother of Helle; carried by ram of Golden Fleece to Colchis.
Pirithous: Son of Ixion; friend of Theseus; tried to carry off Persephone from Hades; bound to enchanted rock by Pluto.
Pleiades: Alcyone, Celaeno, Electra, Maia, Merope, Sterope or Asterope, Taygeta; seven daughters of Atlas; transformed into heavenly constellation, of which six stars are visible (Merope is said to have hidden in shame for loving a mortal).
Pluto (Dis): God of Hades; brother of Zeus.
Plutus: God of wealth.
Pollux: *See* Dioscuri.
Polymnia: *See* Muses.
Polynices: Son of Oedipus; he and his brother Eteocles killed each other; burial rite, forbidden by Creon, performed by his sister Antigone.
Polyphemus: Cyclops; devoured six of Odysseus' men; blinded by Odysseus.
Polyxena: Daughter of Priam; betrothed to Achilles, whom Paris slew at their betrothal; sacrificed to shade of Achilles.
Pomona: Roman goddess of fruits.
Pontus: Sea god; son of Gaea.
Poseidon (Neptune): God of sea; brother of Zeus.
Priam: King of Troy; husband of Hecuba; ransomed Hector's body from Achilles; slain by Neoptolemus.
Priapus: God of regeneration.
Procris: Wife of Cephalus, who accidentally slew her.
Procrustes: Giant; stretched or cut off legs of victims to make them fit iron bed; slain by Theseus.
Proetus: Husband of Anteia; sent Bellerophon to Iobates to be put to death.
Prometheus: Titan; stole fire from heaven for man. Zeus punished him by chaining him to rock in Caucasus where vultures devoured his liver daily.
Proteus: Sea god; assumed various shapes when called on to prophesy.
Psyche: Beloved of Eros; punished by jealous Aphrodite; made immortal and united with Eros.
Pygmalion: King of Cyprus; carved ivory statue of maiden which Aphrodite gave life as Galatea.
Pyramus: Babylonian youth; made love to Thisbe through hole in wall; thinking Thisbe slain by lion, killed himself.
Pyrrhus: *See* Neoptolemus.
Python: Serpent born from slime left by Deluge; slain by Apollo.
Quirinus: Roman war god.
Remus: Brother of Romulus; slain by him.
Rhadamanthus: One of three judges of dead in Hades; son of Zeus and Europa.
Rhea (Ops): Daughter of Uranus and Gaea; wife of Cronus; mother of Zeus; identified with Cybele.
Rivers of Underworld: Acheron (woe), Cocytus (wailing), Lethe (forgetfulness), Phlegethon (fire), Styx (across which souls of dead were ferried by Charon).
Romulus: Founder of Rome; he and Remus suckled in infancy by she-wolf; slew Remus; deified by Romans.
Sarpedon: King of Lycia; son of Zeus and Europa; slain by Patroclus at Troy.
Saturn: *See* Cronus.
Satyrs: Hoofed demigods of woods and fields; companions of Dionysus.
Sciron: Robber; forced strangers to wash his feet, then hurled them into sea where tortoise devoured

them; slain by Theseus.

Scylla: Female monster inhabiting rock opposite Charybdis; menaced passing sailors.

Selene: Goddess of moon.

Semele: Daughter of Cadmus; mother by Zeus of Dionysus; demanded Zeus appear before her in all his splendor and was destroyed by his lightnings.

Sibyls: Various prophetesses; most famous, Cumaean sibyl, accompanied Aeneas into Hades.

Sileni: Minor woodland deities similar to satyrs (singular: silenus). Sometimes Silenus refers to eldest of satyrs, son of Hermes or of Pan.

Silvanus: Roman god of woods and fields.

Sinis: Giant; bent pines, by which he hurled victims against side of mountain; slain by Theseus.

Sirens: Minor deities who lured sailors to destruction with their singing.

Sisyphus: King of Corinth; condemned in Tartarus to roll huge stone to top of hill; it always rolled back down again.

Sol: *See* Helios.

Somnus: *See* Hypnos.

Sphinx: Monster of Thebes; killed those who could not answer her riddle; slain by Oedipus. Name also refers to other monsters having body of lion, wings, and head and bust of woman.

Sterope: *See* Pleiades.

Stheno: *See* Gorgons.

Styx: *See* Rivers.

Symplegades: Clashing rocks at entrance to Black Sea; Argo passed through, causing them to become forever fixed.

Syrinx: Nymph pursued by Pan; changed to reeds, from which he made his pipes.

Tantalus: Cruel king; father of Pelops and Niobe; condemned in Tartarus to stand chin-deep in lake surrounded by fruit branches; as he tried to eat or drink, water or fruit always receded.

Tartarus: Underworld below Hades; often refers to Hades.

Taygeta: *See* Pleiades.

Telemachus: Son of Odysseus; made unsuccessful journey to find his father.

Tellus: Roman goddess of earth.

Terminus: Roman god of boundaries and landmarks.

Terpsichore: *See* Muses.

Terra: Roman earth goddess.

Thalia: *See* Graces; Muses.

Thanatos (Mors): God of death.

Themis: Titan goddess of laws of physical phenomena; daughter of Uranus; mother of Prometheus.

Theseus: Son of Aegeus; slew Minotaur; married and deserted Ariadne; later married Phaedra.

Thisbe: Beloved of Pyramus; killed herself at his death.

Thyestes: Brother of Atreus; Atreus killed three of his sons and served them to him at banquet.

Tiresias: Blind soothsayer of Thebes.

Tisiphone: *See* Furies.

Titans: Early gods from which Olympian gods were derived; children of Uranus and Gaea.

Tithonus: Mortal loved by Eos; changed into grasshopper.

Triton: Demigod of sea; son of Poseidon.

Turnus: King of Rutuli in Italy; betrothed to Lavinia; slain by Aeneas.

Ulysses: *See* Odysseus.

Urania: *See* Muses.

Uranus: Personification of Heaven; husband of Gaea; father of Titans; dethroned by his son Cronus.

Venus: *See* Aphrodite.

Vertumnus: Roman god of fruits and vegetables; husband of Pomona.

Vesta: *See* Hestia.

Vulcan: *See* Hephaestus.

Winds: Aeolus (keeper of winds), Boreas (Aquilo) (north wind), Eurus (east wind), Notus (Auster) (south wind), Zephyrus (Favonius) (west wind).

Zephyrus: *See* Winds.

Zeus (Jupiter): Chief of Olympian gods; son of Cronus and Rhea; husband of Hera.

Norse Mythology

Aesir: Chief gods of Asgard.

Andvari: Dwarf; robbed of gold and magic ring by Loki.

Angerbotha (Angrbotha): Giantess; mother by Loki of Fenrir, Hel, and Midgard serpent.

Asgard (Asgarth): Abode of gods.

Ask (Aske, Askr): First man; created by Odin, Hoenir, and Lothur.

Asynjur: Goddesses of Asgard.

Atli: Second husband of Gudrun; invited Gunnar and Hogni to his court, where they were slain; slain by Gudrun.

Audhumia (Audhumbla): Cow that nourished Ymir, created Buri by licking ice cliff.

Balder (Baldr, Baldur): God of light, spring, peace, joy; son of Odin; slain by Hoth at instigation of Loki.

Bifrost: Rainbow bridge connecting Midgard and Asgard.

Bragi (Brage): God of poetry; husband of Ithunn.

Branstock: Great oak in hall of Volsungs; into it, Odin thrust Gram, which only Sigmund could draw forth.

Brynhild: Valkyrie; wakened from magic sleep by Sigurd; married Gunnar; instigated death of Sigurd; killed herself and was burned on pyre beside Sigurd.

Bur (Bor): Son of Buri; father of Odin, Hoenir, and Lothur.

Buri (Bori): Progenitor of gods; father of Bur; created by Audhumla.

Embla: First woman; created by Odin, Hoenir, and Lothur.

Fafnir: Son of Rodmar, whom he slew for gold in Otter's skin; in form of dragon, guarded gold; slain by Sigurd.

Fenrir: Wolf; offspring of Loki; swallows Odin at Ragnarok and is slain by Vitharr.

Forseti: Son of Balder.

Frey (Freyr): God of fertility and crops; son of Njorth; originally one of Vanir.

Freya (Freyja): Goddess of love and beauty; sister of Frey; originally one of Vanir.

Frigg (Frigga): Goddess of sky; wife of Odin.

Garm: Watchdog of Hel; slays, and is slain by, Tyr at Ragnarok.

Gimle: Home of blessed after Ragnarok.

Giuki: King of Nibelungs; father of Gunnar, Hogni, Guttorm, and Gudrun.

Glathsehim (Gladsheim): Hall of gods in Asgard.

Gram (meaning "Angry"): Sigmund's sword; rewelded by Regin; used by Sigurd to slay Fafnir.

Greyfell: Sigmund's horse; descended from Sleipnir.

Grimhild: Mother of Gudrun; administered magic potion to Sigurd which made him forget Brynhild.

Gudrun: Daughter of Giuki; wife of Sigurd; later wife of Atli and Jonakr.

Gunnar: Son of Giuki; in his semblance Sigurd won Brynhild for him; slain at hall of Atli.

Guttorm: Son of Giuki; slew Sigurd at Brynhild's request.

Heimdall (Heimdallr): Guardian of Asgard.

Hel: Goddess of dead and queen of underworld; daughter of Loki.

Hiordis: Wife of Sigmund; mother of Sigurd.

Hoenir: One of creators of Ask and Embla; son of Bur.

Hogni: Son of Giuki; slain at hall of Atli.

Hoth (Hoder, Hodur): Blind god of night and darkness; slayer of Balder at instigation of Loki.

Ithunn (Ithun, Iduna): Keeper of golden apples of youth; wife of Bragi.

Jonakr: Third husband of Gudrun.

Jormunrek: Slayer of Swanhild; slain by sons of Gudrun.

Jotunnheim (Jotunheim): Abode of giants.

Lif and Lifthrasir: First man and woman after Ragnarok.

Loki: God of evil and mischief; instigator of Balder's death.

Lothur (Lodur): One of creators of Ask and Embla.

Midgard (Midgarth): Abode of mankind; the earth.

Midgard Serpent: Sea monster; offspring of Loki; slays, and is slain by, Thor at Ragnarok.

Mimir: Giant; guardian of well in Jotunnheim at root of Yggdrasill; knower of past and future.

Mjollnir: Magic hammer of Thor.

Nagifar: Ship to be used by giants in attacking Asgard at Ragnarok; built from nails of dead men.
Nanna: Wife of Balder.
Nibelungs: Dwellers in northern kingdom ruled by Giuki.
Niflheim (Nifelheim): Outer region of cold and darkness; abode of Hel.
Njorth: Father of Frey and Freya; originally one of Vanir.
Norns: Demigoddesses of fate: Urth (Urdur) (Past), Verthandi (Verdandi) (Present), Skuld (Future).
Odin (Othin): Head of Aesir; creator of world with Vili and Ve; equivalent to Woden (Wodan, Wotan) in Teutonic mythology.
Otter: Son of Rodmar; slain by Loki; his skin filled with gold hoard of Andvari to appease Rodmar.
Ragnarok: Final destruction of present world in battle between gods and giants; some minor gods will survive, and Lif and Lifthrasir will repeople world.
Regin: Blacksmith; son of Rodmar; foster-father of Sigurd.
Rerir: King of Huns; son of Sigi.
Rodmar: Father of Regin, Otter, and Fafnir; demanded Otter's skin be filled with gold; slain by Fafnir, who stole gold.
Sif: Wife of Thor.
Siggeir: King of Goths; husband of Signy; he and his sons slew Volsung and his sons, except Sigmund; slain by Sigmund and Sinflotli.
Sigi: King of Huns; son of Odin.
Sigmund: Son of Volsung; brother of Signy, who bore him Sinflotli; husband of Hiordis, who bore him Sigurd.
Signy: Daughter of Volsung; sister of Sigmund; wife of Siggeir; mother by Sigmund of Sinflotli.
Sigurd: Son of Sigmund and Hiordis; wakened Brynhild from magic sleep; married Gudrun; slain by Guttorm at instigation of Brynhild.
Sigyn: Wife of Loki.
Sinflotli: Son of Sigmund and Signy.
Skuld: *See* Norns.
Sleipnir (Sleipner): Eight-legged horse of Odin.
Surt (Surtr): Fire demon; slays Frey at Ragnarok.
Svartalfaheim: Abode of dwarfs.
Swanhild: Daughter of Sigurd and Gudrun; slain by Jormunrek.
Thor: God of thunder; oldest son of Odin; equivalent to Germanic deity Donar.
Tyr: God of war; son of Odin; equivalent to Tiu in Teutonic mythology.
Ull (Ullr): Son of Sif; stepson of Thor.
Urth: *See* Norns.
Valhalla (Valhall): Great hall in Asgard where Odin received souls of heroes killed in battle.
Vali: Odin's son: Ragnarok survivor.
Valkyries: Virgins, messengers of Odin, who selected heroes to die in battle and took them to Valhalla; generally considered as nine in number.
Vanir: Early race of gods; three survivors, Njorth, Frey, and Freya, are associated with Aesir.
Ve: Brother of Odin; one of creators of world.
Verthandi: *See* Norns.
Vili: Brother of Odin; one of creators of world.
Vingolf: Abode of goddesses in Asgard.
Vitharr (Vithar): Son of Odin; survivor of Ragnarok.
Volsung: Descendant of Odin, and father of Signy, Sigmund; his descendants were called Volsungs.
Yggdrasill: Giant ash tree springing from body of Ymir and supporting universe; its roots extended to Asgard, Jotunnheim, and Niffheim.
Ymir (Ymer): Primeval frost giant killed by Odin, Vili, and Ve; world created from his body; also, from his body sprang Yggdrasill.

Egyptian Mythology

Aaru: Abode of the blessed dead.
Amen (Amon, Ammdn): One of chief Theban deities; united with sun god under form of Amen-Ra.
Amenti: Region of dead where souls were judged by Osiris.
Anubis: Guide of souls to Amenti; son of Osiris; jackal-headed.
Apis: Sacred bull, an embodiment of Ptah; identified with Osiris as Osiris-Apis or Serapis.
Geb (Keb, Seb): Earth god; father of Osiris; represented with goose on head.
Hathor (Athor): Goddess of love and mirth; cow-headed.
Horus: God of day; son of Osiris and Isis; hawk-headed.
Isis: Goddess of motherhood and fertility; sister and wife of Osiris.
Khepera: God of morning sun.
Khnemu (Khnum, Chnuphis, Chnemu, Chnum): Ram-headed god.
Khonsu (Khensu, Khuns): Son of Amen and Mut.
Mentu (Ment): Solar deity, sometimes considered god of war; falcon-headed.
Min (Khem, Chem): Principle of physical life.
Mut (Maut): Wife of Amen.
Nephthys: Goddess of the dead; sister and wife of Set.
Nu: Chaos from which world was created, personified as a god.
Nut: Goddess of heavens; consort of Geb.
Osiris: God of underworld and judge of dead; son of Geb and Nut.
Ptah (Phtha): Chief deity of Memphis.
Ra: God of the Sun, the supreme god; son of Nut; Pharaohs claimed descent from him; represented as lion, cat, or falcon.
Serapis: God uniting attributes of Osiris and Apis.
Set (Seth): God of darkness or evil; brother and enemy of Osiris.
Shu: Solar deity; son of Ra and Hathor.
Tem (Atmu, Atum, Tum): Solar deity.
Thoth (Dhouti): God of wisdom and magic; scribe of gods; ibis-headed

Modern Wedding Anniversary Gift List

Anniversay	Gift	Anniversay	Gift	Anniversay	Gift
1st	Gold jewelry	10th	Diamond jewelry	19th	Aquamarine
2nd	Garnet	11th	Turquoise	20th	Emerald
3rd	Pearls	12th	Jade	25th	Silver jubilee
4th	Blue topaz	13th	Citrine	30th	Pearl jubilee
5th	Sapphire	14th	Opal	35th	Emerald
6th	Amethyst	15th	Ruby	40th	Ruby
7th	Onyx	16th	Peridot	45th	Sapphire
8th	Tourmaline	17th	Watches	50th	Golden jubilee
9th	Lapis	18th	Cat's–eye	60th	Diamond jubilee

Source: Jewelry Industry Council

Retracing the Footsteps of Evolution:

A rare missing link turns up in a museum drawer

By Kathleen McAuliffe

Most fossil hunters chip away at rock or dig deep trenches in the ground. Oxford University paleontologist Per E. Ahlberg made a stunning discovery in a less arduous way: He launched a dig through museum drawers, emerging from the unorthodox excavation with previously overlooked bones that represent a rare missing link in the transition of life from water to land.

The bones had gathered dust at the university's museum since about 1860, twenty years after the original collector retrieved them from a fossil-rich cliff in Scotland known as Scat Craig. The label on the drawers told generations of scholars that the skeletal parts belonged to ancient lobe-finned fish. But Ahlberg's well-trained eyes spotted something else. One of the jaw bones, he noticed, bore the distinct hallmarks of an early tetrapod—a four-legged creature that developed sometime after lobe-finned fish and before the first fully terrestrial vertebrates. His hunch was later confirmed when he pulled a telltale tibia—a shin bone—from the collection. Since all the bones in those drawers had come from deposits laid down during the upper Devonian period—some 367 million years ago—the fragments were probably almost 10 million years older than any known tetrapod, substantially pushing back the date when life in the water began its progression toward the shores.

It's still not clear whether the tetrapod parts recovered from the Scat Craig collection all came from the same animal. Regardless, the bones speak volumes about a critical juncture in natural history. The sheer size of the skeletal parts presented the first major surprise. Scholars had long assumed that early tetrapods had to be small, lightweight creatures to counter the crushing force of gravity on land. But Ahlberg's discovery tells a different story. The skull he turned up stretches nearly a foot and a half long, and he estimates the full body length of these animals to be about five feet.

Assuming all of the limb bones belonged to the same animal, Ahlberg's tetrapod had well-developed hind limbs and front limbs more like the fins of a fish. This chimera of traits suggests to Ahlberg that water-dwelling organisms must have originally developed legs for some purpose other than walking on land. His theory flies in the face of conventional doctrine, which maintains that vertebrate limbs first evolved to carry fish to a new source of water when their shallow pools began to dry up during the upper-Devonian period.

In fact, on climatic grounds alone, that hallowed notion now seems suspect. "It turns out that the Devonian period had monsoon weather not unlike parts of the Amazon," reports Jennifer Clack, an authority on tetrapods at Cambridge University. "In all likelihood, fish didn't get stranded in shallow pools but simply retreated with the water line during dry spells."

So why did legs evolve? Both Ahlberg and Clack believe the hind limbs were designed to support the animals in shallow water. "The first tetrapods probably hung out in reed-choked riverbeds and used their legs to grab onto weeds on the surface," Clack explains. "Suspended from their perches, they would be less inclined to create vibrations in the water that might alert prey." She points out that the Sargasso frog fish uses fingerlike projections on its back fins for exactly that function today. In the view of the British researchers, tetrapods probably adjusted to a marginal existence on the fringes of swamps for at least 20 million years before embarking on the next major evolutionary step: crawling ashore with a fully developed four-legged gait.

These later tetrapods, of course, needed to breathe on land, but the researchers think they arrived well equipped. "Lobe-finned fish had primitive lungs for gulping air in oxygen-poor water," Ahlberg reports, "so by the time tetrapods appeared millions of years later, lungs were presumably standard equipment."

Ahlberg now wants to determine the true relationship between his tetrapod parts. To figure out which jaw and limbs go together, he needs to see how the bones came to rest in the ground. His most recent excavation at Scat Craig, however, bore no fruit: He and some colleagues from the Royal Museum of Scotland dug around in a likely fossil site—now a woman's garden—and turned up plenty of fish bits but no new tetrapods. □

Biotechnologies' Potential

The biotechnology revolution began in the 1970s and 1980s when scientists learned new techniques to alter precisely the genetic constitution of living organisms. Biotechnology is an ancient practice that includes such familiar applications as the use of yeast in baking bread and cultures in making cheese. The newer, most innovative biotechnologies are tremendously diverse and include gene transfer, embryo manipulation and transfer, plant regeneration, and perhaps the most widely known, recombinant DNA technology (rDNA) or "genetic engineering."

Just a decade and a half after its beginnings, the U.S. biotechnology industry produced pharmaceuticals, diagnostic tests, and agricultural products worth close to $2 billion.

Scientific advances from biotechnology have not been limited to medicines. Biotechnology is expected to play a major role in improving U.S. agriculture and protecting the environment. Cell fusion, the merging of the genetic material of two cells of different species, can accelerate the selective breeding process for producing hardier and more fruitful crops and livestock. Enhancements of certain characteristics in vegetables are expected to provide increased resistance to insects, thus reducing the need for chemical pesticides. Companies are field-testing a variety of crops with enhanced resistance to specific viruses, insect pests, and safer herbicides.

Biotechnology holds great promise for the environment, including products that will clean up the ecosystem, provide alternatives to chemicals, and perform other tasks such as mineral recovery.

Bioremediation is a process that involves the use of microorganisms for cleanup of the environment. Certain microorganisms will feed on and degrade hazardous or toxic chemicals and produce environmentally safe substances as by-products. Recent experiments using bioremediation have demonstrated the value of microbes for cleanup of oil spills. Bioremediation is also used for cleansing soil contaminated with gasoline.

For additional information on the use of biotechnology in plant breeding, *see* article, "Genetically Engineered Foods: Fears and Facts," pages 83–84 in the Nutrition and Health Section. The article discusses the Food and Drug Administration's policy for genetically engineered fruits and vegetables, and their potential environmental risks. □

A Brain Is a Terrible Thing to Waste:

Savings banks for neural tissue are open for deposits

By Nina L. Diamond

Much in demand by researchers, postmortem brains will help reveal secrets of the living mind.

Most people haven't noticed that this country is suffering from a severe brain shortage. "Sure, I've noticed," you may chuckle, pointing a finger at Washington or the local government of your choice. But that's not the kind of brain shortage we're talking about. We mean gray matter, white matter, brain tissue—the stuff in your head that neuroscientists need to investigate a variety of diseases, disorders, and dilemmas.

During the Eighties, investigators learned more about the central nervous system than in all prior human history. The Nineties promise to be even more enlightening. "The brain is the last biological frontier," says neuroscientist Deborah Mash, director of the University of Miami Brain Endowment Bank. Founded in 1986, it's one of only three general brain banks in the nation. "We need to study the human brain postmortem—diseased brains and healthy ones for comparison." The Miami bank has acquired nearly 200 brains in the last six years, and 500 are pledged.

Brain banks provide tissue to researchers looking for new treatments and cures for Parkinson's disease, schizophrenia, Alzheimer's disease, Tourette's syndrome, multiple sclerosis, Huntington's and Lou Gehrig's diseases, Down's syndrome, depression, AIDS, and a host of other illnesses. They're also examining how the brain is affected by internal and external activities: genetics, stress, alcohol, drugs, chemicals, and other toxins. And of course, they're looking to understand the brain.

Individuals who've noted on their drivers licenses that they are organ donors have willed everything *but* the brain, although most are not aware of that. The brain is endowed separately—directly to one of the three banks (Miami, Boston, Los Angeles) that accept all kinds of brains or to one of the handful that specialize in one particular disorder.

"One brain can provide enough tissue for 50 researchers," says neuroscientist Edward Bird, director of the Brain Tissue Resource Center at McLean Hospital of Harvard University, founded in 1978. "We receive ten percent more brains each year than the last, and we always have at least one thousand in our freezers. But the number of researchers and projects is skyrocketing, and the requests will outpace what we have at the moment."

So-called "normal" brains are just as much in demand as unhealthy ones. "We use them as controls to compare to the diseased or impaired brain," explains neuroscientist Wallace Tourtellotte, director of the National Neurological Research Specimen Bank at V.A. Wadsworth Hospital of UCLA, founded in 1961. "All banks have a shortage of normal brains." The L.A. bank has more than 2,000 brains, collects 150 on average each year from donors, and has 1,600 pledged. "When the donor is dying, the next of kin calls to let us know. We've made arrangements for a place to have the brain removed, and we get the donor's medical records, too," Tourtellotte explains.

Although the banks are in dire need of tissue, not just any old brain will do. "The ideal situation is sudden, natural death," says Mash. "Someone brain dead on a respirator is a bad donor, because brain death alters cellular structure, chemistry, and electrical activity." The brain must be removed no later than 12 hours after death. Any later and deterioration will render it useless for research. Brains for donation are removed by pathologists and coroners. After removal, the entire brain is frozen and remains that way in the bank.

Donor awareness is greatest among older Americans, Mash points out, and younger tissue is desperately needed. "We need baby-boomer brains," she says, adding that drug-abuse studies in particular require neural tissue from the 30- to 50-year-old crowd.

Brains of all ages are affected by disease and disorder, and Bird notes that "there's always a shortage of young brains, particularly children's. While families don't like doing autopsies on children, they feel good knowing the tissue is going to a worthwhile cause." Increasing the public's awareness of the need for brain donors is paramount. "People think neuroscientists only work in labs with rats," Bird says.

"Tell the people this is different," Tourtellotte says. "You don't get an immediate return like donating your eyes and giving sight, but the brain tissue will help us understand, treat, and cure disease." The three general and disease-specific brain banks network with each other. "The most exciting aspect of the system," concludes Bird, "is how we can get so many scientists working on a disorder so quickly. All they have to do is call for tissue." □

Table of Geological Periods

It is now generally assumed that planets are formed by the accretion of gas and dust in a cosmic cloud, but there is no way of estimating the length of this process. Our earth acquired its present size, more or less, between 4,000 and 5,000 million years ago. Life on earth originated about 2,000 million years ago, but there are no good fossil remains from periods earlier than the Cambrian, which began about 550 million years ago. The largely unknown past before the Cambrian Period is referred to as the Pre-Cambrian and is subdivided into the Lower (or older) and Upper (or younger) Pre-Cambrian—also called the Archaeozoic and Proterozoic Eras.

The known geological history of the earth since the beginning of the Cambrian Period is subdivided into three "eras," each of which comprises a number of "periods." They, in turn, are subdivided into "subperiods." In a subperiod, a certain section may be especially well known because of rich fossil finds. Such a section is called a "formation," and it is usually identified by a place name.

Paleozoic Era

This era began 550 million years ago and lasted for 355 million years. The name was compounded from Greek *palaios* (old) and zoön *(animal).*

Period	Duration[1]	Subperiods	Events
Cambrian (from *Cambria,* Latin name for Wales)	70	Lower Cambrian Middle Cambrian Upper Cambrian	Invertebrate sea life of many types, proliferating during this and the following period
Ordovician (from Latin *Ordovices,* people of early Britain)	85	Lower Ordovician Upper Ordovician	
Silurian (from Latin *Silures,* people of eary Wales)	40	Lower Silurian Upper Silurian	First known fishes; gigantic sea scorpions
Devonian (from Devonshire in England)	50	Lower Devonian Upper Devonian	Proliferation of fishes and other forms of sea life, land still largely lifeless
Carboniferous (from Latin *carbo* = coal + *fero* = to bear)	85	Lower or Mississippian Upper or Pennsylvanian	Period of maximum coal formation in swampy forests; early insects and first known amphibians
Permian (from district of Perm in Russia)	25	Lower Permian Upper Permian	Early reptiles and mammals; earliest form of turtles

Mesozoic Era

This era began 195 million years ago and lasted for 135 million years. The name was compounded form Greek *mesos* (middle) and *zoön* (animal). Popular name: Age of Reptiles.

Period	Duration[1]	Subperiods	Events
Triassic (from *trias* = triad)	35	Lower or Buntsandstein (from German *bunt* = colorful + *Sandstein* = sandstone) Middle of Muschelkalk (from German *Muschel* = clam + *Kalk* = limestone) Upper or Keuper (old miner's term)	Early saurians
Jurrassic (from Jura Mountains)	35	Lower of Black Jurassic, or Lias (from French *liais* = hard stone) Middle or Brown Jurassic, or Dogger (old provincial English for ironstone) Upper or White Jurasic, or Malm (Middle English for sand)	Many sea-going reptiles; early large dinosaurs; somewhat later, flying reptile (pterosaurs), earliest known birds
Cretaceous (from Latin *creta* = chalk)	65	Lower Cretaceous Upper Cretaceous	Maximum development of dinosaurs; birds proliferating; opossum-like mammals

Cenozoic Era

This era began 60 million years ago and includes the geological present. The name was compounded from Greek *kainos* (new) and *zoön* (animal). Popular name: Age of Mammals.

Period	Duration[1]	Subperiods	Events
Tertiary (originally thought to be the third of only three periods)	c. 60	Palecene (from Greek *palaios* = old + *kainos* = new	First mammals other than marsupials
		Eocene (from Greek *eos* = dawn + *kainos* = new	Formation of amber; rich insect fauna; early bats
		Oligocene (from Greek *oligos* = few + *kainos* = new	Steady increase of large mammals
		Miocene (from Greek *meios* = less + *kainos* = new	
		Pliocene (from Greek *pleios* = more + *kainos* = new	Mammals closely resembling present types; protohumans
Pleistocene (from Greek *pleistos* = most + *kainos* = new) (popular name: Ice Age)	1	Four major glaciations, named Günz, Mindel, Riss, and Würm originally the name of rivers Last glaciation ended 10,000 to 15,000 years ago	Various forms of early man
Holocene (from Greek *holos* = entire + *kainos* = new)		The present	The last 3,000 years are called "history"

1. In millions of years.

Chemical Elements

Element	Symbol	Atomic no.	Atomic weight	Specific gravity	Melting point °C	Boiling point °C	Number of isotopes[1]	Discoverer	Year
Actinium	Ac	89	227[2]	10.07[2]	1050	3200±300	11	Debierne	1899
Aluminum	Al	13	26.9815	2.6989	660.37	2467	8	Wöhler	1827
Americum	Am	95	243[6]	13.67	994 ±4	2607	13[3]	Seaborg et al.	1944
Antimony	Sb	51	121.75	6.61	630.74	1750	29	Early historic times	—
Argon	Ar	18	39.948	1.7837[4]	–189.2	–185.7	8	Rayleigh and Ramsay	1894
Arsenic (gray)	As	33	74.9216	5.73	817 (28 atm.)	613[5]	14	Albertus Magnus	1250?
Astatine	At	85	–210	—	302	337	21	Corson et al.	1940
Barium	Ba	56	137.34	3.5	725	1640	25	Davy	1808
Berkelium	Bk	97	247[6]	14.00[7]	—	—	8[3]	Seaborg et al.	1949
Berylium	Be	4	9.01218	1.848	1278 ±5	2970 (5 mm.)	6	Vauquelin	1798
Bismuth	Bi	83	208.9806	9.747	271.3	1560±5	19	Geoffroy	1753
Boron	B	5	10.81	2.37[8]	2300	2550[5]	6	Gay-Lussac and Thénard; Davy	1808
Bromine	Br	35	79.904	3.12[4]	–7.2	58.78	19	Balard	1826
Cadmium	Cd	48	112.40	8.65	320.9	765	22	Stromeyer	1817
Calcium	Ca	20	40.08	1.55	839 ±2	1484	14	Davy	1808
Californium	Cf	98	251[6]	—	—	—	12[3]	Seaborg et al.	1950
Carbon	C	6	12.011	1.8–3.5[9]	–3550	4827	7	Prehistoric	—
Cerium	Ce	58	140.12	6.771	798 ±3	3257	19	Berzelius and Hisinger; Klaproth	1803
Cesium	Cs	55	132.9055	1.873	28.40	678.4	22	Bunsen and Kirchoff	1860
Chlorine	Cl	17	35.453	1.56[4]	–100.98	–34.6	11	Scheele	1774
Chromium	Cr	24	51.996	7.18–7.20	1857 ±20	2672	9	Vauquelin	1797
Cobalt	Co	27	58.9332	8.9	1495	2870	14	Brandt	c.1735
Copper	Cu	29	63.546	8.96	1083.4±0.2	2567	11	Preshistoric	—
Curium	Cm	96	247[6]	13.51[2]	1340 ±40	—	13[3]	Seaborg et al.	1944
Dysprosium	Dy	66	162.50	8.540	1409	2335	21	Boisbaudran	1886
Einsteinium	Es	99	254[6]	—	—	—	12[3]	Ghiorso et al.	1952
Erbium	Er	68	167.26	9.045	1522	2510	16	Mosander	1843
Europium	Eu	63	151.96	5.283	822 ±5	1597	21	Demarcay	1896
Fermium	Fm	100	257[6]	—	—	—	10[3]	Ghiorso et al.	1953
Fluorine	F	9	18.9984	1.108[4]	–219.62	–188.14	6	Moissan	1886
Francium	Fr	87	223[6]	—	27[2]	677[2]	21	Perey	1938
Gadolinium	Gd	64	157.25	7.898	1311 ±1	3233	17	Marignac	1880
Gallium	Ga	31	69.72	5.904	29.78	2403	14	Boisbaudran	1875
Germanium	Ge	32	72.59	5.323	937.4	2830	17	Winkler	1886
Gold	Au	79	196.9665	19.32	1064.43	2807	21	Prehistoric	—
Hafnium	Hf	72	178.49	13.31	2227 ±20	4602	17	Coster and von Hevesy	1923
Hahnium	Ha	105	262	—	—	—	—	Ghiorso et al.	1970
Helium	He	2	4.00260	0.1785[4]	–272.2 (26 atm.)	–268.934	5	Janssen	1868
Holmium	Ho	67	164.9303	8.781	1470	2720	29	Delafontaine and Soret	1878
Hydrogen	H	1	1.0080	0.070[4]	–259.14	–252.87	3	Cavendish	1766
Indium	In	49	114.82	7.31	156.61	2080	34	Reich and Richter	1863
Iodine	I	53	126.9045	4.93	113.5	184.35	24	Cortois	1811

Element	Symbol	Atomic no.	Atomic weight	Specific gravity	Melting point °C	Boiling point °C	Number of isotopes[1]	Discoverer	Year
Iridium	Ir	77	192.22	22.42	2410	4130	25	Tennant	1803
Iron	Fe	26	55.847	7.894	1535	2750	10	Prehistoric	—
Krypton	Kr	36	83.80	3.733[4]	–156.6	–152.30±0.10	23	Ramsay and Travers	1898
Lanthanum	La	57	138.9055	6.166	920 ±5	3454	19	Mosander	1839
Lawrenceium	Lr	103	257[6]	—	—	—	20[3]	Ghiorso et al.	1961
Lead	Pb	82	207.2	11.35	327.502	1740	29	Prehistoric	—
Lithium	Li	3	6.941	0.534	180.54	1347	5	Arfvedson	1817
Lutetium	Lu	71	174.97	9.835	1656 ±5	3315	22	Urbain	1907
Magnesium	Mg	12	24.305	1.738	648.8±0.5	1090	8	Black	1755
Manganese	Mn	25	54.9380	7.21–7.44[10]	1244 ±3	1962	11	Gahn, Scheele, and Bergman	1774
Mendelevium	Md	101	256[6]	—	—	—	3[3]	Chiorso et al.	1955
Mercury	Hg	80	200.59	13.546	–38.87	356.58	26	Prehistoric	—
Molybdenum	Mo	42	95.94	10.22	2617	4612	20	Scheele	1778
Neodymium	Nd	60	144.24	6.80 & 7.004[10]	1010	3127	16	von Welsbach	1885
Neon	Ne	10	20.179	0.89990 (g/1 0°C/1 atm)	–248.67	–246.048	8	Ramsay and Travers	1898
Neptunium	Np	93	237.0482	20.25	640 ±1	3902	15[3]	McMillan and Abelson	1940
Nickel	Ni	28	58.71	8.902	1453	2732	11	Cronstedt	1751
Niobium (Columbium)	Nb	41	92.9064	8.57	2468 ±10	4742	24	Hatchett	1801
Nitrogen	N	7	14.0067	0.808[4]	–209.86	–195.8	8	Rutherford	1772
Nobelium	No	102	254	—	—	—	7[3]	Ghiorso et al.	1957
Osmium	Os	76	190.2	22.57	3045 ±30	5027±100	19	Tennant	1803
Oxygen	O	8	15.9994	1.14[4]	–218.4	–182.962	8	Preistley	1774
Palladium	Pd	46	106.4	12.02	1552	3140	21	Wollaston	1803
Phosphorous	P	15	30.9738	1.82 (white)	44.1	280	7	Brand	1669
Platinum	Pt	78	195.09	21.45	1772	3827±100	32	Ulloa	1735
Plutonium	Pu	94	244[6]	19.84	641	3232	16[3]	Seaborg et al.	1940
Poionium	Po	84	210[6]	9.32	254	962	34	Curie	1898
Potassium	K	19	39.102	0.862	63.65	774	10	Davy	1807
Praseodymium	Pr	59	140.9077	6.772	931 ±4	3212	15	von Weisbach	1885
Promethium	Pm	61	145[6]	—	≈1080	2460?	14	Marinsky et al.	1945
Protactinium	Pa	91	231.0359	15.37[2]	<1600	—	14	Hahn and Meitner	1917
Radium	Ra	88	226.0254	5.0?	700	1140	15	P. and M. Curie	1898
Radon	Rn	86	222[6]	4.4[4]	–71	–61.8	20	Dorn	1900
Rhenium	Re	75	186.2	21.02	3180	5627[7]	21	Noddack, Berg, and Tacke	1925
Rhodium	Rh	45	102.9055	12.41	1966 ±3	3727±100	20	Wollaston	1803
Rubidium	Rb	37	85.4678	1.532	38.89	688	20	Bunsen and Kirchoff	1861
Rutherfordium	Rf	104	261	—	—	—	—	Ghiorso et al.	1969
Ruthenium	Ru	44	101.07	12.44	2310	3900	16	Klaus	1844
Samarium	Sm	62	150.4	7.536	1072 ±5	1778	17	Boisbaudran	1879
Scandium	Sc	21	44.9559	2.989	1539	2832	15	Nilson	1879
Selenium	Se	34	78.96	4.79 (gray)	217	684.9±1	20	Berzelius	1817
Silicon	Si	14	28.086	2.33	1410	2355	8	Berzelius	1824
Silver	Ag	47	107.868	10.5	961.93	2212	27	Prehistoric	—
Sodium	Na	11	22.9898	0.971	97.81±0.03	882.9	7	Davy	1807
Strontium	Sr	38	87.62	2.54	769	1384	18	Davy	1808
Sulfur	S	16	32.06	2.07[11]	112.8	444.674	10	Prehistoric	—
Tantalum	Ta	73	180.9479	16.654	2996	5425±100	19	Ekeberg	1801
Technetium	Tc	43	98.062	11.50[2]	2172	4877	23	Perrier and Segré	1937
Tellurium	Te	52	127.60	6.24	449.5±0.3	989.8±3.8	29	von Reichenstein	1782
Terbium	Tb	65	158.9254	8.234	1360 ±4	3041	24	Mosander	1843
Thallium	Tl	81	204.37	11.85	303.5	1457±10	28	Crookes	1861
Thorium	Th	90	232.0381	11.72	1750	4790	12	Berzelius	1828
Thulium	Tm	69	168.9342	9.314	1545 ±15	1727	18	Cleve	1879
Tin	Sn	50	118.69	7.31 (white)	231.9681	2270	28	Prehistoric	—
Titanium	Ti	22	47.90	4.55	1660 ±10	3287	9	Gregor	1791
Tungsten (Wolfram)	W	74	183.85	19.3	3410 ±20	5660	22	J. and F. d'Elhuyar	1783
Uranium	U	92	238.029	–18.95	1132.3±0.8	3818	15	Peligot	1841
Vanadium	V	23	50.9414	6.11	1890 ±10	3380	9	del Rio	1801
Xenon	Xe	54	131.30	3.52[4]	–111.9	–107.1±3	31	Ramsay and Travers	1898
Ytterbium	Yb	70	173.04	6.972	824 ±5	1193	16	Marignac	1878
Yttrium	Y	39	88.9059	4.457	1523 ±8	3337	21	Gadolin	1794
Zinc	Zn	30	65.38	7.133	419.58	907	15	Prehistoric	—
Zirconium	Zr	40	91.22	6.506[2]	1852 ±2	4377	20	Klaproth	1789

Elements No. 106, 107, 108, and 109—See NOTE at end of footnotes.

1. Isotopes are different forms of the same element having the same atomic number but different atomic weights. 2. Calculated figure. 3. Artificially produced. 4. Liquid 5. Sublimation point. 6. Mass number of the isotope of longest known life. 7. Estimated. 8. Amorphous. 9. Depending on whether amorphous, graphite or diamond. 10. Depending on allotropic form. 11. Rhombic. ≈ Is approximately. < Is less than. NOTE: There is a dispute between groups at the Lawrence Berkeley Laboratory of the University of California and at the Dubna Laboratory in the Soviet Union concerning the discovery of the unnamed element 106, atomic weight 263. The U.S. laboratory claims that Ghiorso et al. discovered element 106 in 1974. No name has yet been suggested for this element. Names will not be official until the controversy is resolved and they have been approved by the International Union of Pure and Applied Chemistry. In 1992, proposals were made for the names of the three additional elements 107, 108, and 109 discovered by scientists at the Society for Heavy Ion Research (GSI), Darmstadt, Germany, under the direction of Professor Armbruster and Münzenberg. The names are: Nielsbohrium, 107; Hassium, 108; and Meitnerium, 109. The names have to be approved by the International Union of Pure and Applied Chemistry.

INVENTIONS & DISCOVERIES

See also Famous Firsts in Aviation, Nobel Prize Awards

Abacus: *See* Calculating machine
Adding machine: *See* Calculating machine; Computer
Adrenaline: (isolation of) John Jacob Abel, U.S., 1897
Aerosol can: Erik Rotheim, Norway, 1926
Air brake: George Westinghouse, U.S., 1868
Air conditioning: Willis Carrier, U.S., 1911
Airplane: (first powered, sustained, controlled flight) Orville and Wilbur Wright, U.S., 1903. *See also* Jet propulsion
Airship: (non-rigid) Henri Giffard, France, 1852; (rigid) Ferdinand von Zeppelin, Germany, 1900
Aluminum manufacture: (by electrolytic action) Charles M. Hall, U.S., 1866
Anatomy, human: (*De fabrica corporis humani*, an illustrated systematic study of the human body) Andreas Vesalius, 1543; (comparative: parts of an organism are correlated to the functioning whole) Georges Cuvier, 1799–1805
Anesthetic: (first use of anesthetic—ether—on man) Crawford W. Long, U.S., 1842
Antibiotics: (first demonstration of antibiotic effect) Louis Pasteur, Jules-François Joubert, France, 1887; (discovery of penicillin, first modern antibiotic) Alexander Fleming, England, 1928; (penicillin's infection-fighting properties) Howard Florey, Ernst Chain, England, 1940
Antiseptic: (surgery) Joseph Lister, England, 1867
Antitoxin, diphtheria: Emil von Behring, Germany, 1890
Appliances, electric: (fan) Schuyler Wheeler, U.S., 1882; (flatiron) Henry W. Seely, U.S., 1882; (stove) Hadaway, U.S., 1896; (washing machine) Alva Fisher, U.S., 1906
Aqualung: Jacques-Yves Cousteau, Emile Gagnan, France, 1943
Aspirin: Dr. Felix Hoffman,, Germany, 1899
Astronomical calculator: The Antikythera device, first century B.C., Greece. Found off island of Antikythera in 1900
Atom: (nuclear model of) Ernest Rutherford, 1911
Atomic theory: (ancient) Leucippus, Democritus, Greece, c.500 B.C.; Lucretius, Rome, c.100 B.C.; (modern) John Dalton, England, 1808
Automobile: (first with internal combustion engine, 250 rpm) Karl Benz, Germany, 1885; (first with practical high-speed internal combustion engine, 900 rpm) Gottlieb Daimler, Germany, 1885; (first true automobile, not carriage with motor) René Panhard, Emile Lavassor, France, 1891; (carburetor, spray) Charles E. Duryea, U.S., 1892
Autopilot: (for aircraft) Elmer A. Sperry, U.S., c.1910, first successful test, 1912, in a Curtiss flying boat
Avogadro's law: (equal volumes of all gases at the same temperature and pressure contain equal number of molecules) Amedeo Avogadro, 1811
Bacteria: Anton van Leeuwenhoek, The Netherlands, 1683
Bakelite: *See* Plastics
Balloon, hot-air: Joseph and Jacques Montgolfier, France, 1783
Ball-point pen: *See* Pen
Barbed wire: (most popular) Joseph E. Glidden, U.S., 1873
Bar codes: (computer-scanned binary signal code) (retail trade use) Monarch Marking, U.S. 1970; (industrial use) Plessey Telecommunications, England, 1970
Barometer: Evangelista Torricelli, Italy, 1643
Bicycle: Karl D. von Sauerbronn, Germany, 1816; (first modern model) James Starley, England, 1884
Bifocal lens: *See* Lens, bifocal
Big Bang theory: (the universe originated with a huge explosion) Edwin Hubble, U.S., 1929; (confirmed) Arno Penzias, Robert Wilson, 1965
Blood, circulation of: William Harvey, England, 1628
Boyle's law: (relation between pressure and volume in gases) Robert Boyle, Ireland, 1662
Braille: Louis Braille, France, 1829
Bridges: (suspension, iron chains) James Finley, Pa., 1800; (wire suspension) Marc Seguin, Lyons, 1825; (truss) Ithiel Town, U.S., 1820
Bullet: (conical) Claude Minié, France, 1849
Calculating machine: (Abacus) China, c.190; (logarithms: made multiplying easier and thus calculators practical) John Napier, Scotland, 1614; (slide rule) William Oughtred, England, 1632; (digital calculator) Blaise Pascal, 1642; (multiplication machine) Gottfried Leibniz, Germany, 1671; (important 19th-century contributors to modern machine) Frank S. Baldwin, Jay R. Monroe, Dorr E. Felt, W. T. Ohdner, William Burroughs, all U.S.; ("analytical engine" design, included concepts of programming, taping) Charles Babbage, England, 1835. *See also* Computer
Calculus: Isaac Newton, England, 1669; (differential calculus) Gottfried Leibniz, Germany, 1684
Camera: (hand-held) George Eastman, U.S., 1888; (Polaroid Land) Edwin Land, U.S., 1948. *See also* Photography
"Canals" of Mars: Giovanni Schiaparelli, 1877
Carburetor: *See* Automobile
Carpet sweeper: Melville R. Bissell, U.S., 1876
Car radio: William Lear, Elmer Wavering, U.S., 1929, manufactured by Galvin Manufacturing Co., "Motorola"
Celanese: *See* Fibers, man-made
Celluloid: *See* Plastics
Cells: (word used to describe microscopic examination of cork) Robert Hooke, 1665; (theory: cells are common structural and functional unit of all living organisms) Theodor Schwann, Matthias Schleiden, 1838–39
Cement, Portland: Joseph Aspdin, England, 1724
Chewing gum: (spruce-based) John Curtis, U.S., 1848; (chicle-based) Thomas Adams, U.S., 1870
Cholera bacterium: Robert Koch, Germany, 1883
Circuit, integrated: (theoretical) G.W.A. Dummer, England, 1952; (phase-shift oscillator) Jack S. Kilby, Texas Instruments, U.S., 1959
Classification of plants: (first modern, based on comparative study of forms) Andrea Cesalpino, 1583; (classification of plants and animals by genera and species) Carolus Linnaeus, Sweden, 1737–53

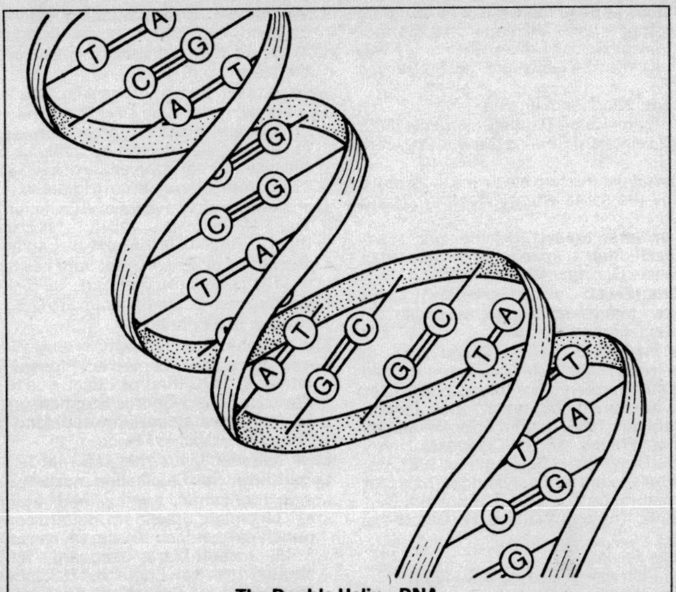

The Double Helix—DNA

Clock, pendulum: Christian Huygens, The Netherlands, 1656

Coca-Cola: John Pemberton, U.S., 1886

Combustion: (nature of) Antoine Lavoisier, France, 1777

Compact disk: RCA, U.S., 1972

Computer: (differential analyzer, mechanically operated) Vannevar Bush, U.S., 1928; (Mark I, first information-processing digital computer) Howard Aiken, U.S., 1944; (ENIAC, Electronic Numerical Integrator and Calculator, first all-electronic) J. Presper Eckert, John W. Mauchly, U.S., 1946; (stored-program concept) John von Neumann, U.S., 1947

Concrete: (reinforced) Joseph Monier, 1877

Condensed milk: Gail Borden, U.S., 1853

Conditioned reflex: Ivan Pavlov, Russia, c.1910

Conservation of electric charge: (the total electric charge of the universe or any closed system is constant) Benjamin Franklin, U.S., 1751–54

Contagion theory: (infectious diseases caused by living agent transmitted from person to person) Girolamo Fracastoro, 1546

Continental drift theory: Antonio Snider-Pellegrini, 1858

Contraceptive, oral: Gregory Pincus, Min Chuch Chang, John Rock, Carl Djerassi, U.S., 1951

Converter, Bessemer: William Kelly, U.S., 1851

Cosmetics: Egypt, c.4000 B.C.

Cotton gin: Eli Whitney, U.S., 1793

Crossbow: China, c.300 B.C.

Cyclotron: Ernest O. Lawrence, U.S., 1931

Deuterium: (heavy hydrogen) Harold Urey, U.S., 1931

Disease: (chemicals in treatment of) crusaded by Philippus Paracelsus, 1527–1541; (germ theory) Louis Pasteur, 1862–77

DNA: (deoxyribonucleic acid) Friedrich Meischer, Germany, 1869; (determination of double-helical structure) F. H. Crick, England, James D. Watson, U.S., 1953

Dyes: (aniline, start of synthetic dye industry) William H. Perkin, 1856

Dynamite: Alfred Nobel, Sweden, 1867

Electric cooking utensil: (first) patented by St. George Lane-Fox, England, 1874

Electric generator (dynamo): (laboratory model) Michael Faraday, England, 1832; Joseph Henry, U.S., c.1832; (hand-driven model) Hippolyte Pixii, France, 1833; (alternating-current generator) Nikola Tesla, U.S., 1892

Electric lamp: (arc lamp) Sir Humphrey Davy, England, 1801; (fluorescent lamp) A.E. Becquerel, France, 1867; (incandescent lamp) Sir Joseph Swann, England, Thomas A. Edison, U.S., contemporaneously, 1870s; (carbon arc street lamp) Charles F. Brush, U.S., 1879; (first widely marketed incandescent lamp) Thomas A. Edison, U.S., 1879; (mercury vapor lamp) Peter Cooper Hewitt, U.S., 1903; (neon lamp) Georges Claude, France, 1911; (tungsten filament) Irving Langmuir, U.S., 1915

Electric motor: *See* Motor

Electrocardiography: demonstrated by Augustus Waller, 1887; (first practical device for recording activity of heart) Willem Einthoven, 1903, Dutch physiologist

Electromagnet: William Sturgeon, England, 1823

Electron: Sir Joseph J. Thompson, England, 1897

Elevator, passenger: (safety device permitting use by passengers) Elisha G. Otis, U.S., 1852; (elevator utilizing safety device) 1857

$E = mc^2$: (equivalence of mass and energy) Albert Einstein, Switzerland, 1907

Engine, internal combustion: No single inventor. Fundamental theory established by Sadi Carnot, France, 1824; (two-stroke) Etienne Lenoir, France, 1860; (ideal operating cycle for four-stroke) Alphonse Beau de Roche, France, 1862; (operating four-stroke) Nikolaus Otto, Germany, 1876; (diesel) Rudolf Diesel, Germany, 1892; (rotary) Felix Wankel, Germany, 1956. *See also* Automobile

Engine, steam: *See* Steam engine

Evolution: (organic) Jean-Baptiste Lamarck, 1809; (by natural selection) Charles Darwin, England, 1859

Exclusion principle: (no two electrons in an atom can occupy the same energy level) Wolfgang Pauli, 1925

Expanding universe theory: (galaxies are receding from each other at speeds proportionate to their distance) George Lemaître, 1927

Falling bodies, law of: Galileo Galilei, Italy, 1590

Fermentation: (micro-organisms as cause of) Louis Pasteur, France, c.1860

Fiber optics: Narinder Kapany, England, 1955

Fibers, man-made: (nitrocellulose fibers treated to change flammable nitrocellulose to harmless cellulose, precursor of rayon) Sir Joseph Swann, England, 1883; (rayon) Count Hilaire de Chardonnet, France, 1889; (Celanese) Henry and Camille Dreyfuss, U.S., ,England, 1921; (research on polyesters and polyamides, basis for modern man-made fibers) U.S., England, Germany, 1930s; (nylon) Wallace H. Carothers, U.S., 1935

Fountain pen: *See* Pen

Frozen food: Clarence Birdseye, U.S. (1924)

Gene transfer: (human) Steven Rosenberg, R. Michael Blaese, W. French Anderson, U.S., 1989

Geometry, elements of: Euclid, Alexandria, Egypt, c.300 B.C.; (analytic) René Descartes, France; and Pierre de Fermat, Switzerland, 1637

Gravitation, law of: Sir Isaac Newton, England, c.1665 (published 1687)

Gunpowder: China, c.700

Gyrocompass: Elmer A. Sperry, U.S., 1905

Gyroscope: Léon Foucault, France, 1852

Halley's Comet: Edmund Halley, 1705

Heart, artificial: Dr. Robert Jarvik, U.S., 1982

Helicopter: (double rotor) Heinrich Focke, Germany, 1936; (single rotor) Igor Sikorsky, U.S., 1939

Helium first observed on sun: Sir Joseph Lockyer, England, 1868

Heredity, laws of: Gregor Mendel, Austria, 1865

Holograph: Dennis Gabor, England, 1947

Home videotape systems (VCR): (Betamax) Sony, Japan, 1975; (VHS) Matsushita, Japan, 1975

Ice age theory: Louis Agassiz, 1840

Induction, electric: Joseph Henry, U.S., 1828

Insulin: Sir Frederick G. Banting, J. J. R. MacLeod, Canada, 1922

Intelligence testing: Alfred Binet, Theodore Simon, France, 1905

Interferon: Alick Isaacs, Jean Lindemann, England, Switzerland, 1957

Isotopes: (concept of) Frederick Soddy, England, 1912; (stable isotopes) J. J. Thompson, England, 1913; (existence demonstrated by mass spectrography) Francis W. Ashton, 1919

Jet propulsion: (engine) Sir Frank Whittle, England, Hans von Ohain, Germany, 1936; (aircraft) *Heinkel He 178*, 1939

Kinetic theory of gases: (molecules of a gas are in a state of rapid motion) Daniel Bernoulli, 1738

Laser: (theoretical work on) Charles H. Townes, Arthur L. Schawlow, U.S., N. Basov, A. Prokhorov, U.S.S.R., 1958; (first working model) T. H. Maiman, U.S., 1960

Lawn mower: Edwin Budding, John Ferrabee, England, 1830 (31)

LCD (liquid crystal display): Hoffmann-La Roche, Switzerland, 1970

Lens, bifocal: Benjamin Franklin, U.S., c.1760

Leyden jar: (prototype electrical condenser) Canon E.G. von Kleist of Kamin, Pomerania, 1745; independently evolved by Cunaeus and P. van Musschenbroek, University of Leyden, Holland, 1746, from where name originated

Light, nature of: (wave theory) Christian Huygens, The Netherlands, 1678; (electromagnetic theory) James Clerk Maxwell, England, 1873

Light, speed of: (theory that light has finite velocity) Olaus Roemer, Denmark, 1675

Lightning rod: Benjamin Franklin, U.S., 1752

Linotype: *See* Printing

Lithography: *See* Printing

Locomotive: (steam powered) Richard Trevithick, England, 1804; (first practical, due to multiple-fire-tube boiler) George Stephenson, England, 1829; (largest steam-powered) Union Pacific's "Big Boy," U.S., 1941

Lock, cylinder: Linus Yale, U.S., 1851

Logarithms: *See* Calculating machine

Loom: (horizontal, two-beamed) Egypt, c.4400 B.C.; (Jacquard drawloom, pattern controlled by punch cards) Jacques de Vaucanson, France, 1745, Joseph-Marie Jacquard, 1801; (flying shuttle) John Kay, England, 1733; (power-driven loom) Edmund Cartwright, England, 1785

Machine gun: James Puckle, England, 1718; Richard J. Gatling, U.S., 1861

Magnet, Earth is: William Gilbert, 1600

Match: (phosphorus) François Derosne, France, 1816; (friction) Charles Sauria, France, 1831; (safety) J. E. Lundstrom, Sweden, 1855

Measles vaccine: John F. Enders, Thomas Peebles, U.S., 1953

Mendelian law: *See* Heredity

Metric system: revolutionary government of France, 1790–1801

Microphone: Charles Wheatstone, England, 1827

Microscope: (compound) Zacharias Janssen, The Netherlands, 1590; (electron) Vladimir Zworykin et al., U.S., Canada, Germany, 1932–1939

Microwave oven: Percy Spencer, U.S., 1947

Motion, laws of: Isaac Newton, England, 1687

Motion pictures: Thomas A. Edison, U.S., 1893

Motion pictures, sound: Product of various inventions. First picture with synchronized musical score: *Don Juan*, 1926; with spoken dialogue: *The Jazz Singer*, 1927; both Warner Bros.

Motor, electric: Michael Faraday, England, 1822; (alternating-current) Nikola Tesla, U.S., 1892

Motor, gasoline: *See* Engine, internal combustion

Motorcycle: (motor tricycle) Edward Butler, England, 1884; (gasoline-engine motorcycle) Gottlieb Daimler, Germany, 1885

National Science Foundation: established by U.S. Congress, 1950 based on report by Vannevar Bush, 1945

Neptune: (discovery of) Johann Galle, 1846

Neptunium: (first transuranic element, synthesis of) Edward M. McMillan, Philip H. Abelson, U.S., 1940

Neutron: James Chadwick, England, 1932

Neutron-induced radiation: Enrico Fermi et al., Italy, 1934

Nitroglycerin: Ascanio Sobrero, Italy, 1846

Bell demonstrating the long-distance capability of his invention at Salem, Mass., on March 15, 1877. A hook-up was made with Boston, 18 miles away, and an extended conversation took place between the two cities.

Nuclear fission: Otto Hahn, Fritz Strassmann, Germany, 1938
Nuclear reactor: Enrico Fermi, et al., 1942
Nylon: *See* Fibers, man-made
Ohm's law: (relationship between strength of electric current, electromotive force, and circuit resistance) Georg S. Ohm, Germany, 1827
Oil well: Edwin L. Drake, Titusville, Pa., 1859
Oxygen: (isolation of) Joseph Priestley, 1774; Carl Scheele, 1773
Ozone: Christian Schöonbein, Germany, 1839
Pacemaker: (internal) Clarence W. Lillehie, Earl Bakk, U.S., 1957
Paper: China, c.100 B.C.
Parachute: Louis S. Lenormand, France, 1783
Pen: (fountain) Lewis E. Waterman, U.S., 1884; (ball-point, for marking on rough surfaces) John H. Loud, U.S., 1888; (ball-point, for handwriting) Lazlo Biro, Argentina, 1944
Penicillin: *See* Antibiotics
Periodic law: (that properties of elements are functions of their atomic weights) Dmitri Mendeleev, Russia, 1869
Periodic table: (arrangement of chemical elements based on periodic law) Dmitri Mendeleev, Russia, 1869
Phonograph: Thomas A. Edison, U.S., 1877
Photography: (first paper negative, first photograph, on metal) Joseph Nicéphore Niepce, France, 1816–1827; (discovery of fixative powers of hyposulfite of soda) Sir John Herschel, England, 1819; (first direct positive image on silver plate, the daguerreotype) Louis Daguerre, based on work with Niepce, France, 1839; (first paper negative from which a number of positive prints could be made) William Talbot, England, 1841. Work of these four men, taken together, forms basis for all modern photography. (First color images) Alexandre Becquerel, Claude Niepce de Saint-Victor, France, 1848–60; (commercial color film with three emulsion layers, Kodachrome) U.S., 1935. *See also* Camera
Photovoltaic effect: (light falling on certain materials can produce electricity) Edmund Becquerel, France, 1839
Piano: (Hammerklavier) Bartolommeo Cristofori, Italy, 1709; (pianoforte with sustaining and damper pedals) John Broadwood, England, 1873
Planetary motion, laws of: Johannes Kepler, Germany, 1609, 1619
Plant respiration and photosynthesis: Jan Ingenhousz, 1779
Plastics: (first material, nitrocellulose softened by vegetable oil, camphor, precursor to Celluloid) Alexander Parkes, England, 1855; (Celluloid, involving recognition of vital effect of camphor) John W. Hyatt, U.S., 1869; (Bakelite, first completely synthetic plastic) Leo H. Baekeland, U.S., 1910; (theoretical background of macromolecules and process of polymerization on which modern plastics industry rests) Hermann Staudinger, Germany, 1922. *See also* Fibers, man-made
Plate tectonics: Alfred Wegener, Germany, 1912–15
Plow, forked: Mesopotamia, before 3000 B.C.

Plutonium, synthesis of: Glenn T. Seaborg, Edwin M. McMillan, Arthur C. Wahl, Joseph W. Kennedy, U.S., 1941

Polaroid Land camera: *See* Camera

Polio, vaccine against: (vaccine made from dead virus strains) Jonas E. Salk, U.S., 1954; (vaccine made from live virus strains) Albert Sabin, U.S., 1960

Positron: Carl D. Anderson, U.S., 1932

Pressure cooker: (early version) Denis Papin, France, 1679

Printing: (block) Japan, c.700; (movable type) Korea, c.1400; Johann Gutenberg, Germany, c.1450 (lithography, offset) Aloys Senefelder, Germany, 1796; (rotary press) Richard Hoe, U.S., 1844; (linotype) Ottmar Mergenthaler, U.S., 1884

Probability theory: René Descartes, France; and Pierre de Fermat, Switzerland, 1654

Programming, information: *See* Calculating machine

Proton: Ernest Rutherford, England, 1919

Psychoanalysis: Sigmund Freud, Austria, c.1904

Pulsars: Jocelyn Bell Bunnell, England, 1968

Quantum theory: (general) Max Planck, Germany, 1900; (sub-atomic) Niels Bohr, Denmark, 1913; (quantum mechanics) Werner Heisenberg, Erwin Schrödinger, Germany, 1925

Quarks: Jerome Friedman, Henry Kendall, Richard Taylor, U.S. (1967)

Quasars: Marten Schmidt, U.S., 1963

Rabies immunization: Louis Pasteur, France, 1885

Radar: (limited to one-mile range) Christian Hulsmeyer, Germany, 1904; (pulse modulation, used for measuring height of ionosphere) Gregory Breit, Merle Tuve, U.S., 1925; (first practical radar—radio detection and ranging) Sir Robert Watson-Watt, England, 1934–35

Radio: (electromagnetism, theory of) James Clerk Maxwell, England, 1873; (spark coil, generator of electromagnetic waves) Henrich Hertz, Germany, 1886; (first practical system of wireless telegraphy) Guglielmo Marconi, Italy, 1895; (vacuum electron tube, basis for radio telephony) Sir John Fleming, England, 1904; (triode amplifying tube) Lee de Forest, U.S., 1906; (regenerative circuit, allowing long-distance sound reception) Edwin H. Armstrong, U.S., 1912; (frequency modulation—FM) Edwin H. Armstrong, U.S., 1933

Radioactivity: (X-rays) Wilhelm K. Roentgen, Germany, 1895; (radioactivity of uranium) Henri Becquerel, France, 1896; (radioactive elements, radium and polonium in uranium ore) Marie Sklodowska-Curie, Pierre Curie, France, 1898; (classification of alpha and beta particle radiation) Pierre Curie, France, 1900; (gamma radiation) Paul-Ulrich Villard, France, 1900; (carbon dating) Willard F. Libby et al., U.S., 1955

Radio signals, extraterrestrial: first known radio noise signals were received by U.S. engineer, Karl Jansky, originating from the Galactic Center, 1931.

Radio waves: (cosmic sources, led to radio astronomy) Karl Jansky, 1932

Rayon: *See* Fibers, man-made

Razor: (safety, successfully marketed) King Gillette, U.S., 1901; (electric) Jacob Schick, U.S., 1928(31)

Reaper: Cyrus McCormick, U.S., 1834

Refrigerator: Alexander Twining, U.S., James Harrison, Australia, 1850; (first with a compressor device) the Domelse, Chicago, U.S., 1913

Refrigerator ship: (first) the *Frigorifique,* 1877, cooling unit designed by Charles Teller, France

Relativity: (special and general theories of) Albert Einstein, Switzerland, Germany, U.S., 1905–53

Revolver: Samuel Colt, U.S., 1835

Richter scale: Charles F. Richter, U.S., 1935

Rifle: (muzzle-loaded) Italy, Germany, c1475; (breech-loaded) England, France, Germany, U.S., c.1866; (bolt-action) Paul von Mauser, Germany, 1889; (automatic) John Browning, U.S., 1918

Rocket: (liquid-fueled) Robert Goddard, U.S., 1926

Roller bearing: (wooden for cartwheel) Germany or France, c.100 B.C.

Rotation of earth: Jean Bernard Foucault, 1851

Royal Observatory, Greenwich: established by Charles II of England, John Flamsteed first Astronomer Royal

Rubber: (vulcanization process) Charles Goodyear, U.S., 1839

Saccharin: Constantine Fuhlberg, Ira Remsen, U.S., 1879

Safety match: *See* Match

Safety pin: Walter Hunt, U.S., 1849

Saturn, ring around: Christian Huygens, The Netherlands, 1659

"Scotch" tape: Richard Drew, U.S., 1929

Screw propeller: Sir Francis P. Smith, England, 1836; John Ericsson, England, worked independently of and simultaneously with Smith, 1837

Seismograph: (first accurate) John Milne, 1880

Sewing machine: Elias Howe, U.S., 1846; (continuous stitch) Isaac Singer, U.S., 1851

Solar energy: first realistic application of solar energy using parabolic solar reflector to drive caloric engine on steam boiler, Jon Ericsson, 1860s

Solar system, universe: (sun-centered universe) Nicolaus Copernicus, Warsaw, 1543; (establishment of planetary orbits as elliptical) Johannes Kepler, Germany, 1609; (infinity of universe) Giordano Bruno, Italian monk, 1584

Spectrum: (heterogeneity of light) Sir Isaac Newton, England, 1665–66

Spectrum analysis: Gustav Kirchoff, Robert Bunsen, 1859

Spermatozoa: Anton van Leeuwenhoek, The Netherlands, 1683

Spinning: (spinning wheel) India, introduced to Europe in Middle Ages; (Saxony wheel, continuous spinning of wool or cotton yarn) England, c.1500–1600; (spinning jenny) James Hargreaves, England, 1764; (spinning frame) Sir Richard Arkwright, England, 1769; (spinning mule, completed mechanization of spinning, permitting production of yarn to keep up with demands of modern looms) Samuel Crompton, England, 1779

Star catalog: (first modern) Tycho Brahe, 1572

Steam engine: (first commercial version based on principles of French physicist Denis Papin) Thomas Savery, England, 1639; (atmospheric steam engine) Thomas Newcomen, England, 1705; (steam engine for pumping water from collieries) Savery, Newcomen, 1725; (modern condensing, doubleacting) James Watt, England, 1782

Steam engine, railroad: *See* Locomotive

Steamship: Claude de Jouffroy d'Abbans, France, 1783; James Rumsey, U.S., 1787; John Fitch,

Johannes Gutenberg.

U.S., 1790. All preceded Robert Fulton, U.S., 1807, credited with launching first commercially successful steamship

Stethoscope: René Laënnec, 1819

Sulfa drugs: (parent compound, para-aminobenzenesulfanomide) Paul Gelmo, Austria, 1908; (antibacterial activity) Gerhard Domagk, Germany, 1935

Superconductivity: (theory) Bardeen, Cooper, Scheiffer, U.S., 1957

Symbolic logic: George Boule, 1854; (modern) Bertrand Russell, Alfred North Whitehead, 1910–13

Syphilis, test for: *See* Wassermann test

Tank, military: Sir Ernest Swinton, England, 1914

Tape recorder: (magnetic steel tape) Valdemar Poulsen, Denmark, 1899

Teflon: DuPont, U.S., 1943

Telegraph: Samuel F.B. Morse, U.S., 1837

Telephone: Alexander Graham Bell, U.S., 1876

Telescope: Hans Lippershey, The Netherlands, 1608; (astronomical) Galileo Galilei, Italy, 1609; (reflecting) Isaac Newton, England, 1668

Television: (mechanical disk-scanning method) successfully demonstrated by J.K. Baird, England, C.F. Jenkins, U.S., 1926; (electronic scanning method) Vladimir K. Zworykin, U.S., 1928; (color, all-electronic) Zworykin, 1926; (color, mechanical disk) Baird, 1928; (color, compatible with black and white) George Valensi, France, 1938; (color, sequential rotating filter) Peter Goldmark, U.S., first introduced, 1951; (color, compatible with black and white) commercially introduced in U.S., National Television Systems Committee, 1953

Thermodynamics: (first law: energy cannot be created or destroyed, only converted from one form to another) Julius von Mayer, Germany, 1842; James Joule, England, 1843; (second law: heat cannot of itself pass from a colder to a warmer body) Rudolph Clausius, Germany, 1850; (third law: the entropy of ordered solids reaches zero at the absolute zero of temperature) Walter Nernst, Germany, 1918

Thermometer: (open-column) Galileo Galilei, c.1593; (clinical) Santorio Santorio, Padua, c.1615; (mercury, also Fahrenheit scale) Gabriel D. Fahrenheit, Germany, 1714; (centigrade scale) Anders Celsius, Sweden, 1742; (absolute-temperature, or Kelvin, scale) William Thompson, Lord Kelvin, England, 1848

Tire, pneumatic: Robert W. Thompson, England, 1845; (bicycle tire) John B. Dunlop, Northern Ireland, 1888

Toilet, flush: Product of Minoan civilization, Crete, c.2000 B.C. Alleged invention by "Thomas Crapper" is untrue.

Tractor: Benjamin Holt, U.S., 1900

Transformer, electric: William Stanley, U.S., 1885

Transistor: John Bardeen, William Shockley, Walter Brattain, U.S., 1948

Tuberculosis bacterium: Robert Koch, Germany, 1882

Typewriter: Christopher Sholes, Carlos Glidden, U.S., 1867

Uncertainty principle: (that position and velocity of an object cannot both be measured exactly, at the same time) Werner Heisenberg, Germany, 1927

Uranus: (first planet discovered in recorded history) William Herschel, 1781

Vaccination: Edward Jenner, England, 1796

Vacuum cleaner: (manually operated) Ives W. McGaffey, 1869; (electric) Hubert C. Booth, England, 19091; (upright) J. Murray Spangler, U.S., 1907

Vacuum tube: *See* Radio

Van Allen (radiation) Belt: (around the earth) James Van Allen, U.S., 1958

Video disk: Philips Co., The Netherlands, 1972

Vitamins: (hypothesis of disease deficiency) Sir F. G. Hopkins, Casimir Funk, England, 1912; (vitamin A) Elmer V. McCollum, M. Davis, U.S., 1912–14; (vitamin B) Elmer V. McCollum, U.S., 1915–16; (thiamin, B_1) Casimir Funk, England, 1912; (riboflavin, B_2) D. T. Smith, E. G. Hendrick, U.S., 1926; (niacin) Conrad Elvehjem, U.S., 1937; (B_6) Paul Gyorgy, U.S., 1934; (vitamin C) C. A. Hoist, T. Froelich, Norway, 1912; (vitamin D) Elmer V. McCollum, U.S., 1922; (folic acid) Lucy Wills, England, 1933

Voltaic pile: (forerunner of modern battery, first source of continuous electric current) Alessandro Volta, 1800

Wallpaper: Europe, 16th and 17th century

Wassermann test: (for syphilis) August von Wassermann, Germany, 1906

Weaving, cloth: *See* Loom

Wheel: (cart, solid wood) Mesopotamia, c.3800–3600 B.C.

Windmill: Persia, c.600

X-ray: *See* Radioactivity

Xerography: Chester Carlson, U.S., 1938

Zero: India, c.600; (absolute zero temperature, cessation of all molecular energy) William Thompson, Lord Kelvin, England, 1848

Zipper, W.L. Judson, U.S., 1891

The National Inventors Hall of Fame

The Inventors Hall of Fame, located in Akron, Ohio, was established in 1973 by the National Council of Patent Law Associations, now the National Council of Intellectual Property Law Associations, and the Patent and Trademark Office of the U.S. Department of Commerce. The year of induction is in parentheses at the end of the entry.

Alexanderson, Ernst 1872–1975 (b. Sweden) HIGH FREQUENCY ALTERNATOR—Alexanderson built a high frequency machine that would operate at high speeds and produce a continuous wave transmission. His inventions included such fields as railway electrification, motors, telephone relays and radio and television. (1983)

Alford, Andrew 1904–1992 (b. Samara, Russia) LOCALIZER ANTENNA SYSTEM—Alford invented and developed antennas for radio navigation systems, including VOR and instrument landing systems, and the "Alford Loop" antenna. (1983)

Alvarez, Luis Walter 1911–1988 (b. San Francisco, Calif.) RADIO DISTANCE AND DIRECTION INDICATOR—Alvarez was awarded the Nobel Prize for Physics in 1968. He helped design a ground-controlled radar system for aircraft landings and with his son developed the meteorite theory of dinosaur extinction. (1978)

Armstrong, Edwin 1890–1954 (b. New York City) METHOD OF RECEIVING HIGH FREQUENCY OSCILLATIONS—Armstrong devised wide-band frequency modulation (FM radio) as a means of reducing background static. He also invented the regenerative circuit, the superheterodyne, and the super-regenerative circuit. (1980)

Baekeland, Leo Hendrik 1863–1944 (b. Ghent, Belgium) SYNTHETIC RESINS—Baekeland developed the thermosetting synthetic resin bakelite which helped found the modern plastics industry. He also invented Velox photographic paper. (1978)

Bardeen, John 1908–1991 (b. Madison, Wisconsin); **Shockley, William Bradford** 1910–1989 (b. London, England); **Brattain, Walter H.** 1902–1987 (b. Amoy, China) TRANSISTOR—Bardeen, Shockley and Brattain shared the 1956 Nobel Prize for Physics for the invention of the transistor. The transistor replaced the vacuum tube and paved the way for the integrated circuit. (1974)

Beckman, Arnold O. 1900– (b. Cullom, Ill.) APPARATUS FOR TESTING ACIDITY—Beckman founded Beckman Instruments, Inc. in 1935 with the development of a pH meter for measuring acidity and alkalinity. He also developed the helical potentiometer, a precision electronic component, and the quartz spectrophotometer, an instrument which pioneered automatic chemical analysis. (1987)

Bell, Alexander Graham 1847–1922 (b. Edinburgh, Scotland) TELEGRAPHY—In addition to the telephone, Bell held patents for the telegraph, photophone, phonograph, aerial vehicles, hydroairplanes, and a selenium cell. He was also noted for his medical research and work in teaching speech to the deaf. (1974)

Bennett, Willard Harrison 1903–1987 (b. Findlay, Ohio) RADIO FREQUENCY MASS SPECTROMETER—Bennett studies in gases ionized by high voltage electricity was used in controlled thermonuclear fusion research. His radio frequency mass spectrometer was the first launched into space to measure the masses of atoms. (1991)

Black, Harold Stephen 1898–1983 (b. Leominster, Mass.) NEGATIVE FEEDBACK AMPLIFIER—Black's negative feedback concept involved feeding systems output back to the input as a method of system control thus helping to eliminate distortion in telecommunications and to extend the frequency range of the amplifier. (1981)

Blumberg, Baruch 1925– (b. New York City); **Millman, Irving** 1923– (b. New York City) TEST AND VACCINE FOR HEPATITIS B—The use of the test reduced the occurrence of hepatitis B after blood transfusions. The vaccine protects people exposed to the hepatitis B virus and has been administered to millions, particularly in Asia and Africa. With hepatitis B an unknown factor associated with the development of liver cancer, the vaccine was the first against a major form of cancer. (1993)

Brattain, Walter H. *See under* Bardeen, John.

Burbank, Luther 1849–1926 (b. Lancaster, Mass.) PEACH—Burbank developed more than 800 new strains and varieties of plants including varieties of potato, plums, prunes, berries, flowers and trees. (1986)

Burroughs, William Seward 1857–1898 (b. Rochester, N.Y.) CALCULATING MACHINE—In 1885 Burroughs submitted his first patent for his "calculating machine." This first model needed a special knack to use and Burroughs was dissatisfied with its durability. His 1892 patent not only improved the machine but added a printer. (1987)

Burton, William Meriam 1865–1954 (b. Cleveland, Ohio) MANUFACTURE OF GASOLINE—Burton developed the high heat and high pressure cracking process of fuel oil which more than doubled the potential yield of gasoline from crude oil. (1984)

Camras, Marvin 1916– (b. Chicago, Ill.) METHOD AND MEANS OF MAGNETIC RECORDING—Camras's inventions are used in modern magnetic tape and wire recorders, including high frequency bias, improved recording heads, wire and tape material, magnetic sound for motion pictures, multi-track tape machines, stereophonic sound reproduction and video tape recording. (1985)

Carlson, Chester F. 1906–1968 (b. Seattle, Wash.) ELECTROPHOTOGRAPHY—Carlson invented xerographic dry-copy printing basing his process on electrostatics as opposed to chemical or photographic processes. (1981)

Carothers, Wallace Hume 1896–1937 (b. Burlington, Iowa) DIAMINE-DICARBOXYLIC ACID SALTS AND PROCESS OF PREPARING SAME AND SYNTHETIC FIBER—Carothers work involved the theory of linear polymerization which culminated in the production of the synthetic material nylon. Nylon was first commercially used in toothbrush bristles. Carothers's work also led others to develop the first successful synthetic rubber, neoprene. (1984)

Carrier, Willis Haviland 1876–1950 (b. Angola, N.Y.) APPARATUS FOR TREATING AIR—Carrier developed the first safe, low pressure centrifugal refrigeration machine using nontoxic, nonflammable refrigerant. By controlling humidity as well as temperature, he invented modern air conditioning. (1985)

Carver, George Washington 1864–1943 (b. Diamond Grove, Mo.) COSMETIC AND PROCESS OF PRODUCING SAME; PAINT AND STAIN AND PROCESS OF PRODUCING THE SAME—When Carver's method of crop rotation produced a surplus of peanuts, sweet potatoes and pecans he devised hundreds of uses for the extra crops, from cooking oil to highway paving material. He also synthesized organic dyes which proved superior to aniline dyes. (1990)

Colton, Frank B. 1923– (b. Poland) ORAL CONTRACEPTIVES—Colton has made many important contributions to medicinal organic chemistry, and particularly to steroid chemistry. His most important research resulted in the discovery of Enovid, the first oral contraceptive. (1988)

Conover, Lloyd H. 1923– (b. Orange, N.J.) TETRACYCLINE—Conover's invention of tetracycline in 1952 was the first creation of an antibiotic made by chemically modifying a naturally-produced drug. Tetracycline quickly became the most prescribed broad spectrum antibiotic in the U.S. 40 years later tetracycline is still being used to combat such serious infections as Rocky Mountain Spotted Fever and Lyme Disease. (1992)

Coolidge, William D. 1873–1974 (b. Hudson, Mass.) VACUUM TUBE—Coolidge invented ductile tungsten, the filament material still used in incandescent lamps. He also invented the "Coolidge tube", the model upon which all X-ray tubes for medical applications are patterned. (1975)

Cottrell, Frederick G. 1877–1948 (b. Oakland, Calif.) ELECTROSTATIC PRECIPITATOR—Cottrell's invention used high voltage electricity to remove from 90 to 98 percent of the ash, dust, and acid which industrial smokestacks spewed into the air. Besides eliminating this particulate pollution, this process also allowed some of the minerals and chemicals to be re-used. (1992)

Damadian, Raymond V. 1936– (b. Forest Hills, N.Y.) APPARATUS AND METHOD FOR DETECTING CANCER IN TISSUE—Damadian invented the magnetic resonance imaging (MRI) scanner that has revolutionized diagnostic medicine. The MRI yields radio signal outputs from the body's tissue that can be either transformed into images or analyzed to provide the chemical composition of the tissue. (1989)

Deere, John 1804–1886 (b. Rutland, Vt.) PLOW—Deere's plow had a cutting part made of steel and a moldboard made of polished wrought iron which proved more effective than implements then in use for cutting and turning prairie soils. (1989)

de Forest, Lee 1873–1961 (b. Council Bluffs, Iowa) AUDION AMPLIFIER—De Forest inserted a third electrode between the cathode and anode to make his audion tube. Radio signals are picked up by connecting an antenna to the tube's grid. (1977)

Diesel, Rudolf 1857–1913 (b. Paris, France) INTERNAL COMBUSTION ENGINE—Diesel is best known for his invention of the pressure-ignited heat engine that bears his name. The Diesel engine was able to supplant the large, expensive, and fuel-wasting steam engine. (1976)

Djerassi, Carl 1923– (b. Vienna, Austria) ORAL CONTRACEPTIVES—Along with developing the oral contraceptive Djerassi's research has included work with steroids, antibiotics, synthesis of antihistamines and anti-inflammatory agents. (1978)

Dow, Herbert Henry 1866–1930 (b. Belleville, Ontario) PROCESS OF EXTRACTING BROMINE—Dow invented an entirely new method of extracting bromine from underground brine. (1983)

Draper, Charles Stark 1901– (b. Windsor, Mo.) GYROSCOPIC APPARATUS—Draper developed a spinning gyroscope, stabilizing U.S. Navy antiaircraft gunsights which led to an inertial guidance system for launching long-range missiles at supersonic jet targets. His Instrumentation Lab at MIT contributed to Project Apollo and men on the moon. (1981)

Durant, Graham J. 1934– (b. Newport, England); **Emmett, John Colin** 1939– (b. Bradford, England); **Ganellin, C. Robin** 1934– (b. London, England) ANTIULCER COMPOUNDS AND COMPOSITIONS—Durant, Emmett and Ganellin discovered the drug cimetidine (trade name Tagamet) which inhibits the production of stomach acid. Cimetidine has the ability to heal stomach ulcers without surgery. (1990)

Eastman, George 1854–1932 (b. Waterville, N.Y.) METHOD AND APPARATUS FOR COATING PLATES FOR USE IN PHOTOGRAPHY—Before Eastman, photographers used glass plates with light-sensitive emulsions on them. Eastman put the emulsions first on paper, then on film rolls. He also developed a stronger motion picture film. (1977)

Edgerton, Harold E. 1903–1990 (b. Fremont, Neb.) STROBOSCOPE—Edgerton's research in the fields of stroboscopy and ultra-high speed photography led to the modern electronic speed flash. He was noted for his photographs revealing operations which move at speeds beyond the capacity of the human eye. (1986)

Edison, Thomas Alva 1847–1931 (b. Milan, Ohio) ELECTRIC LAMP—Edison held 1,093 patents, including those for the incandescent electric lamp, the phonograph, the carbon telephone transmitter, and the motion-picture projector. He also created the world's first industrial research laboratory. (1973)

Elion, Gertrude Belle 1918– (b. New York City) 6-MERCAPTOPURINE—Elion synthesized the leukemia-fighting drug 6-mercaptopurine. Her other developments were drugs used to block organ rejections in kidney transplant patients, for the treatment of gout and to battle herpes virus infections. (1991)

Emmett, John Colin *See under* Durant, Graham

Ericsson, John 1803–1889 (b. Vermland, Sweden) PROPELLER—Ericsson's propeller—still the main form of marine propulsion 150 years later—replaced the inefficient and vulnerable steam-driven oars and paddlewheels. He designed and built the Civil War ironclad *Monitor* which defeated the Confederate *Merrimac*. Ericsson also developed a calorific engine designed to use solar energy. (1993)

Farnsworth, Philo Taylor 1906–1971 (b. Beaver, Utah) TELEVISION SYSTEM—At the age of 20 Farnsworth produced the first all-electronic television image. In addition to his television system he invented the first cold cathode ray tubes and the first simple electronic microscope. He used radio waves to get direction (radar) and black light for seeing at night. (1984)

Fermi, Enrico 1901–1954 (b. Rome, Italy) NEUTRONIC REACTOR—Fermi was awarded the 1938 Nobel Prize for Physics for his work in the field of atomic fission. In 1942 he accomplished the controlled release of nuclear energy via the atomic pile. (1976)

Ford, Henry 1863–1947 (b. Wayne County, Mich.) TRANSMISSION MECHANISM—Ford holds numerous patents on automotive mechanisms and helped devise the factory assembly line method of mass production. (1982)

Forrester, Jay W. 1918– (b. Climax, Nebraska) MULTICOORDINATED DIGITAL INFORMATION STORAGE DEVICE—While working on the Whirlwind, the largest computer project in the late 1940s and early 1950s, Forrester devised the magnetic core memory storage which replaced the unreliable and short-lived electrostatic tubes which had previously been used. (1979)

Ganellin, C. Robin *See under* Durant, Graham

Ginsburg, Charles P. 1920– VIDEOTAPE RECORDER—After World War II audio tape recorders were run at very high speeds to record the very high frequency television signals. Ginsburg developed a new machine that ran much slower for television recording. It was first used by CBS TV in 1956. (1990)

Goddard, Robert Hutchings 1882–1945 (b. Worcester, Mass.) CONTROL MECHANISM FOR ROCKET APPARATUS—Goddard launched the first liquid-fuel rocket in 1926. Other rocket design developments led to the bazooka and rocket-assisted takeoff of carrier planes. (1979)

Goodyear, Charles 1800–1860 (b. New Haven, Conn.) IMPROVEMENT IN INDIA-RUBBER FABRICS—Goodyear discovered the vulcanizing process when some rubber mixed with sulfur accidently dropped on a hot stove. Prior to this, rubber's applications were limited because of its adhesiveness and its inability to withstand temperature extremes. (1976)

Gould, Gordon 1920– (b. New York City) OPTICALLY-PUMPED LASER AMPLIFIERS, GAS-DISCHARGE-EXCITED LIGHT AMPLIFIERS—Gould's lasers are used in 80% of industrial, commercial, and medical applications. He also holds patents on laser uses and fiber optic communications. (1991)

Greatbatch, Wilson 1919– (b. Buffalo, N.Y.) MEDICAL CARDIAC PACEMAKER—Greatbatch's was trained as an electrical engineer but his research combined engineering with medical electronics, agricultural genetics, and the electrochemistry of pacemaker batteries. The first implantable pacemaker was a result of his pacemaker patent. (1986)

Greene, Leonard Michael 1918– (b. New York City) AIRPLANE STALL WARNING DEVICE—Greene developed his airplane stall warning device at a time when more than half of all aviation deaths were called by the stall/spin. He also developed a wind shear warning device for pilots. (1991)

Hall, Charles Martin 1863–1914 (b. Thompson, Ohio) MANUFACTURE OF ALUMINUM—Hall discovered the modern electrolytic method of producing aluminum cheaply which enabled the metal to be put into wide commercial use. (1976)

Hanford, William Edward 1908– (b. Bristol, Pa.); **Holmes, Donald Fletcher** 1910–1980 (b. Woodbury, N.J.) POLYURETHANE—The Hanford and Holmes process is the basis today for the manufacture of all polyurethane. Polyurethane is used as an upholstery material, heat insulating material, in artificial hearts, safety padding in automobiles and in carpeting. (1991)

Hewlett, William R. 1913– (b. Ann Arbor, Mich.) VARIABLE FREQUENCY OSCILLATION GENERATOR—Also known as the "audio oscillator," this was the first practical method of generating high-quality audio frequencies needed in communications, geophysics, medicine, and defense work. Walt Disney Studios ordered eight audio oscillators to use in producing the soundtrack of the film, "Fantasia." (1992)

Higgonnet, Rene Alphonse *See under* Moyroud, Louis Marius.

Hillier, James 1915– (b. Ontario, Canada) ELECTRON LENS CORRECTION DEVICE—Hillier is noted for his contributions to the development of the electron microscope. The electron lens is used to focus a beam of electrons just as an optical lens focuses light rays. In 1937 he helped build a model that magnified 7000 times. (1980)

Hollerith, Herman 1860–1929 (b. Buffalo, N.Y.) ART OF COMPILING STATISTICS—Hollerith invented a punch card tabulation machine system that revolutionized statistical computation. His system enabled the 1890 census to save $5 million and more than two years time. (1990)

Holmes, Donald Fletcher *See under* Hanford, William

Houdry, Eugene 1892–1962 (b. Domont, France) LIQUID FUELS— Up until World War I enough gasoline was produced from crude oil by distillation. Cracking fuel oil, another product of distillation, was necessary to meet increased gasoline demands. Early processes used high heat and pressure but Houdry discovered that a catalyst enabled the process to be done at a lower temperature, more quickly, and more cheaply. He also invented the catalytic muffler which reduces the amount of carbon dioxide and unburned carbons released into the atmosphere. (1990)

Julian, Percy Lavon 1899–1975 (b. Montgomery, Ala.) PREPARATION OF CORTISONE—Julian's notable discoveries were the synthesis of cortisone, used in the treatment of arthritis; Aerofoam, used to suffocate gasoline and oil fires, and the synthesis of physostigmine, a treatment for glaucoma. Physostigmine is also being explored in the treatment of Alzheimer's Disease. (1990)

Keck, Donald *See under* Maurer, Robert.

Kettering, Charles Franklin 1876–1958 (b. Ohio) ENGINE STARTING DEVICES AND IGNITION SYSTEM—Kettering invented the first electrical ignition system and the self-starter for automobiles and the first practical engine-driven generator (the "Delco"). His other scientific work includes research in higher octane gasoline, high compression automobile engines, improved Diesel engine, and a nontoxic and nonflammable refrigerant. (1980)

Kilby, Jack S. 1923– (b. Jefferson City, Mo.) MINIATURIZED ELECTRONIC CIRCUITS—Kilby was responsible for the design and development of thick film integrated circuits, integrated circuit development and applications, and also invented the monolithic integrated circuit widely used in electronic systems. (1982)

Kolff, Willem J. 1911– (b. Netherlands) SOFT SHELL MUSHROOM SHAPED HEART—Kolff invented the artificial kidney dialysis machine and headed a team which invented and tested an artificial heart. (1985)

Land, Edwin 1909–1991 (b. Connecticut) PHOTOGRAPHIC PRODUCT COMPRISING A RUPTURABLE CONTAINING CARRYING A PHOTOGRAPHIC PROCESSING LIQUID—Land developed the first modern light polarizers and also optical devices. His most famous invention, the Polaroid camera, combined positive and negative film with developing chemicals. (1977)

Langmuir, Irving 1881–1957 (b. Brooklyn, N.Y.) INCANDESCENT ELECTRIC LAMP—Langmuir's major inventions were the high-vacuum electron tube and the gas-filled incandescent lamp. He also contributed to the fields of electronics, plasma physics, atomic, and molecular structure. (1989)

Lawrence, Ernest Orlando 1901–1958 (b. Canton, So. Dakota) METHOD AND APPARATUS FOR THE ACCELERATION OF IONS—Lawrence's cyclotron enabled him to study the structure of the atom, transmute certain elements, and produce artificial radioactivity. His research included the use of radiation in biology and medicine and he helped isolate uranium 235 which was used in the first atomic bomb. Lawrence received the 1939 Nobel Prize for Physics. (1982)

Lear, William 1902–1978 (b. Hannibal, Mo.) RADIO APPARATUS–AUTOMOBILE—Lear's design of a practical car radio launched the Motorola Company. He then turned to navigational aids for aircraft and formed Lear, Inc., LearAvia Corp., and then Learjet, a leading supplier of corporate jets. He also designed the eight-track tape player. (1993)

Ledley, Robert S. 1926– (b. New York City) DIAGNOSTIC X-RAY SYSTEMS—Ledley developed the ACTA diagnostic x-ray scanner, the first whole-body computerized tomography (CT) machine. He was the first to do medical imaging, three-dimensional reconstructions and to use CT in radiation therapy planning for cancer patients and the diagnosis of bone disease. (1990)

Maiman, Theodore Harold 1927– (b. Los Angeles, Calif.) RUBY LASER SYSTEMS—In 1960 Maiman built and patented the prototype of the ruby laser. The amplified light of the laser has many uses in industry, surgery, military range finders, as well as bar code scanners and compact disk players. (1984)

Marconi, Guglielmo 1874–1937 (b. Bologna, Italy) TRANSMITTING ELECTRICAL SIGNALS—Marconi's experiments led to practical wireless telegraphy and radio. In 1901 he successfully received signals transmitted from England to Newfoundland. He was awarded the 1909 Nobel Prize for Physics. (1975)

Maurer, Robert 1924– (b. St. Louis, Mo.); **Keck, Donald** 1941– (b. Lansing, Mich.); **Schultz, Peter** 1942– (b. Brooklyn, N.Y.) FUSED SILICA OPTICAL WAVEGUIDE—The inventors designed and produced the first optical fiber with light loss during transmission low enough for wide use in telecommunications. This paved the way for the commercialization of optical fiber and created a revolution in telecommunications. (1993)

McCormick, Cyrus 1809–1884 (b. Rockbridge County, Va.) REAPER—While others had also invented the mechanical grain reaper McCormick's constant improvements and astute business sense enabled him to turn his small family-run business into a worldwide corporation. (1976)

Mergenthaler, Ottmar 1854–1899 (b. Germany) MACHINE FOR PRODUCING PRINTING BARS—Mergenthaler's linotype composing machine allowed one operator to be machinist, typesetter, justifier, typefounder and type distributor by means of a board similar to a typewriter's keyboard. (1982)

Millman, Irving *See under* Blumberg, Baruch.

Morse, Samuel F.B. 1791–1872 (b. Charlestown, Mass.) TELEGRAPH SIGNALS—In 1844 Morse built the first telegraph line between Baltimore and Washington and relayed the first telegraphic message. He also devised the Morse code for his machine. (1975)

Moyer, Andrew J. 1899–1959 (b. Star City, Inc.) METHOD FOR PRODUCTION OF PENICILLIN—Moyer found that by culturing the *Penicillium* mold in a culture broth comprising corn steep liquor and lactose, penicillin yields could be increased many fold over the known methods. His discovery became the model for the development of all other antibiotic fermentations. (1987)

Moyroud, Louis Marius 1914– (b. Moirans, France); **Higonnet, Rene Alphonse** 1902–1983 (b. Valence, France) PHOTO COMPOSING MACHINE—Moyroud and Higgonet developed the first practical phototypesetting machine, the Lumitype—later known as the Photon—which was first demonstrated in 1946 and introduced in America in 1948. (1985)

Noyce, Robert N. 1927–1990 (b. Iowa) SEMICONDUCTOR DEVICE-AND-LEAD STRUCTURE—Noyce, as research director of Fairchild Semiconductor, was responsible for the initial development of silicon mesa and planar transistors, which led to a commercially applicable integrated circuit. He holds 16 patents for semiconductor devices, methods and structures. (1983)

Olsen, Kenneth H. 1926– (b. Stratford, Conn.) MAGNETIC CORE MEMORY—Olsen and his Digital Equipment Corporation developed the first successful minicomputer. Digital also developed the MicroVAX which placed a minicomputer structure on a single microchip. (1990)

Otis, Elisha Graves 1811–1861 (b. Halifax, Vt.) IMPROVEMENT IN HOISTING APPARATUS—Otis built the first modern passenger elevator which used his invention of a safety device which prevented the car from falling if the cables broke. (1988)

Otto, Nicolaus August 1832–1891 (b. Holzhausen, Germany) GAS MOTOR ENGINE—Otto introduced the four-stroke piston cycle on which most modern internal combustion engines are based. (1981)

Parker, Louis W. 1906– (b. Budapest, Hungary) TELEVISION RECEIVER—Parker is best known for the "Intercarrier Sound System" used in all television receivers in the world. He also invented the first color television system using vertical color lines which made it possible to change from the original three color dot system to the simpler vertical color line system. (1988)

Parsons, John T. 1913– (b. Detroit, Mich.) NUMERICAL CONTROL OF MACHINE TOOLS—Parsons built a milling machine which was fed data to automatically activate servo-mechanisms to perform automatic contour cutting. First deveolped for making jet plane wings, the method is now widely used in the manufacture and assembly of many goods, from automobiles to computer chips. (1993)

Pasteur, Louis 1822–1895 (b. France) BREWING BEER AND ALE—Pasteur formulated the fundamental tenets of the germ theory of fermentation and of diseases which led to his pasteurization process of sterilization. He is also known for his pioneer work with vaccines, notably against anthrax and rabies. (1978)

Plank, Charles J. 1915–1989 (b. Calcutta, India); **Rosinski, Edward J.** 1921– (b. Gloucester County, N.J.) CATALYTIC CRACKING OF HYDROCARBONS WITH A CRYSTALLINE ZEOLITE CATALYST COMPOSITE—Plank and Rosinski developed the first commercially useful zeolite catalyst introduced in the petroleum industry for catalytic cracking. (1979)

Plunkett, Roy J. 1910– (b. New Carlisle, Ohio) TETRAFLUOROETHYLENE POLYMERS—Plunkett discovered "Teflon" and also worked on the development of many other fluorochemical products and processes used in the refrigeration, aerosol, electronic and aerospace industries. (1985)

Rosinski, Edward *See under* Plank, Charles J.

Rubin, Benjamin A. 1917– (b. New York City) BIFURCATED VACCINATION NEEDLE—Until 1967 smallpox killed at least 2 million people annually. In 1980 the World Health Organization declared that smallpox had been defeated. Rubin ground down the eyelet of a sewing machine needle to invent the bifurcated vaccination needle which could easily be used by natives under difficult conditions. (1992)

Sarett, Lewis Hastings 1917– (b. Champaign, Ill.) THE PROCESS OF TREATING PREGNENE COMPOUNDS—Sarett prepared the first synthetic cortisone. He and several collaborators developed synthesis from raw materials derived from coal, air, lime and water, leading to the first route which was independent of naturally occurring starting materials. (1980)

Schultz, Peter *See under* Maurer, Robert.

Shockley, William Bradford *See under* Bardeen, John.

Sikorsky, Igor I. 1889–1972 (b. Kiev, Russia) HELICOPTER CONTROLS—Sikorsky's patents covered control and stability improvements. The single rotor helicopter developed by Sikorsky represented a major breakthrough in helicopter technology. (1987)

Sperry, Elmer Ambrose 1860–1930 (b. Cortland, N.Y.) GYROSCOPIC COMPASS—The gyroscope was the basis of Sperry's inventions of an autopilot and an airplane turn indicator that allowed flying without visual reference to the ground. His ideas are used today to stabilize space vehicles. (1991)

Steinmetz, Charles Proteus 1865–1923 (b. Breslau, Germany) SYSTEM OF ELECTRICAL DISTRIBUTION—Steinmetz developed theories for alternating current making possible the expansion of the electric power industry in the United States. (1977)

Stibitz, George R. 1904– (b. York, Pa.) COMPLEX COMPUTER—Stibitz is internationally recognized as the father of the modern digital computer. In 1939 Stibitz helped design the Model I complex number calculator which could add two eight-digit decimal numbers in a tenth of a second. (1983)

Tabern, Donalee L. *See under* Volwiler, Ernest H.

Tesla, Nikola 1856–1943 (b. Smiljan Lika, Croatia) ELECTRO-MAGNETIC MOTOR—Tesla invented the induction motor which had a rotating magnetic field. The electro-magnetic motor was instrumental in converting electrical energy into mechanical energy, enabling electric motors to power machines. (1975)

Tishler, Max 1906–1989 (b. Boston, Mass.) SYNTHESIS OF RIBOFLAVIN AND SULFAQUINOXALINE—Tishler found a new process for the economical and large-scale synthesis of riboflavin (vitamin B_2). He also developed a production process for sulfaquinoxaline, the first effective antibiotic for the prevention and cure of the poultry disease coccidiosis. (1982)

Townes, Charles Hard 1915– (b. Greenville, South Carolina) MASERS—Townes constructed the maser (microwave amplification by stimulated emission of radiation) and also suggested the laser. Both are used in communications, medicine, industry, astronomy and navigation. (1976)

Volwiler, Ernest H. 1893– (b. Hamilton, Ohio); **Tabern, Donalee L.** 1900–1974 (b. Bowling Green, Ohio) THIO-BARBITURIC ACID DERIVATIVES—Volwiler and Tabern came up with Pentothal when they were seeking an anesthetic which could be injected directly into the bloodstream. (1986)

Wang, An 1920–1990 (b. Shanghai, China) MAGNETIC PULSE CONTROLLING DEVICE—Wang's contributions to computer technology included the magnetic pulse controlling device, the principle upon which magnetic core memory is based. He is noted for his innovations in the office automation and information processing field. (1988)

Westinghouse, George 1846–1914 (b. Central Bridge, N.Y.) STEAM-POWER BRAKE DEVICES—Westinghouse invented a system of railroad brakes that would centralize control in the hands of the engineer. Westinghouse, Tesla and other inventors developed alternating current motors and apparatus for the transmission of high tension current leading to large scale municipal lighting. (1989)

Whitney, Eli 1765–1825 (b. Westboro, Mass.) COTTON GIN—Whitney invented the cotton gin, a machine that greatly increased the speed for separating the cotton from its pod and seeds and to clean it. Whitney also adopted the concept of interchangeable parts in manufacturing. (1974)

Williams, Robert R., Jr. 1886–1965 (b. Nellore, India) SYNTHESIS OF VITAMIN B_1—Williams isolated thiamine in crystalline form and synthesized vitamin B_1. He was instrumental in achieving enrichment of flour, cornmeal and other cereal grains, helping to eliminate pellagra and riboflavin deficiency among poor people. He also invented processes for making submarine insulation. (1991)

Wright, Orville 1871–1948 (b. Dayton, Ohio); **Wright, Wilbur** 1867–1912 (b. Millville, Ind.) FLYING MACHINE—The Wright brothers achieved the first powered, sustained and controlled flight of a heavier than air machine at Kitty Hawk, North Carolina in 1903. (1975)

Zworykin, Vladimir Kosma 1889–1982 (b. Murom, Russia) CATHODE RAY TUBE—Zworykin invented the iconoscope, a television transmitting tube and the kinetoscope, a cathode ray tube that projects pictures it receives onto a screen. He also invented an infrared image tube and helped develop an electron microscope. (1977) □

When a New Way to Drink Tea Was Discovered

Ninety years ago, an American institution—iced tea—was invented at the famed Louisiana Purchase Exposition at St. Louis in 1904. A young Englishman, Richard Blechynden, operated a teahouse at the fair in order to popularize his company's special blends of tea. It was a hot, humid summer and visitors seemed uninterested in sampling his free hot drinks.

Blechynden was a bright young fellow and he noted that his teahouse was being passed up in favor of booths selling cooler summer drinks. He had an idea, and quickly obtained enough ice to experiment with cooling his brews. He soon discovered that iced tea tasted just as good as hot tea and offered the newly created thirst quencher to the public. The crowds loved it and a new American summer drink was born.

Another American favorite, the ice cream cone, was first produced at the St. Louis Fair. Several people have taken credit for this invention but Ernest A. Hamivi, an ice cream vendor from Syria is usually given this honor. He began serving ice cream in rolled-up, wafer-life pastry cones when his ice cream concession ran out of plates. The new treat became an instant hit at the Fair and its popularity spread rapidly throughout the United States in the next few years. □

A Look at Major Commercial Information Services

Despite the rise of smaller, specialized on-line services, the industry remains dominated by the big "umbrella" information services—which themselves offer access to numerous, more-targeted services, and bulletin boards. Many computer users first enter the on-line world by way of broad-based commercial information services. Among the better-known are AMERICA ONLINE, COMPUSERVE, DELPHI, GENIE, PRODIGY, and THE SIERRA NETWORK.

Because they differ in the number of service tiers and data base "gateways" they provide, these services are far from the same in what they ultimately make available to their members. But they do begin with a fairly similar on-line mix. The menu typically includes a number of financial management tools; electronic shopping and reservation services; provisions for file transfer, including software downloading; mail and message services; electronic gaming; and an array of computer-linked clubs and bulletin boards. In addition,they all provide access to a variety of data bases with a wide appeal: on-line encyclopedias and other reference works, business files, news, weather, sports updates, and entertainment news. Each of these services can serve as an excellent introduction to many of the things you can accomplish on-line—from tapping an information source to booking a reservation to browsing a bulletin board. It's up to you!

America Online

Like most of the big on-line services, AMERICA ONLINE is accessible via both IBM-PC and Macintosh systems. Its software libraries are stocked with both Macintosh- and PC-compatible programs and shareware, and its bulletin boards support concerns of the wide community of *both* systems' users and vendors.

AMERICA ONLINE makes available a full range of consumer on-line offerings: E-mail, multiplayer interactive games, interactive message boards, worldwide travel reservations, financial and investment information, sports updates, and more. There are classes taught by professional teachers, special-subject conferences with experts of all kinds, a whole nationwide community of users whose areas of interests are as diverse as the offerings of AMERICA ONLINE itself.

Compuserve

Promoting itself as "the information service you won't outgrow," COMPUSERVE has made data base access its long suit. COMPUSERVE is also proud of its highly structured special-interest "forums," which dwell on subjects ranging from cooking to investing and even alternative life-styles. Organized according to special interests, and "emceed" by expert "sysops" (systems operators), COMPUSERVE's forums offer a plethora of special-interest stuff: message boards, on-line discussion fests, member directories, and libraries of freeware and shareware. A free Practice Forum helps new users learn the ropes.

The service's standard tier provides members with a vast array of news, entertainment, travel, health, and business information. There's also an encyclopedia, a shopping service, *Eaasy Sabre*, and a selection of interactive games. Moving up the service tiers, there's a strong emphasis on money management, with guidance from financial stalwarts like Standard & Poor, Value Line, and Dun & Bradstreet. And as with other services, you can also opt for full-text retrieval capability for a broad selection of magazines and journals, including a special library of computer-oriented literature.

In addition, COMPUSERVE accesses hundreds of additional data bases through its IQuest Service, which serves as an on-line hook-up, or gateway, to other information networks. Here, the kind of information available can be quite specific: you can tap into the *Multinational Environment Outlook* data base, for example, or the one devoted to *Advanced Manufacturing Technology.* COMPUSERVE provides numerous other on-line gateways, some of which provide connections to the *National Technical Information Service* and the *Patent Research Center.*

Delphi

User interaction is a prime focus of DELPHI, which takes pride in its international orientation—it touts its far-flung membership, which comes from more than 40 countries. While also offering a basic tier of information and transaction services, DELPHI puts a strong emphasis on its numerous electronically linked clubs. There's one for every conceivable interest—from a divorce support group to a writers' group. Indeed, some are even "private," requiring individual application. And if there isn't a group for your particular interest, DELPHI encourages you to start one.

Electronic gaming is also very popular with DELPHI members. There are often multi-player contests, with scheduled on-line tournaments. And recently, DELPHI took a serious plunge into data-base access when it announced it would offer gateway service to the INTERNET and its labyrinth of participating worldwide research and information networks; to help users find their way, an *INTERNET Support Forum* was launched.

Genie

GENIE, a General Electric product, starts with a service mix similar to the other large services: money matters, news and weather, games and entertainment, and a wide variety of general- and special-interest services. On a premium, business-oriented tier, you can access, among many others, an intriguing service called *Public Opinion On-line*, which shares results of hundreds of recent surveys on virtually every subject that pollsters inquire about.

Like the other large services, GENIE urges its members to interact, and even offers special rates on a *Chat Club* for the talkative. Here, real-time conversations can be purely social, or can center around specific interests. GENIE also gives expert advice to users of specific hardware and software, and with its intensive computer support services, GENIE aims a strong appeal to computer users whose main interest is precisely that—computing—and offers a large trove of downloadable public-domain software and shareware.

Prodigy

PRODIGY stresses the everyday advantages of on-line computing, and its offerings are family-oriented and extensive: movie reviews, games, shopping, etcetera, all via PRODIGY's user-friendly screen format. With PRODIGY, however, you also gain access to various business and market updates, Accu-Weather forecasts, *Eaasy Sabre,* and on-line versions of reference works such as the *Mobil Travel Guide, Grolier's Encyclopedia,* and *Consumer Reports* magazine.

You'll also find a game center, an interactive version of *Sesame Street,* and a broad range of on-line transactions: discount brokerage, travel planning, catalog shopping, floral delivery, and bill paying. In addition, there are expert reports on a host of subjects ranging from rock music to real estate.

One way PRODIGY manages to offer so much service for one small fee is by offering commercial advertising messages that accompany the information flow. In addition to keeping costs down, these commercial messages often provide valuable information like special offers, promotions, and new product information from a variety of companies.

Sierra Network

While not strictly speaking an information services, THE SIERRA NETWORK has had a strong impact on the world of interactive electronic gaming. A subsidiary of SIERRA ON-LINE, THE SIERRA NETWORK offers a broad selection of stylish, imaginative multi-player games, which include *SierraLand* (an adventure arcade and action park); *MedievalLand* (a fantasy role-playing game set in the Dark Ages) and *LarryLand* (an adults-only version of SIERRA's popular *Leisure Suit Larry* that features blackjack, poker, roulette, slots, and other casino games). SIERRA NETWORK members also hook into the service for extensive chat, bulletin board, and electronic-mail capabilities.

• • •

There are numerous other large "vendor" services, as well. These include the business- and research-oriented DIALOG (tel. 800-334-3564); the London-based DATA-STAR, which provides European business information for U.S.-based users (tel. 800-221-7754); MEAD DATA CENTRAL, whose well-known LEXIS service supplies attorneys with legal research data (tel. 800-227-4908); MEAD's NEXIS, a business, news and financial service that also offers access to television transcripts and the full text of more than 800 newspapers and magazines (tel. 800-227-4908); and NEWSNET, which consolidates 350 of the world's best business newsletters, worldwide wire services, and stock-quote services (tel. 800-345-1301).

The Bottom Line on On-Line Costs

NOTE: Depending on the on-line service, numerous factors affect basic billing rates, including special discounts and promotions. Use the prices below as a guide only, and call to verify current pricing and promotions offered.

AMERICA ONLINE. The starter kit is free, and includes software. For IBM users, charges are $7.95 per month, with the first month free; the cost includes five free hours of connect time the first month, two hours free each month thereafter. Connect time after this is $6 per hour. For Macintosh users, charges are $5.95 per month, with the first month free and one free hour of connect time. Connect time after this start at $5 per hour. No extra charge for E-mail (tel. 800-827-6364).

COMPUSERVE. The starter kit costs $49.95, and includes software. There's an $8.95 regular monthly charge which covers unlimited access to 35 basic services; 60 E-mail messages per month are free; and 15 cents each thereafter. Access to more than 1,700 special interest forums and other premium services is additional. (tel. 800-848-8199).

DELPHI. Under the 10/4 plan, the cost is $10 a month for four hours on-line, with the first four hours free. Additional hours are $4 each. The 20/20 plan offers 20 hours on-line each month for $20, with additional hours charged at $1.80 each. (tel. 800-544-4005).

GENIE. The basic service charge is $4.95 per month for non-prime-time user of basic services. Connect charges begin at $6 per hour. (tel. 800-638-9636).

PRODIGY. The starter kit including software and first month is $49.95 (special offers often apply). The regular monthly charge is $14.95, which includes use of bulletin boards and 30 items of E-mail per month. Additional E-mail messages are 25 cents each. (tel. 800-776-3449).

SIERRA NETWORK. The starter kit is free, including software and three hours of on-line time. A $12.95 monthly charge covers 30 hours per month of basic games. Premium games are billed at $4 each per month. The E-mail charge is $2 per month for unlimited use. SIERRA has also just introduced a game/modem package that includes a 2400-baud modem, free connect time, and a starter kit with software, all for less than $50. (tel. 800-743-7721).

Everywhere You Look: Computers in Business

Source: Bureau of Census.

Workers Using Computers by Occupation, 1984 and 1989, Percent

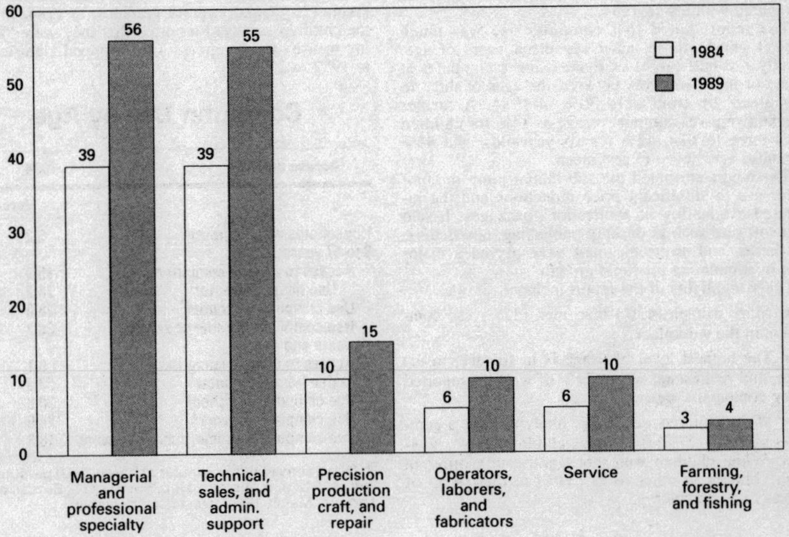

Workers Using Computers by Industry, 1984 and 1989, Percent

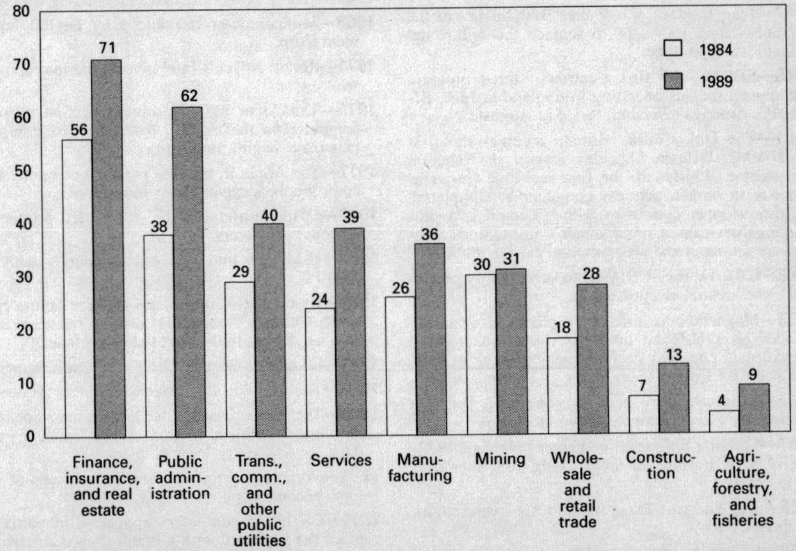

Who Uses Home Computers?

The latest government study on computers focused on the level of use and ownership of computers in American households. It found that nearly ten years after their introduction, almost one-third of the U.S. population uses a computer in some way and that 15% of all households owned a personal computer as compared with 8% in 1984.

The report noted that computer use was much greater among those under seventeen years of age. Nearly one-half (46%) of those using a computer at home or in school were between the ages of three to seventeen, up from only 30% in 1984. A further breakdown gives computer usage as 14% for children ages three to five, 42% for six-year-olds, and 45% for those ages seven to seventeen.

The report attributed the substantial jump in computer use to significant price reductions and the increased availability of applications packages. It said that software such as desktop publishing, newsletters, databases, and electronic mail have played a major role in stimulating the rapid growth.

Other highlights of the report include:

- More women (43%) than men (32%) use computers in the workplace.
- The highest level of usage is in finance, insurance, and real estate, where 71% of workers reported using computers.
- White children were more likely to have a computer at home (27%) than Black children (11%); however, White children were not significantly different from children of other races (28%) in their level of access to a computer.
- For most children, exposure to a computer occurred in the classroom, where usage rose from 28% in 1984 to 46% in 1989.
- The most frequent use of computers by children was for games (84%), homework (40%), word processing (25%), and 12% for graphics. In 1984, 71% of the children surveyed reported that they were "learning to use" the computer. This dropped significantly in 1989 to 25%. □

Computer Use by Age

Access and use	1984	1989
	Percent	
Households with computer	8.2	15.0
3 to 17 years:		
Access to a home computer	15.3	24.2
Use home computer[1]	74.2	71.1
Use computer at school[2]	28.0	46.0
Use computer at home or school	30.2	46.0
18 years and over:		
Access to a home computer	9.1	17.3
Use home computer[1]	53.3	58.4
Use computer at school[2]	30.8	43.6
Use computer at work[3]	24.6	36.8
Use computer at home, school, or work	18.3	28.1

1. Of persons with a computer at home. 2. Of persons enrolled. 3. Of persons with a job. *Source:* U.S. Bureau of the Census, March 1991, latest data available.

A Brief History of Modern Computers

1945—ENIAC designed to calculate ballistic trajectories. One trajectory took a human 3 days to calculate, ENIAC could do it in 20 seconds.

1947—John Bardeen and Walter Brattain invent the point-contact transistor to replace the bulky and fragile vacuum tube.

1949—EDSAC, the first electronic stored program computer, begins operating in England in June. BINAC, America's version, tested in August.

1951—The U.S. Census Bureau receives the first UNIVAC. William Shockley invents the junction transistor. Whirlwind, the first real-time (instantaneous to human actions) computer is completed. Grace Hopper comes up with a compiler, a program that scans a programmer's instructions, produces an organized program, and carries it out.

1952—CBS-TV uses UNIVAC to successfully predict the presidential election result.

1953—Magnetic-core memory replaces electrostatic tubes on Whirlwind doubling speed, quadrupling input data rate, and slashing memory bank maintenance time from 4 hours a day to 2 hours a week.

1955—Silicon Valley gets its start with William Shockley's Semiconductor Laboratory.

1957—The first high-level computer language, FORTRAN, is introduced simplifying computer programming.

1958—Jack Kilby of Texas Instruments creates an integrated circuit.

1959—Robert Noyce invents the planar integrated circuit, opening the door for commercial development.

1961—MIT develops the first time-sharing computer.

1963—Minicomputer introduced by Digital Equipment Corp.

1971—Robert Noyce's Intel invents the microprocessor.

1975—The Altair 8800 becomes the first personal computer on the market. *Byte*, the first computer magazine, begins publication.

1977—The Apple II, the first personal computer with color graphics capability, is introduced.

1978—Epson introduces the dot-matrix printer for personal computers.

1981—IBM gets into personal computers with the IBM PC.

1982—Epson's HX-20 becomes the first laptop computer. Compaq Computer Corp. is founded, challenging IBM with the first IBM PC clone.

1983—Lotus 1-2-3 spreadsheet program is launched.

1984—The user-friendly Macintosh makes its debut.

1985—The Apple LaserWriter laser printer opens up the desktop publishing area. AT&T Bell Labs produce the first fuzzy logic chips.

1988—Notebook computers, smaller versions of laptops, become popular.

1991—Clipboard computers appear. Clipboards replace the keyboard with a liquid crystal screen and electronic stylus.

Computer Terms for Novices

Acoustic Coupler: A portable device for connecting two compatible computers together via the telephone lines using an ordinary telephone. An acoustic coupler is a modem that avoids the need for making a direct connection to the telephone line. (*See* Modem.)

Address: An instruction that identifies where a specific unit of information is stored in the computer's memory. Without the address, it would be nearly impossible to find anything that you have stored.

Alphanumeric: Letters and numbers.

ASCII: American Standard Code for Information Interchange, an encoding system for converting keyboard characters and instructions into the binary number code that the computer understands. (*See* Machine Language.)

BASIC: Beginner's All-Purpose Symbolic Code. This is the most widely used simple and direct language for beginners to use on their home computers. It can inform you when you have made a mistake.

Baud Rate: The speed of data transmission measured in bits per second.

Binary: A numbering system that uses only two digits, 0 and 1. Computers can *only* add and they can only add in 0's and 1's.

Bit: (Stands for binary digit). It is the smallest piece of computer information and is either the number 0 or 1. All information is given to the computer in the binary number system. With proper coding, the computer can "understand" any number, letter, punctuation mark, or symbol through an appropriate combination of the numbers 0 and 1.

Boot: To start up a program.

Bug: A malfunction due to an error in the program or a defect in the equipment.

Byte: Most computers use combinations of eight bits to represent one character of data. These eight-bit combinations are called bytes. Bytes can represent data or instructions. For example, the word "cat" has three characters, and it would be represented by three bytes.

CD-ROM: (Compact Disk Read-Only Memory.) A peripheral system that uses CD-ROM laser disks and a CD-ROM reader (similar to a CD music disk and player) connected to your computer. A single disk can hold an entire library of books such as encyclopedias, and other reference works and multi-media programs for quick, convenient viewing.

Chip: A tiny wafer of silicon containing miniature electric circuits which can store millions of bits of information.

COBOL: Common Ordinary Business-Oriented Language. A programming language for large business computers that is intended for record-keeping functions.

CPU: Central Processing Unit. The "brains" or part of a computer where all the incoming information is controlled and executed by its electronic circuitry.

CRT: Cathode Ray Tube. A visual device similar to your television screen that lets the computer operator see what he is doing.

Cursor: A moving position-indicator displayed on the computer monitor that shows the computer operator where he is working.

Database: A program that enables you to create and update files of information in a well-organized manner.

Debug: Computer slang for finding and correcting in a computer program or equipment malfunction. (*See* Bug.)

Desktop Publishing: Use of a personal computer in combination with text, graphics, and page layout programs to produce publication quality documents.

Directory: A list of files stored in the computer.

Disk: On large computers, disks are hard and are about the same size as a phonograph record. PCs use smaller disks, 5 1/4 or 3 1/2 inches in diameter. Because they are made from a flexible mylar plastic, they are sometimes called *floppy disks*, or *diskettes*.

Disk Drive: The machine that a disk is inserted into so that information may be stored or retrieved from the disk.

Documentation: The instruction manual for a piece of hardware or software.

DOS: Disk Operating System. A program for controlling the storage of information on a disk commonly used in IBM computers and compatibles.

E-mail: Electronic Mail. It can refer to inter-office memos or letters sent by computer or messages sent by users to other computer users.

File: A set of data that is stored in the computer.

Fonts: Sets of typefaces (or characters) that come in different styles and sizes.

Gigabyte (GB): One billion bytes.

Glitch: The cause of an unexpected malfunction.

Graphics: Pictorial matter such as charts, graphs, and diagrams that can be programmed into a computer's video display.

Graphics Terminal: A specially designed CRT that can display intricate, detailed drawings and diagrams in black and white and in color. (*See* Light Pen.)

GUI: Graphical User Interface. A system that simplifies selecting computer commands by enabling the user to point to symbols or illustrations (called "icons") on the computer screen with a mouse.

Hacker: A person with technical expertise who enjoys tinkering with computer systems in order to produce additional features. Also one who intentionally accesses all or part of a computer or a computer system without authorization to do so. (A crime in some states.)

Hard Copy: A permanent record of what you have done on the computer in the form of a paper printout.

Hardware: The physical and mechanical components of a computer system. They include electronic circuitry, chips, screens, disk drives, keyboards, and printers.

Hexidecimal: A machine language written in a 16-base number system. In "Hex," the digits are 0 through 9, plus A, B, C, D, E, and F.

I/O: Input/output. Information into or out of a computer.

Icons: Symbols or illustrations appearing on the computer screen that indicate program files or other computer functions.

Input: Data that goes into a computer device.

Interface: A device that connects a computer with a peripheral so that they can communicate with each other.

Kilobyte (K or KB): Equal to 1,024 bytes. Computer memories are measured in terms of the number of bytes they can store. For example: a 64K memory means that the computer can handle 64 × 1024 or 65,536 bytes.

Language: A special set of symbols, characters, and numbers that you use to communicate with the computer.

Laptop and Notebook: Small, lightweight, portable battery-powered computers that can fit onto your lap. They have a thin, flat, liquid crystal display screen.

Liquid Crystal Display (LCD): The kind of display used to show numerals in digital watches and calculators.

Machine Language: The CPU or "brains" of the computer can only understand instructions written in binary form (bits of 0's and 1's). The commands the operator gives the computer are translated into data by the computer using the two-digit binary number system.

Megabyte (MB): Equal to 1,048,576 bytes, usually rounded off to one million bytes.

Memory: A computer device or series of devices that store information.

Menu: A list of options displayed on the computer terminal that you can choose from.

Merge: To combine two or more files into a single file arrangement.

Microcomputer: A personal computer containing a central processing unit (CPU) and one or more memory circuits.

Microprocessor: A complete central processing unit (CPU) contained on a single silicon chip.

Modem: A device that will connect two compatible computers together by a direct connection to the telephone line. Modems accomplish this by converting the computer's data into an audio signal.

Monitor: A video display terminal.

Mouse: A small hand-held device for controlling the cursor movement on the screen by moving the "mouse" back and forth on a desk.

Multimedia: Software application technology that combines text and graphics with sound and animation. A **multimedia PC** contains the hardware to support these capabilities.

Output: Data that come out of a computer device.

MS-DOS: An operating system developed by Microsoft Corporation.

Network: Computers that are connected to other computers.

OS/2: An operating system for IBM PCs and compatible computers.

PC: Personal computer.

Pen Computer: A type of laptop PC tat uses a stylus (pen) to write directly on the screen rather than using a keyboard.

Peripherals: Extra equipment for the computer that will extend its usefulness and capability. Most peripherals either increase the computer's storage capacity or permit it to communicate with outside devices.

Printer: A mechanical device for making a permanent printed record of your computer's output on paper. The three major types of printers are the **Dot Matrix:** In which individual letters are made up of a series of tiny ink dots. The dots are formed by punching a ribbon with the ends of tiny wires; **Ink Jet:** Sprays tiny droplets of ink particles (which become electrically charged) onto paper and they are formed into characters by a varying electric field; and **Laser:** It uses the principle of dry process office copiers in which a modulated laser beam is used as the light source.

Program: A precise series of instructions written in a computer language that tells the computer what to do and how to do it. Programs are also called "software."

RAM: Random Access Memory. One of two basic types of memory. RAM is a memory that you can add to, retrieve from, or alter at will. RAM is also called Read/Write Memory. (*See* ROM.)

ROM: Read-Only Memory. One of the two basic types of memory. As its name implies, information in it cannot be altered by the computer operator. It can be transferred out, but not transferred in. ROM contains only permanent information put there by the manufacturer. (*See* RAM.)

Scanner: An electronic device that uses light-sensing equipment to scan paper images such as text, photos, and illustrations and translate the images into signals that the computer can understand and copy.

Software: The various computer programs.

Spreadsheets: Software that allows one to calculate numbers in a format that is similar to pages in a conventional ledger.

User: The person who is using the computer.

User Friendly: It means that the system and the instructions for it are supposed to be written in simple language and be easy to operate for people with a nontechnical background.

VGA: Video Graphics Array. A widely used monitor for personal computers.

Virtual Reality (VR): A technology that allows you to experience and interact with the image on the computer screen in a simulated three-dimensional environment. For example, you could design a room in a house on your computer and actually feel that you are walking around in it even though it was never built. (The holodeck in the science fiction TV series "Star Trek: The Next Generation" would be the ultimate virtual reality.) Current technology requires the user to wear a special helmet, viewing goggles, gloves, and other equipment that is wired to the computer.

Virus: An unauthorized piece of computer code attached to a computer program or portions of a computer system that secretly spreads from one computer to another by shared disks and over telephone lines.

Windows: A graphical user interface that enables users to select commands by pointing to illustrations or symbols displayed in a rectangular area on the computer screen with a mouse.

Word Processor: A computer system or program for setting, editing, revising, correcting, storing, and the printing of text.

Worm: An unauthorized independent program that penetrates computers and replicates itself, thereby affecting computers and computer networks. In 1988, Robert T. Morris, a Cornell University graduate student shut down a nationwide computer network with the best-known computer worm in history.

1993 Environmental Quality Index

National Wildlife's annual Environmental Quality Index is a subjective analysis of the state of the nation's natural resources. The information included in each section is based on personal interviews, news reports, and the most current scientific studies. The judgments on resource trends represent the collective thinking of the editors and the National Wildlife Federation staff, based on consultation with government experts, private specialists, and academic researchers.

Wildlife: Worse. Controversy heats up as lawmakers begin the debate over renewal of the expired Endangered Species Act. Throughout 1992 the battlelines were sharply drawn over measures to protect imperiled ecosystems and endangered and threatened species—notably regulations protecting the northern spotted owl of the Pacific Northwest. For several years the bird has been a lightning rod for controversy and 1992 was no different. However, ducks continued to serve as a more traditional indicator of the health of the continent's ecosystem. The U.S. Fish and Wildlife Service estimated that fewer than 30 million ducks flew from Mexico and the southern United States to Canada—a decline of more than 10 million birds since the early 1970s. Overall, the current duck decline is the worst recorded since the 1930s. The worsening figures have raised calls by scientists for the more vigorous protection of wetlands—vital breeding areas for ducks. A recent National Wildlife Federation study noted that wetlands "are being destroyed at the dizzying rate of 35 acres an hour."

Air: Worse. Smog levels decline in some areas, but the United States remains the leading producer of greenhouse gases. A mid-1992 change in the regulations affecting the Clean Air Act would allow large companies to make "minor" changes in their emissions without prior notice or approval. California Congressman Henry A. Waxman accused the administration of "carving the heart out of the new Clean Air Act" with a "knowingly illegal act." In much of the country, cars still account for half of all pollution. To help change this dilemma, the EPA announced stricter vehicle emission inspection programs for 80 major metropolitan areas, and basic testing for 55 cities where it was not required. Carbon dioxide emissions, in contrast to the modest gains against smog, remained high in 1992. Continuing decline of the ozone layer in the upper atmosphere led the U.N. Environment Program and the Bush Administration to move up to 1995 the date for banning CFCs, the chemical thought to be doing the most harm to the ozone layer.

Water: Worse. U.S. rivers continue to be plagued by polluted runoff, while evidence of coastal contamination mounts. The Environmental Protection Agency reported in April 1992 that two-thirds of all surface water in the country meets water quality standards. However, it also noted that contaminated runoff from farms, streets, and lawns has yet to be even partially controlled. Its analysis of more than a half-million miles of rivers (about one-third of the national total) found nearly 50 percent of the river miles too polluted to support their intended uses for recreation, drinking water, or fisheries. About 60 percent of the impairment was traced to agricultural runoff. Coastal pollution (due to dumping of sewage into coastal water) is the principal culprit blamed for a spreading epidemic of blooms of harmful algae that now constitute a "major planetary trend" according to oceanographer Theodore Smayna of the University of Rhode Island. The so-called "red tides" are explosive growths of algae that contain trace amounts of toxins which, after concentrating in the tissues of shellfish and other algae eaters, can become toxic, even fatal, to humans.

Forests: Worse. The administration attempts to settle an ancient-forest dispute by empowering the so-called God-Squad. In the protracted controversy to protect the spotted owl, U.S. Courts took action in 1992 to prevent logging of Northwest ancient forests. However, the situation was further complicated when a committee of federal cabinet members empowered to overrule the Endangered Species Act in cases of severe economic hardship met for the third time in its 14-year history. The so-called God-Squad denied requests by timber interests to open up 31 Oregon old-growth parcels to logging, but voted to overrule the law's provision on 13 tracts, comprising some 1,700 acres of forest under the jurisdiction of the Bureau of Land Management. The decision had no immediate effect because of several impending legal tangles, including a lawsuit brought by environmental groups who were challenging the decision. In June 1992 the Forest Service formalized its intentions to balance timber demands with wildlife habitat and recreation needs.

Energy: Worse. While the Congress finally passes an energy bill the states continue to take positive action. When Congress rejected the President's energy plan that included oil exploration in Alaska's Arctic National Wildlife Refuge, it put itself squarely behind conservation as a major element of future energy strategy. While the final bill sent to the White House made no attempt to raise the tax on gasoline or to increase the efficiency standards of new cars, it did contain a number of measures to improve energy efficiency in homes and commercial buildings. Some states have lost patience with federal dithering about energy policy and have moved ahead with their own strategies. Many electric utilities and their regulators have discovered that reducing demand is cheaper in the long run than increasing their electricity-generating supplies. With expenditures of some $2.5 billion, U.S. utilities promoted more efficient light bulbs and other conservation programs.

Soil: Same. Many U.S. farmers are now embracing conservation tactics, but grazing is taking a toll on public lands. After years of heavy topsoil losses, a survey of American farming practices showed that more farmers than ever before were using conservation tillage methods, which in some areas of the country have become standard practice. In 1991 conservation tillage was being applied to more than 28 percent of the nation's 281 million planted acres. In the Northeast and mid-Atlantic areas it was used on half or more of all planted fields. While acknowledging that the United States has one of the world's best soil conservation programs, a study by the World Resources Institute in Washington, D.C., found that more than a quarter of U.S. cropland is still eroding too rapidly to easily correct. The issues of use—or overuse—of publicly owned western rangelands returned to Congress in 1992 in the form of another attempt to enact higher grazing fees and put the fee receipts into range restoration. A study by the Interior and Agriculture departments estimated the annual losses of the government program at some $52 million. While ranchers paid private landowners an average of $9.66 to graze one cow for a month, the U.S. government rate to ranchers was only $1.92 but its cost for administering the program averaged out to $3.21 per animal per month.

Quality of Life: Worse. As arguments rage over the true cost of pollution control, Americans continue to support cleanup. Recycling is increasing but new EPA data show Americans are producing twice as much garbage today as they did in 1960. American commuters continued to add to the nation's mounting load of air pollutants by avoiding car pooling and mass transit. A surface transportation bill, passed by Congress and signed by President Bush, may help remedy the situation. The act enables states and communities, for the first time, to use federal gasoline taxes to fund mass-transit projects and other alternatives to automobiles. Meanwhile, Americans continue to face serious contamination problems. New evidence confirmed that the number of children at risk from lead exposure is much greater than previously thought. □

Endangered Species

The number of threatened animal taxa identified by International Union for Conservation of Nature and Natural Resources (IUCN) is just over 5,000, comprised of 698 mammals, 1,047 birds, 191 reptiles, 63 amphibians, 762 fishes, and 2,250 invertebrates. However, except for birds, for which International Council for Bird Preservation (ICBP)/IUCN have now attempted a global review, these numbers represent only those taxa whose threatened status is known to IUCN; many, many more taxa, particularly invertebrates, are threatened, and becoming extinct every year undescribed and unknown to the scientific and conservation communities. Thus the number of threatened taxa identified by IUCN represents only the visible fraction of a much greater problem.

The following list comprises some of the more familiar species that are endangered. Due to space limitations, it does not include all mammals, birds, reptiles, amphibians, and fish on the 1990 IUCN Red List nor does it include any clams, crustaceans, snails, insects, or plants.

Some Endangered and Threatened Species of the World[1]

Common Name	Scientific Name	Listed range
MAMMALS		
Bear, Baluchistan	Selenarctos thibetanus gedrosianus	Iran, Pakistan
Bear, Polar[2]	Ursus maritimus	Arctic
Cat, Pardel lynx	Felis pardina	Portugal, Spain
Cat, little spotted[2]	Felis tigrina	Central & South America
Cheetah[2]	Acinonyx jubatus	Africa, Middle East Iran, [India]
Chimpanzee, West African	Pan troglodytes verus	West Africa
Cougar, Florida	Felis concolor coryi	U.S.
Deer, Key[4]	Odocoileus virginiaus clavium	U.S.
Deer, marsh[2]	Blastocerus dichotomus	Central America
Elephant, Indian	Elephas maximus	Asia
Gazelle, Clark's (Dibatag)[2]	Ammodorcas clarkei	Ethiopia, Somalia
Gazelle, slender-horned	Gazella leptoceros	Sahara/Sahel
Gorilla, mountain	Gorilla gorilla beringei	Rwanda, Uganda, Zaire
Ibex, Walia	Capra walie	Ethiopia
Jaguar[2]	Panthera onca	U.S., Central & South America
Leopard[3]	Panthera pardus	Africa, Middle East, Asia
Leopard, snow	Panthera uncia	Asia
Lion, Asiatic	Panthera leo persica	Gujarat (India)

Common Name	Scientific Name	Listed range
Mandrill[2]	Mandrillus sphinx	Cameroon, Congo, Eq. Guinea, Gabon
Monkey, long-haired spider[2]	Ateles belzebuth	South America
Ocelot[2]	Felis pardalis	U.S., Central & South America
Prairie dog, Utah[2]	Cynomys parvidens	U.S.
Pronghorn, Sonoran	Antilocapra americana sonoriensis	Mexico, U.S.
Rat, Morro Bay kangaroo	Dipodomys heermanni morroensis	California
Rhinoceros, great Indian	Rhinoceros unicornis	India, Nepal
Sloth, maned	Bradypus torquatus	Brazil
Tiger	Panthera tigris	Asia
Wallaby, bridled nailtail	Onychogalea fraenata	Australia
Whale, humpback[2]	Megaptera novaeangliae	All oceans
Wolf, gray[2]	Canis lupus	North America, Middle East, Eurasia
Wolf, red	Canis rufus	U.S.
Zebra, Cape Mountain	Equus zebra zebra	South Africa
BIRDS		
Albatross, short-tailed[4]	Diomedea albatrus	Japan
Condor, California	Gymnogyps californianus	U.S.
Crane, whooping	Grus americana	Canada, U.S.
Crow, Hawaiian	Corvus tropicus	Hawaiian Islands
Kestrel, Mauritius	Falco punctatus	Mauritius
Parrot, paradise	Psephotus pulcherrimus	Australia
Stork, oriental white[4]	Ciconia boyciana	China, Japan, South Korea, U.S.S.R.
Woodpecker, ivory-billed	Campephilus principalis	Cuba, U.S.
REPTILES		
Crocodile, American	Crocodylus acutus	Caribbean, Central America, U.S.
Iguana, Anegada ground	Cyclura pinguis	British Virgin Is.
Python, Indian[2]	Python molurus	South & Southeast Asia
Snake, Atlantic saltmarsh[4]	Nerodia fasciata taeniata	U.S.
AMPHIBIANS		
Frog, Israel painted[5]	Discoglossus nigriventer	Israel
Toad, Mount Nimba viviparous[2]	Nectophrynoides occidentalis	Guinea, Cote d'Ivoire
FISH		
Catfish, giant[2]	Pangasianodon gigas	Mekong Basin
Trout, cutthroat[2]	Salmo clarki (subspecies)	U.S.

1. Unless otherwise indicated the species is rated endangered. 2. Vulnerable. 3. Threatened. 4. Rare. 5. Extinct? *[Former distribution] Source: 1990 IUCN Red List of Threatened Animals,* published by the International Union for Conservation of Nature and Natural Resources/United Nations Environment Programme, Avenue du Mont-Blanc, CH-1196 Gland, Switzerland.

Zoological Gardens

North America abounds in zoos from Canada to Mexico. The Metro Toronto Zoo, opened in 1974, is one of the largest in the world. Its six pavilions simulate the animals' natural habitats. So does the Calgary Zoo which also has a children's zoo. Mexico City's Chapultepec Park includes a large zoo featuring one of the few pairs of pandas outside of Red China, and a children's zoo.

The first zoological garden in the United States was established in Philadelphia in 1874. Since that time nearly every large city in the country has acquired a zoo. Among the largest are San Diego's on the West Coast; Chicago's Brookfield Zoo and those of St. Louis and Kansas City in the Middle West; New Orleans' Audubon Park and Zoological Garden in the South; and in the East the New York Zoological Society's park in the Bronx. The National Zoological Park in Washington, D.C., in a beautiful setting of hills, woods, and streams, was established in 1890 by an act of Congress. The major U.S. zoos now have created large naturalhabitat areas for their collections.

In Europe, zoological gardens have long been popular public institutions. The modern concept of zoo keeping may be dated from 1752 with the founding of the Imperial Menagerie at the Schönbrunn Palace in Vienna. It was opened to the public in 1765 and is still in operation. In 1793 the zoological collection of the Jardin des Plantes was established in Paris in the Bois de Boulogne. At Antwerp the Royal Zoological Society founded a large menagerie in 1843. Now its aviary is noted for the principle of lighted and darkened spaces for confining the birds. Germany's famous Tiergarten zoo, in Berlin, was founded in 1841 and officially opened in 1844.

In the British Isles, the Zoological Society of London established its collection in Regent's Park in 1828. It was also responsible for the establishment of the prototype of the openrange zoo, Whipsnade Park, in 1932. Edinburgh's zoo is famous for its collection of penguins, the largest colony in captivity.

U.S. Zoos and Aquariums

Source: The facilities listed are members of, and accredited by, the American Association of Zoological Parks and Aquariums to ensure that they are maintaining professional standards. It also accredits facilities outside of the United States.

Abilene Zoological Gardens, Texas
Akron Zoological Park, Ohio
Alexandria Zoological Park, La.
Aquarium for Wildlife Conservation, The, Brooklyn, N.Y.
Aquarium of the Americas, New Orleans, La.
Arizona-Sonora Desert Museum, Tucson
Audubon Park and Zoological Garden, New Orleans
John Ball Zoological Gardens, Grand Rapids, Mich.
Baltimore Zoo, Md.
Beardsley Zoological Gardens, Bridgeport, Conn.
Belle Isle Zoo and Aquarium, Detroit
Bergen County Zoological Park, Paramus, N.J.
Binder Park Zoo, Battle Creek, Mich.
Blank Park Zoo, Des Moines, Iowa
Brandywine Zoo, Wilmington, Del.
Brookgreen Gardens, Murrells Inlet, S.C.
Buffalo Zoological Gardens, N.Y.
Burnet Park Zoo, Syracuse, N.Y.
Busch Gardens, Tampa, Fla.
Caldwell Zoo, Tyler, Texas
Cape May County Park Zoo, Cape May Court House, N.J.
Central Florida Zoological Park, Lake Monroe, Fla.
Central Park Wildlife Conservation Center, New York, N.Y.
Central Texas Zoo, Waco, Texas
Chaffee Zoological Gardens of Fresno, Calif.
Cheyenne Mountain Zoological Park, Colorado Springs
Chicago Zoological Park, Brookfield, Ill.
Cincinnati Zoo and Botanical Garden, Ohio
Cleveland Metroparks Zoo, Ohio
Columbus Zoological Gardens, Ohio
Dakota Zoo, Bismarck, N.D.
Dallas Zoo, Texas
Denver Zoological Gardens, Colo.
Detroit Zoological Park, Mich.
Dickerson Park Zoo, Springfield, Mo.
Discovery Island Zoological Park, Lake Buena Vista, Fla.
Dreher Park Zoo, West Palm Beach, Fla.
El Paso Zoo, Texas
Emporia Zoo, Kan.
Erie Zoological Gardens, Pa.
Folsom Children's Zoo & Botanical Garden, Lincoln, Neb.
Fort Wayne Children's Zoo, Ind.
Fort Worth Zoological Park, Texas
Fossil Rim Wildlife Center, Glen Rose, Texas
Glen Oak Zoo, Peoria, Ill.
Grassmere Wildlife Park, Nashville, Tenn.
Great Plains Zoo & Musem, Sioux Falls, S.D.
Greater Baton Rouge Zoo, La.
Greenville Zoo, S.C.
Happy Hollow Park and Zoo, San Jose, Calif.
Honolulu Zoo, Hawaii
Houston Zoological Gardens, Texas
Indianapolis Zoo, Ind.
International Crane Foundation, Baraboo, Wis.
International Wildlife Conservation Park (Bronx Zoo), N.Y.
Jackson Zoological Park, Miss.
Jacksonville Zoological Park, Fla.
Kansas City Zoological Gardens, Mo.
Knoxville Zoological Gardens, Tenn.
Lake Superior Zoological Gardens, Duluth, Minn.
Lincoln Park Zoological Gardens, Chicago
Little Rock Zoological Gardens, Ark.
Living Desert, The, Palm Desert, Calif.
Living Seas, The, Lake Buena Vista, Fla.
Los Angeles Zoo, Calif.
Louisville Zoological Garden, Ky.
Lowry Park Zoological Garden, Tampa, Fla.
Marine World Africa USA, Vallejo, Calif.
Memphis Zoological Garden and Aquarium, Tenn.
Mesker Park Zoo, Evansville, Ind.
Metro Washington Park Zoo, Portland, Ore.
Miami Metrozoo, Fla.
Micke Grove Zoo, Lodi, Calif.
Miller Park Zoo, Bloomington, Ill.
Milwaukee County Zoological Gardens, Wis.
Minnesota Zoological Garden, Apple Valley, Minn.
Monterey Bay Aquarium, Calif.
Montgomery Zoo, Ala.
Mystic Marinelife Aquarium, Mystic, Conn.
National Aquarium in Baltimore, Md.
National Zoological Park, Washington, D.C.
New England Aquarium, Boston
North Carolina Aquarium at Fort Fisher, Kure Beach
North Carolina Aquarium at Pine Knoll Shores, Atlantic Beach
North Carolina Aquarium on Roanoke Island, Manteo
North Carolina Zoological Park, Asheboro
Northwest Trek Wildlife Park, Eatonville, Wash.
Oakland Zoo, Calif.
Oglebay's Good Children's Zoo, Wheeling, W.Va.
Oklahoma City Zoological Park, Okla.
Omaha's Henry Doorly Zoo, Neb.
Charles Paddock Zoo, Atascadero, Calif.
Parrot Jungle and Gardens, Miami, Fla.
Clyde Peeling's Reptiland Ltd., Allenwood, Pa.
Philadelphia Zoological Garden, Pa.
Phoenix Zoo, The Ariz.
Pittsburgh Aviary, Pa.
Pittsburgh Zoo, Pa.
Point Defiance Zoo and Aquarium, Tacoma, Wash.
Gladys Porter Zoo, Brownsville, Texas
Potawatomi Zoo, South Bend, Ind.
Potter Park Zoological Gardens, Lansing, Mich.
Pueblo Zoo, Colo.
Racine Zoological Gardens, Wis.
Reid Park Zoo, Tucson, Ariz.
Lee Richardson Zoo, Garden City, Kan.
Rio Grande Zoological Park, Albuquerque, N.M.
Riverbanks Zoological Park, Columbia, S.C.
Riverside Zoo, Scottsbluff, Neb.
Henson Robinson Zoo, Springfield, Ill.
Roosevelt Zoo, Minot, N.D.
Ross Park Zoo, Binghamton, N.Y.
Sacramento Zoo, Calif.
St. Augustine Alligator Farm, Fla.
St. Louis Zoological Park, Mo.
St. Paul's Como Zoo, Minn.
Salisbury Zoological Park, Md.
San Antonio Zoological Gardens and Aquarium, Texas
San Diego Wild Animal Park, Calif.
San Diego Zoo, Calif.
San Francisco Zoological Gardens, Calif.

Santa Ana Zoo, Calif.
Santa Barbara Zoological Gardens, Calif.
Sea Life Park, Waimanalo, Hawaii
Sea World of California, San Diego
Sea World of Florida, Orlando
Sea World of Ohio, Aurora
Sea World of Texas, San Antonio
The Seattle Aquarium, Wash.
Sedgwick County Zoo, Wichita, Kan.
Seneca Park Zoo, Rochester, N.Y.
John G. Shedd Aquarium, Chicago
Staten Island Zoo, N.Y.
Sunset Zoological Park, Manhattan, Kan.
The Texas Zoo, Victoria, Texas
Toledo Zoological Gardens, Ohio
Topeka Zoological Park, Kan.
Tracy Aviary, Salt Lake City, Utah
Trevor Zoo, Millbrook, N.Y.
Ellen Trout Zoo, Lufkin, Texas
Tulsa Zoological Park, Okla.
Utah's Hogle Zoo, Salt Lake City
Utica Zoo, N.Y.
Henry Vilas Zoo, Madison, Wis.
Virginia Zoological Park, Norfolk, Va.
Waikiki Aquarium, Hawaii
Wild Animal Habitat, Kings Island, Ohio
Wildlife Safari, Winston, Ore.
Wildlife World Zoo, Litchfield Park, Ariz.
Roger Williams Park Zoo, Providence, R.I.
Woodland Park Zoological Gardens, Seattle
The ZOO, Gulf Breeze, Fla.
Zoo Atlanta, Ga.
ZOOAMERICA North American Wildlife Park, Hershey, Pa.

Gestation, Incubation, and Longevity of Certain Animals

Animal	Gestation or incubation, in days & (average)	Longevity, in years (& record exceptions)	Animal	Gestation or incubation, in days & (average)	Longeveity, in years (& record exceptions)
Ass	365	18–20 (63)	Horse	329–345 (336)	20–25 (50+)
Bear	180–240[1]	15–30 (47)	Kangaroo	32–39[1]	4–6 (23)
Cat	52–69 (63)	10–12 (26+)	Lion	105–113 (108)	10 (29)
Chicken	22	7–8 (14)	Man	253–303	([2])
Cow	c. 280	9–12 (39)	Monkey	139–270[1]	12–15[1](29)
Deer	197–300[1]	10–15 (26)	Mouse	19–31[1]	1–3 (4)
Dog	53–71 (63)	10–12 (24)	Parakeet (Budgerigar)	17–20 (18)	8 (12+)
Duck	21–35[1](28)	10 (15)	Pig	101–130 (115)	10 (22)
Elephant	510–730 (624)[1]	30–40 (71)	Pigeon	11–19	10–12 (39)
Fox	51–63[1]	8–10 (14)	Rabbit	30–35 (31)	6–8 (15)
Goat	136–160 (151)	12 (17)	Rat	21	3 (5)
Groundhog	31–32	4–9	Sheep	144–152 (151)[1]	12 (16)
Guinea pig	58–75 (68)	3 (6)	Squirrel	44	8–9 (15)
Hamster, golden	15–17	2 (8)	Whale	365–547[1]	—
Hippopotamus	220–255 (240)	30 (49+)	Wolf	60–63	10–12 (16)

1. Depending on kind. 2. For life expectancy charts, *see* Index. *Source:* James Doherty, Curator of Mammals, N.Y. Zoological Society.

Speed of Animals

Most of the following measurements are for maximum speeds over approximate quarter-mile distances. Exceptions—which are included to give a wide range of animals—are the lion and elephant, whose speeds were clocked in the act of charging; the whippet, which was timed over a 200-yard course; the cheetah over a 100-yard distance; man for a 15-yard segment of a 100-yard run; and the black mamba, six-lined race runner, spider, giant tortoise, three-toed sloth, and garden snail, which were measured over various small distances.

Animal	Speed mph	Animal	Speed mph	Animal	Speed mph
Cheetah	70	Mongolian wild ass	40	Man	27.89
Pronghorn antelope	61	Greyhound	39.35	Elephant	25
Wildebeest	50	Whippet	35.5	Black mamba snake	20
Lion	50	Rabbit (domestic)	35	Six-lined race runner	18
Thomson's gazelle	50	Mule deer	35	Squirrel	12
Quarter horse	47.5	Jackal	35	Pig (domestic)	11
Elk	45	Reindeer	32	Chicken	9
Cape hunting dog	45	Giraffe	32	Spider (Tegenearia atrica)	1.17
Coyote	43	White-tailed deer	30	Giant Tortoise	0.17
Gray fox	42	Wart hog	30	Three-toed sloth	0.15
Hyena	40	Grizzly bear	30	Garden snail	0.03
Zebra	40	Cat (domestic)	30		

Source: Natural History Magazine, March 1974, copyright 1974. The American Museum of Natural History; and James Doherty, Curator of Mammals, N.Y. Zoological Society.

Animal Group Terminology

Source: James Doherty, Curator of Mammals, N.Y. Zoological Society, and *Information Please* data.

ants: colony
bears: sleuth, sloth
bees: grist, hive, swarm
birds: flight, volery
cattle: drove
cats: clutter, clowder
chicks: brood, clutch
clams: bed
cranes: sedge, seige
crows: murder
doves: dule
ducks: brace, team
elephants: herd
elks: gang
finches: charm
fish: school, shoal, draught
foxes: leash, skulk
geese: flock, gaggle, skein
gnats: cloud, horde
goats: trip
gorillas: band
hares: down, husk
hawks: cast
hens: brood
hogs: drift
horses: pair, team
hounds: cry, mute, pack
kangaroos: troop
kittens: kindle, litter
larks: exaltation
lions: pride
locusts: plague
magpies: tidings
mules: span
nightingales: watch
oxen: yoke
oysters: bed
parrots: company
partridges: covey
peacocks: muster, ostentation
pheasants: nest, bouquet
pigs: litter
ponies: string
quail: bevy, covey
rabbits: nest
seals: pod
sheep: drove, flock
sparrows: host
storks: mustering
swans: bevy, wedge
swine: sounder
toads: knot
turkeys: rafter
turtles: bale
vipers: nest
whales: gam, pod
wolves: pack, route
woodcocks: fall

Animal Names: Male, Female, and Young

Animal	Male	Female	Young
Ass	Jack	Jenny	Foal
Bear	Boar	Sow	Cub
Cat	Tom	Queen	Kitten
Cattle	Bull	Cow	Calf
Chicken	Rooster	Hen	Chick
Deer	Buck	Doe	Fawn
Dog	Dog	Bitch	Pup
Duck	Drake	Duck	Duckling
Elephant	Bull	Cow	Calf
Fox	Dog	Vixen	Cub
Goose	Gander	Goose	Gosling
Horse	Stallion	Mare	Foal
Lion	Lion	Lioness	Cub
Rabbit	Buck	Doe	Bunny
Sheep	Ram	Ewe	Lamb
Swan	Cob	Pen	Cygnet
Swine	Boar	Sow	Piglet
Tiger	Tiger	Tigress	Cub
Whale	Bull	Cow	Calf
Wolf	Dog	Bitch	Pup

Source: James Doherty, Curator of Mammals, N.Y. Zoological Society.

Record Ozone Hole

According to NASA satellite observations, the seasonal hole in the ozone layer over Antarctica has continued to grow since its discovery in 1985. The hole covered a record area of 8.9 million square miles in September 1992, about three times the area of the 48 U.S. contiguous states. □

Lead in Drinking Water

The U.S. Environmental Protection Agency estimates that drinking water can make up 20% or more of a person's total exposure to lead. Lead in drinking water comes from water supplier pipes and plumbing within the home. It results from water wearing away older pipes, solder, and other plumbing connections. Although lead in drinking water is rarely the single cause of lead poisoning, it can significantly increase a person's total lead exposure. Infants who are fed baby formula or drinks mixed with hot water from the tap are the most vulnerable to lead in drinking water.

Never use hot water from the tap for cooking, drinking, or mixing with food, and never mix hot tap water with infant formula or juice. Hot water is more likely to contain lead than cold water. To be safe, run the water to flush out the pipes for a full minute, especially when the water has not been used for more than six hours.

To find out if your plumbing system contains lead, conduct an inspection. Lead pipes and solder are dull gray, and when scratched look shiny. You may want to ask an experienced professional for help. Have an electrician check your wiring. If grounding wires from the electrical system are attached to your pipes, your water may absorb more lead. Check with a licensed electrician or your local electrical code to determine if your wiring can be grounded elsewhere. *Do not* attempt to change the wiring yourself because improper grounding can cause electric shock and fire hazards.

Testing for lead in drinking water is essential because you cannot see, taste, or smell lead in drinking water. Call your local or state environmental protection agency to request a water test or a list of laboratories that can test your water.

In October 1992, the EPA reported that the results of initial tests for lead in drinking water samples showed that 130 of the nation's 660 large public water systems exceeded the lead "action level" of 15 parts per billion (ppb). These 130 systems provide the drinking water for about 32 million people. □

The National Park System

Source: Department of the Interior, National Park Service.

The National Park System of the United States is administered by the National Park Service, a bureau of the Department of the Interior. Started with the establishment of Yellowstone National Park in 1872, the system includes not only the most extraordinary and spectacular scenic exhibits in the United States but also a large number of sites distinguished either for their historic or prehistoric importance or scientific interest, or for their superior recreational assets. The number and extent of the various types of areas that make up the system follow.

Type of area	Number	Total acreage[1]
International Historic Site	1	35.39
National Battlefields	11	13,142.62
National Battlefield Parks	3	8,727.65
National Battlefield Site	1	1.00
National Historic Sites	72	19,820.70
National Historical Parks	36	159,626.83
National Lakeshores	4	228,745.27
National Memorials	26	7,951.16
National Military Parks	9	37,881.56
National Monuments	76	4,787,743.69
National Parks	51	47,783,680.35
National Parkways	4	170,546.79
National Preserves	14	22,332,829.67
National Recreation Areas	18	3,699,550.55
National Reserves	2	22,407.19
National Rivers	6	362,152.27
National Scenic Trails	3	176,351.97
National Seashores	10	592,531.64
National Wild and Scenic Rivers	9	212,682.12
Parks (other)	11	46,809.00
Total	**367**	**80,663,217.42**

1. Acreages as of May 31, 1992.

National Parks

Name, location, and year authorized	Acreage	Outstanding characteristics
Acadia (Maine), 1919	41,951.06	Rugged seashore on Mt. Desert Island and adjacent mainland
Arches (Utah), 1971	73,373.98	Unusual stone arches, windows, pedestals caused by erosion
Badlands (S.D.), 1978	242,755.94	Arid land of fossils, prairie, bison, deer, bighorn, antelope
Big Bend (Tex.), 1935	801,163.02	Mountains and desert bordering the Rio Grande
Biscayne (Fla.), 1980	172,924.73	Aquatic, coral reef park south of Miami was a national monument, 1968–80
Bryce Canyon (Utah), 1924	35,835.08	Area of grotesque eroded rocks brilliantly colored
Canyonlands (Utah), 1964	337,570.43	Colorful wilderness with impressive red-rock canyons, spires, arches
Capitol Reef (Utah), 1971	241,904.26	Highly colored sedimentary rock formations in high, narrow gorges
Carlsbad Caverns (N.M.), 1930	46,766.45	The world's largest known caves
Channel Islands (Calif.) 1980	249,353.77	Area is rich in marine mammals, sea birds, endangered species and archeology
Crater Lake (Ore.), 1902	183,223.77	Deep blue lake in heart of inactive volcano
Denali (Alaska), 1917	4,741,910.00	Mt. McKinley National Park was renamed and enlarged by Act of Dec. 2, 1980. Contains Mt. McKinley, N. America's highest mountain (20,320 ft)
Dry Tortugas (Fla.), 1992	64,700.00	Formerly Ft. Jefferson National Monument. Located 70 miles off Key West. Features an underwater nature trail.
Everglades (Fla.), 1934	1,506,499.40	Subtropical area with abundant bird and animal life
Gates of the Arctic (Alaska), 1980	7,523,888.00	Diverse north central wilderness contains part of Brooks Range
Glacier Bay (Alaska), 1980	3,225,284.00	Park was a national monument (1925–1980) popular for wildlife, whale-watching, glacier-calving, and scenery
Glacier (Mont.), 1910	1,013,572.42	Rocky Mountain scenery with many glaciers and lakes
Grand Canyon (Ariz.), 1919	1,217,159.32	Mile-deep gorge, 4 to 18 miles wide, 217 miles long
Grand Teton (Wyo.), 1929	309,974.28	Picturesque range of high mountain peaks
Great Basin (Nev.), 1986	77,180.00	Exceptional scenic, biologic, and geologic attractions
Great Smoky Mts. (N.C.-Tenn), 1926	520,269.44	Highest mountain range east of Black Hills; luxuriant plant life
Guadalupe Mountains (Tex.), 1966	86,415.97	Contains highest point in Texas: Guadalupe Peak (8,751 ft)
Haleakala (Hawaii), 1960	28,099.00	World-famous 10,023-ft. Haleakala volcano (dormant)
Hawaii Volcanoes (Hawaii), 1916	229,177.03	Spectacular volcanic area; luxuriant vegetation at lower levels
Hot Springs (Ark.), 1921	5,839.24	47 mineral hot springs said to have therapeutic value
Isle Royale (Mich.), 1931	571.790.11	Largest wilderness island in Lake Superior; moose, wolves, lakes
Katmai (Alaska), 1980	3,586,000.00	Expansion may assure brown bear's preservation. Park was national monument 1918–80; is known for fishing, 1912 eruption, bears

Name, location, and year authorized	Acreage	Outstanding characteristics
Kenai Fjords (Alaska), 1980	689,541.00	Mountain goats, marine mammals, birdlife are features at this seacoast park near Seward
Kings Canyon (Calif.), 1940	461,901.20	Huge canyons; high mountains; giant sequoias
Kobuk Valley (Alaska), 1980	1,750,736.86	Native culture and anthropology center around the broad Kobuk River in northwest Alaska
Lake Clark (Alaska), 1980	2,636,839.00	Park provides scenic and wilderness recreation across Cook Inlet from Anchorage
Lassen Volcanic (Calif.), 1916	106,372.36	Exhibits of impressive volcanic phenomena
Mammoth Cave (Ky.), 1926	52,823.97	Vast limestone labyrinth with underground river
Mesa Verde (Colo.), 1906	52,121.93	Best-preserved prehistoric cliff dwellings in United States
Mount Rainier (Wash.), 1899	235,612.50	Single-peak glacial system; dense forests, flowered meadows
National Park of American Samoa	9,000.00	Samoa National Park, American Samoa: two rain forest preserves and a coral reef on the island of Ofu are home to unique tropical animals. The park also includes several thousand acres on the islands of Tutuila and Ta'u.
North Cascades (Wash.), 1968	504,780.94	Roadless Alpine landscape; jagged peaks; mountain lakes; glaciers
Olympic (Wash.), 1938	922,651.01	Finest Pacific Northwest rain forest; scenic mountain park
Petrified Forest (Ariz.), 1962	93,532.57	Extensive natural exhibit of petrified wood
Redwood (Calif.), 1968	110,232.40	Coastal redwood forests; contains world's tallest known tree (369.2 ft)
Rocky Mountain (Colo.), 1915	265,727.15	Section of the Rocky Mountains; 107 named peaks over 10,000 ft
Sequoia (Calif.), 1890	402,482.38	Giant sequoias; magnificent High Sierra scenery, including Mt. Whitney
Shenandoah (Va.), 1926	196,466.19	Tree-covered mountains; scenic Skyline Drive
Theodore Roosevelt (N.D.), 1978	70,446.59	Scenic valley of Little Missouri River; T.R. Ranch; Wildlife
Virgin Islands (U.S. V.I.), 1956	14,688.87	Beaches; lush hills; prehistoric Carib Indian relics
Voyageurs (Minn.), 1971	218,035.33	Wildlife, canoeing, fishing, and hiking
Wind Cave (S.D.), 1903	28,295.03	Limestone caverns in Black Hills; buffalo herd
Wrangell-St. Elias (Alaska), 1980	7,730,645.18	Largest Park System area has abundant wildlife, second highest peak in U.S. (Mt. St. Elias); adjoins Canadian park
Yellowstone (Wyo.-Mont.-Idaho), 1872	2,219,790.71	World's greatest geyser area; abundant falls, wildlife, and canyons
Yosemite (Calif.), 1890	761,236.20	Mountains; inspiring gorges and waterfalls; giant sequoias
Zion (Utah), 1919	146,597.64	Multicolored gorge in heart of southern Utah desert

NATIONAL HISTORICAL PARKS

Name and location	*Total acreage*
Appomattox Court House (Va.)	1,325.08
Boston (Mass.)	41.03
Chaco Culture (N.M.)	33,974.29
Chesapeake and Ohio Canal (Md.-W.Va.-D.C.).	19,236.60
Colonial (Va.)	9,327.37
Cumberland Gap (Ky.-Tenn.-Va.)	20,445.81
Dayton Aviation Heritage, (Oh.)	.00
George Rogers Clark (Ind.)	26.17
Harpers Ferry (W.Va.-Md.)	2,287.48
Hopewell Culture (Oh.)	1,032.20
Independence (Pa.)	44.85
Jean Lafitte (La.)	20,020.00
Kalaupapa (Hawaii)	10,778.88
Kaloko-Honokohau (Hawaii)	1,160.91
Keewenaw (Mich.)	.00
Klondike Goldrush (Alaska, Wash.)	13,191.35
Lowell (Mass.)	136.86
Lyndon B. Johnson (Tex.)	1,571.93
Marsh–Billings	643.10
Minute Man (Mass.)	789.53
Morristown (N.J.)	1,683.61
Natchez (Miss.)	108.29
Nez Perce (Idaho)	2,109.61
Pecos (N.M.)	6,570.54
Púuchonua o Honaunau (Hawaii)	181.80
Salt River Bay (U.S. V.I.)	912.00
San Antonio Missions (Tex.)	820.01
Name and location	*Total acreage*
San Franisco Maritime (Calif.)	50.00
San Juan Island (Wash.)	1,751.99
Saratoga (N.Y.)	3,392.82
Sitka (Alaska)	106.83
Tumacacori (Ariz.)	46.52
Valley Forge (Pa.)	3,468.06
War in the Pacific (Guam)	1,960.07
Women's Rights (N.Y.)	5.73
Yorktown National Cemetery	2.91
Zuni-Cibola (N.M.)	800.00

NATIONAL MONUMENTS

Agate Fossil Beds (Neb.)	3,055.22
Alibates Flint Quarries (Tex.)	1,370.97
Aniakchak (Alaska)	137,176.00
Aztec Ruins (N.M.)	319.47
Bandelier (N.M.)	32,737.20
Black Canyon (Colo.)	20,766.14
Booker T. Washington (Va.)	223.92
Buck Island Reef (U.S. V.I.)	880.00
Cabrillo (Calif.)	137.06
Canyon de Chelly (Ariz.)	83,840.00
Cape Krusenstern (Alaska)	659,807.00
Capulin Volcano (N.M.)	792.84
Casa Grande (Ariz.)	472.50
Castillo de San Marcos (Fla.)	20.51
Castle Clinton (N.Y.)	1.00
Cedar Breaks (Utah)	6,154.60
Chiricahua (Ariz.)	11,984.80

Name and location	*Total acreage*
Colorado (Colo.)	20,453.93
Congaree Swamp (S.C.)	22,200.00
Craters of the Moon (Idaho)	53,545.05
Custer Battlefield (Mont.)	765.34
Death Valley (Calif.-Nev.)	2,067,627.68
Devils Postpile (Calif.)	798.46
Devils Tower (Wyo.)	1,346.91
Dinosaur (Utah-Colo.)	210,844.02
Effigy Mounds (Iowa)	1,481.39
El Malpais (N.M.)	114,272.09
El Morro (N.M.)	1,278.72
Florissant Fossil Beds (Colo.)	5,998.09
Fort Frederica (Ga.)	216.35
Fort Jefferson (Fla.)	64,700.00
Fort Matanzas (Fla.)	227.76
Fort McHenry (Md.)	43.26
Fort Pulaski (Ga.)	5,623.10
Fort Stanwix (N.Y.)	15.52
Fort Sumter (S.C.)	194.60
Fort Union (N.M.)	720.60
Fossil Butte (Wyo.)	8,198.00
George Washington Birthplace (Va.)	550.23
George Washington Carver (Mo.)	210.00
Gila Cliff Dwellings (N.M.)	533.13
Grand Portage (Minn.)	709.97
Great Sand Dunes (Colo.)	38,662.18
Hagerman Fossil Beds (Idaho)	4,280.00
Hohokam Pima (Ariz.)	1,690.00
Homestead (Neb.)	195.11
Hovenweep (Utah-Colo.)	784.93
Jewel Cave (S.D.)	1,273.51
John Day Fossil Beds (Ore.)	14,014.10
Joshua Tree (Calif.)	559,954.50
Lava Beds (Calif.)	46,559.87
Little Big Horn Battlefield (N.M.)	765.34
Montezuma Castle (Ariz.)	857.69
Mound City Group (Ohio)	270.20
Muir Woods (Calif.)	553.55
Natural Bridges (Utah)	7,636.49
Navajo (Ariz.)	360.00
Ocmulgee (Ga.)	701.54
Oregon Caves (Ore.)	487.98
Organ Pipe Cactus (Ariz.)	330,688.86
Petroglyph (N.M.)	5,195.34
Pinnacles (Calif.)	16,265.44
Pipe Spring (Ariz.)	40.00
Pipestone (Minn.)	281.78
Poverty Point	910.85
Rainbow Bridge (Utah)	160.00
Russell Cave (Ala.)	310.45
Saguaro (Ariz.)	87,687.18
Salinas (N.M.)	1,100.64
Scotts Bluff (Neb.)	3,003.03
Statue of Liberty (N.Y.-N.J.)	58.38
Sunset Crater (Ariz.)	3,040.00
Timpanogos Cave (Utah)	250.00
Tonto (Ariz.)	1,120.00
Tuzigoot (Ariz.)	800.62
Walnut Canyon (Ariz.)	2,249.46
White Sands (N.M.)	143,732.92
Wupatki (Ariz.)	35,253.24
Yucca House (Colo.)	9.60

NATIONAL PRESERVES

Aniakchak (Alaska)	465,603.00
Bering Land Bridge (Alaska)	2,784,960.00
Big Cypress (Fla.)	716,000.00
Big Thicket (Tex.)	85,797.20
Denali (Alaska)	1,334,618.00
Ebey's Landing	17,400.00
Gates of the Arctic (Alaska)	948,629.00

Name and location	*Total acreage*
Glacier Bay (Alaska)	57,884.00
Katmai (Alaska)	374,000.00
Lake Clark (Alaska)	1,407,293.00
Little River Canyon	.00
Noatak (Alaska)	6,574,481.00
Timucuan Ecological and Historic Preserve (Fla.)	46,000.00
Wrangell-St. Elias (Alaska)	4,733,061.09
Yukon-Charley (Alaska)	2,523,509.00

NATIONAL RESERVE

City of Rocks (Idaho)	14.407.19

NATIONAL MILITARY PARKS

Chickamauga and Chattanooga (Ga.-Tenn.)	8,106.04
Fredericksburg and Spotsylvania (Va.)	7,780.73
Fredericksburg National Cemetery	12.00
Gettysburg Nat. Mil. Park (Pa.)	5,875.27
Gettysburg Nat. Cemetery (Pa.)	20.58
Guilford Courthouse (N.C.)	220.25
Horseshoe Bend (Ala.)	2,040.00
Kings Mountain (S.C.)	3,945.29
Pea Ridge (Ark.)	4,300.35
Shiloh Nat. Cemetery (Tenn.)	10.05
Shiloh Nat. Mil. Park (Tenn.)	3,962.82
Vicksburg Nat. Cemetery (Miss.)	116.28
Vicksburg Nat. Mil. Park (Miss.)	1,625.27

NATIONAL BATTLEFIELDS

Antietam (Md.)	3,244.37
Big Hole (Mont.)	655.61
Cowpens (S.C.)	841.56
Fort Donelson (Tenn.)	536.35
Fort Necessity (Pa.)	902.80
Monocacy (Md.)	1,647.01
Moores Creek (N.C.)	86.52
Petersburg (Va.)	2,735.38
Stones River (Tenn.)	719.81
Tupelo (Miss.)	1.00
Wilson's Creek (Mo.)	1,749.00

NATIONAL BATTLEFIELD PARKS

Kennesaw Mountain (Ga.)	2,884.52
Manassas (Va.)	5,071.62
Richmond (Va.)	771.51

NATIONAL BATTLEFIELD SITE

Brices Cross Roads (Miss.)	1.00

NATIONAL HISTORIC SITES

Abraham Lincoln Birthplace (Ky.)	116.50
Adams (Mass.)	9.82
Allegheny Portage Railroad (Pa.)	1,246.97
Andersonville (Ga.)	494.61
Andrew Johnson (Tenn.)	16.68
Bent's Old Fort (Colo.)	799.80
Boston African American (Mass.)	0.00
Carl Sandburg Home (N.C.)	263.52
Charles Pinckney (S.C.)	28.45
Christiansted (V.I.)	27.15
Clara Barton (Md.)	8.59
Edgar Allan Poe (Pa.)	0.52
Edison (N.J.)	21.25
Eisenhower (Pa.)	690.46
Eleanor Roosevelt (N.Y.)	180.50
Eugene O'Neill (Calif.)	13.19
Ford's Theatre (Lincoln Museum) (D.C.)	0.29
Fort Bowie (Ariz.)	1,000.00
Fort Davis (Tex.)	40.00
Fort Laramie (Wyo.)	832.85
Fort Larned (Kan.)	718.39

Name and location	Total acreage
Fort Point (Calif.)	29.00
Fort Raleigh (N.C.)	512.93
Fort Scott (Kan.)	16.69
Fort Smith (Ark.-Okla.)	75.00
Fort Union Trading Post (N.D.-Mont.)	442.45
Fort Vancouver (Wash.)	208.89
Frederick Douglass Home (D.C.)	8.53
Frederick Law Olmsted (Mass.)	1.75
Friendship Hill (Pa.)	674.56
Golden Spike (Utah)	2,735.28
Grant-Kohrs Ranch (Mont.)	1,498.38
Hampton (Md.)	62.04
Harry S Truman (Mo.)	1.41
Herbert Hoover (Iowa)	186.80
Home of F. D. Roosevelt (N.Y.)	290.34
Hopewell Furnace (Pa.)	848.06
Hubbell Trading Post (Ariz.)	160.09
James A. Garfield (Ohio)	7.82
Jimmy Carter (Ga.)	70.54
John F. Kennedy (Mass.)	0.09
John Muir (Calif.)	340.04
Knife River Indian Villages (N.D.)	1,758.35
Lincoln Home (Ill.)	12.24
Longfellow (Mass.)	1.98
M. McLeod Bethune Council House (N.H.)	.07
Maggie L. Walker (Va.)	1.29
Manzanar National Historic Site (Calif.)	500.00
Martin Luther King, Jr. (Ga.)	23.18
Martin Van Buren (N.Y.)	39.58
Mary McLeod Bethune Council House National Historic Site (D.C.)	—
Ninety Six (S.C.)	989.14
Palo Alto Battlefield (Tex.)	3,357.42
Pennsylvania Avenue (D.C.)	0.00
Puukohola Heiau (Hawaii)	80.47
Sagamore Hill (N.Y.)	83.02
Saint-Gaudens (N.H.)	148.23
Saint Paul's Church (N.Y.)	6.13
Salem Maritime (Mass.)	9.02
San Juan (P.R.)	75.13
Saugus Iron Works (Mass.)	8.51
Springfield Armory (Mass.)	54.93
Steamtown (Pa.)	62.48
Theodore Roosevelt Birthplace (N.Y.)	0.11
Theodore Roosevelt Inaugural (N.Y.)	1.03
Thomas Stone (Md.)	328.25
Tuskegee Institute (Ala.)	57.62
Ulysses S. Grant (Mo.)	9.60
Vanderbilt Mansion (N.Y.)	211.65
Weir Farm (Conn.)	58.77
Whitman Mission (Wash.)	98.15
William Howard Taft (Ohio)	3.07

NATIONAL MEMORIALS

Arkansas Post (Ark.)	389.18
Arlington House, the Robert E. Lee Memorial (Va.)	27.91
Chamizal (Tex.)	54.90
Coronado (Ariz.)	4,750.22
De Sota (Fla.)	26.84
Federal Hall (N.Y.)	0.45
Fort Caroline (Fla.)	138.39
Fort Clatsop (Ore.)	125.20
General Grant (N.Y.)	0.76
Hamilton Grange (N.Y.)	0.11
Jefferson National Expansion Memorial (Mo.)	90.96
John F. Kennedy Center for Performing Arts (D.C.)	17.50
Johnstown Flood (Pa.)	164.12
Lincoln Boyhood (Ind.)	199.65
Lincoln Memorial (D.C.)	109.63

Name and location	Total acreage
Lyndon Baines Johnson Memorial Grove on the Potomac (D.C.)	17.00
Mount Rushmore (S.D.)	1,278.45
Perry's Victory and International Peace Memorial (Ohio)	25.38
Roger Williams (R.I.)	4.56
Thaddeus Kosciuszko (Pa.)	0.02
Theodore Roosevelt Island (D.C.)	88.50
Thomas Jefferson Memorial (D.C.)	18.36
USS Arizona Memorial (Hawaii)	0.00
Vietnam Veterans Memorial (D.C.)	2.00
Washington Monument (D.C.)	106.01
Wright Brothers (N.C.)	431.40

NATIONAL CEMETERIES[1]

Antietam (Md.)	11.36
Battleground (D.C.)	1.03
Fort Donelson (Tenn.)	15.30
Poplar Grove (Va.)	8.72
Stones River (Tenn.)	719.81
Yorktown (Va.)	

1. The National Cemeteries are not independent areas of the National Park System; each is part of a military park, battlefield, etc., except Battleground. Their acreage is kept separately. Arlington National Cemetery is under the Department of the Army. *See* Index.

NATIONAL SEASHORES

Assateague Island (Md.-Va.)	39,636.75
Canaveral (Fla.)	57,661.69
Cape Cod (Mass.)	43,569.21
Cape Hatteras (N.C.)	30,319.43
Cape Lookout (N.C.)	28,243.36
Cumberland Island (Ga.)	36,415.09
Fire Island (N.Y.)	19,578.55
Gulf Islands (Fla.-Miss.)	135,624.51
Padre Island (Tex.)	130,434.27
Point Reyes (Calif.)	71,048.78

NATIONAL PARKWAYS

Blue Ridge (Va.-N.C.)	87,782.01
George Washington Memorial (Va.-Md.)	7,247.63
John D. Rockefeller, Jr., Memorial (Wyo.)	23,777.22
Natchez Trace (Miss.-Tenn.-Ala.)	51,739.93

NATIONAL LAKESHORES

Apostle Islands (Wis.)	69,371.89
Indiana Dunes (Ind.)	14,981.31
Pictured Rocks (Mich)	73,174.12
Sleeping Bear Dunes (Mich.)	71,189.15

NATIONAL WILD AND SCENIC RIVERS

Alagnak Wild River (Alaska)	24,038.00
Bluestone National Scenic River (W. Va.)	4,268.00
Delaware (N.Y.-N.J.-Pa.)	1,973.33
St. Croix (Minn.-Wis.)	92,735.85
Missouri National Recreational River (Neb., S.D.)	0.00
Obed Wild & Scenic River (Tenn.)	5,066.94
Rio Grande Wild & Scenic (Tex.)	9,600.00
Upper Delaware (N.Y., N.J.-Pa.)	75,000.00

NATIONAL RIVERS

Big South Fork National River & Recreation Area (Ky.-Tenn.)	125,000.00
Buffalo (Ark.)	94,218.55
Great Egg Harbor River (N.J.)	.00
Mississippi National River & Recreation Area (Minn.)	53,775.00
New River Gorge (W.Va.)	62,143.69
Niobrara/Missouri National Scenic Riverways (Neb.–S.D.)	.00

Name and location	*Total acreage*
Ozark (Mo.)	80,790.04

OTHER PARKS

Catoctin Mountain (Md.)	5,770.22
Constitution Gardens, (D.C.)	52.00
Fort Washington Park (Md.)	341.00
Greenbelt Park (Md.)	1,175.99
Piscataway (Md.)	4,262.52
Prince William Forest (Va.)	18,571.55
Rock Creek Park (D.C.)	1,754.37
Wolf Trap Farm Park for the Performing Arts (Va.)	130.28

NATIONAL RECREATION AREAS

Amistad (Tex.)	58,500.00
Bighorn Canyon (Wyo.-Mont.)	120,296.22
Chattahoochee River (Ga.)	9,259.91
Chickasaw (Okla.)	9,930.95
Coulee Dam (Wash.)	100,390.31
Curecanti (Colo.)	42,114.47
Cuyahoga Valley (Ohio)	32,524.76
Delaware Water Gap (Pa.-N.J.)	67,204.92
Gateway (N.Y.-N.J.)	26,310.93
Gauley River (W. Va.)	10,300.00
Glen Canyon (Ariz.-Utah)	1,236,880.00
Golden Gate (Calif.)	73,179.90
Lake Chelan (Wash.)	61,886.98
Lake Mead (Ariz.-Nev.)	1,495,665.52
Lake Meredith (Tex.)	44,977.63
Ross Lake (Wash.)	117,574.59
Santa Monica Mountains (Calif.)	150,050.00
Whiskeytown-Shasta-Trinity (Calif.)	42,503.46

NATIONAL SCENIC TRAIL

Appalachian (Maine, N.H., Vt., Mass., Conn., N.Y., N.J., Pa., Md., W.Va., Va., N.C., Tenn., Ga.)	165,504.63
Natchez Trace (Ga.-Ala.-Tenn.)	10,995.00
Potomac Heritage (D.C.-Md.-Va.-Pa.)	0.00

NATIONAL MALL

National Mall (D.C.)	146.35

INTERNATIONAL HISTORIC SITE

Saint Croix Island (Maine)	35.39

Name and location	*Total acreage*

AFFILIATED AREAS

(National Historic Sites unless otherwise noted.)

American Memorial Park (N. Mariana Is.)	0.00
Benjamin Franklin (Pa.)[1]	0.00
Blackstone River Valley National Heritage Corridor (Mass., R.I.)	0.00
Chicago Portage (Ill.)	91.20
Chimney Rock (Neb.)	83.36
David Berger (Ohio)[1]	0.00
Delaware and Lehigh Navigation Canal National Heritage Corridor (Pa.)	0.00
Ebey's Landing (Wash.)	8,000.00
Father Marquette (Mich.)[1]	52.00
Gloria Dei Church (Pa.)	3.71
Green Springs Historic District (Va.)	5,490.59
Historic Camden (S.C.)	0.00
Ice Age Scenic Trail (Wis.)	0.00
Ice Age (Wis.)[2]	32,500.00
Iditarod National Historic Trail (Alaska)	0.00
Illinois and Michigan Canal National Heritage Corridor	0.00
International Peace Garden (N.D.)	2,330.30
Jamestown (Va.)	20.63
Lewis & Clark Natl. Historic Trail (Ill., Mo., Kan., Neb., Iowa, Idaho, S.D., N.D., Mont., Ore., Wash.)	39.11
M. McLeod Bethune Council House (D.C.)	0.00
McLaughlin House (Ore.)	0.63
Mormon Pioneer Natl. Historic Trail (Ill., Iowa, Neb., Wyo., Utah)	0.00
North Country Nat'l Scenic Trail (N.Y., Pa., Ohio, Mich., Wis., Minn., N.D.)	0.00
Oregon Natl. Historic Trail (Mo., Kan., Neb., Wyo., Idaho, Ore., Wash.)	0.00
Overmountain Victory Trail (Mo. to Ore.)	0.00
Pinelands Natl. Reserve (N.J.)	0.00
Red Hill Patrick Henry (Va.)[1]	0.00
Roosevelt-Campobello International Park (Canada)	2,721.50
Santa Fe National Historic Trail (Mo. to N.M.)	0.00
Sewell-Belmont House National Historic Site (D.C.)	0.35
Touro Synagogue (R.I.)	0.23
Trail of Tears National Historic Trail (N.C. to Okla.)	0.00

1. National Memorial. 2. National Scientific Reserve.

Water Supply of the World[1]

The Antarctic Icecap is the largest supply of fresh water, nearly 2 percent of the world's total of fresh and salt water. As can be seen from the table below, the amount of water in our atmosphere is over ten times as large as the water in all the rivers taken together. The fresh water actually available for human use in lakes and rivers and the accessible ground water amounts to only about one third of one percent of the world's total water supply.

	Surface area (square miles)	Volume (cubic miles)	Percentage of total
Salt Water			
The oceans	139,500,000	317,000,000	97.2
Inland seas and saline lakes	270,000	25,000	0.008
Fresh Water			
Freshwater lakes	330,000	30,000	0.009
All rivers (average level)	—	300	0.0001
Antarctic Icecap	6,000,000	6,300,000	1.9
Arctic Icecap and glaciers	900,000	680,000	0.21
Water in the atmosphere	197,000,000	3,100	0.001
Ground water within half a mile from surface	—	1,000,000	0.31
Deep-lying ground water	—	1,000,000	0.31
Total (rounded)	—	**326,000,000**	**100.00**

1. All figures are estimated. *Source:* Department of the Interior, Geological Survey.

Three Major Environmental Issues

Acid Rain

Acid rain occurs when sulfur dioxide and nitrogen oxide combine with water in the atmosphere to form harmful compounds that fall to Earth in rain, fog, and snow.

The United States emits almost 20 million tons of sulfur dioxide every year, with three-quarters coming from the burning of fossil fuels by electric utilities. Utility coal consumption has nearly doubled since the mid-1970s.

Coal-burning power plants in the Ohio River Valley and lower Midwest contribute to acidification of lakes as far away as upstate New York, New England, and Canada. Roughly half of the acid rain in Canada results from pollution in the United States.

Acid rain has also damaged high-elevation spruce forests in the eastern United States and it has also accelerated the corrosion of buildings and monuments.

Acid rain apparently facilitates the accumulation of mercury, a toxic metal, in fish. Elevated levels of mercury have led many states—particularly the upper Great Lakes states of Minnesota, Wisconsin, and Michigan—to advise against eating sport fish caught in their inland lakes.

Byproducts of sulfur dioxide, known as sulfates, are recognized as major contributors to regional haze in the East and West. At times, sulfate pollution is so great that people can't see the bottom of the Grand Canyon.

The inhalation of acid aerosols, which are derivatives of sulfur dioxide, may lead to bronchitis in children and decreased lung function in adults, particularly asthmatics.

The 1990 Clean Air Act Amendment enacted by Congress calls for reducing sulfur dioxide emissions below 1980 levels and for making polluters pay for their own cleanup. □

The Greenhouse Warming Controversy

The Earth's atmosphere is composed of oxygen and nitrogen with small amounts of carbon dioxide, methane, and other trace gases. These trace gases, known as "greenhouse gases," trap the sun's heat which is reflected from the Earth. Without this greenhouse effect the Earth would be too cold to be habitable.

Industrialization created the need for massive amounts of energy and resulted in the burning of fossil fuels such as oil, gasoline, or coal. This uses up oxygen and produces carbon dioxide gas. Plants, algae and plankton take in carbon dioxide and produce oxygen.

Our modern society and its need for power create far more carbon dioxide than the planet's vegetation can consume. The excess carbon dioxide rises into the atmosphere to contribute to the greenhouse effect.

Many scientists believe that the increased carbon dioxide will cause an increase in global temperatures. Some predict that within the next 100 years the average surface temperature of the Earth could rise as much as 9° Fahrenheit, causing climate patterns to be dramatically altered.

If these experts are correct, fertile croplands could become deserts and the melting ice caps could cause ocean levels to rise by 3 feet or more, flooding coastal areas where half of the world's population lives. Scientists from the British Antarctic Survey report that the Wordie Ice Shelf off the western coast of Antarctica had disintegrated between 1969 and 1989 because of warmer air.

On the other hand, a minority of scientists disagrees with the global warming theory. One group holds that the sun's output chiefly controls climate, that it is at its maximum, and that its inevitable decline in output will actually cause a cooling trend.

Patrick Michaels of the Intergovernmental Panel on Climate Change claims that surface instruments are too close to urban areas to give accurate readings.

Scientists from the University of Edinburgh (Scotland) believe that the polar ice caps are safe. Any melting of the edges will be compensated by increased precipitation in the interiors which could possibly cause a lowering rather than raising of the ocean levels.

Whether or not greenhouse warming is increasing or not remains an important environmental concern and many nations are unwilling to take strong measures until more data are collected and analyzed. □

The Two Faces of Ozone

Ozone and chlorofluorocarbons (CFCs) together take part in two very different global environmental problems. In the lower atmosphere they are two of the trace gases that contribute to the greenhouse effect. Ozone, one of the ingredients in smog, also irritates breathing passages and damages plants.

But high in the atmosphere, 10 to 30 miles above the Earth, the chemistry changes. Ozone forms a thin layer around the globe that screens out much of the harmful ultraviolet light from the sun. At the same height, CFCs, which are very stable in the lower atmosphere, get broken down by the ultraviolet rays, releasing chlorine, which destroys the protective ozone layer.

The threat to the ozone layer was noticed in the 1970s, and prompted the United States to ban the use of CFCs in aerosols. Then, in 1985, British researchers found that an enormous hole had opened up in the ozone layer over Antarctica in spring, when the frigid temperatures facilitate the breakdown in ozone.

In the last decade, the ozone hole over Antarctica appeared each spring, temporarily lowering ozone levels by about 50 percent. In addition, scientists have recorded decreases in ozone of 2 to 10 percent over the Northern Hemisphere, and there are signs of a hole opening up over the Arctic.

Loss of ozone could dramatically increase the incidence of human skin cancer and cataracts as more cancer-causing rays reach the Earth's surface. Other organisms are also at risk, especially the single-celled plankton that constitute an important link in the food and oxygen cycles.

The production and use of CFCs is now being phased out under a 1987 international agreement known as the Montreal Protocol, which was considerably tightened in 1990 after further evidence of an increasing ozone hole was found. This phasing out will also help to slow the projected climate warming, since CFCs are the most powerful of all the greenhouse gases in trapping heat. But even though the protocol requires that CFCs be eliminated by the year 2000, past emissions ensure that ozone depletion will continue for some time beyond the turn of the century.

The Other Major Air Pollutants

What They Are, Where They Come From, and Their Potential Effects

Source: U.S. Environmental Protection Agency.

Carbon Monoxide. Odorless and colorless gas emitted in the exhaust of motor vehicles and other kinds of engines where there is incomplete fossil fuel combustion.

Sources. Automobiles, buses, trucks, small engines, and some industrial processes. High concentrations can be found in confined spaces like parking garages, poorly ventilated tunnels, or along roadsides during periods of heavy traffic.

Effects. Reduces the ability of blood to deliver oxygen to vital tissues, affecting primarily the cardiovascular and nervous systems. Lower concentrations have been shown to adversely affect individuals with heart disease (e.g.,angina) and to decrease maximal exercise performance in young, healthy men. Higher concentrations can cause symptoms such as dizziness, headaches, and fatigue.

* * *

Nitrogen Dioxide. Light brown gas at lower concentrations; in higher concentrations becomes an important component of unpleasant-looking brown, urban haze.

Sources. Result of burning fuels in utilities, industrial boilers, cars, and trucks.

Effects. One of the major pollutants that causes smog and acid rain. Can harm humans and vegetation when concentrations are sufficiently high. In children, may cause increased respiratory illness such as chest colds and coughing with phlegm. For asthmatics, can cause increased breathing difficulty.

* * *

Particulate Matter. Solid matter or liquid droplets from smoke, dust, fly ash, and condensing vapors that can be suspended in the air for long periods of time.

Sources. Industrial processes, smelters, automobiles, burning industrial fuels, woodsmoke, dust from paved and unpaved roads, construction, and agricultural ground breaking.

Effects. These microscopic particles can affect breathing and respiratory symptoms, causing increased respiratory disease and lung damage and possibly premature death. Children, the elderly, and people suffering from heart or lung disease (like asthma) are especially at risk. Also damages paint, soils clothing, and reduces visibility.

* * *

Sulfur Dioxide. Colorless gas, odorless at low concentrations but pungent at very high concentrations.

Sources. Emitted largely from industrial, institutional, utility, and apartment-house furnaces and boilers, as well as petroleum refineries, smelters, paper mills, and chemical plants.

Effects. One of the major pollutants that causes smog. Can also, at high concentrations, affect human health, especially among asthmatics (who are particularly sensitive to respiratory tract problems and breathing difficulties that SO_2 can induce). Can also harm vegetation and metals. The pollutants it produces can impair visibility and acidify lakes and streams.

* * *

Lead. Lead and lead compounds can adversely affect human health through either ingestion of lead-contaminated soil, dust, paint, etc., or direct inhalation. This is particularly a risk for young children, whose normal hand-to-mouth activities can result in greater ingestion of lead-contaminated soils and dusts.

Sources. Transportation sources using lead in their fuels, coal combustion, smelters, car battery plants, and combustion of garbage containing lead products.

Effects. Elevated lead levels can adversely affect mental development and performance, kidney function, and blood chemistry. Young children are particularly at risk due to their greater chance of ingesting lead and the increased sensitivity of young tissues and organs to lead.

* * *

Toxic Air Pollutants. Includes pollutants such as arsenic, asbestos, and benzene.

Sources. Chemical plants, industrial processes, motor vehicle emissions and fuels, and building materials.

Effects. Known or suspected to cause cancer, respiratory effects, birth defects, and reproductive and other serious health effects. Some can cause death or serious injury if accidentally released in large amounts.

* * *

Stratospheric Ozone Depleters. Chemicals such as chlorofluorocarbons (CFCs), halons, carbon tetrachloride, and methyl chloroform that are used in refrigerants and other industrial processes. These chemicals last a long time in the air, rising to the upper atmosphere where they destroy the protective ozone layer that screens out harmful ultraviolet (UV) radiation before it reaches the earth's surface.

Sources. Industrial household refrigeration, cooling and cleaning processes, car and home air conditioners, some fire extinguishers, and plastic foam products.

Effects. Increased exposure to UV radiation could potentially cause an increase in skin cancer, increased cataract cases, suppression of the human immune response system, and environmental damage.

CALENDAR & HOLIDAYS

1994

JANUARY

S	M	T	W	T	F	S
						1
2	3	4	5	6	7	8
9	10	11	12	13	14	15
16	17	18	19	20	21	22
23	24	25	26	27	28	29
30	31					

1—New Year's Day
6—Epiphany
17—Martin Luther King Jr. Day

FEBRUARY

S	M	T	W	T	F	S
		1	2	3	4	5
6	7	8	9	10	11	12
13	14	15	16	17	18	19
20	21	22	23	24	25	26
27	28					

2—Groundhog Day
12—Lincoln's Birthday
12—1st Day of Ramadan
14—Valentine's Day
16—Ash Wednesday
21—Washington's Birthday Observed
25—Purim

MARCH

S	M	T	W	T	F	S
		1	2	3	4	5
6	7	8	9	10	11	12
13	14	15	16	17	18	19
20	21	22	23	24	25	26
27	28	29	30	31		

17—St. Patrick's Day
27—Palm Sunday
27—1st Day of Passover

APRIL

S	M	T	W	T	F	S
					1	2
3	4	5	6	7	8	9
10	11	12	13	14	15	16
17	18	19	20	21	22	23
24	25	26	27	28	29	30

1—Good Friday
3—Easter
3—Daylight Savings Time begins

MAY

S	M	T	W	T	F	S
1	2	3	4	5	6	7
8	9	10	11	12	13	14
15	16	17	18	19	20	21
22	23	24	25	26	27	28
29	30	31				

8—Mother's Day
12—Ascension Day
16—1st Day of Shavuot
22—Pentecost
30—Memorial Day

JUNE

S	M	T	W	T	F	S
			1	2	3	4
5	6	7	8	9	10	11
12	13	14	15	16	17	18
19	20	21	22	23	24	25
26	27	28	29	30		

14—Flag Day
19—Father's Day

JULY

S	M	T	W	T	F	S
					1	2
3	4	5	6	7	8	9
10	11	12	13	14	15	16
17	18	19	20	21	22	23
24	25	26	27	28	29	30
31						

1—Canada Day
4—Independence Day

AUGUST

S	M	T	W	T	F	S
	1	2	3	4	5	6
7	8	9	10	11	12	13
14	15	16	17	18	19	20
21	22	23	24	25	26	27
28	29	30	31			

SEPTEMBER

S	M	T	W	T	F	S
				1	2	3
4	5	6	7	8	9	10
11	12	13	14	15	16	17
18	19	20	21	22	23	24
25	26	27	28	29	30	

5—Labor day
6—1st Day of Rosh Hashana
15—Yom Kippur

OCTOBER

S	M	T	W	T	F	S
						1
2	3	4	5	6	7	8
9	10	11	12	13	14	15
16	17	18	19	20	21	22
23	24	25	26	27	28	29
30	31					

10—Columbus Day (Observed)
10—Thanksgiving Day (Canada)
30—Daylight Savings Time ends
31—Halloween

NOVEMBER

S	M	T	W	T	F	S
		1	2	3	4	5
6	7	8	9	10	11	12
13	14	15	16	17	18	19
20	21	22	23	24	25	26
27	28	29	30			

1—All Saints Day
8—Election Day
11—Veterans Day
24—Thanksgiving
27—1st Sunday of Advent
28—1st Day of Hanukkah

DECEMBER

S	M	T	W	T	F	S
				1	2	3
4	5	6	7	8	9	10
11	12	13	14	15	16	17
18	19	20	21	22	23	24
25	26	27	28	29	30	31

25—Christmas

Seasons for the Northern Hemisphere, 1994

Eastern Standard Time

March 20, 3:28 p.m., sun enters sign of Aries; spring begins

June 21, 9:48 a.m., sun enters sign of Cancer; summer begins

Sept. 23, 1:19 a.m., sun enters sign of Libra; fall begins

Dec. 21, 9:23 p.m., sun enters sign of Capricorn; winter begins

1993

JANUARY

S	M	T	W	T	F	S
					1	2
3	4	5	6	7	8	9
10	11	12	13	14	15	16
17	18	19	20	21	22	23
24	25	26	27	28	29	30
31						

FEBRUARY

S	M	T	W	T	F	S
	1	2	3	4	5	6
7	8	9	10	11	12	13
14	15	16	17	18	19	20
21	22	23	24	25	26	27
28						

MARCH

S	M	T	W	T	F	S
	1	2	3	4	5	6
7	8	9	10	11	12	13
14	15	16	17	18	19	20
21	22	23	24	25	26	27
28	29	30	31			

APRIL

S	M	T	W	T	F	S
				1	2	3
4	5	6	7	8	9	10
11	12	13	14	15	16	17
18	19	20	21	22	23	24
25	26	27	28	29	30	

MAY

S	M	T	W	T	F	S
2	3	4	5	6	7	8
9	10	11	12	13	14	15
16	17	18	19	20	21	22
23	24	25	26	27	28	29
30	31					

JUNE

S	M	T	W	T	F	S
		1	2	3	4	5
6	7	8	9	10	11	12
13	14	15	16	17	18	19
20	21	22	23	24	25	26
27	28	29	30			

JULY

S	M	T	W	T	F	S
				1	2	3
4	5	6	7	8	9	10
11	12	13	14	15	16	17
18	19	20	21	22	23	24
25	26	27	28	29	30	31

AUGUST

S	M	T	W	T	F	S
1	2	3	4	5	6	7
8	9	10	11	12	13	14
15	16	17	18	19	20	21
22	23	24	25	26	27	28
29	30	31				

SEPTEMBER

S	M	T	W	T	F	S
			1	2	3	4
5	6	7	8	9	10	11
12	13	14	15	16	17	18
19	20	21	22	23	24	25
26	27	28	29	30		

OCTOBER

S	M	T	W	T	F	S
					1	2
3	4	5	6	7	8	9
10	11	12	13	14	15	16
17	18	19	20	21	22	23
24	25	26	27	28	29	30
31						

NOVEMBER

S	M	T	W	T	F	S
	1	2	3	4	5	6
7	8	9	10	11	12	13
14	15	16	17	18	19	20
21	22	23	24	25	26	27
28	29	30				

DECEMBER

S	M	T	W	T	F	S
			1	2	3	4
5	6	7	8	9	10	11
12	13	14	15	16	17	18
19	20	21	22	23	24	25
26	27	28	29	30	31	

1995

JANUARY

S	M	T	W	T	F	S
1	2	3	4	5	6	7
8	9	10	11	12	13	14
15	16	17	18	19	20	21
22	23	24	25	26	27	28
29	30	31				

FEBRUARY

S	M	T	W	T	F	S
			1	2	3	4
5	6	7	8	9	10	11
12	13	14	15	16	17	18
19	20	21	22	23	24	25
26	27	28				

MARCH

S	M	T	W	T	F	S
			1	2	3	4
5	6	7	8	9	10	11
12	13	14	15	16	17	18
19	20	21	22	23	24	25
26	27	28	29	30	31	

APRIL

S	M	T	W	T	F	S
						1
2	3	4	5	6	7	8
9	10	11	12	13	14	15
16	17	18	19	20	21	22
23	24	25	26	27	28	29
30						

MAY

S	M	T	W	T	F	S
	1	2	3	4	5	6
7	8	9	10	11	12	13
14	15	16	17	18	19	20
21	22	23	24	25	26	27
28	29	30	31			

JUNE

S	M	T	W	T	F	S
				1	2	3
4	5	6	7	8	9	10
11	12	13	14	15	16	17
18	19	20	21	22	23	24
25	26	27	28	29	30	

JULY

S	M	T	W	T	F	S
						1
2	3	4	5	6	7	8
9	10	11	12	13	14	15
16	17	18	19	20	21	22
23	24	25	26	27	28	29
30	31					

AUGUST

S	M	T	W	T	F	S
		1	2	3	4	5
6	7	8	9	10	11	12
13	14	15	16	17	18	19
20	21	22	23	24	25	26
27	28	29	30	31		

SEPTEMBER

S	M	T	W	T	F	S
					1	2
3	4	5	6	7	8	9
10	11	12	13	14	15	16
17	18	19	20	21	22	23
24	25	26	27	28	29	30

OCTOBER

S	M	T	W	T	F	S
1	2	3	4	5	6	7
8	9	10	11	12	13	14
15	16	17	18	19	20	21
22	23	24	25	26	27	28
29	30	31				

NOVEMBER

S	M	T	W	T	F	S
			1	2	3	4
5	6	7	8	9	10	11
12	13	14	15	16	17	18
19	20	21	22	23	24	25
26	27	28	29	30		

DECEMBER

S	M	T	W	T	F	S
					1	2
3	4	5	6	7	8	9
10	11	12	13	14	15	16
17	18	19	20	21	22	23
24	25	26	27	28	29	30
31						

Hindu Festival Dates, 1994

Source: Jantri 500, by Pal Singh Purewal.

Jan. 14	Makara Sankranti
Feb. 15	Vasanta Panchami
March 11	Maha Shịvaratri
March 27	Holi (last day)
April 11	Bikarami 2051 Samvat begins
April 11	Chetra Navratras begins
April 13	Vaisakhi
April 20	Ramanavmi
Aug. 21	Raksha Bandhan
Aug. 29	Sri Krishna Jayanti
Sept. 19	Sradhas Begin
Sept. 23	Ganesh Chaturthi
Oct. 5	Asuj Navratras begin
Oct. 14	Dassehra
Oct. 23	Karva Chauth Vrata (Fast)
Nov. 3	Diwali

PERPETUAL CALENDAR

1800 .. 4	1844 .. 9	1888 .. 8	1932 . 13	1976 . 12	2020 . 11
1801 .. 5	1845 .. 4	1889 .. 3	1933 .. 1	1977 .. 7	2021 .. 6
1802 .. 6	1846 .. 5	1890 .. 4	1934 .. 2	1978 .. 1	2022 .. 7
1803 .. 7	1847 .. 6	1891 .. 5	1935 .. 3	1979 .. 2	2023 .. 1
1804 .. 8	1848 . 14	1892 . 13	1936 . 11	1980 . 10	2024 .. 9
1805 .. 3	1849 .. 2	1893 .. 1	1937 .. 6	1981 .. 5	2025 .. 4
1806 .. 4	1850 .. 3	1894 .. 2	1938 .. 7	1982 .. 6	2026 .. 5
1807 .. 5	1851 .. 4	1895 .. 3	1939 .. 1	1983 .. 7	2027 .. 6
1808 . 13	1852 . 12	1896 . 11	1940 .. 9	1984 .. 8	2028 . 14
1809 .. 1	1853 .. 7	1897 .. 6	1941 .. 4	1985 .. 3	2029 .. 2
1810 .. 2	1854 .. 1	1898 .. 7	1942 .. 5	1986 .. 4	2030 .. 3
1811 .. 3	1855 .. 2	1899 .. 1	1943 .. 6	1987 .. 5	2031 .. 4
1812 . 11	1856 . 10	1900 .. 2	1944 . 14	1988 . 13	2032 . 12
1813 .. 6	1857 .. 5	1901 .. 3	1945 .. 2	1989 .. 1	2033 .. 7
1814 .. 7	1858 .. 6	1902 .. 4	1946 .. 3	1990 .. 2	2034 .. 1
1815 .. 1	1859 .. 7	1903 .. 5	1947 .. 4	1991 .. 3	2035 .. 2
1816 .. 9	1860 .. 8	1904 . 13	1948 . 12	1992 . 11	2036 . 10
1817 .. 4	1861 .. 3	1905 .. 1	1949 .. 7	1993 .. 6	2037 .. 5
1818 .. 5	1862 .. 4	1906 .. 2	1950 .. 1	1994 .. 7	2038 .. 6
1819 .. 6	1863 .. 5	1907 .. 3	1951 .. 2	1995 .. 1	2039 .. 7
1820 . 14	1864 . 13	1908 . 11	1952 . 10	1996 .. 9	2040 .. 8
1821 .. 2	1865 .. 1	1909 .. 6	1953 .. 5	1997 .. 4	2041 .. 3
1822 .. 3	1866 .. 2	1910 .. 7	1954 .. 6	1998 .. 5	2042 .. 4
1823 .. 4	1867 .. 3	1911 .. 1	1955 .. 7	1999 .. 6	2043 .. 5
1824 . 12	1868 . 11	1912 .. 9	1956 .. 8	2000 . 14	2044 . 13
1825 .. 7	1869 .. 6	1913 .. 4	1957 .. 3	2001 .. 2	2045 .. 1
1826 .. 1	1870 .. 7	1914 .. 5	1958 .. 4	2002 .. 3	2046 .. 2
1827 .. 2	1871 .. 1	1915 .. 6	1959 .. 5	2003 .. 4	2047 .. 3
1828 . 10	1872 .. 9	1916 . 14	1960 . 13	2004 . 12	2048 . 11
1829 .. 5	1873 .. 4	1917 .. 2	1961 .. 1	2005 .. 7	2049 .. 6
1830 .. 6	1874 .. 5	1918 .. 3	1962 .. 2	2006 .. 1	2050 .. 7
1831 .. 7	1875 .. 6	1919 .. 4	1963 .. 3	2007 .. 2	2051 .. 1
1832 .. 8	1876 . 14	1920 . 12	1964 . 11	2008 . 10	2052 .. 9
1833 .. 3	1877 .. 2	1921 .. 7	1965 .. 6	2009 .. 5	2053 .. 4
1834 .. 4	1878 .. 3	1922 .. 1	1966 .. 7	2010 .. 6	2054 .. 5
1835 .. 5	1879 .. 4	1923 .. 2	1967 .. 1	2011 .. 7	2055 .. 6
1836 . 13	1880 . 12	1924 . 10	1968 .. 9	2012 .. 8	2056 . 14
1837 .. 1	1881 .. 7	1925 .. 5	1969 .. 4	2013 .. 3	2057 .. 2
1838 .. 2	1882 .. 1	1926 .. 6	1970 .. 5	2014 .. 4	2058 .. 3
1839 .. 3	1883 .. 2	1927 .. 7	1971 .. 6	2015 .. 5	2059 .. 4
1840 . 11	1884 . 10	1928 .. 8	1972 . 14	2016 . 13	2060 . 12
1841 .. 6	1885 .. 5	1929 .. 3	1973 .. 2	2017 .. 1	2061 .. 7
1842 .. 7	1886 .. 6	1930 .. 4	1974 .. 3	2018 .. 2	2062 .. 1
1843 .. 1	1887 .. 7	1931 .. 5	1975 .. 4	2019 .. 3	2063 .. 2

DIRECTIONS: The number given with each year in the key above is number of calendar to use for that year

1

JANUARY

S	M	T	W	T	F	S
1	2	3	4	5	6	7
8	9	10	11	12	13	14
15	16	17	18	19	20	21
22	23	24	25	26	27	28
29	30	31				

FEBRUARY

S	M	T	W	T	F	S
			1	2	3	4
5	6	7	8	9	10	11
12	13	14	15	16	17	18
19	20	21	22	23	24	25
26	27	28				

MARCH

S	M	T	W	T	F	S
			1	2	3	4
5	6	7	8	9	10	11
12	13	14	15	16	17	18
19	20	21	22	23	24	25
26	27	28	29	30	31	

APRIL

S	M	T	W	T	F	S
						1
2	3	4	5	6	7	8
9	10	11	12	13	14	15
16	17	18	19	20	21	22
23	24	25	26	27	28	29
30						

MAY

S	M	T	W	T	F	S
	1	2	3	4	5	6
7	8	9	10	11	12	13
14	15	16	17	18	19	20
21	22	23	24	25	26	27
28	29	30	31			

JUNE

S	M	T	W	T	F	S
				1	2	3
4	5	6	7	8	9	10
11	12	13	14	15	16	17
18	19	20	21	22	23	24
25	26	27	28	29	30	

JULY

S	M	T	W	T	F	S
						1
2	3	4	5	6	7	8
9	10	11	12	13	14	15
16	17	18	19	20	21	22
23	24	25	26	27	28	29
30	31					

AUGUST

S	M	T	W	T	F	S
		1	2	3	4	5
6	7	8	9	10	11	12
13	14	15	16	17	18	19
20	21	22	23	24	25	26
27	28	29	30	31		

SEPTEMBER

S	M	T	W	T	F	S
					1	2
3	4	5	6	7	8	9
10	11	12	13	14	15	16
17	18	19	20	21	22	23
24	25	26	27	28	29	30

OCTOBER

S	M	T	W	T	F	S
1	2	3	4	5	6	7
8	9	10	11	12	13	14
15	16	17	18	19	20	21
22	23	24	25	26	27	28
29	30	31				

NOVEMBER

S	M	T	W	T	F	S
			1	2	3	4
5	6	7	8	9	10	11
12	13	14	15	16	17	18
19	20	21	22	23	24	25
26	27	28	29	30		

DECEMBER

S	M	T	W	T	F	S
					1	2
3	4	5	6	7	8	9
10	11	12	13	14	15	16
17	18	19	20	21	22	23
24	25	26	27	28	29	30
31						

2

JANUARY

S	M	T	W	T	F	S
	1	2	3	4	5	6
7	8	9	10	11	12	13
14	15	16	17	18	19	20
21	22	23	24	25	26	27
28	29	30	31			

FEBRUARY

S	M	T	W	T	F	S
				1	2	3
4	5	6	7	8	9	10
11	12	13	14	15	16	17
18	19	20	21	22	23	24
25	26	27	28			

MARCH

S	M	T	W	T	F	S
				1	2	3
4	5	6	7	8	9	10
11	12	13	14	15	16	17
18	19	20	21	22	23	24
25	26	27	28	29	30	31

APRIL

S	M	T	W	T	F	S
1	2	3	4	5	6	7
8	9	10	11	12	13	14
15	16	17	18	19	20	21
22	23	24	25	26	27	28
29	30					

MAY

S	M	T	W	T	F	S
		1	2	3	4	5
6	7	8	9	10	11	12
13	14	15	16	17	18	19
20	21	22	23	24	25	26
27	28	29	30	31		

JUNE

S	M	T	W	T	F	S
					1	2
3	4	5	6	7	8	9
10	11	12	13	14	15	16
17	18	19	20	21	22	23
24	25	26	27	28	29	30

JULY

S	M	T	W	T	F	S
1	2	3	4	5	6	7
8	9	10	11	12	13	14
15	16	17	18	19	20	21
22	23	24	25	26	27	28
29	30	31				

AUGUST

S	M	T	W	T	F	S
			1	2	3	4
5	6	7	8	9	10	11
12	13	14	15	16	17	18
19	20	21	22	23	24	25
26	27	28	29	30	31	

SEPTEMBER

S	M	T	W	T	F	S
						1
2	3	4	5	6	7	8
9	10	11	12	13	14	15
16	17	18	19	20	21	22
23	24	25	26	27	28	29
30						

OCTOBER

S	M	T	W	T	F	S
	1	2	3	4	5	6
7	8	9	10	11	12	13
14	15	16	17	18	19	20
21	22	23	24	25	26	27
28	29	30	31			

NOVEMBER

S	M	T	W	T	F	S
				1	2	3
4	5	6	7	8	9	10
11	12	13	14	15	16	17
18	19	20	21	22	23	24
25	26	27	28	29	30	

DECEMBER

S	M	T	W	T	F	S
						1
2	3	4	5	6	7	8
9	10	11	12	13	14	15
16	17	18	19	20	21	22
23	24	25	26	27	28	29
30	31					

3

JANUARY

S	M	T	W	T	F	S
		1	2	3	4	5
6	7	8	9	10	11	12
13	14	15	16	17	18	19
20	21	22	23	24	25	26
27	28	29	30	31		

FEBRUARY

S	M	T	W	T	F	S
					1	2
3	4	5	6	7	8	9
10	11	12	13	14	15	16
17	18	19	20	21	22	23
24	25	26	27	28		

MARCH

S	M	T	W	T	F	S
					1	2
3	4	5	6	7	8	9
10	11	12	13	14	15	16
17	18	19	20	21	22	23
24	25	26	27	28	29	30
31						

APRIL

S	M	T	W	T	F	S
	1	2	3	4	5	6
7	8	9	10	11	12	13
14	15	16	17	18	19	20
21	22	23	24	25	26	27
28	29	30				

MAY

S	M	T	W	T	F	S
			1	2	3	4
5	6	7	8	9	10	11
12	13	14	15	16	17	18
19	20	21	22	23	24	25
26	27	28	29	30	31	

JUNE

S	M	T	W	T	F	S
						1
2	3	4	5	6	7	8
9	10	11	12	13	14	15
16	17	18	19	20	21	22
23	24	25	26	27	28	29
30						

JULY

S	M	T	W	T	F	S
	1	2	3	4	5	6
7	8	9	10	11	12	13
14	15	16	17	18	19	20
21	22	23	24	25	26	27
28	29	30	31			

AUGUST

S	M	T	W	T	F	S
				1	2	3
4	5	6	7	8	9	10
11	12	13	14	15	16	17
18	19	20	21	22	23	24
25	26	27	28	29	30	31

SEPTEMBER

S	M	T	W	T	F	S
1	2	3	4	5	6	7
8	9	10	11	12	13	14
15	16	17	18	19	20	21
22	23	24	25	26	27	28
29	30					

OCTOBER

S	M	T	W	T	F	S
		1	2	3	4	5
6	7	8	9	10	11	12
13	14	15	16	17	18	19
20	21	22	23	24	25	26
27	28	29	30	31		

NOVEMBER

S	M	T	W	T	F	S
					1	2
3	4	5	6	7	8	9
10	11	12	13	14	15	16
17	18	19	20	21	22	23
24	25	26	27	28	29	30

DECEMBER

S	M	T	W	T	F	S
1	2	3	4	5	6	7
8	9	10	11	12	13	14
15	16	17	18	19	20	21
22	23	24	25	26	27	28
29	30	31				

4

JANUARY

S	M	T	W	T	F	S
			1	2	3	4
5	6	7	8	9	10	11
12	13	14	15	16	17	18
19	20	21	22	23	24	25
26	27	28	29	30	31	

FEBRUARY

S	M	T	W	T	F	S
						1
2	3	4	5	6	7	8
9	10	11	12	13	14	15
16	17	18	19	20	21	22
23	24	25	26	27	28	

MARCH

S	M	T	W	T	F	S
						1
2	3	4	5	6	7	8
9	10	11	12	13	14	15
16	17	18	19	20	21	22
23	24	25	26	27	28	29
30	31					

APRIL

S	M	T	W	T	F	S
		1	2	3	4	5
6	7	8	9	10	11	12
13	14	15	16	17	18	19
20	21	22	23	24	25	26
27	28	29	30			

MAY

S	M	T	W	T	F	S
				1	2	3
4	5	6	7	8	9	10
11	12	13	14	15	16	17
18	19	20	21	22	23	24
25	26	27	28	29	30	31

JUNE

S	M	T	W	T	F	S
1	2	3	4	5	6	7
8	9	10	11	12	13	14
15	16	17	18	19	20	21
22	23	24	25	26	27	28
29	30					

JULY

S	M	T	W	T	F	S
		1	2	3	4	5
6	7	8	9	10	11	12
13	14	15	16	17	18	19
20	21	22	23	24	25	26
27	28	29	30	31		

AUGUST

S	M	T	W	T	F	S
					1	2
3	4	5	6	7	8	9
10	11	12	13	14	15	16
17	18	19	20	21	22	23
24	25	26	27	28	29	30
31						

SEPTEMBER

S	M	T	W	T	F	S
	1	2	3	4	5	6
7	8	9	10	11	12	13
14	15	16	17	18	19	20
21	22	23	24	25	26	27
28	29	30				

OCTOBER

S	M	T	W	T	F	S
			1	2	3	4
5	6	7	8	9	10	11
12	13	14	15	16	17	18
19	20	21	22	23	24	25
26	27	28	29	30	31	

NOVEMBER

S	M	T	W	T	F	S
						1
2	3	4	5	6	7	8
9	10	11	12	13	14	15
16	17	18	19	20	21	22
23	24	25	26	27	28	29
30						

DECEMBER

S	M	T	W	T	F	S
	1	2	3	4	5	6
7	8	9	10	11	12	13
14	15	16	17	18	19	20
21	22	23	24	25	26	27
28	29	30	31			

5

JANUARY

S	M	T	W	T	F	S
				1	2	3
4	5	6	7	8	9	10
11	12	13	14	15	16	17
18	19	20	21	22	23	24
25	26	27	28	29	30	31

FEBRUARY

S	M	T	W	T	F	S
1	2	3	4	5	6	7
8	9	10	11	12	13	14
15	16	17	18	19	20	21
22	23	24	25	26	27	28

MARCH

S	M	T	W	T	F	S
1	2	3	4	5	6	7
8	9	10	11	12	13	14
15	16	17	18	19	20	21
22	23	24	25	26	27	28
29	30	31				

APRIL

S	M	T	W	T	F	S
			1	2	3	4
5	6	7	8	9	10	11
12	13	14	15	16	17	18
19	20	21	22	23	24	25
26	27	28	29	30		

MAY

S	M	T	W	T	F	S
					1	2
3	4	5	6	7	8	9
10	11	12	13	14	15	16
17	18	19	20	21	22	23
24	25	26	27	28	29	30
31						

JUNE

S	M	T	W	T	F	S
	1	2	3	4	5	6
7	8	9	10	11	12	13
14	15	16	17	18	19	20
21	22	23	24	25	26	27
28	29	30				

JULY

S	M	T	W	T	F	S
			1	2	3	4
5	6	7	8	9	10	11
12	13	14	15	16	17	18
19	20	21	22	23	24	25
26	27	28	29	30	31	

AUGUST

S	M	T	W	T	F	S
						1
2	3	4	5	6	7	8
9	10	11	12	13	14	15
16	17	18	19	20	21	22
23	24	25	26	27	28	29
30	31					

SEPTEMBER

S	M	T	W	T	F	S
		1	2	3	4	5
6	7	8	9	10	11	12
13	14	15	16	17	18	19
20	21	22	23	24	25	26
27	28	29	30			

OCTOBER

S	M	T	W	T	F	S
				1	2	3
4	5	6	7	8	9	10
11	12	13	14	15	16	17
18	19	20	21	22	23	24
25	26	27	28	29	30	31

NOVEMBER

S	M	T	W	T	F	S
1	2	3	4	5	6	7
8	9	10	11	12	13	14
15	16	17	18	19	20	21
22	23	24	25	26	27	28
29	30					

DECEMBER

S	M	T	W	T	F	S
		1	2	3	4	5
6	7	8	9	10	11	12
13	14	15	16	17	18	19
20	21	22	23	24	25	26
27	28	29	30	31		

6

JANUARY

S	M	T	W	T	F	S
					1	2
3	4	5	6	7	8	9
10	11	12	13	14	15	16
17	18	19	20	21	22	23
24	25	26	27	28	29	30
31						

FEBRUARY

S	M	T	W	T	F	S
	1	2	3	4	5	6
7	8	9	10	11	12	13
14	15	16	17	18	19	20
21	22	23	24	25	26	27
28						

MARCH

S	M	T	W	T	F	S
	1	2	3	4	5	6
7	8	9	10	11	12	13
14	15	16	17	18	19	20
21	22	23	24	25	26	27
28	29	30	31			

APRIL

S	M	T	W	T	F	S
				1	2	3
4	5	6	7	8	9	10
11	12	13	14	15	16	17
18	19	20	21	22	23	24
25	26	27	28	29	30	

MAY

S	M	T	W	T	F	S
						1
2	3	4	5	6	7	8
9	10	11	12	13	14	15
16	17	18	19	20	21	22
23	24	25	26	27	28	29
30	31					

JUNE

S	M	T	W	T	F	S
		1	2	3	4	5
6	7	8	9	10	11	12
13	14	15	16	17	18	19
20	21	22	23	24	25	26
27	28	29	30			

JULY

S	M	T	W	T	F	S
				1	2	3
4	5	6	7	8	9	10
11	12	13	14	15	16	17
18	19	20	21	22	23	24
25	26	27	28	29	30	31

AUGUST

S	M	T	W	T	F	S
1	2	3	4	5	6	7
8	9	10	11	12	13	14
15	16	17	18	19	20	21
22	23	24	25	26	27	28
29	30	31				

SEPTEMBER

S	M	T	W	T	F	S
			1	2	3	4
5	6	7	8	9	10	11
12	13	14	15	16	17	18
19	20	21	22	23	24	25
26	27	28	29	30		

OCTOBER

S	M	T	W	T	F	S
					1	2
3	4	5	6	7	8	9
10	11	12	13	14	15	16
17	18	19	20	21	22	23
24	25	26	27	28	29	30
31						

NOVEMBER

S	M	T	W	T	F	S
	1	2	3	4	5	6
7	8	9	10	11	12	13
14	15	16	17	18	19	20
21	22	23	24	25	26	27
28	29	30				

DECEMBER

S	M	T	W	T	F	S
			1	2	3	4
5	6	7	8	9	10	11
12	13	14	15	16	17	18
19	20	21	22	23	24	25
26	27	28	29	30	31	

7

JANUARY

S	M	T	W	T	F	S
						1
2	3	4	5	6	7	8
9	10	11	12	13	14	15
16	17	18	19	20	21	22
23	24	25	26	27	28	29
30	31					

FEBRUARY

S	M	T	W	T	F	S
		1	2	3	4	5
6	7	8	9	10	11	12
13	14	15	16	17	18	19
20	21	22	23	24	25	26
27	28					

MARCH

S	M	T	W	T	F	S
		1	2	3	4	5
6	7	8	9	10	11	12
13	14	15	16	17	18	19
20	21	22	23	24	25	26
27	28	29	30	31		

APRIL

S	M	T	W	T	F	S
					1	2
3	4	5	6	7	8	9
10	11	12	13	14	15	16
17	18	19	20	21	22	23
24	25	26	27	28	29	30

MAY

S	M	T	W	T	F	S
1	2	3	4	5	6	7
8	9	10	11	12	13	14
15	16	17	18	19	20	21
22	23	24	25	26	27	28
29	30	31				

JUNE

S	M	T	W	T	F	S
			1	2	3	4
5	6	7	8	9	10	11
12	13	14	15	16	17	18
19	20	21	22	23	24	25
26	27	28	29	30		

JULY

S	M	T	W	T	F	S
					1	2
3	4	5	6	7	8	9
10	11	12	13	14	15	16
17	18	19	20	21	22	23
24	25	26	27	28	29	30
31						

AUGUST

S	M	T	W	T	F	S
	1	2	3	4	5	6
7	8	9	10	11	12	13
14	15	16	17	18	19	20
21	22	23	24	25	26	27
28	29	30	31			

SEPTEMBER

S	M	T	W	T	F	S
				1	2	3
4	5	6	7	8	9	10
11	12	13	14	15	16	17
18	19	20	21	22	23	24
25	26	27	28	29	30	

OCTOBER

S	M	T	W	T	F	S
						1
2	3	4	5	6	7	8
9	10	11	12	13	14	15
16	17	18	19	20	21	22
23	24	25	26	27	28	29
30	31					

NOVEMBER

S	M	T	W	T	F	S
		1	2	3	4	5
6	7	8	9	10	11	12
13	14	15	16	17	18	19
20	21	22	23	24	25	26
27	28	29	30			

DECEMBER

S	M	T	W	T	F	S
				1	2	3
4	5	6	7	8	9	10
11	12	13	14	15	16	17
18	19	20	21	22	23	24
25	26	27	28	29	30	31

8

JANUARY

S	M	T	W	T	F	S
1	2	3	4	5	6	7
8	9	10	11	12	13	14
15	16	17	18	19	20	21
22	23	24	25	26	27	28
29	30	31				

FEBRUARY

S	M	T	W	T	F	S
			1	2	3	4
5	6	7	8	9	10	11
12	13	14	15	16	17	18
19	20	21	22	23	24	25
26	27	28	29			

MARCH

S	M	T	W	T	F	S
				1	2	3
4	5	6	7	8	9	10
11	12	13	14	15	16	17
18	19	20	21	22	23	24
25	26	27	28	29	30	31

APRIL

S	M	T	W	T	F	S
1	2	3	4	5	6	7
8	9	10	11	12	13	14
15	16	17	18	19	20	21
22	23	24	25	26	27	28
29	30					

MAY

S	M	T	W	T	F	S
		1	2	3	4	5
6	7	8	9	10	11	12
13	14	15	16	17	18	19
20	21	22	23	24	25	26
27	28	29	30	31		

JUNE

S	M	T	W	T	F	S
					1	2
3	4	5	6	7	8	9
10	11	12	13	14	15	16
17	18	19	20	21	22	23
24	25	26	27	28	29	30

JULY

S	M	T	W	T	F	S
1	2	3	4	5	6	7
8	9	10	11	12	13	14
15	16	17	18	19	20	21
22	23	24	25	26	27	28
29	30	31				

AUGUST

S	M	T	W	T	F	S
			1	2	3	4
5	6	7	8	9	10	11
12	13	14	15	16	17	18
19	20	21	22	23	24	25
26	27	28	29	30	31	

SEPTEMBER

S	M	T	W	T	F	S
						1
2	3	4	5	6	7	8
9	10	11	12	13	14	15
16	17	18	19	20	21	22
23	24	25	26	27	28	29
30						

OCTOBER

S	M	T	W	T	F	S
	1	2	3	4	5	6
7	8	9	10	11	12	13
14	15	16	17	18	19	20
21	22	23	24	25	26	27
28	29	30	31			

NOVEMBER

S	M	T	W	T	F	S
				1	2	3
4	5	6	7	8	9	10
11	12	13	14	15	16	17
18	19	20	21	22	23	24
25	26	27	28	29	30	

DECEMBER

S	M	T	W	T	F	S
						1
2	3	4	5	6	7	8
9	10	11	12	13	14	15
16	17	18	19	20	21	22
23	24	25	26	27	28	29
30	31					

9

JANUARY

S	M	T	W	T	F	S
	1	2	3	4	5	6
7	8	9	10	11	12	13
14	15	16	17	18	19	20
21	22	23	24	25	26	27
28	29	30	31			

FEBRUARY

S	M	T	W	T	F	S
				1	2	3
4	5	6	7	8	9	10
11	12	13	14	15	16	17
18	19	20	21	22	23	24
25	26	27	28	29		

MARCH

S	M	T	W	T	F	S
					1	2
3	4	5	6	7	8	9
10	11	12	13	14	15	16
17	18	19	20	21	22	23
24	25	26	27	28	29	30
31						

APRIL

S	M	T	W	T	F	S
	1	2	3	4	5	6
7	8	9	10	11	12	13
14	15	16	17	18	19	20
21	22	23	24	25	26	27
28	29	30				

MAY

S	M	T	W	T	F	S
			1	2	3	4
5	6	7	8	9	10	11
12	13	14	15	16	17	18
19	20	21	22	23	24	25
26	27	28	29	30	31	

JUNE

S	M	T	W	T	F	S
						1
2	3	4	5	6	7	8
9	10	11	12	13	14	15
16	17	18	19	20	21	22
23	24	25	26	27	28	29
30						

JULY

S	M	T	W	T	F	S
	1	2	3	4	5	6
7	8	9	10	11	12	13
14	15	16	17	18	19	20
21	22	23	24	25	26	27
28	29	30	31			

AUGUST

S	M	T	W	T	F	S
				1	2	3
4	5	6	7	8	9	10
11	12	13	14	15	16	17
18	19	20	21	22	23	24
25	26	27	28	29	30	31

SEPTEMBER

S	M	T	W	T	F	S
1	2	3	4	5	6	7
8	9	10	11	12	13	14
15	16	17	18	19	20	21
22	23	24	25	26	27	28
29	30					

OCTOBER

S	M	T	W	T	F	S
		1	2	3	4	5
6	7	8	9	10	11	12
13	14	15	16	17	18	19
20	21	22	23	24	25	26
27	28	29	30	31		

NOVEMBER

S	M	T	W	T	F	S
					1	2
3	4	5	6	7	8	9
10	11	12	13	14	15	16
17	18	19	20	21	22	23
24	25	26	27	28	29	30

DECEMBER

S	M	T	W	T	F	S
1	2	3	4	5	6	7
8	9	10	11	12	13	14
15	16	17	18	19	20	21
22	23	24	25	26	27	28
29	30	31				

10

JANUARY

S	M	T	W	T	F	S
		1	2	3	4	5
6	7	8	9	10	11	12
13	14	15	16	17	18	19
20	21	22	23	24	25	26
27	28	29	30	31		

FEBRUARY

S	M	T	W	T	F	S
					1	2
3	4	5	6	7	8	9
10	11	12	13	14	15	16
17	18	19	20	21	22	23
24	25	26	27	28	29	

MARCH

S	M	T	W	T	F	S
						1
2	3	4	5	6	7	8
9	10	11	12	13	14	15
16	17	18	19	20	21	22
23	24	25	26	27	28	29
30	31					

APRIL

S	M	T	W	T	F	S
		1	2	3	4	5
6	7	8	9	10	11	12
13	14	15	16	17	18	19
20	21	22	23	24	25	26
27	28	29	30			

MAY

S	M	T	W	T	F	S
				1	2	3
4	5	6	7	8	9	10
11	12	13	14	15	16	17
18	19	20	21	22	23	24
25	26	27	28	29	30	31

JUNE

S	M	T	W	T	F	S
1	2	3	4	5	6	7
8	9	10	11	12	13	14
15	16	17	18	19	20	21
22	23	24	25	26	27	28
29	30					

JULY

S	M	T	W	T	F	S
		1	2	3	4	5
6	7	8	9	10	11	12
13	14	15	16	17	18	19
20	21	22	23	24	25	26
27	28	29	30	31		

AUGUST

S	M	T	W	T	F	S
					1	2
3	4	5	6	7	8	9
10	11	12	13	14	15	16
17	18	19	20	21	22	23
24	25	26	27	28	29	30
31						

SEPTEMBER

S	M	T	W	T	F	S
	1	2	3	4	5	6
7	8	9	10	11	12	13
14	15	16	17	18	19	20
21	22	23	24	25	26	27
28	29	30				

OCTOBER

S	M	T	W	T	F	S
			1	2	3	4
5	6	7	8	9	10	11
12	13	14	15	16	17	18
19	20	21	22	23	24	25
26	27	28	29	30	31	

NOVEMBER

S	M	T	W	T	F	S
						1
2	3	4	5	6	7	8
9	10	11	12	13	14	15
16	17	18	19	20	21	22
23	24	25	26	27	28	29
30						

DECEMBER

S	M	T	W	T	F	S
	1	2	3	4	5	6
7	8	9	10	11	12	13
14	15	16	17	18	19	20
21	22	23	24	25	26	27
28	29	30	31			

11

JANUARY

S	M	T	W	T	F	S
			1	2	3	4
5	6	7	8	9	10	11
12	13	14	15	16	17	18
19	20	21	22	23	24	25
26	27	28	29	30	31	

FEBRUARY

S	M	T	W	T	F	S
						1
2	3	4	5	6	7	8
9	10	11	12	13	14	15
16	17	18	19	20	21	22
23	24	25	26	27	28	29

MARCH

S	M	T	W	T	F	S
1	2	3	4	5	6	7
8	9	10	11	12	13	14
15	16	17	18	19	20	21
22	23	24	25	26	27	28
29	30	31				

APRIL

S	M	T	W	T	F	S
			1	2	3	4
5	6	7	8	9	10	11
12	13	14	15	16	17	18
19	20	21	22	23	24	25
26	27	28	29	30		

MAY

S	M	T	W	T	F	S
					1	2
3	4	5	6	7	8	9
10	11	12	13	14	15	16
17	18	19	20	21	22	23
24	25	26	27	28	29	30
31						

JUNE

S	M	T	W	T	F	S
	1	2	3	4	5	6
7	8	9	10	11	12	13
14	15	16	17	18	19	20
21	22	23	24	25	26	27
28	29	30				

JULY

S	M	T	W	T	F	S
			1	2	3	4
5	6	7	8	9	10	11
12	13	14	15	16	17	18
19	20	21	22	23	24	25
26	27	28	29	30	31	

AUGUST

S	M	T	W	T	F	S
						1
2	3	4	5	6	7	8
9	10	11	12	13	14	15
16	17	18	19	20	21	22
23	24	25	26	27	28	29
30	31					

SEPTEMBER

S	M	T	W	T	F	S
		1	2	3	4	5
6	7	8	9	10	11	12
13	14	15	16	17	18	19
20	21	22	23	24	25	26
27	28	29	30			

OCTOBER

S	M	T	W	T	F	S
				1	2	3
4	5	6	7	8	9	10
11	12	13	14	15	16	17
18	19	20	21	22	23	24
25	26	27	28	29	30	31

NOVEMBER

S	M	T	W	T	F	S
1	2	3	4	5	6	7
8	9	10	11	12	13	14
15	16	17	18	19	20	21
22	23	24	25	26	27	28
29	30					

DECEMBER

S	M	T	W	T	F	S
		1	2	3	4	5
6	7	8	9	10	11	12
13	14	15	16	17	18	19
20	21	22	23	24	25	26
27	28	29	30	31		

12

JANUARY

S	M	T	W	T	F	S
				1	2	3
4	5	6	7	8	9	10
11	12	13	14	15	16	17
18	19	20	21	22	23	24
25	26	27	28	29	30	31

FEBRUARY

S	M	T	W	T	F	S
1	2	3	4	5	6	7
8	9	10	11	12	13	14
15	16	17	18	19	20	21
22	23	24	25	26	27	28
29						

MARCH

S	M	T	W	T	F	S
	1	2	3	4	5	6
7	8	9	10	11	12	13
14	15	16	17	18	19	20
21	22	23	24	25	26	27
28	29	30	31			

APRIL

S	M	T	W	T	F	S
				1	2	3
4	5	6	7	8	9	10
11	12	13	14	15	16	17
18	19	20	21	22	23	24
25	26	27	28	29	30	

MAY

S	M	T	W	T	F	S
						1
2	3	4	5	6	7	8
9	10	11	12	13	14	15
16	17	18	19	20	21	22
23	24	25	26	27	28	29
30	31					

JUNE

S	M	T	W	T	F	S
		1	2	3	4	5
6	7	8	9	10	11	12
13	14	15	16	17	18	19
20	21	22	23	24	25	26
27	28	29	30			

JULY

S	M	T	W	T	F	S
				1	2	3
4	5	6	7	8	9	10
11	12	13	14	15	16	17
18	19	20	21	22	23	24
25	26	27	28	29	30	31

AUGUST

S	M	T	W	T	F	S
1	2	3	4	5	6	7
8	9	10	11	12	13	14
15	16	17	18	19	20	21
22	23	24	25	26	27	28
29	30	31				

SEPTEMBER

S	M	T	W	T	F	S
			1	2	3	4
5	6	7	8	9	10	11
12	13	14	15	16	17	18
19	20	21	22	23	24	25
26	27	28	29	30		

OCTOBER

S	M	T	W	T	F	S
					1	2
3	4	5	6	7	8	9
10	11	12	13	14	15	16
17	18	19	20	21	22	23
24	25	26	27	28	29	30
31						

NOVEMBER

S	M	T	W	T	F	S
	1	2	3	4	5	6
7	8	9	10	11	12	13
14	15	16	17	18	19	20
21	22	23	24	25	26	27
28	29	30				

DECEMBER

S	M	T	W	T	F	S
			1	2	3	4
5	6	7	8	9	10	11
12	13	14	15	16	17	18
19	20	21	22	23	24	25
26	27	28	29	30	31	

13

JANUARY

S	M	T	W	T	F	S
					1	2
3	4	5	6	7	8	9
10	11	12	13	14	15	16
17	18	19	20	21	22	23
24	25	26	27	28	29	30
31						

FEBRUARY

S	M	T	W	T	F	S
	1	2	3	4	5	6
7	8	9	10	11	12	13
14	15	16	17	18	19	20
21	22	23	24	25	26	27
28	29					

MARCH

S	M	T	W	T	F	S
		1	2	3	4	5
6	7	8	9	10	11	12
13	14	15	16	17	18	19
20	21	22	23	24	25	26
27	28	29	30	31		

APRIL

S	M	T	W	T	F	S
					1	2
3	4	5	6	7	8	9
10	11	12	13	14	15	16
17	18	19	20	21	22	23
24	25	26	27	28	29	30

MAY

S	M	T	W	T	F	S
1	2	3	4	5	6	7
8	9	10	11	12	13	14
15	16	17	18	19	20	21
22	23	24	25	26	27	28
29	30	31				

JUNE

S	M	T	W	T	F	S
			1	2	3	4
5	6	7	8	9	10	11
12	13	14	15	16	17	18
19	20	21	22	23	24	25
26	27	28	29	30		

JULY

S	M	T	W	T	F	S
					1	2
3	4	5	6	7	8	9
10	11	12	13	14	15	16
17	18	19	20	21	22	23
24	25	26	27	28	29	30
31						

AUGUST

S	M	T	W	T	F	S
	1	2	3	4	5	6
7	8	9	10	11	12	13
14	15	16	17	18	19	20
21	22	23	24	25	26	27
28	29	30	31			

SEPTEMBER

S	M	T	W	T	F	S
				1	2	3
4	5	6	7	8	9	10
11	12	13	14	15	16	17
18	19	20	21	22	23	24
25	26	27	28	29	30	

OCTOBER

S	M	T	W	T	F	S
						1
2	3	4	5	6	7	8
9	10	11	12	13	14	15
16	17	18	19	20	21	22
23	24	25	26	27	28	29
30	31					

NOVEMBER

S	M	T	W	T	F	S
		1	2	3	4	5
6	7	8	9	10	11	12
13	14	15	16	17	18	19
20	21	22	23	24	25	26
27	28	29	30			

DECEMBER

S	M	T	W	T	F	S
				1	2	3
4	5	6	7	8	9	10
11	12	13	14	15	16	17
18	19	20	21	22	23	24
25	26	27	28	29	30	31

14

JANUARY

S	M	T	W	T	F	S
						1
2	3	4	5	6	7	8
9	10	11	12	13	14	15
16	17	18	19	20	21	22
23	24	25	26	27	28	29
30	31					

FEBRUARY

S	M	T	W	T	F	S
		1	2	3	4	5
6	7	8	9	10	11	12
13	14	15	16	17	18	19
20	21	22	23	24	25	26
27	28	29				

MARCH

S	M	T	W	T	F	S
			1	2	3	4
5	6	7	8	9	10	11
12	13	14	15	16	17	18
19	20	21	22	23	24	25
26	27	28	29	30	31	

APRIL

S	M	T	W	T	F	S
						1
2	3	4	5	6	7	8
9	10	11	12	13	14	15
16	17	18	19	20	21	22
23	24	25	26	27	28	29
30						

MAY

S	M	T	W	T	F	S
	1	2	3	4	5	6
7	8	9	10	11	12	13
14	15	16	17	18	19	20
21	22	23	24	25	26	27
28	29	30	31			

JUNE

S	M	T	W	T	F	S
				1	2	3
4	5	6	7	8	9	10
11	12	13	14	15	16	17
18	19	20	21	22	23	24
25	26	27	28	29	30	

JULY

S	M	T	W	T	F	S
						1
2	3	4	5	6	7	8
9	10	11	12	13	14	15
16	17	18	19	20	21	22
23	24	25	26	27	28	29
30	31					

AUGUST

S	M	T	W	T	F	S
		1	2	3	4	5
6	7	8	9	10	11	12
13	14	15	16	17	18	19
20	21	22	23	24	25	26
27	28	29	30	31		

SEPTEMBER

S	M	T	W	T	F	S
					1	2
3	4	5	6	7	8	9
10	11	12	13	14	15	16
17	18	19	20	21	22	23
24	25	26	27	28	29	30

OCTOBER

S	M	T	W	T	F	S
1	2	3	4	5	6	7
8	9	10	11	12	13	14
15	16	17	18	19	20	21
22	23	24	25	26	27	28
29	30	31				

NOVEMBER

S	M	T	W	T	F	S
			1	2	3	4
5	6	7	8	9	10	11
12	13	14	15	16	17	18
19	20	21	22	23	24	25
26	27	28	29	30		

DECEMBER

S	M	T	W	T	F	S
					1	2
3	4	5	6	7	8	9
10	11	12	13	14	15	16
17	18	19	20	21	22	23
24	25	26	27	28	29	30
31						

The Calendar

History of the Calendar

The purpose of a calendar is to reckon time in advance, to show how many days have to elapse until a certain event takes place—the harvest, a religious festival, or whatever. The earliest calendars, naturally, were crude, and they must have been strongly influenced by the geographical location of the people who made them. In the Scandinavian countries, for example, where the seasons are pronounced, the concept of the year was determined by the seasons, specifically by the end of winter. The Norsemen, before becoming Christians, are said to have had a calendar consisting of ten months of 30 days each.

But in warmer countries, where the seasons are less pronounced, the Moon became the basic unit for time reckoning; an old Jewish book actually makes the statement that "the Moon was created for the counting of the days." All the oldest calendars of which we have reliable information were lunar calendars, based on the time interval from one new moon to the next—a so-called "lunation." But even in a warm climate there are annual events that pay no attention to the phases of the Moon. In some areas it was a rainy season; in Egypt it was the annual flooding of the Nile. It was, therefore, necessary to regulate daily life and religious festivals by lunations, but to take care of the annual event in some other manner.

The calendar of the Assyrians was based on the phases of the Moon. The month began with the first appearance of the lunar crescent, and since this can best be observed in the evening, the day began with sunset. They knew that a lunation was 29 1/2 days long, so their lunar year had a duration of 354 days, falling eleven days short of the solar year.[1] After three years such a lunar calendar would be off by 33 days, or more than one lunation. We know that the Assyrians added an extra month from time to time, but we do not know whether they had developed a special rule for doing so or whether the priests proclaimed the necessity for an extra month from observation. If they made every third year a year of 13 lunations, their three-year period would cover 1,091 1/2 days (using their value of 29 1/2 days for one lunation), or just about four days too short. In one century this mistake would add up to 133 days by their reckoning (in reality closer to 134 days), requiring four extra lunations per century.

We now know that an eight-year period, consisting of five years with 12 months and three years with 13 months would lead to a difference of only 20 days per century, but we do not know whether such a calendar was actually used.

The best approximation that was possible in antiquity was a 19-year period, with seven of these 19 years having 13 months. This means that the period contained 235 months. This, still using the old value for a lunation, made a total of 6,932 1/2 days, while 19 solar years added up to 6,939.7 days, a difference of just one week per period and about five weeks per century. Even the 19-year period required constant adjustment, but it was the period that became the basis of the religious calendar of the Jews. The Arabs used the same calendar at first, but Mohammed forbade shifting from 12 months to 13 months, so that the Islamic religious calendar, even today, has a lunar year of 354 days. As a result the Islamic religious festivals run through all the seasons of the year three times per century.

The Egyptians had a traditional calendar with 12 months of 30 days each. At one time they added five extra days at the end of every year. These turned into a five-day festival because it was thought to be unlucky to work during that time.

When Rome emerged as a world power, the difficulties of making a calendar were well known, but the Romans complicated their lives because of their superstition that even numbers were unlucky. Hence their months were 29 or 31 days long, with the exception of February, which had 28 days. However, four months of 31 days, seven months of 29 days, and one month of 28 days added up to only 355 days. Therefore, the Romans invented an extra month called Mercedonius of 22 or 23 days. It was added every second year.

Even with Mercedonius, the Roman calendar was so far off that Caesar, advised by the astronomer Sosigenes, ordered a sweeping reform in 45 B.C. One year, made 445 days long by imperial decree, brought the calendar back in step with the seasons. Then the solar year (with the value of 365 days and 6 hours) was made the basis of the calendar. The months were 30 or 31 days in length, and to take care of the six hours, every fourth year was made a 366-day year. Moreover, Caesar decreed, the year began with the first of January, not with the vernal equinox in late March.

This was the Julian calendar, named after Julius Caesar. It is still the calendar of the Eastern Orthodox churches.

However, the year is 11 1/2 minutes shorter than the figure written into Caesar's calendar by Sosigenes, and after a number of centuries, even 11 1/2 minutes add up. *See* table.

While Caesar could decree that the vernal equinox should not be used as the first day of the new year, the vernal equinox is still a fact of Nature that could not be disregarded. One of the first (as far as we know) to become alarmed about this was Roger Bacon. He sent a memorandum to Pope Clement IV, who apparently was not impressed. But Pope Sixtus IV (reigned 1471 to 1484) decided that another reform was needed and called the German astronomer Regiomontanus to Rome to advise him. Regiomontanus arrived in 1475, but one year later he died in an epidemic, one of the recurrent outbreaks of the plague. The Pope himself survived, but his reform plans died with Regiomontanus.

Less than a hundred years later, in 1545, the Council of Trent authorized the then Pope, Paul III, to reform the calendar once more. Most of the mathematical and astronomical work was done by Father Christopher Clavius, S.J. The immediate correction, advised by Father Clavius and ordered by Pope Gregory XIII, was that Thursday, Oct. 4, 1582, was to be the last day of the Julian calendar. The next day was Friday, with the date of October 15. For long-range accuracy, a formula suggested by the Vatican librarian Aloysius Giglio (latinized into Lilius) was adopted: every fourth year is a leap year *unless* it is a century year like 1700 or 1800. Century years can be

1. The correct figures are: lunation: 29 d, 12 h, 44 min, 2.8 sec (29.530585 d); solar year: 365 d, 5 h, 48 min, 46 sec (365.242216 d); 12 lunations: 354 d, 8 h, 48 min, 34 sec (354.3671 d).

Drift of the Vernal Equinox in the Julian Calendar

Date	Julian year	Date	Julian year	Date	Julian Year
March 21	325 A.D.	March 17	837 A.D.	March 13	1349 A.D.
March 20	453 A.D.	March 16	965 A.D.	March 12	1477 A.D.
March 19	581 A.D.	March 15	1093 A.D.	March 11	1605 A.D.
March 18	709 A.D.	March 14	1221 A.D.		

leap years *only* when they are divisible by 400 (e.g., 1600). This rule eliminates three leap years in four centuries, making the calendar sufficiently correct for all ordinary purposes.

Unfortunately, all the Protestant princes in 1582 chose to ignore the papal bull; they continued with the Julian calendar. It was not until 1698 that the German professor Erhard Weigel persuaded the Protestant rulers of Germany and of the Netherlands to change to the new calendar. In England the shift took place in 1752, and in Russia it needed the revolution to introduce the Gregorian calendar in 1918.

The average year of the Gregorian calendar, in spite of the leap year rule, is about 26 seconds longer than the earth's orbital period. But this discrepancy will need 3,323 years to build up to a single day.

Modern proposals for calendar reform do not aim at a "better" calendar, but at one that is more convenient to use, especially for commercial purposes. A 365-day year cannot be divided into equal halves or quarters; the number of days per month is haphazard; the months begin or end in the middle of a week; a holiday fixed by date (e.g., the Fourth of July) will wander through a week; a holiday fixed in another manner (e.g., Easter) can fall on thirty-five possible dates. The Gregorian calendar, admittedly, keeps the calendar dates in reasonable unison with astronomical events, but it still is full of minor annoyances. Moreover, you need a calendar every year to look up dates; an ideal calendar should be one that you can memorize for one year and that is valid for all other years, too.

In 1834 an Italian priest, Marco Mastrofini, suggested taking one day out of every year. It would be made a holiday and *not* be given the name of a weekday. That would make every year begin with January 1 as a Sunday. The leap-year day would be treated the same way, so that in leap years there would be two unnamed holidays at the end of the year.

About a decade later the philosopher Auguste Comte also suggested a 364-day calendar with an extra day, which he called Year Day.

Since then there have been other unsuccessful attempts at calendar reform.

Time and Calendar

The two natural cycles on which time measurements are based are the year and the day. The year is defined as the time required for the Earth to complete one revolution around the Sun, while the day is the time required for the Earth to complete one turn upon its axis. Unfortunately the Earth needs 365 days plus about six hours to go around the Sun once, so that the year does not consist of so and so many days; the fractional day has to be taken care of by an extra day every fourth year.

But because the Earth, while turning upon its axis, also moves around the Sun there are two kinds of days. A day may be defined as the interval between the highest point of the Sun in the sky on two successive days. This, averaged out over the year, produces the customary 24-hour day. But one might also define a day as the time interval between the moments when a certain point in the sky, say a conveniently located star, is directly overhead. This is called:

Sidereal time. Astronomers use a point which they call the "vernal equinox" for the actual determination. Such a sidereal day is somewhat shorter than the "solar day," namely by about 3 minutes and 56 seconds of so-called "mean solar time."

Apparent solar time is the time based directly on the Sun's position in the sky. In ordinary life the day runs from midnight to midnight. It begins when the Sun is invisible by being 12 hours from its zenith. Astronomers use the so-called "Julian Day," which runs from noon to noon; the concept was invented by the astronomer Joseph Scaliger, who named it after his father Julius. To avoid the problems caused by leap-year days and so forth, Scaliger picked a conveniently remote date in the past and suggested just counting days without regard to weeks, months, and years. The Julian Day for 0^h Jan. 31, 1992 is 244 8621.5. The reason for having the Julian Day run from noon to noon is the practical one that astronomical observations usually extend across the midnight hour, which would require a change in date (or in the Julian Day number) if the astronomical day, like the civil day, ran from midnight to midnight.

Mean solar time, rather than apparent solar time, is what is actually used most of the time. The mean solar time is based on the position of a fictitious "mean sun." The reason why this fictitious sun has to be introduced is the following: the Earth turns on its axis regularly; it needs the same number of seconds regardless of the season. But the movement of the Earth around the Sun is not regular because the Earth's orbit is an ellipse. This has the result (as explained in the section The Seasons) that the Earth moves faster in January and slower in July. Though it is the Earth that changes velocity, it looks to us as if the Sun did. In January, when the Earth moves faster, the *apparent* movement of the Sun looks faster. The "mean sun" of time measurements, then, is a sun that moves regularly all year round; the real Sun will be either ahead of or behind the "mean sun." The difference between the real Sun and the fictitious mean sun is called the *equation of time.*

When the real Sun is west of the mean sun we have the "sun fast" condition, with the real Sun crossing the meridian ahead of the mean sun. The opposite is the "sun slow" situation when the real Sun crosses the meridian after the mean sun. Of course, what is observed is the real Sun. The equation of time is needed to establish mean solar time, kept by the reference clocks.

But if all clocks were actually set by mean solar time we would be plagued by a welter of time differences that would be "correct" but a major nuisance. A clock on Long Island, correctly showing mean solar time for its location (this would be *local civil time*), would be slightly ahead of a clock in Newark, N.J. The Newark clock would be slightly ahead of a

The Names of Days

Latin	Saxon	English	French	Italian	Spanish	German
Dies Solis	Sun's Day	Sunday	dimanche	domenica	domingo	Sonntag
Dies Lunae	Moon's Day	Monday	lundi	lunedì	lunes	Montag
Dies Martis	Tiw's Day	Tuesday	mardi	martedì	martes	Dienstag
Dies Mercurii	Woden's Day	Wednesday	mercredi	mercoledì	miércoles	Mittwoch
Dies Jovis	Thor's Day	Thursday	jeudi	giovedì	jueves	Donnerstag
Dies Veneris	Frigg's Day	Friday	vendredi	venerdì	viernes	Freitag
Dies Saturni	Seterne's Day	Saturday	samedi	sabato	sábado	Sonnabend

NOTE: The Romans gave one day of the week to each planet known, the Sun and Moon being considered planets in this connection. The Saxon names are a kind of translation of the Roman names: Tiw was substituted for Mars, Woden (Wotan) for Mercury, Thor for Jupiter (Jove), Frigg for Venus, and Seterne for Saturn. The English names are adapted Saxon. The Spanish, Italian, and French names, which are normally not capitalized, are derived from the Latin. The German names follow the Saxon pattern with two exceptions: Wednesday is Mittwoch (Middle of the Week), and Saturday is Sonnabend (Sunday's Eve).

clock in Trenton, N.J., which, in turn, would be ahead of a clock in Philadelphia. This condition prevailed until 1884, when a system of standard time was adopted by the International Meridian Conference. The earth's surface was divided into 24 zones. The standard time of each zone is the mean astronomical time of one of 24 meridians, 15 degrees apart, beginning at the Greenwich, England, meridian and extending east and west around the globe to the international dateline, (This system was actually put into use a year earlier by the railroad companies of the U.S. and Canada who, until then, had to contend with some 100 conflicting local sun times observed in terminals across the land.)

For practical purposes, this convention is sometimes altered. For example, Alaska, for a time, consisted of four of the eight U.S. time zones: the Pacific Standard Time zone (east of Juneau) and the 6th (Juneau), 7th (Anchorage), and 8th (Nome) zones, encompassing the 135°, 150°, and 165° meridians, respectively. In 1983, by Act of Congress, the entire state (except the westward-most Aleutians) was united into the 6th zone, Alaska Standard Time.

The eight U.S. Standard Time Zones are: Atlantic (includes Puerto Rico and the Virgin Islands), Eastern, Central, Mountain, Pacific, Alaska, Hawaii–Aleutian (includes all of Hawaii and those Aleutians west of the Fox Islands), and Samoa Standard Time.

The date line. While the time zones are based on the natural event of the Sun crossing the meridian, the date must be an arbitrary decision. The meridians are traditionally counted from the meridian of the observatory of Greenwich in England, which is called the zero meridian. The logical place for changing the date is 12 hours, or 180° from Greenwich. Fortunately, the 180th meridian runs mostly through the open Pacific. The date line makes a zigzag in the north to incorporate the eastern tip of Siberia into the Siberian time system and then another one to incorporate a number of islands into the Hawaii-Aleutian time zone. In the south there is a similar zigzag for the purpose of tying a number of British-owned islands to the New Zealand time system. Otherwise the date line is the same as 180° from Greenwich. At points to the east of the date line the calendar is one day earlier than at points to the west of it. A traveller going eastward across the date line from one island to another would not have to re-set his watch because he would stay inside the time zone (provided he does so where the date line does *not* coincide with the 180° meridian), but it would be the same time of the previous day.

The Seasons

The seasons are caused by the tilt of the Earth's axis (23.4°) and not by the fact that the Earth's orbit around the Sun is an ellipse. The average distance of the Earth from the Sun is 93 million miles; the difference between aphelion (farthest away) and perihelion (closest to the Sun) is 3 million miles, so that perihelion is about 91.4 million miles from the Sun. The Earth goes through the perihelion point a few days after New Year, just when the northern hemisphere has winter. Aphelion is passed during the first days in July. This by itself shows that the distance from the Sun is not important within these limits. What is important is that when the Earth passes through perihelion, the northern end of the Earth's axis happens to tilt away from the Sun, so that the areas beyond the Tropic of Cancer receive only slanting rays from a Sun low in the sky.

The Names of the Months

January: named after Janus, protector of the gateway to heaven
February: named after Februalia, a time period when sacrifices were made to atone for sins
March: named after Mars, the god of war, presumably signifying that the campaigns interrupted by the winter could be resumed
April: from *aperire,* Latin for "to open" (buds)
May: named after Maia, the goddess of growth of plants
June: from *juvenis,* Latin for "youth"
July: named after Julius Caesar
August: named after Augustus, the first Roman Emperor
September: from *septem,* Latin for "seven"
October: from *octo,* Latin for "eight"
November: from *novem,* Latin for "nine"
December: from *decem,* Latin for "ten"

NOTE: The earliest Latin calendar was a 10-month one; thus September was the seventh month, October, the eighth, etc. July was originally called Quintilis, as the fifth month; August was originally called Sextilis, as the sixth month.

The tilt of the Earth's axis is responsible for four lines you find on every globe. When, say, the North Pole is tilted away from the Sun as much as possible, the farthest points in the North which can still be reached by the Sun's rays are 23 1/2° from the pole. This is the Arctic Circle. The Antarctic Circle is the corresponding limit 23.4° from the South Pole; the Sun's rays cannot reach beyond this point when we have mid-summer in the North.

When the Sun is vertically above the equator, the day is of equal length all over the Earth. This happens twice a year, and these are the "equinoxes" in March and in September. After having been over the equator in March, the Sun will seem to move northward. The northernmost point where the Sun can be straight overhead is 23.4° north of the equator. This is the Tropic of Cancer; the Sun can never be vertically overhead to the north of this line. Similarly the Sun cannot be vertically overhead to the south of a line 23.4° south of the equator—the Tropic of Capricorn.

This explains the climatic zones. In the belt (the Greek word *zone* means "belt") between the Tropic of Cancer and the Tropic of Capricorn, the Sun can be straight overhead; this is the tropical zone. The two zones where the Sun cannot be overhead but will be above the horizon every day of the year are the two temperate zones; the two areas where the Sun will not rise at all for varying lengths of time are the two polar areas, Arctic and Antarctic.

Holidays

Religious and Secular, 1994

Since 1971, by federal law, Washington's Birthday, Memorial Day, Columbus Day, and Veterans' Day have been celebrated on Mondays to create three-day weekends for federal employees. Many states now observe these holidays on the same Mondays. The dates given for the holidays listed below are the traditional ones.

New Year's Day, Saturday, Jan. 1. A legal holiday in all states and the District of Columbia, New Year's Day has its origin in Roman Times, when sacrifices were offered to Janus, the two-faced Roman deity who looked back on the past and forward to the future.

Epiphany, Thursday, Jan. 6. Falls the twelfth day after Christmas and commemorates the manifestation of Jesus as the Son of God, as represented by the adoration of the Magi, the baptism of Jesus, and the miracle of the wine at the marriage feast at Cana. Epiphany originally marked the beginning of the carnival season preceding Lent, and the evening (sometimes the eve) is known as Twelfth Night.

Martin Luther King, Jr.'s Birthday, Saturday, Jan. 15. Honors the late civil rights leader. Became a legal public holiday in 1986.

Ground-hog Day, Wednesday, Feb. 2. Legend has it that if the ground-hog sees his shadow, he'll return to his hole, and winter will last another six weeks.

Lincoln's Birthday, Saturday, Feb. 12. A legal holiday in many states, this day was first formally observed in Washington, D.C., in 1866, when both houses of Congress gathered for a memorial address in tribute to the assassinated President.

St. Valentine's Day, Monday, Feb. 14. This day is the festival of two third-century martyrs, both named St. Valentine. It is not known why this day is associated with lovers. It may derive from an old pagan festival about this time of year, or it may have been inspired by the belief that birds mate on this day.

Washington's Birthday, Tuesday, Feb. 22. The birthday of George Washington is celebrated as a legal holiday in every state of the Union, the District of Columbia, and all territories. The observance began in 1796.

First Day of Ramadan. Saturday, Feb. 12. This day marks the beginning of a month-long fast which all Moslems must keep during the daylight hours. Only a few are exempt: the sick, those on a journey. It commemorates the first revelation of the Koran.

Shrove Tuesday, Feb. 15. Falls the day before Ash Wednesday and marks the end of the carnival season, which once began on Epiphany but is now usually celebrated the last three days before Lent. In France, the day is known as Mardi Gras (Fat Tuesday), and Mardi Gras celebrations are also held in several American cities, particularly in New Orleans. The day is sometimes called Pancake Tuesday by the English because fats, which were prohibited during Lent, had to be used up.

Ash Wednesday, Feb. 16. The first day of the Lenten season, which lasts 40 days. Having its origin sometime before A.D. 1000, it is a day of public penance and is marked in the Roman Catholic Church by the burning of the palms blessed on the previous year's Palm Sunday. With his thumb, the priest then marks a cross upon the forehead of each worshipper. The Anglican Church and a few Protestant groups in the United States also observe the day, but generally without the use of ashes.

Purim (Feast of Lots), Friday, Feb. 25. A day of joy and feasting celebrating deliverance of the Jews from a massacre planned by the Persian Minister Haman. The Jewish Queen Esther interceded with her husband, King Ahasuerus, to spare the life of her uncle, Mordecai, and Haman was hanged on the same gallows he had built for Mordecai. The holiday is marked by the reading of the Book of Esther (megillah), and by the exchange of gifts, donations to the poor, and the presentation of Purim plays.

St. Patrick's Day, Thursday, March 17. St. Patrick, patron saint of Ireland, has been honored in America since the first days of the nation. There are many dinners and meetings but perhaps the most notable part of the observance is the annual St. Patrick's Day parade on Fifth Avenue in New York City.

Palm Sunday, March 27. Is observed the Sunday

before Easter to commemorate the entry of Jesus into Jerusalem. The procession and the ceremonies introducing the benediction of palms probably had their origin in Jerusalem.

Good Friday, April 1. This day commemorates the Crucifixion, which is retold during services from the Gospel according to St. John. A feature in Roman Catholic churches is the Liturgy of the Passion; there is no Consecration, the Host having been consecrated the previous day. The eating of hot cross buns on this day is said to have started in England.

First Day of Passover (Pesach), Sunday, March 27. The Feast of the Passover, also called the Feast of Unleavened Bread, commemorates the escape of the Jews from Egypt. As the Jews fled they ate unleavened bread, and from that time the Jews have allowed no leavening in the houses during Passover, bread being replaced by matzoh.

Easter Sunday, April 3. Observed in all Christian churches, Easter commemorates the Resurrection of Jesus. It is celebrated on the first Sunday after the full moon which occurs on or next after March 21 and is therefore celebrated between March 22 and April 25 inclusive. This date was fixed by the Council of Nicaea in A.D. 325. The Orthodox Church celebrates Easter on April 18, 1993.

Mother's Day, Sunday, May 8. Observed the second Sunday in May, as proposed by Anna Jarvis of Philadelphia in 1907.

Ascension Day, Thursday, May 12. Took place in the presence of His apostles 40 days after the Resurrection of Jesus. It is traditionally held to have occurred on Mount Olivet in Bethany.

First Day of Shavuot (Hebrew Pentecost), Monday, May 16. This festival, sometimes called the Feast of Weeks, or of Harvest, or of the First Fruits, falls 50 days after Passover and originally celebrated the end of the seven-week grain harvesting season. In later tradition, it also celebrated the giving of the Law to Moses on Mount Sinai.

Memorial Day, Monday, May 30. Also known as Decoration Day, Memorial Day is a legal holiday in most of the states and in the territories, and is also observed by the armed forces. In 1868, Gen. John A. Logan (Retired), Commander in Chief of the Grand Army of the Republic, issued an order designating the day as one in which the graves of soldiers would be decorated. The holiday was originally devoted to honoring the memory of those who fell in the Civil War, but is now also dedicated to the memory of all war dead.

Pentecost (Whitsunday), Sunday, May 22. This day commemorates the descent of the Holy Ghost upon the apostles 50 days after the Resurrection. The sermon by the Apostle Peter, which led to the baptism of 3,000 who professed belief, originated the ceremonies that have since been followed. "Whitsunday" is believed to have come from "white Sunday" when, among the English, white robes were worn by those baptized on the day.

Flag Day, Tuesday, June 14. This day commemorates the adoption by the Continental Congress on June 14, 1777, of the Stars and Stripes as the U.S. flag. Although it is a legal holiday only in Pennsylvania, President Truman, on Aug. 3, 1949, signed a bill requesting the President to call for its observance each year by proclamation.

Father's Day, Sunday, June 19. Observed the third Sunday in June. First celebrated June 19, 1910.

Independence Day, Monday, July 4. The day of the adoption of the Declaration of Independence in 1776, celebrated in all states and territories. The observance began the next year in Philadelphia.

Labor Day, Monday, Sept. 5. Observed the first Monday in September in all states and territories, Labor Day was first celebrated in New York in 1882 under the sponsorship of the Central Labor Union, following the suggestion of Peter J. McGuire, of the Knights of Labor, that the day be set aside in honor of labor.

First Day of Rosh Hashana (Jewish New Year), Tuesday, Sept. 6. This day marks the beginning of the Jewish year 5755 and opens the Ten Days of Penitence closing with Yom Kippur.

Yom Kippur (Day of Atonement), Thursday, Sept. 15. This day marks the end of the Ten Days of Penitence that began with Rosh Hashana. It is described in *Leviticus* as a "Sabbath of rest," and synagogue services begin the preceding sundown, resume the following morning, and continue to sundown.

First Day of Sukkot (Feast of Tabernacles) Tuesday, Sept. 20. This festival, also known as the Feast of the Ingathering, originally celebrated the fruit harvest, and the name comes from the booths or tabernacles in which the Jews lived during the harvest, although one tradition traces it to the shelters used by the Jews in their wandering through the wilderness. During the festival many Jews build small huts in their back yards or on the roofs of their houses.

Simhat Torah (Rejoicing of the Law), Wednesday, Sept. 28. This joyous holiday falls on the eighth day of Sukkot. It marks the end of the year's reading of the Torah (Five Books of Moses) in the synagogue every Saturday and the beginning of the new cycle of reading.

Columbus Day, Wednesday, Oct. 12. A legal holiday in many states, commemorating the discovery of America by Columbus in 1492. Quite likely the first celebration of Columbus Day was that organized in 1792 by the Society of St. Tammany, or Columbian Order, widely known as Tammany Hall.

United Nations Day, Monday, Oct. 24. Marking the founding of the United Nations.

Halloween, Monday, Oct. 31. Eve of All Saints' Day, formerly called All Hallows and Hallowmass. Halloween is traditionally associated in some countries with old customs such as bonfires, masquerading, and the telling of ghost stories. These are old Celtic practices marking the beginning of winter.

All Saints' Day, Tuesday, Nov. 1. A Roman Catholic and Anglican holiday celebrating all saints, known and unknown.

Election Day, (legal holiday in certain states), Tuesday, Nov. 8. Since 1845, by Act of Congress, the first

Tuesday after the first Monday in November is the date for choosing Presidential electors. State elections are also generally held on this day.

Veterans Day, Friday, Nov. 11. Armistice Day was established in 1926 to commemorate the signing in 1918 of the Armistice ending World War I. On June 1, 1954, the name was changed to Veterans Day to honor all men and women who have served America in its armed forces.

Thanksgiving, Thursday, Nov. 24. Observed nationally on the fourth Thursday in November by Act of Congress (1941), the first such national proclamation having been issued by President Lincoln in 1863, on the urging of Mrs. Sarah J. Hale, editor of *Godey's Lady's Book.* Most Americans believe that the holiday dates back to the day of thanks ordered by Governor Bradford of Plymouth Colony in New England in 1621, but scholars point out that days of thanks stem from ancient times.

First Sunday of Advent, Nov. 27. Advent is the season in which the faithful must prepare themselves for the advent of the Saviour on Christmas. The four Sundays before Christmas are marked by special church services.

First Day of Hanukkah (Festival of Lights), Monday, November 28. This festival was instituted by Judas Maccabaeus in 165 B.C. to celebrate the purification of the Temple of Jerusalem, which had been desecrated three years earlier by Antiochus Epiphanes, who set up a pagan altar and offered sacrifices to Zeus Olympius. In Jewish homes, a light is lighted on each night of the eight-day festival.

Christmas (Feast of the Nativity), Sunday, Dec. 25. The most widely celebrated holiday of the Christian year, Christmas is observed as the anniversary of the birth of Jesus. Christmas customs are centuries old. The mistletoe, for example, comes from the Druids, who, in hanging the mistletoe, hoped for peace and good fortune. Use of such plants as holly comes from the ancient belief that such plants blossomed at Christmas. Comparatively recent is the Christmas tree, first set up in Germany in the 17th century, and the use of candles on trees developed from the belief that candles appeared by miracle on the trees at Christmas. Colonial Manhattan Islanders introduced the name Santa Claus, a corruption of the Dutch name for the 4th-century Asia Minor St. Nicholas.

State Observances

January 6, Three Kings' Day: Puerto Rico.
January 8, Battle of New Orleans Day: Louisiana.
January 11, De Hostos' Birthday: Puerto Rico.
January 19, Robert E. Lee's Birthday: Arkansas, Florida, Kentucky, Louisiana, South Carolina, **(third Monday)** Alabama, Mississippi.
January 19, Confederate Heroes Day: Texas.
January (third Monday): Lee-Jackson-King Day: Virginia.
January 30, F.D. Roosevelt's Birthday: Kentucky.
February 15, Susan B. Anthony's Birthday: Florida, Minnesota.
March (first Tuesday), Town Meeting Day: Vermont.
March 2, Texas Independence Day: Texas.
March (first Monday), Casimir Pulaski's Birthday: Illinois.
March 17, Evacuation Day: Massachusetts (in Suffolk County).
March 20 (First Day of Spring), Youth Day: Oklahoma.
March 22, Abolition Day: Puerto Rico.
March 25, Maryland Day: Maryland.
March 26, Prince Jonah Kuhio Kalanianaole Day: Hawaii.
March (last Monday), Seward's Day: Alaska.
April 2, Pascua Florida Day: Florida
April 13, Thomas Jefferson's Birthday: Alabama, Oklahoma.
April 16, De Diego's Birthday: Puerto Rico.
April (third Monday), Patriots' Day: Maine, Massachusetts.
April 21, San Jacinto Day: Texas.
April 22, Arbor Day: Nebraska.
April 22, Oklahoma Day: Oklahoma.
April 26, Confederate Memorial Day: Florida, Georgia.
April (fourth Monday), Fast Day: New Hampshire.
April (last Monday), Confederate Memorial Day: Alabama, Mississippi.
May 1, Bird Day: Oklahoma.
May 8, Truman Day: Missouri.
May 11, Minnesota Day: Minnesota.
May 20, Mecklenburg Independence Day: North Carolina.
June (first Monday), Jefferson Davis's Birthday: Alabama, Mississippi.
June 3, Jefferson Davis's Birthday: Florida, South Carolina.
June 3, Confederate Memorial Day: Kentucky, Louisiana.
June 9, Senior Citizens Day: Oklahoma.
June 11, King Kamehameha I Day: Hawaii.
June 15, Separation Day: Delaware.
June 17, Bunker Hill Day: Massachusetts (in Suffolk County).
June 19, Emancipation Day: Texas.
June 20, West Virginia Day: West Virginia.
July 17, Muñoz Rivera's Birthday: Puerto Rico.
July 24, Pioneer Day: Utah.
July 25, Constitution Day: Puerto Rico.
July 27, Barbosa's Birthday: Puerto Rico.
August (first Sunday), American Family Day: Arizona.
August (first Monday), Colorado Day: Colorado.
August (second Monday), Victory Day: Rhode Island.
August 16, Bennington Battle Day: Vermont.
August (third Friday), Admission Day: Hawaii.
August 27, Lyndon B. Johnson's Birthday: Texas.
August 30, Huey P. Long Day: Louisiana.
September 9, Admission Day: California.
September 12, Defenders' Day: Maryland.
September 16, Cherokee Strip Day: Oklahoma.
September (first Saturday after full moon), Indian Day: Oklahoma.
October 10, Leif Erickson Day: Minnesota.
October 10, Oklahoma Historical Day: Oklahoma.
October 18, Alaska Day: Alaska.
October 31, Nevada Day: Nevada.
November 4, Will Rogers Day: Oklahoma.
November (week of the 16th), Oklahoma Heritage Week: Oklahoma.
November 19, Discovery Day: Puerto Rico.
December 7, Delaware Day: Delaware.

Movable Holidays, 1994–1998

CHRISTIAN AND SECULAR

Year	Ash Wednesday	Easter	Pentecost	Labor Day	Election Day	Thanksgiving	1st Sun. Advent
1994	Feb. 16	April 3	May 22	Sept. 5	Nov. 8	Nov. 24	Nov. 27
1995	March 1	April 16	June 4	Sept. 4	Nov. 7	Nov. 23	Dec. 3
1996	Feb. 21	April 7	May 26	Sept.. 2	Nov. 5	Nov. 28	Dec. 1
1997	Feb. 12	March 30	May 18	Sept. 1	Nov. 4	Nov. 27	Nov. 30
1998	Feb. 25	April 12	May 31	Sept. 7	Nov. 3	Nov. 26	Dec. 6

Shrove Tuesday: 1 day before Ash Wednesday
Palm Sunday: 7 days before Easter
Maundy Thursday: 3 days before Easter
Good Friday: 2 days before Easter
Holy Saturday: 1 day before Easter
Ascension Day: 10 days before Pentecost
Trinity Sunday: 7 days after Pentecost
Corpus Christi: 11 days after Pentecost

NOTE: Easter is celebrated on May 1, 1994, by the Orthodox Church.

JEWISH

Year	Purim[1]	1st day Passover[2]	1st day Shavuot[3]	1st day Rosh Hashana[4]	Yom Kippur[5]	1st day Sukkot[6]	Simhat Torah[7]	1st day Hanukkah[8]
1994	Feb. 25	March 27	May 16	Sept. 6	Sept. 15	Sept. 20	Sept. 28	Nov. 28
1995	March 16	April 15	June 4	Sept. 25	Oct. 4	Oct. 9	Oct. 17	Dec. 18
1996	March 5	April 4	May 24	Sept. 14	Sept. 23	Sept. 28	Oct. 6	Dec. 6
1997	March 23	April 22	June 11	Oct. 3	Oct. 11	Oct. 16	Oct. 24	Dec. 24

1. Feast of Lots. 2. Feast of Unleavened Bread. 3. Hebrew Pentecost; or Feast of Weeks, or of Harvest, or of First Fruits. 4. Jewish New Year. 5. Day of Atonement. 6. Feast of Tabernacles, or of the Ingathering. 7. Rejoicing of the Law. 8. Festival of Lights.

Length of Jewish holidays (O=Orthodox, C=Conservative, R=Reform):

Passover: O & C, 8 days (holy days: first 2 and last 2); R, 7 days (holy days: first and last)
Shavuot: O & C, 2 days; R, 1 day
Rosh Hashana: O & C, 2 days; R, 1 day.
Yom Kippur: All groups, 1 day
Sukkot: All groups, 7 days (holy days: O & C, first 2; R, first only) O & C observe two additional days: Shemini Atseret (Eighth Day of the Feast) and Simhat Torah. R observes Shemini Atseret but not Simhat Torah
Hanukkah: All groups, 8 days

NOTE: All holidays begin at sundown on the evening before the date given.

Islamic 1994

Feb. 12 First day of the month of Ramadan
March 14 'Id al Fitr (Festival of end of Ramadan)
May 21 'Id al-Adha (Festival of Sacrifice at time of annual pilgrimage to Mecca)
June 10 First day of month of Muharram (beginning of liturgical year)
Aug. 20 Mawlid al-Nabi (Anniversary of Prophet Mohammed's birthday)

NOTE: All holidays begin at sundown on the evening before the date given.

Chinese Calendar

The Chinese lunar year is divided into 12 months of 29 or 30 days. The calendar is adjusted to the length of the solar year by the addition of extra months at regular intervals.

The years are arranged in major cycles of 60 years. Each successive year is named after one of 12 animals. These 12-year cycles are continuously repeated. The Chinese New Year is celebrated at the first new moon after the sun enters Aquarius—sometime between Jan. 21 and Feb. 19.

Rat	Ox	Tiger	Cat (Rabbit)	Dragon	Snake	Horse	Sheep (Goat)	Monkey	Rooster	Dog	Pig
1864	1865	1866	1867	1868	1869	1870	1871	1872	1873	1874	1875
1876	1877	1878	1879	1880	1881	1882	1883	1884	1885	1886	1887
1888	1889	1890	1891	1892	1893	1894	1895	1896	1897	1898	1899
1900	1901	1902	1903	1904	1905	1906	1907	1908	1909	1910	1911
1912	1913	1914	1915	1916	1917	1918	1919	1920	1921	1922	1923
1924	1925	1926	1927	1928	1929	1930	1931	1932	1933	1934	1935
1936	1937	1938	1939	1940	1941	1942	1943	1944	1945	1946	1947
1948	1949	1950	1951	1952	1953	1954	1955	1956	1957	1958	1959
1960	1961	1962	1963	1964	1965	1966	1967	1968	1969	1970	1971
1972	1973	1974	1975	1976	1977	1978	1979	1980	1981	1982	1983
1984	1985	1986	1987	1988	1989	1990	1991	1992	1993	1994	1995

National Holidays Around the World, 1994

Afghanistan	Aug. 19
Albania	Nov. 28
Algeria	Nov. 1
Angola	Nov. 11
Antigua and Barbuda	Nov. 1
Argentina	May 25
Armenia	Sept. 21
Australia	Jan. 26
Austria	Oct. 26
Azerbaijan	May 28
Bahamas	July 10
Bahrain	Dec. 16
Bangladesh	March 26
Barbados	Nov. 30
Belarus	July 27
Belgium	July 21
Belize	Sept. 21
Benin	Aug. 1
Bhutan	Dec. 17
Bolivia	Aug. 6
Botswana	Sept. 30
Brazil	Sept. 7
Brunei	Feb. 23
Bulgaria	March 3
Burkina Faso	Aug. 4
Burundi	July 1
Cambodia	June 24
Cameroon	May 20
Canada	July 1
Cape Verde	July 5
Central African Republic	Dec. 1
Chad	June 7
Chile	Sept. 18
China	Oct. 1
Colombia	July 20
Comoros	July 6
Congo	Aug. 15
Costa Rica	Sept. 15
Côte d'Ivoire	Dec. 7
Croatia	May 30
Cuba	Jan. 1
Cyprus	Oct. 1
Czech Republic	Oct. 28
Denmark	April 16
Djibouti	June 27
Dominica	Nov. 3
Dominican Republic	Feb. 27
Ecuador	Aug. 10
Egypt	July 23
El Salvador	Sept. 15
Equatorial Guinea	Oct. 12
Estonia	Feb. 24
Ethiopia	Sept. 12
Fiji	Oct. 10
Finland	Dec. 6
France	July 14
Gabon	Aug. 17
Gambia	Feb. 18
Georgia	May 26
Germany	Oct. 3
Ghana	March 6
Greece	March 25
Grenada	Feb. 7
Guatemala	Sept. 15
Guinea	Oct. 2
Guinea-Bissau	Sept. 24
Guyana	Feb. 23
Haiti	Jan. 1
Honduras	Sept. 15
Hungary	Aug. 20
Iceland	June 17
India	Jan. 26
Indonesia	Aug. 17
Iran	Feb. 11
Iraq	July 17
Ireland	March 17
Israel	April 14[1]
Italy	June 2
Jamaica	Aug. 1[2]
Japan	Dec. 23
Jordan	May 25
Kazakhstan	Dec. 16
Kenya	Dec. 12
North Korea	Sept. 9
South Korea	Aug. 15
Kuwait	Feb. 25
Kyrgyzstan	Aug. 31
Laos	Dec. 2
Latvia	Nov. 18
Lebanon	Nov. 22
Lesotho	Oct. 4
Liberia	July 26
Libya	Sept. 1
Liechtenstein	Aug. 15
Lithuania	Feb. 16
Luxembourg	June 23
Madagascar	June 26
Malawi	July 6
Malaysia	Aug. 31
Maldives	July 26
Mali	Sept. 22
Malta	Sept. 21
Marshall Islands	May 1
Mauritania	Nov. 28
Mauritius	March 12
Mexico	Sept. 16
Micronesia	Nov. 3
Moldova	Aug. 27
Mongolia	July 11
Morocco	March 3
Mozambique	June 25
Myanmar	Jan. 4
Namibia	March 21
Nepal	Dec. 28
Netherlands	April 30
New Zealand	Feb. 6
Nicaragua	Sept. 15
Niger	Dec. 18
Nigeria	Oct. 1
Norway	May 17
Oman	Nov. 18
Pakistan	March 23
Panama	Nov. 3
Papua New Guinea	Sept. 16
Paraguay	May 15
Peru	July 28
Philippines	June 12
Poland	May 3
Portugal	June 10
Qatar	Sept. 3
Romania	Dec. 1
Russia	Nov. 7 & 8
Rwanda	July 1
St. Kitts and Nevis	Sept. 19
St. Lucia	Feb. 22
St. Vincent and the Grenadines	Oct. 27
San Marino	Sept. 3
São Tomé and Príncipe	July 12
Saudi Arabia	Sept. 23
Senegal	April 4
Seychelles	June 5
Sierra Leone	April 27
Singapore	Aug. 9
Slovakia	Aug. 29
Slovenia	June 25
Solomon Islands	July 7
Somalia	Oct. 21
South Africa	May 31
Spain	Oct. 12
Sri Lanka	Feb. 4
Sudan	Jan. 1
Suriname	Nov. 25
Swaziland	Sept. 6
Sweden	June 6
Switzerland	Aug. 1
Syria	April 17
Tajikistan	Sept. 9
Tanzania	April 26
Thailand	Dec. 5
Togo	Jan. 13
Tonga	June 4
Trinidad and Tobago	Aug. 31
Tunisia	March 20
Turkey	Oct. 29
Turkmenistan	Oct. 27
Uganda	Oct. 9
Ukraine	Aug. 24
United Arab Emirates	Dec. 2
United Kingdom	June 11[3]
United States	July 4
Uruguay	Aug. 25
Uzbekistan	Sept. 1
Vanuatu	July 30
Venezuela	July 5
Viet Nam	Sept. 2
Western Samoa	June 1
Yemen, Republic of	May 22
Yugoslavia	April 27
Zaire	June 30
Zambia	Oct. 24
Zimbabwe	April 18

1. Changes yearly according to Hebrew calendar. 2. Celebrated on first Monday in August. 3. Celebrated the second Saturday in June.

Beware of 900-Number Telemarketing Scams

Source: Federal Trade Commission, Bureau of Consumer Affairs.

The 900 number is a new twist in telemarketing—where you may pay for the sales pitch, along with the telephone call.

By dialing a 900 telephone number, you can: order products, hear Santa tell a story, vote in an opinion poll, get financial tips, talk to a willing stranger, and more. To do these things, you pay a flat fee for the entire call or for each minute you stay on the phone.

If you know exactly what you are getting and how much you'll be charged, 900 numbers can be a perfectly good way to do business or get information. But, the Federal Trade Commission (FTC) is investigating complaints that some consumers have been charge excessively for 900-number services or have not received the services advertised.

If you're a victim of a 900-number scam, know that the phone company generally won't disconnect your phone for failure to pay a disputed 900-number charge. In addition, you are protected under the Fair Debt Collection Practices Act if a 900-number information provider tries to collect for a 900-number charge you dispute.

What You Need to Watch Out For

Long-distance 900 numbers, as well as local "976" and long-distance "700" exchanges, are used in many ways. Your best protection against problems may be to watch out for appeals that:

Fail to disclose any costs upfront. Some scams entice you to call a 900 number without first telling you how much you will be charged for the call.

Make it difficult to find out total costs. Some 900-number scams may disclose a cost per minute, but not reveal you must listen for many minutes to hear all the information. Other 900 services use announcers who speak so quickly that you need to call back to understand the message. Some computer-generated calls disclose 900-number costs only at the end of long-winded promotions for "free" gifts. With these, people may hang up before realizing there's a charge for dialing the 900 number to get their "free" gift.

NOTE: Under new Federal Trade Commission rules effective Nov. 1, 1993, 900-number services must clearly disclose their fees, and allow callers grace periods to hang up without charge.

Entice you to call for bogus products or services. Some scams promote 900 numbers for job or housing information. Once you place—and pay for—the call, you are told that the job or house is already taken. Other scams involve pitches for "gold" credit cards. With these, television, newspaper, or telephone ads promoting the scam may reveal the cost of making the 900 call. Unfortunately, only after you place the call are you told about additional charges and limitations on using the card.

Pitch products or services to children and teenagers. Some television promotions encourage children to call 900 numbers for "free" gifts or stories. Teenagers may call 900-number "talklines" to chat with other teens—usually at a cost-per-minute charge. Children may make these calls without telling their parents or understanding that the phone calls cost money. Parents have received phone bills of thousands of dollars.

If You're Caught in a 900-Number Scam

If you have problems with charges on your phone bill for 900 (or 976 or 700)-number scams, write to your telephone company immediately. You can ask the phone company to delete the charge, although it is not legally obligated to do so. AT&T cannot disconnect your phone for failure to pay. For other carriers, call the carrier or the Federal Communications Commission.

You can also write the phone company for the name of the 900-number company charging you and write to that company to delete the charge. The 900-number company could refuse, however, and have a debt collector contact you. In that event, you can write to the collection agency telling it not to contact you.

Under the law, once the collection agency receives your letter, it cannot contact you again except to say there will be no further contact or that some specific action will be taken (if the debt collector or creditor intends to take such action). Because the debt, if not resolved, can remain on your credit record, you are also legally entitled to have your account of the incident included in your credit report.

In addition, you may want to contact the Federal Trade Commission at 6th and Pennsylvania Avenue, N.W., Washington, D.C. 20580. Complaints about 900-number scams help the FTC in its law enforcement efforts.

How to Protect Yourself

900-number scams are constantly changing. In general, you can protect yourself if you:

Deal only with reputable companies. You may see well-known companies or organizations sponsor such 900-number services as opinion surveys or sports information. The costs, usually low, are stated upfront. If you are interested in these services and are willing to pay for them, these are usually legitimate 900-number operations to call.

Know precisely what the 900 call will cost—before you make the call. Companies should state costs upfront as flat rates or—if the cost is per minute—the maximum number of minutes for the call. Unfortunately, even with this information, you may still pay to hear sales pitches for bogus products or services.

Think twice before calling a 900 number for a "free" gift. You may see television ads or receive postcards or phone calls urging you to call 900 numbers for "free" prizes. Know that you pay for those "free" gifts when you make the 900-number call.

Don't confuse 900 numbers with toll-free 800 numbers. You pay for the 900-number call. The company pays for the 800-number call.

Talk to your children. Make sure they understand they shouldn't call 900 number without your permission. □

Credit Card Tips

Source: United States Office of Consumer Affairs.

The following suggestions can help you when selecting a credit card company or using your credit cards.

1. Keep in a safe place a list of your credit card numbers, expiration dates and the phone number of each card issuer.

2. Credit card issuers offer a wide variety of terms (annual percentage rate, methods of calculating the balance subject to the finance charge, minimum monthly payments and actual membership fees). When selecting a card, compare the terms offered by several card issuers to find the card that best suits your needs.

3. When you use your credit card, watch your card after giving it to a clerk. Promptly take back the card after the clerk is finished with it and make sure it's yours.

4. Tear up the carbons when you take your credit card receipt.

5. Never sign a blank receipt; draw a line through any blank spaces above the total when you sign receipts.

6. Save your purchase receipts until the credit card bill arrives. Then, open the bill promptly and compare it with your receipts to check for possible unauthorized charges and billing errors.

7. Write the card issuer promptly to report any questionable charges. Telephone the card issuer to discuss the billing problem **does not** preserve your rights. Do not include written inquiries with your payment. Instead, check the billing statement for the correct address for billing questions. The inquiry must be in writing and must be sent within 60 days to guarantee your rights under the Fair Credit Billing Act.

8. Never give your credit card number over the telephone unless you made the call or have an account with the company calling you. Never put your card number on a post card or on the outside of an envelope.

9. Sign new cards as soon as they arrive. Cut up and throw away expired cards.

10. If any of your credit cards are missing or stolen, report the loss as soon as possible to the card issuer. Check your credit card statement for a telephone number for reporting stolen credit cards. Follow up your phone calls with a letter to each card issuer. The letter should contain your card number, the date the card was missing and the date you called in the loss.

11. If you report the loss before a credit card is used, the issuer cannot hold you responsible for any future unauthorized charges. If a thief uses your card before you report it missing, the most you will owe for unauthorized charges is $50 on each card. A special note of warning: If an automatic teller machine (ATM) card is lost or stolen, the consumer could lose as much as $500 if the card issuer is not notified within two business days after learning of the loss or theft.

12. When writing checks for retail purchases and to protect yourself against fraud, you may refuse to allow a merchant to write your credit card number on your check. However, if you refuse, the merchant might legally refuse to sell you the product. There is probably no harm in allowing a merchant to verify that you hold a major credit card and to note the issuer and the expiration date on the check.

13. If a merchant indicates he or she is using credit cards as back-ups for bounced checks, or refuses your sale because you refuse to provide personal information (including your phone number) on the bankcard sales slip, report the store to the credit card company. The merchant might be violating his or her agreement with the credit card companies. In your letter to the credit card company, provide the name and location of the merchant. □

Copyrights

Source: Library of Congress, Copyright Office.

On March 1, 1989, the United States joined the Berne Union by entering into an international treaty called the Berne Convention, whose full title is the Berne Convention for the Protection of Literary and Artistic Works. Also on that date, amendments to the U.S. copyright law that satisfy U.S. treaty obligations under the Convention took effect and some of them are listed herein. Contact the U.S. Copyright Office for details of Berne Convention obligations.

The U.S. Law continues to govern the protection and registration of works in the United States.

Beginning March 1, 1989, copyright in the works of U.S. authors is protected automatically in all member nations of the Berne Union and the works of foreign authors who are nationals of a Berne Union country, and works first published in a Berne Union country are automatically protected in the United States.

In order to fulfill its Berne Convention obligations, the United States made certain changes in its copyright law by passing the Berne Convention Implementation Act of 1988. These changes are not retroactive and are effective only on and after March 1, 1989.

The copyright law (Title 17 of the United States Code) was amended by the enactment of a statute for its general revision, Public Law 94–553 (90 Stat. 2541), which was signed by the President on October 19, 1976. The new law superseded the copyright act of 1909, as amended, which remained effective until the new enactment took effect on January 1, 1978.

Under the new law, all copyrightable works, whether published or unpublished, are subject to a single system of statutory protection which gives a copyright owner the exclusive right to reproduce the copyrighted work in copies or phonorecords and distribute them to the public by sale, rental, lease, or lending. Among the other rights given to the owner of a copyright are the exclusive rights to prepare derivative works based upon the copyrighted work, to perform the work publicly if it be literary, musical, dramatic, choreographic, a pantomime, motion picture, or other audiovisual work, and in the case of literary, musical, dramatic, and choreographic works, pantomimes, and pictorial, graphic, or sculptural works, including the individual images of a motion picture or other audiovisual work, to display the copyrighted work publicly. All of these rights are subject to certain exceptions, including the principle of "fair use" which the new statute specifically recognizes.

Special provisions are included which permit compulsory licensing for the recording of musical compositions, noncommercial transmissions by public broadcasters of published musical and graphic works, and the secondary transmission of copyrighted works on cable television systems; and voluntary licensing for performances of copyrighted music by jukeboxes.

Copyright protection under the new law extends to original works of authorship fixed in a tangible medium of expression, from which they can be perceived, reproduced, or otherwise communicated, either directly or with the aid of a machine or device. Works of authorship include books, periodicals and other literary works, musical compositions with accompanying lyrics, dramas and dramatico-musical compositions, pantomimes and choreographic works, motion pictures and other audiovisual works, sound recordings, and works of the visual arts.

As a mandatory condition of copyright protection under the law in effect before 1978, all published copies of a work were required to bear a copyright notice. The 1976 Act requires that all visually perceptible copies published in the United States or elsewhere bear a notice of copyright affixed in such manner and location as to give reasonable notice of the claim of copyright. (Abolished in or after March 1, 1989, according to the Berne agreement) The notice consists of the symbol © (the letter C in a circle), the word "Copyright," or the abbreviation "Copr.," and the year of first publication of the work, and the name of the owner of copyright in the work. EXAMPLE: © *1993 John Doe.*

The notice of copyright prescribed for sound recordings consists of the symbol ℗ (the letter P in a circle), the year of first publication of the sound recording, and the name of the owner of copyright in the sound recording, placed on the surface of the phonorecord, or on the phonorecord label or container, in such manner and location as to give reasonable notice of the claim of copyright. EXAMPLE: ℗ *1993 Doe Records, Inc.* Omission or errors in the notice will not immediately result in forfeiture of the copyright, and can be corrected within certain time limits. Innocent infringers misled by the omission or error may be shielded from liability.

In accordance with the Berne agreement, mandatory notice of copyright has been abolished for works published for the first time on or after March 1, 1989. Failure to place a notice of copyright on copies or phonorecords of such works can no longer result in the loss of copyright. Nevertheless, copyright owners must deposit in the Copyright Office two complete copies or phonorecords of the best edition of all works subject to copyright that are publicly distributed in the United States, whether or not the work contains a notice of copyright. In general, this deposit requirement may be satisfied by registration. For more information about mandatory deposit, request Circular 7d.

Voluntary use of notice is encouraged. Placing a notice of copyright on published works is still strongly recommended. One of the benefits is that an infringer will not be able to claim that he or she "innocently infringed" a work. (A successful innocent infringement claim may result in a reduction in damages for infringement that the copyright owner would otherwise receive.)

The notice requirement for works incorporating a predominant portion of U.S. government work has been eliminated as of March 1, 1989. For these works to receive the evidentiary benefit of voluntary notice, in addition to the notice, a statement is required on the copies identifying what is copyrighted.

A sample is: © 1993 Jane Brown. Copyright claimed in Chapters 7–10, exclusive of U.S. government maps.

Notice Unchanged for Works Published Before March 1, 1989

The Berne Convention Implementation Act is not retroactive. Thus, the notice requirements that were in place before March 1, 1989, govern all works first published during that period (regardless of national origin).

- Works first published between January 1, 1978, and February 28, 1989: If a work was first published without notice during this period, it is still necessary to register the work before or within five years after publication and add the notice to copies distributed in the United States after discovery of the omission.
- Works first published before January 1, 1978: If a work was first published without the required notice before 1978, copyright was lost immediately (with the possible exception of works seeking "ad interim" protection). Once copyright is lost, it can never be restored in the United States, except by special legislation.

Registration in the Copyright Office is not a condition of copyright protection but will be a prerequisite to bringing an action in a court of law for infringement. With certain exceptions, the remedies of statutory damages and attorney's fees will not be available for infringements occurring before registration. Most copies or phonorecords published in the United States with notice of copyright are required to be deposited for the collections of the Library of Congress, not as a condition of copyright protection, but under provisions of the law subjecting the copyright owner to certain penalties for failure to deposit after a demand by the Register of Copyrights. Registration is permissive, but may be made either at the time the depository requirements are satisfied or at any other time during the subsistence of the copyright.

For works already under statutory protection, the new law retains the present term of copyright of 28 years from first publication (or from registration in some cases), renewable by certain persons for a second period of protection, but it increases the length of the second period to 47 years.

Copyrights in their first term on January 1, 1978, *may* still be renewed to receive the maximum statutory term of 75 years (a first term of 28 years plus a renewal term of 47 years). Registering such renewal in the Copyright Office during the last (28th) year of the original copyright, or at any time during the renewed and extended term, accrues certain legal benefits:

- The renewal copyright will vest in the name of the renewal claimant on the effective date of the renewal registration;
- The renewal registration will constitute *prima facie* evidence as to the validity of the facts stated in the renewal certificate and the copyright in the renewed and extended term; and,
- The right to utilize the derivative work in the extended term is affected.

However, recent legislation (Public Law 102-307, effective June 26, 1992) has made the renewal of works published or registered between January 1, 1964, and December 31, 1977, *automatic*, and the formality of registering such renewal in the Copyright Office *optional*.

Copyrights in their second term on January 1, 1978, are automatically extended up to a maximum of 75 years. Unpublished works that are already in existence on January 1, 1978, but are not protected by statutory copyright and have not yet gone into the public domain, will generally obtain automatic Federal copyright protection for the author's life, plus an additional 50 years after the author's death, but in any event, for a minimal term of 25 years (that is, until December 31, 2002), and if the work is published before that date, then for an additional term of 25 years, through the end of 2027.

For works created on or after January 1, 1978, the new law provides a term lasting for the author's life, plus an additional 50 years after the author's death. For works made for hire, and for anonymous and pseudonymous works (unless the author's identity is revealed in Copyright Office records), the new term will be 75 years from publication or 100 years from creation, whichever is shorter. The new law provides that all terms of copyright will run through the end of the calendar year in which they would otherwise expire. This will not only affect the duration of copyrights, but also the time-limits for renewal registrations.

Works already in the public domain cannot be protected under the new law. The 1976 Act provides no procedure for restoring protection to works in which copyright has been lost for any reason. In general, works published before January 1, 1918, are not under copyright protection in the United States, at least insofar as any version published before that date is concerned.

Recordation

Recordation as a Prerequisite to an Infringement Suit. The copyright owner no longer has to record a transfer before bringing a copyright lawsuit in that owner's name.

Benefits of recordation. The benefits of recordation in the Copyright Office are unchanged:

- Under certain conditions, recordation establishes priorities between conflicting transfers and nonexclusive licenses;
- Under certain conditions, recordation establishes priority between conflicting transfers; and,
- Recordation establishes a public record of the contents of the transfer or document.

Jukebox Licenses

Section 116 of the 1976 Copyright Act provides for a compulsory license to publicly perform nondramatic musical works by means of coin-operated phonorecord players (jukeboxes). The Berne Convention Implementation Act amends the law to provide for negotiated licenses between the user (the jukebox operator) and the copyright owner. If necessary, the parties are encouraged to submit to arbitration to facilitate negotiated licenses. Such licenses take precedence over the compulsory license.

For detailed information about the amendments to U.S. copyright law under the Berne Convention agreement, request circulars 93, "Highlights of U.S. Adherence to the Berne Convention," and 93a, "The United States Joins The Berne Union" from the Copyright Office.

For publications, call the Forms and Publications Hotline, 202-707-9100, or write:

Copyright Office
Publications Section, LM-455
Library of Congress
Washington, D.C. 20559

To speak with an information specialist or to request further information, call 202-707-3000, or write:

Copyright Office
Information Section, LM-401
Library of Congress
Washington, D.C. 20559

Counterfeit Products

Source: U.S. Office of Consumer Affairs.

Counterfeit products include any product bearing an unauthorized representation of a manufacturer's trademark or trade name. Examples of products which have been counterfeited include prescription and over-the-counter drugs, clothing, credit cards, watches, pacemakers, and machine and automobile replacement parts. Because counterfeit products are often of sub-standard quality, there are potential safety risks which may cause personal injury as well as economic loss.

Avoiding counterfeit products takes practice. The following are usually associated with counterfeit products:

- incorrect, smeared or blurred product packaging
- incorrect spelling of brand name
- no warranty or guarantee available
- "unbelievably" low prices

Unemployment Insurance

Unemployment insurance is managed jointly by the states and the federal government. Most states began paying benefits in 1938 and 1939.

Under What Conditions Can the Worker Collect?

The laws vary from state to state. In general, a waiting period of one week is required after a claim is filed before collecting unemployment insurance; the worker must be able to work, must not have quit without good cause or have been discharged for misconduct; he must not be involved in a labor dispute; above all, he must be ready and willing to work. He may be disqualified if he refuses, without good cause, to accept a job which is suitable for him in terms of his qualifications and experience, unless the wages, hours and working conditions offered are substantially less favorable than those prevailing for similar jobs in the community.

The unemployed worker must go to the local state employment security office and register for work. If that office has a suitable opening available, he must accept it or lose his unemployment payments, unless he has good cause for the refusal. If a worker moves out of his own state, he can still collect at his new residence; the state in which he is now located will act as agent for the other state, which will pay his benefits.

Benefits are paid only to unemployed workers who have had at least a certain amount of recent past employment or earnings in a job covered by the state law. The amount of employment or earnings, and the period used to measure them, vary from state to state, but the intent of the various laws is to limit benefits to workers whose recent records indicate that they are members of the labor force. The amount of benefits an unemployed worker may receive for any week is also determined by application to his past wages of a formula specified in the law. The general objective is to provide a weekly benefit which is about half the worker's customary weekly wages, up to a maximum set by the law (see table). In a majority of states, the total benefits a worker may receive in a 12-month period is limited to a fraction of his total wages in a prior 12-month period, as well as to a stated number of weeks. Thus, not all workers in a state are entitled to benefits for the number of weeks shown in the table.

Who Pays for the Insurance?

The total cost is borne by the employer in all but a few states. Each state has a sliding scale of rates. The standard rate is set at 6.2% of taxable payroll in most states. But employers with records of less unemployment (that is, with fewer unemployment benefits paid to their former workers) are rewarded with rates lower than the standard state rate.

During periods of high unemployment in a state, federal-state extended benefits are available to workers who have exhausted their regular benefits. An unemployed worker may receive benefits equal to the weekly benefit he received under the state program for one half the weeks of his basic entitlement to benefits up to a maximum (including regular benefits) of 39 weeks.

Federal Programs

Amendments to the Social Security Act provided unemployment insurance for Federal civilian employees (1954) and for ex-servicemen (1958). Benefits under these programs are paid by state employment security agencies as agents of the federal government under agreements with the Secretary of Labor. For federal civilian employees and ex-servicemembers, eligibility for benefits and the amount of benefits paid are determined according to the terms and conditions of the applicable state unemployment insurance law.

State Unemployment Compensation Maximums, 1993

State	Weekly benefit[1]	Maximum duration, weeks
Alabama	165	26
Alaska	212–284	26
Arizona	185	26
Arkansas	240	26
California	230	26
Colorado	250	26
Connecticut	306–356	26
Delaware	245	26
D.C.	335	26
Florida	250	26
Georgia	185	26
Hawaii	322	26
Idaho	223	26
Illinois	227–300	26
Indiana	140–181	26
Iowa	200–245	26
Kansas	239	26
Kentucky	217	26
Louisiana	181	26
Maine	198–297	26
Maryland	223	26
Massachusetts	312–468	30
Michigan	293	26
Minnesota	279	26
Mississippi	165	26
Missouri	175	26
Montana	209	26
Nebraska	154	26
Nevada	217	26
New Hampshire	188	26
New Jersey	325	26
New Mexico	191	26
New York	300	26
North Carolina	267	26
North Dakota	212	26
Ohio	228–306	26
Oklahoma	229	26
Oregon	271	26
Pennsylvania	317–325	26
Puerto Rico	133	26
Rhode Island	294–367	26
South Carolina	193	26
South Dakota	154	26
Tennessee	170	26
Texas	245	26
Utah	240	26
Vermont	199	26
Virgin Islands	211	26
Virginia	208	26
Washington	273	30
West Virginia	270	26
Wisconsin	243	26
Wyoming	200	26

1. Maximum amounts. When two amounts are shown, higher includes dependents' allowances. *Source:* Department of Labor, Employment and Training Administration.

Trademarks

Source: Department of Commerce, Patent and Trademark Office.

A trademark may be defined as a word, letter, device, or symbol, as well as some combination of these, which is used in connection with merchandise and which points distinctly to the origin of the goods.

Certificates of registration of trademarks are issued under the seal of the Patent and Trademark Office and may be registered by the owner if he is engaged in interstate or foreign commerce which may lawfully be regulated by Congress since any Federal jurisdiction over trademarks arises under the commerce clause of the Constitution. Effective November 16, 1989, applications to register may also be based on a "bona fide intention to use the mark in commerce." Trademarks may be registered by foreign owners who comply with our law, as well as by citizens of foreign countries with which the U.S. has treaties relating to trademarks. American citizens may register trademarks in foreign countries by complying with the laws of those countries. The right to registration and protection of trademarks in many foreign countries is guaranteed by treaties.

General jurisdiction in trademark cases involving Federal Registrations is given to Federal courts. Adverse decisions of examiners on applications for registration are appealable to the Trademark Trial and Appeal Board, whose affirmances, and decisions in *inter partes* proceedings, are subject to court review. Before adopting a trademark, a person should make a search of prior marks to avoid infringing unwittingly upon them.

The duration of a trademark registration is 10 years, but it may be renewed indefinitely for 10-year periods, provided the trademark is still in use at the time of expiration.

The application fee is $210 per class.

Patents

Source: Department of Commerce, Patent and Trademark Office.

A patent, in the most general sense, is a document issued by a government, conferring some special right or privilege. The term is now restricted mainly to patents for inventions; occasionally, land patents.

The grant of a patent for an invention gives the inventor the privilege, for a limited period of time, of excluding others from making, using, or selling a certain article. However, it does not give him the right to make, use, or sell his own invention.

In the U.S., the law provides that a patent may be granted, for a term of 17 years, to any person who has invented or discovered any new and useful art, machine, manufacture, or composition of matter, as well as any new and useful improvements thereof. A patent may also be granted to a person who has invented or discovered and asexually reproduced a new and distinct variety of plant (other than a tuber-propagated one) or has invented a new, original and ornamental design for an article of manufacture.

A patent is granted only upon a regularly filed application, complete in all respects; upon payment of the fees; and upon determination that the disclosure is complete and that the invention is new, useful, and, in view of the prior art, unobvious to one skilled in the art. The disclosure must be of such nature as to enable others to reproduce the invention.

A complete application, which must be addressed to the Commissioner of Patents and Trademarks, Washington, D.C. 20231, consists of a specification with one or more claims; oath or declaration; drawing (whenever the nature of the case admits of it); and a basic filing fee of $355.[1] The filing fee is not returned to the applicant if the patent is refused. If the patent is allowed, another fee of $585[1] is required before the patent is issued. The fee for design patent application is $145; the issue fee is $205[1]. The fee for a plant patent application is $240; the issue fee is $295. Maintenance fees are required on utility patents at stipulated intervals.

Applications are ordinarily considered in the order in which they are received. Patents are not granted for printed matter, for methods of doing business, or for devices for which claims contrary to natural laws are made. Applications for a perpetual-motion machine have been made from time to time, but until a working model is presented that actually fulfills the claim, no patent will be issued.

1. Fees quoted are for small entities. Fees are double for corporations.

Beware of Illegal Patent Services

It is illegal under patent law (35 USC 33) for anyone to hold himself out as qualified to prepare and prosecute patent applications unless he is registered with the Patent Office. Also, Patent Office regulations forbid registered practitioners advertising for patent business. Some inventors, unaware of this, enter into binding contracts with persons and firms which advertise their assistance in making patent searches, preparing drawings, specifications, and patent applications, only to discover much later that their applications require the services of fully qualified agents or attorneys.

Birthstones

Month	Stone	Month	Stone
January	Garnet	July	Ruby or Star Ruby
February	Amethyst	August	Peridot or Sardonyx
March	Aquamarine or Bloodstone	September	Sapphire or Star Sapphire
April	Diamond	October	Opal or Tourmaline
May	Emerald	November	Topaz or Citrine
June	Pearl, Alexandrite or Moonstone	December	Turquoise, Lapis Lazuli, Blue Zircon or Blue Topaz

Source: Jewelry Industry Council.

How to Write a Complaint Letter

Source: United States Office of Consumer Affairs.

- Include your name, address, and home and work phone numbers.
- Type your letter if possible. If it is handwritten, make sure it is neat and easy to read.
- Make your letter brief and to the point. Include all important facts about your purchase, including the date and place where you made the purchase and any information you can give about the product or service such as serial or model numbers or specific type of service.
- State exactly what you want done about the problem and how long you are willing to wait to get it resolved. Be reasonable.
- Include all documents regarding your problem. Be sure to send COPIES, not originals.
- Avoid writing an angry, sarcastic, or threatening letter. The person reading your letter probably was not responsible for your problem, but may be very helpful in resolving it.
- Keep a copy of the letter for your records.

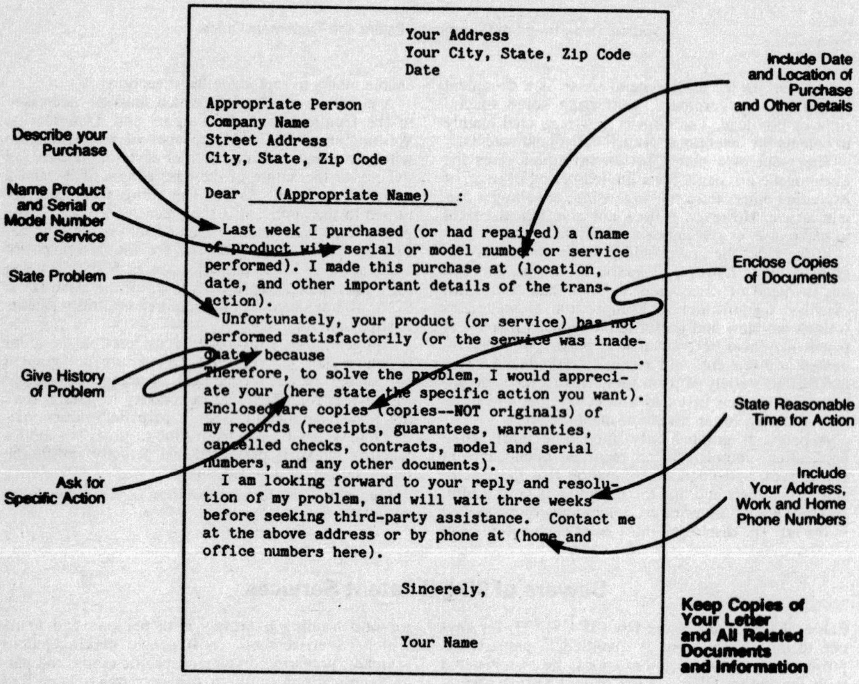

Buying a Used Car

Source: Consumer's Resource Handbook.

Look for and read the "buyer's guide," which must be displayed in the window of all used cars sold by dealers. The buyer's guide explains who must pay for repairs after the purchase. It will tell you if there is a warranty on the car, what the warranty covers, and whether a service contract is available.

Comparison shop for price, condition, warranty, and mileage for the model(s) you are interested in buying. Also compare available interest rates and other terms of financing agreements.

To estimate the total cost of the car, add in any interest rates for financing, the cost of a service contract (if any), and any service or repair expenses you will be likely to pay.

Before buying the car, you might want to consider having a mechanic inspect it.

Check the reliability of the dealer with your state or local consumer protection agency. Also check the local Better Business Bureau to see if there are a large number of complaints against the dealer.

Finally, when purchasing a used car from someone other than a dealer, get a bill of sale, the proper title and registration, and copies of all financial transactions. □

TOLL-FREE NUMBERS

AIDS
CDC National AIDS Hotline
U.S. Public Health Service
1-800-342-2437
Hours: 24 hours, 7 days
SIDA (Spanish line) 1-800-344-7432
Hours: 8:00 a.m.–2:00 a.m. EST, 7 days
TTY (hearing impaired) 1-800-243-7889
Hours: 10:00 a.m.–10:00 p.m. EST, Mon.–Fri.

Provides the latest information to the public about Acquired Immune Deficiency Syndrome (AIDS).

AIDS Drugs Information
National Institute of Allergies and Infectious Diseases
1-800-874-2572
TTY (hearing impaired) 1-800-243-7012
International # 301-217-0023
Hours: 9:00 a.m.–7:00 p.m. EST, Mon.–Fri.

Callers learn the status of research and how to get into a government-sponsored clinical trial.

AUTOMOBILE
Auto Safety Hotline
National Highway Traffic Safety Administration
202-366-0123 (Washington, D.C.)
1-800-424-9393 (Elsewhere)
Hours: 8:00–4:00, EST Mon.–Fri.
Answering service after hours

Handles complaints on safety-related defects, and receives reports of vehicle safety problems. Provides information and in some cases literature on:
•motor vehicle safety recalls •car seats •automobile equipment •tires •motor homes •drunk driving •gas mileage

BANKING
Federal Deposit Insurance Corporation
202-898-3536 (Washington, D.C.)
1-800-934-3422 (Elsewhere)
Hours: 9:00–5:00, EST Mon.–Fri.

Provides general banking information on consumer banking laws. Will refer consumer to proper regulatory agency that supervises institution complaint is being filed against.

BOATING SAFETY HOTLINE
U.S. Coast Guard
1-800-368-5647
Hours: 8:00 a.m.–4:00 p.m. EST Mon.–Fri.

Provides information on boats, safe boating, and associated equipment involved in safety defect (recall) campaigns for past five model years. Takes complaints about possible safety defects. Cannot resolve non-safety problems between consumer and manufacturer and cannot recommend or endorse specific boats or products.

BLIND
National Federation of the Blind
1-800-638-7518,
1-410-659-9314 (Maryland)
Hours: 8:00–5:00 EST, Mon.–Fri.

Provides job information. Concerned about the rights of the blind. Free package of information about blindness.

CHEMICALS
Chemical Referral Center
1-800-262-8200
Hours: 9:00-6:00, EST, Mon.–Fri.

Refers callers to health and safety contacts at chemical manufacturers.

CHILD ABUSE
Parents Anonymous
1-800-352-0386 (California)—machine on 24 hours—can leave message
1-800-421-0353 (Elsewhere) provides referrals for all states
Hours: 8:30–5:00 PST, Mon.–Fri.

CIVICS
National Civic League
1-800-223-6004
303-571-4343 in Colorado
Hours: 8:00–5:00 MST, Mon.–Fri.

Nonprofit organization that seeks to improve state and local governments.

CIVIL RIGHTS
Civil Rights Complaint Hotline
1-800-368-1019

Accepts complaints regarding discrimination on the basis of race, color, national origin, handicap, or age occurring in Health and Human Services programs, i.e., in admission to hospitals, nursing homes, day care centers, or federally funded state health care assistance.

EDUCATION
U.S. Department of Education's Inspector General's Office
1-800-MIS-USED

This number is to report suspected fraud, waste, or abuse involving Federal student aid funds. Callers may remain anonymous.

1-800-433-3243

For complaints on procedure a school is using to distribute financial aid.

DEPARTMENT OF DEFENSE
1-800-424-9098 (Washington, D.C.)
223-5080 (Autovon Line)
693-5080 (FTS)
Hours: 8:00–4:30 EST, Mon.–Fri.

Operated for citizens to report suspected cases of fraud and waste involving the Department of Defense. The anonymity of callers will be respected.

DRUG ABUSE
National Institute on Drug Abuse
1-800-662-HELP
Hours: 9:00 a.m.–3:00 a.m. EST, Mon.–Fri.; 12:00 noon-3:00 a.m., Saturday & Sunday.

Provides information on drug abuse, and treatment referrals.

National Cocaine Hotline
1-800-COCAINE
Hours: 24 hours—7days

Provides information on cocaine and drug-related problems for cocaine abusers.

ALCOHOLISM

National Council on Alcoholism and Drug Dependence Hotline
1-800-622-2255
Hours: 24 hours—7 days

The National Council on Alcoholism, Inc. (NCA), is a national nonprofit organization that combats alcoholism, other drug addictions, and related problems. The council provides an automated referral service for affiliate offices and will mail information. All names and addresses are kept confidential.

Mothers Against Drunk Driving (MADD)
1-800-438-6233
Hours: 24-hours (Business hours: 8 A.M.–5 P.M. Central Time, Mon.–Fri.)
In New York state, call 1-800-245-6233 8:30—5 P.M.

Provides counseling, victim hotline, and nearest chapter referrals. Sends free literature.

"Just Say No Clubs" Hotline (Drug Abuse)
"Just Say No" International
1-800-258-2766
Hours: 7:00 a.m.–5:00 p.m. PCT, Mon.–Fri.

These nationwide clubs provide support and positive peer reinforcement to youngsters through workshops, seminars, newsletters, walk-a-thons, and a variety of other activities. Clubs are organized by schools, communities, and parent groups.

ELECTIONS

Federal Election Commission
Clearinghouse on Election Administration
1-800-424-9530
202-219-3420 (Wash. D.C., Alaska, and Hawaii)
Hours: 8:30–5:30 EST, Mon.–Fri.

Provides information on campaign financing.

ENERGY

Conservation and Renewable Energy Inquiry and Referral Service
1-800-523-2929
Hours: 9:00–5:00 EST, Mon.–Fri.

Provides non-technical information on energy conservation techniques in the home; solar, wind, other energy heating and cooling technologies, and alcohol fuels.

ENVIRONMENT

Hazardous Waste
RCRA Superfund Hotline
Environmental Protection Agency
703-920-9810 (Arlington, Va.)
1-800-424-9346 (Elsewhere)
Hours: 8:30–7:30 EST, Mon.–Fri.

Provides information and interpretation of federal hazardous waste regulations. Will provide referrals regarding other hazardous waste matters.

Pesticide Hotline
National Pesticide Telecommunications Network
1-800-858-7378
Hours: 8:00–6:00 CST, Mon.–Fri.

Provides information on health hazards, cleanup and disposal of pesticides. Will refer callers to human and animal poison control centers in their states if necessary.

FOOD

The Meat and Poultry Hotline
U.S. Department of Agriculture
1-800-535-4555
202-447-3333 in Washington, D.C.
Hours: 10:00 a.m.–4 p.m. EST, Mon.–Fri.

Provides information on proper handling, preparation, storing, and cooking of meat, poultry, and eggs. Answers questions about the safe cooking of poultry and meat in microwave ovens.

GAY & LESBIAN

There is no toll-free number available that can be used on a national level.

HEALTH CARE

Alzheimer's Disease and Related Disorders Association, Inc.
1-800-272-3900
Hours: 8:00–5:00 CST, Mon.–Fri.

Information and referral service. Provides support for patients and their families, aids research efforts, etc.

Cancer Information Service
National Cancer Institute
National Institutes of Health
Department of Health & Human Services
1-800-4-Cancer
Hours: 9:00 a.m.–7:00 p.m. EST, Mon.–Fri.

Provides information on cancer, prevention, treatment and ongoing research; fills requests for pamphlets and other literature on cancer.

National Health Information Center
Department of Health & Human Services
301-565-4167 (Maryland)
1-800-336-4797 (Elsewhere)
Hours: 9:00–5:00 EST, Mon.–Fri.

Provides referrals to sources of information on health-related issues.

Sexually Transmitted Diseases (STDs)
National STD Hotline
Operated by The American Social Health Association
1-800-227-8922
Hours: 8:00 a.m.–11:00 p.m. EST, Mon.–Fri.

Provides latest information about STDs (sometimes called VD) and where to get confidential, free treatment in your area.

HOUSING

Fair Housing Discrimination Hotline
Fair Housing and Equal Opportunity
Department of Housing and Urban Development
202-708-3500 (Washington, D.C.)
1-800-669-9777 (Elsewhere)
Hours: 8:45–5:15 EST, Mon.–Fri.

Receives housing discrimination complaints due to race, color, religion, sex, familial status, handicap, or national origin.

INSURANCE

Federal Crime Insurance
Federal Emergency Management Administration
1-800-638-8780 (National Number)
Hours: 8:30–5:00 EST, Mon.–Fri.
Answering service after hours.

Provides information on federal crime insurance for both homes and businesses which have been robbed or burglarized.

National Insurance Consumer Helpline
Sponsored by insurance industry trade associations
1-800-942-4242
Hours: 8:00–8:00 EST, Mon.–Fri.

Trained personnel provide answers on a wide range of questions about various insurance matters, are able to refer consumer complaints to appropriate sources, and send consumer brochures upon reqeust.

National Flood Insurance
1-800-638-6620
Hours: 8:00 a.m.–8:00 p.m. EST, Mon.–Fri.

Provides information on community participation in the flood program (emergency or regular). If the community does not have a program, it is not eligible for government-subsidized insurance relief. Complaints are referred to the proper office within the agency.

PREGNANCY
Pro-Choice
Abortion Hotline
National Abortion Federation
1-800-772-9100
Hours: 9:30 a.m.–5:30 p.m. EST, Mon.–Fri.

Provides facts about abortion, counseling, and referrals to member clinics.

RIGHT-TO-LIFE
Birthright, Inc. (U.S.A.)
1-800-848-LOVE
1-800-328-LOVE in Canada
Hours: 24 hours, 7-days

Birthright, Inc. provides alternative advice to abortion. Operates crisis centers, and provides help such as pregnancy testing, housing, medical care, and adoption referral.

PRODUCT SAFETY
Consumer Product Safety Commission
1-800-638-2772
Hours: 10:30–4:00 EST, Mon.–Fri.

Provides recorded information on the safety of consumer products. Receives reports of product-related deaths, illnesses, and injuries. Products are not rated or recommended.

RUNAWAYS
Runaway Hotline
1-800-231-6946 (U.S.A. except Texas)
1-800-392-3352 (Texas)
Hours: 24 hours, 7 days

Helps runaways by referring them to shelters, clinics, local hotlines. Will relay messages from the runaway to the parent.

SOCIAL SECURITY AND MEDICARE FRAUD
Inspector General's Hotline
Department of Health and Human Services
1-800-368-5779
Hours: 10:00–4:00 EST, Mon.–Fri.

Takes calls on fraud in Social Security payments or abuse, Medicaid and Medicare fraud and other HHS programs. Recording machine after hours.

1-800-772-1213
Hours: 9:00–4:30 EST, Mon–Fri.

Provides Social Security information.

VIETNAM VETERANS
Vietnam Veterans of America
1-800-424-7275 (answering machine)
202-628-2700 (Washington, D.C.)
Hours: 9:00–5:00 EST, Mon.–Fri.

Answering machine takes messages for information and help. Provides information on Agent Orange, post-traumatic stress disorder, and other maters. Will answer questions on direct line.

Veterans of the Vietnam War, Inc.
1-800-VIETNAM
Hours: 8:00 a.m.–4:30 p.m. EST, Mon.–Fri., (answering service after hours)

Provides information on filing claims against the Agent Orange Settlement, filing claims for veterans benefits with the VA, how to take the VA to court, and information on MIAs and POWs. Veterans newsletter is available, also provides Veterans location services.

Tips For Shopping by Mail, Telephone, or Television

Source: Consumer's Resource Handbook, United States Office of Consumer Affairs.

Be suspicious of exaggerated product claims or very low prices, and read product descriptions carefully—sometimes pictures of products are misleading. If you have any doubt about the company, check with the U.S. Postal Service, your state or local consumer protection agency, or Better Business Bureau before ordering.

Ask about the firm's return policy. If it is not stated, ask before you order. For example, does the company pay charges for shipping and return? Is a warranty or guarantee available? Does the company sometimes substitute comparable goods for the product you want to order?

Keep a record of your order, including the company's name, address, and telephone number, the price of the items ordered, any handling or other charges, the date you mailed (or telephoned) in the order, and your method of payment. Keep copies of canceled checks and/or statements.

If you order by mail, your order should be shipped within 30 days after the company receives your complete order, unless another period is agreed upon when placing the order or is stated in an advertisement. If your order is delayed, a notice of delay should be sent to you within the promised shipping period along with an option to cancel the order.

If you buy a product through a television shopping program, check the cost of the same item sold by other sources, including local stores, catalogs, etc.

If you want to buy a product based on a telephone call from the company, ask for the name, address, and phone number where you can reach the caller after considering the offer. Never give your credit card or social security number over the telephone as proof of your identity.

Postal regulations allow you to write a check payable to the sender, rather than the delivery company, for cash on delivery (C.O.D.) orders. If, after examining the merchandise, you feel there has been a misrepresentation or fraud, you can stop payment on the check and file a complaint with the U.S. Postal Inspector's Office.

You can have a charge removed from your bill if you did not receive the goods or services or if your order was obtained through misrepresentation or fraud. You must notify the credit card company in writing, at the billing/inquiries/disputes address, within 60 days after the charge first appeared on your bill. □

U.S. SOCIETIES & ASSOCIATIONS

Source: Information Please questionnaires to organizations. Names are listed alphabetically according to key word in title; figure in parentheses is year of founding; other figure is membership. An asterisk (*) before a name indicates that up-to-date information has not been provided.

The following is a partial list selected for general readership interest. A comprehensive listing of approximately 20,000 national and international organizations can be found in the **"Encyclopedia of Associations,"** 20th Ed., 1986, Vol. I, Parts 1-3 (Katherine Gruber, Editor; Iris Cloyd, Research Editor), published by Gale Research Company, Book Tower, Detroit, Mich. 48226, available in most public libraries.

AARP (American Association of Retired Persons) (1958): 601 E St. N.W., Washington, D.C. 20049. 33,000,000. Phone: (202) 434-2277.

AAZPA (American Association of Zoological Parks and Aquariums) (1924): Exec. Office/Conservation Center, 7970-D Old Georgetown Rd., Bethesda, Md. 20814-2493. 6,000. Phone: (301) 907-7777.

Abortion Federation, National (1977): 1436 U St. N.W., Suite 103, Washington, D.C. 20009. Phone: (202) 667-5881 or (800) 772-9100.

Accountants, American Institute of Certified Public (1887): 1211 Avenue of the Americas, New York, N.Y. 10036. 304,000. Phone: (212) 596-6200.

Acoustical Society of America (1929): 500 Sunnyside Blvd., Woodbury, N.Y. 11797. 6,800. Phone: (516) 576-2360.

ACSM: American Congress on Surveying and Mapping (1941): 5410 Grosvenor Lane, Bethesda, Md. 20814. 10,000. Phone: (301) 493-0200.

Actors' Equity Association (1913): 165 W. 46th St., New York, N.Y. 10036. Phone: (212) 869-8530.

Actuaries, Society of (1949): 475 N. Martingale Rd., Suite 800, Schaumburg, Ill. 60173-2226. 14,700. Phone: (708) 706-3500.

Adirondack Mountain Club (1922): RR 3, Box 3055, Luzerne Rd., Lake George, N.Y. 12845. 19,000. Phone: (518) 668-4447.

Aeronautic Association, National (1905): 1815 N. Fort Myer Dr., Suite 700, Arlington, Va. 22209. 300,000. Phone: (703) 527-0226.

Aeronautics and Astronautics, American Institute of (1932): The Aerospace Center, 370 L'Enfant Promenade S.W., Washington, D.C. 20024. 40,000+. Phone: (202) 646-7400.

Aerospace Industries Association of America (1919): 1250 Eye St. N.W., Washington, D.C. 20005. 56 companies. Phone: (202) 371-8400.

Aerospace Medical Association (1929): 320 S. Henry St., Alexandria, Va. 22314-3579. 4,000. Phone: (703) 739-2240.

African-American Institute, The (1953): 833 United Nations Plaza, New York, N.Y. 10017. Phone: (212) 949-5666.

AFS Intercultural Programs (American Field Service) (1947): 313 E. 43rd St., New York, N.Y. 10017. 100,000. Phone: (212) 949-4242 or (800) AFS-INFO.

Aging Association, American (1970): 2129 Providence Ave., Chester, Pa. 19013. 500. Phone: (215) 874-7550.

Agricultural Engineers, American Society of (1907): 2950 Niles Rd., St. Joseph, Mich. 49085. 12,000. Phone: (616) 429-0300.

Agricultural History Society (1919): 1301 New York Ave. N.W., Washington, D.C. 20005-4788. 1,400. Phone: (202) 219–0787.

Agronomy, American Society of (1907): 677 S. Segoe Rd., Madison, Wis. 53711-1086. 13,000. Phone: (608) 273-8080.

Air & Waste Management Association (1907): P.O. Box 2861, Pittsburgh, Pa. 15230. 14,000. Phone: (412) 232-3444.

Aircraft Association, Experimental (1953): 3000 Poberezny Rd., Oshkosh, Wis. 54903-3086. 130,000. Phone: (414) 426-4800.

***Aircraft Owners and Pilots Association** (1939): 421 Aviation Way, Frederick, Md. 21701-4798. 300,000. Phone: (301) 695-2000.

Air Force Association (1946): 1501 Lee Highway, Arlington, Va. 22209-1198. 194,000. Phone: (703) 247-5800.

***Air Line Pilots Association** (1931): 1625 Massachusetts Ave. N.W., Washington, D.C. 20036 and 535 Herndon Pkwy., Herndon, Va. 22070. 43,000. Phone: (703) 689-2270.

Air Transport Association of America (1936): 1301 Pennsylvania Ave. N.W., Washington, D.C. 20004-1707. 19 airlines. Phone: (202) 626-4000.

Al-Anon Family Group Headquarters, Inc. For families and friends of alcoholics. (1951): P.O. Box 862, Midtown Station, New York, N.Y. 10018-0862. 31,000 groups worldwide. Phone: (800) 356-9996.

Alateen. For children of alcoholics: P.O. Box 862, Midtown Station, New York, N.Y. 10018-0862. 4,100 groups worldwide. Phone: (800) 356–9996.

Alcoholics Anonymous (1935): General Service Office, A.A. World Services, Inc., 475 Riverside Dr., 11th Floor, New York, N.Y. 10115. 1,800,000. Phone: (212) 870-3400.

Alcoholism and Drug Dependence, National Council on (1944): 12 W. 21st St., New York, N.Y. 10010. 200 affiliates. Phone: (212) 206-6770.

Alcohol Problems, American Council on (1895): 3426 Bridgeland Dr., Bridgeton, Mo. 63044. 3,500. Phone: (314) 739-5944.

Alexander Graham Bell Association for the Deaf (1890): 3417 Volta Place N.W., Washington, D.C. 20007. 6,000. Phone: (202) 337-5220.

Allergy and Immunology, American Academy of (1943): 611 E. Wells St., Milwaukee, Wis. 53202. 4,500. Phone: (414) 272-6071.

Alzheimer's Disease and Related Disorders Association, Inc. (1980): 919 N. Michigan Ave., Suite 1000, Chicago, Ill. 60611-1676. More than 220 Chapters and Affiliates, over 2,000 Family Support Groups. Phone: (312) 335-8700; toll-free (800) 272-3900.

AMBUCS, National Association of American Business Clubs (1922): 3315 No. Main St., High Point, N.C. 27265. 7,000. Phone: (919) 869-2166.

American Alliance for Health, Physical Education, Recreation and Dance (1885): 1900 Association Dr., Reston, Va. 22091. 35,000. Phone: (703) 476-3400.
American Civil Liberties Union (1920): 132 W. 43rd St., New York, N.Y. 10036. 290,000. Phone: (212) 944-9800.
American Contract Bridge League (1927): 2990 Airways Blvd., Memphis, Tenn. 38116-3847. Phone: (901) 332-5586.
American Electroplaters and Surface Finishers Society (AESF) (1909): 12644 Research Pkwy., Orlando, Fla. 32826. 10,000. Phone: (407) 281-6441.
***American Federation of Labor and Congress of Industrial Organizations** (AFL-CIO) (1955): 815 16th St. N.W., Washington, D.C. 20006. 14,100,000. Phone: (202) 637-5010.
American Federation of Musicians of the United States and Canada (1896): 1501 Broadway, Suite 600 Paramount Bldg., New York, N.Y. 10036. Phone: (212) 869-1330.
American Film and Video Association (1943): 8050 Milwaukee Ave., P.O. Box 48659, Niles, Ill. 60714. 1,200. Phone: (708) 698-6440.
American Forests (1875): 1516 P St. N.W., Washington, D.C. 20005. 115,000. Phone: (202) 667-3300.
American Foundrymen's Society, Inc. (1896): 505 State St., Des Plaines, Ill. 60016-8399. 14,000. Phone: (708) 824-0181.
American Friends Service Committee (1917): 1501 Cherry St., Philadelphia, Pa. 19102-1479. Phone: (215) 241-7000.
American Geographical Society, The (1851): 156 Fifth Ave., Suite 600, New York, N.Y. 10010-7002. 1,500. Phone: (212) 242-0214.
American Historical Association (1884): 400 A St. S.E., Washington, D.C. 20003. 19,000. Phone: (202) 544-2422.
American Hospital Association (1898): 840 N. Lake Shore Dr., Chicago, Ill. 60611-2431. 5,800 institutions. Phone: (312) 280-6000.
American Indian Affairs, Association on (1923): 245 Fifth Ave., New York, N.Y. 10016-8728. 35,000. Phone: (212) 689-8720.
American Jail Association (1981): 1000 Day Rd., Suite 100, Hagerstown, Md. 21740-9795. 3,350 jails. Phone: (301) 790-3930.
American Kennel Club (1884): 51 Madison Ave., New York, N.Y. 10010. 485 member clubs. Phone: (212) 696-8200.
American Legion, The (1919): P.O. Box 1055, Indianapolis, Ind. 46206. 3,100,000. Phone: (317) 635-8411.
American Legion Auxiliary (1919): 777 N. Meridian St., Indianapolis, Ind. 46204. 1,000,000. Phone: (317) 635-6291.
American Mensa, Ltd. (1960): 2626 E. 14th St., Brooklyn, N.Y. 11235-3992. 55,000. Phone: (718) 934-3700.
American Montessori Society (1960): 150 Fifth Ave., Suite 203, New York, N.Y. 10011. 12,000. Phone: (212) 924-3209.
American ORT Federation (1922): 817 Broadway, 10th Floor, New York, N.Y. 10003. 160,000. Phone: (212) 677-4400.
American Philosophical Society (1743): 104 S. 5th St., Philadelphia, Pa. 19106-3387. 574 (resident), 126 (foreign). Phone: (215) 440-3400.
American Planning Association (1909): 1776 Massachusetts Ave. N.W., Washington, D.C. 20036 (headquarters). 27,000. Phone: (202) 872-0611. Membership office: 1313 E. 60th St., Chicago, Ill. 60637. Phone: (312) 955-9100.
Americans for Democratic Action, Inc. (1947): 1625 K St. N.W., Suite 210, Washington, D.C. 20006. 70,000. Phone: (202) 785-5980.
American Society for Public Administration (ASPA) (1939): 1120 G St. N.W., Suite 700, Washington, D.C. 20005. 14,000. Phone: (202) 393-7878.
American Society of CLU & ChFC (1928): 270 S. Bryn Mawr Ave., Bryn Mawr, Pa. 19010-2195. Phone: (215) 526-2500.
American Universities, Association of (1900): One Dupont Circle N.W., Suite 730, Washington, D.C. 20036. Phone: (202) 466-5030.
AMIDEAST (America-Mideast Educational and Training Services) (1951): 1100 17th St. N.W., Washington, D.C. 20036-4601. 189 institutional members. Phone: (202) 785-0022.
***Amnesty International/USA** (1961): 322 Eighth Ave., New York, N.Y. 10001-4808. 385,000. Phone: (212) 807-8400.
AMVETS (American Veterans of World War II, Korea, and Vietnam) (1944): 4647 Forbes Blvd., Lanham, Md. 20706-4380. 200,000. Phone: (301) 459-9600.
Animal Protection Institute (1968): 2831 Fruitridge Rd., P.O. Box 22505, Sacramento, Calif. 95822. Phone: (916) 731-5521.
Animals, The American Society for the Prevention of Cruelty to (ASPCA) (1866): 424 E. 92nd St., New York, N.Y. 10128. 400,000+. Phone: (212) 876-7700..
Animals, The Fund For, Inc. (1967): 200 W. 57th St., New York, N.Y. 10019. 175,000. Phone: (212) 246-2096.
Animal Welfare Institute (1951): P.O. Box 3650, Washington, D.C. 20007. 10,000. Phone: (202) 337-2332.
Anthropological Association, American (1902): 4350 N. Fairfax Dr., Suite 640, Arlington, Va. 22203. 11,500. Phone: (703) 528-1902.
Anti-Defamation League of B'nai B'rith (1913): 823 United Nations Plaza, New York, N.Y. 10017-3560. Phone: (212) 490-2525.
Antiquarian Society, American (1812): 185 Salisbury St., Worcester, Mass. 01609. 573. Phone: (508) 755-5221.
Anti-Vivisection Society, The American (1883): 801 Old York Rd., #204, Jenkintown, Pa. 19046-1685. 15,000. Phone: (215) 887-0816.
Appraisers, American Society of (1936): P.O. Box 17265, Washington, D.C. 20041. 6,500. Phone: (800) ASA-VALU or (703) 478-2228.
Arboriculture, International Society of (1924): P.O. Box GG, Savoy, Ill. 61874-1746. 7,500. Phone: (217) 355-9411.
Archaeological Institute of America (1879): 675 Commonwealth Ave., Boston, Mass. 02215-1401. 11,000. Phone: (617) 353-9361.
Architects, The American Institute of (1857): 1735 New York Ave. N.W., Washington, D.C. 20006-5292. 56,000. Phone: (202) 626-7300.
Architectural Historians, Society of (1940): 1232 Pine St., Philadelphia, Pa. 19107-5944. 4,000. Phone: (215) 735-0224.
Army, Association of the United States (1950): 2425 Wilson Blvd., Arlington, Va. 22210-3385. 112,000. Phone: (703) 841-4300.
Arthritis Foundation (1948): 1314 Spring St. N.W., Atlanta, Ga. 30309. 69 local chapters. Phone: (404) 872-7100 or (800) 283-7800.
Arts, National Endowment for the (1965): 1100

Pennsylvania Ave. N.W., Washington, D.C. 20506. Phone: (202) 682-5400.

Arts, The American Federation of (1909): 41 E. 65th St., New York, N.Y. 10021. 525+ institutional members (museums), 600 individual members (patrons). Phone: (212) 988-7700.

Arts and Letters, American Academy of (1898): 633 W. 155th St., New York, N.Y. 10032. 250. Phone: (212) 368-5900.

ASM International® (1913): Materials Park, Ohio 44073-0002. 53,000. Phone: (216) 338-5151.

Association for Investment Management and Research (1947): 5 Boar's Head Lane, P.O. Box 3668, Charlottesville, Va. 22903. 22,500. Phone: (804) 977-6600.

Astronomical Society, American (1899): Dept. of Astronomy. University of Maryland, College Park, Md. 20742. 5,900. Phone: (301) 405–1818.

Astronomical Society of the Pacific (1889): 390 Ashton Ave., San Francisco, Calif. 94112. 6,200. Phone: (415) 337-1100.

Atheists, American (1963): P.O. Box 140195, Austin, Tex. 78714-0195. 40,000 Families. Phone: (512) 458-1244.

Auctioneers Association, National (1949): 8880 Ballentine, Overland Park, Kan. 66214-1985. 5,500. Phone: (913) 541-8084.

Audubon Society, National (1905): 700 Broadway, New York, N.Y. 10003-9501. 600,000. Phone: (212) 979-3000.

***Authors League of America** (1912): 330 W. 42nd St., 29th Floor, New York, N.Y. 10036-6902. 14,000. Phone: (212) 564–8350.

Autism Society of America (1965): 7910 Woodmont Ave., Suite 650, Bethesda, Md. 20814. Phone: (301) 657-0881.

Automobile Association, American (1902): 1000 AAA Dr., Heathrow, Fla., 32746-5063. Phone: (407) 444-7000.

Automobile Club, National (1924): Bayside Plaza, 188 The Embarcadero, #300, San Francisco, Calif. 94105. 300,000. Phone: (415) 777-4000.

Automotive Hall of Fame (1939): P.O. Box 1727, Midland, Mich. 48641-1727. Phone: (517) 631-5760.

Bar Association, American (1878): 750 N. Lake Shore Dr., Chicago, Ill. 60611-4497. 371,000. Phone: (312) 988-5000.

Barber Shop Quartet Singing in America, Society for the Preservation and Encouragement of (SPEBSQSA, Inc.) (1938): 6315 Third Ave., Kenosha, Wis., 53143-5199. 34,000. Phone: (414) 653-8440.

Better Business Bureaus, Council of (1970): 4200 Wilson Blvd., Suite 800, Arlington, Va. 22203-1804. Phone: (703) 276-0100.

Bible Society, American (1816): 1865 Broadway, New York, N.Y. 10023-9980. 200,000. Phone: (212) 408-1200.

Biblical Literature, Society of (1880): 1549 Clairmont Rd., Suite 204, Decatur, Ga. 30033-4635. 5,800 members, 1,200 subscribers. Phone: (404) 636-4744.

Bibliographical Society of America (1904): P.O. Box 397, Grand Central Station, New York, N.Y. 10163. 1,300. Phone: (212) 995-9151.

Bide-A-Wee Home Association, Inc. (1903): 410 E. 38th St., New York, N.Y. 10016. Phone: Adoptions (pets) (212) 532-4455; Clinic and Hospital (212) 532-5884.

Big Brothers/Big Sisters of America (1977): 230 N. 13th St., Philadelphia, Pa. 19107. Phone: (215) 567-7000.

Biochemistry and Molecular Biology, American Society for (1906): 9650 Rockville Pike, Bethesda, Md. 20814. 9,000. Phone: (301) 530-7145.

Biological Sciences, American Institute of (1947): 730 11th St. N.W., Washington, D.C. 20001-4521. 14,000. Phone: (202) 628-1500.

Blind, American Council of the (1961): 1155 15th St. N.W., Suite 720, Washington, D.C. 20005. 30,000. Phone: (202) 467–5081.

Blind, National Federation of the (1940): 1800 Johnson St., Baltimore, Md. 21230. 50,000. Phone: (410) 659-9314.

Blindness, National Society to Prevent (1908): 500 E. Remington Rd., Schaumburg, Ill. 60173-4557. 25 affiliates and divisions. Phone: (708) 843-2020.

Blindness, Research to Prevent (1960): 598 Madison Ave., New York, N.Y. 10022. 1,400. Phone: (212) 752-4333.

***Blue Cross and Blue Shield Association** (1948 and 1946): 676 N. St. Clair St., Chicago, Ill. 60611. 74 Plans. Phone: (312) 440-6000.

B'nai B'rith International (1843): 1640 Rhode Island Ave. N.W., Washington, D.C. 20036-3278. 500,000. Phone: (202) 857-6600.

Booksellers Association, American (1900): 560 White Plains Rd., Tarrytown, N.Y. 10591. 8,200. Phone: (914) 631-7800, (800) 637-0037.

Botanical Gardens & Arboreta, American Association of (1940): 786 Church Rd., Wayne, Pa. 19087. 2,400. Phone: (215) 688-1120.

Boys & Girls Clubs of America (1906): 771 First Ave., New York, N.Y. 10017. 1,850,000. Phone: (212) 351-5900.

Boy Scouts of America (1910): 1325 W. Walnut Hill Lane, P.O. Box 152079, Irving, Tex. 75015-2079. 5,337,905. Phone: (214) 580-2000.

Bridge, Tunnel, and Turnpike Association, International (1932): 2120 L St. N.W., Suite 305, Washington, D.C. 20037-1527. 215 agencies. Phone: (202) 659-4620.

Broadcasters, National Association of (1922): 1771 N St. N.W., Washington, D.C. 20036-2891. 6,500. Phone: (202) 429-5300.

Brookings Institution, The (1916): 1775 Massachusetts Ave. N.W., Washington, D.C. 20036-2188. Phone: (202) 797-6000.

Brooks Bird Club, Inc., The (1932): 707 Warwood Ave., Wheeling, W. Va. 26003. 1,000. Phone: (614) 635-9246.

Business Education Association, National (1946): 1914 Association Dr., Reston, Va. 22091-1596. 14,000. Phone: (703) 860-8300.

Business Women's Association, American (1949): 9100 Ward Parkway, P.O. Box 8728, Kansas City, Mo. 64114-0728. 100,000. Phone: (816) 361-6621.

Campers & Hikers Association, National (1949): 4804 Transit Rd., Bldg. 2, Depew, N.Y. 14043-4906. 24,000 families. Phone: (716) 668-6242.

Camp Fire Boys and Girls (1910): 4601 Madison Ave., Kansas City, Mo. 64112-1278. 600,000. Phone: (816) 756-1950.

Camping Association, The American (1910): 5000 State Rd. 67 N., Martinsville, Ind. 46151-7902. 5,500. Phone: (317) 342-8456.

Cancer Society, American (1913): 1599 Clifton Rd. N.E.., Atlanta, Ga. 30329. 2,646,070 volunteers. Phone: (800) ACS-2345 or check local listings.

CARE, Inc. (1945): 151 Ellis St., Atlanta, Ga. 30303. Programs in 60 developing countries. Phone: ( )

Carnegie Endowment for International Peace

(1910): 2400 N St. N.W., Washington, D.C. 20037. Phone: (202) 862-7900.
Cartoonists Society, National (1946): 157 W. 57th St., Suite 904, New York, N.Y. 10019. Phone: (212) 333-7606.
Catholic Charities USA (1910): 1731 King St., Alexandria, Va. 22314. 3,000 individuals, 1,200 agencies and institutions. Phone: (703) 549-1390.
Catholic Daughters of the Americas (1903): 10 W. 71st St., New York, N.Y. 10023. 140,000. Phone: (212) 877-3041.
Catholic Historical Society, American (1884): 263 S. Fourth St., Philadelphia, Pa. 19106. 950. Phone: (215) 925-5752.
Catholic War Veterans of the U.S.A. Inc. (1935): 441 N. Lee St., Alexandria, Va. 22314. 30,000. Phone: (703) 549-3622.
Ceramic Society, The American (1899): 735 Ceramic Place, Westerville, Ohio 43081-8720.
Cerebral Palsy Associations, Inc., United (1949): 1522 K St. N.W., Suite 1112, Washington, D.C. 20005. 160 affiliates. Phone: (800) USA-5UCP/TT (202) 842-1266.
Chamber of Commerce of the U.S. (1912): 1615 H St. N.W., Washington, D.C. 20062-2000. 215,000. Phone: (202) 659-6000.
Chemical Engineers, American Institute of (1908): 345 E. 47th St., New York, N.Y. 10017. 56,000. Phone: (212) 705-7338.
Chemical Manufacturers Association, Inc. (1872): 2501 M St. N.W., Washington, D.C. 20037. 185 companies. Phone: (202) 887-1100.
Chemical Society, American (1876): 1155 16th St. N.W., Washington, D.C. 20036. 145,579. Phone: (202) 872-4600.
Chemists, The American Institute of (1923): 7315 Wisconsin Ave., Suite 518E, Bethesda, Md. 20814. 5,000. Phone: (301) 652-2447.
Chess Federation, United States (1939): 186 Rt. 9W, New Windsor, N.Y. 12553. 70,000. Phone: (914) 562-8350/(800) 388–KING.
Child Labor Committee, National (1904): 1501 Broadway, Rm. 1111, New York, N.Y. 10036. Phone: (212) 840-1801.
Children's Aid Society, The (1853): 105 E. 22nd St., New York, N.Y. 10010. Child welfare services, community centers, camps and health services. Phone: (212) 949-4800.
Children's Book Council (1945): 568 Broadway, Suite 404, New York, N.Y. 10012. 70 imprints. Phone: (212) 966-1990.
Child Welfare League of America (1920): 440 First St. N.W., Suite 310, Washington, D.C. 20001-2085. Phone: (202) 638-2952.
Chiropractic Association, American (1963): 1701 Clarendon Blvd., Arlington, Va. 22209. 21,300. Phone: (703) 276-8800.
Christians and Jews, National Conference of (1927): 71 Fifth Ave., New York, N.Y. 10003. 200,000. Phone: (212) 206-0006.
Churches of Christ in the USA, National Council of the (1950): 475 Riverside Drive, New York, N.Y. 10115. 32 Protestant and Orthodox communions. Phone: (212) 870-2511.
Cities, National League of (1924): 1301 Pennsylvania Ave. N.W., Washington, D.C. 20004. 16,000 cities and towns. Phone: (202) 626-3000.
Civil Air Patrol (1941): Maxwell AFB, Ala. 36112-6332. 105 S. Hansell St. 55,000. Phone: (205) 953-5463.
Civil Engineers, American Society of (1852): 345 E. 47th St., New York, N.Y. 10017-2398. 115,000. Phone: (212) 705-7496.
Clinical Chemistry, Inc., American Association for (1948): 2029 K St. N.W., 7th Floor, Washington, D.C. 20006. 10,000. Phone (202) 857-0717.
Clinical Pathologists, American Society of (1922): 2100 W. Harrison St., Chicago, Ill. 60612-3798. 52,237. Phone: (312) 738-1336.
Collectors Association, American (1939): Box 39106, Minneapolis, Minn. 55439-0106. Over 3,690 debt collection agencies. Phone: (612) 926-6547.
College Board, The (1900): 45 Columbus Ave., New York, N.Y. 10023-6992. 2,900 institutions. Phone: (212) 713-8000.
College Placement Council (1956): 62 E. Highland Ave., Bethlehem, Pa. 18017. 3,100. Phone: (215) 868-1421.
***Common Cause** (1970): 2030 M St. N.W., Washington, D.C. 20036. 270,000. Phone: (202) 833-1200.
Community Colleges, American Association of (1920): One Dupont Circle N.W., Suite 410, Washington, D.C. 20036-1176. 1,124 institutions. Phone: (202) 728-0200.
Community Cultural Center Association, American (1978): 19 Foothills Dr., Pompton Plains, N.J. 07444. Phone: (201) 835-2661.
Composers, Authors, and Publishers, American Society of (ASCAP) (1914): One Lincoln Plaza, New York, N.Y. 10023. 55,000. Phone: (212) 621-6000.
Composers/USA, National Association of (1932): P.O. Box 49652, Barrington Station, Los Angeles, Calif. 90049. 550. Phone: (310) 541-8213.
Congress of Racial Equality (CORE) (1942): 2111 Nostrand Ave., Brooklyn, N.Y. 11210. Phone: (718) 434-3580. 30 Cooper Square, New York, N.Y. 10003. Phone: (212) 598-4000. Nationwide network of chapters.
Conscientious Objectors, Central Committee for (1948): 2208 South St., Philadelphia, Pa. 19146. Phone: (215) 545-4626.
Conservation Engineers, Association of (1961): Alabama Dept. of Cons. & Natural Resources, Engineering Section, 64 N. Union St., Montgomery, Ala. 36130. Phone: (205) 242-3476.
Consulting Chemists & Chemical Engineers, Inc., Association of (1928): 295 Madison Ave., 27th Floor, New York, N.Y. 10017. 130. Phone: (212) 983-3160.
Consulting Organizations, Council of (1989): 521 Fifth Ave., 35th Floor, New York, N.Y. 10175-3598. 2,200 individuals in the IMC Division, 48 firms in ACME Division. Phone: (212) 697-9693.
Consumer Federation of America (1968): 1424 16th St. N.W., Suit 604, Washington, D.C. 20036. 240 member organizations. Phone: (202) 387-6121.
Consumer Interests, American Council on (1953): 240 Stanley Hall, Univ. of Missouri, Columbia, Mo. 65211. 1,500. Phone: (314) 882-3817.
Consumers League, National (1899): 815 15th St. N.W., Suite 928-N, Washington, D.C. 20005. Phone: (202) 639-8140.
Consumers Union (1936): 101 Truman Ave., Yonkers, N.Y. 10703-1057. 5,000,000 subscribers to *Consumer Reports*. Phone: (914) 378-2000.
Counselors and Family Therapists, National Academy of (1972): 55 Morris Ave., Springfield, N.J. 07081-1422. Phone: (201) 379-7496.
Country Music Association (1958): One Music Circle South, Nashville, Tenn. 37203. 7,000+. Phone: (615) 244-2840.

Credit Management, National Association of (1896): 8815 Centre Park Dr., Suite 200, Columbia, Md. 21045. Phone: (410) 740-5560.

Credit Union National Association (1934): P.O. Box 431, Madison, Wis. 53701. 52 state leagues representing 13,400 credit unions. Phone: (608) 231-4000.

Crime and Delinquency, National Council on (1907): 685 Market St., #620, San Francisco, Calif. 94105. Criminal justice research, nationwide membership. Phone: (415) 896-6223.

CSA/USA, Celiac Sprue Association/United States of America, Inc., P.O. Box 31700, Omaha, Neb. 68131-0700. 6 regions in U.S., 52 chapters, 60 active resource units. Phone: (402) 558-0600.

Dairy Council, National (1915): 10255 W. Higgins Rd., Suite 900, Rosement, Ill. 60018. Phone: (708) 803-2000.

Daughters of the American Revolution, National Society (1890): 1776 D St. N.W., Washington, D.C. 20006. 200,000. Phone: (202) 628-1776.

Daughters of the Confederacy, United (1894): 328 N. Boulevard, Richmond, Va. 23220-4057. 25,000. Phone: (804) 355-1636.

Deaf, National Association of the (1880): 814 Thayer Ave., Silver Spring, Md. 20910. Phone: (301) 587-1788; (301) 587-1789 TDD.

***Defenders of Wildlife** (1947): 1244 19th St. N.W., Washington, D.C. 20036. 84,000 members and supporters. Phone: (202) 659-9510.

Defense Preparedness Association, American (1919): Two Colonial Place, Suite 400, 2101 Wilson Blvd., Arlington, Va. 22201-3061. 29,000 individual, 705 corporate. Phone: (703) 522-1820.

Dental Association, American (1859): 211 E. Chicago Ave., Chicago, Ill. 60611. 140,000. Phone: (312) 440-2500.

Diabetes Association, American (1940): 1660 Duke St., Alexandria, Va. 22314. Phone: (703) 549-1500.

Dignity (1969): 1500 Massachusetts Ave. N.W., Suite 11, Washington, D.C. 20005. 5,000. Phone: (202) 861-0017 and (800) 877-8797.

Disabled American Veterans (1920): 807 Maine Ave. S.W., Washington, D.C. 20024. 1.4 million. Phone: (202) 554-3501.

Dowsers, Inc., The American Society of (1961): P.O. Box 24, Danville, Vt. 05828-0024. 4,500. Phone: (802) 684-3417.

Drug, Chemical & Allied Trades Association, Inc., The (1890): 2 Roosevelt Ave., Syosset, N.Y. 11791. 575. Phone (516) 496-3317.

Ducks Unlimited, Inc. (1937): One Waterfowl Way, Memphis, Tenn. 38120. 550,000. Phone: (901) 758-3825.

Earthwatch (1972): 680 Mt. Auburn St., Box 403N, Watertown, Mass. 02272. 75,000. Phone: (800) 776-0188.

Eastern Star, Order of, General Grand Chapter (1876): 1618 New Hampshire Ave. N.W., Washington, D.C. 20009. 1,378,239. Phone: (202) 667-4737.

Easter Seal Society, The National (1919): 230 W. Monroe, 18th Floor, Chicago, Ill. 60603. 160 state and local affiliate societies and Puerto Rico. Phone: (312) 726-6200 and (312) 726-4258 TDD.

Economic Association, American (1885): 2014 Broadway, Suite 305, Nashville, Tenn. 37203-2418. 21,000. 6,000 inst. subscribers. Phone: (615) 322-2595.

Economic Development, Committee for (1942): 477 Madison Ave., New York, N.Y. 10022. 250 trustees. Phone: (212) 688-2063.

Edison Electric Institute (1933): 701 Pennsylvania Ave. N.W., Washington, D.C. 20004-2696.

Education, American Council on (1918): One Dupont Circle N.W., Washington, D.C. 20036. 1,600 institutions; over 200 organizations. Phone: (202) 939-9300.

Education, Council for Advancement and Support of (CASE) (1974): 11 Dupont Circle N.W., Suite 400, Washington, D.C. 20036-1261. 14,000. Phone: (202) 328-5900.

Educational Exchange, International, Council on (1947): 205 E. 42nd St., New York, N.Y. 10017. 203. Phone: (212) 661-1414.

Educational Research Association, American (1916): 1230 17th St. N.W., Washington, D.C. 20036. 19,514. Phone: (202) 223-9485.

Education Association, National (1857): 1201 16th St. N.W., Washington, D.C. 20036-3290. 2 million. Phone: (202) 833-4000.

Electrochemical Society, The (1902): 10 S. Main St., Pennington, N.J. 08534-2896. 6,301. Phone: (609) 737-1902.

Electronic Industries Association (1924): 2001 Pennsylvania Ave. N.W., Washington, D.C. 20006-1813. 1,000 member companies. Phone: (202) 457-4900.

Elks of the U.S.A., Benevolent and Protective Order of the (1868): 2750 Lake View Ave., Chicago, Ill. 60614. 1,400,000. Phone: (312) 477-2750.

Energy Engineers, Association of (1977): 4025 Pleasantdale Rd., Suite 420, Atlanta, Ga. 30340. 8,500. Phone: (404) 447-5083.

English-Speaking Union of the United States (1920): 16 E. 69th St., New York, N.Y. 10021. 25,000. Phone: (212) 879-6800.

Entomological Society of America (1889): 9301 Annapolis Rd., Lanham, Md. 20706-3115. 9,000. Phone: (301) 731-4535.

Esperanto League for North America, The (1952): P.O. Box 1129, El Cerrito, Calif. 94530. Over 1,000. Phone: (510) 653-0998.

Exceptional Children, The Council for (1922): 1920 Association Dr., Reston, Va. 22091. 54,000. Phone: (703) 620-3660.

Experimental Test Pilots, The Society of (1956): 44814 Elm St., Lancaster, Calif. 93584-0986. 1,800. Phone: (805) 942-9574.

Exploration Geophysicists, Society of (1930): P.O. Box 702740, Tulsa, Okla. 74170-2740. 15,000. Phone: (918) 493-3516.

Family Physicians, American Academy of (1947): 8880 Ward Pkwy., Kansas City, Mo. 64114-2797. 75,000. Phone: (816) 333-9700.

Family Relations, National Council on (1938): 3989 Central Ave. N.E., #550, Minneapolis, Minn. 55421-3921. 3,800. Phone: (612) 781-9331.

Family Service America (1911): 11700 W. Lake Park Dr., Park Place, Milwaukee, Wis. 53224. Approximately 300 member agencies. Phone: (414) 359-1040.

Farm Bureau Federation, American (1919): 225 Touhy Ave., Park Ridge, Ill. 60068. 4.1 million member families. Phone: (312) 399-5700.

Farmer Cooperatives, National Council of (1929): 50 F St. N.W., Washington, D.C. 20001. 135. Phone: (202) 626-8700.

Federal Bar Association (1920): 1815 H St. N.W., Suite 408, Washington, D.C. 20006-3697. 15,000. Phone: (202) 638-0252.

Federal Employees, National Federation of (1917): 1016 16th St. N.W., Washington, D.C. 20036. Rep. 150,000. Phone: (202) 862-4400.

Feline and Canine Friends, Inc. (1973): 505 N. Bush St., Anaheim, Calif. 92805. 1,000. Phone: (714) 635-7975.
Fellowship of Reconciliation (1915): Box 271, Nyack, N.Y. 10960. 36,000. Phone: (914) 358-4601.
Female Executives, National Association for (1972): 127 W. 24th St., New York, N.Y. 10011. 250,000. Phone: (212) 645-0770.
FFA Organization, National (1928): 5632 Mt. Vernon Memorial Hwy., P.O. Box 15160, Alexandria, Va. 22309-0160. 401,574. Phone: (703) 360-3600.
Fire Protection Association, National (1896): One Batterymarch Park, P.O. Box 9101, Quincy, Mass. 02269-9101. 60,000. Phone: (617) 770-3000.
Flag Foundation, National (1968): Flag Plaza, Pittsburgh, Pa. 15219-3630. 3,000+. Phone: (412) 261-1776.
Fleet Reserve Association (1924): 125 N. West St., Alexandria, Va. 22314-2754. 167,000. Phone: (703) 683-1400.
Flight Test Engineers, Society of (1968): P.O. Box 4047, Lancaster, Calif. 93539. 1,100. Phone: (805) 538-9715.
Foreign Policy Association (1918): 729 Seventh Ave., New York, N.Y. 10019. Phone: (212) 764-4050/(800) 477-5836.
Foreign Relations, Council on (1921): 58 E. 68th St., New York, N.Y. 10021. 2,600. Phone: (212) 734-0400.
Foreign Study, American Institute for (1965): 102 Greenwich Ave., Greenwich, Conn. 06830. Phone: (203) 869-9090/(800) 727-AIFS.
Foreign Trade Council, Inc., National (1914): 1270 Avenue of the Americas, New York, N.Y. 10020. Over 550 companies. Phone: (212) 399-7128. Also, 1625 K St. N.W., Washington, D.C. 20006. Phone: (202) 887-0278.
Forensic Sciences, American Academy of (1948): 410 N. 21st St., Suite 203/80904, P.O. Box 669, Colorado Springs, Colo. 80901-0669. 3,850. Phone: (719) 636-1100.
***Forest Council, American** (1932): 1250 Connecticut Ave. N.W., Suite 320, Washington, D.C. 20036. 100. Phone: (202) 463 -2455.
Foresters, Society of American (1900): 5400 Grosvenor Lane, Bethesda, Md. 20814-2198. 19,000. Phone: (301) 897-8720.
Fortean Organization, International (1965): P.O. Box 367, Arlington, Va. 22210-0367. 900. Phone: (703) 522-9232.
4-H Program (early 1900s): Room 3860-S, U.S. Department of Agriculture, Washington, D.C. 20250. 5.6 million. Phone: (202) 720-5853.
Freedom of Information Center (1958): 20 Walter Williams Hall, Univ. of Missouri, Columbia, Mo. 65211. Phone: (314) 882-4856.
French-American Chamber of Commerce in the U.S. Inc. (1896): 509 Madison Ave., Suite 1900, New York, N.Y. 10022. 605. Membership Association. Phone: (212) 371-4466.
French Institute/Alliance Française (1911): 22 E. 60th St., New York, N.Y. 10022-1077. 9,000. Phone: (212) 355-6100.
Friendship and Good Will, International Society of (1978): 211 W. Fourth Ave., P.O. Box 2637, Gastonia, N.C. 28053-2637. 4,137 in 180 countries. Phone: (704) 864-7906.
Friends of Animals Inc. (1957): P.O. Box 1244, Norwalk, Conn. 06856. 120,000. Phone: (203) 866-5223. For low-cost spay/neuter information call: (800) 321-PETS.
Friends of the Earth (1969): 218 D St. S.E., Washington, D.C. 20003. 20,000. Phone: (202) 544-2600.
Future Homemakers of America, Inc. (1945): 1910 Association Dr., Reston, Va. 22091. 275,000. Phone: (703) 476-4900.
Gamblers Anonymous: Box 17173, Los Angeles, Calif. 90017. Phone: (213) 386-8789.
Gay and Lesbian Task Force, National (1973): 1734 14th St., NW, Washington, D.C. 20009. 30,000 members. Phone: (202) 332-6483.
Genealogical Society, National (1903): 4527 17th St. N., Arlington, Va. 22207-2399. 13,000. Phone: (703) 525-0050.
Genetic Association, American (1903): P.O. Box 39, Buckeystown, Md. 21717. 1,000. Phone: (301) 695-9292.
Geographers, Association of American (1904): 1710 16th St. N.W., Washington, D.C. 20009-3198. 6,300. Phone: (202) 234-1450.
Geographic Education, National Council for (1915): Indiana University of Pennsylvania, Indiana, Pa. 15705. 3,700. Phone: (412) 357-6290.
Geographic Society, National (1888): 17th and M Sts. N.W., Washington, D.C. 20036. 9,700,000. Phone: (202) 857-7000.
Geological Institute, American (1948): 4220 King St., Alexandria, Va. 22302-1507. 23 geoscience societies representing 80,000 geoscientists. Phone: (703) 379-2480.
Geological Society of America, Inc. (1888): 3300 Penrose Pl., P.O. Box 9140, Boulder, Colo. 80301. 17,000. Phone: (303) 447-2020.
Geriatrics Society, American (1942): 770 Lexington Ave., Suite 300, New York, N.Y. 10021. 6,200. Phone: (212) 308-1414.
German American National Congress, The (Deutsch-Amerikanischer National Congress—D.A.N.K.) (1958): 4740 N. Western Ave., Chicago, Ill. 60625-2097. 30,000, plus Associates. Phone: (312) 275-1100.
Gideons International, The (1889): 2900 Lebanon Rd., Nashville, Tenn. 37214-0800. 110,000. Phone: (615) 883-8533.
Gifted, The Association for the (1958): The Council for Exceptional Children, 1920 Association Dr., Reston, Va. 22091. 2,200. Phone: (703) 620-3660.
Girl Scouts of the U.S.A. (1912): 420 Fifth Ave., New York, N.Y. 10018. 3.5 million. Phone: (212) 852-8000.
Girls Incorporated (1945): 30 E. 33rd St., New York, N.Y. 10016. 250,000. Phone: (212) 689-3700.
Graphoanalysis Society, International (1929): 111 N. Canal St., Chicago, Ill. 60606. 10,000. Phone: (312) 930-9446.
Gray Panthers Project Fund (1970): 2025 Pennsylvania Ave. N.W., Suite 821, Washington, D.C. 20006. Over 60 chapters (networks). Phone: (202) 466-3132.
Greenpeace (1979): 1436 U St. N.W., Washington, D.C. 20009. 1,800,000. Phone: (202) 462-1177.
Group Psychotherapy Association, American (1942): 25 E. 21st St., 6th Floor, New York, N.Y. 10010. 3,800 Phone: (212) 477-2677.
Guide Dog Foundation for the Blind, Inc. (1946): 371 E. Jericho Turnpike, Smithtown, N.Y. 11787-2976. 40,000. Phone: (516) 265-2121; outside N.Y. city call (800) 548-4337.
Hadassah, The Women's Zionist Organization of America (1912): 50 W. 58th St., New York, N.Y. 10019. 385,000. Phone: (212) 355-7900.
Handgun Control, Inc. (1974): 1225 Eye St. N.W.,

Suite 1100, Washington, D.C. 20005. 300,000. Phone: (202) 898-0792.

Heart Association, American (1924): 7272 Greenville Ave., Dallas, Tex. 75231-4596. 3,500,000 volunteers. Phone: (214) 373-6300.

Heating, Refrigerating, and Air-Conditioning Engineers, Inc., American Society of (1894): 1791 Tullie Circle N.E., Atlanta, Ga. 30329. 50,000. Phone: (404) 636-8400.

Helicopter Association International (1948): 1619 Duke St., Alexandria, Va. 22314-3439. Phone: (703) 683-4646.

Hemispheric Affairs, Council on (1975): 724 9th St. N.W., Rm. 401, Washington, D.C. 20001. Phone: (202) 393-3322.

Historians, The Organization of American (1907): Indiana Univ., 112 N. Bryan St., Bloomington, Ind. 47408. 9,000. Phone: (812) 855-7311.

Historic Preservation, National Trust for (1949): 1785 Massachusetts Ave. N.W., Washington, D.C. 20036. 250,000. Phone: (202) 673-4000.

Home Economics Association, American (1909): 1555 King St., Alexandria, Va. 22314. 20,000. Phone: (703) 706-4600.

Horse Council, Inc., American (1969): 1700 K St. N.W., #300, Washington, D.C. 20006. More than 190 organizations and 2,400 individuals. Phone: (202) 296-4031.

Horse Shows Association, Inc., American (1917): 220 E. 42nd St., New York, N.Y. 10017-5876. 65,000. Phone: (212) 972-2472.

Horticultural Association, National Junior (1935): 401 N. 4th, Durant, Okla. 74701. Phone: (405) 924-0771.

Horticultural Society, American (1922): 7931 East Boulevard Dr., Alexandria, Va. 22308. 20,000. Phone: (703) 768-5700 or (800) 777-7931.

Housing Science, International Association for (1972): P.O. Box 340254, Coral Gables/Miami, Fla. 33114. 500 professionals. Phone: (305) 446-9462.

Humane Association, American (1877): 63 Inverness Drive East, Englewood, Colo. 80112-5117. Phone: (303) 792-9900.

Humane Association, The American Children's Division (1877): 63 Inverness Dr. East, Englewood, Colo. 80112. Phone: (303) 792-9900.

Humane Society of the United States (1954): 2100 L St. N.W., Washington, D.C. 20037. 1,500,000. Phone: (202) 452-1100.

Humanities, National Endowment for the (1965): 1100 Pennsylvania Ave. N.W., Washington, D.C. 20506. Phone: (202) 606-8428.

Hydrogen Energy, International Association for (1975): P.O. Box 248266, Coral Gables, Fla. 33124. 2,500. Phone: (305) 284-4666.

Illustrators, Society of (1901): 128 E. 63rd St., New York, N.Y. 10021. 975. Phone: (212) 838-2560 .

Industrial Engineers, Institute of (1948): 25 Technology Park/Atlanta, Norcross, Ga. 30092. 30,000. Phone: (404) 449-0460.

Interfraternity Conference, National (1909): 3901 W. 86th St., Suite 390, Indianapolis, Ind. 46268-1791. 62. Phone: (317) 872-1112.

International Credit Association (ICA) (1912): P.O. Box 419057, St. Louis, Mo. 63141-1757. 10,000 members, 113 local associations. Phone: (314) 991-3030.

Investigative Pathology, American Society for (1976): 9650 Rockville Pike, Bethesda, Md. 20814-3993. 2,300. Phone: (301) 530-7130.

Iron and Steel Institute, American (1908): 1101 17th St. N.W., Washington, D.C. 20036-4700. 1,200. Phone: (202) 452-7100.

***Izaak Walton League of America** (1922): 1401 Wilson Blvd., Level B, Arlington, Va. 22209. 55,000. Phone: (703) 528-1818.

Jaycees, The United States (The U.S. Junior Chamber of Commerce) (1920): P.O. Box 7, Tulsa, Okla. 74102-0007. 200,000. Phone: (918) 584-2481.

Jewish Community Centers, World Confederation of (1946): 12 Hess St., Jerusalem, Israel 94185. Phone: (02) 231 371/251 265.

Jewish Community Centers Association of North America (1917): 15 E. 26th St., New York, N.Y. 10010-1579. 275 affiliated Jewish Community Centers, YM-YWHAs, and camps. Phone: (212) 532-4949.

***Jewish Congress, American** (1918): 15 E. 84th St., New York, N.Y. 10028. 50,000. Phone: (212) 879-4500.

Jewish Historical Society, American (1892): 2 Thornton Rd., Waltham, Mass. 02154. 3,500. Phone: (617) 891-8110.

Jewish War Veterans of the U.S.A. (1896): 1811 R St. N.W., Washington, D.C. 20009-1659. Phone: (202) 265-6280.

Jewish Women, National Council of (1893): 53 W. 23rd St., New York, N.Y. 10010. 100,000. Phone: (212) 645-4048.

John Birch Society (1958): P.O. Box 8040, Appleton, Wis. 54913. Under 100,000. Phone: (414) 749-3780.

Journalists, Society of Professional, (1909): 16 S. Jackson, Greencastle, Ind. 46135-0077. 14,000. Phone: (317) 653-3333.

Journalists and Authors, American Society of (1948): 1501 Broadway, Suite 302, New York, N.Y. 10036. 800. Phone: (212) 997-0947.

Judaism, American Council for (1943): P.O. Box 9009, Alexandria, Va. 22304. 10,000. Phone: (703) 836-2546.

Junior Achievement Inc. (1919): One Education Way, Colorado Springs, Colo. 80906-4477. 1.5 million. Phone: (719) 540-8000.

Junior Leagues International, Inc., Association of (1921): 660 First Ave., New York, N.Y. 10016-3241. 280 Leagues, 188,000 members. Phone: (212) 683-1515.

Junior Statesmen of America (1934): 650 Bair Island Rd., Suite 201, Redwood City, Calif. 94063. 10,000. Phone: (415) 366-2700.

Kiwanis International (1915): 3636 Woodview Trace, Indianapolis, Ind. 46268-3196. 330,000. Phone: (317) 875-8755.

Knights of Columbus (1882): One Columbus Plaza, New Haven, Conn. 06507-0901. 1,530,283. Phone: (203) 772-2130.

Knights of Pythias, Supreme Lodge (1864): 2785 E. Desert Inn Rd. #150, Las Vegas, Nev. 89121. 85,000. Phone: (702) 735-3302.

Knights Templar, Grand Encampment of (1816): 5097 N. Elston, Suite 101, Chicago, Ill. 60630. 300,000. Phone: (312) 777-3300.

La Leche League International (1956): 9616 Minneapolis Ave., Franklin Park, Ill. 60131-8209. 50,000. Phone: (708) 455-7730.

Law, American Society of International (1906): 2223 Massachusetts Ave. N.W., Washington, D.C. 20008. 4,500. Phone: (202) 265-4313.

League of Women Voters of the U.S. (1920): 1730 M St. N.W., Washington, D.C. 20036. 100,000. Phone: (202) 429-1965.

Legal Aid and Defender Association, National (1911): 1625 K St. N.W., Suite 800, Washington,

D.C. 20006. 5,000. Phone: (202) 452-0620.

Legal Secretaries, National Association of (1950): 2250 E. 73rd St., Suite 550, Tulsa, Okla. 74136-6864. 18,000. Phone: (918) 493-3540.

Lesbians and Gays, Federation of Parents and Friends of (1981): 1012 14th St. NW, Suite 700, Washington, D.C. 20005. 20,000+ members. 320 chapters in 12 countries. Phone: (202) 638-4200.

Leukemia Society of America (1949): 600 Third Ave., 4th Floor, New York, N.Y. 10016. Phone: (212) 573-8484.

Library Association, American (1876): 50 E. Huron St., Chicago, Ill. 60611. 54,735. Phone: (312) 944-6780.

Life Insurance, American Council of (1976): 1001 Pennsylvania Ave. N.W., Washington, D.C. 20004-2599. 617. Phone: (202) 624-2000.

Life Underwriters, National Association of (1890): 1922 F St. N.W., Washington, D.C. 20006-4387. Phone: (202) 331-6000.

Lions Clubs International (1917): 300 22nd St., Oak Brook, Ill. 60521-8842. 1,402,000. Phone: (708) 571-5466.

Lung Association, American (1904): 1740 Broadway, New York, N.Y. 10019-4374. 120 constituent and affiliate associations. Phone: (212) 315-8700.

Magazine Editors, American Society of (1963): 575 Lexington Ave., New York, N.Y. 10022. 700. Phone: (212) 752-0055.

Magazine Publishers of America (1919): 575 Lexington Ave., New York, N.Y. 10022. 317 companies, 1,200+ publications. Phone: (212) 752-0055.

Management Accountants, Institute of (formerly National Association of Accountants) (1919): 10 Paragon Dr., Montvale, N.J. 07645-1760. 90,000. Phone: (201) 573-9000.

Management Association, American (1923): 135 W. 50th St., New York, N.Y. 10020-1201. 75,000. Phone: (212) 586-8100.

Manufacturers, National Association of (1895): 1331 Pennsylvania Ave. N.W., Suite 1500-North, Washington, D.C. 20004-1703. 12,000. Phone: (202) 637-3065.

Manufacturers' Agents National Association (MANA) (1947): 23016 Mill Creek Rd., P.O. Box 3467, Laguna Hills, Calif. 92654. 9,000. Phone: (714) 859-4040.

March of Dimes Birth Defects Foundation (1938): 1275 Mamaroneck Ave., White Plains, N.Y. 10605. 131 chapters. Phone: (914) 428-7100.

Marine Conservation, Center for (1972): 1725 De Sales St. N.W., Suite 500, Washington, D.C. 20036. 110,000. Phone: (202) 429-5609.

Marine Corps Association (1913): Bldg. #715, Marine Corps Base, Quantico, Va. 22134. 100,723. Phone: (703) 640-6161/(800) 336-0291.

Marine Corps League (1923): 8626 Lee Hwy., Fairfax, Va. Correspondence address: P.O. Box 3070, Merrifield, Va. 22116. 35,000. Phone: (703) 207-9588 or (703) 207-9589.

Marine Technology Society (1963): 1828 L St. N.W., Suite 906, Washington, D.C. 20036-5104. 2,700. Phone: (202) 775-5966.

Masons, Ancient and Accepted Scottish Rite, Northern Masonic Jurisdiction, Supreme Council 33 (1813): 33 Marrett Rd., Lexington, Mass. 02173. 385,870. Phone: (617) 862-4410.

Masons, Ancient and Accepted Scottish Rite, Southern Jurisdiction, Supreme Council (1801): 1733 16th St. N.W., Washington, D.C. 20009. 530,000. Phone: (202) 232-3579.

Masons, Royal Arch, General Grand Chapter International (1797): P.O. Box 489, 111 S. Fourth St., Danville, Ky. 40422. 254,071. Phone: (606) 236-0757.

Massachusetts Audubon Society (1896): South Great Rd., Lincoln, Mass. 01773. 52,000 member households. Phone: (508) 259-9500.

Mathematical Association of America (1915): 1529 18th St. N.W., Washington, D.C. 20036. 33,000. Phone: (202) 387-5200.

Mathematical Society, American (1888): P.O. Box 6248, Providence, R.I. 02940-6248. 28,710. Phone: (401) 455-4000.

Mathematical Statistics, Institute of (1935): 3401 Investment Blvd. #7, Hayward, Calif. 94545-3819. 4,000. Phone: (510) 783-8141.

Mayflower Descendants, General Society of (1897): 4 Winslow St., P.O. Box 3297, Plymouth, Mass. 02361. 25,000. Phone: (508) 746-3188.

***Mayors, U.S. Conference of** (1932): 1620 Eye St. N.W., Washington, D.C. 20006. 10 standing committees. Phone: (202) 293-7330.

Mechanical Engineers, American Society of (1880): 345 E. 47th St., New York, N.Y. 10017. 122,000. Phone: (212) 705-7722.

Mechanics, American Academy of (1969): 4205 EBUI, AMES, 0411, University of Calif.–San Diego, 9500 Gilman Dr., La Jolla, Calif. 92093-0411. 1,600. Phone: (619) 534-2036.

Medical Association, American (1847): 515 N. State St., Chicago, Ill. 60610-4377. Phone: (312) 464-5000.

Medical Library Association (1898): Six N. Michigan Ave., Suite 300, Chicago, Ill. 60602. 5,000. Phone: (312) 419-9094.

Mental Health Association, National (1909): 1021 Prince St., Alexandria, Va., 22314-2971. 1,000,000. Phone: (703) 684-7722.

Meteorological Society, American (1919): 45 Beacon St., Boston, Mass. 02108-3693. 10,000. Phone: (617) 227-2425.

Military Chaplains Association of the U.S.A. (1925): P.O. Box 42660, Washington, D.C. 20015-0660. 1,500. Phone: (202) 574-2423.

***Mining, Metallurgy and Exploration, Society for; The Minerals, Metals & Materials Society** (1871): 345 E. 47th St., New York, N.Y. 10017. 4 Member Societies: Society of Mining Engineers, The Minerals, Metals and Materials Society, Iron & Steel Society, Society of Petroleum Engineers. Phone: (212) 705-7695.

Mining and Metallurgical Society of America (1910): 9 Escalle Lane, Larkspur, Calif. 94939. 300. Phone: (415) 924-7441.

Model Aeronautics, Academy of (1936): 5151 East Memorial Dr., Muncie, Ind. 47302. 150,000. Phone: (317) 287-1256.

Modern Language Association of America (1883): 10 Astor Place, New York, N.Y. 10003. 32,000. Phone: (212) 475-9500.

***Modern Woodmen of America** (1883): 1701 1st Ave., Rock Island, Ill. 61201. 675,000. Phone: (309) 786-6481.

Moose International, Inc. (1888): Mooseheart, Ill. 60539. 1,816,054. Phone: (708) 859-2000.

Mothers Against Drunk Driving (MADD) (1980): P.O. box 541688, Dallas, Tex. 75354-1688. 3.2 million. Phone: (214) 744-6233.

Motion Picture & Television Engineers, Society of (1916): 595 W. Hartsdale Ave., White Plains, N.Y. 10607. 9,500. Phone: (914) 761-1100.

Motion Picture Arts & Sciences, Academy of (1927): 8949 Wilshire Blvd., Beverly Hills, Calif. 90211-1972. Phone: (310) 247-3000.

Multiple Sclerosis Society, National (1946): 733

Third Ave., New York, N.Y. 10017-3288. 400,000. Phone: (212) 986-3240.

Muscular Dystrophy Association (1950): 3300 East Sunrise Dr., Tucson, Ariz. 85718. 2,300,000 volunteers. Phone: (602) 529-2000.

Museum of Natural History, American (1869): Central Park West at 79th St., New York, N.Y. 10024-5192. 520,000. Phone: (212) 769-5100.

Museums, American Association of (1906): 1225 Eye St. N.W., Suite 200, Washington, D.C. 20005. 12,400. Phone: (202) 289-1818.

***Music Council, National** (1940): P.O. Box 5551, Englewood, N.J. 07631-5551. 50 National Music Organizations. Phone: (201) 871-9088.

Music Publishers Association, Inc., National (1917): 205 E. 42nd St., New York, N.Y. 10017. Trade Organization/Harry Fox Agency-Licensing Organization. Phone: (212) 370-5330.

Muzzle Loading Rifle Association, National (1933): P.O. Box 67, Friendship, Ind. 47021. 30,000. Phone: (812) 667-5131.

***NAFSA: Association of International Educators** (1948): 1875 Connecticut Ave. N.W., Suite 1000, Washington, D.C. 20009-5728. 6,500. Phone: (202) 462-4811.

***Narcolepsy and Cataplexy Foundation of America** (1975): 445 E. 68th St., Suite 12L, New York, N.Y. 10021. 3,991. Phone: (212) 628-6315.

National Abortion Rights Action League (NARAL) (1969): 1156 15th St. N.W., Washington, D.C. 20005. 500,000. Phone: (202) 973-3000.

***National Association for the Advancement of Colored People** (1909): 4805 Mt. Hope Dr., Baltimore, Md. 21215. 500,000+. Phone: (301) 358-8900.

National Cooperative Business Association (formerly Cooperative League of the U.S.A.) (1916): 1401 New York Ave. N.W., Suite 1100, Washington, D.C. 20005. Phone: (202) 638-6222.

National Grange, The (1867): 1616 H St. N.W., Washington, D.C. 20006-4999. 330,000. Phone: (202) 628-3507.

National PTA (National Congress of Parents and Teachers) (1897): 330 N. Wabash Ave., Chicago, Ill. 60611. 7.0 million. Phone: (312) 951-6782.

National Rifle Association of America (1871): 1600 Rhode Island Ave. N.W., Washington, D.C. 20036. 3,000,000. Phone: (202) 828-6000.

***Natural Science for Youth Foundation** (1961): 130 Azalea Dr., Roswell, Ga. 30075. 350. Phone: (404) 594-9367.

Nature Conservancy, The (1951): 1815 N. Lynn St., Arlington, Va. 22209. 710,000. Phone: (703) 841-5300.

Naval Architects and Marine Engineers, The Society of (1893): 601 Pavonia Ave., Jersey City, N.J. 07306. 11,000. Phone: (201) 798-4800.

Naval Engineers, American Society of (1888): 1452 Duke St., Alexandria, Va. 22314. 7,500. Phone: (703) 836-6727.

Naval Institute, United States (1873): 118 Maryland Ave., Annapolis, Md. 21402-5035. 100,000. Phone: (410) 268-6110.

Navigation, The Institute of (1945): 1800 Diagonal Rd., Suite 480, Alexandria, Va. 22314. 3,800. Phone: (703) 683-7101.

Navy League of the United States (1902): 2300 Wilson Blvd., Arlington, Va. 22201-3308. 72,500; John R. Dalrymple, Rear Admiral, USN (Ret.), Executive Director.

Neurofibromatosis Foundation, The National (1978): 141 Fifth Ave., Suite 7-S, New York, N.Y. 10010. 27,000. Phone: (212) 460-8980; toll-free (800) 323-7938.

Newspaper Association of America (1887): The Newspaper Center, 11600 Sunrise Valley Dr., Reston, Va. 22091-1412. 1,700. Phone: (703) 648-1000.

Newspaper Editors, American Society of (1922): P.O. Box 4090, Reston, Va. 22090-1700. 900. Phone: (703) 648-1144.

Ninety-Second Street Young Men's and Young Women's Hebrew Association (1874): 1395 Lexington Ave., New York, N.Y. 10128. Phone: (212) 996-1100.

Nondestructive Testing, Inc., The American Society for (1941): 1711 Arlingate Lane, P.O. Box 28518, Columbus, Ohio 43228-0518. 10,478. Phone: (800) 222-ASNT.

***North American Shortwave Assn.** (1964): 45 Wildflower Rd., Levittown, Pa. 19057. 1,800. Phone: (215) 945-0543.

NOT SAFE (National Organization Taunting Safety and Fairness Everywhere) (1980): P.O. Box 5743, Montecito, Calif. 93108. 975. Phone: (805) 969-6217.

Nuclear Society, American (1954): 555 N. Kensington Ave., La Grange Park, Ill. 60525. 17,000. Phone: (708) 352-6611.

Numismatic Association, American (1891): 818 N. Cascade Ave., Colorado Springs, Colo. 80903-3279. 30,000. Phone: (719) 632-2646.

Nurses Association, American (1896): 600 Maryland Ave. S.W., Suite 100, Washington, D.C. 20024-2571. 209,000. Phone: (202) 554-4444.

Nutrition, American Institute of (1928): 9650 Rockville Pike, Bethesda, Md. 20814-3990. 2,950. Phone: (301) 530-7050.

Odd Fellows, Sovereign Grand Lodge, Independent Order of (1819): 422 Trade St., Winston-Salem, N.C. 27101-2830. 500,000. Phone: (919) 725-5955.

Olympic Committee, United States (1921): One Olympic Plaza, Colorado Springs, Colo. 80909-5760. Phone: (719) 632-5551.

Optical Society of America (1916): 2010 Massachusetts Ave. N.W., Washington, D.C. 20036. 12,000. Phone: (202) 223-8130.

Optimist International (1919): 4494 Lindell Blvd., St. Louis, Mo. 63108. 170,000. Phone: (314) 371-6000.

Optometric Association, American (1898): 243 N. Lindbergh Blvd., St. Louis, Mo. 63141. 30,000. Phone: (314) 991-4100.

***Organization of American States, General Secretariat** (1890): 1889 F St. N.W., Washington, D.C. 20006. 35 member nations. Phone: (202) 458-3000.

Ornithologists' Union, American (1883): c/o National Museum of Natural History, NHB E607, MRC-116, Smithsonian Institution, Washington, D.C. 20560. 5,000. Phone: (202) 357-2051.

***Overeaters Anonymous** (1960): P.O. Box 92870, Los Angeles, Calif. 90009. 150,000. Phone: (310) 618-8835.

Parents Without Partners (1957): 8807 Colesville Rd., Silver Spring, Md. 20910. 104,060. Phone: (301) 588-9354 or (800) 637-7974.

Parks & Conservation Association, National (1919): 1776 Massachusetts Ave. N.W., Suite 200, Washington, D.C. 20036. 350,000. Phone: (202) 223-6722.

Peace Action (a merger of SANE and the Nuclear Weapons Freeze Campaign) (1957): 1819 H St. N.W., Suite 640, Washington, D.C. 20006-3603. 170,000. Phone: (202) 862-9740.

People for the American Way (1980): 2000 M St. N.W., Suite 400, Washington, D.C. 20036. 300,000. Phone: (202) 467-4999.

Petroleum Geologists, American Association of (1917): P.O. Box 979, Tulsa, Okla. 74101-0979. 33,207. Phone: (918) 584-2555.

Pharmaceutical Association, American (1852): 2215 Constitution Ave. N.W., Washington, D.C. 20037. 40,000. Phone: (202) 628-4410.

Philatelic Society, American (1886): P.O. Box 8000, State College, Pa. 16803. 57,000. Phone: (814) 237-3803.

Photogrammetry and Remote Sensing, American Society for (1934): 5410 Grosvenor Lane, Suite 210, Bethesda, Md. 20814-2160. Phone: (301) 493-0290.

Photographic Society of America (1934): 3000 United Founders Blvd., Suite 103, Oklahoma City, Okla. 73112. Phone: (405) 843-1437.

Photography, International Center of (1974): 1130 Fifth Ave., New York, N.Y. 10128. Midtown branch: 1133 Avenue of the Americas, New York, N.Y. 10036. Phone: (212) 860-1777.

Physical Society, American (1899): 335 E. 45th St., New York, N.Y. 10017-3483. 43,000. Phone: (212) 682-7341.

Physical Therapy Association, American (APTA) (1921): 1111 N. Fairfax St., Alexandria, Va. 22314. 56,000. Phone: (703) 684-2782.

Physics, American Institute of (1931): 335 E. 45th St., New York, N.Y. 10017. 102,500. Phone: (212) 661-9404.

Pilot International (1921): Pilot International Headquarters, 244 College St., P.O. Box 4844, Macon, Ga. 31213-0599. 19,000. Phone: (912) 743-7403.

Planetary Society, The (1979): 65 N. Catalina Ave., Pasadena, Calif. 91106. 120,000. Phone: (818) 793-5100.

Plan International (1937): Box 804, East Greenwich, R.I. 02818-1667. Phone: (401) 826-2500.

Planned Parenthood® Federation of America, Inc., (1916): 810 Seventh Ave., New York, N.Y. 10019. 169 affiliates. Phone: (212) 541-7800.

Plastics Engineers, Society of (1942): 14 Fairfield Dr., Brookfield, Conn. 06804-0403. 37,000. Phone: (203) 775-0471.

Police, American Federation of (1966): Records Center, 3801 Biscayne Blvd., Miami, Fla. 33137. 55,000. Phone: (305) 573-0070.

Police, International Association of Chiefs of (1893): 515 N. Washington St., Alexandria, Va. 22314-2357. 13,000. Phone: (703) 836-6767.

Police Hall of Fame, American (1960): 3801 Biscayne Blvd., Miami, Fla. 33137. 55,000. Phone: (305) 573-0070.

Political and Social Science, American Academy of (1889): 3937 Chestnut St., Philadelphia, Pa. 19104. Phone: (215) 386-4594.

Political Science, Academy of (1880): 475 Riverside Dr., Suite 1274, New York, N.Y. 10115-1274. 9,000. Phone: (212) 870-2500.

Powder Metallurgy Institute, American (1958): 105 College Rd. East, Princeton, N.J. 08540. 2,800. Phone: (609) 452-7700.

Practical Nurse Education and Service, National Association for (1941): 1400 Spring St., Suite 310, Silver Spring, Md. 20910. Phone: (301) 588-2491.

Press Club, National (1908): National Press Bldg., 529 14th St. N.W., Washington, D.C. 20045. 4,500. Phone: (202) 662-7500.

***Professional Engineers, National Society of** (1934): 1420 King St., Alexandria, Va. 22314. 75,000. Phone: (703) 684-2800.

Professional Photographers of America, Inc. (1880): 57 Forsyth St. N.W., Atlanta, Ga. 30303. 17,000. Phone: (800) 786-6277.

Psychiatric Association, American (1844): 1400 K St. N.W., Washington, D.C. 20005. 38,069. Phone: (202) 682-6000.

Psychoanalytic Association, The American (1911): 309 E. 49th St., New York, N.Y. 10017. 3,050 psychoanalysts. Phone: (212) 752-0450.

Psychological Association, American (1892): 750 First St. N.E., Washington, D.C. 20002-4242. 114,000. Phone: (202) 336-5500; TDD: (202) 336-5662.

Public Health Association, American (1872): 1015 15th St. N.W., Washington, D.C. 20005. 50,000+. Phone: (202) 789-5600.

Puppeteers of America (1937): 5 Cricklewood Path, Pasadena, Calif. 91107-1002. Phone: (818) 797-5748.

Quality Control, The American Society for (1946): 611 E. Wisconsin Ave., P.O. Box 3005, Milwaukee, Wis. 53201-3005. 105,000+. Phone: (414) 272-8575.

Railroads, Association of American (1934): 50 F St. N.W., Washington, D.C. 20001-1564. Phone: (202) 639-2100.

Recording Arts and Sciences, Inc., National Academy of (1958): 3402 Pico Blvd., Santa Monica, Calif. 90405. 8,200. Phone: (310) 392-3777.

Red Cross, American (1881): 17th and D Sts. N.W., Washington, D.C. 20006. Over 2,800 chapters. Phone: (202) 737-8300.

Rehabilitation Association, National (1925): 633 S. Washington St., Alexandria, Va. 22314-4193. 18,000. Phone: (703) 836-0850.

Research and Enlightenment, Association for (1931): 67th St. & Atlantic Ave. (P.O. Box 595), Virginia Beach, Va. 23451. 55,000. Phone: (804) 428-3588.

Reserve Officers Association of the United States (1922): 1 Constitution Ave. N.E., Washington, D.C. 20002. 110,000. Phone: (202) 479-2200.

Retired Federal Employees, National Association: 1533 New Hampshire Ave. N.W., Washington, D.C. 20036-1279. 500,000. Phone: (202) 234-0832.

Reye's Syndrome Foundation, National (1974): 426 N. Lewis St., Bryan, Ohio 43506. Phone: (800) 233-7393.

RID-USA (Remove Intoxicated Drivers) (1978): Box 520, Schenectady, N.Y. 12301. Over 150/40 state chapters. Phone: (518) 372-0034.

Right to Life Committee, Inc., National (1973): 419 7th St. N.W., Washington, D.C. 20004. Phone: (202) 626-8800.

Rotary International (1905): One Rotary Center, 1560 Sherman Ave., Evanston, Ill. 60201. 1,157,175 in 187 countries and geographical regions. Phone: (708) 866-3000.

SAE (1905): 400 Commonweatlh Dr., Warrendale, Pa. 15096-0001. 60,000. Phone: (412) 776-4841.

Safety Council, National (1913): 1121 Spring Lake Dr., Itasca, Ill. 60143-3201. Phone: (708) 285-1121.

Salvation Army, The (1865): National Headquarters, 615 Slaters Lane, Alexandria, Va. 22313. 446,403. Phone: (703) 684-5500.

Save-the-Redwoods League (1918): 114 Sansome St., Suite 605, San Francisco, Calif. 94104. 45,000. Phone: (415) 362-2352.

Savings & Community Bankers of America

(1992): 900 19th St. N.W., Suite 400, Washington, D.C. 20006. Phone: (202) 857-3100.

Science, American Association for the Advancement of (1848): 1333 H St. N.W., Washington, D.C. 20005. 133,000. Phone: (202) 326-6400.

Science and Health, American Council on (1978): 1995 Broadway, 2nd Floor, New York, N.Y. 10023-5860. Phone: (212) 362-7044.

Science Fiction Society, World (1939): c/o Southern California Institute for Fan Interests, P.O. Box 8442, Van Nuys, Calif. 91409. 6,000. Phone: (818) 366-3827.

Science Writers, Inc., National Association of (1934): P.O. Box 294, Greenlawn, N.Y. 11740. 1,810. Phone: (516) 757-5664.

Scientists, Federation of American (FAS) (1945): 307 Massachusetts Ave. N.E., Washington, D.C. 20002. 4,000. Phone: (202) 546-3300.

SCRABBLE® Association, National (1972): P.O. Box 700, Front Street Garden, Greenport, N.Y. 11944. 15,000. Phone: (516) 477-0033.

Screen Actors Guild (1933): 5757 Wilshire Blvd., Los Angeles, Calif. 90036. 76,000. Phone: ( )

Sculpture Society, National (1893): 1177 Ave. of the Americas, New York, N.Y. 10036. 4,000. Phone: (212) 764-5645.

Seeing Eye Inc., The (1929): P.O. Box 375. Morristown, N.J. 07963-0375. Phone: (201) 539-4425.

Separationists, Society of (1963): P.O. Box 140195, Austin, Tex. 78714-0195. Phone: (512) 458-1244.

Shriners of North America and Shriners Hospitals for Crippled Children, The (1872): Box 31356, Tampa, Fla. 33631-3356. 750,000. Phone: (813) 281-0300.

Sierra Club (1892): 730 Polk St., San Francisco, Calif. 94109. 650,000. Phone: (415) 776-2211.

SIETAR INTERNATIONAL (The International Society for Intercultural Education, Training and Research) (1974): 808 17th St. N.W., Suite 200, Washington, D.C. 20006-3953. 2,000+. Phone: (202) 466-7883.

Simon Wiesenthal Center (1978): 9760 W. Pico Blvd., Los Angeles, Calif. 90035-4792. 375,000. Phone: (310) 553-9036.

Small Business United, National (1937): 1155 15th St. N.W., #710, Washington, D.C. 20005. 65,000. Phone: (202) 293-8830.

SMYAL, Sexual Minorities Youth Assistance League (1984): 333 1/2 Pennsylvania Ave. SE, Washington, D.C. 20003-1148. 1,000 members. Phone: (202) 546-5940.

Social Work Education, Council on (1952): 1600 Duke St., Alexandria, Va. 22314-3421. Phone: (703) 683-8080.

Social Workers, National Association of (1955): 750 First St. N.E., Suite 700, Washington, D.C. 20002-4241. Phone: (202) 408-8600.

Sociological Association, American (1905): 1722 N St. N.W., Washington, D.C. 20036-2981. 13,000. Phone: (202) 833-3410.

Soil and Water Conservation Society (1945): 7515 N.E. Ankeny Rd., Ankeny, Iowa 50021-9764. 11,000. Phone: (515) 289-2331.

Songwriters Guild of America, The (1931): 276 Fifth Ave., Suite 306, New York, N.Y. 10001. 4,200. Phone: (212) 686-6820.

Sons of Italy in America, Order (1905): 219 E St. N.E., Washington, D.C. 20002. 475,000. Phone: (202) 547-2900.

Sons of the American Revolution, National Society of the (1889): 1000 S. 4th St., Louisville, Ky. 40203. 27,000. Phone: (502) 589-1776.

Soroptimist International of the Americas (1921): 1616 Walnut St., Philadelphia, Pa. 19103. 50,000. Phone: (215) 732-0512.

Southern Early Childhood Association (formerly SACUS) (1948): P.O. Box 56130, Little Rock, Ark. 72215-6130. 17,000. Phone: (501) 663-0353.

Space Education Association, U.S. (1973): Global Operations Center, 231 School Lane, P.O. Box 249, Rheems, Pa. 17570-0249. Voice/Fax: (717) 367-5196.

Space Society, National (1974): 922 Pennsylvania Ave. S.E., Washington, D.C. 20003. 30,000. Phone: (202) 543-1900.

***Special Olympics International, Inc.** (1968): 1350 New York Ave. N.W., Suite 500, Washington, D.C., 20005. 1,000,000. Phone: (202) 628-3630.

Speech-Language-Hearing Association, American (1925): 10801 Rockville Pike, Rockville, Md. 20852. 65,000. Phone: (301) 897-5700.

Sports Car Club of America Inc. (1944): 9033 E. Easter Place, Englewood, Colo. 80112-2105. 54,000. Phone: (303) 694-7222.

State Garden Clubs, Inc., National Council of (1929): 4401 Magnolia Ave., St. Louis, Mo. 63110. 280,992. Phone: (314) 776-7574.

State Governments, The Council of (1933): P.O. Box 11910, Lexington, Ky. 40578-1910. All state officials, all 50 states. Phone: (606) 231-1939.

Statistical Association, American (1839): 1429 Duke St., Alexandria, Va. 22314. 17,500.

Student Association, United States (1947): 815 15th St. N.W. #838, Washington, D.C. 20005. 350 schools (3.5 million students). Phone: (202) 347-8772.

Surgeons, American College of (1913): 55 E. Erie St., Chicago, Ill. 60611-2797. 52,000+. Phone: (312) 664-4050.

Symphony Orchestra League, American (1942): 777 Fourteenth St. N.W., Suite 500, Washington, D.C. 20005. 4,500. Phone: (202) 628-0099.

TASH: The Association for Persons with Severe Handicaps (1973): 11201 Greenwood Ave. N., Seattle, Wash. 98133. 8,500. Phone: (206) 361-8870.

Tax Foundation, Inc. (1937): 1250 H St. N.W., Suite 750, Washington, D.C. 20005. Phone: (202) 783-2760.

Teachers, American Federation of (1916): 555 New Jersey Ave. N.W., Washington, D.C., 20001. 800,000+. Phone: (202) 879-4400.

Testing & Materials, American Society for (1898): 1916 Race St., Philadelphia, Pa. 19103-1187. 33,000. Phone: (215) 299-5400.

The Arc, a national organization on mental retardation (1950): 500 E. Border St., Suite 300, Arlington, Texas 76010. 140,000 members, 1,200 state and local chapters. Phone: (817) 261-6003.

***Theatre Guild, Inc.** (1919): 226 W. 47th St., New York, N.Y. 10036. 72,000. Phone: (212) 869-5470.

Theosophical Society in America, The (1875): P.O. Box 270, Wheaton, Ill. 60189-0270. 4,800. Phone: (708) 668-1571.

Tin Can Sailors, Inc. (1976): P.O. Box 100, Somerset, Mass. 02726. 17,000. Phone: (508) 677-0515.

Toastmasters International (1924): P.O. Box 9052, Mission Viejo, Calif. 92690-7052, and 23182 Arroyo Vista, Rancho Santa Margarita, Calif. 92688. 180,000. Phone: (714) 542-6793 and (714) 858-8255.

TOUGHLOVE International (1977): P.O. Box 1069, Doylestown, Pa. 18901. 750 registered groups. Phone: (215) 348-7090; (800) 333-1069.

TransAfrica Forum (1982): 1744 R St. N.W., Washington, D.C. 20009. Phone: (202) 547-2550.

Travel Agents, American Society of (ASTA) (1931): 1101 King St., Alexandria, Va. 22314. 20,000. Phone: (703) 739-2782.

Travelers Aid Services (1905/1982); 2 Lafayette St., New York, N.Y. 10007. Lucy N. Friedman, Executive Director. (Result of merger of Travelers Aid Society of New York and Victim Services Agency in 1982). Phone: (212) 577-7700. **Client Services:** Times Square Office, 1481 Broadway, Manhattan (212) 944-0013; JFK Airport Office, International Arrivals Bldg. 50, Jamaica, Queens (718) 656-4870; 24-Hour Crime Victims Hotline (212) 577-7777; Immigration Hotline (718) 899-4000.

Tuberous Sclerosis Association, Inc., National (1975): 8000 Corporate Dr., Suite 120, Landover, Md. 20785. 5,000. Phone: (301) 459-9888 or (800) 225-6872.

UFOs, National Investigations Committee on (1967): 14617 Victory Blvd., Suite 4, Van Nuys, Calif. 91411. Phone & FAX: (818) 989-5942.

UNICEF, U.S. Committee for (1947): 333 E. 38th St., New York, N.Y. 10016. 20,000 volunteers. Phone: (212) 686-5522.

Union of Concerned Scientists (1969): 26 Church St., Cambridge, Mass. 02238. 100,000. Phone: (617) 547-5552.

United Jewish Appeal (1939): 99 Park Ave., New York, N.Y. 10016. Phone: (212) 818-9100.

United Negro College Fund Inc. (1944): 500 E. 62nd St., New York, N.Y. 10021. Phone: (212) 326-1100.

United Way of America (1918): 701 N. Fairfax St., Alexandria, Va. 22314-2045. 2,300 local United Ways. Phone: (703) 836-7100.

University Foundation, International (1973): 1301 S. Noland Rd., Independence, Mo. 64055. 67,000. Phone: (816) 461-3633.

University Women, American Association of (1881): 1111 16th St. N.W., Washington, D.C. 20036. 130,000. Phone: (202) 785-7700.

Urban League, National (1910): 500 E. 62nd St., New York, N.Y. 10021. 116. Phone: (212) 310-9000.

***USO (United Service Organizations)** (1941): World Headquarters, 601 Indiana Ave. N.W., Washington, D.C. 20004. Phone: (202) 783-8121.

***Variety Clubs International** (1927): 1560 Broadway, Suite 1209, New York, N.Y. 10036. 15,000. Phone: (212) 704-9872.

Veterans Committee, American (AVC) (1944): 6309 Bannockburn Dr., Bethesda, Md. 20817. 15,000. Phone & FAX: (301) 320-6490.

Veterans of Foreign Wars of the U.S. (1899): 406 W. 34th St., Kansas City, Mo. 64111. VFW and Auxiliary, 2,850,000. Phone: (816) 756-3390.

Veterinary Medical Association, American (1863): 1931 N. Meacham Rd., Suite 100, Schaumburg, Ill. 60173-4360. 53,500. Phone: (708) 925-8070.

Visual Handicaps, Division on (1948): The Council for Exceptional Children, 1920 Association Dr., Reston, Va. 22091. 1,000. Phone: (703) 620-3660.

Volunteers of America (1896): 3813 N. Causeway Blvd., Metairie, La. 70002. Provides human services in more than 300 communities. Phone: (504) 837-2652.

War Resisters League (1923): 339 Lafayette St., New York, N.Y. 10012. 15,000. Phone: (212) 228-0450.

Washington Legal Foundation (1976): 1705 N St. N.W., Washington, D.C. 20036. 200,000. Phone: (202) 857-0240.

Water Quality Association (1974): 4151 Naperville Rd., Lisle, Ill. 60532. Phone: (708) 505-0160.

Water Resources Association, American (1964): 5410 Grosvenor Lane, Suite 220, Bethesda, Md. 20814. 4,000. Phone: (301) 493-8600.

Welding Society, American (1919): 550 N.W. LeJeune Rd., Miami, Fla. 33126. 42,000. Phone: (305) 443-9353; toll free (800) 443-9353.

***Wildlife Federation, National** (1936): 1400 16th St. N.W., Washington, D.C. 20036-2266. 5,600,000. Phone: (202) 797-6800.

Wildlife Fund, World (1961): 1250 24th St. N.W., Washington, D.C. 20037-1175. 1 million. Phone: (202) 293-4800.

Woman's Christian Temperance Union, National (1874): 1730 Chicago Ave., Evanston, Ill. 60201. Under 50,000. Phone: (708) 864-1396.

Women, National Organization for (NOW) (1966): 1000 16th St. N.W., Suite 700, Washington, D.C. 20036-5705. 270,000. Phone: (202) 331-0066.

Women Police, The International Association of (1915): P.O. Box 371008, Decatur, Ga. 30037-1008. 3,000. Phone: (404) 244-2541.

Women's American ORT (1927): 315 Park Ave. South, New York, N.Y. 10010. Over 1,000 Chapters. Phone: (212) 505-7700.

Women's Clubs, General Federation of (1890): 1734 N St., N.W., Washington, D.C. 20036-2990. 350,000. Phone: (202) 347-3168.

Women's Educational and Industrial Union (1877): 356 Boylston St., Boston, Mass. 02116. 1,500. Phone: (617) 536-5651.

***Women's International League for Peace and Freedom** (1915): 1213 Race St., Philadelphia, Pa. 19107-1691. 50,000. Phone: (215) 563-7110.

World Future Society (1966): 7910 Woodmont Ave., Suite 450, Bethesda, Md. 20814. 30,000. Phone: (301) 656-8274.

World Health, American Association for (1953): 1129 20th St. N.W., Washington, D.C. 20036. 800. Phone: (202) 466-5883.

World Peace, International Association of Educators for (1969): P.O. Box 3282, Mastin Lake Station, Huntsville, Ala. 35810-0282. 25,000. Phone: (205) 534-5501.

World Peace Foundation (1910): 22 Batterymarch St., Boston, Mass. 02109. Phone: (617) 482-3875.

Worldwatch Institute (1974): 1776 Massachusetts Ave. N.W., Washington, D.C. 20036. Research organization. Phone: (202) 452-1999.

Writers Union, National (1983): 873 Broadway, Suite 203, New York, N.Y. 10003. 3,500. Phone: (212) 254-0279.

YMCA of the USA (1844): 101 N. Wacker Dr., Chicago, Ill. 60606. 12,800,000. Phone: (312) 977-0031.

Young Women's Christian Association of the U.S.A. (1858 in U.S.A., 1855 in England): 726 Broadway, New York, N.Y. 10003. 1,800,000. Phone: (212) 614-2700.

Youth Hostels, Inc., American—Hostelling International (1934): P.O. Box 37613, Washington, D.C. 20013-7613. 124,000. Phone: (202) 783-6161.

Zero Population Growth (1968): 1400 Sixteenth St. N.W., Suite 320, Washington, D.C. 20036. 50,000. Phone: (202) 332-2200.

Zionist Organization of America (1897): ZOA House, 4 E. 34th St., New York, N.Y. 10016. 110,000. Phone: (212) 481-1500.

Zoologists, American Society of (1890): 401 N. Michigan Ave., Chicago, Ill. 60611. 4,000. Phone: (312) 527-6697.

THE DECLARATION OF INDEPENDENCE

In Congress, July 4, 1776

The unanimous Declaration of the thirteen united States of America.

When in the Course of human events it becomes necessary for one people to dissolve the political bands which have connected them with another, and to assume among the powers of the earth, the separate and equal station to which the Laws of Nature and of Nature's God entitle them, a decent respect to the opinions of mankind requires that they should declare the causes which impel them to the separation.

We hold these truths to be self-evident, that all men are created equal, that they are endowed by their Creator with certain unalienable Rights, that among these are Life, Liberty and the pursuit of Happiness.—That to secure these rights, Governments are instituted among Men, deriving their just powers from the consent of the governed,—That whenever any Form of Government becomes destructive of these ends, it is the Right of the People to alter or to abolish it, and to institute new Government, laying its foundation on such principles and organizing its powers in such form, as to them shall seem most likely to effect their Safety and Happiness. Prudence, indeed, will dictate that Governments long established should not be changed for light and transient causes; and accordingly all experience hath shewn that mankind are more disposed to suffer, while evils are sufferable, than to right themselves by abolishing the forms to which they are accustomed. But when a long train of abuses and usurpations, pursuing invariably the same Object evinces a design to reduce them under absolute Despotism, it is their right, it is their duty, to throw off such Government, and to provide new Guards for their future security.—Such has been the patient sufferance of these Colonies; and such is now the necessity which constrains them to alter their former Systems of Government. The history of the present King of Great Britain is a history of repeated injuries and usurpations, all having in direct object the establishment of an absolute Tyranny over these States. To prove this, let Facts be submitted to a candid world.

He has refused his Assent to Laws, the most wholesome and necessary for the public good.

He has forbidden his Governors to pass Laws of immediate and pressing importance, unless suspended in their operation till his Assent should be obtained; and when so suspended, he has utterly neglected to attend to them.

He has refused to pass other Laws for the accommodation of large districts of people, unless those people would relinquish the right of Representation in the Legislature, a right inestimable to them and formidable to tyrants only.

He has called together legislative bodies at places unusual, uncomfortable, and distant from the depository of their Public Records, for the sole purpose of fatiguing them into compliance with his measures.

He has dissolved Representative Houses repeatedly, for opposing with manly firmness his invasions on the rights of the people.

He has refused for a long time, after such dissolutions, to cause others to be elected; whereby the Legislative Powers, incapable of Annihilation, have returned to the People at large for their exercise; the State remaining in the mean time exposed to all the dangers of invasion from without, and convulsions within.

He has endeavoured to prevent the population of these States; for that purpose obstructing the Laws for Naturalization of Foreigners; refusing to pass others to encourage their migrations hither, and raising the conditions of new Appropriations of Lands.

He has obstructed the Administration of Justice, by refusing his Assent to Laws for establishing Judiciary Powers.

He has made Judges dependent on his Will alone, for the tenure of their offices, and the amount and payment of their salaries.

He has erected a multitude of New Offices, and sent hither swarms of Officers to harass our people, and eat out their substance.

He has kept among us, in times of peace, Standing Armies without the Consent of our legislatures.

He has affected to render the Military independent of and superior to the Civil Power.

He has combined with others to subject us to a jurisdiction foreign to our constitution, and unacknowledged by our laws; giving his Assent to their Acts of pretended Legislation:

For quartering large bodies of armed troops among us:

For protecting them, by a mock Trial, from punishment for any Murders which they should commit on the Inhabitants of these States:

For cutting off our Trade with all parts of the

NOTE: On April 12, 1776, the legislature of North Carolina authorized its delegates to the Continental Congress to join with others in a declaration of separation from Great Britain; the first colony to instruct its delegates to take the actual initiative was Virginia on May 15. On June 7, 1776, Richard Henry Lee of Virginia offered a resolution to the Congress to the effect "that these United Colonies are, and of right ought to be, free and independent States. . . ." A committee, consisting of Thomas Jefferson, John Adams, Benjamin Franklin, Robert R. Livingston, and Roger Sherman was organized to "prepare a declaration to the effect of the said first resolution." The Declaration of Independence was adopted on July 4, 1776.

Most delegates signed the Declaration August 2, but George Wythe (Va.) signed August 27; Richard Henry Lee (Va.), Elbridge Gerry (Mass.), and Oliver Wolcott (Conn.) in September; Matthew Thornton (N.H.), not a delegate until September, in November; and Thomas McKean (Del.), although present on July 4, not until 1781 by special permission, having served in the army in the interim.

world:

For imposing Taxes on us without our Consent:

For depriving us in many cases, of the benefits of Trial by Jury:

For transporting us beyond Seas to be tried for pretended offences:

For abolishing the free System of English Laws in a neighbouring Province, establishing therein an Arbitrary government, and enlarging its Boundaries so as to render it at once an example and fit instrument for introducing the same absolute rule into these Colonies:

For taking away our Charters, abolishing our most valuable Laws and altering fundamentally the Forms of our Governments:

For suspending our own Legislatures, and declaring themselves invested with power to legislate for us in all cases whatsoever.

He has abdicated Government here, by declaring us out of his Protection and waging War against us.

He has plundered our seas, ravaged our Coasts, burnt our towns, and destroyed the lives of our people.

He is at this time transporting large Armies of foreign Mercenaries to compleat the works of death, desolation, and tyranny, already begun with circumstances of Cruelty & Perfidy scarcely paralleled in the most barbarous ages, and totally unworthy the Head of a civilized nation.

He has constrained our fellow Citizens taken Captive on the high Seas to bear Arms against their Country, to become the executioners of their friends and Brethren, or to fall themselves by their Hands.

He has excited domestic insurrections amongst us, and has endeavoured to bring on the inhabitants of our frontiers, the merciless Indian Savages, whose known rule of warfare, is an undistinguished destruction of all ages, sexes and conditions.

In every stage of these Oppressions We have Petitioned for Redress in the most humble terms: Our repeated Petitions have been answered only by repeated injury. A Prince, whose character is thus marked by every act which may define a Tyrant, is unfit to be the ruler of a free people.

Nor have We been wanting in attentions to our Brittish brethren. We have warned them from time to time of attempts by their legislature to extend an unwarrantable jurisdiction over us. We have reminded them of the circumstances of our emigration and settlement here. We have appealed to their native justice and magnanimity, and we have conjured them by the ties of our common kindred to disavow these usurpations, which would inevitably interrupt our connections and correspondence. They too have been deaf to the voice of justice and of consanguinity. We must, therefore, acquiesce in the necessity, which denounces our Separation, and hold them, as we hold the rest of mankind, Enemies in War, in Peace Friends.

We, therefore, the Representatives of the United States of America, in General Congress, Assembled, appealing to the Supreme Judge of the world for the rectitude of our intentions, do, in the Name, and by Authority of the good People of these Colonies, solemnly publish and declare, That these United Colonies are, and of Right ought to be Free and Independent States; that they are Absolved from all Allegiance to the British Crown, and that all political connection between them and the State of Great Britain, is and ought to be totally dissolved; and that as Free and Independent States, they have full Power to levy War, conclude Peace, contract Alliances, establish Commerce, and to do all other Acts and Things which Independent States may of right do.—And for the support of this Declaration, with a firm reliance on the protection of Divine Providence, we mutually pledge to each other our Lives, our Fortunes and our sacred Honor. —John Hancock

New Hampshire
Josiah Bartlett
Wm. Whipple
Matthew Thornton

Rhode Island
Step. Hopkins
William Ellery

Connecticut
Roger Sherman
Sam'el Huntington
Wm. Williams
Oliver Wolcott

New York
Wm. Floyd
Phil. Livingston
Frans. Lewis
Lewis Morris

New Jersey
Richd. Stockton
Jno. Witherspoon
Fras. Hopkinson
John Hart
Abra. Clark

Pennsylvania
Robt. Morris
Benjamin Rush
Benj. Franklin
John Morton
Geo. Clymer
Jas. Smith
Geo. Taylor
James Wilson
Geo. Ross

Massachusetts-Bay
Saml. Adams
John Adams
Robt. Treat Paine
Elbridge Gerry

Delaware
Caesar Rodney
Geo. Read
Tho. M'Kean

Maryland
Samuel Chase
Wm. Paca
Thos. Stone
Charles Carroll of Carrollton

Virginia
George Wythe
Richard Henry Lee
Th. Jefferson
Benj. Harrison
Ths. Nelson, Jr.
Francis Lightfoot Lee
Carter Braxton

North Carolina
Wm. Hooper
Joseph Hewes
John Penn

South Carolina
Edward Rutledge
Thos. Heyward, Junr.
Thomas Lynch, Junr.
Arthur Middleton

Georgia
Button Gwinnett
Lyman Hall
Geo. Walton

Constitution of the United States of America

(Historical text has been edited to conform to contemporary American usage. The bracketed words are designations for your convenience; they are not part of the Constitution.)

The oldest federal constitution in existence was framed by a convention of delegates from twelve of the thirteen original states in Philadelphia in May, 1787, Rhode Island failing to send a delegate. George Washington presided over the session, which lasted until September 17, 1787. The draft (originally a preamble and seven Articles) was submitted to all thirteen states and was to become effective when ratified by nine states. It went into effect on the first Wednesday in March, 1789, having been ratified by New Hampshire, the ninth state to approve, on June 21, 1788. The states ratified the Constitution in the following order:

Delaware	December 7, 1787	South Carolina	May 23, 1788
Pennsylvania	December 12, 1787	New Hampshire	June 21, 1788
New Jersey	December 18, 1787	Virginia	June 25, 1788
Georgia	January 2, 1788	New York	July 26, 1788
Connecticut	January 9, 1788	North Carolina	November 21, 1789
Massachusetts	February 6, 1788	Rhode Island	May 29, 1790
Maryland	April 28, 1788		

[Preamble]

We the people of the United States, in order to form a more perfect Union, establish justice, insure domestic tranquility, provide for the common defence, promote the general welfare, and secure the blessings of liberty to ourselves and our posterity, do ordain and establish this Constitution for the United States of America.

Article I

Section 1

[Legislative powers vested in Congress.] All legislative powers herein granted shall be vested in a Congress of the United States, which shall consist of a Senate and House of Representatives.

Section 2

[Composition of the House of Representatives.—1.] The House of Representatives shall be composed of members chosen every second year by the people of the several States, and the electors in each State shall have the qualifications requisite for electors of the most numerous branch of the State Legislature.

[Qualifications of Representatives.—2.] No Person shall be a Representative who shall not have attained to the age of twenty-five years, and been seven years a citizen of the United States, and who shall not, when elected, be an inhabitant of that State in which he shall be chosen.

[Apportionment of Representatives and direct taxes—census.[1]—3.] (Representatives and direct taxes shall be apportioned among the several States which may be included within this Union, according to their respective numbers, which shall be determined by adding to the whole number of free persons, including those bound to service for a term of years, and excluding Indians not taxed, three fifths of all other persons.) The actual enumeration shall be made within three years after the first meeting of the Congress of the United States, and within every subsequent term of ten years, in such manner as they shall by law direct. The number of Representatives shall not exceed one for every thirty thousand, but each State shall have at least one Representative; and until such enumeration shall be made, the State of New Hampshire shall be entitled to choose three, Massachusetts eight, Rhode-Island and Providence Plantations one, Connecticut five, New York six, New Jersey four, Pennsylvania eight, Delaware one, Maryland six, Virginia ten, North Carolina five, South Carolina five, and Georgia three.

[Filling of vacancies in representation.—4.] When vacancies happen in the representation from any State, the Executive Authority thereof shall issue writs of election to fill such vacancies.

[Selection of officers; power of impeachment.—5.] The House of Representatives shall choose their Speaker and other officers; and shall have the sole power of impeachment.

Section 3[2]

[The Senate.—1.] The Senate of the United States shall be composed of two Senators from each State, chosen by the Legislature thereof, for six years; and each Senator shall have one vote.

[Classification of Senators; filling of vacancies.—2.] Immediately after they shall be assembled in consequence of the first election, they shall be divided as equally as may be into three classes. The seats of the Senators of the first class shall be vacated at the expiration of the second year, of the second class at the expiration of the fourth year, and of the third class at the expiration of the sixth year, so that one-third may be chosen every second year; and if vacancies happen by resignation, or otherwise, during the recess of the Legislature of any State, the Executive thereof may make temporary appointments (until the next meeting of the Legislature, which shall then fill such vacancies).

[Qualification of Senators.—3.] No person shall be a Senator who shall not have attained to the age of thirty years, and been nine years a citizen of the United States, and who shall not, when elected, be an inhabitant of that State for which he shall be chosen.

[Vice President to be President of Senate.—4.] The Vice President of the United States shall be President of the Senate, but shall have no vote, unless they be equally divided.

[Selection of Senate officers; President pro tempore.—5.] The Senate shall choose their other officers, and also a President pro tempore, in the absence of the Vice President, or when he shall exercise the office of President of the United States.

[Senate to try impeachments.—6.] The Senate

shall have the sole power to try all impeachments. When sitting for that purpose, they shall be on oath or affirmation. When the President of the United States is tried, the Chief Justice shall preside: and no person shall be convicted without the concurrence of two thirds of the members present.

[Judgment in cases of Impeachment.—7.] Judgment in cases of impeachment shall not extend further than to removal from office, and disqualification to hold and enjoy any office of honor, trust, or profit under the United States: but the party convicted shall nevertheless be liable and subject to indictment, trial, judgment and punishment, according to Law.

Section 4

[Control of congressional elections.—1.] The times, places, and manner of holding elections for Senators and Representatives, shall be prescribed in each State by the Legislature thereof; but the Congress may at any time by law make or alter such regulations, except as to the places of choosing Senators.

[Time for assembling of Congress[3]—2.] The Congress shall assemble at least once in every year, and such meeting shall be on the first Monday in December, unless they shall by law appoint a different day.

Section 5

[Each house to be the judge of the election and qualifications of its members; regulations as to quorum.—1.] Each House shall be the judge of the elections, returns, and qualifications of its own members, and a majority of each shall constitute a quorum to do business; but a smaller number may adjourn from day to day, and may be authorized to compel the attendance of absent members, in such manner, and under such penalties as each House may provide.

[Each house to determine its own rules.—2.] Each House may determine the rules of its proceedings, punish its members for disorderly behavior, and, with the concurrence of two thirds, expel a member.

[Journals and yeas and nays.—3.] Each House shall keep a journal of its proceedings, and from time to time publish the same, excepting such parts as may in their judgment require secrecy; and the yeas and nays of the members of either House on any question shall, at the desire of one fifth of those present, be entered on the journal.

[Adjournment.—4.] Neither House, during the session of Congress, shall, without the consent of the other, adjourn for more than three days, nor to any other place than that in which the two Houses shall be sitting.

Section 6

[Compensation and privileges of members of Congress.—1.] The Senators and Representatives shall receive a compensation for their services, to be ascertained by law, and paid out of the Treasury of the United States. They shall in all cases, except treason, felony, and breach of the peace, be privileged from arrest during their attendance at the session of their respective Houses, and in going to and returning from the same; and for any speech or debate in either House, they shall not be questioned in any other place.

[Incompatible offices; exclusions.—2.] No Senator or Representative shall, during the time for which he was elected, be appointed to any civil office under the authority of the United States, which shall have been created, or the emoluments whereof shall have been increased during such time; and no person holding any office under the United States shall be a member of either House during his continuance in office.

Section 7

[Revenue bills to originate in House.—1.] All bills for raising revenue shall originate in the House of Representatives; but the Senate may propose or concur with amendments as on other bills.

[Manner of passing bills; veto power of President.—2.] Every bill which shall have passed the House of Representatives and the Senate, shall, before it becomes a law, be presented to the President of the United States; if he approve he shall sign it, but if not he shall return it, with his objections to that House in which it shall have originated, who shall enter the objections at large on their journal, and proceed to reconsider it. If after such reconsideration two thirds of that House shall agree to pass the bill, it shall be sent, together with the objections, to the other House, by which it shall likewise be reconsidered, and if approved by two thirds of that House, it shall become a law. But in all such cases the votes of both Houses shall be determined by yeas and nays, and the names of the persons voting for and against the bill shall be entered on the journal of each house, respectively. If any bill shall not be returned by the President within ten days (Sundays excepted) after it shall have been presented to him, the same shall be a law, in like manner as if he had signed it, unless the Congress by their adjournment prevent its return, in which case it shall not be a law.

[Concurrent orders or resolutions, to be passed by President.—3.] Every order, resolution, or vote to which the concurrence of the Senate and House of Representatives may be necessary (except on a question of adjournment) shall be presented to the President of the United States; and before the same shall take effect, shall be approved by him, or being disapproved by him, shall be repassed by two thirds of the Senate and House of Representatives, according to the rules and limitations prescribed in the case of a bill.

Section 8

[General powers of Congress.[4]]

[Taxes, duties, imposts, and excises.—1.] The Congress shall have power to lay and collect taxes, duties, imposts and excises, to pay the debts and provide for the common defense and general welfare of the United States; but all duties, imposts and excises shall be uniform throughout the United States;

[Borrowing of money.—2.] To borrow money on the credit of the United States;

[Regulation of commerce.—3.] To regulate commerce with foreign nations, and among the several States, and with the Indian tribes;

[Naturalization and bankruptcy.—4.] To establish a uniform rule of naturalization, and uniform laws on the subject of bankruptcies throughout the United States;

[Money, weights and measures.—5.] To coin money, regulate the value thereof, and of foreign coin, and fix the standard of weights and measures;

[Counterfeiting.—6.] To provide for the punishment of counterfeiting the securities and current coin of the United States;

[Post offices.—7.] To establish post offices and post roads;

[Patents and copyrights.—8.] To promote the

progress of science and useful arts, by securing for limited times to authors and inventors the exclusive right to their respective writings and discoveries;

[Inferior courts.—9.] To constitute tribunals inferior to the Supreme Court;

[Piracies and felonies.—10.] To define and punish piracies and felonies committed on the high seas, and offences against the law of nations;

[War; marque and reprisal.—11.] To declare war, grant letters of marque and reprisal, and make rules concerning captures on land and water;

[Armies.—12.] To raise and support armies, but no appropriation of money to that use shall be for a longer term than two years;

[Navy.—13.] To provide and maintain a navy;

[Land and naval forces.—14.] To make rules for the government and regulation of the land and naval forces;

[Calling out militia.—15.] To provide for calling forth the militia to execute the laws of the Union, suppress insurrections, and repel invasions;

[Organizing, arming, and disciplining militia.—16.] To provide for organizing, arming, and disciplining, the militia, and for governing such part of them as may be employed in the service of the United States, reserving to the States, respectively, the appointment of the officers, and the authority of training the militia according to the discipline prescribed by Congress;

[Exclusive legislation over District of Columbia.—17.] To exercise exclusive legislation in all cases whatsoever, over such district (not exceeding ten miles square) as may, by cession of particular States, and the acceptance of Congress, become the seat of the Government of the United States, and to exercise like authority over all places purchased by the consent of the Legislature of the State in which the same shall be, for the erection of forts, magazines, arsenals, dock-yards, and other needful buildings;—And

[To enact laws necessary to enforce Constitution.—18.] To make all laws which shall be necessary and proper for carrying into execution the foregoing powers, and all other powers vested by this Constitution in the Government of the United States, or in any department or officer thereof.

Section 9

[Migration or importation of certain persons not to be prohibited before 1808.—1.] The migration or importation of such persons as any of the States now existing shall think proper to admit, shall not be prohibited by the Congress prior to the year one thousand eight hundred and eight, but a tax or duty may be imposed on such importation, not exceeding ten dollars for each person.

[Writ of habeas corpus not to be suspended; exception.—2.] The privilege of the writ of habeas corpus shall not be suspended, unless when in cases of rebellion or invasion the public safety may require it.

[Bills of attainder and ex post facto laws prohibited.—3.] No bill of attainder or ex post facto law shall be passed.

[Capitation and other direct taxes.—4.] No capitation, or other direct, tax shall be laid, unless in proportion to the census or enumeration herein before directed to be taken.[5]

[Exports not to be taxed.—5.] No tax or duty shall be laid on articles exported from any State.

[No preference to be given to ports of any States; interstate shipping.—6.] No preference shall be given by any regulation of commerce or revenue to the ports of one State over those of another: nor shall vessels bound to, or from, one State, be obliged to enter, clear, or pay duties in another.

[Money, how drawn from treasury; financial statements to be published.—7.] No money shall be drawn from the Treasury, but in consequence of appropriations made by law; and a regular statement and account of the receipts and expenditures of all public money shall be published from time to time.

[Titles of nobility not to be granted; acceptance by government officers of favors from foreign powers.—8.] No title of nobility shall be granted by the United States: and no person holding any office of profit or trust under them, shall, without the consent of the Congress, accept of any present, emolument, office, or title, of any kind whatever, from any king, prince, or foreign state.

Section 10

[Limitations of the powers of the several States.—1.] No State shall enter into any treaty, alliance, or confederation; grant letters of marque and reprisal; coin money; emit bills of credit; make any thing but gold and silver coin a tender in payment of debts; pass any bill of attainder, ex post facto law, or law impairing the obligation of contracts, or grant any title of nobility.

[State imposts and duties.—2.] No State shall, without the consent of the Congress, lay any imposts or duties on imports or exports, except what may be absolutely necessary for executing its inspection laws; and the net produce of all duties and imposts, laid by any State on imports or exports, shall be for the use of the Treasury of the United States; and all such laws shall be subject to the revision and control of the Congress.

[Further restrictions on powers of States.—3.] No State shall, without the consent of Congress, lay any duty of tonnage, keep troops, or ships of war in time of peace, enter into any agreement or compact with another state, or with a foreign power, or engage in war, unless actually invaded, or in such imminent danger as will not admit of delay.

Article II

Section 1

[The President; the executive power.—1.] The executive power shall be vested in a President of the United States of America. He shall hold his office during the term of four years, and, together with the Vice President, chosen for the same term, be elected, as follows

[Appointment and qualifications of presidential electors.—2.] Each State shall appoint, in such manner as the Legislature thereof may direct, a number of electors, equal to the whole number of Senators and Representatives to which the State may be entitled in the Congress: but no Senator or Representative, or person holding an office of trust or profit under the United States, shall be appointed an elector.

[Original method of electing the President and Vice President.[6]] (The electors shall meet in their respective States, and vote by ballot for two persons, of whom one at least shall not be an inhabitant of the same State with themselves. And they shall make a list of all the persons voted for, and of the number of votes for each; which list they shall sign and certify, and transmit sealed to the seat of the Government of the United States, directed to the President of the

Senate. The President of the Senate shall, in the presence of the Senate and House of Representatives, open all the certificates, and the votes shall then be counted. The person having the greatest number of votes shall be the President, if such number be a majority of the whole number of electors appointed; and if there be more than one who have such majority, and have an equal number of votes, then the House of Representatives shall immediately choose by ballot one of them for President; and if no person have a majority, then from the five highest on the list the said House shall in like manner choose the President. But in choosing the President, the votes shall be taken by States, the representation from each State having one vote; A quorum for this purpose shall consist of a member or members from two thirds of the States, and a majority of all the states shall be necessary to a choice. In every case, after the choice of the President, the person having the greatest number of votes of the electors shall be the Vice President. But if there should remain two or more who have equal votes, the Senate should choose from them by ballot the Vice President.)

[Congress may determine time of choosing electors and day for casting their votes.—3.] The Congress may determine the time of choosing the electors, and the day on which they shall give their votes; which day shall be the same throughout the United States.

[Qualifications for the office of President.[7]—4.] No person except a natural born citizen, or a citizen of the United States, at the time of the adoption of this Constitution, shall be eligible to the office of President; neither shall any person be eligible to that office who shall not have attained to the age of thirty-five years, and been fourteen years a resident within the United States.

[Filling vacancy in the office of President.[8]—5.] In case of the removal of the President from office, or of his death, resignation, or inability to discharge the powers and duties of the said office, the same shall devolve on the Vice President, and the Congress may by law provide for the case of removal, death, resignation or inability, both of the President and Vice President, declaring what officer shall then act as President, and such officer shall act accordingly, until the disability be removed, or a President shall be elected.

[Compensation of the President.—6.] The President shall, at stated times, receive for his services, a compensation, which shall neither be increased nor diminished during the period for which he shall have been elected, and he shall not receive within that period any other emolument from the United States, or any of them.

[Oath to be taken by the President.—7.] Before he enter on the execution of his office, he shall take the following oath or affirmation:—"I do solemnly swear (or affirm) that I will faithfully execute the office of President of the United States, and will to the best of my ability, preserve, protect, and defend the Constitution of the United States."

Section 2

[The President to be commander in chief of army and navy and head of executive departments; may grant reprieves and pardons.—1.] The President shall be Commander in Chief of the Army and Navy of the United States, and of the militia of the several States, when called into the actual service of the United States; he may require the opinion, in writing, of the principal officer in each of the executive departments, upon any subject relating to the duties of their respective offices, and he shall have power to grant reprieves and pardons for offences against the United States, except in cases of impeachment.

[President may, with concurrence of Senate, make treaties, appoint ambassadors, etc.; appointment of inferior officers, authority of Congress over.—2.] He shall have power, by and with the advice and consent of the Senate, to make treaties, provided two thirds of the Senators present concur; and he shall nominate, and by and with the advice and consent of the Senate, shall appoint ambassadors, other public ministers and consuls, judges of the Supreme Court, and all other officers of the United States, whose appointments are not herein otherwise provided for, and which shall be established by law: but the Congress may by law vest the appointment of such inferior officers, as they think proper, in the President alone, in the courts of law, or in the heads of departments.

[President may fill vacancies in office during recess of Senate.—3.] The President shall have power to fill up all vacancies that may happen during the recess of the Senate, by granting commissions which shall expire at the end of their session.

Section 3

[President to give advice to Congress; may convene or adjourn it on certain occasions; to receive ambassadors, etc.; have laws executed and commission all officers.] He shall from time to time give to the Congress information of the state of the Union, and recommend to their consideration such measures as he shall judge necessary and expedient; he may, on extraordinary occasions, convene both Houses, or either of them, and in case of disagreement between them, with respect to the time of adjournment, he may adjourn them to such time as he shall think proper; he shall receive ambassadors and other public ministers: he shall take care that the laws be faithfully executed, and shall commission all the officers of the United States.

Section 4

[All civil officers removable by impeachment.] The President, Vice President, and all civil officers of the United States shall be removed from office on impeachment for, and conviction of, treason, bribery, or other high crimes and misdemeanors.

Article III

Section 1

[Judicial powers; how vested; term of office and compensation of judges.] The judicial Power of the United States, shall be vested in one Supreme Court, and in such inferior courts as the Congress may from time to time ordain and establish. The judges, both of the supreme and inferior courts, shall hold their offices during good behavior, and shall, at stated times, receive for their services, a compensation, which shall not be diminished during their continuance in office.

Section 2

[Jurisdiction of Federal courts[9]—1.] The judicial power shall extend to all cases, in law and equity, arising under this Constitution, the laws of the United States, and treaties made, or which shall be made, under their authority; to all cases affecting ambassadors, other public ministers and consuls; to all cases of admiralty and maritime jurisdiction; to controversies to which the United States, shall be a party; to controversies between two or more States; between a State and citizens of another State; between citizens of different States; between citizens of the same State claiming lands under grants of different states, and between a State, or the citizens thereof, and foreign states, citizens, or subjects.

[Original and appellate jurisdiction of Supreme Court.—2.] In all cases affecting ambassadors, other public ministers and consuls, and those in which a State shall be party, the Supreme Court shall have original jurisdiction. In all the other cases before mentioned, the Supreme Court shall have appellate jurisdiction, both as to law and fact, with such exceptions, and under such regulations, as the Congress shall make.

[Trial of all crimes, except impeachment, to be by jury.—3.] The trial of all crimes, except in cases of impeachment, shall be by jury; and such trial shall be held in the State where the said crimes shall have been committed; but when not committed within any State, the trial shall be at such place or places as the Congress may by law have directed.

Section 3

[Treason defined; conviction of.—1.] Treason against the United States, shall consist only in levying war against them, or, in adhering to their enemies, giving them aid and comfort. No person shall be convicted of treason unless on the testimony of two witnesses to the same overt act, or on confession in open court.

[Congress to declare punishment for treason; proviso.—2.] The Congress shall have power to declare the punishment of treason, but no attainder of treason shall work corruption of blood, or forfeiture except during the life of the person attained.

Article IV

Section 1

[Each State to give full faith and credit to the public acts and records of other States.] Full faith and credit shall be given in each State to the public acts, records, and judicial proceedings of every other State. And the Congress may by general laws prescribe the manner in which such acts, records, and proceedings shall be proved, and the effect thereof.

Section 2

[Privileges of citizens.—1.] The citizens of each State shall be entitled to all privileges and immunities of citizens in the several States.

[Extradition between the several States.—2.] A person charged in any State with treason, felony, or other crime, who shall flee from justice, and be found in another State, shall on demand of the Executive authority of the State from which he fled, be delivered up, to be removed to the State having jurisdiction of the crime.

[Persons held to labor or service in one State, fleeing to another, to be returned.—3.] No person held to service or labor in one State, under the laws thereof, escaping into another, shall, in consequence of any law or regulation therein, be discharged from such service or labor, but shall be delivered up on claim of the party to whom such service or labor may be due.

Section 3

[New States.—1.] New States may be admitted by the Congress into this Union; but no new State shall be formed or erected within the jurisdiction of any other State; nor any State be formed by the junction of two or more States, or parts of States, without the consent of the Legislatures of the States concerned as well as of the Congress.

[Regulations concerning territory.—2.] The Congress shall have power to dispose of and make all needful rules and regulations respecting the territory or other property belonging to the United States; and nothing in this Constitution shall be so construed as to prejudice any claims of the United States, or of any particular State.

Section 4

[Republican form of government and protection guaranteed the several States.] The United States shall guarantee to every State in this Union a Republican form of government, and shall protect each of them against invasion; and on application of the Legislature, or of the Executive (when the Legislature cannot be convened) against domestic violence.

Article V

[Ways in which the Constitution can be amended.] The Congress, whenever two thirds of both Houses shall deem it necessary, shall propose amendments to this Constitution, or, on the application of the Legislatures of two thirds of the several States shall call a convention for proposing amendments, which, in either case, shall be valid to all intents and purposes, as part of this Constitution, when ratified by the Legislatures of three fourths of the several States, or by conventions in three fourths thereof, as the one or the other mode of ratification may be proposed by the Congress; provided that no amendment which may be made prior to the year one thousand eight hundred and eight shall in any manner affect the first and fourth clauses in the ninth Section of the first Article; and that no State, without its consent, shall be deprived of its equal suffrage in the Senate.

Article VI

[Debts contracted under the confederation secured.—1.] All debts contracted and engagements entered into, before the adoption of this Constitution, shall be as valid against the United States under this Constitution, as under the Confederation.

[Constitution, laws, and treaties of the United States to be supreme.—2.] This Constitution, and the laws of the United States which shall be made in pursuance thereof; and all treaties made, or which shall be made, under the authority of the United States, shall be the supreme law of the land; and the judges in every State shall be bound thereby, any thing in the Constitution or laws of any State to the

1. The clause included in parentheses is amended by the 14th Amendment, Section 2. 2. The first paragraph of this section and the part of the second paragraph included in parentheses are amended by the 17th Amendment. 3. Amended by the 20th Amendment, Section 2. 4. By the 16th Amendment, Congress is given the power to lay and collect taxes on income. 5. See the 16th Amendment. 6. This clause has been superseded by the 12th Amendment. 7. For qualifications of the Vice President, see 12th Amendment. 8. Amended by the 20th Amendment, Sections 3 and 4. 9. This section is abridged by the 11th Amendment. 10. See the 13th Amendment.

contrary notwithstanding.

[Who shall take constitutional oath; no religious test as to official qualification.—3.] The Senators and Representatives before mentioned, and the members of the several State Legislatures, and all executive and judicial officers, both of the United States and of the several States, shall be bound by oath or affirmation, to support this Constitution; but no religious test shall ever be required as a qualification to any office or public trust under the United States.

Article VII

[Constitution to be considered adopted when ratified by nine States.] The ratification of the conventions of nine States shall be sufficient for the establishment of this Constitution between the States so ratifying the same.

Done in convention by the unanimous consent of the States present the seventeenth day of September in the year of our Lord one thousand seven hundred and eighty seven and of the independence of the United States of America the Twelfth. In witness whereof we have hereunto subscribed our names.

GEORGE WASHINGTON
President and Deputy from Virginia

NEW HAMPSHIRE
John Langdon — Nicholas Gilman

MASSACHUSETTS
Nathaniel Gorham — Rufus King

CONNECTICUT
Wm. Saml. Johnson — Roger Sherman

NEW YORK
Alexander Hamilton

NEW JERSEY
Wil. Livingston — Wm. Paterson
David Brearley — Jona. Dayton

PENNSYLVANIA
B. Franklin — Thomas Mifflin
Robt. Morris — Geo. Clymer
Thos. FitzSimons — Jared Ingersoll
James Wilson — Gouv. Morris

DELAWARE
Geo. Read — Gunning Bedford Jun.
John Dickinson — Richard Bassett
Jaco. Broom

MARYLAND
James McHenry — Dan. of St. Thos. Jenifer
Danl. Carroll

VIRGINIA
John Blair — James Madison, Jr.

NORTH CAROLINA
Wm. Blount — Richd Dobbs Spaight
Hu. Williamson

SOUTH CAROLINA
J. Rutledge — Charles Cotesworth Pinckney
Charles Pinckney — Pierce Butler

GEORGIA
William Few — Abr. Baldwin

Attest: William Jackson, Secretary

Amendments to the Constitution of the United States

(Amendments I to X inclusive, popularly known as the Bill of Rights, were proposed and sent to the states by the first session of the First Congress. They were ratified Dec. 15, 1791.)

Article I

[Freedom of religion, speech, of the press, and right of petition.] Congress shall make no law respecting an establishment of religion, or prohibiting the free exercise thereof; or abridging the freedom of speech, or of the press; or the right of the people peaceably to assemble, and to petition the Government for a redress of grievances.

Article II

[Right of people to bear arms not to be infringed.] A well regulated militia, being necessary to the security of a free State, the right of the people to keep and bear arms, shall not be infringed.

Article III

[Quartering of troops.] No soldier shall, in time of peace be quartered in any house, without the consent of the owner, nor in time of war, but in a manner to be prescribed by law.

Article IV

[Persons and houses to be secure from unreasonable searches and seizures.] The right of the people to be secure in their persons, houses, papers, and effects, against unreasonable searches and seizures, shall not be violated, and no warrants shall issue, but upon probable cause, supported by oath or affirmation, and particularly describing the place to be searched, and the persons or things to be seized.

Article V

[Trials for crimes; just compensation for private property taken for public use.] No person shall be held to answer for a capital, or otherwise infamous crime, unless on a presentment or indictment of a Grand Jury, except in cases arising in the land or naval forces, or in the militia, when in actual service in time of war or public danger; nor shall any person be subject for the same offence to be twice put in jeopardy of life or limb; nor shall be compelled in any criminal case to be a witness, against himself, nor be deprived of life, liberty, or property, without due process of law; nor shall private property be taken for public use, without just compensation.

Article VI

[Civil rights in trials for crimes enumerated.] In all criminal prosecutions, the accused shall enjoy the right to a speedy and public trial, by an impartial jury of the State and district wherein the crime shall have been committed, which district shall have been previously ascertained by law, and to be informed of the nature and cause of the accusation; to be confronted with the witnesses against him; to have compulsory process for obtaining witnesses in his favor, and to have the assistance of counsel for his defense.

Article VII

[Civil rights in civil suits.] In suits at common law, where the value in controversy shall exceed twenty dollars, the right of trial by jury shall be preserved, and no fact tried by a jury, shall be otherwise re-examined in any court of the United States, than according to the rules of the common law.

Article VIII

[Excessive bail, fines, and punishments prohibited.] Excessive bail shall not be required, nor excessive fines imposed, nor cruel and unusual punishments inflicted.

Article IX

[Reserved rights of people.] The enumeration in the Constitution, of certain rights, shall not be construed to deny or disparage others retained by the people.

Article X

[Powers not delegated, reserved to states and people respectively.] The powers not delegated to the United States by the Constitution, nor prohibited by it to the States, are reserved to the States, respectively, or to the people.

Article XI

(The proposed amendment was sent to the states Mar. 5, 1794, by the Third Congress. It was ratified Feb. 7, 1795.)

[Judicial power of United States not to extend to suits against a State.] The judicial power of the United States shall not be construed to extend to any suit in law or equity, commenced or prosecuted against one of the United States by citizens of another State, or by citizens or subjects of any foreign state.

Article XII

(The proposed amendment was sent to the states Dec. 12, 1803, by the Eighth Congress. It was ratified July 27, 1804.)

[Present mode of electing President and Vice-President by electors.[1]] The electors shall meet in their respective states, and vote by ballot for President and Vice President, one of whom, at least, shall not be an inhabitant of the same state with themselves; they shall name in their ballots the person voted for as President, and in distinct ballots the person voted for as Vice President, and they shall make distinct lists of all persons voted for as President, and of all persons voted for as Vice President, and of the number of votes for each, which lists they shall sign and certify, and transmit sealed to the seat of the government of the United States, directed to the President of the Senate; the President of the Senate shall, in the presence of the Senate and House of Representatives, open all the certificates and the votes shall then be counted; the person having the greatest number of votes for President, shall be the President, if such number be a majority of the whole number of electors appointed; and if no person have such majority, then from the persons having the highest numbers not exceeding three on the list of those voted for as President, the House of Representatives shall choose immediately, by ballot, the President. But in choosing the President, the votes shall be taken by states, the representation from each State having one vote; a quorum for this purpose shall consist of a member or members from two thirds of the states, and a majority of all the states shall be necessary to a choice. And if the House of Representatives shall not choose a President whenever the right of choice shall devolve upon them, before the fourth day of March next following, then the Vice President shall act as President, as in the case of the death or other constitutional disability of the President. The person having the greatest number of votes as Vice President, shall be the Vice President, if such number be a majority of the whole number of electors appointed, and if no person have a majority, then from the two highest numbers on the list, the Senate shall choose the Vice President; a quorum for the purpose shall consist of two thirds of the whole number of Senators, and a majority of the whole number shall be necessary to a choice. But no person constitutionally ineligible to the office of President shall be eligible to that of Vice President of the United States.

Article XIII

(The proposed amendment was sent to the states Feb. 1, 1865, by the Thirty-eighth Congress. It was ratified Dec. 6, 1865.)

Section 1

[Slavery prohibited.] Neither slavery nor involuntary servitude, except as a punishment for crime whereof the party shall have been duly convicted, shall exist within the United States, or any place subject to their jurisdiction.

Section 2

[Congress given power to enforce this article.] Congress shall have power to enforce this article by appropriate legislation.

Article XIV

(The proposed amendment was sent to the states June 16, 1866, by the Thirty-ninth Congress. It was ratified July 9, 1868.)

Section 1

[Citizenship defined; privileges of citizens.] All persons born or naturalized in the United States, and subject to the jurisdiction thereof, are citizens of the United States and of the State wherein they reside. No State shall make or enforce any law which shall abridge the privileges or immunities of citizens of the United States; nor shall any State deprive any person of life, liberty, or property, without due process of law; nor deny to any person within its jurisdiction the equal protection of the laws.

Section 2

[Apportionment of Representatives.] Representatives shall be apportioned among the several States according to their respective numbers, counting the whole number of persons in each State, excluding Indians not taxed. But when the right to vote at any election for the choice of electors for President and Vice President of the United States, Representatives in Congress, the executive and judicial officers of a State, or the members of the Legislature thereof, is denied to any of the male inhabitants of such State, being twenty-one years of age, and citizens of the United States, or in any way abridged, except for participation in rebellion, or other crime, the basis of representation therein shall be reduced in the proportion which the number of such male citizens shall bear to the whole number of male citizens twenty-one years of age in such State.

Section 3

[Disqualification for office; removal of disability.] No person shall be a Senator or Representative in Congress, or elector of President and Vice President, or hold any office, civil or military, under the United States, or under any State, who, having previously taken an oath, as a member of Congress, or as an officer of the United States, or as a member of any State Legislature, or as an executive or judicial officer of any State, to support the Constitution of the United States, shall have engaged in insurrection or rebellion against the same, or given aid or comfort to the enemies thereof. But Congress may, by a vote of two thirds of each House, remove such disability.

Section 4

[Public debt not to be questioned; payment of debts and claims incurred in aid of rebellion forbidden.] The validity of the public debt of the United States, authorized by law, including debts incurred for payment of pensions and bounties for services in suppressing insurrection or rebellion, shall not be questioned. But neither the United States nor any State shall assume or pay any debt or obligation incurred in aid of insurrection or rebellion against the United States, or any claim for the loss or emancipation of any slave; but all such debts, obligations, and claims shall be held illegal and void.

Section 5

[Congress given power to enforce this article.] The Congress shall have power to enforce, by appropriate legislation, the provisions of this article.

Article XV

(The proposed amendment was sent to the states Feb. 27, 1869, by the Fortieth Congress. It was ratified Feb. 3, 1870.)

Section 1

[Right of certain citizens to vote established.] The right of citizens of the United States to vote shall not be denied or abridged by the United States or by any State on account of race, color, or previous condition of servitude.

Section 2

[Congress given power to enforce this article.] The Congress shall have power to enforce this article by appropriate legislation.

Article XVI

(The proposed amendment was sent to the states July 12, 1909, by the Sixty-first Congress. It was ratified Feb. 3, 1913.)

[Taxes on income; Congress given power to lay and collect.] The Congress shall have power to lay and collect taxes on incomes, from whatever source derived, without apportionment among the several States, and without regard to any census or enumeration.

Article XVII

(The proposed amendment was sent to the states May 16, 1912, by the Sixty-second Congress. It was ratified April 8, 1913.)

[Election of United States Senators; filling of vacancies; qualifications of electors.] The Senate of the United States shall be composed of two Senators from each State, elected by the people thereof, for six years; and each Senator shall have one vote. The electors in each State shall have the qualifications requisite for electors of the most numerous branch of the State Legislatures.

When vacancies happen in the representation of any State in the Senate, the executive authority of such State shall issue writs of election to fill such vacancies: Provided, that the legislature of any State may empower the executive thereof to make temporary appointment until the people fill the vacancies by election as the legislature may direct.

This amendment shall not be so construed as to affect the election or term of any Senator chosen before it becomes valid as part of the Constitution.

Article XVIII[2]

(The proposed amendment was sent to the states Dec. 18, 1917, by the Sixty-fifth Congress. It was ratified by three quarters of the states by Jan. 16, 1919, and became effective Jan. 16, 1920.)

Section 1

[Manufacture, sale, or transportation of intoxicating liquors, for beverage purposes, prohibited.] After one year from the ratification of this article the manufacture, sale, or transportation of intoxicating liquors within, the importation thereof into, or the exportation thereof from the United States and all territory subject to the jurisdiction thereof for beverage purposes is hereby prohibited.

Section 2

[Congress and the several States given concurrent power to pass appropriate legislation to enforce this article.] The Congress and the several States shall have concurrent power to enforce this article by appropriate legislation.

Section 3

[Provisions of article to become operative, when adopted by three fourths of the States.] This article shall be inoperative unless it shall have been ratified as an amendment to the Constitution by the legislatures of the several States, as provided in the Constitution, within seven years from the date of the submission hereof to the States by Congress.

Article XIX

(The proposed amendment was sent to the states June 4, 1919, by the Sixty-sixth Congress. It was ratified Aug. 18, 1920.)

[The right of citizens to vote shall not be denied because of sex.] The right of citizens of the United States to vote shall not be denied or abridged by the United States or by any State on account of sex.

[Congress given power to enforce this article.] Congress shall have power to enforce this article by appropriate legislation.

Article XX

(The proposed amendment, sometimes called the "Lame Duck Amendment," was sent to the states Mar. 3, 1932, by the Seventy-second Congress. It was ratified Jan. 23, 1933; but, in accordance with Section 5, Sections 1 and 2 did not go into effect until Oct. 15, 1933.)

Section 1

[Terms of President, Vice President, Senators, and Representatives.] The terms of the President and Vice President shall end at noon on the twentieth day of January, and the terms of Senators and Representatives at noon on the third day of January, of the years in which such terms would have ended if this article had not been ratified; and the terms of their successors shall then begin.

Section 2

[Time of assembling Congress.] The Congress shall assemble at least once in every year, and such meeting shall begin at noon on the third day of January, unless they shall by law appoint a different day.

Section 3

[Filling vacancy in office of President.] If, at the time fixed for the beginning of the term of the President, the President-elect shall have died, the Vice President-elect shall become President. If a President shall not have been chosen before the time fixed for the beginning of his term, or if the President-elect shall have failed to qualify, then the Vice President shall have qualified; and the Congress may by law provide for the case wherein neither a President-elect nor a Vice President-elect shall have qualified, declaring who shall then act as President, or the manner in which one who is to act shall be selected, and such person shall act accordingly until a President or Vice President shall have qualified.

Section 4

[Power of Congress in Presidential succession.] The Congress may by law provide for the case of the death of any of the persons from whom the House of Representatives may choose a President whenever the right of choice shall have devolved upon them, and for the case of the death of any of the persons from whom the Senate may choose a Vice President whenever the right of choice shall have devolved upon them.

Section 5

[Time of taking effect.] Sections 1 and 2 shall take effect on the 15th day of October following the ratification of this article.

Section 6

[Ratification.] This article shall be inoperative unless it shall have been ratified as an amendment to the Constitution by the legislatures of three fourths of the several States within seven years from the date of its submission.

Article XXI

(The proposed amendment was sent to the states Feb. 20, 1933, by the Seventy-second Congress. It was ratified Dec. 5, 1933.)

Section 1

[Repeal of Prohibition Amendment.] The eighteenth article of amendment to the Constitution of the United States is hereby repealed.

Section 2

[Transportation of intoxicating liquors.] The transportation or importation into any State, territory, or possession of the United States for delivery or use therein of intoxicating liquors, in violation of the laws thereof, is hereby prohibited.

Section 3

[Ratification.] This article shall be inoperative unless it shall have been ratified as an amendment to the Constitution by convention in the several States, as provided in the Constitution, within seven years from the date of the submission thereof to the States by the Congress.

Article XXII

(The proposed amendment was sent to the states Mar. 21, 1947, by the Eightieth Congress. It was ratified Feb. 27, 1951.)

Section 1

[Limit to number of terms a President may serve.] No person shall be elected to the office of the President more than twice, and no person who has held the office of President, or acted as President, for more than two years of a term to which some other person was elected President shall be elected to the office of the President more than once. But this article shall not apply to any person holding the office of President when this article was proposed by the Congress, and shall not prevent any person who may be holding the office of President, or acting as President, during the term within which this article becomes operative from holding the office of President or acting as President during the remainder of such term.

Section 2

[Ratification.] This article shall be inoperative unless it shall have been ratified as an amendment to the Constitution by the legislatures of three fourths of the several States within seven years from the date of its submission to the States by the Congress.

Article XXIII

(The proposed amendment was sent to the states June 16, 1960, by the Eighty-sixth Congress. It was ratified March 29, 1961.)

Section 1

[Electors for the District of Columbia.] The District constituting the seat of Government of the United States shall appoint in such manner as the Congress may direct: A number of electors of President and Vice President equal to the whole number of Senators and Representatives in Congress to which the District would be entitled if it were a State, but in no event more than the least populous State; they shall be in addition to those appointed by the States, but they shall be considered, for the purposes of the election of President and Vice President, to be electors appointed by a State; and they shall meet in the District and perform such duties as provided by the twelfth article of amendment.

Section 2

[Congress given power to enforce this article.] The Congress shall have the power to enforce this article by appropriate legislation.

Article XXIV

(The proposed amendment was sent to the states Aug. 27, 1962, by the Eighty-seventh Congress. It was ratified Jan. 23, 1964.)

Section 1

[Payment of poll tax or other taxes not to be prerequisite for voting in federal elections.] The right of citizens of the United States to vote in any primary or other election for President or Vice President, for electors for President or Vice President, or for Senator or Representative in Congress, shall not be denied or abridged by the United States or any State by reasons of failure to pay any poll tax or other tax.

Section 2

[Congress given power to enforce this article.] The Congress shall have the power to enforce this article by appropriate legislation.

Article XXV

(The proposed amendment was sent to the states July 6, 1965, by the Eighty-ninth Congress. It was ratified Feb. 10, 1967.)

Section 1

[Succession of Vice President to Presidency.] In case of the removal of the President from office or of his death or resignation, the Vice President shall become President.

Section 2

[Vacancy in office of Vice President.] Whenever there is a vacancy in the office of the Vice President, the President shall nominate a Vice President who shall take office upon confirmation by a majority vote of both Houses of Congress.

Section 3

[Vice President as Acting President.] Whenever the President transmits to the President pro tempore of the Senate and the Speaker of the House of Representatives his written declaration that he is unable to discharge the powers and duties of his office, and until he transmits to them a written declaration to the contrary, such powers and duties shall be discharged by the Vice President as Acting President.

Section 4

[Vice President as Acting President.] Whenever the Vice President and a majority of either the principal officers of the executive departments or of such other body as Congress may by law provide, transmit to the President pro tempore of the Senate and the Speaker of the House of Representatives their written declaration that the President is unable to discharge the powers and duties of his office, the Vice President shall immediately assume the powers and duties of the office as Acting President.

Thereafter, when the President transmits to the President pro tempore of the Senate and the Speaker of the House of Representatives his written declaration that no inability exists, he shall resume the powers and duties of his office unless the Vice President and a majority of either the principal officers of the executive department or of such other body as Congress may by law provide, transmit within four days to the President pro tempore of the Senate and the Speaker of the House of Representatives their written declaration that the President is unable to discharge the powers and duties of his office. Thereupon Congress shall decide the issue, assembling within forty-eight hours for that purpose if not in session. If the Congress, within twenty-one days after receipt of the latter written declaration, or, if Congress is not in session, within twenty-one days after Congress is required to assemble, determines by two thirds vote of both Houses that the President is unable to discharge the powers and duties of his office, the Vice President shall continue to discharge the same as Acting President; otherwise, the President shall resume the powers and duties of his office.

Article XXVI

(The proposed amendment was sent to the states Mar. 23, 1971, by the Ninety-second Congress. It was ratified July 1, 1971.)

Section 1

[Voting for 18-year-olds.] The right of citizens of the United States, who are 18 years of age or older, to vote shall not be denied or abridged by the United States or by any state on account of age.

Section 2

[Congress given power to enforce this article.] The Congress shall have power to enforce this article by appropriate legislation.

Article XXVII

(Ratified May 7, 1992.)

[Congressional raises.] No law, varying the compensation for the services of the Senators and Representatives, shall take effect, until an election of Representativies shall have intervened.

1. Amended by the 20th Amendment, Sections 3 and 4. 2. Repealed by the 21st Amendment.

The White House

Source: Department of the Interior, U.S. National Park Service.

The White House, the official residence of the President, is at 1600 Pennsylvania Avenue in Washington, D.C. 20500. The site, covering about 18 acres, was selected by President Washington and Pierre Charles L'Enfant, and the architect was James Hoban. The design appears to have been influenced by Leinster House, Dublin, and James Gibb's *Book of Architecture*. The cornerstone was laid Oct. 13, 1792, and the first residents were President and Mrs. John Adams in November 1800. The building was fired by the British in 1814.

From December 1948 to March 1952, the interior of the White House was rebuilt, and the outer walls were strengthened.

The rooms for public functions are on the first floor; the second and third floors are used as the residence of the President and First Family. The most celebrated public room is the East Room, where formal receptions take place. Other public rooms are the Red Room, the Green Room, and the Blue Room. The State Dining Room is used for formal dinners. There are 132 rooms.

The Mayflower Compact

On Sept. 6, 1620, the *Mayflower,* a sailing vessel of about 180 tons, started her memorable voyage from Plymouth, England, with about 100[1] pilgrims aboard, bound for Virginia to establish a private permanent colony in North America. Arriving at what is now Provincetown, Mass., on Nov. 11 (Nov. 21, new style calendar), 41 of the passengers signed the famous "Mayflower Compact" as the boat lay at anchor in that Cape Cod harbor. A small detail of the pilgrims, led by William Bradford, assigned to select a place for permanent settlement landed at what is now Plymouth, Mass., on Dec. 21 (n.s.).

The text of the compact follows:

> In the name of God, Amen. We, whose names are underwritten, the Loyal Subjects of our dread Sovereign Lord, King *James,* by the Grace of God, of *Great Britain, France and Ireland,* King, *Defender of the Faith, &*
>
> Having undertaken for the Glory of God, and Advancement of the Christian Faith, and the Honour of our King and Country, a voyage to plant the first colony in the northern Parts of Virginia; do by these Presents, solemnly and mutually in the Presence of God and one of another, covenant and combine ourselves together into a civil Body Politick, for our better Ordering and Preservation, and Furtherance of the Ends aforesaid; And by Virtue hereof to enact, constitute, and frame, such just and equal Laws, Ordinances, Acts, Constitutions and Offices, from time to time, as shall be thought most meet and convenient for the General good of the Colony; unto which we promise all due Submission and Obedience.
>
> In Witness whereof we have hereunto subscribed our names at *Cape Cod* the eleventh of *November,* in the Reign of our Sovereign Lord, King *James* of *England, France* and *Ireland,* the eighteenth, and of *Scotland* the fifty-fourth. *Anno Domini,* 1620

John Carver
Digery Priest
William Brewster
Edmund Margesson
John Alden
George Soule
James Chilton
Francis Cooke
Moses Fletcher
John Ridgate
Christopher Martin
William Mullins
Thomas English
John Howland
Stephen Hopkins
Edward Winslow
Gilbert Winslow
Miles Standish
Richard Bitteridge
Francis Eaton
John Tilly
John Billington
Thomas Tinker
Samuel Fuller
Richard Clark
John Allerton
Richard Warren
Edward Liester
William Bradford
Thomas Williams
Isaac Allerton
Peter Brown
John Turner
Edward Tilly
John Craxton
Thomas Rogers
John Goodman
Edward Fuller
Richard Gardiner
William White
Edward Doten

1. Historians differ as to whether 100, 101, or 102 passengers were aboard.

The Monroe Doctrine

The Monroe Doctrine was announced in President James Monroe's message to Congress, during his second term on Dec. 2, 1823, in part as follows:

"In the discussions to which this interest has given rise, and in the arrangements by which they may terminate, the occasion has been deemed proper for asserting as a principle in which rights and interests of the United States are involved, that the American continents, by the free and independent condition which they have assumed and maintain, are henceforth not to be considered as subjects for future colonization by any European power. . . . We owe it, therefore, to candor and to the amicable relations existing between the United States and those powers to declare that we should consider any attempt on their part to extend their system to any portion of this hemisphere as dangerous to our peace and safety. With the existing colonies or dependencies of any European power we have not interfered and shall not interfere. But with the governments who have declared their independence and maintain it, and whose independence we have, on great consideration and on just principles, acknowledged, we could not view any interposition for the purpose of oppressing them or controlling in any other manner their destiny by any European power in any other light than as the manifestation of an unfriendly disposition toward the United States."

Order of Presidential Succession

1. The Vice President
2. Speaker of the House
3. President pro tempore of the Senate
4. Secretary of State
5. Secretary of the Treasury
6. Secretary of Defense
7. Attorney General
8. Secretary of the Interior
9. Secretary of Agriculture
10. Secretary of Commerce
11. Secretary of Labor
12. Secretary of Health and Human Services
13. Secretary of Housing and Urban Development
14. Secretary of Transportation
15. Secretary of Energy
16. Secretary of Education

NOTE: An official cannot succeed to the Presidency unless that person meets the Constitutional requirements.

The Star-Spangled Banner

Francis Scott Key, 1814

O say, can you see, by the dawn's early light,
What so proudly we hail'd at the twilight's last gleaming?
Whose broad stripes and bright stars, thro' the perilous fight,
O'er the ramparts we watch'd, were so gallantly streaming?
And the rockets' red glare, the bombs bursting in air,
Gave proof thro' the night that our flag was still there.
O say, does that star-spangled banner yet wave
O'er the land of the free and the home of the brave?

On the shore dimly seen thro' the mists of the deep,
Where the foe's haughty host in dread silence reposes,
What is that which the breeze, o'er the towering steep,
As it fitfully blows, half conceals, half discloses?
Now it catches the gleam of the morning's first beam,
In full glory reflected, now shines on the stream:
'T is the star-spangled banner: O, long may it wave
O'er the land of the free and the home of the brave!

And where is that band who so vauntingly swore
That the havoc of war and the battle's confusion,
A home and a country should leave us no more?
Their blood has wash'd out their foul footsteps' pollution.
No refuge could save the hireling and slave
From the terror of flight or the gloom of the grave:
And the star-spangled banner in triumph doth wave
O'er the land of the free and the home of the brave.

O thus be it ever when free-men shall stand
Between their lov'd home and the war's desolation;
Blest with vict'ry and peace, may the heav'n-rescued land
Praise the Pow'r that hath made and preserv'd us a nation!
Then conquer we must, when our cause it is just,
And this be our motto: "In God is our trust!"
And the star-spangled banner in triumph shall wave
O'er the land of the free and the home of the brave!

On Sept. 13, 1814, Francis Scott Key visited the British fleet in Chesapeake Bay to secure the release of Dr. William Beanes, who had been captured after the burning of Washington, D.C. The release was secured, but Key was detained on ship overnight during the shelling of Fort McHenry, one of the forts defending Baltimore. In the morning, he was so delighted to see the American flag still flying over the fort that he began a poem to commemorate the occasion. First published under the title "Defense of Fort M'Henry," and later as "The Star-Spangled Banner," the poem soon attained wide popularity as sung to the tune "To Anacreon in Heaven." The origin of this tune is obscure, but it may have been written by John Stafford Smith, a British composer born in 1750. "The Star-Spangled Banner" was officially made the National Anthem by Congress in 1931, although it had been already adopted as such by the Army and the Navy.

The Emancipation Proclamation

January 1, 1863

By the President of the United States of America:

A Proclamation.

Whereas on the 22d day of September, A.D. 1862, a proclamation was issued by the President of the United States, containing, among other things, the following, to wit:

"That on the 1st day of January, A.D. 1863, all persons held as slaves within any State or designated part of a State the people whereof shall then be in rebellion against the United States shall be then, thenceforward, and forever free; and the executive government of the United States, including the military and naval authority thereof, will recognize and maintain the freedom of such persons and will do not act or acts to repress such persons, or any of them, in any efforts they may make for their actual freedom.

"That the executive will on the 1st day of January aforesaid, by proclamation, designate the States and parts of States, if any, in which the people thereof, respectively, shall then be in rebellion against the United States; and the fact that any State or the people thereof shall on that day be in good faith represented in the Congress of the United States by members chosen thereto at elections wherein a majority of the qualified voters of such States shall have participated shall, in the absence of strong countervailing testimony, be deemed conclusive evidence that such State and the people thereof are not then in rebellion against the United States."

Now, therefore, I, Abraham Lincoln, President of

the United States, by virtue of the power in me vested as Commander-in-Chief of the Army and Navy of the United States in time of actual armed rebellion against the authority and government of the United States, and as a fit and necessary war measure for suppressing said rebellion, do, on this 1st day of January, A.D. 1863, and in accordance with my purpose so to do, publicly proclaimed for the full period of one hundred days from the first day above mentioned, order and designate as the States and parts of States wherein the people thereof, respectively, are this day in rebellion against the United States the following, to wit:

Arkansas, Texas, Louisiana (except the parishes of St. Bernard, Plaquemines, Jefferson, St. John, St. Charles, St. James, Ascension, Assumption, Terrebonne, Lafourche, St. Mary, St. Martin, and Orleans, including the city of New Orleans), Mississippi, Alabama, Florida, Georgia, South Carolina, North Carolina, and Virginia (except the forty-eight counties designated as West Virginia, and also the counties of Berkeley, Accomac, Northhampton, Elizabeth City, York, Princess Anne, and Norfolk, including the cities of Norfolk and Portsmouth), and which excepted parts are for the present left precisely as if this proclamation were not issued.

And by virtue of the power and for the purpose aforesaid, I do order and declare that all persons held as slaves within said designated States and parts of States are, and henceforward shall be, free; and that the Executive Government of the United States, including the military and naval authorities thereof, will recognize and maintain the freedom of said persons.

And I hereby enjoin upon the people so declared to be free to abstain from all violence, unless in necessary self-defense; and I recommend to them that, in all cases when allowed, they labor faithfully for reasonable wages.

And I further declare and make known that such persons of suitable condition will be received into the armed service of the United States to garrison forts, positions, stations, and other places, and to man vessels of all sorts in said service.

And upon this act, sincerely believed to be an act of justice, warranted by the Constitution upon military necessity, I invoke the considerate judgment of mankind and the gracious favor of Almighty God.

The Confederate States of America

State	Seceded from Union	Readmiited to Union[1]	State	Seceded from Union	Readmitted to Union[1]
1. South Carolina	Dec. 20, 1860	July 9, 1868	7. Texas	March 2, 1861	March 30, 1870
2. Mississippi	Jan. 9, 1861	Feb. 23, 1870	8. Virginia	April 17, 1861	Jan. 26, 1870
3. Florida	Jan. 10, 1861	June 25, 1868	9. Arkansas	May 6, 1861	June 22, 1868
4. Alabama	Jan. 11, 1861	July 13, 1868	10. North Carolina	May 20, 1861	July 4, 1868
5. Georgia	Jan. 19, 1861	July 15, 1870[2]	11. Tennessee	June 8, 1861	July 24, 1866
6. Louisiana	Jan. 26, 1861	July 9, 1868			

1. Date of readmission to representation in U.S. House of Representatives. 2. Second readmission date. First date was July 21, 1868, but the representatives were unseated March 5, 1869. NOTE: Four other slave states—Delaware, Kentucky, Maryland, and Missouri—remained in the Union.

Lincoln's Gettysburg Address

The Battle of Gettysburg, one of the most noted battles of the Civil War, was fought on July 1, 2, and 3, 1863. On Nov. 19, 1863, the field was dedicated as a national cemetery by President Lincoln in a two-minute speech that was to become immortal. At the time of its delivery the speech was relegated to the inside pages of the papers, while a two-hour address by Edward Everett, the leading orator of the time, caught the headlines.

The following is the text of the address revised by President Lincoln from his own notes:

Fourscore and seven years ago our fathers brought forth on this continent a new nation conceived in liberty and dedicated to the proposition that all men are created equal. Now we are engaged in a great civil war testing whether that nation, or any nation so conceived and so dedicated, can long endure. We are met on a great battlefield of that war. We have come to dedicate a portion of that field as a final resting-place for those who here gave their lives that that nation might live. It is altogether fitting and proper that we should do this. But, in a larger sense, we cannot dedicate, we cannot consecrate, we cannot hallow this ground. The brave men, living and dead, who struggled here have consecrated it far above our poor power to add or detract. The world will little note nor long remember what we say here, but it can never forget what they did here. It is for us the living rather to be dedicated here to the unfinished work which they who fought here have thus far so nobly advanced. It is rather for us to be here dedicated to the great task remaining before us—that from these honored dead we take increased devotion to that cause for which they gave the last full measure of devotion—that we here highly resolve that these dead shall not have died in vain, that this nation under God shall have a new birth of freedom, and that government of the people, by the people, for the people shall not perish from the earth.

Slavery in the United States

Source: The Reader's Companion to American History.

The Institution of Slavery

Slavery has been of signal importance in American history. During the antebellum period, it undergirded the nation's economy, increasingly dominated its politics, and finally led to civil war between North and South. After that war, the legacy of slavery continued to shape much of American history, from the struggle over Reconstruction in the 1860s and 1870s to the struggle over civil rights a century later.

Forced labor emerged in the American colonies, as it did elsewhere in the New World, to meet a pervasive labor shortage that resulted when settlers sought commercial exploitation of agricultural staples (primarily tobacco in the Upper South and rice in the Lower South) in areas of low population density. Although twenty Africans were sold to settlers in Virginia as early as 1619, throughout most of the seventeenth century white indentured servants were far more numerous in the English mainland colonies than African slaves. Only after 1680, when the flow of indentured migrants from Europe diminished, did European servitude increasingly give way to African slavery,. By the middle of the eighteenth century, slavery existed in all thirteen colonies and formed the heart of the agricultural labor system in the southern colonies.

In the years following the American Revolution, slavery, which had never been so prevalent or economically important in the North as in the South, became the South's "peculiar institution." Between 1774 and 1804 all the northern states undertook to abolish slavery. In some states emancipation was immediate, but more often—as in New York and New Jersey—it was gradual, freeing slaves born after passage of the state's emancipation act when they reached a given age (usually in their twenties). But despite widespread questioning of its morality and a proliferation of private manumissions in the Upper South during the revolutionary era, bondage actually expanded in the southern states. The spread of cotton production following the invention of the cotton gin in 1793 sharply increased the demand for slave labor and made possible the emergence of a vast new slave empire as southerners moved west. At the outbreak of the Revolution, the United States contained about half a million slaves, North and South; on the eve of the Civil War the country held almost 4 million slaves, confined entirely to the South.

Southern slavery was highly diverse. Slaveholdings varied according to size, location, and crops produced. Slavery in cities differed substantially from that in the countryside. Masters exhibited varying temperaments and used diverse methods to run their farms and plantations. Slaves served as skilled craftsmen, preachers, nurses, drivers, and mill workers, as well as field hands and house servants.

Despite these variations, southern slavery displayed some distinctive features. Unlike slavery in the rest of the New World, which depended on the continued importation of Africans, that in the southern United States was self-sustaining: during the half century after the end of legal importation in 1808, the slave population more than tripled. One consequence of this natural population growth was an equal ratio of males to females that—in contrast to the male preponderance in slave societies heavily dependent on imports from Africa—facilitated the formation of strong families. Another was the emergence of a slave population, that, despite its distinctive cultural norms, was increasingly American in birth and character. Slaves adopted the religion of their masters, for example, but adapted it to their own particular needs. In short, Africans became African-Americans.

Equally important was the moderate ratio of slaves to nonslaves, which set the South off both from societies in which slavery was legal but slaves were few and from Caribbean countries like Haiti and Jamaica, where slaves formed over 90 percent of the population, lived on immense estates with hundreds of other slaves, and rarely saw their owners. Throughout the antebellum period, slaves constituted about one-third of the southern population. Most lived on large farms and small plantations—three-quarters on holdings with fewer than fifty slaves—with resident masters who took an active role in directing them and were committed to slavery not just as an economic investment but as a way of life.

The slave-master relationship was intense and unstable. Slaves strove mightily to improve their conditions, sometimes by running away or striking back at hated individuals but more often by focusing on their families, friends, and churches. Although slaves were able to secure a measure of social autonomy in their quarters, that autonomy was severely limited by the masters' pervasive interference in their lives. Owners held Bible readings, nursed the sick, provided material conditions that were relatively high by international standards, and prided themselves on caring for their "people." But they (and their overseers) subjected the slaves to countless arbitrary regulations, resorted frequently to the lash, took sexual liberties with slave women, separated family members more often than they admitted, and strove to keep their human property in a state of complete dependence.

The unique sectional nature of antebellum slavery led to an increasingly bitter political struggle between North and South that culminated in civil war. A militant abolitionist movement, predicated on the sinfulness of slaveholding, emerged in the 1830s. Far more persuasive to most northerners was the "free-labor" argument that slavery was backward, inefficient, and socially degrading and must not be allowed to expand. Southern spokesmen responded with elaborate arguments in defense of slavery, including pseudoscientific demonstrations that blacks were unfit for freedom, reminders that the nation's economic well-being depended on slave labor, assertions that the Bible itself sanctioned the enslavement of the "sons of Ham," and claims that slavery produced a more humane and harmonious social order than the exploitative free-labor system of Great Britain and the North. From the late 1840s, the controversy over slavery increasingly dominated national politics. Finally, Abraham Lincoln's election to the presidency in 1860 on a free-labor Republican platform plunged the country into a secession crisis and civil war as southern politicians defended to the end their peculiar institution.

The chief casualty of the war to preserve slavery was slavery itself. Under the combined pressure of military necessity, growing northern antislavery sentiment, and the self-liberation of slaves who deserted in droves as federal troops neared, northern war aims, originally limited to preserving the Union, evolved to include the destruction of slavery. After Lincoln issued the Emancipation Proclamation that took effect on January 1, 1863, it became clear that northern victory would mean the end of slavery. The Thirteenth Amendment to the Constitution, ratified in 1865, provided legal confirmation. What should replace slavery, however, remained unanswered and would emerge as the primary issue of Reconstruction.

Slave Trade

The Atlantic slave trade began in the fifteenth century incidental to the Portuguese exploration of the African coast. Although trade in slaves dates back to ancient times, the Atlantic trade was marked by its westward direction, huge volume, long duration of the crossing, and racial character. Europe and the Iberian islands made the first imports; not until the second half of the sixteenth century did Latin America become the major market.

Dutch, French, and English colonization in America opened new markets for slave traders. The practice of importing labor from distant Africa sprang from the colonists' failure to develop a work force among Native Americans and white immigrants. Colonists, finding that Africans were cheap and relatively immune to tropical diseases, rationalized slavery on grounds that blacks were racially inferior.

Although the Dutch introduced the first Africans in North America in 1619, only about 20,500 had arrived by 1700. But the expansion of staple agriculture in the eighteenth century, especially tobacco, rice, and indigo, created a rising demand for slave labor: these crops required the performance of many manual tasks and a force that could be relied on to work through the long growing season.

Importation of Africans into the present United States occurred during a relatively short span of time. Only about one-third of the total arrived before 1760, more than one-half in the next half century, and a large influx—over one-sixth—in the decade before importation was abolished in 1808. Perhaps a thousand a year were brought in illegally over the next half century. Total imports, including those into Louisiana after 1761, amounted to some 600,000 persons—about 6 percent of the whole transatlantic traffic.

West Africa, stretching from the Senegal River through the Congo region, provided most of the slave trade's victims. Contrary to some historians, the West Indies did not ship many slaves to North America. A study of Virginia imports, 1727–1769, found that only about a tenth arrived from the West Indies, and another study, of South Carolina imports, 1735–1775, found that a seventh came from there. Most slaves entering the American mainland came directly from Africa, without the "seasoning" in the West Indies described by some writers.

The antebellum argument that New England slavers fastened the practice on the South is a myth. To the contrary, British ships from London, Bristol, and Liverpool introduced most of the slaves, with New England vessels contributing only in a small way to mainland trade.

The leading North American carrier was Newport, the fifth largest colonial port. Rhode Islanders, who were at a disadvantage competing with the more advanced economies of Europe in textiles, metalwares, and guns, had one product of superior quality—the rum they distilled. Often trading the liquor directly with Africans instead of Europeans, Rhode Islanders successfully plied the trade for a century, transporting over 106,000 Africans by 1808.

Rhode Island slavers supplied West Indian markets in far greater proportion than those on the mainland. Before the American Revolution Barbados was their most important destination, and after 1783 Cuba took half of their slave cargoes. The mainland market never averaged more than a third of the Rhode Island trade. New York, which sent out 151 voyages, and other ports, including Boston, Philadelphia, and Charleston, shared in transporting slaves. In general, southerners did not engage in the carrying business.

South Carolina and Virginia were the main markets, the first receiving about twenty thousand slaves between 1735 and 1775, and the second about the same number between 1699 and 1775. The trade virtually ceased during the American Revolution, but South Carolina afterward intermittently imported slaves in large numbers until 1808.

The Middle Passage, as the trip across the Atlantic was called, was undoubtedly horrible, with the frightened Africans mercilessly shackled, stowed, and sometimes cruelly handled and driven to suicide. Modern investigators, however, have lightened a little the grim picture painted by abolitionists by pointing out that traders had a financial stake in delivering slaves alive and healthy. It has been shown that white mortality on ocean voyages, especially in the tropics, was also heavy. Rhode Island averaged a 12 percent loss of slaves, higher than the English rate.

The slave trade came under attack in the egalitarian and anti-British atmosphere of the American Revolution. But in deference to certain objectors, drafters of the Declaration of Independence dropped a proposed condemnation of the practice in that document, and the Framers of the Constitution compromised on the issue. It was agreed that the trade could be abolished as early as 1808, an agreement that was fulfilled with a minimum of dissent. Efforts to end the subsequent illegal traffic were hampered for over half a century by southern objections as well as friction with the British, some of whom were crusading to suppress the traffic entirely. During the Civil War, with southerners out of Congress and an antislavery administration in power, the United States signed a treaty with Great Britain that led to ending the traffic.

The Constitution did not contemplate a ban on interstate slave trading, leaving the issue to the states. The federal government, however, prohibited trade in the District of Columbia and set regulations regarding the size of ships used in coastal trade. The exhaustion of soil in the older states, expansion of the cotton kingdom, and suppression of the foreign trade combined to encourage domestic trading. Many slaves migrated westward with their masters, and others were sold through a system that was well established by the early nineteenth century. The seaboard and border states exported an estimated twenty-five thousand slaves a year, with Virginia the largest resource.

Large-scale traders in the Upper South maintained agencies and representatives in the Lower South. Although water transport was used, slaves more commonly were marched overland, in coffles, to markets where they commanded prices that at least quadrupled between 1800 and 1860. At first only erratically regulated by the states and then unregulated altogether by 1850, the trade led to the breakup of families, which became the particular target of antislavery writers like Harriet Beecher Stowe. □

The Early Congresses

At the urging of Massachusetts and Virginia, the First Continental Congress met in Philadelphia on Sept. 5, 1774, and was attended by representatives of all the colonies except Georgia. Patrick Henry of Virginia declared: "The distinctions between Pennsylvanians, New Yorkers and New Englanders are no more. I am not a Virginian but an American." This Congress, which adjourned Oct. 26, 1774, passed intercolonial resolutions calling for extensive boycott by the colonies against British trade.

The following year, most of the delegates from the colonies were chosen by popular election to attend the Second Continental Congress, which assembled in Philadelphia on May 10. As war had already begun between the colonies and England, the chief problems before the Congress were the procuring of military supplies, the establishment of an army and proper defenses, the issuing of continental bills of credit, etc. On June 15, 1775, George Washington was elected to command the Continental army. Congress adjourned Dec. 12, 1776.

Other Continental Congresses were held in Baltimore (1776–77), Philadelphia (1777), Lancaster, Pa. (1777), York, Pa. (1777–78), and Philadelphia (1778–81).

In 1781, the Articles of Confederation, although establishing a league of the thirteen states rather than a strong central government, provided for the continuance of Congress. Known thereafter as the Congress of the Confederation, it held sessions in Philadelphia (1781–83), Princeton, N.J. (1783), Annapolis, Md. (1783–84), and Trenton, N.J. (1784). Five sessions were held in New York City between the years 1785 and 1789.

The Congress of the United States, established by the ratification of the Constitution, held its first meeting on March 4, 1789, in New York City. Several sessions of Congress were held in Philadelphia, and the first meeting in Washington, D.C., was on Nov. 17, 1800.

Presidents of the Continental Congresses

Name	Elected	Brith and Death Dates	Name	Elected	Birth and Death Dates
Peyton Randolph, Va.	9/5/1774	c.1721–1775	John Hanson, Md.	11/5/1781	1715–1783
Henry Middleton, S.C.	10/22/1774	1717–1784	Elias Boudinot, N.J.	11/4/1782	1740–1821
Peyton Randolph, Va.	5/10/1775	c.1721–1775	Thomas Mifflin, Pa.	11/3/1783	1744–1800
John Hancock, Mass.	5/24/1775	1737–1793	Richard Henry Lee, Va.	11/30/1784	1732–1794
Henry Laurens, S.C.	11/1/1777	1724–1792	John Hancock, Mass.[1]	11/23/1785	1737–1793
John Jay, N.Y.	12/10/1778	1745–1829	Nathaniel Gorham, Mass.	6/6/1786	1738–1796
Samuel Huntington, Conn.	9/28/1779	1731–1796	Arthur St. Clair, Pa.	2/2/1787	1734–1818
Thomas McKean, Del.	7/10/1781	1734–1817	Cyrus Griffin, Va.	1/22/1788	1748–1810

1. Resigned May 29, 1786, never having served, because of continued illness.

The Great Seal of the U.S.

On July 4, 1776, the Continental Congress appointed a committee consisting of Benjamin Franklin, John Adams, and Thomas Jefferson "to bring in a device for a seal of the United States of America." After many delays, a verbal description of a design by William Barton was finally approved by Congress on June 20, 1782. The seal shows an American bald eagle with a ribbon in its mouth bearing the device *E pluribus unum* (One out of many). In its talons are the arrows of war and an olive branch of peace. On the reverse side it shows an unfinished pyramid with an eye (the eye of Providence) above it. Although this description was adopted in 1782, the first drawing was not made until four years later, and no die has ever been cut.

The American's Creed

William Tyler Page

"I believe in the United States of America as a government of the people, by the people, for the people; whose just powers are derived from the consent of the governed; a democracy in a republic; a sovereign Nation of many sovereign States; a perfect union, one and inseparable; established upon those principles of freedom, equality, justice, and humanity for which American patriots sacrificed their lives and fortunes.

"I therefore believe it is my duty to my country to love it, to support its Constitution, to obey its laws, to respect its flag, and to defend it against all enemies."

NOTE: William Tyler Page, Clerk of the U.S. House of Representatives, wrote "The American's Creed" in 1917. It was accepted by the House on behalf of the American people on April 3, 1918.

U.S. Capitol

When the French architect and engineer Maj. Pierre L'Enfant first began to lay out the plans for a new Federal city (now Washington, D.C.), he noted that Jenkins' Hill, overlooking the area, seemed to be "a pedestal waiting for a monument." It was here that the U.S. Capitol would be built. The basic structure as we know it today evolved over a period of more than 150 years. In 1792 a competition was held for the design of a capitol building. Dr. William Thornton, a physician and amateur architect, submitted the winning plan, a simple, low-lying structure of classical proportions with a shallow dome. Later, internal modifications were made by Benjamin Henry Latrobe. After the building was burned by the British in 1814, Latrobe and architect Charles Bulfinch were responsible for its reconstruction. Finally, under Thomas Walter, who was Architect of the Capitol from 1851 to 1865, the House and Senate wings and the imposing cast iron dome topped with the Statue of Freedom were added, and the Capitol assumed the form we see today. It was in the old Senate chamber that Daniel Webster cried out, "Liberty and Union, now and forever, one and inseparable!" In Statuary Hall, which used to be the old House chamber, a small disk on the floor marks the spot where John Quincy Adams was fatally stricken after more than 50 years of service to his country. A whisper from one side of this room can be heard across the vast space of the hall. Visitors can see the original Supreme Court chamber a floor below the Rotunda.

In addition to its historical association, the Capitol Building is also a vast artistic treasure house. The works of such famous artists as Gilbert Stuart, Rembrandt Peale, and John Trumbull are displayed on the walls. The Great Rotunda, with its 180-foot- (54.9-m-) high dome, is decorated with a massive fresco by Constantino Brumidi, which extends some 300 feet (90 m) in circumference. Throughout the building are many paintings of events in U.S. history and sculptures of outstanding Americans. The Capitol itself is situated on a 68-acre (27.5-ha) park designed by the 19th-century landscape architect Frederick Law Olmsted. There are free guided tours of the Capitol, which include admission to the House and Senate galleries. Those who wish to visit the visitors' gallery in either wing without taking the tour may obtain passes from their Senators or Congressmen. Visitors may ride on the monorail subway that joins the House and Senate wings of the Capitol with the Congressional office buildings.

Washington Monument

Construction of this magnificent Washington, D.C., monument, which draws some two million visitors a year, took nearly a century of planning, building, and controversy. Provision for a large equestrian statue of George Washington was made in the original city plan, but the project was soon dropped. After Washington's death it was taken up again, and a number of false starts and changes of design were made. Finally, in 1848, work was begun on the monument that stands today. The design, by architect Robert Mills, then featured an ornate base. In 1854, however, political squabbling and a lack of money brought construction to a halt. Work was resumed in 1880, and the monument was completed in 1884 and opened to the public in 1888. The tapered shaft, faced with white marble and rising from walls 15 feet thick (4.6 m) at the base was modeled after the obelisks of ancient Egypt. The monument, one of the tallest masonry constructions in the world, stands just over 555 feet (169 m). Memorial stones from the 50 States, foreign countries, and organizations line the interior walls. The top, reached only by elevator, commands a panoramic view of the city.

The Liberty Bell

The Liberty Bell was cast in England in 1752 for the Pennsylvania Statehouse (now named Independence Hall) in Philadelphia. It was recast in Philadelphia in 1753. It is inscribed with the words, "Proclaim liberty throughout all the land unto all the inhabitants thereof" (Lev. 25:10). The bell was rung on July 8, 1776, for the first public reading of the Declaration of Independence. Hidden in Allentown during the British occupation of Philadelphia, it was replaced in Independence Hall in 1778. The bell cracked on July 8, 1835, while tolling the death of Chief Justice John Marshall. In 1976 the Liberty Bell was moved to a special exhibition building near Independence Hall.

Arlington National Cemetery

Arlington National Cemetery occupies 612 acres in Virginia on the Potomac River, directly opposite Washington. This land was part of the estate of John Parke Custis, Martha Washington's son. His son, George Washington Parke Custis, built the mansion which later became the home of Robert E. Lee. In 1864, Arlington became a military cemetery. More than 230,000 servicemembers and their dependents are buried there. Expansion of the cemetery began in 1966, using a 180-acre tract of land directly east of the present site.

In 1921, an Unknown American Soldier of World War I was buried in the cemetery; the monument at the Tomb was opened to the public without ceremony in 1932. Two additional Unknowns, one from World War II and one from the Korean War, were buried May 30, 1958. The Unknown Serviceman of Vietnam was buried on May 28, 1984. The inscription carved on the Tomb of the Unknowns reads:

HERE RESTS IN
HONORED GLORY
AN AMERICAN
SOLDIER
KNOWN BUT TO GOD

History of the Flag

Source: Encyclopaedia Britannica.

The first official American flag, the Continental or Grand Union flag, was displayed on Prospect Hill, Jan. 1, 1776, in the American lines besieging Boston. It had 13 alternate red and white stripes, with the British Union Jack in the upper left corner.

On June 14, 1777, the Continental Congress adopted the design for a new flag, which actually was the Continental flag with the red cross of St. George and the white cross of St. Andrew replaced on the blue field by 13 stars, one for each state. No rule was made as to the arrangement of the stars, and while they were usually shown in a circle, there were various other designs. It is uncertain when the new flag was first flown, but its first official announcement is believed to have been on Sept. 3, 1777.

The first public assertion that Betsy Ross made the first Stars and Stripes appeared in a paper read before the Historical Society of Pennsylvania on March 14, 1870, by William J. Canby, a grandson. However, Mr. Canby on later investigation found no official documents of any action by Congress on the flag before June 14, 1777. Betsy Ross's own story, according to her daughter, was that Washington, Robert Morris, and George Ross, as representatives of Congress, visited her in Philadelphia in June 1776, showing her a rough draft of the flag and asking her if she could make one. However, the only actual record of the manufacture of flags by Betsy Ross is a voucher in Harrisburg, Pa., for 14 pounds and some shillings for flags for the Pennsylvania navy.

On Jan. 13, 1794, Congress voted to add two stars and two stripes to the flag in recognition of the admission of Vermont and Kentucky to the Union. By 1818, there were 20 states in the Union, and as it was obvious that the flag would soon become unwieldly, Congress voted April 18 to return to the original 13 stripes and to indicate the admission of a new state simply by the addition of a star the following July 4. The 49th star, for Alaska, was added July 4, 1959; and the 50th star, for Hawaii, was added July 4, 1960.

The first Confederate flag, adopted in 1861 by the Confederate convention in Montgomery, Ala., was called the Stars and Bars; but because of its similarity in colors to the American flag, there was much confusion in the Battle of Bull Run. To remedy this situation, Gen. G. T. Beauregard suggested a battle flag, which was used by the Southern armies throughout the war. The flag consisted of a red field on which was placed a blue cross of St. Andrew separated from the field by a white fillet and adorned with 13[1] white stars for the Confederate states. In May 1863, at Richmond, an official flag was adopted by the Confederate Congress. This flag was white and twice as long as wide; the union, two-thirds the width of the flag, contained the battle flag designed for Gen. Beauregard. A broad transverse stripe of red was added Feb. 4, 1865, so that the flag might not be mistaken for a signal of truce.

1. 11 states formally seceded, and unofficial groups in Kentucky and Missouri adopted ordinances of secession. On this basis, these two states were admitted to the Confederacy, although the official state governments remained in the Union.

The Pledge of Allegiance[1] to the Flag

"I pledge allegiance to the Flag of the United States of America, and to the Republic for which it stands, one Nation under God,[2] indivisible, with liberty and justice for all."

1. The original pledge was published in the Sept. 8, 1892, issue of *The Youth's Companion* in Boston. For years, the authorship was in dispute between James B. Upham and Francis Bellamy of the magazine's staff. In 1939, after a study of the controversy, the United States Flag Association decided that authorship be credited to Bellamy. 2. The phrase "under God" was added to the pledge on June 14, 1954.

The Statue of Liberty

The Statue of Liberty ("Liberty Enlightening the World") is a 225-ton, steel-reinforced copper female figure, 152 ft in height, facing the ocean from Liberty[1] Island in New York Harbor. The right hand holds aloft a torch, and the left hand carries a tablet upon which is inscribed: "July IV MDCCLXXVI."

The statue was designed by Fredéric Auguste Bartholdi of Alsace as a gift to the United States from the people of France to memorialize the alliance of the two countries in the American Revolution and their abiding friendship. The French people contributed the $250,000 cost.

The 150-foot pedestal was designed by Richard M. Hunt and built by Gen. Charles P. Stone, both Americans. It contains steel underpinnings designed by Alexander Eiffel of France to support the statue. The $270,000 cost was borne by popular subscription in this country. President Grover Cleveland accepted the statue for the United States on Oct. 28, 1886.

On Sept. 26, 1972, President Richard M. Nixon dedicated the American Museum of Immigration, housed in structural additions to the base of the statue. In 1984 scaffolding went up for a major restoration and the torch was extinguished on July 4. It was relit with much ceremony July 4, 1986 to mark its centennial.

On a tablet inside the pedestal is engraved the following sonnet, written by Emma Lazarus (1849–1887):

The New Colossus

Not like the brazen giant of Greek fame.
With conquering limbs astride from land to land;
Here at our sea-washed, sunset gates shall stand
A mighty woman with a torch, whose flame
Is the imprisoned lightning, and her name
Mother of Exiles. From her beacon-hand
Glows world-wide welcome; her mild eyes command
The air-bridged harbor that twin cities frame.
"Keep, ancient lands, your storied pomp!" cries she
With silent lips. "Give me your tired, your poor,
Your huddled masses yearning to breathe free,
The wretched refuse of your teeming shore.
Send these, the homeless, tempest-tost to me,
I lift my lamp beside the golden door!"

1. Called Bedloe's Island prior to 1956.

Presidents

Name and (party)[1]	Term	State of birth	Born	Died	Religion	Age at inaug.	Age at death
1. Washington (F)[2]	1789–1797	Va.	2/22/1732	12/14/1799	Episcopalian	57	67
2. J. Adams (F)	1797–1801	Mass.	10/30/1735	7/4/1826	Unitarian	61	90
3. Jefferson (DR)	1801–1809	Va.	4/13/1743	7/4/1826	Deist	57	83
4. Madison (DR)	1809–1817	Va.	3/16/1751	6/28/1836	Episcopalian	57	85
5. Monroe (DR)	1817–1825	Va.	4/28/1758	7/4/1831	Episcopalian	58	73
6. J. Q. Adams (DR)	1825–1829	Mass.	7/11/1767	2/23/1848	Unitarian	57	80
7. Jackson (D)	1829–1837	S.C.	3/15/1767	6/8/1845	Presbyterian	61	78
8. Van Buren (D)	1837–1841	N.Y.	12/5/1782	7/24/1862	Reformed Dutch	54	79
9. W. H. Harrison (W)[3]	1841	Va.	2/9/1773	4/4/1841	Episcopalian	68	68
10. Tyler (W)	1841–1845	Va.	3/29/1790	1/18/1862	Episcopalian	51	71
11. Polk (D)	1845–1849	N.C.	11/2/1795	6/15/1849	Methodist	49	53
12. Taylor (W)[3]	1849–1850	Va.	11/24/1784	7/9/1850	Episcopalian	64	65
13. Fillmore (W)	1850–1853	N.Y.	1/7/1800	3/8/1874	Unitarian	50	74
14. Pierce (D)	1853–1857	N.H.	11/23/1804	10/8/1869	Episcopalian	48	64
15. Buchanan (D)	1857–1861	Pa.	4/23/1791	6/1/1868	Presbyterian	65	77
16. Lincoln (R)[4]	1861–1865	Ky.	2/12/1809	4/15/1865	Liberal	52	56
17. A. Johnson (U)[5]	1865–1869	N.C.	12/29/1808	7/31/1875	([6])	56	66
18. Grant (R)	1869–1877	Ohio	4/27/1822	7/23/1885	Methodist	46	63
19. Hayes (R)	1877–1881	Ohio	10/4/1822	1/17/1893	Methodist	54	70
20. Garfield (R)[4]	1881	Ohio	11/19/1831	9/19/1881	Disciples of Christ	49	49
21. Arthur (R)	1881–1885	Vt.	10/5/1830	11/18/1886	Episcopalian	50	56
22. Cleveland (D)	1885–1889	N.J.	3/18/1837	6/24/1908	Presbyterian	47	71
23. B. Harrison (R)	1889–1893	Ohio	8/20/1833	3/13/1901	Presbyterian	55	67
24. Cleveland (D)[7]	1893–1897	—	—	—	—	55	—
25. McKinley (R)[4]	1897–1901	Ohio	1/29/1843	9/14/1901	Methodist	54	58
26. T. Roosevelt (R)	1901–1909	N.Y.	10/27/1858	1/6/1919	Reformed Dutch	42	60
27. Taft (R)	1909–1913	Ohio	9/15/1857	3/8/1930	Unitarian	51	72
28. Wilson (D)	1913–1921	Va.	12/28/1856	2/3/1924	Presbyterian	56	67
29. Harding (R)[3]	1921–1923	Ohio	11/2/1865	8/2/1923	Baptist	55	57
30. Coolidge (R)	1923–1929	Vt.	7/4/1872	1/5/1933	Congregationalist	51	60
31. Hoover (R)	1929–1933	Iowa	8/10/1874	10/20/1964	Quaker	54	90
32. F. D. Roosevelt (D)[3]	1933–1945	N.Y.	1/30/1882	4/12/1945	Episcopalian	51	63
33. Truman (D)	1945–1953	Mo.	5/8/1884	12/26/1972	Baptist	60	88
34. Eisenhower (R)	1953–1961	Tex.	10/14/1890	3/28/1969	Presbyterian	62	78
35. Kennedy (D)[4]	1961–1963	Mass.	5/29/1917	11/22/1963	Roman Catholic	43	46
36. L. B. Johnson (D)	1963–1969	Tex.	8/27/1908	1/22/1973	Disciples of Christ	55	64
37. Nixon (R)[8]	1969–1974	Calif.	1/9/1913	—	Quaker	56	—
38. Ford (R)	1974–1977	Neb.	7/14/1913	—	Episcopalian	61	—
39. Carter (D)	1977–1981	Ga.	10/1/1924	—	Southern Baptist	52	—
40. Reagan (R)	1981–1989	Ill.	2/6/1911	—	Disciples of Christ	69	—
41. Bush (R)	1989–1993	Mass.	6/12/24	—	Episcopalian	64	—
42. Clinton (D)	1993–	Ark.	8/19/46	—	Baptist	46	—

1. F—Federalist; DR—Democratic-Republican; D—Democratic; W—Whig; R—Republican; U—Union. 2. No party for first election. The party system in the U.S. made its appearance during Washington's first term. 3. Died in office. 4. Assassinated in office. 5. The Republican National Convention of 1864 adopted the name Union Party. It renominated Lincoln for President; for Vice President it nominated Johnson, a War Democrat. Although frequently listed as a Republican Vice President and President, Johnson undoubtedly considered himself strictly a member of the Union Party. When that party broke apart after 1868, he returned to the Democratic Party. 6. Johnson was not a professed church member; however, he admired the Baptist principles of church government. 7. Second nonconsecutive term. 8. Resigned Aug. 9, 1974.

Vice Presidents

Name and (party)[1]	Term	State of birth	Birth and death dates	President served under
1. John Adams (F)[2]	1789–1797	Massachusetts	1735–1826	Washington
2. Thomas Jefferson (DR)	1797–1801	Virginia	1743–1826	J. Adams
3. Aaron Burr (DR)	1801–1805	New Jersey	1756–1836	Jefferson
4. George Clinton (DR)[3]	1805–1812	New York	1739–1812	Jefferson and Madison
5. Elbridge Gerry (DR)[3]	1813–1814	Massachusetts	1744–1814	Madison
6. Daniel D. Tompkins (DR)	1817–1825	New York	1774–1825	Monroe
7. John C. Calhoun[4]	1825–1832	South Carolina	1782–1850	J. Q. Adams and Jackson
8. Martin Van Buren (D)	1833–1837	New York	1782–1862	Jackson
9. Richard M. Johnson (D)	1837–1841	Kentucky	1780–1850	Van Buren
10. John Tyler (W)[5]	1841	Virginia	1790–1862	W. H. Harrison
11. George M. Dallas (D)	1845–1849	Pennsylvania	1792–1864	Polk
12. Millard Fillmore (W)[5]	1849–1850	New York	1800–1874	Taylor
13. William R. King (D)[3]	1853	North Carolina	1786–1853	Pierce
14. John C. Breckinridge (D)	1857–1861	Kentucky	1821–1875	Buchanan

Name and (party)[1]	Term	State of birth	Birth and death dates	President served under
15. Hannibal Hamlin (R)	1861–1865	Maine	1809–1891	Lincoln
16. Andrew Johnson (U)[5]	1865	North Carolina	1808–1875	Lincoln
17. Schuyler Colfax (R)	1869–1873	New York	1823–1885	Grant
18. Henry Wilson (R)[3]	1873–1875	New Hampshire	1812–1875	Grant
19. William A. Wheeler (R)	1877–1881	New York	1819–1887	Hayes
20. Chester A. Arthur (R)[5]	1881	Vermont	1830–1886	Garfield
21. Thomas A. Hendricks (D)[3]	1885	Ohio	1819–1885	Cleveland
22. Levi P. Morton (R)	1889–1893	Vermont	1824–1920	B. Harrison
23. Adlai E. Stevenson (D)	1893–1897	Kentucky	1835–1914	Cleveland
24. Garrett A. Hobart (R)[3]	1897–1899	New Jersey	1844–1899	McKinley
25. Theodore Roosevelt (R)[5]	1901	New York	1858–1919	McKinley
26. Charles W. Fairbanks (R)	1905–1909	Ohio	1852–1918	T. Roosevelt
27. James S. Sherman (R)[3]	1909–1912	New York	1855–1912	Taft
28. Thomas R. Marshall (D)	1913–1921	Indiana	1854–1925	Wilson
29. Calvin Coolidge (R)[5]	1921–1923	Vermont	1872–1933	Harding
30. Charles G. Dawes (R)	1925–1929	Ohio	1865–1951	Coolidge
31. Charles Curtis (R)	1929–1933	Kansas	1860–1936	Hoover
32. John N. Garner (D)	1933–1941	Texas	1868–1967	F. D. Roosevelt
33. Henry A. Wallace (D)	1941–1945	Iowa	1888–1965	F. D. Roosevelt
34. Harry S. Truman (D)[5]	1945	Missouri	1884–1972	F. D. Roosevelt
35. Alben W. Barkley (D)	1949–1953	Kentucky	1877–1956	Truman
36. Richard M. Nixon (R)	1953–1961	California	1913–	Eisenhower
37. Lyndon B. Johnson (D)[5]	1961–1963	Texas	1908–1973	Kennedy
38. Hubert H. Humphrey (D)	1965–1969	South Dakota	1911–1978	Johnson
39. Spiro T. Agnew (R)[6]	1969–1973	Maryland	1918–	Nixon
40. Gerald R. Ford (R)[7]	1973–1974	Nebraska	1913–	Nixon
41. Nelson A. Rockefeller (R)[8]	1974–1977	Maine	1908–1979	Ford
42. Walter F. Mondale (D)	1977–1981	Minnesota	1928–	Carter
43. George Bush (R)	1981–1989	Massachusetts	1924–	Reagan
44. J. Danforth Quayle (R)	1989–1993	Indiana	1947–	Bush
45. Albert A. Gore, Jr. (D)	1993–	Washington, D.C.	1948–	Clinton

1. F—Federalist; DR—Democratic-Republican; D—Democratic; W—Whig; R—Republican; U—Union. 2. No party for first election. The party system in the U.S. made its appearance during Washington's first term as President. 3. Died in office. 4. Democratic-Republican with J. Q. Adams; Democratic with Jackson. Calhoun resigned in 1832 to become a U.S. Senator. 5. Succeeded to presidency on death of President. 6. Resigned Oct. 10, 1973, after pleading no contest to Federal income tax evasion charges. 7. Nominated by Nixon on Oct. 12, 1973, under provisions of 25th Amendment. Confirmed by Congress on Dec. 6, 1973, and was sworn in same day. He became President Aug. 9, 1974, upon Nixon's resignation. 8. Nominated by Ford Aug. 20, 1974; confirmed by Congress on Dec. 19, 1974, and was sworn in same day.

Burial Places of the Presidents

President	Burial place	President	Burial place
Washington	Mt. Vernon, Va.	Grant	New York City
J. Adams	Quincy, Mass.	Hayes	Fremont, Ohio
Jefferson	Charlottesville, Va.	Garfield	Cleveland, Ohio
Madison	Montpelier Station, Va.	Arthur	Albany, N.Y.
Monroe	Richmond, Va.	Cleveland	Princeton, N.J.
J. Q. Adams	Quincy, Mass.	B. Harrison	Indianapolis
Jackson	The Hermitage, nr. Nashville, Tenn.	McKinley	Canton, Ohio
		T. Roosevelt	Oyster Bay, N.Y.
Van Buren	Kinderhook, N.Y.	Taft	Arlington National Cemetery
W. H. Harrison	North Bend, Ohio	Wilson	Washington National Cathedral
Tyler	Richmond, Va.	Harding	Marion, Ohio
Polk	Nashville, Tenn.	Coolidge	Plymouth, Vt.
Taylor	Louisville, Ky.	Hoover	West Branch, Iowa
Fillmore	Buffalo, N.Y.	F. D. Roosevelt	Hyde Park, N.Y.
Pierce	Concord, N.H.	Truman	Independence, Mo.
Buchanan	Lancaster, Pa.	Eisenhower	Abilene, Kan.
Lincoln	Springfield, Ill.	Kennedy	Arlington National Cemetery
A. Johnson	Greeneville, Tenn.	L. B. Johnson	Stonewall, Tex.

"In God We Trust"

"In God We Trust" first appeared on U.S. coins after April 22, 1864, when Congress passed an act authorizing the coinage of a 2-cent piece bearing this motto. Thereafter, Congress extended its use to other coins. On July 30, 1956, it became the national motto.

Wives and Children of the Presidents

President	Wife's name	Year an place of wife's birth	Married	Wife died	Children of President[1] Sons	Daughters
Washington	Martha Dandridge Custis	1732, Va.	1759	1802	—	—
John Adams	Abigail Smith	1744, Mass.	1764	1818	3	2
Jefferson	Martha Wayles Skelton	1748, Va.	1772	1782	1	5
Madison	Dorothy "Dolley" Payne Todd	1768, N.C.	1794	1849	—	—
Monroe	Elizabeth "Eliza" Kortright	1768, N.Y.	1786	1830	—	2
J. Q. Adams	Louisa Catherine Johnson	1775, England	1797	1852	3	1
Jackson	Mrs. Rachel Donelson Robards	1767, Va.	1791	1828	—	—
Van Buren	Hannah Hoes	1788, N.Y.	1807	1819	4	—
W. H. Harrison	Anna Symmes	1775, N.J.	1795	1864	6	4
Tyler	Letitia Christian	1790, Va.	1813	1842	3	4
	Julia Gardiner	1820, N.Y.	1844	1889	5	2
Polk	Sarah Childress	1803, Tenn.	1824	1891	—	—
Taylor	Margaret Smith	1788, Md.	1810	1852	1	5
Fillmore	Abigail Powers	1798, N.Y.	1826	1853	1	1
	Caroline Carmichael McIntosh	1813, N.J.	1858	1881	—	—
Pierce	Jane Means Appleton	1806, N.H.	1834	1863	3	—
Buchanan	(Unmarried)	—	—	—	—	—
Lincoln	Mary Todd	1818, Ky.	1842	1882	4	—
A. Johnson	Eliza McCardle	1810, Tenn.	1827	1876	3	2
Grant	Julia Dent	1826, Mo.	1848	1902	3	1
Hayes	Lucy Ware Webb	1831, Ohio	1852	1889	7	1
Garfield	Lucretia Rudolph	1832, Ohio	1858	1918	5	2
Arthur	Ellen Lewis Herndon	1837, Va.	1859	1880	2	1
Cleveland	Frances Folsom	1864, N.Y.	1886	1947	2	3
B. Harrison	Caroline Lavinia Scott	1832, Ohio	1853	1892	1	1
	Mary Scott Lord Dimmick	1858, Pa.	1896	1948	—	1
McKinley	Ida Saxton	1847, Ohio	1871	1907	—	2
T. Roosevelt	Alice Hathaway Lee	1861, Mass.	1880	1884	—	1
	Edith Kermit Carow	1861, Conn.	1886	1948	4	1
Taft	Helen Herron	1861, Ohio	1886	1943	2	1
Wilson	Ellen Louise Axson	1860, Ga.	1885	1914	—	3
	Edith Bolling Galt	1872, Va.	1915	1961	—	—
Harding	Florence Kling DeWolfe	1860, Ohio	1891	1924	—	—
Coolidge	Grace Anna Goodhue	1879, Vt.	1905	1957	2	—
Hoover	Lou Henry	1875, Iowa	1899	1944	2	—
F. D. Roosevelt	Anna Eleanor Roosevelt	1884, N.Y.	1905	1962	5	1
Truman	Bess Wallace	1885, Mo.	1919	1982	—	1
Eisenhower	Mamie Geneva Doud	1896, Iowa	1916	1979	2	—
Kennedy	Jacqueline Lee Bouvier	1929, N.Y.	1953	—	2	1
L. B. Johnson	Claudia Alta "Lady Bird" Taylor	1912, Tex.	1934	—	—	2
Nixon	Thelma Catherine "Pat" Ryan	1912, Nev.	1940	1993	—	2
Ford	Elizabeth "Betty" Bloomer Warren	1918, Ill.	1948	—	3	1
Carter	Rosalynn Smith	1928, Ga.	1946	—	3	1
Reagan	Jane Wyman	1914, Mo.	1940[2]	—	1[3]	1
	Nancy Davis	1921 (?)[4], N.Y.	1952	—	1	1
Bush	Barbara Pierce	1925, N.Y.	1945	—	4	2
Clinton	Hillary Rodham	1946, Ill.	1975	—	—	1

1. Includes children who died in infancy. 2. Divorced in 1948. 3. Adopted. 4. Birthday officially given as 1923 but her high school and college records show 1921 for year of birth.

Elections

How a President Is Nominated and Elected

The National Conventions of both major parties are held during the summer of a presidential-election year. Earlier, each party selects delegates by primaries, conventions, committees, etc.

For their 1992 National Convention, the Republicans allow each state a base of 6 delegates at large; the District of Columbia, 14; Puerto Rico, 14; Guam and the Virgin Islands, 4 each. In addition, each state receives 3 district delegates for each representative it has in the House of Representatives, regardless of political affiliation. This did not apply to the District of Columbia, Puerto Rico, Guam and the Virgin Islands.

Each state is awarded additional delegates at large on the basis of having supported the Republican candidate for President in 1988 and electing Republican candidates for Senator, Governor, and U.S. Representative between 1988 and 1991 inclusive.

The number of delegates at the 1992 convention, to be held in Houston starting August 17, will be 2,206.[1]

Following is the apportionment of delegates:

Alabama	38	Florida	97	Kentucky	35	Montana	20	Ohio	83	Texas	121
Alaska	19	Georgia	52	Louisiana	38	Nebraska	24	Oklahoma	34	Utah	27
Arizona	37	Guam	4	Maine	22	Nevada	21	Oregon	23	Vermont	19
Arkansas	27	Hawaii	14	Maryland	42	N.H.	23	Pa.	90	V.I.	4
California	201	Idaho	22	Mass.	38	N. Jersey	60	P.R.	14	Virginia	54
Colorado	37	Illinois	85	Michigan	72	New Mexico	25	R.I.	15	Washington	35
Connecticut	35	Indiana	51	Minnesota	32	New York	100	S.C.	36	W. Va.	18
Delaware	19	Iowa	23	Mississippi	32	N.C.	57	S.D.	19	Wisconsin	35
D.C.	14	Kansas	30	Missouri	47	N.D.	17	Tennessee	45	Wyoming	20

1. Includes 4 delegates from American Samoa.

The Democrats base the number of delegates on a state's showing in the 1988 and 1990 elections. At the 1992 convention, to be held in New York starting July 13, there will be 4,313[1,2] delegates casting 4,282 votes. Following is the apportionment by states:

Alabama	62	Florida	160	Kentucky	62	Montana	22	Ohio	167	Texas	214
Alaska	18	Georgia	88	Louisiana	69	Nebraska	31	Oklahoma	52	Utah	28
Arizona	47	Guam	10[1]	Maine	30	Nevada	23	Oregon	53	Vermont	19
Arkansas	43	Hawaii	26	Maryland	80	N. H.	24	Pa.	188	V.I.	10[1]
California	382	Idaho	24	Mass.	107	New Jersey	117	P.R.	57	Virginia	92
Colorado	54	Illinois	183	Michigan	148	New Mexico	33	R.I.	28	Washington	80
Connecticut	61	Indiana	86	Minnesota	87	New York	268	S.C.	50	W. Va.	38
Delaware	19	Iowa	57	Mississippi	45	N.C.	93	S.D.	20	Wisconsin	91
D. C.	29	Kansas	42	Missouri	86	N.D.	20	Tennessee	77	Wyoming	19

1. Fractional votes. 2. Includes 22[1] delegates for Democrats Abroad and 10[1] for American Samoa. As of March 26, 1991.

The Conventions

At each convention, a temporary chairman is chosen. After a credentials committee seats the delegates, a permanent chairman is elected. The convention then votes on a platform, drawn up by the platform committee.

By the third or fourth day, presidential nominations begin. The chairman calls the roll of states alphabetically. A state may place a candidate in nomination or yield to another state.

Voting, again alphabetically by roll call of states, begins after all nominations have been made and seconded. A simple majority is required in each party, although this may require many ballots.

Finally, the vice-presidential candidate is selected. Although there is no law saying that the candidates *must* come from different states, it is, practically, necessary for this to be the case. Otherwise, according to the Constitution (*see* Amendment XII), electors from that state could vote for only one of the candidates and would have to cast their other vote for some person of another state. This could result in a presidential candidate's receiving a majority electoral vote and his running mate's failing to.

The Electoral College

The next step in the process is the nomination of electors in each state, according to its laws. These electors must not be Federal office holders. In the November election, the voters cast their votes for electors, not for President. In some states, the ballots include only the names of the presidential and vice-presidential candidates; in others, they include only names of the electors. Nowadays, it is rare for electors to be split between parties. The last such occurrence was in North Carolina in 1968[1]; the last before that, in Tennessee in 1948. On three occasions (1824, 1876, and 1888), the presidential candidate with the largest popular vote failed to obtain an electoral-vote majority.

Each state has as many electors as it has Senators and Representatives. For the 1992 election, the total electors were 538, based on 100 Senators, 435 Representatives, plus 3 electoral votes from the District of Columbia as a result of the 23rd Amendment to the Constitution.

On the first Monday after the second Wednesday in December, the electors cast their votes in their respective state capitols. Constitutionally they may vote for someone other than the party candidate but usually they do not since they are pledged to one party and its candidate on the ballot. Should the presidential or vice-presidential candidate die between the November election and the December meetings, the electors pledged to vote for him could vote for whomever they pleased. However, it seems certain that the national committee would attempt to get an agreement among the state party leaders for a replacement candidate.

The votes of the electors, certified by the states, are sent to Congress, where the president of the Senate opens the certificates and has them counted in the presence of both Houses on January 6. The new President is inaugurated at noon on January 20.

Should no candidate receive a majority of the electoral vote for President, the House of Representatives chooses a President from among the three highest candidates, voting, not as individuals, but as states, with a majority (now 26) needed to elect. Should no vice-presidential candidate obtain the majority, the Senate, voting as individuals, chooses from the highest two.

1. In 1956, 1 of Alabama's 11 electoral votes was cast for Walter B. Jones. In 1960, 6 of Alabama's 11 electoral votes and 1 of Oklahoma's 8 electoral votes were cast for Harry Flood Byrd. (Byrd also received all 8 of Mississippi's electoral votes.)

National Political Conventions Since 1856

Opening date	Party	Where held
June 17, 1856	Republican	Philadelphia
June 2, 1856	Democratic	Cincinnati
May 16, 1860	Republican	Chicago
April 23, 1860	Democratic	Charleston and Baltimore
June 7, 1864	Republican[1]	Baltimore
Aug. 29, 1864	Democratic	Chicago
May 20, 1868	Republican	Chicago
July 4, 1868	Democratic	New York City
June 5, 1872	Republican	Philadelphia
June 9, 1872	Democratic	Baltimore
June 14, 1876	Republican	Cincinnati
June 28, 1876	Democratic	St. Louis
June 2, 1880	Republican	Chicago
June 23, 1880	Democratic	Cincinnati
June 3, 1884	Republican	Chicago
July 11, 1884	Democratic	Chicago
June 19, 1888	Republican	Chicago
June 6, 1888	Democratic	St. Louis
June 7, 1892	Republican	Minneapolis
June 21, 1892	Democratic	Chicago
June 16, 1896	Republican	St. Louis
July 7, 1896	Democratic	Chicago
June 19, 1900	Republican	Philadelphia
July 4, 1900	Democratic	Kansas City
June 21, 1904	Republican	Chicago
July 6, 1904	Democratic	St. Louis
June 16, 1908	Republican	Chicago
July 7, 1908	Democratic	Denver
June 18, 1912	Republican	Chicago
June 25, 1912	Democratic	Baltimore
June 7, 1916	Republican	Chicago
June 14, 1916	Democratic	St. Louis
June 8, 1920	Republican	Chicago
June 28, 1920	Democratic	San Francisco
June 10, 1924	Republican	Cleveland
June 24, 1924[2]	Democratic	New York City
June 12, 1928	Republican	Kansas City
June 26, 1928	Democratic	Houston
June 14, 1932	Republican	Chicago
June 27, 1932	Democratic	Chicago
June 9, 1936	Republican	Cleveland
June 23, 1936	Democratic	Philadelphia
June 24, 1940	Republican	Philadelphia
July 15, 1940	Democratic	Chicago
June 26, 1944	Republican	Chicago
July 19, 1944	Democratic	Chicago
June 21, 1948	Republican	Philadelphia
July 12, 1948	Democratic	Philadelphia
July 17, 1948	([3])	Birmingham
July 22, 1948	Progressive	Philadelphia
July 7, 1952	Republican	Chicago
July 21, 1952	Democratic	Chicago
Aug. 20, 1956	Republican	San Francisco
Aug. 13, 1956	Democratic	Chicago
July 25, 1960	Republican	Chicago
July 11, 1960	Democratic	Los Angeles
July 13, 1964	Republican	San Francisco
Aug. 24, 1964	Democratic	Atlantic City
Aug. 5, 1968	Republican	Miami Beach
Aug. 26, 1968	Democratic	Chicago
July 10, 1972	Democratic	Miami Beach
Aug. 21, 1972	Republican	Miami Beach
July 12, 1976	Democratic	New York City
Aug. 16, 1976	Republican	Kansas City, Mo.
Aug. 11, 1980	Democratic	New York City
July 14, 1980	Republican	Detroit
Aug. 20, 1984	Republican	Dallas
July 16, 1984	Democratic	San Francisco
July 18, 1988	Democratic	Atlanta
Aug. 15, 1988	Republican	New Orleans
July 13, 1992	Democratic	New York City
Aug. 17, 1992	Republican	Houston

1. The Convention adopted name Union party to attract War Democrats and others favoring prosecution of war. 2. In session until July 10, 1924. 3. States' Rights delegates from 13 Southern states.

National Committee Chairmen Since 1944

Chairman and (state)	Term
REPUBLICAN	
Herbert Brownell, Jr. (N.Y.)	1944–46
Carroll Reece (Tenn.)	1946–48
Hugh D. Scott, Jr. (Pa.)	1948–49
Guy G. Gabrielson (N.J.)	1949–52
Arthur E. Summerfield (Mich.)	1952–53
Wesley Roberts (Kan.)	1953–
Leonard W. Hall (N.Y.)	1953–57
Meade Alcorn (Conn.)	1957–59
Thruston B. Morton (Ky.)	1959–61
William E. Miller (N.Y.)	1961–64
Dean Burch (Ariz.)	1964–65
Ray C. Bliss (Ohio)	1965–69
Rogers C. B. Morton (Md.)	1969–71
Robert Dole (Kan.)	1971–73
George H. Bush (Tex.)	1973–74
Mary Louise Smith (Iowa)	1974–77
William E. Brock III (Tenn.)	1977–81
Richard Richards (Utah)	1981–83
Frank J. Fahrenkopf, Jr. (Nevada)	1983–89
Lee Atwater (S.C.)	1989–91
Clayton K. Yeutter (Neb.)	1991–92
Richard Bond (N.Y.)	1992–93
Haley Barbour (Miss.)	1993–
DEMOCRATIC	
Robert E. Hannegan (Mo.)	1944–47
J. Howard McGrath (R.I.)	1947–49
William M. Boyle, Jr. (Mo.)	1949–51
Frank E. McKinney (Ind.)	1951–52
Stephen A. Mitchell (Ill.)	1952–54
Paul M. Butler (Ind.)	1955–60
Henry M. Jackson (Wash.)	1960–61
John M. Bailey (Conn.)	1961–68
Lawrence F. O'Brien (Mass.)	1968–69
Fred R. Harris (Okla.)	1969–70
Lawrence F. O'Brien (Mass.)	1970–72
Jean Westwood (Utah)	1972
Robert S. Strauss (Tex.)	1972–77
Kenneth M. Curtis (Me.)	1977
John C. White (Tex.)	1977–81
Charles T. Manatt (Calif.)	1981–85
Paul G. Kirk, Jr. (Mass.)	1985–89
Ronald H. Brown (D.C.)	1989–93
David Wilhelm (Ill.)	1993–

Republican National Committee: 310 First St., S.E., Washington, D. C. 20003.
Democratic National Committee: 430 South Capitol St., S.E., Washington, D.C. 20003.

Presidential Elections, 1789 to 1992

For the original method of electing the President and the Vice President (elections of 1789, 1792, 1796, and 1800), see Article II, Section 1, of the Constitution. The election of 1804 was the first one in which the electors voted for President and Vice President on separate ballots. (See Amendment XII to the Constitution.)

Year	Presidential candidates	Party	Electoral vote
1789[1]	George Washington	(no party)	69
	John Adams	(no party)	34
	Scattering	(no party)	35
	Votes not cast		8
1792	George Washington	Federalist	132
	John Adams	Federalist	77
	George Clinton	Anti-Federalist	50
	Thomas Jefferson	Anti-Federalist	4
	Aaron Burr	Anti-Federalist	1
	Votes not cast		6

Year	Vice-presidential candidates	Party	Electoral vote
1796	John Adams	Federalist	71
	Thomas Jefferson	Dem.-Rep.	68
	Thomas Pinckney	Federalist	59
	Aaron Burr	Dem.-Rep.	30
	Scattering		48
1800[2]	Thomas Jefferson	Dem.-Rep.	73
	Aaron Burr	Dem.-Rep.	73
	John Adams	Federalist	65
	Charles C. Pinckney	Federalist	64
	John Jay	Federalist	1

Year	Presidential candidates	Party	Electoral vote	Vice-presidential candidates	Party	Electoral vote
1804	Thomas Jefferson	Dem.-Rep.	162	George Clinton	Dem.-Rep.	162
	Charles C. Pinckney	Federalist	14	Rufus King	Federalist	14
1808	James Madison	Dem.-Rep.	122	George Clinton	Dem.-Rep.	113
	Charles C. Pinckney	Federalist	47	Rufus King	Federalist	47
	George Clinton	Dem.-Rep.	6	John Langdon	Ind. (no party)	9
	Votes not cast		1	James Madison	Dem.-Rep.	3
				James Monroe	Dem.-Rep.	3
				Votes not cast		1
1812	James Madison	Dem.-Rep.	128	Elbridge Gerry	Dem.-Rep.	131
	De Witt Clinton	Federalist	89	Jared Ingersoll	Federalist	86
	Votes not cast		1	Votes not cast		1
1816	James Monroe	Dem.-Rep.	183	Daniel D. Tompkins	Dem.-Rep.	183
	Rufus King	Federalist	34	John E. Howard	Federalist	22
	Votes not cast		4	James Ross	Ind. (no party)	5
				John Marshall	Federalist	4
				Robert G. Harper	Ind. (no party)	3
				Votes not cast		4
1820	James Monroe	Dem-Rep	231	Daniel D. Tompkins	Dem.-Rep.	218
	John Quincy Adams	Ind. (no party)	1	Richard Stockton	Ind. (no party)	8
	Votes not cast		3	Daniel Rodney	Ind. (no party)	4
				Richard Rush	Ind. (no party)	1
				Robert G. Harper	Ind. (no party)	1
				Votes not cast		3
1824[3]	John Quincy Adams	(no party)	84	John C. Calhoun	(no party)	182
	Andrew Jackson	(no party)	99	Nathan Sanford	(no party)	30
	William H. Crawford	(no party)	41	Nathaniel Macon	(no party)	24
	Henry Clay	(no party)	37	Andrew Jackson	(no party)	13
				Martin Van Buren	(no party)	9
				Henry Clay	(no party)	2
				Votes not cast		1
1828	Andrew Jackson	Democratic	178	John C. Calhoun	Democratic	171
	John Quincy Adams	Natl. Rep.	83	Richard Rush	Natl. Rep.	83
				William Smith	Democratic	7
1832	Andrew Jackson	Democratic	219	Martin Van Buren	Democratic	189
	Henry Clay	Natl. Rep.	49	John Sergeant	Natl. Rep.	49
	John Floyd	Ind. (no party)	11	Henry Lee	Ind. (no party)	11
	William Wirt	Antimasonic[4]	7	Amos Ellmaker	Antimasonic	7
	Votes not cast		2	William Wilkins	Ind. (no party)	30
				Votes not cast		2

Year	Presidential candidates	Party	Electoral vote	Vice-presidential candidates	Party	Electoral vote
1836	Martin Van Buren	Democratic	170	Richard M. Johnson[5]	Democratic	147
	William H. Harrison	Whig	73	Francis Granger	Whig	77
	Hugh L. White	Whig	26	John Tyler	Whig	47
	Daniel Webster	Whig	14	William Smith	Ind. (no party)	23
	W. P. Mangum	Ind. (no party)	11			
1840	William H. Harrison[6]	Whig	234	John Tyler	Whig	234
	Martin Van Buren	Democratic	60	Richard M. Johnson	Democratic	48
				L. W. Tazewell	Ind. (no party)	11
				James K. Polk	Democratic	1
1844	James K. Polk	Democratic	170	George M. Dallas	Democratic	170
	Henry Clay	Whig	105	Theo. Frelinghuysen	Whig	105
1848	Zachary Taylor[7]	Whig	163	Millard Fillmore	Whig	163
	Lewis Cass	Democratic	127	William O. Butler	Democratic	127
1852	Franklin Pierce	Democratic	254	William R. King	Democratic	254
	Winfield Scott	Whig	42	William A. Graham	Whig	42
1856	James Buchanan	Democratic	174	John C. Breckinridge	Democratic	174
	John C. Fremont	Republican	114	William L. Dayton	Republican	114
	Millard Fillmore	American[8]	8	A. J. Donelson	American[8]	8
1860	Abraham Lincoln	Republican	180	Hannibal Hamlin	Republican	180
	John C. Breckinridge	Democratic	72	Joseph Lane	Democratic	72
	John Bell	Const. Union	39	Edward Everett	Const. Union	39
	Stephen A. Douglas	Democratic	12	H. V. Johnson	Democratic	12
1864	Abraham Lincoln[9]	Union[10]	212	Andrew Johnson	Union[15]	212
	George B. McClellan	Democratic	21	G. H. Pendleton	Democratic	21
1868	Ulysses S. Grant	Republican	214	Schuyler Colfax	Republican	214
	Horatio Seymour	Democratic	80	Francis P. Blair, Jr.	Democratic	80
	Votes not counted[11]		23	Votes not counted[11]		23

Year	Presidential candidates	Party	Electoral vote	Popular vote	Vice-presidential candidates and party
1872	Ulysses S. Grant	Republican	286	3,597,132	Henry Wilson—R
	Horace Greeley	Dem., Liberal Rep.	([12])	2,834,125	B. Gratz Brown—D, LR—(47)
	Thomas A. Hendricks	Democratic	42		Scattering—(19)
	B. Gratz Brown	Dem., Liberal Rep.	18		Votes not counted—(14)
	Charles J. Jenkins	Democratic	2		
	David Davis	Democratic	1		
	Votes not counted		17		
1876[13]	Rutherford B. Hayes	Republican	185	4,033,768	William A. Wheeler—R
	Samuel J. Tilden	Democratic	184	4,285,992	Thomas A. Hendricks—D
	Peter Cooper	Greenback	0	81,737	Samuel F. Cary—G
1880	James A. Garfield[14]	Republican	214	4,449,053	Chester A. Arthur—R
	Winfield S. Hancock	Democratic	155	4,442,035	William H. English—D
	James B. Weaver	Greenback	0	308,578	B. J. Chambers—G
1884	Grover Cleveland	Democratic	219	4,911,017	Thomas A. Hendricks—D
	James G. Blaine	Republican	182	4,848,334	John A. Logan—R
	Benjamin F. Butler	Greenback	0	175,370	A. M. West—G
	John P. St. John	Prohibition	0	150,369	William Daniel—P
1888	Benjamin Harrison	Republican	233	5,440,216	Levi P. Morton—R
	Grover Cleveland	Democratic	168	5,538,233	A. G. Thurman—D
	Clinton B. Fisk	Prohibition	0	249,506	John A. Brooks—P
	Alson J. Streeter	Union Labor	0	146,935	Charles E. Cunningham—UL
1892	Grover Cleveland	Democratic	277	5,556,918	Adlai E. Stevenson—D
	Benjamin Harrison	Republican	145	5,176,108	Whitelaw Reid—R
	James B. Weaver	People's[15]	22	1,041,028	James G. Field—Peo
	John Bidwell	Prohibition	0	264,133	James B. Cranfill—P

Year	Presidential candidates	Party	Electoral vote	Popular vote	Vice-presidential candidates and party
1896	William McKinley	Republican	271	7,035,638	Garret A. Hobart—R
	William J. Bryan	Dem., People's[15]	176	6,467,946	Arthur Sewall—D—(149)
					Thomas E. Watson—Peo—(27)
	John M. Palmer	Natl. Dem.	0	133,148	Simon B. Buckner—ND
	Joshua Levering	Prohibition	0	132,007	Hale Johnson—P
1900	William McKinley[16]	Republican	292	7,219,530	Theodore Roosevelt—R
	William J. Bryan	Dem., People's[15]	155	6,358,071	Adlai E. Stevenson—D, Peo
	Eugene V. Debs	Social Democratic	0	94,768	Job Harriman—SD
1904	Theodore Roosevelt	Republican	336	7,628,834	Charles W. Fairbanks—R
	Alton B. Parker	Democratic	140	5,084,491	Henry G. Davis—D
	Eugene V. Debs	Socialist	0	402,400	Benjamin Hanford—S
1908	William H. Taft	Republican	321	7,679,006	James S. Sherman—R
	William J. Bryan	Democratic	162	6,409,106	John W. Kern—D
	Eugene V. Debs	Socialist	0	402,820	Benjamin Hanford—S
1912	Woodrow Wilson	Democratic	435	6,286,214	Thomas R. Marshall—D
	Theodore Roosevelt	Progressive	88	4,126,020	Hiram Johnson—Prog
	William H. Taft	Republican	8	3,483,922	Nicholas M. Butler—R[17]
	Eugene V. Debs	Socialist	0	897,011	Emil Seidel—S
1916	Woodrow Wilson	Democratic	277	9,129,606	Thomas R. Marshall—D
	Charles E. Hughes	Republican	254	8,538,221	Charles W. Fairbanks—R
	A. L. Benson	Socialist	0	585,113	G. R. Kirkpatrick—S
1920	Warren G. Harding[18]	Republican	404	16,152,200	Calvin Coolidge—R
	James M. Cox	Democratic	127	9,147,353	Franklin D. Roosevelt—D
	Eugene V. Debs	Socialist	0	917,799	Seymour Stedman—S
1924	Calvin Coolidge	Republican	382	15,725,016	Charles G. Dawes—R
	John W. Davis	Democratic	136	8,385,586	Charles W. Bryan—D
	Robert M. LaFollette	Progressive, Socialist	13	4,822,856	Burton K. Wheeler—Prog S
1928	Herbert Hoover	Republican	444	21,392,190	Charles Curtis—R
	Alfred E. Smith	Democratic	87	15,016,443	Joseph T. Robinson—D
	Norman Thomas	Socialist	0	267,420	James H. Maurer—S
1932	Franklin D. Roosevelt	Democratic	472	22,821,857	John N. Garner—D
	Herbert Hoover	Republican	59	15,761,841	Charles Curtis—R
	Norman Thomas	Socialist	0	884,781	James H. Maurer—S
1936	Franklin D. Roosevelt	Democratic	523	27,751,597	John N. Garner—D
	Alfred M. Landon	Republican	8	16,679,583	Frank Knox—R
	Norman Thomas	Socialist	0	187,720	George Nelson—S
1940	Franklin D. Roosevelt	Democratic	449	27,244,160	Henry A. Wallace—D
	Wendell L. Willkie	Republican	82	22,305,198	Charles L. McNary—R
	Norman Thomas	Socialist	0	99,557	Maynard C. Krueger—S
1944	Franklin D. Roosevelt[19]	Democratic	432	25,602,504	Harry S. Truman—D
	Thomas E. Dewey	Republican	99	22,006,285	John W. Bricker—R
	Norman Thomas	Socialist	0	80,518	Darlington Hoopes—S
1948	Harry S. Truman	Democratic	303	24,179,345	Alben W. Barkley—D
	Thomas E. Dewey	Republican	189	21,991,291	Earl Warren—R
	J. Strom Thurmond	States' Rights Dem.	39	1,176,125	Fielding L. Wright—SR
	Henry A. Wallace	Progressive	0	1,157,326	Glen Taylor—Prog
	Norman Thomas	Socialist	0	139,572	Tucker P. Smith—S
1952	Dwight D. Eisenhower	Republican	442	33,936,234	Richard M. Nixon—R
	Adlai E. Stevenson	Democratic	89	27,314,992	John J. Sparkman—D
1956	Dwight D. Eisenhower	Republican	457	35,590,472	Richard M. Nixon—R
	Adlai E. Stevenson	Democratic	73[20]	26,022,752	Estes Kefauver—D
1960	John F. Kennedy[22]	Democratic	303	34,226,731	Lyndon B. Johnson—D
	Richard M. Nixon	Republican	219[21]	34,108,157	Henry Cabot Lodge—R

Year	Presidential candidates	Party	Electoral vote	Popular vote	Vice-presidential candidates and party
1964	Lyndon B. Johnson	Democratic	486	43,129,484	Hubert H. Humphrey—D
	Barry M. Goldwater	Republican	52	27,178,188	William E. Miller—R
1968	Richard M. Nixon	Republican	301	31,785,480	Spiro T. Agnew—R
	Hubert H. Humphrey	Democratic	191	31,275,166	Edmund S. Muskie—D
	George C. Wallace	American Independent	46	9,906,473	Curtis F. LeMay—AI
1972	Richard M. Nixon[23]	Republican	520 [24]	47,169,911	Spiro T. Agnew—R
	George McGovern	Democratic	17	29,170,383	Sargent Shriver—D
	John G. Schmitz	American	0	1,099,482	Thomas J. Anderson—A
1976	Jimmy Carter	Democratic	297	40,830,763	Walter F. Mondale—D
	Gerald R. Ford	Republican	240 [25]	39,147,973	Robert J. Dole—R
	Eugene J. McCarthy	Independent	0	756,631	None
1980	Ronald Reagan	Republican	489	43,899,248	George Bush—R
	Jimmy Carter	Democratic	49	36,481,435	Walter F. Mondale—D
	John B. Anderson	Independent	0	5,719,437	Patrick J. Lucey—I
1984	Ronald Reagan	Republican	525	54,455,075	George Bush—R
	Walter F. Mondale	Democratic	13	37,577,185	Geraldine A. Ferraro—D
1988	George H. Bush	Republican	426	48,886,097	J. Danforth Quayle—R
	Michael S. Dukakis	Democratic	111 [26]	41,809,074	Lloyd Bentsen—D
1992	William J. Clinton	Democratic	370	44,909,889	Albert A. Gore, Jr.—D
	George H. Bush	Republican	168	39,104,545	J. Danforth Quayle—R
	H. Ross Perot	Independent	0	19,742,267	James B. Stockdale—I

1. Only 10 states participated in the election. The New York legislature chose no electors, and North Carolina and Rhode Island had not yet ratified the Constitution. 2. As Jefferson and Burr were tied, the House of Representatives chose the President. In a vote by states, 10 votes were cast for Jefferson, 4 for Burr; 2 votes were not cast. 3. As no candidate had an electoral-vote majority, the House of Representatives chose the President from the first three. In a vote by states, 13 votes were cast for Adams, 7 for Jackson, and 4 for Crawford. 4. The Antimasonic Party on Sept. 26, 1831, was the first party to hold a nominating convention to choose candidates for President and Vice-President. 5. As Johnson did not have an electoral-vote majority, the Senate chose him 33–14 over Granger, the others being legally out of the race. 6. Harrison died April 4, 1841, and Tyler succeeded him April 6. 7. Taylor died July 9, 1850, and Fillmore succeeded him July 10. 8. Also known as the Know-Nothing Party. 9. Lincoln died April 15, 1865, and Johnson succeeded him the same day. 10. Name adopted by the Republican National Convention of 1864. Johnson was a War Democrat. 11. 23 Southern electoral votes were excluded. 12. See Election of 1872 in *Unusual Voting Results* under Elections, Presidential, in Index. 13. See Election of 1876 in *Unusual Voting Results* under Elections, Presidential, in Index. 14. Garfield died Sept. 19, 1881, and Arthur succeeded him Sept. 20. 15. Members of People's Party were called Populists. 16. McKinley died Sept. 14, 1901, and Roosevelt succeeded him the same day. 17. James S. Sherman, Republican candidate for Vice President, died Oct. 30, 1912, and the Republican electoral votes were cast for Butler. 18. Harding died Aug. 2, 1923, and Coolidge succeeded him Aug. 3. 19. Roosevelt died April 12, 1945, and Truman succeeded him the same day. 20. One electoral vote from Alabama was cast for Walter B. Jones. 21. Sen. Harry F. Byrd received 15 electoral votes. 22. Kennedy died Nov. 22, 1963, and Johnson succeeded him the same day. 23. Nixon resigned Aug. 9, 1974, and Gerald R. Ford succeeded him the same day. 24. One electoral vote from Virginia was cast for John Hospers, Libertarian Party. 25. One electoral vote from Washington was cast for Ronald Reagan. 26. One electoral vote from West Virginia was cast for Lloyd Bentsen.

Gerrymander

Source: "The Reader's Companion to American History," Houghton Mifflin Company.

Gerrymander refers to the drawing of boundaries of legislative districts to benefit one party or group and handicap another. Although the practice dates back to the colonial period, its name is derived from Elbridge Gerry, a signer of the Declaration of Independence, a nonsigning delegate to the Federal Convention of 1787, and a leader of the Jeffersonian Republican party.

In 1812, while Gerry was governor of Massachusetts, the Republican-dominated legislature redrew district lines to weigh representation in favor of Republicans and against Federalists. The Federalists attacked the redistricting, specifically blaming Gerry although he had nothing to do with the project and, in private, opposed it. A Federalist newspaper published a political cartoon depicting the oddly shaped district covering Essex County as a salamander; the cartoonist dubbed his creation a "Gerry-mander." The word quickly passed into common parlance.

Since the 1950s, the federal courts have been increasingly willing to examine states' defining of representative districts to determine their adherence to the principle of "one man, one vote," as enunciated in *Baker* v. *Carr* (1962). Ironically, in light of the term's New England origins, most gerrymanders examined by the Supreme Court have come from southern states, where local legislatures sought to dilute the representation of urban residents and African-Americans. □

Large Voter Turnout

Voter turnout for the presidential election of 1992 was the largest since 1972 with 61% of the voting-age population going to the polls. Furthermore, the 1992 turnout rate was four percentage points higher than in 1988 (57%). □

Qualifications for Voting

The Supreme Court decision of March 21, 1972, declared lengthy requirements for voting in state and local elections unconstitutional and suggested that 30 days was an ample period. Most of the states have changed or eliminated their durational residency requirements to comply with the ruling, as shown.

NO DURATIONAL RESIDENCY REQUIREMENT

Alabama,[6] Arkansas, Connecticut,[13] Delaware,[12] District of Columbia,[16] Florida,[5] Georgia,[2] Hawaii,[2] Iowa,[6] Louisiana,[8] Maine, Maryland, Massachusetts,[3] Missouri,[4] Nebraska,[9] New Hampshire,[17] New Mexico,[7] Oklahoma, South Carolina,[22] South Dakota,[10] Tennessee,[20] Texas, Virginia, West Virginia,[2] Wyoming[2]

30-DAY RESIDENCY REQUIREMENT

Alaska,[18] Arizona,[11] Idaho,[23] Illinois, Indiana, Michigan, Mississippi,[21] Montana, Nevada, New Jersey, New York, North Carolina, North Dakota, Ohio, Pennsylvania, Rhode Island, Utah, Washington

OTHER

California,[19] Colorado,[1] Minnesota[15] and Oregon, 20 days; Kentucky, 28 days; Kansas, 14 days; Vermont, 17 days;[14] Wisconsin, 10 days

1. 25 days immediately preceding the election. 2. 30-day registration requirement. 3. No residency required to register to vote. 4. Must be registered by the fourth Wednesday prior to election. 5. 30-day registration requirement for national elections; 30-day for state elections. 6. 10-day registration requirement. In-person registration by 5 PM, eleven days before election date. 7. Must register 28 days before election. 8. 24 days prior to any election. 9. Registration requirement, 2nd Friday prior to elections. 10. 15-day registration requirement. 11. Residency in the state 29 days next preceding the election. 12. Must reside in Delaware and register by the last day that the books are open for registration. 13. Registration deadline 14th day before election; registration and party enrollment deadline the day before primary. 14. Administrative cut-off date for processing applications 3rd Saturday before the election by 12 noon. 15. Permits registration and voting on election day with approved ID. 16. Registration stops 30 days before any election and until 15 days after. Voters must inform Board of Elections of change of address within 30 days of moving. 17. Registration requirement, 10 days prior to elections. 18. If otherwise qualified but has not been a resident of the election district for at least 30 days preceding the date of a presidential election, is entitled to register and vote for presidential and vice-presidential candidates. 19. 29 days before an election. 20. Must be resident of state for a period of at least 20 days prior to registration. 21. 30 days registration required, 60 days if registration is by mail. 22. Registration certificate not valid for 30 days but if you move within the state you can vote in old precinct during the 30 days. 23. Register 10 days prior to election with County Clerk; 17 days prior registration with precinct registrar. *Source: Information Please* questionnaires to the states.

Facts About Elections

Candidate with highest populate vote: Reagan (1984), 54,455,075.
Candidate with highest electoral vote: Reagan (1984), 525.
Candidate carrying most states: Nixon (1972) and Reagan (1984), 49.
Candidate running most times: Norman Thomas, 6 (1928, 1932, 1936, 1940, 1944, 1948).
Candidate elected, defeated, then reelected: Cleveland (1884, 1888, 1892).

Plurality and Majority

In order to win a plurality, a candidate must receive a greater number of votes than anyone running against him. If he receives 50 votes, for example, and two other candidates receive 49 and 2, he will have a plurality of one vote over his closest opponent.

However, a candidate does not have a majority unless he receives more than 50% of the total votes cast. In the example above, the candidate does not have a majority, because his 50 votes are less than 50% of the 101 votes cast.

Unusual Voting Results

Election of 1872

The presidential and vice-presidential candidates of the Liberal Republicans and the northern Democrats in 1872 were Horace Greeley and B. Gratz Brown. Greeley died Nov. 29, 1872, before his 66 electors voted. In the electoral balloting for President, 63 of Greeley's votes were scattered among four other men, including Brown.

Election of 1876

In the election of 1876 Samuel J. Tilden, the Democratic candidate, received a popular majority but lacked one undisputed electoral vote to carry a clear majority of the electoral college. The crux of the problem was in the 22 electoral votes which were in dispute because Florida, Louisiana, South Carolina, and Oregon each sent in two sets of election returns. In the three southern states, Republican election boards threw out enough Democratic votes to certify the Republican candidate, Hayes. In Oregon, the Democratic governor disqualified a Republican elector, replacing him with a Democrat. Since the Senate was Republican and the House of Representatives Democratic, it seemed useless to refer the disputed returns to the two houses for solution. Instead Congress appointed an Electoral Commission with five representatives each from the Senate, the House, and the Supreme Court. All but one Justice was named, giving the Commission seven Republican and seven Democratic members. The naming of the fifth Justice was left to the other four. He was a Republican who first favored Tilden but, under pressure from his party, switched to Hayes, ensuring his election by the Commission voting 8 to 7 on party lines.

Minority Presidents

Sixteen candidates have become President of the United States with a popular vote less than 50% of the total cast. It should be noted, however, that in elections before 1872, presidential electors were not chosen by popular vote in all states. Adams' election in 1824 was by the House of Representatives, which chose him over Jackson, who had a plurality of both electoral and popular votes, but not a majority in the electoral college.

Besides Jackson in 1824, only two other candidates receiving the largest popular vote have failed to gain a majority in the electoral college—Samuel J. Tilden (D) in 1876 and Grover Cleveland (D) in 1888.

The "minority" Presidents follow:

Vote Received by Minority Presidents

		Electoral	Popular vote
Year	President	Percent	Percent
1824	John Q. Adams	31.8	29.8
1844	James K. Polk (D)	61.8	49.3
1848	Zachary Taylor (W)	56.2	47.3
1856	James Buchanan (D)	58.7	45.3
1860	Abraham Lincoln (R)	59.4	39.9
1876	Rutherford B. Hayes (R)	50.1	47.9
1880	James A. Garfield (R)	57.9	48.3
1884	Grover Cleveland (D)	54.6	48.8
1888	Benjamin Harrison (R)	58.1	47.8
1892	Grover Cleveland (D)	62.4	46.0
1912	Woodrow Wilson (D)	81.9	41.8
1916	Woodrow Wilson (D)	52.1	49.3
1948	Harry S. Truman (D)	57.1	49.5
1960	John F. Kennedy (D)	56.4	49.7
1968	Richard M. Nixon (R)	56.1	43.4
1992	William J. Clinton (D)	68.8	43.0

Percent of Persons Voting in Presidential Elections 1964–1992

(Numbers in thousands. Civilian noninstitutional population.)

United States	1992	1988	1984	1980	1976	1972	1968	1964
Total voting age	**185,684**	**178,098**	**169,963**	**157,085**	**146,548**	**136,203**	**116,535**	**110,604**
Percent voted	61.3	57.4	59.9	59.2	59.2	63.0	67.8	69.3
White	63.6	59.1	61.4	60.9	60.9	64.5	69.1	70.7
Black	54.0	51.5	55.8	50.5	48.7	52.1	57.6	58.5[2]
Hispanic origin[1]	28.9	28.8	32.6	29.9	31.8	37.5	n.a.	n.a.
Male	60.2	56.4	59.0	59.1	59.6	64.1	69.8	71.9
Female	62.3	58.3	60.8	59.4	58.8	62.0	66.0	67.0
18 to 24 years	42.8	36.2	40.8	39.9	42.2	49.6	50.4[3]	50.9[3]
25 to 44 years	58.3	54.0	58.4	58.7	58.7	62.7	66.6	69.0
45 to 64 years	70.0	67.9	69.8	69.3	68.7	70.8	74.9	75.9
65 years and over	70.1	68.8	67.7	65.1	62.2	63.5	65.8	66.3

1. Persons of Hispanic origin may be of any race. 2. Black and other races in 1964. 3. Prior to 1972, includes persons 18 to 20 years old in Georgia and Kentucky, 19 and 20 in Alaska, and 20 years old in Hawaii. n.a. = not available. *Source:* Bureau of the Census, *Current Population Reports,* April 1993.

How a Bill Becomes a Law

When a Senator or a Representative introduces a bill, he sends it to the clerk of his house, who gives it a number and title. This is the *first reading,* and the bill is referred to the proper committee.

The committee may decide the bill is unwise or unnecessary and *table* it, thus killing it at once. Or it may decide the bill is worthwhile and hold hearings to listen to facts and opinions presented by experts and other interested persons. After members of the committee have debated the bill and perhaps offered amendments, a vote is taken; and if the vote is favorable, the bill is sent back to the floor of the house.

The clerk reads the bill sentence by sentence to the house, and this is known as the *second reading.* Members may then debate the bill and offer amendments. In the House of Representatives, the time for debate is limited by a *cloture rule,* but there is no such restriction in the Senate for cloture, where 60 votes are required. This makes possible a *filibuster,* in which one or more opponents hold the floor to defeat the bill.

The *third reading* is by title only, and the bill is put to a vote, which may be by voice or roll call, depending on the circumstances and parliamentary rules. Members who must be absent at the time but who wish to record their vote may be paired if each negative vote has a balancing affirmative one.

The bill then goes to the other house of Congress, where it may be defeated, or passed with or without amendments. If the bill is defeated, it dies. If it is passed with amendments, a joint Congressional committee must be appointed by both houses to iron out the differences.

After its final passage by both houses, the bill is sent to the President. If he approves, he signs it, and the bill becomes a law. However, if he disapproves, he *vetoes* the bill by refusing to sign it and sending it back to the house of origin with his reasons for the veto. The objections are read and debated, and a roll-call vote is taken. If the bill receives less than a two-thirds vote, it is defeated and goes no farther. But if it receives a two-thirds vote or greater, it is sent to the other house for a vote. If that house also passes it by a two-thirds vote, the President's veto is *overridden,* and the bill becomes a law.

Should the President desire neither to sign nor to veto the bill, he may retain it for ten days, Sundays excepted, after which time it automatically becomes a law without signature. However, if Congress has adjourned within those ten days, the bill is automatically killed, that process of indirect rejection being known as a *pocket veto.*

Government Officials

Cabinet Members With Dates of Appointment

Although the Constitution made no provision for a President's advisory group, the heads of the three executive departments (State, Treasury, and War) and the Attorney General were organized by Washington into such a group; and by about 1793, the name "Cabinet" was applied to it. With the exception of the Attorney General up to 1870 and the Postmaster General from 1829 to 1872, Cabinet members have been heads of executive departments.

A Cabinet member is appointed by the President, subject to the confirmation of the Senate; and as his term is not fixed, he may be replaced at any time by the President. At a change in Administration, it is customary for him to tender his resignation, but he remains in office until a successor is appointed.

The table of Cabinet members lists only those members who actually served after being duly commissioned.

The dates shown are those of appointment. "Cont." indicates that the term continued from the previous Administration for a substantial amount of time.

With the creation of the Department of Transportation in 1966, the Cabinet consisted of 12 members. This figure was reduced to 11 when the Post Office Department became an independent agency in 1970 but, with the establishment in 1977 of a Department of Energy, became 12 again. Creation of the Department of Education in 1980 raised the number to 13. Creation of the Department of Veterans' Affairs in 1989 raised the number to 14.

WASHINGTON

Secretary of State	Thomas Jefferson 1789
	Edmund Randolph 1794
	Timothy Pickering 1795
Secretary of the Treasury	Alexander Hamilton 1789
	Oliver Wolcott, Jr. 1795
Secretary of War	Henry Knox 1789
	Timothy Pickering 1795
	James McHenry 1796
Attorney General	Edmund Randolph 1789
	William Bradford 1794
	Charles Lee 1795

J. ADAMS

Secretary of State	Timothy Pickering (Cont.)
	John Marshall 1800
Secretary of the Treasury	Oliver Wolcott, Jr. (Cont.)
	Samuel Dexter 1801
Secretary of War	James McHenry (Cont.)
	Samuel Dexter 1800
Attorney General	Charles Lee (Cont.)
Secretary of the Navy	Benjamin Stoddert 1798

JEFFERSON

Secretary of State	James Madison 1801
Secretary of the Treasury	Samuel Dexter (Cont.)
	Albert Gallatin 1801
Secretary of War	Henry Dearborn 1801
Attorney General	Levi Lincoln 1801
	Robert Smith 1805
	John Breckinridge 1805
	Caesar A. Rodney 1807
Secretary of the Navy	Benjamin Stoddert (Cont.)
	Robert Smith 1801

MADISON

Secretary of State	Robert Smith 1809
	James Monroe 1811
Secretary of the Treasury	Albert Gallatin (Cont.)
	George W. Campbell 1814
	Alexander J. Dallas 1814
	William H. Crawford 1816
Secretary of War	William Eustis 1809
	John Armstrong 1813
	James Monroe 1814
	William H. Crawford 1815
Attorney General	Caesar A. Rodney (Cont.)
	William Pinckney 1811
	Richard Rush 1814
Secretary of the Navy	Paul Hamilton 1809
	William Jones 1813
	B. W. Crowninshield 1814

MONROE

Secretary of State	John Quincy Adams 1817
Secretary of the Treasury	William H. Crawford (Cont.)
Secretary of War	John C. Calhoun 1817
Attorney General	Richard Rush (Cont.)
	William Wirt 1817
Secretary of the Navy	B. W. Crowninshield (Cont.)
	Smith Thompson 1818
	Samuel L. Southard 1823

J. Q. ADAMS

Secretary of State	Henry Clay 1825
Secretary of the Treasury	Richard Rush 1825
Secretary of War	James Barbour 1825
	Peter B. Porter 1828
Attorney General	William Wirt (Cont.)
Secretary of the Navy	Samuel L. Southard (Cont.)

JACKSON

Secretary of State	Martin Van Buren 1829
	Edward Livingston 1831
	Louis McLane 1833
	John Forsyth 1834
Secretary of the Treasury	Samuel D. Ingham 1829
	Louis McLane 1831
	William J. Duane 1833
	Roger B. Taney[3] 1833
	Levi Woodbury 1834
Secretary of War	John H. Eaton 1829
	Lewis Cass 1831
Attorney General	John M. Berrien 1829
	Roger B. Taney 1831
	Benjamin F. Butler 1833
Postmaster General[1]	William T. Barry 1829
	Amos Kendall 1835
Secretary of the Navy	John Branch 1829
	Levi Woodbury 1831
	Mahlon Dickerson 1834

VAN BUREN

Secretary of State	John Forsyth (Cont.)
Secretary of the Treasury	Levi Woodbury (Cont.)
Secretary of War	Joel R. Poinsett 1837
Attorney General	Benjamin F. Butler (Cont.)
	Felix Grundy 1838
	Henry D. Gilpin 1840
Postmaster General	Amos Kendall (Cont.)
	John M. Niles 1840
Secretary of the Navy	Mahlon Dickerson (Cont.)
	James K. Paulding 1838

W. H. HARRISON

Secretary of State	Daniel Webster 1841
Secretary of the Treasury	Thomas Ewing 1841
Secretary of War	John Bell 1841
Attorney General	John J. Crittenden 1841
Postmaster General	Francis Granger 1841
Secretary of the Navy	George E. Badger 1841

TYLER

Secretary of State	Daniel Webster (Cont.)
	Abel P. Upshur 1843
	John C. Calhoun 1844
Secretary of the Treasury	Thomas Ewing (Cont.)
	Walter Forward 1841
	John C. Spencer[3] 1843
	George M. Bibb 1844
Secretary of War	John Bell (Cont.)
	John C. Spencer 1841
	James M. Porter[3] 1843
	William Wilkins 1844
Attorney General	John J. Crittenden (Cont.)
	Hugh S. Legaré 1841
	John Nelson 1843
Postmaster General	Francis Granger (Cont.)
	Charles A. Wickliffe 1841
Secretary of the Navy	George E. Badger (Cont.)
	Abel P. Upshur 1841
	David Henshaw[3] 1843
	Thomas W. Gilmer 1844
	John Y. Mason 1844

POLK

Secretary of State	James Buchanan 1845
Secretary of the Treasury	Robert J. Walker 1845
Secretary of War	William L. Marcy 1845
Attorney General	John Y. Mason 1845
	Nathan Clifford 1846
	Isaac Toucey 1848
Postmaster General	Cave Johnson 1845
Secretary of the Navy	George Bancroft 1845
	John Y. Mason 1846

TAYLOR

Secretary of State	John M. Clayton 1849
Secretary of the Treasury	William M. Meredith 1849
Secretary of War	George W. Crawford 1849
Attorney General	Reverdy Johnson 1849
Postmaster General	Jacob Collamer 1849
Secretary of the Navy	William B. Preston 1849
Secretary of the Interior	Thomas Ewing 1849

FILLMORE

Secretary of State	Daniel Webster 1850
	Edward Everett 1852
Secretary of the Treasury	Thomas Corwin 1850
Secretary of War	Charles M. Conrad 1850
Attorney General	John J. Crittenden 1850
Postmaster General	Nathan K. Hall 1850
	Samuel D. Hubbard 1852
Secretary of the Navy	William A. Graham 1850
	John P. Kennedy 1852
Secretary of the Interior	Thos. M. T. McKennan 1850
	Alex. H. H. Stuart 1850

PIERCE

Secretary of State	William L. Marcy 1853
Secretary of the Treasury	James Guthrie 1853
Secretary of War	Jefferson Davis 1853
Attorney General	Caleb Cushing 1853
Postmaster General	James Campbell 1853
Secretary of the Navy	James C. Dobbin 1853
Secretary of the Interior	Robert McClelland 1853

BUCHANAN

Secretary of State	Lewis Cass 1857
	Jeremiah S. Black 1860
Secretary of the Treasury	Howell Cobb 1857
	Philip F. Thomas 1860
	John A. Dix 1861
Secretary of War	John B. Floyd 1857
	Joseph Holt 1861
Attorney General	Jeremiah S. Black 1857
	Edwin M. Stanton 1860
Postmaster General	Aaron V. Brown 1857
	Joseph Holt 1859
	Horatio King 1861
Secretary of the Navy	Isaac Toucey 1857
Secretary of the Interior	Jacob Thompson 1857

LINCOLN

Secretary of State	William H. Seward 1861
Secretary of the Treasury	Salmon P. Chase 1861
	William P. Fessenden 1864
	Hugh McCulloch 1865
Secretary of War	Simon Cameron 1861
	Edwin M. Stanton 1862
Attorney General	Edward Bates 1861
	James Speed 1864
Postmaster General	Montgomery Blair 1861
	William Dennison 1864
Secretary of the Navy	Gideon Welles 1861
Secretary of the Interior	Caleb B. Smith 1861
	John P. Usher 1863

A. JOHNSON

Secretary of State	William H. Seward (Cont.)
Secretary of the Treasury	Hugh McCulloch (Cont.)
Secretary of War	Edwin M. Stanton (Cont.)
	John M. Schofield 1868
Attorney General	James Speed (Cont.)
	Henry Stanbery 1866
	William M. Evarts 1868
Postmaster General	William Dennison (Cont.)
	Alexander W. Randall 1866
Secretary of the Navy	Gideon Welles (Cont.)
Secretary of the Interior	John P. Usher (Cont.)
	James Harlan 1865
	Orville H. Browning 1866

GRANT

Secretary of State	Elihu B. Washburne 1869
	Hamilton Fish 1869
	George S. Boutwell 1869
	William A. Richardson 1873
	Benjamin H. Bristow 1874
	Lot M. Morrill 1876
Secretary of War	John A. Rawlins 1869
	William W. Belknap 1869
	Alphonso Taft 1876
	James D. Cameron 1876
Attorney General	Ebenezer R. Hoar 1869
	Amos T. Akerman 1870
	George H. Williams 1871
	Edwards Pierrepont 1875
	Alphonso Taft 1876
Postmaster General	John A. J. Creswell 1869
	Marshall Jewell 1874
	James N. Tyner 1876
Secretary of the Navy	Adolph E. Borie 1869
	George M. Robeson 1869
Secretary of the Interior	Jacob D. Cox 1869
	Columbus Delano 1870
	Zachariah Chandler 1875

HAYES

Secretary of State	William M. Evarts 1877
Secretary of the Treasury	John Sherman 1877
Secretary of War	George W. McCrary 1877
	Alexander Ramsey 1879

Attorney General	Charles Devens 1877
Postmaster General	David M. Key 1877
	Horace Maynard 1880
	Richard W. Thompson 1877
	Nathan Goff, Jr. 1881
Secretary of the Interior	Carl Schurz 1877

GARFIELD

Secretary of State	James G. Blaine 1881
Secretary of the Treasury	William Windom 1881
Secretary of War	Robert T. Lincoln 1881
Attorney General	Wayne MacVeagh 1881
Postmaster General	Thomas L. James 1881
Secretary of the Navy	William H. Hunt 1881
Secretary of the Interior	Samuel J. Kirkwood 1881

ARTHUR

Secretary of State	James G. Blaine (Cont.)
	F. T. Frelinghuysen 1881
Secretary of the Treasury	William Windom (Cont.)
	Charles J. Folger 1881
	Walter Q. Gresham 1884
	Hugh McCulloch 1884
Secretary of War	Robert T. Lincoln (Cont.)
Attorney General	Wayne MacVeagh (Cont.)
	Benjamin H. Brewster 1881
Postmaster General	Thomas L. James (Cont.)
	Timothy O. Howe 1881
	Walter Q. Gresham 1883
	Frank Hatton 1884
Secretary of the Navy	William H. Hunt (Cont.)
	William E. Chandler 1882
Secretary of the Interior	Samuel J. Kirkwood (Cont.)
	Henry M. Teller 1882

CLEVELAND

Secretary of State	Thomas F. Bayard 1885
Secretary of the Treasury	Daniel Manning 1885
	Charles S. Fairchild 1887
Secretary of War	William C. Endicott 1885
Attorney General	Augustus H. Garland 1885
Postmaster General	William F. Vilas 1885
	Don M. Dickinson 1888
Secretary of the Navy	William C. Whitney 1885
Secretary of the Interior	Lucius Q. C. Lamar 1885
	William F. Vilas 1888
Secretary of Agriculture	Norman J. Colman 1889

B. HARRISON

Secretary of State	James G. Blaine 1889
	John W. Foster 1892
Secretary of the Treasury	William Windom 1889
	Charles Foster 1891
Secretary of War	Redfield Proctor 1889
	Stephen B. Elkins 1891
Attorney General	William H. H. Miller 1889
Postmaster General	John Wanamaker 1889
Secretary of the Navy	Benjamin F. Tracy 1889
Secretary of the Interior	John W. Noble 1889
Secretary of Agriculture	Jeremiah M. Rusk 1889

CLEVELAND

Secretary of State	Walter Q. Gresham 1893
	Richard Olney 1895
Secretary of the Treasury	John G. Carlisle 1893
Secretary of War	Daniel S. Lamont 1893
Attorney General	Richard Olney 1893
	Judson Harmon 1895
Postmaster General	Wilson S. Bissell 1893
	William L. Wilson 1895
Secretary of the Navy	Hilary A. Herbert 1893
Secretary of the Interior	Hoke Smith 1893
	David R. Francis 1896
Secretary of Agriculture	Julius Sterling Morton 1893

MCKINLEY

Secretary of State	John Sherman 1897
	William R. Day 1898
	John Hay 1898
Secretary of the Treasury	Lyman J. Gage 1897
Secretary of War	Russell A. Alger 1897
	Elihu Root 1899
Attorney General	Joseph McKenna 1897
	John W. Griggs 1898
	Philander C. Knox 1901
Postmaster General	James A. Gary 1897
	Charles E. Smith 1898
Secretary of the Navy	John D. Long 1897
Secretary of the Interior	Cornelius N. Bliss 1897
	Ethan A. Hitchcock 1898
Secretary of Agriculture	James Wilson 1897

T. ROOSEVELT

Secretary of State	John Hay (Cont.)
	Elihu Root 1905
	Robert Bacon 1909
Secretary of the Treasury	Lyman J. Gage (Cont.)
	Leslie M. Shaw 1902
	George B. Cortelyou 1907
Secretary of War	Elihu Root (Cont.)
	William H. Taft 1904
	Luke E. Wright 1908
Attorney General	Philander C. Knox (Cont.)
	William H. Moody 1904
	Charles J. Bonaparte 1906
Postmaster General	Charles E. Smith (Cont.)
	Henry C. Payne 1902
	Robert J. Wynne 1904
	George B. Cortelyou 1905
	George von L. Meyer 1907
Secretary of the Navy	John D. Long (Cont.)
	William H. Moody 1902
	Paul Morton 1904
	Charles J. Bonaparte 1905
	Victor H. Metcalf 1906
	Truman H. Newberry 1908
Secretary of the Interior	Ethan A. Hitchcock (Cont.)
	James R. Garfield 1907
Secretary of Agriculture	James Wilson (Cont.)
Secretary of Commerce and Labor	George B. Cortelyou 1903
	Victor H. Metcalf 1904
	Oscar S. Straus 1906

TAFT

Secretary of State	Philander C. Knox 1909
Secretary of the Treasury	Franklin MacVeagh 1909
Secretary of War	Jacob M. Dickinson 1909
	Henry L. Stimson 1911
Attorney General	George W. Wickersham 1909
Postmaster General	Frank H. Hitchcock 1909
Secretary of the Navy	George von L. Meyer 1909
Secretary of the Interior	Richard A. Ballinger 1909
	Walter L. Fisher 1911
Secretary of Agriculture	James Wilson (Cont.)
Secretary of Commerce and Labor	Charles Nagel 1909

WILSON

Secretary of State	William J. Bryan 1913
	Robert Lansing 1915
	Bainbridge Colby 1920
Secretary of the Treasury	William G. McAdoo 1913
	Carter Glass 1918
	David F. Houston 1920
Secretary of War	Lindley M. Garrison 1913
	Newton D. Baker 1916
Attorney General	James C. McReynolds 1913
	Thomas W. Gregory 1914
	A. Mitchell Palmer 1919
Postmaster General	Albert S. Burleson 1913
Secretary of the Navy	Josephus Daniels 1913
Secretary of the Interior	Franklin K. Lane 1913
	John B. Payne 1920
Secretary of Agriculture	David F. Houston 1913
	Edwin T. Meredith 1920
Secretary of Commerce	William C. Redfield 1913
	Joshua W. Alexander 1919
Secretary of Labor	William B. Wilson 1913

HARDING

Secretary of State	Charles E. Hughes 1921
Secretary of the Treasury	Andrew W. Mellon 1921
Secretary of War	John W. Weeks 1921
Attorney General	Harry M. Daugherty 1921
Postmaster General	Will H. Hays 1921
	Hubert Work 1922

	Harry S. New 1923
Secretary of the Navy	Edwin Denby 1921
Secretary of the Interior	Albert B. Fall 1921
	Hubert Work 1923
Secretary of Agriculture	Henry C. Wallace 1921
Secretary of Commerce	Herbert Hoover 1921
Secretary of Labor	James J. Davis 1921

COOLIDGE

Secretary of State	Charles E. Hughes (Cont.)
	Frank B. Kellogg 1925
Secretary of the Treasury	Andrew W. Mellon (Cont.)
Secretary of War	John W. Weeks (Cont.)
	Dwight F. Davis 1925
Attorney General	Harry M. Daughtery (Cont.)
	Harlan F. Stone 1924
	John G. Sargent 1925
Postmaster General	Harry S. New (Cont.)
Secretary of the Navy	Edwin Denby (Cont.)
	Curtis D. Wilbur 1924
Secretary of the Interior	Hubert Work (Cont.)
	Roy O. West 1928
Secretary of Agriculture	Henry C. Wallace (Cont.)
	Howard M. Gore 1924
	William M. Jardine 1925
Secretary of Commerce	Herbert Hoover (Cont.)
	William F. Whiting 1928
Secretary of Labor	James J. Davis (Cont.)

HOOVER

Secretary of State	Frank B. Kellogg (Cont.)
	Henry L. Stimson 1929
Secretary of the Treasury	Andrew W. Mellon (Cont.)
	Ogden L. Mills 1932
Secretary of War	James W. Good 1929
	Patrick J. Hurley 1929
Attorney General	William D. Mitchell 1929
Postmaster General	Walter F. Brown 1929
Secretary of the Navy	Charles F. Adams 1929
Secretary of the Interior	Ray Lyman Wilbur 1929
Secretary of Agriculture	Arthur M. Hyde 1929
Secretary of Commerce	Robert P. Lamont 1929
	Roy D. Chapin 1932
Secretary of Labor	James J. Davis (Cont.)
	William N. Doak 1930

F. D. ROOSEVELT

Secretary of State	Cordell Hull 1933
	E. R. Stettinius, Jr. 1944
Secretary of the Treasury	William H. Woodin 1933
	Henry Morgenthau, Jr. 1934
Secretary of War	George H. Dern 1933
	Harry H. Woodring 1936
	Henry L. Stimson 1940
Attorney General	Homer S. Cummings 1933
	Frank Murphy 1939
	Robert H. Jackson 1940
	Francis Biddle 1941
Postmaster General	James A. Farley 1933
	Frank C. Walker 1940
Secretary of the Navy	Claude A. Swanson 1933
	Charles Edison 1940
	Frank Knox 1940
	James Forrestal 1944
Secretary of the Interior	Harold L. Ickes 1933
Secretary of Agriculture	Henry A. Wallace 1933
	Claude R. Wickard 1940
Secretary of Commerce	Daniel C. Roper 1933
	Harry L. Hopkins 1938
	Jesse H. Jones 1940
	Henry A. Wallace 1945
Secretary of Labor	Frances Perkins 1933

TRUMAN

Secretary of State	E. R. Stettinius, Jr. (Cont.)
	James F. Byrnes 1945
	George C. Marshall 1947
	Dean Acheson 1949
Secretary of the Treasury	Henry Morgenthau, Jr. (Cont.)
	Frederick M. Vinson 1945
	John W. Snyder 1946
Secretary of Defense	James Forrestal 1947
	Louis A. Johnson 1949
	George C. Marshall 1950
	Robert A. Lovett 1951
Attorney General	Francis Biddle (Cont.)
	Tom C. Clark 1945
	J. Howard McGrath 1949
	James P. McGranery 1952
Postmaster General	Frank C. Walker (Cont.)
	Robert E. Hannegan 1945
	Jesse M. Donaldson 1947
Secretary of the Interior	Harold L. Ickes (Cont.)
	Julius A. Krug 1946
	Oscar L. Chapman 1949
Secretary of Agriculture	Claude R. Wickard (Cont.)
	Clinton P. Anderson 1945
	Charles F. Brannan 1948
Secretary of Commerce	Henry A. Wallace (Cont.)
	W. Averell Harriman 1946
	Charles Sawyer 1948
Secretary of Labor	Frances Perkins (Cont.)
	Lewis B. Schwellenbach 1945
	Maurice J. Tobin 1948
Secretary of War[2]	Henry L. Stimson (Cont.)
	Robert P. Patterson 1945
	Kenneth C. Royall 1947
Secretary of the Navy[2]	James Forrestal (Cont.)

EISENHOWER

Secretary of State	John Foster Dulles 1953
	Christian A. Herter 1959
Secretary of the Treasury	George M. Humphrey 1953
	Robert B. Anderson 1957
Secretary of Defense	Charles E. Wilson 1953
	Neil H. McElroy 1957
	Thomas S. Gates, Jr. 1959
Attorney General	Herbert Brownell, Jr. 1953
	William P. Rogers 1958
Postmaster General	Arthur E. Summerfield 1953
Secretary of the Interior	Douglas McKay 1953
	Frederick A. Seaton 1956
Secretary of Agriculture	Ezra Taft Benson 1953
Secretary of Commerce	Sinclair Weeks 1953
	Lewis L. Strauss[3] 1958
	Frederick H. Mueller 1959
Secretary of Labor	Martin P. Durkin 1953
	James P. Mitchell 1953
Secretary of Health, Education, and Welfare	Oveta Culp Hobby 1953
	Marion B. Folsom 1955
	Arthur S. Flemming 1958

KENNEDY

Secretary of State	Dean Rusk 1961
Secretary of the Treasury	C. Douglas Dillon 1961
Secretary of Defense	Robert S. McNamara 1961
Attorney General	Robert F. Kennedy 1961
Postmaster General	J. Edward Day 1961
	John A. Gronouski 1963
Secretary of the Interior	Stewart L. Udall 1961
Secretary of Agriculture	Orville L. Freeman 1961
Secretary of Commerce	Luther H. Hodges 1961
Secretary of Labor	Arthur J. Goldberg 1961
	W. Willard Wirtz 1962
Secretary of Health, Education, and Welfare	Abraham A. Ribicoff 1961
	Anthony J. Celebrezze 1962

L. B. JOHNSON

Secretary of State	Dean Rusk (Cont.)
Secretary of the Treasury	C. Douglas Dillon (Cont.)
	Henry H. Fowler 1965
	Joseph W. Barr[4] 1968
Secretary of Defense	Robert S. McNamara (Cont.)
	Clark M. Clifford 1968
Attorney General	Robert F. Kennedy (Cont.)
	N. de B. Katzenbach 1965
	Ramsey Clark 1967
Postmaster General	John A. Gronouski (Cont.)
	Lawrence F. O'Brien 1965
	W. Marvin Watson 1968
Secretary of the Interior	Stewart L. Udall (Cont.)
Secretary of Agriculture	Orville L. Freeman (Cont.)

Secretary of Commerce	Luther H. Hodges (Cont.) John T. Connor 1964 A. B. Trowbridge 1967 C. R. Smith 1968
Secretary of Labor	W. Willard Wirtz (Cont.)
Secretary of Health, Education, and Welfare	Anthony J. Celebrezze (Cont.) John W. Gardner 1965 Wilbur J. Cohen 1968
Secretary of Housing and Urban Development	Robert C. Weaver 1966 Robert C. Wood[4] 1969
Secretary of Transportation	Alan S. Boyd 1966

NIXON

Secretary of State	William P. Rogers 1969 Henry A. Kissinger 1973
Secretary of the Treasury	David M. Kennedy 1969 John B. Connally 1971 George P. Shultz 1972 William E. Simon 1974
Secretary of Defense	Melvin R. Laird 1969 Elliot L. Richardson 1973 James R. Schlesinger 1973
Attorney General	John N. Mitchell 1969 Richard G. Kleindienst 1972 Elliot L. Richardson 1973 William B. Saxbe 1974
Postmaster General[5]	William M. Blount 1969
Secretary of the Interior	Walter J. Hickel 1969 Rogers C. B. Morton 1971
Secretary of Agriculture	Clifford M. Hardin 1969 Earl L. Butz 1971
Secretary of Commerce	Maurice H. Stans 1969 Peter G. Peterson 1972 Frederick B. Dent 1973
Secretary of Labor	George P. Shultz 1969 James D. Hodgson 1970 Peter J. Brennan 1973
Secretary of Health, Education, and Welfare	Robert H. Finch 1969 Elliot L. Richardson 1970 Caspar W. Weinberger 1973
Secretary of Housing and Urban Development	George Romney 1969 James T. Lynn 1973
Secretary of Transportation	John A. Volpe 1969 Claude S. Brinegar 1973

FORD

Secretary of State	Henry A. Kissinger (Cont.)
Secretary of the Treasury	William E. Simon (Cont.)
Secretary of Defense	James R. Schlesinger (Cont.) Donald H. Rumsfeld 1975
Attorney General	William B. Saxbe (Cont.) Edward H. Levi 1975
Secretary of the Interior	Rogers C. B. Morton (Cont.) Stanley K. Hathaway 1975 Thomas S. Kleppe 1975
Secretary of Agriculture	Earl L. Butz (Cont.) John Knebel 1976
Secretary of Commerce	Frederick B. Dent (Cont.) Rogers C. B. Morton 1975 Elliot L. Richardson 1976
Secretary of Labor	Peter J. Brennan (Cont.) John T. Dunlop 1975 William J. Usery, Jr. 1976
Secretary of Health, Education, and Welfare	Caspar W. Weinberger (Cont.) F. David Mathews 1975
Secretary of Housing and Urban Development	James T. Lynn (Cont.) Carla A. Hills 1975
Secretary of Transportation	Claude S. Brinegar (Cont.) William T. Coleman, Jr. 1975

CARTER

Secretary of State	Cyrus R. Vance 1977 Edmund S. Muskie 1980
Secretary of the Treasury	W. Michael Blumenthal 1977 G. William Miller 1979
Secretary of Defense	Harold Brown 1977
Attorney General	Griffin B. Bell 1977 Benjamin R. Civiletti 1979
Secretary of the Interior	Cecil D. Andrus 1977
Secretary of Agriculture	Bob S. Bergland 1977
Secretary of Commerce	Juanita M. Kreps 1977 Philip M. Klutznick 1979
Secretary of Labor	F. Ray Marshall 1977
Secretary of Health and Human Services[6]	Joseph A. Califano, Jr. 1977 Patricia Roberts Harris 1979
Secretary of Housing and Urban Development	Patricia Roberts Harris 1977 Moon Landrieu 1979
Secretary of Transportation	Brock Adams 1977 Neil E. Goldschmidt 1979
Secretary of Energy	James R. Schlesinger 1977 Charles W. Duncan, Jr. 1979
Secretary of Education	Shirley Mount Hufstedler 1979

REAGAN

Secretary of State	Alexander M. Haig, Jr. 1981 George P. Shultz 1982
Secretary of the Treasury	Donald T. Regan 1981 James A. Baker 3rd 1985 Nicholas F. Brady 1988
Secretary of Defense	Caspar W. Weinberger 1981 Frank C. Carlucci 1987
Attorney General	William French Smith 1981 Edwin Meese 3rd 1985 Richard L. Thornburgh 1988
Secretary of the Interior	James G. Watt 1981 William P. Clark 1983 Donald P. Hodel 1985
Secretary of Agriculture	John R. Block 1981 Richard E. Lyng 1986
Secretary of Commerce	Malcolm Baldrige 1981 C. William Verity, Jr. 1987
Secretary of Labor	Raymond J. Donovan 1981 William E. Brock 1985 Ann Dore McLaughlin 1987
Secretary of Health and Human Services	Richard S. Schweiker 1981 Margaret M. Heckler 1983 Otis R. Bowen 1985
Secretary of Housing and Urban Development	Samuel R. Pierce, Jr. 1981
Secretary of Transportation	Andrew L. Lewis, Jr. 1981 Elizabeth H. Dole 1983 James H. Burnley 4th 1987
Secretary of Energy	James B. Edwards 1981 Donald P. Hodel 1983 John S. Herrington 1985
Secretary of Education	T. H. Bell 1981 William J. Bennett 1985 Lauro F. Cavazos 1988

BUSH

Secretary of State	James A. Baker 3d 1989 Lawrence S. Eagleburger 1992
Secretary of the Treasury	Nicholas F. Brady (Cont.)
Secretary of Defense	Richard Cheney 1989
Attorney General	Richard L. Thornburgh (Cont.) William P. Barr 1992
Secretary of the Interior	Manuel Lujan Jr. 1989
Secretary of Agriculture	Clayton K. Yeutter 1989 Edward Madigan 1991
Secretary of Commerce	Robert A. Mosbacher Sr. 1989 Barbara H. Franklin 1992
Secretary of Labor	Elizabeth H. Dole 1989 Lynn Martin 1991
Secretary of Health and Human Services	Louis W. Sullivan 1989
Secretary of Housing and Urban Development	Jack F. Kemp 1989
Secretary of Transportation	Samuel K. Skinner 1989 Andrew Card 1992
Secretary of Energy	James D. Watkins 1989
Secretary of Education	Lauro F. Cavazos (Cont.) Lamar Alexander 1991
Secretary of Veterans Affairs	Edward J. Derwinski 1989

CLINTON

Secretary of State	Warren M. Christopher 1993
Secretary of the Treasury	Lloyd Bentsen 1993
Secretary of Defense	Les Aspin 1993
Attorney General	Janet Reno 1993
Secretary of the Interior	Bruce Babbitt 1993
Secretary of Agriculture	Mike Espy 1993
Secretary of Commerce	Ronald H. Brown 1993
Secretary of Labor	Robert B. Reich 1993
Secretary of Health and Human Services	Donna E. Shalala 1993
Secretary of Housing and Urban Development	Henry G. Cisneros 1993
Secretary of Transportation	Federico F. Pena 1993
Secretary of Energy	Hazel R. O'Leary 1993
Secretary of Education	Richard W. Riley 1993
Secretary of Veterans Affairs	Jesse Brown 1993

1. The Postmaster General did not become a Cabinet member until 1829. Earlier Postmasters General were: Samuel Osgood (1789), Timothy Pickering (1791), Joseph Habersham (1795), Gideon Granger (1801), Return J. Meigs, Jr. (1814), and John McLean (1823). 2. On July 26, 1947, the Departments of War and of the Navy were incorporated into the Department of Defense. 3. Not confirmed by the Senate. 4. Recess appointment. 5. The Postmaster General is no longer a Cabinet member. 6. Known as Department of Health, Education, and Welfare until May 1980.

The Beginning of the U.S. Supreme Court

In 1801, Chief Justice John Marshall and his colleagues had to meet in a tiny room in the basement of the Capitol because the planners of Washington, D.C., had forgotten to provide a space for the Supreme Court.

Although the Supreme Court is the most important judicial body in the world in terms of the role it plays within the political order, no one could have predicted this at the time the Constitution was written in 1787. The first chief justice, John Jay, resigned in 1795 to run for governor of New York. Nominated as his successor by President George Washington was John Rutledge, who had been named to the initial Court in 1789, but resigned in 1791, without ever sitting, to go to what was considered the more prestigious South Carolina Supreme Court. Because Rutledge failed to receive Senate confirmation, Oliver Ellsworth was nominated and confirmed in 1796 as chief justice, but he too resigned to accept a diplomatic post in France in 1800. Few decisions of this period were of great significance. The most important, a 1793 decision upholding federal jurisdiction in a suit brought by South Carolina land speculators against the state of Georgia, was met by a storm of protest that resulted in the quick proposal and ratification of the Eleventh Amendment effectively overruling the decision.

The rise in importance of the Supreme Court began with the appointment by President John Adams in 1801 of John Marshall, his secretary of state, to succeed Ellsworth. This appointment was widely interpreted as the symbol of the desire of the Federalists who had lost the recent election to retain control of the judicial branch after Thomas Jefferson and his supporters took over the presidency and Congress. This illustrates the extent to which the institutional mechanisms of checks and balances can help a repudiated political party. Given the lifetime tenure of justices, the Supreme Court is almost by definition a "conservative" force, even if what is being "conserved" is the liberal vision of an earlier party.

Not the least important of Marshall's contributions to the power of the Supreme Court was his establishment of the notion of a single "opinion of the Court" and his efforts, usually successful, to discourage the expression of any dissent from this opinion. Previously, the justices, like members of English courts, delivered separate opinions, with none being designated as the view of the institutional Court.

Marshall's opinion in *Marbury v. Madison* (1803) is famous for exemplifying the Court's power to invalidate even a congressional statute thought to violate the Constitution. Far more important, however, were a number of decisions upholding congressional power or limiting state power.

Most important was *McCulloch* v. *Maryland* (1819), which upheld the power of Congress to charter the (Second) Bank of the United States even though the Constitution contains no language specifically authorizing such an act. (This lack of authorization had led Representative James Madison, when the First Bank of the United States was chartered in 1791, to oppose the act as unconstitutional.) Moreover, the Court invalidated an attempt by Maryland to tax the Bank, viewing such a tax as an impermissible attack on the powers of the national government. What *McCulloch* illustrates is the crucial ability of the Supreme Court to legitimatize the decisions made by other branches of government by reassuring the public that they are, indeed, "constitutional."

Although "judicial review" is analyzed most often in terms of the ability of the Court to invalidate unconstitutional legislation, in fact the Court rarely finds legislation unconstitutional. Most often challenges, especially to federal legislation, fail, and the disputed legislation gains legitimacy from having survived judicial scrutiny.

Also more important than *Marbury*, practically speaking, was the 1810 decision in *Fletcher* v. *Peck*, in which for the first time the Court struck down state legislation as constitutionally invalid. Over the half century following *Marbury*, the combination of the Court's upholding federal legislation and invalidating state legislation deemed offensive to one or another constitutional principle (most often the contract clause or the commerce clause) served to bolster the power of the national government and to provide reins on state powers. □

Figures and Legends in American Folklore

Appleseed, Johnny (John Chapman, 1774–1847): Massachusetts-born nurseryman; reputed to have spread seeds and seedlings from which rose orchards of the Midwest.
Billy the Kid (William H. Bonney, 1859–1881): New York-born desperado; killed his first man before he reached his teens; after short life of crime in Wild West, was gunned down by Sheriff Pat Garrett; symbol of lawless West.
Boone, Daniel (1734–1820): Frontiersman and Indian fighter, about whom legends of early America have been built; figured in Byron's *Don Juan.*
Brodie, Steve (1863–1901): Reputed to have dived off Brooklyn Bridge on July 23, 1886. (Whether he actually did so has never been proved.)
Buffalo Bill (William F. Cody, 1846–1917): Buffalo hunter and Indian scout; much of legend about him and Wild West stems from his own Wild West show, which he operated in late 19th century.
Bunyan, Paul: Mythical lumberjack; subject of tall tales throughout timber country (that he dug Grand Canyon, for example).
Crockett, David (1786–1836): Frontiersman and member of U.S. Congress, about whom legends have been built of heroic feats; died in defense of Alamo.
Fritchie (or Frietchie), Barbara: Symbol of patriotism; in ballad by John Greenleaf Whittier, 90-year-old Barbara Fritchie defiantly waves Stars and Stripes as "Stonewall" Jackson's Confederate troops march through Frederick, Md.
James, Jesse (1847–1882): Bank and train robber; folklore has given him quality of American Robin Hood.
Jones, Casey (John Luther Jones, 1863–1900): Example of heroic locomotive engineer given to feats of prowess; died in wreck with his hand on brake lever when his Illinois Central "Cannonball" express hit freight train at Vaughan, Miss.
Ross, Betsy (1752–1836): Member of Philadelphia flag-making family; reported to have designed and sewn first American flag. (Report is without confirmation.)
Uncle Sam: Personification of United States and its people; origin uncertain; may be based on inspector of government supplies in Revolutionary War and War of 1812.

Assassinations and Attempts in U. S. Since 1865

Cermak, Anton J. (Mayor of Chicago): Shot Feb. 15, 1933, in Miami by Giuseppe Zangara, who attempted to assassinate Franklin D. Roosevelt; Cermak died March 6.

Ford, Gerald R. (President of U.S.): Escaped assassination attempt Sept. 5, 1975, in Sacramento, Calif., by Lynette Alice (Squeaky) Fromm, who pointed but did not fire .45-caliber pistol. Escaped assassination attempt in San Francisco, Calif., Sept. 22, 1975, by Sara Jane Moore, who fired one shot from a .38-caliber pistol that was deflected.

Garfield, James A. (President of U.S.): Shot July 2, 1881, in Washington, D.C., by Charles J. Guiteau; died Sept. 19.

Jordan, Vernon E., Jr. (civil rights leader): Shot and critically wounded in assassination attempt May 29, 1980, in Fort Wayne, Ind.

Kennedy, John F. (President of U.S.): Shot Nov. 22, 1963, in Dallas, Tex., allegedly by Lee Harvey Oswald; died same day. Injured was Gov. John B. Connally of Texas. Oswald was shot and killed two days later by Jack Ruby.

Kennedy, Robert F. (U.S. Senator from New York): Shot June 5, 1968, in Los Angeles by Sirhan Bishara Sirhan; died June 6.

King, Martin Luther, Jr. (civil rights leader): Shot April 4, 1968, in Memphis by James Earl Ray; died same day.

Lincoln, Abraham (President of U.S.): Shot April 14, 1865, in Washington, D.C., by John Wilkes Booth; died April 15.

Long, Huey P. (U.S. Senator from Louisiana): Shot Sept. 8, 1935, in Baton Rouge by Dr. Carl A. Weiss; died Sept. 10.

McKinley, William (President of U.S.): Shot Sept. 6, 1901, in Buffalo by Leon Czolgosz; died Sept. 14.

Reagan, Ronald (President of U.S.): Shot in left lung in Washington by John W. Hinckley, Jr., on March 30, 1981; three others also wounded.

Roosevelt, Franklin D. (President-elect of U.S.): Escaped assassination unhurt Feb. 15, 1933, in Miami. *See* Cermak.

Roosevelt, Theodore (ex-President of U.S.): Escaped assassination (though shot) Oct. 14, 1912, in Milwaukee while campaigning for President.

Seward, William H. (Secretary of State): Escaped assassination (though injured) April 14, 1865, in Washington, D.C., by Lewis Powell (or Paine), accomplice of John Wilkes Booth.

Truman, Harry S. (President of U.S.): Escaped assassination unhurt Nov. 1, 1950, in Washington, D.C., as 2 Puerto Rican nationalists attempted to shoot their way into Blair House.

Wallace, George C. (Governor of Alabama): Shot and critically wounded in assassination attempt May 15, 1972, at Laurel, Md., by Arthur Herman Bremer. Wallace paralyzed from waist down.

Impeachments of Federal Officials

Source: Congressional Directory

The procedure for the impeachment of Federal officials is detailed in Article I, Section 3, of the Constitution. See Index

The Senate has sat as a court of impeachment in the following cases:

William Blount, Senator from Tennessee; charges dismissed for want of jurisdiction, January 14, 1799.
John Pickering, Judge of the U.S. District Court for New Hampshire; removed from office March 12, 1804.

Samuel Chase, Associate Justice of the Supreme Court; acquitted March 1, 1805.
James H. Peck, Judge of the U.S. District Court for Missouri; acquitted Jan. 31, 1831.
West H. Humphreys, Judge of the U.S. District Court for the middle, eastern, and western districts of Tennessee; removed from office June 26, 1862.
Andrew Johnson, President of the United States; acquitted May 26, 1868.
William W. Belknap, Secretary of War; acquitted Aug. 1, 1876.
Charles Swayne, Judge of the U.S. District Court for the northern district of Florida; acquitted Feb. 27, 1905.
Robert W. Archbald, Associate Judge, U.S. Commerce Court; removed Jan. 13, 1913.
George W. English, Judge of the U.S. District Court for eastern district of Illinois; resigned Nov. 4, 1926; proceedings dismissed.
Harold Louderback, Judge of the U.S. District Court for the northern district of California; acquitted May 24, 1933.
Halsted L. Ritter, Judge of the U.S. District Court for the southern district of Florida; removed from office April 17, 1936.
Harry E. Claiborne, Judge of the U.S. District Court for the district of Nevada; removed from office October 9, 1986.
Alcee L. Hastings, Judge of the U.S. District Court for the southern district of Florida; removed from office October 20, 1989.
Walter L. Nixon, Jr., Judge of the U.S. District Court for Mississippi; removed from office November 3, 1989.

Members of the Supreme Court of the United States

	Service		Birth			
Name; apptd. from	Term	Yrs	Place	Date	Died	Religion
CHIEF JUSTICES						
John Jay, N.Y.	1789–1795	5	N.Y.	1745	1829	Episcopal
John Rutledge, S.C.	1795	0	S.C.	1739	1800	Church of England
Oliver Ellsworth, Conn.	1796–1800	4	Conn.	1745	1807	Congregational
John Marshall, Va.	1801–1835	34	Va.	1755	1835	Episcopal
Roger B. Taney, Md.	1836–1864	28	Md.	1777	1864	Roman Catholic
Salmon P. Chase, Ohio	1864–1873	8	N.H.	1808	1873	Episcopal
Morrison R. Waite, Ohio	1874–1888	14	Conn.	1816	1888	Episcopal
Melville W. Fuller, Ill.	1888–1910	21	Me.	1833	1910	Episcopal
Edward D. White, La.	1910–1921	10	La.	1845	1921	Roman Catholic
William H. Taft, Conn.	1921–1930	8	Ohio	1857	1930	Unitarian
Charles E. Hughes, N.Y.	1930–1941	11	N.Y.	1862	1948	Baptist
Harlan F. Stone, N.Y.	1941–1946	4	N.H.	1872	1946	Episcopal
Frederick M. Vinson, Ky.	1946–1953	7	Ky.	1890	1953	Methodist
Earl Warren, Calif.	1953–1969	15	Calif.	1891	1974	Protestant
Warren E. Burger, Va.	1969–1986	17	Minn.	1907	—	Presbyterian
William H. Rehnquist, Ariz.	1986–		Wis.	1924	—	Lutheran
ASSOCIATE JUSTICES						
James Wilson, Pa.	1789–1798	8	Scotland	1742	1798	Episcopal
John Rutledge, S.C.	1790–1791	1	S.C.	1739	1800	Church of England
William Cushing, Mass.	1790–1810	20	Mass.	1732	1810	Unitarian
John Blair, Va.	1790–1796	5	Va.	1732	1800	Presbyterian
James Iredell, N.C.	1790–1799	9	England	1751	1799	Episcopal
Thomas Johnson, Md.	1792–1793	0	Md.	1732	1819	Episcopal
William Paterson, N.J.	1793–1806	13	Ireland	1745	1806	Protestant
Samuel Chase, Md.	1796–1811	15	Md.	1741	1811	Episcopal
Bushrod Washington, Va.	1799–1829	30	Va.	1762	1829	Episcopal
Alfred Moore, N.C.	1800–1804	3	N.C.	1755	1810	Episcopal
William Johnson, S.C.	1804–1834	30	S.C.	1771	1834	Presbyterian
Brockholst Livingston, N.Y.	1807–1823	16	N.Y.	1757	1823	Presbyterian
Thomas Todd, Ky.	1807–1826	18	Va.	1765	1826	Presbyterian
Gabriel Duval, Md.	1811–1835	23	Md.	1752	1844	French Protestant
Joseph Story, Mass.	1812–1845	33	Mass.	1779	1845	Unitarian
Smith Thompson, N.Y.	1823–1843	20	N.Y.	1768	1843	Presbyterian
Robert Trimble, Ky.	1826–1828	2	Va.	1777	1828	Protestant
John McLean, Ohio	1830–1861	31	N.J.	1785	1861	Methodist-Epis.
Henry Baldwin, Pa.	1830–1844	14	Conn.	1780	1844	Trinity Church
James M. Wayne, Ga.	1835–1867	32	Ga.	1790	1867	Protestant
Philip P. Barbour, Va.	1836–1841	4	Va.	1783	1841	Episcopal
John Catron, Tenn.	1837–1865	28	Pa.	1786	1865	Presbyterian
John McKinley, Ala.	1837–1852	14	Va.	1780	1852	Protestant
Peter V. Daniel, Va.	1841–1860	18	Va.	1784	1860	Episcopal
Samuel Nelson, N.Y.	1845–1872	27	N.Y.	1792	1873	Protestant
Levi Woodbury, N.H.	1845–1851	5	N.H.	1789	1851	Protestant
Robert C. Grier, Pa.	1846–1870	23	Pa.	1794	1870	Presbyterian
Benjamin R. Curtis, Mass.	1851–1857	5	Mass.	1809	1874	([2])

Name; apptd. from	Service		Birth		Died	Religion
	Term	Yrs	Place	Date		
John A. Campbell, Ala.	1853–1861	8	Ga.	1811	1889	Episcopal
Nathan Clifford, Maine	1858–1881	23	N.H.	1803	1881	(1)
Noah H. Swayne, Ohio	1862–1881	18	Va.	1804	1884	Quaker
Samuel F. Miller, Iowa	1862–1890	28	Ky.	1816	1890	Unitarian
David Davis, Ill.	1862–1877	14	Md.	1815	1886	(4)
Stephen J. Field, Calif.	1863–1897	34	Conn.	1816	1899	Episcopal
William Strong, Pa.	1870–1880	10	Conn.	1808	1895	Presbyterian
Joseph P. Bradley, N.J.	1870–1892	21	N.Y.	1813	1892	Presbyterian
Ward Hunt, N.Y.	1872–1882	9	N.Y.	1810	1886	Episcopal
John M. Harlan, Ky.	1877–1911	33	Ky.	1833	1911	Presbyterian
William B. Woods, Ga.	1880–1887	6	Ohio	1824	1887	Protestant
Stanley Matthews, Ohio	1881–1889	7	Ohio	1824	1889	Presbyterian
Horace Gray, Mass.	1882–1902	20	Mass.	1828	1902	(3)
Samuel Blatchford, N.Y.	1882–1893	11	N.Y.	1820	1893	Presbyterian
Lucius Q. C. Lamar, Miss.	1888–1893	5	Ga.	1825	1893	Methodist
David J. Brewer, Kan.	1889–1910	20	Asia Minor	1837	1910	Protestant
Henry B. Brown, Mich.	1890–1906	15	Mass.	1836	1913	Protestant
George Shiras, Jr., Pa.	1892–1903	10	Pa.	1832	1924	Presbyterian
Howell E. Jackson, Tenn.	1893–1895	2	Tenn.	1832	1895	Baptist
Edward D. White, La.	1894–1910	16	La.	1845	1921	Roman Catholic
Rufus W. Peckham, N.Y.	1895–1909	13	N.Y.	1838	1909	Episcopal
Joseph McKenna, Calif.	1898–1925	26	Pa.	1843	1926	Roman Catholic
Oliver W. Holmes, Mass.	1902–1932	29	Mass.	1841	1935	Unitarian
William R. Day, Ohio	1903–1922	19	Ohio	1849	1923	Protestant
William H. Moody, Mass.	1906–1910	3	Mass.	1853	1917	Episcopal
Horace H. Lurton, Tenn.	1909–1914	4	Ky.	1844	1914	Episcopal
Charles E. Hughes, N.Y.	1910–1916	5	N.Y.	1862	1948	Baptist
Willis Van Devanter, Wyo.	1910–1937	26	Ind.	1859	1941	Episcopal
Joseph R. Lamar, Ga.	1910–1916	4	Ga.	1857	1916	Ch. of Disciples
Mahlon Pitney, N.J.	1912–1922	10	N.J.	1858	1924	Presbyterian
James C. McReynolds, Tenn.	1914–1941	26	Ky.	1862	1946	Disciples of Christ
Louis D. Brandeis, Mass.	1916–1939	22	Ky.	1856	1941	Jewish
John H. Clarke, Ohio	1916–1922	5	Ohio	1857	1945	Protestant
George Sutherland, Utah	1922–1938	15	England	1862	1942	Episcopal
Pierce Butler, Minn.	1923–1939	16	Minn.	1866	1939	Roman Catholic
Edward T. Sanford, Tenn.	1923–1930	7	Tenn.	1865	1930	Episcopal
Harlan F. Stone, N.Y.	1925–1941	16	N.H.	1872	1946	Episcopal
Owen J. Roberts, Pa.	1930–1945	15	Pa.	1875	1955	Episcopal
Benjamin N. Cardozo, N.Y.	1932–1938	6	N.Y.	1870	1938	Jewish
Hugo L. Black, Ala.	1937–1971	34	Ala.	1886	1971	Baptist
Stanley F. Reed, Ky.	1938–1957	19	Ky.	1884	1980	Protestant
Felix Frankfurter, Mass.	1939–1962	23	Austria	1882	1965	Jewish
William O. Douglas, Conn.	1939–1975	36	Minn.	1898	1980	Presbyterian
Frank Murphy, Mich.	1940–1949	9	Mich.	1890	1949	Roman Catholic
James F. Byrnes, S.C.	1941–1942	1	S.C.	1879	1972	Episcopal
Robert H. Jackson, Pa.	1941–1954	13	N.Y.	1892	1954	Episcopal
Wiley B. Rutledge, Iowa	1943–1949	6	Ky.	1894	1949	Unitarian
Harold H. Burton, Ohio	1945–1958	13	Mass.	1888	1964	Unitarian
Tom C. Clark, Tex.	1949–1967	17	Tex.	1899	1977	Presbyterian
Sherman Minton, Ind.	1949–1956	7	Ind.	1890	1965	Roman Catholic
John M. Harlan, N.Y.	1955–1971	16	Ill.	1899	1971	Presbyterian
William J. Brennan, Jr., N.J.	1956–1990	33	N.J.	1906	—	Roman Catholic
Charles E. Whittaker, Mo.	1957–1962	5	Kan.	1901	1973	Methodist
Potter Stewart, Ohio	1958–1981	23	Mich.	1915	1985	Episcopal
Byron R. White, Colo.	1962–1993	31	Colo.	1917	—	Episcopal
Arthur J. Goldberg, Ill.	1962–1965	2	Ill.	1908	1990	Jewish
Abe Fortas, Tenn.	1965–1969	3	Tenn.	1910	1982	Jewish
Thurgood Marshall, N.Y.	1967–1991	24	Md.	1908	1993	Episcopal
Harry A. Blackmun, Minn.	1970–	—	Ill.	1908	—	Methodist
Lewis F. Powell, Jr., Va.	1972–1987	15	Va.	1907	—	Presbyterian
William H. Rehnquist, Ariz.	1972–1986	14	Wis.	1924	—	Lutheran
John Paul Stevens, Ill.	1975–	—	Ill.	1920	—	Protestant
Sandra Day O'Connor, Ariz.	1981–	—	Tex.	1930	—	Episcopal
Antonin Scalia, D.C.	1986–	—	N.J.	1936	—	Roman Catholic
Anthony M. Kennedy, Calif.	1988–	—	Calif.	1936	—	n.a.
David H. Souter, N.H.	1990–	—	Mass.	1939	—	Episcopal
Clarence Thomas, D.C.	1991–	—	Ga.	1948	—	Roman Catholic
Ruth Bader Ginsburg, D.C.	1993–	—	N.Y.	1933	—	Jewish

1. Congregational; later Unitarian. 2. Unitarian; then Episcopal. 3. Unitarian or Congregational. 4. Not a member of any church. NOTE: n.a. = not available.

Executive Departments and Agencies

Source: Congressional Directory, 1991–1992
Unless otherwise indicated, addresses shown are in Washington, D.C.
*Nominated but not confirmed before Congress recessed in August.

CENTRAL INTELLIGENCE AGENCY (CIA)
Washington, D.C. (20505).
Established: 1947.
Director: R. James Woolsey.

COUNCIL OF ECONOMIC ADVISERS (CEA)
Room 314, Old Executive Office Bldg. (20500).
Members: 3.
Established: Feb. 20, 1946.
Chairman: Laura D. Tyson.

COUNCIL ON ENVIRONMENTAL QUALITY
722 Jackson Pl., N.W. (20503).
Members: 3.
Established: 1969.
Acting Director: Dinah Bear

NATIONAL SECURITY COUNCIL (NSC)
Old Executive Office Bldg. (20506).
Members: 4.
Established: July 26, 1947.
Chairman: The President.
Other members: Vice President; Secretary of State; Secretary of Defense.

OFFICE OF ADMINISTRATION
Old Executive Office Bldg. (20500).
Established: Dec. 12, 1977.
Director: Patsy Thomasson.

OFFICE OF MANAGEMENT AND BUDGET
Old Executive Office Bldg. (20503).
Established: July 1, 1970.
Director: Leon E. Panetta.

OFFICE OF SCIENCE AND TECHNOLOGY POLICY
Executive Office Building (20506).
Established: May 11, 1976.
Director: Dr. John H. Gibbons.

OFFICE OF THE UNITED STATES TRADE REPRESENTATIVE
600 17th St., N.W. (20506).
Established: Jan. 15, 1963.
Trade Representative: Michael Kantor.

OFFICE OF POLICY DEVELOPMENT
1600 Pennsylvania Ave., N.W. (20500).
Established: Jan. 21, 1981.
Acting Director: Kevin Jones.

OFFICE OF NATIONAL DRUG CONTROL POLICY
Suite 1011, 1825 Connecticut Ave., N.W. (20009).
Established: March 13, 1989.
Director: Dr. Lee Brown.

Executive Departments

DEPARTMENT OF STATE
2201 C St., N.W. (20520).
Established: 1781 as Department of Foreign Affairs; reconstituted, 1789, following adoption of Constitution; name changed to Department of State Sept. 15, 1789.
Secretary: Warren Christopher.
Deputy Secretary: Clifford Wharton.
Chief Delegate to U.N.: Madelaine Konibel Albright.

DEPARTMENT OF THE TREASURY
15th St. & Pennsylvania Ave., N.W. (20220).
Established: Sept. 2, 1789.
Secretary: Lloyd Bentsen.
Deputy Secretary: Roger Altman.
Treasurer of the U.S.: Vacancy.
Comptroller of the Currency: Eugene Ludwig.

DEPARTMENT OF DEFENSE
The Pentagon (20301).
Established: July 26, 1947, as National Department Establishment; name changed to Department of Defense on Aug. 10, 1949. Subordinate to Secretary of Defense are Secretaries of Army, Navy, Air Force.
Secretary: Les Aspin.
Deputy Secretary: Donald J. Atwood.
Secretary of Army: Michael P.W. Stone.
Secretary of Navy: Sean O'Keefe.
Secretary of Air Force: Sheila E. Widnall
Commandant of Marine Corps: Carl E. Mundy, Jr.
Joint Chiefs of Staff: Gen. John Shalikashvili*, Chairman; Adm. David E. Jeremiah, Navy; Gen. Merrill A. McPeak, Air Force; Gen. Gordon Russell Sullivan, Army; Gen. John R. Dailey, Marine Corps.

DEPARTMENT OF JUSTICE
Constitution Ave. between 9th & 10th Sts., N.W. (20530).
Established: Office of Attorney General was created Sept. 24, 1789. Although he was one of original Cabinet members, he was not executive department head until June 22, 1870, when Department of Justice was established.
Attorney General: Janet Reno.
Deputy Attorney General: Phillip Heymann.
Solicitor General: Drew Days 3rd
Director of FBI: Louis Joseph Freeh.

DEPARTMENT OF THE INTERIOR
C St. between 18th & 19th Sts., N.W. (20240).
Established: March 3, 1849.
Secretary: Bruce Babbitt.
Under Secretary: Vacancy.

DEPARTMENT OF AGRICULTURE
Independence Ave. between 12th & 14th Sts., S.W. (20250).
Established: May 15, 1862. Administered by Commissioner of Agriculture until 1889, when it was made executive department.
Secretary: Mike Espy.
Deputy Secretary: Richard Roninger.

DEPARTMENT OF COMMERCE
14th St. between Constitution Ave. & E St., N.W. (20230).
Established: Department of Commerce and Labor was created Feb. 14, 1903. On March 4, 1913, all labor activities were transferred out of Department of Commerce and Labor and it was renamed Department of Commerce.
Secretary: Ron Brown.
Deputy Secretary: Tony Das.

DEPARTMENT OF LABOR
200 Constitution Ave., N.W. (20210).
Established: Bureau of Labor was created in 1884 under Department of the Interior; later became independent department without executive rank. Returned to bureau status in Department of Commerce and Labor, but on March 4, 1913, became independent executive department under its present name.
Secretary: Robert Reich.
Deputy Secretary: Thomas P. Glynn.

DEPARTMENT OF HEALTH AND HUMAN SERVICES[1]
200 Independence Ave., S.W. (20201).
Established: April 11, 1953, replacing Federal Security Agency created in 1939.

Secretary: Donna Shalala.
Surgeon General: Dr. Joycelyn Elders.

1. Originally Department of Health, Education and Welfare. Name changed in May 1980 when Department of Education was activated.

DEPARTMENT OF HOUSING AND URBAN DEVELOPMENT
451 7th St., S.W. (20410).
Established: 1965, replacing Housing and Home Finance Agency created in 1947.
Secretary: Henry Cisneros.
Under Secretary: Clarence Duvernay.

DEPARTMENT OF TRANSPORTATION
400 7th St., S.W. (20590).
Established: Oct. 15, 1966, as result of Department of Transportation Act, which became effective April 1, 1967.
Secretary: Frederico Pena.
Deputy Secretary: Mort Downey.

DEPARTMENT OF ENERGY
1000 Independence Ave., S.W. (20585).
Established: Aug. 1977.
Secretary: Hazel R. O'Leary.
Deputy Secretary: William White.

DEPARTMENT OF EDUCATION
400 Maryland Avenue, S.W. (20202).
Established: Oct. 17, 1979.
Secretary: Richard Riley.
Under Secretary: Madeline Kunin.

DEPARTMENT OF VETERANS' AFFAIRS
810 Vermont Avenue, N.W. (20420).
Established: March 15, 1989, replacing Veterans Administration created in 1930.
Secretary: Jesse Brown.
Deputy Secretary: Herschel Gober.

Major Independent Agencies

ACTION
1100 Vermont Ave., N.W. (20525).
Established: July 1, 1971.
Director: Vacancy.

CONSUMER PRODUCT SAFETY COMMISSION
5401 Westbard Ave., Bethesda, Md. (20207).
Members: 5.
Established: Oct. 27, 1972.
Chairman: Jacqueline Jones-Smith.

ENVIRONMENTAL PROTECTION AGENCY (EPA)
401 M St., S.W. (20460).
Established: Dec. 2, 1970.
Administrator: Carol M. Browner.

EQUAL EMPLOYMENT OPPORTUNITY COMMISSION (EEOC)
1801 L St., N.W. (20507).
Members: 5.
Established: July 2, 1965.
Acting Chairman: Tony Gallegos.

FARM CREDIT ADMINISTRATION (FCA)
1501 Farm Credit Dr., McLean, Va. (22102).
Members: 13.
Established: July 17, 1916.
Chairman of Federal Farm Credit Board: Harold B. Steele.

FEDERAL COMMUNICATIONS COMMISSION (FCC)
1919 M St., N.W. (20554).
Members: 7.
Established: 1934.
Acting Chairman: James Quello.

FEDERAL DEPOSIT INSURANCE CORPORATION (FDIC)
550 17th St., N.W. (20429).
Members: 3.
Established: June 16, 1933.
Acting Chairman: Andrew Hove.

FEDERAL ELECTION COMMISSION (FEC)
999 E St., N.W. (20463).
Members: 6.
Established: 1974.
Chairman: Scott E. Thomas.

FEDERAL MARITIME COMMISSION
1100 L St., N.W. (20573).
Members: 5.
Established: Aug. 12, 1961.
Chairman: William D. Hathaway.

FEDERAL MEDIATION AND CONCILIATION SERVICE (FMCS)
2100 K St., N.W. (20427).
Established: 1947.
Director: Bernard E. DeLury.

FEDERAL RESERVE SYSTEM (FRS), BOARD OF GOVERNORS OF
20th St. & Constitution Ave., N.W. (20551).
Members: 7.
Established: Dec. 23, 1913.
Chairman: Alan Greenspan.

FEDERAL TRADE COMMISSION (FTC)
Pennsylvania Ave. at 6th St., N.W. (20580).
Members: 5.
Established: Sept. 26, 1914.
Chairman: Janet D. Steiger.

GENERAL SERVICES ADMINISTRATION (GSA)
18th and F Sts., N.W. (20405).
Established: July 1, 1949.
Administrator: Roger Johnson.

INTERSTATE COMMERCE COMMISSION (ICC)
12th St. & Constitution Ave., N.W. (20423).
Members: 7.
Established: Feb. 4, 1887.
Chairman: Gail C. McDonald.

NATIONAL AERONAUTICS AND SPACE ADMINISTRATION (NASA)
600 Independence Ave. (20546).
Established: 1958.
Administrator: Daniel S. Goldin

NATIONAL FOUNDATION ON THE ARTS AND THE HUMANITIES
1100 Pennsylvania Ave., N.W., (20506).
Established: 1965.
Chairmen: National Endowment for the Arts, Chairman, Jane Alexander*; National Endowment for the Humanities, Chairman, Sheldon Hackney.

NATIONAL LABOR RELATIONS BOARD (NLRB)
1717 Pennsylvania Ave., N.W. (20570).
Members: 5.
Established: July 5, 1935.
Chairman: James M. Stephens.

NATIONAL MEDIATION BOARD
Suite 910, 1425 K St., N.W. (20572).
Members: 3.
Established: June 21, 1934.
Chairman: Kimberly A. Madigan.

NATIONAL SCIENCE FOUNDATION (NSF)
1800 G St., N.W. (20550).
Established: 1950.
Acting Director: Dr. Frederick Bernthal.

NATIONAL TRANSPORTATION SAFETY BOARD
800 Independence Ave., S.W. (20594).
Members: 5.
Established: April 1, 1975.
Chairman: Carl Vogt.

NUCLEAR REGULATORY COMMISSION (NRC)
Rockville, Md. (20852).
Members: 5.
Established: Jan. 19, 1975.
Chairman: Ivan Selin.

OFFICE OF PERSONNEL MANAGEMENT (OPM)
1900 E St., N.W. (20415).
Members: 3.
Established: Jan. 1, 1979.
Director: James B. King.

SECURITIES AND EXCHANGE COMMISSION (SEC)
450 5th St., N.W. (20549).
Members: 5.
Established: July 2, 1934.
Chairman: Richard C. Breeden.

SELECTIVE SERVICE SYSTEM (SSS)
National Headquarters 1023 31st., N.W. (20435).
Established: Sept. 16, 1940.
Director: Robert W. Gambino.

SMALL BUSINESS ADMINISTRATION (SBA)
409 3rd St., N.W. (20416).
Established: July 30, 1953.
Administrator: Erskine J. Bowles.

TENNESSEE VALLEY AUTHORITY (TVA)
400 West Summit Hill Drive, Knoxville, Tenn. (37902).
Washington office: Capitol Hill Office Bldg., 412 First St., S.E. (20444).
Members of Board of Directors: 3.
Established: May 18, 1933.
Director: William Kennoy.

U.S. AGENCY FOR INTERNATIONAL DEVELOPMENT
520 21st St., N.W. (20523).
Established: Oct. 1, 1979.
Administrator: J. Brian Atwood.

U.S. ARMS CONTROL AND DISARMAMENT AGENCY
520 21st St., N.W., (20451).
Established: Sept. 26, 1961.
Acting Director: Thomas Graham.

U.S. COMMISSION ON CIVIL RIGHTS
1121 Vermont Avenue, N.W. (20425).
Members: 8.
Established: 1957.
Chairman: Arthur A. Fletcher.

U.S. INFORMATION AGENCY
301 Fourth St., S.W. (20547).
Established: Aug. 1, 1953. Reorganized April 1, 1978.
Director: Dr. Joseph Duffey.

U.S. INTERNATIONAL TRADE COMMISSION
500 E St., N.W. (20436).
Members: 6.
Established: Sept. 8, 1916.
Chairman: Don E. Newquist.

U.S. POSTAL SERVICE
475 L'Enfant Plaza West, S.W. (20260).
Postmaster General: Marvin T. Runyon.
Deputy Postmaster General: Michael S. Coughlin.
Established: Office of Postmaster General and temporary post office system created in 1789. Act of Feb. 20, 1792, made detailed provisions for Post Office Department. In 1970 became independent agency headed by 11-member board of governors.

Other Independent Agencies

Administrative Conference of the United States—Suite 500, 2120 L St., N.W. (20037).
American Battle Monuments Commission—5127 Pulaski Bldg. 20 Massachusetts Ave., N.W. (20314).
Appalachian Regional Commission—1666 Connecticut Ave., N.W. (20235).
Board for International Broadcasting—Suite 400, 1201 Connecticut Ave., N.W. (20036).
Commission of Fine Arts—Pension Bldg. 441 F St., N.W. (20001).
Commodity Futures Trading Commission—2033 K St., N.W. (20581).
Export-Import Bank of the United States—811 Vermont Ave., N.W. (20571).
Federal Emergency Management Agency—500 C St., S.W. (20472).
Federal Home Loan Bank Board—1700 G St., N.W. (20552).
Federal Labor Relations Authority—500 C St., S.W. (20424).
Inter-American Foundation—1515 Wilson Blvd., Arlington, Va. (22209).
Merit Systems Protection Board—1120 Vermont Ave., N.W. (20419).
National Commission on Libraries and Information Science—Suite 310, 111 18th st., N.W. (20036).
National Credit Union Administration—1776 G St., N.W. (20456).
Occupational Safety and Health Review Commission—1825 K St., N.W. (20006).
Panama Canal Commission—Suite 550, 2000 L St., N.W. (20036).
Peace Corps—1990 K St., N.W. (20526).
Pension Benefit Guaranty Corporation—2020 K St., N.W. (20006).
Postal Rate Commission—Suite 300, 1333 H St., N.W. (20268).
President's Committee on Employment of the Handicapped—1111 20th St., N.W. (20036).
President's Council on Physical Fitness and Sports—450 5th St., N.W. (20001).
Railroad Retirement Board (RRB)—844 Rush St., Chicago, Ill. (60611); Washington Liaison Office: Suite 558, 2000 L St. (20036).
U.S. Parole Commission—Room 420, 5550 Friendship Blvd., Chevy Chase, Md. (20815).

Legislative Department

Architect of the Capitol—U.S. Capitol Building (20515).
General Accounting Office (GAO)—441 G St., N.W. (20548).
Government Printing Office (GPO)—North Capitol & H Sts., N.W. (20401).
Library of Congress—10 First St. S.E. (20540).
Office of Technology Assessment—600 Pennsylvania Ave., S.E. (20510).
United States Botanic Garden—Office of Director, 245 First St., S.W. (20024).

Quasi-Official Agencies

American National Red Cross—430 17th St., N.W. (20006).
Legal Services Corporation—400 Virginia Ave. S.W. (20024).
National Academy of Sciences, National Academy of Engineering, National Research Council, Institute of Medicine—2101 Constitution Ave., N.W. (20418).
National Railroad Passenger Corporation (Amtrak)—60 Massachusetts Ave., N.E. (20002).
Smithsonian Institution—1000 Jefferson Dr., S.W. (20560).

Biographies of the Presidents

GEORGE WASHINGTON was born on Feb. 22, 1732 (Feb. 11, 1731/2, old style) in Westmoreland County, Va. While in his teens, he trained as a surveyor, and at the age of 20 he was appointed adjutant in the Virginia militia. For the next three years, he fought in the wars against the French and Indians, serving as Gen. Edward Braddock's aide in the disastrous campaign against Fort Duquesne. In 1759, he resigned from the militia, married Martha Dandridge Custis, a widow, and settled down as a gentleman farmer at Mount Vernon, Va.

As a militiaman, Washington had been exposed to the arrogance of the British officers, and his experience as a planter with British commercial restrictions increased his anti-British sentiment. He opposed the Stamp Act of 1765 and after 1770 became increasingly prominent in organizing resistance. A delegate to the Continental Congress, Washington was selected as commander in chief of the Continental Army and took command at Cambridge, Mass., on July 3, 1775.

Inadequately supported and sometimes covertly sabotaged by the Congress, in charge of troops who were inexperienced, badly equipped, and impatient of discipline, Washington conducted the war on the policy of avoiding major engagements with the British and wearing them down by harrassing tactics. His able generalship, along with the French alliance and the growing weariness within Britain, brought the war to a conclusion with the surrender of Cornwallis at Yorktown, Va., on Oct. 19, 1781.

The chaotic years under the Articles of Confederation led Washington to return to public life in the hope of promoting the formation of a strong central government. He presided over the Constitutional Convention and yielded to the universal demand that he serve as first President. He was inaugurated on April 30, 1789, in New York, the first national capital. In office, he sought to unite the nation and establish the authority of the new government at home and abroad. Greatly distressed by the emergence of the Hamilton-Jefferson rivalry, Washington worked to maintain neutrality but actually sympathized more with Hamilton. Following his unanimous re-election in 1792, his second term was dominated by the Federalists. His Farewell Address on Sept. 17, 1796 (published but never delivered) rebuked party spirit and warned against "permanent alliances" with foreign powers.

He died at Mount Vernon on Dec. 14, 1799.

JOHN ADAMS was born on Oct. 30 (Oct. 19, old style), 1735, at Braintree (now Quincy), Mass. A Harvard graduate, he considered teaching and the ministry but finally turned to law and was admitted to the bar in 1758. Six years later, he married Abigail Smith. He opposed the Stamp Act, served as lawyer for patriots indicted by the British, and by the time of the Continental Congresses, was in the vanguard of the movement for independence. In 1778, he went to France as commissioner. Subsequently he helped negotiate the peace treaty with Britain, and in 1785 became envoy to London. Resigning in 1788, he was elected Vice President under Washington and was re-elected in 1792.

Though a Federalist, Adams did not get along with Hamilton, who sought to prevent his election to the presidency in 1796 and thereafter intrigued against his administration. In 1798, Adam's independent policy averted a war with France but completed the break with Hamilton and the right-wing Federalists; at the same time, the enactment of the Alien and Sedition Acts, directed against foreigners and against critics of the government, exasperated the Jeffersonian opposition. The split between Adams and Hamilton resulted in Jefferson's becoming the next President. Adams retired to his home in Quincy. He and Jefferson died on the same day, July 4, 1826, the 50th anniversary of the signing of the Declaration of Independence.

His *Defence of the Constitutions of Government of the United States* (1787) contains original and striking, if conservative, political ideas.

THOMAS JEFFERSON was born on April 13 (April 2, old style), 1743, at Shadwell in Goochland (now Albemarle) County, Va. A William and Mary graduate, he studied law, but from the start showed an interest in science and philosophy. His literary skill and political clarity brought him to the forefront of the revolutionary movement in Virginia. As delegate to the Continental Congress, he drafted the Declaration of Independence. In 1776, he entered the Virginia House of Delegates and initiated a comprehensive reform program for the abolition of feudal survivals in land tenure and the separation of church and state.

In 1779, he became governor, but constitutional limitations on his power, combined with his own lack of executive energy, caused an unsatisfactory administration, culminating in Jefferson's virtual abdication when the British invaded Virginia in 1781. He retired to his beautiful home at Monticello, Va., to his family. His wife, Martha Wayles Skelton, whom he married in 1772, died in 1782.

Jefferson's *Notes on Virginia* (1784–85) illustrate his many-faceted interests, his limitless intellectual curiosity, his deep faith in agrarian democracy. Sent to Congress in 1783, he helped lay down the decimal system and drafted basic reports on the organization of the western lands. In 1785 he was appointed minister to France, where the Anglo-Saxon liberalism he had drawn from John Locke, the British philosopher, was stimulated by contact with the thought that would soon ferment in the French Revolution. In 1789, Washington appointed him Secretary of State. While favoring the Constitution and a strengthened central government, Jefferson came to believe that Hamilton contemplated the establishment of a monarchy. Growing differences resulted in Jefferson's resignation on Dec. 31, 1793.

Elected vice president in 1796, Jefferson continued to serve as spiritual leader of the opposition to Federalism, particularly to the repressive Alien and Sedition Acts. He was elected President in 1801 by the House of Representatives as a result of Hamilton's decision to throw the Federalist votes to him rather than to Aaron Burr, who had tied him in electoral votes. He was the first President to be inaugurated in Washington, which he had helped to design.

The purchase of Louisiana from France in 1803, though in violation of Jefferson's earlier constitutional scruples, was the most notable act of his administration. Re-elected in 1804, with the Federalist Charles C. Pinckney opposing him, Jefferson tried desperately to keep the United States out of the Napoleonic Wars in Europe, employing to this end the unpopular embargo policy.

After his retirement to Monticello in 1809, he developed his interest in education, founding the University of Virginia and watching its development with never-flagging interest. He died at Monticello on July 4, 1826. Jefferson had an enormous variety of interests and skills, ranging from education and science to architecture and music.

JAMES MADISON was born in Port Conway, Va., on March 16, 1751 (March 5, 1750/1, old style). A Princeton graduate, he joined the struggle for independence on his return to Virginia in 1771. In the 1770s and 1780s he was active in state politics, where he championed the Jefferson reform program, and in the Continental Congress. Madison was influential in the Constitutional Convention as leader of the group favoring a strong central government and as recorder of the debates; and he subsequently wrote, in collaboration with Alexander Hamilton and John Jay, the *Federalist* papers to aid the campaign for the adoption of the Constitution.

Serving in the new Congress, Madison soon emerged as the leader in the House of the men who opposed Hamilton's financial program and his pro-British leanings in foreign policy. Retiring from Congress in 1797, he continued to be active in Virginia and drafted the Virginia Resolution protesting the Alien and Sedition Acts. His intimacy with Jefferson made him the natural choice for Secretary of State in 1801.

In 1809, Madison succeeded Jefferson as President, defeating Charles C. Pinckney. His attractive wife, Dolley Payne Todd, whom he married in 1794, brought a new social sparkle to the executive mansion. In the meantime, increasing tension with Britain culminated in the War of 1812—a war for which the United States was unprepared and for which Madison lacked the executive talent to clear out incompetence and mobilize the nation's energies. Madison was re-elected in 1812, running against the Federalist De Witt Clinton. In 1814, the British actually captured Washington and forced Madison to flee to Virginia.

Madison's domestic program capitulated to the Hamiltonian policies that he had resisted 20 years before and he now signed bills to establish a United States Bank and a higher tariff.

After his presidency, he remained in retirement in Virginia until his death on June 28, 1836.

JAMES MONROE was born on April 28, 1758, in Westmoreland County, Va. A William and Mary graduate, he served in the army during the first years of the Revolution and was wounded at Trenton. He then entered Virginia politics and later national politics under the sponsorship of Jefferson. In 1786, he married Elizabeth (Eliza) Kortright.

Fearing centralization, Monroe opposed the adoption of the Constitution and, as senator from Virginia, was highly critical of the Hamiltonian program. In 1794, he was appointed minister to France, where his ardent sympathies with the Revolution exceeded the wishes of the State Department. His troubled diplomatic career ended with his recall in 1796. From 1799 to 1802, he was governor of Virginia. In 1803, Jefferson sent him to France to help negotiate the Louisiana Purchase and for the next few years he was active in various negotiations on the Continent.

In 1808, Monroe flirted with the radical wing of the Republican Party, which opposed Madison's candidacy; but the presidential boom came to naught and, after a brief term as governor of Virginia in 1811, Monroe accepted Madison's offer to become Secretary of State. During the War of 1812, he vainly sought a field command and instead served as Secretary of War from September 1814 to March 1815.

Elected President in 1816 over the Federalist Rufus King, and re-elected without opposition in 1820, Monroe, the last of the Virginia dynasty, pursued the course of systematic tranquilization that won for his administrations the name "the era of good feeling." He continued Madison's surrender to the Hamiltonian domestic program, signed the Missouri Compromise, acquired Florida, and with the able assistance of his Secretary of State, John Quincy Adams, promulgated the Monroe Doctrine in 1823, declaring against foreign colonization or intervention in the Americas. He died in New York City on July 4, 1831, the third president to die on the anniversary of Independence.

JOHN QUINCY ADAMS was born on July 11, 1767, at Braintree (now Quincy), Mass., the son of John Adams, the second President. He spent his early years in Europe with his father, graduated from Harvard, and entered law practice. His anti-Jeffersonian newspaper articles won him political attention. In 1794, he became minister to the Netherlands, the first of several diplomatic posts that occupied him until his return to Boston in 1801. In 1797, he married Louisa Catherine Johnson.

In 1803, Adams was elected to the Senate, nominally as a Federalist, but his repeated displays of independence on such issues as the Louisiana Purchase and the embargo caused his party to demand his resignation and ostracize him socially. In 1809, Madison rewarded him for his support of Jefferson by appointing him minister to St. Petersburg. He helped negotiate the Treaty of Ghent in 1814, and in 1815 became minister to London. In 1817 Monroe appointed him Secretary of State where he served with great distinction, gaining Florida from Spain without hostilities and playing an equal part with Monroe in formulating the Monroe Doctrine.

When no presidential candidate received a majority of electoral votes in 1824, Adams, with the support of Henry Clay, was elected by the House in 1825 over Andrew Jackson, who had the original plurality. Adams had ambitious plans of government activity to foster internal improvements and promote the arts and sciences, but congressional obstructionism, combined with his own unwillingness or inability to play the role of a politician, resulted in little being accomplished. After being defeated for re-election by Jackson in 1828, he successfully ran for the House of Representatives in 1830. There though nominally a Whig, he pursued as ever an independent course. He led the fight to force Congress to receive antislavery petitions and fathered the Smithsonian Institution.

Stricken on the floor of the House, he died on Feb. 23, 1848. His long and detailed *Diary* gives a unique picture of the personalities and politics of the times.

ANDREW JACKSON was born on March 15, 1767, in what is now generally agreed to be Waxhaw, S.C. After a turbulent boyhood as an orphan and a British prisoner, he moved west to Tennessee, where he soon qualified for law practice but found time for such frontier pleasures as horse racing, cockfighting, and dueling. His marriage to Rachel Donelson Robards in 1791 was complicated by subsequent legal uncertainties about the status of her divorce. During the 1790s, Jackson served in the Tennessee Constitutional Convention, the United States House of Representatives and Senate, and on the Tennessee Supreme Court.

After some years as a country gentleman, living at the Hermitage near Nashville, Jackson in 1812 was given command of Tennessee troops sent against the Creeks. He defeated the Indians at Horseshoe Bend in 1814; subsequently he became a major general and won the Battle of New Orleans over veteran British troops, though after the treaty of peace had been signed at Ghent. In 1818, Jackson invaded Florida, captured Pensacola, and hanged two Englishmen named Arbuthnot and Ambrister, creating an international incident. A presidential boom began for him in 1821, and to foster it, he returned to the Senate (1823–25). Though he won a plurality of electoral votes in 1824, he lost in the House when Clay threw his strength to Adams. Four years later, he easily defeated Adams.

As President, Jackson greatly expanded the power and prestige of the presidential office and carried through an unprecedented program of domestic reform, vetoing the bill to extend the United States Bank, moving toward a hard-money currency policy, and checking the program of federal internal improvements. He also vindicated federal authority against South Carolina with its doctrine of nullification and against France on the question of debts. The support given his policies by the workingmen of the East as well as by the farmers of the East, West, and South resulted in his triumphant re-election in 1832 over Clay.

After watching the inauguration of his handpicked successor, Martin Van Buren, Jackson retired to the Hermitage, where he maintained a lively interest in national affairs until his death on June 8, 1845.

MARTIN VAN BUREN was born on Dec. 5, 1782, at Kinderhook, N.Y. After graduating from the village school, he became a law clerk, entered practice in 1803, and soon became active in state politics as state senator and attorney general. In 1820, he was elected to the United States Senate. He threw the support of his efficient political organization, known as the Albany Regency, to William H. Crawford in 1824 and to Jackson in 1828. After leading the opposition to Adams's administration in the Senate, he served briefly as governor of New York (1828–29) and resigned to become Jackson's Secretary of State. He was soon on close personal terms with Jackson and played an important part in the Jacksonian program.

In 1832, Van Buren became vice president; in 1836, President. The Panic of 1837 overshadowed his term. He attributed it to the overexpansion of the credit and favored the establishment of an independent treasury as repository for the federal funds. In 1840, he established a 10-hour day on public works. Defeated by Harrison in 1840, he was the leading contender for the Democratic nomination in 1844 until he publicly opposed immediate annexation of Texas, and was subsequently beaten by the Southern delegations at the Baltimore convention. This incident increased his growing misgivings about the slave power.

After working behind the scenes among the anti-slavery Democrats, Van Buren joined in the movement that led to the Free-Soil Party and became its candidate for President in 1848. He subsequently returned to the Democratic Party while continuing to object to its pro-Southern policy. He died in Kinderhook on July 24, 1862. His *Autobiography* throws valuable sidelights on the political history of the times.

His wife, Hannah Hoes, whom he married in 1807, died in 1819.

WILLIAM HENRY HARRISON was born in Charles City County, Va., on Feb. 9, 1773. Joining the army in 1791, he was active in Indian fighting in the Northwest, became secretary of the Northwest Territory in 1798 and governor of Indiana in 1800. He married Anna Symmes in 1795. Growing discontent over white encroachments on Indian lands led to the formation of an Indian alliance under Tecumseh to resist further aggressions. In 1811, Harrison won a nominal victory over the Indians at Tippecanoe and in 1813 a more decisive one at the Battle of the Thames, where Tecumseh was killed.

After resigning from the army in 1814, Harrison had an obscure career in politics and diplomacy, ending up 20 years later as a county recorder in Ohio. Nominated for President in 1835 as a military hero whom the conservative politicians hoped to be able to control, he ran surprisingly well against Van Buren in 1836. Four years later, he defeated Van Buren but caught penumonia and died in Washington on April 4, 1841, a month after his inauguration. Harrison was the first president to die in office.

JOHN TYLER was born in Charles City County, Va., on March 29, 1790. A William and Mary graduate, he entered law practice and politics, serving in the House of Representatives (1817–21), as governor of Virginia (1825–27), and as senator (1827–36). A strict constructionist, he supported Crawford in 1824 and Jackson in 1828, but broke with Jackson over his United States Bank policy and became a member of the Southern state-rights group that co-operated with the Whigs. In 1836, he resigned from the Senate rather than follow instructions from the Virginia legislature to vote for a resolution expunging censure of Jackson from the Senate record.

Elected vice president on the Whig ticket in 1840, Tyler succeeded to the presidency on Harrison's death. His strict-constructionist views soon caused a split with the Henry Clay wing of the Whig party and a stalemate on domestic questions. Tyler's more considerable achievements were his support of the Webster-Ashburton Treaty with Britain and his success in bringing about the annexation of Texas.

After his presidency he lived in retirement in Virginia until the outbreak of the Civil War, when he emerged briefly as chairman of a peace convention and then as delegate to the provisional Congress of the Confederacy. He died on Jan. 18, 1862. He married Letitia Christian in 1813 and, two years after her death in 1842, Julia Gardiner.

JAMES KNOX POLK was born in Mecklenburg County, N.C., on Nov. 2, 1795. A graduate of the University of North Carolina, he moved west to Tennessee, was admitted to the bar, and soon became prominent in state politics. In 1825, he was elected to the House of Representatives, where he opposed Adams and, after 1829, became Jackson's floor leader in the fight against the Bank. In 1835, he became Speaker of the House. Four years later, he was elected governor of Tennessee, but was beaten in tries for re-election in 1841 and 1843.

The supporters of Van Buren for the Democratic

nomination in 1844 counted on Polk as his running mate; but, when Van Buren's stand on Texas alienated Southern support, the convention swung to Polk on the ninth ballot. He was elected over Henry Clay, the Whig candidate. Rapidly disillusioning those who thought that he would not run his own administration, Polk proceeded steadily and precisely to achieve four major objectives—the acquisition of California, the settlement of the Oregon question, the reduction of the tariff, and the establishment of the independent treasury. He also enlarged the Monroe Doctrine to exclude all non-American intervention in American affairs, whether forcible or not, and he forced Mexico into a war that he waged to a successful conclusion.

His wife, Sarah Childress, whom he married in 1824, was a woman of charm and ability. Polk died in Nashville, Tenn., on June 15, 1849.

ZACHARY TAYLOR was born at Montebello, Orange County, Va., on Nov. 24, 1784. Embarking on a military career in 1808, Taylor fought in the War of 1812, the Black Hawk War, and the Seminole War, meanwhile holding garrison jobs on the frontier or desk jobs in Washington. A brigadier general as a result of his victory over the Seminoles at Lake Okeechobee (1837), Taylor held a succession of Southwestern commands and in 1846 established a base on the Rio Grande, where his forces engaged in hostilities that precipitated the war with Mexico. He captured Monterrey in September 1846 and, disregarding Polk's orders to stay on the defensive, defeated Santa Anna at Buena Vista in February 1847, ending the war in the northern provinces.

Though Taylor had never cast a vote for president, his party affiliations were Whiggish and his availability was increased by his difficulties with Polk. He was elected president over the Democrat Lewis Cass. During the revival of the slavery controversy, which was to result in the Compromise of 1850, Taylor began to take an increasingly firm stand against appeasing the South; but he died in Washington on July 9, 1850, during the fight over the Compromise. He married Margaret Mackall Smith in 1810. His bluff and simple soldierly qualities won him the name Old Rough and Ready.

MILLARD FILLMORE was born at Locke, Cayuga County, N.Y., on Jan. 7, 1800. A lawyer, he entered politics with the Anti-Masonic Party under the sponsorship of Thurlow Weed, editor and party boss, and subsequently followed Weed into the Whig Party. He served in the House of Representatives (1833–35 and 1837–43) and played a leading role in writing the tariff of 1842. Defeated for governor of New York in 1844, he became State comptroller in 1848, was put on the Whig ticket with Taylor as a concession to the Clay wing of the party, and became president upon Taylor's death in 1850.

As president, Fillmore broke with Weed and William H. Seward and associated himself with the pro-Southern Whigs, supporting the Compromise of 1850. Defeated for the Whig nomination in 1852, he ran for president in 1856 as candidate of the American, or Know-Nothing Party, which sought to unite the country against foreigners in the alleged hope of diverting it from the explosive slavery issue. Fillmore opposed Lincoln during the Civil War. He died in Buffalo on March 8, 1874.

He was married in 1826 to Abigail Powers, who died in 1853, and in 1858 to Caroline Carmichael McIntosh.

FRANKLIN PIERCE was born at Hillsboro, N.H., on Nov. 23, 1804. A Bowdoin graduate, lawyer, and Jacksonian Democrate, he won rapid political advancement in the party, in part because of the prestige of his father, Gov. Benjamin Pierce. By 1831 he was Speaker of the New Hampshire House of Representatives; from 1833 to 1837, he served in the federal House and from 1837 to 1842 in the Senate. His wife, Jane Means Appleton, whom he married in 1834, disliked Washington and the somewhat dissipated life led by Pierce; in 1842 Pierce resigned from the Senate and began a successful law practice in Concord, N.H. During the Mexican War, he was a brigadier general.

Thereafter Pierce continued to oppose antislavery tendencies within the Democratic Party. As a result, he was the Southern choice to break the deadlock at the Democratic convention of 1852 and was nominated on the 49th ballot. In the election, Pierce overwhelmed Gen. Winfield Scott, the Whig candidate.

As president, Pierce followed a course of appeasing the South at home and of playing with schemes of territorial expansion abroad. The failure of his foreign and domestic policies prevented his renomination; and he died in Concord on Oct. 8, 1869, in relative obscurity.

JAMES BUCHANAN was born near Mercersburg, Pa., on April 23, 1791. A Dickinson graduate and a lawyer, he entered Pennsylvania politics as a Federalist. With the disappearance of the Federalist Party, he became a Jacksonian Democrat. He served with ability in the House (1821–31), as minister to St. Petersburg (1832–33), and in the Senate (1834–45), and in 1845 became Polk's Secretary of State. In 1853, Pierce appointed Buchanan minister to Britain, where he participated with other American diplomats in Europe in drafting the expansionist Ostend Manifesto.

He was elected president in 1856, defeating John C. Frémont, the Republican candidate, and former President Millard Fillmore of the American Party. The growing crisis over slavery presented Buchanan with problems he lacked the will to tackle. His appeasement of the South alientated the Stephen Douglas wing of the Democratic Party without reducing Southern militancy on slavery issues. While denying the right of secession, Buchanan also denied that the federal government could do anything about it. He supported the administration during the Civil War and died in Lancaster, Pa., on June 1, 1868.

The only president to remain a bachelor throughout his term, Buchanan used his charming niece, Harriet Lane, as White House hostess.

ABRAHAM LINCOLN was born in Hardin (now Larue) County, Ky., on Feb. 12, 1809. His family moved to Indiana and then to Illinois, and Lincoln gained what education he could along the way. While reading law, he worked in a store, managed a mill, surveyed, and split rails. In 1834, he went to the Illinois legislature as a Whig and became the party's floor leader. For the next 20 years he practiced law in Springfield, except for a single term (1847–49) in Congress, where he denounced the Mexican War. In 1855, he was a candidate for senator annd the next year he joined the new Republican Party.

A leading but unsuccessful candidate for the vice-presidential nomination with Frémont, Lincoln gained national attention in 1858 when, as Republican candidate for senator from Illinois, he engaged in a series of debates with Stephen A. Douglas, the Democratic candidate. He lost the election, but continued to prepare the way for the 1860 Republican convention and was rewarded with the presidential nomination on the third ballot. He won the election over three opponents.

From the start, Lincoln made clear that, unlike Buchanan, he believed the national government had the power to crush the rebellion. Not an abolitionist, he held the slavery issue subordinate to that of preserving the Union, but soon perceived that the war could not be brought to a successful conclusion without freeing the slaves. His administration was hampered by the incompetence of many Union generals, the inexperience of the troops, and the harassing political tactics both of the Republican Radicals, who favored a hard policy toward the South, and the Democratic Copperheads, who desired a negotiated peace. The Gettysburg Address of Nov. 19, 1863, marks the high point in the record of American eloquence. Lincoln's long search for a winning combination finally brought Generals Ulysses S. Grant and William T. Sherman on the top; and their series of victories in 1864 dispelled the mutterings from both Radicals and Peace Democrats that at one time seemed to threaten Lincoln's re-election. He was re-elected in 1864, defeating Gen. George B. McClellan, the Democratic candidate. His inaugural address urged leniency toward the South: "With malice toward none, with charity for all . . . let us strive on to finish the work we are in; to bind up the nation's wounds . . ." This policy aroused growing opposition on the part of the Republican Radicals, but before the matter could be put to the test, Lincoln was shot by the actor John Wilkes Booth at Ford's Theater, Washington, on April 14, 1865. He died the next morning.

Lincoln's marriage to Mary Todd in 1842 was often unhappy and turbulent, in part because of his wife's pronounced instability.

ANDREW JOHNSON was born at Raleigh, N.C., on Dec. 29, 1808. Self-educated, he became a tailor in Greeneville, Tenn., but soon went into politics, where he rose steadily. He served in the House of Representatives (1843–54), as governor of Tennessee (1853–57), and as a senator (1857–62). Politically he was a Jacksonian Democrat and his specialty was the fight for a more equitable land policy. Alone among the Southern Senators, he stood by the Union during the Civil War. In 1862, he became war governor of Tennessee and carried out a thankless and difficult job with great courage. Johnson became Lincoln's running mate in 1864 as a result of an attempt to give the ticket a nonpartisan and nonsectional character. Succeeding to the presidency on Lincoln's death, Johnson sought to carry out Lincoln's policy, but without his political skill. The result was a hopeless conflict with the Radical Republicans who dominated Congress, passed measures over Johnson's vetoes, and attempted to limit the power of the executive concerning appointments and removals. The conflict culminated with Johnson's impeachment for attempting to remove his disloyal Secretary of War in defiance of the Tenure of Office Act which required senatorial concurrence for such dismissals. The opposition failed by one vote to get the two thirds necessary for conviction.

After his presidency, Johnson maintained an interest in politics and in 1875 was again elected to the Senate. He died near Carter Station, Tenn., on July 31, 1875. He married Eliza McCardle in 1827.

ULYSSES SIMPSON GRANT was born (as Hiram Ulysses Grant) at Point Pleasant, Ohio, on April 27, 1822. He graduated from West Point in 1843 and served without particular distinction in the Mexican War. In 1848 he married Julia Dent. He resigned from the army in 1854, after warnings from his commanding officer about his drinking habits, and for the next six years held a wide variety of jobs in the Middle West. With the outbreak of the Civil War, he sought a command and soon, to his surprise, was made a brigadier general. His continuing successes in the western theaters, culminating in the capture of Vicksburg, Miss., in 1863, brought him national fame and soon the command of all the Union armies. Grant's dogged, implacable policy of concentrating on dividing and destroying the Confederate armies brought the war to an end in 1865. The next year, he was made full general.

In 1868, as Republican candidate for president, Grant was elected over the Democrat, Horatio Seymour. From the start, Grant showed his unfitness for the office. His Cabinet was weak, his domestic policy was confused, many of his intimate associates were corrupt. The notable achievement in foreign affairs was the settlement of controversies with Great Britain in the Treaty of London (1871), negotiated by his able Secretary of State, Hamilton Fish.

Running for re-election in 1872, he defeated Horace Greeley, the Democratic and Liberal Republican candidate. The Panic of 1873 graft scandals close to the presidency created difficulties for his second term.

After retiring from office, Grant toured Europe for two years and returned in time to accede to a third-term boom, but was beaten in the convention of 1880. Illness and bad business judgment darkened his last years, but he worked steadily at the *Personal Memoirs*, which were to be so successful when published after his death at Mount McGregor, near Saratoga, N.Y., on July 23, 1885.

RUTHERFORD BIRCHARD HAYES was born in Delaware, Ohio, on Oct. 4, 1822. A graduate of Kenyon College and the Harvard Law School, he practiced law in Lower Sandusky (now Fremont) and then in Cincinnati. In 1852 he married Lucy Webb. A Whig, he joined the Republican party in 1855. During the Civil War he rose to major general. He served in the House of Representatives from 1865 to 1867 and then confirmed a reputation for honesty and efficiency in two terms as Governor of Ohio (1868–72). His election to a third term in 1875 made him the logical candidate for those Republicans who wished to stop James G. Blaine in 1876, and he was nominated.

The result of the election was in doubt for some time and hinged upon disputed returns from South Carolina, Louisiana, Florida, and Oregon. Samuel J. Tilden, the Democrat, had the larger popular vote but was adjudged by the strictly partisan decisions of the Electoral Commission to have one fewer electoral vote, 185 to 184. The national acceptance of this result was due in part to the general understanding that Hayes would pursue a conciliatory policy toward the South. He withdrew the troops from the South, took a conservative position on financial and labor issues, and urged civil service reform.

Hayes served only one term by his own wish and

spent the rest of his life in various humanitarian endeavors. He died in Fremont on Jan. 17, 1893.

JAMES ABRAM GARFIELD, the last president to be born in a log cabin, was born in Cuyahoga County, Ohio, on Nov. 19, 1831. A Williams graduate, he taught school for a time and entered Republican politics in Ohio. In 1858, he married Lucretia Rudolph. During the Civil War, he had a promising career, rising to major general of volunteers; but he resigned in 1863, having been elected to the House of Representatives, where he served until 1880. His oratorical and parliamentary abilities soon made him the leading Republican in the House, though his record was marred by his unorthodox acceptance of a fee in the DeGolyer paving contract case and by suspicions of his complicity in the Crédit Mobilier scandal.

In 1880, Garfield was elected to the Senate, but instead became the presidential candidate on the 36th ballot as a result of a deadlock in the Republican convention. In the election, he defeated Gen. Winfield Scott Hancock, the Democratic candidate. Garfield's administration was barely under way when he was shot by Charles J. Guiteau, a disappointed office seeker, in Washington on July 2, 1881. He died in Elberton, N.J., on Sept. 19.

CHESTER ALAN ARTHUR was born at Fairfield, Vt., on Oct. 5, 1830. A graduate of Union College, he became a successful New York lawyer. In 1859, he married Ellen Herndon. During the Civil War, he held administrative jobs in the Republican state administration and in 1871 was appointed collector of the Port of New York by Grant. This post gave him control over considerable patronage. Though not personally corrupt, Arthur managed his power in the interests of the New York machine so openly that President Hayes in 1877 called for an investigation and the next year Arthur was suspended.

In 1880 Arthur was nominated for vice president in the hope of conciliating the followers of Grant and the powerful New York machine. As president upon Garfield's death, Arthur, stepping out of his familiar role as spoilsman, backed civil service reform, reorganized the Cabinet, and prosecuted political associates accused of post office graft. Losing machine support and failing to gain the reformers, he was not nominated for a full term in 1884. He died in New York City on Nov. 18, 1886.

STEPHEN GROVER CLEVELAND was born at Caldwell, N.J., on March 18, 1837. He was admitted to the bar in Buffalo, N.Y., in 1859 and lived there as a lawyer, with occasional incursions into Democratic politics, for more than 20 years. He did not participate in the Civil War. As mayor of Buffalo in 1881, he carried through a reform program so ably that the Democrats ran him successfully for governor in 1882. In 1884 he won the Democratic nomination for President. The campaign contrasted Cleveland's spotless public career with the uncertain record of James G. Blaine, the Republican candidate, and Cleveland received enough Mugwump (independent Republican) support to win.

As president, Cleveland pushed civil service reform, opposed the pension grab and attacked the high tariff rates. While in the White House, he married Frances Folsom in 1886. Renominated in 1888, Cleveland was defeated by Benjamin Harrison, polling more popular but fewer electoral votes. In 1892, he was elected over Harrison. When the Panic of 1893 burst upon the country, Cleveland's attempts to solve it by sound-money measures alienated the free-silver wing of the party, while his tariff policy alienated the protectionists. In 1894, he sent troops to break the Pullman strike. In foreign affairs, his firmness caused Great Britain to back down in the Venezuela border dispute.

In his last years Cleveland was an active and much-respected public figure. He died in Princeton, N.J., on June 24, 1908.

BENJAMIN HARRISON was born in North Bend, Ohio, on Aug. 20, 1833, the grandson of William Henry Harrison, the ninth president. A graduate of Miami University in Ohio, he took up the law in Indiana and became active in Republican politics. In 1853, he married Caroline Lavinia Scott. During the Civil War, he rose to brigadier general. A sound-money Republican, he was elected senator from Indiana in 1880. In 1888, he received the Republican nomination for President on the eighth ballot. Though behind on the popular vote, he won over Grover Cleveland in the electoral college by 233 to 168.

As President, Harrison failed to please either the bosses or the reform element in the party. In foreign affairs he backed Secretary of State Blaine, whose policy foreshadowed later American imperialism. Harrison was renominated in 1892 but lost to Cleveland. His wife died in the White House in 1892 and Harrison married her niece, Mary Scott (Lord) Dimmick, in 1896. After his presidency, he resumed law practice. He died in Indianapolis on March 13, 1901.

WILLIAM McKINLEY was born in Niles, Ohio, on Jan. 29, 1843. He taught school, then served in the Civil War, rising from the ranks to become a major. Subsequently he opened a law office in Canton, Ohio, and in 1871 married Ida Saxton. Elected to Congress in 1876, he served there until 1891, except for 1883–85. His faithful advocacy of business interests culminated in the passage of the highly protective McKinley Tariff of 1890. With the support of Mark Hanna, a shrewd Cleveland businessman interested in safeguarding tariff protection, McKinley became governor of Ohio in 1892 and Republican presidential candidate in 1896. The business community, alarmed by the progressivism of William Jennings Bryan, the Democratic candidate, spent considerable money to assure McKinley's victory.

The chief event of McKinley's administration was the war with Spain, which resulted in our acquisition of the Philippines and other islands. With imperialism an issue, McKinley defeated Bryan again in 1900. On Sept. 6, 1901, he was shot at Buffalo, N.Y., by Leon F. Czolgosz, an anarchist, and he died there eight days later.

THEODORE ROOSEVELT was born in New York City on Oct. 27, 1858. A Harvard graduate, he was early interested in ranching, in politics, and in writing picturesque historical narratives. He was a Republican member of the New York Assembly in 1882–84, an unsuccessful candidate for mayor of New York in 1886, a U.S. Civil Service Commissioner under Benjamin Harrison, Police Commissioner of New York City in 1895, and Assistant Secretary of the Navy under McKinley in 1897. He resigned in 1898 to help organize a volunteer regiment, the Rough Riders, and take a more direct part in the war with Spain. He was elected governor of New York in 1898 and vice president in 1900, in spite of lack of enthusiasm on the part of the bosses.

Assuming the presidency of the assassinated McKinley in 1901, Roosevelt embarked on a wide-ranging program of government reform and conservation of natural resources. He ordered antitrust suits against several large corporations, threatened to intervene in the anthracite coal strike of 1902, which prompted the operators to accept arbitration, and, in general, championed the rights of the "little man" and fought the "malefactors of great wealth." He was also responsible for such progressive legislation as the Elkins Act of 1901, which outlawed freight rebates by railroads; the bill establishing the Department of Commerce and Labor; the Hepburn Act, which gave the I.C.C. greater control over the railroads; the Meat Inspection Act; and the Pure Food and Drug Act.

In foreign affairs, Roosevelt pursued a strong policy, permitting the instigation of a revolt in Panama to dispose of Colombian objections to the Panama Canal and helping to maintain the balance of power in the East by bringing the Russo-Japanese War to an end, for which he won the Nobel Peace Prize, the first American to achieve a Nobel prize in any category. In 1904, he decisively defeated Alton B. Parker, his conservative Democratic opponent.

Roosevelt's increasing coldness toward his successor, William Howard Taft, led him to overlook his earlier disclaimer of third-term ambitions and to re-enter politics. Defeated by the machine in the Republican convention of 1912, he organized the Progressive Party (Bull Moose) and polled more votes than Taft, though the split brought about the election of Woodrow Wilson. From 1915 on, Roosevelt strongly favored intervention in the European war. He became deeply embittered at Wilson's refusal to allow him to raise a volunteer division. He died in Oyster Bay, N.Y., on Jan. 6, 1919. He was married twice: in 1880 to Alice Hathaway Lee, who died in 1884, and in 1886 to Edith Kermit Carow.

WILLIAM HOWARD TAFT was born in Cincinnati on Sept. 15, 1857. A Yale graduate, he entered Ohio Republican politics in the 1880s. In 1886 he married Helen Herron. From 1887 to 1890, he served on the Ohio Superior Court; 1890–92, as solicitor general of the United States; 1892–1900, on the federal circuit court. In 1900 McKinley appointed him president of the Philippine Commission and in 1901 governor general. Taft had great success in pacifying the Filipinos, solving the problem of the church lands, improving economic conditions, and establishing limited self-government. His period as Secretary of War (1904–08) further demonstrated his capacity as administrator and conciliator, and he was Roosevelt's hand-picked successor in 1908. In the election, he polled 321 electoral votes to 162 for William Jennings Bryan, who was running for the presidency for the third time.

Though he carried on many of Roosevelt's policies, Taft got into increasing trouble with the progressive wing of the party and displayed mounting irritability and indecision. After his defeat in 1912, he became professor of constitutional law at Yale. In 1921 he was appointed Chief Justice of the United States. He died in Washington on March 8, 1930.

THOMAS WOODROW WILSON was born in Staunton, Va., on Dec. 28, 1856. A Princeton graduate, he turned from law practice to post-graduate work in political science at Johns Hopkins University, receiving his Ph.D. in 1886. He taught at Bryn Mawr, Wesleyan, and Princeton, and in 1902 was made president of Princeton. After an unsuccessful attempt to democratize the social life of the university, he welcomed an invitation in 1910 to be the Democratic gubernatorial candidate in New Jersey, and was elected. His success in fighting the machine and putting through a reform program attracted national attention.

In 1912, at the Democratic convention in Baltimore, Wilson won the nomination on the 46th ballot and went on to defeat Roosevelt and Taft in the election. Wilson proceeded under the standard of the New Freedom to enact a program of domestic reform, including the Federal Reserve Act, the Clayton Antitrust Act, the establishment of the Federal Trade Commission, and other measures designed to restore competition in the face of the great monopolies. In foreign affairs, while privately sympathetic with the Allies, he strove to maintain neutrality in the European war and warned both sides against encroachments on American interests.

Re-elected in 1916 as a peace candidate, he tried to mediate between the warring nations; but when the Germans resumed unrestricted submarine warfare in 1917, Wilson brought the United States into what he now believed was a war to make the world safe for democracy. He supplied the classic formulations of Allied war aims and the armistice of Nov. 11, 1918 was negotiated on the basis of Wilson's Fourteen Points. In 1919 he strove at Versailles to lay the foundations for enduring peace. He accepted the imperfections of the Versailles Treaty in the expectation that they could be remedied by action within the League of Nations. He probably could have secured ratification of the treaty by the Senate if he had adopted a more conciliatory attitude toward the mild reservationists; but his insistence on all or nothing eventually caused the diehard isolationists and diehard Wilsonites to unite in rejecting a compromise.

In September 1919 Wilson suffered a paralytic stroke that limited his activity. After leaving the presidency he lived on in retirement in Washington, dying on Feb. 3, 1924. He was married twice—in 1885 to Ellen Louise Axson, who died in 1914, and in 1915 to Edith Bolling Galt.

WARREN GAMALIEL HARDING was born in Morrow County, Ohio, on Nov. 2, 1865. After attending Ohio Central College, Harding became interested in journalism and in 1884 bought the *Marion* (Ohio) *Star.* In 1891 he married a wealthy widow, Florence Kling De Wolfe. As his paper prospered, he entered Republican politics, serving as state senator (1899–1903) and as lieutenant governor (1904–06). In 1910, he was defeated for governor, but in 1914 was elected to the Senate. His reputation as an orator made him the keynoter at the 1916 Republican convention.

When the 1920 convention was deadlocked between Leonard Wood and Frank O. Lowden, Harding became the dark-horse nominee on his solemn affirmation that there was no reason in his past that he should not be. Straddling the League question, Harding was easily elected over James M. Cox, his Democratic opponent. His Cabinet contained some able men, but also some manifestly unfit for public office. Harding's own intimates were mediocre when they were not corrupt. The impending disclosure of the Teapot Dome scandal in the Interior Department and illegal practices in the Justice Department and Veterans' Bureau, as well as political setbacks, profoundly worried him. On his return from Alaska in 1923, he died unexpectedly in San Francisco on Aug. 2.

JOHN CALVIN COOLIDGE was born in Plymouth, Vt., on July 4, 1872. An Amherst graduate, he went into law practice at Northampton, Mass., in 1897. He married Grace Anna Goodhue in 1905. He entered Republican state politics, becoming successively mayor of Northampton, state senator, lieutenant governor and, in 1919, governor. His use of the state militia to end the Boston police strike in 1919 won him a somewhat undeserved reputation for decisive action and brought him the Republican vice-presidential nomination in 1920. After Harding's death Coolidge handled the Washington scandals with care and finally managed to save the Republican Party from public blame for the widespread corruption.

In 1924, Coolidge was elected without difficulty, defeating the Democrat, John W. Davis, and Robert M. La Follette running on the Progressive ticket. His second term, like his first, was characterized by a general satisfaction with the existing economic order. He stated that he did not choose to run in 1928.

After his presidency, Coolidge lived quietly in Northampton, writing an unilluminating *Autobiography* and conducting a syndicated column. He died there on Jan. 5, 1933.

HERBERT CLARK HOOVER was born at West Branch, Iowa, on Aug. 10, 1874, the first president to be born west of the Mississippi. A Stanford graduate, he worked from 1895 to 1913 as a mining engineer and consultant throughout the world. In 1899, he married Lou Henry. During World War I, he served with distinction as chairman of the American Relief Committee in London, as chairman of the Commission for Relief in Belgium, and as U.S. Food Administrator. His political affiliations were still too indeterminate for him to be mentioned as a possibility for either the Republican or Democratic nomination in 1920, but after the election he served Harding and Coolidge as Secretary of Commerce.

In the election of 1928, Hoover overwhelmed Gov. Alfred E. Smith of New York, the Democratic candidate and the first Roman Catholic to run for the presidency. He soon faced the worst depression in the nation's history, but his attacks upon it were hampered by his devotion to the theory that the forces that brought the crisis would soon bring the revival and then by his belief that there were too many areas in which the federal government had no power to act. In a succession of vetoes, he struck down measures proposing a national employment system or national relief, he reduced income tax rates, and only at the end of his term did he yield to popular pressure and set up agencies such as the Reconstruction Finance Corporation to make emergency loans to assist business.

After his 1932 defeat, Hoover returned to private business. In 1946, President Truman charged him with various world food missions; and from 1947 to 1949 and 1953 to 1955, he was head of the Commission on Organization of the Executive Branch of the Government. He died in New York City on Oct. 20, 1964.

FRANKLIN DELANO ROOSEVELT was born in Hyde Park, N.Y., on Jan. 30, 1882. A Harvard graduate, he attended Columbia Law School and was admitted to the New York bar. In 1910, he was elected to the New York State Senate as a Democrat. Reelected in 1912, he was appointed Assistant Secretary of the Navy by Woodrow Wilson the next year. In 1920, his radiant personality and his war service resulted in his nomination for vice president as James M. Cox's running mate. After his defeat, he returned to law practice in New York. In August 1921, Roosevelt was stricken with infantile paralysis while on vacation at Campobello, New Brunswick. After a long and gallant fight, he recovered partial use of his legs. In 1924 and 1928, he led the fight at the Democratic national conventions for the nomination of Gov. Alfred E. Smith of New York, and in 1928 Roosevelt was himself induced to run for governor of New York. He was elected, and was re-elected in 1930.

In 1932, Roosevelt received the Democratic nomination for president and immediately launched a campaign that brought new spirit to a weary and discouraged nation. He defeated Hoover by a wide margin. His first term was characterized by an unfolding of the New Deal program, with greater benefits for labor, the farmers, and the unemployed, and the progressive estrangement of most of the business community.

At an early stage, Roosevelt became aware of the menace to world peace posed by totalitarian fascism, and from 1937 on he tried to focus public attention on the trend of events in Europe and Asia. As a result, he was widely denounced as a warmonger. He was re-elected in 1936 over Gov. Alfred M. Landon of Kansas by the overwhelming electoral margin of 523 to 8, and the gathering international crisis prompted him to run for an unprecedented third term in 1940. He defeated Wendell L. Willkie.

Roosevelt's program to bring maximum aid to Britain and, after June 1941, to Russia was opposed, until the Japanese attack on Pearl Harbor restored national unity. During the war, Roosevelt shelved the New Deal in the interests of conciliating the business community, both in order to get full production during the war and to prepare the way for a united acceptance of the peace settlements after the war. A series of conferences with Winston Churchill and Joseph Stalin laid down the bases for the postwar world. In 1944 he was elected to a fourth term, running against Gov. Thomas E. Dewey of New York.

On April 12, 1945, Roosevelt died of a cerebral hemorrhage at Warm Springs, Ga., shortly after his return from the Yalta Conference. His wife, Anna Eleanor Roosevelt, whom he married in 1905, was a woman of great ability who made significant contributions to her husband's policies.

HARRY S. TRUMAN was born on a farm near Lamar, Mo., on May 8, 1884. During World War I, he served in France as a captain with the 129th Field Artillery. He married Bess Wallace in 1919. After engaging briefly and unsuccessfully in the haberdashery business in Kansas City, Mo., Truman entered local politics. Under the sponsorship of Thomas Pendergast, Democratic boss of Missouri, he held a number of local offices, preserving his personal honesty in the midst of a notoriously corrupt political machine. In 1934, he was elected to the Senate and was re-elected in 1940. During his first term he was a loyal but quiet supporter of the New Deal, but in his second term, an appointment as head of a Senate committee to investigate war production brought out his special qualities of honesty, common sense, and hard work, and he won widespread respect.

Elected vice president in 1944, Truman became president upon Roosevelt's sudden death in April 1945 and was immediately faced with the problems of winding down the war against the Axis and preparing the nation for postwar adjustment.

The years 1947–48 were distinguished by civil-rights proposals, the Truman Doctrine to contain the spread of Communism, and the Marshall Plan to aid in the economic reconstruction of war-ravaged nations. Truman's general record, highlighted by a vigorous Fair Deal campaign, brought about his unexpected election in 1948 over the heavily favored Thomas E. Dewey.

Truman's second term was primarily concerned with the Cold War with the Soviet Union, the implementing of the North Atlantic Pact, the United Nations police action in Korea, and the vast rearmament program with its accompanying problems of economic stabilization.

On March 29, 1952, Truman announced that he would not run again for the presidency. After leaving the White House, he returned to his home in Independence, Mo., to write his memoirs. He further busied himself with the Harry S. Truman Library there. He died in Kansas City, Mo., on Dec. 26, 1972.

DWIGHT DAVID EISENHOWER was born in Denison, Tex., on Oct. 14, 1890. His ancestors lived in Germany and emigrated to America, settling in Pennsylvania, early in the 18th century. His father, David, had a general store in Hope, Kan., which failed. After a brief time in Texas, the family moved to Abilene, Kan.

After graduating from Abilene High School in 1909, Eisenhower did odd jobs for almost two years. He won an appointment to the Naval Academy at Annapolis, but was too old for admittance. Then he received an appointment in 1910 to West Point, from which he graduated as a second lieutenant in 1915.

He did not see service in World War I, having been stationed at Fort Sam Houston, Tex. There he met Mamie Geneva Doud, whom he married in Denver on July 1, 1916, and by whom he had two sons: Doud Dwight (died in infancy) and John Sheldon Doud.

Eisenhower served in the Philippines from 1935 to 1939 with Gen. Douglas MacArthur. Afterward, Gen. George C. Marshall, the Army Chief of Staff, brought him into the War Department's General Staff and in 1942 placed him in command of the invasion of North Africa. In 1944, he was made Supreme Allied Commander for the invasion of Europe.

After the war, Eisenhower served as Army Chief of Staff from November 1945 until February 1948, when he was appointed president of Columbia University.

In December 1950, President Truman recalled Eisenhower to active duty to command the North Atlantic Treaty Organization forces in Europe. He held his post until the end of May 1952.

At the Republican convention of 1952 in Chicago, Eisenhower won the presidential nomination on the first ballot in a close race with Senator Robert A. Taft of Ohio. In the election, he defeated Gov. Adlai E. Stevenson of Illinois.

Through two terms, Eisenhower hewed to moderate domestic policies. He sought peace through Free World strength in an era of new nationalisms, nuclear missiles, and space exploration. He fostered alliances pledging the United States to resist Red aggression in Europe, Asia, and Latin America. The Eisenhower Doctrine of 1957 extended commitments to the Middle East.

At home, the popular president lacked Republican Congressional majorities after 1954, but he was re-elected in 1956 by 457 electoral votes to 73 for Stevenson.

While retaining most Fair Deal programs, he stressed "fiscal responsibility" in domestic affairs. A moderate in civil rights, he sent troops to Little Rock, Ark., to enforce court-ordered school integration.

With his wartime rank restored by Congress, Eisenhower returned to private life and the role of elder statesman, with his vigor hardly impaired by a heart attack, an ileitis operation, and a mild stroke suffered while in office. He died in Washington on March 28, 1969.

JOHN FITZGERALD KENNEDY was born in Brookline, Mass., on May 29, 1917. His father, Joseph P. Kennedy, was Ambassador to Great Britain from 1937 to 1940.

Kennedy was graduated from Harvard University in 1940 and joined the Navy the next year. He became skipper of a PT boat that was sunk in the Pacific by a Japanese destroyer. Although given up for lost, he swam to a safe island, towing an injured enlisted man.

After recovering from a war-aggravated spinal injury, Kennedy entered politics in 1946 and was elected to Congress. In 1952, he ran against Senator Henry Cabot Lodge, Jr., of Massachusetts, and won.

Kennedy was married on Sept. 12, 1953, to Jacqueline Lee Bouvier, by whom he had three children: Caroline, John Fitzgerald, Jr., and Patrick Bouvier (died in infancy).

In 1957 Kennedy won the Pulitzer Prize for a book he had written earlier, *Profiles in Courage*.

After strenuous primary battles, Kennedy won the Democratic presidential nomination on the first ballot at the 1960 Los Angeles convention. With a plurality of only 118,574 votes, he carried the election over Vice President Richard M. Nixon and became the first Roman Catholic president.

Kennedy brought to the White House the dynamic idea of a "New Frontier" approach in dealing with problems at home, abroad, and in the dimensions of space. Out of his leadership in his first few months in office came the 10-year Alliance for Progress to aid Latin America, the Peace Corps, and accelerated programs that brought the first Americans into orbit in the race in space.

Failure of the U.S.-supported Cuban invasion in April 1961 led to the entrenchment of the Communist-backed Castro regime, only 90 miles from United States soil. When it became known that Soviet offensive missiles were being installed in Cuba in 1962, Kennedy ordered a naval "quarantine" of the island and moved troops into position to eliminate this threat to U.S. security. The world seemed on the brink of a nuclear war until Soviet Premier Khrushchev ordered the removal of the missiles.

A sudden "thaw," or the appearance of one, in the cold war came with the agreement with the Soviet Union on a limited test-ban treaty signed in Moscow on Aug. 6, 1963.

In his domestic policies, Kennedy's proposals for medical care for the aged, expanded area redevelopment, and aid to education were defeated, but on minimum wage, trade legislation, and other measures he won important victories.

Widespread racial disorders and demonstrations led to Kennedy's proposing sweeping civil rights legislation. As his third year in office drew to a close, he also recommended an $11-billion tax cut to bolster the economy. Both measures were pending in Congress when Kennedy, looking forward to a second term, journeyed to Texas for a series of speeches.

While riding in a procession in Dallas on Nov. 22, 1963, he was shot to death by an assassin firing from an upper floor of a building. The alleged assassin, Lee Harvey Oswald, was killed two days later in the Dallas city jail by Jack Ruby, owner of a strip-tease place.

At 46 years of age, Kennedy became the fourth president to be assassinated and the eighth to die in office.

LYNDON BAINES JOHNSON was born in Stonewall, Tex., on Aug. 27, 1908. On both sides of his family he had a political heritage mingled with a Baptist background of preachers and teachers. Both his father and his paternal grandfather served in the Texas House of Representatives.

After his graduation from Southwest Texas State Teachers College, Johnson taught school for two years. He went to Washington in 1932 as secretary to Rep. Richard M. Kleberg. During this time, he married Claudia Alta Taylor, known as "Lady Bird." They had two children: Lynda Bird and Luci Baines.

In 1935, Johnson became Texas administrator for the National Youth Administration. Two years later, he was elected to Congress as an all-out supporter of Franklin D. Roosevelt, and served until 1949. He was the first member of Congress to enlist in the armed forces after the attack on Pearl Harbor. He served in the Navy in the Pacific and won a Silver Star.

Johnson was elected to the Senate in 1948 after he had captured the Democratic nomination by only 87 votes. He was 40 years old. He became the Senate Democratic leader in 1953. A heart attack in 1955 threatened to end his political career, but he recovered fully and resumed his duties.

At the height of his power as Senate leader, Johnson sought the Democratic nomination for president in 1960. When he lost to John F. Kennedy, he surprised even some of his closest associates by accepting second place on the ticket.

Johnson was riding in another car in the motorcade when Kennedy was assassinated in Dallas on Nov. 22, 1963. He took the oath of office in the presidential jet on the Dallas airfield.

With Johnson's insistent backing, Congress finally adopted a far-reaching civil-rights bill, a voting-rights bill, a Medicare program for the aged, and measures to improve education and conservation. Congress also began what Johnson described as "an all-out war" on poverty.

Amassing a record-breaking majority of nearly 16 million votes, Johnson was elected president in his own right in 1964, defeating Senator Barry Goldwater of Arizona.

The double tragedy of a war in Southeast Asia and urban riots at home marked Johnson's last two years in office. Faced with disunity in the nation and challenges within his own party, Johnson surprised the country on March 31, 1968, with the announcement that he would not be a candidate for re-election. He died of a heart attack suffered at his LBJ Ranch on Jan. 22, 1973.

RICHARD MILHOUS NIXON was born in Yorba Linda, Calif., on Jan. 9, 1913, to Midwestern-bred parents, Francis A. and Hannah Milhous Nixon, who raised their five sons as Quakers.

Nixon was a high school debater and was undergraduate president at Whittier College in California, where he was graduated in 1934. As a scholarship student at Duke University Law School in North Carolina, he graduated third in his class in 1937.

After five years as a lawyer, Nixon joined the Navy in August 1942. He was an air transport officer in the South Pacific and a legal officer stateside before his discharge in 1946 as a lieutenant commander.

Running for Congress in California as a Republican in 1946, Nixon defeated Rep. Jerry Voorhis. As a member of the House Un-American Activities Committee, he made a name as an investigator of Alger Hiss, a former high State Department official, who was later jailed for perjury. In 1950, Nixon defeated Rep. Helen Gahagan Douglas, a Democrat, for the Senate. He was criticized for portraying her as a Communist dupe.

Nixon's anti-Communism, his Western base, and his youth figured in his selection in 1952 to run for vice president on the ticket headed by Dwight D. Eisenhower. Demands for Nixon's withdrawal followed disclosure that California businessmen had paid some of his Senate office expenses. He televised rebuttal, known as "the Checkers speech" (named for a cocker spaniel given to the Nixons), brought him support from the public and from Eisenhower. The ticket won easily in 1952 and again in 1956.

Eisenhower gave Nixon substantive assignments, including missions to 56 countries. In Moscow in 1959, Nixon won acclaim for his defense of U.S. interests in an impromptu "kitchen debate" with Soviet Premier Nikita S. Khrushchev.

Nixon lost the 1960 race for the presidency to John F. Kennedy.

In 1962, Nixon failed in a bid for California's governorship and seemed to be finished as a national candidate. He became a Wall Street lawyer, but kept his old party ties and developed new ones through constant travels to speak for Republicans.

Nixon won the 1968 Republican presidential nomination after a shrewd primary campaign, then made Gov. Spiro T. Agnew of Maryland his surprise choice for vice president. In the election, they edged out the Democratic ticket headed by Vice President Hubert H. Humphrey by 510,314 votes out of 73,212,065 cast.

Committed to wind down the U.S. role in the Vietnamese War, Nixon pursued "Vietnamization"—training and equipping South Vietnamese to do their own fighting. American ground combat forces in Vietnam fell steadily from 540,000 when Nixon took office to none in 1973 when the military draft was ended. But there was heavy continuing use of U.S. air power.

Nixon improved relations with Moscow and reopened the long-closed door to mainland China with a good-will trip there in February 1972. In May of that year, he visited Moscow and signed agreements on arms limitation and trade expansion and approved plans for a joint U.S.-Soviet space mission in 1975.

Inflation was a campaign issue for Nixon, but he failed to master it as president. On Aug. 15, 1971, with unemployment edging up, Nixon abruptly announced a new economic policy: a 90-day wage-price freeze, stimulative tax cuts, a temporary 10% tariff, and spending cuts. A second phase, imposing guidelines on wage, price and rent boosts, was announced October 7.

The economy responded in time for the 1972 campaign, in which Nixon played up his foreign-policy achievements. Played down was the burglary on June 17, 1972, of Democratic national headquarters in the Watergate apartment complex in Washington. The Nixon-Agnew re-election campaign cost a record $60 million and swamped the Democratic ticket headed by Senator George McGovern of South Dakota with a plurality of 17,999,528 out of 77,718,554 votes. Only Massachusetts, with 14 electoral votes, and the District of Columbia, with 3, went for McGovern.

In January 1973, hints of a cover-up emerged at the trial of six men found guilty of the Watergate burglary. With a Senate investigation under way, Nixon announced on April 30 the resignations of his top aides, H. R. Haldeman and John D. Ehrlichman, and the dismissal of White House counsel John Dean III. Dean was the star witness at televised Senate hearings that exposed both a White House cover-up of Watergate and massive illegalities in Republican fund-raising in 1972.

The hearings also disclosed that Nixon had routinely tape-recorded his office meetings and telephone conversations.

On Oct. 10, 1973, Agnew resigned as vice president, then pleaded no-contest to a negotiated federal charge of evading income taxes on alleged bribes. Two days later, Nixon nominated the House minority leader, Rep. Gerald R. Ford of Michigan, as the new vice president. Congress confirmed Ford on Dec. 6, 1973.

In June 1974, Nixon visited Israel and four Arab nations. Then he met in Moscow with Soviet leader Leonid I. Brezhnev and reached preliminary nuclear arms limitation agreements.

But, in the month after his return, Watergate ended the Nixon regime. On July 24 the Supreme Court ordered Nixon to surrender subpoenaed tapes. On July 30, the Judiciary Committee referred three impeachment articles to the full membership. On August 5, Nixon bowed to the Supreme Court and released tapes showing he halted an FBI probe of the Watergate burglary six days after it occurred. It was in effect an admission of obstruction of justice, and impeachment appeared inevitable.

Nixon resigned on Aug. 9, 1974, the first president ever to do so. A month later, President Ford issued an unconditional pardon for any offenses Nixon might have committed as president, thus forestalling possible prosecution.

In 1940, Nixon married Thelma Catherine (Pat) Ryan. They had two daughters, Patricia (Tricia) Cox and Julie, who married Dwight David Eisenhower II, grandson of the former president.

GERALD RUDOLPH FORD was born in Omaha, Neb., on July 14, 1913, the only child of Leslie and Dorothy Gardner King. His parents were divorced in 1915. His mother moved to Grand Rapids, Mich., and married Gerald R. Ford. The boy was renamed for his stepfather.

Ford captained his high school football team in Grand Rapids, and a football scholarship took him to the University of Michigan, where he starred as varsity center before his graduation in 1935. A job as assistant football coach at Yale gave him an opportunity to attend Yale Law School, from which he graduated in the top third of his class in 1941.

He returned to Grand Rapids to practice law, but entered the Navy in April 1942. He saw wartime service in the Pacific on the light aircraft carrier *Monterey* and was a lieutenant commander when he returned to Grand Rapids early in 1946 to resume law practice and dabble in politics.

Ford was elected to Congress in 1948 for the first of his 13 terms in the House. He was soon assigned to the influential Appropriations Committee and rose to become the ranking Republican on the subcommittee on Defense Department appropriations and an expert in the field.

As a legislator, Ford described himself as "a moderate on domestic issues, a conservative in fiscal affairs, and a dyed-in-the-wool internationalist." He carried the ball for Pentagon appropriations, was a hawk on the war in Vietnam, and kept a low profile on civil-rights issues.

He was also dependable and hard-working and popular with his colleagues. In 1963, he was elected chairman of the House Republican Conference. He served in 1963–64 as a member of the Warren Commission that investigated the assassination of John F. Kennedy. A revolt by dissatisfied younger Republicans in 1965 made him minority leader.

Ford shelved his hopes for the Speakership on Oct. 12, 1973, when Nixon nominated him to fill the vice presidency left vacant by Agnew's resignation under fire. It was the first use of the procedures for filling vacancies in the vice presidency laid down in the 25th Amendment to the Constitution, which Ford had helped enact.

Congress confirmed Ford as vice president on Dec. 6, 1973. Once in office, he said he did not believe Nixon had been involved in the Watergate scandals, but criticized his stubborn court battle against releasing tape recordings of Watergate-related conversations for use as evidence.

The scandals led to Nixon's unprecedented resignation on Aug. 9, 1974, and Ford was sworn in immediately as the 38th president, the first to enter the White House without winning a national election.

Ford assured the nation when he took office that "our long national nightmare is over" and pledged "openness and candor" in all his actions. He won a warm response from the Democratic 93rd Congress when he said he wanted "a good marriage" rather than a honeymoon with his former colleagues. In December 1974 Congressional majorities backed his choice of former New York Gov. Nelson A. Rockefeller as his successor in the again-vacant vice presidency.

The cordiality was chilled by Ford's announcement on Sept. 8, 1974, that he had granted an unconditional pardon to Nixon for any crimes he might have committed as president. Although no formal charges were pending, Ford said he feared "ugly passions" would be aroused if Nixon were brought to trial. The pardon was widely criticized.

To fight inflation, the new president first proposed fiscal restraints and spending curbs and a 5% tax surcharge that got nowhere in the Senate and House. Congress again rebuffed Ford in the spring of 1975 when he appealed for emergency military aid to help the governments of South Vietnam and Cambodia resist massive Communist offensives.

In November 1974, Ford visited Japan, South Korea, and the Soviet Union, where he and Soviet leader Leonid I. Brezhnev conferred in Vladivostok and reached a tentative agreement to limit the number of strategic offensive nuclear weapons. It was Ford's first meeting as president with Brezhnev, who planned a return visit to Washington in the fall of 1975.

Politically, Ford's fortunes improved steadily in the first half of 1975. Badly divided Democrats in Congress were unable to muster votes to override his vetoes of spending bills that exceeded his budget. He faced some right-wing opposition in his own party, but moved to pre-empt it with an early announcement—on July 8, 1975—of his intention to be a candidate in 1976.

Early state primaries in 1976 suggested an easy victory for Ford despite Ronald Reagan's bitter attacks on administration foreign policy and defense programs. But later Reagan primary successes threatened the President's lead. At the Kansas City convention, Ford was nominated by the narrow margin of 1,187 to 1,070. But Reagan had moved the party to the right, and Ford himself was regarded as a caretaker president lacking in strength and vision. He was defeated in November by Jimmy Carter.

In 1948, Ford married Elizabeth Anne (Betty) Bloomer. They had four children, Michael Gerald, John Gardner, Steven Meigs, and Susan Elizabeth.

JAMES EARL CARTER, JR., was born in the tiny village of Plains, Ga., Oct. 1, 1924, and grew up on the family farm at nearby Archery. Both parents were fifth-generation Georgians. His father, James Earl Carter, was known as a segregationist, but treated his black and white workers equally. Carter's mother, Lillian Gordy, was a matriarchal presence in home and community and opposed the then-prevailing code of racial inequality. The future President was baptized in 1935 in the conservative Southern Baptist Church and spoke often of being a "born again" Christian, although committed to the separation of church and state.

Carter married Rosalynn Smith, a neighbor, in 1946. Their first child, John William, was born a year later in Portsmouth, Va. Their other children are James Earl III, born in Honolulu in 1950; Donnel Jeffrey, born in New London, Conn., in 1952, and Amy Lynn, born in Plains in 1967.

In 1946 Carter was graduated from the U.S. Naval Academy at Annapolis and served in the nuclear-submarine program under Adm. Hyman G. Rickover. In 1954, after his father's death, he resigned from the Navy to take over the family's flourishing warehouse and cotton gin, with several thousand acres for growing seed peanuts.

Carter was elected to the Georgia Senate in 1962. In 1966 he lost the race for Governor, but was elected in 1970. His term brought a state government reorganization, sharply reduced agencies, increased economy and efficiency, and new social programs, all with no general tax increase. In 1972 the peanut farmer-politician set his sights on the Presidency and in 1974 built a base for himself as he criss-crossed the country as chairman of the Democratic Campaign Committee, appealing for revival and reform. In 1975 his image as a typical Southern white was erased when he won support of most of the old Southern civil-rights coalition after endorsement by Rep. Andrew Young, black Democrat from Atlanta, who had been the closest aide to the Rev. Martin Luther King, Jr. At Carter's 1971 inauguration as Governor he had called for an end to all forms of racial discrimination.

In the 1976 spring primaries, he won 19 out of 31 with a broad appeal to conservatives and liberals, black and white, poor and well-to-do. Throughout his campaigning Carter set forth his policies in his soft Southern voice, and with his electric-blue stare faced down skeptics who joked about "Jimmy Who?" His toothy smile became his trademark. He was nominated on the first roll-call vote of the 1976 Bicentennial Democratic National Convention in New York, and defeated Gerald R. Ford in November. Likewise, in 1980 he was renominated on the first ballot after vanquishing Senator Edward M. Kennedy of Massachusetts in the primaries. At the convention he defeated the Kennedy forces in their attempt to block a party rule that bound a large majority of pledged delegates to vote for Carter. In the election campaign, Carter attacked his rivals, Ronald Reagan and John B. Anderson, independent, with the warning that a Reagan Republican victory would heighten the risk of war and impede civil rights and economic opportunity. In November Carter lost to Reagan, who won 489 Electoral College votes and 51% of the popular tally, to 49 electoral votes and 41% for Carter.

In his one term, Carter fought hard for his programs against resistance from an independent-minded Democratic Congress that frustrated many pet projects although it overrode only two vetoes. Many of his difficulties were traced to his aides' brusqueness in dealing with Capitol Hill and insensitivity to Congressional feelings and tradition. Observers generally viewed public dissatisfaction with the "stagflation" economy as a principal factor in his defeat. Others included his jittery performance in the debate Oct. 28 with Reagan and the final uncertainties in the negotiations for freeing the Iranians' hostages, along with earlier staff problems, friction with Congress, long gasoline lines, and the months-long Iranian crisis, including the abortive sally in April 1980 to free the hostages. The President, however, did deflect criticism resulting from the activities of his brother, Billy. Yet, assessments of his record noted many positive elements. There was, for one thing, peace throughout his term, with no American combat deaths and with a brake on the advocates of force. Regarded as perhaps his greatest personal achievements were the Camp David accords between Israel and Egypt and the resulting treaty—the first between Israel and an Arab neighbor. The treaty with China and the Panama Canal treaties were also major achievements. Carter worked for nuclear-arms control. His concern for international human rights was credited with saving lives and reducing torture, and he supported the British policy that ended internecine warfare in Rhodesia, now Zimbabwe. Domestically, his environmental record was a major accomplishment. His judicial appointments won acclaim; the Southerner who had forsworn racism made 265 choices for the Federal bench that included minority members and women. On energy, he ended by price decontrols the practice of holding U.S. petroleum prices far below world levels.

—Arthur P. Reed, Jr.

RONALD WILSON REAGAN rode to the Presidency in 1980 on a tide of resurgent right-wing sentiment among an electorate battered by winds of unwanted change, longing for a distant, simpler era.

He left office in January 1989 with two-thirds of the American people approving his performance during his two terms. It was the highest rating for any retiring President since World War II. In his farewell speech, Reagan exhorted the nation to cling to the revival of patriotism that he had fostered. And he spoke proudly of the economic recovery during his Administrations, although regretting the huge budget deficit, for which, in part, many blamed his policies.

Reagan had retained the public's affection as he applied his political magic to policy goals. His place in history will rest, perhaps, on the short- and intermediate-range missile treaty consummated on a cordial visit to the Soviet Union that he had once reviled as an "evil empire." Its provisions, including a ground-breaking agreement on verification inspection, were formulated in four days of summit talks in Moscow in May 1988 with the Soviet leader, Mikhail S. Gorbachev.

And Reagan can point to numerous domestic achievements: sharp cuts in income tax rates, sweeping tax reform; creating economic growth without inflation, reducing the unemployment rate, among others. He failed, however, to win the "Reagan Revolution" on such issues as abortion and school prayer, and he seemed aloof from "sleazy" conduct by some top officials.

In his final months Reagan campaigned aggressively to win election as President for his two-term Vice President, George Bush.

Reagan's popularity with the public dipped sharply in 1986 when the Iran-Contra scandal broke, shortly after the Democrats gained control of the Senate. Observers agreed that Reagan's presidency had been weakened, if temporarily, by the two unrelated events. Then the weeks-long Congressional hearings in the summer of 1987 heard an array of Administration officials, present and former, tell their tales of a White House riven by deceit and undercover maneuvering. Yet no breath of illegality touched the President's personal reputation; on Aug. 12, 1987, he told the nation that he had not known of questionable activities but agreed that he was "ultimately accountable."

Ronald Reagan, actor turned politician, New Dealer turned conservative, came to the films and politics from a thoroughly Middle-American background—middle class, Middle West and small town. He was born in Tampico, Ill., Feb. 6, 1911, the second son of John Edward Reagan and Nelle Wilson Reagan, and the family later moved to Dixon, Ill. The father, of Irish descent, was a shop clerk and merchant with Democratic sympathies. It was an impoverished family; young Ronald sold homemade popcorn at high school games and worked as a lifeguard to earn money for his college tuition. When the father got a New Deal WPA job, the future President became an ardent Roosevelt Democrat.

Reagan won a B.A. degree in 1932 from Eureka (Ill.) College, where a photographic memory aided in his studies and in debating and college theatricals. In a Depression year, he was making $100 a week as a sports announcer for radio station WHO in Des Moines, Iowa, from 1932 to 1937. His career as a film and TV actor stretched from 1937 to 1966, and his salary climbed to $3,500 a week. As a World War II captain in Army film studios, Reagan recoiled from what he saw as the laziness of Civil Service workers, and moved to the Right. As president of the Screen Actors Guild, he resisted what he considered a Communist plot to subvert the film industry. With advancing age, Reagan left leading-man roles and became a television spokesman for the General Electric Company at $150,000.

With oratorical skill his trademark, Reagan became an active Republican. At the behest of a small group of conservative Southern California businessmen, he ran for governor with a pledge to cut spending, and was elected by almost a million votes over the political veteran, Democratic Gov. Edmund G. Brown, father of the later governor.

In the 1980 election battle against Jimmy Carter, Reagan broadened his appeal by espousing moderate policies, gaining much of his support from disaffected Democrats and blue-collar workers. The incoming Administration immediately set out to "turn the government around" with a new economic program. Over strenuous Congressional opposition, Reagan triumphed on his "supply side" theory to stimulate production and control inflation through tax cuts and sharp reductions in government spending.

The President won high acclaim for his nomination of Sandra Day O'Connor as the first woman on the Supreme Court. His later nominations met increasing opposition but did much to tilt the Court's orientation to the Right.

In 1982, the President's popularity had slipped as the economy declined into the worst recession in 40 years, with persistent high unemployment and interest rates. Initial support for "supply side" economics faded but the President won crucial battles in Congress.

Internationally, Reagan confronted numerous critical problems in his first term. The successful invasion of Grenada accomplished much diplomatically. But the intervention in Lebanon and the withdrawal of Marines after a disastrous terrorist attack were regarded as military failures.

The popular President won reelection in the 1984 landslide, with the economy improving and inflation under control. Domestically, a tax reform bill that Reagan backed became law. But the constantly growing budget deficit remained a constant irritant, with the President and Congress persistently at odds over priorities in spending for defense and domestic programs. His foreign policy met stiffening opposition, with Congress increasingly reluctant to increase spending for the Nicaraguan "Contras" and the Pentagon and to expand the development of the MX missile. But even severe critics praised Reagan's restrained but decisive handling of the crisis following the hijacking of an American plane in Beirut by Moslem extremists. The attack on Libya in April 1986 galvanized the nation, although it drew scathing disapproval from the NATO alliance.

Barely three months into his first term, Reagan was the target of an assassin's bullet; his courageous comeback won public admiration.

Reagan is devoted to his wife, Nancy, whom he married after his divorce from the screen actress Jane Wyman. The children of the first marriage are Maureen, his daughter by Miss Wyman, and Michael, an adopted son. In the present marriage the children are Patricia and Ron.

—*Arthur P. Reed, Jr.*

GEORGE H. BUSH became President on January 20, 1989, with his theme harmony and conciliation after the often-turbulent Reagan years. With his calm and unassuming manner, he emerged from his subordinate Vice-Presidential role with an air of quiet authority. His Inaugural address emphasized "A new breeze is blowing, and the old bipartisanship must be made new again."

In his first months, the President, the nation's 41st, established himself as his own man and all but erased memories of what many had regarded as his fiercely abrasive Presidential election campaign of 1988 and questionable tactics against his Democratic opponent. People liked his easy style and readiness to compromise even as he remained a staunch conservative, although that readiness had disconcerted some conservatives.

Bush's early Cabinet choices reflected a pragmatic desire for an efficient nonideological Government. And with his usual cautious instinct, in 1990 he nominated to the Supreme Court the scholarly David H. Souter, with broadly conservative views. Souter was confirmed without a bruising battle.

In his first year, Bush, a World War II hero, had won plaudits at home and abroad for his confident, competent conduct at the NATO 40th anniversary summit meeting in Brussels, the Paris economic conference, on his tour of Eastern Europe, and at the Malta conference with Gorbachev. Grave challenges in that year were the Lebanese hostage crisis and the ongoing war on the drug traffic.

Domestically, Bush had to cope with such issues as the *Exxon Valdez* oil spill in Alaska and the dispute over flag-burning restrictions, which was resolved, if only for a time, in mid-1990.

But in his second year, 1990, the President confronted a mounting array of problems, the most critical being on the domestic side. Chief among them were the staggering and mushrooming budget deficit and the savings and loan crisis. Other vexing issues were the question of cutting defense expenditures with consequent economic dislocation, the war on drugs and environmental matters.

At home, the President's popularity dipped sharply from its near-record public approval following the invasion of Panama in late 1989. This plunge followed Bush's recantation of his campaign "no new taxes" pledge as he sat down with Congressional leaders to tame the budge deficit and deal with a faltering economy.

In 1991, the 67-year-old President emerged as the leader of an international coalition of Western democracies, Japan, and even some Arab states that freed invaded Kuwait and vanquished, at least for a time, Iraq's President Saddam Hussein and his armies.

A nation grateful at feeling the end of the "Vietnam syndrome" gave the President an over-all rating of 89 percent in a Gallup poll in March after the end of the war. The approval rate fell as the year went on, but a solid majority continued to approve the President's performance, although with growing concern about the faltering economy and other domestic problems. And there were nagging doubts about the Persian Gulf war, its motives and conduct, and about the ensuing refugee crisis.

A major Bush accomplishment in 1991 was the Strategic Arms Reduction Treaty (Start), signed in July with Soviet President Mikhail S. Gorbachev at their fourth summit conference, marking the end of the long weapons buildup. Succeeding events in the Soviet Union and the apparent disintegration of the Communist empire could only enhance his status.

The year also saw the President undergoing treatment for Graves' disease, a thyroid disorder, from which he suffered serious side effects.

Bush, scion of an aristocratic New England family, came to the White House after a long career in public service, in which he held top positions in national and international organizations. As Vice President, he avoided the appearance of direct involvement in the Iran-Contra affair while not seeming to shy away from the President.

Earlier, in the 1960s, Bush won two contests for a Texas Republican seat in the House of Representatives, but lost two bids for a Senate seat and one for the Presidency. After his second race for the Senate, President Nixon appointed him U.S. delegate to the United Nations with the rank of Ambassador and he later became Republican National Chairman. He headed the United States liaison office in Beijing before becoming Director of Central Intelligence.

In 1980 Bush became Reagan's running mate despite earlier criticism of Reagan "voodoo economics" and by the 1984 election had won acclaim for devotion to Reagan's conservative agenda despite his own reputation as somewhat more liberally inclined. Nevertheless, die-hard right-wingers could find satisfaction in Bush's war record and his Government service, particularly with the C.I.A. Throughout he remained influential in White House decisions, particularly in foreign affairs.

In the 1988 campaign, Bush's choice of Senator Dan Quayle of Indiana for Vice President surprised his friends and provoked criticism and ridicule that continued even after the Administration was established in office. Nonetheless Bush strongly defended his choice.

In the 1992 Presidential election, Bush was defeated by Gov. Bill Clinton of Arkansas.

The future President joined the Navy after war broke out and at 18 became the Navy's youngest commissioned pilot, serving from 1942 to 1945. The man later derided by some as a "wimp" fought the Japanese on 58 missions and was shot down once. He won the Distinguished Flying Cross.

Throughout his whole career, Bush had the backing of an established family, headed by his father, the autocratic and wealthy Prescott Bush, who was elected to the Senate from Connecticut in 1952. And his family helped the young patrician became established in his early business ventures, a rich uncle raising most of the capital required for founding a new oil company in Texas.

George Herbert Walker Bush was born June 12, 1924, in Milton, Mass., to Prescott and Dorothy Bush. The family later moved to Connecticut. The youth studied at the elite Phillips Academy in Andover, Mass., before entering the Navy.

After the war, Bush earned an economics degree and a Phi Beta Kappa key in two and a half years at Yale University. While there he captained the baseball team and was initiated into "Skull and Bones," the prestigious Yale secret society.

In 1945 Bush married Barbara Pierce of Rye, N.Y., daughter of a magazine publisher. With his bride, Bush moved to Texas instead of entering his father's investment banking business. There he founded his oil company and in 1980 reported an estimated wealth of $1.4 million.

The Bushes have lived in 17 cities and more than a score of homes and have traveled in as many countries. In her husband's frequent absences during the early years, Mrs. Bush was often matriarch of a family of four boys and a girl. Bush is close to his immediate family and to 10 grandchildren, a sister, and three brothers.

After the Clinton inauguration in January, the Bushes flew to Houston, Texas, where they had rented a home. —*Arthur P. Reed, Jr.*

WILLIAM J. CLINTON became the 42nd U.S. President after a turbulent political campaign, only to face an array of daunting problems, with many setbacks and few victories. Almost immediately after his Inauguration in January 1993 he became embroiled with the military leadership over the politically sensitive issue of his campaign pledge to allow homosexuals to serve openly in the armed forces. He finally agreed to a compromise. And soon the new Administration was rocked by a "Nannygate" scandal, which caused his first two choices for Attorney General to fall victims to allegations concerning their employment of illegal aliens as household workers.

But his third choice, Janet Reno, proved to be a strong and popular nominee, as later did Ruth Bader Ginsburg, named to the Supreme Court. Both were confirmed easily by the Senate. But it was months before Clinton had staffed his Administration on all levels.

A major early defeat was the Congressional rejection of his program for economic stimulus.

The Arkansas Governor, elected on a platform stressing domestic economic issues, soon had to confront the new, to him, field of international affairs. He seemed to be successful, at least for a time, in shoring up Russian President Yeltsin with pledges of economic aid. But the complex and agonizing situation in the former Yugoslavia taxed the full powers of Clinton and his advisers, particularly in view of the reluctance of the Western allies to deal harshly with the aggressors in Bosnia and Hercegovina.

Clinton's popularity soon fell sharply but was bolstered by his success at the Tokyo economic summit conference and in his coping with flood relief in the Middle West disaster zone. He barely escaped a major catastrophe that could have undermined his Presidency when the Senate and House passed his budget package by the narrowest of margins. Other problems before him included health care, campaign practices, lobbying, and welfare reform.

Even democrats in Congress were restive at implementing President Clinton's economic package. Politics was one factor. And conservatives, including Democrats, demanded more spending cuts, fewer taxes, and caps on such "entitlement" programs as Medicare. As the year drew on, the new President found himself increasingly under fire for his stands on the economy, social issues, foreign trade, and the ethnic strife in the Balkans. His critics found him indecisive on many fronts and involved in too many issues at once. Clinton himself recognized this, and conceded that the White House was "out of focus," and that his staff needed improved organization. He soon appointed David Gergen, a columnist, a former Bush–Reagan adviser, to coordinate communications.

After his first six months, Clinton called a news conference at which he claimed an aggressive and largely successful attempt to reinvigorate Government, rejecting allegations that he had been indecisive.

"There is no wavering," he said, and noted that interest rates and unemployment had dropped, housing sales had risen, and that he had been a leader in world affairs.

In a tragic-comic episode, Clinton, who had campaigned as a commoner, found himself the butt of ridicule from friend and foe alike for a $200 haircut from a Hollywood stylist aboard *Air Force I* waiting at the Los Angeles Airport.

Clinton became the Democratic Presidential candidate after fighting back attacks on his personal life and public conduct to win a series of bruising primary contests. As a politician—and as a person—he displayed an empathy for the feelings of others and a genius for compromise that in his thinking and actions blended belief in programs for social welfare with fiscal responsibility and economic growth. These ideas had guided his role in the 1980s in striving to rebuild a Democratic Party that had lost key White House races.

The issue of "character" repeatedly haunted him as he sought the Presidency. He had to rebut allegations of adultery and in a television interview he and his wife reaffirmed their solid relationship.

Another target was Clinton's actions in the Vietnam War, which he actively opposed, and like many young men of his generation faced a series of unpalatable choices. In the event, he chose to sign a letter, much publicized in the primary campaign, signifying his intention of avoiding the draft by joining the Reserve Officers Training Corps. But he canceled his plans when draft calls were reduced.

After a series of primary victories, Clinton was nominated at the Democratic National Convention in New York. The platform reflected the nominee's own instinct for moderation in its appeal to middle-class values. Clinton's acceptance speech denounced years of Republican rule and President Bush's "failed economic policy." The speech reflected Clinton's record as Governor and earlier campaign positions. He had supported the death penalty and the use of force in the Persian Gulf.

He favored laws requiring minors seeking abortion to have the consent of parents or a judge. In the campaign he advocated a 10 percent middle-class tax cut and an $800-per-child tax credit. And he supported job training and health care for welfare recipients.

Clinton was born in Hope, Ark., on August 19, 1946, named William Jefferson Blythe 3rd for his father, who had been killed in an automobile accident before William's birth. His mother, Virginia Kelly, set an example of stamina by training to become a nurse anesthetist. The future Governor later changed his name to that of his stepfather, Roger Clinton, a car dealer. Meanwhile the family had moved to Hot Springs, Ark.

In high school young Clinton thought of becoming a doctor, but politics beckoned after a meeting with President John F. Kennedy in Washington on a Boys' Nation trip. He won a B.S. in international affairs at Georgetown University, where he spent his junior year working for Arkansas Senator J. William Fulbright, graduating in 1968. He was a Rhodes scholar at Oxford 1968–70. He then attended Yale Law School, where he met his future wife, Hillary Rodham, a Wellesley graduate. In 1974–76 he taught at the University of Arkansas and in 1976 was elected state Attorney General.

In 1979 he was elected Governor, at 32 the nation's youngest, but was defeated for re-election by voters irate at a rise in the state's automobile license fees.

In 1982 he was elected again. This time he reined in liberal tendencies to accommodate the conservative bent of the voters.

Hillary retained her maiden name until her husband's defeat for Governor, when it seemed politic to adopt his. The couple have one child, Chelsea, aged 13.

—*Arthur P. Reed, Jr.*

Milestones in the Gay Rights Movement

Source: Excerpted from *The Reader's Companion to American History.*

Late in the [19th] century, as large cities allowed for greater anonymity, as wage labor apart from family became common, and as more women were drawn out of the home, evidence of a new pattern of homosexual expression surfaced. . . .

At first, these individuals developed ways of meeting one another and institutions to foster a sense of identity. . . . By 1915, one participant in this new gay world was referring to it as "a community distinctly organized." For the most part hidden from view because of social hostility, an urban gay subculture had come into existence by the 1920s and 1930s.

World War II served as a critical divide in the social history of homosexuality. Large numbers of the young left families, small towns, and closely knit ethnic neighborhoods to enter a sex-segregated military or to migrate to larger cities for wartime employment. . . .

After the war, many of them made choices designed to support their gay identities. Pat Bond, a woman from Iowa who first met other lesbians while in the military, decided to stay in San Francisco after her discharge. [Donald] Vining remained in New York City rather than return to his small hometown in New Jersey. They, along with countless others, sustained a vibrant gay subculture that revolved around bars and friendship networks. Many cities saw their first gay bars during the 1940s. . . .

This new visibility provoked latent cultural prejudices. . . . Firings from government jobs and purges from the military intensified in the 1950s. President Dwight D. Eisenhower issued an executive order in 1953 barring gay men and lesbians from all federal jobs. Many state and local governments and private corporations followed suit. The FBI began a surveillance program against homosexuals.

The lead taken by the federal government encouraged local police forces to harass gay citizens. Vice officers regularly raided gay bars, sometimes arresting dozens of men and women on a single night. . . . Under these conditions, some gays began to organize politically. In November 1950 in Los Angeles, a small group of men led by Harry Hay and Chuck Rowland met to form what would become the Mattachine Society. Mostly male in membership, it was joined in 1955 by a lesbian organization in San Francisco, the Daughters of Bilitis, founded by Del Martin and Phyllis Lyon. In the 1950s these organizations remained small, but they established chapters in several cities and published magazines that were a beacon of hope to the readers.

In the 1960s, influenced by the model of a militant black civil rights movement, the "homophile movement," as the participants dubbed it, became more visible. Activists, such as Franklin Kameny and Barbara Gittings, picketed government agencies in Washington to protest discriminatory employment policies. In San Francisco, Martin, Lyon, and others targeted police harassment. By 1969, perhaps fifty homophile organizations existed in the United States, with memberships of a few thousand.

Then, on Friday evening, June 27, 1969, the police in New York City raided a Greenwich Village gay bar, the Stonewall Inn. Contrary to expectations, the patrons fought back, provoking three nights of rioting in the area accompanied by the appearance of "gay power" slogans on the buildings. Almost overnight, a massive grassroots gay liberations movement was born. Owing much to the radical protest of blacks, women, and college students in the 1960s, gays challenged all forms of hostility and punishment meted out by society. Choosing to "come out of the closet" and publicly proclaim their identity, they ushered in a social change movement that has grown substantially. By 1973, there were almost eight hundred gay and lesbian organizations in the United States; by 1990, the number was several thousand. By 1970, 5,000 gay men and lesbians marched in New York City to commemorate the first anniversary of the Stonewall Riots; in October 1987, over 600,000 marched in Washington, to demand equality.

The changes were far-reaching. Over the next two decades, half the states decriminalized homosexual behavior, and police harassment was sharply contained. Many large cities included sexual orientation in their civil rights statutes, as did Wisconsin and Massachusetts, first among the states to do so. . . . [In 1975] the Civil Service Commission eliminated the ban on the employment of homosexuals in most federal jobs. Many of the nation's religious denominations engaged in spirited debates about the morality of homosexuality, and some, like Unitarianism and Reformed Judaism, opened their doors to gay and lesbian ministers and rabbis. The lesbian and gay world was no longer an underground subculture but, in larger cities especially, a well-organized community, with businesses, political clubs, social service agencies, community centers, and religious congregations bringing people together. In a number of places, openly gay candidates ran for elective office and won.

These changes spawned opposition. In 1977 the singer Anita Bryant led a campaign to repeal a gay rights ordinance in Dade County, Florida. Her success encouraged others, and by the early 1980s, a well-organized conservative force had materialized to target the gay rights movement. Politicians, such as Senator Jesse Helms of North Carolina, and fundamentalist ministers, such as Jerry Falwell of Lynchburg, Virginia, who formed Moral Majority, Inc., joined forces to slow the progress of the gay movement.

The onset of the AIDS epidemic in the 1980s, although it intensified the antigay rhetoric of the New Right, also stimulated further organizing within the gay community. AIDS made political mobilization a matter of life and death. With a large majority of the cases striking male homosexuals, the gay community in short order created a host of organizations, such as the Gay Men's Health Crisis in New York City, to provide services and assistance to those infected. Local and national gay civil rights groups also grew in size and number, as the community sought to increase funding for research and education and to win protection against discrimination. A personal and social tragedy of immense proportions, AIDS paradoxically strengthened the political arm of the gay movement. □

Firsts in America

This selection is based on our editorial judgment. Other sources may list different firsts.

Admiral in U.S. Navy: David Glasgow Farragut, 1866.

Air–mail route, first transcontinental: Between New York City and San Francisco, 1920.

Assembly, representative: House of Burgesses, founded in Virginia, 1619.

Bank established: Bank of North America, Philadelphia, 1781.

Birth in America to English parents: Virginia Dare, born Roanoke Island, N.C., 1587.

Black newspaper: *Freedom's Journal,* 1827, edited by John B. Russworm.

Black U.S. diplomat: Ebenezer D. Bassett, 1869, minister-resident to Haiti.

Black elected governor of a state: L. Douglas Wilder, Virginia, 1990.

Black elected to U.S. Senate: Hiram Revels, 1870, Mississippi.

Black elected to U.S. House of Representatives: Jefferson Long, Georgia, 1870.

Black associate justice of U.S. Supreme Court: Thurgood Marshall, Oct. 2, 1967.

Black U.S. cabinet minister: Robert C. Weaver, 1966, Secretary of the Department of Housing and Urban Development.

Botanic garden: Established by John Bartram in Philadelphia, 1728 and is still in existence in its original location.

Cartoon, colored: "The Yellow Kid," by Richard Outcault, in *New York World,* 1895.

College: Harvard, founded 1636.

College to confer degrees on women: Oberlin (Ohio) College, 1841.

College to establish coeducation: Oberlin (Ohio) College, 1833.

Electrocution of a criminal: William Kemmler in Auburn Prison, Auburn, N.Y., Aug. 6, 1890.

Five and Ten Cents Store: Founded by Frank Woolworth, Utica, N.Y., 1879 (moved to Lancaster, Pa., same year).

Fraternity: Phi Beta Kappa; founded Dec. 5, 1776, at College of William and Mary.

Gay and lesbian civil rights advocacy organization: National Gay and Lesbian Task Force, founded in New York City, 1973.

Gay Power: Rioting following police raid on NYC gay bar mobilizes gay community and leads to birth of gay liberation movement, June 27, 1969.

Law to be declared unconstitutional by U.S. Supreme Court: Judiciary Act of 1789. Case: *Marbury* v. *Madison,* 1803.

Library, circulating: Philadelphia, 1731.

Newspaper, illustrated daily: *New York Daily Graphic,* 1873.

Newspaper published daily: *Pennsylvania Packet and General Advertiser,* Philadelphia, Sept., 1784.

Newspaper published over a continuous period: *The Boston News–Letter,* April, 1704.

Newsreel: Pathé Frères of Paris, in 1910, circulated a weekly issue of their *Pathé Journal.*

Oil well, commercial: Titusville, Pa., 1859.

Panel quiz show on radio: *Information Please,* May 17, 1938.

Postage stamps issued: 1847.

Public School: Boston Latin School, Boston, 1635.

Radio station licensed: KDKA, Pittsburgh, Pa., Oct. 27, 1920.

Railroad, transcontinental: Central Pacific and Union Pacific railroads, joined at Promontory, Utah, May 10, 1869.

Savings bank: The Provident Institute for Savings, Boston, 1816.

Science museum: Founded by Charleston (S.C.) Library Society, 1773.

Skyscraper: Home Insurance Co., Chicago, 1885 (10 floors, 2 added later).

Slaves brought into America: At Jamestown, Va., 1619, from a Dutch ship.

Sorority: Kappa Alpha Theta, at De Pauw University, 1870.

State to abolish capital punishment: Michigan, 1847.

State to enter Union after original 13: Vermont, 1791.

Steam–heated building: Eastern Hotel, Boston, 1845.

Steam railroad (carried passengers and freight): Baltimore & Ohio, 1830.

Strike on record by union: Journeymen Printers, New York City, 1776.

Subway: Opened in Boston, 1897.

"Tabloid" picture newspaper: *The Illustrated Daily News* (now *The Daily News*), New York City, 1919.

Vaudeville theater: Gaiety Museum, Boston, 1883.

Woman astronaut to ride in space: Dr. Sally K. Ride, 1983.

Woman astronaut to walk in space: Dr. Kathryn D. Sullivan, 1984.

Woman cabinet member: Frances Perkins, Secretary of Labor, 1933.

Woman candidate for President: Victoria Claflin Woodhull, nominated by National Woman's Suffrage Assn. on ticket of Nation Radical Reformers, 1872.

Woman candidate for Vice–President: Geraldine A. Ferraro, nominated on a major party ticket, Democratic Party, 1984.

Woman doctor of medicine: Elizabeth Blackwell; M.D. from Geneva Medical College of Western New York, 1849.

Woman elected governor of a state: Nellie Tayloe Ross, Wyoming, 1925.

Woman elected to U.S. Senate: Hattie Caraway, Arkansas; elected Nov., 1932.

Woman graduate of law school: Ada H. Kepley, Union College of Law, Chicago, 1870.

Woman member of U.S. House of Representatives: Jeannette Rankin; elected Nov., 1916.

Woman member of U.S. Senate: Rebecca Latimer Felton of Georgia; appointed Oct. 3, 1922.

Woman member of U.S. Supreme Court: Sandra Day O'Connor; appointed July 1981.

Woman suffrage granted: Wyoming Territory, 1869.

Written constitution: *Fundamental Orders of Connecticut,* 1639.

NATIVE AMERICANS

Talk Is Chief: When Seattle Spoke, Were Environmentalists Listening?

Celebrating the sentiments of Chief Seattle, the environmental movement's patron saint, may be the thing to do at Earth Day celebrations. But Native American scholars think putting words in the great Chief's mouth is politically incorrect—and exploitative.

By Linda Marsa

Just like Elvis and Marilyn, Chief Seattle's notoriety after his death has eclipsed his fame in life. The eco-sermon this nineteenth-century tribal leader gave in 1854, extolling the virtues of living in harmony with nature, has become part of environmental lore. The speech is quoted everywhere. Even mythologist Joseph Campbell and Prince Philip have referred to it. And this past April [1992], it was reverentially recited by leaders at Earth Day gatherings around the world.

Chief Seattle

No doubt about it. Chief Seattle is the ecology movement's patron saint.

Except for one niggling detail: It's all bogus.

Historians say Chief Seattle, a Suquamish Indian who lived on the Puget Sound outside the city that bears his name, was a skilled diplomat and a great orator. But he never uttered the words credited to him. They were actually penned by Ted Perry, a screenwriter inspired by some writings unwittingly attributed to the Chief, for *Home,* a 1972 ABC film about ecology.

How this myth was perpetuated and how Chief Seattle's original message was distorted is like the kid's game of telephone played out over decades. Environmentalists, of course, see no harm in canonizing Chief Seattle. But Native Americans aren't happy with the cooption of their spiritual ethos by American culture.

Historians have re-created the events surrounding the famous 1854 oration of the 68-year-old Chief during treaty negotiations between the Suquamish and Isaac Stevens, Washington's first territorial governor. But they are divided on the authenticity of surviving texts.

Eyewitness accounts say the Chief, a respected tribal elder, spoke movingly and eloquently in his native dialect about his people and of the inevitability of their displacement by the white settlers. Henry Smith, the frontier doctor who became Chief Seattle's self-appointed Boswell, however, didn't actually publish a translation of the Chief's speech until 1887—more than 30 years later. By that time, the remote outpost had mushroomed into a bustling metropolis of 35,000.

"Smith was well-educated and a minor poet given to flowery images and the romantic verbiage of the Victorian era," says Murray Morgan, a Pacific Northwest historian. What Smith wrote was probably a composite of comments the Chief made at two meetings with Governor Stevens, embellished with Smith's trademark flourishes and warped by the memory lapses that come with time.

In the 1930s, authors tinkered with this version of Chief Seattle's talk. By the time Ted Perry heard it read at the first Earth Day festivities in 1970, the speech had been significantly altered. Impressed, Perry incorporated the essence of Seattle's sentiments into a script that he wrote for the Southern Baptist Radio and Television Commission.

"This is where things got out of hand," says Daniel Miller, a social activist. The film's producer, Christianized Seattle's sensibilities and dropped Perry's name—despite his protests—from the script, which left the impression that these were Seattle's words. But the speech is littered with such anachronisms that the only real mystery is why no one caught on to this artistic license sooner.

Probably the most flagrant: "I have seen a thousand rotting buffaloes on the prairies left by the white man who shot them from a passing train." Bison did not live on Puget Sound, which was a thousand miles from the plains. The speech was given 15 years before the transcontinental railroad connection was completed, and the great buffalo slaughter peaked in 1872, several years after Seattle died. Lines such as, "What is there to life if a man cannot hear the lovely cry of a whippoorwill," are equally ludicrous. Whippoorwills are not indigenous to the Pacific Northwest.

"I'm embarrassed now when I'm seen as someone who put words in Chief Seattle's mouth," says Ted Perry, a tweedy professorial type who teaches film at Vermont's Middlebury College. "That was never my intention." Of course, most people are puzzled by the raging controversy. After all, Chief Seattle is a revered icon. So no harm, no foul. Right?

Wrong, say scholars. "Native American culture is constantly being exploited and appropriated as illustrations of whatever European theory is in fashion," says Jack D. Forbes, a professor of Native American studies at the University of California at Davis. These range from the extreme individualism of the 1983 novel *Hanta Yo* to the New Age spiritualism of Lynn Andrews. "When," asks Forbes, echoing the frustrations of other Native Americans, "will the thefts of our spiritual traditions end?" □

Chief Seattle

The renowned Indian Chief was born into the Salmon fishing tribe of the Suquamish about 1786 and he grew up in the Puget Sound area of the present state of Washington.

The Puget Sound natives frequently had to defend themselves against attack from fellow Indian raiders from the north. Women and children were sometimes carried off as captives to be sold to other tribes. Seattle demonstrated his bravery and great skill in protecting his people and rose to become a famous war chief of the Suquamish and Duwamish and his authority extended along the eastern shore of the Sound. The Chief was a prominent figure when the Hudson Bay fur traders built a new post in the region in 1832. Seattle was a big fellow and the Canadians called him "Le Gros."

He was baptized Noah Sealth by a Catholic missionary and introduced Christian practices to his people. When the Americans arrived in the 1850s, Seattle got along with them and was well liked. The Chief was always interested in trading with the whites and he persuaded Dr. David Maynard, a businessman from Olympia, to open a store in the town of Duwamps (which had been named after the tribe). A leading citizen, Dr. Maynard persuaded the white community to rename the town Seattle after his friend, the Chief.

In January 1854, the territorial governor met with the Duwamish and Suquamish in order to persuade them to give up and sell their land to settlers, sign treaties with the Government, and relocate to reservations and receive Government protection. It was here that Chief Seattle stood up and delivered his famous speech decrying the dark future of his people at the hands of the U.S. Government. The Chief's speech, which was spoken in his native tongue and translated by an interpreter for the governor, has been embellished over the years. A published version written by Dr. Henry Smith from notes taken at the time did not appear until 33 years later. While this version may contain the gist of Seattle's eloquent remarks, it nowhere mentions Chief Seattle talking about the environment, railroads, buffalos, birds, or any other living creatures. Today, no one knows for sure just what Seattle actually said on that historic occasion.

The great Chief retired to live on the newly established Fort Kitsap reservation located in his people's territory on the western shore of the Sound where he died on June 7, 1866.—*Ed.* □

Indigenous People of the Americas

Paleo-Indians

During the last Ice Age massive glaciers locked up so much water that the ocean level dropped. When that happened the Bering Strait between Asia and North America became dry land, a grassy "bridge" 1,000 miles wide between the two continents. The first humans in the Americas were probably hunters who wandered across the land bridge following herds of animals.

It is hard to say precisely when the first Paleo-Indians arrived here from Asia. Some came as early as 20,000 or even 40,000 years ago. Most, however, moved into North America about 12,000 years ago.

At the height of the Ice Age the Paleo-Indians could go no farther than western Alaska, for walls of ice blocked their way. But about 12,000 years ago the climate began to warm up. As the glaciers started melting, great grassy corridors opened up between the mountains of ice. Bands of hunters migrated south through these corridors.

Hunter-Gatherers

As the climate warmed up, North America became drier. Within 2,000 years, the huge game animals became extinct. No one knows why for certain. Whatever happened, about 10,000 years ago the Paleo-Indians had to change their way of life to survive. Instead of depending on the meat of the giant mammoth, they learned to hunt smaller animals like deer. Their tools changed from huge throwing spears to small spears, and finally to the bow and arrow.

In adapting to a new environment, the Indians broadened their food-gathering patterns. Some came to depend on shellfish. Others became skilled at weaving nets to catch fish. People began to dig roots and gather berries, fruits, nuts, and grass seeds.

About 10,000 years ago agriculture began in the river valleys of the Near East with the domestication of both plants and animals. People of the Near East domesticated the wild grasses that became wheat and barley. By 5,000 years ago people had begun to cultivate rice in southern China. At about the same time, people in central Mexico began to sow the seeds of wild corn.

The cobs of this wild corn were tiny, about the size of a strawberry. Through selective breeding, the Indian farmers developed a corn cob like the one today. Although corn was first developed in central Mexico, its cultivation spread south to Peru and north to what is now the United States.

In time the Indians domesticated more than 100 plants. In Mexico people cultivated pumpkins, peppers, beans, and tomatoes. Indians in Peru domesticated gourds, lima beans, and potatoes. Other domestic plants once unique to the Western Hemisphere include pineapple, bananas, peanuts, tobacco, and cacao.

Mesoamerica

The first Indian civilization in the Western Hemisphere developed in Mesoamerica, or Middle America. The "waist" of the Western Hemisphere, this tropical region extends from central Mexico in the north to Panama in the south. It was here that corn was first domesticated.

The "mother culture" of Mesoamerica was that of the Olmecs. The Olmec culture developed on the Gulf of Mexico near the present city of Vera Cruz. About 1000 B.C. the Olmecs introduced traditions and skills that would influence Middle America for centuries.

The Olmecs built, not cities, but large religious centers that featured earthen temple mounds. They were the first in this hemisphere to devise glyphic writing and they may also have been the first to develop a calendar system. The Olmecs conducted a vigorous commerce by land and sea with other parts of the hemisphere.

Among those who learned from the Olmecs were the Mayas, a people living in the tropical rain forest of what is now Guatemala. They too had ceremonial centers, home to the priests and nobles who controlled the surrounding region. The power of these leaders probably came from their knowledge of astronomy and the calendar.

Maya culture in the Guatemala lowlands declined starting about A.D 900. It continued for several centuries more, however, at sites in the Yucatán Peninsula.

Olmec culture also influenced people living in the Valley of Mexico, the site of present-day Mexico City. By A.D 300 they had built the city of Teotihuacán. This was a ceremonial center, but it was also a true city, with neighborhoods for both artisans and merchants. Rising above the city was a pyramid 20 stories high, now called the Pyramid of the Sun. Ranking at the top of the city's 50,000 people were the priest-rulers.

The Aztecs

Waves of war-loving barbarians began swooping out of the north about A.D 700. They burned and plundered Teotihuacán. In time they adopted much of the culture of the conquered, but warriors replaced priests as rulers.

The last of the barbarian waves from the north was that of the Aztecs, who moved into the Valley of Mexico about 1325. There they settled at Tenochitlán[1] an island in Lake Texcoco and proceeded to turn the island into a base of operations from which to conquer neighboring city-states. The conquered peoples were forced to pay the Aztecs tribute in goods and produce.

With tribute flowing in, the Aztecs were free to develop their army and conquer even more peoples. In this way, the Aztecs came to control most of central Mexico. They were a warrior people, whose most important god was the war god Huitzilopochtli. One purpose of war was to collect captives who could be sacrificed to the god. It is said that more than 20,000 people were sacrificed when the temple in Huitzilopochtli was dedicated in 1490.

The Incas

Along the west coast of South America there arose another great civilization. Much of that area was either desert or mountains. Yet there, in what is now Ecuador or Peru, the Indians developed highly efficient farming communities. To make the best use of their land, they farmed on hillside terraces. Large-scale aqueducts carried water from the mountains to fields in the dry coastal valleys. The people also domesticated the llama and the guinea pig.

With time, Peruvian political, social, and religious structures grew in complexity. Powerful city-states developed that were ruled by a class of nobles and priests. One of these city-states was that of the Incas, whose capital was Cuzco. Cuzco, with an altitude of over 11,000 feet, is the oldest continually inhabited city in the Americas.

In 1438 the Incas began to conquer neighboring states. By 1532 their empire stretched for 2,000 miles between the Pacific Ocean and the Andes. In area it was larger than California, Oregon, and Washington combined. Great stone roads knit the empire together. Armies as large as 30,000 enforced Inca authority. Probably about 6 million people lived in the Inca Empire.

Transoceanic Diffusion

Some anthropologists have suggested that peoples from across the ocean—from Asia, Africa, or Europe—might have influenced the development of culture in the Western Hemisphere ("transoceanic diffusion").

To prove that transoceanic migration was possible archeologist Thor Heyerdahl has crossed both the Atlantic (1970) and Pacific (1947) oceans in primitive craft. Diffusionists also point out that the Chinese 2,000 years ago had boats that could sail into the wind. By the fourth century the Chinese were using a compass. The Polynesians too were excellent navigators who colonized islands across the Pacific, including those of Hawaii. To these oceangoing peoples, the ocean was not a barrier but a highway.

Then the diffusionists point to evidence uncovered in the Americas. The earliest examples of pottery in the Western Hemisphere have been found at the site of a village in Ecuador. This is not crude pottery such as one might make accidentally by playing with clay. It reflects a developed craft tradition. It also is almost identical to pottery then being made in Japan.

Furthermore, some of the cultural traditions of the Olmecs were similar to those of the Chinese of the same time. These included placing a piece of jade in the mouth of a dead person to ensure eternal life. Another example of possible Chinese influence is the pottery of Teotihuacán, which is similar to that found in China of the same centuries.

In general, scholars are willing to accept the possibility of Asian influences on Western Hemisphere cultures. They are skeptical, however, about African or European influences because there is less evidence

1. During the 1400s, Tenochitlán, the Aztec capital, had an estimated population of 250,000 people and was larger than any European city.

of these. What evidence there is, however, is intriguing.

The Olmecs carved huge statues of heads with distinctly Negroid features. West African myths tell about people going west across the ocean on rafts. Is it possible that the Olmecs were West African in origin? There is no evidence for this theory, however, other than the features of the carved heads.

Evidence of European influence includes Roman coins found in Venezuela. And on a wall in the once-buried Roman city of Pompeii is a painting of a pineapple, a plant native to the Western Hemisphere. In a twelfth-century tomb in Mexico, archeologists found a clay head that was made in third-century Rome.

Suppose the ancient Europeans or Africans did reach the Americas. Does that mean they influenced the development of Indian cultures? Most scholars say no, the available evidence does not support such a theory.

The Hohokam and Anasazi

Although scholars are still debating transoceanic diffusion, they do not question that Mesoamerican culture influenced Indian peoples to the north. The first influence was agriculture. The desert people of the Southwest began raising corn and squash 4,000 years ago. Later they learned to grow beans. Over time, they developed distinct farming cultures that depended on what the Indians called the Three Sisters—corn, squash, and beans.

The Hohokam people may have migrated from Mexico about 300 B.C. to settle in what is now central Arizona. To get water to their crops, they dug lengthy canals using only digging sticks as tools. The major canals in this system were more than 30 miles long.

The Hohokam culture broke up in the 1400s, perhaps because turbulent times in Mexico cut off trade and contact. The Hohokam people then became more like their neighbors. They survived through hunting, gathering, and a little farming.

During the same centuries the Anasazi people of the Colorado Plateau also developed a culture based on agriculture. Like the Hohokam, they built irrigation ditches to catch water, and they farmed on terraces to prevent erosion. To supplement their crops, they hunted game and gathered wild plants and nuts.

The Anasazi were also traders. Roads 30 feet wide radiated out from Pueblo Bonito in Chaco Canyon. A thousand years ago people traveled these roads carrying wood from the mountains, along with pottery, cloth, baskets, and turquoise. Pieces of the turquoise would end up in the markets of faraway Mexico.

By 1300, however, the Anasazi had abandoned their villages. No one knows exactly why. From the study of tree rings, scientists do know that a terrible, 25-year drought began in 1275. The drought might have been too much for these desert farmers to survive.

Whatever the cause, the Anasazi moved to other sites in the Southwest, including the Rio Grande Valley of New Mexico. Their descendants—the Pueblo Indians—live there still.

Woodland Cultures

To the east, meanwhile, complex cultures were emerging in the Eastern Woodlands—roughly the region between the Mississippi River and the Atlantic Coast. People there developed complex cultures based primarily on trade. As early as 3000 B.C. the Woodland Indians were engaged in long-distance trading of useful and decorative stones, copper tools, and carved beads. The later Crystal River culture along Florida's Gulf Coast, for example, carried on an extensive trade that reached south to the Olmecs of Mexico and north to the Great Lakes.

It is possible that the Crystal River culture was the first civilization north of Mexico to build pyramid mounds. Other Woodland cultures north of Florida also adopted this practice. Elaborate burial mounds became the most distinctive feature of the Hopewell culture, situated in the Ohio Valley. This culture, which emerged about 500 B.C., would last for about 1,200 years.

The Hopewell people began cultivating corn about A.D. 450. With the beginning of agriculture, some say, their trading activities declined and the communities became more isolated from each other. About 300 years later they took to the hills, where they built large defensive earthworks. Obviously there was unrest in the land, perhaps an invading people. These earthworks are the last evidence of the Hopewell culture.

The Mississippian Culture

About A.D. 900 another mound culture emerged in the Southeast and Mississippi Valley. This is known as the Mississippian culture and this culture had clear ties with Mexico.

Communities in the Mississippian culture clustered on the river flood plains where such locations were good for farming because floods constantly renewed the fertility of the soil. Their towns featured large flat-topped mounds on which were built temples, meeting houses, and residences of chiefs and priests. Common symbols in their art were the falcon and the jaguar, both of which had long been revered in Mesoamerica.

The crown jewel of the Mississippian culture was Cahokia, in western Illinois. In its heyday, Cahokia boasted 30,000 residents and more than 1,000 mounds. The tallest mound at Cahokia rises ten stories from a sixteen-acre base, rivaling Mexico's Pyramid of the Sun in size. By the time European explorers arrived in the region, the Mississippians had abandoned Cahokia. The Mississippian culture declined rapidly. Later Indians of the region could not say who had built the mounds. Yet there seems to be little doubt that the major tribes of the Southeast were descendants of the mound builders. These include the Cherokees, Catawbas, Creeks, Chickasaws, and Choctaws.

The first European explorers and settlers in the Americas left vivid accounts of the Indians they encountered, yet these accounts have tended to "freeze" Indians in time and place. This is because they assumed that the Indians had always lived in the same place and in the same way. But that is not true. Indian groups moved from one territory to another. As they did, they changed their way of life when it was necessary to do so.

The Cheyenne, for instance, are usually thought of as Plains Indians who hunted buffalo. Originally, however, they were farmers in southern Minnesota. Once they migrated to the Plains, the Cheyenne continued a life that included both farming and hunting-gathering. Then, when the Spanish brought horses to the Plains in the mid-1500s, the Cheyenne abandoned farming to rely on hunting.

The Indian societies in North America were a diverse lot. Some devoted themselves to warfare. Others were peaceful, fighting only if necessary. Some societies were egalitarian. Others were organized into social classes, often with slaves as the lowest class. Some societies emphasized the importance of individual feats of valor or of possessions to increase status. Others discouraged individualism and personal status-seeking.

Chiefs headed most Indian societies. The chief, either male or female depending on tradition, had only as much authority as the group was willing to give. Important decisions were made in consultation with other village leaders and sometimes a village chief might bow to the authority of the chief of a more powerful neighbor.

The Land

Concerned with survival rather than conservation, Indians did not always live in harmony with the earth. Many scientists, for example, think ancient big-game hunters may have hunted horses to extinction in the Western Hemisphere. They also think the Anasazi stripped large areas of forests and ruined the topsoil.

A major change in the use of the American land came with the rise of agriculture. In the Southwest the Indians adopted methods of irrigation. In the Eastern Woodlands the Indians practiced slash-and-burn farming. To prepare a field, they would kill the trees by cutting away strips of bark from around their trunks. Then they would burn the underbrush. The ashes helped fertilize the soil. Between the dead trees, the Indians used sticks to poke holes in the ground. In the holes they planted corn, beans, and squash, often mixing the seeds together. Whenever the soil became exhausted, usually after eight years, the Woodland Indians would move on to clear another plot and build another village. Meanwhile, forests would retake the old fields, thus renewing the land.

The Woodland Indians also used fire to reshape the forests and groups such as the Algonquin not only lived on the land; they managed it.

Their principal tool of management was fire. They regularly and systematically set fire in the woods to destroy the underbrush. These were low-heat fires that swept through an area quickly, not burning well-established trees. One effect of these fires was to make ashes that added nutrients to the soil. Another effect was that grass and berries were likely to establish themselves on the fire-cleared ground. The grass and berries in turn attracted animals such as deer, bears, and wild turkeys. By firing the woods, therefore, the Indians created an environment more supportive of wildlife.

The Woodland Indians were not alone in using fire to shape the environment. This technique was used throughout the continent. In California, for instance, the Indians set fire to the meadowlands each fall to ensure a good harvest of grass seed for the coming year.

The Clash of Cultures

The Europeans brought deadly new diseases that ravaged the Indians and their attitude toward land use, as well as their technology, destroyed the hunting-gathering environment on which the Indians depended.

The Indians had had no contact with diseases that were commonplace in the rest of the world. These included chicken pox, measles, smallpox, and flu. As a result, what was an ordinary case of flu to a European meant certain death for an Indian. With death rates as high as 90%, the social and economic foundations of whole tribes were wiped out. Millions died. The Indian population of North America dropped from about 10 or 12 million in 1500 to about half a million in 1900.

Differences over the meaning of land ownership became a principal source of conflict between the white and Indian cultures. To a white person, land ownership meant controlling what happened to the land. For the Indians, land ownership meant having access to the things on the land during different seasons of the year. No one could own the land itself, only have rights to its produce.

Disagreements between Indians and white settlers over the use of the land led to war and the settlers won because of their superior numbers and superior technology. □

The Trail of Tears

Source: The Reader's Companion to American History.

The Trail of Tears refers to the route followed by fifteen thousand Cherokee during their 1838 removal and forced march from Georgia to Indian Territory (present-day Oklahoma).

In 1791, a U.S. treaty had recognized Cherokee territory in Georgia as independent, and the Cherokee people had created a thriving republic with a written constitution. For decades, the state of Georgia sought to enforce its authority over the Cherokee Nation, but its efforts had little effect until the election of President Andrew Jackson, a longtime supporter of Indian removal. Although the Supreme Court declared Congress's 1830 Indian removal bill unconstitutional (*Worcester* v. *Georgia,* 1832), the national and state harassment continued, culminating in the rounding up of the Cherokee by troops in 1838.

The Cherokee were forced to abandon their property, livestock, and ancestral burial grounds and move to camps in Tennessee. From there, in the midst of severe winter weather, they were marched another eight hundred miles to Indian Territory. An estimated four thousand people—over 25 percent of the Cherokee Nation—died during the march.

The Trail of Tears, the path the Cherokee followed, became a national monument in 1987, serving as a symbol of the wrongs suffered by Indians at the hands of the U.S. government. □

The Battle of Wounded Knee

Source: The Reader's Companion to American History.

The Battle of Wounded Knee on December 29, 1890, was, in fact, not a battle but a massacre, in which the U.S. Seventh Cavalry Division killed 146 Sioux men, women, and children, after the Sioux warriors refused to surrender their arms.

Two years earlier, on a reservation in Nevada, a Paiute named Wovoka (also known as Jack Wilson) had begun preaching that an Indian Messiah would soon arrive who would restore the American continent to the Indians and reunite them with their dead families. A cult grew from his teachings, centering on the mystical Ghost Dance, and within a year it had spread to dozens of other reservations. Its strength among the Sioux alarmed U.S. officials, who made repeated efforts to suppress the new religion. These efforts culminated in the massacre at the Black Hills Reservation in Wounded Knee, South Dakota, ending the Ghost Dance (or Messiah) War. Wounded Knee was the last military encounter between American Indians and whites. □

LOCATIONS OF LARGEST AMERICAN INDIAN TRIBES AND SELECTED RESERVATIONS

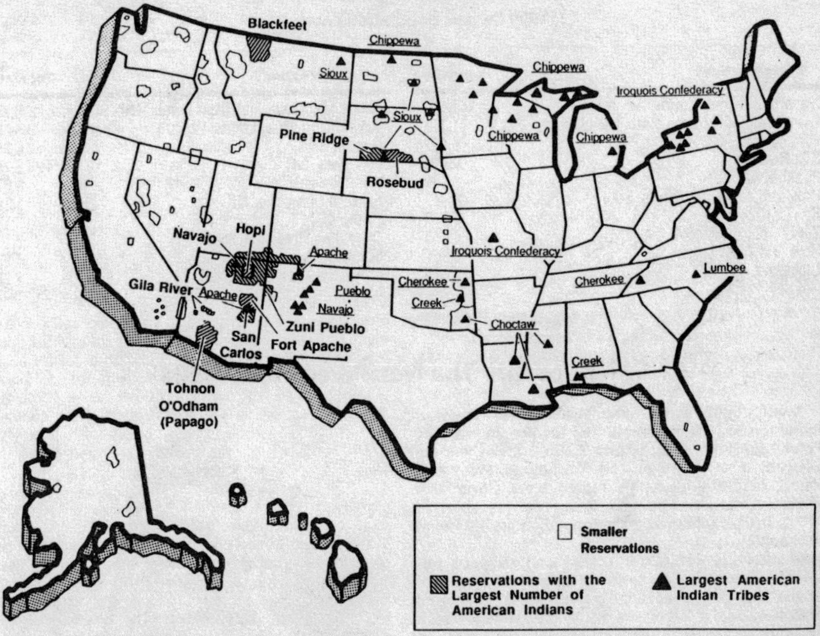

Population of Native Americans By State, 1990

States	American Indian	Eskimo	Aleut	States	American Indian	Eskimo	Aleut
Alabama	16,312	105	89	Montana	47,524	106	49
Alaska	31,245	44,401	10,052	Nebraska	12,344	38	28
Arizona	203,009	284	234	Nevada	19,377	156	104
Arkansas	12,641	80	52	New Hampshire	2,075	45	14
California	236,078	2,552	3,534	New Jersey	14,500	201	269
Colorado	27,271	297	208	New Mexico	134,097	162	96
Connecticut	6,472	83	99	New York	60,855	754	1,042
Delaware	1,982	19	18	North Carolina	79,825	152	178
D.C.	1,432	14	20	North Dakota	25,870	38	9
Florida	35,461	431	443	Ohio	19,859	230	269
Georgia	12,926	223	199	Oklahoma	252,089	202	129
Hawaii	4,738	155	206	Oregon	37,443	545	508
Idaho	13,594	132	54	Pennsylvania	14,210	264	259
Illinois	20,970	414	452	Rhode Island	3,987	42	42
Indiana	12,453	170	97	South Carolina	8,049	106	91
Iowa	7,217	67	65	South Dakota	50,501	62	12
Kansas	21,767	114	84	Tennessee	9,859	96	84
Kentucky	5,614	82	73	Texas	64,349	721	807
Louisiana	18,361	92	88	Utah	24,093	116	74
Maine	5,945	34	19	Vermont	1,650	32	14
Maryland	12,601	169	202	Virginia	14,893	200	189
Massachusetts	11,857	210	174	Washington	77,627	1,791	2,065
Michigan	55,131	253	282	West Virginia	2,385	36	37
Minnesota	49,392	235	282	Wisconsin	38,986	181	220
Mississippi	8,435	50	40	Wyoming	9,426	37	16
Missouri	19,508	173	154	**United States**	**1,878,285**	**57,152**	**23,797**

Source: U.S. Department of Commerce, Bureau of the Census.

Reservations With Largest Number of American Indians

(1990 Census populations over 4,000)

Reservations	Population	Reservations	Population
Navajo and Trust Lands, AZ–NM–UT	143,405	Turtle Mountain and Trust Lands, ND–SD	6,772
Pine Ridge and Trust Lands, NE–SD	11,182	Yakima and Trust Lands, WA	6,307
Fort Apache, AZ	9,825	Osage, OK	6,161
Gila River, AZ	9,116	Fort Peck, MT	5,782
Papago, AZ	8,480	Wind River, WY	5,676
Rosebud and Trust Lands, SD	8,043	Eastern Cherokee, NC	5,388
San Carlos, AZ	7,110	Flathead, MT	5,130
Zuni Pueblo, AZ–NM	7,073	Cheyenne River, SD	5,100
Hopi and Trust Lands, AZ	7,061	Standing Rock, ND–SD	4,870
Blackfeet, MT	7,025	Crow and Trust Lands, MT	4,724

Source: Department of Commerce, Bureau of the Census

Chief Joseph, The Nez Percé (1840–1904)

A tall, dignified, mission-educated North American Indian leader, Chief Joseph, and his people, the Nez Percé,[1] inhabited what is now Central Idaho and the adjacent areas of Oregon and Washington. Many Nez Percé, including Joseph's father, were Christians. From his father, whom he succeeded as chief in 1871, Joseph inherited a determination to hold onto his people's land.

In the early 1800s, fur traders and trappers, followed by missionaries, began penetrating the territory of the Nez Percé. In 1855, a treaty with the United States created a large Nez Percé reservation, which encompassed most of the tribe's traditional land. The discovery of gold in the 1860s, however, and the subsequent influx of thousands of miners, led U.S. commissioners to fraudulently reduce the size of the tribe's reservation by three-fourths. Homesteaders reduced the area even more. Many Nez Percé had never accepted either the old or the new treaties. A series of hostile actions and raids by both whites and Indians led to the Nez Percé War of 1877, as the tribe tried to escape to Canada.

Chief Joseph

For five months, Joseph and about 250 warriors waged a series of battles against 5,000 U.S. troops. The fighting was carried on across more than 1,500 miles, as the tribe made its way through Washington, Oregon, Idaho, Wyoming, and Montana. Joseph and the tribe crossed the Missouri River in northern Montana on September 23. Suffering from hunger and exhaustion, and thinking they had outwitted their pursuers, they stopped to rest about forty miles south of the Canadian border. However, they were surprised by American troops, and on October 5, 1877, Joseph was forced to surrender, delivering perhaps the most famous speech in American Indian history:

"Tell General Howard I know his heart. What he told me before—I have it in my heart. I am tired of fighting. Our chiefs are killed. Looking-glass is dead. *Too-hul-hul-suit*[2] is dead. The old men are all dead. It is the young men, now, who say 'yes' or 'no' [that is, vote in council]. He who led on the young men [Joseph's brother, Ollicut] is dead. It is cold, and we have no blankets. The little children are freezing to death. My people—some of them—have run away to the hills, and have no blankets, no food. No one knows where they are—perhaps freezing to death. I want to have time to look for my children, and to see how many of them I can find; may be I shall find them among the dead. Hear me, my chiefs; my heart is sick and sad. From where the sun *now* stands, I will fight no more forever!"

Instead of being returned to the Northwest as promised, Joseph and his band were sent to a barren reservation Indian Territory (now Oklahoma). There, many of the Indians became sick and died. Although still exiled from their ancestral home, Joseph and the remainder of his tribe were sent to the Colville Reservation in northeastern Washington in 1885. For the rest of his life, Joseph pleaded with federal authorities to allow his people to return to their homeland. Joseph died at Colville in 1904 and was buried there.

Most historians believe that Joseph's role in the Nez Percé retreat has been exaggerated; he was only one of several Indian leaders. Nonetheless, his bravery and humane treatment of others won him high praise. He remains an enduring symbol of Indian resistance. □

1. French for "pierced nose," although the wearing of nose pendants does not seem to have been widespread among the tribe. 2. A Nez Percé chief.

Indian-White Relations

Source: The Reader's Companion to American History.

Indian-white relations in the period following the arrival of Columbus can be seen variously as the continuation of a normal process of migration by humans from one part of the world to another, as a genocidal assault by more powerful intruders upon weaker, more "primitive" peoples, or as the process by which Western civilization and Christianity were transferred from the Old World to the New. Whichever perception is adopted will be in accordance with one's cultural, epistemological, and emotional preconceptions.

The Europeans who followed Leif Eriksson's Norsemen at the turn of the tenth century (and gave us the first recorded account of European relations with the native peoples of North America) and those who followed Columbus at the end of the fifteenth century were greeted warily by the native population (in a friendly fashion in the case of Columbus's first voyage), but relations soon turned to hostility and war. In the Spanish case at least, the source of the hostility was Spanish cruelty and greed spurred by the realization that those living in the Caribbean basin were unable to defend themselves from the technologically superior newcomers. This conclusion derives from the evidence provided by the Spanish themselves, however much these accounts were exploited by Spain's rivals in the New World, whose hypocrisy often concealed similar cruelty and greed.

Spain and Portugal had a century's head start on France, England, Holland, and Sweden in establishing relations with the peoples of the newfound world; thus the two countries had first choice of which lands to conquer, colonize, and exploit. Although we tend to think of Latin America today as a poor third world area, in the sixteenth century these lands were considered the richest and most desirable because of their valuable resources and their extensive populations who were soon forced to serve the Europeans as slaves, servants, or dependent trading partners. The present areas of the United States and Canada were considered by the Iberian powers the least desirable portions of the New World, hardly worth colonizing except to prevent northern European nations from establishing bases from which to harass the Spanish and Portuguese.

Because of the absence of both mineral wealth and subservient populations in the areas north of Mexico, the English, French, Dutch, and Swedish set up colonies at the beginning of the seventeenth century that were primarily extensions of their own societies and dealt only intermittently with the surrounding native populations. The natural growth of these colonies provided increasing military and economic power vis-à-vis the Indians, whose numerical superiority in the first half-century in almost every colony was lost in the second half-century as European diseases and warfare took their toll.

Cruelty and greed were prevalent in the early history of all the northern European nations' dealings with the Indians, but the picture was not entirely one-sided: treachery and cunning existed on both sides. Cultural differences—the failure of each side to understand the assumptions of the other—led to frequent misunderstandings that in turn led to warfare. One of the most elementary forms of misunderstanding, for example, was the anger felt by the Indians over the colonists' allowing their cattle and hogs to roam in unfenced freedom. The consequence was often the destruction of the Indians' corn, which led to the Indians' killing the offending animals, which led to retaliation by the settlers upon the Indians who had killed the animals, and so on. And too often those retaliating failed to discriminate between the Indians who were responsible for the "offense" and those who were not.

While Spain and Portugal exploited the labor (through slavery and serfdom) of the large populations of the areas they settled, the northern Europeans made only limited use of Indian labor. Rather, they wanted land; if it had not been acquired through war or simple occupation, they sought to purchase it. But often the Indians assumed they were conferring on Europeans only the right to use the land without losing their own right to continue to use it for hunting, fishing, or gathering food. Northern European governments soon prohibited their colonists from making such purchases for fear that the contracts would compromise the royal assertions of ultimate sovereignty over all the lands.

With the destruction or subordination of most of the coastal tribes, England and France, the two most successful of the northern European colonial powers, extended their jurisdiction into the interior, the English across the Appalachian Mountains hemming in their coastal settlements, and the French down the St. Lawrence River and up the Mississippi. The French, from their interior position, hoped to confine their English rivals to the coastal regions. The French were more adept at forging alliances with the powerful Indian nations in the interior, though they were not averse to wars of extermination, such as that against the Natchez in the Mississippi valley. Because the French had fewer settlers than the English, they tended to rely on a network of military and trade alliances with the Indians rather than developing agricultural and commercial settlements to match those of the English.

With the destruction of French power in the great war for empire that raged across North America and Europe during the 1750s and 1760s, the situation of the Indians was weakened. They were no longer able to play off one European power against another but had to confront England directly. Only with the coming of the American Revolution did they recover the opportunity to play a balancing role. But, unfortunately, most tribes chose to side with the loser, and the victorious Americans treated the Indian nations who had fought with the British as defeated foes. Great Britain made no attempt to secure Indian rights in treaty negotiations with the Americans, and even the objections of Spain (America's wartime ally) that the area between the Appalachians and the Mississippi River remained Indian territory were dismissed by the victorious revolutionaries. But treating the Indians as defeated enemies was not an entirely successful tactic. After the tribes of the Old Northwest had inflicted a number of stinging setbacks upon the U.S. Army, the new American nation formulated a more moderate policy toward the Indians. The United States recognized the right of the Indian nations to exist as autonomous entities but sought to buy as much of their land as possible. Even the Indian allies of the Americans were pressured to sell off large portions of their lands.

As the United States grew in power in the early nineteenth century, several Indian nations such as the

Cherokee were overwhelmed and sent on forced marches to the so-called Indian Territory (later Oklahoma) with significant loss of life. The "Trail of Tears" of the Cherokee migration to the Indian Territory in the 1830s became an enduring symbol of white injustice toward the Indians, particularly since the removal was carried out despite the Cherokee Nation's legal victory over the state of Georgia in the Supreme Court. Most of the Indians in the eastern United States now moved West, either voluntarily or under duress, with a few remaining in small pockets near their original homelands.

The health and longevity of the Indians had suffered a steady decline since the arrival of the Europeans, for the whites carried diseases, such as smallpox and measles, for which the Indians had no immunity. The diseases and the numbers affected by them is a subject of intense debate among scholars. Estimates of Indian population before the arrival of whites have increased over the years, sometimes by as much as ten times the earlier estimates. Henry Dobyns put the number at some 10 to 12 million in North America north of Mexico and 90 to 112 million for the entire Western Hemisphere. Most scholars have discounted such high estimates, although conceding that earlier estimates (such as the traditional figure of about 1 million for the present area of the United States) were probably too low. In any event, the steady decline of the Indian population in the United States reached its low point of 228,000 in 1890.

This decline coincided with the loss of tribal lands and tribal authority, particularly under the General Allotment Act (Dawes Security Act) of 1887. This act imposed a system of individual land ownership upon many of the Indian tribes with the government selling off the surplus lands to white settlers for the presumed benefit of the tribes (some western tribes were exempted or not forced to comply). Contemporary Indians often cite the Dawes Act as legislation that could and should have been avoided, but that is probably an unrealistic assessment. The vast landholdings of small impotent tribes simply could not have been maintained against the millions of well-armed whites moving west. The land rush in 1889 into the Indian Territory (which became Oklahoma as a result) is an example. Even the staunchest friends of the Indian were convinced that the tribes could not survive unless they gave up much of their land claims and secured a portion in severalty (individual allotments) with the security of a "white man's [fee simple] title."

Although the popular impression during those years was that the Indians were a "disappearing race," the twentieth century saw a dramatic reversal of almost all indexes of decline. Health problems came under increasing control, and diseases like tuberculosis were nearly eliminated. But alcoholism, or alcohol-related events such as car accidents, became the principal cause of death among Indians: no one has determined why Indians seem to be so susceptible to alcoholic stress, and the debate between those favoring a genetic explanation and those a cultural one continues.

The gradual loss of Indian tribal authority was suddenly reversed in 1934 with the passage of the Indian Reorganization Act, which addressed the strengthening of tribal life and government with federal assistance. Although it was subject to bitter debate both at the time and later, the evidence is conclusive that the act, the product of the thinking of John Collier, commissioner of Indian affairs, put Indian communities, then nearing political and cultural dissolution, on the road to recovery and growth. Collier, struck by the strength and viability of Indian communal societies in the Southwest (e.g., the Hopis) and appalled by the destructive effects on tribal societies of the allotment system, sought to restore tribal structures by making the tribes instrumentalities of the federal government. In this way, he asserted, tribes would be "surrounded by the protective guardianship of the federal government and clothed with the authority of the federal government." Indian tribal governments, as Collier foresaw, now exist on a government-to-government basis with the states and the federal government. Although they are financially and legally dependent upon the federal government, they have been able to extend their political and judicial authority in areas nineteenth-century politicians would have found unimaginable.

American Indians, now a rapidly growing minority group, possess a unique legal status (based on treaties and constitutional decisions) and are better educated, in better health, and more prosperous than ever before (despite the persistence of high levels of unemployment, poverty, and disease). The causes of this "Indian Renaissance" have been the subject of much dispute, some attributing it to the well-publicized activities of Indian radicals, others to the commitment and decency of the larger society. Nevertheless, the popular stereotype of the impoverished, drunken, abused Indian has continued to cloud Indian life.

Contemporary issues being fought out in the courts, legislatures, and tribal councils have concerned Indian religious freedom, water rights, and land claims. Demands in the 1980s and 1990s for the return of Indian skeletal remains in museum collections pitted some white museum administrators and archaeologists against Indian religious and political leaders. The Indians seemed to be winning, as the Smithsonian Institution, Stanford University, and other groups promised the repatriation of Indian remains and accompanying grave goods to the tribes claiming them. Water rights continued to be a bitter issue affecting western tribes, but Supreme Court decisions in the 1980s dampened the more optimistic Indian hopes for an increased portion of the limited water resources in the West. Land claims, although settled for the most part by the defunct Indian Claims Commission, were occasionally reasserted in specific instances in the 1980s, as among the Iroquois of New York State.

It has often been assumed that acculturation was a one-way street—that Indians were shaped by whites and not the other way around. But it is clear that the process was one of "transculturization,' as the anthropologist Irving Hallowell put it. Not only did whites adopt aspects of Indian material culture (e.g., maize, moccasins), but spiritually and psychologically the transplanted European society acquired an Indian cast, particularly a taste for individual freedom and a distaste for the constraints of civilization, as D.H. Lawrence, James Adair, Carl Jung, and James Fenimore Cooper all noted. It was not because Indians were despised but because they were admired that their symbolic powers were often appropriated and celebrated by their former foes. □

Eskimos

The Eskimos are the most widely dispersed group in the world still leading a partly aboriginal way of life. They live in a region that spans more than 3,500 miles, including Greenland, the northern fringe of North America, and a sector of eastern Siberia.

Eskimos are racially distinct from American Indians, and are not, as previously believed, merely "Indians transformed." In fact, the Eskimos are most closely related to the Mongolian peoples of eastern Asia. Eskimos consider themselves to be "Inuit" (The People). The Eskimo-Aleut languages are unrelated to any American Indian language groups.

The Eskimo population was approximately 50,000 at the time of the first widespread contact with Europeans. An estimated 2,000 Siberian Eskimos lived near the Bering Strait, the Alaskan Eskimos numbered about 25,000, and the Central Eskimos (who inhabited what is now northern Canada) numbered about 10,000. The Labrador Eskimos totaled about 3,000, while the Greenland Eskimos totaled about 10,000.

The popular conception of the Eskimos—whale hunters dressed in heavy fur clothing and living in dome-shaped ice lodges—is derived from the Eskimos who live farthest north, on the Arctic islands of Canada and along northwestern Greenland. In reality, these northern Arctic dwellers formed a minority among Eskimos as a whole. No single environmental adaptation existed throughout the area of Eskimo occupancy. Eskimos along the Pacific coast probably obtained much of their food by fishing for salmon, while the Central Eskimos of Canada subsisted mainly on caribou. Eskimo groups lived in various types of shelters, including semi-subterranean sod houses and tents made of caribou skins.

At no time did the Eskimos possess a national or even well-defined tribal sense. The emphasis was on the local and familial group rather than on associations of land and territory.

The overall Eskimo population has remained fairly constant over the past several centuries, although not all groups have remained stable in number. According to the 1990 census, there are 57,152 Eskimos and 23,797 Aleuts living in the United States. □

Facts About American Indians Today

Source: U.S. Department of the Interior, Bureau of Indian Affairs.

Reservations. The number of Indian land areas in the U.S. administered as Federal Indian Reservations total 287. The largest is the Navajo Reservation of some 16 million acres of land in Arizona, New Mexico, and Utah. Many of the smaller reservations are less than 1,000 acres with the smallest less than 100 acres. On some reservations, a high percentage of the land is owned and occupied by non-Indians. Some 140 reservations have entirely tribally-owned land.

Indians do not have to live on reservations and are free to move about like all other Americans. Indians also have the right to buy and hold title to land purchased with their own funds. Over half of the total U.S. Indian and Alaska Native population now lives away from reservations. Many return home to participate in family and tribal life and sometimes to retire.

Indian Tribes. There are over 500 Federally recognized tribes in the United States, including about 200 village groups in Alaska. "Federally-recognized" means these tribes and groups have a special, legal relationship to the U.S. government and its agent, The Bureau of Indian Affairs (BIA).

A number of Indian tribes and groups in the U.S. do not have a federally-recognized status, although some are state-recognized. The Bureau of Indian Affairs has a special program to work with those seeking federal recognition status.

Who is an Indian? No single federal or tribal criterion establishes a person's identity as an Indian. Government agencies use differing criteria to determine who is an Indian eligible to participate in their programs. Tribes also have varying eligibility criteria for membership. To be eligible for Bureau of Indian Affairs services, an Indian must (1) be a member of a tribe recognized by the federal government and (2) must, for some purposes, be of one-fourth or more Indian ancestry. By legislative and administrative decision, the Aleuts, Eskimos, and Indians of Alaska are eligible for BIA services.

Tribal membership. A tribe sets up its own criteria, although the U.S. Congress can also establish tribal membership criteria. Becoming a member of a particular tribe requires meeting its membership rules, including adoption. Except for adoption, the amount of blood quantum needed varies, with some tribes requiring only a trace of Indian blood (of the tribe) while others require as much as one-half.

What is an Indian tribe? Originally, an Indian tribe was a body of people bound together by blood ties who were socially, politically, and religiously organized, who lived together in a defined territory, and who spoke a common language or dialect. The establishment of the reservation system created some new tribal groupings when two or three tribes were placed on one reservation, or when members of one tribe were spread over two or three reservations.

Taxes. Indians pay the same taxes as other citizens with the exceptions applying to those Indians living on federal reservations: (1) federal income taxes are not levied on income from trust lands held for them by the United States; (2) state income taxes are not paid on income earned on a federal reservation; (3) state sales taxes are not paid on transactions made on a federal reservation, and (4) local property taxes are not paid on reservation or trust land.

Citizenship. Indians are U.S. citizens and have the same right to vote as other Americans. They also have the right to hold federal, state, and local government offices. Ben Nighthorse Campbell, a member of the Northern Cheyenne Tribe of Montana, was elected to the U.S. House of Representatives in 1986 from the Third District of Colorado and was serving his third term in 1992. □

PEOPLE

Many public figures not listed here may be found elsewhere in the *Information Please Almanac.*

41 Governors
634 Presidents
636 Presidents' Wives
34 Senators
930 Sports Personalities
652 Supreme Court Justices
634 Vice Presidents

A name in parentheses is the original name or form of name. Localities are places of birth. Country name in parenthesis is the present-day name. Dates of birth appear as month/day/year. **Boldface** years in parentheses are dates of **(birth-death).**

Information has been gathered from many sources, including the individuals themselves. However, the *Information Please Almanac* cannot guarantee the accuracy of every individual item.

A

Aalto, Alvar (architect); Kuortane, Finland **(1898-1976)**
Abbado, Claudio (orchestra conductor); Milan, Italy, 1933
Abbott, Bud (William) (comedian); Asbury Park, N.J. **(1898-1974)**
Abbott, George (stage producer); Forestville, N.Y., 6/25/1887
Abel, Walter (actor); St. Paul **(1898-1987)**
Abelard, Peter (theologian); nr. Nantes, France **(1079-1142)**
Abernathy, Ralph (civil rights leader); Linden, Ala., **(1926-1990)**
Acheson, Dean (statesman); Middletown, Conn. **(1893-1971)**
Acuff, Roy Claxton (musician); nr. Maynardsville, Tenm. **(1903-1992)**
Adams, Charles Francis (diplomat); Boston **(1807-1886)**
Adams, Don (actor); New York City, 4/19/1926
Adams, Edie (Edie Enke) (actress); Kingston, Pa., 4/16/1929
Adams, Franklin Pierce (columnist and author); Chicago **(1881-1960)**
Adams, Henry Brooks (historian); Boston **(1838-1918)**
Adams, Joey (comedian); New York City, 1/6/1911
Adams, Mason (actor); New York City, 2/26/19
Adams, Maude (Maude Kiskadden) (actress); Salt Lake City **(1872-1953)**
Adams, Samuel (American Revolutionary patriot); Boston **(1722-1803)**
Adamson, Joy (naturalist); Troppau, Silesia **(1910-1980)**
Addams, Charles (cartoonist); Westfield, N.J., **(1912-1988)**
Addams, Jane (social worker); Cedarville, Ill. **(1860-1935)**
Adderley, Julian "Cannonball" (jazz saxophonist); Tampa, Fla. **(1928-1975)**
Ade, George (humorist); Kentland, Ind. **(1866-1944)**
Adenauer, Konrad (statesman); Cologne, Germany **(1876-1967)**
Adler, Alfred (psychoanalyst); Vienna **(1870-1937)**
Adler, Larry (musician); Baltimore, 2/10/1914
Adler, Richard (songwriter); New York City, 8/3/1921
Adoree, Renée (Renée La Fonte) (actress); Lille, France **(1898-1933)**
Aeschylus (dramatist); Eleusis (Greece) **(525-456 B.C.)**
Aesop (fabulist); birthplace unknown **(lived c. 600 B.C.)**
Aherne, Brian (actor); King's Norton, England **(1902-1986)**
Aiello, Danny (actor); New York City, 6/20/33
Aiken, Conrad (poet); Savannah, Ga. **(1889-1973)**
Ailey, Alvin (c horeographer); Rogers, Tex., **(1931-1989)**
Albanese, Licia (operatic soprano); Bari, Italy, 7/22/1913
Albee, Edward (playwright); Washington, D.C., 3/12/1928
Albers, Josef (painter); Bottrop, Germany (1888-1976)
Albert, Eddie (Edward Albert Heimberger) (actor); Rock Island, Ill., 4/22/1908
Albert, Edward (actor); Los Angeles, 2/20/51
Albertson, Jack (actor); Malden, Mass. **(1910?-1981)**
Albright, Lola (actress); Akron, Ohio, 7/20/1925
Alcott, Louisa May (novelist); Germantown, Pa. **(1832-1888)**
Alda, Alan (actor); New York City, 1/28/1936
Alda, Robert (Alphonso d'Abruzzo) (actor); New York City **(1914-1986)**
Alden, John (American Pilgrim); England **(1599?-1687)**
Alexander, Jane (Quigley) (actress); Boston, 10/28/39
Alexander the Great (monarch and conqueror); Pella, Macedonia (Greece) **(356-323 B.C.)**
Alger, Horatio (author); Revere, Mass. **(1834-1899)**
Algren, Nelson (novelist); Detroit **(1909-1981)**
Allen, Debbie (dancer-choreographer, actress); Houston, Tex., 1/16/50
Allen, Ethan (American Revolutionary soldier); Litchfield, Conn. **(1738-1789)**
Allen, Fred (John Florence Sullivan) (comedian); Cambridge, Mass. **(1894-1956)**
Allen, Gracie (Grace Ethel Cecile Rosalie Allen) (comedienne); San Francisco **(1906-1964)**
Allen, Mel (Melvin Israel) (sportscaster); Birmingham, Ala., 2/14/1913
Allen, Peter (actor, songwriter); Tenterfield, Australia **(1944-1992)**
Allen, Steve (TV entertainer); New York City, 12/26/1921
Allen, Woody (Allen Stewart Konigsberg) (actor, writer, and director); Brooklyn, N.Y., 12/1/1935
Alley, Kirstie (actress); Wichita, Kan., 1/12/55
Allison, Fran (actress); LaPorte City, Iowa, **(1908?-1989)**
Allman, Gregg (singer); Nashville, Tenn., 12/8/1947
Allyson, June (Jan Allyson) (actress); New York City, 10/7/1923
Alonso, Alicia (ballerina); Havana, 12/21/1921(?)
Alpert, Herb (band leader); Los Angeles, 3/31/1935(?)
Alsop, Joseph W., Jr. (journalist); Avon, Conn., **(1910-1989)**
Alsop, Stewart (journalist); Avon, Conn. **(1914-1974)**
Altman, Robert (film director); Kansas City, Mo., 2/20/1925
Amati, Nicola (violin maker); Cremona, Italy **(1596-1684)**
Ambler, Eric (suspense writer); London, 6/28/1909
Ameche, Don (Dominic Amici) (actor); Kenosha, Wis., 5/31/1908
Ames, Leon (actor); Portland, Ind., 1/20/03
Amis, Kingsley (novelist); London, 4/16/1922
Amory, Cleveland (writer and conservationist); Nahant, Mass., 9/2/1917
Amos (Freeman F. Gosden) (radio comedian); Richmond, Va. **(1899-1982)**
Amos, John (actor); Newark, N.J., 12/27/41
Amsterdam, Morey (actor); Chicago, 12/14/1914
Andersen, Hans Christian (author of fairy-tales); Odense, Denmark **(1805-1875)**
Anderson, Eddie. *See* Rochester
Anderson, Harry (actor); Newport, R.I., 10/14/52
Anderson, Ib (ballet dancer); Copenhagen, 12/14/1954
Anderson, Jack (journalist); Long Beach, Calif., 10/19/1922
Anderson, Dame Judith (actress); Adelaide, Australia **(1898-1992)**
Anderson, Lindsay (Gordon) (director); Bangalore, India, 4/17/1923
Anderson, Loni (actress); St. Paul, Minn. 8/5/45
Anderson, Lynn (singer); Grand Forks, N.D., 9/26/1947
Anderson, Marian (contralto); Philadelphia **(1897-1993)**
Anderson, Maxwell (dramatist); Atlantic, Pa. **(1888-1959)**
Anderson, Richard Dean (actor); Minneapolis, Minn., 1/23/50
Anderson, Robert (playwright); New York City, 4/28/1917
Andersson, Bibi (actress); Stockholm, 11/11/1935
Andress, Ursula (actress); Switzerland, 3/19/1938
Andrews, Dana (actor); Collins, Miss. **(1909-1992)**
Andrews, Julie (Julia Wells) (actress and singer); Walton-on-Thames, England, 10/1/1935
Andrews, La Verne (singer); Minneapolis **(1916-1967)**
Andrews, Maxene (singer); Minneapolis, 1/3/1918
Andrews, Patti (singer); Minneapolis, 2/16/1920
Andy (Charles J. Correll) (radio comedian); Peoria, Ill. **(1890-1972)**
Angeles, Victoria de los (Victoria Gamez Cima) (operatic soprano); Barcelona, 11/1/1924
Anka, Paul (singer and composer); Ottawa, 7/30/1941
Ann-Margret (Ann-Margret Olsson) (actress); Valsjobyn, Sweden, 4/28/1941
Annabella (actress); Paris, 1912
Anouilh, Jean (playwright); Bordeaux, France **(1910-1987)**
Anthony, Susan Brownell (woman suffragist); Adams, Mass. **(1820-1906)**
Antonioni, Michelangelo (director); Ferrara, Italy, 9/2 9/1912
Antony, Mark (Marcus Antonius) (statesman); Rome **(83?-30 B.C.)**
Anuszkiewicz, Richard (painter); Erie, Pa., 5/23/1930
Aquinas, St. Thomas (philosopher); nr. Aquino (Italy) **(1225?-1274)**
Arbuckle, Roscoe "Fatty" (actor and director); San Jose, Calif. **(1887-1933)**
Archimedes (physicist and mathematician); Syracuse, Sicily **(287?-212 B.C.)**
Archipenko, Alexandre (sculptor); Kiev, Russia **(1887-1964)**
Arden, Elizabeth (Florence Nightingale Graham) (cosmetics executive); Woodbridge, Canada **(1891-1966)**

Arden, Eve (Eunice Quedens) (actress); Mill Valley, Calif. **(1907–1990)**
Arendt, Hannah (historian); Hannover, Germany **(1906-1975)**
Aristophanes (dramatist); Athens **(448?-380 B.C.)**
Aristotle (philosopher); Stagirus, Macedonia **(384-322 B.C.)**
Arkin, Alan (actor and director); New York City, 3/26/1934
Arledge, Roone (TV executive); Forest Hills, N.Y., 7/8/1931
Arlen, Harold (Hyman Arluck) (composer); Buffalo, N.Y. **(1905-1986)**
Arlen, Richard (actor); Charlottesville, Va. **(1900-1976)**
Arliss, George (actor); London **(1868-1946)**
Armstrong, Louis ("Satchmo") (musician); New Orleans **(1900-1971)**
Armstrong-Jones, Anthony. *See* Snowdon, Earl of
Arnaz, Desi (Desiderio) (actor and producer); Santiago, Cuba **(1917-1986)**
Arness, James (James Aurness) (TV actor); Minneapolis, 5/26/1923
Arno, Peter (cartoonist); New York City **(1904-1968)**
Arnold, Benedict (American Revolutionary War general, charged with treason); Norwich, Conn. **(1741-1801)**
Arnold, Eddy (singer); Henderson, Tenn., 5/15/1918
Arnold, Edward (actor); New York City **(1890-1956)**
Arnold, Matthew (poet and critic); Laleham, England **(1822-1888)**
Arp, Jean (sculptor and painter); Strasbourg (France) **(1887-1966)**
Arpino, Gerald (choreographer); Staten Island, N.Y., 1/14/28
Arquette, Cliff ("Charley Weaver") (actor); Toledo, Ohio **(1905-1974)**
Arquette, Rosanna (actress); New York City, 8/10/59
Arrau, Claudio (pianist); Chillán, Chile **(1903–1991)**
Arroyo, Martina (soprano); New York City, 2/2/1940
Arthur, Bea (Bernice Frankel) (actress); New York City, 5/13/1926(?)
Arthur, Jean (Gladys Greene) (actress); New York City **(1900–1991)**
Asch, Sholem (novelist); Kutno, Poland **(1880-1957)**
Ashcroft, Dame Peggy (actress); Croydon, England **(1907–1991)**
Ashkenazy, Vladimir (concert pianist); Gorki, U.S.S.R., 7/6/1937
Ashley, Elizabeth (actress); Ocala, Fla., 8/30/1939
Ashton, Sir Frederick William Mallandaine (choreographer); Guayaquil, Ecuador **(1904-1988)**
Asimov, Isaac (author); Petrovichi, Russia **(1920-1992)**
Asner, Edward (actor); Kansas City, Mo., 11/15/1929
Astaire, Fred (Frederick Austerlitz) (dancer and actor); Omaha, Neb. **(1899-1987)**
Astin, John (actor, director); Baltimore, Md., 3/30/30
Astor, John Jacob (financier); Waldorf (Germany) **(1763-1848)**
Astor, Mary (Lucile Langhanke) (actress); Quincy, Ill. **(1906-1987)**
Atkins, Chet (guitarist); nr. Luttrell, Tenn., 6/20/1924
Atkinson, Brooks (drama critic); Melrose, Mass. **(1894-1984)**
Attenborough, Richard (actor-director) Cambridge, England, 8/29/1923
Attila (King of Huns, called "Scourge of God") **(406?-453)**
Attlee, Clement Richard (statesman); London **(1883-1967)**
Atwill, Lionel (actor); Croydon, England, **(1885-1946)**
Auberjonois, Rene (actor); New York City, 6/1/40
Auchincloss, Louis (author); Lawrence, N.Y., 9/27/1917
Auden, W(ystan) H(ugh) (poet); York, England **(1907-1973)**
Audubon, John James (naturalist and painter); Haiti **(1785-1851)**
Auer, Leopold (violinist and teacher); Veszprém, Hungary **(1845-1930)**
Auer, Mischa (actor); St. Petersburg, Russia **(1905-1967)**
Augustine, Saint (Aurelius Augustinus) (theologian); Tagaste, Numidia (Algeria) **(354-430)**
Augustus (Gaius Octavius) (Roman emperor); Rome **(63 B.C.-A.D. 14)**
Aumont, Jean-Pierre (actor); Paris, 1/5/1913
Austen, Jane (novelist); Steventon, England **(1775-1817)**
Autry, Gene (singer and actor); Tioga, Tex., 9/29/1907
Avalon, Frankie (singer); Philadelphia, 9/18/1940
Avedon, Richard (photographer); New York City, 5/15/1923
Avery, Milton (painter); Alt mar, N.Y. **(1893-1965)**
Ax, Emanuel (pianist); Lvov, U.S.S.R., 6/8/1949
Axelrod, George (playwright); New York City, 6/9/1922
Ayckbourn, Alan (playwright); London, 4/12/1939
Ayckroyd, Dan (actor); Ottawa, Ont., Canada, 7/1/1952
Ayres, Agnes (actress); Carbondale, Ill. **(1896-1940)**
Ayres, Lew (actor); Minneapolis, 12/28/1908
Aznavour, Charles (singer, composer); Paris, France, 5/22/24

B

Bacall, Lauren (Betty Joan Perske) (actress); New York City, 9/16/1924
Bach, Johann Sebastian (composer); Eisenach, Germany **(1685-1750)**
Bach, Karl Phillipp Emanuel (composer); Weimar, Germany **(1714-1788)**
Bacharach, Burt (songwriter); Kansas City, Mo., 5/12/1929
Backus, Jim (actor); Cleveland **(1913-1989)**
Bacon, Francis (painter); Dublin **(1910-1992)**
Bacon, Francis (philosopher and essayist); London **(1561-1626)**
Bacon, Roger (philosopher and scientist); Ilchester, England **(1214?-1294)**
Baedeker, Karl (travel-guidebook publisher); Essen (Germany) **(1801-1859)**
Baez, Joan (folk singer); Staten Island, N.Y., 1/9/1941
Bagnold, Enid (novelist); Rochester, England **(1889-1981)**
Bailey, F. Lee (lawyer); Waltham, Mass., 6/10/1933
Bailey, Pearl (singer); Newport News, Va. **(1918-1990)**
Bain, Conrad (actor); Lethbridge, Alberta, Canada, 2/4/23
Bainter, Fay (actress); Los Angeles **(1891-1968)**
Baio, Scott (actor); Brooklyn, N.Y., 9/22/61
Baird, Bil (William B.) (puppeteer); Grand Island, Neb. **(1904-1987)**
Baker, Anita (singer); Toledo, Ohio, 1958
Baker, Carroll (actress); Johnstown, Pa., 5/28/1931
Baker, Josephine (singer and dancer); St. Louis **(1906-1975)**
Baker, Russell (columnist); Loudoun County, Va., 8/14/1925
Balanchine, George (choreographer); St. Petersburg, Russia **(1904-1983)**
Balboa, Vasco Nuñez de (explorer); Jerez de los Caballeros (Spain) **(1475-1517)**
Baldwin, Faith (novelist); New Rochelle, N.Y. **(1893-1978)**
Baldwin, James (novelist); New York City **(1924-1987)**
Balenciaga, Cristóbal (fashion designer); Guetaria, Spain **(1895--972)**
Ball, Lucille (Désirée) (actress and producer); Celoron (nr. Jamestown), N.Y. **(1911-1989)**
Ballard, Kaye (Catherine Gloria Balotta) (actress); Cleveland, 11/20/1926
Balmain, Pierre (fashion designer); St.-Jean-de-Maurienne, France **(1914-1982)**
Balsam, Martin (actor); New York City, 11/4/1919
Balzac, Honoré de (novelist); Tours, France **(1799-1850)**
Bancroft, Anne (Annemarie Italiano) (actress); New York City, 9/17/1931
Bancroft, George (actor); Philadelphia **(1882-1956)**
Bankhead, Tallulah (actress); Huntsville, Ala. **(1903-1963)**
Banneker, Benjamin (almanacker and mathematician-astronomer on District of Columbia site survey); Ellicott, Md. **(1731-1806)**
Banting, Fredrick Grant (physiologist); Alliston, Ont., Canada **(1891-1941)**
Bara, Theda (Theodosia Goodman) (actress); Cincinnati **(1890-1955)**
Barber, Red (Walter Lanier) (sportscaster); Columbus, Miss. **(1908-1992)**
Barber, Samuel (composer); West Chester, Pa. **(1910-1981)**
Bardot, Brigitte (actress); Paris, 1935
Barenboim, Daniel (concert pianist and conductor); Buenos Aires, 11/15/1942
Bari, Lynn (actress); Roanoke, Va., 12/18/13 (?)
Barker, Bob (host); Darrington, Wash., 12/12/23
Barnard, Christiaan N. (heart surgeon); Beauford West, South Africa, 1923
Barnes, Priscilla (actress); Fort Dix, N.J., 12/7/55
Barnum, Phineas Taylor (showman); Bethel, Conn. **(1810-1891)**
Barr, Roseanne (actress), Salt Lake City, 11/3/1952
Barrie, Sir James Matthew (author); Kirriemuir, Scotland **(1860-1937)**
Barrie, Wendy (actress); Hong Kong **(1913-1978)**
Barry, Gene (Eugene Klass) (actor); New York City, 6/4/1922
Barry, John (naval officer); County Wexford, Ireland **(1745-1803)**
Barrymore, Diana (actress); New York City **(1921-1960)**
Barrymore, Ethel (Ethel Blythe) (actress); Philadelphia **(1879-1959)**
Barrymore, Georgiana Drew (actress); Philadelphia **(1856-1893)**
Barrymore, John (John Blythe) (actor); Philadelphia **(1882-1942)**
Barrymore, Lionel (Lionel Blythe) (actor); Philadelphia **(1878-1954)**
Barrymore, Maurice (Herbert Blythe) (actor and playwright); Agra, India **(1847-1905)**
Barthelme, Donald (novelist); Philadelphia **(1931 -1989)**
Barthelmess, Richard (actor); New York City **(1897-1963)**
Bartholomew, Freddie (actor); London **(1924-1992)**
Bartók, Béla (composer); Nagyszentmiklos (Romania) **(1881-1945)**
Barton, Clara (founder of American Red Cross); Oxford, Mass. **(1821-1912)**
Baruch, Bernard Mannes (statesman), Camden, S.C. **(1870-1965)**
Baryshnikov, Mikhail Nikolayevich (ballet dancer and artistic director); Riga, Latvia, 1/27/1948
Basehart, Richard (actor); Zanesville, Ohio **(1914-1984)**
Basie, Count (William) (band leader); Red Bank, N.J. **(1904-1984)**
Basinger, Kim (actress); Athens, Ga., 12/8/53
Bassey, Shirley (singer); Cardiff, Wales, 1/8/1937
Batchelor, Clarence Daniel (political cartoonist); Osage City, Kan. **(1888-1977)**
Bateman, Jason (actor); Rye, N.Y. 1/14/69
Bateman, Justine (actress); Rye, N.Y., 2/19/66
Bates, Alan (actor); Allestree, England, 2/17/1934
Battle, Kathleen (soprano); Portsmouth, Ohio, 8/13/48
Baudelaire, Charles Pierre (poet); Paris **(1821-1867)**

Baudouin (King); Palace of Laeken, Belgium, 9/7/1930
Baxter, Anne (actress); Michigan City, Ind. **(1923-1985)**
Baxter, Warner (actor); Columbus, Ohio **(1891-1951)**
Baxter-Birney, Meredith (actress); Los Angeles, 6/21/47
Bean, Orson (Dallas Frederick Burrows) (actor); Burlington, Vt., 7/22/1928
Beardsley, Aubrey Vincent (illustrator); Brighton, England **(1872-1898)**
Beaton, Cecil (photographer and designer); London **(1904-1980)**
Beatty, Clyde (animal trainer); Chillicothe, Ohio **(1903-1965)**
Beatty, Warren (actor and producer); Richmond, Va., 3/30/1937
Beaumont, Francis (dramatist); Grace-Dieu, England **(1584-1616)**
Beavers, Louise (actress); Cincinnati, Ohio **(1902-1962)**
Becket, Thomas à (Archbishop of Canterbury); London **(1118?-1170)**
Beckett, Samuel (playwright); Dublin **(1906-1989)**
Beckmann, Max (painter); Leipzig, Germany **(1884-1950)**
Bede, Saint ("The Venerable Bede") (scholar); Monkwearmouth, England **(673-735)**
Beecham, Sir Thomas (conductor); St. Helens, England **(1879-1961)**
Beecher, Henry Ward (clergyman); Litchfi eld, Conn. **(1813-1887)**
Beerbohm, Sir Max (author); London **(1872-1956)**
Beery, Noah (actor); Kansas City, Mo. **(1884-1946)**
Beery, Noah, Jr. (actor); New York City, 8/10/1916
Beery, Wallace (actor); Kansas City, Mo. **(1886-1949)**
Beethoven, Ludwig von (composer); Bonn (Germany) **(1770-1827)**
Begley, Ed (actor); Hartford, Conn. **(1901-1970)**
Belafonte, Harry (singer and actor); New York City, 3/1/1927
Belafonte-Harper, Shari (actress); New York City, 9/22/54
Belasco, David (dramatist and producer); San Francisco **(1854-1931)**
Bel Geddes, Barbara (actress); New York City, 10/31/22
Bell, Alexander Graham (inventor); Edinburgh, Scotland **(1847-1922)**
Bellamy, Edward (author); Chicopee Falls, Mass. **(1850-1898)**
Bellamy, Ralph (actor); Chicago **(1904-1991)**
Bellini, Giovanni (painter); Venice **(c.1430-1516)**
Bellow, Saul (novelist); Lachine, Quebec, Canada, 6/10/1915
Bellows, George Wesley (painter and lithographer); Columbus, Ohio **(1882-1925)**
Belmondo, Jean-Paul (actor); Neuilly-sur-Seine, France, 4/9/1933
Belushi, Jim (actor); Chicago, 6/15/54
Belushi, John (comedian, actor); Chicago **(1949-1982)**
Benchley, Peter Bradford (novelist); New York City, 5/8/1940
Benchley, Robert Charles (humorist); Worcester, Mass. **(1889-1945)**
Bendix, William (actor); New York City **(1906-1964)**
Benedict, Dirk (actor); Helena, Mont., 3/1/44
Benes, Eduard (statesman); Kozlany (Czechoslovakia) **(1884-1948)**
Benét, Stephen Vincent (poet and story writer); Bethlehem, Pa. **(1898-1943)**
Benét, William Rose (poet and novelist); Ft. Hamilton, Brooklyn, N.Y. **(1886-1950)**
Ben-Gurion, David (David Green) (statesman); Plónsk (Poland) **(1886-1973)**
Benjamin, Richard (actor); New York City, 5/22/1938
Bennett, Constance (actress); New York City **(1905-1965)**
Bennett, Enoch Arnold (novelist and dramatist); Hanley, England **(1867-1931)**
Bennett, James Gordon (editor); Keith, Scotland **(1795-1872)**
Bennett, Joan (actress); Palisades, N.J. **(1910–1990)**
Bennett, Robert Russell (composer); Kansas City, Mo. **(1894-1981)**
Bennett, Tony (Anthony Benedetto) (singer); Astoria, Queens, N.Y., 8/3/1926
Benny, Jack (Benjamin Kubelsky) (comedian); Chicago **(1894-1974)**
Benson, Robby (actor); Dallas, Tex., 1/21/56
Bentham, Jeremy Heinrich (economist); London **(1748-1832)**
Benton, Thomas Hart (painter); Neosho, Mo. **(1889-1975)**
Berg, Alban (composer); Vienna **(1885-1935)**
Berg, Gertrude (writer and actress); New York City **(1899-1966)**
Bergen, Candice (actress); Beverly Hills, Calif., 5/9/1946
Bergen, Edgar (ventriloquist); Chicago, **(1903-1978)**
Bergen, Polly (actress and singer); Knoxville, Tenn., 7/14/1930
Bergerac, Cyrano de (poet); Paris **(1619-1655)**
Bergman, Ingmar (film director); Uppsala, Sweden, 7/14/1918
Bergman, Ingrid (actress); Stockholm **(1918-1982)**
Bergson, Henri (philosopher); Paris **(1859-1941)**
Berkeley, Busby (choreographer, director); Los Angeles **(1885-1976)**
Berle, Milton (Milton Berlinger) (comedian); New York City, 7/12/1908
Berlin, Irving (Israel Baline) (songwriter); Temum, Russia **(1888-1989)**
Berlioz, Louis Hector (composer); La Côte-Saint-André, France **(1803-1869)**
Berman, Lazar (concert pianist); Leningrad, 1930.
Berman, Shelley (Sheldon) (comedian); Chicago, 2/3/1926
Bernardi, Herschel (actor); New York City **(1922-1986)**
Bernhardt, Sarah (Rosine Bernard) (actress); Paris **(1844-1923)**
Bernini, Gian Lorenzo (sculptor and painter); Naples (Italy) **(1598-1680)**
Bernoulli, Jacques (scientist); Basel, Switzerland **(1654-1705)**
Bernsen, Corbin (actor); North Hollywood, Calif., 7/7/?
Bertinelli, Valerie (actress); Wilmington, Del., 4/23/60
Bernstein, Leonard (conductor); Lawrence, Mass. **(1918–1990)**
Berry, Chuck (Charles Edward Berry) (singer and guitarist); San Jose, Calif., 1/15/1926
Berry, Ken (actor); Moline, Ill., 11/3/30
Betjeman, Sir John (Poet Laureate); London **(1906-1984)**
Bettelheim, Bruno (psychoanalyst); Vienna **(1903-1990)**
Bickford, Charles (actor); Cambridge, Mass. **(1889-1967)**
Bierce, Ambrose Gwinnett (journalist); Meigs County, Ohio **(1842-1914?)**
Bikel, Theodore (actor and folk singer); Vienna, 5 /2/1924
Bing, Sir Rudolf (opera manager); Vienna, 1/9/1902
Bingham, George Caleb (painter); Augusta Co., Va. **(1811-1879)**
Bishop, Joey (Joseph Gottlieb) (comedian); New York City, 2/3/1919
Bismarck-Schönhausen, Prince Otto Eduard Leopold von (statesman); Schönhausen, Germany **(1815-1898)**
Bisset, Jacqueline (actress); Weybridge, England, 9/13/1944
Bixby, Bill (actor); San Francisco, 1/22/1934
Bizet, Georges (Alexandre César Léopold Bizet) (composer); Paris **(1838-1875)**
Bjoerling, Jussi (tenor); Stora Tuna, Sweden **(1911-1960)**
Black, Cilla (singer and actress); Liverpool, England, 5/27/1943
Black, Karen (actress); Park Ridge, Ill., 7/1/1942
Black, Shirley Temple (former actress); Santa Monica, Calif., 4/23/1928
Blackmer, Sidney (actor); Salisbury, N.C. **(1898-1973)**
Blackstone, Sir William (jurist); London **(1723-1780)**
Blaine, Vivian (actress and singer); Newark, N.J., 11/21/1924
Blair, Janet (actress); Altoona, Pa., 4/23/1921
Blake, Amanda (Beverly Louise Neill) (actress); Buffalo, N.Y. **(1929-1989)**
Blake, Eubie (James Hubert) (pianist); Baltimore **(1883-1983)**
Blake, Robert (Michael Gubitosi) (actor); Nutley, N.J., 9/18/1933
Blake, William (poet and artist); London **(1757-1827)**
Blanc, Mel(vin Jerome) (actor and voice specialist); San Francisco **(1908-1989)**
Blass, Bill (fashion designer); Fort Wayne, Ind., 6/22/1922
Bloch, Ernest (composer); Geneva **(1880-1959)**
Blondell, Joan (actress); New York City **(1909-1979)**
Bloom, Claire (actress); London, 2/15/1931
Bloomgarden, Kermit (producer); Brooklyn, N.Y. **(1904-1976)**
Blore, Eric (actor); London **(1887-1959)**
Blue, Monte (actor); Indianapolis **(1890-1963)**
Blyth, Ann (actress); New York City, 8/16/1928
Boccaccio, Giovanni (author); Paris **(1313-1375)**
Boccherini, Luigi (Rodolfo) (composer); Lucca, Italy **(1743-1805)**
Boccioni, Umberto (painter and sculptor); Reggio di Calabria, Italy **(1882-1916)**
Bock, Jerry (composer); New Haven, Conn., 11/23/1928
Bogarde, Dirk (Derek Van den Bogaerde) (film actor and director); London, 3/28/1921
Bogart, Humphrey DeForest (actor); New York City **(1899-1957)**
Bogdanovich, Peter (producer and director); Kingston, N.Y., 7/30/1939
Bohlen, Charles E. (diplomat); Clayton, N.Y. **(1904-1974)**
Bohr, Niels (atomic physicist); Copenhagen **(1885-1962)**
Boland, Mary (actress); Philadelphia, Pa. **(1880-1965)**
Boles, John (actor); Greenville, Tex. **(1895-1969)**
Bolger, Ray (dancer and actor); Dorchester, Mass **(1904-1987)**
Bolivar, Simón (South American liberator); Caracas, Venezuela **(1783-1830)**
Bologna, Giovanni da (sculptor); Douai (France) **(1529-1608)**
Bombeck, Erma (author, columnist); Dayton, Ohio 2/21/1927
Bonaparte, Napoleon (Emperor of the French); Ajaccio, Corsica (France) **(1769-1821)**
Bond, Julian (Georgia legislator); Nashville, Tenn., 1/14/1940
Bondi, Beulah (actress); Chicago **(1883-1981)**
Bonet, Lisa (actress); San Francisco, 11/16/67
Bonnard, Pierre (painter); Fontenayaux-Roses, France **(1867-1947)**
Bon Jovi, Jon (musician, songwriter); Sayreville, N.J., 3/2/62
Bono, Sonny (Salvatore) (singer); Detroit, 2/16/1935
Boone, Daniel (frontiersman); nr. Reading, Pa. **(1734-1820)**
Boone, Pat (Charles) (singer); Jacksonville, Fla., 6/1/1934
Boone, Richard (actor); Los Angeles **(1917-1981)**
Booth, Edwin Thomas (actor); Bel Air, Md. **(1833-1893)**
Booth, Evangeline Cory (religious leader); London **(1865-1950)**
Booth, John Wilkes (actor; assassin of Lincoln); Harford County, Md. **(1838-1865)**
Booth, Shirley (Thelma Booth Ford) (actress); New York City **(1898(?)-1992)**
Bordoni, Irene (actress); Ajaccio (France) **(1895-1953)**
Borge, Victor (pianist and comedian); Copenhagen, 1/3/1909

Borgia, Cesare (nobleman and soldier); Rome **(1475?-1507)**
Borgia, Lucrezia (Duchess of Ferrara); Rome **(1480-1519)**
Borgnine, Ernest (actor); Hamden, Conn., 1/24/1917
Borromini, Francesco (architect); Bissone (Italy) **(1599-1667)**
Bosch, Hieronymus (Hieronymus van Aeken) (painter); Hertogenbosch (Netherlands) **(c.1450-1516)**
Bosley, Tom (actor); Chicago, 10/1/1927
Bostwick, Barry (actor); San Mateo, Calif., 2/24/45
Boswel l, Connee (singer); New Orleans **(1907-1976)**
Boswell, James (diarist and biographer); Edinburgh, Scotland **(1740-1795)**
Botticelli, Sandro (Alessandro di Mariano dei Filipepi) (painter); Florence (Italy) **(1444?-1510)**
Bottoms, Joseph (actor); Santa Barbara, Calif., 4/16/33
Bottoms, Timothy (actor); Santa Barbara, Calif., 8/30/50
Boulez, Pierre (conductor); Montbrison, France, 3/26/1925
Bourke-White, Margaret (photographer); New York City **(1906-1971)**
Bow, Clara (actress); Brooklyn, N.Y. **(1905-1965)**
Bowen, Catherine Drinker (biographer); Haverford, Pa. **(1897-1973)**
Bowes, Edward (radio show director); San Francisco **(1874-1946)**
Bowie, David (David Robert Jones) (actor and musician); London, 1/8/1947(?)
Bowie, James (soldier); Burke County, Ga. **(1799-1836)**
Bowles, Chester (diplomat); Springfield, Mass. **(1901-1986)**
Boxleitner, Bruce (actor); Elgin, Ill., 5/12/50
Boyce, William (composer); London? **(1710-1779)**
Boyd, Bill (William) ("Hopalong Cassidy") (actor); Cambridge, Ohio **(1898-1972)**
Boyd, Stephen (Stephen Millar) (actor); Belfast, Northern Ireland **(1928-1977)**
Boyer, Charles (actor); Figeac, France **(1899-1978)**
Boy George (George Alan O'Dowd) (singer); London, 1961
Boyle, Peter (actor); Philadelphia, 10/18/33
Boyle, Robert (scientist); Lismore Castle, Munster, Ireland **(1627-1691)**
Bracken, Eddie (actor); Astoria, Queens, N.Y., 2/7/1920
Bradbury, Ray Douglas (science-fiction writer); Waukegan, Ill., 8/22/1920
Bradlee, Benjamin C. (editor); Boston, 8/26/1921
Bradley, Ed (broadcast journalist); Philadelphia, Pa., 6/22/1941
Bradley, Omar N. (5-star general); Clark, Mo. **(1893-1981)**
Brady, Alice (actress); New York City **(1892-1939)**
Brady, Scott (actor); Brooklyn, N.Y., **(1924-1985)**
Brahe, Tycho (astronomer); Knudstrup, Denmark **(1546-1601)**
Brahms, Johannes (composer); Hamburg **(1833-1897)**
Braille, Louis (teacher of blind); Coupvray, France **(1809-1862)**
Brailowsky, Alexander (pianist); Kiev, Russia **(1896-1976)**
Bramante, Donato D'Agnolo (architect); Monte Asdrualdo (now Fermignano, Italy) **(1444-1514)**
Brancusi, Constantin (sculptor); Pestisansi, Romania **(1876-1957)**
Brando, Marlon (actor); Omaha, Neb., 4/3/1924
Brandt, Willy (Herbert Frahm) (ex-Chancellor); Lübeck, Germany **(1913-1992)**
Braque, Georges (painter); Argenteuil, France **(1882-1963)**
Brazzi, Rossano (actor); Bologna, Italy, 9/18/1916
Brecht, Bertolt (dramatist and poet); Augsburg, Bavaria **(1898-1956)**
Brel, Jacques (singer and composer); Brussels, **(1929-1978)**
Brennan, Walter (actor); Lynn, Mass. **(1894-1974)**
Brent, George (actor); Dublin **(1904-1979)**
Breslin, Jimmy (journalist): Jamaica, Queens, N.Y., 10/17/1930
Breuer, Marcel (architect and designer); Pécs, Hungary **(1902-1981)**
Brewer, Teresa (singer); Toledo, Ohio, 5/7/1931
Brewster, Kingman, Jr. (ex-president of Yale); Longmeadow, Mass. **(1919-1988)**
Brezhnev, Leonid I. (Communist Party Secretary); Dneprodzerzhinsk, Ukraine **(1906-1982)**
Brice, Fanny (Fannie Borach) (comedienne); New York City **(1892-1951)**
Bridges, Beau (actor); Los Angeles, 12/9/1941
Bridges, Jeff (actor); Los Angeles, 12/4/49
Bridges, Lloyd (actor); San Leandro, Calif. 1/15/1913
Brinkley, David (TV newscaster); Wilmington, N.C., 7/10/1920
Britt, May (Maybritt Wilkins) (actress); Sweden, 3/22/1936
Britten, Benjamin (composer); Lowestoft, England **(1913-1976)**
Britton, Barbara (actress); Long Beach, Calif. **(1920-1980)**
Broderick, Helen (actress); Philadelphia, Pa. **(1891-1959)**
Brolin, James (actor); Los Angeles, 7/18/40
Bromfield, Louis (novelist); Mansfield, Ohio **(1896-1956)**
Bronson, Charles (Charles Buchinsky) (actor); Ehrenfield, Pa., 11/3/1922(?)
Brontë, Charlotte (novelist); Thornton, England **(1816-1855)**
Brontë, Emily Jane (novelist); Thornton, England **(1818-1848)**
Bronzino, Agnolo (painter); Monticelli (Italy) **(1503-1572)**
Brook, Peter (director); London, 3/21/1925
Brooke, Rupert (poet); Rugby, England **(1887-1915)**
Brooks, Geraldine (Geraldine Stroock) (actress); New York City **(1925-1977)**
Brooks, Gwendolyn (poet); Topeka, Kan., 6/7/1917
Brooks, Mel (Melvin K aminsky) (writer and film director); Brooklyn, N.Y., 1926(?)
Brosnan, Pierce (actor); County Meath, Ireland, 5/16/52
Brothers, Joyce (Bauer) (psychologist, author, radio-TV personality); New York City, 1927(?)
Broun, Matthew Heywood Campbell (journalist); Brooklyn, N.Y. **(1888-1939)**
Brown, Helen Gurley (author); Green Forest, Ark., 2/18/1922
Brown, James (singer); Augusta, Ga., 5/3/1934
Brown, Joe E. (comedian); Holgate, Ohio **(1892-1973)**
Brown, John (abolitionist); Torrington, Conn. **(1800-1859)**
Brown, John Mason (critic); Louisville, Ky. **(1900-1969)**
Brown, Les (band leader); Reinerton, Pa., 1912
Brown, Pamela (actress); London **(1918-1975)**
Brown, Vanessa (Smylla Brind) (actress); Vienna, 3/24/1928
Browne, Jackson (singer and guitarist); Heidelberg, Germany, 10/9/1948
Browning, Elizabeth Barrett (poet); Durham, England **(1806-1861)**
Browning, Robert (poet); London **(1812-1889)**
Brubeck, Dave (musician); Concord, Calif., 12/6/1920
Bruce, Lenny (comedian); Long Island, N.Y. **(1926-1966)**
Bruce, Nigel (actor); Ensenada, Mexico **(1895-1953)**
Bruce, Virginia (actress); Minneapolis, Minn. **(1910-1982)**
Brueghel, Pieter (painter); nr. Breda, Flanders (Netherlands) **(1520?-1569)**
Bruhn, Erik (Belton Evers) (ballet dancer); Copenhagen **(1928-1986)**
Brunelleschi, Filippo (architect); Florence (Italy) **(1377-1446)**
Bruno, Giordano (philosopher); Nola, Italy **(1548-1600)**
Brutus, Marcus Junius (Roman politician); **(85?-42 B.C.)**
Bryan, William Jennings (orator and politician); Salem, Ill. **(1860-1925)**
Bryant, Anita (singer); Barnsdall, Okla., 3/25/1940
Bryant, William Cullen (poet and editor); Cummington, Mass. **(1794-1878)**
Brynner, Yul (Taidje Khan) (actor); Sakhalin Island, Russia **(1920-1985)**
Brzezinski, Zbigniew (ex-presidential adviser); Warsaw, 3/28/1928
Buber, Martin (philosopher and theologian); Vienna **(1878-1965)**
Bucchanan, Jack (actor); Glasgow, Scotland **(1891-1957)**
Buchanan, Edgar (actor); Humansville, Mo., **(1903-1979)**
Buchholz, Horst (actor); Berlin, 12/4/1933
Buchwald, Art (Arthur) (columnist); Mount Vernon, N.Y., 10/20/1925
Buck, Pearl S(ydenstricker) (author); Hillsboro, W. Va. **(1892-1973)**
Buckley, William F., Jr. (journalist); New York City, 11/24/1925
Buddha. *See* Gautama Buddha
Buffalo Bill (William Frederick Cody) (scout); Scott County, Iowa **(1846-1917)**
Bujold, Genevieve (actress); Montreal, 7/1/1942
Bujones, Fernando (ballet dancer); Miami, Fla., 3/9/1955
Bullins, Ed (playwright); Philadelphia, 7/2/1935
Bullock, Jm J. (actor); Casper Wyom., 2/9/?
Bumbry, Grace (mezzo-soprano); St. Louis, 1/4/1937
Bunche, Ralph J. (statesman); Detroit **(1904-1971)**
Bundy, McGeorge (educator); Boston, 3/30/1919
Bundy, William Putnam (editor); Washington, D.C., 9/24/1917
Buñuel, Luis (film director); Calanda, Spain, **(1900-1983)**
Bunyan, John (preacher and author); Elstow, England **(1628-1688)**
Burbank, Luther (horticulturist); Lancaster, Mass. **(1849-1926)**
Burke, Adm. Arleigh A. (ex-Chief of Naval Operations); Boulder, Colo., 10/19/1901
Burke, Billie (comedienne); Washington, D.C. **(1885-1970)**
Burke, Delta (actress); Orlando, Fla., 7/30/56
Burke, Edmund (statesman); Dublin **(1729-1797)**
Burne-Jones, Edward Coley (painter); Birmingham, England **(1833-1898)**
Burnett, Carol (comedienne); San Antonio, 4/26/1933
Burnette, Smiley (Lester Alvin) (actor); Summum, Ill. **(1911-1967)**
Burney, Fanny (Frances) (writer); King's Lynn, England **(1752-1840)**
Burns, George (Nathan Birnbaum) (comedian); New York City, 1/20/1896
Burns, Robert (poet); Alloway, Scotland **(1759-1796)**
Burr, Aaron (political leader); Newark, N.J. **(1756-1836)**
Burr, Raymond (William Stacey Burr) (actor); New Westminster, British Columbia, Canada, 5/21/1917
Burroughs, Edgar Rice (novelist); Chicago **(1875-1950)**
Burrows, Abe (playwright and director); New York City **(1910-1985)**
Burstyn, Ellen (Edna Rae Gillooly) (actress); Detroit, 12/7/1932
Burton, LaVar (actor); Landsthul, Germany, 2/16/57
Burton, Richard (Richard Jenkins) (actor); Pontrhydfen, Wales **(1925-1984)**
Bush, Vannevar (scientist); Everett, Mass. **(1890-1974)**
Bushman, Francis X. (actor); Baltimore **(1883-1966)**
Butkus, Dick (actor); Chicago, 12/9/42

Butler, Samuel (author); Langar, England **(1835-1902)**
Butterworth, Charles (actor); South Bend, Ind. **(1896-1946)**
Buttons, Red (Aaron Chwatt) (actor); New York City, 2/5/1919
Buzzi, Ruth (comedienne); Wequetequock, Conn., 7/24/1936
Byington, Spring (actress); Colorado Springs, Colo. **(1893-1971)**
Byrd, Richard Evelyn (polar explorer); Winchester, Va. **(1888-1957)**
Byron, George Gordon (6th Baron Byron) (poet); London **(1788-1824)**

C

Caan, James (actor); The Bronx, N.Y., 3/26/1939
Caballé, Montserrat (soprano); Barcelona, Spain, 4/12/33
Cabot, Bruce (actor); Carlsbad, N.M. **(1904-1972)**
Cabot, John (Giovanni Caboto) (navigator); Genoa (?) **(1450-1498)**
Cabot, Sebastian (navigator); Venice **(1476?-1557)**
Cadmus, Paul (painter and etcher); New York City, 12/17/1904
Caesar, Gaius Julius (statesman); Rome **(100?-44** B.C.**)**
Caesar, Sid (comedian); Yonkers, N.Y., 9/8/1922
Cagney, James (actor); New York City **(1899-1986)**
Cahn, Sammy (songwriter); New York City **(1913-1993)**
Caine, Michael (Maurice J. Micklewhite) (actor); London, 3/14/1933
Calder, Alexander (sculptor); Lawnton, Pa. **(1898-1976)**
Calderón del al Barca, Pedro (dramatist); Madrid **(1600-1681)**
Caldwell, Erskine (novelist); White Oak, Ga **(1903-1987)**
Caldwell, Sarah (opera director and conductor); Maryville, Mo., 1928
Caldwell, Taylor (novelist); Manchester, England **(1900-1985)**
Caldwell, Zoe (actress); Hawthorn, Australia, 9/14/1933
Calhern, Louis (Carl Henry Vogt) (actor); Brooklyn, N.Y. **(1895-1956)**
Calhoun, John Caldwell (statesman); nr. Calhoun Mills, S.C. **(1782-1850)**
Calisher, Hortense (novelist); New York City, 12/20/1911
Callas, Maria (Maria Calogeropoulos) (dramatic soprano); New York City **(1923-1977)**
Calloway, Cab (Cabell) (band leader); Rochester, N.Y., 12/25/1907
Calvet, Corinne (actress); Paris, 4/30/1926
Calvin, John (Jean Chauvin) (religious reformer); Noyon, Picardy **(1509-1564)**
Cambridge, Godfrey (comedian); New York City **(1933-1976)**
Cameron, Rod (Rod Cox) (actor); Calgary, Alberta, Canada **(1912-1983)**
Campbell, Glen (singer); nr. Delight, Ark., 4/22/1938
Campbell, Mrs. Patrick (Beatrice Stella Tanner) (actress); London **(1865-1940)**
Camus, Albert (author); Mondovi, Algeria **(1913-1960)**
Canaletto, (Giovanni Antonio Canale); (painter) Venice **(1697-1768)**
Candy, John (actor, comedian); Toronto, Ont., Canada, 10/31/50
Caniff, Milton (cartoonist); Hillsboro, Ohio **(1907-1988)**
Cannon, Dyan (actress); Tacoma, Wash., 1/4/1937
Canova, Judy (comedienne); Jacksonville, Fla. **(1916-1983)**
Cantinflas (Mario Moreno) (comedian); Mexico City **(1911-1993)**
Cantor, Eddie (Edward Iskowitz) (actor); New York City **(1892-1964)**
Cantrell, Lana (singer); Sydney, Australia, 1944
Capote, Truman (novelist); New Orleans **(1924-1984)**
Capp, Al (Alfred Gerald Caplin) (cartoonist); New Haven, Conn. **(1909-1979)**
Capra, Frank (film producer, director); Palermo, Italy **(1897–1991)**
Caravaggio, Michelangelo Merisi da (painter); Caravaggio (Italy) **(1573-1610)**
Cardin, Pierre (fashion designer); nr. Venice, 7/7/1922
Cardinale, Claudia (actress); Tunis, Tunisia, 1939
Carey, Harry (actor); New York City **(1878-1947)**
Carey, Macdonald (actor); Sioux City, Iowa, 3/15/1913
Carlin, George (comedian); Bronx, N.Y., 5/12/1937
Carlisle, Kitty (singer and actress); New Orleans, 9/3/1915
Carlson, Richard (actor); Albert Lea, Minn. **(1912-1977)**
Carlyle, Thomas (essayist and historian); Ecclefechan, Scotland **(1795-1881)**
Carmichael, Hoagy (Hoagland Howard) (songwriter); Bloomington, Ind. **(1899-1981)**
Carne, Judy (Joyce Botterill) (singer); Northampton, England, 1939
Carnegie, Andrew (industrialist); Dunfermline, Scotland **(1835-1919)**
Carney, Art (actor); Mt. Vernon, N.Y., 11/4/1918
Carnovsky, Morris (actor); St. Louis **(1897–1992)**
Caron, Leslie (actress); Paris, 7/1/1931
Carr, Vikki (singer); El Paso, 7/19/1942
Carracci, Annibale (painter); Bologna (Italy) **(1560-1609)**
Carracci, Lodovico (painter); Bologna (Italy) **(1555-1619)**
Carradine, David (actor); Holly wood, Calif., 12/8/1936
Carradine, John (actor); New York City **(1906-1988)**
Carradine, Keith (actor); San Mateo, Calif., 8/8/49
Carreras, José (tenor); Barcelona, Spain, 12/5/1946
Carrillo, Leo (actor); Los Angeles **(1881-1961)**
Carroll, Diahann (Carol Diahann Johnson) (singer and actress); Bronx, N.Y., 7/17/1935
Carroll, Leo G. (actor); Weedon, England **(1892-1972)**
Carroll, Lewis (Charles Lutwidge Dodgson) (author and mathematician); Daresbury, England **(1832-1898)**
Carroll, Madeleine (actress); West Bromwich, England **(1906-1987)**
Carroll, Nancy (actress); New York City **(1904-1965)**
Carroll, Pat (comedienne); Shreveport, La., 5/5/1927
Carson, Jack (actor); Carmen, Man., Canada **(1910-1963)**
Carson, Johnny (TV entertainer); Corning, Iowa, 10/23/1925
Carson, Kit (Christopher) (scout); Madison County, Ky. **(1809-1868)**
Carson, Rachel (biologist and author); Springdale, Pa. **(1907-1964)**
Carter, Dixie (actress); McLemoresville, Tenn., 5/25/39
Carter, Jack (comedian); New York City, 1923
Carter, Lynda (actress); Phoenix, Ariz., 7/24/51
Cartier, Jacques (explorer); Saint-Malo, Brittany (France) **(1491-1557)**
Cartier-Brisson, Henri (photographer); Chanteloup, France, 8/22/1908
Cartland, Barbara (author); England, 7/9/1901
Caruso, Enrico (Errico) (tenor); Naples, Italy **(1873-1921)**
Carver, George Washington (botanist); Missouri **(1864-1943)**
Cary, Arthur Joyce Lunel (novelist); Londonderry, Ireland **(1888-1957)**
Casals, Pablo (cellist); Vendrell, Spain **(1876-1973)**
Casanova de Seingalt, Giovanni Jacopo (adventurer); Venice **(1725-1798)**
Cash, Johnny (singer); nr. Kingsland, Ark., 2/26/1932
Cass, Peggy (comedienne); Boston, 5/21/1924
Cassatt, Mary (painter); Allegheny, Pa. **(1844-1926)**
Cassavetes, John (actor and director); New York City **(1929-1989)**
Cassidy, David (singer); New York City, 4/12/1950
Cassidy, Jack (actor); Richmond Hill, Queens, N.Y. **(1927-1976)**
Cassidy, Shaun (actor); Los Angeles, 9/27/58
Cassini, Oleg (Oleg Lolewski-Cassini) (fashion designer); Paris, 4/11/1913
Castagno, Andrea del (painter); San Martino a Corella (Italy) **(c.1421-1457)**
Castellano, Richard (actor); New York City **(1934-1988)**
Castle, Irene (Irene Foote) (actress and dancer); New Rochelle, N.Y. **(1893-1969)**
Castle, Vernon Blythe (dancer and aviator); Norwich, England **(1887-1918)**
Castro Ruz, Fidel (Premier); Mayari, Oriente, Cuba, 8/13/1926
Cather, Willa Sibert (novelist); Winchester, Va. **(1876-1947)**
Cato, Marcus Porcius (called Cato the Elder) (statesman); Tusculum (Italy) **(234-149** B.C.**)**
Catt, Carrie Chapman Lane (woman suffragist); Ripon, Wis. **(1859-1947)**
Catton, Bruce (historian); Petoskey, Mich. **(1899-1978)**
Cauldfield, Joan (actress); East Orange, N.J. **(1927–1991)**
Cavallaro, Carmen (band leader); New York City **(1913-1989)**
Cavett, Dick (Richard) (TV entertainer); Gibbon, Neb., 11/19/1936
Cellini, Benvenuto (goldsmith and sculptor); Florence (Italy) **(1500-1571)**
Cervantes Saavedra, Miguel de (novelist); Alcalá de Henares, Spain **(1547-1616)**
Cézanne, Paul (painter); Aix-en-Provence, France **(1839-1906)**
Chagall, Marc (painter); Vitebsk, Russia, **(1887-1985)**
Chaliapin, Feodor Ivanovitch (operatic basso); Kazan, Russia **(1873-1938)**
Chamberlain, Arthur Neville (statesman); Edgbaston, England **(1869-1940)**
Chamberlain, Richard (actor); Los Angeles, 3/31/1935(?)
Champion, Gower (choreographer); Geneva, Ill. **(1921-1980)**
Champion, Marge (actress and dancer); Los Angeles, 9/2/1923
Champlain, Samuel de (explorer); nr. Rochefort, France **(1567?-1635)**
Chancellor, John (TV commentator); Chicago, 7/14/1927
Chandler, Jeff (actor); Brooklyn, N.Y. **(1918-1961)**
Chandler, Raymond (writer); Chicago **(1883-1959)**
Chanel, "Coco" (Gabriel Bonheur) (fashion designer); Issoire, France **(1883-1971)**
Chaney, Lon (actor); Colorado Springs, Colo. **(1883-1930)**
Channing, Carol (actress); Seattle, 1/31/1923
Channing, Stockard (actress); New York City, 2/13/44
Chaplin, Geraldine (actress); Santa Monica, Calif., 7/31/1944
Chaplin, Sir Charles (actor); London **(1889-1977)**
Charisse, Cyd (Tula Finklea) (dancer and actress); Amarillo, Tex., 3/8/1923
Charlemagne (Holy Roman Emperor); birthplace unknown **(742-814)**
Charles, Ray (Ray Charles Robinson) (pianist, singer, and songwriter); Albany Ga., 9/23/1930
Charo (Maria Rosario Pilar Martinez) (actress); Murcia, Spain 1/15/51
Chase, Charlie (actor, director); Baltimore, Md. **(1893-1940)**
Chase, Chevy (Cornelius Crane Chase) (comedian); New York City, 10/8/1943

Chase, Ilka (author and actress); New York City **(1905-1978)**
Chase, Lucia (founder Ballet Theatre [now American Ballet Theatre]); Waterbury, Conn. **(1907-1986)**
Chatterton, Ruth (actress); New York City **(1893-1961)**
Chaucer, Geoffrey (poet); London **(1340?-1400)**
Chávez, Carlos (composer); nr. Mexico City **(1899-1978)**
Chavez, Cesar (labor leader); nr. Yuma, Ariz. **(1927-1993)**
Chayefsky, Paddy (Sidney) (playwright); New York City, **(1923-1981)**
Checker, Chubby (Ernest Evans) (performer); Philadelphia, 10/3/1941
Cheever, John (novelist); Quincy, Mass. **(1912-1982)**
Chekhov, Anton Pavlovich (dramatist and short-story writer); Taganrog, Russia **(1860-1904)**
Cher (Cherilyn LaPiere) (singer); El Centro, Calif., 5/20/1946
Cherubini, Luigi (composer); Florence **(1760-1842)**
Chesterton, Gilbert Keith (author); Kensington, England **(1874-1936)**
Chevalier, Maurice (entertainer); Paris **(1888-1972)**
Chiang Kai-shek (Chief of State); Feng-hwa, China **(1887-1975)**
Child, Julia (food expert); Pasadena, Calif., 8/15/1912
Chippendale, Thomas (cabinet-maker); Otley, England **(1718?-1779)**
Chirico, Giorgio de (painter); Vólos, Greece, **(1888-1978)**
Chopin, Frédéric François (composer); nr. Warsaw **(1810-1849)**
Chou En-lai. *See* Zhou Enlai
Christian, Linda (Blanca Rosa Welter) (actress); Tampico, Mexico, 11/13/1924
Christie, Agatha (mystery writer); Torquay, England **(1890-1976)**
Christie, Julie (actress); Chukua, India, 4/14/1941
Christopher, Jordon (actor and musician); Youngstown, Ohio, 1941
Christy, June (singer); Springfield, Ill., 1925
Churchill, Sir Winston Leonard Spencer (statesman); Blenheim Palace, Oxfordshire, England **(1874-1965)**
Cicero, Marcus Tullius (orator and statesman); Arpinum (Italy) **(106-43 B.C.)**
Cid, El (Rodrigo (or Ruy) DíezdeBivar)(Spanish nationl hero); nr. Burgos, Spain **(1040?-1099)**
Cilento, Diane (actress); Queensland, Australia, 10/5/1933
Cimabue, Giovanni (painter); Florence (Italy) **(c.1240-c.1302)**
Cimino, Michael (film director); New York City, 1943(?)
Clair, René (René Chomette) (film director); Paris **(1898-1981)**
Claire, Ina (Ina Fagan) (actress); Washington, D.C. **(1895-1985)**
Clapton, Eric (singer and guitarist); Ripley, England, 3/30/1945
Clark, Bobby (comedian, actor); Springfield, Ohio **(1888-1960)**
Clark, Dane (Barney Zanville) (actor); New York City, 2/18/1915
Clark, Dick (TV personality); Mt. Vernon, N.Y., 11/30/1929
Clark, Mark W. (general); Madison Barracks, N.Y. **(1896-1984)**
Clark, Petula (singer); Epsom, England, 11/15/1934
Clark, Roy (country music artist); Meherrin, Va., 4/15/1933
Clark, William (explorer); Caroline County, Va. **(1770-1838)**
Clarke, Arthur C. (science fiction writer); Minehead, England, 12/16/1917
Clary, Robert (actor); Paris, France, 3/1/26
Claude Lorrain (Claude Gellée) (painter); Champagne, France **(1600-1682)**
Clausewitz, Karl von (military strategist); Burg (East Germany) **(1780-1831)**
Clay, Henry (statesman); Hanover County, Va. **(1777-1852)**
Clay, Lucius D. (banker, ex-general); Marietta, Ga. **(1897-1978)**
Clayburgh, Jill (actress); New York City, 4/30/1944
Cleese, John (writer, actor); Weston-super-Mare, England, 10/27/39
Clemenceau, Georges (statesman); Mouilleron-en-Pareds, Vondée, France **(1841-1929)**
Clemens, Samuel L. *See* Mark Twain
Cleopatra (Queen of Egypt); Alexandria, Egypt **(69-30 B.C.)**
Cliburn, Van (Harvey Lavan Cliburn, Jr.) (concert pianist); Shreveport, La., 7/12/1934
Clifford, Clark M. (ex-Secretary of Defense); Ft. Scott, Kan., 12/25/1906
Clift, Montgomery (actor); Omaha, Neb. **(1920-1966)**
Clooney, Rosemary (singer); Maysville, Ky., 5/23/1928
Close, Glenn (actress); Greenwich, Conn., 3/19/1947
Clurman, Harold (stage producer); New York City **(1901-1980)**
Cobb, Irvin Shrewsbury (humorist); Paducah, Ky. **(1876-1944)**
Cobb, Lee J. (Leo Jacob) (actor); New York City **(1911-1976)**
Coburn, Charles Douville (actor); Savannah, Ga. **(1877-1961)**
Coburn, James (actor); Laurel, Neb., 8/31/1928
Coca, Imogene (comedienne); Philadelphia, 11/18/1908
Cocker, Joe (John Robert Cocker) (singer); Sheffield, England, 5/20/1944
Coco, James (actor); New York City **(1929-1987)**
Cocteau, Jean (author); Maison-Lafitte, France **(1891-1963)**
Cody, W. F. *See* Buffalo Bill
Cohan, George Michael (actor and dramatist); Providence, R.I. **(1878-1942)**
Cohn, Mindy (actress); Los Angeles, 5/20/66
Colbert, Claudette (Lily Chauchoin) (actress); Paris, 9/13/1903
Colby, William E. (ex-Director of CIA); St. Paul, 1/4/1920
Cole, Nat "King" (singer); Montgomery, Ala. **(1919-1965)**
Cole, Natalie (singer); Los Angeles, 2/6/1950
Cole, Thomas (painter); Lancashire, England **(1801-1848)**
Coleman, Dabney (actor); Corpus Christi, Tex., 1/2/32
Coleman, Gary (actor); Zion, Ill., 2/8/68
Coleridge, Samuel Taylor (poet); Ottery St. Mary, England **(1772-1834)**
Colette (Sidonie-Gabrielle Colette) (novelist); St.-Sauveur, France **(c.1873-1954)**
Collier, Constance (actress); Windsor, England **(1878-1955)**
Collingwood, Charles (TV commentator); Three Rivers, Mich. **(1917-1985)**
Collins, Dorothy (Marjorie Chandler) (singer); Windsor, Ontario, Canada, 11/18/1926
Collins, Joan (actress); London 5/23/1933
Collins, Judy (singer); Seattle, 5/1/1939
Colman, Ronald (actor); Richmond, England **(1891-1958)**
Colonna, Jerry (comedian); Boston **(1905-1986)**
Columbo, Russ (singer, bandleader); San Francisco **(1908-1934)**
Columbus, Christopher (Cristoforo Colombo) (discoverer of America); Genoa (Italy) **(1451-1506)**
Comden, Betty (writer); New York City, 5/3/1919
Comenius, Johann Amos (educational reformer) Nivnice, Moravia (Czechoslovakia) **(1592-1670)**
Commager, Henry Steele (historian); Pittsburgh, 10/25/1902
Como, Perry (Pierino) (singer); Canonsburg, Pa., 5/18/1912
Compton, Karl Taylor (phy sicist); Wooster, Ohio **(1887-1954)**
Comte, Auguste (philosopher); Montpellier, France **(1798-1857)**
Conant, James B. (educator and statesman); Dorchester, Mass. **(1893-1978)**
Condon, Eddie (jazz musician); Goodland, Ind. **(1905-1973)**
Confucius (K'ung Fu-tzu) (philosopher); Shantung province, China **(c.551-479 B.C.)**
Congreve, William (dramatist); nr. Leeds, England **(1670-1729)**
Connelly, Marc (playwright); McKeesport, Pa. **(1890-1980)**
Connery, Sean (actor); Edinburgh, Scotland, 8/25/1930
Conniff, Ray (band leader); Attleboro, Mass., 11/6/1916
Connolly, Walter (actor); Cincinnati, Ohio **(1887-1940)**
Connors, Chuck (actor); Brooklyn, N.Y. **(1921-1992)**
Connors, Mike (Krekor Ohanian) (actor); Fresno, Calif., 8/15/1925
Conrad, Joseph (Teodor Jozef Konrad Korzeniowski) (novelist); Berdichev, Ukraine **(1857-1924)**
Conrad, Robert (Conrad Robert Falk) (actor); Chicago, 3/1/1935
Conrad, William (actor); Louisville, Ky., 9/27/1920
Conried, Hans (Frank Foster) (actor); Baltimore **(1915-1982)**
Constable, John (painter); East Bergholt, Suffolk, England **(1776-1837)**
Constantine II (ex-king); Athens, 6/2/1940
Constantine, Michael (actor); Reading, Pa., 5/22/27
Conte, Richard (actor); New York City **(1916-1975)**
Conti, Tom (actor); Paisley, Scotland, 11/22/1941
Converse, Frank (actor); St. Louis, 1938
Convy, Bert (actor, host); St. Louis, Mo. **(1933–1991)**
Conway, Tim (comedian); Chagrin Falls, Ohio, 12/15/1933
Coogan, Jackie (actor); Los Angeles **(1914-1984)**
Cook, Peter (actor, writer); Torquay, England, 11/17/37
Cooke, Alistair (Alfred Alistair); (TV narrator and journalist); Manchester, England, 11/20/1908
Cooley, Denton A(rthur) (heart surgeon); Houston, Tex., 8/22/1920
Coolidge, Rita (singer); Nashville, Tenn., 1944
Cooper, Alice (Vincent Furnier) (rock musician); Detroit, 2/4/1948
Cooper, Gary (Frank James Cooper) (actor); Helena, Mont. **(1901-1961)**
Cooper, Dame Gladys (actress); Lewisham, England **(1898-1971)**
Cooper, Jackie (actor and director); Los Angeles, 9/15/1922
Cooper, James Fenimore (novelist); Burlington, N.J. **(1789-1 851)**
Cooper, Peter (industrialist and philanthropist); New York City **(1791-1883)**
Copernicus, Nicolaus (Mikolaj Kopernik) (astronomer); Thorn, Poland **(1473-1543)**
Copland, Aaron (composer); Brooklyn, N.Y. **(1900–1990)**
Copley, John Singleton (painter); Boston, Mass. **(1738-1815)**
Copperfield, David (illusionist); Matuchen, N.J., 9/16/1956
Coppolla, Francis Ford (film director); Detroit, 4/7/1939
Corelli, Arcangelo (composer); Fusignano, Italy **(1653-1713)**
Corelli, Franco (operatic tenor); Ancona, Italy, 4/8/1923
Corneille, Pierre (dramatist); Rouen, France **(1606-1684)**
Cornell, Katharine (actress); Berlin **(1893-1974)**
Coret, Jean Baptiste Camille (painter); Paris **(1796-1875)**
Correggio, Antonio Allegri da (painter); Correggio (Italy) **(1494-1534)**
Corsaro, Frank (opera director); New York harbor, 12/22/1924
Cortés (or Cortez), Hernando (explorer); Medellin, Spain **(1485-1547)**
Cosby, Bill (actor); Philadelphia, 7/12/1937
Cosell, Howard (Howard Cohen) (sportscaster); Winston-Salem, N.C., 3/25/1920

Costa-Gavras, Henri (Kostantinos Gavras) (film director); Athens, 1933
Costello, Dolores (actress); Pittsburgh, Pa. **(1905-1979)**
Costello, Elvis (Declan Patrick McManus) (singer, musician, songwriter); London, 1954
Costello, Lou (comedian); Paterson, N.J. **(1908-1959)**
Costello, Maurice (actor); Pittsburgh **(1877-1950)**
Cotten, Joseph (actor); Petersburg, Va., 5/15/1905
Couperin, François (composer); Paris **(1668-1733)**
Courbet, Gustave (painter); Ornans, France **(1819-1877)**
Courrsssèges, André (fashion designer); Pau, France, 3/9/1923
Courtenay, Tom (actor); Hull, England, 2/25/1937
Cousins, Norman (publisher); Union Hill, N.J. **(1915–1990)**
Cousteau, Jacques-Yves (marine explorer); St. André-de-Cubzac, France, 6/11/1910
Coward, Sir Noel (playwright and actor); Teddington, England **(1899-1973)**
Cowl, Jane (actress); Boston **(1887-1950)**
Cowles, Gardner, Jr. (newspaper publisher); Algona, Iowa **(1903-1985)**
Cowper, William (poet); Great Berkhamstead, England **(1731-1800)**
Cox, Wally (actor); Detroit, Mich. **(1924-1973)**
Cozzens, James Gould (novelist); Chicago **(1903-1978)**
Crabbe, Buster (Clarence) (actor); Oakland, Calif. **(1908-1983)**
Crain, Jeanne (actress); Barstow, Calif., 5/25/1925
Cranach, Lucas, the elder (painter); Kronach (Germany) **(1472-1553)**
Crane, Hart (poet); Garrettsville, Ohio **(1899-1932)**
Crane, Stephen (novelist and poet); Newark, N.J. **(1871-1900)**
Cranmer, Thomas (churchman); Aslacton, England **(1489-1556)**
Crawford, Broderick (actor); Philadelphia **(1911-1986)**
Crawford, Cheryl (stage producer); Akron, Ohio **(1902-1986)**
Crawford, Joan (Lucille LeSueur) (actress and business executive); San Antonio **(1908-1977)**
Cregar, Laird (actor); Philadelphia, Pa. **(1916-1944)**
Crenna, Richard (actor); Los Angeles, 11/30/1927
Crespin, Régine (operatic soprano); Marseilles, France, 2/23/1929
Crichton, (John) Michael (novelist); Chicago, 10/23/1942
Crisp, Donald (actor); London **(1880-1974)**
Croce, Benedetto (philosopher); Peseasseroli, Aquila, Italy **(1866-1952)**
Croce, Jim (singer); Philadelphia **(1942-1973)**
Crockett, Davy (David) (frontiersman); Greene County, Tenn. **(1786-1836)**
Cromwell, Oliver (statesman); Huntingdon, England **(1599-1658)**
Cronin, A. J. (Archibald J. Cronin) (novelist); Cardross, Scotland **(1896-1981)**
Cronkite, Walter (TV newscaster); St. Joseph, Mo., 11/4/1916
Cronyn, Hume (actor); London, Ontario, Canada, 7/18/1911
Crosby, Bing (Harry Lillis) (singer, actor); Tacoma, Wash. **(1904-1977)**
Crosby, Bob (musician); Spokane, Wash. **(1913-1993)**
Crosby, Cathy Lee (actress); Los Angeles, 12/2/48
Crosby, Norm (comedian); Boston, 9/15/27
Cross, Ben (Bernard) (actor); Paddington, England, 12/16/1947
Cross, Milton (opera commentator); New York City **(1897-1975)**
Crouse, Russel (playwright); Findlay, Ohio **(1893-1966)**
Cruise, Tom (actor); Syracuse, N.Y., 7/3/1962
Crystal, Billy (comedian, actor); Long Beach, L.I., N.Y., 3/14/47
Cugat, Xavier (band leader); Barcelona, Spain **(1900–1990)**
Cukor, George (film director); New York City **(1899-1983)**
Cullen , Bill (William Lawrence Cullen) (radio and TV entertainer); Pittsburgh **(1920-1990)**
Culp, Robert (actor); Berkeley, Calif., 8/16/1930
Cummings, E. E. (Edward Estlin Cummings) (poet); Cambridge, Mass. **(1894-1962)**
Cummings, Robert (actor); Joplin, Mo. **(1908–1990)**
Curie, Marie (Marja Sklodowska) (physical chemist); Warsaw **(1867-1934)**
Curie, Pierre (physicist); Paris **(1859-1906)**
Curtin, Jane (actress); Cambridge, Mass., 9/6/47
Curtin, Phyllis (soprano); Clarksburg, W.Va., 12/3/1927
Curtis, Jamie Lee (actress); Los Angeles, 11/22/58
Curtis, Tony (Bernard Schwartz) (actor); Bronx, N.Y., 6/3/1925
Curzon, Clifford (concert pianist); London **(1907-1982)**
Custer, George Armstrong (army officer); New Rumley, Ohio **(1839-1876)**

D

da Gama, Vasco (explorer); Sines, Portugal **(1460-1524)**
Daguerre, Louis (photographic pioneer); nr. Paris **(1787-1851)**
Dahl, Arlene (actress); Minneapolis, 8/11/1928
Dailey, Dan (actor and dancer); New York City **(1917-1978)**
Dale, Jim (actor, singer, songwriter); Rothwell, England, 8/15/35
Daley, Richard J. (Mayor of Chicago); Chicago **(1902-1976)**
Dali, Salvador (painter); Figueras, Spain **(1904-1989)**
Dalton, Abby (actress); Las Vegas, Nev., 8/15/32
Dalton, John (chemist); nr. Cockermouth, England **(1766-1844)**
Daly, James (actor); Wisconsin Rapids, Wis. **(1918-1978)**
Daly, John (radio and TV news analyst); Johannesburg, South Africa **(1914–1991)**
Daly, Tyne (actress); Madison, Wis. 2/21/19476
d'Amboise, Jacques (ballet dancer); Dedham, Mass., 7/28/1934
Damone, Vic (Vito Farinola) (singer); Brooklyn, N.Y., 6/12/1928
Damrosch, Walter Johannes (orchestra conductor); Breslau (Poland) **(1862-1950)**
Dana, Charles Anderson (editor); Hinsdale, N.H. **(1819-1897)**
Dandridge, Dorothy (actress); Cleveland **(1923-1965)**
Dangerfield, Rodney (comedian); Babylon, L.I., N.Y., 1921
Daniels, Bebe (Virginia Daniels) (actress); Dallas **(1901-1971)**
Daniels, William (actor); Brooklyn, N.Y., 3/31/27
Danilova, Alexandra (ballerina); Peterhof, Russia, 1/20/1904
Dannay, Frederic (novelist, pseudonym Ellery Queen); Brooklyn, N.Y. **(1905-1982)**
Danner, Blythe (actress); Philadelphia, 1944(?)
D'Annunzio, Gabriele (soldier and author); Francaville at Mare, Pescara, Italy **(1863-1938)**
Danson, Ted (actor); San Diego, Calif., 12/29/47
Dante (or Durante) Alighieri (poet); Florence (Italy) **(1265-1321)**
Danton, Georges Jacques (French Revolutionary leader); Arcis-sur-Aube, France **(1759-1794)**
Danza, Tony (actor); Brooklyn, N.Y., 4/21/51
Darnell, Linda (actress); Dallas **(1921-1965)**
Darren, James (actor); Philadelphia, 6/8/1936
Darrieux, Danielle (actress); Bordeaux, France, 5/1/1917
Darrow, Clarence Seward (lawyer); Kinsman, Ohio **(1857-1938)**
Darwell, Jane (actress); Palmyra, Mo. **(1879-1967)**
Darwin, Charles Robert (naturalist); Shrewsbury, England **(1809-1882)**
daSilva, Howard (actor); Cleveland **(1909-1986)**
Dassin, Jules (film director); Middletown, Conn., 12/18/1911
Daumier, Honoré (caricaturist); Marseilles, France **(1808-1879)**
Dauphin, Claude (actor); Corbeil, France **(1903-1978)**
Davenport, Harry (actor); New York City **(1866-1949)**
David, Jacques-Louis (painter); Paris **(1748-1825)**
David (King of Israel and Judah) **(died c. 973 B.C.)**
Davidson, John (singer and actor); Pittsburgh, 12/13/1941
Davies, Marion (Marion Douras) (actress); New York City **(1898?-1961)**
da Vinci, Leonardo (painter and scientist); Vinci, Tuscany (Italy) **(1452-1519)**
Davis, Ann B. (actress); Schenectady, N.Y., 5/5/26
Davis, Bette (actress); Lowell, Mass. **(1908-1989)**
Davis, Elmer Holmes (radio commentator); Aurora, Ind. **(1890-1958)**
Davis, Jefferson (President of the Confederacy); Christian (now Todd) County, Ky. **(1808-1889)**
Davis, Joan (actress); St. Paul, Minn. **(1907-1961)**
Davis, Mac (singer); Lubbock, Tex., 1/21/1942
Davis, Miles (jazz trumpeter); Alton, Ill. **(1926-1991)**
Davis, Ossie (actor and writer); Cogdell, Ga., 12/18/1917
Davis, Sammy, Jr. (actor and singer); New York City **(1925-1990)**
Davis, Skeeter (Mary Francis Penick) (singer); Dry Ridge, Ky., 12/30/1931
Davis, Stuart (painter); Philadelphia **(1894-1964)**
Dawber, Pam (actress); Farmington Hills, Mich., 10/18/51
Dawson, Richard (actor, host); Gosport, Hampshire, England, 11/20/32
Day, Dennis (singer); New York City **(1917-1988)**
Day, Doris (Doris von Kappelhoff) (singer and actress); Cincinnati, 4/3/1924
Day, Laraine (La Raine Johnson) (actress); Roosevelt, Utah, 10/13/1920
Dayan, Moshe (ex-Defense Minister of Israel); Dagania, Palestine **(1915-1981)**
Dean, James (actor); Marion, Ind. **(1931-1955)**
Dean, Jimmy (singer); Seth Ward, nr. Plainview, Tex., 8/10/1928
De Bakey, Michael E. (heart surgeon); Lake Charles, La., 9/7/1908
de Beauvoir, Simone (novelist and philosopher); Paris **(1908-1986)**
Debs, Eugene Victor (Socialist leader); Terre Haute, Ind. **(1855-1926)**
Debussy, Claude Achille (composer); St. Germain-en-Laye, France **(1862-1918)**
DeCamp, Rosemary (actress); Prescott, Ariz., 11/14/14(?)
De Carlo, Yvonne (Peggy Yvonne Middleton) (actress); Vancouver, B.C., Canada, 9/1/1924
de Chirico, Giorgio (painter); Volos, Greece, **(1888-1978)**
Dee, Francis (actress); Los Angeles, 11/26/07
Dee, Ruby (actress); Cleveland, Ohio, 10/27/23(?)
Dee, Sandra (Alexandra Zuck) (actress); Bayonne, N.J., 4/23/1942
Defoe, Daniel (novelist); London **(1659?-1731)**

Defore, Don (actor); Cedar Rapids, Iowa, 8/25/17
Degas, Hilaire Germain Edgar (painter); Paris **(1834-1917)**
de Gaulle, Charles André Joseph Marie (soldier and statesman); Lille, France **(1890-1970)**
DeHaven, Gloria (actress); Los Angeles, 7/23/1925
de Havilland, Olivia (actress); Tokyo, 7/1/1916
Dekker, Albert (actor); Brooklyn, N.Y. **(1904-1968)**
de Kooning, Willem (painter); Rotterdam, 4/24/1904
Delacroix, Eugène (painter); Charenton-St. Maurice, France **(1798-1863)**
de la Renta, Oscar (fashion designer); Santo Domingo, Dominican Republic, 7/22/1932
Delaunay, Robert (painter); Paris **(1885-1941)**
De Laurentiis, Dino (film producer); Torre Annunziata, Bay of Naples, Italy, 8/8/1919
della Robbia, Andrea (sculptor) Florence **(1435-1525)**
della Robbia, Luca (sculptor); Florence **(1400-1482)**
Delon, Alain (actor); Sceaux, France, 11/8/1935
Del Rio, Dolores (Dolores Ansunsolo) (actress); Durango, Mexico **(1905-1983)**
DeLuise, Dom (comedian); Brooklyn, N.Y., 8/1/1933
Demarest, William (actor); St. Paul **(1892-1983)**
de Mille, Agnes (choreographer); New York City 9/18/1905
De Mille, Cecil Blount (film director); Ashfield, Mass. **(1881-1959)**
Demosthenes (orator); Athens **(385?-322 B.C.)**
Deneuve, Catherine (actress); Paris, 10/22/1943
De Niro, Robert (actor); New York City, 8/17/1943
Dennehy, Brian (actor); Brigeport, Conn., 7/9/40
Denning, Richard (actor); Poughkeepsie, N.Y., 3/27/14
Dennis, Sandy (actress); Hastings, Neb. **(1937-1992)**
Denny, Reginald (actor); Richmond, England **(1891-1967)**
Denver, John (Henry John Deutschendorf, Jr.) (singer); Roswell, N.M., 12/31/1943
De Palma, Brian (film director); Newark, N.J., 9/11/1940
Derain, André (painter); Chatou, Seine-et-Oise, France **(1880-1954)**
Derek, John (actor, director); Los Angeles, 8/12/26
Dern, Bruce (actor); Chicago, 6/4/1936
Descartes, René (philosopher and mathematician); La Haye, France **(1596-1650)**
De Seversky, Alexander P. (aviator); Tiflis, Russia **(1894-1974)**
De Sica, Vittorio (film director); Sora, Italy **(1901-1974)**
Desmond, Johnny (composer); Detroit **(1921-1985)**
Desmond, William (actor); Dublin **(1878-1949)**
De Soto, Hernando (explorer); Barcarrota, Spain **(1500?-1542)**
De Valera, Eamon (ex-President of Ireland); New York City **(1882-1975)**
Devane, William (actor); Albany, N.Y., 9/5/39
Devine, Andy (actor); Flagstaff, Ariz. **(1905-1977)**
DeVito, Danny (Daniel Michael); (actor, director); Neptune, N.J., 11/17/1944
De Vries, Peter (novelist); Chicago, 2/27/1910
de Waart, Edo (conductor); Amsterdam, the Netherlands, 6/1/41
Dewey, George (admiral); Montpelier, Vt. **(1837-1917)**
Dewey, John (philosopher and educator); Burlington, Vt. **(1859-1952)**
Dewey, Thomas E. (politician); Owosso, Mich. **(1902-1971)**
Dewhurst, Colleen (actress); Montreal **(1924–1991)**
De Wilde, Brandon (actor); Brookly, N.Y. **(1942-1972)**
DeWitt, Joyce (actress); Wheeling W.Va., 4/23/49
De Wolfe, Billy (actor); Wollaston, Mass. **(1907-1974)**
Dey, Susan (actress); Pekin, Ill., 12/10/52
Diamond, Neil (singer); Brooklyn, N.Y., 1/24/1941
Diana (Diana Frances Spencer) (Princess of Wales); Sandringham, England, 7/1/61
Dichter, Misha (pianist); Shanghai, 9/27/1945
Dickens, Charles John Huffam (novelist); Portsea, England **(1812-1870)**
Dickey, James (poet); Atlanta, 2/2/1923
Dickinson, Angie (Angeline Brown) (actress); Kulm, N.D., 9/30/1932
Dickinson, Emily Elizabeth (poet); Amherst, Mass. **(1830-1886)**
Diddley, Bo (Elias McDaniel) (guitarist); McComb, Miss., 12/30/1928
Diderot, Denis (encyclopedist); Langres, France **(1713-1784)**
Diefenbaker, John G. (ex-Prime Minister); Grey County, Ontario, Canada **(1895-1979)**
Dietrich, Marlene (Maria Magdalena von Losch) (actress); Berlin **(1901-1992)**
Diggs, Dudley (actor); Dublin **(1879-1947)**
Diller, Phyllis (Phyllis Driver) (comedienne); Lima, Ohio, 7/17/1917
Dillman, Bradford (actor); San Francisco, 4/14/1930
Dine, Jim (painter); Cincinnati, 6/16/1935
Diogenes (philosopher); Sinope (Turkey) **(412?-323 B.C.)**
Dion (Dion DiMucci) (singer); Bronx, N.Y., 7/18/1939
Dior, Christian (fashion designer); Granville, France **(1905-1957)**
Disney, Walt(er) Elias (film animator and producer); Chicago **(1901-1966)**
Disraeli, Benjamin (Earl of Beaconsfield) (statesman); London **(1804-1881)**
Dix, Dorothea (civil rights reformer); Hampden, Me. **(1802-1887)**
Dix, Richard (Ernest Carlton Brimmer) (actor); St. Paul **(1894-1949)**
Dixon, Jeane (Jeane Pinckert) (seer); Medford, Wis., 1918
Dobbs, Mattiwilda (soprano); Atlanta, Ga., 7/11/1925
Doctorow, E(dgar) L(aurence) (novelist); New York City, 1/6/1931
Dodgson, C. L. *See* Carroll, Lewis.
Dolin, Anton (dancer); Slinfold, England **(1904-1983)**
Domingo, Placido (tenor); Madrid, 1/21/1941
Domino, Fats (Antoine) (musician); New Orleans, 2/26/1928
Donahue, Phil (television personality); Cleveland, 12/21/1935
Donahue, Troy (actor); New York City, 1/27/36(?)
Donat, Robert (actor); Withington, England **(1905-1958)**
Donatello (Donato Niccolò di Betto Bardi) (sculptor); Florence **(c.1386-1466)**
Donlevy, Brian (actor); Portadown, Ireland **(1899-1972)**
Donovan (Donovan Leitch) (singer and songwriter); Glasgow, Scotland, 2/10/1946
Donne, John (poet); London **(1573-1631)**
Doolittle, James H. (ex-Air Force general); Alameda, Calif., 12/14/1896
Dorati, Antal (orchestra conductor); Budapest **(1906-1988)**
Dorsey, Jimmy (band leader); Shenandoah, Pa. **(1904-1957)**
Dorsey, Tommy (band leader); Mahonoy Plains, Pa. **(1905-1956)**
Dos Passos, John (author); Chicago **(1896-1970)**
Dostoevski, Fyodor Mikhailovich (novelist); Moscow **(1821-1881)**
Dotrice, Roy (actor); Guernsey, Channel Islands, England, 5/26/23
Douglas, Helen Gahagan (ex-Representative); Boonton, N.J. **(1900-1980)**
Douglas, Kirk (Issur Danielovitch) (actor); Amsterdam, N.Y., 12/9/1916
Douglas, Melvyn (Melvyn Hesselberg) (actor); Macon, Ga., **(1901-1981)**
Douglas, Michael (actor; movie producer); New Brunswick, N.J., 9/25/1944
Douglas, Mike (Michael D. Dowd, Jr.) (TV personality); Chicago, 8/11/1925
Douglas, Paul (actor); Philadelphia **(1907-1959)**
Douglas, Stephen Arnold (politician); Brandon, Vt. **(1813-1861)**
Dowling, Eddie (Edward Goucher) (actor and stage producer); Woonsocket, R.I. **(1894-1976)**
Down, Lesley-Anne (actress); London, England, 3/17/54
Downs, Hugh (TV entertainer); Akron, Ohio, 2/14/1921
Doyle, Sir Arthur Conan (novelist and spiritualist); Edinburgh, Scotland **(1859-1930)**
Doyle, David (actor); Omaha, Neb., 12/1/25
Drake, Alfred (singer and actor); New York City **(1914-1992)**
Drake, Sir Francis (navigator); Tavistock, England **(1545-1596)**
Dreiser, Theodore (writer); Terre Haute, Ind. **(1871-1945)**
Dressler, Marie (Leila Koeber) (actress); Cobourg, Ontario, Canada **(1869-1934)**
Dreyfus, Alfred (French army officer); Mulhouse (France) **(1859-1935)**
Dreyfuss, Richard (actor); Brooklyn, N.Y., 10/29/1947
Drury, Allen (novelist); Houston, 9/2/1918
Dryden, John (poet); Northamptonshire, England **(1631-1700)**
Dryer, Fred (actor); Hawthorne, Calif., 7/6/46
Dru, Joan (actress); Logan, W. Va., 1/31/23
Dubček, Alexander (ex-President of Czechoslovakia); Uhroved (Czechoslovakia) **(1921-1992)**
Dubinsky, David (David Dobnievski) (labor leader); Brest-Litovsk (U.S.S.R.) **(1892-1982)**
Duchamp, Marcel (painter); Blainville, France **(1887-1968)**
Duchin, Eddy (pianist, bandleader); Cambridge, Mass. **(1909-1951)**
Duchin, Peter (pianist and band leader); New York City, 7/28/1937
Dufay, Guillaume (composer); Cambrai, France **(c. 1400-1474)**
Duff, Howard (actor); Bremerton, Wash. **(1917-1990)**
Duffy, Julia (actress); Minneapolis, Minn., 6/27/50
Dufy, Raoul (painter); Le Havre, France **(1877-1953)**
Duke, James B. (industrialist); nr. Durham, N.C. **(1856-1925)**
Duke, Patty (Anna Marie Duke) (actress); New York City, 12/14/1946
Dullea, Keir (actor); Cleveland, 5/30/1936(?)
Dulles, Allen Welsh (ex-Director of CIA); Watertown, N.Y. **(1893-1969)**
Dulles, John Foster (statesman); Washington, D.C. **(1888-1959)**
Dumas, Alexandre (called Dumas fils) (novelist); Paris **(1824-1895)**
Dumas, Alexandre (called Dumas père) (novelist); Villers-Cotterets, France **(1802-1870)**
du Maurier, Daphne (novelist); London **(1907-1989)**
du Maurier, George Louis Palmella Busson (novelist); Paris **(1834-1896)**
Dumont, Margaret (actress); **(1889-1965)**
Dunaway, Faye (actress); Bascom, Fla., 1/14/1941
Duncan, Isadora (dancer); San Francisco **(1878-1927)**
Duncan, Sandy (actress); Henderson, Tex., 2/20/1946
Dunham, Katherine (dancer, choreographer); Chicago, 1914

Dunn, James (actor); Santa Monica, Calif. **(1905-1967)**
Dunne, Irene (actress); Louisville, Ky. **(1901?-1990)**
Dunnock, Mildred (actress); Baltimore **(1901–1991)**
Duns Scotus, John (theologian); Duns, Scotland **(1265-1303)**
Du Pont, Pierre S. (economist); Paris **(1739-1817)**
Durante, Jimmy (comedian); New York City **(1893-1980)**
Durbin, Deanna (Edna Mae) (actress); Winnipeg, Canada, 12/4/1922
Dürer, Albrecht (painter and engraver); Nürnberg (Germany) **(1471-1528)**
Durning, Charles (actor); Highland Falls, N.Y., 2/28/1923
Durrell, Lawrence George (novelist); Julundur, India **(1912–1990)**
Duryea, Dan (actor); White Plains, N.Y. **(1907-1968)**
Duse, Eleonora (actress); Chioggia, Italy **(1859-1924)**
Dussault, Nancy (actress); Pensacola, Fla., 6/30/1936
Duvalier, Jean-Claude (ex-President; son of "Papa Doc"); Port-au-Prince, Haiti, 7/3/1951
Duvall, Robert (actor); San Diego, Calif., 1931
Duvall, Shelley (actress); Houston, Tex., 1950
Dvořák, Antonin (composer); Nelahozeves (Czechoslovakia) **(1841-1904)**
Dylan, Bob (Robert Zimmerman) (folk singer and composer); Duluth, Minn., 5/24/1941
Dysart, Richard (actor); Brighton, Mass., 3/30/?

E

Eagels, Joanne (actress); Kansas City, Mo. **(1894-1929)**
Eakins, Thomas (painter and sculptor); Philadelphia **(1844-1916)**
Earhart, Amelia (aviator); Atchison, Kan. **(1898-1937)**
Eastman, George (inventor); Waterville, N.Y. **(1854-1932)**
Eastwood, Clint (actor); San Francisco, 5/31/1930
Ebert, Roger (film critic); Urbana, Ill., 6/18/42
Ebsen, Buddy (Christian Ebsen, Jr.) (actor); Belleville, Ill., 4/2/1908
Eckstine, Billy (singer); Pittsburgh **(1914-1993)**
Eddy, Mary Baker (founder of Christian Science Church); Bow, N.H. **(1821-1910)**
Eddy, Nelson (baritone and actor); Providence, R.I. **(1901-1967)**
Eden, Sir Anthony (Earl of Avon) (ex-Prime Minister); Durham, England **(1897-1977)**
Eden, Barbara (actress); Tucson, Ariz., 8/23/34
Edison, Thomas Alva (inventor); Milan, Ohio **(1847-1931)**
Edwards, Anthony (actor); Santa Barbara, Calif., 7/19/?
Edwards, Blake (film writer-producer); Tulsa, Okla. 7/26/1922
Edwards, Jonathan (theologian); East Windsor, Conn. **(1703-1758)**
Edwards, Ralph (TV and radio producer); Merino, Colo., 1913
Edwards, Vincent (actor); Brooklyn, N.Y., 7/7/1928
Egan, Richard (actor); San Francisco **(1923-1987)**
Eggar, Samantha (actress); London, 5/3/1939
Eglevsky, André (ballet dancer); Moscow **(1917-1977)**
Ehrlich, Paul (bacteriologist); Strzelin (Poland) **(1854-1915)**
Eikenberry, Jill (actress); New Haven, Conn., 1/21/47
Einstein, Albert (physicist); Ulm, Germany **(1879-1955)**
Eisenhower, Milton S. (educator); Abilene, Kan. **(1899-1985)**
Eisenstaedt, Alfred (photographer and photojournalist); Dirschau (Poland), 12/6/1898
Ekberg, Anita (actress); Malmö, Sweden, 9/29/1931
Ekland, Britt (Britt-Marie) (actress); Stockholm, Sweden, 1942
Eldridge, Florence (Florence McKechnie) (actress); Brooklyn, N.Y. **(1901-1988)**
Elgar, Sir Edward (composer); Worcester, England **(1857-1934)**
Elgart, Larry (band leader); New London, Conn., 3/20/1922
El Greco (Domenicos Theotocopoulos) (painter); Candia, Crete (Greece) **(c.1541-1614)**
Eliot, George (Mary Ann Evans) (novelist); Chilvers Coton, England **(1819-1880)**
Eliot, Thomas Stearns (poet); St. Louis **(1888-1965)**
Ellington, Duke (Edward Kennedy) (jazz musician); Washington, D.C. **(1899-1974)**
Elliot, "Mama" Cass (Ellen Naomi Cohen) (singer); Baltimore **(1941-1974)**
Elliott, Denholm (actor); London **(1922-1992)**
Elliott, Sam (actor); Californa, 8/9/44
Elman, Mischa (violinist); Stalnoye, Ukraine **(1891-1967)**
Emerson, Ralph Waldo (philosopher and poet); Boston **(1803-1882)**
Enesco, Georges (composer); Dorohoi, Romania **(1881-1955)**
Engels, Friedrich (Socialist writer); Barmen (Germany) **(1820-1895)**
Englund, Robert (actor); Glendale, Calif., 6/6/49
Entremont, Philippe (concert pianist); Rheims, France, 6/7/1934
Epicurus (philosopher); Samos (Greece) **(341-270 B.C.)**
Epstein, Sir Jacob (sculptor); New York City **(1880-1959)**
Erasmus, Desiderius (Gerhard Gerhards) (scholar); Rotterdam **(1466?-1536)**
Erhard, Ludwig (ex-Chancellor); Furth, Germany **(1897-1977)**
Erickson, Leif (actor); Alameda, Calif. **(1911-1986)**
Ericson, Leif (navigator); **(c. 10th century A.D.)**
Erikson, Erik H. (psychoanalyst); Frankfurt, Germany, 6/15/1902
Ernst, Max (painter); Bruhl, Germany **(1891-1976)**
Erté (Romain de Tirtoff) (artist, designer); St. Petersburg, Russia **(1892-1990)**
Estrada, Erik (actor); New York City, 3/16/1949
Euclid (mathematician); Megara (Greece) **(c. 300 B.C.)**
Euler, Leonhard (mathematician); Basel, Switzerland **(1707-1783)**
Euripides (dramatist); Salamis (Greece) **(c.484-407 B.C.)**
Evans, Dale (Frances Butts) (actress and singer); Uvalde, Tex., 10/31/1912
Evans, Dame Edith (actress); London **(1888-1976)**
Evans, Linda (actress), Hartford, Conn., 11/18/1942
Evans, Maurice (actor); Dorchester, England **(1901-1989)**
Everett, Chad (actor); (Raymon Lee Cramton) South Bend, Ind., 6/11/1936
Evers, Charles (civil rights leader); Decatur, Miss., 9/14/1923(?)
Evers, Medgar (civil rights leader); Decatur, Miss. **(1925-1963)**
Evigan, Greg (actor); South Amboy, N.J., 10/14/1953
Ewell, Tom (Yewell Tompkins) (actor); Owensboro, Ky., 4/29/1909

F

Fabares, Shelley (actress); Santa Monica, Calif., 1/19/1944
Fabian (Fabian Anthony Forte) (singer); Philadelphia, 2/6/1943
Fabray, Nanette (Nanette Fabarés) (actress); San Diego, Calif., 10/27/1922
Fadiman, Clifton (literary critic); Brooklyn, N.Y., 5/15/1904
Fahrenheit, Gabriel (German physicist); Danzig (Poland); **(1686-1736)**
Fairbanks, Douglas (Douglas Ulman) (actor); Denver **(1883-1939)**
Fairbanks, Douglas, Jr. (actor); New York City, 12/9/1909
Fairchild, Morgan (actress); Dallas, Tex., 2/3/1950
Faith, Percy (conductor); Toronto **(1908-1976)**
Falk, Peter (actor); New York City, 9/16/1927
Falla, Manuel de (composer); Cadiz, Spain **(1876-1946)**
Faraday, Michael (physicist); Newington, England **(1791-1867)**
Farber, Barry (radio-TV broadcaster); Baltimore, Md., 1930
Farentino, James (actor); Brooklyn, N.Y., 2/24/1938
Farmer, Frances (actress); Seattle, Wash. **(1913-1970)**
Farmer, James (civil rights leader); Marshall, Tex., 1/12/1920
Farnum, William (actor); Boston **(1876-1953)**
Farr, Jamie (actor); Toledo, Ohio, 7/1/1934
Farrar, Geraldine (soprano, actress); Melrose, Mass. **(1882-1967)**
Farrell, Charles (actor); Onset Bay, Mass. **(1901-1990)**
Farrell, Eileen (operatic soprano); Willimantic, Conn., 2/13/1920
Farrell, Glenda (actress); Enid, Okla. **(1904-1971)**
Farrell, James T. (novelist); Chicago **(1904-1979)**
Farrell, Mike (actor); St. Paul, Minn., 2/6/1939
Farrell, Suzanne (Roberta Sue Ficker) (ballerina); Cincinnati, 8/16/1945
Farrow, Mia (actress); Los Angeles, 2/9/1946
Fasanella, Ralph (painter); New York City, 9/2/1914
Fassbinder, Rainer Werner (film and stage director); Bad Wörishofen, West Germany **(1946-1982)**
Fast, Howard (novelist); New York City, 11/11/1914
Faulkner, William (novelist); New Albany, Miss. **(1897-1962)**
Fauré, Gabriel Urbain (composer); Pamiers, France **(1845-1924)**
Fawcett, Farrah (actress); Corpus Christi, Tex., 2/2/1947(?)
Faye, Alice (Ann Leppert) (actress); New York City, 5/5/1912
Feiffer, Jules (cartoonist); New York City, 1/26/1929
Feininger, Lyonel (painter); New York City **(1871-1956)**
Feldman, Marty (actor, screenwriter, director); London **(1938-1982)**
Feldon, Barbara (actress); Pittsburgh, 3/12/1941
Feliciano, José (singer); Larez, Puerto Rico, 9/10/1945
Felker, Clay S. (editor and publisher); St. Louis, 10/2/1925(?)
Fell, Norman (actor); Philadelphia, 3/24/1923
Fellini, Federico (film director); Rimini, Italy, 1/20/1920
Fender, Freddie (Baldemar Huerta) (singer); San Benito, Tex., 1937
Ferber, Edna (novelist); Kalamazoo, Mich. **(1885-1968)**
Ferguson, Maynard (jazz trumpeter); Verdun, Quebec, Canada, 5/4/1928
Fermi, Enrico (atomic physicist); Rome **(1901-1954)**
Fernandel (Fernand Joseph Desire Contandin) (actor); Marseilles, France **(1903-1971)**
Ferrer, José (actor and director); Santurce, Puerto Rico **(1912-1992)**
Ferrer, Mel (actor); Elberon, N.J., 8/25/1917
Ferrigno, Lou (actor); Brooklyn, N.Y., 11/9/1952
Fetchit, Stepin (Lincoln Theodore Perry) (comedian); Key West, Fla. **(1902-1985)**
Fiedler, Arthur (conductor); Boston **(1894-1979)**
Field, Betty (actress); Boston **(1918-1973)**
Field, Eugene (poet); St. Louis **(1850-1895)**
Field, Marshall (merchant); nr. Conway, Mass. **(1834-1906)**
Field, Sally (actress); Pasadena, Calif., 11/6/1946

Fielding, Henry (novelist); nr. Glastonbury, England **(1707-1754)**
Fields, Gracie (comedienne); Rochdale, England **(1898-1979)**
Fields, Totie (comedienne); Hartford, Conn. **(1931-1978)**
Fields, W. C. (William Claude Dukenfield) (comedian); Philadelphia **(1880-1946)**
Fierstein, Harvey (Forbes) (playwright and actor); Brooklyn, 6/6/1954
Filene, Edward A. (merchant); **(1860-1937)**
Finch, Peter (actor); Kensington, England **(1916-1977)**
Finney, Albert (actor); Salford, England, 5/9/1936
Firkusny, Rudolf (pianist); Napajedia (Czechoslovakia), 2/11/1912
Fischer-Dieskau, Dietrich (baritone); Berlin, 5/28/1925
Fisher, Carrie (actress); Los Angeles, 10/21/1956
Fisher, Eddie (Edwin) (singer); Philadelphia, 8/10/1928
Fitzgerald, Barry (William Joseph Shields) (actor); Dublin **(1888-1961)**
Fitzgerald, Edward (radio broadcaster); Troy, N.Y. **(1898(?)-1982)**
Fitzgerald, Ella (singer); Newport News, Va., 4/25/1918
Fitzgerald, F. Scott (Francis Scott Key) (novelist); St. Paul, Minn. **(1896-1940)**
Fitzgerald, Geraldine (actress); Dublin, 11/24/1914
Fitzgerald, Pegeen (radio broadcaster); Norcatur, Kan. **(1910-1989)**
Flack, Roberta (singer); Black Mountain, N.C., 2/10/1940
Flagstad, Kirsten (Wagnerian soprano); Hamar, Norway **(1895-1962)**
Flatt, Lester Raymond (bluegrass musician); Overton County, Tenn. **(1914-1979)**
Flaubert, Gustave (novelist); Rouen, France **(1821-1880)**
Fleming, Sir Alexander (bacteriologist); Lochfield, Scotland **(1881-1955)**
Fleming, Rhonda (Marilyn Louis) (actress); Los Angeles, 8/10/1923
Fletcher, John (dramatist); Rye? England **(1579-1625)**
Flynn, Errol (actor); Hobart, Tasmania **(1909-1959)**
Foch, Nina (actress); Leyden, Netherlands, 4/20/1924
Fodor, Eugene (violinist); Turkey Creek, Colo., 3/5/1950
Fokine, Michel (dancer, choreographer); St. Petersburg, Russia **(1880-1942)**
Fonda, Henry (actor); Grand Island, Neb. **(1905-1982)**
Fonda, Jane (actress); New York City, 12/21/1937
Fonda, Peter (actor); New York City, 2/23/1939
Fontaine, Frank (singer and comedian); Cambridge, Mass. **(1920-1979)**
Fontaine, Joan (Joan de Havilland) (actress); Tokyo, 10/22/1917
Fontanne, Lynn (actress); London **(1887-1983)**
Fonteyn, Dame Margot (Margaret Hookham) (ballerina); Reigate, England **(1919–1991)**
Forbes, Malcolm S(tevenson) (publisher and sportsman); Brooklyn, N.Y. **(1919-1990)**
Ford, Glenn (Gwyllyn Ford) (actor); Quebec, 5/1/1916
Ford, Harrison (actor); Chicago, 7/13/1942
Ford, Henry (industrialist); Greenfield, Mich. **(1863-1947)**
Ford, Henry, II (auto maker); Detroit **(1917-1987)**
Ford, John (film director); Cape Elizabeth, Me. **(1895-1973)**
Ford, Paul (actor); Baltimore **(1901-1976)**
Ford, Tennessee Ernie (Ernie Jennings Ford) (singer); Bristol, Tenn. **(1919-1991)**
Forrester, Maureen (contralto); Montreal, 7/25/1930
Forsythe, John (actor); Penn's Grove, N.J., 1/29/1918
Fosdick, Harry Emerson (clergyman); Buffalo, N.Y. **(1878-1968)**
Fosse, Bob (Robert Louis) (choreographer and director); Chicago **(1927-1987)**
Foster, Jodie (actress); Bronx, N.Y., 1963
Foster, Preston (actor); Ocean City, N.J. **(1900-1970)**
Foster, Stephen Collins (composer); nr. Pittsburgh **(1826-1864)**
Fox, Michael J. (actor); Edmonton, Alta., Canada, 6/9/1961
Foxx, Redd (John Elroy Sanford) (actor and comedian); St. Louis **(1922-1991)**
Foy, Eddie, Jr. (dancer and actor); New Rochelle, N.Y. **(1905-1983)**
Fra Angelico (Giovanni da Fiesole) (painter); Vicchio in the Mugello, Tuscany (Italy) **(c.1387-1455)**
Fracci, Carla (ballerina); Milan, Italy, 8/20/1936
Fragonard, Jean Honoré (painter); Grasse, France **(1732-1806)**
Frampton, Peter (rock musician); Beckenham, England, 4/20/1950
France, Anatole (Jacques Anatole François Thibault) (author); Paris **(1844-1924)**
Francescatti, Zino (violinist); Marseilles, France **(1902–1991)**
Franciosa, Anthony (Anthony Papaleo) (actor); New York City, 10/25/1928
Francis, Anne (actress); Ossining, N.Y., 7/16/1930
Francis, Arlene (Arlene Francis Kazanjian) (actress); Boston, 10/20/1908
Francis, Connie (Concetta Franconero) (singer); Newark, N.J., 12/12/1938
Francis, Genie (actress); Englewood, N.J., 5/26/1962
Francis, Kay (Katherine Edwina Gibbs) (actress); Oklahoma City **(1903-1968)**
Francis of Assisi, Saint (Giovanni Francesco Barnardone) (founder of Franciscans); Assisi, Italy **(1182-1226)**
Franck, César Auguste (composer); Liège (Belgium) **(1822-1890)**
Franco Bahamonde, Francisco (Chief of State); El Ferrol, Spain **(1892-1975)**
Franklin, Aretha (singer); Memphis, Tenn., 3/25/1942
Franklin, Benjamin (statesman and scientist); Boston **(1706-1790)**
Franklin, Bonnie (actress); Santa Monica, Calif., 1/6/1944
Frann, Mary (actress); St. Louis, Mo., 2/27/1943
Frazer, Sir James George (anthropologist); Glasgow, Scotland **(1854-1941)**
Freud, Sigmund (psychoanalyst); Moravia (Czechoslovakia) **(1856-1939)**
Friedan, Betty (Betty Naomi Goldstein) (feminist); Peoria, Ill., 2/4/1921
Fromm, Erich (psychoanalyst); Frankfurt-am-Main, Germany **(1900-1980)**
Frost, David (TV entertainer); Tenterden, England, 4/7/1939
Frost, Robert Lee (poet); San Francisco **(1874-1963)**
Fry, Christopher (playwright); Bristol, England, 12/18/1907
Frye, David (impressionist); Brooklyn, N.Y., 1934
Fugard, Athol (playwright); Middleburg, South Africa, 6/11/1932
Fuller, R(ichard) Buckminster (Jr.) (architect and educator); Milton, Mass. **(1895-1983)**
Fulton, Robert (inventor); Lancaster County, Pa. **(1765-1815)**
Funicello, Annette (actress); Los Angeles, 10/22/1942
Funt, Allen (TV producer); Brooklyn, N.Y., 9/16/1914
Furness, Betty (Elizabeth) (ex-actress and consumer advocate); New York City, 1/3/1916

G

Gabel, Martin (actor and producer); Philadelphia **(1912-1986)**
Gabin, Jean (actor); Paris **(1904-1976)**
Gable, (William) Clark (actor); Cadiz, Ohio **(1901-1960)**
Gabo, Naum (sculptor); Briansk, Russia **(1890-1977)**
Gabor, Eva (actress); Budapest, 2/11/1926(?)
Gabor, Zsa Zsa (Sari) (actress); Budapest, 2/6/1919(?)
Gabrieli, Giovanni (composer); Venice **(c.1557-1612)**
Gainsborough, Thomas (painter); Sudbury, Suffolk, England **(1727-1788)**
Galbraith, John Kenneth (economist); Iona Station, Ontario, Canada, 10/15/1908
Galilei, Galileo (astronomer and physicist); Pisa (Italy) **(1564-1642)**
Gallico, Paul (novelist); New York City **(1897-1976)**
Gallup, George H. (poll taker); Jefferson, Iowa **(1901-1984)**
Galsworthy, John (novelist and dramatist); Coombe, England **(1867-1933)**
Galway, James (flutist); Belfast, Northern Ireland, 12/8/1939
Gambling, John A. (radio broadcaster); New York City, 1930
Gandhi, Indira (Indira Nehru) (Prime Minister); Allahabad, India **(1917-1984)**
Gandhi, Mohandas Karamchand (called Mahatma Gandhi) (Hindu leader); Porbandar, India **(1869-1948)**
Gannett, Frank E. (editor and publisher); **(1876-1957)**
Garagiola, Joe (Joseph Henry) (sportscaster); St. Louis, 2/12/1926
Garbo, Greta (Greta Gustafsson) (actress); Stockholm **(1905-1990)**
Garcia Lorca, Frederico (author); Fuente Vaqueros, Spain **(1898-1936)**
Garden, Mary (soprano); Aberdeen, Scotland **(1874-1967)**
Gardenia, Vincent (actor); Naples, Italy **(1922-1992)**
Gardner, Ava (actress); Smithfield, N.C. **(1922-1990)**
Gardner, Erle Stanley (novelist); Malden, Mass. **(1889-1970)**
Garfield, John (Jules Garfinkle) (actor); New York City **(1913-1952)**
Garfunkel, Art (Arthur) (singer); Newark, N.J., 11/5/1941
Gargan, William (actor); Brooklyn, N.Y., **(1905-1979)**
Garibaldi, Giuseppe (Italian nationalist leader); Nice, France **(1807-1882)**
Garland, Judy (Frances Gumm) (actress and singer); Grand Rapids, Minn. **(1922-1969)**
Garner, Erroll (jazz pianist); Pittsburgh **(1921-1977)**
Garner, James (James Bumgarner) (actor); Norman, Okla., 4/7/1928
Garner, Peggy Ann (actress); Canton, Ohio **(1932-1984)**
Garr, Teri (actress); Lakewood, Ohio, 12/11/1949
Garrett, Betty (actress); St. Joseph, Mo., 5/23/1919
Garrick, David (actor); Hereford, England **(1717-1779)**
Garrison, William Lloyd (abolitionist); Newburyport, Mass. **(1805-1879)**
Garroway, Dave (TV host); Schenectady, N.Y. **(1913-1982)**
Garson, Greer (actress); County Down, Northern Ireland, 9/29/1912(?)
Gary, John (singer); Watertown, N.Y., 11/29/1932
Gassman, Vittorio (film actor and director); Genoa, Italy, 9/1/1922
Gaudí, Antonio (architect); Reus, Spain **(1852-1926)**
Gauguin, Eugène Henri Paul (painter); Paris **(1848-1903)**
Gautama Buddha (Prince Siddhartha) (philosopher); Kapilavastu (India) **(563?-?483 B.C.)**

Gavin, John (actor, diplomat); Los Angeles, 4/8/1935
Gayle, Crystal (Brenda Gayle Webb) (singer); Paintsville, Ky., 1/9/1951
Gaynor, Janet (actress); Philadelphia **(1906-1984)**
Gaynor, Mitzi (Francesca Mitzi Marlene de Czanyi von Gerber) (actress); Chicago, 9/4/1931
Gazzara, Ben (Biago Anthony Gazzara) (actor); New York City, 8/28/1930
Gebel-Williams, Gunther (animal trainer); Schweidnitz (Poland), 1934
Gedda, Nicolai (tenor); Stockholm, Sweden, 7/11/1925
Geddes, Barbara Bel (actress); New York City, 10/31/1922
Genet, Jean (playwright); Paris **(1910-1986)**
Genghis Khan (Temujin) (conqueror); nr. Lake Baikal, Russia **(1162-1227)**
Genn, Leo (actor); London **(1905-1978)**
Gentry, Bobbie (Roberta Streeter) (singer); Chickasaw Co., Miss., 7/27/1944
George, David Lloyd (statesman); Manchester, England **(1863-1945)**
Gere, Richard (actor); Philadelphia, 1950
Gericault, Jean Louis (painter); Rouen, France **(1791-1824)**
Geronimo (Goyathlay) (Apache chieftain); Arizona **(1829-1909)**
Gershwin, George (composer); Brooklyn, N.Y. **(1898-1937)**
Gershwin, Ira (lyricist); New York City, **(1896-1983)**
Getty, J. Paul (oil executive); Minneapolis **(1892-1976)**
Getz, Stan (saxophonist); Philadelphia **(1927–1991)**
Ghiberti, Lorenzo (goldsmith and sculptor); Florence **(1378-1455)**
Ghostley, Alice (actress); Eve, Mo., 8/14/1926
Giacometti, Alberto (sculptor); Switzerland **(1901-1966)**
Giannini, Giancarlo (actor); La Spezia, Italy, 8/1/1942
Gibbon, Edward (historian); Putney, England **(1737-1794)**
Gibson, Charles Dana (illustrator); Roxbury, Mass. **(1867-1944)**
Gibson, Henry (actor, comedian); Germantown, Pa., 9/21/35
Gibson, Hoot (Edward) (actor); Tememah, Neb. **(1892-1962)**
Gibson, Mel (actor); Peekskill, N.Y., 1/3/1956
Gide, André (author); Paris **(1869-1951)**
Gielgud, Sir John (actor); London, 4/14/1904
Gilbert, John (movie actor); Logan, Utah **(1897-1936)**
Gilbert, Melissa (actress); Los Angeles, 5/8/1964
Gilbert, Sir William Schwenck (librettist); London **(1836-1911)**
Gilels, Emil (concert pianist); Odessa, Ukraine **(1916-1985)**
Gillespie, Dizzy (John Birks Gillespie) (jazz trumpeter); Cheraw, S.C. **(1917-1993)**
Gillette, William (actor); Hartford, Conn. **(1855-1932)**
Gimbel, Bernard F. (merchant); Vincennes, Ind. **(1885-1966)**
Gingold, Hermione (actress and comedienne); London **(1897-1987)**
Ginsberg, Allen (poet); Newark, N.J., 6/3/1926
Giordano, Luca (painter); Naples, Italy **(1632-1705)**
Giorgione (painter); Castelfranco, (Italy) **(c.1477-1510)**
Giotto di Bondone (painter); Vespignamo (Italy) **(c.1266-1337)**
Giovanni, Nikki (poet); Knoxville, Tenn., 6/7/1943
Giroud, Françoise (French government official); Geneva, 9/21/1916
Gish, Dorothy (actress); Massillon, Ohio **(1898-1968)**
Gish, Lillian (Lillian de Guiche) (actress); Springfield, Ohio **(1893-1993)**
Givenchy, Hubert (fashion designer); Beauvais, France, 2/21/1927
Gladstone, William Ewart (statesman); Liverpool, England **(1809-1898)**
Glaser, Paul Michael (actor, director); Cambridge, Mass., 3/25/1943
Glass, Philip (composer); Baltimore, 1/31/1937
Gleason, Jackie (comedian); Brooklyn, N.Y. **(1916-1987)**
Gleason, James (actor); New York City **(1886-1959)**
Gless, Sharon (actress); Los Angeles, 5/31/1943
Gluck, Christoph Willibald (composer); Erasbach (Germany) **(1714-1787)**
Gobel, George (comedian); Chicago **(1920–1991)**
Godard, Jean Luc (film director); Paris, 12/3/1930
Goddard, Robert Hutchings (father of modern rocketry); Worcester, Mass. **(1882-1945)**
Goddard, Paulette (Marion Levy) (actress); Great Neck, N.Y. **(1911?-1990)**
Godfrey, Arthur (entertainer); New York City **(1903-1983)**
Godunov, Alexander (ballet dancer); Sakhalin, U.S.S.R. 11/28/1949
Goebbels, Joseph Paul (Nazi leader); Rheydt, Germany **(1897-1945)**
Goering, Hermann (Nazi leader); Rosenheim, Germany **(1893-1946)**
Goethals, George Washington (engineer); Brooklyn, N.Y. **(1858-1928)**
Goethe, Johann Wolfgang von (poet, playwright, and novelist); Frankfurt-am-Main, Germany **(1749-1832)**
Gogol, Nikolai Vasilievich (novelist); nr. Mirgorod, Ukraine **(1809-1852)**
Goldberg, Rube (cartoonist); San Francisco **(1883-1970)**
Goldberg, Whoopi (actress); New York City, 1949 (?)
Goldblum, Jeff (actor); Pittsburgh, Pa., 10/22/52
Golden, Harry (Harry Goldhurst) (auth or); New York City **(1902-1981)**
Goldsmith, Oliver (dramatist and poet); County Longford, Ireland **(1728-1774)**
Goldwyn, Samuel (Samuel Goldfish) (film producer); Warsaw **(1882-1974)**
Golenpaul, Dan (creator of Information Please radio show and editor of almanac of same name); New York City **(1900-1974)**
Gompers, Samuel (labor leader); London **(1850-1924)**
Goodall, Jane (Baroness van Lawick-Goodall) (ethologist); London, 4/3/1934
Goodman, Benny (clarinetist); Chicago **(1909-1986)**
Goodyear, Charles (inventor); New Haven, Conn. **(1800-1860)**
Gorbachev, Mikhail Sergeyevich (Soviet leader); Privolnoye, U.S.S.R., 3/2/1931
Gordimer, Nadine (novelist and short-story writer); Springs, South Africa, 12/20/1923
Gordon, Max (stage producer); New York City **(1892-1978)**
Gordon, Ruth (actress); Wollaston, Mass. **(1896-1985)**
Gordy, Berry, Jr. (record company executive); Detroit, 11/28/1929
Gore, Lesley (singer); Tenafly, N.J., 1946
Goren, Charles H. (bridge expert); Philadelphia **(1901–1991)**
Gorki, Maxim (Alexei Maximovich Peshkov) (author); Nizhni Novgorod, Russia **(1868-1936)**
Gorky, Arshile (painter); Armenia **(1904-1948)**
Gormé, Eydie (singer); Bronx, N.Y., 8/16/1932
Gorshin, Frank (actor); Pittsburgh, 4/5/1934
Gosden, Freeman F. *See* Amos
Gossett, Louis, Jr. (actor); Brooklyn, N.Y., 5/27/1936
Gottschalk, Louis Moreau (pianist, composer); New Orleans, La. **(1829-1869)**
Gould, Chester (cartoonist); Pawnee, Okla. **(1900-1985)**
Gould, Elliott (Elliott Goldstein) (actor); Brooklyn, N.Y., 8/29/1938
Gould, Glenn (concert pianist); Toronto, **(1932-1982)**
Gould, Morton (composer); Richmond Hill, Queens, N.Y., 12/10/1913
Goulet, Robert (singer); Lawrence, Mass., 11/26/1933
Gounod, Charles François (composer); Paris **(1818-1893)**
Goya y Lucientes, Francisco José de (painter); Fuendetodos, Spain **(1746-1828)**
Grable, Betty (actress); St. Louis **(1916-1973)**
Grace, Princess of Monaco (Grace Kelly) (ex-actress); Philadelphia **(1929-1982)**
Graham, Bill (Wolfgang Grajonca) (rock impresario); Berlin, 1931
Graham, Billy (William F.) (ev angelist); Charlotte, N.C., 11/7/1918
Graham, Katharine Meyer (newspaper publisher); New York City, 6/16/1917
Graham, Martha (choreographer); Pittsburgh **(1894–1991)**
Graham, Virgina (actress,host); Chicago, 7/4/1913
Grahame, Gloria (Gloria Hallwood) (actress); Los Angeles **(1929-1981)**
Grainger, Percy Aldridge (pianist and composer); Melbourne, Australia **(1882-1961)**
Gramm, Donald (Grambach) (bass-baritone); Milwaukee **(1927-1983)**
Granger, Farley (actor); San Jose, Calif., 7/1/1925
Granger, Stewart (James Stewart) (actor); London **(1913-1993)**
Grant, Cary (Alexander Archibald Leach) (actor); Bristol, England **(1904-1986)**
Grant, Kathryn (actress); Houston, Tex. 1933
Grant, Lee (Lyova Haskell Rosenthal) (actress); New York City, 10/31/1930
Granville, Bonita (actress); New York City **(1923-1988)**
Grass, Günter (novelist); Danzig (Poland), 10/16/1927
Grauer, Ben (radio and TV announcer); New York City **(1908-1977)**
Graves, Peter (Peter Arness) (actor); Minneapolis, 3/18/1926
Graves, Robert (writer); London **(1895-1985)**
Gray, Barry (Bernard Yaroslaw) (radio interviewer); Atlantic City, N.J., 7/2/1916
Gray, Dolores (singer and actress); Chicago, 6/7/1930
Gray, Linda (actress); Santa Monica, Calif., 9/12/1940
Gray, Thomas (poet); London **(1716-1771)**
Grayson, Kathryn (Zelma Hednick) (singer and actress); Winston-Salem, N.C., 2/9/1923
Greco, Buddy (singer); Philadelphia, 8/14/1926
Greco, José (dancer); Montorio nei Frentani, Itály, 12/23/1918
Greeley, Horace (journalist and politician); Amherst, N.H. **(1811-1872)**
Green, Adolph (actor and lyricist); New York City, 12/2/1915
Green, Al (singer); Forrest City, Ark., 4/13/1946
Greene, Graham (novelist); Berkhamsted, England **(1904–1991)**
Greene, Lorne (actor); Ottawa **(1915-1987)**
Greene, Martyn (actor); London **(1899-1975)**
Greene, Michele (actress); Las Vegas, Nev., 2/3/?
Greene, Shecky (comedian, actor); Chicago, 4/8/1925
Greenstreet, Sydney (actor); Sandwich, England **(1879-1954)**
Greenwood, Charlotte (actress); Philadelphia, Pa. **(1893-1978)**
Greenwood, Joan (actress and director); London **(19 21-1987)**
Greer, Germaine (feminist); Melbourne, 1/29/1939
Gregory, Cynthia (ballerina); Los Angeles, 7/8/1946
Gregory, Dick (comedian); St. Louis, 1932

Greuze, Jean-Baptiste (painter); Tournus, France **(1725-1805)**
Grey, Joel (Joel Katz) (actor); Cleveland, 4/11/1932
Grey, Zane (author); Zanesville, Ohio **(1875-1939)**
Grieg, Edvard Hagerup (composer); Bergen, Norway **(1843-1907)**
Grier, Roosevelt (entertainer and former athlete); Cuthbert, Ga., 7/14/1932
Griffin, Merv (TV entertainer); San Mateo, Calif., 7/6/1925
Griffith, Andy (actor); Mount Airy, N.C., 6/1/1926
Griffith, David Lewelyn Wark (film producer); La Grange, Ky. **(1875-1948)**
Griffith, Melanie (actress); New York City, 8/9/1957
Grigorovich, Yuri (choreographer); Leningrad, 1/1/1927
Grimes, Tammy (actress); Lynn, Mass., 1/30/1934
Grimm, Jacob (author of fairy tales); Hanau (Germany) **(1785-1863)**
Grimm, Wilhelm (author of fairy tales); Hanau (Germany) **(1786-1859)**
Gris, Juan (José Victoriano González) (painter); Madrid **(1887-1927)**
Grizzard, George (actor); Roanoke Rapids, N.C., 4/1/1928
Grodin, Charles (actor); Pittsburgh, Pa., 4/21/1935
Groh, David (actor); Brooklyn, N.Y., 5/21/1939
Gromyko, Andrei A. (diplomat); Starye Gromyki, Russia **(1909-1989)**
Gropius, Walter (architect); Berlin **(1883-1969)**
Gropper, William (painter, illustrator); New York City **(1897-1977)**
Gross, Michael (actor); Chicago, 6/21/1947
Grosz, George (painter); Germany **(1893-1959)**
Guardino, Harry (actor); New York City, 12/23/1925
Guggenheim, Meyer (capitalist); Langnau, Switzerland **(1828-1905)**
Guillaume, Robert (actor); St. Louis, Mo. 11/30/1927
Guinness, Sir Alec (actor); London, 4/2/1914
Guitry, Sacha (Alexandre) (actor and film director); St. Petersburg, Russia **(1885-1957)**
Gumbel, Bryant Charles (TV newscaster); New Orleans, 9/29/1948
Gunther, John (author); Chicago **(1901-1970)**
Guténberg, Johannes (printer); Mainz (Germany) **(1400?-?1468)**
Guthrie, Arlo (singer); New York City, 7/10/1947
Guthrie, Woody (folk singer and composer); Okemah, Okla. **(1912-1967)**
Gwenn, Edmund (actor); London **(1875-1959)**
Gwynne, Fred (actor); New York City **(1926-1993)**

H

Hackett, Bobby (trumpeter); Providence, R.I. **(1915-1976)**
Hackett, Buddy (Leonard Hacker) (comedian and actor); Brooklyn, N.Y., 8/31/1924
Hackman, Gene (actor); San Bernardino, Calif., 1/30/1931
Hagen, Uta (actress); Göttingen, Germany, 6/12/1919
Haggard, Merle (songwriter); Bakersfield, Calif., 4/6/1937
Hagman, Larry (actor); Weatherford, Tex., 1931
Haig, Alexander Meigs, Jr. (ex-Secretary of State and ex-general); Bala-Cynwyd, Pa., 12/2/1924
Haile Selassie (Ras Tafari Makonnen) (ex-Emperor); Ethiopia **(1892-1975)**
Hailey, Arthur (novelist); Luton, England, 4/5/1920
Halberstam, David (journalist); New York City, 4/10/1934
Hale, Alan (actor, director); Washington, D.C. **(1892-1950)**
Hale, Barbara (actress); DeKalb, Ill., 4/18/1921
Hale, Edward Everett (clergyman and author); Boston **(1822-1909)**
Hale, Nathan (American Revolutionary officer); Coventry, Conn. **(1755-1776)**
Halevi, Judah (Jewish poet); Toledo, Spain **(1085-1140)**
Haley, Alex (writer); Ithaca, N.Y. **(1921-1992)**
Haley, Jack (actor); Boston **(1899-1979)**
Hall, Arsenio (comedian and talk show host); Cleveland, Ohio, 2/12/?
Hall, Donald (Andrew, Jr.) (poet) New Haven, Conn., 9/20/1928
Hall, Huntz (actor); New York City, 1920
Hall, Monty (TV personality); Winnipeg, Canada, 1923
Halley, Edmund (astronomer); London **(1656-1742)**
Hals, Frans (painter); Antwerp (Netherlands) **(1580?-1666)**
Halsey, William Frederick, Jr. (naval officer); Elizabeth, N.J. **(1882-1959)**
Hamel, Veronica (actress); Philadelphia, Pa., 11/20/1943
Hamill, Pete (journalist); Brooklyn, N.Y., 6/24/1935
Hamilton, Alexander (statesman); Nevis, British West Indies **(1757?-1804)**
Hamilton, George (actor); Memphis, Tenn., 8/12/1939
Hamilton, Margaret (actress); Cleveland **(1902-1985)**
Hamlin, Harry (actor); Pasadena, Calif., 10/30/1951
Hamlisch, Marvin (composer and pianist); New York City, 6/2/1944
Hammarskjöld, Dag (U.N. Secretary-General); Jönköping, Sweden **(1905-1961)**
Hammerstein, Oscar, II (librettist and stage producer); New York City **(1895-1960)**
Hampden, Walter (Walter Hampden Dougherty) (actor); Brooklyn, N.Y. **(1879-1955)**
Hampshire, Susan (actress); London, 5/12/1938
Hampton, Lionel (vibraharpist and band leader); Birmingham, Ala., 4/12/1913
Hamsun, Knut (Knut Pedersen) (novelist); Lom, Norway **(1859-1952)**
Hancock, John (statesman); Braintree, Mass. **(1737-1793)**
Hand, Learned (jurist); Albany, N.Y. **(1872-1961)**
Handel, George Frederick (Georg Friedrich Händel) (composer); Halle (East Germany) **(1685-1759)**
Handy, William Christopher (blues composer); Florence, Ala. **(1873-1958)**
Hanks, Tom (actor); Concord, Calif., 7/9/1956
Hannibal (Carthaginian general); North Africa **(247-182** B.C.)
Hanson, Howard (conductor); Wahoo, Neb., **(1896-1981)**
Harburg, E. Y. "Yip" (songwriter); New York City **(1896-1981)**
Harding, Ann (actress); San Antonio, Tex. **(1902-1981)**
Hardwicke, Sir Cedric (actor); Stourbridge, England **(1893-1964)**
Hardy, Oliver (comedian); Atlanta **(1892-1957)**
Hardy, Thomas (novelist); Dorsetshire, England **(1840-1928)**
Harkness, Edward S. (capitalist); Cleveland **(1874-1940)**
Harlow, Jean (Harlean Carpentier) (actress); Kansas City, Mo. **(1911-1937)**
Harnick, Sheldon (lyricist); Chicago, 4/30/1924
Harper, Valerie (actress); Suffern, N.Y., 8/22/1940(?)
Harrell, Lynn (cellist); New York City, 1/30/1944
Harriman, W. (William) Averell (ex-Governor of New York); New York City **(1891-1986)**
Harrington, Pat., Jr. (actor, comedian); New York City, 8/13/1929
Harris, Barbara (actress); Evanston, Ill., 1935
Harris, Emmylou (singer); Birmingham, Ala., 1949
Harris, Julie (actress); Grosse Pointe Park, Mich., 12/2/1925
Harris, Phil (actor and band leader); Linton, Ind., 6/24/1906
Harris, Richard (actor); Limerick, Ireland, 10/1/1933
Harris, Rosemary (actress); Ashby, England, 9/19/1930
Harris, Roy (composer); Lincoln County, Okla. **(1898-1979)**
Harrison, George (singer and songwriter); Liverpool, England, 2/25/1943
Harrison, Gregory (actor); Avalon, Catalina Island, Calif., 5/31/1950
Harrison, Sir Rex (Reginald Carey) (actor); Huyton, England **(1908-1990)**
Hart, Lorenz (lyricist); New York **(1895-1943)**
Hart, Mary (host); Sioux Falls, S.D., c.1950
Hart, Moss (playwright); New York City **(1904-1961)**
Hart, William S. (actor); Newburgh, N.Y. **(1862-1946)**
Harte, Bret (Francis Brett Harte) (author); Albany, N.Y. **(1836-1902)**
Hartford, Huntington (George Huntington Hartford II) (A.&P. heir); New York City, 4/18/1911
Hartford, John (singer and banjoist); New York City, 12/30/1937
Hartley, Mariette (actress); New York City, 6/21/1940
Hartman, David Downs (TV newscaster); Pawtucket, R.I., 5/19/1935
Hartman, Elizabeth (actress); Youngstown, Ohio **(1941-1987)**
Hartman, Lisa (actress); Houston, Tex., 6/1/1956
Harvey, Laurence (Larushka Skikne) (actor); Joniskis, Lithuania **(1928-1973)**
Harvey, William (physician); Folkestone, England **(1578-1657)**
Hasselhoff, David (actor); Baltimore, Md., 7/17/1952
Hasso, Signe (actress); Stockholm, 8/15/1915
Havoc, June (June Hovick) (actress); Seattle, 1916
Haver, June (actress); Rock Island, Ill., 6/10/1926
Hawkins, Jack (actor); London **(1910-1973)**
Hawn, Goldie (actress); Washington, D.C., 11/21/1945
Haworth, Jill (actress); Sussex, England, 1945
Hawthorne, Nathaniel (novelist); Salem, Mass. **(1804-1864)**
Hay, John Milton (statesman); Salem, Ind. **(1838-1905)**
Hayakawa, Sessue (actor); Honshu, Japan **(1890-1973)**
Hayden, Melissa (ballerina); Toronto, 4/25/1923
Hayden, Sterling (Sterling Relyea Walter) (actor and writer); Montclair, N.J. **(1916-1986)**
Haydn, Franz Joseph (composer); Rohrau (Austria) **(1732-1809)**
Hayes, Helen (Helen Hayes Brown) (actress); Washington, D.C. **(1900-1993)**
Hayes, Isaac (composer); Covington, Tenn., 8/20/1942
Hayes, Peter Lind (comedian, singer); San Francisco, 6/25/1915
Haymes, Dick (singer, actor); Buenos Aires **(1916-1980)**
Hayward, Leland (producer); Nebraska City, Neb. **(1902-1971)**
Hayward, Louis (actor); Johannesburg, South Africa **(1909-1985)**
Hayward, Susan (Edythe Marrener) (actress); Brooklyn, N.Y. **(1919?-1975)**
Hayworth, Rita (Margarita Cansino) (actress); New York City **(1918-1987)**
Head, Edith (costume designer); Los Angeles **(1907-1981)**
Hearst, William Randolph (publisher); San Francisco **(1863-1951)**
Hearst, William Randolph, Jr. (publisher); New York City **(1908-1993)**
Heath, Edward (ex-Prime Minister); Broadstairs, England, 7/9/1916
Heatherton, Joey (actress); Rockville Centre, N.Y., 9/14/1944

Hecht, Ben (author); New York City **(1894-1964)**
Heckart, Eileen (actress); Columbus, Ohio, 3/29/1919
Heflin, Van (Emmet Evan Heflin) (actor); Walters, Okla. **(1910-1971)**
Hefner, Hugh (publisher); Chicago, 4/9/1926
Hegel, Georg Wilhelm Friedrich (philosopher); Stuttgart (Germany) **(1770-1831)**
Heifetz, Jascha (concert violinist); Vilna, Russia **(1901-1987)**
Heine, Heinrich (Harry) (poet); Düsseldorf (Germany) **(1797-1856)**
Heinemann, Gustav (ex-President of Germany); Schweim, Germany **(1899-1976)**
Heisenberg, Werner Karl (physicist); Würzburg, Germany **(1901-1976)**
Held, Anna (comedienne); Paris, France **(1873(?)-1918)**
Heller, Joseph (novelist); Brooklyn, N.Y., 5/1/1923
Hellman, Lillian (playwright); New Orleans **(1905-1984)**
Helmond, Katherine (actress); Galveston, Tex., 7/5/1934(?)
Hemingway, Ernest Miller (novelist); Oak Park, Ill. **(1899-1961)**
Hemingway, Margaux (actress); Portland, Ore., Feb. 1955
Hemmings, David (actor); Guilford, England, 11/2/1941
Henderson, Florence (actress); Dale, Ind., 2/14/1934
Henderson, Skitch (Lyle Russell Cedric) (conductor and pianist); Birmingham, England(?), 1/27/1918
Hendrix, Jimi (James Marshall Hendrix) (guitarist); Seattle **(1942-1970)**
Henley, Beth (playwright-actress); Jackson, Miss., 5/8/1952
Henner, Marilu (actress); Chicago, 4/6/1952
Henning, Doug (magician and actor); Winnipeg, Canada, 1947(?)
Henreid, Paul (actor); Trieste **(1908-1992)**
Henri, Robert (painter); Cincinnati **(1865-1926)**
Henry, O. (William Sydney Porter) (story writer); Greensboro, N.C. **(1862-1910)**
Henry, Patrick (statesman); Hanover County, Va. **(1736-1799)**
Henson, Jim (puppeteer); Greenville, Miss. **(1936-1990)**
Hepburn, Audrey (actress); Brussels, Belgium **(1929-1993)**
Hepburn, Katharine (actress); Hartford, Conn., 11/8/1909
Hepplewhite, George (furniture designer); England **(?-1786)**
Hepworth, Barbara (sculptor); Wakefield, England **(1903-1975)**
Herachel, William (Frederich Wilhelm) (astronomer); Hanover, Germany **(1738-1822)**
Herbert, George (poet); Montgomery Castle, Wales **(1593-1633)**
Herbert, Victor (composer); Dublin **(1859-1924)**
Herblock (Herbert L. Block) (political cartoonist); Chicago, 10/13/1909
Herman, Pee-wee (Paul Reubens) (comedian); Peekskill, N.Y., 1952
Herman, Woody (Woodrow Charles) (band leader); Milwaukee **(1913-1987)**
Herod (Herodes) (called Herod the Great) (King of Judea) **(73?-4 60**B.C.**)**
Herodotus (historian); Halicarnassus, Asia Minor (Turkey) **(c. 484-425** B.C.**)**
Herrick, Robert (poet); London? **(1591-1674)**
Hershey, Barbara (actress); Hollywood, Calif., 2/5/1948(?)
Hershfield, Harry (humorist and raconteur); Cedar Rapids, Iowa **(1885-1974)**
Hersholt, Jean (actor); Copenhagen **(1886-1956)**
Hesburgh, Theodore M. (educator); Syracuse, N.Y., 5/2/1917
Hesseman, Howard (actor); Salem, Ore., 2/27/1940
Heston, Charlton (actor); Evanston, Ill., 10/4/1924
Heyerdahl, Thor (ethnologist and explorer); Larvik, Norway, 10/6/1914
Hildegarde (Hildegarde Loretta Sell) (singer); Adell, Wis., 2/1/1906
Hill, Arthur (actor); Melfort, Canada, 8/1/1922
Hill, Benny (comedian); Southampton, England **(1925–1992)**
Hillary, Sir Edmund (mountain climber); New Zealand, 7/20/1919
Hiller, Wendy (actress); Bramhall, England, 8/15/1912
Hillerman, John (actor); Denison, Tex., 12/20(?)/1932
Hilliard, Harriet. *See* Nelson, Harriet
Hindemith, Paul (composer); Hanau, Germany **(1895-1963)**
Hines, Earl "Fatha" (jazz pianist); Duquesne, Pa. **(1905-1983)**
Hines, Gregory (dancer, actor); New York City, 2/14/1946
Hines, Jerome (Jerome Heinz) (basso); Los Angeles, 11/8/1921
Hingle, Pat (actor); Denver, 7/19/1924
Hippocrates (physician); Cos, Greece **(c. 460-c. 377** B.C.**)**
Hirohito (Emperor); Tokyo, **(1901-1989)**
Hiroshige, Ando (pain ter); Edo? (Tokyo) **(1797-1858)**
Hirsch, Judd (actor); New York City, 3/15/1935
Hirschfeld, Al (Albert) (cartoonist); St. Louis, 6/21/1903
Hirschhorn, Joseph Herman (financier, speculator, and art collector); Mitau, Latvia **(1899-1981)**
Hirt, Al (trumpeter); New Orleans, 11/7/1922
Hitchcock, Alfred J. (film director); London **(1899-1980)**
Hitler, Adolf (German dictator); Braunau, Austria **(1889-1945)**
Hitzig, William Maxwell (physician); Austria, 12/15/1904
Hobbes, Thomas (philosopher); Westport, England **(1588-1679)**
Hobson, Laura Z. (Laura K. Zametkin) (novelist); New York City **(1900-1986)**
Hockney, David (artist); Bradford, England, 7/9/1937
Hodges, Eddie (actor); Hattiesburg, Miss., 3/5/1947
Hoffa, James R(iddle) (labor leader); Brazil, Ind. **(1913-75?)**; presumed murdered.
Hoffman, Dustin (film actor and director); Los Angeles, 8/8/1937
Hofmann, Hans (painter); Germany **(1880-1966)**
Hogan, Paul (actor); Lightning Ridge, NSW, Australia, 1941 (?)
Hogarth, William (painter and engraver); London **(1697-1764)**
Hokusai, Katauhika (artist); Yedo, Japan **(1760-1849)**
Holbein, Hans (the Elder) (painter); Augsburg (Germany) **(1465?-1524)**
Holbein, Hans (the Younger) (painter); Augsburg (Germany) **(1497?-1543)**
Holbrook, Hal (actor); Cleveland, 2/17/1925
Holden, William (William Franklin Beedle, Jr.) (actor); O'Fallon, Ill. **(1918-1981)**
Holder, Geoffrey (dancer); Port-of-Spain, Trinidad, 8/1/1930
Holiday, Billie (Eleanora Fagan) (jazz-blues singer); Baltimore **(1915-1959)**
Holliday, Judy (Judith Tuvim) (comedienne); New York City **(1922-1965)**
Holliday, Polly (actress); Jasper, Ala., 7/2/1937
Holliman, Earl (actor); Delhi, La., 9/11/1928
Holloway, Stanley (actor); London **(1890-1982)**
Holloway, Sterling (actor); Cedartown, Ga. **(1905-1992)**
Holm, Celeste (actress); New York City, 4/29/1919
Holmes, Oliver Wendell (jurist); Boston **(1841-1935)**
Holt, Jack (actor); Winchester, Va. **(1888-1951)**
Holt, Tim (actor); Beverly Hills, Calif. **(1918-1973)**
Holtz, Lou (comedian); San Francisco **(1898-1980)**
Home, Lord (Alexander Frederick Douglas-Home) (diplomat); London, 7/2/1903
Homeier, Skip (George Vincent Homeier) (actor); Chicago, 10/5/1930
Homer, Winslow (painter); Boston, Mass. **(1836-1910)**
Homer (Greek poet) **(c.850** B.C.**?)**
Homolka, Oscar (actor); Vienna **(1898-1978)**
Honegger, Arthur (composer); Le Havre, France **(1892-1955)**
Hook, Sidney (philosopher); New York City **(1902-1989)**
Hoover, J. Edgar (FBI director); Washington, D.C. **(1895-1972)**
Hope, Bob (Leslie Townes Hope) (comedian); London, 5/29/1903
Hopkins, Anthony (actor); Port Talbot, Wales, 12/31/1937
Hopkins, Gerald Manley (poet); Stratford, England **(1844-1899)**
Hopkins, Johns (financier); Anne Arundel County, Md. **(1795-1873)**
Hopkins, Miriam (actress); Bainbridge, Ga. **(1902-1972)**
Hopper, Dennis (actor); Dodge City, Kan., 5/17/1936
Hopper, Edward (painter); Nyack, N.Y. **(1882-1967)**
Horace (Quintus Horatius Flaccus) (poet); Venosa (Italy) **(65-8** B.C.**)**
Horne, Lena (singer); Brooklyn, N.Y., 6/30/1917
Horne, Marilyn (mezzo-soprano); Bradford, Pa., 1/16/1934
Horowitz, Vladimir (pianist); Kiev, Russia **(1903-1989)**
Horsley, Lee (actor); Muleshoe, Tex., 5/15/1955
Horton, Edward Everett (comedian); Brooklyn, N.Y. **(1887-1970)**
Hoskins, Bob (actor); Bury St. Edminds, England, 10/26/1942
Houdini, Harry (Ehrich Weiss) (magician); Appleton, Wis. **(1874-1926)**
Houseman, John (Jacques Haussmann) (producer, director, and actor); Bucharest **(1902-1988)**
Housman, A(lfred) E(dward) (poet); Fockburg, England **(1859-1936)**
Houston, Samuel (political leader); Rockbridge County, Va. **(1793-1863)**
Houston, Whitney (singer); Newark, N.J., 8/9/1963
Howard, Ken (actor); El Centro, Calif., 3/28/1944
Howard, Leslie (Leslie Stainer) (actor); London **(1893-1943)**
Howard, Ron (actor, producer, director); Duncan, Okla., 3/1/1954
Howard, Trevor (actor); Kent, England **(1916-1988)**
Howe, Elias (inventor); Spencer, Mass. **(1819-1867)**
Howe, Irving (literary critic); New York City **(1920-1993)**
Howe, Julia Ward (poet and reformer); New York City **(1819-1910)**
Howes, Sally Ann (actress); London, 7/20/1934
Hudson, Henry (English navigator) **(?-1611)**
Hudson, Rock (born Roy Scherer, Jr.; took Roy Fitzgerald as legal name) (actor); Winnetka, Ill. **(1925-1985)**
Hughes, Barnard (actor); Bedford Hills, N.Y., 7/16/15
Hughes, Charles Evans (jurist); Glens Falls, N.Y. **(1862-1948)**
Hughes, Howard (industrialist and film producer); Houston **(1905-1976)**
Hughes, Langston (poet); Joplin, Mo. **(1902-1967)**
Hugo, Victor Marie (author); Besançon, France **(1802-1885)**
Hulce, Tom (actor); Detroit, Mich., 12/6/1953
Hull, Henry (actor); Louisville, Ky. **(1890-1977)**
Hume, David (philosopher); Edinburgh, Scotland **(1711-1776)**
Humperdinck, Engelbert (Arnold Dorsey) (singer); Madras, India, 5/2/1936
Humperdinck, Engelbert (composer); Siegburg (Germany) **(1854-1921)**
Hunt, H. L. (industrialist); nr. Vandalia, Ill. **(1889-1974)**

Hunt, Marsha (actress); Chicago, 10/17/1917
Hunter, Kim (Janet Cole) (actress); Detroit, 11/12/1922
Hunter, Tab (Arthur Andrew Gelien) (actor); New York City, 7/11/1931
Huntley, Chet (TV newscaster); Cardwell, Mont. **(1911-1974)**
Hurok, Sol (Solomon) (impresario); Pogar, Russia **(1884-1974)**
Hurst, Fannie (novelist); Hamilton, Ohio **(1889-1968)**
Hurt, John (actor); Shirebrook, England, 1/22/1940
Hurt, William (actor); Washington, D.C., 3/20/1950
Hus, Jan (Bohemian religious reformer); Husinetz, nr. Budweis (Czechoslovakia) **(c.1369-1415)**
Husing, Ted (sportscaster); New York City **(1901-1962)**
Hussein I (King); Jordan, 11/14/1935
Hussey, Ruth (Ruth Carol O'Rourke) (actress); Providence, R.I., 10/30/1914
Huston, John (film director and writer); Nevada, Mo. **(1906-1987)**
Huston, Walter (Walter Houghston) (actor); Toronto **(1884-1950)**
Hutchins, Robert M. (educator); Brooklyn, N.Y. **(1899-1977)**
Hutton, Barbara (Woolworth heiress); New York City **(1912-1979)**
Hutton, Betty (Betty Thornburg) (actress); Battle Creek, Mich., 2/26/1921
Hutton, Lauren (actress, model); Charleston, S.C., 11/17/1943
Hutton, Timothy (actor); Los Angeles, 8/16/1960
Huxley, Aldous (au thor); Godalming, England **(1894-1963)**
Huxley, Sir Julian S. (biologist and author); London **(1887-1975)**
Huxley, Thomas Henry (biologist); Ealing, England **(1825-1895)**

I

Ian, Janis (singer); New York City, 5/7/1951
Ibsen, Henrik (dramatist); Skien, Norway **(1828-1906)**
Inge, William (playwright); Independence, Kan. **(1913-1973)**
Ingres, Jean Auguste Dominique (painter); Montauban, France **(1780-1867)**
Inness, George (painter); nr. Newburgh, N.Y. **(1825-1894)**
Ionesco, Eugene (playwright); Slatina, Romania, 11/26/1912
Ireland, Jill (actress); London, **(1936-1990)**
Ireland, John (actor); Vancouver, B.C., Canada **(1914-1992)**
Irons, Jeremy (actor); Cowes, Isle of Wight, England, 9/19/1948
Irving, Amy (actress); Palo Alto, Calif., 9/10/1953
Irving, John (Winslow) (writer), Exeter, N.H., 3/2/1942
Irving, Washington (author); New York City **(1783-1859)**
Isherwood, Christopher (novelist and playwright); nr. Dilsey and High Lane, England **(1904-1986)**
Iturbi, José (concert pianist); Valencia, Spain **(1895-1980)**
Ives, Burl (Icle Ivanhoe) (singer); Hunt, Ill., 6/14/1909
Ives, Charles E(dward) (composer); Danbury, Conn. **(1874-1954)**

J

Jackson, Anne (actress); Millvale, Pa., 9/3/1926
Jackson, Glenda (actress); Hoylake, England, 1937(?)
Jackson, Gordon (actor); Glasgow, Scotland, **(1923-1990)**
Jackson, Rev. Jesse (civil rights leader); Greenville, S.C., 10/8/1941
Jackson, Kate (actress); Birmingham, Ala., 10/29/1949
Jackson, Mahalia (gospel singer); New Orleans **(1911-1972)**
Jackson, Michael (singer); Gary, Ind., 8/29/1958
Jackson, Thomas Jonathan ("Stonewall") (general); Clarksburg, Va. (now W. Va.) **(1824-1863)**
Jacobi, Derek (actor); Leytonstone, England, 10/22/1938
Jacobi, Lou (actor); Toronto, 12/26/1913
Jacobs, Jane (urbanologist); Scranton, Pa., 5/1/1916
Jaffe, Sam (actor); New York City **(1891-1984)**
Jagger, Dean (actor); Lima, Ohio **(1903–1991)**
Jagger, Mick (Michael Phillip) (singer); Dartford, England, 7/26/1943
James, Harry (trumpeter); Albany, Ga. **(1916-1983)**
James, Henry (novelist); New York City **(1843-1916)**
James, Jesse Woodson (outlaw); Clay County, Mo. **(1847-1882)**
James, William (psychologist); New York City **(1842-1910)**
Jameson, (Margaret) Storm (novelist); Whitby, England **(1897-1986)**
Janis, Byron (pianist); McKeesport, Pa., 3/24/1928
Janis, Conrad (actor, musician); New York City, 2/11/1928
Jannings, Emil (actor); Brooklyn, N.Y. **(1886-1950)**
Janssen, David (David Meyer) (actor); Naponee, Neb. **(1930-1980)**
Jay, John (statesman and jurist); New York City **(1745-1829)**
Jeanmaire, Renée (dancer); Paris, 4/29/1924
Jenner, Edward (physician); Berkeley, England **(1749-1823)**
Jennings, Waylon (singer); Littlefield, Tex., 1937
Jessel, George (entertainer); New York City **(1898-1981)**
Jessup, Philip C. (diplomat); New York City **(1897-1986)**
Jiang Qing (political leader); Chucheng, China **(1913(?)-1991)**
Jillian, Ann (actress); Cambridge, Mass., 1/29/1951
Joan of Arc (Jeanne d'Arc) (saint and patriot); Domremy-la-Pucelle, France **(1412-1431)**
Joel, Billy (singer); New York City, 5/9/1949
Joffrey, Robert (Abdullah Jaffa Bey Khan) (choreographer); Seattle **(1930-1988)**
John, Elton (Reginald Kenneth Dwight) (singer and pianist); Pinner, England, 3/25/1947
Johns, Glynis (actress); Pretoria, South Africa, 10/5/1923
Johns, Jasper (painter and sculptor); Augusta, Ga., 5/15/1930
Johnson, Don (actor); Flatt Creek, Mo., 12/15/1949
Johnson, James Weldon (author and educator); Jacksonville, Fla. **(1871-1938)**
Johnson, Philip Cortalyou (architect); Cleveland, Ohio, 7/8/1906
Johnson, Samuel (lexicographer and author); Lichfield, England **(1709-1784)**
Johnson, Van (actor); Newport, R.I., 8/20/1916
Joliot-Curie, Frédéric (physicist); Paris **(1900-1958)**
Joliot-Curie, Irène (Irène Curie) (physicist); France **(1897-1956)**
Jolliet (or Joliet), Louis (explorer); Beaupré, Canada **(1645-1700)**
Jolson, Al (Asa Yoelson) (actor and singer); St. Petersburg, Russia **(1886-1950)**
Jones, Allan (singer, actor); Old Forge, Pa. **(1908-1992)**
Jones, Buck (Charles Frederick Gebhart) (actor); Vincennes, Ind. **(1889-1942)**
Jones, Carolyn (singer and actress); Amarillo, Tex., **(1933-1983)**
Jones, Dean (actor); Morgan County, Ala., 1/25/1935
Jones, George (singer); Saratoga, Tex., 9/12/1931
Jones, Inigo (architect); London **(1573-1652)**
Jones, James (novelist); Robinson, Ill. **(1921-1977)**
Jones, James Earl (actor); Arkabutla, Miss., 1/17/1931
Jones, Jennifer (Phyllis Isley) (actress); Tulsa, Okla., 3/2/1919
Jones, John Paul (John Paul) (naval officer); Scotland **(1747-1792)**
Jones, Quincy (composer); Chicago, 3/14/1933
Jones, Shirley (singer and actress); Smithtown, Pa., 3/31/1934
Jones, Spike (host, orchestra leader); Long Beach, Calif. **(1911-1965)**
Jones, Tom (Thomas Jones Woodward) (singer); Pontypridd, Wales, 6/7/1940
Jong, Erica (writer); New York City, 3/26/1942
Jonson, Ben (Benjamin) (poet and dramatist); Westminster, England **(1572-1637)**
Joplin, Janis (singer); Port Arthur, Tex. **(1943-1970)**
Joplin, Scott (ragtime pianist and composer); Texarkansas, Tex. **(1868-1917)**
Jordan, James Edward (radio actor-Fibber McGee); Peoria, Ill. **(1896-1988)**
Jordan, Marian (radio actress-Molly of Fibber McGee and Molly); Peoria, Ill. **(1898-1961)**
Jory, Victor (actor); Dawson City, Yukon, Canada **(1902-1982)**
Josquin des Prés (usually known as Josquin) (composer); Conde-sur-L'Escaut?, Hainaut (France or Belgium) **(c.1445-1521)**
Jourdan, Louis (Louis Gendre) (actor); Marseilles, France, 6/19/1920
Joyce, James (novelist); Dublin **(1882-1941)**
Juárez, Benito Pablo (statesman); Guelatao, Mexico **(1806-1872)**
Julia, Raul (Raúl Rafael Carlos Julia y Arcelay) (actor); San Juan, Puerto Rico, 3/9/1940
Juliana (Queen); The Hague, Netherlands, 4/30/1909
Jung, Carl Gustav (psychoanalyst); Basel, Switzerland **(1875-1961)**
Jurado, Katy (actress); Guadalajara, Mexico, 1927

K

Kabalevsky, Dmitri (composer); St. Petersburg, Russia **(1904-1987)**
Kafka, Franz (author); Prague **(1883-1924)**
Kádár, János (Communist Party leader); Hungary **(1912-1989)**
Kahn, Gus (songwriter); Coblenz, Germany **(1886-1941)**
Kahn, Louis I. (architect); Oesel Island, Estonia **(1901-1974)**
Kahn, Madeline (actress); Boston, 9/29/1942
Kaminska, Ida (actress); Odessa, Russia **(1899-1980)**
Kandinsky, Wassily (painter); Moscow **(1866-1944)**
Kane, Helen (actress, singer); Bronx, N.Y. **(1903-1966)**
Kanin, Garson (playwright); Rochester, N.Y., 11/24/1912
Kant, Immanuel (philosopher); Königsberg (Kaliningrad, U.S.S.R.) **(1724-1804)**
Kantor, MacKinlay (novelist); Webster City, Iowa **(1904-1977)**
Kaplan, Gabe (Gabriel) (actor); Brooklyn, N.Y., 3/31/1945
Karloff, Boris (William Henry Pratt) (actor); London **(1887-1969)**
Kasem, Casey (disc jockey); Detroit, Mich., 4/27/1932
Katt, William (actor); Los Angeles, 2/16/1950
Kaufman, George S. (playwright); Pittsburgh **(1889-1961)**
Kavner, Julie (actress); Los Angeles, 9/7/1951
Kaye, Danny (David Daniel Kominski) (comedian); Brooklyn, N.Y. **(1913-1987)**
Kaye, Sammy (band leader); Cleveland **(1910-1987)**
Kazan, Elia (director); Constantinople, Turkey, 9/7/1909
Kazan, Lainie (Levine) (singer); New York City, 5/15/1940
Keach, Stacy (actor); Savannah, Ga., 6/2/1941

Kean, Edmund (actor); London **(1787-1833)**
Keaton, Buster (Joseph Frank Keaton) (comedian); Piqua, Kan. **(1896-1966)**
Keaton, Diane (actress); Los Angeles, 1/5/1946
Keats, John (poet); London **(1795-1821)**
Keel, Howard (singer and actor); Gillespie, Ill., 4/13/1919
Keeler, Ruby (Lehy Keeler) (actress and dancer); Halifax, Nova Scotia, Canada **(1910-1993)**
Kefauver, Estes (legislator); Madisonville, Tenn. **(1903-1963)**
Keith, Brian (actor); Bayonne, N.J., 11/14/1921
Keller, Helen Adams (author and educator); Tuscumbia, Ala. **(1880-1968)**
Kellerman, Sally (actress); Long Beach, Calif., 6/2/1938
Kelley, DeForest (actor); Atlanta, Ga., 1/20/1920
Kelly, Emmett (clown); Sedan, Kan., **(1898-1979)**
Kelly, Gene (dancer and actor); Pittsburgh, 8/23/1912
Kelly, Grace. *See* Grace, Princess of Monaco.
Kelly, Nancy (actress); Lowell, Mass., 3/25/1921
Kelly, Patsy (actress and comedienne); Brooklyn, N.Y. **(1910-1981)**
Kelly, Walt (cartoonist); Philadelphia **(1913-1973)**
Kemal Ataturk (Mustafa Kemal) (Turkish soldier and statesman); Salonika (Greece) **(1881-1938)**
Kemble, Fanny (F rances Anne) (actress); London **(1809-1893)**
Kempis, Thomas à (mystic); Kempis, Prussia (Germany) **(1380-1471)**
Kennan, George F. (diplomat); Milwaukee, 2/16/1904
Kennedy, Arthur (actor); Worcester, Mass. **(1914-1990)**
Kennedy, George (actor); New York City, 2/18/1925
Kennedy, Jacqueline. *See* Onassis, Jacqueline
Kennedy, Joseph P. (financier); Boston **(1888-1969)**
Kennedy, Robert Francis (legislator); Brookline, Mass. **(1925-1968)**
Kennedy, Rose Fitzgerald (President's mother); Boston, 7/22/1890
Kent, Allegra (ballerina); Santa Monica, Calif., 8/11/1938
Kent, Rockwell (painter); Tarrytown Heights, N.Y. **(1882-1971)**
Kenton, Stan (Stanley Newcomb) (jazz musician); Wichita, Kan. **(1912-1979)**
Kepler, Johannes (astronomer); Weil (Germany) **(1571-1630)**
Kercheval, Ken (actor); Wolcottville, Ind., 7/15/1935
Kerensky, Alexander Fedorovich (statesman); Simbirks, Russia **(1881-1970)**
Kern, Jerome David (composer); New York City **(1885-1945)**
Kerns, Joanna (actress); San Francisco, 2/12/1953
Kerr, Deborah (actress); Helensburgh, Scotland, 9/30/1921
Kettering, Charles F. (engineer and inventor); nr. Loudonville, Ohio **(1876-1958)**
Key, Francis Scott (lawyer and author of national anthem); Frederick (now Carroll) County, Md. **(1779-1843)**
Keyes, Frances Parkinson (novelist); Charlottesville, Va. **(1885-1970)**
Keynes (1st Baron of Tilton) (John Maynard Keynes) (economist); Cambridge, England **(1883-1946)**
Khachaturian, Aram (composer); Tiflis, Russia **(1903-1978)**
Khrushchev, Nikita S. (Soviet leader); Kalinovka, nr. Kursk, Ukraine **(1894-1971)**
Kibbee, Guy (actor); El Paso **(1886-1956)**
Kidd, Michael (choreographer); Brooklyn, N.Y., 1917
Kidd, William (called Captain Kidd) (pirate); Greenock, Scotland **(1645?-1701)**
Kidder, Margot (actress); Yellowknife, N.W.T., Canada, 10/17/1948
Kiepura, Jan (tenor); Sosnowiec, Poland **(1904(?)-1966)**
Kieran, John (writer); New York City **(1892-1981)**
Kierkegaard, Sören Aalys (philosopher); Copenhagen **(1813-1855)**
Kiesinger, Kurt Georg (diplomat); Ebingen, Germany **(1904-1988)**
Kiley, Richard (actor and singer); Chicago, 3/31/1922
Kilmer, Alfred Joyce (poet); New Brunswick, N.J. **(1886-1918)**
King, Alan (Irwin Alan Kniberg) (entertainer); Brooklyn, N.Y., 12/26/1927
King, B.B. (Riley King) (guitarist); Itta Bena, Miss., 9/16/1925
King, Carole (singer and songwriter); Brooklyn, N.Y., 2/9/1941
King, Coretta Scott (civil rights leader); Marion, Ala., 4/27/1927
King, Dennis (actor, singer); Coventry, England **(1897-1971)**
King, Martin Luther, Jr. (civil rights leader); Atlanta **(1929-1968)**
King, Pee Wee (Frank) (singer); Abrams, Wis., 2/18/1914
King, Stephen (writer); Portland, Maine, 9/21/1947
Kingsley, Ben (Krishna Bhanji) (actor); Snainton, England, 12/31/1943
Kingsley, Sidney (Sidney Kirschner) (playwright); New York City, 10/18/1906
Kinski, Nastassja (Nastassja Nakszynski) (actress); West Berlin, 1/24/1961
Kipling, Rudyard (author); Bombay **(1865-1936)**
Kipnis, Alexander (basso); Ukraine, **(1891-1978)**
Kirby, George (comedian); Chicago, 1923(?)
Kirk, Grayson (educator); Jeffersonville, Ohio, 10/12/1903
Kirk, Lisa (actress and singer); Charleroi, Pa. **(1925–1990)**
Kirk, Phyllis (actress); Plainfield, N.J., 9/18/1930
Kirkland, Gelsey (ballerina); Bethlehem, Pa., 12/29/1952
Kirkpatrick, Jeane Jordan (educator-public affairs); Duncan, Okla., 11/19/1926
Kirkpatrick, Ralph (harpsichordist); Leominster, Mass. **(1911-1984)**
Kirkwood, James (actor); Grand Rapids, Mich. **(1883-1963)**
Kirsten, Dorothy (soprano); Montclair, N.J. **(1910-1992)**
Kissinger, Henry (Heinz Alfred Kissinger) (ex-Secretary of State); Furth, Germany, 5/27/1923
Kitt, Eartha (singer); North, S.C., 1/26/1928
Klee, Paul (painter); Münchenbuchsee, nr. Bern, Switzerland **(1879-1940)**
Klein, Calvin (fashion designer); Bronx, N.Y., 11/19/1942
Klein, Robert (comedian); New York City, 2/8/1942
Kline, Kevin (actor); St. Louis, Mo., 10/24/1947
Kleist, Henrich von (poet); Frankfurt an der Oder (East Germany) **(1777-1811)**
Klemperer, Otto (conductor); Breslau (Poland) **(1885-1973)**
Klemperer, Werner (actor); Cologne, Germany, 3/22/1920
Klugman, Jack (actor); Philadelphia, 4/27/1922
Knievel, Evel (Robert Craig) (daredevil motorcyclist); Butte, Mont., 10/17/1938
Knight, Gladys (singer); Atlanta, 5/28/1944
Knight, Ted (Tadeus Wladyslaw Konopka) (actor); Terryville, Conn., **(1923-1986)**
Knight, John S. (publisher); Bluefield, W. Va. **(1894-1981)**
Knopf, Alfred A. (publisher); New York City, **(1892-1984)**
Knotts, Don (actor); Morgantown, W.Va., 7/21/1924
Knox, John (religious reformer); Haddington, East Lothian, Scotland **(1505-1572)**
Koch, Robert (physician); Klausthal (Germany) **(1843-1910)**
Koestler, Arthur (novelist); Budapest **(1905-1983)**
Kokoschka, Oskar (painter); Póchlarn Austria **(1886-1980)**
Kooper, Al (singer and pianist); Brooklyn, N.Y., 2/5/1944
Kopell, Bernie (actor); New York City, 6/21/1933
Koppel, Ted (broadcast journalist); Lancashire, England, 2/8/1940
Korman, Harvey (actor); Chicago, 2/15/1927
Kosciusko, Thaddeus (Tadeusz Andrzej Bonawentura Kosciuszko) (military officer); Grand Duchy of Lithuania **(1746-1817)**
Kossuth, Lajos (patriot); Monok, Hungary **(1802-1894)**
Kostelanetz, André (orchestra conductor); St. Petersburg, Russia **(1901-1980)**
Kosygin, Aleksei N. (Premier); St. Petersburg, Russia **(1904-1980)**
Koussevitzky, Serge (Sergei) Alexandrovitch (orchestra conductor); Vishni Volochek, Tver, Russia **(1874-1951)**
Kovacs, Ernie (comedian); Trenton, N.J. **(1919-1962)**
Kramer, Stanley E. (film producer and director); New York City, 9/29/1913
Kràus, Lili (pianist); Budapest **(1905-1986)**
Kreisler, Fritz (violinist and composer); Vienna **(1875-1962)**
Kresge, S. S. (merchant); Bald Mount, Pa. **(1867-1966)**
Krips, Josef (orchestra conductor); Vienna **(1902-1974)**
Kristofferson, Kris (singer); Brownsville, Tex., 6/22/1936
Kruger, Otto (actor); Toledo, Ohio **(1885-1974)**
Krupa, Gene (drummer); Chicago **(1909-1973)**
Krupp, Alfred (munitions magnate); Essen, Germany **(1812-1887)**
Kubelik, Rafael (conductor); Bychory (Czechoslovakia), 6/29/1914
Kublai Khan (Mongol conqueror) **(1216-1294)**
Kubrick, Stanley (producer and director); New York City, 7/26/1928
Kuralt, Charles (TV journalist); Wilmington, N.C., 9/10/1934
Kurosawa, Akira (film director); Tokyo, 3/23/1910
Kurtz, Efrem (conductor); St. Petersburg, Russia, 11/7/1900
Kurtz, Swoosie (actress); Omaha, Neb., 9/6/1944
Ky, Nguyen Cao (ex-Vice President of South Vietnam); Son Tay (Vietnam), 9/8/1930

L

LaBelle, Patti (singer, actress); Philadelphia, Pa., 5/24/1944
Ladd, Alan (actor); Hot Springs, Ark. **(1913-1964)**
Ladd, Cheryl (Cheryl Stoppelmoor) (actress); Huron, S.D., 7/12/1951
Ladd, Diane (actress); Meridian, Miss., 11/29/1932
Lafayette, Marquis de (Marie Joseph Paul Yves Roch Gilbert du Motier) (military officer); Auvergne, France **(1757-1834)**
Lafitte, Jean (pirate); Bayonne? France **(1780-1826)**
La Follette, Robert Marin (politician); Primrose, Wis. **(1855-1925)**
La Guardia, Fiorello Henry (Mayor of New York); New York City **(1882-1947)**
Lahr, Bert (Irving Lahrheim) (comedian); New York City **(1895-1967)**
Laine, Cleo (Clementina Dinah Campbell) (singer, actress); Southall, England, 10/28/1927
Laine, Frankie (Frank Paul LoVecchio) (singer); Chicago, 3/30/1913
Laird, Melvin (ex-Secretary of Defense); Omaha, Neb., 9/1/1922
Lake, Veronica (actress); Brooklyn, N.Y. **(1919-1973)**
Lamarck, Chevalier de (Jean Baptiste Pierre Antoine de Monet) (naturalist); Bazantin, France **(1744-1829)**
Lamarr, Hedy (Hedwig Kiesler) (actress); Vienna, 1915

Lamas, Fernando (actor); Buenos Aires, **(1915-1982)**
Lamas, Lorenzo (actor); Los Angeles, 1/20/1958
Lamb, Charles (Elia) (essayist); London **(1775-1834)**
L'Amour, Louis (author); Jamestown, N.D. **(1908-1988)**
Lamour, Dorothy (Dorothy Kaumeyer) (actress); New Orleans, 10/10/1914
Lancaster, Burt (actor); New York City, 11/2/1913
Lanchester, Elsa (Elsa Sullivan) (actress); London **(1902-1986)**
Landau, Martin (actor); Brooklyn, N.Y., 1934
Landers, Ann (columnist); Sioux City, Iowa, 7/4/1918
Landon, Michael (Eugene Maurice Orowitz) (actor); Forest Hills, Queens, N.Y. **(1936–1991)**
Lane, Abbe (singer); New York City, 1933
Lang, Fritz (film director); Vienna **(1890-1976)**
Lang, Paul Henry (music critic); Budapest **(1901-1991)**
Lange, Hope (actress); Redding Ridge, Conn., 11/28/1933
Lange, Jessica (actress); Cloquet, Minn., 4/20/1949
Langella, Frank (actor); Bayonne, N.J., 1/1/1940
Langford, Frances (singer); Lakeland, Fla., 4/4/1913
Langmuir, Irving (chemist); Brooklyn, N.Y. **(1881-1957)**
Langtry, Lillie (Emily Le Breton) (actress); Island of Jersey **(1852-1929)**
Lansbury, Angela (actress); London, 10/16/1925
Lansing, Robert (Robert Howell Brown) (actor); San Diego, Calif., 6/5/1928
Lanza, Mario (Alfred Arnold Cocozza) (singer and actor); Philadelphia **(1921-1959)**
Lao-Tzu (or Lao-Tse) (Li Erh) (philosopher); Honan Province, China **(c. 604-531** B.C.)
Lardner, Ring (Ringgold Wilmar Lardner) (story writer); Niles, Mich. **(1885-1933)**
La Rouchefoucauld, Francois duc de (author); Paris **(1613-1680)**
Larroquette, John (actor); New Orleans, 11/25/1947
La Salle, Sieur de (Robert Cavelier) (explorer); Rouen, France **(1643-1687)**
Lasser, Louise (actress); New York City, 1940(?)
Lauder, Sir Harry (Harry MacLennan) (singer); Portobello, Scotland **(1870-1950)**
Laughton, Charles (actor); Scarborough, England **(1899-1962)**
Lauper, Cyndi (singer); New York City, 6/20/1953
Laurel, Stan (Arthur Jefferson) (comedian); Ulverston, England **(1890-1965)**
Laurents, Arthur (playwright); New York City, 7/14/1918
Laurie, Piper (Rosetta Jacobs) (actress); Detroit, 1/22/1932
Lavin, Linda (actress); Portland, Me., 10/15/1937
Lavoisier, Antoine-Laurent (chemist); Paris **(1743-1794)**
Lawford, Peter (actor); London **(1923-1984)**
Lawrence, David Herbert (novelist); Nottingham, England **(1885-1930)**
Lawrence, Gertrude (Gertrud Klasen) (actress); London **(1900-1952)**
Lawrence, Marjorie (singer); Deans Marsh, Australia **(1908-1979)**
Lawrence, Steve (Sidney Leibowitz) (singer); Brooklyn, N.Y., 7/8/1935
Lawrence of Arabia (Thomas Edward Lawrence, later changed to Shaw) (author and soldier); Tremadoc, Wales **(1888-1935)**
Lawrence, Vicki (actress); Inglewood, Calif., 3/26/1949
Leach, Robin (host, producer); London, c.1941
Leachman, Cloris (actress); Des Moines, Iowa, 4/30/1926(?)
Lean, David (film director); Croydon, En gland **(1908–1991)**
Lear, Edward (nonsense poet); London **(1812-1888)**
Lear, Evelyn (Shulman) (soprano); Brooklyn, N.Y., 1/8/1929(?)
Lear, Norman (TV producer); New Haven, Conn., 7/27/1922
Learned, Michael (actress); Washington, D.C., 4/9/1939
le Carré, John (David John Moore Cornwell) (novelist); Poole, England, 10/19/1931
Le Corbusier (Charles Edouard Jeanneret) (architect); La Chaux-de-Fonds, Switzerland **(1887-1965)**
Lederer, Francis (actor); Prague, 11/6/1906
Lee, Christopher (actor); London, 5/27/1922
Lee, Gypsy Rose (Rose Louise Hovick) (entertainer); Seattle **(1914-1970)**
Lee, Manfred B. (novelist, pseudonym Ellery Queen); Brooklyn, N.Y. **(1905-1971)**
Lee, Michele (actress, singer); Los Angeles, 6/24/1942
Lee, Peggy (Norma Engstrom) (singer); Jamestown, N.D., 5/26/1920
Lee, Robert Edward (Confederate general); Stratford Estate, Va. **(1807-1870)**
Leeuwenhoek, Anton van (zoologist); Delft (Netherlands) **(1632-1723)**
Le Gallienne, Eva (actress); London **(1899–1991)**
Lehár Franz (composer); Komárom (Czechoslovakia) **(1870-1948)**
Lehman, Herbert H. (Governor and Senator); New York City **(1878-1963)**
Lehmann, Lotte (soprano); Perleberg (Germany) **(1888-1976)**
Leibniz, Gottfried W. von (scientist); Leipzig (East Germany) **(1646-1716)**
Leigh, Janet (Jeanetta Morrison) (actress); Merced, Calif., 7/6/1927
Leigh, Vivien (Vivien Mary Hartley) (actress); Darjeeling, India **(1913-1967)**
Leighton, Margaret (actress); nr. Birmingham, England **(1922-1976)**
Leinsdorf, Erich (conductor); Vienna, 2/4/1912
Lemmon, Jack (actor); Boston, 2/8/1925
Lenin, Vladimir (Vladimir Ilich Ulyanov) (Soviet leader); Simbirsk, Russia **(1870-1924)**
Lennon, Dianne (singer); Los Angeles, 12/1/1939
Lennon, Janet (singer); Culver City, Calif., 11/15/1946
Lennon, John (singer and songwriter); Liverpool, England **(1940-1980)**
Lennon, Kathy (singer); Santa Monica, Calif., 8/22/1942
Lennon, Peggy (singer); Los Angeles, 4/8/1941
Leno, Jay (comedian, T.V. host); New Rochelle, N.Y., 4/28/1950
Lenya, Lotte (Karoline Blamauer) (singer and actress); Vienna, Austria **(1898-1981)**
Leonard, Sheldon (act or and director); New York City, 2/22/1907
Lerner, Alan Jay (lyricist); New York City **(1918-1986)**
Lerner, Max (columnist); Minsk, Russia **(1902-1992)**
Le Roy, Mervyn (film producer); San Francisco **(1900-1987)**
Leslie, Joan (actress); Detroit, 1/26/1925
Lessing, Doris (novelist); Kermanshah, Iran, 10/22/1919
Lester, Mark (actor); Richmond, England, 1958
Letterman, David (TV personality); Indianapolis, 1947
Levant, Oscar (pianist); Pittsburgh **(1906-1972)**
Levene, Sam (actor); New York City **(1905-1980)**
Levenson, Sam (humorist); New York City **(1911-1980)**
Levi, Carlo (novelist); Turin, Italy **(1902-1975)**
Levine, James (music director, Metropolitan Opera); Cincinnati, 6/23/1943
Levine, Joseph E. (film producer); Boston **(1905-1987)**
Lewis, Jerry (Joseph Levitch) (comedian and film director); Newark, N.J., 3/16/1926
Lewis, Jerry Lee (singer); Ferriday, La., 9/29/1935
Lewis, John Llewellyn (labor leader); Lucas, Iowa **(1880-1969)**
Lewis, Meriwether (explorer); Albemarle Co., Va. **(1774-1809)**
Lewis, Shari (Shari Hurwitz) (puppeteer); New York City, 1/17/1934
Lewis, Sinclair (novelist); Sauk Centre, Minn. **(1885-1951)**
Lewis, Ted (entertainer); Circleville, Ohio **(1891-1971)**
Ley, Willy (science writer); Berlin **(1906-1969)**
Liberace (Wladziu Liberace) (pianist); West Allis, Wis. **(1919-1987)**
Lichtenstein, Roy (painter); New York City, 10/27/1923
Lie, Trygve Halvdan (first U.N. Secretary-General); Oslo **(1896-1968)**
Light, Judith (actress); Trenton, N.J., 2/9/1949
Lightfoot, Gordon (singer and songwriter); Orillia, Ontario, Canada, 11/17/1938
Lillie, Beatrice (Lady Peel) (actress and comedienne); Toronto **(1898-1989)**
Lin Yutang (author); Changchow, China **(1895-1976)**
Lind, Jenny (Johanna Maria Lind) (soprano); Stockholm **(1820-1887)**
Lindbergh, Anne Morrow (author); Englewood, N.J., 6/22/1906
Lindbergh, Charles A. (aviator); Detroit **(1902-1974)**
Linden, Hal (Harold Lipshitz) (actor); New York City, 3/20/1931
Lindfors, Viveca (actress); Uppsala, Sweden, 12/29/1920
Lindsay, Howard (playwright); Waterford, N.Y. **(1889- 1968)**
Lindsay, John Vliet (ex-Mayor of New York City); New York City, 11/24/1921
Lindstrom, Pia (TV newscaster); Stockholm, 11/?/1938
Linkletter, Art (radio-TV personality); Moose Jaw, Saskatchewan, Canada, 7/17/1912
Linnaeus, Carolus (Carl von Linné (botanist); Råshult, Sweden **(1707-1778)**
Lipchitz, Jacques (sculptor); Druskieniki, Latvia **(1891-1973)**
Lippi, Fra Filippo (painter); Florence **(1406-1469)**
Lippmann, Walter (columnist, author, and political analyst); New York City **(1889-1974)**
Lister, (1st Baron of Lyme Regis) (Joseph Lister) (surgeon); Upton, England **(1827-1912)**
Liszt, Franz (composer and pianist); Raiding (Hungary) **(1811-1886)**
Lithgow, John (actor); Rochester, N.Y., 6/6/1945
Little, Cleavon (actor and comedian); Chickasha, Okla. **(1939-1992)**
Little, Rich (impressionist); Ottawa, 11/26/1938
Livesey, Roger (actor); Barry, Wales **(1906-1976)**
Livingstone, David (missionary and explorer); Lanarkshire, Scotland **(1813-1873)**
Livingstone, Mary (Sadye Marks) (comedienne); Seattle **(1909-1983)**
Llewellyn, Richard (novelist); St. David's, Wales **(1906-1983)**
Lloyd, Harold (comedian); Burchard, Neb. **(1894-1971)**
Lloyd George, David (Earl of Dwyfor) (statesman); Manchester, England **(1863-1945)**
Lloyd Webber, Andrew (composer); London, England, 3/22/1948
Locke, John (philosopher); Somersetshire, England **(1632-1704)**
Lockhart, Gene (actor); London, Ontario, Canada **(1891-1957)**
Lockhart, June (actress); New York City, 6/25/1925
Lockwood, Margaret (actress); Karachi (Pakistan) **(1916-1990)**

Lodge, Henry Cabot (legislator); Boston **(1850-1924)**
Lodge, Henry Cabot, Jr. (diplomat); Nahant, Mass. **(1902-1985)**
Loesser, Frank (composer); New York City **(1910-1969)**
Loewe, Frederick (composer); Vienna **(1901-1988)**
Logan, Joshua (director and producer); Texarkana, Tex. **(1908-1988)**
Lollobrigida, Gina (actress); Subiaco, Italy, 1928
Lombard, Carole (Carol Jane Peters) (actress); Ft. Wayne, Ind. **(1908-1942)**
Lombardo, Guy (band leader); London, Ontario, Canada **(1902-1977)**
London, George (baritone); Montreal **(1920-1985)**
London, Jack (John Griffith London) (novelist); San Francisco **(1876-1916)**
London, Julie (Julie Peck) (singer and actress); Santa Rosa, Calif., 9/26/1926
Long, Huey Pierce (politician); Winnfield, La. **(1893-1935)**
Long, Shelly (actress); Fort Wayne, Ind., 8/23/1949
Longfellow, Henry Wadsworth (poet); Portland, Me. **(1807-1882)**
Longworth, Alice Roosevelt (social figure); New York City **(1884-1980)**
Loos, Anita (novelist); Sissons, Calif., **(1888-1981)**
Lopez, Trini (singer); Dallas, Tex., 5/15/1937
Lopez, Vincent (band leader); Brooklyn, N.Y. **(1895-1975)**
Lord, Jack (John Joseph Ryan) (actor); New York City, 12/30/1930
Loren, Sophia (Sofia Scicolone) (actress); Rome, 9/20/1934
Lorre, Peter (Laszlo Löewenstein) (actor); Rosenberg (Czechoslovakia) **(1904-1964)**
Loudon. Dorothy (actress, singer); Boston, 9/17/1933
Louise, Tina (actress); New York City, 2/11/1937
Lovecraft, Howard Phillips (author); Providence, R.I., **(1890-1937)**
Lowe, Edmund (actor); San Jose, Calif. **(1892-1971)**
Lowell, Amy (poet); Brookline, Mass. **(1874-1925)**
Lowell, James Russell (poet); Cambridge, Mass. **(1819-1891)**
Lowell, Robert (poet); Boston **(1917-1977)**
Loy, Myrna (Myrna Williams) (actress); nr. Helena, Mont., 8/2/1905
Loyola, St. Ignatius of (Iñigo de Oñez y Loyola) (founder of Jesuits); Gúipuzcoa Province, Spain **(1491-1556)**
Lubitsch, Ernst (film director); Berlin **(1892-1947)**
Lucas, George (film director); Modesto, Calif., 5/14/1944
Lucci, Susan (actress); Scarsdale, N.Y., 12/23/1948
Luce, Clare Boothe (playwright and former Ambassador); New York City **(1903-1987)**
Luce, Henry Robinson (editor and publisher); Tengchow, China **(1898-1967)**
Ludlum, Robert (author); New York City, 5/25/1927
Lugosi, Bela (Bela Lugosi Blasko) (actor); Logos, Hungary **(1888-1956)**
Lukas, Paul (actor); Budapest **(1895-1971)**
Lully, Jean Baptiste (French composer); Florence **(1639-1687)**
Lumet, Sidney (film and TV director); Philadelphia, 6/25/1924
Lunden, Joan (TV host); Fair Oaks, Calif., 9/19/1950
Lunt, Alfred (actor); Milwaukee **(1892-1977)**
Lupino, Ida (actress and director); London, 2/4/1918
LuPone, Patti (actress; singer); Northport, N.Y., 4/21/1949
Luther, Martin (religious reformer); Eisleben (East Germany) **(1483-1546)**
Lynde, Paul (comedian); Mt. Vernon, Ohio **(1926-1982)**
Lynley, Carol (actress); New York City, 2/13/1942
Lynn, Jeffrey (actor); Auburn, Mass., 1909
Lynn, Loretta (singer); Butcher's Hollow, Ky., 4/14/1935

M

Ma, Yo-Yo (cellist); Paris, 10/7/1955
Maazel, Lorin (conductor); Neuilly, France, 3/5/1930
MacArthur, Charles (playwright); Scranton, Pa. **(1895-1956)**
MacArthur, Douglas (five-star general); Little Rock Barracks, Ark. **(1880-1964)**
MacArthur, James (actor); Los Angeles, 12/8/1937
Macaulay, Thomas Babington (author); Rothley Temple, England **(1800-1859)**
MacCorkindale, Simon (actor); Ely, England, 2/12/1953
MacDermot, Galt (composer); Montreal, 12/19/1928
MacDonald, James Ramsay (statesman); Lossiemouth, Scotland **(1866-1937)**
MacDonald, Jeanette (actress and soprano); Philadelphia **(1907-1965)**
Macdonald, Ross (Kenneth Millar) (mystery writer); Los Gatos, Calif. **(1915-1983)**
MacDowell, Edward Alexander (composer); New York City **(1861-1908)**
Macfadden, Bernarr (physical culturist); nr. Mill Spring, Mo. **(1868-1955)**
MacGraw, Ali (actress); New York City, 4/1/1939
Machaut, Guillaume de (composer); Marchault, France **(1300-1377)**
Machiavelli, Niccolò (political philosopher); Florence (Italy) **(1469-1527)**
Mack, Ted (TV personality); Greeley, Colo. **(1904-1976)**
MacKenzie, Gisele (Marie Marguerite Louise Gisele LaFleche) (singer and actress); Winnipeg, Manitoba, Canada, 1/10/1927
Mackie, Bob (designer); Monterey Park, Calif., 3/24/1940
MacLaine, Shirley (Shirley MacLean Beatty) (actress); Richmond, Va., 4/24/1934
MacLeish, Archibald (poet); Glencoe, Ill. **(1892-1982)**
Macmillan, Harold (ex-Prime Minister); London **(1894-1986)**
MacMurray, Fred (actor); Kankakee, Ill. **(1908-1991)**
MacNeil, Cornell (baritone); Minneapolis, 1925
MacRae, Gordon (singer); East Orange, N.J. **(1921-1986)**
MacRae, Sheila (comedienne); London, 9/24/1924
Madison, Guy (Robert Moseley) (actor); Bakersfield, Calif., 1/19/1922
Madonna (Madonna Louise Ciccone) (singer); Bay City, Mich., 8/16/1958
Maeterlinck, Count Maurice (author); Ghent, Belgium **(1862-1949)**
Magellan, Ferdinand (Fernando de Magalhaes) (navigator); Sabrosa, Portugal **(1480?-1521)**
Magnani, Anna (actress); Rome **(1908-1973)**
Magritte, René (painter); Belgium **(1898-1967)**
Magsaysay, Ramón (statesman); Iba, Luzon, Philippines **(1907-1957)**
Mahan, Alfred Thayer (naval historian); West Point, N.Y. **(1840-1914)**
Mahler, Gustav (composer and conductor); Kalischt (Czechoslovakia) **(1860-1911)**
Mailer, Norman (novelist); Long Branch, N.J., 1/31/1923
Mailloi, Aristide (sculptor); Banyuls-sur-Mer, Rousillion, France **(1861-1944)**
Maimonides, Moses (Jewish philosopher); Cordoba, Spain **(1135-1204)**
Main, Marjorie (Mary Tomlinson Krebs) (actress); Acton, Ind. **(1890-1975)**
Mainbocher (Main Rousseau Bocher) (fashion designer); Chicago **(1891-1976)**
Majors, Lee (actor); Wyandotte, Mich., 4/23/1940
Makarova, Natalia (ballerina); Leningrad, 11/21/1940
Makeba, Miriam (singer); Johannesburg, South Africa, 3/4/1932
Malamud, Bernard (novelist); Brooklyn, N.Y., **(1914-1986)**
Malden, Karl (Miaden Sekulovich) (actor); Chicago, 3/22/1913
Malkovich, John (actor); Christopher, Ill., 12/9/1953
Malle, Louis (director); Thumeries, France, 10/30/1932
Malone, Dorothy (actress); Chicago, 1/30/1925
Malraux, André (author); Paris **(1901-1976)**
Malthus, Thomas Robert (economist); nr. Dorking, England **(1766-1834)**
Mamet, David (playwright); Chicago, 11/30/1947
Manchester, Melissa (singer); Bronx, N.Y., 2/15/1951
Manchester, William (writer); Attleboro, Mass., 4/1/1922
Mancini, Henry (composer and conductor); Cleveland, 4/16/1924
Mandela, Nelson (Rolihlahla) (South African political activist) Umtata, Transkei, 1918
Mandela, Winnie (Nomzamo) (South African political activist), Pondoland district of the Transkei, 1936(?)
Mandrell, Barbara (singer); Houston, 12/25/1948
Manet, Edouard (painter); Paris **(1832-1883)**
Mangano, Silvana (actress); Rome **(1930-1989)**
Mangione, Chuck (hornist, pianist, and composer); Rochester, N.Y., 11/29/1940
Manilow, Barry (singer); Brooklyn, N.Y., 6/17/1946
Mankiewicz, Frank F. (columnist); New York City, 5/16/1924
Mankiewicz, Joseph L. (film writer and director); Wilkes-Barre, Pa. **(1909-1993)**
Mann, Horace (educator); Franklin, Mass. **(1796-1859)**
Mann, Thomas (novelist); Lübeck, Germany **(1875-1955)**
Mannes, Marya (writer); New York City, 11/14/1904
Mansfield, Jayne (Jayne Palmer) (actress); Bryn Mawr, Pa. **(1932-1967)**
Mansfield, Katherine (story writer); Wellington, New Zealand **(1888-1923)**
Mantovani, Annunzio (conductor); Venice **(1905-1980)**
Mao Zedong (Tse-tung) (Chinese leader); Shao Shan, China **(1893-1976)**
Mapplethorpe, Robert (photographer); Floral Park, Queens, N.Y. **(1946-1989)**
Marat, Jean Paul (French revolutionist); Boudry, Neuchâtei, Switzerland **(1743-1793)**
Marceau, Marcel (mime); Strasbourg, France, 3/22/1923
March, Fredric (Frederick Bickel) (actor); Racine, Wis. **(1897-1975)**
Marchand, Nancy (actress); Buffalo, N.Y., 6/19/1923
Marconi, Guglielmo (inventor); Bologna, Italy **(1874-1937)**
Marcus Aurelius (Marcus Annius Verus) (Roman emperor); Rome **(121-180)**
Marcuse, Herbert (philosopher); Berlin, **(1898-1979)**
Margaret Rose (Princess); Glamis Castle, Angus, Scotland,

8/21/1930
Margrethe II (Queen); Copenhagen, 4/16/1940
Marie Antoinette (Josephe Jeanne Marie Antoinette) (Queen of France); Vienna **(1755-1793)**
Marisol (sculptor); Venezuela, 1930
Markham, Edwin (poet); Oregon City, Ore. **(1852-1940)**
Markova, Dame Alicia (Lilian Alice Marks) (ballerina); London 12/1/1910
Marley, Bob (reggae singer and songwriter); Kingston, Jamaica **(1945-1981)**
Marlowe, Christopher (dramatist); Canterbury, England **(1564-1593)**
Marlowe, Julia (Sarah Frances Frost) (actress); Cumberlandshire, England **(1866-1950)**
Marquand, J(ohn) P(hillips) (novelist); Wilmington, Del. **(1893-1960)**
Marquette, Jacques (missionary and explorer); Laon, France **(1637-1675)**
Marriner, Neville (conductor); Lincoln, England, 4/15/1924
Marsalis, Wynton (musician); New Orleans, La., 10/18/1961
Marsh, Jean (actress); Stoke Newington, England, 7/1/1934
Marshall, E.G. (actor); Owatonna, Minn., 6/18/1910
Marshall, George Catlett (general); Uniontown, Pa. **(1880-1959)**
Marshall, Herbert (actor); London **(1890-1968)**
Marshall, John (jurist); nr. Germantown, Va. **(1755-1835)**
Marshall, Penny (actress); New York City, 10/15/1942
Martin, Dean (Dino Crocetti) (singer and actor); Steubenville, Ohio, 6/17/1917
Martin, Mary (singer and actress); Weatherford, Tex. **(1913–1990)**
Martin, Steve (comedian); Waco, Tex., 1945(?)
Martin, Tony (Alvin Morris) (singer); San Francisco, 12/25/1913
Martinelli, Giovanni (tenor); Montagnana, Italy **(1885-1969)**
Martins, Peter (dancer-choreographer); Copenhagen, 10/27/1945
Marvell, Andrew (poet); Winestead, England **(1621-1678)**
Marvin, Lee (actor); New York City **(1924-1987)**
Marx, Chico (Leonard) (comedian); New York City **(1891-1961)**
Marx, Groucho (Julius) (comedian); New York City **(1890-1977)**
Marx, Harpo (Arthur) (comedian); New York City **(1893-1964)**
Marx, Karl (Socialist writer); Treves (Germany) **(1818-1883)**
Marx, Zeppo (Herbert) (comedian); New York City **(1901-1979)**
Mary Stuart (Queen of Scotland); Linlithgow, Scotland **(1542-1587)**
Masaryk, Jan Garrigue (statesman); Prague (Czechoslovakia) **(1886-1948)**
Masaryk, Thomas Garrigue (statesman); Hodonin (Czechoslovakia) **(1850-1937)**
Masefield, John (poet); Ledbury, England **(1878-1967)**
Masekela, Hugh (trumpeter); Wilbank, South Africa, 4/4/1939
Mason, Jackie (comedian); Sheboygan, Wis., 6/9/1930(?)
Mason, James (actor); Huddersfield, England **(1909-1984)**
Mason, Marsha (actress); St. Louis, Mo., 4/3/1942
Massenet, Jules Emile Frédéric (composer); Montaud, France **(1842-1912)**
Massey, Raymond (actor); Toronto **(1896-1983)**
Massine, Léonide (choreographer); Moscow **(1895-1979)**
Masters, Edgar Lee (poet); Garnett, Kan. **(1869-1950)**
Mastroianni, Marcello (actor); Fontana Liri, Italy, 9/28/1924
Mather, Cotton (clergyman); Boston **(1663-1728)**
Mathis, Johnny (singer); San Francisco, 9/30/1935
Matisse, Henri (painter); Le Cateau, France **(1869-1954)**
Matthau, Walter (Walter Matuschanskayasky) (actor); New York City, 10/1/1920
Mature, Victor (actor); Louisville, Ky., 1/19/1916
Maugham, W(illiam) Somerset (author); Paris **(1874-1965)**
Mauldin, Bill (political cartoonist); Mountain Park, N.M., 10/29/1921
Maupassant, Henri René Albert Guy de (story writer); Normandy, France **(1850-1893)**
Maurois, André (Emile Herzog) (author); Elbauf, France **(1885-1967)**
Maximilian (Ferdinand Maximilian Joseph) (Emperor of Mexico); Vienna **(1832-1867)**
Maxwell, James Clerk (physicist); Edinburgh, Scotland **(1831-1879)**
May, Elaine (Elaine Berlin) (entertainer-writer); Philadelphia, 4/21/1932
May, Rollo (psychologist); Ada, Ohio, 4/21/1909
Mayall, John (singer and songwriter); Manchester, England, 11/29/1933
Mayer, Louis B. (motion picture executive); Minsk, Russia **(1885-1957)**
Mayo, Charles H. (surgeon); Rochester, Minn. **(1865-1939)**
Mayo, Charles W. (surgeon); Rochester, Minn. **(1898-1968)**
Mayo, Virginia (Jones) (actress); St. Louis, 1920
Mayo, William J. (surgeon); Le Sueur, Minn. **(1861-1939)**
Mayron, Melanie (actress); Philadelphia, 10/20/1952
Mazzini, Giuseppe (patriot); Genoa **(1805-1872)**
McBride, Mary Margaret (radio personality); Paris, Mo. **(1899-1976)**
McBride, Patricia (ballerina); Teaneck, N.J., 8/23/1942
McCallum, David (actor); Glasgow, Scotland, 9/19/1933
McCambridge, Mercedes (actress); Joliet, Ill., 3/17/1918
McCarthy, Eugene J. (ex-Senator); Watkins, Minn., 3/29/1916
McCarthy, Joseph Raymond (Senator); Grand Chute, Wis. **(1908-1957)**
McCarthy, Kevin (actor); Seattle, 2/15/1914
McCarthy, Mary (novelist); Seattle **(1912-1989)**
McCartney, Paul (singer and songwriter); Liverpool, England, 6/18/1942
McClanahan, Rue (actress); Healdton, Okla., 2/21/1935
McClellan, George Brinton (general); Philadelphia **(1826-1885)**
McClintock, Barbara (geneticist); Hartford, Conn. **(1902–1992)**
McCloy, John J. (lawyer and banker); Philadelphia **(1895-1989)**
McClure, Doug (actor); Glendale, Calif., 5/11/1938
McCormack, John (tenor); Athlone, Ireland **(1884-1945)**
McCormack, John W. (ex-Speaker of House); Boston **(1891-1980)**
McCormack, Patty (actress); New York City, 8/21/1945
McCormick, Cyrus Hall (inventor); Rockbridge County, Va. **(1809-1884)**
McCormick, Myron (actor); Albany, Ind. **(1907-1962)**
McCoy, Col. Tim (actor); Saginaw, Mich. **(1891-1978)**
McCracken, James (dramatic tenor); Gary, Ind. **(1926-1988)**
McCrea, Joel (actor); Los Angeles **(1905–1990)**
McCullers, Carson (novelist); Columbus, Ga. **(1917-1967)**
McDaniel, Hattie (actress); Wichita, Kan. **(1895-1952)**
McDowall, Roddy (actor); London, 9/17/1928
McDowell, Malcolm (actor); Leeds, England, 6/19/1943
McFarland, Spanky (George Emmett) (actor); Fort Worth, Tex. **(1928-1993)**
McGavin, Darren (actor); San Joaquin, Calif., 5/7/1922
McGinley, Phyllis (poet and writer); Ontario, Ore. **(1905-1978)**
McGoohan, Patrick (actor); Astoria, Queens, N.Y., 1928
McGovern, Maureen (singer); Youngstown, Ohio, 7/27/1949
McGuire, Dorothy (actress); Omaha, Neb. 6/14/1919
McKellen, Ian (actor); Burnley, England, 5/25/1939
McKenna, Siobhan (actress); Belfast, Northern Ireland **(1923-1986)**
McKuen, Rod (singer and composer); Oakland, Calif., 4/29/1933
McLaglen, Victor (actor); Tunbridge Wells, Kent, England **(1886-1959)**
McLaughlin, John (guitarist); Yorkshire, England, 1942
McLean, Don (singer and songwriter); New Rochelle, N.Y., 10/2/1945
McLuhan, Marshall (Herbert Marshall) (communications writer); Edmonton, Canada **(1911-1980)**
McMahon, Ed (TV personality); Detroit, 3/6/1923
McNamara, Robert S. (former president of World Bank); San Francisco, 6/9/1916
McQueen, Butterfly (Thelma) (actress); Tampa, Fla., 1/8/1911
McQueen, Steve (Terence Stephen McQueen) (actor); Indianapolis **(1930-1980)**
McRaney, Gerald (actor); Collins, Miss., 8/19/1947
Mead, Margaret (anthropologist); Philadelphia, **(1901-1978)**
Meadows, Audrey (actress); Wu Chang, China, 1922(?)
Meadows, Jayne (actress); Wu Chang, China 9/27/1926
Meany, George (labor leader); New York City **(1894-1980)**
Meara, Anne (actress); New York City, 1929
Medici, Lorenzo de' (called Lorenzo the Magnificent) (Florentine ruler); Florence (Italy) **(1449-1492)**
Meek, Donald (actor); Glasgow, Scotland **(1880-1946)**
Meeker, Ralph (Ralph Rathgeber) (actor); Minneapolis, **(1920-1988)**
Mehta, Zubin (conductor); Bombay, 4/29/1936
Meir, Golda (Golda Myerson, nee Mabovitz) (ex-Premier of Israel); Kiev, Russia **(1898-1978)**
Melanie (Melanie Safka) (singer and songwriter); New York City, 2/3/1947
Melba, Dame Nellie (Helen Porter Mitchell) (soprano); nr. Melbourne **(1861-1931)**
Melchior, Lauritz (Lebrecht Hommel) (heroic tenor); Copenhagen **(1890-1973)**
Mellon, Andrew William (financier); Pittsburgh **(1855-1937)**
Melville, Herman (novelist); New York City **(1819-1891)**
Mencken, Henry Louis (writer); Baltimore **(1880-1956)**
Mendel, Gregor Johann (geneticist); Heinzendorf, Austrian Silesia **(1822-1884)**
Mendeleyev, Dmitri Ivanovich (chemist); Tobolsk, Russia **(1834-1907)**
Mendelssohn-Bartholdy, Jakob Ludwig Felix (composer); Hamburg **(1809-1847)**
Mendès-France, Pierre (ex-Premier); Paris **(1905-1982)**
Menjou, Adolphe (actor); Pittsburgh **(1890-1963)**
Mennin, Peter (Peter Mennini) (composer); Erie, Pa. **(1923-1983)**
Menninger, William C. (psychiatrist); Topeka, Kan. **(1899-1966)**
Menotti, Gian Carlo (composer); Cadegliano, Italy, 7/7/1911
Menuhin, Yehudi (violinist and conductor); New York City, 4/22/1916
Menzies, Robert Gordon (ex-Prime Minister); Jeparit, Australia **(1894-1978)**
Mercer, Johnny (songwriter); Savannah, Ga. **(1909-1976)**
Mercer, Mabel (singer); Burton-on-Trent, England **(1900-1984)**
Mercer, Marian (actress, singer); Akron, Ohio, 11/26/1935
Mercouri, Melina (actress); Athens, 10/18/1925

Meredith, Burgess (actor); Cleveland, 11/16/1908
Merkel, Una (actress); Covington, Ky. **(1903-1986)**
Merman, Ethel (Ethel Zimmerman) (singer and actress); Astoria, Queens, N.Y. **(1909-1984)**
Merrick, David (David Margulois) (stage producer); St. Louis, 11/27/1912
Merrill, Dina (actress); New York City, 12/9/1925
Merrill, Gary (actor); Hartford, Conn. **(1915-1990)**
Merrill, Robert (baritone); Brooklyn, N.Y., 6/4/1919
Merton, Thomas (clergyman and writer); France **(1915-1968)**
Mesmer, Franz Anton (physician); Itzmang, nr. Constance (Germany) **(1733-1815)**
Mesta, Perle (social figure); Sturgis, Mich. **(1889-1975)**
Metternich, Prince Klemens Wenzel Nepomuk Lothar von (statesman); Coblenz (Germany) **(1773-1859)**
Michelangelo Buonarroti (painter, sculptor, and architect); Caprese (Italy) **(1475-1564)**
Michener, James A. (novelist); New York City, 2/3/1907
Mickiewicz, Adam (Polish poet); Zozie, Belorussia (U.S.S.R.) **(1798-1855)**
Midler, Bette (singer); Honolulu, 1945
Mielziner, Jo (stage designer); Paris **(1901-1976)**
Mies van der Rohe, Ludwig (architect and designer); Aachen, Germany **(1886-1969)**
Mikoyan, Anastas I. (diplomat); Sanain, Armenia, **(1895-1978)**
Miles, Sarah (actress); Essex, England, 12/31/1943
Miles, Sylvia (actress); New York City, 9/9/1932
Miles, Vera (Vera Ralston) (actress); nr. Boise City, Okla., 8/23/1930
Milhaud, Darius (composer); Aix-en-Provence, France **(1892-1974)**
Mill, John Stuart (philosopher); London, **(1806-1873)**
Milland, Ray (Reginald Truscott-Jones) (actor); Neath, Wales **(1907-1986)**
Millay, Edna St. Vincent (poet); Rockland, Me. **(1892-1950)**
Miller, Ann (Lucille Ann Collier) (dancer and actress); Cherino, Tex., 4/12/1923
Miller, Arthur (playwright); New York City, 10/17/1915
Miller, Glenn (band leader); Clarinda, Iowa **(1904-1944)**
Miller, Henry (novelist); New York City **(1891-1980)**
Miller, Jason (John Miller) (playwright); New York City, 1939(?)
Miller, Marilyn (dancer-singer, actress); Evansville, Ind. **(1898-1936)**
Miller, Mitch (Mitchell) (musician); Rochester, N.Y., 7/4/1911
Miller, Roger (singer); Fort Worth **(1936-1992)**
Millet, Jean François (painter); Gruchy, France **(1814-1875)**
Millett, Kate (feminist); St. Paul, 9/14/1934
Millikan, Robert A. (physicist); Morrison, Ill. **(1869-1953)**
Mills, Donna (actress); Chicago, 12/11/1941
Mills, Hayley (actress); London, 4/18/1946
Mills, John (actor); Felixstowe, England, 2/22/1908
Mills, Juliet (actress); London, 11/21/1941
Milne, A(lan) A(lexander) (author); London **(1882-1956)**
Milner, Martin (actor); Detroit, Mich., 12/28/1931
Milnes, Sherrill (baritone); Downers Grove, Ill., 1/10/1935
Milstein, Nathan (concert violinist); Odessa, Russia **(1904-1992)**
Milton, John (poet); London **(1608-1674)**
Mimieux, Yvette (actress); Hollywood, Calif., 1/8/1941
Mineo, Sal (actor); New York City **(1939-1976)**
Minnelli, Liza (singer and actress); Hollywood, Calif., 3/12/1946
Minnelli, Vincente (film director); Chicago **(1913-1986)**
Minuit, Peter (Governor of New Amsterdam); Wesel (Germany) **(1580-1638)**
Miranda, Carmen (Maria do Carmo da Cunha) (singer and dancer); Lisbon **(1913-1955)**
Miró Joan (painter); Barcelona **(1893-1983)**
Mitchell, Cameron (actor); Dallastown, Pa., 4/11/1918
Mitchell, Guy (actor); Detroit, 2/27/1927
Mitchell, John N. (former Attorney General); Detroit **(1913-1988)**
Mitchell, Joni (Roberta Joan Anderson) (singer and songwriter); Ft. Macleod, Canada, 11/7/1943
Mitchell, Margaret (novelist); Atlanta **(1900-1949)**
Mitchell, Thomas (actor); Elizabeth, N.J. **(1892-1962)**
Mitchum, Robert (actor); Bridgeport, Conn., 8/6/1917
Mitropoulos, Dimitri (orchestra conductor); Athens **(1896-1960)**
Mix, Tom (actor); Mix Run, Pa. **(1880-1940)**
Modigliani, Amedeo (painter); Leghorn, Italy **(1884-1920)**
Moffo, Anna (soprano); Wayne, Pa., 6/27/1934
Mohammed (prophet); Mecca (Saudi Arabia) **(570-632)**
Molière (Jean Baptiste Poquelin) (dramatist); Paris **(1622-1673)**
Moll, Richard (actor); Pasadena, Calif. 1/13/(?)
Molnar, Ferenc (dramatist); Budapest **(1878-1952)**
Molotov, Vyacheslav M. (V. M. Skryabin) (diplomat); Kukarka, Russia **(1890-1986)**
Mondrian, Piet (painter); Amersfoort, Netherlands **(1872-1944)**
Monet, Claude (painter); Paris **(1840-1926)**
Monk, Meredith (choreographer-composer-performing artist); Lima, Peru, 11/20/1942
Monk, Thelonious (pianist); Rocky Mount, N.C. **(1918-1982)**
Monroe, Marilyn (Norma Jean Mortenson or Baker) (actress); Los Angeles **(1926-1962)**
Monroe, Vaughn (Wilton) (band leader); Akron, Ohio **(1912-1973)**
Monsarrat, Nicholas (novelist); Liverpool, England **(1910-1979)**
Montaigne, Michel Eyquem de (essayist); nr. Bordeaux, France **(1533-1592)**
Montalban, Ricardo (actor); Mexico City, 11/25/1920
Montand, Yves (Yvo Montand Livi) (actor and singer); Monsummano, Italy **(1921-1991)**
Montesquieu, Charles-Louis de Secondat, baron de La Brède and de, (philosopher) nr. Borleaux, France **(1689-1755)**
Monteux, Pierre (conductor); Paris **(1875-1964)**
Monteverdi, Claudio (composer); Cremona? Italy **(1567-1643)**
Montez, Maria (actress); Dominican Republican **(1918-1951)**
Montezuma II (Aztec emperor); Mexico **(1480?-1520)**
Montgomery, Elizabeth (actress); Hollywood, Calif., 4/15/1933
Montgomery, George (George Montgomery Letz) (actor); Brady, Mont., 8/29/1916
Montgomery, Robert (Henry, Jr.) (actor); Beacon, N.Y. **(1904-1981)**
Montgomery of Alamein, 1st Viscount of Hindhead (Sir Bernard Law Montgomery) (military leader); London **(1887-1976)**
Montoya, Carlos (guitarist); Madrid **(1903-1993)**
Moore, Clement Clarke (author); New York City **(1779-1863)**
Moore, Dudley (actor-writer-musician); Dagenham, England, 4/19/1935
Moore, Garry (Thomas Garrison Morfit) (TV personality); Baltimore, 1/31/1915
Moore, Grace (soprano); Jellico, Tenn. **(1901-1947)**
Moore, Henry (sculptor); Castleford, England **(1898-1986)**
Moore, Marianne (poet); Kirkwood, Mo. **(1887-1972)**
Moore, Mary Tyler (actress); Brooklyn, N.Y., 12/29/1937
Moore, Melba (Beatrice) (singer and actress); New York City, 10/27/1945
Moore, Roger (actor); London, 10/14/1927(?)
Moore, Thomas (poet); Dublin **(1779-1852)**
Moore, Victor (actor); Hammonton, N.J. **(1876-1962)**
Moorehead, Agnes (actress); Clinton, Mass. **(1906-1974)**
More, Henry (philosopher); Grantham, England **(1614-1687)**
More, Sir Thomas (statesman and author); London **(1478-1535)**
Moreau, Jeanne (actress); Paris, 1/23/1928
Moreno, Rita (Rosita Dolores Alverio) (actress); Humacao, Puerto Rico, 12/11/1931
Morgan, Dennis (actor); Prentice, Wis., 12/10/1920
Mo rgan, Frank (actor); New York City **(1890-1949)**
Morgan, Harry (actor); Detroit, 4/10/1915
Morgan, Helen (singer); Danville, Ohio **(1900?-1941)**
Morgan, Henry (comedian); New York City, 3/31/1915
Morgan, Jane (Florence Currier) (singer); Boston, 1920
Morgan, John Pierpont (financier); Hartford, Conn. **(1837-1913)**
Morgan, Ralph (actor); New York City **(1882-1956)**
Moriarty, Michael (actor); Detroit, 4/5/1941
Morini, Erica (concert violinist); Vienna, 1/5/1910
Morison, Samuel Eliot (historian); Boston **(1887-1976)**
Morley, Christopher Darlington (novelist); Haverford, Pa. **(1890-1957)**
Morley, Robert (actor); Semley, England **(1908-1992)**
Morris, Chester (actor); New York City **(1901-1970)**
Morris, Wayne (actor); Los Angeles, Calif. **(1914-1959)**
Morrison, Jim (James Douglas Morrison) (singer and songwriter); Melbourne, Fla. **(1943-1971)**
Morse, Marston (mathematician); Waterville, Me. **(1892-1977)**
Morse, Robert (actor); Newton, Mass., 5/18/1931
Morse, Samuel Finley Breese (painter and inventor); Charlestown, Mass. **(1791-1872)**
Moses, Grandma (Mrs. Anna Mary Robertson Moses) (painter); Greenwich, N.Y. **(1860-1961)**
Moses, Robert (urban planner); New Haven, Conn., **(1888-1981)**
Mostel, Zero (Samuel Joel Mostel) (actor); Brooklyn, N.Y. **(1915-1977)**
Moussorgsky, Modest Petrovich (composer); Karev, Russia **(1839-1881)**
Mowbray, Alan (actor); London **(1896-1969)**
Moyers, Bill D. (Billy Don) (journalist); Hugo, Okla., 6/5/1934
Moynihan, Daniel Patrick (New York Senator); Tulsa, Okla., 3/16/1927
Mozart, Wolfgang Amadeus (Johannes Chrysostomus Wolfgangus Theophilus Mozart) (composer); Salzburg (Austria) **(1756-1791)**
Mudd, Roger (TV newscaster); Washington, D.C., 2/9/1928
Muggeridge, Malcolm (Thomas) (writer); Croydon, England **(1903–1990)**
Muhammad, Elijah (Elijah Poole) (religious leader); Sandersville, Ga. **(1897-1975)**
Mulgrew, Kate (actress); Dubuque, Iowa, 4/?/1929
Mulhare, Edward (actor); Ireland, 1923
Mumford, Lewis (cultural historian and city planner); Flushing, Queens, N.Y. **(1895-1990)**

Munch, Edvard (painter); Löt en, Norway **(1863-1944)**
Munchhausen, Karl Friedrick Hieronymus, baron von (anecdotist); Hanover, Germany **(1720-1797)**
Muni, Paul (Muni Weisenfreund) (actor); Lemburg (Ukraine) **(1895-1967)**
Munsel, Patrice (soprano); Spokane, Wash., 5/14/1925
Murdoch, Iris (novelist); Dublin, 7/15/1919
Murdoch, Rupert (publisher); Melbourne, 3/11/1931
Murillo, Bartolomé Esteban (painter); Seville, Spain **(1617-1682)**
Murphy, Audie (actor and war hero); Kingston, Tex. **(1924-1971)**
Murphy, Eddie (actor-comedian); Brooklyn, N.Y. 4/3/1961
Murphy, George (actor, dancer, and ex-Senator); New Haven, Conn. **(1902-1992)**
Murray, Arthur (dance teacher); New York City **(1895–1991)**
Murray, Bill (actor-comedian); Wilmette, Ill. 9/21/1950
Murray, Kathryn (dance teacher); Jersey City, N.J., 1906
Murray, Ken (Don Court) (producer); Nyack, N.Y. **(1903-1988)**
Murray, Mae (Marie Adrienne Koenig) (actress); Portsmouth, Va. **(1890-1965)**
Murrow, Edward R. (commentator and government official); Greensboro, N.C. **(1908-1965)**
Mussolini, Benito (Italian dictator); Dovia, Forli, Italy **(1883-1945)**
Muti, Riccardo (orchestra conductor); Naples, Italy, 7/28/1941
Mutter, Anne-Sophie (violinist); Rheinfelden, West Germany, 6/29/1963
Myerson, Bess (consumer advocate); Bronx, N.Y., 1924
Myrdal, Gunnar (sociologist and economist); Gustaf Parish, Sweden **(1898-1987)**

N

Nabokov, Vladimir (novelist); St. Petersburg, Russia **(1899-1977)**
Nabors, Jim (actor and singer); Sylacauga, Ala., 6/12/1932
Nader, Ralph (consumer advocate); Winsted, Conn., 2/27/1934
Nagel, Conrad (actor); Keokuk, Iowa **(1897-1970)**
Naish, J. Carrol (actor); New York City **(1900-1973)**
Naldi, Nita (Anita Donna Dooley) (actress); New York City **(1899-1961)**
Napoleon Bonaparte. *See* Bonaparte, Napoleon
Nash, Graham (singer); Blackpool, England, 1942
Nash, Ogden (poet); Rye, N.Y. **(1902-1971)**
Nasser, Gamal Abdel (statesman); Beni Mor, Egypt **(1918-1970)**
Nast, Thomas (cartoonist); Landau (Germany) **(1840-1902)**
Nation, Carry Amelia (temperance leader); Garrard County, Ky. **(1846-1911)**
Natwick, Mildred (actress); Baltimore, 6/19/1908
Nazimova, Alla (actress); Yalta, Crimea, Russia **(1879-1945)**
Neagle, Anna (Marjorie Robertson) (actress); London **(1908-1986)**
Neal, Patricia (actress); Packard, Ky., 1/20/1926
Neff, Hildegarde (actress); Ulm, Germany, 12/28/1925
Negri, Pola (Apolina Mathias-Chalupec) (actress); Bromberg (Poland) **(1899-1987)**
Nehru, Jawaharlal (first Prime Minister of India); Allahabad, India **(1889-1964)**
Nelligan, Kate (actress); London, Ont., Canada, 3/16/1951
Nelson, Barry (Neilsen) (actor); San Francisco, 1920
Nelson, David (actor); New York City, 10/24/1936
Nelson, Harriet Hilliard (Peggy Lou Snyder) (actress); Des Moines, Iowa, 1914
Nelson, Ozzie (Oswald) (actor); Jersey City, N.J. **(1907-1975)**
Nelson, Ricky (Eric) (singer and actor); Teaneck, N.J. **(1940-1985)**
Nelson, Viscount Horatio (naval officer); Burnham Thorpe, England **(1758-1805)**
Nelson, Willie (singer); Waco, Texas, 4/30/1933
Nenni, Pietro (Socialist leader); Faenza, Italy **(1891-1980)**
Nero (Nero Claudius Caesar Drusus Germanicus) (Roman emperor); Antium (Italy) **(37-68)**
Nero, Peter (pianist); New York City, 5/22/1934
Nesbitt, Cathleen (actress); Cheshire, England **(1889-1982)**
Nevelson, Louise (sculptor); Kiev, Russia **(1899-1988)**
Newhart, Bob (entertainer); Chicago, 9/5/1929
Newhouse, Samuel I. (publisher); New York City **(1895-1979)**
Newley, Anthony (actor and song writer); London, 9/24/1931
Newman, Edwin (news commentator); New York City, 1/25/1919
Newman, John Henry (prelate); London **(1801-1890)**
Newman, Paul (actor and director); Cleveland, 1/26/1925
Newman, Randy (singer); Los Angeles, 11/28/1943
Newton, Huey (black activist); New Orleans **(1942-1989)**
Newton, Sir Isaac (mathematician and scientist); nr. Grantham, England **(1642-1727)**
Newton, Wayne (singer); Norfolk, Va., 4/3/1942
Newton-John, Olivia (singer); Cambridge, England, 9/26/1948
Nichols, Mike (Michael Peschkowsky) (stage and film director); Berlin, 11/6/1931
Nicholson, Jack (actor); Neptune, N.J., 4/22/1937
Nietzsche, Friedrich Wilhelm (philosopher); nr. Lützen Saxon y (East Germany) **(1844-1900)**
Nightingale, Florence (nurse); Florence (Italy) **(1820-1910)**
Nijinsky, Vaslav (ballet dancer); Warsaw **(1890-1950)**
Nilsson, Birgit (soprano); West Karup, Sweden, 5/17/1923
Nilsson, Harry (singer and songwriter); Brooklyn, N.Y., 6/15/1941
Nimitz, Chester W. (naval officer); Fredericksburg, Tex. **(1885-1966)**
Nimoy, Leonard (actor); Boston, 3/26/1931
Nin, Anais (author and diarist); Neuilly, France **(1903-1977)**
Niven, David (actor); Kirriemuir, Scotland, **(1910-1983)**
Nizer, Louis (lawyer and author); London, 2/6/1902
Nobel, Alfred Bernhard (industrialist); Stockholm **(1833-1896)**
Noguchi, Isamu (sculptor); Los Angeles **(1904-1988)**
Nolan, Lloyd (actor); San Francisco **(1902-1985)**
Nolte, Nick (actor); Omaha, Neb., 1942
Norell, Norman (Norman Levinson) (fashion designer); Noblesville, Ind. **(1900-1972)**
Norman, Jessye (soprano); Augusta, Ga., 9/15/1945
Norman, Marsha (Marsha Williams) (playwright); Louisville, Ky., 9/21/1947
Normand, Mabel (actress); Boston **(1894-1930)**
Norstad, Gen. Lauris (ex-commander of NATO forces); Minneapolis **(1907-1988)**
North, John Ringling (circus director); Baraboo, Wis. **(1903-1985)**
North, Sheree (actress); Los Angeles, 1/17/1933
Norton, Eleanor Holmes (New York City government official, lawyer); Washington, D.C., 6/13/1937
Nostradamus (Michel de Notredame) (astrologer); St. Rémy, France **(1503-1566)**
Novaes, Guiomar (pianist); São João de Boa Vista, Brazil **(1895-1979)**
Novak, Kim (Marilyn Novak) (actress); Chicago, 2/13/1933
Novarro, Ramon (Ramon Samaniegoes) (actor); Durango, Mexico **(1899-1968)**
Novello, Ivor (actor, playwright, composer); Cardiff, Wales **(1893-1951)**
Nugent, Elliott (actor and director); Dover, Ohio, **(1899-1980)**
Nureyev, Rudolf (ballet dancer); Siberia **(1938-1993)**
Nuyen, France (actress); Marseilles, France, 7/31/1939
Nyro, Laura (singer and songwriter); Bronx, N.Y., 1947

O

Oakie, Jack (actor); Sedalia, Mo. **(1903-1978)**
Oakley, Annie (Phoebe Anne Oakley Mozee) (markswoman); Darke County, Ohio **(1860-1926)**
Oates, Joyce Carol (novelist); Lockport, N.Y., 6/16/1938
Oberon, Merle (Estelle Merle O'Brien Thompson) (actress); Calcutta, India **(1911-1979)**
Oberth, Hermann (rocketry and space flight pioneer); Hermannstadt, Romania **(1894-1989)**
O'Brian, Hugh (Hugh J. Krampe) (actor); Rochester, N.Y., 4/19/1930
O'Brien, Edmond (actor); New York City **(1915-1985)**
O'Brien, Margaret (Angela Maxine O'Brien) (actress); San Diego, Calif., 1/15/1937
O'Brien, Pat (William Joseph O'Brien, Jr.) (actor); Milwaukee **(1899-1983)**
O'Casey, Sean (playwright); Dublin **(1881-1964)**
Ochs, Adolph Simon (publisher); Cincinnati **(1858-1935)**
O'Connor, Carroll (actor); New York City, 8/2/1924
O'Connor, Donald (actor); Chicago, 8/28/1925
Odets, Clifford (playwright); Philadelphia **(1906-1963)**
Odetta (Odetta Holmes) (folk singer and actress); Birmingham, Ala., 12/31/1930
Offenbach, Jacques (composer); Cologne, Germany **(1819-1880)**
O'Hara, John (novelist); Pottsville, Pa. **(1905-1970)**
O'Hara, Maureen (Maureen FitzSimons) (actress); Dublin, 8/17/1921
Ohlsson, Garrick (pianist); Bronxville, N.Y., 4/3/1948
Ohrbach, Jerry (actor-singer); Bronx, N.Y., 10/20/1935
Oistrakh, David (concert violinist); Odessa, Russia **(1908-1974)**
O'Keefe, Dennis (actor); Fort Madison, Iowa **(1908-1968)**
O'Keeffe, Georgia (painter); Sun Prairie, Wis. **(1887-1986)**
Oland, Warner (actor); Umea, Sweden **(1880-1938)**
Oldenburg, Claes (painter); Stockholm, Sweden, 1/28/1929
Oliver, Edna May (actress); Malden, Mass. **(1883-1942)**
Olivier, Lord (Laurence) (actor); Dorking, England **(1907-1989)**
Olmsted, Frederick Law (landscape architect); Hartford, Conn. **(1822-1903)**
Olsen, Ole (John Sigvard Olsen) (comedian); Peru, Ind. **(1892-1963)**
Omar Khayyam (poet and astronomer); Nishapur (Iran) **(died c. 1123)**
Onassis, Aristotle (shipping executive); Smyrna, Turkey **(1906-1975)**
Onassis, Christina (shipping executive); New York City **(1950-1988)**

Onassis, Jacqueline Kennedy (Jacqueline Bouvier) (President's widow); Southampton, N.Y., 7/28/1929
O'Neal, Ryan (Patrick) (actor); Los Angeles, 4/20/1941
O'Neal, Tatum (actress); Los Angeles, Calif., 11/5/1963
O'Neill, Eugene Gladstone (playwright); New York City **(1888-1953)**
O'Neill, Jennifer (actress); Rio de Janeiro, 2/20/1949
Oppenheimer, J. Robert (nuclear physicist); New York City **(1904-1967)**
Orff, Carl (composer); Munich, Germany **(1895-1982)**
Orlando, Tony (Michael Anthony Orlando Cassavitis) (singer); New York City, 4/3/1944
Ormandy, Eugene (conductor); Budapest **(1899-1985)**
Orozco, José Clemente (painter); Zapotlán, Jalisco, Mexico **(1883-1949)**
Orwell, George (Eric Arthur Blair) (British author); Motihari, India **(1903-1950)**
Osborn, Paul (playwright); Evansville, Ind. **(1901-1988)**
Osborne, John (playwright); London, 12/12/1929
Osler, Sir William (physician); Bondhead, Ontario, Canada **(1849-1919)**
Osmond, Donny (singer); Ogden, Utah, 12/9/1957
Osmond, Marie (singer); Ogden, Utah, 1959
O'Sullivan, Maureen (actress); County Roscommon, Ireland, 5/17/1911
Otis, Elisha (inventor); Halifax, Vt. **(1811-1861)**
O'Toole, Peter (actor); Connemara, Ireland, 8/2/1933
Ouspenskaya, Maria (actress); Tula, Russia **(1876-1949)**
Ovid (Publius Ovidius Naso) (poet); Sulmona (Italy) **(43 B.C.-?A.D. 17)**
Owen, Reginald (actor); Wheathampstead, England **(1887-1972)**
Owens, Buck (Alvis Edgar Owens) (singer); Sherman, Tex., 8/12/1929
Ozawa, Seiji (orchestra conductor); Fentian (Shenyan), Manchura, 7/1/1935

P

Paar, Jack (TV personality); Canton, Ohio, 5/1/1918
Pacino, Al (Alfred) (actor); New York City, 4/25/1940
Packard, Vance (author); Granville Summit, Pa., 5/22/1914
Paderewski, Ignace Jan (pianist and statesman); Kurylowka, Russian Podolia **(1860-1941)**
Paganini, Nicolò (violinist); Genoa (Italy) **(1782-1840)**
Page, Geraldine (actress); Kirksville, Mo. **(1924-1987)**
Page, Patti (Clara Ann Fowler) (singer and entertainer); Claremore, Okla., 11/8/1927
Paige, Janis (actress); Tacoma, Wash., 9/16/1922
Paine, Thomas (political philosopher); Thetford, England **(1737-1809)**
Palance, Jack (Walter Palanuik) (actor); Lattimer, Pa., 2/18/1920
Palestrina, Giovanni Pierluigi da (composer); Palestrina, Italy **(1526-1594)**
Paley, William S. (broadcasting executive); Chicago **(1901–1990)**
Palladio, Andrea (architect); Padua or Vicenza (Italy) **(1508-1580)**
Pallette, Eugene (actor); Winfield, Kan. **(1889-1954)**
Palmer, Betsy (actress); East Chicago, Ind., 1929
Palmer, Lilli (Lilli Peiser) (actress); Posen (Germany) **(1914-1986)**
Palmerston, Henry John Templeton (3rd Viscount) (statesman); Broadlands, England **(1784-1865)**
Pangborn, Franklin (actor); Newark, N.J. **(1893-1958)**
Papanicolaou, George N. (physician); Coumi, Greece **(1883-1962)**
Papas, Irene (actress); Chiliomodion, Greece, 1929
Papp, Joseph (Joseph Papirofsky) (stage producer and director); Brooklyn, N.Y. **(1921-1991)**
Paracelaus, Philippus (Aureolus Theophrastus Bombastus von Hohenheim) (physican); Einsiedeln, Switzerland **(1493-1541)**
Park, Chung Hee (President of South Korea); Sangmo-ri, Korea **(1917-1979)**
Parker, Dorothy (Dorothy Rothschild) (author); West End, N.J. **(1893-1967)**
Parker, Eleanor (actress); Cedarville, Ohio, 6/26/1922
Parker, Fess (actor); Fort Worth, Tex., 1925
Parker, Jean (actress); Butte, Mont., 8/11/1912
Parker, Suzy (model and actress); San Antonio, 10/28/1933
Parkinson, C(yril) Northcote (historian); Durham, England **(1909-1993)**
Parks, Bert (Bert Jacobson) (entertainer); Atlanta **(1914-1992)**
Parks, Gordon (film director); Ft. Scott, Kan., 11/30/1912
Parnell, Charles Stewart (statesman); Avondale, Ireland **(1846-1891)**
Parnis, Mollie (Mollie Parnis Livingston) (fashion designer); New York City **(1905(?)-1992)**
Parsons, Estelle (actress); Marblehead, Mass., 11/20/1927
Parton, Dolly (singer); Locust Ridge, Tenn. 1/19/1946
Pascal, Blaise (philosopher); Clermont, France **(1623-1662)**
Pasternak, Boris Leonidovich (author); Moscow **(1890-1960)**
Pasternak, Joseph (film producer); Silagy-Somlyo, Romania **(1901–1991)**
Pasteur, Louis (chemist); Dôle, France **(1822-1895)**
Pastor, Tony (Antonio) (actor, theater manager); New York City **(1837-1908)**
Paton, Alan (author): Pietermaritzburg, South Africa **(1903-1988)**
Patti, Adelina (soprano); Madrid **(1843-1919)**
Patton, George Smith, Jr. (general); San Gabriel, Calif., **(1885-1945)**
Paul, Les (Lester William Polfus) (guitarist); Waukesha, Wis., 6/9/1915
Paul VI (Giovanni Battista Montini) (Pope); Concesio, nr. Brescia, Italy **(1897-1978)**
Pauley, Jane (TV newscaster); Indianapolis, 10/31/1950
Pauling, Linus Carl (chemist); Portland, Ore., 2/28/1901
Pavarotti, Luciano (tenor); Modena, Italy, 10/12/1935
Pavlov, Ivan Petrovich (physiologist); Ryazan district, Russia **(1849-1936)**
Pavlova, Anna (ballerina); St. Petersburg, Russia **(1885-1931)**
Paxinou, Katina (actress); Piraeus, Greece **(1900-1973)**
Payne, John (actor); Roanoke, Va. **(1912-1989)**
Peale, Norman Vincent (clergyman); Bowersville, Ohio, 5/31/1898
Pearl, Minnie (Sarah Ophelia Colley Cannon) (comedienne and singer); Centerville, Tenn., 10/25/1912
Pears, Peter (tenor); Farnham, England **(1910-1986)**
Pearson, Drew (Andrew Russel Pearson) (columnist); Evanston, Ill. **(1897-1969)**
Pearson, Lester B. (statesman); Toronto **(1897-1972)**
Peary, Robert Edwin (explorer); Cresson, Pa. **(1856-1920)**
Peck, Gregory (actor); La Jolla, Calif., 4/5/1916
Peckinpah, Sam (film director); Fresno, Calif. **(1925-1984)**
Peerce, Jan (tenor); New York City **(1904-1984)**
Pegler, (James) Westbrook (columnist); Minneapolis **(1894-1969)**
Pei, I(eoh) M(ing) (architect); Canton, China, 4/26/1917
Penn, Arthur (stage and film director); Philadelphia, 9/27/1922
Penn, William (American colonist); London **(1644-1718)**
Penner, Joe (comedian); Hungary **(1904-1941)**
Penney, James C. (merchant); Hamilton, Mo. **(1875-1971)**
Peppard, George (actor); Detroit, 10/1/1928
Pepys, Samuel (diarist); Bampton, England **(1633-1703)**
Perelman, S(idney) J(oseph) (writer); Brooklyn, N.Y. **(1904-1979)**
Pergolesi, Giovanni Battista (composer); Jesi, Italy **(1710-1736)**
Pericles (statesman); Athens **(died 429 B.C.)**
Perkins, Osgood (actor); West Newton, Mass. **(1892-1937)**
Perkins, Anthony (actor); New York City **(1932–1992)**
Perlman, Itzhak (violinist); Tel Aviv, Israel, 8/31/1945
Perlman, Rhea (actress); Brooklyn, N.Y., 3/31/1948
Perón, Isabel (María Estela Martínez Cartas) (former chief of state); La Rioja, Argentina, 2/4/1931
Perón, Juan D. (statesman); nr. Lobos, Argentina **(1895-1974)**
Perón, Maria Eva Duarte de (political leader); Los Toldos, Argentina **(1919-1952)**
Perrine, Valerie (actress and dancer); Galveston, Tex., 9/3/1943
Pershing, John Joseph (general); Linn County, Mo. **(1860-1948)**
Pestalozzi, Johann (educator); Zurich, Switzerland **(1746-1827)**
Peters, Bernadette (Bernadette Lazzara) (actress); New York City, 2/28/1944
Peters, Brock (actor-singer); New York City, 7/2/1927
Peters, Jean (actress); Canton, Ohio, 10/15/1926
Peters, Roberta (Roberta Peterman) (soprano); New York City, 5/4/1930
Petit, Roland (choreographer and dancer); Villemombe, France, 1924
Petrarch (Francesco Petrarca) (poet); Arezzo (Italy) **(1304-1374)**
Pfeiffer, Michelle (actress); Santa Ana, Calif., 4/29/1958
Philip (Philip Mountbatten) (Duke of Edinburgh); Corfu, Greece, 6/10/1921
Piaf, Edith (Edith Gassion) (chanteuse); Paris **(1916-1963)**
Piatigorsky, Gregor (cellist); Ekaterinoslav, Russia **(1903-1976)**
Piazza, Ben (actor); Little Rock, Ark., 7/30/1934
Piazza, Marguerite (soprano); New Orleans, 5/6/1926
Picasso, Pablo (painter and sculptor); Málaga, Spain **(1881-1973)**
Pickford, Jack (Jack Smith) (actor); Toronto **(1896-1933)**
Pickford, Mary (Gladys Mary Smith) (actress); Toronto **(1893-1979)**
Picon, Molly (actress); New York City **(1898-1992)**
Pidgeon, Walter (actor); East St. John, New Brunswick, Canada **(1898-1984)**
Pinter, Harold (playwright); London, 10/10/1930
Pinza, Ezio (basso); Rome **(1892-1957)**
Pirandello, Luigi (dramatist and novelist); nr. Girgenti, Italy **(1867-1936)**
Piranesi, Giambattista (artist); Mestre, Italy **(1720-1778)**
Pissaro, Camille Jacob (painter); St. Thomas (U.S. Virgin Islands) **(1830-1903)**
Piston, Walter (composer); Rockland, Me. **(1894-1976)**
Pitman, Sir (Isaac) James (educator a nd publisher); Bath, England, 8/14/1901
Pitt, William ("Younger Pitt") (statesman); nr. Bromley, England **(1759-1806)**
Pitts, ZaSu (actress); Parsons, Kan. **(1898-1963)**

Pius XII (Eugenio Pacelli) (Pope); Rome **(1876-1958)**
Pizarro, Francisco (explorer); Trujillo, Spain **(1470?-1541)**
Planck, Max (physicist); Kiel, Germany **(1858-1947)**
Plato (Aristocles) (philosopher); Athens (?) **(427?-347 B.C.)**
Pleasence, Donald (actor); Worksop, England, 10/5/1919
Pleshette, Suzanne (actress); New York City, 1/31/1937
Plimpton, George (author); New York City, 3/18/1927
Plisetskaya, Maya (ballerina); Moscow, 11/20/1925
Plowright, Joan (actress); Brigg, England, 10/28/1929
Plummer, Christopher (actor); Toronto, 12/13/1929
Plutarch (biographer); Chaeronea (Greece) **(46?-?120)**
Pocahontas (Matoaka) (American Indian princess); Virginia (?) **(1595?-1617)**
Podhoretz, Norman (author); Brooklyn, N.Y., 1/16/1930
Poe, Edgar Allan (poet and story writer); Boston, Mass. **(1809-1849)**
Poitier, Sidney (film actor and director); Miami, Fla., 2/20/1927
Polanski, Roman (film director); Paris, 8/18/1933
Pollard, Michael J. (actor); Passaic, N.J., 5/30/1939
Pollock, Jackson (painter); Cody, Wyo. **(1912-1956)**
Polo, Marco (traveler); Venice **(1254?-?1324)**
Pompadour, Mme. de (Jeanne Antoinette Poisson) (courtesan); Versailles **(1721-1764)**
Pompey (Gnaeus Pompeius Magnus) (general); Rome (?) **(106-48 B.C.)**
Ponce de León, Juan (explorer); Servas, Spain **(1460?-1521)**
Pons, Lily (coloratura soprano); Cannes, France **(1904-1976)**
Ponselle, Rosa (soprano); Meriden, Conn. **(1897-1981)**
Ponti, Carlo (director); Milan, Italy, 12/11/1913
Pope, Alexander (poet); London **(1688-1744)**
Porter, Cole (songwriter); Peru, Ind. **(1891-1964)**
Porter, Katherine Anne (novelist); Indian Creek, Tex. **(1891-1980)**
Post, Wiley (aviator); Grand Plain, Tex. **(1900-1935)**
Poston, Tom (actor); Columbus, Ohio, 10/17/1927
Potëmkin, Grigori Aleksandrovich, Prince (statesman); Khizovo (Khizov, Belorussia, U.S.S.R.) **(1739-1791)**
Potok, Chaim (author); New York City, 2/17/1929
Poulenc, Francis (composer); Paris **(1899-1963)**
Pound, Ezra (poet); Hailey, Idaho **(1885-1972)**
Poussin, Nicolas (painter); Villers, France **(1594-1665)**
Powell, Adam Clayton, Jr. (Congressman); New Haven, Conn. **(1908-1972)**
Powell, Dick (actor); Mt. View, Ark. **(1904-1963)**
Powell, Eleanor (actress and tap dancer); Springfield, Mass. **(1912-1982)**
Powell, Jane (Suzanne Burce) (actress and singer); Portland, Ore., 4/1/1929
Powell, William (actor); Pittsburgh, **(1892-1984)**
Power, Tyrone (actor); Cincinnati, Ohio **(1914-1958)**
Powers, Stephanie (Taffy Paul) (actress); Hollywood, Calif., 11/12/1942
Praxiteles (sculptor); Athens **(c.370-c.330 B.C.)**
Preminger, Otto (film director and producer); Vienna **(1906-1986)**
Prentiss, Paula (Paula Ragusa) (actress); San Antonio, 1939
Presley, Elvis (singer and actor); Tupelo, Miss. **(1935-1977)**
Presley, Priscilla (actress); Brooklyn, N.Y., 5/24/1945
Preston, Robert (Robert Preston Meservey) (actor); Newton Highlands, Mass **(1918-1987)**
Previn, André (conductor); Berlin, 4/6/1929
Previn, Dory (singer); Rahway, N.J., 10/22/1929(?)
Price, Leontyne (Mary) (soprano); Laurel, Miss., 2/10/1927
Price, Ray (country music artist); Perryville, Tex., 1/12/1926
Price, Vincent (actor); St. Louis, 5/27/1911
Pride, Charley (singer); Sledge, Miss., 3/18/1938(?)
Priestley, J. B. (John B.) (author); Bradford, England **(1894-1984)**
Priestley, Joseph (chemist); nr. Leeds, England **(1733-1804)**
Primrose, William (violist); Glasgow, Scotland **(1904-1982)**
Prince (Prince Roger Nelson) (singer); Minneapolis, 6/7/58
Prince, Harold (stage producer); New York City, 1/30/1928
Principal, Victoria (actress); Fukuoka, Japan, 1/3/1945(?)
Prinze, Freddie (actor); New York City **(1954-1977)**
Pritchett, V(ictor) S(awdon) (literary critic); Ipswich, England, 12/16/1900
Procter, William (scientist); Cincinnati **(1872-1951)**
Prokofiev, Sergei Sergeevich (composer); St. Petersburg, Russia **(1891-1953)**
Proust, Marcel (novelist); Paris **(1871-1922)**
Provine, Dorothy (actress); Deadwood, S. Dak., 1/20/1937
Prowse, Juliet (actress); Bombay, 9/25/1936
Pryor, Richard (comedian); Peoria, Ill., 12/1/1940
Ptolemy (Claudius Ptolemaeus) (astronomer and geographer); Ptolemais Hermii (Egypt) **(2nd century A.D.)**
Pucci, Emilio (Marchese di Barsento) (fashion designer); Naples, Italy **(1914-1992)**
Puccini, Giacomo (composer); Lucca, Italy **(1858-1924)**
Puente, Tito (band leader); New York City, 4/20/1923
Pulaski, Casimir (military officer); Podolia, Poland **(1748-1779)**
Pulitzer, Joseph (publisher); Makó (Hungary) **(1847-1911)**
Pullman, George (inventor); Brockton, N.Y. **(1831-1897)**
Purcell, Henry (composer); London **(1658-1695)**
Pusey, Nathan M. (educator); Council Bluffs, Iowa, 4/4/1907
Pushkin, Alexander Sergeevich (poet and dramatist); Moscow **(1799-1837)**
Puzo, Mario (novelist); New York City, 10/15/1921
Pyle, Ernest Taylor (journalist); Dana, Ind. **(1900-1945)**
Pythagoras (mathematician and philosopher); Samos (Greece) **(6th century B.C.)**

Q

Quaid, Randy, (actor); Houston, Texas, 10/1/1950
Quayle, Anthony (actor); Ainsdale, England **(1913-1989)**
Queen, Ellery: pen name of the late Frederic Dannay and the late Manfred B. Lee
Queler, Eve (conductor); New York City, 1/1/1936
Quennell, Peter Courtney (biographer); Bromley, England, 3/9/1905
Quinn, Anthony (actor); Chihuahua, Mexico, 4/21/1916

R

Rabe, David (playwright); Dubuque, Iowa, 3/10/1940
Rabelais, François (satirist); nr. Chinon, France **(1494?-1553)**
Rabi, I(sidor) I(saac) (physicist); Rymanow (Poland) **(1898-1988)**
Rachmaninoff, Sergei Wassilievitch (pianist and composer); Oneg Estate, Novgorod, Russia **(1873-1943)**
Racine, Jean Baptiste (dramatist); La Ferté-Milon, France **(1639-1699)**
Radner, Gilda (comedienne); Detroit **(1946-1989)**
Raft, George (actor); New York City **(1895-1980)**
Rainer, Luise (actress); Vienna, 1912
Raines, Ella (actress); Snoqualmie Falls, Wash. **(1921-1988)**
Rainier III (Prince); Monaco, 5/31/1923
Rains, Claude (actor); London **(1889-1967)**
Raitt, Bonnie (singer); Burbank, Calif., 11/8/1949
Raitt, John (actor,singer); Santa Ana, Calif., 1/29(?)/17
Raleigh, Sir Walter (courtier and navigator); London **(1552?-1618)**
Rambeau, Marjorie (actress); San Francisco **(1889-1970)**
Rameau, Jean-Philippe (composer); Dijon? France **(1683-1764)**
Rampal, Jean-Pierre (Louis) (flutist); Marseilles, France, 7/1/22
Randall, Tony (Leonard Rosenberg) (actor); Tulsa, Okla., 2/26/1920
Randolph, A(sa) Philip (labor leader); Crescent City, Fla. **(1889-1979)**
Raphael (Raffaello Santi) (painter and architect); Urbino (Italy) **(1483-1520)**
Rasputin, Grigori Efimovich (monk); Tobolsk Province, Russia **(1871?-1916)**
Rathbone, Basil (actor); Johannesburg, South Africa **(1892-1967)**
Rather, Dan (TV newscaster); Wharton, Tex., 10/31/1931
Ratoff, Gregory (film director); St. Petersburg, Russia **(1897-1960)**
Rattigan, Terence (playwright); London **(1911-1977)**
Rauschenberg, Robert (painter); Port Arthur, Tex., 10/22/1925
Ravel, Maurice Joseph (composer); Ciboure, France **(1875-1937)**
Ray, Aldo (DaRe) (actor); Pen Argyl, Pa. **(1926–1991)**
Ray, Gene Anthony (actor, dancer); Harlem, N.Y., 5/24/1963
Ray, Man (painter); Philadelphia **(1890-1976)**
Ray, Satyajat (film director); Calcutta **(1921-1992)**
Rayburn, Gene (TV personality); Christopher, Ill., 12/22/1917
Raye, Martha (Margie Yvonne Reed) (comedienne and actress); Butte, Mont., 8/27/1916
Raymond, Gene (actor); New York City, 8/13/1908
Reasoner, Harry (TV commentator); Dakota City, Iowa **(1923–1991)**
Redding, Otis (singer); Dawson, Ga. **(1941-1967)**
Reddy, Helen (singer); Melbourne, 10/25/1941
Redford, Robert (Charles Robert Redford, Jr.) (actor); Santa Monica, Calif., 8/18/1937
Redgrave, Lynn (actress); London, 3/8/1943
Redgrave, Sir Michael (actor); Bristol, England **(1908-1985)**
Redgrave, Vanessa (actress); London, 1/30/1937
Reed, Donna (actress); Denison, Iowa **(1921-1986)**
Reed, Rex (critic); Ft. Worth, 10/2/1940
Reed, Walter (army surgeon); Belroi, Va. **(1851-1902)**
Reese, Della (Deloreese Patricia Early) (singer); Detroit, 7/6/1932
Reeve, Christopher (actor); New York City, 9/25/1952
Reeves, Jim (singer); Panola County, Tex. **(1923-1964)**
Reich, Steve (composer): New York City, 10/3/1936
Reid, Wallace (actor); St. Louis **(1891-1923)**
Reiner, Carl (actor); New York City, 3/20/1922
Reiner, Fritz (conductor); Budapest **(1888-1963)**
Reiner, Robert (actor); Bronx, N.Y., 1945
Reinhardt, Max (Max Goldmann) (theater producer); nr. Vienna **(1873-1943)**

Remarque, Erich Maria (novelist); Osnabrük, Germany **(1898-1970)**
Rembrandt (Rembrandt Harmensz van Rijn) (painter); Leyden (Netherlands) **(1605-1669)**
Remick, Lee (Ann) (actress); Boston **(1935–1991)**
Rennert, Günther (opera director and producer); Essen, Germany, 4/1/1911
Rennie, Michael (actor); Bradford, England **(1909-1971)**
Renoir, Jean (film director and writer); Paris, **(1894-1979)**
Renoir, Pierre Auguste (painter); Limoges, France **(1841-1919)**
Resnais, Alain (film director); Vannes, France, 6/3/1922
Resnik, Regina (mezzo-soprano); New York City, 8/30/1922
Respighi, Ottorino (composer); Bologna, Italy **(1879-1936)**
Reston, James (journalist); Clydebank, Scotland, 11/3/1909
Reuther, Walter (labor leader); Wheeling, W. Va. **(1907-1970)**
Revere, Paul (silversmith and hero of famous ride); Boston **(1735-1818)**
Revson, Charles (business executive); Boston **(1906-1975)**
Reynolds, Burt (actor); Waycross, Ga., 2/11/1936
Renolds, Debbie (Marie Frances Reynolds) (actress); El Paso, 4/1/1932
Reynolds, Sir Joshua (painter); nr. Plymouth, England **(1723-1792)**
Reynolds, Marjorie (Goodspeed) (actress); Buhl, Idaho, 8/12/1921
Rhodes, Cecil John (South African statesman); Bishop Stortford, England **(1853-1902)**
Rice, Elmer (playwright); New York City **(1892-1967)**
Rice, Grantland (sports writer); Murfreesboro, Tenn. **(1880-1954)**
Rich, Buddy (Bernard) (drummer); Brooklyn, N.Y. **(1917-1987)**
Rich, Charlie (singer); Colt, Ark., 12/14/1932
Richardson, Elliot L. (ex-Cabinet member); Boston, 7/20/1920
Richardson, Sir Ralph (actor); Cheltenham, England **(1902-1983)**
Richardson, Tony (director); Shipley, England **(1928-1991)**
Richelieu, Duc de (Armand Jean du Plessis) (cardinal); Paris **(1585-1642)**
Richie, Lionel (singer-songwriter); Tuskegee, Ala., 1949 (?)
Richter, Charles Francis (seismologist); Hamilton, Canada **(1900-1985)**
Richter, Sviatosiav (pianist); Zhitomir, Ukraine, 3/20/1914
Rickenbacker, Edward V. (aviator); Columbus, Ohio **(1890-1973)**
Rickles, Don (comedian); New York City, 5/8/1926
Rickover, Vice Admiral Hyman G. (atomic energy expert); Russia **(1900-1986)**
Riddle, Nelson (composer); Hackensack, N.J. **(1921-1985)**
Ride, Sally K(risten) (astronaut, astrophysicist); Encino, Calif., 5/26/1951
Ridgway, General Matthew B. (ex-Army Chief of Staff); Ft. Monroe, Va. **(1895-1993)**
Rigg, Diana (actress); Doncaster, England, 7/20/1938
Riley, James Whitcomb (poet); Greenfield, Ind. **(1849-1916)**
Rimsky-Korsakov, Nikolai Andreevich (composer); Tikhvin, Russia **(1844-1908)**
Rinehart, Mary (née Roberts) (novelist); Pittsburgh **(1876-1958)**
Ritchard, Cyril (actor and director); Sydney, Australia **(1898-1977)**
Ritter, John (Jonathan) (actor); Burbank, Calif., 9/17/1948
Ritter, Tex (Woodward Maurice Ritter) (singer); Panola County, Tex., **(1905-1973)**
Ritter, Thelma (actress); Brooklyn, N.Y. **(1905-1969)**
Rivera, Chita (Dolores Conchita Figuero del Rivero) (dancer-actress-singer); Washington, D.C. 1/23/1933
Rivera, Diego (painter); Guanajuato, Mexico **(1886-1957)**
Rivera, Geraldo (Miguel) (TV newscaster); New York City, 7/3/1943
Rivers, Joan (comedienne); Brooklyn, N.Y., 6/8/1933
Rivers, Larry (Yitzroch Loiza Grossberg) (painter); New York City, 8/17/1923
Roach, Hal (film producer); Elmira, N.Y., 1/14/1892
Robards, Jason, Jr. (actor); Chicago, 7/26/1922
Robards, Jason, Sr. (actor); Hillsdale, Mich. **(1892-1963)**
Robbins, Harold (Harold Rubin) (novelist); New York City, 5/21/1916
Robbins, Jerome (Jerome Rabinowitz) (choreographer); New York City, 10/11/1918
Robbins, Marty (singer); Glendale, Ariz., **(1925-1982)**
Roberts, Eric (actor); Bilox, Miss., 4/18/1956
Roberts, (Granville) Oral (evangelist and publisher); nr. Ada, Okla., 1/24/1918
Robertson, Cliff (actor); La Jolla, Cal if., 9/9/1925
Robertson, Dale (Dayle) (actor); Oklahoma City, 7/14/1923
Robeson, Paul (singer and actor); Princeton, N.J., **(1898-1976)**
Robespierre, Maximilien François Marie Isidore de (French Revolutionist); Arras, France **(1758-1794)**
Robinson, Bill "Bojangles" (Luther) (dancer); Richmond, Va. **(1878-1949)**
Robinson, Edward G. (Emanuel Goldenberg) (actor); Bucharest **(1893-1973)**
Robinson, Edwin Arlington (poet); Head Tide, Me. **(1869-1935)**
Robson, Dame Flora (actress); South Shields, England **(1902-1984)**
Robson, May (actress); Melbourne, Australia **(1858-1942)**
Rochester (Eddie Anderson) (actor); Oakland, Calif. **(1905-1977)**
Rockefeller, David (banker); New York City, 6/12/1915
Rockefeller, John Davison (capitalist); Richford, N.Y. **(1839-1937)**
Rockefeller, John Davison, Jr. (industrialist); Cleveland **(1874-1960)**
Rockefeller, John D., 3rd (philanthropist); New York City **(1906-1978)**
Rockefeller, Laurance S. (conservationist); New York City, 5/26/1910
Rockwell, Norman (painter and illustrator); New York City **(1894-1978)**
Rodgers, Jimmie (singer); Meridian, Miss. **(1897-1933)**
Rodgers, Richard (composer); New York City **(1902-1979)**
Rodin, François Auguste René (sculptor); Paris **(1840-1917)**
Rodzinski, Artur (conductor); Spalato, Dalmatia **(1894-1958)**
Roentgen, Wilhelm Konrad (physicist); Lennep, Prussia **(1845-1923)**
Rogers, Buddy (Charles) (actor); Olathe, Kan., 8/13/1904
Rogers, Fred (Television producer, host): Latrobe, Pa., 3/20/1928
Rogers, Ginger (Virginia McMath) (dancer and actress); Independence, Mo., 7/16/1911
Rogers, Kenny (singer); Houston, 1939(?)
Rogers, Roy (Leonard Slye) (actor); Cincinnati, 11/5/1912
Rogers, Wayne (actor); Birmingham, Ala. 4/7/1933
Rogers, Will (William Penn Adair Rogers) (humorist); Oologah, Okla. **(1879-1935)**
Rogers, William P. (ex-Secretary of State); Norfolk, N.Y., 6/23/1913
Roland, Gilbert (actor); Juarez, Mexico, 12/11/1905
Rolland, Romain (author); Clamecy, France **(1866-1944)**
Rollins, Sonny (saxophonist); New York City, 9/7/1930
Romberg, Sigmund (comp oser); Szeged (Hungary) **(1887-1951)**
Rome, Harold (composer); Hartford, Conn., 5/27/1908
Romero, Cesar (actor); New York City, 2/15/1907
Romney, George W. (ex-Secretary of HUD); Chihuahua, Mexico, 7/8/1907
Romulo, Carlos P. (diplomat and educator); Manila **(1899-1985)**
Ronsard, Pierre de (poet); La Possonnière nr. Couture (Couture-sur-Loir, France) **(1524-1585)**
Ronstadt, Linda (singer); Tucson, Ariz., 7/30/1946
Rooney, Andy (TV personality); Albany, N.Y., 1/14/1919
Rooney, Mickey (Joe Yule, Jr.) (actor); Brooklyn, N.Y., 9/23/1920
Roosevelt, Anna Eleanor (reformer and humanitarian); New York City **(1884-1962)**
Rorem, Ned (composer); Richmond, Ind., 10/23/1923
Rose, Billy (showman); New York City **(1899-1966)**
Rose, Leonard (concert cellist); Washington, D.C. **(1918-1984)**
Ross, Betsy (Betsey Griscom) (flagmaker); Philadelphia **(1752-1836)**
Ross, Diana (singer); Detroit, 3/26/1944
Ross, Katharine (actress); Hollywood, Calif., 1/29/1943
Rossellini, Isabella (model, actress); Rome, Italy, 6/18/1952
Rossellini, Roberto (film director); Rome **(1906-1977)**
Rossetti, Dante Gabriel (painter and poet); London **(1828-1882)**
Rossini, Gioacchino Antonio (composer); Pesaro (Italy) **(1792-1868)**
Rostand, Edmond (dramatist); Marseilles, France **(1868-1918)**
Rostow, Walt Whitman (economist); New York City, 10/7/1916
Rostropovich, Mstislav (cellist and conductor); Baku, U.S.S.R., 3/27/1927
Roth, Lillian (singer); Boston **(1910-1980)**
Roth, Philip (novelist); Newark, N.J., 3/19/1933
Rothko, Mark (Marcus Rothkovich) (painter); Russia **(1903-1970)**
Rouault, Georges (painter); Paris **(1871-1958)**
Roundtree, Richard (actor); New Rochelle, N.Y., 9/7/1942
Rousseau, Henri (painter); Laval, France **(1844-1910)**
Rousseau, Jean Jacques (philosopher); Geneva **(1712-1778)**
Rovere, Richard H. (journalist); Jersey City, N.J., 5/5/1915
Rowan, Dan (comedian); Beggs, Okla. **(1922-1987)**
Rowlands, Gena (actress); Cambria, Wis., 6/19/1936(?)
Rubens, Sir Peter Paul (painter); Siegen (Germany) **(1577-1640)**
Rubinstein, Arthur (concert pianist); Lódz (Poland) **(1887-1982)**
Rubinstein, Helena (cosmetics executive); Krakow (Poland) **(1882?-1965)**
Rubinstein, John (actor, composer); Los Angeles, 12/8/1946
Rudel, Julius (conductor); Vienna, 3/6/1921
Ruffo, Titta (baritone); Italy **(1878-1953)**
Ruggles, Charles (actor); Los Angeles **(1892-1970)**
Rule, Janice (actress); Norwood, Ohio, 8/15/1931
Runcie, Robert (Alexander Kennedy) (Archbishop of Canterbury); Liverpool, England, 10/2/1921
Runyon, (Alfred) Damon (journalist); Manhattan, Kan. **(1884-1945)**
Rusk, Dean (ex-Sec. of State); Cherokee County, Ga., 2/9/1909
Ruskin, John (art critic); London **(1819-1900)**
Russell, Lord Bertrand (Arthur William) (mathematician and philosopher); Trelleck, Wales **(1872-1970)**
Russell, Jane (actress); Bemidji, Minn., 6/21/1921
Russell, Ken (film director); Southhampton, England, 4/3/1927
Russell, Leon (pianist and singer); Lawton, Okla., 4/2/1941
Russell, Lillian (Helen Louise Leonard) (soprano); Clinton, Iowa **(1861-1965)**
Russell, Mark (satirist); Buffalo, N.Y., 8/23/1932

Russell, Nipsy (comedian); Atlanta, 1924(?)
Russell, Rosalind (actress); Waterbury, Conn. **(1912-1976)**
Rustin, Bayard (civil rights leader); West Chester, Pa. **(1910-1987)**
Rutherford, Dame Margaret (actress); London **(1892-1972)**
Ryan, Robert (actor); Chicago **(1909-1973)**
Rydell, Bobby (singer); Philadelphia, 1942
Rysanek, Leonie (dramatic soprano); Vienna, 11/14/1928

S

Saarinen, Eero (architect); Finland **(1910-1961)**
Sabin, Albert B. (polio researcher); Bialystok (Poland) **(1906-1993)**
Sabu (Dastagir) (actor); Karapur, India **(1924-1963)**
Sadat, Anwar el- (President); Egypt **(1918-1981)**
Sade, Marquis de (Donatien Alphonse Francois, Comte de Sade) (libertine and writer); Paris **(1740-1814)**
Safer, Morley (TV newscaster); Toronto, 11/8/1931
Sagan, Carl (Edward) (astronomer, astrophysicist); New York City, 11/9/1934
Sagan, Françoise (novelist); Cajarc, France, 6/21/1935
Sahl, Mort (Morton Lyon Sahl) (comedian); Montreal, 5/11/1927
Saint, Eva Marie (actress); Newark, N.J., 7/4/1924
Saint-Gaudens, Augustus (sculptor); Dublin **(1848-1907)**
St. Denis, Ruth (dancer,choreographer); Newark, N.J. **(1878-1968)**
St. James, Susan (Susan Miller) (actress); Los Angeles, 8/14/1946
St. John, Jill (actress); Los Angeles, 8/19/1940
St. Johns, Adela Rogers (journalist and author); Los Angeles **(1894-1988)**
Saint-Laurent, Yves (Henri Donat Mathieu) (fashion designer); Oran, Algeria, 8/1/1936
Saint-Saens, Charles Camille (composer); Paris **(1835-1921)**
Sainte-Marie, Buffy (Beverly) (folk singer); Craven, Saskatchewan, Canada, 2/20/1942(?)
Sales, Soupy (Milton Hines); Franklinton, N.C., 1/6/1926
Salinger, J(erome) D(avid) (novelist); New York City, 1/1/1919
Salisbury, Harrison E. (journalist); Minneapolis **(1908-1993)**
Salk, Jonas (polio researcher); New York City, 10/28/1914
Salk, Leo (psychologist); New York City, 1926
Salomon, Haym (American Revolution financier); Leszno, Poland **(1740-1785)**
Sand, George (Amandine Lucille Aurore Dudevant, née Dupin) (novelist); Paris **(1804-1876)**
Sandburg, Carl (poet and biographer); Galesburg, Ill. **(1878-1967)**
Sanders, George (actor); St. Petersburg, Russia **(1906-1972)**
Sands, Tommy (singer); Chicago, 8/27/1937
Sanger, Margaret (birth control leader); Corning, N.Y. **(1883-1966)**
Santayana, George (philosopher); Madrid **(1863-1952)**
Sappho (poet); Lesbos (Greece) (lived c. 600 B.C.)
Sargent, John Singer (painter); Florence, Italy **(1856-1925)**
Sarnoff, David (radio executive); Minsk, Russia **(1891-1971)**
Saroyan, William (novelist); Fresno, Calif. **(1908-1981)**
Sarrazin, Michael (actor); Quebec, 5/22/1940
Sarto, Andrea del (Andrea Domenico d'Agnolo di Francesco) (painter); Florence (Italy) **(1486-1531)**
Sartre, Jean-Paul (existentialist writer); Paris **(1905-1980)**
Sassoon, Vidal (hair stylist); London, 1/(?)/1928
Saul (King of Israel) **(11th century B.C.)**
Savalas, Telly (Aristoteles) (actor); Garden City, N.Y., 1/21/1924(?)
Savonarola, Girolamo (religious reformer); Ferrara, Italy **(1452-1498)**
Sawyer, Diane (broadcast journalist); Glasgow, Ky., 12/22/1945
Sayão, Bidú (soprano); Rio de Janeiro, 5/11/1902
Scaasi, Arnold (Arnold Isaacs) (fashion designer); Montreal
Scarlatti, Alessandro (composer); Palermo, Italy **(1659-1725)**
Scarlatti, Domenico (composer); Naples, Italy **(1685-1757)**
Scavullo, Francesco (photographer); Staten Island, N.Y. 1/16/1929
Schary, Dore (producer and writer); Newark, N.J. **(1905-1980)**
Schell, Maria (actress); Vienna, 1/15/1926
Schell, Maximilian (actor); Vienna, 12/8/1930
Schiaparelli, Elsa (fashion designer); Rome **(1890?-1973)**
Schiff, Dorothy (newspaper publisher); New York City **(1903-1989)**
Schildkraut, Joseph (actor); Vienna **(1896-1964)**
Schiller, Johann Christoph Friedrich von (dramatist and poet); Marbach (Germany) **(1759-1805)**
Schipa, Tito (tenor); Lecce, Italy **(1890-1965)**
Schippers, Thomas (conductor); Kalamazoo, Mich. **(1930-1977)**
Schlegel, Friedrich von (philosopher); Hanover? Germany **(1772-1829)**
Schlesinger, Arthur M., Jr. (historian); Columbus, Ohio, 10/15/1917
Schnabel, Artur (pianist,composer); Lipnik, Austria **(1882-1951)**
Schneider, Romy (Rose-Marie Albach) (actress); Vienna **(1938-1982)**
Schoenberg, Arnold (composer); Vienna **(1874-1951)**
Schopenhauer, Arthur (philosopher); Danzig (Poland) **(1788-1860)**
Schubert, Franz Peter (composer); Vienna **(1797-1828)**
Schulberg, Budd (novelist); New York City, 3/27/1914
Schulz, Charles M. (cartoonist); Minneapolis, 11/26/1922
Schuman, Robert (statesman); Luxembourg **(1886-1963)**
Schuman, William (composer); New York City **(1910-1992)**
Schumann, Robert Alexander (composer); Zwickau (East Germany) **(1810-1856)**
Schumann-Heink, Ernestine (contralto); near Prague **(1861-1936)**
Schwartz, Arthur (song writer); Brooklyn, N.Y. **(1900-1984)**
Schwarzenegger, Arnold (bodybuilder, actor); Graz, Austria, 7/30/1947
Schwarzkopf, Elisabeth (soprano); Jarotschin, Poznán (Poland), 12/9/1915
Schweitzer, Albert (humanitarian); Kaysersburg, Upper Alsace **(1875-1965)**
Scofield, Paul (actor); Hurstpierpoint, England, 1/21/1922
Scorsese, Martin (film director); Flushing, N.Y., 11/17/1942
Scott, George C. (actor); Wise, Va., 10/18/1927
Scott, Hazel (singer, pianist); Port of Spain, Trinidad **(1920-1981)**
Scott, Lizabeth (Emma Matso) (actress); Scranton, Pa., 1923
Scott, Martha (actress); Jamesport, Mo., 9/22/1914
Scott, Randolph (Randolph Crane) (actor); Orange County, Va **(1898-1987)**
Scott, Robert Falcon (explorer); Devonport, England **(1868-1912)**
Scott, Sir Walter (novelist); Edinburgh, Scotland **(1771-1832)**
Scott, Zachary (actor); Austin, Tex. **(1914-1965)**
Scotto, Renata (operatic soprano); Savona, Italy, 2/?/1936?
Scruggs, Earl Eugene (bluegrass musician); Cleveland County, N.C., 1/6/1924
Sebastian, John (composer); New York City, 3/17/1944
Seberg, Jean (actress); Marshalltown, Iowa **(1938-1979)**
Sedaka, Neil (singer); Brooklyn, N.Y., 3/13/1939
Seeger, Pete (folk singer); New York City, 5/3/1919
Segal, Erich (novelist); Brooklyn, N.Y., 6/16/1937
Segal, George (actor); New York City, 2/13/1936
Segovia, Andrés (guitarist); Linares, Spain **(1893-1987)**
Selleck, Tom (actor); Detroit, 1/29/1945
Sellars, Peter (theater director): Pittsburgh, Pa., 1958 (?)
Sellers, Peter (actor); Southsea, England **(1925-1980)**
Selznick, David O. (film producer); Pittsburgh **(1902-1965)**
Sendak, Maurice (Bernard) (children's book author and illustrator); Brooklyn, N.Y., 6/10/1928
Sennett, Mack (Michael Sinnott) (film producer); Richmond, Quebec, Canada **(1880-1960)**
Serkin, Peter (pianist): New York City, 7/24/1947
Serkin, Rudolf (pianist); Eger (Hungary) **(1903–1991)**
Serling, Rod (story writer); Syracuse, N.Y. **(1924-1975)**
Sessions, Roger (composer); Brooklyn, N.Y. **(1896-1985)**
Seurat, Georges (painter); Paris **(1859-1891)**
Seuss, Dr. (Theodor Seuss Geisel) (author and illustrator); Springfield, Mass. **(1904-1991)**
Sevareid, Eric (TV commentator); Velva, N.D. **(1912-1992)**
Severinsen, Doc (Carl) (band leader); Arlington, Ore., 7/7/1927
Sexton, Anne (poet); Newton, Mass. **(1928-1974)**
Seymour, Jane (actress); Wimbledon, England, 2/15/1951
Shaffer, Peter (playwright); Liverpool, England, 5/15/1926
Shahn, Ben(jamin) (painter); Kaunas, Lithuania **(1898-1969)**
Shakespeare, William (dramatist); Stratford on Avon, England **(1564-1616)**
Shandling, Garry (comedian); Chicago, Ill., 1950
Shankar, Ravi (sitar player); Benares, India, 4/7/1920
Sharif, Omar (Michael Shalhoub) (actor); Alexandria, Egypt, 4/10/1932
Shatner, William (actor); Montreal, 3/22/1931
Shaw, Artie (Arthur Arshawsky) (band leader); New York City, 5/23/1910
Shaw, George Bernard (dramatist); Dublin, **(1856-1950)**
Shaw, Irwin (novelist); Brooklyn, N.Y., **(1913-1984)**
Shaw, Robert (actor); Lancashire, England **(1927-1978)**
Shaw, Robert (chorale conductor); Red Bluff, Calif., 4/30/1916
Shawn, Ted (Edwin Myers Shawn) (dancer,choreographer); Kansas City, Mo. **(1891-1972)**
Shearer, Moira (ballerina); Dunfermline, Scotland, 1/17/1926
Shearer, Norma (actress); Montreal, **(1902?-1983)**
Shearing, George (pianist); London, 8/13/1920
Sheen, Fulton J. (Peter Sheen) (Roman Catholic bishop); El Paso, Ill. **(1895-1979)**
Sheen, Martin (Ramon Estevez) (actor); Dayton, Ohio, 8/3/1940
Shelley, Percy Bysshe (poet); nr. Horsham, England **(1792-1822)**
Shepard, Sam (playwright); Ft. Sheridan, Ill. 11/5/1943
Shepherd, Cybill (actress); Memphis, Tenn., 2/18/1950
Sheraton, Thomas (furniture designer); Stockton-on-Tees, England **(1751-1806)**
Sheridan, Ann (actress); Denton, Tex. **(1915-1967)**
Sheridan, Philip (army officer); Albany, N.Y. **(1831-1888)**
Sheridan, Richard Brinsley (dramatist); Dublin **(1751-1816)**
Sherman, William Tecumseh (army officer); Lancaster, Ohio

(1820-1891)
Sherwood, Robert Emmet (playwright); New Rochelle, N.Y. **(1896-1955)**
Shevardnadze, Eduard Amvrosiyevich (State Council Chairman, Georgia); Mamati, Georgia, U.S.S.R. 1/25/1928
Shields, Brooke (actress); New York City, 5/31/1965
Shire, Talia (Coppola) (actress) Lake Success, N.Y. 4/25/1946(?)
Shirer, William L. (journalist and historian); Chicago, 2/23/1904
Shirley, Anne (actress); New York City **(1918-1993)**
Sholokhov, Mikhail (novelist); Veshenskaya, Russia **(1905-1984)**
Shore, Dinah (Frances Rose Shore) (singer); Winchester, Tenn., 3/1/1917(?)
Short, Bobby (Robert Waltrip Short) (singer and pianist); Danville, Ill., 9/15/1924
Shostakovich, Dmitri (composer); St. Petersburg, Russia **(1906-1975)**
Shriner, Herb (humorist,host); Toledo, Ohio **(1918-1970)**
Shriver, Maria (TV co-host); Chicago, 11/6/1955
Shriver, Sargent (Robert Sargent Shriver, Jr.) (business executive); Westminster, Md., 11/9/1915
Shulman, Max (novelist); St. Paul **(1919-1988)**
Sibelius, Jean (Johann Julius Christian Sibelius) (composer); Tavastehus (Finland) **(1865-1957)**
Siddons, Sarah (Sarah Kemble) (actress); Wales **(1755-1831)**
Sidney, Sylvia (actress); New York City, 8/8/1910
Siepi, Cesare (basso); Milan, Italy, 2/10/1923
Signoret, Simone (Simone Kaminker) (actress); Wiesbaden, Germany **(1921-1985)**
Sikorsky, Igor I. (inventor); Kiev, Russia **(1889-1972)**
Sills, Beverly (Belle Silverman) (soprano, opera director); Brooklyn, N.Y., 5/25/1929
Sills, Milton (actor); Chicago **(1882-1930)**
Silone, Ignazio (Secondo Tranquilli) (novelist); Pescina del Marsi, Italy **(1900-1978)**
Silverman, Fred (broadcasting executive); New York City, 9/13/1937
Silver, Ron (actor); New York City, 7/2/1946
Silvers, Phil (Philip Silversmith) (comedian); Brooklyn, N.Y. **(1912-1985)**
Sim, Alastair (actor); Edinburgh, Scotland **(1900-1976)**
Simenon, Georges (Georges Sim) (mystery writer); Liège, Belgium **(1903-1989)**
Simmons, Jean (actress); Crouch Hill, London, 1/31/1929
Simon, Carly (singer and songwriter); New York City, 6/25/1945
Simon, Neil (playwright); Bronx, N.Y., 7/4/1927
Simon, Norton (business executive); Portland, Ore. **(1907-1993)**
Simon, Paul (singer and songwriter); Newark, N.J., 11/5/1942
Simon, Simone (actress); Marseilles, France, 4/23/1914
Simone, Nina (Eunice Kathleen Waymoa) (singer and pianist); Tryon, N.C., 2/21/1933
Sinatra, Frank (Francis Albert) (singer and actor); Hoboken, N.J., 12/12/1915
Sinclair, Upton Beall (novelist); Baltimore **(1878-1968)**
Singer, Isaac Bashevis (novelist); Radzymin (Poland) **(1904–1991)**
Siqueiros, David (painter); Chihuahua, Mexico **(1896-1974)**
Sisley, Alfred (painter); Paris **(1839-1899)**
Sitting Bull (Prairie Sioux Indian Chief); on Grand River, S.D. **(c. 1835-1890)**
Skelton, Red (Richard) (comedian); Vincennes, Ind., 7/18/1913
Skinner, B(urrhus) F(rederic) (psychologist); Susquehanna, Pa. **(1904-1990)**
Skinner, Cornelia Otis (writer and actress); Chicago, **(1901-1979)**
Skinner, Otis (actor); Cambridge, Mass. **(1858-1942)**
Slatkin, Leonard (conductor): Los Angeles, 9/1/1944
Slezak, Walter (actor); Vienna **(1902-1983)**
Sloan, Alfred P., Jr. (industrialist); New Haven, Conn. **(1875-1965)**
Sloan, John (painter); Lock Haven, Pa. **(1871-1951)**
Smetana, Bedrich (composer); Litomysl (Czechoslovakia) **(1824-1884)**
Smith, Adam (economist); Kirkaldy, Scotland **(1723-1790)**
Smith, Alexis (actress); Penticon, Canada **(1921-1993)**
Smith, Alfred Emanuel (politician); New York City **(1873-1944)**
Smith, Sir C. Aubrey (actor); London **(1863-1948)**
Smith, David (sculptor); Decatur, Ind. **(1906-1965)**
Smith, H. Allen (humorist); McLeansboro, Ill. **(1907-1976)**
Smith, Howard K. (TV commentator); Ferriday, La., 5/12/1914
Smith, Jaclyn (actress); Houston, 10/26/1947
Smith, John (American colonist); Willoughby, Lincolnshire, England **(1580-1631)**
Smith, Joseph (religious leader); Sharon, Vt. **(1805-1844)**
Smith, Kate (Kathryn) (singer); Greenville, Va. **(1909-1986)**
Smith, Dame Maggie (actress); Ilford, England, 12/28/1934
Smith, Red (Walter) (sports columnist); Green Bay, Wis. **(1905-1982)**
Smits, Jimmy (actor); New York City, 7/9/1958
Smollet, Tobias (novelist); Dalquhurn, Scotland **(1721-1771)**
Smothers, Dick (Richard) (comedian); Governors Island, New York City, 11/20/1939
Smothers, Tom (Thomas) (comedian); Governors Island, New York City, 2/2/1937
Snow, Lord (Charles Percy) (author); Leicester, England **(1905-1980)**
Snowdon, Earl of (Anthony Armstrong-Jones) (photographer); London, 3/7/1930
Snyder, Tom (TV personality); Milwaukee, 5/12/1936
Socrates (philosopher); Athens **(469-399 B.C.)**
Solomon (King of Israel); Jerusalem (?) **(died c. 933 B.C.)**
Solon (lawgiver); Salamis (Greece) **(638?-559 B.C.)**
Solti, Sir Georg (conductor); Budapest, 10/21/1912
Solzhenitsyn, Aleksandr (novelist); Kislovodsk, Russia, 12/11/1918
Somers, Suzanne (Suzanne Mahoney) (actress); San Bruno, Calif., 10/16/1946
Somes, Michael (ballet dancer); Horsley, England, 1917
Sommer, Elke (Elke Schletz) (actress); Berlin, 11/5/1942
Sondheim, Stephen (composer); New York City, 3/22/1930
Sontag, Susan (author and film director); New York City, 1/28/1933
Sophocles (dramatist); nr. Athens **(496?-406 B.C.)**
Sothern, Ann (Harriette Lake) (actress); Valley City, N.D., 1/22/1909
Soul, David (David Solberg) (actor); Chicago, 8/28/(?)
Sousa, John Philip (composer); Washington, D.C. **(1854-1932)**
Soyer, Raphael (painter); Borisoglebsk, Russia **(1899-1987)**
Spaak, Paul-Henri (statesman); Brussels **(1899-1972)**
Spacek, Sissy (Mary Elizabeth) (actress); Quitman, Tex., 12/25/1949
Spark, Muriel (novelist); Edinburgh, Scotland, 2/1/1918
Sparks, Ned (actor); Ontario **(1883-1957)**
Spector, Phil (rock producer); Bronx, N.Y., 12/25/1940
Spencer, Herbert (philosopher); Derby, England **(1820-1903)**
Spender, Stephen (poet); nr. London, 2/28/1909
Spengler, Oswald (philosopher); Blankenburg, (East Germany) **(1880-1936)**
Spenser, Edmund (poet); London **(1552?-1599)**
Spewack, Bella (playwright); Hungary **(1899-1990)**
Spiegel, Sam (producer); Jaroslaw (Poland) **(1901-1985)**
Spielberg, Steven (film director); Cincinnati, 12/18/1947
Spillane, Mickey (Frank Spillane) (mystery writer); Brooklyn, N.Y., 3/9/1918
Spinoza, Baruch (philosopher); Amsterdam (Netherlands) **(1632-1677)**
Spitalny, Phil (orchestra leader); **(1890-1970)**
Spivak, Lawrence (TV producer); Brooklyn, N.Y., 1900
Spock, Benjamin (pediatrician); New Haven, Conn., 5/2/1903
Springsteen, Bruce (singer and songwriter); Freehold, N.J., 9/23/1949
Sproul, Robert G. (educator); San Francisco **(1891-1975)**
Stack, Robert (actor); Los Angeles, 1/13/1919
Stafford, Jo (singer); Coalinga, Calif., 1918
Stalin, Joseph Vissarionovich (Iosif V. Dzhugashvili) (Soviet leader); nr. Tiflis, Russia **(1879-1953)**
Stallone, Sylvester (actor and writer); New York City, 7/6/1946
Stamp, Terrence (actor); London, 1938
Stander, Lionel (actor); New York City, 1/11/1908
Standing, Sir Guy (actor); London **(1873-1937)**
Stang, Arnold (comedian); Chelsea, Mass., 1925
Stanislavski (Konstantin Sergeevich Alekseev) (stage producer); Moscow **(1863-1938)**
Stanley, Sir Henry Morton (John Rowlands) (explorer); Denbigh, Wales **(1841-1904)**
Stanley, Kim (Patricia Reid) (actress); Tularosa, N.M., 2/11/1925
Stans, Maurice H. (ex-Secretary of Commerce); Shakope, Minn., 3/22/1908
Stanton, Frank (broadcasting executive); Muskegon, Mich., 3/20/1908
Stanwyck, Barbara (Ruby Stevens) (actress); Brooklyn, N.Y. **(1907-1990)**
Stapleton, Jean (Jeanne Murray) (actress); New York City, 1/19/1923
Stapleton, Maureen (actress); Troy, N.Y., 6/21/1925
Starker, Janós (cellist); Budapest, 7/5/1926
Starr, Kay (Starks) (singer); Dougherty, Okla., 7/21/1922
Starr, Ringo (Richard Starkey) (singer and songwriter); Liverpool, England, 7/7/1940
Stassen, Harold E. (ex-government official); West St. Paul, Minn., 4/13/1907
Steber, Eleanor (soprano); Wheeling, W. Va., 7/17/1916
Steegmuller, Francis (biographer); New Haven, Conn., 7/3/1906
Steele, Tommy (singer); London, 12/17/1936
Stegner, Wallace (Earle) (novelist and critic); Lake Mills, Iowa **(1909-1993)**
Steichen, Edward Jean (photographer, artist); Luxembourg **(1879-1973)**
Steiger, Rod (Rodney) (actor); Westhampton, N.Y., 4/14/1925
Stein, Gertrude (author); Allegheny, Pa. **(1874-1946)**
Steinbeck, John Ernst (novelist); Salinas, Calif. **(1902-1968)**
Steinberg, David (comedian); Winnipeg, Manitoba, Canada, 8/19/1942

Steinberg, William (conductor); Cologne, Germany **(1899-1978)**
Steinem, Gloria (feminist); Toledo, Ohio, 3/25/1934
Steinmetz, Charles (electrical engineer); Breslau (Poland) **(1865-1923)**
Stendhal (Marie Henri Beyle) (novelist); Grenoble, France **(1783-1842)**
Sterling, Jan (actress); New York City, 4/3/1923
Stern, Isaac (concert violinist); Kreminlecz, Russia, 7/21/1920
Sterne, Laurence (novelist); Clonmel, Ireland **(1713-1768)**
Stevens, Cat (Steven Georgiou) (singer and songwriter); London, 7/?/1947
Stevens, Connie (Concetta Ingolia) (singer); Brooklyn, N.Y., 8/8/1938
Stevens, George (film director); Oakland, Calif. **(1905-1975)**
Stevens, Risë (mezzo-soprano); New York City, 6/11/1913
Stevens, Stella (actress); Yazoo City, Miss., 10/1/1936
Stevenson, Adlai Ewing (statesman); Los Angeles **(1900-1965)**
Stevenson, McLean (actor); Bloomington, Ill., 11/14/1929(?)
Stevenson, Parker (actor); Philadelphia, Pa., 6/4/1952
Stevenson, Robert Louis Balfour (novelist and poet); Edinburgh, Scotland **(1850-1894)**
Stewart, James (actor); Indiana, Pa., 5/20/1908
Stewart, Rod (Roderick David) (singer); London, 1/10/1945
Stickney, Dorothy (actress); Dickinson, N.D. 6/21/1903
Stieglitz, Alfred (photographer); Hoboken, N.J. **(1864-1946)**
Stiers, David Ogden (actor); Peoria, Ill., 10/31/1942
Stiller, Jerry (actor); Brooklyn, N.Y., 6/8/1929
Stills, Stephen (singer and songwriter); Dallas, 1/3/1945
Sting (Gordon Matthew Sumner) (singer and composer): Wallsend, England, 10/2/1951
Stockwell, Dean (actor); North Hollywood, Calif., 3/5/1936
Stokes, Carl (TV newscaster); Cleveland, 6/21/1927
Stokowski, Leopold (conductor); London **(1882-1977)**
Stone, Edward Durell (architect); Fayetteville, Ark. **(1902-1978)**
Stone, Ezra (actor and producer); New Bedford, Mass., 12/2/1917
Stone, I(sidor) F(einstein) (journalist); Philadelphia **(1907-1989)**
Stone, Irving (Irving Tennenbaum) (novelist); San Francisco **(1903-1989)**
Stone, Lewis (actor); Worcester, Mass. **(1879-1953)**
Stone, Lucy (woman suffragist); nr. West Brookfield, Mass. **(1818-1893)**
Stone, Sly (Sylvester) (rock musician); 1944
Stoppard, Tom (Thomas Straussler) (playwright); Zlin, Czechoslovakia, 7/3/1937
Storm, Gale (actress); Bloomington, Tex., 1922
Stout, Rex (mystery writer); Noblesville, Ind. **(1886-1975)**
Stowe, Harriet Elizabeth Beecher (novelist); Litchfield, Conn. **(1811-1896)**
Stradivari, Antonio (violinmaker); Cremona (Italy) **(1644-1737)**
Straight, Beatrice (actress); Old Westbury, N.Y., 8/2/1916(?)
Strasberg, Lee (stage director); Budanov, Austria **(1901-1982)**
Strasberg, Susan (actress); New York City, 5/22/1938
Stratas, Teresa (soprana); Toronto, Ont., Canada, 5/26/1938
Straus, Oskar (composer); Vienna **(1870-1954)**
Strauss, Johann (composer); Vienna **(1825-1899)**
Strauss, Lewis L. (naval officer and scientist); Charleston, W. Va. **(1896-1974)**
Strauss, Peter (actor); New York City, 2/20/1947
Strauss, Richard (composer); Munich, Germany **(1864-1949)**
Stravinsky, Igor (composer); Orlenbaum, Russia **(1882-1971)**
Streep, Meryl (Mary Louise) (actress); Summit, N.J., 6/22/1949
Streisand, Barbra (singer and actress); Brooklyn, N.Y., 4/24/1942
Stritch, Elaine (actress); Detroit, 2/2/1925(?)
Struthers, Sally Ann (actress); Portland, Ore., 7/28/1948
Stuart, Gilbert Charles (painter); Rhode Island **(1755-1828)**
Stuart, James Ewell Brown (known as Jeb) (Confederate army officer); Patrick County, Va. **(1833-1864)**
Sturges, Preston (director, screenwriter, playwright); Chicago **(1898-1959)**
Stuyvesant, Peter (Governor of New Amsterdam); West Friesland (Netherlands) **(1592-1672)**
Styne, Jule (Julius Kerwin Stein) (songwriter); London, 12/31/1905
Styron, William (William Clark Styron, Jr.) (novelist); Newport News, Va., 6/11/1925
Sullavan, Margaret Brooke (actress); Norfolk, Va. **(1911-1960)**
Sullivan, Sir Arthur Seymour (composer); London **(1842-1900)**
Sullivan, Barry (Patrick Barry) (actor); New York City, 8/29/1912
Sullivan, Ed (columnist and TV personality); New York City **(1901-1974)**
Sullivan, Frank (Francis John) (humorist); Saratoga Springs, N.Y. **(1892-1976)**
Sullivan, Louis Henry (architect); Boston, Mass. **(1856-1924)**
Sulzberger, Arthur Ochs (newspaper publisher); New York City, 2/5/1926
Sumac, Yma (singer); Ichocan, Peru, 9/10/1927
Summer, Donna (La Donna Andrea Gaines) (singer); Boston, 12/31/1948
Summerville, Slim (George) (actor); Albuquerque, N.M. **(1892-1946)**
Sun Yat-sen (statesman); nr. Macao **(1866-1925)**
Susann, Jacqueline (novelist); Philadelphia **(1926?-1974)**
Susskind, David (TV producer); New York City **(1920-1987)**
Sutherland, Donald (actor); St. John, N.B., Canada, 7/17/34
Sutherland, Joan (soprano); Sydney, Australia, 11/7/1926
Suzuki, Pat (actress); Cressey, Calif., 1931
Swados, Elizabeth (composer, playwright); Buffalo, N.Y., 2/5/1951
Swanson, Gloria (Gloria May Josephine Svensson) (actress); Chicago **(1899-1983)**
Swarthout, Gladys (soprano); Deepwater, Mo. **(1904-1969)**
Swayze, John Cameron (news commentator); Wichita, Kan., 4/4/1906
Swayze, Patrick (actor, dancer); Houston, Tex., 8/18/1954
Swendenborg, Emanuel (scientist, philosopher, mystic); Stockholm **(1688-1772)**
Swift, Jonathan (satirist); Dublin **(1667-1745)**
Swinburne, Algernon Charles (poet); London **(1837-1909)**
Swit, Loretta (actress); Passaic, N.J., 11/4/1937
Swope, Herbert Bayard (journalist); St. Louis **(1882-1958)**
Sydow, von, Max (Carl Adolf von Sydow) (actor); Lund, Sweden, 4/10/1929
Synge, John Millington (dramatist); nr. Dublin **(1871-1909)**
Szilard, Leo (physicist); Budapest **(1898-1964)**

T

Taft, Robert Alphonso (legislator); Cincinnati **(1889-1953)**
Tagore, Sir Rabindranath (poet); Calcutta **(1861-1941)**
Tallchief, Maria (ballerina); Fairfax, Okla., 1/24/1925
Talleyrand-Pèrigord, Charles Maurice de (statesman); Paris **(1754-1838)**
Talmadge, Norma (actress); Niagara Falls, N.Y. **(1897-1957)**
Talvela, Martti (basso); Hiitola, Finalnd **(1935-1989)**
Tamerlane (Timur) (Mongol conqueror); nr. Samarkand (U.S.S.R.) **(1336?-1405)**
Tamiroff, Akim (actor) Baku, Russia **(1899-1972)**
Tandy, Jessica (actress); London, 6/7/1909
Tarkington, (Newton) Booth (novelist); Indianapolis **(1869-1946)**
Tate, Allen (John Orley) (poet and critic); Winchester, Ky., **(1899-1979)**
Tate, Sharon (actress); Dallas **(1943-1969)**
Tati, Jacques (Jacques Tatischeff) (actor); Pecq, France **(1908-1982)**
Taylor, Deems (composer); New York City **(1885-1966)**
Taylor, Elizabeth (actress); London, 2/27/1932
Taylor, Estelle (actress); Wilmington, Del. **(1899-1958)**
Taylor, Harold (educator); Toronto, 9/28/1914
Taylor, James (singer and songwriter); Boston, 3/12/1948
Taylor, (Joseph) De ems (composer); New York City **(1885-1966)**
Taylor, Laurette (Laurette Cooney) (actress); New York City **(1884-1946)**
Taylor, Gen. Maxwell D. (former Army Chief of Staff); Keytesville, Mo **(1901-1987)**
Taylor, Robert (Spangler Arlington Brugh) (actor); Filley, Neb. **(1911-1969)**
Taylor, Rod (actor); Sydney, Australia, 1/11/1930
Tchaikovsky, Peter (Pëtr) Ilich (composer); Votkinsk, Russia **(1840-1893)**
Teasdale, Sara (poet); St. Louis **(1884-1933)**
Tebaldi, Renata (lyric soprano); Pesaro, Italy, 1/2/1922
Tecumseh (Shawnee Indian chief); nr. Springfield, Ohio **(1768?-1813)**
Te Kanawa, Kiri (soprano); Gisborne, New Zealand, 1946(?)
Telemann, Georg Philipp (composer); Magdeburg (East Germany) **(1681-1767)**
Teller, Edward (atomic physicist); Budapest, 1/15/1908
Temple, Shirley. *See* Black, Shirley Temple
Templeton, Alec Andrew (pianist, composer); Cardiff, Wales **(1910-1963)**
Tennille, Toni (singer); Montgomery, Ala., 5/8/1943
Tennyson, Alfred (1st Baron Tennyson) (poet); Somersby, England **(1809-1892)**
Terhune, Albert Payson (novelist and journalist); Newark, N.J. **(1872-1942)**
Terkel, Studs (writer-interviewer); New York City, 5/16/1912
Terry, Ellen Alicia (actress); Coventry, England **(1848-1928)**
Terry-Thomas (Thomas Terry Hoar Stevens) (actor); London **(1911-1990)**
Tesla, Nikola (electrical engineer and inventor); Smiljan (Yugoslavia) **(1856-1943)**
Thackeray, William Makepeace (novelist); Calcutta **(1811-1863)**
Thalberg, Irving G. (producer); Brooklyn, N.Y. **(1899-1936)**
Thant, U (U.N. statesman); Pantanaw (Burma) **(1909-1974)**
Tharp, Twyla (dancer and choreographer); Portland, Ind., 7/1/1941(?)

Thatcher, Margaret (Prime Minister); Grantham, England, 10/13/1925
Thaxter, Phyllis (actress); Portland, Me., 1921
Thebom, Blanche (mezzo-soprano); Monessen, Pa., 9/19/1919
Theodorakis, Mikis (composer); Chios, Greece, 7/29/1925
Thicke, Alan (actor); Kirland Lake, Ont., Canada, 3/1/1947
Thieu, Nguyen Van (ex-President of South Vietnam); Trithuy (Vietnam) 4/5/1923
Thomas, Danny (Amos Jacobs) (entertainer and TV producer); Deerfield, Mich. **(1912–1991)**
Thomas, Dylan Marials (poet); Carmarthenshire, Wales **(1914-1953)**
Thomas, Lowell (explorer, commentator); Woodington, Ohio **(1892-1981)**
Thomas, Marlo (actress); Detroit, 11/21/1943
Thomas, Michael Tilson (conductor); Hollywood, Calif., 12/21/1944
Thomas, Norman Mattoon (Socialist leader): Marion, Ohio **(1884-1968)**
Thomas, Philip Michael (actor); Columbus, Ohio, 5/26/1949
Thomas, Richard (actor); New York City, 6/13/1951
Thompson, Dorothy (writer); Lancaster, N.Y. **(1894-1961)**
Thompson, Hunter (Stockton) (writer); Louisville, Ky. 7/18/1939
Thompson, Sada (actress); Des Moines, Iowa, 9/27/1929
Thomson, Virgil (Garnett) (composer); Kansas City, Mo. **(1896-1989)**
Thoreau, Henry David (naturalist and author); Concord, Mass. **(1817-1862)**
Thorndike, Dame Sybil (actress); Gainsborough, England **(1882-1976)**
Thurber, James Grover (author and cartoonist); Columbus, Ohio **(1894-1961)**
Tibbett, Lawrence (baritone); Bakersfield, Calif. **(1896-1960)**
Tiegs, Cheryl (model,actress); Minnesota, 9/25/1947
Tierney, Gene (actress); Brooklyn, N.Y. **(1920-1991)**
Tiffin, Pamela (actress); Oklahoma City, 10/13/1942
Tillstrom, Burr (puppeteer); Chicago **(1917-1985)**
Tintoretto, Il (Jacopo Robusti) (painter); Venice **(1518-1594)**
Tiny Tim (Herbert Khaury) (entertainer); New York City, 1923(?)
Tiomkin, Dmitri (composer); St. Petersburg, Russia **(1894-1979)**
Titian (Tiziano Vecelli) (painter); Pieve di Cadore (Italy) **(1477-1576)**
Tito (Josip Broz or Brozovich) (President of Yugoslavia); Croatia (Yugoslavia) **(1892-1980)**
Tocqueville, Alexis de (writer); Verneuil, France **(1805-1859)**
Todd, Ann (actress); Hartford, England **(1909-1993)**
Todd, Michael (producer); Minneapolis, Minn. **(1907-1958)**
Todd, Richard (actor); Dublin, Ireland, 6/11/1919
Todd, Thelma (actress); Lawrence, Mass. **(1905-1935)**
Tolstoi, Count Leo (Lev) Nikolaevich (novelist); Tula Province, Russia **(1828-1910)**
Tomlin, Lily (comedienne); Detroit, 1939(?)
Tone, Franchot (actor); Niagara Falls, N.Y. **(1905-1968)**
Toomey, Regis (actor); Pittsburgh, Pa. **(1902-1991)**
Tormé, Mel (Melvin) (singer); Chicago, 9/13/1925
Torn, Rip (Elmore Torn, Jr.) (actor and director); Temple, Tex., 2/6/1931
Torquamada, Tomásde (Spanish Inquisitor); Vlladolid, Spain **(1420-1498)**
Toscanini, Arturo (orchestra conductor); Parma, Italy **(1867-1957)**
Toulouse-Lautrec (Henri Marie Raymond de Toulouse-Lautrec Monfa) (painter); Albi, France **(1864-1901)**
Toynbee, Arnold J. (historian); London **(1889-1975)**
Tracy, Lee (actor); Atlanta, Ga. **(1898-1968)**
Tracy, Spencer (actor); Milwaukee **(1900-1967)**
Traubel, Helen (Wagnerian soprano); St. Louis **(1903-1972)**
Travanti, Daniel J. (actor); Kenosha, Wis., 3/7/1940
Travolta, John (actor); Englewood, N.J., 2/18/1954
Treacher, Arthur (actor); Brighton, England **(1894-1975)**
Tree, Sir Herbert Beerbolm (actor-manager); London **(1853-1917)**
Trevor, Claire (actress); New York City, 1911
Trigère, (Pauline (fashion designer); Paris, 11/4/1912
Trilling, Lionel (author and educator); New York City **(1905-1975)**
Trotsky, Leon (Lev Davidovich Bronstein) (statesman); Elisavetgrad, Russia **(1879-1940)**
Troyanos, Tatiana (mezzo-soprano); New York City **(1938-1993)**
Trudeau, Garry (cartoonist); New York City, 1948
Trudeau, Pierre Elliott (former Prime Minister); Montreal, 10/18/1919
Truffaut, François (film director); Paris **(1932-1984)**
Trujillo y Molina, Rafael Leonidas (Dominican Republic dictator); San Cristóbal, Dominican Republic **(1891-1961)**
Truman, Margaret (author); Independence, Mo., 2/17/1924
Tryon, Thomas (actor and novelist); Hartford, Conn. **(1926–1991)**
Tsiolkovsky, Konstantin E. (father of cosmonautics); Izhevskoye, Russia **(1857-1935)**
Tuchman, Barbara (Wertheim) (historian, author); New York City **(1912-1989)**
Tucker, Forrest (actor); Plainfield, Ind. **(1919-1986)**
Tucker, Richard (tenor); New York City **(1914-1975)**
Tucker, Sophie (Sophie Abuza) (singer); Europe **(1884?-1966)**
Tudor, Antony (choreographer); London **(1909-1987)**
Tune, Tommy (dancer-choreographer); Wichita Falls, Tex., 2/28/1939
Turgenev, Ivan Sergeevich (novelist); Orel, Russia **(1818-18 83)**
Turner, Ike (singer); Clarksdale, Miss., 11/?/1931
Turner, Joseph M.W. (painter); London **(1775-1851)**
Turner, Kathleen (actress); Springfield, Mo., 1956 (?)
Turner, Lana (Julia Jean Mildred Frances Turner) (actress); Wallace, Idaho, 2/8/1920
Turner, Nat (civil rights leader); Southampton County, Va. **(1800-1831)**
Turner, Tina (Annie Mae Bullock) (singer); nr. Brownsville, Tex., 11/25/1940(?)
Turpin, Ben (comedian); New Orleans **(1874-1940)**
Tushingham, Rita (actress); Liverpool, England, 3/14/1942
Twain, Mark (Samuel Langhorne Clemens) (author); Florida, Mo. **(1835-1910)**
Tweed, William Marcy (politician); New York City **(1823-1878)**
Twiggy (Leslie Hornby) (model); London, 9/19/1949
Twining, Gen. Nathan F. (former Air Force Chief of Staff); Monroe, Wis. **(1897-1982)**
Twitty, Conway (Harold Lloyd Jenkins) (singer and guitarist); Friars Point, Miss. **(1933-1993)**
Tyson, Cicely (actress); New York City, 12/19/1939(?)

U

Udall, Stewart L. (ex-Secretary of the Interior); St. Johns, Ariz., 1/31/1920
Uggams, Leslie (singer and actress); New York City, 5/25/1943
Ulanova, Galina (ballerina); St. Petersburg, Russia, 1/10/1910
Ullman, Tracey (actress, singer); Slough, England, 12/30/1959
Ullmann, Liv (actress); Tokyo, 12/16/1939
Ulric, Lenore (actress); New Ulm, Minn. **(1894-1970)**
Untermeyer, Louis (anthologist and poet); New York City **(1885-1977)**
Updike, John (novelist); Shillington, Pa., 3/18/1932
Urey, Harold C. (physicist); Walkerton, Ind. **(1893-1981)**
Uris, Leon (novelist); Baltimore, 8/3/1924
Ustinov, Peter (actor and producer); London, 4/16/1921
Utrillo, Maurice (painter); Paris **(1883-1955)**

V

Vaccaro, Brenda (actress); Brooklyn, N.Y., 11/18/1939
Vadim, Roger (Roger Vadim Plemiannikov) (film director); Paris, 1/26/1928
Valentine, Karen (actress); Santa Rosa, Calif., 1947
Valentino, Rudolph (Rodolpho d'Antonguolla) (actor); Castellaneta, Italy **(1895-1926)**
Valentino (Valentino Garavani) (fashion designer); nr. Milan, Italy, 5/11/1932
Vallee, Rudy (Hubert Prior Rudy Vallée) (band leader and singer); Island Pond, Vt. **(1901-1986)**
Valli, Frankie (Frank Castellaccio) (singer); Newark, N.J., 5/3/1937
Van Allen, James Alfred (space physicist); Mt. Pleasant, Iowa, 9/7/1914
Van Buren, Abigail (Mrs. Morton Phillips) (columnist); Sioux City, Iowa, 7/4/1918
Vance, Vivian (actress); Cherryvale, Kan. **(1912-1979)**
Vanderbilt, Alfred G. (sportsman); London, 9/22/1912
Vanderbilt, Cornelius (financier); Port Richmond, N.Y. **(1794-1877)**
Vanderbilt, Gloria (fashion designer) New York City, 2/20/1924
Van Doren, Carl (writer and educator); Hope, Ill. **(1885-1950)**
Van Doren, Mamie (actress); Rowena, S.D., 2/6/1933
Van Dyke, Dick (actor); West Plains, Mo., 12/13/1925
Vandyke (or Van Dyck), Sir Anthony (painter); Antwerp (Belgium) **(1599-1641)**
Van Eyck, Jan (painter); Maeseyck (Belgium) **(c.1390-1441)**
Van Fleet, Jo (actress); Oakland, Calif., 12/30/1919
van Gogh, Vincent (painter); Groot Zundert, Brabant **(1853-1890)**
van Hamel, Martine (ballerina); Brussels, 11/16/1945
Van Heusen, Jimmy (Edward Chester Babcock) (songwriter); Syracuse, N.Y. **(1913-1990)**
Van Patten, Dick (actor); Richmond Hill, N.Y., 12/9/1928
Van Peebles, Melvin (playwright); Chicago, 9/21/1932
Vaughan, Sarah (singer); Newark, N.J. **(1924-1990)**
Vaughan Williams, Ralph (composer); Down Ampney, England **(1872-1958)**
Vaughn, Robert (actor); New York City, 11/22/1932
Veidt, Conrad (actor); Potsdam, Germany **(1893-1943)**
Velázquez, Diego Rodriguez de Silva y (painter); Seville, Spain **(1599-1660)**
Velez, Lupe (Guadelupe Velez de Villalobos) (actress); San Luis Potosi, Mexico **(1908-1944)**

Venturi, Robert (Charles) (architect); Philadelphia, 6/25/1925
Verdi, Giuseppe (composer); Roncole (Italy) **(1813-1901)**
Verdon, Gwen (actress); Culver City, Calif., 1/13/1925
Vereen, Ben (actor and singer); Miami, Fla., 10/10/1946
Vermeer, Jan (or Jan van der Meer van Delft) (painter); Delft (Netherlands) **(1632-1675)**
Verne, Jules (author); Nantes, France **(1828-1905)**
Veronese, Paolo (Paolo Cagliari) (painter); Verona **(1528-1588)**
Verrazano, Giovanni da (navigator); Florence (Italy) **(1485?-1528)**
Verrett, Shirley (mezzo-soprano); New Orleans, 5/31/1933
Vesalius, Andreas (anatomist); Brussels, Belgium **(1515-1564)**
Vespucci, Amerigo (navigator); Florence (Italy) **(1454-1512)**
Vickers, Jon (tenor); Prince Albert, Sask, Canada, 10/29/1926
Vico, Giovanni Battista (philosopher); Naples, Italy **(1668-1744)**
Vidal, Gore (novelist); West Point, N.Y., 10/3/1925
Vidor, King (film director and producer); Galveston, Tex. **(1895-1982)**
Vigoda, Abe (actor); New York City, 2/24/1921
Villa, Pancho (Doroteo Arango) (revolutionary); Hacienda de Rio Grande, San Juan del Rio, Meixco **(1877-1923)**
Villella, Edward (ballet dancer); Bayside, Queens, N.Y., 10/1/1936
Villon, François (François de Montcorbier) (poet); Paris **(1431-1463)**
Vincent, Helen (actress); Beaumont, Tex., 9/17/1907
Vinton, Bobby (singer); Canonsburg, Pa., 4/16/1935(?)
Virgil (or Vergil) (Publius Vergilius Maro) (poet); nr. Mantua (Italy) **(70-19 B.C.)**
Vishnevskaya, Galina (soprano); Leningrad, 10/25/1926
Vivaldi, Antonio (composer); Venice **(1678-1741)**
Vlaminck, Maurice de (painter); Paris **(1876-1958)**
Voight, Jon (actor); Yonkers, N.Y., 12/29/1938
Volta, Alessandro (scientist); Como, Italy **(1745-1827)**
Voltaire (François Marie Arouet) (author); Paris **(1694-1778)**
von Aroldingen, Karin (Karin Awny Hannelore Reinbold von Aroedingen and Eltzinger) (ballet dancer); Greiz (East Germany) 7/9/1941
von Braun, Wernher (rocket scientist); Wirsitz, Germany **(1912-1977)**
von Furstenberg, Betsy (Elizabeth Caroline Maria Agatha Felicitas Therese von Furstenberg-Hedringen) (actress); Nelheim-Heusen, Germany, 8/16/1935
von Fürstenberg, Diane (Diane Simone Michelle Halfin) (fashion designer); Brussels, 12/31/1946
von Hindenburg, Paul (statesman): Posen (Poland) **(1847-1934)**
von Karajan, Herbert (conductor); Salzburg (Austria) **(1908-1989)**
Vonnegut, Kurt, Jr. (novelist); Indianapolis, 11/11/1922
Von Stade, Frederica (mezzo-soprano); Somerville, N.J., 1945
Von Stroheim, Erich Oswald Hans Carl Maria von Nordenwall (film actor and director); Vienna **(1885-1957)**
Von Zell, Harry (announcer); Indianapolis, Ind. **(1906-1981)**
Vreeland, Diana (Diana Da Iziel) (fashion journalist and museum consultant); Paris **(1903?-1989)**

W

Wagner, Lindsay (actress); Los Angeles, 6/22/1949
Wagner, Robert (actor); Detroit, 2/10/1930
Wagner, Robert F. (ex-Mayor of New York City); New York City **(1910–1991)**
Wagner, Wilhelm Richard (composer); Leipzig (East Germany) **(1813-1883)**
Waldheim, Kurt (ex-U.N. Secretary-General); St. Andrae-Wörden, Austria, 12/21/1918
Walker, Nancy (Ann Myrtle Swoyer); (actress and comedienne); Philadelphia **(1922-1992)**
Walker, Robert (actor); Salt Lake City, Utah **(1918-1951)**
Wallace, DeWitt (publisher); St. Paul **(1889-1981)**
Wallace, George C. (ex-govenor); Clio, Ala. 8/25/1919
Wallace, Irving (novelist); Chicago **(1916-1990)**
Wallace, Mike (Myron Wallace) (TV interviewer and commentator); Brookline, Mass., 5/9/1918
Wallach, Eli (actor); Brooklyn, N.Y., 12/7/1915
Wallenstein, Alfred (conductor); Chicago **(1898-1983)**
Waller, Thomas "Fats" (pianist); New York City **(1904-1943)**
Wallis, Hal (film producer); Chicago **(1899-1986)**
Walpole, Horace (statesman and novelist); London **(1717-1797)**
Waltari, Mika (novelist); Helsinki, Finland, **(1903-1979)**
Walter, Bruno (Bruno Walter Schlesinger) (orchestra conductor); Berlin **(1876-1962)**
Walters, Barbara (TV commentator); Boston, 9/25/1931
Walton, Izaak (author); Stafford, England **(1593-1683)**
Wambaugh, Joseph (author and screenwriter); East Pittsburgh, Pa., 1/22/1937
Wanamaker, John (merchant); Philadelphia **(1838-1922)**
Wanamaker, Sam (actor,director); Chicago, 6/14/1919
Ward, Barbara (economist); York, England **(1914-1981)**
Warhol, Andy (artist and producer); Pennsylvania **(1928(?)-1987)**
Waring, Fred (band leader); Tyrone, Pa. **(1900-1984)**
Warner, H. B. (Henry Bryan Warner Lickford) (actor); London **(1876-1958)**
Warren, Lesley Ann (actress); New York City, 8/16/1946
Warren, Robert Penn (novelist); Guthrie, Ky. **(1905-1989)**
Warrick, Ruth (actress) St. Joseph, Mo., 6/29/1915
Warwick, Dionne (singer); East Orange, N.J., 1941
Washington, Booker Taliaferro (educator); Franklin County, Va. **(1856-1915)**
Waters, Ethel (actr ess and singer); Chester, Pa. **(1896-1977)**
Waters, Muddy (McKinley Morganfield) (singer and guitarist); Rolling Fork, Miss. **(1915-1983)**
Waterson, Sam (actor); Cambridge, Mass., 11/15/1940
Watson, Thomas John (industrialist); Campbell, N.Y. **(1874-1956)**
Watt, James (inventor); Greenock, Scotland **(1736-1819)**
Watteau, Jean-Antoine (painter); Valanciennes, France **(1684-1721)**
Wattleton, Faye (family planning advocate); St. Louis, Mo., 7/8/1943
Watts, André (concert pianist); Nuremberg, Germany, 6/20/1946
Waugh, Alec (Alexander Raban Waugh) (novelist); London **(1898-1981)**
Waugh, Evelyn (satirist); London **(1903-1966)**
Wayne, Anthony (military officer); Waynesboro (family farm), nr. Paoli, Pa. **(1745-1796)**
Wayne, David (David McMeekan); (actor); Traverse City, Mich., 1/30/1914
Wayne, John (Marion Michael Morrison) (actor); Winterset, Iowa **(1907-1979)**
Weaver, Dennis (actor); Joplin, Mo., 6/4/1925
Weaver, Fritz (actor); Pittsburgh, Pa., 1/19/1926
Weaver, Sigourney (actress); New York City, 10/8/1949
Webb, Clifton (Webb Parmelee Hollenbeck) (actor); Indianapolis **(1893-1966)**
Webb, Jack (film actor and producer); Santa Monica, Calif. **(1920-1982)**
Weber, Karl Maria Friedrich Ernst von (composer); nr. Lübeck (Germany) **(1786-1826)**
Webster, Daniel (statesman); Salisbury, N.H. **(1782-1852)**
Webster, Margaret (producer, director, actress); New York City **(1905-1973)**
Webster, Noah (lexicographer); West Hartford, Conn. **(1758-1843)**
Weill, Kurt (composer); Dessau, (East Germany) **(1900-1950)**
Weir, Peter (film director); Sydney, Australia, 8/21/1944
Weizmann, Chaim (statesman); Grodno Province, Russia **(1874-1952)**
Welch, Raquel (Raquel Tejada) (actress); Chicago, 9/5/1942
Weld, Tuesday (Susan) (actress); New York City, 8/27/1943
Welk, Lawrence (band leader); Strasburg, N.D. **(1903-1992)**
Welles, Orson (actor and producer); Kenosha, Wis. **(1915-1985)**
Wellington, Duke of (Arthur Wellesley) (statesman); Ireland **(1769-1852)**
Wells, H(erbert) G(eorge) (author); Bromley, England **(1866-1946)**
Welty, Eudora (novelist); Jackson, Miss., 4/13/1909
Werfel, Franz (novelist); Prague **(1890-1945)**
Werner, Oskar (Josef Schliessmayer) (film actor and director); Vienna **(1922-1984)**
Wertmuller, Lina (film director); Rome, 1926(?)
Wesley, John (religious leader); Epworth Rectory, Lincolnshire, England **(1703-1791)**
West, Dame Rebecca (Cicily Fairfield); (novelist); County Kerry, Ireland **(1892-1983)**
West, Jessamyn (novelist); nr. North Vernon, Ind. **(1902-1984)**
West, Mae (actress); Brooklyn, N.Y. **(1893-1980)**
West, Nathanael (Nathan Weinstein) (novelist); New York City **(1902-1940)**
Westheimer, Ruth (Karola Ruth Siegel) (psychologist, author, broadcaster); Frankfurt, Germany, 1928
Westinghouse, George (inventor); Central Bridge, N.Y. **(1846-1914)**
Westmoreland, William Childs (ex-Army Chief of Staff); Saxon, S.C., 3/26/1914
Wharton, Edith Newbold (née Jones) (novelist); New York City **(1862-1937)**
Wheeler, Bert (Albert Jerome Wheeler) (comedian); Paterson, N.J. **(1895-1968)**
Whistler, James Abbott McNeill (painter and etcher); Lowell, Mass. **(1834-1903)**
White, Betty (actress); Oak Park, Ill., 1/17/1924(?)
White, E(lwyn) B(rooks) (author); Mt. Vernon, N.Y. **(1899-1985)**
White, Pearl (actress); Green Ridge, Mo. **(1889-1938)**
White, Stanford (architect); New York City **(1853-1906)**
White, Theodore H. (historian); Boston **(1915-1986)**
White, Vanna (TV personality); Conway, S.C., 2/18/1957
White, William Allen (journalist); Emporia, Kan. **(1868-1944)**
Whitehead, Alfred North (mathematician and philosopher); Isle of Thanet, England **(1861-1947)**

Whiteman, Paul (band leader); Denver **(1891-1967)**
Whiting, Margaret (singer, actress); Detroit, Mich., 7/22/1924
Whitman, Walt (Walter) (poet); West Hills, N.Y. **(1819-1892)**
Whitmore, James (actor); White Plains, N.Y., 10/1/1921
Whitney, Cornelius Vanderbilt (sportsman); New York City **(1899-1992)**
Whitney, Eli (inventor); Westboro, Mass. **(1765-1825)**
Whitney, John Hay (publisher); Ellsworth, Me. **(1904-1982)**
Whittier, John Greenleaf (poet); Haverhill, Mass. **(1807-1892)**
Whitty, Dame May (actr ess); Liverpool, England **(1865-1948)**
Widmark, Richard (actor); Sunrise, Minn., 12/26/1914
Wiesel, Elie (Eliezer) (author); Signet, Romania, 9/30/1928
Wilde, Cornel (film actor and producer); New York City **(1915-1989)**
Wilde, Oscar Fingal O'Flahertie Wills (author); Dublin **(1854-1900)**
Wilder, Billy (film producer and director); Vienna, 6/22/1906
Wilder, Gene (Jerome Silberman) (actor); Milwaukee, 6/11/1935(?)
Wilder, Thornton (author); Madison, Wis. **(1897-1975)**
Wilding, Michael (actor); Westcliff, England **(1912-1979)**
Wilkins, Roy (civil rights leader); St. Louis **(1901-1981)**
Williams, Andy (singer); Wall Lake, Iowa, 12/3/1930
Williams, Billy Dee (actor); New York City, 4/6/1937
Williams, Cindy (actress); Van Nuys, Calif., 8/22/(?)
Williams, Edward Bennett (lawyer); Hartford, Conn. **(1920-1988)**
Williams, Emlyn (actor and playwright); Mostyn, Wales **(1905-1987)**
Williams, Esther (actress); Los Angeles, 8/8/1923
Williams, Gluyas (cartoonist); San Francisco **(1888-1982)**
Williams, Hank, Sr. (Hiram King Williams) (singer); Georgiana, Ala. **(1923-1953)**
Williams, Joe (singer); Cordele, Ga., 12/12/1918
Williams, Paul (singer, composer, actor); Omaha, Neb., 9/19/1940
Williams, Robin (comedian); Chicago, 7/?/1952
Williams, Roger (clergyman); London **(1603?-1683)**
Williams, Tennessee (Thomas L. Williams) (playwright); Columbus, Miss. **(1911-1983)**
Williams, William Carlos (physician and poet); Rutherford, N.J. **(1883-1963)**
Williamson, Nicol (actor); Hamilton, Scotland, 9/14/38
Willkie, Wendell Lewis (lawyer); Elwood, Ind. **(1892-1944)**
Willis, Bruce (actor); Germany, 3/19/1955
Willson, Meredith (composer); Mason City, Iowa **(1902-1984)**
Wilson, August (poet, writer, playwright); Pittsburgh, Pa., 1945
Wilson, Don (radio and TV announcer); Lincoln, Neb. **(1900-1982)**
Wilson, Dooley (actor, musician); Tyler, Tex. **(1894-1953)**
Wilson, Edmund (literary critic and author); Red Bank, N.J. **(1895-1972)**
Wilson, Flip (Clerow) (comedian); Jersey City, N.J., 12/8/1933
Wilson, Harold (ex-Prime Minister); Huddersfield, England, 3/11/1916
Wilson, Marie (actress); Anaheim, Calif. **(1916-1972)**
Wilson, Nancy (singer); Chillicothe, Ohio, 2/20/1937
Wilson, Sloan (novelist); Norwalk, Conn., 5/8/1920
Winchell, Walter (columnist); New York City **(1897-1972)**
Windsor, Duchess of (Bessie Wallis Warfield); Blue Ridge Summit, Pa. **(1896-1986)**
Windsor, Duke of (formerly King Edward VIII of England); Richmond Park, England **(1894-1972)**
Winfrey, Oprah (talk show hostess, actress); Kosciuska, Miss., 1/29/1954
Winger, Debra (actress); Cleveland, Ohio, 1955
Winkler, Henry (actor); New York City, 10/30/1945
Winninger, Charles (actor); Athen, Wis. **(1884-1969)**
Winningham, Mare (actress); Phoenix, Ariz., 5/16/1959
Winter, Johnny (guitarist); Leland, Miss., 2/23/1944
Winters, Jonathan (comedian); Dayton, Ohio, 11/11/1925
Winters, Shelley (Shirley Schrift) (actress); East St. Louis, Ill., 8/18/1922
Winthrop, John (first Governor, Massachusetts Bay Colony); Suffolk, England **(1588-1649)**
Wise, Stephen Samuel (rabbi); Budapest **(1874-1949)**
Withers, Jane (actress); Atlanta, 1927
Wittgenstein, Ludwig (Josef Johann) (philosopher); Vienna **(1889-1951)**
Wodehouse, P(elham) G(renville) (novelist); Guildford, England **(1881-1975)**
Wolfe, Thomas Clayton (novelist); Asheville, N.C. **(1900-1938)**
Wolfe, Tom (journalist); Richmond, Va., 3/2/1931
Wolsey, Thomas (prelate and statesman); Ipswich, England **(1475?-1530)**
Wonder, Stevie (Steveland Judkins, later Steveland Morris) (singer and songwriter); Saginaw, Mich., 5/13/1950
Wong, Anna May (Lu Tsong Wong) (actress); Los Angeles **(1907-1961)**
Wood, Grant (painter); Anamosa, Iowa **(1892-1942)**
Wood, Natalie (Natasha Gurdin) (film actress); San Francisco **(1938-1981)**
Wood, Peggy (Margaret) (actress); Brooklyn, N.Y. **(1892-1978)**
Woodhouse, Barbara (Blackburn) (dog trainer, author, TV personality): Rathfarnham, Ireland **(1910-1988)**
Woodward, Edward (actor); Croydon, England, 6/1/1930
Woodward, Joanne (film actress); Thomasville, Ga., 2/27/1930
Woolf, Adeline Virginia (née Stephens) (novelist); London **(1882-1941)**
Woollcott, Alexander (author-critic); Phalanx, N.J. **(1887-1943)**
Woolley, Monty (Edgar Montillion Woolley) (actor); New York City **(1888-1963)**
Woolworth, Frank (merchant); Rodman, N.Y. **(1852-1919)**
Wopat, Tom (actor); Lodi, Wis., 9/9/1950
Wordsworth, William (poet); Cockermouth, England **(1770-1850)**
Wouk, Herman (novelist); New York City, 5/27/1915
Wray, Fay (actress); Alberta, Canada, 1907
Wren, Sir Christopher (architect); East Knoyle, England **(1632-1723)**
Wright, Frank Lloyd (architect); Richland Center, Wis. **(1869-1959)**
Wright, Martha (singer); Seattle, Wash., 3/23/1926
Wright, Orville (inventor); Dayton, Ohio **(1871-1948)**
Wright, Richard (novelist); nr. Natchez, Miss. **(1908-1960)**
Wright, Teresa (actress); New York City, 10/27/1918
Wright, Wilbur (inventor); Millville, Ind. **(1867-1912)**
Wyatt, Jane (film actress); Campgaw, N.J., 8/12/1912
Wycliffe, John (church reformer); Hipswell, England **(1320-1384)**
Wyeth, Andrew (painter); Chadds Ford, Pa., 7/12/1917
Wyler, William (film director); Mulhouse (France), **(1902-1981)**
Wyman, Jane (Sarah Jane Fulks) (actress); St. Joseph, Mo., 1/4/1914
Wynette, Tammy (Wynette Pugh) (singer); Tupelo, Miss. 5/5/1942
Wynn, Ed (Isaiah Edwin Leopold) (comedian); Philadelphia **(1886-1966)**
Wynn, Keenan (actor); New York City **(1916-1986)**
Wynter, Dana (actress); London, 6/8/1930

X

Xavier, St. Francis (Jesuit missionary); Pamplona, Navarre (Spain) **(1506-1552)**
Xenophon (soldier, historian and essayist): Athens, Greece **(434(?)-355(?)** B.C.**)**
Xerxes, the Great (king): Persian Empire **(519(?)-465** B.C.**)**

Y

Yeats, William Butler (poet); nr. Dublin **(1865-1939)**
Yevtushenko, Yevgeny (poet); Zima, U.S.S.R., 7/18/1933
York, Alvin Cullun (Sergeant York, World War I hero): Tennessee **(1887-1964)**
York, Michael (actor); Fulmer, England, 3/27/1942
York, Susannah (Fletcher) (actress); London, 1/9/1942
Yorty, Samuel W. (ex-Mayor of Los Angeles); Lincoln, Neb., 10/1/1909
Yothers, Tina (actress); Whittier, Calif., 5/5/1973
Young, Alan (actor); North Shield, England, 11/19/1919
Young, Brigham (religious leader); Whitingham, Vt. **(1801-1877)**
Young, Gig (Byron Barr) (actor); St. Cloud, Minn. **(1917-1978)**
Young, Loretta (Gretchen Young) (actress); Salt Lake City, Utah, 1/6/1913
Young, Neil (singer and songwriter); Toronto, 11/12/1945
Young, Robert (actor); Chicago, 2/22/1907
Young, Roland (actor); London **(1887-1953)**
Youngman, Henny (comedian); Liverpool, England, 1/12/1906

Z

Zanuck, Darryl F. (film producer); Wahoo, Neb. **(1902-1979)**
Zappa, Frank (Francis Vincent Zappa, Jr.) (singer and songwriter); Baltimore, 12/21/1940
Zeffirelli, Franco (director); Florence, Italy, 2/12/1923
Zenger, John Peter (printer and journalist): Germany, **(1697-1746)**
Zhou Enlai (Premier); Hualyin, China **(1898-1976)**
Ziegfeld, Florenz (theatrical producer); Chicago **(1869-1932)**
Zimbalist, Efrem (concert violinist); Rostov-on-Don, Russia **(1889-1985)**
Zimbalist, Efrem, Jr. (actor); New York City, 11/30/1923
Zimbalist, Stephanie (actress); New York City, 10/8/56
Zola, Emile (novelist); Paris **(1840-1902)**
Zoroaster (religious leader); Persian Empire **(c. 6th century** B.C.**)**
Zukerman, Pinchas (violinist); Tel Aviv, Israel, 7/16/1948
Zukor, Adolph (film executive); Risce, Hungary **(1873-1976)**
Zweig, Stefan (author); Vienna **(1881-1942)**
Zwingli, Huldrych (humanist); Wildaus, Switzerland **(1484-1531)**

Nobel Prizes

The Nobel prizes are awarded under the will of Alfred Bernhard Nobel, Swedish chemist and engineer, who died in 1896. The interest of the fund is divided annually among the persons who have made the most outstanding contributions in the fields of physics, chemistry, and physiology or medicine, who have produced the most distinguished literary work of an idealist tendency, and who have contributed most toward world peace.

In 1968, a Nobel Prize of economic sciences was established by Riksbank, the Swedish bank, in celebration of its 300th anniversary. The prize was awarded for the first time in 1969.

The prizes for physics and chemistry are awarded by the Swedish Academy of Science in Stockholm, the one for physiology or medicine by the Caroline Medical Institute in Stockholm, that for literature by the academy in Stockholm, and that for peace by a committee of five elected by the Norwegian Storting. The distribution of prizes was begun on December 10, 1901, the anniversary of Nobel's death. The amount of each prize varies with the income from the fund and currently is about $190,000. No Nobel prizes were awarded for 1940, 1941, and 1942; prizes for Literature were not awarded for 1914, 1918, and 1943.

PEACE

1901 Henri Dunant (Switzerland); Frederick Passy (France)
1902 Elie Ducommun and Albert Gobat (Switzerland)
1903 Sir William R. Cremer (England)
1904 Institut de Droit International (Belgium)
1905 Bertha von Suttner (Austria)
1906 Theodore Roosevelt (U.S.)
1907 Ernesto T. Moneta (Italy) and Louis Renault (France)
1908 Klas P. Arnoldson (Sweden) and Frederik Bajer (Denmark)
1909 Auguste M. F. Beernaert (Belgium) and Baron Paul H. B. B. d'Estournelles de Constant de Rebecque (France)
1910 Bureau International Permanent de la Paix (Switzerland)
1911 Tobias M. C. Asser (Holland) and Alfred H. Fried (Austria)
1912 Elihu Root (U.S.)
1913 Henri La Fontaine (Belgium)
1915 No award
1916 No award
1917 International Red Cross
1919 Woodrow Wilson (U.S.)
1920 Léon Bourgeois (France)
1921 Karl H. Branting (Sweden) and Christian L. Lange (Norway)
1922 Fridtjof Nansen (Norway)
1923 No award
1924 No award
1925 Sir Austen Chamberlain (England) and Charles G. Dawes (U.S.)
1926 Aristide Briand (France) and Gustav Stresemann (Germany)
1927 Ferdinand Buisson (France) and Ludwig Quidde (Germany)
1928 No award
1929 Frank B. Kellogg (U.S.)
1930 Lars O. J. Söderblom (Sweden)
1931 Jane Addams and Nicholas M. Butler (U.S.)
1932 No award
1933 Sir Norman Angell (England)
1934 Arthur Henderson (England)
1935 Karl von Ossietzky (Germany)
1936 Carlos de S. Lamas (Argentina)
1937 Lord Cecil of Chelwood (England)
1938 Office International Nansen pour les Réfugiés (Switzerland)
1939 No award
1944 International Red Cross
1945 Cordell Hull (U.S.)
1946 Emily G. Balch and John R. Mott (U.S.)
1947 American Friends Service Committee (U.S.) and British Society of Friends' Service Council (England)
1948 No award
1949 Lord John Boyd Orr (Scotland)
1950 Ralph J. Bunche (U.S.)
1951 Léon Jouhaux (France)
1952 Albert Schweitzer (French Equatorial Africa)
1953 George C. Marshall (U.S.)
1954 Office of U.N. High Commissioner for Refugees
1955 No award
1956 No award
1957 Lester B. Pearson (Canada)
1958 Rev. Dominique Georges Henri Pire (Belgium)
1959 Philip John Noel-Baker (England)
1960 Albert John Luthuli (South Africa)
1961 Dag Hammarskjöld (Sweden)
1962 Linus Pauling (U.S.)
1963 Intl. Comm. of Red Cross; League of Red Cross Societies (both Geneva)
1964 Rev. Dr. Martin Luther King, Jr. (U.S.)
1965 UNICEF (United Nations Children's Fund)
1966 No award
1967 No award
1968 René Cassin (France)
1969 International Labour Organization
1970 Norman E. Borlaug (U.S.)
1971 Willy Brandt (West Germany)
1972 No award
1973 Henry A. Kissinger (U.S.); Le Duc Tho (North Vietnam)[1]
1974 Eisaku Sato (Japan); Sean MacBride (Ireland)
1975 Andrei D. Sakharov (U.S.S.R.)
1976 Mairead Corrigan and Betty Williams (both Northern Ireland)
1977 Amnesty International
1978 Menachem Begin (Israel) and Anwar el-Sadat (Egypt)
1979 Mother Teresa of Calcutta (India)
1980 Adolfo Pérez Esquivel (Argentina)
1981 Office of the United Nations High Commissioner for Refugees
1982 Alva Myrdal (Sweden) and Alfonso García Robles (Mexico)
1983 Lech Walesa (Poland)
1984 Bishop Desmond Tutu (South Africa)
1985 International Physicians for the Prevention of Nuclear War
1986 Elie Wiesel (U.S.)
1987 Oscar Arias Sánchez (Costa Rica)
1988 U.N. Peacekeeping Forces
1989 Dalai Lama (Tibet)
1990 Mikhail S. Gorbachev (U.S.S.R.)
1991 Daw Aung San Suu Kyi (Myanmar)
1992 Rigoberta Menchú (Guatemala)

1. Le Duc Tho refused prize, charging that peace had not yet been really established in South Vietnam.

LITERATURE

1901 René F. A. Sully Prudhomme (France)
1902 Theodor Mommsen (Germany)
1903 Björnstjerne Björnson (Norway)
1904 Frédéric Mistral (France) and José Echegaray (Spain)
1905 Henryk Sienkiewicz (Poland)
1906 Giosuè Carducci (Italy)
1907 Rudyard Kipling (England)
1908 Rudolf Eucken (Germany)
1909 Selma Lagerlöf (Sweden)
1910 Paul von Heyse (Germany)
1911 Maurice Maeterlinck (Belgium)
1912 Gerhart Hauptmann (Germany)
1913 Rabindranath Tagore (India)
1915 Romain Rolland (France)
1916 Verner von Heidenstam (Sweden)
1917 Karl Gjellerup (Denmark) and Henrik Pontoppidan (Denmark)
1919 Carl Spitteler (Switzerland)
1920 Knut Hamsun (Norway)
1921 Anatole France (France)
1922 Jacinto Benavente (Spain)
1923 William B. Yeats (Ireland)
1924 Wladyslaw Reymont (Poland)
1925 George Bernard Shaw (Ireland)
1926 Grazia Deledda (Italy)
1927 Henri Bergson (France)
1928 Sigrid Undset (Norway)
1929 Thomas Mann (Germany)
1930 Sinclair Lewis (U.S.)
1931 Erik A. Karlfeldt (Sweden)
1932 John Galsworthy (England)
1933 Ivan G. Bunin (Russia)
1934 Luigi Pirandello (Italy)
1935 No award
1936 Eugene O'Neill (U.S.)
1937 Roger Martin du Gard (France)
1938 Pearl S. Buck (U.S.)
1939 Frans Eemil Sillanpää (Finland)
1944 Johannes V. Jensen (Denmark)
1945 Gabriela Mistral (Chile)
1946 Hermann Hesse (Switzerland)
1947 André Gide (France)
1948 Thomas Stearns Eliot (England)
1949 William Faulkner (U.S.)
1950 Bertrand Russell (England)
1951 Pär Lagerkvist (Sweden)
1952 François Mauriac (France)
1953 Sir Winston Churchill (England)
1954 Ernest Hemingway (U.S.)
1955 Halldór Kiljan Laxness (Iceland)
1956 Juan Ramón Jiménez (Spain)
1957 Albert Camus (France)
1958 Boris Pasternak (U.S.S.R.) (declined)
1959 Salvatore Quasimodo (Italy)
1960 St-John Perse (Alexis St.-Léger Léger) (France)
1961 Ivo Andric (Yugoslavia)
1962 John Steinbeck (U.S.)
1963 Giorgios Seferis (Seferiades) (Greece)
1964 Jean-Paul Sartre (France) (declined)
1965 Mikhail Sholokhov (U.S.S.R.)
1966 Shmuel Yosef Agnon (Israel) and Nelly Sachs (Sweden)
1967 Miguel Angel Asturias (Guatemala)
1968 Yasunari Kawabata (Japan)
1969 Samuel Beckett (Ireland)
1970 Aleksandr Solzhenitsyn (U.S.S.R.)
1971 Pablo Neruda (Chile)
1972 Heinrich Böll (Germany)
1973 Patrick White (Australia)
1974 Eyvind Johnson and Harry Martinson (both Sweden)
1975 Eugenio Montale (Italy)
1976 Saul Bellow (U.S.)
1977 Vicente Aleixandre (Spain)
1978 Isaac Bashevis Singer (U.S.)
1979 Odysseus Elytis (Greece)
1980 Czeslaw Milosz (U.S.)
1981 Elias Canetti (Bulgaria)
1982 Gabriel García Márquez (Colombia)
1983 William Golding (England)
1984 Jaroslav Seifert (Czechoslovakia)
1985 Claude Simon (France)
1986 Wole Soyinka (Nigeria)
1987 Joseph Brodsky (U.S.)
1988 Naguib Mahfouz (Egypt)
1989 Camilo José Cela (Spain)
1990 Octavio Paz (Mexico)
1991 Nadine Gordimer (South Africa)
1992 Derek Walcott (Trinidad)

PHYSICS

1901 Wilhelm K. Roentgen (Germany), for discovery of Roentgen rays
1902 Hendrik A. Lorentz and Pieter Zeeman (Netherlands), for work on influence of magnetism upon radiation
1903 A. Henri Becquerel (France), for work on spontaneous radioactivity; and Pierre and Marie Curie (France), for study of radiation
1904 John Strutt (Lord Rayleigh) (England), for discovery of argon in investigating gas density
1905 Philipp Lenard (Germany), for work with cathode rays
1906 Sir Joseph Thomson (England), for investigations on passage of electricity through gases
1907 Albert A. Michelson (U.S.), for spectroscopic and metrologic investigations
1908 Gabriel Lippmann (France), for method of reproducing colors by photography
1909 Guglielmo Marconi (Italy) and Ferdinand Braun (Germany), for development of wireless
1910 Johannes D. van der Waals (Netherlands), for work with the equation of state for gases and liquids
1911 Wilhelm Wien (Germany), for his laws governing the radiation of heat
1912 Gustaf Dalén (Sweden), for discovery of automatic regulators used in lighting lighthouses and light buoys
1913 Heike Kamerlingh-Onnes (Netherlands), for work leading to production of liquid helium
1914 Max von Laue (Germany), for discovery of diffraction of Roentgen rays passing through crystals
1915 Sir William Bragg and William L. Bragg (England), for analysis of crystal structure by X rays
1916 No award
1917 Charles G. Barkla (England), for discovery of Roentgen radiation of the elements
1918 Max Planck (Germany), discoveries in connection with quantum theory
1919 Johannes Stark (Germany), discovery of Doppler effect in Canal rays and decomposition of spectrum lines by electric fields
1920 Charles E. Guillaume (Switzerland), for discoveries of anomalies in nickel steel alloys
1921 Albert Einstein (Germany), for discovery of the law of the photoelectric effect
1922 Niels Bohr (Denmark), for investigation of structure of atoms and radiations emanating from them
1923 Robert A. Millikan (U.S.), for work on elementary charge of electricity and photoelectric phenomena
1924 Karl M. G. Siegbahn (Sweden), for investigations in X-ray spectroscopy
1925 James Franck and Gustav Hertz (Germany), for discovery of laws governing impact of electrons upon atoms

1926 Jean B. Perrin (France), for work on discontinuous structure of matter and discovery of the equilibrium of sedimentation
1927 Arthur H. Compton (U.S.), for discovery of Compton phenomenon; and Charles T. R. Wilson (England), for method of perceiving paths taken by electrically charged particles
1928 In 1929, the 1928 prize was awarded to Sir Owen Richardson (England), for work on the phenomenon of thermionics and discovery of the Richardson Law
1929 Prince Louis Victor de Broglie (France), for discovery of the wave character of electrons
1930 Sir Chandrasekhara Raman (India), for work on diffusion of light and discovery of the Raman effect
1931 No award
1932 In 1933, the prize for 1932 was awarded to Werner Heisenberg (Germany), for creation of the quantum mechanics
1933 Erwin Schrödinger (Austria) and Paul A. M. Dirac (England), for discovery of new fertile forms of the atomic theory
1934 No award
1935 James Chadwick (England), for discovery of the neutron
1936 Victor F. Hess (Austria), for discovery of cosmic radiation; and Carl D. Anderson (U.S.), for discovery of the positron
1937 Clinton J. Davisson (U.S.) and George P. Thomson (England), for discovery of diffraction of electrons by crystals
1938 Enrico Fermi (Italy), for identification of new radioactivity elements and discovery of nuclear reactions effected by slow neutrons
1939 Ernest Orlando Lawrence (U.S.), for development of the cyclotron
1943 Otto Stern (U.S.), for detection of magnetic momentum of protons
1944 Isidor Isaac Rabi (U.S.), for work on magnetic movements of atomic particles
1945 Wolfgang Pauli (Austria), for work on atomic fissions
1946 Percy Williams Bridgman (U.S.), for studies and inventions in high-pressure physics
1947 Sir Edward Appleton (England), for discovery of layer which reflects radio short waves in the ionosphere
1948 Patrick M. S. Blackett (England), for improvement on Wilson chamber and discoveries in cosmic radiation
1949 Hideki Yukawa (Japan), for mathematical prediction, in 1935, of the meson
1950 Cecil Frank Powell (England), for method of photographic study of atom nucleus, and for discoveries about mesons
1951 Sir John Douglas Cockcroft (England) and Ernest T. S. Walton (Ireland), for work in 1932 on transmutation of atomic nuclei
1952 Edward Mills Purcell and Felix Bloch (U.S.), for work in measurement of magnetic fields in atomic nuclei
1953 Fritz Zernike (Netherlands), for development of "phase contrast" microscope
1954 Max Born (England), for work in quantum mechanics; and Walther Bothe (Germany), for work in cosmic radiation
1955 Polykarp Kusch and Willis E. Lamb, Jr. (U.S.), for atomic measurements
1956 William Shockley, Walter H. Brattain, and John Bardeen (U.S.), for developing electronic transistor
1957 Tsung Dao Lee and Chen Ning Yang (China), for disproving principle of conservation of parity
1958 Pavel A. Cherenkov, Ilya M. Frank, and Igor E. Tamm (U.S.S.R.), for work resulting in development of cosmic-ray counter
1959 Emilio Segre and Owen Chamberlain (U.S.), for demonstrating the existence of the anti-proton
1960 Donald A. Glaser (U.S.), for invention of "bub-ble chamber" to study subatomic particles
1961 Robert Hofstadter (U.S.), for determination of shape and size of atomic nucleus; Rudolf Mössbauer (Germany), for method of producing and measuring recoil-free gamma rays
1962 Lev D. Landau (U.S.S.R.), for his theories about condensed matter
1963 Eugene Paul Wigner, Maria Goeppert Mayer (both U.S.), and J. Hans D. Jensen (Germany), for research on structure of atom and its nucleus
1964 Charles Hard Townes (U.S.), Nikolai G. Basov, and Aleksandr M. Prochorov (both U.S.S.R.), for developing maser and laser principle of producing high-intensity radiation
1965 Richard P. Feynman, Julian S. Schwinger (both U.S.), and Shinichiro Tomonaga (Japan), for research in quantum electrodynamics
1966 Alfred Kastler (France), for work on energy levels inside atom
1967 Hans A. Bethe (U.S.), for work on energy production of stars
1968 Luis Walter Alvarez (U.S.), for study of subatomic particles
1969 Murray Gell-Mann (U.S.), for study of subatomic particles
1970 Hannes Alfvén (Sweden), for theories in plasma physics; and Louis Néel (France), for discoveries in antiferromagnetism and ferrimagnetism
1971 Dennis Gabor (England), for invention of holographic method of three-dimensional imagery
1972 John Bardeen, Leon N. Cooper, and John Robert Schrieffer (all U.S.), for theory of superconductivity, where electrical resistance in certain metals vanishes above absolute zero temperature
1973 Ivar Giaever (U.S.), Leo Esaki (Japan), and Brian D. Josephson (U.K.), for theories that have advanced and expanded the field of miniature electronics
1974 Antony Hewish (England), for discovery of pulsars; Martin Ryle (England), for using radiotelescopes to probe outer space with high degree of precision
1975 James Rainwater (U.S.) and Ben Mottelson and Aage N. Bohr (both Denmark), for showing that the atomic nucleus is asymmetrical
1976 Burton Richter and Samuel C. C. Ting (both U.S.), for discovery of subatomic particles known as J and psi
1977 Philip W. Anderson and John H. Van Vleck (both U.S.), and Nevill F. Mott (U.K.), for work underlying computer memories and electronic devices
1978 Arno A. Penzias and Robert W. Wilson (both U.S.), for work in cosmic microwave radiation; Piotr L. Kapitsa (U.S.S.R.), for basic inventions and discoveries in low-temperature physics
1979 Steven Weinberg and Sheldon L. Glashow (both U.S.) and Abdus Salam (Pakistan), for de-veloping theory that electromagnetism and the "weak" force, which causes radioactive decay in some atomic nuclei, are facets of the same phenomenon
1980 James W. Cronin and Val L. Fitch (both U.S.), for work concerning the assymetry of subatomic particles
1981 Nicolaas Bloembergen and Arthur L. Schawlow (both U.S.) and Kai M. Siegbahn (Sweden), for developing technologies with lasers and other devices to probe the secrets of complex forms of matter
1982 Kenneth G. Wilson (U.S.), for analysis of changes in matter under pressure and temperature
1983 Subrahmanyam Chandrasekhar and William A. Fowler (both U.S.) for complementary research on processes involved in the evolution of stars
1984 Carlo Rubbia (Italy) and Simon van der Meer (Netherlands), for their role in discovering three subatomic particles, a step toward developing a single theory to account for all natural forces

1985 Klaus von Klitzing (Germany), for developing an exact way of measuring electrical conductivity
1986 Ernst Ruska, Gerd Binnig (both Germany) and Heinrich Rohrer (Switzerland) for work on microscopes
1987 K. Alex Müller (Switzerland) and J. Georg Bednorz (Germany) for their discovery of high-temperature superconductors.
1988 Leon M. Lederman, Melvin Schwartz, and Jack Steinberger (all U.S.) for research that improved the understanding of elementary particles and forces.
1989 Norman F. Ramsey (U.S.), for work leading to development of the atomic clock, and Hans G. Dehmelt (U.S.) and Wolfgang Paul (Germany) for developing methods to isolate atoms and subatomic particles.
1990 Dr. Richard E. Taylor (Canada) and Dr. Jerome I. Friedman and Dr. Henry W. Kendall (both U.S.), for their "breakthrough in our understanding of matter" which confirmed the reality of quarks.
1991 Dr. Pierre-Gilles de Gennes (France) for his discoveries about the ordering of molecules in substances ranging from "super" glue to an exotic form of liquid helium.
1992 Dr. George Charpak (France)

CHEMISTRY

1901 Jacobus H. van't Hoff (Netherlands), for laws of chemical dynamics and osmotic pressure in solutions
1902 Emil Fischer (Germany), for experiments in sugar and purin groups of substances
1903 Svante A. Arrhenius (Sweden), for his electrolytic theory of dissociation
1904 Sir William Ramsay (England), for discovery and determination of place of inert gaseous elements in air
1905 Adolf von Baeyer (Germany), for work on organic dyes and hydroaromatic combinations
1906 Henri Moissan (France), for isolation of fluorine, and introduction of electric furnace
1907 Eduard Buchner (Germany), discovery of cell-less fermentation and investigations in biological chemistry
1908 Sir Ernest Rutherford (England), for investigations into disintegration of elements
1909 Wilhelm Ostwald (Germany), for work on catalysis and investigations into chemical equilibrium and reaction rates
1910 Otto Wallach (Germany), for work in the field of alicyclic compounds
1911 Marie Curie (France), for discovery of elements radium and polonium
1912 Victor Grignard (France), for reagent discovered by him; and Paul Sabatier (France), for methods of hydrogenating organic compounds
1913 Alfred Werner (Switzerland), for linking up atoms within the molecule
1914 Theodore W. Richards (U.S.), for determining atomic weight of many chemical elements
1915 Richard Willstätter (Germany), for research into coloring matter of plants, especially chlorophyll
1916 No award
1917 No award
1918 Fritz Haber (Germany), for synthetic production of ammonia
1919 No award
1920 Walther Nernst (Germany), for work in thermochemistry
1921 Frederick Soddy (England), for investigations into origin and nature of isotopes
1922 Francis W. Aston (England), for discovery of isotopes in nonradioactive elements and for discovery of the whole number rule
1923 Fritz Pregl (Austria), for method of microanalysis of organic substances discovered by him
1924 No award
1925 In 1926, the 1925 prize was awarded to Richard Zsigmondy (Germany), for work on the heterogeneous nature of colloid solutions
1926 Theodor Svedberg (Sweden), for work on disperse systems
1927 In 1928, the 1927 prize was awarded to Heinrich Wieland (Germany), for investigations of bile acids and kindred substances
1928 Adolf Windaus (Germany), for investigations on constitution of the sterols and their connection with vitamins
1929 Sir Arthur Harden (England) and Hans K. A. S. von Euler-Chelpin (Sweden), for research of fermentation of sugars
1930 Hans Fischer (Germany), for work on coloring matter of blood and leaves and for his synthesis of hemin
1931 Karl Bosch and Friedrich Bergius (Germany), for invention and development of chemical high-pressure methods
1932 Irving Langmuir (U.S.), for work in realm of surface chemistry
1933 No award
1934 Harold C. Urey (U.S.), for discovery of heavy hydrogen
1935 Frédéric and Irène Joliot-Curie (France), for synthesis of new radioactive elements
1936 Peter J. W. Debye (Netherlands), for investigations on dipole moments and diffraction of X rays and electrons in gases
1937 Walter N. Haworth (England), for research on carbohydrates and Vitamin C; and Paul Karrer (Switzerland), for work on carotenoids, flavins, and Vitamins A and B
1938 Richard Kuhn (Germany), for carotinoid study and vitamin research (declined)
1939 Adolf Butenandt (Germany), for work on sexual hormones (declined the prize); and Leopold Ruzicka (Switzerland), for work with polymethylenes
1943 Georg Hevesy De Heves (Hungary), for work on use of isotopes as indicators
1944 Otto Hahn (Germany), for work on atomic fission
1945 Artturi Illmari Virtanen (Finland), for research in the field of conservation of fodder
1946 James B. Sumner (U.S.), for crystallizing enzymes; John H. Northrop and Wendell M. Stanley (U.S.), for preparing enzymes and virus proteins in pure form
1947 Sir Robert Robinson (England), for research in plant substances
1948 Arne Tiselius (Sweden), for biochemical discoveries and isolation of mouse paralysis virus
1949 William Francis Giauque (U.S.), for research in thermodynamics, especially effects of low temperature
1950 Otto Diels and Kurt Alder (Germany), for discovery of diene synthesis enabling scientists to study structure of organic matter
1951 Glenn T. Seaborg and Edwin H. McMillan (U.S.), for discovery of plutonium
1952 Archer John Porter Martin and Richard Laurence Millington Synge (England), for development of partition chromatography
1953 Hermann Staudinger (Germany), for research in giant molecules
1954 Linus C. Pauling (U.S.), for study of forces holding together protein and other molecules
1955 Vincent du Vigneaud (U.S.), for work on pituitary hormones
1956 Sir Cyril Hinshelwood (England) and Nikolai N. Semenov (U.S.S.R.), for parallel research on chemical reaction kinetics
1957 Sir Alexander Todd (England), for research with chemical compounds that are factors in heredity

1958 Frederick Sanger (England), for determining molecular structure of insulin
1959 Jaroslav Heyrovsky (Czechoslovakia), for development of polarography, an electrochemical method of analysis
1960 Willard F. Libby (U.S.), for "atomic time clock" to measure age of objects by measuring their radioactivity
1961 Melvin Calvin (U.S.), for establishing chemical steps during photosynthesis
1962 Max F. Perutz and John C. Kendrew (England), for mapping protein molecules with X-rays
1963 Carl Ziegler (Germany) and Giulio Natta (Italy), for work in uniting simple hydrocarbons into large molecule substances
1964 Dorothy Mary Crowfoot Hodgkin (England), for determining structure of compounds needed in combating pernicious anemia
1965 Robert B. Woodward (U.S.), for work in synthesizing complicated organic compounds
1966 Robert Sanderson Mulliken (U.S.), for research on bond holding atoms together in molecule
1967 Manfred Eigen (Germany), Ronald G. W. Norrish, and George Porter (both Eng land), for work in high-speed chemical reactions
1968 Lars Onsager (U.S.), for development of system of equations in thermodynamics
1969 Derek H. R. Barton (England) and Odd Hassel (Norway), for study of organic molecules
1970 Luis F. Leloir (Argentina), for discovery of sugar nucleotides and their role in biosynthesis of carbohydrates
1971 Gerhard Herzberg (Canada), for contributions to knowledge of electronic structure and geometry of molecules, particularly free radicals
1972 Christian Boehmer Anfinsen, Stanford Moore, and William Howard Stein (all U.S.), for pioneering studies in enzymes
1973 Ernst Otto Fischer (W. Germany) and Geoffrey Wilkinson (U.K.), for work that could solve problem of automobile exhaust pollution
1974 Paul J. Flory (U.S.), for developing analytic methods to study properties and molecular structure of long-chain molecules
1975 John W. Cornforth (Australia) and Vladimir Prelog (Switzerland), for research on structure of biological molecules such as antibiotics and cholesterol
1976 William N. Lipscomb, Jr. (U.S.), for work on the structure and bonding mechanisms of boranes
1977 Ilya Prigogine (Belgium), for contributions to nonequilibrium thermodynamics, particularly the theory of dissipative structures
1978 Peter Mitchell (U.K.), for contributions to the understanding of biological energy transfer
1979 Herbert C. Brown (U.S.) and Georg Wittig (West Germany), for developing a group of substances that facilitate very difficult chemical reactions
1980 Paul Berg and Walter Gilbert (both U.S.) and Frederick Sanger (England), for developing methods to map the structure and function of DNA, the substance that controls the activity of the cell
1981 Roald Hoffmann (U.S.) and Kenichi Fukui (Japan), for applying quantum-mechanics theories to predict the course of chemical reactions
1982 Aaron Klug (U.K.), for research in the detailed structures of viruses and components of life
1983 Henry Taube (U.S.), for research on how electrons transfer between molecules in chemical reactions
1984 R. Bruce Merrifield (U.S.) for research that revolutionized the study of proteins
1985 Herbert A. Hauptman and Jerome Karle (both U.S.) for their outstanding achievements in the development of direct methods for the determination of crystal structures
1986 Dudley R. Herschback, Yuan T. Lee (both U.S.), and John C. Polanyi (Canada) for their work on "reaction dynamics"
1987 Donald J. Cram and Charles J. Pedersen (both U.S.) and Jean-Marie Lehn (France), for wide-ranging research that has included the creation of artificial molecules that can mimic vital chemical reactions of the processes of life.
1988 Johann Deisenhofer, Robert Huber, and Hartmut Michel (all West Germany) for unraveling the structure of proteins that play a crucial role in photosynthesis.
1989 Thomas R. Cech and Sidney Altman (both U.S.) for their discovery, independently, that RNA could actively aid chemical reactions in the cells.
1990 Dr. Elias James Corey (U.S.) for developing new ways to synthesize complex molecules ordinarily found in nature.
1991 Dr. Richard R. Ernst (Switzerland) for refinements he developed in nuclear magnetic resonance spectroscopy.
1992 Dr. Rudolph A. Marcus (U.S.)

PHYSIOLOGY OR MEDICINE

1901 Emil A. von Behring (Germany), for work on serum therapy against diptheria
1902 Sir Ronald Ross (England), for work on malaria
1903 Niels R. Finsen (Denmark), for his treatment of lupus vulgaris with concentrated light rays
1904 Ivan P. Pavlov (U.S.S.R.), for work on the physiology of digestion
1905 Robert Koch (Germany), for work on tuberculosis
1906 Camillo Golgi (Italy) and Santiago Ramón y Cajal (Spain), for work on structure of the nervous system
1907 Charles L. A. Laveran (France), for work with protozoa in the generation of disease
1908 Paul Ehrlich (Germany), and Elie Metchnikoff (U.S.S.R.), for work on immunity
1909 Theodor Kocher (Switzerland), for work on the thyroid gland
1910 Albrecht Kossel (Germany), for achievements in the chemistry of the cell
1911 Allvar Gullstrand (Sweden), for work on the dioptrics of the eye
1912 Alexis Carrel (France), for work on vascular ligature and grafting of blood vessels and organs
1913 Charles Richet (France), for work on anaphylaxy
1914 Robert Bárány (Austria), for work on physiology and pathology of the vestibular system
1915-1918 No award
1919 Jules Bordet (Belgium), for discoveries in connection with immunity
1920 August Krogh (Denmark), for discovery of regulation of capillaries' motor mechanism
1921 No award
1922 In 1923, the 1922 prize was shared by Archibald V. Hill (England), for discovery relating to heat-production in muscles; and Otto Meyerhof (Germany), for correlation between consumption of oxygen and production of lactic acid in muscles
1923 Sir Frederick Banting (Canada) and John J. R. Macleod (Scotland), for discovery of insulin
1924 Willem Einthoven (Netherlands), for discovery of the mechanism of the electrocardiogram
1925 No award
1926 Johannes Fibiger (Denmark), for discovery of the Spiroptera carcinoma
1927 Julius Wagner-Jauregg (Austria), for use of malaria inoculation in treatment of dementia paralytica
1928 Charles Nicolle (France), for work on typhus exanthematicus
1929 Christiaan Eijkman (Netherlands), for discovery of the antineuritic vitamins; and Sir Frederick Hopkins (Eng-

land), for discovery of growth-promoting vitamins

1930 Karl Landsteiner (U.S.), for discovery of human blood groups

1931 Otto H. Warburg (Germany), for discovery of the character and mode of action of the respiratory ferment

1932 Sir Charles Sherrington (England) and Edgar D. Adrian (U.S.), for discoveries of the function of the neuron

1933 Thomas H. Morgan (U.S.), for discoveries on hereditary function of the chromosomes

1934 George H. Whipple, George R. Minot, and William P. Murphy (U.S.), for discovery of liver therapy against anemias

1935 Hans Spemann (Germany), for discovery of the organizer-effect in embryonic development

1936 Sir Henry Dale (England) and Otto Loewi (Germany), for discoveries on chemical transmission of nerve impulses

1937 Albert Szent-Györgyi von Nagyrapolt (Hungary), for discoveries on biological combustion

1938 Corneille Heymans (Belgium), for determining importance of sinus and aorta mechanisms in the regulation of respiration

1939 Gerhard Domagk (Germany), for antibacterial effect of prontocilate

1943 Henrik Dam (Denmark) and Edward A. Doisy (U.S.), for analysis of Vitamin K

1944 Joseph Erlanger and Herbert Spencer Gasser (U.S.), for work on functions of the nerve threads

1945 Sir Alexander Fleming, Ernst Boris Chain, and Sir Howard Florey (England), for discovery of penicillin

1946 Herman J. Muller (U.S.), for hereditary effects of X-rays on genes

1947 Carl F. and Gerty T. Cori (U.S.), for work on animal starch metabolism; Bernardo A. Houssay (Argentina), for study of pituitary

1948 Paul Mueller (Switzerland), for discovery of insect-killing properties of DDT

1949 Walter Rudolf Hess (Switzerland), for research on brain control of body; and Antonio Caetano de Abreu Freire Egas Moniz (Portugal), for development of brain operation

1950 Philip S. Hench, Edward C. Kendall (both U.S.), and Tadeus Reichstein (Switzerland), for discoveries about hormones of adrenal cortex

1951 Max Theiler (South Africa), for development of anti-yellow-fever vaccine

1952 Selman A. Waksman (U.S.), for co-discovery of streptomycin

1953 Fritz A. Lipmann (Germany-U.S.) and Hans Adolph Krebs (Germany-England), for studies of living cells

1954 John F. Enders, Thomas H. Weller, and Frederick C. Robbins (U.S.), for work with cultivation of polio virus

1955 Hugo Theorell (Sweden), for work on oxidation enzymes

1956 Dickinson W. Richards, Jr., André F. Cournand (both U.S.), and Werner Forssmann (Germany), for new techniques in treating heart disease

1957 Daniel Bovet (Italy), for development of drugs to relieve allergies and relax muscles during surgery

1958 Joshua Lederberg (U.S.), for work with genetic mechanisms; George W. Beadie and Edward L. Tatum (U.S.), for discovering how genes transmit hereditary characteristics

1959 Severo Ochoa and Arthur Kornberg (U.S.), for discoveries related to compounds within chromosomes, which play a vital role in heredity

1960 Sir Macfarlane Burnet (Australia) and Peter Brian Medawar (England), for discovery of acquired immunological tolerance

1961 Georg von Bekesy (U.S.), for discoveries about physical mechanisms of stimulation within cochlea

1962 James D. Watson (U.S.), Maurice H. F. Wilkins, and Francis H. C. Crick (England), for determining structure of deoxyribonucleic acid (DNA)

1963 Alan Lloyd Hodgkin, Andrew Fielding Huxley (both England), and Sir John Carew Eccles (Australia), for research on nerve cells

1964 Konrad E. Bloch (U.S.) and Feodor Lynen (Germany), for research on mechanism and regulation of cholesterol and fatty acid metabolism

1965 François Jacob, André Lwolff, and Jacques Monod (France), for study of regulatory activities in body cells

1966 Charles Brenton Huggins (U.S.), for studies in hormone treatment of cancer of prostate; Francis Peyton Rous (U.S.), for discovery of tumor-producing viruses

1967 Haldan K. Hartline, George Wald, and Ragnar Granit (U.S.), for work on human eye

1968 Robert W. Holley, Har Gobind Khorana, and Marshall W. Nirenberg (U.S.), for studies of genetic code

1969 Max Delbruck, Alfred D. Hershey, and Salvador E. Luria (U.S.), for study of mechanism of virus infection in living cells

1970 Julius Axelrod (U.S.), Ulf S. von Euler (Swed-en), and Sir Bernard Katz (England), for studies of how nerve impulses are transmitted within the body

1971 Earl W. Sutherland, Jr. (U.S.), for research on how hormones work

1972 Gerald M. Edelman (U.S.), and Rodney R. Porter (U.K.), for research on the chemical structure and nature of antibodies

1973 Karl von Frisch and Konrad Lorenz (Austria), and Nikolaas Tinbergen (Netherlands), for their studies of individual and social behavior patterns

1974 George E. Palade and Christian de Duve (both U.S.) and Albert Claude (Belgium), for contributions to understanding inner workings of living cells

1975 David Baltimore, Howard M. Temin, and Renato Dulbecco (all U.S.), for work in interaction between tumor viruses and genetic material of the cell

1976 Baruch S. Blumberg and D. Carleton Gajdusek (U.S.), for discoveries concerning new mechanisms for the origin and dissemination of infectious diseases

1977 Rosalyn S. Yalow, Roger C. L. Guillemin, and Andrew V. Schally (all U.S.), for research in role of hormones in chemistry of the body

1978 Daniel Nathans and Hamilton Smith (both U.S.) and Werner Arber (Switzerland), for discovery of restriction enzymes and their application to problems of molecular genetics

1979 Allan McLeod Cormack (U.S.) and Godfrey Newbold Hounsfield (England), for developing computed axial tomography (CAT scan) X-ray technique

1980 Baruj Benacerraf and George D. Snell (both U.S.) and Jean Dausset (France), for discoveries that explain how the structure of cells relates to organ transplants and diseases

1981 Roger W. Sperry and David H. Hubel (both U.S.) and Torsten N. Wiesel (Sweden), for studies vital to understanding the organization and functioning of the brain

1982 Sune Bergstrom and Bengt Samuelsson (Sweden) and John R. Vane (U.K.), for research in prostaglandins, a hormonelike substance involved in a wide range of illnesses

1983 Barbara McClintock (U.S.), for her discovery of mobile genes in the chromosomes of a plant that change the future generations of plants they produce

1984 Cesar Milstein (U.K./Argentina) Georges J.F. Kohler (West Germany), and Niels K. Jerne (U.K./Denmark) for their work in immunology

1985 Michael S. Brown and Joseph L. Goldstein (both U.S.) for their work which has drastically widened our understanding of the cholesterol metabolism and increased our possibilities to prevent and treat atherosclerosis and heart attacks

1986 Rita Levi-Montalcini (dual U.S./Italy) and Stanley Cohen (U.S.) for their contributions to the understanding of substances that influence cell growth

1987 Susumu Tonegawa (Japan), for his discoveries of how the body can suddenly marshal its immunological defenses against millions of different disease agents that it has never encountered before.

1988 Gertrude B. Elion, George H. Hitchings (both U.S.) and Sir James Black (U.K.) for their discoveries of important principles for drug treatment.

1989 J. Michael Bishop and Harold E. Varmus (both U.S.) for their unifying theory of cancer development.

1990 Dr. Joseph E. Murray and Dr. E. Donnall Thomas (both U.S.), for their pioneering work in transplants.

1991 Dr. Erwin Neher and Dr. Bert Sakmann (both Germany) for their research, particularly for the development of a technique called patch clamp.

1992 Dr. Edmond H. Fischer and Dr. Edwin G. Kerbs (U.S.)

ECONOMIC SCIENCE

1969 Ragnar Frisch (Norway) and Jan Tinbergen (Netherlands), for work in econometrics (application of mathematics and statistical methods to economic theories and problems)

1970 Paul A. Samuelson (U.S.), for efforts to raise the level of scientific analysis in economic theory

1971 Simon Kuznets (U.S.), for developing concept of using a country's gross national product to determine its economic growth

1972 Kenneth J. Arrow (U.S.) and Sir John R. Hicks (U.K.), for theories that help to assess business risk and government economic and welfare policies

1973 Wassily Leontief (U.S.), for devising the input–output technique to determine how different sectors of an economy interact

1974 Gunnar Myrdal (Sweden) and Friedrich A. von Hayek (U.K.), for pioneering analysis of the in terdependence of economic, social and institutional phenomena

1975 Leonid V. Kantorovich (U.S.S.R.) and Tjalling C. Koopmans (U.S.), for work on the theory of optimum allocation of resources

1976 Milton Friedman (U.S.), for work in consumption analysis and monetary history and theory, and for demonstration of complexity of stabilization policy

1977 Bertil Ohlin (Sweden) and James E. Meade (U.K.), for contributions to theory of international trade and international capital movements

1978 Herbert A. Simon (U.S.), for research into the decision-making process within economic organizations

1979 Sir Arthur Lewis (England) and Theodore Schultz (U.S.), for work on economic problems of developing nations

1980 Lawrence R. Klein (U.S.), for developing models for forecasting economic trends and shaping policies to deal with them

1981 James Tobin (U.S.), for analyses of financial markets and their influence on spending and saving by families and businesses

1982 George J. Stigler (U.S.), for work on government regulation in the economy and the functioning of industry

1983 Gerard Debreu (U.S.), in recognition of his work on the basic economic problem of how prices operate to balance what producers supply with what buyers want.

1984 Sir Richard Stone (U.K.), for his work to develop the systems widely used to measure the performance of national economics

1985 Franco Modigliani (U.S.) for his pioneering work in analyzing the behavior of household savers and the functioning of financial markets

1986 James M. Buchanan (U.S.) for his development of new methods for analyzing economic and political decision-making

1987 Robert M. Solow (U.S.), for seminal contributions to the theory of economic growth.

1988 Maurice Allais (France) for his pioneering development of theories to better understand market behavior and the efficient use of resources.

1989 Trygve Haavelmo (Norway) for his pioneering work in methods for testing economic theories.

1990 Harry M. Markowitz, William F. Sharpe, and Merton H. Miller (all U.S.), whose work provided new tools for weighing the risks and rewards of different investments and for valuing corporate stocks and bonds.

1991 Ronald Coase (U.S.) for his pioneering work in how property rights and the cost of doing business affect the economy.

1992 Gary S. Becker (U.S.)

Motion Picture Academy Awards (Oscars)

1928

Picture: *Wings,* Paramount
Director: Frank Borzage, *Seventh Heaven;* Lewis Milestone, *Two Arabian Nights*
Actress: Janet Gaynor, *Seventh Heaven, Street Angel, Sunrise*
Actor: Emil Jannings, *The Way of All Flesh, The Last Command*

1929

Picture: *The Broadway Melody,* M–G–M
Director: Frank Lloyd, *The Divine Lady*
Actress: Mary Pickford, *Coquette*
Actor: Warner Baxter, *In Old Arizona*

1930

Picture: *All Quiet on the Western Front,* Universal
Director: Lewis Milestone, *All Quiet on the Western Front*
Actress: Norma Shearer, *The Divorcee*
Actor: George Arliss, *Disraeli*

1931

Picture: *Cimarron:* RKO Radio
Director: Norman Taurog, *Skippy*
Actress: Marie Dressler, *Min and Bill*
Actor: Lionel Barrymore, *A Free Soul*

1932

Picture: *Grand Hotel,* M–G–M
Director: Frank Borzage, *Bad Girl*
Actress: Helen Hayes, *The Sin of Madelon Claudet*
Actor: Fredric March, *Dr. Jekyll and Mr. Hyde,* and Wallace Beery, *The Champ*

1933

Picture: *Cavalcade,* Fox
Director: Frank Lloyd, *Cavalcade*
Actress: Katharine Hepburn, *Morning Glory*
Actor: Charles Laughton, *The Private Life of Henry VIII*

1934

Picture: *It Happened One Night,* Columbia
Director: Frank Capra, *It Happened One Night*
Actress: Claudette Colbert, *It Happened One Night*
Actor: Clark Gable, *It Happened One Night*

1935
Picture: *Mutiny on the Bounty,* MGM
Director: John Ford, *The Informer*
Actress: Bette Davis, *Dangerous*
Actor: Victor McLaglen, *The Informer*

1936
Picture: *The Great Ziegfeld,* M–G–M
Director: Frank Capra, *Mr. Deeds Goes to Town*
Actress: Luise Rainer, *The Great Ziegfeld*
Actor: Paul Muni, *The Story of Louis Pasteur*
Supporting Actress: Gale Sondergaard, *Anthony Adverse*
Supporting Actor: Walter Brennan, *Come and Get It*

1937
Picture: *The Life of Emile Zola,* Warner Bros.
Director: Leo McCarey, *The Awful Truth*
Actress: Luise Rainer, *The Good Earth*
Actor: Spencer Tracy, *Captains Courageous*
Supporting Actress: Alice Brady, *In Old Chicago*
Supporting Actor: Joseph Schildkraut, *The Life of Emile Zola*

1938
Picture: *You Can't Take It with You,* Columbia
Director: Frank Capra, *You Can't Take It with You*
Actress: Bette Davis, *Jezebel*
Actor: Spencer Tracy, *Boys Town*
Supporting Actress: Fay Bainter, *Jezebel*
Supporting Actor: Walter Brennan, *Kentucky*

1939
Picture: *Gone with the Wind,* SelznickM–G–M
Director: Victor Fleming, *Gone with the Wind*
Actress: Vivien Leigh, *Gone with the Wind*
Actor: Robert Donat, *Goodbye, Mr. Chips*
Supporting Actress: Hattie McDaniel, *Gone with the Wind*
Supporting Actor: Thomas Mitchell, *Stagecoach*

1940
Picture: *Rebecca,* Selznick–UA
Director: John Ford, *The Grapes of Wrath*
Actress: Ginger Rogers, *Kitty Foyle*
Actor: James Stewart, *The Philadelphia Story*
Supporting Actress: Jane Darwell, *The Grapes of Wrath*
Supporting Actor: Walter Brennan, *The Westerner*

1941
Picture: *How Green Was My Valley,* 20th CenturyFox
Director: John Ford, *How Green Was My Valley*
Actress: Joan Fontaine, *Suspicion*
Actor: Gary Cooper, *Sergeant York*
Supporting Actress: Mary Astor, *The Great Lie*
Supporting Actor: Donald Crisp, *How Green Was My Valley*

1942
Picture: *Mrs. Miniver,* M–G–M
Director: William Wyler, *Mrs. Miniver*
Actress: Greer Garson, *Mrs. Miniver*
Actor: James Cagney, *Yankee Doodle Dandy*
Supporting Actress: Teresa Wright, *Mrs. Miniver*
Supporting Actor: Van Heflin, *Johnny Eager*

1943
Picture: *Casablanca,* Warner Bros.
Director: Michael Curtiz, *Casablanca*
Actress: Jennifer Jones, *The Song of Bernadette*
Actor: Paul Lukas, *Watch on the Rhine*
Supporting Actress: Katina Paxinou, *For Whom the Bell Tolls*
Supporting Actor: Charles Coburn, *The More the Merrier*

1944
Picture: *Going My Way,* Paramount
Director: Leo McCarey, *Going My Way*
Actress: Ingrid Bergman, *Gaslight*
Actor: Bing Crosby, *Going My Way*
Supporting Actress: Ethel Barrymore, *None But the Lonely Heart*
Supporting Actor: Barry Fitzgerald, *Going My Way*

1945
Picture: *The Lost Weekend,* Paramount
Director: Billy Wilder, *The Lost Weekend*
Actress: Joan Crawford, *Mildred Pierce*
Actor: Ray Milland, *The Lost Weekend*
Supporting Actress: Anne Revere, *National Velvet*
Supporting Actor: James Dunn, *A Tree Grows in Brooklyn*

1946
Picture: *The Best Years of Our Lives,* Goldwyn–RKO Radio
Director: William Wyler, *The Best Years of Our Lives*
Actress: Olivia de Havilland, *To Each His Own*
Actor: Fredric March, *The Best Years of Our Lives*
Supporting Actress: Anne Baxter, *The Razor's Edge*
Supporting Actor: Harold Russell, *The Best Years of Our Lives*

1947
Picture: *Gentleman's Agreement,* 20th CenturyFox
Director: Elia Kazan, *Gentleman's Agreement*
Actress: Loretta Young, *The Farmer's Daughter*
Actor: Ronald Colman, *A Double Life*
Supporting Actress: Celeste Holm, *Gentleman's Agreement*
Supporting Actor: Edmund Gwenn, *Miracle on 34th Street*

1948
Picture: *Hamlet,* Rank–Two Cities–UI
Director: John Huston, *Treasure of Sierra Madre*
Actress: Jane Wyman, *Johnny Belinda*
Actor: Laurence Olivier, *Hamlet*
Supporting Actress: Claire Trevor, *Key Largo*
Supporting Actor: Walter Huston, *Treasure of Sierra Madre*

1949
Picture: *All the King's Men,* Rossen–Columbia
Director: Joseph L. Mankiewicz, *A Letter to Three Wives*
Actress: Olivia de Havilland, *The Heiress*
Actor: Broderick Crawford, *All the King's Men*
Supporting Actress: Mercedes McCambridge, *All the King's Men*
Supporting Actor: Dean Jagger, *Twelve O'Clock High*

1950
Picture: *All About Eve,* 20th Century–Fox
Director: Joseph L. Mankiewicz, *All About Eve*
Actress: Judy Holliday, *Born Yesterday*
Actor: José Ferrer, *Cyrano de Bergerac*
Supporting Actress: Josephine Hull, *Harvey*
Supporting Actor: George Sanders, *All About Eve*

1951
Picture: *An American in Paris,* M–G–M
Director: George Stevens, *A Place in the Sun*
Actress: Vivien Leigh, *A Streetcar Named Desire*
Actor: Humphrey Bogart, *The African Queen*
Supporting Actress: Kim Hunter, *A Streetcar Named Desire*
Supporting Actor: Karl Malden, *A Streetcar Named Desire*

1952
Picture: *The Greatest Show on Earth,* DeMille–Paramount
Director: John Ford, *The Quiet Man*
Actress: Shirley Booth, *Come Back, Little Sheba*
Actor: Gary Cooper, *High Noon*
Supporting Actress: Gloria Grahame, *The Bad and the Beautiful*
Supporting Actor: Anthony Quinn, *Viva Zapata!*

1953

Picture: *From Here to Eternity,* Columbia
Director: Fred Zinnemann, *From Here to Eternity*
Actress: Audrey Hepburn, *Roman Holiday*
Actor: William Holden, *Stalag 17*
Supporting Actress: Donna Reed, *From Here to Eternity*
Supporting Actor: Frank Sinatra, *From Here to Eternity*

1954

Picture: *On the Waterfront,* Horizon–American Corp., Columbia
Director: Elia Kazan, *On the Waterfront*
Actress: Grace Kelly, *The Country Girl*
Actor: Marlon Brando, *On the Waterfront*
Supporting Actress: Eva Marie Saint, *On the Waterfront*
Supporting Actor: Edmond O'Brien, *The Barefoot Contessa*

1955

Picture: *Marty,* Hecht and Lancaster, United Artists
Director: Delbert Mann, *Marty*
Actress: Anna Magnani, *The Rose Tattoo*
Actor: Ernest Borgnine, *Marty*
Supporting Actress: Jo Van Fleet, *East of Eden*
Supporting Actor: Jack Lemmon, *Mister Roberts*

1956

Picture: *Around the World in 80 Days,* Michael Todd Co., Inc.–U.A.
Director: George Stevens, *Giant*
Actress: Ingrid Bergman, *Anastasia*
Actor: Yul Brynner, *The King and I*
Supporting Actress: Dorothy Malone, *Written on the Wind*
Supporting Actor: Anthony Quinn, *Lust for Life*

1957

Picture: *The Bridge on the River Kwai,* Horizon Picture, Columbia
Director: David Lean, *The Bridge on the River Kwai*
Actress: Joanne Woodward, *The Three Faces of Eve*
Actor: Alec Guinness, *The Bridge on the River Kwai*
Supporting Actress: Miyoshi Umeki, *Sayonara*
Supporting Actor: Red Buttons, *Sayonara*

1958

Picture: *Gigi,* Arthur Freed Productions, Inc., M–G–M
Director: Vincente Minnelli, *Gigi*
Actress: Susan Hayward, *I Want to Live!*
Actor: David Niven, *Separate Tables*
Supporting Actress: Wendy Hiller, *Separate Tables*
Supporting Actor: Burl Ives, *The Big Country*

1959

Picture: *BenHur,* M–G–M
Director: William Wyler, *BenHur*
Actress: Simone Signoret, *Room at the Top*
Actor: Charlton Heston, *BenHur*
Supporting Actress: Shelley Winters, *The Diary of Anne Frank*
Supporting Actor: Hugh Griffith, *BenHur*

1960

Picture: *The Apartment,* Mirisch Co., Inc., United Artists
Director: Billy Wilder, *The Apartment*
Actress: Elizabeth Taylor, *Butterfield 8*
Actor: Burt Lancaster, *Elmer Gantry*
Supporting Actress: Shirley Jones, *Elmer Gantry*
Supporting Actor: Peter Ustinov, *Spartacus*

1961

Picture: *West Side Story,* Mirisch Pictures, Inc., and B and P Enterprises, Inc., United Artists
Director: Robert Wise and Jerome Robbins, *West Side Story*
Actress: Sophia Loren, *Two Women*
Actor: Maximillian Schell, *Judgment at Nuremberg*
Supporting Actress: Rita Moreno, *West Side Story*
Supporting Actor: George Chakiris, *West Side Story*

1962

Picture: *Lawrence of Arabia,* Horizon Pictures, Ltd.–Columbia
Director: David Lean, *Lawrence of Arabia*
Actress: Anne Bancroft, *The Miracle Worker*
Actor: Gregory Peck, *To Kill a Mockingbird*
Supporting Actress: Patty Duke, *The Miracle Worker*
Supporting Actor: Ed Begley, *Sweet Bird of Youth*

1963

Picture: *Tom Jones,* A Woodfall Production, UA–Lopert Pictures
Director: Tony Richardson, *Tom Jones*
Actress: Patricia Neal, *Hud*
Actor: Sidney Poitier, *Lilies of the Field*
Supporting Actress: Margaret Rutherford, *The V.I.P.s*
Supporting Actor: Melvyn Douglas, *Hud*

1964

Picture: *My Fair Lady,* Warner Bros.
Director: George Cukor, *My Fair Lady*
Actress: Julie Andrews, *Mary Poppins*
Actor: Rex Harrison, *My Fair Lady*
Supporting Actress: Lila Kedrova, *Zorba the Greek*
Supporting Actor: Peter Ustinov, *Topkapi*

1965

Picture: *The Sound of Music,* Argyle Enterprises Production, 20th CenturyFox
Director: Robert Wise, *The Sound of Music*
Actress: Julie Christie, *Darling*
Actor: Lee Marvin, *Cat Ballou*
Supporting Actress: Shelley Winters, *A Patch of Blue*
Supporting Actor: Martin Balsam, *A Thousand Clowns*

1966

Picture: *A Man for All Seasons,* Highland Films, Ltd., Production, Columbia
Director: Fred Zinnemann, *A Man for All Seasons*
Actress: Elizabeth Taylor, *Who's Afraid of Virginia Woolf?*
Actor: Paul Scofield, *A Man for All Seasons*
Supporting Actress: Sandy Dennis, *Who's Afraid of Virginia Woolf?*
Supporting Actor: Walter Matthau, *The Fortune Cookie*

1967

Picture: *In the Heat of the Night,* Mirisch Corp. Productions, United Artists
Director: Mike Nichols, *The Graduate*
Actress: Katharine Hepburn, *Guess Who's Coming to Dinner*
Actor: Rod Steiger, *In the Heat of the Night*
Supporting Actress: Estelle Parsons, *Bonnie and Clyde*
Supporting Actor: George Kennedy, *Cool Hand Luke*

1968

Picture: *Oliver!,* Columbia Pictures
Director: Sir Carol Reed, *Oliver!*
Actress: Katharine Hepburn, *The Lion in Winter* and Barbara Streisand, *Funny Girl*
Actor: Cliff Robertson, *Charly*
Supporting Actress: Ruth Gordon, *Rosemary's Baby*
Supporting Actor: Jack Albertson, *The Subject Was Roses*

1969

Picture: *Midnight Cowboy,* Jerome Hellman-John Schlesinger Production, United Artists
Director: John Schlesinger, *Midnight Cowboy*
Actress: Maggie Smith, *The Prime of Miss Jean Brodie*
Actor: John Wayne, *True Grit*
Supporting Actress: Goldie Hawn, *Cactus Flower*
Supporting Actor: Gig Young, *They Shoot Horses Don't They?*

1970

Picture: *Patton,* Frank McCarthy–Franklin J. Schaffner Production, 20th Century Fox
Director: Franklin J. Schaffner, *Patton*
Actress: Glenda Jackson, *Women in Love*
Actor: George C. Scott, *Patton*
Supporting Actress: Helen Hayes, *Airport*
Supporting Actor: John Mills, *Ryan's Daughter*

1971

Picture: *The French Connection,* D'Antoni Productions, 20th CenturyFox
Director: William Friedkin, *The French Connection*
Actress: Jane Fonda, *Klute*
Actor: Gene Hackman, *The French Connection*
Supporting Actress: Cloris Leachman, *The Last Picture Show*
Supporting Actor: Ben Johnson, *The Last Picture Show*

1972

Picture: *The Godfather,* Albert S. Ruddy Production, Paramount
Director: Bob Fosse, *Cabaret*
Actress: Liza Minnelli, *Cabaret*
Actor: Marlon Brando, *The Godfather*
Supporting Actress: Eileen Heckart, *Butterflies Are Free*
Supporting Actor: Joel Gray, *Cabaret*

1973

Picture: *The Sting,* Universal-Bill-Phillips-George Roy Hill Production, Universal
Director: George Roy Hill, *The Sting*
Actress: Glenda Jackson, *A Touch of Class*
Actor: Jack Lemmon, *Save the Tiger*
Supporting Actress: Tatum O'Neal, *Paper Moon*
Supporting Actor: John Houseman, *The Paper Chase*

1974

Picture: *The Godfather, Part II,* Coppola Co. Production, Paramount
Director: Francis Ford Coppola, *The Godfather, Part II*
Actress: Ellen Burstyn, *Alice Doesn't Live Here Anymore*
Actor: Art Carney, *Harry and Tonto*
Supporting Actress: Ingrid Bergman, *Murder on the Orient Express*
Suppo rting **Actor:** Robert De Niro, *The Godfather, Part II*

1975

Picture: *One Flew Over the Cuckoo's Nest,* Fantasy Films Production, United Artists
Director: Milos Forman, *One Flew Over the Cuckoo's Nest*
Actress: Louise Fletcher, *One Flew Over the Cuckoo's Nest*
Actor: Jack Nicholson, *One Flew Over the Cuckoo's Nest*
Supporting Actress: Lee Grant, *Shampoo*
Supporting Actor: George Burns, *The Sunshine Boys*

1976

Picture: *Rocky,* Robert Chartoff–Irwin Winkler Production, United Artists
Director: John G. Avildsen, *Rocky*
Actress: Faye Dunaway, *Network*
Actor: Peter Finch, *Network*
Supporting Actress: Beatrice Straight, *Network*
Supporting Actor: Jason Robards, *All the President's Men*

1977

Picture: *Annie Hall,* Jack Rollins–Charles H. Joffe Production, United Artists
Director: Woody Allen, *Annie Hall*
Actress: Diane Keaton, *Annie Hall*
Actor: Richard Dreyfuss, *The Goodbye Girl*
Supporting Actress: Vanessa Redgrave, *Julia*
Supporting Actor: Jason Robards, *Julia*

1978

Picture: *The Deer Hunter,* Michael Cimino Film Production, Universal
Director: Michael Cimino, *The Deer Hunter*
Actress: Jane Fonda, *Coming Home*
Actor: Jon Voight, *Coming Home*
Supporting Actress: Maggie Smith, *California Suite*
Supporting Actor: Christopher Walken, *The Deer Hunter*

1979

Picture: *Kramer vs. Kramer,* Stanley Jaffe Production, Columbia Pictures
Director: Robert Benton, *Kramer vs. Kramer*
Actress: Sally Field, *Norma Rae*
Actor: Dustin Hoffman, *Kramer vs. Kramer*
Supporting Actress: Meryl Streep, *Kramer vs. Kramer*
Supporting Actor: Melvyn Douglas, *Being There*

1980

Picture: *Ordinary People,* Wildwood Enterprises Production, Paramount
Director: Robert Redford, *Ordinary People*
Actress: Sissy Spacek, *Coal Miner's Daughter*
Actor: Robert De Niro, *Raging Bull*
Supporting Actress: Mary Steenburgen, *Melvin and Howard*
Supporting Actor: Timothy Hutton, *Ordinary People*

1981

Picture: *Chariots of Fire,* Enigma Productions, Ladd Company/Warner Bros.
Director: Warren Beatty, *Reds*
Actress: Katharine Hepburn, *On Golden Pond*
Actor: Henry Fonda, *On Golden Pond*
Supporting Actress: Maureen Stapleton, *Reds*
Supporting Actor: John Gielgud, *Arthur*

1982

Picture: *Gandhi,* Indo–British Films Production/Columbia
Director: Richard Attenborough, *Gandhi*
Actress: Meryl Streep, *Sophie's Choice*
Actor: Ben Kingsley, *Gandhi*
Supporting Actress: Jessica Lange, *Tootsie*
Supporting Actor: Louis Gossett, Jr., *An Officer and a Gentleman*

1983

Picture: *Terms of Endearment,* Paramount
Director: James L. Brooks, *Terms of Endearment*
Actress: Shirley MacLaine, *Terms of Endearment*
Actor: Robert Duvall, *Tender Mercies*
Supporting Actress: Linda Hunt, *The Year of Living Dangerously*
Supporting Actor: Jack Nicholson, *Terms of Endearment*

1984

Picture: *Amadeus,* Orion Pictures
Director: Milos Forman, *Amadeus*
Actress: Sally Field, *Places in the Heart*
Actor: F. Murray Abraham, *Amadeus*
Supporting Actress: Dame Peggy Ashcroft, *A Passage to India*
Supporting Actor: Haing S. Ngor, *The Killing Fields*

1985

Picture: *Out of Africa,* Universal
Director: Sydney Pollack, *Out of Africa*
Actress: Geraldine Page, *The Trip to Bountiful*
Actor: William Hurt, *Kiss of the Spider Woman*
Supporting Actress: Anjelica Huston, *Prizzi's Honor*
Supporting Actor: Don Ameche, *Cocoon*

1986

Picture: *Platoon,* Orion Pictures
Director: Oliver Stone, *Platoon*
Actress: Marlee Matlin, *Children of a Lesser God*
Actor: Paul Newman, *The Color of Money*
Supporting Actress: Dianne Wiest, *Hannah and Her Sisters*
Supporting Actor: Michael Caine, *Hannah and Her Sisters*

1987

Picture: *The Last Emperor,* Columbia Pictures
Director : Bernardo Bertolucci, *The Last Emperor*
Actress: Cher, *Moonstruck*
Actor: Michael Douglas, *Wall Street*
Supporting Actress: Olympia Dukakis, *Moonstruck*
Supporting Actor: Sean Connery, *The Untouchables*

1988

Picture: *Rain Man,* United Artists
Director: Barry Levinson, *Rain Man*
Actress: Jodie Foster, *The Accused*
Actor: Dustin Hoffman, *Rain Man*
Supporting Actress: Geena Davis, *The Accidental Tourist*

Supporting Actor: Kevin Kline: *A Fish Called Wanda*

1989

Picture: *Driving Miss Daisy,* Warner Brothers
Director: Oliver Stone, *Born on the Fourth of July*
Actress: Jessica Tandy, *Driving Miss Daisy*
Actor: Daniel Day-Lewis, *My Left Foot*
Supporting Actress: Brenda Fricker, *My Left Foot*
Supporting Actor: Denzel Washington, *Glory*

1990

Picture: *Dances With Wolves,* Orion
Director: Kevin Costner, *Dances With Wolves*
Actress: Kathy Bates, *Misery*
Actor: Jeremy Irons, *Reversal of Fortune*
Supporting Actress: Whoopi Goldberg, *Ghost*
Supporting Actor: Joe Pesci, *Goodfellas*

1991

Picture: *The Silence of the Lambs,* Orion
Director: Jonathan Demme, *The Silence of the Lambs*
Actress: Jodie Foster, *The Silence of the Lambs*
Actor: Anthony Hopkins, *The Silence of the Lambs*
Supporting Actress: Mercedes Ruehl, *The Fisher King*
Supporting Actor: Jack Palance, *City Slickers*

1992

Picture: *Unforgiven,* Warner Brothers
Director: Clint Eastwood, *Unforgiven*
Actress: Emma Thompson, *Howards End*
Actor: Al Pacino, *Scent of a Woman*
Supporting Actress: Marisa Tomei, *My Cousin Vinny*
Supporting Actor: Gene Hackman, *Unforgiven*

Other Academy Awards for 1992

Art Direction: Luciana Arrighi, art direction, and Ian Whittaker, set decoration, *Howards End*
Cinematography: Philippe Rousselot, *A River Runs Through It*
Costume Design: Eiko Ishioka, *Bram Stoker's "Dracula"*
Documentary (feature): *The Panama Deception;* **(short subject):** *Educating Peter*
Editing: Joel Cox, *Unforgiven*
Foreign-language film: *Indochine,* France
Makeup: Greg Cannom, Michele Burke, and Matthew W. Mungle, *Bram Stoker's "Dracula"*
Music (original score): Alan Menken, *Aladdin;* **(song):** Alan Menken and Tim Rice, "Whole New World" from *Aladdin*
Screenplay, Original: Neil Jordan, *The Crying Game*
Screenplay, Adapted: Ruth Prawer Jhabvala, *Howards End*
Short subject (live action): *Omnibus;* **(animated):** *Mona Lisa Descending a Staircase*
Sound: Chris Jenkins, Doug Hemphill, Mark Smith, and Simon Kaye, *The Last of the Mohicans*
Sound effects editing: Tom C. McCarthy and David E. Stone, *Bram Stoker's "Dracula"*
Visual effects: Ken Ralston, Doug Chiang, Doug Smythe, and Tom Woodruff, Jr., *Death Becomes Her*
Honorary Award: Federico Fellini
Jean Hersholt Humanitarian Award: Audrey Hepburn (posthumously) and Elizabeth Taylor
Academy Award of Merit: (technical) Chadwell O'Connor
Gordon E. Sawyer Award: (technical) Erich Kaestner

George Foster Peabody Awards for Broadcasting, 1992

Radio

KJLH, Los Angeles: coverage of the riots following acquittal of officers in the Rodney King trial.
National Public Radio, Washington, D.C.: *Prisoners in Bosnia.*
National Public Radio and WBUR, Boston: *Car Talk.*
KFFA, Helena, Ark.: *King Biscuit Time.*
David Isay, independent producer: *American Folklife Radio Project.*

Television

KTTV, Los Angeles: coverage of the Rodney G. King case.
WTVJ, Miami: coverage of Hurricane Andrew.
WGBH, Boston: *The Health Quarterly: The AIDS Report Series.*
WGBH, Boston: *The American Experience.*
WGBH, Boston: *The Machine That Changed the World.*
WGBH, Boston and WQED, Pittsburgh: *Where in the World is Carmen Sandiego?*
ABC News, New York: *Nightline: 72 Hours to Victory.*
ABC News, New York: *Nightline: Moment of Crisis—Anatomy of a Riot.*
Propaganda Films and Fox Broadcasting: *Rock the Vote.*
KIRO, Seattle: *When the Salmon Runs Dry.*
KNME and the Institute for American Indian Arts, Albuquerque, N.M.: *Surviving Columbus.*
Signifyin' Works, Berkeley, Calif. and PBS: *Color Adjustment.*
Canamedia Productions Ltd. and TV Ontario, Toronto: *Threads of Hope.*
HKO Media Inc. and WKBD, Detroit: *Close to Home: The Tommy Boccomino Story.*
GPN–Nebraska ETV, Lincoln: *Reading Rainbow: The Wall.*
WCVB, Needham, Mass.: *The Incredible Voyage of Bill Pinkney.*
NBC: *The More You Know.*
MTV: *Choose or Lose Campaign.*
CBS and Finnegan–Pinchuk Co. in association with **Brand–Falsey Productions:** *Northern Exposure: Cicely.*
CNN, Atlanta: *Larry King Live Election Coverage 1992.*
CBS and Granada Television, London: *Age Seven in America.*

Personal Awards

Daniel Schorr for a lifetime of uncompromising reporting of the highest integrity.

Fred Rogers in recognition of 25 years of beautiful days in the neighborhood.

Institutional Awards

BBC Radio for the consistency, range, variety, intelligence, and humor provided to English-speaking audiences worldwide.

C-SPAN for ongoing, sustained, honest, and frequently compelling coverage of the democratic process in action.

Pulitzer Prize Awards

(For years not listed, no award was made.)

Source: Columbia University.

Pulitzer Prizes in Journalism

MERITORIOUS PUBLIC SERVICE

1918 *New York Times;* also special award to Minna Lewinson and Henry Beetle Hough
1919 *Milwaukee Journal*
1921 *Boston Post*
1922 *New York World*
1923 *Memphis Commercial Appeal*
1924 *New York World*
1926 *Columbus* (Ga.) *Enquirer Sun*
1927 *Canton* (Ohio) *Daily News*
1928 *Indianapolis Times*
1929 *New York Evening World*
1931 *Atlanta Constitution*
1932 *Indianapolis News*
1933 *New York World-Telegram*
1934 *Medford* (Ore.) *Mail Tribune*
1935 *Sacramento Bee*
1936 *Cedar Rapids* (Iowa) *Gazette*
1937 *St. Louis Post-Dispatch*
1938 *Bismarck* (N.D.) *Tribune*
1939 *Miami Daily News*
1940 *Waterbury* (Conn.) *Republican* and *American*
1941 *St. Louis Post-Dispatch*
1942 *Los Angeles Times*
1943 *Omaha World-Herald*
1944 *New York Times*
1945 *Detroit Free Press*
1946 *Scranton* (Pa.) *Times*
1947 *Baltimore Sun*
1948 *St. Louis Post-Dispatch*
1949 (Lincoln) *Nebraska State Journal*
1950 *Chicago Daily News;* and *St. Louis Post-Dispatch*
1951 *Miami Herald;* and *Brooklyn Eagle*
1952 *St. Louis Post-Dispatch*
1953 *Whiteville* (N.C.) *News Reporter;* and *Tabor City* (N.C.) *Tribune*
1954 *Newsday* (Garden City, L.I.)
1955 *Columbus* (Ga.) *Ledger* and *Sunday Ledger-Enquirer*
1956 *Watsonville* (Calif.) *Register-Pajaronian*
1957 *Chicago Daily News*
1958 (Little Rock) *Arkansas Gazette*
1959 *Utica* (N.Y.) *Observer Dispatch* and *Utica Daily Press*
1960 *Los Angeles Times*
1961 *Amarillo* (Tex.) *Globe-Times*
1962 *Panama City* (Fla.) *News-Herald*
1963 *Chicago Daily News*
1964 *St. Petersburg* (Fla.) *Times*
1965 *Hutchinson* (Kan.) *News*
1966 *Boston Globe*
1967 *Louisville Courier-Journal* and *Milwaukee Journal*
1968 *Riverside* (Calif.) *Press-Enterprise*
1969 *Los Angeles Times*
1970 *Newsday* (Garden City, L.I.)
1971 *Winston-Salem* (N.C.) *Journal and Sentinel*
1972 *New York Times*
1973 *Washington Post*
1974 *Newsday* (Garden City, L.I.)
1975 *Boston Globe*
1976 *Anchorage* (Alaska) *Daily News*
1977 *Lufkin* (Tex.) *News*
1978 *Philadelphia Inquirer*
1979 *Point Reyes* (Calif.) *Light*
1980 Gannett News Service
1981 *Charlotte* (N.C.) *Observer*
1982 *Detroit News*
1983 *Jackson* (Miss.) *Clarion-Ledger*
1984 *Los Angeles Times*
1985 *The Fort Worth Star-Telegram*
1986 *Denver Post*
1987 Andrew Schneider and Matthew Brelis, *Pittsburgh Press*
1988 *Charlotte* (N.C.) *Observer*
1989 *Anchorage Daily News*
1990 *Philadelphia Inquirer* and *Washington* (N.C.) *Daily News*
1991 *Des Moines Register,* reporting by Jane Schorer
1992 *Sacramento Bee* for "The Sierra in Peril" series by Tom Knudson
1993 *Miami Herald*

EDITORIAL

1917 *New York Tribune*
1918 *Louisville Courier-Journal*
1920 Harvey E. Newbranch *(Omaha Evening World-Herald)*
1922 Frank M. O'Brien *(New York Herald)*
1923 William Allen White *(Emporia* [Kan.] *Gazette)*
1924 *Boston Herald* (Frank Buxton); special prize: Frank I. Cobb *(New York World)*
1925 *Charleston* (S.C.) *News and Courier*
1926 *New York Times* (Edward M. Kingsbury)
1927 *Boston Herald* (F. Lauriston Bullard)
1928 Grover Cleveland Hall *(Montgomery* [Ala.] *Advertiser)*
1929 Louis Isaac Jaffe *(Norfolk Virginian-Pilot)*
1931 Charles S. Ryckman *(Fremont* [Neb.] *Tribune)*
1933 *Kansas City* (Mo.) *Star*
1934 E. P. Chase *(Atlantic* [Iowa] *News Telegraph)*
1936 Felix Morley *(Washington Post);* George B. Parker (Scripps-Howard Newspapers)
1937 John W. Owens *(Baltimore Sun)*
1938 W. W. Waymack *(Des Moines Register and Tribune)*
1939 Ronald G. Callvert *(Portland Oregonian)*
1940 Bart Howard *(St. Louis Post-Dispatch)*
1941 Reuben Maury *(New York Daily News)*
1942 Geoffrey Parsons *(New York Herald Tribune)*
1943 Forrest W. Seymour *(Des Moines Register and Tribune)*
1944 *Kansas City* (Mo.) *Star* (Henry J. Haskell)
1945 George W. Potter *(Providence* [R.I.] *Journal-Bulletin)*
1946 Hodding Carter ([Greenville, Miss.] *Delta Democrat-Times*)
1947 William H. Grimes *(Wall Street Journal)*
1948 Virginius Dabney *(Richmond Times-Dispatch)*
1949 John H. Crider *(Boston Herald);* Herbert Elliston *(Washington Post)*

1950 Carl M. Saunders (*Jackson* [Mich.] *Citizen Patriot*)
1951 William H. Fitzpatrick (*New Orleans States*)
1952 Louis LaCoss (*St. Louis Globe-Democrat*)
1953 Vermont C. Royster (*Wall Street Journal*)
1954 *Boston Herald* (Don Murray)
1955 *Detroit Free Press* (Royce Howes)
1956 Lauren K. Soth (*Des Moines Register and Tribune*)
1957 Buford Boone (*Tuscaloosa* [Ala.] *News*)
1958 Harry S. Ashmore (*Arkansas Gazette*)
1959 Ralph McGill (*Atlanta Constitution*)
1960 Lenoir Chambers (*Virginian-Pilot*)
1961 William J. Dorvillier (*San Juan* [P.R.] *Star*)
1962 Thomas M. Storke (*Santa Barbara* [Calif.] *News-Press*)
1963 Ira B. Harkey, Jr. (*Pascagoula* [Miss.] *Chronicle*)
1964 Hazel Brannon Smith (*Lexington* [Miss.] *Advertiser*)
1965 John R. Harrison (*Gainesville* [Fla.] *Daily Sun*)
1966 Robert Lasch (*St. Louis Post-Dispatch*)
1967 Eugene Patterson (*Atlanta Constitution*)
1968 John S. Knight (Knight Newspapers)
1969 Paul Greenberg (*Pine Bluff* [Ark.] *Commercial*)
1970 Phillip L. Geyelin (*Washington Post*)
1971 Horance G. Davis, Jr. (*Gainesville* [Fla.] *Sun*)
1972 John Strohmeyer (*Bethlehem* [Pa.] *Globe Times*)
1973 Roger Bourne Linscott (*Berkshire Eagle* [Pittsfield, Mass.])
1974 F. Gilman Spencer (*Trenton* [N.J.] *Trentonian*)
1975 John Daniell Maurice (*Charleston* [W. Va.] *Daily Mail*)
1976 Philip P. Kerby (*Los Angeles Times*)
1977 Warren L. Lerude, Foster Church and Norman F. Cardoza (*Reno* [Nev.] *Gazette* and *Nevada State Journal*)
1978 Meg Greenfield (*Washington Post*)
1979 Edwin M. Yoder, Jr. (*Washington Star*)
1980 Robert L. Bartley (*Wall Street Journal*)
1981 Not awarded
1982 Jack Rosenthal (*New York Times*)
1983 *Miami Herald*
1984 Albert Scardino (*Georgia Gazette*)
1985 Richard Aregood (*Philadelphia Daily News*)
1986 Jack Fuller (*Chicago Tribune*)
1987 Jonathan Freedman (*San Diego Tribune*)
1988 Jane E. Healy (*Orlando Sentinel*)
1989 Lois Wille (*Chicago Tribune*)
1990 Thomas J. Hylton (*Pottstown* [Pa.] *Mercury*)
1991 Ron Casey, Harold Jackson, and Joey Kennedy (*Birmingham* [Ala.] *News*)
1992 Maria Henson (*Lexington* [Ky.] *Herald-Leader*)

CORRESPONDENCE

1929 Paul Scott Mowrer (*Chicago Daily News*)
1930 Leland Stowe (*New York Herald Tribune*)
1931 H. R. Knickerbocker (*Philadelphia Public Ledger* and *New York Evening Post*)
1932 Walter Duranty (*New York Times*); Charles G. Ross (*St. Louis Post-Dispatch*)
1933 Edgar Ansel Mowrer (*Chicago Daily News*)
1934 Frederick T. Birchall (*New York Times*)
1935 Arthur Krock (*New York Times*)
1936 Wilfred C. Barber (*Chicago Tribune*)
1937 Anne O'Hare McCormick (*New York Times*)
1938 Arthur Krock (*New York Times*)
1939 Louis P. Lochner (Associated Press)
1940 Otto D. Tolischus (*New York Times*)
1941 Group award[1]
1942 Carlos P. Romulo (*Philippines Herald*)
1943 Hanson W. Baldwin (*New York Times*)
1944 Ernie Pyle (Scripps-Howard Newspaper Alliance)
1945 Harold V. (Hal) Boyle (Associated Press)
1946 Arnaldo Cortesi (*New York Times*)
1947 Brooks Atkinson (*New York Times*)
1948 Discontinued

1. For the public services and the individual achievements of American news reporters in the war zones.

EDITORIAL CARTOONING

1922 Rollin Kirby (*New York World*)
1924 Jay Norwood Darling (*New York Tribune*)
1925 Rollin Kirby (*New York World*)
1926 D. R. Fitzpatrick (*St. Louis Post-Dispatch*)
1927 Nelson Harding (*Brooklyn Eagle*)
1928 Nelson Harding (*Brooklyn Eagle*)
1929 Rollin Kirby (*New York World*)
1930 Charles R. Macauley (*Brooklyn Eagle*)
1931 Edmund Duffy (*Baltimore Sun*)
1932 John T. McCutcheon (*Chicago Tribune*)
1933 H. M. Talburt (*Washington Daily News*)
1934 Edmund Duffy (*Baltimore Sun*)
1935 Ross A. Lewis (*Milwaukee Journal*)
1937 C. D. Batchelor (*New York Daily News*)
1938 Vaughn Shoemaker (*Chicago Daily News*)
1939 Charles G. Werner (*Daily Oklahoman* [Oklahoma City])
1940 Edmund Duffy (*Baltimore Sun*)
1941 Jacob Burck (*Chicago Times*)
1942 Herbert L. Block (NEA Service)
1943 Jay Norwood Darling (*New York Herald Tribune*)
1944 Clifford K. Berryman (*Washington Evening Star*)
1945 Bill Mauldin (United Features Syndicate)
1946 Bruce Alexander Russell (*Los Angeles Times*)
1947 Vaughn Shoemaker (*Chicago Daily News*)
1948 Reuben L. Goldberg (*New York Sun*)
1949 Lute Pease (*Newark Evening News*)
1950 James T. Berryman (*Washington Evening Star*)
1951 Reg (Reginald W.) Manning (*Arizona Republic* [Phoenix])
1952 Fred L. Packer (*New York Mirror*)
1953 Edward D. Kuekes (*Cleveland Plain Dealer*)
1954 Herbert L. Block (*Washington Post* and *Times-Herald*)
1955 Daniel R. Fitzpatrick (*St. Louis Post-Dispatch*)
1956 Robert York (*Louisville Times*)
1957 Tom Little (*Nashville Tennessean*)
1958 Bruce M. Shanks (*Buffalo Evening News*)
1959 Bill Mauldin (*St. Louis Post-Dispatch*)
1961 Carey Orr (*Chicago Tribune*)
1962 Edmund S. Valtman (*Hartford Times*)
1963 Frank Miller (*Des Moines Register*)
1964 Paul Conrad (formerly of *Denver Post*, later on *Los Angeles Times*)
1966 Don Wright (*Miami News*)
1967 Patrick B. Oliphant (*Denver Post*)
1968 Eugene Gray Payne (*Charlotte* [N.C.] *Observer*)
1969 John Fischetti (*Chicago Daily News*)
1970 Thomas F. Darcy (*Newsday* [Garden City, L.I.])
1971 Paul Conrad (*Los Angeles Times*)
1972 Jeffrey K. MacNelly (*Richmond* [Va.] *News Leader*)
1974 Paul Szep (*Boston Globe*)
1975 Garry Trudeau (Universal Press Syndicate)
1976 Tony Auth (*Philadelphia Inquirer*)
1977 Paul Szep (*Boston Globe*)
1978 Jeffrey K. MacNelly (*Richmond* [Va.] *News Leader*)
1979 Herbert L. Block (*Washington Post*)
1980 Don Wright (*Miami News*)
1981 Mike Peters (*Dayton* [Ohio] *Daily News*)
1982 Ben Sargent (*Austin* [Tex.] *American-Statesman*)
1983 Richard Locher (*Chicago Tribune*)
1984 Paul Conrad (*Los Angeles Times*)
1985 Jeff MacNelly (*Chicago Tribune*)
1986 Jules Feiffer (*Village Voice*)
1987 Berke Breathed (*Washington Post* Writers Group)
1988 Doug Marlette (*Atlanta Constitution* and *Charlotte* [N.C.] *Observer*)
1989 Jack Higgins (*Chicago Sun-Times*)
1990 Tom Toles (*Buffalo News*)

1991 Jim Borgman *(Cincinnati Inquirer)*
1992 Signe Wilkinson, *(Philadelphia Daily News)*
1993 Stephen R. Benson *(Arizona Republic)*

NEWS PHOTOGRAPHY

1942 Milton Brooks *(Detroit News)*
1943 Frank Noel (Associated Press)
1944 Frank Filan (Associated Press); Earle L. Bunker *(Omaha World-Herald)*
1945 Joe Rosenthal (Associated Press)
1947 Arnold Hardy
1948 Frank Cushing *(Boston Traveler)*
1949 Nat Fein *(New York Herald Tribune)*
1950 Bill Crouch *(Oakland Tribune)*
1951 Max Desfor (Associated Press)
1952 John Robinson and Don Ultang *(Des Moines Register & Tribune)*
1953 William M. Gallagher *(Flint* [Mich.] *Journal)*
1954 Mrs. Walter M. Schau
1955 John L. Gaunt, Jr. *(Los Angeles Times)*
1956 *New York Daily News*
1957 Harry A. Trask *(Boston Traveler)*
1958 William C. Beall *(Washington Daily News)*
1959 William Seaman *(Minneapolis Star)*
1960 Andrew Lopez (United Press International)
1961 Yasushi Nagao (Mainichi Newspapers, Tokyo)
1962 Paul Vathis (Harrisburg [Pa.] bureau of Associated Press)
1963 Hector Rondon (*La Republica*, Caracas, Venezuela)
1964 Robert H. Jackson *(Dallas Times Herald)*
1965 Horst Faas (Associated Press)
1966 Kyoichi Sawada (United Press International)
1967 Jack R. Thornell (Associated Press)
1968 News: Rocco Morabito *(Jacksonville* [Fla.] *Journal)*; features: Toshio Sakai (United Press International)
1969 Spot news: Edward T. Adams (Associated Press); features: Moneta Sleet, Jr.
1970 Spot news: Steve Starr (Associated Press); features: Dallas Kinney *(Palm Beach Post)*
1971 Spot news: John Paul Filo (*Valley Daily News* and *Daily Dispatch* [Tarentum and New Kensington, Pa.]); features: Jack Dykinga *(Chicago Sun-Times)*
1972 Spot news: Horst Faas and Michel Laurent (Associated Press); features: Dave Kennerly (United Press International)
1973 Spot news: Huynh Cong Ut *(Associated Press)*; features: Brian Lanker *(Topeka Capital-Journal)*
1974 Spot news: Anthony K. Roberts (Associated Press); features: Slava Veder (Associated Press)
1975 Spot news: Gerald H. Gay *(Seattle Times)*; features: Matthew Lewis *(Washington Post)*
1976 Spot news: Stanley J. Forman *(Boston Herald-American)*; features: photographic staff of *Louisville Courier-Journal* and *Times*
1977 Spot news: Neal Ulevich (Associated Press) and Stanley J. Forman *(Boston Herald-American)*; features: Robin Hood *(Chattanooga News-Free Press)*
1978 Spot news: John Blair, freelance, Evansville, Ind.; features: J. Ross Baughman (Associated Press)
1979 Spot news: Thomas J. Kelly, 3rd *(Pottstown* [Pa.] *Mercury)*; features: photographic staff of *Boston Herald-American*
1980 Features: Erwin H. Hagler *(Dallas Times Herald)*
1981 Spot news: Larry C. Price *(Fort Worth Star-Telegram)*; features: Taro M. Yamasaki *(Detroit Free Press)*
1982 Spot news: Ron Edmonds (Associated Press); features: John H. White *(Chicago Sun-Times)*
1983 Spot news: Bill Foley (Associated Press); features: James B. Dickman *(Dallas Times Herald)*
1984 Spot news: Stan Grossfeld *(Boston Globe)*; features: Anthony Suau *(Denver Post)*
1985 Spot news: photographic staff of *Register,* Santa Ana, Calif.; features: Stan Grossfeld *(Boston Globe)*
1986 Spot news: Michel duCille and Carol Guzy *(Miami Herald)*; features: Tom Gralish *(Philadelphia Inquirer)*
1987 Spot news: Kim Komenich *(San Francisco Examiner)*; features: David Peterson *(Des Moines Register)*
1988 Spot news: Scott Shaw *(Odessa* [Texas] *American)*; features: Michel duCille *(Miami Herald)*
1989 Spot news: Ron Olshwanger *(St. Louis Post-Dispatch)*; features: Manny Crisostomo *(Detroit Free Press)*
1990 Spot news: *Oakland Tribune*; features: David C. Turnley *(Detroit Free Press)*
1991 Spot news: Greg Marinovich (Associated Press); features: William Snyder *(Dallas Morning News)*
1992 Spot news: Associated Press staff; features: John Kaplan *(Herald* [Monterey, Calif.] and *Pittsburgh Post-Gazette)*
1993 Spot news: William Snyder and Ken Geiger *(Dallas Morning News)*; features: Associated Press

NATIONAL TELEGRAPHIC REPORTING

1942 Louis Stark *(New York Times)*
1944 Dewey L. Fleming *(Baltimore Sun)*
1945 James Reston *(New York Times)*
1946 Edward A. Harris *(St. Louis Post-Dispatch)*
1947 Edward T. Folliard *(Washington Post)*

NATIONAL REPORTING

1948 Bert Andrews *(New York Herald Tribune)*; Nat S. Finney *(Minneapolis Tribune)*
1949 C. P. Trussell *(New York Times)*
1950 Edwin O. Guthman *(Seattle Times)*
1952 Anthony Leviero *(New York Times)*
1953 Don Whitehead (Associated Press)
1954 Richard Wilson (Cowles Newspapers)
1955 Anthony Lewis *(Washington Daily News)*
1956 Charles L. Bartlett *(Chattanooga Times)*
1957 James Reston *(New York Times)*
1958 Relman Morin (Associated Press) and Clark Mollenhoff *(Des Moines Register & Tribune)*
1959 Howard Van Smith *(Miami News)*
1960 Vance Trimble (Scripps-Howard Newspaper Alliance)
1961 Edward R. Cony *(Wall Street Journal)*
1962 Nathan G. Caldwell and Gene S. Graham *(Nashville Tennessean)*
1963 Anthony Lewis *(New York Times)*
1964 Merriman Smith (United Press International)
1965 Louis M. Kohlmeier *(Wall Street Journal)*
1966 Haynes Johnson *(Washington Evening Star)*
1967 Stanley Penn and Monroe Karmin *(Wall Street Journal)*
1968 Howard James *(Christian Science Monitor)*; Nathan K. (Nick) Kotz *(Des Moines Register* and *Minneapolis Tribune)*
1969 Robert Cahn *(Christian Science Monitor)*
1970 William J. Eaton *(Chicago Daily News)*
1971 Lucinda Franks and Thomas Powers (United Press International)
1972 Jack Anderson *(United Feature Syndicate)*
1973 Robert Boyd and Clark Hoyt *(Knight Newspapers)*
1974 Jack White *(Providence* [R.I.] *Journal-Bulletin)*; and James R. Polk *(Washington Star-News)*
1975 Donald L. Barlett and James B. Steele *(Philadelphia Inquirer)*
1976 James Risser *(Des Moines Register)*
1977 Walter Mears (Associated Press)
1978 Gaylord D. Shaw *(Los Angeles Times)*
1979 James Risser *(Des Moines Register)*
1980 Bette Swenson Orsini and Charles Stafford *(St. Petersburg Times)*
1981 John M. Crewdson *(New York Times)*
1982 Rick Atkinson *(Kansas City* [Mo.] *Times)*
1983 *Boston Globe*
1984 John N. Wilford *(New York Times)*

1985 Thomas J. Knudson (*Des Moines Register*)
1986 Craig Flournoy and George Rodrigue (*Dallas Morning News*) and Arthur Howe (*Philadelphia Inquirer*)
1987 *Miami Herald*, staff; *New York Times*, staff
1988 Tim Weiner (*Philadelphia Inquirer*)
1989 Donald L. Barlett and James B. Steele (*Philadelphia Inquirer*)
1990 Ross Anderson, Bill Dietrich, Mary Ann Gwinn, and Eric Nalder (*Seattle Times*)
1991 Marjie Lundstrom and Rochelle Sharpe (Gannett News Service)
1992 Jeff Taylor and Mike McGraw (*Kansas City Star*)
1993 David Marannis (*Washington Post*)

INTERNATIONAL TELEGRAPHIC REPORTING

1942 Laurence Edmund Allen (Associated Press)
1943 Ira Wolfert (North American Newspaper Alliance, Inc.)
1944 Daniel De Luce (Associated Press)
1945 Mark S. Watson (*Baltimore Sun*)
1946 Homer W. Bigart (*New York Herald Tribune*)
1947 Eddy Gilmore (Associated Press)

INTERNATIONAL REPORTING

1948 Paul W. Ward (*Baltimore Sun*)
1949 Price Day (*Baltimore Sun*)
1950 Edmund Stevens (*Christian Science Monitor*)
1951 Keyes Beech and Fred Sparks (*Chicago Daily News*); Homer Bigart and Marguerite Higgins (*New York Herald Tribune*); Relman Morin and Don Whitehead (Associated Press)
1952 John M. Hightower (Associated Press)
1953 Austin C. Wehrwein (*Milwaukee Journal*)
1954 Jim G. Lucas (Scripps-Howard Newspapers)
1955 Harrison E. Salisbury (*New York Times*)
1956 William Randolph Hearst, Jr. and Frank Conniff (Hearst Newspapers) and Kingsbury Smith (INS)
1957 Russell Jones (United Press)
1958 *New York Times*
1959 Joseph Martin and Philip Santora (*New York Daily News*)
1960 A. M. Rosenthal (*New York Times*)
1961 Lynn Heinzerling (Associated Press)
1962 Walter Lippmann (New York Herald Tribune Syndicate)
1963 Hal Hendrix (*Miami News*)
1964 Malcolm W. Browne (Associated Press) and David Halberstam (*New York Times*)
1965 J. A. Livingston (*Philadelphia Bulletin*)
1966 Peter Arnett (Associated Press)
1967 R. John Hughes (*Christian Science Monitor*)
1968 Alfred Friendly (*Washington Post*)
1969 William Tuohy (*Los Angeles Times*)
1970 Seymour M. Hersh (Dispatch News Service)
1971 Jimmie Lee Hoagland (*Washington Post*)
1972 Peter R. Kann (*Wall Street Journal*)
1973 Max Frankel (*New York Times*)
1974 Hedrick Smith (*New York Times*)
1975 William Mullen and Ovie Carter (*Chicago Tribune*)
1976 Sydney H. Schanberg (*New York Times*)
1978 Henry Kamm (*New York Times*)
1979 Richard Ben Cramer (*Philadelphia Inquirer*)
1980 Joel Brinkley and Jay Mather (*Louisville Courier-Journal*)
1981 Shirley Christian (*Miami Herald*)
1982 John Darnton (*New York Times*)
1983 Thomas L. Friedman (*New York Times*)
1984 Karen E. House (*Wall Street Journal*)
1985 Josh Friedman, Dennis Bell, and Ozier Muhammad (*Newsday*)
1986 Lewis M. Simons, Pete Carey, and Katherine Ellison (*San Jose Mercury News*)
1987 Michael Parks (*Los Angeles Times*)
1988 Thomas L. Friedman (*New York Times*)
1989 Bill Keller (*New York Times*); Glenn Frankel (*Washington Post*)
1990 Nicholas D. Kristof and Sheryl WuDunn (*New York Times*)
1991 Caryle Murphy (*Washington Post*) and Serge Schmemann (*New York Times*)
1992 Patrick J. Sloyan (*Newsday*)
1993 John F. Burns (*New York Times*) and Roy Gutman (*Newsday*)

REPORTING

1917 Herbert B. Swope (*New York World*)
1918 Harold A. Littledale (*New York Evening Post*)
1920 John J. Leary, Jr. (*New York World*)
1921 Louis Seibold (*New York World*)
1922 Kirke L. Simpson (Associated Press)
1923 Alva Johnston (*New York Times*)
1924 Magner White (*San Diego Sun*)
1925 James W. Mulroy and Alvin H. Goldstein (*Chicago Daily News*)
1926 William Burke Miller (*Louisville Courier-Journal*)
1927 John T. Rogers (*St. Louis Post-Dispatch*)
1929 Paul Y. Anderson (*St. Louis Post-Dispatch*)
1930 Russell D. Owen (*New York Times*); special award: W. O. Dapping (*Auburn* [N.Y.] *Citizen*)
1931 A. B. MacDonald (*Kansas City* [Mo.] *Star*)
1932 W. C. Richards, D. D. Martin, J. S. Pooler, F. D. Webb, J. N. W. Sloan (all of *Detroit Free Press*)
1933 Francis A. Jamieson (Associated Press)
1934 Royce Brier (*San Francisco Chronicle*)
1935 William H. Taylor (*New York Herald Tribune*)
1936 Lauren D. Lyman (*New York Times*)
1937 John J. O'Neill (*New York Herald Tribune*); William Leonard Laurence (*New York Times*); Howard W. Blakeslee (Associated Press); Gobind Behari Lal (Universal Service); David Dietz (Scripps-Howard Newspapers)
1938 Raymond Sprigle (*Pittsburg Post-Gazette*)
1939 Thomas L. Stokes (*New York World-Telegram*)
1940 S. Burton Heath (*New York World-Telegram*)
1941 Westbrook Pegler (*New York World-Telegram*)
1942 Stanton Delaplane (*San Francisco Chronicle*)
1943 George Weller (*Chicago Daily News*)
1944 Paul Schoenstein and associates (*New York Journal-American*)
1945 Jack S. McDowell (*San Francisco Call-Bulletin*)
1946 William Leonard Laurence (*New York Times*)
1947 Frederick Woltman (*New York World-Telegram*)
1948 George E. Goodwin (*Atlanta Journal*)
1949 Malcolm Johnson (*New York Sun*)
1950 Meyer Berger (*New York Times*)
1951 Edward S. Montgomery (*San Francisco Examiner*)
1952 George de Carvalho (*San Francisco Chronicle*)
1953 Editorial staff (*Providence Journal and Evening Bulletin*);[1] Edward J. Mowery (*New York World-Telegram and Sun*)[2]
1954 *Vicksburg* (Miss.) *Sunday Post-Herald*;[1] Alvin Scott McCoy (*Kansas City* [Mo.] *Star*)[2]
1955 Mrs. Caro Brown (*Alice* [Tex.] *Daily Echo*);[1] Roland Kenneth Towery (*Cuero* [Tex.] *Record*)[2]
1956 Lee Hills (*Detroit Free Press*);[1] Arthur Daley (*New York Times*)[2]
1957 *Salt Lake Tribune*;[1] Wallace Turner and William Lambert (*Portland Oregonian*)[2]
1958 *Fargo* [N.D.] *Forum*;[1] George Beveridge (*Washington* [D.C.] *Evening Star*)[2]
1959 Mary Lou Werner (*Washington* [D.C.] *Evening Star*);[1] John Harold Brislin (*Scranton* [Pa.] *Tribune & Scrantonian*)[2]
1960 Jack Nelson (*Atlanta Constitution*);[1] Miriam Ottenberg (*Washington Evening Star*)[2]
1961 Sanche de Gramont (*New York Herald Tribune*);[1] Edgar May (*Buffalo Evening News*)[2]

1962 Robert D. Mullins (*Deseret News*, Salt Lake City);[1] George Bliss *(Chicago Tribune)*[2]
1963 Sylvan Fox, Anthony Shannon, and William Longgood *(New York World-Telegram and Sun)*;[1] Oscar Griffin, Jr. (former editor of *Pecos* [Tex.] *Independent and Enterprise*, now on staff of *Houston Chronicle*)[2]

1. Reporting under pressure of edition deadlines. 2. Reporting not under pressure of edition deadlines.

GENERAL LOCAL REPORTING

1964 Norman C. Miller *(Wall Street Journal)*
1965 Melvin H. Ruder (*Hungry Horse News*, Columbia Falls, Mont.)
1966 Staff of *Los Angeles Times*
1967 Robert V. Cox *(Chambersburg* [Pa.] *Public Opinion)*
1968 Staff of *Detroit Free Press*
1969 John Fetterman *(Louisville Times* and *Courier-Journal)*
1970 Thomas Fitzpatrick *(Chicago Sun-Times)*
1971 Staff of *Akron* (Ohio) *Beacon*
1972 Richard Cooper and John Machacek *(Rochester* [N.Y.] *Times-Union)*
1973 *Chicago Tribune*
1974 Arthur M. Petacque and Hugh F. Hough *(Chicago Sun-Times)*
1975 *Xenia* (Ohio) *Daily Gazette*
1976 Gene Miller *(Miami Herald)*
1977 Margo Huston *(Milwaukee Journal)*
1978 Richard Whitt *(Louisville Courier-Journal)*
1979 Staff of *San Diego* (Calif.) *Evening Tribune*
1980 Staff of *Philadelphia Inquirer*
1981 *Longview* (Wash.) *Daily News*
1982 *Kansas City* (Mo.) *Star* and *Kansas City* (Mo.) *Times*
1983 *Fort Wayne* (Ind.) *News-Sentinel*
1984 *Newsday*

GENERAL NEWS REPORTING

1985 Thomas Turcol (*Virginian-Pilot and Ledger-Star*)
1986 Edna Buchanan *(Miami Herald)*
1987 *Akron Beacon Journal*, staff
1988 *Alabama Journal* (Montgomery), staff, *Lawrence* (Mass.) *Eagle-Tribune*, staff
1989 *Louisville Courier-Journal* staff
1990 *San Jose* (Calif.) *Mercury News*

SPOT NEWS REPORTING

1991 *Miami Herald* staff
1992 *New York Newsday* staff
1993 *Los Angeles Times* staff

SPECIAL LOCAL REPORTING

1964 James V. Magee, Albert V. Gaudiosi, and Frederick A. Meyer (*Philadelphia Bulletin*)
1965 Gene Goltz (*Houston Post*)
1966 John A. Frasca *(Tampa Tribune)*
1967 Gene Miller *(Miami Herald)*
1968 J. Anthony Lukas *(New York Times)*
1969 Albert L. Delugach and Denny Walsh *(St. Louis Globe-Democrat)*
1970 Harold Eugene Martin *(Montgomery Advertiser)*
1971 William Hugh Jones *(Chicago Tribune)*
1972 Timothy Leland, Gerard N. O'Neill, Stephen A. Kurkjian, and Ann DeSantis *(Boston Globe)*
1973 Sun Newspapers of Omaha, Neb.
1974 William Sherman *(New York Daily News)*
1975 *Indianapolis Star*
1976 *Chicago Tribune*
1977 Acel Moore and Wendell Rawls, Jr. *(Philadelphia Inquirer)*
1978 Anthony R. Dolan *(Stamford* [Conn.] *Advocate)*
1979 Gilbert M. Gaul and Elliot G. Jaspin *(Pottsville* [Pa.] *Republican)*
1980 Nils J. Bruzelius, Alexander B. Hawes, Jr., Stephen A. Kurkjian, Robert M. Porterfield, and Joan Vennochi *(Boston Globe)*
1981 Clark Hallas and Robert B. Lowe (*Arizona Daily Star*, Tucson)
1982 Paul Henderson *(Seattle Times)*
1983 Loretta Tofani *(Washington Post)*
1984 *Boston Globe*

INVESTIGATIVE REPORTING

1985 Lucy Morgan and Jack Reed (*St. Petersburg* [Fla.] *Times*) and William K. Marimow (*Philadelphia Inquirer*)
1986 Jeffrey A. Marx and Michael M. York *(Lexington* [Ky.] *Herald Leader)*
1987 Daniel R. Biddle, H.G. Bissinger, and Fredric N. Tulsky *(Philadelphia Inquirer)*
1988 Dean Baquet, William C. Gaines, and Ann Marie Lipinski *(Chicago Tribune)*
1989 Bill Dedman *(Atlanta Journal and Constitution)*
1990 Lou Kilzer and Chris Ison *(Minneapolis-St. Paul Star Tribune)*
1991 Joseph T. Hallinan and Susan M. Headden *(Indianapolis Star)*
1992 Lorraine Adams and Dan Malone *(Dallas Morning News)*
1993 Jeff Brazil and Steve Berry *(Orlando* [Fla.] *Sentinel)*

FEATURE WRITING

1979 Jon D. Franklin *(Baltimore Evening Sun)*
1980 Madeleine Blais *(Miami Herald)*
1981 Teresa Carpenter (*Village Voice*, New York)
1982 Saul Pett (Associated Press)
1983 Nan Robertson *(New York Times)*
1984 Peter M. Rinearson *(Seattle Times)*
1985 Alice Steinbach (*Baltimore Sun*)
1986 John Camp *(St. Paul Pioneer Press and Dispatch)*
1987 Steve Twomey *(Philadelphia Inquirer)*
1988 Jacqui Banasz ynski *(St. Paul Pioneer Press Dispatch)*
1989 David Zucchino *(Philadelphia Inquirer)*
1990 Dave Curtin *(Colorado Springs Gazette Telegraph)*
1991 Sheryl James, *(St. Petersburg* [Fla.] *Times)*
1992 Howell Raines *(New York Times)*
1993 George Lardner, Jr. *(Washington Post)*

COMMENTARY

1970 Marquis W. Childs *(St. Louis Post-Dispatch)*
1971 William A. Caldwell (*Record* [Hackensack, N.J.])
1972 Mike Royko *(Chicago Daily News)*
1973 David S. Broder *(Washington Post)*
1974 Edwin A. Roberts, Jr. *(National Observer)*
1975 Mary McGrory *(Washington Star)*
1976 Walter W. (Red) Smith *(New York Times)*
1977 George F. Will (*Washington Post* Writers Group)
1978 William Safire *(New York Times)*
1979 Russell Baker *(New York Times)*
1980 Ellen H. Goodman *(Boston Globe)*
1981 Dave Anderson *(New York Times)*
1982 Art Buchwald (*Los Angeles Times* Syndicate)
1983 Claude Sitton *(Raleigh* [N.C.] *News & Observer)*
1984 Vermont Royster *(Wall Street Journal)*
1985 Murray Kempton (*Newsday*)
1986 Jimmy Breslin *(New York Daily News)*
1987 Charles Krauthammer (*Washington Post* Writers Group)
1988 Dave Barry *(Miami Herald)*
1989 Clarence Page *(Chicago Tribune)*
1990 Jim Murray *(Los Angeles Times)*
1991 Jim Hoagland *(Washington Post)*
1992 Anna Quindlen *(New York Times)*
1993 Liz Balmaseda *(Mami Herald)*

CRITICISM

1970 Ada Louise Huxtable *(New York Times)*

1971 Harold C. Schonberg *(New York Times)*
1972 Frank Peters, Jr. *(St. Louis Post-Dispatch)*
1973 Ronald Powers *(Chicago Sun-Times)*
1974 Emily Genauer (Newsday Syndicate)
1975 Roger Ebert *(Chicago Sun-Times)*
1976 Alan M. Kriegsman *(Washington Post)*
1977 William McPherson *(Washington Post)*
1978 Walter Kerr *(New York Times)*
1979 Paul Gapp *(Chicago Tribune)*
1980 William A. Henry, 3rd *(Boston Globe)*
1981 Jonathan Yardley *(Washington Star)*
1982 Martin Bernheimer *(Los Angeles Times)*
1983 Manuela Hoelterhoff *(Wall Street Journal)*
1984 Paul Goldberger *(New York Times)*
1985 Howard Rosenberg (*Los Angeles Times*)
1986 Donal Henahan *(New York Times)*
1987 Richard Eder *(Los Angeles Times)*
1988 Tom Shales *(Washington Post)*
1989 Michael Skube (*News and Observer,* Raleigh, N.C.)
1990 Allan Temko *(San Francisco Chronicle)*
1991 David Shaw *(Los Angeles Times)*
1993 Michael Dirda *(Washington Post)*

EXPLANATORY JOURNALISM

1985 Jon Franklin (*Baltimore Evening Sun*)
1986 *New York Times*
1987 Jeff Lyon and Peter Gorner *(Chicago Tribune)*
1988 Daniel Hertzberg and James B. Stewart *(Wall Street Journal)*
1989 David Hanners, William Snyder, and Karen Blessen *(Dallas Morning News)*
1990 David A. Vise and Coll *(Washington Post)*
1991 Susan C. Faludi *(Wall Street Journal)*
1992 Robert S. Capers and Eric Lipton *(Hartford Courant)*
1993 Mike Toner *(Atlanta Journal–Constitution)*

SPECIALIZED REPORTING

1985 Randall Savage and Jackie Crosby (*Macon* [Ga.] *Telegraph and News*)
1986 Andrew Schneider and Mary Pat Flaherty *(Pittsburgh Press)*
1987 Alex S. Jones *(New York Times)*
1988 Walt Bogdanich *(Wall Street Journal)*
1989 Edward Humes *(Orange County Register)*
1990 Tamar Stieber *(Albuquerque* (N.M.) *Journal)*

BEAT REPORTING

1991 Natalie Angier *(New York Times)*
1992 Deborah Blum *(Sacramento Bee)*
1993 Paul Ingrassia and Joseph B. White, *(Wall Street Journal)*

SPECIAL CITATIONS

1938 *Edmonton* (Alberta) *Journal,* special bronze plaque for editorial leadership in defense of freedom of press in Province of Alberta.
1941 *New York Times* for the public educational value of its foreign news report.
1944 Byron Price, Director of the Office of Censorship, for the creation and administration of the newspaper and radio codes. Mrs. William Allen White, for her husband's interest and services during the past seven years as a member of the Advisory Board of the Graduate School of Journalism, Columbia University. Richard Rodgers and Oscar Hammerstein II for their musical *Oklahoma!*
1945 The cartographers of the American press for their war maps.
1947 (Pulitzer centennial year.) Columbia University and the Graduate School of Journalism for their efforts to maintain and advance the high standards governing the Pulitzer Prize awards. The *St. Louis Post-Dispatch* for its unswerving adherence to the public and professi onal ideals of its founder and its leadership in American journalism.
1948 Dr. Frank D. Fackenthal for his interest and service.
1951 Cyrus L. Sulzberger *(New York Times)* for his exclusive interview with Archbishop Stepinac in a Yugoslav prison.
1952 *Kansas City Star* for coverage of 1951 floods; Max Kase *(New York Journal-American)* for exposures of bribery in college basketball.
1953 *New York Times* for its 17-year publication of "News of the Week in Review"; and Lester Markel, its founder.
1957 Kenneth Roberts for his historical novels.
1958 Walter Lippmann *(New York Herald Tribune)* for his "wisdom, perception and high sense of responsibility" in his commentary on national and international affairs.
1960 Garrett Mattingly, for *The Armada.*
1961 *American Heritage Picture History of the Civil War,* as distinguished example of American book publishing.
1964 Gannett Newspapers, Rochester, N.Y.
1973 James Thomas Flexner for his biography *George Washington.*
1974 Roger Sessions for his "life's work in music."
1976 John Hohenberg for "services for 22 years as administrator of the Pulitzer Prizes"; Scott Joplin for his contributions to American music.
1977 Alex Haley for his novel, *Roots.*
1978 E.B. White of *New Yorker* magazine and Richard L. Strout of *Christian Science Monitor.*
1982 Milton Babbitt, "for his life's work as a distinguished and seminal American composer."
1984 Theodor Seuss Geisel (Dr. Seuss) for "books full of playful rhymes, nonsense words and strange illustrations."
1985 William H. Schuman for "more than a half century of contribution to American music as a composer and educational leader."
1987 Joseph Pulitzer Jr., "for extraordinary services to American journalism and letters during his 31 years as chairman of the Pulitzer Prize Board and for his accomplishments as an editor and publisher."

Pulitzer Prizes in Letters

FICTION[1]

1918 *His Family.* Ernest Poole
1919 *The Magnificent Ambersons.* Booth Tarkington
1921 *The Age of Innocence.* Edith Wharton
1922 *Alice Adams.* Booth Tarkington
1923 *One of Ours.* Willa Cather
1924 *The Able McLaughlins.* Margaret Wilson
1925 *So Big.* Edna Ferber
1926 *Arrowsmith.* Sinclair Lewis
1927 *Early Autumn.* Louis Bromfield
1928 *The Bridge of San Luis Rey.* Thornton Wilder
1929 *Scarlet Sister Mary.* Julia Peterkin
1930 *Laughing Boy.* Oliver La Farge
1931 *Years of Grace.* Margaret Ayer Barnes
1932 *The Good Earth.* Pearl S. Buck
1933 *The Store.* T. S. Stribling
1934 *Lamb in His Bosom.* Caroline Miller
1935 *Now in November.* Josephine Winslow Johnson
1936 *Honey in the Horn.* Harold L. Davis
1937 *Gone With the Wind.* Margaret Mitchell
1938 *The Late George Apley.* John Phillips Marquand
1939 *The Yearling.* Marjorie Kinnan Rawlings
1940 *The Grapes of Wrath.* John Steinbeck

1. Before 1948, award was for novels only.

1942 *In This Our Life.* Ellen Glasgow
1943 *Dragon's Teeth.* Upton Sinclair
1944 *Journey in the Dark.* Martin Flavin
1945 *A Bell for Adano.* John Hersey
1947 *All the King's Men.* Robert Penn Warren
1948 *Tales of the South Pacific.* James A. Michener
1949 *Guard of Honor.* James Gould Cozzens
1950 *The Way West.* A. B. Guthrie, Jr.
1951 *The Town.* Conrad Richter
1952 *The Caine Mutiny.* Herman Wouk
1953 *The Old Man and the Sea.* Ernest Hemingway
1955 *A Fable.* William Faulkner
1956 *Andersonville.* MacKinlay Kantor
1958 *A Death in the Family.* James Agee
1959 *The Travels of Jaimie McPheeters.* Robert Lewis Taylor
1960 *Advise and Consent.* Allen Drury
1961 *To Kill a Mockingbird.* Harper Lee
1962 *The Edge of Sadness.* Edwin O'Connor
1963 *The Reivers.* William Faulkner
1965 *The Keepers of the House.* Shirley Ann Grau
1966 *Collected Stories of Katherine Anne Porter.* Katherine Anne Porter
1967 *The Fixer.* Bernard Malamud
1968 *The Confessions of Nat Turner.* William Styron
1969 *House Made of Dawn.* N. Scott Momaday
1970 *Collected Stories.* Jean Stafford
1972 *Angle of Repose.* Wallace Stegner
1973 *The Optimist's Daughter.* Eudora Welty
1975 *The Killer Angels.* Michael Shaara
1976 *Humboldt's Gift.* Saul Bellow
1978 *Elbow Room.* James Alan McPherson
1979 *The Stories of John Cheever.* John Cheever
1980 *The Executioner's Song.* Norman Mailer
1981 *A Confederacy of Dunces.* John Kennedy Toole
1982 *Rabbit Is Rich.* John Updike
1983 *The Color Purple.* Alice Walker
1984 *Ironweed.* William Kennedy
1985 *Foreign Affairs,* Alison Lurie
1986 *Lonesome Dove,* Larry McMurtry
1987 *A Summons to Memphis,* Peter Taylor
1988 *Beloved,* Toni Morrison
1989 *Breathing Lessons,* Anne Tyler
1990 *The Mambo Kings Play Songs of Love,* Oscar Hijeulos
1991 *Rabbit at Rest,* John Updike
1992 *A Thousand Acres,* Jane Smiley
1993 *A Good Scent From a Strange Mountain,* Robert Olen Butler

DRAMA

1918 *Why Marry?* Jesse Lynch Williams
1920 *Beyond the Horizon.* Eugene O'Neill
1921 *Miss Lulu Bett.* Zona Gale
1922 *Anna Christie.* Eugene O'Neill
1923 *Icebound.* Owen Davis
1924 *Hell-Bent Fer Heaven.* Hatcher Hughes
1925 *They Knew What They Wanted.* Sidney Howard
1926 *Craig's Wife.* George Kelly
1927 *In Abraham's Bosom.* Paul Green
1928 *Strange Interlude.* Eugene O'Neill
1929 *Street Scene.* Elmer L. Rice
1930 *The Green Pastures.* Marc Connelly
1931 *Alison's House.* Susan Glaspell
1932 *Of Thee I Sing.* George S. Kaufman, Morrie Ryskind, and Ira Gershwin
1933 *Both Your Houses.* Maxwell Anderson
1934 *Men in White.* Sidney Kingsley
1935 *The Old Maid.* Zöe Akins
1936 *Idiot's Delight.* Robert E. Sherwood
1937 *You Can't Take It With You.* Moss Hart and George S. Kaufman
1938 *Our Town.* Thornton Wilder
1939 *Abe Lincoln in Illinois.* Robert E. Sherwood
1940 *The Time of Your Life.* William Saroyan
1941 *There Shall Be No Night.* Robert E. Sherwood
1943 *The Skin of Our Teeth.* Thornton Wilder
1945 *Harvey.* Mary Chase
1946 *State of the Union.* Russel Crouse and Howard Lindsay
1948 *A Streetcar Named Desire.* Tennessee Williams
1949 *Death of a Salesman.* Arthur Miller
1950 *South Pacific.* Richard Rodgers, Oscar Hammerstein II, and Joshua Logan
1952 *The Shrike.* Joseph Kramm
1953 *Picnic.* William Inge
1954 *The Teahouse of the August Moon.* John Patrick
1955 *Cat on a Hot Tin Roof.* Tennessee Williams
1956 *The Diary of Anne Frank.* Frances Goodrich and Albert Hackett
1957 *Long Day's Journey Into Night.* Eugene O'Neill
1958 *Look Homeward, Angel.* Ketti Frings
1959 *J.B.* Archibald MacLeish
1960 *Fiorello!* George Abbott, Jerome Weidman, Jerry Bock, and Sheldon Harnick
1961 *All the Way Home.* Tad Mosel
1962 *How to Succeed in Business Without Really Trying.* Frank Loesser and Abe Burrows
1965 *The Subject Was Roses.* Frank D. Gilroy
1967 *A Delicate Balance.* Edward Albee
1969 *The Great White Hope.* Howard Sackler
1970 *No Place to Be Somebody.* Charles Gordone
1971 *The Effect of Gamma Rays on Man-in-the-Moon Marigolds.* Paul Zindel
1973 *That Championship Season.* Jason Miller
1975 *Seascape.* Edward Albee
1976 *A Chorus Line.* Conceived by Michael Bennett
1977 *The Shadow Box.* Michael Cristofer
1978 *The Gin Game.* Donald L. Coburn
1979 *Buried Child.* Sam Shepard
1980 *Talley's Folly.* Lanford Wilson
1981 *Crimes of the Heart.* Beth Henley
1982 *A Soldier's Play.* Charles Fuller
1983 *'Night, Mother.* Marsha Norman
1984 *Glengarry Glen Ross.* David Mamet
1985 *Sunday in the Park with George.* Stephen Sondheim and James Lapine
1987 *Fences.* August Wilson
1988 *Driving Miss Daisy.* Alfred Uhry
1989 *The Heidi Chronicles,* Wendy Wasserstein
1990 *The Piano Lesson,* August Wilson
1991 *Lost in Yonkers,* Neil Simon
1992 *The Kentucky Cycle,* Robert Schenkkan
1993 *Angels in America: Millennium Approaches,* Tony Kushner

HISTORY OF UNITED STATES

1917 *With Americans of Past and Present Days.* J. J. Jusserand, Ambassador of France to United States
1918 *A History of the Civil War, 1861–1865.* James Ford Rhodes
1920 *The War With Mexico.* Justin H. Smith
1921 *The Victory at Sea.* William Sowden Sims in collaboration with Burton J. Hendrick
1922 *The Founding of New England.* James Truslow Adams
1923 *The Supreme Court in United States History.* Charles Warren
1924 *The American Revolution—A Constitutional Interpretation.* Charles Howard McIlwain
1925 *A History of the American Frontier.* Frederic L. Paxson
1926 *The History of the United States.* Edward Channing
1927 *Pinckney's Treaty.* Samuel Flagg Bemis
1928 *Main Currents in American Thought.* Vernon Louis Parrington

1929 *The Organization and Administration of the Union Army, 1861–1865.* Fred Albert Shannon
1930 *The War of Independence.* Claude H. Van Tyne
1931 *The Coming of the War: 1914.* Bernadotte E. Schmitt
1932 *My Experiences in the World War.* John J. Pershing
1933 *The Significance of Sections in American History.* Frederick J. Turner
1934 *The People's Choice.* Herbert Agar
1935 *The Colonial Period of American History.* Charles McLean Andrews
1936 *The Constitutional History of the United States.* Andrew C. McLaughlin
1937 *The Flowering of New England.* Van Wyck Brooks
1938 *The Road to Reunion, 1865–1900.* Paul Herman Buck
1939 *A History of American Magazines.* Frank Luther Mott
1940 *Abraham Lincoln: The War Years.* Carl Sandburg
1941 *The Atlantic Migration, 1607–1860.* Marcus Lee Hansen
1942 *Reveille in Washington.* Margaret Leech
1943 *Paul Revere and the World He Lived In.* Esther Forbes
1944 *The Growth of American Thought.* Merle Curti
1945 *Unfinished Business.* Stephen Bonsal
1946 *The Age of Jackson.* Arthur M. Schlesinger, Jr.
1947 *Scientists Against Time.* James Phinney Baxter, 3rd
1948 *Across the Wide Missouri.* Bernard DeVoto
1949 *The Disruption of American Democracy.* Roy Franklin Nichols
1950 *Art and Life in America.* Oliver W. Larkin
1951 *The Old Northwest, Pioneer Period 1815–1840.* R. Carlyle Buley
1952 *The Uprooted.* Oscar Handlin
1953 *The Era of Good Feelings.* George Dangerfield
1954 *A Stillness at Appomattox.* Bruce Catton
1955 *Great River: The Rio Grande in North American History.* Paul Horgan
1956 *The Age of Reform.* Richard Hofstadter
1957 *Russia Leaves the War: Soviet-American Relations, 1917–1920.* George F. Kennan
1958 *Banks and Politics in America: From the Revolution to the Civil War.* Bray Hammond
1959 *The Republican Era: 1869–1901.* Leonard D. White, assisted by Jean Schneider
1960 *In the Days of McKinley.* Margaret Leech
1961 *Between War and Peace: The Potsdam Conference.* Herbert Feis
1962 *The Triumphant Empire, Thunder-Clouds Gather in the West.* Lawrence H. Gipson
1963 *Washington, Village and Capital, 1800–1878.* Constance McLaughlin Green
1964 *Puritan Village: The Formation of a New England Town.* Sumner Chilton Powell
1965 *The Greenback Era.* Irwin Unger
1966 *Life of the Mind in America.* Perry Miller
1967 *Exploration and Empire: The Explorer and Scientist in the Winning of the American West.* William H. Goetzmann
1968 *The Ideological Origins of the American Revolution.* Bernard Bailyn
1969 *Origins of the Fifth Amendment.* Leonard W. Levy
1970 *Present at the Creation: My Years in the State Department.* Dean Acheson
1971 *Roosevelt: The Soldier of Freedom.* James McGregor Burns
1972 *Neither Black Nor White. Slavery and Race Relations in Brazil and the United States.* Carl N. Degler
1973 *People of Paradox: An Inquiry Concerning the Origin of American Civilization.* Michael Kammen
1974 *The Americans: The Democratic Experience, Vol. 3.* Daniel J. Boorstin
1975 *Jefferson and His Time.* Dumas Malone
1976 *Lamy of Santa Fe.* Paul Horgan
1977 *The Impending Crisis: 1841–1861.* David M. Potter (posth)
1978 *The Invisible Hand: The Managerial Revolution in American Business.* Alfred D. Chandler, Jr.
1979 *The Dred Scott Case: Its Significance in Law and Politics.* Don E. Fehrenbacher
1980 *Been in the Storm So Long.* Leon F. Litwack
1981 *American Education: The National Experience; 1783–1876.* Lawrence A. Cremin
1982 *Mary Chestnut's Civil War.* C. Vann Woodward, editor
1983 *The Transformation of Virginia, 1740–1790.* Rhys L. Isaac
1985 *The Prophets of Regulation.* Thomas K. McCraw
1986 *. . . the Heavens and the Earth: A Political History of the Space Age.* Walter A. McDougall
1987 *Voyagers to the West: A Passage in the Peopling of America on the Eve of the Revolution.* Bernard Bailyn
1988 *The Launching of Modern American Science 1846–1876.* Robert V. Bruce
1989 *Parting the Waters,* Taylor Branch; *Battle Cry of Freedom,* James M. McPherson
1990 *In Our Image: America's Empire in the Philippines,* Stanley Karnow
1991 *A Midwife's Tale: The Life of Martha Ballard, Based on Her Diary 1785–1812,* Laurel Thatcher Ulrich
1992 *The Fate of Liberty: Abraham Lincoln and Civil Liberties,* Mark E. Neely, Jr.
1993 *The Radicalism of the American Revolution,* Gordon S. Wood

BIOGRAPHY OR AUTOBIOGRAPHY

1917 *Julia Ward Howe.* Laura E. Richards and Maude Howe Elliott, assisted by Florence Howe Hall
1918 *Benjamin Franklin, Self-Revealed.* William Cabell Bruce
1919 *The Education of Henry Adams.* Henry Adams
1920 *The Life of John Marshall.* Albert J. Beveridge
1921 *The Americanization of Edward Bok.* Edward Bok
1922 *A Daughter of the Middle Border.* Hamlin Garland
1923 *The Life and Letters of Walter H. Page,* Burton J. Hendrick
1924 *From Immigrant to Inventor.* Michael Idvorsky Pupin
1925 *Barrett Wendell and His Letters.* M. A. DeWolfe Howe
1926 *The Life of Sir William Osler.* Harvey Cushing
1927 *Whitman.* Emory Holloway
1928 *The American Orchestra and Theodore Thomas.* Charles Edward Russell
1929 *The Training of an American. The Earlier Life and Letters of Walter H. Page.* Burton J. Hendrick
1930 *The Raven.* Marquis James
1931 *Charles W. Eliot.* Henry James
1932 *Theodore Roosevelt.* Henry F. Pringle
1933 *Grover Cleveland.* Allan Nevins
1934 *John Hay.* Tyler Dennett
1935 *R. E. Lee.* Douglas S. Freeman
1936 *The Thought and Character of William James.* Ralph Barton Perry
1937 *Hamilton Fish.* Allan Nevins
1938 *Pedlar's Progress.* Odell Shepard; *Andrew Jackson.* Marquis James
1939 *Benjamin Franklin.* Carl Van Doren
1940 *Woodrow Wilson. Life and Letters,* Vols. VII and VIII. Ray Stannard Baker
1941 *Jonathan Edwards.* Ola E. Winslow
1942 *Crusader in Crinoline.* Forrest Wilson
1943 *Admiral of the Ocean Sea.* Samuel Eliot Morison
1944 *The American Leonardo: The Life of Samuel F. B. Morse.* Carleton Mabee
1945 *George Bancroft: Brahmin Rebel.* Russel Blaine Nye
1946 *Son of the Wilderness.* Linnie Marsh Wolfe
1947 *The Autobiography of William Allen White*
1948 *Forgotten First Citizen: John Bigelow.* Margaret Clapp

1949 *Roosevelt and Hopkins.* Robert E. Sherwood
1950 *John Quincy Adams and the Foundations of American Foreign Policy.* Samuel Flagg Bemis
1951 *John C. Calhoun: American Portrait.* Margaret Louise Coit
1952 *Charles Evans Hughes.* Merlo J. Pusey
1953 *Edmund Pendleton, 1721–1803.* David J. Mays
1954 *The Spirit of St. Louis.* Charles A. Lindbergh
1955 *The Taft Story.* William S. White
1956 *Benjamin Henry Latrobe.* Talbot F. Hamlin
1957 *Profiles in Courage.* John F. Kennedy
1958 *George Washington.* Douglas Southall Freeman (Vols. 1–6) and John Alexander Carroll and Mary Wells Ashworth (Vol. 7)
1959 *Woodrow Wilson, American Prophet.* Arthur Walworth
1960 *John Paul Jones.* Samuel Eliot Morison
1961 *Charles Sumner and the Coming of the Civil War.* David Donald
1963 *Henry James: Vol. II, The Conquest of London, 1870–1881; Vol. III, The Middle Years, 1881–1895.* Leon Edel
1964 *John Keats.* Walter Jackson Bate
1965 *Henry Adams* (3 Vols.). Ernest Samuels
1966 *A Thousand Days.* Arthur M. Schlesinger, Jr.
1967 *Mr. Clemens and Mark Twain.* Justin Kaplan
1968 *Memoirs, 1925–1950.* George F. Kennan
1969 *The Man From New York.* B. L. Reid
1970 *Huey Long.* T. Harry Williams
1971 *Robert Frost: The Years of Triumph, 1915–1938.* Lawrence Thompson
1972 *Eleanor and Franklin: The Story of Their Relationship Based on Eleanor Roosevelt's Private Papers.* Joseph P. Lash
1973 *Luce and His Empire.* W. A. Swanberg
1974 *O'Neill, Son and Artist.* Louis Sheaffer
1975 *The Power Broker: Robert Moses and the Fall of New York.* Robert A. Caro
1976 *Edith Wharton: A Biography.* Richard W. B. Lewis
1977 *A Prince of Our Disorder.* John E. Mack
1978 *Samuel Johnson.* Walter Jackson Bate
1979 *Days of Sorrow and Pain: Leo Baeck and the Berlin Jews.* Leonard Baker
1980 *The Rise of Theodore Roosevelt.* Edmund Morris
1981 *Peter the Great.* Robert K. Massie
1982 *Grant: A Biography.* William S. McFeely
1983 *Growing Up.* Russell Baker
1984 *Booker T. Washington.* Louis R. Harlan
1985 *The Life and Times of Cotton Mather,* Kenneth Silverman
1986 *Louise Bogan: A Portrait,* Elizabeth Frank
1987 *Bearing the Cross: Martin Luther King Jr. and the Southern Christian Leadership Conference,* David J. Garrow
1988 *Look Homeward: A Life of Thomas Wolfe.* David Herbert Donald
1989 *Oscar Wilde.* Richard Ellmann
1990 *Machiavelli in Hell,* Sebastian de Grazia
1991 *Jackson Pollock: An American Saga,* Steven Naifeh and Gregory White Smith
1992 *Fortunate Son: The Healing of a Vietnam Vet,* Lewis B. Puller, Jr.
1993 *Truman,* David McCullough

POETRY[1]

1918 *Love Songs.* Sara Teasdale
1919 *Old Road to Paradise.* Margaret Widdemer; *Corn Huskers.* Carl Sandburg
1922 *Collected Poems.* Edwin Arlington Robinson
1923 *The Ballad of the Harp-Weaver; A Few Figs from Thistles;* eight sonnets in *American Poetry, 1922, A Miscellany.* Edna St. Vincent Millay
1924 *New Hampshire: A Poem With Notes and Grace Notes.* Robert Frost
1925 *The Man Who Died Twice.* Edwin Arlington Robinson
1926 *What's O'Clock.* Amy Lowell
1927 *Fiddler's Farewell.* Leonora Speyer
1928 *Tristram.* Edwin Arlington Robinson
1929 *John Brown's Body.* Stephen Vincent Benét
1930 *Selected Poems.* Conrad Aiken
1931 *Collected Poems.* Robert Frost
1932 *The Flowering Stone.* George Dillon
1933 *Conquistador.* Archibald MacLeish
1934 *Collected Verse.* Robert Hillyer
1935 *Bright Ambush.* Audrey Wurdemann
1936 *Strange Holiness.* Robert P. T. Coffin
1937 *A Further Range.* Robert Frost
1938 *Cold Morning Sky.* Marya Zaturenska
1939 *Selected Poems.* John Gould Fletcher
1940 *Collected Poems.* Mark Van Doren
1941 *Sunderland Capture.* Leonard Bacon
1942 *The Dust Which Is God.* William Rose Benét
1943 *A Witness Tree.* Robert Frost
1944 *Western Star.* Stephen Vincent Benét
1945 *V-Letter and Other Poems.* Karl Shapiro
1947 *Lord Weary's Castle.* Robert Lowell
1948 *The Age of Anxiety.* W. H. Auden
1949 *Terror and Decorum.* Peter Viereck
1950 *Annie Allen.* Gwendolyn Brooks
1951 *Complete Poems.* Carl Sandburg
1952 *Collected Poems.* Marianne Moore
1953 *Collected Poems, 1917–1952.* Archibald MacLeish
1954 *The Waking.* Theodore Roethke
1955 *Collected Poems.* Wallace Stevens
1956 *Poems—North & South.* Elizabeth Bishop
1957 *Things of This World.* Richard Wilbur
1958 *Promises: Poems, 1954–1956.* Robert Penn Warren
1959 *Selected Poems, 1928–1958.* Stanley Kunitz
1960 *Heart's Needle.* William Snodgrass
1961 *Times Three: Selected Verse From Three Decades.* Phyllis McGinley
1962 *Poems.* Alan Dugan
1963 *Pictures From Breughel.* William Carlos Williams
1964 *At the End of the Open Road.* Louis Simpson
1965 *77 Dream Songs.* John Berryman
1966 *Selected Poems.* Richard Eberhart
1967 *Live or Die.* Anne Sexton
1968 *The Hard Hours.* Anthony Hecht
1969 *Of Being Numerous.* George Oppen
1970 *Untitled Subjects.* Richard Howard
1971 *The Carrier of Ladders.* William S. Merwin
1972 *Collected Poems.* James Wright
1973 *Up Country.* Maxine Winokur Kumin
1974 *The Dolphin.* Robert Lowell
1975 *Turtle Island.* Gary Snyder
1976 *Self-Portrait in a Convex Mirror.* John Ashbery
1977 *Divine Comedies.* James Merrill
1978 *Collected Poems.* Howard Nemerov
1979 *Now and Then: Poems, 1976–1978.* Robert Penn Warren.
1980 *Selected Poems.* Donald Rodney Justice
1981 *The Morning of the Poem.* James Schuyler
1982 *The Collected Poems.* Sylvia Plath
1983 *Selected Poems.* Galway Kinnell
1984 *American Primitive.* Mary Oliver
1985 *Yin,* Carolyn Kizer
1986 *The Flying Change,* Henry Taylor
1987 *Thomas and Beulah,* Rita Dove
1988 *Partial Accounts: New and Selected Poems.* William Meredith
1989 *New and Collected Poems.* Richard Wilbur
1990 *The World Doesn't End,* Charles Simic
1991 *Near Changes,* Mona Van Duyn

1. This prize was established in 1922. The 1918 and 1919 awards were made from gifts provided by the Poetry Society.

1992 *Selected Poems,* James Tate
1993 *The Wild Iris,* Louise Gluck

GENERAL NONFICTION

1962 *The Making of the President, 1960.* Theodore H. White
1963 *The Guns of August.* Barbara W. Tuchman
1964 *Anti-Intellectualism in American Life.* Richard Hofstadter
1965 *O Strange New World.* Howard Mumford Jones
1966 *Wandering Through Winter.* Edwin Way Teale
1967 *The Problem of Slavery in Western Culture.* David Brion Davis
1968 *Rousseau and Revolution.* Will and Ariel Durant
1969 *So Human an Animal.* Rene Jules Dubos; *The Armies of the Night.* Norman Mailer
1970 *Gandhi's Truth.* Erik H. Erikson
1971 *The Rising Sun.* John Toland
1972 *Stilwell and the American Experience in China, 1911–1945.* Barbara W. Tuchman
1973 *Fire in the Lake: The Vietnamese and the Americans in Vietnam.* Frances FitzGerald; and *Children of Crisis* (Vols. 1 and 2). Robert M. Coles
1974 *The Denial of Death.* Ernest Becker
1975 *Pilgrim at Tinker Creek.* Annie Dillard
1976 *Why Survive? Being Old in America.* Robert N. Butler
1977 *Beautiful Swimmers: Watermen, Crabs and the Chesapeake Bay.* William W. Warner
1978 *The Dragons of Eden.* Carl Sagan
1979 *On Human Nature.* Edward O. Wilson
1980 *Gödel, Escher, Bach: An Eternal Golden Braid.* Douglas R. Hofstadter
1981 *Fin-de-Siecle Vienna: Politics and Culture.* Carl E. Schorske
1982 *The Soul of a New Machine.* Tracy Kidder
1983 *Is There No Place on Earth for Me?* Susan Sheehan
1984 *Social Transformation of American Medicine.* Paul Starr
1985 *The Good War: An Oral History of World War II,* Studs Terkel
1986 *Move Your Shadow: South Africa, Black and White,* Joseph Lelyveld; *Common Ground: A Turbulent Decade in the Lives of Three American Families,* J. Anthony Lukas
1987 *Arab and Jew: Wounded Spirits in a Promised Land,* David K. Shipler
1988 *The Making of the Atomic Bomb.* Richard Rhodes
1989 *A Bright Shining Lie.* Neil Sheehan
1990 *And Their Children After Them,* Dale Maharidge and Michael Williamson
1991 *The Ants,* Bert Holldobler and Edward O. Wilson
1992 *The Prize: The Epic Quest for Oil, Money and Power,* Daniel Yergin
1993 *Lincoln at Gettysburg: The Words That Remade America,* Garry Wills

PULITZER PRIZES IN MUSIC

1943 *Secular Cantata No. 2, A Free Song.* William Schuman
1944 *Symphony No. 4* (Op. 34). Howard Hanson
1945 *Appalachian Spring.* Aaron Copland
1946 *The Canticle of the Sun.* Leo Sowerby
1947 *Symphony No. 3.* Charles Ives
1948 *Symphony No. 3.* Walter Piston
1949 *Louisiana Story* music. Virgil Thomson
1950 *The Consul.* Gian Carlo Menotti
1951 Music for opera *Giants in the Earth.* Douglas Stuart Moore
1952 *Symphony Concertante.* Gail Kubik
1954 *Concerto for Two Pianos and Orchestra.* Quincy Porter
1955 *The Saint of Bleecker Street.* Gian Carlo Menotti
1956 *Symphony No. 3.* Ernst Toch
1957 *Meditations on Ecclesiastes.* Norman Dello Joio
1958 *Vanessa.* Samuel Barber
1959 *Concerto for Piano and Orchestra.* John La Montaine
1960 *Second String Quartet.* Elliott Carter
1961 *Symphony No. 7.* Walter Piston
1962 *The Crucible.* Robert Ward
1963 *Piano Concerto No. 1.* Samuel Barber
1966 *Variations for Orchestra.* Leslie Bassett
1967 *Quartet No. 3.* Leon Kirchner
1968 *Echoes of Time and the River.* George Crumb
1969 *String Quartet No. 3.* Karel Husa
1970 *Time's Encomium.* Charles Wuorinen
1971 *Synchronisms No. 6 for Piano and Electronic Sound.* Mario Davidowsky
1972 *Windows.* Jacob Druckman
1973 *String Quartet No. 3.* Elliott Carter
1974 *Notturno.* Donald Martino
1975 *From the Diary of Virginia Woolf.* Dominick Argento
1976 *Air Music.* Ned Rorem
1977 *Visions of Terror and Wonder.* Richard Wernick
1978 *Déjà Vu for Percussion Quartet and Orchestra.* Michael Colgrass
1979 *Aftertones of Infinity.* Joseph Schwantner
1980 *In Memory of a Summer Day.* David Del Tredici
1981 Not awarded
1982 *Concerto for Orchestra.* Roger Sessions
1983 *Three Movements for Orchestra.* Ellen T. Zwilich
1984 *Canti del Sole.* Bernard Rands
1985 *Symphony RiverRun,* Stephen Albert
1986 *Wind Quintet IV,* George Perle
1987 *The Flight Into Egypt,* John Harbison
1988 *12 New Etudes for Piano.* William Bolcom
1989 *Whispers Out of Time,* Roger Reynolds
1990 *Duplicates: A Concerto for Two Pianos and Orchestra,* Mel Powell
1991 *Symphony,* Shulamit Ran
1992 *The Face of the Night, The Heart of the Dark,* Wayne Peterson
1993 *Trombone Concerto,* Christopher Rouse

SPECIAL AWARD

1992 *Maus,* Art Spiegelman

National Society of Film Critics Awards, 1992

Best Film: *Unforgiven*
Best Actress: Emma Thompson, *Howards End*
Best Actor: Stephen Rea, *The Crying Game*
Best Supporting Actress: Judy Davis, *Husbands and Wives*
Best Supporting Actor: Gene Hackman, *Unforgiven*
Best Director: Clint Eastwood, *Unforgiven*
Best Screenwriter: David Webb, *Unforgiven*
Best Cinematography: Zhao Fei, *Raise the Red Lantern*
Best Documentary: *American Dream,* Barbara Kopple
Best Foreign Film: *Raise the Red Lantern,* Zhang Yimou
Best Experimental Film: *Another Girl, Another Planet,* Michael Almereyda

1993 Bancroft Prizes in American History

Margaret Fuller: An American Romantic Life, Volume I, The Private Years, by Charles Capper (Oxford University Press)

A Preponderance of Power: National Security, the Truman Administration and the Cold War, by Melvyn P. Leffler (Stanford University Press)

Winners of Bollingen Prize in Poetry

($5,000[1] award is given biennially. It is administered by Yale University and the Bollingen Foundation.)

1949 Ezra Pound
1950 Wallace Stevens
1951 John Crowe Ransom
1952 Marianne Moore
1953 Archibald MacLeish and William Carlos Williams
1954 W. H. Auden
1955 Léonie Adams and Louise Bogan
1956 Conrad Aiken
1957 Allen Tate
1958 E.E. Cummings
1959 Theodore Roethke
1960 Delmore Schwartz
1961 Yvor Winters
1962 John Hall Wheelock and Richard Eberhart
1963 Robert Frost
1965 Horace Gregory
1967 Robert Penn Warren
1969 John Berryman and Karl Shapiro
1971 Richard Wilbur and Mona Van Duyn
1973 James Merrill
1975 Archie Randolph Ammons
1977 David Ignatow
1979 W. S. Merwin
1981 Howard Nemerov and May Swenson
1983 Anthony Hecht and John Hollander
1985 John Ashbery and Fred Chappell
1987 Stanley Kunitz
1989 Edgar Bowers
1991 Laura Riding Jackson and Donald Justin
1993 Mark Strand

1. Beginning 1989 award increased to $10,000.

1993 Obie Award Winners

Performance: Jane Alexander and Robert Klein, *The Sisters Rosensweig;* Frances Conroy, *The Last Yankee;* David Drake, *The Night Larry Kramer Kissed Me;* Giancarlo Esposito, *Distant Fires;* Geoffrey C. Ewing, *Ali;* Hallie Foote, *The Roads to Home;* Edward Hibbert, *Jeffrey;* Bill Irwin, *Texts for Nothing;* John Cameron Mitchell, *The Destiny of Me;* and Linda Stephens, *Wings*

Sustained Excellence in Performance: Miriam Colon and Ellen Parker

Playwriting: Harry Kondoleon, *The Houseguests;* Larry Kramer, *The Destiny of Me;* Jose Rivera, *Marisol;* and Paul Rudnick, *Jeffrey*

Direction: Christopher Ashley, *Jeffrey;* Michael Maggio, *Wings;* and Frederick Zollo, *Aven'U Boys*

Sustained Excellence of Set Design: Loy Arcenas

Sustained Excellence of Lighting Design: Howard Thies

Citations: Cirque du Soleil; Betty Corwin, New York Public Library Archives; Ensemble Studio Theater, One-Act Play Marathon; The International Festival of Puppet Theater; Ariane Mnouchkine, *Les Atrides;* Serious Fun!

Sustained Achievement: Joanne Akalaitis

Grants: Nuyorican Poets Cafe and Pearl Theater

New York Drama Critics' Circle Awards

1935–36
Winterset, Maxwell Anderson
1936–37
***High Tor,* Maxwell Anderson**
1937–38
Of Mice and Men, John Steinbeck
Shadow and Substance, Paul Vincent Carroll[1]
1938–39
(No award) *The White Steed,* Paul Vincent Carroll[1]
1939–40
The Time of Your Life, William Saroyan
1940–41
Watch on the Rhine, Lillian Hellman
The Corn Is Green, Emlyn Williams[1]
1941–42
(No award) *Blithe Spirit,* Noel Coward[1]
1942–43
The Patriots, Sidney Kingsley
1943–44
(No award) *Jacobowsky and the Colonel.* Franz Werfel and S. N. Behrman[1]
1944–45
The Glass Menagerie, Tennessee Williams
1945–46
(No award) *Carousel,* Richard Rodgers and Oscar Hammerstein II[2]
1946–47
All My Sons, Arthur Miller
No Exit, Jean-Paul Sartre[1]
Brigadoon, Alan Jay Lerner and Frederick Loewe[2]
1947–48
A Streetcar Named Desire, Tennessee Williams
The Winslow Boy, Terence Rattigan[1]
1948–49
Death of a Salesman, Arthur Miller
The Madwoman of Chaillot, Jean Giraudoux and Maurice Valency[1]
South Pacific, Richard Rodgers, Oscar Hammerstein II, and Joshua Logan[2]
1949–50
The Member of the Wedding, Carson McCullers
The Cocktail Party, T. S. Eliot[1]
The Consul, Gian Carlo Menotti[2]
1950–51
Darkness at Noon, Sidney Kingsley[3]
The Lady's Not for Burning, Christopher Fry[1]
Guys and Dolls, Abe Burrows, Jo Swerling, and Frank Loesser[2]
1951–52
I Am a Camera, John Van Druten[4]
Venus Observed, Christopher Fry[1]
Pal Joey, Richard Rodgers, Lorenz Hart, and John O'Hara[2]
Don Juan in Hell, George B. Shaw[5]
1952–53
Picnic, William Inge *The Love of Four Colonels,* by Peter Ustinov[1]
Wonderful Town, Joseph Fields, Jerome Chodorov, Betty Comden, Adolph Green, and Leonard Bernstein[2]
1953–54
The Teahouse of the August Moon, John Patrick
Ondine, Jean Giraudoux[1]
The Golden Apple, John Latouche and Jerome Moross[2]
1954–55
Cat on a Hot Tin Roof, Tennessee Williams
Witness for the Prosecution, Agatha Christie[1]
The Saint of Bleecker Street, Gian Carlo Menotti[2]

1955–56
The Diary of Anne Frank, Frances Goodrich and Albert Hackett
Tiger at the Gates, Jean Giraudoux and Christopher Fry[1]
My Fair Lady, Frederick Loewe and Alan Jay Lerner[2]
1956–57
Long Day's Journey Into Night, Eugene O'Neill
Waltz of the Toreadors, Jean Anouilh[1]
The Most Happy Fella, Frank Loesser[2 6]
1957–58
Look Homeward, Angel, Ketti Frings[7]
Look Back in Anger, John Osborne[1]
The Music Man, Meredith Willson[2]
1958–59
A Raisin in the Sun, Lorraine Hansberry
The Visit, Friedrich Duerrenmatt-Maurice Valency[1]
La Plume de ma Tante, Robert Dhery and Gerard Calvi[2]
1959–60
Toys in the Attic, Lillian Hellman
Five Finger Exercise, Peter Shaffer[1]
Fiorello], Jerome Weidman, George Abbott, Jerry Bock, and Sheldon Harnick[2]
1960–61
All the Way Home, Tad Mosel[3]
A Taste of Honey, Shelagh Delaney[1]
Carnival, Michael Stewart[2]
1961–62
The Night of the Iguana, Tennessee Williams
A Man for All Seasons, Robert Bolt[1]
How to Succeed in Business Without Really Trying, Abe Burrows, Jack Weinstock, Willie Gilbert, and Frank Loesser[2] 9
1962–63
Who's Afraid of Virginia Woolf?, Edward Albee
Beyond the Fringe, Alan Bennett, Peter Cook, Jonathan Miller, and Dudley Moore[10]
1963–64
Luther, John Osborne
Hello, Dolly], Michael Stewart and Jerry Herman[2 11]
The Trojan Women, Euripides[10 12]
1964–65
The Subject Was Roses, Frank D. Gilroy
Fiddler on the Roof, Joseph Stein, Jerry Bock, and Sheldon Harnick[2 13]
1965–66
The Persecution and Assassination of Marat as Performed by the Inmates of the Asylum of Charenton Under the Direction of the Marquis de Sade, Peter Weiss
The Man of La Mancha, Dale Wasserman, Mitch Leigh, and Joe Darion
1966–67
The Homecoming, Harold Pinter
Cabaret, Joe Masteroff, John Kander, and Fred Ebb[2 14]
1967–68
Rosencrantz and Guildenstern Are Dead, Tom Stoppard
Your Own Thing, Donald Driver, Hal Hester, and Danny Apolinar[2]
1968–69
The Great White Hope, Howard Sackler
1776, Sherman Edwards and Peter Stone[2]
1969–70
Borstal Boy, Frank McMahon[15]
The Effect of Gamma Rays on Man-in-the-Moon Marigolds, Paul Zindel[16]
Company, George Furth and Stephen Sondheim[2]
1970–71
Home, David Storey
The House of Blue Leaves, John Guare[16]
Follies, James Goldman and Stephen Sondheim[2]
1971–72
That Championship Season, Jason Miller
Two Gentlemen of Verona, adapted by John Guare and Mel Shapiro[2]
The Screens, Jean Genet[1]
1972–73
The Changing Room, David Storey
The Hot l Baltimore, by Lanford Wilson[16]
A Little Night Music, Hugh Wheeler and Stephen Sondheim[2]
1973–74
The Contractors, David Storey
Short Eyes, Miguel Piñero[16]
Candide, Leonard Bernstein, Hugh Wheeler, and Richard Wilbur[2]
1974–75
Equus, Peter Shaffer
The Taking of Miss Janie, Ed Bullins[16]
A Chorus Line, James Kirkwood and Nicholas Dante[2]
1975–76
Travesties, Tom Stoppard
Streamers, David Rabe[16]
Pacific Overtures, Stephen Sondheim, John Weidman, and Hugh Wheeler[2]
1976–77
Otherwise Engaged, Simon Gray
American Buffalo, David Mamet[16]
Annie, Thomas Meehan, Charles Strouse, and Martin Charnin[2]
1977–78
Da, Hugh Leonard
Ain't Misbehavin', conceived by Richard Maltby, Jr.[2]
1978–79
The Elephant Man, Bernard Pomerance
Sweeney Todd, Hugh Wheeler and Stephen Sondheim[2]
1979–80
Talley's Folly, Lanford Wilson
Evita,[2] Andrew Lloyd Webber and Tim Rice
Betrayal, Harold Pinter[1]
1980–81
A Lesson From Aloes, Athol Fugard
Crimes of the Heart, Beth Henley[16]
1981–82
The Life and Adventures of Nicholas Nickleby, adapted by David Edgar
A Soldier's Play, Charles Fuller[16]
1982–83
Brighton Beach Memoirs, Neil Simon
Plenty, David Hare[1]
Little Shop of Horrors, Alan Menken and Howard Ashman[2 17]
1983–84
The Real Thing, Tom Stoppard
Glengarry Glen Ross, David Mamet[16]
Sunday in the Park with George, Stephen W Sondheim and James Lapine[2]
1984–85
Ma Rainey's Black Bottom, August Wilson
(No award for best musical or foreign play)
1985–86
Lie of the Mind, Sam Shepard
Benefactors, Michael Frayn[1]
The Search for Signs of Intelligent Life in the Universe, Lily Tomlin and Jane Wagner[10]
(No award for best musical)
1986–87
Fences, August Wilson
Les Liaisons Dangereuses, Christopher Hampton[1]
Les Miserables, Claude-Michel Schonberg and Alain Boublil[2]
1987–88
Joe Turner's Come and Gone, August Wilson
The Road to Mecca, Athol Fugard[1]
Into the Woods, Stephen Sondheim and James Lapine[2]

1988–89
The Heidi Chronicles, Wendy Wasserstein
Aristocrats, Brian Friel[1]
Largely New York, Bill Irwin[10]
(No award for best musical)
1989–90
The Piano Lesson, August Wilson
Privates on Parade, Peter Nichols[1]
City of Angels, Larry Gelbart, Cy Coleman, and David Zippel[2]
1990–91
Six Degrees of Separation, John Guare
Our Country's Good, Timberlake Wertenbaker[1]
The Will Rogers Follies, Cy Coleman, Peter Stone, Betty Comden, and Adolph Green[2]
Eileen Atkins, *A Room of One's Own*[10]
1991–92
Dancing at Lughnasa, Brian Friel
Two Trains Running, August Wilson[16]
(No award for best musical)
1992-93
Angels in America: Millennium Approaches, Tony Kushner
Someone Who'll Watch Over Me, Frank McGuinness[1]
Kiss of the Spider Woman, John Kander, Fred Ebb and Terrence McNally[2]

1. Citation for best foreign play. 2. Citation for best musical. 3. Based on a novel by Arthur Koestler. 4. Based on Christopher Isherwood's *Berlin Stories.* 5. For "distinguished and original contribution to the theater." 6. Based on Sidney Howard's *They Knew What They Wanted.* 7. Based on a novel by Thomas Wolfe. 8. Based on James Agee's *A Death in the Family.* 9. Based on a book by Shepherd Mead. 10. Special citation. 11. Based on Thornton Wilder's *The Matchmaker.* 12. Translated by Edith Hamilton. 13. Based on Sholem Aleichem's Tevye stories, translated by Arnold Perl. 14. Based on John Van Druten's *I Am a Camera,* which won the award for the best play in 1951–52. 15. Based on Brendan Behan's autobiography. 16. Citation for best American play. 17. Based on a story by Roger Corman.

Antoinette Perry (Tony) Awards, 1993

Dramatic Play: *Angels in America,* Tony Kushner
Musical: *Kiss of the Spider Woman*
Actor (play): Ron Leibman, *Angels in America*
Actress (play): Madeline Kahn, *The Sisters Rosensweig*
Actor, featured (play): Stephen Spinella, *Angels in America*
Actress, featured (play): Debra Monk, *Redwood Curtain*
Actor (musical): Brent Carver, *Kiss of the Spider Woman*
Actress (musical): Chita Rivera, *Kiss of the Spider Woman*
Actor, featured (musical): Anthony Crivello, *Kiss of the Spider Woman*
Actress, featured (musical): Andrea Martin, *My Favorite Year*
Director (play): George C. Wolfe, *Angels in America*
Director (musical): Des McAnuff, *Tommy*
Best book of musical: Terrence McNally, *Kiss of the Spider Woman*
Best original musical score: John Kander and Fred Ebb, *Kiss of the Spider Woman* and Pete Townshend, *Tommy*
Scenic design: John Arnone, *Tommy*
Costume design: Florence Klotz, *Kiss of the Spider Woman*
Lighting design: Chris Parry, *Tommy*
Choreography: Wayne Cilento, *Tommy*
Revival: *Anna Christie*
Special Award: *Oklahoma!* in recognition of its 50th anniversary
Regional theater: La Jolla Playhouse, California
Honors for excellence in the theater: Broadway Cares/Equity Fights AIDS and International Alliance of Theatrical Stage Employees and Moving Picture Machine Operators of the United States and Canada

Awards of the Society of Professional Journalists, 1992

(Sigma Delta Chi)

Deadline reporting: Laurie Becklund and Stephanie Chavez, *Los Angeles Times*
Non-deadline reporting: Deborah Scroggins and Jean Shifrin, *Atlanta Journal–Constitution*
Investigative reporting: Dave Davis and Ted Wendling, *Plain Dealer,* Cleveland
Feature writing: Barry Bearak, *Los Angeles Times*
Editorial writing: Sara Engram, *Baltimore Sun*
Washington correspondence: Frank Aukofer, *Milwaukee Journal*
Foreign correspondence: Scott Kraft, *Los Angeles Times*
Public service in newspaper journalism: *Miami Herald* (circulation greater than 100,000); *Albuquerque Tribune* (circulation less than 100,000)
Magazine reporting: Eileen McNamara, *Boston Globe*
Public service in magazine journalism: *Fortune*
Photography: Ron Tarver, *Philadelphia Inquirer*
Editorial cartoons: Robert Ariail, *The State*
Radio spot-news: KTRH News Radio-News team, Houston
Radio editorial: Nicholas DeLuca, KCBS Radio, San Francisco
Radio investigative reporting: Bruce Gellerman, WBUR-FM, Boston
Radio feature reporting: Andy Bowers, NPR
Public service in radio journalism: Minnesota Public Radio–KLSE/KZSE
Television spot-news reporting: Cable News Network
Television editorials: Chuck Kraemer, WCVB, Boston
Television investigative reporting: Steve Eckert, Patrick Weiland, Julie Kramer, Gary Feblowitz, and Joe Berglove, WCCO, Minneapolis
Television feature reporting: Janice Tomlin, Tom Jarriel, and Victor Neufeld, ABC News 20/20
Public service in television journalism: WCPO, Cincinnati (top 40 market); KREM, Spokane (other markets)
Public service in newsletter journalism: United Communications Group
Research about journalism: Beverly G. Hawk, *Africa's Media Image*

Poets Laureate of the United States

The post was established in 1985. Appointment is for a one-year term, but is renewable.

Robert Penn Warren	1986–1987
Richard Wilbur	1987–1988
Howard Nemerov	1988–1990
Mark Strand	1990–1991
Joseph Brodsky	1991–1992
Mona Van Duyn	1992–1993
Rita Dove	1993–

Alfred I. du Pont-Columbia University Broadcast News Awards

(For work broadcast between July 1, 1991, and June 30, 1992)

Gold Baton Award: National Public Radio for its coverage of the Los Angeles riots, several series—including "Morning Edition," "All Things Considered" and "American Folklife"—and its reporting of the Senate hearings on the nomination of Clarence Thomas to the Supreme Court.

Silver Baton Awards: ABC News "Nightline" for its coverage of the Los Angeles riots; CBS' "60 Minutes" for "Made in China"; PBS' "The American Experience" for "LBJ," "Frontline" for "Who Killed Adam Mann?" and "P.O.V." for the independent film "Berkeley in the Sixties"; HBO for "Abortion: Desperate Choices" and Nickelodeon for "Nick News." Awards also went to these stations: KTTV, Los Angeles; WCVB-TV, Boston; KCNC-TV, Denver; WCPO-TV, Cincinnati; KSTP-TV, St. Paul and Louisiana Public Broadcasting stations.

Silver Baton : To Bill Leonard, former CBS News President for five decades of distinguished work in broadcast news.

National Book Awards, 1992

Established by Association of American Publishers

(American Book Awards 1980–86. Reverted to original name in 1987.)

Fiction: *All the Pretty Horses,* by Cormac McCarthy (Knopf)

Nonfiction: *Becoming a Man: Half a Life Story,* by Paul Monette (Harcourt Brace Jovanovich)

Poetry: *New and Selected Poems,* by Mary Oliver (Beacon Press)

The National Book Foundation Medal for Distinguished Contribution to American Letters: James Laughlin, the founder and publisher of New Directions.

Enrico Fermi Award

Named in honor of Enrico Fermi, the atomic pioneer, the $100,000 award is given in recognition of "exceptional and altogether outstanding" scientific and technical achievement in atomic energy.

1954 Enrico Fermi
1956 John von Neumann
1957 Ernest O. Lawrence
1958 Eugene P. Wigner
1959 Glenn T. Seaborg
1961 Hans A. Bethe
1962 Edward Teller
1963 J. Robert Oppenheimer
1964 Hyman G. Rickover
1966 Otto Hahn, Lise Meitner, and Fritz Strassman
1968 John A. Wheeler
1969 Walter H. Zinn
1970 Norris E. Bradbury
1971 Shields Warren and Stafford L. Warren
1972 Manson Benedict
1976 William L. Russell
1978 Harold M. Agnew and Wolfgang K.H. Panofsky
1980 Alvin M. Weinberg and Rudolf E. Peirls
1981 W. Bennett Lewis
1982 Herbert Anderson and Seth Neddermeyer
1983 Alexander Hollaender and John Lawrence
1984 Robert R. Wilson and Georges Vendryès
1985 Norman C. Rasmussen and Marshall N. Rosenblath
1986 Ernest D. Courant and M. Stanley Livingston
1987 Luis W. Alvarez and Gerald F. Tape
1988 Richard B. Setlow and Victor F. Weisskopf
1989 Award not given
1990 George A. Cowan and Robley D. Evans
1991 Award not given
1992 Leon M. Lederman, Harold Brown, and John S. Foster, Jr.

1993 Christopher Awards

Adult Books

The Book of the Just: The Unsung Heroes Who Rescued Jews from Hitler, by Eric Silver (Grove Press)

Choteau Creek: A Sioux Reminiscence, by Joseph Iron Eye Dudley (University of Nebraska Press)

Fritz Eichenberg: Works of Mercy, edited by Robert Ellsberg (Orbis Books)

The Measure of Our Success: A Letter to My Children and Yours, by Marian Wright Edelman (Beacon Press)

There's a Boy in Here, by Judy Barron and Sean Barron (Simon & Schuster)

A Year in Saigon, by Katie Kelly (Simon & Schuster)

Young People's Books

The Rainbow Fish, by Marcus Pfister, translated by J. Alison James (North–South Books)

Rosie & The Yellow Ribbon, by Paula DePaolo, pictures by Janet Wolf (Little, Brown)

Letters from Rifka, by Karen Hesse (Henry Holt)

Mississippi Challenge, by Mildred Pitts Walter (Bradbury Press)

Television Specials

Against Her Will: An Incident in Baltimore (CBS)
The Broken Cord (ABC)
Father/Son (Independent Network)
Jonathan: The Boy Nobody Wanted (NBC)
Miles from Nowhere (CBS)
Sr. Thea: Her Own Story (NBC)
A Town Torn Apart (NBC)

Films

Enchanted April (Miramax Films)
Howards End (Sony Picture Classics)
Lorenzo's Oil (Universal)
Sarafina! (Hollywood Pictures and Miramax Fillms)

James Keller Youth Award

Vincent J. Fontana, M.D., The New York Foundling Hospital's Medical Director, for his determined commitment to children and for his pioneering efforts and advocacy in child abuse prevention.

Life Achievement Award

Robert G. Schwartz, The Metropolitan Life Insurance Company's Chairman, President, and CEO, for outstanding corporate leadership and community service.

Recipients of Kennedy Center Honors

The Kennedy Center for the Performing Arts in Washington, D.C., created its Honors awards in 1978 to recognize the achievements of five distinguished contributors to the performing arts. Following are the recipients:

1978: Marian Anderson (contralto), Fred Astaire (dancer-actor), Richard Rodgers (Broadway composer), Arthur Rubinstein (pianist), George Balanchine (choreographer).

1979: Ella Fitzgerald (jazz singer), Henry Fonda (actor), Martha Graham (dancer-choreographer), Tennessee Williams (playwright), Aaron Copland (composer).

1980: James Cagney (actor), Leonard Bernstein (composer-conductor), Agnes de Mille (choreographer), Lynn Fontanne (actress), Leontyne Price (soprano).

1981: Count Basie (jazz composer-pianist), Cary Grant (actor), Helen Hayes (actress), Jerome Robbins (choreographer), Rudolf Serkin (pianist).

1982: George Abbott (Broadway producer), Lillian Gish (actress), Benny Goodman (jazz clarinetist), Gene Kelly (dancer-actor), Eugene Ormandy (conductor).

1983: Katherine Dunham (dancer-choreographer), Elia Kazan (director-author), James Stewart (actor), Virgil Thomson (music critic-composer), Frank Sinatra (singer).

1984: Lena Horne (singer), Danny Kaye (comedian-actor), Gian Carlo Menotti (composer), Arthur Miller (playwright), Isaac Stern (violinist).

1985: Merce Cunningham (dancer-choreographer), Irene Dunne (actress), Bob Hope (comedian), Alan Jay Lerner (lyricist-playwright), Frederick Loewe (composer), Beverly Sills (soprano and opera administrator).

1986: Lucille Ball (comedienne), Ray Charles (musician), Yehudi Menuhin (violinist), Antony Tudor (choreographer), Hume Cronyn and Jessica Tandy (husband-and-wife acting team).

1987: Perry Como (singer), Bette Davis (actress), Sammy Davis Jr. (entertainer), Nathan Milstein (violinist), Alwin Nikolais (choreographer).

1988: Alvin Ailey (choreographer), George Burns (comedian-actor), Myrna Loy (actress), Alexander Schneider (violinist), Roger L. Stevens (theatrical producer and the Kennedy Center's founding chairman).

1989: Harry Belafonte (singer-actor), Claudette Colbert (actress), Alexandra Danilova (ballerina-teacher), Mary Martin (actress), William Schuman (composer)

1990: Dizzy Gillespie (jazz trumpeter), Katharine Hepburn (actress), Risë Stevens (mezzo-soprano), Jule Styne (composer), Billy Wilder (director-author)

1991: Roy Acuff (country songwriter and singer), Betty Comden and Adloph Green (co-authors of books and lyrics of musicals), the brothers Fayard and Harold Nicholas (dancers), Gregory Peck (actor), Robert Shaw (choral director).

1992: Lionel Hampton (jazz musician), Paul Newman (actor), Joanne Woodward (actress), Ginger Rogers (dancer–actress), Mstislav Rostropovich (cellist–conductor), Paul Taylor (dancer–choreographer).

National Book Critics Circle Awards, 1993

Fiction: *All the Pretty Horses* by Cormac McCarthy (Knopf)
General nonfiction: *Young Men and Fire* by Norman Maclean (University of Chicago Press)
Poetry: *Collected Poems 1946–1991* by Hayden Carruth (Copper Canyon Press)
Criticism: *Lincoln at Gettysburg: The Words That Remade America* by Garry Wills (Simon & Schuster)
Biography/Autobiography: *Writing Dangerously: Mary McCarthy and Her World* by Carol Brightman (Clarkson N. Potter)

American Library Association Awards for Children's Books, 1993

(For books published in 1992)

John Newbery Medal for best book: *Missing May,* Cynthia Rylant (Orchard Books)
Newbery Honor Books: *The Dark-Thirty: Southern Tales of the Supernatural,* Patricia McKissak, illustrated by Brian Pinkey (Alfred A. Knopf); *Somewhere in the Darkness,* Walter Dean Myers (Scholastic Hardcover) and *What Hearts,* Bruce Brooks (a Laura Geringer book for Harper Collins)
Randolph Caldecott Medal for best picture book: *Mirette on the High Wire,* Emily Arnold McCully (G.P. Putnam's)
Caldecott Honor Books: *Seven Blind Mice,* illustrated and written by Ed Young (Philomel Books); *The Stinky Cheese Man and Other Fairly Stupid Tales,* illustrated by Lane Smith, written by Jon Sciezka and edited by Regina Hayes (Viking) and *Working Cotton,* illustrated by Carole Byard and written by Sherley Anne Williams (Harcourt Brace Jovanovich)

Poets Laureate of England

Edmund Spenser	1591–1599	Laurence Eusden	1718–1730	Alfred Lord Tennyson	1850–1892
Samuel Daniel	1599–1619	Colley Cibber	1730–1757	Alfred Austin	1896–1913
Ben Jonson	1619–1637	William Whitehead	1757–1785	Robert Bridges	1913–1930
William Davenant	1638–1668	Thomas Warton	1785–1790	John Masefield	1930–1967
John Dryden[1]	1670–1689	Henry James Pye	1790–1813	C. Day Lewis	1967–1972
Thomas Shadwell	1689–1692	Robert Southey	1813–1843	Sir John Betjeman	1972–1984
Nahum Tate	1692–1715	William Wordsworth	1843–1850	Ted Hughes	1984–
Nicholas Rowe	1715–1718				

1. First to bear the title officially. *Source: Encyclopaedia Britannica.*

Major Grammy Awards for Recording in 1992

Source: National Academy of Recording Arts and Sciences.

Record: "Tears in Heaven," Eric Clapton
Album: "Unplugged," Eric Clapton
Song: "Tears in Heaven," Eric Clapton
New Artist: Arrested Development
Pop Vocalists: (Female) K.D. Lang, "Constant Craving"; (Male) Eric Clapton, "Tears in Heaven"
Pop Duo or Group: Celine Dion and Peabo Bryson, "Beauty and the Beast"
Traditional Pop: Tony Bennett, "Perfectly Frank"
Rock Vocalists: (Female) Melissa Etheridge, "Ain't It Heavy"; (Male) Eric Clapton, "Unplugged"
Rock Duo or Group: U2, "Achtung Baby"
Rock Instrumental: Stevie Ray Vaughan and Double Trouble, "Little Wing" (from the album "The Sky is Falling")
Hard Rock: Red Hot Chili Peppers, "Give It Away"
Metal: Nine-Inch Nails, "Wish"
Rhythm-and-Blues Vocalists: (Female) Chaka Khan, "The Woman I Am"; (Male) Al Jarreau, "Heaven and Earth"
Rhythm-and-Blues Duo or Group: Boyz II Men, "End of the Road"
Rhythm-and-Blues Song: L.A. Reid, Babyface and Daryl Simmons, "End of the Road"
Traditional Blues: Dr. John, "Goin' Back to New Orleans"
Contemporary Blues: Stevie Ray Vaughan and Double Trouble, "The Sky Is Crying"
Rap, Solo: Sir Mix-a-Lot, "Baby Got Back"
Rap Duo or Group: Arrested Development, "Tennessee"
New Age: Enya, "Shepherd Moons"
Contemporary Jazz (Instrumental): Pat Metheny, "Secret Story:
Jazz Vocalist: Bobby McFerrin, " 'Round Midnight" from the album "Play"
Jazz Instrumentalists: (Solo) Joe Henderson, "Lush Life"; (Individual or Group) Branford Marsalis, "I Heard You Twice the First Time"
Large Jazz Ensemble: McCoy Tyner Big Band, "The Turning Point"
Country Vocalists: (Female) Mary-Chapin Carpenter, "I Feel Lucky"; (Male) Vince Gill, "I Still Believe in You"
Country Duo or Group: Emmylou Harris and the Nash Ramblers
Country Instrumental: "Sneakin' Around" (album), Chet Atkins and Jerry Reed
Country Song: "I Still Believe in You," Vince Gill; John Barlow Jarvis, and Vince Gill, songwriters
Rock/Contemporary Gospel: "Unseen Power," Petra
Pop Gospel: "The Great Adventure," Steven Curtis Chapman
Southern Gospel: "Sometimes Miracles Hide," Bruce Carroll
Traditional Soul-Gospel: "He's Working It Out for You," Shirley Caeser
Contemporary Soul-Gospel: Various artists on "Handel's Messiah: A Soulful Celebration," Vickie Winans
Gospel Choir or Chorus: "Edwin Hawkins Music and Arts Seminar Mass Choir: Recorded Live in Los Angeles," Music and Arts Seminar Mass Choir
Latin Pop: Jon Secada, "Otro Dia Mas Sin Verte"
Tropical Latin: Linda Ronstadt, "Frenesi"
Mexican-American Album: Linda Ronstadt, "Mas Conciones"
Traditional Folk: The Chieftains, "An Irish Evening Live in the Grand Opera House, Belfast"
Contemporary Folk: The Chieftains, "Another Country"
Best Polka: Walter Ostanek, "35th Anniversary"
Reggae: Shabba Ranks, "X-Tra Naked"
For Children: "Beauty and the Beast: Original Motion Picture Soundtrack," various artists
Comedy: Peter Schickele, "P.D.Q. Bach: Music for an Awful Lot of Winds and Percussion"
Spoken Word or Nonmusical: "What Can You Do to Avoid AIDS," Earvin (Magic) Johnson and Robert O'Keefe
Musical Show Album: "Guys and Dolls: The New Broadway Recording"
Instrumental Composition: "Harlem Renaissance Suite," Benny Carter (from the album "Harlem Renaissance")
Instrumental Composition Written for a Motion Picture or for Television: "Beauty and the Beast," Alan Menken
Instrumental Arrangement: "Strike Up the Band," (from the album "Brassy and Sassy") Rob McConnell, arranger
Music Video—Short Form: "Digging in the Dirt," Peter Gabriel; John Downer, video director and video line producer
Music Video—Long Form: "Diva," Annie Lennox; Sophie Muller, video director; Rob Small, video line producer
Historical Album: "The Complete Capitol Recordings of the Nat King Cole Trio," Nat King Cole Trio; Michael Cuscuna, album producer
Classical Album: "Mahler's Symphony No. 9," Leonard Bernstein conductor, Berlin Philharmonic Orchestra
Orchestral Performance, Opera: "R. Strauss: Die Frau Ohne Schatten," Vienna Philharmonic, Sir Georg Solti, conductor
Classic Soloist with Orchestra: Yo-Yo Ma, cellist, "Prokofiev: Sinfonia Concertante/Tchaikovsky: Variations on a Rococo Theme," Lorin Maazel, conductor, Pittsburgh Symphony Orchestra; **Without Orchestra:** Vladimir Horowitz, pianist, "Horowitz: Discovered Treasures (Chopin, Clementi, Liszt, Scarlatti, Scriabin)"
Chamber Music: Yo-Yo Ma, cellist and Emanuel Ax, pianist, "Brahms: Sonatas for Cello and Piano"
Classical Vocal Performance: "Kathleen Battle at Carnegie Hall (Handel, Mozart, Liszt, Strauss, Charpentier, etc.)" Kathleen Battle, soprano
Classical Choral: "Orff: Carmina Burana," Herbert Blomstedt, conductor, San Francisco Girls/Boys Chorus, The San Francisco Chorus and Symphony Orchestra
Contemporary Classic Composition: "Barber: The Lovers," Samuel Barber
Producers: Non-Classical: A tie: Daniel Lanois and Brian Eno; **ClassicaL** Michael Fine
Engineers: Non-Classical: Bruce Swedien and Teddy Riley, "Dangerous"; **Classical:** Stanley Goodall, "Orff: Carmina Burana"

1993 Jefferson Awards

The Jefferson Awards, to honor the highest ideals and achievements in the field of public service, are sponsored by the American Institute for Public Service. The Institute was founded in 1972 and the first awards were presented in 1973.

Beginning in 1990, through an agreement with *Weekly Reader*, elementary school students became eligible for the award.

The Greatest Public Service Performed by an Elected or Appointed Official: Carla Hills, former U.S. Trade Representative, for protecting vital U.S. trade interests throughout the world and securing America's position as a major global competitor.

The Greatest Public Service Performed by a Private Citizen: James Burke, Chairman, Partnership for a Drug-Free America, for leading a $1 billion campaign against drug abuse in America.

The Greatest Public Service Benefiting the Disadvantaged: Arthur Ashe, tennis champion and activist, for fighting to end discrimination and oppression throughout the world.

The Greatest Public Service Performed by an Individual Thirty-Five or Under: Mary Taylor, nurse and relief worker, for devoting her life to care for the sick and starving populations around the globe.

Greatest Public Service Benefiting Local Communities: Leatrice (Chick) Big Crow, Sioux Falls, S.D.; Ella M. Jones, Sacramento, Calif.; Rev. Herschel C. Smith, Houston, Texas; Christy Todd, Phoenix, Ariz.; and Dr. James Withers, Pittsburgh, Pa.

Outstanding Public Service Performed by Students: Melinda Kummer, Gaithersburg, Md., and Brian Mulhollen, Jacksonville, Ore.

Templeton Foundation Prize for Progress in Religion

The Templeton Prize, an award to encourage progress in religion, was established in 1972 by Sir John Templeton, a Tennessee-born financial analyst and Presbyterian layman, and first presented in 1973. Its value has increased over the years and by 1992 it exceeded $1 million.

Winners to date are:

1973 Mother Teresa of Calcutta, founder of the Missionaries of Charity
1974 Brother Roger, Founder and Prior of the Taize Community in France
1975 Dr. Sarvepalli Radhakrishnan, former President of India and Oxford Professor of Eastern Religions and Ethics
1976 H.E. Leon Joseph Cardinal Suenens, Archbishop of Malines-Brussels
1977 Chiara Lubich, Founder of the Focolare Movement, Italy
1978 Prof. Thomas F. Torrance, President of International Academy of Religion and Sciences, Scotland
1979 Nikkyo Niwano, Founder of Rissho Kosel Kai and World Conferences on Religion and Peace, Japan
1980 Prof. Ralph Wendell Burhoe, Founder and Editor of *Zygon,* Chicago
1981 Dame Cicely Saunders, Originator of Modern Hospice Movement, England
1982 The Rev'd Dr. Billy Graham, Founder, The Billy Graham Evangelistic Association
1983 Aleksandr Solzhenitsyn, U.S.A.
1984 The Rev'd Michael Bourdeaux, Founder of Keston College, England
1985 Sir Alister Hardy, Oxford, England
1986 Rev'd Dr. James McCord, Princeton, N.J.
1987 Rev'd Professor Stanley L. Jaki, Princeton, N.J.
1988 Dr. Inamullah Khan, Secretary-general of the World Moslem Congress
1989 The Very Reverend Lord MacLeod of the Iona Community, Scotland, and Professor Carl Friedrich von Weizsäcker of Starnberg, West Germany
1990 Baba Amte, India, and Professor Charles Birch, Sydney, Australia
1991 The Rt. Hon. Lord Jakobovits, Chief Rabbi of Great Britain and the Commonwealth
1992 Dr. Kyung-Chik Han, Founder of Seoul's Young Nak Presbyterian Church
1993 Charles W. Colson, Founder, Prison Fellowship, Virginia

1993 MacArthur Foundation Awards

Nancy D. Cartwright, professor at the London School of Economics and Political Science
Demetrios Christodoulou, mathematics professor at Princeton University
Maria Luisa Crawford, geology professor at Bryn Mawr College
Stanley Crouch, critic, essayist, and playwright
Nora C. England, anthropology professor at the University of Iowa
Paul Edward Farmer, anthropologist and doctor at Brigham and Women's Hospital at Harvard University
Victoria Elizabeth Foe, research associate professor at the University of Washington, specializing in developmental biology
Ernest J. Gaines, novelist and professor of English and creative writing at the University of Southwest Louisiana
Pedro Jose Greer, Jr., founder and medical director of the Camillus Health Concern, a Miami, Fla., clinic for homeless people.
Thom Gunn, poet, literary critic, and senior lecturer at the University of California–Berkeley
Ann Hamilton, visual artist
Sokoni Karania, founder and president of the Center for New Horizons, a Chicago organization that aided the black community
Ann Lauterbach, poet and creative writing professor at the City College of New York
Stephen Lee, associate professor of chemistry at the University of Michigan
Carol Levine, director of the Orphan Project in New York City, an organization researching children orphaned as a result of AIDS
Amory Bloch Lovins, founder and director of the Rocky Mountain Institute, a Colorado environmental organization
Jane Lubchenco, zoology professor at Oregon State University
Ruth Watson Lubic, nurse-midwife and founder of the National Association of Childbearing Center
Jim Powell, poet, translator, and literary critic
Margie Profet, research associate in a field combining evolutionary biology and health sciences at the University of California at Berkeley
Thomas M. Scanlon, philosophy professor at Harvard University
Aaron Shirley, doctor in charge of the Jackson–Hinds Comprehensive Health Care Center in Mississippi
William H. Siemering, radio producer who was a major force in the creation of National Public Radio
Ellen Kovner Silbergeld, toxics specialist at the Environmental Defense Fund and professor at the University of Maryland Medical School
Leonard van der Kuijp, associate professor of Buddhist and Tibetan studies at the University of Washington
Frank von Hippel, professor at Princeton University's Woodrow Wilson School of Public and International Affairs
John Edgar Wideman, novelist and professor at the University of Massachusetts at Amherst
Heather Williams, assistant professor of biology at Williams College
Marion Williams, gospel singer
Robert H. Williams, senior research physicist at the Center for Energy and Environmental Studies at Princeton University
Henry Tutwiler Wright, professor of archaeology at the University of Michigan

Presidential Medal of Freedom

The nation's highest civilian award, the Presidential Medal of Freedom, was established in 1963 by President John F. Kennedy to continue and expand Presidential recognition of meritorious service which, since 1945, had been granted as the Medal of Freedom. Kennedy selected the first recipients, but was assassinated before he could make the presentations. They were made by President Johnson. NOTE: An asterisk following a year denotes a posthumous award.

SELECTED BY PRESIDENT KENNEDY

Marian Anderson (contralto)	1963
Ralph J. Bunche (statesman)	1963
Ellsworth Bunker (diplomat)	1963
Pablo Casals (cellist)	1963
Genevieve Caulfield (educator)	1963
James B. Conant (educator)	1963
John F. Enders (bacteriologist)	1963
Felix Frankfurter (jurist)	1963
Karl Horton (youth authority)	1963
Robert J. Kiphuth (athletic director)	1963
Edwin H. Land (inventor)	1963
Herbert H. Lehman (statesman)	1963*
Robert A. Lovett (statesman)	1963
J. Clifford MacDonald (educator)	1963*
John J. McCloy (banker and statesman)	1963
George Meany (labor leader)	1963
Alexander Meiklejohn (philosopher)	1963
Ludwig Mies van der Rohe (architect)	1963
Jean Monnet (European statesman)	1963
Luis Muñoz-Marin (Governor of Puerto Rico)	1963
Clarence B. Randall (industrialist)	1963
Rudolf Serkin (pianist)	1963
Edward Steichen (photographer)	1963
George W. Taylor (educator)	1963
Alan T. Waterman (scientist)	1963
Mark S. Watson (journalist)	1963
Annie D. Wauneka (public health worker)	1963
E. B. White (author)	1963
Thornton N. Wilder (author)	1963
Edmund Wilson (author and critic)	1963
Andrew Wyeth (artist)	1963

AWARDED BY PRESIDENT BUSH

James A. Baker 3d (government service)	1991
Lucille Ball (entertainer)	1989*
William F. Buckley, Jr. (editor, columnist)	1991
Dick Cheney (government service)	1991
Javier Perez De Cuellar (Secretary General, UN)	1991
C. Douglas Dillon (public servant)	1989
James H. Doolittle (aviation pioneer)	1989
Luis A. Ferre (public servant)	1991
Elizabeth Ford (public servant)	1991
Hanna Holburn Gray (educator)	1991
Friedrich August von Hayek (economist)	1991
George F. Kennen (public servant and author)	1989
Thomas P. O'Neill, Jr. (public servant)	1991
Claude D. Pepper (public servant)	1989
Gen. Colin L. Powell (soldier)	1991
Ronald Reagan (former President of U.S.)	1993
Gen. H. Norman Schwarzkopf (soldier)	1991
Brent Scowcroft (government service)	1991
Margaret Chase Smith (public servant)	1989
Leon Sullivan (civil rights leader)	1991
Margaret Thatcher (former Prime Minister of U.K.)	1991
Russell E. Train (environmentalist)	1991
Lech Walesa (human rights champion)	1989
Vernon A. Walters (diplomat)	1991
Sam Walton (businessman)	1992
Theodore S. (Ted) Williams (baseball legend)	1991

1993 National Magazine Awards

Feature writing: *The New Yorker* for "Whose Art Is It?" by Jane Kramer
Fiction: *The New Yorker* for "A Wilderness Station," by Alice Munro; "Parachute Silk," by Emily Carter; and "Career Move," by Martin Amis
Reporting: *IEEE Spectrum* for "Seeking Nuclear Safeguards"
Essays and criticism: *The American Lawyer* for "Maybe the Jury was Right," by Roger Parloff
Personal service: *Good Housekeeping* for its articles that give practical guidance in dealing with the realities of everyday life and *Philadelphia* magazine for a collection of witty, personal essays
Public interest: *The Family Therapy Network* for writing about the daunting problems of the homeless, drug victims, and family pathology among the poor.
Single-topic issue: *Newsweek* for "How We Won: The Untold Story of Bill Clinton's Triumph"
Design: *Harper's Bazaar* for borrowing on its past to create a design of thoroughly modern excellence
Photography: *Harper's Bazaar* for its irresistible blend of elegance, clarity, and wit
General excellence: (for magazines with a circulation of more than one million): *Newsweek* for reinventing the spirit of the news magazine. **Others:** *The Atlantic Monthly* for its respect for language, reasonableness and careful thought, graphic elegance, and a capacity to surprise and entertain; *American Photo* for celebrating the art of photography not its technique; and *Lingua Franca* because while it is written for academics it ventures well beyond the ivory tower in a tone that is irreverent, if not downright sassy.

American Academy of Arts and Letters Literature Awards 1993

The Gold Medal for Belles Lettres and Criticism: Elizabeth Hardwick
Academy Awards in Literature: Ellen Akins, Richard Bausch, Vance Bourjaily, Deborah Eisenberg, Rolf Fjelde, Tina Howe, Denis Johnson, A.G. Mojtabai
Michael Braude Award for Light Verse: Turner Cassity
Witter Bynner Prize for Poetry: Patricia Storace
E.M. Forster Award in Literature: Sean O'Brien
Sue Kaufman Prize for First Fiction: Francisco Goldman, *The Long Night of White Chickens*
Rome Fellowship in Literature: Thomas Bolt
Richard and Hinda Rosenthal Foundation Award in Literature: Robert Olen Bulter, *A Good Scent from a Strange Mountain*
Jean Stein Award for Nonfiction: Stanley Crouch
Harold D. Vursell Memorial Award in Literature: T. Coraghessan Boyle
Morton Dauwen Zabel Award in Fiction: James Purdy

ENTERTAINMENT & CULTURE

U.S. Symphony Orchestras and Their Music Directors

(With expenses over $1,050,000)

Source: American Symphony Orchestra League.

Alabama Symphony: Paul Polivnick
American Symphony Orchestra (New York City): Leon Botstein
Atlanta Symphony: Yoel Levi
Austin Symphony: Sung Kwak
Baltimore Symphony: David Zinman
Boston Symphony: Seiji Ozawa
Brooklyn Philharmonic: Dennis Russell Davies
Buffalo Philharmonic: Maximiano Valdes
Charleston Symphony: David Stahl
Charlotte Symphony: Leo B. Driehuys
Chattanooga Symphony & Opera Assn.: Robert Bernhardt
Chicago Symphony: Daniel Barenboim
Cincinnati Symphony: Jesus Lopez-Cobos
Cleveland Orchestra: Christoph von Dohnanyi
Colorado Springs Symphony: Christopher P. Wilkins
Colorado Symphony (Denver): David T. Abosch[1]
Columbus Symphony: Alessandro Siciliani[1]
Concerto Soloists Chamber Orchestra (Philadelphia): Marc S. Mostovoy
Dallas Symphony: Eduardo Mata
Dayton Philharmonic: Isaiah Jackson
Delaware Symphony: Stephen Gunzenhauser
Detroit Symphony: Neeme Jarvi
Florida Philharmonic Orchestra: James Judd
Florida Orchestra: Jahja Ling
Florida Symphony: Joseph Silverstein[2]
Florida Symphonic Pops: Mark Azzolina[1]
Fort Wayne Philharmonic: Ronald Ondrejka
Fort Worth Symphony: John Giordano
Grand Rapids Symphony: Catherine Comet
Grant Park Symphony (Chicago): Catherine M. Cahill[3]
Handel and Haydn Society (Boston): Christopher Hogwood[2]
Hartford Symphony: Michael Lankester
Honolulu Symphony Society: Donald Johanos
Houston Symphony: Christoph Eschenbach
Hudson Valley Philharmonic (Poughkeepsie): Randall Craig Fleischer
Indianapolis Symphony: Raymond Leppard
Jacksonville Symphony: Roger Nierenberg
Kansas City Symphony: William McGlaughlin
Knoxville Symphony: Kirk Trevor
Long Beach Symphony: JoAnn Falletta
Long Island Philharmonic: Marin Alsop
Los Angeles Chamber Orchestra: Christof Perick
Los Angeles Philharmonic: Esa-Pekka Salonen[4]
Louisville Orchestra: Lawrence Leighton Smith
Memphis Symphony: Alan Balter
Milwaukee Symphony: Zdenek Macal
Minnesota Orchestra: Edo de Waart
Mississippi Symphony: Colman Pearce
Naples Philharmonic: Timothy W. Russell
Nashville Symphony: Kenneth D. Schermerhorn
National Symphony (D.C.): Mstislav Rostropovich
New Haven Symphony: Michael Palmer
New Jersey Symphony: Zdenek Macal[5]
New Mexico Symphony: Neal H. Stulberg
New World Symphony (Fla.): Michael Tilson Thomas[1]
New York Chamber Symphony of the 92nd St. Y: Gerard Schwarz
New York Philharmonic: Kurt Masur
North Carolina Symphony: Gerhardt Zimmermann
Ohio Chamber Orchestra: Not designated
Oklahoma City Philharmonic: Joel A. Levine
Omaha Symphony: Bruce B. Hangen
Oregon Symphony: James DePreist
Pacific Symphony (Calif.): Carl St. Clair
Philadelphia Orchestra: Wolfgang Sawallisch
Phoenix Symphony: James Sadares
Pittsburgh Symphony: Lorin Maazel
Portland Symphony: Toshiyuki Shimada
Rhode Island Philharmonic: Zuohuang Chen
Richmond Symphony: George Manahan
Rochester Philharmonic: Mark Elder
Sacramento Symphony: Alasdair P. Neale[5]
St. Louis Symphony: Leonard Slatkin
St. Paul Chamber Orchestra: Hugh Wolff
San Antonio Symphony: Christopher Wilkins
San Diego Symphony: Yoav Talmi
San Francisco Symphony: Herbert Blomstedt
San Jose Symphony: Leonid Grin
Savannah Symphony: Philp B. Greenberg
Seattle Symphony: Gerard Schwarz
Spokane Symphony: Vakhtang Jordania
Springfield Symphony (Mass.): Raymond C. Harvey
Syracuse Symphony: Kazuyoshi Akiyama
Toledo Symphony: Andrew Massey
Tucson Symphony: Robert E. Bernhardt
Tulsa Philharmonic: Bernard Rubenstein
Utah Symphony: Joseph Silverstein
Virginia Symphony: JoAnn Falletta
West Virginia Symphony: Thomas B. Conlin
Wichita Symphony: Zuohuang Chen
Winston-Salem Symphony Assn.: Peter J. Perret

1. Artistic Director. 2. Music Adviser. 3. General Manager/Artistic Director. 4. Music Director Designate. 5. Artistic Adviser.

Remembering Balanchine

To mark the tenth anniversary of the death of George Balanchine, the New York City Ballet, which he founded with Lincoln Kirstein and for which he was ballet master and principal choreographer, staged a Balanchine Celebration May 4 to June 27, 1993.

Devoting eight weeks of its ten-week spring season to the celebration, the company performed 73 of the master's works chronologically from the earliest, the 1928 *Apollo* to music by Stravinsky to his last, the 1981 *Mozartiana* to the Tchaikovsky score of the same name.

The gala finale spanned afternoon and evening performances with a break for dinner. It featured excerpts from the previously performed ballets. An added highlight was the appearance of dancers from other U.S. and foreign companies who knew the ballets from dancing Balanchine works with their home companies. PBS taped the program for broadcasting nationally at a later date.

Major Public Libraries

City (branches)	Volumes	Circulation	Budget (in millions)
Akron–Summit County, Ohio (17)	1,376,153	3,404,343	$12.5
Albuquerque, N.M. (12)	953,087	2,821,609	6.5
Annapolis, Md. (14)	1,152,331	5,167,669	9.7
Atlanta–Fulton County (31)	1,862,000	3,036,000	15.5
Austin, Tex. (16)	1,005,651	2,755,556	8.5
Baltimore (29)	2,217,508	1,625,000	15.7
Baton Rouge, La. (9)	914,815	2,362,340	9.4
Birmingham, Ala. (19)	906,590	1,953,105	9.6
Boston (25)	6,000,000	3,500,000	28.4
Buffalo–Erie County, N.Y. (58)	3,915,223[1]	8,107,398	21.8
Charleston–Kanawna County, W. Va. (8)	588,928	962,486	3.7[2]
Charlotte, N.C. (21)	1,236,413	4,196,394	12.8
Chicago (82)	8,166,421	8,008,213	72.0
Cincinnati (41)	4,423,432	10,995,062	30.1
Cleveland (28)	2,672,396	5,798,260	34.2
Columbus Metropolitan, Ohio (21)	2,072,353	9,642,350	32.4
Dallas (19)	2,452,000	4,451,083	15.2
Dayton–Montgomery County, Ohio (20)	1,600,000	6,358,683	13.0
Denver (21)	4,243,162	4,416,154	15.1
Des Moines, Iowa (5)	559,259	1,336,147	4.1
Detroit (25)	2,791,796	1,589,458	23.5
D.C. (27)	1,870,923	2,183,579	21.3
El Paso (10)	1,418,523[3]	1,542,824	5.2[4]
Erie, Pa. (6)	436,199	1,680,096	2.8
Evansville–Vanderburgh Ind. (7)	931,493	1,576,485	5.1
Fairfax County, Va. (22)	1,800,000	8,500,000	15.1
Fort Wayne–Allen County, Ind. (14)	2,247,973	3,743,848	10.7
Fort Worth (10)	1,860,694	4,475,127	5.9
Grand Rapids, Mich. (5)	1,062,710	1,093,040	4.0
Greenville City–County, S.C. (11)	631,598[5]	1,632,948	5.2
Hawaii State Public Library System (49)[6]	2,857,090[7]	6,699,876[7]	23.6[7]
Houston (33)	3,982,539	6,334,647	22.0
Independence, Mo. (26)	1,985,243	5,161,151	16.5
Indianapolis–Marion County (21)	1,738,641	7,399,635	21.2
Jackson–Hinds County, Miss. (15)	550,000	850,000	2.2
Jacksonville, Fla. (18)	2,363,181	2,942,763	11.1
Kansas City, Mo. (9)	1,867,065	2,256,725	10.1
Knoxville, Tenn. (16)	611,211	1,834,340	4.3
Lincoln, Neb. (7)	585,183	1,971,474	3.5
Long Beach, Calif. (11)	1,080,032	2,739,843	11.4
Los Angeles (County) (98)	5,784,785[1]	16,095,328	$64.6
Louisville, Ky. (15)	841,773[5]	2,362,891[5]	9.8
Madison, Wic. (8)	670,000	2,765,000	6.2
Memphis, Tenn. (22)	1,682,008	3,482,460	12.5
Miami-Dade County, Fla. (31)	3,554,437	6,806,454	30.9
Milwaukee (12)	2,408,882	3,046,884	17.0
Minneapolis (14)	2,022,162	3,334,739	15.2
Nashville–Davidson County, Tenn. (16)	656,537[7]	2,034,664	8.9[9]
Newark, N.J. (11)	1,400,000	1,000,000	9.5
New Orleans (15)	909,841	1,289,863	5.9
New York City:			
*New York Public Library Branches (82)	4,400,000	9,908,640	73.0
Research	11,300,000	—	62.7
Brooklyn Public Library (60)	5,474,809	8,452,880	36.9
Queens Borough Public Library (62)	9,271,960	13,237,878[2]	52.0[10]
Norfolk, Va. (11)	909,565	717,903	3.7
Oklahoma City–County (10)	925,631	4,591,599	8.7
Omaha, Neb. (9)	655,719	2,115,565	6.7
Philadelphia (52)	5,062,771	6,103,990	46.7
Phoenix, Ariz. (11)	1,759,723	6,036,235	13.6
Pittsburgh (20)	1,942,704	2,999,206	14.3
Portland–Multnomah County, Ore. (14)	1,587,291	6,087,001	17.2
Providence, R.I. (9)	886,798	701,576	4.3
Richmond, Va. (10)	819,778[11]	928,085	3.7
Rochester, N.Y. (11)	1,251,495	1,537,176	9.5
Sacramento, Calif. (22)	1,627,138	3,846,177	19.2
St. Louis (12)	1,406,969	2,007,975	10.5
St. Paul (12)	903,575[12]	2,529,222	6.4
St. Petersburg, Fla. (5)	420,000	1,100,000	2.9
Salt Lake City–County, Utah (15)	1,235,017	4,796,417	12.3
San Antonio (17)	2,704,762	3,090,671	8.8
San Diego, Calif. (33)	1,938,998[1]	5,364,276	24.1[13]
San Francisco (26)	3,814,386	2,921,207	20.1
San Jose, Calif. (18)	1,460,000	4,500,450	18.2
Seattle (22)	2,110,610[1]	4,308,192	21.9
Springfield, Mass. (9)	680,977	1,046,764	4.3
Tampa, Fla. (17)	1,995,026	3,528,299	12.3[14]
Tucson, Ariz. (19)	1,200,000	5,200,000	11.2
Tulsa City–County, Okla. (21)	918,887	3,652,550	10.2
Wichita, Kan. (11)	893,465[15]	1,639,947	4.7
Winston-Salem–Forsyth County, N.C. (9)	400,000	2,100,000	5.0
Worcester, Mass. (2)	511,030	604,095	2.3
Youngstown–Mahoning County, Ohio (22)	667,732	1,604,756	8.2

1. Includes books and audio-visual materials. 2. Fiscal 1992–93. 3. Includes books, periodicals, records, films, government documents. 4. Budget includes both general and bond funds. 5. Book collection only. 6. State-wide system. 7. Fiscal 1991–92. 8. Includes capital. 9. Includes benefits. 10. Fiscal 1993–94. 11. Estimate June 30, 1993. 12. Includes books, audiovisual materials, government documents, musical scores, etc. 13. Includes capital improvements, grant-funded services, and gifts. 14. Plus $950,000 building fund. 15. Includes CDs, films, cassettes, pamphlets, periodicals, and microforms. *Includes Manhattan, Bronx, and Staten Island.

Glossary of Art Movements

Abstract Expressionism. American art movement of the 1940s that emphasized form and color within a nonrepresentational framework. Jackson Pollock initiated the revolutionary technique of splattering the paint directly on canvas to achieve the subconscious interpretation of the artist's inner vision of reality.

Art Deco. A 1920s style characterized by setbacks, zigzag forms, and the use of chrome and plastic ornamentation. New York's Chrysler Building is an architectural example of the style.

Art Nouveau. An 1890s style in architecture, graphic arts, and interior decoration characterized by writhing forms, curving lines, and asymmetrical organization. Some critics regard the style as the first stage of modern architecture.

Ashcan School. A group of New York realist artists, formed in 1908, who abandoned decorous subject matter and portrayed the more common as well as the sordid aspects of city life.

Assemblage (Collage). Forms of modern sculpture and painting utilizing readymades, found objects, and pasted fragments to form an abstract composition. Louise Nevelson's boxlike enclosures, each with its own composition of assembled objects, illustrate the style in sculpture. Pablo Picasso developed the technique of cutting and pasting natural or manufactured materials to a painted or unpainted surface.

Barbizon School (Landscape Painting). A group of painters who, around the middle of the 19th century, reacted against classical landscape and advocated a direct study of nature. They were influenced by English and Dutch landscape masters. Theodore Rousseau, one of the principal figures of the group, led the fight for outdoor painting. In this respect, the school was a forerunner of Impressionism.

Baroque. European art and architecture of the 17th and 18th centuries. Giovanni Bernini, a major exponent of the style, believed in the union of the arts of architecture, painting, and sculpture to overwhelm the spectator with ornate and highly dramatized themes. Although the style originated in Rome as the instrument of the Church, it spread throughout Europe in such monumental creations as the Palace of Versailles.

Beaux Arts. Elaborate and formal architectural style characterized by symmetry and an abundance of sculptured ornamentation. New York's old Custom House at Bowling Green is an example of the style.

Black or Afro-American Art. The work of American artists of African descent produced in various styles characterized by a mood of protest and a search for identity and historical roots.

Classicism. A form of art derived from the study of Greek and Roman styles characterized by harmony, balance, and serenity. In contrast, the Romantic Movement gave free rein to the artist's imagination and to the love of the exotic.

Constructivism. A form of sculpture using wood, metal, glass, and modern industrial materials expressing the technological society. The mobiles of Alexander Calder are examples of the movement.

Cubism. Early 20th-century French movement marked by a revolutionary departure from representational art. Pablo Picasso and Georges Bracque penetrated the surface of objects, stressing basic abstract geometric forms that presented the object from many angles simultaneously.

Dada. A product of the turbulent and cynical post-World War I period, this anti-art movement extolled the irrational, the absurd, the nihilistic, and the nonsensical. The reproduction of Mona Lisa adorned with a mustache is a famous example. The movement is regarded as a precursor of Surrealism. Some critics regard HAPPENINGS as a recent development of Dada. This movement incorporates environment and spectators as active and important ingredients in the production of random events.

Expressionism. A 20th-century European art movement that stresses the expression of emotion and the inner vision of the artist rather than the exact representation of nature. Distorted lines and shapes and exaggerated colors are used for emotional impact. Vincent Van Gogh is regarded as the precursor of this movement.

Fauvism. The name "wild beasts" was given to the group of early 20th-century French painters because their work was characterized by distortion and violent colors. Henri Matisse and Georges Roualt were leaders of this group.

Futurism. This early 20th-century movement originating in Italy glorified the machine age and attempted to represent machines and figures in motion. The aesthetics of Futurism affirmed the beauty of technological society.

Genre. This French word meaning "type" now refers to paintings that depict scenes of everyday life without any attempt at idealization. Genre paintings can be found in all ages, but the Dutch productions of peasant and tavern scenes are typical.

Impressionism. Late 19th-century French school dedicated to defining transitory visual impressions painted directly from nature, with light and color of primary importance. If the atmosphere changed, a totally different picture would emerge. It was not the object or event that counted but the visual impression as caught at a certain time of day under a certain light. Claude Monet and Camille Pissarro were leaders of the movement.

Mannerism. A mid-16th century movement, Italian in origin, although El Greco was a major practitioner of the style. The human figure, distorted and elongated, was the most frequent subject.

Neoclassicism. An 18th-century reaction to the excesses of Baroque and Rococo, this European art movement tried to recreate the art of Greece and Rome by imitating the ancient classics both in style and subject matter.

Neoimpressionism. A school of painting associated with George Seurat and his followers in late 19th-century France that sought to make Impressionism more precise and formal. They employed a technique of juxtaposing dots of primary colors to achieve brighter secondary colors, with the mixture left to the eye to complete (pointillism).

Op Art. The 1960s movement known as Optical Painting is characterized by geometrical forms that create an optical illusion in which the eye is required to blend the colors at a certain distance.

Pop Art. In this return to representational art, the artist returns to the world of tangible objects in a reaction against abstraction. Materials are drawn from the everyday world of popular culture—comic strips, canned goods, and science fiction.

Realism. A development in mid-19th-century France lead by Gustave Courbet. Its aim was to depict the customs, ideas, and appearances of the time using scenes from everyday life.

Rococo. A French style of interior decoration developed during the reign of Louis XV consisting mainly of asymmetrical arrangements of curves in paneling, porcelain, and gold and silver objects. The characteristics of ornate curves, prettiness, and gaiety can also be found in the painting and sculpture of the period.

Surrealism. A further development of Collage, Cubism, and Dada, this 20th-century movement stresses the weird, the fantastic, and the dreamworld of the subconscious.

Symbolism. As part of a general European movement in the latter part of the 19th century, it was closely allied with Symbolism in literature. It marked a turning away from painting by observation to transforming fact into a symbol of inner experience. Gauguin was an early practitioner.

Top 10 Videocassettes Sales, 1992

1. **Fantasia** (Walt Disney Home Video)
2. **101 Dalmations** (Walt Disney Home Video)
3. **The Jungle Book** (Walt Disney Home Video)
4. **Robin Hood: Prince of Thieves** (Warner Home Video)
5. **Cherfitness: A New Attitude** (FoxVideo)
6. **Fievel Goes West** (MCA/Universal Home Video)
7. **1992 Playboy Video Playmate Calendar** (Uni Dist. Corp.)
8. **Home Alone** (FoxVideo)
9. **The Rescuers Down Under** (Walt Disney Home Video)
10. **Playboy: Sexy Lingerie IV** (Uni Dist. Corp.)

Source: © 1993 BPI Communications, Inc. Used with permission from *Billboard.*

Top 10 Classical Crossover Albums, 1992

1. **Hush,** Yo-Yo Ma/Bobby McFerrin (Sony Masterworks)
2. **The Wind Beneath My Wings,** James Galway (RCA)
3. **Pavarotti Songbook,** Luciano Pavarotti (London)
4. **Spirituals in Concert,** Kathleen Battle, Jessye Norman (Levine) (DG)
5. **Diva!** Lesley Garrett (Silva America)
6. **Kiri Sidetracks,** Kiri Te Kanawa (Phillips)
7. **Lucky To Be Me,** Jessye Norman (Phillips)
8. **Amazing Grace,** Jessye Norman (Phillips)
9. **Songs of the Cat,** Fredrica Von Stade, Garrison Keillor (RCA)
10. **Opening Night—The Overtures,** Hollywood Bowl Orchestra (Mauceri) (Phillips)

Source: © 1992 BPI Communications. Used with permission from *Billboard.*

Top 10 Music Videocassettes, 1992

1. **We Will Rock You,** Queen (Strand Home Video)
2. **Garth Brooks,** Garth Brooks (Capitol Video)
3. **The Three Tenors in Concert,** Carreras-Domingo-Pavarotti (PolyGram Video)
4. **Live at the El Mocambo,** Stevie Ray Vaughan (SMV Enterprises)
5. **This Is Garth Brooks,** Garth Brooks (Liberty Home Video)
6. **Two Rooms,** Various artists (PolyGram Video)
7. **Unplugged + 3,** Mariah Carey (SMV Enterprises)
8. **Sexy MF,** Prince & the N.P.G. (Warner Reprise Video)
9. **Soul and Passion,** Michael Bolton (SMV Enterprises)
10. **The Heart In Motion Video,** Amy Grant (PolyGram Video)

Source: © 1993 BPI Communications, Inc. Used with permission from *Billboard.*

VCR &TV Sales to Retailers, 1992

Color TV[1]	21,356,000 (est)
Monochrome TV[1]	1,158,000(est.)
Projection TV	404,000
VCR decks	12,329,000
Camcorders	2,815,000

1. Includes LCD (liquid crystal displays). *Source:* Electronic Industries Association Consumer Electronics Group.

Top 10 Kid Videocassettes, 1992

1. **Fantasia** (Walt Disney Home Video)
2. **The Jungle Book** (Walt Disney Home Video)
3. **The Rescuers Down Under** (Walt Disney Home Video)
4. **101 Dalmations** (Walt Disney Home Video)
5. **Fievel Goes West** (MCA/Universal Home Video)
6. **An American Tail** (MCA/Universal Home Video)
7. **Peter Pan** (Walt Disney Home Video)
8. **Dumbo** (Walt Disney Home Video)
9. **Robin Hood** (Walt Disney Home Video)
10. **Charlotte's Web** (Paramount Home Video)

Source: © 1993 BPI Communications, Inc. Used with permission from *Billboard.*

Top 10 Videocassettes Rentals, 1992

1. **Thelma and Louise** (MGM/UA Home Video)
2. **The Silence of the Lambs** (Orion Home Video)
3. **The Fisher King** (Columbia TriStar Home Video)
4. **City Slickers** (Columbia TriStar Home Video)
5. **Backdraft** (MCA/Universal Home Video)
6. **Cape Fear** (MCA/Universal Home Video)
7. **The Hand That Rocks the Cradle** (Hollywood Home Video)
8. **Father of the Bride** (Touchstone Home Video)
9. **Deceived** (Touchstone Home Video)
10. **What About Bob?** (Touchstone Home Video)

Source: © 1993 BPI Communications, Inc. Used with permission from *Billboard.*

15 Top-Grossing Concerts

1. **Genesis,** $6,515,992, Niedersachsenstadion, Hannover, Germany, July 10–11, 13.
2. **Bruce Springsteen,** $6,295,707, Meadowlands Arena, East Rutherford, N.J. July 23, 25–26, 28, 30–31, Aug. 2, 4, 6–7, 10.
3. **Elton John/Eric Clapton, Curtis Stigers,** Shea Stadium, Flushing, N.Y. Aug. 21–22.
4. **U2, Primus, Disposable Heroes of Hiphoprisy,** Foxboro Stadium, Foxboro, Mass., Aug. 20, 22–23.
5. **Neil Diamond,** $4,060,744, Wembley Arena, London, England, July 16–19, 21–22, 24–25.
6. **Elton John,** $4,006,410, Azteca Stadium, Mexico City, Mexico, Nov. 13–14.
7. **"Jesus Christ Superstar—The Concert,"** $3,809,741, Sydney Entertainment Centre, Sydney, Australia, Sept. 5–6, 8–11, 20–22, 24–27.
8. **Neil Diamond,** $3,682,208, Sydney Entertainment Centre, Sydney, Australia, April 13–16, 18, May 3–5, 7–8.
9. **Elton John/Eric Clapton, Curtis Stigers,** $3,422,520, Dodger Stadium, Los Angeles, Calif., Aug. 29–30.
10. **Elton John,** $3,345,477, Madison Square Garden, New York, Oct. 2–3, 5, 7, 9–10.
11. **Harry Connick, Jr.,** $3,287,399, The Paramount, New York, N.Y., March 19–21, 23–24, 26–28, 30–31, April 2–4, 6–7.
12. **Neil Diamond,** $3,281,923, Great Western Forum, Inglewood, Calif., March 11–16, 22–23.
13. **U2, Primus, Disposable Heroes of Hiphoprisy,** Giants Stadium, East Rutherford, N.J., Aug. 12–13.
14. **U2, Public Enemy, Sugarcubes,** $3,250,710, Dodger Stadium, Los Angeles, Oct. 30–31.
15. **Frank Sinatra/Shirley MacLaine,** $3,225,585, Radio City Music Hall, New York, Oct. 8–12, 14–15, 30–31, Nov. 1.

Source: © 1992 by *Amusement Business* magazine. Reprinted by permission.

Top 10 Classical Albums, 1992

1. **In Concert,** Jose Carreras, Placido Domingo, Luciano Pavarotti (Mehta) (London)
2. **Baroque Duet,** Kathleen Battle, Wynton Marsalis (Sony Classical)
3. **Pieces of Africa,** Kronos Quartet (Nonesuch)
4. **The Bach Album,** Kathleen Battle, Itzhak Perlman (DG)
5. **McCartney/Davis: Liverpool Oratorio,** Kiri Te Kanawa, Jerry Hadley, Royal Liverpool Philharmonic (Davis) (EMI Classics)
6. **Gorecki: Symphony No. 3,** Dawn Upshaw, London Sinfonietta (Zinman) (Nonesuch)
7. **Mozart: Arias,** Cecilia Bartoli (London)
8. **Favorite Arias by World's Favorite,** Jose Carreras, Placido Domingo, Luciano Pavarotti (Sony Classical)
9. **Corigliano: Symphony No. 1,** Chicago Symphony (Barenboim) (Erato)
10. **Rossini Heroines,** Cecilia Bartoli (London)

Source: © 1992 BPI Communications. Used with permission from *Billboard.*

Artists of the Year, 1992

Single of the Year: End of the Road (from Boomerang), Boyz II Men
Album of the Year: Ropin' the Wind, Garth Brooks
Female Artist of the Year: Mariah Carey
Male Artist of the Year: Garth Brooks
Group of the Year: Guns N' Roses
New Artist of the Year: Kris Kross
Country Artist of the Year: Garth Brooks
Rhythm & Blues Artist of the Year: Jodeci
Adult Contemporary Artist ofthe Year: Richard Marx
Jazz Artist of the Year: Shirley Horn
Classical Artist of the Year: Carreras, Domingo & Pavarotti

Source: © 1992 BPI Communications. Used with permission from *Billboard.*

Top 10 Pop Single Recordings, 1992

1. **End of the Road (From Boomerang),** Boyz II Men (Biv 10)
2. **Baby Got Back,** Sir Mix-A-Lot (Def American)
3. **Jump,** Kris Kross (Ruffhouse)
4. **Save the Best for Last,** Vanessa Williams (Wing)
5. **Baby-Baby-Baby,** TLC (LaFace)
6. **Tears in Heaven,** Eric Clapton (Reprise)
7. **My Lovin' (You're Never Gonna Get It),** En Vogue (Atco EastWest)
8. **Under the Bridge,** Red Hot Chili Peppers (Warner Bros.)
9. **All 4 Love,** Color Me Badd (Giant)
10. **Just Another Day,** Jon Secada (SBK)

Source: © 1992 BPI Communications. Used with permission from *Billboard*/SoundScan, Inc./Broadcast Data Systems.

Manufacturers' Dollar[1] Shipments of Recordings (in millions)

	1989	1990	1991	1992
Singles	116.4	94.4	63.9	66.4
LP's/EP's	220.3	86.5	29.4	13.5
CD's	2,587.7	3,451.6	4,337.7	5,326.5
Cassettes	3,345.8	3,472.4	3,019.6	3,116.3
Cassette singles	194.6	257.9	230.4	298.8
CD singles	–.7	6.0	35.1	45.1
Music videos	115.4	172.3	118.1	157.4

1. List price value. *Source:* Recording Industry Association of America, Inc.

Top 10 Country Single Recordings, 1992

1. **I Saw the Light,** Wynonna (Curb/MCA)
2. **Achy Breaky Heart,** Billy Ray Cyrus (Mercury)
3. **Is There Life Out There,** Reba McIntire (MCA)
4. **What She's Doing Now,** Garth Brooks (Liberty)
5. **We Tell Ourselves,** Clint Black (RCA)
6. **Dallas,** Alan Jackson (Arista)
7. **Boot Scootin' Boogie,** Brooks & Dunn (Arista)
8. **I Still Believe in You,** Vince Gill (MCA)
9. **Neon Moon,** Brooks & Dunn (Arista)
10. **Some Girls Do,** Sawyer Brown (Curb)

Source: © 1992 BPI Communications, Inc. Used with permission from *Billboard*/SoundScan, Inc.

Top 10 Pop Albums, 1992

1. **Ropin' the Wind,** Garth Brooks (Liberty)
2. **Dangerous,** Michael Jackson (Epic)
3. **Nevermind,** Nirvana (DGC)
4. **Some Gave All,** Billy Ray Cyrus (Mercury)
5. **Achtung Baby,** U2 (Island)
6. **No Fences,** Garth Brooks (Liberty)
7. **Metallica,** Metallica (Elektra)
8. **Time, Love and Tenderness,** Michael Bolton (Columbia)
9. **Too Legit to Quit,** Hammer (Capitol)
10. **Totally Krossed Out,** Kris Kross (Ruffhouse)

Source: © 1992 BPI Communications, Inc. Used with permission from *Billboard*/SoundScan, Inc.

Top 10 Rhythm & Blues Single Recordings, 1992

1. **Come & Talk to Me,** Jodeci (Uptown)
2. **Honey Love,** R. Kelly & Public Announcement (Jive)
3. **You Remind Me (From Strictly Business),** Mary J. Blige (Uptown)
4. **End of the Road (From Boomerang),** Boyz II Men (Biv 10)
5. **Tell Me What You Want Me to Do,** Tevin Campbell (Qwest)
6. **Breakin' My Heart (Pretty Brown Eyes),** Mint Condition (Perspective)
7. **Baby-Baby-Baby,** TLC (LaFace)
8. **Somebody Loves You Baby (You Know Who It Is),** Patti LaBelle (MCA)
9. **Tennessee,** Arrested Development (Chrysalis)
10. **Stay,** Jodeci (Uptown)

Source: © 1992 BPI Communications, Inc. Used with permission from *Billboard*/SoundScan, Inc./Broadcast Data Systems.

Top 15 Regularly Scheduled Network Programs, 1992–93[1]

Rank	Program name (network)	Total percent of TV households
1.	60 Minutes (CBS)	21.6
2.	Roseanne (ABC)	20.8
3.	Home Improvement (ABC)	19.2
4.	Murphy Brown (CBS)	17.9
5.	Murder, She Wrote (CBS)	17.6
6.	Coach (ABC)	17.5
7.	NFL Monday Night Football (ABC)	16.8
8.	CBS Sunday Movie	16.1
8.	Cheers (NBC)	16.1
10.	Full House (ABC)	15.8
11.	Northern Exposure (CBS)	15.2
12.	Rescue: 911 (CBS)	15.1
13.	20/20 (ABC)	14.9
14.	CBS Tuesday Movie	14.7
14.	Love & War (CBS)	14.7
Total U.S. TV households 93,100,000		

1. Sept. 21, 1992, through April 18, 1993. NOTE: Percentages are calculated from average audience viewings, 5 minutes or longer and 2 or more telecasts. *Source:* Nielsen Media Research. Copyright 1993, Nielsen Media Research.

Top 15 Syndicated TV Programs 1992–93 Season

Rank	Program	Rating (% U.S.)[1]
1.	Wheel of Fortune	14.0
2.	Star Trek	12.3
3.	Jeopardy	12.1
4.	Star Trek: Deep Space Nine	11.1
5.	Oprah Winfrey Show	10.4
6.	Entertainment Tonight	8.7
7.	Magic II	8.2
8.	Married With Children	7.8
9.	Wheel of Fortune, Weekend	7.7
10.	Current Affair	7.5
10.	Inside Edition	7.5
12.	Tri Star Showcase III	7.3
13.	National Geographic on Assignment	7.1
14.	Buena Vista I	7.0
15.	Warner Brothers Volume 29	6.9

1. 8/31/92–4/11/93. *Source:* Nielsen Syndication Service National TV Ratings. Copyright 1993, Nielsen Media Research.

Top Sports Shows 1992–93[1]

Rank	Program name (network)	Rating (% of TV households)
1.	Super Bowl XXVII Game (NBC)	45.1
2.	NFC Championship Game (CBS)	33.3
3.	AFC Championship Game (NBC)	25.5
4.	NFC Playoff Game (CBS)	25.0
5.	AFC Playoff Game (NBC)	23.1
6.	NFC Playoff Game (CBS)	22.7
6.	World Series Game Toronto at Atlanta (CBS)	22.7
8.	NFC Wild Card Game (CBS)	22.5
9.	NFL Monday Night Football (ABC)	22.3
10.	NCAA Basketball Championship (CBS)	22.2

1. Sept. 21, 1992, through April 18, 1993. *Source:* Nielsen Media Research. Copyright 1993, Nielsen Media Research.

Top Specials 1992–93[1]

Rank	Program name (network)	Rating (% of TV households)
1.	Last Call: A Cheers Celebration (NBC)	39.6
2.	Michael Jackson Talks with Oprah (ABC)	39.3
3.	65th Academy Awards (ABC)	31.2
4.	Jackson's American Dream (ABC)	23.9
5.	CBS Movie—Queen, part 3	22.8

1. Sept. 21, 1992, through April 18, 1993. *Source:* Nielsen Media Research. Copyright 1993, Nielsen Media Research.

Persons Viewing Prime Time[1] (in millions)

	Total persons
Monday	101.5
Tuesday	96.7
Wednesday	98.8
Thursday	96.5
Friday	88.0
Saturday	88.4
Sunday	109.6
Total average	**97.7**

1. Average minute audiences Nov. 1992. NOTE: Prime time is 8–11 p.m. (EST) except Sun. 7–11 pm. *Source:* Nielsen Media Research. Copyright 1993, Nielsen Media Research.

Top Rated Movies 1992–93[1]

Rank	Program name (network)	Rating (% of TV households)
1.	Queen, Part 1 (CBS)	24.7
2.	Queen, Part 2 (CBS)	24.1
3.	Queen, Part 3 (CBS)	22.8
4.	The Jacksons: American Dream (ABC)	21.1
5.	Man with Three Wives (CBS)	20.7
6.	Hallmark: Skylark (CBS)	19.9
7.	Family of Strangers (CBS)	19.8
8.	Men Don't Tell (CBS)	19.7
9.	The Amy Fisher Story (ABC)	19.5
10.	Amy Fisher: My Story (NBC)	19.1

1. Sept. 21, 1992, through June 20, 1993. *Source:* Nielsen Media Research. Copyright 1993, Nielsen Media Research.

Average Hours of Household TV Usage

(In hours and minutes per day)

	Yearly average	February	July
1983–84	7 h 08 min	7 h 38 min	6 h 26 min
1984–85	7 h 07 min	7 h 49 min	6 h 34 min
1985–86	7 h 10 min	7 h 48 min	6 h 37 min
1986–87	7 h 05 min	7 h 35 min	6 h 32 min
1987–88	6 h 55 min	7 h 38 min	6 h 31 min
1988–89	7 h 02 min	7 h 32 min	6 h 27 min
1989–90	6 h 55 min	7 h 16 min	6 h 24 min
1990–91	6 h 56 min	7 h 30 min	6 h 26 min
1991–92	7 h 04 min	7 h 32 min	6 h 39 min

Source: Nielsen Media Research, copyright 1993, Nielsen Media Research.

Weekly TV Viewing by Age

(in hours and minutes)

	Time per week	
	Nov. 1992	Nov. 1991
Women 18–24 years old	28 h 54 min	28 h 54 min
Women 25–54	31 h 05 min	32 h 05 min
Women 55 and over	44 h 11 min	43 h 31 min
Men 18–24	23 h 31 min	23 h 01 min
Men 25–54	28 h 44 min	28 h 04 min
Men 55 and over	38 h 28 min	39 h 49 min
Female Teens	21 h 00 min	22 h 11 min
Male Teens	22 h 39 min	22 h 41 min
Children 6–11	21 h 20 min	21 h 10 min
Children 2–5	25 h 32 min	26 h 23 min

Source: Nielsen Media Research, copyright 1993, Nielsen Media Research.

Television Network Addresses

American Broadcasting Companies (ABC)
77 W. 66th Street
New York, N.Y. 10023
Cable News Network (CNN)
100 International Blvd., ICNN Center
Atlanta, Ga. 30348
Canadian Broadcasting Corporation (CBC)
1500 Bronson Avenue
Ottawa, Ontario, Canada K1G 3J5
Columbia Broadcasting System (CBS)
51 W. 52nd Street
New York, N.Y. 10019
Fox Television
10201 W. Pico Blvd.
Los Angeles, Calif. 90064
National Broadcasting Company (NBC)
30 Rockefeller Plaza
New York, N.Y. 10020
Public Broadcasting Service (PBS)
1320 Braddock Place
Alexandra, Va. 22314
Turner Network Television (TNT)
100 International Blvd., ICNN Center
Atlanta, Ga. 30348
Westinghouse Broadcasting (Group W)
250 Harbor Dr.
Stamford, Conn. 06902

Television Set Ownership

(Nielsen estimate as of Jan. 1, 1993)

Homes with	Number	Percent
Color TV sets	91,238,000	98.0
B&W only	1,862,000	02.0
2 or more sets	59,584,000	64.0
One set	33,516,000	36.0
Cable[1]	57,200,340	61.0
Total TV households	**93,100,000**	**98.0**

1. May 1993. *Source:* Nielsen Media Research, copyright 1993, Nielsen Media Research.

Audience Composition by Selected Program Type[1]

(Average Minute Audience)

	General drama	Suspense and mystery drama	Situation comedy	Informational[2] 6-7 p.m.	Feature films	All regular network programs 7–11 p.m.
Women (18 and over)	7,300,000	8,080,000	8,170,000	7,220,000	9,730,000	8,230,000
Men (18 and over)	4,420,000	6,240,000	5,420,000	5,650,000	6,050,000	6,010,000
Teens (12–17)	1,120,000	680,000	1,510,000	390,000	1,110,000	1,140,000
Children (2–11)	1,280,000	1,160,000	2,510,000	650,000	1,410,000	1,650,000
Total persons (2+)	**14,120,000**	**16,160,000**	**17,610,000**	**13,910,000**	**18,300,000**	**17,040,000**

1. All figures are estimated for the period Nov. 1992. 2. Multiweekly viewing. *Source:* Nielsen Media Research, copyright 1993, Nielsen Media Research.

Hours of TV Usage Per Week by Household Income

	Under $30,000	$30,000+	$40,000+	$50,000+	$60,000+
Nov. 1990	n.a.	48 h 03 min	47 h 35 min	47 h 24 min	46 h 12 min
Nov. 1991	52 h 57 min	52 h 25 min	50 h 04 min (includes $50,000+)		47 h 13 min
Nov. 1992	53 h 35 min	52 h 05 min	50 h 24 min (includes ($50,000+)		47 h 13 min

Source: Nielsen Media Research, copyright 1993, Nielsen Media Research. NOTE: n.a. = not available.

Source of Household Viewing—Prime Time

Pay Cable, Basic Cable, and Non-Cable Households

(Mon.-Sun. 8–11 pm)

	Nov. 1992			Nov. 1991			Nov. 1990		
	Pay cable	Basic cable	Non-cable	Pay cable	Basic cable	Non-cable	Pay cable	Basic cable	Non-cable
% TV Usage	68.7	62.6	55.5	69.0	61.6	56.8	66.3	59.6	54.5
Pay Cable	10.0	—	—	9.5	—	—	9.9	—	—
Cable-originated programming	20.5	20.3	—	20.5	19.5	—	15.9	15.5	—
Other-on-air stations	7.1	7.5	11.1	6.9	7.1	10.9	14.1	14.0	17.5
Network affiliated stations	43.8	42.7	48.2	44.5	41.5	49.9	37.0	35.8	42.0
Network share	(64)	(68)	(87)	(64)	(67)	(88)	(56)	(60)	(75)

Source: Nielsen Media Research, copyright 1993, Nielsen Media Research.

Major U.S. Fairs and Expositions

1853 Crystal Palace Exposition, New York City: modeled on similar fair held in London.

1876 Centennial Exposition, Philadelphia: celebrating 100th year of independence.

1893 World's Columbian Exposition, Chicago: commemorating 400th anniversary of Columbus' voyage to America.

1894 Midwinter International Exposition, San Francisco: promoting business revival after Depression of 1893.

1898 Trans-Mississippi and International Exposition, Omaha, Neb.: exhibiting products, resources, industries, and civilization of states and territories west of the Mississippi River.

1901 Pan-American Exposition, Buffalo, N.Y.: promoting social and commercial interest of Western Hemisphere nations.

1904 Louisiana Purchase Exposition, St. Louis: marking 100th anniversary of major land acquisition from France and opening up of the West.

1905 Lewis and Clark Centennial Exposition, Portland, Ore.: commemorating 100th anniversary of exploration of a land route to the Pacific.

1907 Jamestown Tercentennial Exposition, Hampton Roads, Va.: marking 300th anniversary of first permanent English settlement in America.

1909 Alaska-Yukon-Pacific Exposition, Seattle: celebrating growth of the Puget Sound area.

1915–16 Panama-Pacific International Exposition, San Francisco: celebrating opening of the Panama Canal.

1915–16 Panama-California Exposition, San Diego: promoting resources and opportunities for development and commerce of the Western states.

1926 Sesquicentennial Exposition, Philadelphia: marking 150th year of independence.

1933–34 Century of Progress International Exposition, Chicago: celebrating 100th anniversary of incorporation of Chicago as a city.

1935 California Pacific International Exposition, San Diego: marking 400 years of progress since the first Spaniard landed on the West Coast.

1939–40 New York World's Fair, New York City: "The World of Tomorrow," symbolized by Trylon and Perisphere. Officially commemorating 150th anniversary of inauguration of George Washington as President in New York.

1939–1940 Golden Gate International Exposition, Treasure Island, San Francisco: celebrating new Golden Gate Bridge and Oakland Bay Bridge.

1962 The Century 21 Exposition, Seattle: "Man in the Space Age," symbolized by 600-foot steel space needle.

1964–65 New York World's Fair, New York City: "Peace Through Understanding."

1974 Expo '74, Spokane: "Tomorrow's Fresh, New Environment."

1982 World's Fair, Knoxville, Tenn.: "Energy Turns the World," symbolized by the bronze-globed Sunsphere.

1984 Louisiana World Exposition, New Orleans: "The World of Rivers."

Longest Broadway Runs[1]

1.	A Chorus Line (M) (1975–90)	6,137
2.	Oh, Calcutta (M) (1976–89)	5,959
3.	Cats (M) (1982–)	4,517
4.	42nd Street (M) (1980–89)	3,486
5.	Grease (M) (1972–80)	3,388
6.	Fiddler on the Roof (1964–72)	3,242
7.	Life with Father (1939–47)	3,224
8.	Tobacco Road (1933–41)	3,182
9.	Hello, Dolly! (M) (1964–71)	2,844
10.	My Fair Lady (M) (1956–62)	2,717
11.	Les Miserables (M) (1987–)	2,604
12.	Annie (M) (1977–83)	2,377
13.	Oklahoma (M) (1943–48)	2,377
14.	Man of La Mancha (M) (1965–71)	2,328
15.	Abie's Irish Rose (1922–27)	2,327
16.	Phantom of the Opera (1988–)	2,303
17.	Pippin (M) (1971–77)	1,994
18.	South Pacific (M) (1949–54)	1,925
19.	Magic Show (M) (1974–78)	1,920
20.	Deathtrap (1978–82)	1,792
21.	Gemini (1977–81)	1,788
22.	Harvey (1944–49)	1,775
23.	Dancin' (M) (1978–82)	1,774
24.	Cage aux Folles (M) (1983–87)	1,761
25.	Hair (M) (1968–72)	1,750

1. As of Aug. 1, 1993. M = musical. Years are those of opening and closing.

Motion Picture Revenues

All-Time Top Money Makers[1]

1.	E.T. The Extra-Terrestrial (Universal, 1982)	$228,618,939
2.	Star Wars (20th Century-Fox, 1977)	193,777,000
3.	Return of the Jedi (20th Century-Fox, 1983)	169,193,000
4.	Batman (Warner Brothers, 1989)	150,500,000
5.	The Empire Strikes Back (20th Century-Fox, 1980)	141,672,000
6.	Home Alone (20th Century-Fox, 1990)	140,099,000
7.	Ghostbusters (Columbia, 1984)	132,720,000
8.	Jaws (Universal, 1975)	129,549,325
9.	Raiders of the Lost Ark (Paramount, 1981)	115,598,000
10.	Indiana Jones and the Last Crusade (Paramount, 1989)	115,500,000
11.	Terminator 2 (TriStar, 1991)	112,500,000
12.	Indiana Jones and the Temple of Doom (Paramount, 1984)	109,000,000
13.	Beverly Hills Cop (Paramount, 1984)	108,000,000
14.	Back to the Future (Universal, 1985)	105,496,267
15.	Home Alone 2 (20th Century–Fox)	102,000,000
16.	Batman Returns (Warner Brothers, 1992)	100,100,000
17.	Ghost (Paramount, 1990)	98,200,000
18.	Grease (Paramount, 1978)	96,300,000
19.	Tootsie (Columbia, 1982)	94,910,000
20.	The Exorcist (Warner Brothers, 1973)	89,000,000
21.	Rain Man (United Artists, 1988)	86,813,000
22.	The Godfather (Paramount, 1972)	86,275,000
23.	Robin Hood: Prince of Thieves (Warner Brothers, 1991)	86,000,000
24.	Superman (Warner Brothers, 1978)	82,800,000
25.	Close Encounters of the Third Kind (Columbia, 1977)	82,750,000

Top Rentals 1992[2]

1.	Home Alone 2: Lost in New York (20th Century–Fox)	$102,000,000
2.	Batman Returns (Warner Brothers)	100,100,000
3.	Lethal Weapon 3 (Warner Brothers)	80,000,000
4.	Sister Act (Buena Vista)	62,420,000
5.	Aladdin (Buena Vista)	60,000,000
6.	Wayne's World (Paramount)	54,000,000
7.	A League of Their Own (Columbia)	53,100,000
8.	Basic Instinct (TriStar)	53,000,000
9.	The Bodyguard (Warner Brothers)	52,900,000
10.	A Few Good Men (Columbia)	52,000,000
11.	Bram Stoker's Dracula (Columbia)	47,200,000
12.	The Hand That Rocks the Cradle (Buena Vista)	39,334,000
13.	Patriot Games (Paramount)	37,500,000
14.	Fried Green Tomatoes (Universal)	37,402,827
15.	Unforgiven (Warner Brothers)	36,000,000
16.	White Men Can't Jump (20th Century–Fox)	34,115,000
17.	Boomerang (Paramount)	34,000,000
18.	Under Siege (Warner Brothers)	33,000,000
19.	Alien 3 (20th Century–Fox)	31,762,000
20.	The Last of the Mohicans (20th Century–Fox)	31,491,000
21.	Death Becomes Her (Universal)	30,433,483
22.	Beauty and the Beast (continuing run)	30,415,000
23.	Housesitter (Universal)	30,390,622
24.	Far and Away (Universal)	28,910,698
25.	Honey, I Blew Up the Kid (Buena Vista)	27,417,000

NOTE: United States and Canada only. 1. Figures are not to be confused with gross box-office receipts from sale of tickets. 2. Figures are total rentals collected by film distributors as of Dec. 31, 1992. *Source:* Reprinted with permission from *Variety Inc.*

Miss America Winners

1921 Margaret Gorman, Washington, D.C.
1922-23 Mary Campbell, Columbus, Ohio
1924 Ruth Malcolmson, Philadelphia, Pa.
1925 Fay Lamphier, Oakland, Calif.
1926 Norma Smallwood, Tulsa, Okla.
1927 Lois Delaner, Joliet, Ill.
1933 Marion Bergeron, West Haven, Conn.
1935 Henrietta Leaver, Pittsburgh, Pa.
1936 Rose Coyle, Philadelphia, Pa.
1937 Bette Cooper, Bertrand Island, N.J.
1938 Marilyn Meseke, Marion, Ohio
1939 Patricia Donnelly, Detroit, Mich.
1940 Frances Marie Burke, Philadelphia, Pa.
1941 Rosemary LaPlanche, Los Angeles, Calif.
1942 JoCaroll Dennison, Tyler, Texas
1943 Jean Bartel, Los Angeles, Calif.
1944 Venus Ramey, Washington, D.C.
1945 Bess Myerson, New York, N.Y.
1946 Marilyn Buferd, Los Angeles, Calif.
1947 Barbara Walker, Memphis, Tenn.
1948 BeBe Shopp, Hopkins, Minn.
1949 Jacque Mercer, Litchfield, Ariz.
1951 Yolande Betbeze, Mobile, Ala.
1952 Coleen Kay Hutchins, Salt Lake City, Utah
1953 Neva Jane Langley, Macon, Ga.
1954 Evelyn Margaret Ay, Ephrata, Pa.
1955 Lee Meriwether, San Francisco, Calif.
1956 Sharon Ritchie, Denver, Colo.
1957 Marian McKnight, Manning, S.C.
1958 Marilyn Van Derbur, Denver, Colo.
1959 Mary Ann Mobley, Brandon, Miss.
1960 Lynda Lee Mead, Natchez, Miss.
1961 Nancy Fleming, Montague, Mich.
1962 Maria Fletcher, Asheville, N.C.
1963 Jacquelyn Mayer, Sandusky, Ohio
1964 Donna Axum, El Dorado, Ark.
1965 Vonda Kay Van Dyke, Phoenix, Ariz.
1966 Deborah Irene Bryant, Overland Park, Kan.
1967 Jane Anne Jayroe, Laverne, Okla.
1968 Debra Dene Barnes, Moran, Kan.
1969 Judith Anne Ford, Belvidere, Ill.
1970 Pamela Anne Eldred, Birmingham, Mich.
1971 Phyllis Ann George, Denton, Texas
1972 Laurie Lea Schaefer, Columbus, Ohio
1973 Terry Anne Meeuwsen, DePere, Wis.
1974 Rebecca Ann King, Denver, Colo.
1975 Shirley Cothran, Fort Worth, Texas
1976 Tawney Elaine Godin, Yonkers, N.Y.
1977 Dorothy Kathleen Benham, Edina, Minn.
1978 Susan Perkins, Columbus, Ohio
1979 Kylene Baker, Galax, Va.
1980 Cheryl Prewitt, Ackerman, Miss.
1981 Susan Powell, Elk City, Okla.
1982 Elizabeth Ward, Russellville, Ark.
1983 Debra Maffett, Anaheim, Calif.
1984 Vanessa Williams, Milwood, N.Y.[1]
Suzette Charles, Mays Landing, N.J.
1985 Sharlene Wells, Salt Lake City, Utah
1986 Susan Akin, Meridian, Miss.
1987 Kellye Cash, Memphis, Tenn.
1988 Kaye Lani Rae Rafko, Toledo, Ohio
1989 Gretchen Elizabeth Carlson, Anoka, Minn.
1990 Debbye Turner, Mexico, Mo.
1991 Marjorie Judith Vincent, Oak Park, Ill.
1992 Carolyn Suzanne Sapp
1993 Leanza Cornett
1994 (*See* Current Events)

1. Resigned July 23, 1984.

U.S. Opera Companies

(Budgets $200,000 and over)

Arizona Opera Company (Tucson), Glynn Ross, Gen. Dir.
Aspen Music Festival (Colo.), Robert Hirth, President & CEO
Baltimore Opera Company (Md.), Michael Harrison, Gen. Dir.
Central City Opera House Association (Colo.), Daniel R. Rule, Gen. Mgr.
Cincinnati Opera Association (Ohio), James de Blasis, Art. Dir.
Civic Light Opera (Pittsburgh), Charles Gray, Exec. Dir. & Gen. Mgr.
Cleveland Opera (Ohio), David Bamberger, Gen. Dir.
Dallas Opera, The (Texas), Plato S. Karayanis, Gen. Dir.
Florentine Opera Company (Milwaukee), Dennis W. Hanthorne, Gen. Dir.
Greater Miami Opera Association (Fla.), Robert M. Heuer, Gen. Dir.
Gimmerglass Opera (Cooperstown, N.Y.), Paul Kellogg, Gen. Dir.
Goodspeed Opera House (East Haddan, Conn.), Michael Price, Exec. Dir.
Houston Grand Opera Association (Texas), R. David Gockley, Gen. Dir.
Kentucky Opera (Louisville), Thomson Smillie, Gen. Dir.
Long Beach Civic Light Opera (Calif.), Barry Brown, Producer & CEO
Los Angeles Music Center Opera (Calif.), Peter Hemmings, Gen. Dir.
Lyric Opera of Chicago (Ill.), Ardis Krainik, Gen. Dir.
Lyric Opera of Dallas, The (Texas), John Burrows, Art. Dir.
Lyric Opera of Kansas City (Mo.), Russell Patterson, Gen. & Art. Dir.
Metro Lyric Opera, (Allenhurst, N.J.), Era M. Tognoli, Gen. & Art. Dir.
Metropolitan Opera Association, James Levine, Art. Dir.
Michigan Opera Theatre (Detroit), David di Chiera, Gen. Dir.
Minnesota Opera, The (Minneapolis), Kevin Smith, President & Gen. Dir.
New York City Opera (N.Y.), Christopher Keene, Gen. Dir.
Ohio Light Opera (Wooster), James Stuart, Art. Dir.
Opera Colorado (Denver), Nathaniel Merrill Harrison, President & Gen. Dir.
Opera Company of Philadelphia (Pa.), Robert B. Driver, Gen. Dir.
Opera Pacific (Costa Mesa, Calif.), David Di Chiera, Gen. Dir.
Opera Theatre of St. Louis (Mo.), Charles MacKay, Gen. Dir.
Pittsburgh Opera, Inc. (Pa.), Tito Capobianco, Gen. Dir.
Portland Opera Association (Ore.), Robert Bailey, Gen. Dir.
San Diego Civic Light Opera Association (Calif.), C.E. Franks, Exec. Dir.
San Diego Opera (Calif.), Ian D. Campbell, Gen. Dir.
San Jose Civic Light Opera (Calif.), Dianna Schuster, Art. Dir.
San Francisco Opera (Calif.), Lofti Mansouri, Gen. Dir.
San Francisco Opera Center (Calif.), Christine Bullin, Dir.
Santa Fe Opera (N.M.), John Crosby, Gen. Dir.
Seattle Opera Association (Wash.), Speight Jenkins, Gen. Dir.
Virginia Opera (Norfolk), Peter Mark, Gen. Dir.
Utah Opera Company (Salt Lake City), Anne Ewers, Gen. Dir.
Washington Opera, The (D.C.), Martin Feinstein, Gen. Dir.

Major U.S. Dance Companies

(Figure in parentheses is year of founding)

Alvin Ailey American Dance Theatre (1958): Dir.: Judith Jamison
American Ballet Theatre (1940): Art Dir.: Kevin McKenzie
Ballet West (1968[1]): Art. Dir.: John Hart
Boston Ballet (1964): Art. Dir.: Bruce Marks
Dance Theatre of Harlem (1968): Art. Dir.: Arthur Mitchell
Feld Ballet NY (1974): Dir.: Eliot Feld
Houston Ballet (1968): Art. Dir.: Ben Stevenson
Joffrey Ballet (1954): Art. Dir.: Gerald Arpino
Jose Limon Dance Company (1946): Art. Dir.: Carla Maxwell
Lar Lubovitch Dance Company (1968): Dir.: Lar Lubovitch
Laura Dean Dancers and Musicians (1974): Dir.: Laura Dean
Lucinda Childs Dance Company (1973): Dir.: Lucinda Childs
Martha Graham Dance Company (1927): Gen. Dir.: Ron Protas
Merce Cunningham Dance Company (1952): Dir.: Merce Cunningham
Miami City Ballet (1986): Art. Dir.: Edward Villella
New York City Ballet (1948): Peter Martins, Ballet Master in Chief
Nikolais Dance Theatre (1948): Art. Dir.: Murray Louis
Pacific Northwest Ballet (1972): Art. Dirs.: Kent Stowell and Francia Russell
Pennsylvania Ballet (1963): Art. Dir.: Christopher d'Amboise
Pilobolus Dance Theatre (1971): Manager: Susan Mandler
Pittsburgh Ballet Theater (1970): Art. Dir.: Patricia Wilde
San Francisco Ballet (1933): Art. Dir.: Helgi Tomasson
Washington Ballet (1962): Dir.: Mary Day

1. Prior company founded 1963, name changed to Ballet West in 1968.

Holocaust Museum Opens

In the four-month period from its opening in April 1993, approximately a half million people have visited the United States Holocaust Memorial Museum in Washington, D.C. The museum, which was chartered by a unanimous act of Congress in 1980, is dedicated to presenting the history of the persecution and murder of six million Jews and millions of other victims of Nazi tyranny from 1933 to 1945.

It is located near the national Mall in a neighborhood of museums and is open free to the public daily from 10 a.m. to 5:30 p.m.

U.S. STATES

States and Territories

Sources for state populations, populations under 18, over 65, median age, largest cities and counties, and population by race are latest data provided by the U.S. Census Bureau. NOTE: Persons of Hispanic origin can be of any race. The population counts set forth herein by the Census Bureau are subject to possible correction for undercount or overcount. They include Armed Forces residing in each state. 1992 State populations are for July 1, 1992. Largest cities include incorporated places only, as defined by the U.S. Census Bureau. They do not include adjacent or suburban areas as do the Metropolitan Statistical Areas found in the "U.S. Statistics" section of this Almanac. For secession and readmission dates of the former Confederate states, *see* Index. For lists of Governors, Senators, and Representatives, *see* Index. For additional state information, *see* the sections on "Business and the Economy," "Elections," "Taxes," and "U.S. Statistics."

ALABAMA

Capital: Montgomery
Governor: Jim E. Folsom, Jr., R (to Jan. 1995)
Lieut. Governor: (Vacant)
Secy. of State: Billy Joe Camp, D (to Jan. 1995)
Treasurer: George C. Wallace, Jr., D (to Jan. 1995)
Atty. General: James H. Evans, D (to Jan. 1995)
Auditor: Terry Ellis, D (to Jan. 1995)
Organized as territory: March 3, 1817
Entered Union & (rank): Dec. 14, 1819 (22)
Present constitution adopted: 1901
Motto: *Audemus jura nostra defendere* (We dare defend our rights)
STATE SYMBOLS: flower, Camellia (1959); **bird,** Yellowhammer (1927); **song,** "Alabama" (1931); **tree,** Southern pine (longleaf) (1949); **salt water fish,** Tarpon (1955); **fresh water fish,** Largemouth bass (1975); **horse,** Racking horse; **mineral,** Hematite (1967); **rock,** Marble (1969); **game bird,** Wild turkey (1980); **dance,** Square dance (1981); **nut,** Pecan (1982); **fossil,** species *Basilosaurus Cetoides* (1984).
Nickname: Yellowhammer State
Origin of name: May come from Choctaw meaning "thicket-clearers" or "vegetation-gatherers"
10 largest cities (1990 census): Birmingham, 265,968; Mobile, 196,278; Montgomery, 187,106; Huntsville, 159,789; Tuscaloosa, 77,759; Dothan, 53,589; Decatur, 48,761; Gadsden, 42,523; Hoover, 39,788; Florence, 36,426
Land area & (rank): 50,750 sq mi. (131,443 sq km) (28)
Geographic center: In Chilton Co., 12 mi. SW of Clanton
Number of counties: 67
Largest county (1990 census): Jefferson, 651,525
State forests: 21 (48,000 ac.)
State parks: 22 (45,614 ac.)
1992 resident population est.: 4,136,000
1990 census population, sex, & (rank): 4,040,587 (22). **Male:** 1,936,162; **Female:** 2,104,425. **White:** 2,975,797 (73.6%); **Black:** 1,020,705 (25.3%); **American Indian, Eskimo, or Aleut:** 16,506 (0.4%); **Asian or Pacific Islander:** 21,797 (0.5%); **Other race:** 5,782 (0.1%); **Hispanic:** 24,629 (0.6%). **1990 percent population under 18:** 26.2; **65 and over:** 12.9; **median age:** 33.0.

Spanish explorers are believed to have arrived at Mobile Bay in 1519, and the territory was visited in 1540 by the explorer Hernando de Soto. The first permanent European settlement in Alabama was founded by the French at Fort Louis de la Mobile in 1702. The British gained control of the area in 1763 by the Treaty of Paris, but had to cede almost all the Alabama region to the U.S. after the American Revolution. The Confederacy was founded at Montgomery in February 1861 and, for a time, the city was the Confederate capital.

During the last part of the 19th century, the economy of the state slowly improved. At Tuskegee Institute, founded in 1881 by Booker T. Washington, Dr. George Washington Carver carried out his famous agricultural research.

In the 1950s and '60s, Alabama was the site of such landmark civil-rights actions as the bus boycott in Montgomery (1955–56) and the "Freedom March" from Selma to Montgomery (1965).

Today paper, chemicals, rubber and plastics, apparel and textiles, and primary metals comprise the leading industries of Alabama. Continuing as a major manufacturer of coal, iron, and steel, Birmingham is also noted for its world-renowned medical center, especially for heart surgery. The state ranks high in the production of poultry, soybeans, milk, vegetables, livestock, wheat, cattle, cotton, peanuts, fruits, hogs, and corn.

Points of interest include the Space and Rocket Center at Huntsville, the White House of the Confederacy, the restored state Capitol, and Shakespeare Festival Theater Complex in Montgomery, and Russell Cave near Bridgeport, and the Gulf Coast area.

Famous natives and residents: Hank Aaron, baseball player; Ralph Abernathy, civil rights activist; Tallulah Bankhead, actress; Hugo L. Black, jurist; George Washington Carver, educator, agricultural chemist; Nat "King" Cole, entertainer; Marva Collins, educator; Kenneth Gibson, first Black mayor of major eastern city (Newark); Lionel Hampton, jazz musician; W.C. Handy, composer; Kate Jackson, actress; Helen Keller, author and educator Coretta Scott King, civil rights leader; Harper Lee, writer; Joe Louis, boxer; Willie Mays, baseball player; Jim Nabors, actor; Jesse Owens, athlete; Rosa Parks, civil rights activist; Wayne Rogers, actor; Tuscaloosa, Choctaw chief; George Wallace, ex-governor; William Weatherford (Red Eagle), Creek leader

ALASKA

Capital: Juneau
Governor: Walter J. Hickel, Ind-R[1] (to Dec. 1994)
Lieut. Governor: John B. "Jack" Coghill, Ind.-R[1] (to Dec. 1994)
Commissioner of Administration: Millett Keller, R (to Dec. 1994)
Atty. General: Charles E. Cole,R (to Dec. 1994)
Organized as territory: 1912
Entered Union & (rank): Jan. 3, 1959 (49)
Constitution ratified: April 24, 1956
Motto: North to the Future
STATE SYMBOLS: flower, Forget-me-not (1949); **tree,** Sitka spruce (1962); **bird,** Willow ptarmigan (1955); **fish,** King salmon (1962); **song,** "Alaska's Flag" (1955); **gem,** Jade (1968); **marine mammal,** Bowhead Whale (1983); **fossil,** Woolly Mammoth (1986); **mineral,** Gold (1968); **sport,** Dog Mushing (1972)

Nickname: The state is commonly called "The Last Frontier" or "Land of the Midnight Sun"
Origin of name: Corruption of Aleut word meaning "great land" or "that which the sea breaks against"
10 largest cities: Anchorage, 226,338; Fairbanks, 30,843; Juneau, 26,751; Sitka, 8,588; Ketchikan, 8,263; Kodiak, 6,365; Kenai, 6,327
Land area & (rank): 570,374 sq mi. (1,477,267 sq km) (1)
Geographic center: 60 mi. NW of Mt. McKinley
Number of boroughs: 12
Largest borough (1990 census): Fairbanks North Star, 77,720
State forests: None
State parks: 5; 59 waysides and areas (3.3 million ac.)
1992 resident population est.: 587,000
1990 resident census populationm, sex, & (rank): 550,043 (49). **Male:** 289,867; **Female:** 260,176. **White:** 415,492 (75.5%); **Black:** 22,451 (4.1%); **American Indian, Eskimo, or Aleut:** 85,698 (15.6%); **Asian or Pacific Islander:** 19,728 (3.6%); **Other race:** 6,675 (1.2%); **Hispanic:** 17,803 (3.2%). **1990 percent population under 18:** 31.3; **65 and over:** 4.1; **median age:** 29..4

1. Independent–Republican.

Vitus Bering, a Dane working for the Russians, and Alexei Chirikov discovered the Alaskan mainland and the Aleutian Islands in 1741. The tremendous land mass of Alaska—equal to one fifth of the continental U.S.—was unexplored in 1867 when Secretary of State William Seward arranged for its purchase from the Russians for $7,200,000. The transfer of the territory took place on Oct. 18, 1867. Despite a price of about two cents an acre, the purchase was widely ridiculed as "Seward's Folly." The first official census (1880) reported a total of 33,426 Alaskans, all but 430 being of aboriginal stock. The Gold Rush of 1898 resulted in a mass influx of more than 30,000 people. Since then, Alaska has returned billions of dollars' worth of products to the U.S.

In 1968, a large oil and gas reservoir near Prudhoe Bay on the Arctic Coast was found. The Prudhoe Bay reservoir, with an estimated recoverable 10 billion barrels of oil and 27 trillion cubic feet of gas, is twice as large as any other oil field in North America. The Trans-Alaska pipeline was completed in 1977 at a cost of $7.7 billion. On June 20, oil started flowing through the 800-mile-long pipeline from Prudhoe Bay to the port of Valdez.

Other industries important to Alaska's economy are fisheries, wood and wood products, and furs, and tourism.

Denali National Park and Mendenhall Glacier in North Tongass National Forest are of interest, as is the large totem pole collection at Sitka National Historical Park. The Katmai National Park includes the "Valley of Ten Thousand Smokes," an area of active volcanoes.

Famous natives and residents: Clarence L. Andrews, author; Aleksandr Baranov, first governor of Russian America; Margaret Elizabeth Bell, author; Benny Benson, designed state flag at age 13; Vitus Bering, explorer; Charles E. Bunnell, educator; Susan Butcher, sled-dog racer; William A. Egan, first state governor; Carl Ben Eielson, pioneer pilot; Henry E. Gruennig, political leader; B. Frank Heintzleman, territorial governor; Walter J. Hickel, governor; Sheldon Jackson, educator and missionary; Joe Juneau, prospector; Austin Lathrop, industrialist; Sydney Lawrence, painter; Ray Mala, actor; Virgil F. Partch, cartoonist; Joe Redington, Sr., sled-dog musher and promoter; Peter Trinble Rowe, first Episcopal bishop; Ivan Popov-Veniaminov (St. Innocent), Russian Orthodox missionary; Ferdinand Wrangel, educator; Samuel Hall Young, founder of first American church

ARIZONA

Capital: Phoenix
Governor: Fife Symington, R (to Jan. 1995)
Secy. of State: Richard Mahoney, D (to Jan. 1995)
Atty. General: Grant Woods, R (to Jan. 1995)
State Treasurer: Tony West, R (to Jan. 1995)
Organized as territory: Feb. 24, 1863
Entered Union & (rank): Feb. 14, 1912 (48)
Present constitution adopted: 1911
Motto: *Ditat Deus* (God enriches)
STATE SYMBOLS: flower: Flower of saguaro cactus (1931); **bird:** Cactus wren (1931); **colors:** Blue and old gold (1915); **song:** "Arizona March Song" (1919); **tree:** Palo Verde (1954); **neckwear,** Bolo tie (1973); **fossil,** Petrified wood (1988); **gemstone,** Turquoise (1974); **animals, mammal,** Ringtail; **reptile,** Arizona ridgenose rattlesnake; **fish,** Arizona trout; **amphibian,** Arizona tree frog (1986)
Nickname: Grand Canyon State
Origin of name: From the Indian "Arizonac," meaning "little spring"
10 largest cities (1990 census): Phoenix, 983,403; Tucson, 405,390; Mesa, 288,091; Glendale, 148,134; Tempe, 141,865; Scottsdale, 130,069; Chandler, 90,533; Yuma, 54,923; Peoria, 50,618; Flagstaff, 45,857
Land area & (rank): 114,000 sq mi. (296,400 sq km) (6)
Geographic center: In Yavapai Co., 55 mi. ESE of Prescott
Number of counties: 15
Largest county (1990 census): Maricopa, 2,122,101
State forests: None
State parks: 24
1992 resident population est.: 3,832,000
1990 resident census population, sex, & (rank): 3,665,228 (24). **Male:** 1,810,691; **Female:** 1,854,537. **White:** 2,963,186 (80.8%); **Black:** 110,524 (3.0%); **American Indian, Eskimo, or Aleut:** 203,527 (5.6%); **Asian or Pacific Islander:** 55,206 (1.5%); **Other race:** 332,785 (9.1%); **Hispanic:** 688,338 (18.8%). **1990 percent population under 18:** 26.8; **65 and over:** 13.1; **median age:** 32.2

Marcos de Niza, a Spanish Franciscan friar, was the first European to explore Arizona. He entered the area in 1539 in search of the mythical Seven Cities of Gold. Although he was followed a year later by another gold seeker, Francisco Vásquez de Coronado, most of the early settlement was for missionary purposes. In 1775 the Spanish established Fort Tucson. In 1848, after the Mexican War, most of the Arizona territory became part of the U.S., and the southern portion of the territory was added by the Gadsden Purchase in 1853.

In 1973 one of the world's most massive dams, the New Cornelia Tailings, was completed near Ajo.

Arizona history is rich in legends of America's Old West. It was here that the great Indian chiefs Geronimo and Cochise led their people against the frontiersmen. Tombstone, Ariz., was the site of the West's most famous shoot-out—the gunfight at the O.K. Corral. Today, Arizona has the largest U.S. Indian population; more than 14 tribes are represented on 20 reservations.

Manufacturing has become Arizona's most important industry. Principal products include electrical, communications, and aeronautical items. The state produces over half the country's copper. Agriculture is also important to the state's economy.

State attractions include such famous scenery as the Grand Canyon, the Petrified Forest, and the Painted Desert. Hoover Dam, Lake Mead, Fort Apache, and the reconstructed London Bridge at Lake Havasu City are of particular interest.

Famous natives and residents: Apache Kid, Indian outlaw; Cesar Chavez, labor leader; Cochise, Apache chief; Joan Ganz Cooney, children's television executive; Lewis W. Douglas, public official; Max Ernst, painter; Geronimo (Goyathlay), Apache chief; Barry Goldwater, politician; Zane Grey, novelist; Carl Trumbull Hayden, politician; George Wylie Hunt, first state governor; Helen Hull Jacobs, tennis champion, writer; Ulysses S. Kay, composer; Eusebio Kino, missionary; Percival Lowell, astronomer; Frank Luke, Jr., WWI fighter ace; Charles Mingus, jazz musician, composer; Carlos Montezuma, doctor and Indian spokesman; William O'Neill, frontier sheriff; Alexander M. Patch, general; William H. Pickering, astronomer; Linda Ronstadt, singer; Clyde W. Tombaugh, astronomer; Stewart Udall, ex-Secretary of the Interior; Pauline Weaver, mountain man

ARKANSAS

Capital: Little Rock
Governor: Jim Guy Tucker, D (to Jan. 1995)
Lieut. Governor: (Vacant)
Secy. of State: W. J. McCuen, D (to Jan. 1995)
Atty. General: Winston Bryant, D (to Jan. 1995)
Auditor of State: Julia Hughes Jones, D (to Jan. 1995)
Treasurer of State: Jimmie Lou Fisher Lumpkin, D (to Jan. 1995)
Land Commissioner: Charles Daniels, D (to Jan. 1995)
Organized as territory: March 2, 1819
Entered Union & (rank): June 15, 1836 (25)
Present constitution adopted: 1874
Motto: *Regnat populus* (The people rule)
STATE SYMBOLS: flower, Apple Blossom (1901); **tree,** Pine (1939); **bird,** Mockingbird (1929); **insect,** Honeybee (1973); **song,** "Arkansas" (1963)
Nickname: Land of Opportunity
Origin of name: From the Quapaw Indians
10 largest cities (1990 census): Little Rock, 175,795; Fort Smith, 72,798; North Little Rock, 61,741; Pine Bluff, 57,140; Jonesboro, 46,535; Fayetteville, 42,099; Hot Springs, 32,462; Springdale, 29,941; Jacksonville, 29,101; West Memphis, 28,259
Land area & (rank): 52,075 sq mi. (134,875 sq km) (27)
Geographic center: In Pulaski Co., 12 mi. NW of Little Rock
Number of counties: 75
Largest county (1990 census): Pulaski, 349,660
State forests: None
State parks: 44
1992 resident population est.: 2,399,000
1990 resident population, sex, & rank: 2,350,725 (33). **Male:** 1,133,076; **Female:** 1,217,649. **White:** 1,944,744 (82.7%); **Black:** 373,912 (15.9%); **American Indian, Eskimo, or Aleut:** 12,773 (0.5%); **Asian or Pacific Islander:** 12,530 (0.5%); **Other race:** 6,766 (0.3%); **Hispanic:** 19,876 (0.8%). **1990 percent population under 18:** 26.4; **65 and over:** 14.9; **median age:** 33.8.

Hernando de Soto, in 1541, was among the early European explorers to visit the territory. It was a Frenchman, Henri de Tonti, who in 1686 founded the first permanent white settlement—the Arkansas Post. In 1803 the area was acquired by the U.S. as part of the Louisiana Purchase.

Food products are the state's largest employing sector, with lumber and wood products a close second. Arkansas is also a leader in the production of cotton, rice, and soybeans. It also has the country's only active diamond mine; located near Murfreesboro, it is operated as a tourist attraction.

Hot Springs National Park, and Buffalo National River in the Ozarks are major state attractions.

Blanchard Springs Caverns, the Arkansas Territorial Restoration at Little Rock, and the Arkansas Folk Center in Mountain View are of interest.

Famous natives and residents: G.M. "Broncho Billy" Anderson, actor; Maya Angelou, author, poet; Katharine Susan Anthony, author; Helen Gurley Brown, author; Glen Campbell, singer; Hattie Caraway, first woman senator; Johnny Cash, singer; Eldridge Cleaver, Black activist; William Jefferson Clinton, 42nd President; Dizzy Dean, baseball player; Orval Faubus, governor; John Gould Flecher, writer; James W. Fulbright, senator; John H. Johnson, publisher; Alan Ladd, actor; Douglas MacArthur, 5-star general; John Paul McConnell, U.S. Air Force officer; Ben Murphy, actor; Frank Pace, Jr., public official; Ben Piazza, actor; Albert Pike, pioneer teacher, lawyer; Dick Powell, actor; Opie P. Read, writer; Jenny D. Rice-Meyrowitz, painter; Brehon Burke Somervell, World Wars I and II U.S. Army officer; Mary Steenburgen, actress; Edward Durrell Stone, architect; Sam Walton, Wal-Mart founder; William C. Warfield, concert singer, actor

CALIFORNIA

Capital: Sacramento
Governor: Pete Wilson, R (to Jan. 1995)
Lieut. Governor: Leo McCarthy, D (to Jan. 1995)
Secy. of State: March Fong Eu, D (to Jan. 1995)
Controller: Gray Davis, D (to Jan. 1995)
Atty. General: Dan Lungren, R (to Jan. 1995)
Treasurer: Kathleen Brown, D (to Jan. 1995)
Acting Supt. of Public Instruction: William D. Dawson
Entered Union & (rank): Sept. 9, 1850 (31)
Present constitution adopted: 1879
Motto: *Eureka* (I have found it)
STATE SYMBOLS: flower, Golden poppy (1903); **tree,** California redwoods (*Sequoia sempervirens & Sequoia gigantea)* (1937 % 1953); **bird,** California valley quail (1931); **animal,** California grizzly bear (1953); **fish,** California golden trout (1947); **colors,** Blue and gold (1951); **song,** "I Love You, California" (1951)
Nickname: Golden State
Origin of name: From a book, *Las Sergas de Esplandián,* by Garcia Ordóñez de Montalvo, c. 1500
10 largest cities (1990 census): Los Angeles, 3,485,398; San Diego, 1,110,549; San Jose, 782,248; San Francisco, 723,959; Long Beach, 429,433; Oakland, 372,242; Sacramento, 369,365; Fresno, 354,202; Santa Ana, 293,742; Anaheim, 266,406
Land area & (rank): 155,973 sq mi. (403,970 sq km) (3)
Geographic center: In Madera Co., 35 mi. NE of Madera
Number of counties: 58
Largest county (1990 census): Los Angeles, 8,863,164
State forests: 8 (70,283 ac.)
State parks and beaches: 180 (723,000 ac.)
1992 resident population est.: 30,3867,000
1990 resident population, sex, & (rank): 29,760,021 (1). **Male:** 14,897,627; **Female:** 14,862,394. **White:** 20,524,327 (69.9%); **Black:** 2,208,801 (7.4%); **American Indian, Eskimo, or Aleut:** 242,164 (0.8%); **Asian or Pacific Islander,** 2,845,659 (9.6%); **Other race:** 3,939,070 (13.2%); **Hispanic,** 7,687,938 (25.8%). **1990 percent population under 18:** 26.0; **65 and over:** 10.5; **median age:** 31.5.

Although California was sighted by Spanish navigator Juan Rodríguez Cabrillo in 1542, its first Spanish mission (at San Diego) was not established until 1769. California became a U.S. Territory in 1847 when Mexico surrendered it to John C. Frémont. On Jan. 24, 1848, James W. Marshall discovered gold at Sutter's Mill, starting the California Gold Rush and bringing settlers to the state in large numbers.

In 1964, the U.S. Census Bureau estimated that California had become the most populous state, surpassing New York. California also leads the country in personal income and consumer expenditures.

Leading industries include manufacturing (transportation equipment, machinery, and electronic equipment), agriculture, biotechnology, and tourism. Principal natural resources include timber, petroleum, cement, and natural gas.

More immigrants settle in California than any other state—more than 30% of the nation's total in 1990. Asian-Pacific Islanders led the influx.

Death Valley, in the southeast, is 282 feet below sea level, the lowest point in the nation; and Mt. Whitney (14,491 ft) is the highest point in the contig-uous 48 states. Lassen Peak is one of two active U.S. volcanos outside of Alaska and Hawaii; its last eruptions were recorded in 1917. The General Sherman Tree in Sequoia National Park is estimated to be about 3,500 years old and a stand of bristlecone pine trees in the White Mountains may be over 4,000 years old.

Other points of interest include Yosemite National Park, Disneyland, Hollywood, the Golden Gate bridge, San Simeon State Park, and Point Reyes National Seashore.

Famous natives and residents: Gertrude Atherton, author; David Belasco, playwright and producer; Shirley Temple Black, actress, ambassador; Dave Brubeck, musician; Luther Burbank, horticulturalist; Julia Child, chef; Joe DiMaggio, baseball player; James H. Doolittle, Air Force general, Isadora Duncan, dancer; John Frémont, explorer; Robert Frost, poet; Henry George, economist; Richard "Pancho" Gonzales, tennis player; George E. Hale, astronomer; Bret Harte, writer; William Randolph Hearst, publisher; Sidney Howard, playwright; Collis Potter Huntington, financier; Helen Hunt Jackson, writer; Robinson Jeffers, poet; Anthony M. Kennedy, jurist; Jack London, author; James W. Marshall, first discovered gold; Aimee Semple McPherson, evangelist; Marilyn Monroe, actress; John Muir, naturalist; Richard M. Nixon, President; Isamu Noguchi, sculptor; Frank Norris, novelist; Kathleen Norris, novelist; George S. Patton, Jr, general; Robert Redford, actor; Sally K. Ride, astronaut; William Saroyan, author; Junípero Serra, missionary; Upton Sinclair, novelist; Leland Stanford, railroad magnate; Lincoln Steffens, journalist, author; John Steinbeck, author; Adlai Stevenson, statesman; Johann Sutter, pioneer; Michael Tilson Thomas, conductor; Earl Warren, jurist

COLORADO

Capital: Denver
Governor: Roy Romer, D (to Jan. 1995)
Lieut. Governor: Michael Callihan, D (to Jan. 1995)
Secy. of State: Natalie Meyer, R (to Jan 1995)
Treasurer: Gail Schoettler, D (to Jan. 1995)
Controller: Cliff Hall, R (appointed)
Atty. General: Gale Norton, R (to Jan. 1995)
Organized as territory: Feb. 28, 1861
Entered Union & (rank): Aug. 1, 1876 (38)
Present constitution adopted: 1876
Motto: *Nil sine Numine* (Nothing without Providence)
STATE SYMBOLS: flower, Rocky Mountain columbine (1899); **tree,** Colorado blue spruce (1939); **bird,** Lark bunting (1931); **animal,** Rocky Mountain bighorn sheep (1961); **gemstone,** Aquamarine (1971); **colors,** Blue and white (1911); **song,** "Where the Columbines Grow" (1915); **fossil,** Stegosaurus (1991)
Nickname: Centennial State
Origin of name: From the Spanish, "ruddy" or "red"
10 largest cities (1990 census): Denver, 467,610; Colorado Springs, 281,140; Aurora, 222,103; Lakewood, 126,481; Pueblo, 98,640; Arvada, 89,235; Fort Collins, 87,758; Boulder, 83,312; Westminster, 74,625; Greeley, 60,536
Land area & (rank): 103,730 sq mi. (268,660 sq km) (8)
Geographic center: In Park Co., 30 mi. NW of Pikes Peak
Number of counties: 63
Largest county (1990 census): Denver, 467,610
State forests: 1 (71,000 ac.)
State parks: 44
1992 resident population est.: 3,470,000
1990 resident census population, sex, & (rank): 3,294,394 (26). **Male:** 1,631,295; **Female:** 1,663,099. **White:** 2,095,474 (88.2%); **Black:** 133,146 (4.0%); **American Indian, Eskimo, or Aleut:** 27,776 (0.8%); **Asian or Pacific Islander,** 59,862 (1.8%); **Other race:** 168,136 (5.1%); **Hispanic:** 424,302 (12.9%). **1990 percent population under 18:** 26.1; **65 and over:** 10.0; **median age:** 32.5

First visited by Spanish explorers in the 1500s, the territory was claimed for Spain by Juan de Ulibarri in 1706. The U.S. obtained eastern Colorado as part of the Louisiana Purchase in 1803, the central portion in 1845 with the admission of Texas as a state, and the western part in 1848 as a result of the Mexican War.

Colorado has the highest mean elevation of any state, with more than 1,000 Rocky Mountain peaks over 10,000 feet high and 54 towering above 14,000 feet. Pikes Peak, the most famous of these mountains, was discovered by U.S. Army Lieut. Zebulon M. Pike in 1806.

Once primarily a mining and agricultural state, Colorado's economy is now driven by the service-producing industries, which provide jobs for approximately 82.4% of the state's non-farm work force. Tourism expenditures in the state total approximately 6 billion dollars annually. Tourist expenditures on the ski industry account for 1.8 billion dollars annually, approximately 1/3 of the total tourist expenditures. The main tourist attractions in the state include Rocky Mountain National Park, Curecanti National Recreation Area, Mesa Verde National Park, the Great Sand Dunes and Dinosaur National Monuments, Colorado National Monument, and the Black Canyon of the Gunnison National Monument.

The two primary facets of Colorado's manufacturing industry are food and kindred products, and printing and publishing.

The mining industry, which includes oil and gas, coal, and metal mining, was important to Colorado's economy, but it now employs only 1.2 percent of the state's workforce. Denver is home to companies that control half of the nation's gold production. The farm industry, which is primarily concentrated in livestock, is also an important element of the state's economy. The primary crops in Colorado are corn, hay, and wheat.

Famous natives and residents: William E. Barrett, writer; William Bent, fur trader and pioneer; Charles F. Brannan, lawyer and public official; M. Scott Carpenter, astronaut; Lon Chaney, actor; Mary Coyle Chase, playwright; Jack Dempsey, boxer; Ralph Edwards, entertainer; John Evans, physician, educator; Douglas Fairbanks, actor; John Thomas Fante, writer; Eugene Fodor, violinist; Gene Fowler, writer; Erick Hawkins, choreographer; Homer Lea, soldier, writer; Ted Mack, TV host; Jaye P. Morgan, singer; Peg Murray, actress; Ouray, Ute Indian chief; Anne Parrish, writer; Barbara Rush, actress; Horace A. Tabor, silver king, Lieut.-Governor; Lowell Thomas, commentator and author; Dalton Trumbo, screenwriter, novelist; Byron R. White, jurist; Paul Whiteman, conductor; Don Wilson, announcer

CONNECTICUT

Capital: Hartford
Governor: Lowell P. Weicker, Jr., ACP[1] (to Jan. 1995)
Lieut. Governor: Eunice S. Groark, ACP[1] (to Jan. 1995)
Secy. of State: Pauline R. Kezer, R (to Jan. 1995)
Comptroller: William E. Curry, Jr., D (to Jan. 1995)
Treasurer: Joseph M. Suggs, Jr., D (to Jan. 1995)
Atty. General: Richard Blumenthal, D (to Jan. 1995)
Entered Union & (rank): Jan. 9, 1788 (5)
Present constitution adopted: Dec. 30, 1965
Motto: *Qui transtulit sustinet* (He who transplanted still sustains)
STATE SYMBOLS: flower, Mountain Laurel (1907); **tree,** White Oak (1947); **animal,** Sperm Whale (1975); **bird,** American Robin (1943); **hero,** Nathan Hale (1985); **insect,** Praying Mantis (1977); **mineral,** Garnet (1977); **song,** "Yankee Doodle" (1978); **ship,** USS Nautilus (SSN571) (1983); **shellfish,** Eastern Oyster (1989); **fossil,** Eubrontes Giganteus (1991)
Official designation: *Constitution State* (1959)
Nickname: Nutmeg State
Origin of name: From an Indian word (Quinnehtukqut) meaning "beside the long tidal river"
10 largest cities (1990 census): Bridgeport, 141,686; Hartford, 139,739; New Haven, 130,474; Waterbury, 108,961; Stamford, 108,056; Norwalk, 78,331; New Britain, 75,491; Danbury, 65,585; Bristol, 60,640; Meriden, 59,479
Land area & (rank): 4,845 sq mi. (12,550 sq km) (48)
Geographic center: In Hartford Co., at East Berlin
Number of counties: 8
Largest town (1990 census): West Hartford 60,110
State forests: 30 (142,010 ac.)
State parks: 98 (31,247 ac.)
1992 resident population est.: 3,281,000
1990 resident population, sex, & (rank): 3,287,116 (27). **Male:** 1,592,873; **Female:** 1,694,243. **White:** 2,859,353 (87.0%); **Black:** 274,269 (8.3%); **American Indian, Eskimo, or Aleut:** 6,654 (0.2%); **Asian or Pacific Islander:** 50,698 (1.5%); **Other race:** 96,142 (2.9%); **Hispanic:** 213,116 (6.5%). **1990 percent population under 18:** 22.8; **65 and over:** 13.6; **median age:** 34.4.

1. A Connecticut Party.

The Dutch navigator, Adriaen Block, was the first European of record to explore the area, sailing up the Connecticut River in 1614. In 1633, Dutch colonists built a fort and trading post near presentday Hartford, but soon lost control to English Puritans migrating south from the Massachusetts Bay Colony.

English settlements, established in the 1630s at Windsor, Wethersfield, and Hartford, united in 1639 to form the Connecticut Colony and adopted the *Fundamental Orders,* considered the world's first written constitution.

The colony's royal charter of 1662 was exceptionally liberal. When Gov. Edmund Andros tried to seize it in 1687, it was hidden in the Hartford Oak, commemorated in Charter Oak Place.

Connecticut played a prominent role in the Revolutionary War, serving as the Continental Army's major supplier. Sometimes called the "Arsenal of the Nation," the state became one of the most industrialized in the nation.

Today, Connecticut factories produce weapons, sewing machines, jet engines, helicopters, motors, hardware and tools, cutlery, clocks, locks, ball bearings, silverware, and submarines. Hartford, which has the oldest U.S. newspaper still being published—the *Hartford Courant,* established 1764—is the insurance capital of the nation.

Poultry, fruit, and dairy products account for the largest portion of farm income, and Connecticut's shade-grown tobacco is acknowledged to be the state's most valuable crop per acre.

Connecticut is a popular resort area with its 250-mile Long Island Sound shoreline and many inland lakes. Among the major points of interest are Yale University's Gallery of Fine Arts and Peabody Museum. Other famous museums include the P.T. Barnum, Winchester Gun, and American Clock and Watch. The town of Mystic features a recreated 19th-century New England seaport and the Mystic Marinelife Aquarium.

Famous natives and residents: Dean Acheson, statesman; Ethan Allan, American Revolutionary soldier; Benedict Arnold, American Revolutionary general; Wadsworth Atheneum; P.T. Barnum, showman; Henry Ward Beecher, clergyman; John Brown, abolitionist; Oliver Ellsworth, jurist; Eileen Farrell, soprano; Charles Goodyear, inventor; Nathan Hale, American Revolutionary officer; Dorothy Hamill, ice skater; Katharine Hepburn, actress; Charles Ives, composer; Edwin H. Land, inventor; John Pierpont Morgan, financier; Frederick Law Olmsted, landscape planner; Rosa Ponselle, soprano; Adam Clayton Powell, Jr., congressman; Benjamin Spock, pediatrician; Harriet Beecher Stowe, author; Morris R. Waite, jurist; Noah Webster, lexicographer

DELAWARE

Capital: Dover
Governor: Thomas R. Carver, D (to Jan. 1997)
Lieut. Governor: Ruth Ann Minner, D (to Jan. 1997)
Secy. of State: William T. Quillen, D (Pleasure of Governor)
State Treasurer: Janet C. Rzewnicki, R (to Jan. 1995)
Atty. General: Charles M. Oberly III, D (to Jan. 1995)
Entered Union & (rank): Dec. 7, 1787 (1)
Present constitution adopted: 1897
Motto: Liberty and independence
STATE SYMBOLS: colors, Colonial blue and buff; **flower,** Peach blossom (1895); **tree,** American holly (1939); **bird,** Blue Hen chicken (1939); **insect,** Ladybug (1974); **fish,** Weakfish, *Cynoscion regalis* (1981); **song,** "Our Delaware"
Nicknames: Diamond State; First State; Small Wonder
Origin of name: From Delaware River and Bay; named in turn for Sir Thomas West, Lord De La Warr
10 largest cities (1990 census): Wilmington, 71,529; Dover, 27,630; Newark, 26,464; Milford, 6,040; Elsmere Town, 5,935; Seaford, 5,689; Smyrna Town, 5,213; New Castle 4,837; Middletown Town, 3,834; Georgetown Town, 3,732
Land area & (rank): 1,982 sq mi. (5,153 sq km) (49)
Geographic center: In Kent Co., 11 mi. S of Dover
Number of counties: 3
Largest county (1990 census): New Castle, 441,946
State forests: 3 (6,149 ac.)
State parks: 12
1992 resident population est.: 689,000
1990 resident census population, sex, & (rank): 666,168 (46). **Male:** 322,968; **Female:** 343,200. **White:** 535,094 (80.3%); **Black:** 112,460 (16.9%); **American Indian, Eskimo, or Aleut:** 2,019 (0.3%); **Asian or Pacific Islander:** 9,057 (1.4%); **Other race:** 7,538 (1.1%); **Hispanic:** 15,820 (2.4%). **1990 percent population under 18:** 24.5; **65 and over:** 12.1; **median age:** 32.9.

Henry Hudson, sailing under the Dutch flag, is credited with Delaware's discovery in 1609. The following year, Capt. Samuel Argall of Virginia named Delaware for his colony's governor, Thomas West,

Baron De La Warr. An attempted Dutch settlement failed in 1631. Swedish colonization began at Fort Christina (now Wilmington) in 1638, but New Sweden fell to Dutch forces led by New Netherlands' Gov. Peter Stuyvesant in 1655.

England took over the area in 1664 and it was transferred to William Penn as the southern Three Counties in 1682. Semiautonomous after 1704, Delaware fought as a separate state in the American Revolution and became the first state to ratify the constitution in 1787.

During the Civil War, although a slave state, Delaware did not secede from the Union.

In 1802, Ëleuthère Irénée du Pont established a gunpowder mill near Wilmington that laid the foundation for Delaware's huge chemical industry. Delaware's manufactured products now also include vulcanized fiber, textiles, paper, medical supplies, metal products, machinery, machine tools, and automobiles.

Delaware also grows a great variety of fruits and vegetables and is a U.S. pioneer in the food-canning industry. Corn, soybeans, potatoes, and hay are important crops. Delaware's broiler chicken farms supply the big Eastern markets, fishing and dairy products are other important industries.

Points of interest include the Fort Christina Monument, Hagley Museum, Holy Trinity Church (erected in 1698, the oldest Protestant church in the United States still in use), and Winterthur Museum, in and near Wilmington; central New Castle, an almost unchanged late 18th-century capital; and the Delaware Museum of Natural History.

Popular recreation areas include Cape Henlopen, Delaware Seashore, Trapp Pond State Park, and Rehoboth Beach.

Famous natives and residents: Richard Allen, founder of African Methodist Episcopal Church; Valerie Bertinelli, actress; Robert Montgomery Bird, playwright and novelist; Henry S. Canby, editor and author; Annie Jump Cannon, astronomer; Elizabeth Margaret Chandler, author; Felix Darley, artist; John Dickinson, statesman; E.I. du Pont, industrialist; Oliver Evans, inventor; Thomas Garrett, abolitionist; Henry Heimlich, surgeon, inventor; Wilham Julius "Judy" Johnson, basketball player; J.P. Marquand, novelist; Howard Pyle, artist and author; George Read, jurist, signer of Declaration of Independence; Jay Saunders Redding, educator and author; Caesar Rodney, patriot, signer of Declaration of Independence; Frank Stephens, sculptor; Estelle Taylor, actress; George Alfred Townsend, journalist and author

DISTRICT OF COLUMBIA

See listing at end of *50 Largest Cities of the United States.*

FLORIDA

Capital: Tallahassee
Governor: Lawton Chiles, D (to Jan. 1995)
Lieut. Governor: Buddy McKay, D (to Jan. 1995)
Secy. of State: Jim Smith, R (to Jan. 1995)
Comptroller: Gerald Lewis, D (to Jan. 1995)
Commissioner of Agriculture: Bob Crawford, D (to Jan. 1995)
Atty. General: Bob Butterworth, D (to Jan. 1995)
Organized as territory: March 30, 1822
Entered Union & (rank): March 3, 1845 (27)
Present constitution adopted: 1969
Motto: In God we trust (1868)
STATE SYMBOLS: flower, Orange blossom (1909); **bird,** Mockingbird (1927); **song,** "Suwannee River" (1935)
Nickname: Sunshine State (1970)
Origin of name: From the Spanish, meaning "feast of flowers" (Easter)
10 largest cities (1990 census): Jacksonville (CC[1]), 672,971; Miami, 358,548; Tampa, 280,015; St. Petersburg, 238,629; Hialeah, 188,004; Orlando, 164,693; Fort Lauderdale, 149,377; Tallahassee, 124,773; Hollywood, 121,697; Clearwater, 98,784
Land area & (rank): 53,997 sq mi. (139,852 sq km) (26)
Geographic center: In Hernando Co., 12 mi. NNW of Brooksville
Number of counties: 67
Largest county (1990 census): Dade, 1,937,094
State forests: 3 (306,881 ac.)
State parks: 105 (215,820 ac.)
1992 resident population est.: 13,488,000
1990 resident census population, sex, & (rank): 12,937,926 (4). **Male:** 6,261,719; **Female:** 6,676,207. **White:** 10,749,285 (83.1%); **Black:** 1,759,534 (13.6%); **American Indian, Eskimo, or Aleut:** 36,335 (0.3%); **Asian or Pacific Islander:** 154,302 (1.2%); **Other race:** 238,470 (1.8%); **Hispanic:** 1,574,143 (12.2%). **1990 percent population under 18:** 22.2; **65 and over:** 18.3; **median age:** 36.4.

1. Consolidated City (Coextensive with Duval County).

In 1513, Ponce De Leon, seeking the mythical "Fountain of Youth," discovered and named Florida, claiming it for Spain. Later, Florida would be held at different times by Spain and England until Spain finally sold it to the United States in 1819. (Incidentally, France established a colony named Fort Caroline in 1564 in the state that was to become Florida.)

Florida's early 19th-century history as a U.S. territory was marked by wars with the Seminole Indians that did not end until 1842, although a treaty was actually never signed.

One of the nation's fastest-growing states, Florida's population has gone from 2.8 million in 1950 to more than 12.9 million in 1990.

Florida's economy rests on a solid base of tourism (in 1992 the state entertained more than 40.5 million visitors from all over the world), manufacturing, agriculture, and international trade.

In recent years, oranges, grapefruit and tomatoes lead Florida's crop list, followed by vegetables, potatoes, melons, strawberries, sugar cane, dairy products, cattle and calves, and forest products.

Major tourist attractions are Miami Beach, Palm Beach, St. Augustine (founded in 1565, thus the oldest permanent city in the U.S.), Daytona Beach, and Fort Lauderdale on the East Coast. West Coast resorts include Sarasota, Tampa, Key West and St. Petersburg. The Orlando area, where Disney World is located on a 27,000-acre site, is Florida's most popular tourist destination.

Also drawing many visitors are the NASA Kennedy Space Center's Spaceport USA, located in the town of Kennedy Space Center, Everglades National Park, and the Epcot Center.

Famous natives and residents: Julian "Cannonball" Adderley, jazz saxophonist; Pat Boone, singer; Fernando Bujones, ballet dancer; Steve Carlton, baseball player; Fay Dunaway, actress; Stepin Fetchit (Lincoln Theodore Perry), comedian; Lue Gim Gong, horticulturist; Dwight Gooden, baseball player; James Weldon Johnson, author and educator; Frances Langford, singer; Butterfly McQueen, actress; Jim Morrison, singer; Osceola, Seminole Indian leader; Sidney Poitier, actor; A. Philip Randolph, labor leader; Marjorie Kinnan Rawlings, author; Charles and John Ringling, circus entrepreneurs; Joseph W. Stilwell, army general; Ben Vereen, actor

GEORGIA

Capital: Atlanta
Governor: Zell Miller, D (to Jan. 1995)
Lieut. Governor: Pierre Howard, D (to Jan. 1995)
Secy. of State: Max Cleland, D (to Jan. 1995)
Insurance Commissioner: Tim Ryles, D (to Jan. 1995)
Atty. General: Michael J. Bowers, D (to Jan. 1995)
Entered Union & (rank): Jan. 2, 1788 (4)
Present constitution adopted: 1977
Motto: Wisdom, justice, and moderation
STATE SYMBOLS: flower, Cherokee rose (1916); **tree,** Live oak (1937); **bird,** Brown thrasher (1935); **song,** "Georgia on My Mind" (1922)
Nicknames: Peach State, Empire State of the South
Origin of name: In honor of George II of England
10 largest cities (1990 census): Atlanta, 394,017; Columbus[1], 179,278; Savannah, 137,560; Macon, 106,612; Albany, 78,122; Roswell, 47,923; Athens, 45,734; Augusta, 44,639; Marietta, 44,129; Warner Robins, 43,726.
Land area & (rank): 57,919 sq mi. (150,010 sq km) (21)
Geographic center: In Twiggs Co., 18 mi. SE of Macon
Number of counties: 159
Largest county (1990 census): Fulton, 648,951
State forests: 25,258,000 ac. (67% of total state area)
State parks: 53 (42,600 ac.)
1992 resident population est.: 6,751,000
1990 resident census population, sex, & (rank): 6,478,216 (11). **Male:** 3,144,503; **Female:** 3,333,713. **White:** 4,600,148 (71.0%); **Black:** 1,746,565 (27.0%); **American Indian, Eskimo, or Aleut:** 13,348 (0.2%); **Asian or Pacific Islander:** 75,781 (1.2%); **Other race:** 42,374 (0.7%); **Hispanic:** 108,922 (1.7%). **1990 percent population under 18:** 26.7; **65 and over:** 10.1; **median age:** 31.6.

1. Consolidated City (Coextensive with Muscogee County).

Hernando de Soto, the Spanish explorer, first traveled parts of Georgia in 1540. British claims later conflicted with those of Spain. After obtaining a royal charter, Gen. James Oglethorpe established the first permanent settlement in Georgia in 1733 as a refuge for English debtors. In 1742, Oglethorpe defeated Spanish invaders in the Battle of Bloody Marsh.

A Confederate stronghold, Georgia was the scene of extensive military action during the Civil War. Union General William T. Sherman burned Atlanta and destroyed a 60-mile wide path to the coast where he captured Savannah in 1864.

The largest state east of the Mississippi, Georgia is typical of the changing South with an ever-increasing industrial development. Atlanta, largest city in the state, is the communications and transportation center for the Southeast and the area's chief distributor of goods.

Georgia leads the nation in the production of paper and board, tufted textile products, and processed chicken. Other major manufactured products are transportation equipment, food products, apparel, and chemicals.

Important agricultural products are corn, cotton, tobacco, soybeans, eggs, and peaches. Georgia produces twice as many peanuts as the next leading state. From its vast stands of pine come more than half the world's resins and turpentine and 74.4% of the U.S. supply. Georgia is also a leader in the production of marble, kaolin, barite, and bauxite.

Principal tourist attractions in Georgia include the Okefenokee National Wildlife Refuge, Andersonville Prison Park and National Cemetery, Chickamauga and Chattanooga National Military Park, the Little White House at Warm Springs where Pres. Franklin D. Roosevelt died in 1945, Sea Island, the enormous Confederate Memorial at Stone Mountain, Kennesaw Mountain National Battlefield Park, and Cumberland Island National Seashore.

Famous natives and residents: Conrad Aiken, poet; James Bowie, soldier; James Brown, singer; Jim Brown, actor and athlete; Erskine Caldwell, writer; James E. Carter, President; Ray Charles, singer; Lucius D. Clay, banker, ex-general; Ty Cobb, baseball player; Ossie Davis, actor & writer; James Dickey, poet; Mattiwilda Dobbs, soprano; Melvyn Douglas, actor; Rebecca Latimer Felton, first woman U.S. senator; Roosevelt Grier, entertainer and ex-athlete; Oliver Hardy, comedian; Joel Chandler Harris, journalist and author; Larry Holmes, boxer; Miriam Hopkins, actress; Harry James, trumpeter; Jasper Johns, painter and sculptor; Bobby Jones, golfer; Stacy Keach, actor; DeForest Kelley, actor; Martin Luther King, Jr., civil rights leader; Gladys Knight, singer; Joseph R. Lamar, jurist; Juliette Gordon Low, U.S. Girl Scouts founder; Carson McCullers, novelist; Johnny Mercer, songwriter; Margaret Mitchell, novelist; Elijah Muhammad, religious leader; Jessye Norman, soprano; Otis Redding, singer; Burt Reynolds, actor; Jackie Robinson, baseball player; Dean Rusk, ex-Secretary of State; Nipsey Russell, comedian; Alice Walker, author; Joanne Woodward, actress

HAWAII

Capital: Honolulu (on Oahu)
Governor: John Waihee, D (to Dec. 1994)
Lieut. Governor: Ben Cayetano, D (to Dec. 1994)
Comptroller: Robert Takushi (to Dec. 1994)
Atty. General: Robert A. Marts (to Dec. 1994)
Organized as territory: 1900
Entered Union & (rank): Aug. 21, 1959 (50)
Motto: *Ua Mau Ke Ea O Ka Aina I Ka Pono* (The life of the land is perpetuated in righteousness)
STATE SYMBOLS: flower, Hibiscus (yellow) 1988); **song,** "Hawaii Ponoi" (1967); **bird,** Nene (hawaiian goose) (1957); **tree,** Kukui (Candlenut) (1959)
Nickname: Aloha State (1959)
Origin of name: Uncertain. The islands may have been named by Hawaii Loa, their traditional discoverer. Or they may have been named after Hawaii or Hawaiki, the traditional home of the Polynesians.
10 largest cities[1] (1990 census): Honolulu, 377,059; Hilo, 37,808; Kailua, 36,818; Kaneohe, 35,448; Waipahu, 31,435; Pearl City, 30,993; Waimalu, 29,967; Mililani Town, 29,359; Schofield Barracks, 19,597; Wahiawa, 17,386
Land area & (rank): 6,423.4 sq mi. (16,636.5 sq km) (47)
Geographic center: Between islands of Hawaii and Maui
Number of counties: 4 plus one non-functioning county (Kalawao)
Largest county (1990 census): Honolulu, 836,231
State parks and historic sites: 77
1992 resident population est.: 1,160,000
1990 resident census population, sex, & (rank): 1,108,229 (40). **Male:** 563,891; **Female:** 544,338. **White:** 369,616 (33.4%); **Black:** 27,195 (2.5%); **American Indian, Eskimo, or Aleut:** 5,099 (0.5%); **Asian or Pacific Islander:** 685,236 (61.8%); **Other race:** 21,083 (1.9%); **Hispanic:** 81,390 (7.3%). **1990 percent population under 18:** 25.3; **65 and over:** 11.3; **median age:** 32.6

1. Census Designated Place. There are no political boundaries to Honolulu or any other place, but statistical boundaries are assigned under state law.

First settled by Polynesians sailing from other Pacific islands between 300 and 600 A.D., Hawaii was visited in 1778 by British Captain James Cook who called the group the Sandwich Islands.

Hawaii was a native kingdom throughout most of the 19th century when the expansion of the vital sugar industry (pineapple came after 1898) meant increasing U.S. business and political involvement. In 1893, Queen Liliuokalani was deposed and a year later the Republic of Hawaii was established with Sanford B. Dole as president. Then, following its annexation in 1898, Hawaii became a U.S. Territory in 1900.

The Japanese attack on the naval base at Pearl Harbor on Dec. 7, 1941, was directly responsible for U.S. entry into World War II.

Hawaii, 2,397 miles west-southwest of San Francisco, is a 1,523-mile chain of islets and eight main islands—Hawaii, Kahoolawe, Maui, Lanai, Molokai, Oahu, Kauai, and Niihau. The Northwestern Hawaiian Islands, other than Midway, are administratively part of Hawaii.

The temperature is mild and Hawaii's soil is fertile for tropical fruits and vegetables. Cane sugar and pineapple are the chief products. Hawaii also grows coffee, bananas and nuts. The tourist business is Hawaii's largest source of outside income.

Hawaii's highest peak is Mauna Kea (13,796 ft.). Mauna Loa (13,679 ft.) is the largest volcanic mountain in the world in cubic content.

Among the major points of interest are Hawaii Volcanoes National Park (Hawaii), Haleakala National Park (Maui), Puuhonua o Honaunau National Historical Park (Hawaii), Polynesian Cultural Center (Oahu), the U.S.S. *Arizona* Memorial at Pearl Harbor, and Iolani Palace (the only royal palace in the U.S.), Bishop Museum, and Waikiki Beach (all in Honolulu).

Famous natives and residents: Salevaa Antinoe (Konishiki), sumo wrestler; George Ariyoshi, first Japanese-American elected governor; Hiram Bingham, missionary; Charles R. Bishop, banker and philanthropist; Tia Carrere, singer, actress; Samuel N. Castle, missionary, founder of Castle & Cooke Ltd. with Amos S. Cooke, missionary and educator; Father Damien, leper colony worker; Sanford B. Dole, territorial governor; Jean Erdman, dancer, choreographer; Hiram L. Fong, first Chinese-American senator; Don Ho, entertainer; Daniel K. Inouye, senator; Gerrit P. Judd, advisor of Hawaiian king; Keahumanu, female chief; Duke Paoa Kahanamoku, Olympic swimming champion; Kamehameha I, first Hawaiian king; Kamehameha V, last of the dynasty; George Parsons Lathrop, journalist and poet; Liliuokalani, queen, last Hawaiian monarch; Bette Midler, singer; Ellison Onizuka, astronaut; Kawaipuna Prejean, Hawaiian activist, proponent of Hawaiian sovereignty; Harold Sakata, actor; Carolyn Suzanne Sapp, 1991 Miss America; James Shigeta, actor; Claus Spreckels, developer of Hawaiian sugar industry; Don Stroud, actor

IDAHO

Capital: Boise
Governor: Cecil D. Andrus, D (to Jan. 1995)
Lieut. Governor: C. L. "Butch" Otter, R (to Jan. 1995)
Secy. of State: Pete T. Cenarrusa, R (to Jan. 1995)
State Auditor: J.D. Williams, D (to Jan. 1995)
Atty. General: Larry Echohawk, D (to Jan. 1995)
Treasurer: Lydia Justice Edwards, R (to Jan. 1995)
Organized as territory: March 3, 1863
Entered Union & (rank): July 3, 1890 (43)
Present constitution adopted: 1890
Motto: *Esto perpetua* (It is forever)
STATE SYMBOLS: flower, Syringa (1931); **tree,** White pine (1935); **bird,** Mountain bluebird (1931); **horse,** Appaloosa (1975); **gem,** Star garnet (1967); **song,** "Here We Have Idaho"; **folk dance,** Square Dance; **fish,** Cutthroat trout (1990); **fossil,** Hagerman horse fossil (1988)
Nicknames: Gem State; Spud State; Panhandle State
Origin of name: Unknown. It is an invented name and has no Indian translation meaning "Gem of the Mountains." Meaning of name, if any, is unknown.
10 largest cities (1990 census): Boise, 125,738; Pocatello, 46,080; Idaho Falls, 43,929; Nampa, 28,365; Lewiston, 28,082; Twin Falls, 27,591; Coeur d'Alene, 24,563, Moscow, 18,519; Caldwell, 18,400; Rexburg, 14,302
Land area & (rank): 82,751 sq mi. (214,325 sq km) (11)
Geographic center: In Custer Co., at Custer, SW of Challis
Number of counties: 44, plus small part of Yellowstone National Park
Largest county (1991 est.): Ada, 215,865
State forests: 881,000 ac.
State parks: 22 (44,177 ac.)
1992 resident population est.: 1,067,250
1990 resident census population, sex, & (rank): 1,006,749 (42). **Male:** 500,956; **Female:** 505,793. **White:** 950,451 (94.4%); **Black:** 3,370 (0.3%); **American Indian, Eskimo, or Aleut:** 13,780 (1.4%); **Asian or Pacific Islander:** 9,365 (0.9%); **Other race:** 29,783 (3.0%); **Hispanic:** 52,927 (5.3%). **1990 percent population under 18:** 30.6; **65 and over:** 12.0; **median age:** 31.5.

After its acquisition by the U.S. as part of the Louisiana Purchase in 1803, the region was explored by Meriwether Lewis and William Clark in 1805–06. Northwest boundary disputes with Great Britain were settled by the Oregon Treaty in 1846 and the first permanent U.S. settlement in Idaho was established by the Mormons at Franklin in 1860.

After gold was discovered on Orofino Creek in 1860, prospectors swarmed into the territory, but left little more than a number of ghost towns.

In the 1870s, growing white occupation of Indian lands led to a series of battles between U.S. forces and the Nez Percé, Bannock, and Sheepeater tribes.

Mining, lumbering, and irrigation farming have been important for years. Idaho produces more than one fifth of all the silver mined in the U.S. It also ranks high among the states in antimony, lead, cobalt, garnet, phosphate rock, vanadium, zinc, mercury, and gold.

Idaho's most impressive growth began when World War II military needs made processing agricultural products a big industry, particularly the dehydrating and freezing of potatoes. The state produces about one fourth of the nation's potato crop, as well as wheat, apples, corn, barley, sugar beets, and hops.

With the growth of winter sports, tourism now outranks mining in dollar revenue. Idaho's many streams and lakes provide fishing, camping, and boating sites. The nation's largest elk herds draw hunters from all over the world and the famed Sun Valley resort attracts thousands of visitors to its swimming and skiing facilities.

Other points of interest are the Craters of the Moon National Monument; Nez Percé National Historic Park, which includes many sites visited by Lewis and Clark; and the State Historical Museum in Boise.

Famous natives and residents: Joe Albertson, grocery chain founder; T.H. Bell, educator; Ezra Taft Benson, Eisenhower's Secretary of Agriculture, pres. LDS church, marketing specialist; William E. Borah, senator; Gutzon Borglum, Mt. Rushmore sculptor; Carol R. Brink, author; Frank F. Church, senator; Fred Dubois, senator; Vardis Fisher, novelist; Lawrence H. Gipson, historian; Ernest Hemingway, author; Mariel Hemingway, actress; Chief Joseph, Nez Percé chief; Harmon Killebrew, baseball player; Jerry Kramer, football player, author; Ezra Pound, poet; Sacagawea, Shoshonean guide; J.R. Simplot, industrialist; Robert E. Smylie, political leader; Henry Spalding, missionary; Frank Steunenberg, governor; David Tompson, founded first trading post; Lana Turner, actress

ILLINOIS

Capital: Springfield
Governor: Jim Edgar, R (to Jan. 1995)
Lieut. Governor: Bob Kustra, R (to Jan. 1995)
Atty. General: Roland W. Burris, D (to Jan. 1995)
Secy. of State: George H. Ryan, R (to Jan. 1995)
Comptroller: Dawn Clark Netsch, D (to Jan. 1995)
Treasurer: Patrick Quinn, D (to Jan. 1995)
Organized as territory: Feb. 3, 1809
Entered Union & (rank): Dec. 3, 1818 (21)
Present constitution adopted: 1970
Motto: State sovereignty, national union
STATE SYMBOLS: flower, Violet (1908); **tree,** White oak (1973); **bird,** Cardinal (1929); **animal,** White-tailed deer (1982); **fish,** Bluegill (1987); **insect,** Monarch butterfly (1975); **song,** "Illinois" (1925); **mineral,** Fluorite (1965)
Nickname: Prairie State
Origin of name: From an Indian word and French suffix meaning "tribe of superior men"
10 largest cities (1990 census): Chicago, 2,783,726; Rockford, 139,426; Peoria, 113,504; Springfield, 105,227; Aurora, 99,581; Naperville, 85,351; Decatur, 83,885; Elgin, 77,010; Joliet, 76,836; Arlington Heights Village, 75,460
Land area & (rank): 55,593 sq mi. (143,987 sq kkm) (24)
Geographic center: In Logan County 28 mi. NE of Springfield
Number of counties: 102
Largest county (1990 census): Cook, 5,105,067
Public use areas: 187 (275,000 ac.), incl. state parks, memorials, forests and conservation areas
1992 resident population est.: 11,631,000
1990 resident census population, sex, & (rank): 11,430,602 (6). **Male:** 5,552,233; **Female:** 5,878,369. **White:** 8,952,978 (78.3%); **Black:** 1,694,273 (14.8%); **American Indian, Eskimo, or Aleut:** 21,836 (0.2%); **Asian or Pacific Islander:** 285,311 (2.5%); **Other race:** 476,204 (4.2%); **Hispanic:** 904,446 (7.9%). **1990 percent population under 18:** 25.8; **65 and over:** 12.6; **median age:** 32.8.

French explorers Marquette and Joliet, in 1673, were the first Europeans of record to visit the region. In 1699 French settlers established the first permanent settlement at Cahokia, near present-day East St. Louis.

Great Britain obtained the region at the end of the French and Indian War in 1763. The area figured prominently in frontier struggles during the Revolutionary War and in Indian wars during the early 19th century.

Significant episodes in the state's early history include the growing migration of Eastern settlers following the opening of the Erie Canal in 1825; the Black Hawk War, which virtually ended the Indian troubles in the area; and the rise of Abraham Lincoln from farm laborer to President-elect.

Today, Illinois stands high in manufacturing, coal mining, agriculture, and oil production. The sprawling Chicago district (including a slice of Indiana) is a great iron and steel producer, meat packer, grain exchange, and railroad center. Chicago is also famous as a Great Lakes port.

Illinois ranks third in the nation in export of agricultural products, first in soybeans, and second in corn and hog production. An important dairying state, Illinois is also a leader in corn, oats, wheat, barley, rye, truck vegetables, and the nursery products.

The state manufactures a great variety of industrial and consumer products: railroad cars, clothing, furniture, tractors, liquor, watches, and farm implements are just some of the items made in its factories and plants.

Central Illinois is noted for shrines and memorials associated with the life of Abraham Lincoln. In Springfield are the Lincoln Home, the Lincoln Tomb, and the restored Old State Capitol. Other points of interest are the home of Mormon leader Joseph Smith in Nauvoo and, in Chicago: the Art Institute, Field Museum, Museum of Science and Industry, Shedd Aquarium, Adler Planetarium, Merchandise Mart, and Chicago Portage National Historic Site.

Famous natives and residents: Franklin Pierce Adams, author; Jane Addams, social worker; Mary Astor, actress; Jack Benny, comedian; Black Hawk, Sauk Indian chief; Harry A. Blackmun, jurist; Ray Bradbury, author; William Jennings Bryan, orator and politician; Edgar Rice Burroughs, novelist; Gower Champion, choreographer; John Chancellor, TV commentator; Raymond Chandler, writer; Jimmy Connors, tennis champion; James Gould Cozzens, novelist; Richard J. Daley, mayor of Chicago; Miles Davis, musician; Peter DeVries, novelist; Walt Disney, film animator and produceer; John Dos Passos, author; James T. Farrell, novelist; Betty Friedan, feminist; Benny Goodman, musician; John Gunther, author; Ernest Hemingway, author; Charlton Heston, actor; Wild Bill Hickok, scout; William Holden, actor; Rock Hudson, actor; Burl Ives, singer; James Jones, novelist; John Jones, civil rights leader; Quincy Jones, composer; Keokuk (Watchful Fox), chief of the Sac and Fox Indians; Walter Kerr, drama critic; Archibalt MacLeish, poet; David Mamet, playwright; Robert A. Millikan, physicist; Sherrill Milnes, baritone; Bill Murray, actor; Bob Newhart, actor, comedian; William S. Paley, broadcasting executive; Drew Pearson, columnist; Richard Pryor, comedian, actor; Ronald Reagan, President; Carl Sandburg, poet; Sam Shepard, playwright; William L. Shirer, author and historian; John Paul Stevens, jurist; McLean Stevenson, actor; Preston Sturges, director; Gloria Swanson, actress; Carl Van Doren, writer and educator; Melvin Van Peebles, playwright; Irving Wallace, novelist; Alfred Wallenstein, conductor; Raquel Welch, actress; Florenz Ziegfield, theatrical producer

INDIANA

Capital: Indianapolis
Governor: Birch Evans Bayh III, D (to Jan. 1997)
Lieut. Governor: Frank O'Bannon, D (to Jan. 1997)
Secy. of State: Joseph H. Hogsett, D (to Dec. 1994)
Treasurer: Majorie H. O'Laughlin, R (to Feb. 1995)
Atty. General: Pamela Carter, D (to Jan. 1997)
Auditor: Ann G. Devore, R (to Dec. 1994)
Organized as territory: May 7, 1800
Entered Union & (rank): Dec. 11, 1816 (19)
Present constitution adopted: 1851
Motto: The Crossroads of America
STATE SYMBOLS: flower: Peony (1957); **tree,** Tulip tree (1931); **bird,** Cardinal (1933); **song,** "On the Banks of the Wabash, Far Away" (1913)
Nickname: Hoosier State
Origin of name: Meaning "land of Indians"
10 largest cities (1990 census): Indianapolis, 731,327; Fort Wayne, 173,072; Evansville, 126,272; Gary, 116,646; South Bend, 105,511; Hammond, 84,236; Muncie, 71,035; Bloomington, 60,633; Anderson, 59,459; Terre Haute, 57,483
Land area & (rank): 35,870 sq mi. (92,904 sq km) (38)

Geographic center: In Boone Co., 14 mi. NNW of Indianapolis
Number of Counties: 92
Largest county (1990 census): Marion, 797,159
State parks: 20 (56,806 ac.)
State memorials: 16 (941.977 ac.)
1992 resident population est.: 5,662,000
1990 census population, sex, & (rank): 5,544,159 (14). **Male:** 2,688,281; **Female:** 2,855,878. **White:** 5,020,700 (90.6%); **Black:** 432,092 (7.8%); **American Indian, Eskimo, or Aleut:** 12,720 (0.2%); **Asian or Pacific Islander:** 37,617 (0.7%); **Other race:** 41,030 (0.7%); **Hispanic:** 98,788 (1.8%). **1990 percent population under 18:** 26.3; **65 and over:** 12.6; **median age:** 32.8.

First explored for France by La Salle in 1679–80, the region figured importantly in the Franco-British struggle for North America that culminated with British victory in 1763.

George Rogers Clark led American forces against the British in the area during the Revolutionary War and, prior to becoming a state, Indiana was the scene of frequent Indian uprisings until the victory of Gen. William Henry Harrison at Tippecanoe in 1811.

Indiana's 41-mile Lake Michigan waterfront—one of the world's great industrial centers—turns out iron, steel, and oil products. Products include automobile parts and accessories, mobile homes and recreational vehicles, truck and bus bodies, aircraft engines, farm machinery, and fabricated structural steel. Phonograph records, wood office furniture, and pharmaceuticals are also manufactured.

The state is a leader in agriculture with corn the principal crop. Hogs, soybeans, wheat, oats, rye, tomatoes, onions, and poultry also contribute heavily to Indiana's agricultural output. Much of the building limestone used in the U.S. is quarried in Indiana which is also a large producer of coal.

Wyandotte Cave, one of the largest in the U.S., is located in Crawford County in southern Indiana and West Baden and French Lick are well known for their mineral springs. Other attractions include Indiana Dunes National Lakeshore, Indianapolis Motor Speedway, Lincoln Boyhood National Memorial, and the George Rogers Clark National Historical Park.

Famous natives and residents: George Ade, humorist; Leon Ames, actor; Anne Baxter, actress; Albert J. Beveridge, political leader; Bill Blass, fashion designer; Frank Borman, astronaut; Hoagy Carmichael, songwriter; James Dean, actor; Eugene V. Debs, Socialist leader; Lloyd C. Douglas, author; Theodore Dreiser, writer; Bernard F. Gimbel, merchant; Virgil Grissom, astronaut; Phil Harris, actor and band leader; John Milton Hay, statesman; James R. Hoffa, labor leader; Michael Jackson, singer; Buck Jones, actor; Alfred C. Kinsey, zoologist; David Letterman, TV host, comedian; Eli Lilly, pharmaceuticals manufacturer; Carole Lombard, actress; Shelley Long, actress; Marjorie Main, actress; James McCracken, tenor; Joaquin Miller, poet; Paul Osborn, playwright; Cole Porter, songwriter; Gene Stratton Porter, naturalist and author; Ernest Taylor Pyle, journalist; James Whitcomb Riley, poet; Knute Rockne, football coach; Ned Rorem, composer; Red Skelton, comedian; Rex Stout, mystery writer; Booth Tarkington, author; Twyla Tharp, dancer and choreographer; Forrest Tucker, actor; Harold C. Urey, physicist; Jessamyn West, novelist; Wendell Willkie, lawyer; Wilbur Wright, inventor

IOWA

Capital: Des Moines
Governor: Terry E. Branstad, R (to Jan. 1995)
Lieut. Governor: Joy Corning, R (to Jan. 1995)
Secy. of State: Elaine Baxter, D (to Jan. 1995)
Treasurer: Michael L. Fitzgerald, D (to Jan. 1995)
Atty. General: Bonnie Campbell, D (to Jan. 1995)
Organized as territory: June 12, 1838
Entered Union & (rank): Dec. 28, 1846 (29)
Present constitution adopted: 1857
Motto: Our liberties we prize and our rights we will maintain
STATE SYMBOLS: flower, Wild rose (1897); **bird,** Eastern goldfinch (1933); **colors,** Red, white, and blue (in state flag); **song,** "Song of Iowa"
Nickname: Hawkeye State
Origin of name: Probably from an Indian word meaning "I-o-w-a, this is the place," or "The Beautiful Land"
10 largest cities (1990 census): Des Moines, 193,187; Cedar Rapids, 108,751; Davenport, 95,333; Sioux City, 80,505; Waterloo, 66,467; Iowa City, 59,738; Dubuque, 57,546; Council Bluffs, 54,315; Ames, 47,198; Cedar Falls, 34,298
Land area & (rank): 55,875 sq mi. (144,716 sq km) (23)
Geographic center: In Story Co., 5 mi. NE of Ames
Number of counties: 99
Largest county (1990 census): Polk, 327,140
State forests: 5 (28,000 ac.)
State parks: 84 (49,237)
1992 resident population est.: 2,812,000
1990 resident census population, sex, & (rank): 2,776,755 (30). **Male:** 1,344,802; **Female:** 1,431,953. **White:** 2,683,090 (96.6%); **Black:** 48,090 (1.7%); **American Indian, Eskimo, or Aleut:** 7,349 (0.3%); **Asian or Pacific Islander:** 25,476 (0.9%); **Other race:** 12,750 (0.5%); **Hispanic:** 32,647 (1.2%). **1990 percent population under 18:** 25.9; **65 and over:** 15.3; **median age:** 34.0

The first Europeans to visit the area were the French explorers, Father Jacques Marquette and Louis Joliet in 1673. The U.S. obtained control of the area in 1803 as part of the Louisiana Purchase.

During the first half of the 19th century, there was heavy fighting between white settlers and Indians. Lands were taken from the Indians after the Black Hawk War in 1832 and again in 1836 and 1837.

When Iowa became a state in 1846, its capital was Iowa City; the more centrally located Des Moines became the new capital in 1857. At that time, the state's present boundaries were also drawn.

Although Iowa produces a tenth of the nation's food supply, the value of Iowa's manufactured products is twice that of its agriculture. Major industries are food and associated products, non-electrical machinery, electrical equipment, printing and publishing, and fabricated products.

Iowa stands in a class by itself as an agricultural state. Its farms sell over $10 billion worth of crops and livestock annually. Iowa leads the nation in all corn, soybeans, livestock, and hog marketings, with about 25% of the pork supply and 8% of the grain-fed cattle. Iowa's forests produce hardwood lumber, particularly walnut, and its mineral products include cement, limestone, sand, gravel, gypsum, and coal.

Tourist attractions include the Herbert Hoover birthplace and library near West Branch; the Amana Colonies; Fort Dodge Historical Museum, Fort, and Stockade; the Iowa State Fair at Des Moines in August; and the Effigy Mounds National Monument at Marquette, a prehistoric Indian burial site.

Famous natives and residents: Bix Beiderbecke, jazz musician; Norman Borlang, plant pathologist and geneticist, Nobel Peace Prize winner; William "Buffalo Bill" F. Cody, scout; Johnny Carson, TV entertainer; Gardner Cowles, Jr., publisher; Simon Estes, bass-baritone; William Frawley, actor; George H. Gallup, poll taker; Susan Glaspell, writer; Herbert Hoover, President; MacKinlay Kantor, novelist; Charles A. Kettering, inventor; Ann Landers, columnist; Cloris Leachman, actress; John L. Lewis, labor leader; Glenn L. Martin, aviator, manufacturer; Elsa Maxwell, writer; Frederick L. Maytag, inventor and manufacturer; Glenn Miller, bandleader; Harriet Nelson, actress; Nathan M. Pusey, educator; David Rabe, playwright; Harry Reasoner, TV commentator; Donna Reed, actress; Lillian Russell, soprano; Robert Schiller, evangelist; Wallace Stegner, novelist and critic; Billy Sunday, evangelist; James A. Van Allen, space physicist; Abigail Van Buren, columnist; Henry A. Wallace, statesman and vice president; John Wayne, actor; Andy Williams, singer; Meredith Willson, composer; Grant Wood, painter

KANSAS

Capital: Topeka
Governor: Joan Finney, D (to Jan. 1995)
Lieut. Governor: James Francisco, D (to Jan. 1995)
Secy. of State: Bill Graves, R (to Jan. 1995)
Treasurer: Sally Thompson, D (to Jan. 1995)
Atty. General: Robert T. Stephan, R (to Jan. 1995)
Commission of Insurance: Ron Todd, R (to Jan. 1995)
Organized as territory: May 30, 1854
Entered Union & (rank): Jan. 29, 1861 (34)
Present constitution adopted: 1859
Motto: *Ad astra per aspera* (To the stars through difficulties)
STATE SYMBOLS: flower, Sunflower (1903); **tree,** Cottonwood (1937); **bird,** Western meadowlark (1937); **animal,** Buffalo (1955); **song,** "Home on Range" (1947)
Nicknames: Sunflower State; Jayhawk State
Origin of name: From a Siouan word meaning "people of the south wind"
10 largest cities (1990 census): Wichita, 304,011; Kansas City, 149,767; Topeka, 119,883; Overland Park, 111,790; Lawrence, 65,608; Olathe, 63,352; Salina, 42,303; Hutchinson, 39,308; Leavenworth, 38,495; Shawnee, 37,993
Land area & (rank): 81,823 sq mi. (211,922 sq km) (13)
Geographic center: In Barton Co., 15 mi. NE of Great Bend
Number of counties: 105
Largest county (1990 census): Sedgwick, 403,662
State parks: 22 (14,394 ac.)
1992 resident population est.: 2,523,000
1990 resident census population, sex, & (rank): 2,477,574 (32). **Male:** 1,214,645; **Female:** 1,262,929. **White:** 2,231,986 (90.1%); **Black:** 143,076 (5.8%); **American Indian, Eskimo, or Aleut:** 21,965 (0.9%); **Asian or Pacific Islander:** 31,750 (1.3%); **Other race:** 48,797 (2.0%); **Hispanic:** 93,670 (3.8%). **1990 percent population under 18:** 26.7; **65 and over:** 13.8; **median age:** 32.9.

Spanish explorer Francisco de Coronado, in 1541, is considered the first European to have traveled this region. La Salle's extensive land claims for France (1682) included present-day Kansas. Ceded to Spain by France in 1763, the territory reverted back to France in 1800 and was sold to the U.S. as part of the Louisiana Purchase in 1803.

Lewis and Clark, Zebulon Pike, and Stephen H. Long explored the region between 1803 and 1819. The first permanent settlements in Kansas were outposts—Fort Leavenworth (1827), Fort Scott (1842), and Fort Riley (1853)—established to protect travelers along the Santa Fe and Oregon Trails.

Just before the Civil War, the conflict between the pro- and anti-slavery forces earned the region the grim title "Bleeding Kansas."

Today, wheat fields, oil well derricks, herds of cattle, and grain storage elevators are chief features of the Kansas landscape. A leading wheat-growing state, Kansas also raises corn, sorghums, oats, barley, soy beans, and potatoes. Kansas stands high in petroleum production and mines zinc, coal, salt, and lead. It is also the nation's leading producer of helium.

Wichita is one of the nation's leading aircraft manufacturing centers, ranking first in production of private aircraft. Kansas City is an important transportation, milling, and meat-packing center.

Points of interest include the new Kansas Museum of History at Topeka, the Eisenhower boyhood home and the new Eisenhower Memorial Museum and Presidential Library at Abilene, John Brown's cabin at Osawatomie, recreated Front Street in Dodge City, Fort Larned (once the most important military post on the Santa Fe Trail), and Fort Leavenworth and Fort Riley.

Famous natives and residents: Roscoe "Fatty" Arbuckle, actor; Clarence D. Batchelor, political cartoonist; Gwendolyn Brooks, poet; Walter P. Chrysler, auto manufacturer; Clark M. Clifford, ex-Secretary of Defense; John Steuart Curry, painter; Amelia Earhart, aviator; Milton S. Eisenhower, educator; Gary Hart, politician; William Inge, playwright; Walter Johnson, baseball pitcher; Osa L. Johnson, documentary film producer; Buster Keaton, comedian; Emmett Kelly, clown; Stan Kenton, jazz musician; James Lehrer, broadcast journalist; Edgar Lee Masters, poet; Mary McCarthy, actress; Hattie McDaniel, actress; William C. Menninger, psychiatrist; Gordon Parks, film director; Zasu Pitts, actress; Samuel Ramey, opera singer; Charles Robinson, statesman and first governor; Charles (Buddy) Rogers, actor; Damon Runyon, journalist; Eugene W. Smith, photojournalist; Milburn Stone, actor; John Cameron Swayze, news commentator; William Allen White, journalist; Charles E. Whittaker, jurist; Jess Willard, boxer

KENTUCKY

Capital: Frankfort
Governor: Brereton C. Jones, D (to Dec. 1995)
Lieut. Governor: Paul E. Patton, D (to Dec. 1995)
Secy. of State: Bob Babbage, D (to Jan. 1996)
State Treasurer: Frances Jones Mills, D (to Jan. 1996)
State Auditor: Ben Chandler, D (to Jan. 1996)
Atty. General: Chris Gorman, D (to Jan. 1996)
Entered Union & (rank): June 1, 1792 (15)
Present constitution adopted: 1891
Motto: United we stand, divided we fall
STATE SYMBOLS: tree, Coffeetree; **flower,** Goldenrod; **bird,** Kentucky cardinal; **song,** "My Old Kentucky Home"
Nickname: Bluegrass State
Origin of name: From an Iroquoian word "Ken-tah-ten" meaning "land of tomorrow"
10 largest cities (1990 census): Louisville, 269,063; Lexington-Fayette, 225,366; Owensboro, 53,549; Covington, 43,264; Bowling Green, 40,641; Hopkinsville, 29,809; Paducah, 27,256; Frankfort, 25,968; Henderson, 25,945; Ashland, 23,622
Land area & (rank): 39,732 sq mi. (102,907 sq km) (36)
Geographic center: In Marion Co., 3 mi. NNW of Lebanon
Number of counties: 120
Largest county (1990 census): Jefferson, population 664,937
State forests: 9 (44,173 ac.)
State parks: 43 (40,574 ac.)
1992 resident population est.: 3,755,000

1990 resident census population, sex, & (rank): 3,685,296 (23). **Male:** 1,785,235; **Female:** 1,900,061. **White:** 3,391,832 (92.0%); **Black:** 262,907 (7.1%); **American Indian, Eskimo, or Aleut:** 5,769 (0.2%); **Asian or Pacific Islander:** 17,812 (0.5%); **Other race:** 6,976 (0.2%); **Hispanic:** 21,984 (0.6%). **1990 percent population below age 18:** 25.9; **65 and over:** 12.7; **median age:** 33.0.

Kentucky was the first region west of the Allegheny Mountains settled by American pioneers. James Harrod established the first permanent settlement at Harrodsburg in 1774; the following year Daniel Boone, who had explored the area in 1767, blazed the Wilderness Trail and founded Boonesboro.

Politically, the Kentucky region was originally part of Virginia, but early statehood was gained in 1792.

During the Civil War, as a slaveholding state with a considerable abolitionist population, Kentucky was caught in the middle of the conflict, supplying both Union and Confederate forces with thousands of troops.

In recent years, manufacturing has shown important gains, but agriculture and mining are still vital to Kentucky's economy. Kentucky prides itself on producing some of the nation's best tobacco, horses, and whiskey. Corn, soybeans, wheat, fruit, hogs, cattle, and dairy farming are also important.

Among the manufactured items produced in the state are furniture, aluminum ware, brooms, shoes, lumber products, machinery, textiles, and iron and steel products. Kentucky also produces significant amounts of petroleum, natural gas, fluorspar, clay, and stone. However, coal accounts for 90% of the total mineral income.

Louisville, the largest city, famed for the Kentucky Derby at Churchill Downs, is also the location of a large state university, whiskey distilleries, and cigarette factories. The Bluegrass country around Lexington is the home of some of the world's finest race horses. Other attractions are Mammoth Cave, the George S. Patton, Jr., Military Museum at Fort Knox, and Old Fort Harrod State Park.

Famous natives and residents: John Adair, pioneer and political leader; Muhammad Ali, boxer; Alben W. Barkley, vice president; Louis D. Brandeis, jurist; John Mason Brown, critic; Kit Carson, scout; Champ Clark, politician; Rosemary Clooney, singer; Irvin S. Cobb, humorist; Jefferson Davis, President of Confederacy; Irene Dunne, actress; Crystal Gayle, singer; David W. Griffith, film producer; John M. Harlan, jurist; Elizabeth Hardwick, writer; Casey Jones, celebrated locomotive engineer; Abraham Lincoln, President; Loretta Lynn, singer; Carry Amelia Nation, temperance leader; Patrician Neal, actress; George Reeves, actor; Wiley B. Rutledge, jurist; Diane Sawyer, broadcast journalist; Phil Simms, football player; Adlai Stevenson, vice president; Allen Tate, poet and critic; Hunter Thompson, writer, Frederick M. Vinson, jurist; Robert Penn Warren, novelist

LOUISIANA

Capital: Baton Rouge
Governor: Edwin W. Edwards, D (to Jan. 1996)
Lieut. Governor: Melinda Schwegman, D (to Jan. 1996)
Secy. of State: W. Fox McKeithen, R (to Jan. 1996)
Treasurer: Mary L. Landieu, D (to Jan. 1996)
Atty. General: Richard P. Ieyoub, D (to Jan. 1996)
Organized as territory: March 26, 1804
Entered Union & (rank): April 30, 1812 (18)
Present constitution adopted: 1974
Motto: Union, justice, and confidence
STATE SYMBOLS: flower, Magnolia (1900); **tree,** Bald cypress (1963); **bird,** Pelican (1958); **songs,** "Give Me Louisiana" and "You Are My Sunshine"
Nicknames: Pelican State; Sportsman's Paradise; Creole State; Sugar State
Origin of name: In honor of Louis XIV of France
10 largest cities (1990 census): New Orleans, 496,938; Baton Rouge, 219,531; Shreveport, 198,525; Lafayette, 94,440; Kenner, 72,033; Lake Charles, 70,580; Monroe, 54,909; Bossier City, 52,721; Alexandria, 49,188; New Iberia, 31,828
Land area & (rank): 43,566 sq mi. (112,836 sq km) (33)
Geographic center: In Avoyelles Parish, 3 mi. SE of Marksville
Number of parishes (counties): 64
Largest parish (1990 census): Jefferson, 448,306
State forests: 1 (8,000 ac.)
State parks: 30 (13,932 ac.)
1992 resident population est.: 4,287,000
1990 resident census population, sex, & (rank): 4,219,973 (21). **Male:** 2,031,386; **Female:** 2,188,587. **White:** 2,839,138 (67.3%); **Black:** 1,299,281 (30.8%); **American Indian, Eskimo, or Aleut:** 18,541 (0.4%); **Asian or Pacific Islander:** 41,099 (1.0%); **Other race:** 21,914 (0.5%); **Hispanic:** 93,044 (2.2%). **1990 percent population under 18:** 29.1; **65 and over:** 11.1; **median age:** 31.0.

Louisiana has a rich, colorful historical background. Early Spanish explorers were Piñeda, 1519; Cabeza de Vaca, 1528; and de Soto in 1541. La Salle reached the mouth of the Mississippi and claimed all the land drained by it and its tributaries for Louis XIV of France in 1682.

Louisiana became a French crown colony in 1731, was ceded to Spain in 1763, returned to France in 1800, and sold by Napoleon to the U.S. as part of the Louisiana Purchase (with large territories to the north and northwest) in 1803.

In 1815, Gen. Andrew Jackson's troops defeated a larger British army in the Battle of New Orleans, neither side aware that the treaty ending the War of 1812 had been signed.

As to total value of its mineral output, Louisiana is a leader in natural gas, salt, petroleum, and sulfur production. Much of the oil and sulfur comes from offshore deposits. The state also produces large crops of sweet potatoes, rice, sugar cane, pecans, soybeans, corn, and cotton.

Leading manufactures include chemicals, processed food, petroleum and coal products, paper, lumber and wood products, transportation equipment, and apparel.

Louisiana marshes supply most of the nation's muskrat fur as well as that of opossum, raccoon, mink, and otter, and large numbers of game birds.

Major points of interest include New Orleans with its French Quarter and Superdome, plantation homes near Natchitoches and New Iberia, Cajun country in the Mississippi delta region, Chalmette National Historical Park, and the state capital at Baton Rouge.

Famous natives and residents: Louis Armstrong, musician; Geoffrey Beene, fashion designer; Truman Capote, writer; Kitty Carlisle, singer and actress; Van Cliburn, concert pianist; Michael De Bakey, heart surgeon; Fats Domino, musician; Louis Moreau Gottschalk, pianist, composer; Bryant Gumbel, TV newscaster; Lillian Hellman, playwright; Al Hirt, trumpeter; Mahalia Jackson, gospel singer; Jean Laffite, privateer; Dorothy Lamour, actress; John A. Lejeune, Marine Corps general; Elmore Leonard, author; Jerry Lee Lewis, singer; Huey P. Long, politician; Wynton Marsalis, musician; Jelly Roll Morton, jazz musician and composer; Huey Newton, black activist; Marguerite Piazza, soprano; Paul Prudhomme, chef; Howard K. Smith, TV commentator; Ben Turpin, comedian; Ray Walston, actor; Edward Douglas White, jurist

MAINE

Capital: Augusta
Governor: John R. McKernan, Jr., R (to Jan. 1995)
Secy. of State: G. William Diamond, D (to Jan. 1995)
Controller: David A. Bourne, R (term indefinite)
Atty. General: Michael E. Carpenter, D (to Jan. 1995)
Entered Union & (rank): March 15, 1820 (23)
Present constitution adopted: 1820
Motto: *Dirigo* (I direct)
STATE SYMBOLS: flower, White pine cone and tassel (1895); **tree,** White pine tree (1945); **bird,** Chickadee (1927); **fish,** Landlocked salmon (1969); **mineral,** Tourmaline (1971); **song,** "State of Maine Song" (1937)
Nickname: Pine Tree State
Origin of name: First used to distinguish the mainland from the offshore islands. It has been considered a compliment to Henrietta Maria, Queen of Charles I of England. She was said to have owned the province of Mayne in France.
10 largest cities (1990 census): Portland, 64,358; Lewiston, 39,757; Bangor, 33,181; Auburn, 24,309; South Portland, 23,163; Augusta, 21,325; Biddeford, 20,710; Waterville, 17,173; Westbrook, 16,121; Saco, 15,181
Land area & (rank): 30,865 sq mi. (79,939 sq km) (39)
Geographic center: In Piscataquis Co., 18 mi. N of Dover–Foxcroft
Number of counties: 16
Largest town (1990 census): Brunswick, 20,906
State forests: 1 (21,000 ac.)
State parks: 26 (247,627 ac.)
State historic sites: 18 (403 ac.)
1992 resident population est.: 1,235,000
1990 resident census population, sex, & (rank): 1,227,928 (38). **Male:** 597,850; **Female:** 630,078. **White:** 1,208,360 (98.4%); **Black:** 5,138 (0.4%); **American Indian, Eskimo, or Aleut:** 5,998 (0.5%); **Asian or Pacific Islander:** 6,683: (0.5%); **Other race:** 1,749 (0.1%); **Hispanic:** 6,829 (0.6%).

John Cabot and his son, Sebastian, are believed to have visited the Maine coast in 1498. However, the first permanent English settlements were not established until more than a century later, in 1623.

The first naval action of the Revolutionary War occurred in 1775 when colonials captured the British sloop *Margaretta* off Machias on the Maine coast. In that same year, the British burned Falmouth (now Portland).

Long governed by Massachusetts, Maine became the 23rd state as part of the Missouri Compromise in 1820.

Maine produces 98% of the nation's low-bush blueberries. Farm income is also derived from apples, potatoes, dairy products, and vegetables, with poultry and eggs the largest items.

The state is one of the world's largest pulp-paper producers. It ranks second in boot-and-shoe manufacturing. With almost 89% of its area forested, Maine turns out wood products from boats to toothpicks.

Maine leads the world in the production of the familiar flat tins of sardines, producing more than 75 million of them annually. Lobstermen normally catch 51% of the nation's true total of lobsters.

A scenic seacoast, beaches, lakes, mountains, and resorts make Maine a popular vacationland. There are more than 2,500 lakes and 5,000 streams, plus 26 state parks, to attract hunters, fishermen, skiers, and campers.

Major points of interest are: Bar Harbor, Allagash National Wilderness Waterway, the Wadsworth-Longfellow House in Portland, Roosevelt Campobello International Park, and the St. Croix Island National Monument.

Famous natives and residents: F. Lee Bailey, defense attorney; Charles F. Browne (Artemus Ward), humorist; Cyrus Curtis, publisher; Dorothea Dix, civil rights reformer; John Ford, film director; Melville Fuller, jurist; Marsden Hartley, painter; Henry Wadsworth Longfellow, poet; Sarah Orne Jewett, author; Stephen King, writer; Linda Lavin, actress; Edna St. Vincent Millay, poet; Marston Morse, mathematician; Frank Munsey, publisher; Walter Piston, composer; George Putnam, publisher; Kenneth Roberts, historical novelist; Edwin Arlington Robinson, poet; Margaret Chase Smith, politician; Samantha Smith, peacemaker, actress; John Hay Whitney, publisher

MARYLAND

Capital: Annapolis
Governor: William Donald Schaefer, D (to Jan. 1995)
Lieut. Gov.: Melvin A. Steinberg, D (to Jan. 1995)
Secy. of State: Tyras S. Athey, D (appointed by governor) (to Jan. 1995)
Comptroller of the Treasury: Louis L. Goldstein, D (to Jan. 1995)
Treasurer: Lucille Maurer, D (to Jan. 1995)
Atty. General: J. Joseph Curran, Jr., D (to Jan. 1995)
Entered Union & (rank): April 28, 1788 (7)
Present constitution adopted: 1867
Motto: *Fatti maschii, parole femine* (Manly deeds, womanly words)
STATE SYMBOLS: flower, Black-eyed susan (1918); **tree,** White oak (1941); **bird,** Baltimore oriole (1947); **dog,** Chesapeake Bay retriever (1964); **fish,** Rockfish (1965); **crustacean,** Maryland Blue Crab (1989); **insect,** Baltimore checkerspot butterfly (1973); **boat,** Skipjack (1985); **sport,** Jousting (1962); **song,** "Maryland! My Maryland!" (1939)
Nicknames: Free State; Old Line State
Origin of name: In honor of Henrietta Maria (Queen of Charles I of England)
10 largest cities (1990 census): Baltimore, 736,014; Rockville, 44,835; Frederick, 40,148; Gaithersburg, 39,542; Bowie, 37,589; Hagerstown, 35,445; Annapolis, 33,187; Cumberland, 23,706; College Park, 21,927; Greenbelt, 21,096
Land area & (rank): 9,775 sq mi. (25,316 sq km) (42)
Geographic center: In Prince Georges Co., 4 1/2 mi. NW of Davidsonville
Number of counties: 23, and 1 independent city
Largest county (1990 census): Montgomery, 757,027
State forests: 13 (132,944 ac.)
State parks: 47 (87,670 ac.)
1992 resident population est.: 4,908,000
1990 resident census population, sex, & (rank): 4,781,468 (19). **Male:** 2,318,671; **Female:** 2,462,797. **White:** 3,393,964 (71.0%); **Black:** 1,189,899 (24.9%); **American Indian, Eskimo, or Aleut:** 12,972 (0.3%); **Asian or Pacific Islander:** 139,719 (2.9%); **Other race:** 44,914 (0.9%); **Hispanic:** 125,102 (2.6%). **1990 percent population under 18:** 24.3; **65 and over:** 10.8; **median age:** 33.0

Maryland was inhabited by Indians as early as c. 10,000 B.C., and permanent Indian villages were established by c. 1,000 A.D.

In 1608, Capt. John Smith explored Chesapeake Bay. Charles I granted a royal charter for Maryland to Cecil Calvert, Lord Baltimore, in 1632, and English settlers, many of whom were Roman Catholic, landed on St. Clement's (now Blakistone) Island in 1634. Religious freedom, granted all Christians in the Toleration Act passed by the Maryland assembly in 1649, was ended by a Puritan revolt, 1654–58.

From 1763 to 1767, Charles Mason and Jeremiah Dixon surveyed Maryland's northern boundary line with Pennsylvania. In 1791, Maryland ceded land to form the District of Columbia.

In 1814, when the British unsuccessfully tried to capture Baltimore, the bombardment of Fort McHenry inspired Francis Scott Key to write *The Star Spangled Banner.*

The Baltimore clipper ship trade developed during the 19th century. During the Civil War, Maryland remained a Union state even while the battles of South Mountain (1862), Antietam (1862), and Monocacy (1864) were fought on her soil.

In 1904, the Great Fire of Baltimore occurred. In 1937, the City of Greenbelt, a New Deal model community, was chartered.

Maryland's Eastern Shore and Western Shore embrace the Chesapeake Bay, and the many estuaries and rivers create one of the longest waterfronts of any state. The Bay produces more seafood—oysters, crabs, clams, fin fish—than any comparable body of water. Important agricultural products, in order of cash value, are chickens, dairy products, cattle, soy beans, eggs, corn, hogs, vegetables, and tobacco. Maryland is a leader in vegetable canning. Sand, gravel, lime and cement, stone, coal, and clay are the chief mineral products.

Manufacturing industries produce missiles, airplanes, steel, clothing, and chemicals. Baltimore, home of The Johns Hopkins University and Hospital, ranks as the nation's second port in foreign tonnage. Annapolis, site of the U.S. Naval Academy, has one of the earliest state houses (1772–79) still in regular use by a State government.

Among the popular attractions in Maryland are the Fort McHenry National Monument; Harpers Ferry and Chesapeake and Ohio Canal National Historic Parks; Antietam National Battlefield; National Aquarium, USS *Constellation,* and Maryland Science Center at Baltimore's Inner Harbor; Historic St. Mary's City; Jefferson Patterson Historical Park and Museum at St. Leonard; U.S. Naval Academy in Annapolis; Goddard Space Flight Center at Greenbelt; Assateague Island National Park Seashore; Ocean City beach resort; and Catoctin Mountain, Fort Frederick, and Piscataway parks.

Famous natives and residents: Benjamin Banneker, almanacker, mathetmatician-astronomer; Eubie Blake, musician; John Wilkes Booth, actor, Lincoln assassin; Francis X. Bushman, actor; James M. Cain, writer; Samuel Chase, jurist; Frederick Douglass, abolitionist; John Hurst Fletcher, Methodist bishop and educator; Christopher Gist, frontiersman; Philip Glass, composer; Billie Holiday, jazz-blues singer; Johns Hopkins, financier; Reverdy Johnson, lawyer and statesman; Thomas Johnson, political leader; Francis Scott Key, laywer, author of National Anthem; Thurgood Marshall, jurist; H.L. Mencken, writer; Mildred Natwick, actress; Charles Wilson Peale, painter; Frank Perdue, farmer, businessman; James R. Randall, journalist, wrote state song; Lisette Reese, poet and author; Babe Ruth, baseball player; Upton Sinclair, novelist; Roger B. Taney, jurist; Harriet Tubman, abolistionist; Leon Uris, novelist; Frank Zappa, singer

MASSACHUSETTS

Capital: Boston
Governor: William F. Weld, R (to Jan. 1995)
Lieut. Governor: Paul Cellucci, R (to Jan. 1995)
Secy. of the Commonwealth: Michael Joseph Connolly, D (to Jan. 1995)
Treasurer & Receiver-General: Joseph Malone, R (to Jan. 1995)
Auditor of the Commonwealth: A. Joseph DeNucci, D (to Jan. 1995)
Atty. General: L. Scott Harshbarger, D (to Jan. 1995)
Present constitution drafted: 1780 (oldest U.S. state constitution in effect today)
Entered Union & (rank): Feb. 6, 1788 (6)
Motto: *Ense petit placidam sub libertate quietem* (By the sword we seek peace, but peace only under liberty)
STATE SYMBOLS: flower, Mayflower (1918); **tree.** American elm (1941); **bird,** Chickadee (1941); **colors,** Blue and gold; **song,** "All Hail to Massachusetts" (1966); **beverage,** Cranberry juice (1970); **insect,** Ladybug (1974); **muffin,** corn muffin
Nicknames: Bay State; Old Colony State
Origin of name: From two Indian words meaning "Great mountain place"
10 largest cities (1990 census): Boston, 574,283; Worcester, 169,759; Springfield, 156,983; Lowell, 103,439; New Bedford, 99,922; Cambridge, 95,802; Brockton, 92,788; Fall River, 92,703; Quincy, 84,985; Newton, 82,585
Land area & (rank): 7,838 sq mi. (20,300 sq km) (45)
Geographic center: In Worcester Co., in S part of city of Worcester
Number of counties: 14
Largest county (1990 census): Middlesex, 1,398,468
State forests and parks: 129 (242,000 ac.)[1]
1992 resident population est.: 5,998,000
1990 resident census population, sex, & (rank): 6,016,425 (13). **Male:** 2,888,745; **Female:** 3,127,680. **White:** 5,405,374 (89.8%); **Black:** 300,130 (5.0%); **American Indian, Eskimo, or Aleut:** 12,241 (0.2%); **Asian or Pacific Islander:** 143,392 (2.4%); **Other race:** 155,288 (2.6%); **Hispanic:** 287,549 (4.8%). **1990 percent population under 18:** 22.5; **65 and over:** 13.6; **median age:** 33.6.

1. The Metropolitan District Commission, an agency of the Commonwealth serving municipalities in the Boston area, has about 14,000 acres of parkways and reservations under its jurisdiction.

Massachusetts has played a significant role in American history since the Pilgrims, seeking religious freedom, founded Plymouth Colony in 1620.

As one of the most important of the 13 colonies, Massachusetts became a leader in resisting British oppression. In 1773, the Boston Tea Party protested unjust taxation. The Minutemen started the American Revolution by battling British troops at Lexington and Concord on April 19, 1775.

During the 19th century, Massachusetts was famous for the vigorous intellectual activity of famous writers and educators and for its expanding commercial fishing, shipping, and manufacturing interests.

Massachusetts pioneered in the manufacture of textiles and shoes. Today, these industries have been replaced in importance by activity in the electronics and communications equipment fields.

The state's cranberry crop is the nation's largest. Also important are dairy and poultry products, nursery and greenhouse produce, vegetables, and fruit.

Tourism has become an important factor in the economy of the state because of its numerous recreational areas and historical landmarks.

Cape Cod has summer theaters, water sports, and an artists' colony at Provincetown. Tanglewood, in the Berkshires, features the summer concerts of the Boston Symphony.

Among the many other points of interest are Old Sturbridge Village in Sturbridge in central Massachusetts, Minuteman National Historical Park between Lexington and Concord, and, in Boston: Old North Church, Old State House, Faneuil Hall, the USS *Constitution* and the John F. Kennedy Library.

Famous natives and residents: John Adams, President; John Quincy Adams, President; Samuel Adams, patriot; Horatio Alger, novelist; Susan B. Anthony, woman suffragist; Clara Barton, American Red Cross founder; Leonard Bernstein, conductor; George Bush, President; William Cullen Bryan, poet and editor; Luther Burbank, horticulturalist; John Cheever, novelist; John Singleton Copley, painter; E.E. Cummings, poet; Jacques d'Amboise, ballet dancer; Bette Davis, actress; Cecil B. De Mille, film director; Emily Dickinson, poet; Ralph Waldo Emerson, philosopher and poet; Geraldine Farrar, soprano, actress; Benjamin Franklin, statesman and scientist; Buckminster Fuller, architect and educator; Robert Goddard, father of modern rocketry; John Hancock, statesman; Nathaniel Hawthorne, novelist; Oliver Weldell Holmes, jurist; Winslow Homer, painter; Elias Howe, inventor; John F. Kennedy, President; Amy Lowell, poet; James Russell Lowell, poet; Robert Lowell, poet; Horace Mann, educator; Cotton Mather, clergyman; Samuel F.B. Morse, painter and inventor; Edgar Allan Poe, writer; Paul Revere, silversmith, hero of ride; Dr. Seuss (Theodore Geisel), author and illustrator; David Souter, jurist; Lucy Stone, woman suffragist; Louis Henry Sullivan, architect; Henry David Thoreau, author; Barbara Walters, TV commentator; James McNeill Whistler, painter; Eli Whitney, inventor; John Greenleaf Whittier, poet

MICHIGAN

Capital: Lansing
Governor: John M. Engler, R (to Jan. 1995)
Lieut. Governor: Connie Binsfeld, R (to Jan. 1995)
Secy. of State: Richard H. Austin, D (to Jan. 1995)
Atty. General: Frank J. Kelley, D (to Jan. 1995)
Organized as territory: Jan. 11, 1805
Entered Union & (rank): Jan. 26, 1837 (26)
Present constitution adopted: April 1, 1963, (effective Jan. 1, 1964)
Motto: *Si quaeris peninsulam amoenam circumspice* (If you seek a pleasant peninsula, look around you)
STATE SYMBOLS: flower, Apple blossom (1897); **bird,** Robin (1931); **fishes,** Trout (1965), Brook trout (1988); **gem,** Isle Royal Greenstone (Chlorastrolite) (1972); **stone,** Petoskey Stone (1965); **tree,** White pine (1955); **soil,** Kalkaska Soil series (1990); **flag,** "Blue charged with the arms of the state" (1911)
Nickname: Wolverine State
Origin of name: From Indian word "Michigana" meaning "great or large lake"
10 largest cities (1990 census): Detroit, 1,027,974; Grand Rapids, 189,126; Warren, 144,864; Flint, 140,761; Lansing, 127,321; Sterling Heights, 117,810; Ann Arbor, 109,592; Livonia, 100,850; Dearborn, 89,286; Westland, 84,724
Land area & (rank): 58,110 sq mi. (151,086 sq km) (22)
Geographic center: In Wexford Co., 5 mi. NNW of Cadillac
Number of counties: 83
Largest county (1990 census): Wayne, 2,111,687
State parks and recreation areas: 82 (250,000 ac.)
1992 resident population est.: 9,437,000
1990 resident census population, sex, & (rank): 9,295,297 (8). **Male:** 4,512,781; **Female:** 4,787,516. **White:** 7,756,086 (83.4%); **Black:** 1,291,706 (13.9%); **American Indian, Eskimo, or Aleut:** 55,638 (0.6%); **Asian or Pacific Islander:** 104,983 (1.1%); **Other race:** 86,884 (0.9%); **Hispanic:** 201,596 (2.2%). **1990 percent population under 18:** 26.5; **65 and over:** 11.9; **median age:** 32.6.

Indian tribes were living in the Michigan region when the first European, Etienne Brulé of France, arrived in 1618. Other French explorers, including Marquette, Joliet, and La Salle, followed, and the first permanent settlement was established in 1668 at Sault Ste. Marie. France was ousted from the territory by Great Britain in 1763, following the French and Indian War.

After the Revolutionary War, the U.S. acquired most of the region, which remained the scene of constant conflict between the British and U.S. forces and their respective Indian allies through the War of 1812.

Bordering on four of the five Great Lakes, Michigan is divided into Upper and Lower Peninsulas by the Straits of Mackinac, which link Lakes Michigan and Huron. The two parts of the state are connected by the Mackinac Bridge, one of the world's longest suspension bridges. To the north, connecting Lakes Superior and Huron are the busy Sault Ste. Marie Canals.

While Michigan ranks first among the states in production of motor vehicles and parts, it is also a leader in many other manufacturing and processing lines including prepared cereals, machine tools, airplane parts, refrigerators, hardware, steel springs, and furniture.

The state produces important amounts of iron, copper, iodine, gypsum, bromine, salt, lime, gravel, and cement. Michigan's farms grow apples, cherries, beans, pears, grapes, potatoes, and sugar beets. Michigan's forests contribute significantly to the state's economy. Forest-based industries (wood product industry, tourism, and recreation) support nearly 180,000 jobs and contribute over $1.8 billion to the state economy. With 10,083 inland lakes and 3,288 miles of Great Lakes' shoreline, Michigan is a prime area for both commercial and sport fishing.

Points of interest are the automobile plants in Dearborn, Detroit, Flint, Lansing, and Pontiac; Mackinac Island; Pictured Rocks and Sleeping Bear Dunes National Lakeshores, Greenfield Village in Dearborn; and the many summer resorts along both the inland and Great Lakes.

Famous natives and residents: Nelsen Algren, novelist; Ralph J. Bunche, statesman, Ellen Burstyn, actress; Bruce Catton, historian; Roger Chaffee, astronaut; Francis Ford Coppola, film director; Thomas E. Dewey, politician; Edna Ferber, novelist; Gerald R. Ford, U.S. President (1974–77); Henry Ford, industrialist; Ali Haji-Sheikh, football player; Julie Harris, actress; Earvin "Magic" Johnson, basketball player; Ring Lardner, story writer; Charles A. Lindbergh, aviator; Madonna, singer; Dick Martin, comedian; John N. Mitchell, former Attorney General; Gilda Radner, comedienne; Della Reese, singer; Jason Robards, Sr., actor; Diana Ross, singer; Thomas Schippers, conductor; Potter Stewart, jurist; Danny Thomas, entertainer; Margaret Whiting, singer; Stevie Wonder, singer

MINNESOTA

Capital: St. Paul
Governor: Arne Carlson, R (to Jan. 1995)
Lieut. Governor: Joanell Dyrstad, R (to Jan. 1995)
Secy. of State: Joan Anderson Growe, D (to Jan. 1995)
State Auditor: Mark Dayton, D (to Jan. 1995)
Atty. General: Hubert H. Humphrey III, D (to Jan. 1995)
State Treasurer: Michael McGrath, D (to Jan. 1995)
Organized as territory: March 3, 1849
Entered Union & (rank): May 11, 1858 (32)
Present constitution adopted: 1858
Motto: L'Etoile du Nord (The North Star)
STATE SYMBOLS: flower, Showy lady slipper (1902); **tree,** Red (or Norway) pine (1953); **bird,** Common loon (also called Great Northern Diver) (1961); **song,** "Hail Minnesota" (1945); **fish,** Walleye (1965); **mushroom,** Morel (1984)
Nicknames: North Star State; Gopher State; Land of 10,000 Lakes

Origin of name: From a Dakota Indian word meaning "sky-tinted water"
10 largest cities (1991 est. population): Minneapolis, 368,993; St. Paul, 272,537; Bloomington, 86,453; Duluth, 85,382; Rochester, 72,480; Brooklyn Park, 57,359; Coon Rapids, 54,518; Plymouth, 52,492; Burnsville, 51,743; St. Cloud, 49,350
Land area & (rank): 79,617 sq mi. (206,207 sq km) (14)
Geographic center: In Crow Wing Co., 10 mi. SW of Brainerd
Number of counties: 87
Largest county (1991 est. population): Hennepin, 1,039,099
State forests: 56 (3,200,000+ ac.)
State parks: 66 (226,000 ac.)
1992 resident population est.: 4,480,034
1990 resident census population, sex, & (rank): 4,375,099 (20). **Male:** 2,145,183; **Female:** 2,229,916. **White:** 4,130,395 (94.4%); **Black:** 94,944 (2.2%); **American Indian, Eskimo, or Aleut:** 49,909 (1.1%); **Asian or Pacific Islander:** 77,886 (1.8%); **Other race:** 21,965 (0.5%); **Hispanic:** 53,884 (1.2%). **1990 percent population under 18:** 26.7; **65 and over:** 12.5; **median age:** 32.5.

Following the visits of several French explorers, fur traders, and missionaries, including Marquette and Joliet and La Salle, the region was claimed for Louis XIV by Daniel Greysolon, Sieur Duluth, in 1679.

The U.S. acquired eastern Minnesota from Great Britain after the Revolutionary War and 20 years later bought the western part from France in the Louisiana Purchase of 1803. Much of the region was explored by U.S. Army Lt. Zebulon M. Pike before cession of the northern strip of Minnesota bordering Canada by Britain in 1818.

The state is rich in natural resources. A few square miles of land in the north in the Mesabi, Cuyuna, and Vermillion ranges, produce more than 75% of the nation's iron ore. The state's farms rank high in yields of corn, wheat, rye, alfalfa, and sugar beets. Other leading farm products include butter, eggs, milk, potatoes, green peas, barley, soy beans, oats, and livestock.

Minnesota's factory production includes nonelectrical machinery, fabricated metals, flour-mill products, plastics, electronic computers, scientific instruments, and processed foods. It is also one of the nation's leaders in the printing and paper products industries.

Minneapolis is the trade center of the Northwest; and the headquarters of the world's largest super computer and grain distributor. St. Paul is the nation's biggest publisher of calendars and law books. These "twin cities" are the nation's third largest trucking center. Duluth has the nation's largest inland harbor and now handles a significant amount of foreign trade. Rochester is the home of the Mayo Clinic, an internationally famous medical center.

Today, tourism is a major revenue producer in Minnesota, with arts, fishing, hunting, water sports, and winter sports bringing in millions of visitors each year.

Among the most popular attractions are the St. Paul Winter Carnival; the Tyrone Guthrie Theatre, the Institute of Arts, Walker Art Center, and Minnehaha Park, in Minneapolis; Boundary Waters Canoe Area; Voyageurs National Park; North Shore Drive; and the Minnesota Zoological Gardens and the state's more than 10,000 lakes.

Famous natives and residents: LaVerne, Maxene, and Patti Andrews, singers; Warren E. Burger, jurist; William E. Colby, ex-director of CIA; William Demarest, actor; William O. Douglas, jurist; Bob Dylan, singer and composer; F. Scott Fitzgerald, novelist; Judy Garland, singer and actress; J. Paul Getty, oil executive; Cass Gilbert, architect; Duane Hanson, sculptor; Hubert H. Humphrey, senator and vice president; Jessica Lange, actress; Sinclair Lewis, novelist; Cornell MacNeil, baritone; Roger Maris, baseball player; E.G. Marshall, actor; Charles H. Mayo, surgeon, William J. Mayo, surgeon; Eugene J. McCarthy, senator; Kate Millett, feminist; Gen. Lauris Norstad, ex-commander of NATO forces; Westbrook Pegler, columnist; John Sargent Pillsbury, flour milling; Marion Ross, actress; Jane Russell, actress; Harrison E. Salisbury, journalist; Charles M. Schulz, cartoonist; Max Shulman, novelist; Maurice H. Stans, ex-Secretary of Commerce; Harold E. Stassen, ex-government official; Michael Todd, producer; Frederick Weyerhaeuser, lumbering; Gig Young, actor

MISSISSIPPI

Capital: Jackson
Governor: Kirk Fordice, R (to Jan. 1996)
Lieut. Governor: Eddie Briggs, R (to Jan. 1996)
Secy. of State: Dick Molpus, D (to Jan. 1996)
Treasurer: Marshall Bennett, D (to Jan. 1996)
Atty. General: Mike Moore, D (to Jan. 1996)
Organized as Territory: April 7, 1798
Entered Union & (rank): Dec. 10, 1817 (20)
Present constitution adopted: 1890
Motto: *Virtute et armis* (By valor and arms)
STATE SYMBOLS: flower, Flower or bloom of the magnolia or evergreen magnolia (1952); **tree,** Magnolia (1938); **bird,** Mockingbird (1944); **song,** "Go, Mississippi" (1962); **stone,** Petrified wood (1976); **fish,** Largemouth or black bass (1974); **insect,** Honeybee (1980); **shell,** Oyster shell (1974); **water mammal,** Bottle-nosed dolphin or porpoise (1974); **fossil,** Prehistoric whale (1981); **land mammal,** White-tailed deer (1974); **waterfowl,** Wood duck (1974); **beverage,** Milk (1984)
Nickname: Magnolia State
Origin of name: From an Indian word meaning "Father of Waters"
10 largest cities (1990 census): Jackson, 196,637; Biloxi, 46,319; Greenville, 45,226; Hattiesburg, 41,882; Meridian, 41,036; Gulfport, 40,775; Tupelo, 30,685; Pascagoula, 25,899; Columbus, 23,799; Clinton, 21,847
Land area & (rank): 46,914 sq mi. (121,506 sq km) (31)
Geographic center: In Leake Co., 9 mi. WNW of Carthage
Number of counties: 82
Largest county (1990 census): Hinds, 254,441
State forests: 1 (1,760 ac.)
State parks: 27 (16,763 ac.)
1992 resident population est.: 2,614,000
1990 resident census population, sex, & (rank): 2,573,216 (31). **Male:** 1,230,617; **Female:** 1,342,599. **White:** 1,633,461 (63.5%); **Black:** 915,057 (35.6%); **American Indian, Eskimo, or Aleut:** 8,525 (0.3%); **Asian or Pacific Islander:** 13,016 (0.5%); **Other race:** 3,157 (0.1%); **Hispanic:** 15,931 (0.6%). **1990 percent population under 18:** 29.0; **65 and over:** 12.5; **median age:** 31.2.

First explored for Spain by Hernando de Soto who discovered the Mississippi River in 1540, the region was later claimed by France. In 1699, a French group under Sieur d'Iberville established the first permanent settlement near present-day Ocean Springs.

Great Britain took over the area in 1763 after the French and Indian War, ceding it to the U.S. in 1783 after the Revolution. Spain did not relinquish its claims until 1798, and in 1810 the U.S. annexed West Florida from Spain, including what is now southern Mississippi.

For a little more than one hundred years, from shortly after the state's founding through the Great Depression, cotton was the undisputed king of Mississippi's largely agrarian economy. Over the last half-century, however, Mississippi has progressively deepened its commitment to diversification by balancing agricultural output with increased industrial activity.

Today, agriculture continues as a major segment of the state's economy. While the most acreage is devoted to soybeans, cotton is the largest cash crop—Mississippi remains third in the nation in cotton production. The state's farmlands yield important harvests of corn, peanuts, pecans, rice, sugar cane, sweet potatoes, soybeans and food grains as well as poultry, eggs, meat animals, dairy products, feed crops and horticultural crops. Mississippi remains the world's leading producer of pond-raised catfish. The total acres of catfish ponds nationwide is approximately 140,000 acres whereas Mississippi alone has 100,000 acres of the total nationwide figure.

The state abounds in historical landmarks and is the home of the Vicksburg National Military Park. Other National Park Service areas are Brices Cross Roads National Battlefield Site, Tupelo National Battlefield, and part of Natchez Trace National Parkway. Pre-Civil War mansions are the special pride of Natchez, Oxford, Columbus, Vicksburg, and Jackson.

Famous natives and residents: Red Barber, sportscaster; Craig Claiborne, columnist and restaurant critic; Bo Diddley, guitarist; Charles Evers, civil rights leader; Medgar Evers, civil rights leader; William Faulkner, novelist; Beth Henley, playwright and actress; Jim Henson, puppeteer; James Earl Jones, actor; B.B. King, guitarist; Mary Ann Mobley, actress; Willie Morris, writer; Elvis Presley, singer and actor; Leontyne Price, soprano; Jerry Rice, football player; Jimmie Rodgers, singer; Muddy Waters, singer and guitarist; Eudora Welty, novelist; Tennessee Williams, playwright; Oprah Winfrey, talk show host and actress; Richard Wright, novelist

MISSOURI

Capital: Jefferson City
Governor: Mel Carnahan, D (to Jan. 1997)
Lieut. Governor: Roger Wilson, D (to Jan. 1997)
Secy. of State: Judith K. "Judi" Moriarty, D (to Jan. 1997)
Auditor: Margaret Kelly, R (to Jan. 1995)
Treasurer: Bob Holden, D (to Jan. 1997)
Atty. General: William Jay Nixon, D (to Jan. 1997)
Organized as territory: June 4, 1812
Entered Union & (rank): Aug. 10, 1821 (24)
Present constitution adopted: 1945
Motto: *Salus populi suprema lex esto* (The welfare of the people shall be the supreme law)
STATE SYMBOLS: flower, Hawthorn (1923); **bird,** Bluebird (1927); **song,** "Missouri Waltz" (1949); **fossil,** Crinoidea (1989); **musical instrument,** Fiddle (1987); **rock,** Mozarkite (1967); **mineral,** Galena (1967); **insect,** Honeybee (1985); **tree,** Flowering dogwood (1955); **tree nut,** black walnut (1990)
Nickname: Show-me State
Origin of name: Named after a tribe called Missouri Indians. "Missouri" means "town of the large canoes."
10 largest cities (1990 census): Kansas City, 435,146; St. Louis, 396,685; Springfield, 140,494; Independence, 112,301; St. Joseph, 71,852; Columbia, 69,101; St. Charles, 54,555; Florissant, 51,206; Lee's Summit, 46,418; St. Peter's, 45,779
Land area & (rank): 68,898 sq mi. (178,446 sq km) (18)
Geographic center: In Miller Co., 20 mi. SW of Jefferson City
Number of counties: 114, plus 1 independent city
Largest county (1990 census): St. Louis, 993,529
Conservation areas[1]: 343 (602,272 ac.)
Conservation accesses: 218 (9,457 ac.)
State parks and historic sites: 79 (126,072 ac.)
1992 resident population est.: 5,193,000
1990 resident census population, sex, & (rank): 5,117,073 (15). **Male:** 2,464,315; **Female:** 2,652,758. **White:** 4,486,228 (87.7%); **Black:** 548,208 (10.7%); **American Indian, Eskimo, or Aleut:** 19,835 (0.4%); **Asian or Pacific Islander:** 41,277 (0.8%); **Other race:** 21,525 (0.4%); **Hispanic:** 61,702 (1.2%). **1990 percent population under 18:** 25.7; **65 and over:** 14.0; **median age:** 33.5.

1. Includes wildlife areas, natural history areas, state forests, and tower sites.

De Soto visited the Missouri area in 1541. France's claim to the entire region was based on La Salle's travels in 1682. French fur traders established Ste. Genevieve in 1735 and St. Louis was first settled in 1764.

The U.S. gained Missouri from France as part of the Louisiana Purchase in 1803, and the territory was admitted as a state following the Missouri Compromise of 1820. Throughout the pre-Civil War period and during the war, Missourians were sharply divided in their opinions about slavery and in their allegiances, supplying both Union and Confederate forces with troops. However, the state itself remained in the Union.

Historically, Missouri played a leading role as a gateway to the West, St. Joseph being the eastern starting point of the Pony Express, while the much-traveled Santa Fe and Oregon Trails began in Independence. Now a popular vacationland, Missouri has 11 major lakes and numerous fishing streams, springs, and caves. Bagnell Dam, across the Osage River in the Ozarks, completed in 1931, created one of the largest man-made lakes in the world, covering 65,000 acres of surface area.

Manufacturing, paced by the aerospace industry, provides more income and jobs than any other segment of the economy. Missouri is also a leading producer of transportation equipment, shoes, lead, and beer. Among the major crops are grain sorghum, hay, corn, soybeans, wheat, oats, barley, potatoes, tobacco, grapes, rice, and cotton. Missouri ranks second nationally in cattle production.

Points of interest include Mark Twain's boyhood home and Mark Twain Cave (Hannibal), the Harry S Truman Library and Museum (Independence), the house where Jesse James was killed in St. Joseph, Jefferson National Expansion Memorial (St. Louis), and the Ozark National Scenic Riverway.

Famous natives and residents: Robert Altman, film director; Burt Bacharach, songwriter; Josephine Baker, singer and dancer; Wallace Beery, actor; Robert Russell Bennett, composer; Yogi Berra, baseball player; Thomas Hart Benton, painter; Bill Bradley, basketball player and N.J. senator; Omar N. Bradley, 5-star general; Grace Bumbry, soprano; William Burroughs, writer; Sarah Caldwell, opera director and conductor; Martha Jane Canary (Calamity Jane), frontierswoman; Walter Cronkhite, TV newscaster; Robert Cummings, actor; Jane Darwell, actress; Jeanne Eagels, actress; T.S. Eliot, poet; Eugene Field, poet; Redd Foxx, actor and comedian; Betty Grable, actress; Dick Gregory, comic and activist; Jean Harlow, actress; George Hearn, actor; Al Hirschfeld, artist; Langston Hughes, poet; John Huston, film director; Jesse James, outlaw; Bernarr MacFadden, physical culturist; Mary Margaret McBride, TV hostess; Marianne Moore, poet; Geraldine Page, actress; James C. Penney, merchant; Marlin Perkins, TV host, zoo director; John Joseph Pershing, general; Vincent Price, actor; Doris Roberts, actress; Ginger Rogers, dancer and actress; Ted Shawn, dancer and choreographer; Casey Stengel, baseball; Gladys Swarthout, soprano; Sara Teasdale, poet; Virgil Thomson, composer; Harry S Truman, President; Mark Twain, author; Dick Van Dyke, actor; Ruth Warrick, actress; Dennis Weaver, actor; Pearl White, actress; Mary Wickes, actress; Roy Wilkins, civil rights leader

MONTANA

Capital: Helena
Governor: Marc Racirot, R (to Jan. 1997)
Lieut. Governor: Dennis R. Rehberg, R (to Jan. 1997)
Secy. of State: Mike Cooney, D (to Jan. 1997)
Auditor: Mark O'Keefe, D (to Jan. 1997)
Atty. General: Joe Mazurek, D (to Jan. 1997)
Organized as territory: May 26, 1864
Entered Union & (rank): Nov. 8, 1889 (41)
Present constitution adopted: 1972
Motto: *Oro y plata* (Gold and silver)
STATE SYMBOLS: flower, Bitterroot (1895); **tree,** Ponderosa pine (1949); **stones,** Sapphire and agate (1969); **bird,** Western meadowlark (1981); **song,** "Montana" (1945)
Nickname: Treasure State
Origin of name: Chosen from Latin dictionary by J. M. Ashley. It is a Latinized Spanish word meaning "mountainous."
10 largest cities (1990 census): Billings, 81,151; Great Falls, 55,097; Missoula, 42,918; Butte-Silver Bow[1], 33,941; Helena, 24,569; Bozeman, 22,660; Kalispell, 11,917; Anaconda-Deer Lodge County, 10,278; Havre, 10,201; Miles City, 8,461
Land area & (rank): 145,556 sq mi. (376,991 sq km) (4)
Geographic center: In Fergus Co., 12 mi. W of Lewistown
Number of counties: 56, plus small part of Yellowstone National Park
Largest county (1990 census): Yellowstone, 113,419
State forests: 7 (214,000 ac.)
State parks and recreation areas: 110 (18,273 ac.)
1992 resident population est.: 824,000
1990 resident census population, sex, & (rank): 799,065 (44). **Male:** 395,769; **Female:** 403,296. **White:** 741,111 (92.7%); **Black:** 2,381 (0.3%); **American Indian, Eskimo, or Aleut:** 47,679 (6.0%); **Asian or Pacific Islander:** 4,259 (0.5%); **Other race:** 3,635 (0.5%); **Hispanic:** 12,174 (1.5%). **1990 percent population under 18:** 27.8; **65 and over:** 13.3; **median age:** 33.8.

1. Consolidated City.

First explored for France by François and Louis-Joseph Verendrye in the early 1740s, much of the region was acquired by the U.S. from France as part of the Louisiana Purchase in 1803. Before western Montana was obtained from Great Britain in the Oregon Treaty of 1846, American trading posts and forts had been established in the territory.

The major Indian wars (1867–1877) included the famous 1876 Battle of the Little Big Horn, better known as "Custer's Last Stand," in which Cheyennes and Sioux killed George A. Custer and more than 200 of his men in southeastern Montana.

Much of Montana's early history was concerned with mining with copper, lead, zinc, silver, coal, and oil as principal products.

Butte is the center of the area that once supplied half of the U.S. copper.

Fields of grain cover much of Montana's plains; it ranks high among the states in wheat and barley, with rye, oats, flaxseed, sugar beets, and potatoes other important crops. Sheep and cattle raising make significant contributions to the economy.

Tourist attractions include hunting, fishing, skiing, and dude ranching. Glacier National Park, on the Continental Divide, is a scenic and vacation wonderland with 60 glaciers, 200 lakes, and many streams with good trout fishing.

Other major points of interest include the Custer Battlefield National Monument, Virginia City, Yellowstone National Park, Museum of the Plains Indians at Browning, and the Fort Union Trading Post and Grant-Kohr's Ranch National Historic Sites.

Famous natives and residents: Dorothy Baker, author; Dirk Benedict, actor; W.A. (Tony) Boyle, labor union official; Gary Cooper, actor; John Cowan, prospector and founder of Last Chance Gulch (now Helena); Alfred Bertram Guthrie, Pulitzer Prize-winning author; Chet Huntley, TV newscaster; Will James, writer and artist; Dorothy Johnson, author; Evel Knievel, daredevil motorcyclist; Myrna Loy, actress; David Lynch, filmmaker; Mike Mansfield, senator; George Montgomery, actor; Jeannette Rankin, first woman elected to Congress; Martha Raye, actress; Charles M. Russell, Old West painter; Michael Smuin, choreographer; Lester C. Thurow, economist, educator

NEBRASKA

Capital: Lincoln
Governor: Ben Nelson, D (to Jan. 1995)
Lieut. Governor: Maxine Moul, D (to Jan. 1995)
Secy. of State: Allen J. Beermann, R (to Jan. 1995)
Atty. General: Don Stenberg, R (to Jan. 1995)
Auditor: John Breslow, D (to Jan. 1995)
Treasurer: Dawn Rockey, D (to Jan. 1995)
Organized as territory: May 30, 1854
Entered Union & (rank): March 1, 1867 (37)
Present constitution adopted: Nov. 1, 1875 (extensively amended 1919–20)
Motto: Equality before the law
STATE SYMBOLS: flower, Goldenrod (1895); **tree,** Cottonwood (1972); **bird,** Western meadowlark (1929); **insect,** Honeybee (1975); **gemstone,** Blue agate (1967); **rock,** Prairie agate (1967); **fossil;** Mammoth (1967); **song,** "Beautiful Nebraska" (1967); **soil,** Typie Arguistolls, Holdrege Series (1979); **mammal,** Whitetail deer (1981)
Nicknames: Cornhusker State (1945); Beef State; The Tree Planter State (1895)
Origin of name: From an Oto Indian word meaning "flat water"
10 largest cities (1990 census): Omaha, 335,795; Lincoln, 191,972; Grand Island, 39,386; Bellevue, 30,982; Kearney, 24,396; Fremont, 23,680; Hastings, 22,837; North Platte, 22,605; Norfolk, 21,476; Columbus, 19,480
Land area & (rank): 76,878 sq mi. (199,113 sq km) (15)
Geographic center: In Custer Co., 10 mi. NW of Broken Bow
Number of counties: 93
Largest county (1990 census): Douglas, 416,444
State forests: None
State parks: 86 areas, historical and recreational; 8 major areas
1992 resident population est.: 1,606,000
1990 resident census population, sex, & (rank): 1,578,385 (36). **Male:** 769,439; **Female:** 808,946. **White:** 1,480,558 (93.8%); **Black:** 57,404 (3.6%); **American Indian, Eskimo, or Aleut:** 12,410 (0.8%); **Asian or Pacific Islander:** 12,422 (0.8%); **Other race:** 15,591 (1.0%); **Hispanic:** 36,969 (2.3%). **1990 percent population under 18:** 27.2; **65 and over:** 14.1; **median age:** 33.0.

French fur traders first visited Nebraska in the early 1700s. Part of the Louisiana Purchase in 1803, Nebraska was explored by Lewis and Clark in 1804–06.

Robert Stuart pioneered the Oregon Trail across Nebraska in 1812–13 and the first permanent settlement was established at Bellevue in 1823. Western Nebraska was acquired by treaty following the Mexican War in 1848. The Union Pacific began its transcontinental railroad at Omaha in 1865. In 1937, Nebraska became the only state in the Union to have a unicameral (one-house) legislature. Members are elected to it without party designation.

Nebraska is a leading grain-producer with bumper crops of rye, corn, and wheat. More varieties of grass, valuable for forage, grow in this state than in any other in the nation.

The state's sizable cattle and hog industries make Dakota City and Lexington among the nation's largest meat-packing centers.

Manufacturing has become diversified in Nebraska, strengthening the state's economic base. Firms making electronic components, auto accessories, pharmaceuticals, and mobile homes have joined such older industries as clothing, farm machinery, chemicals, and transportation equipment. Oil was discovered in 1939 and natural gas in 1949.

Among the principal attractions are Agate Fossil Beds, Homestead, and Scotts Bluff National Monuments; Chimney Rock National Historic Site; a recreated pioneer village at Minden; SAC Museum at Bellevue; the Stuhr Museum of the Prairie Pioneer with 57 original 19th-century buildings near Grand Island; the Sheldon Memorial Art Gallery at the University of Nebraska in Lincoln; and the Lied Center for the Performing Arts located on the University of Nebraska campus in Lincoln.

Famous natives and residents: Grace Abbott, social worker; Fred Astaire, dancer and actor; Max Baer, boxer; Bil Baird, puppeteer; George Beadle, geneticist; Marlon Brando, actor; Dick Cavett, TV entertainer; Richard B. Cheney, Secretary of Defense; Montgomery Clift, actor; James Coburn, actor; Sandy Dennis, actress; Mignon Eberhart, author; Ruth Etting, singer, actress; Henry Fonda, actor; Gerald Ford, President; Bob Gibson, baseball player; Hoot Gibson, actor; Howard Hanson, conductor; Leland Hayward, producer; Susette La Flesche, Omaha Indian artist; Francis La Flesche, ethnologist; Melvin Laird, politician, Secretary of Defense; Frank W. Leahy, football coach; Harold Lloyd, actor; David Janssen, actor; Irish McCalla, actress; Dorothy McGuire, actress; Julius Sterling Morton, politician, journalist, originated Arbor Day; Nick Nolte, actor; Inga Swenson, actress; Robert Taylor, actor; Paul Williams, singer, composer, actor; Julie Wilson, singer and actress; Daryl F. Zanuck, film producer

NEVADA

Capital: Carson City
Governor: Robert J. Miller, D (to Jan. 1995)
Lieut. Governor: Sue Wagner, R (to Jan. 1995)
Secy. of State: Cheryl Lau, R (to Jan. 1995)
Treasurer: Bob Seale, R (to Jan. 1995)
Controller: Darrel R. Daines, R (to Jan. 1995)
Atty. General: Frankie Sue Del Papa, D (to Jan. 1995)
Organized as territory: March 2, 1861
Entered Union & (rank): Oct. 31, 1864 (36)
Present constitution adopted: 1864
Motto: All for Our Country
STATE SYMBOLS: flower, Sagebrush (1959); **trees,** Single-leaf pinon (1953) and Bristlecone pine (1987); **bird,** Mountain bluebird (1967); **animal,** Desert bighorn sheep (1973); **colors,** Silver and blue (1983); **song,** "Home Means Nevada" (1933); **rock,** Sandstone (1987); **precious gemstone,** Virgin Valley Black Fire Opal (1987); **semiprecious gemstone,** Nevada Turquoise (1987); **grass,** Indian Ricegrass (1977); **metal,** Silver (1977); **fossil,** Ichthyosaur (1977); **fish,** Lahontan Cutthroat Trout (1981); **reptile,** Desert tortoise (1989)
Nicknames: Sagebrush State; Silver State; Battle-born State
Origin of name: Spanish: "snowcapped"
10 largest cities (1990 census): Las Vegas, 258,295; Reno, 133,850; Henderson, 64,942; Sparks, 53,367; North Las Vegas, 47,707; Carson City, 40,443; Elko, 14,736; Boulder City, 12,567; Fallon, 6,438; Winnemucca, 6,134
Land area & (rank): 109,806 sq mi. (284,397 sq km) (7)
Geographic center: In Lander Co., 26 mi. SE of Austin
Number of counties: 16, plus 1 independent city
Largest county (1990 census): Clark, 741,459
State forests: None
State parks: 20 (150,000 ac., including leased lands)
1992 resident population est.: 1,327,000
1990 resident census population, sex, & (rank): 1,201,833 (39). **Male:** 611,880; **Female:** 589,953. **White:** 1,012,695 (84.3%); **Black:** 78,771 (6.6%); **American Indian, Eskimo, or Aleut:** 19,637 (1.6%); **Asian or Pacific Islander:** 38,127 (3.2%); **Other race:** 52,603 (4.4%); **Hispanic:** 124,419 (10.4%). **1990 percent population under 18:** 24.7; **65 and over:** 10.6; **median age:** 33.3.

Trappers and traders, including Jedediah Smith, and Peter Skene Ogden, entered the Nevada area in the 1820s. In 1843–45, John C. Fremont and Kit Carson explored the Great Basin and Sierra Nevada.

In 1848 following the Mexican War, the U.S. obtained the region and the first permanent settlement was a Mormon trading post near present-day Genoa.

The driest state in the nation with an average annual rainfall of only about 7 inches,[1] much of Nevada is uninhabited, sagebrush-covered desert.

Nevada was made famous by the discovery of the fabulous Comstock Lode in 1859 and its mines have produced large quantities of gold, silver, copper, lead, zinc, mercury, barite, and tungsten. Oil was discovered in 1954. Gold now far exceeds all other minerals in value of production.

In 1931, the state created two industries, divorce and gambling. For many years, Reno and Las Vegas were the "divorce capitals of the nation." More liberal divorce laws in many states have ended this distinction, but Nevada is the gambling and entertainment capital of the U.S. State gambling taxes account for 40.1% of general fund tax revenues. Although Nevada leads the nation in per capita gambling revenue, it ranks only fourth in total gambling revenue.

Near Las Vegas, on the Colorado River, stands Hoover Dam, which impounds the waters of Lake Mead, one of the world's largest artificial lakes.

The state's agricultural crop consists mainly of hay, alfalfa seed, barley, wheat, and potatoes.

Nevada manufactures gaming equipment; lawn and garden irrigation devices; titanium products; seismic and machinery monitoring devices; and specialty printing.

Major resort areas flourish in Lake Tahoe, Reno, and Las Vegas. Recreation areas include those at Pyramid Lake, Lake Tahoe, and Lake Mead and Lake Mohave, both in Lake Mead National Recreation Area. Among the other attractions are Hoover Dam, Virginia City, and Great Basin National Park (includes Lehman Caves).

Famous natives and residents: Eva Adams, director of U.S. Mint; Andre Agassi, tennis player; Raymond T. Baker, director of U.S. Mint; Helen Delich Bentley, government official, newspaperwoman; Robert Caples, painter; Walter Van Tilburg Clark, writer; Henry Comstock, prospector of "Comstock Lode" fame; Abby Dalton, actress; Michele Greene, actress; Sarah Winnemucca Hopkins, Paiute interpreter and peacemaker, author; Jack Kramer, tennis player; Paul Laxalt, politician; William Lear, aviation inventor; Robert C. Lynch, surgeon; John W. Mackay, benefactor, one of Big Four of Comstock Lode; Emma Nevada, opera singer; Thelma "Pat" Nixon, First Lady; James W. Nye, territory governor, U.S. senator; Lute Pease, cartoonist, Pulitzer Prize winner; Edna Purviance, actress; Jack Wilson, Paiute Indian prophet; George Wingfield, mining millionaire

1. Wettest part of state receives about 40 inches of precipitation per year, while driest spot has less than four inches per year.

NEW HAMPSHIRE

Capital: Concord
Governor: Stephen E. Merrill, R (to Jan. 1995)
Treasurer: Georgie A. Thomas, R (to Dec. 1994)
Secy. of State: William M. Gardner, D (to Dec. 1994)
Commissioner: Patrick Duffy
Atty. General: Jeffrey R. Howard, R (to Mar. 1997)
Entered Union & (rank): June 21, 1788 (9)
Present constitution adopted: 1784
Motto: Live free or die
STATE SYMBOLS: flower, Purple lilac (1919); **tree,** White birch (1947); **bird,** Purple finch (1957); **songs,** "Old New Hampshire" (1949) and "New Hampshire, My New Hampshire" (1963)
Nickname: Granite State
Origin of name: From the English county of Hampshire
10 largest cities (1990 census): Manchester, 99,567; Nashua, 79,662; Concord, 36,006; Rochester, 26,630; Portsmouth, 25,925; Dover, 25,042; Keene, 22,430; Laconia, 15,743; Claremont, 13,902; Lebanon, 12,183
Land area & (rank): 8,969 sq mi. (23,231 sq km) (44)
Geographic center: In Belknap Co., 3 mi. E of Ashland
Number of counties: 10
Largest county (1990 census): Hillsborough, 336,073
State forests & parks: 175 (96,975 ac.)
1992 resident population est.: 1,111,000
1990 resident census population, sex, & (rank): 1,109,252 (41). **Male:** 543,544; **Female:** 565,708. **White:** 1,087,433 (98.0%); **Black:** 7,198 (0.6%); **American Indian, Eskimo, or Aleut:** 2,134 (0.2%); **Asian or Pacific Islander:** 9,343 (0.8%); **Other race:** 3,144 (0.3%); **Hispanic:** 11,333 (1.0%). **1990 percent population under 18:** 25.1; **65 and over:** 11.3; **median age:** 32.8.

Under an English land grant, Capt. John Smith sent settlers to establish a fishing colony at the mouth of the Piscataqua River, near present-day Rye and Dover, in 1623. Capt. John Mason, who participated in the founding of Portsmouth in 1630, gave New Hampshire its name.

After a 38-year period of union with Massachusetts, New Hampshire was made a separate royal colony in 1679. As leaders in the revolutionary cause, New Hampshire delegates received the honor of being the first to vote for the Declaration of Independence on July 4, 1776. New Hampshire is the only state that ever played host at the formal conclusion of a foreign war when, in 1905, Portsmouth was the scene of the treaty ending the Russo-Japanese War.

Abundant water power early turned New Hampshire into an industrial state and manufacturing is the principal source of income in the state. The most important industrial products are electrical and other machinery, textiles, pulp and paper products, and stone and clay products.

Dairy and poultry farming and growing fruit, truck vegetables, corn, potatoes, and hay are the major agricultural pursuits.

Tourism, because of New Hampshire's scenic and recreational resources, now brings over $3.5 billion into the state annually.

Vacation attractions include Lake Winnipesaukee, largest of 1,300 lakes and ponds; the 724,000-acre White Mountain National Forest; Daniel Webster's birthplace near Franklin; Strawbery Banke, restored building of the original settlement at Portsmouth; and the famous "Old Man of the Mountain" granite head profile, the state's official emblem, at Franconia.

Famous natives and residents: Sherman Adams, governor and presidential advisor; Salmon P. Chase, jurist; Charles Anderson Dana, editor; Mary Baker Eddy, founder of Christian Science Church; Dustin Farnum, actor; Thomas Green Fessenden, journalist and satirical poet; Daniel Chester French, sculptor; Horace Greeley, journalist and politician; Sarah J. Hale, editor; John Irving, writer; Benjamin F. Keith, theater entrepreneur; Jackson Hall Kelly, promoter of Oregon settlement; John Langdon, political leader; Sharon Christa McAuliffe, teacher and astronaut; Franklin Pierce, President; Augustus Saint-Gaudens, sculptor; Alan Shepard, astronaut; Harlan F. Stone, jurist; Daniel Webster, statesman; Henry Wilson, politician and U.S. vice president; Noah Worcester, clergyman and pacifist

NEW JERSEY

Capital: Trenton
Governor: James J. Florio, D (to Jan. 1994)
Secy. of State: Daniel Dalton, D (to Jan. 1994)
Treasurer: Samuel Crane, D (to Jan. 1994)
Atty. General: Robert Del Tufo, D (to Jan. 1994)
Entered Union & (rank): Dec. 18, 1787 (3)
Present constitution adopted: 1947
Motto: Liberty and prosperity
STATE SYMBOLS: flower, Purple violet (1913); **bird,** Eastern goldfinch (1935); **insect,** Honeybee (1974); **tree,** Red oak (1950); **animal,** Horse (1977); **colors,** Buff and blue (1965)
Nickname: Garden State
Origin of name: From the Channel Isle of Jersey
10 largest cities (1990 census)[1]: Newark, 275,221; Jersey City, 228,537; Paterson, 140,891; Elizabeth, 110,002; Edison[2], 88,680; Trenton, 88,675; Camden, 87,492; East Orange, 73,552; Clifton, 71,742; Cherry Hill[2], 69,319
Land area & (rank): 7,419 sq mi. (19,215 sq km) (46)
Geographic center: In Mercer Co., 5 mi. SE of Trenton
Number of counties: 21
Largest county (1990 census): Bergen, 825,380
State forests: 11
State parks: 35 (67,111 ac.)
1992 resident population est.: 7,789,000
1990 resident census population, sex, & (rank): 7,730,188 (9). **Male:** 3,735,685; **Female:** 3,994,503. **White:** 6,130,465 (79.3%); **Black:** 1,036,825 (13.4%); **American Indian, Eskimo, or Aleut:** 14,970 (0.2%); **Asian or Pacific Islander:** 272,521 (3.5%); **Other race:** 275,407 (3.6%); **Hispanic:** 739,861 (9.6%). **1990 percent population under 18:** 23.3; **65 and over:** 13.4; **median age:** 34.5.

1. These are the official 1990 census largest cities. However, the townships of Woodbridge, 93,086, and Hamilton, 86,553, are also legal municipalities or cities. 2. Census Designated Place.

New Jersey's early colonial history was involved with that of New York (New Netherlands), of which it was a part. One year after the Dutch surrender to England in 1664, New Jersey was organized as an English colony under Gov. Philip Carteret.

In the late 1600s the colony was divided between Carteret and William Penn; later it would be administered by the royal governor of New York. Finally, in 1738, New Jersey was separated from New York under its own royal governor, Lewis Morris.

Because of its key location between New York City and Philadelphia, New Jersey saw much fighting during the American Revolution.

Today, New Jersey, an area of wide industrial diversification, is known as the Crossroads of the East. Products from over 15,000 factories can be delivered overnight to almost 60 million people, representing 12 states and the District of Columbia. The greatest single industry is chemicals and New Jersey is one of the foremost research centers in the world. Many large oil refineries are located in northern New Jersey and other important manufactures are pharmaceuticals, instruments, machinery, electrical goods, and apparel.

Of the total land area, 37% is forested. Farmland is declining. In 1991 there were about 8,300 farms, with over 880,000 acres under harvest. The state ranks high in production of almost all garden vegetables. Tomatoes, asparagus, corn, and blueberries are important crops, and poultry farming and dairying make significant contributions to the state's economy.

Tourism is the second largest industry in New Jersey. The state has numerous resort areas on 127 miles of Atlantic coastline. In 1977, New Jersey voters approved legislation allowing legalized casino gambling in Atlantic City. Points of interest include the Walt Whitman House in Camden, the Delaware Water Gap, the Edison National Historic Site in West Orange, Princeton University, and the N.J. State Aquarium in Camden (opened 1992).

Famous natives and residents: Bud Abbott, comedian, Charles Addams, cartoonist; Edwin Aldrin, astronaut; Count Basie, band leader; Joan Bennett, actress; Jon Bon Jovi, musician; William J. Brennan, jurist; Aaron Burr, political leader; James Fenimore Cooper, novelist; Lou Costello, comedian; Stephen Crane, writer; Helen Gahagan Douglas, ex-Representative; Allen Ginsberg, poet; William Frederick Halsey, Jr., admiral; Alfred Joyce Kilmer, poet; Ernie Kovacs, comedian; Jerry Lewis, comedian, film director; Anne Morrow Lindbergh, author; Norman Mailer, novelist; Patricia McBride, ballerina; Richard Nixon, President; Dorothy Parker, author; Joe Piscopo, comedian, actor; Paul Robeson, singer and actor; Philip Roth, novelist; Ruth St. Denis, dancer and choreographer; Antonin Scalia, jurist; H. Norman Schwarzkopf, general; Frank Sinatra, singer and actor; Bruce Springsteen, musician; Alfred Stieglitz, photographer; Albert Payson Terhune, journalist and novelist; Sarah Vaughan, singer; William Carlos Williams, physician and poet; Edmund Wilson, literary crtic and author

NEW MEXICO

Capital: Santa Fe
Governor: Bruce King, D (to Jan. 1995)
Lieut. Governor: Casey Luna, D (to Jan. 1995)
Secy. of State: Stephanie Gonzales, D (to Jan. 1995)
Atty. General: Tom Udall, D (to Jan. 1995)
State Auditor: Robert E. Vigil, D (to Jan. 1995)
State Treasurer: David W. King, D (to Jan. 1995)
Commissioner of Public Lands: Jim Baca, D (to Jan. 1995)
Organized as territory: Sept. 9, 1850
Entered Union & (rank): Jan. 6, 1912 (47)
Present constitution adopted: 1911
Motto: *Crescit eundo* (It grows as it goes)
STATE SYMBOLS: flower, Yucca (1927); **tree,** Pinon (1949); **animal,** Black bear (1963); **bird,** Roadrunner (1949); **fish,** Cutthoroat trout (1955); vegetables, Chili and frijol (1965); **gem,** Turquoise (1967); **colors,** Red and yellow of old Spain (1925); **song,** "O Fair New Mexico" (1917); **Spanish language song,** "Asi Es Nuevo Méjico" (1971); **poem,** A Nuevo México (1991); **grass,** Blue gramma; **fossil,** Coelophysis; **cookie,** Bizcochito (1989); **insect,** Tarantula hawk wasp (1989)
Nicknames: Land of Enchantment; Sunshine State
Origin of name: From the country of Mexico
10 largest cities (1990 census): Albuquerque, 384,736; Las Cruces, 62,126; Santa Fe, 55,859; Roswell, 44,654; Farmington, 33,997; Rio Rancho, 32,505; Clovis, 30,954; Hobbs, 29,115; Alamogordo, 27,596; Carlsbad, 24,952
Land area & (rank): 121,365 sq mi. (314,334 sq km) (5)
Geographic center: In Torrance Co., 12 mi. SSW of Willard
Number of counties: 33
Largest county (1990 census): Bernalillo, 480,577
State-owned forested land: 933,000 ac.
State parks: 29 (105,012 ac.)
1992 resident population est.: 1,581,000
1990 resident census population, sex, & (rank): 1,515,069 (37). **Male:** 745,253; **Female:** 769,816. **White:** 1,146,028 (75.6%); **Black:** 30,210 (2.0%); **American Indian, Eskimo, or Aleut:** 134,355 (8.9%); **Asian or Pacific Islander:** 14,124 (0.9%); **Other race:** 190,352 (12.6%); **Hispanic:** 579,224 (38.2%). **1990 percent population under 18:** 29.5; **65 and over:** 10.8; **median age:** 31.3.

Francisco Vásquez de Coronado, Spanish explorer searching for gold, traveled the region that became New Mexico in 1540–42. In 1598 the first Spanish settlement was established on the Rio Grande River by Juan de Onate and in 1610 Santa Fe was founded and made the capital of New Mexico.

The U.S. acquired most of New Mexico in 1848, as a result of the Mexican War, and the remainder in the 1853 Gadsden Purchase. Union troops captured the territory from the Confederates during the Civil War. With the surrender of Geronimo in 1886, the Apache Wars and most of the Indian troubles in the area were ended.

Since 1945, New Mexico has been a leader in energy research and development with extensive experiments conducted at Los Alamos Scientific Laboratory and Sandia Laboratories in the nuclear, solar, and geothermal areas.

Minerals are the state's richest natural resource and New Mexico is one of the U.S. leaders in output of uranium and potassium salts. Petroleum, natural gas, copper, gold, silver, zinc, lead, and molybdenum also contribute heavily to the state's income.

The principal manufacturing industries include food products, chemicals, transportation equipment, lumber, electrical machinery, and stone-clay-glass products. More than two thirds of New Mexico's farm income comes from livestock products, especially sheep. Cotton, pecans, and sorghum are the most important field crops. Corn, peanuts, beans, onions, chile, and lettuce are also grown.

Tourist attractions in New Mexico include the Carlsbad Caverns National Park, Inscription Rock at El Morro National Monument, the ruins at Fort Union, Billy the Kid mementos at Lincoln, the White Sands and Gila Cliff Dwellings National Monuments, and the Chaco Culture National Historical Park.

Famous natives and residents: Ernest L. Blumenshein, artist; William "Billy the Kid" Bonney, outlaw; Bruce Cabot, actor; Kit Carson, Army scout and trapper; Dennis Chavez, Congressman; John Chisum, cattle king; Mangus Coloradas, Apache leader; Edward Condon, physicist; John Denver, singer; Patrick Garrett, lawman; William Hanna, animator; Carl Hatch, senator; Conrad Hilton, hotel executive; Peter Hurd, artist; Preston Jones, playwright, actor; Ralph Kiner, baseball player, sportscaster; Nancy Lopez, golfer; Maria Martínez, San Ildefonso Pueblo potter; Bill Mauldin, political cartoonist; Popé, San Juan Pueblo medicine man, leader; Harrison Schmitt, astronaut; Kim Stanley, actress; Slim Summerville, actor; Al Unser, Bobby Unser, auto racers; Victorio, Apache chief; Kathy Whitworth, golfer

NEW YORK

Capital: Albany
Governor: Mario M. Cuomo, D (to Jan. 1995)
Lieut. Governor: Stan Lundine, D (to Jan. 1995)
Secy. of State: Gail S. Shaffer, D (to Jan. 1995)
Comptroller: Edward V. Regan, R (to Jan. 1995)
Atty. General: Robert Abrams, D (to Jan. 1995)
Entered Union & (rank): July 26, 1788 (11)
Present constitution adopted: 1777 (last revised 1938)
Motto: *Excelsior* (Ever upward)
STATE SYMBOLS: animal, Beaver (1975); **fish,** Brook trout (1975); **gem,** Garnet (1969); **flower,** Rose (1955); **tree,** Sugar maple (1956); **bird,** Bluebird (1970); **insect,** Ladybug (1989); **song,** "I Love New York" (1980)
Nickname: Empire State
Origin of name: In honor of the English Duke of York
10 largest cities (1990 census): New York, 7,322,564; Buffalo, 328,123; Rochester, 231,636; Yonkers, 188,082; Syracuse, 163,860; Albany, 101,082; Utica, 68,637; New Rochelle, 67,265; Mount Vernon, 67,153; Schenectady, 65,566
Land area & (rank): 47,224 sq mi. (122,310 sq km) (30)
Geographic center: In Madison Co., 12 mi. S of Oneida and 26 mi. SW of Utica
Number of counties: 62
Largest county (1990 census): Kings, 2,300,664
State forest preserves: Adirondacks, 2,500,000 ac., Catskills, 250,000 ac.
State parks: 150 (250,000 ac.)
1992 resident population est.: 18,119,000
1990 resident census population, sex, & (rank): 17,990,455 (2). **Male:** 8,625,673; **Female:** 9,364,782. **White:** 13,385,255 (74.4%); **Black:** 2,859,055 (15.9%); **American Indian, Eskimo, or Aleut:** 62,651 (0.3%); **Asian or Pacific Islander:** 693,760 (3.9%); **Other race:** 989,734 (5.5%); **Hispanic:** 2,214,026 (12.3%). **1990 percent population under 18:** 23.7; **65 and over:** 13.1; **median age:** 33.9,.

Giovanni da Verrazano, Italian-born navigator sailing for France, discovered New York Bay in 1524. Henry Hudson, an Englishman employed by the Dutch, reached the bay and sailed up the river now bearing his name in 1609, the same year that northern New York was explored and claimed for France by Samuel de Champlain.

In 1624 the first permanent Dutch settlement was established at Fort Orange (now Albany); one year later Peter Minuit is said to have purchased Manhattan Island from the Indians for trinkets worth about $24 and founded the Dutch colony of New Amsterdam (now New York City), which was surrendered to the English in 1664.

For a short time, New York City was the U.S. capital and George Washington was inaugurated there as first President on April 30, 1789.

New York's extremely rapid commercial growth may be partly attributed to Governor De Witt Clinton, who pushed through the construction of the Erie Canal (Buffalo to Albany), which was opened in 1825. Today, the 559-mile Governor Thomas E. Dewey Thruway connects New York City with Buffalo and with Connecticut, Massachusetts, and Pennsylvania express highways. Two toll-free superhighways, the Adirondack Northway (linking Albany with the Canadian border) and the North-South-Expressway (crossing central New York from the Pennsylvania border to the Thousand Islands) have been opened.

New York, with the great metropolis of New York City, is the spectacular nerve center of the nation. It is a leader in manufacturing, foreign trade, commercial and financial transactions, book and magazine publishing, and theatrical production.

New York City is not only a national but an international leader. A leading seaport, its John F. Kennedy International Airport is one of the busiest airports in the world. It is the largest manufacturing center in the country and its apparel industry is the city's largest manufacturing employer, with printing and publishing second.

Nearly all the rest of the state's manufacturing is done on Long Island, along the Hudson River north to Albany and through the Mohawk Valley, Central New York, and Southern Tier regions to Buffalo. The St. Lawrence seaway and power projects have opened the North Country to industrial expansion and have given the state a second seacoast.

The state ranks third in the nation in manufacturing with 1,057,100 employees in 1991. The principal industries are apparel, printing and publishing, leather products, instruments and electronic equipment.

The convention and tourist business is one of the state's most important sources of income.

New York farms are famous for raising cattle and calves, producing corn for grain, poultry, and the raising of vegetables and fruits. The state is a leading wine producer.

Among the major points of interest are Castle Clinton, Fort Stanwix, and Statue of Liberty National Monuments; Niagara Falls; U.S. Military Academy at West Point; National Historic Sites that include homes of Franklin D. Roosevelt at Hyde Park and Theodore Roosevelt in Oyster Bay and New York City; National Memorials, including Grant's Tomb and Federal Hall in New York City; Fort Ticonderoga; the Baseball Hall of Fame in Cooperstown; and the United Nations, skyscrapers, museums, theaters, and parks in New York City.

Famous natives and residents: Kareem Abdul-Jabbar, basketball player; Lucille Ball, actress; Humphrey Bogart, actor; James Cagney, actor; Maria Callas, soprano; Benjamin N. Cardozo, jurist; Paddy Chayefsky, playwright; Peter Cooper, industrialist and philanthropist; Aaron Copland, composer; Sammy Davis, Jr., actor and singer; Agnes de Mille, choreographer; Eamon De Valera, ex-President of Ireland; George Eastman, inventor; Millard Fillmore, President; Lou Gehrig, baseball plyer; George Gershwin, composer; Learned Hand, jurist; Edward Hopper, painter; Julia Ward Howe, poet and reformer; Charles Evans Hughes, jurist; Washington Irving, author; Henry James, novelist; John Jay, jurist; Michael Jordan, basketball; Jerome Kern, composer; Rockwell Kent, painter; Vince Lombardi, football coach; Chico, Groucho, Harpo, Zeppo Marx, comedians; Herman Melville, author; Ethel Merman, singer and actress; Ogden Nash, poet; Eugene O'Neill, playwright; Red Jacket, Seneca chief; John D. Rockefeller, industrialist; Norman Rockwell, painter and illustrator; Mickey Rooney, actor; Anna Eleanor Roosevelt, reformer and humanitarian; Franklin D. Roosevelt, President; Theodore Roosevelt, President; Jonas Salk, polio researcher; Margaret Sanger, birth control leader; Barbara Stanwyck, actress; Risë Stevens, mezzo-soprano; Richard Tucker, tenor; Martin Van Buren, President; Mae West, actress; Walt Whitman, poet; Edith Wharton, novelist

NORTH CAROLINA

Capital: Raleigh
Governor: James B. Hunt, Jr., D (to Jan. 1997)
Lieut. Governor: Dennis A. Wicker, D (to Jan. 1997)
Secy. of State: Rufus L. Edmisten, D (to Jan. 1997)
Treasurer: Harlan E. Boyles, D (to Jan. 1997)
Auditor: Ralph Campbell, D (to Jan. 1997)
Atty. General: Michael Easley, D (to Jan. 1997)
Entered Union & (rank): Nov. 21, 1789 (12)
Present constitution adopted: 1971
Motto: *Esse quam videri* (To be rather than to seem)
STATE SYMBOLS: flower, Dogwood (1941); **tree,** Pine (1963); **bird,** Cardinal (1943); **mammal,** Gray squirrel (1969); **insect,** Honeybee (1973); **reptile,** Eastern box turtle (1979); **gemstone,** Emerald (1973); **shell,** Scotch bonnet (1965); **historic boat,** Shad Boat (1987); **beverage,** Milk (1987); **rock,** Granite (1979); **dog,** Plott Hound (1989); **song,** "The Old North State" (1927); **colors,** Red and blue (1945)
Nickname: Tar Heel State
Origin of name: In honor of Charles I of England
10 largest cities (1990 census): Charlotte, 395,934; Raleigh, 207,951; Greensboro, 183,521; Winston-Salem, 143,485; Durham, 136,611; Fayetteville, 75,695; High Point, 69,496; Asheville, 61,607; Wilmington, 55,530; Gastonia, 54,732
Land area & (rank): 48,718 sq mi. (126,180 sq km) (29)
Geographic center: In Chatham Co., 10 mi. NW of Sanford
Number of counties: 100
Largest county (1990 census): Mecklenburg, 511,433
State forests: 1
State parks: 30 (125,000 ac.)
1992 resident population est.: 6,843,000
1990 resident census population, sex, & (rank): 6,628,637 (10). **Male:** 3,214,290; **Female:** 3,414,347. **White:** 5,008,491 (75.6%); **Black:** 1,456,323 (22.0%); **American Indian, Eskimo, or Aleut:** 80,155 (1.2%); **Asian or Pacific Islander:** 52,166 (0.8%); **Other race:** 31,502 (0.5%); **Hispanic:** 76,726 (1.2%). **1990 percent population under 18:** 24.2; **65 and over:** 12.1; **median age:** 33.1.

English colonists, sent by Sir Walter Raleigh, unsuccessfully attempted to settle Roanoke Island in 1585 and 1587. Virginia Dare, born there in 1587, was the first child of English parentage born in America.

In 1653 the first permanent settlements were established by English colonists from Virginia near the Roanoke and Chowan Rivers.

The region was established as an English proprietary colony in 1663–65 and its early history was the scene of Culpepper's Rebellion (1677), the Quaker-led Cary Rebellion of 1708, the Tuscarora Indian War in 1711–13, and many pirate raids.

During the American Revolution, there was relatively little fighting within the state, but many North Carolinians saw action elsewhere. Despite considerable pro-Union, anti-slavery sentiment, North Carolina joined the Confederacy.

North Carolina is the nation's largest furniture, tobacco, brick, and textile producer. It holds second place in the Southeast in population and first place in the value of its industrial and agricultural production. This production is highly diversified, with metalworking, chemicals, and paper constituting enormous industries. Tobacco, corn, cotton, hay, peanuts, and truck and vegetable crops are of major importance. It is the country's leading producer of mica and lithium.

Tourism is also important, with travelers and vacationers spending more than $1 billion annually in North Carolina. Sports include year-round golfing, skiing at mountain resorts, both fresh and salt water fishing, and hunting.

Among the major attractions are the Great Smoky Mountains, the Blue Ridge National Parkway, the Cape Hatteras and Cape Lookout National Seashores, the Wright Brothers National Memorial at Kitty Hawk, Guilford Courthouse and Moores Creek National Military Parks, Carl Sandburg's home near Hendersonville, and the Old Salem Restoration in Winston-Salem.

Famous natives and residents: David Brinkley, TV newscaster; Howard Cosell, sportscaster; Virginia Dare, first person born in America to English parents; James B. Duke, industrialist; Roberta Flack, singer; Ava Gardner, actress; Richard Gatling, inventor; Billy Graham, evangelist; Kathryn Grayson, singer and actress; Jesse Helms, politician; O. Henry, story writer; Barbara Howar, broadcaster, writer; Andrew Johnson, President; Charles Kuralt, TV journalist; Sugar Ray Leonard, boxer; Dolley Madison, First Lady; Ronni Milsap, country music singer; Theolonious Monk, pianist; Alfred Moore, jurist; Edward R. Murrow, commentator and government official; Walter Hines Page, journalist and ambassador; Floyd Patterson, boxer; Richard Petty, auto racer; James K. Polk, President; Soupy Sales, comedian; Earl Scruggs; bluegrass musician; Randy Travis, musician; John Scott Trotter, orchestra leader; Thomas Wolfe, novelist

NORTH DAKOTA

Capital: Bismarck
Governor: Edward Schafer, R (to Dec. 15, 1996)
Lieut. Governor: Rosemarie Myrdal, R (to Dec. 15, 1996)
Secy. of State: Alvin A. Jaeger, R (to Dec. 31, 1996)
Auditor: Robert W. Peterson, R (to Dec. 31, 1996)
State Treasurer: Kathi Gilmore, D (to Dec. 31, 1996)
Atty. General: Heidi Heitkamp, D (to Dec. 31, 1996)
Organized as territory: March 2, 1861
Entered Union & (rank): Nov. 2, 1889 (39)
Present constitution adopted: 1889
Motto: Liberty and union, now and forever: one and inseparable
STATE SYMBOLS: tree, American elm (1947); **bird,** Western meadowlark (1947); **song,** "North Dakota Hymn" (1947)
Nickname: Sioux State; Flickertail State, Peace Garden State
Origin of name: From the Dakotah tribe, meaning "allies"
10 largest cities (1990 census): Fargo, 74,111; Grand Forks, 49,425; Bismarck, 49,256; Minot, 34,544; Dickinson, 16,097; Jamestown, 15,571; Mandan, 15,177; Williston, 13,131; West Fargo, 12,287; Wahpeton, 8,751
Land area & (rank): 68,994 sq mi. (178,695 sq km) (17)
Geographic center: In Sheridan Co., 5 mi. SW of McClusky
Number of counties: 53
Largest county (1990 census): Cass, 102,874
State forests: None
State parks: 14 (14,922.6 ac.)
1992 resident population est.: 636,000
1990 resident census population, sex, & (rank): 638,800 (47). **Male:** 318,201; **Female:** 320,599. **White:** 604,142 (94.6%); **Black:** 3,524 (0.6%); **American Indian, Eskimo, or Aleut:** 25,917 (4.1%); **Asian or Pacific Islander:** 3,462 (0.5%); **Other race:** 1,755 (0.3%); **Hispanic:** 4,665 (0.7%). **1990 percent population under 18:** 27.5; **65 and over:** 14.3; **median age:** 32.4.

North Dakota was explored in 1738–40 by French Canadians led by La Verendrye. In 1803, the U.S. acquired most of North Dakota from France in the Louisiana Purchase. Lewis and Clark explored the region in 1804–06 and the first settlements were made at Pembina in 1812 by Scottish and Irish families while this area was still in dispute between the U.S. and Great Britain.

In 1818, the U.S. obtained the northeastern part of North Dakota by treaty with Great Britain and took possession of Pembina in 1823.

North Dakota is the most rural of all the states, with farms covering more than 90% of the land. North Dakota ranks first in the Nation's production of spring and durum wheat, and the state's coal and oil reserves are plentiful.

Other agricultural products include barley, rye, sunflowers, dry edible beans, honey, oats, flaxseed, sugar beets, and hay; beef cattle, sheep, and hogs.

Recently, manufacturing industries have grown, especially food processing and farm equipment. The state also produces natural gas, lignite, salt, clay, sand, and gravel.

The Garrison Dam on the Missouri River provides extensive irrigation and produces 400,000 kilowatts of electricity for the Missouri Basin areas.

Known for its waterfowl, grouse, and deer hunting and bass, trout, and northern pike fishing, North Dakota has 20 state parks and recreation areas. Points of interest include the International Peace Garden near Dunseith, Fort Union Trading Post National Historic Site, the State Capitol at Bismarck, the Badlands, and Fort Lincoln, now a state park, from which Gen. George Custer set out on his last campaign in 1876.

Famous natives and residents: Lynn Anderson, singer; Maxwell Anderson, playwright; Angie Dickinson, actress; William H. Gass, writer, philosopher; Louis L'Amour, author; Peggy Lee, singer; William Lemke, U.S. Representative; Roger Maris, baseball player; Marquis de Mores, cattleman, established Medora; Gerald P. Nye, U.S. Senator; Arthur Peterson, radio and TV actor; James Rosenquist, paitner; Eric Sevareid, TV commentator; Ann Sothern, actress; Tommy Tucker, band leader; Lawrence Welk, band leader; Larry Woiwode, writer

OHIO

Capital: Columbus
Governor: George V. Voinovich, R (to Jan. 1995)
Lieut. Governor: R. Michael DeWine, R (to Jan. 1995)
Secy. of State: Bob Taft, R (to Jan. 1995)
Auditor: Thomas E. Ferguson, D (to Jan. 1995)
Treasurer: Mary Ellen Withrow, D (to Jan. 1995)
Atty. General: Lee I. Fisher, D (to Jan. 1995)
Entered Union & (rank): March 1, 1803 (17)
Present constitution adopted: 1851
Motto: With God, all things are possible
STATE SYMBOLS: flower, Scarlet carnation (1904); **tree,** Buckeye (1953); **bird,** Cardinal (1933); **insect,** Ladybug (1975); **gemstone,** Flint (1965); **song,** "Beautiful Ohio" (1969); **drink,** Tomato juice (1965)
Nickname: Buckeye State
Origin of name: From an Iroquoian word meaning "great river"
10 largest cities (1990 census): Columbus, 632,910; Cleveland, 505,616; Cincinnati, 364,040; Toledo, 332,943; Akron, 223,019; Dayton, 182,044; Youngstown, 95,732; Parma, 87,876; Canton, 84,161; Lorain, 71,245
Land area & (rank): 40,953 sq mi. (106,067 sq km) (35)
Geographic center: In Delaware Co., 25 mi. NNE of Columbus
Number of counties: 88
Largest county (1990 census): Cuyahoga, 1,412,140
State forests: 19 (172,744 ac.)
State parks: 71 (198,027 ac.)
1992 resident population est.: 11,016,000
1990 resident census population, sex, & (rank): 10,847,115 (7). **Male:** 5,226,340; **Female:** 5,620,775. **White:** 9,521,756 (87.8%); **Black:** 1,154,826 (10.6%); **American Indian, Eskimo, or Aleut:** 20,358 (0.2%); **Asian or Pacific Islander:** 91,179 (0.8%); **Other race:** 58,996 (0.5%); **Hispanic:** 139,696 (1.3%). **1990 percent population under 18:** 25.8; **65 and over:** 13.0; **median age:** 33.3.

First explored for France by La Salle in 1669, the Ohio region became British property after the French and Indian War. Ohio was acquired by the U.S. after the Revolutionary War in 1783 and, in 1788, the first permanent settlement was established at Marietta, capital of the Northwest Territory.

The 1790s saw severe fighting with the Indians in Ohio; a major battle was won by Maj. Gen. Anthony Wayne at Fallen Timbers in 1794. In the War of 1812, Commodore Oliver H. Perry defeated the British in the Battle of Lake Erie on Sept. 10, 1813.

Ohio is one of the nation's industrial leaders, ranking third in the value of manufactured products. Important manufacturing centers are located in or near Ohio's major cities. Akron is known for rubber; Canton for roller bearings; Cincinnati for jet engines and machine tools; Cleveland for auto assembly and parts, refining, and steel; Dayton for office machines, refrigeration, and heating and auto equipment; Youngstown and Steubenville for steel; and Toledo for glass and auto parts.

The state's thousands of factories almost overshadow its importance in agriculture and mining. Its fertile soil produces soybeans, corn, oats, grapes, and clover. More than half of Ohio's farm receipts come from dairying and sheep and hog raising. Ohio is the top state in lime production and among the leaders in coal, clay, salt, sand, and gravel. Petroleum, gypsum, cement, and natural gas are also important.

Tourism is a valuable revenue producer, bringing in $8.5 billion in 1992, and ranking 10th among the 50 states. Attractions include the Indian burial grounds at Mound City Group National Monument, Perry's Victory International Peace Memorial, the Pro Football Hall of Fame at Canton, and the homes of Presidents Grant, Taft, Hayes, Harding, and Garfield.

Famous natives and residents: Neil Armstrong, astronaut; Kathleen Battle, soprano; George Bellows, painter and lithographer; Ambrose Bierce, journalist; Erma Bombeck, columnist; Bill Boyd (Hopalong Cassidy), actor; Milton Caniff, cartoonist; Hart Crane, poet; George Armstrong Custer, army officer; Dorothy Dandridge, actress; Doris Day, singer and actress; Clarence Darrow, lawyer; Ruby Dee, actress; Rita Dove, U.S. Poet Laureate; Hugh Downs, TV broadcaster; Thomas A. Edison, inventor; Clark Gable, actor; James A. Garfield, President; Lillian Gish, actress; John Glenn, astronaut and senator; Ulysses S. Grant, President; Warren G. Harding, President; Rutherford Hayes, President; Benjamin Harrison, President; William Dean Howells, novelist and critic; Zane Grey, author; Robert Henri, painter; Kenisaw Mountain Landis, first baseball commissioner; Dean Martin, singer and actor; William McKinley, President; Paul Newman, actor; Jack Nicklaus, golfer; Annie Oakley, markswoman; Norman Vincent Peale, clergyman; Tyrone Power, actor; Judith Resnik, astronaut; Eddie Rickenbacker, aviator; Arthur M. Schlesinger, Jr., historian; William Tecumseh Sherman, army general; Gloria Steinem, feminist; William H. Taft, President; Tecumseh, Shawnee Indian chief; Lowell Thomas, explorer and commentator; James Thurber, author and cartoonist; Orville Wright, inventor; Cy Young, baseball player

OKLAHOMA

Capital: Oklahoma City
Governor: David Walters, D (to Jan. 1995)
Lieut. Governor: Jack Mildren, D (to Jan. 1995)
Secy. of State: John Kennedy, D (to Jan. 1995)
Treasurer: Claudette Henry, R (to Jan. 1995)
Atty. General: Susan Brimer-Loving, D (to Jan. 1995)
Organized as territory: May 2, 1890
Entered Union & (rank): Nov. 16, 1907 (46)
Present constitution adopted: 1907
Motto: *Labor omnia vincit* (Labor conquers all things)
STATE SYMBOLS: flower, Mistletoe (1893); **tree,** Redbud (1937); **bird,** Scissor-tailed flycatcher (1951); **animal,** Bison (1972); **reptile,** Mountain boomer lizard (1969); **stone,** Rose Rock (barite rose) (1968); **colors,** Green and white (1915); **song,** "Oklahoma" (1953)
Nickname: Sooner State
Origin of name: From two Choctaw Indian words meaning "red people"
10 largest cities (1990 census): Oklahoma City, 444,719; Tulsa, 367,302; Lawton, 80,561; Norman, 80,071; Broken Arrow, 58,043; Edmond, 52,315; Midwest City, 52,267; Enid, 45,309; Moore, 40,318; Muskogee, 37,708
Land area & (rank): 68,679 sq mi. (177,877 sq km) (19)
Geographic center: In Oklahoma Co., 8 mi. N of Oklahoma City
Number of counties: 77
Largest county (1990 census): Oklahoma, 599,611
State forests: None
State parks: 36 (57,487 ac.)
1992 resident population est.: 3,212,000
1990 resident census population, sex, & (rank): 3,145,585 (28). **Male:** 1,530,819; **Female:** 1,614,766. **White:** 2,583,512 (82.1%); **Black:** 233,801 (7.4%); **American Indian, Eskimo, or Aleut:** 252,420 (8.0%); **Asian or Pacific Islander:** 33,563 (1.1%); **Other race:** 42,289 (1.3%); **Hispanic:** 86,160 (2.7%). **1990 percent population under 18:** 26.6; **65 and over:** 13.5; **median age:** 33.2.

Francisco Vásquez de Coronado first explored the region for Spain in 1541. The U.S. acquired most of Oklahoma in 1803 in the Louisiana Purchase from France; the Western Panhandle region became U.S. territory with the annexation of Texas in 1845.

Set aside as Indian Territory in 1834, the region was divided into Indian Territory and Oklahoma Territory on May 2, 1890. The two were combined to make a new state, Oklahoma, on Nov. 16, 1907.

On April 22, 1889, the first day homesteading was permitted, 50,000 people swarmed into the area. Those who tried to beat the noon starting gun were called "Sooners." Hence the state's nickname.

Oil made Oklahoma a rich state, but natural gas production has now surpassed it. Oil refining, meat packing, food processing, and machinery manufacturing (especially construction and oil equipment) are important industries.

Other minerals produced in Oklahoma include helium, gypsum, zinc, cement, coal, copper, and silver.

Oklahoma's rich plains produce bumper yields of wheat, as well as large crops of sorghum, hay, cotton, and peanuts. More than half of Oklahoma's annual farm receipts are contributed by livestock products, including cattle, dairy products, and broilers.

Tourist attractions include the National Cowboy Hall of Fame in Oklahoma City, the Will Rogers Memorial in Claremore, the Cherokee Cultural Center with a restored Cherokee village, the restored Fort Gibson Stockade near Muskogee, and the Lake Texoma recreation area, Pari-Mutual horse racing at Remington Park in Oklahoma City, and Blue Ribbon Downs in Sallisaw.

Famous natives and residents: Johnny Bench, baseball player; John Berryman, poet; Iron Eyes Cody, Cherokee actor; L. Gordon Cooper, astronaut; Ralph Ellison, writer; James Garner, actor; Chester Gould, cartoonist; Woody Guthrie, singer and composer; Roy Harris, composer; Paul Harvey, broadcaster; Van Heflin, actor; Ron Howard, actor and director; Ben Johnson, actor; Jennifer Jones, actress; Jeane Kirkpatrick, educator and public affairs; Wilma P. Mankiller, Principal Chief of Cherokee Nation of Oklahoma; Mickey Mantle, baseball player; Bill Moyers, journalist; Daniel Patrick Moynihan, N.Y. Senator; Patti Page, singer; Mary Kay Place, actress and writer; Tony Randall, actor; Oral Roberts, evangelist; Dale Robertson, actor; Will Rogers, humorist; Dan Rowan, comedian; Maria Tallchief, ballerina; Jim Thorpe, athlete; Alfre Woodard, actress

OREGON

Capital: Salem
Governor: Barbara Roberts, D (to Jan. 1995)
Secy. of State: Phil Keisling, D (to Jan. 1997)
Treasurer: James A. Hill, D (to Jan. 1997)
Atty. General: Theodore R. Kulongoski, D (to Jan. 1997)
Organized as territory: Aug. 14, 1848
Entered Union & (rank): Feb. 14, 1859 (33)
Present constitution adopted: 1859
Motto: "Alis volat Propriis" ("She flies with her own wings") (1987)
STATE SYMBOLS: flower, Oregon grape (1899); **tree,** Douglas fir (1939); **animal,** Beaver (1969); **bird,** Western meadowlark (1927); **fish,** Chinook salmon (1961); **rock,** Thunderegg (1965); **colors,** Navy blue and gold (1959); **song,** "Oregon, My Oregon" (1927)
Nickname: Beaver State
Poet Laureate: William E. Stafford (1974)
Origin of name: Unknown. However, it is generally accepted that the name, first used by Jonathan Carver in 1778, was taken from the writings of Maj. Robert Rogers, an English army officer.
10 largest cities (1990 census): Portland, 437,319; Eugene, 112,669; Salem, 107,786; Gresham, 68,235; Beaverton, 53,310; Medford, 46,951; Corvallis, 44,757; Springfield, 44,683; Hillsboro, 37,520; Lake Oswego, 30,576
Land area & (rank): 96,003 sq mi. (248,647 sq km) (10)
Geographic center: In Crook Co., 25 mi. SSE of Prineville
Number of counties: 36
Largest county (1990 census): Multnomah, 583,887
State forests: 820,000 ac.
State parks: 240 (93,330 ac.)
1992 resident population est.: 2,977,000
1990 resident census population, sex, & (rank): 2,842,321 (29). **Male:** 1,397,073; **Female:** 1,445,248. **White:** 2,636,787 (92.8%); **Black:** 46,178 (1.6%); **American Indian, Eskimo, or Aleut:** 38,496 (1.4%); **Asian or Pacific Islander:** 69,269 (2.4%); **Other race:** 51,591 (1.8%); **Hispanic:** 112,707 (4.0%). **1990 percent population under 18:** 25.5; **65 and over:** 13.8; **median age:** 34.5.

Spanish and English sailors are believed to have sighted the Oregon coast in the 1500s and 1600s. Capt. James Cook, seeking the Northwest Passage, charted some of the coastline in 1778. In 1792, Capt. Robert Gray, in the *Columbia,* discovered the river named after his ship and claimed the area for the U.S.

In 1805 the Lewis and Clark expedition explored the area and John Jacob Astor's fur depot, Astoria, was founded in 1811. Disputes for control of Oregon between American settlers and the Hudson Bay Company were finally resolved in the 1846 Oregon Treaty in which Great Britain gave up claims to the region.

Oregon has a $3.1 billion lumber and wood products industry. Its salmon-fishing industry is one of the world's largest.

In agriculture, the state leads in growing peppermint, winter pears, fresh plums, prunes, blackberries, boysenberries, filberts, Blue Lake beans, and cover seed crops, and also raises strawberries, hops, wheat and other grains, sugar beets, potatoes, green peas, fiber flax, dairy products, livestock and poultry, apples, pears, and cherries. Oregon is the source of all the nickel produced in the U.S.

With the low-cost electric power provided by Bonneville Dam, McNary Dam, and other dams in the Pacific Northwest, Oregon has developed steadily as a manufacturing state. Leading manufactures are lumber and plywood, metalwork, machinery, aluminum, chemicals, paper, food packing, and electronic equipment.

Crater Lake National Park, Mount Hood, and Bonneville Dam on the Columbia are major tourist attractions. Oregon Dunes National Recreation Area has been established near Florence. Other points of interest include the Oregon Caves National Monument, Cape Perpetua in Siuslaw National Forest, Columbia River Gorge between The Dalles and Troutdale, and Hells Canyon.

Famous natives and residents: James Beard, food expert; Raymond Carver, writer, poet; Homer C. Davenport, political cartoonist; David Douglas, botanist; Abigail Scott Duniway, women's suffrage advocate; John E. Frohnmeyer, Chairman National Endowment of the Arts; Robert Gray, sea captain, discoverer of Columbia River; Matt Groening, cartoonist; Mark Hatfield, senator; Donald P. Hodel, Secretary of the Interior; Chief Joseph, Nez Percé chief; Dave Kingman, baseball player; Ursula LeGuin, writer; Edwin Markham, poet; Phyllis McGinley, author; Linus Pauling, chemist; Jane Powell, actress and singer; John Reed, poet and author; Harvey W. Scott, editor; Doc Severinsen, band leader; Norton Simon, business executive; Paul M. Simon, Illinois senator; Sally Struthers, actress

PENNSYLVANIA

Capital: Harrisburg
Governor: Robert P. Casey, D (to Jan. 1995)
Lieut. Governor: Mark S. Singel, D (to Jan. 1995)
Secy. of the Commonwealth: Brenda K. Mitchell, D (at the pleasure of the Governor)
Auditor General: Barbara Hafer, R (to Jan. 1997)
Atty. General: Ernest D. Preate, Jr., R (to Jan. 1997)
Entered Union & (rank): Dec. 12, 1787 (2)
Present constitution adopted: 1968
Motto: Virtue, liberty, and independence
STATE SYMBOLS: flower, Mountain laurel (1933); **tree,** Hemlock (1931); **bird,** Ruffed grouse (1931); **dog,** Great Dane (1965); **colors,** Blue and gold (1907); **song,** "Pennsylvania" (1990)
Nickname: Keystone State
Origin of name: In honor of Adm. Sir. William Penn, father of William Penn. It means "Penn's Woodland."
10 largest cities (1990 census): Philadelphia, 1,585,577; Pittsburgh, 369,879; Erie, 108,718; Allentown, 105,090; Scranton, 81,805; Reading, 78,380; Bethlehem, 71,428; Lancaster, 55,551; Harrisburg, 52,376; Altoona, 51,881
Land area & (rank): 44,820 sq mi. (116,083 sq km) (32)
Geographic center: In Centre Co., 2 1/2 mi. SW of Bellefonte
Number of counties: 67
Largest county (1990 census): Allegheny, 1,336,449
State forests: 1,930,108 ac.
State parks: 120 (297,438 ac.)
1992 resident population est.: 12,009,000
1990 resident census population, sex, & (rank): 11,881,643 (5). **Male:** 5,694,265; **Female:** 6,187,378. **White:** 10,520,201 (88.5%); **Black:** 1,089,795 (9.2%); **American Indian, Eskimo, or Aleut:** 14,733 (0.1%); **Asian or Pacific Islander:** 137,438 (1.2%); **Other race:** 119,476 (1.0%); **Hispanic:** 232,262 (2.0%). **1990 percent population under 18:** 23.5; **65 and over:** 15.4; **median age:** 35.

Rich in historic lore, Pennsylvania territory was disputed in the early 1600s among the Dutch, the Swedes, and the English. England acquired the region in 1664 with the capture of New York and in 1681 Pennsylvania was granted to William Penn, a Quaker, by King Charles II.

Philadelphia was the seat of the federal government almost continuously from 1776 to 1800; there the Declaration of Independence was signed in 1776 and the U.S. Constitution drawn up in 1787. Valley Forge, of Revolutionary War fame, and Gettysburg, the turning-point of the Civil War, are both in Pennsylvania. The Liberty Bell is located in a glass pavilion across from Independence Hall in Philadelphia.

With the decline of the coal, steel and railroad industries, Pennsylvania's industry has diversified, though the state still leads the country in the production of specialty steel. Pennsylvania is a leader in the production of chemicals, food, and electrical machinery and produces 10% of the nations's cement. Also important are brick and tiles, glass, limestone, and slate. Data processing is also increasingly important.

Pennsylvania's nine million agricultural acres (6 million acres for crops and pasture, 3 million acres in farm woodlands) produce a wide variety of crops and its 55,535 farms are the backbone of the state's economy. Leading products are milk, poultry and eggs, a variety of fruits, sweet corn, potatoes, mushrooms, cheese, beans, hay, maple syrup, and even Christmas trees.

Pennsylvania has the largest rural population in the nation. The state's farmers sell more than $3.3 billion in crops and livestock annually and agribusiness and food-related industries account for another $35 billion in economic activity annually.

Tourists now spend approximately $6 billion in Pennsylvania annually. Among the chief attractions: the Gettysburg National Military Park, Valley Forge National Historical Park, Independence National Historical Park in Philadelphia, the Pennsylvania Dutch region, the Eisenhower farm near Gettysburg, and the Delaware Water Gap National Recreation Area.

Famous natives and residents: Louisa May Alcott, novelist; Marian Anderson, contralto; Maxwell Anderson, dramatist; Samuel Barber, composer; John Barrymore, actor; Donald Barthelme, author; Stephen Vincent Benet, poet and story writer; Daniel Boone, frontiersman; Ed Bradley, TV anchorman; James Buchanan, President; Alexander Calder, sculptor; Rachel Carson, biologist and author; Mary Cassatt, painter; Henry Steele Commager, historian; Bill Cosby, actor; Stuart Davis, painter; Jimmy & Tommy Dorsey, band leaders; W.C. Fields, comedian; Stephen Foster, composer; Robert Fulton, inventor; Grace, Princess of Monaco; Martha Graham, choreographer; Alexander Haig, ex-Secretary of State; Marilyn Horne, mezzo-soprano; Lee Iacocca, auto executive; Reggie Jackson, baseball player; Gene Kelly, dancer and actor; Gelsey Kirkland, ballerina; S.S. Kresge, merchant; Mario Lanza, actor and singer; George C. Marshall, 5-star general; George McClellan, general; Margaret Mead, anthropologist; Andrew Mellon, financier; Tom Mix, actor; Arnold Palmer, golfer; Robert E. Peary, explorer; Man Ray, painter; Mary Roberts Rinehart, novelist; Betsy Ross, flagmaker; B.F. Skinner, psychologist; John Sloan, painter; Gertrude Stein, author; James Stewart, actor; John Updike, novelist; Honus Wagner, baseball player; Fred Waring, band leader; Ethel Waters, singer and actress; Anthony Wayne, military officer; August Wilson, poet, writer, and playwright; Duchess of Windsor (Wallis Warfield); Andrew Wyeth, painter

RHODE ISLAND

Capital: Providence
Governor: Bruce G. Sundlun, R (to Jan. 1995)
Lieut. Governor: Robert A. Weygand, D (to Jan. 1995)
Secy. of State: Barbara M. Leonard, D (to Jan. 1995)
Atty. General: Jeffery B. Pine, D (to Jan. 1995)
General Treasurer: Nancy J. Mayer, D (to Jan. 1995)
Entered Union & (rank): May 29, 1790 (13)
Present constitution adopted: 1843
Motto: Hope
STATE SYMBOLS: flower, Violet (unofficial) (1968); **tree,** Red maple (official) (1964); **bird,** Rhode Island Red (official) (1954); **shell,** Quahog (official); **mineral,** Bowenite; **stone,** Cumberlandite; **colors,** Blue, white, and gold (in state flag); **song,** "Rhode Island" (1946)
Nickname: The Ocean State
Origin of name: From the Greek Island of Rhodes
10 largest cities (1990 census): Providence, 160,728; Warwick, 85,427; Cranston, 70,060; Pawtucket, 72,644; East Providence, 50,380; Woonsocket, 43,877; Newport, 28,227; Central Falls, 17,637
Land area & (rank): 1,045 sq mi. (2,706 sq km) (50)
Geographic center: In Kent Co., 1 mi. SSW of Crompton
Number of counties: 5
Largest town (1990 census): North Providence, 32,090
State forests: 11 (20,900 ac.)
State parks: 17 (8,200 ac.)
1992 resident population est.: 1,005,000
1990 resident census population, sex, & (rank): 1,003,464 (43). **Male:** 481,496; **Female:** 521,968. **White:** 917,375 (91.4%); **Black:** 38,861 (3.9%); **American Indian, Eskimo, or Aleut:** 4,071 (0.4%); **Asian or Pacific Islander:** 18,325 (1.8%); **Other race:** 24,832 (2.5%); **Hispanic:** 45,752 (4.6%). **1990 percent population under 18:** 22.5; **65 and over:** 15.0; **median age:** 34.

From its beginnings, Rhode Island has been distinguished by its support for freedom of conscience and action, started by Roger Williams, who was exiled by the Massachusetts Bay Colony Puritans in 1636, and was the founder of the present state capital, Providence. Williams was followed by other religious exiles who founded Pocasset, now Portsmouth, in 1638 and Newport in 1639.

Rhode Island's rebellious, authority-defying nature was further demonstrated by the burnings of the British revenue cutters *Liberty* and *Gaspee* prior to the Revolution, by its early declaration of independence from Great Britain in May 1776, its refusal to participate actively in the War of 1812, and by Dorr's Rebellion of 1842, which protested property requirements for voting.

Rhode Island, smallest of the fifty states, is densely populated and highly industrialized. It is a primary center for jewelry manufacturing in the United States. Electronics, metal, plastic products, and boat and ship construction are other important industries. Non-manufacturing employment includes research in health and medical areas, and the ocean environment. Providence is a wholesale distribution center for New England.

Two of New England's fishing ports are at Galilee and Newport. Rural areas of the state support small-scale farming including grapes for local wineries, turf grass and nursery stock.

Tourism is one of Rhode Island's largest industries, generating over a billion dollars a year in revenue.

Newport became famous as the summer capital of society in the mid-19th century. Touro Synagogue (1763) is the oldest in the U.S. Other points of interest include the Roger Williams National Memorial in Providence, Samuel Slater's Mill in Pawtucket, the General Nathanael Greene Homestead in Coventry and Block Island.

Famous natives and residents: Harry Anderson, actor; George M. Cohan, actor and dramatist; Eddie Dowling, actor and stage producer; Nelson Eddy, baritone and actor; Ann Smith Franklin, printer and almanac publisher; Charles Gorham, silversmith; Spalding Gray, writer, performance artist; Bobby Hackett, trumpeter; David Hartman, TV newscaster; Ruth Hussey, actress; Anne Hutchinson, religious leader; Thomas H. Ince, film producer; Wilbur John, Quaker leader; Van Johnson, actor; Clarence King, first director of the U.S. Geological Survey; Galway Kinnell, poet; Oliver LaFarge, writer; Irving R. Levine, news correspondent; H.P. Lovecraft, author; Ida Lewis, lighthouse keeper; John McLaughlin, political commentator, broadcaster; Dana C. Munro, educator and historian; Matthew C. Perry, naval officer; Oliver Hazard Perry, naval officer; King Philip (Metacomet), Indian leader; Gilbert Stuart, painter; Sarah Helen (Power) Whitman, poet; Jemima Wilkinson, religious leader; Roger Williams, clergyman and founder of Rhode Island; Leonard Woodcock, labor union official

SOUTH CAROLINA

Capital: Columbia
Governor: Carroll A. Campbell, Jr., R (to Jan. 1995)
Lieut. Governor: Nick Theodore, D (to Jan. 1995)
Secy. of State: Jim Miles, R (to Jan. 1995)
Comptroller General: Earle E. Morris, Jr., D (to Jan. 1995)
Atty. General: T. Travis Medlock, D (to Jan. 1995)
Entered Union & (rank): May 23, 1788 (8).
Present constitution adopted: 1895
Mottoes: *Animis opibusque parati* (Prepared in mind and resources) and *Dum spiro spero* (While I breathe, I hope)
STATE SYMBOLS: flower, Carolina yellow jessamine (1924); **tree,** Palmetto tree (1939); **bird,** Carolina wren (1948); **song,** "Carolina" (1911)
Nickname: Palmetto State
Origin of name: In honor of Charles I of England
10 largest cities (1990 census): Columbia, 98,052; Charleston, 80,414; North Charleston, 70,218; Greenville, 58,282; Spartanburg, 43,467; Sumter, 41,943; Rock Hill, 41,643; Mount Pleasant Town, 30,108; Florence, 29,813; Anderson, 26,184
Land area & (rank): 30,111 sq mi. (77,988 sq km) (40)
Geographic center: In Richland Co., 13 mi. SE of Columbia
Number of counties: 46
Largest county (1990 census): Greenville, 320,167
State forests: 4 (124,052 ac.)
State parks: 50 (61,726 ac.)
1992 resident population est.: 3,603,000
1990 resident census population, sex, & (rank): 3,486,703 (25). **Male:** 1,688,510; **Female:** 1,798,193. **White:** 2,406,974 (69.0%); **Black:** 1,039,884 (29.8%); **American Indian, Eskimo, or Aleut:** 8,246 (0.2%); **Asian or Pacific Islander:** 22,382 (0.6%); **Other race:** 9,217 (0.3%); **Hispanic:** 30,551 (0.9%) **1990 percent population under 18:** 26.4; **65 and over:** 11.4; **median age: 32.0**

Following exploration of the coast in 1521 by De Gordillo, the Spanish tried unsuccessfully to establish a colony near present-day Georgetown in 1526 and the French also failed to colonize Parris Island near Fort Royal in 1562.

The first English settlement was made in 1670 at Albemarle Point on the Ashley River, but poor conditions drove the settlers to the site of Charleston (originally called Charles Town). South Carolina, officially separated from North Carolina in 1729, was the scene of extensive military action during the Revolution and again during the Civil War. The Civil War began in 1861 as South Carolina troops fired on federal Fort Sumter in Charleston Harbor and the state was the first to secede from the Union.

Once primarily agricultural, South Carolina has built so many large textile and other mills that today its factories produce eight times the output of its farms in cash value. Charleston makes asbestos, wood, pulp, and steel products; chemicals, machinery, and apparel are also important.

Farms have become fewer but larger in recent years. South Carolina grows more peaches than any other state except California; it ranks fifth in overall tobacco production. Other farm products include cotton, peanuts, sweet potatoes, soybeans, corn, and oats. Poultry and dairy products are also important revenue producers.

Points of interest include Fort Sumter National Monument, Fort Moultrie, Fort Johnson, and aircraft carrier USS *Yorktown* in Charleston Harbor; the Middleton, Magnolia, and Cypress Gardens in Charleston; Cowpens National Battlefield; and the Hilton Head resorts.

Famous natives and residents: Bernard Baruch, statesman; Mary McLeod Bethune, educator; James F. Byrnes, senator, jurist, Secretary of State; John C. Calhoun, statesman; Mark Clark, general; Joe Frazier, prize fighter; Althea Gibson, tennis champion; Dizzy Gillespie, jazz trumpeter; DuBose Heyward, poet, playwright, novelist; Andrew Jackson, President; Jesse Jackson, civil rights leader; Eartha Kitt, singer; Francis Marion "Swamp Fox," Revolutionary general; Ronald McNair, astronaut; John Rutledge, jurist; Strom Thurmond, politician; Charles Townes, physicist; William Westmoreland, ex-Army Chief of Staff; Vanna White, television personality

SOUTH DAKOTA

Capital: Pierre
Governor: Walter Dale Miller, R (to Jan. 1995)
Lieut. Governor: (Vacant)
Atty. General: Mark Barnett, R (to Jan. 1995)
Secy. of State: Joyce Hazeltine, R (to Jan. 1995)
State Auditor: Vern Larson, R (to Jan. 1995)
State Treasurer: G. Homer Harding, R (to Jan. 1995)
Organized as territory: March 2, 1861
Entered Union & (rank): Nov. 2, 1889 (40)
Present constitution adopted: 1889
Motto: Under God the people rule
STATE SYMBOLS: flower, American pasqueflower (1903); **grass,** Western wheat grass (1970); **soil,** Houdek (1990); **tree,** Black Hills spruce (1947); **bird,** Ring-necked pheasant (1943); **insect,** Honeybee (1978); **animal,** Coyote (1949); **mineral stone,** Rose quartz (1966); **gemstone,** Fairburn agate (1966); **colors,** Blue and gold (in state flag); **song,** "Hail! South Dakota" (1943); **fish,** Walleye (1982); **musical instrument,** Fiddle (1989); **soil,** Houdek soil (1990)
Nicknames: Mount Rushmore State; Coyote State
Origin of name: Same as for North Dakota
10 largest cities (1990 census): Sioux Falls, 100,814; Rapid City, 54,523; Aberdeen, 24,927; Watertown, 17,592; Brookings, 16,270; Mitchell, 13,798; Pierre, 12,906; Yankton, 12,703; Huron, 12,448; Vermillion, 10,034
Land area & (rank): 75,898 sq mi. (196,575 sq km) (16)
Geographic center: In Hughes Co., 8 mi. NE of Pierre
Number of counties: 67 (64 county governments)
Largest county (1990 census): Minnehaha, 123,809
State forests: None[1]
State parks: 13 plus 39 recreational areas (87,269 ac.)[2]
1992 resident population est.: 711,000
1990 resident census population, sex, & (rank): 696,004 (45). **Male:** 342,498; **Female:** 353,506. **White:** 637,515 (91.6%); **Black:** 3,258 (0.5%); **American Indian, Eskimo, or Aleut:** 50,575 (7.3%); **Asian or Pacific Islander:** 3,123 (0.4%); **Other race:** 1,533 (0.2%); **Hispanic:** 5,252 (0.8%). **1990 percent population under 18:** 28.5; **65 and over:** 14.7; **median age:** 32.5.

1. No designated state forests; about 13,000 ac. of state land is forestland. 2. Acreage includes 39 recreation areas and 80 roadside parks, in addition to 12 state parks.

Exploration of this area began in 1743 when Louis-Joseph and François Verendrye came from France in search of a route to the Pacific.

The U.S. acquired the region as part of the Louisiana Purchase in 1803 and it was explored by Lewis and Clark in 1804–06. Fort Pierre, the first permanent settlement, was established in 1817 and, in 1831, the first Missouri River steamboat reached the fort.

Settlement of South Dakota did not begin in earnest until the arrival of the railroad in 1873 and the discovery of gold in the Black Hills the following year.

Agriculture is the state's leading industry. South Dakota leads the nation in the production of oats and ranks second among the states in the production of rye, flaxseed, and sunflower seed.

South Dakota is the nation's second leading producer of gold and the Homestake Mine is the richest in the U.S. Other minerals produced include berylium, bentonite, granite, silver, petroleum, and uranium.

Processing of foods produced by farms and ranches is the largest South Dakota manufacturing industry, followed by lumber, wood products, and machinery, including farm equipment.

The Black Hills are the highest mountains east of the Rockies. Mt. Rushmore, in this group, is famous for the likenesses of Washington, Jefferson, Lincoln, and Theodore Roosevelt, which were carved in granite by Gutzon Borglum. A memorial to Crazy Horse is also being carved in granite near Custer.

Other tourist attractions include the Badlands; the World's Only Corn Palace in Mitchell; and the city of Deadwood where Wild Bill Hickok was killed in 1876 and where gambling was recently legalized to truly recapture the city's Old West flavor.

Famous natives and residents: Sparky Anderson, baseball manager; Gertrude Bonnin (Zitkala-Sa), Sioux writer and pan-Indian activist; Tom Brokaw, TV newscaster; Robert Casey, writer; Myron Floren, accordionist; Joseph J. Foss, WW II Marine fighter ace; Mary Hart, host; Crazy Horse, Oglala chief; Oscar Howe, Sioux artist; Hubert H. Humphrey, Vice President; Cheryl Ladd, actress; Ernest Orlando Lawrence, physicist; Russell Means, American Indian activist; George McGovern, politician; Arthur C. Mellette, first governor; Dorothy Provine, actress; Rain-in-the-Face, Hunkpapa Sioux chief; Red Cloud, chief of the Oglala Sioux; Ben Reifel, Brulé Sioux Congressman; Ole Edvart Rölvaag, writer; Sitting Bull, Chief of Hunkpappa Sioux; Norm Van Brocklin, football player; Mamie Van Doren, actress

TENNESSEE

Capital: Nashville
Governor: Ned Ray McWherter, D (to Jan. 1995)
Lieut. Governor: John S. Wilder, D (to Jan. 1997)
Secy. of State: Riley C. Darnell, D (to Jan. 1997)
Atty. General: Charles W. Burson, D (to Aug. 1998)
State Treasurer: Steve Adams, D (to Jan. 1993)
Entered Union & (rank): June 1, 1796 (16)
Present constitution adopted: 1870; amended 1953, 1960, 1966, 1972, 1978
Motto: "Agriculture and Commerce" (1987)
Slogan: "Tennessee—America at its best!" (1965)
STATE SYMBOLS: flower, Iris (1933); **tree,** Tulip poplar (1947); **bird,** Mockingbird (1933); **horse,** Tennessee walking horse; **animal,** Raccoon (1971); **wild flower,** Passion flower (1973); **song,** "Tennessee Waltz" (1965)
Nickname: Volunteer State
Origin of name: Of Cherokee origin; the exact meaning is unknown
10 largest cities (1990 census): Memphis, 610,337; Nashville-Davidson (CC[1]), 510,784; Knoxville, 165,121; Chattanooga, 152,466; Clarksville, 75,494; Johnson City, 49,381; Jackson, 48,949; Murfreesboro, 44,922; Kingsport, 36,365; Germantown, 32,893
Land area & (rank): 41,220 sq mi. (106,759 sq km) (34)
Geographic center: In Rutherford Co., 5 mi. NE of Murfreesboro
Number of counties: 95
Largest county (1990 census): Shelby, 826,330
State forests: 14 (155,752 ac.)
State parks: 21 (130,000 ac.)
1992 resident population est.: 5,024,000
1990 resident census population, sex, & (rank): 4,877,185 (17). **Male:** 2,348,928; **Female:** 2,528,257. **White:** 4,048,068 (83.0%); **Black:** 778,035 (16.0%); **American Indian, Eskimo, or Aleut:** 10,039 (0.2%); **Asian or Pacific Islander:** 31,839 (0.7%); **Other race:** 9,204 (0.2%); **Hispanic:** 32,741 (0.7%). **1990 percent population under 18:** 24.9; **65 and over:** 12.7; **median age:** 33.6.

1. Consolidated City.

First visited by the Spanish explorer de Soto in 1540, the Tennessee area would later be claimed by both France and England as a result of the 1670s and 1680s explorations of Marquette and Joliet, La Salle, and the Englishmen James Needham and Gabriel Arthur.

Great Britain obtained the region following the French and Indian War in 1763 and it was rapidly occupied by settlers moving in from Virginia and the Carolinas.

During 1784–87, the settlers formed the "state" of Franklin, which was disbanded when the region was allowed to send representatives to the North Carolina legislature. In 1790 Congress organized the territory south of the Ohio River and Tennessee joined the Union in 1796.

Although Tennessee joined the Confederacy during the Civil War, there was much pro-Union sentiment in the state, which was the scene of extensive military action.

The state is now predominantly industrial; the majority of its population lives in urban areas. Among the most important products are chemicals, textiles, apparel, electrical machinery, furniture, and leather goods. Other lines include food processing, lumber, primary metals, and metal products. The state is known as the U.S. hardwood-flooring center and ranks first in the production of marble, zinc, pyrite, and ball clay.

Tennessee is one of the leading tobacco-producing states in the nation and its farming income is also derived from livestock and dairy products as well as corn, cotton, and soybeans.

With six other states, Tennessee shares the extensive federal reservoir developments on the Tennessee and Cumberland River systems. The Tennessee Valley Authority operates a number of dams and reservoirs in the state.

Among the major points of interest: the Andrew Johnson National Historic Site at Greenville, American Museum of Atomic Energy at Oak Ridge, Great Smoky Mountains National Park, The Hermitage (home of Andrew Jackson near Nashville), Rock City Gardens near Chattanooga, and three National Military Parks.

Famous natives and residents: James Agee, writer; Eddy Arnold, singer; Chet Atkins, guitarist; Julian Bond, Georgia legislator; Davy Crockett, frontiersman; David G. Farragut, first American admiral; Lester Flatt, bluegrass musician; Tennessee Ernie Ford, singer; Abe Fortas, jurist; Aretha Franklin, singer; Nikki Giovanni, poet; Isaac Hayes, composer; Benjamin L. Hooks, civil rights activist; Red Grooms, artist; Estes Kefauver, legislator; Anita Kerr, singer; Grace Moore, soprano; Dolly Parton, singer; Minnie Pearl, singer and comedienne; Grantland Rice, sportswriter; Carl Rowan, journalist; Wilma Rudolph, sprinter; Sequoya, Cherokee scholar and educator; Cybil Shepherd, actress; Dinah Shore, actress, singer; Alvin York, World War I hero

TEXAS

Capital: Austin
Governor: Ann Richards, D (to Jan. 1995)
Lieut. Governor: Bob Bullock, D (to Jan. 1995)
Secy. of State: John Hannah, Jr., D (Apptd. by Gov.)
Treasurer: Martha Whitehead, R (Apptd. by Gov.)
Comptroller: John Sharp, D (to Jan. 1995)
Atty. General: Dan Morales, D (to Jan. 1995)
Entered Union & (rank): Dec. 29, 1845 (28)
Present constitution adopted: 1876
Motto: Friendship
STATE SYMBOLS: flower, Bluebonnet (1901); **tree,** Pecan (1919); **bird,** Mockingbird (1927); **song,** "Texas, Our Texas" (1929); **fish,** Guadalupe bass (1989); **seashell,** Lightning whelk (1987)
Nickname: Lone Star State
Origin of name: From an Indian word meaning "friends"
10 largest cities (1990 census): Houston, 1,630,553, 1993: 1,630,864; Dallas, 1,006,877, 1993: 1,007,617; San Antonio, 935,933; El Paso, 515,342; Austin, 465,622; Fort Worth, 447,619; Arlington, 261,721; Corpus Christi, 257,453; Lubbock, 186,206; Garland, 180,650
Land area & (rank): 261,914 sq mi. (678,358 sq km) (2)
Geographic center: In McCulloch Co., 15 mi. NE of Brady
Number of counties: 254
Largest county (1990 census): Harris, 2,818,199
State forests: 5 (7,609 ac.)
State parks: 218 (206 developed)
1992 resident population est.: 17,656,000
1990 resident census population, sex, & (rank): 16,986,510 (3). **Male:** 8,365,963; **Female:** 8,620,547. **White:** 12,774,762 (75.2%); **Black:** 2,021,632 (11.9%); **American Indian, Eskimo, or Aleut:** 65,877 (0.4%); **Asian or Pacific Islander:** 319,459 (1.9%); **Other race:** 1,804,780 (10.6%); **Hispanic:** 4,339,905 (25.5%). **1990 percent population under 18:** 28.5; **65 and over:** 10.1; **median age:** 30.8.

Spanish explorers, including Cabeza de Vaca and Coronado, were the first to visit the region in the 16th and 17th centuries, settling at Ysleta near El Paso in 1682. In 1685, La Salle established a short-lived French colony at Matagorda Bay.

Americans, led by Stephen F. Austin, began to settle along the Brazos River in 1821 when Texas was controlled by Mexico, recently independent from Spain. In 1836, following a brief war between the American settlers in Texas and the Mexican government, and famous for the battles of the Alamo and San Jacinto, the Independent Republic of Texas was proclaimed with Sam Houston as president.

After Texas became the 28th U.S. state in 1845, border disputes led to the Mexican War of 1846–48.

Today, Texas, second only to Alaska in land area, leads all other states in such categories as oil, cattle, sheep, and cotton. Possessing enormous natural resources, Texas is a major agricultural state and an industrial giant.

Sulfur, salt, helium, asphalt, graphite, bromine, natural gas, cement, and clays give Texas first place in mineral production. Chemicals, oil refining, food processing, machinery, and transportation equipment are among the major Texas manufacturing industries.

Texas ranches and farms produce beef cattle, poultry, rice, pecans, peanuts, sorghum, and an extensive variety of fruits and vegetables.

Millions of tourists spend well over $20.6 billion annually visiting more than 70 state parks, recreation areas, and points of interest such as the Gulf Coast resort area, the Lyndon B. Johnson Space Center in Houston, the Alamo in San Antonio, the state capital in Austin, and the Big Bend and Guadalupe Mountains National Parks.

Famous natives and residents: Alvin Ailey, choreographer; Mary Kay Ash, cosmetics entrepreneur; Steven Fuller Austin, founding father of Texas; Gene Autry, singer and actor; Carol Burnett, comedienne; Cyd Charisse, actress and dancer; Denton A. Cooley, heart surgeon; Joan Crawford, actress; Dwight David Eisenhower, President, general; A.J. Foyt, auto racer; Ben Hogan, golfer; Howard Hughes, industrialist and film producer; Jack Johnson, boxer; Lyndon B. Johnson, President; George Jones, singer; Scott Joplin, composer; Trini Lopez, singer; Mary Martin, singer and actress; Spanky McFarland, actor; Audie Murphy, actor and war hero; Chester Nimitz, admiral; Sandra Day O'Connor, jurist; Buck Owens, singer; Katherine Anne Porter, novelist; Wiley Post, aviator; Dan Rather, TV newscaster; Robert Rauschenberg, painter; Tex Ritter, singer; Rip Torn, actor and director; Tommy Tune, dancer and choreographer; Tina Turner, singer; Dooley Wilson, actor and musician; Babe Didrikson Zaharias, athlete, golfer

UTAH

Capital: Salt Lake City
Governor: Norman H. Bangerter, R (to Jan. 1997)
Lieut. Governor: Arlene S. Walker, R (to Jan. 1997)
Atty. General: Jon Graham, D (to Jan. 1997)
Organized as territory: Sept. 9, 1850
Entered Union & (rank): Jan. 4, 1896 (45)
Present constitution adopted: 1896
Motto: Industry
STATE SYMBOLS: flower, Sego lily (1911); **tree,** Blue spruce (1933); **bird,** Seagull (1955); **emblem,** Beehive (1959); **song,** "Utah, We Love Thee" (1953)
Nickname: Beehive State
Origin of name: From the Ute tribe, meaning "people of the mountains"
10 largest cities (1990 census): Salt Lake City, 159,936; West Valley City, 86,976; Provo, 86,835; Sandy, 75,058; Orem, 67,561; Ogden, 63,909; Taylorsville-Bennion, 52,351; West Jordan, 42,892; Layton, 41,784; Bountiful, 36,659
Land area & (rank): 82,168 sq mi. (212,816 sq km) (12)
Geographic center: In Sanpete Co., 3 mi. N. of Manti
Number of counties: 29
Largest county (1990 census): Salt Lake, 725,956
National parks: 5
National monuments: 6
State parks/forests: 44 (64,097 ac.)
1992 resident population est.: 1,813,000
1990 resident census population, sex, & (rank): 1,722,850 (35). **Male:** 855,759; **Female:** 867,091. **White:** 1,615,845 (93.8%); **Black:** 11,576 (0.7%); **American Indian, Eskimo, or Aleut:** 24,283 (1.4%); **Asian or Pacific Islander:** 33,371 (1.9%); **Other race:** 37,775 (2.2%); **Hispanic:** 84,597 (4.9%). **1990 percent population under 18:** 36.4; **65 and over:** 8.7; **median age:** 26.2.

The region was first explored for Spain by Franciscan friars, Escalante and Dominguez in 1776. In 1824 the famous American frontiersman Jim Bridger discovered the Great Salt Lake.

Fleeing the religious persecution encountered in eastern and middle-western states, the Mormons reached the Great Salt Lake in 1847 and began to build Salt Lake City. The U.S. acquired the Utah region in the treaty ending the Mexican War in 1848 and the first transcontinental railroad was completed with the driving of a golden spike at Promontory Summit in 1869.

Mormon difficulties with the federal government about polygamy did not end until the Mormon Church renounced the practice in 1890, six years before Utah became a state.

Rich in natural resources, Utah has long been a leading producer of copper, gold, silver, lead, zinc, and molybdenum. Oil has also become a major product; with Colorado and Wyoming, Utah shares what have been called the world's richest oil shale deposits.

Ranked eighth among the states in number of sheep in 1989, Utah also produces large crops of alfalfa, winter wheat, and beans. Utah's farmlands and crops require extensive irrigation.

Utah's traditional industries of agriculture and mining are being complemented by increased tourism business and growing aerospace, biomedical, and computer-related businesses. Utah is home to computer software giants Novell and WordPerfect.

Utah is a great vacationland with 11,000 miles of fishing streams and 147,000 acres of lakes and reservoirs. Among the many tourist attractions are Arches, Bryce Canyon, Canyonlands, Capitol Reef, and Zion National Parks; Dinosaur, Natural Bridges, and Rainbow Bridge National Monuments; the Mormon Tabernacle in Salt Lake City; and Monument Valley.

Famous natives and residents: Maude Adams, actress; Roseanne Arnold, actress; Frank Borzage, film director and producer; John M. Browning, inventor; Butch Cassidy, outlaw; Laraine Day, actress; Bernard De Voto, writer; Avard Fairbanks, sculptor; Philo Farnsworth, television pioneer; Jake Garn, senator; John Gilbert, actor; J, Willard Marriott, restaurant and hotel chain founder; Peter Skene Ogden, fur trader, trapper; Merlin Olsen, football player; Donny Osmond, Marie Osmond, singers; Ivy Baker Priest, U.S. treasurer; Lee Greene Richards, painter; Leroy Robertson, composer; Brent Scowcroft, business executive, consultant; Reed Smoot, first Morman elected to U.S. Senate; Mack Swain, actor; Everett Thorpe, painter; Robert Walker, actor; James Woods, actor; Brigham Young, territory governor and religious leader; Loretta Young, actress

VERMONT

Capital: Montpelier
Governor: Howard B. Dean, D (to Jan. 1995)
Lieut. Governor: Barbara W. Snelling, R (to Jan. 1995)
Secy. of State: Donald M. Hooper, D (to Jan. 1995)
Treasurer: Paul W. Ruse, Jr., D (to Jan. 1995)
Auditor of Accounts: Edward S. Flanagan D (to Jan. 1995)
Atty. General: Jeffrey L. Amestoy, R (to Jan. 1995)
Entered Union & (rank): March 4, 1791 (14)
Present constitution adopted: 1793
Motto: Vermont, Freedom, and Unity
STATE SYMBOLS: flower, Red clover (1894); **tree,** Sugar maple (1949); **bird,** Hermit thrush (1941); **animal,** Morgan horse (1961); **insect,** Honeybee (1978); **song,** "Hail, Vermont!" (1938)
Nickname: Green Mountain State
Origin of name: From the French "vert mont," meaning "green mountain"
10 largest cities (1990 census): Burlington, 39,127; Rutland, 18,230; South Burlington, 12,809; Barre, 9,482; Essex Junction, 8,396; Montpelier, 8,247; St. Albans, 7,339; Winooski, 6,649; Newport, 4,434; Bellows Falls, 3,313
Land area & (rank): 9,249 sq mi. (23,956 sq km) (43)
Geographic center: In Washington Co., 3 mi. E of Roxbury
Number of counties: 14
Largest county (1990 census): Chittenden, 131,761
State forests: 34 (113,953 ac.)
State parks: 45 (31,325 ac.)
1992 resident population est.: 570,000
1990 resident census population, sex, & (rank): 562,758 (48). **Male:** 275,492; **Female:** 287,266. **White:** 555,088 (98.6%); **Black:** 1,951 (0.3%); **American Indian, Eskimo, or Aleut:** 1,696 (0.3%); **Asian or Pacific Islander:** 3,215 (0.6%); **Other race:** 808 (0.1%); **Hispanic:** 3,661 (0.7%). **1990 percent population under 18:** 25.4; **65 and over:** 11.8; **median age:** 33.0.

The Vermont region was explored and claimed for France by Samuel de Champlain in 1609 and the first French settlement was established at Fort Ste. Anne in 1666. The first English settlers moved into the area in 1724 and built Fort Drummer on the site of present-day Brattleboro. England gained control of the area in 1763 after the French and Indian War.

First organized to drive settlers from New York out of Vermont, the Green Mountain Boys, led by Ethan Allen, won fame by capturing Fort Ticonderoga from the British on May 10, 1775, in the early days of the Revolution.

In 1777 Vermont adopted its first constitution abolishing slavery and providing for universal male suffrage without property qualifications. In 1791 Vermont became the first state after the original 13 to join the Union.

Vermont leads the nation in the production of monument granite, marble, and maple syrup. It is also a leader in the production of talc.

In ratio to population, Vermont keeps more dairy cows than any other state. Vermont's soil is devoted to dairying, truck farming, and fruit growing because the rugged, rocky terrain discourages extensive farming.

Principal industrial products include electrical equipment, fabricated metal products, printing and publishing, and paper and allied products.

Tourism is a major industry in Vermont. Vermont's many famous ski areas include Stowe, Killington, Mt. Snow, Bromley, Jay Peak, and Sugarbush. Hunting and fishing also attract many visitors to Vermont each year. Among the many points of interest are the Green Mountain National Forest, Bennington Battle Monument, the Calvin Coolidge Homestead at Plymouth, and the Marble Exhibit in Proctor.

Famous natives and residents: Chester A. Arthur, President; Orson Bean, actor; Calvin Coolidge, President; George Dewey, admiral; John Dewey, philosopher and educator; Stephen A. Douglas, politician; James Fisk, financial speculator; Wilbur Fisk, clergyman and educator; Richard Morris Hunt, architect; William Morris Hunt, painter; Elisha Otis, inventor; Moses Pendleton, choreographer; Joseph Smith, religious leader; Ernest Thompson, actor, writer; Rudy Vallee, singer and band leader; Henry Wells, pioneer entrepreneur (Wells Fargo & Co.); Brigham Young, religious leader

VIRGINIA

Capital: Richmond
Governor: L. Douglas Wilder, D (to Jan. 1994)
Lieut. Governor: Donald S. Beyer, Jr., D (to Jan. 1994)
Secy. of the Commonwealth: Pamela M. Wornack (apptd. by governor)
Comptroller: Edward J. Mazur (apptd. by governor)
Atty. General: Mary Sue Terry, D (to Jan. 1994)
Entered Union & (rank): June 25, 1788 (10)
Present constitution adopted: 1970
Motto: *Sic semper tyrannis* (Thus always to tyrants)
STATE SYMBOLS: flower, American dogwood (1918); **bird,** Cardinal (1950); **dog,** American foxhound (1966); **shell,** Oyster shell (1974); **song,** "Carry Me Back to Old Virginia" (1940)
Nicknames: The Old Dominion; Mother of Presidents
Origin of name: In honor of Elizabeth "Virgin Queen" of England
10 largest cities (1990 census): Virginia Beach, 393,069; Norfolk, 261,229; Richmond, 203,056; Newport News, 170,045; Chesapeake, 151,976; Hampton, 133,793; Alexandria, 111,183; Portsmouth, 103,907; Roanoke, 96,907; Lynchburg, 66,049
Land area & (rank): 39,598 sq mi. (102,558 sq km) (37)
Geographic center: In Buckingham Co., 5 mi. SW of Buckingham
Number of counties: 95, plus 41 independent cities
Largest county (1990 census): Fairfax, 818,384
State forests: 8 (49,566 ac.)
State parks and recreational parks: 27, plus 3 in process of acquisition and/or development (42,722 ac.)[1]
1992 resident population est.: 6,377,000
1990 resident census population, sex, & (rank): 6,187,358 (12). **Male:** 3,033,974; **Female:** 3,153,384. **White:** 4,791,739 (77.4%); **Black:** 1,162,994 (18.8%); **American Indian, Eskimo, or Aleut:** 15,282 (0.2%); **Asian or Pacific Islander:** 159,053 (2.6%); **Other race:** 58,290 (0.9%); **Hispanic:** 160,288 (2.6%). **1990 percent population under 18:** 24.3; **65 and over:** 10.7; **median age:** 32.6.

1. Does not include portion of Breaks Interstate Park (Va.-Ky., 1,200 ac.) which lies in Virginia.

The history of America is closely tied to that of Virginia, particularly in the Colonial period. Jamestown, founded in 1607, was the first permanent English settlement in North America and slavery was introduced there in 1619. The surrenders ending both the American Revolution (Yorktown) and the Civil War (Appomattox) occurred in Virginia. The state is called the "Mother of Presidents" because eight chief executives of the United States were born there.

Today, Virginia has a large number of diversified manufacturing industries including transportation equipment, textiles, food processing and printing. Other important lines are electronic and other electric equipment, chemicals, apparel, lumber and wood products, furniture, and industrial machinery and equipment.

Agriculture remains an important sector in the Virginia economy and the state ranks among the top 10 in the U.S. in tomatoes, tobacco, peanuts, summer potatoes, turkeys, apples, broilers, and sweet potatoes. Other crops include corn, vegetables, and barley. Famous for Smithfield hams, Virginia also has a large dairy industry.

Coal mining accounts for roughly 75% of Virginia's mineral output, and lime, kyanite, and stone are also mined.

Points of interest include Mt. Vernon and other places associated with George Washington; Monticello, home of Thomas Jefferson; Stratford, home of the Lees; Richmond, capital of the Confederacy and of Virginia; and Williamsburg, the restored Colonial capital.

The Chesapeake Bay Bridge-Tunnel spans the mouth of Chesapeake Bay, connecting Cape Charles with Norfolk. Consisting of a series of low trestles, two bridges and two mile-long tunnels, the complex is 18 miles (29 km) long. It was opened in 1964.

Other attractions are the Shenandoah National Park, Fredericksburg and Spotsylvania National Military Park, the Booker T. Washington birthplace near Roanoke, Arlington House (the Robert E. Lee Memorial), the Skyline Drive, and the Blue Ridge National Parkway.

Famous natives and residents: Richard Arlen, actor; Arthur Ashe, tennis player; Pearl Bailey, singer; Russell Baker, columnist; Warren Beatty, actor; George Bingham, painter; Richard E. Byrd, polar explorer; Willa Cather, novelist; Roy Clark, country music artist; William Clark, explorer; Henry Clay, statesman; Joseph Cotten, actor; Ella Fitzgerald, singer; William H. Harrison, President; Patrick Henry, statesman; Sam Houston, political leader; Thomas Jefferson, President; Robert E. Lee, Confederate general; Meriwether Lewis, explorer; Shirley MacLaine, actress; James Madison, President; John Marshall, jurist; Cyrus McCormick, inventor; James Monroe, President; Opechancanough, Powhatan leader; John Payne, actor; Walter Reed, army surgeon; Matthew Ridgway, ex-Army Chief of Staff; Bill "Bojangles" Robinson, dancer; George C. Scott, actor; Sam Snead, golfer; James "Jeb" Stuart, Confederate army officer; Zachary Taylor, President; Nat Turner, civil rights leader; John Tyler, President; Booker T. Washington, educator; George Washington, first President; Woodrow Wilson, President; Tom Wolfe, journalist

WASHINGTON

Capital: Olympia
Governor: Mike Lowry, D (to 1997)
Lieut. Governor: Joel Pritchard, R (to 1997)
Secy. of State: Ralph Munro, R (to 1997)
State Treasurer: Daniel K. Grimm, D (to 1997)
Atty. General: Christine Gregoire, D (to 1997)
Organized as territory: March 2, 1853
Entered Union & (rank): Nov. 11, 1889 (42)
Present constitution adopted: 1889
Motto: *Al-Ki* (Indian word meaning "by and by")
STATE SYMBOLS: flower, Coast Rhododendron (1949); **tree,** Western hemlock (1947); **bird,** Willow goldfinch (1951); **fish,** Steelhead trout (1969); **gem,** Petrified wood (1975); **colors,** Green and gold (1925); **song,** "Washington, My Home" (1959); **folk song,** "Roll On Columbia, Roll On" (1987); **dance,** Square dance (1979)
Nicknames: Evergreen State; Chinook State
Origin of name: In honor of George Washington
10 largest cities (1990 census): Seattle, 516,259; Spokane, 177,196; Tacoma, 176,664; Bellevue, 86,874; Everett, 69,961; Yakima, 54,827; Bellingham, 42,155; Renton, 41,688
Land area & (rank): 66,582 sq mi. (172,447 sq km) (20)
Geographic center: In Chelan Co., 10 mi. WSW of Wenatchee
Number of counties: 39
Largest county (1991 census): King, 1,542,300
State forest lands: 1,922,880 ac.
State parks: 215 (231,861 ac.)[1]
1992 resident population est.: 5,136,000
1990 resident census population, sex, & (rank): 4,866,692 (18). **Male:** 2,413,747; **Female:** 2,452,945. **White:** 4,308,937 (88.5%); **Black:** 149,801 (3.1%); **American Indian, Eskimo, or Aleut:** 81,483 (1.7%); **Other race:** 115,513 (2.4%); **Hispanic:** 214,570 (4.4%). **1990 percent population under 18:** 25.9; **65 and over:** 11.8; **median age:** 33.1.

1. Parks and undeveloped areas administered by State Parks and Recreation Commission. Dept. of Wildlife administers wildlife and recreation areas totaling 428,989.5 acres.

As part of the vast Oregon Country, Washington territory was visited by Spanish, American, and British explorers—Bruno Heceta for Spain in 1775, the American Capt. Robert Gray in 1792, and Capt. George Vancouver for Britain in 1792–94. Lewis and Clark explored the Columbia River region and coastal areas for the U.S. in 1805–06.

Rival American and British settlers and conflicting territorial claims threatened war in the early 1840s. However, in 1846 the Oregon Treaty set the boundary at the 49th parallel and war was averted.

Washington is a leading lumber producer. Its rugged surface is rich in stands of Douglas fir, hemlock, ponderosa and white pine, spruce, larch, and cedar. The state holds first place in apples, lentils, dry edible peas, hops, pears, red raspberries, spearmint oil, and sweet cherries, and ranks high in apricots, asparagus, grapes, peppermint oil, and potatoes. Livestock and livestock products make important contributions to total farm revenue and the commercial fishing catch of salmon, halibut, and bottomfish makes a significant contribution to the state's economy.

Manufacturing industries in Washington include aircraft and missiles, shipbuilding and other transportation equipment, lumber, food processing, metals and metal products, chemicals, and machinery.

The Columbia River contains one third of the potential water power in the U.S., harnessed by such dams as the Grand Coulee, one of the greatest power producers in the world. Washington has over 1,000 dams built for a variety of purposes including irrigation, power, flood control, and water storage. Its abundance of electrical power makes Washington one of the nation's major producers of refined aluminum.

Among the major points of interest: Mt. Rainier, Olympic, and North Cascades. In 1980, Mount St. Helens, a peak in the Cascade Range in Southwestern Washington erupted on May 18th. Also of interest are National Parks; Whitman Mission and Fort Vancouver National Historic Sites; and the Pacific Science Center and Space Needle in Seattle.

Famous natives and residents: Bob Barker, TV host; Dyan Cannon, actress; Carol Channing, actress; Judy Collins, singer; Bing Crosby, singer, actor; Bob Crosby, musician; Merce Cunningham, choreographer; Howard Duff, actor; Frances Farmer, actress; Jimi Hendrix, guitarist; Frank Herbert, writer; Robert Joffrey, choreographer; Gypsy Rose Lee, entertainer; Hank Ketcham, cartoonist; Mary McCarthy, novelist; Guthrie McClintic, theatrical producer and director; John McIntire, actor; Robert Motherwell, artist; Patrice Munsel, soprano;

Ella Raines, actress; Jimmy Rogers, singer; Francis Scobee, astronaut; Seattle, Dwamish, Suquamish chief; Jeff Smith, TV cook; Smohalla, Indian prophet and chief; Adam West, actor; Martha Wright, singer; Audrey Wurdemann, poet

WEST VIRGINIA

Capital: Charleston
Governor: Gaston Caperton, D (to Jan. 1997)
Secy. of State: Ken Heckler, D (to Jan. 1997)
State Auditor: Glen Gainer (to Jan. 1997)
Atty. General: Darrell McGraw, D (to Jan. 1997)
Entered Union & (rank): June 20, 1863 (35)
Present constitution adopted: 1872
Motto: *Montani semper liberi* (Mountaineers are always free)
STATE SYMBOLS: flower, Rhododendron (1903); **tree,** Sugar maple (1949); **bird,** Cardinal (1949); **animal,** Black bear (1973); **colors,** Blue and gold (official) (1863); **songs,** "West Virginia, My Home Sweet Home," "The West Virginia Hills," and "This Is My West Virginia" (adopted by Legislature in 1947, 1961, and 1963 as official state songs)
Nickname: Mountain State
Origin of name: Same as for Virginia
10 largest cities (1990 census): Charleston, 57,287; Huntington, 54,844; Wheeling, 34,882; Parkersburg, 33,862; Morgantown, 25,879; Weirton, 22,124; Fairmont, 20,210; Beckley, 18,296; Clarksburg, 18,059; Martinsburg, 14,073
Land area & (rank): 24,087 sq mi. (62,384 sq km) (41)
Geographic center: In Braxton Co., 4 mi. E of Sutton
Number of counties: 55
Largest county (1990 census): Kanawha, 207,619
State forests: 9 (79,502 ac.)
State parks: 34 (74,508 ac.)
1992 resident population est.: 1,812,000
1990 resident census population, sex, & (rank): 1,793,477 (34). **Male:** 861,536; **Female:** 931,941. **White:** 1,725,523 (96.2%); **Black:** 56,295 (3.1%); **American Indian, Eskimo, or Aleut:** 2,458 (0.1%); **Asian or Pacific Islander:** 7,459 (0.4%); **Other race:** 1,742 (0.1%); **Hispanic:** 8,489 (0.5%). **1990 percent population under 18:** 24.7; **65 and over:** 15.0; **median age:** 35.4.

West Virginia's early history from 1609 until 1863 is largely shared with Virginia, of which it was a part until Virginia seceded from the Union in 1861. Then the delegates of 40 western counties formed their own government, which was granted statehood in 1863.

First permanent settlement dates from 1731 when Morgan Morgan founded Mill Creek. In 1742 coal was discovered on the Coal River, an event that would be of great significance in determining West Virginia's future.

The state usually ranks 3rd in total coal production with about 15% of the U.S. total. It also is a leader in steel, glass, aluminum, and chemical manufactures; natural gas, oil, quarry products, and hardwood lumber.

Major cash farm products are poultry and eggs, dairy products, apples, and feed crops. Nearly 80% of West Virginia is covered with forests.

Tourism is increasingly popular in mountainous West Virginia and visitors spent $2.475 billion in 1990. More than a million acres have been set aside in 34 state parks and recreation areas and in 9 state forests, and national forests.

Major points of interest include Harpers Ferry and New River Gorge National River, The Greenbrier and Berkeley Springs resorts, the scenic railroad at Cass, and the historic homes in the Eastern Panhandle.

Famous natives and residents: George Brett, baseball player; Pearl S. Buck, author; Phyllis Curtin, soprano; Martin R. Delany, first Black Army major; Billy Dixon, frontiersman and scout; Joanne Dru, actress; Thomas "Stonewall" Jackson, Confederate general; John S. Knight, publisher; Don Knotts, actor; Peter Marshall, TV host; Whitney D. Morrow, banker and diplomat; Mary Lou Retton, gymnast; Walter Reuther, labor leader; Eleanor Steber, soprano; Lewis L. Strauss, naval officer and scientist; Cyrus Vance, government official; William Lyne Wilson, legislator and university president; Chuck Yeager, test pilot and Air Force general

WISCONSIN

Capital: Madison
Governor: Tommy G. Thompson, R (to Jan. 1995)
Lieut. Governor: Scott McCallum, R (to Jan. 1995)
Secy. of State: Douglas J. La Follette, D (to Jan. 1995)
State Treasurer: Cathy S. Zeuske, R (to Jan. 1995)
Atty. General: James E. Doyle, D (to Jan. 1995)
Superintendent of Public Instruction: John Benson Nonpartisan (to July 1997)
Organized as territory: July 4, 1836
Entered Union & (rank): May 29, 1848 (30)
Present constitution adopted: 1848
Motto: Forward
STATE SYMBOLS: flower, Wood violet (1949); **tree,** Sugar maple (1949); **grain,** corn (1990); **bird,** Robin (1949); **animal,** Badger; **"wild life" animal,** White-tailed deer (1957); **"domestic" animal,** Dairy cow (1971); **insect,** Honeybee (1977); **fish,** Musky (Muskellunge) (1955); **song,** "On Wisconsin"; **mineral,** Galena (1971); **rock,** Red Granite (1971); **symbol of peace:** Mourning Dove (1971); **soil,** Antigo Silt Loam (1983); **fossil,** Trilobite (1985); **dog,** American Water Spaniel (1986); **beverage,** Milk (1988)
Nickname: Badger State
Origin of name: French corruption of an Indian word whose meaning is disputed
10 largest cities (1990 census): Milwaukee, 628,088; Madison, 191,262; Green Bay, 96,466; Racine, 84,298; Kenosha, 80,352; Appleton, 65,695; West Allis, 63,221; Waukesha, 56,958; Eau Claire, 56,856; Oshkosh, 55,006
Land area & (rank): 54,314 sq mi. (140,673 sq km) (25)
Geographic center: In Wood Co., 9 mi. SE of Marshfield
Number of counties: 72
Largest county (1990 census): Milwaukee, 959,275
State forests: 9 (476,004 ac.)
State parks & scenic trails: 49 parks, 13 trails (66,185 ac.)
1992 resident population est.: 5,007,000
1990 resident census population, sex, & (rank): 4,891,769 (16). **Male:** 2,392,935; **Female:** 2,498,834. **White:** 4,512,523 (92.2%); **Black:** 244,539 (5.0%); **American Indian, Eskimo, or Aleut:** 39,387 (0.8%); **Asian or Pacific Islander:** 53,583 (1.1%); **Other race:** 41,737 (0.9%); **Hispanic:** 93,194 (1.9%). **1980 percent population under 18:** 26.4; **65 and over:** 13.3; **median age:** 32.9.

The Wisconsin region was first explored for France by Jean Nicolet, who landed at Green Bay in 1634. In 1660 a French trading post and Roman Catholic mission were established near present-day Ashland.

Great Britain obtained the region in settlement of the French and Indian War in 1763; the U.S. acquried it in 1783 after the Revolutionary War. However, Great Britain retained actual control until after the War of 1812. The region was successively governed as part of the territories of Indiana, Illinois, and Michigan between 1800 and 1836, when it became a separate territory.

Wisconsin leads the nation in milk and cheese production. In 1991 the state ranked first in the number of milk cows (1,675,000) and produced 16.2% of the nation's total output of milk. Other important farm products are peas, beans, corn, potatoes, oats, hay, and cranberries.

The chief industrial products of the state are automobiles, machinery, furniture, paper, beer, and processed foods. Wisconsin ranks second among the 47 paper-producing states.

Wisconsin pioneered in social legislation, providing pensions for the blind (1907), aid to dependent children (1913), and old-age assistance (1925). In labor legislation, the state was the first to enact an unemployment compensation law (1932) and the first in which a workman's compensation law actually took effect. Wisconsin had the first state-wide primary-election law and the first successful income-tax law. In April 1984, Wisconsin became the first state to adopt the Uniform Marital Property Act. The act took effect on January 1, 1986.

The state has over 8,500 lakes, of which Winnebago is the largest. Water sports, ice-boating, and fishing are popular, as are skiing and hunting. Public parks and forests take up one seventh of the land, with 49 state parks, 9 state forests, 13 state trails, 3 recreational areas, and 2 national forests.

Among the many points of interest are the Apostle Islands National Lakeshore; Ice Age National Scientific Reserve; the Circus World Museum at Baraboo; the Wolf, St. Croix, and Lower St. Croix national scenic riverways; and the Wisconsin Dells.

Famous natives and residents: Don Ameche, actor; Ray Chapman Andrews, naturalist and explorer; Walter Annenberg, media tycoon and philanthropist; Carrie Catt, woman suffragist; Tyne Daly, actress; August Derleth, author; Jeanne Dixon, seer; Zona Gale, novelist; Eric Heiden, skater; Woody Herman, band leader; Hildegarde, singer; Harry Houdini, magician; Hans V. Kaltenborne, journalist; Pee Wee King, singer; George F. Kennan, diplomat; Robert La Follette, politician; Liberace, pianist; Charles Litel, actor; Allen Ludden, TV host; Alfred Lunt, actor; Frederic March, actor; Jackie Mason, comedian; John Ringling North, circus director; Pat O'Brien, actor; Georgia O'Keeffe, painter; Charlotte Rae, actress; William H. Rehnquist, jurist; Gena Rowlands, actress; Tom Snyder, newscaster; Spencer Tracy, actor; Thorstein Veblen, economist; Orson Welles, actor and producer; Thornton Wilder, author; Charles Winninger, actor; Frank Lloyd Wright, architect.

WYOMING

Capital: Cheyenne
Governor: Michael J. Sullivan, D (to Jan. 1995)
Secy. of State: Kathy Karpan, D (to Jan. 1995)
Auditor: Dave Ferrari, R (to Jan. 1995)
Supt. of Public Instruction: Diana Ohman, R (to Jan. 1995)
Treasurer: Stanford S. Smith, R (to Jan. 1995)
Atty. General: Joseph B. Meyer, D (apptd. by Governor)
Organized as territory: May 19, 1869
Entered Union & (rank): July 10, 1890 (44)
Present constitution adopted: 1890
Motto: Equal rights (1955)
STATE SYMBOLS: flower, Indian paintbrush (1917); **tree,** Cottonwood (1947); **bird,** Meadowlark (1927); **gemstone,** Jade (1967); **insignia,** Bucking horse (unofficial); **song,** "Wyoming" (1955)
Nickname: Equality State
Origin of name: From the Delaware Indian word, meaning "mountains and valleys alternating"; the same as the Wyoming Valley in Pennsylvania
10 largest cities (1990 census): Cheyenne, 50,008; Casper, 46,742; Laramie, 26,687; Rock Springs, 19,050; Gillette, 17,635; Sheridan, 13,900; Green River, 12,711; Evanston, 10,903; Rawlins, 9,380; Riverton, 9,202
Land area & (rank): 97,105 sq mi. (251,501 sq km) (9)
Geographic center: In Fremont Co., 58 mi. ENE of Lander
Number of counties: 23, plus Yellowstone National Park
Largest county (1990 census): Laramie, 73,142
State forests: None
State parks and historic sites: 17 (58,498 ac.)
1992 resident population est.: 466,000
1990 resident census population, sex, & (rank): 453,588 (50). **Male:** 227,007; **Female:** 226,581. **White:** 427,061 (94.2%); **Black:** 3,606 (0.8%); **American Indian, Eskimo, or Aleut:** 9,479 (2.1%); **Asian or Pacific Islander:** 2.806 (0.6%); **Other race:** 10,636 (2.3%); **Hispanic:** 25,751 (5.7%). **1990 percent population under 18:** 29.9; **65 and over:** 10.4; **median age:** 32.0.

The U.S. acquired the territory from France as part of the Louisiana Purchase in 1803. John Colter, a fur-trapper, is the first white man known to have entered present Wyoming. In 1807 he explored the Yellowstone area and brought back news of its geysers and hot springs.

Robert Stuart pioneered the Oregon Trail across Wyoming in 1812–13 and, in 1834, Fort Laramie, the first permanent trading post in Wyoming, was built. Western Wyoming was obtained by the U.S. in the 1846 Oregon Treaty with Great Britain and as a result of the treaty ending the Mexican War in 1848.

When the Wyoming Territory was organized in 1869 Wyoming women became the first in the nation to obtain the right to vote. In 1925 Mrs. Nellie Tayloe Ross was elected first woman governor in the United States.

Wyoming's towering mountains and vast plains provide spectacular scenery, grazing lands for sheep and cattle, and rich mineral deposits.

Mining, particularly oil and natural gas, is the most important industry. Wyoming has the world's largest sodium carbonate (natrona) deposits and has the nation's second largest uranium deposits.

Wyoming ranks second among the states in wool production. In January 1991, its sheep numbered 830,000, exceeded only by Texas and California; it also had 1,190,000 cattle. Principal crops include wheat, oats, sugar beets, corn, potatoes, barley, and alfalfa.

Second in mean elevation to Colorado, Wyoming has many attractions for the tourist trade, notably Yellowstone National Park. Cheyenne is famous for its annual "Frontier Days" celebration. Flaming Gorge, the Fort Laramie National Historic Site, and Devils Tower and Fossil Butte National Monuments are other National points of interest.

Famous natives and residents: James Bridger, trapper, guide, storyteller; Dick Cheney, ex-Secretary of Defense; Buffalo Bill Cody; John Colter, trader and first white man to enter Wyoming; June E. Downey, educator; Thomas Fitzpatrick, mountain man and guide; Curt Gowdy, sportscaster; Tom Horn, detective; Isabel Jewell, actress; Velma Linford, writer; Esther Morris, first woman judge; Ted Olson, writer; John "Portugee" Phillips, frontiersman; Jackson Pollock, painter; Nellie Tayloe Ross, first woman elected governor of a state; Alan K. Simpson, senator; Jedediah S. Smith, mountain man and first American to reach California from the East; Alan Swallow, publisher, author; Willis Van Devanter, Supreme Court justice; Francis E. Warren, first state governor; Chief Washakie, chief of the Shoshone; James G. Watt, ex-Secretary of the Interior

U.S. Territories and Outlying Areas

PUERTO RICO

(Commonwealth of Puerto Rico)
Governor: Pedro Rosselló, New Progressive Party (to 1996)
Capital: San Juan
Land area: 3,459 sq mi. (8,959 sq km)
Song: "La Borinqueña"
1990 census population: 3,522,037
Languages: Spanish and English
Literacy rate: 89%
Labor force (1992): 1,140,000; 20% government, 17% commerce, 14% manufacturing, 5% construction, 5% communications and transportation, 39% other
Ethnic divisions: Almost entirely Hispanic.

10 largest municipios (1990 census): San Juan, 437,745; Bayamón, 220,262; Ponce, 187,749; Carolina, 177,806; Caguas, 133,447; Mayagüez, 100,371; Arecibo, 93,385; Guaynabo, 92,886; Toa Baja, 89,454; Trujillo Alto, 61,120

Gross product (FY 1992): $23.6 billion; per capita, $6,625; real growth rate, 1.2%

Land use: 13% cropland, 41% meadows and pastures, 20% forest and woodland, 26% other.

Environment: Subtropical marine climate; high central mountain range circled by coastal plains; abundant agricultural production and foliage fostered by natural irrigation in all regions except relatively arid south coast.

The Commonwealth of Puerto Rico is located in the Caribbean Sea, about 1,000 miles east southeast of Miami, Florida. A possession of the United States, it consists of the island of Puerto Rico—smallest of the Greater Antilles, measuring about 100 miles from east to west and 35 miles across—plus the adjacent islets of Vieques, Culebra and Mona.

Discovered by Christopher Columbus in 1493, Puerto Rico subsequently became the only New World colony of Spain that never waged a war for independence. Despite this lack of animosity toward Madrid, however, Puerto Ricans warmly welcomed invading United States troops during the Spanish-American War of 1898. Since then, Puerto Rico has remained an unincorporated U.S. territory. Its people were granted American citizenship in 1917; were permitted to elect their own governor, beginning in 1948; and now fully administer their internal affairs under a constitution approved by the U.S. Congress in 1952.

From 1940 to 1968, Puerto Rican politics was dominated by a party advocating voluntary association with the U.S. But during the past quarter century, a party favoring U.S. statehood has won four of seven gubernatorial elections—including that of 1992. Statehooders currently control two-thirds of the legislative seats and 54 of 78 mayoralties.

Under commonwealth status, residents of Puerto Rico lack voting representation in Congress and the right to participate in Presidential elections. Also, funding caps limit their access to several key Federal programs. As U.S. citizens, Puerto Ricans are subject to military service and most Federal laws. Residents of the Commonwealth pay no Federal income tax on locally-generated earnings, but Puerto Rico government income tax rates are set at a level that closely parallels Federal-plus-state levies on the mainland.

Puerto Rico is a major hub of Caribbean commerce, finance, tourism, and communications. San Juan is one of the world's busiest cruise ship ports, and Puerto Rico hosts hundreds of modern manufacturing facilities. Its population's standard of living is among the highest in the hemisphere.

Famous natives and residents: Pablo Casals, cellist; Roberto Clemente, baseball player; Angel Cordero, jockey and trainer; Justino Diaz, opera star; Beatriz "Gigi" Fernández, U.S. Olympic tennis gold medalist; Luis Ferré, political leader, philanthropist; José Ferrer, actor; Juan Igor González, baseball player; José Luis González, writer; Raúl Juliá, actor; Jacobo Morales, filmmaker; Rita Moreno, actress; Luis Muñoz-Marín, political leader; Antonia Novello, U.S. Surgeon General; Miguel Piñero, dramatist; Chita Rivera, actress; Juan "Chi Chi" Rodríguez, golfer; José Serrano, chair of Congressional Hispanic Caucus; Dayanara Torres, Miss Universe 1993; Juan Torruella, U.S. appeals court judge

GUAM

(Territory of Guam)
Governor: Joseph F. Ada
Capital: Agaña
Land area: 209 sq mi. (541 sq km)
1990 census population: 133,152
1989 net migration: 7 migrants per 1,000 population
Ethnic divisions: Chamorro, 43%; Filipino, 23%; Caucasian, 14%; Asian, 7%; other, 13%
Language: English and Chamorro, most residents bilingual; Japanese also widely spoken
Literacy rate: 90%
Labor force (1991): 66,390; 30% government, 70% private
Gross national product (1988 est.): $1.0 billion, per capita $7,675; real growth rate 20%

Guam, the largest of the Mariana Islands, is independent of the trusteeship assigned to the U.S. in 1947. It was acquired by the U.S. from Spain in 1898 (occupied 1899) and was placed under the Navy Department.

In World War II, Guam was seized by the Japanese on Dec. 11, 1941; but on July 21, 1944, it was once more in U.S. hands.

On Aug. 1, 1950, President Truman signed a bill which granted U.S. citizenship to the people of Guam and established self-government. However, the people do not vote in national elections. In 1972 Guam elected its first delegate to the U.S. Congress. The Executive Branch of the Guam government is under the general supervision of the U.S. Secretary of the Interior. In November 1970, Guam elected its first Governor.

Currently, Guam is an unincorporated, organized territory of the United States. It is "unincorporated" because not all of the provisions of the U.S. constitution apply to the territory. It is an "organized" territory because the Congress provided the territory with an Organic Act in 1950 which organized the government much as a constitution would.

Guam's economy is based on two main sources of revenue: tourism and U.S. military spending (U.S. Naval and Air Force bases on Guam). Federal expenditures (most military) in 1989 amounted to more than $680 million, of which more than $300 million went for salaries and more than $100 million for purchases in the local economy.

The world's strongest earthquake in over four years, measuring 8.2 on the Richter scale, struck Guam on Aug. 8, 1993. About 40 people were injured.

U.S. VIRGIN ISLANDS

(Virgin Islands of the United States)
Governor: Alexander A. Farrelly
Capital: Charlotte Amalie (on St. Thomas)
1990 population: 101,809 (St. Croix, 50,139; St. Thomas, 48,166; St. John, 3,504)
Land area: 132 sq mi (342 sq km): St. Croix, 84 sq. mi. (218 sq km), St. Thomas, 32 sq mi (83 sq km), St. John, 20 sq mi. (52 sq km)
1989 net migration rate: –1 migrants per 1,000 population
Ethnic divisions: West Indian, 74% (45% born in the Virgin Islands and 29% born elsewhere in the West Indies), U.S. mainland, 13%; Puerto Rican, 5%; other, 8%; black, 80%, white, 15%, other, 5%; 14% of Hispanic origin.
Language: English (official), but Spanish and various dialects are widely spoken.
Literacy rate: 90%
Labor force (1992): 48,620
Gross domestic product (1989): $1.34 billion, per capita $11,052
Aid: Western (non-U.S.) countries, official development assistance and other official flows, and bilateral commitments (1970–1987): $33.5 million.

The Virgin Islands, consisting of nine main islands and some 75 islets, were discovered by Columbus in 1493. Since 1666, England has held six of the main islands; the other three (St. Croix, St. Thomas, and St. John), as well as about 50 of the islets, were eventually acquired by Denmark, which named them the Danish West Indies. In 1917, these islands were purchased by the U.S. from Denmark for $25 million.

Congress granted U.S. citizenship to Virgin Islanders in 1927; and, in 1931, administration was transferred from the Navy to the Department of the Interior. Universal suffrage was given in 1936 to all persons who could read and write the English language. The Governor was elected by popular vote for the first time in 1970; previously he had been appointed by the President of the U.S. A unicameral 15-man legislature serves the Virgin Islands, and Congressional legislation gave the islands a non-voting Representative in Congress.

The "Constitution" of the Virgin Islands is the Revised Organic Act of 1954 in which the U.S. Congress defines the three branches of the territorial government, i.e., the Executive Branch, the Legislative Branch, and the Judicial Branch. Residents of the islands substantially enjoy the same rights as those enjoyed by mainlanders with one important exception: citizens of the U.S. who are residents may not vote in presidential elections.

Tourism is the primary economic activity, accounting for more than 70% of the GDP and 70% of employment. Tourist expenditures are estimated to be over $791.5 million annually. In 1992, 1,963,800 tourists arrived in the Virgin Islands; about two-thirds were day visitors on cruise ships. The manufacturing sector consists of textile, electronics, pharmaceutical, and watch assembly plants. The agricultural sector is small with most food imported. International business and financial services are a small but growing component of the economy. The world's largest petroleum refinery is at St. Croix.

AMERICAN SAMOA

(Territory of American Samoa)
Governor: A.P. Lutali
Lieut. Governor: Tauese Pita Sunia
Capital: Pago Pago
1990 census population: 46,638
1989 net migration rate: –11 migrants per 1,000 population
Ethnic divisions: Samoan (Polynesian) 90%; Caucasian, 2%; Tongan 2%; other 6%
Language: Samoan (closely related to Hawaiian and other Polynesian languages) and English; most people are bilingual
Literacy rate: 99%
Labor force (1990): 13,250
Land area: 77 sq mi (199 sq km)
Gross national product (1985): $190 million; per capita, $5,210
Aid (1989): $20.1 million in operational funds and $5.8 million in construction for capital-improvement projects from the U.S. Department of Interior.

American Samoa, a group of five volcanic islands and two coral atolls located some 2,600 miles south of Hawaii in the South Pacific Ocean, is an unincorporated, unorganized territory of the U.S., administered by the Department of the Interior.

By the Treaty of Berlin, signed Dec. 2, 1899, and ratified Feb. 16, 1900, the U.S. was internationally acknowledged to have rights extending over all the islands of the Samoa group east of longitude 1715 west of Greenwich. On April 17, 1900, the chiefs of Tutuila and Aunu'u ceded those islands to the U.S. In 1904, the King and chiefs of Manu'a ceded the islands of Ofu, Olosega and Tau (composing the Manu'a group) to the U.S. Swains Island, some 214 miles north of Samoa, was included as part of the territory by Act of Congress March 4, 1925; and on Feb. 20, 1929, Congress formally accepted sovereignty over the entire group and placed the responsibility for administration in the hands of the President. From 1900 to 1951, by Presidential direction, the Department of the Navy governed the territory. On July 1, 1951, administration was transferred to the Department of the Interior. The first Constitution for the territory was signed on April 27, 1960, and was revised in 1967.

Congress has provided for a non-voting delegate to sit in the House of Representatives in 1981.

The people of American Samoa are U.S. nationals, not U.S. citizens. Like U.S. citizens, they owe allegiance to the United States.

Fish processing is the main economic activity. In 1988, American Samoa generated approximately $368 million worth of exports, almost exclusively by tuna canneries located in Pago Pago. The canneries are the second largest employer on the islands. Other principal products are fish, pet food, fish meal, mats, and handicrafts.

BAKER, HOWLAND, AND JARVIS ISLANDS

These Pacific islands were not to play a role in the extraterritorial plans of the U.S. until May 13, 1936. President F. D. Roosevelt, at that time, placed them under the control and jurisdiction of the Secretary of the Interior for administration purposes.

The three islands have a tropical climate with scant rainfall, constant wind, and a burning sun.

Baker Island is a saucer-shaped atoll with an area of approximately one square mile. It is about 1,650 miles from Hawaii.

Howland Island, 36 miles to the northwest, is approximately one and a half miles long and half a mile wide. It is a low-lying, nearly level, sandy, coral island surrounded by a narrow fringing reef.

Howland Island is related to the tragic disappearance of Amelia Earhart and Fred J. Noonan during the round-the-world flight in 1937. They left New Guinea on July 2, 1937, for Howland, but were never seen again.

Jarvis Island is several hundred miles to the east and is approximately one and three quarter miles long by one mile wide. It is a sandy coral island surrounded by a a narrow fringing reef.

Baker, Howland, and Jarvis have been uninhabited since 1942. In 1974, these islands became part of the National Wildlife Refuge System, administered by the U.S. Fish & Wildlife Service, Department of the Interior.

JOHNSTON ATOLL

Johnston is a coral atoll about 700 miles southwest of Hawaii. It consists of four small islands—Johnston Island, Sand Island, Hikina Island, and Akau Island—which lie on a reef about 9 miles long in a northeast-southwest direction.

The atoll was discovered by Capt. Charles James Johnston of *H.M.S. Cornwallis* in 1807. In 1858 it was claimed by Hawaii, and later became a U.S. possession.

Johnston Atoll is a Naval Defensive Sea Area and Airspace Reservation and is closed to the public. The airspace entry control has been suspended but is subject to immediate reinstatement without notice. The administration of Johnston Atoll is under the jurisdiction of the Defense Nuclear Agency, Commander, Johnston Atoll (FCDNA), APO San Francisco, CA 96305.

KINGMAN REEF

Kingman Reef, located about 1,000 miles south of Hawaii, was discovered by Capt. E. Fanning in 1798, but named for Capt. W. E. Kingman, who rediscovered it in 1853. The reef, drying only on its northeast, east and southeast edges, is of atoll character. The reef is triangular in shape, with its apex northward; it is about 9.5 miles long, east and west, and 5 miles wide, north and south, within the 100-fathom curve. The island is uninhabited.

A United States possession, Kingman Reef is a Naval Defensive Sea Area and Airspace Reservation, and is closed to the public. The Airspace Entry Control has been suspended, but is subject to immediate reinstatement without notice. No vessel, except those authorized by the Secretary of the Navy, shall be navigated in the area within the 3-mile limit.

MIDWAY ISLANDS

Midway Islands, lying about 1,150 miles west-northwest of Hawaii, were discovered by Captain N. C. Brooks of the Hawaiian bark *Gambia* on July 5, 1859, in the name of the United States. The atoll was formally declared a U.S. possession in 1867, and in 1903 Theodore Roosevelt made it a naval reservation. The island was renamed "Midway" by the U.S. Navy in recognition of its geographic location on the route between California and Japan.

Midway Islands consist of a circular atoll, 6 miles in diameter, and enclosing two islands. Eastern Island, on its southeast side, is triangular in shape, and about 1.2 miles long. Sand Island on its south side, is about 2.25 miles long in a northeast-southwest direction.

A National Wildlife Refuge was set up on Midway under an agreement with the Fish and Wildlife Service of the U.S. Dept. of the Interior.

The Midway Islands are within a Naval Defensive Sea Area. The Navy Department maintains an installation and has jurisdiction over the atoll. Permission to enter the Naval Defensive Sea Area must be obtained in advance from the Commander Third Fleet (N31), Pearl Harbor, HI 96860.

Midway has no indigenous population. It is currently populated with several U.S. military personnel.

WAKE ISLAND

Total area: 2.5 sq mi. (6.5 sq km)
Comparative size: about 11 times the size of The Mall in Washington, D.C.
Population (Jan. 1990): no indigenous inhabitants; temporary population consists of 11 U.S. Air Force personnel, 27 U.S. civilians, and 151 Thai contractors.
Economy: The economic activity is limited to providing services to U.S. military personnel and contractors on the island. All food and manufactured goods must be imported.

Wake Island, about halfway between Midway and Guam, is an atoll comprising the three islets of Wilkes, Peale, and Wake. They were discovered by the British in 1796 and annexed by the U.S. in 1899. The entire area comprises 3 square miles and has no native population. In 1938, Pan American Airways established a seaplane base and Wake Island has been used as a commercial base since then. On Dec. 8, 1941, it was attacked by the Japanese, who finally took possession on Dec. 23. It was surrendered by the Japanese on Sept. 4, 1945.

The President, acting pursuant to the Hawaii Omnibus Act, assigned responsibility for Wake to the Secretary of the Interior in 1962. The Department of Transportation exercised civil administration of Wake through an agreement with the Department of the Interior until June 1972, at which time the Department of the Air Force assumed responsibility for the Territory.

CAROLINE ISLANDS

The Caroline Islands, east of the Philippines and south of the Marianas, include the Yap, Truk, and the Palau groups and the islands of Ponape and Kusqie, as well as many coral atolls.

The islands are composed chiefly of volcanic rock, and their peaks rise 2,000 to 3,000 feet above sea level. Chief exports of the islands are copra, fish products, and handicrafts.

Formerly members of the U.S. Trust Territory of the Pacific, all of the group but Palau joined the Federated States of Micronesia.

MARIANA ISLANDS

(The Commonwealth of The Northern Mariana Islands)

Governor: Lorenzo I. De Leon Guerrero (1989)
1990 population: 43,345. The population of the Commonwealth of the Northern Mariana Islands (CNMI) is concentrated on the three largest inhabited islands: Saipan, the government seat and commerce center, 39,090; Rota, 2,311; and Tinian, 2,118. The CNMI's northern islands have a population of 36. Of

the CNMI's total population, approximately 22,063 are registered aliens, a 670% increase since 1980.

Language: English is the official language, but Chamorro and Carolinian are the spoken native tongues. Japanese is also spoken in many of the hotels and shops, reflecting a heavy tourism industry.

Gross Island Product (1989): $512 million

Economy: The government of the CNMI benefits substantially from U.S. financial assistance. A seven-year financial agreement with the U.S.for the years 1986–1992 entitles the Commonwealth to $228 million for capital development, government operations, and special programs. A new agreement for $120 million for capital development is now pending before Congress. In addition, the CNMI is eligible for categorical federal programs provided to the 50 states.

The Mariana Islands, east of the Philippines and south of Japan, include the islands of Guam, Rota, Saipan, Tinian, Pagan, Guguan, Agrihan, and Aguijan. Guam, the largest, is independent of the trusteeship, having been acquired by the U.S. from Spain in 1898. (For more information, *see* the entry on Guam in this section.) The remaining islands, referred to as the Commonwealth of the Northern Mariana Islands (CNMI) became part of the United States pursuant to P.L. 94-241 as of November 3, 1986.

Tourism is the leading earning export with total visitor expenditures equaling about 37% of the GIP. Seventy-five percent of the tourists are Japanese.

Agricultural products are coffee, coconuts, fruits, tobacco, and cattle.

Trust Territory of the Pacific Islands

REPUBLIC OF PALAU

Capital: Koror

Total area: 177 sq mi (458 sq km)

Comparative size: slightly more than 2.5 times the size of Washington, D.C.

1990 population: 15,122, growth rate: 0.7%

Gross domestic product (1986): $31.6 million, per capita $2,260

Economy: The economy consists primarily of subsistence agriculture and fishing. Tourism provides some foreign exchange. The Government relies heavily on financial assistance from the United States.

Ethnic divisions: Palauans are a composite of Polynesian, Malayan, and Melanesian races.

Language: Palauan is the official language, though English is commonplace.

Palau is the last member of the Trust Territory of the Pacific Islands and is administered by the United States. The islands are located 528 mi. (850 km) southeast of the Philippines.

The islands vary geologically from the high mountainous main island of Babelthuap to low, coral islands usually fringed by large barrier reefs.

Tabulated Data on State Governments

State	Governor		Legislature[1]						Highest Court[2]		
	Term, years	Annual salary	Membership U[3]	Membership L[4]	Term, yrs. U[3]	Term, yrs. L[4]	Salaries of members[5]		Members	Term, years	Annual salary
Alabama	4[10]	70,222[16]	35	105	4	4	50.00	per diem[21]	9	6	83,880[6]
Alaska	4	92,988	20	40	4	2	24,012	per annum	5	([8])	99,504
Arizona	4	75,000	30	60	2	2	15,000	per annum	5	6	91,728[6]
Arkansas	4	60,000	35	100	4	2	12,500	per annum	7	8	81,772[6]
California	4	114,000[29]	40	80	2	3	52,500	per annum	7	12	121,207[6]
Colorado	4	70,000	35	65	4	2	17,500	per annum	7	10	84,000[6, 25]
Connecticut	4	78,000	36	151	2	2	16,760	per annum	7	8	101,479[6]
Delaware	4[9]	95,000	21	41	4	2	24,900[5]	per annum	5	12	106,700
Florida	4[10]	103,909	40	120	4	2	21,684	per annum	7	6	100,444
Georgia[10]	4	92,088	56	180	2	2	10,641	per annum	7	6	93,774
Hawaii	4	94,780	25	51	4	2	27,000	per year	5	10	93,780[6]
Idaho	4	75,000	35	70	2	2	12,000[35]	per annum[5]	5	6	79,183[6]
Illinois	4	100,681	59	118	4-2	2	38,496	per annum	7	10	100,681
Indiana	4[10]	77,200	50	100	4	2	11,600	per annum	5	([24])	81,000
Iowa	4	76,700	50	100	4	2	18,100	per annum	9	8	90,100[6]
Kansas	4	65,000	40	125	4	2	119	per diem[22]	7	6	58,000
Kentucky	4[7]	81,647	38	100	4	2	100	per diem[36]	7	8	78,273[6]
Louisiana	4	73,440	39	105	4	4	16,800[5]	per annum	7	10	66,566
Maine	4	70,000[16]	35	151	2	2	10,500[37]	per annum[16]	7	7	77,300
Maryland	4[10]	120,000	47	141	4	4	28,000[5]	per annum	7	10	99,000[6]
Massachusetts	4	75,000	40	160	2	2	30,000	per annum	7	([13])	90,450[6]
Michigan	4	112,024[16]	38	110	4	2	47,722[38]	per annum	7	8	111,940
Minnesota	4	109,053	67	134	4[32]	2	27,979[5]	per annum[16]	7	6	94,395[6]
Mississippi	4	75,600	52	122	4	4	10,000	per session[5]	9	8	76,000[6]
Missouri	4[10]	90,312	34	163	4[39]	2	22,862[5]	per annum	7	12	91,594
Montana	4	53,006	50	100	4	2	55.40	per diem[16]	7	8	56,452
Nebraska	4[10]	65,000	49[11]	—	4[10,11]	—	12,000	per annum	7	6	88,157
Nevada	4	90,000	21	42	4	2	7,800[5]	per biennium	5	6	85,000
New Hampshire	2	79,542	24	([12])	2	2	200	per biennium	5	([13])	88,200[6]
New Jersey[27]	4[10]	130,000	40	80	4[14]	2	35,000[30]	per annum	7	7[15]	112,000[6]
New Mexico	4[40]	90,000	42	70	4	2	75	per diem	5	8	75,000[6]
New York	4	130,000	61	150	2	2	57,500	per annum	7	14	120,000[6]

State	Governor: Term, years	Governor: Annual salary	Legislature[1]: Membership U[3]	Membership L[4]	Term, yrs. U[3]	Term, yrs. L[4]	Salaries of members[5]		Highest Court[2]: Members	Term, years	Annual salary
North Carolina	4[41]	91,938[16]	50	120	2	2	13,026	per annum[16]	7	8	89,532[6]
North Dakota	4	68,280[16]	49	98	4	2	90	per diem[16 23]	5	10	71,555[6]
Ohio	4	105,000	33	99	4	2	43,834[34]	per annum	7	6	101,150[6]
Oklahoma	4	70,000	48	101	4	2	32,000[16]	per annum	([19])	6	81,874[6]
Oregon	4[10]	80,000	30	60	4	2	989[42]	per month	7	6	76,400[6]
Pennsylvania	4[10]	105,000	50	203	4	2	47,000	per annum	7	10	105,000
Rhode Island	2	69,900	50	100	2	2	5	per diem[17]	5	([18])	117,373
South Carolina	4	99,960	46	124	4	2	10,400	per annum	5	10	91,163[6]
South Dakota	4[10]	72,475	35	70	2	2	8,000	per biennium	5	3[26]	72,079
Tennessee	4	85,000	33	99	4	2	16,500	per annum	5	8	93,540[6]
Texas	4	93,432	31	150	4	2	7,200[5]	per annum	([20])	9	89,250
Utah	4	77,250	29	75	4	2	85	per diem[16]	5	([33])	89,300[6]
Vermont	2	85,977	30	150	2	2	510	per week[28]	5	6	71,355[6]
Virginia	4[7]	110,000	40	100	4	2	17,640[31]	per annum	7	12	102,700[6]
Washington	4[43]	121,000	49	98	4[44]	2	25,900	per annum	9	6	107,200
West Virginia	4[10]	72,000	34	100	4	2	6,500[16]	per annum	5	12	72,000
Wisconsin	4	92,283	33	99	4	2	35,070	per annum	7	10	91,252
Wyoming	4	70,000	30	60	4	2	60[16]	per diem	5	8	72,000

1. Known as *General Assembly* in Ark., Colo., Conn., Del., Ga., Iowa, Ind., Ky., Md., Mo., N.C., Ohio, Pa., R.I., S.C., Tenn., Vt., Va.; *Legislative Assembly* in N.D., Ore.; *General Court* in Mass., N.H.; *Legislature* in other states. Meets biennially in Calif., Ky., Me., Mont., Nev., N.J., N.C., N.D., Ore., Pa., Texas. Wyoming Legislature has regular general session on odd numbered years and a budget session on even numbered years. Arkansas General Assembly meets every other year for 60 days in odd numbered years. Legislative bodies meet annually in other states. 2. Known as *Court of Appeals* in Md., N.Y.; *Supreme Court of Virginia* in Va.; *Supreme Judicial Court* in Me., Mass.; *Supreme Court* in other states. 3. Upper house: *Senate* in all states. 4. Lower house: *Assembly* in Calif., Nev., N.Y., Wis.; *House of Delegates* in Md., Va., W.Va.; *General Assembly* in N.J.; *House of Representatives* in other states. 5. Base salary. Does not include additional payments for expenses, mileage, special sessions, etc., or additional per diem payments. 6. Chief Justice receives a higher salary. 7. Cannot succeed himself. 8. Appointed for 3 years; thereafter subject to approval or rejection on a nonpartisan ballot for 10-year term. 9. May serve only 2 terms, consecutive or otherwise. 10. May not serve 3rd consecutive term. 11. Unicameral legislature. 12. Constitutional number: 375-400. 13. Until 70 years old. 14. When term begins in Jan. of 2nd year following U.S. census, term shall be 2 years. 15. 2nd term receive tenure, mandatory retirement at 70. 16. Plus expense allowance. 17. For 60 days only. 18. Term of good behavior. 19. Nine members in Supreme Court, highest in civil cases; five in Court of Criminal Appeals. 20. Nine members in Supreme Court, highest in civil cases; nine in Court of Criminal Appeals. 21. Five days a week when the Legislature is in session plus $2,280 per month in expenses. 22. When in session, plus $600/mo. when not in session. 23. Plus $180 per month when not in session. 24. Appointed for 2 years; thereafter elected popularly for 10-year term. 25. Beginning FY 1993. 26. Subsequent terms, 8 years. 27. Governor has refused to accept the raise because of budget crisis. 28. To limit of $13,000 per biennium; $100 per diem for Special Session. 29. Governor remitted $6,000 for his salary to the state for current fiscal year. 30. Each legislator receives $70,000 annually for appointment of personal staff aides. 31. Senate $18,000. 32. Every 10 years (the year after census) term is only for 2 years. 33. Appointed by governor. Up for re-election at first general election that takes place at least 3 years after appointment. After that, face a retention election every 10 years. 34. Senator's salary higher. 35. $3,000 additional for speaker and president pro tem of the senate. 36. When in session, plus $950 a month when not in session. 37. $10,500 per annum first year, $7,500 per annum second year. 38. Expense accounts. 39. Legislators may serve only eight years in each house, 16 combined. 40. May serve two terms in office; after that ineligible to be governor until one term has expired. 41. May only serve two consecutive terms. 42. Plus $73 per day for expenses during session. 43. No person is eligible who would have served during eight of the previous 14 years. 44. Have term limitations. NOTE: Salaries are rounded to nearest dollar. *Source: Information Please* questionnaires to the states.

A Majority of Americans Are Shore Dwellers

According to a recent Census Bureau report, 54 percent of Americans (135 million people) live in the 672 counties adjacent to the Atlantic and Pacific Oceans, the Gulf of Mexico, and the Great Lakes. This coastal population has increased by almost 41 million (43 percent) over the last 30 years, slightly faster than the United States as a whole.

Don Starsinic, who compiled the tabulation on coastal populations, said, "Our earliest settlements were located along the Atlantic coast, and even today nearly a quarter of our population (60 million) live in coastal counties along the Atlantic Ocean. The region's population has increased by about a third since 1960."

However, the most rapid coastal growth during the last 30 years occurred along the Pacific coast and the Gulf of Mexico. Thirty-four million people lived along the Pacific coast in 1991 and 16 million lived along the Gulf coast. This is nearly double the number who lived there in 1960.

The fourth major coastal area rims the five Great Lakes. This industrial region of 26 million people has hardly grown since 1960, while the interior of the United States, with 117 million people in 1991, has increased about 38 percent since 1960.

Over half the population in 18 states and the District of Columbia live in coastal counties. They are: Rhode Island, Connecticut, Delaware, District of Columbia, Hawaii (at 100%); Maine, Massachusetts, New Jersey, Maryland, Florida (90% or more); California, Alaska, Washington, Michigan (85–89%); and New Hampshire, New York, Virginia, Oregon, Louisiana (51–84%). □

Land and Water Area of States, 1990

(in square miles)

State	Rank (total area)	Land[1] area	Water[2] area	Total area
Alabama	30	50,750.23	1,672.71	52,422.94
Alaska	1	570,373.55	86,050.59	656,424.14
Arizona	6	113,642.26	364.00	114,006.26
Arkansas	29	52,075.29	1,107.07	53,182.36
California	3	155,973.09	7,734.06	163,707.15
Colorado	8	103,729.54	370.78	104,100.32
Connecticut	48	4,845.39	698.26	5,543.65
Delaware	49	1,954.62	534.76	2,489.38
Dist. of Columbia	—	61.41	6.95	68.36
Florida	22	53,997.08	11,761.00	65,758.08
Georgia	24	57,918.73	1,522.49	59,441.22
Hawaii	43	6,423.34	4,508.24	10,931.58
Idaho	14	82,750.93	822.84	83,573.77
Illinois	25	55,593.29	2,324.55	57,917.84
Indiana	38	35,870.18	549.91	36,420.09
Iowa	26	55,874.90	400.64	56,275.54
Kansas	15	81,823.02	458.98	82,282.00
Kentucky	37	39,732.31	678.93	40,411.24
Louisiana	31	43,566.03	8,277.44	51,843.47
Maine	39	30,864.55	4,522.78	35,387.33
Maryland	42	9,774.65	2,632.80	12,407.45
Massachusetts	44	7,837.98	2,716.81	10,554.79
Michigan	11	56,809.18	40,001.04	96,810.22
Minnesota	12	79,616.66	7,326.05	86,942.71
Mississippi	32	46,913.64	1,519.95	48,433.59
Missouri	21	68,898.01	810.80	69,708.81
Montana	4	145,556.34	1,489.82	147,046.16
Nebraska	16	76,877.73	480.67	77,358.40
Nevada	7	109,805.89	761.02	110,566.91
New Hampshire	46	8,969.36	381.57	9,350.93
New Jersey	47	7,418.84	1,303.11	8,721.95
New Mexico	5	121,364.54	233.69	123,598.23
New York	27	47,223.85	7,250.71	54,474.56
North Carolina	28	48,718.08	5,103.27	53,821.35
North Dakota	19	68,994.24	1,709.59	70,703.83
Ohio	34	40,952.59	3,874.94	44,827.53
Oklahoma	20	68,678.57	1,224.33	69,902.90
Oregon	9	96,002.58	2,383.17	98,385.75
Pennsylvania	33	44,819.61	1,238.63	46,058.24
Rhode Island	50	1,044.98	500.12	1,545.10
South Carolina	40	30,111.12	1,895.99	32,007.11
South Dakota	17	75,897.74	1,223.72	77,121.46
Tennessee	36	41,219.52	926.49	42,146.01
Texas	2	261,914.26	6,686.70	268,600.96
Utah	13	82,168.15	2,735.97	84,904.12
Vermont	45	9,249.33	365.67	9,615.00
Virginia	35	39,597.79	3,171.09	42,768.88
Washington	18	66,581.95	4,720.70	71,302.65
West Virginia	41	24,086.55	144.89	24,231.44
Wisconsin	23	54,313.71	11,189.50	65,503.21
Wyoming	10	97,104.55	713.56	97,818.11
U.S. Total		**3,536,341.73**	**251,083.35**	**3,787,425.08**

1. Dry land and land temporarily or partially covered by water, such as marshland, swamps, etc.; streams and canals under one-eighth statute mile wide; and lakes, reservoirs, and ponds under 40 acres. 2. Permanent inland water surface, such as lakes, reservoirs, and ponds having an area of 40 acres or more; streams, sloughs, estuaries, and canals one-eighth statute mile or more in width; deeply indented embayments and sounds, and other coastal waters behind or sheltered by headlands or islands separated by less than 1 nautical mile of water, and islands under 40 acres in area. Excludes areas of oceans, bays, sounds, etc. lying within U.S. jurisdiction but not defined as inland water. *Source:* Department of Commerce, Bureau of the Census.

The Great Flood of 1993

State by State Summary as of August 1, 1993

Source: Storm Phillips, STORMFAX, Inc.

Illinois: Deaths: 4. Estimated property damage: $2 billion. Estimated crop loss: $565 million. Number of evacuations: 12,700 people. Number of homes damaged: 6,000. Acreage flooded: 580,000. Number of counties declared disaster areas: 26—state, 12—federal.

Iowa: Deaths: 5. Estimated property and crop loss: $2.7 billion. Number of evacuations: At least 6,000 people. Number of homes damaged: 12,229. Acreage flooded: 2 million. Number of counties declared disaster areas: all 99—federal.

Kansas: Deaths: 1. Estimated property and crop loss: $350 million. Number of evacuations: 1,600. Number of homes damaged: N.A. Acreage flooded: N.A.

Kentucky: Deaths: none. Estimated property and crop loss: $15 million. Number of evacuations: 2 homes. Number of homes damaged: none. Acreage flooded: 40,000. Number of counties declared disaster areas: none.

Minnesota: Deaths: 4. Estimated property damage: $18.4 million. Estimated crop loss: $1.7 billion. Number of evacuations: 1,100. Number of homes damaged: 10,000. Acreage flooded: 2.2 million. Number of counties declared disaster areas: 25—federal.

Missouri: Deaths: 24. Estimated property and crop loss: $2.7 billion. Number of evacuations: 19,000 people. Number of homes damaged: N.A. Acreage flooded: 1.7 million. Number of counties declared disaster areas: 49—federal, including the city of St. Louis.

Nebraska: Deaths: 2. Estimated property damage: $50 million. Estimated crop loss: $288 million. Number of evacuations: 2,700. Number of homes damaged: 662. Acreage flooded: 3 million. Number of counties declared disaster areas: 3—state.

North Dakota: Deaths: 2. Estimated property damage: $100 million. Estimated crop loss: $400 million. Number of evacuations: 1 family. Number of homes damaged: 300 (Fargo), 300 (Bismarck). Acreage flooded: N.A.

South Dakota: Deaths: 3. Estimated property damage: $596 million. Estimated crop loss: $572 million. Number of evacuations: 2,200. Number of homes damaged: 1,000. Acreage flooded: 3.3 million. Number of counties declared disaster areas: 17—state, plus 33 declared agricultural emergency areas.

Wisconsin: Deaths: 2. Estimated property damage: $133 million. Estimated crop loss: $800 million. Number of evacuations: 700 people. Number of homes damaged: 1,600. Acreage flooded: N.A. Number of counties declared disaster areas: 37—state and federal.

Top 50 Cities in the United States

(According to the 1990 Census)

Size 1990	Rank 1980	Rank by percent change	City and state	1990 Population	1980 Population	Change Number	Change Percent
1	1	114	New York, NY	7,322,564	7,071,639	250,925	3.5
2	3	66	Los Angeles, CA	3,485,398	2,968,528	516,870	17.4
3	2	177	Chicago, IL	2,783,726	3,005,072	–221,346	–7.4
4	5	125	Houston, TX	1,630,553	1,595,138	35,415	2.2
5	4	171	Philadelphia, PA	1,585,577	1,688,210	–102,633	–6.1
6	8	49	San Diego, CA	1,110,549	875,538	235,011	26.8
7	6	191	Detroit, MI	1,027,974	1,203,368	–175,394	–14.7
8	7	80	Dallas, TX	1,006,877	904,599	102,278	11.3
9	9	51	Phoenix, AZ	983,403	789,704	193,699	24.5
10	11	61	San Antonio, TX	935,933	785,940	149,993	19.1
11	17	52	San Jose, CA	782,248	629,400	152,848	24.3
12	12	111	Indianapolis, IN (consolidated city)	741,952	711,539	30,413	4.3
13	10	173	Baltimore, MD	736,014	786,741	–50,727	–6.4
14	13	99	San Francisco, CA	723,959	678,974	44,985	6.6
15	19	65	Jacksonville, FL (consolidated city)	672,971	571,003	101,968	17.9
16	20	74	Columbus, OH	632,910	565,021	67,889	12.0
17	16	146	Milwaukee, WI	628,088	636,297	–8,209	–1.3
18	14	167	Memphis, TN	610,337	646,174	–35,837	–5.5
19	15	164	Washington, DC	606,900	638,432	–31,532	–4.9
20	21	127	Boston, MA	574,283	562,994	11,289	2.0
21	23	110	Seattle, WA	516,259	493,846	22,413	4.5
22	28	57	El Paso, TX	515,342	425,259	90,083	21.2
23	25	96	Nashville-Davidson, TN (consolidated city)	510,784	477,811	32,973	6.9
24	18	188	Cleveland, OH	505,616	573,822	–68,206	–11.9
25	22	186	New Orleans, LA	496,938	557,927	–60,989	–10.9
26	24	165	Denver, CO	467,610	492,686	–25,076	–5.1
27	42	32	Austin, TX	465,622	345,890	119,732	34.6
28	33	69	Fort Worth, TX	447,619	385,164	62,455	16.2
29	31	85	Oklahoma City, OK	444,719	404,014	40,705	10.1
30	35	63	Portland, OR	437,319	368,148	69,171	18.8
31	27	153	Kansas City, MO	435,146	448,028	–12,882	–2.9
32	37	62	Long Beach, CA	429,433	361,498	67,935	18.8
33	45	55	Tucson, AZ	405,390	330,537	74,853	22.6
34	26	189	St. Louis, MO	396,685	452,801	–56,116	–12.4
35	47	50	Charlotte, NC	395,934	315,474	80,460	25.5
36	29	176	Atlanta, GA	394,017	425,022	–31,005	–7.3
37	56	17	Virginia, Beach, VA	393,069	262,199	130,870	49.9
38	44	71	Albuquerque, NM	384,736	332,920	51,816	15.6
39	43	87	Oakland, CA	372,242	339,337	32,905	9.7
40	30	190	Pittsburgh, PA	369,879	423,959	–54,080	–12.8
41	52	34	Sacramento, CA	369,365	275,741	93,624	34.0
42	34	145	Minneapolis, MN	368,383	370,951	–2,568	–0.7
43	38	128	Tulsa, OK	367,302	360,919	6,383	1.8
44	36	137	Honolulu CDP, HI	365,272	365,048	224	0.1
45	32	166	Cincinnati, OH	364,040	385,409	–21,369	–5.5
46	41	117	Miami, FL	358,548	346,681	11,867	3.4
47	65	9	Fresno, CA	354,202	217,491	136,711	62.9
48	48	95	Omaha, NE	335,795	313,939	21,856	7.0
49	40	172	Toledo, OH	332,943	354,635	–21,692	–6.1
50	39	179	Buffalo, NY	328,123	357,870	–29,747	–8.3

Source: U.S. Bureau of the Census.

195 Cities Have Populations Over 100,000

The 1990 census showed that 195 American cities had populations of 100,000 or more. Mesa, Arizona, was the greatest percentage gainer in the Nation, growing by 89% from 152,404 in 1980 to 288,091 in 1990. Others in the top ten in growth were Rancho Cucamonga, California (84%); Plano, Texas (78%); Irvine, California (78%); Escondido, California (69%); Oceanside, California (67%); Bakersfield, California (66%); Arlington, Texas (64%); Fresno, California (63%); and Chula Vista, California (61%).

Two of the California cities over 100,000—Santa Clarita in Los Angeles County and Moreno Valley in Riverside County—were not incorporated cities in 1980.

Five cities fell from the ranks of 100,000-plus cities since 1980: Columbia, South Carolina; Davenport, Iowa; Pueblo, Colorado; Roanoke, Virginia; and Youngstown, Ohio.

50 Largest Cities of the United States

(According to the 1990 Census)

Data supplied by Bureau of the Census and by the cities in response to *Information Please* questionnaires. Ranking of 50 largest cities (April 1990 census data). Civilian labor force and unemployment figures (Annual averages, 1992); per capita personal income (1989); average daily temperature: *(County and City Data Book)*. NOTE: Persons of Hispanic origin may be of any race.

ALBUQUERQUE, N.M.

Mayor: Louis E. Saavedra (to Dec. 1993)
1990 census population, sex & (rank): 384,736 (38); **% change,** 15.6; **Male,** 186,584; **Female,** 198,152; **White,** 301,010; **Black,** 11,484 (3.0%); **American Indian, Eskimo, or Aleut,** 11,708 (3.0%); **Asian or Pacific Islander,** 6,660 (1.7%); **Other race,** 53.874; **Hispanic origin,** 132,706 (34.5%). **1990 percent population under 18:** 25.0%; **65 and over:** 11.1%; **median age:** 32.5.
Land area: 137 sq mi. (356.2 sq km); **Alt.:** 4,958 ft.
Avg. daily temp: Jan., 34.8° F; July, 78.8° F
Churches: 211; **City-owned parks:** 169; **Radio stations:** 43 (AM, 19; FM, 24); **Television stations:** 11
CIVILIAN LABOR FORCE: 224,003; **Unemployed:** 10,305, **Percent:** 4.6; **Per capita personal income:** $15,806
Chamber of Commerce: Greater Albuquerque Chamber of Commerce, 401 2nd St., N.W., Albuquerque, N.M. 87102. Albuquerque Hispano Chamber of Commerce, 1520 Central Ave., S.E., Albuquerque, N.M. 87106

Albuquerque is the largest city in New Mexico and the seat of Bernalillo county. It is situated in west central New Mexico on the upper Rio Grande River. Early Spanish settlers arrived there in the mid-1600s. The old town was founded in 1706 by Don Francisco Cuervo y Valdés, the Governor of New Mexico, and named after the Duke of Alburquerque, the viceroy of New Spain. During the Civil War, Confederate forces briefly occupied the city in 1862. The new town section was founded in 1880. In 1883, Albuquerque became the county seat and was incorporated as a city in 1891.

The city is noted as a center for health and medical services in the region, and government agencies, nuclear research, banking, and tourism are important to the economy. There is a growing high-tech center in Albuquerque and Intel Corp.'s largest manufacturing facility is located there.

Famous natives: Erna Fergusson, author; Annabeth Gish, actress; Fred Haney, baseball player, executive; Slim Summerville, actor; Al and Bobby Unser, auto racers

ATLANTA, GA.

Mayor: Maynard Jackson (to Jan. 1994)
1990 census population, sex, & (rank): 394,017 (36); **% change,** –7.3; **Male,** 187,877; **Female,** 206,140; **White,** 122,327; **Black,** 264,262 (67.1%); **American Indian, Eskimo, or Aleut,** 563 (0.1%); **Asian or Pacific Islander,** 3,498 (0.9%); **Other race,** 3,367; **Hispanic origin,** 7,525 (1.9%). **1990 percent population under 18:** 24.1; **65 and over:** 11.3; **median age:** 31.5.
City land area: 136 sq mi. (352.2 sq km); **Alt.:** Highest, 1,050 ft; lowest, 940
Avg. daily temp.: Jan., 41.9° F; July, 78.6° F
Churches (18-county area): 1,500; **City-owned parks:** 277 (3,178 ac.); **Radio stations (18-county area):** AM, 7; FM, 20; **Television stations (18-county area):** 7 commercial; 2 PBS
CIVILIAN LABOR FORCE: 182,703; **Unemployed:** 18,197, **Percent:** 10.0; **Per capita personal income:** $19,055
Chamber of Commerce: Atlanta Chamber of Commerce, 235 International Blvd., Atlanta, Ga. 30301; Information is gathered on the 20-county MSA

Atlanta, the largest city and capital of Georgia, is the seat of Fulton county. It is situated in the northwest part of the state at the base of the Blue Ridge Mountains near the Chattahoochee River. The first European settler was Hardy Ivy who built a cabin there in 1833.

The town was founded as Terminus in 1837 as the end of the Georgia railroad line (Western and Atlantic Railroad) and became incorporated as Marthasville in 1843 in honor of ex-governor Lumpkin's daughter Martha. It was renamed Atlanta in 1845 and incorporated as a city in 1847. Its name was suggested by the railroad's chief engineer, J. Edgar Thomson, and was derived from its location at the end of the Georgia and Atlantic railroad line. The city later became the capital of Georgia in 1868.

During the Civil War, the city was burned and almost completely destroyed by General W.T. Sherman in November 1864. It was quickly rebuilt after the war and it grew rapidly due to the expansion of the railroads in the southwest. Atlanta's diverse economy is led by the service industries, retail trade, manufacturing, and finance and insurance. The convention business is also important, and the 1996 Summer Olympic Games will be held there.

Famous natives: Hank Aaron, baseball player; Arrested Development, recording artists; Jimmy Carter, former President; Ray Charles, singer; James Dickey, poet; Mattivilda Dobbs, soprano; Walt Frazier, basketball player; Oliver Hardy, comedian; Evander Holyfield, boxer; Allan Jackson, singer; Bobby Jones, golfer; DeForest Kelley, actor; Martin Luther King, Jr., civil rights leader, Nobel Peace Prize winner; Gladys Knight, singer; Kriss Kross, recording artists; Margaret Mitchell, novelist; Bert Parks, entertainer; Eric Roberts, actor; Julia Roberts, actress; Ferroll Sams, author; Doug Stone, singer; Pamela Stone, comedienne; Gwen Torrence, Olympic athlete; Lee Tracy, actor; Travis Tritt, singer; Ted Turner, TBS, CNN founder; Jane Withers, actress; Joanne Woodward, actress; Andrew Young, civil rights activist

AUSTIN, TEX.

Mayor: Bruce Todd (to May 1994)
1990 census population, sex, & (rank): 465,622 (27); **% change,** 34.6; **Male,** 232,473; **Female,** 233,149; **White,** 328,542; **Black,** 57,868 (12.4%); **American Indian, Eskimo, or Aleut:,** 1,756 (0.4%); **Asian or Pacific Islander,** 14,141 (3.0%); **Other race,** 63,315; **Hispanic origin,** 106,868 (23.0%). **1990 percent population under 18:** 23.1%; **65 and over:** 7.4%; **median age:** 28.9
Land area: 116 sq mi. (300 sq km); **Alt.:** From 425 ft. to over 1000 ft. elevation

Avg. daily temp.: Jan., 49.1° F; July, 84.7° F
Churches: 353 churches, representing 45 denominations; **City-owned parks and playgrounds**: 169 (11,800 ac.); **Radio stations**: AM, 6; FM, 12; **Television stations**: 3 commercial; 1 PBS; 1 independent
CIVILIAN LABOR FORCE: 285,190; **Unemployed**: 16,115, **Percent**: 5.7; **Per capita personal income**: $16,113
Chamber of Commerce: Greater Austin Chamber of Commerce, P.O. Box 1967, Austin, Tex. 78767

Austin, the capital and seat of Travis county, is the fifth largest city in Texas. It is situated in the south central part of the state on the Colorado River. The site was called Waterloo in 1838 and in 1839 was incorporated as a city and chosen to become the capital of the independent Republic of Texas. Waterloo was renamed Austin in honor of Stephen F. Austin, the founder of the Texas Republic. It became the permanent capital of the state of Texas in 1870.

Austin's growth was spurred by several developments after the Civil War—the railroads reached the city in the 1870s; it was crossed by the important Chisholm cattle trail, and it became the seat of the state university in 1883.

Austin, the state capital, has a growing commercial and diversified manufacturing sectors. Civilian government employment is 28% of the labor force and is important to the economy. As home to the University of Texas, Austin is a major research and development, and nationally-recognized high technology center. The city has a new convention center downtown.

Famous natives: Don Baylor, baseball player, manager; Earl Campbell, football player; Liz Carpenter, author; Dabney Coleman, actor; Ben Crenshaw, golfer; Michael Dell, founder Dell Computer Corp.; Tobe Hooper, film director; Lady Bird Johnson, former First Lady; Tom Kite, golfer; James Michener, author; Willie Nelson, musician; Amado Pena, artist; Darrell Royal, legendary UT football coach; Zachary Scott, actor; Jerry Jeff Walker, musician; Dalhart Windberg, artist

BALTIMORE, MD.

Mayor: Kurt L. Schmoke (to Dec. 1994)
1990 census population, sex, & (rank): 736,014 (13); **% change**, –6.4; **Male**, 343,513; **Female**: 392,501; **White**: 287,753; **Black**: 435,768 (59.2%); **American Indian, Eskimo, or Aleut**: 2,555 (0.3%); **Asian or Pacific Islander**: 7,942 (1.1%); **Other race**: 1,996; **Hispanic origin**: 7,602 (1.0%). **1990 percent population under 18**: 24.4; **65 and over**: 13.7; **Median age**: 32.6.
Land area: 80.3 sq mi. (208 sq km); **Alt.**: Highest, 490 ft; lowest, sea level
Avg. daily temp.: Jan., 35.5° F; July, 79.9° F
Churches: Roman Catholic, 72; Jewish, 50; Protestant and others, 344; **City-owned parks**: 347 park areas and tracts (6,314 ac.); **Radio stations**: AM, 10; FM, 11; **Television stations**: 7 (including Home Shopping Network)
CIVILIAN LABOR FORCE: 333,043; **Unemployed**: 35,531, **Percent**: 10.7; **Per capita personal income**: $20,267
Chamber of Commerce: Greater Baltimore Committee, 111 S. Calvert St., Ste. 1500, Baltimore, Md. 21202

Baltimore is the largest city in Maryland and is situated in the northern part of the state on the Patapsco River estuary, an arm of Chesapeake Bay. The city is independent and is in no county.

The site was settled in the early 17th century and founded as a town in 1729. The town was named after Lord Baltimore, the founder of Maryland, and was incorporated as a city in 1797. It has an excellent harbor and has been a principal port since the 18th century. Baltimore was a pioneer ship-building center and the Baltimore clipper was one of the best sailing ships of its day and was used extensively in world trade. It ranks today as the nation's second port in foreign tonnage.

Baltimore's economy is focused on manufacturing, in steel, heavy and light industries, ship construction, and scientific research and development.

Famous natives: Larry Adler, musician; John Astin, actor; Eubie Blake, pianist; Francis X. Bushman, actor; Charlie Chase, actor; Hans Conried, actor; Mildred Dunnock, actress; "Mama" Cass Elliot, singer; Barry Farber, broadcaster; Paul Ford, actor; Philip Glass, composer; Billy Holiday, singer; Barry Levinson, director; H.L. Mencken, writer; Babe Ruth, baseball player; Upton Sinclair, novelist; Leon Uris, novelist; Frank Zappa, musician

BOSTON, MASS.

Acting Mayor: Thomas Menino
1990 census population, sex, & (rank): 574,283 (20); **% change**, 2.0; **Male**, 275,972; **Female**, 298,311; **White**, 360,875; **Black**, 146,945 (25.6%); **American Indian, Eskimo, or Aleut**, 1,884 (0.3%); **Asian or Pacific Islander**, 30,388 (5.3%); **Other race**, 34,191; **Hispanic origin**, 61,955 (10.8%). **1990 percent population under 18**: 19.1; **65 and over**: 11.5; **median age**: 30.3.
Land area: 47.2 sq mi. (122 sq km); **Alt.**: Highest, 330 ft; lowest, sea level
Avg. daily temp.: Jan., 29.6° F; July, 73.5° F
Churches: Protestant, 187; Roman Catholic, 72; Jewish, 28; others, 100; **City-owned parks, playgrounds, etc.**: 2,276.36 ac.; **Radio stations**: AM, 9; FM, 12; **Television stations**: 10
CIVILIAN LABOR FORCE: 294,320; **Unemployed**: 23,032, **Percent**: 7.8; **Per capita personal income**: $23,746[1]
Chamber of Commerce: Boston Chamber of Commerce, 600 Atlantic Ave., Boston, Mass. 02210
1. Boston-Lawrence-Salem-Lowell-Brockton NECMA.

Boston is the capital and seat of Suffolk county and the largest city in Massachusetts. It is located in the eastern part of the state at the head of Boston Bay. It was incorporated as a city in 1822. No city in the U.S. is richer in historical associations than Boston, and no city has retained more of its original buildings as memorials to America's past.

Puritans from England settled at Boston in 1630, only ten years after the Pilgrims had landed at Plymouth in 1620. They named their new town Boston, after the former home of many of the Pilgrims in Lincolnshire, England. Fourteen years later, the pioneer Bostonians set aside the first public park in the U.S.—the Boston Common. The following year, 1635, they opened the first free public school in America. Today, Boston is home to 65 colleges and universities.

Boston is a major industrial, financial, and educational hub and has one of the finest ports in the world. The Port of Boston ships more than $8 billion worth of goods each year.

Although the city's banking and financial services, insurance, and real estate sectors have declined in recent years other industries continue to grow, especially in the health care field. Boston has 25 medical research institutions, more than any other U.S. city, and its health care industry is growing at a rate of about 3% a year. The city's unique cultural and historic heritage makes it a center of tourism and its hotel industry ranks first in the nation in occupancy. Boston's other businesses are in high-technology, biotechnology, software, and electronics.

Famous natives: Samuel Adams, patriot; John Singleton Copley, painter; Ralph Waldo Emerson, philosopher and poet; Arthur Fiedler, conductor; Benjamin Franklin; Edward Everett Hale, clergyman, author; Oliver Wendell Holmes, jurist; Winslow Homer, painter; Joseph P. and Rose Fitzgerald Kennedy; Jack Lemmon, actor; Robert Lowell, poet; Edgar Allan Poe, writer; Paul Revere, patriot, silversmith; John L. Sullivan, boxer; Barbara Walters, TV journalist

BUFFALO, N.Y.

Mayor: James Griffin (to Dec. 1993)
1990 census population, sex, & (rank): 328,123 (50); **% change,** –8.3; **Male,** 153,050; **Female,** 175,073; **White,** 212,449; **Black,** 100,579 (30.7%); **American Indian, Eskimo, or Aleut:** 2,547 (0.8%); **Asian or Pacific Islander,** 3,261 (1.0%); **Other race,** 9,287; **Hispanic origin,** 16,129 (4.9%). **1990 percent population under 18:** 24.2%; **65 and over:** 14.8%; **median age:** 32.0.
Land area: 42.67 sq. mi. (109 sq. km); **Alt.:** Highest 705 ft; lowest 571.84 ft
Avg. daily temp (1991).: Jan., 26.0° F; July, 71.9° F
Churches: 60 denominations, with over 1,100 churches; **County-owned parks:** 9 public parks (3,000 ac.); **Radio stations:** AM 14; FM 17; **Television stations:** 8 (plus reception from 3 Canadian stations)
CIVILIAN LABOR FORCE: 143,120; **Unemployed:** 17,232, **Percent:** 12.0; **Per capita personal income:** $18,305[1]
Chamber of Commerce: Greater Buffalo Partnership, 300 Main Place Tower, Buffalo, New York 14202.
1. PMSA.

Buffalo is the second largest city in New York state and the seat of Erie county, situated in the western part of the state at the eastern end of Lake Erie and at the head of the Niagara River. It was named after Buffalo Creek which runs into Lake Erie. The origin of the city's name is in dispute and may have been a mispronunciation of "beau fleuve," French for "beautiful river."

The first ship to sail the Great Lakes—the *Griffon*—was built near the present site of Buffalo by La Salle in 1679. The town was laid out in 1803 at the site of the present-day city by Joseph Ellicot for the Holland Land Company and was known as New Amsterdam (but popularly called Buffalo). Buffalo was still a relatively small town in 1813 when the British captured it and set its homes and buildings afire. Two years later, the town was rebuilt, and it began to thrive with the coming of the Erie Canal. Buffalo was incorporated as a village in 1816 and became the seat of Erie county in 1821. The city was incorporated in 1832.

Buffalo is a major Great Lakes port of entry, especially for grain distribution, and is an important milling (chiefly wheat) center. The city has one of the most diversified economies in the U.S. Major manufacturing products include automotive components, chemicals, fabricated metals, food processing, industrial machinery, medical instruments, and printing. In addition, Buffalo's economy is centered on trade, tourism, and finance.

Famous natives: Harold Arlen, composer; Michael Bennett, choreographer; Amanda Blake, actress; Don Criqui, television sportscaster; Diane English, television writer, producer; Tom Fontana, television writer; Harry Emerson Fosdick, clergyman; Wilson Greatbatch, pacemaker inventor; Orel Hershiser, baseball player; Christian Laettner, basketball player; Bob Lanier, basketball player; Nancy Marchand, actress; Cliff Robinson, basketball player; Susan Rothenberg, painter; Mark Russell, satirist; Warren Spahn, baseball player; Elizabeth Swados, composer, playwright

CHARLOTTE, N.C.

Mayor: Richard Vinroot (to Nov. 1993)
1990 census population, sex, & (rank): 395,934 (35); **% change,** 25.5; **Male,** 188,088; **Female,** 207,846; **White,** 259,760; **Black,** 125,827 (31.8%); **American Indian, Eskimo, or Aleut:** 1,425 (0.4%); **Asian or Pacific Islander:** 7,211 (1.8%); **Other race,** 1,711; **Hispanic origin,** 5,571 (1.4%). **1990 percent population under 18:** 24.2%; **65 and over:** 9.8%; **median age:** 32.1.
Land area: 192 sq mi. (499.2 sq km); **Alt.:** 765 ft
Avg. daily temp.: Jan., 40.5° F; July, 78.5° F
Churches: Protestant, over 400; Roman Catholic, 8; Jewish, 3; Greek Orthodox, 1; **City-owned parks and parkways:** 120; **Radio stations:** AM, 7; FM, 13; **Television stations:** 4 commercial; 2 PBS
CIVILIAN LABOR FORCE: 231,210; **Unemployed:** 12,606, **Percent:** 5.5; **Per capita personal income:** $17,377[1]
Chamber of Commerce: Charlotte Chamber, P.O. Box 32785, Charlotte, N.C., 28232
1. Charlotte-Gastonia Rock Hill, N.C.–S.C. MSA.

Charlotte, North Carolina's largest city and seat of Mecklenburg county, is located in the southern part of the state near the South Carolina border. It was named for King George III of England's wife, Charlotte Sophia of Mecklenburg-Strelitz.

Settled about 1750, Charlotte was incorporated as a city in 1768 and made the county seat in 1774. Charlotte was a leading Confederate city during the Civil War and was the last meeting place of the full Confederate cabinet.

From 1800 to 1848, Charlotte was the center of U.S. gold production and a branch of the U.S. mint operated from there from 1837 to 1913.

The city has a highly diversified economy and is a foremost center for distribution, retailing, technology, and manufacturing. It is the third largest banking center in the U.S. It is the seat of the University of North Carolina at Charlotte.

Famous natives: Romare Bearden, artist; Richard G. Darman, government official; Billy Graham, evangelist; Charles Gwathmey, architect; Hamilton Jordan, government official; Donald Schollander, swimmer; Randolph Scott, actor

CHICAGO, ILL.

Mayor: Richard M. Daley (to April 1995)
1990 census population, sex, & (rank): 2,783,726 (3); **% change,** –7.4; **Male,** 1,334,705; **Female,** 1,449,021; **White,** 1,263,524; **Black,** 1,087,711 (39.1%); **American Indian, Eskimo, or Aleut,** 7,064 (0.3%); **Asian or Pacific Islander,** 104,118 (3.7%); **Other race,** 321,309; **Hispanic origin,** 545,852 (19.6%). **1990 percent population under 18:** 26.0%; **65 and over:** 11.9%; **median age:** 31.3.
Land area: 228.469 sq mi. (592 sq km); **Alt.:** Highest, 672 ft; lowest, 578.5
Avg. daily temp.: Jan., 21.4° F; July, 73.0° F
Churches: Protestant, 850; Roman Catholic, 252; Jewish, 51; **City-owned parks:** 550; **Radio stations:** AM, 15; FM, 24; **Television stations:** 14
CIVILIAN LABOR FORCE: 1,356,716; **Unemployed:** 124,195, **Percent:** 9.2; **Per capita personal income:** $20,349[1]
Chamber of Commerce: Chicagoland Chamber of Commerce, 200 N. LaSalle, Chicago, Ill. 60601
1. PMSA.

Chicago is the largest city in Illinois and the seat of Cook county. Built directly on a lake front, it stretches for 22 miles along the southwestern shore of Lake Michigan.

The first white men known to have visited Chicago were Joliet and Father Marquette in 1673. The first permanent white settler in the area was John Kinzie, sometimes called the father of Chicago, who took over a trading post in 1796 that had been established 1791 by Jean Baptiste Point Sable, a French-speaking black fur trapper. Fort Dearborn, a blockhouse and stockade, was built in 1804, but was evacuated in 1812, with more than half of its garrison massacred at what is now the foot of 18th Street. Not until 1830 was the town laid out. The name Chicago is thought to come from the Algonquian Indian word Chicagou meaning "strong" or "powerful." Some early Frenchmen believed that the name was derived from the Algonquian word for "onion place" because wild onions grew there.

Forty-one years later it was destroyed in the great Chicago fire of 1871. Chicago was incorporated as a village in 1833 and as a city in 1837.

Chicago is a major Great Lakes port and the commercial, financial, industrial, and cultural center of the Midwest. The manufacturing industries dominate the wholesale and retail trade, and trade in agricultural commodities is important to the economy. The Chicago Mercantile Exchange is the largest in the world.

Famous natives: Jack Benny, comedian; Edgar Rice Burroughs, author; Raymond Chandler, author; Michael Crichton, author; Walt Disney, filmmaker; John Dos Passos, author; Bobby Fischer, chess player; Bob Fosse, choreographer, director; Benny Goodman, clarinetist; Dorothy Hamill, figure skater; Quincy Jones, composer; Gene Krupa, drummer; Dorothy Malone, actress; David Mamet, playwright; Bob Newhart, comedian; Kim Novak, actress; Donald O'Connor, actor; William L. Shirer, journalist, historian; Preston Sturges, film director; Gloria Swanson, actress; Melvin Van Peebles, playwright; Alfred Wallenstein, conductor; Robin Williams, comedian, actor; Robert Young, actor

CINCINNATI, OHIO

Mayor: Dwight Tillery (to Nov. 1993)
City Manager: Frank Dawson
1990 census population, sex, & (rank): 364,040 (45); **% change,** –5.5; **Male,** 169,305; **Female,** 194,735; **White,** 220,285; **Black,** 138,1312 (37.9%); **American Indian, Eskimo, or Aleut,** 660 (0.2%); **Asian or Pacific Islander,** 4,030 (1.1%); **Other race,** 933; **Hispanic origin,** 2,386 (0.7%). **1990 percent population under 18:** 25.1%; **65 and over:** 13.9%; **median age:** 30.9.
Land area: 78.1 sq mi. (202 sq km); **Alt.:** Highest, 960 ft; lowest, 441
Avg. daily temp.: Jan., 30.3° F; July, 76.1° F
Churches: 850; **City-owned parks:** 96 (4,345 ac.); **Radio stations:** AM, 10; FM, 15 (Greater Cincinnati); **Television stations:** 8
CIVILIAN LABOR FORCE: 188,161; **Unemployed:** 14,318, **Percent:** 7.6; **Per capita personal income:** $17,624[1]
Chamber of Commerce: Cincinnati Chamber of Commerce, 441 Vine St. Suite 300, Cincinnati, Ohio 45202
1. PMSA.

Cincinnati is the third largest city in Ohio and the seat of Hamilton county. It is located on the Ohio River.

Cincinnati began as part of the Miami Purchase of 1788. The first settlement, Columbia, was begun by Benjamin Stites that same year. The town of Losantiville was founded in 1788 on a plateau above the Ohio River by Mathias Denman, Robert Patterson, and Israel Ludlow. Its strategic location in the Western Territory led to the building of Ft. Washington, the most ambitious military establishment in the territory,. The community of Losantiville that grew up around the fort was renamed Cincinnati in 1790 by Gen. Arthur St. Clair, Commander of Ft. Washington and first governor of the Northwest Territory, after the Revolutionary officers' Society of the Cincinnati, founded by George Washington. It was incorporated as a village in 1802 and chartered as a city in 1819.

The city began to flourish as a commercial hub with the arrival of the first steamboat in 1811, the completion of the Miami and Erie Canal in 1827, and the coming of the first railroad in 1843.

Cincinnati is a port of entry and more than 46 million tons pass through the Port of Cincinnati each year. The city has a diverse economy and is a major center for manufacturing, wholesaling, and retailing, as well as insurance and finance companies and health services. Prominent manufacturing groups include transportation equipment, which includes aircraft engines and auto parts, food and kindred products, metal working, general industrial machinery, chemicals, fabricated metal products, printing, and publishing.

Famous natives: Eddie Arcaro, jockey; Theda Bara, actress; Doris Day, actress; Jim Dine, painter; Suzanne Farrell, ballerina; Robert Henri, painter; James Levine, music director; Adolph Ochs, publisher; Tyrone Power, actor; William Procter, scientist; Roy Rogers, actor; Pete Rose, baseball player; Steven Spielberg, filmmaker; Roger Staubach, football player; Robert A. Taft, legislator; William Howard Taft, president

CLEVELAND, OHIO

Mayor: Michael R. White (to Dec. 1993)
1990 census population, sex, & (rank): 505,616 (24); **% change,** –11.9; **Male,** 237,211; **Female,** 268,405; **White,** 250,234; **Black,** 235,405 (46.6%); **American Indian, Eskimo, or Aleut,** 1,562 (0.3%); **Asian or Pacific Islander,** 5,115 (1.0%); **Other race,** 13,300; **Hispanic origin,** 23,197 (4.6%). **1990 percent population under 18:** 26.9; **65 and over:** 14.0; **median age:** 31.9.
Land area: 79 sq mi. (205 sq km); **Alt.:** Highest, 1048 ft.; lowest, 573
Avg. daily temp.: Jan., 25.5° F; July, 71.6° F
Churches: [1] Protestant, 980; Roman Catholic, 187; Jewish, 31; Eastern Orthodox, 22; **City-owned parks:** 41 (1,930 ac.); **Radio stations:** AM, 15; FM, 17; **Television stations:** 7
CIVILIAN LABOR FORCE: 219,836; **Unemployed:** 27,583, **Percent:** 12.5; **Per capita personal income:** $19,395[1]
Chamber of Commerce: Greater Cleveland Growth Association, 200 Tower City Center, Cleveland, Ohio 44113
1. PMSA.

Cleveland is the second largest city in Ohio and the seat of Cuyahoga county. It is located in the northeastern part of the state on Lake Erie. In the Colonial era, the Cleveland area was known as the Connecticut Western Reserve, part of a land grant made to Connecticut by King Charles II in 1662. The city was founded in 1796 by Gen. Moses Cleaveland, who was the head surveyor of the Connecticut Land Company. This company had bought three million acres in what is now northern Ohio. A permanent settlement was founded in 1799, named after the General, and the spelling was shortened to Cleveland. The city was incorporated in 1836.

Cleveland's industrial growth was stimulated by the opening of the Ohio and Erie Canals in 1832 and, later, the advent of the Civil War with the corresponding demand for machinery, railroad equipment, ships, and other items.

The Port of Cleveland is the largest overseas general cargo port on Lake Erie. Greater Cleveland has long been famous as a diversified durable goods manufacturing area. Following the national trend, Cleveland has been shifting to a more services-based economy. Greater Cleveland is a world corporate center for leading national and multinational companies, including transportation, insurance, retailing, utilities, and commercial banking and finance.

Famous natives: Jim Backus, actor; Dorothy Dandridge, actress; Ruby Dee, actress; Phil Donahue, talk show host; Joel Grey, actor; Arsenio Hall, talk show host; Margaret Hamilton, actress; Philip Johnson, architect; Henry Mancini, composer; Burgess Meredith, actor; Paul Newman, actor; Carl Stokes, judge; Andy Warhol, artist

COLUMBUS, OHIO

Mayor: Gregory S. Lashutka (to Jan. 1996)
1990 census population, sex, & (rank): 632,910 (16); **% change,** 12.0; **Male,** 305,574; **Female,** 327,336; **White,** 471,025; **Black,** 142,748 (22.6%); **American Indian, Eskimo, or Aleut,** 1,469 (0.2%); **Asian or Pacific Islander,** 14,993 (2.4%); **Other race,** 2,675; **Hispanic origin,** 6,741 (1.1%). **1990 percent population under 18:** 23.7; **65 and over:** 9.2; **median age:** 29.4.
Land area: 197.81 sq mi. (514.31 sq km); **Alt.:** Highest, 902 ft; lowest, 702
Avg. daily temp.: Jan., 27.1° F; July, 73.8° F
Churches: Protestant, 436; Roman Catholic, 62; Jewish, 5; Other, 8; **City-owned parks:** 200 (12,293 ac.); **Radio stations:** AM, 10; FM, 16; **Television stations:** 8 commercial, 3 PBS
CIVILIAN LABOR FORCE: 359,574; **Unemployed:** 20,725, **Percent:** 5.8; **Per capita personal income:** $17,178
Chamber of Commerce: Columbus Area Chamber of Commerce, P.O. Box 1527, Columbus, Ohio 43216

Columbus, the largest city in Ohio, is the state capital and seat of Franklin county and is located in central Ohio on the Scioto River.

The first structures near downtown Columbus were earthen mounds constructed by Indian tribes known as the Mound Builders. The Indians lived alone in Central Ohio until the 1700s when the first explorers entered the Midwest. The first permanent settlement was founded by a surveyor from Kentucky, Lucas Sullivant, in 1797 and was named Franklinton. The site was laid out as the state capital in 1812 and named to honor Christopher Columbus and became the capital in 1816. Columbus was chartered as a city in 1834 and annexed Franklinton in 1870. The city's growth was stimulated by the development of transportation facilities—a feeder to the Ohio Canal completed in 1832, the National Road in 1833, and the arrival of the railroad in 1850.

Columbus is a port of entry and a major industrial, commercial, manufacturing, and cultural center. It is the seat of Ohio University. The city has enjoyed steady growth over the years due largely in part to its economic diversity—there is no single activity that dominates the economy.

Famous natives: Warner Baxter, actor; George Bellows, painter; Michael Feinstein, singer, pianist; Eileen Heckart, actress; Jack Nicklaus, golfer; Tom Poston, actor; Eddie Rickenbacker, aviator; Arthur M. Schlesinger, historian; James Thurber, writer

DALLAS, TEX.

Mayor: Steve Bartlett
City Manager: Jan Hart (apptd. April 1990)
1990 census population, sex, & (rank): 1,006,877 (8); **% change,** 11.3; **Male,** 495,141; **Female,** 511,736; **White,** 556,760; **Black,** 296,994 (29.5%); **American Indian, Eskimo, or Aleut,** 4,792 (0.5%); **Asian or Pacific Islander,** 21,952 (2.2%); **Other race,** 126,379; **Hispanic origin,** 210,240 (20.9%). **1990 percent population under 18:** 25.0; **65 and over:** 9.7; **median age:** 30.6.
Land area: 378 sq mi. (979 sq km); **Alt.:** Highest, 750 ft; lowest, 375
Avg. daily temp.: Jan., 45.0° F; July, 86.3° F
Churches: 1,974 (in Dallas Co.); **City-owned parks:** 296 (47,025 ac.); **Radio stations:** AM, 19; FM, 30; **Television stations:** 10 commercial, 1 PBS
CIVILIAN LABOR FORCE: 570,661; **Unemployed:** 50,526, **Percent:** 8.9; **Per capita personal income:** $19,485[1]
Chamber of Commerce: Dallas Chamber of Commerce, 1201 Elm, Dallas, Tex. 75270
1. PMSA.

Dallas is the second largest city in Texas and is the seat of Dallas county. It is situated 185 miles northeast of Austin on the Trinity River near the junction of its three forks. It was first settled by Tennessee lawyer John Neely Bryan as a trading post on the Trinity River in 1841. Many historians believe that John Neely Bryan named the city after George Mifflin Dallas, Vice President under James K. Polk but there is no official agreement on this. It was incorporated as a town in 1856 and a city in 1871. The city developed as a cotton market in the 1870s and became the chief cotton producing region of Texas.

The economy is highly diversified and the city is the leading commercial, marketing, and industrial center of the southwest. The insurance business is important, and the service sector has experienced rapid growth. Dallas is also a popular tourist and convention city.

Famous natives: Tex Avery, animator, director; Robby Benson, actor; Ernie Banks, baseball player; Bebe Daniels, acteress; Linda Darnell, actress; Lee Elder, golfer; Morgan Fairchild, actress; Trini Lopez, singer; Aaron Spelling, producer; Stephen Stills, singer; Sharon Tate, actress; Lee Trevino, golfer

DENVER, COLO.

Mayor: Wellington Webb (to July 1995)
1990 census population, sex, & (rank): 467,610 (26); **% change,** –5.1; **Male,** 227,517; **Female,** 240,093; **White,** 337,198; **Black,** 60,046 (12.8%); **American Indian, Eskimo, or Aleut,** 5,381 (1.2%); **Asian or Pacific Islander,** 11,005 (2.4%); **Other race,** 53,980; **Hispanic origin,** 107,382 (23.0%); **1990 percent population under 18:** 22.0; **65 and over:** 13.9; **median age:** 33.9
Land area: 154.63 sq mi. (400.5 sq km); **Alt.:** Highest, 5,494 ft; lowest, 5,140
Avg. daily temp.: Jan., 29.5° F; July, 73.3° F
Churches:[1] Protestant, 859; Roman Catholic, 60; Jewish, 13; **City-owned parks:** 205 (4,166 ac.); **City-owned mountain parks:** 40 (13,600 ac.); **Radio stations:** AM, 23; FM, 20[1]; **Television stations:** 17[1]
CIVILIAN LABOR FORCE: 245,495[2]; **Unemployed:** 17,527[2]; **Percent:** 7.1[2]; **Per capita personal income:** $19,231[3]
Chamber of Commerce: Greater Denver Chamber of Commerce, 1445 Market Street, Denver, Colo. 80202
1. Metropolitan area. 2. Denver City/County. 3. PMSA.

Denver is the largest city and capital of Colorado and the seat of Denver county. It lies at the foot of the Rocky Mountains and is situated at the junction of the South Platte River and Cherry Creek. The city was born in 1858 when gold was discovered in the sands of Cherry Creek and it began as a tough village of cabins, shacks, and tents. It was incorporated as a city in 1861. In 1867, Denver became the territorial capital. The city is named for James W. Denver, governor of the Kansas Territory which included part of Colorado. The city prospered from the famous gold and silver mines of the 1870s and the 1880s.

Denver is an important cultural, industrial, transportation, tourist, and major marketing center. It is also a regional center for many federal government agencies and a leader in the development of western energy resources.

Denver's fastest growing industries include contract construction, real estate, retail trade, and federal government.

Famous natives: Tim Allen, comedian, actor; Ward Bond, actor; Douglas Fairbanks, Sr., actor; John Hart, newsman; Pat Hingle, actor; Ted Mack, TV host; Barbara Rush, actress; Alan K. Simpson, senator; Paul Whiteman, bandleader; Don Wilson, announcer

DETROIT, MICH.

Mayor: Coleman A. Young (to Jan. 1994)
1990 census population, sex, & (rank): 1,027,974 (7); % **change,** –14.6; **Male,** 476,814; **Female,** 551,160; **White,** 222,316; **Black,** 777,916 (75.7%); **American Indian, Eskimo, or Aleut,** 3,655 (0.4%); **Asian or Pacific Islander,** 8,461 (0.8%); **Other race,** 15,626; **Hispanic origin,** 28,473 (2.8%). **1990 percent population under 18:** 29.4; **65 and over:** 12.2; **median age:** 30.8.
Land area: 143 sq mi. (370 sq km); **Alt.:** Highest, 685 ft; lowest, 574
Avg. daily temp.: Jan., 23.4° F; July, 71.9° F
Churches:[1] Protestant, 1,165; Roman Catholic, 89; Jewish, 2; **City-owned parks:** 56 parks (3,843 ac.); 393 sites (5,838 ac.); **Radio stations:** AM, 27; FM, 30 (includes 3 in Windsor, Ont.); **Television stations:** 8[2] (includes 1 in Windsor, Ont.)
CIVILIAN LABOR FORCE: 393,083; **Unemployed:** 64,712, **Percent:** 16.5; **Per capita personal income:** $19,660
Chamber of Commerce: Greater Detroit Chamber of Commerce, 622 W. Lafayette, Detroit, Mich. 48226

1. Six-county metropolitan area. 2. Within four counties of Metro Detroit.

Detroit, the largest city in Michigan, is situated in the southeastern part of the state on the Detroit River. It is the seat of Wayne county. Detroit was incorporated as a city in 1815 and reincorporated in 1824.

Detroit is the oldest city of any size west of the seaboard colonies, having been founded by Antoine de la Mothe Cadillac on July 24, 1701, more than a century before Chicago was founded. The French were the first settlers and they gave the city its name from their word meaning "straight." They referred to the 27-mile-long Detroit River which connects Lake Erie and Lake St. Clair. The river forms part of the international boundary, and marks the only point where Canada lies directly south of U.S. territory.

Because of its strategic location, Detroit was fought over by the French, the British, and the Indians. It was the headquarters for the British forces in the Northwest during the American Revolutionary War.

The first steam vessel, the *Walk-in-the-Water*, made its appearance on the Great Lakes in 1818, and Detroit was the western terminus for most of its voyages from Buffalo. Its link to all the important cities on the Great Lakes made it a major exporting port. Detroit was incorporated as a city in 1824.

Detroit is one of the largest manufacturing cities in the U.S. and is the center of the automobile manufacturing industry, which has experienced a decline to foreign competition in the past decade. The health and medical care sector is important to the economy, and employment in the finance, insurance, and real estate industries has inched up in the Detroit metropolitan area since 1991.

Famous natives: Ralph Bunche, statesman; Francis Ford Coppola, director; Charles Lindbergh, aviator; Madonna, singer; John Mitchell; U.S. Attorney General; George Peppard, actor; Gilda Radner, comedian; Della Reese, singer; Sugar Ray Robinson, boxer; Diana Ross, singer; Tom Selleck, actor; Margaret Whiting, singer

EL PASO, TEX.

Mayor: Bill Tilney
1990 census population, sex, & (rank): 515,342 (22); % **change,** 21.2; **Male,** 247,163; **Female,** 268,179; **White,** 396,122; **Black,** 17,708 (3.4%); **American Indian, Eskimo, or Aleut,** 2,239 (0.4%); **Asian or Pacific Islander,** 5,956 (1.2%); **Other race,** 93,317; **Hispanic origin,** 355,669 (69.0%). **1990 percent population under 18:** 31.9; **65 and over:** 8.7; **median age:** 28.7
Land area: 247.4 sq mi. (641 sq km); **Alt.:** 4,000 ft
Avg. daily temp.: Jan., 44.2° F; July, 82.5° F
Churches: Protestant, 320; Roman Catholic, 39; Jewish, 3; others, 20; **City-owned parks:** 116[1] (1,180 ac.); **Radio Stations:** AM, 18; FM, 17; **Television stations:** 6
CIVILIAN LABOR FORCE: 234,891; **Unemployed:** 24,273, **Percent:** 10.3; **Per capita personal income:** $10,735
Chamber of Commerce: El Paso Chamber of Commerce, 10 Civic Center Plaza, El Paso, Tex. 79944

1. Includes 109 developed and 7 undeveloped parks.

El Paso, the fourth largest city in Texas and the seat of El Paso county, is located in the far western part of the state on the north bank of the Rio Grande River opposite the Mexican city of Ciudad Juárez on the south bank.

In 1581, Spanish explorers came through the Pass of the North to test the missionary and mining possibilities of New Mexico. The area had been inhabited for centuries by various Indian groups. On April 30, 1598, Juan de Onate took formal possession of the area for King Philip II of Spain and subsequently crossed the Rio Grande river near a site west of the present downtown El Paso which he called "El Paso del Rio del Norte," meaning the crossing of the river—the first use of the name "El Paso." In 1659, the mission of Nuestra Senora de Guadalupe was founded on a site that is present day downdown Ciudad Juárez; the mission is still in use today. In 1682, Spanish colonists from Mexico founded the settlement of Ysleta within the site of the present-day city. However, it wasn't until 1827 that the first permanent settlement at El Paso was established by Juan María Ponce de León. The city's real growth started with the arrival of the Southern Pacific Railroad in 1881. El Paso was incorporated as a city in 1873.

In 1888, Mexico changed the name of Paso del Norte to Ciudad Juárez in honor of Benito Juárez. Later in 1967, the United States agreed to cede a long disputed part of El Paso to Mexico due to changes in the course of the Rio Grande which forms the international boundary between the two countries. El Paso and its sister city of Ciudad Juárez across the U.S./Mexico border are inexorably joined by culture and economy. El Paso and Juárez make up the largest international metroplex in the world.

El Paso is an important port of entry to the U.S. from Mexico. The apparel industry plays a major role in the El Paso area. The high technology, medical device manufacturing, plastics, refining, automotive, food processing, and defense-related industries are important to the economy. El Paso's service sector has experienced the healthiest growth since 1983. El Paso is also a major tourist resort.

Famous natives: Manuel Acosta, artist; Don Bluth, animation director; Vicki Carr, singer; Sam Donaldson, newsman; Judith Ivey, actress; Guy Kibbee, actor; Sandra Day O'Connor, Supreme Court justice; Debbie Reynolds, actress; Irene Ryan, actress

FORT WORTH, TEX.

Mayor: Kay Granger (to May 1993)
City Manager: Bob Terrell
1990 census population, sex, & (rank): 447,619 (28); **% change,** 16.2; **Male,** 220,268; **Female:** 227,351; **White,** 285,549; **Black,** 98,532 (22.0%); **American Indian, Eskimo, or Aleut,** 1,914 (0.4%); **Asian or Pacific Islander,** 8,910 (2.0%); **Other race,** 52,714; **Hispanic origin,** 87,345 (19.5%). **1990 percent population under 18:** 26.6; **65 and over:** 11.2; **median age:** 30.3.
Land area: 295.301 sq mi. (765 sq km); **Alt.:** Highest, 780 ft; lowest, 520
Avg. daily temp.: Jan., 44.2° F; July, 82.5° F
Churches: 941, representing 72 denominations; **City-owned parks:** 171 (8,189 ac.; 3,500 ac. in Nature Center); **Radio stations:** AM, 5; FM, 20; **Television stations:** 15 (9 local)
CIVILIAN LABOR FORCE: 235,212; **Unemployed:** 21,653, **Percent:** 9.2; **Per capita personal income:** $17,259[1]
Chamber of Commerce: Fort Worth Chamber of Commerce, 777 Taylor Street, Suit 900, Fort Worth, Tex. 76102

1. Fort Worth–Arlington MSA.

Fort Worth, seat of Tarrant county, is situated in the north central part of Texas on the Trinity River.

The city was founded by Major Ripley Arnold in 1849 as a military outpost on the Trinity River to protect settlers moving westward from frequent Indian attacks. It was named after Gen. William J. Worth, the commander of the Texas army. Fort Worth was incorporated in 1873. Its growth was stimulated in the 1870s by the proximity to the Chisholm cattle trail. It prospered as a meat packing and shipping center when the Texas and Pacific Railway arrived in 1876, and later experienced a new boom when oil was discovered nearby in 1917. The establishment of military installations in the area during both world wars also spurred the economy.

Ft. Worth has traditionally been a diverse center of manufacturing and is not dependent on the oil or financial sectors. The city's industries range from clothing and food products to jet fighters, helicopters, computers, pharmaceuticals, and plastics. Ft. Worth is a national leader in aviation products, electronic equipment, and refrigeration equipment. It is home to a multitude of major corporate headquarters, office, and distribution centers.

Famous natives: Robert Bass, financier; Kate Capshaw, actress; Sandra Heynie, golfer; Patricia Highsmith, writer; Spanky McFarland, actor; R. Bruce Merrifield, Nobelist in chemistry; Roger Miller, singer; Fess Parker, actor; Rex Reed, critic; Johnny Rutherford, auto racer; Liz Smith, columnist

FRESNO, CALIF.

Mayor: Jim Patterson (to May 1997)
City Manager: Michael A. Bierman
1990 census population, sex, & (rank): 354,202 (47); **% change,** 62.9; **Male,** 172,241; **Female,** 181,961; **White,** 209,604; **Black,** 29,409 (8.3%); **American Indian, Eskimo, or Aleut,** 3,729 (1.1%); **Asian or Pacific Islander,** 44,358 (12.5%); **Other race,** 67,102; **Hispanic origin,** 105,787 (29.9%). **1990 percent population under 18:** 31.7; **65 and over:** 10.1; **median age:** 28.4.
Land area: 99.38 sq mi. (257.39 sq km); **Alt.:** 328 ft
Avg. daily temp.: Jan., 45.5° F; July, 81.0° F
Churches: 450 (approximate); **City-owned parks:** 38 (690 ac.); **Radio stations:** AM 11[1]; FM 13[1]; Bilingual 1; **Television stations:** 8[1]
CIVILIAN LABOR FORCE: 174,496; **Unemployed:** 22,708, **Percent:** 13.0; **Per capita personal income:** $15,927
Chamber of Commerce: Fresno County and City Chamber of Commerce, P.O. Box 1469, 2331 Fresno St., Fresno, CA 93716

1. Metropolitan area.

Fresno is located in central California, 184 miles southeast of San Francisco and 222 miles northwest of Los Angeles. It is the seat of Fresno county. Fresno was incorporated as a city in 1885.

Fresno began as a station for the Central Pacific Railroad in 1872 and was made the seat of Fresno county in 1874. The city's name is Spanish for the ash trees that the early explorers found in the area.

Fresno is the world capital of the agri-business with 250 different crops produced by 7,500 farmers on 1.9 million irrigated acres, worth $3 billion a year. Fresno county's top five leading crops are grapes, cotton, tomatoes, cattle and calves, and turkeys. The city is also a trade, financial, media, and commercial center. Its diverse industries include agricultural chemicals, farm equipment, canned fruit and vegetables, clothing, computer software, electric wire, pumps, glass, and plastic products.

Famous natives: Mike Connors, actor; Maynard Dixon, painter; Bruce Furniss, swimmer; Jon Hall, actor; Daryle Lamonica, football player; Sam Peckinpah, director; William Saroyan, novelist; Tom Seaver, baseball player

HONOLULU, HAWAII

Mayor: Frank F. Fasi (to Jan. 1997)
1990 census population, sex, & (rank): 365,272 (44)[1]; **% change,** 0.1; **Male,** 180,357; **Female,** 184,915; **White,** 97,527; **Black,** 4,821 (1.3%); **American Indian, Eskimo, or Aleut,** 1,126 (0.3%); **Asian or Pacific Islander,** 257,552 (70.5%); **Other race,** 4,246; **Hispanic origin,** 16,704 (4.6%). **1990 percent population under 18:** 19.1; **65 and over:** 16.0; **median age:** 36.9.
Land area: 600 sq mi. (1,554 sq km)[2]; **Alt.:** Highest, 4,025 ft; lowest, sea level
Avg. daily temp.: Jan., 72.6° F; July, 80.1° F
Churches: Roman Catholic, 34; Buddhist, 35; Jewish, 2; Protestant and others, 329; **City-owned parks:** 5,835 ac.; **Radio stations:** AM, 18; FM, 15; **Television stations:** 10
CIVILIAN LABOR FORCE: 408,196[2]; **Unemployed:** 14,168[2], **Percent:** 3.5[2]; **Per capita personal income:** $19,171
Chamber of Commerce: Chamber of Commerce of Hawaii, 735 Bishop St., Honolulu, Hawaii 96813

1. City only. 2. City and county. The census bureau does not include the entire city and county in its census of Honolulu. If it did, the 1990 census and rank would be 836,231 (12).

Honolulu is the capital (on Oahu) and largest city in Hawaii. It is the seat of Honolulu county. The city and government of Honolulu include the entire island of Oahu, the major island of the state of Hawaii. It is situated in the central Pacific Ocean 2,397 miles west-southwest of San Francisco. Honolulu's name means "sheltered harbor" and derives from the native words hono meaning "a bay" and lulu meaning "sheltered."

Honolulu's early history was one of turbulence and conflict. One of the last areas on the globe to be discovered and exploited (visited by British Captain James Cook 1778), Hawaii was subject to strong pressures from every world power, from American missionaries who arrived in 1820, and from the opportunism of whalers. These whalers built Honolulu originally, bringing trade, commerce, and prosperity that led to expansion into the sugar and pineapple industries.

As early as 1814, Russia tried to move in and Russian soldiers built a bastion at the harbor's edge. The British flag was raised there in 1843 and French forces occupied Honolulu in 1849. Each time control was given back to the independent kingdom without bloodshed. In 1898, a group of Americans completed a project attempted at intervals during the previous 65 years—annexation to the United States. Honolulu was incorporated as a city in 1907.

Honolulu was bombed by Japan in a surprise attack on the unprepared U.S. naval base at Pearl Harbor on Dec. 7, 1941. This action forced the United States to enter World War II and "Remember Pearl Harbor," became a famous American wartime slogan.

Hawaiian statehood in 1959 and the arrival of fast jet air travel to the island brought boom times to Honolulu. Tourism is the city's principal industry, followed by defense establishments and agricultural exports (chiefly sugar and pineapples).

Famous natives: Hiram Bingham, explorer, senator; Jean Erdman, dancer, choreographer; Kam Fong, actor; Daniel Inouye, senator; Bette Midler, actress; Kelly Preston, actress; Louise Morgan Sill, author; Don Stroud, actor; Merlin D. Tuttle, biologist, wildlife photographer

HOUSTON, TEX.

Mayor: Robert C. Lanier (to Dec. 1993)
1990 census population, sex, & (rank): 1,630,553 (4); **% change,** 2.2; **Male,** 809,048; **Female,** 821,505; **White,** 859,069; **Black,** 457,990 (28.1%); **American Indian, Eskimo, or Aleut,** 4,126 (0.3%); **Asian or Pacific Islander,** 67,113 (4.1%); **Other race,** 242,255; **Hispanic origin,** 450,483 (27.6%). **1990 percent population under 18:** 26.7; **65 and over:** 8.3; **median age:** 30.4.
Land area: 581.44 sq mi. (1,506 sq km); **Alt.:** Highest, 120 ft; lowest, sea level
Avg. daily temp.: Jan., 51.4° F; July, 83.1° F
Churches: 1,750[2]; **City-owned parks:** 334 (32,500 ac.); **Radio stations:** AM, 25; FM, 29[1]; **Television stations:** 10 commercial, 1 PBS
Poet Laureate: HUY-LUC Khoi Tien Bui
CIVILIAN LABOR FORCE: 883,777; **Unemployed:** 77,160, **Percent:** 8.7; **Per capita personal income:** $17,598[3]
Chamber of Commerce: Greater Houston Partnership, 1100 Milam Building, 25th Fl., Houston, Tex. 77002

1. Includes annexations since 1970. 2. Harris County. 3. PSMA

Houston, the largest city in Texas and seat of Harris county, is located in the southeastern part of the state near the Gulf of Mexico.

Sam Houston was the commander in chief of the Texas troops who fought a successful war of rebellion against the domination by Mexico, which had been in possession of Texas. On April 21, 1836, Houston's men won a decisive victory in which the Mexican dictator, Gen. Santa Anna, was taken prisoner, and signed the treaty which launched the Republic of Texas. In September, a constitution was ratified, and Houston was elected President. The Texas Republic was recognized by the U.S. and by the major European powers. The present city of Houston was incorporated in 1837 and named after Sam Houston, who was president of the erstwhile republic. This was its first capital.

The port of Houston leads the U.S. in foreign tonnage handled. The city is a major business, financial, science, and technology center. Houston is outstanding in oil and natural gas production and is the energy capital of the world. It is the home of one of the largest medical facilities in the world—The Texas Medical Center—and the focus of the aerospace industry. The Lyndon B. Johnson Space Center is the nation's headquarters for manned spaceflight.

Famous natives: Debbie Allen, choreographer; Lance Alworth, football player; Denton Cooley, heart surgeon; Jim Demaret, golfer; Allen Drury, noveslit; Shelly Duvall, actress; A.J. Foyt, auto racer; Howard Hughes, industrialist; Barbara C. Jordan, educator, lawyer, politician; Barbara Mandrell, singer; Annette O'Toole, actress; Dennis and Randy Quaid, actors; Kenny Rogers, singer; Patrick Swayze, actor, dancer;

INDIANAPOLIS, IND.

Mayor: Stephen Goldsmith (to Dec. 31, 1995)
1990 census population, sex, & (rank)[2]: 741,952 (12); **% change,** 4.3; **Male,** 352,309; **Female,** 389,643; **White,** 564,447; **Black,** 166,031 (22.4%); **American Indian, Eskimo, or Aleut,** 1,580 (0.2%); **Asian or Pacific Islander,** 6,943 (0.9%); **Other race,** 2,951; **Hispanic origin,** 7,790 (1.0%). **1990 percent population under 18:** 25.6%; **65 and over:** 11.5; **median age:** 31.8.
Land area: 352 sq mi. (912 sq km); **Alt.:** Highest, 840 ft; lowest, 700
Avg. daily temp.: Jan., 26.0 F; July, 75.1° F
Churches: 1,200[1]; **City-owned parks:** 130 (9,375 ac.); **Radio stations:** AM, 8[3]; FM, 17[3]; **Television stations:** 7[1]
CIVILIAN LABOR FORCE: 399,477 **Unemployed:** 23,771, **Percent:** 6.0; **Per capita personal income:** $19,522
Chamber of Commerce: Indianapolis Chamber of Commerce, 320 N Meridian St., Indianapolis, Ind. 46204

1. Marion County. 2. Consolidated city. 3. Metropolitan area.

Indianapolis, the largest city in Indiana and seat of Marion county, is located in the central part of the state on the West Fork of the White River. Its name derives from combining "Indiana" with "polis," the Greek word for city.

Indianapolis was settled in 1820 and, in 1825, its site was chosen as the state capital and it was incorporated as a city in 1832 and reincorporated in 1838. The city's growth began when the railroad reached it in 1847. Toward the end of the 19th century, the discovery of nearby natural gas and the start of the automobile industry hastened its industrial expansion. On Jan. 1, 1970, Indianapolis merged with the surrounding Marion county.

Indianapolis is an important center of a rich agricultural region and a major grain and livestock market. It is also a focal point of commerce, transportation, and manufacturing for the region. Some leading industries are electronics, pharmaceuticals, and food processing. The financial sector, and service and insurance industries are growing rapidly.

Indianapolis is the site of the world-famous 500-mile automobile race and the Indiana State Fair.

Famous natives: Monte Blue, actor; David Letterman, TV host; Steve McQueen, actor; Jane Pauley, TV newscaster; Booth Tarkington, author; Kurt Vonnegut, Jr., author; Harry Von Zell, announcer; Clifton Webb, actor

JACKSONVILLE, FLA.

Mayor: Ed Austin (to June 30, 1995)
1990 census population, sex, & (rank)[1]: 672,971 (15); **% change,** 17.9; **Male,** 328,737; **Female,** 344,234; **White,** 489,604; **Black,** 163,902 (24.4%); **American Indian, Eskimo, or Aleut,** 1,904 (0.3%); **Asian or Pacific Islander,** 12,940 (1.9%); **Other race,** 4,621; **Hispanic origin,** 17,333 (2.6%). **1990 percent population under 18:** 25.9; **65 and over:** 10.7; **median age:** 31.5.
Land area: 759.6 sq mi. (1,967 sq km); **Alt.:** Highest, 71 ft; lowest, sea level
Avg. daily temp.: Jan., 53.2° F; July, 81.3° F
Churches: Protestant, 794; Roman Catholic, 21; Jewish, 5; others, 22; **City-owned parks and playgrounds:** 138 (1,522 ac.); **Radio stations:** AM, 14; FM, 16; **Television stations:** 6 commercial, 1 PBS, 1 religious
CIVILIAN LABOR FORCE: 328,211; **Unemployed:** 24,051, **Percent:** 7.3; **Per capita personal income:** $16,215
Chamber of Commerce: Jacksonville Area Chamber of Commerce, Jacksonville, Fla. 32202

1. Consolidated city.

Jacksonville, Florida's largest city, is located in Duval county in the northeast corner of Florida on the banks of the St. Johns River and adjacent to the Atlantic Ocean. It is the largest metropolitan area in northeast Florida and southeast Georgia.

Starting in the 16th century, French, Spanish, and English explorers and colonists were attracted to the region by the St. Johns River. The site was settled by Lewis Hogan in 1816. Jacksonville was laid out in 1822 and was named after Gen. Andrew Jackson, the first military governor of Florida. It was incorporated as a city in 1832.

During the Civil War, much of the city was destroyed by Union forces who occupied Jacksonville four times. The city was rebuilt and, following the development of its harbor and the railroads, fast became the transportation hub and leading industrial city in Florida by the 1880s. In 1968, Jacksonville annexed Duval county.

Jacksonville is the transportation hub and distribution focal point in the state. The strength of the city's economy lies in its broad diversification. The area's economic structure is composed of a balance between distribution, financial services, biomedical, consumer goods, information services, manufacturing, and other industries. Jacksonville has the largest deepwater port in the South Atlantic and is the leading port in the U.S. for automobile imports.

Famous natives: Pat Boone, singer; Judy Canova, comedian; Merion C. Cooper, producer, director; Bob Hayes, athlete; Wanda Hendrix, actress; James Weldon Johnson, author, educator; John Rosamond Johnson, musician, composer; Leeroy Yarbrough, auto racer

KANSAS CITY, MO.

Mayor: Emanuel Cleaver II (to April 1995)
City Manager: David H. Olson (apptd. Nov. 1984)
1990 census population, sex, & (rank): 435,146 (31); **% change:** –2.9; **Male,** 206,965; **Female,** 228,181; **White,** 290,572; **Black,** 128,768 (29.6%); **American Indian, Eskimo, or Aleut,** 2,144 (0.5%); **Asian or Pacific Islander,** 5,239 (1.2%); **Other race,** 8,423; **Hispanic origin,** 17,017 (3.9%). **1990 percent population under 18:** 24.8; **65 and over:** 12.9; **median age:** 32.8.
Land area: 317 sq mi. (821 sq km); **Alt.:** Highest, 1,014 ft; lowest, 722
Avg. daily temp.: Jan., 28.4° F; July, 80.9 F
Churches: 1,100 churches of all denominations[1]; **City-owned parks and playgrounds:** 187 (10,386 ac.); **Radio stations:** AM, 14; FM, 19[1]; **Television stations:** 7[1]
CIVILIAN LABOR FORCE: 236,800; **Unemployed:** 15,315, **Percent:** 6.5; **Per capita personal income:** $17,899[2]
Chamber of Commerce: Chamber of Commerce of Greater Kansas City, 920 Main St., Kansas City, Mo. 64105

1. Metropolitan area. 2. Kansas City, Mo.–Kan. MSA.

Kansas City is the largest city in Missouri. It is located in the western part of the state, at the junction of the Missouri and Kansas Rivers. Kansas City is located in Jackson, Clay, Platte, and Cass counties.

In 1821, the year Missouri entered the Union, French trader François Chouteau came from St. Louis to establish a trading post on the site of the present city to take advantage of the growing fur trade with the Kansa, Osage, Wyandotte, and other tribes. In 1833, a settlement was laid out by John Calvin McCoy and developed, called the town of Westport Landing. The community became the Town of Kansas and was incorporated as a city in 1850 and renamed Kansas City in 1889. The city's name reflects its Native American heritage—its site was within the territory of the Kansa or Kaw Indians.

The city grew rapidly in the mid-1880s as the starting point for gold prospectors and settlers heading westward. The coming of the Missouri-Pacific railroad in 1865 and the spanning of the Missouri River by the Hannibal Bridge in 1869 also contributed to the city's growth, and it prospered as a center for the nation's cattle business.

The Kansas City metropolitan area once known primarily for agriculture and manufacturing, has expanded its economic base to include strong growth in areas of telecommunications, banking and finance, and the service industry. A transportation hub since the 1800s, the area enjoys a national and regional prominence as a distribution and manufacturing center. Kansas City ranks nationally as first in greeting card publishing, frozen food storage and distribution, and first in hard winter wheat marketing, second in wheat flour production, and third in auto and truck assembly. The area is one of ten federal regional centers and employs over 25,000 in local, state, and federal government. The city is also a regional center for health care, employing over 55,000 in this industry.

Famous natives: Robert Altman, director; Edward Asner, actor; Burt Bacharach, composer; Noah and Wallace Beery, actors; Robert Russell Bennett, composer; Jeanne Eagels, actress; Jean Harlow, actress; Ted Shawn, dancer, choreographer; Casey Stengel, baseball; Virgil Thompson, composer; Tom Watson, golfer

LONG BEACH, CALIF.

Mayor: Ernie Kell (to third Tuesday of 1994)
City Manager: James C. Hankla
1990 census population, sex, & (rank): 429,433 (32); **% change,** 18.8; **Male,** 216,685; **Female,** 212,748; **White,** 250,716; **Black,** 58,761 (13.7%); **American Indian, Eskimo, or Aleut,** 2,781 (0.6%); **Asian or Pacific Islander,** 58,266 (13.6%); **Other race,** 58,909; **Hispanic origin,** 101,419 (23.6%). **1990 percent population under 18:** 25.5; **65 and over:** 10.8; **median age:** 30.0.
Land area: 49.8 sq mi. (129 sq km); **Alt.:** Highest, 170 ft; lowest, sea level
Avg. daily temp.: Jan., 55.2 F; July, 72.8° F
Churches: 236; **City-owned parks:** 48 (2,000 ac.); **Radio stations:** AM, 2; FM, 2; **Television stations:** 8 (metro area)

CIVILIAN LABOR FORCE: 211,137; **Unemployed:** 18,929, **Percent:** 9.0; **Per capita personal income:** $19,906[1]
Chamber of Commerce: Long Beach Area Chamber of Commerce, One World Trade Center, Suite 350, Long Beach, CA 90831-0350
1. Los Angeles-Long Beach MSA.

Long Beach is the fifth largest city in California and is situated on San Pedro Bay, south of Los Angeles, in Los Angeles county.

The town was laid out and settled in 1881 by developer W.E. Willmore who sold lots in the site as a seaside resort community called Willmore City. It was renamed Long Beach for its 8 1/2-mi. beach in 1884. The city was incorporated in 1888 and reincorporated in 1897.

Long Beach is a major industrial port. The services and manufacturing industries together account for over 50% of the local economy. Retail trade and government are the next largest sectors, accounting for an additional 30% of employment. Tourism is also important to the economy. Minor industries include transportation, communication and utilities, wholesale trade, finance, insurance, and real estate. Long Beach's economy has been adversely affected by cutbacks in the defense and aircraft production industries.

Famous natives: Jack Anderson, journalist; Jennifer Bartlett, artist; Barbara Britton, actress; Nicholas Cage, actor; Spike Jones, orchestra leader; Sally Kellerman, actress; Billie Jean King, tennis player; Martha Rae Watson, track; Heather Watts, dancer

LOS ANGELES, CALIF.

Mayor: Richard Riordan (to June 1997)
1990 census population, sex, & (rank): 3,485,398 (2); **% change,** 17.4; **Male,** 1,750,055; **Female,** 1,735,343; **White,** 1,841,182; **Black,** 487,674 (14.0%); **American Indian, Eskimo, or Aleut,** 16,379 (0.5%); **Asian or Pacific Islander,** 341,807 (9.8%); **Other race,** 798,356; **Hispanic origin,** 1,391,411 (39.9%). **1990 percent population under 18:** 24.8; **65 and over:** 10.0; **median age:** 30.7.
Land area: 467.4 sq mi. (1,210.57 sq km); **Alt.:** Highest, 5,081 ft; lowest, sea level
Avg. daily temp.: Jan., 57.2° F; July, 74.1° F
Churches: 2,000 of all denominations; **City-owned parks:** 355 (15,357 ac.); **Radio stations:** AM, 35; FM, 53; **Television stations:** 19
CIVILIAN LABOR FORCE: 1,827,505; **Unemployed:** 198,626, **Percent:** 10.9; **Per capita personal income:** $19,906[1]
Chamber of Commerce: Los Angeles Chamber of Commerce, 404 S Bixel St., Los Angeles, Calif. 90017
1. Los Angeles-Long Beach MSA.

Los Angeles is the largest city in California and the second largest urban area in the nation. It is located in the southern part of the state on the Pacific Ocean. It is the seat of Los Angeles county. Geographically, it extends more than 40 miles from the mountains to the sea.

The Spanish explorer, Gaspar de Portolá visited the site in 1769. On Sept. 4, 1781, the Mexican Provincial Governor, Filipe de Neve, founded "El Pueblo de Nuestra Señora la Reina de Los Angeles"—meaning "The Village of Our Lady, the Queen of the Angels." The pueblo became the capital of the Mexican province, Alta California, and it was the last place to surrender to the U.S. at the time of the American occupation in 1847. By the Treaty of Guadalupe Hidalgo in 1848, Mexico ceded California to the United States and Los Angeles was incorporated as a city in 1850.

The city's phenomenal growth was brought about primarily by its equable climate which attracted people and industry from all parts of the nation; the development of its citrus-fruit industry; the discovery of oil in the area during the early 1890s; the development of its man-made harbor—its port is one of the busiest in the U.S.; and the growth of the motion picture industry in the early 20th century. Today, Hollywood is a suburb of Los Angeles.

Los Angeles is a major hub of shipping, manufacturing, industry, and finance, and is world renowned in the entertainment and communications fields. It is a favorite vacation destination and attracts millions of tourists to the area each year from all over the world.

Los Angeles county is the nation's largest manufacturing center, surpassing Chicago, New York, and Detroit. The Ports of Los Angeles and Long Beach are second only to New York as the largest customs district in the United States.

Major employer in the Los Angeles Five-County area is the business and management sector. Growth in the key wholesale industries—apparel and textiles, furniture, jewelry, and toys, and the boom in industrial trade have been forecast for the region in the nineties. Other important sectors are health services and international trade and investment. The aerospace and technology industries have declined due to defense cutbacks but are still expected to be a viable part of the region's economy.

Famous natives: Busby Berkeley, choreographer, director; Marge Champion, dancer, choreographer; Jackie Coogan, actor; Jackie Cooper, actor; Linda Fratianne, figure skater; Jodie Foster, actress, director; John Gavin, actor, diplomat; Pancho Gonzalez, tennis player; Cynthia Gregory, ballerina; Jerome Hines, basso; Dustin Hoffman, actor; Theodore Harold Maiman, laser inventor; Marilyn Monroe, actress; Isamu Noguchi, sculptor; Leonard Slotkin, conductor; Duke Snider, baseball player; Adlai E. Stevenson, statesman; Madeleine Stowe, actress; Darryl Strawberry, baseball player;

MEMPHIS, TENN.

Mayor: W.W. Herenton (to Oct. 1994)
1990 census population, sex, & (rank): 610,337 (18); **% change,** –5.5; **Male,** 285,010; **Female,** 325,327; **White,** 268,600; **Black,** 334,737 (54.8%); **American Indian, Eskimo, or Aleut,** 960 (0.2%); **Asian or Pacific Islander,** 4,805 (0.8%); **Other race,** 1,235; **Hispanic origin,** 4,455 (0.7%). **1990 percent population under 18:** 26.9; **65 and over:** 12.2; **median age:** 31.5.
Land area: 281 sq mi. (728 sq km); **Alt.:** Highest, 331 ft
Avg. daily temp.: Jan., 39.6° G; July, 82.1° F
Churches: 800; **Parks and playgrounds:** 172 (5,363 ac.); **Radio stations:** AM, 12; FM, 8; **Television stations:** 6
CIVILIAN LABOR FORCE: 283,850; **Unemployed:** 19,098, **Percent:** 6.7; **Per capita personal income:** $16,484[1]
Chamber of Commerce: Memphis Area Chamber of Commerce, P.O. Box 224, Memphis, Tenn. 38103
1. Memphis, Tenn.–Ark.–Miss. MSA.

Memphis, the largest city in Tennessee and the seat of Shelby county, is located in the southwestern corner of the state, on the Mississippi River.

The first settlers of Memphis were the Chickasaw Indians, who had a village named Chisca there on the bluffs overlooking the Mississippi River. Hernando de Soto, in 1541, is said to have had his first glimpse of the Mississippi from the site of Memphis; and in the next century, Joliet and Marquette stopped there to trade with the Indians. The French explorer Sieur de La Salle tried to claim the region for France in 1682 and built Fort Prudhomme there. The area was ceded to the United States by the Chickasaw Indians in 1818. Memphis was officially established in 1819 by three enterprising businessmen from Nashville, James Winchester, John Overton, and future-President Andrew Jackson. Jackson named it after the ancient Egyptian city because of its Nilelike site on the Mississippi River. Memphis was incorporated as a city in 1826 and became an important Mississippi River port.

During the Civil War, Memphis was a Confederate military center. In 1862, Federal forces won a gunboat battle on the river at Memphis and General Sherman was enabled to take the city.

Memphis's population was devastated by several yellow-fever epidemics during the 1870s and the city did not recover its prosperity until the end of the 19th century.

Memphis is one of the country's largest inland ports and is known as "America's Distribution Center" serving the northeast, southeast, and southwest regions of the country. Memphis is a leader in agribusiness, cultivating soybeans, rice, grain sorghum, winter wheat, corn, and livestock raising. The city is the world's largest trading center for spot cotton, handling over 40% of the nation's spot cotton crops annually. It is the largest hardwood lumber trading and processing center in the world and is estimated to be the nation's third largest total food processor.

Health care and related activities such as medical education and biomedical research is Memphis's largest industry bringing over $2.5 billion a year to the local economy. Also important are high tech communications.

Famous natives: Kathy Bates, actress; Rosalind Cash, singer; Aretha Franklin, singer; Morgan Freeman, actor; George Hamilton, actor; Benjamin Hooks, organization official; Hal Needham, director; Cybill Shepherd, actress; Robert Siodmak, director

MIAMI, FLA.

Mayor: Xavier L. Suarez (to Nov. 1993)
City manager: Cesar Odio (apptd. Dec. 1985)
1990 census population, sex, & (rank): 358,548 (46); **% change,** 3.4; **Male,** 173,223; **Female,** 185,325; **White,** 235,358; **Black,** 98,207 (27.4%); **American Indian, Eskimo, or Aleut,** 545 (0.2%); **Asian or Pacific Islander,** 2,272 (0.6%); **Other race,** 22,166; **Hispanic origin,** 223,964 (62.5%). **1990 percent population under 18:** 23.0; **65 and over,** 16.6; **median age,** 36.0.
Land area: 34.3 sq mi. (89 sq km); **Water area:** 19.5 sq mi.; **Alt.:** Average, 12 ft
Avg. daily temp.: Jan., 67.1° F; July, 82.4° F
Churches (Dade County): Protestant, 700; Roman Catholic, 61; Jewish, 60; **City-owned parks (Miami):** 109; **Radio stations (Dade County):** 17; **Television stations (Dade County):** 11
CIVILIAN LABOR FORCE: 172,619 **Unemployed:** 24,578, **Percent:** 14.2; **Per capita personal income:** $9,799
Chamber of Commerce: Greater Miami Chamber of Commerce, 1601 Biscayne Blvd., Miami, Fla. 33132

Miami, the second largest city in Florida and seat of Dade county, is located in the southeastern part of the state, on Biscayne Bay.

The area was once the home of the Tequesta Indians until they were nearly wiped out by European diseases and warfare brought on by two centuries of Spanish control of Florida. Miami was founded in 1870 near the site of Ft. Dallas built in 1835 during the Seminole Indian wars. The city's name is probably derived from "Mayaimi," the Indian word for "big water."

Miami is the only U.S. city to have been conceived by a woman. Julia Tuttle, a Clevelander, arrived there in 1891 and bought several hundred acres on the bank of the Miami River. She convinced New York financier Henry M. Flagler of the area's vast potential and persuaded him to extend his Florida East Coast Railroad to Miami in 1896, the year the city was incorporated. Flagler dredged Miami harbor, built the renowned Royal Palm Hotel which opened Jan. 1, 1897, and promoted the area as a winter playground. Tourists flocked there and, by 1910, the city was a thriving recreational area. Miami survived the collapse of a land speculation boom in the 1920s and severe hurricanes in 1926 and 1935 and continued to grow in the aftermath of these disasters.

Miami experienced one of its most monumental population boosts during the 1960s when about 260,000 Cuban refugees arrived on its shore seeking freedom. They made a great impact on Miami, now a bilingual metropolis, and spurred economic growth.

Miami is an international banking and finance center and the city has the greatest concentration of international and Edge Act banks[1] in North America which constitute a major employment base. Greater Miami[2] has a highly diversified economy with over 170 multinational Miami-based companies, a bevy of Fortune 500 companies, and a rapidly growing manufacturing and distribution center. Miami ranks number one in Florida for total manufacturing income, employment, and number of manufacturing establishments. Greater Miami is the nation's leader in biomedical technology and the health care sector is a major industry. It is also part of an area known as the Computer Coast of Florida, and its growing technologies include computers, electrical engineering, and plastics manufacturing.

Miami is one of the world's leading year-round resort centers with tourism contributing over 60% of the area's economy. The city is a major transportation hub and the port of Miami is the world's largest cruise port and a major seaport for cargo. The famous island resort of Miami Beach, incorporated in 1915, is part of Greater Miami and is connected to Miami by four causeways.

1. Edge Act banks may make only foreign loans and accept foreign deposits. 2. Greater Miami is made up of 27 municipalities of which the City of Miami is the largest.

Famous natives: Fernando Bujones, dancer; Steve Carlton, baseball player; Debbie Harry, singer; Dick Howser, baseball player and manager; Sidney Poitier, actor; Janet Reno, Attorney General of the U.S.; Ben Vereen, actor; Ellen Zwilich, composer

MILWAUKEE, WIS.

Mayor: John O. Norquist (to April 1996)
1990 census population, sex, & (rank): 628,088 (17); **% change,** –1.3; **Male,** 296,837; **Female,** 331,251; **White,** 398,033; **Black,** 191,255 (30.5%); **American Indian, Eskimo, or Aleut,** 5,858 (0.9%); **Asian or Pacific Islander,** 11,817 (1.9%); **Other race,** 21,125; **Hispanic origin,** 39,409 (6.3%). **1990 percent population under 18:** 27.4; **65 and over:** 12.4; **median age:** 30.3.
Land area: 95.8 sq mi. (248 sq km); **Alt.:** 580.60 ft
Avg. daily temp.: Jan., 18.7° F; July, 70.5° F
Churches: 411; **County-owned parks:** 14,758 ac.; **Radio stations:** AM, 15; FM, 8; **Television stations:** 10
CIVILIAN LABOR FORCE: 302,993; **Unemployed:** 17,468, **Percent:** 5.8; **Per capita personal income:** $18,842[1]

Chamber of Commerce: Metropolitan Milwaukee Association of Commerce, 828 N. Broadway, Milwaukee, Wis. 53202; Milwaukee Minority Chamber of Commerce, 2821 N. 4th St., Milwaukee, Wis. 53212; Hispanic Chamber of Commerce, 1125 W. National Ave., Milwaukee, Wis. 53204

1. PMSA.

Milwaukee, the largest city in Wisconsin and seat of Milwaukee county, is located in the southeastern part of the state on Lake Michigan.

French missionaries visited the site of Milwaukee in the seventeenth century, but it was not until 1795 that Jacques Vieau established a fur-trading post there. The first permanent white settler, Vieau's son-in-law, Solomon Juneau, an agent of the American Fur Company, made his home there in 1818. The settlement merged with several neighboring villages in 1838 to form Milwaukee, and the city was incorporated in 1846. Its name is derived from an Algonquian Indian word Milo-aki meaning "beautiful land." A large wave of German immigrants arrived after 1848 and contributed greatly to the city's political, economic, and cultural development.

Milwaukee is one of the great industrial centers in the country and one of the largest Great Lakes ports. Currently, port commerce runs over 2 million tons per year.

Its economy was forged by heavy industries but is now diversified. Manufacturing remains strong and Milwaukee manufacturers are national leaders in lithographic commercial printing and the production of medical diagnostic instruments, small gasoline engines, malt beverages, iron and steel forgings, mining and construction machinery, robotics, speed changers and drives, and electronic controls. Milwaukee's high-tech manufacturing community is the ninth-largest among the nation's 31 major metropolitan areas. Once known as a "beer town," less than one percent of Milwaukee's workforce is involved in beer production. However, beer still plays an important role and almost 11% of the nation's malt beverage is produced there.

Tourism is important to the economy and about 5 million people visit Milwaukee every year.

Famous natives: Donald Gramm, bass-baritone; Woody Herman, band leader; Al Jarreau, singer; George F. Kennan, diplomat; Alfred Lunt, actor; Pat O'Brien, actor; Tom Snyder, TV personality; Speech, member of rap group, "Arrested Development;" Spencer Tracy, actor; Gene Wilder, actor

MINNEAPOLIS, MINN.

Mayor: Donald M. Fraser (to Jan. 1994)

1990 census population, sex, & (rank): 368,383 (42); **% change,** –0.7; **Male,** 178,671; **Female,** 189,712; **White,** 288,967; **Black,** 47,948 (13.0%); **American Indian, Eskimo, or Aleut,** 12,335 (3.3%); **Asian or Pacific Islander,** 15,723 (4.3%); **Other race,** 3,410; **Hispanic origin,** 7,900 (2.1%). **1990 percent population under 18:** 20.6; **65 and over:** 13.0; **median age:** 31.7

Land area: 58.7 sq mi. (143 sq km); **Alt.:** Highest, 945 ft; lowest, 695

Avg. daily temp.: Jan., 11.2° F; July, 73.1° F

Churches: 419; **City-owned parks:** 153; **Radio stations:** AM, 17; FM, 15 (metro area); **Television stations:** 6 (metro area)

CIVILIAN LABOR FORCE: 204,477; **Unemployed:** 9,905, **Percent:** 4.8; **Per capita personal income:** $20,227[1]

Chamber of Commerce: Greater Minneapolis Chamber of Commerce, Young Quinlan Building, 81 S. Ninth Street, Suite 200, Minneapolis, Minn. 55402-3223

1. Minneapolis-St. Paul Minn.–Wis. MSA.

Minneapolis, the largest city in Minnesota and seat of Hennepin county, is located in the southeast central part of the state on the Mississippi River. It is adjacent to its "twin city" of St. Paul. The Minneapolis-St. Paul Standard Metropolitan Statistical Area is the 15th largest in the United States.

In 1680, Father Louis Hennepin visited the future site of Minneapolis and gave the Falls of St. Anthony their name. Lieutenant Zebulon Pike made a treaty with the Sioux Indians in 1805–06 by which they ceded to the whites land including the Falls of St. Anthony and the site of Minneapolis. Fort Snelling was built in 1819–20 and, in 1823, the government built a lumber and flour mill. Flour milling became the major industry of early Minneapolis and made the city the milling capital of the world. The town of St. Anthony was established on the east bank of the Mississippi in 1848 and the town of Minneapolis grew up on the opposite bank of the river. The name Minneapolis is a combination of the Dakota Sioux word "minna" for water and the Greek word "polis" for city. Minneapolis was incorporated as a city in 1867 and, in 1872, the city of St. Anthony (chartered in 1860) was annexed to it. After the spread of the railroads in the 1870s, Minneapolis became the gateway to the Northern Great Plains.

Minneapolis is a center of industry and commerce serving a large agricultural region. During the 20th century, manufacturing, food processing, milling, computers, health services, and graphic arts developed as Minneapolis's major industries. Fifteen Fortune 500 industrial and 17 Fortune service companies are headquartered there. The city is the home of the world's largest cash grain market and is the headquarters of the Ninth Federal Reserve Bank.

Famous natives: La Verne, Maxene, Patti Andrews, singers; James Arness, actor; Lew Ayres, actor; Patty Berg, golfer; Virginia Bruce, actress; J. Paul Getty, oil executive; Peter Graves, actor; George Roy Hill, director; Cornell MacNeil, baritone; Ralph Meeker, actor; Gen. Lauris Norstad; Westbrook Pegler, columnist; Prince, singer; Harrison Salisbury, journalist; Charles Schulz, cartoonist; Anne Tyler, writer; Bud Wilkinson, football player; David Winfield, baseball player

NASHVILLE-DAVIDSON, TENN.

Mayor: Philip N. Bredesen

1900 census population, sex, & (rank)[1]: 510,784 (23); **% change,** 6.9; **Male,** 242,492; **Female,** 268,292; **White,** 381,740; **Black,** 119,273 (23.4%); **American Indian, Eskimo, or Aleut,** 1,162 (0.2%); **Asian or Pacific Islander,** 7,081 (1.4%); **Other race,** 1,528; **Hispanic origin,** 4,775 (0.9%). **1900 percent population under 18:** 22.8; **65 and over:** 11.6; **median age:** 32.6.

Land area: 533 sq mi. (1,380 sq km); **Altitude:** Highest, 1,100 ft; lowest, approx. 400 ft

Avg. daily temp.: Jan., 36.7° F; July, 76.6° F

Churches: Protestant, 781; Roman Catholic, 18; Jewish, 3; **City-owned parks:** 76 (6,650 ac.); **Radio stations:** AM, 11; FM, 8; **Television stations:** 7

CIVILIAN LABOR FORCE: 267,724; **Unemployed:** 12,893, **Percent:** 4.8; **Per capita personal income:** $17,333

Chamber of Commerce: Nashville Area Chamber of Commerce, 161 Fourth Ave. North, Nashville, Tenn. 37219

1. Consolidated city.

The consolidated city of Nashville–Davidson is the capital and second largest city in Tennessee and is located in the north central part of the state on the Cumberland River. It is the seat of Davidson county.

During the winter of 1779–80, James Robertson and John Donelson founded a settlement at Big Salt Lick by the Cumberland River at the present site of the city. They built forts on both sides of the river naming one of them Fort Nashborough in honor of Francis Nash, a Revolutionary War general. In 1784, the town was named Nashville and was incorporated as a city in 1806.

Nashville became the capital of Tennessee in 1843 and was the seat of Davidson county until 1963 when it merged with the county to become Nashville–Davidson.

Nashville's best known industries are recording, publishing, and the distribution of music, especially country music. The city is a port of entry and an important industrial and commercial center serving the Upper South. Its diverse economy includes chemicals, wearing apparel, publishing, insurance, and banking. Auto manufacturing and health care management are also important industries. Nashville is the home of several religious organizations and is a major tourist attraction and convention center.

Famous natives: Gregg Allman, singer; Julian Bond, legislator; Rita Coolidge, singer; Red Grooms, artist; Barbara Howar, hostess, writer; Annie Potts, actress; Paula Robeson, flutist; Dawn Upshaw, soprano

NEW ORLEANS, LA.

Mayor: Sidney J. Barthelemy (to May 1994)
1990 census population, sex, & (rank): 496,938 (25); **% change,** –10.9; **Male,** 230,883; **Female,** 266,055; **White,** 173,554; **Black,** 307,728 (61.9%); **American Indian, Eskimo, or Aleut,** 759 (0.2%); **Asian or Pacific Islander,** 9,678 (1.9%); **Other race,** 5,219; **Hispanic origin,** 17,238 (3.5%). **1990 percent population under 18:** 27.5; **65 and over,** 13.0; **median age,** 31.6.
Land area: 199.4 sq mi. (516 sq km); **Alt.:** Highest, 15 ft; lowest, –4
Avg. daily temp.: Jan., 52.4° F; July, 77° F
Churches: 712; **City-owned parks:** 165 (299 ac.); **Radio stations:** AM, 12; FM, 14; **Television stations:** 7
CIVILIAN LABOR FORCE: 205,610[1]; **Unemployed:** 15,055[1], **Percent:** 7.3[1]; **Per capita personal income:** $14,745
Chamber of Commerce: The Chamber/New Orleans and the River Region, 301 Camp Street, New Orleans, La. 70130

1. New Orleans City/Orleans Parish.

New Orleans, the largest city in Louisiana and seat of Orleans Parish, is located in the southeastern part of the state, between the Mississippi River and Lake Ponchartrain.

One of the few cities of the nation that has been under three flags, New Orleans has belonged to Spain, France, and the U.S. The French founded it in 1718 and named it in honor of the Duke of Orleans. In 1762, France ceded the city and the territory to Spain. On 1800, the territory was returned to France, but government authorities did not take over until 1803, only 20 days before the region became part of the U.S. in the Louisiana Purchase.

As a memento of the old days, New Orleans has its famous French Quarter which has a fascination for tourists and gourmets. The most spectacular and gayest festival in the U.S. is held in New Orleans—The Mardi Gras—which involves a week of carnival before the beginning of Lent.

New Orleans is one of the world's greatest international ports, the second largest in the nation, and it is a major focus of the city's economy. New Orleans is home to the corporate offices of oil companies with major offshore operations in the Gulf of Mexico, as well as the distribution and service centers of offshore equipment suppliers and fabricators. Refining of petroleum and a broad range of petrochemicals is a leading manufacturing industry. The shipbuilding/repair and aerospace equipment sectors are the largest manufacturing industries in terms of jobs. The New Orleans region also functions as a mining, processing, and transportation center for other minerals, principally sulfur. The information services (telecommunications) industry is one of the fastest growing in the area. The largest service sector in terms of jobs is the health care industry and the region is a leading center of medical service and health care in the southern United States.

Tourism has grown rapidly in recent years and New Orleans hosts more than seven million visitors annually.

Famous natives: Louis Armstrong, musician; Truman Capote, author; Fats Domino, musician; Louis Gottschalk, pianist, composer; Bryant Gumbel, TV personality; Lillian Hellman, playwright, author; Al Hirt, musician; Mahalia Jackson, singer; Dorothy Lamour, actress; Wynton Marsalis, musician; Huey Newton, activist; Marguerite Piazza, soprano; Rusty Staub, baseball player; Ben Turpin, comedian; Shirley Verrett, mezzo-soprano; Carl Weathers, actor; Del Williams, football player

NEW YORK, N.Y.

Mayor: David N. Dinkins (to Dec. 31, 1993)
Borough Presidents: Bronx, Fernando Ferrer; Brooklyn, Howard Golden; Manhattan, Ruth W. Messinger; Queens, Claire Shulman; Staten Island, Guy V. Molinari
1990 census population, sex, & (rank): 7,322,564 (1)[1]: **% change,** 3.5; **Male,** 3,437,687; **Female,** 3,884,877; **White,** 3,827,088; **Black,** 2,102,512 (28.7%); **American Indian, Eskimo, or Aleut,** 27,531 (0.4%); **Asian or Pacific Islander,** 512,719 (7.0%); **Other race,** 852,714; **Hispanic origin,** 1,783,511 (24.4%).[2] **1990 percent population under 18:** 23.0; **65 and over:** 13.0; **median age:** 33.7.
Land area: 321.8 sq mi. (826.68 sq km) (Queens, 112.1; Brooklyn, 81.8; Staten Island, 60.2; Bronx, 44.0 Manhattan, 23.7); **Alt.:** Highest, 410 ft; lowest, sea level
Avg. daily temp.: Jan., 31.8° F; July, 76.7° F
Churches: Protestant, 1,766; Jewish, 1,256; Roman Catholic, 437; Orthodox, 66; **City-owned parks:** 1,701 (26,295 ac.); **Radio stations:** AM, 13; FM, 18; **Television stations:** 6 commercial, 1 public
CIVILIAN LABOR FORCE: 3,311,000; **Unemployed:** 359,000, **Percent:** 10.8; **Per capita personal income:** $22,0645[1]
Chamber of Commerce: New York Chamber of Commerce and Industry, 65 Liberty St., New York, N.Y. 10005

1. PMSA. 2. Race breakdown figures according to N.Y.C. Dept. of City Planning: White, non-Hispanic, 3,163,125; Black, non-Hispanic, 1,847,049; American Indian, Eskimo and Aleut, non-Hispanic, 17,871; Asian and Pacific Islander, non-Hispanic, 489,157; Hispanic, 1,783,511.

New York City is the largest city in the United States. It is located in the southern part of New York State, at the mouth of the Hudson River (also known as North River as it passes Manhattan Island).

In 1609, Henry Hudson, who worked for the Dutch East India Company, sailed up the river that now bears his name and went as far as Albany. Five years later, a permanent settlement was established at what is now New York, but it was originally called New Amsterdam by the Dutch governors. One of them, Peter Minuit, was said to have bought Manhattan Island from the Indians for $24 worth of beads, buttons, and trinkets. In 1664, Great Britain's Duke of York sent a fleet which quietly seized the settlement from the Dutch, without bloodshed, and rechristened the colony in honor of the Duke.

Control of New York passed to the young U.S. at the end of the Revolutionary War, and George Washington was inaugurated President in New York's old City Hall. Congress met in New York from 1785 to 1790.

In 1898, when Greater New York was chartered, the city expanded to include the following five boroughs which are also counties in New York State: Manhattan (New York county); Brooklyn (Kings county); Bronx (Bronx county); Queens (Queens county); and Staten Island (Richmond county).

There is a growing effort among Staten Island residents to separate from Greater New York and become an independent city of Staten Island. In November 1993, Staten Islanders will vote on succession from the rest of the city in a referendum.

Today, the Big Apple is the most populous city in the United States, a major world capital, and the world leader in finance, the arts, and communications. The city is also the center of advertising, fashion, publishing, and radio broadcasting in the United States. New York has innumerable museums, art galleries, and educational institutions. The port of New York is one of the finest in the world. The city is the home of the United Nations and is headquarters for some of the world's largest corporations.

Famous natives: Kareem Abdul-Jabbar, basketball player; Woody Allen, actor, director; Robert Anderson, playwright; Martina Arroyo, soprano; Jean Arthur, actress; Lauren Bacall, actress; James Baldwin, novelist; Harry Belafonte, singer, actor; Humphrey Bogart, actor; James Cagney, actor; Maria Callas, soprano; Paddy Chayefsky, playwright; Aaron Copland, composer; Sammy Davis, Jr., singer, actor; Agnes de Mille, choreographer; Robert De Niro, actor; Eamon De Valera, President of Ireland; Gertrude Elion, Nobel Prize in medicine; Lou Gehrig, baseball player; George Gershwin, composer; Ira Gershwin, lyricist; Jackie Gleason, actor; Rita Hayworth, actress; Lena Horne, singer; Julia Ward Howe, poet, reformer; Washington Irving, author; Henry James, novelist; John Jay, statesman, jurist; Michael Jordan, basketball player; Jerome Kern, composer; Michael Landon, actor; Roy Lichtenstein, painter; Vince Lombardi, football player, coach; Chico, Groucho, Harpo, Zeppo Marx, comedians; Herman Melville, novelist; Yehudi Menuhin, violinist; Ethel Merman, singer, actress; James Michener, novelist; Arthur Miller, playwright; Eugene O'Neill, playwright; J. Robert Oppenheimer, nuclear physicist; Al Pacino, actor; Jan Peerce, tenor; Roberta Peters, soprano; Elmer Rice, playwright; Jerome Robbins, choreographer; Norman Rockwell, painter, illustrator; Eleanor Roosevelt, reformer, humanitarian; Theodore Roosevelt, President; Jonas Salk, polio researcher; Beverly Sills, soprano; Neil Simon, playwright; Risë Stevens, mezzo-soprano; Barbra Streisand, singer, actress; Ed Sullivan, TV personality; Fats Waller, pianist; Mae West, actress; Edith Wharton, novelist; Rosalyn Yalow, Nobel Prize in medicine

OAKLAND, CALIF.

Mayor: Elihu Mason Harris (to Jan. 1995)
City Manager: Henry L. Gardner (apptd. June 1981)
1990 census popultion, sex, & (rank): 372,242 (39); **% change,** 9.7; **Male,** 178,824; **Female,** 193,418; **White,** 120,849; **Black,** 163,335 (43.9%); **American Indian, Eskimo, or Aleut,** 2,371 (0.6%); **Asian or Pacific Islander,** 54,931 (14.8%); **Other race,** 30,756; **Hispanic origin,** 51,711 (13.9%). **1990 percent population under 18,** 24.9; **65 and over,** 12.0; **median age:** 32.7.
Land area: 53.9 sq mi. (140 sq km); **Alt.:** Highest, 1,700 ft; lowest, sea level
Avg. daily temp.: Jan., 49.0° F; July, 63.7° F
Churches: 374, representing over 78 denominations in the City; over 500 churches in Alameda County; **City-owned parks:** 2,196 ac.; **Radio stations:** AM, 1; **Television stations:** 1 commercial
CIVILIAN LABOR FORCE: 180,624; **Unemployed:** 18,148, **Percent:** 10.0; **Per capita personal income:** $22,249[1]
Chamber of Commerce: Oakland Chamber of Commerce, 475 Fourteenth St., Oakland, Calif. 94612-1903

1. PMSA.

Oakland is located in the west central part of California on the east side of San Francisco Bay. It is the seat of Alameda county.

Don Luis Peralta first settled the site of Oakland in 1820 when he established the Rancho San Antonio. The gold rush of 1849 attracted more people to the area and the city's population continued to grow after a ferry service to San Francisco was started in 1851. Oakland was incorporated as a town in 1852 and as a city in 1854. It was named after the numerous oak trees found in the area. Oakland became the western terminus of the Central Pacific Railroad in 1869 and the seat of Alameda county in 1873.

During the latter part of the 19th century and also in 1910, additional territory was annexed to Oakland and the city assumed its present size. In 1906, thousands of people fled to Oakland in the aftermath of the San Francisco earthquake and settled there permanently, furthering the city's growth. Oakland's economic development continued to rise with the opening of the San Francisco–Oakland Bay Bridge in 1936.

Oakland is a major center of culture and commerce. It is an important container shipping port and the terminus of three transcontinental railroads. Oakland's industries include shipbuilding, food processing, chemicals, pharmaceuticals, electrical and high technology manufacturing. Oakland is also a leading importer of foreign cars. The city is the headquarters of many national and international corporations.

Famous natives: Buster Crabbe, actor; Frederick Cottrell, inventor; Dennis Eckersley, athlete; Hammer, singer, dancer, songwriter; Rod McKuen, singer, composer; Russ Meyer, producer, director; (Eddie Anderson) Rochester, actor; George Stevens, director; Amy Tan, writer; Jo Van Fleet, actress

OKLAHOMA CITY, OKLA.

Mayor: Ron Norick (to April 1996)
City Manager: Don Brown
1990 census population, sex, & (rank): 444,719 (29); **% change,** 10.1; **Male,** 214,466; **Female,** 230,253; **White,** 332,539; **Black,** 71,064 (16.0%); **American Indian, Eskimo, or Aleut,** 18,794 (4.2%); **Asian or Pacific Islander,** 10,491 (2.4%); **Other race,** 11,831; **Hispanic origin,** 22,033 (5.0%). **1990 percent population under 18:** 26.0; **65 and over:** 11.9; **median age:** 32.4.
Land area: 623 sq mi. (1,614 sq km); **Alt.:** Highest, 1,320 ft; lowest, 1,140
Avg. daily temp.: Jan., 35.9° F; July, 82.1° F

Churches: Roman Catholic, 25; Jewish, 2; Protestant and others, 741; **City-owned parks:** 138 (3,944 ac.); **Television stations:** 8; **Radio stations:** AM, 10; FM, 14
CIVILIAN LABOR FORCE: 230,226; **Unemployed:** 13,059, **Percent:** 5.7; **Per capita personal income:** $15,536
Chamber of Commerce: Oklahoma City Chamber of Commerce, 1 Santa Fe Plaza, Oklahoma City, Okla. 73102

Oklahoma City, the state capital and seat of Oklahoma county, is the largest city in Oklahoma. It is located in the central part of the state on the North Canadian River.

Oklahoma City sprang into being almost overnight. On April 22, 1889, the government threw open the territory for settlement, and there was a classic rush across the line to stake claims. Within a short time, a sprawling tent city sprang up near the Santa Fe railroad railroad tracks and Oklahoma City was a bustling town of 10,000. The city was incorporated in 1890 and replaced Guthrie as the state capital in 1910. Oil was discovered in the city in 1928 and petroleum production became a mainstay of the city's economy.

Oklahoma City is the wholesale and distributing center for the state, and the city's stockyards are the largest stocker and feeder cattle market in the world. Following the decline of the energy sector, Oklahoma City is fostering a private entrepreneurial environment and a more diversified economy. Within the service sector, health services are projected to grow, followed by retail trade and business services. Aerospace, distribution, and telecommunications have been targeted for business attraction. Nearby Tinker Air Force Base, one of the world's largest air depots, is a major city employer.

Famous natives: Johnny Bench, baseball; Lon Chaney, Jr., actor; Ralph Ellison, writer; Kay Francis, actress; Dale Robertson, actor; Ted Shackleford, actor; Pamela Tiffin, actress

OMAHA, NEB.

Mayor: P.J. Morgan (to June 1993)
1990 census population, sex, & (rank): 335,795 (48); **% change,** 7.0; **Male,** 160,392; **Female,** 175,403; **White,** 281,603; **Black,** 43,989 (13.1%); **American Indian, Eskimo, or Aleut,** 2,274 (0.7%); **Asian or Pacific Islander,** 3,412 (1.0%); **Other race,** 4,517; **Hispanic origin,** 10,288 (3.1%). **1990 percent population under 18:** 25.4; **65 and over:** 12.9; **median age:** 32.2.
Land area: 104.49 sq mi. (271.7 sq km); **Alt.:** Highest, 1,270 ft
Avg. daily temp.: Jan., 20.2° F; July, 77.7° F
Churches: Protestant, 246; Roman Catholic, 44; Jewish, 4; **City-owned parks:** 159 (over 7,000 ac.); **Radio stations:** AM, 7; FM, 13; **Television stations:** 4
CIVILIAN LABOR FORCE: 188,900; **Unemployed:** 6,914, **Percent:** 3.7; **Per capita personal income:** $16,753[1]
Chamber of Commerce: Omaha Chamber of Commerce, 1301 Harney St., Omaha, Neb. 68102

1. Omaha, Neb.–Iowa MSA.

Omaha, the largest city in Nebraska and the seat of Douglas county, is located in the eastern part of the state on the west bank of the Missouri River opposite Council Bluffs, Iowa.

The area was visited by the Lewis and Clark expedition in 1804, and the U.S. Army built Ft. Atkinson nearby in 1819. Pierre Cabanne established a fur-trading post at the site in 1825. The first Mormon migrants wintered there in 1846–47 on their way to Utah. The city grew rapidly as the most northerly supply point for overland wagons to the Far West.

The city was officially founded in 1854 after the Nebraska Territory was opened for settlement. It was named for the Omaha Indians living nearby, whose tribal name means "those who go upstream or against the current." Omaha was incorporated as a city in 1857 and was the capital of the Nebraska Territory from 1855 to 1867. The city continued to thrive as a point of entry and a major transportation center when the Union Pacific trans-continental railroad arrived in 1869.

Omaha is a major market for food processing, telecommunications, and insurance. Other important industries include electrical equipment, finance, as well as printing and publishing.

Famous natives: Fred Astaire, dancer, actor; Max Baer, boxer; Ronald Boone, former NBA professional; Robert Boozer, former NBA professional; Marlon Brando, actor; Montgomery Clift, actor; David Doyle, actor; Gerald Ford, President; Bob Gibson, baseball; Swoosie Kurtz, actress; Melvin Laird, Secretary of Defense; Dorothy McGuire, actress; Nick Nolte, actor; Gale Sayers, football; Malcolm X, political activist; Paul Williams, singer, composer

PHILADELPHIA, PA.

Mayor: Edward G. Rendell (to first Monday, January 1996)
1990 census population, sex, & (rank): 1,585,577 (5); **% change,** –6.1; **Male,** 737,763; **Female,** 847,814; **White,** 848,586; **Black,** 631,936 (39.9%); **American Indian, Eskimo, or Aleut,** 3,454 (0.2%); **Asian or Pacific Islander,** 43,522 (2.7%); **Other race,** 58,079; **Hispanic origin,** 89,193 (5.6%). **1990 percent population under 18:** 23.9; **65 and over:** 15.2; **median age:** 33.2.
Land area: 136 sq mi. (352 sq km); **Alt.:** Highest, 440 ft; lowest, sea level
Avg. daily temp.: Jan., 31.2° F; July, 76.5° F
Churches: Roman Catholic, 133; Jewish, 55; Protestant and others, 830; **City-owned parks:** 630 (10,252 ac.); **Radio stations:** AM, 40[1]; FM, 43[1]; **Television stations:** 14[1]
CIVILIAN LABOR FORCE: 699,391[2]; **Unemployed:** 61,403[2], **Percent:** 8.8[2]; **Per capita personal income:** $19,750[1]
Chamber of Commerce: Philadelphia Chamber of Commerce, 1234 Market Street, Suite 1800, Philadelphia, Pa. 19107

1. PMSA. 2. Philadelphia City/County.

Philadelphia, the largest city in Pennsylvania and seat of Philadelphia county (coterminous), is located in the southeastern part of the state at the junction of the Schuylkill and Delaware Rivers.

Philadelphia, the "City of Brotherly Love," was settled in 1681 by Capt. William Markham, who, with a small band of colonists, was sent out by his cousin, William Penn. Penn arrived the following year.

In the period before the American Revolution, the city outstripped all others in the colonies in education, arts, science, industry, and commerce. In 1774–76, the First and Second Continental Congresses met in Philadelphia; and, from 1781–83, the city was the capital of the U.S. under the Articles of Confederation. In 1790, it became the nation's capital under the Constitution and remained so until the seat of the federal government moved to Washington in 1800.

Within a half-century of the founding of the nation at Independence Hall, Philadelphia had emerged as the "world's greatest workshop." The steam locomotives and hat factories of the 19th century have been replaced by diverse manufacturing specialties such as chemicals, including pharmaceuticals, medical devices, transportation equipment, and printing and publishing. In the services sector, Philadelphia is a major net "exporter" in subsectors such as health services, insurance carriers, legal services, and architecture and engineering services.

The city abounds in landmarks of early American history, including Independence Hall and the Liberty Bell.

Famous natives: Marian Anderson, contralto; John, Lionel, and Ethel Barrymore, actors; Wilt Chamberlain, basketball player; Bill Cosby, actor; Stuart Davis, painter; Thomas Eakins, painter, sculptor; W.C. Fields, comedian; Stan Getz, saxophonist; Grace (Kelly), Princess of Monaco; Walt Kelly, cartoonist; Jack Klugman, actor; Mario Lanza, singer, actor; George McClellan, general; Margaret Mead, anthropologist; Anna Quindlen, writer, Pulitzer Prize winner; Man Ray, painter; Betsy Ross, flagmaker; Jacqueline Susann, novelist; Robert Venturi, architect

PHOENIX, ARIZ.

Mayor: Paul Johnson (to Jan. 1996)
City Manager: Frank Fairbanks (appt. May 1990)
1990 census population, sex, & (rank): 983,403 (9); **% change,** 24.5; **Male,** 487,589; **Female,** 495,814; **White,** 803,332; **Black,** 51,053 (5.2%); **American Indian, Eskimo, or Aleut,** 18,225 (1.9%); **Asian or Pacific Islander,** 16,303 (1.7%); **Other race,** 94,490; **Hispanic origin,** 197,103 (20.0%). **1990 percent population under 18:** 27.2; **65 and over,** 9.7; **median age,** 31.1.
Land area: 431.6 sq mi. (1,112 sq km); **Alt.:** Highest, 2,740 ft.; lowest, 1,017
Avg. daily temp.: Jan., 53.2° F; July, 92.3° F
City-owned parks: 187 (30,314 ac.); **Radio stations:** AM, 20; FM, 20; **Television stations:** 9 commercial; 1 PBS
CIVILIAN LABOR FORCE: 508,989; **Unemployed:** 35,757, **Percent:** 7.0; **Per capita personal income:** $18,042
Chamber of Commerce: Phoenix Chamber of Commerce, 34 W. Monroe St., Phoenix, Ariz. 85003

Phoenix, the capital of Arizona and seat of Maricopa county, is the largest city in the state. It is located in the center of Arizona on the Salt River.

The prehistoric Hohokam Indians first settled the area about 300 B.C. and dug a system of extensive irrigation canals for farming. The Indian culture mysteriously broke up in the 1400s. The site was permanently resettled again by Jack Swilling and "Lord Darrell" Duppa about 1867. Because the city was founded on the ruins of the ancient civilization, it was named Phoenix after the legendary Phoenix bird that could regenerate itself. The irrigation canals were restored for farming, and ranching and prospecting began in the surrounding area. The city quickly grew as an important trading center.

Phoenix was incorporated as a city in 1881 and was made the territorial capital in 1889. It became the state capital when Arizona was admitted to the Union in 1912.

Phoenix is a center of agriculture and commerce. Major industries include agricultural products, aerospace technology, electronics, air-conditioning, leather goods, and Indian arts and crafts.

Famous natives: Lynda Carter, actress; Joan Ganz Cooney, TV executive; Mare Cunningham, actress; Arthur A. Fletcher, government official; Barry Goldwater, politician; Charles S. Robb, politician

PITTSBURGH, PA.

Mayor: Sophie Masloff (to Jan. 1994)
1990 census population, sex, & (rank): 369,879 (40); **% change,** −12.8; **Male,** 171,722; **Female,** 198,157; **White,** 266,791; **Black,** 95,362 (25.8%); **American Indian, Eskimo, or Aleut,** 671 (0.2%); **Asian or Pacific Islander,** 5,937 (1.6%); **Other race,** 1,118; **Hispanic origin,** 3,468 (0.9%). **1990 percent population under 18:** 19.8; **65 and over,** 17.9; **median age:** 34.6.
Land area: 55.5 sq mi. (144 sq km); **Alt.:** Highest, 1,240 ft; lowest, 715
Avg. daily temp.: Jan., 26.7° F; July, 72.0° F
Churches: Protestant, 348; Roman Catholic, 86; Jewish, 28; Orthodox, 26; **City-owned parks and playgrounds:** 270 (2,572 ac.); **Radio stations:** AM, 12; FM, 20; **Television stations:** 8
CIVILIAN LABOR FORCE: 176,754; **Unemployed:** 11,613, **Percent:** 6.6; **Per capita personal income:** $17,763[1]
Chamber of Commerce: The Chamber of Commerce of Greater Pittsburgh, 3 Gateway Center, Pittsburgh, Pa. 15222

1. PMSA.

Pittsburgh, the second largest city in Pennsylvania and seat of Allegheny county, is located in the southwestern part of the state at the junction where the Allegheny and Monongahela Rivers join to form the Ohio River.

Some of the first inhabitants of the area were the Shawnee, Seneca, Delaware, and Iroquois Indians who had left the area by 1754. That year a detachment of troops from Virginia put a fort on the site of present Pittsburgh (Ft. Prince George) considering it a strategic spot. Following the original Virginia settlers, the French seized the spot and named it Ft. Duquesne; and, in 1758, the British took it away from the French. The British built a new fort and named it after the British Prime Minister, William Pitt. A town developed around the fort and was incorporated as Pittsburgh in 1816.

By the end of the 19th century, Pittsburgh had become a world leader in iron and steelmaking. However, in the early 1980s, the country's domestic steel industry collapsed causing major upheavals in Pittsburgh's manufacturing sector.

The Pittsburgh region underwent a successful diversified economic transition, shifting from heavy industries to light manufacturing, advanced technologies such as industrial automation, advanced materials, software engineering and biomedical technology, medicine, education, finance, and corporate services. Pittsburgh is a national leader in health care services and is the world's leading center for organ transplantation. The city is a hub of international business and ranks fifth as a major corporate headquarters center.

Pittsburgh is also a major U.S. transportation center and is the nation's largest inland port in terms of tonnage.

Famous natives: Henry Steele Commager, historian; Bill Cullen, radio and TV entertainer; John Davidson, singer, actor; Billy Eckstine, singer; Erroll Garner, jazz pianist; Scott Glenn, actor; Martha Graham, dancer, choreographer; George S. Kaufman, playwright; Michael Keaton, actor; Gene Kelly, actor, dancer; Oscar Levant, pianist; Andrew Mellon, financier; Adolphe Menjou, actor; William Powell, actor; Mary Roberts Rinehart, novelist; Peter Sellars, theater director; David O. Selznick, producer; Joseph Wambaugh, novelist; August Wilson, playwright

PORTLAND, ORE.

Mayor: Vera Katz (till Jan. 1997)
1992 population est.: 458,275
1990 census population, sex, & (rank): 437,319 (30); **% change,** 18.8; **Male,** 211,914; **Female,** 225,405; **White,** 370,135; **Black,** 33,530 (7.7%); **American Indian, Eskimo, or Aleut,** 5,399 (1.2%); **Asian or Pacific Islander,** 23,185 (5.3%); **Other race,** 5,070; **Hispanic origin,** 13,874 (3.2%). **1990 percent population under 18:** 21.9; **65 and over,** 14.6; **median age:** 34.5.
Land area: 138.8 sq mi. (357 sq km.); **Alt.:** Highest, 1073 ft; lowest, sea level
Avg. daily temp.: Jan., 38.9° F; July, 67.7° F
Churches: Protestant, 450; Roman Catholic, 48; Jewish, 9; Buddhist, 6; other, 190; **City-owned parks:** 200 (over 9,400 ac.); **Radio stations:** AM: 14, FM: 14; **Television stations:** 5 commercial, 1 public
CIVILIAN LABOR FORCE: 248,724; **Unemployed:** 18,372, **Percent:** 7.4; **Per capita personal income:** $18,163[1]
Chamber of Commerce: Portland Chamber of Commerce, 221 NW 2nd Ave., Portland, Ore. 97209
1. PMSA.

Portland, the largest city in Oregon and seat of Multnomah county, is located in the northwestern part of the state on the Willamette River.

Lewis and Clark camped at the site of Portland in 1805 on their expedition across the continent. Portland was founded in 1845 and was almost called Boston after the city in Massachusetts. Its two founders, Amos Lovejoy from Massachusetts and Francis Pettygrove from Maine, flipped a coin to decide the name of the new town. Pettygrove won the toss and named the place Portland after his hometown in Maine. Portland was incorporated as a city in 1851.

Portland's growth was stimulated during the 1850s as a supply base for the California gold rush, the development of its salmon and lumber industries, and by the arrival of the railroad in 1883. The city continued to grow during 1879 to 1900 as a supply point for the Alaska gold rush and as the site of the Lewis and Clark Centennial Exposition in 1905.

The Port of Portland leads the west in grain exports and is among the top five auto import centers in the United States. The Port ranks third in overall volume behind Los Angeles and Long Beach.

Portland has a diverse economy with a broad base of manufacturing, distribution, wholesale and retail trade, regional government, and business services. Major manufacturing industries include machinery, electronics, metals, transportation equipment, and lumber and wood products. High technology is a thriving part of Portland's economy with over 500 high tech companies located in the metropolitan area. Tourism is also important to Portland's economy.

Famous natives: James Beard, food expert; Pietro Belluschi, architect; Richard Fosbury, high jumper; Matt Groening, cartoonist; Margaux Hemingway, actress; Phil Knight, founder of Nike; Terrance Knox, actor; Jeff Lorber, jazz musician; Linus Pauling, chemist; Jane Powell, singer, actress; Ahmad Rashad, football player, sportscaster; Susan Ruttan, actress; Pat Schroeder, congressperson; Doc Severinson, band leader; Norton Simon, business executive; Sally Ann Struthers, actress; Gus Van Sant, film director; Lindsay Wagner, actress; Mitch Williams, baseball pitcher

SACRAMENTO, CALIF.

Mayor: Joe Serna, Jr.
1992 population est.: 391,122; **1990 census population, sex, & (rank):** 369,365 (41); **% change,** 34.0; **Male,** 178,737; **Female,** 190,628; **White,** 221,963; **Black,** 56,521 (15.3%); **American Indian, Eskimo, or Aleut,** 4,561 (1.2%); **Asian or Pacific Islander,** 55,426 (15.0%); **Other race,** 30,894; **Hispanic origin,** 60,007 (16.2%). **1990 percent population under 18:** 26.2; **65 and over,** 12.1; **median age:** 31.8.
Land area: 98 sq mi. (254 sq km);
Avg. daily temp.: Jan., 47.1° F; July, 76.6° F
City park & recreational facilities: 131+ (1,427+ ac.); **Television stations:** 7
CIVILIAN LABOR FORCE: 185,885; **Unemployed:** 17,484, **Percent:** 9.4; **Per capita personal income:** $18,299; **Chamber of Commerce:** Sacramento Chamber of Commerce, 917 7th St., Sacramento, Calif. 95814; West Sacramento Chamber of Commerce, 834-C Jefferson Blvd., Sacramento, Calif. 95691

Sacramento is the capital and seventh largest city in California and is the seat of Sacramento county. It is located in the north central part of the state at the confluence of the Sacramento and American Rivers.

In 1839, German-born Swiss citizen John Augustus Sutter obtained a grant from the Mexican governor to establish a colony for fellow Swiss emigrants on a large tract of land in the vicinity which he named New Helvetia (New Switzerland) and established Fort Sutter there as a trading post.

After gold was discovered on Sutter's property in 1848, the settlement rapidly expanded as the prominent supply point for gold prospectors coming from the East. Sacramento was laid out in 1848 and named after the principal river in California which ran beside it. The river's name in Spanish honors the Holy Sacrament. It became incorporated as a city in 1849 and was made the state capital in 1854. Sacramento was the terminus of the first railroad in 1856 and the western terminus of the Pony Express in 1860.

The city has always been a hub of river transportation and is a major deep-water port connected to the Pacific Ocean. Sacramento's economy is highly diversified and, along with state government and military installations, its industries include aerospace, high technology, furniture, chemicals, pharmaceuticals, meat packing, and food processing of crops from the Central Valley.

The defense sector of the economy is declining and Mather Air Force Base and the Army Depot are scheduled for closure a few years from now.

Famous natives: Joan Didion, author; Mark Goodson, TV producer; Henry Hathaway, director; Anthony M. Kennedy, Supreme Court justice; Molly Ringwald, actress

ST. LOUIS, MO.

Mayor: Freeman Boskly, Jr. (to April 1997)
1990 census population, sex, & (rank): 396,685 (34); **% change,** –12.4; **Male,** 180,680; **Female,** 216,005; **White,** 202,085; **Black,** 188,408 (47.5%); **American Indian, Eskimo, or Aleut,** 950 (0.2%); **Asian or Pacific Islander,** 3,733 (0.9%); **Other race,** 1,509; **Hispanic origin,** 5,124 (1.3%). **1990 percent population under 18:** 25.2; **65 and over:** 16.6; **median age:** 32.8.
Land area: 61.4 sq mi. (159 sq km); **Alt.:** Highest, 616 ft; lowest, 413
Avg. daily temp.: Jan., 28.8° F; July, 78.9° F
Churches: 900[1]; **City-owned parks:** 89 (2,639 ac.); **Radio stations:** AM, 21; FM 27[1]; **Television stations:** 6 commercial; 1 PBS
CIVILIAN LABOR FORCE: 179,278; **Unemployed:** 14,379, **Percent:** 8.0; **Per capita personal income:** $18,957[2]

Chamber of Commerce: St. Louis Regional Commerce and Growth Association, 100 S. Fourth St., Ste. 500, St. Louis, Mo. 63102

1. Metropolitan area. 2. St. Louis, Mo.–Ill. MSA.

St. Louis, the second largest city in Missouri, is located in the east central part of the state on the Mississippi River. The city is independent and is in no county.

St. Louis was founded by the French in 1764 when Auguste Chouteau established a fur-trading post and Pierre Laclède Liguest, a New Orleans merchant, founded a town in February 1764 at the present site of the city and named it after King Louis XV of France and his patron saint, Louis IX of France. From 1770 to 1803, St. Louis was a Spanish possession and retroceded to France in 1803 in accordance with the Treaty of San Ildefonso (1800), only to be acquired by the U.S. as part of the Louisiana purchase that year.

The town was incorporated in 1809. From 1812 to 1821, St. Louis was the capital of the Missouri Territory and was incorporated as a city in 1822.

John Jacob Astor opened the Western branch of the American Fur Company in 1819 and the city prospered during the early part of the 19th century as a center for the transportation of the fur trade. St. Louis's commercial growth continued as a major transportation hub with the development of steamboat traffic and the later expansion of the railroads in the 1850s. The world-famous Louisiana Purchase Exposition was held here in 1904.

Manufacturing is important to the city's economy, and its highly developed industries include automobiles, aircraft and space technology, metal fabrication, beer, steelmaking, chemicals, food processing, and storage and distribution.

The giant stainless steel Gateway Arch, 630 feet high, standing on the banks of the Mississippi symbolizes St. Louis as the Gateway to the West.

Famous natives: Josephine Baker, singer; Yogi Berra, baseball player; Grace Bumbry, mezzo-soprano; Morris Carnovsky, actor; T.S. Eliot, poet; Eugene Field, poet; Redd Foxx, comedian; Joe Garagiola, baseball player; John Goodman, actor; Betty Grable, actress; Dick Gregory, comedian; Al Hirschfeld, cartoonist; Kevin Kline, actor; David Merrick, producer; Vincent Price, actor; Judy Rankin, golfer; Leon Spinks, boxer; Herbert Bayard Swope, journalist; Sara Teasdale, peot; Helen Traubel, soprano; Roy Wilkins, civil rights leader

SAN ANTONIO, TEX.

Mayor: Nelson Wolff (to May 1995)
City Manager: Alexander E. Briseno (apptd. April 27, 1990)
1990 census population, sex, & (rank): 935,933 (10); **% change,** 19.1; **Male,** 450,695; **Female,** 485,238; **White,** 676,082; **Black,** 65,884 (7.0%); **American Indian, Eskimo, or Aleut,** 3,303 (0.4%); **Asian or Pacific Islander,** 10,703 (1.1%); **Other race,** 179,961; **Hispanic origin,** 520,282 (55.6%). **1990 percent population under 18:** 29.0; **65 and over:** 10.5; **median age:** 29.8.
Land area: 342.17 sq mi. (889.6 sq km); **Alt.:** 700 ft
Avg. daily temp.: Jan., 50.4° F; July, 84.6° F
City-owned parks: Approximately 6,536 ac.; **Radio stations:** AM, 21; FM, 20; **Television stations:** 9
CIVILIAN LABOR FORCE: 449,773; **Unemployed:** 33,207, **Percent:** 7.4; **Per capita personal income:** $14,144
Chamber of Commerce: Greater San Antonio Chamber of Commerce, P.O. Box 1628, 602 E Commerce, San Antonio, Tex. 78296

San Antonio, the third largest city in Texas and seat of Bexar county, is located in the south central part of the state, on the San Antonio River.

The site of San Antonio was first visited in 1691 by a Franciscan friar on the feast day of St. Anthony and was named San Antonio de Padua in his honor. San Antonio was permanently settled on May 1, 1718, when the Spanish governor of Coahuila and Texas, Martin de Alarcón, founded the presidio (a fort) of San Antonio de Bejar (Bexar) and the mission of San Antonio de Valero (later called the Alamo[1]) on the site of a Coahuiltecan Indian village. San Antonio remained almost continuously under Spanish rule until 1812 when Mexico won its independence from Spain.

During the outbreak of the Texas revolution (1835) against the tyranny of Mexican dictator General Santa Anna, San Antonio was captured by a small band of rebels who occupied the fortified mission of the Alamo in December 1835. The historic battle of the Alamo was fought there (Feb. 24 to March 6, 1836) and its 183 besieged defenders were massacred by Santa Anna's troops. Their heroism aroused the anger and fighting spirit of Texans to shout their famous battle cry "Remember the Alamo!" and defeat the Mexicans six weeks later (April 21, 1836) at the battle of San Jacinto. Texas became an independent republic in 1836 and San Antonio was incorporated as a city on Jan. 5, 1837.

After the Civil War, San Antonio prospered as a major shipping point for cattle with the arrival of the railroad in 1877. The city has been an important military center since World War II and is the home to five of the largest military installations in the nation, including Fort Sam Houston constructed in 1876. San Antonio is a leading livestock center and one of the largest produce exchange markets. The city's industries are highly diversified and tourism is important to the economy.

1. Spanish for the cottonwood tree.

Famous natives: Carol Burnett, comedienne; Joan Crawford, actress; Cito Gaston, baseball manager; Ann Harding, actress; Oliver North, military officer, government official; Suzy Parker, model, actress; Paula Prentiss, actress; Kyle Rote, football player; David R. Scott, astronaut; John Silber, university president; Edward H. White, astronaut

SAN DIEGO, CALIF.

Mayor: Susan Golding
City Manager: Jack McGrory (apptd. April 1991)
1990 census population, sex, & (rank): 1,110,549 (6); **% change,** 26.8; **Male,** 566,464; **Female,** 544,085; **White,** 745,406; **Black,** 104,261 (9.4%); **American Indian, Eskimo, or Aleut,** 6,800 (0.6%); **Asian or Pacific Islander,** 130,945 (11.8%); **Other race,** 123,137; **Hispanic origin,** 229,519 (20.7%). **1990 percent population under 18:** 23.1; **65 and over:** 10.2; **median age:** 30.5.
Land area: 330.7 sq miles (857 sq km); **Alt.:** Highest, 1,591 ft; lowest, sea level
Avg. daily temp.: Jan., 56.8° F; July, 70.3° F
Churches: Roman Catholic, 39; Jewish, 9; Protestant, 334; Eastern Orthodox, 8; other, 18; **City park and recreation facilities:** 164 (17,207 ac.); **Radio stations:** AM, 8; FM, 18; **Television stations:** 9
CIVILIAN LABOR FORCE: 548,687; **Unemployed:** 41,301, **Percent:** 7.5; **Per capita personal income:** $18,651
Chamber of Commerce: San Diego Chamber of Commerce, 402 West Broadway, Suite 1000, San Diego, Calif. 92101

San Diego is the second largest city in California. It is located in the southwestern part of the state, on San Diego Bay.

Portuguese navigator Juan Rodríguez Cabrillo discovered the bay in 1542 and claimed the area for Spain. The site was named San Miguel by Cabrillo. On Nov. 12, 1602, Don Sebastian de Viscaíno came ashore with his party on the day of St. Didacus (San Diego in Spanish) and celebrated a mass in the saint's honor. By coincidence, Viscaíno's flagship was named *San Diego*. He renamed the place San Diego after the 15th century saint.

In 1769, Franciscan Father Junípero Serra established the first California mission there—San Diego del Alcala. In 1822, Mexico won control of the town after it declared its independence from Spain. In 1846, during the Mexican War, San Diego was seized by the United States and incorporated into a city in 1850 after California joined the Union that same year.

Today, San Diego's excellent natural harbor is a busy commercial port and a hub of U.S. naval operations. However, the naval training center at San Diego is slated to be closed due to defense cutbacks. Other leading industries are electronics, aerospace and missiles, medical and scientific research, oceanography, and agriculture. Its magnificent climate and proximity to Mexico have made tourism a significant part of the city's economy.

Famous natives: Billy Casper, golfer; Florence Chadwick, swimmer; Dennis Conner, yacht racer; Ted Danson, actor; Robert Duvall, actor; Nanette Fabray, actress; Robert Lansing, actor; Margaret O'Brien, actress; Carol Vaness, soprano; Ted Williams, baseball player; Mickey Wright, golfer

SAN FRANCISCO, CALIF.

Mayor: Frank Jordan (to Jan. 1996)

1990 census population, sex, & (rank): 723,959 (14); **% change,** 6.6; **Male,** 362,497; **Female,** 361,462; **White,** 387,783; **Black,** 79,039 (10.9%); **American Indian, Eskimo, or Aleut,** 3,456 (0.5%); **Asian or Pacific Islander,** 210,876 (29.1%); **Other race,** 42,805; **Hispanic origin,** 100,717 (13.9%). **1990 percent population under 18:** 16.1; **65 and over:** 14.6; **median age:** 35.8.

Land area: 46.1 sq mi. (120 sq km); **Alt.:** Highest, 925 ft; lowest, sea level

Avg. daily temp.: Jan., 48.5° F; July, 62.2° F

Churches: 540 of all denominations; **City-owned parks and squares:** 225; **Radio stations:** 29; **Television stations:** 10

CIVILIAN LABOR FORCE: 396,584[1]; **Unemployed:** 27,795[1], **Percent:** 7.0[1]; **Per capita personal income:** $28,170[2]

Chamber of Commerce: Greater San Francisco Chamber of Commerce, 465 California St., San Francisco, Calif. 94104

1. San Francisco City/County. 2. PMSA.

San Francisco, the fourth largest city in California, is coextensive with San Francisco county. It is located in the northern part of the state between the Pacific Ocean and San Francisco Bay. A narrow arm of land embraces San Francisco Bay, the largest landlocked harbor in the world, and shelters it from the Pacific Ocean. On this arm of land is San Francisco, a city on hills, almost surrounded by water.

A Franciscan father who was sailing with Sebastián Rodríguez Cermeño named the bay San Francisco on Nov. 7, 1595. In 1776, the Spaniards established a presidio, or military post, and a Franciscan mission on the end of the beautiful peninsula. In the following year, a little town called Yerba Buena, Spanish for "Good Herb," because mint grew in abundance, was founded around the mission.

In 1846, during the Mexican War, Yerba Buena was taken over by the United States. It was renamed San Francisco in 1847 and became incorporated as a city in 1850.

When gold was discovered in California in 1848, the city's population jumped to 10,000, and it experienced turbulent years until order was established by Vigilance Committees, first in 1851, and again in 1856. Then followed a period of more orderly growth and the foundations of the great commerce and industry of today were laid.

In 1906, San Francisco experienced the nation's worst earthquake which, together with the fire that followed, practically destroyed the city. The city was quickly rebuilt and grew rapidly as a leading transportation, industrial, and cultural center. In the 19th century, the American explorer and soldier, John C. Frémont, known as The Pathfinder, named the entrance to the bay, the Golden Gate, and the famous bright orange Golden Gate Bridge was dedicated in May 1937.

San Francisco's outstanding port, together with the San Francisco Bay area, is the largest seaport on the Pacific Coast and trade with the Pacific Rim countries accounts for about two-thirds of general cargo through the Port of San Francisco.

San Francisco inspires entrepreneurs to start their own businesses, and small businesses have a very important place in the economy. More than90% of the city's 33,800 businesses have fewer than 15 employees. The high-tech industries of electronics and biotechnology are well represented throughout the Bay Area. With nearly 30% of the worldwide biotechnology labor force, the Bay Area has been appropriately called "Bionic Bay." Tourism is one of San Francisco's largest industries and the largest employer of city residents. Nearly 8.2 million persons visit San Francisco each year and spend an average of $10 million per day.

The military has played an important role in the San Francisco and the Bay Area's economy, but its impact will decline due to defense cutbacks.

San Francisco is also the banking and financial center of the West and is home to a Federal Reserve Bank and a United States Mint. More than 60 foreign banks maintain offices there.

Famous natives: Gracie Allen, comedienne; Luis Walter Alvarez, Nobel Prize in physics; David Belasco, dramatist, producer; Mel Blanc, actor, voice specialist; Rosemary Casals, tennis player; Isadora Duncan, dancer; Clint Eastwood, actor; Robert Frost, poet; Rube Goldberg, cartoonist; William Randolph Hearst, publisher; Bruce Lee, actor; Mervyn LeRoy, director; Jack London, novelist; Johnny Mathis, singer; Lloyd Nolan, actor; O.J. Simpson, football player; Robert G. Sproul, educator; Irving Stone, novelist; Natalie Wood, actress

SAN JOSE, CALIF.

Mayor: Susan Hammer (to Dec. 31, 1994)

City Manager: Leslie R. White (apptd. May 1989)

1993 population (est): 822,013

1990 census population, sex, & (rank): 782,248 (11); **% change,** 24.3; **Male,** 397,709; **Female,** 384,539; **White,** 491,280; **Black,** 36,790 (4.7%); **American Indian, Eskimo, or Aleut,** 5,416 (0.7%); **Asian or Pacific Islander,** 152,815 (19.5%); **Other race,** 95,947; **Hispanic origin,** 208,388 (26.6%). **1990 percent population under 18:** 26.7; **65 and over:** 7.2; **median age:** 30.4.

Land area: 173.6 sq mi. (450 sq km); **Alt.:** Highest, 4,372 ft.; lowest, sea level

Avg. daily temp.: Jan., 49.5° F; July, 68.8° F
Churches: 403; **City-owned parks and playgrounds:** 152 (3,136 ac.); **Radio stations:** 14; **Television stations:** 4
CIVILIAN LABOR FORCE: 420,686; **Unemployed:** 33,484, **Percent:** 8.0; **Per capita personal income:** $24,581[1]
Chamber of Commerce: San Jose Chamber of Commerce, One Paseo de San Antonio, San Jose, Calif. 95113
1. PMSA.

San Jose, the third largest city in California and seat of Santa Clara county, is located in the western part of the state in the Santa Clara Valley on the South San Francisco Bay, 50 miles south of downtown San Francisco.

San Jose was founded on Nov. 29, 1777, by Spanish colonizers who named the settlement Pueblo de San José de Guadalupe in honor of Saint Joseph and after the Guadalupe River on which the pueblo (town) was situated. The town was the first city to be established in California.

After California became a U.S. territory in 1847, San Jose became the first state capital from December 1849 to 1852 and was incorporated as a city in 1850. The city developed commercially as a supply base for gold prospectors and, when the railroad connected it with San Francisco in 1864, it became the distribution point for agricultural products from the Santa Clara Valley.

Today, the city continues to be the distribution and food-processing center for the surrounding rich agricultural region producing seasonal fruits and grapes. More than 50 wineries grace the Valley.

Computers are big business here and San Jose is the capital of Silicon Valley (Santa Clara), the nation's center of high technology where more than 3,000 high tech companies are located. Silicon Valley is also one of the world's leading centers for medical treatment and research. Heart transplants, gene splicing, and transportable baby incubators were developed there.

San Jose has healthy retail, transportation, and tourism industries as well and is the primary center for real estate and industrial development in the area.

Famous natives: "Fatty" Arbuckle, actor; Chuck Berry, singer, guitarist; Cesar Chavez, labor leader; Peggy Fleming, figure skater; Farley Granger, actor; Edmund Lowe, actor; Jim Plunkett, football player

SEATTLE, WASH.

Mayor: Norman B. Rice (to Dec. 31, 1993)
1990 census population, sex, & (rank): 516,259 (21); **% change,** 4.5; **Male,** 252,042; **Female,** 264,217; **White,** 388,858; **Black,** 51,948 (10.1%); **American Indian, Eskimo, or Aleut,** 7,326 (1.4%); **Asian or Pacific Islander,** 60,819 (11.8%); **Other race,** 7,308; **Hispanic origin,** 18,349 (3.6%). **1990 percent population under 18:** 16.5; **65 and over:** 15.2; **median age:** 34.9.
Land area: 144.6 sq mi. (375 sq km); **Alt.:** Highest, 540 ft; lowest, sea level
Avg. daily temp.: Jan., 40.6° F; July, 65.3° F
Churches: Roman Catholic, 36; Jewish, 13; Protestant and others, 535; **City-owned parks, playgrounds, etc.:** 278 (4,773.4 ac.); **Radio stations:** AM, 22; FM, 26; **Television stations:** 3 commercial; 1 educational
CIVILIAN LABOR FORCE: 311,437; **Unemployed:** 22,190, **Percent:** 7.1; **Per capita personal income:** $21,137[1]
Chamber of Commerce: Seattle Chamber of Commerce, 1200 One Union Square, Seattle, Wash. 98101
1. PMSA.

Seattle is the largest city in Washington and the seat of King county. A city of steep hills, Seattle lies in western Washington between two bodies of water—Puget Sound on the west and Lake Washington on the east. Its fine land-locked harbor has made Seattle one of the major ports in the United States.

Seattle was first settled by five pioneer families from Illinois at Alki Point at the south end of Elliott Bay in 1851. They moved in 1852 to the eastern shore of the bay and laid out a town in 1853. It was named Seattle after a friendly Suquamish Indian Chief (Seattle is only an approximation of his name).

Seattle successfully withstood an Indian attack in 1856 and was incorporated as a city in 1869. A disastrous fire almost destroyed the entire business district in 1889. When the Great Northern Railway arrived in 1893, the city became a major rail terminus and it grew rapidly. It was a boom town during the Alaska gold rush of 1897 and continued to prosper as a major Pacific port of entry with the opening of the Panama Canal in 1914.

Seattle is the region's commercial and transportation hub and the center of manufacturing, trade, and finance. Its important diversified industries include aircraft, lumber and forest products, fishing, food processing, boat building, machinery, fabricated metals, chemicals, pharmaceuticals, and apparel.

Famous natives: Chester Carlson, Xerox inventor; Carol Channing, actress; Judy Collins, singer; Fred Couples, golfer; Gail Devers, athlete; Frances Farmer, actress; William Gates, corporation executive; June Havoc, actress; Jimi Hendrix, guitarist; Robert Joffrey, choreographer; Gypsy Rose Lee, entertainer; Mary Livingstone, comedienne; Kevin McCarthy, actor; Mary McCarthy, novelist; Jeff Smith, food expert; Martha Wright, singer

TOLEDO, OHIO

Mayor: John McHugh (to Dec. 1993)
City Manager: Thomas R. Hoover
1990 census population, sex, & (rank): 332,943 (49); **% change,** –6.1; **Male,** 157,941; **Female,** 175,002; **White,** 256,239; **Black,** 65,598 (19.7%); **Americn Indian, Eskimo, or Aleut,** 920 (0.3%); **Asian or Pacific Islander,** 3,487 (1.0%); **Other race,** 6,699; **Hispanic origin,** 13,207 (4.0%). **1990 percent population under 18:** 26.2; **65 and over:** 13.6; **median age:** 31.7.
Land area: 84.2 sq mi. (218 sq km); **Alt.:** 630 ft
Avg. daily temp.: Jan., 23.1° F; July, 71.8° F
Churches: Protestant, 301; Roman Catholic, 55; Jewish, 4; others, 98; **City-owned parks and playgrounds:** 134 (2,650.90 ac.); **Radio stations:** AM, 8; FM, 8; **Television stations:** 6
CIVILIAN LABOR FORCE: 161,168; **Unemployed:** 15,660, **Percent:** 9.7; **Per capita personal income:** $16,893
Chamber of Commerce: Toledo Area Chamber of Commerce, 218 Huron St., Toledo, Ohio 43604

Toledo, the fourth largest city in Ohio and seat of Lucas county, is located in the northwestern part of the state on the Maumee River at Lake Erie.

The first European to visit the area was the French explorer Étienne Brulé in 1615. The first white settlement in the area was at Fort Industry built by Gen. "Mad Anthony" Wayne in 1794, after he defeated the Indians at the Battle of Fallen Timbers fought nearby. The village of Port Lawrence was established next to the fort in 1817 and the village of Vistula was established nearby in 1832. The two villages were united in 1833 and named Toledo after the city in Spain. They became incorporated as a city in 1837.

Both Michigan and Ohio claimed the Toledo area which at the time was part of Michigan Territory. The bloodless dispute (Toledo War of 1835) was settled by Congress which awarded the city to Ohio. In return, Michigan received the Upper Peninsula and admission to the Union.

The city developed as a transportation center with the arrival of the railroad in 1836 and the opening of canals in the 1840s. It continued to prosper with the development of the Ohio coalfields, the tapping of gas and oil deposits, and the establishment of the glassworks by Edward Libbey in 1888.

Toledo is a leading commercial and manufacturing center and a major Great Lakes port. Total annual tonnage through the Port of Toledo ranges from 10 to 15 million tons and includes three distinct types of cargo: coal and iron ore, grain, and a wide range of general cargoes.

Toledo is the home of numerous major corporate headquarters and has 13 financial institutions in the area. Major diversified manufacturing industries include Jeeps, glass and plastic containers, fiberglass, automotive components, petroleum refining, coal products, and natural gas distribution. Other important industries are printing and publishing, food products, furniture, and fabricated metal products.

Famous natives: Cliff Arquette, actor; Anita Baker, singer; Teresa Brewer, singer; Jamie Farr, actor; Otto Kruger, actor; Herb Shriner, humorist; Gloria Steinem, feminist

TUCSON, ARIZ.

Mayor: George Miller (to Dec. 1995)
1990 census population, sex, & (rank): 405,390 (33); **% change,** 22.6; **Male,** 197,319; **Female,** 208,071; **White,** 305,055; **Black,** 17,366 (4.3%); **American Indian, Eskimo, or Aleut,** 6,464 (1.6%); **Asian or Pacific Islander,** 8,901 (2.2%); **Other race,** 67,604; **Hispanic origin,** 118,595 (29.3%). **1990 percent population under 18:** 24.5; **65 and over:** 12.6; **median age:** 30.6.
Land area: 156.04 sq mi. (404 sq km); **Alt.:** 2,400 ft
Avg. daily temp.: Jan., 51.1° F; July, 86.2° F
Churches: Protestant, 340; Roman Catholic, 42; other, 150; **City-owned parks and parkways:** (25,349 ac.); **Radio stations:** AM, 16; FM, 11; **Television stations:** 3 commercial; 1 educational; 3 other
CIVILIAN LABOR FORCE: 200,298; **Unemployed:** 11,577, **Percent:** 5.8; **Per capita personal income:** $17,103
Chamber of Commerce: Tucson Metropolitan Chamber of Commerce, P.O. Box 991, Tucson, Ariz. 85702

Tucson is the second largest city in Arizona and the seat of Pima county. It is located in the southeastern part of the state on the Santa Cruz River.

The site was originally settled by the prehistoric Hohokam Indians (300 B.C.–1400s A.D.). The first Europeans to visit the area were Spanish missionaries in the 17th century. In 1700, the Jesuit missionary explorer Father Eusebio Francisco Kino founded the mission of San Xavier del Bac close by the Papago Indian village of Stjukshon (later called Tucson). Stjukshon is an Indian word meaning "village of the dark spring at the foot of the mountain." The Papago Indians are descendants of the ancient Hohakam peoples.

In 1776, Spanish colonists from Mexico constructed a presidio (fort) at Tucson as protection against the hostile Apache Indians and also established the mission of San Jose de Tucson nearby. Tucson remained a military outpost under Spanish rule and later Mexican control until the area was sold to the United States as part of the Gadsden Purchase in 1853. Tucson was the capital of the Arizona Territory from 1867 to 1877. It was incorporated as a city in 1877. The town grew rapidly when the Southern Pacific Railroad arrived in 1880 and silver and copper deposits were discovered nearby.

Tucson is a popular vacation and health resort due to its sunny, mild, and dry climate and unique desert location. Tourism is important to the city's economy. Major industries are aerospace and missile production, high technology, and electronics. Tucson is also the commercial center for the surrounding area's agriculture and mining industries.

Famous natives: Rose E. Bird, jurist; Dennis De Concini, senator; Barbara Eden, actress; Linda Ronstadt, singer

TULSA, OKLA.

Mayor: M. Susan Savage (to May 1994)
1990 census population, sex, & (rank): 367,302 (43); **% change,** 1.8; **Male,** 175,538; **Female,** 191,764; **White,** 291,444; **Black,** 49,825 (13.6%); **American Indian, Eskimo, or Aleut,** 17,091 (4.7%); **Asian or Pacific Islander,** 5,133 (1.4%); **Other race,** 3,809; **Hispanic origin,** 9,564 (2.6%). **1990 percent population under 18:** 24.4; **65 and over:** 12.7; **median age:** 33.1.
Land area: 192.24 sq mi. (499 sq km); **Alt.:** 674 ft
Avg. daily temp.: Jan., 35.2° F; July, 83.2° F
Churches: Protestant, 593; Roman Catholic, 32; Jewish, 2; others, 4; **City parks and playgrounds:** 121 (6,050 ac.); **Radio stations:** AM, 7; FM, 15; **Television stations:** 7 commercial; 1 PBS; 1 cable
CIVILIAN LABOR FORCE: 184,297; **Unemployed:** 10,935, **Percent:** 5.9; **Per capita personal income:** $16,016
Chamber of Commerce: Metropolitan Tulsa Chamber of Commerce, 616 S Boston, Tulsa, Okla. 74119

Tulsa, the second largest city in Oklahoma and seat of Tulsa county, is located in the northeastern part of the state on the Arkansas River.

Tulsa was settled in the 1830s by Creek Indians from Alabama who were forcibly sent to the area (then part of Indian Territory) under the Indian Removal Act of 1830. Creek medicine-men planted ashes from their old home at the new site and the Creeks named their new village "Tulsy" meaning old town in memory of their former home in Tallassee, Alabama. In time, the village became the town of Tulsa.

The coming of the first railroad in 1882 attracted white settlers to Tulsa and the town developed into a cattle shipping center. When enormous oil deposits were discovered at nearby Red Fork in 1901 and at Glenn Pool in 1905, the city experienced rapid growth as a center of a booming petroleum industry. Tulsa was incorporated as a city in 1898 and chartered in 1908.

Tulsa is the center of the state's petroleum industry and has a diversified economy. Important industries include aerospace, chemicals, computer parts, automobile glass, fabricated metals, and industrial machinery. The city became a major inland port when the Tulsa Port of Catoosa opened in 1971. It is the national headquarters of the U.S. Junior Chamber of Commerce (Jaycees).

Famous natives: Garth Brooks, singer; Blake Edwards, director; Paul Harvey, commentator; Jennifer Jones, actress; Henry R. Kravis, investment banker; Daniel Patrick Moynihan, senator; Rony Randall, actor; Alfre Woodard, actress; Judy Woodruff, journalist

VIRGINIA BEACH, VA.

Mayor: Meyera E. Obendorf (to June 30, 1996)
1993 population: 410,607
1990 census population, sex, & (rank): 393,069 (37); **% change,** 49.9; **Male,** 199,571; **Female,** 193,498; **White,** 316,408; **Black,** 54,671 (13.9%); **American Indian, Eskimo, or Aleut,** 1,384 (0.4%); **Asian or Pacific Islander,** 17,025 (4.3%); **Other race,** 3,581; **Hispanic origin,** 12,137 (3.1%); **1990 percent population under 18:** 28.0; **65 and over:** 5.9; **median age:** 28.9.
Land area: 258.7 sq mi. (670 sq km); **Alt.:** 12 ft
Avg. daily temp.: Jan., 39.9° F; July, 78.4° F
Churches: Protestant, 159; Catholic, 8; Jewish, 4; **City-owned parks:** 182 (1,748 ac.); **Radio stations:** AM 18, FM 26; **Television stations:** 4 commercial, 1 PBS, 1 cable
CIVILIAN LABOR FORCE: 194,579; **Unemployed:** 11,541, **Percent:** 5.9; **Per capita personal income:** $15,721[1]
Chamber of Commerce: Hampton Roads Chamber of Commerce, 4512 Virginia Beach Blvd., Virginia Beach, Va., 23456

1. Norfolk-Virginia Beach-Newport News MSA.

Virginia Beach, the largest city in Virginia, is located in the southeasternmost portion of the state on the Atlantic coastline. It is independent and is not part of any county.

The first English settlers to set foot in America landed at Cape Henry at the tip of Virginia Beach on April 29, 1607. They were led by John Smith on his way to establishing Jamestown. The first permanent settlement within the city limits was made at Lynnhaven Bay in 1621. Cape Henry became an important port for British merchant ships calling on America, and it was here that the French Fleet led by Admiral Comte de Grasse blockaded the British Fleet during the American Revolution.

Virginia Beach gained its reputation as a famous vacation resort in the 19th century, following the building of a railroad connecting its oceanfront with Norfolk and the construction of its first hotel in 1883. Virginia Beach was incorporated as a town in 1906 and as a city in 1952. In 1963, Princess Anne County and Virginia Beach merged and gave the present city an area of 310 square miles of oceanfront.

Tourism is the mainstay of the economy and 2.5 million people visit Virginia Beach overnight each year. Four nearby military bases contribute to the city's employment and economy. There are 165 farms in the city and agribusiness is also an important industry. Diversified industries include computer software and engineering and technical services.

Famous natives and residents: V.C. Andrews, novelist; Raymond Brian Buckland, occult writer; Edgar Cayce, psychic; Ann Woodruff Compton, news correspondent; D.J. Dozier, football and baseball player; George Eastman, inventor; Scott McKenzie, singer; Juice Newton, singer; Kenneth S. Reightler, Jr., astronaut; Pat Robertson, evangelist; Grace Sherwood, accused witch; Henry Walke, naval officer in Mexican and Civil Wars; Pernell "Sweet Pea" Whitaker, boxer; Skip Wilkins, wheelchair athlete

WASHINGTON, D.C.

Created municipal corporation: Feb. 21, 1871
Mayor: Sharon Pratt Dixon (to Jan. 1995)
Motto: *Justitia omnibus* (Justice to all)
Flower: American beauty rose; **Tree:** Scarlet oak
1991 resident population est.: 598,000
1990 census population, sex, & (rank): 606,900 (19); **% change,** –4.9, **Male,** 282,970, **Female,** 323,930, **White,** 179,667, **Black,** 399,604 (65.8%), **American Indian, Eskimo, or Aleut,** 1,466 (0.2%); **Asian or Pacific Islander,** 11,214 (1.8%); **Other race,** 14,949; **Hispanic origin,** 32,710 (5.4%)
Land area: 68.25 sq mi. (177 sq km); **Alt.:** Highest, 420 ft; lowest, sea level
Avg. daily temp.: Jan., 35.2° F; July, 78.9° F
Churches: Protestant, 610; Roman Catholic, 132; Jewish, 9; **City parks:** 753 (7,725 ac.); **Radio stations:** AM, 9; FM, 38; **Television stations:** 19
CIVILIAN LABOR FORCE: 276,000; **Unemployed:** 23,000, **Percent:** 8.4; **Per capita personal income:** $24,845[1]
Board of Trade: Greater Washington Board of Trade, 1129 20th Street, N.W., Washington, D.C. 20036
Chamber of Commerce: D.C. Chamber of Commerce, 1319 F St., NW, Washington, D.C. 20004

1. Washington, D.C.–Md.–Va. MSA.

The District of Columbia—identical with the City of Washington—is the capital of the United States and the first carefully planned capital in the world. It is located between Virginia and Maryland on the Potomac River. The district is named after Columbus.

D.C. history began in 1790 when Congress directed selection of a new capital site, 100 miles square, along the Potomac. When the site was determined, it included 30.75 square miles on the Virginia side of the river. In 1846, however, Congress returned that area to Virginia, leaving the 68.25 square miles ceded by Maryland in 1788. The seat of government was transferred from Philadelphia to Washington on Dec. 1, 1800, and President John Adams became the first resident in the White House.

The city was planned and partly laid out by Major Pierre Charles L'Enfant, a French engineer. This work was perfected and completed by Major Andrew Ellicott and Benjamin Banneker, a freeborn black man, who was an astronomer and mathematician. In 1814, during the War of 1812, a British force fired the capital including the White House.

Until Nov. 3, 1967, the District of Columbia was administered by three commissioners appointed by the President. On that day, a government consisting of a mayor-commissioner and a 9-member Council, all appointed by the President with the approval of the Senate, took office. On May 7, 1974, the citizens of the District of Columbia approved a Home Rule Charter, giving them an elected mayor and 13-member council—their first elected municipal government in more than a century. The District also has one non-voting member in the House of Representatives and an elected Board of Education.

On Aug. 22, 1978, Congress passed a proposed constitutional amendment to give Washington, D.C., voting representation in the Congress. The amendment had to be ratified by at least 28 state legislatures within seven years to become effective. As of 1985 it died.

A petition asking for the District's admission to the Union as the 51st State was filed in Congress on September 9, 1983. The District is continuing this drive for statehood.

The federal government and tourism are the mainstays of the city's economy, and many unions, business, professional and nonprofit organizations are headquartered there.

Famous natives: Edward Albee, playwright; Billie Burke, comedienne; Ina Claire, actress; John Foster Dulles, statesman; Duke Ellington, musician; Jane Greer, actress; Goldie Hawn, actress; Helen Hayes, actress; J. Edgar Hoover, F.B.I. director; William Hurt, actor; Noor al-Hussein, Queen of Jordan; Michael Learned, actress; Roger Mudd, newscaster; Eleanor Holmes Norton, government official; Chita Rivera, dancer, actress; Leonard Rose, cellist; John Philip Sousa, composer; Frances Sternhagen, actress

Tabulated Data on City Governments

City	Mayor: Term, years	Mayor: Salary[1]	City manager's salary[2]	Council or Commission: Name	Members	Term, years	Salary[3]
Albuquerque, N.M.	4	$64,355	—	Council	9	4	$6,435
Atlanta	4	100,000	—	Council	19	4	22,000[27]
Austin, Tex.	3	35,006	113,880	Council	6	3	30,014
Baltimore	4	60,000	—	Council	19	4	29,000[21]
Boston	4	100,000	—	Council	13	2	45,000
Buffalo, N.Y.	4	79,000	—	Council	13	2[5]	41,895
Charlotte, N.C.	2	14,800	118,900	Council	11	2	8,000
Chicago	4	115,000	—	Council	50	4	55,000
Cincinnati	2	46,608	125,000	Council	9	2	43,108
Cleveland	4	90,000	—	Council	21	4	40,093[3]
Columbus, Ohio	4	92,000	—	Council	7	4	25,000[15]
Dallas	2	50[6]	—	Council	15	2	50[6]
Denver	4	90,705	—	Council	13	4	35,196[28]
Detroit	4	130,000	—	Council	9	4	60,000[29]
El Paso	2	25,000	—	Council	7[7]	2	15,000
Fort Worth	2	75[8]	104,000	Council	8	2	75[8]
Fresno, Calif.	4	49,800	120,000	Council	7[7]	4	28,800[23]
Honolulu	4	100,000	84,500	Council	9	4	38,500[3]
Houston	2	133,552	—	Council	14	2	35,614
Indianapolis	4	83,211	—	Council	29	4	14,817[10]
Jacksonville, Fla.	4	100,613	105,000[11]	Council	19	4	24,000[3]
Kansas City, Mo.	4	55,020	101,220	Council	13[7]	4	22,020
Long Beach, Calif.	4	74,438	150,667[25]	Council	9	4	19,837
Los Angeles	4	117,884	166,539[4]	Council	15	4	90,680
Memphis, Tenn.	4	100,000	—	Council	13	4	6,000
Miami, Fla.	4	5,000[13]	140,000	Commission	5	4	5,000
Milwaukee	4	97,661	—	Council	17	4	42,996
Minneapolis	4	71,000	89,915	Council	13	4	52,500
Nashville, Tenn.	4	75,000	—	Council	41	4	5,400
New Orleans	4	88,027	57,900[38]	Council	7	4	42,500
New York	4	130,000	112,000[14]	Council	51	4	55,000[26]
Oakland, Calif.	4	80,012	129,660	Council	9[7]	4	15,280[37]
Oklahoma City	4	2,000	100,000	Council	8	4	20[17]
Omaha, Neb.	4	76,303	—	Council	7	4	20,440[3]
Philadelphia	4	110,000	95,000[18]	Council	17	4	65,000[16]
Phoenix, Ariz.	4	37,500	119,860	Council	9[7]	4	18,000
Pittsburgh	4	72,300	—	Council	9	4	41,339
Portland, Ore.	4	77,938	—	Council	4	4	65,708
Sacramento	4	23,700[30]	118,429	Council	9[12]	4	19,500
St. Louis	4	71,266	—	Board of Aldermen	29	4	18,500[32]
San Antonio	2	3,000[19]	107,000	Council	11[7]	2	20[20]
San Diego, Calif.	4	65,300	126,375	Council	8	4	49,000
San Francisco	4	138,669	137,521[33]	Bd. of Supvrs.	11	4	23,924
San Jose, Calif.	4	80,000[34]	136,529[34]	Council	10	4	52,800[34]
Seattle	4	106,000	—	Council	9	4	67,087[39]
Toledo, Ohio	2	36,000	83,639	Council	9[12]	2	7,800[36]
Tucson, Ariz.	4	24,000	100,000	Council	7[7]	4	12,000
Tulsa, Okla.	4	70,000	—	Council	9	2	12,000
Virginia Beach, Va.	4	20,000	108,000[24]	Council	11	4	18,000
Washington, D.C.	4	90,705	90,605[35]	Council	13	4	71,885[22]

1. Annual salary unless otherwise indicated. 2. Annual salary. City Manager's term is indefinite and at will of Council (or Mayor). 3. Annual salary unless otherwise indicated. In some cities, President of Council receives a higher salary. 4. City Administrative Officer appointed by Mayor, approved by Council. 5. For 9 District Councilmen; 4 years for President and 3 Councilmen-at-Large. 6. Per Council meeting; not over $2,600 per year. 7. Including Mayor. 8. Per week and per Council meeting. 9. Managing Director appointed by Mayor; Council approval required. 10. $9,985 base plus $107 per council meeting (22 scheduled); $62 per committee meeting at a maximum of 40 meetings. President gets $1,982 extra, majority leader gets $1,320 extra and the Chairman gets $797 extra. 11. Chief Administrative Officer appointed by Mayor; not subject to Council confirmation. 12. Including Mayor and Vice-Mayor. 13. Plus expense account. 14. No City Manager; salary is for Deputy Mayors. 15. Per member. President earns $29,993. 16. Per member. President earns $80,000. 17. Per Council meeting; not to exceed 5 meetings a month. 18. Appointed by Mayor, with title of Managing Director. 19. Plus Council pay. 20. Per Council meeting; not over $1,040 per year. 21. Per member. President earns $53,000. 22. Council Chairman receives $81,885. 23. Mayor Pro Tempore, $31,200. 24. Plus $4,000 in travel expenses. 25. Plus $1,200 per month expense account. 26. Council President receives $105,000. 27. Council President earns $25,000; Vice President earns $30,500. 28. Council President receives $44,464. 29. Council President receives $63,000. 30. Plus $4,800 annual expense account, $4,800 annual secretary expense allowance and $4,800 annual vehicle expense allowance. 31. Plus $3,600 annual expense account and $4,800 annual vehicle expense allowance. 32. For 12 Aldermen $18,500, 16 Aldermen $21,460. 33. Chief Administrative Officer. 34. Plus $4,200 annual vehicle expense allowance for Mayor/Council and $6,000 for City Manager. 35. City Administrator/Deputy Mayor for operations. 36. Members of Council get $1,200 per year expense account. 37. Council also serves as the Redevelopment Agency for which there is additional compensation. 38. Minimum entrance base salary reported. 39. Salary is $58,457 for members elected on 1/1/90. *Source: Information Please* questionnaires to the cities.

U.S. Telephone Area Codes and Time Zones

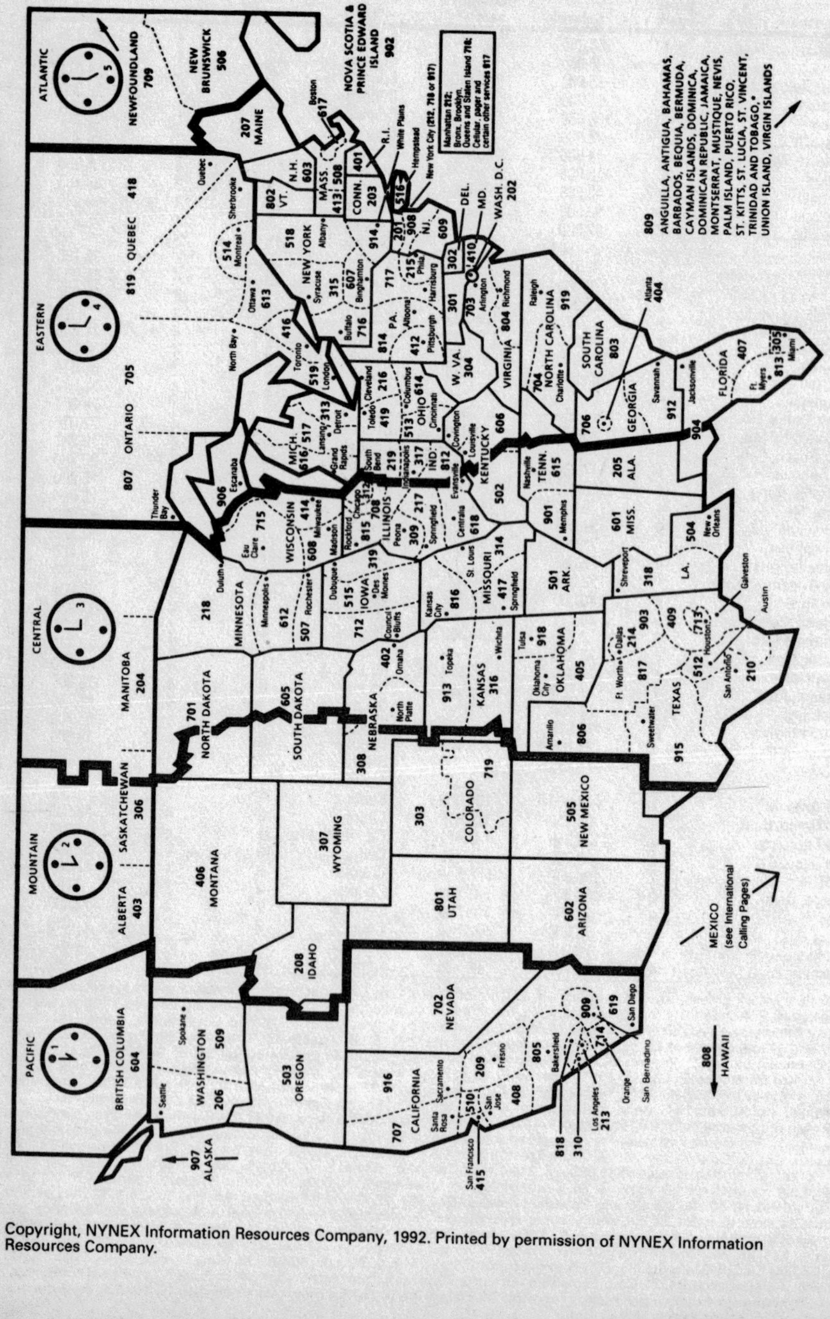

U.S. Cities Over 25,000 Population

Asterisk denotes more than one ZIP code for a city and refers to Postmaster. To find the ZIP code for a particular address, consult the ZIP code directory available in every post office. The ZIP codes printed herein were obtained either from the "National Five-Digit Zip Code & Post Office Directory," published by the U.S. Postal Service or from phone calls made to the postmaster in the areas where they were not listed in the Directory. We have tried to accurately list all the pertinent ZIP codes that were available. If there are any questions regarding the exact ZIP code for a particular street address, you should contact your local post office. NOTE: Census Designated Place (CDP)—A statistical area comprising a densely settled concentration of population that is not incorporated but which resembles an incorporated place in that local people can identify it with a name.

City and major zip code	1990 census	1990 rank
ALABAMA		
Anniston city (36201*)	26,623	1210
Auburn city (36830*)	33,830	904
Bessemer city (35020*)	33,497	921
Birmingham city (35203*)	265,968	60
Decatur city (35601*)	48,761	575
Dothan city (36302*)	53,589	496
Florence city (35630*)	36,426	828
Gadsden city (35902*)	42,523	685
Hoover city (35203*)	39,788	748
Huntsville city (35813*)	159,789	110
Mobile city (36601*)	196,278	79
Montgomery city (36119*)	187,106	86
Phenix City city (36867*)	25,312	1281
Prichard city (36610)	34,311	886
Tuscaloosa city (35401*)	77,759	287
ALASKA		
Anchorage city (99501*)	226,338	69
Fairbanks city (99701*)	30,843	1023
Juneau city (99801)	26,751	1204
ARIZONA		
Chandler city (85225*)	90,533	230
Flagstaff city (86004*)	45,857	627
Gilbert town (85234)	29,188	1090
Glendale city (85301*)	148,134	119
Mesa city (85201*)	288,091	53
Peoria city (85345*)	50,618	547
Phoenix city (85026*)	983,403	9
Prescott city (86301*)	26,455	1220
Scottsdale city (85251*)	130,069	141
Sierra Vista city (85635*)	32,983	938
Sun City CDP (85351*)	38,126	784
Tempe city (85282*)	141,865	124
Tucson city (85726*)	405,390	33
Yuma city (85364*)	54,923	471
ARKANSAS		
Conway city (72032)	26,481	1218
Fayetteville city (72701*)	42,099	694
Fort Smith city (72917*)	72,798	316
Hot Springs city (71901)	32,462	955
Jacksonville city (72076)	29,101	1096
Jonesboro city (72401)	46,535	613
Little Rock city (72231*)	175,795	96
North Little Rock city (72114*)	61,741	403
Pine Bluff city (71601*)	57,140	446
Springdale city (72764*)	29,941	1059
West Memphis city (72301*)	28,259	1132
CALIFORNIA		
Alameda city (94501)	76,459)	292
Alhambra city (91715*)	82,106	271
Altadena CDP (91001*)	42,658	680
Anaheim city (92803*)	266,406	59
Antioch city (94509*)	62,195	395
Apple Valley town (92307*)	46,079	623
Arcadia city (91006*)	48,290	589
Arden-Arcade CDP (95825*)	92,040	228
Azusa city (91702)	41,333	710
Bakersfield city (93380*)	174,820	97
Baldwin Park city (91706)	69,330	343
Bell city (90201)	34,365	885
Bellflower city (90706*)	61,815	401
Bell Gardens city (90201)	42,355	687
Berkeley city (94704*)	102,724	194
Beverly Hills city (90210*)	31,971	974
Brea city (92622*)	32,873	945
Buena Park city (90622*)	68,784	347
Burbank city (91505*)	93,643	221
Burlingame city (94010*)	26,801	1201
Camarillo city (93010*)	52,303	519
Campbell city (95008*)	36,048	839
Carlsbad city (92008*)	63,126	391
Carmichael CDP (95608*)	48,702	579
Carson city (90745*)	83,995	266
Casa de Oro-Mount Helis CDP (91977*)	30,727	1030
Castro Valley CDP (94546)	48,619	582
Cathedral City city (92234*)	30,085	1053
Ceres city (95307)	26,314	1227
Cerritos city (90703)	53,240	503
Chico city (95926*)	40,079	742
Chino city (91710*)	59,682	423
Chino Hills CDP (91710)	27,608	1164
Chula Vista city (92010*)	135,163	133
Citrus Heights CDP (95621)	107,439	183
Claremont city (91711)	32,503	954
Clovis city (93612)	50,323	552
Colton city (92324)	40,213	735
Compton city (90221*)	90,454	231
Concord city (94520*)	111,348	167
Corona city (91720*)	76,095	294
Coronado city (92118*)	26,540	1215
Costa Mesa city (92628*)	96,357	212
Covina city (91722*)	43,207	669
Culver City city (90230*)	38,793	769
Cupertino city (95014*)	40,263	734
Cypress city (90630)	42,655	681
Daly City city (94015*)	92,311	227
Dana Point city (92629)	31,896	978
Danville city (94526*)	31,306	999
Davis city (95616*)	46,209	619
Diamond Bar city (91765)	53,672	494
Downey city (90241*)	91,444	229
East Los Angeles CDP (90055)	126,379	146
El Cajon city (92020*)	88,693	236
El Centro city (92244*)	31,384	997
El Monte city (91731*)	106,209	186
El Toro CDP (92630)	62,685	393
Encinitas city (92024*)	55,386	463
Escondido city (92025*)	108,635	180
Eureka city (95501*)	27,025	1193
Fairfield city (94533)	77,211	289
Fair Oaks CDP (95628)	26,867	1198
Florence-Graham CDP (90052*)	57,147	445
Fontana city (92335*)	87,535	241
Foster City city (94404)	28,176	1137
Fountain Valley city (92708*)	53,691	493
Fremont city (94537*)	173,339	98
Fresno city (93706*)	354,202	47
Fullerton city (92634*)	114,144	160
Folsom city (95630)	29,802	1066

City and major zip code	1990 census	1990 rank
Gardena city (90247*)	49,847	557
Garden Grove city (92642*)	142,050	122
Gilroy city (95020*)	31,487	994
Glendale city (92109*)	180,038	92
Glendora city (91740)	47,828	593
Hacienda Heights CDP (91745)	52,354	515
Hanford city (93230*)	30,897	1020
Hawthorne city (90250*)	71,349	327
Hayward city (94544*)	111,498	166
Hemet city (92343*)	36,094	838
Hesperia city (92345)	50,418	550
Highland city (92346)	34,439	881
Huntington Beach city (92647*)	181,519	90
Huntington Park city (90255)	56,065	456
Imperial Beach city (92032)	26,512	1216
Indio city (92201*)	36,793	821
Inglewood city (90311*)	109,602	173
Irvine city (92713*)	110,330	171
Laguna Hills CDP (92654*)	46,731	610
Laguna Niguel city (92607)	44,400	650
La Habra city (90631*)	51,266	535
Lakeside CDP (92040)	39,412	754
Lakewood city (90714*)	73,557	311
La Mesa city (92041*)	52,931	509
La Mirada city (90638*)	40,452	729
Lancaster city (93534*)	97,291	209
La Puente city (91744*)	36,955	816
La Verne city (91750)	30,897	1020
Lawndale city (90260)	27,331	1180
Livermore city (94550*)	56,741	451
Lodi city (95240*)	51,874	526
Lompoc city (93436*)	37,649	803
Long Beach city (90809*)	429,433	32
Los Altos city (94022*)	26,303	1228
Los Angeles city (90052*)	3,485,398	2
Los Gatos town (95030*)	27,357	1176
Lynwood city (90262)	61,945	397
Madera city (93638*)	29,281	1084
Manhattan Beach city (90266)	32,063	970
Manteca city (95336)	40,773	723
Marina city (93933)	26,436	1222
Martinez city (94553)	31,808	983
Maywood city (90270)	27,850	1151
Menlo Park city (94025*)	28,040	1146
Merced city (95340*)	56,216	454
Milpitas city (95035*)	50,686	544
Mission Viejo city (92690*)	72,820	315
Modesto city (95350*)	164,730	104
Monrovia city (91016*)	35,761	844
Montclair city (91763)	28,434	1124
Montebello city (90640)	59,564	425
Monterey city (93940*)	31,954	975
Monterey Park city (91754)	60,738	411
Moorpark city (93021)	25,494	1273
Moreno Valley city (92388*)	118,779	155
Mountain View city (94041*)	67,460	357
Napa city (94558*)	61,842	399
National City city (92050)	54,249	486
Newark city (94560)	37,861	792
Newport Beach city (92658*)	66,643	363
North Highlands CDP (95660)	42,105	693
Norwalk city (90650*)	94,279	220
Novato city (94947*)	47,585	596
Oakland city (94615*)	372,242	39
Oceanside city (92054*)	128,398	143
Oildale CDP (93308*)	26,553	1214
Ontario city (91761*)	133,179	136
Orange city (92613*)	110,658	169
Orangevale CDP (95662)	26,266	1233
Oxnard city (93030*)	142,216	123

City and major zip code	1990 census	1990 rank
Pacifica city (94044)	37,670	802
Palmdale city (93550*)	68,842	346
Palm Springs city (92263*)	40,181	736
Palo Alto city (94303*)	55,900	458
Paradise town (95969*)	25,408	1276
Paramount city (90723)	47,669	595
Parkway-South Sacramento CDP (95823*)	31,903	977
Pasadena city (91109*)	131,591	139
Petaluma city (94952*)	43,184	671
Pico Rivera city (90660)	59,177	429
Pittsburg city (94565)	47,564	597
Placentia city (92670)	41,259	711
Pleasant Hill city (94523)	31,585	992
Pleasanton city (94566*)	50,553	548
Pomona city (91768*)	131,723	138
Porterville city (93257*)	29,563	1073
Poway city (92064)	43,516	665
Rancho Cordova CDP (95670*)	48,731	577
Rancho Cucamonga city (91739*)	101,409	196
Rancho Palos Verdes (90274)	41,659	706
Redding city (96049*)	66,462	366
Redlands city (92373*)	60,394	417
Redondo Beach city (92077*)	60,167	418
Redwood City city (94063*)	66,072	368
Rialto city (92376*)	72,388	319
Richmond city (94802*)	87,425	243
Ridgecrest city (93555*)	27,725	1154
Riverside city (92517*)	226,505	68
Rohnert Park city (94928*)	36,326	831
Rosemead city (91770)	51,638	528
Roseville city (95678*)	44,685	645
Rowland Heights CDP (91748)	42,647	682
Sacramento city (95813*)	369,365	41
Salinas city (93907*)	108,777	177
San Bernardino city (92403*)	164,164	106
San Bruno city (94066)	38,961	765
San Buenaventura (Ventura) city (93001*)	92,575	226
San Carlos city (94070)	26,167	1241
San Clemente city (92674*)	41,100	714
San Diego city (92199*)	1,110,549	6
San Dimas city (91773)	32,397	957
San Francisco city (94188*)	723,959	14
San Gabriel city (91776*)	37,120	812
San Jose city (95101*)	782,248	11
San Juan Capistrano city (92690*)	26,183	1240
San Leandro city (94577*)	68,223	351
San Luis Obispo city (93401*)	41,958	698
San Marcos city (92069)	38,974	764
San Mateo city (94402*)	85,486	254
San Pablo city (94806)	25,158	1287
San Rafael city (94901*)	48,404	587
San Ramon city (94583)	35,303	861
Santa Ana city (92799*)	293,742	52
Santa Barbara city (93102*)	85,571	252
Santa Clara city (95050*)	93,613	222
Santa Clarita city (91380*)	110,642	170
Santa Cruz city (95060*)	49,040	570
Santa Maria city (93454*)	61,284	408
Santa Monica city (90406*)	86,905	246
Santa Paula city (93060)	25,062	1294
Santa Rosa city (95402*)	113,313	162
Santee city (92071*)	52,902	510
Saratoga city (95070*)	28,061	1145
Seal Beach city (90740)	25,098	1289
Seaside city (93955)	38,901	768
Simi Valley city (93065*)	100,217	200
South Gate city (90280)	86,284	250
South San Francisco (94080*)	54,312	484
South Whittier CDP (90601)	49,514	561
Spring Valley CDP (92078)	55,331	465

City and major zip code	1990 census	1990 rank
Stanton city (90680)	30,491	1042
Stockton city (95213*)	210,943	74
Sunnyvale city (94086*)	117,229	157
Temecula city (92390)	27,099	1189
Temple City city (91780)	31,100	1005
Thousand Oaks city (91359*)	104,352	190
Torrance city (90510*)	133,107	137
Tracy city (95376*)	33,558	918
Tulare city (93274*)	33,249	930
Turlock city (95380*)	42,198	689
Tustin city (92681*)	50,689	543
Union City city (94587)	53,762	491
Upland city (91786*)	63,374	388
Vacaville city (95687*)	71,479	325
Vallejo city (94590*)	109,199	175
Victorville city (92392*)	40,674	725
Visalia city (93277*)	75,636	300
Vista city (92083*)	71,872	321
Walnut city (91789*)	29,105	1095
Walnut Creek city (94596*)	60,569	414
Watsonville city (95076*)	31,099	1006
West Covina city (91790*)	96,086	214
West Hollywood city (90046)	36,118	837
Westminster city (92684*)	78,118	286
Westmont CDP (90250*)	31,044	1008
West Sacramento city (95691)	28,898	1101
Whittier city (90605*)	77,671	288
Willowbrook CDP (90223)	32,772	949
Woodland city (31365*)	39,802	747
Yorba Linda city (92686*)	52,422	513
Yuba City city (95991*)	27,437	1175
Yucaipa city (92399)	32,824	948
COLORADO		
Arvada city (80001*)	89,235	235
Aurora city (80010*)	222,103	72
Boulder city (80302*)	83,312	268
Colorado Springs city (80910*)	281,140	54
Denver city (80201*)	467,610	26
Englewood city (80110*)	29,387	1079
Fort Collins city (80521*)	87,758	240
Grand Junction city (81501*)	29,034	1099
Greeley city (80631*)	60,536	416
Lakewood city (80215*)	126,481	145
Littleton city (80120*)	33,685	912
Longmont city (80501*)	51,555	529
Loveland city (80538*)	37,352	809
Northglenn city (80233*)	27,195	1186
Pueblo city (81003*)	98,640	207
Southglenn CDP (80122*)	43,087	672
Thornton city (80229*)	55,031	468
Westminster city (80030)	74,625	309
Wheat Ridge city (80033*)	29,419	1078
CONNECTICUT		
Bridgeport city (06602*)	141,686	125
Bristol city (06010*)	60,640	412
Central Manchester CDP (06040*)	30,934	1018
Danbury city (06810*)	65,585	374
East Hartford CDP (06118*)	50,452	549
East Haven CDP (06512)	26,144	1242
Hartford city (06101*)	139,739	129
Meriden city (06450)	59,479	426
Middletown city (06457)	42,762	678
Milford city (remainder) (06460)	48,168	590
Naugatuck borough (06770)	30,625	1034
New Britain city (06050*)	75,491	302
New Haven city (06511*)	130,474	140
Newington CDP (06111*)	29,208	1086
New London city (06320)	28,540	1122
Norwalk city (06856*)	78,331	284
Norwich city (06360)	37,391	808
Shelton city (06484)	35,418	856
Stamford city (06910*)	108,056	181
Stratford CDP (06497)	49,389	565
Torrington city (06790)	33,687	911
Trumbull CDP (06611)	32,000	972
Waterbury city (06701*)	108,961	176
West Hartford CDP (06107*)	60,110	419
West Haven city (06516)	54,021	489
Wethersfield CDP (06109*)	25,651	1265
DELAWARE		
Dover city (19901*)	27,630	1160
Newark city (19711*)	25,098	1289
Wilmington city (19850*)	71,529	324
DISTRICT OF COLUMBIA		
Washington city (20066*)	606,900	19
FLORIDA		
Altamonte Springs city (32714*)	34,879	871
Boca Raton city (33431*)	61,492	405
Boynton Beach city (33436*)	46,194	620
Bradenton city (34206*)	43,779	658
Brandon CDP (33511*)	57,985	438
Cape Coral city (33990)	74,991	306
Carol City CDP (33055)	53,331	500
Clearwater city (34618*)	98,784	206
Coconut Creek city (33063)	27,485	1173
Coral Gables city (33114)	40,091	740
Coral Springs city (33075)	79,443	282
Davie town (33329)	47,217	601
Daytona Beach city (32114*)	61,921	398
Deerfield Beach city (33441*)	46,325	617
Delray Beach city (33444*)	47,181	603
Deltona CDP (32725*)	50,828	541
Dunedin city (34698*)	34,012	896
Ferry Pass CDP (32501*)	26,301	1230
Fort Lauderdale city (33310*)	149,377	118
Fort Myers city (33907*)	45,206	637
Fort Pierce city (34950*)	36,830	819
Gainesville city (32602*)	84,770	258
Golden Glades CDP (33054*)	25,474	1274
Hallandale city (33010*)	30,996	1010
Hialeah city (33010*)	188,004	85
Hollywood city (33022*)	121,697	152
Homestead city (33030*)	26,866	1199
Jacksonville city (32203*)	635,230	15
Kendale Lakes CDP (33152*)	48,524	584
Kendall CDP (33256)	87,271	244
Kissimmee city (34744*)	30,050	1054
Lakeland city (33805*)	70,576	334
Lakeside CDP	29,137	1092
Lake Worth city (33461*)	28,564	1121
Largo city (34640*)	65,674	372
Lauderdale Lakes city (33152*)	27,341	1178
Lauderhill city (33152*)	49,708	559
Margate city (33063)	42,985	673
Melbourne city (32901*)	59,646	424
Merritt Island CDP (32953*)	32,886	944
Miami city (33152*)	358,548	46
Miami Beach city (33119)	92,639	225
Miramar city (33023)	40,663	726
North Fort Myers CDP (33903)	30,027	1056
North Lauderdale city (33060*)	26,506	1217
North Miami city (33261)	49,998	556
North Miami Beach city (33160)	35,359	857
Oakland Park city (33334*)	26,326	1226
Ocala city (32678*)	42,045	695
Olympia Heights CDP (33265)	37,792	797

City and major zip code	1990 census	1990 rank
Orlando city (32862*)	164,693	105
Ormond Beach city (32176*)	29,721	1070
Palm Bay city (32901*)	62,632	394
Palm Harbor CDP (34683*)	50,256	553
Panama City city (32401*)	34,378	884
Pembroke Pines city (33084)	65,452	376
Pensacola city (32501*)	58,165	434
Pine Hills CDP (32862*)	35,322	858
Pinellas Park city (34665*)	43,426	667
Plantation city (33318)	66,692	361
Pompano Beach city (33060*)	72,411	318
Port Charlotte CDP (33949)	41,535	708
Port Orange city (32129)	35,317	859
Port St. Lucie city (34985)	55,866	459
Riviera Beach city (33419)	27,639	1158
St. Petersburg city (33730*)	238,629	65
Sanford city (32771*)	32,387	959
Sarasota city (34230*)	50,961	539
South Miami Heights CDP (33152*)	30,030	1055
Spring Hill CDP (34606*)	31,117	1004
Sunrise city (33322)	64,407	381
Tallahassee city (32301*)	124,773	149
Tamarac city (33320)	44,822	643
Tamiami CDP (33144)	33,845	901
Tampa city (33630*)	280,015	55
Titusville city (32780*)	39,394	756
Town 'n' Country CDP (33685)	60,946	409
Westchester CDP (33165)	29,883	1063
West Little River CDP (33152*)	33,575	916
West Palm Beach city (33406*)	67,643	354
GEORGIA		
Albany city (31706*)	78,122	285
Athens city (30601*)	45,734	629
Atlanta city (30304*)	394,017	36
Augusta city (30901*)	44,639	648
Candler-McAfee CDP (30304*)	29,491	1075
Columbus city (remainder) (31908*)	178,681	93
Dunwoody CDP (30304*)	26,302	1229
East Point city (30304*)	34,402	883
La Grange city (30240*)	25,597	1268
Mableton CDP (30059)	25,725	1262
Macon city (31201*)	106,612	185
Marietta city (30060*)	44,129	653
Martinez CDP (30907)	33,731	908
North Atlanta CDP (30319)	27,812	1152
Rome city (30161*)	30,326	1045
Roswell city (30075*)	47,923	591
Sandy Springs CDP (30304*)	67,842	353
Savannah city (31402*)	137,560	131
Smyrna city (30080*)	30,981	1014
South Augusta CDP (30901*)	55,998	457
Tucker CDP (30084*)	25,781	1260
Valdosta city (31603*)	39,806	746
Warner Robins city (31088*)	43,726	661
West Augusta CDP (30901*)	27,637	1159
HAWAII		
Hilo CDP (96720*)	37,808	796
Honolulu CDP (96820*)	365,272	44
Kailua CDP (96734)	36,818	820
Kaneohe CDP (96744)	35,448	854
Mililani Town CDP (96789)	29,359	1080
Pearl City CDP (96782)	30,993	1011
Waimalu CDP (96701)	29,967	1058
Waipahu CDP (96797)	31,435	996
IDAHO		
Boise City city (83708*)	125,738	148
Idaho Falls city (83401*)	43,929	654
Lewiston city (83501)	28,082	1144

City and major zip code	1990 census	1990 rank
Nampa city (83651*)	28,365	1127
Pocatello city (83201*)	46,080	622
Twin Falls city (83301*)	27,591	1167
ILLINOIS		
Addison village (60101)	32,058	971
Alton city (62002)	32,905	941
Arlington Heights village (60005*)	75,460	303
Aurora city (60505*)	99,581	203
Belleville city (62220*)	42,785	677
Berwyn city (60402)	45,426	633
Bloomington city (61701*)	51,972	524
Bolingbrook village (60440)	40,843	720
Buffalo Grove village (60089)	36,427	827
Burbank city (60459)	27,600	1165
Calumet City city (60409)	37,840	793
Carbondale city (62901*)	27,033	1192
Carol Stream village (60188)	31,716	987
Champaign city (61820*)	63,502	387
Chicago city (60607*)	2,783,726	3
Chicago Heights city (60411)	33,072	936
Cicero town (60650)	67,436	358
Danville city (61832*)	33,828	905
Decatur city (62523*)	83,885	267
De Kalb city (60115)	34,925	869
Des Plaines city (60018*)	53,223	504
Downers Grove village (60515*)	46,858	608
East St. Louis city (62201*)	40,944	718
Elgin city (60120*)	77,010	290
Elk Grove Village village (60007*)	33,429	924
Elmhurst city (60126)	42,029	696
Evanston city (60201*)	73,233	313
Freeport city (61032)	25,840	1258
Galesburg city (61401*)	33,530	919
Glendale Heights village (60139)	27,973	1147
Glenview village (60025)	37,093	813
Granite City city (62040)	32,862	946
Hanover Park village (60103)	32,895	942
Harvey city (60426)	29,771	1067
Highland Park city (60035)	30,575	1037
Hoffman Estates village (60195)	46,561	612
Joliet city (60436*)	76,836	291
Kankakee city (60901)	27,575	1168
Lansing village (60438)	28,086	1143
Lombard village (60148)	39,408	755
Maywood village (60153)	27,139	1187
Moline city (61265)	43,202	670
Mount Prospect village (60056)	53,170	505
Naperville city (60540*)	85,351	256
Niles village (60648)	28,284	1131
Normal town (61761)	40,023	744
Northbrook village (60062*)	32,308	963
North Chicago city (60064)	34,978	868
Oak Forest city (60452)	26,203	1238
Oak Lawn village (60455*)	56,182	455
Oak Park village (60301*)	53,648	495
Orland Park village (60462)	35,720	846
Palatine village (60067*)	39,253	760
Park Ridge city (60068)	36,175	835
Pekin city (61554*)	32,254	965
Peoria city (61601*)	113,504	161
Quincy city (62301*)	39,681	751
Rockford city (61125*)	139,426	130
Rock Island city (61201*)	40,552	728
Schaumburg village (60194*)	68,586	349
Skokie village (60077*)	59,432	428
Springfield city (62703*)	105,227	188
Streamwood village (60107)	30,987	1012
Tinley Park village (60477)	37,121	811
Urbana city (61801)	36,344	830
Waukegan city (60085*)	69,392	342

City and major zip code	1990 census	1990 rank
Wheaton city (60187*)	51,464	530
Wheeling village (60090)	29,911	1061
Wlimette village (60091)	26,690	1207
Woodridge village (60517)	26,256	1235
INDIANA		
Anderson city (46011*)	59,459	427
Bloomington city (47408*)	60,633	413
Carmel city (46032)	25,380	1279
Columbus city (47201*)	31,802	984
East Chicago city (46312)	33,892	899
Elkhart city (46515*)	43,627	663
Evansville city (47708*)	126,272	147
Fort Wayne city (46802*)	173,072	99
Gary city (46401*)	116,646	158
Greenwood city (46142*)	26,265	1234
Hammond city (46320*)	84,236	263
Indianapolis (46206*)	731,327	13
Kokomo city (46902*)	44,962	640
Lafayette city (47901*)	43,764	659
Lawrence city (46226)	26,763	1203
Marion city (46952*)	32,618	951
Merrillville town (46410)	27,257	1183
Michigan City city (46360)	33,822	907
Mishawaka city (46544*)	42,608	684
Muncie city (47302*)	71,035	330
New Albany city (47150*)	36,322	832
Portage city (46368)	29,060	1097
Richmond city (47374*)	38,705	772
South Bend city (46624*)	105,511	187
Terre Haute city (47808*)	57,483	442
West Lafayette city (47906*)	25,907	1252
IOWA		
Ames city (50010)	47,198	602
Bettendorf city (52722)	28,132	1141
Burlington city (52601)	27,208	1185
Cedar Falls city (50613)	34,298	887
Cedar Rapids city (52401*)	108,751	178
Clinton city (52732)	29,201	1089
Council Bluffs city (51501*)	54,315	483
Davenport city (52802*)	95,333	218
Des Moines city (50318*)	193,187	80
Dubuque city (52001*)	57,546	441
Fort Dodge city (50501)	25,894	1254
Iowa City city (52240*)	59,738	421
Marshalltown city (50158)	25,178	1286
Mason City city (50401)	29,040	1098
Sioux City city (51101*)	80,505	276
Waterloo city (50703*)	66,467	365
West Des Moines city (50265)	31,702	988
KANSAS		
Emporia city (66801)	25,512	1272
Hutchinson city (67501*)	39,308	759
Kansas City city (66106*)	149,767	116
Lawrence city (66044*)	65,608	373
Leavenworth city (66048)	38,495	775
Lenexa city (66215)	34,034	895
Manhattan city (66502)	37,712	800
Olathe city (66061*)	63,352	389
Overland Park city (66204)	111,790	165
Salina city (67401*)	42,303)	688
Shawnee city (66203)	37,993	788
Topeka city (66603*)	119,883	153
Wichita city (67276*)	304,011	51
KENTUCKY		
Bowling Green city (42101*)	40,641	727
Covington city (41011*)	43,264	668
Frankfort city (40601*)	25,968	1249
Henderson city (42420)	25,945	1250

City and major zip code	1990 census	1990 rank
Hopkinsville city (42240*)	29,809	1065
Lexington-Fayette (40511*)	225,366	70
Louisville city (40231*)	269,063	58
Owensboro city (42301*)	53,549	497
Paducah city (42003*)	27,256	1184
Pleasure Ridge Park CDP (40268)	25,131	1288
LOUISIANA		
Alexandria city (71301*)	49,188	569
Baton Rouge city (70821*)	219,531	73
Bossier City city (71111*)	52,721	511
Chalmette CDP (70043*)	31,860	979
Houma city (70360*)	30,495	1041
Kenner city (70062*)	72,033	320
Lafayette city (70501*)	94,440	219
Lake Charles city (70601*)	70,580	333
Marerro CDP (70072*)	36,671	825
Metairie (70009*)	149,428	117
Monroe city (71203*)	54,909	472
New Iberia city (70560*)	31,828	981
New Orleans city (70113*)	496,938	24
Shreveport city (71102*)	198,525	77
MAINE		
Bangor city (04401*)	33,181	932
Lewiston city (04240*)	39,757	749
Portland city (04101*)	64,358	382
MARYLAND		
Annapolis city (21401*)	33,187	931
Aspen Hill CDP (20916)	45,494	632
Baltimore city (21233*)	736,014	12
Bel Air South CDP (21014*)	26,421	1223
Bethesda CDP (20814*)	62,936	392
Bowie city (20715*)	37,589	804
Carney CDP (21234)	25,578	1269
Catonsville CDP (21228)	35,233	863
Chillum CDP (20783)	31,309	998
Columbia CDP (21045*)	75,883	297
Dundalk CDP (21222*)	65,800	370
Ellicott City CDP (21043)	41,396	709
Essex CDP (21221)	40,872	719
Frederick city (21701*)	40,148	739
Gaithersburg city (20877*)	39,542	752
Germantown CDP (20874*)	41,145	713
Glen Burnie CDP (21061*)	37,305	810
Hagerstown city (21740*)	35,445	855
Lochearn CDP (21207)	25,240	1285
Montgomery Village CDP (20886)	32,315	961
North Bethesda CDP (20850)	29,656	1072
Oxon Hill-Glassmanor (20790*)	35,794	843
Parkville CDP (21234)	31,617	990
Potomac CDP (20859)	45,634	630
Randallstown CDP (21133)	26,277	1231
Rockville city (20850*)	44,835	642
St. Charles CDP (20601)	28,717	1111
Severna Park CDP (21146)	25,879	1255
Silver Spring CDP (20907*)	76,046	296
South Gate CDP (21061)	27,564	1169
Suitland-Silver Mill (20790*)	35,111	865
Towson CDP (21285)	49,445	563
Wheaton-Glenmont CDP (20915)	53,720	492
Woodlawn CDP (21207)	32,907	940
MASSACHUSETTS		
Arlington CDP (02174)	44,630	649
Attleboro city (02703)	38,383	777
Beverly city (01915)	38,195	779
Boston city (02205*)	574,283	20
Braintree CDP (02184)	33,836	903
Brockton city (02402*)	92,788	223

City and major zip code	1990 census	1990 rank
Brookline CDP (02147*)	54,718	479
Cambridge city (02139*)	95,802	215
Chelmsford CDP (01824)	32,388	958
Chelsea city (02150)	28,710	1113
Chicopee city (01020*)	56,632	452
Everett city (02149)	35,701	849
Fall River city (02720*)	92,703	224
Fitchburg city (01420)	41,194	712
Framingham CDP (01701)	64,994	379
Gloucester city (01930*)	28,716	1112
Haverhill city (01830*)	51,418	532
Holyoke city (01040*)	43,704	662
Lawrence city (01842*)	70,207	338
Leominster city (01453)	38,145	782
Lexington CDP (02173)	28,974	1100
Lowell city (01853*)	103,439	193
Lynn city (10901*)	81,245	273
Malden city (02148)	53,884	490
Marlborough city (01752)	31,813	982
Medford city (02155)	57,407	443
Melrose city (02176)	28,150	1139
Milton CDP (02186)	25,725	1262
Needham CDP (02194*)	27,557	1170
New Bedford city (02740*)	99,922	201
Newton city (02164*)	82,585	269
Northampton city (01060*)	29,289	1083
Norwood CDP (02062)	28,700	1115
Peabody city (01960*)	47,039	605
Pittsfield city (01201*)	48,622	581
Quincy city (02369*)	84,985	257
Randolph CDP (02368)	30,093	1052
Revere city (02151)	42,786	676
Salem city (01970*)	48,091	786
Saugus CDP (01906)	25,549	1271
Somerville city (02143*)	76,210	293
Springfield city (01101*)	156,983	112
Taunton city (02780)	49,832	558
Waltham city (02154)	57,878	439
Watertown CDP (02172)	33,284	929
Wellesley CDP (02181)	26,615	1211
Westfield city (01085*)	38,372	778
West Springfield CDP (01089*)	27,537	1172
Weymouth CDP (02188*)	54,063	487
Woburn city (01801)	35,943	841
Worcester city (01613*)	169,759	102
MICHIGAN		
Allen Park city (48101)	31,092	1007
Ann Arbor city (48103*)	109,592	174
Battle Creek city (49016*)	53,540	498
Bay City city (48707*)	38,936	766
Bloomfield Township CDP (48302)	42,137	692
Burton city (48529*)	27,617	1162
Canton CDP (48185*)	57,047	447
Clinton city (48043)	85,866	251
Dearborn city (48120*)	89,286	234
Dearborn Heights city (48127*)	60,838	410
Detroit city (48283*)	1,027,974	7
East Detroit city (48021)	35,283	862
East Lansing city (48823*)	50,677	545
Farmington Hills city (48333*)	74,652	308
Ferndale city (48220)	25,084	1292
Flint city (48502*)	140,761	127
Garden City city (48135)	31,846	980
Grand Rapids city (49501*)	189,126	83
Holland city (49423*)	30,745	1028
Inkster city (48141)	30,772	1025
Jackson city (49201*)	37,446	806
Kalamazoo city (49001*)	80,277	279
Kentwood city (49518)	37,826	794
Lansing city (48924*)	127,321	144
Lincoln Park city (48146)	41,832	702
Livonia city (48150*)	100,850	198
Madison Heights city (48071)	32,196	967
Midland city (48640*)	38,053	787
Muskegon city (49440*)	40,283	733
Novi city (48376*)	32,998	937
Oak Park city (48237)	30,462	1043
Pontiac city (48343*)	71,166	329
Portage city (49081)	41,042	715
Port Huron city (48061*)	33,694	910
Redford CDP (48231*)	54,387	482
Rochester Hills city (48309)	61,766	402
Roseville city (48066)	51,412	533
Royal Oak city (48068*)	65,410	377
Saginaw city (48605*)	69,512	340
St. Clair Shores city (48080*)	68,107	352
Shelby CDP (48318*)	48,655	580
Southfield city (48037*)	75,728	298
Southgate city (48195)	30,771	1026
Sterling Heights city (48311*)	117,810	156
Taylor city (48180)	70,811	331
Troy city (48099*)	72,884	314
Warren city (48090*)	144,864	120
Waterford CDP (48329*)	66,692	361
West Bloomfield Township (48343*)	54,843	475
Westland city (48185)	84,724	259
Wyandotte city (48192)	30,938	1017
Wyoming city (49509)	63,891	384
MINNESOTA		
Apple Valley city (55124)	34,598	876
Blaine city (55434)	38,975	763
Bloomington city (55431*)	86,335	249
Brooklyn Center city (55429*)	28,887	1102
Brooklyn Park city (55429*)	56,381	453
Burnsville city (55337)	51,288	534
Coon Rapids city (55433)	52,978	508
Duluth city (55806*)	85,493	253
Eagan city (55121)	47,409	599
Eden Prairie city (55344*)	39,311	758
Edina city (55424)	46,070	624
Fridley city (55432)	28,335	1128
Mankato city (56001*)	31,477	995
Maple Grove city (55369)	38,736	770
Maplewood city (55109)	30,954	1015
Minneapolis city (55401*)	368,383	42
Minnetonka city (55345)	48,370	588
Moorhead city (56560*)	32,295	964
Plymouth city (55441*)	50,889	540
Richfield city (55423)	35,710	847
Rochester city (55901*)	70,745	332
Roseville city (55113)	33,485	922
St. Cloud city (56301*)	48,812	574
St. Louis Park city (55426)	43,787	657
St. Paul city (55101*)	272,235	57
Winona city (55987)	25,399	1278
MISSISSIPPI		
Biloxi city (39530*)	46,419	618
Greenville city (38701*)	45,226	635
Gulfport city (39503*)	40,775	722
Hattiesburg city (39402*)	41,882	700
Jackson city (39205*)	196,637	78
Meridian city (39301*)	41,036	716
Pascagoula city (39567*)	25,899	1253
Tupelo city (38801*)	30,685	1033
MISSOURI		
Blue Springs city (64015*)	40,153	738
Cape Girardeau city (63701*)	34,438	882
Chesterfield city (63017*)	37,991	789

City and major zip code	1990 census	1990 rank
Columbia city (65201*)	69,101	345
Florissant city (63033*)	51,206	536
Gladstone city (64108*)	26,243	1236
Independence city (64050*)	112,301	164
Jefferson City city (65101*)	35,481	853
Joplin city (64801*)	40,961	717
Kansas City city (64108*)	435,146	31
Kirkwood city (63122)	27,291	1182
Lee's Summit city (64063*)	46,418	615
Maryland Heights city (64043)	25,407	1277
Mehlville CDP (63129)	27,557	1170
Oakville CDP (63129)	31,750	985
Raytown city (64108*)	30,601	1035
St. Charles city (63301*)	54,555	480
St. Joseph city (64501*)	71,852	322
St. Louis city (63155*)	396,685	34
St. Peters city (63376)	45,779	628
Springfield city (65801*)	140,494	128
University City city (63130)	40,087	741
MONTANA		
Billings city (59101*)	81,151	274
Butte-Silver Bow (remainder) (59701*)	33,336	928
Great Falls city (59401*)	55,097	466
Missoula city (59801*)	42,918	674
NEBRASKA		
Bellevue city (68005)	30,982	1013
Grand Island city (68802*)	39,386	757
Lincoln city (68501*)	191,972	81
Omaha city (68108*)	335,795	48
NEVADA		
Carson City (89701*)	40,443	730
Henderson city (89015*)	64,942	380
Las Vegas city (89199*)	258,295	63
North Las Vegas city (89030*)	47,707	594
Paradise CDP (89109*)	124,682	150
Reno city (89510*)	133,850	134
Sparks city (89431*)	53,367	499
Spring Valley CDP (89117*)	51,726	527
Sunrise Manor CDP (89110*)	95,362	217
NEW HAMPSHIRE		
Concord city (03301*)	36,006	840
Dover city (03820)	25,042	1295
Manchester city (03103*)	99,567	204
Nashua city (03060*)	79,662	281
Portsmouth city (03801*)	25,925	1251
Rochester city (03867*)	26,630	1209
NEW JERSEY		
Atlantic City city (08401*)	37,986	790
Bayonne city (07002)	61,444	406
Belleville CDP (07109)	34,213	890
Bloomfield CDP (07003)	45,061	638
Brick Township CDP (08723*)	66,473	364
Camden city (08101*)	87,492	242
Cherry Hill CDP (08034*)	69,319	344
Clifton city (07015*)	71,742	323
East Brunswick CDP (08816)	43,548	664
East Orange city (07019*)	73,552	312
Edison CDP (08818*)	88,680	237
Elizabeth city (07207*)	110,002	172
Ewing CDP (08650*)	34,185	892
Fair Lawn borough (07410)	30,548	1038
Fort Lee borough (07024)	31,997	973
Garfield city (07026)	26,727	1205
Hackensack city (07602*)	37,049	815
Hoboken city (07030)	33,397	926
Irvington CDP (07111)	59,774	420
Jersey City city (07303*)	228,537	67
Kearny town (07032)	34,874	872
Lakewood CDP (08701)	26,095	1243
Linden city (07036)	36,701	823
Livingston CDP (07039)	26,609	1212
Long Branch city (07740)	28,658	1117
Mercerville-Hamilton Square CDP (08619)	26,873	1197
Millville city (08332)	25,992	1248
Montclair CDP (07042*)	37,729	799
Newark city (07102*)	275,221	56
New Bunswick city (08901*)	41,711	704
North Bergen CDP (07047)	48,414	586
North Brunswick Township (08902)	31,287	1001
Nutley CDP (07110)	27,099	1189
Orange CDP (07051*)	29,925	1060
Paramus borough (07652*)	25,067	1293
Parsippany-Troy Hill (07054)	48,478	585
Passaic city (07055)	58,041	436
Paterson city (07510*)	140,891	126
Pennsauken CDP (08110)	34,733	874
Perth Amboy city (08861*)	41,967	697
Plainfield city (07061*)	46,567	611
Rahway city (07065)	25,325	1280
Sayreville borough (08872*)	34,986	867
Teaneck CDP (07666)	37,825	795
Trenton city (08650*)	88,675	238
Union CDP (07083)	50,024	554
Union City city (07087)	58,012	437
Vineland city (08360)	54,780	477
Wayne CDP (07470*)	47,025	606
Westfield town (07091*)	28,870	1103
West Milford CDP (07480)	25,430	1275
West New York town (07093)	38,125	785
West Orange CDP (07052)	39,103	762
Willingboro CDP (08046)	36,291	833
NEW MEXICO		
Alamogordo city (88310*)	27,596	1166
Albuquerque city (87101*)	384,736	38
Clovis city (88101*)	30,954	1015
Farmington city (87401*)	33,997	897
Hobbs city (88240*)	29,115	1094
Las Cruces city (88001*)	62,126	396
Rio Rancho city (87124)	32,505	953
Roswell city (88201*)	44,654	647
Santa Fe city (87501*)	55,859	460
South Valley CDP (87101*)	35,701	849
NEW YORK		
Albany city (12288*)	101,082	197
Auburn city (13021*)	31,258	1003
Binghamton city (13902*)	53,008	507
Brentwood CDP (11717)	45,218	636
Brighton CDP (14610)	34,455	880
Buffalo city (14240*)	328,123	50
Centereach CDP (11720)	26,720	1206
Central Islip CDP (11722)	26,028	1245
Cheektowaga CDP (14225)	84,387	261
Commack CDP (11725)	36,124	836
Coram CDP (11727)	30,111	1049
Deer Park CDP (11729)	28,840	1105
Dix Hills CDP (11746)	25,849	1257
East Meadow CDP (11554)	36,909	818
Elmira city (14901*)	33,724	909
Elmont CDP (11003)	28,612	1119
Franklin Square CDP (11010)	28,205	1136
Freeport village (11520)	39,894	745
Hempstead village (11551*)	49,453	562
Hicksville CDP (11805*)	40,174	737
Holbrook CDP (11741)	25,273	1284
Huntington Station CDP (11746)	28,247	1133
Irondequoit CDP (14617)	52,322	517

City and major zip code	1990 census	1990 rank
Ithaca city (14850*)	29,541	1074
Jamestown city (14701*)	34,681	875
Levittown CDP (11756)	53,286	502
Lindenhurst village (11757)	26,879	1196
Long Beach city (11561)	33,510	920
Mount Vernon city (10551*)	67,153	360
Newburgh city (12550*)	26,454	1221
New City CDP (10956)	33,673	913
New Rochelle city (10802*)	67,265	359
New York city (10199*)	7,322,564	1
Brooklyn (11256*)	2,300,664	
Bronx (10451*)	1,203,789	
Manhattan (10199*)	1,487,536	
Queens	1,951,598	
Staten Island (10314*)	378,977	
Niagara Falls city (14302*)	61,840	400
North Tonawanda city (14120)	34,989	866
Oceanside CDP (11572)	32,423	956
Plainview CDP (11803)	26,207	1237
Poughkeepsie city (12601*)	28,844	1104
Rochester city (14692*)	231,636	66
Rome city (13440)	44,350	652
Saratoga Springs city (12866)	25,001	1296
Schenectady city (12305*)	65,566	375
Smithtown CDP (11787)	25,638	1266
Syracuse city (13220*)	163,860	107
Tonawanda CDP (14150*)	65,284	378
Troy city (12180*)	54,269	485
Utica city (13504*)	68,637	348
Valley Stream village (11582*)	33,946	898
Watertown city (13601*)	29,429	1077
West Babylon CDP (11707)	42,410	686
West Islip CDP (11795)	28,419	1125
West Seneca CDP (14224)	47,866	592
White Plains city (10602*)	48,718	578
Yonkers city (10702*)	188,082	84
NORTH CAROLINA		
Asheville city (28810*)	61,607	404
Burlington city (27215*)	39,498	753
Camp Lejeune Central (28542)	36,716	822
Cary town (27511*)	43,858	656
Chapel Hill town (27514*)	38,719	771
Charlotte city (28228*)	395,934	35
Concord city (28025*)	27,347	1177
Durham city (27701*)	136,611	132
Fayetteville city (28302*)	75,695	299
Fort Bragg CDP (28307)	34,744	873
Gastonia city (28052*)	54,732	478
Goldsboro city (27530*)	40,709	724
Greensboro city (27420*)	183,521	88
Greenville city (27834*)	44,972	639
Hickory city (28603*)	28,301	1130
High Point city (27260*)	69,496	341
Jacksonville city (28540*)	30,013	1057
Kannapolis city (28081*)	29,696	1071
Kinston city (28501*)	25,295	1282
Raleigh city (27611*)	207,951	75
Rocky Mount city (27801*)	48,997	571
Wilmington city (28402*)	55,530	462
Wilson city (27893*)	36,930	817
Winston-Salem city (27102*)	143,485	121
NORTH DAKOTA		
Bismarck city (58501*)	49,256	568
Fargo city (58102*)	74,111	310
Grand Forks city (58201*)	49,425	564
Minot city (58701*)	34,544	878
OHIO		
Akron city (44309*)	223,019	71
Austintown CDP (44515)	32,371	960

City and major zip code	1990 census	1990 rank
Barberton city (44203)	27,623	1161
Beavercreek city (45430*)	33,626	914
Boardman CDP (44512*)	38,596	774
Bowling Green city (43402)	28,176	1137
Brunswick city (44212)	28,230	1134
Canton city (44711*)	84,161	264
Cincinnati city (45234*)	364,040	45
Cleveland city (44101*)	505,616	23
Cleveland Heights city (44118)	54,052	488
Columbus city (43216*)	632,910	16
Cuyahoga Falls city (44222*)	48,950	572
Dayton city (45401*)	182,044	89
East Cleveland city (44112)	33,096	935
Elyria city (44035*)	56,746	450
Euclid city (44117)	54,875	473
Fairborn city (45324)	31,300	1000
Fairfield city (45014)	39,729	750
Findlay city (45840*)	35,703	848
Gahanna city (43230)	27,791	1153
Garfield Heights city (44125)	31,739	986
Hamilton city (45011*)	61,368	407
Huber Heights city (45424)	38,696	773
Kent city (44240)	28,835	1106
Kettering city (45429)	60,569	414
Lakewood city (44107)	59,718	422
Lancaster city (43130)	34,507	879
Lima city (45802*)	45,549	631
Lorain city (44052*)	71,245	328
Mansfield city (44901*)	50,627	546
Maple Heights city (44137)	27,089	1191
Marion city (43302*)	34,075	894
Massillon city (44646*)	31,007	1009
Mentor city (44060*)	47,358	600
Middletown city (45042*)	46,022	625
Newark city (43055*)	44,389	651
North Olmsted city (44070)	34,204	891
Parma city (44129)	87,876	239
Reynoldsburg city (43068)	25,748	1261
Sandusky city (44870*)	29,764	1068
Shaker Heights city (44120)	30,831	1024
Springfield city (45501*)	70,487	335
Stow city (44224)	27,702	1155
Stongsville city (44136)	35,308	860
Toledo city (43601*)	332,943	49
Upper Arlington city (43221)	34,128	893
Warren city (44481*)	50,793	542
Westerville city (43081)	30,269	1046
Westlake city (44145)	27,018	1194
Youngstown city (44501*)	95,732	216
Zanesville city (43701*)	26,778	1202
OKLAHOMA		
Bartlesville city (74003*)	34,256	889
Broken Arrow city (74012*)	58,043	435
Edmond city (73034*)	52,315	518
Enid city (73701*)	45,309	634
Lawton city (73501*)	80,561	275
Midwest City city (73125*)	52,267	520
Moore city (73125*)	40,318	732
Muskogee city (74401*)	37,708	801
Norman city (73069*)	80,071	280
Oklahoma City city (73125*)	444,719	29
Ponca City city (74601*)	26,359	1225
Shawnee city (74801*)	26,017	1246
Stillwater city (74074*)	36,676	824
Tulsa city (74103*)	367,302	43
OREGON		
Albany city (97321)	29,462	1076
Aloha CDP (97006*)	34,284	888
Beaverton city (97005*)	53,310	501
Corvallis city (97333*)	44,757	644

City and major zip code	1990 census	1990 rank
Eugene city (97401*)	112,669	163
Gresham city (97030*)	68,235	350
Hillsboro city (97123*)	37,520	805
Lake Oswego city (97034*)	30,576	1036
Medford city (97501*)	46,951	607
Portland city (97208*)	437,319	30
Powellhurst-Centennial CDP (97208*)	28,756	1109
Salem city (97301*)	107,786	182
Springfield city (97477)	44,683	646
Tigard city (97208*)	29,344	1081
PENNSYLVANIA		
Allentown city (18101*)	105,090	189
Altoona city (16601*)	51,881	525
Bethel Park borough (15102)	33,823	906
Bethlehem city (18016*)	71,428	326
Chester city (19013*)	41,856	701
Drexel Hill CDP (19026)	29,744	1069
Easton city (18042*)	26,276	1232
Erie city (16515*)	108,718	179
Harrisburg city (17107*)	52,376	514
Johnstown city (15901*)	28,134	1140
Lancaster city (17604*)	55,551	461
Levittown CDP (19053*)	55,362	464
McCandless Township CDP (15237*)	28,781	1107
McKeesport city (15134*)	26,016	1247
Mount Lebanon CDP (15228)	33,362	927
Municipality of Monroeville borough (15146*)	29,169	1091
New Castle city (16108*)	28,334	1129
Norristown borough (19401*)	30,749	1027
Penn Hills CDP (15235)	51,430	531
Philadelphia city (19104*)	1,585,577	5
Pittsburgh city (15290*)	369,879	40
Plum borough (15239)	25,609	1267
Radnor Township CDP (19087)	28,705	1114
Reading city (19612*)	78,380	283
Ross Township CDP (15290*)	33,482	923
Scranton city (18505*)	81,805	272
Shaler Township CDP (15290*)	30,533	1040
State College borough (16801*)	38,923	767
Wilkes-Barre city (18701*)	47,523	598
Williamsport city (17701*)	31,933	976
York city (17405*)	42,192	690
RHODE ISLAND		
Cranston city (02920*)	76,060	295
East Providence city (02914)	50,380	551
Newport city (02840)	28,227	1135
Pawtucket city (02860*)	72,644	317
Providence city (02904*)	160,728	108
North Providence CDP (02908)	32,090	969
Warwick city (02886*)	85,427	255
West Warwick CDP (02886*)	29,268	1085
Woonsocket city (02895)	43,877	655
SOUTH CAROLINA		
Anderson city (29621*)	26,184	1239
Charleston city (29423*)	80,414	277
Columbia city (29292*)	98,052	208
Florence city (29501*)	29,813	1064
Greenville city (29602*)	58,282	433
Mount Pleasant town (29464*)	30,108	1050
North Charleston city (29406*)	70,218	337
Rock Hill city (29730*)	41,643	707
St. Andrews CDP (29407*)	25,692	1264
Spartanburg city (29301*)	43,467	666
Sumter city (29150*)	41,943	699
SOUTH DAKOTA		
Rapid City city (57701*)	54,523	481

City and major zip code	1990 census	1990 rank
Sioux Falls city (57101*)	100,814	199
TENNESSEE		
Bartlett town (38101*)	26,989	1195
Chattanooga city (37421*)	152,466	114
Clarksville city (37040*)	75,494	301
Cleveland city (37311*)	30,354	1044
Columbia city (38401*)	28,583	1120
Germantown city (38183)	32,893	943
Hendersonville city (37075*)	32,188	968
Jackson city (38301*)	48,949	573
Johnson City city (37601*)	49,381	566
Kingsport city (37660*)	36,365	829
Knoxville city (37950*)	165,121	103
Memphis city (38101*)	610,337	18
Murfreesboro city (37130*)	44,922	641
Nashville-Davidson (37229*)	488,374	25
Oak Ridge city (37830*)	27,310	1181
TEXAS		
Abilene city (79604*)	106,654	184
Amarillo city (79120*)	157,615	111
Arlington city (76010*)	261,721	61
Austin city (78710*)	465,622	27
Baytown city (77520*)	63,850	385
Beaumont city (77707*)	114,323	159
Bedford city (76021*)	43,762	660
Brownsville city (78520*)	98,962	205
Bryan city (77801*)	55,002	470
Carrollton city (75006*)	82,169	270
Channelview CDP (77530)	25,564	1270
College Station city (77840*)	52,456	512
Conroe city (77301*)	27,610	1163
Corpus Christi (78469*)	257,453	64
Dallas city (75260*)	1,006,877	8
Deer Park city (77536)	27,652	1157
Del Rio city (78840*)	30,705	1032
Denton city (76201*)	66,270	367
DeSoto city (75115)	30,544	1039
Duncanville city (75138*)	35,748	845
Edinburg city (78539*)	29,885	1062
El Paso city (79910*)	515,342	22
Euless city (76039*)	38,149	781
Fort Hood CDP (76541*)	35,580	851
Fort Worth city (76161*)	447,619	28
Galveston city (77550*)	59,070	430
Garland city (75040*)	180,650	91
Grand Prairie city (75051*)	99,616	202
Grapevine city (96051*)	29,202	1088
Haltom City city (76117)	32,856	947
Harlingen city (78550*)	48,735	576
Houston city (77201*)	1,630,553	4
Huntsville city (77340*)	27,925	1149
Hurst city (76053*)	33,574	917
Irving city (75015*)	155,037	113
Killeen city (76541*)	63,535	386
Kingsville city (78363*)	25,276	1283
Kingwood CDP (77338*)	37,397	807
La Porte city (77571*)	27,910	1150
Laredo city (78041*)	122,899	151
League City city (77573*)	30,159	1048
Lewisville city (75067*)	46,521	614
Longview city (75602*)	70,311	336
Lubbock city (79402*)	186,206	87
Lufkin city (75901*)	30,206	1047
McAllen city (78501*)	82,021	265
Mesquite city (75149*)	101,484	195
Midland city (79711*)	89,443	233
Mission city (78572)	28,653	1118
Missouri City city (77489*)	36,176	834
Nacogdoches city (75961*)	30,872	1022

City and major zip code	1990 census	1990 rank
New Braunfels city (78130*)	27,334	1179
North Richland Hills city (76182)	45,895	626
Odessa city (79761*)	89,699	232
Pasadena city (77501*)	119,363	154
Pharr city (78577)	32,921	939
Plano city (75075*)	128,713	142
Port Arthur city (77640*)	58,724	431
Richardson city (75080*)	74,840	307
Round Rock city (78681*)	30,923	1019
San Angelo city (76902*)	84,474	260
San Antonio city (78284*)	935,933	10
San Marcos city (78666*)	28,743	1110
Sherman city (75090*)	31,601	991
Spring CDP (77373*)	33,111	933
Temple city (76501*)	46,109	621
Texarkana city (75501*)	31,656	989
Texas City city (77590*)	40,822	721
The Woodlands CDP (77373*)	29,205	1087
Tyler city (75712*)	75,450	304
Victoria city (77901*)	55,076	467
Waco city (76702*)	103,590	192
Wichita Falls city (76307*)	96,259	213
UTAH		
Bountiful city (80410*)	36,659	826
Cottonwood Heights CDP (84121)	28,766	1108
Kearns CDP (84118)	28,374	1126
Layton city (84041*)	41,784	703
Logan city (84321)	32,762	950
Millcreek CDP (84109)	32,230	966
Murray city (84199*)	31,282	1002
Ogden city (84401*)	63,909	383
Orem city (84057*)	67,561	355
Provo city (84601*)	86,835	248
St. George city (84770*)	28,502	1123
Salt Lake City city (84199*)	159,936	109
Sandy city (84070*)	75,058	305
Taylorsville-Bennion (84107*)	52,351	516
West Jordan city (84084*)	42,892	675
West Valley City city (84199*)	86,976	245
VERMONT		
Burlington city (05401*)	39,127	761
VIRGINIA		
Alexandria city (22313*)	111,183	168
Annandale CDP (22003)	50,975	538
Arlington CDP (22210*)	170,936	100
Blacksburg town (24060*)	34,590	877
Burke CDP (22015)	57,734	440
Centreville CDP (22020)	26,585	1213
Chantilly CDP (22030*)	29,337	1082
Charlottesville city (22906*)	40,341	731
Chesapeake city (23320*)	151,976	115
Dale City CDP (22191*)	47,170	604
Danville city (24541*)	53,056	506
Hampton city (23670*)	133,793	135
Harrisonburg city (22801)	30,707	1031
Jefferson CDP (22030*)	25,782	1259
Lynchburg city (24506*)	66,049	369
Manassas city (22110*)	27,957	1148
McLean CDP (22101*)	38,168	780
Mount Vernon CDP (22121)	27,485	1173
Newport News city (23607*)	170,045	101
Norfolk city (23501*)	261,229	62
Petersburg city (23804*)	38,386	776
Portsmouth city (23707*)	103,907	191
Reston CDP (22090)	48,556	583
Richmond city (23232*)	203,056	76
Roanoke city (24022*)	96,397	211
Suffolk city (23434*)	52,141	522
Tuckahoe CDP (23232*)	42,629	683
Virginia Beach city (23450*)	393,069	37
West Springfield CDP (22152)	28,126	1142
Woodbridge CDP (22191*)	26,401	1224
WASHINGTON		
Auburn city (98002*)	33,102	934
Bellevue city (98009*)	86,874	247
Bellingham city (98225*)	52,179	521
Bremerton city (98310*)	38,142	783
Burien CDP (98166)	25,089	1291
Cascade-Fairwood CDP	30,107	1051
East Hill-Meridian CDP	42,696	679
Edmonds city (98020*)	30,744	1029
Everett city (98201*)	69,961	339
Inglewood-Finn Hill (98011*)	29,132	1093
Federal Way CDP (98063)	67,554	356
Kennewick city (99336*)	42,155	691
Kent city (98031*)	37,960	791
Kirkland city (98033*)	40,052	743
Lakewood CDP (98259)	58,412	432
Longview city (98632)	31,499	993
Lynnwood city (98036*)	28,695	1116
Olympia city (98501*)	33,840	902
Redmond city (98052*)	35,800	842
Renton city (98058*)	41,688	705
Richland city (99352)	32,315	961
Richmond Heights CDP (98177)	26,037	1244
Seattle city (98109*)	516,259	21
Spokane city (99210*)	177,196	94
Tacoma city (98413*)	176,664	95
University Place CDP	27,701	1156
Vancouver city (98661*)	46,380	616
Walla Walla city (99362)	26,748	1219
Yakima city (98903*)	54,827	476
WEST VIRGINIA		
Charleston city (25301*)	57,287	444
Huntington city (25704*)	54,844	474
Morgantown city (26505*)	25,879	1255
Parkersburg city (26101*)	33,862	900
Wheeling city (26003)	34,882	870
WISCONSIN		
Appleton city (54911*)	65,695	371
Beloit city (53511*)	35,573	852
Brookfield city (53045*)	35,184	864
Eau Claire city (54703*)	56,856	449
Fond du Lac city (54935*)	37,757	798
Green Bay city (54303*)	96,466	210
Greenfield city (53220)	33,403	925
Janesville city (53545*)	52,133	523
Kenosha city (53140*)	80,352	278
La Crosse city (54601*)	51,003	537
Madison city (53714*)	191,262	82
Manitowoc city (54220*)	32,520	952
Memomonee Falls village (53051*)	26,840	1200
Milwaukee city (53203*)	628,088	17
New Berlin city (53186*)	33,592	915
Oshkosh city (54901*)	55,006	469
Racine city (53403*)	84,298	262
Sheboygan city (53081*)	49,676	560
Superior city (54836)	27,134	1188
Waukesha city (53186*)	56,958	448
Wausau city (54401*)	37,060	814
Wauwatosa city (53213*)	49,366	567
West Allis city (53214)	63,221	390
WYOMING		
Casper city (82601*)	46,742	609
Cheyenne city (82001*)	50,008	555
Laramie city (82070)	26,687	1208

Demographic State of the Nation: 1993

Source: U.S. Bureau of the Census

Population Projections

Under the middle series projection, the Nation's population would increase by 50% from 255 million in 1992 to 383 million in 2050. The middle series assumes 2.1 births per woman, average life expectancy increasing to 82.1 years by 2050, and an annual net immigration of 880,000 by the turn of the century. The age group with the largest increase (35%) is expected to be persons 45 to 54, from 27.4 million in 1992 to 37.1 million in 2000.

Asian and Pacific Islanders are expected to be the fastest-growing race group with annual growth rates that may exceed 4% in the 1990s. This population would rise from 9 million in 1992 (3% of the total) to 41 million in 2050 (11% of the total). The Hispanic population is expected to rise from 24 million in 1992 (9% of the total) to 81 million in 2050 (21% of the total). Immigration is expected to account for a large part of the growth of these two groups.

Households Increase

There were an estimated 95.7 million households in 1992, up from 94.3 million in 1991, 80.8 million in 1980, and 63.4 million in 1970. The average number of persons per household in 1992 was 2.62, not significantly different from the averages since 1989, but down from 2.76 in 1980 and 3.14 in 1970.

In 1992, married-couple families constituted 55% (52.5 million) of all households, compared to 15% (14.7 million) for families maintained by a householder with no spouse present, and 30% (28.5 million) for nonfamily households. (Families have at least two members, including at least one relative of the householder.) People living alone represented 84% of nonfamily households.

The number of single parents with one or more own children under 18 rose from 3.8 million in 1970 to 10.5 million in 1992, and the vast majority (86%) were mothers. Among single-parents, 8.3 million lived in their own households, whereas 2.2 million lived in households maintained by relatives or nonrelatives.

About 62% of Black family groups with children were single-parent families in 1992. The corresponding figures for Whites and Hispanics were 24% and 34%, respectively.

Education Turns Up

In 1990, 25.2% of persons 18 years or older had obtained a degree beyond high school (either academic or vocational), significantly higher than in 1987 (23.3%) or 1984 (20.7%). Across sex, race, and age groups (except for persons under 25), a higher proportion of persons had a degree beyond high school in 1990 than in 1984.

In 1990, a larger proportion of Whites (26.4%) than of Blacks (14.0%) or Hispanics (11.6%) had degrees beyond high school. Also, a larger proportion of men 26.9%) than women (23.8%) had degrees beyond high school.

A larger proportion of Whites (6.2%) than of Blacks (2.7%) or Hispanics (2.5%) had advanced degrees (the difference was not significant between Blacks and Hispanics).

In general, higher educational attainment leads to higher earnings. However, the mean monthly earnings of persons 18 years or older with a professional degree ($4,961) was higher than persons 18 or older with a doctorate degree.

Financial Support

In 1988, 8 million persons 18 years or older provided financial support (such as child support, alimony, and money for living expenses) to 12.4 million persons not living in the same household with them. Providers contributed $2,980, on average. Forty-nine percent supported only children, 45% supported only adults (not different from 49%), and 6% supported both.

Among providers, 4% were under 25, 58% were 25 to 44, 29% were 45 to 64, and 9% were 65 years or older. Of providers 25 to 44, 73% supported children; of providers 45 to 64, 71% supported dependent adult relatives and 34% supported children; and of providers 65 years and older, 93% supported adults only.

Three times as many men (76%) as women (24%) provided financial assistance. Almost 60% of the men, compared with 16% of the women, supported only children. Support payments by men to former or current spouses averaged 11% of their family income or $4,583 annually.

Among recipients, 44% were adults, with about one-third of them being the providers' parents. About 47% of adult recipients (children 21 and over receiving payments from parents) and 8% of children under 21 received lump-sum payments.

Health Insurance

In the fourth quarter of 1990, 13% of the population (32 million persons) did not have some type of health insurance. The 1990 rate was 12% for Whites, 18% for Blacks, and 28% for Hispanics. Almost one-half of the uninsured were under 25, an age group that accounts for 36% of the total population.

Ten percent of persons with a work disability and receiving retirement or disability income lacked health insurance. The rate was 24% for persons who did not receive these income supplements. Almost 40% of persons receiving unemployment compensation were uninsured at the close of 1990.

Household Income

Median household income declined by 3.5% in real terms between 1990 and 1991 from $31,203 to $30,126. This decline in income is the effect of the most recent recessionary period which began in July of 1990 and ended in March of 1991.

The real median income of White households declined by 3.0% to $31,569, and for Asian and Pacific Islander households by 9.0% to $36,449. The median income of Black households ($18,807) and of Hispanic origin households ($22,691) showed no significant change.

The real median earnings of male year-round, full-time workers with earnings increased between 1990 and 1991 by 2.0% to $29,421. This increase was accompanied by composition changes in the male work force and a decline of 1.3 million year-round, full-time workers. Real median earnings of women working year-round, full-time with earnings, on the other hand, remained unchanged at $20,553. As a result, the female-to-male earnings ratio decreased to .70. The ratio had increased from .60 in 1980 to a record high of .72 in 1990.

Poverty Increased

There were 35.7 million persons (14.2%) below the official government poverty level in 1991, up from 33.6 million (13.5%) in 1990. The 1991 poverty rate for Whites (11.3%) was higher than in 1990, whereas the 1991 rates for Blacks (32.7%) and Hispanics (28.7%) did not change significantly.

The poverty rate for children under 18 continued to be the highest of all age groups (since 1975) at 21.8%. The corresponding figure for persons 18 to 64 and for persons 65 years or older was 11.4% and 12.4%, respectively.

Between 1990 and 1991, the poverty rate for families increased from 10.7% to 11.5%, representing an increase of 613,000 poor families. About two-thirds of this increase was due to the rise in the number of female householder families with no husband present below the poverty level

The poverty rates for Whites, related children under 18, and persons in households maintained by females with no husband present increased significantly from 1990 to 1991. However, significant increases did not occur for Blacks, Hispanics, elderly persons, or persons in married-couple families.

One-Person Households

In 1989, there were 22.4 million single-person households, representing almost a quarter of all occupied housing units. About 53% of householders living alone were renters (representing 35% of all renters) and 47% owned their own homes (representing 18% of all homeowners).

For homeowners living alone, the median age of their homes was 31 years, compared to the median age of 25 years for all owner-occupied homes. Women living alone tended to own older homes (median age of 33 years) than those owned by men living alone (median age of 28 years). The median value of homes owned by persons living alone was $59,800, 21% lower than the $75,400 median for all owner-occupied units.

Homeownership

In 1991, 64% of households were owner occupied. The homeownership rate ranged from a low of 15% for householders under 25, to a high of 81% for householders 65 to 69. The homeownership rate was 79% for persons 70 to 74 years or older.

The homeownership rate for married-couple families in 1991 was 79%. The corresponding rates for families maintained by a male with no wife present and female with no husband present were 54% and 44%, respectively. Among one-person households, the homeownership rate was 43% for males and 54% for females.

Among States, homeownership rates in 1991 rates ranged from 53% in New York to 74% in Pennsylvania. The homeownership rate in the District of Columbia was 35%.

There were 107.3 million housing units in the Nation in 1991: 61 million were owner occupied, 34.2 million were renter occupied, and 12 million were vacant. □

Persons Below Poverty Level by Age, Region, Race, and Hispanic Origin, 1991

Age and region	Number below poverty level				Percent below poverty level			
	All races[2]	White	Black	Hispanic origin[1]	All races[2]	White	Black	Hispanic origin[1]
Under 18 years	14,341	8,848	4,755	3,094	21.8	16.8	45.9	40.4
18 to 21	2,441	1,646	661	466	18.0	15.0	32.8	30.3
22 to 44	10,838	7,399	2,878	8,677	11.7	9.5	25.3	22.9
45 to 54	2,167	1,541	544	328	8.0	6.6	19.5	18.1
55 to 59	1,019	716	246	113	9.6	7.9	21.3	17.0
60 to 64	1,120	796	278	115	10.6	8.7	27.5	19.6
65 and over	3,781	2,802	880	237	12.4	10.3	33.8	20.8
Northeast	6,177	4,389	1,546	1,217	12.2	10.0	28.1	36.3
Midwest	7,989	5,242	2,380	346	13.2	9.9	37.7	23.5
South	13,783	7,837	5,716	1,765	16.0	11.7	33.6	26.1
West	7,759	6,279	600	3,012	14.3	13.5	24.0	28.8
Total	**35,708**	**23,747**	**10,242**	**6,339**	**14.2**	**11.3**	**32.7**	**28.7**

1. Persons of Hispanic origin may be of any race. 2. Includes race not shown separately. *Source:* U.S. Bureau of the Census.

Population

Colonial Population Estimates (in round numbers)

Year	Population	Year	Population	Year	Population	Year	Population
1610	350	1660	75,100	1710	331,700	1760	1,593,600
1620	2,300	1670	111,900	1720	466,200	1770	2,148,100
1630	4,600	1680	151,500	1730	629,400	1780	2,780,400
1640	26,600	1690	210,400	1740	905,600		
1650	50,400	1700	250,900	1750	1,170,800		

National Censuses[1]

Year	Resident population[2]	Land area, sq mi.	Pop. per sq mi.	Year	Resident population[2]	Land area, sq mi.	Pop. per sq mi.
1790	3,929,214	864,746	4.5	1900	75,994,575	2,969,834	25.6
1800	5,308,483	864,746	6.1	1910	91,972,266	2,969,565	31.0
1810	7,239,881	1,681,828	4.3	1920	105,710,620	2,969,451	35.6
1820	9,638,453	1,749,462	5.5	1930	122,775,046	2,977,128	41.2
1830	12,866,020	1,749,462	7.4	1940	131,669,275	2,977,128	44.2
1840	17,069,453	1,749,462	9.8	1950	150,697,361	2,974,726	50.7
1850	23,191,876	2,940,042	7.9	1960	179,323,175	3,540,911	50.6
1860	31,443,321	2,969,640	10.6	1970	203,302,031	3,540,023	57.4
1870	39,818,449	2,969,640	13.4	1980	226,545,805	3,539,289	64.0
1880	50,155,783	2,969,640	16.9	1990	248,709,873	3,536,278	70.3
1890	62,947,714	2,969,640	21.2				

1. Beginning with 1960, figures include Alaska and Hawaii. 2. Excludes armed forces overseas. *Source:* Department of Commerce, Bureau of the Census.

Population Distribution by Age, Race, Nativity, and Sex

	Age						Race and Nativity				
							White[1]				
Year	Total	Under 5	5–19	20–44	45–64	65 and over	Total	Native born	Foreign born	Black	Other races[1]
PERCENT DISTRIBUTION											
1860[2]	100.0	15.4	35.8	35.7	10.4	2.7	85.6	72.6	13.0	14.1	0.3
1870[2]	100.0	14.3	35.4	35.4	11.9	3.0	87.1	72.9	14.2	12.7	0.2
1880[2]	100.0	13.8	34.3	35.9	12.6	3.4	86.5	73.4	13.1	13.1	0.3
1890[3]	100.0	12.2	33.9	36.9	13.1	3.9	87.5	73.0	14.5	11.9	0.3
1900	100.0	12.1	32.3	37.7	13.7	4.1	87.9	74.5	13.4	11.6	0.5
1910	100.0	11.6	30.4	39.0	14.6	4.3	88.9	74.4	14.5	10.7	0.4
1920	100.0	10.9	29.8	38.4	16.1	4.7	89.7	76.7	13.0	9.9	0.4
1930	100.0	9.3	29.5	38.3	17.4	5.4	89.8	78.4	11.4	9.7	0.5
1940	100.0	8.0	26.4	38.9	19.8	6.8	89.8	81.1	8.7	9.8	0.4
1950	100.0	10.7	23.2	37.6	20.3	8.1	89.5	82.8	6.7	10.0	0.5
1960	100.0	11.3	27.1	32.2	20.1	9.2	88.6	83.4	5.2	10.5	0.9
1970[2]	100.0	8.4	29.5	31.7	20.6	9.8	87.6	83.4	4.3	11.1	1.4
1980	100.0	7.2	24.8	37.1	19.6	11.3	83.1	n.a.	n.a.	11.7	5.2
1990	100.0	7.6	21.3	40.1	18.6	12.5	83.9	n.a.	n.a.	12.3	3.8
MALES PER 100 FEMALES											
1860[2]	104.7	102.4	101.2	107.9	111.5	98.3	105.3	103.7	115.1	99.6	260.8
1870[2]	102.2	102.9	101.2	99.2	114.5	100.5	102.8	100.6	115.3	96.2	400.7
1880[2]	103.6	103.0	101.3	104.0	110.2	101.4	104.0	102.1	115.9	97.8	362.2
1890[3]	105.0	103.6	101.4	107.3	108.3	104.2	105.4	102.9	118.7	99.5	165.2
1900	104.4	102.1	100.9	105.8	110.7	102.0	104.9	102.8	117.4	98.6	185.2
1910	106.0	102.5	101.3	108.1	114.4	101.1	106.6	102.7	129.2	98.9	185.6
1920	104.0	102.5	100.8	102.8	115.2	101.3	104.4	101.7	121.7	99.2	156.6
1930	102.5	103.0	101.4	100.5	109.1	100.5	102.9	101.1	115.8	97.0	150.6
1940	100.7	103.2	102.0	98.1	105.2	95.5	101.2	100.1	111.1	95.0	140.5

Year	Age						Race and Nativity				
							White[1]				
	Total	Under 5	5–19	20–44	45–64	65 and over	Total	Native born	Foreign born	Black	Other races[1]
1950	98.6	103.9	102.5	96.2	100.1	89.6	99.0	98.8	102.0	93.7	129.7
1960	97.1	103.4	102.7	95.6	95.7	82.8	97.4	97.6	94.2	93.3	109.7
1970[2]	94.8	104.0	103.3	95.1	91.6	72.1	95.3	95.9	83.8	90.8	100.2
1980	94.5	104.7	104.0	98.1	90.7	67.6	94.8	n.a.	n.a.	89.6	100.3
1990	95.1	104.8	105.0	99.8	92.5	67.2	95.9	n.a.	n.a.	89.8	96.5

1. The 1980 and 1990 census data for white and other races categories are not directly comparable to those shown for the preceding years because of the changes in the way some persons reported their race, as well as changes in procedures relating to racial classification. 2. Excludes persons for whom age is not available. 3. Excludes persons enumerated in the Indian Territory and on Indian reservations. NOTES: Data exclude Armed Forces overseas. Beginning in 1960, includes Alaska and Hawaii. n.a. = not available. *Source:* Department of Commerce, Bureau of the Census.

Population and Rank of Large Metropolitan Areas, 1990

(12/31/92 definition[1])
(over 100,000)

Rank	Standard metropolitan statistical area	Population
1	New York–Northern New Jersey–Long Island–NY–NJ–CT–PA	19,342,013
	New York, Newark, NY–NJ–PA	16,937,653
	Nassau–Suffolk, NY	2,609,212
	Bergen–Passaic, NJ	1,278,440
	Middlesex–Somerset–Hunterdon, NJ	1,019,835
	Bridgeport, CT	443,722
	Stamford–Norwalk, CT	329,935
	Trenton, NJ	325,824
	Orange County, NY	307,647
	Danbury, CT	207,590
2	Los Angeles–Riverside–Orange County, CA	14,531,529
	Los Angeles–Long Beach, CA	8,863,164
	Riverside–San Bernardino, CA	2,588,793
	Orange County, CA	2,410,556
	Ventura, CA	669,016
3	Chicago–Gary–Kenosha, IL–IN–WI	8,239,820
	Chicago, IL	7,410,858
	Gary, IN	604,526
	Kenosha, WI	128,181
	Kankakee, IL	96,255
4	Washington–Baltimore, DC–MD–VA–WV	6,727,050
	Washington, DC	4,223,485
	Baltimore, MD	2,382,172
5	San Francisco–Oakland–San Jose, CA	6,253,311
	Oakland, CA	2,082,914
	San Francisco, CA	1,603,678
	San Jose, CA	1,497,577
	Vallejo–Fairfield–Napa, CA	451,186
	Santa Rosa–Petaluma, CA	388,222
	Santa Cruz, CA	229,734
6	Philadelphia–Wilmington–Atlantic City, PA–NJ–DE–MD	5,892,937
	Philadelphia, PA–NJ	4,922,175
	Wilmington–Newark, DE–MD	513,293
	Atlantic–Cape May, NJ	319,416
	Vineland–Millville–Bridgeton, NJ	138,053
7	Boston–Brockton–Nashua, MA–NH	5,455,403
	Boston, MA	5,050,761
	Brockton, MA	236,409
	Nashua, NH	168,233
8	Detroit–Ann Arbor–Flint, MI	5,187,171
	Detroit, MI	4,266,654
	Ann Arbor, MI	490,058
	Flint, MI	430,459
9	Dallas–Fort Worth, TX	4,037,282
	Dallas, TX	2,676,248
	Fort Worth–Arlington, TX	1,361,034
10	Houston–Galveston–Brazoria, TX	3,731,131
	Houston, TX	3,322,025
	Galveston–Texas City, TX	217,399
	Brazoria, TX	191,707
11	Miami–Fort Lauderdale, FL	3,192,582
	Miami, FL	1,937,094
	Fort Lauderdale, FL	1,255,488
12	Seattle–Tacoma–Bremerton, WA	2,970,328
	Seattle–Bellevue–Everett, WA	2,033,156
	Tacoma, WA	586,203
	Bremerton, WA	189,731
	Olympia, WA	161,238
13	Atlanta, GA	2,959,950
14	Cleveland–Akron, OH	2,859,644
	Cleveland–Lorain–Elyria, OH	2,202,069
	Akron, OH	657,575
15	Minneapolis–St. Paul. MN–WI	2,538,834
16	San Diego, CA	2,498,016
17	St. Louis, MO–IL	2,492,525
18	Pittsburgh, PA	2,394,811
19	Phoenix–Mesa, AZ	2,238,840
20	Tampa–St. Petersburg–Clearwater, FL	2,067,959
21	Denver–Boulder–Greeley, CO	1,980,140
	Denver, CO	1,622,980
	Boulder–Longmont, CO	225,339
	Greeley, CO	131,821
22	Cincinnati–Hamilton, OH–KY–IN	1,817,571
	Cincinnati, OH–KY–IN	1,526,092
	Hamilton–Middletown, OH	291,479
23	Portland–Salem, OR–WA	1,793,476
	Portland–Vancouver, OR–WA	1,515,452
	Salem, OR	278,024
24	Milwaukee–Racine, WI	1,607,183
	Milwaukee–Waukesha, WI	1,432,149
	Racine, WI	175,034
25	Kansas City, MO–KS	1,582,875
26	Sacramento–Yolo, CA	1,481,102

Rank	Standard metropolitan statistical area	Population
27	Norfolk–Virginia Beach–Newport News, VA–NC	1,443,244
28	Columbus, OH	1,345,450
29	Indianapolis, IN	1,380,491
30	San Antonio, TX	1,324,749
31	New Orleans, LA	1,285,270
32	Orlando, FL	1,224,852
33	Buffalo–Niagara Falls, NY	1,189,288
	Buffalo, NY	968,532
	Niagara Falls, NY	220,756
34	Charlotte–Gastonia–Rock Hill, NC–SC	1,162,093
35	Hartford, CT	1,157,585
36	Providence–Fall River–Warwick, RI–MA	1,134,350
37	Salt Lake City–Ogden, UT	1,072,227
38	Rochester, NY	1,062,470
39	Greensboro–Winston-Salem–High Point, NC	1,050,304
40	Memphis, TN–AR–MS	1,007,306
41	Nashville, TN	985,026
42	Oklahoma City, OK	958,839
43	Dayton–Springfield, OH	951,270
44	Louisville, KY–IN	948,829
45	Grand Rapids–Muskegon–Holland, MI	937,891
46	Jacksonville, FL	906,727
47	Richmond–Petersburg, VA	865,640
48	West Palm Beach–Boca Raton, FL	863,518
49	Albany–Schenectady–Troy, NY	861,424
50	Raleigh–Durham–Chapel Hill, NC	855,545
51	Las Vegas, NV–AZ	852,737
52	Austin–San Marcos, TX	846,227
53	Birmingham, AL	840,140
54	Honolulu, HI	836,231
55	Greenville–Spartanburg–Anderson, SC	830,563
56	Fresno, CA	755,580
57	Syracuse, NY	742,177
58	Tulsa, OK	708,954
59	Tucson, AZ	666,880
60	Omaha, NE–IA	639,580
61	Toledo, OH	614,128
62	Youngstown–Warren, OH	600,895
63	El Paso, TX	591,610
64	Albuquerque, NM	589,131
65	Harrisburg–Lebanon–Carlisle, PA	587,986
66	Springfield, MA	587,884
67	Knoxville, TN	585,960
68	Bakersfield, CA	543,477
69	New Haven–Meriden, CT	530,180
70	Little Rock–North Little Rock, AR	513,117
71	Charleston–North Charleston, SC	506,875
72	Sarasota–Bradenton, FL	489,483
73	Wichita, KS	485,270
74	Stockton–Lodi, CA	480,628
75	Mobile, AL	476,923
76	Baton Rouge, LA	470,050
77	Fort Wayne, IN	456,281
78	Columbia, SC	453,331
79	Worcester, MA	436,905
80	Johnson City–Kingsport–Bristol, TN–VA	436,047
81	Lansing–East Lansing, MI	432,674
82	Kalamazoo–Battle Creek, MI	429,453
83	Lancaster, PA	422,822
84	Lexington, KY	405,936
85	Lakeland–Winter Haven, FL	405,382
86	Chattanooga, TN	399,487
87	Daytona Beach, FL	399,413
88	Saginaw–Bay City–Midland, MI	399,320
89	Melbourne–Titusville–Palm Bay, FL	398,978
90	Colorado Springs, CO	397,014
91	Jackson, MS	395,396
92	Augusta–Aiken, GA–SC	395,065
93	Canton–Massillon, OH	394,106
94	Des Moines, IA	392,928
95	McAllen–Edinburg–Mission, TX	383,545
96	Shreveport–Bossier City, LA	376,330
97	Modesto, CA	370,522
98	Santa Barbara–Santa Maria–Lompoc, CA	369,608
99	Madison, WI	367,085
100	Spokane, WA	361,364
101	Beaumont–Port Arthur, TX	361,226
102	Salinas, CA	355,660
103	Davenport–Rock Island–Moline, IA–IL	350,861
104	Corpus Christi, TX	349,894
105	Lafayette, LA	344,953
106	Pensacola, FL	344,406
107	Peoria–Pekin, IL	339,172
108	Reading, PA	336,523
109	Fort Myers–Cape Coral, FL	335,113
110	Rockford, IL	329,676
111	Utica–Rome, NY	316,633
112	Appleton–Oshkosh–Neenah, WI	315,121
113	Biloxi–Gulfport–Pascagoula, MS	312,368
114	Visalia–Tulare–Porterville, CA	311,921
115	Boise City, ID	295,851
116	Huntsville, AL	293,047
117	Montgomery, AL	292,517
118	Hickory–Morganton, NC	292,409
119	Macon, GA	290,909
120	New London–Norwich, CT–RI	290,734
121	Eugene–Springfield, OR	282,912
122	Evansville–Henderson, IN–KY	278,990
123	Salem, OR	278,024
124	Erie, PA	275,572
125	Fayetteville, NC	274,566
126	Binghamton, NY	264,497
127	Springfield, MO	264,346
128	Provo–Orem, UT	263,590
129	Columbus, GA–AL	260,860
130	Brownsville–Harlingen–San Benito, TX	260,120
131	Poughkeepsie, NY	259,462
132	Savannah, GA	258,060
133	Killeen–Temple, TX	255,301
134	Reno, NV	254,667
135	Fort Pierce–Port St. Lucie, FL	251,071
136	Charleston, WV	250,454
137	South Bend, IN	247,052
138	Johnstown, PA	241,247
139	Duluth–Superior, MN–WI	239,971
140	Tallahassee, FL	233,598
141	Anchorage, AK	226,338
142	Odessa–Midland, TX	225,545
143	Roanoke, VA	224,477
144	Portsmouth–Dover–Rochester, NH–ME	223,578
145	Lubbock, TX	222,636
146	Portland, ME	221,095
147	Lincoln, NE	213,641
148	Bradenton, FL	211,707
149	Fayetteville–Springdale–Rogers, AR	210,908
150	Danbury, CT	207,590
151	Waterbury, CT	205,811

NOTE: A standard metropolitan statistical area is one of a large population nucleus together with adjacent communities that have a high degree of economic and social integration with that nucleus. 1. Component areas are subject to change in the future. *Source:* Bureau of the Census.

The EXPANSION of the UNITED STATES
CANADA
Atlantic Ocean
ORIGINAL THIRTEEN STATES
THE UNITED STATES 1783
LOUISIANA PURCHASE
Purchased from France 1803
REPUBLIC OF TEXAS
Annexed 1845
FLORIDA
Purchased from Spain, 1819
Claimed by Spain to 1795
1810 1813
Area claimed by Texas and ceded by Mexico 1848
Ceded by Mexico 1848
Gadsden Purchase 1853
OREGON COUNTRY
U.S. Claim recognized by Great Britain, by Treaty of 1846
ROCKY MOUNTAINS
Mississippi R.
Missouri R.
Colorado
Gila R.
Columbia
Rio Grande
St. Lawrence R.
L. Superior
L. Michigan
L. Huron
L. Erie
L. Ontario
Limit of British claim
St. Mary's R.
Perdido R.
BAHAMA ISLANDS (British)
CUBA
Gulf of Mexico
MEXICO
Pacific Ocean
Present State Boundaries
Scale of Miles
0 100 300 500

Population by State

State	1990	Percent change, 1980–90	Pop. per sq mi., 1990	Pop. rank, 1990	1980	1950	1900	1790
Alabama	4,040,587	+3.8	79.6	22	3,893,888	3,061,743	1,828,697	—
Alaska	550,403	+36.9	1.0	49	401,851	128,643	63,592	—
Arizona	3,665,228	+34.8	32.3	24	2,718,215	749,587	122,931	—
Arkansas	2,350,725	+2.8	45.1	33	2,286,435	1,909,511	1,311,564	—
California	29,760,021	+25.7	190.4	1	23,667,902	10,586,223	1,485,053	—
Colorado	3,294,394	+14.0	31.8	26	2,889,964	1,325,089	539,700	—
Connecticut	3,287,116	+5.8	674.7	27	3,107,576	2,007,280	908,420	237,946
Delaware	666,168	+12.1	344.8	46	594,338	318,085	184,735	59,096
D.C.	606,900	–4.9	—	—	638,333	802,178	278,718	—
Florida	12,937,926	+32.7	238.9	4	9,746,324	2,771,305	528,542	—
Georgia	6,478,216	+18.6	109.9	11	5,463,105	3,444,578	2,216,331	82,548
Hawaii	1,108,229	+14.9	172.5	41	964,691	499,794	154,001	—
Idaho	1,006,749	+6.7	12.2	42	943,935	588,637	161,772	—
Illinois	11,430,602	0.0	205.4	6	11,426,518	8,712,176	4,821,550	—
Indiana	5,544,159	+1.0	154.2	14	5,490,224	3,934,224	2,516,462	—
Iowa	2,776,755	–4.7	49.6	30	2,913,808	2,621,073	2,231,853	—
Kansas	2,477,574	+4.8	30.3	32	2,363,679	1,905,299	1,470,495	—
Kentucky	3,685,296	+0.7	92.9	23	3,660,777	2,944,806	2,147,174	73,677
Louisiana	4,219,973	+0.3	94.8	21	4,205,900	2,683,516	1,381,625	—
Maine	1,227,928	+9.2	39.6	38	1,124,660	913,774	694,466	96,540
Maryland	4,781,468	+13.4	486.0	19	4,216,975	2,343,001	1,188,044	319,728
Massachusetts	6,016,425	+4.9	768.9	13	5,737,037	4,690,514	2,805,346	378,787
Michigan	9,295,297	+0.4	163.2	8	9,262,078	6,371,766	2,420,982	—
Minnesota	4,375,099	+7.3	55.0	20	4,075,970	2,982,483	1,751,394	—
Mississippi	2,573,216	+2.1	54.5	31	2,520,638	2,178,914	1,551,270	—
Missouri	5,117,073	+4.1	74.2	15	4,916,686	3,954,653	3,106,665	—
Montana	799,065	+1.6	5.5	44	786,690	591,024	243,329	—
Nebraska	1,578,385	+0.5	20.6	36	1,569,825	1,325,510	1,066,300	—
Nevada	1,201,833	+50.1	10.9	39	800,493	160,083	42,335	—
New Hampshire	1,109,252	+20.5	123.3	40	920,610	533,242	411,588	141,885
New Jersey	7,730,188	+5.0	1,035.1	9	7,364,823	4,835,329	1,883,669	184,139
New Mexico	1,515,069	+16.3	12.5	37	1,302,894	681,187	195,310	—
New York	17,990,455	+2.5	379.7	2	17,558,072	14,830,192	7,268,894	340,120
North Carolina	6,628,637	+12.7	135.7	10	5,881,766	4,061,929	1,893,810	393,751
North Dakota	638,800	–2.1	9.0	47	652,717	619,636	319,146	—
Ohio	10,847,115	+0.5	264.5	7	10,797,630	7,946,627	4,157,545	—
Oklahoma	3,145,585	+4.0	45.8	28	3,025,290	2,233,351	790,391[1]	—
Oregon	2,842,321	+7.9	29.5	29	2,633,105	1,521,341	413,536	—
Pennsylvania	11,881,643	+0.1	264.7	5	11,863,895	10,498,012	6,302,115	434,373
Rhode Island	1,003,464	+5.9	951.1	43	947,154	791,896	428,556	68,825
South Carolina	3,486,703	+11.7	115.4	25	3,121,820	2,117,027	1,340,316	249,073
South Dakota	696,004	+0.8	9.1	45	690,768	652,740	401,570	—
Tennessee	4,877,185	+6.2	118.5	17	4,591,120	3,291,718	2,020,616	35,691
Texas	16,986,510	+19.4	64.8	3	14,229,191	7,711,194	3,048,710	—
Utah	1,722,850	+17.9	20.9	35	1,461,037	688,862	276,749	—
Vermont	562,758	+10.0	60.7	48	511,456	377,747	343,641	85,425
Virginia	6,187,358	+15.7	155.8	12	5,346,818	3,318,680	1,854,184	747,610[2]
Washington	4,866,692	+17.8	73.1	18	4,132,156	2,378,963	518,103	—
West Virginia	1,793,477	–8.0	73.8	34	1,949,644	2,005,552	958,800	—
Wisconsin	4,891,769	+4.0	89.9	16	4,705,767	3,434,575	2,069,042	—
Wyoming	453,588	–3.4	4.7	50	469,557	290,529	92,531	—
Total U.S.	**248,709,873**	**+9.8**	—	—	**226,545,805**	**151,325,798**	**76,212,168**	**3,929,214**

1. Includes population of Indian Territory: 1900, 392,960. 2. Until 1863, Virginia included what is now West Virginia. *Source:* Department of Commerce, Bureau of the Census.

Householders Grow Younger and Older

Though the median age of the population has steadily risen in recent years, the median age of householders was significantly lower in 1992 than in 1970 (45.7 years compared with 48.1 years). During the 1970s and 1980s, many Baby Boomers formed households as they moved into their twenties, thirties, and early forties. Their disproportionately large numbers caused the median age for householders to drop.

At the opposite end of the householder age spectrum, the number of householders age 75 years and over has risen from 6.4 million, or 8 percent of all households in 1980, to 8.9 million, or 9 percent of the total in 1992. Again, changes in age structure of the population along with continued preference and ability to live independently have contributed to the increase in these households.

Territorial Expansion

Accession	Date	Area[1]
United States	—	3,536,278
Territory in 1790	—	891,364
Louisiana Purchase	1803	831,321
Florida	1819	69,866
Texas	1845	384,958
Oregon	1846	283,439
Mexican Cession	1848	530,706
Gadsden Purchase	1853	29,640
Alaska	1867	591,004
Hawaii	1898	6,471
Other territory	—	4,664
Philippines	1898	115,600[2]
Puerto Rico	1899	3,426
Guam	1899	209
American Samoa	1900	77
Canal Zone[3]	1904	553
Virgin Islands of U.S.	1917	134
Trust Territory of Pacific Islands	1947	177[4]
All other	—	14
Total, 1990	—	**3,540,315**

1. Total land and water area in square miles. 2. Became independent in 1946. 3. Reverted to Panama. 4. Land area only; Palau only Trust Territory remaining. *Source:* Department of Commerce, Bureau of the Census.

Total Population

Area	1990	1980	1970
50 states of U.S.	248,709,873	226,545,805	203,302,031
48 conterminous	247,051,601	225,179,263	202,229,535
Alaska	550,043	401,851	302,583
Hawaii	1,108,229	964,691	769,913
American Samoa	46,773	32,297	27,159
Canal Zone	(1)	(1)	44,198
Corn Islands	—	—	(2)
Guam	133,152	105,979	84,996
Johnston Atoll	n.a.	327	1,007
Midway	(3)	453	2,220
Puerto Rico	3,522,037	3,196,520	2,712,033
Swan Islands	n.a.	n.a.	22
Trust Ter. of Pac. Is.	15,122[5]	132,929[4]	90,940
Virgin Is. of U.S.	101,809	96,569	62,468
Wake Island	(3)	302	1,647
Population abroad	922,819	995,546	1,737,836
Armed forces	910,611	515,408	1,057,776
Total	253,451,585	**231,106,727**	**208,066,557**

1. Reverted to Panama. 2. Returned to Nicaragua April 25, 1971. 3. No indigenous population. 4. Includes Northern Mariana Islands. 5. Palau only Trust Territory remaining. NOTE: n.a. = not available. *Source:* Department of Commerce, Bureau of the Census.

Change in Population, by Age Group, Sex, Race, and Hispanic Origin: July 1, 1981 to July 1, 1991

(Numbers in thousands. Consistent with the 1980 and 1990 decennial enumerations)

Age, sex, race, and Hispanic origin	Estimates, July 1		Population change, 1981–1991		Average annual percent change
	1981	1991	Number	Percent	
Under 5 years	16,893	19,222	2,329	13.8	1.3
5 to 13 years	30,711	32,500	1,789	5.8	0.6
14 to 17 years	15,608	13,423	–2,185	–14.0	–1.5
18 to 24 years	30,245	26,385	–3,860	–12.8	–1.4
25 to 34 years	38,901	42,876	3,976	10.2	1.0
35 to 44 years	26,394	39,273	12,878	48.8	4.0
45 to 54 years	22,580	25,739	3,160	14.0	1.3
55 to 64 years	21,914	21,005	–909	–4.1	–0.4
65 to 74 years	15,890	18,280	2,390	15.0	1.4
75 to 84 years	7,982	10,314	2,332	29.2	2.6
85 years and over	2,349	3,160	811	34.5	3.0
Total all ages	229,466	252,177	22,711	9.0	0.9
Male	111,503	122,979	11,476	10.3	1.0
Female	117,963	129,198	11,235	9.5	0.9
White	196,635	210,899	14,264	7.3	0.7
Black	27,133	31,164	4,031	14.9	1.4
American Indian, Eskimo, and Aleut	1,483	2,117	634	42.8	3.6
Asian and Pacific Islander	4,214	7,996	3,782	89.7	6.4
Hispanic origin (any race)	15,560	23,350	7,790	50.1	4.1
White, not Hispanic	181,974	189,568	7,594	4.2	0.4
Black, not Hispanic	26,532	29,910	3,378	12.7	1.2
American Indian, Eskimo, and Aleut, not Hispanic	1,377	1,845	468	34.0	2.9
Asian and Pacific Islander, not Hispanic	4,022	7,504	3,482	86.6	6.2

Source: U.S. Bureau of the Census.

How Much Living Space for How Much?

Even if you have lower monthly housing costs than other homeowners you might *really* be paying more. More, that is, per *square foot* of living space. Housing costs and living space are not uniform across the country. Single-family detached homes were largest in the Northeast (a median of 2,189 square feet), followed by the Midwest (1,969), West (1,745), and South (1,673).

Though home values were highest in the Northeast ($122,859, compared with $110,317 in the runner-up West), western homes—square foot for square foot—were more expensive. Their median value per square foot was $63.04 compared to $57.60 for the Northeast.

Immigrants to U.S. by Country of Origin

(Figures are totals, not annual averages, and were tabulated as follows: 1820–67, alien passengers arrived; 1868–91 and 1895–97, immigrant aliens arrived; 1892–94 and 1898 to present, immigrant aliens admitted. 1989 and 1990 totals include legalized immigrants. (Data before 1906 relate to country whence alien came; 1906–80, to country of last permanent residence; 1981 to present data based on country of birth.)

Countries	1992	1820–1992	1981–90	1971–80	1961–70	1951–60	1941–50	1820–1940
Europe: Albania[1]	682	3,914	479	329	98	59	85	2,040
Austria[2]	701	2,662,608	4,636	9,478	20,621	67,106	24,860	2,534,617
Belgium	780	210,501	5,706	5,329	9,192	18,575	12,189	158,205
Bulgaria[3]	1,049	72,156	2,342	1,188	619	104	375	65,856
Czechoslovakia[1]	1,181	152,411	11,500	6,023	3,273	918	8,347	120,013
Denmark	764	371,787	5,380	4,439	9,201	10,984	5,393	335,025
Estonia[1]	194	1,511	137	91	163	185	212	506
Finland[1]	525	38,222	3,265	2,868	4,192	4,925	2,503	19,593
France	3,288	784,096	23,124	25,069	45,237	51,121	38,809	594,998
Germany[2]	9,888	7,078,012	70,111	74,414	190,796	477,765	226,578	6,021,951
Great Britain	19,973	5,135,957	142,123	137,374	213,822	202,824	139,306	4,266,561
Greece	1,858	698,594	29,130	92,369	85,969	47,608	8,973	430,608
Hungary[2]	1,304	1,673,817	9,764	6,550	5,401	36,637	3,469	1,609,158
Ireland	12,226	4,742,999	32,823	11,490	32,966	48,362	14,789	4,580,557
Italy	2.592	5,343,689	32,894	129,368	214,111	185,491	57,661	4,719,223
Latvia[1]	419	3,486	359	207	510	352	361	1,192
Lithuania[1]	353	4,928	482	248	562	242	683	2,201
Luxembourg[1]	25	3,214	234	307	556	684	820	565
Netherlands	1,586	376,821	11,958	10,492	30,606	52,277	14,860	253,759
Norway[4]	665	754,607	3,901	3,941	15,484	22,935	10,100	697,095
Poland[5]	25,504	665,177	97,390	37,234	53,539	9,985	7,571	414,755
Portugal	2,748	508,122	40,020	101,710	76,065	19,588	7,423	256,044
Romania[6]	6,500	227,543	39,963	12,393	2,531	1,039	1,076	156,945
Spain	1,631	283,893	15,698	39,141	44,659	7,894	2,898	170,123
Sweden[4]	1,463	1,393,971	10,211	6,531	17,116	21,697	10,665	1,325,208
Switzerland	1,023	359,385	7,076	8,235	18,453	17,675	10,547	295,680
Former U.S.S.R.[7]	43,614	3,570,704	84,081	38,961	2,465	671	571	3,343,361
Former Yugoslavia[3]	2,604	142,008	19,182	30,540	20,381	8,225	1,576	56,787
Other Europe	252	61,383	2,661	4,049	4,904	9,799	3,447	36,060
Total Europe	145,392	37,325,766	705,630	800,368	1,123,492	1,325,727	621,147	32,468,776
Asia: China[8]	38,907	1,028,247	388,686	124,326	34,764	9,657	16,709	382,173
India	36,755	548,690	261,841	164,134	27,189	1,973	1,761	9,873
Israel	5,104	138,905	36,353	37,713	29,602	25,476	476	—
Japan[9]	11,028	474,484	43,248	49,775	39,988	46,250	1,555	277,591
Turkey	2,488	414,953	20,843	13,399	10,142	3,519	798	361,236
Other Asia	262,673	4,208,748	2,042,025	1,198,831	285,957	66,374	15,729	44,053
Total Asia[10]	356,955	6,813,937	2,066,455	1,588,178	427,642	153,249	37,028	1,074,926
America: Canada and Newfoundland[11]	15,205	4,286,560	119,204	169,939	413,310	377,952	171,718	3,005,728
Central America	57,558	979,044	458,753	134,640	101,330	44,751	21,665	49,154
Mexico[12]	213,802	5,046,105	1,653,250	640,294	453,937	299,811	60,589	778,255
South America	55,308	1,379,675	455,977	295,741	257,954	91,628	21,831	121,302
West Indies	94,806	2,955,159	892,392	741,126	470,213	123,091	49,725	446,971
Other America[12]	2,676	117,078	1,352	995	19,630	59,711	29,276	56
Total America	439,355	14,763,521	3,580,928	1,982,735	1,716,374	996,944	354,804	4,401,466
Africa	27,086	412,729	192,212	80,779	28,954	14,092	7,367	26,060
Australia and New Zealand	3,205	149,303	20,169	23,788	19,562	11,506	13,805	54,437
Pacific Islands[13]	89	57,664	21,041	17,454	5,560	1,470	746	11,089
Countries not specified[14]	1,895	272,238	196	12	93	12,491	142	253,689
Total all countries	**973,977**	**59,795,158**	**7,338,062**	**4,493,314**	**3,321,677**	**2,515,479**	**1,035,039**	**38,290,443**

1. Countries established since beginning of World War I are included with countries to which they belonged. 2. Data for Austria–Hungary not reported until 1861. Austria and Hungary recorded separately after 1905, Austria included with Germany 1938–45. 3. Bulgaria, Serbia, Montenegro first reported in 1899. Bulgaria reported separately since 1920. In 1920, separate enumeration for Kingdom of Serbs, Croats, Slovenes; since 1922, recorded as Yugoslavia. 4. Norway included with Sweden 1820–68. 5. Included with Austria–Hungary, Germany, and Russia 1899–1919. 6. No record of immigration until 1880. 7. From 1931–63, the U.S.S.R. was broken down into European U.S.S.R. and Asian U.S.S.R. Since 1964, total U.S.S.R. has been reported in Europe. 8. Beginning in 1957, China includes Taiwan. 9. No record of immigration until 1861. 10. From 1934, Asia included Philippines; before 1934, recorded in separate tables as insular travel. 11. Includes all British North American possessions, 1820–98. 12. No record of immigration, 1886–93. 13. Included with "Countries not specified" prior to 1925. 14. Includes 32,897 persons returning in 1906 to their homes in U.S. *Source:* Department of Justice, Immigration and Naturalization Service. NOTE: Data are latest available.

The Foreign Born Population in the United States: 1990 and 1980

25 Largest Places of Birth

1990 Rank	Place of Birth	Number	Percent	1980 Rank	Place of Birth	Number	Percent
	United States	**19,767,316**	**100.0**		**United States**	**14,079,906**	**100.0**
1	Mexico	4,298,014	21.7	1	Mexico	2,199,221	15.6
2	Philippines	912,674	4.6	2	Germany	849,384	6.0
3	Canada	744,830	3.8	3	Canada	842,859	6.0
4	Cuba	736,971	3.7	4	Italy	831,922	5.9
5	Germany	711,929	3.6	5	United Kingdom	669,149	4.8
6	United Kingdom	640,145	3.2	6	Cuba	607,814	4.3
7	Italy	580,592	2.9	7	Philippines	501,440	3.6
8	Korea	568,397	2.9	8	Poland	418,128	3.0
9	Vietnam	543,262	2.7	9	Soviet Union	406,022	2.9
10	China	529,837	2.7	10	Korea	289,885	2.1
11	El Salvador	465,433	2.4	11	China	286,120	2.0
12	India	450,406	2.3	12	Vietnam	231,120	1.6
13	Poland	388,328	2.0	13	Japan	221,794	1.6
14	Dominican Republic	347,858	1.8	14	Portugal	211,614	1.5
15	Jamaica	334,140	1.7	15	Greece	210,998	1.5
16	Soviet Union	333,725	1.7	16	India	206,087	1.5
17	Japan	290,128	1.5	17	Ireland	197,817	1.4
18	Colombia	286,124	1.4	18	Jamaica	196,811	1.4
19	Taiwan	244,102	1.2	19	Dominican Republic	169,147	1.2
20	Guatemala	225,739	1.1	20	Yugoslavia	152,967	1.1
21	Haiti	225,393	1.1	21	Austria	145,607	1.0
22	Iran	210,941	1.1	22	Hungary	144,368	1.0
23	Portugal	210,122	1.1	23	Colombia	143,508	1.0
24	Greece	177,398	0.9	24	Iran	121,505	0.9
25	Laos	171,577	0.9	25	France	120,215	0.9

Source: U.S. Bureau of the Census, 1993.

Ancestry of U.S. Population by Rank, 1990 Census

1990 Rank	Ancestry group	Number	Percent
	Total population	**248,709,873**	**100.0**
1	German	57,947,873	23.3
2	Irish	38,735,539	15.6
3	English	32,651,788	13.1
4	Afro American	23,777,098	9.6
5	Italian	14,664,550	5.9
6	American	12,395,999	5.0
7	Mexican	11,586,983	4.7
8	French	10,320,935	4.1
9	Polish	9,366,106	3.8
10	American Indian	8,708,220	3.5
11	Dutch	6,227,089	2.5
12	Scotch-Irish	5,617,773	2.3
13	Scottish	5,393,581	2.2
14	Swedish	4,680,863	1.9
15	Norwegian	3,869,395	1.6
16	Russian	2,952,987	1.2
17	French Canadian	2,167,127	0.9
18	Welsh	2,033,893	0.8
19	Spanish	2,024,004	0.8
20	Puerto Rican	1,955,323	0.8
21	Slovak	1,882,897	0.8
22	White	1,799,711	0.7
23	Danish	1,634,669	0.7
24	Hungarian	1,582,302	0.6
25	Chinese	1,505,245	0.6
26	Filipino	1,450,512	0.6
27	Czech	1,296,411	0.5
28	Portuguese	1,153,351	0.5
29	British	1,119,154	0.4
30	Hispanic	1,113,259	0.4
31	Greek	1,110,373	0.4
32	Swiss	1,045,495	0.4
33	Japanese	1,004,645	0.4
34	Austrian	864,783	0.3
35	Cuban	859,739	0.3
36	Korean	836,987	0.3
37	Lithuanian	811,865	0.3
38	Ukrainian	740,803	0.3
39	Scandinavian	678,880	0.3
40	Acadian/Cajun	668,271	0.3
41	Finnish	658,870	0.3
42	United States	643,561	0.3
43	Asian Indian	570,322	0.2
44	Canadian	549,990	0.2
45	Croatian	544,270	0.2
46	Vietnamese	535,825	0.2
47	Dominican	505,690	0.2
48	Salvadoran	499,153	0.2
49	European	466,718	0.2
50	Jamaican	435,024	0.2
51	Lebanese	394,180	0.2
52	Belgian	380,498	0.2
53	Romanian	365,544	0.1
54	Spaniard	360,935	0.1
55	Colombian	351,717	0.1
56	Czechoslovakian	315,285	0.1
57	Armenian	308,096	0.1
58	Pennsylvania German	305,841	0.1
59	Haitian	289,521	0.1
60	Yugoslavian	257,994	0.1
61	Hawaiian	256,081	0.1
62	African	245,845	0.1
63	Guatemalan	241,559	0.1
64	Iranian	235,521	0.1
65	Ecuadorian	197,374	0.1

1990 Rank	Ancestry group	Number	Percent	1990 Rank	Ancestry group	Number	Percent
66	Taiwanese	192,973	0.1	132	Alsatian	16,465	0.0
67	Nicaraguan	177,077	0.1	133	Tongan	16,019	0.0
68	Peruvian	161,866	0.1	134	Aleut	15,816	0.0
69	West Indies	159,167	0.1	135	Amerasian	15,523	0.0
70	Laotian	146,930	0.1	136	Uruguayan	14,641	0.0
71	Cambodian	134,955	0.1	137	Sri Lankan	14,448	0.0
72	Syrian	129,606	0.1	138	Eurasian	14,177	0.0
73	Arab	127,364	0.1	139	Flemish	14,157	0.0
74	Slovene	124,437	0.1	140	North American	12,618	0.0
75	Serbian	116,635	0.0	141	Bangladeshi	12,486	0.0
76	Honduran	116,635	0.0	142	Pacific Islander	11,330	0.0
77	Thai	112,117	0.0	143	Grenadian	11,188	0.0
78	Asian	107,172	0.0	144	South American	10,867	0.0
79	Latvian	100,331	0.0	145	Polynesian	10,854	0.0
80	Pakastani	99,974	0.0	146	Okinawan	10,554	0.0
81	Nigerian	91,688	0.0	147	Central American	10,310	0.0
82	Panamanian	88,649	0.0	148	German Russian	10,153	0.0
83	Hmong	84,823	0.0	149	Liberian	8,797	0.0
84	Turkish	83,850	0.0	150	Burmese	8,646	0.0
85	Israeli	81,677	0.0	151	New Zealand	7,742	0.0
86	Guyanese	81,665	0.0	152	Soviet Union	7,729	0.0
87	Egyptian	78,574	0.0	153	Middle Eastern	7,656	0.0
88	Slavic	76,931	0.0	154	US Virgin Islander	7,621	0.0
89	Trinidad & Tobagonian	76,270	0.0	155	Basque, Spanish	7,620	0.0
90	Northern European	65,993	0.0	156	Carpath Russian	7,602	0.0
91	Brazilian	65,875	0.0	157	Fijian	7,472	0.0
92	Argentinian	63,176	0.0	158	Antigua	7,364	0.0
93	Dutch West Indian	61,530	0.0	159	Manx	6,317	0.0
94	Chilean	61,465	0.0	160	Basque, French	6,001	0.0
95	Samoan	55,419	0.0	161	Hong Kong	5,774	0.0
96	Eskimo	52,920	0.0	162	Vincent/Grenadine Islander	5,773	0.0
97	Australian	52,133	0.0	163	Tirol	5,748	0.0
98	Costa Rican	51,771	0.0	164	Rom	5,693	0.0
99	Assyrian	51,765	0.0	165	Central European	5,604	0.0
100	Cape Verdean	50,772	0.0	166	Nova Scotian	5,489	0.0
101	Sicilian	50,389	0.0	167	Paraguayan	5,415	0.0
102	Luxemburger	49,061	0.0	168	Newfoundland	5,412	0.0
103	Palestinian	48,019	0.0	169	Bermudan	4,941	0.0
104	Basque	47,958	0.0	170	Cypriot	4,897	0.0
105	Albanian	47,710	0.0	171	Kenyan	4,639	0.0
106	Indonesian	43,969	0.0	172	Sierra Leone	4,627	0.0
107	Latin American	43,521	0.0	173	Saxon	4,519	0.0
108	Western European	42,409	0.0	174	Saudi Arabian	4,486	0.0
109	Icelander	40,529	0.0	175	Chamorro	4,427	0.0
110	Venezuelan	40,331	0.0	176	Bavarian	4,348	0.0
111	Maltese	39,600	0.0	177	Azorean	4,310	0.0
112	Guamanian	39,237	0.0	178	Belorussian	4,277	0.0
113	British West Indian	37,819	0.0	179	Eritrean	4,270	0.0
114	Barbadian	35,455	0.0	180	Yemeni	4,011	0.0
115	Bolivian	33,738	0.0	181	Northern Irish	4,009	0.0
116	Afghanistan	31,301	0.0	182	Cornish	3,991	0.0
117	Ethiopian	30,581	0.0	183	West German	3,885	0.0
118	Celtic	29,652	0.0	184	Moravian	3,781	0.0
119	Bulgarian	29,595	0.0	185	Ruthenian	3,776	0.0
120	Malaysian	27,800	0.0	186	Sudanese	3,623	0.0
121	Estonian	26,762	0.0	187	Mongolian	3,507	0.0
122	Prussian	25,469	0.0	188	St. Lucia	3,415	0.0
123	Cantonese	25,020	0.0	189	Micronesian	3,406	0.0
124	Iraqi	23,212	0.0	190	Algerian	3,215	0.0
125	Belizean	22,922	0.0	191	Windish	3,189	0.0
126	Bahamian	21,081	0.0	192	Khmer	2,979	0.0
127	Jordanian	20,656	0.0	193	Kitts/Nevis Islander	2,811	0.0
128	Macedonian	20,365	0.0	194	Ugandan	2,681	0.0
129	Ghanian	20,066	0.0	195	Nepali	2,516	0.0
130	Moroccan	19,089	0.0	196	Singaporean	2,419	0.0
131	South African	17,992	0.0	197	Cypriot, Greek	2,197	0.0

NOTE: Data are based on a sample and subject to sampling variability. Since persons who reported multiple ancestries were included in more than one group, the sum of the persons reporting the ancestry is greater than the total; for example, a person reporting "English-French" was tabulated in both the "English" and "French" categories. Ancestry groups with fewer than 2,000 persons were not included in this report. *Source:* U.S. Bureau of the Census, 1993.

Spanish Leads Foreign Languages Spoken by U.S. Residents

According to the latest census studies released in April 1993, over 31.8 million people—14% of the nation's population five years or over—spoke a language other than English in 1990, compared with 23.1 million (or 11%) in 1980. After English, Spanish was the most common language spoken. About 4.5 million Americans spoke an Asian or Pacific Island language and nearly 332,000 spoke a Native North American language.

More than half of all non-English language speakers in 1990 lived in three states: California (8.6 million), New York (3.9 million), and Florida (4 million). New Mexico had the largest percentage of non-English language speakers at 36%, followed by California with 32 percent.

Spanish was the prevailing language in 39 states and the District of Columbia. The next most widely used language varied by region—Italian and German in the Northeast and Midwest, and French and Chinese in the South and West. French was most used in Louisiana, Maine, New Hampshire, and Vermont; and German in Montana, Minnesota, and North and South Dakota. In Rhode Island, Portuguese was first; in Alaska, it was Yupik; and in Hawaii, Japanese was the language of most non-English language speakers. □

Number of Non-English Language Speaking Americans, 1990

Top 50 languages spoken at home, ranked for persons five years old and over

Language	1990 Population 5 years and over	1980 Population 3 years and over	Percent change
United States	230,445,777	216,384,403	6.5
Total	31,844,979	23,711,574	34.3
Spanish	17,339,172	11,549,333	50.1
French	1,702,176	1,572,275	8.3
German	1,547,099	1,606,743	–3.7
Italian	1,308,648	1,633,279	–19.9
Chinese	1,249,213	631,737	97.7
Tagalog[1]	843,251	451,962	86.6
Polish	723,483	826,150	–12.4
Korean	626,478	275,712	127.2
Vietnamese	507,069	203,268	149.5
Portuguese	429,860	361,101	19.0
Japanese	427,657	342,205	25.0
Greek	388,260	410,462	–5.4
Arabic	355,150	225,597	57.4
Hindi and related	331,484	129,968	155.1
Russian	241,798	174,623	38.5
Yiddish	213,064	320,380	–33.5
Thai	206,266	89,052	131.6
Persian	201,865	109,293	84.7
French Creole	187,658	24,885	654.1
Armenian	149,694	102,301	46.3
Navaho	148,530	123,169	20.6
Hungarian	147,902	180,083	–17.9
Hebrew	144,292	99,166	45.4
Dutch	142,684	146,429	–2.6
Mon-Khmer[2]	127,441	16,417	676.3
Gujarathi[3]	102,418	36,865	177.8
Ukrainian	96,568	122,300	–21.0
Czech	92,485	123,059	–24.8
Pennsylvania Dutch	83,525	68,202	22.5
Miao[4]	81,877	16,189	405.8
Norwegian	80,723	113,227	–28.7
Slovak	80,388	87,941	–8.6
Swedish	77,511	100,886	–23.2
Serbocroatian	70,964	83,216	–14.7
Kru[5]	65,848	24,506	168.7
Rumanian	65,265	32,502	100.8
Lithuanian	55,781	73,234	–23.8
Finnish	54,350	69,386	–21.7
Panjabi	50,005	19,298	159.1
Formosan	46,044	13,661	237.0
Croatian	45,206	42,479	6.4
Turkish	41,876	27,459	52.5
Ilocano[6]	41,131	25,301	62.6
Bengali	38,101	13,180	189.1
Danish	35,639	43,251	–17.6
Syriac	35,146	10,020	250.8
Samoan	34,914	27,475	27.1
Malayalam[7]	33,949	11,385	198.2
Cajun	33,670	9,374	259.2
Amharic[8]	31,505	11,892	164.9

NOTE: The data for 1980 in this table are for the population 3 years old and over; for 1990 they are for persons 5 years and over. *Source:* Census data published April 1993. 1. Filipino language of Manila and adjacent provinces. 2. Language spoken in southeast Asia, mostly in Cambodia. 3. Language of Gujarat region of western India. 4.Language of Hmong people of mountainous regions of southern China and adjacent areas of Vietnam, Laos, and Thailand. 5. Language spoken in Western Africa, chiefly in Liberia. 6. Philippine language of northern Luzon. 7. Language of the state of Kerala in India. 8. Official language of Ethiopia.

A Quarter of Nation's Foreign Born Arrived Since 1985

Nearly one-fourth of the United States' nearly 20 million foreign-born residents entered the country between 1985 and 1990, according to tabulations from the 1990 census.

The listing shows that the number of foreign-born persons entering the United States has increased steadily since the early 1960s, from 1.5 million in 1960–64, to a peak of 5.6 million in 1985–90.

About 7.9 percent of the nation's population was foreign born in 1990, the highest proportion in the past four decades.

California was home to one-third of the nation's foreign-born population. Other states with large concentrations include New York, 14 percent; Florida and Texas, 8 percent each; and New Jersey and Illinois, 5 percent each.

Immigrant and Nonimmigrant Aliens Admitted to U.S.

Period[1]	Immigrants	Non-immigrants[2]	Total	Period[1]	Immigrants	Non-immigrants[2]	Total
1901–10	8,795,386	1,007,909	9,803,295	1984	543,903	9,426,759	9,970,662
1911–20	5,735,811	1,376,271	7,112,082	1985	570,009	9,675,650	10,245,659
1921–30	4,107,209	1,774,896	5,882,090	1986	601,708	10,471,024	11,072,732
1931–40	528,431	1,574,071	2,102,502	1987	601,516	12,272,866	12,874,382
1941–50	1,035,039	2,461,359	3,496,398	1988	643,025	14,591,735	15,234,760
1951–60	2,515,479	7,113,023	9,628,502	1989	1,090,924[3]	16,144,576	17,235,500
1961–70	3,321,677	24,107,224	27,428,901	1990	1,536,483[3]	17,145,680	18,682,163
1971–77	2,797,209	45,236,597	48,033,806	1991	1,827,167[3]	18,962,520	20,789,687
1983[2]	559,763	9,849,458	10,409,221	1992	973,977[4]	20,793,846	21,767,823

1. Fiscal year ending June 30 prior to 1977. After 1977 for fiscal year ending Sept. 30. 2. Nonimmigrant aliens include visitors for business or pleasure, students, foreign government officials, and others temporarily in the U.S. 3. Includes immigrants and legalized immigrants. 4. Includes immigrants and 163,342 legalized immigrants. *Source:* Department of Justice, Immigration and Naturalization Service.

Persons Naturalized Since 1907

Period[1]	Civilian	Military	Total	Period[1]	Civilian	Military	Total
1907–30	2,713,389	300,506	3,013,895	1987	224,100	2,402	227,008[2]
1930–40	1,498,573	19,891	1,518,464	1988	239,541	2,296	242,063[3]
1941–50	1,837,229	149,799	1,987,028	1989	231,198	1,954	233,777[4]
1951–60	1,148,241	41,705	1,189,946	1990	246,845	1,630	270,101[5]
1961–70	1,084,195	36,068	1,120,263	1991	299,373	1,804	308,058[6]
1971–80	1,397,846	66,926	1,464,772	1907–91	12,134,365	645,016	12,816,691[7]

1. Fiscal year ending June 30. Starting 1977, fiscal year ending Sept. 30. 2. Including 506 unidentified. 3. Including 226 unidentified. 4. Including 625 unidentified. 5. Including 21,626 unidentified. 6. Includes 6,881 unidentified. 7. Includes 37,310 unidentified. *Source:* Department of Justice, Immigration and Naturalization Service. NOTE: Data are latest available.

Marriage and Divorce

Marriages and Divorces

	Marriage		Divorce[1]			Marriage		Divorce[1]	
Year	Number	Rate[2]	Number	Rate[2]	Year	Number	Rate[2]	Number	Rate[2]
1900	709,000	9.3	55,751	.7	1969	2,145,438	10.6	639,000	3.2
1905	842,000	10.0	67,976	.8	1970	2,158,802	10.6	708,000	3.5
1910	948,166	10.3	83,045	.9	1971	2,190,481	10.6	773,000	3.7
1915	1,007,595	10.0	104,298	1.0	1972	2,282,154	11.0	845,000	4.1
1920	1,274,476	12.0	170,505	1.6	1973	2,284,108	10.9	915,000	4.4
1925	1,188,334	10.3	175,449	1.5	1974	2,229,667	10.5	977,000	4.6
1930	1,126,856	9.2	195,961	1.6	1975	2,152,662	10.1	1,036,000	4.9
1935	1,327,000	10.4	218,000	1.7	1976	2,154,807	10.0	1,083,000	5.0
1940	1,595,879	12.1	264,000	2.0	1977	2,178,367	10.1	1,091,000	5.0
1945	1,612,992	12.2	485,000	3.5	1978	2,282,272	10.5	1,130,000	5.2
1950	1,667,231	11.1	385,144	2.6	1979	2,341,799	10.6	1,181,000	5.4
1955	1,531,000	9.3	377,000	2.3	1980	2,406,708	10.6	1,182,000	5.2
1957	1,518,000	8.9	381,000	2.2	1981	2,438,000	10.6	1,219,000	5.3
1958	1,451,000	8.4	368,000	2.1	1982	2,495,000	10.8	1,180,000	5.1
1959	1,494,000	8.5	395,000	2.2	1983	2,444,000	10.5	1,179,000	5.0
1960	1,523,000	8.5	393,000	2.2	1984	2,487,000	10.5	1,155,000	4.9
1961	1,548,000	8.5	414,000	2.3	1985	2,425,000	10.2	1,187,000	5.0
1962	1,577,000	8.5	413,000	2.2	1986	2,400,000	10.0	1,159,000	4.8
1963	1,654,000	8.8	428,000	2.3	1987	2,421,000	9.9	1,157,000	4.8
1964	1,725,000	9.0	450,000	2.4	1988	2,389,000	9.7	1,183,000	4.8
1965	1,800,000	9.3	479,000	2.5	1989	2,404,000	9.7	1,163,000	4.7
1966	1,857,000	9.5	499,000	2.5	1990	2,448,000	9.8	1,175,000	4.7
1967	1,927,000	9.7	523,000	2.6	1991	2,371,000	9.4	1,187,000	4.7
1968	2,069,258	10.4	584,000	2.9	1992[3]	2,362,000	9.2	1,215,000	4.7

1. Includes annulments. 2. Per 1,000 population. Divorce rates for 1941–46 are based on population including armed forces overseas. Marriage rates are based on population excluding armed forces overseas. 3. Provisional. NOTE: Marriage and divorce figures for most years include some estimated data. Alaska is included beginning 1959, Hawaii beginning 1960. *Source:* Department of Health and Human Services, National Center for Health Statistics.

Percent of Population Never Married

Age group	All races 1992	All races 1980	All races 1970	White 1992	White 1980	White 1970	Black 1992	Black 1980	Black 1970
Males: 20 t0 24	80.3	68.8	54.6	78.5	67.0	54.5	88.3	79.3	56.1
25 to 29	48.7	33.1	19.1	45.8	31.4	17.8	65.2	44.2	28.4
30 to 34	29.4	15.9	9.4	26.8	14.2	9.2	47.8	30.0	9.2
35 to 39	18.4	7.8	7.2	16.3	6.6	6.1	36.0	18.5	15.8
40 to 44	9.2	7.1	6.3	8.7	6.7	5.7	13.9	10.8	11.2
45 to 54	7.3	6.1	7.5	6.7	5.6	7.1	14.4	11.7	10.4
55 to 64	5.6	5.3	7.8	4.9	5.2	7.6	12.0	5.9	9.1
65 and over	4.2	4.9	7.5	4.0	4.8	7.4	6.5	5.5	5.7
Females: 20 to 24	65.7	50.2	35.8	62.7	47.2	34.6	80.3	68.5	43.5
25 to 29	33.2	20.9	10.5	28.5	18.3	9.2	60.4	37.2	18.8
30 to 34	18.8	9.5	6.2	15.1	8.1	5.5	41.0	19.0	10.8
35 to 39	12.6	6.2	5.4	9.7	5.2	4.6	32.1	12.2	12.1
40 to 44	8.4	4.8	4.9	7.3	4.3	4.8	16.5	9.0	6.9
45 to 54	5.3	4.7	4.9	4.5	4.4	4.9	11.5	7.7	4.4
55 to 64	4.0	4.5	6.8	3.5	4.4	7.0	8.2	5.7	4.7
65 and over	4.9	5.9	7.7	4.8	6.1	8.0	5.7	4.5	4.2

Source: U.S. Burea of the Census, Current Population Reports, Series P-20, No. 468, *Marital Status and Living Arrangements: March 1992.*

Persons Living Alone, by Sex and Age

(numbers in thousands)

Sex and Age[1]	1992 Number	1992 Percent	1991 Number	1991 Percent	1990 Number	1990 Percent	1980 Number	1980 Percent	1970 Number	1970 Percent
BOTH SEXES										
15 to 24 years	1,156	4.8	1,140	4.8	1,210	5.3	1,726	9.4	556	5.1
25 to 44 years	7,404	30.9	7,518	31.9	7,110	30.9	4,729	25.8	1,604	14.8
45 to 64 years	5,890	24.6	5,550	23.5	5,502	23.9	4,514	24.7	3,622	33.4
65 years and over	9,523	39.7	9,381	39.8	9,176	39.9	7,328	40.1	5,071	46.7
Total, 15 years and over	**23,974**	**100.0**	**23,590**	**100.0**	**22,999**	**100.0**	**18,296**	**100.0**	**10,851**	**100.0**
MALE										
15 to 24 years	601	6.2	622	6.6	674	7.4	947	13.6	274	2.5
25 to 44 years	4,443	46.2	4,499	47.6	4,231	46.8	2,920	41.9	933	8.6
45 to 64 years	2,483	25.8	2,319	24.5	2,203	24.3	1,613	23.2	1,152	10.6
65 years and over	2,086	21.7	2,010	21.3	1,942	21.5	1,486	21.3	1,174	10.8
Total, 15 years and over	**9,613**	**100.0**	**9,450**	**100.0**	**9,049**	**100.0**	**6,966**	**100.0**	**3,532**	**32.5**
FEMALE										
15 to 24 years	555	3.9	518	3.7	536	3.8	779	6.9	282	2.6
25 to 44 years	2,962	20.6	3,020	21.3	2,881	20.7	1,809	16.0	671	6.2
45 to 64 years	3,408	23,7	3,232	22.8	3,300	23.7	2,901	25.6	2,470	22.8
65 years and over	7,437	51.8	7,370	52.1	7,233	51.8	5,842	51.6	3,897	35.9
Total, 15 years and over	**14,361**	**100.0**	**14,141**	**100.0**	**13,950**	**100.0**	**11,330**	**100.0**	**7,319**	**67.5**

1. Prior to 1980, data are for persons 14 years and older. NOTE: Details may not add because of rounding. *Source:* Department of Commerce, Bureau of the Census.

Characteristics of Unmarried–Couple Households, 1992

(number in thousands)

Characteristics	Number	Percent	Characteristics	Number	Percent
Unmarried–couple households	3,308	100.0	Presence of children:		
			No children under 15 years	2,187	66.1
Age of householders:			Some children under 15 years	1,121	33.9
Under 25 years	661	20.0			
25–44 years	2,026	61.2	Sex of householders:		
45–64 years	475	14.4	Male	1,881	56.9
65 years and over	146	4.4	Female	1,427	43.1

Source: U.S. Bureau of the Census.

Households, Families, and Married Couples

Date	Households: Number	Households: Average population per household	Families: Number	Families: Average population per family	Maried couples: Number
June 1890	12,690,000	4.93	—	—	—
April 1930	29,905,000	4.11	—	—	25,174,000
April 1940	34,949,000	3.67	32,166,000	3.76	28,517,000
March 1950	43,554,000	3.37	39,303,000	3.54	36,091,000
April 1955	47,874,000	3.33	41,951,000	3.59	37,556,000
March 1960[1]	52,799,000	3.33	45,111,000	3.67	40,200,000
March 1965	57,436,000	3.29	47,956,000	3.70	42,478,000
March 1970	63,401,000	3.14	51,586,000	3.58	45,373,000
March 1975	71,120,000	2.94	55,712,000	3.42	47,547,000
March 1980	80,776,000	2.76	59,550,000	3.29	49,714,000
March 1985	86,789,000	2.69	62,706,000	3.23	51,114,000
March 1990	93,347,000	2.63	66,090,000	3.17	53,256,000
March 1992	95,669,000	2.62	67,173,000	3.17	52,457,000

1. First year in which figures for Alaska and Hawaii are included. *Source:* Department of Commerce, Bureau of the Census.

Families Maintained by Women, With No Husband Present
(numbers in thousands)

	1992 Number	1992 Percent	1990 Number	1990 Percent	1980 Number	1980 Percent	1970 Number	1970 Percent	1960 Number	1960 Percent
Age of women:										
Under 35 years	3,874	33.1	3,699	34.0	3,015	34.6	1,364	24.4	796	17.7
35 to 44 years	3,230	27.6	2,929	26.9	1,916	22.0	1,074	19.2	940	20.9
45 to 64 years	3,040	26.0	2,790	25.6	2,514	28.9	2,021	36.1	1,731	38.5
65 years and over	1,547	13.1	1,471	13.5	1,260	14.5	1,131	20.2	1,027	22.9
Median age	40.9	—	40.7	—	41.7	—	48.5	—	50.1	—
Presence of children:										
No own children under 18 years	4,648	39.8	4,290	39.4	3,260	37.4	2,665	47.7	2,397	53.3
With own children under 18 years	7,043	60.2	6,599	60.6	5,445	62.6	2,926	52.3	2,097	46.7
Total own children under 18 years	12,604	—	11,378	—	10,204	—	6,694	—	4,674	—
Average per family	1.08	—	1.04	—	1.17	—	1.20	—	1.04	—
Average per family with children	1.79	—	1.72	—	1.87	—	2.29	—	2.24	—
Race:										
White	7,726	66.1	7,306	67.1	6,052	69.5	4,165	74.5	3,547	78.9
Black[1]	3,582	30.6	3,275	30.1	2,495	28.7	1,382	24.7	947	21.1
Other	384	3.3	309	2.8	158	1.8	44	0.8	n.a.	n.a.
Marital status:										
Married, husband absent	2,049	17.5	1,947	17.9	1,769	20.3	1,326	23.7	1,099	24.5
Widowed	2,458	21.0	2,536	23.3	2,570	29.5	2,396	42.9	2,325	51.7
Divorced	4,285	36.6	3,949	36.3	3,008	34.6	1,259	22.5	694	15.4
Never married	2,900	24.8	2,457	22.6	1,359	15.6	610	10.9	376	8.4
Total families maintained by women	**11,692**	**100.0**	**10,890**	**100.0**	**8,705**	**100.0**	**5,591**	**100.0**	**4,494**	**100.0**

1. Includes other races in 1960. NOTE: n.a. = not available. (—) as shown in this table, means "not applicable." *Source:* Department of Commerce, Bureau of the Census.

Median Age at First Marriage

Year	Males	Females	Year	Males	Females	Year	Males	Females	Year	Males	Females
1900	25.9	21.9	1930	24.3	21.3	1960	22.8	20.3	1990	26.1	23.9
1910	25.1	21.6	1940	24.3	21.5	1970	23.2	20.8	1991	26.3	24.1
1920	24.6	21.2	1950	22.8	20.3	1980	24.7	22.0	1992	26.5	24.4

Source: Department of Commerce, Bureau of the Census.

Selected Family Characteristics

Characteristics[1]	1991 Number (thous.)	1991 Median income
ALL RACES		
All families	67,173	$35,939
Type of residence		
Nonfarm	65,834	36,002
Farm	1,339	32,889
Location of residence		
Inside metropolitan areas	51,677	38.370
1,000,000 or more	32,854	41,033
Inside central cities	11,706	31,655
Outside central cities	21,147	46,061
Under 1,000,000	18,824	34,402
Inside central cities	7,328	30,918
Outside central cities	11,496	36,381
Outside metropolitan areas	15,496	29,127
Region		
Northeast	13,428	40,265
Midwest	16,170	36,759
South	23,679	31,940
West	13,897	37,171
Type of family		
Married-couple family	52,457	40,995
Wife in paid labor force	30,923	48,169
Wife not in paid labor force	21,534	30,075
Male householder, no wife present	3,025	28,351
Female householder, no husband present	11,692	16,692
Number of earners		
No earners	10,158	15,631
1 earner	18,500	25,960
2 earners or more	38,515	46,835
2 earners	29,681	43,623
3 earners	6,542	55,871
4 earners or more	2,293	70,019
Size of family		
2 persons	28,202	30,175
3 persons	15,594	37,923
4 persons	14,162	43,056
5 persons	6,030	40,881
6 persons	1,986	36,762
7 persons or more	1,200	33,187
WHITE		
All families	57,224	37,783
Type of residence		
Nonfarm	55,922	37,911
Farm	1,302	33,237
Location of residence		
Inside metropolitan areas	43,255	40,671
1,000,000 or more	26,866	43,700
Inside central cities	8,012	35,874
Outside central cities	18,854	47,035
Under 1,000,000	16,389	36,203
Inside central cities	5,854	33,930
Outside central cities	10,535	37,149
Outside metropolitan areas	13,969	30,447
Region		
Northeast	11,777	41,815
Midwest	14,347	38,224
South	19,023	35,226
West	12,078	37,610
Type of family		
Married-couple family	47,124	41,506
Wife in paid labor force	27,463	$48,802
Wife not in paid labor force	19,661	30,792
Male householder, no wife present	2,374	28,924
Female householder, no husband present	7,726	19,547
Number of earners		
No earners	8,355	18,183
1 earner	15,245	28,095
2 earners or more	33,623	47,872
2 earners	25,946	44,711
3 earners	5,658	56,583
4 earners or more	2,019	70,354
Size of family		
2 persons	24,828	31,578
3 persons	13,097	40,100
4 persons	11,997	45,229
5 persons	4,953	42,694
6 persons	1,534	40,248
7 persons or more	815	37,641
BLACK		
All families	7,716	21,548
Type of residence		
Nonfarm	7,695	21,587
Farm	22	(B)
Location of residence		
Inside metropolitan areas	6,486	23,226
1,000,000 or more	4,507	24,741
Inside central cities	3,018	20,559
Outside central cities	1,489	32,722
Under 1,000,000	1,979	20,659
Inside central cities	1,225	19,591
Outside central cities	754	23,695
Outside metropolitan areas	1,230	15,709
Region		
Northeast	1,291	25,533
Midwest	1,554	20,860
South	4,253	20,124
West	618	28,298
Type of family		
Married-couple family	3,631	33,307
Wife in paid labor force	2,420	41,353
Wife not in paid labor force	1,210	20,288
Male householder, no wife present	504	24,508
Female householder, no husband present	3,582	11,414
Number of earners		
No earners	1,547	6,480
1 earner	2,640	15,912
2 earners or more	3,529	37,618
2 earners	2,724	34,060
3 earners	647	46,221
4 earners or more	159	60,126
Size of family		
2 persons	2,680	18,056
3 persons	2,007	22,270
4 persons	1,582	26,158
5 persons	836	23,337
6 persons	341	24,871
7 persons or more	272	22,938

Characteristics[1]	1991 Number (thous.)	1991 Median income
HISPANIC ORIGIN OF HOUSEHOLDER[2]		
All families	5,177	$23,895
Type of residence		
Nonfarm	5,162	23,885
Farm	14	(B)
Location of residence		
Inside metropolitan areas	4,804	24,288
1,000,000 or more	3,676	25,499
Inside central cities	2,007	22,104
Outside central cities	1,668	29,722
Under 1,000,000	1,129	20,641
Inside central cities	667	20,217
Outside central cities	461	21,115
Outside metropolitan areas	372	20,903
Region		
Northeast	856	21,437
Midwest	355	26,942
South	1,651	23,708
West	2,314	24,317
Type of family		
Married-couple family	3,532	28,594
Wife in paid labor force	1,845	$35,655
Wife not in paid labor force	1,687	21,923
Male householder, no wife present	383	21,759
Female householder, no husband present	1,261	12,132
Number of earners		
No earners	719	8,264
1 earner	1,714	17,058
2 earners or more	2,743	34,065
2 earners	1,946	30,802
3 earners	545	38,763
4 earners or more	252	51,680
Size of family		
2 persons	1,266	20,653
3 persons	1,209	22,349
4 persons	1,238	26,294
5 persons	752	25,973
6 persons	387	25,211
7 persons or more	324	26,480

1. Family data as of March 1992. 2. Persons of Hispanic origin may be of any race. (B) Base less than 75,000. *Source:* Department of Commerce, Bureau of the Census. NOTE: Data are the latest available.

Births

Live Births and Birth Rates

Year	Births[1]	Rate[2]	Year	Births[1]	Rate[2]	Year	Births[1]	Rate[2]
1910	2,777,000	30.1	1958[3]	4,255,000	24.5	1975	3,144,198	14.8
1915	2,965,000	29.5	1959[3]	4,295,000	24.3	1976	3,167,788	14.8
1920	2,950,000	27.7	1960[3]	4,257,850	23.7	1977	3,326,632	15.4
1925	2,909,000	25.1	1961[3]	4,268,326	23.3	1978	3,333,279	15.3
1930	2,618,000	21.3	1962[3]	4,167,362	22.4	1979	3,494,398	15.9
1935	2,377,000	18.7	1963[3]	4,098,020	21.7	1980	3,612,258	15.9
1940	2,559,000	19.4	1964[3]	4,027,490	21.0	1982	3,680,537	15.9
1945	2,858,000	20.4	1965[3]	3,760,358	19.4	1983	3,638,933	15.5
1949	3,649,000	24.5	1966[3]	3,606,274	18.4	1984	3,669,141	15.5
1950	3,632,000	24.1	1967[4]	3,520,959	17.8	1985	3,760,561	15.8
1951[3]	3,823,000	24.9	1968[3]	3,501,564	17.5	1986	3,731,000	15.5
1952[3]	3,913,000	25.1	1969[3]	3,600,206	17.8	1987	3,829,000	15.7
1953[3]	3,965,000	25.1	1970[3]	3,731,386	18.4	1988	3,913,000	15.9
1954[3]	4,078,000	25.3	1971[3]	3,555,970	17.2	1989	4,021,000	16.2
1955	4,104,000	25.0	1972	3,258,411	15.6	1990	4,179,000	16.7
1956[3]	4,218,000	25.2	1973	3,136,965	14.9	1991	4,111,000	16.2
1957[3]	4,308,000	25.3	1974	3,159,958	14.9	1992[5]	4,084,000	15.9

1. Figures through 1959 include adjustment for underregistration; beginning 1960, figures represent number registered. For comparison, the 1959 registered count was 4,245,000. 2. Rates are per 1,000 population estimated as of July 1 for each year except 1940, 1950, 1960, 1970, and 1980, which are as of April 1, the census date; for 1942–46 based on population including armed forces overseas. 3. Based on 50% sample of births. 4. Based on a 20 to 50% sample of births. 5. Provisional. NOTE: Alaska is included beginning 1959; Hawaii beginning 1960. Since 1972, based on 100% of births in selected states and on 50% sample in all other states. *Sources:* Department of Health and Human Services, National Center for Health Statistics.

College-Educated Mothers Return to Work Sooner

Labor force participation among women with newborn children is dramatically higher for college-educated women than for women with only a high school diploma or less than a high school education.

A recent report of a 1992 survey from the Census Bureau Population Division found that, among women 15–44 years old who had given birth in the last year and had a graduate or professional degree, 72 percent were in the labor force, as compared with 30 percent for mothers with less than a high school education.

Possible explanations for these differences are greater job commitment or available resources to purchase child care services.

Live Births by Age of Mother

Year[1] and race	Total	Age of Mother: Under 15 yr	15–19 yr	20–24 yr	25–29 yr	30–34 yr	35–39 yr	40–44 yr	45 yr and over
1940	2,558,647	3,865	332,667	799,537	693,268	431,468	222,015	68,269	7,558
1945	2,858,449	4,028	298,868	832,746	785,299	554,906	296,852	78,853	6,897
1950	3,631,512	5,413	432,911	1,155,167	1,041,360	610,816	302,780	77,743	5,322
1955	4,014,112	6,181	493,770	1,290,939	1,133,155	732,540	352,320	89,777	5,430
1960	4,257,850	6,780	586,966	1,426,912	1,092,816	687,722	359,908	91,564	5,182
1965	3,760,358	7,768	590,894	1,337,350	925,732	529,376	282,908	81,716	4,614
1970	3,731,386	11,752	644,708	1,418,874	994,904	427,806	180,244	49,952	3,146
1975	3,144,198	12,642	582,238	1,093,676	936,786	375,500	115,409	26,319	1,628
1980	3,612,258	10,169	552,161	1,226,200	1,108,291	550,354	140,793	23,090	1,200
1985	3,760,561	10,220	467,485	1,141,320	1,201,350	696,354	214,336	28,334	1,162
1988	3,909,510	10,588	478,353	1,067,472	1,239,256	803,547	269,518	39,349	1,427
1989	4,040,958	11,486	506,503	1,077,598	1,263,098	842,395	293,878	44,401	1,599
1990	4,158,212	11,657	521,826	1,093,730	1,277,108	886,063	317,583	48,607	1,638
White	3,290,273	4,974	354,482	837,572	1,051,760	739,209	261,787	39,309	1,180
Black	684,336	6,338	151,613	217,274	168,217	99,514	35,592	5,581	207
Other	183,603	345	15,731	38,884	57,131	47,340	20,204	3,717	251

1. Data for 1940–55 are adjusted for underregistration. Beginning 1960, registered births only are shown. Data for 1960–70 based on a 50% sample of births. For 1972–84, based on 100% of births in selected states and on 50% sample in all other states. Beginning 1960, including Alaska and Hawaii. For 1988 and prior years births were tabulated by race of child. Beginning 1989 births are tabulated by race of mother. NOTE: Data refer only to births occurring within the U.S. Figures are shown to the last digit as computed for convenience in summation. They are not assumed to be accurate to the last digit. Figures for age of mother not stated are distributed. *Source:* Department of Health and Human Services, National Center for Health Statistics.

Births to Unmarried Women
(in thousands, except as indicated)

Age and race	1990	1985	1980	1975	1970	1965	1960	1955	1950
By age of mother:									
Under 15 years	10.7	9.4	9.0	11.0	9.5	6.1	4.6	3.9	3.2
15–19 years	350.0	270.9	262.8	222.5	190.4	123.1	87.1	68.9	56.0
20–24 years	403.9	300.4	237.3	134.0	126.7	90.7	68.0	55.7	43.1
25–29 years	230.0	152.0	99.6	50.2	40.6	36.8	32.1	28.0	20.9
30–34 years	118.2	67.3	41.0	19.8	19.1	19.6	18.9	16.1	10.8
35–39 years	44.1	24.0	13.2	8.1	9.4	11.4	10.6	8.3	6.0
40 years and over	8.5	4.1	2.9	2.3	3.0	3.7	3.0	2.4	1.7
By race:[1]									
White	669.7	433.0	320.1	186.4	175.1	123.7	82.5	64.2	53.5
Black and other	495.7	395.2	345.7	261.6	223.6	167.5	141.8	119.2	88.1
Total of above births	**1,165.4**	**828.2**	**665.8**	**447.9**	**398.7**	**291.2**	**224.3**	**183.4**	**141.6**
Percent of all births[2]	28.0	22.0	18.4	14.2	10.7	7.7	5.3	4.5	3.9
Rate[3]	43.8	32.8	29.4	24.8	26.4	23.4	21.8	19.3	14.1

1. For 1988 and prior years births were tabulated by race of child. Beginning 1989, births are tabulated by race of mother. 2. Through 1955, based on data adjusted for underregistration; thereafter, registered births. 3. Rate per 1,000 unmarried (never married, widowed, and divorced) women, 15–44 years old. *Source:* Department of Health and Human Services, National Center for Health Statistics. NOTE: Data are latest available.

Dual-Employed Families Continue to Rise

Continued increases in women's labor force participation continue to alter the structure of American family life. The traditional family, where the husband worked and wife stayed at home to look after the children, is changing to a family where both parents are employed, creating a family type that might be referred to as dual-employed with kids.

Of 29.5 million wives who were between 15 and 44 years in 1992, 60 percent were in families where both spouses were employed. Dual-employed couples increased from 45 percent of married couples in 1976 to 60 percent in 1992.

Dual-employed spouses in 1992 who were childless represented 13 percent of all married couples while those with at least one child represented almost one-half (47 percent) of all married couples. The proportion of dual-employed spouses with children steadily increased during the latter 1970s and through most of the 1980s, from 33 percent in 1976 to 47 percent in 1992.

In general, dual-employed married couples with children were older than dual-employed married couples without children: 81 percent of couples with children were 30 years old or over compared to 50 percent without children. One in six of the couples with children were college graduates, compared to one out of four who were childless.

Live Births and Birth Rates

State	1991[1] number	1991[1] rate	1990[2] number	1990[2] rate
Alabama	60,513	14.6	68,200	16.5
Alaska	11,245	21.1	11,647	22.0
Arizona	67,656	18.3	68,749	18.9
Arkansas	34,588	14.2	36,109	14.9
California	605,694	19.8	617,989	20.7
Colorado	53,968	16.1	52,913	15.9
Connecticut	48,282	14.8	52,315	16.1
Delaware	11,175	16.0	11,282	16.4
D.C.	9,971	17.0	10,928	18.4
Florida	194,457	14.6	199,641	15.3
Georgia	110,024	16.6	112,899	17.3
Hawaii	20,014	17.5	20,413	18.1
Idaho	17,233	16.6	16,594	16.2
Illinois	193,987	16.5	196,107	16.7
Indiana	84,707	14.9	85,227	15.1
Iowa	36,011	12.6	39,127	13.7
Kansas	37,300	14.6	40,074	15.8
Kentucky	54,913	14.7	57,791	15.5
Louisiana	74,562	17.2	71,704	16.4
Maine	16,581	13.2	16,908	13.6
Maryland	84,452	17.5	83,664	17.6
Massachusetts	86,321	14.5	93,222	15.7
Michigan	153,359	16.4	159,346	17.1
Minnesota	67,020	15.1	68,378	15.5
Mississippi	43,522	16.6	43,849	16.7
Missouri	77,991	15.0	81,157	15.7
Montana	11,544	14.3	11,758	14.6
Nebraska	23,933	14.7	24,010	14.8
Nevada	22,973	18.8	21,255	18.2
New Hampshire	16,060	13.9	17,199	15.2
New Jersey	117,789	15.1	124,082	16.0
New Mexico	28,160	18.0	28,654	18.5
New York	292,400	16.2	301,209	16.7
North Carolina	102,442	15.2	104,715	15.7
North Dakota	9,071	14.0	9,517	14.6
Ohio	158,638	14.4	164,619	15.0
Oklahoma	47,312	14.7	47,250	14.7
Oregon	42,807	14.6	44,408	15.4
Pennsylvania	168,584	13.9	170,888	14.1
Rhode Island	14,591	14.5	14,963	14.9
South Carolina	57,742	16.0	59,075	16.6
South Dakota	11,042	15.4	10,912	15.2
Tennessee	73,104	14.5	72,747	14.6
Texas	325,562	18.8	325,752	19.0
Utah	35,070	20.1	36,216	21.0
Vermont	7,712	13.2	8,282	14.4
Virginia	96,610	15.4	99,942	16.2
Washington	75,734	15.2	78,106	16.0
West Virginia	22,195	12.2	22,202	12.1
Wisconsin	71,736	14.5	72,969	14.9
Wyoming	6,801	14.6	6,984	14.9
Total	**4,095,158**	**16.0**	**4,193,947**	**16.6**

1. Provisional. NOTE: 2. Revised. Provisional data by place of residence. Rates are per 1,000 population. *Source:* Department of Health and Human Services, National Center for Health Statistics.

Live Births by Race or National Origin of Mother

Race	1990	1989
White	3,290,273	3,192,355
Black	684,336	673,124
American Indian[1]	39,051	39,478
Japanese	8,674	8,689
Chinese	22,737	20,982
Filipino	25,770	24,585
Other[2]	84,454	78,819
Total[3]	**4,158,212**	**4,040,958**

1. Includes Eskimos and Aleuts. 2. Hawaiian and other Asian or Pacific Islander. 3. Includes births of other races not shown separately. Data are latest available. *Source:* Department of Health and Human Services, National Center for Health Statistics.

Live Births by Sex and Sex Ratio[1]

Year	Total[2]			White[3]			Black[3]		
	Male	Female	Males per 1,000 females	Male	Female	Males per 1,000 females	Male	Female	Males per 1,000 females
1981[4]	1,860,272	1,768,966	1,052	1,494,437	1,414,232	1,057	297,864	289,933	1,027
1982[4]	1,885,676	1,794,861	1,051	1,509,704	1,432,350	1,054	301,121	291,520	1,033
1983[4]	1,865,553	1,773,380	1,052	1,492,385	1,411,865	1,057	297,011	289,016	1,028
1984[4]	1,879,490	1,789,651	1,050	1,500,326	1,423,176	1,054	300,951	291,794	1,031
1985	1,927,983	1,832,578	1,052	1,536,646	1,454,727	1,056	308,575	299,618	1,030
1986	1,924,868	1,831,679	1,051	1,523,914	1,446,525	1,053	315,788	305,433	1,034
1987	1,951,153	1,858,241	1,050	1,535,517	1,456,971	1,054	325,259	316,308	1,028
1988	2,002,424	1,907,086	1,050	1,562,675	1,483,487	1,053	341,441	330,535	1,033
1989	2,069,490	1,971,468	1,050	1,606,757	1,525,234	1,053	360,131	349,264	1,031
1990	2,129,495	2,028,717	1,050	1,654,928	1,570,415	1,054	367,455	357,121	1,029

1. Excludes births to nonresidents of U.S. 2. Includes races other than white and black. 3. Race of child. 4. Based on 100% of births for selected states and 50% sample in all others. *Source:* Department of Health and Human Services, National Center for Health Statistics. NOTE: Data are latest available.

Abortions and Abortion Rates

State	Number of Abortions 1988	1987	1985	Abortion occurrence rate[1] 1988	1987	1985	Change 1985–88
Alabama	18,220	19,630	19,380	18.7	20.2	20.2	–1.5
Alaska	2,390	2,560	3,450	18.2	19.7	27.7	–9.5
Arizona	23,070	22,130	22,330	28.8	28.2	29.9	–1.1
Arkansas	6,250	7,030	5,420	11.6	13.1	10.1	1.5
California	311,720	300,830	304,130	45.9	45.0	47.9	–2.1
Colorado	18,740	18,850	24,350	22.4	22.4	28.8	–6.4
Connecticut	23,630	22,380	21,850	31.2	29.4	29.3	1.8
Delaware	5,710	5,680	4,590	35.7	35.9	30.9	4.8
District of Columbia	26,120	25,840	23,910	163.3	158.5	145.9	17.4
Florida	82,850	80,560	76,650	31.5	31.2	31.8	–0.3
Georgia	36,720	36,030	38,340	23.5	23.3	26.1	–2.6
Hawaii	11,170	11,290	11,160	43.0	44.1	43.7	–0.7
Idaho	1,920	1,980	2,660	8.2	8.5	11.1	–2.8
Illinois	72,570	72,180	64,960	26.4	26.2	23.8	2.6
Indiana	15,760	14,750	16,090	11.9	11.2	12.2	–0.2
Iowa	9,420	8,900	9,930	14.6	13.8	15.0	–0.4
Kansas	11,440	11,430	10,150	20.1	20.2	18.2	2.0
Kentucky	11,520	11,550	9,820	13.0	13.1	11.0	2.0
Louisiana	17,340	16,550	19,240	16.3	15.4	17.4	–1.1
Maine	4,620	4,950	4,960	16.2	17.7	18.6	–2.4
Maryland	32,670	31,240	29,480	28.6	27.6	26.9	1.7
Massachusetts	43,720	41,490	40,310	30.2	28.7	29.3	0.9
Michigan	63,410	61,060	64,390	28.5	27.3	28.7	–0.3
Minnesota	18,580	17,810	16,850	18.2	17.5	16.6	1.6
Mississippi	5,120	5,430	5,890	8.4	8.9	9.7	–1.3
Missouri	19,490	20,190	20,100	16.4	17.0	17.3	–0.9
Montana	3,050	3,280	3,710	16.5	17.7	19.0	–2.5
Nebraska	6,490	6,580	6,680	17.7	18.0	18.2	–0.4
Nevada	10,190	10,710	9,910	40.3	43.9	40.5	–0.2
New Hampshire	4,710	4,680	7,030	17.5	17.8	29.0	–11.5
New Jersey	63,900	63,570	69,190	35.1	34.9	39.6	–4.5
New Mexico	6,810	6,650	6,110	19.1	18.6	17.4	1.8
New York	183,980	184,420	195,120	43.3	43.3	47.4	–4.0
North Carolina	39,720	37,630	34,180	25.4	24.2	22.6	2.8
North Dakota	2,230	2,560	2,850	14.9	17.0	18.5	–3.6
Ohio	53,400	51,490	57,360	21.0	20.2	22.4	–1.4
Oklahoma	12,120	11,000	13,100	16.2	14.5	17.1	–0.9
Oregon	15,960	14,370	15,230	23.9	21.8	22.3	1.7
Pennsylvania	51,830	51,800	57,370	18.9	18.9	21.3	–2.4
Rhode Island	7,190	7,390	7,770	30.6	31.3	35.5	–4.9
South Carolina	14,160	12,770	11,200	16.7	15.2	13.7	3.1
South Dakota	900	860	1,650	5.7	5.5	10.6	–4.9
Tennessee	22,090	22,050	22,350	18.9	18.9	19.1	–0.2
Texas	100,690	100,210	100,820	24.8	24.7	25.5	–0.7
Utah	5,030	4,830	4,440	12.8	12.4	11.1	1.7
Vermont	3,580	3,690	3,430	25.8	26.9	26.2	–0.5
Virginia	35,420	34,410	34,180	23.7	23.3	24.0	–0.3
Washington	31,220	29,840	30,990	27.6	26.9	28.0	–0.4
West Virginia	3,270	2,990	4,590	7.5	6.8	10.1	–2.6
Wisconsin	18,040	18,330	17,830	16.0	16.3	15.7	0.2
Wyoming	600	680	1,070	5.1	5.7	7.9	–2.8
Total	**1,590,750**	**1,559,110**	**1,588,550**	**27.3**	**26.9**	**28.0**	**–0.7**

1. Rate per 1,000 women aged 15–44. NOTES: Number of abortions are rounded to nearest 10. Data are latest available. *Source:* Reproduced with the permission of The Alan Guttmacher Institute from Stanley K. Henshaw and Jennifer Van Vort, "Abortion Services in the United States, 1987 and 1988," *Family Planning Perspectives,* Volume 22, Number 3, May/June 1990.

Single Mothers Are on the Rise

Nearly a quarter of single women age 18 to 44 had borne a child by June 1992, up from 15 percent a decade earlier. The proportion of single mothers increased regardless of education, more than doubling for college-educated women and almost doubling for those with high school diplomas. It also increased for those without high school diplomas—the highest proportion of single mothers—from just over 35 percent to more than 48 percent.

About 5 percent of teenagers in 1992 had borne a child. Among women in their thirties, over one-third had a child out-of-wedlock. The incidence of out-of-wedlock childbearing increased primarily among women in their twenties and their thirties: about 36 percent of never married women in their thirties in 1992 had a child, whereas in 1982 only 24 percent had a child.

Mortality

Death Rates for Selected Causes

Cause of death	1992[1]	1991	1990	1980	1950	1945–49	1920–24[4]	1900–04[4]
	Death rates per 100,000							
Typhoid fever	n.a.	n.a.	*	0.0	0.1	0.2	7.3	26.7
Communicable diseases of childhood	—	—	—	0.0	1.3	2.3	33.8	65.2
Measles	*	*	0.0	0.0	0.3	0.6	7.3	10.0
Scarlet fever	n.a.	n.a.	*	0.0	0.2	0.1	4.0	11.8
Whooping cough	*	*	*	0.0	0.7	1.0	8.9	10.7
Diphtheria	n.a.	n.a.	*	0.0	0.3	0.7	13.7	32.7
Pneumonia and influenza	29.6	29.6	32.8	23.3	31.3	41.3	140.3	184.3
Influenza	0.4	0.4	0.8	1.1	4.4	5.0	34.8	22.8
Pneumonia	29.1	29.2	31.1	22.0	26.9	37.2	105.5	161.5
Tuberculosis	0.5	0.6	0.7	0.8	22.5	33.3	96.7	184.7
Cancer	203.1	203.7	203.2	182.5	139.8	134.0	86.9	67.7
Diabetes mellitus	19.6	19.7	19.2	15.0	16.2	24.1	17.1	12.2
Major cardiovascular diseases	355.9	358.5	368.3	434.5	510.8	493.1	369.9	359.5
Diseases of the heart	280.5	282.3	289.5	335.2	356.8	325.1	169.8	153.0
Cerebrovascular diseases	55.9	56.3	57.9	74.6	104.0	93.8	93.5	106.3
Nephritis and nephrosis	9.0	9.0	8.3	7.6	16.4	48.4	81.5	84.3
Syphilis	*	0.1	0.0	0.1	5.0	8.4	17.6	12.9
Appendicitis	0.1	0.2	0.2	0.3	2.0	3.5	14.0	9.4
Accidents, all forms	32.9	35.1	37.0	46.0	60.6	67.6	70.8	79.2
Motor vehicle accidents	16.0	17.4	18.8	23.0	23.1	22.3	12.9	n.a.
Infant mortality[2]	n.a.	n.a.	9.2	12.5	29.2	33.3	76.7	n.a.
Neonatal mortality[2]	n.a.	n.a.	5.8	8.4	20.5	22.9	39.7	n.a.
Fetal mortality[3]	n.a.	n.a.	n.a.	9.2	19.2	21.6	n.a	n.a.
Maternal mortality[2]	0.1	0.1	8.2	0.1	0.8	1.4	6.9	n.a.
All causes	**853.3**	**853.9**	**863.8**	**883.4**	**960.1**	**1,000.6**	**1,157.4**	**1,621.6**

1. Provisional, based on a 10% sample of deaths. 2. Rates per 1,000 live births. 3. Ratio per 1,000 births. 4. Includes only deaths occurring within the registration areas. Beginning with 1933, area includes the entire United States; Alaska included beginning in 1959 and Hawaii in 1960. Rates per 100,000 population residing in areas, enumerated as of April 1 for 1940, 1950, and 1980 and estimated as of July 1 for all other years. Due to changes in statistical methods, death rates are not strictly comparable. Beginning in 1989 an asterisk is shown in place of a rate based on fewer than 20 deaths for final data and on 100 or fewer estimated deaths for provisional data. n.a. = not available. *Source:* Department of Health and Human Services, National Center for Health Statistics.

Accident Rates, 1991

Class of accident		One every	Class of accident		One every
All accidents	Deaths	6 minutes	Workers off-job	Deaths	16 minutes
	Injuries	4 seconds		Injuries	13 seconds
Motor-vehicle	Deaths	12 minutes	Home	Deaths	26 minutes
	Injuries	20 seconds		Injuries	10 seconds
Work	Deaths	53 minutes	Public non-motor-vehicle	Deaths	29 minutes
	Injuries	19 seconds		Injuries	14 seconds

NOTE: Data are latest available. *Source:* National Safety Council.

Improper Driving as Factor in Accidents, 1991

Kind of improper driving	Fatal accidents			Injury accidents			All accidents		
	Total	Urban	Rural	Total	Urban	Rural	Total	Urban	Rural
Improper driving	**52.4**	**50.0**	**55.2**	**66.8**	**68.5**	**61.6**	**66.2**	**67.3**	**62.8**
Speed too fast or unsafe	17.9	17.6	18.3	15.7	15.1	17.8	15.9	15.2	18.4
Right of way	12.3	14.3	10.2	22.0	24.0	15.7	21.3	23.2	14.6
Failed to yield	7.7	8.6	6.8	15.6	16.6	12.5	15.9	17.1	12.0
Passed stop sign	2.5	2.9	2.1	1.9	2.0	1.5	1.6	1.7	1.3
Disregarded signal	2.1	2.8	1.3	4.5	5.4	1.7	3.8	4.4	1.3
Drove left of center	6.6	5.4	7.9	1.9	1.4	3.3	1.9	1.5	3.4
Improper overtaking	1.2	0.8	1.6	0.8	0.7	1.1	1.2	1.1	1.6
Made improper turn	2.4	2.0	2.8	2.8	2.6	3.3	4.2	4.2	4.2
Followed too closely	0.6	0.8	0.4	5.1	6.0	2.6	6.3	7.3	3.0
Other improper driving	11.4	9.1	14.0	18.5	18.7	17.8	15.4	14.8	17.6
No improper driving stated	**47.6**	**50.0**	**44.8**	**33.2**	**31.5**	**38.4**	**33.8**	**32.7**	**37.2**

Source: Motor-vehicle reports from 14 state traffic authorities to National Safety Council. NOTE: Figures are latest available.

Motor–Vehicle Deaths by Type of Accident

Year	Deaths from collisions with— Pedestrians	Other motor vehicles	Railroad trains	Pedalcycles	Animal-drawn vehicle, animal, or streetcars	Fixed objects	Deaths from non-collision accidents	Total deaths[1]
1975	8,400	19,550	979	1,000	100	3,130	12,700	45,853
1980	9,700	23,000	739	1,200	100	3,700	14,700	53,172
1985	8,300	19,900	500	1,100	100	2,800	12,900	45,600
1988	8,800	21,200	600	1,100	100	3,300	13,900	49,000
1989	7,200	19,900	700	1,000	100	13,100	4,900	46,900
1990	7,400	19,400	600	1,000	100	12,900	4,900	46,300
1991	7,000	18,500	500	800	100	12,100	4,500	43,500

1. Totals do not equal sums of various types because totals are estimated. NOTE: Figures are latest available. *Source:* National Safety Council.

Accidental Deaths by Principal Types

Year	Motor vehicle	Falls	Drowning	Fire burns	Ingestion of food or object	Firearms	Poison (solid, liquid)	Poison by gas
1984	46,263	11,937	5,388	5,010	3,541	1,668	3,808	1,103
1985	45,600	11,700	5,300	4,900	3,600	1,800	3,600	1,000
1986	47,900	11,000	5,600	4,800	3,600	1,800	4,000	900
1987	48,700	11,300	5,300	4,800	3,200	1,400	4,400	1,000
1988	49,000	12,000	5,000	5,000	3,600	1,400	5,300	1,000
1989	46,900	12,400	4,600	4,400	3,900	1,600	5,600	900
1990	46,300	12,400	5,200	4,300	3,200	1,400	5,700	800
1991	43,500	12,200	4,600	4,200	2,900	1,400	5,600	800

NOTE: Figures are latest available. *Source:* National Safety Council.

Deaths and Death Rates

State	Total deaths 1991 number	Total deaths 1991 rate[1]	Motor vehicle traffic deaths 1991 number	Motor vehicle traffic deaths 1991 rate[2]
Alabama	38,027	9.2	1,108	2.6
Alaska	2,145	4.0	100	2.9
Arizona	29,329	7.9	816	2.3
Arkansas	24,230	10.0	608	2.9
California	218,735	7.2	4,649	1.8
Colorado	22,334	6.7	542	2.0
Connecticut	27,745	8.5	310	1.2
Delaware	5,880	8.4	103	1.6
D.C.	6,961	11.9	63	1.9
Florida	135,280	10.1	2,519	2.3
Georgia	52,708	7.9	1,393	1.9
Hawaii	6,715	5.9	135	1.7
Idaho	7,789	7.5	263	2.7
Illinois	104,389	8.9	1,451	1.9
Indiana	51,780	9.1	1,020	1.9
Iowa	25,906	9.1	491	2.1
Kansas	22,511	8.8	404	1.8
Kentucky	35,281	9.5	828	2.5
Louisiana	38,290	8.8	824	2.2
Maine	10,952	8.7	202	1.7
Maryland	37,982	7.9	708	1.8
Massachusetts	51,366	8.6	550	1.2
Michigan	79,972	8.6	1,409	1.7
Minnesota	35,270	7.9	534	1.4
Mississippi	25,625	9.8	701	2.9
Missouri	53,461	10.3	1,010	2.0
Montana	7,071	8.8	200	2.4
Nebraska	14,665	9.0	275	2.0
Nevada	9,243	7.5	297	2.9
New Hampshire	8,513	7.4	144	1.5
New Jersey	69,983	9.0	785	1.4
New Mexico	11,116	7.1	469	2.9
New York	166,795	9.2	1,973	1.9
North Carolina	58,909	8.7	1,365	2.2
North Dakota	5,648	8.7	94	1.6
Ohio	99,104	9.0	1,544	1.8
Oklahoma	30,349	9.5	643	2.0
Oregon	25,205	8.8	483	1.8
Pennsylvania	123,536	10.2	1,661	1.9
Rhode Island	9,294	9.2	88	1.3
South Carolina	29,983	8.3	890	2.6
South Dakota	6,594	9.2	143	2.0
Tennessee	45,351	9.0	1,112	2.4
Texas	128,926	7.4	3,079	1.9
Utah	9,199	5.3	273	1.8
Vermont	4,541	7.7	106	1.9
Virginia	49,151	7.8	937	1.6
Washington	37,682	7.6	682	1.5
West Virginia	19,801	10.9	414	2.7
Wisconsin	43,749	8.9	794	1.8
Wyoming	3,167	6.8	122	2.2
Total	**2,168,238**	**8.5**	**43,500**	**2.0**

1. Provisional rates per 1,000 population, by place of occurrence. 2. Per 100 million vehicle–miles. *Sources:* Department of Health and Human Services, National Center for Health Statistics; National Safety Council.

Annual Death Rates

Year	Rate	Year	Rate	Year	Deaths	Rate
1900	17.2	1945	10.6	1969	1,921,990	9.5
1905	15.9	1946	10.0	1970[1]	1,921,031	9.5
1910	14.7	1947	10.1	1971	1,927,542	9.3
1915	13.2	1948	9.9	1972	1,963,944	9.4
1920	13.0	1949	9.7	1973	1,973,003	9.3
1925	11.7	1950	9.6	1974	1,934,388	9.1
1928	12.0	1951	9.7	1975	1,892,879	8.8
1929	11.9	1952	9.6	1976	1,909,440	8.8
1930	11.3	1953	9.6	1977	1,899,597	8.6
1931	11.1	1954	9.2	1978	1,927,788	8.7
1932	10.9	1955	9.3	1979	1,913,841	8.5
1933	10.7	1956	9.4	1980	1,989,841	8.7
1934	11.1	1957	9.6	1982	1,974,797	8.5
1935	10.9	1958	9.5	1983	2,019,201	8.6
1936	11.6	1959	9.4	1984	2,039,369	8.6
1937	11.3	1960	9.5	1985	2,086,440	8.7
1938	10.6	1962	9.5	1986	2,099,000	8.7
1939	10.6	1963	9.6	1987	2,127,000	8.7
1940	10.8	1964	9.4	1988	2,171,000	8.8
1941	10.5	1965	9.4	1989	2,155,000	8.7
1942	10.3	1966	9.5	1990	2,162,000	8.6
1943	10.9	1967	9.4	1991	2,165,000	8.5
1944	10.6	1968	9.7	1992[1]	2,177,000	8.5

1. First year for which deaths of nonresidents are excluded. 2. Provisional. NOTE: Includes only deaths occurring within the registration states. Beginning with 1933, area includes entire U.S.; with 1959 includes Alaska, and with 1960 includes Hawaii. Excludes fetal deaths. Rates per 1,000 population residing in area, as of April 1 for 1940, 1950, 1960, 1970, and 1980, and estimated as of July 1 for all other years. *Sources:* Department of Health and Human Services, National Center for Health Statistics.

Death Rates by Age, Race, and Sex

Age	1991[1]	1990	1989	1980	1970[2]	1960	1991[1]	1990	1989	1980	1970[2]	1960
	White males						White females					
Under 1 year	8.5	9.0	9.0	12.3	21.1	26.9	6.5	7.0	7.1	9.6	16.1	20.1
1–4	0.4	0.5	0.4	0.7	0.8	1.0	0.4	0.4	0.3	0.5	0.8	0.9
5–14	0.3	0.3	0.2	0.4	0.5	0.5	0.2	0.2	0.1	0.2	0.3	0.3
15–24	1.4	1.3	1.3	1.7	1.7	1.4	0.5	0.5	0.4	0.5	0.6	0.5
25–34	2.0	1.8	1.7	1.7	1.8	1.6	0.6	0.6	0.6	0.7	0.8	0.9
35–44	2.7	2.7	2.6	2.6	3.4	3.3	1.1	1.2	1.1	1.2	1.9	1.9
45–54	5.4	5.5	5.5	7.0	8.8	9.3	3.0	3.1	3.0	3.7	4.6	4.6
55–64	14.3	14.7	14.8	17.3	22.0	22.3	8.1	8.2	8.2	8.8	10.1	10.8
65–74	32.5	34.0	33.6	40.4	48.1	48.5	19.2	19.2	19.4	20.7	24.7	27.8
75–84	76.9	78.4	79.1	88.3	101.0	103.0	48.4	48.4	50.0	54.0	67.0	77.0
85 and over	176.2	183.0	179.7	191.0	185.5	217.5	136.0	144.0	142.4	149.8	159.8	194.8
	All other males						All other females					
Under 1 year	16.2	18.1	19.1	23.5	40.2	51.9	13.3	15.0	16.2	19.4	31.7	40.7
1–4	0.7	0.8	0.8	1.0	1.4	2.1	0.7	0.6	0.6	0.8	1.2	1.7
5–14	0.4	0.4	0.3	0.4	0.6	0.8	0.3	0.3	0.2	0.3	0.4	0.5
15–24	2.4	2.2	2.1	2.0	3.0	2.1	0.7	0.6	0.6	0.7	1.1	1.1
25–34	3.6	3.5	3.5	3.6	5.0	3.9	1.3	1.3	1.3	1.4	2.2	2.6
35–44	6.0	5.6	6.0	5.9	8.7	7.3	2.5	2.4	2.5	2.9	4.9	5.5
45–54	10.0	10.2	10.6	13.1	16.5	15.5	5.0	5.4	5.3	6.9	9.8	11.4
55–64	20.1	22.2	21.4	26.1	30.5	31.5	12.0	13.0	12.3	14.2	18.9	24.1
65–74	38.1	43.4	40.9	47.5	54.7	56.6	24.1	26.0	25.2	28.6	36.8	39.8
75–84	74.2	83.2	81.0	86.9	89.8	86.6	51.0	53.1	55.3	58.6	63.9	67.1
85 and over	133.0	160.8	145.1	157.7	114.1	152.4	111.0	129.0	118.5	119.2	102.9	128.7

1. Provisional. Based on a 10% sample of deaths. 2. Beginning 1970 excludes deaths of nonresidents of U.S. NOTE: Excludes fetal deaths. Rates are per 1,000 population in each group, enumerated as of April 1 for 1960, 1970, and 1980, and estimated as of July 1 for all other years. *Sources:* Department of Health and Human Services, National Center for Health Statistics.

Expectation of Life

Expectation of Life in the United States

Calendar period	Age 0	10	20	30	40	50	60	70	80
WHITE MALES									
1850[1]	38.3	48.0	40.1	34.0	27.9	21.6	15.6	10.2	5.9
1890[1]	42.50	48.45	40.66	34.05	27.37	20.72	14.73	9.35	5.40
1900–1902[2]	48.23	50.59	42.19	34.88	27.74	20.76	14.35	9.03	5.10
1909–1911[2]	50.23	51.32	42.71	34.87	27.43	20.39	13.98	8.83	5.09
1919–1921[3]	56.34	54.15	45.60	37.65	29.86	22.22	15.25	9.51	5.47
1929–1931	59.12	54.96	46.02	37.54	29.22	21.51	14.72	9.20	5.26
1939–1941	62.81	57.03	47.76	38.80	30.03	21.96	15.05	9.42	5.38
1949–1951	66.31	58.98	49.52	40.29	31.17	22.83	15.76	10.07	5.88
1959–1961[5]	67.55	59.78	50.25	40.98	31.73	23.22	16.01	10.29	5.89
1969–1971[6]	67.94	59.69	50.22	41.07	31.87	23.34	16.07	10.38	6.18
1979–1981	70.82	61.98	52.45	43.31	34.04	25.26	17.56	11.35	6.76
1988	72.3	63.2	53.6	44.4	35.2	26.3	18.4	11.8	6.8
1989	72.7	63.6	54.0	44.7	35.6	26.7	18.7	12.1	7.1
1990	72.7	63.5	54.0	44.7	35.6	26.7	18.7	12.1	7.1
WHITE FEMALES									
1850[1]	40.5	47.2	40.2	35.4	29.8	23.5	17.0	11.3	6.4
1890[1]	44.46	49.62	42.03	35.36	28.76	22.09	15.70	10.15	5.75
1900–1902[2]	51.08	52.15	43.77	36.42	29.17	21.89	15.23	9.59	5.50
1909–1911[2]	53.62	53.57	44.88	36.96	29.26	21.74	14.92	9.38	5.35
1919–1921[3]	58.53	55.17	46.46	38.72	30.94	23.12	15.93	9.94	5.70
1929–1931	62.67	57.65	48.52	39.99	31.52	23.41	16.05	9.98	5.63
1939–1941	67.29	60.85	51.38	42.21	33.25	24.72	17.00	10.50	5.88
1949–1951	72.03	64.26	54.56	45.00	35.64	26.76	18.64	11.68	6.59
1959–1961[5]	74.19	66.05	56.29	46.63	37.13	28.08	19.69	12.38	6.67
1969–1971[6]	75.49	66.97	57.24	47.60	38.12	29.11	20.79	13.37	7.59
1979–1981	78.22	69.21	59.44	49.76	40.16	30.96	22.45	14.89	8.65
1988	78.9	69.7	59.9	50.2	40.6	31.2	22.6	15.0	8.7
1989	79.2	70.0	60.2	50.5	40.9	31.5	22.9	15.3	8.9
1990	79.4	70.1	60.3	50.6	41.0	31.6	23.0	15.4	9.0
ALL OTHER MALES[4]									
1900–1902[2]	32.54	41.90	35.11	29.25	23.12	17.34	12.62	8.33	5.12
1909–1911[2]	34.05	40.65	33.46	27.33	21.57	16.21	11.67	8.00	5.53
1919–1921[3]	47.14	45.99	38.36	32.51	26.53	20.47	14.74	9.58	5.83
1929–1931	47.55	44.27	35.95	29.45	23.36	17.92	13.15	8.78	5.42
1939–1941	52.33	48.54	39.74	32.25	25.23	19.18	14.38	10.06	6.46
1949–1951	58.91	52.96	43.73	35.31	27.29	20.25	14.91	10.74	7.07
1959–1961[5]	61.48	55.19	45.78	37.05	28.72	21.28	15.29	10.81	6.87
1969–1971[6]	60.98	53.67	44.37	36.20	28.29	21.24	15.35	10.68	7.57
1979–1981	65.63	57.40	47.87	39.13	30.64	22.92	16.54	11.36	7.22
1988	67.1	58.6	49.1	40.3	32.0	24.1	17.2	11.6	7.2
1989	67.1	58.6	49.2	40.4	32.1	24.3	17.5	11.8	7.3
1990	67.0	58.5	49.0	40.3	31.9	23.9	17.0	11.4	7.0
ALL OTHER FEMALES[4]									
1900–1902[2]	35.04	43.02	36.89	30.70	24.37	18.67	13.60	9.62	6.48
1909–1911[2]	37.67	42.84	36.14	29.61	23.34	17.65	12.78	9.22	6.05
1919–1921[3]	46.92	44.54	37.15	31.48	25.60	19.76	14.69	10.25	6.58
1929–1931	49.51	45.33	37.22	30.67	24.30	18.60	14.22	10.38	6.90
1939–1941	55.51	50.83	42.14	34.52	27.31	21.04	16.14	11.81	8.00
1949–1951	62.70	56.17	46.77	38.02	29.82	22.67	16.95	12.29	8.15
1959–1961[5]	66.47	59.72	50.07	40.83	32.16	24.31	17.83	12.46	7.66
1969–1971[6]	69.05	61.49	51.85	42.61	33.87	25.97	19.02	13.30	9.01
1979–1981	74.00	65.64	55.88	46.39	37.16	28.59	20.49	14.44	9.17
1988	75.1	66.4	56.7	47.1	37.9	29.2	21.3	14.5	8.8
1989	75.2	66.6	56.9	47.4	38.2	29.4	21.4	14.6	9.0
1990	75.2	66.6	56.8	47.3	38.1	29.2	21.3	14.5	8.8

1. Massachusetts only; white and nonwhite combined, the latter being about 1% of the total. 2. Original Death Registration States. 3. Death Registration States of 1920. 4. Data for periods 1900–1902 to 1929–1931 relate to blacks only. 5. Alaska and Hawaii included beginning in 1959. 6. Deaths of nonresidents of the United States excluded starting in 1970. *Sources:* Department of Health and Human Services, National Center for Health Statistics.

Expectation of Life and Mortality Probabilities, 1990

	Expectation of life in years					Mortality probability per 1,000				
		White		All other			White		All other	
Age	Total persons	Male	Female	Male	Female	Total persons	Male	Female	Male	Female
0	75.4	72.7	79.4	67.0	75.2	9.3	8.5	6.6	7.0	14.1
1	75.1	72.3	78.9	67.2	75.3	0.7	0.7	0.5	1.1	0.8
2	74.1	71.4	78.0	66.2	74.4	0.5	0.5	0.4	0.8	0.6
3	73.1	70.4	77.0	65.3	73.4	0.4	0.4	0.3	0.6	0.5
4	72.2	69.4	76.0	64.3	72.5	0.3	0.3	0.2	0.5	0.4
5	71.2	68.5	75.0	63.4	71.5	0.3	0.3	0.2	0.4	0.3
6	70.2	67.5	74.1	62.4	70.5	0.2	0.3	0.2	0.4	0.3
7	69.2	66.5	73.1	61.4	69.5	0.2	0.2	0.2	0.4	0.2
8	68.2	65.5	72.1	60.4	68.5	0.2	0.2	0.1	0.3	0.2
9	67.3	64.5	71.1	59.4	67.6	0.2	0.2	0.1	0.2	0.2
10	66.3	63.5	70.1	58.5	66.6	0.1	0.1	0.1	0.2	0.2
11	65.3	62.6	69.1	57.5	65.6	0.1	0.1	0.1	0.2	0.2
12	64.3	61.6	68.1	56.5	64.6	0.2	0.2	0.2	0.3	0.2
13	63.3	60.6	67.1	55.5	63.6	0.3	0.4	0.2	0.5	0.3
14	62.3	59.6	66.2	54.5	62.6	0.5	0.6	0.3	0.8	0.3
15	61.3	58.6	65.2	53.6	61.7	0.6	0.8	0.4	1.2	0.4
16	60.4	57.7	64.2	52.6	60.7	0.8	1.0	0.4	1.5	0.5
17	59.4	56.7	63.2	51.7	59.7	0.9	1.2	0.5	1.8	0.5
18	58.5	55.8	62.3	50.8	58.7	1.0	1.3	0.5	2.0	0.6
19	57.5	54.9	61.3	49.9	57.8	1.0	1.4	0.5	2.2	0.6
20	56.6	54.0	60.3	49.0	56.8	1.0	1.4	0.5	2.3	0.6
21	55.7	53.0	59.3	48.1	55.8	1.1	1.4	0.5	2.5	0.7
22	54.7	52.1	58.4	47.3	54.9	1.1	1.5	0.4	2.6	0.7
23	53.8	51.2	57.4	46.4	53.9	1.1	1.5	0.5	2.7	0.8
24	52.8	50.3	56.4	45.5	53.0	1.1	1.5	0.5	2.8	0.8
25	51.9	49.3	55.4	44.6	52.0	1.2	1.5	0.5	2.9	0.9
26	51.0	48.4	54.5	43.8	51.0	1.2	1.5	0.5	3.0	1.0
27	50.0	47.5	53.5	42.9	50.1	1.2	1.6	0.5	3.1	1.1
28	49.1	46.6	52.5	42.0	49.2	1.3	1.6	0.6	3.2	1.2
29	48.1	45.6	51.6	41.2	48.2	1.3	1.7	0.6	3.4	1.3
30	47.2	44.7	50.6	40.3	47.3	1.4	1.8	0.6	3.5	1.4
31	46.3	43.8	49.6	39.4	46.3	1.5	1.8	0.6	3.7	1.5
32	45.3	42.9	48.7	38.6	45.4	1.5	1.9	0.7	3.9	1.6
33	44.4	41.9	47.7	37.7	44.5	1.6	2.0	0.7	4.1	1.7
34	43.5	41.0	46.7	36.9	43.5	1.7	2.1	0.8	4.4	1.8
35	42.6	40.1	45.8	36.0	42.6	1.8	2.2	0.8	4.6	1.9
36	41.6	39.2	44.8	35.2	41.7	1.9	2.3	0.9	4.9	2.0
37	40.7	38.3	43.8	34.4	40.8	2.0	2.4	0.9	5.1	2.1
38	39.8	37.4	42.9	33.5	39.9	2.1	2.5	1.0	5.3	2.2
39	38.9	36.5	41.9	32.7	39.0	2.2	2.6	1.1	5.5	2.3
40	38.0	35.6	41.0	31.9	38.1	2.2	2.7	1.2	5.7	2.5
41	37.0	34.7	40.0	31.1	37.1	2.4	2.8	1.3	5.9	2.6
42	36.1	33.8	39.1	30.3	36.2	2.5	3.0	1.4	6.2	2.8
43	35.2	32.9	38.1	29.4	35.3	2.7	3.2	1.5	6.5	3.0
44	34.3	32.0	37.2	28.6	34.4	2.9	3.4	1.7	7.0	3.3
45	33.4	31.1	36.2	27.8	33.6	3.1	3.7	1.9	7.5	3.6
46	32.5	30.2	35.3	27.0	32.7	3.4	4.0	2.1	8.0	3.9
47	31.6	29.3	34.4	26.3	31.8	3.7	4.3	2.4	8.5	4.3
48	30.7	28.4	33.5	25.5	30.9	4.1	4.7	2.6	9.1	4.7
49	29.9	27.6	32.5	24.7	30.1	4.4	5.1	2.9	9.7	5.1
50	29.0	26.7	31.6	23.9	29.2	4.9	5.6	3.2	10.4	5.5
51	28.1	25.8	30.7	23.2	28.4	5.3	6.1	3.5	11.1	6.0
52	27.3	25.0	29.8	22.4	27.6	5.8	6.8	3.9	11.9	6.6
53	26.4	24.2	29.0	21.7	26.7	6.4	7.5	4.3	13.0	7.2
54	25.6	23.3	28.1	21.0	25.9	7.0	8.2	4.7	14.2	7.8
55	24.8	22.5	27.2	20.3	25.1	7.7	9.1	5.1	15.4	8.5
56	24.0	21.7	26.4	19.6	24.3	8.4	10.0	5.6	16.8	9.2
57	23.2	21.0	25.5	18.9	23.6	9.2	11.1	6.2	18.2	10.0
58	22.4	20.2	24.7	18.3	22.8	10.1	12.2	6.8	19.6	10.9
59	21.6	19.4	23.8	17.6	22.0	11.1	13.5	7.6	21.1	11.8
60	20.8	18.7	23.0	17.0	21.3	12.2	15.0	8.3	22.7	12.8
61	20.1	18.0	22.2	16.4	20.6	13.3	16.5	9.2	24.4	13.8
62	19.4	17.3	21.4	15.8	19.9	14.5	18.0	10.0	26.2	15.0
63	18.6	16.6	20.6	15.2	19.1	15.7	19.6	10.9	28.1	16.1
64	17.9	15.9	19.8	14.6	18.5	16.9	21.4	11.8	30.0	17.4
65	17.2	15.2	19.1	14.0	17.8	18.2	23.0	12.8	32.0	18.7

Age	Expectation of life in years: Total persons	White: Male	White: Female	All other: Male	All other: Female	Mortality probability per 1,000: Total persons	White: Male	White: Female	All other: Male	All other: Female
66	16.5	14.6	18.3	13.5	17.1	19.7	24.8	13.8	34.1	20.1
67	15.9	13.9	17.5	12.9	16.4	21.3	27.0	15.0	36.5	21.6
68	15.2	13.3	16.8	12.4	15.8	23.1	29.4	16.5	39.1	23.1
69	14.5	12.7	16.1	11.9	15.2	25.1	32.2	18.0	41.9	24.7
70	13.9	12.1	15.4	11.4	14.5	27.3	35.1	19.8	45.0	26.4
71	13.3	11.5	14.7	10.9	13.9	29.7	38.3	21.7	48.3	28.1
72	12.7	11.0	14.0	10.5	13.3	32.2	41.7	23.7	51.6	30.1
73	12.1	10.4	13.3	10.0	12.7	34.9	45.5	25.9	55.0	32.2
74	11.5	9.9	12.6	9.5	12.1	37.9	49.5	28.4	58.4	34.6
75	10.9	9.4	12.0	9.1	11.5	41.1	53.9	31.1	62.0	37.1
76	10.4	8.9	11.4	8.7	10.9	44.5	58.6	34.1	65.9	40.0
77	9.8	8.4	10.8	8.3	10.4	48.3	63.7	37.4	70.2	43.1
78	9.3	7.9	10.2	7.8	9.8	52.5	69.3	41.1	75.0	46.6
79	8.8	7.5	9.6	7.4	9.3	57.1	75.4	45.2	80.3	50.6
80	8.3	7.1	9.0	7.0	8.8	62.2	82.0	49.9	86.2	55.1
81	7.8	6.7	8.4	6.7	8.2	67.9	89.3	55.3	92.6	60.3
82	7.4	6.3	7.9	6.3	7.7	74.4	97.2	61.4	99.7	66.3
83	6.9	5.9	7.4	5.9	7.3	81.6	106.0	68.6	107.2	73.4
84	6.5	5.5	6.9	5.6	6.8	90.0	115.7	77.0	115.2	81.8
85	6.1	5.2	6.4	5.3	6.4	—	—	—	—	—

Source: Department of Health and Human Services, National Center for Health Statistics.

Living Arrangements of the Elderly, 1991
(in thousands, except as indicated)

Living arrangement and age	All races: Total	All races: Men	All races: Women	White: Total	White: Men	White: Women	Black: Total	Black: Men	Black: Women
65 years and over	30,093	12,547	17,546	26,898	11,235	15,663	2,547	1,031	1,516
Living									
Alone	31.2	16.0	42.0	31.3	15.5	42.6	32.7	23.3	39.1
With spouse	54.1	74.3	39.7	55.7	76.2	41.0	38.1	55.2	26.5
With relatives	12.5	7.4	16.2	10.9	6.3	14.2	25.9	16.0	32.6
With nonrelatives only	2.2	2.3	2.1	2.0	2.0	2.1	3.4	5.5	1.9
Percent	100.0	100.0	100.0	100.0	100.0	100.0	100.0	100.0	100.0
65 to 74 years	18,237	8,156	10,081	16,209	7,267	8,942	1,581	694	887
Living									
Alone	24.6	13.4	33.7	24.3	12.7	33.7	30.5	23.3	36.1
With spouse	63.7	79.0	51.4	65.7	81.1	53.2	44.3	57.3	34.0
With relatives	9.9	5.5	13.4	8.5	4.6	11.6	21.3	13.4	27.5
With nonrelatives only	1.8	2.0	1.6	1.6	1.7	1.5	3.9	5.9	2.4
Percent	100.0	100.0	100.0	100.0	100.0	100.0	100.0	100.0	100.0
75 years and over	11,855	4,391	7,464	10,689	3,968	6,721	966	337	629
Living									
Alone	41.2	20.8	53.2	42.0	20.8	54.5	36.1	22.8	43.2
With spouse	39.4	65.6	24.0	40.6	67.3	24.9	28.0	50.7	15.7
With relatives	16.6	10.9	20.0	14:6	9.4	17.7	33.4	21.7	39.7
With nonrelatives only	2.8	2.7	2.8	2.7	2.6	2.8	2.5	4.7	1.3
Percent	100.0	100.0	100.0	100.09	100.0	100.0	100.0	100.0	100.0

Source: U.S. Bureau of the Census, Current Population Reports, Series P-20, No. 461, *Marital Status and Living Arrangements: March 1991.*

More Older Women Live Alone

As they age, there is an increasing likelihood that women will live alone. This fact is related to the traditionally shorter life expectancies of men and the tendency of women to marry men older than themselves.

Today's young-old (65–74) are more likely to be in relatively good health and to be able to afford to live alone than was true in the past. In many ways the current generation of elderly women are pacesetters as they defy stereotypes of aging.

For elderly women with protective social networks, living alone does not necessarily mean lonely. Most have families nearby and other companionship. About three in five have lived in the same place for 10 or more years. They also have a greater tendency to use community services than do those living with others.

First National Report on Hate Crime

Although the survey did not include all of the Nation's police agencies, it served to define the nature of this type of violence

The Federal Government published the first data compiled from the F.B.I.'s statistical program on hate crimes in January 1993. This program was initiated in response to the Hate Crimes Statistics Act of 1990 and is being implemented by law enforcement agencies across the Nation. The data cover the calendar year 1991 and were supplied by nearly 3,000 law enforcement agencies in 32 states. The reporting of the information was voluntary and, because all of the law enforcement agencies did not participate, the data give an incomplete picture of the extent of bias crimes. However, it was an important first step.

A total of 4,558 hate crimes were reported in 1991. Among the offenses measured, intimidation was the most frequently reported hate crime, accounting for one-third of the offenses. Following were destruction/damage/vandalism of property, 27 percent; simple assault, 17%; aggravated assault, 16 percent; and robbery, 3 percent.

The remaining offense types: murder, forcible rape, burglary, larceny-theft, motor vehicle theft, and arson, each accounted for one percent or less of the total.

Racial bias motivated six of ten offenses reported; religious bias, two out of ten; and ethnic and sexual-orientation bias, each one out of ten. Among the specific bias types, anti-black offenses accounted for the highest percentage, 36 percent of the total.

Anti-white and anti-Jewish motivations followed with 19 and 17 percent, respectively. Considering incidents for which suspected race of the offender was reported, 65 percent of the hate crimes were committed by whites, 30 percent by blacks, and 2 percent by persons of other races. The remainder of the incidents were committed by groups of offenders not all of the same races.

Hate Crime Offense Codes Reported, 1991

Crime	Number	Percent*
Murder	12	.3
Forcible rape	7	.1
Robbery	119	2.5
Aggravated assault	773	16.3
Burglary	56	1.2
Larceny–theft	22	0.5
Motor vehicle theft	0	0.0
Arson	55	1.2
Simple assault	796	16.7
Intimidation	1,614	33.9
Destruction/Damage/ Vandalism of property	1,301	27.4
Total number of offense types	4,755	100.0

*Because of rounding, percentages do not add to total.

F.B.I. officials acknowledged the lack of complete information about the full extent of these crimes, but stated that it was done on a voluntary basis and that many of the police agencies and local governments did not have the resources to compile the necessary data.

The accompanying tables provide specific hate crime data. A more comprehensive report on these offenses is planned in the future.

Suspected Race of Offenders in Hate Crimes, 1991

Suspected Race of Offender	Number of Incidents	Percent
White	1,679	46.8
Black	769	16.9
American Indian/ Alaskan native	12	0.3
Asian/Pacific Islander	47	1.0
Multi-racial group	77	1.7
Unknown	1,974	43.3
Total incidents	**4,558 ***	**100.0**

*A single incident may involve more than one offense.

Hate Crime Bias–Motivations Reported, 1991

Bias–Motivation	Number	Percent*
RACE	**2,963**	**62.3**
Anti-white	888	18.7
Anti-black	1,689	35.5
Anti-American Indian/ Alaskan native	11	0.2
Anti-Asian/Pacific Islander	287	6.0
Anti-multi-racial group	88	1.9
ETHNICITY	**450**	**9.5**
Anti-Hispanic	242	5.1
Anti-other ethnicity/ national origin	208	4.4
RELIGION	**917**	**19.3**
Anti-Jewish	792	16.7
Anti-Catholic	23	0.5
Anti-Protestant	26	0.5
Anti-Islamic (Moslem)	10	0.2
Anti-other religion	51	1.1
Anti-multi-religious group	11	0.2
Anti-atheism/agnosticism/etc.	4	0.1
SEXUAL ORIENTATION	**425**	**8.9**
Anti-homosexual	421	8.9
Anti-heterosexual	3	0.1
Anti-bisexual	1	0.0
Total	**4,755**	**100.0**

*Because of rounding, percentages do not add to total.

Crime Rates for Selected Large Cities: 1990

(Offenses known to the police per 100,000 population.)

City ranked by population size, 1990[1]	Violent crime: Murder	Forcible rape	Robbery	Aggravated assault	Property crime: Burglary	Larceny–theft	Motor vehicle theft
New York, NY	31	43	1,370	941	1,638	3,668	2,009
Los Angeles, CA	28	58	1,036	1,283	1,477	3,519	1,825
Chicago, IL	31	(2)	1,335	1,477	1,803	4,670	1,747
Houston, TX	35	82	792	479	2,636	4,808	2,506
Philadelphia, PA	32	46	808	463	1,523	2,689	1,632
San Diego, CA	12	40	390	643	1,503	4,375	2,183
Detroit, MI	57	161	1,266	1,216	2,536	4,002	2,955
Dallas, TX	44	134	1,049	1,211	3,275	7,372	2,435
Phoenix, AZ	13	52	344	675	2,510	5,381	1,782
San Antonio, TX	22	46	306	238	2,780	7,495	1,590
San Jose, CA	5	53	132	411	735	2,996	538
Baltimore, MD	41	93	1,288	1,015	2,004	4,807	1,347
Indianapolis, IN	12	112	340	824	1,629	2,833	1,000
San Francisco, CA	14	58	974	665	1,467	4,915	1,569
Jacksonville, FL	28	111	622	1,070	2,753	4,931	949
Columbus, OH	14	102	560	434	2,343	5,117	1,338
Milwaukee, WI	25	79	660	237	1,482	4,709	2,108
Memphis, TN	32	136	680	640	2,544	3,763	2,078
Washington, DC	78	50	1,214	1,117	1,983	4,997	1,336
Boston, MA	25	94	1,049	1,212	1,783	5,162	2,527
Seattle, WA	10	93	522	882	2,166	7,656	1,273
El Paso, TX	7	50	268	668	1,856	7,298	1,094
Cleveland, OH	33	167	973	645	2,017	3,024	2,256
New Orleans, LA	61	73	1,217	908	2,742	4,992	2,443
Nashville–Davidson, TN	13	111	433	821	1,780	4,027	694
Denver, CO	14	80	281	524	1,997	3,591	1,269
Austin, TX	10	60	314	331	2,442	7,722	836
Fort Worth, TX	29	97	626	997	3,418	7,754	2,057
Oklahoma City, OK	15	95	314	658	2,572	5,769	1,187
Portland, OR	8	97	581	1,106	2,050	5,930	1,328
Kansas City, MO	28	119	1,033	1,370	2,678	5,344	2,381
Long Beach, CA	25	69	976	886	2,017	3,937	1,662
Tucson, AZ	7	72	223	606	1,951	8,412	609
St. Louis, MO	45	83	1,187	2,134	2,907	6,192	2,123
Charlotte, NC	24	97	810	1,373	2,751	6,858	682
Atlanta, GA	59	176	1,550	2,300	3,939	8,380	2,832
Virginia Beach, VA	4	38	108	80	1,012	4,208	330
Albuquerque, NM	9	58	268	997	2,468	5,752	513
Oakland, CA	39	139	868	524	2,284	5,125	1,927
Pittsburgh, PA	(2)	(2)	(2)	(2)	(2)	(2)	(2)
Sacramento, CA	12	57	485	524	1,886	4,391	1,773
Minneapolis, MN	(2)	(2)	(2)	(2)	(2)	(2)	(2)
Tulsa, OK	16	104	419	795	2,233	3,900	2,069
Honolulu, HI	4	33	106	145	1,170	4,247	397
Cincinnati, OH	14	107	443	666	1,620	4,246	461
Miami, FL	36	83	2,279	1,954	3,767	8,233	2,671
Fresno, CA	19	73	450	701	2,015	5,258	2,015
Omaha, NE	3	65	180	687	1,248	4,466	401
Toledo, OH	11	127	525	401	1,883	5,278	1,386
Buffalo, NY	11	108	662	826	2,488	3,719	1,079
Wichita, KS	6	106	355	254	2,049	5,444	714
Santa Ana, CA	15	25	529	338	1,217	4,132	1,334
Mesa, AZ	3	33	96	467	1,348	4,272	868
Colorado Springs, CO	3	72	92	255	1,446	5,198	411
Tampa, FL	22	131	1,130	2,044	4,316	7,131	2,352
Newark, NJ	41	119	2,188	1,535	2,449	4,555	5,369
St. Paul, MN	7	99	287	623	1,864	4,404,	851
Louisville, KY	15	45	405	383	1,771	3,228	577
Anaheim, CA	8	35	366	268	1,583	3,664	1,245
Birmingham, AL	47	100	676	753	2,616	5,162	1,907
Arlington, TX	3	53	224	437	1,719	5,041	1,048
Norfolk, VA	24	84	533	451	1,608	6,485	1,070

1. Data are not available for Pittsburgh, PA, and Minneapolis, MN. 2. The rates for forcible rape, violent crime, and crime index are not shown because the forcible rape figures were not in accordance with national Uniform Crime Reporting guidelines. *Source: Statistical Abstract of the United States, 1992.*

Estimated Arrests, 1991[1]

Murder and non-negligent manslaughter	24,050	Weapons—carrying, possession, etc.	232,300
Forcible rape	40,120	Prostitution and commercial vice	98,900
Robbery	173,820	Sex offenses, except forcible rape and prostitution	108,000
Aggravated assault	480,900	Drug abuse violations	1,010,000
Burglary	436,500	Gambling	16,600
Larceny—theft	1,588,300	Offenses against family and children	99,400
Motor vehicle theft	207,700	Driving under the influence	1,771,400
Arson	20,000	Liquor laws	624,100
Total violent crime	718,890	Drunkenness	881,100
Total property crime	2,252,500	Disorderly conduct	757,700
Other assaults	1,041,200	Vagrancy	38,500
Forgery and counterfeiting	103,700	All other offenses, except traffic	3,240,000
Fraud	427,800	Curfew and loitering law violations	93,400
Embezzlement	14,000	Runaways	177,300
Stolen property—buying, receiving, possessing	170,000	**Total**[2]	**14,211,900**
Vandalism	335,100		

1. Arrest totals based on all reporting agencies and estimates for unreported areas. 2. Because of rounding, items may not add to totals. *Source:* Department of Justice, Federal Bureau of Investigation, *Uniform Crime Reports for the United States, 1991*, released 1992.

Number of Arrests by Sex and Age

Offense	Male				Female			
	Total		Under 18		Total		Under 18	
	1991	1990	1991	1990	1991	1990	1991	1990
Murder[1]	15,308	16,387	2,352	2,423	1,758	1,911	113	132
Forcible rape	26,318	30,630	4,035	4,546	300	336	59	82
Robbery	118,485	125,015	30,559	30,168	11,088	11,285	2,951	2,799
Aggravated assault	286,496	326,780	39,942	43,454	45,197	50,137	7,071	7,713
Burglary—breaking or entering	265,410	311,220	88,359	103,314	26,570	29,972	8,293	9,123
Larceny—theft	717,967	843,851	225,220	266,916	339,180	397,385	90,922	105,217
Motor vehicle theft	131,346	151,449	56,266	65,029	14,523	16,889	7,123	7,901
Arson	11,261	13,024	5,501	5,940	1,699	1,950	540	620
Violent crime[2]	446,607	498,812	76,888	80,591	58,343	63,669	10,194	10,726
Other assaults	573,138	672,455	80,812	91,334	113,037	128,970	24,889	27,724
Forgery and counterfeiting	44,213	48,667	3,686	4,532	23,717	25,726	1,842	2,228
Fraud	149,977	156,120	7,149	6,629	108,815	123,656	2,616	2,839
Embezzlement	5,651	7,083	447	532	3,492	4,972	238	332
Stolen property—buying, receiving, possessing	102,699	115,864	28,268	30,813	13,789	15,792	3,154	3,274
Vandalism	194,424	228,872	84,863	95,070	23,921	27,686	7,675	8,684
Weapons—carrying, possessing, etc.	147,686	163,055	31,339	30,055	11,359	13,082	2,146	1,936
Prostitution and commercialized vice	25,628	32,770	455	587	50,242	58,323	516	694
Sex offenses, except forcible rape and prostitution	67,215	78,291	11,725	12,594	5,232	6,561	850	913
Drug abuse violations	581,184	723,329	48,153	57,457	116,248	145,826	5,872	7,283
Gambling	10,265	13,314	759	761	1,582	2,129	24	37
Offenses against family and children	46,315	54,216	1,668	1,700	11,302	11,776	855	911
Driving under the influence	925,267	1,213,216	9,364	13,567	139,795	117,690	1,497	2,205
Liquor laws	290,936	448,898	60,499	87,646	68,030	103,141	23,018	34,401
Drunkenness	542,380	644,594	12,573	16,379	62,882	71,910	2,274	2,965
Disorderly conduct	391,517	469,055	67,963	76,246	99,710	110,619	17,776	19,753
Vagrancy	26,360	27,307	1,753	2,116	3,170	3,930	266	415
All other offenses, except traffic	1,788,508	2,144,717	170,647	196,664	373,181	427,774	46,348	52,071
Curfew and loitering law violations	45,931	46,471	45,931	46,471	16,725	18,097	16,725	18,097
Runaways	51,121	60,189	51,121	60,189	67,853	77,966	67,853	77,966
Total	**7,583,006**	**9,181,930**	**1,171,409**	**1,355,638**	**1,754,397**	**2,068,153**	**343,506**	**398,904**

1. Includes non-negligent manslaughter. 2. Violent crimes are offenses of murder, forcible rape, robbery, and aggravated assault. NOTE: 10,206 agencies reporting; 1990 estimated population 193,507,000. *Source:* Department of Justice, Federal Bureau of Investigation, *Uniform Crime Reports for the United States, 1991*, released 1992.

Arrests by Race, 1991

Offense	White	Black	Other[1]	Total
Murder[2]	7,861	9,924	311	18,096
Forcible rape	16,306	12,960	501	29,767
Robbery	51,217	83,146	1,813	136,176
Aggravated assault	218,628	139,407	6,215	364,250
Burglary	222,817	94,688	6,165	323,670
Larceny–theft	792,895	368,053	29,089	1,190,037
Motor vehicle theft	93,728	62,918	3,457	160,103
Arson	11,309	3,164	265	14,738
Violent crimes[3]	294,012	245,437	8,840	548,289
Property crimes[4]	1,120,749	528,823	38,976	1,688,548
Other assaults	498,497	257,121	16,398	772,016
Forgery and counterfeiting	48,535	25,264	1,070	74,869
Fraud	197,643	91,230	2,655	291,528
Embezzlement	7,202	3,195	168	10,565
Stolen property—buying, receiving, possessing	73,908	54,011	1,690	129,609
Vandalism	189,474	55,014	4,764	249,252
Weapons—carrying, possession, etc.	98,609	72,137	2,744	173,490
Prostitution and commercial vice	47,517	29,943	1,319	78,779
Sex offenses, except forcible rape and prostitution	63,185	15,985	1,668	80,838
Drug abuse violation	443,596	312,997	6,747	763,340
Gambling	5,581	5,843	1,040	12,464
Offenses against family and children	47,304	20,942	2,699	70,954
Driving under the influence	1,129,876	115,724	25,113	1,270,713
Liquor laws	391,991	43,576	13,313	448,880
Drukenness	507,571	102,307	15,249	625,127
Disorderly conduct	365,765	182,414	10,325	558,504
Vagrancy	15,735	14,341	679	30,755
All other offenses except traffic	1,542,890	831,857	53,293	2,428,040
Suspicion	4,150	5,964	70	10,184
Curfew and loitering law violations	55,389	14,819	1,829	72,037
Runaways	102,683	20,355	4,589	127,627
Total	**7,251,862**	**3,049,299**	**215,238**	**10,516,399**

1. Includes American Indian, Alaskan Native, and Asian or Pacific Islander. 2. Includes non–negligent manslaughter. 3. Violent crimes are offenses of murder, forcible rape, robbery, and aggravated assault. 4. Property crimes are offenses of burglary, larceny-theft, motor vehicle theft. NOTE: Figures represent arrests reported by 10,110 agencies serving a total 1990 population of 192,939,000 as estimated by FBI. *Source:* Department of Justice, Federal Bureau of Investigation, *Uniform Crime Reports for the United States, 1991*, released 1992.

Total Arrests, by Age Groups, 1991

Age	Arrests	Age	Arrests	Age	Arrests	Age	Arrests	Age	Arrests
Under 15	527,137	18	387,803	22	321,984	30–34	1,175,491	50–54	141,268
15	273,039	19	396,882	23	303,605	35–39	789,840	55 and over	196,740
16	326,658	20	394,039	24	293,590	40–44	474,171		
17	348,343	21	363,232	25–29	1,405,060	45–49	247,641	**Total**	**8,366,524**

NOTE: Based on reports furnished to the FBI by 10,206 agencies covering a 1990 estimated population of 193,507,000. *Source:* Department of Justice, Federal Bureau of Investigation, *Uniform Crime Reports for the United States, 1991*, released 1992.

Federal Prosecutions of Public Corruption: 1981 to 1990

(Prosecution of persons who have corrupted public office in violation of Federal Criminal Statutes. As of Dec. 31, 1990)

Prosecution status	1990	1989	1988	1987	1986	1985	1984	1983	1982	1981
Total:[1] Indicted	1,176	1,349	1,274	1,340	1,192	1,182	936	1,073	729	878
Convicted	1,084	1,444	1,067	1,075	1,027	997	934	972	671	730
Awaiting trial	300	375	288	368	246	256	269	222	186	231
Federal officials: Indicted	615	695	629	651	596	563	408	460[2]	158	198
Convicted	583	610	529	545	523	470	429	424[2]	147	159
Awaiting trial	103	126	86	118	83	90	77	58	38	23
State officials: Indicted	96	71	66	102	88	79	58	81	4	87
Convicted	79	54	69	76	71	66	52	65	43	66
Awaiting trial	28	18	14	26	24	20	21	26	18	36
Local officials: Indicted	257	269	276	246	232	248	203	270	257	244
Convicted	225	201	229	204	207	221	196	226	232	211
Awaiting trial	98	122	79	89	55	49	74	61	58	102

1. Includes individuals who are neither public officials nor employees, but who were involved with public officials or employees in violating the law, now shown separately. 2. Increases in the number indicted and convicted between 1982 and 1983 resulted from a greater focus on federal corruption nationwide and more consistent reporting of cases involving lower–level employees. NOTE: Figures are latest available. *Source:* U.S. Department of Justice, *Federal Prosecutions of Corrupt Public Officials, 1970–1980*, and *Report to Congress on the Activities and Operations of the Public Integrity Section*, annual from *Statistical Abstract of the United States 1992.*

Law Enforcement Officers Killed or Assaulted: 1981 to 1990

(Covers officers killed feloniously and accidentally in line of duty; includes federal officers.)

	1990	1989	1988	1987	1986	1985	1984	1983	1982	1981
Northeast	13	23	17	24	15	19	21	20	17	17
Midwest	20	22	18	31	19	23	22	26	41	29
South	68	68	77	51	62	64	69	64	75	80
West	23	23	39	40	29	29	32	34	27	27
Puerto Rico	8	8	1	1	6	10	3	6	3	3
Total killed	**132**[6]	**146**[5]	**155**[5]	**147**	**131**	**148**[4]	**147**	**152**[3]	**164**[2]	**157**[1]
Assaults										
Population (1,000)[7]	199,065	189,641	186,418	190,025	196,030	198,935	195,794	198,341	176,563	177,836
Number of—										
Agencies	9,483	9,023	8,866	8,957	9,755	9,906	10,002	9,908	8,829	9,019
Police officers	412,314	380,232	369,743	378,977	380,249	389,808	372,268	377,620	319,101	332,856
Firearm	3,662	3,154	2,759	2,789	2,852	2,793	2,654	3,067	2,642	3,330
Knife or cutting instrument	1,641	1,379	1,367	1,561	1,614	1,715	1,662	1,829	1,452	1,733
Other dangerous weapon	7,390	5,778	5,573	5,685	5,721	5,263	5,148	5,527	4,879	4,800
Hands, fists, feet, etc.	59,101	51,861	49,053	53,807	54,072	51,953	50,689	51,901	46,802	47,253
Total assaulted	**71,794**	**62,172**	**58,752**	**63,842**	**64,259**	**61,724**	**60,153**	**62,324**	**55,775**	**57,116**

1. Includes one officer in American Samoa. 2. Includes one officer in Mariana Islands. 3. Includes one officer each in Guam and Mariana Islands. 4. Includes one officer in Guam and 2 in foreign locations. 5. Includes one officer in American Samoa and 2 in foreign locations. 6. Includes 1 officer killed in Guam and 1 Federal officer killed in Peru. 7. Represents the number of persons covered by agencies shown. NOTE: Data are latest available. *Source: Statistical Abstract of the United States, 1992.*

Full–Time Law Enforcement Employees, 1991

City	Officers	Civilians	Total	1990 Total
Atlanta	1,533	568	2,101	1,933
Baltimore	2,893	562	3,455	3,390
Birmingham, Ala.	724	210	934	937
Boston	1,989	627	2,616	2,662
Buffalo, N.Y.	973	139	1,112	1,171
Chicago	12,132	3,126	15,258	13,535
Cincinnati	964	225	1,189	1,184
Cleveland	1,682	362	2,044	2,082
Columbus, Ohio	1,403	338	1,741	1,735
Dallas	2,857	809	3,666	3,592
Denver	1,361	262	1,623	1,562
Detroit	3,954	618	4,572	5,113
El Paso	768	232	1,000	1,050
Fort Worth	949	343	1,292	1,260
Honolulu	1,887	425	2,312	2,257
Houston	4,077	1,655	5,732	5,653
Indianapolis	988	380	1,368	1,369
Jacksonville, Fla.	1,253	892	2,145	2,084
Kansas City, Mo.	1,167	613	1,780	1,764
Long Beach, Calif.	664	345	1,009	981
Los Angeles	8,198	2,666	10,864	11,190
Louisville, Ky.	603	246	849	829
Memphis, Tenn.	1,390	415	1,805	1,798
Miami, Fla.	1,069	322	1,391	1,418
Milwaukee	1,895	455	2,350	2,281

City	Officers	Civilians	Total	1990 Total
Minneapolis	818	142	960	899
New Orleans	n.a.	n.a.	n.a.	1,734
New York	26,856	9,371	36,227	36,407
Newark, N.J.	1,111	156	1,267	1,225
Norfolk, Va.	676	86	762	768
Oakland, Calif.	671	403	1,074	958
Oklahoma City	897	318	1,215	1,182
Omaha, Neb.	608	149	757	755
Philadelphia	6,424	894	7,318	7,586
Phoenix, Ariz.	1,982	672	2,654	2,628
Pittsburgh	1,135	259	1,394	1,181
Portland, Ore.	829	199	1,028	1,006
Rochester, N.Y.	649	127	776	765
St. Louis	1,516	624	2,140	2,272
St. Paul	515	171	686	674
San Antonio	1,571	326	1,897	1,855
San Diego, Calif.	1,886	722	2,608	2,568
San Francisco	1,840	476	2,316	2,276
San Jose, Calif.	1,170	465	1,635	1,469
Seattle	1,228	461	1,689	1,819
Tampa, Fla.	830	257	1,087	1,126
Toledo, Ohio	668	47	715	723
Tucson, Ariz.	741	237	978	1,003
Tulsa, Okla.	735	182	917	877
Washington, D.C.	4,502	646	5,148	5,521

NOTE: As of Oct. 31, 1990. n.a. = not available. *Source:* Department of Justice, Federal Bureau of Investigation, *Uniform Crime Reports for the United States, 1991,* released 1992.

Adolescent Drug Dealers

Most of them are not necessarily involved in other or more serious criminal activity. Most sell marijuana, amphetamines, and tranquilizers less than once a month to support their own use. Their buyers are almost always known to them and they typically distribute drugs in homes or cars, not in public places. They do not consider these activities "serious crimes." □

U.S. District Courts—Criminal Cases Commenced and Defendants Disposed of, by Nature of Offense: 1989 and 1990

[For years ending June 30]

Nature of offense	1990 cases commenced[1]	Disposition of defendants, 1990									1989	
			Not convicted		Convicted[2]			Sentenced				
		Disposed	Total	Acquitted	Total	Guilty plea[3]	Court or jury	Imprisonment	Probation	Fine and other	Cases commenced[1]	Defendants disposed of
General offenses:												
Homicide	176	162	33	8	129	90	37	106	11	12	174	166
Robbery	1,379	1,340	111	26	1,229	1,060	165	1,207	21	1	1,309	1,206
Assault	562	559	173	42	386	279	105	254	106	26	567	579
Burglary	104	122	9	2	113	101	12	99	12	2	107	103
Larceny—theft	3,391	3,574	675	70	2,899	2,640	220	1,088	1,571	240	3,474	4,065
Embezzlement and fraud	9,579	10,774	1,202	183	9,572	8,759	756	4,134	5,113	325	8,958	10,982
Auto theft	243	319	47	10	272	243	28	198	72	2	233	462
Forgery, counterfeiting	1,514	1,774	217	18	1,557	1,444	105	805	729	23	1,505	1,733
Sex offenses	433	333	62	16	271	223	47	185	83	3	324	348
DAPCA[4]	12,592	19,271	3,083	473	16,188	13,036	3,121	13,838	2,135	215	11,855	16,834
Misc. general offenses	13,265	12,504	3,323	627	9,181	7,437	1,243	3,212	2,514	3,455	16,385	18,165
Total	**47,962**	**56,519**	**9,794**	**1,601**	**46,725**	**39,734**	**6,273**	**27,796**	**14,196**	**4,733**	**44,891**	**54,643**

1. Excludes transfers. 2. Convicted and sentenced. 3. Includes nolo contendere. 4. All marijuana, narcotics, and controlled substances under the Drug Abuse Prevention and Control Act. NOTE: Data are latest available. *Source: Statistical Abstract of the United States, 1992.*

Murder Victims by Weapons Used

Year	Murder victims, total	Weapons used or cause of death						
		Guns						
		Total	Percent	Cutting or stabbing	Blunt object[1]	Strangulation, hands, fists, feet or pushing	Arson[3]	All other[2]
1965	8,773	5,015	57.2	2,021	505	894	226	112
1970	13,649	9,039	66.2	2,424	604	1,031	353	198
1972	15,832	10,379	65.6	2,974	672	1,291	331	185
1973	17,123	11,249	65.7	2,985	848	1,445	173	423
1974	18,632	12,474	66.9	3,228	976	1,417	153	384
1975	18,642	12,061	64.7	3,245	1,001	1,646	193	496
1980	21,860	13,650	62.0	4,212	1,094	1,666	291	947
1981	20,053	12,523	62.4	3,886	1,038	1,469	258	658
1982	19,485	11,721	60.2	4,065	957	1,657	279	630
1983	18,673	10,895	58.0	4,075	1,062	1,656	216	769
1984	16,689	9,819	58.8	3,540	973	1,407	192	758
1985	17,545	10,296	58.7	3,694	972	1,491	243	849
1986	19,257	11,381	59.1	3,957	1,099	1,651	230	939
1987	17,963	10,612	59.1	3,643	1,045	1,525	200	938
1988	17,971	10,895	60.6	3,457	1,126	1,426	255	812
1989	18,954	11,832	62.4	3,458	1,128	1,416	234	886
1990	20,045	12,847	64.1	3,503	1,075	1,424	287	909
1991	21,505	14,265	66.3	3,405	1,082	1,519	194	1,040

1. Refers to club, hammer, etc. 2. Includes poison, explosives, unknown, drowning, asphyxiation, narcotics, other means, and weapons not stated. 3. Before 1973, includes drowning. *Source:* Department of Justice, Federal Bureau of Investigation, *Uniform Crime Reports for the United States, 1991.*

Women Drug Offenders

Women offenders are not likely to be high-rate robbers or assaulters, but about one-third of addicted women offenders are prostitutes. Others commit many thefts. Few become top-level or even mid-level drug dealers. Over half, however, play an active role in the lowest levels of the drug trade and facilitate as many sales as men also involved at the lowest levels.

Many of the seriously drug-involved women have children. Those who continue to inject drugs during pregnancy may have infants born addicted. Additionally, because they frequently share needles with other addicts, they are at high risk of contracting AIDS and their children are also at high risk of contracting AIDS. □

Crime Rates for Population Groups and Selected Cities, 1990

(offenses known to the police per 100,000 population, as of July 1)

	Violent Crime					Property crime				
Group and City	Murder	Forcible rape	Robbery	Aggravated assault	Total	Burglary—breaking or entering	Larceny—theft	Motor vehicle theft	Total	Total all crimes
MSA's (Metropolitan Statistical Areas)	11	46	322	478	856	1,356	3,533	801	5,691	6,547
Other Cities	5	33	63	357	458	1,053	3,559	232	4,845	5,303
Rural Areas	6	22	16	163	207	671	1,024	121	1,815	2,022
Selected Cities:										
Baltimore	41	93	1,288	1,015	2,438	2,004	4,807	1,347	8,158	10,596
Chicago	31	(1)	1,335	1,477	(1)	1,803	4,670	1,747	8,220	(1)
Dallas	44	134	1,049	1,211	2,438	3,275	7,372	2,435	13,082	15,520
Detroit	57	161	1,266	1,216	2,699	2,536	4,002	2,955	9,493	12,192
Houston	35	82	792	479	1,388	2,636	4,808	2,506	9,950	11,338
Indianapolis	12	112	340	824	1,287	1,629	2,833	1,000	5,462	6,749
Los Angeles	28	58	1,036	1,283	2,405	1,477	3,519	1,825	6,821	9,225
Memphis	32	136	680	640	1,488	2,544	3,763	2,078	8,384	9,872
New York	31	43	1,370	941	2,384	1,638	3,668	2,009	7,316	9,699
Philadelphia	32	46	808	463	1,349	1,523	2,689	1,632	5,843	7,192
Phoenix	13	52	344	675	1,085	2,510	5,381	1,782	9,672	10,756
San Antonio	22	46	306	238	612	2,780	7,495	1,590	11,865	12,477
San Diego	12	40	390	643	1,085	1,503	4,375	2,183	8,061	9,145
San Francisco	14	58	974	665	1,711	1,467	4,915	1,569	7,951	9,662
Washington, D.C.	78	50	1,214	1,117	2,458	1,983	4,997	1,336	8,316	10,774

1. The rates for 1990 forcible rape, violent crime, and total crime are not shown because the forcible rape figures were not in accordance with national Uniform Crime Reporting guidelines. NOTE: Data are latest available. *Source: Statistical Abstract of the United States 1992.*

Selected Type and Value of Property Stolen and Recovered, 1991

	Value of property (millions of dollars)		
Type of property	Stolen	Recovered	Percent recovered
Jewelry, metals, currency	$2,224.7	$103.1	4.6
Televisions, radios, stereos	1,106.9	51.8	4.7
Office equipment	320.4	29.0	9.1
Livestock	28.0	3.2	11.6
Motor vehicles	7,671.5	4,866.2	63.4
Consumable goods	114.5	13.9	12.1
Total, all property	**14,972.8**	**5,360.5**	**38.4**

NOTE: Ninety-four percent of police agencies reporting. *Source:* U.S. Department of Justice, Federal Bureau of Investigation, *Uniform Crime Reports, 1991.*

Reported Child Neglect and Abuse Cases: 1985 to 1987

		Total number of reports (1,000)			Reports per 1,000 population		
Division	Percent change 1986–87	1987	1986	1985	1987	1986	1985
New England	4.0	99.8	95.8	59.9	7.8	7.5	4.7
Middle Atlantic	6.3	242.5	228.1	152.2	6.5	6.1	4.1
North Central	–1.2	515.2	521.4	316.4	18.2	19.3	11.1
South Atlantic	–1.9	293.4	299.2	225.0	7.0	7.3	5.6
South Central	–3.0	302.4	311.7	249.9	14.8	15.1	12.9
Mountain	29.6	128.2	98.9	77.6	9.7	7.6	6.1
Pacific	6.1	443.7	418.3	218.4	12.1	11.7	6.2
U.S. Total	**2.6**	**2,025.2**	**1,973.4**	**1,299.4**	**8.3**	**8.2**	**5.4**

NOTE: Figures are latest available. *Source: Statistical Abstract of the United States, 1991.*

Prisoners Under Sentence of Death

Characteristic	1990	1989	1988
White	1,375	1,308	1,235
Black and other	981	935	882
Under 20 years	8	6	11
20–24 years	168	191	195
25–34 years	1,110	1,080	1,048
35–54 years	1,006	917	823
55 years and over	64	56	47
Schooling completed:			
7 years or less	178	183	180
8 years	186	178	184
9–11 years	775	739	692
12 years	729	695	657
More than 12 years	209	192	180
Unknown	279	263	231
Marital status:			
Never married	998	956	898
Married	632	610	594
Divorced or separated[2]	726	684	632
Time elapsed since sentencing:			
Less than 12 months	231	231	293
12–47 months	753	809	812
48–71 months	438	408	409
72 months and over	934	802	610
Legal status at arrest:			
Not under sentence	1,345	1,301	1,207
On parole or probation	578	585[3]	545[3]
In prison or escaped	128	94	93
Unknown	305	270	279
Total	**2,356**	**2,243**	**2,117**

1. For 1988 and 1989 revisions to the total number of prisoners were not carried to the characteristics except for race. 2. Includes widows, widowers, and unknown. 3. Includes persons on mandatory conditional release, work release, leave, AWOL, or bail covers 24 for 1988 and 1989. NOTE: As of Dec. 31. Excludes prisoners under sentence of death confined in local correctional systems pending appeal or who had not been committed to prison. *Source:* U.S. Bureau of Justice Statistics, *Capital Punishment*, annual, from *Statistical Abstract of the United States, 1992.*

Methods of Execution[1]

State	Method
Alabama	Electrocution
Alaska	No death penalty
Arizona	Lethal injection[9]
Arkansas	Lethal injection or electrocution
California	Lethal gas
Colorado	Lethal injection[6]
Connecticut	Electrocution
Delaware	Lethal injection[2]
D.C.	No death penalty
Florida	Electrocution
Georgia	Electrocution
Hawaii	No death penalty
Idaho	Lethal injection[8]
Illinois	Lethal injection
Indiana	Electrocution
Iowa	No death penalty
Kansas	No death penalty
Kentucky	Electrocution
Louisiana	Lethal injection
Maine	No death penalty
Maryland	Lethal gas
Massachusetts	No death penalty
Michigan	No death penalty
Minnesota	No death penalty
Mississippi	Lethal injection[7]
Missouri	Lethal injection
Montana	Hanging, or lethal injection[5]
Nebraska	Electrocution
Nevada	Lethal injection
New Hampshire	Lethal injection
New Jersey	Lethal injection[4]
New Mexico	Lethal injection
New York	No death penalty
North Carolina	Lethal gas or injection
North Dakota	No death penalty
Ohio	Electrocution
Oklahoma	Lethal injection
Oregon	Lethal injection[4]
Pennsylvania	Lethal injection
Rhode Island	No death penalty
South Carolina	Electrocution
South Dakota	Lethal injection
Tennessee	Electrocution
Texas	Lethal injection
Utah	Firing squad or lethal injection
Vermont	No death penalty
Virginia	Electrocution
Washington[6]	Hanging or lethal injection
West Virginia	No death penalty
Wisconsin	No death penalty
Wyoming	Lethal injection
U.S. (Fed. Govt.)	([3])
American Samoa	No death penalty
Guam	No death penalty
Puerto Rico	No death penalty
Virgin Islands	No death penalty

1. On July 1, 1976, by a 7–2 decision, the U.S. Supreme Court upheld the death penalty as not being "cruel or unusual." However, in another ruling the same day, the Court, by a 5–4 vote, stated that states may not impose "mandatory" capital punishment on every person convicted of murder. These decisions left uncertain the fate of condemned persons throughout the U.S. On Oct. 4, the Court refused to reconsider its July ruling, which allows some states to proceed with executions of condemned prisoners. The first execution in this country since 1967 was in Utah on Jan. 17, 1977. Gary Mark Gilmore was executed by shooting. 2. Prisoners originally sentenced to death prior to June 1986 may opt instead to hang. Those sentenced after June 1986 have no choice but lethal injection. 3. Is that of the state in which the execution takes place. 4. Death penalty has been passed, but not been used. 5. Defendant may choose between hanging and a lethal injection. 6. Applies to offenses committed on or after July, 1 1988. Prior to that date the method of execution is lethal gas. 7. Prisoners sentenced prior to July 1, 1984, shall be executed by lethal gas. 8. If the director of the Idaho Department of Corrections finds it impractical to carry out a lethal injection, he may instead use a firing squad. 9. Defendant sentenced to death for an offense committed before Nov. 23, 1992, shall choose either lethal injection or lethal gas. *Source: Information Please* questionnaires to the states.

Motor Vehicle Laws, 1992

	Age for license		Age for driver's license[1]					
State	Motor-cycle	Moped	Regular	Learner's	Restrictive	Driver's license duration	Fee	Annual safety inspection required
Alabama	14	14	16	15[8]	14[11]	4 yrs.	$15.00	no[16]
Alaska	16	14	16	14	14[6, 11]	5	10.00	no[16]
Arizona	16	16	18	15 7 mo.[3, 6]	16[6]	4	7.00	no[17, 18]
Arkansas	16	10[19]	16	14–16[5]	14[6, 9]	4	14.25	yes
California	18[21]	16[21]	18	15[4, 7]	16[4]	4	12.00	no[18]
Colorado	16	16	21	15 9 mo.[5]	15.5[4]	5	15.00	no[18]
Connecticut	16	16	16[4]	16[4]	16[4]	2 or 4	28.50/43.50	no
Delaware	18[21]	16	18	15 10 mo.[5, 6]	16[4, 6]	5	12.50	yes
D.C.	16	16	18	([5, 7])	16[6]	4	20.00	yes[19]
Florida	15	15	16	15[5]	15[6]	4 or 6	20.00	no[18]
Georgia	16	15	21	15	16[6]	4	4.50	no[18]
Hawaii	15	15	18	([5])	15[6]	4[13]	6/12.00	yes
Idaho	16[21]	16[21]	16	16[5]	15[4]	4	19.50	no
Illinois	18	16[21]	18	([5])	16[4, 6]	4 or 5	10.00	no[18]
Indiana	16	15	18	16[8, 20]	16 1 mo.[4, 6]	4[14]	6.00	no[18]
Iowa	16[21]	14	18	14	14[4, 6]	4[2]	8/16.00	no[16]
Kansas	14	14	16	([5])	14	4	8/14.00	no[16]
Kentucky	16	16	18	([5])	16[6]	4	8.00	no
Louisiana	15	15	16	16[6]	17[3]	4	18.00	yes
Maine	16[4]	15[4]	17	([5])	16[4]	4	20.00	yes[19]
Maryland	18[21]	16	18	15 9 mo.[4, 6]	16[4, 6]	5	20.00	no[18, 22]
Massachusetts	17	16	18	([5])	16.5[4, 6]	5	63.75	yes[19]
Michigan	18[21]	15	18		16[4, 6]	2 or 4	6/12.00	no[15]
Minnesota	18[25]	15	18	([5])	16[4]	4	15/34.00	no[16]
Mississippi	15	15	15	([5])		4	20.00	yes
Missouri	15.5[4]	16	16	15[9]	15.5[7]	3	7.50	yes[18]
Montana	15[4]	15[4]	18	([5])	15[4, 6]	4	16/24.00	no
Nebraska	16	16	16	15[9]	14	4	10.00	no
Nevada	16	15.5	18	15.5[5]		4	14/19.00	no[18]
New Hampshire	18[21]	16[4]	18		16[4]	4	30/32.00	yes[19]
New Jersey	17	15	17		16	4	16/17.50	yes
New Mexico	16	13	16	15[4]	14[20]	4	10.00	no
New York	17	16	17[4]	16	16[6]	4	22.25	yes
North Carolina	18	16	18	15[4, 6, 20]	16	4	10.00	yes
North Dakota	16	14	16	([5])	14[4, 6]	4	10.00	no[16]
Ohio	18	14	18	16[5, 6]	14[11]	4	6.50	no[18]
Oklahoma	16		16	([8])	15.5[4]	4	18.00	yes
Oregon	16[21]	16	16	15[5]	14	4	26.25	no[16]
Pennsylvania	16	16	16	16[6, 7]	16[6]	4	22.00	yes
Rhode Island	16	16	16	([5])	16[4]	5	30.00	yes
South Carolina	16	14	16	15[9]	15	4	10.00	yes
South Dakota	16	14	16		14[9]	4	6.00	no
Tennessee	16	14	18	15[7]	15	4	16.00	no
Texas	18[21]	15	16[4]	15	15[4, 7]	4	16.00	yes
Utah	16	16	16[4, 6]	16	15 9 mo.[9, 12]	5	15/20.00	yes[18]
Vermont	18	16	18	15[5, 20]	16[7]	2 or 4	12/20.00	yes
Virginia	18[21]	16	18	15 8 mo.[5, 6, 7]	16[4, 6]	5	12.00	yes
Washington	18[21]	16	18	15[7]	16[4]	4	14.00	no[23]
West Virginia	18[21]	16	18	15[5]	15[6]	4	10.50	yes
Wisconsin	18[21]	16	18[4]	15.5[5]	16[4, 6]	4	15.00	no[15]
Wyoming	18	15[24]	18	15[6, 7]	15[6, 7]	4	10.00	no

1. Full driving privileges at age given in "Regular" column. A license restricted or qualified in some manner may be obtained at age given in "Restricted" column. 2. 2 years if under 18 or over 70. 3. Hours of operation restricted. 4. Must have completed approved driver education course. 5. Learner's permit required. 6. Guardian's or parental consent required. 7. Driver with learner's permit must be accompanied by locally licensed operator 18 years or older. 8. Must be enrolled in driver education course. 9. Driver with learner's permit must be accompanied by locally licensed operator 21 years or older. 10. Up to 50 cc. 11. Restricted to mopeds. 12. For use while enrolled in driver education course. Must be accompanied by instructor. 13. 2 years if 15–24 or over 65. 14. 3 years if over 75. 15. Individual inspection upon reasonable grounds. 16. State troopers are authorized to inspect at their discretion. 17. Arizona emission inspection fee $5.40. 18. Annual emissions test in some counties. 19. Annual emissions test. 20. Must be accompanied by licensed operator 25 years or older or a school driver training instructor. 21. 18; 16, if approved driver training course completed. 22. All used vehicles upon resale or transfer. 23. Required on out-of-state or salvaged vehicles. Emissions tested in some counties. 24. May obtain instruction permit with motorcycle endorsement. 25. Required for drivers and passengers under 18. NOTES: A driver's license is required in every state. All states have an *implied consent* Chemical Test Law for alcohol. *Source:* American Automobile Association.

EDUCATION

School Enrollment, October 1992

(in thousands)

Age	White Enrolled	White Percent	Black Enrolled	Black Percent	Hispanic origin[1] Enrolled	Hispanic origin[1] Percent	All races Enrolled	All races Percent
3 and 4 years	2,473	40.1	446	38.6	286	28.8	3,063	39.7
5 and 6 years	5,774	95.4	1,143	95.9	896	96.0	7,252	95.5
7 to 9 years	8,869	99.4	1,673	99.4	1,347	99.5	11,106	99.4
10 to 13 years	11,682	99.3	2,253	99.7	1,599	99.1	14,662	99.4
14 and 15 years	5,462	99.2	1,089	99.4	774	98.8	6,861	99.1
16 and 17 years	4,982	94.2	994	93.0	630	87.2	6,272	94.1
18 and 19 years	3,212	61.7	566	56.2	418	53.7	4,012	61.4
20 and 21 years	2,530	45.3	335	33.3	230	30.1	3,027	44.0
22 to 24 years	2,069	23.3	305	20.3	176	14.5	2,577	23.7
25 to 29 years	1,553	9.6	203	7.9	143	6.7	1,907	9.8
30 to 34 years	1,104	6.0	144	5.3	100	4.7	1,344	6.1
Total	**49,710**	**50.7**	**9,151**	**53.0**	**6,598**	**49.2**	**62,084**	**51.4**

1. Persons of Hispanic origin may be of any race. NOTE: Figures include persons enrolled in nursery school, kindergarten, elementary school, high school, and college. *Source:* Department of Commerce, Bureau of the Census.

Persons Not Enrolled in School, October 1992

(in thousands)

Age	Population	Total not enrolled Number	Total not enrolled Percent	High school graduate Number	High school graduate Percent	Not high school graduate (dropouts)[1] Number	Not high school graduate (dropouts)[1] Percent
14 and 15 years	6,921	60	0.9	2	0	58	0.8
16 and 17 years	6,666	394	5.9	66	1.0	327	4.9
18 and 19 years	6,535	2,523	38.6	1,742	26.7	780	11.9
20 and 21 years	6,884	3,857	56.0	2,915	42.4	942	13.7
22 to 24 years	10,859	8,282	76.3	6,922	63.7	1,361	12.5

1. Persons who are not enrolled in school and who are not high school graduates are considered dropouts. *Source:* Department of Commerce, Bureau of the Census.

School Enrollment by Grade, Control, and Race

(in thousands)

Grade level and type of control	White Oct 1992[3]	White Oct. 1990[3]	White Oct. 1980[4]	Black Oct. 1992[3]	Black Oct. 1990[3]	Black Oct. 1980[4]	All races[1] Oct. 1992[3]	All races[1] Oct. 1990[3]	All races[1] Oct. 1980[4]
Nursery school: Public	785	896	432	250	283	180	1,098	1,212	633
Private	1,602	1,961	1,205	124	148	115	1,801	2,188	1,354
Kindergarten: Public	2,727	2,609	2,172	625	574	440	3,507	3,322	2,690
Private	529	472	423	63	62	50	623	567	486
Grades 1–8: Public	21,207	20,997	19,743	4,492	4,431	4,058	27,054	26,615	24,398
Private	2,718	2,359	2,768	230	199	202	3,099	2,676	3,051
Grades 9–12: Public	9,578	9,429	12,056[2]	2,039	1,937	2,200[2]	12,158	11,911	14,556[2]
Private	833	810	—	68	65	—	947	906	—
College: Public	9,199	9,049	8,875[2]	1,139	1,120	1,007[2]	11,065	10,754	10,180[2]
Private	2,511	2,439	—	285	274	—	2,970	2,869	—
Total: Public	43,496	42,954	—	8,545	8,344	—	54,882	53,823	—
Private	5,682	8,041	—	770	748	—	9,440	9,204	—
Grand Total	**49,178**	**50,995**	**47,673**	**9,315**	**9,092**	**8,251**	**64,322**	**63,027**	**57.348**

1. Includes persons of Spanish origin. 2. Total public and private. Breakdown not available. 3. Estimates controlled to 1980 census base. 4. Estimates controlled to 1970 census base. *Source:* Department of Commerce, Bureau of the Census.

State Compulsory School Attendance Laws

State	Enactment[1]	Age limits
Alabama	1915	7–16
Alaska[2]	1929	7–16
Arizona[3]	1899	8–16
Arkansas	1909	5–18
California	1874	6–16
Colorado	1889	7–16
Connecticut	1872	7–16
Delaware	1907	5–16
D. C.	1864	7–17
Florida[4]	1915	6–16
Georgia	1916	7–16
Hawaii	1896	6–18
Idaho	1887	7–16
Illinois	1883	7–16
Indiana[5]	1897	7–16
Iowa	1902	7–16
Kansas	1874	7–16
Kentucky[6]	1896	6–16
Louisiana	1910	7–17
Maine	1875	7–17
Maryland	1902	6–16
Massachusetts	1852	6–16
Michigan	1871	6–16
Minnesota[6]	1885	7–16
Mississippi	1918	6–14
Missouri	1905	7–16
Montana[7]	1883	7–16
Nebraska	1887	7–16
Nevada	1873	7–17
New Hampshire	1871	6–16
New Jersey	1875	6–16
New Mexico	1891	6–18
New York[8]	1874	6–16
North Carolina	1907	7–16
North Dakota	1883	7–16
Ohio	1877	6–18
Oklahoma	1907	7–18
Oregon	1889	7–18
Pennsylvania	1895	8–17
Rhode Island	1883	6–16
South Carolina[9]	1915	5–17
South Dakota[7]	1883	7–16
Tennessee	1905	7–17
Texas[10]	1915	7–17
Utah	1890	6–18
Vermont	1867	7–16
Virginia[11]	1908	5–17
Washington	1871	8–18
West Virginia	1897	6–16
Wisconsin[12]	1879	6–18
Wyoming	1876	7–16

1. Date of enactment of first compulsory attendance law. 2. Ages 7 to 16 or high school graduation. 3. Ages 8 to 16 or tenth grade completion. 4. Ages 6 to 16 or age 4 with parental approval. 5. Students between 16 and 18 are required to submit to an exit interview and have written parental approval before leaving high school. 6. Must have parental signature for leaving school between ages of 16 and 18. 7. May leave after completion of eighth grade. 8. The ages are 6 to 17 for New York City and Buffalo. 9. Permits parental waiver of kindergarten at age 5. 10. Information last updated in 1989. 11. Information last updated in 1990. 12. Ages 6 to 18 or high school graduation. *Source:* Department of Education, National Center for Educational Statistics, which prepared this table March 1992.

High School and College Graduates

School Year	High School			College[1]		
	Men	Women	Total	Men	Women	Total
1900	38,075	56,808	94,883	22,173	5,237	27,410
1910	63,676	92,753	156,429	28,762	8,437	37,199
1920	123,684	187,582	311,266	31,980	16,642	48,622
1929–30	300,376	366,528	666,904	73,615	48,869	122,484
1939–40	578,718	642,757	1,221,475	109,546	76,954	186,500
1949–50	570,700	629,000	1,199,700	328,841	103,217	432,058
1959–60	898,000	966,000	1,864,000	254,063	138,377	392,440
1969–70	1,433,000	1,463,000	2,896,000	484,174	343,060	827,234
1974–75	1,541,000	1,599,000	3,140,000	533,797	425,052	978,849
1975–76	1,554,000	1,601,000	3,155,000	557,817	430,578	988,395
1976–77	1,548,000	1,606,000	3,154,000	547,919	435,989	983,908
1977–78	1,535,000	1,599,000	3,134,000	487,000	434,000	921,000
1978–79	1,531,800	1,602,400	3,134,200	529,996	460,242	990,238
1979–80	1,500,000	1,558,000	3,058,000	526,327	473,221	999,548
1980–81	1,483,000	1,537,000	3,020,000	470,000	465,000	935,000
1981–82	1,474,000	1,527,000	3,001,000	473,000	480,000	953,000
1982–83	1,437,000	1,451,000	2,888,000	479,140	490,370	969,510
1983–84	n.a.	n.a.	2,767,000	482,319	491,990	974,309
1984–85	n.a.	n.a.	2,677,000	482,528	496,949	979,477
1985–86	n.a.	n.a.	2,643,000	485,923	501,900	987,823
1986–87	n.a.	n.a.	2,694,000	480,854	510,485	991,339
1987–88	n.a.	n.a.	2,773,000	477,203	517,626	994,829
1988–89	n.a.	n.a.	2,727,000	483,346[2]	535,409[2]	1,018,755[2]
1989–90	n.a.	n.a.	2,587,000	491,488[3]	558,169[3]	1,049,657[3]
1990–91	n.a.	n.a.	2,511,000	498,000[4]	586,000[4]	1,084,000[4]
1991–92	n.a.	n.a.	2,485,000	509,000[4]	596,000[4]	1,105,000[4]

1. Bachelors's degrees. Includes first-professional degrees for years 1900–1960. 2. Revised from previously published data. 3. Preliminary data. 4. Estimated. n.a. = not available. NOTE: Includes graduates from public and private schools. Beginning in 1959–60, figures include Alaska and Hawaii. Because of rounding, details may not add to totals. Most recent data available. *Source:* Department of Education, Center for Education Statistics.

Federal Funds for Some Major Programs for Education, Fiscal Year 1994[1]

Program	Amount in thousands
Elementary-secondary	
Educationally disadvantaged	$7,110,000
School improvement programs	1,573,000
Bilingual education	231,000
School assistance in federally affected areas	689,000
Higher education	
Student financial assistance	7,518,000
Higher education facliities loans	8,000
College housing loans	52,000
Vocational and adult education	$1,455,000
Education for the handicapped	
Special education	3,088,000
Rehabilitation services and disability research	2,251,000
All other	308,000
Indian education	84,000
Education research and improvement	467,000
Total	**$24,834,000**

1. Estimated outlay for fiscal year 1994. *Source: Budget of the United States Government,* Fiscal Year 1994.

Funding for Public Elementary and Secondary Education, 1983–84 to 1989–90

(In thousands except percent)

School year	Total	Federal	State	Local[1]	% Federal	& State	% Local[1]
1983–84	126,055,419	8,576,547	60,232,981	57,245,892	6.8	47.8	45.4
1984–85	137,294,678	9,105,569	67,168,684	61,020,425	6.6	48.9	44.4
1985–86	149,127,779	9,975,622	73,619,575	65,532,582	6.7	49.4	43.9
1986–87	158,523,693	10,146,013	78,830,437	69,547,243	6.4	49.7	43.9
1987–88	169,561,974	10,716,687	84,004,415	74,840,873	6.3	49.5	44.1
1988–89	191,210,310	11,872,419	91,158,363	88,179,529	6.2	47.4	46.1
1989–90	207,583,910	12,750,530	98,059,659	96,773,720	6.1	47.2	46.6

1. Includes a relatively small amount from nongovernmental sources (gifts and tuition and transportation fees from patrons). *Source:* U.S. Department of Education, National Center for Education Statistics.

Major U.S. College and University Libraries—1991–92

(Top 50 based on number of volumes in library)

Institution	Volumes	Microforms[1]
Harvard	12,394,894	6,335,484
Yale	9,173,981	4,020,003
U of Illinois–Urbana	8,096,040	3,897,360
U of California–Berkeley	7,854,630	4,666,786
U of Texas	6,680,406	4,779,137
U of Michigan	6,598,574	4,495,426
Columbia	6,262,162	4,460,914
U of California–Los Angeles	6,247,320	6,377,470
Stanford	6,127,388	4,119,839
Cornell	5,468,870	5,833,564
U of Chicago	5,448,621	1,939,074
U of Wisconsin	5,317,380	3,755,241
Indiana	5,264,138	2,971,921
U of Washington	5,163,302	5,730,164
Princeton	4,965,358	2,813,879
U of Minnesota	4,908,982	3,936,564
Ohio State	4,603,310	3,549,712
Duke	4,134,361	1,719,587
North Carolina	3,956,238	3,462,277
U of Arizona	3,915,913	4,326,629
U of Pennsylvania	3,844,414	2,626,937
U of Virginia	3,842,344	4,871,904
Northwestern	3,607,533	2,539,884
Rutgers	3,367,663	4,314,783
Pennsylvania State	3,318,118	3,333,266
Iowa	3,253,141	4,873,174
New York	3,224,145	3,074,824
U of Georgia	3,048,491	4,865,800
U of Kansas	3,043,964	2,510,217
U of Pittsburgh	3,041,139	2,811,102
U of Florida	2,974,962	4,876,516
Johns Hopkins	2,961,160	1,842,302
Michigan State	2,860,874	4,610,166
Arizona State	2,826,679	4,410,042
Rochester	2,774,892	3,661,525
U of Southern California	2,764,865	3,765,719
SUNY–Buffalo	2,724,222	4,093,112
Washington U–St. Louis	2,703,584	2,469,803
Wayne State	2,667,088	3,271,271
Louisiana State	2,654,485	3,923,432
U of Hawaii	2,651,257	5,242,164
U of California–Davis	2,588,728	3,082,956
U of Missouri	2,579,253	5,012,692
Brown	2,551,187	1,236,258
South Carolina	2,526,408	3,777,699
U of Massachusetts	2,511,558	1,911,953
U of Kentucky	2,459,497	4,861,232
U of Colorado	2,427,603	4,524,983
U of Oklahoma	2,381,304	3,216,398
U of Connecticut	2,372,350	3,228,043

1. Includes reels of microfilm and number of microcards, microprint sheets, and microfiches. *Source:* Association of Research Libraries.

College and University Endowments, 1991–92
(top 75 in millions of dollars)

Institution	Endowment (market value)	Voluntary support[1]	Expenditures[2]
Harvard U	$5,118.1	$206.2	$1,191.6
Yale U	2,838.2	144.0	725.2
Princeton U	2,770.3	86.9	346.2
Stanford U	2,424.1	185.3	536.4
Emory U	1,715.9	38.9	382.4
Columbia U	1,707.9	111.2	921.6
Texas A&M	1,671.4	59.9	319.3
Massachusetts Inst. of Tech.	1,600.0	95.2	681.9
Washington U (Mo.)	1,565.9	69.4	656.0
Northwestern U	1,530.0	102.6	602.0
Rice U	1,254.4	23.2	145.4
U of Chicago	1,151.3	73.6	574.0
Cornell U	1,078.3	177.8	892.4
U of Pennsylvania	974.4	156.6	751.2
Mayo Foundation	917.2	59.3	171.0
Dartmouth C	737.0	69.3	231.6
Vanderbilt U	668.7	59.1	418.0
New York U	663.1	107.4	831.4
U of Notre Dame	652.2	47.2	207.5
U of California–Berkeley	645.8	105.0	784.3
Johns Hopkins U	641.0	101.5	435.2
U of Minnesota	633.9	127.2	1,075.8
U of Rochester	627.7	38.6	350.6
U of Michigan	626.8	84.8	1,079.7
Duke U	590.8	127.2	512.9
U of Southern California	588.8	105.5	763.3
U of Texas–Austin	580.7	85.1	615.6
California Inst. of Tech.	580.5	80.8	227.0
U of Virginia	559.4	51.5	388.8
Rockefeller U	552.3	28.6	91.7
Case Western Reserve U	498.8	58.4	282.6
Macalester C	485.2	5.9	34.7
U of Cincinnati	470.1	30.3	422.0
Purdue U	456.6	72.1	608.5
Brown U	455.4	39.2	214.2
Wellesley C	426.6	32.7	71.6
Princeton Theol. Sem.	426.4	3.2	19.5
Ohio State U	416.1	71.5	911.3
Southern Methodist U	405.8	21.0	139.7
U of California–Los Angeles	399.1	90.4	1,091.5
Swarthmore C	390.5	14.0	51.3
Smith C	387.8	32.0	90.2
U of Delaware	387.0	19.5	262.3
Texas Christian U	384.4	11.4	77.8
Wiliams C	380.2	23.3	60.1
Loyola U of Chcago	376.7	51.0	199.7
Wake Forest U	361.6	29.6	282.6
Carnegie–Mellon U	361.1	39.1	306.3
Boston C	355.7	17.1	189.4
Grinnell C	344.2	11.6	33.4
Pomona C	339.4	10.9	44.1
Indiana U	339.3	110.0	871.3
U of Richmond	328.8	14.8	60.0
Trinity U	317.4	14.8	44.0
Berea C	312.2	13.9	22.6
George Washington U (DC)	297.5	18.2	287.0
Georgetown U	296.9	36.7	354.0
Lehigh U	294.4	26.5	123.1
Boston U	293.4	33.1	591.1
Vassar C	292.1	22.7	63.1
Amherst C	291.2	13.5	49.5
Baylor U	289.8	26.1	113.1
Wesleyan U	289.6	7.0	86.8
U of Wisconsin–Madison	286.0	141.2	956.2
U of Kansas	271.0	31.6	249.5
Georgia Inst. of Tech.	264.3	38.1	298.0
U of Tennessee	259.1	34.9	614.4
Rensselaer Poly. Tech.	254.8	25.0	156.9
Middlebury C	254.8	7.6	70.6
Oberlin C	254.0	11.9	64.4
Lafayette C	252.8	9.0	46.2
Pennsylvania State U	250.6	63.0	904.5
U of North Carolina–Chapel Hill	250.0	59.2	552.7
Tulane U of Louisiana	247.3	27.3	258.7
U of Washington	235.4	103.8	854.7

1. Gifts from business, alumni, religious denominations, and others. 2. Figure represents about 80% of typical operating budget. Does not include auxiliary enterprises and capital outlays. NOTE: C = College; U = University. *Source:* Council for Aid to Education.

Institutions of Higher Education—Average Salaries and Fringe Benefits for Faculty Members, 1970–1991[1]
(in thousands of dollars)

Control and Acadmic Rank	1991	1990	1989	1988	1987	1986	1985	1984	1980	1975	1970
Average Salaries											
Public: All ranks	44.0	41.6	39.6	37.2	35.8	33.4	31.2	29.4	22.1	16.6	13.1
Professor	55.8	53.2	50.1	47.2	45.3	42.3	39.6	37.1	28.8	21.7	17.3
Associate professor	42.2	40.3	37.9	35.6	34.2	32.2	30.2	28.4	21.9	16.7	13.2
Assistant professor	35.2	33.5	31.7	29.6	28.5	26.7	25.0	23.5	18.0	13.7	10.9
Instructor	26.3	25.0	23.9	22.2	21.8	20.9	19.5	19.1	14.8	11.2	9.1
Private:[2] All ranks	47.0	45.1	42.4	39.7	37.8	35.4	33.0	31.1	22.1	16.6	13.1
Professor	61.6	59.6	55.9	52.2	50.3	47.0	44.1	41.5	30.1	22.4	17.8
Associate professor	43.2	41.2	38.8	36.6	34.9	32.9	30.9	29.4	21.0	16.0	12.6
Assistant professor	35.5	34.0	31.9	28.3	26.8	25.0	23.7	22.1	13.0	10.3	
Instructor	26.2	26.0	24.1	22.7	20.4	19.8	19.0	18.4	13.3	10.9	8.6
Average Fringe Benefits—All Ranks Combined											
Public	10.5	9.8	9.0	8.2	7.8	7.3	7.0	6.0	3.9	2.5	1.9
Private[2]	11.6	10.9	10.0	9.2	8.6	8.0	7.2	6.4	4.1	2.8	2.2

1. Figures are for 9 months teaching for full-time faculty members in four-year colleges and universities. 2. Excludes church-related colleges and universities. *Source:* Maryse Eymonerie Associates/American Association of University Professors. Washington, D.C. *AAUP Annual Report on the Economic Status of the Profession.* From *Statistical Abstract of the United States: 1992.* NOTE: Data are latest available.

Accredited U.S. Senior Colleges and Universities

Source: The Guidance Information System (trademark), a product of The Riverside Publishing Company, a Houghton Mifflin company.

Schools listed are four-year institutions that offer at least a Bachelor's degree and are fully accredited by one of the institutional and professional accrediting associations. Included are accredited colleges outside the U.S.

Tuition, room, and board listed are average annual figures (including fees) subject to fluctuation, usually covering two semesters, two out of three trimesters, or three out of four quarters, depending on the school calendar.

For further information, write to the Registrar of the school concerned.

NOTE: n.a. = information not available. — = does not apply. Enrollment figures are approximate. (C) = Coeducational, (M) = primarily for men, (W) = primarily for women.

Abbreviations used for controls: P Private Pub Public

Institution and location	Enrollment	Control	Tuition ($) Res.	Tuition ($) Nonres.	Rm/Bd ($)
Abilene Christian University; Abilene, Tex. 79699	3,375 (C)	P	6,944	6,944	3,200
Academy of Art College; San Francisco, Calif. 94108–3893	2,156 (C)	P	6,000	6,000	6,000
Academy of the New Church College; Bryn Athyn, Pa. 19009	97 (C)	P	3,990	3,990	3,351
Adams State College; Alamosa, Colo. 81102	2,125 (C)	Pub	1,544	4,132	2,754
Adelphi University; Garden City, N.Y. 11530	4,153 (C)	P	11,370	11,370	5,640
Adrian College; Adrian, Mich. 49221	1,144 (C)	P	10,800	10,800	3,540
Aeronautics, College of; Flushing, N.Y. 11371	1,100 (C)	P	7,000	7,000	n.a.
Aero-Space Institute; Chicago, Ill. 60605-1116	102 (C)	P	7,000	7,000	n.a.
Agnes Scott College; Decatur, Ga. 30030	591 (W)	P	11,625	11,625	4,825
Akron, University of; Akron, Ohio 44325-2001	22,755 (C)	Pub	2,841	7,498	3,486
Alabama, University of; Tuscaloosa, Ala. 35487-0132	15,943 (C)	Pub	2,008	5,016	3,288
Alabama, University of–Birmingham; Birmingham, Ala. 35294	10,616 (C)	Pub	2,314	4,552	3,679
Alabama, University of-Huntsville; Huntsville, Ala. 35899	6,113 (C)	Pub	2,244	4,488	4,260
Alabama A&M University; Normal, Ala. 35762	3,956 (C)	Pub	1,550	3,100	2,350
Alabama State University; Montgomery, Ala. 36101-0271	4,181 (C)	Pub	1,500	3,000	2,110
Alaska, University of-Anchorage; Anchorage, Alas. 99508	19,624 (C)	Pub	1,428	4,014	3,830
Alaska, University of-Fairbanks; Fairbanks, Alas. 99701	7,393 (C)	Pub	1,870	4,510	3,100
Alaska Southeast, University of; Juneau, Alas. 99801	2,544 (C)	Pub	1,525	4,421	3,450
Alaska Bible College; Glennallen, Alas. 99588	61 (C)	P	2,918	2,918	3,250
Alaska Pacific University; Anchorage, Alas. 99508	442 (C)	P	7,200	7,200	4,020
Albany College of Pharmacy; Albany, N.Y. 12208	644 (C)	P	8,600	8,600	4,500
Albany State College; Albany, Ga. 31705	2,355 (C)	Pub	1,731	4,413	2,574
Albertson College; Caldwell, Idaho 83605	734 (C)	P	12,942	12,942	3,000
Albertus Magnus College; New Haven, Conn. 06511	646 (C)	P	11,007	11,007	5,080
Albion College; Albion, Mich. 49224	1,652 (C)	P	13,676	13,676	4,588
Albright College; Reading, Pa. 19612-5234	1,102 (C)	P	14,850	14,850	4,250
Alcorn State University; Lorman, Miss. 39096	3,244 (C)	Pub	2,367	4,334	2,000
Alderson-Broaddus College; Philippi, W. Va. 26416	746 (C)	P	9,452	9,452	3,000
Alfred University; Alfred, N.Y. 14802	1,936 (C)	P	14,998	14,998	4,735
Alice Lloyd College; Pippa Passes, Ky. 41844	548 (C)	P	4,230	7,590	2,480
Allegheny College; Meadville, Pa. 16335	1,783 (C)	P	16,700	16,700	4,320
Allen University; Columbia, S.C. 29204	n.a.	n.a.	n.a.	n.a.	n.a.
Allentown College of St. Francis de Sales; Center Valley, Pa. 18034-9568	854 (C)	P	9,270	9,270	4,620
Alma College; Alma, Mich. 48801-1599	1,295 (C)	P	12,046	12,046	4,334
Alvernia College; Reading, Pa. 19607–1799	1,354 (C)	P	8,374	8,374	4,000
Alverno College; Milwaukee, Wis. 53234-3922	2,514 (W)	P	7,332	7,332	3,250
Ambassador College; Big Sandy, Tex. 75755	1,176 (C)	P	2,700	2,700	2,750
Amber University; Garland, Tex. 75041	722 (C)	P	4,500	4,500	n.a.
American Baptist College; Nashville, Tenn. 37207	163 (C)	P	2,000	2,000	1,984
American College for the Applied Arts, The; Atlanta, Ga. 30326–1016	635 (C)	P	8,340	8,340	5,450
American College for the Applied Arts, The; Los Angeles, Calif. 90024	472 (C)	P	9,090	9,090	3,825
American College of Switzerland; Switzerland	120 (C)	P	20,367	20,367	5,282
American Conservatory of Music; Chicago, Ill. 60602–4792	124 (C)	P	9,360	9,360	n.a.
American International College; Springfield, Mass. 01109	1,076 (C)	P	8,992	8,992	4,336
American University; Washington, D.C. 20016	5,373 (C)	P	14,383	14,383	6,014
American University in Cairo; New York, N.Y. 10017	3,084 (C)	P	7,560	7,560	3,580
American University of Beirut; Beirut, Lebanon	4,371 (C)	P	4,000	4,000	1,750
American University of Paris; 75007 Paris, France	1,024 (C)	P	13,526	13,526	n.a.
American Universtity of Puerto Rico; Bayamon, P.R. 00621	4,208 (C)	P	2,300	2,300	n.a.
Amherst College; Amherst, Mass. 01002	1,575 (C)	P	17,900	17,900	4,800
Anderson College; Anderson, SC 29621	1,172 (C)	P	8,320	8,320	3,900
Anderson University; Anderson, Ind. 46012	2,050 (C)	P	8,780	8,780	3,120
Andrews University; Berrien Springs, Mich. 49104	2,009 (C)	P	9,645	9,645	3,810
Angelo State University; San Angelo, Tex. 76909	6,003 (C)	Pub	1,495	5,610	3,490
Anna Maria College for Men and Women; Paxton, Mass. 01612	662 (C)	P	9,980	9,980	4,650
Antillian Adventist University; Mayaguez, P.R. 00709	854 (C)	P	2,620	2,620	2,300

Institution and location	Enrollment	Control	Tuition ($)		Rm/Bd ($)
			Res.	Nonres.	
Antioch College; Yellow Springs, Ohio 45387	675 (C)	P	14,038	14,038	4,272
Antioch School for Adult & Experiential Learning; Yellow Springs, Ohio 45387	231 (C)	P	6,480	6,480	n.a.
Antioch Seattle; Seattle, Wash. 98121	115 (C)	P	7,575	7,575	n.a.
Antioch–Southern California at Los Angeles; Marina Del Rey, Calif. 90292	202 (C)	P	8,100	8,100	n.a.
Antioch–Southern California at Santa Barbara; Santa Barbara, Calif. 93101	77 (C)	P	7,200	7,200	n.a.
Appalachian Bible College; Bradley, W. Va. 25818	186 (C)	P	3,840	3,840	2,600
Appalachian State University; Boone, N.C. 28608	10,726 (C)	Pub	1,445	7,117	2,370
Aquinas College; Grand Rapids, Mich. 49506–1799	1,978 (C)	P	9,722	9,722	4,070
Arizona, University of; Tucson, Ariz. 85721	26,352 (C)	Pub	1,590	6,986	3,968
Arizona College of the Bible; Phoenix, Ariz. 85021	90 (C)	P	4,575	4,575	3,020
Arizona State University; Tempe, Ariz. 85287-0112	31,906 (C)	Pub	1,594	7,000	4,000
Arkansas, Univ. of; Fayetteville, Ark. 72701	11,310 (C)	Pub	1,838	4,718	3,225
Arkansas, Univ. of-Little Rock; Little Rock, Ark. 72204	10,596 (C)	Pub	2,106	5,106	n.a.
Arkansas, Univ. of–Medical Sciences; Little Rock, Ark. 72205–7199	n.a.	n.a.	n.a.	n.a.	n.a.
Arkansas, Univ. of-Monticello; Monticello, Ark. 71655	1,854 (C)	Pub	1,500	3,240	2,130
Arkansas, Univ. of-Pine Bluff; Pine Bluff, Ark. 71601–2799	3,709 (C)	Pub	1,542	3,366	2,180
Arkansas Baptist College; Little Rock, Ark. 72202	233 (C)	P	3,736	3,736	2,420
Arkansas College; Batesville, Ark. 72501	701 (C)	P	8,060	8,060	3,536
Arkansas State University; State University, Ark. 72467	9,716 (C)	Pub	1,640	3,090	2,330
Arkansas Tech. University; Russellville, Ark. 72801–2222	4,159 (C)	Pub	1,560	3,060	2,410
Arlington Baptist College; Arlington, Tex. 76012	179 (C)	P	4,420	4,420	2,920
Armstrong State College; Savannah, Ga. 31419	4,170 (C)	Pub	1,521	4,203	3,144
Armstrong University; Berkeley, Calif. 94704	60 (C)	P	5,940	5,940	n.a.
Art Academy of Cincinnati; Cincinnati, Ohio 45202	238 (C)	P	7,900	7,900	n.a.
Art Center College of Design; Pasadena, Calif. 91103	1,268 (C)	P	12,565	12,565	n.a.
Art Institute of Chicago, School of the; Chicago, Ill. 60603	1,324 (C)	P	12,450	12,450	n.a.
Art Institute of Southern California; Laguna Beach, Calif. 92651	130 (C)	P	8,100	8,100	n.a.
Arts, The University of the; Philadelphia, Pa. 19102	1,306 (C)	P	11,700	11,700	3,700
Asbury College; Wilmore, Ky. 40390	1,053 (C)	P	7,740	7,740	2,676
Ashland University; Ashland, Ohio 44805	2,692 (C)	P	10,563	10,563	4,367
Associated Arts, College of; St. Paul., Minn. 55102–2199	175 (C)	P	7,600	7,600	n.a.
Assumption College; Worcester, Mass. 01615-0005	1,734 (C)	P	10,470	10,470	5,240
Athens State College; Athens, Ala. 35611	2,770 (C)	Pub	1,700	3,400	2,800
Atlanta Christian College; East Point, Ga. 30344	169 (C)	P	3,680	3,680	2,730
Atlanta College of Art; Atlanta, Ga. 30309	420 (C)	P	8,246	8,246	2,856
Atlantic, College of the; Bar Harbor, Maine 04609	246 (C)	P	12,425	12,425	3,390
Atlantic Union College; South Lancaster, Mass. 01561	938 (C)	P	10,300	10,300	3,370
Auburn University; Auburn University, Ala. 36849	18,680 (C)	Pub	1,950	5,850	3,320
Auburn University-Montgomery; Montgomery, Ala. 36117–3596	5,503 (C)	Pub	1,800	5,400	3,190
Audrey Cohen College; New York, N.Y. 10014	1,052 (C)	P	7,040	7,040	n.a.
Augsburg College; Minneapolis, Minn. 55454	1,487 (C)	P	10,853	10,853	4,022
Augusta College; Augusta, Ga. 30910	4,992 (C)	Pub	1,542	4,224	n.a.
Augustana College; Rock Island, Ill. 61201	2,080 (C)	P	12,852	12,852	4,017
Augustana College; Sioux Falls, S.D. 57197	1,890 (C)	P	10,300	10,300	3,120
Aurora University; Aurora, Ill. 60506	1,600 (C)	P	9,180	9,180	3,558
Austin College; Sherman, Tex. 75090	1,147 (C)	P	10,865	10,865	4,134
Austin Peay State University; Clarksville, Tenn. 37040	4,784 (C)	Pub	1,726	5,328	2,760
Averett College; Danville, Va. 24541-3692	1,205 (C)	P	9,090	9,090	3,900
Avila College; Kansas City, Mo. 64145	1,205 (C)	P	8,450	8,450	3,600
Azusa Pacific University; Azusa, Calif. 91702-7000	1,975 (C)	P	9,400	9,400	3,600
Babson College; Wellesley, Mass. 02157	1,679 (C)	P	15,810	15,810	6,715
Baker College of Flint; Flint, Mich. 48507	4,179 (C)	P	5,376	5,376	3,175
Baker University; Baldwin City, Kan. 66006	860 (C)	P	7,631	7,631	3,800
Baldwin-Wallace College; Berea, Ohio 44017	4,087 (C)	P	10,980	10,980	4,230
Ball State University; Muncie, Ind. 47306	18,099 (C)	Pub	2,464	5,872	3,168
Baltimore, University of; Baltimore, Md. 21201	3,101 (C)	Pub	2,746	4,878	n.a.
Baltimore Hebrew University; Baltimore, Md. 21215	612 (C)	P	2,230	2,230	n.a.
Baptist Bible College; Springfield, Mo. 65803	793 (C)	P	2,244	2,244	2,600
Baptist Bible College of Pennsylvania; Clarks Summit, Pa. 18411	494 (C)	P	6,118	6,118	3,484
Barat College; Lake Forest, Ill. 60045	719 (C)	P	9,280	9,280	3,800
Barber-Scotia College; Concord, N.C. 28025	704 (C)	P	4,200	4,200	2,612
Barclay College; Haviland, Kan. 67059	101 (C)	P	3,000	3,000	2,650
Bard College; Annandale-on-Hudson, N.Y. 12504	1,023 (C)	P	17,700	17,700	5,830
Barnard College of Columbia University; New York, N.Y. 10027	2,190 (W)	P	17,756	17,756	7,736
Barry University; Miami Shores, Fla. 33161	4,466 (C)	P	9,990	9,990	5,200
Bartlesville Wesleyan College; Bartlesville, Okla. 74006	502 (C)	P	6,200	6,200	3,050
Barton College; Wilson, N.C. 27893	1,702 (C)	P	7,063	7,063	3,326
Bassist College; Portland, Ore. 97201	164 (C)	P	8,920	8,920	5,800
Bates College; Lewiston, Maine 04240	1,515 (C)	P	22,850	22,850	—
Bayamon Central University; Bayamon, P.R. 00621	n.a.	n.a.	n.a.	n.a.	n.a.
Bay Path College; Longmeadow, Me. 01106	613 (W)	P	10,200	10,200	6,100
Baylor University; Waco, Tex. 76798-7008	10,421 (C)	P	7,020	7,020	3,920
Beaver College; Glenside, Pa. 19038	1,168 (C)	P	11,450	11,450	4,900

Institution and location	Enrollment	Control	Tuition ($)		Rm/Bd ($)
			Res.	Nonres.	
Becker College; Worcester, Mass. 01609	n.a.	n.a.	n.a.	n.a.	n.a.
Behrend College. *See* Pennsylvania State–Erie					
Beirut University College; Beirut, Lebanon	2,026 (C)	P	4,500	4,500	1,500
Belhaven College; Jackson, Miss. 39202	1,056 (C)	P	6,470	6,470	2,420
Bellarmine College; Louisville, Ky. 40205–0671	1,729 (C)	P	8,072	8,072	2,660
Bellevue College; Bellevue, Neb. 68005	1,956 (C)	P	2,916	2,916	n.a.
Bellin College of Nursing; Green Bay, Wis. 54305-3400	199 (C)	P	6,340	10,525	n.a.
Belmont Abbey College; Belmont, N.C. 28012	1,016 (C)	P	8,444	8,444	4,170
Belmont University; Nashville, Tenn. 37212	2,603 (C)	P	7,300	7,300	3,490
Beloit College; Beloit, Wis. 53511	1,172 (C)	P	14,250	14,250	3,420
Bemidji State University; Bemidji, Minn. 56601	4,836 (C)	Pub	2,440	4,158	2,628
Benedict College; Columbia, S.C. 29204	1,448 (C)	P	5,484	5,484	2,892
Benedictine College; Atchison, Kan. 66002	1,203 (C)	P	9,080	9,080	3,950
Bennett College; Greensboro, N.C. 27401	568 (W)	P	5,725	5,725	2,775
Bennington College; Bennington, Vt. 05201	519 (C)	P	19,780	19,780	4,100
Bentley College; Waltham, Mass. 02254	3,389 (C)	P	12,830	12,830	5,200
Berea College; Berea, Ky. 40404	1,589 (C)	P	177	177	2,457
Berklee College of Music; Boston, Mass. 02215	2,362 (C)	P	10,600	10,600	6,560
Bernard M. Baruch Coll. *See* New York, City Univ. of					
Berry College; Mount Berry, Ga. 30149	1,714 (C)	P	7,500	7,500	3,740
Bethany Bible College; Scotts Valley, Calif. 95066–2898	533 (C)	P	6,210	6,210	3,000
Bethany College; Bethany, W. Va. 26032	751 (C)	P	13,655	13,655	4,717
Bethany College; Lindsborg, Kan. 67456	702 (C)	P	8,000	8,000	3,225
Bethel College; McKenzie, Tenn. 38201	496 (C)	P	5,250	5,,250	2,650
Bethel College; Mishawaka, Ind. 46545	959 (C)	P	8,500	8,500	2,950
Bethel College; North Newton, Kan. 67117	625 (C)	P	7,980	7,980	3,350
Bethel College; St. Paul, Minn. 55112	1,832 (C)	P	10,540	10,540	3,790
Beth–El College of Nursing; Colorado Springs, Colo. 80909	285 (C)	Pub	4,350	4,350	n.a.
Bethune-Cookman College; Daytona Beach, Fla. 32015	2,301 (C)	P	4,965	4,965	3,243
Biola University; La Mirada, Calif. 90639	2,065 (C)	P	10,756	10,756	5,000
Birmingham-Southern College; Birmingham, Ala. 35254	1,669 (C)	P	10,306	10,306	3,970
Blackburn College; Carlinville, Ill. 62626	508 (C)	P	7,750	7,750	1,000
Black Hills State University; Spearfish, S.D. 57783	2,765 (C)	Pub	2,127	3,687	2,290
Bloomfield College; Bloomfield, N.J. 07003	2,036 (C)	P	8,050	8,050	4,100
Bloomsburg University of Pennsylvania; Bloomsburg, Pa. 17815	6,978 (C)	Pub	2,798	5,062	2,754
Bluefield College; Bluefield, Va. 24605	642 (C)	P	5,940	5,940	3,860
Bluefield State College; Bluefield, W. Va. 24701	2,907 (C)	Pub	1,700	3,800	n.a.
Blue Mountain College; Blue Mountain, Miss. 38610	398 (W)	P	3,788	3,788	2,090
Bluffton College; Bluffton, Ohio 45817	697 (C)	P	8,685	8,685	3,513
Bob Jones University; Greenville, S.C. 29614	3,629 (C)	P	4,405	4,405	3,540
Boise State University; Boise, Idaho 83725	10,725 (C)	Pub	1,518	4,168	3,069
Boricua College; New York, N.Y. 10032	1,146 (C)	P	5,229	5,229	n.a.
Boston Architecture Center School of Architecture; Boston, Mass. 02115	656 (C)	P	3,166	3,166	n.a.
Boston College; Chestnut Hill, Mass. 02167	8,667 (C)	P	16,006	16,006	6,700
Boston Conservatory; Boston, Mass. 02215	385 (C)	P	12,300	12,300	5,700
Boston University; Boston, Mass. 02215	14,403 (C)	P	16,837	16,837	6,320
Bowdoin College; Brunswick, Me. 04011	1,410 (C)	P	17,355	17,355	5,855
Bowie State University; Bowie, Md. 20715	2,965 (C)	Pub	2,495	4,709	3,504
Bowling Green State University; Bowling Green, Ohio 43403	15,608 (C)	Pub	3,334	7,308	2,900
Bradford College; Bradford, Mass. 01835	500 (C)	P	13,220	13,220	6,120
Bradley University; Peoria, Ill. 61625	5,258 (C)	P	9,728	9,728	4,160
Brandeis University; Waltham, Mass. 02254	2,915 (C)	P	17,000	17,000	6,500
Brescia College; Owensboro, Ky. 42301	840 (C)	P	6,260	6,260	2,790
Brewton-Parker College; Mount Vernon, Ga. 30445	1,972 (C)	P	3,895	3,895	2,370
Briar Cliff College; Sioux City, Iowa 51104-2100	938 (C)	P	9,780	9,780	3,544
Bridgeport, University of; Bridgeport, Conn. 06601	731 (C)	P	12,020	12,020	6,350
Bridgeport Engineering Institute; Fairfield, Conn. 06430	830 (C)	P	5,450	5,450	n.a.
Bridgewater College; Bridgewater, Va. 22812	1,007 (C)	P	10,135	10,135	4,355
Bridgewater State College; Bridgewater, Mass. 02325	5,559 (C)	Pub	2,976	6,840	3,860
Brigham Young University; Provo, Utah 84602	28,282 (C)	P	3,180	3,180	3,200
Brigham Young University-Hawaii; Laie, Oahu, Hawaii 96762	2,119 (C)	P	2,400	2,400	2,780
Brooklyn College. *See* New York, City University of					
Bristol University; Bristol, Tenn. 37625	700 (C)	P	6,000	6,000	n.a.
Brooks Institute of Photography; Santa Barbara, Calif. 93108	616 (C)	P	11,800	11,800	n.a.
Brown University; Providence, R.I. 02912	5,804 (C)	P	18,105	18,105	5,488
Bryan College; Dayton, Tenn. 37321	421 (C)	P	7,690	7,690	3,950
Bryant College; Smithfield, R.I. 02917	2,744 (C)	P	12,120	12,120	6,215
Bryn Mawr College; Bryn Mawr, Pa. 19010	1,177 (W)	P	16,165	16,165	6,150
Bucknell University; Lewisburg, Pa. 17837	3,380 (C)	P	16,670	16,670	4,110
Buena Vista College; Storm Lake, Iowa 50588	971 (C)	P	11,663	11,663	3,327
Burlington College; Burlington, Vt. 05401	184 (C)	P	7,280	7,280	n.a.

Institution and location	Enrollment	Control	Tuition ($) Res.	Tuition ($) Nonres.	Rm/Bd ($)
Butler University; Indianapolis, Ind. 46208	2,525 (C)	P	11,340	11,340	3,930
Cabrini College; Radnor, Pa. 19087–3699	775 (C)	P	9,500	9,500	5,790
Caldwell College; Caldwell, N.J. 07006	1,338 (C)	P	8,400	8,400	4,400
California, University of; Berkeley, Calif. 94720:					
UC-Berkeley; Berkeley, Calif. 94720	22,262 (C)	Pub	3,250	11,176	5,730
UC-Davis; Davis, Calif. 95616	17,877 (C)	Pub	2,980	10,679	5,015
UC-Irvine; Irvine, Calif. 92717	13,811 (C)	Pub	3,074	10,773	5,383
UC-Los Angeles; Los Angeles, Calif. 90024	23,649 (C)	Pub	2,904	10,603	5,410
UC-Riverside; Riverside, Calif. 92521	7,217 (C)	Pub	2,943	10,644	5,430
UC-San Diego; La Jolla, Calif. 92093	14,654 (C)	Pub	3,015	10,716	7,000
UC–San Francisco; San Francisco, Calif. 94143–0244	n.a.	n.a.	n.a.	n.a.	n.a.
UC-Santa Barbara; Santa Barbara, Calif. 93106	15,975 (C)	Pub	3,000	10,500	5,800
UC-Santa Cruz; Santa Cruz, Calif. 95064	9,161 (C)	Pub	3,129	10,828	6,036
California Baptist College; Riverside, Calif. 92504	678 (C)	P	7,170	7,170	3,894
California College of Arts and Crafts; Oakland, Calif. 94618	1,095 (C)	P	12,330	12,330	3,900
California Institute of Technology; Pasadena, Calif. 91125	862 (C)	P	15,160	15,160	4,676
California Institute of the Arts; Valencia, Calif. 91355	668 (C)	P	12,875	12,875	4,500
California Lutheran University; Thousand Oaks, Calif. 91360	1,834 (C)	P	10,950	10,950	5,000
California Maritime Academy; Vallejo, Calif. 94590	454 (C)	Pub	2,299	6,889	4,770
California Polytechnic State University; San Luis Obispo, Calif. 93407	16,318 (C)	Pub	1,242	7,146	4,575
California State Polytechnic University-Pomona; Pomona, Calif. 91768	16,525 (C)	Pub	1,492	8,872	4,589
California State University-Bakersfield; Bakersfield, Calif. 93311-1099	3,852 (C)	Pub	1,455	8,835	3,685
California State University-Chico; Chico, Calif. 95929	13,727 (C)	Pub	1,574	7,478	4,274
California St. Univ.-Dominguez Hills; Carson, Calif. 90747	6,158 (C)	Pub	1,459	8,839	4,022
California State Univ.-Fresno; Fresno, Calif. 93740	15,279 (C)	Pub	1,446	7,390	4,141
California State Univ.-Fullerton; Fullerton, Calif. 92634	21,274 (C)	Pub	1,480	8,860	5,076
California State Univ.-Hayward; Hayward, Calif. 94542	9,888 (C)	Pub	1,425	8,805	4,445
California State Univ.-Long Beach; Long Beach, Calif. 90840	25,480 (C)	Pub	1,433	8,813	4,800
California State Univ.-Los Angeles; Los Angeles, Calif. 90032	16,094 (C)	Pub	1,431	8,811	4,671
California State Univ.-Northridge; Northridge, Calif. 91330	24,125 (C)	Pub	1,128	5,904	5,500
California State Univ.-Sacramento; Sacramento, Calif. 95819	19,406 (C)	Pub	1,460	8,840	4,658
California State Univ.-San Bernardino; San Bernardino, Calif. 92407-2397	9,192 (C)	Pub	1,128	8,508	4,564
California State Univ.–San Marcos; San Marcos, Calif. 92096	1,998 (C)	Pub	1,496	8,876	n.a.
California State Univ.-Stanislaus; Turlock, Calif. 95380	5,791 (C)	Pub	1,434	6,238	4,250
California Univ. of Pennsylvania; California, Pa. 15419-1394	5,865 (C)	Pub	3,488	6,782	3,460
Calumet College of St. Joseph; Whiting, Ind. 46394	1,086 (C)	P	4,200	4,200	n.a.
Calvary Bible College; Kansas City, Mo. 64147	297 (C)	P	3,560	3,560	2,630
Calvin College; Grand Rapids, Mich. 49506	3,537 (C)	P	9,450	9,450	3,570
Cameron University; Lawton, Okla. 73505	5,988 (C)	Pub	1,500	3,025	2,344
Campbellsville College; Campbellsville, Ky. 42718	1,010 (C)	P	5,400	5,400	2,880
Campbell University; Buies Creek, N.C. 27506	4,803 (C)	P	7,550	7,550	2,690
Canisius College; Buffalo, N.Y. 14208	3,533 (C)	P	9,950	9,950	5,240
Capital University; Columbus, Ohio 43209	1,403 (C)	P	12,500	12,500	3,910
Capitol College; Laurel, Md. 20708	610 (C)	P	7,344	7,344	4,200
Cardinal Stritch College; Milwaukee, Wis. 53217	2,667 (C)	P	7,360	7,360	3,360
Caribbean University; Bayamon, P.R. 00619	n.a.	n.a.	n.a.	n.a.	n.a.
Carleton College; Northfield, Minn. 55057	1,707 (C)	P	20,900	20,900	n.a.
Carlow College; Pittsburgh, Pa. 15213	1,669 (W)	P	9,190	9,190	4,000
Carnegie Mellon University; Pittsburgh, Pa. 15213	4,327 (C)	P	17,060	17,060	5,540
Carroll College; Helena, Mont. 59625	1,382 (C)	P	7,825	7,825	3,650
Carroll College; Waukesha, Wis. 53186	1,336 (C)	P	11,680	11,680	3,700
Carson-Newman College; Jefferson City, Tenn. 37760	2,022 (C)	P	7,400	7,400	3,050
Carthage College; Kenosha, Wis. 53140–1994	1,329 (C)	P	12,400	12,400	3,595
Case Western Reserve University; Cleveland, Ohio 44106	3,486 (C)	P	15,200	15,200	4,590
Castleton State College; Castleton, Vt. 05735	1,658 (C)	Pub	3,776	7,688	4,462
Catawba College; Salisbury, N.C. 28144	936 (C)	P	8,130	8,130	3,850
Catholic University of America; Washington, D.C. 20064	2,975 (C)	P	12,881	12,881	5,970
Cayey University College. *See* Puerto Rico, University of					
Cazenovia College; Cazenovia, N.Y. 13035	1,042 (C)	P	8,980	8,980	4,608
Cedar Crest College; Allentown, Pa. 18104-6196	1,342 (W)	P	12,940	12,940	5,110
Cedarville College; Cedarville, Ohio 45314	2,172 (C)	P	6,402	6,402	3,579
Centenary College; Hackettstown, N.J. 07840	399 (C)	P	10,815	10,815	5,130
Centenary College of Louisiana; Shreveport, La. 71104	847 (C)	P	7,770	7,770	3,250
Center for Creative Studies, College of Art and Design; Detroit, Mich. 48202	862 (C)	P	10,440	10,440	4,150
Central Arkansas, University of; Conway, Ark. 72032	8,100 (C)	Pub	1,546	2,966	2,460
Central Baptist College; Conway, Ark. 72032	250 (C)	P	2,500	2,500	2,040
Central Bible College; Springfield, Mo. 65803	935 (C)	P	3,590	3,590	2,800
Central Christian College of the Bible; Moberly, Mo. 65270	76 (C)	P	3,323	3,323	2,390
Central College; Pella, Iowa 50219	1,599 (C)	P	10,238	10,238	3,660
Central Connecticut State University; New Britain, Conn. 06050	6,739 (C)	Pub	2,728	6,914	4,154

Institution and location	Enrollment	Control	Tuition ($) Res.	Tuition ($) Nonres.	Rm/Bd ($)
Central Florida, University of; Orlando, Fla. 32816	17,684 (C)	Pub	1,713	6,472	4,145
Central Methodist College; Fayette, Mo. 65248	1,002 (C)	P	8,050	8,050	3,370
Central Michigan University; Mt. Pleasant, Mich. 48859	14,515 (C)	Pub	2,485	6,557	3,724
Central Missouri State University; Warrensburg, Mo. 64093	10,239 (C)	Pub	2,176	3,040	2,900
Central Oklahoma, University of; Edmond, Okla. 73034-0127	12,042 (C)	Pub	1,283	3,210	2,150
Central State University; Wilberforce, Ohio 45384	3,263 (C)	Pub	2,679	5,898	4,293
Central Texas, University of; Killeen, Tex. 76540	336 (C)	P	3,660	3,660	n.a.
Central Washington University; Ellensburg, Wash. 98926	7,406 (C)	Pub	2,919	8,715	3,415
Central Wesleyan College; Central, S.C. 29630	970 (C)	P	7,500	7,500	3,080
Centre College; Danville, Ky. 40422–1394	904 (C)	P	11,600	11,600	4,200
Chadron State College; Chadron, Neb. 69337	2,062 (C)	Pub	1,575	2,670	2,666
Chaminade University of Honolulu; Honolulu, Hawaii 96816	2,704 (C)	P	7,600	8,500	4,040
Chapman University; Orange, Calif. 92666	1,658 (C)	P	15,396	15,396	5,346
Charles R. Drew University; Los Angeles, Calif. 90059	n.a.	n.a.	n.a.	n.a.	n.a.
Charleston, College of; Charleston, S.C. 29424	7,821 (C)	Pub	2,950	5,900	3,300
Charleston Southern University; Charleston, S.C. 29411	2,413 (C)	P	6,880	6,880	2,990
Charleston, University of; Charleston, W. Va. 25304	1,340 (C)	P	8,700	8,700	3,330
Charter Oak State College; Farmington, Conn. 06032-1934	1,145 (C)	Pub	314	451	n.a.
Chatham College; Pittsburgh, Pa. 15232	630 (W)	P	11,840	11,840	5,030
Chestnut Hill College; Philadelphia, Pa. 19118-2695	856 (W)	P	8,950	8,950	4,450
Cheyney University of Pennsylvania; Cheyney, Pa. 19319	1,210 (C)	Pub	2,938	6,332	3,340
Chicago, University of—The College; Chicago, Ill. 60637	3,398 (C)	P	17,910	17,910	6,130
Chicago State University; Chicago, Ill. 60628	6,542 (C)	Pub	2,198	5,894	n.a.
Chowan College; Murfreesboro, N.C. 27855	n.a. (C)	P	8,880	8,880	3,180
Christendom College; Front Royal, Va. 22630	144 (C)	P	8,350	8,350	3,400
Christian Brothers University; Memphis, Tenn. 38104	1,085 (C)	P	8,880	8,800	3,180
Christian Heritage College; El Cajon, Calif. 92019	310 (C)	P	7,980	7,980	3,900
Christian Life College; Stockton, Calif. 95210	173 (C)	P	2,140	2,140	2,400
Christopher Newport University; Newport News, Va. 23606-2998	4,780 (C)	Pub	2,860	6,852	n.a.
Cincinnati, University of; Cincinnati, Ohio 45221	13,506 (C)	Pub	3,372	8,049	4,431
Cincinnati Bible College; Cincinnati, Ohio 45204	633 (C)	P	3,872	3,872	3,124
Cincinnati College of Mortuary Science; Cincinnati, Ohio 45207	82 (C)	P	7,020	7,020	4,500
Circleville Bible College; Circleville, Ohio 43113	186 (C)	P	4,127	4,127	2,964
Citadel-The Military College of South Carolina; Charleston, S.C. 29409	1,960 (M)	Pub	9,188	12,898	—
City College (NYC). *See* New York, City University of					
City University; Bellevue, Wash. 98004	1,442 (C)	P	6,840	6,840	n.a.
Claflin College; Orangeburg, S.C. 29115	756 (C)	P	6,413	6,413	2,140
Claremont Colleges:					
Claremont McKenna College; Claremont, Calif. 91711-6420	854 (C)	P	15,620	15,620	5,480
Harvey Mudd College; Claremont, Calif. 91711-5990	616 (C)	P	15,920	15,920	6,160
Pitzer College; Claremont, Calif. 91711	750 (C)	P	17,158	17,158	5,764
Pomona College; Claremont, Calif. 91711	1,375 (C)	P	15,830	15,830	6,625
Scripps College; Claremont, Calif. 91711	634 (W)	P	15,612	15,612	6,668
Clarion University of Pennsylvania; Clarion, Pa. 16214	5,753 (C)	Pub	3,328	6,810	2,786
Clark Atlanta University; Atlanta, Ga. 30314	2,339 (C)	P	7,100	7,100	3,752
Clarke College; Dubuque, Iowa 52001	927 (C)	P	10,455	10,455	3,545
Clarkson College; Omaha, Neb. 68131–2739	450 (C)	P	5,808	5,808	3,275
Clarkson University; Potsdam, N.Y. 13676	2,605 (C)	P	15,060	15,060	5,326
Clark University; Worcester, Mass. 01610	2,151 (C)	P	16,867	16,867	4,500
Clayton State College; Morrow, Ga. 30260–1221	4,548 (C)	Pub	1,440	4,122	n.a.
Clearwater Christian College; Clearwater, Fla. 34619–9997	431 (C)	P	4,600	4,600	3,200
Cleary College; Ypsilanti, Mich. 48197	940 (C)	P	5,815	5,815	n.a.
Clemson University; Clemson, S.C. 29634	13,305 (C)	Pub	2,778	7,394	3,474
Cleveland College of Jewish Studies; Beachwood, Ohio 44122	350 (C)	P	3,900	3,900	n.a.
Cleveland Institute of Art; Cleveland, Ohio 44106	465 (C)	P	10,800	10,800	4,390
Cleveland Institute of Music; Cleveland, Ohio 44106	175 (C)	P	12,775	12,775	4,800
Cleveland State University; Cleveland, Ohio 44115	13,408 (C)	Pub	2,976	5,952	3,885
Clinch Valley College. *See* Virginia, University of					
Coe College; Cedar Rapids, Iowa 52402	1,285 (C)	P	12,680	12,680	4,280
Cogswell College; Cupertino, Calif. 95014	350 (C)	P	6,600	6,600	4,400
Cogswell College North; Cupertino, Calif. 95014	235 (C)	P	6,880	6,880	n.a.
Coker College; Hartsville, S.C. 29550	772 (C)	P	8,921	8,921	3,576
Colby College; Waterville, Me. 04901	1,747 (C)	P	17,610	17,610	5,480
Colby-Sawyer College; New London, N.H. 03257	650 (C)	P	13,376	13,376	5,120
Coleman College; La Mesa, Calif. 92041	736 (C)	P	7,400	7,400	n.a.
Colgate University; Hamilton, N.Y. 13346	2,670 (C)	P	18,620	18,620	5,400
College Misericordia; Dallas, Pa. 18612	900 (C)	P	9,050	9,050	4,870
College of West Virginia, The; Beckley, W. Va. 25802	1,670 (C)	P	3,000	3,000	n.a.
Colorado, University of; Boulder, Colo. 80309:					
U. of Colorado-Boulder; Boulder, Colo. 80309	20,407 (C)	Pub	2,540	11,332	3,664
U. of Colorado-Colorado Springs; Colorado Springs, Colo. 80933	4,155 (C)	Pub	2,187	6,865	n.a.
U. of Colorado-Denver; Denver, Colo. 80204	6,128 (C)	Pub	1,706	7,854	n.a.
U. of Colorado–Health Sciences Center; Denver, Colo. 80262	n.a.	n.a.	n.a.	n.a.	n.a.
Colorado Christian University; Lakewood, Colo. 80226	980 (C)	P	6,350	6,350	3,400

Institution and location	Enrollment	Control	Tuition ($) Res.	Tuition ($) Nonres.	Rm/Bd ($)
Colorado College; Colorado Springs, Colo. 80903	1,903 (C)	P	14,760	14,760	3,820
Colorado School of Mines; Golden, Colo. 80401	1,991 (C)	Pub	4,288	11,204	3,860
Colorado State University; Fort Collins, Colo. 80523	17,572 (C)	Pub	2,505	7,671	3,816
Colorado Technical College; Colorado Springs, Colo. 80907	1,261 (C)	P	4,635	4,635	n.a.
Columbia Bible College and Seminary; Columbia, S.C. 29230	425 (C)	P	6,150	6,150	3,262
Columbia Christian College; Portland, Ore. 97216	250 (C)	P	6,270	6,270	2,930
Columbia College; Chicago, Ill. 60605	6,729 (C)	P	6,644	6,664	n.a.
Columbia College; Columbia, Mo. 65216	706 (C)	P	7,166	7,166	3,236
Columbia College; Columbia, S.C. 29203	1,228 (W)	P	9,750	9,750	3,770
Columbia College-Hollywood; Los Angeles, Calif. 90038	249 (C)	P	6,350	6,350	n.a.
Columbia Union College; Takoma Park, Md. 20912	1,159 (C)	P	9,760	9,760	3,450
Columbia University-Columbia College; New York, N.Y. 10027	3,325 (C)	P	16,781	16,781	6,536
Columbia University School of Engineering and Applied Science; New York, N.Y. 10027	n.a.	n.a.	n.a.	n.a.	n.a.
Columbia University School of General Studies; New York, N.Y. 10027	1,200 (C)	P	15,080	15,080	10,440
Columbus College; Columbus, Ga. 31993	4,454 (C)	Pub	1,545	4,227	n.a.
Columbus College of Art and Design; Columbus, Ohio 43215	1,631 (C)	P	8,900	8,900	4,800
Conception Seminary College; Conception, Mo. 64433	76 (M)	P	4,704	4,704	2,974
Concord College; Athens, W. Va. 24712	2,960 (C)	Pub	1,736	3,866	3,018
Concordia College; Ann Arbor, Mich. 48105	521 (C)	P	8,500	8,500	3,740
Concordia College; Bronxville, N.Y. 10708	560 (C)	P	9,370	9,370	4,330
Concordia College; Irvine, Calif. 92715	625 (C)	P	10,440	10,440	4,230
Concordia College; Moorhead, Minn. 56562	2,933 (C)	P	9,105	9,105	2,900
Concordia College; Portland, Ore. 97211	997 (C)	P	8,700	8,700	2,700
Concordia College; St. Paul, Minn. 55104	1,258 (C)	P	9,720	9,720	3,480
Concordia College; Seward, Neb. 68434	783 (C)	P	7,896	7,896	3,270
Concordia Lutheran College; Austin, Tex. 78705	694 (C)	P	6,580	6,580	3,500
Concordia University; River Forest, Ill. 60305	1,280 (C)	P	8,496	8,496	4,035
Concordia University Wisconsin; Mequon, Wis. 53092	2,091 (C)	P	8,700	8,700	3,400
Connecticut, University of; Storrs, Conn. 06269	12,059 (C)	Pub	3,902	10,374	4,878
Connecticut College; New London, Conn. 06320	1,619 (C)	P	17,200	17,200	5,700
Conservatory of Music of Puerto Rico; Hato Rey, P.R. 00918	264 (C)	Pub	390	390	n.a.
Converse College; Spartanburg, S.C. 29301	782 (W)	P	12,050	12,050	3,700
Cooper Union; New York, N.Y. 10003	983 (C)	P	300	300	6,145
Coppin State College; Baltimore, Md. 21216	2,638 (C)	Pub	2,605	4,677	4,395
Corcoran School of Art; Washington, D.C. 20006	268 (C)	P	9,980	9,980	5,120
Cornell College; Mt. Vernon, Iowa 52314	1,162 (C)	P	14,228	14,228	4,197
Cornell University; Ithaca, N.Y. 14853	7,856 (C)	P	17,276	17,276	5,676
Cornish College of the Arts; Seattle, Wash. 98102	556 (C)	P	8,650	8,650	n.a.
Corpus Christi State Univ.; Corpus Christi, Tex. 78412	3,220 (C)	Pub	1,186	4,450	2,650
Covenant College; Lookout Mountain, Ga. 30750	707 (C)	P	8,600	8,600	3,650
Creighton University; Omaha, Neb. 68178	3,883 (C)	P	9,670	9,670	4,000
Crichton College; Memphis, Tenn. 38175-7830	358 (C)	P	4,376	4,376	1,500
Crown College; St. Bonifacius, Minn. 55375-9001	495 (C)	P	7,580	7,580	3,590
Culver-Stockton College; Canton, Mo. 63435	1,145 (C)	P	7,650	7,650	3,500
Cumberland College; Williamsburg, Ky. 40769	1,670 (C)	P	5,880	5,880	3,176
Cumberland University of Tennessee; Lebanon, Tenn. 37087	775 (C)	P	5,200	5,200	2,830
Curry College; Milton, Mass. 02186	970 (C)	P	13,000	13,000	4,900
Curtis Institute of Music; Philadelphia, Pa. 19103	119 (C)	P	1,195	1,195	n.a.
C. W. Post. *See* Long Island Univ. Center					
Daemen College; Amherst, N.Y. 14226	1,707 (C)	P	8,270	8,270	4,150
Dakota State University; Madison, S.D. 57042	1,465 (C)	Pub	1,922	1,922	2,270
Dakota Wesleyan University; Mitchell, S.D. 57301	766 (C)	P	7,110	7,110	2,530
Dallas, University of; Irving, Tex. 75062	1,116 (C)	P	10,200	10,200	4,508
Dallas Baptist University; Dallas, Tex. 75211	2,240 (C)	P	6,000	6,000	3,130
Dallas Christian College; Dallas, Tex. 75234	132 (C)	P	2,568	2,568	2,790
Dana College; Blair, Neb. 68008-1099	572 (C)	P	8,050	8,050	2,930
Daniel Webster College; Nashua, N.H. 03063–1300	488 (C)	P	11,188	11,188	4,454
Dartmouth College; Hanover, N.H. 03755	4,210 (C)	P	17,345	17,345	6,086
Davenport College; Grand Rapids, Mich. 49503	4,077 (C)	P	8,208	8,208	3,750
David Lipscomb University; Nashville, Tenn. 37204-3951	2,412 (C)	P	6,270	6,270	3,190
Davidson College; Davidson, N.C. 28036	1,555 (C)	P	14,950	14,950	4,470
Davis and Elkins College; Elkins, W. Va. 26241	922 (C)	P	8,850	8,850	4,250
Dayton, University of; Dayton, Ohio 45469	6,100 (C)	P	10,670	10,670	4,030
Deaconess College of Nursing; St. Louis, Mo. 63139	n.a.	n.a.	n.a.	n.a.	n.a.
Defiance College, The; Defiance, Ohio 43512	965 (C)	P	9,386	9,386	3,420
Delaware, University of; Newark, Del. 19716	14,645 (C)	P	3,686	9,346	3,756
Delaware State College; Dover, Del. 19901	2,624 (C)	Pub	1,788	4,346	3,464
Delaware Valley College of Science and Agriculture; Doylestown, Pa. 18901	1,286 (C)	P	11,645	11,645	4,800
Delta State University; Cleveland, Miss. 38732	3,330 (C)	Pub	2,194	4,154	1,770
Denison University; Granville, Ohio 43023	2,003 (C)	P	16,730	16,730	4,420
Denver, University of; Denver, Colo. 80208	2,765 (C)	P	13,770	13,770	4,200
CWC Campus Weekend College-Women's Program; Denver, Colo. 80220	419 (W)	P	9,565	9,565	n.a

Institution and location	Enrollment	Control	Tuition ($) Res.	Tuition ($) Nonres.	Rm/Bd ($)
DePaul University; Chicago, Ill. 60604	9,783 (C)	P	10,514	10,514	4,809
DePauw University; Greencastle, Ind. 46135	2,171 (C)	P	13,000	13,000	4,640
Deree College-Division of the American College of Greece; Athens, Greece GR-153 42	4,157 (C)	P	4,600	4,600	n.a.
Design Institute of San Diego; San Diego, Calif. 92121	200 (C)	P	6,400	6,400	n.a.
Detroit College of Business; Dearborn, Mich. 48126	5,111 (C)	P	5,040	5,040	n.a.
Detroit Mercy, University of; Detroit, Mich. 48221	4,788 (C)	P	10,080	10,080	3,600
DeVry Institute of Technology; Chicago, Ill. 60618-5994	3,331 (C)	P	5,249	5,249	n.a.
DeVry Institute of Technology; City of Industry, Calif. 91746-3495	1,884 (C)	P	5,249	5,249	n.a.
DeVry Institute of Technology; Columbus, Ohio 43209-2764	2,745 (C)	P	5,249	5,249	n.a.
DeVry Institute of Technology; Decatur, Ga. 30030-2198	3,133 (C)	P	5,249	5,249	n.a.
DeVry Institute of Technology; Irving, Tex. 75038-4299	2,240 (C)	P	5,249	5,249	n.a.
DeVry Institute of Technology; Kansas City, Mo. 64131-3626	1,814 (C)	P	5,249	5,249	n.a.
DeVry Institute of Technology; Lombard, Ill. 60148-4892	2,564 (C)	P	5,249	5,249	n.a.
DeVry Institute of Technology; Phoenix, Ariz. 85021-2995	2,719 (C)	P	5,249	5,249	n.a.
Dickinson College; Carlisle, Pa. 17013	2,047 (C)	P	17,660	17,660	4,930
Dickinson State University; Dickinson, N.D. 58601	1,605 (C)	Pub	1,706	4,256	1,850
Dillard University; New Orleans, La. 70122–3097	1,200 (C)	P	6,100	6,100	3,450
District of Columbia, Univ. of the; Washington, D.C. 20008	10,899 (C)	Pub	800	2,880	n.a.
Divine Word College; Epworth, Iowa 52045	62 (M)	P	5,200	5,200	1,200
Doane College; Crete, Neb. 68333	826 (C)	P	8,770	8,770	2,700
Dominican College of Blauvelt; Orangeburg, N.Y. 10962	1,495 (C)	P	7,478	7,478	5,430
Dominican College of San Rafael; San Rafael, Calif. 94901-8008	515 (C)	P	11,070	11,070	5,410
Dominican School of Philosophy and Theology; Berkeley, Calif. 94709	8 (C)	P	5,065	5,065	n.a.
Dordt College; Sioux Center, Iowa 51250	1,077 (C)	P	9,000	9,000	2,500
Dowling College; Oakdale, N.Y. 11769	3,242 (C)	P	8,160	8,160	4,100
Drake University; Des Moines, Iowa 50311	4,260 (C)	P	12,780	12,780	4,415
Drew University-College of Liberal Arts; Madison, N.J. 07940	1,290 (C)	P	17,299	17,299	5,092
Drexel University; Philadelphia, Pa. 19104	6,189 (C)	P	11,000	11,000	5,800
Dr. Martin Luther College; New Ulm, Minn. 56073	509 (C)	P	3,585	3,585	1,770
Drury College; Springfield, Mo. 65802	1,083 (C)	P	8,760	8,760	3,280
Dubuque, University of; Dubuque, Iowa 52001	880 (C)	P	9,940	9,940	3,365
Duke University; Durham, N.C. 27706	6,095 (C)	P	16,121	16,121	5,243
Duquesne University; Pittsburgh, Pa. 15282	4,788 (C)	P	10,470	10,470	4,874
Dyke College; Cleveland, Ohio 44115	1,319 (C)	P	5,200	5,200	n.a.
D'Youville College; Buffalo, N.Y. 14201	1,337 (C)	P	8,340	8,340	3,940
Earlham College; Richmond, Ind. 47374	1,057 (C)	P	14,403	14,403	3,894
East Carolina University; Greenville, N.C. 27834	13,883 (C)	Pub	1,296	6,918	3,030
East Central University; Ada, Okla. 74820-6899	4,473 (C)	Pub	1,215	3,210	1,988
Eastern College; St. Davids, Pa. 19087-3696	1,376 (C)	P	9,850	9,850	4,130
Eastern Connecticut State Univ.; Willimantic, Conn. 06226	2,695 (C)	Pub	2,946	7,658	4,020
Eastern Illinois University; Charleston, Ill. 61920	9,826 (C)	Pub	2,533	6,228	2,856
Eastern Kentucky University; Richmond, Ky. 40475	14,922 (C)	Pub	1,540	4,220	2,896
Eastern Mennonite College; Harrisonburg, Va. 22801	958 (C)	P	8,600	8,600	3,400
Eastern Michigan University; Ypsilanti, Mich. 48197	19,715 (C)	Pub	2,529	6,114	3,850
Eastern Montana College; Billings, Mont. 59101	3,377 (C)	Pub	1,835	5,139	2,810
Eastern Nazarene College; Quincy, Mass. 02170	595 (C)	P	8,765	8,765	3,400
Eastern New Mexico University; Portales, N.M. 88130	3,360 (C)	Pub	1,359	4,917	2,410
Eastern Oregon State College; La Grande, Ore. 97850	2,171 (C)	Pub	2,400	2,400	3,360
Eastern Washington University; Cheney, Wash. 99004	6,990 (C)	Pub	1,785	6,297	3,618
Eastman School of Music; Rochester, N.Y. 14604	458 (C)	P	15,347	15,347	6,256
East Stroudsburg University of Pennsylvania; East Stroudsburg, Pa. 18301	4,642 (C)	Pub	3,352	6,746	3,039
East Tennessee State University; Johnson City, Tenn. 37614	9,923 (C)	Pub	1,554	4,156	2,600
East Texas Baptist University; Marshall, Tex. 75670	1,204 (C)	P	5,150	5,150	2,760
East Texas State University; Commerce, Tex. 75429	5,106 (C)	Pub	1,272	5,412	3,760
East Texas State University at Texarkana; Texarkana, Texas 75505–0518	n.a.	n.a.	n.a.	n.a.	n.a.
East-West University; Chicago, Ill. 60605	238 (C)	P	5,910	5,910	n.a.
Eckerd College; St. Petersburg, Fla. 33711	1,368 (C)	P	13,815	13,815	3,500
Edgewood College; Madison, Wis. 53711	1,690 (C)	P	8,100	8,100	3,600
Edinboro University of Pennsylvania; Edinboro, Pa. 16444	7,537 (C)	Pub	3,061	6,555	3,460
Edward Waters College; Jacksonville, Fla. 32209	686 (C)	P	3,476	3,476	3,400
Electronic Data Processing College of Puerto Rico; Hato Rey, P.R. 00918	1,176 (C)	P	2,310	2,310	2,400
Elizabeth City State University; Elizabeth City, N.C. 27909	1,694 (C)	Pub	1,273	5,261	2,549
Elizabethtown College; Elizabethtown, Pa. 17022	1,548 (C)	P	13,600	13,600	4,250
Elmhurst College; Elmhurst, Ill. 60126-3296	1,604 (C)	P	9,050	9,050	3,678
Elmira College; Elmira, N.Y. 14901	1,001 (C)	P	12,700	12,700	4,100
Elms College; Chicopee, Mass. 01013-2839	550 (W)	P	10,375	10,375	4,665
Elon College; Elon College, N.C. 27244	3,221 (C)	P	8,110	8,110	3,485
Embry-Riddle Aeronautical Univ.-Daytona Beach Campus; Daytona Beach, Fla. 32114	4,350 (C)	P	7,340	7,340	3,196
Prescott Campus; Prescott, Ariz. 86301	1,509 (C)	P	7,340	7,340	3,196
Emerson College; Boston, Mass. 02116	2,038 (C)	P	13,504	13,504	7,288

Institution and location	Enrollment	Control	Tuition ($) Res.	Tuition ($) Nonres.	Rm/Bd ($)
Emmanuel College; Boston, Mass. 02115	997 (W)	P	11,241	11,241	5,528
Emmanuel College; Franklin Springs, Ga. 30639	527 (C)	P	4,000	4,000	2,944
Emory and Henry College; Emory, Va. 24327	844 (C)	P	7,320	7,320	4,160
Emory University; Atlanta, Ga. 30322	4,779 (C)	P	16,820	16,820	5,110
Emporia State University; Emporia, Kan. 66801	4,476 (C)	Pub	1,585	4,470	2,880
Endicott College; Beverly, Mass. 01915	755 (W)	P	10,910	10,910	5,890
Erskine College; Due West, S.C. 29639	536 (C)	P	10,630	10,630	3,680
Escuela De Artes Plasticas Instituto De Cultura Puertorriquena; San Juan, P.R. 00905	n.a.	n.a.	n.a.	n.a.	n.a.
Esther Boyer College of Music; Philadelphia, Pa. 19122	300 (C)	Pub	4,900	9,000	5,000
ETI Technical College; Cleveland, Ohio 44114	900 (C)	P	4,185	4,185	2,995
Eugene Bible College; Eugene, Ore. 97405	195 (C)	P	3,585	3,585	2,610
Eureka College; Eureka, Ill. 61530	525 (C)	P	10,955	10,955	3,450
Evangel College; Springfield, Mo. 65802	1,420 (C)	P	6,730	6,730	3,090
Evansville, University of; Evansville, Ind. 47722	2,803 (C)	P	11,130	11,130	4,170
Evergreen State College; Olympia, Wash. 98505	3,108 (C)	Pub	1,785	6,297	4,000
Fairfield University; Fairfield, Conn. 06430	3,000 (C)	P	13,730	13,730	5,350
Fairhaven College-Western Washington University; Bellingham, Wash. 98225	336 (C)	Pub	1,911	6,417	3,732
Fairleigh Dickinson Univ.-Madison; Madison, N.J. 07940	2,501 (C)	P	10,517	10,517	6,000
Fairleigh Dickinson Univ.-Rutherford; Rutherford, N.J. 07070	1,505 (C)	P	10,517	10,517	6,000
Fairleigh Dickinson Univ.-Teaneck; Teaneck, N.J. 07666	4,402 (C)	P	10,517	10,517	6,000
Fairmont State College; Fairmont, W. Va. 26554	6,613 (C)	Pub	1,700	4,020	3,150
Faith Baptist Bible College and Theological Seminary; Ankeny, Iowa 50021	225 (C)	P	4,224	4,224	2,964
Faulkner University; Montgomery, Ala. 36109–3398	1,995 (C)	P	5,400	5,400	2,900
Fayetteville State University; Fayetteville, N.C. 28301	2,972 (C)	Pub	1,268	6,322	2,250
Felician College; Lodi, N.J. 07644	1,010 (C)	P	7,890	7,890	n.a.
Ferris State University; Big Rapids, Mich. 49307	12,461 (C)	Pub	2,970	6,015	3,707
Ferrum College; Ferrum, Va. 24088	1,236 (C)	P	8,210	8,210	3,730
Findlay, University of; Findlay, Ohio 45840	3,136 (C)	P	10,002	10,002	4,545
Fisk University; Nashville, Tenn. 37208	900 (C)	P	5,510	5,510	3,355
Fitchburg State College; Fitchburg, Mass. 01420	4,453 (C)	Pub	3,206	7,070	3,232
Five Towns College; Dix Hills, N.Y. 11746–6055	684 (C)	P	6,750	6,750	4,600
Flagler College; St. Augustine, Fla. 32085	1,282 (C)	P	4,920	4,920	3,070
Flaming Rainbow University; Stilwell, Okla. 74960	94 (C)	P	3,400	3,400	n.a.
Florida, University of; Gainesville, Fla. 32611	27,302 (C)	Pub	1,580	6,030	3,950
Florida A&M University; Tallahassee, Fla. 32307	8,292 (C)	Pub	1,669	6,429	2,698
Florida Atlantic University; Boca Raton, Fla. 33431-0991	11,390 (C)	Pub	1,350	4,850	3,450
Florida Baptist Theological College; Graceville, Fla. 32440	498 (C)	P	1,884	1,884	3,000
Florida Christian College; Kissimmee, Fla. 34744	131 (C)	P	3,390	3,390	3,388
Florida Institute of Technology; Melbourne, Fla. 32901–6988	2,624 (C)	P	11,400	11,400	3,465
Florida International University; Miami, Fla. 33199	18,636 (C)	Pub	1,600	6,400	4,800
Florida Memorial College; Miami, Fla. 33054	1,750 (C)	P	4,450	4,450	2,800
Florida Southern College; Lakeland, Fla. 33801	1,760 (C)	P	7,080	7,080	4,400
Florida State University; Tallahassee, Fla. 32306	21,116 (C)	Pub	1,679	6,438	3,880
Fontbonne College; St. Louis, Mo. 63105	1,532 (C)	P	8,090	8,090	4,100
Fordham University; Bronx, N.Y. 10458	6,393 (C)	P	12,105	12,105	6,840
Forsyth School for Dental Hygienists; Boston, Mass. 02115	108 (C)	P	12,425	12,425	6,800
Fort Hays State University; Hays, Kan. 67601	4,346 (C)	Pub	1,635	4,,515	3,339
Fort Lauderdale College; Fort Lauderdale, Fla. 33304	1,300 (C)	P	4,780	4,780	2,700
Fort Lewis College; Durango, Colo. 81301	4,096 (C)	Pub	1,705	6,059	3,220
Fort Valley State College; Fort Valley, Ga. 31030	2,046 (C)	Pub	1,722	4,404	2,370
Framingham State College; Framingham, Mass. 01701	3,248 (C)	Pub	3,177	7,037	3,466
Franciscan University of Steubenville; Steubenville, Ohio 43952	1,533 (C)	P	9,180	9,180	4,200
Francis Marion University; Florence, S.C. 29501–0547	3,742 (C)	Pub	2,440	4,880	3,078
Franklin and Marshall College; Lancaster, Pa. 17604-3003	1,744 (C)	P	18,350	18,350	3,980
Franklin College; Franklin, Ind. 46131	904 (C)	P	9,590	9,590	3,650
Franklin College; Switzerland	220 (C)	P	19,388	19,388	7,970
Franklin Pierce College; Rindge, N.H. 03461	1,235 (C)	P	11,890	11,890	4,250
Franklin University; Columbus, Ohio 43215-5399	3,990 (C)	P	4,371	4,371	n.a.
Freed-Hardeman University; Henderson, Tenn. 38340	1,131 (C)	P	5,940	5,940	3,020
Free Will Baptist Bible College; Nashville, Tenn. 37205	269 (C)	P	3,160	3,160	2,970
Fresno Pacific College; Fresno, Calif. 93702	488 (C)	P	8,200	8,200	3,300
Friends University; Wichita, Kan. 67213	1,154 (C)	P	7,695	7,695	2,830
Friends World Program. *See* Long Island University					
Frostburg State University; Frostburg, Md. 21532	4,468 (C)	Pub	2,222	4,210	4,000
Furman University; Greenville, S.C. 29613–0645	2,474 (C)	P	12,480	12,480	4,184
Gallaudet University, Washington, D.C. 20002	1,787 (C)	P	4,570	4,570	5,110
Gannon University; Erie, Pa. 16541	3,635 (C)	P	9,838	9,838	4,540
Gannon University–Villa Marie Campus; Erie, Pa. 16505	699 (W)	P	8,830	8,830	3,500
Gardner-Webb College; Boiling Springs, N.C. 28017	1,460 (C)	P	7,180	7,180	3,800
General Motors Institute. *See* GMI Engineering and Management Institute					

Institution and location	Enrollment	Control	Tuition ($) Res.	Tuition ($) Nonres.	Rm/Bd ($)
Geneva College; Beaver Falls, Pa. 15010	1,541 (C)	P	8,164	8,164	3,980
George Fox College; Newberg, Ore. 97132	1,213 (C)	P	11,600	11,600	3,890
George Mason University; Fairfax, Va. 22030	13,329 (C)	Pub	3,336	8,604	4,750
Georgetown College; Georgetown, Ky. 40324	1,156 (C)	P	7,340	7,440	3,600
Georgetown University; Washington, D.C. 20057	6,082 (C)	P	16,589	16,589	6,018
George Washington University, The; Washington, D.C. 20052	6,629 (C)	P	16,205	16,205	6,310
Georgia, University of; Athens, Ga. 30602	22,385 (C)	Pub	2,175	5,757	3,405
Georgia Baptist College of Nursing; Atlanta, Ga. 30312-1239	277 (W)	P	2,670	6,810	2,500
Georgia College; Milledgeville, Ga. 31061	4,378 (C)	Pub	1,632	4,312	2,490
Georgia Institute of Technology; Atlanta, Ga. 30332	9,319 (C)	Pub	2,205	6,531	4,308
Georgian Court College; Lakewood, N.J. 08701	1,833 (W)	P	8,450	8,450	3,850
Georgia Southern University; Statesboro, Ga. 30458	12,220 (C)	Pub	1,638	4,038	2,790
Georgia Southwestern College; Americus, Ga. 31709	2,303 (C)	Pub	1,578	4,158	2,370
Georgia State University; Atlanta, Ga. 30303	17,161 (C)	Pub	1,950	6,280	n.a.
Gettysburg College; Gettysburg, Pa. 17325–1484	2,100 (C)	P	18,870	18,870	4,090
Glassboro State College; Glassboro, N.J. 08028	5,427 (C)	Pub	2,700	3,750	4,515
Glenville State College; Glenville, W. Va. 26351	2,345 (C)	Pub	1,606	3,820	2,928
GMI Engineering & Management Institute; Flint, Mich. 48504	2,367 (C)	P	10,910	10,910	3,158
Goddard College; Plainfield, Vt. 05667	256 (C)	P	13,000	13,000	4,380
God's Bible School and College; Cincinnati, Ohio 45210	189 (C)	P	3,010	3,010	2,450
Golden Gate University; San Francisco, Calif. 94105	2,027 (C)	P	5,216	5,216	n.a.
Goldey Beacom College; Wilmington, Del. 19808	1,724 (C)	P	5,550	5,550	4,357
Gonzaga University; Spokane, Wash. 99258	2,928 (C)	P	12,200	12,200	4,150
Gordon College, Wenham, Mass 01984	1,192 (C)	P	11,600	11,600	3,750
Goshen College; Goshen, Ind. 46526	1,057 (C)	P	8,770	8,770	3,590
Goucher College; Baltimore, Md. 21204	940 (C)	P	13,446	13,446	5,873
Governors State University; University Park, Ill. 60466	2,830 (C)	Pub	1,978	5,674	n.a.
Grace Bible College; Grand Rapids, Mich. 49509	100 (C)	P	4,450	4,450	3,100
Grace College; Winona Lake, Ind. 46590	652 (C)	P	7,512	7,512	3,480
Grace College of the Bible; Omaha, Neb. 68108	259 (C)	P	4,100	4,100	2,500
Graceland College; Lamoni, Iowa 50140	1,058 (C)	P	8,680	8,680	2,920
Grambling State University; Grambling, La. 71245	6,828 (C)	Pub	2,038	3,588	2,636
Grand Canyon University; Phoenix, Ariz. 85017	1,641 (C)	P	6,730	6,730	2,800
Grand Rapids Baptist College; Grand Rapids, Mich. 49505	777 (C)	P	5,852	5,852	3,630
Grand Valley State University; Allendale, Mich. 49401-9401	10,527 (C)	Pub	2,658	5,860	3,800
Grand View College; Des Moines, Iowa 50316	1,477 (C)	P	9,105	9,105	3,200
Gratz College; Melrose Park , Pa. 19126	65 (C)	P	4,200	4,200	n.a.
Great Falls, College of; Great Falls, Mont. 59405	1,237 (C)	P	4,650	4,650	2,870
Great Lakes Christian College; Lansing, Mich. 48917	213 (C)	P	4,305	4,305	2,750
Green Mountain College; Poultney, Vt. 05764	621 (C)	P	10,425	10,425	2,870
Greensboro College; Greensboro, N.C. 27401	1,035 (C)	P	7,240	7,240	3,504
Greenville College; Greenville, Ill. 62246	864 (C)	P	9,910	9,910	4,360
Griffin College; Seattle, Wash. 98121-1443	1,700 (C)	P	5,500	5,500	n.a.
Grinnell College; Grinnell, Iowa 50112	1,291 (C)	P	14,532	14,532	4,138
Grove City College; Grove City, Pa. 16127	2,173 (C)	P	4,770	4,770	2,780
Guam, University of; Mangilao, Guam 96913	2,626 (C)	Pub	1,500	2,528	2,905
Guilford College; Greensboro, N.C. 27410	1,403 (C)	P	11,610	11,610	4,784
Gustavus Adolphus College; St. Peter, Minn. 56082	2,255 (C)	P	13,400	13,400	3,500
Gwynedd-Mercy College; Gwynedd Valley, Pa. 19437	1,837 (C)	P	9,450	9,450	4,900
Hahnemann University School of Health Sciences and Humanities; Philadelphia, Pa. 19102	917 (C)	P	8,260	8,260	5,000
Hamilton College; Clinton, N.Y. 13323	1,710 (C)	P	18,650	18,650	4,850
Hamline University; St. Paul, Minn. 55104	1,432 (C)	P	13,465	13,465	3,895
Hampden-Sydney College; Hampden-Sydney, Va. 23943	972 (M)	P	12,253	12,253	4,148
Hampshire College; Amherst, Mass. 01002	1,173 (C)	P	18,385	18,385	4,875
Hampton University, Hampton, Va. 23668	5,700 (C)	P	7,006	7,006	3,120
Hannibal-LaGrange College; Hannibal, Mo. 63401	760 (C)	P	5,236	5,236	2,300
Hanover College; Hanover, Ind. 47243	1,055 (C)	P	7,450	7,450	3,200
Harding University; Searcy, Ark. 72143	3,463 (C)	P	5,566	5,566	3,186
Hardin-Simmons University; Abilene, Tex. 79698	1,802 (C)	P	6,000	6,000	2,710
Harrington Institute of Interior Design; Chicago, Ill. 60605	404 (C)	P	7,980	7,980	n.a.
Harris Stowe State College; St. Louis, Mo. 63103	1,480 (C)	Pub	1,728	3,404	n.a.
Hartford, University of; West Hartford, Conn. 06117	5,182 (C)	P	14,228	14,228	6,922
Hartford College for Women; Hartford, Conn. 06105	276 (W)	P	10,400	10,400	5,140
Hartwick College; Oneonta, N.Y. 13820	1,465 (C)	P	16,300	16,300	4,550
Harvard and Radcliffe Colleges; Cambridge, Mass. 02138	6,677 (C)	P	17,674	17,674	5,840
Harvey Mudd College. *See* Claremont Colleges					
Hastings College; Hastings, Neb. 68901	925 (C)	P	8,720	8,720	3,010
Haverford College; Haverford, Pa. 19041-1392	1,138 (C)	P	18,000	18,000	5,950
Hawaii, Univ. of-Hilo; Hilo, Hawaii 96720-4091	2,670 (C)	Pub	440	2,730	3,751
Hawaii, University of-Manoa; Honolulu, Hawaii 96822	13,245 (C)	Pub	1,497	4,357	4,129
Hawaii, University of-West Oahu; Pearl City, Hawaii 96782	667 (C)	Pub	860	2,690	n.a.
Hawaii Pacific University; Kaneohe, Hawaii 96744	538 (C)	P	9,000	9,000	5,200
Hawaii Pacific University; Honolulu, Hawaii 96813	6,140 (C)	P	5,900	5,900	6,400
Health Sciences, University of-The Chicago Medical School; North Chicago, Ill. 60064	77 (C)	P	10,794	10,794	n.a.

Institution and location	Enrollment	Control	Tuition ($) Res.	Tuition ($) Nonres.	Rm/Bd ($)
Hebrew Theological College; Skokie, Ill. 60077	218 (C)	P	5,620	5,620	4,340
Heidelberg College; Tiffin, Ohio 44883	1,229 (C)	P	12,999	12,999	4,158
Hellenic College; Brookline, Mass. 02146	65 (C)	P	5,720	5,720	4,180
Henderson State University; Arkadelphia, Ark. 71923	3,223 (C)	Pub	1,520	2,940	2,500
Hendrix College; Conway, Ark. 72023	1,029 (C)	P	7,710	7,710	2,895
Herbert H. Lehman College. *See* New York, City University of					
Heritage College; Toppenish, Wash. 98948	740 (C)	P	5,155	5,155	n.a.
High Point University; High Point, N.C. 27262-3598	2,326 (C)	P	7,760	7,760	3,700
Hillsdale College; Hillsdale, Mich. 49242	1,101 (C)	P	10,460	10,460	4,440
Hillsdale Free Will Baptist College; Moore, Okla. 73153	152 (C)	P	3,150	3,150	3,020
Hiram College; Hiram, Ohio 44234	866 (C)	P	13,825	13,825	4,515
Hobart and William Smith Colleges; Geneva, N.Y. 14456	1,939 (C)	P	17,994	17,994	5,616
Hofstra University; Hempstead, N.Y. 11550	8,164 (C)	P	9,750	9,750	5,780
Hollins College; Roanoke, Va. 24020	826 (W)	P	12,200	12,200	4,950
Holy Apostles College and Seminary; Cromwell, Conn. 06416	54 (C)	P	3,550	3,550	5,050
Holy Cross, College of the; Worcester, Mass. 01610	2,742 (C)	P	17,200	17,200	6,300
Holy Family College; Philadelphia, Pa. 19914	1,066 (C)	P	8,300	8,300	n.a.
Holy Names College; Oakland, Calif. 94619	603 (C)	P	9,986	9,986	4,528
Hong Kong Baptist College; Kowloon, Hong Kong	3,652 (C)	Pub	2,200	2,200	n.a.
Hood College; Frederick, Md 21701	1,104 (W)	P	12,208	12,208	5,675
Hope College, Holland, Mich. 49423	2,755 (C)	P	11,472	11,472	4,156
Houghton College, Houghton, N.Y. 14744	1,163 (C)	P	9,720	9,720	3,400
Houston, Univ. of; Houston, Tex. 77294-2161	25,052 (C)	Pub	1,470	5,550	4,385
Houston, Univ. of-Clear Lake; Houston, Tex. 77058	3,556 (C)	Pub	1,340	5,480	n.a.
Houston, Univ. of-Downtown; Houston, Tex .77002	8,056 (C)	Pub	1,154	4,466	n.a.
Houston, Univ. of-Victoria; Victoria, Tex. 77901	480 (C)	Pub	1,152	4,464	n.a.
Houston Baptist University; Houston, Tex. 77074	1,700 (C)	P	7,265	7,265	2,430
Howard Payne University; Brownwood, Tex. 76801–2794	1,247 (C)	P	4,330	4,330	2,845
Howard University; Washington, D.C. 20059	8,097 (C)	P	7,000	7,000	3,984
Humboldt State University; Arcata, Calif. 95521	6,245 (C)	Pub	1,468	8,848	4,500
Humphreys College; Stockton, Calif. 95207	652 (C)	P	4,704	4,704	5,010
Hunter College. *See* New York, City University of					
Huntingdon College; Montgomery, Ala. 36194	760 (C)	P	7,640	7,640	3,760
Huntington College; Huntington, Ind. 46750	555 (C)	P	8,480	8,480	3,480
Huron University; Huron, S.D. 57350	452 (C)	P	6,450	6,450	2,940
Husson College; Bangor, Me. 04401	1,868 (C)	P	7,650	7,650	3,880
Huston-Tillotson College; Austin, Tex. 78702	502 (C)	P	4,650	4,650	3,449
Idaho, University of; Moscow, Idaho 83843	7,413 (C)	Pub	1,296	4,196	3,060
Idaho State University; Pocatello, Idaho 83209	8,427 (C)	Pub	1,454	4,104	2,870
Illinois, Univ. of, at Chicago; Chicago, Ill. 60680	16,263 (C)	Pub	3,242	7,436	4,846
Illinois, Univ. of, at Urbana-Champaign; Urbana, Ill. 61801	25,846 (C)	Pub	3,328	7,580	4,058
Illinois Benedictine College; Lisle, Ill. 60532	2,015 (C)	P	10,080	10,080	3,982
Illinois College; Jacksonville, Ill. 62650	926 (C)	P	7,050	7,050	3,450
Illinois Institute of Technology; Chicago, Ill. 60616	2,458 (C)	P	13,070	13,070	4,500
Illinois State University; Normal, Ill. 61761	18,637 (C)	Pub	2,937	7,425	2,910
Illinois Wesleyan University; Bloomington, Ill. 61702	1,809 (C)	P	13,295	13,295	3,985
Immaculata College; Immaculata, Pa. 19345	2,050 (W)	P	9,600	9,600	5,100
Incarnate Word College; San Antonio, Tex. 78209	2,282 (C)	P	8,250	8,250	4,050
Indiana Institute of Technology; Fort Wayne, Ind. 46803	936 (C)	P	6,600	6,660	3,240
Indianapolis, University of; Indianapolis, Ind. 46227	2,870 (C)	P	10,590	10,590	3,920
Indiana State University; Terre Haute, Ind. 47809	10,650 (C)	Pub	2,452	5,960	3,470
Indiana University of Pennsylvania; Indiana, Pa. 15705	13,000 (C)	Pub	3,157	6,551	2,834
Indiana University-Bloomington; Bloomington, Ind. 47405	25,312 (C)	Pub	2,533	8,292	3,565
Indiana University-East; Richmond, Ind. 47374	2,389 (C)	Pub	1,772	4,967	n.a.
Indiana University-Kokomo; Kokomo, Ind. 46904–9003	3,442 (C)	Pub	1,916	4,874	n.a.
Indiana University-Northwest; Gary, Ind. 46408	4,933 (C)	Pub	2,156	5,264	n.a.
Indiana University-Purdue University at Fort Wayne; Fort Wayne, Ind. 46805	12,090 (C)	Pub	2,583	5,161	n.a.
Indiana University-Purdue University at Indianapolis; Indianapolis, Ind. 46202-5143	21,446 (C)	Pub	2,417	7,278	3,000
Indiana University-South Bend; South Bend, Ind. 46634	6,157 (C)	Pub	2,376	5,810	n.a.
Indiana University-Southeast; New Albany, Ind. 47150	5,182 (C)	Pub	2,069	5,264	n.a.
Indiana Wesleyan University; Marion, Ind. 46953	1,656 (C)	P	8,120	8,120	3,764
Industrial Engineering College of Chicago; Chicago, Ill. 60601	120 (C)	P	10,320	10,320	n.a.
Insurance, College of; New York, N.Y. 10007	900 (C)	P	9,360	9,360	6,560
Inter-American University of Puerto Rico-Arecibo Campus; Arecibo, P.R. 00613	4,509 (C)	P	2,734	2,734	4,416
Inter–American University of Puerto Rico–Metropolitan Campus; Rio Piedras, P.R. 00919	n.a.	n.a.	n.a.	n.a.	n.a.
Inter–American University of Puerto Rico–San German Campus; San German, P.R. 00753	n.a.	n.a.	n.a.	n.a.	n.a.
International Institute of A.C.E.; Lewisville, Tex. 75067	75 (C)	P	2,000	2,000	2,800
International Training, School for; Brattleboro, Vt. 05301	60 (C)	P	9,900	9,900	4,036
Iona College; New Rochelle, N.Y. 10801	4,710 (C)	P	9,420	9,420	6,000
Iowa, University of; Iowa City, Iowa 52242	18,917 (C)	Pub	2,088	7,052	3,206

Institution and location	Enrollment	Control	Tuition ($) Res.	Tuition ($) Nonres.	Rm/Bd ($)
Iowa State University; Ames, Iowa 50011	20,757 (C)	Pub	2,192	7,226	3,104
Iowa Wesleyan College; Mount Pleasant, Iowa 52641	996 (C)	P	9,200	9,200	3,200
Ithaca College; Ithaca, N.Y. 14850	6,315 (C)	P	12,870	12,870	5,512
ITT Technical Institute; West Covina, Calif. 91790-2767	700 (C)	P	7,253	7,253	n.a.
Jackson State University; Jackson, Miss. 39217	6,051 (C)	Pub	2,230	4,190	2,766
Jacksonville State University; Jacksonville, Ala. 36265-9982	7,106 (C)	Pub	1,600	2,400	2,400
Jacksonville University; Jacksonville, Fla. 32211	2,242 (C)	P	9,600	9,600	4,250
James Madison University; Harrisonburg, Va. 22807	9,787 (C)	Pub	3,576	7,240	4,284
Jamestown College; Jamestown, N.D. 58401	1,020 (C)	P	7,270	7,270	2,980
Jarvis Christian College; Hawkins, Tex. 75765	560 (C)	P	4,015	4,015	2,999
Jersey City State College; Jersey City, N.J. 07305	5,888 (C)	Pub	2,678	3,638	4,700
Jewish Theological Seminary of America; New York, N.Y. 10027	118 (C)	P	6,230	6,230	6,292
John Brown University; Siloam Springs, Ark. 72761	1,018 (C)	P	6,520	6,520	3,360
John Carroll University; University Heights, Ohio 44118	3,532 (C)	P	11,060	11,060	5,450
John F. Kennedy University; Orinda, Calif. 94563	374 (C)	P	6,936	6,936	n.a.
John Jay Coll. of Criminal Justice. *See* New York, City Univ. of					
Johns Hopkins University; Baltimore, Md. 21218	3,297 (C)	P	17,900	17,900	6,460
School of Nursing; Baltimore, Md. 21205	214 (C)	P	13,000	13,000	7,800
The Peabody Institute; Baltimore, Md. 21202-2397	256 (C)	P	13,000	13,000	5,450
School of Continuing Education; Baltimore, Md. 21218	n.a.	n.a.	n.a.	n.a.	n.a.
Johnson and Wales University; Providence, R.I. 02903	7,365 (C)	P	8,646	8,646	4,182
Johnson Bible College; Knoxville, Tenn. 37998	436 (C)	P	3,950	3,950	2,900
Johnson C. Smith University; Charlotte, N.C. 28216	1,278 (C)	P	6,138	6,138	2,191
Johnson State College; Johnson, Vt. 05656	1,298 (C)	Pub	3,676	7,588	4,462
John Wesley College; High Point, N.C. 27265	77 (C)	P	4,142	4,142	2,800
Jones College—Jacksonville; Jacksonville, Fla. 32211	1,700 (C)	P	3,900	3,900	n.a.
Jordan College; Cedar Springs, Mich. 49319	2,118 (C)	P	5,640	5,640	n.a.
Judson College; Elgin, Ill. 60123	605 (C)	P	9,183	9,183	4,423
Judson College; Marion, Ala. 36756	490 (W)	P	5,190	5,190	3,240
Juilliard School; New York, N.Y. 10023	505 (C)	P	11,250	11,250	5,900
Juniata College; Huntingdon, Pa. 16652	1,038 (C)	P	14,150	14,150	4,240
Kalamazoo College; Kalamazoo, Mich. 49006-3295	1,271 (C)	P	13,785	13,785	4,307
Kansas, University of; Lawrence, Kan. 66045	20,007 (C)	Pub	1,798	5,970	3,080
Kansas City Art Institute; Kansas City, Mo. 64111	533 (C)	P	12,910	12,910	4,090
Kansas City College and Bible School; Overland Park, Kan. 66204	51 (C)	P	2,275	2,275	2,450
Kansas Newman College; Wichita, Kan. 67213	1,189 (C)	P	8,064	8,064	3,792
Kansas State University; Manhattan, Kan. 66506	16,814 (C)	Pub	1,957	6,493	3,120
Kansas Wesleyan University; Salina, Kan. 67401	738 (C)	P	7,420	7,420	3,100
Kean College of New Jersey; Union, N.J. 07083	10,907 (C)	Pub	2,613	3,385	3,690
Keene State College; Keene, N.H. 03431	3,838 (C)	Pub	2,865	7,345	3,772
Kendall College; Evanston, Ill. 60201	371 (C)	P	7,355	7,355	4,645
Kendall College of Art and Design; Grand Rapids, Mich. 49503	632 (C)	P	8,850	8,850	n.a.
Kennesaw College, Marietta, Ga. 30061	11,670 (C)	Pub	1,512	4,194	n.a.
Kent State University; Kent, Ohio 44242-0001	19,335 (C)	Pub	3,596	7,192	3,394
Kentucky, University of; Lexington, Ky. 40506	17,658 (C)	Pub	1,904	5,268	3,054
Kentucky Christian College; Grayson, Ky. 41143	505 (C)	P	3,360	3,360	3,110
Kentucky State University; Frankfurt, Ky. 40601	2,425 (C)	Pub	1,452	4,051	2,468
Kentucky Wesleyan College; Owensboro, Ky. 42301	767 (C)	P	7,600	7,600	3,950
Kenyon College; Gambier, Ohio 43022	1,486 (C)	P	17,610	17,610	3,570
Keuka College; Keuka Park, N.Y. 14478	808 (C)	P	9,280	9,280	4,350
King College; Bristol, Tenn. 37620	508 (C)	P	8,250	8,250	3,250
King's College; Wilkes-Barre, Pa 18711	2,285 (C)	P	10,600	10,600	4,900
King's College, The; Briarcliff Manor, N.Y. 10510	413 (C)	P	8,310	8,310	3,920
Knox College; Galesburg, Ill. 61401	943 (C)	P	13,842	13,842	3,858
Knoxville College; Knoxville, Tenn. 37921	1,225 (C)	P	5,355	5,355	2,600
Kutztown University; Kutztown, Pa. 19530	6,784 (C)	Pub	3,160	6,639	2,840
Laboratory Institute of Merchandising; New York, N.Y. 10022	176 (C)	P	9,300	9,300	n.a.
Lafayette College; Easton, Pa. 18042	1,970 (C)	P	16,795	16,795	5,190
LaGrange College; LaGrange, Ga. 30240	999 (C)	P	6,161	6,161	3,482
Lake Erie College; Painesville, Ohio 44077	692 (C)	P	8,960	8,960	4,180
Lake Forest College; Lake Forest, Ill. 60045	1,017 (C)	P	16,175	16,175	3,785
Lakeland College; Sheboygan, Wis. 53082	2,631 (C)	P	9,145	9,145	3,700
Lake Superior State University; Sault Ste. Marie, Mich. 49783	3,054 (C)	Pub	2,694	5,250	3,815
Lakeview College of Nursing; Danville, Ill. 61832	222 (C)	P	4,575	4,575	n.a.
Lamar University; Beaumont, Tex. 77710	11,488 (C)	Pub	1,298	5,438	3,600
Lambuth College; Jackson, Tenn. 38301	819 (C)	P	4,634	4,634	3,160
Lancaster Bible College; Lancaster, Pa. 17601	440 (C)	P	6,840	6,840	3,000
Lander University; Greenwood S.C. 29649	2,195 (C)	Pub	2,920	4,168	2,880
Lane College; Jackson, Tenn. 38301	525 (C)	P	4,487	4,487	2,486
Langston University; Langston, Okla. 73050	2,103 (C)	Pub	1,419	3,448	2,400
Laredo State University; Laredo, Tex. 78040-9960	780 (C)	Pub	930	2,595	3,302
La Roche College; Pittsburgh, Pa. 15237	1,868 (C)	P	7,780	7,780	4,208
La Salle University; Philadelphia, Pa. 19141	3,156 (C)	P	10,970	10,970	5,140
Lasell College; Newton, Mass. 02166	489 (W)	P	10,850	10,850	6,000
LaSierra University; Riverside, Calif. 92515	1,310 (C)	P	10,830	10,830	3,585

Institution and location	Enrollment	Control	Tuition ($) Res.	Tuition ($) Nonres.	Rm/Bd ($)
La Verne, University of; La Verne, Calif 91750	1,489 (C)	P	11,165	11,165	4,835
Lawrence Technological University; Southfield, Mich. 48075	4,886 (C)	P	6,570	6,570	4,138
Lawrence University; Appleton, Wis. 54912	1,202 (C)	P	16,341	16,341	3,555
Lebanon Valley College; Annville, Pa. 17003	1,369 (C)	P	13,325	13,325	4,600
Lee College; Cleveland, Tenn. 37311	1,922 (C)	P	4,560	4,560	3,160
Lee College at the University of Judaism; Los Angeles, Calif. 90077	89 (C)	P	8,790	8,790	5,850
Lees–McRae College; Banner Elk, N.C. 28604	n.a.	n.a.	n.a.	n.a.	n.a.
Lehigh University; Bethlehem, Pa. 18015	4,493 (C)	P	16,700	16,700	5,240
Le Moyne College; Syracuse, N.Y. 13214-1399	2,403 (C)	P	10,605	10,605	4,540
Le Moyne-Owen College; Memphis, Tenn. 38126	1,018 (C)	P	4,200	4,200	3,600
Lenoir-Rhyne College; Hickory, N.C. 28603	1,422 (C)	P	10,220	10,220	3,848
Lesley College; Cambridge, Mass. 02138-2790	575 (W)	P	11,150	11,150	5,125
LeTourneau University; Longview, Tex. 75607	858 (C)	P	7,940	7,940	3,860
Lewis and Clark College; Portland, Ore. 97219	1,767 (C)	P	15,051	15,051	4,929
Lewis Clark State College; Lewiston, Idaho 83501	2,316 (C)	Pub	1,118	3,216	2,700
Lewis University; Romeoville, Ill. 60441	3,378 (C)	P	10,112	10,112	4,450
Liberty University; Lynchburg, Va. 24506	3,603 (C)	P	6,600	6,600	4,380
L.I.F.E. Bible College; San Dimas, Calif. 91773–3298	370 (C)	P	4,140	4,140	3,150
L.I.F.E. Bible College East; Christiansburg, V.A. 24073	105 (C)	P	2,560	2,560	2,240
Lifelong Learning, School for; Durham, N.H. 03824–3545	1,686 (C)	Pub	2,574	2,814	n.a.
Limestone College, Gaffney, S.C. 29340	283 (C)	P	7,100	7,100	3,500
Lincoln Christian College; Lincoln, Ill. 62656	327 (C)	P	3,965	3,965	2,470
Lincoln Memorial University; Harrogate, Tenn. 37752	1,610 (C)	P	5,530	5,530	2,688
Lincoln University; San Francisco, Calif. 94118	194 (C)	P	3,360	3,360	n.a.
Lincoln University; Jefferson City, Mo. 65101	4,031 (C)	Pub	1,632	3,264	2,728
Lincoln University; Lincoln University, Pa. 19352	1,279 (C)	Pub	2,960	4,380	2,800
Lindenwood College; St. Charles, Mo. 63301–4949	2,143 (C)	P	8,880	8,880	4,680
Lindsey Wilson College; Columbia, Ky. 42728	1,327 (C)	P	5,552	5,552	3,280
Linfield College; McMinnville, Ore. 97128	1,528 (C)	P	12,510	12,510	3,970
Livingstone College; Salisbury, N.C. 28144	683 (C)	P	5,200	5,200	3,400
Livingston University; Livingston, Ala. 35470	1,823 (C)	Pub	1,809	1,809	2,205
Lock Haven University of Pennsylvania; Lock Haven, Pa. 17745	3,878 (C)	Pub	3,260	6,654	3,524
Long Island University:					
Brooklyn Campus; Brooklyn, N.Y. 11201	4,193 (C)	P	9,600	9,600	8,250
C.W. Post Campus; Greenvale, N.Y. 11548	4,799 (C)	P	10,810	10,810	5,060
Friends World Program–Southampton Campus; Southampton, N.Y. 11968	140 (C)	P	10,850	10,850	5,480
Southampton Campus; Southampton, N.Y. 11968	1,294 (C)	P	11,600	11,600	5,792
Longwood College; Farmville, Va. 23909	2,915 (C)	Pub	3,664	7,990	3,586
Loras College; Dubuque, Iowa 52001	1,807 (C)	P	9,900	9,900	3,470
Louisiana College; Pineville, La. 71359	1,026 (C)	P	4,870	4,870	2,944
Louisiana State Univ. and A&M Coll.; Baton Rouge, La. 70803	21,243 (C)	Pub	2,173	5,473	2,900
Louisiana State University Medical Center; New Orleans, La. 70112–2223	n.a.	n.a.	n.a.	n.a.	n.a.
Louisiana State University-Shreveport; Shreveport, La. 71115	4,017 (C)	Pub	1,820	4,460	n.a.
Louisiana Tech University; Ruston, La. 71272	9,283 (C)	Pub	1,871	3,026	2,115
Louisville, University of; Louisville, Ky, 40292	18,078 (C)	Pub	1,880	5,720	3,000
Lourdes College; Sylvania, Ohio 43560	1,242 (C)	P	4,928	4,928	n.a.
Loyola College; Baltimore, Md. 21210	3,330 (C)	P	11,100	11,100	5,580
Loyola Marymount University; Los Angeles, Calif. 90045	4,047 (C)	P	12,182	12,182	5,930
Loyola University; New Orleans, La. 70118	3,514 (C)	P	10,400	10,400	5,000
Loyola University of Chicago; Chicago, Ill. 60611	5,757 (C)	P	9,900	9,900	5,154
Lubbock Christian University; Lubbock, Tex. 79407	1,147 (C)	P	6,800	6,800	2,800
Lutheran Bible Institute of Seattle; Issaquah, Wash. 98027	164 (C)	P	2,470	2,470	3,400
Lutheran College of Health Professions; Fort Wayne, Ind. 46807–1698	n.a.	n.a.	n.a.	n.a.	n.a.
Luther College; Decorah, Iowa 52101	2,327 (C)	P	12,375	12,375	3,525
Lycoming College; Williamsport, Pa. 17701	1,478 (C)	P	13,000	13,000	4,200
Lynchburg College; Lynchburg, Va. 24501	1,905 (C)	P	10,900	10,900	5,250
Lyndon State College; Lyndonville, Vt. 05851	1,201 (C)	Pub	3,802	7,714	4,462
Lynn University; Boca Raton, Fla. 33431	1,025 (C)	P	12,900	12,900	5,100
Macalester College; St. Paul, Minn. 55105	1,735 (C)	P	14,105	14,105	4,208
MacMurray College; Jacksonville, Ill. 62650	691 (C)	P	9,160	9,160	3,640
Madonna University; Livonia, Mich. 48150	4,055 (C)	P	4,410	4,410	3,462
Maharishi International University; Fairfield, Iowa 52557-1155	1,968 (C)	P	7,890	7,890	2,760
Maine, Univ. of, at Augusta; Augusta, Me. 04330	4,972 (C)	Pub	2,460	6,000	n.a.
Maine, Univ. of, at Farmington; Farmington, Me. 04938	2,267 (C)	Pub	2,460	6,000	3,790
Maine, Univ. of, at Fort Kent; Fort Kent, Me. 04743-1292	641 (C)	Pub	2,460	3,690	3,545
Maine, Univ. of, at Machias; Machias, Me. 04654	958 (C)	Pub	2,,460	6,000	3,410
Maine, Univ. of, at Orono; Orono, Me. 04469	10,728 (C)	Pub	3,086	7,976	4,362
Maine, Univ. of, at Presque Isle; Presque Isle, Me. 04769	1,511 (C)	Pub	2,460	6,000	3,396
Maine Maritime Academy—The Ocean College; Castine, Me. 04420	640 (C)	Pub	3,750	6,695	4,396
Malone College; Canton, Ohio 44709	1,515 (C)	P	8,490	8,490	3,150

Institution and location	Enrollment	Control	Tuition ($) Res.	Tuition ($) Nonres.	Rm/Bd ($)
Manchester College; North Manchester, Ind. 46962	1,113 (C)	P	8,960	8,960	3,440
Manhattan Christian College; Manhattan, Kan. 66502	259 (C)	P	3,980	3,980	2,670
Manhattan College; Riverdale, N.Y. 10471	2,762 (C)	P	11,800	11,800	6,250
Manhattan School of Music; New York, N.Y. 10027	456 (C)	P	12,000	12,000	6,100
Manhattanville College; Purchase, N.Y. 10577	980 (C)	P	13,435	13,435	6,200
Mankato State University; Mankato, Minn. 56001	12,338 (C)	Pub	2,321	4,310	2,640
Mannes College of Music; New York, N.Y. 10024	104 (C)	P	11,000	11,000	6,600
Mansfield University of Pennsylvania; Mansfield, Pa. 16933	3,223 (C)	Pub	3,474	6,461	2,988
Marian College; Indianapolis, Ind. 46222	1,233 (C)	P	8,484	8,484	3,412
Marian College of Fond du Lac; Fond du Lac, Wis. 54935	1,342 (C)	P	8,120	8,120	3,300
Marietta College; Marietta, Ohio 45750	1,231 (C)	P	12,370	12,370	3,620
Marist College; Poughkeepsie, N.Y. 12601	2,950 (C)	P	9,980	9,980	5,540
Marlboro College; Marlboro, Vt. 05344	252 (C)	P	17,175	17,175	5,680
Marquette University; Milwaukee, Wis. 53233	8,409 (C)	P	9,900	9,900	4,350
Marshall University; Huntington, W. Va. 25755	10,341 (C)	Pub	1,792	4,678	4,000
Mars Hill College; Mars Hill, N.C. 28754	1,323 (C)	P	7,000	7,000	3,550
Martin University; Indianapolis, Ind. 46218	510 (C)	P	6,000	6,000	n.a.
Mary, University of; Bismarck, N.D. 58504	1,700 (C)	P	6,340	6,340	2,570
Mary Baldwin College; Staunton, Va. 24401	800 (W)	P	10,654	10,654	7,046
Marygrove College; Detroit, Mich. 48221	1,139 (C)	P	7,106	7,106	3,706
Mary Hardin-Baylor, University of; Belton, Tex. 76513	1,833 (C)	P	4,950	4,950	2,780
Maryland, Univ. of–Baltimore; Baltimore, Md. 21201	n.a.	n.a.	n.a.	n.a.	n.a.
Maryland, Univ. of-Baltimore County; Baltimore, Md. 21228	9,084 (C)	Pub	2,910	8,228	4,173
Maryland, Univ. of-College Park; College Park, Md. 20742	23,630 (C)	Pub	3,179	8,783	5,003
Maryland, Univ. of-Eastern Shore; Princess Anne, Md. 21853	2,266 (C)	Pub	2,450	6,739	4,173
Maryland, Univ. of, University College; College Park, Md. 20742	11,266 (C)	Pub	4,350	4,650	n.a.
Maryland Institute-College of Art; Baltimore, Md. 21217	850 (C)	P	11,450	11,450	3,700
Marylhurst College; Marylhurst, Ore. 97036	1,048 (C)	P	7,605	7,605	n.a.
Marymount College; Tarrytown, N.Y. 10591	1,115 (W)	P	11,150	11,150	6,200
Marymount Manhattan College; New York, N.Y. 10021	1,406 (W)	P	9,820	9,820	4,500
Marymount Univ.; Arlington, Va. 22207	2,132 (C)	P	10,804	10,804	5,126
Maryville College; Maryville, Tenn. 37801	855 (C)	P	9,580	9,580	3,865
Maryville University-St. Louis; St. Louis, Mo. 63141	3,038 (C)	P	8,700	8,700	4,200
Mary Washington College; Fredericksburg, Va. 22401	3,426 (C)	Pub	2,896	6,752	4,552
Marywood College; Scranton, Pa. 18509	1,858 (C)	P	9,600	9,600	4,200
Massachusetts, Univ. of-Amherst; Amherst, Mass. 01003	17,212 (C)	Pub	5,062	11,165	3,693
Massachusetts, Univ. of-Boston; Boston, Mass. 02125-3393	9,509 (C)	Pub	4,052	8,237	n.a.
Massachusetts, Univ. of-Dartmouth; North Dartmouth, Mass. 02747	4,884 (C)	Pub	3,163	8,049	4,400
Massachusetts, Univ. of–Lowell; Lowell, Mass. 01854	11,325 (C)	Pub	4,513	9,424	4,223
Massachusetts College of Art; Boston, Mass. 02115	1,080 (C)	Pub	3,789	8,529	5,287
Massachusetts College of Pharmacy and Allied Health Sciences; Boston, Mass. 02115	785 (C)	P	10,276	10,276	6,255
Massachusetts Institute of Technology; Cambridge, Mass. 02139	4,389 (C)	P	18,000	18,000	6,000
Massachusetts Maritime Academy; Buzzards Bay, Mass. 02532	686 (C)	Pub	3,203	7,943	3,610
Master's College, The; Newhall, Calif. 91322	819 (C)	P	8,134	8,134	4,472
Mayville State University; Mayville, N.D. 58257	764 (C)	Pub	1,755	4,305	1,954
McKendree College; Lebanon, Ill. 62258	1,450 (C)	P	7,460	7,460	3,440
McMurry College; Abilene, Tex. 79697	1,497 (C)	P	6,255	6,255	3,130
McNeese State University; Lake Charles, La. 70609	7,316 (C)	Pub	1,934	3,484	2,310
McPherson College; McPherson, Kan. 67460	462 (C)	P	7,500	7,500	3,420
Medaille College; Buffalo, N.Y. 14214	1,215 (C)	P	7,950	7,950	n.a.
Medcenter One College of Nursing; Bismarck, N.D. 58501	96 (C)	Pub	2,031	5,613	2,664
Medical College of Georgia; Augusta, Ga. 30912	885 (C)	Pub	2,031	5,613	2,644
Medical University of South Carolina; Charleston, S.C. 29425	995 (C)	Pub	2,120	5,300	3,300
Medicine and Dentistry of New Jersey, Univ. of–School of Health Related Professions; Newark, N.J. 07107–3006	n.a.	n.a.	n.a.	n.a.	n.a.
Memphis College of Art; Memphis, Tenn. 38112	236 (C)	P	8,950	8,950	4,100
Memphis State University; Memphis, Tenn. 38152	15,767 (C)	Pub	1,652	5,254	3,174
Menlo College; Atherton, Calif. 94027-4185	490 (C)	P	13,310	13,310	6,030
Mennonite College of Nursing; Bloomington, Ill. 61701	n.a.	n.a.	n.a.	n.a.	n.a.
Mercer University; Macon, Ga. 31207	2,255 (C)	P	9,450	9,450	3,780
Mercy College; Dobbs Ferry, N.Y. 10522	5,283 (C)	P	7,200	7,200	n.a.
Mercyhurst College; Erie, Pa. 16546	2,259 (C)	P	9,823	9,823	3,600
Meredith College; Raleigh, N.C. 27607-5298	2,100 (W)	P	6,340	6,340	3,100
Merrimack College; North Andover, Mass. 01845	2,952 (C)	P	11,000	11,000	6,100
Mesa State College; Grand Junction, Colo. 81502	4,600 (C)	Pub	1,620	4,442	3,257
Messiah College; Grantham, Pa. 17027	2,259 (C)	P	9,070	9,070	4,550
Methodist College; Fayettesville, N.C. 28311-1499	1,508 (C)	P	8,850	8,850	3,550
Metropolitan State College of Denver; Denver, Colo. 80204	17,818 (C)	Pub	1,709	5,669	n.a.
Metropolitan State University; St. Paul, Minn. 55101	5,444 (C)	Pub	2,086	4,075	n.a.
Miami, University of; Coral Gables, Fla. 33124	8,584 (C)	P	15,880	15,880	6,227
Miami Christian College; Miami, Fla. 33101–9674	341 (C)	P	5,990	5,990	3,120
Miami University; Oxford, Ohio 45056	14,374 (C)	Pub	4,096	8,686	3,620

Institution and location	Enrollment	Control	Tuition ($) Res.	Tuition ($) Nonres.	Rm/Bd ($)
Michigan, Univ. of-Ann Arbor; Ann Arbor, Mich. 48109	23,121 (C)	Pub	4,365	14,069	4,478
Michigan, Univ. of-Dearborn; Dearborn, Mich. 48128	7,111 (C)	Pub	2,886	9,354	n.a.
Michigan, Univ. of-Flint; Flint, Mich. 48502	6,168 (C)	Pub	2,700	8,900	n.a.
Michigan Christian College; Rochester Hills, Mich. 48307	319 (C)	P	4,800	4,800	2,800
Michigan State University; East Lansing, Mich. 48824	31,176 (C)	Pub	3,876	9,648	3,568
Michigan Technological University; Houghton, Mich. 49931	6,360 (C)	Pub	3,249	7,326	3,604
Mid-America Bible College; Oklahoma City, Okla. 73170	290 (C)	P	3,912	3,912	2,596
Mid-America Nazarene College; Olathe, Kan. 66061	1,324 (C)	P	6,270	6,270	3,542
Middlebury College; Middlebury, Vt. 05753–6002	1,950 (C)	P	24,400	24,400	—
Middle Tennessee State University; Murfreesboro, Tenn. 37132	12,744 (C)	Pub	1,580	5,182	2,102
Midland Lutheran College; Fremont, Neb. 68025	962 (C)	P	9,550	9,550	2,860
Midway College; Midway, Ky. 40347	718 (W)	P	6,140	6,140	3,700
Midwestern State University; Wichita Falls, Tex. 76308	5,056 (C)	Pub	1,030	3,352	3,026
Miles College; Birmingham, Ala. 35208	566 (C)	P	3,760	3,760	2,300
Millersville University of Pennsylvania; Millersville, Pa. 17551-0302	6,950 (C)	Pub	3,488	6,982	3,450
Milligan College; Milligan College, Tenn. 37682	696 (C)	P	7,020	7,020	3,136
Millikin University; Decatur, Ill. 62522	1,892 (C)	P	11,240	11,240	4,168
Millsaps College; Jackson, Miss. 39210	1,280 (C)	P	10,280	10,280	6,100
Mills College; Oakland, Calif. 94613	772 (W)	P	15,600	15,600	6,000
Milwaukee Institute of Art and Design; Milwaukee, Wis. 53202	487 (C)	P	8,360	8,360	n.a.
Milwaukee School of Engineering; Milwaukee, Wis. 53201-0644	2,772 (C)	P	10,800	10,800	3,180
Minneapolis Coll. of Art and Design; Minneapolis, Minn. 55404	585 (C)	P	11,050	11,050	3,400
Minnesota, Univ. of-Duluth; Duluth, Minn. 55812	7,347 (C)	Pub	3,047	8,613	3,213
Minnesota, Univ. of-Morris; Morris, Minn. 56267	1,915 (C)	Pub	3,223	10,000	3,030
Minnesota, Univ. of-Twin Cities; Minneapolis, Minn. 55455-0213	27,106 (C)	Pub	3,242	8,811	3,477
Minnesota Bible College; Rochester, Minn. 55902	120 (C)	P	4,500	4,500	3,385
Minot State University; Minot, N.D. 58707	3,246 (C)	Pub	1,710	4,260	1,912
Mississippi, University of; University, Miss. 38677	8,471 (C)	Pub	2,435	4,394	2,830
Mississippi, Univ. of, Medical Center; Jackson, Miss. 39216	472 (C)	Pub	6,710	12,710	n.a.
Mississippi College; Clinton, Miss. 39058	2,078 (C)	P	5,500	5,500	2,620
Mississippi State University; Mississippi State, Miss. 39762	11,471 (C)	Pub	2,474	4,432	3,200
Mississippi University for Women; Columbus, Miss. 39701	2,491 (C)	Pub	2,239	4,199	2,217
Mississippi Valley State University; Itta Bena, Miss. 38941	2,207 (C)	Pub	1,978	3,440	2,025
Missouri, Univ. of-Columbia; Columbia, Mo. 65211	17,386 (C)	Pub	2,934	8,010	3,320
Missouri, Univ. of-Kansas City; Kansas City, Mo. 64110	5,896 (C)	Pub	3,152	8,582	3,574
Missouri, Univ. of-Rolla; Rolla, Mo. 65401	4,126 (C)	Pub	3,000	7,500	3,500
Missouri, Univ. of-St. Louis; St. Louis, Mo. 63121	9,339 (C)	Pub	2,500	6,851	3,964
Missouri Baptist College; St. Louis, Mo. 63141	1,429 (C)	P	6,200	6,200	2,800
Missouri Southern State College; Joplin, Mo. 64801	5,640 (C)	Pub	1,754	3,082	2,996
Missouri Valley College; Marshall, Mo. 65340	1,153 (C)	P	8,650	8,650	4,950
Missouri Western State College; St. Joseph, Mo. 64507	5,093 (C)	Pub	1,822	3,460	2,328
Mobile College; Mobile, Ala. 36613	1,032 (C)	P	5,010	5,010	2,920
Molloy College; Rockville Centre, N.Y. 11570	2,481 (C)	P	8,400	8,400	n.a.
Monmouth College; Monmouth, Ill. 61462	724 (C)	P	12,950	12,950	3,580
Monmouth College; West Long Branch, N.J. 07764	2,826 (C)	P	11,160	11,160	4,840
Montana, University of; Missoula, Mont. 59812	8,576 (C)	Pub	1,900	5,600	3,600
Montana College of Mineral Science and Technology; Butte, Mont. 59701	1,871 (C)	Pub	1,697	5,421	3,210
Montana State University; Bozeman, Mont. 59717	9,697 (C)	Pub	2,302	6,026	3,462
Montclair State College; Upper Montclair, N.J. 07043-1624	10,349 (C)	Pub	2,720	3,840	4,368
Monterey Institute of Intl. Studies; Monterey, Calif. 93940	108 (C)	P	12,545	12,545	n.a.
Montevallo, University of; Montevallo, Ala. 35115	2,648 (C)	Pub	2,100	4,140	2,934
Montreat-Anderson College; Montreat, N.C. 28757	318 (C)	P	7,600	7,600	3,372
Montserrat College of Art; Beverly, Mass. 01915	220 (C)	P	7,800	7,800	n.a.
Moody Bible Institute; Chicago, Ill. 60610	1,422 (C)	P	754	754	4,060
Moore College of Art and Design; Philadelphia, Pa. 19103	440 (W)	P	13,476	13,476	4,864
Moorhead State University; Moorhead, Minn. 56560	8,214 (C)	Pub	2,299	4,289	2,644
Moravian College; Bethlehem, Pa. 18018	1,174 (C)	P	14,460	14,460	4,470
Morehead State University; Morehead, Ky. 40351	7,532 (C)	Pub	1,520	4,200	2,800
Morehouse College; Atlanta, Ga. 30314	2,992 (M)	P	7,430	7,430	4,980
Morgan State University; Baltimore, Md. 21239	5,200 (C)	Pub	2,438	4,780	4,640
Morningside College; Sioux City, Iowa 51106	1,169 (C)	P	10,376	10,376	3,520
Morris Brown College; Atlanta, Ga. 30314	2,000 (C)	P	6,550	6,550	3,800
Morris College; Sumter, S.C. 29150	792 (C)	P	4,136	4,136	2,434
Morrison College/Reno Business College; Reno, Nev. 89503	400 (C)	P	9,600	9,600	n.a.
Mount Aloysius College; Cresson, Pa. 16630	1,066 (C)	P	6,790	6,790	3,160
Mount Holyoke College; South Hadley, Mass. 01075	1,975 (W)	P	16,970	16,970	4,980
Mount Ida College; Newton Centre, Mass. 02159	2,100 (C)	P	9,510	9,510	6,540
Mount Marty College; Yankton, S.D. 57078	1,050 (C)	P	7,470	7,470	2,980
Mount Mary College; Milwaukee, Wis. 53222	1,526 (W)	P	8,100	8,100	2,898
Mount Mercy College; Cedar Rapids, Iowa 52402	1,392 (C)	P	9,880	9,880	3,800
Mount Olive College; Mount Olive, N.C. 28365	806 (C)	P	7,100	7,100	2,550
Mount St. Joseph, College of; Mount St. Joseph, Ohio 45233-9314	2,420 (C)	P	8,740	8,740	4,080
Mount Saint Mary College; Newburgh, N.Y. 12550	1,329 (C)	P	7,470	7,470	4,600

Institution and location	Enrollment	Control	Tuition ($) Res.	Tuition ($) Nonres.	Rm/Bd ($)
Mount Saint Mary's College; Emmitsburg, Md. 21727	1,340 (C)	P	11,725	11,725	6,100
Mount St. Clare College; Clinton, Iowa 52732	411 (C)	P	8,400	8,400	3,400
Mount St. Mary's College; Los Angeles, Calif. 90049	1,156 (W)	P	10,830	10,830	4,500
Mount Saint Vincent, College of; New York, N.Y. 10471	1,045 (C)	P	10,400	10,400	5,250
Mount Senario College; Ladysmith, Wis. 54848	672 (C)	P	7,600	7,600	3,250
Mount Union College; Alliance, Ohio 44601	1,410 (C)	P	12,320	12,320	3,530
Mount Vernon College; Washington, D.C. 20007	400 (W)	P	13,110	13,110	6,445
Mount Vernon Nazarene College; Mount Vernon, Ohio 43050	1,061 (C)	P	6,575	6,575	3,090
Muhlenberg College; Allentown, Pa. 18104	1,636 (C)	P	15,740	15,740	4,260
Multnomah School of the Bible; Portland, Ore. 97220	521 (C)	P	5,790	5,790	3,310
Murray State University; Murray, Ky. 42071	6,972 (C)	Pub	1,540	4,220	2,700
Museum of Fine Arts, School of the-Tufts University; Boston, Mass. 02115	690 (C)	P	12,395	12,395	n.a.
Museum Art School, Portland. *See* Pacific Northwest College of Art					
Muskingum College; New Concord, Ohio 43762	1,015 (C)	P	12,397	12,397	3,580
NAES College; Chicago, Ill. 60659	119 (C)	P	4,330	4,330	n.a.
Naropa Institute; Boulder, Colo. 80302	140 (C)	P	7,950	7,950	n.a.
Nathaniel Hawthorne College. *See* Hawthorne College					
National College; Rapid City, S.D. 57709	502 (C)	P	5,118	5,118	4,680
National College-Albuquerque; Albuquerque, N.M. 87110-7439	122 (C)	P	6,288	6,288	n.a.
National College, Colorado Springs Branch; Colorado Springs, Colo. 80909	280 (C)	P	4,716	4,716	n.a.
National-Louis University; Evanston, Ill. 60201	3,231 (C)	P	8,550	8,550	4,489
National University; San Diego, Calif. 92108–4194	7,121 (C)	P	5,820	5,820	n.a.
Nazarene Bible College; Colorado Springs, Colo. 80935	404 (C)	P	3,160	3,160	n.a.
Nazareth College of Rochester; Rochester, N.Y. 14610	1,303 (C)	P	10,140	10,140	4,900
Nebraska, University of–Kearney; Kearney, Neb. 68849	7,120 (C)	Pub	1,720	2,770	2,380
Nebraska, University of-Lincoln; Lincoln, Neb. 68588-0415	19,746 (C)	Pub	2,187	5,367	2,915
Nebraska, University of–Medical Center; Omaha, Neb. 68198–4230	1,098 (C)	Pub	2,833	5,633	n.a.
Nebraska, University of-Omaha; Omaha, Neb. 68182	14,352 (C)	Pub	1,805	4,677	n.a.
Nebraska Christian College; Norfolk, Neb. 68701	134 (C)	P	3,610	3,610	2,440
Nebraska Methodist College of Nursing and Allied Health; Omaha, Neb. 68114	134 (C)	P	3,610	3,610	2,440
Nebraska Wesleyan University; Lincoln, Neb. 68504	1,694 (C)	P	8,894	8,894	3,200
Neumann College; Aston, Pa. 19014	1,187 (C)	P	9,166	9,166	n.a.
Nevada, University of-Las Vegas; Las Vegas, Nev. 89154	16,812 (C)	Pub	1,665	5,715	4,780
Nevada, University of-Reno; Reno, Nev. 89557	11,909 (C)	Pub	1,665	5,965	4,070
Newberry College; Newberry, S.C. 29108	701 (C)	P	7,900	7,900	3,100
Newbury College; Brookline, Mass. 02146	n.a.	n.a.	n.a.	n.a.	n.a.
New College of California; San Francisco, Calif. 94110	180 (C)	P	6,200	6,200	n.a.
New College of the University of South Florida; Sarasota, Fla. 34243-2197	504 (C)	Pub	1,855	7,567	3,612
New England, University of; Biddeford, Me. 04005	801 (C)	P	10,600	10,600	4,750
New England College; Henniker, N.H. 03242	1,000 (C)	P	12,070	12,070	4,970
New England College-Arundel Campus; England	220 (C)	P	12,070	12,070	4,970
New England Conservatory of Music; Boston, Mass. 02115	358 (C)	P	13,600	13,600	6,600
New England Institute of Technology; Warwick, R.I. 02886	1,950 (C)	P	8,325	8,325	n.a.
New Hampshire, University of; Durham, N.H. 03824	10,704 (C)	Pub	3,941	11,001	3,728
New Hampshire, Univ. of at Manchester; Manchester, N.H. 03102	543 (C)	Pub	2,703	7,423	n.a.
New Hampshire College; Manchester, N.H. 03104	1,897 (C)	P	9,948	9,948	4,635
New Haven, University of; West Haven, Conn. 06516	3,404 (C)	P	10,160	10,160	4,800
New Jersey Institute of Technology; Newark, N.J. 07102–9938	5,063 (C)	Pub	4,524	8,642	4,980
New Mexico, University of; Albuquerque, N.M. 87131	19,937 (C)	Pub	1,656	5,880	3,279
New Mexico Highlands University; Las Vegas, N.M. 87701	2,003 (C)	Pub	1,344	4,920	2,380
New Mexico Inst. of Mining & Technology; Socorro, N.M. 87801	1,264 (C)	Pub	1,666	5,084	3,406
New Mexico State University; Las Cruces, N.M. 88003-0001	12,957 (C)	Pub	1,756	5,686	2,818
New Orleans, University of; New Orleans, La. 70148	12,435 (C)	Pub	1,924	4,616	2,972
New Rochelle, College of-School of Arts & Sciences and School of Nursing; New Rochelle, N.Y. 10805	881 (W)	P	10,200	10,200	4,620
New Rochelle, College of–School of New Resources; New Rochelle, N.Y. 10805–2308	3,248 (C)	P	4,800	4,800	n.a.
New School for Social Research Eugene Lang College; New York, N.Y. 10011	350 (C)	P	12,790	12,790	7,614
New York, City University of; New York, N.Y. 10021:					
Baruch College; New York, N.Y. 10010	12,730 (C)	Pub	2,507	5,107	n.a.
Brooklyn College; Brooklyn, N.Y. 11210	11,326 (C)	Pub	2,005	4,605	n.a.
City College; New York, N.Y. 10031	11,541 (C)	Pub	2,297	5,097	n.a.
College of Staten Island; Staten Island, N.Y. 10301	11,000 (C)	Pub	2,556	5,156	n.a.
Hunter College; New York, N.Y. 10021	14,077 (C)	Pub	1,450	5,050	3,400
John Jay College of Criminal Justice; New York, N.Y. 10019	7,918 (C)	Pub	1,950	4,550	5,050
Lehman College; Bronx, N.Y. 10468	8,517 (C)	Pub	2,562	5,162	n.a.
Medgar Evers College; Brooklyn, N.Y. 11225–2201	2,823 (C)	Pub	2,154	2,714	n.a.
New York City Technical College; Brooklyn, N.Y. 11201–2983	10,323 (C)	Pub	2,498	4,898	n.a.
Queens College; Flushing, N.Y. 11367	14,478 (C)	Pub	2,635	2,635	n.a.
York College; Jamaica, N.Y. 11451	5,455 (C)	Pub	2,534	5,135	n.a.

Institution and location	Enrollment	Control	Tuition ($) Res.	Tuition ($) Nonres.	Rm/Bd ($)
New York, State University of; Albany, N.Y. 12246:					
SUNY-Albany; Albany, N.Y. 12222	11,870 (C)	Pub	2,883	6,783	3,860
SUNY-Binghamton; Binghamton, N.Y. 13901	8,928 (C)	Pub	2,957	6,857	4,760
SUNY-Buffalo; Buffalo, N.Y. 14214	16,785 (C)	Pub	3,100	7,000	4,578
SUNY-College at Brockport; Brockport, N.Y. 14420	7,490 (C)	Pub	2,915	6,765	4,060
SUNY-College at Buffalo; Buffalo, N.Y. 14222	10,204 (C)	Pub	2,835	6,735	3,680
SUNY-College at Cortland; Cortland, N.Y. 13045	3,467 (C)	Pub	2,950	6,850	4,070
SUNY-College at Fredonia; Fredonia, N.Y. 14063	4,428 (C)	Pub	2,926	6,826	3,880
SUNY-College at Geneseo; Geneseo, N.Y. 14454-1471	4,956 (C)	Pub	2,955	6,855	3,554
SUNY-College at New Paltz; New Paltz, N.Y. 12561–2499	4,874 (C)	Pub	2,921	6,821	4,240
SUNY-College at Old Westbury; Old Westbury, N.Y. 11568	3,999 (C)	Pub	2,898	6,798	4,120
SUNY-College at Oneonta; Oneonta, N.Y. 13820	5,283 (C)	Pub	2,896	6,500	4,400
SUNY-College at Oswego; Oswego, N.Y. 13126	7,473 (C)	Pub	2,650	6,550	4,230
SUNY-College at Plattsburgh; Plattsburgh, N.Y. 12901	5,530 (C)	Pub	3,045	6,945	3,692
SUNY-College at Potsdam; Potsdam, N.Y. 13676	3,946 (C)	Pub	2,650	6,550	4,510
SUNY-College of Agriculture and Life Sciences at Cornell University; Ithaca, N.Y. 14853	3,098 (C)	Pub	7,056	13,306	5,676
SUNY-College of Environmental Science and Forestry; Syracuse, N.Y. 13210	1,202 (C)	Pub	2,937	6,837	5,920
SUNY-College of Human Ecology at Cornell University; Ithaca, N.Y. 14853	1,279 (C)	Pub	7,056	13,306	5,676
SUNY–College of Technology at Alfred; Alfred, N.Y. 14802–1196	n.a.	n.a.	n.a.	n.a.	n.a.
SUNY-College of Technology-Farmingdale; Farmingdale, N.Y. 11735	8,800 (C)	Pub	2,925	6,825	4,600
SUNY-Empire State College; Saratoga Springs, N.Y. 12866	7,072 (C)	Pub	2,917	6,817	n.a.
SUNY-Fashion Institute of Technology; New York, N.Y. 10001-5992	4,443 (C)	Pub	2,240	4,890	4,600
SUNY–Health Science Center at Stony Brook; Stony Brook, N.Y. 11794–8276	n.a.	n.a.	n.a.	n.a.	n.a.
SUNY-Health Science Center at Syracuse; Syracuse, N.Y. 13210	380 (C)	Pub	2,865	5,975	4,200
SUNY-Institute of Technology at Utica/Rome; Utica, N.Y. 13054-3050	2,271 (C)	Pub	2,735	6,375	4,560
SUNY-Maritime College; Throggs Neck, N.Y. 10465	631 (C)	Pub	2,650	6,556	4,345
SUNY-Purchase; Purchase, N.Y. 10577	4,456 (C)	Pub	2,650	6,550	4,250
SUNY-School of Industrial and Labor Relations at Cornell University; Ithaca, N.Y. 14853	628 (C)	Pub	7,056	13,306	5,676
SUNY-Stony Brook; Stony Brook, N.Y. 11794	11,513 (C)	Pub	2,818	6,718	4,403
New York, University of the State of, Regents College Degrees; Albany, N.Y. 12203	12,668 (C)	P	480	480	n.a.
New York City Technical Coll. *See* New York, City Univ. of					
New York Institute of Technology; Old Westbury, N.Y. 11568	6,428 (C)	P	8,140	8,140	n.a.
New York Institute of Technology Central Islip Campus; Central Islip, N.Y. 11722	1,616 (C)	P	8,140	8,140	6,845
New York Institute of Technology, Metropolitan Center; New York, N.Y. 10023	2,841 (C)	P	8,140	8,140	n.a.
New York School of Interior Design; New York, N.Y. 10022	613 (C)	P	10,560	10,560	n.a.
New York University; New York, N.Y. 10011	15,092 (C)	P	16,650	16,650	6,680
Niagara University; Niagara University, N.Y. 14109	2,386 (C)	P	9,150	9,150	4,600
Nicholls State University; Thibodaux, La. 70310	6,775 (C)	Pub	1,861	3,661	2,550
Nichols College; Dudley, Mass. 01570	722 (C)	P	8,940	8,940	5,160
Norfolk State University; Norfolk, Va. 23504	7,728 (C)	Pub	2,530	5,760	3,400
North Adams State College; North Adams, Mass. 01247	1,694 (C)	Pub	3,430	7,294	4,051
North Alabama, University of; Florence, Ala. 35632	5,006 (C)	Pub	1,620	1,914	4,000
North Carolina, Univ. of-Asheville; Asheville, N.C. 28804	3,226 (C)	Pub	1,190	6,208	3,120
North Carolina, Univ. of-Chapel Hill; Chapel Hill, N.C. 27599-2200	15,295 (C)	Pub	1,296	7,880	3,950
North Carolina, Univ. of-Charlotte; Charlotte, N.C. 28223	13,087 (C)	Pub	1,191	6,863	2,842
North Carolina, Univ. of-Greensboro; Greensboro, N.C. 27412	9,337 (C)	Pub	1,540	8,124	3,475
North Carolina, Univ. of-Wilmington; Wilmington, N.C. 28403	7,486 (C)	Pub	1,344	7,016	3,570
North Carolina Agricultural and Technical State University; Greensboro, N.C. 27411	6,693 (C)	Pub	1,270	6,942	2,960
North Carolina Central University; Durham, N.C. 27707	4,070 (C)	Pub	1,315	6,999	2,915
North Carolina School of the Arts; Winston-Salem, N.C. 27127-2189	414 (C)	Pub	1,800	8,259	3,163
North Carolina State University-Raleigh; Raleigh, N.C. 27695-7103	22,483 (C)	Pub	1,344	7,928	3,200
North Carolina Wesleyan College; Rocky Mount, N.C. 27801	724 (C)	P	7,640	7,640	3,790
North Central Bible College; Minneapolis, Minn. 55404	1,103 (C)	P	5,415	5,415	3,080
North Central College; Naperville, Ill. 60566-7063	2,122 (C)	P	11,241	11,241	3,939
North Dakota, University of; Grand Forks, N.D. 58202	10,027 (C)	Pub	2,166	5,754	2,500
North Dakota State University; Fargo, N.D. 58105	9,269 (C)	Pub	1,946	5,197	2,397
Northeastern Illinois University, Chicago, Ill. 60625	7,866 (C)	Pub	2,310	6,945	n.a.
Northeastern State Univ.; Tahlequah, Okla. 74464	9,008 (C)	Pub	1,360	3,550	2,280
Northeastern University; Boston, Mass. 02115	22,283 (C)	P	10,148	10,148	6,705
Northeast Louisiana University; Monroe, La. 71209	10,617 (C)	Pub	1,626	3,210	1,980
Northeast Missouri State University; Kirksville, Mo. 63501	5,742 (C)	Pub	2,235	3,939	2,864
Northern Arizona University; Flagstaff, Ariz. 86011	14,056 (C)	Pub	1,590	6,242	2,780

Institution and location	Enrollment	Control	Tuition ($) Res.	Tuition ($) Nonres.	Rm/Bd ($)
Northern Colorado, University of; Greeley, Colo. 80639	8,615 (C)	Pub	2,027	6,888	3,676
Northern Illinois University; De Kalb, Ill. 60115	17,437 (C)	Pub	3,025	7,381	2,956
Northern Iowa, University of; Cedar Falls, Iowa 50614	11,825 (C)	Pub	2,352	5,994	2,620
Northern Kentucky University; Highland Heights, Ky. 41099–7010	10,827 (C)	Pub	1,720	4,720	2,900
Northern Michigan University; Marquette, Mich. 49855	7,895 (C)	Pub	2,496	4,640	3,700
Northern Montana College; Havre, Mont. 59501	1,742 (C)	Pub	1,701	5,021	3,216
Northern State University; Aberdeen, S.D. 57401	2,869 (C)	Pub	2,000	3,540	2,000
North Florida, University of; Jacksonville, Fla. 32216	6,803 (C)	Pub	2,176	7,276	4,002
Northland College; Ashland, Wis. 54806	547 (C)	P	9,190	9,190	3,620
North Texas, University of; Denton, Tex. 76203	19,633 (C)	Pub	1,420	5,560	3,510
Northwest Christian College; Eugene, Ore. 97401	251 (C)	P	6,614	6,614	3,550
Northwest College; Kirkland, Wash. 98083-0579	687 (C)	P	6,646	6,646	3,250
Northwestern College; Orange City, Iowa 51041	1,038 (C)	P	9,300	9,300	2,950
Northwestern College; St. Paul, Minn. 55113	1,174 (C)	P	9,825	9,825	2,745
Northwestern College; Watertown, Wis. 53094	n.a.	n.a.	n.a.	n.a.	n.a.
Northwestern Oklahoma State University; Alva, Okla. 73717	2,065 (C)	Pub	1,411	3,467	1,864
Northwestern State Univ. of Louisiana; Natchitoches, La. 71497	7,626 (C)	Pub	1,801	3,601	2,320
Northwestern University; Evanston, Ill. 60201-3060	7,424 (C)	P	15,804	15,804	5,289
Northwest Missouri State University; Maryville, Mo. 64468	5,300 (C)	Pub	2,010	3,570	3,000
Northwest Nazarene College; Nampa, Idaho 83686	1,095 (C)	P	8,160	8,160	2,715
Northwood Institute of Florida; West Palm Beach, Fla. 33409	524 (C)	P	8,490	8,490	4,890
Northwood University; Cedar Hill, Tex. 75104	280 (C)	P	8,592	8,592	4,095
Northwood Institute of Michigan; Midland, Mich. 48640	1,701 (C)	P	8,620	8,620	4,065
Norwich University; Northfield, Vt. 05663	2,244 (C)	P	12,820	12,820	5,020
Notre Dame, College of, Belmont, Calif. 94002–1997	752 (C)	P	11,750	11,750	5,700
Notre Dame, University of; Notre Dame, Ind. 46556	7,600 (C)	P	14,850	14,850	3,900
Notre Dame College; Manchester, N.H. 03104	650 (C)	P	8,790	8,790	4,635
Notre Dame College of Ohio; Cleveland, Ohio 44121	789 (W)	P	7,400	7,400	3,690
Notre Dame of Maryland, College of; Baltimore, Md. 21210	645 (W)	P	10,650	10,650	5,400
Nova University; Ft. Lauderdale, Fla. 33314	3,401 (C)	P	7,630	7,630	3,850
Nyack College; Nyack, N.Y. 10960	513 (C)	P	8,010	8,010	3,600
Oakland City College; Oakland City, Ind. 47660	757 (C)	P	6,900	6,900	2,840
Oakland University; Rochester, Mich. 48063	10,551 (C)	Pub	2,600	7,400	3,560
Oakwood College; Huntsville, Ala. 35896	1,245 (C)	P	6,216	6,216	3,663
Oberlin College; Oberlin, Ohio 44074	2,827 (C)	P	17,723	17,723	5,370
Oblate College; Washington, D.C. 20017	8 (C)	P	4,050	4,050	n.a.
Occidental College; Los Angeles, Calif. 90041–3393	1,677 (C)	P	15,525	15,525	5,121
Oglala Lakota College; Kyle, S.D. 57752	800 (C)	Pub	1,720	1,720	n.a.
Oglethorpe University; Atlanta, Ga. 30319	1,147 (C)	P	11,150	11,150	4,200
Ohio Dominican College; Columbus, Ohio 43219	1,510 (C)	P	7,370	7,370	3,930
Ohio Northern University; Ada, Ohio 45810	2,436 (C)	P	14,775	14,775	3,885
Ohio State University–Columbus; Columbus, Ohio 43210	38,958 (C)	Pub	2,799	8,292	3,918
Ohio State University-Lima; Lima, Ohio 45804	1,261 (C)	Pub	2,700	8,193	n.a.
Ohio State University-Mansfield; Mansfield, Ohio 44906	1,327 (C)	Pub	2,700	8,193	n.a.
Ohio State University-Marion; Marion, Ohio 43302	1,011 (C)	Pub	2,700	8,193	n.a.
Ohio State University-Newark; Newark, Ohio 43055	1,626 (C)	Pub	2,700	8,193	n.a.
Ohio University; Athens, Ohio 45701	15,323 (C)	Pub	3,234	6,897	3,816
Ohio University-Chillicothe; Chillicothe, Ohio 45601-0629	1,738 (C)	Pub	2,613	6,276	n.a.
Ohio University-Lancaster; Lancaster, Ohio 43130	1,500 (C)	Pub	2,613	6,276	n.a.
Ohio University-Zanesville, Zanesville, Ohio 43701	1,190 (C)	Pub	2,628	6,291	n.a.
Ohio Valley College; Parkersburg, W.Va. 26101	231 (C)	P	4,800	4,800	3,334
Ohio Wesleyan University; Delaware, Ohio 43015	1,940 (C)	P	15,726	15,726	5,382
Oklahoma, University of-Health Sciences Center; Oklahoma City, Okla. 73190	1,183 (C)	Pub	1,620	5,003	n.a.
Oklahoma, University of-Norman; Norman, Okla. 73019	14,980 (C)	Pub	1,750	4,941	3,358
Oklahoma Baptist University; Shawnee, Okla. 74801	2,260 (C)	P	5,036	5,036	2,940
Oklahoma Christian University of Science and Arts; Oklahoma City, Okla. 73136-1100	1,636 (C)	P	5,080	5,080	2,840
Oklahoma City University; Oklahoma City, Okla. 73106	2,119 (C)	P	6,210	6,210	3,630
Oklahoma Panhandle State University; Goodwell, Okla. 73939	1,276 (C)	Pub	1,348	3,276	1,640
Oklahoma State University; Stillwater, Okla. 74078	14,786 (C)	Pub	1,767	4,958	3,070
Old Dominion University; Norfolk, Va. 23529-0050	11,624 (C)	Pub	3,514	8,644	4,134
Olivet College; Olivet, Mich. 49076	766 (C)	P	8,291	8,291	2,890
Olivet Nazarene University; Kankakee, Ill. 60901	1,566 (C)	P	7,048	7,048	3,825
O'More College of Design; Franklin, Tenn. 37604	147 (C)	P	6,250	6,250	n.a.
Oral Roberts University; Tulsa, Okla. 74171	3,250 (C)	P	6,900	6,900	3,300
Oregon, University of; Eugene, Ore. 97403	13,094 (C)	Pub	2,721	7,851	3,229
Oregon Health Sciences University; Portland, Ore. 97201	400 (C)	Pub	3,704	7,655	1,728
Oregon Institute of Technology; Klamath Falls, Ore. 97601	2,759 (C)	Pub	2,595	6,678	3,490
Oregon State University; Corvallis, Ore. 97331	12,070 (C)	Pub	2,691	6,972	3,306
Orlando College; Orlando, Fla. 32810	2,600 (C)	P	5,125	5,125	n.a.
Otis/Parsons School of Art and Design; Los Angeles, Calif. 90057	725 (C)	P	11,730	11,730	2,650

Institution and location	Enrollment	Control	Tuition ($) Res.	Tuition ($) Nonres.	Rm/Bd ($)
Ottawa University; Ottawa, Kan. 66067	545 (C)	P	7,245	7,245	2,900
Ottawa University-Phoenix Center; Phoenix, Ariz. 85021	825 (C)	P	3,360	3,360	n.a.
Otterbein College; Westerville, Ohio 43081	2,439 (C)	P	12,192	12,192	4,310
Ouachita Baptist University; Arkadelphia, Ark. 71998-0001	1,350 (C)	P	5,370	5,370	2,300
Our Lady of Holy Cross College; New Orleans, La. 70131-7399	1,033 (C)	P	4,500	4,500	n.a.
Our Lady of the Lake-University of San Antonio; San Antonio, Tex. 78207–4689	2,112 (C)	P	7,450	7,450	3,496
Ozark Christian College; Joplin, Mo. 64801	558 (C)	P	3,195	3,195	2,850
Ozarks, College of the; Point Lookout, Mo. 65726	1,583 (C)	P	—	—	1,700
Ozarks, University of the; Clarksville, Ark. 72830	570 (C)	P	4,800	4,800	2,850
Pace University; New York, N.Y. 10038	5,492 (C)	P	10,150	10,150	4,660
Pace University-College of White Plains; White Plains, N.Y. 10603	1,313 (C)	P	10,150	10,150	4,660
Pace University-Pleasantville-Briarcliff; Pleasantville, N.Y. 10570	3,778 (C)	P	10,150	10,150	4,660
Pacific, University of the; Stockton, Calif. 95211	3,802 (C)	P	14,990	14,990	5,300
Pacific Christian College; Fullerton, Calif. 92631	466 (C)	P	6,500	6,500	2,960
Pacific Lutheran University; Tacoma, Wash. 98447	2,964 (C)	P	12,672	12,672	4,272
Pacific Northwest College of Art; Portland, Ore. 97205	223 (C)	P	7,700	7,700	n.a.
Pacific Oaks College; Pasadena, Calif. 91103	150 (C)	P	10,695	10,695	n.a.
Pacific States University; Los Angeles, Calif. 90006	300 (C)	P	7,040	7,040	n.a.
Pacific Union College; Angwin, Calif. 94508	1,509 (C)	P	10,680	10,680	3,525
Pacific University; Forest Grove, Ore. 97116	929 (C)	P	12,490	12,490	3,533
Paier College of Art, Inc.; Hamden, Conn. 06511	309 (C)	P	9,800	9,800	n.a.
Paine College; Augusta, Ga. 30910	686 (C)	P	5,468	5,468	2,739
Palm Beach Atlantic College; West Palm Beach, Fla. 33401	1,635 (C)	P	7,200	7,200	3,500
Park College; Parkville, Mo. 64152	490 (C)	P	7,160	7,160	3,600
Parks College of St. Louis University; Cahokia, Ill. 62206	1,070 (C)	P	8,460	8,460	3,900
Parsons School of Design; New York, N.Y. 10011	1,800 (C)	P	14,060	14,060	7,000
Patten College; Oakland, Calif. 94601	589 (C)	P	4,340	4,340	4,575
Paul Quinn College; Waco, Tex. 75241	509 (C)	P	3,710	3,710	2,950
Pembroke State University; Pembroke, N.C. 28372	2,702 (C)	Pub	948	5,966	2,360
Pennsylvania, University of; Philadelphia, Pa. 19104	9,949 (C)	P	15,198	15,198	6,330
Pennsylvania State Erie –The Behrend College; Erie, Pa. 16563	2,975 (C)	Pub	4,618	9,644	3,790
Pennsylvania State Harrisburg–The Capital College; Middletown, Pa. 17057	2,314 (C)	Pub	4,618	9,664	3,790
Pennsylvania State University Park; University Park, Pa. 16802	31,732 (C)	Pub	4,618	9,664	3,790
Pepperdine University School of Business and Management; Culver City, Calif. 90230	451 (C)	P	15,475	15,475	n.a.
Pepperdine University-Seaver College; Malibu, Calif. 90263-4392	2,762 (C)	P	17,050	17,050	6,250
Peru State College; Peru, Neb. 68421	1,381 (C)	Pub	1,594	2,689	2,500
Pfeiffer College; Misenheimer, N.C. 28109	807 (C)	P	8,190	8,190	3,480
Philadelphia College of Bible; Langhorne, Pa. 19047	699 (C)	P	7,140	7,140	4,060
Philadelphia College of Pharmacy and Science; Philadelphia, Pa. 19104	1,654 (C)	P	10,245	10,245	4,386
Philadelphia College of Textiles and Science; Philadelphia, Pa. 19144	1,670 (C)	P	10,344	10,344	4,798
Philander Smith College; Little Rock, Ark. 72202	572 (C)	P	2,620	2,620	2,415
Phillips University; Enid, Okla. 73701	808 (C)	P	8,124	8,124	2,820
Phoenix, University of; Phoenix, Ariz. 85040	3,023 (C)	P	5,670	5,670	n.a.
Piedmont Bible College; Winston-Salem, N.C. 27101	285 (C)	P	3,590	3,590	2,600
Piedmont College; Demorest, Ga. 30535	640 (C)	P	4,920	4,920	3,620
Pikeville College; Pikeville, Ky. 41501	1,000 (C)	P	4,900	4,900	2,500
Pillsbury Baptist Bible College; Owatonna, Minn. 55060	338 (C)	P	4,606	4,606	3,024
Pine Manor College; Chestnut Hill, Mass. 02167	450 (W)	P	14,900	14,900	6,050
Pittsburgh, University of; Pittsburgh, Pa. 15260	18,250 (C)	Pub	4,922	10,066	4,130
Pittsburgh, University of-Bradford; Bradford, Pa. 16701-2898	1,241 (C)	Pub	4,920	10,064	3,710
Pittsburgh, University of-Greensburg; Greensburg, Pa. 15601	1,454 (C)	Pub	4,886	10,030	3,450
Pittsburgh, University of-Johnstown; Johnstown, Pa. 15904	3,243 (C)	Pub	4,966	10,110	3,544
Pittsburg State University; Pittsburg, Kan. 66762	5,100 (C)	Pub	1,564	4,444	2,704
Pitzer College. *See* Claremont Colleges.					
Plymouth State College; Plymouth, N.H. 03264	3,508 (C)	Pub	2,926	7,306	3,756
Point Loma Nazarene College; San Diego, Calif. 92106	2,035 (C)	P	8,704	8,706	3,830
Point Park College; Pittsburgh, Pa. 15222	2,742 (C)	P	8,580	8,580	4,220
Polytechnic University; Brooklyn, N.Y. 11201	1,568 (C)	P	15,000	15,000	4,700
Polytechnic University-Long Island Campus; Farmingdale, N.Y. 11735-3995	396 (C)	P	14,500	14,500	4,000
Pomona College. *See* Claremont Colleges.					
Pontifical Catholicc University of Puerto Rico; Ponce, P.R. 00732	11,234 (C)	P	2,520	2,520	2,473
Pontifical College Josephinum; Columbus, Ohio 43235-1498	58 (M)	P	4,891	4,891	3,300
Portland, University of; Portland, Ore. 97203	2,251 (C)	P	10,040	10,040	3,790
Portland School of Art; Portland, Me. 04101	306 (C)	P	10,013	10,013	4,765
Portland State University; Portland, Ore. 97207–0751	10,778 (C)	Pub	2,658	6,939	4,168
Potsdam Coll. of Arts & Science. *See* New York, State Univ. of					
Prairie View A&M University; Prairie View, Tex. 77446	4,905 (C)	Pub	1,316	5,456	3,420

Institution and location	Enrollment	Control	Tuition ($) Res.	Tuition ($) Nonres.	Rm/Bd ($)
Pratt Institute; Brooklyn, N.Y. 11205	2,241 (C)	P	11,966	11,966	5,940
Presbyterian College; Clinton, S.C. 29325	1,167 (C)	P	11,984	11,984	3,416
Prescott College; Prescott, Ariz. 86301	670 (C)	P	8,600	8,600	n.a.
Presentation College; Anerdeen, S.D. 57401	486 (C)	P	6,480	6,480	2,480
Princeton University; Princeton, N.J. 08544–0430	4,524 (C)	P	18,050	18,050	5,517
Principia College; Elsah, Ill. 62028	587 (C)	P	11,910	11,910	4,890
Providence College; Providence, R.I. 02918	3,814 (C)	P	12,860	12,860	5,600
Puerto Rico, University of–Arecibo Campus; Arecibo, P.R. 00613	3,307 (C)	Pub	970	([1])	n.a.
Puerto Rico, University of–Bayamon Technological University College; Bayamon, P.R. 00619–1919	n.a.	n.a.	n.a.	n.a.	n.a.
Puerto Rico, University of-Cayey University College; Cayey, P.R. 00633	3,243 (C)	Pub	900	2,400	n.a.
Puerto Rico, University of-Humacao University College; Humacao, P.R. 00661	3,884 (C)	Pub	1,289	1,289	n.a.
Puerto Rico, University of-Mayaguez Campus; Mayaguez, P.R. 00708	9,594 (C)	Pub	1,284	1,284	n.a.
Puerto Rico, University of-Medical Science Campus; San Juan, P.R. 00936	996 (C)	Pub	([2])	([1])	n.a.
Puerto Rico, University of–Ponce Technological University College; Ponce, P.R. 00732	2,192 (C)	Pub	1,458	([1])	n.a.
Puerto Rico, University of–Rio Piedras Campus; Rio Piedras, P.R. 00931	15,668 (C)	Pub	1,286	([1])	2,100
Puget Sound, University of; Tacoma, Wash. 98416	2,824 (C)	P	15,220	15,220	4,300
Puget Sound Christian College; Edmonds, Wash. 98020	76 (C)	P	4,650	4,650	3,150
Purdue University; West Lafayette, Ind. 47907	29,311 (C)	Pub	2,520	8,192	3,650
Purdue University-Calumet; Hammond, Ind. 46323	9,160 (C)	Pub	2,226	5,166	n.a.
Purdue University-North Central; Westville, Ind. 46391	3,505 (C)	Pub	2,020	4,960	n.a.
Queens College; Charlotte, N.C. 28274	1,369 (C)	P	9,850	9,850	4,550
Queens College (NYC). *See* New York, City University of					
Quincy University; Quincy, Ill. 62301	1,177 (C)	P	9,742	9,742	3,904
Quinnipiac College; Hamden, Conn. 06518	3,166 (C)	P	11,070	11,070	5,430
Rabbinical College of America; Morristown, N.J. 07960	230 (M)	P	13,000	13,000	—
Rabbinical Seminary of America; Forest Hills, N.Y. 11375	120 (M)	P	4,000	4,000	2,600
Radcliffe College. *See* Harvard and Radcliffe Colleges					
Radford University; Radford, Va. 24142	8,142 (C)	Pub	2,746	6,270	3,922
Ramapo College of New Jersey, Mahwah, N.J. 07403	4,711 (C)	Pub	3,024	4,911	4,950
Randolph-Macon College; Ashland, Va. 23005	1,118 (C)	P	11,400	11,400	4,700
Randolph-Macon Woman's College; Lynchburg, Va. 24503	750 (W)	P	12,450	12,450	5,500
Ray College of Design; Chicago, Ill. 60611	625 (C)	P	8,238	8,238	n.a.
Redlands, University of; Redlands, Calif. 92373-0999	1,433 (C)	P	14,880	14,880	5,720
Reed College; Portland, Ore. 97202	1,230 (C)	P	18,060	18,060	4,980
Reformed Bible College; Grand Rapids, Mich. 49506-9749	176 (C)	P	5,696	5,696	3,100
Regis College; Weston, Mass. 02193	1,096 (W)	P	11,850	11,850	5,600
Regis University; Denver, Colo. 80221	1,097 (C)	P	11,700	11,700	5,500
Reinhardt College; Waleska, Ga. 30183	560 (C)	P	4,350	4,350	3,525
Rensselaer Polytechnic Institute; Troy, N.Y. 12180	4,398 (C)	P	17,325	17,325	5,742
Research College of Nursing; Kansas City, Mo. 64110-2508	160 (C)	P	8,810	8,810	3,492
Rhode Island, University of; Kingston, R.I. 02881	11,770 (C)	Pub	3,540	9,974	5,030
Rhode Island, University of, College of Continuing Education; Providence, R.I. 02908-5090	4,400 (C)	Pub	110/credit	332/credit	n.a.
Rhode Island College; Providence, R.I. 02908	6,983 (C)	Pub	2,498	6,457	4,980
Rhode Island School of Design; Providence, R.I. 02903	1,844 (C)	P	15,135	15,135	6,100
Rhodes College; Memphis, Tenn. 38112	1,414 (C)	P	14,916	14,916	4,708
Rice University; Houston, Tex. 77251	2,741 (C)	P	8,825	8,825	5,200
Richmond, University of; Richmond, Va. 23173	2,889 (C)	P	13,540	13,540	3,160
Richmond College, The American International University in London; Richmond, Surrey, TW10 6JP England	960 (C)	P	11,155	11,155	5,800
Rider College; Lawrenceville, N.J. 08648-3099	2,870 (C)	P	12,100	12,100	4,962
Ringling School of Art and Design; Sarasota, Fla. 34234	620 (C)	P	9,665	9,665	5,100
Ripon College; Ripon, Wis. 54971	820 (C)	P	14,340	14,340	3,810
Rivier College; Nashua, N.H. 03060	940 (C)	P	9,580	9,580	4,600
Roanoke Bible College; Elizabeth City, N.C. 27909	141 (C)	P	3,236	3,236	2,520
Roanoke College; Salem, Va. 24153	1,677 (C)	P	12,000	12,000	4,150
Robert Morris College; Coraopolis, Pa. 15108	4,749 (C)	P	6,670	6,670	4,106
Roberts Wesleyan College; Rochester, N.Y. 14624	938 (C)	P	9,951	9,951	3,366
Rio Grande, University of; Rio Grande, Ohio 45674	2,014 (C)	P	3,015	5,082	3,300
Rochester, University of; Rochester, N.Y. 14627	4,985 (C)	P	17,345	17,349	6,296
Rochester Institute of Technology; Rochester, N.Y. 14623	10,789 (C)	P	12,525	12,525	5,355
Rockford College; Rockford, Ill. 61108	1,127 (C)	P	11,000	11,000	3,800
Rockhurst College; Kansas City, Mo. 64110–2561	2,044 (C)	P	8,870	8,870	3,870
Rocky Mountain College; Billings, Mont. 59102	748 (C)	P	8,933	8,933	3,327
Rocky Mountain College of Art and Design; Denver, Co. 80224–2359	n.a.	n.a.	n.a.	n.a.	n.a.
Roger Williams College; Bristol, R.I. 02809	2,111 (C)	P	10,560	10,560	5,120
Rollins College; Winter Park, Fla. 32789	1,445 (C)	P	15,495	15,495	4,925

Institution and location	Enrollment	Control	Tuition ($) Res.	Tuition ($) Nonres.	Rm/Bd ($)
Roosevelt University; Chicago, Ill. 60605	4,344 (C)	P	6,348	6,348	4,806
Rosary College; River Forest, Ill. 60305-1099	855 (C)	P	10,500	10,500	4,490
Rose-Hulman Institute of Technology; Terre Haute, Ind. 47803	1,320 (M)	P	12,600	12,600	3,900
Rosemont College; Rosemont, Pa. 19010	620 (W)	P	10,700	10,700	5,700
Rush University Colleges of Nursing and Health Sciences; Chicago, Ill. 60612	175 (C)	P	8,355	8,355	5,940
Russell Sage College; Troy, N.Y. 12180	961 (W)	P	11,270	11,270	4,720
Rust College; Holly Springs, Miss. 38635	1,129 (C)	P	4,552	4,552	2,048
Rutgers, The State University of New Jersey–Camden College of Arts and Sciences; Camden, N.J. 08102	2,672 (C)	Pub	3,857	7,227	4,200
Rutgers, The State University of New Jersey–College of Engineering; New Brunswick, N.J. 08903	2,454 (C)	Pub	4,381	8,118	4,200
Rutgers, The State University of New Jersey–College of Nursing-Newark; Newark, N.J. 07102	391 (C)	Pub	3,864	7,234	4,200
Rutgers, The State University of New Jersey–College of Pharmacy; New Brunswick, N.J. 08903	822 (C)	Pub	4,381	8,118	4,200
Rutgers, The State Universit of New Jersey–Cook College; New Brunswick, N.J. 08903	2,908 (C)	Pub	4,375	8,112	4,200
Rutgers, The State University of New Jersey–Douglass College; New Brunswick, N.J. 08903	3,181 (W)	Pub	3,978	7,348	4,200
Rutgers, The State University of New Jersey–Livingston College; New Brunswick, N.J. 08903	3,645 (C)	Pub	4,055	7,425	4,200
Rutgers, The State University of New Jersey–Mason Gross School of the Arts; New Brunswick, N.J. 08903	436 (C)	Pub	4,023	7,393	4,200
Rutgers, The State University of New Jersey–Newark College of Arts and Sciences; Newark, N.J. 07102	3,782 (C)	Pub	3,871	7,241	4,200
Rutgers, The State University of New Jersey–Rutgers College; New Brunswick, N.J. 08903	8,550 (C)	Pub	4,040	7,410	4,200
Rutgers, The State University of New Jersey–University College–Camden; Camden, N.J. 08102	851 (C)	Pub	([3])	([4])	n.a.
Rutgers, The State University of New Jersey–University College–New Brunswick; New Brunswick, N.J. 08903	3,249 (C)	Pub	([3])	([4])	n.a.
Rutgers, The State University of New Jersey–University College–Newark; Newark, N.J. 07102	2,000 (C)	Pub	([3])	([4])	n.a.
Sacred Heart, Univ. of the; Santurce, P.R. 00924	4,753 (C)	P	4,500	4,500	2,000
Sacred Heart Major Seminary; Detroit, Mich. 48206	220 (C)	P	3,675	3,675	4,000
Sacred Heart University; Fairfield, Conn. 06432	1,444 (C)	P	9,740	9,740	5,110
Saginaw Valley State University; University Center, Mich. 48710	5,263 (C)	Pub	2,535	5,213	3,535
Saint Ambrose University; Davenport, Iowa 52803	1,716 (C)	P	9,850	9,850	3,830
Saint Andrews Presbyterian College; Laurinburg, N.C. 28352	631 (C)	P	9,410	9,410	4,155
Saint Anselm College; Manchester, N.H. 03102	1,857 (C)	P	10,870	10,870	5,200
Saint Augustine's College; Raleigh, N.C. 27610–2298	1,716 (C)	P	5,300	5,300	3,400
St. Benedict, College of; St. Joseph, Minn. 56374-2099	1,787 (W)	P	11,340	11,340	4,030
St. Bonaventure University; St. Bonaventure, N.Y. 14778-2284	2,131 (C)	P	9,981	9,981	4,828
St. Catherine, College of; St. Paul, Minn. 55105	2,638 (W)	P	10,120	10,120	5,510
St. Cloud State University; St. Cloud, Minn. 56301	14,475 (C)	Pub	2,289	4,067	2,689
St. Edward's University; Austin, Tex. 78704	2,653 (C)	P	8,256	8,256	3,700
St. Elizabeth, College of; Convent Station, N.J. 07961	1,202 (W)	P	10,200	10,200	4,700
St. Francis, College of; Joliet, Ill. 60435	1,025 (C)	P	9,100	9,100	3,970
St. Francis College; Brooklyn Heights, N.Y. 11201	2,099 (C)	P	6,400	6,400	n.a.
St. Francis College; Fort Wayne, Ind. 46808	709 (C)	P	8,300	8,300	3,630
St. Francis College; Loretto, Pa. 15940	1,136 (C)	P	11,074	11,074	4,720
St. Francis Medical Center College of Nursing; Peoria, Ill. 61603	153 (C)	P	6,343	6,343	2,750
St. Hyacinth College and Seminary; Granby, Mass. 01033	24 (M)	P	3,780	3,780	4,500
St. John Fisher College; Rochester, N.Y. 14618	1,713 (C)	P	9,470	9,470	5,500
St. John's College; Annapolis, Md. 21404	408 (C)	P	16,150	16,150	5,450
St. John's College; Santa Fe, N.M. 87501	400 (C)	P	15,400	15,400	5,200
St. John's College; Springfield, Ill. 62702	110 (C)	P	5,730	5,730	2,590
St. John's Seminary College; Camarillo, Calif. 93012	86 (M)	P	4,000	4,000	—
St. John's Seminary College of Liberal Arts; Brighton, Mass. 02135	31 (M)	P	4,400	4,400	2,600
St. John's University; Collegeville, Minn. 56321	1,812 (M)	P	11,428	11,428	3,936
St. John's University; Jamaica, N.Y. 11439	13,881 (C)	P	8,230	8,230	n.a.
St. John Vianney College Seminary; Miami, Fla. 33165	50 (M)	P	6,500	6,500	3,500
St. Joseph College; West Hartford, Conn. 06117	1,231 (W)	P	11,000	11,000	4,380
St. Joseph College of Nursing; Joliet, Ill. 60435	148 (C)	P	6,180	6,180	n.a.
St. Joseph in Vermont, College of; Rutland, Vt. 05701	377 (C)	P	7,550	7,550	4,420
Saint Joseph's College; Rensselaer, Ind. 47978	1,000 (C)	P	10,430	10,430	3,700
St. Joseph's College; Brooklyn, N.Y. 11205	827 (C)	P	6,600	6,600	n.a.
St. Joseph's College-Suffolk; Patchogue, N.Y. 11772	1,841 (C)	P	7,166	7,166	n.a.
Saint Joseph's College; Windham, Me. 04062-1198	820 (C)	P	8,995	8,995	4,550
St. Joseph Seminary College; St. Benedict, La. 70457	50 (M)	P	5,400	5,400	4,200
Saint Joseph's University; Philadelphia, Pa. 19131	2,546 (C)	P	11,200	11,200	4,850
St. Lawrence University; Canton, N.Y. 13617	2,017 (C)	P	17,770	17,770	5,530
Saint Leo College; Saint Leo, Fla. 33574	944 (C)	P	8,810	8,810	3,880
St. Louis Christian College; Florissant, Mo. 63033	137 (C)	P	3,630	3,630	2,420

Institution and location	Enrollment	Control	Tuition ($) Res.	Tuition ($) Nonres.	Rm/Bd ($)
St. Louis College of Pharmacy; St. Louis, Mo. 63110	717 (C)	P	6,360	6,360	3,900
St. Louis University; St. Louis, Mo. 63103	7,338 (C)	P	10,820	10,820	4,610
St. Martin's College; Lacey, Wash. 98503–1297	577 (C)	P	9,605	9,605	3,720
St. Mary, College of; Omaha, Neb. 68124	1,304 (W)	P	8,920	8,920	3,320
Saint Mary College; Leavenworth, Kan. 66048	1,023 (C)	P	7,300	7,300	3,700
St. Mary-of-the-Woods Coll.; St. Mary-of-the-Woods, Ind. 47876	1,208 (W)	P	9,920	9,920	4,100
St. Mary's College; Notre Dame, Ind. 46556	1,576 (W)	P	11,770	11,770	4,244
St. Mary's College; Orchard Lake, Mich. 48324	430 (C)	P	4,800	4,800	3,150
St. Mary's College; Winona, Minn. 55987	1,312 (C)	P	10,380	10,380	3,470
St. Mary's College of California; Moraga, Calif. 94575	2,583 (C)	P	11,800	11,800	5,600
St. Mary's College of Maryland; St. Mary's City, Md. 20686	1,510 (C)	Pub	4,400	6,700	4,500
St. Mary's University of San Antonio; San Antonio, Tex. 78228	2,595 (C)	P	8,186	8,186	3,440
Saint Meinrad College; St. Meinrad, Ind. 47577	121 (M)	P	5,793	5,793	4,064
Saint Michael's College; Colchester, Vt. 05439	1,728 (C)	P	11,900	11,900	5,400
St. Norbert College; De Pere, Wis. 54115	1,965 (C)	P	11,465	11,465	4,245
St. Olaf College; Northfield, Minn. 55057	3,015 (C)	P	13,500	13,500	3,700
Saint Paul's College; Lawrenceville, Va. 23868	651 (C)	P	4,636	4,636	3,857
Saint Peter's College; Jersey City, N.J. 07306	3,189 (C)	P	8,905	8,905	5,008
St. Scholastica, College of; Duluth, Minn. 55811	1,760 (C)	P	11,205	11,205	3,588
St. Thomas, University of; Houston, Tex. 77006	1,105 (C)	P	5,486	5,486	3,620
St. Thomas, University of; St. Paul, Minn. 55105	5,188 (C)	P	11,168	11,168	3,850
St. Thomas Aquinas College; Sparkill, N.Y. 10968	1,910 (C)	P	7,350	7,350	4,500
Saint Thomas University; Miami, Fla. 33054	1,652 (C)	P	8,550	8,550	4,300
Saint Vincent College; Latrobe, Pa. 15650	1,248 (C)	P	9,300	9,300	3,562
St. Xavier University; Chicago, Ill. 60655	2,177 (C)	P	8,820	8,820	3,692
Salem College; Winston-Salem, N.C. 27108	757 (W)	P	9,290	9,290	5,770
Salem State College; Salem, Mass. 01970	5,450 (C)	Pub	3,073	6,937	3,535
Salem-Teikyo University; Salem, W.Va. 26426	650 (C)	P	8,194	8,194	3,952
Salisbury State University, Salisbury, Md. 21801	5,397 (C)	Pub	3,026	5,694	4,490
Salve Regina University; Newport, R.I. 02840-4192	1,730 (C)	P	13,800	13,800	6,300
Samford University; Birmingham, Ala. 35229	3,194 (C)	P	6,074	6,074	3,436
Sam Houston State University; Huntsville, Tex. 77341	10,837 (C)	Pub	1,456	4,516	2,880
Samuel Merritt College; Oakland, Calif. 94609	262 (C)	P	11,865	11,965	5,520
San Antonio Art Institute; San Antonio, Texas, 78209–0092	n.a.	n.a.	n.a.	n.a.	n.a.
San Diego, University of; San Diego, Calif. 92110	3,914 (C)	P	12,990	12,990	5,900
San Diego State University; San Diego, Calif. 92182	24,162 (C)	Pub	1,500	7,404	5,273
Imperial Valley Campus; Calexico, Calif. 92231	253 (C)	Pub	926	5,859	n.a.
San Francisco, University of; San Francisco, Calif. 94117	2,807 (C)	P	11,816	11,816	5,480
San Francisco Art Institute; San Francisco, Calif. 94133	582 (C)	P	12,300	12,300	n.a.
San Francisco Conservatory of Music; San Francisco, Calif. 94122	147 (C)	P	12,250	12,250	n.a.
San Francisco State Univ.; San Francisco, Calif. 94132	20,492 (C)	Pub	1,504	8,888	4,938
Sangamon State University; Springfield, Ill. 62708	2,645 (C)	Pub	1,884	5,216	2,555
San Jose Christian College; San Jose, Calif. 95108	246 (C)	P	5,532	5,532	3,240
San Jose State University; San Jose, Calif. 95192-0009	23,642 (C)	Pub	1,184	7,088	4,658
Santa Clara University; Santa Clara, Calif. 95053	4,079 (C)	P	12,879	12,879	5,904
Santa Fe, College of; Santa Fe, N.M. 87501	1,337 (C)	P	9,830	9,830	3,822
Sarah Lawrence College; Bronxville, N.Y. 10708	1,000 (C)	P	17,280	17,280	4,550
Savannah College of Art and Design; Savannah, Ga. 31401	2,090 (C)	P	9,180	9,180	5,500
Savannah State College; Savannah, Ga. 31404	1,754 (C)	Pub	1,686	4,368	2,205
Schiller International University; 6900 Heidelberg, Germany	1,280 (C)	P	10,740	10,740	5,600
Schreiner College; Kerrville, Tex. 78028	612 (C)	P	8,610	8,610	5,670
Science and Arts, University of, of Oklahoma; Chickasha, Okla. 73018	1,619 (C)	Pub	1,290	3,315	1,920
Scranton, University of; Scranton, Pa. 18510-4699	4,304 (C)	P	10,715	10,715	5,122
Scripps College. *See* Claremont Colleges					
Seattle Pacific University; Seattle, Wash. 98119	2,277 (C)	P	11,979	11,979	4,525
Seattle University; Seattle, Wash. 98122	3,193 (C)	P	12,150	12,150	4,600
Seaver College. *See* Pepperdine University					
Selma University; Selma, Ala. 36701	217 (C)	P	2,380	2,380	1,740
Seton Hall University; South Orange, N.J. 07079	5,446 (C)	P	11,654	11,654	5,958
Seton Hill College; Greensburg, Pa. 15601	1,012 (W)	P	10,340	10,340	4,040
Shawnee State University; Portsmouth, Ohio 45662	3,449 (C)	Pub	2,409	3,945	1,600
Shaw University; Raleigh, N.C. 27611	1,500 (C)	P	4,894	4,894	3,282
Sheldon Jackson College; Sitka, Alaska 99835	322 (C)	P	9,000	9,000	4,800
Shenandoah University; Winchester, Va. 22601-9986	1,043 (C)	P	8,550	8,550	4,000
Shepherd College; Shepherdstown, W. Va. 25443	3,505 (C)	Pub	1,954	4,474	3,500
Shimer College; Waukegan, Ill. 60085-0500	88 (C)	P	9,200	9,200	3,145
Shippensburg University of Pennsylvania; Shippensburg, Pa. 17257	5,619 (C)	Pub	3,388	6,782	3,200
Shorter College; Rome, Ga. 30165	821 (C)	P	6,220	6,220	3,670
Siena College; Loudonville, N.Y. 12211	3,492 (C)	P	9,500	9,500	4,680
Siena Heights College; Adrian, Mich. 49221	1,726 (C)	P	8,100	8,100	3,550
Sierra Nevada College; Incline Village, Nev. 89450	415 (C)	P	8,250	8,250	4,200

Institution and location	Enrollment	Control	Tuition ($) Res.	Tuition ($) Nonres.	Rm/Bd ($)
Silver Lake College; Manitowoc, Wis. 54220	857 (C)	P	8,280	8,280	n.a.
Simmons Bible College; Louisville, Ky. 40210	103 (C)	P	520	520	n.a.
Simmons College; Boston, Mass. 02115	1,332 (W)	P	15,794	15,794	6,740
Simon's Rock of Bard College; Great Barrington, Mass. 01230	298 (C)	P	16,590	16,590	5,620
Simpson College; Indianola, Iowa 50125	1,752 (C)	P	10,230	10,230	3,670
Simpson College; Redding, Calif. 96003	316 (C)	P	6,738	6,738	3,570
Sinte Gleska College; Rosebud, S.D. 57570	653 (C)	P	1,930	1,930	n.a.
Sioux Falls College; Sioux Falls, S.D. 57105	861 (C)	P	8,450	8,450	3,090
Skidmore College; Saratoga Springs, N.Y. 12866	2,145 (C)	P	16,650	16,650	5,270
Slippery Rock Univ. of Pennsylvania; Slippery Rock, Pa. 16057	7,162 (C)	Pub	3,287	6,681	3,084
Smith College; Northampton, Mass. 01063	2,523 (W)	P	16,850	16,850	6,100
Sojourner-Douglass College; Baltimore, Md. 21205	298 (C)	P	3,300	3,300	n.a.
Sonoma State University; Rohnert Park, Calif. 94928	6,086 (C)	Pub	1,534	7,380	5,121
South, University of the; Sewanee, Tenn. 37375-1000	1,142 (C)	P	14,060	14,060	3,700
South Alabama, University of; Mobile, Ala. 36688	10,282 (C)	Pub	2,295	2,895	2,793
Southampton College. *See* Long Island Univ. Center					
South Carolina, University of; Columbia, S.C. 29208	16,059 (C)	Pub	2,843	7,071	3,218
South Carolina, Univ. of-Aiken; Aiken, S.C. 29801	3,108 (C)	Pub	2,120	5,300	2,100
South Carolina, Univ. of-Coastal Carolina; Myrtle Beach, S.C. 29578	4,023 (C)	Pub	2,270	5,674	3,690
South Carolina, Univ. of-Spartanburg; Spartanburg, S.C. 29303	3,526 (C)	Pub	2,120	5,300	n.a.
South Carolina State University; Orangeburg, S.C. 29117–0001	3,531 (C)	Pub	2,200	5,380	6,972
South Dakota, University of; Vermillion, S.D. 57069	5,878 (C)	Pub	2,190	4,027	2,310
South Dakota School of Mines and Technology; Rapid City, S.D. 57701	2,177 (C)	Pub	3,555	4,676	2,300
South Dakota State University; Brookings, S.D. 57007	8,550 (C)	Pub	2,100	3,822	2,014
Southeast Missouri State Univ.; Cape Girardeau, Mo. 63701	6,388 (C)	Pub	1,900	3,380	3,080
Southeastern Baptist College; Laurel, Miss. 39440	83 (C)	P	2,220	2,220	1,700
Southeastern Bible College; Birmingham, Ala. 35243	138 (C)	P	4,200	4,200	2,700
Southeastern College; Lakeland, Fla. 33801	1,209 (C)	P	3,168	3,168	2,948
Southeastern Louisiana University; Hammond, La. 70402	10,313 (C)	Pub	1,705	3,505	2,280
Southeastern Oklahoma State Univ.; Durant, Okla. 74701	3,634 (C)	Pub	1,340	3,369	2,699
Southeastern University; Washington, D.C. 20024	559 (C)	P	5,688	5,688	n.a.
Southern Arkansas University; Magnolia, Ark. 71753	2,850 (C)	Pub	1,420	2,200	2,100
Southern California, Univ. of; Los Angeles, Calif. 90089-0911	15,500 (C)	P	15,730	15,730	6,370
Southern California College; Costa Mesa, Calif. 92626	835 (C)	P	8,164	8,164	3,640
Southern California Institute of Architecture; Los Angeles, Calif. 90066	420 (C)	P	10,450	10,450	n.a.
Southern College of Seventh-Day Adventists; Collegedale, Tenn. 37315	1,494 (C)	P	7,988	7,988	3,360
Southern College of Technology; Marietta, Ga. 30060	3,829 (C)	Pub	1,548	4,230	3,219
Southern Colorado, University of; Pueblo, Colo. 81001	4,338 (C)	Pub	1,833	6,385	3,680
Southern Connecticut State Univ.; New Haven, Conn. 06515	6,441 (C)	Pub	2,570	6,756	4,204
Southern Illinois Univ. at Carbondale; Carbondale, Ill. 62901	20,485 (C)	Pub	3,006	7,506	3,038
Southern Illinois Univ. at Edwardsville; Edwardsville, Ill. 62026	8,910 (C)	Pub	2,590	6,042	3,300
Southern Indiana, University of; Evansville, Ind. 47714	7,430 (C)	Pub	2,062	4,703	3,582
Southern Maine, University of; Gorham, Me. 04038	8,645 (C)	Pub	2,850	7,720	4,188
Southern Methodist University; Dallas, Tex. 75275	5,434 (C)	P	12,688	12,688	4,832
Southern Mississippi, Univ. of; Hattiesburg, Miss. 39406	9,841 (C)	Pub	2,392	4,352	2,470
Southern Nazarene Univ.; Bethany, Okla. 73008	1,425 (C)	P	5,835	5,835	3,299
Southern Oregon State College; Ashland, Ore. 97520	4,519 (C)	Pub	2,487	5,988	3,350
Southern University at New Orleans; New Orleans, La. 70126	3,200 (C)	Pub	1,451	3,009	n.a.
Southern University-Baton Rouge; Baton Rouge, La. 70813	9,914 (C)	Pub	1,588	3,110	2,866
Southern Utah State University; Cedar City, Utah 84720	4,300 (C)	Pub	1,497	4,143	2,505
Southern Vermont College; Bennington, Vt. 05201	743 (C)	P	8,370	8,370	4,304
South Florida, University of; Tampa, Fla. 33620	23,033 (C)	Pub	1,600	5,760	3,300
Southwest, College of the; Hobbs, N.M. 88240	352 (C)	P	3,700	3,700	4,044
Southwest Baptist University; Bolivar, Mo. 65613	2,804 (C)	P	6,401	6,401	2,385
Southwestern Adventist College; Keene, Tex. 76059	879 (C)	P	7,064	7,064	3,466
Southwestern Assemblies of God College; Waxahachie, Tex. 75165	761 (C)	P	2,900	2,900	2,762
Southwestern College; Winfield, Kan. 67156	737 (C)	P	6,500	6,500	3,532
Southwestern Conservative Baptist Bible College; Phoenix, Ariz. 85032	152 (C)	P	4,920	4,920	2,200
Southwestern Louisiana, University of; Lafayette, La. 70504	16,195 (C)	Pub	1,578	3,378	2,054
Southwestern Oklahoma State Univ.; Weatherford, Okla. 73096	5,453 (C)	Pub	1,320	3,450	1,980
Southwestern University; Georgetown, Tex. 78626	1,204 (C)	P	11,000	11,000	4,484
Southwest Missouri State Univ.; Springfield, Mo. 65804	17,430 (C)	Pub	2,356	4,576	2,630
Southwest State University; Marshall, Minn. 56258	2,742 (C)	Pub	2,650	4,650	2,750
Southwest Texas State Univ.; San Marcos, Tex. 78666	21,743 (C)	Pub	1,208	4,448	3,700
Spalding University; Louisville, Ky. 40203	835 (C)	P	7,896	7,896	2,600
Spelman College; Atlanta, Ga. 30314	1,905 (W)	P	7,394	7,394	5,000
Spring Arbor College; Spring Arbor, Mich. 49283	884 (C)	P	8,706	8,706	3,550
Springfield College; Springfield, Mass. 01109	2,210 (C)	P	9,870	9,870	4,300
Spring Hill College; Mobile, Ala. 36608	1,062 (C)	P	11,400	11,400	4,600
Stanford University; Stanford, Calif. 94305	6,505 (C)	P	16,536	16,536	6,314

Institution and location	Enrollment	Control	Tuition ($) Res.	Tuition ($) Nonres.	Rm/Bd ($)
Staten Island, Coll. of (NYC). *See* New York, City Univ. of					
Stephen F. Austin State Univ. Nacogdoches, Tex. 75962	11,319 (C)	Pub	1,388	5,528	3,424
Stephens College; Columbia, Mo. 65215	1,045 (W)	P	13,410	13,410	5,040
Sterling College; Sterling, Kan. 67579	480 (C)	P	7,230	7,230	3,100
Stetson University; DeLand, Fla. 32720	2,113 (C)	P	11,110	11,110	4,275
Stevens Institute of Technology; Hoboken, N.J. 07030	1,293 (C)	P	15,400	15,400	5,050
Stillman College; Tuscaloosa, Ala. 35403	770 (C)	P	4,460	4,460	2,754
Stockton State College; Pomona, N.J. 08240	5,683 (C)	Pub	2,696	3,336	3,974
Stonehill College; North Easton, Mass. 02357	1,986 (C)	P	10,970	10,970	5,674
Strayer College; Washington, D.C. 20005	2,288 (C)	P	5,400	5,400	n.a.
Suffolk University; Boston, Mass. 02108-2770	3,003 (C)	P	9,800	9,800	n.a.
Sul Ross State University; Alpine, Texas 79832	1,558 (C)	Pub	1,321	5,461	2,860
Sul Ross State University–Uvalde Study Center; Uvalde, Texas 78801	291 (C)	Pub	1,196	5,336	n.a.
Sullivan College; Louisville, Ky. 40232	1,914 (C)	P	7,200	7,200	4,210
Summit Christian College; Fort Wayne, Ind. 46807	376 (C)	P	7,500	7,500	3,000
Susquehanna University; Selinsgrove, Pa. 17870–1001	1,465 (C)	P	14,500	14,500	4,400
Swarthmore College; Swarthmore, Pa. 19081	1,269 (C)	P	17,646	17,646	5,844
Sweet Briar College; Sweet Briar, Va. 24595	600 (W)	P	13,890	13,890	5,755
Syracuse University; Syracuse, N.Y. 13244	10,948 (C)	P	13,714	13,714	6,212
Tabor College; Hillsboro, Kan. 67063	460 (C)	P	7,320	7,320	3,200
Talladega College; Talladega, Ala. 35160	912 (C)	P	5,166	5,166	2,664
Tampa, University of; Tampa, Fla. 33606	2,026 (C)	P	11,685	11,685	4,200
Tampa College; Tampa, Fla. 33614	1,440 (C)	P	4,975	4,975	n.a.
Tarleton State University; Stephensville, Tex. 76402	5,600 (C)	Pub	1,322	5,462	2,650
Taylor University; Upland, Ind. 46989	1,817 (C)	P	10,650	10,650	3,800
Teikyo Marycrest University; Davenport, Iowa 52804	1,053 (C)	P	8,996	8,996	3,280
Teikyo Post College; Waterbury, Conn. 06723-2540	1,964 (C)	P	10,900	10,900	5,200
Teikyo Westmar University; Le Mars, Iowa 51031	761 (C)	P	9,500	9,500	3,350
Temple University, Philadelphia, Pa. 19122	22,859 (C)	Pub	4,868	9,082	4,868
Temple University-Ambler; Ambler, Pa. 19002	4,242 (C)	Pub	4,696	8,636	4,775
Tennessee, Univ. of-Chattanooga; Chattanooga, Tenn. 37403	7,024 (C)	Pub	1,670	5,270	4,572
Tennessee, Univ. of-Knoxville; Knoxville, Tenn. 37996-0230	19,342 (C)	Pub	1,898	5,498	3,166
Tennessee, Univ. of-Martin; Martin, Tenn. 38238	5,660 (C)	Pub	1,728	5,328	2,800
Tennessee, Univ. of-Memphis, The Health Science Center; Memphis, Tenn. 38163	380 (C)	Pub	2,448	5,808	4,243
Tennessee State University; Nashville, Tenn. 37203	7,012 (C)	Pub	1,632	5,234	3,020
Tennessee Technological Univ.; Cookeville, Tenn. 38505	6,755 (C)	Pub	1,634	5,236	3,424
Tennessee Temple University; Chattanooga, Tenn. 37404	951 (C)	P	3,930	3,930	3,370
Tennessee Wesleyan College; Athens, Tenn. 37303	632 (C)	P	6,520	6,520	3,340
Texas, University of-Arlington; Arlington, Tex. 76019	20,405 (C)	Pub	917	4,157	4,050
Texas, University of-Austin; Austin, Tex. 78712	35,911 (C)	Pub	1,375	5,515	3,800
Texas, University of-Dallas; Richardson, Tex. 75083-0688	4,841 (C)	Pub	1,096	4,408	2,363
Texas, University of-El Paso; El Paso, Tex. 79968	14,603 (C)	Pub	1,588	5,672	3,300
Texas, University of–Health Science Center at Houston; Houston, Tex. 77225	n.a.	n.a.	n.a.	n.a.	n.a.
Texas, University of-Health Science Center-San Antonio; San Antonio, Tex. 78284	843 (C)	Pub	845	3,965	n.a.
Texas, University of, Medical Branch-Galveston; Galveston, Tex. 77555-1305	916 (C)	Pub	1,590	7,710	4,815
Texas, University of–Pan American; Edinburg, Tex. 78539	9,000 (C)	Pub	991	3,487	1,906
Texas, University of-Permian Basin; Odessa, Tex. 79762	1,456 (C)	Pub	1,200	4,240	3,435
Texas, University of-San Antonio; San Antonio, Tex. 78249-0616	13,849 (C)	Pub	1,182	3,840	3,958
Texas, University of, Southwestern Medical Center at Dallas; Dallas, Tex. 75235	379 (C)	Pub	1,275	6,171	n.a.
Texas, University of-Tyler; Tyler, Tex. 75701	2,307 (C)	Pub	1,008	4,320	n.a.
Texas A&I University-Kingsville; Kingsville, Tex. 78363	5,302 (C)	Pub	1,221	4,341	2,816
Texas A&M University; College Station, Tex. 77843	33,479 (C)	Pub	1,526	5,606	4,062
Texas A&M University-Galveston; Galveston, Tex. 77553	1,213 (C)	Pub	1,515	5,655	3,235
Texas Christian University; Fort Worth, Tex. 76129	5,692 (C)	P	8,570	8,570	2,730
Texas College; Tyler, Tex. 75702–2404	353 (C)	P	3,605	3,605	2,430
Texas Lutheran College; Seguin, Tex. 78155	1,091 (C)	P	7,420	7,420	3,280
Texas Southern University; Houston, Tex. 77004	7,179 (C)	Pub	1,170	5,310	3,250
Texas Tech University; Lubbock, Tex. 79409	19,611 (C)	Pub	1,490	5,630	3,452
Texas Wesleyan University; Fort Worth, Tex. 76105	1,493 (C)	P	6,150	6,150	3,230
Texas Woman's University; Denton, Tex. 76204	5,319 (W)	Pub	1,016	3,608	2,828
Thiel College; Greenville, Pa. 16125	918 (C)	P	9,775	9,775	4,505
Thomas Aquinas College; Santa Paula, Calif. 93060	203 (C)	P	11,980	11,980	4,960
Thomas College; Thomasville, Ga. 31792–7499	357 (C)	P	2,925	2,925	n.a.
Thomas College; Waterville, Me. 04901	450 (C)	P	8,400	8,400	4,450
Thomas Edison State College, Trenton, N.J. 08608-1176	8,019 (C)	Pub	330	660	n.a.
Thomas Jefferson University, College of Allied Health Sciences; Philadelphia, Pa. 19107	1,333 (C)	P	12,300	12,300	3,600
Thomas More College; Crestview Hills, Ky. 41017	1,268 (C)	P	8,400	8,400	3,600

Institution and location	Enrollment	Control	Tuition ($) Res.	Tuition ($) Nonres.	Rm/Bd ($)
Tiffin University; Tiffin, Ohio 44883	958 (C)	P	7,100	7,100	3,700
Toccoa Falls College; Toccoa Falls, Ga. 30598	911 (C)	P	5,784	5,784	3,566
Toledo, University of; Toledo, Ohio 43606	21,162 (C)	Pub	3,073	7,378	3,053
Tougaloo College; Tougaloo, Miss. 39174	1,003 (C)	P	5,090	5,090	1,840
Touro College; New York, N.Y. 10001-4103	4,298 (C)	P	7,030	7,030	6,100
Towson State University; Towson, Md. 21204-7097	13,404 (C)	Pub	3,118	5,620	4,430
Transylvania University; Lexington, Ky. 40508-1797	974 (C)	P	10,240	10,240	4,300
Trenton State College; Trenton, N.J. 08650–4700	6,018 (C)	Pub	3,687	5,289	5,027
Trevecca Nazarene College; Nashville, Tenn. 37210	1,067 (C)	P	6,220	6,220	3,660
Tri-State University; Angola, Ind. 46703	1,060 (C)	P	8,298	8,298	3,600
Trinity Bible College; Ellendale, N.D. 58436–7150	443 (C)	P	4,779	4,779	2,994
Trinity Christian College; Palos Heights, Ill. 60463	571 (C)	P	9,460	9,460	3,800
Trinity College; Burlington, Vt. 05401	1,040 (W)	P	10,024	10,024	4,952
Trinity College; Deerfield, Ill. 60015	882 (C)	P	9,200	9,200	4,030
Trinity College; Hartford, Conn. 06106	2,013 (C)	P	17,830	17,830	5,160
Trinity College; Washington, D.C. 20017	882 (W)	P	11,230	11,230	6,430
Trinity University; San Antonio, Tex. 78212	2,281 (C)	P	11,720	11,720	4,930
Troy State University; Troy, Ala. 36082	4,088 (C)	Pub	1,617	2,518	2,834
Troy State University-Dothan; Dothan, Ala. 36303	1,740 (C)	Pub	1,697	2,777	n.a.
Troy State University-Montgomery; Montgomery, Ala. 36103-4419	2,718 (C)	Pub	1,617	3,234	n.a.
Tufts University; Medford, Mass. 02155	4,432 (C)	P	18,793	18,793	5,693
Tulane University; New Orleans, La. 70118	6,762 (C)	P	18,735	18,735	5,730
Tulsa, University of; Tulsa, Okla. 74104	3,315 (C)	P	9,380	9,380	3,600
Turabo University; Caguas, P.R. 00658	n.a.	n.a.	n.a.	n.a.	n.a.
Tusculum College; Greeneville, Tenn. 37743	930 (C)	P	7,100	7,100	3,300
Tuskegee University; Tuskegee, Ala. 36088	3,191 (C)	P	6,535	6,535	3,270
Union College; Barbourville, Ky. 40906	638 (C)	P	6,200	6,200	2,710
Union College; Lincoln, Neb. 68506	614 (C)	P	8,000	8,000	2,750
Union College; Schenectady, N.Y. 12308	1,894 (C)	P	16,748	16,748	5,722
Union Institute, The; Cincinnati, Ohio 45206–1947	300 (C)	P	6,525	6,525	n.a.
Union University; Jackson, Tenn. 38305	1,928 (C)	P	5,380	5,380	2,700
U.S. Air Force Academy; Colorado Springs, Colo. 80840	4,440 (C)	Pub	—	—	—
U.S. Coast Guard Academy; New London, Conn. 06320	911 (C)	Pub	—	—	—
U.S. International University; San Diego, Calif. 92131	355 (C)	P	10,125	10,125	4,800
U.S. Merchant Marine Academy; Kings Point, N.Y. 11024	844 (C)	Pub	3,450	3,450	—
U.S. Military Academy; West Point, N.Y. 10996	4,392 (C)	Pub	—	—	—
U.S. Naval Academy; Annapolis, Md. 21402	4,200 (C)	Pub	—	—	—
Unity College; Unity, Me. 04988	433 (C)	P	7,400	8,500	4,525
Universidad de las Americas—Puebla; Puebla, Mexico 72820	5,481 (C)	P	3,400	3,400	3,000
Universidad Metropolitana; Rio Piedras, P.R. 00918	n.a.	n.a.	n.a.	n.a.	n.a.
Universidad Politecnica de Puerto Rico; Hato Rey, San Juan, P.R. 00918	4,322 (C)	P	3,270	3,270	n.a.
Upper Iowa University; Fayette, Iowa 52142	2,641 (C)	P	8,840	8,840	3,060
Upsala College; East Orange, N.J. 07019	920 (C)	P	11,500	11,500	5,000
Urbana Univ.; Urbana, Ohio 43078-2091	952 (C)	P	8,437	8,437	4,140
Ursinus College; Collegeville, Pa. 19426	1,113 (C)	P	13,240	13,240	4,800
Ursuline College; Pepper Pike, Ohio 44124	1,464 (C)	P	9,000	9,000	4,000
Utah, University of; Salt Lake City, Utah 84112	22,036 (C)	Pub	2,100	6,100	3,600
Utah State University; Logan, Utah 84322	12,854 (C)	Pub	1,821	4,983	3,105
Utica College of Syracuse University; Utica, N.Y. 13502	1,700 (C)	P	11,890	11,890	4,640
Valdosta State College; Valdosta, Ga. 31698	6,730 (C)	Pub	1,689	4,371	2,850
Valley City State University; Valley City, N.D. 58072	1,003 (C)	Pub	1,707	4,257	2,220
Valley Forge Christian College; Phoenixville, Pa. 19460	511 (C)	P	3,678	3,678	2,684
Valparaiso University; Valparaiso, Ind. 46383	2,993 (C)	P	11,720	11,720	3,090
Vanderbilt University; Nashville, Tenn. 37203	5,547 (C)	P	17,999	17,999	5,764
Vandercook College of Music; Chicago, Ill. 60616	82 (C)	P	8,600	8,600	4,500
Vassar College; Poughkeepsie, N.Y. 12601	2,250 (C)	P	18,456	18,456	5,750
Vennard College; University Park, Iowa 52595	143 (C)	P	5,042	5,042	2,430
Vermont, University of; Burlington, Vt. 05401-3596	7,992 (C)	Pub	6,140	14,740	4,588
Villa Julie College; Stevenson, Md. 21153	1,681 (C)	P	6,320	6,320	n.a.
Villanova University; Villanova, Pa. 19085	6,400 (C)	P	13,560	13,560	5,770
Virginia, University of; Charlottesville, Va. 22906	11,371 (C)	Pub	3,890	10,826	3,470
Virginia, University of—Clinch Valley College; Wise, Va. 24293	1,840 (C)	Pub	2,650	6,024	3,200
Virginia Commonwealth University; Richmond, Va. 23284-2526	15,699 (C)	Pub	3,529	9,625	3,860
Virginia Intermont College; Bristol, Va. 24201-4298	637 (C)	P	8,270	8,270	3,980
Virginia Military Institute; Lexington, Va. 24450	1,265 (M)	Pub	4,640	10,290	3,690
Virginia Polytechnic Institute and State University; Blacksburg, Va. 24061–0202	18,819 (C)	Pub	3,538	8,986	2,876
Virginia State University; Petersburg, Va. 23806	4,260 (C)	Pub	2,913	6,315	4,127
Virginia Union University; Richmond, Va. 23220	1,209 (C)	P	10,194	10,194	3,384
Virginia Wesleyan College; Norfolk-Virginia Beach, Va. 23502	1,513 (C)	P	10,150	10,150	4,800
Virgin Islands, University of the; St. Thomas, V.I. 00802	2,668 (C)	Pub	1,590	4,590	4,300
Visual Arts, School of; New York, N.Y. 10010	2,293 (C)	P	10,680	10,680	6,300
Viterbo College; La Crosse, Wis. 54601	1,160 (C)	P	8,300	8,300	3,250
Voorhees College; Denmark, S.C. 29042	574 (C)	P	6,632	6,632	2,578

Institution and location	Enrollment	Control	Tuition ($) Res.	Tuition ($) Nonres.	Rm/Bd ($)
Wabash College; Crawfordsville, Ind. 47933	770 (M)	P	12,450	12,450	4,000
Wadhams Hall Seminary—College; Ogdensburg, N.Y. 13669-9308	58 (C)	P	3,550	3,550	3,400
Wagner College; Staten Island, N.Y. 10301	1,248 (C)	P	11,250	11,250	5,000
Wake Forest University; Winston-Salem, N.C. 27109	3,746 (C)	P	13,000	13,000	4,300
Walla Walla College; College Place, Wash. 99324	1,561 (C)	P	9,555	9,555	3,105
Walsh College; North Canton, Ohio 44720	1,331 (C)	P	7,710	7,710	3,930
Walsh College of Accountancy and Business Administration; Troy, Mich. 48007	1,830 (C)	P	3,576	3,576	n.a.
Warner Pacific College; Portland, Ore. 97215	591 (C)	P	7,511	7,511	3,840
Warner Southern College; Lake Wales, Fla. 33853	441 (C)	P	5,640	5,640	4,370
Warren Wilson College; Ashville, N.C. 28815	490 (C)	P	9,500	9,500	2,852
Wartburg College; Waverly, Iowa 50677	1,445 (C)	P	11,080	11,080	3,450
Warwick, University of; Coventry, CV4 7AL, England	6,706 (C)	Pub	3,799	3,799	2,047
Washburn University; Topeka, Kan. 66621	5,913 (C)	Pub	2,492	4,232	3,000
Washington, University of; Seattle, Wash. 98195	25,092 (C)	Pub	2,253	6,345	3,852
Washington and Jefferson College; Washington, Pa. 15301	1,144 (C)	P	15,360	15,360	3,740
Washington and Lee University; Lexington, Va. 24450	1,594 (C)	P	13,100	13,100	4,510
Washington Bible College; Lanham, Md. 20706	325 (C)	P	5,278	5,278	3,180
Washington College; Chestertown, Md. 21620-9926	886 (C)	P	13,226	13,226	5,128
Washington State University; Pullman, Wash. 99164	14,893 (C)	Pub	2,274	6,345	3,730
Washington University; St. Louis, Mo. 63130	4,896 (C)	P	17,776	17,776	5,731
Washington University–University College; St. Louis, Mo. 63130	n.a.	n.a.	n.a.	n.a.	n.a.
Wayland Baptist University; Plainview, Tex. 79072	2,382 (C)	P	4,916	4,916	2,868
Waynesburg College; Waynesburg, Pa. 15370	1,308 (C)	P	8,580	8,580	3,380
Wayne State College; Wayne, Neb. 68787	3,018 (C)	Pub	1,599	2,694	2,550
Wayne State University; Detroit, Mich. 48202	21,085 (C)	Pub	2,956	7,648	n.a.
Webber College; Babson Park, Fla. 33827	370 (C)	P	5,770	5,770	2,900
Webb Institute of Naval Architecture; Glen Cove, N.Y. 11542	78 (C)	P	—	—	4,800
Weber State University; Ogden, Utah 84408	14,837 (C)	Pub	1,542	4,332	3,000
Webster University; St. Louis, Mo. 63119	3,239 (C)	P	8,560	8,560	4,090
Wellesley College; Wellesley, Mass. 02181	2,271 (W)	P	17,610	17,610	6,000
Wells College; Aurora, N.Y. 13026	400 (W)	P	13,800	13,800	5,300
Wentworth Institute of Technology; Boston, Mass. 02115	2,412 (C)	P	8,750	8,750	5,950
Wesleyan College; Macon, Ga. 31297	501 (W)	P	11,195	11,195	4,250
Wesleyan University; Middletown, Conn. 06457	2,724 (C)	P	18,780	18,780	5,390
Wesley College; Dover, Del. 19901	1,346 (C)	P	8,755	8,755	4,000
Wesley College; Florence, Miss. 39073–0070	65 (C)	P	1,900	1,900	2,200
Westbrook College; Portland, Me. 04103	387 (C)	P	11,000	11,000	4,900
West Chester Univ. of Pennsylvania; West Chester, Pa. 19383	9,961 (C)	Pub	3,158	6,552	3,630
West Coast University; Los Angeles, Calif. 90020-1765	850 (C)	P	9,145	9,145	n.a.
Western Baptist College; Salem, Ore. 97301	478 (C)	P	8,700	8,700	3,700
Western Carolina University; Cullowhee, N.C. 28723	5,106 (C)	Pub	1,375	6,429	2,268
Western Connecticut State University; Danbury, Conn. 06810	4,792 (C)	Pub	2,521	6,251	3,562
Western Illinois University; Macomb, Ill. 61455-1383	10,802 (C)	Pub	2,455	6,135	3,060
Western International University; Phoenix, Ariz. 85021	982 (C)	P	5,400	5,400	n.a.
Western Kentucky University; Bowling Green, Ky. 42101	13,711 (C)	Pub	1,602	4,602	3,106
Western Maryland College; Westminster, Md. 21157	1,227 (C)	P	13,750	13,750	5,240
Western Michigan University; Kalamazoo, Mich. 49008	20,675 (C)	Pub	2,810	6,620	3,830
Western Montana College; Dillon, Mont. 59725	905 (C)	Pub	1,274	2,945	3,100
Western New England College; Springfield, Mass. 01119	2,993 (C)	P	9,174	9,174	5,400
Western New Mexico University; Silver City, N.M. 88061	1,790 (C)	Pub	1,204	4,384	2,110
Western Oregon State College; Monmouth, Ore. 97361	3,554 (C)	Pub	2,481	5,982	3,166
Western School of Christian Ministries; Fresno, Calif. 93710	274 (C)	P	2,904	2,904	3,170
Western State College of Colorado; Gunnison, Colo. 81230	2,662 (C)	Pub	1,667	5,057	3,180
Western Washington University; Bellingham, Wash. 98225	9,183 (C)	Pub	1,860	6,297	3,488
Westfield State College; Westfield, Mass. 01086	3,162 (C)	Pub	3,023	6,890	3,842
West Florida, University of; Pensacola, Fla. 32514	6,408 (C)	Pub	1,654	6,413	3,360
West Georgia College; Carrollton, Ga. 30118	5,586 (C)	Pub	2,268	5,844	3,352
West Liberty State College; West Liberty, W. Va. 26074	2,377 (C)	Pub	1,590	3,660	2,650
West Los Angeles, University of, School of Paralegal Studies; Los Angeles, Calif. 90066	267 (C)	P	4,350	4,350	n.a.
Westminster College; Fulton, Mo. 65251	761 (C)	P	9,150	9,150	3,550
Westminster College; New Wilmington, Pa. 16172	1,347 (C)	P	11,365	11,365	3,285
Westminster Coll. of Salt Lake City; Salt Lake City, Utah 84105	1,711 (C)	P	8,220	8,220	3,880
Westmont College; Santa Barbara, Calif. 93108	1,317 (C)	P	12,766	12,766	4,850
West Suburban College of Nursing; Oak Park, Ill. 60302	222 (C)	P	8,496	8,496	4,035
West Texas State University; Canyon, Tex. 79016	4,813 (C)	Pub	2,010	4,208	2,686
West Virginia Institute of Technology; Montgomery, W. Va. 25136	3,027 (C)	Pub	1,784	3,954	3,752
West Virginia State College; Institute, W. Va. 25112	4,986 (C)	Pub	1,712	4,002	3,050
West Virginia University; Morgantown, W. Va. 26506-6009	16,282 (C)	Pub	1,928	5,486	4,016
West Virginia University at Parkersburg; Parkersburg, W. Va. 26101-9577	3,979 (C)	Pub	864	2,880	n.a.
West Virginia Wesleyan College; Buckhannon, W. Va. 26201	1,529 (C)	P	12,605	12,605	3,350
Wheaton College; Norton, Mass. 02766	1,319 (C)	P	17,670	17,670	6,050
Wheaton College; Wheaton, Ill. 60187-5593	2,304 (C)	P	10,640	10,640	4,070

Institution and location	Enrollment	Control	Tuition ($) Res.	Tuition ($) Nonres.	Rm/Bd ($)
Wheeling Jesuit College; Wheeling, W. Va. 26003	1,290 (C)	P	10,000	10,000	4,370
Wheelock College; Boston, Mass. 02215	771 (C)	P	11,776	11,776	5,224
White Plains, Coll. of, of Pace Univ. *See* Pace Univ.					
Whitman College; Walla Walla, Wash. 99362	1,205 (C)	P	15,805	15,805	4,790
Whittier College; Whittier, Calif. 90608	1,159 (C)	P	16,181	16,181	5,480
Whitworth College; Spokane, Wash. 99251	1,400 (C)	P	11,965	11,965	4,300
Wichita State University; Wichita, Kan. 67208	15,120 (C)	Pub	1,904	6,074	2,800
Widener University; Chester, Pa. 19013	2,403 (C)	P	11,120	11,120	4,830
Wilberforce University; Wilberforce, Ohio 45384	758 (C)	P	6,646	6,646	3,392
Wiley College; Marshall, Tex. 75670	505 (C)	P	3,450	3,450	2,544
Wilkes University; Wilkes-Barre, Pa. 18766	1,965 (C)	P	9,500	9,500	5,000
Willamette University; Salem, Ore. 97301	1,623 (C)	P	13,030	13,030	4,150
William and Mary, College of; Williamsburg, Va. 23185	5,356 (C)	Pub	4,048	11,428	3,900
William Carey College; Hattiesburg, Miss. 39401	1,546 (C)	P	4,555	4,555	2,250
William Jewell College; Liberty, Mo. 64068	1,366 (C)	P	8,970	8,970	2,750
William Paterson College; Wayne, N.J. 07470	7,864 (C)	Pub	2,832	3,728	4,510
William Penn College; Oskaloosa, Iowa 52577	750 (C)	P	9,870	9,870	2,990
Williams Baptist College; Walnut Ridge, Ark. 72476	612 (C)	P	3,662	3,662	2,796
Williams College; Williamstown, Mass. 01267	1,985 (C)	P	17,840	17,840	5,410
William Smith College. *See* Hobart and William Smith Colleges					
William Tyndale College; Farmington Hills, Mich. 48108	360 (C)	P	4,890	4,890	3,400
William Woods College; Fulton, Mo. 65251	823 (W)	P	9,825	9,825	4,200
Wilmington College; New Castle, Del. 19720	1,773 (C)	P	4,945	4,945	n.a.
Wilmington College of Ohio; Wilmington, Ohio 45177	995 (C)	P	9,830	9,830	3,870
Wilson College; Chambersburg, Pa. 17201-1285	901 (W)	P	11,546	11,546	5,084
Wingate College; Wingate, N.C. 28174	1,386 (C)	P	6,740	6,740	3,050
Winona State University; Winona, Minn. 55987	7,000 (C)	Pub	2,300	4,300	2,700
Winston-Salem State University; Winston-Salem, N.C. 27110	2,604 (C)	Pub	1,254	6,272	2,762
Winthrop University; Rock Hill, S.C. 29733	4,107 (C)	Pub	3,112	5,512	3,132
Wisconsin, University of-Eau Claire; Eau Claire, Wis. 54701	9,891 (C)	Pub	2,034	6,219	2,704
Wisconsin, University of-Green Bay; Green Bay, Wis. 54302	4,679 (C)	Pub	1,995	6,180	2,600
Wisconsin, University of-La Crosse; La Crosse, Wis. 54601	8,177 (C)	Pub	1,954	5,800	2,190
Wisconsin, University of-Madison; Madison, Wis. 53706	29,248 (C)	Pub	2,290	7,480	3,850
Wisconsin, University of-Milwaukee; Milwaukee, Wis. 53201	19,715 (C)	Pub	2,393	7,679	4,076
Wisconsin, University of-Oshkosh; Oshkosh, Wis. 54901	9,536 (C)	Pub	1,922	5,700	2,110
Wisconsin, University of-Parkside; Kenosha, Wis. 53141–2000	4,896 (C)	Pub	1,990	6,175	3,200
Wisconsin, University of-Platteville; Platteville, Wis. 53818	4,381 (C)	Pub	2,087	6,271	2,518
Wisconsin, University of-River Falls; River Falls, Wis. 54022	5,021 (C)	Pub	2,025	6,210	2,318
Wisconsin, University of-Stevens Point; Stevens Point, Wis. 54481	8,269 (C)	Pub	2,080	6,265	2,858
Wisconsin, University of-Stout; Menomonie, Wis. 54751	6,803 (C)	Pub	2,054	6,238	2,462
Wisconsin, University of-Superior; Superior, Wis. 54880	2,112 (C)	Pub	1,917	6,102	2,470
Wisconsin, University of-Whitewater; Whitewater, Wis. 53190	9,222 (C)	Pub	2,039	6,224	2,292
Wisconsin Lutheran College; Milwaukee, Wis. 53226	322 (C)	P	8,680	8,680	3,500
Wittenberg University; Springfield, Ohio 45501	2,279 (C)	P	15,726	15,726	4,272
Wofford College; Spartanburg, S.C. 29303-3663	1,127 (C)	P	11,480	11,480	4,150
Women's College of Brenau University, The; Gainesville, Ga. 30501	503 (W)	P	8,364	8,364	5,536
Woodbury University; Burbanks, Calif. 91510-7846	933 (C)	P	11,190	11,190	5,340
Wooster, College of; Wooster, Ohio 44691	1,785 (C)	P	14,380	14,380	4,400
Worcester Polytechnic Institute; Worcester, Mass. 01609	2,786 (C)	P	15,290	15,290	5,060
Worcester State College; Worcester, Mass. 01602–2597	3,600 (C)	Pub	2,532	6,396	3,690
World College West; Petaluma, Calif. 94952	134 (C)	P	10,200	10,200	4,400
Wright State University; Dayton, Ohio 45435	13,699 (C)	Pub	2,934	5,868	3,579
Wyoming, University of; Laramie, Wyo. 82071	9,293 (C)	Pub	1,426	4,498	3,313
Xavier University; Cincinnati, Ohio 45207	3,996 (C)	P	10,970	10,970	4,470
Xavier University of Louisiana; New Orleans, La. 70125	2,916 (C)	P	6,615	6,615	3,800
Yale University; New Haven, Conn. 06520	5,194 (C)	P	18,630	18,630	6,480
Yeshiva University; New York, N.Y. 10033-3299	1,852 (C)	P	11,550	11,550	3,950
York College of Pennsylvania; York, Pa. 17405	2,975 (C)	P	4,714	4,714	3,161
Youngstown State Univ.; Youngstown, Ohio 44555	13,569 (C)	Pub	2,589	4,389	3,555

1. Varies. 2. $23 per credit. 3. $106 per credit. 4. $215 per credit.

Why Do Teachers Leave Teaching?

Of the 2.3 million public school teachers in the 1987–88 school year, 6 percent had left teaching by the following year. For the 300,000 private school teachers, the respective figure was 13 percent. Why did they leave?

The largest share (35 percent of public and 47 percent of private school teachers) cited either family or personal reasons, health, or pregnancy/childbearing as the main reason.

The data are obtained from the Teacher Followup Survey (TFS) conducted by the Census Bureau and sponsored by the National Center for Education Statistics (NCES). The survey is conducted at 3-year intervals: the first TFS was during 1988–89 and the latest during the 1991–92 school year.

Results from the 1988–89 TFS have been released by NCES. Products from the 1991–92 TFS were to begin coming out late in 1993.

Selected Degree Abbreviations

A.B. Bachelor of Arts
AeEng. Aeronautical Engineer
A.M.T. Master of Arts in Teaching
B.A. Bachelor of Arts
B.A.E. Bachelor of Arts in Education, or Bachelor of Art Education, Aeronautical Engineering, Agricultural Engineering, or Architectural Engineering
B.Ag. Bachelor of Agriculture
B.A.M. Bachelor of Applied Mathematics
B.Arch. Bachelor of Architecture
B.B.A. Bachelor of Business Administration
B.C.E. Bachelor of Civil Engineering
B.Ch.E. Bachelor of Chemical Engineering
B.C.L. Bachelor of Canon Law
B.D. Bachelor of Divinity
B.E. Bachelor of Education or Bachelor of Engineering
B.E.E. Bachelor of Electrical Engineering
B.F. Bachelor of Forestry
B.F.A. Bachelor of Fine Arts
B.J. Bachelor of Journalism
B.L.S. Bachelor of Liberal Studies or Bachelor of Library Science
B.Lit. Bachelor of Literature
B.M. Bachelor of Medicine or Bachelor of Music
B.M.S. Bachelor of Marine Science
B.N. Bachelor of Nursing
B.Pharm. Bachelor of Pharmacy
B.R.E. Bachelor of Religious Education
B.S. Bachelor of Science
B.S.Ed. Bachelor of Science in Education
C.E. Civil Engineer
Ch.E. Chemical Engineer
D.B.A. Doctor of Business Administration
D.C. Doctor of Chiropractic
D.D. Doctor of Divinity[1]
D.D.S. Doctor of Dental Surgery or Doctor of Dental Science
D.L.S. Doctor of Library Science
D.M.D. Doctor of Dental Medicine
D.O. Doctor of Osteopathy
D.M.S. Doctor of Medical Science
D.P.A. Doctor of Public Administration[2]
D.P.H. Doctor of Public Health
D.R.E. Doctor of Religious Education
D.S.W. Doctor of Social Welfare or Doctor of Social Work
D.Sc. Doctor of Science[3]
D.V.M. Doctor of Veterinary Medicine
Ed.D. Doctor of Education[2]
Ed.S. Education Specialist
E.E. Electrical Engineer
E.M. Engineer of Mines
E.Met. Engineer of Metallurgy
I.E. Industrial Engineer or Industrial Engineering
J.D. Doctor of Laws[2]
J.S.D. Doctor of Juristic Science
L.H.D. Doctor of Humane Letters[3]
Litt.B. Bachelor of Letters
Litt.M. Master of Letters[4]
LL.B. Bachelor of Laws
LL.D. Doctor of Laws[3]
LL.M. Master of Laws
M.A. Master of Arts
M.Aero.E. Master of Aeronautical Engineering
M.B.A. Master of Business Administration
M.C.E. Master of Christian Education or Master of Civil Engineering
M.C.S. Master of Computer Science
M.D. Doctor of Medicine
M.Div. Master of Divinity
M.E. Master of Engineering
M.Ed. Master of Education
M.Eng. Master of Engineering
M.F.A. Master of Fine Arts
M.H.A. Master of Hospital Administration
M.L.S. Master of Library Science
M.M. Master of Music
M.M.E. Master of Mechanical Engineering or Master of Music Education
M.Mus. Master of Music
M.N. Master of Nursing
M.R.E. Master of Religious Education
M.S. Master of Science
M.S.W. Master of Social Work
M.Th. Master of Theology
Nuc.E. Nuclear Engineer
O.D. Doctor of Optometry
Pharm.D. Doctor of Pharmacy[2]
Ph.B. Bachelor of Philosophy
Ph.D. Doctor of Philosophy
S.B. Bachelor of Science
Sc.D. Doctor of Science[3]
S.J.D. Doctor of Juridical Science or Doctor of the Science of Law
S.Sc.D. Doctor of Social Science
S.T.B. Bachelor of Sacred Theology
S.T.D. Doctor of Sacred Theology
S.T.M. Master of Sacred Theology
Th.B. Bachelor of Theology
Th.D. Doctor of Theology
Th.M. Master of Theology

1. Honorary. 2. Earned and honorary. 3. Usually honorary. 4. Sometimes honorary.

Academic Costume: Colors Associated With Fields

Field	Color	Field	Color
Agriculture	Maize	Medicine	Green
Arts, Letters, Humanities	White	Music	Pink
Commerce, Accountancy, Business	Drab	Nursing	Apricot
Dentistry	Lilac	Oratory (Speech)	Silver gray
Economics	Copper	Pharmacy	Olive green
Education	Light blue	Philosophy	Dark blue
Engineering	Orange	Physical Education	Sage green
Fine Arts, Architecture	Brown	Public Admin. including Foreign Service	Peacock blue
Forestry	Russet	Public Health	Salmon pink
Journalism	Crimson	Science	Golden yellow
Law	Purple	Social Work	Citron
Library Science	Lemon	Theology	Scarlet
		Veterinary Science	Gray

THE OLYMPIC GAMES

(W)—Site of Winter Games. (S)—Site of Summer Games

1896 Athens
1900 Paris
1904 St. Louis
1906 Athens
1908 London
1912 Stockholm
1920 Antwerp
1924 Chamonix (W)
1924 Paris (S)
1928 St. Moritz (W)
1928 Amsterdam (S)
1932 Lake Placid (W)
1932 Los Angeles (S)
1936 Garnisch–Partenkirchen (W)
1936 Berlin (S)
1948 St. Moritz (W)
1948 London (S)
1952 Oslo (W)
1952 Helsinki (S)
1956 Cortina d'Ampezzo, Italy (W)
1956 Melbourne (S)
1960 Squaw Valley, Calif. (W)
1960 Rome (S)
1964 Innsbruck, Austria (W)
1964 Tokyo (S)
1968 Grenoble, France (W)
1968 Mexico City (S)
1972 Sapporo, Japan (W)
1972 Munich (S)
1976 Innsbruck, Austria (W)
1976 Montreal (S)
1980 Lake Placid (W)
1980 Moscow (S)
1984 Sarajevo, Yugoslavia (W)
1984 Los Angeles (S)
1988 Calgary, Alberta (W)
1988 Seoul, South Korea (S)
1992 Albertville, France (W)
1992 Barcelona, Spain (S)
1994 Lillehammer, Norway (W)
1996 Atlanta, Ga. (S)

The first Olympic Games of which there is record were held in 776 B.C., and consisted of one event, a great foot race of about 200 yards held on a plain by the River Alpheus (now the Ruphia) just outside the little town of Olympia in Greece. It was from that date the Greeks began to keep their calendar by "Olympiads," the four–year spans between the celebrations of the famous games.

The modern Olympic Games, which started in Athens in 1896, are the result of the devotion of a French educator, Baron Pierre de Coubertin, to the idea that, since young people and athletics have gone together through the ages, educaiton and athletics might go hand–in–hand toward a better international understanding.

The principal organization responsible for the staging of the Games every four years is the International Olympic Committee (IOC). Other important roles are played by the National Olympic Committees in each participating country, international sports federations, and the organizing committee of the host city.

The headquarters of the 89–member International Olympic Committee are in Lausanne, Switzerland. The president of the IOC is Juan Antonio Samaranch of Spain.

The Olympic motto is "Citius, Altius, Fortius,"–"Faster, Higher, Stronger." The Olympic symbol is five interlocking circles colored blue, yellow, black, green, and red, on a white background, representing the five continents. At least one of those colors appears in the national flag of every country.

Unified Team, United Germany Dominate 1992 Winter Games

Everything new was old again at the 1992 Winter Olympics in Albertville, France.

The changing world political scene presented the Games with some major changes.

East and West Germany competed as one country for the first time since 1936. Athletes from the republics of the former Soviet Union remained tied together under the Olympic banner and competed as something called The Unified Team.

Yet, when the Games were concluded, the results looked very familiar.

Germany stood atop the medals standing with a total of 26—10 gold, 10 silver, six bronze. The Unified Team finished second with 23 medals—nine gold, six silver, eight bronze.

In both 1988 and 1984, those two countries also finished 1–2, with the Soviet Union on top in both cases.

Overall, more than 2,000 athletes from 64 nations participated in competition held in a mountainous region spanning 650 square miles.

The United States' hero was Bonnie Blair, a double gold medal winner in speedskating. The Champaign, Ill., skater won both the 500-meter and 1,000-meter races.

The United States fared a bit better in these games than it had during recent Winter Olympics. Americans brought home 11 medals, 5 of them gold. That equalled the finest performance ever by a U.S. team on foreign soil. The United States also won 11 medals at Oslo in 1952.

The total of 11 was one off the American standard of 12 set at the 1980 Games in Lake Placid, N.Y.

The United States hockey team created some excitement early in the Games, emerging undefeated from preliminary play into the medal round. The American hockey team, trying to duplicate the surprise gold medal won by the U.S. team in 1980, fell short of its goal, finishing fourth.

Figure skater Kristi Yamaguchi lived up to pre-Olympic predictions by capturing the women's gold medal.

Donna Weinbrecht of New Jersey won a gold medal in the new Olympic sport of mogul skiing. American Nelson Carmichael won a bronze in that event.

Two American Alpine skiers—Diann Roffe and Hilary Lindh—won silver medals in the giant slalom and downhill, respectively.

The American success, though modest by international standards, left the U.S. team with hope for an even better showing in 1994, when the Winter Games will be held in Lillehammer, Norway.

The U.S. cause may be aided in 1994 by the addition of some new sports. The U.S. won demonstration bronze medals in freestyle ballet skiing and curling at Albertville. There will be men's and women's competitions in both sports in 1994, along with men's and women's speed skiing. *—Dennis Lyons*

Winter Games

FIGURE SKATING–MEN

1908	Ulrich Salchow, Sweden
1920	Gillis Grafstrom, Sweden
1924	Gillis Grafstrom, Sweden
1928	Gillis Grafstrom, Sweden
1932	Karl Schaefer, Austria
1936	Karl Schaefer, Austria
1948	Richard Button, United States
1952	Richard Button, United States
1956	Hayes Alan Jenkins, United States
1960	David Jenkins, United States
1964	Manfred Schnelldorfer, Germany
1968	Wolfgang Schwartz, Austria
1972	Ondrej Nepela, Czechoslovakia
1976	John Curry, Great Britain
1980	Robin Cousins, Great Britain
1984	Scott Hamilton, United States
1988	Brian Boitano, United States
1992	Viktor Petrenko, Unified Team*

*Former Soviet Union team.

FIGURE SKATING–WOMEN

1908	Madge Syers, Britain
1920	Magda Julin–Maurey, Sweden
1924	Herma Szabo–Planck, Austria
1928	Sonja Henie, Norway
1932	Sonja Henie, Norway
1936	Sonja Henle, Norway
1948	Barbara Ann Scott, Canada
1952	Jeannette Altwegg, Great Britain
1956	Tenley Albright, United States
1960	Carol Heiss, United States
1964	Sjoukje Dijkstra, Netherlands
1968	Peggy Fleming, United States
1972	Beatrix Schuba, Austria
1976	Dorothy Hamill, United States
1980	Anett Poetzsch, East Germany
1984	Katarina Witt, East Germany
1988	Katarina Witt, East Germany
1992	Kristi Yamaguchi, United States

SPEED SKATING–MEN

(U.S. winners only)

500 Meters

1924	Charles Jewtraw	44.0
1932	John A. Shea	43.4
1952	Kenneth Henry	43.2
1964	Terrence McDermott	40.1
1980	Eric Heiden	38.03

1,000 Meters

1976	Peter Mueller	1:19.32
1980	Eric Heiden	1:15.18

1,500 Meters

1932	John A. Shea	2:57.5
1980	Eric Heiden	1:55.44

5,000 Meters

1932	Irving Jaffee	9:40.8
1980	Eric Heiden	7:02.29

10,000 Meters

1932	Irving Jaffee	19:13.6
1980	Eric Heiden	14:28.13

SPEED SKATING–WOMEN

500 Meters

1972	Anne Henning	43.33
1976	Sheila Young	42.76
1988	Bonnie Blair	39.10[1]
1992	Bonnie Blair	40.33

1,000 Meters

1992	Bonnie Blair	1:21.90

1,500 Meters

1972	Dianne Holum	2:20.85

1. World Record

SKIING, ALPINE–MEN

Downhill

1948	Henri Oreiller, France	2m55.0s
1952	Zeno Colo, Italy	2m30.8s
1956	Anton Sailer, Austria	2m52.2s
1960	Jean Vuarnet, France	2m06.2s
1964	Egon Zimmermann, Austria	2m18.16s
1968	Jean–Claude Killy, France	1m59.85s
1972	Bernhard Russi, Switzerland	1m51.43s
1976	Franz Klammer, Austria	1m45.72s
1980	Leonhard Stock, Austria	1m45.50s
1984	Bill Johnson, United States	1m45.59s
1988	Pirmin Zurbriggen, Switzerland	1m59.63s
1992	Patrick Ortlieb, Austria	1m50.37s

Slalom

1948	Edi Reinalter, Switzerland	2m10.3s
1952	Othmar Schneider, Austria	2m00.0s
1956	Anton Sailer, Austria	194.7 pts.
1960	Ernst Hinsterseer, Austria	2m08.9s
1964	Josef Stiegler, Austria	2m10.13
1968	Jean–Claude Killy, France	1m39,73s
1972	Francisco Fernandez Ochoa, Spain	1m49.27s
1976	Piero Gros, Italy	2m03.29s
1980	Integmar Stenmark, Sweden	1m44.26s
1984	Phil Mahre, United States	1m39.41s
1988	Alberto Tomba, Italy	1m39.47s
1992	Finn Christian, Norway	1m44.39s

Giant Slalom

1952	Stein Eriksen, Norway	2m25.0s
1956	Anton Sailer, Austria	3m00.1s
1960	Roger Staub, Switzerland	1m48.3s
1964	François Bonlieu, France	1m46.71s
1968	Jean-Claude Killy, France	3m29.28s
1972	Gustavo Thoeni, Italy	3m09.52s
1976	Heini Hemmi, Switzerland	3m26.97s
1980	Ingemar Stenmark, Sweden	2m40.74s
1984	Max Julen, Switzerland	1m20.54s
1988	Alberto Tomba, Italy	2m06.37s
1992	Alberto Tomba, Italy	2m06.98s

SKIING, ALPINE–WOMEN

Downhill

1948	Hedi Schlunegger, Switzerland	2m28.3s
1952	Trude Jochum–Beiser, Austria	1m47.1s
1956	Madeleine Berthod, Switzerland	1m40.1s
1960	Heidi Biebl, Germany	1m37.6s
1964	Christi Haas, Austria	1m55.39s
1968	Olga Pall, Austria	1m40.87s

1972	Marie–Therese Nadig, Switzerland	1m36.68s
1976	Rosi Mittermeier, West Germany	1m46.16s
1980	Annemarie Proell Moser, Austria	1m37.52s
1984	Michela Figini, Switzerland	1m13.36s
1988	Marina Kiehl, West Germany	1m25.86s
1992	Kerrin Lee-Gartner, Canada	1m52.55s

Slalom

1948	Gretchen Fraser, United States	1m57.2s
1952	Andrea Mead Lawrence, United States	2m10.6s
1956	Renee Colliard, Switzerland	112.3 pts.
1960	Anne Heggtveigt, Canada	1m49.6s
1964	Christine Goitschel, France	1m29.86s
1968	Marielle Goitschel, France	1m25.86s
1972	Barbara Cochran, United States	1m31.24s
1976	Rosi Mittermeier, West Germany	1m30.54s
1980	Hanni Wenzel, Liechtenstein	1m25.09s
1984	Paoletta Magoni, Italy	1m36.47s
1988	Vreni Schneider, Switzerland	1m36.69s
1992	Petra Kronberger, Austria	1m32.68s

Giant Slalom

1952	Andrea M. Lawrence, United States	2m06.8s
1956	Ossi Reichert, Germany	1m56.5s
1960	Yvonne Ruegg, Switzerland	1m39.9s
1964	Marielle Goitschel, France	1m52.24s
1968	Nancy Greene, Canada	1m51.97s
1972	Marie–Therese Nadig, Switzerland	1m29.90s
1976	Kathy Kreiner, Canada	1m29.13s
1980	Hanni Wenzel, Liechtenstein	2m41.66s
1984	Debbie Armstrong, United States	2m20.98s
1988	Vreni Schneider, Switzerland	2m06.49s
1992	Pernilla Wiberg, Sweden	2m12.74s

1992 UNITED STATES MEDALISTS

Alpine Skiing

Women Downhill—SILVER—Hilary Lindh, Juneau, Alaska
Women Giant Slalom—SILVER—Diann Roffe, Potsdam, N.Y.

Figure Skating

Men—SILVER—Paul Wylie, Denver
Women—GOLD—Kristi Yamaguchi, Fremont, Calif.
Women—BRONZE—Nancy Kerrigan, Stoneham, Mass.

Freestyle Skiing

Men Moguls—BRONZE—Nelston Carmichael, Steamboat Springs, Colo.
Women Moguls—GOLD—Donna Weinbrecht, West Milford, N.J.

Short Track Speedskating

Women—GOLD—Cathy Turner, Rochester, N.Y.
Women 3,000 Relay—SILVER—United States (Cathy Turner, Hilton, N.Y.; Amy Peterson, Maplewood, Minn.; Darci Dohnal, Wauwatosa, Wis.; Nikki Ziegelmeyer, Imperial, Mo.)

Speedskating

Women 500—GOLD—Bonnie Blair, Champaign, Ill.
Women 1,000—GOLD—Bonnie Blair, Champaign, Ill.

ICE HOCKEY

1920	Canada	1964	U.S.S.R.
1924	Canada	1968	U.S.S.R.
1928	Canada	1972	U.S.S.R.
1932	Canada	1976	U.S.S.R.
1936	Great Britain	1980	United States
1948	Canada	1984	U.S.S.R.
1952	Canada	1988	U.S.S.R.
1956	U.S.S.R.	1992	Unified Team*
1960	United States		

*Former Soviet Union team.

DISTRIBUTION OF MEDALS 1992 WINTER GAMES

(Albertville, France)

	Gold	Silver	Bronze	Total
Germany	10	10	6	26
Unified Team	9	6	8	23
Austria	6	7	8	21
Norway	9	6	5	20
Italy	4	6	4	14
United States	5	4	2	11
France	3	5	1	9
Finland	3	1	3	7
Canada	2	3	2	7
Japan	1	2	4	7
South Korea	2	1	1	4
The Netherlands	1	1	2	4
Sweden	1	0	3	4
Switzerland	1	0	2	3
China	0	3	0	3
Czechoslovakia	0	0	3	3
Luxembourg	0	2	0	2
New Zealand	0	1	0	1
North Korea	0	1	0	1
Spain	0	0	1	1

FINAL 1992 OLYMPIC HOCKEY STANDINGS

	W	L	T
1. Unified Team	8	0	0
2. Canada	7	1	0
3. Czechoslovakia	6	2	0
United States	5	2	1

1. Won gold medal 2. Won silver medal 3. Won bronze medal

Championship
Unified Team 3, Canada 1

Third Place
Czechoslovakia 6, United States 1

Fifth Place
Sweden 4, Germany 3

Seventh Place
Finland 4, France 1

Ninth Place
Norway 5, Switzerland 2

1994 Winter Games Headed for Another Small Town

When the nations of the world convene for the 1994 Winter Olympics in Lillehammer, Norway, they will be coming to a town with a population of about 23,000.

Lillehammer is actually one of the few Norwegian towns of any size in the interior of the Scandinavian country. Norway's total population is 4.2 million.

The Lillehammer games will begin on Feb. 12, 1994—less than two full years after the conclusion of the most recent Winter Games in Albertville, France.

The 1994 Winter Games will be the beginning of the International Olympic Committee's new cycle of having the Winter Games and Summer Games two years apart, instead of in the same year, as has been the tradition since the Winter Games began in 1924.

The idea is that the Winter Games will get more attention when they aren't staged the same year as the bigger Summer Games.

The next Summer Games won't be held until 1996 in Atlanta, Ga.

Other 1992 Winter Olympic Games Champions

Biathlon

10-kilometer—Mark Kirchner, Germany
20-kilometer—Evgeni Redkine, Unified Team
30-kilometer relay—Germany

Bobsledding

2-man—Switzerland
4-man—Austria I

Figure Skating

Pairs—Natalia Mishkutienuk and Artur Dmitriev, Unified Team
Dance—Marina Klimova and Sergei Ponomarenko, Unified Team

Speed Skating–Men

500m—Uwe-Jens Mey, Germany
1,000m—Olaf Zinke, Germany
1,500m—Johann Koss, Norway
5,000m—Geir Karlstad, Norway
10,000m—Bart Veldkamp, The Netherlands

Speed Skating–Women

500m—Bonnie Blair, United States
1,000m—Bonnie Blair, United States
1,500m—Jacqueline Boerner, Germany
3,000m—Gunda Niemann, Germany
5,000m—Gunda Niemann, Germany

Luge

Men's singles—Georg Hacki, Germany
Men's doubles—Stefan Krausse and Jan Behrendt, Germany

Skiing, Nordic–Men

Combined team—Japan
Combined—Fabrice Guy, France
Men's 10-kilometer—Vegard Ulvang, Norway
Men's 15-kilometer—Bjorn Dahlie, Norway.
Men's 30-kilometer—Vegard Uvang, Norway
Men's 50-kilometer—Bjorn Dahlie, Norway
40-kilometer relay—Norway
90-m jump—Ernst Vettori, Austria
120-m jump—Toni Nieminen, Finland

Skiing, Nordic–Women

Women's 5-kilometer—Marjut Lukkarinen, Finland
Women's 10-kilometer—Lyubov Egornova, Unified Team
Women's 15-kilometer—Lyubov Egornova, Unified Team
Women's 30-kilometer—Stafania Belmondo, Italy
20-kilometer relay—Unified Team

Summer Games

TRACK AND FIELD–MEN

100-Meter Dash

1896	Thomas Burke, United States	12s
1900	Francis W. Jarvis, United States	10.8s
1904	Archie Hahn, United States	11s
1906	Archie Hahn, United States	11.2s
1908	Reginald Walker, South Africa	10.8s
1912	Ralph Craig, United States	10.8s
1920	Charles Paddock, United States	10.8s
1924	Harold Abrahams, Great Britain	10.6s
1928	Percy Williams, Canada	10.8s
1932	Eddie Tolan, United States	10.3s
1936	Jesse Owens, United States	10.3s [1]
1948	Harrison Dillard, United States	10.3s
1952	Lindy Remigino, United States	10.4s
1956	Bobby Morrow, United States	10.5s
1960	Armin Hary, Germany	10.2s
1964	Robert Hayes, United States	10s
1968	James Hines, United States	9.9s
1972	Valery Borzow, U.S.S.R.	10.14s
1976	Hasely Crawford, Trinidad and Tobago	10.06s
1980	Allan Wells, Britain	10.25s
1984	Carl Lewis, United States	9.99s
1988	Carl Lewis, United States	9.92s [2]
1992	Linford Christie, Great Britain	09.96s

1. Wind assisted. 2. Lewis was awarded the gold medal when Ben Johnson of Canada, the original winner in 09.79s, was stripped of the medal after testing positive for steroid use.

200-Meter Dash

1900	John Tewksbury, United States	22.2s
1904	Archie Hahn, United States	21.6s
1908	Robert Kerr, Canada	22.6s
1912	Ralph Craig, United States	21.7s
1920	Allan Woodring, United States	22s
1924	Jackson Scholz, United States	21.6s
1928	Percy Williams, Canada	21.8s
1932	Eddie Tolan, United States	21.2s
1936	Jesse Owens, United States	20.7s
1948	Melvin E. Patton, United States	21.1s
1952	Andrew Stanfield, United States	20.7s
1956	Bobby Morrow, United States	20.6s
1960	Livio Berruti, Italy	20.5s
1964	Henry Carr, United States	20.3s
1968	Tommie Smith, United States	19.8s
1972	Vallery Borzov, U.S.S.R.	20s
1976	Don Quarrie, Jamaica	20.23s
1980	Pietro Mennea, Italy	20.19s
1984	Carl Lewis, United States	19.80s
1988	Joe DeLoach, United States	19.75s
1992	Mike Marsh, United States	20.01s

400-Meter Dash

1896	Thomas Burke, United States	54.2s
1900	Maxwell Long, United States	49.4s
1904	Harry Hillman, United States	49.2s
1906	Paul Pilgrim, United States	53.2s
1908	Wyndham Halswelle, Great Britain (walkover)	50s
1912	Charles Reidpath, United States	48.2s
1920	Bevil Rudd, South Africa	49.6s
1924	Eric Liddell, Great Britain	47.6s
1928	Ray Barbuti, United States	47.8s
1932	William Carr, United States	46.2s
1936	Archie Williams, United States	46.5s
1948	Arthur Wint, Jamaica, B.W.I.	46.2s
1952	George Rhoden, Jamaica, B.W.I.	45.9s
1956	Charles Jenkins, United States	46.7s
1960	Otis Davis, United States	44.9s

1964	Mike Larrabee, United States	45.1s
1968	Lee Evans, United States	43.8s
1972	Vincent Matthews, United States	44.66s
1976	Alberto Juantorena, Cuba	44.26s
1980	Viktor Markin, U.S.S.R.	44.60s
1984	Alonzo Babers, United States	44.27s
1988	Steve Lewis, United States	43.87s
1992	Quincy Watts, United States	43.50s

800–Meter Run

1896	Edwin Flack, Australia	2m11s
1900	Alfred Tysoe, Great Britain	2m1.4s
1904	James Lightbody, United States	1m56s
1906	Paul Pilgrim, United States	2m1.2s
1908	Mel Sheppard, United states	1m52.8s
1912	Ted Meredith, United States	1m51.9s
1920	Albert Hill, Great Britain	1m53.4s
1924	Douglas Lowe, Great Britain	1m52.4s
1928	Douglas Lowe, Great Britain	1m51.8s
1932	Thomas Hampson, Great Britain	1m49.8s
1936	John Woodruff, United States	1m52.9s
1948	Malvin Whitfield, United States	1m49.2s
1952	Malvin Whitfield, United States	1m49.2s
1956	Tom Courtney, United States	1m47.7s
1960	Peter Snell, New Zealand	1m46.3s
1964	Peter Snell, New Zealand	1m45.1s
1968	Ralph Doubell, Australia	1m44.3s
1972	David Wottle, United States	1m45.9s
1976	Alberto Juantorena, Cuba	1m43.5s
1980	Steve Ovett, Britain	1m45.4s
1984	Joaquin Cruz, Brazil	1m43.0s
1988	Paul Ereng, Kenya	1m43.45s
1992	WilliamTanui, Kenya	1m43.66s

1,500–Meter Run

1896	Edwin Flack, Australia	4m33.2s
1900	Charles Bennett, Great Britain	4m6s
1904	James Lightbody, United States	4m5.4s
1906	James Lightbody, United States	4m12s
1908	Mel Sheppard, United States	4m3.4s
1912	Arnold Jackson, Great Britain	3m56.8s
1920	Albert Hill, Great Britain	4m1.8s
1924	Paavo Nurmi, Finland	3m53.6s
1928	Harry Larva, Finland	3m53.2s
1932	Luigi Becali, Italy	3m51.2s
1936	Jack Lovelock, New Zealand	3m47.8s
1948	Henri Eriksson, Sweden	3m49.8s
1952	Joseph Barthel, Luxembourg	3m45.2s
1956	Ron Delany, Ireland	3m41.2s
1960	Herb Elliott, Australia	3m35.6s
1964	Peter Snell, New Zealand	3m38.1s
1968	Kipchoge Keino, Kenya	3m34.9s
1972	Pekka Vasala, Finland	3m36.3s
1976	John Walker, New Zealand	3m39.17s
1980	Sebastian Coe, Britain	3m38.4s
1984	Sebastian Coe, Britain	3m32.53s
1988	Peter Rono, Kenya	3m35.96s
1992	Fermin Cacho Ruiz, Spain	3m40.12s

5,000-Meter Run

1912	Hannes Kolehmainen, Finland	14m36.6s
1920	Joseph Guillemot, France	14m55.6s
1024	Paavo Nurmi, Finland	14m31.2s
1928	Willie Ritola, Finland	14m38s
1932	Lauri Lehtinen, Finland	14m30s
1936	Gunnar Hockert, Finland	14m22.2s
1948	Gaston Reiff, Belgium	14m17.6s
1952	Emil Zatopek, Czechoslovakia	14m6.6s
1956	Vladimir Kuts, U.S.S.R.	13m39.6s
1960	Murray Halberg, New Zealand	13m43.4s
1964	Bob Schul, United States	13m48.8s
1968	Mohamed Gammoudi, Tunisia	14m.05s
1972	Lasse Viren, Finland	13m26.4s
1976	Lasse Viren, Finland	13m24.76s
1980	Miruts Yifter, Ethiopia	13m21s
1984	Saud Aouita, Morocco	13m5.59s
1988	John Ngugi, Kenya	13m11.70s
1992	Dieter Baumann, Germany	13m12.52s

10,000–Meter Run

1912	Hannes Kolehmainen, Finland	31m20.8s
1920	Paavo Nurmi, Finland	31m45.8s
1924	Willie Ritola, Finland	30m23.2s
1928	Paavo Nurmi, Finland	30m18.8s
1932	Janusz Kusocinski, Poland	30m11.4s
1936	Ilmari Salminen, Finland	30m15.4s
1948	Emil Zatopek, Czechoslovakia	29m59.6s
1952	Emil Zatopek, Czechoslovakia	29ml7s
1956	Vladimir Kuts, U.S.S.R.	28m45.6s
1960	Peter Bolotnikov, U.S.S.R.	28m32.2s
1964	Billy Mills, United States	28m24.4s
1968	Nartali Temu, Kenya	29m27.4s
1972	Lasse Viren, Finland	27m38.4s
1976	Lasse Viren, Finland	27m40.38s
1980	Miruts Yifter, Ethiopia	27m42.7s
1984	Alberto Cova, Italy	27m47.5s
1988	Mly Brahim Boutaib, Morocco	27m21.46s
1992	Khalid Skah, Morocco	27m47.70s

Marathon

1896	Spiridon Loues, Greece	2h58m50s
1900	Michel Teato, France	2h59m45s
1904	Thomas Hicks, United States	3h28m53s
1906	William J. Sherring, Canada	2h51m23.65s
1908	John J. Hayes, United States	2h55m18.4s
1912	Kenneth McArthur, South Africa	2h36m54.8s
1920	Hannes Kolehmainen, Finland	2h32m35.8s
1924	Albin Stenroos, Finland	2h41m22.6s
1928	A.B. El Quafi, France	2h32m57s
1932	Juan Zabala, Argentina	2h31m36s
1936	Kitei Son, Japan	2h29m19.2s
1948	Delfo Cabrera, Argentina	2h34m51.6s
1952	Emil Zatopek, Czechoslovakia	2h23m3.2s
1956	Alain Mimoun, France	2h25m
1960	Abebe Bikila, Ethiopia	2h15m16.2s
1964	Abebe Bikila, Ethiopia	2h12m11.2s
1968	Mamo Wold, Ethiopia	2h20m26.4s
1972	Frank Shorter, United States	2h12m19.8s
1976	Walter Cierpinski, East Germany	2h09m55s
1980	Walter Cierpinski, East Germany	2h11m3s
1984	Carlos Lopes, Portugal	2h9m.55s
1988	Gelindo Bordin, Italy	2hr10m47s
1992	Hwang Young-Cho, South Korea	2h13m23s

110–Meter Hurdles

1896	Thomas Curtis, United States	17.6s
1900	Alvin Kraenzlein, United States	15.4s
1904	Frederick Schule, United States	16s
1906	R.G. Leavitt, United States	16.2s
1908	Forrest Smithson, United States	15s
1912	Frederick Kelly, United States	15.1s
1920	Earl Thomson, Canada	14.8s
1924	Daniel Kinsey, United States	15s
1928	Sydney Atkinson, South Africa	14.8s
1932	George Saling, United States	14.6s
1936	Forrest Towns, United States	14.2s
1948	William Porter, United States	13.9s
1952	Harrison Dillard, United States	13.7s
1956	Lee Calhoun, United States	13.5s
1960	Lee Calhoun, United States	13.8s
1964	Hayes Jones, United States	13.6s
1968	Willie Davenport, United States	13.3s
1972	Rodney Milburn, United States	13.24s
1976	Guy Drut, France	13.30s
1980	Thomas Munkett, East Germany	13.20s
1984	Roger Kingdom, United States	13.20s

1988	Roger Kingdom, United States	12.98s
1992	Mark McCoy, Canada	13.12s

200-Meter Hurdles

1900	Alvin Kraenzlein, United States	25.4s
1904	Harry Hillman, United States	24.6s

400-Meter Hurdles

1900	John Tewksbury, United States	57.6s
1904	Harry Hillman, United States	53s
1908	Charles Bacon, United States	55s
1920	Frank Loomis, United States	54s
1924	F. Morgan Taylor, United States	52.6s
1928	Lord David Burghley, Great Britain	53.4s
1932	Robert Tisdall, Ireland	51.8s [1]
1936	Glenn Hardin, United States	52.4s
1948	Roy Cochran, United States	51.1s
1952	Charles Moore, United States	50.8s
1956	Glenn Davis, United States	50.1s
1960	Glenn Davis, United States	49.3s
1964	Rex Cawley, United States	49.6s
1968	David Hemery, Great Britain	48.1s
1972	John Akii-Bua, Uganda	47.8s
1976	Edwin Moses, United States	47.64s
1980	Volker Beck, East Germany	48.70s
1984	Edwin Moses, United States	47.75s
1988	Andre Phillips, United States	47.19s
1992	Kevin Young, United States	46.78s

1. Record not allowed.

2,500-Meter Steeplechase

1900	George Orton, United States	7m34s
1904	James Lightbody, United States	7m39.6s

3,000-Meter Steeplechase

1920	Percy Hodge, Great Britain	10m0.4s
1924	Willie Ritola, Finland	9m33.6s
1928	Toivo Loukola, Finland	9m21.8s
1932	Volmari Iso-Hollo, Finland	10m33.4s [1]
1936	Volmari Iso-Hollo, Finland	9m3.8s
1948	Thure Sjoestrand, Sweden	9m4.6s
1952	Horace Ashenfelter, United States	8m45.4s
1956	Chris Brasher, Great Britain	8m41.2s
1960	Zdzislaw Krzyskowiak, Poland	8m34.2s
1964	Gaston Roelants, Belgium	8m30.8s
1968	Amos Biwott, Kenya	8m51s
1972	Kipchoge Keino, Kenya	8m23.6s
1976	Anders Gardervd, Sweden	8m08.02s
1980	Bronislaw Malinowski, Poland	8m9.7s
1984	Julius Korir, Kenya	8m11.80s
1988	Julius Karluki, Kenya	8m05.51s
1992	Matthew Birir, Kenya	8m08.84s

1. About 3,450 meters-extra lap by error.

10,000-Meter Walk

1912	George Goulding, Canada	46m28.4s
1920	Ugo Frigerio, Italy	48m6.2s
1924	Ugo Frigerio, Italy	47m49s
1948	John Mikaelsson, Sweden	45m13.2s
1952	John Mikaelsson, Sweden	45m2.8s

20,000-Meter Walk

1956	Leonid Spirin, U.S.S.R.	1h31m27.4s
1960	Vladimir Golubnichy, U.S.S.R.	1h34m7.2s
1964	Ken Mathews, Great Britain	1h29m34s
1968	Vladimir Golubnichy, U.S.S.R.	1h33m58.4s
1972	Peter Frenkel, East Germany	1h26m42.4s
1976	Daniel Bautista, Mexico	1h24m40.6s
1980	Maurizio Damiliano, Italy	1h23m35.5s
1984	Ernesto Conto, Mexico	1m23.13s
1988	Jozef Pribilinec, Czechoslovakia	1h19m57s
1992	Daniel Plaza, Spain	1h21m45s

50,000-Meter Walk

1932	Thomas W. Green, Great Britain	4h50m10s
1936	Harold Whitlock, Great Britain	4h30m41.1s
1948	John Ljunggren, Sweden	4h41m52s
1952	Giuseppe Dordoni, Italy	4h28m7.8s
1956	Norman Read, New Zealand	4h30m42.8s
1960	Donald Thompson, Great Britain	4h25m30s
1964	Abdon Pamich, Italy	4h11m12.4s
1968	Christoph Hohne, East Germany	4h20m13.6s
1972	Bern Kannernberg, West Germany	3h56m11.6s
1980	Hartwig Guader, East Germany	3h49m24s
1984	Raul Gonzalez, Mexico	3hr37m26s
1988	Viacheslau Ivanenko, U.S.S.R.	3h438m29s
1992	Andrei Perlov, Unified Team	3h50m13s

400-Meter Relay (4x100)

1912	Great Britain	42.4s
1920	United States	42.2s
1924	United States	41s
1928	United States	41s
1932	United States	40s
1936	United States	39.8s
1948	United States	40.6s
1952	United States	40.1s
1956	United States	39.5s
1960	Germany	39.5s
1964	United States	39s
1968	United States	38.2s
1972	United States	38.19s
1976	United States	38.33s
1980	U.S.S.R.	38.26s
1984	United States	37.83s
1988	U.S.S.R.	38.19s
1992	United States	37.40s[1]

1. World record.

1,600-Meter Relay (4x400)

1912	United States	3m16.6s
1920	Great Britain	3m22.2s
1924	United States	3m16s
1928	United States	3m14.2s
1932	United States	3m8.2s
1936	Great Britain	3m9s
1948	United States	3m10.4s
1952	Jamaica, B.W.I.	3m3.9s
1956	United States	3m4.8s
1960	United States	3m2.2s
1964	United States	3m0.7s
1968	United States	2m56.1s
1972	Kenya	2m59.8s
1976	United States	2m58.65s
1980	U.S.S.R.	3m01.1s
1984	United States	2m57.91s
1988	United States	2m56.16s
1992	United States	2m55.74s[1]

1. World record.

Team Race

		Pts
1900	Great Britain (5,000 meters)	26
1904	United States (4 miles)	27
1908	Great Britain (3 miles)	6
1912	United States (3,000 meters)	9
1920	United States (3,000 meters)	10
1924	Finland (3,000 meters)	9

Standing High Jump

1900	Ray Ewry, United States	5 ft 5 in.
1904	Ray Ewry, United States	4 ft. 11 in.
1906	Ray Ewry, United States	5 ft 1 5/8 in.
1908	Ray Ewry, United States	5 ft 2 in.
1912	Platt Adams, United States	5 ft 4 1/8 in.

Running High Jump

1896	Ellery Clark, United States	5 ft 11 1/4 in.
1900	Irving Baxter, United States	6 ft 2 3/4 in.
1904	Samuel Jones, United States	5 ft 11 in.
1906	Con Leahy, Ireland	5 ft 9 7/8 in.
1908	Harry Porter, United States	6 ft 3 in.
1912	Alma Richards, United States	6 ft 4 in.
1920	Richmond Landon, United States	6 ft 4 1/4 in.
1924	Harold Osborn, United States	6 ft 5 15/16 in.
1928	Robert W. King, United States	6 ft 4 3/8 in.
1932	Duncan McNaughton, Canada	6 ft 5 5/8 in.
1936	Cornelius Johnson, United States	6 ft 7 15/16 in.
1948	John Winter, Australia	6 ft 6 in.
1952	Walter David, United States	6 ft 8 5/16 in.
1956	Charles Dumas, United States	6 ft 11 1/4 in.
1960	Robert Shavlakadze, U.S.S.R.	7 ft 1 in.
1964	Valeri Brumel, U.S.S.R.	7 ft 1 3/4 in.
1968	Dick Fosbury, United States	7 ft 4 1/4 in.
1972	Yuri Tarmak, U.S.S.R.	7 ft 3 3/4 in.
1976	Jacek Wszola, Poland	(2.25m) 7 ft 4 1/2 in.
1980	Gerd Wessig, East Germany	7 ft 8 3/4 in.
1984	Dietmar Mogenburg, West Germany	7 ft 8 1/2 in.
1988	Guennadi Avdeenko, U.S.S.R.	7 ft 9 1/2 in.
1992	Javier Sotomayer, Cuba	7ft 8 1/4 in.

Long Jump

1896	Ellery Clark, United States	20 ft 9 3/4 in.
1900	Alvin Kraenzlein, United States	23 ft 6 7/8 in.
1904	Myer Prinstein, United States	24 ft 1 in.
1906	Myer Prinstein, United States	23 ft 7 1/2 in.
1908	Frank Irons, United States	24 ft 6 1/2 in.
1912	Albert Gutterson, United States	24 ft 11 1/4 in.
1920	William Petterssen, Sweden	23 ft 5 1/2 in.
1924	DeHart Hubbard, United States	24 ft 5 1/8 in.
1928	Edward B. Hamm, United States	25 ft 4 3/4 in.
1932	Edward Gordon, United States	25 ft 3/4 in.
1936	Jesse Owens, United States	26 ft 5 5/16 in.
1948	Willie Steele, United States	25 ft 8 in.
1952	Jerome Biffle, United States	24 ft 10 in.
1956	Gregory Bell, United States	25 ft 8 1/4 in.
1960	Ralph Boston, United States	26 ft 7 3/4 in.
1964	Lynn Davies, Great Britain	26 ft 5 3/4 in.
1968	Bob Beamon, United States	29 ft 2 1/2 in.
1972	Randy Williams, United States	27 ft 1/2 in.
1976	Arnie Robinson, United States	(8.35m) 24 ft 7 3/4 in.
1980	Lutz Dombrowski, E. Germany	28 ft 1/4 in.
1984	Carl Lewis, United States	28 ft 1/4 in.
1988	Carl Lewis, United States	28 ft 7 1/4 in.
1992	Carl Lewis, United States	28 ft 5 1/2 in.

Triple Jump

1896	James B. Connolly, United States	45 ft
1900	Myer Prinstein, United States	47 ft 4 1/4 in.
1904	Myer Prinstein, United States	47 ft
1906	P.G. O'Connor, Ireland	46 ft 2 in.
1908	Timothy Ahearne, Great Britain	48 ft 11 1/4 in.
1912	Gustaf Lindblom, Sweden	48 ft 5 1/8 in.
1920	Vilho Tuulos, Finland	47 ft 6 7/8 in.
1924	Archie Winter, Australia	50 ft 11 1/8 in.
1928	Mikio Oda, Japan	49 ft 10 13/16 in.
1932	Chuhei Nambu, Japan	51 ft 7 in.
1936	Naoto Tajima, Japan	52 ft 5 7/8 in.
1948	Arne Ahman, Sweden	50 ft 6 1/4 in.
1952	Adhemar da Silva, Brazil	53 ft 2 1/2 in.
1956	Adhemar da Silva, Brazil	53 ft 7 1/2 in.
1960	Jozef Schmidt, Poland	55 ft 1 3/4 in.
1964	Jozef Schmidt, Poland	55 ft 3 1/4 in.
1968	Viktor Saneyev, U.S.S.R.	57 ft 3/4 in.
1972	Viktor Saneyev, U.S.S.R.	56 ft 11 in.
1976	Viktor Saneyev, U.S.S.R.	(17.29m) 56 ft 8 3/4 in.
1980	Jaak Uŭdmae, U.S.S.R.	56 ft 11 1/8 in.
1984	Al Joyner, United States	56 ft 7 1/2 in.
1988	Hristo Markov, Bulgaria	57 ft 9 1/4 in.
1992	Mike Conley, United States	59 ft 7 1/2 in.

Pole Vault

1896	William Hoyt, United States	10 ft 9 3/4 in.
1900	Irving Baxter, United States	10 ft 9 7/8 in.
1904	Charles Dvorak, United States	11 ft 6 in.
1906	Fernand Gouder, France	11 ft 6 in.
1908	Alfred Gilbert, United States, and Edward Cook, United States (tie)	12 ft 2 in.
1912	Harry Babcock, United States	12 ft 11 1/2 in.
1920	Frank Foss, United States	13 ft 5 9/16 in.
1924	Lee Barnes, United States	12 ft 11 1/2 in.
1928	Sabin W. Carr, United States	13 ft 9 3/8 in.
1932	William Miller, United States	14 ft 1 7/8 in.
1936	Earle Meadows, United States	14 ft 3 1/4 in.
1948	Guinn Smith, United States	14 ft 1 1/4 in.
1952	Robert Richards, United States	14 ft 11 1/8 in.
1956	Robert Richards, United States	14 ft 11 1/2 in.
1960	Don Bragg, United States	15 ft 5 1/8 in.
1964	Fred Hansen, United States	16 ft 8 3/4 in.
1968	Bob Seagren, United States	17 ft 8 1/2 in.
1972	Wolfgang Nordwig, East Germany	18 ft 1/2 in.
1976	Tadeusz Slusarski, Poland	(5.50m) 18 ft 1/2 in.
1980	Wladyslaw Kozakiewics, Poland	18 ft 11 1/2 in.
1984	Pierre Quinon, France	18 ft 10 1/4 in.
1988	Sergei Bubka, U.S.S.R.	18 ft 4 1/4 in.
1992	Maxim Tarassov, Unified Team	19 ft 0 1/4 in.

16–lb Shot–Put

1896	Robert Garrett, United States	36 ft 9 3/4 in.
1900	Richard Sheldon, United States	46 ft 3 1/8 in.
1904	Ralph Rose, United States	48 ft 7 in.
1906	Martin Sheridan, United States	40 ft 4 4/5 in.
1908	Ralph Rose, United States	46 ft 7 1/2 in.
1912	Pat McDonald, United States	50 ft 4 in.
1920	Ville Porhola, Finland	48 ft 7 1/8 in.
1924	Clarence Houser, United States	49 ft 2 1/2 in.
1928	John Kuck, United States	52 ft 11 11/16 in.
1932	Leo Sexton, United States	52 ft 6 3/16 in.
1936	Hans Woellke, Germany	53 ft 1 3/4 in.
1948	Wilbur Thompson, United States	56 ft 2 in.
1952	Parry O'Brien, United States	57 ft 1 1/2 in.
1956	Parry O'Brien, United States	60 ft 11 in.
1960	Bill Nieder, United States	64 ft 6 3/4 in.
1964	Dallas Long, United States	66 ft 8 1/4 in.
1968	Randy Matson, United States	67 ft 4 3/4 in.
1972	Wladyslaw Komar, Poland	69 ft 6 in.
1976	Udo Beyer, East Germany	(21.05m) 69 ft 3/4 in.
1980	Vladmir Kiselyov, U.S.S.R.	70 ft 1/2 in.
1984	Alessandro Andrei, Italy	69 ft 9 in.
1988	Uhf Timmerman, East Germany	73 ft 8 3/4 in.
1992	Michael Stulze, United States	71 ft 2 1/2 in.

Discus Throw

1896	Robert Garrett, United States	95 ft 7 1/2 in.
1900	Rudolf Bauer, Hungary	118 ft 2 7/8 in.
1904	Martin Sheridan, United States	128 ft 10 1/2 in.
1906	Martin Sheridan, United States	136 ft 1/3 in.
1908	Martin Sheridan, United States	134 ft 2 in.
1912	Armas Taipale, Finland	145 ft 9/16 in.
1920	Elmer Niklander, Finland	146 ft 7 in.
1924	Clarence Houser, United States	151 ft 5 1/4 in.
1928	Clarence Houser, United States	155 ft 2 4/5 in.
1932	John Anderson, United States	162 ft 4 7/8 in.
1936	Ken Carpenter, United States	165 ft 7 3/8 in.
1948	Adolfo Consolini, Italy	173 ft 2 in.
1952	Simeon Iness, United States	180 ft 6 1/2 in.
1956	Al Oerter, United States	184 ft 10 1/2 in.
1960	Al Oerter, United States	194 ft 2 in.
1964	Al Oerter, United States	200 ft 1 1/2 in.
1968	Al Oerter, United States	212 ft 6 in.
1972	Ludvik Danek, Czechoslovakia	211 ft 3 in.

1976	Mac Wilkins, United States	(67.5m) 221 ft 5 in.
1980	Viktor Rashchupkin, U.S.S.R.	218 ft 8 in.
1984	Rolf Dannenberg, West Germany	218 ft 6 in.
1988	Jurgen Schult, East Germany	225 ft 9 1/4 in.
1992	Romas Ubartas, Lithuania	213 ft 7 3/4 in.

Javelin Throw

1906	Eric Lemming, Sweden	175 ft 6 in.
1908	Eric Lemming, Sweden	179 ft 10 1/2 in.
1912	Eric Lemming, Sweden	198 ft 11 1/4 in.
1920	Jonni Myyra, Finland	215 ft 9 3/4 in.
1924	Jonni Myyra, Finland	206 ft 6 3/4 in.
1928	Eric Lundquist, Sweden	218 ft 6 1/8 in.
1932	Matti Jarvinen, Finland	238 ft 7 in.
1936	Gerhard Stoeck, Germany	235 ft 8 5/16 in.
1948	Kaj Rautavaara, Finland	228 ft 10 1/2 in.
1952	Cy Young, United States	242 ft 3/4 in.
1956	Egil Danielsen, Norway	281 ft 2 1/4 in.
1960	Viktor Tsibuelnko, U.S.S.R.	277 ft 8 3/8 in.
1964	Pauli Nevala, Finland	271 ft 2 1/4 in.
1968	Janis Lusis, U.S.S.R.	295 ft 7 in.
1972	Klaus Wolfermann, West Germany	296 ft 10 in.
1976	Miklos Nemeth, Hungary	(94.58m) 310 ft 4 in.
1980	Dainis Kula, U.S.S.R.	299 ft 2 3/8 in.
1984	Arto Haerkoenen, Finland	284 ft 8 in.
1988	Tapio Korjus, Finland	276 ft 6 in.
1992	Jan Zelezny, Czechoslovakia	294 ft 2 in.

16-lb Hammer Throw

1900	John Flanagan, United States	167 ft 4 in.
1904	John Flanagan, United States	168 ft 1 in.
1908	John Flanagan, United States	170 ft 4 1/4 in.
1912	Matt McGrath, United States	179 ft 7 1/8 in.
1920	Pat Ryan, United States	173 ft 5 5/8 in.
1924	Fred Tootell, United States	174 ft 10 1/4 in.
1928	Patrick O'Callaghan, Ireland	168 ft 7 1/2 in.
1932	Patrick O'Callaghan, Ireland	176 ft 11 1/8 in.
1936	Karl Hein, Germany	185 ft 4 in.
1948	Imre Nemeth, Hungary	183 ft 11 1/2 in.
1952	Jozsef Csermak, Hungary	197 ft 11 9/16 in.
1956	Harold Connolly, United States	207 ft 2 3/4 in.
1960	Vasily Rudenkov, U.S.S.R.	220 ft 1 5/8 in.
1964	Romuald Klim, U.S.S.R.	228 ft 9 1/2 in.
1968	Gyula Zsivotzky, Hungary	240 ft 8 in.
1972	Anatoly Bondarchuk, U.S.S.R.	247 ft 8 1/2 in.
1976	Yuri Sedykh, U.S.S.R.	(77.52m)254 ft 4 in.
1980	Yuri Sedykh, U.S.S.R.	(81.80m 268 ft 4 1/2 in.
1984	Juha Tiainen, Finland	256 ft 2 in.
1988	Sergei Litvinov, U.S.S.R.	278 ft 2 1/2 in.
1992	Andrey Abduvaliyev, Unified Team	270 ft 9 1/2 in.

Decathlon

1912	Jim Thorpe, United States	—
	Hugo Wieslander, Sweden	—
1920	Helge Lovland, Norway	6,804.35 pts.
1924	Harold Osborn, United States	7,710.775 pts.
1928	Paavo Yrjola, Finland	8,053.29 pts.
1932	James Bausch, United States	8,462.23 pts.
1936	Glenn Morris, United States	7,900 pts.[1]
1948	Robert B. Mathias, United States	7,139 pts.
1952	Robert B. Mathias, United States	7,887 pts.
1956	Milton Campbell, United States	7,937 pts.
1960	Rafer Johnson, United States	8,392 pts.
1964	Willi Holdorf, Germany	7,887 pts.[1]
1968	Bill Toomey, United States	8,193 pts.
1972	Nikolai Avilov, U.S.S.R.	8,454 pts.
1976	Bruce Jenner, United States	8,618 pts.
1980	Daley Thompson, Britain	8,495 pts.
1984	Daley Thompson, Britain	8,797 pts.
1988	Christian Schenk, East Germany	8,488 pts.
1992	Robert Zmelik, Czechoslovakia	8,611 pts.

1. Point system revised.

TRACK AND FIELD–WOMEN

100-Meter Dash

1928	Elizabeth Robinson, United States	12.2s
1932	Stella Walsh, Poland	11.9s
1936	Helen Stephens, United States	11.5s
1948	Fanny Blankers–Koen, Netherlands	11.9s
1952	Marjorie Jackson, Australia	11.5s
1956	Betty Cuthbert, Australia	11.5s
1960	Wilma Rudolph, United States	11s
1964	Wyomia Tyus, United States	11.4s
1968	Wyomia Tyus, United States	11s
1972	Renate Stecher, East Germany	11.07s
1976	Annegret Richter, West Germany	11.08s
1980	Lyudmila Kondratyeva, U.S.S.R.	11.06s
1984	Evelyn Ashford, United States	10.97s
1988	Florence Griffith–Joyner, United States	10.54s
1992	Gail Devers, United States	10.82s

200-Meter Dash

1948	Fanny Blankers–Koen, Netherlands	24.4s
1952	Marjorie Jackson, Australia	23.7s
1956	Betty Cuthbert, Australia	23.4s
1960	Wilma Rudolph, United States	24s
1964	Edith McGuire, United States	23s
1968	Irena Szewinska, Poland	22.5s
1972	Renate Stecher, East Germany	22.4s
1976	Baerbel Eckert, East Germany	22.37s
1980	Barbara Wockel, East Germany	22.03s
1984	Valerie Brisco–Hooks, United States	21.81s
1988	Florence Griffith–Joyner, United States	21.34s
1992	Gwen Torrence, United States	21.81s

400-Meter Dash

1964	Betty Cuthbert, Australia	52s
1968	Colette Besson, France	52s
1972	Monika Zehrt, East Germany	51.08s
1976	Irena Szewinska, Poland	49.29s
1980	Marita Koch, East Germany	48.88s
1984	Valerie Brisco–Hooks, United States	48.83s
1988	Olga Bryzguina, U.S.S.R.	48.65s
1992	Marie Jose-Perec, France	48.83s

800-Meter Run

1928	Lina Radke, Germany	2m16.8s
1960	Ljudmila Shevcova, U.S.S.R.	2m4.3s
1964	Ann Packer, Great Britain	2m1.1s
1968	Madeline Manning, United States	2m0.9s
1972	Hildegard Falck, West Germany	1m58.6s
1976	Tatiana Kazankina, U.S.S.R.	1m54.94s
1980	Nadezhda Olizarenko, U.S.S.R.	1m53.5s
1984	Doina Melinte, Romania	1m57.60s
1988	Sigrun Wodars, East Germany	1m56.10s
1992	Ellen Van Langen, Netherlands	1m55.54s

1,500-Meter Run

1972	Ludmila Bragina, U.S.S.R.	4m01.4s
1976	Tatiana Kazankina, U.S.S.R.	4m05.48s
1980	Tatiana Kazankina, U.S.S.R.	3m56.6s
1984	Gabriella Dorio, Italy	4m03.25s
1988	Paula Ivan, Romania	3m53.96s
1992	Hassiba Boulmerka, Algeria	3m55.30s

3,000-Meter Run

1984	Maricica Puica, Romania	8m35.96s
1988	Tatiana Samolenko, U.S.S.R.	8m26.53s
1992	Elena Romanova, Unified Team	8m46.04s

10,000-Meter Run

1992	Derartu Tulu, Ethiopia	31m6.02s

80–Meter Hurdles

1932	Mildred Didrikson, United States	11.7s
1936	Trebisonda Valla, Italy	11.7s
1948	Fanny Blankers–Koen, Netherlands	11.2s
1952	Shirley S. de la Hunty, Australia	10.9s
1956	Shirley S. de la Hunty, Australia	10.7s
1960	Irina Press, U.S.S.R.	10.8s
1964	Karin Balzer, Germany	10.5s[1]
1968	Maureen Caird, Australia	10.3s

1. Wind assisted.

100–Meter Hurdles

1972	Annelie Ehrhardt, East Germany	12.59s
1976	Johanna Schaller, East Germany	12.77s
1980	Vera Komisova, U.S.S.R.	12.56s
1984	Benita Fitzgerald–Brown, United States	12.84s
1988	Jordanka Donkova, Bulgaria	12.38s
1992	Paraskevi Patoulidou, Greece	12.64s

400–Meter Hurdles

1984	Nawai El Moutawakel, Morocco	54.61s
1988	Debra Flintoff–King, Australia	53.17s
1992	Sally Gunnell, Great Britain	53.23s

400–Meter Relay

1928	Canada	48.4s
1932	United States	47s
1936	United States	46.9s
1948	Netherlands	47.5s
1952	United States	45.9s
1956	Australia	44.5s
1960	United States	44.5s
1964	Poland	43.6s
1968	United States	42.8s
1972	West Germany	42.81s
1976	East Germany	42.55s
1980	East Germany	41.60s
1984	United States	41.65s
1988	United States	41.98s
1992	United States	42.11s

1,600–Meter Relay

1972	East Germany	3m23s
1976	East Germany	3m19.23s
1980	U.S.S.R.	3m20.2s
1984	United States	3m18.29s
1988	U.S.S.R.	3m15.18s
1992	Unified Team	3m20.20s

10,000-Meter Walk

1992	Chen Yueling, China	44m32s

Marathon

1984	Joan Benoit, United States	2 hr 24 m 52s
1988	Rose Mota, Portugal	2 hr 25 m 40s
1992	Valentina Yegorova, Unified Team	2h32m41s

Running High Jump

1928	Ethel Catherwood, Canada	5 ft 3 in.
1932	Jean Shiley, United States	5 ft 5 1/4 in.
1936	Ibolya Csak, Hungary	5 ft 3 in.
1948	Alice Coachman, United States	5 ft 6 1/8 in.
1952	Ester Brand, South Africa	5 ft 5 3/4 in.
1956	Mildred McDaniel, United States	5 ft 9 1/4 in.
1960	Iolanda Balas, Romania	6 ft 3/4 in.
1964	Iolanda Balas, U.S.S.R.	6 ft 2 3/4 in.
1968	Miloslava Rezkova, Czechoslovakia	5 ft 11 3/4 in.
1972	Ulrike Meyfarth, West Germany	6 ft 3 5/8 in.
1976	Rosemarie Ackerman, E. Germany	(1.93m) 6 ft 4 in.
1980	Sara Simeoni, Italy	6 ft 5 1/2 in.
1984	Ulrike Meyfarth, West Germany	6 ft 7 1/2 in.
1988	Louise Ritter, United States	6 ft 8 in.
1992	Heike Henkel, Germany	6 ft 7 1/2 in.

Long Jump

1948	Olga Gyarmati, Hungary	18 ft 8 1/4 in.
1952	Yvette Williams, New Zealand	20 ft 5 3/4 in.
1956	Elzbieta Krzesinska, Poland	20 ft 9 3/4 in.
1960	Vera Krepkina, U.S.S.R.	20 ft 10 3/4 in.
1964	Mary Rand, Great Britain	22 ft 2 in.
1968	Viorica Ciscopoleanu, Romania	22 ft 4 1/2 in.
1972	Heidemarie Rosendahl, West Germany	22 ft 3 in.
1976	Angela Voigt, East Germany	(6.72m) 22 ft 1/2 in.
1980	Tatiana Kolpakova, U.S.S.R.	23 ft 2 in.
1984	Anisoara Stanciu, Romania	22 ft 10 in.
1988	Jackie Joyner–Kersee, United States	24 ft 3 1/2 in.
1992	Heike Drechsler, Germany	23 ft 5 1/4 in.

Shot–Put

1948	Micheline Ostermeyer, France	45 ft 1 1/2 in.
1952	Galina Zybina, U.S.S.R.	50 ft 1 1/2 in.
1956	Tamara Tishkyevich, U.S.S.R.	54 ft 5 in.
1960	Tamara Press, U.S.S.R.	56 ft 9 7/8 in.
1964	Tamara Press, U.S.S.R.	59 ft 6 in.
1968	Margitta Gummel, East Germany	64 ft 4 in.
1972	Nadezhda Chizhova, U.S.S.R.	69 ft
1976	Ivanka Christova, Bulgaria	(21.16m) 69 ft 5 in.
1980	Ilona Sluplanek, East Germany	73 ft 6 in.
1984	Claudia Losch, West Germany	67 ft 2 1/4 in.
1988	Natalya Lisovskaya, U.S.S.R.	72 ft 11 1/2 in.
1992	Svetlana Kriveleva, Unified Team	69 ft 1 1/4 in.

Discus Throw

1928	Helena Konopacka, Poland	129 ft 11 7/8 in.
1932	Lillian Copeland, United States	133 ft 2 in.
1936	Gisela Mauermayer, Germany	156 ft 3 3/16 in.
1948	Micheline Ostermeyer, France	137 ft 6 1/2 in.
1956	Olga Fikotova, Czechoslovakia	176 ft 1 1/2 in.
1960	Nina Ponomareva, U.S.S.R.	180 ft 8 1/4 in.
1964	Tamara Press, U.S.S.R.	187 ft 10 3/4 in.
1968	Lia Manoliu, Romania	191 ft 2 1/2 in.
1972	Faina Melnik, U.S.S.R.	218 ft 7 in.
1976	Evelin Schlaak, East Germany	(69.0m) 226 ft 4 in.
1980	Evelin Jahl, East Germany	229 ft 6 1/2 in.
1984	Ria Stalman, Netherlands	214 ft 5 in.
1988	Martina Hellmann, East Germany	237 ft 2 1/4 in.
1992	Maritza Marten, Cuba	229 ft 10 1/4 in.

Javelin Throw

1932	Mildred Didrikson, United States	143 ft 4 in.
1936	Tilly Fleischer, Germany	148 ft 2 3/4 in.
1948	Herma Bauma, Austria	149 ft 6 in.
1952	Dana Zatopek, Czechoslovakia	165 ft 7 in.
1956	Inessa Janzeme, U.S.S.R.	176 ft 8 in.
1960	Elvira Ozolina, U.S.S.R.	183 ft 8 in.
1964	Mihaela Penes, Romania	198 ft 7 1/2 in.
1968	Angela Nemeth, Hungary	198 ft 0 in.
1972	Ruth Fuchs, East Germany	209 ft 7 in.
1976	Ruth Fuchs, East Germany	(65.94m) 216 ft 4 in.
1980	Maria Colon, Cuba	224 ft 5 in.
1984	Tessa Sanderson, Britain	228 ft 2 in.
1988	Petra Felke, East Germany	245 ft
1992	Silke Renke, Germany	224 ft 2 1/2 in.

Pentathlon

1964	Irina Press, U.S.S.R.	5,246 pts.
1968	Ingrid Becker, West Germany	5,098 pts.
1972	Mary Peters, Britain	4,801 pts.
1976	Siegrun Siegl, East Germany	4,745 pts.
1980	Nadyeszhda Tkachenko, U.S.S.R.	5,083 pts.
1984	Daniele Masala, Italy	5,469 pts.
1988	Jackie Joyner–Kersee, United States	7,291 pts.

Heptathlon

1992	Jackie Joyner-Kersee, United States	7,044 pts.

SWIMMING–MEN

50 Meter Freestyle

1988	Matt Biondi, United States	22.14s
1992	Alexandre Popov, Unified Team	21.91s

100 Meter Freestyle

1896	Alfred Hajos, Hungary	1m22.2s
1904	Zoltan de Halmay, Hungary	1m2.8s [1]
1906	Charles Daniels, United States	1m13s
1908	Charles Daniels, United States	1m5.6s
1912	Duke P. Kahanamoku, United States	1m3.4s
1920	Duke P. Kahanamoku, United States	1m1.4s
1924	John Weissmuller, United States	59s
1928	John Weissmuller, United States	58.6s
1932	Yasuji Miyazaki, Japan	58.2s
1936	Ferenc Csik, Hungary	57.6s
1948	Walter Ris, United States	57.3s
1952	Clarke Scholes, United States	57.4s
1956	Jon Henricks, Australia	55.4s
1960	John Devitt, Australia	55.2s
1964	Don Schollander, United States	53.4s
1968	Michael Wenden, Australia	52.2s
1972	Mark Spitz, United States	51.22s
1976	Jim Montgomery, United States	49.99s
1980	Jorg Woithe, East Germany	50.40s
1984	Rowdy Gaines, United States	49.80s
1988	Matt Biondi, United States	48.63s
1992	Alexandre Popov, Unified Team	49.02s

1. 100 yards.

200–Meter Freestyle

1900	Frederick Lane, Australia	2m25.2s
1904	Charles Daniels, United States	2m44.2s [1]
1968	Michael Wenden, Australia	1m55.2s
1972	Mark Spitz, United States	1m52.78s
1976	Bruce Furniss, United States	1m50.29s
1980	Sergei Kopiliakov, U.S.S.R.	4m49.81s
1984	Michael Gross, West Germany	1m47.44s
1988	Duncan Armstrong, Australia	1m47.25s
1992	Evgueni Sadovyi, Unified Team	1m46.70s

1. 220 yards

400–Meter Freestyle

1896	Paul Neumann, Austria	8m12.6s [1]
1904	Charles Daniels, United States	6m16.2s [2]
1906	Otto Sheff, Austria	6m23.8s
1908	Henry Taylor, Great Britain	5m36.8s
1912	George Hodgson, Canada	5m24.4s
1920	Norman Ross, United States	5m26.8s
1926	John Weissmuller, United States	5m4.2s
1928	Albert Zorilla, Argentina	5m1.6s
1932	Clarence Crabbe, United States	4m48.4s
1936	Jack Medica, United States	4m44.5s
1948	William Smith, United States	4m41s
1952	Jean Boiteux, France	4m30.7s
1956	Murray Rose, Australia	4m27.3s
1960	Murray Rose, Australia	4m18.3s
1964	Don Schollander, United States	4m12.2s
1968	Mike Burton, United States	4m9s
1972	Bradford Cooper, Australia	4m00.27s [3]
1976	Brian Goodell, United States	3m51.93s
1980	Vladimir Salnikov, U.S.S.R.	3m51.31s
1984	George DiCarlo, United States	3m51.23s
1988	Uwe Dassier, East Germany	3m46.95s
1992	Evgueni Sadovyi, Unified Team	3m45.00s [4]

1. 500 meters. 2. 440 yards. 3. Rich DeMont, United States, won but was disqualified following day for medical reasons. 4. World record.

1,500 Meter Freestyle

1904	Emil Rausch, Germany	27m18.2s [1]
1906	Henry Taylor, Great Britain	28m28s [2]
1908	Henry Taylor, Great Britain	22m48.4s
1912	George Hodgson, Canada	22m
1920	Norman Ross, United States	22m23.2s
1924	Andrew Charlton, Australia	20m6.6s
1928	Arne Borg, Sweden	19m51.8s
1932	Kusuo Kitamura, Japan	19m12.4s
1936	Noboru Terada, Japan	19m13.7s
1948	James McLane, United States	19m18.5s
1952	Ford Konno, United States	18m30s
1956	Murray Rose, Australia	17m58.9s
1960	Jon Konrads, Australia	17m19.6s
1964	Robert Windle, Australia	17m1.7s
1968	Michael Burton, United States	16m38.9s
1972	Michael Burton, United States	15m52.58s
1976	Brian Goodell, United States	15m02.4s
1980	Vladimir Salnikov, U.S.S.R.	14m58.27s
1984	Michael O'Brien, United States	15m05.2s
1988	Vladimir Salnikov, U.S.S.R.	15m00.4s
1992	Kieren Perkins, Australia	14m43.48s

1. One mile. 2. 1,600 meters

100–Meter Backstroke

1904	Walter Brack, Germany	1m16.8s [1]
1908	Arno Bieberstein, Germany	1m24.6s
1912	Harry Hebner, United States	1m21.2s
1920	Warren Kealoha, United States	1m15.2s
1924	Warren Kealoha, United States	1m13.2s
1928	George Kojac, United States	1m8.2s
1932	Masaji Kiyokawa, Japan	1m8.6s
1936	Adolph Kiefer, United States	1m5.9s
1948	Allen Stack, United States	1m6.4s
1952	Yoshinobu Oyakawa, United States	1m5.4s
1956	David Thiele, Australia	1m2.2s
1960	David Thiele, Australia	1m1.9s
1968	Roland Matthes, East Germany	58.7s
1972	Roland Matthes, East Germany	56.58s
1976	John Naber, United States	55.49s
1980	Bengt Baron, Sweden	56.53s
1984	Rick Carey, United States	55.79s
1988	Daichi Suzuki, Japan	55.05s
1992	Mark Tewksbury, Canada	53.98s

1. 100 yards

200–Meter Backstroke

1900	Ernst Hoppenberg, Germany	2m47s
1964	Jed Graef, United States	2m10.3s
1968	Roland Matthes, East Germany	2m9.6s
1972	Roland Matthes, East Germany	2m2.82s
1976	John Naber, United States	1m59.19s
1980	Sandor Wladar, Hungary	2:01.93s
1984	Rick Carey, United States	2m00.23s
1988	Igor Polianski, U.S.S.R.	1m59.37s
1992	Martin Lopez Zubero, Spain	1m58.47s

100–Meter Breaststroke

1968	Donald McKenzie, United States	1m7.7s
1972	Nobutaka Taguchi, Japan	1m4.94s
1976	John Hencken, United States	1m03.11s
1980	Duncan Goodhew, Britain	1m03.34s
1984	Steve Lindquist, United States	1m01.65s
1988	Adrian Moorhouse, Great Britain	1m02.04s
1992	Nelson Diebel, United States	1m01.50s

200–Meter Breaststroke

1908	Frederick Holman, Great Britain	3m9.2s
1912	Walter Bathe, Germany	3m1.8s
1920	Haken Malmroth, Sweden	3m4.4s
1924	Robert Skelton, United States	2m56.6s
1928	Yoshiyuki Tsuruta, Japan	2m48.8s
1932	Yoshiyuki Tsuruta, Japan	2m45.4s
1936	Tetsuo Hamuro, Japan	2m41.5s
1948	Joseph Verdeur, United States	2m39.3s

1952	John Davies, Australia	2m34.4s
1956	Masaura Furukawa, Japan	2m34.7s
1960	Bill Muliken, United States	2m37.4s
1964	Ian O'Brien, Australia	2m27.8s
1968	Felipe Munoz, Mexico	2m28.7s
1972	John Hencken, United States	2m21.55s
1976	David Willkie, Britain	2m15.11s
1980	Robertas Zulpa, U.S.S.R.	2m15.85s
1984	Victor Davis, Canada	2m13.34s
1988	Jozef Szabo, Hungary	2m13.52s
1992	Mike Barrowman, United States	2m10.16s

100–Meter Butterfly

1968	Douglas Russell, United States	55.9s
1972	Mark Spitz, United States	54.27s
1976	Matt Vogel, United States	54.35s
1980	Par Arvidsson, Sweden	54.92s
1984	Michael Gross, West Germany	53.08s
1988	Anthony Nesty, Surinam	53.0s
1992	Pablo Morales, United States	53.32s

200–Meter Butterfly

1956	Bill Yorzyk, United States	2m19.3s
1960	Mike Troy, United States	2m12.8s
1964	Kevin Berry, Australia	2m6.6s
1968	Carl Robie, United States	2m8.7s
1972	Mark Spitz, United States	2m00.7s
1976	Mike Bruner, United States	1m59.23s
1980	Sergei Fesenko, U.S.S.R.	1m59.76s
1984	Jon Sieben, Australia	1m57.0s
1988	Michael Gross, East Germany	1m56.94s
1992	Mel Stewart, United States	1m56.26s

200–Meter Individual Medley

1968	Charles Hickcox, United States	2m12s
1972	Gunnar Larsson, Sweden	2m7.17s
1988	Tamas Darnyi, Hungary	2m0.17s
1992	Tamas Darnyi, Hungary	2m00.76s

400–Meter Individual Medley

1964	Dick Roth, United States	4m45.4s
1968	Charles Hickox, United States	4m48.4s
1972	Gunnar Larsson, Sweden	4m31.98s
1976	Rod Strachan, United States	4m23.68s
1980	Aleksandr Sidorenko, U.S.S.R.	4m22.8s
1984	Alex Baumann, Canada	4m17.41s
1988	Tamas Darnyi, Hungary	4m14.75s
1992	Tamas Darnyi, Hungary	4m14.23s

400–Meter Freestyle Relay

1964	United States	3m32.2s
1968	United States	3m31.7s
1972	United States	3m26.42s
1988	United States	3m16.52s
1992	United States	3m16.74s

800–Meter Freestyle Relay

1908	Great Britain	10m55.6s
1912	Australia	10m11.2s
1920	United States	10m4.4s
1924	United States	9m53.4s
1928	United States	9m36.2s
1932	Japan	8m58.4s
1936	Japan	8m51.5s
1948	United States	8m46.1s
1952	United States	8m31.1s
1956	Australia	8m23.6s
1960	United States	8m10.2s
1964	United States	7m52.1s
1968	United States	7m52.3s
1972	United States	7m35.78s
1976	United States	7m23.22s
1980	U.S.S.R.	7m23.50s
1984	United States	7m16.59s
1988	United States	7m12.51s
1992	Unified Team	7m11.95s

400–Meter Medley Relay

1960	United States	4m5.4s
1964	United States	3m58.4s
1968	United States	3m54.9s
1972	United States	3m48.16s
1976	United States	3m42.22s
1980	Australia	3m45.70s
1984	United States	3m39.30s
1988	United States	3m36.93s
1992	United States	3m36.93s[1]

1. World record.

Springboard Dive

		Points
1908	Albert Zuerner, Germany	85.5
1912	Paul Guenther, Germany	79.23
1920	Louis Kuehn, United States	675
1924	Albert White, United States	696.4
1928	Pete Desjardins, United States	185.04
1932	Michael Galitzen, United States	161.38
1936	Richard Degener, United States	163.57
1948	Bruce Harlan, United States	163.64
1952	David Browning, United States	205.59
1956	Robert Clotworthy, United States	159.56
1960	Gary Tobian, United States	170.00
1964	Ken Sitzberger, United States	159.90
1968	Bernard Wrightson, United States	170.15
1972	Vladimir Vasin, U.S.S.R.	594.09
1976	Phil Boggs, United States	619.05
1980	Alexsandr Portnov, U.S.S.R.	905.02
1984	Greg Louganis, United States	754.41
1988	Greg Louganis, United States	730.80
1992	Mark Lenzi, United States	676.53

Platform Dive

		Points
1904	G.E. Sheldon, United States	12.75
1906	Gottlob Walz, Germany	156
1908	Hialmar Johansson, Sweden	83.75
1912	Erik Adlerz, Sweden	73.94
1920	Clarence Pinkston, United States	100.67
1924	Albert White, United States	487.3
1928	Pete Desjardins, United States	98.74
1932	Harold Smith, United States	124.80
1936	Marshall Wayne, United States	113.58
1948	Samuel Lee, United States	130.05
1952	Samuel Lee, United States	156.28
1956	Joaquin Capilla, Mexico	152.44
1960	Bob Webster, United States	165.56
1964	Bob Webster, United States	148.58
1968	Klaus Dibiasi, Italy	164.18
1972	Klaus Dibiasi, Italy	504.12
1976	Klaus Dibiasi, Italy	600.51
1980	Falk Hoffman, E. Germany	835.65
1984	Greg Louganis, United States	710.91
1988	Greg Louganis, United States	638.61
1992	Sun Shuwei, China	677.31

SWIMMING–WOMEN

50–Meter Freestyle

1988	Kristin Otto, East Germany	25.49s
1992	Yang Wenyi, China	24.79s

100–Meter Freestyle

1912	Fanny Durack, Australia	1m22.2s
1920	Ethelda Bleibtrey, United States	1m13.6s
1924	Ethel Lackie, United States	1m12.4s
1928	Albina Osipowich, United States	1m11s
1932	Helene Madison, United States	1m6.8s

1936	Hendrika Mastenbroek, Netherlands	1m5.9s
1948	Greta Andersen, Denmark	1m6.3s
1952	Katalin Szoke, Hungary	1m6.8s
1956	Dawn Fraser, Australia	1m2s
1960	Dawn Fraser, Australia	1m1.2s
1964	Dawn Fraser, Australia	59.5s
1968	Marge Jan Henne, United States	1m
1972	Sandra Neilson, United States	58.59s
1976	Kornelia Ender, East Germany	55.65s
1980	Barbara Krause, East Germany	54.79s
1984	Carrie Steinseifer, United States	55.92s
1988	Kristin Otto, East Germany	54.93s
1992	Zhuang Yong, China	54.64s

200-Meter Freestyle

1968	Debbie Meyer, United States	2m10.5s
1972	Shane Gould, Australia	2m3.56s
1976	Kornelia Ender, East Germany	1m59.26s
1980	Barbara Krause, East Germany	1m58.33s
1984	Mary Wayle, United States	1m59.23s
1988	Heike Friedrich, East Germany	1m57.65s
1992	Nicole Haislett, United States	1m57.90s

400-Meter Freestyle

1920	Ethelda Bleibtrey, United States	4m34s [1]
1924	Martha Norelius, United States	6m2.2s
1928	Martha Norelius, United States	5m42.8s
1932	Helene Madison, United States	5m28.5s
1936	Hendrika Mastenbroek, Netherlands	5m26.4s
1948	Ann Curtis, United States	5m17.8s
1952	Valerie Gyenge, Hungary	5m12.1s
1956	Lorraine Crapp, Australia	4m54.6s
1960	Chris von Saltza, United States	4m50.6s
1964	Ginny Duenkel, United States	4m43.3s
1968	Debbie Meyer, United States	4m31.8s
1972	Shane Gould, Australia	4m19.04s
1976	Petra Thumer, East Germany	4m09.89s
1980	Ines Diers, East Germany	4m08.76s
1984	Tiffany Cohen, United States	4m07.10s
1988	Janet Evans, United States	4m03.85s
1992	Dagmar Hase, Germany	4m07.18s

1. 300 meters.

800-Meter Freestyle

1968	Debbie Meyer, United States	9m24s
1972	Keena Rothhammer, United States	8m53.68s
1976	Petra Thumer, East Germany	8m37.14s
1980	Michelle Ford, Australia	8m28.90s
1984	Tiffany Cohen, United States	8m24.95s
1988	Janet Evans, United States	8m20.20s
1992	Janet Evans, United States	8m25.52s

100-Meter Backstroke

1924	Sybil Bauer, United States	1m23.2s
1928	Marie Braun, Netherlands	1m22s
1932	Eleanor Holm, United States	1m19.4s
1936	Dina Senff, Netherlands	1m18.9s
1948	Karen Harup, Denmark	1m14.4s
1952	Joan Harrison, South Africa	1m14.3s
1956	Judy Grinham, Great Britain	1m12.9s
1960	Lynn Burke, United States	1m9.3s
1964	Cathy Ferguson, United States	1m7.7s
1968	Kaye Hall, United States	1m6.2s
1972	Melissa Belote, United States	1m5.78s
1976	Ulrike Richter, East Germany	1m01.83s
1980	Rica Reinisch, East Germany	1m00.86s
1984	Theresa Andrews, United States	1m02.55s
1988	Kristin Otto, East Germany	1m0.89s
1992	Kristina Egerszegí, Hungary	1m0.68s

200-Meter Backstroke

1968	Pokey Watson–United States	2m24.8s
1972	Melissa Belote, United States	2m19.19s

DISTRIBUTION OF MEDALS 1992 SUMMER GAMES

Country	Gold	Silver	Bronze	Total
Unified Team	45	38	29	112
United States	37	34	37	108
Germany	33	21	28	82
China	16	22	16	54
Cuba	14	6	11	31
Hungary	11	12	7	30
South Korea	12	5	12	29
France	8	5	16	29
Australia	7	9	11	27
Spain	13	7	2	22
Japan	3	8	11	22
Britain	5	3	12	20
Italy	6	5	8	19
Poland	3	6	10	19
Canada	6	5	7	18
Romania	4	6	8	18
Bulgaria	3	7	6	16
Netherlands	2	6	7	15
Sweden	1	7	4	12
New Zealand	1	4	5	10
North Korea	4	0	5	9
Kenya	2	4	2	8
Czechoslovakia	4	2	1	7
Norway	2	4	1	7
Turkey	2	2	2	6
Denmark	1	1	4	6
Indonesia	2	2	1	5
Finland	1	2	2	5
Jamaica	0	3	1	4
Nigeria	0	3	1	4
Brazil	2	1	0	3
Morocco	1	1	1	3
Ethiopia	1	0	2	3
Latvia	0	2	1	3
Belgium	0	1	2	3
Croatia	0	1	2	3
Iran	0	1	2	3
Yugoslavs	0	1	2	3
Greece	2	0	0	2
Ireland	1	1	0	2
Algeria	1	0	1	2
Estonia	1	0	1	2
Lithuania	1	0	1	2
Austria	0	2	0	2
Namibia	0	2	0	2
South Africa	0	2	0	2
Israel	0	1	1	2
Mongolia	0	0	2	2
Slovenia	0	0	2	2
Switzerland	1	0	0	1
Peru	0	1	0	1
Mexico	0	1	0	1
Taiwan	0	1	0	1
Argentina	0	0	1	1
Bahamas	0	0	1	1
Colombia	0	0	1	1
Ghana	0	0	1	1
Malaysia	0	0	1	1
Pakistan	0	0	1	1
Philippines	0	0	1	1
Puerto Rico	0	0	1	1
Qatar	0	0	1	1
Suriname	0	0	1	1
Thailand	0	0	1	1

1976	Ulrike Richter, East Germany	2m13.43s
1980	Rica Reinisch, East Germany	2m11.77s
1984	Jolanda DeRover, Netherlands	2m12.38s
1988	Krisztina Egerszegi, Hungary	2m09.29s
1992	Krisztina Egerszegí, Hungary	2m07.06s

100–Meter Breaststroke

1968	Djurdjica Bjedov, Yugoslavia	1m15.8s
1972	Catherine Carr, United States	1m13.58s
1976	Hannelore Anke, East Germany	1m11.16s
1980	Ute Geweniger, East Germany	1m10.22s
1984	Petra Van Staveren, Netherlands	1m09.88s
1988	Tainia Dangalakova, Bulgaria	1m07.95s
1992	Elena Roudkovskaia, Unified Team	1m08.00s

200–Meter Breaststroke

1924	Lucy Morton, Great Britain	3m33.2s
1928	Hilde Schrader, Germany	3m12.6s
1932	Clare Dennis, Australia	3m6.3s
1936	Hideko Maehata, Japan	3m3.6s
1948	Nel van Vliet, Netherlands	2m57.2s
1952	Eva Szekely, Hungary	2m51.7s
1956	Ursala Happe, Germany	2m53.1s
1960	Anita Lonsbrough, Great Britain	2m49.5s
1964	Galina Prozumenschikova, U.S.S.R.	2m46.4s
1968	Sharon Wichman, United States	2m44.4s
1972	Beverly Whitfield, Australia	2m41.71s
1976	Marina Koshevaia, U.S.S.R.	2m33.35s
1980	Lina Kachushite, U.S.S.R.	2m29.54s
1984	Anne Ottenbrite, Canada	2m30.38s
1988	Silke Hoerner, East Germany	2m26.71s
1992	Kyoko Iwasaki, Japan	2m26.65s

100–Meter Butterfly

1956	Shelley Mann, United States	1m11s
1960	Carolyn Schuler, United States	1m9.5s
1964	Sharon Stouder, United States	1m4.7s
1968	Lynn McClements, Australia	1m5.5s
1972	Mayumi Aoki, Japan	1m3.34s
1976	Kornelia Ender, East Germany	1m00.13s
1980	Caren Metschuck, East Germany	1m00.42s
1984	Mary Meagher, United States	59.26s
1988	Kristin Otto, East Germany	59s
1992	Qian Hong, China	58.62s

200–Meter Butterfly

1968	Ada Kok, Netherlands	2m24.7s
1972	Karen Moe, United States	2m15.57s
1976	Andrea Pollack, East Germany	2m11.41s
1980	Ines Geissler, East Germany	2m10.44s
1984	Mary Meagher, United States	2m06.90s
1988	Kathleen Nord, East Germany	2m9.51s
1992	Summer Sanders, United States	2m06.67s

200–Meter Individual Medley

1968	Claudia Kolb, United States	2m24.7s
1972	Shane Gould, Australia	2m23.07s
1984	Tracy Caulkins, United States	2m12.64s
1988	Daniela Hunger, East Germany	2m12.59s
1992	Lin Lee, China	2m11.55s[1]

1. World record.

400–Meter Individual Medley

1964	Donna de Varona, United States	5m18.7s
1968	Claudia Kolk, United States	5m8.5s
1972	Gail Neall, Australia	5m2.97s
1976	Ulrike Tauber, East Germany	4m42.77s
1980	Petra Schneider, East Germany	4m36.29s
1984	Tracy Caulkins, United States	4m39.21s
1988	Janet Evans, United States	4m37.76s
1992	Krisztina Egerszegi, Hungary	4m36.54s

400–Meter Freestyle Relay

1912	Great Britain	5m52.8s
1920	United States	5m11.6s
1924	United States	4m58.8s
1928	United States	4m47.6s
1932	United States	4m38s
1936	Netherlands	4m36s
1948	United States	4m29.2s
1952	Hungary	4m24.4s
1956	Australia	4m17.1s
1960	United States	4m8.9s
1964	United States	4m3.8s
1968	United States	4m2.5s
1972	United States	3m55.19s
1976	United States	3m44.82s
1980	East Germany	3m42.71s
1984	United States	3m44.43s
1988	East Germany	3m40.63s
1992	United States	3m39.46s[1]

1. World record.

400–Meter Medley Relay

1960	United States	4m41.1s
1964	United States	4m33.9s
1968	United States	4m28.3s
1972	United States	4m20.75s
1976	East Germany	4m07.95s
1980	East Germany	4m06.67s
1984	United States	4m08.34s
1988	East Germany	4m03.74s
1992	United States	4m02.54s[1]

1. World record.

Springboard Dive

		Points
1920	Aileen Riggin, United States	539.90
1924	Elizabeth Becker, United States	474.5
1928	Helen Meany, United States	78.62
1932	Georgia Coleman, United States	87.52
1936	Marjorie Gestring, United States	89.27
1948	Victoria M. Draves, United States	108.74
1952	Patricia McCormick, United States	147.30
1956	Patricia McCormick, United States	142.36
1960	Ingrid Kramer, Germany	155.81
1964	Ingrid Kramer Engel, Germany	145.00
1968	Sue Gossick, United States	150.77
1972	Micki King, United States	450.03
1976	Jennifer Chandler, United States	506.19
1980	Irina Kalinina, U.S.S.R.	725.91
1984	Sylvie Bernier, Canada	530.70
1988	Gao Min, China	580.23
1992	Gao Min, China	572.40

Platform Dive

		Points
1912	Greta Johansson, Sweden	39.9
1920	Stefani Fryland, Denmark	34.60
1924	Caroline Smith, United States	166
1928	Elizabeth B. Pinkston, United States	31.60
1932	Dorothy Poynton, United States	40.26
1936	Dorothy Poynton Hill, United States	33.92
1948	Victoria M. Draves, United States	68.87
1952	Patricia McCormick, United States	79.37
1956	Patricia McCormick, United States	84.85
1960	Ingrid Kramer, Germany	91.28
1964	Lesley Bush, United States	99.80
1968	Milena Duchkova, Czechoslovakia	109.59
1972	Ulrika Knape, Sweden	390.00
1976	Elena Vaytsekhovskaia, U.S.S.R.	406.59
1980	Martina Jaschke, East Germany	596.25
1984	Zhou Jihong, China	435.51
1988	Xu Yanmei, China	445.20
1992	Fu Mingxia, China	461.43

BASKETBALL–MEN

1904 United States
1936 United States
1948 United States
1952 United States
1956 United States
1960 United States
1964 United States
1968 United States
1972 U.S.S.R.
1976 United States
1980 Yugoslavia
1984 United States
1988 U.S.S.R.
1992 United States

BASKETBALL–WOMEN

1976 U.S.S.R.
1980 U.S.S.R.
1984 United States
1988 United States
1992 Unified Team

BOXING

(U.S. winners only)

(U.S. boycotted Olympics in 1980)

Flyweight–112 pounds (51 kilograms)

1904 George v. Finnegan
1920 Frank De Genaro
1924 Fidel La Barba
1952 Nate Brooks
1976 Leo Randolph
1984 Steve McCrory

Bantamweight–119 (54 kg)

1904 O.L. Kirk
1988 Kennedy McKinney

Featherweight–126 pounds (57 kg)

1904 O.L. Kirk
1924 Jackie Fields
1984 Meldrick Taylor

Lightweight–132 pounds (60 kg)

1904 H.J. Spanger
1920 Samuel Mosberg
1968 Ronnie Harris
1976 Howard Davis
1984 Pernell Whitaker
1992 Oscar De La Hoya

Light Welterweight–140 pounds (63.5 kg)

1952 Charles Adkins
1972 Ray Seales
1976 Ray Leonard
1984 Jerry Page

Welterwight–148 pounds (67 kg)

1904 Al Young
1932 Edward Flynn
1984 Mark Breland

Light Middleweight–157 pounds (71 kg)

1960 Wilbert McClure
1984 Frank Tate

Middleweight–165 pounds (75 kg)

1904 Charles Mayer
1932 Carmen Barth
1952 Floyd Patterson
1960 Eddie Cook
1976 Michael Spinks

Light Heavyweight–179 pounds (81 kg)

1920 Edward Eagan
1952 Norvel Lee
1956 James Boyd
1960 Cassius Clay
1976 Leon Spinks
1988 Andrew Maynard

Heavyweight–201 pounds

1904 Sam Berger
1952 Edward Sanders
1956 Pete Rademacher
1964 Joe Frazier
1968 George Foreman
1984 Henry Tilman
1988 Ray Mercer

Super Heavyweight (unlimited)

1984 Tyrell Biggs

Other 1992 Summer Olympic Games Champions

Archery
Men—Sebastien Flute, France
Men's Team—Spain
Women—Cho Youn-Jeong, South Korea
Women's Team—South Korea

Baseball
Men—Cuba

Canoe-Kayak—Men
Single Canoe Slalom—Lukas Pollert, Czechoslovakia
Double Canoe Slalom—United States (Scott Strausbaugh and Joe Jacobi)
Single Kayak Slalom—Pierpaolo Ferrazzi, Italy
Kayak 500m singles—Mikko Yrjoe Kolehmainen, Finland
Kayak 500m doubles—Germany (Kay Bluhm, Torsten Rene Gutsche)
Kayak 1,000m singles—Clint Robinson, Australia
Kayak 1,000m doubles—Germany (Kay Bluhm, Torsten Rene Gutsche)
Kayak 1,000m fours—Germany (Mario Von Appen, Oliver Kegel, Thomas Reineck, Andre Wohllebe)
Canoe 500m singles—Nikolai Boukhalov, Bulgaria
Canoe 500m doubles—Unified Team (Alexandre Masseikov, Dmitri Dovgalenok)
Canoe 1,000m singles—Nikolai Boukhalov, Bulgaria
Canoe 1,000m doubles—Germany (Ulrich Papke, Ingo Spelly)

Kayak—Women
Kayak slalom—Elisabeth Micheler, Germany
Kayak 500m singles—Birgit Schmidt, Germany
Kayak 500m doubles—Germany (Ramona Porturch, Anke Von Sek)
Kayak 500m fours—Hungary

Cycling—Men
4,000m individual pursuit—Chris Boardman, Great Britain
1,000m individual pursuit—Jens Fieldler, Germany
Individual points race—Giovanni Lombardi, Italy
Individual road race—Fabio Casartelli, Italy
1 km time trial—Jose Moreno, Spain
4,000m team pursuit—Germany
Team time trial—Germany

Cycling—Women
Individual road race—Kathryn Watt, Australia
1,000m individual sprint—Erika Salumae, Estonia
3,000m individual pursuit—Petra Rossner, Germany

Equestrian
Individual jumping—Ludger Beerbaum, Germany
Team jumping—Netherlands
Individual dressage—Nicole Uphoff, Germany
Team dressage—Germany
Individual three-day event—Matthew Ryan, Australia
Team three-day event—Australia

Fencing—Men
Individual foil—Philippe Omnes, France
Team foil—Germany
Individual sabre—Bence Szabo, Hungary
Team sabre—Unified Team
Individual épée—Eric Srecki, France
Team épée—Germany

Fencing—Women
Individual foil—Giovanna Trillini, Italy
Team foil—Italy

Field Hockey
Men—Germany
Women—Spain

Gymnastics—Men
All-around—Vitali Scherbo, Unified Team
Floor exercise—Li Xiaosqhuang, China
Horizontal bar—Trent Dimas, United States
Parallel bars—Vitali Scherbo, Unified Team
Pommel horse—Vitali Scherbo, Unified Team
Rings—Vitali Scherbo, Unified Team
Vault—Vitali Scherbo, Unified team
Team—Unified Team

Gymnastics—Women
All-around—Tatiana Gutsu, Unified Team
Balance beam—Tatiana Lisenko, Unified Team
Floor exercise—Lavania Milosovici, Romania
Uneven bars—Lu Li, China
Vault—Henrietta Onodi, Hungary and Lavinia Milosovici, Romania
Team—Unified Team

Judo—Men
132 lb—Nazim Gousseinov, Unified Team
143 lb—Rogerio Sampaio Cardoso, Brazil
157 lb—Toshihiko Koga, Japan
172 lb—Hidehiko Yoshida, Japan
198 lb—Waldemar Legein, Poland
209 lb—Antal Kovacs, Hungary
Over 209 lb—David Khakhaleichvili, Unified Team

Judo—Women
106 lb—Cecile Nowak, France
115 lb—Almudena Martinez, Spain
123 lb—Miriam Blasco Soto, Spain
134 lb—Catherine Fleury, France
146 lb—Odalis Reve, Cuba
159 lb—Kim Mi-Jung, South Korea
Over 159 lb—Zhuang Xiaoyan, China

Modern Pentathlon
Individual—Arkadiusz Skrzypaszek, Poland
Team—Poland

Rowing—Men
Singles—Thomas Lange, Germany
Doubles—Australia
Quadruples—Germany
Pairs—Great Britain
Pairs with coxswain—Great Britain
Fours—Australia
Fours with coxswain—Romania
Eights—Canada

Rowing—Women
Singles—Elisabeta Lipa, Romania
Doubles—Germany
Pairs—Canada
Fours with coxswain—Canada
Quadruple sculls—Germany
Eights—Canada

Shooting—Men
Skeet—Zhang Shan, China
Trap—Petr Hrdlicka, Czechoslovakia
Air pistol—Wang Yifu, China
Free pistol—Konstantine Loukqchik, Unified Team
Rapid-fire pistol—Ralf Schumann, Germany
Running game target—Michael Jakosits, Germany
Air rifle—Iouri Fedkine, Unified Team
Free rifle—Lee Eun Chui, South Korea
Three-position rifle—Gratchia Petikiane, Unified Team

Shooting—Women
Sport pistol—Marina Logvinenko, Unified Team
Air pistol—Marina Logvinenko, Unified Team
Air rifle—Yeo Kab Soon, South Korea
Three-position rifle—Launi Meili, United States

Synchronized Swimming
Solo—Kristin Babb-Sprague, United States
Duet—United States (Karen and Sarah Josephson)

Table Tennis
Men's singles—Jan Waldner, Sweden
Men's doubles—China (Lu Lin and Wang Tao)
Women's singles—Deng Yaping, China
Women's doubles—China (Deng Yaping and Qiao Hong)

Tennis
Men's singles—Marc Rosset, Switzerland
Men's doubles—Germany (Boris Becker and Michael Stich)
Women's singles—Jennifer Capriati, United States
Women's doubles—United States (Gigi Fernandez and Mary Jo Fernandez)

Weightlifting
115 lb—Ivan Ivanov, Bulgaria
123 lb—Chun Byung-Kwan, South Korea
132 lb—Naim Suleymanoglu, Turkey
148 lb—Israel Militossian, Unified Team
165 lb—Fedor Kassapu, Unified Team
181 lb—Pyrros Dimas, Greece
198 lb—Kakhi Kakhiachvili, Unified Team
220 lb—Victor Tregoubov, Unified Team
243 lb—Ronny Weller, Germany
Over 243 lb—Alexandre Fourlovitch, Unified Team

Wrestling—Freestyle
105.5 lb—Kim Il, North Korea
114.5 lb—Li Hak Son, South Korea
125.5 lb—Alejandro Puerto, Cuba
136.5 lb—John Smith, United States
149.5 lb—Arsen Fadzaev, Unified Team
163 lb—Park Jang Soon, South Korea
181 lb—Kevin Jackson, United States
198.5 lb—Makharbek Khadartsev, Unified Team
220 lb—Leri Khabelov, Unified Team
286 lb—Bruce Baumgartner, United States

Wrestling—Greco-Roman
105.5 lb—Oleg Koutherenko, Unified Team
114.5 lb—Joe Ronningen, Norway
125.5 lb—An Han-Bong, South Korea
136.5 lb—M. Akif Pirim, Turkey
149.5 lb—Attila Repka, Hungary
163 lb—Mnatsakan Iskandarian, Unified Team
181.5 lb—Peter Farkas, Hungary
198 lb—Malik Bullmann, Germany
220 lb—Hector Millian, Cuba
286 lb—Alexander Karelin, Unified Team

Yachting
Men's sailboard—Franck David, France
Women's sailboard—Barbara Kendall, New Zealand
Men's 470—Spain
Women's 470—Spain
Finn—Jose Van Der Ploeg, Spain
Europe—Linda Anderson, Norway
Flying Dutchman—Spain
Solins—Denmark
Star—United States (Mark Reynolds, Hal Haenel)
Tornado—France

Other Champions
Water polo—Italy
Volleyball, men—Brazil
Volleyball, women—Cuba
Soccer—Spain
Rhythmic gymnastics—Alexandra Timoshenka, Unified Team

FOOTBALL

The pastime of kicking around a ball goes back beyond the limits of recorded history. Ancient savage tribes played football of a primitive kind. There was a ball-kicking game played by Athenians, Spartans, and Corinthians 2500 years ago, which the Greeks called *Episkuros*. The Romans had a somewhat similar game called *Harpastum* and are supposed to have carried the game with them when they invaded the British Isles in the First Century, B.C.

Undoubtedly the game known in the United States as Football traces directly to the English game of Rugby, though the modifications have been many. Informal football was played on college lawns well over a century ago, and an annual Freshman-Sophomore series of "scrimmages" began at Yale in 1840. The first formal intercollegiate football game was the Princeton-Rutgers contest at New Brunswick, N.J. on Nov. 6, 1869, with Rutgers winning by 6 goals to 4.

In those days, games were played with 25, 20, 15, or 11 men on a side. In 1880, there was a convention at which Walter Camp of Yale persuaded the delegates to agree to a rule calling for 11 players on a side.

The first professional game was played in 1895 at Latrobe, Pa. The National Football League was founded in 1921. The All-American Conference went into action in 1946. At the end of the 1949 season the two circuits merged, retaining the name of the older league. In 1960, the American Football League began operations. In 1970, the leagues merged. The United States Football League played its first season in 1983, from March to July. It suspended spring operation after the 1985 season, and planned a 1986 move to fall, but suspended operations again.

In 1991, another effort at spring football was launched, but this time it had the backing of the National Football League. The World League of American Football debuted in March 1991 with 10 teams. Three of them were in Europe—London, Barcelona, and Frankfurt. The other seven were in North America, including the Montreal Machine in Canada and six United States teams. With television contracts signed with ABC and USA Cable Network, the league seemed to be on sound footing from the beginning. But after just two seasons, it was gone, too.

College Football

NATIONAL COLLEGE FOOTBALL CHAMPIONS

The "National Collegiate A.A. Football Guide" recognizes as unofficial national champion the team selected each year by press association polls. If the Associated Press Poll (of writers) did not agree with the United Press International poll (of coaches) through 1991 or the USA Today–CNN poll from 1992, the guide lists both teams selected.

1937	Pittsburgh
1938	Texas Christian
1939	Texas A & M
1940	Minnesota
1941	Minnesota
1942	Ohio State
1943	Notre Dame
1944	Army
1945	Army
1946	Notre Dame
1947	Notre Dame
1948	Michigan
1949	Notre Dame
1950	Oklahoma
1951	Tennessee
1952	Mich. State
1953	Maryland
1954	Ohio State and U.C.L.A.
1955	Oklahoma
1956	Oklahoma
1957	Auburn and Ohio State
1958	Louisiana State
1959	Syracuse
1960	Minnesota
1961	Alabama
1962	So. California
1963	Texas
1964	Alabama
1965	Alabama and Mich. State
1966	Notre Dame
1967	So. California
1968	Ohio State
1969	Texas
1970	Texas and Nebraska
1971	Nebraska
1972	So. California
1973	Notre Dame and U. of Ala.
1974	Oklahoma and So. California
1975	Oklahoma
1976	Pittsburgh
1977	Notre Dame
1978	Alabama and So. California
1979	Alabama
1980	Georgia
1981	Clemson
1982	Penn State
1983	Miami
1984	Brigham Young
1985	Oklahoma
1986	Penn State
1987	Miami
1988	Notre Dame
1989	Miami
1990	Colorado and Georgia Tech
1991	Miami and Washington
1992	Alabama

RECORD OF ANNUAL MAJOR COLLEGE FOOTBALL BOWL GAMES

Rose Bowl

(At Pasadena, Calif.)

1902	Michigan 49, Stanford 0
1916	Washington State 14, Brown 0
1917	Oregon 14, Pennsylvania 0
1918	Mare Island Marines 19, Camp Lewis 7
1919	Great Lakes 17, Mare Island Marines 0
1920	Harvard 7, Oregon 6
1921	California 28, Ohio State 0
1922	Washington and Jefferson 0, California 0
1923	So. California 14, Penn State 3
1924	Navy 14, Washington 14
1925	Notre Dame 27, Stanford 10
1926	Alabama 20, Washington 19
1927	Alabama 7, Stanford 7
1928	Stanford 7, Pittsburgh 6
1929	Georgia Tech 8, California 7
1930	So. California 47, Pittsburgh 14
1931	Alabama 24, Wash. State 0
1932	So. California 21, Tulane 12
1933	So. California 35, Pittsburgh 0
1934	Columbia 7, Stanford 0
1935	Alabama 29, Stanford 13
1936	Stanford 7, So. Methodist 0
1937	Pittsburgh 21, Washington 0
1938	California 13, Alabama 0
1939	So. California 7, Duke 3
1940	So. California 14, Tennessee 0
1941	Stanford 21, Nebraska 13
1942	Oregon State 20, Duke 16[1]
1943	Georgia 9, U.C.L.A. 0
1944	So. California 29, Washington 0
1945	So. California 25, Tennessee 0
1946	Alabama 34, So. California 14
1947	Illinois 45, U.C.L.A. 14
1948	Michigan 49, So. California 0
1949	Northwestern 20, California 14
1950	Ohio State 17, California 14
1951	Michigan 14, California 6
1952	Illinois 40, Stanford 7
1953	So. California 7, Wisconsin 0
1954	Michigan State 28, U.C.L.A. 20
1955	Ohio State 20, So. California 7
1956	Michigan State 17, U.C.L.A. 14
1957	Iowa 35, Oregon State 19
1958	Ohio State 10, Oregon 7
1959	Iowa 38, California 12
1960	Washington 44, Wisconsin 8
1961	Washington 17, Minnesota 7
1962	Minnesota 21, U.C.L.A. 3
1963	So. California 42, Wisconsin 37
1964	Illinois 17, Washington 7
1965	Michigan 34, Oregon State 7
1966	U.C.L.A. 14, Michigan State 12
1967	Purdue 14, So. California 13
1968	So. California 14, Indiana 3
1969	Ohio State 27, So. California 16
1970	So. California 10, Michigan 3
1971	Stanford 27, Ohio State 17

1972 Stanford 13, Michigan 12
1973 So. California 42, Ohio State 17
1974 Ohio State 42, So. California 21
1975 So. California 18, Ohio State 17
1976 U.C.L.A. 23, Ohio State 10
1977 So. California 14, Michigan 6
1978 Washington 27, Michigan 20
1979 So. California 17, Michigan 10
1980 So. California 17, Ohio State 16
1981 Michigan 23, Washington 6
1982 Washington 28, Iowa 0
1983 U.C.L.A. 24, Michigan 14
1984 U.C.L.A. 45, Illinois 9
1985 USC 20, Ohio St. 17
1986 U.C.L.A. 45, Iowa 28
1987 Arizona State 22, Michigan 15
1988 Michigan State 20, USC 17
1989 Michigan 22, So. California 14
1990 USC 17, Michigan 10
1991 Washington 46, Iowa 34
1992 Washington 34, Michigan 14
1993 Michigan 38, Washington 31

1. Played at Durham, N.C.

Orange Bowl
(At Miami)

1933 Miami (Fla.) 7, Manhattan 0
1934 Duquesne 33, Miami (Fla.) 7
1935 Bucknell 26, Miami (Fla.) 0
1936 Catholic 20, Mississippi 19
1937 Duquesne 13, Mississippi State 12
1938 Auburn 6, Michigan State 0
1939 Tennessee 17, Oklahoma 0
1940 Georgia Tech 21, Missouri 7
1941 Mississippi State 14, Georgetown 7
1942 Georgia 40, Texas Christian 26
1943 Alabama 37, Boston College 21
1944 Louisiana State 19, Texas A&M 14
1945 Tulsa 26, Georgia Tech 12
1946 Miami (Fla.) 13, Holy Cross 6
1947 Rice 8, Tennessee 0
1948 Georgia Tech 20, Kansas 14
1949 Texas 41, Georgia 28
1950 Santa Clara 21, Kentucky 13
1951 Clemson 15, Miami (Fla.) 14
1952 Georgia Tech 17, Baylor 14
1953 Alabama 61, Syracuse 6
1954 Oklahoma 7, Maryland 0
1955 Duke 34, Nebraska 7
1956 Oklahoma 20, Maryland 6
1957 Colorado 27, Clemson 21
1958 Oklahoma 48, Duke 21
1959 Oklahoma 21, Syracuse 6
1960 Georgia 14, Missouri 0
1961 Missouri 21, Navy 14
1962 Louisiana State 25, Colorado 7
1963 Alabama 17, Oklahoma 0
1964 Nebraska 13, Auburn 7
1965 Texas 21, Alabama 17
1966 Alabama 39, Nebraska 28
1967 Florida 27, Georgia Tech 12
1968 Oklahoma 26, Tennessee 24
1969 Penn State 15, Kansas 14
1970 Penn State 10, Missouri 3
1971 Nebraska 17, Louisiana State 12
1972 Nebraska 38, Alabama 6
1973 Nebraska 40, Notre Dame 6
1974 Penn State 16, Louisiana State 9
1975 Notre Dame 13, Alabama 11
1976 Oklahoma 14, Michigan 6
1977 Ohio State 27, Colorado 10
1978 Arkansas 31, Oklahoma 6
1979 Oklahoma 31, Nebraska 24
1980 Oklahoma 24, Florida State 7
1981 Oklahoma 18, Florida State 17
1982 Clemson 22, Nebraska 15
1983 Nebraska 21, Louisiana State 20
1984 Miami 31, Nebraska 30
1985 Washington 28, Oklahoma 17
1986 Oklahoma 25, Penn St. 10
1987 Oklahoma 42, Arkansas 8
1988 Miami 20, Oklahoma 14
1989 Miami 23, Nebraska 3
1990 Notre Dame 21, Colorado 6
1991 Colorado 10, Notre Dame 9
1992 Miami 22, Nebraska 0
1993 Florida State 27, Nebraska 14

Sugar Bowl
(At New Orleans)

1935 Tulane 20, Temple 14
1936 Texas Christian 3, Louisiana State 2
1937 Santa Clara 21, Louisiana State 14
1938 Santa Clara 6, Louisiana State 0
1939 Texas Christian 15, Carnegie Tech 7
1940 Texas A & M 14, Tulane 13
1941 Boston College 19, Tennessee 13
1942 Fordham 2, Missouri 0
1943 Tennessee 14, Tulsa 7
1944 Georgia Tech 20, Tulsa 18
1945 Duke 29, Alabama 26
1946 Oklahoma A & M 33, St. Mary's (Calif.) 13
1947 Georgia 20, North Carolina 10
1948 Texas 27, Alabama 7
1949 Oklahoma 14, North Carolina 6
1950 Oklahoma 35, Louisiana State 0
1951 Kentucky 13, Oklahoma 7
1952 Maryland 28, Tennessee 13
1953 Georgia Tech 24, Mississippi 7
1954 Georgia Tech 42, West Virginia 19
1955 Navy 21, Mississippi 0
1956 Georgia Tech 7, Pittsburgh 0
1957 Baylor 13, Tennessee 7
1958 Mississippi 39, Texas 7
1959 Louisiana State 7, Clemson 0
1960 Mississippi 21, Louisiana State 0
1961 Mississippi 14, Rice 6
1962 Alabama 10, Arkansas 3
1963 Mississippi 17, Arkansas 13
1964 Alabama 12, Mississippi 7
1965 Louisiana State 13, Syracuse 10
1966 Missouri 20, Florida 18
1967 Alabama 34, Nebraska 7
1968 Louisiana State 20, Wyoming 13
1969 Arkansas 16, Georgia 2
1970 Mississippi 27, Arkansas 22
1971 Tennessee 34, Air Force Academy 13
1972 Oklahoma 40, Auburn 22
1973 Oklahoma 14, Penn State 0
1974 Notre Dame 24, Alabama 23
1975 Nebraska 13, Florida 10
1976 Alabama 13, Penn State 6
1977 Pittsburgh 27, Georgia 3
1978 Alabama 35, Ohio State 6
1979 Alabama 14, Penn State 7
1980 Alabama 24, Arkansas 9
1981 Georgia 17, Notre Dame 10
1982 Pittsburgh 24, Georgia 20
1983 Penn State 27, Georgia 23
1984 Auburn 9, Michigan 7
1985 Nebraska 28, LSU 10
1986 Tennessee 35, Miami, Fla. 7
1987 Nebraska 30, Louisiana State 15
1988 Syracuse 16, Auburn 16 (tie)
1989 Florida State 13, Auburn 7
1990 Miami 33, Alabama 25
1991 Tennessee 23, Virginia 22
1992 Notre Dame 39, Florida 28
1993 Alabama 34, Miami 13

Cotton Bowl
(At Dallas)

1937 Texas Christian 16, Marquette 6
1938 Rice 28, Colorado 14
1939 St. Mary's (Calif.) 20, Texas Tech. 13
1940 Clemson 6, Boston College 3
1941 Texas A & M 13, Fordham 12
1942 Alabama 29, Texas A & M 21
1943 Texas 14, Georgia Tech 7
1944 Randolph Field 7, Texas 7
1945 Oklahoma A & M 34, Texas Christian 0
1946 Texas 40, Missouri 27
1947 Louisiana State 0, Arkansas 0
1948 So. Methodist 13, Penn State 13
1949 So. Methodist 21, Oregon 13
1950 Rice 27, North Carolina 13
1951 Tennessee 20, Texas 14
1952 Kentucky 20, Texas Christian 7
1953 Texas 16, Tennessee 0
1954 Rice 28, Alabama 6
1955 Georgia Tech 14, Arkansas 6
1956 Mississippi 14, Texas Christian 13
1957 Texas Christian 28, Syracuse 27
1958 Navy 20, Rice 7
1959 Air Force 0, Texas Christian 0
1960 Syracuse 23, Texas 14
1961 Duke 7, Arkansas 6
1962 Texas 12, Mississippi 7
1963 Louisiana State 13, Texas 0
1964 Texas 28, Navy 6
1965 Arkansas 10, Nebraska 7
1966 Louisiana State 14, Arkansas 7
1967 Georgia 24, So. Methodist 9
1968 Texas A & M 20, Alabama 16
1969 Texas 36, Tennessee 13
1970 Texas 21, Notre Dame 17
1971 Notre Dame 24, Texas 11
1972 Penn State 30, Texas 6
1973 Texas 17, Alabama 13
1974 Nebraska 19, Texas 3
1975 Penn State 41, Baylor 20
1976 Arkansas 31, Georgia 10
1977 Houston 30, Maryland 21
1978 Notre Dame 38, Texas 10
1979 Notre Dame 35, Houston 34
1980 Houston 17, Nebraska 14
1981 Alabama 30, Baylor 2
1982 Texas 14, Alabama 12
1983 Southern Methodist 7, Pittsburgh 3
1984 Georgia 10, Texas 9
1985 Boston College 45, Houston 28
1986 Texas A & M 36, Auburn 16
1987 Ohio State 28, Texas A & M 12
1988 Texas A & M 35, Notre Dame 10
1989 UCLA 17, Arkansas 3
1990 Tennessee 31, Arkansas 27
1991 Miami 46, Texas 3
1992 Florida State 10, Texas A&M 2
1993 Notre Dame 28, Texas A&M 3

Gator Bowl

(At Jacksonville, Fla.)

1953	Florida 14, Tulsa 13
1954	Texas Tech 35, Auburn 13
1955	Auburn 33, Baylor 13
1956	Vanderbilt 25, Auburn 13
1957	Georgia Tech 21, Pittsburgh 14
1958	Tennessee 3, Texas A & M 0
1959	Mississippi 7, Florida 3
1960	Arkansas 14, Georgia Tech 7
1961	Florida 13, Baylor 12
1962	Penn State 30, Georgia Tech 15
1963	Florida 17, Penn State 7
1964	No. Carolina 35, Air Force 0
1965	Florida State 36, Oklahoma 19
1966	Georgia Tech 31, Texas Tech 21
1967	Tennessee 18, Syracuse 12
1968	Penn State 17, Florida State 17
1969	Missouri 35, Alabama 10
1970	Florida 14, Tennessee 13
1971	Auburn 35, Mississippi 28
1972	Georgia 7, North Carolina 3
1973	Auburn 24, Colorado 3
1974	Texas Tech 28, Tennessee 19
1975	Auburn 27, Texas 3
1976	Maryland 13, Florida 0
1977	Notre Dame 20, Penn State 9
1978	Pittsburgh 34, Clemson 3
1979	Clemson 17, Ohio State 15
1980	North Carolina 17, Michigan 15
1981	Pittsburgh 37, South Carolina 9
1982	North Carolina 31, Arkansas 27
1983	Florida State 31, West Virginia 12
1984	Florida 14, Iowa 6
1985	Oklahoma St. 21, South Carolina 14
1986	Florida State 34, Oklahoma St. 23
1987	Clemson 27, Stanford 21
1988	LSU 30, South Carolina 13
1989	Georgia 34, Michigan St. 27
1990	Clemson 27, West Virginia 7
1991	Michigan 35, Mississippi 3
1992	Oklahoma 38, Virginia 14
1993	Florida 27, No. Carolina St. 10

RESULTS OF OTHER 1992 SEASON BOWL GAMES

Aloha (Honolulu, Hawaii, Dec. 25, 1992)—Kansas 23, Brigham Young 20

Blockbuster (Miami, Jan. 1, 1993)—Stanford 24, Penn State 3

Copper (Tucson, Ariz., Dec. 29, 1992)—Washington State 31, Utah 28

Fiesta (Tempe, Ariz., Jan. 1, 1993)—Syracuse 26, Colorado 22

Florida Citrus (Orlando, Jan. 1, 1993)—Georgia 21, Ohio State 14

Freedom (Anaheim, Calif., Dec. 29, 1992)—Fresno State 24, USC 7

Hall of Fame (Tampa, Fla., Jan. 1, 1993)—Tennessee 38, Boston College 23

Holiday (San Diego, Dec. 30, 1992)—Hawaii 27, Illinois 17

Independence (Shreveport, La., Dec. 31, 1992)—Wake Forest 39, Oregon 35

John Hancock (El Paso, Tex., Dec. 31, 1992)—Baylor 20, Arizona 15

Las Vegas (Las Vegas, Nev., Dec. 18, 1992)—Bowling Green 35, Nevada (Reno) 34

Liberty (Memphis, Dec. 31, 1992)—Mississippi 13, Air Force 0

Peach (Atlanta, Jan. 2, 1993)—North Carolina 21, Mississippi State 17

HEISMAN MEMORIAL TROPHY WINNERS

The Heisman Memorial Trophy is presented annually by the Downtown Athletic club of New York City to the nation's outsanding college football player, as determined by a poll of sportswriters and sportscasters.

1935	Jay Berwanger, Chicago
1936	Larry Kelley, Yale
1937	Clinton Frank, Yale
1938	Davey O'Brien, Texas Christian
1939	Nile Kinnick, Iowa
1940	Tom Harmon, Michigan
1941	Bruce Smith, Minnesota
1942	Frank Sinkwich, Georgia
1943	Angelo Bertelli, Notre Dame
1944	Leslie Horvath, Ohio State
1945	Felix Blanchard, Army
1946	Glenn Davis, Army
1947	Johnny Lujack, Notre Dame
1948	Doak Walker, So. Methodist
1949	Leon Hart, Notre Dame
1950	Vic Janowicz, Ohio State
1951	Dick Kazmaier, Princeton
1952	Billy Vessels, Oklahoma
1953	Johnny Lattner, Notre Dame
1954	Alan Ameche, Wisconsin
1955	Howard Cassady, Ohio State
1956	Paul Hornung, Notre Dame
1957	John Crow, Texas A & M
1958	Pete Dawkins, Army
1959	Billy Cannon, Louisiana State
1960	Joe Bellino, Navy
1961	Ernie Davis, Syracuse
1962	Terry Baker, Oregon State
1963	Roger Staubach, Navy
1964	John Huarte, Notre Dame
1965	Mike Garrett, Southern California
1966	Steve Spurrier, Florida
1967	Gary Beban, U.C.L.A.
1968	O.J. Simpson, Southern California
1969	Steve Owens, Oklahoma
1970	Jim Plunkett, Stanford
1971	Pat Sullivan, Auburn
1972	Johnny Rodgers, Nebraska
1973	John Cappelletti, Penn State
1974–75	Archie Griffin, Ohio State
1976	Tony Dorsett, Pittsburgh
1977	Earl Campbell, Texas
1978	Billy Sims, Oklahoma
1979	Charles White, Southern California
1980	George Rogers, South Carolina
1981	Marcus Allen, Southern California
1982	Hershel Walker, Georgia
1983	Mike Rozier, Nebraska
1984	Doug Flutie, Boston College
1985	Bo Jackson, Auburn
1986	Vinnie Testeverde, Miami
1987	Tim Brown, Notre Dame
1988	Barry Sanders, Oklahoma State
1989	Andre Ware, Houston
1990	Ty Detmer, Brigham Young
1991	Desmond Howard, Michigan
1992	Gino Torretta, Miami

1992 N.C.A.A. CHAMPIONSHIP PLAYOFFS

DIVISION I–AA

Quarterfinals

Marshall 35, Middle Tenn. State 21
Delaware 41, Northeast Louisiana 18
Youngstown State 42, The Citadel 17
Northern Iowa 29, McNeese State 7

Semifinals

Marshall 28, Delaware 7
Youngstown State 19, Northern Iowa 7

Championship

Marshall 31, Youngstown State 28

DIVISION II

Quarterfinals

Jacksonville (Ala.) St. 14, No. Ala. 12
New Haven (Conn.) 35, Ferris St. 13
Pittsburg (Kan.) St. 38, North Dakota State 37 (OT)
Portland (Ore.) State 35, Texas A&I 30

Semifinals

Jacksonville (Ala.) State 46, New Haven (Conn.) 35
Pittsburg (Kan.) State 41, Portland (Ore.) State 38

Championship

Jacksonville (Ala.) State 17, Pittsburg (Kan.) State 13

DIVISION III

Quarterfinals

Wisconsin–LaCrosse 34, Central (Iowa) 9
Mt. Union (Ohio) 49, Ill. Wesleyan 27
Washington & Jefferson (Pa.) 51, Emory & Henry 15
Rowan (N.J.) 28, Buffalo St. 19

Semifinals

Wisc.–LaCrosse 29, Mt. Union (Oh.) 24
Washington & Jefferson (Pa.) 18, Rowan (N.J.) 13

Championship

Wisconsin–LaCrosse 16, Washington & Jefferson 12

1992 NATIONAL ASSOCIATION OF INTERCOLLEGIATE ATHLETICS CHAMPIONSHIPS

DIVISION I

Quarterfinals

Central (Ohio) State 34, Harding (Ark.) 0
Central Arkansas 14, Southwestern Oklahoma 2
Gardner–Webb (N.C.) 28, Concord (W. Va.) 21
Shepard (W. Va.) 6, Carson–Newman (Tenn.) 3

Semifinals

Central (Ohio) State 30, Central Arkansas 23
Gardner–Webb (N.C.) 22, Shepard (W. Va.) 7

Championship

Central (Ohio) State 19, Gardner–Webb (N.C.) 16

DIVISION II

Quarterfinals

Findlay (Ohio) 13, Westminster (Pa.) 7
Minot State (N.D.) 21, Hardin Simmons (Texas) 14
Benedictine (Kan.) 21, Baker (Kan.) 14
Linfield (Ohio) 44, Pacific Lutheran (Wash.) 30

Semifinals

Findlay 27, Benedictine 24
Linfield 47, Minot State 12

Championship

Findlay 26, Linfield 13

COLLEGE FOOTBALL HALL OF FAME

(Kings Island, Interstate 71, Kings Mills, Ohio) (Date given is player's last year of competition)

Players

Abell, Earl—Colgate, 1915
Agase, Alex—Purdue/Illinois, 1946
Agganis, Harry—Boston Univ., 1952
Albert, Frank—Stanford, 1941
Aldrich, Chas. (Ki)—T.C.U., 1938
Aldrich, Malcolm—Yale, 1921
Alexander, John—Syracuse, 1920
Alworth, Lance—Arkansas, 1961
Ameche, Alan (Horse)—Wisconsin, 1954
Amling, Warren—Ohio State, 1946
Anderson, Dick—Colorado, 1967
Anderson, Donny—Texas Tech, 1965
Andderson, H. (Hunk)—Notre Dame, 1921
Atkins, Doug—Tennessee, 1952
Bacon, C. Everett—Wesleyan, 1912
Bagnell, Francis (Reds)—Penn, 1950
Baker, Hobart (Hobey)—Princeton, 1913
Baker, John—So. Calif., 1931
Baker, Terry—Oregon State, 1962
Ballin, Harold—Princeton, 1914
Banker, Bill—Tulane, 1929
Banonis, Vince—Detroit, 1941
Barnes, Stanley—S. California, 1921
Barrett, Charles—Cornell, 1915
Baston, Bert—Minnesota, 1916
Battles, Cliff—W. Va. Wesleyan, 1931
Baugh, Sammy—Texas Christian U., 1936
Baughan, Maxie—Georgia Tech, 1959
Bausch, James—Kansas, 1930
Beagle, Ron—Navy, 1955
Beban, Gary—UCLA, 1967
Bechtol, Hub—Texas Tech, 1946
Beckett, John—Oregon, 1913
Bednariok, Chuck—Pennsylvania 1948
Behm, Forrest—Nebraska, 1940
Bell, Bobby—Minnesota, 1962
Bellino, Joe—Navy, 1960
Below, Marty—Wisconsin, 1923
Benbrook, A.—Michigan, 1911
Bertelli, A.—Notre Dame, 1943
Berry, Charlie—Lafayette, 1924
Berwanger, John (Jay)—Chicago, 1935
Bettencourt, Larry—St. Mary's, 1927
Biletnikoff, Fred—Florida State, 1964
Blanchard, Felix (Doc)—Army, 1946
Bock, Ed—Iowa State, 1938
Bomar, Lynn—Vanderbilt, 1924
Bomeisler, Doug (Bo)—Yale, 1913
Booth, Albie–Yale, 1931
Borries, Fred—Navy, 1934
Bosely, Bruce—West Virginia, 1955
Bosseler, Don—Miami, Fla., 1956
Bottari, Vic—California, 1939
Boynton, Ben—Williams, 1920
Bozis, Al—Georgetown, 1941
Brewer, Charles—Harvard, 1895
Bright, John—Drake, 1951
Brodie, John—Stanford, 1956
Brooke, George—Pennsylvania, 1895
Brown, Bob—Nebraska, 1963
Brown, George—Navy, San Diego St., 1947
Brown, Gordon—Yale, 1900
Brown, John, Jr.—Navy, 1913
Brown, Johnny Mack—Alabama, 1925
Brown, Raymond (Tay)—So. Calif., 1932
Bunker, Paul—Army, 1902
Burton, Ron—Northwestern, 1956
Butkus, Dick—Illinois, 1964
Butler, Robert—Wisconsin, 1912
Cafego, George—Tennessee, 1939
Cagle, Chris—SW La. / Army, 1929
Cain, John—Alabama, 1932
Cameron, Eddie—Wash. & Lee, 1924
Campbell, David C.—Harvard, 1901
Campbell, Earl—Texas, 1977
Cannon, Billy—L.S.U., 1959
Cannon, Jack—Notre Dame, 1929
Cappelletti, John—Penn State, 1973
Carideo, Frank—Notre Dame, 1930
Caroline, J.C.—Illinois, 1954
Carney, Charles—Illinois, 1921
Carpenter, Bill—Army, 1959
Carpenter, C. Hunter—VPI, 1905
Carroll, Charles—Washington, 1928
Casey, Edward L.—Harvard, 1919
Cassady, Howard—Ohio State, 1955
Chamberlain, Guy—Nebraska, 1915
Chapman, Sam—Cal.-Berkeley, 1938
Chappuis, Bob—Michigan, 1947
Christman, Paul—Missouri, 1940
Clark, Earl (Dutch)—Colo. College, 1929
Cleary, Paul—USC, 1947
Clevenger, Zora—Indiana, 1903
Cloud, Jack—William & Mary, 1948
Cochran, Gary—Princeton, 1895
Cody, Josh—Vanderbilt, 1920
Coleman, Don—Mich. State, 1951
Conerly, Chuck—Mississippi, 1947
Connor, George—Notre Dame, 1947
Corbin, W.—Yale, 1888
Corbus, William—Stanford, 1933
Cowan, Hector—Princeton, 1889
Coy, Edward H. (Tad)—Yale, 1909
Crawford, Fred—Duke, 1933
Crow, John D.—Texas A&M, 1957
Crowley, James—Notre Dame, 1924
Csonka, Larry—Syracuse, 1967
Cutter, Slade—Navy, 1934
Czarobski, Ziggie—Notre Dame, 1947
Dale, Carroll—Virginia Tech, 1959
Dalrymple, Gerald—Tulane, 1931
Daniell, James—Ohio State, 1941
Dalton, John—Navy, 1912
Daly, Charles—Harvard/Army, 1902
Daniell, Averell—Pittsburgh, 1936
Davies, Tom—Pittsburgh, 1921
Davis, Ernest—Syracuse, 1961
Davis, Glenn—Army, 1946
Davis, Robert T.—Georgia Tech, 1947
Dawkins, Pete—Army, 1958
DeLong, Steve—Tennessee, 1964
De Rogatis, Al—Duke, 1940
DesJardien, Paul—Chicago 1914
Devino, Aubrey—Iowa, 1921
DeWitt, John—Princeton, 1903
Dial, Buddy—Rice, 1958
Ditka, Mike—Pittsburgh, 1960
Dobbs, Glenn—Tulsa, 1942
Dodd, Bobby—Tennessee, 1930
Donan, Holland—Princeton, 1950
Donchess, Joseph—Pittsburgh, 1929
Dougherty, Nathan—Tennessee, 1909
Drahos, Nick—Cornell, 1940
Driscoll, Paddy—Northwestern, 1917
Drury, Morley—So. California, 1927
Dudley, William (Bill)—Virginia, 1941
Easley, Ken—UCLA, 1980
Eckersall, Walter—Chicago, 1906
Edwards, Turk—Washington State, 1931
Edwards, William—Princeton, 1900
Eichenlaub, R.—Notre Dame, 1913
Elliott, Chalmers—Purdue, 1944 & Mich., 1947
Evans, Ray—Kansas, 1947
Exendine, Albert—Carlisle, 1908
Falaschi, Nello—Santa Clara, 1937
Fears, Tom—Santa Clara/UCLA, 1947
Feathers, Beattie—Tennessee, 1933
Fenimore, Robert—Oklahoma State, 1947
Fenton, G.E. (Doc)—La. State U., 1910
Ferraro, John—So. California, 1944
Fesler, Wesley—Ohio State, 1930
Fincher, Bill—Georgia Tech, 1920
Fischer, Bill—Notre Dame, 1948
Fish, Hamilton—Harvard, 1909
Fisher, Robert—Harvard, 1911
Flowers, Abe—Georgia Tech, 1920
Fortmann, Daniel—Colgate, 1935
Francis, Sam—Nebraska, 1936
Franco, Edmund (Ed)—Fordham, 1937
Frank, Clint—Yale, 1937
Franz, Rodney—California, 1949
Friedman, Benny—Michigan, 1926
Gabriel, Roman—North Carolina St., 1961
Gain, Bob—Kentucky, 1950
Galiffa, Arnold—Army, 1949
Gallarneau, Hugh—Stanford, 1941
Garbisch, Edgar—Army, 1924
Garrett, Mike—USC, 1965
Gelbert, Charles—Pennsylvania, 1896
Geyer, Forest—Oklahoma, 1915
Giel, Paul—Minnesota, 1953
Gifford, Frank—So. California, 1951
Gilbert, Walter—Auburn, 1936
Gilmer, Harry—Alabama, 1947
Gipp, George—Notre Dame, 1920
Gladchuk, Chet—Boston College, 1940
Glass, Bill—Baylor, 1956
Goldberg, Marshall—Pittsburgh, 1938
Goodreault, Gene—Boston College, 1940
Gordon, Walter—California, 1918
Governale, Paul—Columbia, 1942
Graham, Otto—Northwestern, 1943
Grange, Harold (Red)—Illinois, 1925
Grayson, Roberty—Stanford, 1935
Green, Joe—North Texas State, 1968
Griese, Bob—Purdue, 1966
Griffin, Archie—Ohio State, 1975

Gulick, Merel—Hobart, 1929
Guyon, Joe—Georgia Tech, 1919
Hale, Edwin—Mississippi Col, 1921
Hall, Parker—Mississippi, 1938
Ham, Jack—Penn State, 1970
Hamilton, Robert (Bones)—Stanford, 1935
Hamilton, Tom—Navy, 1925
Hanson, Vic—Syracuse, 1926
Harder, Pat—Wisconsin, 1942
Hardwick, H. (Tack)—Harvard, 1914
Hare, T. Truxton—Pennsylvania, 1900
Harley, Chick—Ohio State, 1919
Harmon, Tom—Michigan, 1940
Harpster, Howard—Carnegie Tech, 1928
Hart, Edward J. Princeton, 1911
Hart, Leon—Notre Dame, 1949
Hartman, Bill—Georgia, 1937
Hazel, Homer—Rutgers, 1924
Healey, Ed—Dartmouth, 1916
Heffelfiner, W. (Pudge)—Yale, 1891
Hein, Mel—Washington State, 1930
Heinrich, Don—Washington, 1952
Hendricks, Ted—Miami, 1968
Henry, Wilbur—Wash. & Jefferson, 1919
Herschberger, Clarence—Chicago, 1899
Herwig, Robert—California, 1937
Heston, Willie—Michigan, 1904
Hickman, Herman—Tennessee, 1931
Hickok, William—Yale, 1895
Hill, Dan—Duke, 1938
Hillebrand, A.R. (Doc)—Princeton, 1900
Hinkey, Frank—Yale, 1894
Hinkle, Carl—Vanderbilt, 1937
Hinkle, Clark—Bucknell, 1932
Hirsch, Elroy—Wis. / Mich., 1943
Hitchcock, James—Auburn, 1932
Hoffman, Frank—Notre Dame, 1931
Hogan, James J.—Yale, 1904
Holland, Jerome (Brud)—Cornell, 1938
Holleder, Don—Army, 1955
Hollenbeck, William—Penn., 1908
Holovak, Michael—Boston College, 1942
Holub, E.J.—Texas Tech, 1960
Hornung, Paul—Notre Dame, 1956
Horrell, Edwin—California, 1924
Horvath, Les—Ohio State, 1944
Howe Arthur—Yale, 1911
Howell, Millard (Dixie)—Alabama, 1934
Hubbard, Cal—Centenary, 1926
Hubbard, John—Amherst, 1906
Hubert, Allison—Alabama, 1925
Huff, Robert Lee (Sam)—W. Va., 1955
Humble, Weldon G.—Rice, 1946
Hunt, Joel—Texas A&M, 1927
Huntington, Ellery—Colgate, 1914
Hutson, Don—Alabama, 1934
Ingram, James—Navy, 1906
Isbell, Cecil—Purdue, 1937
Jablonsky, Harvey—Wash. U./Army, 1933
Janowicz, Vic—Ohio State, 1951
Jenkins, Darold—Missouri, 1941
Jensen, Jack—Cal-Berkeley, 1948
Joesting, Herbert—Minnesota, 1927
Johnson, James—Carlisle, 1903
Johnson, Robert—Tennessee, 1967
Johnson, Ron—Michigan, 1968
Jones, Calvin—Iowa, 1955
Jones, Gormer—Ohio State, 1935
Jordan, Lee Roy—Alabama, 1962
Juhan, Frank—Univ. of South, 1910
Justice, Charlie—North Carolina, 1949
Kaer, Mort—So. California, 1926
Karras, Alex—Iowa, 1957
Kavanaugh, Kenneth—La. State U., 1939
Kaw, Edgar—Cornell, 1922
Kazmaier, Richard—Princeton, 1951
Keck, James—Princeton, 1921
Kelley, Larry—Yale, 1936
Kelly, William—Montana, 1926
Kenna, Ed—Syracuse, 1966
Kern, George—Boston College, 1941
Ketcham, Henry—Yale, 1913
Keyes, Leroy—Purdue, 1968
Killinger, William—Penn State, 1922
Kimbrough, John—Texas A&M, 1940
Kinard, Frank—Mississippi, 1937
King, Philip—Princeton, 1893
Kinnick, Nile—Iowa, 1939
Kipke, Harry—Michigan, 1923
Kirkpatrick, John Reed—Yale, 1910
Kitzmiller, John—Oregon, 1929
Koch, Barton—Baylor, 1931
Kitner, Malcolm—Texas, 1942
Kramer, Ron—Michigan, 1956
Krueger, Charlie—Texas A&M, 1957
Kwalick, Ted—Penn State, 1968
Lach, Steve—Duke, 1941
Lane, Myles—Dartmouth, 1927
Lattner, Joseph J.—Notre Dame, 1953
Lauricella, Hank—Tennessee, 1952
Lautenschlaeger—Tulane, 1925
Layden, Elmer—Notre Dame, 1924
Layne, Bobby—Texas, 1947
Lea, Langdon—Princeton, 1895
LeBaron, Eddie—Univ. of Pacific, 1949
Leech, James—Va. Mil. Insst., 1920
Lester, Darrell—Texas Christian, 1935
Lilly, Bob—Texas Christian, 1960
Little, Floyd—Syracuse, 1966
Lio, Augie—Georgetown, 1940
Locke, Gordon—Iowa, 1922
Lourie, Don—Princeton, 1921
Lucas, Richard—Penn State, 1959
Luckman, Sid—Columbia, 1938
Lujack, John—Notre Dame, 1947
Lund, J.L. (Pug)—Minnesota, 1934
Lynch, Jim—Notre Dame, 1966
Macomber, Bart—Illinois, 1915
MacLeod, Robert—Dartmouth, 1938
Maegle, Dick—Rice, 1954
Mahan, Edward W.—Harvard, 1915
Majors, John—Tennessee, 1956
Mallory, William—Yale, 1893
Mancha, Vaughn—Alabama, 1947
Mann, Gerald—So. Methodist, 1927
Manning, Archie—Mississippi, 1970
Manske, Edgar—Northwestern, 1933
Marinaro, Ed—Cornell, 1971
Markov, Vic—Washinton, 1937
Marshall, Robert—Minnesota, 1907
Matson, Ollie—San Fran. U., 1952
Matthews, Ray—Texas Christ. U., 1928
Maulbetsch, John—Michigan, 1914
Mauthe, J.L. (Pete)—Penn State, 1912
Maxwell, Robert—Chi./Swarthmore, 1906
McAfee, George—Duke, 1939
McClung, Thomas L.—Yale, 1891
McColl, William F.—Stanford, 1951
McCormick, James B.—Princeton, 1907
McDonald, Tom—Oklahoma, 1956
McDowall, Jack—No. Car. State, 1927
McElhenny, Hugh—Washington, 1951
McEver, Gene—Tennessee, 1931
McEwan, John—Minn./Army, 1916
McFadden, J.B.—Clemson, 1939
McFadin, Bud—Texas, 1950
McGee, Mike—Duke, 1959
McGinley, Edward—Pennsylvania, 1924
McGovern, J.—Minnesota, 1910
McGraw, Thurman—Colorado State, 1949
McKeever, Mike—USC, 1960
McLaren, George—Pittsburgh, 1918
McMillan, Dan—U.S.C./Calif., 1922
McMillin, A.N. (Bo)—Centre, 1921
McWhorter, Robert—Georgia, 1913
Mercer, Leroy—Pennsylvania, 1912
Meredith, Don—Southern Methodist, 1959
Metzger, Bert—Notre Dame, 1930
Meyland, Wayne—Nebraska, 1967
Michaels, Lou—Kentucky, 1957
Mickal, Abe—La. State U., 1935
Miller, Creighton—Notre Dame, 1943
Miller, Don—Notre Dame, 1925
Miller, Edgar (Rip)—Notre Dame, 1924
Miller, Eugene—Penn State, 1913
Miller, Fred—Notre Dame, 1928
Millner, Wayne—Notre Dame, 1935
Milstead, Century—Wabash, Yale, 1923
Minds, John—Pennsylvania, 1897
Minisi, Anthony—Navy, Pennsylvania, 1947
Modzelewski, Dick—Maryland, 1952
Moffatt, Alex—Princeton, 1884
Molinski, Ed—Tennessee, 1940
Montgomery, Cliff—Columbia, 1933
Moomaw, Donn—U.C.L.A., 1952
Morley, William—Columbia, 1903
Morris, George—Georgia Tech, 1952
Morris, Larry—Georgia Tech., 1954
Morton, Craig—California, 1964
Morton, William—Dartmouth, 1931
Moscrip, Monk—Stanford, 1935
Muller, Harold (Brick)—Calif., 1922
Nagurski, Bronko—Minnesota, 1929
Nevers, Ernie—Stanford, 1925
Newell, Marshall—Harvard, 1893
Newman, Harry—Michigan, 1932
Nobis, Tommy—Texas, 1965
Nomellini, Leo—Minnesota, 1949
Oberland, Andrew—Dartmouth, 1925
O'Brien, Davey—Texas Chrtist. U., 1938
O'Dea, Pat-Wisconsin, 1899
Odell, Robert—Pennsylvania, 1943
O'Hearn, J.—Cornell, 1915
Olds, Robin—Army, 1942
Oliphant, Elmer—Purdue/Army, 1917
Olsen, Merlin—Utah State, 1961
Oosterbaan, Ben—Michigan, 1927
O'Rourke, Charles—Boston College, 1940
Orsi, John—Colgate, 1931
Osgood, W.D.—Cornell/Penn, 1895
Osmanski, William—Holy Cross, 1938
Owen, George—Harvard, 1922
Owens, Jim—Oklahoma, 1949
Owens, Steve—Oklahoma, 1969
Page, Alan—Notre Dame, 1966
Pardee, Jack—Texas A&M, 1956
Parilli, Vito (Babe)—Kentucky, 1951
Parker, Clarence (Ace)—Duke, 1936
Parker, Jackie—Miss. State, 1953
Parker, James—Ohio State, 1956
Pazzetti, V.J.—Wes./Lehigh, 1912
Peabody, Endicott—Harvard, 1941
Peck, Robert—Pittsburgh, 1916
Pennock, Stanley B.—Harvard, 1914
Pfann, George—Cornell, 1923
Phillips, H.D.—U. of South, 1904
Phillips, Loyd—Arkansas, 1966
Pingel, John—Michigan State, 1938
Pihos, Pete—Indiana, 1945
Pinckert, Ernie—So. California, 1931
Plunkett, Jim—Stanford, 1970
Poe, Arthur—Princeton, 1899
Pollard, Fritz—Brown, 1916
Poole, Barney—Miss./Army, 1947
Pregulman, Merv—Michigan, 1943
Price, Eddie—Tulane, 1949
Pund, Henry—Georgia Tech, 1928
Ramsey, Gerrard—Wm. & Mary, 1942
Reeds, Claude—Oklahoma, 1913
Reid, Mike—Penn St., 1970
Reid, Steve—Northwestern, 1936
Reid, William—Harvard, 1900
Renfro, Mel—Oregon, 1963
Rentner, Ernest—Northwestern, 1932
Reynolds, Robert—Nebraska, 1952
Reynolds, Robert—Stanford, 1935
Richter, Les—California, 1951
Riley, John—Northwestern, 1931
Rinehart, Charles—Lafayette, 1897
Roberts, J.D.—Oklahoma, 1953
Rodgers, Ira—West Virginia, 1919
Rogers, Edward L.—Minnesota, 1903
Romig, Joe—Colorado, 1961
Rosenberg, Aaron—So. California, 1934
Rote, Kyle—So. Methodist, 1950
Routt, Joe—Texas A&M, 1937
Salmon, Louis—Notre Dame, 1904
Sauer, George—Nebraska, 1933
Savitsky, George—Pennsylvania, 1947
Sayers Gale—Kansas, 1964
Scarbath, Jack—Maryland, 1952
Scarlett, Hunter—Pennsylvania, 1909

Schloredt, Bob—Washington, 1960
Schoonover, Wear—Arkansas, 1929
Schreiner, Dave—Wisconsin, 1942
Schultz, Adolf (Germany)—Mich., 1908
Schwab, Frank—Lafayette, 1922
Schwartz, Marchmont—Notre Dame, 1931
Schwegler, Paul—Washington, 1931
Scott, Clyde—Arkansas, 1949
Scott, Richard—Navy, 1947
Scott, Tom—Virginia, 1953
Seibels, HHenry—Sewanee, 1899
Sellers, Ron—Florida State, 1968
Selmon, Lee Roy—Oklahoma, 1975
Shakespeare, Bill—Notre Dame, 1935
Shelton, Murray—Cornell, 1915
Shevlin, Tom—Yale, 1905
Shively, Bernie—Illinois, 1926
Simons, Claude—Tulane, 1934
Simpson, O.J.—So. Calif., 1968
Sington, Fred—Alabama, 1930
Sinkwich, Frank—Georgia, 1942
Sitko, Emil—Notre Dame, 1949
Skladany, Joe—Pittsburgh, 1933
Slater, F.F. (Duke)—Iowa, 1921
Smith, Bruce—Minnesota, 1941
Smith, Bubba—Michigan State, 1966
Smith, Ernie—So. California, 1932
Smith, Harry—So. California, 1939
Smith, Jim Ray—Baylor, 1954
Smith, John (Clipper)—Notre Dame, 1927
Smith, Riley—Alabama, 1935
Smith, Vernon—Georgia, 1931
Snow, Neil—Michigan, 1901
Sparlis, Al—U.C.L.A., 1945
Spears, Clarence W.—Dartmouth, 1915
Spears, W.D.—Vanderbilt, 1927
Sprackling, William—Brown, 1911
Sprague, M. (Bud)—Texas/Army, 1928
Spurrier, Steve—Florida, 1966
Stafford, Harrison—Texas, 1932
Stagg, Amos Alonzo—Yale, 1889
Starcevich, Max—Washington, 1936
Staubach, Roger—Navy, 1963
Steffen, Walter—Chicago, 1908
Steffy, Joe—Army, 1947
Stein, Herbert—Pittsburgh, 1921
Steuber, Robert—Missouri, 1943
Stevens, Mal—Yale, 1923
Stevenson, Vincent—Pennsylvania, 1905
Stillwagon, Jim—Ohio State, 1970
Stinchcomb, Gaylord—Ohio State, 1920
Strom, Brock—Air Force, 1959
Strong, Ken—New York Univ., 1928
Strupper, George—Georgia Tech, 1917
Stuhldreher, Harry—Notre Dame, 1924
Stydahar, Joe—West Virginia, 1935
Suffridge, Robert—Tennessee, 1940
Suhey, Steve—Pennsylvania State, 1947
Sullivan, Pat—Auburn, 1971
Sundstrom, Frank—Cornell, 1923
Swann, Lynn—USC, 1973
Swanson, Clarence—Nebraska, 1921
Swiacki, Bill—Holy Cross/Colombia, 1947
Swink, Jim—Texas Christian, 1956
Taliafarro, George—Indiana, 1948
Tarkenton, Fran—Georgia, 1960
Tavener, John—Indiana, 1944
Taylor, Charles—Stanford, 1942
Thomas, Aurelius—Ohio St., 1957
Thompson, Joe—Pittsburgh, 1907
Thorne, Samuel B.—Yale, 1906
Thorpe, Jim—Carlisle, 1912
Ticknor, Ben—Harvard, 1930
Tigert, John—Vanderbilt, 1904
Tinsley, Gaynell—La. State U., 1936
Tipton, Eric—Duke, 1938
Tonnemaker, Clayton—Minnesota, 1949
Torrey, Robert—Pennsylvania, 1906
Travis, Ed Tarkio—Missouri, 1920
Trippi, Charles—Georgia, 1946
Tryon, J. Edward—Colgate, 1925
Utay, Joe—Texas A&M, 1907
Van Brocklin, Norm—Oregon, 1948
Van Sickel, Dale—Florida, 1929
Van Surdam, Henderson—Wesleyan, 1905
Very, Dexter—Penn Stste, 1912
Vessels, Billy—Oklahoma, 1952
Vick, Ernie—Michigan, 1921
Wagner, Huber—Pittsburgh, 1913
Walker, Doak—So. Methodist, 1949
Wallace, Bill—Rice, 1935
Walsh, Adam—Notre Dame, 1924
Warburton, I. (Cotton)—So. Calif., 1934
Ward, Robert (Bob)—Maryland, 1951
Warner, William—Cornell, 1903
Washington, Ken—U.C.L.A., 1939
Weatherall, Jim—Oklahoma, 1951
Webster, George—Michigan St., 1966
Wedemeyer, Herman J.—St. Mary's, 1947
Weekes, Harold—Columbia, 1902
Weiner, Art—North Carolina, 1949
Weir, Ed—Nebraska, 1925
Welch, Gus—Carlisle, 1914
Weller, John—Princeton, 1935
Wendell, Percy—Harvard, 1913
West, D. Belford—Colgate, 1919
Westfall, Bob—Michigan, 1941
Weyand, Alex—Army, 1915
Wharton, Charles—Pennsylvania, 1896
Wheeler, Arthur—Princeton, 1894
White, Byron (Whizzer)—Colorado, 1937
Whitmire, Don—Alabama/Navy, 1944
Wickhorst, Frank—Navy, 1926
Widseth, Ed—Minnesota, 1936
Wildung, Richard—Minnesota, 1942
Williams, Bob—Notre Dame, 1950
Williams, James—Rice, 1949
Willis, William—Ohio State, 1945
Wilson, George—Washington, 1925
Wilson, George—Lafayette, 1928
Wilson, Harry—Penn State/Army, 1923
Wistert, Albert A.—Michigan, 1942
Wistert, Al—Michigan, 1942
Wistert, Frank (Whitey)—Mich., 1933
Wood, Barry—Harvard, 1931
Wojciechowicz, Alex—Fordham, 1936
Wyant, Andrew—Bucknell/Chicago, 1894
Wyatt, Bowden—Tennessee, 1938
Wyckoff, Clint—Cornell, 1896
Yarr, Tom—Notre Dame, 1931
Yary, Ron—USC, 1968
Yoder, Lloyd—Carnegie Tech, 1926
Young, Claude (Buddy)—Illinois, 1946
Young, Harry—Wash. & Lee, 1916
Young, Walter—Oklahoma, 1938
Youngblood, Jack—Florida, 1970
Zarnas, Gus—Ohio State, 1937

Coaches

Bill Alexander
Dr. Ed Anderson
Ike Armstrong
Earl Banks
Harry Baujan
Matty Bell
Hugo Bezdek
Dana X. Bible
Bernie Bierman
Bob Blackman
Earl (Red) Blaik
Frank Broyles
Paul "Bear" Bryant
Charles W. Caldwell
Walter Camp
Len Casanova
Frank Cavanaugh
Richard Colman
Fritz Crisler
Duffy Daugherty
Bob Devaney
Dan Devine
Gil Dobie
Bobby Dodd
Michael Donohue
Gus Dorais
Bill Edwards
Charles (Rip) Engle
Don Faurot
Jake Gaither
Sid Gillman
Ernest Godfrey
Ray Graves
Andy Gustafson
Jack Harding
Edward K. Hall
Richard Harlow
Jesse Harper
Percy Haughton
Woody Hayes
John W. Heisman
R.A. (Bob) Higgins
Orin E. Hollingberry
Frank Howard
William Ingram
Morley Jennings
Howard Jones
L. (Biff) Jones
Thomas (Tad) Jones
Ralph (Shug) Jordan
Andy Kerr
Frank Leahy
George E. Little
Lou Little
El (Slip) Madigan
Dave Maurer
Charley McClendon
Herbert McCracken
Daniel McGugin
John McKay
Allyn McKeen
DeOrmond (Tuss) McLaughry
L.R. (Dutch) Meyer
Bernie Moore
Scrappy Moore
Jack Mollenkopf
Ray Morrison
George A. Munger
Clarence Munn
Frank Murray
William Murray
Ed (Hooks) Mylin
Earle (Greasy) Neale
Jess Neely
David Nelson
Robert Neyland
Homer Norton
Frank (Buck) O'Neill
Bennie Owen
Ara Parseghian
Doyt LPerry
James Phalea
Tommy Prothro
John Ralston
E.N. Robinson
Knute Rockne
E.L. (Dick) Romney
William W. Roper
Darrell Royal
George F. Sanford
Bo Schembechler
Francis A. Schmidt
Floyd (Ben) Schwart-zwalder
Clark Shaughnessy
Buck Shaw
Andrew L. Smith
Carl Snavely
Amos A. Stagg
Jock Sutherland
James Tatum
Frank W. Thomas
Thad Vann
John H. Vaught
Wallace Wade
Lynn Waldorf
Glenn (Pop) Warner
E.E. (Tad) Wieman
John W. Wilce
Bud Wilkinson
Henry L. Williams
George W. Woodruff
Warren Woodson
Fielding H. Yost
Robert Zuppke

Professional Football

NATIONAL FOOTBALL LEAGUE FINAL STANDINGS 1992

AMERICAN FOOTBALL CONFERENCE

Eastern Division

	W	L	T	Pct	Pts	Op
Miami[1]	11	5	0	.688	340	281
Buffalo[2]	11	5	0	.688	381	283
Indianapolis	9	7	0	.563	216	302
New York Jets	4	12	0	.250	220	315
New England	2	14	0	.125	205	363
Central Division						
Pittsburgh[1]	11	5	0	.688	299	225
Houston[2]	10	6	0	.625	352	258
Cleveland	7	9	0	.438	272	275
Cincinnati	5	11	0	.313	274	364
Western Division						
San Diego[1]	11	5	0	.688	335	241
Kansas City[2]	10	6	0	.625	348	282
Denver	8	8	0	.500	262	329
Los Angeles Raiders	7	9	0	.438	249	281
Seattle	2	14	0	.125	140	312

1. Division champion. 2. Wild card qualifier for playoffs. Playoffs: Buffalo 41, Houston 38 (OT); San Diego 17, Kansas City 0; Buffalo 24, Pittsburgh 3; Miami 31, San Diego 0. Conference championship: Buffalo 29, Miami 10.

NATIONAL FOOTBALL CONFERENCE

Eastern Division

	W	L	T	Pct	Pts	Op
Dallas[1]	13	3	0	.813	409	243
Philadelphia[2]	11	5	0	.688	354	245
Washington[2]	9	7	0	.563	300	255
New York Giants	6	10	0	.375	306	367
Phoenix	4	12	0	.250	243	332
Central Division						
Minnesota[1]	11	5	0	.688	374	249
Green Bay	9	7	0	.563	276	296
Detroit	5	11	0	.313	273	332
Tampa Bay	5	11	0	.313	267	365
Chicago	5	11	0	.313	295	361
Western Division						
San Francisco[1]	14	2	0	.875	431	236
New Orleans[2]	12	4	0	.750	330	202
Atlanta	6	10	0	.375	327	414
Los Angeles Rams	6	10	0	.375	313	383

1. Division champion. 2. Wild card qualifier for playoffs. Playoffs: Washington 24, Minnesota 7; Philadelphia 36, New Orleans 20; San Francisco 20, Washington 13; Dallas 34, Philadelphia 10. Conference championship: Dallas 30, San Francisco 20.

LEAGUE CHAMPIONSHIP—SUPER BOWL XXVII

(January 31, 1993 at The Rose Bowl, Pasadena, Calif.; Attendance: 98,374)

Scoring

	1st Q	2nd Q	3rd Q	4th Q	Final
Buffalo (AFC)	7	3	7	0	—17
Dallas (NFC)	14	14	3	21	—52

First Quarter: Buffalo: Thomas, 2-yard run (Christie kick) 5:00; Dallas: Novacek, 23-yard pass from Aikman (Elliott kick) 13:24; J. Jones, 2-yard fumble return (Elliott kick) 13:39.

Second Quarter: Buffalo: FG, Christie, 21 yards, 11:36; Dallas: Irvin, 19-yard pass from Aikman (Elliott kick) 13:06; Irvin, 18-yard pass from Aikman (Elliott kick) 13:24.

Third Quarter: Dallas: FG, Elliott, 20, 6:39; Buffalo: Beebe, 40-yard pass from Reich (Christie kick) 15:00.

Fourth Quarter: Dallas: Harper, 45-yard pass from Aikman (Elliott kick) 4:56; E. Smith, 10-yard run (Elliott kick) 6:54; Norton, 10-yard fumble return (Elliott kick) 7:29.

Statistics of the Game

	Buffalo	Dallas
First downs	22	20
Return yardage	0	70
Penalties—yards	4–30	8–53
Time of possession	28:48	31:12

Individual Statistics

Rushing: BUFFALO—K. Davis 15–86, Thomas 11–19, Gardner 1–3, Reich 2–0. DALLAS—E. Smith 22–108; Aikman 3–28, Gainer 2–1, Johnston 1–0, Beuerlein 1–0.

Receiving: BUFFALO—Reed 8–152, Thomas 4–10, K. Davis 3–16, Beebe 2–50, Tasker 2–30, Metzelaars 2–12, McKeller 1–6. DALLAS—Novacek 7–72, Irvin 6–114, E. Smith 6–27, Johnston 2–15, Harper 1–45.

Passing

Player	Att	Cmp	Yds	TD	Int
BUFFALO					
Kelly	7	4	82		2
Reich	31	18	194	1	2
DALLAS					
Aikman	30	22	273	4	0
Beuerlein	0	0	0	0	0

SUPER BOWLS I–XXVII

Game	Date	Winner	Loser	Site	Attendance
XXVII	Jan. 31, 1993	Dallas (NFC) 52	Buffalo (AFC) 17	Rose Bowl, Pasadena, Calif.	98,374
XXVI	Jan. 26, 1992	Washington (NFC) 37	Buffalo (AFC) 24	Metrodome, Minneapolis, Minn.	63,130
XXV	Jan. 27, 1991	Giants (NFC) 20	Buffalo (AFC) 19	Tampa Stadium, Tampa, Fla.	73,813
XXIV	Jan. 28, 1990	San Francisco (NFC) 55	Denver (AFC) 10	Superdome, New Orleans	72,919
XXIII	Jan. 22, 1989	San Francisco (NFC) 20	Cincinnati (AFC) 16	Joe Robbie Stadium, Miami, Fla.	75,179
XXII	Jan. 31, 1988	Washington (NFC) 42	Denver (AFC) 10	Jack Murphy Stadium, San Diego, Calif.	73,302
XXI	Jan. 25, 1987	Giants (NFC) 39	Denver (AFC) 20	Rose Bowl, Pasadena, Calif.	101,063
XX	Jan. 26, 1986	Chicago (NFC) 46	New England (AFC) 10	Superdome, New Orleans	73,818
XIX	Jan. 20, 1985	San Francisco (NFC) 38	Miami (AFC) 16	Stanford Stadium, Palo Alto, Calif.	84,059
XVIII	Jan. 22, 1984	Los Angeles Raiders (AFC) 38	Washington (NFC) 9	Tampa Stadium, Tampa, Fla	72,920
XVII	Jan. 30, 1983	Washington (NFC) 27	Miami (AFC) 17	Rose Bowl, Pasadena, Calif.	103,667
XVI	Jan. 24, 1982	San Francisco (NFC) 26	Cincinnati (AFC) 21	Silverdome, Pontiac, Mich.	81,270
XV	Jan. 25, 1981	Oakland (AFC) 27	Philadelphia (NFC) 10	Superdome, New Orleans	75,500

Game	Date	Winner	Loser	Site	Attendance
XIV	Jan. 20, 1980	Pittsburgh (AFC) 31	Los Angeles (NFC) 19	Rose Bowl, Pasadena	103,985
XIII	Jan. 21, 1979	Pittsburgh (AFC) 35	Dallas (NFC) 31	Orange Bowl, Miami	79,484
XII	Jan. 15, 1978	Dallas (NFC) 27	Denver (AFC) 10	Superdome, New Orleans	75,583
XI	Jan. 9, 1977	Oakland (AFC) 32	Minnesota (NFC) 14	Rose Bowl, Pasadena	103,424
X	Jan. 18, 1976	Pittsburgh (AFC) 21	Dallas (NFC) 17	Orange Bowl, Miami	80,187
IX	Jan. 12, 1975	Pittsburgh (AFC) 16	Minnesota (NFC) 6	Tulane Stadium, New Orleans	80,997
VIII	Jan. 13, 1974	Miami (AFC) 24	Minnesota (NFC) 7	Rice Stadium, Houston	71,882
VII	Jan. 14, 1973	Miami (AFC) 14	Washington (NFC) 7	Memorial Coliseum, Los Angeles	90,182
VI	Jan. 16, 1972	Dallas (NFC) 24	Miami (AFC) 3	Tulane Stadium, New Orleans	81,591
V	Jan. 17, 1971	Baltimore (AFC) 16	Dallas (NFC) 13	Orange Bowl, Miami	79,204
IV	Jan. 11, 1970	Kansas City (AFL) 23	Minnesota (NFL) 7	Tulane Stadium, New Orleans	80,562
III	Jan. 12, 1969	New York (AFL) 16	Baltimore (NFL) 7	Orange Bowl, Miami	75,389
II	Jan. 14, 1968	Green Bay (NFL) 33	Oakland (AFL) 14	Orange Bowl, Miami	75,546
I	Jan. 15, 1967	Green Bay (NFL) 35	Kansas City (AFL) 10	Memorial Coliseum, Los Angeles	61,946

NOTE: Super Bowls I to IV were played before the American Football League and National Football League merged into the NFL, which was divided into two conferences, the NFC and AFC.

NATIONAL LEAGUE CHAMPIONS

Year	Champion (W–L–T)
1921	Chicago Bears (Staley's) (10–1–1)
1922	Canton Bulldogs (10–0–2)
1923	Canton Bulldogs (11–0–1)
1924	Cleveland Indians (7–1–1)
1925	Chicago Cardinals (11–2–1)
1926	Frankford Yellow Jackets!(14–1–1)
1927	New York Giants (11–1–1)
1928	Providence Steamrollers (8–1–2)
1929	Green Bay Packers (12–0–1)
1930	Green Bay Packers (10–3–1)
1931	Green Bay Packers (12–2–0)
1932	Chicago Bears (7–1–6)

Year	Eastern Conference winners (W–L–T)	Western Conference winners (W–L–T)	League champion playoff results
1933	New York Giants (11–3–0)	Chicago Bears (10–2–1)	Chicago Bears 23, New York 21
1934	New York Giants (8–5–0)	Chicago Bears (13–0–0)	New York 30, Chicago Bears 13
1935	New York Giants (9–3–0)	Detroit Lions (7–3–2)	Detroit 26, New York 7
1936	Boston Redskins (7–5–0)	Green Bay Packers (10–1–1)	Green Bay 21, Boston 6
1937	Washington Redskins (8–3–0)	Chicago Bears (9–1–1)	Washington 28, Chicago Bears 21
1938	New York Giants (8–2–1)	Green Bay Packers (8–3–0)	New York 23, Green Bay 17
1939	New York Giants (9–1–1)	Green Bay Packers (9–2–0)	Green Bay 27, New York 0
1940	Washington Redskins (9–2–0)	Chicago Bears (8–3–0)	Chicago Bears 73, Washington 0
1941	New York Giants (8–3–0)	Chicago Bears (10–1–1)[2]	Chicago Bears 37, New York 9
1942	Washington Redskins (10–1–1)	Chicago Bears (11–0–0)	Washington 14, Chicago Bears 6
1943	Washington Redskins (6–3–1)[2]	Chicago Bears (8–1–1)	Chicago Bears 41, Washington 21
1944	New York Giants (8–1–1)	Green Bay Packers (8–2–0)	Green Bay 14, New York 7
1945	Washington Redskins (8–2–0)	Cleveland Rams (9–1–0)	Cleveland 15, Washington 14
1946	New York Giants (7–3–1)	Chicago Bears (8–2–1)	Chicago Bears 24, New York 14
1947	Philadelphia Eagles (8–4–0)[2]	Chicago Cardinals (9–3–0)	Chicago Cardinals 28, Philadelphia 21
1948	Philadelphia Eagles (9–2–1)	Chicago Cardinals (11–1–0)	Philadelphia 7, Chicago Cardinals 0
1949	Philadelphia Eagles (11–1–0)	Los Angeles Rams (8–2–2)	Philadelphia 14, Los Angeles 0
1950[1]	Cleveland Browns (10–2–0)[2]	Los Angeles Rams (9–3–0)[2]	Cleveland 30, Los Angeles 28
1951[1]	Cleveland Browns (11–1–0)	Los Angeles Rams (8–4–0)	Los Angeles 24, Cleveland 17
1952[1]	Cleveland Browns (8–4–0)	Detroit Lions (9–3–0)[2]	Detroit 17, Cleveland 7
1953	Cleveland Browns (11–1–0)	Detroit Lions (10–2–0)	Detroit 17, Cleveland 16
1954	Cleveland Browns (9–3–0)	Detroit Lions (9–2–1)	Cleveland 56, Detroit 10
1955	Cleveland Browns (9–2–1)	Los Angeles Rams (8–3–1)	Cleveland 38, Los Angeles 14
1956	New York Giants (8–3–1)	Chicago Bears (9–2–1)	New York 47, Chicago Bears 7
1957	Cleveland Browns (9–2–1)	Detroit Lions (8–4–0)[2]	Detroit 59, Cleveland 14
1958	New York Giants (9–3–0)[2]	Baltimore Colts (9–3–0)	Baltimore 23, New York 17[3]
1959	New York Giants (10–2–0)	Baltimore Colts (9–3–0)	Baltimore 31, New York 16
1960	Philadelphia Eagles (10–2–0)	Green Bay Packers (8–4–0)	Philadelphia 17, Green Bay 13
1961	New York Giants (10–3–1)	Green Bay Packers (11–3–0)	Green Bay 37, New York 0
1962	New York Giants (12–2–0)	Green Bay Packers (13–1–0)	Green Bay 16, New York 7
1963	New York Giants (11–3–0)	Chicago Bears (11–1–2)	Chicago 14, New York 10
1964	Cleveland Browns (10–3–1)	Baltimore Colts (12–2–0)	Cleveland 27, Baltimore 0
1965	Cleveland Browns (11–3–0)	Green Bay Packers (11–3–1)[2]	Green Bay 23, Cleveland 12
1966	Dallas Cowboys (10–3–1)	Green Bay Packers (12–2–0)	Green Bay 34, Dallas 27
1967	Dallas Cowboys (9–5–0)[2]	Green Bay Packers (9–4–1)[2]	Green Bay 21, Dallas 17
1968	Cleveland Browns (10–4–0)[2]	Baltimore Colts (13–1–0)[2]	Baltimore 34, Cleveland 0
1969	Cleveland Browns (10–3–1)2	Minnesota Vikings (12–2–0)[2]	Minnesota 27, Cleveland 7

1. League was divided into American and National Conferences, 1950–52 and again in 1970, when leagues merged. 2. Won divisional playoff. 3. Won at 8:15 of sudden death overtime period.

NATIONAL CONFERENCE CHAMPIONS

Year	Eastern Division	Central Division	Western Division	Champion
1970	Dallas Cowboys (10–4–0)	Minnesota Vikings (12–2–0)	San Francisco 49ers (10–3–1)	Dallas
1971	Dallas Cowboys (11–3–0)	Minnesota Vikings (11–3–0)	San Francisco 49ers (9–5–0)	Dallas
1972	Washington Redskins (11–3–0)	Green Bay Packers (10–4–0)	San Francisco 49ers (8–5–1)	Washington
1973	Dallas Cowboys (10–4–0)	Minnesota Vikings (12–2–0)	Los Angeles Rams (12–2–0)	Minnesota
1974	St. Louis Cardinals (10–4–0)	Minnesota Vikings (10–4–0)	Los Angeles Rams (10–4–0)	Minnesota
1975	St. Louis Cardinals (11–3–0)	Minnesota Vikings (12–2–0)	Los Angeles Rams (10–4–0)	Dallas
1976	Dallas Cowboys (11–3–0)	Minnesota Vikings (11–2–1)	Los Angeles Rams (10–3–1)	Minnesota
1977	Dallas Cowboys (12–2–0)	Minnesota Vikings (9–5–0)	Los Angeles Rams (10–4–0)	Dallas
1978	Dallas Cowboys (12–4–0)	Minnesota Vikings (8–7–1)	Los Angeles Rams (12–4–0)	Dallas
1979	Dallas Cowboys (11–5–0)	Tampa Bay Buccaneers (10–6–0)	Los Angeles Rams (9–7–0)	Los Angeles
1980	Philadelphia Eagles (12–4–0)	Minnesota Vikings (9–7–0)	Atlanta Falcons (12–4–0)	Philadelphia
1981	Dallas Cowboys (12–4–0)	Tampa Bay Buccaneers (9–7–0)	San Francisco 49ers (13–3–0)	San Francisco
1982*	Washington Redskins won conference title and also had best regular–season record (8–1–0)			
1983	Washington Redskins (14–2–0)	Detroit Lions (8–8–0)	San Francisco 49ers (10–6–0)	Washington
1984	Washington Redskins (11–5–0)	Chicago Bears (10–6–0)	San Francisco 49ers (15–1–0)	San Francisco
1985	Dallas Cowboys (10–6–0)	Chicago Bears (15–1–0)	Los Angeles Rams (11–5–0)	Chicago
1986	New York Giants (14–2–0)	Chicago Bears (14–2–0)	San Francisco 49ers (10–5–1)	New York
1987	Washington Redskins (11–4–0)	Chicago Bears (11–4–0)	San Francisco 49ers (13–2–0)	Washington
1988	Philadelphia Eagles (10–6–0)	Chicago Bears (12–4–0)	San Francisco 49ers (10–6–0)	San Francisco
1989	New York Giants (12–4–0)	Minnesota Vikings (10–6–0)	San Francisco 49ers (14–2–0)	San Francisco
1990	New York Giants (13–3–0)	Chicago Bears (11–5–0)	San Francisco 49ers (14–2–0)	New York
1991	Washington (14–2–0)	Detroit Lions (12–4–0)	New Orleans Saints (11–5–0)	Washington
1992	Dallas (13–3–0)	Minnesota (11–5–0)	San Francisco (14–2–0)	Dallas

*Schedule reduced to 9 games from usual 16, with no standings kept in Eastern, Central, and Western Divisions, because of 57–day player strike.

AMERICAN CONFERENCE CHAMPIONS

Year	Eastern Division	Central Division	Western Division	Champion
1970	Baltimore Colts (11–2–1)	Cincinnati Bengals (8–6–0)	Oakland Raiders (8–4–2)	Baltimore
1971	Miami Dolphins (10–3–1)	Cleveland Browns (9–5–0)	Kansas City Chiefs (10–3–1)	Miami
1972	Miami Dolphins (14–0–0)	Pittsburgh Steelers (11–3–0)	Oakland Raiders (10–3–1)	Miami
1973	Miami Dolphins (12–2–0)	Cincinnati Bengals (10–4–0)	Oakland Raiders (9–4–1)	Miami
1974	Miami Dolphins (11–3–0)	Pittsburgh Steelers (10–3–1)	Oakland Raiders (12–2–0)	Pittsburgh
1975	Baltimore Colts (10–4–0)	Pittsburgh Steelers (12–2–0)	Oakland Raiders (12–2–0)	Pittsburgh
1976	Baltimore Colts (11–3–0)	Pittsburgh Steelers (10–4–0)	Oakland Raiders (13–1–0)	Oakland
1977	Baltimore Colts (10–4–0)	Pittsburgh Steelers (9–5–0)	Denver Broncos (12–2–0)	Denver
1978	New England Patriots (11–5–0)	Pittsburgh Steelers (14–2–0)	Denver Broncos (10–6–0)	Pittsburgh
1979	Miami Dolphins (10–6–0)	Pittsburgh Steelers (12–4–0)	San Diego Chargers (12–4–0)	Pittsburgh
1980	Buffalo Bills (11–5–0)	Cleveland Browns (11–5–0)	San Diego Chargers (11–5–0)	Oakland
1981	Miami Dolphins (11–4–1)	Cincinnati Bengals (12–4–0)	San Diego Chargers (10–6–0)	Cincinnati
1982*	Miami Dolphins won the conference title, but the Los Angeles Raiders had best regular–season record (8–1–0).			
1983	Miami (12–4–0)	Pittsburgh (10–6–0)	Los Angeles Raiders (12–4–0)	Los Angeles
1984	Miami (14–2–0)	Pittsburgh (9–7–0)	Denver (13–3–0)	Miami
1985	Miami (12–4–0)	Cleveland (8–8)	Los Angeles Raiders (12–4–0)	New England
1986	New England (11–5–0)	Cleveland (12–4–0)	Denver (11–5–0)	Denver
1987	Indianapolis Colts (9–6–0)	Cleveland Browns (10–5–0)	Denver Broncos (10–4–1)	Denver
1988	Buffalo Bills (12–4–0)	Cincinnati Bengals (12–4–0)	Seattle Seahawks (9–7–0)	Cincinnati
1989	Buffalo Bills (9–7–0)	Cleveland Browns (9–6–1)	Denver Broncos (11–5–0)	Denver
1990	Buffalo Bills (13–3–0)	Cincinnati Bengals (9–7–0)	Los Angeles Raiders (12–4–0)	Buffalo
1991	Buffalo Bills (13–3–0)	Houston Oilers (11–5–0)	Denver Broncos (12–4–0)	Buffalo
1992	Miami Dolphins (11–5–0)	Pittsburgh Steelers (11–5–0)	San Diego Chargers (11–5–0)	Buffalo

*Schedule reduced to 9 games from usual 16, with no standings kept in Eastern, Central, and Western Divisions, because of 57–day player strike.

AMERICAN LEAGUE CHAMPIONS

Year	Eastern Division (W–L–T)	Western Division (W–L–T)	League champion, playoff results
1960	Houston Oilers (10–4–0)	Los Angeles Chargers (10–4–0)	Houston 24, Los Angeles 16
1961	Houston Oilers (10–3–1)	San Diego Chargers (12–2–0)	Houston 10, San Diego 3
1962	Houston Oilers (11–3–0)	Dallas Texans (11–3–0)	Dallas 20, Houston 17[1]
1963	Boston Patriots (8–6–1)[2]	San Diego Chargers (11–3–0)	San Diego 51, Boston 10
1964	Buffalo Bills (12–2–0)	San Diego Chargers (8–5–1)	Buffalo 20, San Diego 7
1965	Buffalo Bills (10–3–1)	San Diego Chargers (9–2–3)	Buffalo 23, San Diego 0
1966	Buffalo Bills (9–4–1)	Kansas City Chiefs (11–2–1)	Kansas City 31, Buffalo 7
1967	Houston Oilers (9–4–1)	Oakland Raiders (13–1–0)	Oakland 40, Houston 7
1968	New York Jets (11–3–0)	Oakland Raiders (12–2–0)[2]	New York 27, Oakland 23
1969	New York Jets (10–4–0)	Oakland Raiders (12–1–1)	Kansas City 17, Oakland 7[3]

1. Won at 2:45 of second sudden death overtime period. 2. Won divisional playoff. 3. Kansas City defeated New York, 13–6, and Oakland defeated Houston, 56–7, in interdivisional playoffs.

PRO FOOTBALL HALL OF FAME

(National Football Museum, Canton, Ohio)

Teams named are those with which player is best identified; figures in parentheses indicate number of playing seasons.

Adderley, Herb, defensive back, Packers, Cowboys (12)	1961–72
Alworth, Lance, wide receiver, Chargers, Cowboys (12)	1962–72
Atkins, Doug, defensive end, Browns, Bears, Saints (17)	1953–69
Badgro, Morris, end, N.Y. Yankees, Giants, Bklyn. Dodgers (8)	1927, 1930–36
Barney, Lem, defensive back, Lions (11)	1967–78
Battles, Cliff, back, Redskins (6)	1932–37
Bednarik, Chuck, center–lineback, Eagles (14)	1949–62
Bell, Bert, N.F.L. founder, Eagles and Steelers, N.F.L. Commissioner	1946–59
Bell, Bobby, linebacker, Chiefs (12)	1963–74
Berry, Raymond, end, Colts (13)	1955–67
Bidwell, Charles W., owner Chicago Cardinals	1933–47
Biletnikoff, Fred, wide receiver, Raiders (14)	1965–1978
Blanda, George, quarterback–kicker, Bears, Oilers, Raiders (27)	1949–75
Blount, Mel, cornerback, Pittsburgh Steelers (14)	1970–83
Bradshaw, Terry, quarterback, Pittsburgh Steelers (14)	1970–83
Brown, Jim, fullback, Browns (9)	1957–65
Brown, Paul E., coach, Browns (1946–62), Bengals (1968–75)	1946–75
Brown, Roosevelt, tackle, Giants (13)	1953–65
Brown, Willie, cornerback, Broncos, Raiders (16)	1963–78
Buchanan, Buck, tackle, Chiefs (11)	1963–73
Butkus, Dick, linebacker, Bears (9)	1965–73
Campbell, Earl, running back, Oilers, Saints (8)	1978–85
Canadeo, Tony, back, Packers (11)	1941–52
Carr, Joe, president N.F.L. (18)	1921–39
Chamberlin, Guy, end 4 teams (9)	1919–27
Christiansen, Jack, defensive back, Lions (8)	1951–58
Clark, Earl (Dutch), Qback, Spartans, Lions (7)	1931–38
Connor, George, tackle, linebacker, Bears (8)	1948–55
Conzelman, Jimmy, Qback 5 teams (10), owner	1921–48
Csonka, Larry, back, Dolphins, Giants (11)	1968–79
Davis, Al, owner, Raiders, coach, general manager	1963–present
Davis, Willie, defensive end, Packers (10)	1960–69
Dawson, Len, quarterback, Steelers, Browns, Texans, Chiefs (19)	1957–75
Ditka, Mike, tight end, Bears, Eagles, Cowboys (12)	1961–72
Donovan, Art, defensive tackle, Colts (12)	1950–61
Driscoll, John (Paddy), Qback, Cards, Bears (11)	1919–29
Dudley, Bill, back, Steelers, Lions, Redskins (9)	1942–53
Edwards, Albert Glen (Turk), tackle, Redskins (9)	1932–40
Ewbank, Weeb, coach Colts, Jets (20)	1954–73
Fears, Tom, end, Rams (9); coach, Saints	1948–56
Flaherty, Ray, end, Yankees, Giants (9); coach, Redskins, Yankees (14)	1928–49
Ford, Len, end, def. end, Browns, Packers (11)	1948–58
Fouts, Dan, quarterback, Chargers (15)	1973–87
Fortmann, Daniel J., guard, Bears (8)	1936–43
Gatski, Frank, offensive lineman, Browns (12)	1946–57
George, Bill, linebacker, Bears, Rams (15)	1952–66
Gifford, Frank, back, Giants (12)	1952–64
Gillman, Sid, coach, Rams, Chargers, Oilers (18)	1955–70, 73–74
Graham, Otto, quarterback, Browns (10)	1946–55
Grange, Harold (Red), back, Bears, Yankees (9)	1925–34
Greene, Joe, defensive tackle, Steelers (13)	1968–81
Gregg, Forrest, tackle, Packers (15)	1956–71
Griese, Bob, quarterback, Dolphins (14)	1967–80
Groza, Lou, place–kicker, tackle, Browns (21)	1946–67
Guyon, Joe, back, 6 teams (8)	1919–27
Halas, George, N.F.L. founder, owner and coach, Staleys and Bears, end (11)	1919–27
Ham, Jack, linebacker, Steelers (13)	1970–82
Hannah, John, guard, Patriots (13)	1973–85
Harris, Franco, running back, Steelers, Seahawks (13)	1972–84
Healey, Ed, Tackle, Bears (8)	1920–27
Hein, Mel, center, Giants (15)	1931–45
Hendricks, Ted, linebacker, Colts, Packers, Raiders (15)	1969–83
Henry, Wilbur (Pete), tackle, Bulldogs, Giants (8)	1920–28
Herber, Arnie, Qback, Packers, Giants (13)	1930–45
Hewitt, Bill, end, Bears, Eagles (9)	1932–43
Hinkle, Clarke, fullback, Packers (10)	1932–41
Hirsch, Elroy (Crazy Legs), back, end, Rams (12)	1946–57
Hornung, Paul, running back, Packers (9)	1957–62, 64–66
Houston, Ken, def. bck, Oilers, Redskins (14)	1967–80
Hubbard, R. (Cal), tackle, Giants, Packers (9)	1927–36
Huff, Sam, linebacker, Giants, Redskins (13)	1956–67, 1969
Hunt, Lamar, Founder A.F.L., owner Texans, Chiefs	1959–
Hutson, Don, end, Packers (11)	1935–45
Johnson, John Henry, back, 49ers, Lions, Steelers, Oilers (13)	1954–66
Jones, David (Deacon), defensive end, Rams, Chargers, Redskins (14)	1961–74
Jones, Stan, defensive tackle, Bears, Redskins (13)	1954–66
Jurgensen, Sonny, quarterback, Eagles, Redskins (18)	1957–74
Kiesling, Walt, guard 6 teams (13)	1926–38
Kinard, Frank (Bruiser), tackle, Dodgers (9)	1938–47
Lambeau, Earl (Curly), N.F.L. founder, coach, end, back, Packers (11)	1919–53
Lambert, Jack, linebacker, Steelers (11)	1974–84
Landry, Tom, coach, Cowboys (29)	1960–88
Lane, Richard (Night Train), defensive back, Rams, Cardinals, Lions (14)	1952–65
Langer, Jim, center, Dolphins, Vikings (12)	1970–81
Lanier, Willie, linebacker, Chiefs (11)	1967–77
Lary, Yale, defensive back, punter, Lions (11)	1952–64
Laveill, Dante, end, Browns (11)	1946–56
Layne, Bobby, Qback, Bears, Lions, Steelers (15)	1948–62
Leemans, Alphonse (Tuffy), back, Giants (8)	1936–43
Lilly, Bob, defensive tackle, Cowboys (14)	1961–74
Little, Larry, guard, Dolphins, Chargers (14)	1967–80
Lombardi, Vince, coach, Packers, Redskins (11)	1959–70
Luckman, Sid, quarterback, Bears (12)	1939–50
Lyman, Roy (Link), tackle, Bulldogs, Bears (11)	1922–34
Mackey, John, tight end, Colts, Chargers (10)	1963–72
Mara, Tim, N.F.L. founder, owner Giants	1925–59
Marchetti, Gino, defensive end, Colts (14)	1952–66
Marshall, George P., N.F.L. founder, owner, Redskins	1932–65
Matson, Ollie, back, Cardinals, Rams, Lions, Eagles (14)	1952–66
Maynard, Don, receiver, Giants, Jets, Cardinals (15)	1958–73
McAfee, George, back, Bears (8)	1940–50
McCormack, Mike, tackle, N.Y. Yankees, Cleveland Browns (10)	1951–62
McElhenny, Hugh, back, 49ers, Vikings, Giants (13)	1952–64
McNally, John (Blood), back, 7 teams (15)	1925–39
Michalske, August, guard, Yankees, Packers (11)	1926–37
Millner, Wayne, end, Redskins (7)	1936–45
Mitchell, Bobby, wide receiver, Browns, Redskins (11)	1958–68
Mix, Ron, tackle, Chargers (11)	1960–71
Moore, Lenny, back, Colts (12)	1956–67
Motley, Marion, fullback, Browns, Steelers (9)	1946–55
Musso, George, guard–tackle, Bears (12)	1933–44
Nagurski, Bronko, fullback, Bears (9)	1930–43
Namath, Joe, quarterback, Jets, Rams (13)	1965–77
Neale, Earle (Greasy), coach, Eagles	1941–50
Nevers, Ernie, fullback, Chicago Cardinals (5)	1926–31
Nitschke, Ray, linebackers, Packers (15)	1958–72
Noll, Chuck, coach, Steelers (23)	1969–91
Nomellini, Leo, defensive tackle, 49ers (14)	1950–63
Olsen, Merlin, defensive tackle, Rams (15)	1962–76
Otto, Jim, center, Raiders (15)	1960–74
Owen, Steve, tackle, Giants (9), coach, Giants (13)	1924–53
Page, Alan, defensive tackle, Vikings, Bears (15)	1967–81
Parker, Clarence (Ace), quarterback, Dodgers (7)	1937–46
Parker, Jim, guard, tackle, Colts (11)	1957–67
Payton, Walter, running back, Bears (13)	1977–89
Perry, Joe, fullback, 49ers, Colts (16)	1948–63
Pihos, Pete, end, Eagles (9)	1947–55
Ray, Hugh, Shorty, N.F.L. advisor	1938–52
Reeves, Dan, owner Rams	1941–71
Riggins, John, running back, Jets, Redskins (14)	1971–84
Ringo, Jim, center, Packers (15)	1953–67
Robustelli, Andy, def. end, Rams, Giants (14)	1951–64
Rooney, Art, N.F.L. founder, owner Steelers	1933–
Rozelle, Pete, commissioner, NFL,	1960–89
St. Claire, Bob, tackle, 49ers (11)	1953–63
Sayers, Gale, back, Bears (7)	1965–71
Schmidt, Joe, linebacker, Lions (13)	1953–65
Schramm, Tex, administrator Rams, Cowboys (42)	1947–89
Shell, Art, tackle, Raiders (15)	1968–82
Simpson, O.J., back, Bills, 49ers (11)	1969–79
Starr, Bart, quarterback, coach, Packers (16)	1956–71
Staubach, Roger, quarterback, Cowboys (11)	1969–79
Stautner, Ernie, defensive tackle, Steelers (14)	1950–63
Stenerud, Jan, placekicker, Chiefs, Packers, Vikings (19)	1967–85

Strong, Ken, back, Giants, Yankees (14)	1929–47
Stydahar, Joe, tackle, Bears (9); coach, Rams, Cardinals (5)	1936–54
Tarkenton, Fran, quarterback, Vikings, Giants (18)	1961–78
Taylor, Charlie, wide receiver, Redskins (14)	1964–77
Taylor, Jim, fullback, Packers, Saints (10)	1958–67
Thorpe, Jim, back, 7 teams (12)	1915–28
Tittle, Y.A., Qback, Colts, 49ers, Giants (17)	1948–64
Trafton, George, center, Bears (13)	1920–32
Trippi, Charley, back, Chicago Cardinals (9)	1947–55
Tunnell, Emlen, def. back, Giants, Packers (14)	1948–61
Turner, Clyde (Bulldog), center, Bears (13)	1940–52
Unitas, John, quarterback, Colts (18)	1956–73
Upshaw, Gene, guard, Raiders (15)	1967–81
Van Brocklin, Norm, Qback, Rams, Eagles (12)	1949–60
Van Buren, Steve, back, Eagles (8)	1944–51
Walker, Doak, running back, def. back, kicker, Lions (6)	1950–55
Walsh, Bill, coach, 49ers (10)	1979–88
Warfield, Paul, wide receiver, Browns, Dolphins (13)	1964–74, 76–77
Waterfield, Bob, quarterback, Rams (8)	1945–52
Weinmeister, Arnie, tackle, N.Y. Yankees, Giants (6)	1948–53
Willis, Bill, guard, Browns (8)	1946–53
Wilson, Larry, defensive back, Cardinals (13)	1960–72
Wood, Willie, safety, Packers (12)	1960–71
Wojciechowicz, Alex, center, Lions, Eagles (13)	1938–50

NFL TEAM NICKNAMES AND HOME FIELD CAPACITIES

AMERICAN CONFERENCE

Eastern Division

Buffalo Bills	Rich Stadium (AT)	80,020
Indianapolis Colts[1]	Hoosier Dome (AT)	61,500
Miami Dolphins	Joe Robbie Stadium (G)	75,000
New England Patriots	Sullivan Stadium (ST)	61,297
New York Jets[2]	Giants Stadium (AT)	76,891

Central Division

Cincinnati Bengals	Riverfront Stadium (AT)	59,754
Cleveland Browns	Municipal Stadium (G)	80,322
Houston Oilers	Astrodome (AT)	50,496
Pittsburgh Steelers	Three Rivers Stadium (AT)	59,000

Western Division

Denver Broncos	Mile High Stadium (G)	75,103
Kansas City Chiefs	Arrowhead Stadium (TT)	78,067
Los Angeles Raiders[3]	Memorial Coliseum (G)	92,498
San Diego Chargers	Jack Murphy Stadium (G)	53,675
Seattle Seahawks	Kingdome (AT)	64,757

1. Moved franchise from Baltimore prior to 1984 season. 2. Moved to Giants Stadium; East Rutherford, N.J. prior to 1984 season. 3. Moved franchise to Los Angeles for 1982 season.

NATIONAL CONFERENCE

Eastern Division

Dallas Cowboys	Texas Stadium (TT)	65,101
New York Giants	Giants Stadium (AT)[1]	76,891
Philadelphia Eagles	Veterans Stadium (AT)	72,204
Phoenix Cardinals	Sun Devil Stadium (G)	70,491
Washington Redskins	R.F. Kennedy Stadium (G)	55,045

Central Division

Chicago Bears	Soldier Field (AT)	65,793
Detroit Lions	Pontiac Silverdome (AT)	80,638
Green Bay Packers	Lambeau Field (G)	56,189
	Milwaukee Stadium (G)	55,958
Minnesota Vikings	Hubert Humphrey Metrodome (ST)	62,212
Tampa Bay Buccaneers	Tampa Stadium (G)	72,812

Western Division

Atlanta Falcons	Georgia Dome (AT)	71,500
Los Angeles Rams	Anaheim Stadium (G)	69,007
New Orleans Saints	Louisiana Superdome (AT)	71,330
San Francisco 49ers	Candlestick Park (G)	61,185

1. At East Rutherford, N.J. NOTE: Stadium playing surfaces in parentheses: (AT) Astro Turf; (G) Grass; (ST) Super Turf; (TT) Tartan Turf.

CHAMPIONS OF LEAGUES THAT NO LONGER EXIST

No professional league in American sports has had to contend with more pretenders to the throne than the NFL. Seven times in as many decades a rival league has risen up to challenge the NFL and six of them went under in less than five seasons. Only the fourth American Football League (1960–69) succeeded, forcing the older league to sue for peace and a full partnership in 1966.

Of the six leagues that didn't make it, only the All-America Football Conference (1946–49) lives on—the Cleveland Browns and San Francisco 49ers joined the NFL after the AAFC folded in 1949.

The champions of leagues past are listed below.

American Football League I

Year		Head Coach
1926	Philadelphia Quakers	Bob Folwell

American Football League II

Year		Head Coach
1936	Boston Shamrocks	George Kennedy
1937	Los Angeles Bulldogs	Gus Henderson

American Football League III

Year		Head Coach
1940	Columbus Bullies	Phil Bucklew
1941	Columbus Bullies	Phil Bucklew

All-America Football Conference

Year	Championship Game	Head Coach
1946	At Cleve. Browns 14, NY Yankees 9	Paul Brown
1947	Cleve. Browns 14, at NY Yankees 3	Paul Brown
1948	At Cleve. Browns 49, Buffalo 7	Paul Brown
1949	At Cleve. Browns 21, S.F. 49ers 7	Paul Brown

World Football League

Year	World Bowl	Head Coach
1974	At Birmingham 22, Florida 21	Jack Gotta
1975	Folded mid-season	

United States Football League

Year	Championship Game	Head Coach
1983	Michigan 24, Philadelphia Stars 22	Jim Stanley
1984	Philadelphia Stars 23, Arizona 3	Jim Mora
1985	Baltimore Stars 28, Oakland 14	Jim Mora

USFL Championship Game sites: Denver (1983), Tampa (1984), East Rutherford, N.J. (1985)

N.F.L. INDIVIDUAL LIFETIME, SEASON, AND GAME RECORDS

(American Football League records were incorporated into N.F.L. records after merger of the leagues) Players listed in boldface were active during the 1992 season. Players listed in capital letters are members of the Pro Football Hall of Fame. The All-America Football Conference (AAFC) existed from 1946 to 1949. The 49ers, Browns, and Colts merged with the NFL in 1949.

All-Time Leading Touchdown Scorers

(Through 1992)

Player	Yrs	Rush.	Rec.	Returns	TD
Jim Brown	9	106	20	0	126
Walter Payton	13	110	15	0	125
John Riggins	14	104	12	0	116
Lenny Moore	12	63	48	2	113
Jerry Rice	8	5	103	0	108
Don Hutson	11	3	99	3	105
Steve Largent	14	1	100	0	101
Franco Harris	13	91	9	0	100
Marcus Allen	11	79	18	1	98
Eric Dickerson	10	90	6	0	96
Jim Taylor	10	83	10	0	93
Tony Dorsett	12	77	13	1	91
Bobby Mitchell	11	18	65	8	91

All-Time Leading Receivers

(Through 1992)

Player	League	Yrs.	No.	Yds.	Avg.	TD
Art Monk	NFL	13	847	11,628	13.7	63
Steve Largent	NFL	14	819	13,089	16.0	100
Charlie Joiner	AFL–NFL	18	750	12,146	16.2	65
James Lofton	NFL	15	750	13,821	18.4	75
Ozzie Newsom	NFL	13	662	7,980	12.1	47
CHARLEY TAYLOR	NFL	13	649	9,110	14.0	79
DON MAYNARD	NFL–AFL	15	633	11,834	18.7	88
RAYMOND BERRY	NFL	13	631	9,275	14.7	68
Jerry Rice	NFL	8	610	10,273	16.8	103
Drew Hill	NFL	13	600	9,447	15.7	60
Harold Carmichael	NFL	14	590	8,985	15.2	79
FRED BILETNIKOFF	AFL–NFL	14	589	8,974	15.2	76
Harold Jackson	NFL	16	579	10,372	17.9	76

All-Time Leading Passers

(Minimum 1,500 attempts. Through 1992)

Rank	Player	League	Yrs	Comp	Atts	Yds	TDs	Int	Rating*
1.	**Joe Montana**	NFL	13	2,929	4,600	35,124	244	123	93.5
2.	**Steve Young**	NFL	8	908	1,506	11,877	76	42	90.4
3.	**Dan Marino**	NFL	10	3,128	5,284	39,502	290	165	87.7
4.	**Jim Kelly**	NFL	7	1,824	3,024	23,031	161	108	86.9
5.	OTTO GRAHAM	AAFC–NFL	10	1,464	2,626	23,584	174	135	86.6
6.	**Mark Rypien**	NFL	5	1,078	1,888	14,414	97	65	84.3
7.	ROGER STAUBACH	NFL	11	1,685	2,958	22,700	153	109	83.4
8.	Neil Lomax	NFL	8	1,817	3,153	22,771	136	90	82.7
9.	SONNY JURGENSEN	NFL	18	2,433	4,262	32,224	255	189	82.6
10.	LEN DAWSON	AFL–NFL	19	2,136	3,741	28,711	239	183	82.5
11.	**Dave Krieg**	NFL	13	2,326	3,989	29,247	210	160	82.1
12.	Ken Anderson	NFL	16	2,654	4,475	32,838	197	160	81.9
13.	**Bernie Kosar**	NFL	8	1,774	3,012	21,097	111	78	81.84
14.	**Boomer Esiason**	NFL	9	1,897	3,378	25,671	174	129	81.80
15.	Danny White	NFL	13	1,761	2,950	21,959	155	132	81.7

* Minimum 1,500 attempts.

All-Time Leading Scorers

(Through 1992)

Rank	Player	Yrs	TD	PAT	FG	Pts
1.	GEORGE BLANDA	26	9	943	335	2,002
2.	JAN STENERUD	19	0	580	373	1,699
3.	LOU GROZA	21	1	810	264	1,608
4.	Pat Leahy	18	0	558	304	1,470
5.	Jim Turner	16	1	521	304	1,439
6.	Mark Moseley	16	0	482	300	1,382
7.	Jim Bakken	17	0	534	282	1,380
8.	**Nick Lowery**	14	0	449	306	1,367
9.	Fred Cox	15	0	519	282	1,365
10.	Chris Bahr	14	0	490	241	1,213
11.	**Jim Breech**	13	0	486	224	1,158
12.	Gino Cappelletti	11	42	350	176	1,130
13.	Ray Wersching	15	0	456	222	1,122
14.	**Eddie Murray**	12	0	381	244	1,113
15.	Don Cockroft	13	0	432	216	1,080

All-Time Leading Rushers

(Through 1992)

Rank	Player	Yrs	Att.	Yds	Avg	TDs
1.	WALTER PAYTON	13	3,838	16,726	4.4	110
2.	**Eric Dickerson**	10	2,970	13,168	4.4	110
3.	Tony Dorsett	12	2,936	12,739	4.3	77
4.	JIM BROWN	9	2,359	12,312	5.2	106
5.	FRANCO HARRIS	13	2,949	12,120	4.1	91
6.	JOHN RIGGINS	14	2,916	11,352	3.9	104
7.	O.J. SIMPSON[1]	11	2,404	11,236	4.7	61
8.	**O.J. Anderson**	14	2,562	10,273	4.0	81
9.	JOE PERRY[2]	16	1,929	9,723	5.0	71
10.	EARL CAMPBELL	8	2,187	9,407	4.3	74
11.	JIM TAYLOR	10	1,941	8,597	4.4	83
12.	**Marcus Allen**	11	2,090	8,545	4.1	79
13.	Gerald Riggs	10	1,989	8,188	4.1	69
14.	LARRY CSONKA[1]	11	1,891	8,081	4.3	64
15.	**Freeman McNeil**	12	1,798	8,074	4.5	38

NOTE: All players NFL unless noted. 1. AFL–NFL. 2. AAFC–NFL.

Scoring

Most points scored, lifetime—2,002, George Blanda, Chicago Bears, 1949–58; Baltimore, 1950; Houston, 1960–66; Oakland, 1967–75 (9tds, 943 pat, 335 fgs).

Most points, season—176, Paul Hornung, Green Bay, 1960 (15 td, 41 pat, 15 fg).

Most points, game—40, Ernie Nevers, Chicago Cardinals, 1929 (6 td, 4 pat).

Most points, per quarter—29, Don Hutson, Green Bay, 1945 (4 td, 5 pat).

Most touchdowns, lifetime—126, Jim Brown, Cleveland, 1957–65

Most touchdowns, season—24, John Riggins, Washington, 1983

Most touchdowns, game—6, Ernie Nevers, Chicago Cardinals, 1929; William Jones, Cleveland, 1951; Gale Sayers, Chicago Bears, 1965.

Most points after touchdown, lifetime—943, George Blanda, Chicago Bears, 1949–58; Baltimore, 1950; Houston, 1960–66; Oakland, 1967–75.

Most points after touchdown, game—9, Pat Harder, Chicago Cardinals, 1948; Bob Waterfield, Los Angeles, 1950; Charlie Gogolak, Washington, 1966.

Most consecutive points after touchdown—234, Tommy Davis, San Francisco, 1959–65.

Most points after touchdown, no misses, season—56, Danny Villanueva, Dallas, 1966; Ray Wersching, San Francisco, 1984; Chip Lohmiller, Washington, 1991.
Most field goals, lifetime—373, Jan Stenerud, Kansas City Chiefs, 1967–79; Green Bay Packers, 1980–83; Minnesota Vikings, 1984–85.
Most field goals, season—35, Ali Haji-Sheikh, N.Y. Giants, 1983.
Most field goals, game—7, Jim Bakken, St. Louis, 1967; and Rick Karlis, Minnesota, 1989.
Longest field goal—63 yards, Tom Dempsey, New Orleans, 1970.

Rushing
Most yards gained, lifetime—16,726, Walter Payton, Chicago Bears, 1975–1987.
Most yards gained, season—2,105, Eric Dickerson, Los Angeles, 1984.
Most yards gained, game—275, Walter Payton, Chicago, 1977.
Most touchdowns, lifetime—110, Walter Payton, Chicago, 1975–1987.
Most touchdowns, season—24, John Riggins, Washington, 1983.
Most touchdowns, game—6, Ernie Nevers, Chicago Cardinals, 1929; Dub Jones, Cleveland Browns, 1951; Gale Sayers, Chicago Bears, 1968.
Longest run from scrimmage—99 yards, Tony Dorsett, Dallas, Jan. 3, 1983.

Passing
Most touchdown passes, lifetime—342, Fran Tarkenton, Minnesota, 1961–66, 72–78; New York Giants, 1967–71.
Most touchdown passes, season—48, Dan Marino, Miami, 1984.
Most touchdown passes, game—7, Sid Luckman, Chicago Bears, 1943; Adrian Burk, Philadelphia, 1954; George Blanda, Houston, 1961; Y.A. Tittle, New York Giants, 1963; Joe Kapp, Minnesota, 1969.
Most consecutive games, touchdown passes—47, John Unitas, Baltimore, 1956–60.
Most consecutive passes attempted, none intercepted—308, Bernie Kosar, Cleveland, 1990–91.
Longest pass completion—99 yards, Frank Filchock (to Andy Farkas), Washington, 1939; George Izo (to Bob Mitchell), Washington, 1963; Karl Sweetan (to Pat Studstill), Detroit, 1966; Sonny Jurgensen (to Gerry Allen), Washington, 1968; Jim Plunkett (to Cliff Branch) L.A. Raiders, 1985; Ron Jaworksi (to Mike Quick), Philadelphia, 1985.

Receiving
Most pass receptions, lifetime—847, Art Monk[1], Washington, 1980–92.
Most pass receptions, season—108, Sterling Sharpe,[1] Green Bay, 1992.
Most pass receptions, game—18, Tom Fears, Los Angeles, 1950.
Most consecutive games, pass receptions—177, Steve Largent, 1976–1989.
Most yards gained, pass receptions, lifetime—13,821, James Lofton,[1] Green Bay, 1978–86; L.A. Raiders, 1987–88; Buffalo, 1989–92.
Most yards gained receptions, season—1,746, Charley Hennigan, Houston, 1961.
Most yards gained receptions, game—336, Willie Anderson, Los Angeles Rams, Nov. 26, 1989 vs. New Orleans.
Most touchdown receptions, lifetime—103, Jerry Rice, San Francisco, 1985–92.
Most touchdown pass receptions, season—22, Jerry Rice, San Francisco 49ers, 1987.
Most touchdown pass receptions, game—5, Bob Shaw, Chicago Cards, 1950; Kellen Winslow, San Diego Chargers, 1981; Jerry Rice, San Francisco 49ers, 1990.
Most consecutive games, touchdown pass receptions—13, Jerry Rice, San Francisco 49ers, 1986–87.
Most pass interceptions, lifetime—81, Paul Krause, Washington, 1964–67; Minnesota, 1968–79.
Most pass interceptions, season—14, Richard (Night Train) Lane, Los Angeles, 1952.
Most pass interceptions, game—4, by 17 players.
Longest pass interception return—103 yards, Venice Glenn, San Diego, vs. Denver, Nov. 29, 1987.

1. Still active coming into 1993 season.

Kicking
Longest punt—98 yrds, Steve O'Neal, New York Jets, 1969.
Highest average punting, lifetime—45.16 yards, Sammy Baugh, Washington, 1937–52.
Longest punt return—98 yards, Gil LeFebvre, Cincinnati Reds, 1933; Charlie West, Minnesota, 1968; Dennis Morgan, Dallas, 1974; Terrence Mathis, N.Y. Jets, 1990.
Longest kick-off return—106 yards, Roy Green, St. Louis, 1979; Al Carmichael, Green Bay, 1956; Noland Smith, Kansas City, 1967.
Most punts lifetime—1,154, Dave Jennings, N.Y. Giants 1974–84; N.Y. Jets, 1985–87.

Passing
Most passes completed, lifetime—3,686, Fran Tarkenton, Minnesota, 1961–66, 72–78; New York Giants, 1967–71.
Most passes completed, season—404, Warren Moon, 1991.
Most passes completed, game—42, Richard Todd, New York Jets, 1980.
Most consecutive passes completed—22, Joe Montana, San Francisco, 1987.
Most yards gained, lifetime—47,003, Fran Tarkenton, Minnesota, 1961–66, 72–78; New York Giants, 1967–71.
Most yards gained, season—5,084, Dan Marino, Miami, 1984.
Most yards gained, game—554, Norm Van Brocklin, Los Angeles, 1951.

NFL GOVERNMENT

Paul Tagliabue, Commissioner; Neil Austrian, President; Jay Moyer, Executive Vice President and League Counsel; Harold Henderson, Executive Vice President for Labor Relations/Chairman NFLMC; Joe Browne, Vice President of Communications & Development; Val Pinchbeck, Jr., Vice President of Broadcasting & Productions; Tom Sullivan, Treasurer; Jim Steeg, Executive Director for Special Events; Roger Goodell, Executive Director for Club Relations and International Development; Dennis Curran, General Counsel/Management Council; Pete Abitante, Director of Information; Greg Aiello, Director of Communications; Phil Ayoub, Comptroller; Nancy Behar, Assistant Director of Broadcasting and Productions; Joel Bussert, Director of Player Personnel; John Buzzeo, Director of Administration; David Cornwell, Director of Equal Emploument and Assistant Counsel; Joe Ellis, Assistant Director of Club Administration; Bill Granholm, Director of Special Projects; Leslie Hammond, Director of Information, AFC; Charlie Jackson, Assistant Director of Security; John Jones, Director of Labor Operations; Dick Maxwell, Director of Broadcasting Services; Susan McCann Minogue, Assistant Director of Special Events; Jack Reader, Assistant Director of Officiating; Reggie Roberts, Director of Information, NFC; Peter Ruocco, Director of Planning for Player Employment; Jerry Seeman, Director of Officiating; Jan Van Duser, Director of Game Operations; Don Weiss, Director of Planning; Warren Welsh, Director of Security.

BASKETBALL

Basketball may be the one sport whose exact origin is definitely known. In the winter of 1891–92, Dr. James Naismith, an instructor in the Y.M.C.A. Training College (now Springfield College) at Springfield, Mass., deliberately invented the game of basketball in order to provide indoor exercise and competition for the students between the closing of the football season and the opening of the baseball season. He affixed peach baskets overhead on the walls at opposite ends of the gymnasium and organized teams to play his new game in which the purpose was to toss an association (soccer) ball into one basket and prevent the opponents from tossing the ball into the other basket. The game is fundamentally the same today, though there have been improvements in equipment and some changes in rules.

Because Dr. Naismith had eighteen available players when he invented the game, the first rule was: "There shall be nine players on each side." Later the number of players became optional, depending upon the size of the available court, but the five-player standard was adopted when the game spread over the country. United States soldiers brought basketball to Europe in World War I, and it soon became a world-wide sport.

College Basketball

NATIONAL COLLEGIATE A.A. CHAMPIONS

1939	Oregon	1952	Kansas	1965	U.C.L.A.	1983	North Carolina State
1940	Indiana	1953	Indiana	1966	Texas Western	1984	Georgetown
1941	Wisconsin	1954	La Salle	1967–73	U.C.L.A.	1985	Villanova
1942	Stanford	1955	San Francisco	1974	No. Carolina State	1986	Louisville
1943	Wyoming	1956	San Francisco	1975	U.C.L.A.	1987	Indiana
1944	Utah	1957	North Carolina	1976	Indiana	1988	Kansas
1945	Oklahoma A & M	1958	Kentucky	1977	Marquette	1989	Michigan
1946	Oklahoma A & M	1959	California	1978	Kentucky	1990	Nevada–Las Vegas
1947	Holy Cross	1960	Ohio State	1979	Michigan State	1991	Duke
1948	Kentucky	1961	Cincinnati	1980	Louisville	1992	Duke
1949	Kentucky	1962	Cincinnati	1981	Indiana	1993	North Carolina
1950	C.C.N.Y.	1963	Loyola (Chicago)	1982	North Carolina		
1951	Kentucky	1964	U.C.L.A.				

NATIONAL INVITATION TOURNAMENT (NIT) CHAMPIONS

1939	Long Island U.	1954	Holy Cross	1968	Dayton	1982	Bradley
1940	Colorado	1955	Duquesne	1969	Temple	1983	Fresno State
1941	Long Island U.	1956	Louisville	1970	Marquette	1984	Michigan
1942	West Virginia	1957	Bradley	1971	North Carolina	1985	U.C.L.A.
1943–44	St. John's (N.Y.C.)	1958	Xavier (Cincinnati)	1972	Maryland	1986	Ohio State
1945	DePaul	1959	St. John's (N.Y.C.)	1973	Virginia Tech	1987	So. Mississippi
1946	Kentucky	1960	Bradley	1974	Purdue	1988	Connecticut
1947	Utah	1961	Providence	1975	Princeton	1989	St. John's
1948	St. Louis	1962	Dayton	1976	Kentucky	1990	Vanderbilt
1949	San Francisco	1963	Providence	1977	St. Bonaventure	1991	Stanford
1950	C.C.N.Y.	1964	Bradley	1978	Texas	1992	Virginia
1951	Brigham Young	1965	St. John's (N.Y.C.)	1979	Indiana	1993	Minnesota
1952	La Salle	1966	Brigham Young	1980	Virginia		
1953	Seton Hall	1967	So. Illinois	1981	Tulsa		

N.C.A.A. MAJOR COLLEGE INDIVIDUAL SCORING RECORDS

Single Season Averages

Player, Team	Year	G	FG	FT	Pts	Avg
Pete Maravich, Louisiana State	1969–70	31	522[1]	337	1381[1]	44.5[1]
Pete Maravich	1968–69	26	433	282	1148	44.2
Pete Maravich	1967–68	26	432	274	1138	43.8
Frank Selvy, Furman	1953–54	29	427	355[1]	1209	41.7
Johnny Neumann, Mississippi	1970–71	23	366	191	923	40.1
Freeman Williams, Portland State	1976–77	26	417	176	1010	38.8
Billy McGill, Utah	1961–62	26	394	221	1009	38.8
Calvin Murphy, Niagara	1967–68	24	337	242	916	38.2
Austin Carr, Notre Dame	1969–70	29	444	218	1106	38.1

1. Record.

N.C.A.A. CAREER SCORING TOTALS

Division I

Player, Team	Last year	G	FG	FT	Pts	Avg
Pete Maravich, Louisiana State	1970	83	1387[1]	893[1]	3667[1]	44.2[1]
Austin Carr, Notre Dame	1971	74	1017	526	2560	34.6
Oscar Robertson, Cincinnati	1960	88	1052	869	2973	33.8
Calvin Murphy, Niagara	1970	77	947	654	2548	33.1
Dwight Lamar[2]	1973	57	768	326	1862	32.7
Frank Selvy, Furman	1954	78	922	694	2538	32.5
Rick Mount, Purdue	1970	72	910	503	2323	32.3
Darrel Floyd, Furman	1956	71	868	545	2281	32.1
Nick Werkman, Seton Hall	1964	71	812	649	2273	32.0

1. Record. 2. Also played two seasons in college division.

Division II

Player, Team	Last year	G	FG	FT	Pts	Avg
Travis Grant, Kentucky State	1972	121	1760[1]	525	4045[1]	33.4[1]
John Rinka, Kenyon	1970	99	1261	729	3251	32.8
Florindo Vierira, Quinnipiac	1957	69	761	741	2263	32.8
Willie Shaw, Lane	1964	76	960	459	2379	31.3
Mike Davis, Virginia Union	1969	89	1014	730	2758	31.0
Henry Logan, Western Carolina	1968	107	1263	764	3290	30.7
Willie Scott, Alabama State	1969	103	1277	601	3155	30.6
Gregg Northington, Alabama State	1972	75	894	403	2191	29.2
Bob Hopkins, Grambling	1956	126	1403	953	3759	29.8

1. Record.

TOP SINGLE-GAME SCORING MARKS

Player, Team (Opponent)	Yr	Pts
Selvy, Furman (Newberry)	1954	100[1]
Williams, Portland State (Rocky Mtn.)	1978	81
Mlkvy, Temple (Wilkes)	1951	73
Williams, Portland State (So. Oregon)	1977	71
Maravich, LSU (Alabama)	1970	69
Murphy, Niagara (Syracuse)	1969	68
Floyd, Furman (Morehead)	1955	67
Maravich, LSU (Tulane)	1969	66
Handlan, W & L (Furman)	1951	66
Roberts, Oral Roberts (N.C. A&T)	1977	66
Williams, Portland State (Geo. Fox Coll.)	1978	66
Roberts, Oral Roberts (Oregon)	1977	65

1. Record.

MEN'S N.C.A.A. BASKETBALL CHAMPIONSHIPS—1993

DIVISION I

First Round—East
North Carolina 85, East Carolina 65
Rhode Island 74, Purdue 68
St. John's 85, Texas Tech 67
Arkansas 94, Holy Cross 64
Virginia 78, Manhattan 66
Massachusetts 54, Penn 50
New Mexico State 93, Nebraska 79
Cincinnati 93, Coppin State 66

First Round—Southeast
Kentucky 96, Rider 52
Utah 86, Pittsburgh 65
Wake Forest 81, Tenn.–Chattanooga 58
Iowa 82, Northeast Louisiana 69
Tulane 55, Kansas State 53
Florida State 82, Evansville 70
Western Kentucky 55, Memphis State 52
Seton Hall 81, Tennessee State 59

First Round—Midwest
Indiana 97, Wright State 54
Xavier 73, New Orleans 55
Oklahoma State 74, Marquette 62
Louisville 76, Delaware 70
California 66, LSU 64
Duke 105, Southern Illinois 70
BYU 80, SMU 71
Kansas 94, Ball State 72

First Round—West
Michigan 84, Coastal Carolina 53
UCLA 81, Iowa State 70
George Washington 82, New Mexico 68
Southern 93, Georgia Tech 78
Illinois 75, Long Beach State 72
Vanderbilt 92, Boise State 72
Temple 75, Missouri 61
Santa Clara 64, Arizona 61

Second Round—East
North Carolina 112, Rhode Island 67
Arkansas 80, St. John's 74
Virginia 71, Massachusetts 56
Cincinnati 92, New Mexico State 55

Second Round—Southeast
Kentucky 83, Utah 62
Wake Forest 84, Iowa 78
Florida State 94, Tulane 63
Western Kentucky 72, Seton Hall 68

Second Round—Midwest
Indiana 73, Xavier 70
Louisville 78, Oklahoma State 63
California 82, Duke 77
Kansas 90, BYU 76

Second Round—West
Michigan 86, UCLA 84 (OT)
George Washington 90, Southern 80
Vanderbilt 85, Illinois 68
Temple 68, Santa Clara 57

Third Round—East
North Carolina 80, Arkansas 74
Cincinnati 71, Virginia 54

Third Round—Southeast
Kentucky 103, Wake Forest 69
Florida State 81, West. Kentucky 78 (OT)

Third Round—Midwest
Indiana 82, Louisville 69
Kansas 93, California 76

Third Round—West
Michigan 72, George Washington 64
Temple 67, Vanderbilt 59

Regional Finals
East: No. Carolina 75, Cincinnati 68 (OT)
Southeast: Kentucky 106, Florida St. 81
Midwest: Kansas 83, Indiana 77
West: Michigan 77, Temple 72

National Semifinals
(Sat., April 3, 1993 at New Orleans)
Michigan 81, Kentucky 78 (OT)
North Carolina 78, Kansas 68

National Final
(Mon., April 5, 1993 at New Orleans)
North Carolina 77, Michigan 71

DIVISION II

Semifinals
Cal–State Bakersfield 61, Wayne State 57
Troy State 126, New Hampshire Coll. 123

Championship
Cal–State Bakersfield 85, Troy State 72

DIVISION III

Semifinals
Ohio Northern 74, Mass.–Dartmouth 73
Augustana (Ill.) 83, Rowan (N.J.) 81

Championship
Ohio Northern 71, Augustana 68

WOMEN'S N.C.A.A. BASKETBALL CHAMPIONSHIPS—1993

DIVISION I

First Round—East
Rutgers 80, Vermont 74
Miami 61, St. Peter's 44
Georgetown 76, Northern Illinois 74
Florida 69, Bowling Green 67

First Round—Mideast
Northwestern 90, Georgia Tech 62
Alabama 102, Georgia Southern 70
Louisville 74, Connecticut 71
Old Dominion 77, Tennessee Tech 60

First Round—Midwest
California 62, Kansas 47
Clemson 70, Xavier 64
Louisiana Tech 70, DePaul 59
Southwest Missouri St. 86, Oklahoma State 71

First Round—West
Georgia 85, San Diego State 68
Cal–Santa Barbara 88, BYU 79
Nebraska 81, San Diego 58
Washington 80, Montana State 51

Second Round—East
Ohio State 91, Rutgers 60
Western Kentucky 78, Miami 63
Georgetown 68, Penn State 67
Virginia 69, Florida 55

Second Round—Mideast
Tennessee 89, Northwestern 66
North Carolina 74, Alabama 73 (OT)
Auburn 66, Louisville 61
Iowa 82, Old Dominion 56

Second Round—Midwest
Vanderbilt 82, California 63
S.F. Austin 89, Clemson 78
Louisiana Tech 82, Texas 78
Southwest Missouri St. 86, Maryland 82

Second Round—West
Stanford 93, Georgia 60
Colorado 81, Cal–Santa Barbara 54
Southern California 78, Nebraska 60
Texas Tech 70, Washington 64

Third Round—East
Ohio State 86, Western Kentucky 73
Virginia 77, Georgetown 57

Third Round—Mideast
Tennessee 74, North Carolina 54
Iowa 63, Auburn 50

Third Round—Midwest
Vanderbilt 59, S.F. Austin 56
Louisiana Tech 59, Southwest Missouri St. 43

Third Round—West
Colorado 80, Stanford 67
Texas Tech 79, Southern California 54

Regional Finals
East: Ohio State 75, Virginia 73
Mideast: Iowa 72, Tennessee 56
Midwest: Vanderbilt 58, Louisiana Tech 53
West: Texas Tech 79, Colorado 54

National Semifinals
(April 3, 1993, at Atlanta, Ga.)
Ohio State 73, Iowa 72 (OT)
Texas Tech 60, Vanderbilt 46

National Championship
(April 4, 1993, at Atlanta, Ga.)
Texas Tech 84, Ohio State 82

DIVISION II

Semifinals
Delta State (Miss.) 71, Michigan Tech 67
North Dakota State 79, Bentley (Mass.) 57

Championship
North Dakota State 94, Delta State 63

DIVISION III

Semifinals
Capital (Ohio) 65, Scranton (Pa.) 61
Central Iowa 60, St. Benedict (Minn.) 59

Championship
Central Iowa 71, Capital 63

LEADING N.C.A.A. SCORERS—1992–93

Division I

	TFG	3FG	FT	Pts	Avg
1. Grey Guy, Tex.–Pan American	189	67	111	556	29.3
2. J.R. Rider, Nevada–Las Vegas	282	55	195	814	29.1
3. John Best, Tennessee Tech.	296	4	203	799	28.5
4. Vin Baker, Hartford	305	32	150	792	28.3
5. Lindsey Hunter, Jackson St.	320	112	155	907	26.7
6. Alphonso Ford, Miss. Val. St.	252	76	148	728	26.0
7. Bill Edwards, Wright St.	288	43	138	757	25.2
8. Billy Ross, Appalachian St.	232	93	126	683	24.4
9. Glenn Robinson, Purdue	246	32	152	676	24.1
10. Kenneth Sykes, Grambling	242	37	123	644	23.9
11. Tony Dumas, Mo.–Kansas City	238	45	122	643	23.8
12. Eddie Benton, Vermont	176	82	185	619	23.8
13. Tony Dunkin, Coastal Caro.	263	64	169	759	23.7
14. Damian Johnson, Central Conn. St.	236	0	133	605	23.3
15. Stan Rose, Weber St.	240	0	170	650	23.2
16. Jesse Ratcliff, North Texas	207	60	127	601	23.1
17. Lucious Harris, Long Beach St.	251	73	164	739	23.1
18. Darnell Sneed, Charleston So.	218	25	161	622	23.0
18. Devin Boyd, Towson St.	177	54	214	622	23.0
20. Anfernee Hardaway, Memphis St.	249	73	158	729	22.8
21. Brian Gilgeous, American	205	49	177	636	22.7
22. Demetrius Dudley, Hofstra	184	81	141	590	22.7
23. Kareem Townes, La Salle	203	97	104	607	22.5
24. Calbert Cheaney, Indiana	303	47	132	785	22.4

NATIONAL ASSOCIATION OF INTERCOLLEGIATE ATHLETICS—1993

MEN'S TOURNAMENT

Division I

First Round
Belmont (N.C.) 87, Findlay (Ohio) 73
Lenoir–Rhyne (N.C.) 77, Wisconsin–Stevens Point 74
Central Washington 78, Central Arkansas 66
Urbana (Ohio) 95, Incarnate Word (Texas) 77
Briar Cliff (Iowa) 74, Cumberland (Ky.) 70
Midwestern State (Texas) 73, Geneva (Pa.) 63
Georgetown (Ky.) 92, Presbyterian (S.C.) 79
Ozarks 87, Pfeiffer (N.C.) 81
Salem–Telkyo (W. Va.) 64, Taylor (Ind.) 62 (OT)
Hawaii Pacific 92, Kennesaw, Ga. 71
Life (Ga.) 97, Benedict (S.C.) 62
David Lipscomb (Tenn.) 87, McKendree, Ill. 72
Oklahoma Baptist 79, Tri-State (Ind.) 71
Birmingham Southern (Ala.) 76, Drury (Mo.) 70
Oklahoma City 84, Spring Hill (Ala.) 79
Minnesota Morris 83, Azusa Pacific 68

Second Round
Lenoir–Rhyne 85, Oklahoma City 67
Georgetown 77, Birmingham Southern 72
Midwestern State 78, Central Washington 74
Urbana 126, Ozarks 104
Hawaii Pacific 83, Briar Cliff 79
Oklahoma Baptist 84, Salem–Telkyo 74
David Lipscomb 94, Life 89
Minnesota Morris 66, Belmont 59

Quarterfinals
Hawaii Pacific 79, Lenoir–Rhyne 76
Oklahoma Baptist 83, Urbana 76
Georgetown 101, David Lipscomb 91
Midwestern 88, Minnesota–Morris 76

Semifinals
Oklahoma Baptist 83, Georgetown 69
Hawaii Pacific 85, Midwestern 84

Championship
Hawaii Pacific 88, Oklahoma Baptist 83

Division II

Semifinals

Northern State (S.D.) 87, William Jewell (Mo.) 59
Willamette (Ore.) 77, Northwest Nazarene (Idaho) 72 (OT)

Championship

Willamette (Ore.) 63, Northern State (S.D.) 56

WOMEN'S TOURNAMENT

Quarterfinals

Arkansas Tech 75, St. Edward's (Texas) 69
SW Oklahoma 60, David Lipscomb (Tenn.) 58
Southern Nazarene (Okla.) 79, Wayland Baptist (Texas) 77
Union (Tenn.) 81, Montevallo (Ala.) 70

Semifinals

Arkansas Tech 81, Southern Nazarene 79
Union 54, SW Oklahoma 53

Championship

Arkansas Tech 76, Union (Tenn.) 75

NATIONAL INVITATION TOURNAMENT (N.I.T.)—1993

Semifinals

(March 29, 1993 at Madison Square Garden, N.Y.)

Minnesota 76, Providence 70
Georgetown 45, Alabama–Birmingham 41

Championship

(March 31, 1993 at Madison Square Garden, N.Y.)

Minnesota 62, Georgetown 61

FINAL 1993 N.C.A.A. REBOUNDING LEADERS

	Games	No.	Av
1. Warren Kidd, Middle Tenn. St.	26	386	14.
2. Jervaughn Scales, Southern–B.R.	31	393	12.
3. Reggie Jackson, Nicholls St.	26	325	12.
4. Spencer Dunkley, Delaware	30	367	12.
5. Dan Callahan, Northeastern	28	340	12.
6. Ervin Johnson, New Orleans	29	346	11.
7. Carlos Rogers, Tennessee St.	29	339	11.
8. Malik Rose, Drexel	29	330	11.
9. Michael Smith, Providence	33	375	11.
10. Darren Brown, Colgate	28	317	11.
11. Keith Bullock, Manhattan	30	332	11.
12. DeLon Turner, Florida A&M	26	287	11.
13. Clifford Rozier, Louisville	31	338	10.
14. Will Flemons, Texas Tech.	30	324	10.
15. Lee Matthews, Siena	29	313	10.
16. Ashraf Amaya, Southern Ill.	33	354	10.
17. Vin Baker, Hartford	28	300	10.
18. Josh Grant, Utah	31	331	10.
19. Sascha Hupmann, Evansville	23	244	10.
20. Sharone Wright, Clemson	30	314	10.
21. Jesse Ratliff, North Texas	26	269	10.
22. Glen Whisby, Southern Miss.	27	279	10.
23. Yinka Dare, Geo. Washington	30	308	10.
24. Malcolm Mackey, Georgia Tech.	30	306	10.
25. Geert Hammink, Louisiana St.	32	325	10.
26. Leonard White, Southern–B.R.	30	302	10.1
27. Chris Webber, Michigan	36	362	10.1
28. Bryant Reeves, Oklahoma St.	29	291	10.0
29. Bo Outlaw, Houston	30	301	10.0
30. Johnny McDowell, Texas–Arlington	28	280	10.0
31. Mike Peploswki, Michigan St.	28	279	10.0

HANDBALL

U.S.H.A. NATIONAL FOUR-WALL CHAMPIONS

Singles

1960	Jimmy Jacobs
1961	John Sloan
1962–63	Oscar Obert
1964–65	Jimmy Jacobs
1966–67	Paul Haber
1968	Simon (Stuffy) Singer
1969–71	Paul Haber
1972	Fred Lewis
1973	Terry Muck
1974	Fred Lewis
1975	Jay Bilyeu
1976	Vern Roberts, Jr.
1977	Naty Alvarado
1978	Fred Lewis
1979	Naty Alvarado
1980	Naty Alvarado
1981	Fred Lewis
1982	Naty Alvarado
1983	Naty Alvarado
1984	Naty Alvarado
1985	Naty Alvarado
1986	Naty Alvarado
1987	Naty Alvarado
1988	Naty Alvarado[1]
1989	Ponch Monreal
1990	Naty Alvarado
1991	John Bike
1992	Octavio Silveyra
1993	David Chapman[2]

Doubles

1960	Jimmy Jacobs–Dick Weisman
1961	John Sloan–Vic Hershkowitz
1962–63	Jimmy Jacobs–Marty Decatur
1964	John Sloan–Phil Elbert
1965	Jimmy Jacobs–Marty Decatur
1966	Pete Tyson–Bob Lindsay
1967–68	Jimmy Jacobs–Marty Decatur
1969	Lou Kramberg–Lou Russo
1970	Karl and Ruby Obert
1971	Ray Neveau–Simie Fein
1972	Kent Fusselman–Al Drews
1973–74	Ray Neveau–Simie Fein
1975	Marty Decatur–Steve Lott
1976	Gary Rohrer–Dan O'Connor
1977	Skip McDowell–Matt Kelly
1978	Stuffy Singer–Marty Decatur
1979	Stuffy Singer–Marty Decatur
1980	Skip McDowell–Harry Robertson
1981	Tom Kopatich–Jack Roberts
1982	Naty Alvarado–Vern Roberts
1983	Naty Alvarado–Vern Roberts
1984	Naty Alvarado–Vern Roberts
1985	Naty Alvarado–Vern Roberts
1986–87	Jon Kemdler–Poncho Monreal
1988	Doug Glatt–Dennis Haynes
1989	Danny Bell—Charlie Kalil
1990	Doug Glatt–Rod Prince
1991	John Bike–Octavio Silveyra
1992	David Chapman–Naty Alvarado, Jr.
1993	David Chapman[2]–Naty Alvarado, Jr.

1. 10th time—American record. 2. Chapman, at 17, is the youngest to win the singles and doubles championship in the same year.

Professional Basketball

NATIONAL BASKETBALL ASSOCIATION CHAMPIONS

Source: National Basketball Association.

The National Basketball Association was originally the Basketball Association of America. It took its current name in 1949 when it merged with the National Basketball League.

Season	Eastern Conference (W–L)	Western Conference (W–L)	Playoff Champions[1]
1946–47	Washington Capitols (49–11)	Chicago Stags (39–22)	Philadelphia Warriors
1947–48	Philadelphia Warriors (27–21)	St. Louis Bombers (29–19)	Baltimore Bullets
1948–49	Washington Capitols (38–22)	Rochester Royals (45–15)	Minneapolis Lakers
1949–50	Syracuse Nationals (51–13)	Indianapolis Olympians (39–25)	Minneapolis Lakers
1950–51	Philadelphia Warriors (40–26)	Minneapolis Lakers (44–24)	Rochester Royals
1951–52	Syracuse Nationals (40–26)	Rochester Royals (41–25)	Minneapolis Lakers
1952–53	New York Knickerbockers (47–23)	Minneapolis Lakers (48–22)	Minneapolis Lakers
1953–54	New York Knickerbockers (44–28)	Minneapolis Lakers (46–26)	Minneapolis Lakers
1954–55	Syracuse Nationals (43–29)	Ft. Wayne Pistons (43–29)	Syracuse Nationals
1955–56	Philadelphia Warriors (45–27)	Ft. Wayne Pistons (37–35)	Philadelphia Warriors
1956–57	Boston Celtics (44–28)	St. Louis Hawks (38–34)	Boston Celtics
1957–58	Boston Celtics (48–23)	St. Louis Hawks (41–31)	St. Louis Hawks
1958–59	Boston Celtics (52–20)	St. Louis Hawks (49–23)	Boston Celtics
1959–60	Boston Celtics (59–16)	St. Louis Hawks (46–29)	Boston Celtics
1960–61	Boston Celtics (57–22)	St. Louis Hawks (51–28)	Boston Celtics
1961–62	Boston Celtics (60–20)	Los Angeles Lakers (54–26)	Boston Celtics
1962–63	Boston Celtics (58–22)	Los Angeles Lakers (53–27)	Boston Celtics
1963–64	Boston Celtics (59–21)	San Francisco Warriors (48–32)	Boston Celtics
1964–65	Boston Celtics (62–18)	Los Angeles Lakers (49–31)	Boston Celtics
1965–66	Philadelphia 76ers (55–25)	Los Angeles Lakers (45–35)	Boston Celtics
1966–67	Philadelphia 76ers (68–13)	San Francisco Warriors (44–37)	Philadelphia 76ers
1967–68	Philadelphia 76ers (62–20)	St. Louis Hawks (56–26)	Boston Celtics
1968–69	Baltimore Bullets (57–25)	Los Angeles Lakers (55–27)	Boston Celtics
1969–70	New York Knickerbockers (60–22)	Atlanta Hawks (48–34)	New York Knicks
1970–71	Baltimore Bullets (42–40)	Milwaukee Bucks (66–16)	Milwaukee Bucks
1971–72	New York Knickerbockers (48–34)	Los Angeles Lakers (69–13)	Los Angeles Lakers
1972–73	New York Knickerbockers (57–25)	Los Angeles Lakers (60–22)	New York Knicks
1973–74	Boston Celtics (56–26)	Milwaukee Bucks (59–23)	Boston Celtics
1974–75	Washington Bullets (60–22)	Golden State Warriors (48–34)	Golden State Warriors
1975–76	Boston Celtics (54–28)	Phoenix Suns (42–40)	Boston Celtics
1976–77	Philadelphia 76ers (50–32)	Portland Trail Blazers (49–33)	Portland Trail Blazers
1977–78	Washington Bullets (44–38)	Seattle Super Sonics (47–35)	Washington Bullets
1978–79	Washington Bullets (54–28)	Seattle Super Sonics (52–30)	Seattle Super Sonics
1979–80	Philadelphia 76ers (59–23)	Los Angeles Lakers (60–22)	Los Angeles Lakers
1980–81	Boston Celtics (62–20)	Houston Rockets (40–42)	Boston Celtics
1981–82	Philadelphia 76ers (58–24)	Los Angeles Lakers (57–25)	Los Angeles Lakers
1982–83	Philadelphia 76ers (65–17)	Los Angeles Lakers (58–24)	Philadelphia 76ers
1983–84	Boston Celtics (56–26)	Los Angeles Lakers (58–24)	Boston Celtics
1984–85	Boston Celtics (63–19)	Los Angeles Lakers (62–20)	Los Angeles Lakers
1985–86	Boston Celtics (67–15)	Houston Rockets (51–31)	Boston Celtics
1986–87	Boston Celtics (59–23)	Los Angeles Lakers (65–17)	Los Angeles Lakers
1987–88	Detroit Pistons (54–28)	Los Angeles Lakers (62–20)	Los Angeles Lakers
1988–89	Detroit Pistons (63–18)	Los Angeles Lakers (57–25)	Detroit Pistons
1989–90	Detroit Pistons (59–23)	Portland Trail Blazers (59–23)	Detroit Pistons
1990–91	Chicago Bulls (61–21)	Los Angeles Lakers (58–24)	Chicago Bulls
1991–92	Chicago Bulls (67–15)	Portland Trail Blazers (57–25)	Chicago Bulls
1992–93	Chicago Bulls (57–25)	Phoenix Suns (62–20)	Chicago Bulls

1. Playoffs may involve teams other than conference winners.

INDIVIDUAL N.B.A. SCORING CHAMPIONS

Season	Player, Team	G	FG	FT	Pts	Avg
1953–54	Neil Johnston, Philadelphia Warriors	72	591	577	1759	24.4
1954–55	Neil Johnston, Philadelphia Warriors	72	521	589	1631	22.7
1955–56	Bob Pettit, St. Louis Hawks	72	646	557	1849	25.7
1956–57	Paul Arizin, Philadelphia Warriors	71	613	591	1817	25.6
1957–58	George Yardley, Detroit Pistons	72	673	655	2001	27.8
1958–59	Bob Pettit, St. Louis Hawks	72	719	667	2105	29.2
1959–60	Wilt Chamberlain, Philadelphia Warriors	72	1065	577	2707	37.6
1960–61	Wilt Chamberlain, Philadelphia Warriors	79	1251	531	3033	38.4
1961–62	Wilt Chamberlain, Philadelphia Warriors	80	1597	835	4029	50.4
1962–63	Wilt Chamberlain, San Francisco Warriors	80	1463	660	3586	44.8

Season	Player, Team	G	FG	FT	Pts	Avg
1963–64	Wilt Chamberlain, San Francisco Warriors	80	1204	540	2948	36.9
1964–65	Wilt Chamberlain, San Francisco Warriors–Phila. 76ers	73	1063	408	2534	34.7
1965–66	Wilt Chamberlain, Philadelphia 76ers	79	1074	501	2649	33.5
1966–67	Rick Barry, San Francisco Warriors	78	1011	753	2775	35.6
1967–68	Dave Bing, Detroit Pistons	79	835	472	2142	27.1
1968–69	Elvin Hayes, San Diego Rockets	82	930	467	2327	28.4
1969–70	Jerry West, Los Angeles Lakers	74	831	647	2309	31.2
1970–71	Lew Alcindor,[1] Milwaukee Bucks	82	1063	470	2596	31.7
1971–72	Kareem Abdul–Jabbar, Milwaukee Bucks	81	1159	504	2822	34.8
1972–73	Nate Archibald, Kansas City–Omaha Kings	80	1028	663	2719	34.0
1973–74	Bob McAdoo, Buffalo Braves	74	901	459	2261	30.8
1974–75	Bob McAdoo, Buffalo Braves	82	1095	641	2831	34.5
1975–76	Bob McAdoo, Buffalo Braves	78	934	559	2427	31.1
1976–77	Pete Maravich, New Orleans Jazz	73	886	501	2273	31.1
1977–78	George Gervin, San Antonio Spurs	82	864	504	2232	27.2
1978–79	George Gervin, San Antonio Spurs	80	947	471	2365	29.6
1979–80	George Gervin, San Antonio Spurs	78	1024	505	2585	33.1
1980–81	Adrian Dantley, Utah Jazz	80	909	632	2452	30.7
1981–82	George Gervin, San Antonio Spurs	79	993	555	2551	32.3
1982–83	Alex English, Denver Nuggets	82	959	406	2326	28.4
1983–84	Adrian Dantley, Utah Jazz	79	802	813	2418	30.6
1984–85	Bernard King, New York Knicks	55	691	426	1809	32.9
1985–86	Dominique Wilkins, Atlanta Hawks	78	888	527	2366	30.3
1986–87	Michael Jordan, Chicago Bulls[2]	82	1098	833	3041	37.1
1987–88	Michael Jordan, Chicago Bulls[3]	82	1069	723	2868	35.0
1988–89	Michael Jordan, Chicago Bulls[4]	81	966	674	2633	32.5
1989–90	Michael Jordan, Chicago Bulls[5]	82	1034	593	2753	33.6
1990–91	Michael Jordan, Chicago Bulls[6]	82	990	571	2580	31.5
1991–92	Michael Jordan, Chicago Bulls[7]	80	943	491	2404	30.1
1992–93	Michael Jordan, Chicago Bulls[8]	78	992	476	2541	32.6

1. (Kareem Abdul–Jabbar). 2. Also had 12 3–point field goals. 3. Also had 7 3–point field goals. 4. Also had 27 3–point field goals. 5. Also had 92 3–point field goals. 6. Also had 29 3-point-field goals. 7. Also had 27 3-pt field goals in 1991–92. 8. Also had 81 3-pt field goals in 1992–93.

N.B.A. LIFETIME LEADERS

(Through 1992–93 season)

NBA and ABA records combined

Most Games Played

Kareem Abdul–Jabbar	1,560
Moses Malone[1]	1,383
Robert Parish[1]	1,339
Artis Gilmore	1,329
Elvin Hayes	1,303
Caldwell Jones	1,299
John Havlicek	1,270
Paul Silas	1,254
Julius Erving	1,243
Dan Issel	1,218

Free Throw Percentage

(1,200 free throws made, minimum)

	FT%	FTA	FT
Mark Price[1]	.908	1,648	1,497
Rick Barry	.893	6,397	5,713
Calvin Murphy	.892	3,864	3,445
Larry Bird	.886	4,471	3,960
Bill Sharman	.883	3,559	3,143
Ricky Pierce[1]	.876	3,142	2,751
Jeff Malone[1]	.874	3,045	2,662
Reggie Miller[1]	.872	2,753	2,400
Kiki Vandeweghe[1]	.872	3,997	3,484
Mike Newlin	.870	3,456	3,005

Blocked Shots

Kareem Abdul–Jabbar	3,189
Mark Eaton[1]	3,064
Artis Gilmore	2,497
Tree Rollins	2,471
Hakeem Olajuwon[1]	2,444
Caldwell Jones	2,297
Robert Parish[1]	2,156
George T. Johnson	2,082
Manute Bol[1]	2,061
Larry Nance[1]	1,972

Scoring Average

(400 games or 10,000 points minimum)

	Avg	Pts	G
Michael Jordan[1]	32.3	21,541	667
Wilt Chamberlain	30.1	31,419	1,045
Elgin Baylor	27.4	23,149	846
Jerry West	27.0	25,192	932
Dominique Wilkins[1]	26.5	22,096	833
Bob Pettit	26.4	20,880	792
Karl Malone[1]	26.1	16,987	652
Oscar Robertson	25.7	26,710	1,040
George Gervin	25.1	26,595	1,060
Rick Barry	24.8	25,273	1,020

Steals

Maurice Cheeks[1]	2,310
Julius Erving	2,091
Alvin Robertson[1]	1,946
John Stockton[1]	1,932
Don Buse	1,918
Michael Jordan[1]	1,815
Isiah Thomas[1]	1,793
Magic Johnson	1,698
Gus Williams	1,638
Clyde Drexler[1]	1,623

Rebounds

Wilt Chamberlain	23,924
Bill Russell	21,620
Moses Malone[1]	17,562
Kareem Abdul–Jabbar	17,440
Artis Gilmore	16,330
Elvin Hayes	16,279
Nate Thurmond	14,464
Walt Bellamy	14,241
Wes Unseld	13,769
Robert Parish	13,431

1. Active going into 1993–94 season.

Field Goal Percentage
(2,000 field goals made, minimum)

	FG%	FGA	FG
Artis Gilmore	.582	16,158	9,403
Steve Johnson[1]	.572	4,965	2,841
Darryl Dawkins	.572	6,079	3,477
James Donaldson[1]	.570	5,368	3,061
Charles Barkley[1]	.569	10,098	5,741
Jeff Ruland	.564	3,734	2,105
Bobby Jones	.560	7,953	4,451
Kareem Abdul-Jabbar	.559	28,307	15,837
Buck Williams[1]	.554	9,674	5,362
Otis Thorpe[1]	.554	8,033	4,449

1. Active going into 1993–94 season.

Assists

Magic Johnson	9,921
Oscar Robertson	9,887
Isiah Thomas[1]	8,662
John Stockton[1]	8,352
Maurice Cheeks[1]	7,392
Lenny Wilkens	7,211
Bob Cousy	6,955
Guy Rodgers	6,917
Nate Archibald	6,476
John Lucas	6,454

NATIONAL BASKETBALL ASSOCIATION FINAL STANDINGS—1992–93

EASTERN CONFERENCE

Atlantic Division

	W	L	Pct	Games behind
y–New York Knicks	60	22	.732	—
y–Boston Celtics	48	34	.585	12
y–New Jersey Nets	43	39	.524	17
Orlando Magic	41	41	.500	19
Miami Heat	36	46	.439	24
Philadelphia 76ers	26	56	.317	34
Washington Bullets	22	60	.268	38

Central Division

	W	L	Pct	Games behind
y–Chicago Bulls	57	25	.695	—
y–Cleveland Cavaliers	54	28	.663	3
y–Charlotte Hornets	44	38	.537	13
y–Atlanta Hawks	43	39	.530	14
y–Indiana Pacers	41	41	.500	16
Detroit Pistons	40	42	.488	17
Milwaukee Bucks	28	54	.341	29

y—Secured playoff berth.

WESTERN CONFERENCE

Midwest Division

	W	L	Pct	Games behind
y–Houston Rockets	55	27	.671	—
y–San Antonio Spurs	49	33	.598	6
y–Utah Jazz	47	35	.573	8
Denver Nuggets	36	46	.439	19
Minnesota Timberwolves	19	63	.232	36
Dallas Mavericks	11	71	.134	44

Pacific Division

	W	L	Pct	Games behind
y–Phoenix Suns	62	20	.756	—
y–Seattle SuperSonics	55	27	.671	7
y–Portland Trail Blazers	51	31	.622	11
y–L.A. Clippers	41	41	.500	21
y–L.A. Lakers	39	43	.476	23
Golden State Warriors	34	48	.415	28
Sacramento Kings	25	57	.305	37

N.B.A. PLAYOFFS—1993

EASTERN CONFERENCE

First Round
(Best 3 out of 5)

New York defeated Indiana, 3 games to 1
Cleveland defeated New Jersey, 3 games to 2
Chicago defeated Atlanta, 3 games to 0
Charlotte defeated Boston, 3 games to 1

Second Round

Chicago defeated Cleveland, 4 games to 0
New York defeated Charlotte, 4 games to 1

Conference Finals

Chicago defeated New York, 4 games to 2
May 23—NEW YORK 98, Chicago 90
May 25—NEW YORK 96, Chicago 91
May 29—CHICAGO 103, New York 83
May 31—CHICAGO 105, New York 95
June 2—Chicago 97, NEW YORK 94
June 4—CHICAGO 96, New York 88

WESTERN CONFERENCE

First Round
(Best 3 out of 5)

Phoenix defeated L.A. Lakers, 3 games to 2
Houston defeated L.A. Clippers, 3 games to 2
Seattle defeated Utah, 3 games to 2
San Antonio defeated Portland, 3 games to 1

Second Round

Phoenix defeated San Antonio, 4 games to 2
Seattle defeated Houston, 4 games to 3

Conference Finals

Phoenix defeated Seattle, 4 games to 3
May 24—PHOENIX 105, Seattle 91
May 26—Seattle 103, PHOENIX 99
May 28—Phoenix 104, SEATTLE 97
May 30—SEATTLE 120, Phoenix 101
June 1—PHOENIX 120, Seattle 114
June 3—SEATTLE 118, Phoenix 102
June 5—PHOENIX 123, Seattle 110

CHAMPIONSHIP

Chicago defeated Phoenix, 4 games to 2
June 9—Chicago 100, PHOENIX 92
June 11—Chicago 111, PHOENIX 108
June 13—Phoenix 129, CHICAGO 121 (3 OT)
June 16—CHICAGO 111, Phoenix 105
June 18—Phoenix 108, CHICAGO 98
June 20—Chicago 99, PHOENIX 98

NOTE: All caps denotes home team

N.B.A. INDIVIDUAL RECORDS

(Through 1992–93 season)

Most points, game—100, Wilt Chamberlain, Philadelphia vs. New York at Hershey, Pa. 1962
Most points, quarter—33, George Gervin, San Antonio, 1978
Most points, half—59, Wilt Chamberlain, Philadelphia, 1962
Most free throws, game—28, Wilt Chamberlain, Philadelphia vs. New York at Hershey, Pa. 1962; 28, Adrian Dantley, Utah vs. Houston, 1984
Most free throws, quarter—14, Rick Barry, San Francisco, 1966
Most free throws, half—19, Oscar Robertson, Cincinnati, 1964
Most field goals, game—36, Wilt Chamberlain, Philadelphia, 1962
Most consecutive field goals, game—18, Wilt Chamberlain, San Franciscco, 1963; Wilt Chamberlain, Philadelphia, 1967
Most assists, game—30, Scott Skiles, Orlando vs. Denver, 1990
Most rebounds, game—55, Wilt Chamberlain, Philadelphia vs. Boston, 1960
Most 3-pt. field goals, game—10, Brian Shaw, Miami vs. Milwaukee, 1993

N.B.A. MOST VALUABLE PLAYERS

1956	Bob Pettit
1957	Bob Cousy
1958	Bill Russell
1959	Bob Pettit
1960	Wilt Chamberlain
1961–63	Bill Russell
1964	Oscar Robertson
1965	Bill Russell
1966–68	Wilt Chamberlain
1969	Wes Unseld
1970	Willis Reed
1971–72	Lew Alcindor (Kareem Abdul–Jabbar)
1973	Dave Cowens
1974	Kareem Abdul–Jabbar, Milwaukee
1975	Bob McAdoo, Buffalo
1976–77	Kareem Abdul–Jabbar, Los Angeles
1978	Bill Walton, Portland
1979	Moses Malone, Houston
1980	Kareem Abdul–Jabbar, Los Angeles
1981	Julius Erving, Philadelphia
1982	Moses Malone, Houston
1983	Moses Malone, Philadelphia
1984	Larry Bird, Boston
1985	Larry Bird, Boston
1986	Larry Bird, Boston
1987	Earvin Johnson, Los Angeles
1988	Michael Jordan, Chicago
1989	Earvin Johnson, Los Angeles
1990	Earvin Johnson, Los Angeles
1991	Michael Jordan, Chicago
1992	Michael Jordan, Chicago
1993	Charles Barkley, Phoenix

N.B.A. TEAM RECORDS

Most points, game—186, Detroit vs. Denver, 3 overtimes, 1983
Most points, quarter—58, Buffalo vs. Boston, 1968
Most points, half—97, Atlanta vs. San Diego, 1970
Most points, overtime period—22, Detroit vs. Cleveland, 1973
Most field goals, game—74, Detroit, 1983
Most field goals, quarter—23, Boston, 1959; Buffalo, 1972
Most field goals, half—40, Boston, 1959; Syracuse, 1963; Atlanta, 1979
Most assists, game—53, Milwaukee, 1978
Most rebounds, game—109, Boston, 1960
Most points, both teams, game—370 (Detroit 186, Denver 184) 3 overtimes, Denver, December 13, 1983
Most points, both teams, quarter—96 (Boston 52, Minneapolis 44), 1959; (Detroit 53, Cincinnati 43), 1972
Most points, both teams, half—170 (Philadelphia 90, Cincinnati 80), Philadelphia, 1971
Longest winning streak—33, Los Angeles, 1971–72
Longest losing streak—20, Philadelphia, 1973
Longest winning streak at home—36, Philadelphia, 1966–67
Most games won, season—69, Los Angeles, 1971–72
Most games lost, season—73, Philadelphia, 1972–73
Highest average points per game—126.5, Denver, 1981–82

LEADING SCORERS—1992–1993

	GP	Pts	Avg
Michael Jordan, Chicago	78	2541	32.6
Dominique Wilkins, Atlanta	71	2121	29.9
Karl Malone, Utah	82	2217	27.0
Hakeem Olajuwon, Houston	82	2140	26.1
Charles Barkley, Phoenix	76	1944	25.6
Patrick Ewing, New York	81	1959	24.2
Joe Dumars, Detroit	77	1809	23.5
Shaquille O'Neal, Orlando	81	1893	23.4
David Robinson, San Antonio	82	1916	23.4
Danny Manning, L.A. Clippers	79	1800	22.8
Drazen Petrovic, New Jersey	70	1564	22.3
Larry Johnson, Charlotte	82	1812	22.1
Tim Hardaway, Golden State	66	1419	21.5
Reggie Miller, Indiana	82	1736	21.2
Alonzo Mourning, Charlotte	78	1639	21.0
Reggie Lewis, Boston	80	1666	20.8
Derrick Coleman, New Jersey	76	1572	20.7
Hersey Hawkins, Philadelphia	81	1643	20.3
Brad Daugherty, Cleveland	71	1432	20.2
Nick Anderson, Orlando	79	1574	19.9

STEALS LEADERS—1992–1993

(minimum 70 games or 125 steals)

	G	Stl	Avg
Michael Jordan, Chicago	78	221	2.8
Mookie Blaylock, Atlanta	80	203	2.5
John Stockton, Utah	82	199	2.4
Nate McMillan, Seattle	73	173	2.4
Alvin Robertson, Detroit	69	155	2.2
Ron Harper, L.A. Clippers	80	182	2.2
Erick Murdock, Milwaukee	79	174	2.2
Micheal Williams, Minnesota	76	165	2.2
Gary Payton, Seattle	82	177	2.2
Scottie Pippen, Chicago	81	173	2.1
Tyrone Bogues, Charlotte	81	161	2.0
Chris Morris, New Jersey	77	144	1.9
Hakeem Olajuwon, Houston	82	150	1.8
Sedale Threatt, L.A. Lakers	82	142	1.7

ASSISTS LEADERS—1992–1993

(minimum 70 games or 400 assists)

	G	No.	Avg
John Stockton, Utah	82	987	12.0
Tim Hardaway, Golden State	66	699	10.6
Scott Skiles, Orlando	78	735	9.4

	G	No.	Avg
Mark Jackson, L.A. Clippers	82	724	8.8
Tyrone Bogues, Charlotte	81	711	8.8
Micheal Williams, Minnesota	76	661	8.7
Isiah Thomas, Detroit	79	671	8.5
Mookie Blaylock, Atlanta	80	671	8.4
Kenny Anderson, New Jersey	55	449	8.2
Mark Price, Cleveland	75	602	8.0
Pooh Richardson, Indiana	74	573	7.7
Eric Murdock, Milwaukee	79	603	7.6
Michael Adams, Washington	70	526	7.5
Avery Johnson, San Antonio	75	561	7.5
Rod Strickland, Portland	78	559	7.2

BLOCKED-SHOTS LEADERS—1992–1993

(minimum 70 games or 100 blocked shots)

	G	No.	Avg
Hakeem Olajuwon, Houston	82	342	4.2
Shaquille O'Neal, Orlando	81	286	3.5
Dikembe Mutombo, Denver	82	287	3.5
Alonzo Mourning, Charlotte	78	271	3.5
David Robinson, San Antonio	82	264	3.2
Larry Nance, Cleveland	77	198	2.6
Pervis Ellison, Washington	49	108	2.2
Manute Bol, Philadelphia	58	119	2.1
Cliff Robinson, Portland	82	163	2.0
Patrick Ewing, New York	81	161	2.0
Andrew Lang, Philadelphia	73	141	1.9
Shawn Kemp, Seattle	78	146	1.9
Stanley Roberts, L.A. Clippers	77	141	1.8
Dale Davis, Indiana	82	148	1.8
Oliver Miller, Phoenix	56	100	1.8

FIELD GOAL PERCENTAGE LEADERS—1992–1993

(minimum 300 FG made)

	G	FG	FGA	Pct
Cedric Ceballos, Phoenix	74	381	662	.576
Brad Daugherty, Cleveland	71	520	911	.571
Dale Davis, Indiana	82	304	535	.568
Shaquille O'Neal, Orlando	81	733	1304	.562
Otis Thorpe, Houston	72	385	690	.558
Karl Malone, Utah	82	797	1443	.552
Larry Nance, Cleveland	77	533	971	.549
Frank Brickowski, Milwaukee	66	456	836	.545
Larry Stewart, Washington	81	306	564	.543
Antoine Carr, San Antonio	71	379	705	.538
A.C. Green, L.A. Lakers	82	379	706	.537
Robert Parish, Boston	79	416	777	.535
Hakeem Olajuwon, Houston	82	848	1603	.529
Stanley Roberts, L.A. Clippers	77	375	711	.527
Larry Johnson, Charlotte	82	728	1385	.526

FREE-THROW PERCENTAGE LEADERS—1992–1993

(minimum 125 FT made)

	G	FTM	FTA	Pct
Mark Price, Cleveland	75	289	305	.948
Chris Jackson, Denver	81	217	232	.935
Eddie Johnson, Seattle	82	234	257	.911
Micheal Williams, Minnesota	76	419	462	.907
Scott Skiles, Orlando	78	289	324	.892
Ricky Pierce, Seattle	77	313	352	.889
Reggie Miller, Indiana	82	427	485	.880
Kenny Smith, Houston	82	195	222	.878
Drazen Petrovic, New Jersey	70	315	362	.870
Reggie Lewis, Boston	80	326	376	.867
Dell Curry, Charlotte	80	136	157	.866
Jeff Hornacek, Philadelphia	79	250	289	.865
Joe Dumars, Detroit	77	343	397	.864
B.J. Armstrong, Chicago	82	130	151	.861
Rod Higgins, Sacramento	69	130	151	.861

REBOUND LEADERS—1992–1993

(minimum 70 games or 700 rebounds)

	G	Reb	Avg
Dennis Rodman, Detroit	62	1132	18.3
Shaquille O'Neal, Orlando	81	1122	13.9
Dikembe Mutombo, Denver	82	1070	13.0
Hakeem Olajuwon, Houston	82	1068	13.0
Kevin Willis, Atlanta	80	1028	12.9
Charles Barkley, Phoenix	76	928	12.2
Patrick Ewing, New York	81	980	12.1
Roy Seikaly, Miami	72	846	11.8
David Robinson, San Antonio	82	956	11.7
Derrick Coleman, New Jersey	76	852	11.2
Karl Malone, Utah	82	919	11.2
Shawn Kemp, Seattle	78	833	10.7
Larry Johnson, Charlotte	82	864	10.5
Alonzo Mourning, Charlotte	78	805	10.3
Brad Daugherty, Cleveland	71	726	10.2

3-POINT FIELD GOAL LEADERS 1992–1993

(minimum 50 made)

	G	3FG	3FGA	Pct
B.J. Armstrong, Chicago	82	63	139	.453
Chris Mullin, Golden State	46	60	133	.451
Drazen Petrovic, New Jersey	70	75	167	.449
Kenny Smith, Houston	82	96	219	.438
Jim Les, Sacramento	73	66	154	.429
Mark Price, Cleveland	75	122	293	.416
Terry Porter, Portland	81	143	345	.414
Danny Ainge, Phoenix	79	150	372	.403
Dennis Scott, Orlando	54	108	268	.403
Steve Smith, Miami	48	53	132	.402
Dell Curry, Charlotte	80	95	237	.401
Dale Ellis, San Antonio	82	119	297	.401
Reggie Miller, Indiana	82	167	419	.399
Hersey Hawkins, Philadelphia	81	122	307	.397
Trent Tucker, Chicago	69	53	131	.397

DEFUNCT NBA TEAMS

Teams that once played in the BAA and NBA, but no longer exist.

Anderson (Ind.)—Packers (1949–50); **Baltimore**—Bullets (1947–55); **Chicago**—Stags (1946–50); **Cleveland**—Rebels (1946–47); **Denver**—Nuggets (1949–50); **Detroit**—Falcons (1946–47); **Indianapolis**—Jets (1948–49) and Olympians (1949–53); **Pittsburgh**—Ironmen (1946–47); **Providence**—Steamrollers (1946–49); **St. Louis**—Bombers (1946–50); **Sheboygan (Wisc.)**—Redskins (1949–50); **Toronto**—Huskies (1946–47); **Washington**—Capitals (1946–51); **Waterloo (Iowa)**—Hawks (1949–50).

Sports Personalities

A name in parentheses is the original name or form of name. Localities are places of birth. Dates of birth appear as month/day/year. **Boldface** years in parentheses are dates of **(birth–death)**.
Information has been gathered from many sources, including the individuals themselves. However, the *Information Please Almanac* cannot guarantee the accuracy of every individual item.

Aaron, Hank (Henry) (baseball); Mobile, Ala., 2/5/1934
Aaron, Tommie (baseball); Mobile, Ala., **(1939–1984)**
Abdul-Jabbar, Kareem (Lewis Ferdinand Alcindor, Jr.) (basketball); New York City, 4/16/1947
Adderly, Herbert A. (football); Philadelphia, 6/8/1939
Affleck, Francis (auto racing) **(1951–1985)**
Alcindor, Lew. *See* Abdul-Jabbar.
Ali, Muhammad (Cassius Clay) (boxing); Louisville, Ky., 1/18/1942
Allen, Dick (Richard Anthony) (baseball); Wampum, Pa., 3/8/1942
Allen, George (football) **(1918–1990)**
Allison, Bobby (Robert Arthur) (auto racing); Hueytown, Ala., 12/3/1937
Alston, Walter (baseball); Venice, Ohio **(1911–1984)**
Alworth, Lance (football); Houston, 8/3/1940
Ameche, Alan (football); Houston, Tex., **(1933–1988)**
Anderson, Donny (Gary Donny) (football); Brooklyn, N.Y., 4/3/1949
Anderson, Ken (football); Batavia, Ill., 2/15/1949
Anderson, Sparky (George) (baseball); Bridgewater, S.D., 2/22/1934
Andretti, Mario (auto racing); Montona, Trieste, Italy, 2/28/1940
Anthony, Earl (bowling); Kent, Wash., 4/27/1938
Appling, Luke (baseball); High Point, N.C **(1907–1990)**
Arcaro, Eddie (George Edward) (jockey); Cincinnati, 2/19/1916
Ashe, Arthur (tennis); Richmond, Va. **(1943–1993)**
Ashford, Evelyn (track & field); Shreveport, La., 4/15/1957
Austin, Tracy (tennis); Rolling Hills, Calif., 12/2/1962
Averill, Earl (baseball); Everett, Wash. **(1915–1983)**
Babashoff, Shirley (swimming); Whittier, Calif., 1/31/1957
Baer, Max (boxing); Omaha, Neb. **(1909–1959)**
Bakken, Jim (James Leroy) (football); Madison, Wis., 11/2/1940
Banks, Ernie (baseball); Dallas, 1/31/1931
Bannister, Roger (runner); Harrow, England, 3/24/1929
Barkley, Charles (basketball); Leeds, Ala., 2/20/1963
Barry, Rick (Richard) (basketball); Elizabeth, N.J., 3/28/1944
Bauer, Hank (Henry) (baseball); East St. Louis, Ill., 7/31/1922
Baugh, Sammy (football); Temple, Tex., 3/17/1914
Bayi, Filbert (runner); Karratu, Tanganyika, 6/23/1953
Baylor, Elgin (basketball); Washington, D.C., 9/16/1934
Beamon, Bob (long jumper); New York City, 8/2/1946
Becker, Boris (tennis); Leiman, W. Germany, 11/22/1967
Bee, Clair (basketball); Cleveland, Ohio **(1896–1983)**
Beliveau, Jean (hockey); Three Rivers, Quebec, Canada, 8/31/1931
Bell, Rickey (football); Inglewood, Calif. **(1949–1984)**
Beman, Deane (golf); Washington, D.C., 4/22/1938
Bench, Johnny (Johnny Lee) (baseball); Oklahoma City, 12/7/1947
Berg, Patty (Patricia Jane) (golf); Minneapolis, 2/13/1918
Berning, Susie Maxwell (golf); Pasadena, Calif., 7/22/1941
Berra, Yogi (Lawrence) (baseball); St. Louis, 5/12/1925
Biletnikoff, Frederick (football); Erie, Pa., 2/23/1943
Bing, Dave (basketball); Washington, D.C., 11/24/1943
Bird, Larry (basketball); French Lick, Ind., 12/7/1956
Blaik, Earl H. (football); Detroit **(1897–1989)**
Blanda, George Frederick (football); Youngwood, Pa., 9/17/1927
Blue, Vida (baseball); Mansfield, La., 7/28/1949
Bonds, Barry (baseball); Riverside, Calif., 7/24/1964
Borg, Björn (tennis); Stockholm, 6/6/1956
Boros, Julius (golf); Fairfield, Conn., 3/3/1920
Bossy, Mike (hockey); Montreal, 1/22/1957
Boston, Ralph (long jumper); Laurel, Miss., 5/9/1939
Bradley, Bill (William Warren) (basketball); Crystal City, Mo., 7/28/1943
Bradshaw, Terry (football); Shreveport, La., 9/2/1948
Brathwaite, Chris (track); Eugene, Ore. **(1949–1984)**
Breedlove, Craig (Norman) (speed driving); Los Angeles, 3/23/1938
Brett, George (baseball); Glendale, W. Va., 5/15/1953
Brewer, James (Jim) (baseball); Merced, Calif. **(1937–1987)**
Brock, Louis Clark (baseball); El Dorado, Ark., 6/18/1939
Brown, Jimmy (football); St. Simon Island, Ga., 2/17/1936
Brown, Larry (football); Clairton, Pa., 9/19/1947
Brumel, Valeri (high jumper); Tolbuzino, Siberia, 4/14/1942
Bryant, Paul "Bear" (football); Tuscaloosa, Ala., **(1913–1983)**
Bryant, Rosalyn Evette (track); Chicago, 1/7/1956
Burton, Michael (swimming); Des Moines, Iowa, 7/3/1947
Butkus, Dick (Richard Marvin) (football); Chicago, 12/9/1942
Campanella, Roy (baseball); Homestead, Pa. **(1921–1993)**
Campbell, Earl (football); Tyler, Tex., 3/29/1955
Canseco, Jose (baseball); Havana, Cuba, 7/2/1964
Caponi, Donna Maria (golf); Detroit, 1/29/1945
Cappelletti, Gino (football); Keewatin, Minn., 3/26/1934
Carew, Rod (Rodney Cline) (baseball); Gatun, Panama, 10/1/1945
Carlos, John (sprinter); New York City, 6/5/1945
Carlton, Steven Norman (baseball); Miami, Fla., 12/22/1944
Carner, Joanne Gunderson, Mrs. Don (golf); Kirkland, Wash., 3/4/1939
Casals, Rosemary (tennis); San Francisco, 9/16/1948
Casper, Billy (golf); San Diego, Calif., 6/24/1931
Caulkins, Tracy (swimming); Winona, Minn., 1/11/1963
Cauthen, Steve (jockey); Covington, Ky., 5/1/1960
Chamberlain, Wilt (Wilton) (basketball); Philadelphia, 8/21/1936
Chandler, A.B. (Happy) (baseball); Louisville, Ky. **(1899–1991)**
Chandler, Spud (baseball); Commerce, Ga., **(1907–1990)**
Chapot, Frank (equestrian); Camden, N.J., 2/24/1934
Chinaglia, Giorgio (soccer); Carrara, Italy, 1/24/1947
Clarke, Bobby (Robert Earle) (hockey); Flin Flon, Manitoba, Canada, 8/13/1949
Clay, Cassius. *See* Ali, Muhammad
Clemens, Roger (baseball); Dayton, Ohio, 8/4/1962
Clemente, Roberto Walker (baseball); Carolina, Puerto Rico **(1934–1972)**
Cobb, Ty (Tyrus Raymond) (baseball); Narrows, Ga., **(1886–1961)**
Cochran, Barbara Ann (skiing); Claremont, N.H., 1/14/1951
Cochran, Marilyn (skiing); Burlington, Vt., 2/7/1950
Cochran, Robert (skiing); Claremont, N.H., 12/11/1951
Coe, Sebastian Newbold (track); London, England, 9/29/1956
Colavito, Rocky (Rocco Domenico) (baseball); New York City, 8/10/1933
Comaneci, Nadia (gymnast); Onesti, Romania, 11/12/1961
Conigliaro, Tony (baseball); Revere, Mass., **(1945–1990)**
Connors, Jimmy (James Scott) (tennis); East St. Louis, Ill., 9/2/1952
Cordero, Angel (jockey); Santurce, Puerto Rico, 5/8/1942
Cournoyer, Yvan Serge (hockey); Drummondville, Quebec, Canada, 11/22/1943
Court, Margaret Smith (tennis); Albury, New South Wales, Australia, 7/16/1942
Cousy, Bob (basketball); New York City, 8/9/1928
Crabbe, Buster (swimming); Scottsdale, Ariz. **(1908–1983)**
Crenshaw, Ben (golf); Austin, Tex., 1/11/1952
Cronin, Joe (baseball executive); San Francisco, **(1906–1984)**
Cruyff, Johan (soccer); Amsterdam, Netherlands, 4/25/47
Csonka, Larry (Lawrence Richard) (football); Stow, Ohio, 12/25/1946
Dancer, Stanley (harness racing); New Egypt, N.J., 7/25/1927
Dantley, Adrian (basketball); Washington, D.C., 2/28/1956
Dark, Alvin (baseball); Comanche, Okla., 1/7/1922
Davenport, Willie (track); Troy, Ala., 6/6/1943
Dawson, Leonard Ray (football); Alliance, Ohio, 6/20/1935
Dean, Dizzy (Jay Hanna) (baseball); Lucas, Ark. **(1911–1974)**
DeBusschere, Dave (basketball); Detroit, 10/16/1940
Delvecchio, Alex Peter (hockey); Fort William, Ontario, Canada, 12/4/1931
Demaret, Jim (golf); Houston **(1910–1983)**
Dempsey, Jack (William H.) (boxing); Manassa, Colo. **(1895–1983)**
DeVicenzo, Roberto (golf); Buenos Aires, 4/14/1923
Dibbs, Edward George (tennis); Brooklyn, New York, 2/23/1951
Dietz, James W. (rowing); New York, N.Y., 1/12/1949
DiMaggio, Joe (baseball); Martinez, Calif., 11/25/1914
Dionne, Marcel (hockey); Drummondville, Quebec, Canada, 8/3/1951
Dominguín, Luis Miguel (matador); Madrid, 12/9/1926
Dorsett, Tony (football); Rochester, Pa., 4/7/1954
Dryden, Kenneth (hockey); Hamilton, Ontario, Canada, 8/4/1947
Drysdale, Don (baseball); Van Nuys, Calif. **(1936–1993)**
Duran, Roberto (boxing); Panama City, 6/16/1951
Durocher, Leo (baseball); West Springfield, Mass. **(1906–1991)**
Durr, Francois (tennis); Algiers, Algeria, 12/25/1942
El Cordobés, (Manuel Benitez Pérez) (matador); Palma del Rio, Córdoba, Spain, 5/4/1936(?)
Elder, Lee (golf); Dallas, 7/14/1934
Emerson, Roy (tennis); Kingsway, Australia, 11/3/1936
Ender, Kornelia (swimming); Plauen, East Germany, 10/25/1958
Erving, "Dr. J" (Julius) (basketball); Roosevelt, N.Y., 2/22/1950
Espinosa, Nino (baseball); Villa Altagracia, Dominican Republic **(1953–1988)**

Esposito, Phil (Philip Anthony) (hockey); Sault Ste. Marie, Ontario, Canada, 2/20/1942
Evans, Lee (runner); Mandena, Calif., 2/25/1947
Everett, Chris (tennis); Fort Lauderdale, Fla., 12/21/1954
Ewbank, Weeb (football); Richmond, Ind., 5/6/1907
Ewing, Patrick (basketball); Kingston, Jamaica, 8/5/1962
Feller, Robert (Bobby) (baseball); Van Meter, Iowa, 11/3/1918
Feuerbach, Allan Dean (track); Preston, Iowa, 1/12/1948
Finley, Charles O. (sportsman); Ensley, Ala., 2/22/1918
Fischer, Bobby (chess); Chicago, 3/9/1943
Fitzsimmons, Bob (Robert Prometheus) (boxing); Cornwall, England **(1862–1917)**
Fleming, Peggy Gale (ice skating); San Jose, Calif., 7/27/1948
Ford, Whitey (Edward) (baseball); New York City, 10/21/1928
Foreman, George (boxing); Marshall, Tex., 1/10/1949
Fosbury, Richard (high jumper); Portland, Ore., 3/6/1947
Fox, Nellie (Jacob Nelson) (baseball); St. Thomas, Pa. **(1927–1975)**
Foxx, James Emory (baseball); Sudlersville, Md. **(1907–1967)**
Foyt, A. J. (auto racing); Houston, 1/16/1935
Francis, Emile (hockey); North Battleford, Sask., Canada, 9/13/1926
Fratianne, Linda (figure skating); Los Angeles, 8/2/1960
Frazier, Joe (boxing); Beauford, S.C., 1/17/1944
Frazier, Walt (basketball); Atlanta, 3/29/1945
Frick, Ford C. (baseball); Wawaka, Ind. **(1894–1978)**
Furillo, Carl (baseball); Stony Creek Mills, Pa. **(1922–1989)**
Furniss, Bruce (swimming); Fresno, Calif., 5/27/1957
Gable, Dan (wrestling); Waterloo, Iowa, 10/25/1945
Gabriel, Roman (football); Wilmington, N.C., 8/5/1940
Gallagher, Michael Donald (skiing); Yonkers, N.Y., 10/3/1941
Garms, Debs (baseball); Glen Rose, Tex. **(1908–1984)**
Garvey, Steve (baseball); Tampa, Fla., 12/22/1948
Gehrig, Lou (Henry Louis) (baseball); New York City **(1903–1941)**
Gehringer, Charlie (baseball); Fowlerville, Mich., 5/11/1903
Gervin, George (basketball); Long Beach, Calif., 4/27/52
Geoffrion, "Boom Boom" (Bernie) (hockey); Montreal, 2/14/1931
Gerulaitis, Vitas (tennis); Brooklyn, N.Y., 7/26/1954
Giacomin, Ed (hockey); Sudbury, Ontario, Canada, 6/6/1939
Giamatti, A. Bartlett (baseball); South Hadley, Mass. **(1938–1989)**
Gibson, Bob (baseball); Omaha, Neb., 11/9/1935
Gifford, Frank (football); Santa Monica, Calif., 8/16/1930
Gilbert, Rod (Rodrique) (hockey); Montreal, 7/1/1941
Giles, Warren (baseball executive); Tiskilwa, Ill. **(1896–1979)**
Gilmore, Artis (basketball); Chipley, Fla., 9/21/1949
Glance, Harvey (track); Phenix City, Ala., 3/28/1957
Gonzalez, Pancho (tennis); Los Angeles, 5/9/1928
Goodell, Brian Stuart (swimming); Stockton, Calif., 4/2/1959
Gooden, Dwight (baseball); Tampa, Fla., 11/16/1964
Goodrich, Gail (basketball); Los Angeles, 4/23/1943
Goolagong, Cawley, Evonne (tennis); Griffith, Australia, 7/31/1951
Gossage, "Goose" (Rich) (baseball); Colorado Springs, Colo., 4/5/1951
Gottfried, Brian (tennis); Baltimore, Md., 1/27/1952
Graf, Steffi (tennis); Mannheim, W. Germany, 6/14/1969
Graham, David (golf); Windson, Australia, 5/23/1946
Graham, Otto Everett (football); Waukegan, Ill., 12/6/1921
Grange, Red (Harold) (football); Forksville, Pa. **(1904–1991)**
Green, Hubert (golf); Birmingham, Ala., 12/28/1946
Greene, Charles E. (sprinter); Pine Bluff, Ark., 3/21/1945
Greene, "Mean" (Joe); (football); Temple, Tex., 9/24/1946
Gretzky, Wayne (hockey); Brantford, Ont., 1/26/1961
Griese, Bob (Robert Allen) (football); Evansville, Ind., 2/3/1945
Groebli, "Mr. Frick" (Werner) (ice skating); Basil, Switzerland, 4/21/1915
Grove, Lefty (Robert Moses) (baseball); Lonaconing, Md., **(1900–1975)**
Groza, Lou (football); Martins Ferry Ohio, 1/25/1924
Guidry, Ronald Ames (baseball); Lafayette, La., 8/28/1950
Gunter, Nancy Richey (tennis); San Angelo, Tex., 8/23/1942
Halas, George (football); Chicago **(1895–1983)**
Hall, Gary (swimming); Fayetteville, N.C., 8/7/1951
Hamill, Dorothy (figure skating); Chicago, 1956(?)
Hamilton, Scott (figure skating); Bowling Green, Ohio, 8/28/1958
Hammond, Kathy (runner); Sacramento, Calif., 11/2/1951
Harris, Franco (football); Ft. Dix, N.J., 3/7/1950
Hartack, William, Jr. (jockey); Colver, Pa., 12/9/1932
Haughton, William (harness racing); Gloversville, N.Y. **(1923–1986)**
Havlicek, John (basketball); Martins Ferry, Ohio, 4/8/1940
Hayes, Elvin (basketball); Rayville, La., 11/17/1945
Hayes, Woody (football); Upper Arlington, Ohio **(1913–1987)**
Haynie, Sandra (golf); Fort Worth, 6/4/1943
Heiden, Eric (speed skating); Madison, Wis., 6/14/1958
Hencken, John (swimming); Culver City, Calif., 5/29/1954
Henderson, Rickey (baseball); Chicago, 12/25/1958
Henie, Sonja (ice skater); Oslo **(1912–1969)**
Herman, Floyd Caves (Babe) (baseball); Buffalo, N.Y. **(1903–1987)**
Hernandez, Keith (baseball); San Francisco, 10/20/1953
Hershiser, Orel (baseball); Buffalo, N.Y., 9/16/1958
Hickcox, Charles (swimming); Phoenix, Ariz., 2/6/1947
Hines, James (sprinter); Dumas, Ark., 9/10/1946
Hodges, Gil (baseball); Princeton, Ind. **(1924–1972)**
Hogan, Ben (golf); Dublin, Tex., 8/13/1912
Holmes, Larry (boxing); Cuthert, Ga., 11/3/1949
Hornsby, Rogers (baseball); Winters, Tex. **(1896–1963)**
Hornung, Paul (football); Louisville, Ky., 12/23/1935
Houk, Ralph (baseball); Lawrence, Kan., 8/9/1919
Howard, Elston (baseball); St. Louis **(1929–1980)**
Howe, Gordon (hockey); Floral, Sask., Canada, 3/31/1928
Howell, Jim Lee (football); Lonoke, Ark., 9/27/1914
Howser, Dick (baseball); Miami, Fla. **(1937–1987)**
Hubbell, Carl (baseball); Carthage, Mo. **(1903–1988)**
Huff, Sam (Robert Lee) (football); Morgantown, W. Va., 10/4/1934
Hull, Bobby (hockey); Point Anne, Ontario, Canada, 1/3/1939
Hunter, "Catfish" (Jim) (baseball); Hertford, N.C., 4/8/1946
Huntley, Joni (track); McMinnville, Ore., 8/4/1956
Hutson, Donald (football); Pine Bluff, Ark., 1/31/1913
Insko, Del (harness racing); Amboy, Minn., 7/10/1931
Irwin, Hale (golf); Joplin, Mo., 6/3/1945
Jackson, Reggie (baseball); Wyncote, Pa., 5/18/1946
Jeffries, James J. (boxing); Carroll, Ohio **(1875–1953)**
Jenkins, Ferguson Arthur (baseball); Chatham, Ontario, Canada, 12/13/1943
Jenner, (W.) Bruce (track); Mt. Kisco, N.Y., 10/28/1949
Jezek, Linda (swimming); Palo Alto, Calif., 3/10/1960
Johnson, "Magic" (Earvin) (basketball); E. Lansing, Mich., 8/14/1959
Johnson, Anthony (rowing); Washington, D.C., 11/16/1940
Johnson, Jack (John Arthur) (boxing); Galveston, Tex. **(1876–1946)**
Johnson, Rafer (decathlon); Hillsboro, Tex., 8/18/1935
Johnson, Wilham Julius (Judy) (baseball); Wilmington, Del. **(1899–1989)**
Jones, Deacon (David) (football); Eatonville, Fla., 12/9/1938
Jordan, Michael (basketball); Brooklyn, N.Y., 2/17/1963
Joyner, Florence Griffith (sprinter); Mojave Desert, Calif., 12/21/1959
Joyner-Kersee, Jackie (track); East St. Louis, Ill., 3/3/1962
Juantoreno, Alberto (track); Santiago, Cuba, 12/3/1951
Jurgensen, Sonny (football); Wilmington, N.C., 8/23/1934
Kaat, Jim (baseball); Zeeland, Mich., 11/7/1938
Kaline, Al (Albert) (baseball); Baltimore, 12/19/1934
Keino, Kipchoge (runner); Kapchemoiymo, Kenya 1/?/1940
Kelly, Leroy (football); Philadelphia, 5/20/1942
Kelly, Red (Leonard Patrick) (hockey); Simcoe, Ontario, Canada, 7/9/1927
Killebrew, Harmon (baseball); Payette, Idaho, 6/29/1936
Killy, Jean-Claude (skiing); Saint-Cloud, France, 8/30/1943
Kilmer, Bill (William Orland) (football); Topeka, Kan., 9/5/1939
King, Bille Jean (Bille Jean Moffitt) (tennis); Long Beach, Calif., 11/22/1943
Kinsella, John (swimming); Oak Park, Ill., 8/26/1952
Kluszeewski, Ted (baseball); Argo, Ill. **(1924–1988)**
Kodes, Jan (tennis); Prague, 3/1/1946
Kolb, Claudia (swimming); Hayward, Calif., 12/19/1949
Koosman, Jerry Martin (baseball); Appleton, Minn., 12/23/1942
Korbut, Olga (gymnast); Grodno, Byelorussia, U.S.S.R., 5/16/1955
Koufax, Sandy (Sanford) (baseball); Brooklyn, N.Y., 12/30/1935
Kramer, Jack (tennis); Las Vegas, Nev., 8/1/1921
Kramer, Jerry (football); Jordan, Mont., 1/23/1936
Kuenn, Harvey (baseball); West Allis, Wis. **(1930–1988)**
Kuhn, Bowie Kent (baseball); Takoma Park, Md., 10/28/1926
Kwalik, Ted (Thaddeus John) (football); McKees Rocks, Pa., 4/15/1947
Lafleur, Guy Damien (hockey); Thurson, Quebec, Canada, 8/20/1951
Laird, Ronald (walker); Louisville, Ky., 5/31/1935
Lamonica, Daryle (football); Fresno, Calif., 7/17/1941
Landis, Kenesaw Mountain (1st baseball commissioner); Millville, Ohio **(1866–1944)**
Landry, Tom (football); Mission, Tex., 9/11/1924
Landy, John (runner); Australia, 4/4/1930
Larrieu, Francie (track); Palo Alto, Calif., 11/28/1952
Lasorda, Tom (baseball); Norristown, Pa., 9/22/1927
Laver, Rod (tennis); Rockhampton, Australia, 8/9/1938
Layne, Bobby (football); Lubbock, Texas **(1927–1986)**
Lemieux, Mario (hockey); Montreal, Quebec, Canada, 10/5/1965
Lendl, Ivan (tennis); Prague, 3/7/1960
Leonard, Benny (Benjamin Leiner) (boxing); New York City **(1896–1947)**
Leonard, Sugar Ray (boxing); Wilmington, N.C., 5/17/1956
Lewis, Carl (track); Willingboro, N.J., 7/1/1961
Linehan, Kim (swimming); Bronxville, N.Y., 12/11/1962

Liquori, Marty (runner); Montclair, N.J., 9/11/1949
Little, Floyd Douglas (football); New Haven, Conn., 7/4/1942
Little, Lou (football); Leominster, Mass., **(1893–1979)**
Littler, Gene (golf); La Jolla, Calif., 7/21/1930
Lombardi, Vince (football); Brooklyn, N.Y. **(1913–1970)**
Longden, Johnny (horse racing); Wakefield, England, 2/14/1907
Lopat, Eddie (baseball); New York, N.Y. **(1918–1992)**
Lopez, Al (baseball); Tampa, Fla., 8/20/1908
Lopez, Nancy (golf); Torrance, Calif., 1/6/1957
Louis, Joe (Joe Louis Barrow) (boxing); Lafayette, Ala. **(1914–1981)**
Lynn, Frederic Michael (baseball); Chicago, Ill., 2/3/1952
Lynn, Janet (figure skating); Rockford, Ill., 4/6/1953
Mack, Connie (Cornelius Alexander McGillicuddy) (baseball executive); East Brookfield, Mass. **(1862–1956)**
Mackey, John (football); New York City, 9/24/1941
Mahovlich, Frank (Francis William) (hockey); Timmins, Ontario, Canada, 1/10/1938
Mahre, Phil (skiiing); White Pass, Wash., 5/10/1957
Malone, Moses (basketball); Petersburg, Va., 3/23/1955
Mandlikova, Hana (tennis); Prague, Czechoslovakia, 2/1962
Mann, Carol (golf); Buffalo, N.Y., 2/3/1941
Manning, Madeline (runner); Cleveland, 1/11/1948
Mantle, Mickey Charles (baseball); Spavinaw, Okla., 10/20/1931
Maravich, "Pistol Pete" (Peter); Aliquippa, Pa. **(1948–1988)**
Marble, Alice (tennis); Palm Springs, Calif. **(1913–1990)**
Marciano, Rocky (boxing); Brockton, Mass. **(1923–1969)**
Marichal, Juan (baseball); Laguna Verde, Montecristi, Dominican Republic, 10/20/1937
Maris, Roger (baseball); Hibbing, Minn. **(1934–1985)**
Martin, Billy (Alfred Manuel) (baseball); Berkeley, Calif. **(1928–1989)**
Martin, Rick (Richard Lionel) (hockey); Verdun, Quebec, Canada, 7/26/1951
Mathews, Ed (Edwin) (baseball); Texarkana, Tex., 10/13/1931
Matson, Randy (shot putter); Kilgore, Tex., 3/5/1945
Mays, Willie (baseball); Westfield, Ala., 5/6/1931
McAdoo, Bob (basketball); Greensboro, N.C., 9/25/1951
McCarthy, Joe (Joseph Vincent) (baseball); Philadelphia **(1887–1978)**
McCovey, Willie Lee (baseball); Mobile, Ala., 1/10/1938
McDonald, Lanny (hockey); Hanna, Alberta, Canada, 2/16/1953
McDowell, Jack (baseball); Van Nuys, Calif., 1/16/1966
McEnroe, John Patrick, Jr. (tennis); Wiesbaden, Germany, 2/16/1959
McGraw, John Joseph (baseball); Truxton, N.Y. **(1873–1934)**
McLain, Dennis (baseball); Chicago, 3/24/1944
McMillan, Kathy Laverne (track); Raeford, N.C., 11/7/1957
Merrill, Janice (track); New London, Conn., 6/18/1962
Meyer, Deborah (swimming); Haddonfield, N.J., 8/14/1952
Middlecoff, Cary (golf); Halls, Tenn., 1/6/1921
Mikita, Stan (hockey); Sokolce, Czechoslovakia, 5/20/1940
Milburn, Rodney, Jr. (hurdler); Opelousas, La., 5/18/1950
Miller, Johnny (golf); San Francisco, 4/29/1947
Montgomery, Jim (swimming); Madison, Wis., 1/24/1955
Moore, Archie (boxing); Benoit, Miss., 12/13/1916
Morgan, Joe Leonard (baseball); Bonham, Tex., 9/19/1943
Morrall, Earl (football); Muskegon, Mich., 5/17/1934
Morton, Craig L. (football); Flint, Mich., 2/5/1943
Mosconi, Wilie (pocket billiards); Philadelphia, 6/27/1913
Moser, Annemarie. *See* Proell, Annemarie.
Moses, Edward Corley (track); Dayton, Ohio, 8/31/1958
Mungo, Van Lingo (baseball); Pageland, S.C. **(1911–1985)**
Munson, Thurman (baseball); Akron, Ohio **(1947–1979)**
Murphy, Calvin (basketball); Norwalk, Conn., 5/9/1948
Musial, Stan (baseball); Donora, Pa., 11/21/1920
Myers, Linda (archery); York, Pa., 6/19/1947
Naber, John (swimming); Evanston, Ill., 1/20/1956
Namath, Joe (Joseph William) (football); Beaver Falls, Pa., 5/31/1943
Nastase, Ilie (tennis); Bucharest, 7/19/1946
Navratilova, Martina (tennis); Prague, 10/18/1956
Nehemiah, Renaldo (track); Newark, N.J., 3/24/1959
Nelson, Cindy (skiing); Lutsen, Minn., 8/19/1955
Newcombe, John (tennis); Sydney, Australia, 5/23/1943
Niekro, Phil (baseball); Lansing, Ohio, 4/1/1939
Nicklaus, Jack (golf); Columbus, Ohio, 1/21/1940
Norman, Gregory (golf); Mount Isa, Australia, 2/10/1955
North, Lowell (yachting); Springfield, Mo., 12/2/1929
Oerter, Al (discus thrower); New York City, 9/19/1936
Okker, Tom (tennis); Amsterdam, 2/22/1944
Oldfield, Barney (racing driver); Fulton County, Ohio **(1878–1946)**
Oliva, Tony (Pedro) (baseball); Pinar Del Rio, Cuba, 7/20/1940
Olsen, Merlin Jay (football); Logan, Utah, 9/15/1940
O'Malley, Walter (baseball executive); New York City **(1903–1979)**
Orantes, Manuel (tennis); Granada, Spain, 2/6/1949
Orr, Bobby (hockey); Parry Sound, Ontario, Canada, 3/20/1948
Ovett, Steve (track); Brighton, England, 10/9/1955
Owens, Jesse (track); Decatur, Ala. **(1914–1980)**
Pace, Darrell (archery); Cincinnati, 10/23/1956
Paige, Satchell (Leroy) (baseball); Mobile, Ala. **(1906–1982)**
Palmer, Arnold (golf); Latrobe, Pa., 9/10/1929
Palmer, James Alvin (baseball); New York City, 10/15/1945
Parent, Bernard Marcel (hockey); Montreal, 4/3/1945
Park, Brad (Douglas Bradford) (hockey); Toronto, Ontario, Canada, 7/6/1948
Parseghian, Ara (football); Akron, Ohio, 5/21/1923
Pasarell, Charles (tennis); San Juan, Puerto Rico, 2/12/1944
Patterson, Floyd (boxing); Waco, N.C., 1/4/1935
Peete, Calvin (golf); Detroit, Mich., 7/18/1943
Pelé (Edson Arantes do Nascimento) (soccer); Tres Coracoes, Brazil, 10/23/1940
Perry, Gaylord (baseball); Williamston, N.C., 9/15/1938
Perry, Jim (baseball); Williamston, N.C., 10/30/1936
Pettit, Bob (basketball); Baton Rouge, La., 12/12/1932
Petty, Richard Lee (auto racing); Randleman, N.C., 7/2/1937
Pincay, Laffit, Jr. (jockey); Panama City, Panama, 12/29/1946
Plager, Barclay (ice hockey); Kirkland Lake, Ontario **(1941–1988)**
Plante, Jacques (hockey); Sahwinigan Falls, Quebec, Canada, 1/17/1929
Player, Gary (golf); Johannesburg, South Africa, 11/1/1935
Plunkett, Jim (football); San Jose, Calif., 12/5/1947
Potvin, Denis Charles (hockey); Hull, Quebec, Canada, 10/29/1953
Powell, Boog (John) (baseball); Lakeland, Fla., 8/17/1941
Powell, Mike (track); Philadelphia, 11/10/1963
Prefontaine, Steve Roland (runner); Coos Bay, Ore. **(1951–1975)**
Prince, Bob (baseball announcer); Pittsburgh **(1917–1985)**
Proell, Annemarie Moser (Alpine skier); Kleinarl, Austria, 3/27/1953
Ralston, Dennis (tennis); Bakersfield, Calif., 7/27/1942
Rankin, Judy Torluemke (golf); St. Louis, Mo., 2/18/1945
Raschi, Vic (baseball); West Springfield, Mass. **(1919–1988)**
Ratelle, Jean (Joseph Gilbert Yvon Jean) (hockey); St. Jean, Quebec, Canada, 10/29/1953
Rawls, Betsy (Elizabeth Earle) (golf); Spartanburg, S.C., 5/4/1928
Reed, Willis (basketball); Hico, La., 6/25/1942
Reese, Pee Wee (Harold) (baseball); Ekron, Ky., 7/23/1919
Resch, Glenn "Chico" (hockey); Moose Jaw, Saskatchewan, Canada, 7/10/1948
Richard, Maurice (hockey); Montreal, 8/14/1924
Riessen, Martin (tennis); Hinsdale, Ill., 12/4/1941
Rigney, William (baseball); Alameda, Calif., 1/29/1918
Rizzuto, Phil (baseball); New York City, 9/25/1918
Roark, Helen Willis Moody (tennis); Centerville, Calif., 10/6/1906
Robertson, Oscar (basketball); Charlotte, Tenn., 11/24/1938
Robinson, Arnie (track); San Diego, Calif., 4/7/1948
Robinson, Brooks (baseball); Little Rock, Ark., 5/18/1937
Robinson, Dave (basketball); Key West, Fla., 8/6/1965
Robinson, Frank (baseball); Beaumont, Tex., 8/31/1935
Robinson, Jackie (baseball); Cairo, Ga. **(1919–1972)**
Robinson, Larry Clark (hockey); Marvelville, Ontario, Canada, 6/2/1951
Robinson, "Sugar" Ray (boxing); Detroit **(1920–1989)**
Rockne, Knute Kenneth (football); Voss, Norway **(1888–1931)**
Rockwell, Martha (skiing); Providence, R.I., 4/26/1944
Rono, Harry (track); Kiptaragon, Kenya, 2/12/1952
Rooney, Art (football); Pittsburgh, Pa. **(1901–1988)**
Rose, Pete (Peter Edward) (baseball); Cincinnati, 4/14/1942
Rosenbloom, Maxie (boxing); New York City **(1904–1976)**
Rosewall, Ken (tennis); Sydney, Australia, 11/2/1934
Rote, Kyle (football); San Antonio, 10/27/1928
Roush, Edd (baseball); Oakland City, Ind. **(1893–1988)**
Rozelle, Pete (Alvin Ray) (commissioner of National Football League); South Gate, Calif., 3/1/1926
Rudolph, Wilma Glodean (sprinter); St. Bethlehem, Tenn., 6/23/1940
Russell, Bill (basketball); Monroe, La., 2/12/1934
Ruth, Babe (George Herman Ruth) (baseball); Baltimore **(1895–1948)**
Rutherford, Johnny (auto racing); Fort Worth, 3/12/1938
Ryan, Nolan (Lynn Nolan, Jr.) (baseball); Refugio, Tex., 1/31/1947
Ryon, Luann (archery); Long Beach, Calif., 1/13/1953
Ryun, Jim (runner); Wichita, Kan., 4/29/1947
Salazar, Alberto (track); Havana, 8/7/1958
Samuels, Howard (horse racing soccer); New York City **(1920–1984)**
Santana, Manuel (Manuel Santana Martinez) (tennis); Chamartin, Spain, 5/10/1938
Sayers, Gale (football); Wichita, Kan., 5/30/1943
Schmidt, Mike (baseball); Dayton, Ohio, 9/27/1949

Shoendienst, Al (Albert) (baseball); Germantown, Ill., 2/2/1923
Schollander, Donald (swimming); Charlotte, N.C., 4/30/1946
Seagren, Bob (Robert Lloyd) (pole vaulter); Pomona, Calif., 10/17/1946
Seaver, Tom (baseball); Fresno, Calif., 11/17/1944
Seidler, Maren (track); Brooklyn, N.Y., 6/11/1962
Selke, Frank (ice hockey); Canada **(1893–1985)**
Sewell, Joe (baseball); Titus, Ala., **(1898–1990)**
Shepherd, Lee (auto racing) **(1945–1985)**
Shero, Fred (hockey); Camden, N.J. **(1945–1990)**
Shoemaker, Willie (jockey); Fabens, Tex., 8/19/1931
Shore, Eddie (ice hockey); Saskatchewan, Canada **(1902–1985)**
Shorter, Frank (runner); Munich, Germany, 10/31/1947
Shriver, Pam (tennis); Baltimore, 7/4/1962
Shula, Don (Donald Francis) (football); Grand River, Ohio, 1/4/1930
Silvester, Jay (discus thrower); Tremonton, Utah, 2/27/1937
Simpson, O.J. (Orenthal James) (football); San Francisco, 7/9/1947
Sims, Billy (football); St. Louis, 9/18/1955
Smith, Bubba (Charles Aaron) (football); Orange, Tex., 2/28/1945
Smith, Ronnie Ray (sprinter); Los Angeles, 3/28/1949
Smith, Stanley Roger (tennis); Pasadena, Calif., 12/14/1946
Smith, Tommie (sprinter); Clarksville, Tex., 6/5/1944
Smoke, Marcia Jones (canoeing); Oklahoma City, 7/18/1941
Snead, Sam (golf); Hot Springs, Va., 5/27/1912
Sneva, Tom (auto racing); Spokane, Wash., 6/1/1948
Snider, Duke (Edwin) (baseball); Los Angeles, 9/19/1926
Solomon, Harold (tennis); Washington, D.C., 9/17/1952
Spahn, Warren (baseball); Buffalo, N.Y., 4/23/1921
Speaker, Tristram (baseball); Hubbard City, Tex. **(1888–1958)**
Spencer, Brian (ice hockey); Fort St. James, British Columbia **(1949–1988)**
Spinks, Leon (boxing); St. Louis, 7/11/1953
Spitz, Mark (swimming); Modesto, Calif., 2/10/1950
Stabler, Kenneth (football); Foley, Ala., 12/25/1945
Stagg, Amos Alonzo (football); West Orange, N.J. **(1862–1965)**
Stargell, Willie (Wilver Dornell) (baseball); Earlsboro, Okla., 3/6/1941
Starr, Bart (football); Montgomery, Ala., 1/9/1934
Staub, "Rusty" (Daniel) (baseball); New Orleans, 4/4/1944
Staubach, Roger (football); Cincinnati, 2/5/1942
Steinkraus, William C. (equestrian); Cleveland, 10/12/1925
Stenerud, Jan (football); Fetsund, Norway, 11/26/1942
Stengel, Casey (Charles Dillon) (baseball); Kansas City, Mo. **(1891–1975)**
Stenmark, Ingemar (Alpine skier); Tarnaby, Sweden, 3/18/1956
Stockton, Richard LaClede (tennis); New York City, 2/18/1951
Stones, Dwight Edwin (track); Los Angeles, 12/6/1953
Strawberry, Darryl (baseball); Los Angeles, 3/12/1962
Sullivan, John Lawrence (boxing); Boston **(1858–1918)**
Sutton, Don (Donald Howard) (baseball); Clio, Ala., 4/2/1945
Swann, Lynn (football); Alcoa, Tenn., 3/7/1952
Tanner, Leonard Roscoe III (tennis); Chattanooga, Tenn., 10/15/1951
Tarkenton, Fran (Francis) (football); Richmond, Va., 2/3/1940
Tebbetts, Birdie (George R.) (baseball); Nashua, N.H., 11/10/1914
Theismann, Joe (football); New Brunswick, N.J., 9/9/1946
Thoeni, Gustavo (Alpine skier); Trafoi, Italy, 2/28/1951
Thomas, Isiah (basketball); Chicago, Ill., 4/30/1961
Thompson, David (basketball); Shelby, N.C., 7/13/1954
Thorpe, Jim (James Francis) (all-around athlete); nr. Prague, Okla. **(1888–1953)**
Tilden, William Tatem II (tennis); Philadelphia **(1893–1953)**
Tittle, Y. A. (Yelberton Abraham) (football); Marshall, Tex., 10/24/1926
Toomey, William (decathlon); Philadelphia, 1/10/1939
Trevino, Lee (golf); Dallas, 12/1/1939
Trottier, Bryan (hockey); Val Marie, Sask., Canada, 7/17/1956
Tunney, Gene (James J.) (boxing); New York City **(1898–1978)**
Tyus, Wyomia (runner); Griffin, Ga., 8/29/1945
Ueberroth, Peter (baseball); Evanston, Ill., 9/2/1937
Unitas, John (football); Pittsburgh, 5/7/1933
Unser, Al (auto racing); Albuquerque, N. Mex., 5/29/1939
Unser, Bobby (auto racing); Albuquerque, N. Mex., 2/20/1934
Valenzuela, Fernando (baseball); Sonora, Mexico, 11/1/1960
Van Brocklin, Norm (football); Eagle Butte, S. Dak. **(1926–1983)**
Vilas, Guillermo (tennis); Mar del Plata, Argentina, 8/17/1952
Viola, Frank (baseball); Hempstead, N.Y., 4/19/1960
Viren, Lasse (track); Myrskyla, Finland, 7/12/1949
Wade, Virginia (tennis); Bournemouth, England, 7/10/1945
Wagner, Honus (John Peter Honus) (baseball); Carnegie, Pa. **(1867–1955)**
Waitz, Grete (Andersen) (running); Oslo, Norway, 10/1/1953
Wakefield, Dick (baseball); Chicago **(1921–1985)**
Walcott, Jersey Joe (Arnold Cream) (boxing); Merchantville, N.J., 1/31/1914
Walsh, Adam (football) **(1902–1985)**
Walton, Bill (basketball); La Mesa, Calif., 11/5/1952
Waterfield, Bob (football); Burbank, Calif **(1921–1983)**
Watson, Martha Rae (track); Long Beach, Calif., 8/19/1946
Watson, Tom (golf); Kansas City, Mo., 9/4/1949
Weaver, Earl (baseball); St. Louis, 8/14/1930
Webster, Alex (football); Kearny, N.J., 4/19/1931
Weiskopf, Tom (golf); Massillon, Ohio, 11/9/1942
Weiss, George (baseball executive); New Haven, Conn. **(1895–1972)**
Weissmuller, Johnny (swimmer and actor); Windber, Pa. **(1904–1984)**
Weld, Philip (sailing); Cambridge, Mass. **(1915–1984)**
West, Jerry (basketball); Cheylan, W. Va., 5/28/1938
White, Willye B. (long jumper); Money, Miss., 1/1/1936
Whitworth, Kathy (golf); Monahans, Tex., 9/27/1939
Widing, Juha (ice hockey); Vancouver, Canada **(1948–1985)**
Wilkens, Mac Maurice (track); Eugene, Ore., 11/15/1950
Wilkins, Lennie (basketball); 11/25/1937
Wilkinson, Bud (football); Minneapolis, 4/23/1916
Williams, Del (football); New Orleans **(1945–1984)**
Williams, Dick (baseball); St. Louis, 5/7/1929
Williams, Ted (baseball); San Diego, Calif., 8/30/1918
Wills, Maury (baseball); Washington, D.C., 10/2/1932
Winfield, Dave (baseball); St. Paul, Minn., 10/3/1951
Wohlhuter, Richard C. (runner); Geneva, Ill., 12/23/1945
Wood, "Smokey" (Joseph) (baseball); Kansas City, Mo. **(1890–1985)**
Woodhead, Cynthia (swimming); Riverside, Calif., 2/7/1964
Wottle, David James (runner); Canton, Ohio, 8/7/1950
Wright, Mickey (Mary Kathryn) (golf); San Diego, Calif., 2/14/1935
Yarborough, Cale (William Caleb) (auto racing); Timmonsville, S.C., 3/27/1939
Yarbrough, Leeroy (auto racing); Jacksonville, Fla. **(1938–1984)**
Yastrzemski, Carl (baseball); Southampton, N.Y., 8/22/1939
Young, Cy (Denton True) (baseball); Gilmore, Ohio **(1867–1955)**
Young, Shelia (speed skater, bicycle racer); Detroit, 10/14/1950
Zaharias, Babe Didrikson (golf); Port Arthur, Tex. **(1913–1956)**

Yachting

The word "yacht" is of Dutch origin and the first "yacht race" of record in the English language was a sailing contest from Greenwich to Gravesend and return in 1662 between a Dutch yacht and an English yacht designed and, at some part of the race, sailed by Charles II of England. The royal yacht won the contest.

The first yacht club was organized at Cork, Ireland, in 1720 under the name of the Cork Harbour Water Club, later changed to the Royal Cork Yacht Club. The Royal Yacht Squadron was organized at Cowes in 1812 and the name changed to the Royal Yacht Club in 1820. The New York Yacht Club was organized aboard the Stevens schooner "Gimcrack" on July 30, 1844, and a clubhouse erected at Elysian Fields, Hoboken, N.J., the following year.

International yacht racing was launched in 1851 when England's Royal Yacht Squadron staged a 60-mile regatta around the Isle of Wight and offered a silver trophy to the winner. The 101-foot schooner *America*, sent over by the New York Yacht Club, won the race and the prize. Originally called the Hundred-Guinea Cup, the trophy was renamed The America's Cup after the winning boat's owners deeded it to the NYYC with instructions to defend it whenever challenged.

From 1870–1980, the NYYC successfully defended the Cup 25 straight times; first in large schooners and J-class boats that measured up to 140 feet in overall length, then in 12-meter boats.

HOCKEY

Ice hockey, by birth and upbringing a Canadian game, is an offshoot of field hockey. Some historians say that the first ice hockey game was played in Montreal in December 1879 between two teams composed almost exclusively of McGill University students, but others assert that earlier hockey games took place in Kingston, Ontario, or Halifax, Nova Scotia. In the Montreal game of 1879, there were fifteen players on a side, who used an assortment of crude sticks to keep the puck in motion. Early rules allowed nine men on a side, but the number was reduced to seven in 1886 and later to six.

The first governing body of the sport was the Amateur Hockey Association of Canada, organized in 1887. In the winter of 1894–95, a group of college students from the United States visited Canada and saw hockey played. They became enthused over the game and introduced it as a winter sport when they returned home. The first professional league was the International Hockey League, which operated in northern Michigan in 1904–06.

Until 1910, professionals and amateurs were allowed to play together on "mixed teams," but this arrangement ended with the formation of the first "big league," the National Hockey Association, in eastern Canada in 1910. The Pacific Coast League was organized in 1911 for western Canadian hockey. The league included Seattle and later other American cities. The National Hockey League replaced the National Hockey Association in 1917. Boston, in 1924, was the first American city to join that circuit. The league expanded to include western cities in 1967. The Stanley Cup was competed for by "mixed teams" from 1894 to 1910, thereafter by professionals. It was awarded to the winner of the N.H.L. playoffs from 1926–67 and now to the league champion. The World Hockey Association was organized in October 1972 and was dissolved after the 1978–79 season when the N.H.L. absorbed four of the teams.

The National Hockey League Players Association staged a 10-day strike near the end of the 1991–92 season, the first strike in the league's 75-year history.

The agreement which settled the strike extended the regular season from 80 to 84 games beginning with the 1992–93 season, with owners and players sharing revenues from the final two games on a partnership basis.

The agreement also increased the players' playoff fund from $7.5 million to $9 million and the minimum salary to $100,000.

In addition, free agency for the players was made less restrictive and owners' contributions to the pension fund increased.

Shortly after the 1992 Stanley Cup playoffs concluded, John Ziegler, president of the NHL since 1977, resigned under pressure from the league's owners. Gil Stein was named as interim president and a search begun to name the league's first commissioner.

The search ended in 1993 when Gary Bettman was named to the position. Bettman served as an assistant to National Basketball Association Commissioner David Stern for 12 years.

STANLEY CUP WINNERS

Emblematic of World Professional Championship; N.H.L. Championship after 1967

1894	Montreal A.A.A.	1924	Montreal Canadiens	1953	Montreal Canadiens
1895	Montreal Victorias	1925	Victoria Cougars	1954–55	Detroit Red Wings
1896	Winnipeg Victorias	1926	Montreal Maroons	1956–60	Montreal Canadiens
1897–99	Montreal Victorias	1927	Ottawa Senators	1961	Chicago Black Hawks
1900	Montreal Shamrocks	1928	N.Y. Rangers	1962–64	Toronto Maple Leafs
1901	Winnipeg Victorias	1929	Boston Bruins	1965–66	Montreal Canadiens
1902	Montreal A.A.A.	1930–31	Montreal Candiens	1967	Toronto Maple Leafs
1903–05	Ottawa Silver Seven	1932	Toronto Maple Leafs	1968–69	Montreal Canadiens
1906	Montreal Wanderers	1933	N.Y. Rangers	1970	Boston Bruins
1907	Kenora Thistles[1]	1934	Chicago Black Hawks	1971	Montreal Canadiens
1907	Mont. Wanderers[2]	1935	Montreal Maroons	1972	Boston Bruins
1908	Montreal Wanderers	1936–37	Detroit Red Wings	1973	Montreal Canadiens
1909	Ottawa Senators	1938	Chicago Black Hawks	1974–75	Philadelphia Flyers
1910	Montreal Wanderers	1939	Boston Bruins	1976–79	Montreal Canadiens
1911	Ottawa Senators	1940	N.Y. Rangers	1980–83	New York Islanders
1912–13	Quebec Bulldogs	1941	Boston Bruins	1984	Edmonton Oilers
1914	Toronto	1942	Toronto Maple Leafs	1985	Edmonton Oilers
1915	Vancouver Millionaries	1943	Detroit Red Wings	1986	Montreal Canadiens
1916	Montreal Canadiens	1944	Montreal Canadiens	1987	Edmonton Oilers
1917	Seattle Metropolitans	1945	Toronto Maple Leafs	1988	Edmonton Oilers
1918	Toronto Arenas	1946	Montreal Canadiens	1989	Calgary Flames
1919	No champion	1947–49	Toronto Maple Leafs	1990	Edmonton Oilers
1920–21	Ottawa Senators	1950	Detroit Red Wings	1991	Pittsburgh Penguins
1922	Toronto St. Patricks	1951	Toronto Maple Leafs	1992	Pittsburgh Penguins
1923	Ottawa Senators	1952	Detroit Red Wings	1993	Montreal Canadiens

1. January. 2. March.

M.J. O'Brien Trophy

Donated by Canadian mining magnate M.J. O'Brien, whose son Ambrose founded the National Hockey Assn. in 1910. Originally presented to the NHA champion until the league's demise in 1917, the trophy then passed to the NHL champion through 1927. It was awarded to the NHL's Canadian Division winner from 1927–38 and the Stanley Cup runner-up from 1939–50 before being retired in 1950.

NHA winners included the Montreal Wanderers (1910), Ottawa Senators (1911 and '15), Quebec Bulldogs (1912 and '13), Toronto Blueshirts (1914) and Montreal Canadiens (1916 and '17).

NATIONAL HOCKEY LEAGUE YEARLY TROPHY WINNERS

The Hart Trophy—Most Valuable Player

1924 Frank Nighbor, Ottawa
1925 Billy Burch, Hamilton
1926 Nels Stewart, Montreal Maroons
1927 Herb Gardiner, Montreal Canadiens
1928 Howie Morenz, Montreal Canadiens
1929 Roy Worters, N.Y. Americans
1930 Nels Stewart, Montreal Maroons
1931–32 Howie Morenz, Montreal Canadiens
1933 Eddie Shore, Boston
1934 Aurel Joliat, Montreal Canadiens
1935–36 Eddie Shore, Boston
1937 Babe Siebert, Montreal Canadiens
1938 Eddie Shore, Boston
1939 Toe Blake, Montreal Canadiens
1940 Eddie Goodfellow, Detroit
1941 Bill Cowley, Boston
1942 Tom Anderson, N.Y. Americans
1943 Bill Cowley, Boston
1944 Babe Pratt, Toronto
1945 Elmer Lach, Montreal Canadiens
1946 Max Bentley, Chicago
1947 Maurice Richard, Montreal Canadiens
1948 Buddy O'Connor, N.Y. Rangers
1949 Sid Abel, Detroit
1950 Chuck Rayner, N.Y. Rangers
1951 Milt Schmidt, Boston
1952–53 Gordon Howe, Detroit
1954 Al Rollins, Chicago
1955 Ted Kennedy, Toronto
1956 Jean Belveau, Montreal Canadiens
1957–58 Gordon Howe, Detroit
1959 Andy Bathgate, N.Y. Rangers
1960 Gordon Howe, Detroit
1961 Bernie Geoffrion, Montreal Canadiens
1962 Jacques Plante, Montreal Canadiens
1963 Gordon Howe, Detroit
1964 Jean Beliveau, Montreal Canadiens
1965–66 Bobby Hull, Chicago
1967–68 Stan Mikita, Chicago
1969 Phil Esposito, Boston
1970–72 Bobby Orr, Boston
1973 Bobby Clarke, Philadelphia
1974 Phil Esposito, Boston
1975–76 Bobby Clarke, Philadelphia
1977–78 Guy Lafleur, Montreal
1979 Bryan Trottier, N.Y. Islanders
1980 Wayne Gretzky, Edmonton
1981 Wayne Gretzky, Edmonton
1982 Wayne Gretzky, Edmonton
1983 Wayne Gretzky, Edmonton
1984 Wayne Gretzky, Edmonton
1985 Wayne Gretzky, Edmonton
1986 Wayne Gretzky, Edmonton
1987 Wayne Gretzky, Edmonton
1988 Mario Lemieux, Pittsburgh
1989 Wayne Gretzky, Los Angeles
1990 Mark Messier, Edmonton
1991 Brett Hull, St. Louis
1992 Mark Messier, N.Y. Rangers
1993 Mario Lemieux, Pittsburgh

Vezina Trophy—Leading Goalkeeper

1956–60 Jacques Plante, Montreal
1961 Johnny Bower, Toronto
1962 Jacques Plante, Montreal
1963 Glenn Hall, Chicago
1964 Charlie Hodge, Montreal
1965 Terry Sawchuk—Johnny Bower, Toronto
1966 Lorne Worsley—Charlie Hodge, Montreal
1967 Glen Hall—Denis DeJordy, Chicago
1968 Lorne Worsley—Rogatien Vachon, Montreal
1969 Glen Hall—Jacques Plante, St. Louis
1970 Tony Esposito, Chicago
1971 Ed Giacomin—Gilles Villemure, New York
1972 Tony Esposito—Gary Smith, Chicago
1973 Ken Dryden, Montreal
1974 Bernie Parent, Philadelphia and Tony Esposito, Chicago
1975 Bernie Parent, Philadelphia
1976 Ken Dryden, Montreal
1977–79 Ken Dryden—Michel Larocque, Montreal
1980 Bob Sauve—Don Edwards, Buffalo
1981 Richard Sevigny, Denis Herron and Michel Larocque, Montreal
1982 Billy Smith, New York Islanders
1983 Pete Peeters, Boston
1984 Tom Barrasso, Buffalo
1985 Pelle Lindbergh, Philadelphia
1986 John Vanbiesbrouck, New York Rangers
1987 Ron Hextall, Philadelphia
1988 Grant Fuhr, Edmonton
1989 Patrick Roy, Montreal
1990 Patrick Roy, Montreal
1991 Ed Belfour, Chicago
1992 Patrick Roy, Montreal
1993 Ed Belfour, Chicago

James Norris Trophy—Defenseman

1954 Red Kelly, Detroit
1955–58 Doug Harvey, Montreal
1959 Tom Johnson, Montreal
1960–62 Doug Harvey, Montreal; New York (62)
1963–65 Pierre Pilote, Chicago
1966 Jacques Laperriere, Montreal
1967 Harry Howell, New York
1968–75 Bobby Orr, Boston
1976 Denis Potvin, N.Y. Islanders
1977 Larry Robinson, Montreal
1978–79 Denis Potvin, N.Y. Islanders
1980 Larry Robinson, Montreal
1981 Randy Carlyle, Pittsburgh
1982 Doug Wilson, Chicago
1983–84 Rod Langway, Washington
1985 Paul Coffey, Edmonton
1986 Paul Coffey, Edmonton
1987 Ray Bourque, Boston
1988 Ray Bourque, Boston
1989 Chris Chelios, Montreal
1990 Ray Bourque, Boston
1991 Ray Bourque, Boston
1992 Brian Leetch, N.Y. Rangers
1993 Chris Chelios, Chicago

Lady Byng Trophy—Sportsmanship

1960 Don McKenney, Boston
1961 Red Kelly, Detroit
1962–63 Dave Keon, Toronto
1964 Ken Wharram, Chicago
1965 Bobby Hull, Chicago
1966 Alex Delvecchio, Detroit
1967–68 Stan Mikita, Chicago
1969 Alex Delvecchio, Detroit
1970 Phil Goyette, St. Louis
1971 John Bucyk, Boston
1972 Jean Ratelle, New York
1973 Gil Perrault, Buffalo
1974 John Bucyk, Boston
1975 Marcel Dionne, Detroit
1976 Jean Ratelle, N.Y. Rangers–Boston
1977 Marcel Dionne, Los Angeles
1978 Butch Goring, Los Angeles
1979 Bob MacMillan, Atlanta
1980 Wayne Gretzky, Edmonton
1981 Rick Kehoe, Pittsburgh
1982 Rick Middleton, Boston
1983–84 Mike Bossy, N.Y. Islanders
1985 Jari Kurri, Edmonton
1986 Mike Bossy, N.Y. Islanders
1987 Joe Mullen, Calgary
1988 Mats Naslund, Montreal
1989 Joe Mullen, Calgary
1990 Brett Hull, St. Louis
1991 Wayne Gretzky, Los Angeles
1992 Wayne Gretzky, Los Angeles
1993 Pierre Turgeon, N.Y. Islanders

Calder Trophy—Rookie

1962 Bobby Rousseau, Montreal
1963 Kent Douglas, Toronto
1964 Jacques Laperriere, Montreal
1965 Roger Crozier, Detroit
1966 Brit Selby, Toronto
1967 Bobby Orr, Boston
1968 Derek Sanderson, Boston
1969 Danny Grant, Minnesota
1970 Tony Esposito, Chicago
1971 Gilbert Perrault, Buffalo
1972 Ken Dryden, Montreal
1973 Steve Vickers, New York Rangers
1974 Denis Potvin, N.Y. Islanders
1975 Eric Vail, Atlanta
1976 Bryan Trottier, N.Y. Islanders

1977	Willi Plett, Atlanta
1978	Mike Bossy, N.Y. Islanders
1979	Bobby Smith, Minnesota
1980	Ray Bourque, Boston
1981	Peter Stastny, Quebec
1982	Dale Hawerchuk, Winnipeg
1983	Steve Larmer, Chicago
1984	Tom Barrasso, Buffalo
1985	Mario Lemieux, Pittsburgh
1986	Gary Suter, Calgary
1987	Luc Robitaille, Los Angeles
1988	Joe Niewendyk, Calgary
1989	Brian Leetch, N.Y. Rangers
1990	Sergei Makarov, Calgary
1991	Ed Belfour, Chicago
1992	Pavel Bure, Vancouver
1993	Teemu Selanne, Winnipeg

Art Ross Trophy—Leading scorer

1955	Bernie Geoffrion, Montreal
1956	Jean Beliveau, Montreal
1957	Gordie Howe, Detroit
1958–59	Dickie Moore, Montreal
1960	Bobby Hull, Chicago
1961	Bernie Geoffrion, Montreal
1962	Bobby Hull, Chicago
1963	Gordie Howe, Detroit
1964–65	Stan Mikita, Chicago
1966	Bobby Hull, Chicago
1967–68	Stan Mikita, Chicago
1969	Phil Esposito, Boston
1970	Bobby Orr, Boston
1971–74	Phil Esposito, Boston
1975	Bobby Orr, Boston
1976–78	Guy Lafleur, Montreal
1979	Bryan Trottier, N.Y. Islanders
1980	Marcel Dionne, Los Angeles
1981–87	Wayne Gretzky, Edmonton
1988	Mario Lemieux, Pittsburgh
1989	Mario Lemieux, Pittsburgh
1990	Wayne Gretzky, Los Angeles
1991	Wayne Gretzky, Los Angeles
1992	Mario Lemieux, Pittsburgh
1993	Mario Lemieux, Pittsburgh

N.H.L. CHAMPIONS

Wales Trophy

1939	Boston
1940	Boston
1941	Boston
1942	New York
1943	Detroit
1944–47	Montreal
1948	Toronto
1948–55	Detroit
1956	Montreal
1957	Detroit
1958–62	Montreal
1963	Toronto
1964	Montreal
1965	Detroit
1966	Montreal
1967	Chicago

Eastern Division

1968–69	Montreal
1970	Chicago
1971	Boston
1972	Boston
1973	Montreal
1974	Boston

Wales Conference

1975	Buffalo
1976–79	Montreal
1980	Buffalo
1981	Montreal
1982	New York Islanders
1983	New York Islanders
1984	New York Islanders
1985	Philadelphia
1986	Montreal
1987	Philadelphia
1988	Boston
1989	Montreal
1990	Boston
1991	Pittsburgh
1992	Pittsburgh
1993	Montreal

CAMPBELL BOWL

Western Division

1968	Philadelphia
1969	St. Louis
1970	St. Louis
1971–73	Chicago
1974	Philadelphia

Campbell Conference

1975	Philadelphia
1976–77	Philadelphia
1978–79	N.Y. Islanders
1980	Philadelphia
1981	New York Islanders
1982	Edmonton
1983	Edmonton
1984	Edmonton
1985	Edmonton
1986	Calgary
1987	Edmonton
1988	Edmonton
1989	Calgary
1990	Edmonton
1991	Minnesota
1992	Chicago
1993	Los Angeles

Stanley Cup Playoffs—1993

DIVISION SEMIFINALS

Patrick Division

New York Islanders defeated Washington Capitals, 4 games to 2

Pittsburgh Penguins defeated New Jersey Devils, 4 games to 1

Adams Division

Buffalo Sabres defeated Boston Bruins, 4 games to 0

Montreal Canadiens defeated Quebec Nordiques, 4 games to 2

Norris Division

St. Louis Blues defeated Chicago Black Hawks, 4 games to 0

Toronto Maple Leafs defeated Detroit Red Wings, 4 games to 3

Smythe Division

Vancouver Canucks defeated Winnipeg Jets, 4 games to 2

Los Angeles Kings defeated Calgary Flames, 4 games to 2

DIVISION FINALS

Patrick Division

New York Islanders defeated Pittsburgh Penguins, 4 games to 3

Adams Division

Montreal Canadiens defeated Buffalo Sabres, 4 games to 0

Norris Division

Toronto Maple Leafs defeated St. Louis Blues, 4 games to 3

Smythe Division

Los Angeles Kings defeated Vancouver Canucks, 4 games to 2

NOTE: Home teams are in capitals.

CONFERENCE FINALS (League Semifinals)

Prince of Wales Conference

Montreal Canadiens defeated New Islanders, 4 games to 1

May 16—MONTREAL 4, N.Y. Islanders 1
May 18—MONTREAL 4, N.Y. Islanders 3 (2 OT)
May 20—Montreal 2, N.Y. ISLANDERS 1 (OT)
May 22—N.Y. ISLANDERS 4, Montreal 1
May 24—MONTREAL 5, N.Y. Islanders 2

Clarence Campbell Conference

Los Angeles Kings defeated Toronto Maple Leafs, 4 games to 3

May 17—TORONTO 4, Los Angeles 1
May 19—Los Angeles 3, TORONTO 2
May 21—LOS ANGELES 4, Toronto 2
May 23—Toronto 4, LOS ANGELES 2
May 25—TORONTO 3, Los Angeles 2 (OT)
May 27—LOS ANGELES 5, Toronto 4 (OT)
May 29—Los Angeles 5, TORONTO 4

STANLEY CUP CHAMPIONSHIP FINALS

Montreal Canadiens defeated Los Angeles Kings, 4 games to 1

June 1—Los Angeles 4, MONTREAL 1
June 3—MONTREAL 3, Los Angeles 2 (OT)
June 5—Montreal 4, LOS ANGELES 3 (OT)
June 7—Montreal 3, LOS ANGELES 2 (OT)
June 9—MONTREAL 4, Los Angeles 1

NATIONAL HOCKEY LEAGUE
FINAL STANDINGS OF THE CLUBS—1992–93

PRINCE OF WALES CONFERENCE

Patrick Division

	W	L	T	Pts	GF	GA
x–Pittsburgh Penguins	56	21	7	119	367	268
x–Washington Capitals	43	34	7	93	325	286
x–New York Islanders	40	37	7	87	335	297
x–New Jersey Devils	40	37	7	87	308	299
Philadelphia Flyers	36	37	11	83	319	319
New York Rangers	34	39	11	79	304	308

Adams Division

	W	L	T	Pts	GF	GA
x–Boston Bruins	51	26	7	109	332	268
x–Quebec Nordiques	47	27	10	104	351	300
x–Montreal Canadiens	48	30	6	102	326	280
x–Buffalo Sabres	38	36	10	86	335	297
Hartford Whalers	26	52	6	58	284	369
Ottawa Senators	10	70	4	24	202	395

CLARENCE CAMPBELL CONFERENCE

Norris Division

	W	L	T	Pts	GF	GA
x–Chicago Black Hawks	47	25	12	106	279	230
x–Detroit Red Wings	47	28	9	103	369	280
x–Toronto Maple Leafs	44	29	11	99	288	241
x–St. Louis Blues	37	36	11	85	282	278
Minnesota North Stars	36	38	10	82	272	293
Tampa Bay Lightning	23	54	7	53	245	332

Smythe Division

	W	L	T	Pts	GF	GA
x–Vancouver Canucks	46	29	9	101	346	278
x–Calgary Flames	43	30	11	97	322	282
x–Los Angeles Kings	39	35	10	88	338	340
x–Winnipeg Jets	40	37	7	87	322	320
Edmonton Oilers	26	50	8	60	242	337
San Jose Sharks	11	71	2	24	218	414

x—Secured playoff berth.

N.H.L. LEADING GOALTENDERS—1992–93

(Minimum 1,300 minutes played)

	GP	Mins	GA	Avg
Felix Potvin, Toronto	48	2781	116	2.50
Ed Belfour, Chicago	71	4106	177	2.59
Tom Barrasso, Pittsburgh	63	3702	186	3.01
Curtis Joseph, St. Louis	68	3890	196	3.02
Kay Whitmore, Vancouver	31	1817	94	3.10

OTHER N.H.L. AWARDS—1993

Frank Selke Trophy (top defensive forward)—Doug Gilmour, Toronto

King Clancy Award (Humanitarian)—Dave Poulin, Boston

Jack Adam Trophy (Coach of the Year)—Pat Burns, Toronto

Bill Masterson Trophy (Sportsmanship)—Mario Lemieux, Pittsburgh

N.H.L. LEADING SCORERS—1992–93

	Team	GP	G
Alexander Mogilny	Buffalo	77	76
Teemu Selanne	Winnipeg	84	76
Mario Lemieux	Pittsburgh	60	69
Luc Robitaille	Los Angeles	84	63
Pavel Bure	Vancouver	83	60
Pierre Turgeon	N.Y. Islanders	83	58
Steve Yzerman	Detroit	84	58
Kevin Stevens	Pittsburgh	72	55
Brett Hull	St. Louis	80	54
Dave Andreychuk	Buffalo/Toronto	83	54
Pat LaFontaine	Buffalo	84	53
Mark Recchi	Philadelphia	84	53
Brendan Shanahan	St. Louis	71	51
Jeremy Roenick	Chicago	84	50
Joe Sakic	Quebec	78	48

N.H.L. CAREER SCORING LEADERS

(Through 1992–93 season)

	Yrs	Games	G	A	Pts
Wayne Gretzky[1]	14	1,044	764	1,563	2,328
Gordie Howe	26	1,767	801	1,049	1,850
Marcel Dionne	18	1,348	731	1,040	1,771
Phil Esposito	18	1,282	717	873	1,590
Stan Mikita	22	1,394	541	926	1,467
Brian Trottier[1]	17	1,238	520	890	1,410
John Bucyk	23	1,540	556	813	1,369
Guy Lafleur	17	1,126	560	793	1,363
Gilbert Perreault	17	1,191	512	814	1,326
Alex Delvecchio	24	1,549	456	825	1,281
Jean Ratelle	21	1,281	491	776	1,267
Mark Messier[1]	14	1,005	452	780	1,232
Norm Ullman	20	1,410	490	739	1,229
Peter Stasny[1]	13	954	444	777	1,221
Jean Beliveau	20	1,125	507	712	1,219
Dale Hawerchuk[1]	12	951	449	763	1,212
Bobby Clarke	15	1,144	358	852	1,210
Paul Coffey[1]	13	953	330	871	1,201
Denis Savard[1]	13	946	423	769	1,192
Jari Kurri[1]	12	909	524	666	1,190
Bobby Hull	16	1,063	610	560	1,170
Bernie Federko	14	1,000	389	761	1,130
Mike Bossy	10	752	573	553	1,126
Darryl Sittler	15	1,096	484	637	1,121
Frank Mahovlich	18	1,181	533	570	1,103

1. Still active in the N.H.L.

Defunct NHL Teams

Teams that once played in the NHL, but no longer exist.

Brooklyn—Americans (1941–42, formerly N.Y. Americans from 1925–41); **Cleveland**—Barons (1976–78; originally California–Oakland Seals from 1967–76); **Hamilton (Ont.)**—Tigers (1920–25, originally Quebec Bulldogs from 1919–20); **Montreal**—Maroons (1924–38) and Wanderers (1917–18); **New York**—Americans (1925–42, later Brooklyn Americans for 1941–42); **Oakland**—Seals (1967–76, also known as California Seals and Golden Seals and later Cleveland Barons from 1976–78); **Ottawa**—Senators (1917–31 and 1932–34, later St. Louis Eagles for 1934–35); **Philadelphia**—Quakers (1930–31, originally Pittsburgh Pirates from 1925–30); **Pittsburgh**—Pirates (1925–30; later Philadelphia Quakers for 1930–31); **Quebec**—Bulldogs (1919–20, later Hamilton Tigers from 1920–25); **St. Louis**—Eagles (1934–35), originally Ottawa Senators (1917–31 and 1932–34).

BOWLING

The game of bowling in the United States is an indoor development of the more ancient outdoor game that survives as lawn bowling. The outdoor game is prehistoric in origin and probably goes back to Primitive Man and round stones that were rolled at some target. It is believed that a game something like nine-pins was popular among the Dutch, Swiss and Germans as long ago as A.D. 1200 at which time the game was played outdoors with an alley consisting of a single plank 12 to 18 inches wide along which was rolled a ball toward three rows of three pins each placed at the far end of the alley. When the first indoor alleys were built and how the game was modified from time to time are matters of dispute.

It is supposed that the early settlers of New Amsterdam (New York City) being Dutch, they brought their two bowling games with them. About a century ago the game of nine-pins was flourishing in the United States but so corrupted by gambling on matches that it was barred by law in New York and Connecticut. Since the law specifically barred "nine-pins," it was eventually evaded by adding another pin and thus legally making it a new game.

Various organizations were formed to make rules for bowling and supervise competition in the United States but none was successful until the American Bowling Congress, organized Sept. 9, 1895, became the ruling body.

AMERICAN BOWLING CONGRESS CHAMPIONS

Year	Singles	All-events
1959	Ed Lubanski	Ed Lubanski
1960	Paul Kulbaga	Vince Lucci
1961	Lyle Spooner	Luke Karen
1962	Andy Renaldo	Billy Young
1963	Fred Delello	Bus Owalt
1964	Jim Stefanich	Les Zikes, Jr.
1965	Ken Roeth	Tom Hathaway
1966	Don Chapman	John Wilcox
1967	Frank Perry	Gary Lewis
1968	Wayne Kowalski	Vince Mazzanti
1969	Greg Campbell	Eddie Jackson
1970	Jake Yoder	Mike Berlin
1971	Al Cohn	Al Cohn
1972	Bill Pointer	Mac Lowry
1973	Ed Thompson	Ron Woolet
1974	Gene Krause	Bob Hart
1975	Jim Setser	Bobby Meadows
1976	Mike Putzer	Jim Lindquist
1977	Frank Gadaleto	Bud Debenham
1978	Rich Mersek	Chris Cobus
1979	Rick Peters	Bob Basacchi
1980	Mike Eaton	Steve Fehr
1981	Rob Vital	Rod Toft
1982	Bruce Bohm	Rich Wonders
1983	Rick Kendrick	Tony Cariello
1984	Bob Antczak and Neal Young (tie)	Bob Goike
1985	Glen Harbison	Barry Asher
1986	Jess Mackey	Ed Marazka
1987	Terry Taylor	Ryan Schafer
1988	Steve Hutkowski	Rick Steelsmith
1989	Paul Tetreault	George Hall
1990	Bob Hochrein	Mike Neumann
1991	Ed Deines	Tom Howery
1992	Bob Youker and Gary Blatchford (tie)	Mike Tucker
1993	Dan Bock	Jeff Nimke

PROFESSIONAL BOWLERS ASSOCIATION

National Championship Tournament

1960	Don Carter
1961	Dave Soutar
1962	Carmen Salvino
1963	Billy Hardwick
1964	Bob Strampe
1965	Dave Davis
1966	Wayne Zahn
1967	Dave Davis
1968	Wayne Zahn
1969	Mike McGrath
1970	Mike McGrath
1971	Mike Lemongello
1972	Johnny Guenther
1973	Earl Anthony
1974	Earl Anthony
1975	Earl Anthony
1976	Paul Colwell
1977	Tommy Hudson
1978	Warren Nelson
1979	Mike Aulby
1980	Johnny Petraglia
1981	Earl Anthony
1982	Earl Anthony
1983	Earl Anthony
1984	Bob Chamberlain
1985	Mike Aulby
1986	Tom Crites
1987	Randy Pedersen
1988	Brian Voss
1989	Pete Weber
1990	Jim Pencak
1991	Mike Miller
1992	Eric Forkel
1993	Ron Palombi

BOWLING PROPRIETORS' ASSOCIATION OF AMERICA—MEN

United States Open[1]

1971	Mike Lemongello
1972	Don Johnson
1973	Mike McGrath
1974	Larry Laub
1975	Steve Neff
1976	Paul Moser
1977	Johnny Petraglia
1978	Nelson Burton, Jr.
1979	Joe Berardi
1980	Steve Martin
1981	Marshall Holman
1982	Dave Husted
1983	Gary Dickinson
1984	Mark Roth
1985	Marshall Holman
1986	Steve Cook
1987	Del Ballard
1988	Pete Weber
1989	Mike Aulby
1990	Ron Palumbi, Jr.
1991	Pete Weber
1992	Robert Lawrence
1993	Del Ballard, Jr.

1. Replaced All-Star tournament and is rolled as part of B.P.A. tour.

WOMEN'S INTERNATIONAL BOWLING CONGRESS CHAMPIONS

Year	Singles	All-events	Year	Singles	All-events
1959	Mae Bolt	Pat McBride	1978	Mae Bolt	Annese Kelly
1960	Marge McDaniels	Judy Roberts	1979	Betty Morris	Betty Morris
1961	Elaine Newton	Evelyn Teal	1980	Betty Morris	Cheryl Robinson
1962	Martha Hoffman	Flossie Argent	1981	Virginia Norton	Virginia Norton
1963	Dot Wilkinson	Helen Shablis	1982	Gracie Freeman	Aleta Rzepecki
1964	Jean Havlish	Jean Havlish	1983	Aleta Rzepecki	Virginia Norton
1965	Doris Rudell	Donna Zimmerman	1984	Freida Gates	Shinobu Saitoh
1966	Gloria Bouvia	Kate Helbig	1985	Polly Schwarzel	Aleta Sill
1967	Gloria Paeth	Carol Miller	1986	Dana Stewart	Robin Romeo Maria Lewis (tie)
1968	Norma Parks	Susie Reichley			
1969	Joan Bender	Helen Duval	1987	Regi Junak	Leanne Barrette
1970	Dorothy Fothergill	Dorothy Fothergill	1988	Michelle Meyer-Welty	Lisa Wagner
1971	Mary Scruggs	Lorrie Nichols	1989	Lorraine Anderson	Nancy Fehn
1972	D. D. Jacobson	Mildred Martorella	1990	Dana Miller-Mackie and Paula Carter	Carol Norman
1973	Bobby Buffaloe	Toni Calvery			
1974	Shirley Garms	Judy C. Soutar	1991	Debbie Kuhn	Debbie Kuhn
1975	Barbara Leicht	Virginia Norton	1992	Patty Ann	Mitsuko Tokimoto
1976	Bev Shonk	Betty Morris	1993	Karen Collura and Kari Murph (tie)	Bertha Blackshur and Sharon Davis (tie)
1977	Akiko Yamaga	Akiko Yamaga			

BOWLING PROPRIETORS' ASSOCIATION OF AMERICA—WOMEN

United States Open

1971	Paula Carter	1977	Betty Morris	1983	Dana Miller	1989	Robin Romeo
1972	Lorrie Nichols	1978	Donna Adamek	1984	Karen Ellingsworth	1990	Dana Miller-Mackie
1973	Mildred Martorella	1979	Diana Silva	1985	Pat Mercatanti	1991	Anne Marie Duggan
1974	Pat Costello (Calif.)	1980	Pat Costello (Calif.)	1986	Wendy MacPherson	1992	Tish Johnson
1975	Paula Carter	1981	Donna Adamek	1987	Carol Nurman	1993	Dede Davidson
1976	Patty Costello (Pa.)	1982	Shinobu Saitoh	1988	Lisa Wagner		

WIBC QUEENS TOURNAMENT CHAMPIONS

1961	Janet Harman	1970	Mildred Martorella	1978	Loa Boxberger	1986	Cora Fiebig
1962	Dorothy Wilkinson	1971	Mildred Martorella	1979	Donna Adamek	1987	Cathy Almeida
1963	Irene Monterosso	1972	Dorothy Fothergill	1980	Donna Adamek	1988	Wendy McPherson
1964	D.D. Jacobson	1973	Dorothy Fothergill	1981	Katsuko Sugimoto	1989	Carol Gianotti
1965	Betty Kuczynski	1974	Judy Soutar	1982	Katsuko Sugimoto	1990	Patty Ann
1966	Judy Lee	1975	Cindy Powell	1983	Aleta Rzepecki	1991	Dede Davidson
1967	Mildred Martorella	1976	Pamela Buckner	1984	Kazue Inahashi	1992	Cindy Coburn-Carroll
1968	Phyllis Massey	1977	Dana Stewart	1985	Aleta Sill	1993	Jan Schmidt
1969	Ann Feigel						

PROFESSIONAL BOWLERS ASSOCIATION Championship—1993

(Toledo, Ohio, Feb. 21–27, 1993)

Winner—Ron Palombi, Erie, Pa., defeated Eugene Mccune, Munster, Ind., 237–224
3. Philip Ringner, Big Spring, Texas
4. Adam Apo, Honolulu, Hawaii
King of the Hill—Ron Williams, Ft. Worth, Tex., defeated Ron Palombi, Erie, Pa., 185–179

WOMEN'S INTERNATIONAL BOWLING CONGRESS QUEENS TOURNAMENT

(Baton Rouge, La., May 9–13, 1993)

Winner—Jan Schmidt, Rochelle, Ill., defeated Pat Costello, Lantana, Fla., 201–163 in title match.
3. Jeanne Naccarato, Tacoma, Wash
4. Wendy MacPherson-Papnos, Henderson, Nev.
5. Linda Kelly, Huber Heights, Ohio

AMERICAN BOWLING CONGRESS TOURNAMENT—1993

(Tulsa, Okla., Feb. 13–June 6, 1993)

Regular Division

Singles—Dan Bock, Owatonna, Minn.	798
Doubles—Darrin Lindsey and Rick Fangman, Waterloo, Iowa Terry Saccone and Dave Callery, Cincinnati, Ohio Randy and Ron Wild, Green Bay, Wisc. (tie)	1498
All Events—Jeff Nimke, Kenosha, Wisc.	2254
Team—Bruegger's Bagels No. 1, Albany, N.Y.	3537

Booster Division

Team—Schooner Lane	2891
Doubles—Glen Humbert and Rich Leskanich, Dwight, Ill.	1185
Singles—Gary Kuhfus, Radcliffe, Iowa	669

SKIING

HISTORY OF SKIING IN THE UNITED STATES

Skis were devised for utility, to aid those who had to travel over snow. The Norwegians, Swedes, Lapps, and other inhabitants of northern lands used skis for many centuries before skiing became a sport. Emigrants from these countries brought skis to the United States with them. The first skier of record in the United States was a mailman by the name of "Snowshoe" Thompson, born and raised in Telemarken, Norway, who came to the United States and, beginning in 1850, used skis through 20 successive winters in carrying mail from Northern California to Carson Valley, Idaho.

Ski clubs sprang up over 100 years ago where there were Norwegian and Swedish settlers in Wisconsin and Minnesota and ski contests were held in that territory in 1886. On Feb. 21, 1904, at Ishpening, Mich., a small group of skiers organized the National Ski Association. In 1961 it was renamed the United States Ski Association.

ALPINE WORLD CUP OVERALL WINNERS

Year	Men	Women	Team
1967	Jean–Claude Killy, France	Nancy Greene, Canada	France
1968	Jean–Claude Killy, France	Nancy Greene, Canada	France
1969	Karl Schranz, Austria	Gertrude Gabl, Austria	Austria
1970	Karl Schranz, Austria	Michel Jacot, France	France
1971	Gustavo Thoeni, Italy	Annemarie Proell, Austria	France
1972	Gustavo Thoeni, Italy	Annemarie Proell, Austria	France
1973	Gustavo Thoeni, Italy	Annemarie Proell Moser, Austria	France
1974	Piero Gros, Italy	Annemarie Proell Moser, Austria	Austria
1975	Gustavo Thoeni, Italy	Annemarie Proell Moser, Austria	Austria
1976	Ingemar Stenmark, Sweden	Rosi Mittermaier, West Germany	Austria
1977	Ingemar Stenmark, Sweden	Lise–Marie Morerod, Switzerland	Austria
1978	Ingemar Stenmark, Sweden	Hanni Wenzel, Liechtenstein	Austria
1979	Peter Luescher, Switzerland	Annemarie Proell Moser, Austria	Austria
1980	Andreas Wenzel, Liechtenstein	Hanni Wenzel, Liechtenstein	Liechtenstein
1981	Phil Mahre, United States	Marie–Theres Nadig, Switzerland	Switzerland
1982	Phil Mahre, United States	Erika Hess, Switzerland	Austria
1983	Phil Mahre, United States	Tamara McKinney, United States	Switzerland
1984	Pirmin Zurbriggen, Switzerland	Erika Hess, Switzerland	Switzerland
1985	Marc Girardelli, Luxembourg	Michela Figini, Switzerland	Switzerland
1986	Marc Girardelli, Luxembourg	Maria Walliser, Switzerland	Switzerland
1987	Pirmin Zubriggen, Switzerland	Maria Walliser, Switzerland	Switzerland
1988	Pirmin Zubriggen, Switzerland	Michela Figini, Switzerland	Switzerland
1989	Marc Girardelli, Luxembourg	Vreni Schneider, Switzerland	Switzerland
1990	Pirmin Zubriggen, Switzerland	Petra Kronberger, Austria	Switzerland
1991	Marc Girardelli, Luxembourg	Petra Kronberger, Austria	Austria
1992	Paul Accola, Switzerland	Petra Kronberger, Austria	Austria
1993	Marc Girardelli, Luxembourg	Anita Wachter, Austria	Switzerland

Austria

1993 UNITED STATES ALPINE CHAMPIONSHIPS

(Winter Park, Colorado, Feb.18–22, 1993)

Men's Downhill

1. Cary Mullen, Canada	1:11:53
2. Tommy Moe, U.S.A.	1:11.60
3. AJ Kitt, U.S.A.	1:11.73
4. Chad Fleischer, U.S.A.	1:12.38
5. Murray Smith, Canada	1:12.42

Women's Downhill

1. Lindsey Roberts, Canada	1:15.98
2. Edith Thys, U.S.A.	1:16.10
3. Picabo Street, U.S.A.	1:16.11
4. Megan Gerety, U.S.A.	1:16.12
5. Krista Schmidinger, U.S.A.	1:16.20

Men's Slalom

1. Matthew Grosjean, U.S.A.	1:39.44
2. Ron Crossan, Canada	1:39.84
3. Eric Villiard, Canada	1:41.91
4. Scott Wither, U.S.A.	1:42.77
5. Christopher Puckett, U.S.A.	1:43.06

Women's Slalom

1. Kristi Terzian, U.S.A.	1:17.81
2. Carrie Sheinberg, U.S.A.	1:18.22
3. Julie Parisien, U.S.A.	1:18.41
4. Heidi Voelker, U.S.A.	1:19.00
5. D. Roffe-Steinrotter, U.S.A.	1:19.64

Men's Giant Slalom

1. Thomas Grandi, Canada	2:13.68
2. Cary Mullen, Canada	2:14.37
3. Sean Valentine, Canada	2:14.73
4. Christopher Puckett, U.S.A.	2:14.74
5. Rob Crossan, Canada	2:15.37

Women's Giant Slalom

1. D. Roffe-Steinrotter, U.S.A.	2:08.04
2. Julie Parisien, U.S.A.	2:09.12
3. Heidi Voelker, U.S.A.	2:09.57
4. Edith Thys, U.S.A.	2:09.69
5. Carrie Sheinberg, U.S.A.	2:11.71

Men's Super G

1. Cary Mullen, Canada	1:14.48
2. Tommy Moe, U.S.A.	1:15.25
3. Roman Torn, Canada	1:15.52
4. Reggie Crist, U.S.A.	1:15.73
5. AJ Kitt, U.S.A.	1:16.21

Women's Super G

1. Picabo Street, U.S.A.	1:23.15
2. Julie Parisien, U.S.A.	1:23.34
3. Lindsey Roberts, Canada	1:23.40
4. D. Roffe-Steinrotter, U.S.A.	1:23.55
5. Krista Schmidinger, U.S.A.	1:24.02

Men's Combined

1. Christopher Puckett, U.S.A.	86.24
2. Toni Standteiner, U.S.A.	107.42
3. Tommy Moe, U.S.A.	111.42
4. Scott Wither, U.S.A.	132.42
5. Bill Hudson, U.S.A.	154.94

Women's Combined

1. Julie Parisien, U.S.A.	25.66
2. Picabo Street, U.S.A.	56.03
3. Kristi Terzian, U.S.A.	87.38
4. Heidi Voelker, U.S.A.	104.46
5. Monique Pelletier, U.S.A.	111.17

1993 ALPINE WORLD CUP CHAMPIONS

Men	Pts
Overall—Marc Girardelli, Luxembourg	1379
Downhill—Franz Heinzer, Switzerland	527
Slalom—Tomas Fogdoe, Sweden	545
Giant Slalom—Kjetil Andre Aamodt, Norway	410
Super G—Kjetil Andre Aamodt, Norway	420
Combined—Marc Girardelli, Luxembourg	300
Women	
Overall—Anita Wachter, Austria	1286
Downhill—Katja Seizinger, Germany	604
Slalom—Vreni Schneider, Switzerland	490
Giant Slalom—Carole Merle, France	480
Super G—Katja Seizinger, Germany	371
Combined—Anita Wachter, Austria	150

NCAA RESULTS—1993

(March 10–13, 1993, Steamboat Springs, Colo.)

Men

Slalom—Mark Bonnell, University of Utah	1:32.56
Giant Slalom—Sean Ramsden, Univ. of Colorado	1:43.16
10-k Classical—Luke Bodensteiner, Univ. of Utah	31:41.10
20-k Freestyle—Peter Vordenberg, Univ. of N. Mex.	55:27.7

Women

Slalom—Gibson La Fountaine, Univ. of Vermont	1:41.49
Giant Slalom—Karianne Eriksen, Univ. of Utah	1:53.48
5-k Classical—Anette Skjolden, Univ. of Colorado	15:43.90
15-k Freestyle—Ivana Radlova, Univ. of N. Mexico	47:41.10

Final Team Standings

1. University of Utah	783
2. University of Vermont	700.5
3. University of New Mexico	685
4. University of Colorado	628
5. University of Alaska–Anchorage	543

WORLD CUP SKI JUMPING FINAL STANDINGS—1993

1. Andreas Goldberger, Austria	206
2. Jaroslav Sakala, Czech Republic	185
3. Noriaki Kasai, Japan	172
4. Werner Rathmayr, Austria	171
5. Espen Bredesen, Norway	151
6. Chrisoph Duffner, Germany	121
7. Didier Mollard, France	114
8. Stefan Horngacher, Austria	78
9. Werner Haim, Austria	71
10. Bjorn Myrbakken, Norway	63

WORLD CUP NORDIC COMBINED—1993

1. Kenji Ogiwara, Japan	185
2. Fred Borre Lundberg, Norway	115
3. Takanori Kono, Japan	112
4. Masashi Abe, Japan	94
5. Allar Levandi, Estonia	62
6. Knut Tore Apeland, Norway	48
7. Trond Einar Elden, Norway	44
8. Jean-Yves Cuendet, Switzerland	41
9. Andreas Schaad, Switzerland	40
10. Fabrice Guy, France	39

1993 UNITED STATES NORDIC CHAMPIONS

Men's Cross Country

10-k classic—Benjamin Husaby	0:25:53.0
15-k classic—Benjamin Husaby	0:34:03.5
20-k classic—Benjamin Husaby	0:53:35.4
50 kilometers—Audun Endestad	2:20:11.6

Women's Cross Country

5-k classic—Nancy Fiddler	0:15:38.5
10-k freestyle—Leslie Thompson	0:28:08.1
15-k classic—Leslie Thompson	0:40:26.3
30 kilometers—Laura McCabe	1:26:19.1
50 kilometers—Kerrin Petty	2:51:16.0

NORDIC WORLD CHAMPIONSHIPS—1993

Men

30-k classic—Bjorn Daehlie, Norway	1:17:33.6
10-k classic—Sture Sivertsen, Norway	24:51.6
50-k freestyle—Torgny Mogren, Sweden	2:03:36.8
Pursuit—Bjorn Daehlie, Norway	1:01:45.0
Relay—Norway	1:44:14.9

Women

5-k classic—Larissa Lazutina, Russia	14:07.6
15-k classic—Elena Vaelhe, Russia	44:49.1
30-k freestyle—Stefanie Belmendo, Italy	1:22:41.3
Pursuit—Stefanie Belmendo, Italy	40:19.0
Relay—Russia	54:15.7

Jumping	Pts
Large Hill—Espen Bredesen, Norway	241.4
Normal Hill—Mashiko Harada, Japan	237.8
Large Hill Team—Norway	821.5

Nordic Combined Final Standings

1. Kenji Ogiwara, Japan
2. K. Tore Apeland, Norway
3. T. Einar-Elden, Norway
4. B. Engen Vik, Norway
5. Takanori Kono, Japan

Best United States finish: 27th—Dave Jarrett

SPEED SKATING

U.S. OUTDOOR CHAMPIONS (LONG TRACK)

Men

1959–60	Ken Bartholomew
1961	Ed Rudolph
1962	Floyd Bedbury
1963	Tom Gray
1964	Neil Blatchford
1965–66	Rich Wurster
1967	Mike Passarella
1968–70	Peter Cefalu
1971	Jack Walters
1972	Barth Levy
1973	Mike Woods
1974	Leigh Barczewski, Mike Passarella
1975	Rich Wurster
1976	John Wurster
1977	Jim Chapin
1978	Bill Heinkel
1979	Erik Henriksen
1980	Greg Oly
1981	Tom Grannes
1982	Greg Oly
1983	Michael Ralston
1984	Michael Ralston
1985	Andy Gabel
1986	Eric Klein
1987	Dave Paulicic
1988	Patrick Wentland
1989	Matt Trimble
1990	Andy Zak
1991	Pat Seltsam
1992	Dan Jansen
1993	Brian Smith

Women

1960	Mary Novak
1961	Jean Ashworth
1962	Jean Omelenchuk
1963	Jean Ashworth
1964	Diane White
1965	Jean Omelenchuk
1966	Diane White
1967	Jean Ashworth
1968	Helen Lutsch
1969	Sally Blatchford
1970–71	Sheila Young
1972	Ruth Moore, Nancy Thorne
1973	Nancy Class
1974	Kris Garbe
1975	Nancy Swider
1976	Connie Carpenter
1977	Liz Crowe
1978	Paula Class, Betsy Davis
1979	Gretchen Byrnes
1980	Shari Miller
1981	Lisa Merrifield
1982	Lisa Merrifield
1983	Janet Hainstock
1984	Janet Hainstock
1985	Betsy Davis
1986	Deb Perkins
1987	Laura Zuckerman
1988	Elise Brinich
1989	Liza Merrifield
1990	Jane Eickhoff
1991	Liza Dennehy
1992	Hilary Mills
1993	Chantal Bailey

WORLD SPEED SKATING RECORDS

Distance	Time	Skater	Place	Year
Men				
500m	0:36.41	Dan Jansen, United States	Davos, Switzerland	1992
1000m	1:12.58	Pavel Pegov, Soviet Union	Medeo, U.S.S.R.	1983
1000m	1:12.58	Igor Zhelezovski	Heerenveen, The Netherlands	1989
1500m	1:52.50	Andre Hoffmann, East Germany	Calgary, Canada	1988
3000m	3:57.52	Johann Olav Koss, Norway	Heerenveen, The Netherlands	1990
5000m	6:41.73	Johann Olav Koss, Norway	Heerenveen, The Netherlands	1991
10,000m	13:43.54	Johann Olav Koss, Norway	Heerenveen, The Netherlands	1991
All-around	160.807	Victor Shasherin, Soviet Union	Medeo, U.S.S.R.	1984
Women				
500m	0:39.10	Bonnie Blair, United States	Calgary, Canada	1988
1000m	1:17.65	Christa Rothenburger, E. Germany	Calgary, Canada	1988
1500m	2:00.68	Yvonne Van Gennip, Netherlands	Calgary, Canada	1988
3000m	4:11.94	Yvonne Van Gennip, Netherlands	Calgary, Canada	1988
5000m	7:14:13	Yvonne Van Gennip, Netherlands	Calgary, Canada	1988
All-around	171.760	Andrea Schone, East Germany	Medeo, U.S.S.R.	1984

WORLD SPRINT CHAMPIONSHIPS—1993

(Ikaho, Japan, Feb. 27–28, 1993)

Men

500m—Yasunori Miyabe, Japan 0:37.18
1000m—Igor Zhelezovski, Belarus 117.05
Overall—Igor Zhelezovski, Belarus 151.025 pts

Women

500m—Ye Qiaobo, China 0:40.46
1000m—Ernese Hunyady, Austria 1:24.45
Overall—1. Ye Qiaobo, China 165.925 pts
2. Bonnie Blair, United States 166.475 pts

U.S. JUNIOR OUTDOOR (LONG TRACK) CHAMPIONS—1993

Boys (13–14) 1,000 meters—Chris Sylvester, Lake Placid, N.Y. 1:30.98
Boys (13–14) 3,000 meters—Lucas Mills, Evanston, Ill. 5:17.41
Boys (15–18) 1,500 meters—Mike Witty, West Allis, Wis. 2:01.07
Boys (15–18) 5,000 meters—Brian Kretschmann, Milwaukee, Wis. 7:39.42
Girls 1,000 meters—Christine Witty, West Allis, Wis. 1:24.34
Girls 3,000 meters—Christine Witty, West Allis, Wis. 4:55.11

U.S. OUTDOOR (LONG TRACK) CHAMPIONS—1993

Men

Overall—Brian Smith, Cedar Rapids, Iowa 168.045 pts
500 meters—Dan Jansen, Greenfield, Wis. 0:37.61
1,000 meters—Dan Jansen, Greenfield, Wis. 1:16.28
1,500 meters—Brian Wanek, Mequon, Wis. 1:57.99
10,000 meters—David Tamburrino, Saratoga Springs, N.Y. 15:05.99

Women

Overall—Chantal Bailey, Boulder, Colo. 183.756 pts
500 meters—Bonnie Blair, Champaign, Ill. 0:40.80
1,000 meters—Bonnie Blair, Champaign, Ill. 1:24.22
1,500 meters—Chantal Bailey, Boulder, Colo. 2:11.49
5,000 meters—Chantal Bailey, Boulder, Colo. 8:14.06

WORLD CHAMPIONSHIPS—1993

(at Heerenveen, The Netherlands)

Men

500 meters—Dan Jansen, United States	229 pts
1,500 meters—Rintje Ritsma, Netherlands	112 pts
10,000 meters—Bart Veld Kamp, Netherlands	141 pts

Women

500 meters—Ye Qiaobo, China	175 pts
1,500 meters—Gunda Niemann, Germany	100 pts
5,000 meters—Gunda Niemann, Germany	175 pts

FIGURE SKATING

WORLD CHAMPIONS

Men

1960	Alain Giletti, France
1961	No competition
1962	Donald Jackson, Canada
1963	Don McPherson, Canada
1964	Manfred Schnelldorfer, West Germany
1965	Alain Calmat, France
1966–68	Emmerich Danzer, Austria
1969–70	Tim Wood, United States
1971–73	Ondrej Nepela, Czechoslovakia
1974	Jan Hoffman, East Germany
1975	Sergei Yolkov, U.S.S.R.
1976	John Curry, Britain
1977	Vladimir Kovalev, U.S.S.R.
1978	Charles Tickner, United States
1979	Vladimir Kovalev, U.S.S.R.
1980	Jan Hoffman, East Germany
1981	Scott Hamilton, United States
1982	Scott Hamilton, United States
1983	Scott Hamilton, United States
1984	Scott Hamilton, United States
1985	Alexandr Fadeev, U.S.S.R.
1986	Brian Boitano, United States
1987	Brian Orser, Canada
1988	Brian Boitano, United States
1989	Kurt Browning, Canada
1990	Kurt Browning, Canada
1991	Kurt Browning, Canada
1992	Viktor Petrenko, Unified Team
1993	Kurt Browning, Canada

Women

1956–60	Carol Heiss, United States
1961	No competition
1962–64	Sjoukje Dijkstra, Netherlands
1965	Petra Burka, Canada
1966–68	Peggy Fleming, United States
1969–70	Gabriele Seyfert, East Germany
1971–72	Beatrix Schuba, Austria
1973	Karen Magnusson, Canada
1974	Christine Errath, East Germany
1975	Dianne de Leeuw, Netherlands
1976	Dorothy Hamill, United States
1977	Linda Fratianne, United States
1978	Anett Poetzsch, East Germany
1979	Linda Fratianne, United States
1980	Anett Poetzsch, East Germany
1981	Denise Beillmann, Switzerland
1982	Elaine Zayak, United States
1983	Rosalynn Sumners, United States
1984	Katarina Witt, East Germany
1985	Katarina Witt, East Germany
1986	Debi Thomas, United States
1987	Katarina Witt, East Germany
1988	Katarina Witt, East Germany
1989	Midori Ito, Japan
1990	Jill Trenary, United States
1991	Kristi Yamaguchi, United States
1992	Kristi Yamaguchi, United States
1993	Oksana Baivl, Ukraine

U.S. CHAMPIONS

Men

1946–52	Richard Button
1953–56	Hayes Jenkins
1957–60	David Jenkins
1961	Bradley Lord
1962	Monty Hoyt
1963	Tommy Liz
1964	Scott Allen
1965	Gary Visconti
1966	Scott Allen
1967	Gary Visconti
1968–70	Tim Wood
1971	John M. Petkevich
1972	Ken Shelley
1973–75	Gordon McKellen
1976	Terry Kubicka
1977–80	Charles Tickner
1981	Scott Hamilton
1982	Scott Hamilton
1983	Scott Hamilton
1984	Scott Hamilton
1985	Brian Boitano
1986	Brian Boitano
1987	Brian Boitano
1988	Brian Boitano
1989	Christopher Bowman
1990	Todd Eldredge
1991	Todd Eldredge
1992	Christopher Bowman
1993	Scott Davis

Women

1943–48	Gretchen Merrill
1949–50	Yvonne Sherman
1951	Sonya Klopfer
1952–56	Tenley Albright
1957–60	Carol Heiss
1961	Laurence Owen
1962	Barbara Roles Pursley
1963	Lorraine Hanlon
1964–68	Peggy Fleming
1969–73	Janet Lynn
1974–76	Dorothy Hamill
1977–80	Linda Fratianne
1981	Elaine Zayak
1982	Rosalynn Sumners
1983	Rosalynn Sumners
1984	Rosalynn Sumners
1985	Tiffany Chin
1986	Debi Thomas
1987	Jill Trenary
1988	Debi Thomas
1989	Jill Trenary
1990	Jill Trenary
1991	Tonya Harding
1992	Kristi Yamaguchi
1993	Nancy Kerrigan

UNITED STATES CHAMPIONSHIPS—1993

(Jan. 17–24, Phoenix, Arizona)

Senior men—Scott Davis, Great Falls, Mont.
Senior women—Nancy Kerrigan, Stoneham, Mass.
Senior pairs—Calla Urbanski, Chicago, and Rocky Marvel, New Egypt, N.J.
Senior dance—Renee Roca, Rochester, N.Y., and Gorsha Sur, Russia
Junior men—Michael Weiss, Fairfax, Va.
Junior women—Michelle Cho, Costa Mesa, Calif.
Junior pairs—Stephanie Stiegler, Manhattan Beach, Calif., and Lance Travis, Greensboro, N.C.
Junior dance—Kim Hartley, Roseville, Minn., and Michael Sklutousky, Indianapolis, Ind.
Novice men—Ryan Jahnke, Grosse Point Farms, Mich.

WORLD CHAMPIONSHIPS—1993

(Prague, Czech Republic, March 9–14, 1993)

Men's singles—Kurt Browning, Canada
Women's singles—Oksana Baivl, Ukraine
Pairs—Isabelle Brasseur and Lloyd Eisler, Canada
Dance—Maya Usova and Alexandr Zhulin, Russia

SWIMMING

WORLD RECORDS—MEN

(Through September 19, 1993)
Approved by the International Swimming Federation (F.I.N.A.)
(F.I.N.A. discontinued acceptance of records in yards in 1968)
Source: United States Swim Team

Distance	Record	Holder	Country	Date
Freestyle				
50 meters	0:21.81	Tom Jager	United States	March 24, 1990
100 meters	0:48.42	Matt Biondi	United States	August 9, 1988
200 meters	1:46.69	Georgio Lamberti	Italy	Aug. 15, 1989
400 meters	3:45.00	Evgueni Sadovyi	Unified Team	July 29, 1992
800 meters	7:46.60	Kieren Perkins	Australia	Feb. 14, 1992
1,500 meters	14:43.48	Kieren Perkins	Australia	July 31, 1992
Backstroke				
100 meters	53.86	Jeff Rouse	United States	July 31, 1992
200 meters	1:57.30	Martin Zubero	Spain	Aug. 13, 1991
Breaststroke				
100 meters	1:00.95	Karolyi Guttler	Hungary	Aug. 5, 1993
200 meters	2:10.16	Mike Barrowman	United States	July 29, 1992
Butterfly				
100 meters	0:52.84	Pablo Morales	United States	June 23, 1986
200 meters	1:55.69	Melvin Stewart	United States	Jan. 12, 1991
Individual Medley				
200 meters	1:59.36	Tamas Darnyi	Hungary	Jan. 13, 1991
400 meters	4:12.36	Tamas Darnyi	Hungary	Jan. 18, 1991
Freestyle Relay				
400 meters	3:16.53	United States	National Team	Sept. 23, 1988
800 meters	7:11.95	Unified Team	Former Soviet Union	July 27, 1992
Medley Relay				
400 meters	3:36.93	United States	National Team	Sept. 25, 1988

WORLD RECORDS—WOMEN

Distance	Record	Holder	Country	Date
Freestyle				
50 meters	0:24.79	Yang Wenyi	China	July 31, 1992
100 meters	0:54.48	Jenny Thompson	United States	March 1, 1992
200 meters	1:57.55	Heike Friedrich	East Germany	June 16, 1986
400 meters	4:03.85	Janet Evans	United States	Sept. 22, 1988
800 meters	8:16.22	Janet Evans	United States	Aug. 20, 1989
1,500 meters	15:52.10	Janet Evans	United States	March 26, 1988
Backstroke				
100 meters	1:00.31	Kristina Egerszegi	Hungary	Aug. 20, 1991
200 meters	2:06.62	Kristina Egerszegi	Hungary	Aug. 26, 1991
Breaststroke				
100 meters	1:07.91	Silke Hoerner	East Germany	Aug. 21, 1987
200 meters	2:25.35	Anita Nall	United States	March 2, 1992
Butterfly				
100 meters	0:57.93	Mary T. Meagher	United States	Aug. 16, 1981
200 meters	2:05.96	Mary T. Meagher	United States	Aug. 13, 1981
Individual Medley				
200 meters	2:11.65	Lin Li	China	July 30, 1992
400 meters	4:36.10	Petra Schneider	East Germany	Aug. 1, 1982
Freestyle Relay				
400 meters	3:39.46	United States	National Team	July 28, 1992
800 meters	7:55.47	East Germany	National Team	Aug. 18, 1987
Medley Relay				
400 meters	4:02.54	United States	National Team	July 30, 1992

AMERICAN SWIMMING RECORDS

(As of September 19, 1993)

Distance	Holder	Record	Date
MEN			
Freestyle			
50 meters	Tom Jager	0:21.81	March 24, 1990
100 meters	Matt Biondi	0:48.42	August 10, 1988
200 meters	Matt Biondi	1:47.72	August 15, 1989
400 meters	Matt Cetlinski	3:48.06	August 11, 1988
800 meters	Sean Killion	7:52.45	July 27, 1987
1500 meters	George DiCarlo	15:01.51	June 30, 1984
Backstroke			
100 meters	Jeff Rouse	0:53.86	July 31, 1992
200 meters	Rick Carey	1:58.86	June 27, 1984
Breaststroke			
100 meters	Steve Lundquist	1:01.65	July 29, 1984
200 meters	Mike Barrowman	2:10.16	July 29, 1992
Butterfly			
100 meters	Pablo Morales	0:52.84	June 23, 1986
200 meters	Melvin Stewart	1:55.69	January 12, 1991
Individual Medley			
200 meters	David Wharton	2:00.11	August 20, 1989
400 meters	Eric Namesnik	4:14.50	July 26, 1993
Freestyle Relay			
400 meters	US National Team	3:16.53	September 23, 1988
800 meters	US National Team	7:12.51	September 21, 1988
Medley Relay			
400 meters	US National Team	3:36.93	July 31, 1992
	US National Team	3:36.93	September 25, 1988

Distance	Holder	Record	Date
WOMEN			
Freestyle			
50 meters	Jenny Thompson	0:25.20	July 31, 1992
100 meters	Jenny Thompson	0:54.48	March 1, 1992
200 meters	Nicole Haislett	1:57.55	March 27, 1992
400 meters	Janet Evans	4:03.85	September 22, 1988
800 meters	Janet Evans	8:16.22	August 20, 1989
1500 meters	Janet Evans	15:52.10	March 26, 1988
Backstroke			
100 meters	Lea Loveless	1:00.82	July 30, 1992
200 meters	Betsy Mitchell	2:08.60	June 27, 1986
Breaststroke			
100 meters	Anita Nall	1:08.17	July 29, 1992
200 meters	Anita Nall	2:25.35	March 3, 1992
Butterfly			
100 meters	Mary T. Meagher	0:57.93	August 16, 1981
200 meters	Mary T. Meagher	2:05.96	August 13, 1981
Individual Medley			
200 meters	Summer Sanders	2:11.91	July 30, 1992
400 meters	Summer Sanders	4:37.58	July 26, 1992
Freestyle Relay			
400 meters	US National Team	3:39.46	July 28, 1992
800 meters	US National Team	8:02.12	August 17, 1986
Medley Relay			
400 meters	US National Team	4:02.54	July 30, 1992

YMCA NATIONAL CHAMPIONSHIPS—1993

(April 5–8, 1993, Ft. Lauderdale, Fla.)

Women's Events

50-meter freestyle—Melissa Stone	0:23.43
100-meter freestyle—K. Robinson	0:50.85
200-meter freestyle—Lindsay Benko	1:48.68
500-meter freestyle—Jamie White	4:51.90
1,650-meter freestyle—Suzanne Blak	16:35.41
100-meter backstroke—Alegra Breaux	0:55.63
200-meter backstroke—S. Toledo	1:58.86
100-meter breaststroke—R. Gustin	1:03.24
200-meter breaststroke—R. Gustin	2:17.13
100-meter butterfly—K. Campbell	0:56.24
200-meter butterfly—Talor Bendel	2:00.48
200-meter individual medley—Alegra Breaux	2:01.98
400-meter individual medley—S. Maggio	4:22.01
200-meter medley relay—Houston, Texas	1:45.19
400-meter medley relay—Houston, Texas	3:45.71
200-meter freestyle relay—Birmingham, Mich.	1:35.49
400-meter freestyle relay—Upper Main Line, Pa.	3:30.68
800-meter freestyle relay—M.E. Lyons, Ohio	7:30.30
1-meter dive—Kortney Schell	330.35 pts
3-meter dive—Jennifer Allesandra	393.65 pts

Team standings: 1. Houston, Texas 311
2. M.E. Lyons, Ohio 277
3. Upper Main Line, Pa. 276

Men's Events

50-meter freestyle—Jess Withey	0:20.85
100-meter freestyle—Dod Wales	0:45.42
200-meter freestyle—Dod Wales	1:40.36
500-meter freestyle—Kent Willis	4:31.65
1,650-meter freestyle—Kent Willis	15:40.54
100-meter backstroke—M. Thomson	0:50.98
200-meter backstroke—Jason Crowder	1:50.41
100-meter breaststroke—Jeremy Linn	0:56.13
200-meter breaststroke—Jeremy Linn	2:04.25
100-meter butterfly—Dod Wales	0:49.23
200-meter butterfly—Jason Davis	1:53.31
200-meter individual medley—M. Thomson	1:52.02
400-meter individual medley—M. Thomson	3:59.09
200-meter medley relay—M.E. Lyons, Ohio	1:34.15
400-meter medley relay—M.E. Lyons, Ohio	3:27.37
200-meter freestyle relay—M.E. Lyons, Ohio	1:24.91
400-meter freestyle relay—M.E. Lyons, Ohio	3:03.88
800-meter freestyle relay—M.E. Lyons, Ohio	6:47.99
1-meter dive—Adam Terrell	513.50 pts
3-meter dive—Jeffrey Moss	477.25 pts

Team Standings—1. M.E. Lyons, Ohio 371.5
2. Houston, Texas 325.5
3. Rochester, Minn. 181.5

Combined Team Champions—1. M.E. Lyons, Ohio 648.5
2. Houston, Texas 636.5
3. Upper Main Line, Pa. 352

PHILLIPS 66 NATIONAL SWIMMING CHAMPIONSHIPS—1993

(July 26–30, 1993, Austin, Texas)

Men's Events

50-meter freestyle—David Fox	0:22.49
100-meter freestyle—Jon Olsen	0:49.33
200-meter freestyle—Joe Hudepohl	1:49.22
400-meter freestyle—Chard Carvin	3:50.89
800-meter freeestyle—Peter Wright	7:58.90
1,500-meter freestyle—Carlton Brunner	15:16.21
100-meter backstroke—Jeff Rouse	0:54.21
200-meter backstroke—Royce Sharp	1:58.81
100-meter breaststroke—Tyler Mayfield	'1:02.31
200-meter breaststroke—Eric Wunderlich	2:14.45
100-meter butterfly—Mark Henderson	0:53.62
200-meter butterfly—Melvin Stewart	1:58.11
200-meter individual medley—Greg Burgess	2:00.84
400-meter individual medley—Eric Namesnik	4:15.35
400-meter medley relay—Stanford "A"	3:39.26
400-meter freestyle relay—Ft. Lauderdale "A"	3:22.46
800-meter freestyle relay—Stanford	7:28.09

Women's Events

50-meter freestyle—Angel Martino	0:25.63
100-meter freestyle—Jenny Thompson	0:55.34
200-meter freestyle—Nicole Haislett	1:59.38
400-meter freestyle—Janet Evans	4:05.85
800-meter freestyle—Janet Evans	8:23.61
1,500- meter freeestyle—Janet Evans	15:59.44
100-meter backstroke—B.J. Bedford	1:01.58
200-meter backstroke—Lea Loveless	2:11.69
100-meter breaststroke—Anita Nall	1:09.65
200-meter breaststroke—Anita Nall	2:27.79
100-meter butterfly—Jenny Thompson	0:59.49
200-meter butterfly—Paige Wilson	2:12.89
200-meter individual medley—Allison Wagner	2:14.34
400-meter individual medley—Allison Wagner	4:41.93
400-meter medley relay—Ft. Lauderdale "A"	4:12.80
400-meter freestyle relay—Ft. Lauderdale "A"	3:48.54
800-meter freestyle relay—Badger Dolphins	8:20.08

Team Standings

Combined—1. Ft. Lauderdale, 2. Stanford, 3. Florida Atlantic.

Men	**Women**
1. Stanford	1. Ft. Lauderdale
2. Ft. Lauderdale	2. Badger Dolphins
3. Club Wolverine	3. Florida Atlantic

U.S. DIVING CHAMPIONSHIPS—1993

INDOOR

(April 20–24, 1993, Austin, Texas)

Women's Events

1-meter—Carrie Zarse, unattached	438.39
3-meter—Veronica Ribot-Canales, Miami, Fla.	475.89
Platform—Mary Ellen Clark, Ft. Lauderdale, Fla.	412.26

Men's Events

1-meter—Dean Panaro, Miami, Fla.	593.13
3-meter—M. Bradshaw, Ohio State	651.99
Platform—Russ Bertram, Ft. Lauderdale, Fla.	567.42

OUTDOOR

(Aug. 15, 1993, Los Angeles, Calif.)

Women's Events

1-meter—Carrie Zarse, Kimball Divers	430.41
3-meter—Eileen Richetelli, Stanford Divers	476.82
Platform—Mary Ellen Clark, Ft. Lauderdale Divers	412.38

Men's Events

1-meter—Mark Lenzi, Kimball Divers	618.66
3-meter—Mark Bradshaw, Ohio State	648.08
Platform—Patrick Jeffrey, Ft. Lauderdale Divers	565.02

3OXING

Whether it be called pugilism, prize fighting or boxing, ıere is no tracing "the Sweet Science" to any definite ource. Tales of rivals exchanging blows for fun, fame or ıoney go back to earliest recorded history and classical ːgend. There was a mixture of boxing and wrestling alled the "pancratium" in the ancient Olympic Games nd in such contests the rivals belabored one another with ıands fortified with heavy leather wrappings that were ometimes studded with metal. More than one Olympic ːompetitor lost his life at this brutal exercise.

There was little law or order in pugilism until Jack 3roughton, one of the early champions of England, lrew up a set of rules for the game in 1743. Broughton, ːalled "the father of English boxing," also is credited with having invented boxing gloves. However, these gloves—or "mufflers" as they were called—were used only in teaching "the manly art of self–defense" or in training bouts. All professional championship fights were contested with "bare knuckles" until 1892, when John L. Sullivan lost the heavyweight championship of the world to James J. Corbett in New Orleans in a bout in which both contestants wore regulation gloves.

The Broughton rules were superseded by the London Prize Ring Rules of 1838. The 8th Marquis of Queensberry, with the help of John G. Chambers, put forward the "Queensberry Rules" in 1866, a code that called for gloved contests. Amateurs took quickly to the Queensberry Rules, the professionals slowly.

HISTORY OF WORLD HEAVYWEIGHT CHAMPIONSHIP FIGHTS

(Bouts in which a new champion was crowned)

Date	Where held	Winner, weight, age	Loser, weight, age	Rounds	Referee
Sept. 7, 1892	New Orleans, La.	James J. Corbett, 178 (26)	John L. Sullivan, 212 (33)	21	Prof. John Duffy
March 17, 1897	Carson City, Nev.	Bob Fitzsimmons, 167 (34)	James J. Corbett, 183 (30)	KO 14	George Siler
June 9, 1899	Coney Island, N.Y.	James J. Jeffries, 206 (24)[1]	Bob Fitzsimmons, 167 (37)	KO 11	George Siler
Feb. 23, 1906	Los Angeles	Tommy Burns, 180 (24)[2]	Marvin Hart, 188 (29)	20	James J. Jeffries
Dec. 26, 1908	Sydney, N.S.W.	Jack Johnson, 196 (30)	Tommy Burns, 176 (27)	KO 14	Hugh McIntosh
April 5, 1915	Havana, Cuba	Jess Willard, 230 (33)	Jack Johnson, 205 1/2 (37)	KO 26	Jack Welch
July 4, 1919	Toledo, Ohio	Jack Dempsey, 187 (24)	Jess Willard, 245 (37)	KO 3	Ollie Pecord
Sept. 23, 1926	Philadelphia	Gene Tunney, 189 (28)[3]	Jack Dempsey, 190 (31)	10	Pop Reilly
June 12, 1930	New York	Max Schmeling, 188 (24)	Jack Sharkey, 197 (27)	WF 4	Jim Crowley
June 21, 1932	Long Island City	Jack Sharkey, 205 (29)	Max Schmeling, 188 (26)	15	Gunboat Smith
June 29, 1933	Long Island City	Primo Carnera, 260 1/2 (26)	Jack Sharkey, 201 (30)	KO 6	Arthur Donovan
June 14, 1934	Long Island City	Max Baer, 209 1/2 (25)	Primo Carnera, 263 1/4 (27)	KO 11	Arthur Donovan
June 13, 1935	Long Island City	Jim Braddock, 193 3/4 (29)	Max Baer, 209 1/2 (26)	15	Jack McAvoy
June 22, 1937	Chicago	Joe Louis, 197 1/4 (23)	Jim Braddock, 197 (31)	KO 8	Tommy Thomas
June 22, 1949	Chicago	Ezzard Charles, 181 3/4 (27)[4]	Joe Walcott, 195 1/2 (35)	15	Davey Miller
Sept. 27, 1950	New York	Ezzard Charles, 184 1/2 (29)[5]	Joe Louis, 218 (36)	15	Mark Conn
July 18, 1951	Pittsburgh	Joe Walcott, 194 (37)	Ezzard Charles, 182 (30)	KO 7	Buck McTiernan
Sept. 23, 1952	Philadelphia	Rocky Marciano, 184 (29)[6]	Joe Walcott, 196 (38)	KO13	Charley Daggert
Nov. 30, 1956	Chicago	Floyd Patterson, 182 1/4 (21)	Archie Moore, 187 3/4 (42)	KO 5	Frank Sikora
June 26, 1959	New York	Ingemar Johansson, 196 (26)	Floyd Patterson, 182 (24)	KO 3	Ruby Goldstein
June 20, 1960	New York	Floyd Patterson, 190 (25)	Ingemar Johansson, 194 3/4 (27)	KO 5	Arthur Mercante
Sept. 25, 1962	Chicago	Sonny Liston, 214 (28)	Floyd Patterson, 189 (27)	KO 1	Frank Sikora
Feb. 25, 1964	Miami Beach, Fla.	Cassius Clay, 210 (22)[7]	Sonny Liston, 218 (30)	KO 7	Barney Felix
March 4, 1968	New York	Joe Frazier, 204 1/2 (24)[8]	Buster Mathis, 243 1/2 (23)	KO 11	Arthur Mercante
April 27, 1968	Oakland, Calif.	Jimmy Ellis, 197 (28)[9]	Jerry Quarry, 195 (22)	15	Elmer Costa
Feb. 16, 1970	New York	Joe Frazier, 205 (26)[10]	Jimmy Ellis, 201 (29)	KO 5	Tony Perez
Jan. 22, 1973	Kingston, Jamaica	George Foreman, 217 1/2 (24)	Joe Frazier, 214 (29)	KO 2	Arthur Mercante
Oct. 30, 1974	Kinshasa, Zaire	Muhammad Ali, 216 1/2 (32)	George Foreman, 220 (26)	KO 8	Zack Clayton
Feb. 15, 1978	Las Vegas, Nev.	Leon Spinks, 197 (25)	Muhammad Ali, 224 1/2 (36)	15	Howard Buck
June 9, 1978	Las Vegas, Nev.	Larry Holmes, 212 (28)[11]	Ken Norton, 220 (32)	15	Mills Lans
Sept. 15, 1978	New Orleans	Muhammad Ali, 221 (36)[12]	Leon Spinks, 201 (25)	15	Lucien Joubert
Oct. 20, 1979	Pretoria, S. Africa	John Tate, 240 (24)[13]	Gerrie Coetzee, 222 (24)	15	Carlos Berrocal
March 31, 1980	Knoxville, Tenn.	Mike Weaver, 207 1/2 (27)	John Tate, 232 (25)	KO 15	Ernesto Magana Ansorena
Dec. 10, 1982	Las Vegas, Nev.	Michael Dokes, 216 (24)	Mike Weaver, 209 1/2 (30)	KO 1	Joey Curtis
Sept. 23, 1983	Richfield, Ohio	Gerrie Coetzee, 215 (28)	Michael Dokes, 217 (25)	KO 10	Tony Perez
March 9, 1984	Las Vegas, Nev.	Tim Witherspoon, 2201/2 (26)[14]	Greg Page, 239 1/2 (25)	12	Mills Lane
August 31, 1984	Las Vegas, Nev.	Pinklon Thomas, 216 (26)	Tim Witherspoon, 217 (26)	12	Richard Steele
Nov. 9, 1984	Las Vegas, Nev.	Larry Holmes, 221 1/2 (35)[15]	James Smith 227 (31)	KO 12	Dave Pearl
Dec. 1, 1984	Sun City, S. Africa	Greg Page, 236 (25)[16]	Gerry Coetzee, 217 (29)	KO 8	unavailable
April 29, 1985	Buffalo, N.Y.	Tony Tubbs, 229 (26)[16]	Greg Page, 239 1/2 (26)	15	unavailable.
Sept. 21,1985	Las Vegas, Nev.	Michael Spinks, 200 (29)	Larry Holmes, 221 (35)	15	Carlos Padilla
Jan. 17, 1986	Atlanta, Ga.	Tim Witherspoon, 227 (28)	Tony Tubbs, 229 (27)	15	unavailable
Nov. 23, 1986	Las Vegas, Nev.	Mike Tyson, 217 (20)[17]	Trevor Berbick, 220 (29)	KO 2	unavailable
Dec. 12, 1986	New York, N.Y.	James Smith, 230 (33)[16]	Tim Witherspoon, 218 (29)	KO 1	unavailable

Date	Where held	Winner, weight, age	Loser, weight, age	Rounds	Referee
March 7, 1987	Las Vegas, Nev.	Mike Tyson, 217 (20)[16]	James Smith, 230 (33)	12	unavailable
Feb. 10, 1990	Tokyo	James "Buster" Douglas,[18] 231 1/2 (29)	Mike Tyson (220) (23)	KO 10	Octavio Meyrom
Oct. 25, 1990	Las Vegas, Nev.	Evander Holyfield, 208 (28)	James "Buster" Douglas, 246 (30)	KO 3	Mills Lane
Nov. 13, 1992	Las Vegas, Nev.	Riddick Bowe,[19] 235 (25)	Evander Holyfield, 205 (30)	12	Joe Cortez

1. Jeffries retired as champion in March 1905. He named Marvin Hart and Jack Root as leading contenders and agreed to referee their fight in Reno, Nev., on July 3, 1905, with the stipulation that he would term the winner the champion. Hart, 190 (28), knocked out Root, 171 (29), in the 12th round. 2. Burns claimed the title after defeating Hart. 3. Tunney retired as champion after defeating Tom Heeney on July 26, 1928. 4. After Louis announced his retirement as champion on March 1, 1949, Charles won recognition from the National Boxing Association as champion by defeating Walcott. 5. Charles gained undisputed recognition as champion by defeating Louis, who came out of retirement. 6. Retired as Champion April 27, 1956. 7. The World Boxing Association later withdrew its recognition of Clay as champion and declared the winner of a bout between Ernie Terrell and Eddie Machen would gain its version of the title. Terrell, 199 (25), won a 15-round decision from Machen, 192 (32), in Chicago on March 5, 1965. Clay, 212 1/4 (25) and Terrell, 212 1/2 (27) met in Houston on Feb. 6, 1967, Clay winning a 15-round decision. 8. Winner recognized by New York, Massachusetts, Maine, Illinois, Texas and Pennsylvania to fill vacated title when Clay was stripped of championship for failing to accept U. S. Induction. 9. Bout was final of eight-man tournament to fill Clay's place and is recognized by World Boxing Association. 10. Bout settled controversy over title. 11. Holmes won World Boxing Council title after WBC had withdrawn recognition of Spinks, March 18, 1978, and awarded its title to Norton. WBC said Spinks had reneged on agreement to fight Norton 12. Ali regained World Boxing Association championship. 13. Tate won WBA title after Ali retired and left it vacant. 14. Tim Witherspoon and Greg Page fought for the WBC heavyweight title vacated by Larry Holmes, who could not come to agreement on a deal to fight Page, the No. 1 contender. Holmes declared he would fight under the banner of the International Boxing Federation. Several dates were set and postponed for fights between Holmes and Gerry Coetzee, the WBA champ, the latest being Nov. 16, 1984. 15. First fight under banner of International Boxing Federation. 16. New W.B.A. champion. 17. New W.B.C. champion. 18. New undisputed champion. 19. The W.B.C. stripped Bowe of its version of the title in December 1992 and named Lennox Lewis champion.

OTHER WORLD BOXING TITLEHOLDERS

(Through Aug. 16, 1993)

Light Heavyweight

1903 Jack Root, George Gardner
1903–05 Bob Fitzsimmons
1905–12 Philadelphia Jack O'Brien[1]
1912–16 Jack Dillon
1916–20 Battling Levinsky
1920–22 Georges Carpentier
1923 Battling Siki
1923–25 Mike McTigue
1925–26 Paul Berlenbach
1926–27 Jack Delaney[2]
1927 Mike McTigue
1927–29 Tommy Loughran
1930 Jimmy Slattery
1930–34 Maxie Rosenbloom
1934–35 Bob Olin
1935–39 John Henry Lewis
1939 Melio Bettina
1939–41 Billy Conn[2]
1941 Anton Christoforidis (NBA)
1941–48 Gus Lesnevich
1948–50 Freddie Mills
1950–52 Joey Maxim
1952–61 Archie Moore[3]
1961–63 Harold Johnson
1963–65 Willie Pastrano
1965–66 José Torres
1966–67 Dick Tiger
1968 Dick Tiger, Bob Foster
1969–70 Bob Foster
1971 Vicente Rondon (WBA), Bob!Foster (WBC)
1972-73 Bob Foster (WBA, WBC)
1974 John Conteh (WBA), Bob Foster (WBC)[1,4]
1975–76 Victor Galindez (WBA), John Conteh (WBC)
1977 Victor Galindez (WBA), John Conteh (WBC)[4] Miguel Cuello (WBC)
1978 Victor Galindez (WBA), Mike Rossman (WBA), Miguel Cuello (WBC), Mate Parlov (WBC), Marvin Johson (WBC)
1979 Mike Rossman (WBA), Victor Galindez (WBA), Marvin Johnson (WBC), Matthew (Franklin) Saad Muhammad (WBC)
1980 Matthew Saad Muhammad (WBC), Marvin Johnson (WBA), Eddie (Gregory), Mustafa Muhammad (WBA)
1981 Matthew Saad Muhammad (WBC), Eddie Mustafa Muhammad (WBA), Michael Spinks (WBA), Dwight Braxton (WBC)
1982 Dwight Braxton (WBC), Michael Spinks (WBA)
1983 Michael Spinks (undisputed)
1984 Michael Spinks (undisputed)
1985 Michael Spinks (undisputed)[5]
1986 Marvin Johnson (WBA) Dennis Andries (WBC)
1987 Thomas Hearns (WBC), Virgil Hill (WBA), Bobby Czyz (IBF)
1988 Charles Williams (IBF), Virgil Hill (WBA), Donny Lalonde (WBC), Sugar Ray Leonard (WBC)
1989 Dennis Andries (WBC), Virgil Hill (WBA), Charles Williams (IBF), Jeff Harding (WBC)
1990 Virgil Hill (WBA), Charles Williams (IBF), Jeff Harding (WBC), Dennis Andries (WBC)
1991 Virgil Hall (WBA), Thomas Hearns (WBA), Dennis Andries (WBC), Charles Williams (IBF)
1992 Charlie Williams (IBF), James Waring (IBF), Jeff Harding (WBC)
1993 Virgil Hill (WBA), Jeff Harding (WBC), Henry Maske (IBF)

1. Retired. 2. Abandoned title. 3. NBA withdrew recognition in 1961, New York Commission in 1962; recognized thereafter only by California and Europe. 4. WBC withdrew recognition. 5. Spinks relinquished title in 1985 to fight for heavyweight title.

Middleweight

1867–72 Tom Chandler
1872–81 George Rooke
1881–82 Mike Donovan[1]
1884–91 Jack (Nonpareil) Dempsey
1891–97 Bob Fitzsimmons[2]
1908 Stanley Ketchel, Billy Papke

1908–10 Stanley Ketchel[3]
1913 Frank Klaus
1913–14 George Chip
1914–17 Al McCoy
1917–20 Mike O'Dowd
1920–23 Johnny Wilson
1923–26 Harry Greb
1926 Tiger Flowers
1926–31 Mickey Walker[2]
1931–41 Gorilla Jones, Ben Jeby, Marcel Thil, Lou Brouillard, Vince Dundee, Teddy Yarosz, Babe Risko, Freddy Steele, Al Hostak, Solly Kreiger, Fred Apostoli, Cerferino Garcia, Ken Overlin, Billy Soose, Tony Zale[4]
1941–47 Tony Zale
1947–48 Rocky Graziano
1948 Tony Zale
1948–49 Marcel Cerdan
1949–51 Jake LaMotta
1952 Ray Robinson, Randy Turpin
1951–52 Ray Robinson[1]
1953–55 Carl Olson
1955–57 Ray Robinson[5]
1957 Gene Fullmer, Ray Robinson
1957–58 Carmen Basilio
1958–60 Ray Robinson[6]
1960–61 Paul Pender[7]
1959–62 Gene Fullmer (NBA)
1961–62 Terry Downes[1]
1962 Paul Pender[1]
1962–63 Dick Tiger
1963–65 Joey Giardello
1965–66 Dick Tiger
1966 Emile Griffith
1967 Nino Benvenuti, Emile Griffith
1968 Emile Griffith, Nino Benvenuti
1969 Nino Benvenuti
1970 Nino Benvenuti, Carlos Monzon
1971–73 Carlos Monzon
1974–75 Carlos Monzon (WBA), Rodrigo Valdez (WBC)
1976 Carlos Monzon (WBA, WBC), Rodrigo Valdez (WBC)
1977 Carlos Monzon (WBA,WBC)[1], Rodrigo Valdez (WBA, WBC)
1978 Rodrigo Valdez, Hugo Corro
1979 Hugo Corro, Vito Antuofermo
1980 Vito Antuofermo, Alan Minter, Marvin Hagler
1981 Marvin Hagler
1982–86 Marvelous Marvin Hagler (undisputed)
1987 Marvin Hagler (undisputed) Sugar Ray Leonard (undisputed)
1988 Sumbu Kalambay (WBA), Thomas Hearns (WBC), Iran Barkley (WBC), Frank Tate (IBF), Michael Nunn (IBF), James Kinchen (NABF)
1989 Michael Nunn (IBF), Mike McCallum (WBA), Iran Barkley (WBC), Roberto Duran (WBC)
1990 Michael McCallum (WBA), Michael Nunn (IBF), Iran Barkley (WBC)
1991 Michael Nunn (IBF), James Toney (IBF), Michael McCallum (WBA)
1992 James Toney (IBF), Julian Jackson (WBC), Reggie Johnson (WBA)
1993 Reggie Johnson (WBA), Gerald McClellan (WBC), Roy Jones (IBF)

1. Retired. 2. Abandoned title. 3. Died. 4. National Boxing Association and New York Commission disagreed on champions. Those listed were accepted by one or the other until Zale gained world-wide recognition. 5. Ended retirement in 1954. 6. NBA withdrew recognition. 7. Recognized by New York, Massachusetts, and Europe.

Welterweight

1892–94 Mysterious Billy Smith
1894–96 Tommy Ryan
1896 Kid McCoy[2]
1896–1900 Mysterious Billy Smith
1900 Rube Ferns
1900–01 Matty Matthews
1901 Ruby Ferns
1901–04 Joe Walcott
1904 Dixie Kid[2]
1904–06 Joe Walcott
1906–07 Honey Mellody
1907 Mike (Twin) Sullivan[2]
1915–19 Ted Lewis
1919–22 Jack Britton
1922–26 Mickey Walker
1926–27 Pete Latzo
1927–29 Joe Dundee
1929–30 Jackie Fields
1930 Young Jack Thompson
1930–31 Tommy Freeman
1931 Young Jack Thompson
1931–32 Lou Brouillard
1932–33 Jackie Fields
1933 Young Corbett 3rd
1933–34 Jimmy McLarnin, Barney Ross
1934–35 Jimmy McLarnin
1935–38 Barney Ross
1938–40 Henry Armstrong
1940–41 Fritzie Zivic
1941–46 Freddie Cochrane
1946 Marty Servo[1]
1946–51 Ray Robinson[2]
1951 Johnny Bratton (NBA)
1951–54 Kid Gavilan
1954–55 Johnny Saxton
1955 Tony DeMarco
1955–56 Carmen Basilio
1956 Johnny Saxton
1956–57 Carmen Basilio[2]
1958 Virgil Akins
1959–60 Don Jordan
1960–61 Benny (Kid) Paret
1961 Emile Griffith
1961–62 Benny (Kid) Paret
1962–63 Emile Griffith, Luis Rodriguez
1963–66 Emile Griffith[2]
1966-69 Curtis Cokes
1969 Curtis Cokes, José Napoles
1970 José Napoles, Billy Backus
1971 Billy Backus, José Napoles
1972–74 José Napoles
1975 José Napoles (WBA, WBC),[3] Angel Espada (WBA), John Stracey (WBC)
1976 Angel Espada (WBA), José Cuevas (WBA), John Stracey (WBC), Carlos Palomino
1977–78 José Cuevas (WBA), Carlos Palomino (WBC)
1979 José Cuevas (WBA), Carlos Palomino (WBC), Wilfredo Benitez (WBC)
1980 José Cuevas (WBA), Ray Leonard (WBC), Roberto Duran (WBC), Thomas Hearns (WBA)
1981 Ray Leonard (WBC), Thomas Hearns (WBA), Ray Leonard (WBC,WBA)
1982 Ray Leonard
1983–85 Donald Curry (WBA)
1983–85 Milton McCrory (WBC)
1985–86 Donald Curry (undisputed)
1987 Mark Breland (WBA) Marlon Starling (WBA) Lloyd Honeychan (IBF)
1988 Marlon Starling (WBA), Tomas Molinares (WBA), Lloyd Honeyghan (WBC), Simon Brown (IBF)
1989 Mark Breland (WBA), Marlon Starling (WBC), Simon Brown (IBF)
1990 Mark Breland (WBA), Aaron Davis (WBA), Simon Brown (IBF), Marlon Starling (WBC), Maurice Blocker (WBC)
1991 Meldrick Taylor (WBA), Simon Brown (IBF, WBC)
1992 Meldrick Taylor (WBA), James "Buddy" McGirt (WBC), Maurice Blocker (IBF)
1993 Cristianto Espana (WBA), Pernell Whitaker (WBC), Felix Trinidad (IBF)

1. Retired. 2. Abandoned title. 3. WBA withdrew recognition.

Lightweight

1869–99 Kid Lavigne
1899–1902 Frank Erne
1902–08 Joe Gans
1908–10 Battling Nelson
1910–12 Ad Wolgast
1912–14 Willie Ritchie
1914–17 Freddy Welsh
1917–25 Benny Leonard[1]
1925 Jimmy Goodrich
1925–26 Rocky Kansas
1926–30 Sammy Mandell
1930 Al Singer
1930–33 Tony Canzoneri
1933–35 Barney Ross[2]
1935–36 Tony Canzoneri
1936–38 Lou Ambers
1938–39 Henry Armstrong
1939–40 Lou Ambers
1940–41 Lew Jenkins
1941–42 Sammy Angott[1]
1943–47 Beau Jack (N.Y.), Bob Montgomery (N.Y.), Sammy Angott (NBA), Juan Zurita (NBA), Ike Williams (NBA)
1947–51 Ike Williams
1951–52 James Carter
1952 Lauro Salas
1952–54 James Carter
1954 Paddy DeMarco
1954–55 James Carter
1955–56 Wallace Smith
1956–62 Joe Brown
1962–65 Carlos Ortiz
1965 Ismael Laguna
1965–68 Carlos Ortiz
1968 Teo Cruz
1969 Teo Cruz, Mando Ramos
1970 Mando Ramos, Ismael Laguna, Ken Buchanan
1971 Ken Buchanan (WBA), Mando Ramos (WBC), Pedro Carrasco (WBC)
1972 Ken Buchanan (WBA), Roberto Duran (WBA), Pedro Carrasco (WBC), Mando Ramos (WBC), Chango Carmona (WBC), Rodolfo Gonzalez (WBC)
1973 Roberto Duran (WBA), Rodolfo Gonzalez (WBC)
1974 Roberto Duran (WBA), Rodolfo Gonzalez (WBC), Guts Ishimatsu (WBC)
1975 Roberto Duran (WBA), Guts Ishimatsu (WBC)
1976 Roberto Duran (WBA), Guts Ishimatsu (WBC), Esteban!De Jesus (WBC)
1977 Roberto Duran (WBA), Esteban De Jesus (WBC)
1978 Roberto Duran (WBA, WBC)
1979 Roberto Duran[2], Jim Watt (WBC), Ernesto Espana (WBA)
1980 Ernesto Espana (WBA), Hilmer Kenty (WBA), Jim Watt (WBC)
1981 Hilmer Kenty (WBA), Sean O'Grady (WBA), James Watt (WBC), Alexis Arguello (WBC), Arturo Frias (WBA)
1982 Arturo Frias (WBA), Ray Mancini (WBA), Alexis Arguello (WBC)
1983 Edwin Rosario (WBC), Ray Mancini (WBA)
1984 Edwin Rosario (WBC), Livingstone Bramble (WBA)
1985 Jose Luis Ramirez (WBC) Hector Camacho (WBC) Livingstone Bramble (WBA)
1986 Hector Camacho (WBC) Livingstone Bramble (WBA) Jim Paul (IBF)
1987 Edwin Rosario (WBA) Jose Luis Ramirez (WBC), Greg Haugen (IBF)
1988 Jose Luis Ramirez (WBC), Julio Cesar Chavez (WBA), Greg Haugen (IBF), Julius Cesar Chavez (WBC & WBA title unified)
1989 Pernell Whitaker (IBF, WBC), Edwin Rosario (WBA)
1990 Pernell Whitaker (IBF, WBC) Juan Nazario (WBA)
1991 Pernell Whitaker (IBF, WBA, WBC)
1992 Pernell Whitaker (IBF, WBA, WBC)[3], Joey Gamache (WBA).
1993 Dingaan Thobela (WBA), Angel Gonzalez (WBC), Freddie Pendleton (IBF)

1. Retired. 2. Abandoned title. 3. Moving up in weight class, so resigned titles.

Featherweight

1889 Dal Hawkins[1]
1890 Billy Murphy
1892–1900 George Dixon
1900–01 Terry McGovern
1901 Young Corbett[1]
1901–12 Abe Attell
1912–23 Johnny Kilbane
1923 Eugene Criqui
1923–25 Johnny Dundee[1]
1925–27 Louis (Kid) Kaplan[1]
1927–28 Benny Bass
1928 Tony Canzoneri
1928–29 Andre Routis
1929–32 Battling Battalino[1]
1932 Tommy Paul (NBA), Kid Chocolate (N.Y.)
1933–36 Freddie Miller
1936–37 Petey Sarron
1937–38 Henry Armstrong[1]
1938–40 Joey Archibald
1940–41 Harry Jefra, Joey Archibald
1941–42 Chalky Wright
1942–48 Willie Pep
1948–49 Sandy Saddler[2]
1949–50 Willie Pep
1950–57 Sandy Saddler
1957–59 Kid Bassey
1959–63 Davey Moore
1963–64 Sugar Ramos
1964–67 Vicente Saldivar[2]
1968 Howard Winstone, José Legra,[3] Paul Rojas (WBA), Sho Saijo (WBA)
1969 Sho Saijo (WBA), Johnny Famechon[3]
1970 Sho Saijo (WBA), Johnny Famechon,[3] Vicente Salvidar,[3] Kuniaki Shibata[3]
1971 Sho Saijo (WBA), Antonio Gomez (WBA), Kuniaki Shibata (WBC)
1972 Antonio Gomez (WBA), Ernesto Marcel (WBA), Kuniaki Shibata (WBC), Clemente Sanchez (WBC), José Legra (WBC)
1973 Ernesto Marcel (WBA), José Legra (WBC), Eder Jofre (WBC)
1974 Ernesto Marcel (WBA)[2], Ruben Olivares (WBA), Alexis Arguello (WBA), Eder Jofre (WBC), Bobby Chacon (WBC)
1975 Alexis Arguello (WBA), Bobby Chacon (WBC), Ruben Olivares (WBC), David Kotey (WBC)
1976 Alexis Arguello (WBA),[2] David Kotey (WBC), Danny Lopez (WBC)
1977 Rafael Ortega (WBA), Danny Lopez (WBC)
1978 Rafael Ortega (WBA), Cecilio Lastra (WBA), Eusebio Pedroza (WBA), Danny Lopez (WBC)
1979 Eusebio Pedroza (WBA), Danny Lopez (WBC)
1980 Eusebio Pedroza (WBA), Danny Lopez (WBC), Salvador Sanchez (WBC)
1981 Eusebio Pedroza (WBA), Salvador Sanchez (WBC)
1982 Eusebio Pedroza (WBA), Salvador Sanchez (WBC)[4]
1983 Juan Laporte (WBC), Eusebio Pedroza (WBA)
1984 Wilfred Gomez (WBC), Eusebio Pedroza (WBA)
1985 Eusebio Pedroza (WBA) Barry McGuigan (WBA) Azumah Nelson (WBC)
1986 Barry McGuigan (WBA) Stevie Cruz (WBA) Azumah Nelson (WBC)
1987 Azumah Nelson (WBC) Antonio Esparragoza (WBA)
1988 Calvin Grove (IBF), Jorge Paez (IBF), Antonio Esparragoza (WBA), Jeff Fenech (WBC)
1989 Jorge Paez (IBF), Antonio Esparragoza (WBA), Jeff Fenech (WBC)
1990 Marcos Villasana (WBC), Antonio Esparragoza (WBA), Jorge Paez (IBF)

1991 Park Young-Kyun (WBA), Troy Dorsey (IBF), Marcos Villagana (WBC)
1992 Paul Hodkinson (WBC), Manuel Medina (IBF), Yung Kyun Park (WBA)
1993 Yung-Kyun Park (WBA), Goyo Vargas (WBC), Tom Johnson (IBF)

1. Abandoned title. 2. Retired. 3. Recognized in Europe, Mexico, and Orient. 4. Killed in auto accident.

Bantamweight

1890–92 George Dixon[1]
1894–99 Jimmy Barry[2]
1899–
1900 Terry McGovern[1]
1901 Harry Harris[1]
1902–03 Harry Forbes
1903–04 Frankie Neil
1904 Joe Bowker[1]
1905–07 Jimmy Walsh[1]
1910–14 Johnny Coulon
1914–17 Kid Williams
1917–20 Pete Herman
1920 Joe Lynch
1920–21 Joe Lynch, Pete Herman, Johnny Buff
1922 Johnny Buff, Joe Lynch
1923 Joe Lynch
1924 Joe Lynch, Abe Goldstein
1924 Abe Goldstein, Eddie (Cannonball) Martin
1925 Eddie (Cannonball) Martin, Charlie (Phil) Rosenberg[3]
1927–28 Bud Taylor (NBA)[1]
1929–34 Al Brown
1935 Al Brown, Baltazar Sangchili
1936 Baltazar Sangchili, Tony Marino, Sixto Escobar
1937 Sixto Escobar, Harry Jeffra
1938 Harry Jeffra, Sixto Escobar
1939–40 Sixto Escobar[2]
1940–42 Lou Salica
1942–46 Manuel Ortiz
1947 Manuel Ortiz, Harold Dade
1948–50 Manuel Ortiz
1950–52 Vic Toweel
1952–54 Jimmy Carruthers[2]
1954–55 Robert Cohen
1956 Robert Cohen, Mario D'Agata, Raul Macias (NBA)
1957 Mario D'Agata, Alphonse Halimi
1958–59 Alphonse Halimi
1959–60 Jose Becerra[2]
1960–61 Alphonse Halimi[4]
1961–62 Johnny Caldwell[4]
1961–65 Eder Jofre
1965–68 Masahika (Fighting) Harada
1968 Masahika (Fighting) Harada, Lionel Rose
1969 Lionel Rose, Ruben Olivares
1970 Ruben Olivares, Chucho Castillo
1971 Chucho Castillo, Ruben Olivares
1972 Ruben Olivares, Rafael Herrera, Enrique Pinder
1973 Enrique Pinder (WBA), Romeo Anaya (WBA), Arnold Taylor (WBA), Rodolfo Martinez (WBC), Rafael Herrera
1974 Arnold Taylor (WBA), Soo Hwan Hong (WBA), Rafael Herrera (WBC), Rodolfo Martinez (WBC)
1975 Soo Hwan Hong (WBA), Alfonso Zamora (WBA), Rodolfo Martinez (WBC)
1976 Alfonso Zamora (WBA), Rodolfo Martinez (WBC), Carlos Zarate (WBC)
1977 Alfonso Zamora (WBA), Jorge Lujan (WBA), Carlos Zarate (WBC)
1978 Jorge Lujan (WBA), Carlos Zarate (WBC)
1979 Jorge Lujan (WBA), Carlos Zarate (WBC), Lupe Pintor (WBC)
1980 Jorge Lujan (WBA), Lupe Pintor (WBC), Julian Solis (WBA), Jeff Chandler (WBA)
1981 Lupe Pintor (WBC), Jeff Chandler (WBA)
1982 Lupe Pintor (WBC), Jeff Chandler (WBA)
1983 Jeff Chandler (WBA), Albert Dauila (WBC)
1984 Richie Sandqual (WBA), Albert Dauila (WBC)
1985 Richard Sandoval (WBA) Daniel Zaragoza (WBC) Miguel Lora (WBC)
1986 Richard Sandoval (WBA) Bernardo Pinango (WBA) Jeff Fenech (IBF)
1987 Bernardo Pinango (WBA) Takuya Muguruma (WBA) Miguel Lora (WBC)
1988 Wilfred Vasquez (WBA), Jibaro Perez (WBC), Moon Sung–gil (WBA) Orlando Canizales (IBF)
1989 Jibaro Perez (WBC), Moon Sung–gil (WBA), Orlando Canizales (IBF) Kaokor Galaxy (WBA), Luis Espinosa (WBA)
1990 Orlando Canizales (IBF), Jibaro Perez (WBC), Luis Espinosa (WBA)
1991 Greg Richardson (WBC), Orlando Canizales (IBF), Luis Espinosa (WBA)
1992 Joichiro Tatsuyoshi (WBC), Victor Manuel Rabanales (WBC), Eddie Cook (WBA), Orlando Gonzales (IBF)
1993 Jorge Julio (WBA), Byun-Jong-il (WBC), Orlando Canizales (IBF)

1. Abandoned title. 2. Retired. 3. Deprived of title for failing to make weight. 4. Recognized in Europe.

Flyweight

1916–23 Jimmy Wilde
1923–25 Pancho Villa[1]
1925 Frankie Genaro
1925–27 Fidel La Barba[2]
1927–31 Corporal Izzy Schwartz, Frankie Genaro, Emile (Spider) Pladner, Midget Wolgast, Young Perez[3]
1932–35 Jackie Brown
1935–38 Bennie Lynch[4]
1939 Peter Kane[4]
1943–47 Jackie Paterson[1]
1947–50 Rinty Monaghan[2]
1950 Terry Allen
1950–52 Dado Marino
1952–54 Yoshio Shirai
1954–60 Pascual Perez
1960–62 Pone Kingpetch
1962–63 Masahika (Fighting) Harada
1963–64 Hiroyuki Ebihara
1964–65 Pone Kingpetch
1965–66 Salvatore Burrini
1966 Walter McGown, Chartchai Chionoi
1966–68 Charchai Chionoi
1969 Bernabe Villacampa, Efran Torres (WBA)
1970 Bernabe Villacampa, Chartchai Chionoi, Erbito Salavarria, Berkrerk Chartvanchai (WBA) Masao Ohba (WBA)
1971 Masao Ohba (WBA), Erbito Salavarria (WBC)
1972 Masao Ohba (WBA), Erbito Salavarria (WBC), Betulio Gonzalez (WBC), Venice Borkorsor (WBC)
1973 Masao Ohba (WBA), Chartchai Chionoi (WBA), Venice Borkorsor (WBC), Betulio Gonzalez (WBC)
1974 Chartchai Chionoi (WBA), Susumu Hanagata (WBA), Betulio Gonzalez (WBC), Shoji Oguma (WBC)
1975 Susumu Hanagata (WBA), Erbito Salavarria (WBA), Shoji Oguma (WBC), Miguel Canto (WBC)
1976 Erbito Salavarria (WBA), Alfonso Lopez (WBA), Guty Espadas (WBA), Miguel Canto (WBC)
1977 Guty Espadas (WBA), Miguel Canto (WBC)
1978 Guty Espadas (WBA), Betulio Gonzalez (WBA), Miguel Canto (WBC)
1979 Betulio Gonzalez (WBA), Miguel Canto (WBC), Park Chan–Hee (WBC)
1980 Luis Ibarra (WBA), Kim Tae Shik (WBA), Park Chan–Hee (WBC), Shoji Oguma (WBC)
1983 Frank Cedeno (WBC), Santos Lacia (WBA)
1984 Koji Kobayashy (WBA), Gabriel Bernal (WBC), Santos Laciar (WBA)

1985 Sot Chitlada (WBC) Santos Laciar (WBA)
1986 Hilario Zapata (WBA) Julio Cesar–Chevez (WBC)
1987 Shin Hi Sop (IBF) Chang Ho Choi (IBF) Sot Chitlada (WBC)
1988 Sot Chitlada (WBC), Kim Young Kang (WBC), Duke McKenzie (IBF), Fidel Bassa (WBA)
1989 Kim Young–gang (WBC), Sot Chitlada (WBC), Lee Yol–woo (WBA), Duke McKenzie (IBF), Dave McAuley (IBF) Jesus Rojas (WBA)
1990 Sot Chitlada (WBC), Kim Bong–Jung (WBA), Lee Yul–woo (WBA), Dave McAuley (IBF), Leopard Tamakuma (WBA)
1991 Muangchai Kittasem (WBC), Kim-Young-Kang (WBC), Elvis Alvarez (WBA), Dave McAuley (IBF)
1992 Kim Young-Kang (WBA), Yuri Arbachakov (WBC), Rodolfo Blanco (IBF)
1993 David Griman (WBA), Yuri Arbachakov (WBC), P. Sitbangprachan (IBF)

1. Died. 2. Retired. 3. Claimants to NBA and New York Commission titles. 4. Abandoned title.

WEIGHTLIFTING

U.S. WEIGHTLIFTING FEDERATION

MEN'S NATIONAL CHAMPIONSHIPS

(May 7, 1993, Peoria, Ill.)

	Snatch	C&J[1]	Total[2]
54 kg—Chad Ikai	95.0	117.5	212.5
59 kg—Bryan Alan Jacob	80.0	110.0	190.0
64 kg—Tim Lenard McRee	135.0	165.0	300.0
70 kg—Michael Jacques	115.0	145.0	260.0
76 kg—Dean Goad	130.0	172.5	302.5
83 kg—Jeffrey Macy	135.0	165.0	300.0
91 kg—Paul Fleschier	152.5	192.5	345.0
99 kg—Wesley Barnett	150.0	195.0	345.0
108 kg—Richard Schutz	160.0	190.0	350.0
Over 108 kg—Mark Henry	175.0	210.0	385.0

1. Clean and jerk. 2. All results in kilograms.

WOMEN'S NATIONAL CHAMPIONSHIPS

(May 7, 1993, Peoria, Ill.)

	Snatch	C&J[1]	Total[2]
46 kg—Sibby Flowers	62.5	80.0	142.5
50 kg—Christy Byrd	57.5	70.0	127.5
54 kg—Robin Byrd	80.0	97.5	177.5
59 kg—Stephanie Bodie	72.5	82.5	155.0
64 kg—Giselle Shepatin	75.0	95.0	170.0
70 kg—Arlya Johnson	80.0	105.0	185.0
76 kg—Kerri Ann Hanebrink	82.5	97.5	180.0
83 kg—Decia Stenzel	87.5	107.5	195.0
Over 83 kg—Carla Garrett	102.5	132.5	235.0

WRESTLING

N.C.A.A. CHAMPIONSHIPS—1993

(University of Iowa, Ames, Iowa)

Division I

118 lb—Sam Henson, Clemson, decisioned Chad Zaputil, Iowa, 3–2

126 lb—Tony Purter, Nebraska, dec. Shawn Charles, Arizona State, 7–5

134 lb—T.J. Jaworsky, North Carolina, dec. Cary Kolat, Penn State, 6–4

142 lb—Lincoln McIlravy, Iowa, dec. Gerry Abas, Fresno State, 16–15

150 lb—Terry Steiner, Iowa, dec. Troy Sunderland, Penn State, 8–7

158 lb—Markus Mollica, Arizona State, dec. Josh Robbins, Penn State, 6–4

167 lb—Ray Miller, Arizona State, dec. Shaon Fry, Missouri, 6–2

177 lb—Kevin Randleman, Ohio State, dec. Corey Olson, Nebraska, 5–2

190 lb—Rex Holman, Ohio State, dec. Joel Sharratt, Iowa, 7–5

Heavyweight—Sylvester Terkay, North Carolina State, pinned down Don Whipp, Michigan State, 1:43

Team Champions

1. Iowa, 123.75; 2. Penn State, 87.50; 3. Nebraska, 79.50; 4. Arizona St., 72.50; 5. Ohio St., 64.00

WORLD WRESTLING CHAMPIONSHIPS—1993

(Aug. 26–28, 1993, Toronto, Canada)

Freestyle

105.5 lb (48 kg)—Alexis Vila, Cuba
114.5 lb (52 kg)—Valentin Jordanov, Bulgaria
125.5 lb (57 kg)—Terry Brands, Iowa City, Ia.
136.5 lb (62 kg)—Tom Brands, Iowa City, Ia.
149.5 lb (68 kg)—Ali Akhbar Falla, Iran
163.0 lb (74 kg)—Park Jang–Soon, South Korea
180.5 lb (82 kg)—Sebhattin Ozturk, Turkey
198.0 lb (90 kg)—Abbas Jadidi, Iran
220.0 lb (100 kg)—Leri Khabelov, Russia
286 lb (130 kg)—Bruce Baumgartner, Cambridge Springs, Pa.

Team

1. United States, 74; 2. Russia, 52; 3. Turkey, 51; 4. South Korea, 40; 5. China, 38.

WORLD CUP—1993

Freestyle

105.5 lb (48 kg)—Petr Umshanov, Russia
114.5 lb (52 kg)—Zeke Jones, United States
125.5 lb (57 kg)—Bagaudin Umakhanov, Russia
136.5 ln (62 kg)—Gadhi Rachidov, Russia
149.5 lb (68 kg)—Chris Wilson, Canada
163.0 lb (74 kg)—Rob Koll, United States
180.5 lb (82 kg)—Kevin Jackson, United States
198.0 lb (90 kg)—Vitali Gizoev, Russia
220.0 lb (100 kg)—Oleg Ladik, Canada
266.0 lb (121 kg)—Andrei Shumilin, Russia

HORSE RACING

Ancient drawings on stone and bone prove that horse racing is at least 3000 years old, but Thoroughbred Racing is a modern development. Practically every thoroughbred in training today traces its registered ancestry back to one or more of three sires that arrived in England about 1728 from the Near East and became known, from the names of their owners, as the Byerly Turk, the Darley Arabian, and the Godolphin Arabian. The Jockey Club (English) was founded at Newmarket in 1750 or 1751 and became the custodian of the Stud Book as well as the court of last resort in deciding turf affairs.

Horse racing took place in this country before the Revolution, but the great lift to the breeding industry came with the importation in 1798, by Col. John Hoomes of Virginia, of Diomed, winner of the Epsom Derby of 1780. Diomed's lineal descendants included such famous stars of the American turf as American Eclipse and Lexington. From 1800 to the time of the Civil War there were race courses and breeding establishments plentifully scattered through Virginia, North Carolina, South Carolina, Tennessee, Kentucky, and Louisiana.

The oldest stake event in North America is the Queen's Plate, a Canadian fixture that was first run in the Province of Quebec in 1836. The oldest stake event in the United States is The Travers, which was first run at Saratoga in 1864. The gambling that goes with horse racing and trickery by jockeys, trainers, owners, and track officials caused attacks on the sport by reformers and a demand among horse racing enthusiasts for an honest and effective control of some kind, but nothing of lasting value to racing came of this until the formation in 1894 of The Jockey Club.

"TRIPLE CROWN" WINNERS IN THE UNITED STATES[1]

(Kentucky Derby, Preakness and Belmont Stakes)

Year	Horse	Owner	Year	Horse	Owner
1919	Sir Barton	J. K. L. Ross	1946	Assault	Robert J. Kleberg
1930	Gallant Fox	William Woodward	1948	Citation	Warren Wright
1935	Omaha	William Woodward	1973	Secretariat	Meadow Stable
1937	War Admiral	Samuel D. Riddle	1977	Seattle Slew	Karen Taylor
1941	Whirlaway	Warren Wright	1978	Affirmed	Louis Wolfson
1943	Count Fleet	Mrs. John Hertz			

KENTUCKY DERBY

Churchill Downs; 3-year-olds; 1 1/4 miles.

Year	Winner	Jockey	Wt.	Win val.	Year	Winner	Jockey	Wt.	Win val.
1875	Aristides	O. Lewis	100	$2,850	1909	Wintergreen	V. Powers	117	$4,850
1876	Vagrant	R. Swim	97	2,950	1910	Donau	F. Herbert	117	4,850
1877	Baden Baden	W. Walker	100	3,300	1911	Meridian	G. Archibald	117	4,850
1878	Day Star	J. Carter	100	4,050	1912	Worth	C. H. Shilling	117	4,850
1879	Lord Murphy	C. Schauer	100	3,550	1913	Donerail	R. Goose	117	5,475
1880	Fonso	G. Lewis	105	3,800	1914	Old Rosebud	J. McCabe	114	9,125
1881	Hindoo	J. McLaughlin	105	4,410	1915	Regret	J. Notler	112	11,450
1882	Apollo	B. Hurd	102	4,560	1916	George Smith	J. Loftus	117	9,750
1883	Leonatus	W. Donohue	105	3,760	1917	Omar Khayyam	C. Borel	117	16,600
1884	Buchanan	I. Murphy	110	3,990	1918	Exterminator	W. Knapp	114	14,700
1885	Joe Cotton	E. Henderson	110	4,630	1919	Sir Barton	J. Loftus	1121/2	20,825
1886	Ben Ali	P. Duffy	118	4,890	1920	Paul Jones	T. Rice	126	30,375
1887	Montrose	I. Lewis	118	4,200	1921	Behave Yourself	C. Thompson	126	38,450
1888	Macbeth II	G. Covington	115	4,740	1922	Morvich	A. Johnson	126	46,775
1889	Spokane	T. Kiley	118	4,970	1923	Zev	E. Sande	126	53,600
1890	Riley	I. Murphy	118	5,460	1924	Black Gold	J. D. Mooney	126	52,775
1891	Kingman	I. Murphy	122	4,680	1925	Flying Ebony	E. Sande	126	52,950
1892	Azra	A. Clayton	122	4,230	1926	Bubbling Over	A. Johnson	126	50,075
1893	Lookout	E. Kunze	122	4,090	1927	Whiskery	L. McAtee	126	51,000
1894	Chant	F. Goodale	122	4,020	1928	Reigh Count	C. Lang	126	55,375
1895	Halma	J. Perkins	122	2,970	1929	Clyde Van Dusen	L. McAtee	126	53,950
1896	Ben Brush	W. Simms	117	4,850	1930	Gallant Fox	E. Sande	126	50,725
1897	Typhoon H	F. Garner	117	4,850	1931	Twenty Grand	C. Kurtsinger	126	48,725
1898	Plaudit	W. Simms	117	4,850	1932	Burgoo King	E. James	126	52,350
1899	Manuel	F. Taral	117	4,850	1933	Brokers Tip	D. Meade	126	48,925
1900	Lieut. Gibson	J. Boland	117	4,850	1934	Cavalcade	M. Garner	126	28,175
1901	His Eminence	J. Winkfield	117	4,850	1935	Omaha	W. Saunders	126	39,525
1902	Alan-a-Dale	J. Winkfield	117	4,850	1936	Bold Venture	I. Hanford	126	37,725
1903	Judge Himes	H. Booker	117	4,850	1937	War Admiral	C. Kurtsinger	126	52,050
1904	Elwood	F. Prior	117	4,850	1938	Lawrin	E. Arcaro	126	47,050
1905	Agile	J. Martin	122	4,850	1939	Johnstown	J. Stout	126	46,350
1906	Sir Huon	R. Troxler	117	4,850	1940	Gallahadion	C. Bierman	126	60,150
1907	Pink Star	A. Minder	117	4,850	1941	Whirlaway	E. Arcaro	126	61,275
1908	Stone Street	A. Pickens	117	4,850	1942	Shut Out	W. D. Wright	126	64,225

Year	Winner	Jockey	Wt.	Win val.
1943	Count Fleet	J. Longden	126	$60,725
1944	Pensive	C. McCreary	126	64,675
1945	Hoop Jr.	E. Arcaro	126	64,850
1946	Assault	W. Mehrtens	126	96,400
1947	Jet Pilot	E. Guerin	126	92,160
1948	Citation	E. Arcaro	126	83,400
1949	Ponde	S. Brooks	126	91,600
1950	Middleground	W. Boland	126	92,650
1951	Count Turf	C. McCreary	126	98,050
1952	Hill Gail	E. Arcaro	126	96,300
1953	Dark Star	H. Moreno	126	90,050
1954	Determine	R. York	126	102,050
1955	Swaps	W. Shoemaker	126	108,400
1956	Needles	D. Erb	126	123,450
1957	Iron Liege	W. Hartack	126	107,950
1958	Tim Tam	I. Valenzuela	126	116,400
1959	Tomy Lee	W. Shoemaker	126	119,650
1960	Venetian Way	W. Hartack	126	114,850
1961	Carry Back	J. Sellers	126	120,500
1962	Decidedly	W. Hartack	126	119,650
1963	Chateauguay	B. Baeza	126	108,900
1964	Northern Dancer	W. Hartack	126	114,300
1965	Lucky Debonair	W. Shoemaker	126	112,000
1966	Kauai King	D. Brumfield	126	120,500
1967	Proud Clarion	R. Ussery	126	119,700
1968	Forward Pass[1]	I. Valenzuela	126	122,600
1969	Majestic Prince	W. Hartack	126	$113,200
1970	Dust Commander	M. Manganello	126	127,800
1971	Canonero II	G. Avila	126	145,500
1972	Riva Ridge	R. Turcotte	126	140,300
1973	Secretariat	R. Turcotte	126	155,050
1974	Cannonade	A. Cordero, Jr.	126	274,000
1975	Foolish Pleasure	J. Vasquez	126	209,600
1976	Bold Forbes	A. Cordero, Jr.	126	165,200
1977	Seattle Slew	J. Cruguet	126	214,700
1978	Affirmed	S. Cauthen	126	186,900
1979	Spectacular Bid	R. Franklin	126	228,650
1980	Genuine Risk	J. Vasquez	126	250,550
1981	Pleasant Colony	J. Velasquez	126	317,200
1982	Gato del Sol	E. Delahoussaye	126	417,600
1983	Sunny's Halo	E. Delahoussaye	126	426,000
1984	Swale	L. Pincay, Jr.	126	537,400
1985	Spend a Buck	A. Cordero, Jr.	126	406,800
1986	Ferdinand	W. Shoemaker	126	609,400
1987	Alysheba	C. McCarron	126	618,600
1988	Winning Colors	Gary Stevens	126	611,200
1989	Sunday Silence	Patrick Valenzuela	126	574,200
1990	Unbridled	Craig Perret	126	581,000
1991	Strike the Gold	Chris Antley	126	655,800
1992	Lil E. Tee	P. Day	126	724,800
1993	Sea Hero	Jerry Bailey	126	735,900

1. Dancer's Image finished first but was disqualified after traces of drug were found in system.

PREAKNESS STAKES

Pimlico; 3–year–olds; 1 3/16 miles; first race 1873.

Year	Winner	Jockey	Wt.	Win val.
1919	Sir Barton	J. Loftus	126	$24,500
1930	Gallant Fox	E. Sande	126	51,925
1931	Mate	G. Ellis	126	48,225
1932	Burgoo King	E. James	126	50,375
1933	Head Play	C. Kurtsinger	126	26,850
1934	High Quest	R. Jones	126	25,175
1935	Omaha	W. Saunders	126	25,325
1936	Bold Venture	G. Woolf	126	27,325
1937	War Admiral	C. Kurtsinger	126	45,600
1938	Dauber	M. Peters	126	51,875
1939	Challedon	G. Seabo	126	53,710
1940	Bimelech	F.A. Smith	126	53,230
1941	Whirlaway	E. Arcaro	126	49,365
1942	Alsab	B. James	126	58,175
1943	Count Fleet	J. Longden	126	43,190
1944	Pensive	C. McCreary	126	60,075
1945	Polynesian	W.D. Wright	126	66,170
1946	Assault	W. Mehrtens	126	96,620
1947	Faultless	D. Dodson	126	98,005
1948	Citation	E. Arcaro	126	91,870
1949	Capot	T. Atkinson	126	79,985
1950	Hill Prince	E. Arcaro	126	56,115
1951	Bold	E. Arcaro	126	83,110
1952	Blue Man	C. McCreary	126	86,135
1953	Native Dancer	E. Guerin	126	65,200
1954	Hasty Road	J. Adams	126	91,600
1955	Nashua	E. Arcaro	126	67,550
1956	Fabius	W. Hartack	126	84,250
1957	Bold Ruler	E. Arcaro	126	65,250
1958	Tim Tam	I. Valenzuela	126	97,900
1959	Royal Orbit	W. Harmatz	126	136,200
1960	Bally Ache	R. Ussery	126	121,000
1961	Carry Back	J. Sellers	126	126,200
1962	Greek Money	J. Rotz	126	$135,800
1963	Candy Spots	W. Shoemaker	126	127,500
1964	Northern Dancer	W. Hartack	126	124,200
1965	Tom Rolfe	R. Turcotte	126	128,100
1966	Kauai King	D. Brumfield	126	129,000
1967	Damascus	W. Shoemaker	126	141,500
1968	Forward Pass	I. Valenzuela	126	142,700
1969	Majestic Prince	W. Hartack	126	129,500
1970	Personality	E. Belmonte	126	151,300
1971	Canonero II	G. Avila	126	137,400
1972	Bee Bee Bee	E. Nelson	126	135,300
1973	Secretariat	R. Turcotte	126	129,900
1974	Little Current	M. Rivera	126	156,000
1975	Master Derby	D. McHargue	126	158,100
1976	Elocutionist	J. Lively	126	129,700
1977	Seattle Slew	J. Cruguet	126	138,600
1978	Affirmed	S. Cauthen	126	136,200
1979	Spectacular Bid	R. Franklin	126	165,300
1980	Codex	A. Cordero	126	180,600
1981	Pleasant Colony	J. Velasquez	126	270,800
1982	Aloma's Ruler	J. Kaenel	126	209,900
1983	Deputed Testimony	D. Miller	126	251,200
1984	Gate Dancer	A. Cordero	126	243,600
1985	Tank's Prospect	Pat Day	126	423,200
1986	Snow Chief	A. Solis	126	411,900
1987	Alysheba	C. McCarron	126	421,100
1988	Risen Star	E. Delahoussaye	126	413,700
1989	Sunday Silence	P. Valenzuela	126	438,230
1990	Summer Squall	Pat Day	126	445,900
1991	Hansel	Jerry Bailey	126	432,770
1992	Pine Bluff	C. McCarron	126	484,120
1993	Prairie Bayou	Mike Smith	126	471,835

BELMONT STAKES

Belmont Park; 3–year–olds; 1 1/2 miles.

Run at Jerome Park 1867 to 1890; at Morris Park 1890–94; at Belmont Park 1905–62; at Aqueduct 1963–67. Distance 1 5/8 miles prior to 1874; reduced to 1 1/2 miles, 1874; reduced to 1 1/4 miles, 1890; reduced to 1 1/8 miles, 1893; increased to 1 1/4 miles, 1895; increased to 1 3/8 miles, 1896; reduced to 1 1/4 miles in 1904; increased to 1 1/2 miles, 1926.

Year	Winner	Jockey	Wt.	Win val.
1919	Sir Barton	J. Loftus	126	$11,950
1930	Gallant Fox	E. Sande	126	66,040
1931	Twenty Grand	C. Kurtsinger	126	58,770
1932	Faireno	T. Malley	126	55,120
1933	Hurryoff	M. Garner	126	49,490
1934	Peace Chance	W.D. Wright	126	43,410
1935	Omaha	W. Saunders	126	35,480
1936	Granville	J. Stout	126	29,800
1937	War Admiral	C. Kurtsinger	126	38,020
1938	Pasteurized	J. Stout	126	34,530
1939	Johnstown	J. Stout	126	37,020
1940	Bimelech	F.A. Smith	126	35,030
1941	Whirlaway	E. Arcaro	126	39,770
1942	Shut Out	E. Arcaro	126	44,520
1943	Count Fleet	J. Longden	126	35,340
1944	Bounding Home	G.L. Smith	126	55,000
1945	Pavot	E. Arcaro	126	56,675
1946	Assault	W. Mehrtens	126	75,400
1947	Phalanx	R. Donoso	126	78,900
1948	Citation	E. Arcaro	126	77,700
1949	Capot	T. Atkinson	126	60,900
1950	Middleground	W. Boland	126	61,350
1951	Counterpoint	D. Gorman	126	82,000
1952	One Count	E. Arcaro	126	82,400
1953	Native Dancer	E. Guerin	126	82,500
1954	High Gun	E. Guerin	126	89,000
1955	Nashua	E. Arcaro	126	83,700
1956	Needles	D. Erb	126	83,600
1957	Gallant Man	W. Shoemaker	126	77,300
1958	Cavan	P. Anderson	126	73,440
1959	Sword Dancer	W. Shoemaker	126	93,525
1960	Celtic Ash	W. Hartack	126	96,785
1961	Sherluck	B. Baeza	126	104,900
1962	Jaipur	W. Shoemaker	126	109,550
1963	Chateauguay	B. Baeza	126	$101,700
1964	Quadrangle	M. Ycaza	126	110,850
1965	Hail to All	J. Sellers	126	104,150
1966	Amberoid	W. Boland	126	117,700
1967	Damascus	W. Shoemaker	126	104,950
1968	Stage Door Johnny	H. Gustines	126	117,700
1969	Arts and Letters	B. Baeza	126	104,050
1970	High Echelon	J. Rotz	126	115,000
1971	Pass Catcher	R. Blum	126	97,710
1972	Riva Ridge	R. Turcotte	126	93,540
1973	Secretariat	R. Turcotte	126	90,120
1974	Little Current	M. Rivera	126	101,970
1975	Avatar	W. Shoemaker	126	116,160
1976	Bold Forbes	A. Cordero, Jr.	126	117,000
1977	Seattle Slew	J. Cruguet	126	109,080
1978	Affirmed	S. Cauthen	126	110,580
1979	Coastal	R. Hernandez	126	161,400
1980	Temperence Hill	E. Maple	126	176,220
1981	Summing	G. Martens	126	170,580
1982	Conquistador Cielo	L. Pincay, Jr.	126	159,720
1983	Caveat	L. Pincay, Jr.	126	215,100
1984	Swale	L. Pincay, Jr.	126	310,020
1985	Creme Fraiche	Eddie Maple	126	307,740
1986	Danzig Connection	C. McCarron	126	338,640
1987	Bet Twice	C. Perret	126	329,160
1988	Risen Star	E. Delahoussaye	126	303,720
1989	Easy Goer	P. Day	126	413,520
1990	Go And Go	Michael Kinane	126	411,600
1991	Hansel	Jerry Bailey	126	417,480
1992	A.P. Indy	E. Delahoussay	126	458,880
1993	Colonial Affair	Julie Krone	126	444,450

TRIPLE CROWN RACES—1993

Kentucky Derby (Churchill Downs, Louisville, Ky., May 1, 1993). Gross purse: $985,900. Distance: 1 1/4 miles. Order of finish: 1. Sea Hero (Bailey), mutuel return: $27.80, $12.80, $8.00. 2. Prairie Bayou (Smith) $7.20, $4.80. 3. Wild Gale (Sellers) $4.20. 4. Personal Hope (Stevens). 5. Diazo (Desormeaux). 6. Corby (McCarron). 7. Kissin Kris (Santos). 8. Silver of Silver (Vasquez). 9. Ragtime Rebel (Lester). 10. Truth of it All (Velasquez). 11. Bull in the Heather (Ramos). 12. Dixieland Heat (Romero). 13. Wallenda (Day). 14. Mi Cielo (Gryder). 15. Union City (Valenzuela). 16. Storm Tower (Wilson). 17. Rockamundo (Borel). 18. El Bakan (Perret). 19. Tossofthecoin (Pincay). Winner's purse: $745,900. Margin of victory: 2 1/2 lengths. Time of race: 2:02 2/5.

Preakness Stakes (Pimlico, Md., May 15, 1993). Gross purse: $725,900. Distance: 1 3/16 miles. Order of finish: 1. Prairie Bayou (Smith), mutuel return: $6.40, $3.60, $3.40. 2. Cherokee Run (Day) $7.20, $5.20. 3. El Bakan (Perret) $14.60. 4. Personal Hope (Stevens). 5. Sea Hero (Bailey). 6. Woods of Windsor (Wilson). 7. Rockamundo (Prado). 8. Wild Gale (Sellers). 9. Hegar (Ferrer). 10. Koluctoo Jimmy Al (McCarron). 11. Too Wild (McCauley). Did not finish: Union City (Valenzuela). Winner's purse: $471,835. Margin of victory: 1 1/2 lengths. Time of race: 1:56 3/5.

Belmont Stakes (Elmont, N.Y., June 5, 1993). Gross purse: $740,900. Distance: 1 1/2 miles. Order of finish: 1. Colonial Affair (Krone), mutuel return: $29.80, $14.80, $9.40. 2. Kissin Kris (Santos) $11.20, $7.20. 3. Wild Gale (Sellers) $14.00. 4. Silver of Silver (Vasquez). 5. Virginia Rapids (Maple). 6. Cherokee Run (Antley). 7. Sea Hero (Bailey). 8. Bull in the Heather (Chavez). 9. Antrim Rd. (Migliore). 10. Raglan Road (Pincay). 11. Only Alpha (Davis). 12. Arinthod (Desormeaux). Did not finish: Prairie Bayou (Smith). Winner's purse: $444,450. Margin of victory: 2 1/4 lengths. Time of race: 2:29 4/5.

ECLIPSE AWARDS—1992

(Presented February 1993)

Horse of the Year	AP Indy
4-year-old and up colt, horse, or gelding	Pleasant Tap
3-year-old colt or gelding	AP Indy
3-year-old filly	Saratoga Dew
4-year-old and up filly or mare	Paseana
Jockey	Kent Desormeaux
Trainer	Ron McAnally
Breeder	William S. Farish III
Owner	Juddmonte Farms
Apprentice jockey	Jesus A. Bracho
2-year-old colt	Gilded Time
2-year-old filly	Eliza
Sprinter	Rubiano
Male turf horse	Sky Classic
Female turf horse	Flawlessly
Steeplechase	Lonesome Glory

(Based on vote by the Thoroughbred Racing Associations, the *Daily Racing Form*, and the National Turf Writers Association.)

TRACK AND FIELD

WORLD RECORDS—MEN

Source: USA Track & Field
(Through Sept. 13, 1993)

Recognized by the International Athletic Federation.
The I.A.A.F. decided late in 1976 not to recognize records in yards except for the one-mile run.
The I.A.A.F. also requires automatic timing for all records for races of 400 meters or less.

Event	Record	Holder	Home Country	Where Made	Date
Running					
100 m	0:09.86	Carl Lewis	United States	Tokyo, Japan	Aug. 25, 1991
200 m	0:19.72	Pietro Mennea	Italy	Mexico City	Sept. 17, 1979
400 m	0:43.29	Butch Reynolds	United States	Indianapolis, Ind.	Aug. 17, 1988
800 m	1:41.80	Sebastian Coe	England	Florence, Italy	June 10, 1981
1,000 m	2:12.40	Sebastian Coe	England	Oslo, Norway	July 11, 1981
1,500 m	3:29.45	Said Aouita	Morocco	Berlin	August 23, 1985
1 mile	3:44.39	Noureddine Morceli	Algeria	Rieti, Italy	Sept. 5, 1993
2,000 m	4:50.81	Said Aouita	Morocco	Paris	July 16, 1987
3,000 m	7:28.96	Moses Kiptanui	Kenya	Cologne	Aug. 16, 1992
3,000 m steeplechase	8:02.08	Moses Kiptanui	Kenya	Zurich	Aug. 19, 1992
5,000 m	12:58.39	Said Aouita	Morocco	Rome	July 22, 1987
10,000 m	26:58.38	Yobes Ondieki	Kenya	Oslo, Norway	July 10, 1993
25,000 m	1:13:55.80	Toshihiko Seko	Japan	Christchurch, N.Z.	March 22, 1981
30,000 m	1:29:18.80	Toshihiko Seko	Japan	Christchurch, N.Z.	March 22, 1981
20,000 m	56:55.60	Arturo Barrios	Mexico	La Fleche, France	March 30, 1991
1 hour	21,101 m	Arturo Barrios	Mexico	La Fleche, France	March 30, 1991
Marathon	2:06.50	Belayneh Densimo	Ethiopia	Rotterdam	April 17, 1988
Walking					
20,000 m	1:18:35.20	Stefan Johansson	Sweden	Fana, Norway	May 15, 1992
2 hours	17 mi. 1,092 yd	Ralph Kowalsky	East Germany	East Berlin	March 28, 1982
30,000 m	2:06:27.00	Maurizio Damilano	Italy	Milanese, Italy	May 5, 1985
50,000 m	3:41.39	Raul Gonzales	Mexico	Bergen, Norway	May 25, 1979
Hurdles					
110 m	0:12.91	Colin Jackson	Great Britain	Stuttgart, Germany	Aug. 20, 1993
400 m	0:46.78	Kevin Young	United States	Barcelona	Aug. 6, 1992
Relay Races					
400 m (4 × 100)	0:37.40	United States		Stuttgart, Germany	Aug. 21, 1993
800 m (4 × 200)	1:19.11	Santa Monica T.C.	United States	Philadelphia	April 25, 1992
1,600 m (4 × 400)	2:54.29	United States		Stuttgart, Germany	Aug. 21, 1993
3,200 m (4 × 800)	7:03.89	National Team (Peter Elliot, Garry Cook, Steve Cram, Sebastian Coe)	Britain	London	Aug. 30, 1982
Field Events					
High Jump	8 ft 1/2 in.	Javier Sotomayor	Cuba	Salamanca, Spain	July 27, 1993
Long jump	29 ft 4 1/2 in.	Mike Powell	United States	Tokyo, Japan	Aug. 30, 1991
Triple Jump	58 ft 11 1/2 in.	Willie Banks	Los Angeles, Ca.	Indianapolis	June 16, 1985
Pole vault	20 ft 1 in.	Sergey Bubka	Unified Team	Padua	Aug. 30, 1992
Shot-put	75 ft 10 1/4 in.	Randy Barnes	United States	Los Angeles	May 20, 1990
Discus throw	243 ft 0 in.	Juergen Schult	East Germany	Neubrandenburg	June 6, 1986
Hammer throw	284 ft 7 in.	Yuriy Syedikh	U.S.S.R.	Stuttgart	Aug. 28, 1986
Javelin throw	313 ft 10 in.	Jon Zelezny	Czech Republic	Sheffield, Great Britain	Aug. 29, 1993
Decathlon	8,798 pts.	Jurgen Hingsen	W. Germany	Mannheim, W. Ger.	June 8–9, 1984

WORLD RECORDS—WOMEN

Source: USA Track & Field
(Through Sept. 13, 1993)

Event	Record	Holder	Home Country	Where Made	Date
Running					
100 m	0:10.49	Florence Griffith-Joyner	United States	Indianapolis, Ind.	July 16, 1988
200 m	0:21.56	Florence Griffith-Joyner	United States	Seoul, South Korea	Oct. 1, 1988
400 m	0:47.60	Martina Koch	East Germany	Canberra	Oct. 6, 1985
800 m	1:53.28	Jarmila Kratochvilova	Czechoslovakia	Munich, W. Ger.	July 26, 1983
1,500 m	3:50.46	Qu Yunxia	China	Beijing, China	Sept. 11, 1993
1 mile	4:15.61	Paula Ivan	Romania	Nice, Italy	July 10, 1989
3,000 m	8:06.11	Wang Junxia	China	Beijing, China	Sept. 13, 1993
5,000 m	14:37.33	Ingrid Kristiansen	Norway	Stockholm	Aug. 5, 1986

10,000 m	29:31.78	Wang Junxia	China	Beijing, China	Sept. 8, 1993
Marathon	2:21:06.0	Ingrid Kristiansen	Norway	London	April 21, 1985
Walking					
5,000 m	20:07.52	Beate Anders	East Germany	Rostock	June 23, 1990
10,000 m	41:30.00	Ileana Salvador	Italy	Livorno, Italy	July 10, 1993
Hurdles					
100–m hurdles	0:12.25	Ginka Zagorcheva	Bulgaria	Greece	August 8, 1987
400 m	0:52.74	Sally Gunnell	Great Britain	Stuttgart, Germany	Aug. 19, 1993
Relay Races					
400 m (4 × 100)	0:41.53	East Germany	E. Germany	Berlin, E. Ger.	July 31, 1983
800 m (4 × 200)	1:28.15	East Germany	E. Germany	Jena, E. Ger.	Aug. 9, 1980
1,600 m (4 × 400)	3:15.18	Soviet Union	Soviet Union	Seoul, South Korea	Oct. 1, 1988
3,200 m (4 × 800)	7:52.3	U.S.S.R.	U.S.S.R.	Podolsk, U.S.S.R.	Aug. 16, 1976
Field Events					
High jump	6 ft 10 1/4 in.	Stefka Kostadinova	Bulgaria	Rome	August 30, 1987
Long jump	24 ft 8 1/4 in.	Galina Chistyakova	Soviet Union	Leningrad	June 11, 1988
Triple jump	49 ft 6 1/4 in.	Ana Biryukova	Russia	Stuttgart, Germany	Aug. 21, 1993
Shot–put	74 ft 3 in.	Natalya Lisovskaya	U.S.S.R.	Moscow	June 7, 1987
Discus throw	252 ft 0 in.	Gabriele Reinsch	East Germany	Neubrandenburg, E. Ger.	July 9, 1988
Javelin throw	262 ft 5 in.	Petra Felke	East Germany	Potsdam	Sept. 9, 1988
Heptathlon	7,291 pts	Jackie Joyner–Kersee	United States	Seoul, South Korea	Sept. 24, 1988

AMERICAN RECORDS—MEN

Source: USA Track & Field

(Through Sept. 13, 1993)

Event	Record	Holder	Where Made	Date
Running				
100 m	0:09.86	Carl Lewis	Tokyo, Japan	Aug. 25, 1991
200 m	0:19.73	Mike Marsh	Barcelona	Aug. 5, 1992
400 m	0:43.29	Butch Reynolds	Indianapolis, Ind.	Aug. 17, 1988
800 m	1:42.60	Johnny Gray	Koblenz, W. Ger.	Aug. 29, 1985
1,000 m	2:13.9	Richard Wohlhuter	Oslo, Norway	July 30, 1974
1,500 m	3:29.77	Sydney Maree	Cologne, W. Ger.	Aug. 25, 1985
1 mile	3:47.69	Steve Scott	Oslo, Norway	July 7, 1982
2,000 m	4:54.71	Steve Scott	Ingelhelm, W. Ger.	Aug. 31, 1982
3,000 m	7:35.84	Doug Padilla	Oslo, Norway	July 9, 1983
5,000 m	13:01.15	Sydney Maree	Oslo, Norway	July 27, 1985
10,000 m	27:20.56	Mark Nenow	Brussels	Sept. 5, 1986
20,000 m	58:15.0	Bill Rodgers	Boston, Mass.	Aug. 9, 1977
25,000 m	1:14:11.8	Bill Rodgers	Saratoga, Cal.	Feb. 21, 1979
30,000 m	1:31:49.0	Bill Rodgers	Saratoga, Cal.	Feb. 21, 1979
1 hour	12 mi., 1351 yds	Bill Rodgers	Boston, Mass.	Aug. 9, 1977
3,000–m steeplechase	8:09.17	Henry Marsh	Koblenz, W. Ger.	Aug. 29, 1985
Hurdles				
110 m	0:12.92	Roger Kingdom	Berlin	Aug. 16, 1989
400 m	0:46.78	Kevin Young	Barcelona	Aug. 6, 1992
Relay Races				
400 m (4 × 100)	0:37.40	USA National Team	Stuttgart, Germany	Aug. 21, 1993
800 m (4 × 200)	1:19.11	Santa Monica T.C.	Philadelphia	April 25, 1992
1,600 m (4 × 400)	2:54.29	USA National Team	Stuttgart, Germany	Aug. 22, 1993
3,200 m (4 × 800)	7:06.50	Santa Monica T.C.	Walnut	Apr. 26, 1986
Field Events				
High jump	7 ft 10 1/2 in.	Charles Austin	Zurich	Aug. 7, 1991
Long jump	29 ft 4 1/2 in.	Mike Powell	Tokyo, Japan	Aug. 30, 1991
Triple jump	58 ft 11 1/2 in.	Willie Banks	Indianapolis, Ind.	June 16, 1985
Pole vault	19 ft 6 1/2 in.	Joe Dial	Norman	June 18, 1987
Shot–put	75 ft 10 1/4 in.	Randy Barnes	Los Angeles	May 20, 1990
Discus throw	237 ft 4 in.	Ben Plucknett	Stockholm, Swe.	July 7, 1981
Javelin throw	281 ft 2 in.	Tom Pukstys	Kourtane, Finland	June 26, 1993
Hammer throw	268 ft 8 in.	Judd Logan	University Park, Pa.	April 23, 1988
Decathlon	8,812 pts	Dan O'Brien	Tokyo, Japan	Aug. 29–30, 1991

AMERICAN RECORDS—WOMEN

Source: USA Track & Field (Through Sept. 13, 1993)

Event	Record	Holder	Where Made	Date
Running				
100 m	0:10.49	Florence Griffith–Joyner	Indianapolis, Ind.	July 16, 1988
200 m	0:21.56	Florence Griffith–Joyner	Seoul, South Korea	Oct. 1, 1988
400 m	0:48.83	Valerie Brisco–Hooks	Los Angeles, Cal.	Aug. 6, 1984
800 m	1:56.90	Mary Decker Slaney	Bern	Aug. 16, 1985
1,500 m	3:57.12	Mary Decker Slaney	Stockholm, Swe.	July 26, 1983
1000 m	2:34.8	Mary Decker Slaney	Eugene, Ore.	July 4, 1985
1 mile	4:16.71	Mary Decker Slaney	Zurich	Aug. 21, 1985
3,000 m	8:29.69	Mary Decker Slaney	Cologne	Aug. 25, 1985
5,000 m	14:56.07	Annette Peters	Berlin, Germany	Aug. 27, 1993
10,000 m	31:28.92	Francie L. Smith	Austin, Texas	April 4, 1991
Hurdles				
100 m hurdles	0:12.46	Gail Devers	Stuttgart, Germany	Aug. 20, 1993
400 m hurdles	0:52.79	Sandra Farmer–Patrick	Stuttgart, Germany	Aug. 19, 1993
Relay Races				
400 m (4 × 100)	0:41.49	U.S. National Team	Stuttgart, Germany	Aug. 22, 1993
800 m (4 × 200)	1:32.57	Louisiana State	Des Moines, Iowa	April 28, 1989
1,600 m (4 × 400)	3:15.51	U.S. Olympic Team	Seoul, South Korea	Oct. 1, 1988
Field Events				
High jump	6 ft 8 in.	Louise Ritter	Austin, Tex.	July 9, 1988
Long jump	24 ft. 5 1/2 in.	Jackie Joyner–Kersee	Indianapolis	August 12, 1987
Triple jump	46 ft. 8 1/4 in.	Sheila Hudson	New Orleans	June 20, 1992
Shot–put	66 ft. 2 1/2 in.	Ramon Pagel	San Diego, Calif.	June 25, 1988
Discus throw	216 ft 10 in.	Carol Cady	San Jose, Calif.	May 31, 1986
Javelin throw	227 ft 5 in.	Kate Schmidt	Furth, W. Ger.	Sept. 10, 1977
Heptathlon	7,291 pts	Jackie Joyner–Kersee	Seoul, South Korea	Sept. 23–24, 1988

HISTORY OF THE RECORD FOR THE MILE RUN

Source: USA Track & Field

Time	Athlete	Country	Year	Location
4:36.5	Richard Webster	England	1865	England
4:29.0	William Chinnery	England	1868	England
4:28.8	Walter Gibbs	England	1868	England
4:26.0	Walter Slade	England	1874	England
4:24.5	Walter Slade	England	1875	London
4:23.2	Walter George	England	1880	London
4:21.4	Walter George	England	1882	London
4:18.4	Walter George	England	1884	Birmingham, England
4:18.2	Fred Bacon	Scotland	1894	Edinburgh, Scotland
4:17.0	Fred Bacon	Scotland	1895	London
4:15.6	Thomas Conneff	United States	1895	Travers Island, N.Y.
4:15.4	John Paul Jones	United States	1911	Cambridge, Mass.
4:14.4	John Paul Jones	United States	1913	Cambridge, Mass.
4:12.6	Norman Taber	United States	1915	Cambridge, Mass.
4:10.4	Paavo Nurmi	Finland	1923	Stockholm
4:09.2	Jules Ladoumegue	France	1931	Paris
4:07.6	Jack Lovelock	New Zealand	1933	Princeton, N.J.
4:06.8	Glenn Cunningham	United States	1934	Princeton, N.J.
4:06.4	Sydney Wooderson	England	1937	London
4:06.2	Gundar Hägg	Sweden	1942	Goteborg, Sweden
4:06.2	Arne Andersson	Sweden	1942	Stockholm
4:04.6	Gunder Hägg	Sweden	1942	Stockholm
4:02.6	Arne Andersson	Sweden	1943	Goteborg, Sweden
4:01.6	Arne Andersson	Sweden	1944	Malmo, Sweden
4:01.4	Gunder Hägg	Sweden	1945	Malmo, Sweden
3:59.4	Roger Bannister	England	1954	Oxford, England
3:58.0	John Landy	Australia	1954	Turku, Finland
3:57.2	Derek Ibbotson	England	1957	London
3:54.5	Herb Elliott	Australia	1958	Dublin
3:54.4	Peter Snell	New Zealand	1962	Wanganui, N.Z.
3:54.1	Peter Snell	New Zealand	1964	Auckland, N.Z.
3:53.6	Michel Jazy	France	1965	Rennes, France
3:51.3	Jim Ryun	United States	1966	Berkeley, Calif.
3:51.1	Jim Ryun	United States	1967	Bakersfield, Calif.
3:51.0	Filbert Bayi	Tanzania	1975	Kingston, Jamaica
3:49.4	John Walker	New Zealand	1975	Goteborg, Sweden
3:49.0	Sebastian Coe	England	1979	Oslo

3:48.8	Steve Ovett	England	1980	Oslo
3:48.53	Sebastian Coe	England	1981	Zurich, Switzerland
3:48.40	Steve Ovett	England	1981	Koblenz, W. Ger.
3:47.33	Sebastian Coe	England	1981	Brussels
3:46.31	Steve Cram	England	1985	Oslo
3:44.39	Noureddine Morceli	Algeria	1993	Rieti, Italy

TOP TEN WORLD'S FASTEST OUTDOOR MILES

Source: USA Track & Field

Time	Athlete	Country	Date	Location
3:44.39	Noureddine Morceli	Algeria	Sept. 5, 1993	Rieti, Italy
3:46.31	Steve Cram	England	July 27, 1985	Oslo
3:47.33	Sebastian Coe	England	Aug. 28, 1981	Brussels
3:47.69	Steve Scott	United States	July 7, 1982	Oslo
3:47.79	Jose Gonzalez	Spain	July 27, 1985	Oslo
3:48.40	Steve Ovett	England	Aug. 26, 1981	Koblenz, W. Ger.
3:48.53	Sebastian Coe	England	Aug. 19, 1981	Zurich
3:48.53	Steve Scott	United States	June 26, 1982	Oslo
3:48.8	Steve Ovett	England	July 1, 1980	Oslo
3:48.83	Sydney Maree	United States	Sept. 9, 1981	Rieti, Italy

NOTE: Professional marks not included.

TOP TEN WORLD'S FASTEST INDOOR MILES

Source: USA Track & Field

Time	Athlete	Country	Date	Location
3:49.78	Eamonn Coghlan	Ireland	Feb. 27, 1983	East Rutherford, N.J.
3:50.6	Eamonn Coghlan	Ireland	Feb. 20, 1981	San Diego
3:50.7	Noureddine Morceli	Algeria	Feb. 20, 1993	Birmingham, England
3:50.94	Marcus O'Sullivan	Ireland	Feb. 13, 1988	East Rutherford, N.J.
3:51.2	Ray Flynn[1]	Ireland	Feb. 27, 1983	East Rutherford, N.J.
3:51.66	Marcus O'Sullivan	Ireland	Feb. 10, 1989	East Rutherford, N.J.
3:51.8	Steve Scott[1]	United States	Feb. 20, 1981	San Diego
3:52.28	Steve Scott[2]	United States	Feb. 27, 1983	East Rutherford, N.J.
3:52:30	Frank O'Mara	Ireland	Feb. 1986	New York
3:52.37	Eamonn Coughlan	Ireland	Feb. 9, 1985	East Rutherford, N.J.

1. Finished second. 2. Finished third.

WORLD CHAMPIONSHIPS—1993

(Stuttgart, Germany, Aug. 14–22, 1993)

Men's Events

100 m—Linford Christie, Great Britain	0:09.87
200 m—Frank Fredericks, Namibia	0:19.85
400 m—Michael Johnson, United States	0:43.65
800 m—Paul Ruto, Kenya	1:44.71
1,500 m—Noureddine Morceli, Algeria	3:34.24
3,000 m steeplechase—Moses Kiptanui, Kenya	8:06.36
5,000 m—Ismael Kirui, Kenya	13:02.75
10,000 m—Haile Gebresilasie, Ethiopia	27:46.02
Marathon—Mark Plaatjes, United States	2:13:57.00
110-m hurdles—Colin Jackson, Great Britain	0:12.91*
400-m hurdles—Kevin Young, United States	0:47.18
20–k walk—Valentin Massana, Spain	1:22.31
50–k walk—Jesus Angel Garcia, Spain	3:41.41
400–m relay—United States (John Drummond, Andre Cason, Dennis Mitchell, Leroy Burrell)	0:37.48
1,600–m relay—United States (Andrew Valmon, Quincy Watts, Butch Reynolds, Michael Johnson)	2:54.29*
High jump—Javier Sotomayor, Cuba	7 ft 10 1/2 in.
Pole vault—Sergei Bubka, Ukraine	19 ft 8 1/4 in.
Long jump—Mike Powell, United States	28 ft 2 1/4 in.
Triple jump—Mike Conley, United States	58 ft 7 1/4 in.
Shot-put—Werner Gunthor, Switzerland	72 ft 1 in.
Discus—Lars Riedel, Germany	222 ft 2 in.
Hammer throw—Andrey Abduvaliyev, Tajikistan	267 ft 10 in.
Javelin—Jan Zelezny, Czech Republic	282 ft 1 in.
Decathlon—Dan O'Brien, United States	8,817 pts

Women's Events

100 m—Gail Devers, United States	0:10.82
200 m—Merlene Ottey, Jamaica	0:21.98
400 m—Jearl Miles, United States	0:49.82
800 m—Maria Mutola, Mozambique	1:55.43
1,500 m—Dong Liu, China	4:00.50
3,000 m—Yunxia Qu, China	8:28.71
10,000 m—Junxia Wang, China	30:49.30
Marathon—Junko Asari, Japan	2:30:03.00
10-k walk—Sari Essayah, Finland	42:59.00
100-m hurdles—Gail Devers, United States	0:12.46
400-m hurdles—Sally Gunnell, Great Britain	0:52.74*
400-m relay—Russia	0:41.49
1,600-m relay—United States (Gwen Torrance, Maicel Malone, Natasha Kaiser-Brown, Jearl Miles)	3:16.71
High jump—Ioamnet Quintero, Cuba	6 ft 6 1/4 in.
Long jump—Heike Dreschler, Germany	23 ft 4 in.
Triple jump—Ana Biryukova, Russia	49 ft 6 1/4 in.*
Shot-put—Zhihong Huang, China	67 ft 6 in.
Discus—Olga Buruova, Russia	221 ft 1 in.
Javelin—Trine Hattesstad, Norway	227 ft 0 in.
Heptathlon—Jackie Joyner-Kersee, United States	5,785 pts

*World record.

USA/MOBIL OUTDOOR TRACK & FIELD CHAMPIONSHIP—1993

(June 15–19, 1993, University of Oregon, Eugene, Ore.)

Men's Events

100 m—Andre Cason	0:09.85
200 m—Michael Marsh	0:19.97
400 m—Michael Johnson	0:43.74
800 m—Mark Everett	1:44.43
1,500 m—William Burke	3:42.74
3,000 m—Marc Davis	8:20.93
5,000 m—Matt Giusto	13:23.60
10,000 m—Todd Williams	28:02.05
110-m hurdles—Jack Pierce	0:13.19
400-m hurdles—Kevin Young	0:47.69
20-k walk—Allen James	1:29:09.00
High jump—Hollis Conway	7 ft 7 in.
Pole vault—Scott Huffman	18 ft 8 1/4 in.
Long jump—Mike Powell	28 ft 0 in.
Triple jump—Mike Conley	58 ft 1/2 in.
Shot-put—Randy Barnes	69 ft 9 3/4 in.
Discus—Anthony Washington	207 ft 6 in.
Javelin—Tom Pukstys	272 ft 6 in.
Hammer throw—Lance Deal	256 ft 3 in.
Decathlon—Dan O'Brien	8,331 pts

Team—1. Reebok Track Club, 58.5. 2. Nike International, 45.5. 3. Santa Barbara Track Club, 45.0.

Women's Events

100 m—Gail Devers	0:10.82
200 m—Gwen Torrence	0:22.57
400 m—Jearl Miles	0:50.43
800 m—Joetta Clark	2:01.47
1,500 m—Annette Peters	4:11.53
2,000 m steeplechase—Maris Sutera	7:27.30
3,000 m—Annette Peters	8:48.59
5,000 m—Christine McNamara	16:11.85
10,000 m—Lynn Jennings	31:57.83
100-m hurdles—Lynda Tolbert	0:12.82
400-m hurdles—Sandra Patrick-Farmer	0:53.96
10,000-m walk—Debbi Lawrence	45:55.00
High jump—Tanya Hughes	6 ft 2 3/4 in.
Long jump—Jackie Joyner-Kersee	23 ft 1/2 in.
Triple jump—Claudia Haywood	45 ft 5 3/4 in.
Shot-put—Connie Price-Smith	62 ft 5 in.
Discus—Connie Price-Smith	208 ft 5 in.
Javelin—Donna Mayhew	206 ft 7 in.
Hammer throw—Sonja Fitts	190 ft 2 in.
Heptathlon—Jackie Joyner-Kersee	6,770 pts

Team—1. Reebok Track Club, 58. 2. Nike Coast Track Club, 53.5. 3. Nike Track Club, 30.

N.C.A.A. CHAMPIONSHIPS—1993

OUTDOOR

(June 2–5, 1993, at Tulane University)

Men's Events

100 m—Michael Green, Clemson	0:10.09
200 m—Chris Nelloms, Ohio State	0:20.27
400 m—Calvin Davis, Arkansas	0:45.04
800 m—Jose Parrilla, Tennessee	1:46.51
1,500 m—Marko Korers, Illinois	3:38.50
3,000 m–steeplechase—Donovan Bergstrom, Wisconsin	8:29.08
5,000 m—Jon Dennis, South Florida	13:59.0
10,000 m—Jonah Koech, Iowa State	28:28.67
110-m hurdles—Glenn Terry, Indiana	0:13.43
400-m hurdles—Bryan Bronson, Rice	0:49.07
400-m relays—Louisiana State	0:38.70
1,600-m relays—Ohio State	3:00.82
Pole vault—Mark Buse, Indiana	18 ft 4 1/2 in.
High jump—Randy Jenkins, Tennessee	7 ft 5 3/4 in.
Long jump—Eric Walder, Arkansas	28 ft
Triple jump—Tyrell Taitt, No. Carolina State	55 ft 5 3/4 in.
Shot-put—Brent Noon, Georgia	66 ft 11 1/2 in.
Discus—Brian Milne, Penn State	200 ft 5 in.
Javelin—Erik Smith, UCLA	259 ft 10 in.
Hammer—Balazs Kiss, Southern California	246 ft 10 in.
Decathlon—Chris Huffins, California	8,007 pts

Team—1. Arkansas, 69; 2. Louisiana State, 45; 2. Ohio State, 45.

Women's Events

100 m—Holly Hyche, Indiana State	0:11.14
200 m—Holly Hyche, Indiana State	0:22.34
400 m—Juliet Campbell, Auburn	0:50.58
800 m—Kim Sherman, Wisconsin	2:02.99
1,500 m—Claire Eichner, Wisconsin	4:20.12
3,000 m—Claire Eichner, Wisconsin	9:03.06
5,000 m—Kay Gooch, Oklahoma	16:31.02
10,000 m—Carole Zajac, Villanova	34:18.14
100-m hurdles (wind aided)—Gillian Russell, Miami–Florida	0:13.02
400-m hurdles—Debbie Ann Parris, Louisiana State	0:56.37
400-m relay—Louisiana State	0:43.49
1,600-m relay—Louisiana State	3:27.97
High jump—Tanya Hughes, Arizona	6 ft 3 1/2 in.
Long jump—Daphne Saunders, Louisiana State	22 ft 2 1/2 in.
Triple jump—Claudia Haywood, Rice	44 ft 5 1/4 in.
Shot-put—Dawn Dumble, UCLA	56 ft 4 in.
Discus—Danyel Mitchell, Louisiana State	186 ft 6 in.
Javelin—Ashley Selmen, Oregon	188 ft 5 in.
Heptathlon—Kelly Blair, Oregon	6,038 pts

Team—1. Louisiana State, 93 pts; 2. Wisconsin, 44; 3. UCLA, 38.

QUARTER HORSE RACING—1993

All American Futurity—A Classic Dash

1993 Leading Horses by Money Earned

		ST	W	P	S	Earnings
1.	A Classic Dash	8	7	1	0	$1,078,617
2.	Treacherously	9	8	0	1	548,000
3.	Heza Fast Man	6	4	2	0	349,654
4.	Zipuino	2	2	0	0	230,080
5.	Four Forty Blast	8	7	0	1	194,233
6.	Royal Down Dash	10	6	0	1	182,038
7.	Refrigerator	3	3	0	0	179,636
8.	Md Hammertime	6	2	2	0	165,199
9.	King Khalid	7	5	1	0	150,952
10.	Coup De Main	8	1	2	1	127,588

As of September 21.

All-Time Leading Horses by Money Earned

		ST	W	P	S	Earnings
1.	Eastex	13	4	5	4	$1,869,406
2.	Mr. Master Bug	25	17	4	3	1,793,718
3.	Ronas Ryon	23	18	4	0	1,777,977
4.	Refrigerator	25	18	6	1	1,770,507
5.	Dashingly	25	18	5	0	1,754,323
6.	Higheasterjet	30	20	2	2	1,633,035
7.	Merganser	23	13	3	2	1,373,704
8.	Strawberry Silk	17	11	3	0	1,266,264
9.	Dash For Speed	30	22	3	2	1,225,337
10.	Special Effort	14	13	0	1	1,219,950

Source: American Quarter Horse Association.

TENNIS

Lawn tennis is a comparatively modern modification of the ancient game of court tennis. Major Walter Clopton Wingfield thought that something like court tennis might be played outdoors on lawns, and in December, 1873, at Nantclwyd, Wales, he introduced his new game under the name of *Sphairistike* at a lawn party. The game was a success and spread rapidly, but the name was a total failure and almost immediately disappeared when all the players and spectators began to refer to the new game as "lawn tennis." In the early part of 1874, a young lady named Mary Ewing Outerbridge returned from Bermuda to New York, bringing with her the implements and necessary equipment of the new game, which she had obtained from a British Army supply store in Bermuda. Miss Outerbridge and friends played the first game of lawn tennis in the United States on the grounds of the Staten Island Cricket and Baseball Club in the spring of 1874.

For a few years, the new game went along in haphazard fashion until about 1880, when standard measurements for the court and standard equipment within definite limits became the rule. In 1881, the U.S. Lawn Tennis Association (whose name was changed in 1975 to U.S. Tennis Association) was formed and conducted the first national championship at Newport, R.I. The international matches for the Davis Cup began with a series between the British and United States players on the courts of the Longwood Cricket Club, Chestnut Hill, Mass., in 1900, with the home players winning.

Professional tennis, which got its start in 1926 when the French star Suzanne Lenglen was paid $50,000 for a tour, received full recognition in 1968. Staid old Wimbledon, the London home of what are considered the world championships, let the pros compete. This decision ended a long controversy over open tennis and changed the format of the competition. The United States championships were also opened to the pros and the site of the event, long held at Forest Hills, N.Y., was shifted to the National Tennis Center in Flushing Meadows, N.Y., in 1978. Pro tours for men and women became worldwide in play that continued throughout the year.

DAVIS CUP CHAMPIONSHIPS

No matches in 1901, 1910, 1915–18, and 1940–45.

1900	United States 3, British Isles 0
1902	United States 3, British Isles 2
1903	British Isles 4, United States 1
1904	British Isles 5, Belgium 0
1905	British Isles 5, United States 0
1906	British Isles 5, United States 0
1907	Australasia 3, British Isles 2
1908	Australasia 3, United States 2
1909	Australasia 5, United States 0
1911	Australasia 5, United States 0
1912	British Isles 3, Australasia 2
1913	United States 3, British Isles 2
1914	Australasia 3, United States 2
1919	Australasia 4, British Isles 1
1920	United States 5, Australasia 0
1921	United States 5, Japan 0
1922	United States 4, Australasia 1
1923	United States 4, Australasia 1
1924	United States 5, Australasia 0
1925	United States 5, France 0
1926	United States 4, France 1
1927	France 3, United States 2
1928	France 4, United States 1
1929	France 3, United States 2
1930	France 4, United States 1
1931	France 3, Great Britain 2
1932	France 3, United States 2
1933	Great Britain 3, France 2
1934	Great Britain 4, United States 1
1935	Great Britain 5, United States 0
1936	Great Britain 3, Australia 2
1937	United States 4, Great Britain 1
1938	United States 3, Australia 2
1939	Australia 3, United States 2
1946	United States 5, Australia 0
1947	United States 4, Australia 1
1948	United States 5, Australia 0
1949	United States 4, Australia 1
1950	Australia 4, United States 1
1951	Australia 3, United States 2
1952	Australia 4, United States 1
1953	Australia 3, United States 2
1954	United States 3, Australia 2
1955	Australia 5, United States 0
1956	Australia 5, United States 0
1957	Australia 3, United States 2
1958	United States 3, Australia 2
1959	Australia 3, United States 2
1960	Australia 4, Italy 1
1961	Australia 5, Italy 0
1962	Australia 5, Mexico 0
1963	United States 3, Australia 2
1964	Australia 3, United States 2
1965	Australia 4, Spain 1
1966	Australia 4, India 1
1967	Australia 4, Spain 1
1968	United States 4, Australia 1
1969	United States 5, Romania 0
1970	United States 5, West Germany 0
1971	United States 3, Romania 2
1972	United States 3, Romania 2
1973	Australia 5, United States 0
1974	South Africa (Default by India)
1975	Sweden 3, Czechoslovakia 2
1976	Italy 4, Chile 1
1977	Australia 3, Italy 1
1978	United States 4, Britain 1
1979	United States 5, Italy 0
1980	Czechoslovakia 3, Italy 2
1981	United States 3, Argentina 1
1982	United States 3, France 0
1983	Australia 3, Sweden 2
1984	Sweden 4, United States 1
1985	Sweden 3, West Germany 2
1986	Australia 3, Sweden 2
1987	Sweden 5, Austria 0
1988	West Germany 4, Sweden 1
1989	West Germany 3, Sweden 2
1990	United States 3, Australia 2
1991	France 3, United States 1
1992	United States 3, Switzerland 1

FEDERATION CUP CHAMPIONSHIPS

World team competition for women conducted by International Lawn Tennis Federation.

1963	United States 2, Australia 1
1964	Australia 2, United States 1
1965	Australia 2, United States 1
1966	United States 3, West Germany 0
1967	United States 2, Britain 0
1968	Australia 3, Netherlands 0
1969	United States 2, Australia 1
1970	Australia 3, West Germany 0
1971	Australia 3, Britain 0
1972	South Africa 2, Britain 1
1973	Australia 3, South Africa 0
1974	Australia 2, United States 1
1975	Czechoslovakia 3, Australia 0
1976	United States 2, Australia 1
1977	United States 2, Australia 1
1978	United States 2, Australia 1
1979	United States 3, Australia 0
1980	United States 3, Australia 0
1981	United States 3, Britain 0
1982	United States 3, West Germany 0
1983	Czechoslovakia 2, West Germany 1

1984 Czechoslovakia 2, Australia 1
1985 Czechoslovakia 2, United States 1
1986 United States 3, Czechoslovakia 0
1987 West Germany 2, United States 1
1988 Czechoslovakia 2, Soviet Union 1
1989 United States 3, Spain 0
1990 United States 2, Soviet Union 1
1991 Spain 2, United States 1
1992 Germany 2, Spain 1
1993 Spain 3, Australia 0

U.S. CHAMPIONS

Singles—Men

NATIONAL

1881–87 Richard D. Sears
1888–89 Henry Slocum, Jr.
1890–92 Oliver S. Campbell
1893–94 Robert D. Wrenn
1895 Fred H. Hovey
1896–97 Robert D. Wrenn
1898–1900 Malcolm Whitman
1901–02 William A. Larned
1903 Hugh L. Doherty
1904 Holcombe Ward
1905 Beals C. Wright
1906 William J. Clothier
1907–11 William A. Larned
1912–13 Maurice McLoughlin[1]
1914 R. N. Williams II
1915 William Johnston
1916 R. N. William II
1917–18 R. Lindley Murray[2]
1919 William Johnston
1920–25 Bill Tilden
1926–27 Jean Rene Lacoste
1928 Henri Cochet
1929 Bill Tilden
1930 John H. Doeg
1931–32 Ellsworth Vines
1933–34 Fred J. Perry
1935 Wilmer L. Allison
1936 Fred J. Perry
1937–38 Don Budge
1939 Robert L. Riggs
1940 Donald McNeill
1941 Robert L. Riggs
1942 Fred Schroeder
1943 Joseph Hunt
1944–45 Frank Parker
1946–47 Jack Kramer
1948–49 Richard Gonzales
1950 Arthur Larsen
1951–52 Frank Sedgman
1953 Tony Trabert
1954 Vic Seixas
1955 Tony Trabert
1956 Ken Rosewall
1957 Mal Anderson
1958 Ashley Cooper
1959–60 Neale Fraser
1961 Roy Emerson
1962 Rod Laver
1963 Rafael Osuna
1964 Roy Emerson
1965 Manuel Santana
1966 Fred Stolle
1967 John Newcombe
1968 Arthur Ashe
1969 Rod Laver

OPEN

1968 Arthur Ashe
1969 Rod Laver
1970 Ken Rosewall
1971 Stan Smith
1972 Ilie Nastase
1973 John Newcombe
1974 Jimmy Connors
1975 Manuel Orantes
1976 Jimmy Connors
1977 Guillermo Vilas
1978 Jimmy Connors
1979 John McEnroe
1980–81 John McEnroe
1982 Jimmy Connors
1983 Jimmy Connors
1984 John McEnroe
1985–87 Ivan Lendl
1988 Mats Wilander
1989 Boris Becker
1990 Pete Sampras
1991 Stefan Edberg
1992 Stefan Edberg
1993 Pete Sampras

Singles—Women

NATIONAL

1887 Ellen F. Hansel
1888–89 Bertha Townsend
1890 Ellen C. Roosevelt
1891–92 Mabel E. Cahill
1893 Aline M. Terry
1894 Helen R. Helwig
1895 Juliette P. Atkinson
1896 Elisabeth H. Moore
1897–98 Juliette P. Atkinson
1899 Marion Jones
1900 Myrtle McAteer
1901 Elisabeth H. Moore
1902 Marion Jones
1903 Elisabeth H. Moore
1904 May Sutton
1905 Elisabeth H. Moore
1906 Helen Homans
1907 Evelyn Sears
1908 Maud Bargar–Wallach
1909–11 Hazel V. Hotchkiss
1912–14 Mary K. Browne
1915–18 Molla Bjurstedt
1919 Hazel Hotchkiss Wightman
1920–22 Molla Bjurstedt Mallory
1923–25 Helen N. Wills
1926 Molla B. Mallory
1927–29 Helen N. Wills
1930 Betty Nuthall
1931 Helen Wills Moody
1932–35 Helen Jacobs
1936 Alice Marble
1937 Anita Lizana
1938–40 Alice Marble
1941 Sarah Palfrey Cooke
1942–44 Pauline Betz
1945 Sarah Cooke
1946 Pauline Betz
1947 Louise Brough
1948–50 Margaret Osborne duPont
1951–53 Maureen Connolly
1954–55 Doris Hart
1956 Shirley Fry
1957–58 Althea Gibson
1959 Maria Bueno
1960–61 Darlene Hard
1962 Margaret Smith
1963–64 Maria Bueno
1965 Margaret Smith
1966 Maria Bueno
1967 Billie Jean King
1968–69 Margaret Smith Court[3]

OPEN

1968 Virginia Wade
1969–70 Margaret Court
1971–72 Billie Jean King
1973 Margaret Court
1974 Billie Jean King
1975–78 Chris Evert
1979 Tracy Austin
1980 Chris Evert–Lloyd
1981 Tracy Austin
1982 Chris Evert–Lloyd
1983–84 Martina Navratilova
1985 Hana Mandlikova
1986–87 Martina Navratilova
1988 Steffi Graf
1989 Steffi Graf
1990 Grabriela Sabatini
1991 Monica Seles
1992 Monica Seles
1993 Steffi Graf

Doubles—Men

NATIONAL

1920	Bill Johnston–C. J. Griffin
1921–22	Bill Tilden–Vincent Richards
1923	Bill Tilden–B. I. C. Norton
1924	H. O. Kinsey—R. G. Kinsey
1925–26	Vincent Richards—R. N. Williams II
1927	Bill Tilden—Frank Hunter
1928	G. M. Lott, Jr.–V. Hennessy
1929–30	G. M. Lott, Jr.–J. H. Doeg
1931	W. L. Allison–John Van Ryn
1932	E. H. Vines, Jr.–Keith Gledh
1933–34	G. M. Lott, Jr.–L. R. Stoefen
1935	W. L. Allison–John Van Ryn
1936	Don Budge—Gene Mako
1937	G. von Cramm–H. Henkel
1938	Don Budge–Gene Mako
1939	A. K. Quist–J. E. Bromwich
1940–41	Jack Kramer–F. R. Schroeder
1942	Gardnar Mulloy–Bill Talbert
1943	Jack Kramer—Frank Parker
1944	Don McNeill—Bob Falkenburg
1945	Gardnar Mulloy–Bill Talbert
1946	Gardnar Mulloy–Bill Talbert
1947	Jack Kramer–Fred Schroeder
1948	Gardnar Mulloy–Bill Talbert
1949	John Bromwich–William Sidwell
1950	John Bromwich–Frank Sedgman
1951	Frank Sedgman–Ken McGregor
1952	Vic Seixas–Mervyn Rose
1953	Mervyn Rose–Rex Hartwig
1954	Vic Seixas–Tony Trabert
1955	Kosei Kamo–Atsushi Miyagi
1956	Lewis Hoad–Ken Rosewall
1957	Ashley Cooper–Neale Fraser
1958	Ham Richardson–Alex Olmedo
1959–60	Neale Fraser–Roy Emerson
1961	Chuck McKinley–Dennis Ralston
1962	Rafael Osuna–Antonio Palafox
1963–64	Chuck McKinley–Dennis Ralston
1965–66	Fred Stolle–Roy Emerson
1967	John Newcombe–Tony Roche
1968	Stan Smith–Bob Lutz[3]
1969	Richard Crealy–Allan Stone[3]

OPEN

1968	Stan Smith–Bob Lutz
1969	Fred Stolle–Ken Rosewall
1970	Nikki Pilic–Fred Barthes
1971	John Newcombe–Roger Taylor
1972	Cliff Drysdale–Roger Taylor
1973	John Newcombe–Owen Davidson
1974	Bob Lutz–Stan Smith
1975	Jimmy Connors–Ilie Nastase
1976	Marty Riessen–Tom Okker
1977	Frew McMillan–Bob Hewitt
1978	Bob Lutz–Stan Smith
1979	John McEnroe–Peter Fleming
1980	Stan Smith–Bob Lutz
1981	John McEnroe–Peter Fleming
1982	Kevin Curren–Steve Denton
1983	John McEnroe–Peter Fleming
1984	John Fitzgerald–Tomas Smid
1985	Ken Flach–Robert Seguso
1986	Andres Gomez–Slobodan Zivojinovic
1987	Stefan Edberg–Anders Jarryd
1988	Sergio Casal–Emilio Sanchez
1989	John McEnroe–Mark Woodforde
1990	Pieter Aldrich–Danie Visser
1991	John Fitzgerald–Anders Jarryd
1992	Jim Grabb–Richey Reneberg
1993	Ken Flach–Rick Leach

1. Challenge round abandoned in 1912. 2. Patriotic Tournament in 1917. 3. With the inaugural of the Open Tournament in 1968, the United States Lawn Tennis Association held a national championship at Longwood, Chestnut Hill, Mass. which barred contract professionals in 1968 and 1969.

Doubles—Women

NATIONAL

1924	G. W. Wightman–Helen Wills
1925	Mary K. Browne–Helen Wills
1926	Elizabeth Ryan–Eleanor Goss
1927	L. A. Godfree–Ermyntrude Harvey
1928	Hazel Hotchkiss Wightman–Helen Wills
1929	Phoebe Watson–L. R. C. Michell
1930	Betty Nuthall–Sarah Palfrey
1931	Betty Nuthall–E. B. Wittingstall
1932	Helen Jacobs–Sarah Palfrey
1933	Betty Nuthall–Freda James
1934	Helen Jacobs–Sarah Palfrey
1935	Helen Jacobs–Sarah Palfrey Fabyan
1936	Marjorie G. Van Ryn–Carolin Babcock
1937–40	Sarah Palfrey Fabyan–Alice Marble
1941	Sarah Palfrey Cooke–Margaret Osborne
1942–47	A. Louise Brough–Margaret Osborne
1948–50	A. Louise Brough–Margaret O. duPont
1951–54	Doris Hart–Shirley Fry
1955–57	A. Louise Brough–Margaret O. duPont
1958–59	Darlene Hard–Jeanne Arth
1960	Darlene Hard–Maria Bueno
1961	Darlene Hard–Lesley Turner
1962	Darlene Hard–Maria Bueno
1963	Margaret Smith–Robyn Ebbern
1964	Karen Hantze Susman–Billie Jean Moffitt
1965	Nancy Richey–Carole Caldwell Graebner
1966	Nancy Richey–Maria Bueno
1967	Billie Jean King–Rosemary Casals
1968	Margaret Court–Maria Bueno[3]
1969	Margaret Court–Virginia Wade[3]

OPEN

1968	Maria Bueno–Margaret Court
1969	Darlene Hard–Francoise Durr
1970	Margaret Court–Judy Dalton
1971	Rosemary Casals–Judy Dalton
1972	Francoise Durr–Betty Stove
1973	Margaret Court–Virginia Wade
1974	Billie Jean King–Rosemary Casals
1975	Margaret Court–Virginia Wade
1976	Linky Boshoff–Ilana Kloss
1977	Martina Navratilova–Betty Stove
1978	Billie Jean King–Martina Navratilova
1979	Betty Stove–Wendy Turnbull
1980	Billie Jean King–Martina Navratilova
1981	Kathy Jordan–Anne Smith
1982	Rosemary Casals–Wendy Turnbull
1983–84	Martina Navratilova–Pam Shriver
1985	Claudia Khode–Kilsch–Helena Sukova

1986–87 Martina Navratilova–Pam Shriver
1988 Gigi Fernandez–Robin White
1989 Hana Mandlikova–Martina Navratilova
1990 Gigi Fernandez–Martina Navratilova
1991 Pam Shriver–Natalia Zvereva
1992 Gigi Fernandez–Natalia Zvereva
1993 Arantxa Sanchez Vicario–Helena Sukova

1. Challenge round abandoned in 1912. 2. Patriotic Tournament in 1917. 3. With the inaugural of the Open Tournament in 1968, the United States Lawn Tennis Association held a national championship at Longwood, Chestnut Hill, Mass. which barred contract professionals in 1968 and 1969.

BRITISH (WIMBLEDON) CHAMPIONS

(Amateur from inception in 1877 through 1967)

Singles—Men

1908–09 Arthur Gore
1910–13 A. F. Wilding
1914 N. E. Brookes
1919 G. L. Patterson
1920–21 Bill Tilden
1922 G. L. Patterson
1923 William Johnston
1924 Jean Borotra
1925 Rene Lacoste
1926 Jean Borotra
1927 Henri Cochet
1928 Rene Lacoste
1929 Jean Cochet
1930 Bill Tilden
1931 S. B. Wood
1932 Ellsworth Vines
1933 J. H. Crawford
1934–36 Fred Perry
1937–38 Don Budge
1939 Robert L. Riggs
1946 Yvon Petra
1947 Jack Kramer
1948 R. Falkenburg
1949 Fred Schroeder
1950 Budge Patty
1951 Richard Savitt
1952 Frank Sedgman
1953 Vic Siexas
1954 Jaroslav Drobny
1955 Tony Trabert
1956–57 Lewis Hoad
1958 Ashley Cooper
1959 Alex Olmedo
1960 Neale Fraser
1961–62 Rod Laver
1963 Chuck McKinley
1964–65 Roy Emerson
1966 Manuel Santana
1967 John Newcombe
1968–69 Rod Laver
1970–71 John Newcombe
1972 Stan Smith
1973 Jan Kodes
1974 Jimmy Connors
1975 Arthur Ashe
1976–80 Bjorn Borg
1981 John McEnroe
1982 Jimmy Connors
1983–84 John McEnroe
1985–86 Boris Becker
1987 Pat Cash
1988 Stefan Edberg
1989 Boris Becker
1990 Stefan Edberg
1991 Michael Stich
1992 Andre Agassi
1993 Peter Sampras

Singles—Women

1919–23 Lenglen
1924 Kathleen McKane
1925 Lenglen
1926 Godfree
1927–29 Helen Wills
1930 Helen Wills Moody
1931 Frl. C. Aussen
1932–33 Helen Wills Moody
1934 D. E. Round
1935 Helen Wills Moody
1936 Helen Jacobs
1937 D. E. Round
1938 Helen Wills Moody
1939 Alice Marble
1946 Pauline M. Betz
1947 Margaret Osborne
1948–50 A. Louise Brough
1951 Doris Hart
1952–54 Maureen Connolly
1955 A. Louise Brough
1956 Shirley Fry
1957–58 Althea Gibson
1959–60 Maria Bueno
1961 Angela Mortimer
1962 Karen Susman
1963 Margaret Smith
1964 Maria Bueno
1965 Margaret Smith
1966–67 Billie Jean King
1968 Billie Jean King
1969 Ann Jones
1970 Margaret Court
1971 Evonne Goolagong
1972–73 Billie Jean King
1974 Chris Evert
1975 Billie Jean King
1976 Chris Evert
1977 Virginia Wade
1978–79 Martina Navratilova
1980 Evonne Goolagong Cawley
1981 Chris Evert–Lloyd
1982–87 Martina Navratilova
1988–89 Steffi Graf
1990 Martina Navratilova
1991 Steffi Graf
1992 Monica Seles
1993 Steffi Graf

Doubles—Men

1953 K. Rosewall–L. Hoad
1954 R. Hartwig–M. Rose
1955 R. Hartwig–L. Hoad
1956 L. Hoad–K. Rosewall
1957 Gardnar Mulloy–Budge Patty
1958 Sven Davidson–Ulf Schmidt
1959 Roy Emerson–Neale Fraser
1960 Dennis Ralston–Rafael Osuna
1961 Roy Emerson–Neale Fraser
1962 Fred Stolle–Bob Hewitt
1963 Rafael Osuna–Antonio Palafox
1964 Fred Stolle–Bob Hewitt
1965 John Newcombe–Tony Roche
1966 John Newcombe–Ken Fletcher
1967 Bob Hewitt–Frew McMillan
1968–70 John Newcombe–Tony Roche
1971 Rod Laver–Roy Emerson
1972 Bob Hewitt–Frew McMillan
1973 Jimmy Connors–Ilie Nastase
1974 John Newcombe–Tony Roche
1975 Vitas Gerulaitis–Sandy Mayer
1976 Brian Gottfried–Raul Ramirez
1977 Ross Case–Geoff Masters
1978 Fred McMillan–Bob Hewitt
1979 Peter Fleming–John McEnroe
1980 Peter McNamara–Paul McNamee
1981 John McEnroe–Peter Fleming
1982 Paul McNamee–Peter McNamara
1983–84 John McEnroe–Peter Fleming
1985 Heinz Gunthardt–Balazs Taroczy
1986 Joakim Nystrom–Mats Wilander
1987 Ken Flach–Robert Seguso
1988 Ken Flach–Robert Seguso
1989 John Fitzgerald–Anders Jarryd
1990 Rick Leach–Jim Pugh
1991 Anders Jarryd–John Fitzgerald
1992 John McEnroe–Michael Stich
1993 Todd Woodbridge—Mark Woodforde

Doubles–Women

1956 Althea Gibson–Angela Buxton
1957 Althea Gibson–Darlene Hard
1958 Althea Gibson–Maria Bueno
1959 Darlene Hard–Jeanne Arth
1960 Darlene Hard–Maria Bueno
1961 Karen Hantze–Billie Jean Moffitt
1962 Karen Hantze Susman–Billie Jean Moffitt
1963 Darlene Hard–Maria Bueno
1964 Margaret Smith–Les Turnerley
1965 Billie Jean Moffitt–Maria Bueno
1966 Nancy Richey–Maria Bueno
1967–68 Billie Jean King–Rosemary Casals

1969	Margaret Court–Judy Tegart		Navratilova	1986	Pam Shriver–Martina Navratilova
1970–71	Billie Jean King–Rosemary Casals	1977	Helen Cawley–JoAnne Russell	1987	Claudia Khode–Kilsch–Helena Sukova
1972	Billie Jean King–Betty Stove	1978	Wendy Turnbull–Kerry Reid	1988	Steffi Graf–Gabriela Sabatini
1973	Billie Jean King–Rosemary Casals	1979	Billie Jean King–Martina Navratilova	1989	Jana Novotna–Helena Sukova
1974	Evonne Goolagong–Peggy Michel	1980	Kathy Jordan–Anne Smith	1990	Jana Novotna–Helena Sukova
1975	Ann Kiyomura–Kazuko Sawamatsu	1981	Martina Navratilova–Pam Shriver	1991	Pam Shriver–Natalia Zvereva
1976	Chris Evert–Martina	1982–84	Pam Shriver–Martina Navratilova	1992	Gigi Fernandez–Natalia Zvereva
		1985	Kathy Jordan–Elizabeth Smylie	1993	Gigi Fernandez–Natalia Zvereva

UNITED STATES CHAMPIONS—1993

United States Open

(Flushing Meadow, Aug. 30–Sept. 12, 1993)

Men's singles—Pete Sampras, Tampa, Fla., defeated Cedric Pioline, France, 6–4, 6–4, 6–3.

Women's singles—Steffi Graf, Germany, defeated Helena Sukova, Czech Republic, 6–3, 6–3.

Men's doubles—Ken Flach, Alpharetta, Ga., and Rick Leach, Laguna Beach, Calif., defeated Karel Novacek and Martin Damm, Czech Republic, 6–7 (3–7), 6–4, 6–2.

Women's doubles—Arantxa Sanchez Vicario, Spain, and Helena Sukova, Czech Republic, defeated Amanda Coetzer, South Africa, and Ines Gorrochategui, Argentina, 6–4, 6–2.

Other U.S. Open Champions

Mixed doubles—Helena Sukova, Czech Republic, and Todd Woodbridge, Australia

Senior men's singles—Gene Mayer, Woodmere, N.Y.

Senior men's doubles—Marty Riessen, Dallas, and Sherwood Stewart, The Woodlands, Texas.

Senior women's doubles—Betsy Nagelson, Kapalua Bay, Hawaii, and Joanne Russell, Kingsmill, Va.

Senior mixed doubles—Kathy May, Beverly Hills, Calif., and Jaime Fillol, Chile.

Junior boys' singles—Marcelo Rios, Chile.

Junior boys' doubles—Neville Godwin and Gareth Williams, South Africa.

Junior girls' singles—Francesca Bentivoglio, Italy.

Junior girls' doubles—Nicole London, Rolling Hills, Calif., and Julie Steven, Wichita, Kansas.

United States Hardcourts—Men

(Aug. 17–22, 1993, Indianapolis, Ind.)

Singles—Jim Courier, Dade City, Fla., defeated Boris Becker, Germany, 7–5, 6–3.

Doubles—Scott Davis, Newport Beach, Calif., and Todd Martin, Lansing, Mich., defeated Ken Flach, Alpharetta, Ga., and Rick Leach, Laguna Beach, Calif., 6–4, 6–4.

United States Hardcourts—Women

(July 27–Aug. 1, 1993, Stratton Mountain, Vt.)

Singles—Conchita Martinez, Spain, defeated Zina Garrison–Jackson, Houston, 6–3, 6–2.

Doubles—Helena Sukova, Czech Republic, and Liz Smylie, Australia, defeated Manuela Maleeva–Fragniere, Switzerland, and Mercedes Paz, Argentina, 6–1, 6–2.

Hall of Fame Championships

(July 6–11, 1993)

Men's singles—Greg Rusedski, Canada, defeated Javier Frana, Argentina, 7–5, 6–7 (9–7), 7–6 (7–5).

Women's singles—Rosalyn Fairbank–Nideffer, South Africa, defeated Zina Garrison–Jackson, Houston, 6–4, 3–6, 6–4.

International Players Championships

(March 9–21, 1993, Key Biscayne, Fla.)

Men's singles—Pete Sampras, Tampa, Fla., defeated Mali Vai Washington, Ponte Verdra Beach, Fla., 6–3, 6–2.

Women's singles—Arantxa Sanchez Vicario, Spain, defeated Steffi Graf, Germany, 6–4, 3–6, 6–3.

Women's doubles—Larisa Neiland, Latvia, and Jana Novotna, Czech Republic, defeated Jill Hetherington, Canada, and Kathy Rinaldi, Amelia Island, Fla., 6–2, 7–5.

Men's doubles—Richard Krajicek and Jan Siemerink, Netherlands, defeated Jonathan Stark, Medford, Ore., and Patrick McEnroe, Oyster Bay, N.Y., 6–3, 6–2.

U.S. Indoor

(Feb. 16–21, 1993, Philadelphia, Pa.)

Singles—Mark Woodforde, Australia, defeated Ivan Lendl, Greenwich, Conn., 5–4 (Lendl retired with an injury).

Doubles—Jim Grabb, Tampa, Fla., and Richey Reneberg, Houston, defeated Marcos Ondruska, South Africa, and Brad Pearce, Provo, Utah, 6–7 (4–7), 6–3, 6–0.

OTHER 1993 CHAMPIONS

Australian Open

Men's singles—Jim Courier, Dade City, Fla., defeated Stefan Edberg, Sweden, 6–2, 6–1, 2–6, 7–5..

Women's singles—Monica Seles, Yugoslavia, defeated Steffi Graf, Germany, 4–6, 6–3, 6–2.

Men's doubles—Danie Visser, South Africa, and Laurie Warder, Australia, defeated John Fitzgerald, Australia, and Anders Jarryd, Sweden, 6–4, 6–3, 6–4.

Women's doubles—Gigi Fernandez, Aspen, Colo., and Natalia Zvereva, Belarus, defeated Pam Shriver, Baltimore, Md., and Elizabeth Smylie, Australia, 6–4, 6–3.

Mixed doubles—Arantxa Sanchez Vicario, Spain, and Todd Woodbridge, Australia, defeated Zina Garrison–Jackson, Houston, and Rick Leach, Laguna Beach, Calif., 7–5, 6–4.

Wimbledon Open

Men's singles—Pete Sampras, Tampa, Fla., defeated Jim Courier, Dade City, Fla., 7–6 (7–3), 7–6 (8–6), 3–6, 6–3.

Women's singles—Steffi Graf, Germany, defeated Jana Novotna, Czech Republic, 7–6 (8–6), 1–6, 6–4.

Men's doubles—Todd Woodbridge and Mark Woodforde, Australia, defeated Grant Connell, Canada, and Patrick Galbraith, Tacoma, Wash., 7–5, 6–3, 7–6 (7–4).

Women's doubles—Gigi Fernandez, Aspen, Colo., and Natalia Zvereva, Belarus, defeated Larisa Neiland, Latvia, and Jana Novotna, Czech Republic, 6–4, 6–7 (4–7), 6–4.
Mixed doubles—Mark Woodforde, Australia, and Martina Navratilova, Aspen, Colo., defeated Tom Nijssen and Manon Bollegraf, Netherlands, 6–3, 6–4.

French Open
Men's singles—Sergi Bruguera, Spain, defeated Jim Courier, Dade City, Fla., 6–4, 2.6, 6–2, 3–6, 6–3.
Women's singles—Steffi Graf, Germany, defeated Mary Jo Fernandez, Miami, Fla., 4–6, 6–2, 6–4.
Men's doubles—Luke Jensen and Murphy Jensen, Ludington, Mich., defeated Marc Goellner and David Prinosil, Germany, 6–4, 6–7 (4–7), 6–4.
Women's doubles—Gigi Fernandez, Aspen, Colo., and Natalia Zvereva, Belarus, defeated Larisa Neiland, Latvia and Jana Novotna, Czech Republic, 6–4, 7–5.
Mixed doubles—Eugenia Maniokova and Andrei Olhovskly, Russia, defeated Elna Reinach and Danie Visser, South Africa, 6–2, 4–6, 6–4.

MEN'S MONEY LEADERS—1993
(Through Sept. 1, 1993)

Men—1. Jim Courier (United States), $1,670,336; 2. Pete Sampras (United States), $1,459,525; 3. Sergei Bruguera (Spain), $1,263,724; 4. Michael Stich (Germany), $1,248,141; 5. Stefen Edberg (Sweden), $927,169; 6. Michael Chang (United States), $824,089; 7. Andrei Medvedev (Ukraine), $781,968; 8. Peter Korda (Czech Republic), $674,629; 9. Boris Becker (Germany), $665,039; 10. Richard Krajicek (Netherlands) $652,443.

DAVIS CUP RESULTS—1992
United States 3, Switzerland 1
(Dec. 4–6, at Fort Worth, Texas)

Singles—Andre Agassi, United States, defeated Jakob Hlasek, Switzerland, 6–1, 6–2, 6–2; Marc Rosset, Switzerland, defeated Jim Courier, United States, 6–3, 6–7 (9–11), 3–6, 6–4, 6–4; Jim Courier, United States, defeated Jakob Hlasek, Switzerland, 6–3, 3–6, 6–3, 6–4.
Doubles—John McEnroe and Pete Sampras, United States, defeated Jakob Hlasek and Marc Rosset, Switzerland, 6–7 (5–7), 6–7 (7–9), 7–5, 6–1, 6–2.

WOMEN'S MONEY LEADERS—1993
(Through Sept. 1, 1993)

Women—1. Steffi Graf (Germany), $1,893,837; 2. Arantxa Sanchez Vicario (Spain), $971,889; 3. Conchita Martinez (Spain), $681,220; 4. Jana Novotna (Czech Republic), $656,696; 5. Martina Navratilova (United States), $608,044; 6. Mary Joe Fernandez (United States), $577,731; 7. Natalia Zvereva (Belarus), $546,810; 8. Gabriela Sabatini (Argentina), $477,430; 9. Gigi Fernandez (United States), $463,963; 10. Monica Seles (Yugoslavia), $437,588.

ROWING

Rowing goes back so far in history that there is no possibility of tracing it to any particular aboriginal source. The oldest rowing race still on the calendar is the "Doggett's Coat and Badge" contest among professional watermen of the Thames (England) that began in 1715. The first Oxford-Cambridge race was held at Henley in 1829. Competitive rowing in the United States began with matches between boats rowed by professional oarsmen of the New York waterfront. They were oarsmen who rowed the small boats that plied as ferries from Manhattan Island to Brooklyn and return, or who rowed salesmen down the harbor to meet ships arriving from Europe. Since the first salesman to meet an incoming ship had some advantage over his rivals, there was keen competition in the bidding for fast boats and the best oarsmen. This gave rise to match races.

Amateur boat clubs sprang up in the United States between 1820 and 1830 and seven students of Yale joined together to purchase a four-oared lap-streak gig in 1843. The first Harvard-Yale race was held Aug. 3, 1852, on Lake Winnepesaukee, N.H. The first time an American college crew went abroad was in 1869 when Harvard challenged Oxford and was defeated on the Thames. There were early college rowing races on Lake Quinsigamond, near Worcester, Mass., and on Saratoga Lake, N.Y., but the Intercollegiate Rowing Association in 1895 settled on the Hudson, at Poughkeepsie, as the setting for the annual "Poughkeepsie Regatta." In 1950 the I.R.A. shifted its classic to Marietta, Ohio, and in 1952 it was moved to Syracuse, N.Y. The National Association of Amateur Oarsmen, organized in 1872, has conducted annual championship regattas since that time.

INTERCOLLEGIATE ROWING ASSOCIATION REGATTA
(Varsity Eight-Oared Shells)

Rowed at 4 miles, Poughkeepsie, N.Y., 1895–97, 1899–1916, 1925–32, 1934–41. Rowed at 3 miles, Saratoga, N.Y., 1898; Poughkeepsie, 1921–24, 1947–49; Syracuse, N.Y., 1952–1963, 1965–67. Rowed at 2,000 meters, Syracuse, N.Y., 1964 and from 1968 on. Rowed at 2 miles, Ithaca, N.Y., 1920; Marietta, Ohio, 1950–51. Suspended 1917–19, 1933, 1942–46.

Year	Time	First	Second
1895	21:25	Columbia	Cornell
1896	19:59	Cornell	Harvard
1897	20:47 4/5	Cornell	Columbia
1898	15:51 1/2	Pennsylvania	Cornell
1899	20:04	Pennsylvania	Wisconsin
1900	19:44 3/5	Pennsylvania	Wisconsin
1901	18:53 1/5	Cornell	Columbia
1902	19:03 3/5	Cornell	Wisconsin
1903	18:57	Cornell	Georgetown
1904	20:22 3/5	Syracuse	Cornell
1905	20:29	Cornell	Syracuse
1906	19:36 4/5	Cornell	Pennsylvania
1907	20:02 2/5	Cornell	Columbia
1908	19:24 1/5	Syracuse	Columbia
1909	19:02	Cornell	Columbia
1910	20:42 1/5	Cornell	Pennsylvania
1911	20:10 4/5	Cornell	Columbia
1912	19:31 2/5	Cornell	Wisconsin
1913	19:28 3/5	Syracuse	Cornell
1914	19:37 4/5	Columbia	Pennsylvania
1915	19:36 3/5	Cornell	Stanford
1916	20:15 2/5	Syracuse	Cornell

Year	Time	First	Second
1920	11:02 3/5	Syracuse	Cornell
1921	14:07	Navy	California
1922	13:33 3/5	Navy	Washington
1923	14:03 1/5	Washington	Navy
1924	15:02	Washington	Wisconsin
1925	19:24 4/5	Navy	Washington
1926	19:28 3/5	Washington	Navy
1927	20:57	Columbia	Washington
1928	18:35 4/5	California	Columbia
1929	22:58	Columbia	Washington
1930	21:42	Cornell	Syracuse
1931	18:54 1/5	Navy	Cornell
1932	19:55	California	Cornell
1934	19:44	California	Washington
1935	18:52	California	Cornell
1936	19:09 3/5	Washington	California
1937	18:33 3/5	Washington	Navy
1938	18:19	Navy	California
1939	18:12 3/5	California	Washington
1940	22:42	Washington	Cornell
1941	18:53 3/10	Washington	California
1947	13:59 1/5	Navy	Cornell
1948	14:06 2/5	Washington	California
1949	14:42 3/5	California	Washington
1950	8:07.5	Washington	California
1951	7:50.5	Wisconsin	Washington
1952	15:08.1	Navy	Princeton
1953	15:29.6	Navy	Cornell
1954	16:04.4	Navy[1]	Cornell
1955	15:49.9	Cornell	Pennsylvania
1956	16:22.4	Cornell	Navy
1957	15:26.6	Cornell	Pennsylvania
1958	17:12.1	Cornell	Navy
1959	18:01.7	Wisconsin	Syracuse
1960	15:57	California	Navy
1961	16:49.2	California	Cornell
1962	17:02.9	Cornell	Washington
1963	17:24	Cornell	Navy
1964	6:31.1	California	Washington
1965	16:51.3	Navy	Cornell
1966	16:03.4	Wisconsin	Navy
1967	16:13.9	Pennsylvania	Wisconsin
1968	6:15.6	Pennsylvania	Washington
1969	6:30.4	Pennsylvania	Dartmouth
1970	6:39.3	Washington	Wisconsin
1971	6:06	Cornell	Washington
1972	6:22.6	Pennsylvania	Brown
1973	6:21	Wisconsin	Brown
1974	6:33	Wisconsin	M.I.T.
1975	6:08.2	Wisconsin	M.I.T.
1976	6:31	California	Princeton
1977	6:32.4	Cornell	Pennsylvania
1978	6:39.5	Syracuse	Brown
1979	6:26.4	Brown	Wisconsin
1980	6:46	Navy	Northeastern
1981	5:57.3	Cornell	Navy
1982	5:57.5	Cornell	Princeton
1983	6:14.4	Brown	Navy
1984	5:54.7	Navy	Pennsylvania
1985	5:49.9	Princeton	Brown
1986	5:50.2	Brown	Pennsylvania
1987	6:02.9	Brown	Wisconsin
1988	6:14.0	Northeastern	Brown
1989	5:56.0	Penn	Wisconsin
1990	5:55.5	Wisconsin	Pennsylvania
1991	6:05.2	Northeastern	Pennsylvania
1992	6:10.5	Dartmouth	Harvard
1993	5::59.1	Brown	Pennsylvania

1. Disqualified.

JAMES E. SULLIVAN MEMORIAL AWARD WINNERS

(Amateur Athlete of Year Chosen in Amateur Athletic Union Poll)

1930	Robert Tyre Jones, Jr.	Golf
1931	Bernard E. Berlinger	Track and field
1932	James A. Bausch	Track and field
1933	Glenn Cunningham	Track and field
1934	William R. Bonthron	Track and field
1935	W. Lawson Little, Jr.	Golf
1936	Glenn Morris	Track and field
1937	J. Donald Budge	Tennis
1938	Donald R. Lash	Track and field
1939	Joseph W. Burk	Rowing
1940	J. Gregory Rice	Track and field
1941	Leslie MacMitchell	Track and field
1942	Cornelius Warmerdam	Track and field
1943	Gilbert L. Dodds	Track and field
1944	Ann Curtis	Swimming
1945	Felix (Doc) Blanchard	Football
1946	Y. Arnold Tucker	Football
1947	John B. Kelly, Jr.	Rowing
1948	Robert B. Mathias	Track and field
1949	Richard T. Button	Figure skating
1950	Fred Wilt	Track and field
1951	Robert E. Richards	Track and field
1952	Horace Ashenfelter	Track and field
1953	Major Sammy Lee	Diving
1954	Malvin Whitfield	Track and field
1955	Harrison Dillard	Track and field
1956	Patricia McCormick	Diving
1957	Bobby Jo Morrow	Track and Field
1958	Glenn Davis	Track and field
1959	Parry O'Brien	Track and field
1960	Rafer Johnson	Track and field
1961	Wilma Rudolph Ward	Track and field
1962	Jim Beatty	Track and field
1963	John Pennel	Track and field
1964	Don Schollander	Swimming
1965	Bill Bradley	Basketball
1966	Jim Ryun	Track and field
1967	Randy Matson	Track and field
1968	Debbie Meyer	Swimming
1969	Bill Toomey	Decathlon
1970	John Kinsella	Swimming
1971	Mark Spitz	Swimming
1972	Frank Shorter	Marathon
1973	Bill Walton	Basketball
1974	Rick Wohlhuter	Track
1975	Tim Shaw	Swimming
1976	Bruce Jenner	Track and field
1977	John Naber	Swimming
1978	Tracy Caulkins	Swimming
1979	Kurt Thomas	Gymnastics
1980	Eric Heiden	Speed skating
1981	Carl Lewis	Track and field
1982	Mary Decker Tabb	Track and field
1983	Edwin Moses	Track and field
1984	Greg Louganis	Diving
1985	Joan Benoit–Samuelson	Marathon
1986	Jackie Joyner–Kersee	Heptathlon
1987	Jim Abbott	Baseball
1988	Florence Griffith–Joyner	Track and field
1989	Janet Evans	Swimming
1990	John Smith	Wrestling
1991	Mike Powell	Track and field
1992	Bonnie Blair	Speed skating

HARNESS RACING

Oliver Wendell Holmes, the famous Autocrat of the Breakfast Table, wrote that the running horse was a gambling toy but the trotting horse was useful and, furthermore, "horse–racing is not a republican institution; horse–trotting is." Oliver Wendell Holmes was a born–and–bred New Englander, and New England was the nursery of the harness racing sport in America. Pacers and trotters were matters of local pride and prejudice in Colonial New England, and, shortly after the Revolution, the Messenger and Justin Morgan strains produced many winners in harness racing "matches" along the turnpikes of New York, Connecticut, Rhode Island, Massachusetts, Vermont, and New Hampshire.

There was English thoroughbred blood in Messenger and Justin Morgan, and, many years later, it was blended in Rysdyk's Hambletonian, foaled in 1849. Hambletonian was not particularly fast under harness but his descendants have had almost a monopoly of prizes, titles, and records in the harness racing game. Hambletonian was purchased as a foal with its dam for a total of $124 by William Rysdyk of Goshen, N.Y., and made a modest fortune for the purchaser.

Trotters and pacers often were raced under saddle in the old days, and, in fact, the custom still survives in some places in Europe. Dexter, the great trotter that lowered the mile record from 2:19 3/4 to 2:17 1/4 in 1867, was said to handle just as well under saddle as when pulling a sulky. But as sulkies were lightened in weight and improved in design, trotting under saddle became less common and finally faded out in this country.

WORLD RECORDS

Established in a race or against time at one mile. *Source:* United States Trotting Association (Through Sept. 19, 1993)

Trotting on Mile Track

	Record	Holder	Driver	Where Made	Year
All Age	1:52 1/5	Mack Lobell	John Campbell	Springfield, Ill.	1987
	1:52 4/5	Peace Corps	John Campbell	Du Quoin, Ill.	1989
	1:53	Express Ride	Berndt Lindstedt	Lexington, Ky.	1987
	* 1:55 1/4	Greyhound	Sep Palin	Lexington, Ky.	1938
2–year–old	* 1:55	Noxie Hanover	Jim Simpson	Lexington, Ky.	1988
	1:55 3/5	Mack Lobell	John Campbell	Lexington, Ky.	1986
	1:57 2/5	I'm Impeccable	Dave Rankin	Lexington, Ky.	1989
3–year–old	1:52 1/5	Mack Lobell	John Campbell	Springfield, Ill.	1987
	1:52 4/5	Peace Corps	John Campbell	Du Quoin, Ill.	1989
	1:56	Nuclear Arsenal	Dave Magee	Springfield, Ill.	1989
4–year–old	1:53	Express Ride	Berndt Lindstedt	Lexington, Ky.	1987
	1:54 1/5	Imperfection	D. Magee	Balmoral, Illinois	1993
	* 1:55 2/5	Classical Way	John Simpson Jr.	Lexington, Ky.	1980
5–year–old and older	1:54 1/5	Napoletano	Stig Johansson	East Rutherford, N.J.	1989
	1:54 4/5	Kit Lobell	Berndt Lindstedt	East Rutherford, N.J.	1990
	1:55	Franconia	John Campbell	East Rutherford, N.J.	1987
	* 1:55 1/4	Greyhound	Sep Palin	Lexington, Ky.	1938

Trotting on Five-Eighths-Mile Track

	Record	Holder	Driver	Where Made	Year
All Age	1:54 1/5	Mack Lobell	John Campbell	Pompano Beach, Fla.	1987
2–year–old	1:57 3/5	Royal Troubador	Carl Allen	Pompano Beach, Fla.	1989
3–year–old	1:54 1/5	Mack Lobell	John Campbell	Pompano Beach, Fla.	1987
4–year–old	1:54 4/5	Mack Lobell	John Campbell	Solvalla, Sweden	1988
5–year–old and older	1:54 3/5	Mack Lobell	John Campbell	Pompano Beach, Fla.	1991

Trotting on Half-Mile Track

	Record	Holder	Driver	Where Made	Year
All Age	1:56	Mack Lobell	John Campbell	Saratoga Springs, N.Y.	1988
2–year–old	1:58 1/5	Royal Troubador	Carl Allen	Delaware, Ohio	1989
3–year–old	1:56 4/5	Editor In Chief	John Campbell	Delaware, Ohio	1988
4–year–old	1:56	Mack Lobell	John Campbell	Saratoga Springs, N.Y.	1988
5–year–old and older	1:57 3/5	Atkinson Ridge	H. Filion	Yonkers, N.Y.	1992
	1:57 3/5	Chief Litigator	J. Marsh, Jr.	Yonkers, N.Y.	1992

Pacing on a Mile Track

	Record	Holder	Driver	Where Made	Year
All Age	* 1:48 2/5	Matt's Scooter	Michel Lachance	Lexington, Ky.	1988
	1:49 2/5	Artsplace	C. Manzi	East Rutherford, N.J.	1992
	1:49 4/5	Dorunrun	J. Schwind	East Rutherford, N.J.	1992
2–year–old	1:51 4/5	America's Pasttime	W. Hennessey	East Rutherford, N.J.	1992
	1:52	L Dees Trish	Michel Lachance	Lexington, Ky.	1988
	1:52 1/5	Raque Bogart	Bill Fahy	Lexington, Ky.	1988
3–year–old	* 1:48 2/5	Matt's Scooter	Michel Lachance	Lexington, Ky.	1988
	1:50 4/5	Western Hanover	W. Fahy	East Rutherford, N.J.	1992
	* 1:51 2/5	Trini Hanover	Ron Waples	Springfield, Ill.	1987
	1:51 4/5	Indian Alert	Larry Noggle	Lexington, Ky.	1987
4–year–old	1:49 2/5	Artsplace	C. Manzi	East Rutherford, N.J.	1992
	* 1:49 2/5	Jaguar Spur	Dick Stillings	Lexington, Ky.	1988
	* 1:50 4/5	Fan Hanover	Glen Garnsey	Lexington, Ky.	1982
	1:51 1/5	Indian Alert	Jack Moiseyev	East Rutherford, N.J.	1988
5–year–old and older	1:49 4/5	Dorunrun	J. Schwind	East Rutherford, N.J.	1992

Pacing on Five-Eighths-Mile Track					
All Age	1:50 4/5	In the Pocket	John Campbell	Meadow Lands, Pa.	1990
2–year–old	1:53 2/5	Kentucky Spur	Dick Stillings	Pompano Beach, Fla.	1988
3–year–old	1:50 4/5	In the Pocket	John Campbell	Meadow Lands, Pa.	1990
	1:51 1/5	Goalie Jeff	Michel Lachance	Montreal, Canada	1989
4–year–old	1:51	Falcon Seelster	Tom Harmer	Meadow Lands, Pa.	1986
	1:51	Matt's Scooter	Michel Lachance	Campbellville, Ont., Canada	1989
5–year–old and older	1:52 2/5	Ring of Light	James Morand	Laurel, Md.	1988
Pacing on a Half-Mile Track					
All Age	1:51	Falcon Seelster	Tom Harmer	Delaware, Ohio	1985
2–year–old	1:54 1/5	Tooter Scooter	Bill Fahy	Louisville, Ky.	1990
	1:54 1/5	W.R.H.	John Campbell	Delaware, Ohio	1990
3–year–old	1:51	Falcon Seelster	Tom Harmer	Delaware, Ohio	1985
4–year–old	1:53 1/5	Falcon Seelster	Tom Harmer	Maywood, Ill.	1986
5–year–old and older	1:54 1/5	Port Stanley	John Reese	Maywood, Ill.	1988

*Set in a time trial.

HARNESS RACING RECORDS FOR THE MILE

Trotters Time	Trotter, age, driver	Year	Pacers Time	Pacer, age, driver	Year
2:00	Lou Dillon, 5, Millard Sanders	1903	2:00 1/2	John R. Gentry, 7, W.J. Andrews	1896
1:58 1/2	Lou Dillon, 5, Millard Sanders	1903	1:59 1/4	Star Pointer, 8, D. McClary	1897
1:58	Uhlan, 8, Charles Tanner	1912	1:59	Dan Patch, 7, M. E. McHenry	1903
1:58	Peter Manning, 5, T. W. Murphy	1921	1:56 1/4	Dan Patch, 7, M. E. McHenry	1903
1:57 3/4	Peter Manning, 5, T. W. Murphy	1921	1:56	Dan Patch, 8, H. C. Hersey	1904
1:57	Peter Manning, 6, T. W. Murphy	1922	1:55	Billy Direct, 4, Vic Fleming	1938
1:56 3/4	Peter Manning, 6, T. W. Murphy	1922	1:55	Adios Harry, 4, Luther Lyons	1955
1:56 3/4	Greyhound, 5, Sep Palin	1937	1:54 3/5	Adios Butler, 4, Paige West	1960
1:56	Greyhound, 5, Sep Palin	1937	1:54	Bret Hanover, 4, Frank Ervin	1966
1:55 1/4	Greyhound, 6, Sep Palin	1938	1:53 3/5	Bret Hanover, 4, Frank Ervin	1966
1:54 4/5	Nevele Pride, 4, Stanley Dancer	1969	1:52	Steady Star, 4, Joe O'Brien	1971
1:54 4/5	Lindy's Crown, 4, Howard Beissinger	1980	1:49 1/5	Niatross, 3, Clint Galbraith	1980
1:54	Arndon, 3, Del Miller	1982	1:48 2/5	Matt's Scooter, 3, Michel Lachance	1989
1:52 1/5	Mack Lobell, 3, John Campbell	1987	1:46 1/5	Cambest, 5, W. Hennessey	1993

HISTORY OF TRADITIONAL HARNESS RACING STAKES

The Hambletonian

Three–year–old trotters. One mile. Guy McKinney won first race at Syracuse in 1926; held at Goshen, N.Y., 1930–1942, 1944–1956; at Yonkers, N.Y., 1943; at Du Quoin, Ill., 1957–1980. Since 1981, the race has been held at The Meadowlands in East Rutherford, N.J.

Year	Winner	Driver	Best time	Total purse
1967	Speedy Streak	Del Cameron	2:00	$122,650
1968	Nevele Pride	Stanley Dancer	1:59 2/5	116,190
1969	Lindy's Pride	Howard Beissinger	1:57 3/5	124,910
1970	Timothy T.	John Simpson, Jr.	1:58 2/5[1]	143,630
1971	Speedy Crown	Howard Beissinger	1:57 2/5	129,770
1972	Super Bowl	Stanley Dancer	1:56 2/5	119,090
1973	Flirth	Ralph Baldwin	1:57 1/5	144,710
1974	Christopher T	Billy Haughton	1:58 3/5	160,150
1975	Bonefish	Stanley Dancer	1:59[2]	232,192
1976	Steve Lobell	Billy Haughton	1:56 2/5	263,524
1977	Green Speed	Billy Haughton	1:55 3/5	284,131
1978	Speedy Somolli	Howard Beissinger	1:55[3]	241,280
1979	Legend Hanover	George Sholty	1:56 1/5	300,000
1980	Burgomeister	Billy Haughton	1:56 3/5	293,570
1981	Shiaway St. Pat	Ray Remmen	2:01 1/5[4]	838,000
1982	Speed Bowl	Tommy Haughton	1:56 4/5	875,750
1983	Duenna	Stanley Dancer	1:57 2/5	1,000,000
1984	Historic Free	Ben Webster	1:56 2/5	1,219,000
1985	Prakas	Bill O'Donnell	1:54 3/5	1,272,000
1986	Nuclear Kosmos	Ulf Thoresen	1:56	1,172,082
1987	Mack Lobell	John Campbell	1:53 3/5	1,046,300
1988	Armbro Goal	John Campbell	1:54 3/5	1,156,800
1989	Park Avenue Joe	Ron Waples	1:55 3/5	1,131,000
1990	Embassy Lobell	Michel Lachance	1:56 1/5	1,346,000
1991	Giant Victory	Jack Moiseyev	1:54 4/5	1,238,000
1992	Alf Palema	Mickey McNichol	1:56 3/5	1,288,000
1993	American Winner	Ron Pierce	1:53 1/5	1,200,000

1. By Formal Notice. 2. By Yankee Bambino. 3. By Speedy Somolli and Florida Pro. 4. By Super Juan.

Little Brown Jug

Three-year-old pacers. One Mile. Raced at Delaware County Fair Grounds, Delaware, Ohio.

Year	Winner	Driver	Best time	Total purs
1967	Best of All	Jim Hackett	1:59[1]	$84,77
1968	Rum Customer	Billy Haughton	1:59 3/5	104,22
1969	Laverne Hanover	Billy Haughton	2:00 2/5	109,73
1970	Most Happy Fella	Stanley Dancer	1:57 1/5	100,11
1971	Nansemond	Herve Filion	1:57 2/5	102,99
1972	Strike Out	Keith Waples	1:56 3/5	104,91
1973	Melvin's Woe	Joe O'Brien	1:57 3/5	120,00
1974	Ambro Omaha	Billy Haughton	1:57	132,63
1975	Seatrain	Ben Webster	1:57[2]	147,81
1976	Keystone Ore	Stanley Dancer	1:56 4/5[3]	153,79
1977	Governor Skipper	John Chapman	1:56 1/5	150,00
1978	Happy Escort	William Popfinger	1:55 2/5[4]	186,76
1979	Hot Hitter	Herve Filion	1:55 3/5	226,45
1980	Niatross	Clint Galbraith	1:54 4/5	207,36
1981	Fan Hanover	Glen Garnsey	1:56[5]	243,79
1982	Merger	John Campbell	1:56 3/5	328,90
1983	Ralph Hanover	Ron Waples	1:55 3/5	358,80
1984	Colt 46	Norman Boring	1:53 3/5	366,717
1985	Nihilator	Bill O'Donnell	1:52 1/5	350,73
1986	Barberry Spur	Bill O'Donnell	1:52 4/5	407,684
1987	Jaguar Spur	Richard Stillings	1:55 3/5	412,330
1988	B.J. Scoot	Michel Lachance	1:52 3/5	486,050
1989	Goalie Jeff	Michel Lachance	1:54 1/5	500,200
1990	Beach Towel	Ray Remmen	1:53 3/5	253,049
1991	Precious Bunny	Jack Moiseyev	1:54 1/5	575,150
1992	Fake Left	Ron Waples	1:54 2/5	556,210
1993	Life Sign	John Campbell	1:52	465,500

1. By Nardin's Byrd. 2. By Albert's Star. 3. By Armbro Ranger. 4. By Falcon Almahurst. 5. By Seahawk Hanover.

HARNESS HORSE OF THE YEAR

Chosen in poll conducted by United States Trotting Association in conjunction with the U.S. Harness Writers Assn.

1959	Bye Bye Byrd, Pacer	1974	Delmonica Hanover, Trotter	1984	Fancy Crown, Trotter
1960–61	Adios Butler, Pacer	1975	Savoir, Trotter	1985	Nihilator, Trotter
1962	Su Mac Lad, Trotter	1976	Keystone Ore, Pacer	1986	Forrest Skipper
1963	Speedy Scot, Trotter	1977	Green Speed, Trotter	1987–88	Mack Lobell
1964–66	Bret Hanover, Pacer	1978	Abercrombie, Pacer	1989	Matt's Scooter
1967–69	Nevele Pride, Trotter	1979–80	Niatross, Pacer	1990	Beach Towell
1970	Fresh Yankee, Trotter	1981	Fan Hanover, Pacer	1991	Precious Bunny
1971–72	Albatross, Pacer	1982–83	Cam Fella, Pacer	1992	Artsplace
1973	Sir Dalrae, Pacer				

RODEO

THE COWBOY SPORT

A rodeo was originally a contest held after a roundup where the cowboys competed among themselves in contests such as horse racing, steer riding, and calf roping. This display of cowboy skills originated in Mexico and the word "rodeo" comes from the Spanish word *rodear* which means a cattle roundup. The first real rodeo is commonly believed to have been held in Kansas in 1882 and was organized by Col. George Miller of the famous 101 Ranch. Others think that the first organized rodeo was held in Pecos, Texas, in 1883.

These cowboy displays of skill developed into the annual rodeo events held in the West today where millions of people watch professional rodeo performers compete. The Rodeo Cowboy Association was founded in 1936 to establish uniform regulations for the sport. There are five standard events in a modern rodeo. They are saddle bronc riding, bareback riding, bull riding, calf roping, and steer wrestling or "bulldogging."

PROFESSIONAL RODEO COWBOY ASSOCIATION, ALL AROUND COWBOY

1953	Bill Linderman	1963–65	Dean Oliver	1976–79	Tom Ferguson	1986	Lewis Field
1954	Buck Rutherford	1966–70	Larry Mahan	1980	Paul Tierney	1987	Lewis Field
1955	Casey Tibbs	1971–72	Phil Lyne	1981	Jimmie Cooper	1988	Dave Appleton
1956–59	Jim Shoulders	1973	Larry Mahan	1982	Chris Lybbert	1989	Ty Murray
1960	Harry Tompkins	1974	Tom Ferguson	1983	Roy Cooper	1990	Ty Murray
1961	Benny Reynolds	1975	Leo Camarillo and Tom Ferguson	1984	Dee Pickett	1991	Ty Murray
1962	Tom Nesmith			1985	Lewis Field	1992	Ty Murray

NOTE: 1993 Championship scheduled after *Information Please Almanac* went to press.

GOLF

It may be that golf originated in Holland—historians believe it did—but certainly Scotland fostered the game and is famous for it. In fact, in 1457 the Scottish Parliament, disturbed because football and golf had lured young Scots from the more soldierly exercise of archery, passed an ordinance that "futeball and golf be utterly cryit doun and nocht usit." James I and Charles I of the royal line of Stuarts were golf enthusiasts, whereby the game came to be known as "the royal and ancient game of golf."

The golf balls used in the early games were leather-covered and stuffed with feathers. Clubs of all kinds were fashioned by hand to suit individual players. The great step in spreading the game came with the change from the feather ball to the guttapercha ball about 1850. In 1860, formal competition began with the establishment of an annual tournament for the British Open championship. There are records of "golf clubs" in the United States as far back as colonial days but no proof of actual play before John Reid and some friends laid out six holes on the Reid lawn in Yonkers, N.Y., in 1888 and played there with golf balls and clubs brought over from Scotland by Robert Lockhart. This group then formed the St. Andrews Golf Club of Yonkers, and golf was established in this country.

However, it remained a rather sedate and almost aristocratic pastime until a 20-year-old ex-caddy, Francis Ouimet of Boston, defeated two great British professionals, Harry Vardon and Ted Ray, in the United States Open championship at Brookline, Mass., in 1913. This feat put the game and Francis Ouimet on the front pages of the newspapers and stirred a wave of enthusiasm for the sport. The greatest feat so far in golf history is that of Robert Tyre Jones, Jr., of Atlanta, who won the British Open, the British Amateur, the U.S. Open, and the U.S. Amateur titles in one year, 1930.

THE MASTERS TOURNAMENT WINNERS

Augusta National Golf Club, Augusta, Ga.

Year	Winner	Score	Year	Winner	Score	Year	Winner	Score
1934	Horton Smith	284	1955	Cary Middlecoff	279	1974	Gary Player	278
1935	Gene Sarazen[1]	282	1956	Jack Burke	289	1975	Jack Nicklaus	276
1936	Horton Smith	285	1957	Doug Ford	283	1976	Ray Floyd	271
1937	Byron Nelson	283	1958	Arnold Palmer	284	1977	Tom Watson	276
1938	Henry Picard	285	1959	Art Wall, Jr.	284	1978	Gary Player	277
1939	Ralph Guldahl	279	1960	Arnold Palmer	282	1979	Fuzzy Zoeller[1]	280
1940	Jimmy Demaret	280	1961	Gary Player	280	1980	Severiano Ballesteros	275
1941	Craig Wood	280	1962	Arnold Palmer[1]	280	1981	Tom Watson	280
1942	Byron Nelson[1]	280	1963	Jack Nicklaus	286	1982	Craig Stadler[1]	284
1943–45	No Tournaments		1964	Arnold Palmer	276	1983	Severiano Ballesteros	280
1946	Herman Keiser	282	1965	Jack Nicklaus	271	1984	Ben Crenshaw	277
1947	Jimmy Demaret	281	1966	Jack Nicklaus[1]	288	1985	Bernhard Langer	282
1948	Claude Harmon	279	1967	Gay Brewer, Jr.	280	1986	Jack Nicklaus	279
1949	Sam Snead	282	1968	Bob Goalby	277	1987	Larry Mize[1]	285
1950	Jimmy Demaret	283	1969	George Archer	281	1988	Sandy Lyle	281
1951	Ben Hogan	280	1970	Billy Casper[1]	279	1989	Nick Faldo[1]	283
1952	Sam Snead	286	1971	Charles Coody	279	1990	Nick Faldo	278
1953	Ben Hogan	274	1972	Jack Nicklaus	286	1991	Ian Woosnam	277
1954	Sam Snead[1]	289	1973	Tommy Aaron	283	1992	Fred Couples	275
						1993	Bernard Langer	277

1. Winner in playoff.

U.S. OPEN CHAMPIONS

Year	Winner	Score	Where played	Year	Winner	Score	Where played
1895	Horace Rawlins	173	Newport	1915	Jerome D. Travers[2]	297	Baltusrol
1896	James Foulis	152	Shinnecock Hills	1916	Charles Evans, Jr.[2]	286	Minikahda
1897	Joe Lloyd	162	Chicago	1917–18	No tournaments[4]		
1898[3]	Fred Herd	328	Myopia	1919	Walter Hagen[2]	301	Brae Burn
1899	Willie Smith	315	Baltimore	1920	Edward Ray	295	Inverness
1900	Harry Vardon	313	Chicago	1921	Jim Barnes	289	Columbia
1901	Willie Anderson[1]	331	Myopia	1922	Gene Sarazen	288	Skokie
1902	Laurie Auchterlonie	307	Garden City	1923	R. T. Jones, Jr.[1 2]	296	Inwood
1903	Willie Anderson[1]	307	Baltusrol	1924	Cyril Walker	297	Oakland Hills
1904	Willie Anderson	303	Glen View	1925	Willie Macfarlane[1]	291	Worcester
1905	Willie Anderson	314	Myopia	1926	R. T. Jones, Jr.[2]	293	Scioto
1906	Alex Smith	295	Onwentsia	1927	Tommy Armour[1]	301	Oakmont
1907	Alex Ross	302	Philadelphia	1928	Johnny Farrell[1]	294	Olympia Fields
1908	Fred McLeod[1]	322	Myopia	1929	R. T. Jones, Jr.[1 2]	294	Winged Foot
1909	George Sargent	290	Englewood	1930	R. T. Jones, Jr.[2]	287	Interlachen
1910	Alex Smith[1]	298	Philadelphia	1931	Billy Burke[1]	292	Inverness
1911	John McDermott[1]	307	Chicago	1932	Gene Sarazen	286	Fresh Meadow
1912	John McDermott	294	Buffalo	1933	John Goodman[2]	287	North Shore
1913	Francis Ouimet[1 2]	304	Brookline	1934	Olin Dutra	293	Merion
1914	Walter Hagen	290	Midlothian	1935	Sam Parks, Jr.	299	Oakmont

Year	Winner	Score	Where played	Year	Winner	Score	Where played
1936	Tony Manero	282	Baltusrol	1967	Jack Nicklaus	275	Baltusrol
1937	Ralph Guldahl	281	Oakland Hills	1968	Lee Trevino	275	Oak Hill
1938	Ralph Guldahl	284	Cherry Hills	1969	Orville Moody	281	Champions G. C.
1939	Byron Nelson[1]	284	Philadelphia	1970	Tony Jacklin	281	Hazeltine
1940	Lawson Little[1]	287	Canterbury	1971	Lee Trevino[1]	280	Merion
1941	Craig Wood	284	Colonial	1972	Jack Nicklaus	290	Pebble Beach
1942–45	No tournaments[5]			1973	Johnny Miller	279	Oakmont
1946	Lloyd Mangrum[1]	284	Canterbury	1974	Hale Irwin	287	Winged Foot
1947	Lew Worsham[1]	282	St. Louis	1975	Lou Graham[1]	287	Medinah
1948	Ben Hogan	276	Riviera	1976	Jerry Pate	277	Atlanta A.C.
1949	Cary Middlecoff	286	Medinah	1977	Hubert Green	278	Southern Hills
1950	Ben Hogan[1]	287	Merion	1978	Andy North	285	Cherry Hills
1951	Ben Hogan	287	Oakland Hills	1979	Hale Irwin	284	Inverness
1952	Julius Boros	281	Northwood	1980	Jack Nicklaus	272	Baltusrol
1953	Ben Hogan	283	Oakmont	1981	David Graham	273	Merion
1954	Ed Furgol	284	Baltusrol	1982	Tom Watson	282	Pebble Beach
1955	Jack Fleck[1]	287	Olympic	1983	Larry Nelson	280	Oakmont
1956	Cary Middlecoff	281	Oak Hill	1984	Fuzzy Zoeller[1]	276	Winged Foot
1957	Dick Mayer[1]	298	Inverness	1985	Andy North	279	Oakland Hills
1958	Tommy Bolt	283	Southern Hills	1986	Ray Floyd	279	Shinnecock Hills
1959	Bill Casper, Jr.	282	Winged Foot	1987	Scott Simpson	277	Olympic Golf Club
1960	Arnold Palmer	280	Cherry Hills	1988	Curtis Strange[1]	278	The Country Club
1961	Gene Littler	281	Oakland Hills	1989	Curtis Strange	278	Oak Hill Country Club
1962	Jack Nicklaus[1]	283	Oakmont				
1963	Julius Boros[1]	293	Country Club	1990	Hale Irwin[1]	280	Medinah C.C.
1964	Ken Venturi	278	Congressional	1991	Payne Stewart[1]	282	Hazeltine
1965	Gary Player[1]	282	Bellerive	1992	Tom Kite	285	Pebble Beach
1966	Bill Casper[1]	278	Olympic	1993	Lee Janzen	272	Baltusrol

1. Winner in playoff. 2. Amateur. 3. In 1898, competition was extended to 72 holes. 4. In 1917, Jock Hutchison, with a 292 won an Open Patriotic Tournament for the benefit of the American Red Cross at Whitemarsh Valley Country Club. 5. In 1942, Ben Hogan, with a 271 won a Hale American National Open Tournament for the benefit of the Navy Relief Society and USO at Ridgemoor Country Club.

U.S. AMATEUR CHAMPIONS

1895	Charles B. Macdonald	1923	Max R. Marston	1951	Billy Maxwell	1973[3]	Craig Stadler
		1924–25	R. T. Jones, Jr.	1952	Jack Westland	1974	Jerry Pate
1896–97	H. J. Whigham	1926	George Von Elm	1953	Gene Littler	1975	Fred Ridley
1898	Findlay S. Douglas	1927–28	R. T. Jones, Jr.	1954	Arnold Palmer	1976	Bill Sander
1899	H. M. Harriman	1929	H. R. Johnston	1955–56	Harvie Ward	1977	John Fought
1900–01	Walter J. Travis	1930	R. T. Jones, Jr.	1957	Hillman Robbins	1978	John Cook
1902	Louis N. James	1931	Francis Ouimet	1958	Charles Coe	1979	Mark O'Meara
1903	Walter J. Travis	1932	Ross Somerville	1959	Jack Nicklaus	1980	Hal Sutton
1904–05	H. Chandler Egan	1933	G. T. Dunlap, Jr.	1960	Deane Beman	1981	Nathaniel Crosby
1906	Eben M. Byers	1934–35	Lawson Little	1961	Jack Nicklaus	1982	Jay Sigel
1907–08	Jerome D. Travers	1936	John W. Fischer	1962	Labron Harris, Jr.	1983	Jay Sigel
1909	Robert A. Gardner	1937	John Goodman	1963	Deane Beman	1984	Scott Verplank
1910	W. C. Fownes, Jr.	1938	Willie Turnesa	1964	Bill Campbell	1985	Sam Randolph
1911	Harold H. Hilton	1939	Marvin H. Ward	1965[2]	Robert Murphy, Jr.	1986	Buddy Alexander
1912–13	Jerome D. Travers	1940	R. D. Chapman	1966	Gary Cowan[1]	1987	Bill Mayfair
1914	Francis Ouimet	1941	Marvin H. Ward	1967	Bob Dickson	1988	Eric Meeks
1915	Robert A. Gardner	1946	Ted Bishop	1968	Bruce Fleisher	1989	Chris Patton
1916	Charles Evans, Jr.	1947	Robert Riegel	1969	Steven Melnyk	1990	Phil Mickelson
1919	S. D. Herron	1948	Willie Turnesa	1970	Lanny Wadkins	1991	Mitch Voges
1920	Charles Evans, Jr.	1949	Charles Coe	1971	Gary Cowan	1992	Justin Leonard
1921	Jesse P. Guilford	1950	Sam Urzetta	1972	Vinny Giles 3d	1993	John Harris
1922	Jess W. Sweetser						

1. Winner in playoff. 2. Tourney switched to medal play through 1972. 3. Return to match play.

U.S. P.G.A. CHAMPIONS

1916	Jim Barnes	1930	Tommy Armour	1938	Paul Runyan	1946	Ben Hogan
1919	Jim Barnes	1931	Tom Creavy	1939	Henry Picard	1947	Jim Ferrier
1920	Jock Hutchison	1932	Olin Dutra	1940	Byron Nelson	1948	Ben Hogan
1921	Walter Hagen	1933	Gene Sarazen	1941	Victor Ghezzi	1949	Sam Snead
1922–23	Gene Sarazen	1934	Paul Runyan	1942	Sam Snead	1950	Chandler Harper
1924–27	Walter Hagen	1935	Johnny Revolta	1944	Bob Hamilton	1951	Sam Snead
1928–29	Leo Diegel	1936–37	Denny Shute	1945	Byron Nelson	1952	Jim Turnesa

1953	Walter Burkemo	1964	Bobby Nichols	1974	Lee Trevino	1984	Lee Trevino
1954	Chick Harbert	1965	Dave Marr	1975	Jack Nicklaus	1985	Hubert Green
1955	Doug Ford	1966	Al Geiberger	1976	Dave Stockton	1986	Bob Tway
1956	Jack Burke, Jr.	1967	Don January[1]	1977	Lanny Wadkins[1]	1987	Larry Nelson
1957	Lionel Hebert	1968	Julius Boros	1978	John Mahaffey	1988	Jeff Sluman
1958[2]	Dow Finsterwald	1969	Ray Floyd	1979	David Graham[1]	1989	Payne Stewart
1959	Bob Rosburg	1970	Dave Stockton	1980	Jack Nicklaus	1990	Mac Grady
1960	Jay Hebert	1971	Jack Nicklaus	1981	Larry Nelson	1991	John Daly
1961	Jerry Barber[1]	1972	Gary Player	1982	Ray Floyd	1992	Nick Price
1962	Gary Player	1973	Jack Nicklaus	1983	Hal Sutton	1993	Paul Azinger[1]
1963	Jack Nicklaus						

1. Winner in playoff. 2. Switched to medal play.

U.S. WOMEN'S AMATEUR CHAMPIONS

1916	Alexa Stirling	1938	Patty Berg	1960	JoAnne Gunderson	1975	Beth Daniel
1919–20	Alexa Stirling	1939–40	Betty Jameson	1961	Anne Quast Decker	1976	Donna Horton
1921	Marion Hollins	1941	Mrs. Frank Newell	1962	JoAnne Gunderson	1977	Beth Daniel
1922	Glenna Collett	1946	Mildred Zaharias	1963	Anne Quast Welts	1978	Cathy Sherk
1923	Edith Cummings	1947	Louise Suggs	1964	Barbara McIntire	1979	Carolyn Hill
1924	Dorothy Campbell Hurd	1948	Grace Lenczyk	1965	Jean Ashley	1980	Juli Inkster
1925	Glenna Collett	1949	Mrs. D. G. Porter	1966	JoAnne Gunderson	1981	Juli Inkster
1926	Helen Stetson	1950	Beverly Hanson	1967	Lou Dill	1982	Juli Inkster
1927	Mrs. M. B. Horn	1951	Dorothy Kirby	1968	JoAnne G. Carner	1983	Joanne Pacillo
1928–30	Glenna Collett	1952	Jacqueline Pung	1969	Catherine LaCoste	1984	Deb Richard
1931	Helen Hicks	1953	Mary Lena Faulk	1970	Martha Wilkinson	1985	Michiko Hattori
1932–34	Virginia Van Wie	1954	Barbara Romack	1971	Laura Baugh	1986	Kay Cockerill
1935	Glenna Collett Vare	1955	Patricia Lesser	1972	Mary Ann Budke	1987	Kay Cockerill
1936	Pamela Barton	1956	Marlene Stewart	1973	Carol Semple	1988	Pearl Sinn
1937	Mrs. J. A. Page, Jr.	1957	JoAnne Gunderson	1974	Cynthia Hill	1989	Vicki Goetze
		1958	Anne Quast			1990	Pat Hurst
		1959	Barbara McIntire			1991	Amy Fruhwirth
						1992	Vicki Goetze
						1993	Jill McGill

U.S. WOMEN'S OPEN CHAMPIONS

Year	Winner	Score	Year	Winner	Score	Year	Winner	Score
1946	Patty Berg (match play)	—	1962	Murle Lindstrom	301	1978	Hollis Stacy	289
1947	Betty Jameson	295	1963	Mary Mills	289	1979	Jerilyn Britz	284
1948	Mildred D. Zaharias	300	1964	Mickey Wright[1]	290	1980	Amy Alcott	280
1949	Louise Suggs	291	1965	Carol Mann	290	1981	Pat Bradley	279
1950	Mildred D. Zaharias	291	1966	Sandra Spuzich	297	1982	Janet Alex	283
1951	Betsy Rawls	293	1967	Catherine LaCoste[2]	294	1983	Jan Stephenson	290
1952	Louise Suggs	284	1968	Susie Berning	289	1984	Hollis Stacy	290
1953	Betsy Rawls[1]	302	1969	Donna Caponi	294	1985	Kathy Baker	280
1954	Mildred D. Zaharias	291	1970	Donna Caponi	287	1986	Jane Geddes[1]	287
1955	Fay Crocker	299	1971	JoAnne Carner	288	1987	Laura Davies[1]	285
1956	Katherine Cornelius[1]	302	1972	Susie Berning	299	1988	Liselotte Neumann	277
1957	Betsy Rawls	299	1973	Susie Berning	290	1989	Betsy King	278
1958	Mickey Wright	290	1974	Sandra Haynie	295	1990	Betsy King	284
1959	Mickey Wright	287	1975	Sandra Palmer	295	1991	Meg Mallon	283
1960	Betsy Rawls	291	1976	JoAnne Carner[1]	292	1992	Patty Sheehan	280
1961	Mickey Wright	293	1977	Hollis Stacy	292	1993	Lauri Merten	280

1. Winner in playoff. 2. Amateur.

BRITISH OPEN CHAMPIONS

(First tournament, held in 1860, was won by Willie Park, Sr.)

Year	Winner	Score	Year	Winner	Score	Year	Winner	Score
1920	George Duncan	303	1928	Walter Hagen	292	1936	A. H. Padgham	287
1921	Jock Hutchison[1]	296	1929	Walter Hagen	292	1937	Henry Cotton	290
1922	Walter Hagen	300	1930	R. T. Jones, Jr.	291	1938	R. A. Whitcombe	295
1923	A. G. Havers	295	1931	Tommy Armour	296	1939	R. Burton	290
1924	Walter Hagen	301	1932	Gene Sarazen	283	1940	Sam Snead	290
1925	Jim Barnes	300	1933	Denny Shute1	292	1947	Fred Daly	294
1926	R. T. Jones, Jr.	291	1934	Henry Cotton	283	1948	Henry Cotton	283
1927	R. T. Jones, Jr.	285	1935	A. Perry	283	1949	Bobby Locke[1]	283

1. Winner in playoff.

Year	Winner	Score	Year	Winner	Score	Year	Winner	Score
1950	Bobby Locke	279	1965	Peter Thomson	285	1980	Tom Watson	271
1951	Max Faulkner	285	1966	Jack Nicklaus	282	1981	Bill Rogers	276
1952	Bobby Locke	287	1967	Roberto de Vicenzo	278	1982	Tom Watson	284
1953	Ben Hogan	282	1968	Gary Player	289	1983	Tom Watson	275
1954	Peter Thomson	283	1969	Tony Jacklin	280	1984	Severiano Ballesteros	276
1955	Peter Thomson	281	1970	Jack Nicklaus[1]	283	1985	Sandy Lyle	282
1956	Peter Thomson	286	1971	Lee Trevino	278	1986	Greg Norman	280
1957	Bobby Locke	279	1972	Lee Trevino	278	1987	Nick Faldo	279
1958	Peter Thomson[1]	278	1973	Tom Weiskopf	276	1988	Seve Ballesteros	273
1959	Gary Player	284	1974	Gary Player	282	1989	Mark Calcavecchia	275
1960	Kel Nagle	278	1975	Tom Watson[1]	279	1990	Nick Faldo	270
1961	Arnold Palmer	284	1976	Johnny Miller	279	1991	Ian Baker-Finch	272
1962	Arnold Palmer	276	1977	Tom Watson	268	1992	Nick Faldo	272
1963	Bob Charles[1]	277	1978	Jack Nicklaus	281	1993	Greg Norman	267
1964	Tony Lema	279	1979	Severiano Ballesteros	283			

1. Winner in playoff.

OTHER 1993 PGA TOUR WINNERS

(Through August 23, 1993)

Buick Open—Larry Mize (272)	$180,000
St. Jude Classic—Nick Price (266)	198,000
New England Classic—Paul Azinger (268)	180,000
Anheuser Busch Classic—J. Gallagher (269)	198,000
Western Open—Nick Price (269)	216,000
Greater Hartford Open—Nick Price (271)	180,000
Buick Classic—Vijay Singh (280)	180,000
The Memorial—Paul Azinger (274)	252,000
Colonial Classic—Fulton Allem (264)	234,000
Kemper Open—Grant Waite (275)	234,000
Byron Nelson Classic—Scott Simpson (270)	216,000
Bell South Classic—Nolan Henke (271)	216,000
Houston Open—Jim McGovern (199)	234,000
Greater Greensboro Open—Rocco Mediate (281)	270,000
Heritage Classic—David Edwards (273)	202,500
Deposit Guaranty Classic—Greg Kraft (287)	54,000
Freeport McMoran Classic—Mike Standly (279)	180,000
Players Championship—Nick Price (270)	450,000
Nestle Invitational—Ben Crenshaw (280)	180,000
Honda Classic—Fred Couples (207)	198,000
Doral Open—Greg Norman (265)	252,000
Los Angeles Open—Tom Kite (206)	180,000
Buick Invitational—Phil Mickelson (278)	180,000
Bob Hope Classic—Tom Kite (325)	198,000
National Pro-Am—Brett Ogle (276)	225,000
Phoenix Open—Lee Janzen (273)	180,000
Northern Telecom Open—Larry Mize	198,000
Hawaiian Open—Howard Twitty (269)	216,000
Tournament of Champions—Davis Love III (272)	144,000
International—Phil Mickelson (45 pts)	234,000

OTHER 1993 LPGA TOUR WINNERS

(Through August 23, 1993)

McCall's Classic—D. Lofland-Dorman (275)	$ 75,000
Ping-Welch's Championship—Meg Mallon (272)	60,000
Big Apple Classic—Hiromi Kobayashi (278)	144,000
Youngstown-Warren Classic—Nancy Lopez (275)	90,000
Toledo Classic—Brandie Burton (201)	67,500
Shop Rite Classic—Shelley Hamlin (204)	67,500
Rochester International—Tammie Green (276)	75,000
LPGA Championship—Patty Sheehan (275)	150,000
Oldsmobile Classic—Jan Geddes (277)	82,500
Corning Classic—Kelly Robins (277)	75,000
Lady Keystone Open—Val Skinner (210)	60,000
McDonald's Championship—Laura Davies (277)	135,000
Sara Lee Classic—Meg Mallon (205)	78,750
Sprint Classic—Kristi Albers (279)	180,000
Atlanta Championship—Trish Johnson (282)	90,000
Las Vegas LPGA—Trish Johnson (209)	67,500
LPGA Dinah Shore—Helen Alfredsson (284)	105,000
Standard Register Ping—Patty Sheehan (275)	105,000
Hawaiian Ladies Open—Lisa Walters (210)	67,500
Palm Beach Classic—Tammie Green (208)	60,000
Minnesota LPGA Classic—Hiromi Kobayashi (205)	67,500

FENCING

World Champions—1993

(Essen, Germany, July 1–10, 1993)

Men's epee—Pavel Kolobkov, Russia
Men's foil—Alexander Koch, Germany
Men's sabre—Grigory Kirienko, Russia
Women's epee—Oksana Jermakova, Estonia
Women's foil—Francesca Bortolozzi, Italy
Men's foil team—Germany
Men's epee team—Italy
Men's sabre team—Hungary
Women's foil team—Germany
Women's epee team—Hungary

United States Champions—1993

(Ft. Myers, Fla., June 5–13, 1993)

Men's foil—Michael Marx, South Bend, Ind.
Women's foil—Felicia Zimmerman, Rush, N.Y.
Men's epee—Benjamin Atkins, New York, N.Y.
Women's epee—Leslie Marx, South Bend, Ind.
Men's sabre—David Mandell, New York, N.Y.

SOCCER

The early history of the sport is uncertain. A form of the game in which a leather ball was dribbled was played in China as early as the 4th century B.C. The Romans played a variation of soccer which eventually spread throughout Europe. British schools and universities played soccer (known as football) during the 1800s, however, each school used different sets of rules and the number of players varied. This difficulty was corrected on Oct. 26, 1863 when the Football Association (FA) was formed in London for the purpose of unifying the rules of the game.

The Federation of International Football Associations (FIFA) was created in 1913 as a world governing body to coordinate all of the national associations in the world. The FIFA held the first World Cup Championship tournament in 1930 in Montevideo, Uruguay. Today, soccer is the world's most popular sport.

WORLD CUP

1930 Uruguay
1934 Italy
1938 Italy
1942 No competition
1946 No competition
1950 Uruguay
1954 West Germany
1958 Brazil
1962 Brazil
1966 England
1970 Brazil
1974 West Germany
1978 Argentina
1982 Italy
1986 Argentina
1990 West Germany
1994 To be held in United States

WORLD CUP—1990

SEMIFINALS

1. Argentina 1, Italy 1 (at Naples, Italy, July 3, 1990) (Argentina wins, on 4–3 penalty kick shootout)

2. West Germany 1, England 1 (at Turin, Italy, July 4, 1990) (West Germany wins, on 4–3 penalty kick shootout)

THIRD PLACE

Italy 2, England 1 (at Bari, Italy, July 7, 1990)

FINALS

West Germany 1, Argentina 0 (at Rome, Italy, July 8, 1990)

West Germany (Group D)
W. Germany 4, Yugoslavia 1
W. Germany 5, United Arab Emirates 1
W. Germany 1, Colombia 1 (tie)
West Germany 2, Netherlands 1
West Germany 1, Czechoslovakia 0

Argentina (Group B)
Cameroon 1, Argentina 0
Argentina 2, Soviet Union 0
Argentina 1, Romania 1 (tie)
Argentina 1, Brazil 0
Argentina 0, Yugoslavia 0 (Argentina wins, 3–2, on a penalty shootout)

England (Group F)
England 1, Ireland 1 (tie)
England 0, Netherlands 0 (tie)
England 1, Egypt 0
England 1, Belgium 0 (extra time)
England 3, Cameroon 2 (OT)

Italy (Group A)
Italy 1, Austria 0
Italy 1, United States 0
Italy 2, Czechoslovakia 0
Italy 2, Uruguay 0
Italy 1, Ireland 0

WEST GERMANY WINS WORLD CUP ON A PENALTY KICK

Andreas Brehme's penalty kick in the 84th minute gave West Germany a 1–0 victory over Argentina in the World Cup championship game played in Rome, Italy. The championship was West Germany's third in the 60–year history of the event, tying that country for first in the all–time World Cup standings with Brazil.

West Germany dominated the final against an Argentine team crippled by injuries and the eventual expulsion of two players, which forced the defending champions to play with nine men at the end.

The shutout was the first in World Cup championship game history. Argentina had defeated West Germany, 3–2, in the 1986 World Cup championship game.

A crowd of 73,603 witnessed the championship, televised in America by Turner Network Television, a cable company.

The winning goal came with six minutes remaining in regulation. Midfielder Lothar Matthaeus passed the ball to forward Rudi Voeller. Voeller carried the ball into the box with Argentina's Roberto Sensini shadowing him. When Sensini reached in with his right leg, he was called for tripping Voeller, and West Germany was awarded the penalty kick.

Brehme was the choice to take it. He pushed the ball up, just inside the left post and just beyond the reach of Argentina's goalkeeper, Sergio Goycoechea.

The United States made a bit of World Cup history by qualifying for the first time since 1950. Though the U.S. went winless in the tournament's first round—losing to Czechoslovakia 5–1, Italy 1–0, and Austria 2–1—the experience gave the American team much–needed help in getting ready for its role as host of the 1994 World Cup.

U.S. GAINS 1994 WORLD CUP

It was both fitting and a bit ironic that the Federation Internationale de Football Association picked July 4, 1989, to award the United States the 1994 World Cup competition.

The World Cup, arguably the No. 1 sports event in the world, thus comes to a country where soccer has struggled for a national foothold.

The 1990 World Cup was held in Italy, and 113 countries from around the world competed, including the United States.

The right to stage the World Cup is a prize the United States Soccer Federation had been seeking for many years. In 1983, the U.S. Federation bid for the 1986 tournament, but it was rejected by FIFA, which did not feel the necessary fan support existed in the United States.

What likely put the United States over the top was the total attendance of more than 1.4 million for soccer at the 1984 Summer Olympics in Los Angeles.

A new organization, World Cup USA 1994 was formed, with Paul Stiehl as director and financial backing from sponsors including Coca-Cola, Gillette, Anheuser-Busch, and American Express.

MAJOR SOCCER LEAGUE TEAM STANDINGS—1992[1]

	W	L	Pct	GB
San Diego	26	14	.650	—
Dallas	22	18	.550	4
Cleveland	20	20	.500	6
Baltimore	19	21	.475	7
Wichita	18	22	.450	8
Tacoma	18	22	.450	8
St. Louis	17	23	.425	9

1. League suspended operations after 1992 season.

1992 PLAYOFF RESULTS DALLAS SIDEKICKS VS. SAN DIEGO SOCKERS, MSL CHAMPIONSHIP SERIES

(Best of seven)

Game 1, Thursday, April 30—San Diego 7, Dallas 3
Game 2, Saturday, May 2—San Diego 9, Dallas 7
Game 3, Tuesday, May 5—San Diego 5, Dallas 4 (OT)
Game 4, Friday, May 8—Dallas 10, San Diego 6
Game 5, Saturday, May 9—Dallas 4, San Diego 2
Game 6, Tuesday, May 12—San Diego 8, Dallas 7
San Diego wins series, 4–2 and eighth Major Soccer League title.

NORTH AMERICAN SOCCER LEAGUE CHAMPIONS

1968—Atlanta Chiefs
1969—Kansas City Stars
1970—Rochester Lancers
1971—Dallas Tornado
1972—New York Cosmos
1973—Philadelphia Atoms
1974—Los Angeles Aztecs
1975—Tampa Bay Rowdies
1976—Toronto Metro–Croatia
1977—New York Cosmos
1978—New York Cosmos
1979—Vancouver Whitecaps
1980—New York Cosmos
1981—Chicago Sting
1982—New York Cosmos
1983—Tulsa Roughnecks
1984—Chicago Sting

YACHTING

AMERICA'S CUP RECORD

First race in 1851 around Isle of Wight, Cowes, England. First defense and all others through 1920 held 30 miles off New York Bay. Races since 1930 held 30 miles off Newport, R.I. Conducted as one race only in 1851 and 1870; best four–of–seven basis, 1871; best two–of–three, 1876–1887; best three–of–five, 1893–1901; best four–of–seven, since 1930. Figures in parentheses indicate number of races won.

Year	Winner and owner	Loser and owner
1851	AMERICA (1), John C. Stevens, U.S.	AURORA, T. Le Marchant, England[1]
1870	MAGIC (1), Franklin Osgood, U.S.	CAMBRIA, James Ashbury, England[2]
1871	COLUMBIA (2), Franklin Osgood, U.S.[3] SAPPHO (2), William P. Douglas, U.S.	LIVONIA (1), James Ashbury, England
1876	MADELEINE (2), John S. Dickerson, U.S.	COUNTESS OF DUFFERIN, Chas. Gifford, Canada
1881	MISCHIEF (2), J. R. Busk, U.S.	ATALANTA, Alexander Cuthbert, Canada
1885	PURITAN (2), J. M. Forbes–Gen. Charles Paine, U.S.	GENESTA, Sir Richard Sutton, England
1886	MAYFLOWER (2), Gen. Charles Paine, U.S.	GALATEA, Lt. William Henn, England
1887	VOLUNTEER (2), Gen. Charles Paine, U.S.	THISTLE, James Bell et al., Scotland
1893	VIGILANT (3), C. Oliver Iselin et al., U.S.	VALKYRIE II, Lord Dunraven, England
1895	DEFENDER (3), C. O. Iselin–W. K. Vanderbilt–E. D. Morgan, U.S	VALKYRIE III, Lord Dunraven–Lord Lonsdale–Lord Wolverton, England
1899	COLUMBIA (3), J. P. Morgan–C. O. Iselin, U.S.	SHAMROCK I, Sir Thomas Lipton, Ireland
1901	COLUMBIA (3), Edwin D. Morgan, U.S.	SHAMROCK II, Sir Thomas Lipton, Ireland
1903	RELIANCE (3), Cornelius Vanderbilt et al., U.S.	SHAMROCK III, Sir Thomas Lipton, Ireland
1920	RESOLUTE (3), Henry Walters et al., U.S.	SHAMROCK IV (2), Sir Thomas Lipton, Ireland
1930	ENTERPRISE (4), Harold S. Vanderbilt et al., U.S.	SHAMROCK V, Sir Thomas Lipton, Ireland
1934	RAINBOW (4), Harold S. Vanderbilt, U.S.	ENDEAVOUR (2), T. O. M. Sopwith, England
1937	RANGER (4), Harold S. Vanderbilt, U.S.	ENDEAVOUR II, T. O. M. Sopwith, England
1958	COLUMBIA (4), Henry Sears et al., U.S.	SCEPTRE, Hugh Goodson et al., England
1962	WEATHERLY (4), Henry D. Mercer et al., U.S.	GRETEL (1), Sir Frank Packer et al., Australia
1964	CONSTELLATION (4), New York Y.C. Syndicate, U.S.	SOVEREIGN (0), J. Anthony Bowden, England
1967	INTREPID (4), New York Y.C. Syndicate, U.S.	DAME PATTIE (0), Sydney (Aust.) Syndicate
1970	INTREPID (4), New York Y.C. Syndicate, U.S.	GRETEL II (1), Sydney (Aust.) Syndicate
1974	COURAGEOUS (4), New York, N.Y. Syndicate, U.S.	SOUTHERN CROSS (0), Sydney (Aust.) Syndicate
1977	COURAGEOUS (4), New York, N.Y. Syndicate, U.S.	AUSTRALIA (0), Sun City (Aust.) Syndicate
1980	FREEDOM (4), New York, N.Y. Syndicate, U.S.	AUSTRALIA (1), Alan Bond et al, Australia
1983	AUSTRALIA II (4) Alan Bond et al., Australia,	LIBERTY (3) New York, N.Y. Syndicate, U.S.
1987	STARS & STRIPES (4), Dennis Conner et al., United States	KOOKABURRA III (0), Iain Murray et al., Australia
1988[4]	STARS & STRIPES, Dennis Conner, et al., United States	NEW ZEALAND Michael Fay, et al., New Zealand
1992	AMERICA 3, Bill Koch et al., United States	IL MORO DI VENEZIA, Paul Cayard, et al., Italy

1. Fourteen British yachts started against America; Aurora finished second. 2. Cambria sailed against 23 U.S. yachts and finished tenth. 3. Columbia was disabled in the third race, after winning the first two; Sappho substituted and won the fourth and fifth. 4. Shortly after Dennis Conner and his 60–foot, twin–hulled catamaran easily defeated the challenge of the New Zealand, a 133–foot, single–hulled yacht in the waters off San Diego in early September 1988, a New York State Supreme Court judge ruled that the Americans did not live up to the America's Cup Deed of Gift, which means competing boats must be similar. The judge ruled that the Americans had an unfair advantage over the monohulled ship, and awarded the Cup to New Zealand. However, an Appeal awarded the Cup to the United States.

AUTO RACING

INDIANAPOLIS 500

Year	Winner	Car	Time	mph	Second place
1911	Ray Harroun	Marmon	6:42:08	74.59	Ralph Mulford
1912	Joe Dawson	National	6:21:06	78.72	Teddy Tetzloff
1913	Jules Goux	Peugeot	6:35:05	75.93	Spencer Wishart
1914	René Thomas	Delage	6:03:45	82.47	Arthur Duray
1915	Ralph DePalma	Mercedes	5:33:55.51	89.84	Dario Resta
1916[1]	Dario Resta	Peugeot	3:34:17	84.00	Wilbur D'Alene
1919	Howard Wilcox	Peugeot	5:40:42.87	88.05	Eddie Hearne
1920	Gaston Chevrolet	Monroe	5:38:32	88.62	René Thomas
1921	Tommy Milton	Frontenac	5:34:44.65	89.62	Roscoe Sarles
1922	Jimmy Murphy	Murphy Special	5:17:30.79	94.48	Harry Hartz
1923	Tommy Milton	H. C. S. Special	5:29.50.17	90.95	Harry Hartz
1924	L. L. Corum–Joe Boyer	Dusenberg Special	5:05:23.51	98.23	Earl Cooper
1925	Peter DePaolo	Dusenberg Special	4:56:39.45	101.13	Dave Lewis
1926[2]	Frank Lockhart	Miller Special	4:10:14.95	95.904	Harry Hartz
1927	George Souders	Dusenberg Special	5:07:33.08	97.54	Earl DeVore
1928	Louis Meyer	Miller Special	5:01:33.75	99.48	Lou Moore
1929	Ray Keech	Simplex Special	5:07:25.42	97.58	Louis Meyer
1930	Billy Arnold	Miller–Hartz Special	4:58:39.72	100.448	Shorty Cantlon
1931	Louis Schneider	Bowes Special	5:10:27.93	96.629	Fred Frame
1932	Fred Frame	Miller–Hartz Special	4:48:03.79	104.144	Howard Wilcox
1933	Louis Meyer	Tydol Special	4:48:00.75	104.162	Wilbur Shaw
1934	Bill Cummings	Boyle Products Special	4:46:05.20	104.863	Mauri Rose
1935	Kelly Petillo	Gilmore Special	4:42:22.71	106.240	Wilbur Shaw
1936	Louis Meyer	Ring Free Special	4:35:03.39	109.069	Ted Horn
1937	Wilbur Shaw	Shaw–Gilmore Special	4:24:07.80	113.580	Ralph Hepburn
1938	Floyd Roberts	Burd Piston Ring Special	4:15:58.40	117.200	Wilbur Shaw
1939	Wilbur Shaw	Boyle Special	4:20:47.39	115.035	Jimmy Snyder
1940	Wilbur Shaw	Boyle Special	4:22:31.17	114.277	Rex Mays
1941	Floyd Davis–Mauri Rose	Noc–Out Hose Clamp Special	4:20:36.24	115.117	Rex Mays
1946	George Robson	Thorne Engineering Special	4:21:26.71	114.820	Jimmy Jackson
1947	Mauri Rose	Blue Crown Special	4:17:52.17	116.338	Bill Holland
1948	Mauri Rose	Blue Crown Special	4:10:23.33	119.814	Bill Holland
1949	Bill Holland	Blue Crown Special	4:07:15.97	121.327	Johnny Parsons
1950[3]	Johnnie Parsons	Wynn's Friction Proof Special	2:46:55.97	124.002	Bill Holland
1951	Lee Wallard	Belanger Special	3:57:38.05	126.244	Mike Nazaruk
1952	Troy Ruttman	Agajanian Special	3:52:41.88	128.922	Jim Rathmann
1953	Bill Vukovich	Fuel Injection Special	3:53:01.69	128.740	Art Cross
1954	Bill Vukovich	Fuel Injection Special	3:49:17.27	130.840	Jim Bryan
1955	Bob Sweikert	John Zink Special	3:53:59.13	128.209	Tony Bettenhausen
1956	Pat Flaherty	John Zink Special	3:53:28.84	128.490	Sam Hanks
1957	Sam Hanks	Belond Exhaust Special	3:41:14.25	135.601	Jim Rathmann
1958	Jimmy Bryan	Belond A–P Special	3:44:13.80	133.791	George Amick
1959	Rodger Ward	Leader Card 500 Roadster	3:40:49.20	135.857	Jim Rathmann
1960	Jim Rathmann	Ken–Paul Special	3:36:11.36	138.767	Rodger Ward
1961	A. J. Foyt	Bowes Special	3:35:37.49	139.130	Eddie Sachs
1962	Rodger Ward	Leader Card Special	3:33:50.33	140.293	Len Sutton
1963	Parnelli Jones	Agajanian Special	3:29:35.40	143.137	Jim Clark
1964	A. J. Foyt	Sheraton–Thompson Spl.	3:23:35.83	147.350	Rodger Ward
1965	Jim Clark	Lotus–Ford	3:19:05.34	150.686	Parnelli Jones
1966	Graham Hill	Red Ball Lola–Ford	3:27:52.53	144.317	Jim Clark
1967[4]	A. J. Foyt	Sheraton-Thompson Coyote–Ford	3:18:24.22	151.207	Al Unser
1968	Bobby Unser	Rislone Eagle–Offenhauser	3:16:13.76	152.882	Dan Gurney
1969	Mario Andretti	STP Hawk–Ford	3:11:14.71	156.867	Dan Gurney
1970	Al Unser	Johnny Lightning P. J. Colt–Ford	3:12:37.04	155.749	Mark Donohue
1971	Al Unser	Johnny Lightning P. J. Colt–Ford	3:10:11.56	157.735	Peter Revson
1972	Mark Donohue	Sunoco McLaren–Offenhauser	3:04:05.54	162.962	Al Unser
1973[5]	Gordon Johncock	STP Eagle–Offenhauser	2:05:26.59	159.036	Bill Vukovich, Jr.
1974	Johnny Rutherford	McLaren–Offenhauser	3:09:10.06	158.589	Bobby Unser
1975[6]	Bobby Unser	Jorgensen Eagle–Offenhauser	2:54:55.08	149.213	Johnny Rutherford
1976[7]	Johnny Rutherford	Hy-gain McLaren–Offenhauser	1:42:52.48	148.725	A. J. Foyt
1977	A. J. Foyt	Gilmore Coyote–Foyt	3:05:57.16	161.331	Tom Sneva
1978	Al Unser	1st Nat'l City Lola–Cosworth	3:05:54.99	161.363	Tom Sneva
1979	Rick Mears	Gould Penske–Cosworth	3:08:27.97	158.899	A. J. Foyt
1980	Johnny Rutherford	Pennzoil Chaparral–Cosworth	3:29:59.56	142.862	Tom Sneva
1981[8]	Bobby Unser	Norton Penske–Cosworth	3:35:41.78	139.029	Mario Andretti
1982	Gordon Johncock	STP Wildcat–Cosworth	3:05:09.14	162.029	Rick Mears
1983	Tom Sneva	Texaco Star March–Cosworth	3:05:03.06	162.117	Al Unser
1984	Rick Mears	Pennzoil March–Cosworth	3:03:21.00	162.962	Roberto Guerrero

Year	Winner	Car	Time	mph	Second place
1985	Danny Sullivan	Miller March–Cosworth	3:16:06.069	152.982	Mario Andretti
1986	Bobby Rahal	Budweiser March–Cosworth	2:55:43.48	170.722	Kevin Cogan
1987	Al Unser, Sr.	Cummins March–Cosworth	3:04:59.147	162.175	Roberto Guerrero
1988	Rick Mears	Pennzoil Penske P.C.17–Chevrolet	3:27:10.204	144.809	Emerson Fittipaldi
1989	Emerson Fittipaldi	Marlboro Penske-Cosworth	2:59:01.04	167.581	Al Unser, Jr.
1990	Arie Luyendyk	Domino's Pizza Lola–Cosworth	·2:41:18.248	185.987	Bobby Rahal
1991	Rick Mears	Marlboro Penske–Cosworth	2:50:01.018	176.460	Michael Andretti
1992	Al Unser, Jr.	Valvoline–Chevrolet	3:43.05.148	134.477	Scott Goodyear
1993	Emerson Fittipaldi	Penske–Chevrolet	3:10:49.860	157.207	Arie Luyendyk

1. 300 miles. 2. Race ended at 400 miles because of rain. 3. Race ended at 345 miles because of rain. 4. Race, postponed after 18 laps because of rain on May 30, was finished on May 31. 5. Race postponed May 28 and 29 was cut to 332.5 miles because of rain, May 30. 6. Race ended at 435 miles because of rain. 7. Race ended at 255 miles because of rain. 8. Andretti was awarded the victory the day after the race after Bobby Unser, whose car finished first, was penalized one lap and dropped from first place to second for passing other cars illegally under a yellow caution flag. Unser appealed the decision to the U.S. Auto Club and was upheld. A panel ruled the penalty was too severe and instead fined Unser $40,000, but restored the victory to him.

INDY CAR NATIONAL CHAMPIONS

1910	Ray Harroun	1928–29	Louis Meyer	1953	Sam Hanks	1975	A. J. Foyt
1911	Ralph Mulford	1930	Billy Arnold	1954	Jimmy Bryan	1976	Gordon Johncock
1912	Ralph DePalma	1931	Louis Schneider	1955	Bob Sweikert	1977–78	Tom Sneva
1913	Earl Cooper	1932	Bob Carey	1956–57	Jimmy Bryan	1979	Rick Mears (CART)
1914	Ralph DePalma	1933	Louis Meyer	1958	Tony Bettenhausen		A.J. Foyt (USAC)[1]
1915	Earl Cooper	1934	Bill Cummings	1959	Rodger Ward	1980	Johnny Rutherford
1916	Dario Resta	1935	Kelly Petillo	1960–61	A. J. Foyt	1981–82	Rick Mears
1917	Earl Cooper	1936	Mauri Rose	1962	Rodger Ward	1983	Al Unser
1918	Ralph Mulford	1937	Wilbur Shaw	1963–64	A. J. Foyt	1984	Mario Andretti
1919	Howard Wilcox	1938	Floyd Roberts	1965–66	Mario Andretti	1985	Al Unser
1920	Gaston Chevrolet	1939	Wilbur Shaw	1967	A. J. Foyt	1986–87	Bobby Rahal
1921	Tommy Milton	1940–41	Rex Mays	1968	Bobby Unser	1988	Danny Sullivan
1922	James Murphy	1946–48	Ted Horn	1969	Mario Andretti	1989	Emerson Fittipaldi
1923	Eddie Hearne	1949	Johnnie Parsons	1970	Al Unser	1990	Al Unser Jr.
1924	James Murphy	1950	Henry Banks	1971–72	Joe Leonard	1991	Michael Andretti
1925	Peter DePaolo	1951	Tony Bettenhausen	1973	Roger McCluskey	1992	Bobby Rahal
1926	Harry Hartz	1952	Chuck Stevenson	1974	Bobby Unser	1993	Nigel Mansell
1927	Peter DePaolo						

1. Two separate series were held in 1979. NOTE: There have been three sanctioning bodies for the series: the Automobile Association of America (1909–1955), the U.S. Auto Club (1956–1979), and the Championship Auto Racing Team (CART), 1979–present.

WORLD GRAND PRIX DRIVER CHAMPIONS

1950 Giuseppe Farina, Italy, Alfa Romeo
1951 Juan Fangio, Argentina, Alfa Romeo
1952 Alberto Ascari, Italy, Ferrari
1953 Alberto Ascari, Italy, Ferrari
1954 Juan Fangio, Argentina, Maserati, Mercedes–Benz
1955 Juan Fangio, Argentina, Mercedes–Benz
1956 Juan Fangio, Argentina, Lancia–Ferrari
1957 Juan Fangio, Argentina, Masserati
1958 Mike Hawthorn, England, Ferrari
1959 Jack Brabham, Australia, Cooper
1960 Jack Brabham, Australia, Cooper
1961 Phil Hill, United States, Ferrari
1962 Graham Hill, England, BRM
1963 Jim Clark, Scotland, Lotus–Ford
1964 John Surtees, England, Ferrari
1965 Jim Clark, Scotland, Lotus–Ford
1966 Jack Brabham, Australia, Brabham–Repco
1967 Denis Hulme, New Zealand, Brabham–Repco
1968 Graham Hill, England, Lotus–Ford
1969 Jackie Stewart, Scotland, Matra–Ford
1970 Jochen Rindt, Austria, Lotus–Ford
1971 Jackie Stewart, Scotland, Tyrrell–Ford
1972 Emerson Fittipaldi, Brazil, Lotus–Ford
1973 Jackie Stewart, Scotland, Tyrrell–Ford
1974 Emerson Fittipaldi, Brazil, McLaren–Ford
1975 Niki Lauda, Austria, Ferrari
1976 James Hunt, Britain, McLaren–Ford
1977 Niki Lauda, Austria, Ferrari
1978 Mario Andretti, United States, Lotus
1979 Jody Scheckter, South Africa, Ferrari
1980 Alan Jones, Australia, Williams–Ford
1981 Nelson Piquet, Brazil, Brabham–Ford
1982 Kiki Rosberg, Finland, Williams–Ford
1983 Nelson Piquet, Brazil. Brabham–BMW
1984 Nikki Lauda, Austria, McLaren–Porsche
1985 Alain Prost, France, McLaren–Porsche
1986 Alain Prost, France, McLaren–Porsche
1987 Nelson Piquet, Brazil, Williams–Honda
1988 Aryton Senna, Brazil, McLaren–Honda
1989 Alain Prost, France, McLaren–Honda
1990 Ayrton Senna, Brazil, McLaren–Honda
1991 Aryton Senna, Brazil, McLaren–Honda
1992 Nigel Mansell, Britain, Williams–Renault
1993 Champion to be determined after *Information Please* went to press

NATIONAL ASSOCIATION FOR STOCK CAR AUTO RACING WINSTON CUP CHAMPIONS

1949	Red Byron	1960	Rex White	1971–72	Richard Petty	1984	Terry Labonte
1950	Bill Rexford	1961	Ned Jarrett	1973	Benny Parsons	1985	Darrell Waltrip
1951	Herb Thomas	1962–63	Joe Weatherly	1974–75	Richard Petty	1986	Dale Earnhardt
1952	Tim Flock	1964	Richard Petty	1976–78	Cale Yarborough	1987	Dale Earnhardt
1953	Herb Thomas	1965	Ned Jarrett	1979	Richard Petty	1988	Bill Elliott
1954	Lee Petty	1966	David Pearson	1980	Dale Earnhardt	1989	Rusty Wallace
1955	Tim Flock	1967	Richard Petty	1981	Darrell Waltrip	1990	Dale Earnhardt
1956–57	Buck Baker	1968–69	David Pearson	1982	Darrell Waltrip	1991	Dale Earnhardt
1958–59	Lee Petty	1970	Bobby Isaac	1983	Bobby Allison	1992	Alan Kulwicki[1]

1. Kulwicki was killed in a plane crash in April 1993.

1992 NASCAR LEADING MONEY WINNERS

1. Alan Kulwicki	$2,322,561
2. Davey Allison	1,955,628
3. Bill Elliott	1,692,381
4. Harry Gant	1,122,776
5. Kyle Petty	1,107,063
6. Mark Martin	1,000,571
7. Ernie Irvan	996,885
8. Dale Earnhardt	915,463
9. Darrell Waltrip	876,492
10. Rickey Rudd	793,903

1992 WINSTON CUP POINT LEADERS

1. Alan Kulwicki	4078	11. Ernie Irvan	3580
2. Bill Elliott	4068	12. Dale Earnhardt	3574
3. Davey Allison	4015	13. Rusty Wallace	3556
4. Harry Gant	3955	14. Morgan Shepherd	3549
5. Kyle Petty	3945	15. Brett Bodine	3491
6. Mark Martin	3887	16. Geoff Bodine	3437
7. Rickey Rudd	3735	17. Ken Schrader	3404
8. Terry Labonte	3674	18. Ted Musgrave	3315
9. Darrell Waltrip	3659	19. Dale Jarrett	3251
10. Sterling Marlin	3603	20. Dick Trickle	3097

TOP 10 1992 INDY CAR WORLD SERIES PERFORMANCES

Driver	Points	Purse	Driver	Points	Purse
1. Al Unser, Jr.	169	$2,324,654	6. Danny Sullivan	99	$859,975
2. Bobby Rahal	196	2,235,298	7. John Andretti	94	826,212
3. Michael Andretti	192	1,903,572	8. Mario Andretti	105	824,086
4. Scott Goodyear	108	1,361,480	9. Eddie Cheever	80	798,915
5. Emerson Fittipaldi	151	1,352,793	10. Paul Tracy	59	625,625

LACROSSE

NATIONAL INTERCOLLEGIATE CHAMPIONS

1946	Navy	1961	Army, Navy	1981	North Carolina
1947–48	Johns Hopkins	1962–66	Navy	1982	North Carolina
1949	Johns Hopkins, Navy	1967	Johns Hopkins, Maryland, Navy	1983	Syracuse
1950	Johns Hopkins	1968	Johns Hopkins	1984	Johns Hopkins
1951	Army, Princeton	1969	Army, Johns Hopkins	1985	Johns Hopkins
1952	Virginia, R.P.I.	1970	Johns Hopkins, Navy, Virginia	1986	North Carolina
1953	Princeton	1971[1]	Cornell	1987	Johns Hopkins
1954	Navy	1972	Virginia	1988	Syracuse
1955–56	Maryland	1973	Maryland	1989	Syracuse
1957	Johns Hopkins	1974	Johns Hopkins	1990	Syracuse
1958	Army	1975	Maryland	1991	North Carolina
1959	Army, Johns Hopkins, Maryland	1976–77	Cornell	1992	Princeton
1960	Navy	1978–80	Johns Hopkins	1993	Syracuse

1. First year of N.C.A.A. Championship Tournaments.

1993 N.C.A.A. LACROSSE

DIVISION I
Men's Championships
Quarterfinals
North Carolina 14, Army 5
Johns Hopkins 14, Virginia 10
Syracuse 20, Hofstra 8
Princeton 12, Loyola, Md. 6

Championship
(at College Park, Md., May 31, 1993)
Syracuse 13, North Carolina 12

Women's Championships

Championship
(at College Park, Md., May 16, 1993)
Virginia 8, Princeton 6 (OT)

DIVISION III
Championship

Trenton State 10, William Smith 9

SOFTBALL

Source: Amateur Softball Association.

AMATEUR CHAMPIONS

1959	Aurora (Ill.) Sealmasters
1960	Clearwater (Fla.) Bombers
1961	Aurora (Ill.) Sealmasters
1962–63	Clearwater (Fla.) Bombers
1964	Burch Gage & Tool, Detroit
1965	Aurora (Ill.) Sealmasters
1966	Clearwater (Fla.) Bombers
1967	Aurora (Ill.) Sealmasters
1968	Clearwater (Fla.) Bombers
1969–70	Raybestos Cardinals, Stratford, Conn.
1971	Welty Way, Cedar Rapids, Iowa
1972	Raybestos Cardinals, Stratford, Conn.
1973	Clearwater (Fla.) Bombers
1974	Santa Rosa (Calif.)
1975	Rising Sun Hotel, Reading, Pa.
1976	Raybestos Cardinals, Stratford, Conn.
1977	Billard Barbell, Reading, Pa.
1978	Reading, Pa.
1979	Midland, Mich.
1980	Peterbilt Western, Seattle
1981	Archer Daniels Midland, Decatur, Ill.
1982	Peterbilt Western, Seattle
1983	Franklin Cardinals, West Haven, Conn.
1984	California Coors Kings, Merced, Calif.
1985	Pay 'n Pak, Bellevue, Wash.
1986	Pay 'n Pak, Bellevue, Wash.
1987	Pay 'n Pak, Bellevue, Wash.
1988	TransAire, Elkhart, Ind.
1989	Penn Corp., Sioux City, Iowa
1990	Penn Corp., Sioux City, Iowa
1991	Guanella Brothers, Rohnert Park, Calif.
1992	National Health Care, Sioux City, Iowa
1993	National Health Care, Sioux City, Iowa

AMATEUR SOFTBALL ASSOCIATION CHAMPIONS—1993

Adult Champions

Men's Major Fast Pitch—National Health Care Discount, Sioux City, Iowa
Women's Major Fast Pitch—Redding Rebels, Redding, Calif.
Men's Class A Fast Pitch—Bow Valley Travelers, Broken Arrow, Neb.
Women's Class A Fast Pitch—Southern California Jazz, Downey, Calif.
Men's Class B Fast Pitch—Bakersfield Rebels, Bakersfield, Calif.
Women's Class B Fast Pitch—Creative Awards, Tucson, Ariz.
Men's Class C Fast Pitch—Frank's/Dr. Dobney, Lorain, Ohio
Women's Class C Fast Pitch—SOMA, Montgomery, Ala.
Men's Masters 40-Over Fast Pitch—Nor Cal Merchants, Stockton, Calif.
Women's 35-Over Fast Pitch—Chico Peppers, Chico, Calif.
Men's 23-Under Fast Pitch—Da Boys, Geneva, Minn.
Women's Major Modified Pitch—PA Club, Methuen, Mass.
Men's Class A Modified Pitch—Fleetwood Heating, Easton, Md.
Men's Super Slow Pitch—Ritch's/Superior, Windsor Locks, Conn.
Men's Major Slow Pitch—Back Porch/Destin Roofing, Destin, Fla.
Women's Major Slow Pitch—UPI, Cookeville, Tenn.
Men's Class A Slow Pitch—UPI, Cookeville, Tenn.
Men's Major Industrial Slow Pitch—Sikorsky, Shelton, Conn.
Women's Major Industrial Slow Pitch—Southern Lites, Birmingham, Ala.
Men's Class A Industrial Slow Pitch—Olympic Steel, Milford, Conn.
Women's Class A Industrial Slow Pitch—Hutcheson Medical Center, Ft. Oglethorpe, Ga.
Men's Major Church Slow Pitch—Rehoboth Presbyterian, Lilburn, Ga.
Women's Major Church Slow Pitch—Hillcrest Baptist, Jacksonville, Fla.
Men's Class A Church Slow Pitch—Central Park, Decatur, Ala.
Women's Class A Church Slow Pitch—Sharon Baptist, Benton, Ark.
Women's Masters 35-Over Slow Pitch—Winner's Bracket, Tulsa, Okla.
Men's Masters 40-Over Slow Pitch—Nothdurft, Clinton Township, Mich.
Men's Senior 50-Over Slow Pitch—Betty and Jake's Tavern, Baltimore, Md.
Men's Senior 55-Over Slow Pitch—Nothdurft Softball Club, Clinton Township, Mich.
Men's Masters 60-Over Slow Pitch—Forrest Park, Tyron, Ga.
Men's Major 16-Inch Slow Pitch—Lettuce, Chicago, Ill.
Coed Class A Slow Pitch—David Fong's, Bloomington, Minn.

Junior Champions

Boys' 18-under Fast Pitch—GM Contracting, Lake Crystal, Minn.
Boys' 18-under Slow Pitch—Playmakers, Luverne, Ala.
Girls' 18-under Slow Pitch—Flames, Euclid, Ohio
Girls' 18-under Fast Pitch—Gordon's Panthers, Cypress, Calif.
Boys' 16-under Slow Pitch—Swampfrogs, Pembroke Pines, Fla.
Boys' 16-under Fast Pitch—KL Sports Black, Salt Lake City, Utah
Girls' 16-under Slow Pitch—Davie Dolphins, Davie, Fla.
Girls' 16-under Fast Pitch—Fresno Force, Fresno,Calif.
Boys' 14-under Fast Pitch—Ebert's Construction, Sioux Falls, S.D.
Girls' 14-under Slow Pitch—Mustangs, Fort Smith, Ark.
Girls' 14-under Fast Pitch—So. California Crunch, Chino, Calif.
Boys' 12-under Slow Pitch—Al's Trophy Shop, Satellite Beach, Fla.
Boys' 12-under Fast Pitch—Reiner's Auto, Hartford, S.D.
Girls' 12-under Slow Pitch—Lake Lytal Cougars, West Palm Beach, Fla.
Girls' 12-under Fast Pitch—California Cruisers, Irvine, Calif.

MEDIA

(Courtesy of *Information Please Sports Almanac.*)

DAILY NEWSPAPER

USA Today
1000 Wilson Blvd., Arlington, Va. 22229
(703) 276-3400

WEEKLY MAGAZINE

Sports Illustrated
Time & Life Bldg., Rockefeller Ctr., New York, N.Y. 10020
(212) 586-1212

TELEVISION

ABC Sports
47 West 66th St., 13th Floor, New York, N.Y. 10023
(212) 887-4867

CBS Sports
51 West 52nd St., 30th Floor, New York, N.Y. 10019
(212) 975-5230

ESPN
ESPN Plaza, Bristol, Conn. 06010
(203) 585-2000

HBO Sports
1100 Ave. of the Americas, New York, N.Y. 10036
(212) 512-1000

NBC Sports
30 Rockefeller Plaza, New York, N.Y. 10112
(212) 664-4444

Prime Network
5251 Gulfton St., Houston, Texas 77081
(713) 661-0078

SportsChannel America
3 Crossways Park West, Woodbury, N.Y. 11797
(516) 921-3764

Turner Sports
One CNN Center, Suite 1300, Atlanta, Ga. 30303
(404) 827-1735

USA Network
1230 Ave. of the Americas, New York, N.Y. 10020
(212) 408-8895

BASEBALL

The popular tradition that baseball was invented by Abner Doubleday at Cooperstown, N.Y., in 1839 has been enshrined in the Hall of Fame and National Museum of Baseball erected in that town, but research has proved that a game called "Base Ball" was played in this country and England before 1839. The first team baseball as we know it was played at the Elysian Fields, Hoboken, N.J., on June 19, 1846, between the Knickerbockers and the New York Nine. The next fifty years saw a gradual growth of baseball and an improvement of equipment and playing skill.

Historians have it that the first pitcher to throw a curve was William A. (Candy) Cummings in 1867. The Cincinnati Red Stockings were the first all-professional team, and in 1869 they played 64 games without a loss. The standard ball of the same size and weight, still the rule, was adopted in 1872. The first catcher's mask was worn in 1875. The National League was organized in 1876. The first chest protector was worn in 1885. The three-strike rule was put on the books in 1887, and the four-ball ticket to first base was instituted in 1889. The pitching distance was lengthened to 60 feet 6 inches in 1893, and the rules have been modified only slightly since that time.

The American League, under the vigorous leadership of B. B. Johnson, became a major league in 1901. Judge Kenesaw Mountain Landis, by action of the two major leagues, became Commissioner of Baseball in 1921. Peter Ueberroth became baseball's fifth commissioner and took office Oct. 1, 1984.

Ueberroth did not seek a new term in 1989 and was succeded by Bart Giamatti who died suddenly on Sept. 1, 1989. Francis T. Vincent, Jr., replaced him on Sept. 13, 1989.

Vincent, under pressure from owners to relinquish some of his powers, resigned in late 1992. Bud Selig, principal owner of the Milwaukee Brewers, headed a baseball executive committee that ruled baseball while the search for a new commissioner extended late into 1993.

MAJOR LEAGUE ALL-STAR GAME

Year	Date	Winning league and manager	Runs	Losing league and manager	Runs	Winning pitcher	Losing pitcher	Site	Paid attendance
1933	July 6	A.L. (Mack)	4	N.L. (McGraw)	2	Gomez	Hallahan	Chicago A.L.	47,595
1934	July 10	A.L. (Cronin)	9	N.L. (Terry)	7	Harder	Mungo	New York N.L.	48,363
1935	July 8	A.L. (Cochrane)	4	N.L. (Frisch)	1	Gomez	Walker	Cleveland A.L.	69,831
1936	July 7	N.L. (Grimm)	4	A.L. (McCarthy)	3	J. Dean	Grove	Boston N.L.	25,556
1937	July 7	A.L. (McCarthy)	8	N.L. (Terry)	3	Gomez	J. Dean	Washington A.L.	31,391
1938	July 6	N.L. (Terry)	4	A.L. (McCarthy)	1	Vander Meer	Gomez	Cincinnati N.L.	27,067
1939	July 11	A.L. (McCarthy)	3	N.L. (Hartnett)	1	Bridges	Lee	New York A.L.	62,892
1940	July 9	N.L. (McKechnie)	4	A.L. (Cronin)	0	Derringer	Ruffing	St. Louis N.L.	32,373
1941	July 8	A.L. (Baker)	7	N.L. (McKechnie)	5	E. Smith	Passeau	Detroit A.L.	54,674
1942	July 6	A.L. (McCarthy)	3	N.L. (Durocher)	1	Chandler	Cooper	New York N.L.	34,178
1943	July 13[1]	A.L. (McCarthy)	5	N.L. (Southworth)	3	Leonard	Cooper	Philadelphia A.L.	31,938
1944	July 11[1]	N.L. (Southworth)	7	A.L. (McCarthy)	1	Raffensberger	Hughson	Pittsburgh N.L.	29,589
1946	July 9	A.L. (O'Neill)	12	N.L. (Grimm)	0	Feller	Passeau	Boston A.L.	34,906
1947	July 8	A.L. (Cronin)	2	N.L. (Dyer)	1	Shea	Sain	Chicago N.L.	41,123
1948	July 13	A.L. (Harris)	5	N.L. (Durocher)	2	Raschi	Schmitz	St. Louis A.L.	34,009
1949	July 12	A.L. (Boudreau)	11	N.L. (Southworth)	7	Trucks	Newcombe	Brooklyn N.L.	32,577
1950	July 11	N.L. (Shotton)	4	A.L. (Stengel)	3[3]	Blackwell	Gray	Chicago A.L.	46,127
1951	July 10	N.L. (Sawyer)	8	A.L. (Stengel)	3	Maglie	Lopat	Detroit A.L.	52,075
1952	July 8	N.L. (Durocher)	3	A.L. (Stengel)	2[4]	Rush	Lemon	Philadelphia N.L.	32,785
1953	July 14	N.L. (Dressen)	5	A.L. (Stengel)	1	Spahn	Reynolds	Cincinnati N.L.	30,846
1954	July 13	A.L. (Stengel)	11	N.L. (Alston)	9	Stone	Conley	Cleveland A.L.	68,751
1955	July 12	N.L. (Durocher)	6	A.L. (Lopez)	5[5]	Conley	Sullivan	Milwaukee N.L.	45,643
1956	July 10	N.L. (Alston)	7	A.L. (Stengel)	3	Friend	Pierce	Washington A.L.	28,843
1957	July 9	A.L. (Stengel)	6	N.L. (Alston)	5	Bunning	Simmons	St. Louis N.L.	30,693
1958	July 8	A.L. (Stengel)	4	N.L. (Haney)	3	Wynn	Friend	Baltimore A.L.	48,829
1959[2]	July 7	N.L. (Haney)	5	A.L. (Stengel)	4	Antonelli	Ford	Pittsburgh N.L.	35,277
	Aug. 3	A.L. (Stengel)	5	N.L. (Haney)	3	Walker	Drysdale	Los Angeles N.L.	55,105
1960[2]	July 11	N.L. (Alston)	5	A.L. (Lopez)	3	Friend	Monbouquette	Kansas City A.L.	30,619
	July 13	N.L. (Alston)	6	A.L. (Lopez)	0	Law	Ford	New York A.L.	38,362
1961[2]	July 11	N.L. (Murtaugh)	5	A.L. (Richards)	4[6]	Miller	Wilhelm	San Francisco N.L.	44,115
	July 31	N.L (Murtaugh)	1	A.L. (Richards)	1[7]	—	—	Boston A.L.	31,851
1962[2]	July 10	N.L. (Hutchinson)	3	A.L. (Houk)	1	Marichal	Pascual	Washington A.L.	45,480
	July 30	A.L. (Houk)	9	N.L. (Hutchinson)	4	Herbert	Mahaffey	Chicago N.L.	38,359
1963	July 9	N.L. (Dark)	5	A.L. (Houk)	3	Jackson	Bunning	Cleveland A.L.	44,160
1964	July 7	N.L. (Alston)	7	A.L. (Lopez)	4	Marichal	Radatz	New York N.L.	50,850
1965	July 13	N.L. (March)	6	A.L. (Lopez)	5	Koufax	McDowell	Minnesota A.L.	46,706
1966	July 12	N.L. (Alston)	2	A.L. (Mele)	1[6]	Perry	Rickert	St. Louis N.L.	49,926
1967	July 11	N.L. (Alston)	2	A.L. (Bauer)	1[8]	Drysdale	Hunter	Anaheim A.L.	46,309
1968	July 9	N.L. (Schoendienst)	1	A.L. (Williams)	0	Drysdale	Tiant	Houston N.L.	48,321
1969	July 23	N.L. (Schoendienst)	9	A.L. (M. Smith)	3	Carlton	Stottlemyre	Washington A.L.	45,259
1970	July 14	N.L. (Hodges)	5	A.L. (Weaver)	4	Osteen	Wright	Cincinnati N.L.	51,838
1971	July 13	A.L. (Weaver)	6	N.L. (Anderson)	4	Blue	Ellis	Detroit A.L.	53,559

1972	July 25	N.L. (Murtaugh)	4	A.L. (Weaver)	3[6]	McGraw	McNally	Atlanta N.L.	53,107
1973	July 24[1]	N.L. (Anderson)	7	A.L. (Williams)	1	Wise	Blyleven	Kansas City A.L.	40,849
1974	July 23[1]	N.L. (Berra)	7	A.L. (Williams)	2	Brett	Tiant	Pittsburgh N.L.	50,706
1975	July 15[1]	N.L. (Alston)	6	A.L. (Dark)	3	Matlack	Hunter	Milwaukee A.L.	51,540
1976	July 13	N.L. (Anderson)	7	A.L. (D. Johnson)	1	R. Jones	Fidrych	Philadelphia N.L.	63,974
1977	July 19[1]	N.L. (Anderson)	7	A.L. (Martin)	5	Sutton	Palmer	New York A.L.	56,683
1978	July 11[1]	N.L. (Lasorda)	7	A.L. (Martin)	3	Sutter	Gossage	San Diego N.L.	51,549
1979	July 17[1]	N.L. (Lasorda)	7	A.L. (Lemon)	6	Sutter	Kern	Seattle A.L.	58,905
1980	July 8[1]	N.L. (Tanner)	4	A.L. (Weaver)	2	Reuss	John	Los Angeles N.L.	56,088
1981	Aug. 9[1]	N.L. (Green)	5	A.L. (Frey)	4	Blue	Fingers	Cleveland* A.L.	72,086
1982	July 13[1]	N.L. (Lasorda)	4	A.L. (Martin)	1	Rogers	Eckersley	Montreal N.L.	59,057
1983	July 6[1]	A.L. (Kuenn)	13	N.L. (Herzog)	3	Steib	Soto	Chicago A.L.	43,801
1984	July 11[1]	N.L. (Owens)	3	A.L. (Altobelli)	1	Leg	Steib	San Francisco, N.L.	57,756
1985	July 16[1]	N.L. (Williams)	6	A.L. (Anderson)	1	Hoyt	Morris	Minneapolis, A.L.	54,960
1986	July 15[1]	A.L. (Howser)	3	N.L. (Herzog)	2	Clemens	Gooden	Houston, N.L.	45,774
1987	July 14[1]	N.L. (Johnson)	2	A.L. (McNamara)	0	Smith	Howell	Oakland, A.L.	49,671
1988	July 12[1]	A.L. (Kelly)	2	N.L. (Herzog)	1	Viola	Gooden	Cincinnati, N.L	55,837
1989	July 11[1]	A.L. (LaRussa)	5	N.L. (Lasorda)	3	Ryan	Smoltz	California, A.L.	64,036
1990	July 10[1]	A.L. (LaRussa)	2	N.L. (Craig)	0	Saberhagen	Brantley	Chicago, N.L.	39,071
1991	July 9[1]	A.L. (LaRussa)	4	N.L. (Piniella)	2	Key	Martinez	Toronto, A.L.	52,383
1992	July 14	A.L. (Kelly)	13	N.L. (Cox)	6	Brown	Glavine	San Diego, N.L.	59,372
1993	July 13	A.L. (Gaston)	9	N.L. (Cox)	3	McDowell	Burkett	Baltimore, A.L.	48,147

1. Night game. 2. Two games. 3. Fourteen innings. 4. Five innings, rain. 5. Twelve innings. 6. Ten innings. 7. Called because of rain after nine innings. 8. Fifteen innings. NOTE: No game in 1945. *Game was originally scheduled for July 14, but was put off because of players' strike.

NATIONAL BASEBALL HALL OF FAME

Cooperstown, N.Y.

Fielders

Member	Active years
Aaron, Henry (Hank)	1954–1976
Anson, Adrian (Cap)	1876–1897
Aparicio, Luis	1956–1973
Appling, Lucius (Luke)	1930–1950
Averill, H. Earl	1929–1941
Baker, J. Frank (Home Run)	1908–1922
Bancroft, David	1915–1930
Banks, Ernest	1953–1971
Beckley, Jacob	1888–1907
Bell, James (Cool Papa)[1]	1920–1947
Bench, John	1967–1983
Berra, Lawrence (Yogi)	1946–1965
Bottomley, James	1922–1937
Boudreau, Louis	1938–1952
Bresnahan, Roger	1897–1915
Brock, Lou	1961–1980
Brouthers, Dennis	1879–1896
Burkett, Jesse	1890–1905
Campanella, Roy	1948–1957
Carew, Rod	1967–1985
Carey, Max	1910–1929
Chance, Frank	1898–1914
Charleston, Oscar[1]	1915–1954
Clarke, Fred	1894–1915
Clemente, Roberto	1955–1972
Cobb, Tyrus	1905–1928
Cochrane, Gordon (Mickey)	1925–1937
Collins, Edward	1906–1930
Collins, James	1895–1908
Comiskey, Charles	1882–1894
Combs, Earle	1924–1935
Connor, Roger	1880–1897
Crawford, Samuel	1899–1917
Cronin, Joseph	1926–1945
Cuyler, Hazen (Kiki)	1921–1938
Dandridge, Ray[1]	1933–1953
Delahanty, Edward	1888–1903
Dickey, William	1928–1946
Dihigo, Martin[1]	1923–1945
DiMaggio, Joseph	1936–1951
Doerr, Bobby	1937–1951
Member	**Active years**
Duffy, Hugh	1888–1906
Ewing, William	1880–1897
Eyers, John	1902–1919
Flick, Elmer	1898–1910
Foxx, James	1925–1945
Frisch, Frank	1919–1937
Gehrig, H. Louis (Lou)	1923–1939
Gehringer, Charles	1924–1942
Gibson, Josh[1]	1929–1946
Goslin, Leon (Goose)	1921–1938
Greenberg, Henry (Hank)	1933–1947
Hafey, Charles (Chick)	1924–1937
Hamilton, William	1888–1901
Hartnett, Charles (Gabby)	1922–1941
Heilmann, Harry	1914–1932
Herman, William	1931–1947
Hooper, Harry	1909–1925
Hornsby, Rogers	1915–1937
Irvin, Monford (Monte)[1]	1939–1956
Jackson, Reggie	1967–1987
Jackson, Travis	1922–1936
Jennings, Hugh	1891–1918
Johnson, William (Judy)[1]	1921–1937
Kaline, Albert W.	1953–1974
Keeler, William (Wee Willie)	1892–1910
Kell, George	1943–1957
Kelley, Joseph	1891–1908
Kelly, George	1915–1932
Kelly, Michael (King)	1878–1893
Killebrew, Harmon	1954–1975
Kiner, Ralph	1946–1955
Klein, Charles H. (Chuck)	1928–1944
Lajoie, Napoleon	1896–1916
Lazzeri, Tony	1926–1939
Leonard, Walter (Buck)[1]	1933–1955
Lindstrom, Frederick	1924–1936
Lloyd, John Henry[1]	1905–1931
Lombardi, Ernie	1932–1947
Mantle, Mickey	1951–1968
Manush, Henry (Heinie)	1923–1939
Maranville, Walter (Rabbit)	1912–1935
Matthews, Edwin	1952–1968
Member	**Active years**
Mays, Willie	1951–1973
McCarthy, Thomas	1884–1896
McGraw, John J.	1891–1906
McCovey, Willie	1959–1980
Medwick, Joseph (Ducky)	1932–1948
Mize, John (The Big Cat)	1936–1953
Morgan, Joe	1963–1984
Musial, Stanley	1941–1963
O'Rourke, James	1876–1894
Ott, Melvin	1926–1947
Reese, Harold (Pee Wee)	1940–1958
Rice, Edgar (Sam)	1915–1934
Robinson, Brooks	1955–1977
Robinson, Frank	1956–1976
Robinson, Jack	1947–1956
Robinson, Wilbert	1886–1902
Roush, Edd	1913–1931
Ruth, George (Babe)	1914–1935
Schalk, Raymond	1912–1929
Schoendienst, Red	1945–1963
Sewell, Joseph	1920–1933
Simmons, Al	1924–1944
Sisler, George	1915–1930
Slaughter, Enos	1938–1959
Snider, Edwin D. (Duke)	1947–1964
Speaker, Tristram	1907–1928
Stargell, Willie	1962–1982
Terry, William	1923–1936
Thompson, Samuel	1885–1906
Tinker, Joseph	1902–1916

Traynor, Harold (Pie)	1920–1937	Waner, Paul	1926–1945	Williams, Theodore	1939–1960
Vaughan, Arky	1932–1948	Ward, John (Monte)	1878–1894	Wilson, Lewis R. (Hack)	1923–1934
Wagner, John (Honus)	1897–1917	Wheat, Zachariah	1909–1927	Yastrzemski, Carl	1961–1983
Wallace, Roderick (Bobby)	1894–1918	Williams, Billy	1959–1976	Youngs, Ross (Pep)	1917–1926
Waner, Lloyd	1927–1945				

1. Negro League player selected by special committee.

Pitchers

Alexander, Grover	1911–1930	Grove, Robert (Lefty)	1925–1941	Palmer, Jim	1965–1984
Bender, Charles (Chief)	1903–1925	Haines, Jesse	1918–1937	Pennock, Herbert	1912–1934
Brown, Mordecai (3–Finger)	1903–1916	Hoyt, Waite	1918–1938	Perry, Gaylord	1962–1983
Chesbro, John	1899–1909	Hubbell, Carl	1928–1943	Plank, Edward	1901–1917
Clarkson, John	1882–1894	Hunter, Jim (Catfish)	1965–1979	Radbourn, Charles (Hoss)	1880–1891
Coveleski, Stanley	1912–1928	Jenkins, Ferguson	1965–1983	Rixey, Eppa	1912–1933
Dean, Jerome (Dizzy)	1930–1947	Johnson, Walter	1907–1927	Roberts, Robert (Robin)	1948–1966
Drysdale, Don	1956–1969	Joss, Adrian	1902–1910	Ruffing, Charles (Red)	1924–1947
Faber, Urban (Red)	1914–1933	Keefe, Timothy	1880–1893	Rusie, Amos	1889–1901
Feller, Robert	1936–1956	Koufax, Sanford (Sandy)	1955–1966	Seaver, Tom	1967–1986
Ferrell, Rick	1929–1947	Lemon, Robert	1946–1958	Spahn, Warren	1942–1965
Fingers, Rollie	1968–1985	Lyons, Theodore	1923–1946	Vance, Arthur (Dazzy)	1915–1935
Ford, Edward (Whitey)	1950–1967	Marichal, Juan	1960–1975	Waddell, George	1897–1910
Foster, Andrew (Rube)	1897–1926	Marquard, Richard (Rube)	1908–1924	Walsh, Edward	1904–1917
Galvin, James (Pud)	1876–1892	Mathewson, Christopher	1900–1916	Welch, Michael (Mickey)	1880–1892
Gibson, Bob	1959–1975	McGinnity, Joseph	1899–1908	Wilhelm, Hoyt	1952–1972
Gomez, Vernon (Lefty)	1930–1943	Neuhouser, Hal	1939–1955	Wynn, Early	1939–1963
Griffith, Clark	1891–1914	Nichols, Charles (Kid)	1890–1906	Young, Denton (Cy)	1890–1911
Grimes, Burleigh	1916–1934	Paige, Leroy (Satchel)[1]	1926–1965		

1. Negro League player selected by special committee.

Officials and Others

Alston, Walter[1]
Barlick, Al[4]
Barrow, Edward[1, 2]
Bulkeley, Morgan G.[2]
Cartwright, Alexander[2]
Chadwick, Henry[3]
Chandler, A.B.[6]
Comiskey, Charles[1]
Conlan, John[2]
Connolly, Thomas[4]
Cummings, William A.[5]
Evans, William G.[4, 2]
Foster, Rube[2]
Frick, Ford C.[6, 2]
Giles, Warren C.[2]
Harridge, William[2]
Harris, Stanley R.[7]
Hubbard, R. Calvin[4]
Higgins, Miller J.[1]
Johnson, B. Bancroft[2]
Klem, William[4]
Landis, Kenesaw M.[6]
Lopez, Alfonso R.[7]
Mack, Connie[1, 2]
MacPhail, Leland S.[2]
McCarthy, Joseph V.[1]
McGowan, Bill[4]
McKechnie, William B.[1]
Rickey, W. Branch[1, 2]
Spalding, Albert G.[4]
Stengel, Charles D.[7]
Veeck, Bill[2]
Weiss, George M.[2]
Wright, George[5]
Wright, Harry[5, 1]
Yawkey, Thomas[2]

1. Manager. 2. Executive. 3. Writer-statistician. 4. Umpire. 5. Early player. 6. Commissioner. 7. Player-manager.

BASEBALL SUFFERS THROUGH TWO STRIKES AND A LOCKOUT

Major League baseball endured a strike by players for the second time since 1981 in August 1985. Unlike the 1981 strike, which lasted seven weeks and canceled 713 games, this one was ended quickly. The players walked on Aug. 6, and were back on the field three days later.

While in 1981 the major issue was over compensation for free agent signings to the club losing players, the 1985 strike was primarily over the pension fund, and how much of the reported $1.1 billion the owners receive through network television agreements would go into the plan.

The players were seeking an increase of $45 million over the $15 million they'd been receiving under the contract signed in 1981. The owners were adamant in refusing such a large increase.

There were other matters at question, including the issue of arbitration. Under the 1981 agreement, a player with two years of major league service who couldn't come to terms with ownership could take his case to binding arbitration. The owners were looking to increase the number of years vested service required to three years, and pointed to substantial operating losses caused,in part, by large salaries granted by arbitrators and the increasing spiral of free agent salaries.

In the end, the players wound up with approximately $35 million for their pension fund, and the owners got their desired three years for arbitration, albeit the rule did not take effect until 1987.

The games canceled by the strike were rescheduled for later in the season, unlike the 1981 affair when far too many games were lost to be made up.

The 1981 strike settlement had been complicated by the decision to play a split season—awarding divisional championships to the teams in first place before the strike began, and starting a new second season to crown four additional champions. Those eight teams played off in a preliminary series. The survivors played for the league title and the right to move on to the World Series.

With the contract expiring with the 1989 season, the owners locked the players out of spring training camps in 1990 and the regular season was delayed a week in starting. Spring training was reduced to three weeks. A new three-year contract was negotiated. Late in the 1993 season, there had still been no negotiations with the players.

LIFETIME BATTING, PITCHING, AND BASE-RUNNING RECORDS

(An asterisk indicates active player)

Source: The Complete Handbook of Baseball, published and copyrighted by New American Library, New York, N.Y. 10019. All records through 1992 unless noted.

(Records Through 1992)

Hits (3,000 or more)

Pete Rose	4,256
Ty Cobb	4,190
Henry Aaron	3,771
Stan Musial	3,630
Tris Speaker	3,515
Carl Yastrzemski	3,419
Honus Wagner	3,418
Eddie Collins	3,311
Willie Mays	3,283
Nap Lajoie	3,244
Paul Waner	3,152
Rod Carew	3,053
Robin Yount	3,025
Lou Brock	3,023
Al Kaline	3,007
George Brett	3,005
Cap Anson	3,000
Roberto Clemente	3,000

Earned Run Average

(Minimum 1,500 innings pitched)

Ed Walsh	1.82
Addie Joss	1.88
Joe Wood	2.03
Three Finger Brown	2.06
Christy Mathewson	2.13
Rube Waddell	2.16
Walter Johnson	2.17
Orvie Overall	2.23
Ed Ruelbach	2.28
Jim Scott	2.32
Ed Plank	2.34
Ed Cicotte	2.37
Ed Killian	2.38
Doc White	2.38
Nap Rucker	2.42
Jeff Tesreau	2.43
Chief Bender	2.46
Sam Leaver	2.47

Runs Scored

Ty Cobb	2,245
Henry Aaron	2,174
Babe Ruth	2,174
Pete Rose	2,165
Willie Mays	2,062
Stan Musial	1,949
Lou Gehrig	1,888
Tris Speaker	1,881
Mel Ott	1,859
Frank Robinson	1,829
Eddie Collins	1,816
Carl Yastrzemski	1,816
Ted Williams	1,798
Charlie Gehringer	1,774
Jimmie Foxx	1,751
Honus Wagner	1,740
Willie Keeler	1,720
Cap Anson	1,712
Jesse Burkett	1,708
Billy Hamilton	1,690
Mickey Mantle	1,677
John McPhee	1,674
George Van Haltren	1,650

Strikeouts, Pitching

Nolan Ryan**	5,668
Steve Carlton	4,136
Bert Blyleven**	3,701
Tom Seaver	3,640
Don Sutton	3,569
Gaylord Perry	3,534
Walter Johnson	3,509
Phil Niekro	3,342
Ferguson Jenkins	3,192
Bob Gibson	3,117
Jim Bunning	2,855
Mickey Lolich	2,832
Cy Young	2,819
Frank Tanana**	2,657
Warren Spahn	2,583
Bob Feller	2,581
Jerry Koosman	2,556
Tim Keefe	2,538
Christy Mathewson	2,505

Home Runs (350 or More)

Henry Aaron	755
Babe Ruth	714
Willie Mays	660
Frank Robinson	586
Harmon Killebrew	573
Reggie Jackson	563
Mike Schmidt	548
Mickey Mantle	536
Jimmie Foxx	534
Ted Williams	521
Willie McCovey	521
Eddie Mathews	512
Ernie Banks	512
Mel Ott	511
Lou Gehrig	493
Stan Musial	475
Willie Stargell	475
Carl Yastrzemski	452
Dave Kingman	442
Dave Winfield**	432
Billy Williams	426
Darrell Evans	414
Eddie Murray**	414
Duke Snider	406
Andre Dawson**	399
Al Kaline	399
Dale Murphy**	398
Johnny Bench	389
Frank Howard	382
Jim Rice	382
Orlando Cepeda	379
Norm Cash	377
Carlton Fisk**	375
Rocky Colavito	374
Tony Perez	371
Gil Hodges	370
Ralph Kiner	369
Joe DiMaggio	361
Lee May	360
Johnny Mize	359
Yogi Berra	358
Dick Allen	351

Shutouts

Walter Johnson	110
Grover Alexander	90
Christy Mathewson	83
Cy Young	77
Ed Plank	64
Warren Spahn	63
Nolan Ryan**	61
Bert Blyleven**	60
Tom Seaver	60
Ed Walsh	58
Don Sutton	58
James Galvin	57
Bob Gibson	56
Steve Carlton	55
Bert Blyleven	55
Jim Palmer	53
Gaylord Perry	53
Juan Marichal	52

Strikeouts, Batting

Reggie Jackson	2,597
Willie Stargell	1,936
Mike Schmidt	1,883
Tony Perez	1,867
Dave Kingman	1,816
Bobby Bonds	1,757
Dale Murphy**	1,733
Lou Brock	1,730
Mickey Mantle	1,710
Harmon Killebrew	1,699
Dwight Evans	1,697
Lee May	1,570
Dick Allen	1,566
Willie McCovey	1,550
Dave Parker	1,537
Frank Robinson	1,532
Willie Mays	1,526

Bases on Balls

Babe Ruth	2,056
Ted Williams	2,019
Joe Morgan	1,865
Carl Yastrzemski	1,845
Mickey Mantle	1,734
Mel Ott	1,708
Eddie Yost	1,614
Darrell Evans	1,605
Stan Musial	1,599
Pete Rose	1,566
Harmon Killebrew	1,559
Lou Gehrig	1,508
Mike Schmidt	1,507
Eddie Collins	1,503
Willie Mays	1,463
Jimmie Foxx	1,452
Eddie Mathews	1,444
Frank Robinson	1,420
Henry Aaron	1,402

**Active coming into 1993 season

BASEBALL'S PERFECTLY PITCHED GAMES[1]

(no opposing runner reached base)

John Richmond—Worcester vs. Cleveland (NL) June 12, 1880	(1–0)
John M. Ward—Providence vs. Buffalo (NL) June 17, 1880	(5–0)
Cy Young—Boston vs. Philadelphia (AL) May 5, 1904	(3–0)
Addie Joss—Cleveland vs. Chicago (AL) Oct. 2, 1908	(1–0)
Ernest Shore[2]—Boston vs. Washington (AL) June 23, 1917	(4–0)
Charles Robertson—Chicago vs. Detroit (AL) April 30, 1922	(2–0)
Don Larsen[3]—New York (AL) vs. Brooklyn (NL) Oct. 8, 1956	(2–0)
Jim Bunning—Philadelphia vs. New York (NL) June 21, 1964	(6–0)
Sandy Koufax—Los Angeles vs. Chicago (NL) Sept. 9, 1965	(1–0)
Jim Hunter—Oakland vs. Minnesota (AL) May 8, 1968	(4–0)
Len Barker—Cleveland vs. Toronto (AL) May 15, 1981	(3–0)
Mike Witt—California vs. Texas (AL) Sept. 30, 1984	(1–0)
Tom Browning—Cincinnati vs. Los Angeles (NL) Sept. 16, 1988	(1–0)
Dennis Martinez—Montreal vs. Los Angeles (NL) July 28, 1991	(2–0)

1. Harvey Haddix, of Pittsburgh, pitched 12 perfect innings against Milwaukee (NL), May 26, 1959 but lost game in 13th on error and hit. 2. Shore, relief pitcher for Babe Ruth who walked first batter before being ejected by umpire, retired 26 batters who faced him and baserunner was out stealing. 3. World Series.

RECORD OF WORLD SERIES GAMES

(Through 1992)

Source: The Book of Baseball Records, published by Seymour Siwoff, New York City.

Figures in parentheses for winning pitchers (WP) and losing pitchers (LP) indicate the game number in the series.

1903—Boston A.L. 5 (Jimmy Collins); Pittsburgh N.L. 3 (Fred Clarke). WP—Bos.: Dinneen (2, 6, 8), Young (5, 7); Pitts.: Phillippe (1, 3, 4). LP—Bos.: Young (1), Hughes (3), Dinneen (4); Pitts.: Leever (2, 6), Kennedy (5), Phillippe (7, 8).

1904—No series.

1905—New York N.L. 4 (John J. McGraw); Philadelphia A.L. 1 (Connie Mack). WP—N.Y.: Mathewson (1, 3, 5); McGinnity (4); Phila.: Bender (2). LP—N.Y.: McGinnity (2); Phila.: Plank (1, 4), Coakley (3), Bender (5).

1906—Chicago A.L. 4 (Fielder Jones); Chicago N.L. 2 (Frank Chance). WP—Chi.: A.L.: Altrock (1), Walsh (3, 5), White (6); Chi.: N.L.: Reulbach (2), Brown (4). LP—Chi. A.L.: White (2), Altrock. (4); Chi.: N.L.: Brown (1, 6), Pfeister (3, 5).

1907—Chicago N.L. 4 (Frank Chance); Detroit A.L. 0 (Hugh Jennings). First game tied 3–3, 12 innings. WP—Pfeister (2), Reulbach (3), Overall (4), Brown (5). LP—Mullin (2, 5), Siever (3), Donovan (4).

1908—Chicago N.L. 4 (Frank Chance); Detroit A.L. 1 (Hugh Jennings). WP—Chi.: Brown (1, 4), Overall (2, 5); Det.: Mullin (3). LP—Chi.: Pfeister (3); Det.: Summers (1, 4), Donovan (2, 5).

1909—Pittsburgh N.L. 4 (Fred Clarke); Detroit A.L. 3 (Hugh Jennings). WP—Pitts.: Adams (1, 5, 7), Maddox (3); Det.: Donovan (2), Mullin (4, 6). LP—Pitts.: Camnitz (2), Leifield (4), Willis (6); Det.: Mullin (1), Summers (3, 5), Donovan (7).

1910—Philadelphia A.L. 4 (Connie Mack); Chicago N.L. 1 (Frank Chance). WP—Phila.: Bender (1), Coombs (2, 3, 5); Chi.: Brown (4). LP—Phila.: Bender (4); Chi.: Overall (1), Brown (2, 5), McIntyre (3).

1911—Philadelphia A.L. 4 (Connie Mack); New York N.L. 2 (John J. McGraw). WP—Phila.: Plank (2), Coombs (3), Bender (4, 6); N.Y.: Mathewson (1), Crandall (5). LP—Phila.: Bender (1), Plank (5); N.Y.: Marquard (2), Mathewson (3, 4), Ames (6).

1912—Boston A.L. 4 (J. Garland Stahl); New York N.L. 3 (John J. McGraw). Second game tied, 6–6, 11 innings. WP—Bos.: Wood (1, 4, 8), Bedient (5); N.Y.: Marquard (3, 6), Tesreau (7). LP—Bos.: O'Brien (3, 6), Wood (7); N.Y.: Tesreau (1, 4), Mathewson (5, 8).

1913—Philadelphia A.L. 4 (Connie Mack); New York N.L. 1 (John J. McGraw). WP—Phila.: Bender (1, 4), Bush (3), Plank (5); N.Y.: Mathewson (2); LP—Phila.: Plank (2); N.Y.: Marquard (1), Tesreau (3), Demaree (4), Mathewson (5).

1914—Boston N.L. 4 (George Stallings); Philadelphia A.L. 0 (Connie Mack). WP—Rudolph (1, 4), James (2, 3). LP—Bender (1), Plank (2), Bush (3), Shawkey (4).

1915—Boston A.L. 4 (Bill Carrigan); Philadelphia N.L. 1 (Pat Moran). WP—Bos.: Foster (2, 5), Leonard (3), Shore (4); Phila.: Alexander (1). LP—Bos.: Shore (1); Phila.: Mayer (2), Alexander (3), Chalmers (4), Rixey (5).

1916—Boston A.L. 4 (Bill Carrigan); Brooklyn N.L. 1 (Wilbert Robinson). WP—Bos.: Shore (1, 5), Ruth (2), Leonard (4); Bklyn.: Coombs (3). LP—Bos.: Mays (3); Bklyn.: Marquard (1, 4), Smith (2), Pfeffer (5).

1917—Chicago A.L. 4 (Clarence Rowland); New York N.L. 2 (John J. McGraw). WP—Chi.: Cicotte (1), Faber (2, 5, 6); N.Y.: Benton (3), Schupp (4), LP—Chi.: Cicotte (3), Faber (4); N.Y.: Sallee (1, 5), Anderson (2), Benton (6).

1918—Boston A.L. 4 (Ed Barrow); Chicago N.L. 2 (Fred Mitchell). WP—Bos.: Ruth (1, 4), Mays (3, 6); Chi.: Tyler (2), Vaughn (5). LP—Bos.: Bush (2), Jones (5); Chi.: Vaughn (1, 3), Douglas (4), Tyler (6).

1919—Cincinnati N.L. 5 (Pat Moran); Chicago A.L. 3 (William Gleason). WP—Cin.: Ruether (1), Sallee (2), Ring (4), Eller (5, 8); Chi.: Kerr (3, 6), Cicotte (7). LP—Cin.: Fisher (3), Ring (6), Sallee (7); Chi.: Cicotte (1, 4), Williams (2, 5, 8).

1920—Cleveland A.L. 5 (Tris Speaker); Brooklyn N.L. 2 (Wilbert Robinson). WP—Cleve.: Coveleski (1, 4, 7), Bagby (5), Mails (6); Bklyn.: Grimes (2), Smith (3). LP—Cleve.: Bagby (2), Caldwell (3). Bklyn.: Marquard (1), Cadore (4), Grimes (5, 7), Smith (6).

1921—New York N.L. 5 (John J. McGraw); New York A.L. 3 (Miller Huggins). WP—N.Y. N.L.: Barnes (3, 6), Douglas (4, 7), Nehf (8); N.Y. A.L.: Mays (1), Hoyt (2, 5). LP—N.Y. N.L.: Nehf (2, 5), Douglas (1). N.Y. A.L.: Quinn (3), Mays (4, 7), Shawkey (6), Hoyt (8).

1922—New York N.L. 4 (John J. McGraw); New York A.L. 0 (Miller Huggins). Second game tied 3–3, 10 innings. WP—Ryan (1), Scott (3), McQuillan (4), Nehf (5); LP—Bush (1, 5), Hoyt (3), Mays (4).

1923—New York A.L. 4 (Miller Huggins); New York N.L. 2 (John J. McGraw). WP—N.Y. A.L.: Pennock (2, 6), Shawkey (4), Bush (5); N.Y. N.L.: Ryan (1), Nehf (3). LP—N.Y. A.L.: Bush (1), Jones (3); N.Y. N.L.: McQuillan (2), Scott (4), Bentley (5), Nehf (6).

1924—Washington A.L. 4 (Bucky Harris); New York N.L. 3 (John J. McGraw). WP—Wash.: Zachary (2, 6), Mogridge (4), Johnson (7); N.Y.: Nehf (1), McQuillan (3), Bentley (5). LP—Wash.: Johnson (1, 5), Marberry (3); N.Y.: Bentley (2, 7), Barnes (4), Nehf (6).

1925—Pittsburgh N.L. 4 (Bill McKechnie); Washington A.L. 3 (Bucky Harris). WP—Pitts.: Aldridge (2, 5), Kremer (6, 7); Wash.: Johnson (1, 4), Ferguson (3). LP—Pitts.: Meadows (1), Kremer (3), Yde (4); Wash.: Coveleski (2, 5), Ferguson (6), Johnson (7).

1926—St. Louis N.L. 4 (Rogers Hornsby); New York A.L. 3 (Miller Huggins). WP—St. L.: Alexander (2, 6), Haines (3, 7); N.Y.: Pennock (1, 5), Hoyt (4). LP—St. L.: Sherdel (1, 5), Reinhart (4); N.Y.: Shocker (2), Ruether (3), Shawkey (6), Hoyt (7).

1927—New York A.L. 4 (Miller Huggins); Pittsburgh N.L. 0 (Donie Bush). WP—Hoyt (1), Pipgras (2), Pennock (3), Moore (4). LP—Kremer (1), Aldridge (2), Meadows (3), Miljus (4).

1928—New York A.L. 4 (Miller Huggins); St. Louis N.L. 0 (Bill McKechnie). WP—Hoyt (1, 4), Pipgras (2), Zachary (3). LP—Sherdel (1, 4), Alexander (2), Haines (3).

1929—Philadelphia A.L. 4 (Connie Mack); Chicago N.L. 1 (Joe McCarthy). WP—Phila.: Ehmke (1), Earnshaw (2), Rommel (4), Walberg (5); Chi.: Bush (3). LP—Phila.: Earnshaw (3) Chi.: Root (1), Malone (2, 5), Blake (4).

1930—Philadelphia A.L. 4 (Connie Mack); St. Louis N.L. 2 (Gabby Street). WP—Phila.: Grove (1, 5), Earnshaw (2, 6); St. L.: Hallahan (3), Haines (4). LP—Phila.: Walberg (3), Grove (4); St. L.: Grimes (1, 5), Rhem (2), Hallahan (6).

1931—St. Louis N.L. 4 (Gabby Street); Philadelphia A.L. 3 (Connie Mack). WP—St. L.: Hallahan (2, 5), Grimes (3, 7); Phila.: Grove (1, 6), Earnshaw (4). LP—St. L.: Derringer (1, 6), Johnson (4); Phila.: Earnshaw (2, 7), Grove (3), Hoyt (5).

1932—New York A.L. (Joe McCarthy); Chicago N.L. 0 (Charles Grimm). WP—Ruffing (1), Gomez (2), Pipgras (3), Moore (4). LP—Bush (1), Warneke (2), Root (3), May (4).

1933—New York N.L. 4 (Bill Terry); Washington A.L. 1 (Joe Cronin.). WP—N.Y.: Hubbell (1, 4), Schumacher (2), Luque (5); Wash.: Whitehill (3). LP—N.Y.: Fitzsimmons (3); Wash.: Stewart (1), Crowder (2), Weaver (4), Russell (5).

1934—St. Louis N.L. 4 (Frank Frisch); Detroit A.L. 3 (Mickey Cochrane). WP—St. L.: J. Dean (1, 7), P. Dean (3, 6); Det.: Rowe (2), Auker (4), Bridges (5). LP—St. L.: W. Walker (2, 4), J. Dean (5); Det.: Crowder (1), Bridges (3), Rowe (6), Auker (7).

1935—Detroit A.L. 4 (Mickey Cochrane); Chicago N.L. 2 (Charles Grimm). WP—Det.: Bridges (2, 6), Rowe (3), Crowder (4); Chi.: Warneke (1, 5); LP—Det.: Rowe (1, 5), Chi.: Root (2), French (3, 6), Carleton (4).

1936—New York A.L. 4 (Joe McCarthy); New York N.L. 2 (Bill Terry). WP—N.Y. A.L.: Gomez (2, 6), Hadley (3), Pearson (4); N.Y. N.L.: Hubbell (1), Schumacher (5); LP—N.Y. A.L.: Ruffing (1), Malone (5); N.Y. N.L.: Schumacher (2), Fitzsimmons (3, 6), Hubbell (4).

1937—New York A.L. 4 (Joe McCarthy); New York N.L. 1 (Bill Terry). WP—N.Y. A.L.: Gomez (1, 5), Ruffing (2), Pearson (3); N.Y. N.L.: Hubbell (4). LP—N.Y. A.L.: Hadley (4); N.Y. N.L.: Hubbell (1), Melton (2, 5), Schumacher (3).

1938—New York A.L. 4 (Joe McCarthy); Chicago N.L. 0 (Gabby Hartnett). WP—Ruffing (1, 4), Gomez (2), Pearson (3) LP—Lee (1, 4), Dean (2), Bryant (3).

1939—New York A.L. 4 (Joe McCarthy); Cincinnati N.L. 0 (Bill McKechnie). WP—Ruffing (1), Pearson (2), Hadley (3), Murphy (4). LP—Derringer (1), Walters (2, 4), Thompson (3).

1940—Cincinnati N.L. 4 (Bill McKechnie); Detroit A.L. 3

(Del Baker). WP—Cin.: Walters (2, 6), Derringer (4, 7); Det.: Newsom (1, 5), Bridges (3). LP—Cin.: Derringer (1), Turner (3), Thompson (5); Det.: Rowe (2, 6), Trout (4), Newsom (7).

1941—New York A.L. 4 (Joe McCarthy); Brooklyn N.L. 1 (Leo Durocher). WP—N.Y.: Ruffing (1), Russo (3), Murphy (4), Bonham (5); Bklyn: Wyatt (2). LP—N.Y.: Chandler (2); Bklyn: Davis (1), Casey (3, 4), Wyatt (5).

1942—St. Louis N.L. 4 (Billy Southworth); New York A.L. 1 (Joe McCarthy). WP—St. L.: Beazley (2, 5), White (3), Lanier (4); N.Y.: Ruffing (1). LP—St. L.: Cooper (1); N.Y.: Bonham (2), Chandler (3), Donald (4), Ruffing (5).

1943—New York A.L. 4 (Joe McCarthy); St. Louis N.L. 1 (Billy Southworth). WP—N.Y.: Chandler (1, 5), Borowy (3), Russo (4); St. L.: Cooper (2). LP—N.Y.: Bonham (2); St. L.: Lanier (1), Brazle (3), Brecheen (4), Cooper (5).

1944—St. Louis N.L. 4 (Billy Southworth); St. Louis A.L. 2 (Luke Sewell). WP—St. L. N.L.: Donnelly (2), Brecheen (4), Cooper (5), Lanier (6); St. L. A.L.: Galehouse (1), Kramer (3). LP—St. L. N.L.: Cooper (1), Wilks (3); St. L. A.L.: Muncrief (2), Jakucki (4), Galehouse (5), Potter (6).

1945—Detroit A.L. 4 (Steve O'Neill); Chicago N.L. 3 (Charles Grimm). WP—Det.: Trucks (2), Trout (4), Newhouser (5, 7); Chi.: Borowy (1, 6), Passeau (3). LP—Det.: Newhouser (1), Overmire (3), Trout (6); Chi.: Wyse (2), Prim (4), Borowy (5, 7).

1946—St. Louis N.L. 4 (Eddie Dyer); Boston A.L. 3 (Joe Cronin). WP—St. L.: Brecheen (2, 6, 7), Munger (4); Bos.: Johnson (1), Ferriss (3), Dobson (5). LP—St. L.: Pollet (1), Dickson (3), Brazle (5); Bos.: Harris (2, 6), Hughson (4), Klinger (7).

1947—New York A.L. 4 (Bucky Harris); Brooklyn N.L. 3 (Burt Shotton). WP—N.Y.: Shea (1, 5), Reynolds (2), Page (7); Bklyn.: Casey (3, 4), Branca (6). LP—N.Y.: Newsom (3), Bevens (4), Page (6); Bklyn.: Branca (1), Lombardi (2), Barney (5), Gregg (7).

1948—Cleveland A.L. 4 (Lou Boudreau); Boston N.L. 2 (Billy Southworth). WP—Cleve.: Lemon (2, 6), Bearden (3), Gromek (4); Bos.: Sain (1), Spahn (5). LP—Cleve.: Feller (1, 5); Bos.: Spahn (2), Bickford (3), Sain (4), Voiselle (6).

1949—New York A.L. 4 (Casey Stengel); Brooklyn N.L. 1 (Burt Shotton). WP—N.Y.: Reynolds (1), Page (3), Lopat (4), Raschi (5); Bklyn.: Roe (2). LP—N.Y.: Raschi (2); Bklyn.: Newcombe (1, 4), Branca (3), Barney (5).

1950—New York A.L. 4 (Casey Stengel); Philadelphia N.L. 0 (Eddie Sawyer). WP—Raschi (1), Reynolds (2), Ferrick (3), Ford (4). LP—Konstanty (1), Roberts (2), Meyer (3), Miller (4).

1951—New York A.L. 4 (Casey Stengel); New York N.L. 2 (Leo Durocher). WP—N.Y. A.L.: Lopat (2, 5), Reynolds (4), Raschi (6); N.Y. N.L.: Koslo (1), Hearn (3). LP—N.Y. A.L.: Reynolds (1), Raschi (3); N.Y. N.L.: Jansen (2, 5), Maglie (4), Koslo (6).

1952—New York A.L. 4 (Casey Stengel); Brooklyn N.L. 3 (Chuck Dressen). WP—N.Y.: Raschi (2, 6), Reynolds (4, 7); Bklyn.: Black (1), Roe (3), Erskine (5). LP—N.Y.: Reynolds (1), Lopat (3), Sain (5); Bklyn.: Erskine (2), Black (4, 7), Loes (6).

1953—New York A.L. 4 (Casey Stengel); Brooklyn N.L. 2 (Chuck Dressen). WP—N.Y.: Sain (1), Lopat (2), McDonald (5), Reynolds (6); Bklyn.: Erskine (3), Loes (4). LP—N.Y.: Raschi (3), Ford (4); Bklyn.: Labine (1, 6), Roe (2), Podres (5).

1954—New York N.L. 4 (Leo Durocher); Cleveland A.L. 0 (Al Lopez). WP—Grissom (1), Antonelli (2), Gomez (3), Liddie (4). LP—Lemon (1, 4), Wynn (2), Garcia (3).

1955—Brooklyn N.L. 4 (Walter Alston); New York A.L. 3 (Casey Stengel). WP—Bklyn.: Podres (3, 7), Labine (4), Craig (5); N.Y.: Ford (1, 6), Byrne (2). LP—Bklyn.: Newcombe (1), Loes (2), Spooner (6); N.Y.: Turley (3), Larsen (4), Grim (5), Byrne (7).

1956—New York A.L. 4 (Casey Stengel); Brooklyn N.L. 3 (Walter Alston). WP—N.Y.: Ford (3), Sturdivant (4), Larsen (5), Kucks (7); Bklyn.: Maglie (1), Bessent (2), Labine (6). LP—N.Y.: Ford (1), Morgan (2), Turley (6); Bklyn.: Craig (3), Erskine (4), Maglie (5), Newcombe (7).

1957—Milwaukee N.L. 4 (Fred Haney); New York A.L. 3 (Casey Stengel). WP—Mil.: Burdette (2, 5, 7), Spahn (4); N.Y.: Ford (1), Larsen (3), Turley (6). LP—Mil.: Spahn (1), Buhl (3), Johnson (6); N.Y.: Shantz (2), Grim (4), Ford (5), Larsen (7).

1958—New York A.L. 4 (Casey Stengel); Milwaukee N.L. 3 (Fred Haney). WP—N.Y.: Larsen (3), Turley (5, 7), Duren (6); Mil.: Spahn (1, 4), Burdette (2). LP—N.Y.: Duren (1), Turley (2), Ford (4); Mil.: Rush (3), Burdette (5, 7), Spahn (6).

1959—Los Angeles N.L. 4 (Walter Alston); Chicago A.L. 2 (Al Lopez). WP—L.A.: Podres (2), Drysdale (3), Sherry (4, 6); Chi.: Wynn (1), Shaw (5). LP—L.A.: Craig (1), Koufax (5); Chi.: Shaw (2), Donovan (3), Staley (4), Wynn (6).

1960—Pittsburgh N.L. 4 (Danny Murtaugh); New York A.L. 3 (Casey Stengel). WP—Pitts.: Law (1, 4), Haddix (5, 7); N.Y.: Turley (2), Ford (3, 6). LP—Pitts.: Friend (2, 6), Mizell (3); N.Y.: Ditmar (1, 5), Terry (4, 7).

1961—New York A.L. 4 (Ralph Houk); Cincinnati N.L. 1 (Fred Hutchinson). WP—N.Y.: Ford (1, 4), Arroyo (3), Daley (5); Cin.: Jay (2). LP—N.Y.: Terry (2); Cin.: O'Toole (1, 4), Purkey (3), Jay (5).

1962—New York A.L. 4 (Ralph Houk); San Francisco N.L. 3 (Al Dark). WP—N.Y.: Ford (1), Stafford (3), Terry (5, 7); S.F. Sanford (2), Larsen (4), Pierce (6). LP—N.Y.: Terry (2), Coates (4), Ford (6); S.F.: O'Dell (1), Pierce (3), Sanford (5, 7).

1963—Los Angeles N.L. 4 (Walter Alston); New York A.L. 0 (Ralph Houk). WP—Koufax (1, 4), Podres (2), Drysdale (3). LP—Ford (1, 4), Downing (2), Bouton (3).

1964—St. Louis N.L. 4 (Johnny Keane); New York A.L. 3 (Yogi Berra). WP—St. L.: Sadecki (1), Craig (4), Gibson (5, 7); N.Y.: Stottlemyre (2), Bouton (3, 6). LP—St. L.: Gibson (2), Schultz (3), Simmons (6); N.Y.: Ford (1), Downing (4), Mikkelsen (5), Stottlemyre (7).

1965—Los Angeles N.L. 4 (Walter Alston); Minnesota A.L. 3 (Sam Mele). WP—L.A.: Osteen (3), Drysdale (4), Koufax (5, 7); Minn.: Grant (1, 6), Kaat (2). LP—L.A.: Drysdale (1), Koufax (2), Osteen (6); Minn.: Pascual (3), Grant (4), Kaat (5, 7).

1966—Baltimore A.L. 4 (Hank Bauer); Los Angeles N.L. 0 (Walter Alston). WP—Drabowsky (1), Palmer (2), Bunker (3), McNally (4). LP—Drysdale (1, 4), Koufax (2), Osteen (3).

1967—St. Louis N.L. 4 (Red Schoendienst); Boston A.L. 3 (Dick Williams). WP—St. L.: Gibson (1, 4, 7), Briles (3); Bos.: Lonborg (2, 5); Wyatt (6). LP—St. L.: Hughes (2), Carlton (5), Lamabe (6); Bos.: Santiago (1, 4), Bell (3), Lonborg (7).

1968—Detroit A.L. 4 (Mayo Smith); St. Louis N.L. 3 (Red Schoendienst). WP—Det.: Lolich (2, 5, 7), McLain (6); St. L.: Gibson (1, 4), Washburn (3), LP—Det.: McLain (1, 4), Wilson (3); St. L.: Briles (2), Hoerner (5), Washburn (6), Gibson (7).

1969—New York N.L. 4 (Gil Hodges); Baltimore A.L. 1 (Earl Weaver). WP—N.Y.: Koosman (2, 5), Gentry (3), Seaver (4); Balt.: Cuellar (1). LP—N.Y.: Seaver (1); Balt.: McNally (2), Palmer (3), Hall (4), Watt (5).

1970—Baltimore A.L. 4 (Earl Weaver); Cincinnati N.L. 1 (Sparky Anderson) 1. WP—Balt.: Palmer (1), Phoebus (2), McNally (3), Cuellar (5); Cin.: Carroll (4). LP—Cin.: Nolan (1), Wilcox (2), Cloninger (3), Merritt (5); Balt.: Watt (4).

1971—Pittsburgh N.L. 4 (Danny Murtaugh); Baltimore A.L. 3 (Earl Weaver). WP—Pitts.: Blass (3, 7), Kison (4), Briles (5); Balt.: McNally (1, 6), Palmer (2). LP—Pitts.: Ellis (1), R. Johnson (2), Miller (6); Balt.: Cuellar (3, 7), Watt (4) McNally (5).

1972—Oakland A.L. 4 (Dick Williams); Cincinnati N.L. (Sparky Anderson) 3. WP—Oakland: Holtzman (1), Hunter (2, 7), Fingers (4); Cincinnati: Billingham (3), Grimsley (5, 6). LP—Oakland: Odom (3), Fingers (5), Blue (6); Cincinnati: Nolan (1), Grimsley (2), Carroll (4), Borbon (7).

1973—Oakland A.L. 4 (Dick Williams): New York N.L. 3 (Yogi Berra). WP—Oakland: Holtzman (1, 7), Lindblad (3), Hunter (6). New York: McGraw (2), Matlack (4), Koosman (5). LP—Oakland: Fingers (2), Holtzman (4), Blue (5). New York: Matlack (1, 7) Parker (3), Seaver (6).

1974—Oakland A.L. 4 (Al Dark); Los Angeles N.L. 1 (Walter Alston). WP—Oakland: Fingers (1), Hunter (3), Holtzman (4), Odom (5). Los Angeles: Sutton (2). LP—Oakland: Blue (2), Los Angeles: Messersmith (1, 4), Downing (3), Marshall (5).

1975—Cincinnati N.L. 4 (Sparky Anderson); Boston A.L. 3 (Darrell Johnson). WP—Cincinnati: Eastwick (2, 3), Gullett (5), Carroll (7); Boston: Tiant (1, 4), Wise (6). LP—Cincinnati: Gullett (1), Norman (4), Darcy (6); Boston: Drago (2), Willoughby (3), Cleveland (5), Burton (7).

1976—Cincinnati N.L. 4 (Sparky Anderson); New York A.L. 0 (Billy Martin). WP—Gullett (1), Billingham (2), Zachry (3), Nolan (4). LP—Alexander (1), Hunter (2), Ellis (3), Figueroa (4).

1977—New York A.L. 4 (Billy Martin); Los Angeles N.L. 2

(Tom Lasorda). WP—New York: Lyle (1), Torrez (3, 6), Guidry (4); Los Angeles: Hooton (2), Sutton (5). LP—New York: Hunter (2), Gullett (5); Los Angeles: Rhoden (1), John (3), Rau (4), Hooton (6).

1978—New York A.L. 4 (Bob Lemon), Los Angeles N.L. 2 (Tom Lasorda); WP—New York: Guidry (3), Gossage (4); Beattie (5), Hunter (6); Los Angeles: John (1), Hooton (2). LP—New York: Figueroa (1), Hunter (2); Los Angeles: Sutton (3, 6), Welch (4), Hooton (5).

1979—Pittsburgh N.L. 4 (Chuck Tanner), Baltimore A.L. 3 (Earl Weaver); WP—Pittsburgh: D. Robinson (2), Blyleven (5), Candelaria (6), Jackson (7); Baltimore: Flanagan (1), McGregor (3), Stoddard (4). LP—Pittsburgh: Kison (1), Candelaria (3), Tekulve (4); Baltimore: Stanhouse (2), Flanagan (5), Palmer (6), McGregor (7).

1980—Philadelphia N.L. 4 (Dallas Green), Kansas City A.L. 2 (Jim Frey); WP—Philadelphia: Walk (1), Carlton (2), McGraw (5), Carlton (6); Kansas City: Quisenberry (3), Leonard (4). LP—Philadelphia: McGraw (3), Christenson (4); Kansas City: Leonard (1), Quisenberry (2), Quisenberry (5), Gale (6).

1981—Los Angeles N.L. 4 (Tom Lasorda), New York A.L. 2 (Bob Lemon); WP—Los Angeles: Valenzuela (3), Howe (4), Reuss (5), Hooton (6); New York: Guidry (1), John (2). LP—Los Angeles: Reuss (1), Hooton (2); New York: Frazier (3), Frazier (4), Guidry (5), Frazier (6).

1982—St. Louis N.L. 4 (Whitey Herzog), Milwaukee A.L. 3 (Harvey Kuenn); WP—St. Louis: Sutter (2), Andujar (3), Stuper (6), Andujar (7). Milwaukee: Caldwell (1), Slaton (4), Caldwell (5). LP—St. Louis: Forsch (1), Bair (4), Forsch (5). Milwaukee: McClure (2), Vuckovich (3), Sutton (6), McClure (7).

1983—Baltimore A.L. 4 (Joe Altobelli), Philadelphia N.L. 1 (Paul Owens); WP—Baltimore: Boddicker (2), Palmer (3), Davis (4), McGregor (5). Philadelphia: Denny (1).

1984—Detroit A.L. 4 (Sparky Anderson), San Diego N.L. 1 (Dick Williams); WP—Det.: Morris (1,4), Wilcox (3), Lopez (5), San Diego: Hawkins (2). LP—Det.: Petry (2), San Diego: Thurmond (1), Lollar (3), Show (4), Hawkins (5).

1985—Kansas City A.L. 4 (Dick Howser), St. Louis N.L. 3 (Whitey Herzog); WP—KC: Saberhagen (3,7) Quisenberry (6), Jackson (5). St. Louis: Tudor (1,4) Dayley (2). LP—KC: Jackson (1), Leibrandt (2), Black (4); St. Louis: Andujar (3), Forsch (5), Worrell (6), Tudor (7).

1986—New York N.L. 4 (Dave Johnson); Boston A.L. (John McNamara) 3 WP—N.Y.—Ojeda (3), Darling (4), Aguilera (6), McDowell (7), Bos: Hurst (1), (5), Crawford (2). LP—N.Y. Darling (1), Gooden (2, 5).

1987—Minnesota, A.L. 4 (Tom Kelly); St. Louis N.L. (Whitey Herzog) 3. WP—Minn. Viola (1, 7), Blyleven (2), Schatzeder (6), St. Louis: Tudor (3), Forsch (4), Cox (5). LP—Minn. Berenguer (3), Viola (4), Blyleven (5); St. Louis: Magrane (1), Cox (2, 7), Tudor (6).

1988—Los Angeles N.L. 4 (Tommy Lasorda); Oakland A.L. (Tony LaRussa) 1. WP—Los Angeles: Hershiser (2, 5), Pena (1), Belcher (4); Oakland: Honeycutt (3). LP—Los Angeles: Howell (3); Oakland: Davis (2, 5), Eckersley (1), Stewart (4).

1989—Oakland, A.L. 4 (Tony LaRussa); San Francisco N.L. 0 (Roger Craig). WP—Oakland: Dave Stewart (1, 3), Mike Moore (2, 4). LP—San Francisco: Scott Garrelts (1, 3), Don Robinson (4), Rick Reuschel (2).

1990—Cincinnati N.L. 4 (Lou Piniella); Oakland A.L. 0 (Tony LaRussa). WP—Cincinnati: Jose Rijo (1, 4), Rob Dibble (2), Tom Browning (3). LP—Oakland: Dave Stewart (1, 4), Dennis Eckersley (2), Mike Moore (3).

1991—Minnesota, A.L. 4 (Tom Kelly); Atlanta, N.L. 3 (Bobby Cox). WP—Minnesota: Morris (1,7), Tapani (2), Aguilera (6). Atlanta: Clancy (3), Stanton (4), Glavine (5). LP—Minnesota: Aguilera (3), Gurhtie (4), Tapani (5). Atlanta: Leibrandt (1, 6), Glavine (2), Pena (7).

1992—Toronto, A.L. 4 (Cito Gaston), Atlanta, N.L. 2 (Bobby Cox); WP—Toronto: Ward (2, 3), Key (4, 6). Atlanta: Glavine (1), Smoltz (5). LP—Toronto: Morris (1, 5). Atlanta: Leibrandt (6), Reardon (2), Avery (3), Glavine (4).

Before the World Series

Source: Information Please Sports Almanac

The NL–American Assn. Series, 1882–90

When the National League met the American League for the first time in the 1903 World Series, it was not the N.L.'s first venture into post-season play.

From 1882–90, the N.L. pennant winner engaged in a championship series with the champion of the American Association. The Nationals won four of the eight series, lost once, and tied three times.

Year	Champion	Loser	Series
1882	Chicago (NL) & Cincinnati (AA)	—	1–1
1883	No series		
1884	Providence (NL)	New York (AA)	3–0
1885	Chicago (NL) & St. Louis (AA)	—	3–3–1
1886	St. Louis (AA)	Chicago (NL)	4–2
1887	Detroit (NL)	St. Louis (AA)	10–5
1888	New York (NL)	St. Louis (AA)	6–4
1889	New York (NL)	Brooklyn (AA)	6–3
1890	Brooklyn (NL) & Louisville (AA)	—	3–3–1

Early NL and AL Pennant Winners

The National League had been around 27 years before the 1903 World Series. The AL, however, was only in its third season when the two leagues met. The following lists account for the pennant winners in those pre-World Series years and in 1904 when the NL champion New York Giants refused to play Boston.

NL Pennant Winners, 1876–1902, '04

Year	Winner	Manager
1876	Chicago	Al Spalding
1877	Boston	Harry Wright
1878	Boston	Harry Wright
1879	Providence	George Wright
1880	Chicago	Cap Anson
1881	Chicago	Cap Anson
1882	Chicago	Cap Anson
1883	Boston	John Morrill
1884	Providence	Frank Bancroft
1885	Chicago	Cap Anson
1886	Chicago	Cap Anson
1887	Detroit	Bill Watkins
1888	New York	Jim Mutrie
1889	New York	Jim Mutrie
1890	Brooklyn	Bill McGunnigle
1891	Boston	Frank Selee
1892	Boston	Frank Selee
1893	Boston	Frank Selee
1894	Baltimore	Ned Hanlon
1895	Baltimore	Ned Hanlon
1896	Baltimore	Ned Hanlon
1897	Boston	Frank Selee
1898	Boston	Frank Selee
1899	Brooklyn	Ned Hanlon
1900	Brooklyn	Ned Hanlon
1901	Pittsburgh	Fred Clarke
1902	Pittsburgh	Fred Clarke
1904	New York	John McGraw

AL Pennant Winners, 1901–02, '04

Year	Winner	Manager
1901	Chicago	Clark Griffith
1902	Philadelphia	Connie Mack
1904	Boston	Jimmy Collins

WORLD SERIES CLUB STANDING
(Through 1992)

	Series	Won	Lost	Pct.
Toronto (A)	1	1	0	1.000
Pittsburgh (N)	7	5	2	.714
New York (A)	33	22	11	.667
Oakland (A)	6	4	2	.667
Cleveland (A)	3	2	1	.667
Minnesota (A)	3	2	1	.667
New York (N–Mets)	3	2	1	.667
Philadelphia (A)	8	5	3	.625
St. Louis (N)	15	9	6	.600
Boston (A)	9	5	4	.550
Los Angeles (N)	9	5	4	.550
Cincinnati (N)	9	5	4	.550
Milwaukee (N)	2	1	1	.500
Boston (N)	2	1	1	.500
Chicago (A)	4	2	2	.500
Baltimore (A)	6	3	3	.500
Kansas City (A)	2	1	1	.500
Detroit (A)	9	4	5	.444
New York (N–Giants)	14	5	9	.357
Washington (A)	3	1	2	.333
Philadelphia (N)	4	1	3	.250
Chicago (N)	10	2	8	.200
Brooklyn (N)	9	1	8	.111
St. Louis (A)	1	0	1	.000
San Francisco (N)	2	0	2	.000
Milwaukee (A)	1	0	1	.000
San Diego (N)	1	0	1	.000
Atlanta (N)	2	0	2	.000

Recapitulation

	Won
American League	51
National League	36

LIFETIME WORLD SERIES RECORDS
(Through 1992)

Most hits—71, Yogi Berra, New York A.L., 1947, 1949–53, 1955–58, 1960–63.

Most runs—42, Mickey Mantle, New York A.L., 1951–53, 1955–58, 1960–64.

Most runs batted in—40, Mickey Mantle, New York A.L., 1951–53, 1955–58, 1960–64.

Most home runs—18, Mickey Mantle, New York A.L., 1951–53, 1955–58, 1960–64.

Most bases on balls—43, Mickey Mantle, New York A.L., 1951–53, 1955–58, 1960–64.

Most strikeouts—54, Mickey Mantle, New York A.L., 1951–53, 1955–58, 1960–64.

Most stolen bases—14, Eddie Collins, Philadelphia A.L. 1910–11, 13–14; Chicago A.L., 1917, 1919. Lou Brock, St. Louis N.L., 1964, 67–68.

Most victories, pitcher—10, Whitey Ford, New York A.L., 1950, 1953, 1955–58, 1960–64.

Most times member of winning team—10, Yogi Berra, New York A.L., 1947, 1949–53, 1956, 1958, 1961–62.

Most victories, no defeats—6, Vernon Gomez, New York A.L., 1932, 1936(2), 1937(2), 1938.

Most shutouts—4, Christy Mathewson, New York N.L., 1905 (3), 1913.

Most innings pitched—146, Whitey Ford, New York A.L., 1950, 1953, 1955–58, 1960–1964

Most consecutive scoreless innings—33 2/3, Whitey Ford, New York A.L., 1960 (18), 1961 (14), 1962 (1 2/3).

Most strikeouts by pitcher—94, Whitey Ford, New York A.L., 1950, 1953, 1955–58, 1960–64.

SINGLE GAME AND SINGLE SERIES RECORDS
(Through 1992)

Most hits game—5, Paul Molitor, Milwaukee A.L., first game vs. St. Louis, N.L., 1982.

Most 4-hit games, series—2, Robin Yount, Milwaukee A.L., first and fifth games vs. St. Louis N.L., 1982.

Most hits inning—2, held by many players.

Most hits series—13 (7 games) Bobby Richardson, New York A.L., 1964; Lou Brock, St. Louis N.L., 1968; 12 (6 games) Billy Martin, New York A.L., 1953; 12 (8 games) Buck Herzog, New York N.L., 1912; Joe Jackson, Chicago A.L., 1919; 10 (4 games) Babe Ruth, New York A.L., 1928; 9 (5 games) held by 8 players.

Most home runs, series—5 (6 games) Reggie Jackson, New York A.L., 1977; 4 (7 games) Babe Ruth, New York A.L., 1926; Duke Snider, Brooklyn N.L., 1952, 1955; Hank Bauer, New York A.L., 1958; Gene Tenace, Oakland A.L., 1972; 4 (4 games) Lou Gehrig, New York A.L., 1928; 3 (6 games) Babe Ruth, New York A.L., 1923; Ted Kluszewski, Chicago A.L., 1959; 3 (5 games) Donn Clendenon, New York Mets N.L., 1969.

Most home runs, game—3, Babe Ruth, New York A.L., 1926 and 1928; Reggie Jackson, New York A.L., 1977.

Most strikeouts, series—12 (6 games) Willie Wilson, Kansas City A.L., 1980; 11 (7 games) Ed Mathews, Milwaukee N.L., 1958; Wayne Garrett, New York N.L., 1973: 10 (8 games) George Kelly, New York N.L., 1921; 9 (6 games) Jim Bottomley, St. Louis N.L., 1930; 9 (5 games) Carmelo Martinez, San Diego, N.L., 1984; Duke Snider, Brooklyn N.L., 1949; 7 (4 games) Bob Muesel, New York A.L., 1927.

Most stolen bases, game—3, Honus Wagner, Pittsburgh N.L., 1909; Willie Davis, Los Angeles N.L., 1965; Lou Brock, St. Louis N.L., 1967 and 1968.

Most strikeouts by pitcher, game—17, Bob Gibson, St. Louis N.L. 1968.

Most strikeouts by pitcher in succession—6, Horace Eller, Cincinnati N.L., 1919; Moe Drabowsky, Baltimore A.L., 1966.

Most strikeouts by pitcher, series—35 (7 games) Bob Gibson, St. Louis N.L., 1968; 28 (8 games) Bill Dinneen, Boston A.L., 1903; 23 (4 games) Sandy Koufax, Los Angeles, 1963; 20 (6 games) Chief Bender, Philadelphia A.L., 1911; 18 (5 games) Christy Mathewson, New York N.L., 1905.

Most bases on balls, series—11 (7 games) Babe Ruth, New York A.L., 1926; Gene Tenace, Oakland A.L., 1973; 9 (6 games) Willie Randolph, New York A.L., 1981; 7 (5 games) James Sheckard, Chicago N.L., 1910; Mickey Cochrane, Philadelphia A.L., 1929; Joe Gordon, New York A.L., 1941; 7 (4 games) Hank Thompson, New York N.L., 1954.

Most consecutive scoreless innings one series—27, Christy Mathewson, New York N.L., 1905.

AMERICAN LEAGUE HOME RUN CHAMPIONS

Year	Player, team	No.
1901	Nap Lajoie, Phila.	13
1902	Ralph Seybold, Phila.	16
1903	Buck Freeman, Bost.	13
1904	Harry Davis, Phila.	10
1905	Harry Davis, Phila.	8
1906	Harry Davis, Phila.	12
1907	Harry Davis, Phila.	8
1908	Sam Crawford, Det.	7
1909	Ty Cobb, Det.	9
1910	J. Garland Stahl, Bost.	10
1911	Franklin Baker, Phila.	9
1912	Franklin Baker, Phila.	10
1913	Franklin Baker, Phila.	12
1914	Franklin Baker, Phila., and Sam Crawford, Det.	8
1915	Robert Roth, Chi.–Cleve.	7
1916	Wally Pipp, N.Y.	12
1917	Wally Pipp, N.Y.	9
1918	Babe Ruth, Bost., and Clarence Walker, Phila.	11
1919	Babe Ruth, Bost.	29
1920	Babe Ruth, N.Y.	54
1921	Babe Ruth, N.Y.	59
1922	Ken Williams, St. L.	39
1923	Babe Ruth, N.Y.	41
1924	Babe Ruth, N.Y.	46
1925	Bob Meusel, N.Y.	33
1926	Babe Ruth, N.Y.	47
1927	Babe Ruth, N.Y.	60
1928	Babe Ruth, N.Y.	54
1929	Babe Ruth, N.Y.	46
1930	Babe Ruth, N.Y.	49
1931	Lou Gehrig, N.Y., and Babe Ruth, N.Y.	46
1932	Jimmy Foxx, Phila.	58
933	Jimmy Foxx, Phila.	48
1934	Lou Gehrig, N.Y.	49
1935	Jimmy Foxx, Phila., and Hank Greenberg, Det.	36
1936	Lou Gehrig, N.Y.	49
1937	Joe DiMaggio, N.Y.	46
1938	Hank Greenberg, Det.	58
1939	Jimmy Foxx, Bost.	35
1940	Hank Greenberg, Det.	41
1941	Ted Williams, Bost.	37
1942	Ted Williams, Bost.	36
1943	Rudy York, Det.	34
1944	Nick Etten, N.Y.	22
1945	Vern Stephens, St. L.	24
1946	Hank Greenberg, Det.	44
1947	Ted Williams, Bost.	32
1948	Joe DiMaggio, N.Y.	39
1949	Ted Williams, Bost.	43
1950	Al Rosen, Cleve.	37
1951	Gus Zernial, Chi.–Phila.	33
1952	Larry Doby, Cleve.	32
1953	Al Rosen, Cleve.	43
1954	Larry Doby, Cleve.	32
1955	Mickey Mantle, N.Y.	37
1956	Mickey Mantle, N.Y.	52
1957	Roy Sievers, Wash.	42
1958	Mickey Mantle, N.Y.	42
1959	Rocky Colavito, Cleve., and Harmon Killebrew, Wash.	42
1960	Mickey Mantle, N.Y.	40
1961	Roger Maris, N.Y.	61
1962	Harmon Killebrew, Minn.	48
1963	Harmon Killebrew, Minn.	45
1964	Harmon Killebrew, Minn.	49
1965	Tony Conigliaro, Bost.	32
1966	Frank Robinson, Balt.	49
1967	Carl Yastrzemski, Bost., and Harmon Killebrew, Minn.	44
1968	Frank Howard, Wash.	44
1969	Harmon Killebrew, Minn.	49
1970	Frank Howard, Wash.	44
1971	Bill Melton, Chicago	33
1972	Dick Allen, Chicago	37
1973	Reggie Jackson, Oak.	32
1974	Dick Allen, Chicago	32
1975	Reggie Jackson, Oak., and George Scott, Mil.	36
1976	Graig Nettles, N.Y.	32
1977	Jim Rice, Boston	39
1978	Jim Rice, Boston	46
1979	Gorman Thomas, Milwaukee	45
1980	Reggie Jackson, N.Y., and Ben Oglivie, Mil.	41
1981*	Tony Armas, Oak., Dwight Evans, Bost., Bobby Grich, Calif., and Eddie Murray, Balt. (tie)	22
1982	Gorman Thomas, Mil., and Reggie Jackson, Calif.	39
1983	Jim Rice, Boston	39
1984	Tony Armas, Boston	43
1985	Darrell Evans, Detroit	40
1986	Jesse Barfield, Toronto	40
1987	Mark McGwire, Oakland	49
1988	Jose Canseco, Oakland	42
1989	Fred McGriff, Toronto	36
1990	Cecil Fielder, Detroit	51
1991	Jose Canseco, Oakland Cecil Fielder, Detroit (tie)	44
1992	Juan Gonzalez, Texas	43
1993	Juan Gonzalez, Texas	46

AMERICAN LEAGUE BATTING CHAMPIONS

Year	Player, team	Avg
1901	Nap Lajoie, Phila.	.422
1902	Ed Delahanty, Wash.	.376
1903	Nap Lajoie, Cleve.	.355
1904	Nap Lajoie, Cleve.	.381
1905	Elmer Flick, Cleve.	.306
1906	George Stone, St. L.	.358
1907	Ty Cobb, Det.	.350
1908	Ty Cobb, Det.	.324
1909	Ty Cobb, Det.	.377
1910	Ty Cobb, Det.	.385
1911	Ty Cobb, Det.	.420
1912	Ty Cobb, Det.	.410
1913	Ty Cobb, Det.	.390
1914	Ty Cobb, Det.	.368
1915	Ty Cobb, Det.	.369
1916	Tris Speaker, Cleve.	.386
1917	Ty Cobb, Det.	.383
1918	Ty Cobb, Det.	.382
1919	Ty Cobb, Det.	.384
1920	George Sisler, St. L.	.407
1921	Harry Heilmann, Det.	.394
1922	George Sisler, St. L.	.420
1923	Harry Heilmann, Det.	.403
1924	Babe Ruth, N.Y.	.378
1925	Harry Heilmann, Det.	.393
1926	Heinie Manush, Det.	.378
1927	Harry Heilmann, Det.	.398
1928	Goose Goslin, Wash.	.379
1929	Lew Fonseca, Cleve.	.369
1930	Al Simmons, Phila.	.381
1931	Al Simmons, Phila.	.390
1932	Dale Alexander, Det.–Bost.	.367
1933	Jimmy Foxx, Phila.	.356
1934	Lou Gehrig, N.Y.	.363
1935	Buddy Myer, Wash.	.349
1936	Luke Appling, Chi.	.388
1937	Charley Gehringer, Det.	.371
1938	Jimmy Foxx, Bost.	.349
1939	Joe DiMaggio, N.Y.	.381
1940	Joe DiMaggio, N.Y.	.352
1941	Ted Williams, Bost.	.406
1942	Ted Williams, Bost.	.356
1943	Luke Appling, Chi.	.328
1944	Lou Boudreau, Cleve.	.327
1945	George Sternweiss, N.Y.	.309
1946	Mickey Vernon, Wash.	.353
1947	Ted Williams, Bost.	.343
1948	Ted Williams, Bost.	.369
1949	George Kell, Det.	.343
1950	Billy Goodman, Bost.	.354
1951	Ferris Fain, Phila.	.344
1952	Ferris Fain, Phila.	.327
1953	Mickey Vernon, Wash.	.337
1954	Bobby Avila, Cleve.	.341
1955	Al Kaline, Det.	.340
1956	Mickey Mantle, N.Y.	.353
1957	Ted Williams, Bost.	.388
1958	Ted Williams, Bost.	.328
1959	Harvey Kuenn, Det.	.353
1960	Pete Runnels, Bost.	.320
1961	Norman Cash, Det.	.361
1962	Pete Runnels, Bost.	.326
1963	Carl Yastrzemski, Bost.	.321
1964	Tony Oliva, Minn.	.323
1965	Tony Oliva, Minn.	.321
1966	Frank Robinson, Balt.	.316
1967	Carl Yastrzemski, Bost.	.326
1968	Carl Yastrzemski, Bost.	.301
1969	Rod Carew, Minn.	.332
1970	Alex Johnson, Calif.	.329
1971	Tony Oliva, Minn.	.337
1972	Rod Carew, Minn.	.318
1973	Rod Carew, Minn.	.350
1974	Rod Carew, Minn.	.364
1975	Rod Carew, Minn.	.359
1976	George Brett, Kansas City	.333
1977	Rod Carew, Minn.	.388
1978	Rod Carew, Minn.	.333
1979	Fred Lynn, Boston	.333

*Split season because of player strike.

Year	Player, team	Avg
1980	George Brett, Kansas City	.390
1981*	Carney Lansford, Bost.	.336
1982	Willie Wilson, Kansas City	.332
1983	Wade Boggs, Boston	.361
1984	Don Mattingly, New York	.343
1985	Wade Boggs, Boston	.368
1986	Wade Boggs, Boston	.357
1987	Wade Boggs, Boston	.363
1988	Wade Boggs, Boston	.366
1989	Kirby Puckett, Minnesota	.339
1990	George Brett, Kansas City	.328
1991	Julio Franco, Texas	.341
1992	Edgar Martinez, Seattle	.343
1993	John Olerud, Toronto	.363

NATIONAL LEAGUE HOME RUN CHAMPIONS

Year	Player, team	No.
1876	George Hall, Phila. Athletics	5
1877	George Shaffer, Louisville	3
1878	Paul Hines, Providence	4
1879	Charles Jones, Bost.	9
1880	James O'Rourke, Bost., and Harry Stovey, Worcester	6
1881	Dan Brouthers, Buffalo	8
1882	George Wood, Det.	7
1883	William Ewing, N.Y.	10
1884	Ed Williamson, Chi.	27
1885	Abner Dalrymple, Chi.	11
1886	Arthur Richardson, Det.	11
1887	Roger Connor, N.Y., and Wm. O'Brien, Wash.	17
1888	Roger Connor, N.Y.	14
1889	Sam Thompson, Phila.	20
1890	Tom Burns, Bklyn, and Mike Tiernan, N.Y.	13
1891	Harry Stovey, Bost., and Mike Tiernan, N.Y.	16
1892	Jim Holliday, Cin.	13
1893	Ed Delahanty, Phila.	19
1894	Hugh Duffy, Bost., and Robert Lowe, Bost.	18
1895	Bill Joyce, Wash.	17
1896	Ed Delahanty, Phila., and Sam Thompson, Phila.	13
1897	Nap Lajoie, Phila.	10
1898	James Colins, Bost.	14
1899	John Freeman, Wash.	25
1900	Herman Long, Bost.	12
1901	Sam Crawford, Con.	16
1902	Tom Leach, Pitts.	6
1903	James Sheckard, Bklyn.	9
1904	Harry Lumley, Bklyn.	9
1905	Fred Odwell, Cin.	9
1906	Tim Jordan, Bklyn	12
1907	David Brain, Bost.	10
1908	Tim Jordan, Bklyn.	12
1909	John Murray, N.Y.	7
1910	Fred Beck, Bost., and Frank Schulte, Chi.	10
1911	Frank Schulte, Chi.	21
1912	Henry Zimmerman, Chi.	14
1913	Cliff Cravath, Phila.	19
1914	Cliff Cravath, Phila.	19
1915	Cliff Cravath, Phila.	24
1916	Davis Robertson, N.Y., and Fred Williams, Chi.	12
1917	Davis Robertson, N.Y., and Cliff Cravath, Phila.	12
1918	Cliff Cravath, Phila.	8
1919	Cliff Cravath, Phila.	12
1920	Cy Williams, Phila.	15
1921	George Kelly, N.Y.	23
1922	Rogers Hornsby, St. L.	42
1923	Cy Williams, Phila.	41
1924	Jacques Fournier, Bklyn.	27
1925	Rogers Hornsby, St. L.	39
1926	Hack Wilson, Chi.	21
1927	Hack Wilson, Chi., and Cy Williams, Phila.	30
1928	Hack Wilson, Chi., and Jim Bottomley, St. L.	31
1929	Chuck Klein, Phila.	43
1930	Hack Wilson, Chi.	56
1931	Chuck Klein, Phila.	31
1932	Chuck Klein, Phila., and Mel Ott, N.Y.	38
1933	Chuck Klein, Phila.	28
1934	Mel Ott, N.Y., and Rip Collins, St. L.	35
1935	Wally Berger, Bost.	34
1936	Mel Ott, N.Y.	33
1937	Mel Ott, N.Y., and Joe Medwick, St. L.	31
1938	Mel Ott, N.Y.	36
1939	John Mize, St. L.	28
1940	John Mize, St. L.	43
1941	Dolph Camilli, Bklyn.	34
1942	Mel Ott, N.Y.	30
1943	Bill Nicholson, Chi.	29
1944	Bill Nicholson, Chi.	33
1945	Tommy Holmes, Bost.	28
1946	Ralph Kiner, Pitts.	23
1947	Ralph Kiner, Pitts., and John Mize, N.Y.	51
1948	Ralph Kiner, Pitts., and John Mize, N.Y.	40
1949	Ralph Kiner, Pitts.	54
1950	Ralph Kiner, Pitts.	47
1951	Ralph Kiner, Pitts.	42
1952	Ralph Kiner, Pitts., and Hank Sauer, Chi.	37
1953	Ed Mathews, Mil.	47
1954	Ted Kluszewski, Cin.	49
1955	Willie Mays, N.Y.	51
1956	Duke Snider, Bklyn.	43
1957	Henry Aaron, Mil.	44
1958	Ernie Banks, Chi.	47
1959	Ed Mathews, Mil.	46
1960	Ernie Banks, Chi.	41
1961	Orlando Cepeda, San Fran.	46
1962	Willie Mays, San Fran.	49
1963	Henry Aaron, Mil., and Willie McCovey, San Fran.	44
1964	Willie Mays, San Fran.	47
1965	Willie Mays, San Fran.	52
1966	Henry Aaron, Atlanta	44
1967	Henry Aaron, Atlanta	39
1968	Willie McCovey, San Fran.	36
1969	Willie McCovey, San Fran.	45
1970	Johnny Bench, Cin.	45
1971	Willie Stargell, Pitts.	48
1972	Johnny Bench, Cin.	40
1973	Willie Stargell, Pitts.	44
1974	Mike Schmidt, Phila.	36
1975	Mike Schmidt, Phila.	38
1976	Mike Schmidt, Phila.	38
1977	George Foster, Cin.	52
1978	George Foster, Cin.	40
1979	Dave Kingman, Chicago	48
1980	Mike Schmidt, Phila.	48
1981*	Mike Schmidt, Phila.	31
1982	Dave Kingman, N.Y.	37
1983	Mike Schmidt, Phila.	40
1984	Mike Schmidt, Phila. and Dale Murphy, Atlanta	36
1985	Dale Murphy, Atlanta	37
1986	Mike Schmidt, Phila.	37
1987	Andre Dawson, Chicago	49
1988	Darryl Strawberry, N.Y.	39
1989	Kevin Mitchell, San Francisco	47
1990	Ryne Sandberg, Chicago	40
1991	Howard Johnson, N.Y.	38
1992	Fred McGriff, San Diego	35
1993	Barry Bonds, San Francisco	46

*Split season because of player strike.

NATIONAL LEAGUE BATTING CHAMPIONS

Year	Player, team	Avg
1876	Roscoe Barnes, Chicago	.404
1877	Jim White, Boston	.385
1878	Abner Dalrymple, Mil.	.356
1879	Cap Anson, Chicago	.407
1880	George Gore, Chicago	.365
1881	Cap Anson, Chicago	.399
1882	Dan Brouthers, Buffalo	.367
1883	Dan Brouthers, Buffalo	.371
1884	James O'Rourke, Buffalo	.350
1885	Roger Connor, N. Y.	.371
1886	King Kelly, Chicago	.388
1887	Cap Anson, Chicago	.421
1888	Cap Anson, Chicago	.343
1889	Dan Brouthers, Boston	.373
1890	John Glasscock, N. Y.	.336
1891	William Hamilton, Phila.	.338
1892	Dan Brouthers, Bklyn., and Clarence Childs, Cleve.	.335
1893	Hugh Duffy, Boston	.378
1894	Hugh Duffy, Boston	.438
1895	Jesse Burkett, Cleveland	.423
1896	Jesse Burkett, Cleveland	.410
1897	Willie Keeler, Baltimore	.432
1898	Willie Keeler, Baltimore	.379
1899	Ed Delahanty, Phila.	.408
1900	Honus Wagner, Pittsburgh	.381
1901	Jesse Burkett, St. Louis	.382
1902	Clarence Beaumont, Pitts.	.357
1903	Honus Wagner, Pittsburgh	.355
1904	Honus Wagner, Pittsburgh	.349
1905	Cy Seymour, Cincinnati	.377
1906	Honus Wagner, Pittsburgh	.339
1907	Honus Wagner, Pittsburgh	.350

Year	Player, team	Avg
1908	Honus Wagner, Pittsburgh	.354
1909	Honus Wagner, Pittsburgh	.339
1910	Sherwood Magee, Phila.	.331
1911	Honus Wagner, Pittsburgh	.334
1912	Henry Zimmerman, Chicago	.372
1913	Jake Daubert, Brooklyn	.350
1914	Jake Daubert, Brooklyn	.329
1915	Larry Doyle, New York	.320
1916	Hal Chase, Cincinnati	.339
1917	Edd Roush, Cincinnati	.341
1918	Zack Wheat, Brooklyn	.335
1919	Edd Roush, Cincinnati	.321
1920	Rogers Hornsby, St. Louis	.370
1921	Rogers Hornsby, St. Louis	.397
1922	Rogers Hornsby, St. Louis	.401
1923	Rogers Hornsby, St. Louis	.384
1924	Rogers Hornsby, St. Louis	.424
1925	Rogers Hornsby, St. Louis	.403
1926	Gene Hargrave, Cincinnati	.353
1927	Paul Waner, Pittsburgh	.380
1928	Rogers Hornsby, Boston	.387
1929	Lefty O'Doul, Phila.	.398
1930	Bill Terry, N.Y.	.401
1931	Chick Hafey, St. Louis	.349
1932	Lefty O'Doul, Brooklyn	.368
1933	Chuck Klein, Phila.	.368
1934	Paul Waner, Pittsburgh	.362
1935	Arky Vaughan, Pittsburgh	.385
1936	Paul Waner, Pittsburgh	.373
1937	Joe Medwick, St. Louis	.374
1938	Ernie Lombardi, Cin.	.342
1939	John Mize, St. Louis	.349
1940	Debs Garms, Pittsburgh	.355
1941	Pete Reiser, Brooklyn	.343
1942	Ernie Lombardi, Boston	.330
1943	Stan Musial, St. Louis	.357
1944	Dixie Walker, Brooklyn	.357
1945	Phil Cavarretta, Chicago	.355
1946	Stan Musial, St. Louis	.365
1947	Harry Walker, St. L.–Phila.	.363
1948	Stan Musial, St. Louis	.376
1949	Jackie Robinson, Brooklyn	.342
1950	Stan Musial, St. Louis	.346
1951	Stan Musial, St. Louis	.355
1952	Stan Musial, St. Louis	.336
1953	Carl Furillo, Brooklyn	.344
1954	Willie Mays, N. Y.	.345
1955	Richie Ashburn, Phila.	.338
1956	Henry Aaron, Mil.	.328
1957	Stan Musial, St. Louis	.351
1958	Richie Ashburn, Phila.	.350
1959	Henry Aaron, Mil.	.355
1960	Dick Groat, Pittsburgh	.325
1961	Roberto Clemente, Pitts.	.351
1962	Tommy Davis, L. A.	.346
1963	Tommy Davis, L. A.	.326
1964	Roberto Clemente, Pitts.	.339
1965	Roberto Clemente, Pitts.	.329
1966	Matty Alou, Pittsburgh	.342
1967	Roberto Clemente, Pitts.	.357
1968	Pete Rose, Cincinnati	.335
1969	Pete Rose, Cincinnati	.348
1970	Rico Carty, Atlanta	.366
1971	Joe Torre, St. Louis	.363
1972	Billy Williams, Chicago	.333
1973	Pete Rose, Cincinnati	.338
1974	Ralph Garr, Atlanta	.353
1975	Bill Madlock, Chicago	.354
1976	Bill Madlock, Chicago	.339
1977	Dave Parker, Pittsburgh	.338
1978	Dave Parker, Pittsburgh	.334
1979	Keith Hernandez, St. Louis	.344
1980	Bill Buckner, Chicago	.324
1981*	Bill Madlock, Pittsburgh	.341
1982	Al Oliver, Montreal	.331
1983	Bill Madlock, Pittsburgh	.323
1984	Tony Gwynn, San Diego	.351
1985	Willie McGee, St. Louis	.353
1986	Tim Raines, Montreal	.334
1987	Tony Gwynn, San Diego	.370
1988	Tony Gwynn, San Diego	.313
1989	Tony Gwynn, San Diego	.336
1990	Willie McGee, St. Louis	.335
1991	Terry Pendleton, Atlanta	.319
1992	Gary Sheffield, San Diego	.330
1993	Andres Galarraga, Colorado	.370

AMERICAN LEAGUE PENNANT WINNERS

Year	Club	Manager	Won	Lost	Pct
1901	Chicago	Clark C. Griffith	83	53	.610
1902	Philadelphia	Connie Mack	83	53	.610
1903[1]	Boston	Jimmy Collins	91	47	.659
1904[2]	Boston	Jimmy Collins	95	59	.617
1905	Philadelphia	Connie Mack	92	56	.622
1906[1]	Chicago	Fielder A. Jones	93	58	.616
1907	Detroit	Hugh A. Jennings	92	58	.613
1908	Detroit	Hugh A. Jennings	90	63	.588
1909	Detroit	Hugh A. Jennings	98	54	.645
1910[1]	Philadelphia	Connie Mack	102	48	.680
1911[1]	Philadelphia	Connie Mack	101	50	.669
1912[1]	Boston	J. Garland Stahl	105	47	.691
1913[1]	Philadelphia	Connie Mack	96	57	.627
1914	Philadelphia	Connie Mack	99	53	.651
1915[1]	Boston	William F. Carrigan	101	50	.669
1916[1]	Boston	William F. Carrigan	91	63	.591
1917[1]	Chicago	Clarence H. Rowland	100	54	.649
1918[1]	Boston	Ed Barrow	75	51	.595
1919	Chicago	William Gleason	88	52	.629
1920[1]	Cleveland	Tris Speaker	98	56	.636
1921	New York	Miller J. Huggins	98	55	.641
1922	New York	Miller J. Huggins	94	60	.610
1923[1]	New York	Miller J. Huggins	98	54	.645
1924[1]	Washington	Stanley R. Harris	92	62	.597
1925	Washington	Stanley R. Harris	96	55	.636
1926	New York	Miller J. Huggins	91	63	.591
1927[1]	New York	Miller J. Huggins	110	44	.714
1928[1]	New York	Miller J. Huggins	101	53	.656
1929[1]	Philadelphia	Connie Mack	104	46	.693
1930[1]	Philadelphia	Connie Mack	102	52	.662
1931	Philadelphia	Connie Mack	107	45	.704
1932[1]	New York	Joseph V. McCarthy	107	47	.695
1933	Washington	Joseph E. Cronin	99	53	.651
1934	Detroit	Gordon Cochrane	101	53	.656
1935[1]	Detroit	Gordon Cochrane	93	58	.616
1936[1]	New York	Joseph V. McCarthy	102	51	.667
1937[1]	New York	Joseph V. McCarthy	102	52	.662
1938[1]	New York	Joseph V. McCarthy	99	53	.651
1939[1]	New York	Joseph V. McCarthy	106	45	.702
1940	Detroit	Delmar D. Baker	90	64	.584
1941[1]	New York	Joseph V. McCarthy	101	53	.656
1942	New York	Joseph V. McCarthy	103	51	.669
1943[1]	New York	Joseph V. McCarthy	98	56	.636
1944	St. Louis	Luke Sewell	89	65	.578
1945[1]	Detroit	Steve O'Neill	88	65	.575
1946	Boston	Joseph E. Cronin	104	50	.675
1947[1]	New York	Stanley R. Harris	97	57	.630
1948[1]	Cleveland	Lou Boudreau	97	58	.626
1949[1]	New York	Casey Stengel	97	57	.630
1950[1]	New York	Casey Stengel	98	56	.636
1951[1]	New York	Casey Stengel	98	56	.636
1952[1]	New York	Casey Stengel	95	59	.617
1953[1]	New York	Casey Stengel	99	52	.656
1954	Cleveland	Al Lopez	111	43	.721
1955	New York	Casey Stengel	96	58	.623
1956[1]	New York	Casey Stengel	97	57	.630
1957	New York	Casey Stengel	98	56	.636
1958[1]	New York	Casey Stengel	92	62	.597
1959	Chicago	Al Lopez	94	60	.610
1960	New York	Casey Stengel	97	57	.630
1961[1]	New York	Ralph Houk	109	53	.673
1962[1]	New York	Ralph Houk	96	66	.593
1963	New York	Ralph Houk	104	57	.646
1964	New York	Yogi Berra	99	63	.611
1965	Minnesota	Sam Mele	102	60	.630
1966[1]	Baltimore	Hank Bauer	97	53	.606
1967	Boston	Dick Williams	92	70	.568
1968[1]	Detroit	Mayo Smith	103	59	.636
1969	Baltimore[3]	Earl Weaver	109	53	.673
1970[1]	Baltimore[3]	Earl Weaver	108	54	.667
1971	Baltimore[4]	Earl Weaver	101	57	.639
1972[1]	Oakland[5]	Dick Williams	93	62	.600
1973[1]	Oakland[6]	Dick Williams	94	68	.580
1974[1]	Oakland[6]	Alvin Dark	90	72	.556

Year	Club	Manager	Won	Lost	Pct
1975	Boston[4]	Darrell Johnson	95	65	.594
1976	New York[7]	Billy Martin	97	62	.610
1977[1]	New York[7]	Billy Martin	100	62	.617
1978[1]	New York[7]	Billy Martin and Bob Lemon	100	63	.613
1979	Baltimore[8]	Earl Weaver	102	57	.642
1980	Kansas City[9]	Jim Frey	97	65	.599
1981	New York[10]	Gene Michael–Bob Lemon	59	48	.551 *
1982	Milwaukee[11]	Harvey Kuenn	95	67	.586
1983[1]	Baltimore[12]	Joe Altobelli	98	64	.605
1984[1]	Detroit[13]	Sparky Anderson	104	58	.642
1985[1]	Kansas City[14]	Dick Howser	91	71	.562
1986	Boston[11]	John McNamara	95	66	.590
1987	Minnesota[15]	Tom Kelly	85	77	.525
1988	Oakland[16]	Tony LaRussa	104	58	.642
1989	Oakland[17]	Tony LaRussa	99	63	.611
1990	Oakland[18]	Tony LaRussa	103	59	.636
1991	Minnesota[19]	Tom Kelly	95	67	.586
1992	Toronto[10]	Cito Gaston	96	66	.593
1993	Toronto[12]	Cito Gaston	95	67	.586

*Split season because of player strike. 1. World Series winner. 2. No World Series. 3. Defeated Minnesota, Western Division winner, in playoff. 4. Defeated Oakland, Western Division Leader, in playoff. 5. Defeated Detroit, Eastern Division winner, inplayoff. 6. Defeated Baltimore, Eastern Division winner, in playoff. 7. Defeated Kansas City, Western Division winner, in playoff. 8. Defeated California, Western Division winner, in playoff. 9. Defeated New York, Eastern Division winner, in playoff. 10. Defeated Oakland, Western Division winner, in playoff. 11. Defeated California, Western Division winner, in playoff. 12. Defeated Chicago, Western Division winner in playoff. 13. Defeated Kansas City, Western Division winner, in playoff. 14. Defeated Toronto, Eastern Division winner, in playoff. 15. Defeated Detroit, Eastern winner, in playoff. 16. Defeated Boston, Eastern division winner, in playoffs. 17. Defeated Toronto, Eastern Division winner, in playoffs. 18. Defeated Boston, Eastern Division winner, in playoffs. 19. Defeated Toronto, Eastern Division winner, in playoffs.

NATIONAL LEAGUE PENNANT WINNERS

Year	Club	Manager	Won	Lost	Pct
1876	Chicago	Albert G. Spalding	52	14	.788
1877	Boston	Harry Wright	31	17	.646
1878	Boston	Harry Wright	41	19	.683
1879	Providence	George Wright	55	23	.705
1880	Chicago	Adrian C. Anson	67	17	.798
1881	Chicago	Adrian C. Anson	56	28	.667
1882	Chicago	Adrian C. Anson	55	29	.655
1883	Boston	John F. Morrill	63	35	.643
1884	Providence	Frank C. Bancroft	84	28	.750
1885	Chicago	Adrian C. Anson	87	25	.777
1886	Chicago	Adrian C. Anson	90	34	.726
1887	Detroit	W. H. Watkins	79	45	.637
1888	New York	James J. Mutrie	84	47	.641
1889	New York	James J. Mutrie	83	43	.659
1890	Brooklyn	Wm. H. McGunnigle	86	43	.667
1891	Boston	Frank G. Selee	87	51	.630
1892	Boston	Frank G. Selee	102	48	.680
1893	Boston	Frank G. Selee	86	44	.662
1894	Baltimore	Edward H. Hanlon	89	39	.695
1895	Baltimore	Edward H. Hanlon	87	43	.669
1896	Baltimore	Edward H. Hanlon	90	39	.698
1897	Boston	Frank G. Selee	93	39	.705
1898	Boston	Frank G. Selee	102	47	.685
1899	Brooklyn	Edward H. Hanlon	88	42	.677
1900	Brooklyn	Edward H. Hanlon	82	54	.603
1901	Pittsburgh	Fred C. Clarke	90	49	.647
1902	Pittsburgh	Fred C. Clarke	103	36	.741
1903	Pittsburgh	Fred C. Clarke	91	49	.650
1904	New York[2]	John J. McGraw	106	47	.693
1905	New York[1]	John J. McGraw	105	48	.686
1906	Chicago	Frank L. Chance	116	36	.763
1907	Chicago[1]	Frank L. Chance	107	45	.704
1908	Chicago[1]	Frank L. Chance	99	55	.643
1909	Pittsburgh[1]	Fred C. Clarke	110	42	.724
1910	Chicago	Frank L. Chance	104	50	.675
1911	New York	John J. McGraw	99	54	.647
1912	New York	John J. McGraw	103	48	.682
1913	New York	John J. McGraw	101	51	.664
1914	Boston[1]	George T. Stallings	94	59	.614
1915	Philadelphia	Patrick J. Moran	90	62	.592
1916	Brooklyn	Wilbert Robinson	94	60	.610
1917	New York	John J. McGraw	98	56	.636
1918	Chicago	Fred L. Mitchell	84	45	.651
1919	Cincinnati[1]	Patrick J. Moran	96	44	.686
1920	Brooklyn	Wilbert Robinson	93	61	.604
1921	New York[1]	John J. McGraw	94	59	.614
1922	New York[1]	John J. McGraw	93	61	.604
1923	New York	John J. McGraw	95	58	.621
1924	New York	John J. McGraw	93	60	.608
1925	Pittsburgh[1]	Wm. B. McKechnie	95	58	.621
1926	St. Louis[1]	Rogers Hornsby	89	65	.578
1927	Pittsburgh	Donie Bush	94	60	.610
1928	St. Louis	Wm. B. McKechnie	95	59	.617
1929	Chicago	Joseph V. McCarthy	98	54	.645
1930	St. Louis	Gabby Street	92	62	.597
1931	St. Louis[1]	Gabby Street	101	53	.656
1932	Chicago	Charles J. Grimm	90	64	.584
1933	New York[1]	William H. Terry	91	61	.599
1934	St. Louis[1]	Frank F. Frisch	95	58	.621
1935	Chicago	Charles J. Grimm	100	54	.649
1936	New York	William H. Terry	92	62	.597
1937	New York	William H. Terry	95	57	.625
1938	Chicago	Gabby Hartnett	89	63	.586
1939	Cincinnati	Wm. B. McKechnie	97	57	.630
1940	Cincinnati[1]	Wm. B. McKechnie	100	53	.654
1941	Brooklyn	Leo E. Durocher	100	54	.649
1942	St. Louis[1]	Wm. H. Southworth	106	48	.688
1943	St. Louis	Wm. H. Southworth	105	49	.682
1944	St. Louis[1]	Wm. H. Southworth	105	49	.682
1945	Chicago	Charles J. Grimm	98	56	.636
1946	St. Louis[1]	Edwin H. Dyer	98	58	.628
1947	Brooklyn	Burton E. Shotton	94	60	.610
1948	Boston	Wm. H. Southworth	91	62	.595
1949	Brooklyn	Burton E. Shotton	97	57	.630
1950	Philadelphia	Edwin M. Sawyer	91	63	.591
1951	New York	Leo E. Durocher	98	59	.624
1952	Brooklyn	Charles W. Dressen	96	57	.630
1953	Brooklyn	Charles W. Dressen	105	49	.682
1954	New York[1]	Leo E. Durocher	97	57	.630
1955	Brooklyn[1]	Walter Alston	98	55	.641
1956	Brooklyn	Walter Alston	93	61	.604
1957	Milwaukee1	Fred Haney	95	59	.617
1958	Milwaukee	Fred Haney	92	62	.597
1959	Los Angeles[1]	Walter Alston	88	68	.564
1960	Pittsburgh[1]	Danny Murtaugh	95	59	.617
1961	Cincinnati	Fred Hutchinson	93	61	.604
1962	San Francisco	Alvin Dark	103	62	.624
1963	Los Angeles[1]	Walter Alston	99	63	.611
1964	St. Louis[1]	Johnny Keane	93	69	.574
1965	Los Angeles[1]	Walter Alston	97	65	.599
1966	Los Angeles	Walter Alston	95	67	.586
1967	St. Louis[1]	Red Schoendienst	101	60	.627
1968	St. Louis	Red Schoendienst	97	65	.599
1969	New York[1,3]	Gil Hodges	100	62	.617

Year	Club	Manager	Won	Lost	Pct	Year	Club	Manager	Won	Lost	Pct
1970	Cincinnati[4]	Sparky Anderson	102	60	.630	1982[1]	St. Louis[3]	Whitey Herzog	92	70	.568
1971	Pittsburgh[1 5]	Danny Murtaugh	97	65	.599	1983	Philadelphia[11]	Paul Owens	90	72	.556
1972	Cincinnati[4]	Sparky Anderson	95	59	.617	1984	San Diego[12]	Dick Williams	92	70	.568
1973	New York[6]	Yogi Berra	82	79	.509	1985	St. Louis[11]	Whitey Herzog	101	61	.623
1974	Los Angeles[4]	Walter Alston	102	60	.630	1986	New York[8]	Dave Johnson	108	54	.667
1975	Cincinnati[1 4]	Sparky Anderson	108	54	.667	1987	St. Louis[5]	Whitey Herzog	95	67	.586
1976	Cincinnati[7 1]	Sparky Anderson	102	60	.630	1988	Los Angeles[10]	Tom Lasorda	94	67	.584
1977	Los Angeles[7]	Tom Lasorda	98	64	.605	1989	San Francisco[12]	Roger Craig	92	70	.568
1978	Los Angeles[7]	Tom Lasorda	95	67	.586	1990	Cincinnati[4]	Lou Piniella	91	71	.562
1979[1]	Pittsburgh[6]	Chuck Tanner	98	64	.605	1991	Atlanta[4]	Bobby Cox	94	68	.580
1980[1]	Philadelphia[8]	Dallas Green	91	71	.562	1992	Atlanta[4]	Bobby Cox	98	64	.605
1981	Los Angeles[1 9]	Tom Lasorda	63	47	.573*	1993	Philadelphia[3]	Jim Fregosi	97	65	.599

*Split season because of player strike. 1. World Series winner. 2. No World Series. 3. Defeated Atlanta, Western Division winner, in playoff. 4. Defeated Pittsburgh, Eastern Division winner, in playoff. 5. Defeated San Francisco, Western Division winner, in playoff. 6. Defeated Cincinnati, Western Division winner, in playoff. 7. Defeated Philadelphia, Eastern Division winner, in playoff. 8. Defeated Houston, Western Division winner, in playoff. 9. Defeated Montreal, Eastern Division winner, in playoff. 10. Defeated New York, Eastern Division winner, in playoff. 11. Defeated Los Angeles, Western Division in playoff. 12. Defeated Chicago, Eastern Division champion in playoff.

MOST VALUABLE PLAYERS

(Baseball Writers Association selections)

American League

1931	Lefty Grove, Philadelphia
1932–33	Jimmy Foxx, Philadelphia
1934	Mickey Cochrane, Detroit
1935	Hank Greenberg, Detroit
1936	Lou Gehrig, New York
1937	Charlie Gehringer, Detroit
1938	Jimmy Foxx, Boston
1939	Joe DiMaggio, New York
1940	Hank Greenberg, Detroit
1941	Joe DiMaggio, New York
1942	Joe Gordon, New York
1943	Spurgeon Chandler, New York
1944–45	Hal Newhouser, Detroit
1946	Ted Williams, Boston
1947	Joe DiMaggio, New York
1948	Lou Boudreau, Cleveland
1949	Ted Williams, Boston
1950	Phil Rizzuto, New York
1951	Yogi Berra, New York
1952	Bobby Shantz, Philadelphia
1953	Al Rosen, Cleveland
1954–55	Yogi Berra, New York
1956–57	Mickey Mantle, New York
1958	Jackie Jensen, Boston
1959	Nellie Fox, Chicago
1960–61	Roger Maris, New York
1962	Mickey Mantle, New York
1963	Elston Howard, New York
1964	Brooks Robinson, Baltimore
1965	Zoilo Versalles, Minnesota
1966	Frank Robinson, Baltimore
1967	Carl Yastrzemski, Boston
1968	Dennis McLain, Detroit
1969	Harmon Killebrew, Minnesota
1970	John (Boog) Powell, Baltimore
1971	Vida Blue, Oakland
1972	Dick Allen, Chicago
1973	Reggie Jackson, Oakland
1974	Jeff Burroughs, Texas
1975	Fred Lynn, Boston
1976	Thurman Munson, New York
1977	Rod Carew, Minnesota
1978	Jim Rice, Boston
1979	Don Baylor, California
1980	George Brett, Kansas City
1981	Rollie Fingers, Milwaukee
1982	Robin Yount, Milwaukee
1983	Cal Ripken, Jr., Baltimore
1984	Willie Hernandez, Detroit
1985	Don Mattingly, New York
1986	Roger Clemens, Boston
1987	George Bell, Toronto
1988	Jose Canseco, Oakland
1989	Robin Yount, Milwaukee
1990	Rickey Henderson, Oakland
1991	Cal Ripken, Jr., Baltimore
1992	Dennis Eckersley, Oakland

National League

1931	Frank Frisch, St. Louis
1932	Chuck Klein, Philadelphia
1933	Carl Hubbell, New York
1934	Dizzy Dean, St. Louis
1935	Gabby Hartnett, Chicago
1936	Carl Hubbell, New York
1937	Joe Medwick, St. Louis
1938	Ernie Lombardi, Cincinnati
1939	Bucky Walters, Cincinnati
1940	Frank McCormick, Cincinnati
1941	Dolph Camilli, Brooklyn
1942	Mort Cooper, St. Louis
1943	Stan Musial, St. Louis
1944	Marty Marion, St. Louis
1945	Phil Cavarretta, Chicago
1946	Stan Musial, St. Louis
1947	Bob Elliott, Boston
1948	Stan Musial, St. Louis
1949	Jackie Robinson, Brooklyn
1950	Jim Konstanty, Philadelphia
1951	Roy Campanella, Brooklyn
1952	Hank Sauer, Chicago
1953	Roy Campanella, Brooklyn
1954	Willie Mays, New York
1955	Roy Campanella, Brooklyn
1956	Don Newcombe, Brooklyn
1957	Henry Aaron, Milwaukee
1958–59	Ernie Banks, Chicago
1960	Dick Groat, Pittsburgh
1961	Frank Robinson, Cincinnati
1962	Maury Wills, Los Angeles
1963	Sandy Koufax, Los Angeles
1964	Ken Boyer, St. Louis
1965	Willie Mays, San Francisco
1966	Roberto Clemente, Pittsburgh
1967	Orlando Cepeda, St. Louis
1968	Bob Gibson, St. Louis
1969	Willie McCovey, San Francisco
1970	Johnny Bench, Cincinnati
1971	Joe Torre, St. Louis
1972	Johnny Bench, Cincinnati
1973	Pete Rose, Cincinnati
1974	Steve Garvey, Los Angeles
1975–76	Joe Morgan, Cincinnati
1977	George Foster, Cincinnati
1978	Dave Parker, Pittsburgh
1979	Willie Stargell, Pittsburgh
1979	Keith Hernandez, St. Louis
1980	Mike Schmidt, Philadelphia
1981	Mike Schmidt, Philadelphia
1982	Dale Murphy, Atlanta
1983	Dale Murphy, Atlanta
1984	Ryne Sandberg, Chicago
1985	Willie McGee, St. Louis
1986	Mike Schmidt, Philadelphia
1987	Andre Dawson, Chicago
1988	Kirk Gibson, Los Angeles
1989	Kevin Mitchell, San Francisco
1990	Barry Bonds, Pittsburgh
1991	Terry Pendleton, Atlanta
1992	Barry Bonds, Pittsburgh

CY YOUNG AWARD

1956 Don Newcombe, Brooklyn N.L.
1957 Warren Spahn, Milwaukee N.L.
1958 Bob Turley, New York A.L.
1959 Early Wynn, Chicago A.L.
1960 Vernon Law, Pittsburgh, N.L
1961 Whitey Ford, New York A.L.
1962 Don Drysdale, Los Angeles N.L.
1963 Sandy Koufax, Los Angeles N.L.
1964 Dean Chance, Los Angeles A.L.
1965 Sandy Koufax, Los Angeles N.L.
1966 Sandy Koufax, Los Angeles N.L.
1967 Jim Lonborg, Boston A.L.; Mike McCormick, San Francisco N.L.
1968 Dennis, McLain, Detroit A.L.; Bob Gibson, St. Louis N.L.
1969 Mike Cuellar, Baltimore, and Dennis McLain, Detroit, tied in A.L.; Tom Seaver, N.Y. N.L.
1970 Jim Perry, Minnesota A.L; Bob Gibson, St. Louis N.L.
1971 Vida Blue, Oakland A.L.; Ferguson Jenkins, Chicago N.L.
1972 Gaylord Perry, Cleveland A.L.; Steve Carlton, Phila. N.L.
1973 Jim Palmer, Baltimore A.L.; Tom Seaver, New York N.L.
1974 Catfish Hunter, Oakland A.L.; Mike Marshall, Los Angeles N.L.
1975 Jim Palmer, Baltimore A.L.; Tom Seaver, New York N.L.
1976 Jim Palmer, Baltimore A.L.; Randy Jones, San Diego N.L.
1977 Sparky Lyle, N.Y., A.L.; Steve Carlton, Philadelphia N.L.
1978 Ron Guidry, N.Y., A.L.; Gaylord Perry, San Diego N.L.
1979 Mike Flanagan, Baltimore, A.L.; Bruce Sutter, Chicago, N.L.
1980 Steve Stone, Baltimore, A.L.; Steve Carlton, Philadelphia, N.L.
1981 Rollie Fingers, Milwaukee, A.L.; Fernando Valenzuela, Los Angeles, N.L.
1982 Pete Vuckovich, Milwaukee, A.L.; Steve Carlton, Philadelphia, N.L.
1983 LaMarr Hoyt, Chicago, A.L.; John Denny, Philadelphia, N.L.
1984 Willie Hernandez, Detroit, A.L.; Rick Sutcliffe, Chicago, N.L.
1985 Bret Saberhagen, A.L.; Dwight Gooden, N.L.
1986 Roger Clemens, A.L.; Mike Scott, N.L.
1987 Roger Clemens, A.L.; Steve Bedrosian, N.L.
1988 Frank Viola, A.L.; Orel Hershiser, N.L.
1989 Bret Saberhagen, A.L.; Mark Davis, N.L.
1990 Bob Welch, A.L.; Doug Drabek, N.L.
1991 Roger Clemens, A.L.; Tom Glavine, N.L.
1992 Dennis Eckersley, A.L.; Greg Maddox, N.L.

MAJOR LEAGUE LIFETIME RECORDS

(Through 1992)

Leading Pitchers—Wins

* Indicates left-handed pitcher.

		Yrs	GS	W	L	Pct
1.	Cy Young	22	815	511	313	.620
2.	Walter Johnson	21	666	416	279	.599
3.	Christy Mathewson	17	551	373	188	.665
	Grover Alexander	20	598	373	208	.642
5.	Warren Spahn*	21	665	363	245	.597
6.	Kid Nichols	15	561	361	208	.634
	Pud Galvin	14	682	361	308	.540
8.	Tim Keefe	14	594	342	225	.603
9.	Steve Carlton*	24	709	329	244	.574
10.	Eddie Plank*	17	527	327	193	.629
11.	John Clarkson	12	518	326	177	.648
12.	Don Sutton	23	756	324	256	.559
13.	**Nolan Ryan**	26	760	319	287	.526
14.	Phil Niekro	24	716	318	274	.537
15.	Gaylord Perry	22	690	314	265	.542
16.	Old Hoss Radbourn	12	503	311	194	.616
	Tom Seaver	20	647	311	205	.603
18.	Mickey Welch	13	549	308	209	.596
19.	Lefty Grove*	17	456	300	141	.680
	Early Wynn	23	612	300	244	.551
21.	Tommy John*	26	700	288	231	.555
22.	**Bert Blyleven**	22	685	287	250	.534
23.	Robin Roberts	19	609	286	245	.539
24.	Tony Mullane	13	505	285	220	.564
25.	Ferguson Jenkins	19	594	284	226	.557

NOTE: Players active in 1993 in boldfaces.

Pitchers Active in 1993

		Yrs	GS	W	L	Pct
1.	Nolan Ryan	26	760	319	287	.526
2.	Bert Blyleven	22	685	287	250	.534
3.	Jack Morris	16	477	237	168	.585
4.	Frank Tanana	20	585	233	219	.515
5.	Charlie Hough	23	385	202	191	.514
6.	Bob Welch	15	426	199	129	.607
7.	Dennis Martinez	17	442	193	156	.553
8.	Dennis Eckersley	18	361	181	145	.555
9.	John Candelaria	18	356	177	119	.598
10.	Dave Stieb	14	405	174	132	.569

Leading Batters, by Average

* Indicates left-handed hitter.

		Years	AB	H	Avg
1.	Ty Cobb*	24	11,429	4191	.367
2.	Rogers Hornsby	23	8,137	2930	.358
3.	Joe Jackson*	13	4,981	1774	.356
4.	Ed Delahanty	16	7,502	2591	.345
5.	Ted Williams*	19	7,706	2654	.344
6.	Tris Speaker*	22	10,208	3515	.344
7.	Billy Hamilton*	14	6,284	2163	.344
8.	Willie Keeler*	19	8,585	2947	.343
9.	Dan Brouthers*	19	6,711	2296	.342
10.	Babe Ruth*	22	8,399	2873	.342
11.	Harry Heilmann	17	7,787	2660	.342
12.	Pete Browning	13	4,820	1646	.341
13.	Bill Terry*	14	6,428	2193	.341
14.	George Sisler*	15	8,267	2812	.340
15.	Lou Gehrig*	17	8,001	2721	.340
16.	Jesse Burkett*	16	8,413	2853	.339
17.	Nap Lajoie	21	9,592	3244	.338
18.	**Wade Boggs***	11	6,213	2098	.338
19.	Riggs Stephenson	14	4,508	1515	.336
20.	Al Simmons	20	8,761	2927	.334
21.	Paul Waner*	20	9,459	3152	.333
22.	Eddie Collins*	25	9,949	3311	.333
23.	Stan Musial*	22	10,972	3630	.331
24.	Sam Thompson*	14	6,005	1986	.331
25.	Heinie Manush*	17	7,653	2524	.330

NOTE: Players active in 1993 in boldfaces.

Players Active in 1993

		Years	AB	H	Avg
1.	Wade Boggs*	11	6,213	2098	.338
2.	Tony Gwynn*	11	5,701	1864	.327
3.	Kirby Puckett	9	5,645	1812	.321
4.	Don Mattingly*	11	5,643	1754	.311
5.	George Brett*	20	9,789	3005	.307
6.	Mike Greenwell*	8	2,980	912	.306
7.	Paul Molitor	15	7,520	2281	.303
8.	Will Clark	7	3,778	1139	.301
9.	Ken Griffey, Jr.	4	2,165	652	.301
10.	Julio Franco	11	5,416	1630	.301

MAJOR LEAGUE INDIVIDUAL ALL-TIME RECORDS

(Through 1993)

Highest Batting Average—.442, James O'Neill, St. Louis, A.A., 1887; .438, Hugh Duffy, Boston, N.L., 1894 (Since 1900—.424, Rogers Hornsby, St. Louis, N.L., 1924; .422, Nap Lajoie, Phil., A.L., 1901)

Most Times at Bat—12,364, Henry Aaron, Milwaukee N.L., 1954–65; Atlanta N.L., 1966–74; Milwaukee A.L., 1975–76.

Most Years Batted .300 or Better—23, Ty Cobb, Detroit A.L., 1906–26, Philadelphia A.L., 1927–28.

Most hits—4,256, Pete Rose, Cincinnati 1963–79, Philadelphia 1980–83, Montreal 1984, Cincinnati 1984–86.

Most Hits, Season—257, George Sisler, St. Louis A.L., 1920.

Most Hits, Game (9 innings)—7, Wilbert Robinson, Baltimore N.L., 6 singles, 1 double, 1892. Rennie Stennett, Pittsburgh N.L., 4 singles, 2 doubles, 1 triple, 1975.

Most Hits, Game (extra innings)—9, John Burnett, Cleveland A.L., 18 innings, 7 singles, 2 doubles, 1932.

Most Hits in Succession—12, Mike Higgins, Boston A.L., in four games, 1938; Walt Dropo, Detroit A.L., in three games, 1952.

Most Consecutive Games Batted Safely—56, Joe DiMaggio, New York A.L., 1941.

Most Runs—2,244, Ty Cobb, Detroit A.L., 1905–26, Philadelphia A.L., 1927–28.

Most Runs, Season—196, William Hamilton, Philadelphia N.L., 1894. (Since 1900—177, Babe Ruth, New York A.L., 1921.)

Most Runs, Game—7, Guy Hecker, Louisville A.A., 1886. (Since 1900—6, by Mel Ott, New York N.L., 1934, 1944; Johnny Pesky, Boston A.L., 1946; Frank Torre, Milwaukee N.L., 1957.)

Most Runs Batted in—2,297, Henry Aaron, Milwaukee N.L., 1954–1965; Atlanta N.L., 1966–74; Milwaukee A.L., 1975–76.

Most Runs Batted in, Season—190, Hack Wilson, Chicago N.L., 1930.

Most Runs Batted In, Game—12, Jim Bottomley, St. Louis N.L., 1924, and Mark Whiten, St. Louis N.L., 1993.

Most Home Runs—755, Henry Aaron, Milwaukee N.L., 1954–1965; Atlanta N.L., 1966–74; Milwaukee A.L., 1975–76.

Most Home Runs, Season—61, Roger Maris, New York A.L., 1961 (162–game season); 60, Babe Ruth, New York A.L., 1927 (154–game season)

Most Home Runs with Bases Filled—23, Lou Gehrig, New York A.L., 1927–39.

Most 2–Base Hits—793, Tris Speaker, Boston A.L., 1907–15, Cleveland A.L., 1916–26, Washington A.L., 1927, Philadelphia A.L., 1928.

Most 2–Base Hits, Season—67, Earl Webb, Boston A.L., 1931.

Most 2–base Hits, Game—4, by many.

Most 3–Base Hits—312, Sam Crawford, Cincinnati N.L., 1899–1902, Detroit A.L., 1903–17.

Most 3–Base Hits, Season—36, Owen Wilson, Pittsburgh N.L., 1912.

Most 3–Base Hits, Game—4, George Strief, Philadelphia A.A., 1885; William Joyce, New York N.L., 1897. (Since 1900—3, by many.)

Most Games Played—3,562, Pete Rose, Cincinnati N.L., Philadelphia N.L., Montreal N.L., 1964–86

Most Consecutive Games Played—2,130, Lou Gehrig, New York A.L., 1925–39.

Most Bases on Balls—2,056, Babe Ruth, Boston A.L., 1914–19; New York A.L., 1920–34, Boston N.L., 1935.

Most Bases on Balls, Season—170, Babe Ruth, New York A.L., 1923.

Most bases on Balls, Game—6, Jimmy Foxx, Boston A.L., 1938.

Most Strikeouts, Season—189, Bobby Bonds, San Francisco N.L., 1970.

Most Strikeouts, Game (9 innings)—5, by many.

Most Strikeouts, Game (extra innings)—6, Carl Weilman, St Louis A.L., 15 innings, 1913; Don Hoak, Chicago N.L., 17 innings, 1956; Fred Reichardt, California A.L., 17, innings, 1966; Billy Cowan, California A.L., 20, 1971; Cecil Cooper, Boston A.L., 15, 1974.

Most pinch—hits, lifetime—150, Manny Mota, S.F., 1962; Pitt., 1963–68; Montreal, 1969; L.A., 1969–80, N.L.

Most Pinch–hits, season—25, Jose Morales, Montreal N.L., 1976.

Most consecutive pinch–hits—9, Dave Philley, Phil., N.L., 1958 (8), 1959 (1).

Most pinch–hit home runs, lifetime—18, Gerald Lynch, Pitt.–Cin. N.L., 1957–66.

Most pinch–hit home runs, season—6, Johnny Frederick, Brooklyn, N.L., 1932.

Most stolen bases, lifetime (since 1900)—1,042, Rickey Henderson,* 1979–84 Oakland, 1985–89 New York (A.L.), 1989–92 Oakland

Most stolen bases, season—156, Harry Stovey, Phil., A.A., 1888. Since 1900: 130, Rickey Henderson, Oak., A.L., 1982; 118, Lou Brock, St. Louis, N.L., 1974.

Most stolen bases, game—7, George Gore, Chicago N.L. 1881; William Hamilton, Philadelphia N.L. 1894. (Since 1900—6, Eddie Collins, Philadelphia A.L., 1912.) and Otis Nixon*, Atlanta N.L., 1991.

Most time stealing home, lifetime—35, Ty Cobb, Detroit–Phil. A.L., 1905–28.

*Still active coming into 1994 season.

MAJOR LEAGUE ALL–TIME PITCHING RECORDS

(Through 1993)

Most Games Won—511, Cy Young, Cleveland N.L., 1890–98, St. Louis N.L., 1899–1900, Boston A.L., 1901–08, Cleveland A.L., 1909–11, Boston N.L., 1911.

Most Games Won, Season—60, Hoss Radbourne, Providence N.L., 1884. (Since 1900—41, Jack Chesbro, New York A.L., 1904.)

Most Consecutive Games Won—24, Carl Hubbell, New York N.L., 1936 (16) and 1937 (8).

Most Consecutive Games Won, Season—19, Tim Keefe, New York N.L., 1888; Rube Marquard, New York N.L., 1912.

Most Years Won 20 or More Games—16, Cy Young, Cleveland N.L., 1891–98, St. Louis N.L., 1899–1900, Boston A.L., 1901–04, 1907–08.

Most Shutouts—113, Walter Johnson, Wash. A.L., 1907–27.

Most Shutouts, Season—16, Grover Alexander, Philadelphia N.L., 1916.

Most Consecutive Shutouts—6, Don Drysdale, Los Angeles, N.L., 1968.

Most Consecutive Scoreless Innings—59, Orel Hershiser, Los Angeles Dodgers, 1988.

Most Strikeouts—5,714, Nolan Ryan, New York N.L., California A.L., Houston N.L., 1968–1988 Texas, 1989–93.

Most Strikeouts, Season—505, Matthew Kilroy, Baltimore A.A., 1886. (Since 1900—383, Nolan Ryan, California, A.L., 1973.)

Most Strikeouts, Game—21, Tom Cheney, Washington A.L., 1962, 16 innings. Nine innings: 20, Roger Clemens, Boston, A.L., 1986; 19, Charles McSweeney, Providence N.L., 1884; Hugh Dailey, Chicago U.A., 1884. (Since 1900—19, Steve Carlton, St. Louis N.L. vs. New York, Sept. 15, 1969; Tom Seaver, New York N.L. vs. San Diego, April 22, 1970; Nolan Ryan, California A.L. vs. Boston, Aug. 12, 1974; David Cone, New York N.L. vs. Philadelphia, Oct. 6, 1991.)

Most Consecutive Strikeouts—10, Tom Seaver, New York N.L. vs. San Diego, April 22, 1970.

Most Games, Season—106, Mike Marshall, Los Angeles, N.L., 1974.

Most Complete Games, Season—74, William White, Cincinnati N.L., 1879. (Since 1900—48, Jack Chesbro, New York A.L., 1904.)

ROOKIE OF THE YEAR

(Baseball Writers Association selections)

American League

1949 Roy Sievers, St. Louis
1950 Walt Dropo, Boston
1951 Gil McDougald, New York
1952 Harry Byrd, Philadelphia
1953 Harvey Kuenn, Detroit
1954 Bob Grim, New York
1955 Herb Score, Cleveland
1956 Luis Aparicio, Chicago
1957 Tony Kubek, New York
1958 Albie Pearson, Washington
1959 Bob Allison, Washington
1960 Ron Hansen, Baltimore
1961 Don Schwall, Boston
1962 Tom Tresh, New York
1963 Gary Peters, Chicago
1964 Tony Oliva, Minnesota
1965 Curt Blefary, Baltimore
1966 Tommy Agee, Chicago
1967 Rod Carew, Minnesota
1968 Stan Bahnsen, New York
1969 Lou Piniella, Kansas City
1970 Thurman Munson, New York
1971 Chris Chambliss, Cleveland
1972 Carlton Fisk, Boston
1973 Alonzo Bumbry, Baltimore
1974 Mike Hargrove, Texas
1975 Fred Lynn, Boston
1976 Mark Fidrych, Detroit
1977 Eddie Murray, Baltimore
1978 Lou Whitaker, Detroit
1979 Alfredo Griffin, Toronto
1979 John Castino, Minnesota
1980 Joe Charboneau, Cleveland
1981 Dave Righetti, New York
1982 Cal Ripken, Jr., Baltimore
1983 Ron Kittle, Chicago
1984 Alvin Davis, Seattle
1985 Ozzie Guillen, Chicago
1986 Jose Canseco, Oakland
1987 Mark McGwire, Oakland
1988 Walter Weiss, Oakland
1989 Gregg Olson, Baltimore
1990 Sandy Alomar Jr., Cleveland
1991 Chuck Knoblauch, Minnesota
1992 Pat Listach, Milwaukee

National League

1949 Don Newcombe, Brooklyn
1950 Sam Jethroe, Boston
1951 Willie Mays, New York
1952 Joe Black, Brooklyn
1953 Jim Gilliam, Brooklyn
1954 Wally Moon, St. Louis
1955 Bill Virdon, St. Louis
1956 Frank Robinson, Cincinnati
1957 Jack Sanford, Philadelphia
1958 Orlando Cepeda, San Francisco
1959 Willie McCovey, San Francisco
1960 Frank Howard, Los Angeles
1961 Billy Williams, Chicago
1962 Ken Hubbs, Chicago
1963 Pete Rose, Cincinnati
1964 Richie Allen, Philadelphia
1965 Jim Lefebvre, Los Angeles
1966 Tommy Helms, Cincinnati
1967 Tom Seaver, New York
1968 Johnny Bench, Cincinnati
1969 Ted Sizemore, Los Angeles
1970 Carl Morton, Montreal
1971 Earl Williams, Atlanta
1972 Jon Matlack, New York
1973 Gary Matthews, San Francisco
1974 Bake McBride, St. Louis
1975 John Montefusco, San Francisco
1976 Pat Zachry, Cincinnati
1976 Bruce Metzger, San Diego
1977 Andre Dawson, Montreal
1978 Bob Horner, Atlanta
1979 Rick Sutcliffe, Los Angeles
1980 Steve Howe, Los Angeles
1981 Fernando Valenzuela, Los Angeles
1982 Steve Sax, Los Angeles
1983 Darryl Strawberry, New York
1984 Dwight Gooden, New York
1985 Vince Coleman, St. Louis
1986 Todd Worrell, St. Louis
1987 Benito Santiago, San Diego
1988 Chris Sabo, Cincinnati
1989 Jerome Walton, Chicago
1990 Dave Justice, Atlanta
1991 Jeff Baguell, Houston
1992 Eric Karros, Los Angeles

MAJOR LEAGUE ATTENDANCE RECORDS

(Through 1993)

Single game—78,672, San Francisco at Los Angeles (N.L.), April 18, 1958. (At Memorial Coliseum.)

Doubleheader—84,587, New York at Cleveland (A.L.), Sept. 12, 1954.

Night—78,382, Chicago at Cleveland (A.L.), Aug. 20, 1948.

Season, home—4,483,350, Colorado (N.L.), 1993.

Season, league—36,912,502, National League, 1993.

Season, both leagues—70,257,938, 1993.

Season, road—2,461,240, New York (A.L.), 1980.

World Series, single game—92,706, Chicago (A.L.) at Los Angeles (N.L.), Oct. 6, 1959.

World Series, all games (6)—420,784, Chicago (A.L.) and Los Angeles (N.L.), 1959.

MOST HOME RUNS IN ONE SEASON
(45 or More)

HR	Player/Team	Year
61	Roger Maris, New York (AL)	1961
60	Babe Ruth, New York (AL)	1927
59	Babe Ruth, New York (AL)	1921
58	Jimmy Foxx, Philadelphia (AL)	1932
58	Hank Greenberg, Detroit (AL)	1938
56	Hack Wilson, Chicago (NL)	1930
54	Babe Ruth, New York (AL)	1920
54	Babe Ruth, New York (AL)	1928
54	Ralph Kiner, Pittsburgh (NL)	1949
54	Mickey Mantle, New York (AL)	1961
52	Mickey Mantle, New York (AL)	1956
52	Willie Mays, San Francisco (NL)	1965
52	George Foster, Cincinnati (NL)	1977
51	Ralph Kiner, Pittsburgh (NL)	1947

HR	Player/Team	Year
51	John Mize, New York (NL)	1947
51	Willie Mays, New York (NL)	1955
51	Cecil Fielder (AL)	1990
50	Jimmy Foxx, Boston (AL)	1938
49	Babe Ruth, New York (AL)	1930
49	Lou Gehrig, New York (AL)	1934
49	Lou Gehrig, New York (AL)	1936
49	Ted Kluszewski, Cincinnati (NL)	1954
49	Willie Mays, San Francisco (NL)	1962
49	Harmon Killebrew, Minnesota (AL)	1964
49	Frank Robinson, Baltimore (AL)	1966
49	Harmon Killebrew, Minnesota (AL)	1969
49	Mark McGwire, Oakland (AL)	1987
49	Andre Dawson, Chicago (NL)	1987
48	Jimmy Foxx, Philadelphia (AL)	1933
48	Frank Howard, Washington (AL)	1969
48	Harmon Killebrew, Minnesota (AL)	1962
48	Willie Stargell, Pittsburgh (NL)	1971
48	Dave Kingman, Chicago (NL)	1979
48	Mike Schmidt, Philadelphia (NL)	1980
47	Babe Ruth, New York (AL)	1926
47	Ralph Kiner, Pittsburgh (NL)	1950
47	Ed Mathews, Milwaukee (NL)	1953
47	Ernie Banks, Chicago (NL)	1958
47	Willie Mays, San Francisco (NL)	1964
47	Henry Aaron, Atlanta (NL)	1971
47	Reggie Jackson, Oakland (AL)	1969
47	George Bell, Toronto (AL)	1987
47	Kevin Mitchell, San Francisco (NL)	1989
46	Babe Ruth, New York (AL)	1924
46	Babe Ruth, New York, (AL)	1929
46	Babe Ruth, New York (AL)	1931
46	Lou Gehrig, New York (AL)	1931
46	Joe DiMaggio, New York (AL)	1937
46	Ed Mathews, Milwaukee (NL)	1959
46	Orlando Cepeda, San Francisco (NL)	1961
46	Jim Rice, Boston (AL)	1978
46	Juan Gonzalez, Texas (AL)	1993
46	Barry Bonds, San Francisco (NL)	1993
45	Harmon Killebrew, Minnesota (AL)	1963
45	Willie McCovey, San Francisco (NL)	1969
45	Johnny Bench, Cincinnati (NL)	1970
45	Gorman Thomas, Milwaukee (AL)	1979
45	Henry Aaron, Milwaukee (NL)	1962
45	Ken Griffey, Jr., Seattle (AL)	1993

MAJOR LEAGUE BASEBALL—1993

AMERICAN LEAGUE

(Final Standing—1993)

EASTERN DIVISION

Team	W	L	Pct	GB
Toronto Blue Jays	95	67	.586	—
New York Yankees	88	74	.543	7
Baltimore Orioles	85	77	.525	10
Detroit Tigers	85	77	.525	10
Boston Red Sox	80	82	.494	15
Cleveland Indians	76	86	.469	19
Milwaukee Brewers	69	93	.426	26

WESTERN DIVISION

Team	W	L	Pct	GB
Chicago White Sox	94	68	.580	—
Texas Rangers	86	76	.531	8
Kansas City Royals	84	78	.519	10
Seattle Mariners	82	80	.506	12
California Angels	71	91	.438	23
Minnesota Twins	71	91	.438	23
Oakland Athletics	68	94	.420	26

AMERICAN LEAGUE LEADERS—1993

Batting—John Olerud, Toronto	.363
Runs—Rafael Palmeiro, Texas	124
Hits—Paul Molitor, Toronto	211
Runs batted in—Albert Belle, Cleveland	129
Triples—Lance Johnson, Chicago	14
Doubles—John Olerud, Toronto	54
Home runs—Juan Gonzalez, Texas	46
Stolen bases—Kenny Lofton, Cleveland	70
Total bases—Ken Griffey, Jr., Seattle	359
Slugging percentage—Juan Gonzalez, Texas	.632
On-base percentage—John Olerud, Toronto	.473

Pitching

Victories—Jack McDowell, Chicago	22
Earned run average—Kevin Appier, Kansas City	2.56
Strikeouts—Randy Johnson, Seattle	308
Shutouts—Jack McDowell, Chicago	4
Complete games—Chuck Finley, California	13
Saves—Jeff Montgomery, Kansas City and Duane Ward, Toronto	45
Innings pitched—Cal Eldred, Milwaukee	258

NATIONAL LEAGUE

(Final Standing—1993)

EASTERN DIVISION

Team	W	L	Pct	GB
Philadelphia Phillies	97	65	.599	—
Montreal Expos	94	68	.580	3
St. Louis Cardinals	87	75	.537	10
Chicago Cubs	84	78	.519	13
Pittsburgh Pirates	75	87	.463	22
Florida Marlins	64	98	.395	33
New York Mets	59	103	.364	38

WESTERN DIVISION

Team	W	L	Pct	GB
Atlanta Braves	104	58	.642	—
San Francisco Giants	103	59	.636	1
Houston Astros	85	77	.525	19
Los Angeles Dodgers	81	81	.500	23
Cincinnati Reds	73	89	.451	31
Colorado Rockies	67	95	.414	37
San Diego Padres	61	101	.377	43

NATIONAL LEAGUE LEADERS—1993

Batting—Andres Galarraga, Colorado	..370
Runs—Lenny Dykstra, Philadelphia	143
Hits—Lenny Dykstra, Philadelphia	194
Runs batted in—Barry Bonds, San Francisco	123
Triples—Steve Finley, Houston	13
Doubles—Charlie Hayes, Colorado	45
Home runs—Barry Bonds, San Francisco	46
Stolen bases—Chuck Carr, Florida	58
Total bases—Barry Bonds, San Francisco	365
Slugging percentage—Barry Bonds, San Francisco	.677
On-base percentage—Barry Bonds, San Francisco	.458

Pitching

Victories—Tom Glavine, Atlanta and John Burkett, San Francisco	22
Earned run average—Greg Maddux, Atlanta	2.36
Strikeouts—Jose Rijo, Cincinnati	227
Shutouts—Pete Harnisch, Houston	4
Complete games—Greg Maddux, Atlanta	8
Saves—Randy Myers, Chicago	53
Innings pitched—Greg Maddux, Atlanta	267

AMERICAN LEAGUE AVERAGES—1993

Team Batting

	AB	R	H	HR	RBI	Pct
New York	5615	821	1568	178	793	.279
Toronto	5579	847	1556	159	796	.278
Detroit	5620	899	1546	178	853	.275
Cleveland	5619	790	1547	141	747	.275
Texas	5510	835	1472	181	780	.267
Baltimore	5508	786	1470	157	744	.266
Chicago	5483	776	1454	162	731	.265
Minnesota	5601	693	1480	121	642	.264
Boston	5496	686	1451	114	644	.264
Kansas City	5522	675	1455	125	641	.263
Seattle	5494	734	1429	161	681	.260
California	5391	684	1399	114	644	.259
Milwaukee	5525	733	1426	125	688	.258
Oakland	5543	715	1408	158	679	.254

Individual Batting

(Based on 315 plate appearances.)

Player/Team	AB	R	H	HR	RBI	Avg
Olerud Tor	551	109	200	24	107	.363
James NY	343	62	114	7	36	.332
Molitor Tor	636	121	211	22	111	.332
Trammell Det	401	72	132	12	60	.329
RAlomar Tor	589	109	192	17	93	.326
Lofton Cle	569	116	185	1	42	.325
Baerga Cle	624	105	200	21	114	.321
Thomas Chi	549	106	174	41	128	.317
Greenwell Bos	540	77	170	13	72	.315
Phillips Det	566	113	177	7	57	.313
Baines Bal	416	64	130	20	78	.312
LJohnson Chi	540	75	168	0	47	.311
O'Neill NY	498	71	155	20	75	.311
Gonzalez Tex	536	105	166	46	118	.310
Hoiles Bal	419	80	130	29	82	.310
Hamilton Mil	520	74	161	9	48	.310
Griffey Jr Sea	582	113	180	45	109	.309
TFernandez Tor	353	45	108	4	50	.306
Raines Chi	415	75	127	16	54	.306
Stanley NY	423	70	129	26	84	.305
Harper Min	530	52	161	12	73	.304
Pagliarulo Bal	370	55	112	9	44	.303
Boggs NY	560	83	169	2	59	.302
Fryman Det	607	98	182	22	97	.300
Gwynn KC	287	36	86	1	25	.300
MVaughn Bos	539	86	160	29	101	.297
Puckett Min	622	89	184	22	89	.296
Palmeiro Tex	597	124	176	37	105	.295

Individual Pitching

(Based on 12 decisions)

Player/Club	IP	H	BB	SO	W	L	ERA
Montgomery KC	87	65	23	66	7	5	2.27
Appier KC	238	183	81	186	18	8	2.56
Alvarez Chi	207	168	122	155	15	8	2.95
Key NY	236	219	43	173	18	6	3.00
Cox Tor	83	73	29	84	7	6	3.12
Fernandez Chi	247	221	67	169	18	9	3.13
Viola Bos	183	180	72	91	11	8	3.14
Finley Cal	251	243	82	187	16	14	3.15
Langston Cal	256	220	85	196	16	11	3.20
RJohnson Sea	255	185	99	308	19	8	3.24
Darwin Bos	229	196	49	130	15	11	3.26
Cone KC	254	205	114	191	11	14	3.33
McDowell Chi	256	261	69	158	22	10	3.37
McDonald Bal	220	185	86	171	13	14	3.39
Pavlik Tex	166	151	80	131	12	6	3.41
Moyer Bal	152	154	38	90	12	9	3.43
Bosio Sea	164	138	59	119	9	9	3.45
Hanson Sea	215	215	60	163	11	12	3.47
Bere Chi	142	109	81	129	12	5	3.47
Gordon KC	155	125	77	143	12	6	3.58
Brown Tex	233	228	74	142	15	12	3.59
Harris Bos	112	95	60	103	6	7	3.77
Frohwirth Bal	96	91	44	50	6	7	3.83
Hentgen Tor	216	215	74	122	19	9	3.87
Quantrill Bos	138	151	44	66	6	12	3.91
Guzman Tor	221	211	110	194	14	3	3.99
Eldred Mil	258	232	91	180	16	16	4.01
Banks Min	171	186	78	138	11	12	4.04

Team Pitching

	ERA	H	ER	BB	SO	ShO	SA
Chicago	3.70	1398	598	566	974	11	48
Boston	3.77	1379	609	552	997	11	44
Kansas City	4.04	1379	649	571	985	6	48
Seattle	4.20	1421	679	605	1083	10	41
Toronto	4.20	1441	674	620	1023	11	50
Texas	4.27	1476	684	562	957	6	45
Baltimore	4.31	1427	691	579	900	10	42
California	4.34	1482	690	550	843	6	41
New York	4.34	1467	695	552	899	13	38
Milwaukee	4.45	1511	716	522	810	6	29
Cleveland	4.57	1591	735	591	888	8	45
Detroit	4.64	1547	742	542	828	7	36
Minnesota	4.71	1591	756	514	901	3	44
Oakland	4.90	1551	791	680	864	2	42

NATIONAL LEAGUE AVERAGES—1993

Team Batting

	AB	R	H	HR	RBI	Pct
San Francisco	5557	808	1534	168	759	.276
Philadelphia	5685	877	1555'	156	811	.273
Colorado	5517	758	1507	142	704	.273
St. Louis	5551	758	1508	118	724	.271
Chicago	5627	738	1521	161	706	.270
Pittsburgh	5549	707	1482	110	664	.267
Houston	5464	716	1459	138	656	.267
Cincinnati	5517	722	1457	137	669	.264
Atlanta	5515	767	1444	169	712	.261
Los Angeles	5588	675	1458	130	639	.260
Montreal	5493	732	1410	122	682	.256
San Diego	5502	679	1386	153	633	.251
New York	5448	672	1350	158	632	.247
Florida	5475	581	1356	94	542	.247

Individual Batting

(Based on 315 plate appearances.)

Player/Team	AB	R	H	HR	RBI	Avg
Galarraga Col	470	71	174	22	98	.370
Gwynn SD	489	70	175	7	59	.358
Jefferies StL	544	89	186	16	83	.342
Mitchell Cin	323	56	110	19	64	.341
Bonds SF	539	129	181	46	123	.336
Grace Chi	594	86	193	14	98	.325
Bagwell Hou	535	76	171	20	88	.320
Kelly Cin	320	44	102	9	35	.319
Piazza LA	547	81	174	35	112	.318
Eisenreich Phi	362	51	115	7	54	.318
Morris Cin	379	48	120	7	49	.317
Kruk Phi	535	100	169	14	85	.316
Larkin Cin	384	57	121	8	51	.315
Merced Pit	447	68	140	8	70	.313
RbThompson SF	494	85	154	19	65	.312
Bichette Col	538	93	167	21	89	.310
JBell Pit	604	102	187	9	51	.310
VanSlyke Pit	323	42	100	8	50	.310
Sandberg Chi	456	67	141	9	45	.309
Gilkey StL	557	99	170	16	70	.305
Hayes Col	573	89	175	25	98	.305
Blauser Atl	597	110	182	15	73	.305
Dykstra Phi	637	143	194	19	66	.305

	AB	R	H	HR	RBI	Pct
Wilkins Chi	446	78	135	30	73	.303
McGee SF	475	53	143	4	46	.301
Gonzalez Hou	540	82	162	15	72	.300
DSmith Chi	310	51	93	11	35	.300
Slaught Pit	377	34	113	10	55	.300
Grissom Mon	630	104	188	19	95	.298

Individual Pitching
(Based on 12 decisions)

Player/Team	IP	H	BB	SO	W	L	ERA
Wetteland Mon	85	58	28	113	9	3	1.37
Fassero Mon	149	119	54	140	12	5	2.29
Gott LA	77	71	17	67	4	8	2.32
GMaddux Atl	267	228	52	197	20	10	2.36
Rijo Cin	257	218	62	227	14	9	2.48
PJMartinez LA	107	76	57	119	10	5	2.61
Portugal Hou	208	194	77	131	18	4	2.77
Swift SF	232	195	55	157	21	8	2.82
Bautista Chi	111	105	27	63	10	3	2.82
Avery Atl	223	216	43	125	18	6	2.94
Rojas Mon	88	80	30	48	5	8	2.95
Harnisch Hou	217	171	79	185	16	9	2.98
MJackson SF	77	58	24	70	6	6	3.03
GeHarris SD	59	57	37	39	6	6	3.03
Candiotti LA	213	192	71	155	8	10	3.12
Glavine Atl	239	236	90	120	22	6	3.20
KHill Mon	183	163	74	90	9	7	3.23
Mulholland Phi	191	177	40	116	12	9	3.25
Saberhagen NY	139	131	17	93	7	7	3.29
Aquino Fla	110	115	40	67	6	8	3.42
TGreene Phi	200	175	62	167	16	4	3.42
RMartinez LA	211	202	104	127	10	12	3.44
Gooden NY	208	188	61	149	12	15	3.45
Kile Hou	171	152	69	141	15	8	3.51
Astacio LA	186	165	68	122	14	9	3.57
Hershiser LA	215	201	72	141	12	14	3.59
TWilson SF	110	110	40	57	7	5	3.60
Smoltz Atl	243	208	100	208	15	11	3.62

Team Pitching

	ERA	H	ER	BB	SO	ShO	SA
Atlanta	3.13	1297	507	480	1036	16	46
Houston	3.49	1363	559	467	1056	14	42
Los Angeles	3.50	1406	573	567	1043	9	36
Montreal	3.54	1369	574	521	934	7	61
San Francisco	3.61	1385	585	442	982	9	50
Philadelphia	3.95	1419	647	573	1117	11	46
New York	4.04	1483	647	434	867	8	22
St. Louis	4.08	1553	660	383	775	7	54
Florida	4.13	1437	661	598	945	5	48
Chicago	4.18	1514	674	470	905	5	56
San Diego	4.22	1470	675	558	957	6	32
Cincinnati	4.50	1510	718	508	996	8	37
Pittsburgh	4.76	1557	766	485	832	5	34
Colorado	5.40	1664	860	609	913	0	35

MAJOR LEAGUE BASEBALL—1993

AMERICAN LEAGUE PLAYOFFS—1993
(Toronto Blue Jays Win Series, 4 Games to 2)

1st game, Chicago, Ill., Oct. 5, 1993

Toronto	000	230	200	—	7	17	1
Chicago	000	300	000	—	3	6	1

Guzman, Cox, Ward; McDowell, DeLeon, Radinsky, McCaskill.
Winner: Guzman. Loser: McDowell. Attendance: 46,246.

2nd game, Chicago, Ill., Oct. 6, 1993

Toronto	100	200	000	—	3	8	0
Chicago	100	000	000	—	1	7	2

Stewart, Leiter, Ward; Fernandez, Hernandez.
Winner: Stewart. Loser: Fernandez. Attendance: 46,101.

3rd game, Toronto, Canada, Oct. 8, 1993

Chicago	005	100	000	—	6	12	0
Toronto	001	000	000	—	1	7	1

Alvarez; Hentgen, Cox, Eichhorn, Castillo.
Winner: Alvarez. Loser: Hentgen. Attendance: 51,783.

4th game, Toronto, Canada, Oct. 9, 1993

Chicago	020	003	101	—	7	11	0
Toronto	003	001	000	—	4	9	0

Bere, Belcher, McCaskill, Radinsky, Hernandez; Stottlemyre, Leiter, Timlin.
Winner: Belcher. Loser: Stottlemyre. Attendance: 51,889.

5th game, Toronto, Canada, Oct. 10, 1993

Chicago	000	010	002	—	3	5	1
Toronto	111	100	10x	—	5	14	0

McDowell, DeLeon, Radinsky, Hernandez; Guzman, Castillo, Ward.
Winner: Guzman. Loser: McDowell. Attendance: 51,375

6th game, Chicago, Ill., Oct. 12, 1993

Toronto	020	100	003	—	6	10	0
Chicago	002	000	001	—	3	5	3

Stewart, Ward; Fernandez, McCaskill, Radinsky, Hernandez.
Winner: Stewart. Loser: Fernandez. Attendance: 45,527.

NATIONAL LEAGUE PLAYOFFS—1993
(Philadelphia Wins Series, 4 Games to 2)

1st game, Philadelphia, Pa., Oct. 6, 1993

Atlanta	001	100	001	0—	3	9	0
Philadelphia	100	101	000	1—	4	9	1

Avery, Mercker, McMichael; Schilling, Williams.
Winner: Williams. Loser: McMichael. Attendance: 62,012

2nd game, Philadelphia, Pa., Oct. 7, 1993

Atlanta	206	010	041	—	14	16	0
Philadelphia	000	200	001	—	3	7	2

Maddux, Stanton, Wohlers; Greene, Thigpen, Rivera, Mason, West, Andersen.
Winner: Maddux. Loser: Greene. Attendance: 62,436

3rd game, Atlanta, Ga., Oct. 9, 1993

Philadelphia	000	101	011	—	4	10	1
Atlanta	000	005	40x	—	9	12	0

Mulholland, Mason, Andersen, West, Thigpen; Glavine, Mercker, McMichael.
Winner: Glavine. Loser: Mulholland. Attendance: 52,032

4th game, Atlanta, Ga., Oct. 10, 1993

Philadelphia	000	200	000	—	2	8	1
Atlanta	010	000	000	—	1	10	1

Jackson, Williams; Smoltz, Mercker, Wohlers.
Winner: Jackson. Loser: Smoltz. Attendance: 52,032.

5th game, Atlanta, Ga., Oct. 11, 1993

Philadelphia	100	100	001	1—	4	6	1
Atlanta	000	000	003	0—	3	7	1

Schilling, Williams, Andersen; Avery, Mercker, McMichael, Wohlers.
Wiinner: Williams. Loser: Wohlers. Attendance: 52,032

6th game, Philadelphia, Pa., Oct. 13, 1993

Atlanta	000	010	200	—	3	5	3
Philadelphia	002	022	00x	—	6	7	1

Maddux, Mercker, McMichael, Wohlers; Greene, West, Williams.
Winner: Greene. Loser: Maddux. Attendance: 62,502

WORLD SERIES—1993

1st Game—Toronto, Oct. 16
Toronto 8, Philadelphia 5

PHILADELPHIA (N)	AB	R	H	RBI	TORONTO (A)	AB	R	H	RBI
Dykstra cf	4	1	1	0	RHenderson lf	3	1	1	0
Duncan 2b	5	2	3	0	White cf	4	3	2	2
Kruk 1b	4	2	3	2	RAlomar 2b	4	0	1	2
DHollins 3b	4	0	0	0	Carter rf	3	1	1	1
Daulton c	4	0	1	1	Olerud 1b	3	2	2	1
Eisenreich rf	5	0	1	1	Molitor dh	4	0	1	1
RJordan dh	5	0	1	0	TFernandez ss	3	0	0	1
MThompson lf	3	0	0	0	Sprague 3b	4	0	1	0
Incaviglia ph-lf	1	0	0	0	Borders c	4	1	1	0
Stocker ss	3	0	1	0					
Totals	**38**	**5**	**11**	**4**	**Totals**	**32**	**8**	**10**	**8**

Philadelphia	201	010	001	—	5	11	1
Toronto	021	011	30x	—	8	10	3

E—MThompson (1), RAlomar (1), Carter (1), Sprague (1). LOB—Philadelphia 11, Toronto 4. 2B—White (1), RAlomar (1). 3B—Duncan (1). HR—White (1) off Schilling, Olerud (1) off Schilling. RBI—Kruk 2 (2), Daulton (1), Eisenreich (1), White 2 (2). RAlomar 2 (2), Carter (1), Olerud (1), Molitor (1), TFernandez (1). SB—Dykstra (1), Duncan (1), RAlomar (1). CS—TFernandez (1). SF—Carter. GIDP—MThompson, White. RLISP—Philadelphia 5, Toronto 2. RMU—DHollins, TFernandez. DP—Philadelphia 1, Toronto 1.

	IP	H	R	ER	BB	SO	NP	ERA
Philadelphia								
Schilling L, 0–1	6 1/3	8	7	6	2	3	99	8.53
West	0	2	1	1	0	0	12	
Andersen	2/3	0	0	0	1	1	7	0.00
Mason	1	0	0	0	0	1	11	0.00
Toronto								
Guzman	5	5	4	4	4	6	116	7.20
ALeiter W, 1–0	2 2/3	4	0	0	1	2	56	0.00
DWard S, 1	1 1/3	2	1	0	0	3	30	0.00

West pitched to 2 batters in the 7th. Inherited runners scored—West 2–2, Andersen 1–0, DWard 2–0. IBB—off Andersen (Olerud) 1, off Guzman (Daulton) 1. WP—Guzman. PB—Daulton. Time of game—3:27. Attendance—52,011.

2nd Game—Toronto, Oct. 17
Philadelphia 6, Toronto 4

PHILADELPHIA (N)	AB	R	H	RBI	TORONTO (A)	AB	R	H	RBI
Dykstra cf	4	2	2	1	RHenderson lf	3	0	0	0
Duncan 2b	4	1	1	0	White cf	4	0	1	0
Kruk 2b	5	1	2	1	Molitor dh	3	2	2	0
DHollins 3b	4	1	2	1	Carter rf	4	1	1	2
Batiste 3b	0	0	0	0	Olerud 1b	3	0	0	1
Daulton c	5	0	1	0	RAlomar 2b	3	1	1	0
Eisenreich rf	4	1	1	3	TFernandez ss	3	0	2	1
Incaviglia lf	4	0	1	0	Sprague 3b	4	0	0	0
MThompson					Griffin pr	0	0	0	0
pr-lf	0	0	0	0	Borders c	4	0	1	0
RJordan dh	4	0	1	0					
Stocker ss	3	0	1	0					
Totals	**37**	**6**	**12**	**6**	**Totals**	**31**	**4**	**8**	**4**

Philadelphia	005	000	100	—	6	12	0
Toronto	000	201	010	—	4	8	0

LOB—Philadelphia 9, Toronto 5. 2B—White (2), Molitor (1), TFernandez (1). HR—Carter (1) off Mulholland, Dykstra (1) off Castillo, Eisenreich (1) off Stewart. RBI—Dykstra (1), Kruk (3), DHollins (1), Eisenreich 3 (4), Carter 2 (3), Olerud (2), TFernandez (2). SB—Molitor (1), RAlomar (2). CS—Stocker (1), RHenderson (1), RAlomar (1). SF—Olerud. GIDP—Eisenreich, Borders. RLISP—Philadelphia 6, Toronto 2. RMU—Kruk, Daulton 2, RJordan. DP—Philadelphia 1, Toronto 1.

	IP	H	R	ER	BB	SO	NP	ERA
Philadelphia								
Mulholland W, 1–0	5 2/3	7	3	3	2	4	105	4.76
Mason	1 2/3	1	1	1	0	2	24	3.38
MtWilliams S, 1	1 2/3	0	0	0	2	0	31	0.00
Toronto								
Stewart L, 0–1	6	6	5	5	4	6	122	7.50
Castillo	1	3	1	1	0	0	21	9.00
Eichhorn	1/3	1	0	0	1	0	15	0.00
Timlin	1 2/3	2	0	0	0	2	22	0.00

Inherited runners scored—Mason 1–0, MtWilliams 1–1, Timlin 2–0. WP—Stewart. Balk—Stewart. Time of game—3:35. Attendance—52,062.

3rd Game—Philadelphia, Oct. 19
Toronto 10, Philadelphia 3

TORONTO (A)	AB	R	H	RBI	PHILADELPHIA (N)	AB	R	H	RBI
RHenderson lf	4	2	2	0	Dykstra cf	5	0	1	0
White cf	4	2	1	1	Duncan 2b	5	0	2	1
Molitor 1b	4	3	3	3	Kruk 1b	3	1	2	0
Carter rf	4	1	1	1	Dhollins 3b	3	0	0	0
RAlomar 2b	5	2	4	2	Daulton c	3	0	0	0
TFernandez ss	3	0	2	2	Eisenreich rf	4	0	1	1
Sprague 3b	4	0	0	1	Incaviglia lf	3	0	0	0
Borders c	4	0	0	0	Thigpen p	0	0	0	0
Hentgen p	3	0	0	0	Morandini ph	0	0	0	0
Cox p	1	0	0	0	Andersen p	0	0	0	0
DWard p	0	0	0	0	Stocker ss	4	0	1	0
					DnJackson p	1	0	0	0
					Chamberlain ph	1	0	0	0
					Rivera p	0	0	0	0
					MThompson lf	2	2	2	1
Totals	**36**	**10**	**13**	**10**	**Totals**	**34**	**3**	**9**	**3**

Toronto	301	001	302	—	10	13	1
Philadelphia	000	001	101	—	3	9	0

E—Carter (2). LOB—Toronto 7, Philadelphia 9. 2B—RHenderson (1), Kruk (1). 3B—White (1), Molitor (1), RAlomar (1). HR—MThompson (1) off DWard, Molitor (1) off DnJackson. RBI—White (3), Molitor 3 (4), Carter (4), RAlomar 2 (4), TFernandez 2 (4), Sprague (1), Duncan (1), Eisenreich (5), MThompson (1). SB—RAlomar 2 (4). SF—Carter, TFernandez, Sprague. GIDP—DHollins, Chamberlain. RLISP—Toronto 3, Philadelphia 6.

	IP	H	R	ER	BB	SO	NP	ERA
Toronto								
Hentgen W, 1–0	6	5	1	1	3	6	99	1.50
Cox	2	3	1	1	2	2	29	4.50
DWard	1	1	1	1	0	2	18	3.86
Philadelphia								
DnJackson L, 0–1	5	6	4	4	1	1	89	7.20
Rivera	1 1/3	4	4	4	2	3	50	27.00
Thigpen	1 2/3	0	0	0	1	0	27	0.00
Andersen	1	3	2	2	0	0	28	10.80

Inherited runners scored—Thigpen 2–1. HPB—by Thigpen (RHenderson). Time of game—3:16. Attendance—62,689.

4th Game—Philadelphia, Oct. 20
Toronto 15, Philadelphia 14

TORONTO (A)	AB	R	H	RBI	PHILADELPHIA (N)	AB	R	H	RBI
RHenderson lf	5	2	2	2	Dykstra cf	5	4	3	4
White cf	5	2	3	4	Duncan 2b	6	1	3	1
RAlomar 2b	6	1	2	1	Kruk 1b	5	0	0	0
Carter rf	6	2	3	0	DHollins 3b	4	3	2	0
Olerud 1b	4	2	1	0	Daulton c	3	2	1	3
Molitor 3b	4	2	1	1	Eisenreich rf	4	2	1	1
Griffin 3b	0	0	0	0	MThompson lf	5	1	3	5
TFernandez ss	6	2	3	5	Stocker ss	4	0	0	0
Borders c	4	1	1	1	TGreene p	1	1	1	0
Stottlemyre p	0	0	0	0	Mason p	1	0	0	0

Butler ph	1	1	0	0	RJordan ph	1	0	0	0
ALeiter p	1	0	1	0	West p	0	0	0	0
Castillo p	1	0	0	0	Chamberlain ph	1	0	0	0
Sprague ph	1	0	0	0	Andersen p	0	0	0	0
Timlin p	0	0	0	0	MtWilliams p	0	0	0	0
DWard p	0	0	0	0	Morandini ph	1	0	0	0
					Thigpen p	0	0	0	0
Totals	**44**	**15**	**17**	**14**	**Totals**	**41**	**14**	**14**	**14**

Toronto	304	002	060	—	15	17	0
Philadelphia	420	151	100	—	14	14	1

E—DHollins (1). LOB—Toronto 10, Philadelphia 8. 2B—RHenderson (2), White (3), Carter (1), ALeiter (1), Dykstra (1), DHollins (1), MThompson (1). 3B—White (2), MThompson (1). HR—Dykstra (2) off Stottlemyre, Dykstra (3) off ALeiter, Daulton (1) off ALeiter. RBI—RHenderson 2 (2), White 4 (7), RAlomar (5), Molitor (5), TFernandez 5 (9), Borders (1), Dykstra 4 (5), Duncan (2), Daulton 3 (4), Eisenreich (6), MThompson 5 (6). SB—RHenderson (1), White (1), Dykstra (2), Duncan (2). RLISP—Toronto 8, Philadelphia 5. RMU—Olerud, TFernandez, Butler.

	IP	H	R	ER	BB	SO	NP	ERA
Toronto								
Stottlemyre	2	3	6	6	4	1	53	27.00
ALeiter	2 2/3	8	6	6	0	1	52	10.13
Castillo W, 1–0	2 1/3	3	2	2	3	1	54	8.10
Timlin	2/3	0	0	0	0	2	8	0.00
DWard S, 2	1 1/3	0	0	0	0	2	14	2.45
Philadelphia								
TGreene	2 1/3	7	7	7	4	1	66	27.00
Mason	2 2/3	2	0	0	1	2	38	1.69
West	1	3	2	2	0	0	19	27.00
Andersen	1 1/3	1	3	1	1	2	26	9.00
MtWilliams L, 0–1	2/3	3	3	3	1	1	20	11.57
Thigpen	1	1	0	0	0	0	17	0.00

Inherited runners scored—Castillo 1–0, Mason 2–2, MtWilliams 2–2. HBP—by Castillo (Daulton), by West (Molitor). Time of game—4:14. Attendance: 62,731.

5th Game—Philadelphia, Oct. 21
Philadelphia 2, Toronto 0

TORONTO (A)	AB	R	H	RBI	PHILADELPHIA (N)	AB	R	H	RBI
RHenderson lf	3	0	0	0	Dykstra cf	2	1	0	0
White cf	3	0	0	0	Duncan 2b	4	0	0	0
RAlomar 2b	3	0	1	0	Kruk 1b	3	0	1	1
Carter rf	4	0	0	0	DHollins 3b	3	0	1	0
Olerud 1b	4	0	0	0	Batiste 3b	0	0	0	0
Molitor 3b	4	0	1	0	Daulton c	4	1	1	0
TFernandez ss	3	0	0	0	Eisenreich rf	4	0	0	0
Borders c	3	0	2	0	MThompson lf	3	0	0	0
Canate pr	0	0	0	0	Stocker ss	2	0	1	1
Knorr c	0	0	0	0	Schilling p	2	0	1	0
Guzman p	2	0	0	0					
Butler ph	1	0	1	0					
Cox p	0	0	0	0					
Totals	**30**	**0**	**5**	**0**	**Totals**	**27**	**2**	**5**	**2**

Toronto	000	000	000	—	0	5	1
Philadelphia	110	000	00x	—	2	5	1

E—Borders (1), Duncan (1). LOB—Toronto 6, Philadelphia 8. 2B—Daulton (1), Stocker (1). RBI—Kruk (4), Stocker (1). SB—Dykstra (3). CS—RAlomar (2). S—Schilling. GIDP—RAlomar, Guzman, Duncan. RLISP—Toronto 2, Philadelphia 5. RMU—RHenderson, Kruk, Eisenreich. DP—Toronto 1, Philadelphia 3.

	IP	H	R	ER	BB	SO	NP	ERA
Toronto								
Guzman L, 0–1	7	5	2	1	4	6	101	3.75
Cox	1	0	0	0	2	3	24	3.00
Philadelphia								
Schilling W, 1–1	9	5	0	0	3	6	148	3.52

IBB—off Guzman (Dykstra) 1. Time of game—2:53. Attendance—62,706.

6th Game—Toronto, Oct. 23
Toronto 8, Philadelphia 6

PHILADELPHIA (N)	AB	R	H	RBI	TORONTO (A)	AB	R	H	RBI
Dykstra cf	3	1	1	3	RHenderson lf	4	1	0	0
Duncan dh	5	1	1	0	White cf	4	1	0	0
Kruk 1b	3	0	0	0	Molitor dh	5	3	3	2
DHollins 3b	5	1	1	1	Carter rf	4	1	1	4
Batiste 3b	0	0	0	0	Olerud 1b	3	1	1	0
Daulton c	4	1	1	0	Griffin pr-3b	0	0	0	0
Eisenreich rf	5	0	2	1	RAlomar 2b	4	1	3	1
MThompson lf	3	0	0	0	TFernandez ss	3	0	0	0
Incaviglia ph-lf	0	0	0	1	Sprague 3b-1b	2	0	0	1
Stocker ss	3	1	0	0	Borders c	4	0	2	0
Morandini 2b	4	1	1	0					
Totals	**35**	**6**	**7**	**6**	**Totals**	**33**	**8**	**10**	**8**

Philadelphia	000	100	500	–	6	7	0
Toronto	300	110	003	–	8	10	2

One out when winning run scored. E–RAlomar (2), Sprague (2). LOB–Philadelphia 9, Toronto 7. 2B–Daulton (2), Olerud (1), RAlomar (2). 3B–Molitor (2). HR–Molitor (2) off Mulholland, Carter (2) off MTWilliams, Dykstra (4) off Stewart. RBI–Dykstra 3 (8), DHollins (2), Eisenreich (7), Incaviglia (1), Molitor 2 (8), Carter 4 (8), RAlomar (6), Sprague (2). SB–Dykstra (4), Duncan (3). SF–Incaviglia, Carter, Sprague. RLISP–Philadelphia 4, Toronto 2. RMU–RAlomar, TFernandez.

	IP	H	R	ER	BB	SO	NP	ERA
Philadelphia								
Mulholland	5	7	5	5	1	1	70	6.75
Mason	2 1/3	1	0	0	0	2	27	1.17
West	0	0	0	0	1	0	5	27.00
Andersen	2/3	0	0	0	1	0	27	12.27
MtWilliams L, 0-2	1/3	2	3	3	1	0	21	20.25
Toronto								
Stewart	6	4	4	4	4	2	120	6.75
Cox	1/3	3	2	2	1	1	24	8.10
ALeiter	1 2/3	0	0	0	1	2	21	7.71
DWard W, 1-0	1	0	0	0	0	0	7	1.93

Stewart pitched to 3 batters in the 7th. West pitched to 1 batter in the 8th. Inherited runners scored–Andersen 1-0, ALeiter 3-1. HBP–by Andersen (TFernandez). Time of game–3:26. Attendance–52,195.

JORDAN'S RETIREMENT SHOCKS SPORTS WORLD

Michael Jordan, arguably the best to ever play in the National Basketball Association, surprised the sports world just before the start of the 1993–94 NBA season by announcing his retirement.

"I've reached the pinnacle of my career," Jordan said. "I just feel that I don't have anything else for myself to prove."

The NBA's three-time MVP won seven scoring titles, led the Bulls to three straight championships and has two Olympic gold medals.

In his nine years in Chicago, Jordan became the Bulls' all-time leading scorer.

Among his many accomplishments:

- Member of the United States' gold medal-winning Olympic basketball teams in both 1984 and 1992.
- Named NBA Rookie of the Year after averaging 28.2 points in the 1984–85 season.
- Scored a playoff-record 63 points in a first-round game against Boston in 1986.
- Won seven straight NBA scoring titles.
- Only player in NBA history to record at least 200 steals (236) and at least 100 blocked shots (125) in the same season.
- Named All-NBA first team seven straight seasons.
- Named NBA Finals MVP for a record three straight seasons.

—*Dennis Lyons*

BADMINTON

WORLD BADMINTON CHAMPIONSHIPS

(June 7, 1993, Birmingham, England)

Men

Singles—Joko Suprianto, Indonesia, defeated Hermawan Susanto, Indonesia, 15–5, 15–11

Doubles—Ricky Subagja and Rudy Gunawan, Indonesia, defeated Cheah Soon Kit and Soo Beng Kiang, Malaysia, 15–11, 15–3

Women

Singles—Susi Susanti, Indonesia, defeated Bang Soo-Hyun, South Korea, 7–11, 11–9, 11–3

Doubles—Nong Qunhua and Zhou Lei, China, defeated Chen Ying and Wu Yuhong, China, 15–5, 15–10

Mixed doubles—Thomas Lund, Denmark, and Catrine Bengtsson, Sweden, defeated Jon Holst-Christensen and Greta Mogensen, Denmark, 10–15, 15–6, 15–12

IDITAROD

21ST IDITAROD TRAIL SLED DOG RACE—1993

(Alaska, March 6–17, 1993)

The annual 1,159-mile race stretches from Anchorage to Nome, Alaska. Begun in 1973, the course follows an old frozen river mail route and is named after a deserted mining town along the way. The Iditarod also commemorates a famous midwinter emergency mission to get medical supplies to Nome during a 1925 diphtheria epidemic. Men and women mushers compete together.

Course: 1,159 miles, Anchorage to Nome.

1993 Champion—Jeff King, 37, of Denali Park, Alaska won in 10 days, 15 hours, and 30 minutes, breaking Martin Buser's 1992 record of 10 days, 19 hours, and 17 minutes. Second—Dee Dee Jonroe, 33, of Willlow, Alaska, finished second, about 30 minutes behind King.

Winner's purse: $50,000.

Winning times since 1980: 1980, Joe May, 14 days–7 hours–11 minutes; 1981, Swenson, 12–8–45; 1982, Swenson, 16–4–40; 1983, Rick Mackey, 12–14–10; 1984, Dean Osmar, 12–15–7; 1985, Libby Riddles, 18–00–20; 1986, Butcher, 11–15–6; 1987, Butcher, 11–2–5; 1988, Butcher, 11–11–41; 1989, Joe Runyan, 11–5–24; 1990, Butcher, 11–1–53; 1991, Swenson, 12–16–34; 1992, Martin Buser, 10–19–17; 1993, Jeff King, 10–15–30.

CURLING

UNITED STATES CHAMPIONSHIPS—1993

Men (St. Paul, Minn., Feb. 21–27, 1993)—Bemidji, Minn., Scott Baird skip, defeated Seattle, Wash., Doug Jones, skip, 7–3 in final

Women (St. Paul, Minn., Feb. 21–27, 1993)—Denver, Colo., Bev Behnke, skip, defeated Detroit, Mich., Kathy Frankowiak, skip, 9–5 in final

WORLD CHAMPIONSHIPS—1993

Men (Geneva, Switzerland, March 28–April 5, 1993)—Canada, Russ Howard, skip, defeated Scotland, Dave Smith, skip, 8–4 in final

Women (Geneva, Switzerland, March 28–April 5, 1993)—Canada, Sandra Peterson, skip, defeated Germany, Janet Strayer, skip, 5–3 in final

AMATEUR BOXING

U.S. CHAMPIONSHIPS—1993

(Results at Broadmoor World Arena)

106 pounds—Albert Guardado, Topeka, Kan., dec. Bradley Martinez, Army–Fort Huachuca, Ariz., 39–17.

112—Russell Roberts, Gretna, La., def. Arturo Hoffman, Dade City, Fla., RSC–1 (2:34).

119—Aristead Clayton, Jr., Baker, La., dec. Mark Burse, St Louis, 63–33.

125—Julian Wheeler, Navy–Virginia Beach, dec. Frank Carmona, Los Angeles, 47–22.

132—Abayomi Miller, Toledo, Ohio, dec. Larry Nicholson, Tyler Texas, 34–31.

139—Lupe Suazo, Tucson, Ariz., dec. Yagim Abdullah, Syracuse, N.Y., 44–27.

147—Hector Colon, Milwaukee, def. Jesse Briseno, Kalamazoo, Mich., RSC–1 (1:13).

156—Wayne Blair, Miami, dec. Antwun Echols, Davenport, Iowa, 30–29.

165—Eric Wright, Army–Fort Hood, Texas, dec. Shane Swartz, Fort Collins, Colo., 40–39.

178—Antonio Tarver, Orlando, dec. Frank Vassar, Spokane, Wash., 50–21.

201—Derrell Dixon, Lynnwood, Wash., dec. Javier Alvarez, San Antonio, 19–15.

201 plus—Joel Scott, Albany, N.Y. dec. Rodney Harris, Cleveland, 29–10.

(RSC—Referee Stopped Contest)

BICYCLING

TOUR DE FRANCE

(July 3–25, 1993)

Race in 21 days covering 2,312 miles

Final standings

1. Miguel Indurain, Spain, Banesto, 95 hours, 57 minutes, 9 seconds. 2. Tony Rominger, Switzerland, CLAS, 4 minutes, 59 seconds behind. 3. Zenon Jaskula, Poland, GB–MG, 5:48. 4. Alvaro Merjia, Colombia, Motorola, 7:29. 5. Bjarne Riis, Denmark, Ariostea, 16:26. 6. Claudio Chiappucci, Italy, Carerra, 17:18. 7. Johan Bruyneel, Belgium, ONCE, 18:04. 8. Andy Hampsten, U.S., Motorola, 20:14., 9. Pedro Delgado, Spain, Banesto, 23:57. 10. Vladimir Poulnikov, Ukraine, Carrera, 25:29. 11. Gianni Faresin, Italy, MOB, 29:05. 12. Antonio Martin, Spain, Amaya, 29:51. 13. Stephen Roche, Ireland, Carrera, 29:53. 14. Roberto Conti, Italy, Ariostea, 30:05. 15. Jean-Phulippe Dojwa, France, Festina, 30:24.

WORLD CHAMPIONSHIPS—1993

(Aug. 29, 1993, Oslo, Norway)

Final results from the 159.7-mile professional road race: 1. Lance Armstrong, Plano, Texas, 6 hours, 17 minutes, 10 seconds, avg. speed, 25.407 mph. 2. Miguel Indurain, Spain, 19 seconds behind. 3. Olaf Ludwig, Germany, same time. 4. Johan Musseuw, Belgium, same time. 5. Maurizio Fondriest, Italy, same time. 6. Andrei Tchemile, Moldova, same time. 7. Dag Otto Lauritzen, Norway, same time. 8. Gerard Rue, France, same time. 9. Bjarne Riis, Denmark, same time. 10. Frans Maassen, Netherlands, same time. 11. Marco Giovannetti, Italy, same time. 12. Claudio Chiappucci, Italy, 24 seconds behind. 13. Andreas Kappes, Germany, 1:17 behind. 14. Adrie van der Poel, Netherlands, same time. 15. Laurent Jalabert, France, 1:47 minutes behind.

CHESS

WORLD CHAMPIONS

1894–1921	Emanuel Lasker, Germany
1921–27	Jose R. Capablanca, Cuba
1927–35	Alexander A. Alekhine, U.S.S.R.
1935–37	Dr. Max Euwe, Netherlands
1937–46	Alexander A. Alekhine, U.S.S.R.[1]
1948–57	Mikhail Botvinnik, U.S.S.R.
1957–58	Vassily Smyslov, U.S.S.R.
1958–60	Mikhail Botvinnik, U.S.S.R.
1960–61	Mikhail Tal, U.S.S.R.
1961–63	Mikhail Botvinnik, U.S.S.R.
1963–68	Tigran Petrosian, U.S.S.R.
1969–71	Boris Spassky, U.S.S.R.
1972–74	Bobby Fischer, Los Angeles
1975	Bobby Fischer[2], Anatoly Karpov, U.S.S.R.
1976–85	Anatoly Karpov, U.S.S.R.[3]
1985–93[4]	Gary Kasparov, U.S.S.R.

1. Alekhine, a French citizen, died while champion. 2. Relinquished title. 3. In 1978, Karpov defeated Viktor Korchnoi 6 games to 5. 4. Next World Championship scheduled for September, 1993, after *Information Please Almanac* copy deadline.

UNITED STATES CHAMPIONS

1909–36	Frank J. Marshall, New York
1936–44	Samuel Reshevsky, New York[1]
1944–46	Arnold S. Denker, New York
1946	Samuel Reshevsky, Boston
1948	Herman Steiner, Los Angeles
1951–52	Larry Evans, New York
1954–57	Arthur Bisguier, New York
1958–61	Bobby Fischer, Brooklyn, N.Y.
1962	Larry Evans, New York
1963–67	Bobby Fischer, New York
1968	Larry Evans, New York
1969–71	Samuel Reshevsky, Spring Valley, N.Y.
1972	Robert Byrne, Ossining, N.Y.
1973	Lubomir Kavelek, Washington; John Grefe, San Francisco
1974–77	Walter Browne, Berkeley, Calif.
1978–79	Lubomir Kavalek, New York
1980	Tie, Walter Browne, Berkeley, Calif. Larry Christiansen, Modesto, Calif. Larry Evans, Reno, Nev.
1981–82[2]	Tie, Walter Browne, Berkeley, Calif. Yasser Seirawan, Seattle, Wash.
1983	Tie, Walter Browne, Berkeley, Calif. Larry Christiansen, Los Angeles, Calif., Roman Dzindzichashvili, Corona, N.Y.
1984–85	Lev Alburt, New York City
1986	Yasser Seirawan, Seattle, Wash.
1987	Tie—Nick Defirmian, San Francisco, and Joel Benjamin, Brooklyn, N.Y.
1988	Michael Wilder, Princeton, N.J.
1989	Tie, Stuart Rachels, Birmingham, Ala. Yasser Seirawan, Seattle, Wash. Roman Dzindzichashvili, New York, N.Y.
1990–91	Lev Alburt, New York, N.Y.
1992	Gata Kamsky, Brooklyn, N.Y. Patrick Wolff, Summerville, Mass.

1. In 1942, Isaac I. Kashdan of New York was co-champion for a while because of a tie with Reshevsky in that year's tournament. Reshevsky won the play-off. 2. Championship not contested in 1982. NOTE: 1993 United States Championships to be held in December, after *Information Please Almanac* went to press.

GYMNASTICS

WORLD CHAMPIONSHIPS—1993

(April 14–18, Birmingham, England)

Men	Pts
Floor exercise—1. Grigori Misutin, Ukraine	9.400
2. Neil Thomas, Great Britain	9.350
3. Vitaly Scherbo, Belarus	9.350
Pommel horse—1. Gil Su Poe, North Korea	9.750
2. Andreas Wecker, Germany	9.425
3. Karoly Schupkegel, Hungary	9.400
Rings—1. Yuri Chechi, Italy	9.625
2. Andreas Wecker, Germany	9.575
3. Ivan Ivankov, Belarus	9.500
Vault—1. Vitaly Scherbo, Belarus	9.612
2. Chang Peng Chih, Taiwan	9.487
3. Ok-ryul Yoo, South Korea	9.418
Uneven bars—1. Vitaly Scherbo, Belarus	9.600
2. Igor Korobchinski, Ukraine	9.525
3. Valeri Belenki, Azerbaijan	9.475
High bar—1. Sergei Charkov, Russia	9.450
2. Marius Gherman, Romania	9.375
3. Zoltan Supila, Hungary	9.350
All-Around Champion—Vitaly Scherbo, Belarus	

Women	Pts
Vault—1. Yelana Piskoun, Belarus	9.762
2. Lavinia Milosovici, Romania	9.737
3. Oksana Chusovitina, Ukraine	9.718
Uneven bars—1. Shannon Miller, United States	9.887
2. Dominique Dawes, United States	9.800
3. Andrea Cacovean, Romania	9.787
Balance beam—1. Lavinia Milosovici, Romania	9.850
2. Dominque Dawes, United States	9.725
3. Gina Gogean, Romania	9.650
Floor exercise—1. Shannon Miller, United States	9.787
2. Gina Gogean, Romania	9.737
3. Natalia Bobrova, Russia	9.712
All-Around Champion—Shannon Miller, United States	

UNITED STATES CHAMPIONSHIPS

(Aug. 26–29, 1993, Salt Lake City, Utah)

Men (Listed with college affiliation)
All-around—1. John Roethlisberger, University of Minnesota
2. Chainey Umphrey, UCLA
3. Scott Keswick, UCLA
Floor exercise—1. Kerry Huston, University of Minnesota
2. Bill Roth, Temple University
3. Jarrod Hanks, University of Oklahoma
Rings—1. John Roethlisberger, University of Minnesota
2. Chainey Umphrey, UCLA
3. Scott Keswick, UCLA
Pommel horse—1. Chris Waller, UCLA
2. Brian Yee, University of Minnesota
3. Scott Keswick, UCLA
Vault—1. Bill Roth, Temple University
2. Richard Grace, Nebraska
3. Scott Keswick, UCLA
Horizontal bar—1. Steve McCain, UCLA
2. Chainey Umphrey, UCLA and Scott Keswick, UCLA (tie)
Parallel bars—1. Chainey Umphrey, UCLA
2. Scott Keswick, UCLA
3. John Roethlisberger, University of Minnesota

Women (Listed with club affiliation)
All-around—1. Shannon Miller, Dynamo Gymnastics
2. Dominique Dawes, Hill's Angels
3. Kerri Strug, Dynamo Gymnastics
Vault—1. Dominique Dawes, Hill's Angels
2. Shannon Miller, Dynamo Gymnastics
3. Kim Arnold, Desert Devils
Uneven bars—1. Shannon Miller, Dynamo Gymnastics
2. Kerri Strug, Dynamo Gymnastics
3. Dominique Dawes, Hill's Angels
Beam—1. Dominique Dawes, Hill's Angels
2. Kellee Davis, American Twisters
3. Shannon Miller, Dynamo Gymnastics
Floor exercise—1. Shannon Miller, Dynamo Gymnastics
2. Dominique Dawes, Hill's Angels
3. Kerri Strug, Dynamo Gymnastics

SPORTS ORGANIZATIONS AND BUREAUS

(Note: Addresses are subject to change)

Amateur Athletic Union of the U.S. 3400 West 86th St., P.O. Box 68207, Indianapolis, Ind. 46268–0207

Amateur Softball Association/USA SOFTBALL. 2801 N.E. 50th St., Oklahoma City, Okla. 73111

American Amateur Racquetball Association/International Racquetball Federation/Pan American Racquetball Confederation. 815 N. Weber St., Colorado Springs, Colo. 80903-2947

American Association of Professional Baseball Clubs. 401 E. McMillan, Cincinnati, Ohio 45206

American Bowling Congress. 5301 South 76th St., Greendale, Wis. 53129–1127

American Hockey League. 425 Union St., Springfield, Mass. 01089

American Horse Shows Association. 220 E. 42nd St., New York, N.Y. 10017–5876

American Kennel Club Inc. 51 Madison Ave., New York, N.Y. 10010

American League (baseball). 350 Park Ave., New York, N.Y. 10022

American Sportcasters Association, The. 5 Beekman St., New York, N.Y. 10038

Athletics Congress/USA, The. One Hoosier Dome, Ste. 140, Indianapolis, Ind. 46225

Baseball Hall of Fame. P.O. Box 590, Cooperstown, N.Y. 13326

Big Ten Conference, Inc. (1896). 1500 W. Higgins Rd., Park Ridge, Ill. 60068-6300

Football Hall of Fame (college). Kings Island, Ohio 45034

International Game Fish Association. 1301 E. Atlantic Blvd., Pompano Beach, Fla. 33060

International League of Professional Baseball Clubs, Inc. 55 S. High St., Ste. 202, Dublin, Ohio 43017

International Olympic Committee. Chateau de Vidy, Case Postale 356, 1001 Lausanne, Switzerland

International Tennis Hall of Fame. National Historic Landmark, Newport Casino, 194 Bellevue Ave., Newport, R.I. 02840

Little League Baseball. P.O. Box 3485, Williamsport, Pa. 17701

National Archery Association. 1750 E. Boulder St., Colorado Springs, Colo. 80909-5788

National Association for Stock Car Auto Racing. P.O. Box 2875, Daytona Beach, Fla. 32120-2875

National Association of Intercollegiate Athletics. 1221 Baltimore Ave., Kansas City, Mo. 64105

National Baseball Congress. P.O. Box 1420, Wichita, Kan. 67201

National Collegiate Athletic Association. 6201 College Blvd., Overland Park, Kan. 66211-2422

National Duckpin Bowling Congress. 4991 Fairview Ave., Linthicum, Md. 29090

National Field Archery Association. 31407 Outer I–10, Redlands, Calif. 92373

National Football Foundation and College Hall of Fame. 1865 Palmer Ave., Larchmont, N.Y. 10538. ***See also:*** Football Hall of Fame (college)

National Football League. 410 Park Ave., New York, N.Y. 10022

National Hockey League. 75 International Blvd., Ste. 300, Rexdale, Ont., Canada M9W 6L9

National Horseshoe Pitchers Association. Box 7927, Columbus, Ohio 43207-7927

National Hot Rod Association. P.O. Box 5555, Glendora, Calif. 91740-0750

National Junior College Athletic Association. P.O. Box 7305, Colorado Springs, Colo. 80933-7305

National Rifle Association of America. 1600 Rhode Island Ave., N.W., Washington, D.C. 20036

National Shuffleboard Association. *Summer:* 2508 Westmoor Rd., Findlay, Ohio 45840. *Winter:* 704 52nd Dr. W., Bradenton, Fla. 34207.

National Skeet Shooting Association. P.O. Box 680007, San Antonio, Tex. 78268–0007

National Sporting Clays Association. P.O. Box 680007, San Antonio, Tex. 78268-0007

New York Racing Association. P.O. Box 90, Jamaica, N.Y. 11417

New York State Athletic Commission (boxing and wrestling). 270 Broadway, New York, N.Y. 10007

PGA TOUR, Inc. 112 TPC Blvd., Sawgrass, Ponte Vedra, Fla. 32082

Pro Football Hall of Fame. 2121 George Halas Drive, N.W., Canton, Ohio 44708

Roller Skating Associations. P.O. Box 81846, Lincoln, Neb. 68501

Thoroughbred Racing Assns. of N. America. 420 Fair Hill Dr., Ste. 1, Elkton, Md. 21921-2573

United States Amateur Boxing, Inc. One Olympic Plaza, Colorado Springs, Colo. 80909

United States Amateur Confederation of Roller Skating. P.O. Box 6579, Lincoln, Neb. 68506

United States Auto Club. 4910 West 16th St., Speedway, Ind. 46224

United States Gymnastics Federation. 201 S. Capitol, Ste. 300, Indianapolis, Ind. 46225

United States–International Professional Shuffleboard. 1901 S.W. 87th Terrace, Fort Lauderdale, Fla. 33324

United States Sailing Association. P.O. Box 209, Newport, R.I. 02840

USA Baseball. 2160 Greenwood Ave., Trenton, N.J. 08609

USA Basketball. 1750 East Boulder St., Colorado Springs, Colo. 80909-5777

USA Hockey, Inc. 4965 N. 30th St., Colorado Springs, Colo. 80919

USA Track & Field. One Hoosier Dome, Ste. 140, Indianapolis, Ind. 46225.

U.S. Chess Federation. 186 Route 9W, New Windsor, N.Y. 12553

U.S. Cycling Federation. One Olympic Plaza, Colorado Springs, Colo. 80909

U.S. Fencing Assn. 1750 E. Boulder St., Colorado Springs, Colo. 80909-5774

U.S. Figure Skating Association. 20 First St., Colorado Springs, Colo. 80906

U.S. Golf Association. Golf House, P.O. Box 708, Far Hills, N.J. 07931–0708

U.S. Handball Association. 930 N. Benton Ave., Tucson, Ariz. 85711

U.S. Olympic Committee. One Olympic Plaza, Colorado Springs, Colo. 80909-5760

U.S. Orienteering Federation. Box 1444, Forest Park, Ga. 30051

U.S. Rowing Assn. Pan American Plaza, 201 S. Capitol Ave., Ste. 400, Indianapolis, Ind. 46225

U.S. Soccer Federation. 1801-1811 S. Prairie Ave., Chicago, Ill. 60616

U.S. Tennis Association. 70 W. Red Oak Lane, White Plains, N.Y. 10604

U.S. Trotting Association. 750 Michigan Ave., Columbus, Ohio 43215

Women's International Bowling Congress. 5301 S. 76th St., Greendale, Wis. 53129-1191

STANDARD MEASUREMENTS IN SPORTS

BASEBALL

Home plate to pitcher's box: 60 feet 6 inches.
Plate to second base: 127 feet 3 3/8 inches.
Distance from base to base (home plate included): 90 feet.
Size of bases: 15 inches by 15 inches.
Pitcher's plate: 24 inches by 6 inches.
Batter's box: 4 feet by 6 feet.
Home plate: Five-sided, 17 inches by 8 1/2 inches by 8 1/2 inches by 12 inches by 12 inches, cut to a point at rear.
Home plate to backstop: Not less than 60 feet (recommended).
Weight of ball: Not less than 5 ounces nor more than 5 1/4 ounces.
Circumference of ball: Not less than 9 inches nor more than 9 1/4 inches.
Bat: Must be one piece of solid wood, round, not over 2 3/4 inches in diameter at thickest part, nor more than 42 inches in length.070

BASKETBALL

(National Collegiate A.A. Men's Rules)
Playing court: College: 94 feet long by 50 feet wide (ideal dimensions). High School: 84 feet long by 50 feet wide (ideal inside dimensions).
Baskets: Rings 18 inches in inside diameter, with white cord 12-mesh nets, 15 to 18 inches in length. Each ring is made of metal, is not more than 5/8 of an inch in diameter, and is bright orange in color.
Height of basket: 10 feet (upper edge).
Weight of ball: Not less than 20 ounces nor more than 22.
Circumference of ball: Not greater than 30 inches and not less than 29 1/2.
Free-throw line: 15 feet from the face of the backboard, 2 inches wide.
Three-point field goal line: 19 feet, 9 inches from the center of the basket. In the National Basketball Association, the distance is 23 feet.

BOWLING

Lane dimensions: Overall length 62 feet 10 3/16 inches, measuring from foul line to pit (not including tail plank), with + or – 1/2 inch tolerance permitted. Foul line to center of No. 1 pinspot 60 feet, with + or – 1/2 inch tolerance permitted. Lane width, 41 1/2 inches with a tolerance of + or – 1/2 inch permitted. Approach, not less than 15 feet. Gutters, 9 5/16 inches wide with plus 3/16 inch or minus 5/16 inch tolerances permitted.
Ball: Circumference, not more than 27.002 inches. Weight, 16 pounds maximum.

BOXING

Ring: Professional matches take place in an area not less than 18 nor more than 24 feet square including apron. It is enclosed by four covered ropes, each not less than one inch in diameter. The floor has a 2-inch padding of Ensolite (or equivalent) underneath ring cover that extends at least 6 inches beyond the roped area in the case of elevated rings. For USA Boxing or Olympic-style boxing, not less than 16 nor more than 20 feet square within the ropes. The floor must extend beyond the ring ropes not less than 2 feet. The ring posts shall be connected to the four ring ropes with the extension not shorter than 18 inches and must be properly padded.
Gloves: In professional fights, not less than 8-ounce gloves generally are used. USA Boxing, 10 ounces for boxers 106 pounds through 156 pounds; 12-ounce for boxers 165 pounds through 201+ pounds; for international competition, 8 ounces for lighter classes, 10 ounces for heavier divisions.
Headguards: Mandatory in Olympic-style boxing.

FOOTBALL

(N.C.A.A.)
Length of field: 120 yards (including 10 yards of end zone at each end).
Width of field: 53 1/3 yards (160 feet).
Height of goal posts: At least 30 feet.
Height of crossbar: 10 feet.
Width of goal posts (above crossbar): 18 feet 6 inches, inside to inside.
Length of ball: 10 7/8 to 11 7/16 inches (long axis).
Circumference of ball: 20 3/4 to 21 1/4 inches (middle); 27 3/4 to 28 1/2 inches (long axis).

GOLF

Specifications of ball: Broadened to require that the ball be designed to perform as if it were spherically symmetrical. The weight of the ball shall not be greater than 1.620 ounces avoirdupois, and the size shall not be less than 1.680 inches in diameter.
Velocity of ball: Not greater than 250 feet per second when tested on U.S.G.A. apparatus, with 2 percent tolerance.
Hole: 4 1/4 inches in diameter and at least 4 inches deep.
Clubs: 14 is the maximum number permitted.
Overall distance standard: A brand of ball shall not exceed a distance of 280 yards plus 6% when tested on USGA apparatus under specified conditions, on an outdoor range at USGA Headquarters.

HOCKEY

Size of rink: 200 feet long by 85 feet wide surrounded by a wooden wall not less than 40 inches and not more than 48 inches above level of ice.
Size of goal: 6 feet wide by 4 feet in height.
Puck: 1 inch thick and 3 inches in diameter, made of vulcanized rubber; weight 5 1/2 to 6 ounces.
Length of stick: Not more than 60 inches from heel to end of shaft nor more than 12 1/2 inches from heel to end of blade. Blade should not be more than 3 inches in width but not less than 2 inches—except goal keeper's stick, which shall not exceed 3 1/2 inches in width except at the heel, where it must not exceed 4 1/2 inches, nor shall the goalkeeper's stick exceed 15 1/2 inches from the heel to the end of the blade.

TENNIS

Size of court: 120 feet long by 60 feet wide, with rectangle marked off at 78 feet long by 27 feet wide (singles) and 78 feet long by 36 feet wide (doubles).
Height of net: 3 feet in center, gradually rising to reach 3-foot 6-inch posts at a point 3 feet outside each side of court.
Ball: Shall be more than 2 1/2 inches and less than 2 5/8 inches in diameter and weigh more than 2 ounces and less than 2 1/16 ounces.
Service line: 21 feet from net.

Russia and Eastern Europe, 1993

By Arthur P. Reed, Jr.

Events in Russia and former Yugoslavia overshadowed developments elsewhere. In Russia, reformers and former old-line Communists struggled over policy, with progress at times seeming to be set back, at others to be gaining. And inflation remained a perennial threat.

In the Balkans, it was another story—especially of raging civil war in Bosnia and Hercegovina that pitted ethnic groups against each other, with women and children ruthlessly slain. Cease-fires were agreed to and promptly broken by cynical leaders. The West kept aloof except for diplomatic maneuvering and United Nations troops sent to guard supply lines.

Peace had seemed near when the three entities involved—Serb, Croat, and Muslim—considered a proposal drafted by Lord Owen of the European Community and Thorvald Stoltenberg of the United Nations. This would have divided Bosnia into three autonomous republics—Serb, Croat, and Muslim. The Muslim share would have been increased to 30 percent of the territory, with 52 percent for the Serbs, and 18 percent for the Croats. But talks at Geneva collapsed when the Serbs and Croats rejected Muslim demands for more territory in eastern Bosnia and northwestern Bosnia and for rights to Neum, Bosnia's only port on the Adriatic Sea.

Russia's battle to tame inflation was achieving some results as 1993 wore on after the shocking 2,000 percent inflation rate for all of 1992. For that, loose monetary and fiscal policies had been blamed. In April, after his victory in a popular referendum, President Boris Yeltsin did much to control prices by reducing spending, raising energy prices, and cutting subsidies to state-owned enterprises.

And the Central Bank reduced interest rates.

But in mid-summer the bank set off a panic by announcing that it was withdrawing all bank notes issued before the beginning of the year. Economists feared wide difficulties for businesses in Russia and for other former Soviet republics still using the Russian ruble. The bank's decision caused a serious split in the Government. Finally, President Yeltsin, responding to wide popular discontent and sharp opposition from the reform wing of the Government, greatly modified the drastic currency revision. Among diplomats the ruble frenzy caused some second thoughts about the fragility of Russia's economic reforms and the value of continued foreign aid.

Such aid from the West, however, was an important factor in the Russian economy during the year. The West had come to realize the necessity to global stability of a healthy economy in the successor states to the once-feared Soviet Union. And President Bill Clinton was a driving force in the endeavor. At a summit meeting with Yeltsin at Vancouver, B.C., in April, Clinton pledged $1.6 billion in assistance. In another major move to strengthen Yeltsin's position, an emergency meeting in Tokyo of the seven leading industrial nations agreed on $28 billion in aid for Russia, most of it linked to austerity measures by Moscow. Most of the package was to come from international lending agencies. However, it included $2 billion in credits or loan guarantees to pay for Russian imports of American goods. At the meeting in Tokyo in July, the seven nations approved Clinton's plan to help privatize Russian business and industry.

In April the International Monetary Fund announced a program to provide billions of dollars in loans to Russia and the other nations of the former Soviet bloc under somewhat relaxed conditions. Also in April, the World Bank announced an agreement to help finance a $1-billion project to increase Russian oil production.

In his running battle with die-hard conservatives, Yeltsin chalked up some gains and some losses. In April a public referendum gave him an impressive vote of confidence, with new opportunities to push his reforms, as well as new challenges in his perennial contest with the holdover Soviet-era legislature, the Congress of Peoples' Deputies. The Parliament flexed its muscles before adjourning for the summer recess by voting measures aimed at undermining Yeltsin. The actions would disrupt the economy, interfere with privatization, and otherwise frustrate the Yeltsin agenda. But the measures were subject to veto by the President or could simply be ignored, as similar ones had been. There was, however, an ominous footnote: The increasingly influential extreme Right was stirring its witch's brew of anti-democracy, virulent anti-Semitism, and a general appeal to traditional prejudices and xenophobia.

The 15 former Soviet republics struggled, meanwhile, with attempts to cooperate in solving their common economic problems. In mid-year the three big Slavic states that had dominated the Soviet Union—Russia, Ukraine, and Belarus—moved to form an economic union. They agreed on principles of economic integration and "a single economic space." The three comprise more than 70 percent of the population of the old Soviet Union and contain even more of its industrial wealth and modern technology. They have held the door open to the former Soviet nations of Central Asia, who have been gravitating toward their Islamic kin in Turkey and the Middle East. Earlier nine of the 15 former Soviet republics signed a declaration of intent to form an economic union, but the move lagged.

Civil war raged in Central Asia, particularly in the Republic of Azerbaijan. There, the Armenian enclave of Nagorno-Karabakh has fought a major battle for independence.

Among the former Communist states, Poland and Albania stood out as examples of opposites—Poland for its successes, Albania for its pitiful economic wretchedness. Poland, in fact, has been rated by experts as Eastern Europe's most flourishing economy. Small enterprises, run by imaginative developers, are at the heart of this success. A three percent growth in the economy was projected for 1993, continuing the trend of 1992, the opposite of others in the region. While the economy is strong—more than 50 percent of its workers employed in private enterprise, and inflation seems tamed—political uncertainty clouded the future as the year drew on. Prime Minister Hanna Suchocka faced new elections after her coalition Government lost a vote of confidence in Parliament.

Post-Communist Albania resembled a disaster zone, according to reports from correspondents. Indeed, the United Nations classified it as a "least-developed nation"—the only one in Europe. Albania was dependent on the West, estimated to receive more foreign aid than any other country. Hundreds of thousands of residents had fled to find jobs abroad, with the unemployment rate about 40 percent. News reports have painted a grim picture: no rail service and few buses, hospitals without vital equipment. Tragically, hundreds of schools had been destroyed, and those remaining had no textbooks and parents had no money to clothe their children for school.

The picture in other nations of Eastern Europe was less gloomy, although still far from bright.

The Czech Republic has taken major steps toward free-market capitalism and away from the Communist-era central planning and state ownership. Private investors could trade in the newly opened Prague Stock Exchange. Other signs of the new era were investment funds, corporate boards, calls for job elimination, and other cost-cutting measures—and company meetings. And Volkswagen A.C. acquired the Skoda automobile plant in a move to show that the region can yield a profit. But newly independent Slovakia, faced with economic uncertainties, had not been so fortunate.

Among other East European nations, Hungary and Romania reached a surprising ethnic agreement. At a conference in Romania the two traditionally hostile nations settled on sweeping measures to improve the lot of the Hungarian minority in Romania.

In May the Hungarian Parliament ratified a treaty confirming the existing border with Ukraine and protecting the rights of Ukraine's Hungarian minority.

Greece and Bulgaria in February agreed on steps to keep Balkan unrest from spreading to Macedonia. And Bulgaria and Albania signed a friendship pact calling for a highway from the Bulgarian Black Sea Coast through Macedonia to the Albanian port of Durres.

What the future holds for East Europe and the former Soviet empire no one can say. But the past has irrevocably vanished.

One cheering note: The last Russian troops stationed in Lithuania left the Baltic republic at the end of August. Thus ended more than half a century of Soviet and Russian military presence. In celebration, the Roman Catholic Church ordered bells to be rung throughout the country. At Kaunas, Lithuania's second-largest city, the remaining 30 soldiers at the paratroop base left after the yellow, red, and green Lithuanian flag was hoisted in farewell. With its Baltic neighbors, Estonia and Latvia, Lithuania was annexed by the Soviet Union under the secret Hitler-Stalin treaty. Estonia and Latvia had still to reach an agreement for Russian withdrawal.

Western Europe, 1993

By Arthur P. Reed, Jr.

The dream of a unified Europe had faded in 1993. It was still alive, and the vision was still bright among the 12 nations of the European Community. Indeed, formal ratification of the Maastricht Treaty was virtually complete with approval by Britain and Denmark. But jarring realities and the persistent economic blight—the worst since World War II—served to dim its luster. Related problems were unemployment that strained welfare programs and a racist backlash as hundreds of thousands of refugees from Southeastern Europe fled unstable and nationalist regimes.

British ratification of the treaty was delayed when the opposition Labor Party pressed for an amendment to scrap a special protocol to the treaty. The protocol was a compromise that would exempt Britain from the "Social Chapter" on labor relations, which Prime Minister John Major opposed as being potentially burdensome to British business. In April the Government succeeded in blocking an opposition move to submit the treaty to a referendum. But in May the Government was forced to accept an amendment removing mention of the "Social Chapter." Finally, Commons—292–112—approved ratification on its third reading, with 41 Conservatives voting against.

The citizens of Denmark, in a referendum May 18, voted to ratify the treaty, reversing its narrow defeat in 1992. The Copenhagen Government had won several concessions allowing it to "opt out" of certain moves to closer union, including cooperation on defense policies and on monetary matters.

In Germany, the Government, supporting the treaty, expected the Constitutional Court to reject 18 challenges, most concerning the legality of transferring powers to E.C. institutions. Treaty opponents argued that these were not democratically controlled.

A major threat to European unity was the crumbling of the European Monetary System, once seen as the first step toward a common currency, as envisioned at Maastricht, the Netherlands town where the treaty was agreed upon in December 1991. In large part this was because of high German interest rates. In a turbulent midsummer market upset, the French franc, with the Danish, Belgian, Spanish, and Portuguese currencies, lost ground against the strong German mark and the Dutch guilder. And the result was that the finance ministers of Western Europe announced in August that they had virtually given up hope for the 14-year-old plan for curbing currency fluctuations. Some observers felt that the free flow of money had actually fueled the activities of currency speculators seeking the most profitable investments. And not only speculators were involved; also seeking to avoid losses were corporations, mutual and pension funds, and banks. The lagging economy in Western Europe had its repercussions. With tax revenues falling, each nation had to seek ways to cope. Generous wages and benefits had priced goods out of many markets. In Germany, for example, perquisites for employees have been, to American thinking, unbelievably high—such as six weeks' vacation time and an extra week's pay at Christmas, along with health insurance, pensions, and unemployment compensation—all required by law. It was no wonder that many nations sought to reduce benefits, often in the face of protests from organized labor. Economists pointed to the available supply of cheap, trained workers from the East as an argument for reducing labor costs to keep the West's economy competitive.

The end of the Cold War and the threat from the Soviet Union had a sharp and bitter impact on the social structure of Western Europe. The refugee crisis has been especially acute in Germany, already struggling with the problems resulting from reunification. There were more than a million refugees and asylum-seekers. General resentment against them fueled a spate of violence—including firebombings and beatings.

In six months of 1993 the Government reported eight deaths, 30 percent more than in the like 1992 period. In all, there were more than a thousand attacks. And this was despite the official war on right-wing extremists and neo-Nazi groups.

And a constant specter was the slaughter in the Balkans, the tinder box of Europe, as Serbs, Croats, and Muslims fought for pieces of Bosnia and Hercegovina.

The Clinton Health Care Program

By Arthur P. Reed, Jr.

President Clinton's program for universal health insurance was sweeping, complex, and to many, difficult to comprehend. Hillary Rodham Clinton directed a panel during months of development that saw countless proposals examined and rejected. As laid out in the secret, unauthorized—but apparently authentic—copy finally available to Congress and the press, it would call for a combination of Government regulation and free-market competition.

Briefly, in the President's words, his program "enhances the security of the American people," who would not lose health coverage when becoming ill or losing jobs. The plan would expand Federal power to control private spending on medical care. In the "bootlegged" draft, Clinton predicted that the plan, phased in over the decade, would cut $91 billion from budget deficits over seven years. The states could start the system by January 1995 and must by January 1997. The program would require approval by Congress, which is certain to add its own touches; the Republicans were quick to offer their own, different, proposals—and in conciliatory terms.

Following are key provisions of the President's program:

- Package would cover all citizens and legal residents, with minimum benefits continuing despite illness or change of employment. (Illegal immigrants would continue to be eligible for emergency and other services.)
- Range of services would include hospital care, emergency services, doctors and other health professionals, pregnancy-related services (abortion not mentioned), hospice and home health care, ambulances, outpatient laboratory tests, and prescription drugs.
- Expanded home-care service for the disabled.
- Free preventive care, including immunizations, screening procedures and, ultimately, medical examinations.
- New Medicare benefit for prescription drugs.
- Choice between traditional fee-for-service and other plans.

Operation of Plan: All Americans would get a national health identification card guaranteeing access to services. Most would be enrolled in regional health alliances that buy care from networks of doctors, hospitals, and insurance companies. Those now under Medicare would continue, but later could join alliances. Medicaid recipients would be enrolled in alliances. Companies with more than 5,000 employees could provide care by creating corporate alliances and contracting directly with health-care providers.

Payment: Average standard premium $1,800 a year for individuals and $4,200 for families. Businesses required to pay 80 percent of average premium. There would be options for the plan selected. Companies with fewer than 50 employees and those with many low-wage workers eligible for Government subsidies and payment caps.

Payment directly or by withholding. Self-employed and unemployed responsible for entire premium unless eligible for assistance based on income. Different provisions for options in choice of doctor for high-, low-, and combination-cost plans.

Cost Control: A National Health Board to oversee system and set a national health budget to limit rate of increase of health-care spending to inflation rate. If this does not reduce growth, mandatory limits on growth of annual premiums, forcing plans to spend less. The Health Board could not set drug prices, but would publicize the cost of new drugs and could investigate costs of existing drugs it considers overpriced. The plan does not allow for costs resulting from new technology or increased use of medical services—major factors in health-care costs. But states would get broad powers to regulate and tax health-benefit plans of the biggest corporations, hitherto exempt.

In a gesture to political reality, the plan would avoid appreciable new taxes, and would emphasize competition to control costs. □

Gays in the Military

By Arthur P. Reed, Jr.

Early in his term, President Clinton had to deal with the delicate issue of homosexuals in the military. A compromise with the Pentagon leadership and the gay element, completely satisfactory to neither, resolved the question, at least for the time.

Bill Clinton had promised in his 1992 campaign to lift the ban with an executive order immediately following his inauguration. But he met unexpected opposition from Congress and the Joint Chiefs of Staff. In an immediate compromise with Senate Democrats, the President made two changes: Recruits were not to be questioned about their orientation; open homosexuals in the service were to be placed on reserve status. A permanent arrangement was to be worked out in six months. In July the White House announced that the President had agreed with the Pentagon, the Justice Department, and the Joint Chiefs on the arrangement under which "don't ask, don't tell, don't pursue" was codified. While the plan fell short of the campaign pledge, officials felt it was the best possible in view of the conservative resistance, and a start toward further relaxation of the ban. After final adjustments and a review by the Justice Department, Clinton promulgated the compromise in an executive order. Key elements of the Pentagon's new guidelines were:

- Sexual orientation no bar to service unless manifested by conduct.
- No investigations solely to determine sexual orientation.
- Bodily contact with homosexual intent a cause for separation.
- Mere allegations not a cause for separation.
- Hostile treatment or violence not to be tolerated.

Thus, weeks of negotiations involving nearly 30 lawyers created a "private zone" for gay men and lesbians. Officials indicated that under the "don't pursue" rubric persons would not be investigated and discharged solely for their nature. Permissible conduct, it was indicated, would include such actions as drinking in a gay bar, reading gay publications, marching in a gay-pride parade, or displaying a same-sex picture. It would allow private revelations of homosexuality to one other person.

Inevitably, the compromise aroused resentment in both pro and anti camps. Conservatives denounced "special treatment" for homosexuals. Liberals charged that the President had reneged on his campaign pledge. And even the conservative leader, Gary L. Bauer, president of the Family Research Council, said people would have respected Clinton more if he had kept his campaign promise. □

What Happened in 1993

Highlights of the important events of the year from January to October 1993, organized month by month, in three categories for easy reference. The Countries of the World section (starting on page 143) covers specific international events, country by country.

JANUARY 1993

International

Crowds in Africa Protest U.N. Chief (Jan. 3): Angry throngs in Somalia capital demonstrate against Secretary General Boutros Boutros-Ghali.

Rape of 20,000 by Serbs Reported (Jan. 8): European Community inquiry says Muslim women have been deliberate target of abuse aimed at driving them from homes in Bosnia and Hercegovina.

Serbian Draftee Slays a Top Bosnian Official (Jan. 8): Hakija Turajlic, one of three deputy prime ministers, shot after U.N. vehicle is halted. **(Jan. 10):** Leader of Serbian forces involved apologizes for assassination. Young draftee arrested as suspect.

Erich Honecker Released From Prison (Jan. 13): Germany frees former East German leader because of failing health. He leaves to join wife in Chile.

Death Toll Past 550 in Bombay Clashes (Jan. 13): Troops seek to curb violence in nine days of fighting between Hindus and Moslems.

Iraq Removes Missiles From No-Fly Zone (Jan. 6): U.S. and U.N. allies give Baghdad 48 hours to remove surface-to-air weapons threatening planes patrolling southern region. **(Jan. 9):** White House says Iraq has "backed down" and removed missiles.

Allies Raid Targets in Iraq (Jan. 13): Warplanes from U.S., Britain, and France bomb missile sites in south. After Iraq incursion into Kuwait, Bush dispatches troops to prevent further forays. **(Jan. 17):** Navy ships launch 40 cruise missiles at Iraqi industrial complex in Baghdad suburb. One hits Baghdad hotel. Two civilians killed and several wounded. **(Jan. 18):** Allied warplanes renew bombing raids in north and south.

First U.S. Combat Troops Leave Somalia (Jan. 19): More than 500 Marines embark for California in symbolic redeployment. Operation began Dec. 9, 1992.

Iraq Orders Cease-Fire Against U.S. Planes (Jan. 19): Extends good-will gesture to Clinton. Also admits U.N. inspectors to Baghdad without interference.

Vaclav Havel Elected as Czech President (Jan. 26): Playwright who led Czechoslovakia's transition from Communism chosen by Parliament of new Czech Republic. Slovakia Premier suffers setback.

National

103rd Congress Convenes (Jan. 5): Democratic leaders hasten to give priority to measures vetoed by President Bush. There is wrangling over rules.

Shortcut Impeachment Trials Ruled Legal (Jan. 13): Supreme Court decides, 9–0, Senate can use committee procedure to remove two federal judges.

Supreme Court Voids Use of Klan Law (Jan. 13): Justices rule, 6–3, Reconstruction Era civil rights statute does not give federal judges right to bar anti-abortion protesters from blocking clinics.

No Evidence of Hostage Deal in 1980 (Jan. 13): House inquiry clears Reagan Administration officials of secret arrangement with Iran.

Senate Confirms First Clinton Nominees (Jan. 20): Without opposition, approves Warren M. Christopher for Secretary of State, Rep. Lee Aspin of Wisconsin for Secretary of Defense, and Senator Lloyd Bentsen of Texas for Secretary of Treasury.

Clinton Inaugurated as 42nd President (Jan. 20): Takes oath in Washington ceremony as thousands watch. In address, he stresses theme of renewal and calls for sacrifice to safeguard country's future.

Senate Confirms 14 Clinton Appointments (Jan. 21): Ronald H. Brown approved for Commerce Secretary after agreeing to sever ties with law firm and avoid decisions savoring of conflict of interest.

Clinton Removes Abortion Restrictions (Jan. 22): Reverses decade of Republican policies in signing five memoranda on 20th anniversary of Roe v. Wade decision. Lifts ban on counseling and removes curbs on research using fetal tissue.

Clinton Withdraws Zoë Baird Nomination (Jan. 22): Acts after nominee for Attorney General draws public and Congressional ire for hiring illegal aliens. President admits he erred in selection.

Clinton Agrees to Compromise on Military Gay Ban (Jan. 29): Temporarily suspends formal discharge of homosexuals in concession to opponents. Orders Pentagon to produce policy in six months. Action follows public and Congressional outcry.

General

Twenty-five Killed in Mexico Bus Crash (Jan. 3): Fourteen Americans among victims when excursion vehicle hits high-tension power line on slippery road.

Tanker Spills Oil Off Shetland Islands (Jan. 5): The *Braer*, battered by hurricane-force winds, goes aground on rocks. Loaded with 26 million gallons of crude oil. Imperils one of Europe's largest seabird and wildlife colonies. Miles of coastline polluted. **(Jan. 7):** Slick spreads toward salmon farms, a major industry. **(Jan. 12):** Tanker breaks up in heavy storms. Rest of oil spilled.

Dying Man Gets Baboon's Liver (Jan. 10): Patient, 62, afflicted with hepatitis B virus that has destroyed organ. Transplant at University of Pittsburgh is part of effort to overcome species barrier.

Judge Stays Colorado Ban on Gay Rights Laws (Jan. 15): Holds up enforcement until hearing on whether statute violates Federal or state constitutions.

Seven Killed in Indiana Train Wreck (Jan. 18): Dozens injured as two commuter trains traveling in opposite directions sideswipe each other on narrow bridge at Gary.

U.S. Launches 53rd Shuttle Mission (Jan. 13): *Endeavour* orbited with five astronauts from Cape Canaveral, Fla. Members of crew: Air Force Col. John H. Casper, commander; Air Force Lieut. Col. Donald R. McMonagle, pilot; Navy Lieut. Comdr. Mario Runco, Jr.; Gregory Harbaugh, a civilian, and Air Force Maj. Susan J. Helms, only space rookie. **(Jan. 19):** *Endeavour* lands at Cape Canaveral after six-day mission that included space walk, release of $200 million relay satellite, science show for children, and ringing of Liberty Bell replica for inauguration of President Clinton.

FEBRUARY 1993

International

China Frees Two Political Prisoners (Feb. 1): Announces release of dissidents in apparent gesture to improve relations with U.S.

U.N. Suspends Aid Flights to Sarajevo (Feb. 13): Acts to counter Bosnian Government's refusal to accept relief supplies for capital.

Halt in Bosnia U.N. Relief Brings Rebuff (Feb. 17): Agency official suspends most of operations until opposing factions allow convoys to pass. **(Feb. 19):** U.N. Secretary-General rebuffs official and orders immediate resumption of operations. **(Feb. 21):** Relief convoy finally arrives at besieged Muslim area.

China Releases Prominent Dissident (Feb. 17): Frees Wang Dan, 24, student who symbolized pro-democracy movement behind Tiananamen Square demonstration.

Mandela Group Accepts Power Sharing (Feb. 18): African National Congress agrees to have minority parties share in governing for five years after end of white minority domination.

Russian-Aid Coordinator Named (Feb. 22): State Department appoints Thomas W. Simons, Jr., career diplomat and an expert on Russia.

U.N. Head Endorses Clinton Air-Drop Plan (Feb. 23): Secretary-General assured relief proposal will be coordinated with U.N. Bosnia operation.

Iraqis Challenge U.N. Inspectors (Feb. 23): Aim guns at two helicopters seeking Scud missiles.

Canada's 18th Prime Minister Resigns (Feb. 24): Brian Mulroney hurt by weak economy, high unemployment, and low support in polls. He furthered free trade with U.S. but failed to achieve national unity.

Warlord's Supporters Riot in Somali Capital (Feb. 24): Thousands storm streets, paralyzing Mogadishu in orgy of looting and destruction. **(Feb. 25):** Mobs fire weapons for six hours in challenge to foreign military presence. U.N. forces return attack.

South Korea Gets Civilian Leader (Feb. 25): Kim Young Sam first nonmilitary leader in more than three decades. Vows to end "Dark political night" of corruption and economic blight.

Police in India Block Hindu Rally (Feb. 25): Riot force thwarts nationalists demanding resignation of Government of Prime Minister P.V. Narasimha Rao. More than 1,000 Hindu militants arrested.

U.S. Begins Airdrop of Aid to Bosnia (Feb. 28): Three C-130 transports fly from base in Germany to bring supplies to besieged towns.

National

Clinton Rescinds Two Bush Orders on Labor Policy (Feb. 2): Revokes edicts on union membership and political use of funds, measures hated by labor.

Second Clinton Nominee Withdraws Name (Feb. 5): Judge Kimba M. Wood halts consideration for Attorney General post after Administration learns she had hired illegal immigrant before it was illegal.

Clinton Signs His First Legislation (Feb. 6): Approves Family and Medical Leave Act, passed by Congress. Law gives workers right to take unpaid leaves for family emergencies, such as child care.

Clinton Names Third Choice as Attorney General (Feb. 11): Appoints Janet Reno, 54, veteran Miami prosecutor, to end turmoil over first two choices.

Clinton Outlines Economic Program (Feb. 17): In speech to joint session of Congress, he proposes tax increases and spending cuts to trim Federal deficit by $500 billion, 38 percent, over four years. New taxes would hit business and wealthy most.

Clinton to Still Two Cold War Voices (Feb. 20): Deficit reduction plan to shut down Radio Free Europe and Radio Liberty and merge them into U.S. Information Agency with savings of millions.

Supreme Court Restricts Criminal Defendants (Feb. 23): Unanimously rules that false testimony on stand may constitutionally add to prison terms.

General

Dinosaur Fossil Ruled U.S. Property (Feb. 3): Federal judge rules rare Tyrannosaurus rex fossil was excavated illegally from site held for Indians.

Amtrak Wins Agreement for High-Speed Trains (Feb. 3): Freight railroads permit travel by fast European trains on their tracks outside Northeast.

Baseball Magnate Punished for Ethnic Slurs (Feb. 3): Major league executive council suspends Marge Schott, owner of Cincinnati Reds, for a year and fines her $25,000. She was accused of using such terms as "nigger" and "money-grubbing Jews."

Russian Space Mirror Reflects Sunlight (Feb. 4): Scientists send narrow beam across dark side of Earth. Era of wide illumination predicted.

G.M. Held Negligent on Pickup Trucks (Feb. 4): Jury in Atlanta finds company knew of defective fuel-tank design that caused death of teen-ager but failed to correct it. Awards $105.2 million in damages to parents of youth burned to death.

Dutch Parliament Approves Mercy Deaths (Feb. 9): Votes, 90–45, for law to sanction euthanasia under strict conditions after two decades of debate.

Shark Tissue Yields Antibiotic Compound (Feb. 14): Scientists report extracting substance that is powerful killer of bacteria, fungi, and parasites.

Hundreds Lost as Haiti Ferry Capsizes (Feb. 17): Overloaded freighter sinks off southern peninsula. **(Feb. 19):** Red Cross accounts for 285 survivors. Total passenger count placed from 800 to 1,200.

Two Boys Accused in Child's Killing (Feb. 20): England shocked as two 10-year-olds in Liverpool are charged with murder and kidnapping in death of 2-year-old abducted from shopping mall.

CBS Buys Theater to Keep Letterman (Feb. 21): Ed Sullivan house to be new studio for late-night show when David Letterman leaves NBC.

Five Missing Skiers Safe in Rockies (Feb. 23): Found after three days fighting sub-zero cold.

Blast Shakes World Trade Center; Five Dead (Feb. 26): Hundreds injured as explosion laid to bomb collapses walls and floors, starts fires, and darkens New York City's largest building. City's economy and transportation disrupted. Trade center closed indefinitely for repairs and safety checkup.

Four Federal Officers Killed in Gun Battle (Feb. 28): Fourteen others injured in attempt to arrest leader of heavily armed religious cult in fortified compound ten miles outside of Waco, Texas.

MARCH 1993

International

Bosnia Conclave Falls After U.S. Airdrop (March 2): Besieged Muslim community of Cerska in east taken by Serbian nationalist forces as relief supplies arrive too late.

New Corruption Scandal Rocks Japan (March 9): Investigators find hundreds of pounds of gold bars and $50 million in cash and securities in home and office of Shin Kanemaru, 78, political power broker under arrest on tax evasion charges.

Egypt Combats Muslim Extremists (March 10): Twenty-one killed and two dozen wounded in nine raids on militants in Cairo and Aswan.

Three Italian Industrialists Arrested (March 11): In Milan raids police round up heads of subsidiaries of state-owned energy corporation linked to investigation of bribery and corruption.

Russian Congress Rebukes Yeltsin (March 13): Congress of Peoples Deputies rejects President's bid for national referendum and adjourns after four-day session criticizing him and his reforms.

U.N. Inquiry Accuses El Salvadoran Officers (March 14): Blames active and retired military men for killing thousands of civilians, including Archbishop of San Salvador. Names defense minister as one of group that ordered killing of six Jesuit priests.

Parliament Sets Back Polish Reforms (March 18): Vote is 203–181 against Warsaw bill to convert 600 state companies into private enterprises.

U.S. and Russian Submarines Collide (March 20): American Grayling attack vessel involved with Delta-class sub, normally equipped with 16 ocean-spanning nuclear-tipped missiles, in Arctic Ocean.

French Conservatives Rout Socialist Regime (March 21): Socialists suffer crushing defeat in first round of parliamentary elections. **(March 28):** Runoff returns give Union for France coalition 487 seats in 577-member National Assembly.

South Africa Reveals Destruction of Nuclear Arsenal (March 24): President F.W. de Klerk says nation built six crude atomic bombs and was at work on seventh when it scrapped program in 1989.

Bosnian Muslim Leader Accepts Peace Plan (March 25): Agrees to map dividing Bosnia and Hercegovina into 10 autonomous provinces.

Somali Leaders Agree on Government (March 27): Fifteen parties reach fragile accord on transitional national council pending formation of national government within two years. U.N. optimistic.

Food Convoy Reaches Besieged Bosnian Town (March 28): Relieves threat of starvation for thousands of sick and malnourished persons in Muslim Srebrenica.

Russian Congress Agrees on Referendum (March 29): Peoples Deputies accept Yeltsin call for national vote of confidence on leadership but with conditions that threaten indecisive result.

Two Serbs Doomed for Killing and Rapes (March 30): Military court in Sarajevo sentences men to firing squad for genocide against Muslims.

Cyrus R. Vance Resigning as Balkan Mediator (March 31): Announces plan to leave U.N. post.

National

Senate, 98–0, Confirms Attorney General (March 11): Approves Janet Reno, 54, chief prosecutor of Dade County, Fla., as first woman in post. Applause follows vote. **(March 12):** Ms. Reno sworn in.

Boston Mayor to be Envoy to Vatican (March 16): Raymond L. Flynn says Clinton will appoint him.

Congress Approves Clinton's Budget Outline (March 18): House, 243–183, gives President victory on measure to cut spending and raise taxes. **(March 25):** Senate, 54–45, approves five-year program, first step in Congressional budget process.

Panel Recommends Drug for Alzheimer's Disease (March 18): F.D.A. advisory group unanimously votes for approval of tacrine. It would be first on market to treat disease, but would not be a cure.

Justice Byron R. White, 75, to Retire (March 19): Only remaining appointee of a Democratic President announces plan to resign from Supreme Court.

Pamela Harriman Named Envoy to Paris (March 23): President picks widow of New York Gov. Averell Harriman. At 73, she will be one of first women to head a major American mission abroad.

Attorney General Demands All U.S. Prosecutors to Resign (March 23): Accelerates routine procedure. But U.S. attorney in District of Columbia suggests order is linked to his investigation of Representative Dan Rostenkowski, a Clinton ally.

Clinton Shifts on Federal Land Policy (March 30): Bows to pressure from Western Senators opposed to change in grazing and royalty standards.

General

Law Agents Besiege Texas Cult (March 1 et seq.): Nearly 400 Federal agents and local police officers mass near compound of religious body day after six are killed in raid. Man who says he is Jesus Christ in control of followers and massive cache of legal and illegal weapons. Standoff continues throughout month. Tactics in raid questioned.

Seventy-seven Feared Dead in Macedonia Jet Crash (March 5): Pal Air Fokker 100 explodes while taking off at Skopje Airport in snowstorm.

Doctor Slain in Anti-Abortion Protest (March 10): Demonstrator shoots David Gunn, 47, outside his clinic at Pensacola, Fla. Authorities call slaying first of its kind in the nation.

Blasts Kill Hundreds in Bombay (March 12): Hundreds wounded as series of explosions rocks India's financial capital. First blast hits Stock Exchange, where about 50 perish, including brokers and crowds around food stands and teas stalls. Blasts also wreck other major structures. Police hint aim was to disrupt commerce and spread terror.

Heavy Storm Batters East Coast (March 13): "Blizzard of '93" attacks Northeast after battering Atlantic Seaboard and causing deadly tornadoes and six-foot high snowdrifts in South. Storm cuts power to millions of homes. Thousands flee flooded coastal areas. All activities disrupted over Northeast. **(March 14):** Death toll put at about 100 as stricken areas dig out.

Blast Kills 45 in Calcutta (March 17): Levels two apartment buildings in central residential area four days after Bombay explosion killed 232.

Scientists Locate Gene Behind Brain Disorder (March 23): International team reports discovering key to understanding Huntington's disease, a neurodegenerative malady that afflicts and kills thousands.

Several Arrested in Trade Center Bombing (March 28): Five in custody and sixth sought in massive explosion that killed six. A major suspect, Egyptian-born cab driver, was returned to New York after capture in Cairo. Letter to *New York Times* ascribed bombing to deep resentment against U.S. policy in Middle East.

Baseball Owners Step Up Minority Hiring (March 29): In policy change, major leagues announce new initiatives to be enforced by sanctions.

APRIL 1993

International

Bosnia Serbs Reject Peace Plan (April 2): Nationalists bar even conditional acceptance of proposals already approved by Croats and Muslims.

Clinton and Yeltsin Confer at Summit (April 3–4): Two Presidents hold first meeting at Vancouver, B.C. Clinton pledges $1.6-billion aid package to support Russian leader's reforms. Package includes credits for increased food and medical assistance, with funds for industries and technical advisers.

U.S. Jets Bomb Iraqi Antiaircraft Guns (April 9): Retaliate against batteries that reportedly fired on routine surveillance mission in north.

Russia Agrees to Limited Growth of Monetary Supply (April 10): Government and central bank bow to pressure from West and I.M.F. to limit granting of low- or no-cost loans as condition of aid.

A Black Leader Slain in South Africa (April 10): Chris Hani, Communist Party head, shot. White man arrested. Death is blow to African National Congress in negotiations to end white minority rule.

Vietnam P.O.W. "Report" Called Fake (April 11): Secret document found in Moscow says Hanoi lied on total of American prisoners of war. Vietnam officials impugn authenticity. **(April 21):** Special U.S. envoy to Vietnam gives Clinton evidence that Moscow document was not authentic.

Allied Planes Patrol Skies Over Bosnia (April 12): U.S., Dutch, and French aircraft enforce U.N. ban on unauthorized flights. French Mirage jet reported to have crashed on return from mission.

Serb Attacks Break Two-Week Bosnia Cease-Fire (April 12): Nationalists aim heavy artillery fire on Sarajevo and besieged Muslim enclave of Srebrenica. **(April 13):** More than 50 civilians reported killed. High U.N. officials, ending restraint, condemn shellings.

Industrial Nations Vote Aid to Russia (April 15): Group of Seven, at Tokyo conference, agrees on $28 billion to bolster President Yeltsin. Much relief depends on austerity steps that may baffle Moscow.

Croat Nationalists Battle Bosnia Army (April 19): Two nominal allies against Serbians launch full-scale war marked by terrorist tactics.

Italians Vote for Political Change (April 19): Referendum repudiates leadership after months of scandal, recession, and Government paralysis.

Twelve in State Dept. Demand Action Against Serbs (April 22): Top Balkan experts tell Secretary of State diplomacy has failed and ask military blow.

I.R.A. Bomb Damages London Financial District (April 24): Kills one, wounds 44 others and causes hundreds of millions of dollars in destruction.

Yeltsin Wins Large Majority in Referendum (April 25): Russian President and economic reforms win popular victory over Congress of People's Deputies in 65.7% turnout. But impasse is unresolved.

National

F.C.C. Orders Cuts in Cable TV Prices (April 1): Also bids companies cancel any increases imposed since Congress voted to regulate the industry.

Attorney General Names Top Aides (April 2): Janet Reno includes two Carter Administration officials and close friend of Hillary Rodham Clinton.

Navy's Top Admiral Backs Combat Role for Women (April 4): Also recommends immediate expansion of positions aboard ships that are open to them.

President Offers $1.52-Trillion Budget (April 8): Clinton gives Congress proposals for reducing Government deficit while increasing expenditures for public works, education, and retraining jobless.

G.O.P. Senators Kill Clinton Economic Plan (April 21): Democrats bow to filibuster and agree to limit bill to $4 billion to extend unemployment benefits.

Clinton Backs Two Environmental Policies (April 21): In departure from Bush, President plans timetable to reduce global warming and to sign international treaty protecting rare and endangered species.

Museum Honors Holocaust Dead (April 22): U.S. Holocaust Memorial Museum dedicated in Washington. World leaders and survivors gather to hail it as debt to Nazis' victims and warning to the future.

Tailhook Report Accuses Naval Officers (April 23): Pentagon inquiry says 175 may face disciplinary action for drinking, debauchery, and sexual abuse at aviators' convention in 1991.

Women to Get Combat Roles (April 27): Defense Secretary Aspin announces order to military to drop most restrictions in aerial and naval warfare.

General

U.S. Indicts Four Palestinians (April 1): Charges plot to kill Jews and blow up Israeli Embassy as part of Abu Nidal terrorist network.

G.M. Asked to Recall Trucks with Fire Risk (April 9): U.S. requests voluntary action against millions of pickup vehicles regarded as hazardous.

Church Leader Named N.A.A.C.P. Head (April 9): Rev. Benjamin R. Chavis, Jr., an official of the United Church of Christ, chosen as director. He has a strong background in the civil rights movement.

Survey Finds 1% of Men Are Homosexual (April 14): New study finds figure considerably lower than 10% published in Kinsey Report in 1948.

Ten Dead in Ohio Prison Siege (April 13): Hundreds of inmates seize cellblock at Lucasville and hold eight guards as hostages. **(April 21):** Siege ends after nine days. Inmates promise to release hostages and return to cells. **(April 22):** Death toll set at nine prisoners and a guard.

Two Convicted in Los Angeles Beating (April 17): U.S. jury finds Sgt. Stacey C. Koon and Officer Laurence M. Powell guilty of civil rights violation in arrest of Rodney G. King. Two other officers acquitted.

Fire Kills 72 as Cult Standoff Ends (April 19): Officials say blaze set within destroyed compound near Waco, Texas, where David Koresh and his Branch Davidian followers had defied Federal agents for 51 days. Fires started after Federal agents began battering buildings and injecting tear gas.

Gays and Lesbians March on Washington (April 24): Estimated 300,000 protesters demand end to military ban on gays and equal rights for homosexuals.

Shuttle Launched on German Space Mission (April 26): *Columbia* starts nine-day schedule of biological and materials-testing experiments. Research directors are Dr. Ulrich Walter and Hans William Schlegel, both German physicists. Other crew members: Commander, Air Force Col. Steven R. Nagel; other astronauts, Col. Terence T. Henricks, Col. Jerry L. Ross, and Maj. Charles J. Precourt, all of Air Force, and Dr. Bernard A. Harris, Jr., a physician.

Woman Tennis Star Stabbed in Hamburg (April 30): Monica Seles, 19, world's top-ranking female player, slightly injured by spectator.

MAY 1993

International

President of Sri Lanka Assassinated (May 1): Man with explosives strapped to body kills Ranasinghe Premadasa and 10 others during May Day political rally at Colombo, the capital, a week after leading opposition politician was gunned down.

U.N. Takes Over Somalia Relief Operation (May 4): Lieut. Gen. Robert Johnston of U.S. Marines ends U.S. leadership. Turkish Lieut. Gen. Cevik Bir to head U.N. force expected to reach 28,000 troops.

Christopher Fails in Mission on Bosnia (May 7): Returns to U.S. without support of Europeans for Clinton plan to use military force against Serbs.

Europeans Reject Clinton Plan to Aid Bosnians (May 10): Governments refuse to back arms for Muslim-dominated regime and to approve threat to mount air strike against Bosnian Serb targets.

Bosnian Serbs Reject Peace Plan (May 16): Radovan Karadzic, leader, says failure of referendum on Vance-Owen proposal opens way for "Greater Serbia" with no Bosnia. **(May 19):** Bosnia Serb leaders meet to ratify ballot, confident that U.S. and other Western governments will accept result.

Danish Voters Back European Union (May 18): Reversing 1992 action, they overwhelmingly ratify greater economic and political unity. Ballot bolsters Continent's hopes. Denmark result aided by exemptions on common currency and other matters.

Iraqi Says He Led Attempt to Kill Bush (May 19): Suspect held in Kuwait tells F.B.I. he acted for Iraqi Government in plot to assassinate former President. Implicates other members of 10-man team.

U.S. to Recognize Angolan Government (May 18): Clinton decides to end years of hostility, including support for guerrilla insurgent group.

British Commons Approves European Unity Pact (May 20): House votes, 292–112, after months of debate to move Britain closer to being 12th and final nation to support stronger European Community.

Egyptian Court Dooms Six Muslim Militants (May 22): Military tribunal sentences two others to life in prison for attacks against tourists and plotting to assassinate Information Minister.

U.S. and Allies Agree on Bosnia Strategy (May 22): Washington conference approves plan for containing fighting and to guard enclaves of Muslim civilians besieged by Serbian nationalists. U.S. would use airpower to protect United Nations peacekeeping forces guarding six towns.

Eritrea Marks Independence (May 24): Northern province of Ethiopia formally declares itself a nation after winning 30-year struggle.

Germany Raises Bars to Asylum Seekers (May 26): Bonn Parliament votes to keep out thousands of foreigners who say they suffer persecution in own nations.

Bomb Kills Six Outside Florence Art Gallery (May 27): Destroys or damages dozens of works in Uffizi's priceless collection. Terrorists or Mafia blamed.

National

Clinton Compromises on Vaccination Plan (May 4): Bows to Congressional opposition to proposal for buying up and distributing all childhood vaccines in U.S.

Clinton Offers Plan to Curb Campaign Spending (May 7): Proposes public TV subsidies for Congressional candidates and seeks to reduce influence of lobbyists and political action committees.

Post Office Killing Toll Reaches 29 (May 7): Officials inquire into shootings in California and Michigan in which two persons were killed and three were wounded. Disgruntled employees blamed.

Congress Passes Voting Measure (May 11): Senate Democrats break G.O.P. filibuster and send Clinton bill to direct states to provide registration facilities at motor vehicle offices, military recruiting offices, and welfare offices.

Clinton Backs Trust Fund for Budget (May 12): Endorses proposal that money raised by tax increases and saved by spending cuts be used solely to cut deficit.

"Star Wars" Program Officially Dead (May 13): Administration downgrades Reagan-era Strategic Defense Initiative. Proposed anti-missile shield cost nearly $30 billion over ten years. Research to continue on small-scale renamed program.

White House Ousts Seven-Person Travel Staff (May 19): Charges failure to account for thousands of dollars and calls on F.B.I. to examine books. **(May 20):** Administration acknowledges that action came after close friend of Clinton sought White House business for colleagues in travel industry. **(May 21):** Arkansas travel agency with close ties to Clinton withdraws from work for White House.

House Hands President Victory on Budget (May 19): Clinton quells revolt by conservative Democrats demanding deeper spending cuts. **(May 27):** House approves heart of program to lower budget deficit by raising taxes of almost all except poor, with new steps to reduce spending. Battle in Senate is likely.

Chief Justice Scolds Library of Congress (May 25): Rehnquist charges bad judgment in releasing papers of Justice Thurgood Marshall so soon after death.

Naval Airman Gets Life in Killing (May 27): Court-martial sentences Terry M. Helvey in beating of Radioman Allen R. Schindler. Navy releases papers showing Helvey stalked homosexual victim.

Former Reagan Adviser to Aid Clinton (May 29): President names David R. Gergen, magazine columnist, to improve communications operation.

Clinton Speaks at Vietnam Memorial (May 31): President booed and cheered by thousands of veterans at Memorial Day observance. President, who avoided service, asks that differences "not divide us."

General

Scientists Find Gene Causing Cancer (May 5): Helsinki team near to locating gene that triggers colon cancer and several other varieties of disease.

Space Shuttle Columbia Lands (May 6): Returns to Earth with seven-man crew at Edwards Air Force Base, Calif., after ten-day German research mission.

More Than 200 Perish in Thailand Factory Fire (May 10): Doll factory collapses in flames. About 500 injured. Toll believed greatest in any factory fire.

French Police Save Nursery Hostages (May 15): Rescue six children by killing sleeping captor.

Dr. Kevorkian Helps in Another Suicide (May 16): Apparently defies new Michigan law by being at side of lung cancer victim in Detroit suburb.

Three Rivals Agree on Advanced TV System (May 24): Top competitors to collaborate on development of high-definition television.

White House Reinstates Five of Seven Travel Aides (May 25): Chief of Staff blamed for controversy over dismissal of group charged with incompetence and over involvement of the F.B.I.

Miami Police Officer Acquitted in Killings (May 28): William Lozano, 33, Hispanic, cleared by jury in second trial in deaths of two young black men. Case had aroused racial tensions in Florida.

JUNE 1993

International

Ruling Party Defeated in Cambodia (May 31): Royalist opposition victorious over Vietnamese-installed Cambodian People's Party in election sponsored by United Nations. **(June 14):** New National Assembly votes wide powers to Prince Norodom Sihanouk, former monarch, opposition leader.

Mortar Shells Kill 12 at Sarajevo Soccer Game (June 1): Wound 80 in tournament at Bosnian capital. Attack one of the worst in year of bombardment of city by Bosnian Serb forces.

Guatemalan Army Restores Democracy (June 1): Forces President Jorge Serrano Elias from office eight days after he seized virtual dictatorial powers. Political parties, businessmen, and civic groups support agreement to restore constitutional government.

Date Set for South African Election (June 3): Government and most opposition parties agree on April 27, 1994, for black majority to cast first votes to end more than three centuries of white rule.

U.N. Authorizes Air Strikes Against Serbs (June 4): Security Council votes overwhelmingly to allow U.S. and allies to attack forces besieging six Muslim enclaves in Bosnia and Hercegovina.

Twenty-Two U.N. Troops Killed in Somalia (June 5): Pakistan peacekeeping soldiers killed in fighting. Other Pakistanis and Americans injured. **(June 6):** U.N. officials blame Somali warlord.

Ship with Illegal Chinese Immigrants Goes Aground (June 6): Hundreds aboard smuggling vessel wrecked in surf off Queens, N.Y. At least seven are killed and 16 injured. About 30 missing. **(June 7):** U.S. charges captain and crew with smuggling aliens.

Mexicans Capture Drug Leader in Cardinal's Death (June 10): Officials term trafficker, Joaquin Guzmán Loera, a key figure in killing of Juan Jesùs Cardinal Posadas Ocampo and six others at airport.

U.S. Attacks Somali Warlord's Power Base (June 11): With allies, delivers pounding air and ground attack against leader in Mogadishu blamed for ordering deadly ambush of U.N. peacekeepers. **(June 14):** In three days of attacks against Gen. Mohammed Farah Aidid, gunships have blasted weapons sites, helicopters have attacked radio station, and attack helicopter has demolished rocket launcher.

Serb Shells Kill 50 at Bosnian First-Aid Center (June 13): Heavy artillery bombards Gorazde, designated by U.N. as safe center. Toll highest in single attack since Bosnian fighting began in 1992.

Canada Gets First Woman Prime Minister (June 13): Defense Minister Kim Campbell, 46, elected to head Progressive Conservative Party and nation.

Death Toll Near 600 in Liberian Massacre (June 16): Interim Government orders two investigations into killings of civilians in farm area. Rebel National Patriotic Front blamed.

Japanese Government Toppled (June 18): Rebels in party of Prime Minister Kiichi Miyazawa join opposition in no-confidence vote. Premier dissolves Parliament and calls for new elections.

U.S. Attacks Iraqi Intelligence Center (June 28): Launches missiles on Baghdad in retaliation for attempt to assassinate former President George Bush during visit to Kuwait in April.

National

Clinton Cancels Civil Rights Nomination (June 3): Concedes he would not have chosen Lani Guinier after reading her legal writings on increasing the political power of black voters.

Public Schools Opened to Church Groups (June 7): Supreme Court rules unanimously that religious bodies must have same right of access as community groups.

Disabled Get Access to Jobs and Health Benefits (June 8): Equal Employment Opportunity Commission rules employers cannot refuse to hire them because of insurance costs and must grant insurance.

Justices Overrule Ban on Animal Sacrifices (June 11): Supreme Court rules unanimously that Florida city's statute violates sect's religious freedom.

High Court Upholds Stiff Sentences for Hate Crimes (June 11): Justices rule unanimously that states may impose harsher sentences on criminals who pick victims on basis of race, religion, or other personal characteristics.

Rights Advocate Named to Supreme Court (June 14): President chooses Appeals Court Judge Ruth Bader Ginsburg. She is known for her litigation for women's rights. If confirmed, she would be second woman on Supreme Court and first Jew since 1969.

Interpreter in Parochial School Approved (June 18): Supreme Court, 5–4, rules Constitution permits government to pay for sign-language interpreter to accompany deaf child in religious setting.

Air Force Ousts General Who Attacked Clinton (June 18): Maj. Gen. Harold N. Campbell fined $7,000 and forced to retire for calling President "dope smoking," "draft dodging" Commander in Chief.

Justices Uphold Interception of Haitians (June 21): Supreme Court, 8–1, approves Bush and Clinton policy of halting fugitives at sea and returning them without hearings on asylum status.

Mrs. Clinton Ruled "de Facto" Federal Official (June 22): U.S. Appeals Court upholds secrecy of task force on health care, accepting her views on role and powers as First Lady.

Justices Rule on Job-Bias Cases (June 25): Supreme Court, 5–4, decides employees must prove discrimination is real reason for employer action.

House Votes to Halt Work on Supercollider (June 24): Rejects $11-billion proton-smasher in Texas in defeat for expensive scientific research.

Four Networks Agree to TV Warning on Violence (June 29): Move to avert federally imposed ratings system.

Clinton Backs Logging Compromise (June 30): President approves plan to reduce harvesting on U.S. lands in Northwest and provide more than $1 billion to retrain workers and help distressed timber communities. Proposals attacked from all sides.

General

Psychoanalyst Wins New Yorker Lawsuit (June 2): San Francisco jury decides Jeffrey M. Masson was libeled in articles by Janet Malcolm. Deadlocked on damages in $7.5-million action.

Woody Allen Loses Child Custody Battle (June 7): New York judge awards custody of three children to mother, Mia Farrow. Judge brands Allen "untrustworthy."

Japanese Royal Wedding Blends Traditions (June 9): Crown Prince Naruhito and Masako Owada married in Shinto ritual. In a precedent, Princess has had thriving career in diplomacy.

Publisher Makes Record Gift to Private Schools (June 19): Walter Annenberg announces $365 million in cash grants to three universities and obscure preparatory school in Hightstown, N.J. It is largest one-time such gift in American history.

Terrorist Ring Smashed in New York (June 24): Federal agents seize eight alleged Muslim extremists planning campaign of bombings and political assassinations. Wired informer aided coup.

JULY 1993

International

U.N. Inspectors Leave Iraq (July 4): Weapons inspectors withdraw after Baghdad refuses to allow installation of monitoring cameras at missile sites.

Economic Summit Convened in Tokyo (July 7): President Clinton joins other leaders of seven major industrial democracies. Hails limited agreement to lower tariffs. **(July 10):** Clinton and Japanese Prime Minister Kiichi Miyazawa reach major accord on "framework" for resolving trade disputes.

U.S. Troops Join Forces Guarding Macedonia (July 12): Three hundred ground forces part of U.N. contingent seeking to prevent Balkan warfare from spreading to former Yugoslav republic.

U.N. Forces Attack Somali Clan Leader's Base (July 12): Fire on Gen. Mohammed Farah Aidid's command center. Angry mob kills two journalists.

Mexico Accepts Chinese Refugees (July 14): Agrees to be responsible for 659 aboard three ships intercepted by U.S. Coast Guard 60 miles off Mexican coast while headed for United States.

Chinese Refugees Sent Back Home (July 17): First 100 board plane for China within hours after two ships dock at Ensenada, Mexico.

Egypt Hangs Five Islamic Militants (July 17): Executes five more in campaign that officials say has caused worst damage to Fundamentalists in 18 months.

Ruling Party Defeated in Japan (July 18): Liberal Democrats lose majority in Parliament for first time. Keep enough seats to wield influence.

Iraq Accepts U.N. Weapons Monitoring (July 19): Bows to diplomatic and military pressure designed to prevent building weapons of mass destruction.

Serbs Close in on Sarajevo (July 21): Nationalist forces in Bosnia battle to close off key roads that would cut off retreat of Muslim defenders.

Major Wins Key Vote on European Treaty (July 23): Gains vote of confidence that insures British Parliament's final approval of Treaty on European Union.

Russia Parliament Flouts Yeltsin Program (July 23): Lawmakers vote extraordinary measures that threaten to disrupt the economy and undermine the transfer of public property to private interests. President expected to veto or ignore actions.

Russia Cancels Currency Revision (July 24): Central Bank moves to reassert control over money supply. With government support withdraws all bank notes issued before beginning of year. Announcement sets off panic. **(July 26):** President Yeltsin modifies drastic currency revision, responding to popular dissatisfaction and protests from market-oriented wing of his government.

Israelis Bomb Guerrilla Bases in Lebanon (July 25): Jets pound targets in retaliation for rocket attacks that killed seven Israeli soldiers. **(July 26):** Israelis step up bombing, artillery, and gunboat attacks on southern Lebanon targets. But pro-Iranian militiamen aim more rocket attacks on Israeli settlements. Civilians on both sides forced to flee or take shelter in bunkers.

Car Bombs Rock Milan and Rome (July 27): Explosion kills at least five in downtown Milan. Shortly afterward, bomb injures 24 in heart of Rome and damages basilica of St. John Lateran, the Pope's See.

Japanese Coalition Chooses Leader (July 29): Opposition parties select Morihiro Hosokawa, conservative populist, to become prime minister. In drastic change, he has pledged to reduce government's role.

Israel Court Frees John Demjanjuk (July 29): Supreme tribunal finds "reasonable doubt" that he was "Ivan the Terrible," sadistic Nazi death camp guard.

European Monetary System Threatened (July 30): Speculators attack franc. Parity with mark near collapse as currency traders mount drive against both French and German central banks.

Cease-Fire Reached in South Lebanon (July 31): Israel and pro-Iranian guerrillas agree to U.S. proposal to cease fighting after seven days of shelling and air attacks. Syria the main power broker.

National

White House Critical of Travel Staff Dismissals (July 2): Report rebukes four for ousters and for appearing to pressure F.B.I. into action.

Clinton Dismisses F.B.I. Director (July 19): William S. Sessions had refused to resign after internal ethics report severely critical of his conduct.

President Presents Plan for Gays in Military (July 19): Generals and admirals support compromise proposals for easing ban on homosexuals. Plan limits ability of commanders to open investigations.

Representative Rostenkowski Accused (July 19): Former House of Representatives Postmaster says he helped powerful Democrat embezzle $21,300.

Clinton Appoints New F.B.I. Director (July 20): Names Judge Louis J. Freeh of Manhattan Federal District Court to succeed William S. Sessions.

Supreme Court Justice Rejects Adoption Plea (July 26): John Paul Stevens refuses to allow Michigan couple to keep two-year-old girl they had raised since birth and sought to bar return to biological parents.

Homosexuals Sue Over Service Compromise (July 27): Seven gay and lesbian members of armed forces resort to Federal Court in fight to overturn new regulations agreed to by Clinton. Contend that their treatment violates Constitution.

General

Sheik Surrenders in Bombing Inquiry (July 2): Omar Abdel Rahman, Islamic Fundamentalist, arrested by Federal agents outside Brooklyn, N.Y., mosque. His followers linked to bombing conspiracies.

Compact to Clear Up Everglades Reached (July 13): Federal and Florida officials announce agreement with agricultural interests on $465-million plan to improve water quantity and quality.

Earthquake Devastates Japan Area (July 14): Strongest temblor in 25 years hits coastal communities. Seventy-nine reported dead, hundreds missing.

President Again Visits Midwest Flood Area (July 17): Makes third trip to region and confers with officials on ways to clean up damage and relieve suffering in one of nation's worst natural disasters.

Friend of Clinton Apparent Suicide (July 22): Justice Department seeks motive in death of Vincent W. Foster, Jr., a senior White House lawyer.

Monsoon Kills More Than 500 in India (July 22): Rains drive hundreds of thousands from homes and farms. Agricultural losses in hundreds of millions.

Flood Loss Expected to Pass $10 Billion (July 24): Damage estimate raised as rains keep falling in devastated areas of Midwest inundated by Mississippi and other rivers. Bankers, farmers, state officials, and Federal Reserve analysts see mounting damage to the nation's economy.

New I.B.M. Chairman Announces Drastic Cuts (July 27): Louis V. Gerstner announces $8.9-billion program to revive world's largest computer maker. Plans to eliminate 60,000 jobs and reduce factories.

AUGUST 1993

International

Brother to Succeed King of Belgium (Aug. 1): Prince Albert, 59, to take ceremonial post. Monarch for 42 years dead of heart attack in Spain.

Italian Electoral System Abolished (Aug. 4): Parliament, after 45 years, votes to replace it with direct ballot expected to make politicians more accountable. Minor parties will still have seats.

Reformer Named Japanese Prime Minister (Aug. 6): Morihiro Hosokawa, 55, first in office in 38 years who is not a member of Liberal Democratic Party. He is second youngest premier since World War II.

Buckingham Palace Open to Public (Aug. 7): Once protected royal sanctuary finally admits tourists after nearly two centuries. Income from admissions to help defray cost of royal establishment.

Four U.S. Soldiers Killed in Somalia (Aug. 8): Victims of explosion part of U.N. peacekeeping force. Other soldiers attacked after blast. Deaths bring American casualties in country to 12.

C.I.A. Agent Killed Near Tbilisi, Georgia (Aug. 8): Fred Woodruff, 45, shot while riding in car with chief bodyguard of President Shevardnadze.

Hotel Collapse Kills 88 in Thailand (Aug. 13): More than 200 injured in wreckage of building in northeastern area. **(Aug. 14):** Scores believed trapped.

Egyptian Official Survives Bombing Attack (Aug. 18): New security chief wounded in assassination attempt by Islamic militants in center of Cairo. Four killed and at least 15 wounded.

Islamic Militants Kill Eight Israeli Soldiers (Aug. 19): Launch two separate bombing attacks against patrols in South Lebanon. Israeli planes retaliate.

Brazil Gold Miners Kill Indians (Aug. 21): Death toll from attack on Yanomami reservation Aug. 15 mounts to 73, nation's largest massacre of century. **(Aug. 22):** As public outrage grows, President seeks to enlist help of military in tracking down killers.

U.S. Imposes Sanctions on China (Aug. 26): Bans exports of almost $1 billion in high-technology goods for two years as penalty for Beijing's selling of sensitive missile technology to Pakistan in violation of international arms control agreements.

U.N. Suspends Oil Embargo Against Haiti (Aug. 27): Lifts sanctions harmful to economy after military agrees to end rule and let President return.

Israeli-Palestinian Accord Reached (Aug. 28): Leaders agree in principle on Palestinian authority over Gaza Strip and Jericho on West Bank as first step to self-rule in Israeli-occupied territories.

Bosnian Parliament, 65–0, Rejects U.N. Peace Plan (Aug. 28): Muslim-dominated body votes to return negotiators to Geneva to work for changes.

Last Russian Troops Leave Lithuania (Aug. 31): Complete former Soviet Army's withdrawal. Baltic republic celebrates end of more than half century of Soviet and Russian military presence. Church bells ring.

National

Nobel Laureate Nominated to Science Post (Aug. 3): White House names Dr. Harold E. Varmus of University of California to head National Institutes of Health, with wide power over research.

U.S. Appeals Court Backs Demjanjuk (Aug. 3): Rules former citizen acquitted by Israeli court of Nazi camp role must be allowed to return.

U.S. Top Expert on Bosnia Resigns (Aug. 4): Marshall Freeman Harris charges Clinton Administration is putting too much pressure on government of Bosnia and Hercegovina to agree to partition.

Congress Narrowly Approves Clinton's Budget (Aug. 5): House, 218–216, approves $496-billion deficit reduction program after day of frantic maneuvering. **(Aug. 6):** Senate approves compromise measure 51–50, with Bob Kerrey, Nebraska Democrat, providing key vote and Vice President Gore breaking tie. Administration had won over skeptical key Democrats only by promising more spending cuts.

New Head of Joint Chiefs Named (Aug. 11): President appoints Gen. John Shalikashvili, NATO commander, to succeed Gen. Colin L. Powell. New chairman a critic of Western inaction on Bosnia.

President Voids Ban on Air-Controller Rehiring (Aug. 12): Cancels Reagan policy on F.A.A. employees in symbolic gesture to organized labor.

Rigging of "Star Wars" Test Revealed (Aug. 17): Former Reagan officials say project officials also faked other data in move to deceive Soviet Union but that also misled Congress into increasing spending.

State Department Expert on Bosnia Resigns (Aug. 23): Stephen W. Walker fourth to quit over U.S. policy he believes sanctions genocide and aggression.

General

Two Sentenced in Rodney King Beating (Aug. 4): U.S. judge in Los Angeles metes 2 1/2 years to police officers. Explains lenient penalty because he considered that King had provoked violence.

Midwest Floods Rage Two Months; 50 Dead (Aug. 9): Nearly 70,000 homeless. Property and agricultural damage estimated at $12 billion in Mississippi River area. Flood-control policies debated.

Pope Travels to North America (Aug. 11): On his 60th overseas tour, John Paul II arrives in Mexico and criticizes injustice against indigenous peoples. **(Aug. 12):** At Denver, in first face-to-face meeting with Clinton, Pope expresses opposition to President's stand on abortion and challenges Americans to revive "high moral vision." **(Aug. 14):** In celebrating Roman Catholic World Youth Day, Pontiff denounces "false morality" of today, condemning abortion and euthanasia. **(Aug. 15):** Youthful crowd of nearly 400,000 from around world join in prayer, song, dance, and cheering for mass celebrated by Pope in dusty field 14 miles from Denver.

Robert A. Altman Acquitted (Aug. 14): Washington lawyer cleared by jury of fraud charges in case involving Bank of Credit and Commerce International.

Suicide Doctor Charged Under Michigan Law (Aug. 17): Dr. Jack Kevorkian, as he wished, is first person accused under statute banning assisted suicides. He faces penalty up to four years in prison.

Florida Teen-ager Wins Family-Rights Suit (Aug. 18): Judge upholds right of child switched at birth to sever contacts with biological parents.

Scientists Monitor Deep-Sea Volcano (Aug. 19): For first time, they use Navy's super-secret underwater listening system to follow explosion of eruption below surface of ocean. New era of exploration seen.

Siamese Twin Survives Separation (Aug. 20): Angela Lakeberg rests comfortably after sister gives life to save her in rarely performed operation by surgeons at Children's Hospital of Pennsylvania.

Sheik Indicted in New York Bombing (Aug. 25): Egyptian clergyman, Omar Abdel Rahman, charged by U.S. with being a leader of group behind World Trade Center bombing plot to blow up New York structures and killing of Rabbi Meir Kahane, Jewish militant. Sheik known for fiery Islamic sermons.

Mars Observer Lost in Space (Aug. 26): Officials and engineers seek new ways to explore red planet after losing communication with spacecraft.

Israel and P.L.O. Reach Peace Agreement (Sept. 9): Recognize each other's legitimacy. Yasir Arafat, leader of Palestine Liberation Organization, renounces use of terrorism. Israel's Prime Minister Yitzhak Rabin agrees to begin peace negotiations. **(Sept. 13):** On White House lawn, Arafat and Rabin shake hands in President Clinton's presence to seal first agreement to end conflict and sign "Declaration of Principles" on Palestinian self-government in Israeli-occupied Gaza Strip and West Bank.

SEPTEMBER 1993

South Africa to Share Transition Powers (Sept. 7): White Government to give first formal voice to disenfranchised blacks in multiparty committee subjecting Government functions to predominantly black interim council leading to universal election.

Miss America Receives Crown (Sept. 18): Kimberly Clarice Aiken from Columbia, S.C., is the new titleholder.

Yeltsin Dissolves Russian Parliament (Sept. 21): Charges opposition blocks his reforms and ability to govern. Calls elections in December for new legislature. Supreme Soviet votes to dépose Yeltsin and swears in Vice President Alexsandr V. Rutskoi as acting president. Clinton supports Yeltsin.

Railroad Crash Kills 47 in Alabama (Sept. 22): Amtrak train with 206 passengers plunges off 12-foot-high trestle near Mobile into bayou, trapping sleeping victims in deep water. Accident is worst in Amtrak's 23-year history. Stray barge had rammed bridge just before crash. Sensor use had been rejected.

Olympic Committee Picks Sydney for 2000 Games (Sept. 23): International body administers unexpected rebuff to China in rejecting bid by Beijing. China's human-rights record cited by opponents.

Clinton Offers Sweeping Health-Care Program (Sept. 22): President warmly applauded in historic address to joint session of Congress. He calls for giving "every American health security—health care that's always there—health care that can never be taken away." Outlines six principles as "guiding stars": security, simplicity, savings, choice, quality, and responsibility. Extensive discussion begins.

Earthquake Kills Thousands in Central India (Sept. 30): Most devastating earthquake in India in more than 50 years rocks remote sugar-cane-growing region.

Hillary Clinton Testifies on Health Care (Sept. 30): First Lady wins praise of Senators and Representatives in five Congressional hearings in three days as she explains and answers questions about President's plan for universal coverage.

Major Emmy Awards for TV, 1993

(Sept. 19, 1993)

Drama Series: *Picket Fences* (CBS)
- **Actress:** Kathy Baker, *Picket Fences* (CBS)
- **Actor:** Tom Skerritt, *Picket Fences* (CBS)
- **Supporting actress:** Mary Alice, *I'll Fly Away* (NBC)
- **Supporting actor:** Chad Lowe, *Life Goes On* (ABC)

Comedy series: *Seinfeld* (NBC)
- **Actress:** Roseanne Arnold, *Roseanne* (ABC)
- **Actor:** Ted Danson, *Cheers* (NBC)
- **Supporting actress:** Laurie Metcalf, *Roseanne* (ABC)
- **Supporting actor:** Michael Richards, *Seinfeld* (NBC)

Variety, Music or Comedy Series: *Saturday Night Live* (NBC)

Variety, Music or Comedy Special: *Bob Hope: The First 90 Years* (NBC)

Miniseries or Special: *Mystery! Prime Suspect 2* (PBS)
- **Actress:** Holly Hunter, *The Positively True Adventures of the Alleged Texas Cheerleader-Murdering Mom* (HBO)
- **Actor:** Robert Morse, *Tru (American Playhouse)* (PBS)
- **Supporting actress:** Mary Tyler Moore, *Stolen Babies* (Lifetime)
- **Supporting actor:** Beau Bridges, *The Positively True Adventures of the Alleged Texas Cheerleader-Murdering Mom* (HBO)

Made for TV Movie: *Barbarians at the Gates* (HBO); *Stalin* (HBO)

Individual Performance, Variety or Music Program: Dana Carvey, *Saturday Night Live's Presidential Bash* (NBC)

OCTOBER 1993
(Through October 17)

International

Leaders of Israel and Jordan Shake Hands (Oct. 1): After 45 years of secret talks, they meet at White House to confirm normal relationships.

Twelve G.I.'s Killed in Somalia Fighting (Oct. 3): A 13th American is fatally injured as Somali militia shoot down two U.S. helicopters during U.N. military operations in Mogadishu, nation's capital. About 20 backers of Gen. Mohammad Farah Aidid, fugitive fighter, seized. **(Oct. 4):** Clinton sends hundreds of fresh troops and heavy armor to Somalia. **(Oct. 7):** President promises to have all U.S. forces home within six months.

Yeltsin Crushes Revolt by Opposition (Oct. 4): Thousands of enemies take up arms to break his blockade of rebel Parliament. Tanks and troops loyal to President crush uprising. Parliament "White House" in flames. **(Oct. 5):** Yeltsin moves to consolidate power, banning opposition parties and newspapers and censoring major publications. **(Oct. 6):** He affirms new parliamentary elections for Dec. 12.

China Breaks Nuclear Test Moratorium (Oct. 5): Despite plea from President Clinton, explodes device beneath western desert. Clinton orders preparations for resuming American testing.

Benazir Bhutto Claims Parliamentary Win (Oct. 7): Ms. Bhutto's Pakistan Peoples Party wins plurality but not a majority of seats and she faces the task of forming a coalition government.

Former Greek Premier Restored (Oct. 10): Andreas Papandreou's Pan-Hellenic Socialist Movement triumphs four years after he was driven from office.

German Court Upholds Maastricht Pact (Oct. 12): It rules treaty on European union does not violate the German constitution, clearing the way for it to go into effect on Nov. 1, 1993.

Haitian Mobs Block U.S. Troops (Oct. 11): Forces on U.N. mission kept from landing by armed demonstrators believed to be directed by security groups opposed to return of President Aristide. **(Oct. 13):** U.N. Security Council reimposes oil and arms embargo. **(Oct. 14):** Gunmen slay Justice Minister and two aides. **(Oct. 15):** President Clinton orders six American warships to Haiti to enforce embargo.

Serbs Resume Shelling (Oct. 16): After a lull of several weeks Serbian nationalist forces bombard Sarajevo with heavy artillery. **(Oct. 17):** NATO planes fly low level sorties over gun positions as warning to Serbs not to resume attacks.

National

U.S. Agents Blamed in Waco, Tex., Siege (Oct. 1): Justice Department report says mid- and lower-grade officials recommended that negotiations be ended and asked a tear-gas assault on Davidian cult.

Secretary Aspin Saves Top Admiral (Oct. 4): Defense head overrules Navy Secretary and keeps Frank B. Kelso as chief of Naval Operations despite criticism over Tailhook sex scandal. **(Oct. 15):** Navy Secretary Dalton censures three admirals in the Tailhook affair and takes milder administrative action against 30 other senior officers, including Admiral Kelso.

Pentagon Suspends New Gay-Troops Policy (Oct. 8): U.S. judge in Los Angeles allows homosexual service people to serve openly while Government appeals ruling against "don't ask, don't tell" policy.

General

World Trade Center Trial Begins (Oct. 4): Prosecutor opens with a tale of horror bolstered by the trial's first witness, Charles J. Maikish, director of the Port Authority's World Trade department. The defense attacks tactic as inflammatory.

Former Priest Admits Child Abuse (Oct. 4): James R. Porter, 58, pleads guilty in Boston court to molesting 28 when a Roman Catholic clergyman.

India Earthquake Toll Past 10,000 (Oct. 6): Some estimate deaths September 30 as high as 30,000, with 120,000 homeless. Amateur radio operators form communications network to help victims.

Bank Robbery Fugitive Sentenced (Oct. 6): Katherine Ann Power, once antiwar radical, faces 8–12 years in Massachusetts prison for role in slaying of Boston policeman in 1970. Judge bars leniency.

Michael Jordan Retires From Basketball (Oct. 6): Star of Chicago Bulls, aged 30, considered world's greatest player, sees "no more challenges."

Scientologists Gain Tax Exemption (Oct. 13): Ending a 39-year legal dispute, the Internal Revenue Service agrees to the exemption.

Medical Manufacturer Admits Fraud (Oct. 15): C.R. Bard Inc. agrees to plead guilty to more than 390 counts of fraud and human experimentation for selling untested heart catheters.

1993 Nobel Prize Winners

Peace: F.W. de Klerk and Nelson Mandela (South Africans) for negotiating the end of the apartheid state and collaborating in the quest for a nonracial democracy. Mr. de Klerk is South Africa's president and Mr. Mandela is head of the African National Congress.

Literature: Toni Morrison (American), novelist, for her work which "gives life to an essential aspect of American reality" in novels "characterized by visionary force and poetic import."

Medicine: Dr. Phillip A. Sharp (American) and Dr. Richard J. Roberts (English) for their independent discovery in 1977 of "split genes." Dr. Sharp is head of the biology department at the Massachusetts Institute of Technology and Dr. Roberts is research director for New England Biolabs.

Economics: Robert W. Fogel and Douglass C. North (Americans) for their work in economic history "applying economic theory and quantitative methods" to historical puzzles. Professor Fogel is on the faculty of the University of Chicago and Professor North is affiliated with Washington University, in St. Louis.

Physics: Dr. Joseph H. Taylor and Dr. Russell A. Hulse (Americans) for their discovery of a binary pulsar that had an especially powerful impact on the study of gravity. Dr. Taylor is a professor of physics at Princeton University and Dr. Hulse conducts research in hydrogen fusion at Princeton Plasma Physics Laboratory.

Chemistry: Dr. Kary B. Mullis (American) and Dr. Michael Smith (Canadian) for their contributions to the science of genetics. Dr. Mullis is the inventor of a technique for making many copies of a single gene fragment called the polymerase chain reaction (P.C.R.). Dr. Smith, British born, invented a method used to splice foreign components into genetic molecules. He is a professor of biochemistry at the University of British Columbia.

Deaths in 1992–1993

(As of September 5, 1993)

Acuff, Roy, 89: singer and fiddler known as King of Country Music to thousands of listeners to Grand Ole Opry. Nov. 23, 1992.

Anderson, Marian, 96: Black contralto famed across the world. Helped to topple racial bars in the arts. April 8, 1993.

Ashe, Arthur, 49: tennis champion who fought discrimination in sport. Only black to win Wimbledon and U.S. and Australian Opens. In last year, fought for public awareness of AIDS. Feb. 6, 1993.

Banky, Vilma, about 90: Hungarian-born film actress, a major Hollywood star of 1920s. March 18, 1991.

Barber, Red (Walter Lanier), 84: rated as greatest baseball sportscaster of his age. Known as voice of Brooklyn Dodgers. Oct. 22, 1992.

Baudouin I, King of Belgium, 62: reclusive monarch reigned in Brussels for 42 years. July 31, 1993.

Bazelon, David L., 83: Federal Appeals Court judge for three decades. Landmark decisions broadened rights of individuals and rights of criminal defendants. Feb. 19, 1993.

Bloom, Allan, 62: professor of political philosophy whose book "The Closing of the American Mind," attacked new educational values. Oct. 7, 1992.

Booth, Shirley, 94: star of stage, screen, radio, and television won both a Tony and an Oscar for her performance in "Come Back, Little Sheba." Also won two Emmys for her role of Hazel in the TV series of that name. Oct. 16, 1992.

Boyle, Kay, 90: novelist and short-story writer known for keen insights into human nature. Dec. 27, 1992.

Brandt, Willy, 78: Social Democratic leader of West Germany from 1969 to 1974. Won Nobel Peace Prize for efforts to end Cold War division of Europe. Oct. 8, 1992.

Burdett, Winston M., 79: journalist, CBS news correspondent on radio and television. He was a protégé of Edward R. Murrow. A target of the House Un-American Activities Committee, he was permanently assigned to CBS bureau in Rome. May 19, 1993.

Burkitt, Dr. Denis P., 82: missionary surgeon in Africa. In his late 40s turned to research and made important findings on cancer and nutrition. March 23, 1993.

Cahn, Sammy, 79: lyricist who collaborated with such composers as Jule Styne and Jimmy Van Heusen. "Three Coins in the Fountain," "All the Way," and "Call Me Irresponsible" are some of his memorable titles. Jan. 15, 1993.

Campanella, Roy, 71: top National League catcher of day. Joined Brooklyn Dodgers in 1948 as one of first black major league players. June 26, 1993.

Cantinflas (Mario Moreno), 81: Mexico's most famous comic actor. Was costar as valet in "Around the World in 80 Days." April 20, 1993.

Chavez, Cesar, 66: founder of America's first successful union of farm workers, the United Farm Workers of America. April 23, 1993.

Christoff, Boris, 79: famed Bulgarian operatic bass. Known for roles in "Boris Godounov," other Russian works, Verdi operas, and others. June 28, 1993.

Connally, John B., 76: former Governor of Texas. Served in two Presidential Administrations. Wounded when President Kennedy was assassinated. June 15, 1993.

Connors, Chuck, 71: former professional basketball and baseball player who later starred in TV series "The Rifleman." Nov., 10, 1992.

Crosby, Bob, 80: popular swing-era band leader and younger brother of Bing Crosby. March 10, 1993.

Diebenkorn, Richard, 70: a leading American post-war painter known for lyrical abstractions of light and spaces in California. March 30, 1993.

Donner, Frank J., 82: civil liberties lawyer. Director for American Civil Liberties Union's Project on Political Surveillance. June 11, 1993.

Dubcek, Alexander, 70: Czechoslovak leader. Soviet-led Warsaw Pact troops crushed his attempt in 1968 to give country "socialism with a human face." Nov. 7, 1992.

Fine, Reuben, 79: one of greatest U.S. chess geniuses. Psychologist and author of many books about chess and psychology. March 26, 1993.

Gallo, Julio, 83: a founder and longtime president of E.&J. Gallo Winery, one of world's largest wine-makers. May 2, 1993.

Garrison, Jim, 70: New Orleans District Attorney who won notoriety with charges of widespread conspiracy and cover-up in assassination of President John F. Kennedy. Oct. 22, 1992.

Gesell, Gerhard A., 82: Federal judge who presided over major cases in Watergate scandals, release of secret Pentagon Papers, Iran-Contra affair, and legalization of abortion. Feb. 19, 1993.

Gillespie, Dizzy (John Birks), 75: trumpet virtuoso. Pioneer of jazz innovations and identified with bebop revolution. Jan. 6, 1993.

Gish, Lillian, 91: last of great stars of silent-film era. Appeared for more than 85 years in movies, theater, and television. Feb. 27, 1993.

Gleason, Thomas W., 92: labor union official and former president of the International Longshoremen's Association, which controlled stevedores in all Atlantic and Gulf ports. Dec. 24, 1992.

Golding, Sir William, 81: British author and poet. Nobel prize-winning author of "Lord of the Flies" and other works exploring dark side of human nature. June 19, 1993.

Granger, Stewart, 80: swashbuckling star of such films as "King Solomon's Mines" and "Scaramouche." Aug. 16, 1993.

Hallinan, Vincent W., 95: West Coast lawyer who defended Harry Bridges and other unpopular causes and reformed San Francisco's corrupt jury system. Oct. 2, 1992.

Harken, Dwight, 83: pioneer in heart surgery and creator of intensive-care units for critically ill patients. Aug. 27, 1993.

Hayes, Helen, 92: actress called First Lady of American theater. Lifetime of acting included roles as Queen Victoria, Mary Queen of Scots, and other regal women. March 17, 1993.

Hearst, William Randolph, Jr., 85: Pulitzer prize-winning journalist. Editor-in-chief of publishing empire founded by father. May 14, 1993.

Hepburn, Audrey, 63: actress who epitomized an elegance that looked effortless in such films as "Roman Holiday," "Breakfast at Tiffany's," and "My Fair Lady." In recent years she won respect for her work as a goodwill ambassador for UNICEF. Jan. 20, 1993.

Hersey, John, 78: novelist and journalist. "A Bell for Adano" won Pulitzer fiction prize in 1945. Nonfiction "Hiroshima" alerted Americans to horrors of nuclear warfare. March 24, 1993.

Horszowski, Mieczyslaw, 100: virtuoso pianist with career of more than nine decades. Known for elegance and clarity of performances. May 22, 1993.

Howe, Irving, 72: literary critic and founding editor of *Dissent* magazine. Wrote essays on culture and literature, the advocacy of democratic socialism, and the Jewish experience in America. May 5, 1993.

Janeway, Eliot, 80: political economist and author. Critical of policies of Presidents from Franklin D. Roosevelt to Ronald Reagan. Feb. 8, 1993.

Jonas, Hans, 89: influential philosophy professor who fled Nazi Germany. Won wide attention for repudiating early mentor for being pro-Hitler. Feb. 5, 1993.

Keeler, Ruby, 82: tap-dancing and singing actress of Depression era. Appeared in nine Warner Brothers musicals. Introduced "42nd Street" and "Shuffle Off to Buffalo." Feb. 28, 1993.

Kempner, Robert M.W., 93: lawyer who was deputy chief counsel for United States at Nuremberg war-crimes trials. Wrote about Nazi era. Aug. 15, 1993.

Kirsten, Dorothy, 82: American lyric soprano who sang leading roles at Metropolitan Opera for 30 years. Sang on radio and television. Nov. 18, 1992.

Mankiewicz, Joseph L., 83: Hollywood writer, director, and producer. Won four Academy Awards and other prizes for sophisticated comedies. Feb. 5, 1993.

Mayer, Dr. Jean, 72: widely known for work as nutritionist clarifying nature of hunger and obesity. Chancellor and former president of Tufts University. Jan. 1, 1993.

Marshall, Thurgood, 84: first black Justice of Supreme Court. A pioneer of civil rights movement and creator of legal strategy that ended official segregation. Jan. 24, 1993.

McFarland, George (Spanky), 64: memorable child actor in the "Our Gang" comedies of the 1930s. June 30, 1993.

Milstein, Nathan, 88: Russian-born violin virtuoso. Regarded as a leading exponent of 19th century romantic repertory. Dec. 21, 1992.

Montoya, Carlos, 89: guitarist and composer. Transformed flamenco from Spanish folk dance into international style. March 3, 1993.

Morris, Dr. John McLean, 78: gynecologic researcher who discovered "morning-after" contraceptive pill and contributed to cancer treatment. April 8, 1993.

Nikolais, Alwin, 82: modern-dance director, choreographer, teacher, designer, composer of electronic dance music, and a trailblazer in multimedia dance. May 8, 1993.

Nixon, Patricia Ryan, 81: wife of former President Richard M. Nixon and his supporter through victory and disgrace. June 22, 1993.

Nureyev, Rudolf, 54: ballet dancer who defected from the Soviet Union to the West. Regarded as one of the most popular and creative ballet artists of century. Jan. 6, 1993.

Nye, Russell, 80: retired professor and historian of American culture and literature. Awarded a Pulitzer Prize for biography in 1945. Sept. 2, 1993.

Parkinson, C. Northcote, 83: British historian and writer. Author of "Parkinson's Law" that work expands to occupy time of people needed for its completion. March 8, 1993.

Pucci, Emilio, 78: Italian fashion designer noted for his brilliantly colored prints that were the rage in the 1960s and recently saw a worldwide revival. Nov. 29, 1992.

Pulitzer, Joseph, Jr., 80: chairman of Pulitzer Publishing Company, owner of one of world's finest collections of modern art. May 26, 1993.

Ridgway, Gen. Matthew B., 98: soldier-diplomat who became Army Chief of Staff after leading American forces in Normandy and U.N. troops in Korea. Planned and executed Army's first airborne assault, into Sicily in World War II. July 26,1993.

Roach, Hal (Harold Eugene), 100 (cq): film writer, producer, and director, pioneer in shaping film comedy. Executive producer of nearly 1,000 films. Helped the rise to stardom of Will Rogers, Harold Lloyd, and other comedians. Nov. 2, 1992.

Rockefeller, Blanchette Ferry Hooker, 83: widow of John D. Rockefeller 3rd. Philanthropist and major benefactor of New York Museum of Modern Art. Nov. 29, 1992.

Ross, Steven J., 65: founder of Time-Warner Inc., world's largest media and entertainment company. Dec. 20, 1992.

Sabin, Dr. Albert B., 86: pioneering researcher on viruses and viral diseases. Best known for developing live-virus polio vaccine. March 3, 1993.

Salisbury, Harrison E., 84: won Pulitzer Prizes as correspondent for *New York Times*. Later became a top editor at the newspaper and author of 29 books. July 5, 1993.

Schneider, Alexander, 84: Eminent violinist, conductor, and teacher, survivor of Romantic tradition. Nurtured generations of musicians. Feb. 2, 1993.

Shawn, William, 85: quiet but strong-willed editor of *New Yorker* magazine for 35 years. Dec. 8, 1992.

Simon, Norton, 86: California industrialist who spent more than $100 million in amassing a major art collection. Outspoken public figure in California. June 2, 1993.

Slayton, Donald K. (Deke), 69: one of seven original American astronauts and an influential manager in space agency. June 13, 1993.

Stark, Dame Freya, 100 (cq): scholarly author of 24 travel books and autobiographies. First Westerner to travel through many regions of Middle East. May 9, 1993.

Stegner, Wallace, 84: novelist and short-story writer. Won highest awards for works celebrating American West. April 13, 1993.

Swanberg, William A., 84: author of 10 biographies of public figures. Won Pulitzer Prize for "Luce and His Empire," life of co-founder of Time Inc. Sept. 17, 1992.

Tambo, Oliver R., 75: leader of African National Congress in decades of its banishment and guerrilla war against South African government. April 24, 1993.

Troyanos, Tatiana, 54: mezzo-soprano whose repertory covered entire operatic history. Sang in wide range of roles at Metropolitan Opera and elsewhere. Aug. 21, 1993.

Van Fleet, Gen. James A., 100 (cq): veteran of four decades in Army. Led major campaigns in World War II and Korea. Sept. 23, 1992.

Warburg, Edward M., 84: philanthropist and benefactor of the arts. Helped found American Ballet (Balanchine's first American company) and Museum of Modern Art. Nov. 21, 1992.

Weng, Will, 86: editor of *New York Times* crossword puzzles for more than 10 years. May 2, 1993.

Whitney, Cornelius Vanderbilt, 93: a founder of Pan American Airways and a Truman Administration official. Was a prominent figure in horse racing and a patron of the arts. Dec. 14, 1992.

Domestic Mail Service 1993

First Class

First-class consists of letters and written and sealed matter. The rate is 29¢ for the first oz; 23¢ for each additional oz, or fraction of an oz, up to 11 oz. Pieces over 11 oz are subject to priority-mail (heavy pieces) rates. Single postcards, 19¢; double postcards, 38¢ (19¢ for each half). The post office sells prestamped single and double postal cards. Consult your postmaster for information on business-reply mail and presort rates.

The weight limit for first-class mail is 70 lb.

Weight not exceeding	Rates
1 oz	$ .29
2 oz	.52
3 oz	.75
4 oz	.98
5 oz	1.21
6 oz	1.44
7 oz	1.67
8 oz	1.90
9 oz	2.13
10 oz	2.36
11 oz	2.59
Over 11 ounces, *see* Priority Mail.	

Priority Mail (over 11 oz to 70 lb)

The zone rate applies to mailable matter over 11 oz of any class carried by air. Your local post office will supply free official zone tables appropriate to your location.

Airmail

First-class and priority mail receive airmail service.

Express Mail

Express Mail Service is available for any mailable article up to 70 lb in weight and 108 in. in combined length and girth, 7 days a week, 365 days a year. Call 800-333-8777 for pick-up service; there is a single charge of $4.50, no matter how many pieces. Flat rates: letter rate (up to 8 ounces), $9.95; up to 2 lb, $13.95; over 2 lb and up to 70 lb, consult your postmaster.

The flat-rate envelope (whatever the weight, the item goes for the same 2-lb rate) may be used by paying the appropriate 2-lb postage rate for the level of service desired. Other service features include: noon delivery between major business markets; merchandise and document reconstruction insurance; Express Mail shipping containers; shipment receipt; special collection boxes; and such options as return receipt service; COD service; waiver of signature; and pickup service.

Consult Postmaster for other Express Mail Services and rates.

The Postal Service will refund, upon application to originating office, the postage for any Express Mail shipments not meeting the service standard, except for those delayed by strike or work stoppage.

Second Class

Second-class mail is used primarily by newspapers, magazines, and other periodicals with second-class mailing privileges. For copies mailed by the public, the rate is the applicable Express Mail, Priority Mail, or single-piece first-, third- or fourth-class rate.

Third Class (under 16 oz)

Third-class mail is used for circulars, books, catalogs, printed matter, merchandise, seeds, cuttings, bulbs, roots, scions, and plants. There are two rate structures for this class, a single-piece and a bulk rate. Regular and special bulk rates are available only to authorized mailers—consult postmaster for details.

Third-Class, Single-Piece Rates

Weight not exceeding	Rates	Weight not exceeding	Rates
1 oz	$ .29	10 oz	$ 1.44
2 oz	.52	12 oz	1.56
3 oz	.75	14 oz	1.67
4 oz	.98	Over 14 oz but less than 16 oz	1.79
6 oz	1.21		
8 oz	1.33		

Fourth Class (Parcel Post—16 oz and over)

Fourth-class mail is used for merchandise, books, printed matter, and all other mailable matter not in first, second, or third class. Special fourth-class rates apply to books, library books, publications or records for the blind, and certain controlled-circulation publications.

Packages should be taken to your local post office, where the postage will be determined according to the weight of the package and the distance it is being sent. Information on weight and size limits for fourth-class mail may be obtained there.

Special Services

Registered Mail. When you use registered mail service, you are buying security—the safest way to send valuables. The full value of your mailing must be declared when mailed. You receive a receipt and the movement of your mail is controlled throughout the postal system. For an additional fee, a return receipt showing to whom, when, and where delivered may be obtained.

Fees for articles (in addition to postage)

Value			With insurance	Without insurance
$0.01	to	$ 100	$4.50	$4.40
100.01	to	500	4.85	4.70
500.01	to	1,000	5.25	5.05

For higher values, consult your postmaster.

Certified Mail. Certified mail service provides for a receipt to the sender and a record of delivery at the post office of address. No record is kept at the post office where mailed. It is for First-Class and Priority Mail only.

Fee in addition to postage, $1.00

Return Receipts. Available for COD, Express Mail, and certified, insured (for over $50), and registered mail. Requested at time of mailing:

Showing to whom and date delivered	$1.00
Showing to whom, date, and address where delivered	1.35
Requested after mailing:	
Showing to whom and date delivered	6.00

C.O.D. Mail. Maximum value for service is $600. Consult your postmaster for fees and conditions of mailing.

Insured Mail. Fees, in addition to postage, for coverage against loss or damage:

Liability	Fees
$ .01 to $50	$ .75
$ 50.01 to $100	1.60
$ 100.01 to $200	2.40
$ 200.01 to $300	3.50
$ 300.01 to $400	4.60
$ 400.01 to $500	5.40
$ 500.01 to $600	6.20

Special Delivery. The payment of the special-delivery fee entitles mail to the most expeditious transportation and delivery. The fee is in addition to the regular postage.

	Weight/Fees		
Class of mail	Not more than 2 lb	More than 2 lb but not more than 10 lb	More than 10 lb
First-class	$7.65	$7.95	$8.55
All other classes	8.05	8.65	9.30

Special Handling. Payment of the special-handling fee entitles third- and fourth-class matter to the most expeditious handling and transportation, but not special delivery. The fee is in addition to the regular postage.

Weight	Fees
Not more than 10 lb	$1.80
More than 10 lb	2.50

Money Orders. Money orders are used for the sa transmission of money.

Amount of money order	Fee
$ .01 to $700	$1.0

Minimum Mail Sizes

All mail must be at least 0.007 in. thick and ma that is 1/4 in. or less in thickness must be at least 1/2 in. in height, at least 5 in. long, and rectangul in shape (except keys and identification devices NOTE: Pieces greater than 1/4 in. thick can b mailed even if they measure less than 3 1/2 by inches.

Adhesive Stamps Available

Purpose	Form	Prices and denomination
Regular postage	Single or sheet	1, 2, 3, 4, 5, 6, 7, 8, 9, 10, 15, 19, 20, 22, 23, 25, 28, 29, 30, 35, 40, 45, 50, 52, 65, 75¢, $1, $2, $2.90, $5, $9.95.
	Booklets	10 at 29 cents ($2.90) 20 at 29 cents ($5.80) 20 at 19 cents ($3.80)
	Coil of 100	19, 25, and 29¢ (dispenser and stamp affixer for use with these coils are also available).
	Coil of 500	1, 2, 3, 4, 5, 10, 15, 19, 20, 23, 25, 29¢, and $1.
	Coil of 3000	1, 2, 3, 4, 5, 10, 15, 19, 20, 23, 25, 29¢.
	Coil of 10,000	29¢.
International airmail postage	Single or sheet	40 and 50¢

Note: Denominations listed are currently in stock. Others may be available until supplies are exhausted.

Regular envelopes are available prestamped for 29¢ and 34¢ each (less than 500). For bulk prices, consult postmaster.

Single postcards are available prestamped for 19¢ each. Reply postcards (19¢ each half) are 38¢ each.

Non-Standard Mail

All first-class mail (except presort first-class and carrier route first-class weighing one ounce or less) and all single-piece rate third-class mail weighing one ounce or less is nonstandard (and subject to a 10¢ surcharge in addition to the applicable postage and fees) if any of the following dimensions are exceeded: length—11 1/2 inches; height—6 1/8 inches; thickness—1/4 inch, or the piece has a height to length (aspect) ratio which does not fall between 1 to 1.3 and 1 to 2.5 inclusive. (The aspect ratio is found by dividing the length by the height. If the answer is between 1.3 and 2.5 inclusive, the piece has a standard aspect ratio).

International Mail Service, 1993

Letters and Letter Packages

Items of mail containing personal handwritten or ypewritten communications having the character of urrent correspondence must be sent as letters or letter ackages. Unless prohibited by the country of destination, merchandise or other articles within the applicable weight and size limits may also be mailed at the etter rate of postage. Weight limit for all countries, 4 ounds. For rates, consult your local post office.

Letters and Letter Packages—Airmail Rates

All Countries other than Canada & Mexico

Weight not over	Rate	Weight not over	Rate
Oz		*Oz*	
0.5	$ 0.50	24.5	$19.28
1.0	0.95	25.0	19.67
1.5	1.34	25.5	20.06
2.0	1.73	26.0	20.45
2.5	2.12	26.5	20.84
3.0	2.51	27.0	21.23
3.5	2.90	27.5	21.62
4.0	3.29	28.0	22.01
4.5	3.68	28.5	22.40
5.0	4.07	29.0	22.79
5.5	4.46	29.5	23.18
6.0	4.85	30.0	23.57
6.5	5.24	30.5	23.96
7.0	5.63	31.0	24.35
7.5	6.02	31.5	24.74
8.0	6.41	32.0	25.13
8.5	6.80	33	25.52
9.0	7.19	34	25.91
9.5	7.58	35	26.30
10.0	7.97	36	26.69
10.5	8.36	37	27.08
11.0	8.75	38	27.47
11.5	9.14	39	27.86
12.0	9.53	40	28.25
12.5	9.92	41	28.64
13.0	10.31	42	29.03
13.5	10.70	43	29.42
14.0	11.09	44	29.81
14.5	11.48	45	30.20
15.0	11.87	46	30.59
15.5	12.26	47	30.98
16.0	12.65	48	31.37
16.5	13.04	49	31.76
17.0	13.43	50	32.15
17.5	13.82	51	32.54
18.0	14.21	52	32.93
18.5	14.60	53	33.32
19.0	14.99	54	33.71
19.5	15.38	55	34.10
20.0	15.77	56	34.49
20.5	16.16	57	34.88
21.0	16.55	58	35.27
21.5	16.94	59	35.66
22.0	17.33	60	36.05
22.5	17.72	61	36.44
23.0	18.11	62	36.83
23.5	18.50	63	37.22
24.0	18.89	64	37.61

Post and Postal Cards

Canada $0.30 All other—surface $0.35
Mexico $0.30 All other—air $0.40

Aerogrammes—$0.45 each.

Canada and Mexico—Surface Rates

All Countries other than Canada & Mexico

Weight not over Lb	Oz	Canada	Mexico	Weight not over Lb	Oz	Canada	Mexico
0	0.5	$.40	$.35	0	10	2.47	2.65
0	1	.40	.45	0	11	2.70	2.90
0	1.5	.63	.55	0	12	2.93	3.15
0	2	.63	.65	1	0	3.25	4.15
0	3	.86	.90	1	8	3.85	6.15
0	4	1.09	1.15	2	0	4.45	8.15
0	5	1.32	1.40	2	8	5.38	10.15
0	6	1.55	1.65	3	0	6.31	12.15
0	7	1.78	1.90	3	8	7.24	14.15
0	8	2.01	2.15	4	0	8.17	16.15
0	9	2.24	2.40				

Weight Limit—4 Pounds*

Note: Mail paid at this rate receives First-Class service in the United States and air service in Canada and Mexico. *Registered letters to Canada may weigh up to 66 pounds. The rate for over 4 pounds to 66 pounds is $1.80 per pound or fraction of a pound.

Countries Other Than Canada and Mexico—Surface Rates

Letters and Letter Packages

Weight not over Lb	Oz	Rate	Weight not over Lb	Oz	Rate
0	1	0.70	0	11	3.95
0	2	0.95	0	12	3.95
0	3	1.20	1	0	5.55
0	4	1.45	1	8	7.65
0	5	1.70	2	0	9.75
0	6	1.95	2	8	11.85
0	7	2.20	3	0	13.95
0	8	2.45	3	8	16.05
0	9	3.95	4	0	18.15
0	10	3.95			

Weight limit—4 pounds.

United Nations Stamps

United Nations stamps are issued in three different currencies, namely, U.S. dollars, Swiss francs, and Austrian schillings. Stamps in all three currencies are available at face value at each of the U.N. Postal Administration offices in New York, Geneva, and Vienna. They may be purchased over the counter, by mail, or by opening a Customer Deposit Account.

Mail orders for mint (unused) stamps and postal stationery may be sent to the U.N. Postal Administration in New York, Geneva, and Vienna. Write to: United Nations Postal Administration, P.O. Box 5900, Grand Central Station, New York, N.Y. 10017.

Authorized 2-Letter State Abbreviations

When the Post Office instituted the ZIP Code for mail in 1963, it also drew up a list of two-letter abbreviations for the states which would gradually replace the traditional ones in use. Following is the official list, including the District of Columbia, Guam, Puerto Rico, and the Virgin Islands (note that only capital letters are used):

Alabama	AL	Kentucky	KY	Ohio	OH
Alaska	AK	Louisiana	LA	Oklahoma	OK
Arizona	AZ	Maine	ME	Oregon	OR
Arkansas	AR	Maryland	MD	Pennsylvania	PA
California	CA	Massachusetts	MA	Puerto Rico	PR
Colorado	CO	Michigan	MI	Rhode Island	RI
Connecticut	CT	Minnesota	MN	South Carolina	SC
Delaware	DE	Mississippi	MS	South Dakota	SD
Dist. of Columbia	DC	Missouri	MO	Tennessee	TN
Florida	FL	Montana	MT	Texas	TX
Georgia	GA	Nebraska	NE	Utah	UT
Guam	GU	Nevada	NV	Vermont	VT
Hawaii	HI	New Hampshire	NH	Virginia	VA
Idaho	ID	New Jersey	NJ	Virgin Islands	VI
Illinois	IL	New Mexico	NM	Washington	WA
Indiana	IN	New York	NY	West Virginia	WV
Iowa	IA	North Carolina	NC	Wisconsin	WI
Kansas	KS	North Dakota	ND	Wyoming	WY

International Surface Parcel Post

Other Than Canada

Weight through lb	Mexico Central America, Caribbean Islands, Bahamas, Bermuda, St. Pierre and Miquelon	All other countries
2	$6.00 $1.85 each additional lb or fraction	$6.55 $2.10 each additional lb or fraction

Consult your postmaster for weight/size limits of individual countries.

For other international services and rates consult your local postmaster.

Canada Surface Parcel Post

Up to 2 lb $4.85, $1.45 for each additional lb up to the maximum weight of 66 lb. Minimum weight is 1 lb.

International Money Order Fees

This service available only to certain countries. Consult post office. Fee: $3.00. Maximum amount for a single money order is $700.

How to Complain About a Postal Problem

When you have a problem with your mail service, complete a Consumer Service Card which is available from letter carriers and at post offices. This will help your postmaster respond to your problem. If you wish to telephone a complaint, a postal employee will fill out the card for you.

The Consumer Advocate represents consumers at the top management level in the Postal Service. If your postal problems cannot be solved by your local post office, then write to the Consumer Advocate. His staff stands ready to serve you.

Write to: The Consumer Advocate, U.S. Postal Service, Washington, D.C. 20260-6320. Or phone: 1-202-268-2284.

The Mail Order Merchandise Rule

The mail order rule adopted by the Federal Trade Commission in October 1975 provides that when you order by mail:

You must receive the merchandise when the seller says you will.

If you are not promised delivery within a certain time period, the seller must ship the merchandise to you no later than 30 days after your order comes in.

If you don't receive it shortly after that 30-day period, you can cancel your order and get your money back.

How the Rule Works

The seller must notify you if the promised delivery date (or the 30-day limit) cannot be met. The seller must also tell you what the new shipping date will be and give you the option to cancel the order and receive a full refund or agree to the new shipping date. The seller must also give you a free way to send back your answer, such as a stamped envelope or a postage-paid postcard. *If you don't answer, it means that you agree to the shipping delay.*

The seller must tell you if the shipping delay is going to be more than 30 days. You then can agree to the delay or, if you do not agree, the seller must return your money by the end of the first 30 days of the delay.

If you cancel a prepaid order, the seller must mail you the refund within seven business days. Where there is a credit sale, the seller must adjust your account within one billing cycle.

It would be impossible, however, for one rule to apply uniformly to such a varied field as mail order merchandising. For example, the rule does not apply to mail order photo finishing, magazine subscriptions, and other serial deliveries (except for the initial shipment); to mail order seeds and growing plants; to COD orders; or to credit orders where the buyer's account is not charged prior to shipment of the merchandise.